sadržaj • содержание • contents • inhalt • sommaire • sumario • indice • innehåll • 目 次 • المحتويات

saradnici • сотрудники • contributors • mitarbeiter • collaborateurs • colaboradores • collaboratori • medarbetare • 協力者 • المعاونون

Argentina

O. PANNO g

Armenia

V. AKOPIAN g
S. LPUTIAN g
A. NADANIAN
T. NALBANDIAN f
A. PETROSIAN g
R. VAGANIAN g

Australia

D. JOHANSEN m
I. ROGERS g

Azerbeidzhan

I. BADŽARANI
E. MAGERRAMOV g

Belarus'

E. AGREST m
V. DYDYŠKO m
B. GEL'FAND g
JU. ZEZJUL'KIN m

Belgique

M. GEENEN f
M. GUREVICH g
R. MEULDERS f
L. WINANTS m

B"lgarija

I. BALINOV
KIR. GEORGIEV g
J. IVANOV m
M. VOJSKA g

Bosna i Hercegovina

I. SOKOLOV g

Brasil

D. LIMA m

Česko

P. HÁBA m
V. JANSA g
P. LAURENC
J. SMEJKAL g

China

DENG KONGLIANG m

Colombia

R. HENAO m
A. ZAPATA g

Cuba

M. ANDRÉS m
J. BECERRA RIVERA f
H. ELIZART CARDENAS f
G. ESTÉVEZ m
JÓ. HERNÁNDEZ
J. HERNÁNDEZ RUÍZ f
I. HERRERA m
J. NOGUEIRAS g
F. PÉREZ CRUZ
N. PÉREZ PASCUAL
PUJOLS
E. PUPO f
E. RAVELO GIL f
L. VALDÉS f

Danmark

L. BO HANSEN g

Deutschland

A. BANGIEV
G. HERTNECK g
R. HÜBNER g
S. KINDERMANN g
R. KNAAK g
A. LAGUNOV m
W. UHLMANN g

Eesti

J. EHLVEST g
U. LAUK
O. SEPP

England

M. ADAMS g
M. CHANDLER g
A. MILES g
J. NUNN g
N. SHORT g
J. SPEELMAN g

España

J. DE LA VILLA GARCÍA m
M. ILLESCAS CÓRDOBA g
F. OCHOA DE ECHAGÜEN m

France

M. APICELLA m
I. DORFMAN g
J. LAUTIER g
M. LESKI m
E. RELANGE
A. VAÏSSER g

Georgia

G. GEORGADZE m
E. GUFEL'D g
E. UBILAVA g

Greece

V. KOTRONIAS g
K. NIKOLAIDIS
S. SKEMBRIS g
A. VOULDIS

India

V. ANAND g
V. KOSHI
D. PRASAD m
P. THIPSAY m

Ísland

J. HJARTARSON g
M. PÉTURSSON g
H. STEFÁNSSON g

Israel

B. ALTERMAN g
FAERMAN
L. GOFSHTEIN m
J. KAGAN
I. KHENKIN g
V. LŐWY f
V. MIKHALEVSKI
V. MILOV m
L. PSAKHIS g
I. SMIRIN g
MA. TSEITLIN m
A. VYDESLAVER
L. YUDASIN g

Italia

E. MINERVA
L. PANTALEONI

Japan

H. NISHIMURA

Jugoslavija

D. ĆIRIĆ g
S. CVETKOVIĆ m
B. DAMLJANOVIĆ g
M. DRAŠKO g
S. GLIGORIĆ g
Z. ILINČIĆ m
S. JOCIĆ
M. KNEŽEVIĆ g
D. KOSIĆ m
B. MAKSIMOVIĆ m
A. MARIĆ g
M. MATULOVIĆ g

ШАХМАТНЫЙ ИНФОРМАТОР

CHESS INFORMANT

SCHACH-INFORMATOR

INFORMATEUR D'ECHECS

INFORMADOR AJEDRECISTICO

INFORMATORE SCACCHISTICO

SCHACK-INFORMATOR

チェス新報

دليــل الشـطرنج

šahovski informator

57

II – V 1993

ISBN: 84-87301-87-8

Depósito Legal: M-21.770-1993

Izdavač • Издатель • Publisher • Herausgeber • Editeur • Editorial • Editore • Utgivare • 出版社 • الناشر

S. I. Chess Informant Ltd.

2, Sofouli Str., Chanteclair Bldg., Office 205
Nicosia, Cyprus

Ediciones Eseuve, S.A.

Batalla del Salado, 34 - 1.º A
28045 Madrid, España

B. MILJANIĆ m
S. MIRKOVIĆ m
N. NIKČEVIĆ m
M. PAVLOVIĆ m
D. RAJKOVIĆ g
A. STRIKOVIĆ m
G. M. TODOROVIĆ m
M. VUKIĆ g
M. ZAFIROVSKI

Latvija

A. GIPSLIS g
A. ŠIROV g

Lietuva

A. KVEINYS g
E. ROZENTALIS g
D. RUZELE m
D. ZAGORSKIS m
A. ZAPOLSKIS m

Magyarország

A. ADORJÁN g
A. CHERNIN g
GY. FEHÉR m
P. HARDICSAY m
P. LÉKÓ m
P. LUKÁCS g
J. POLGÁR g
ZSU. POLGÁR g
Z. RIBLI g
GY. SAX g

Moldova

V. BOLOGAN g
V. KOMLIAKOV m
V. NEVEDNIČIJ g
D. ROGOZENKO m

Nederland

F. NIJBOER g
JE. PIKET g
J. TIMMAN g
J. VAN DER WIEL g
L. VAN WELY g

Polska

J. GDAŃSKI m
M. KAMIŃSKI m
M. KRASENKOV g
W. SAPIS m

România

CO. IONESCU m
A. ISTRĂŢESCU m
M. MARIN g
F. MATEI
D. POPESCU
G. SCHWARTZMAN m
V. STOICA m
R. SZUHANEK
D. VLAD m

Rossija

N. ANDRIANOV m
B. ARHANGEL'SKIJ
K. ASEEV g
E. BAREEV g
V. ČEHOV g
MI. CEJTLIN g
K. ČERNIŠOV
V. CEŠKOVSKIJ g
JU. CIMMERMAN
JU. DOHOJAN g
S. DOLMATOV g
A. DREEV g
V. EPIŠIN g
V. GAGARIN m
S. GALAHOV
A. GAVRILOV m
I. GLEK g
A. GOL'DIN g
S. GULIEV
A. HALIFMAN g
A. HARLOV g
R. HOLMOV g
S. IONOV m
SE. IVANOV m
I. JAGUPOV m
JU. JAKOVIČ g
V. JANDEMIROV m
V. JURKOV
A. JUSUPOV g
G. KAJDANOV g
S. KALINIČEV m
AN. KARPOV g
G. KASPAROV g
S. KIBALNIČENKO
S. KISELËV m
S. KIŠNËV m
V. KRAMNIK g
A. KUZ'MIN m
I. KUZNECOV
A. LUKIN m
A. LYSENKO

M. MAKAROV g
A. MOROZEVIČ m
G. NESIS
A. NIKITIN
M. NOVIK
A. OBUHOV m
JU. PISKOV g
A. POLULJAHOV m
B. POSTOVSKIJ
S. PRUDNIKOVA g
A. RAECKIJ m
JU. RAZUVAEV g
V. RUBAN g
K. SAKAEV g
V. SALOV g
B. ŠČIPKOV
A. SEREBRJANIK
S. ŠEVELËV m
S. ŠIPOV m
S. SMAGIN g
V. SMYSLOV g
A. SOKOLOV g
E. SOLOŽENKIN m
A. SUĖTIN g
A. ŠVEDČIKOV m
E. SVEŠNIKOV g
S. TIVJAKOV g
L. TOCKIJ
N. TOLSTIH
P. TREGUBOV m
G. TUNIK m
M. ULYBIN g
I. UMANSKAJA m
A. VAULIN m
N. VLASSOV
A. VUL'
A. VYŽMANAVIN g
I. ZAJCEV g
V. ZINOV

Schweiz

V. KORTCHNOI g

Scotland

B. McCAMON

Slovensko

J. FRANZEN m
Ľ. FTÁČNIK g
I. ŠTOHL g

Sverige

TH. ERNST g

Turkey

S. ATALIK m
T. HAMARAT

Ukrajina

A. BELJAVSKIJ g
V. BOGDANOV
I. ČELUŠKINA g
V. ĖJNGORN g
A. FROLOV m
V. GOLOD m
M. GOLUBEV m
A. HUZMAN g
V. IVANČUK g
D. KOMAROV m
F. LEVIN m
V. MALANJUK g
A. MIHAL'ČIŠIN g
V. MOSKALENKO g
S. SAVČENKO g
L. ŠMUTER m
B. TABOROV
V. TUKMAKOV g
K. TYŠKOVEC
A. VAJSMAN

USA

L. ALBURT g
J. BENJAMIN g
P. BENKÖ g
W. BROWNE g
R. BYRNE g
L. CHRISTIANSEN g
J. DONALDSON m
I. GUREVICH m
ALEXA. IVANOV g
G. KAMSKY g
Ľ. KAVÁLEK g
E. MEDNIS g
F. RHINE
V. SEGAL
Y. SEIRAWAN g
J. VATNIKOV m
J. WAITZKIN
A. YERMOLINSKY g

Uzbekistan

A. BLODŠTEJN
S. NADYRHANOV m
A. NENAŠEV g
G. SERPER g
S. ZAGREBEL'NYJ g

deset najboljih partija prethodnog toma • десять лучших партий предыдущего тома • the best ten games of the preceding volume • die zehn besten schachpartien aus dem vorigen band • les dix meilleures parties du volume précédent • las diez mejores partidas del tomo precedente • le dieci migliori partite del volume precedente • de tio bästa partierna i föregående volym • 前巻のベスト十局 •

الأشواط العشرة الأهم الواردة في العدد السابق

predlog redakcije
предложение редакции
editorial selection
vorschlag der redaktion
proposition de la rédaction
proposicion de la redacción
proposta della redazione
redaktionens förslag
編集部推薦局
مقترح هيئة التحرير

		MURRAY CHANDLER	LARRY CHRISTIANSEN	ĽUBOMIR KAVÁLEK	VIKTOR KORTCHNOI	MILAN MATULOVIĆ	OSCAR PANNO	ZOLTÁN RIBLI	JAN SMEJKAL	JONATHAN SPEELMAN	
1. **AN. KARPOV** – KAMSKY	527	–	–	9	6	10	10	10	10	–	**55**
2. **KRAMNIK** – LPUTIAN	449	10	–	7	–	9	3	–	9	8	**46**
3. **J. POLGÁR** – SPASSKY	388	7	4	8	9	–	7	1	7	–	**43**
4. **A. CHERNIN** – ŠTOHL	543	8	–	1	3	6	6	5	5	–	**34**
5. NUNN – KRAMNIK	219	6	10	–	–	1	4	–	–	9	**30**
6. WAHLS – JUSUPOV	333	9	7	–	–	–	–	3	–	10	**29**
7. **IVANČUK** – KAMSKY	379	4	9	–	–	7	8	–	–	–	**28**
8. TUKMAKOV – **HENKIN**	471	3	–	–	10	3	–	9	–	1	**26**
9. **N. SHORT** – TIMMAN	369	–	–	–	–	–	9	2	8	7	**26**
10. G. GEORGADZE – **ADORJÁN**	535	2	5	5	–	4	–	8	–	2	**26**
11. KUPREJČIK – **SKEMBRIS**	326	–	2	10	4	–	–	–	4	–	**20**
12. **VYŽMANAVIN** – ŠIROV	487	–	6	–	8	–	–	–	6	–	**20**
13. **KRASENKOV** – JANOVSKIJ	406	–	–	–	2	8	1	6	–	–	**17**
14. M. GUREVICH – **SVEŠNIKOV**	23	1	–	6	–	–	–	7	–	–	**14**
15. P. NIKOLIĆ – **ŠIROV**	472	–	8	–	–	–	–	–	–	5	**13**
16. I. SOKOLOV – **VAN DER WIEL**	621	–	–	–	7	2	–	4	–	–	**13**
17. HERTNECK – **JUSUPOV**	98	–	–	4	–	–	5	–	2	–	**11**
18. **KASPAROV** – IVANČUK	335	–	–	–	–	–	2	–	3	4	**9**
19. TIMMAN – **KAMSKY**	399	5	3	–	–	–	–	–	–	–	**8**
20. **ANASTASIAN** – SMIRIN	24	–	1	–	5	–	–	–	1	–	**7**
21. A. ROTŠTEJN – **SERPER**	13	–	–	–	–	–	–	–	–	6	**6**
22. **B. GEL'FAND** – ŠTOHL	544	–	–	–	–	5	–	–	–	–	**5**
23. **M. GUREVICH** – CU. HANSEN	690	–	–	3	1	–	–	–	–	–	**4**
24. I. SOKOLOV – SMIRIN	69	–	–	–	–	–	–	–	–	3	**3**
25. ŠIROV – **KAMSKY**	548	–	–	2	–	–	–	–	–	–	**2**
26. NOVIK – DVOJRIS	45	–	–	–	–	–	–	–	–	–	**0**
27. **ADAMS** – CVITAN	245	–	–	–	–	–	–	–	–	–	**0**
28. DREEV – **SVEŠNIKOV**	499	–	–	–	–	–	–	–	–	–	**0**
29. HENKIN – **LAUTIER**	591	–	–	–	–	–	–	–	–	–	**0**
30. RAZUVAEV – **I. SOKOLOV**	672	–	–	–	–	–	–	–	–	–	**0**

najbolju partiju nagrađuje
лучшая партия получает премию
the best game prize awarded by
die beste partie erhielt einen preis von
la meilleure partie primée par
la mejor partida premiada por
la partita migliore premiata da
det bästa partiet uppsatt av
すまし致彰表を者勝優が
افضل جولة حائزة على جائزة من :

56/527. **D 79**

AN. KARPOV 2715 – KAMSKY 2655
Moskva 1992

1. d4 ♘f6 2. c4 g6 3. ♘f3 ♗g7 4. g3 c6 5. ♗g2 d5 6. cd5 cd5 7. ♘c3 0–0 8. ♘e5 e6 9. 0–0 ♘fd7 10. f4 ♘c6 11. ♗e3 ♘b6 12. ♗f2 ♗d7 13. e4 ♘e7 14. ♘d7 ♕d7 15. e5 ♖ac8 N [15... ♖fc8 – 44/(557)] **16. ♖c1 a6 17. b3!? ♖c7 18. ♕d2 ♖fc8 19. g4 ♗f8**

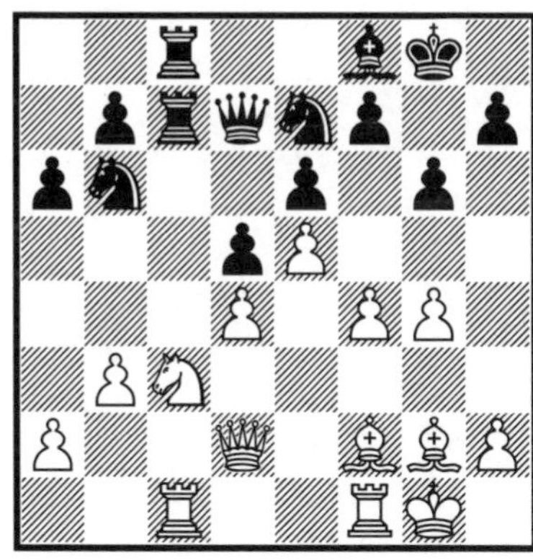

20. ♕e3! [20. ♘e2 ♖c1 21. ♖c1 (21. ♘c1 ♕c7⇆) ♖c1 22. ♘c1 ♘c6 23. ♘d3±] **♘c6 21. f5 ♗a3** [21... ef5 22. gf5 ♕f5 23. ♗h3 ♕h5 24. ♗c8 ♗h6 25. ♕h3 ♗c1 26. ♕h5 gh5 27. ♗b7±] **22. ♖cd1 ♘b4 23. ♕h6!** [23. ♘b1 ♘c2! 24. ♕h6 ♗f8] **♕e8** [23... ♘c2 24. ♘e2±; 23... ♕e7 24. ♘b1 ♗b2 25. ♗h4 ♕f8 26. ♕d2 ♖c2 27. ♕e1] **24. ♘b1! ♗b2 25. ♕d2 ♘c2** [25... a5 26. a3 (26. ♕b2? ♖c2 27. ♕a3 ♖a2) ♘c2 (26... ♖c2 27. ♕e1 ♕b5 28. ab4 ♖e2 29. ♕e2 ♕e2 30. ba5 ♘d7 31. ♖d2+–) 27. ♕a5±] **26. ♔h1 ♕e7 27. ♗g1 ♘d7 28. ♖f3 ♕b4** [28... b5 29. ♖h3 ♕f8 30. ♖f1±] **29. ♕h6!** [29. ♕f4 ♗d4 30. ♗d4 ♘d4 31. ♖d4 ♖c1 32. ♖f1 ♖f1 33. ♗f1 ♕e1 34. ♘d2 ♘e5⇆] **♕f8 30. ♕g5! ♕g7 31. ♕d2 b6 32. ♖df1 a5 33. h4 ♘b4 34. a3 ♖c2 35. ♕f4 ♘c6 36. ♗h3! ♘d8 37. ♗e3 b5 38. ♖3f2!± b4 39. ab4 ab4 40. ♖c2 ♖c2 41. ♖f2 ♖f2 42. ♕f2 ♗a3** [42... ♗c3 43. f6 ♕f8 44. ♕c2+–] **43. ♕c2 ♘e5** [43... ♘b8 44. ♘d2 (44. ♕c8!? ♘bc6 45. ♗g5 ♕f8 46. ♗d8 ♘d8 47. ♘d2 ♗b2 48. ♘f3+–) ♘dc6 45. ♘f3] **44. de5 ♕e5 45. ♕c8! ♕e4 46. ♗g2 ♕b1 47. ♔h2 ♗b2 48. ♕d8 ♔g7 49. f6 ♗f6 50. ♗h6 ♔h6 51. ♕f6 ♕c2 52. g5 ♔h5 53. ♔g3** [53. ♔h3? ♕f5 54. ♕f5 gf5 55. ♗f3 ♔g6] **♕c7 54. ♔h3 1 : 0 [An. Karpov]**

deset najvažnijih teorijskih novosti prethodnog toma • десять важнейших теоретических партий предыдущего тома • the ten most important theoretical novelties of the preceding volume • die zehn wichtigsten theoretischen neuerungen aus dem vorigen band • les dix nouveautés théoriques les plus importantes du volume précédent • las diez novedades teóricas más importantes del tomo precedente • le dieci importantissime novitá teoriche del volume precedente • de tio mest betydelsefulla teoretiska nyheterna i föregående volym •

前巻のベスト新手十局 • المبتكرات النظرية العشرة الأهم الواردة في العدد السابق

predlog redakcije
предложение редакции
editorial selection
vorschlag der redaktion
proposition de la rédaction
proposicion de la redacción
proposta della redazione
redaktionens förslag
編集部推薦局
مقترح هيئة التحرير

		VISWANATHAN ANAND	EVGENIJ BAREEV	ĽUBOMIR FTÁČNIK	SVETOZAR GLIGORIĆ	JOHANN HJARTARSON	LEV PSAKHIS	VALERIJ SALOV	JAN TIMMAN	ELIZBAR UBILAVA	
1. KRAMNIK – **ŠIROV**	669	7	7	10	5	7	10	10	3	10	**69**
2. **KASPAROV** – VAGANIAN	453	8	5	–	8	6	8	8	10	8	**61**
3. **IVANČUK** – KAMSKY	379	10	9	6	10	4	4	–	–	1	**44**
4. **KRAMNIK** – ADORJÁN	536	–	8	–	4	10	–	9	1	6	**38**
5. YE JIANGCHUAN – **DOLMATOV**	(294)	5	–	3	2	5	9	5	7	–	**36**
6. **KASPAROV** – IVANČUK	335	–	–	–	9	9	6	4	–	5	**33**
7. **M. GUREVICH** – CU. HANSEN	690	9	1	1	3	–	–	7	8	4	**33**
8. **ILLESCAS CÓRDOBA** – JUDASIN	46	6	10	2	–	–	7	–	–	7	**32**
9. **KORTCHNOI** – TUKMAKOV	39	–	2	8	–	8	2	1	2	3	**26**
10. ŠIROV – **KAMSKY**	548	–	–	–	–	–	–	3	9	9	**21**
11. CVITAN – **A. CHERNIN**	506	4	3	9	–	–	–	–	–	–	**16**
12. **M. GUREVICH** – WAN WELY	708	–	–	7	–	2	5	–	–	–	**14**
13. **SVEŠNIKOV** – OLLS	147	3	–	–	–	–	–	2	6	–	**11**
14. **SISNIEGA** – MATAMOROS	291	2	–	5	–	–	–	–	4	–	**11**
15. **AN. KARPOV** – NUNN	671	–	–	–	7	1	–	–	–	–	**8**
16. G. GEORGADZE – **ADORJÁN**	535	–	–	4	–	3	1	–	–	–	**8**
17. LANDA – **P. TREGUBOV**	196	–	6	–	–	–	–	–	–	–	**6**
18. IVANČUK – **LANKA**	218	–	–	–	–	–	–	6	–	–	**6**
19. NUNN – **JE. PIKET**	347	–	–	–	6	–	–	–	–	–	**6**
20. V. SALOV – **TIMMAN**	48	–	–	–	1	–	–	–	5	–	**6**
21. SAX – **HJARTARSON**	386	–	4	–	–	–	–	–	–	–	**4**
22. **JUSUPOV** – DOHOJAN	474	–	–	–	–	–	3	–	–	–	**3**
23. **SPEELMAN** – VAN DER OUDEWEETERING	497	–	–	–	–	–	–	–	–	2	**2**
24. FTÁČNIK – **LOBRON**	597	1	–	–	–	–	–	–	–	–	**1**
25. BOLOGAN – **VAN DER WIEL**	225	–	–	–	–	–	–	–	–	–	**0**
26. VAN DER WIEL – **BRUNNER**	281	–	–	–	–	–	–	–	–	–	**0**
27. SMIRIN – **N. SHORT**	317	–	–	–	–	–	–	–	–	–	**0**
28. **G. M. TODOROVIĆ** – PETRONIĆ	354	–	–	–	–	–	–	–	–	–	**0**
29. GYÓRKÖS – **ADORJÁN**	550	–	–	–	–	–	–	–	–	–	**0**
30. PSAKHIS – **LOBRON**	595	–	–	–	–	–	–	–	–	–	**0**

najznačajniju novost nagrađuje
лучшая новинка получает премию
the most important novelty prize awarded by
die wichtigste neurung erhielt einen preis von
la nouveauté plus importante primée par
la novedad más importante premiada por
la novità più importante premiata da
den mest betydelsefulla nyheten uppsatt av
すまし致彰表を者勝優が
افضل حولة حائزة على جائزة من :

56/669. !N **E 81**

KRAMNIK 2625 – ŠIROV 2710
Deutschland 1992

1. d4 ♘f6 2. c4 g6 3. ♘c3 ♗g7 4. e4 d6 5. f3 0–0 6. ♗e3 c5 7. dc5 dc5 8. ♕d8 ♖d8 9. ♗c5 ♘c6 10. ♗a3 a5 11. ♖d1 ♗e6 12. ♘d5

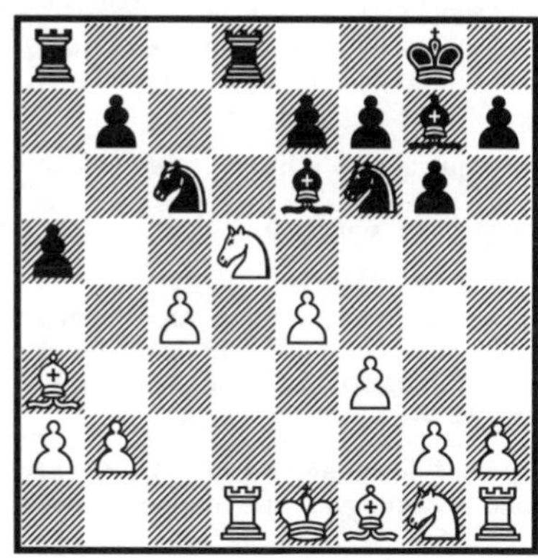

12... ♘b4! N [12... ♗d5?± – 55/593, 594] **13. ♘e7** [13. ♗b4? ab4 14. ♘b4 ♘d7! 15. ♖d2 ♘c5∓] **♔h8 14. ♖d8** [14. ♘d5!? *a)* 14... ♘c2 15. ♔f2 ♘a3 16. ba3 *a1)* 16... b5 17. ♘h3 bc4 18. ♗c4 ♖ac8 19. ♘b6!? (19. ♗b3 a4 20. ♗a4 ♘d5 21. ed5 ♗d5=) ♖d1 20. ♖d1 ♖c4 21. ♖d8 ♘g8 22. ♘c4 ♗c4∞; *a2)* 16... ♗f8!? 17. ♖b1 ♘d7!=/∞ Kramnik; *b)* 14... b5!? 15. ♗b4 ab4 16. ♘b4 ♖d1 17. ♔d1 ♗f8! 18. ♘d5 ♖a2! 19. ♔c2! ♗g7 20. ♔b1! ♖b2!? 21. ♔b2 ♘e4!? (21... ♘d5 22. ♔c1! ♗h6 23. ♔b1 ♘e3 24. ♘e2 ♗c4 25. ♘g3 ♗f1 26. ♘f1 ♘g2±) 22. ♔c2 (22. ♘c3? ♘c3!) ♘f2=; 20... ♖a7!?=/∞] **♖d8 15. ♘d5** [15. ♗b4? ab4 16. ♘d5 ♖a8 17. ♘b4 ♘d7!∓] **♘c2 16. ♔d2** [16. ♔f2!? ♘a3 17. ba3 b5 (17... ♘d7!?=/∞ Kramnik) 18. ♘h3 ♖c8!? (18... bc4 19. ♗c4 ♖c8! 20. ♗b3 a4 21. ♗a4 ♘d5 22. ed5 ♗d5= △ 23. ♗b3 ♗b3 24. ab3 ♖c2) 19. ♘hf4 (19. ♘f6?! ♗f6 20. cb5 ♗d4 21. ♔e2 ♖c1!=/∞) bc4 20. ♘e6 fe6 21. ♘b6 ♘e4! 22. ♔e3! ♖c6 23. ♔e4 ♖b6 24. ♗c4 ♖c6! 25. ♔d3 (25. ♗b5 ♖c2; 25. ♗d3 ♗b2 26. a4 ♖c1=) ♗f8 26. a4 ♔g7=] **♘a3 17. ba3 b5 18. ♘h3** [18... bc4 19. ♗c4 ♘d5 20. ed5 ♗d5 21. ♗d5 ♖d5 22. ♔e2=] **1/2 : 1/2**
[Širov]

sistem znakova • система знаков • code system • zeichenerklärung • système de symboles • sistema de signos • spiegazione dei segni • teckenförklaring • 解説記号 • نظام الرموز

± beli stoji nešto bolje • у белых несколько лучше • white stands slightly better • Weiss steht etwas besser • les blancs sont un peu mieux • el blanco está algo mejor • il bianco sta un po' meglio • vit står något bättre • 白やゝ優勢 • وضع الابيض افضل نوعا ما

∓ crni stoji nešto bolje • у черных несколько лучше • black stands slightly better • Schwarz steht etwas besser • les noirs sont un peu mieux • el negro está algo mejor • il nero sta un po' meglio • svart står något bättre • 黒やゝ優勢 • وضع الاسود أفضل نوعا ما

± beli stoji bolje • у белых лучше • white has the upper hand • Weiss steht besser • les blancs sont mieux • el blanco está mejor • il bianco sta meglio • vit står bättre • 白 優勢 • الابيض في وضع مسيطر

∓ crni stoji bolje • у черных лучше • black has the upper hand • Schwarz steht besser • les noirs sont mieux • el negro está mejor • il nero sta meglio • svart står bättre • 黒 優勢 • الاسود في وضع مسيطر

+— beli ima odlučujuću prednost • у белых решающее преимущество • white has a decisive advantage • Weiss hat entscheidenden Vorteil • les blancs ont un avantage décisif • el blanco tiene una ventaja decisiva • il bianco é in vantaggio decisivo • vit har avgörande fördel • 白 勝勢 • الابيض يتمتع بأفضلية حاسمة

—+ crni ima odlučujuću prednost • у черных решающее преимущество • black has a decisive advantage • Schwarz hat entscheidenden Vorteil • les noirs ont un avantage décisif • el negro tiene una ventaja decisiva • il nero é in vantaggio decisivo • svart har avgörande fördel • 黒 勝勢 • الاسود يتمتع بأفضلية حاسمة

= jednako • равно • even • ausgeglichen • égalité • igual • equivalente • lika • 形勢互角 • تكافوء

∞ neizvesno • неизвестно • unclear • unklar • incertain • incierto • incerto • oklar • 形勢不明 • غير واضح

$\overline{\infty}$ kompenzacija za materijal • компенсация за материал • with compensation for the material • mit Kompensation für den materiellen Nachteil • avec compensation pour le matériel • con compensación por el material • con compenso per il vantaggio materiale avversario • med kompensation för materialet • 駒損不利なし • مع تعويض خسارة القطع

↻ razvojna prednost • преимущество в развитии • development advantage • Entwicklungsvorsprung • avantage de développement • ventaja de desarrollo • vantaggio di sviluppo • utvecklingsförsprång • 展開よし • افضلية للتطور

○ prostorna prednost • преимущество в пространстве • greater board room • beherrscht mehr Raum • avantage d'espace • ventaja de espacio • maggior vantaggio spaziale • terrängfördel • 模様大 • افضلية مكانية على الرقعة

→ sa napadom • с атакой • with attack • mit Angriff • avec attaque • con ataque • con attacco • med angrepp • 攻勢 • مع الهجوم

↑ sa inicijativom • с инициативой • with initiative • mit Initiative • avec initiative • con iniciative • con iniziativa • med initiativ • 主導権あり • مع المبادرة

⇆ sa protivigrom • с контригрой • with counter-play • mit Gegenspiel • avec contre-jeu • con contrajuego • con controgioco • med motspel • 反撃 • مع لعب مضاد

⊙ iznudica • цугцванг • zugzwang • Zugzwang • zugzwang • zugzwang • zugzwang • dragtvång • ツーク、ツワング • زوغزوانغ

mat • мат • mate • matt • mat • mate • matto • matt • メイト • اماتة الشاه

! vrlo dobar potez • очень хороший ход • a very good move • ein sehr guter Zug • très bon coup • muy buena jugada • buona mossa • ett bra drag • 好 手 • نقلة جيدة جدا

!! odličan potez • отличный ход • an excellent move • ein ausgezeichneter Zug • excellent coup • excelente jugada • mossa ottima • ett utmärkt drag • 妙 手 • نقلة ممتازة

? slab potez • слабый ход • a mistake • ein schwacher Zug • coup faible • mala jugada • mossa debole • ett dåligt drag • 疑 問 手 • نقلة خطا

?? gruba greška • грубая ошибка • a blunder • ein grober Fehler • erreur grave • grave error • grave errore • ett grovt fel • 悪 手 • نقلة سيئة جدا

!? potez zaslužuje pažnju • ход заслуживающий внимания • a move deserving attention • ein beachtenswerter Zug • coup qui mérite l'attention • jugada que merece atención • mossa degna di considerazione • ett drag som förtjänar uppmärksamhet • 注 目 手 • نقلة تستحق الانتباه

?! sumnjiv potez • сомнительный ход • a dubious move • ein Zug von zweifelhaftem Wert • coup de valeur douteuse • jugada de dudoso valor • mossa dubbia • ett tvivelaktigt drag • 鬼 手 • نقلة مشكوك في نتيجتها

△ sa idejom • с идеей • with the idea • mit der Idee • avec l'idée • con idea • con l'idea • med idén • 狙いは…… • يتصور

□ jedini potez • единственный ход • only move • der einzig spielbare Zug • le seul coup • unica jugada • unica mossa • enda draget • 絶 対 手 • النقلة الوحيدة

⌓ bolje je • лучше • better is • besser ist • meilleur est • es mejor • è meglio • bättre är • 正 着 は • الافضل هو

♔ ♕ ♖ ♗ ♘

⇔ linija • линия • file • Linie • colonne • linea • linea • linje • 横 列 • الرتل

⇗ dijagonala • диагональ • diagonal • Diagonale • diagonale • diagonal • diagonal • diagonal • 斜 筋 • القطر

⊞ centar • центр • centre • Zentrum • centre • centro • centro • centrum • 中 央 • المركز

» kraljevo krilo • королевский фланг • king's side • Königsflügel • aile-roi • flanco de rey • lato di R • kungsflygeln • キング側 • جناح الملك

« damino krilo • ферзевый фланг • queen's side • Damenflügel • aile-dame • flanco de dama • lato di D • damflygeln • クイン側 • جناح الملكة

× slaba tačka • слабый пункт • weak point • schwacher Punkt • point faible • punto débil • punto debole • svaghet • 弱 点 • نقطة ضعف

⊥ završnica • эндшпиль • ending • Endspiel • finale • final • finale • slutspel • 収 局 • المرحلة النهائية

⧉ lovački par • два слона • pair of bishops • Läuferpaar • paire de fous • pareja de alfiles • la coppia degli alfieri • löparpar • 双ビショップ • الفيلان

⧉ raznobojni lovci • разноцветные слоны • bishops of opposite color • ungleichfarbige Läufer • fous de couleurs opposées • alfiles de distinto color • alfieri di colore diverso • löpare med olika färg • 異色ビショップ • فيلان من لونين مختلفين

⧉ istobojni lovci • одноцветные слоны • bishops of the same color • gleichfarbige Läufer • fous de même couleur • alfiles del mismo color • alfieri di colore uguale • löpare med samma färg • 同色ビショップ • فيلان من نفس اللون

oo vezani pešaci • связанные пешки • united pawns • verbundene Bauern • pions liés • peones unidos • pedoni uniti • garderade bönder • 連ポーン • بيادق مرتبطة

o-o razdvojeni pešaci • изолированные пешки • separated pawns • isolierte Bauern • pions isolés • peones aislados • pedoni isolati • isolerade bönder • 離ポーン • بيادق منفصلة

8 udvojeni pešaci • сдвоенные пешки • double pawns • Doppelbauern • pions doublés • peones dobles • pedoni doppi • dubbel bönder • 重ポーン • بيادق مزدوجة

♙ slobodan pešak • проходная пешка • passed pawn • Freibauer • pion passé • peón pasado • pedone libero • fribonde • 失ったポーン • بيدق حر

\> prednost u broju pešaka • преимущество в числе пешек • advantage in number of pawns • im Bauernmehrbesitz • avantage quantitatif en pions • ventaja en el número de peones • vantaggio quantitativo dei pedoni • fördel i antal bönder • ポーン数での優勢 • الأفضلية بعدد البيادق

⊕ vreme • время • time • Zeit • temps • tiempo • tempo • tid • 時間切迫 • الوقت

♔ ♕ ♖ ♗ ♘

7/113, 48/241... Šahovski informator • Шахматный информатор • Chess Informant • Schach-informator • Informateur d'échecs • Informador ajedrecistico • Informatore scacchistico • Schack-informator • チェス新報巻/局 • دليل الشطرنج

A 30, B 17, C 92... Enciklopedija šahovskih otvaranja • Энциклопедия шахматных дебютов • Encyclopaedia of Chess Openings • Enzyklopädie der Schacheröffnungen • Encyclopédie des ouvertures d'échecs • Enciclopedia de aperturas de ajedrez • Enciclopedia delle aperture negli scacchi • Encyklopedi över spelöppningar i schack • 布局大成 • موسوعة افتتاحيات الشطرنج

♙ 3/c3, ♖ 3/d... Enciklopedija šahovskih završnica • Энциклопедия шахматных окончаний • Encyclopaedia of Chess Endings • Enzyklopädie der Schachendspiele • Encyclopédie des finales d'échecs • Enciclopedia de finales de ajedrez • Enciclopedia dei finali negli scacchi • Encyklopedi över slutspel i schack • 収局大成 • موسوعة نهائيات الشطرنج

N novost • новинка • a novelty • eine Neuerung • nouveauté • novedad • un'innovazione • nyhet • 新 手 • حديد مبتكر

♔ ♕ ♖ ♗ ♘

(ch) šampionat • чемпионат • championship • Meisterschaft • championnat • campeonato • campionato • mästerskap • 世界チャンピオン戦 • البطولة

(izt) međuzonski turnir • межзональный турнир • interzonal tournament • Interzonenturnier • tournoi interzonal • torneo interzonal • torneo interzonale • interzonturnering • インター・ゾーン • دورة مباريات للمناطق

(ct) turnir kandidata • турнир претендентов • candidates' tournament • Kandidatenturnier • tournoi des candidats • torneo de candidatos • torneo dei candidati • kandidatturnering • 挑戦者決定戦 • دورة مباريات للمرشحين

(m) meč • матч • match • Wettkampf • match • encuentro • match • match • マッチ • مباراة

(ol) olimpijada • олимпиада • olympiad • Olympiade • olympiade • olimpiada • olimpiade • olympiad • オリンピック • الاولمبياد

corr. dopisna partija • партия по переписке • correspondence game • Fernpartie • partie par correspondance • partida por correspondencia • partita per corrispondenza • korrespondensparti • 通信戦 • لعبة أو مباراة بالمراسلة

RR primedba redakcije • примечание редакции • editorial comment • Anmerkung der Redaktion • remarque de la rédaction • nota de la redacción • nota redazionale • redaktionens anmärkning • 編集部評 • تعليق هيئة التحرير

R razni potezi • разные ходы • various moves • verschiedene Züge • différents coups • diferentes movidas • mosse varie • olika drag • 変 化 手 • نقلات متنوعة

∟ sa • с • with • mit • avec • con • con • med • 以下の手順となるもの • مع

⌟ bez • без • without • ohne • sans • sin • senza • utan • 以下の手順とならないもの • بدون

|| itd. • и.т.д. • etc • usw. • etc. • etc • ecc • o.s.v. • 等 々 • الخ

— vidi • смотри • see • siehe • voir • ved • vedi • se • 参 照 • انظر

partije • партии • games • partien • parties • partidas • partite • partier • 棋譜 • الاشواط

klasifikacija otvaranja • классификация дебютов • classification of openings • klassifizierung der eröffnungen • classification des ouvertures • clasificación de las aperturas • classificazione delle aperture • klassifikation av öppningar • 布局大分類 • تصنيف الافتتاحيات

A – R ⌟ 1. e4, 1. d4
– 1. d4 R ⌟ 1... d5, 1... ♘f6
– 1. d4 ♘f6 R ⌟ 2. c4
– 1. d4 ♘f6 2. c4 R ⌟ 2... e6, 2... g6

B – 1. e4 R ⌟ 1... c5, 1... e6, 1... e5
– 1. e4 c5

C – 1. e4 e6
– 1. e4 e5

D – 1. d4 d5
– 1. d4 ♘f6 2. c4 g6 ⌞ 3... d5

E – 1. d4 ♘f6 2. c4 e6
– 1. d4 ♘f6 2. c4 g6 ⌟ 3... d5

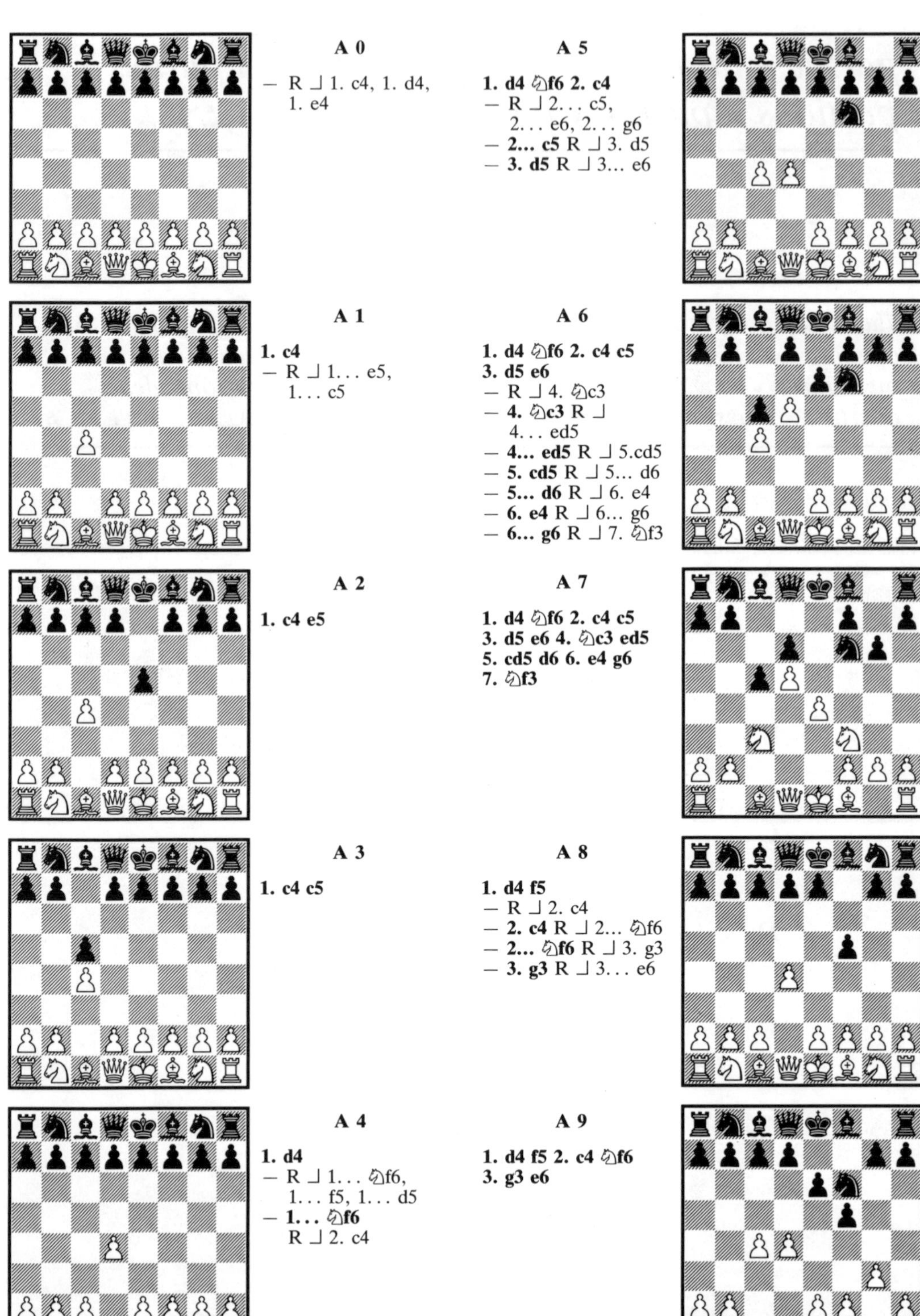

A 0

— R ┘ 1. c4, 1. d4, 1. e4

A 1

1. c4
— R ┘ 1. . . e5, 1. . . c5

A 2

1. c4 e5

A 3

1. c4 c5

A 4

1. d4
— R ┘ 1. . . ♘f6, 1. . . f5, 1. . . d5
— **1. . . ♘f6** R ┘ 2. c4

A 5

1. d4 ♘f6 2. c4
— R ┘ 2. . . c5, 2. . . e6, 2. . . g6
— **2... c5** R ┘ 3. d5
— **3. d5** R ┘ 3... e6

A 6

1. d4 ♘f6 2. c4 c5 3. d5 e6
— R ┘ 4. ♘c3
— **4. ♘c3** R ┘ 4. . . ed5
— **4... ed5** R ┘ 5.cd5
— **5. cd5** R ┘ 5... d6
— **5... d6** R ┘ 6. e4
— **6. e4** R ┘ 6... g6
— **6... g6** R ┘ 7. ♘f3

A 7

1. d4 ♘f6 2. c4 c5 3. d5 e6 4. ♘c3 ed5 5. cd5 d6 6. e4 g6 7. ♘f3

A 8

1. d4 f5
— R ┘ 2. c4
— **2. c4** R ┘ 2... ♘f6
— **2... ♘f6** R ┘ 3. g3
— **3. g3** R ┘ 3. . . e6

A 9

1. d4 f5 2. c4 ♘f6 3. g3 e6

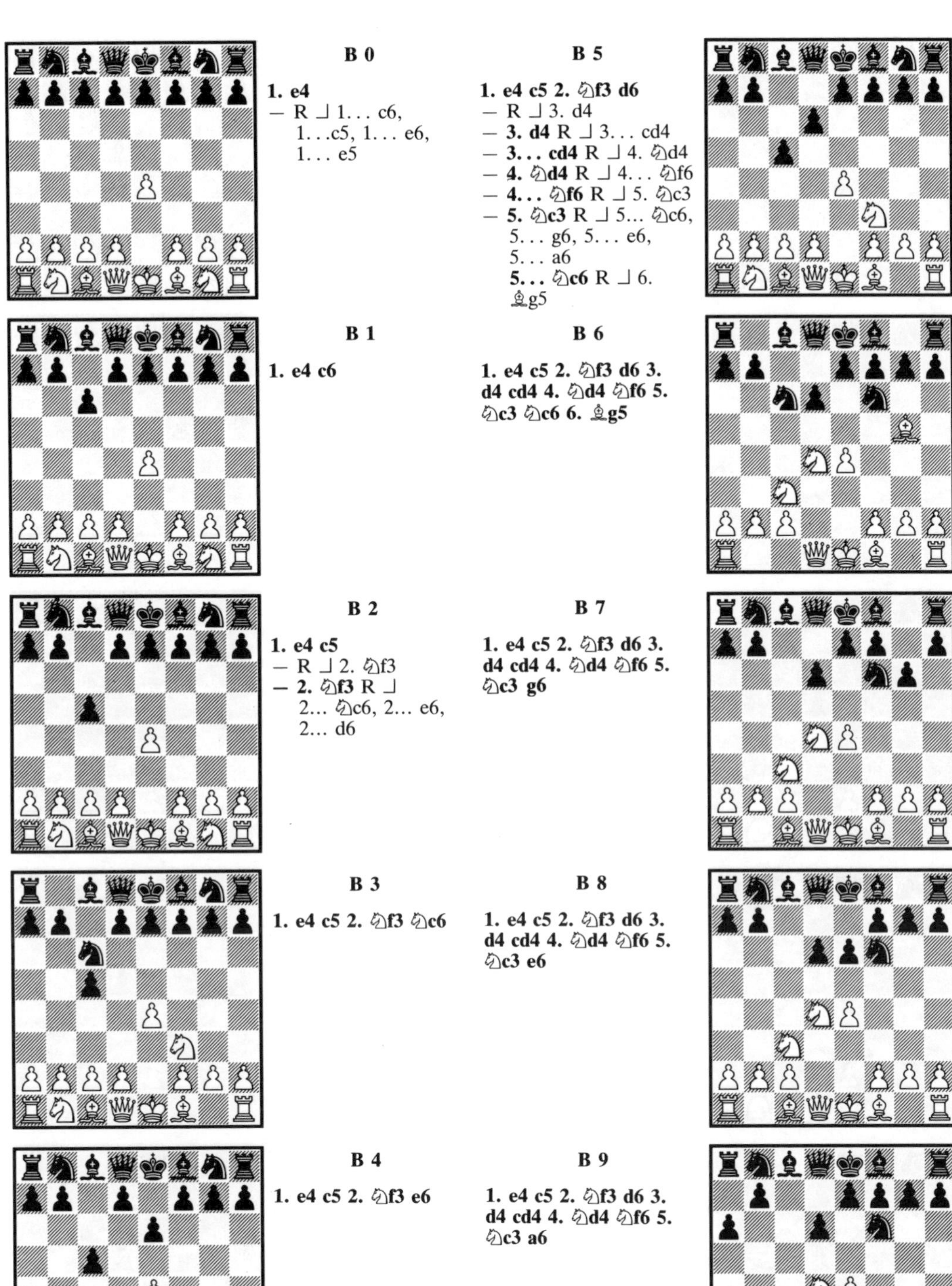

B 0

1. e4
– R ┘ 1... c6, 1...c5, 1... e6, 1... e5

B 1

1. e4 c6

B 2

1. e4 c5
– R ┘ 2. ♘f3
– **2. ♘f3** R ┘ 2... ♘c6, 2... e6, 2... d6

B 3

1. e4 c5 2. ♘f3 ♘c6

B 4

1. e4 c5 2. ♘f3 e6

B 5

1. e4 c5 2. ♘f3 d6
– R ┘ 3. d4
– **3. d4** R ┘ 3... cd4
– **3... cd4** R ┘ 4. ♘d4
– **4. ♘d4** R ┘ 4... ♘f6
– **4... ♘f6** R ┘ 5. ♘c3
– **5. ♘c3** R ┘ 5... ♘c6, 5... g6, 5... e6, 5... a6
5... ♘c6 R ┘ 6. ♗g5

B 6

1. e4 c5 2. ♘f3 d6 3. d4 cd4 4. ♘d4 ♘f6 5. ♘c3 ♘c6 6. ♗g5

B 7

1. e4 c5 2. ♘f3 d6 3. d4 cd4 4. ♘d4 ♘f6 5. ♘c3 g6

B 8

1. e4 c5 2. ♘f3 d6 3. d4 cd4 4. ♘d4 ♘f6 5. ♘c3 e6

B 9

1. e4 c5 2. ♘f3 d6 3. d4 cd4 4. ♘d4 ♘f6 5. ♘c3 a6

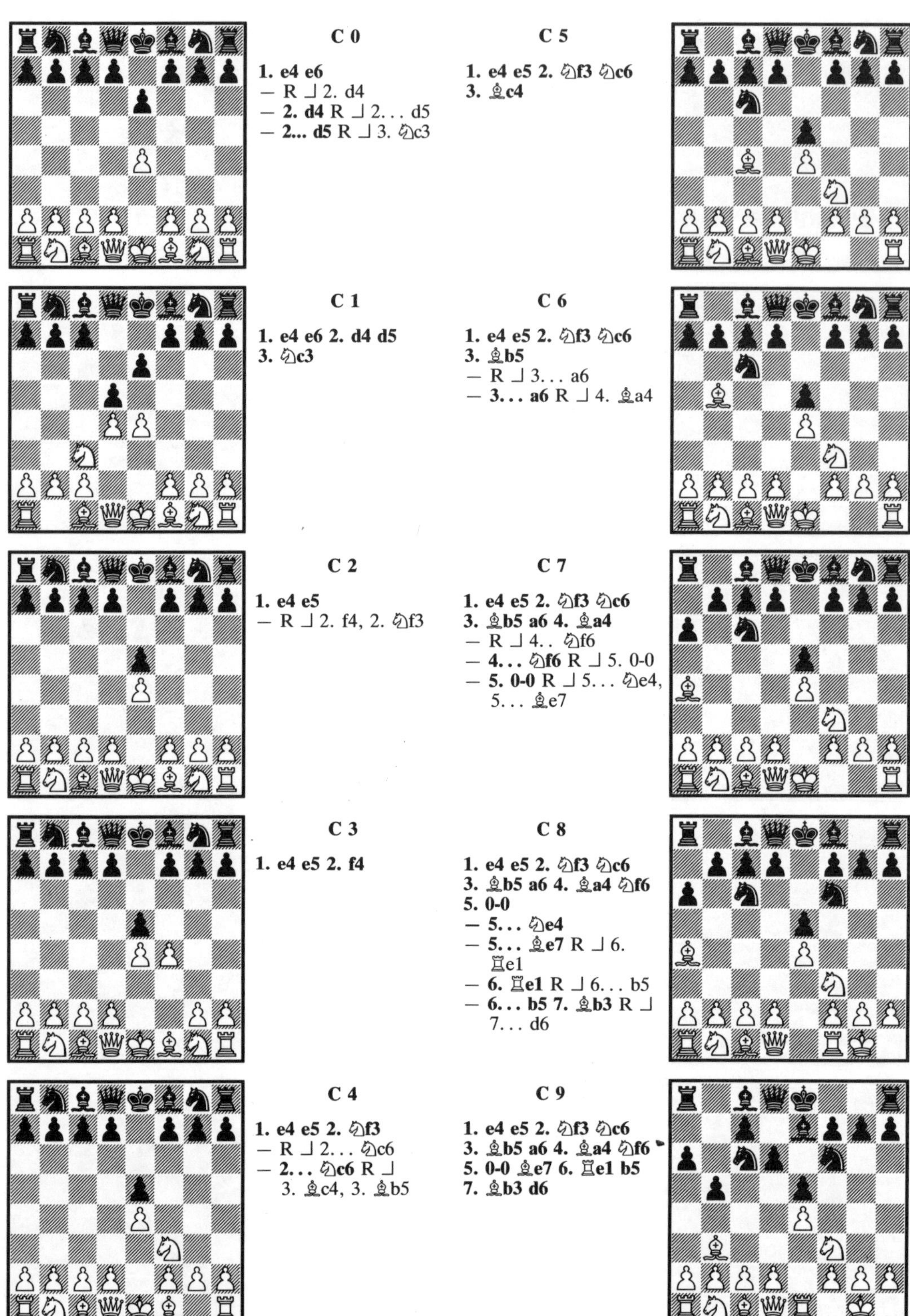

C 0

1. e4 e6
— R ┘ 2. d4
— **2. d4** R ┘ 2. . . d5
— **2... d5** R ┘ 3. ♘c3

C 1

1. e4 e6 2. d4 d5
3. ♘c3

C 2

1. e4 e5
— R ┘ 2. f4, 2. ♘f3

C 3

1. e4 e5 2. f4

C 4

1. e4 e5 2. ♘f3
— R ┘ 2. . . ♘c6
— **2. . . ♘c6** R ┘ 3. ♗c4, 3. ♗b5

C 5

1. e4 e5 2. ♘f3 ♘c6
3. ♗c4

C 6

1. e4 e5 2. ♘f3 ♘c6
3. ♗b5
— R ┘ 3. . . a6
— **3. . . a6** R ┘ 4. ♗a4

C 7

1. e4 e5 2. ♘f3 ♘c6
3. ♗b5 a6 4. ♗a4
— R ┘ 4. . ♘f6
— **4. . . ♘f6** R ┘ 5. 0-0
— **5. 0-0** R ┘ 5. . . ♘e4, 5. . . ♗e7

C 8

1. e4 e5 2. ♘f3 ♘c6
3. ♗b5 a6 4. ♗a4 ♘f6
5. 0-0
— **5. . . ♘e4**
— **5. . . ♗e7** R ┘ 6. ♖e1
— **6. ♖e1** R ┘ 6. . . b5
— **6. . . b5 7. ♗b3** R ┘ 7. . . d6

C 9

1. e4 e5 2. ♘f3 ♘c6
3. ♗b5 a6 4. ♗a4 ♘f6
5. 0-0 ♗e7 6. ♖e1 b5
7. ♗b3 d6

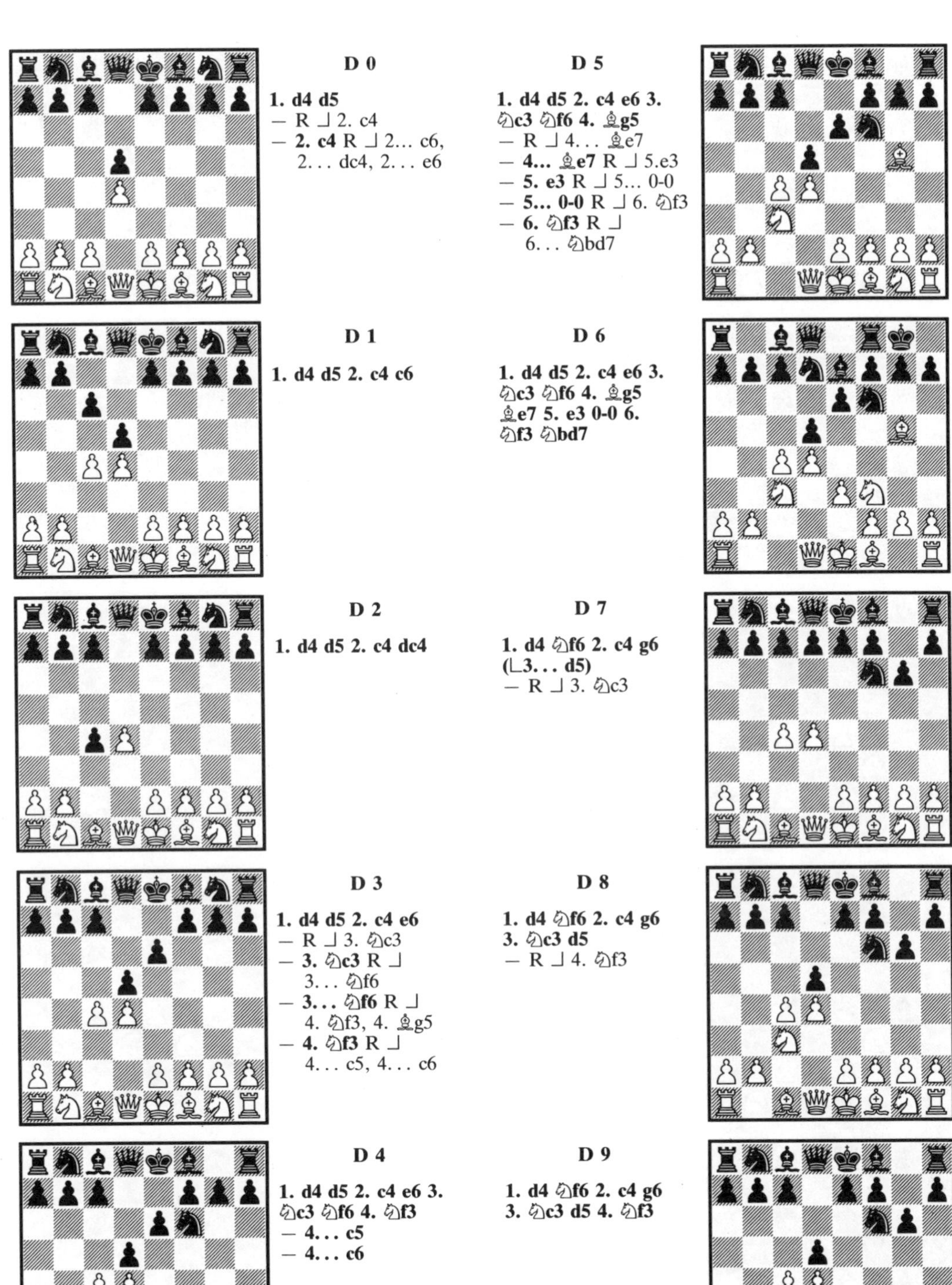

D 0

1. d4 d5
— R ┘ 2. c4
— **2. c4** R ┘ 2... c6, 2. . . dc4, 2. . . e6

D 1

1. d4 d5 2. c4 c6

D 2

1. d4 d5 2. c4 dc4

D 3

1. d4 d5 2. c4 e6
— R ┘ 3. ♘c3
— **3. ♘c3** R ┘ 3. . . ♘f6
— **3. . . ♘f6** R ┘ 4. ♘f3, 4. ♗g5
— **4. ♘f3** R ┘ 4. . . c5, 4. . . c6

D 4

1. d4 d5 2. c4 e6 3. ♘c3 ♘f6 4. ♘f3
— **4. . . c5**
— **4. . . c6**

D 5

1. d4 d5 2. c4 e6 3. ♘c3 ♘f6 4. ♗g5
— R ┘ 4. . . ♗e7
— **4... ♗e7** R ┘ 5.e3
— **5. e3** R ┘ 5... 0-0
— **5... 0-0** R ┘ 6. ♘f3
— **6. ♘f3** R ┘ 6. . . ♘bd7

D 6

1. d4 d5 2. c4 e6 3. ♘c3 ♘f6 4. ♗g5 ♗e7 5. e3 0-0 6. ♘f3 ♘bd7

D 7

1. d4 ♘f6 2. c4 g6 (└3. . . d5)
— R ┘ 3. ♘c3

D 8

1. d4 ♘f6 2. c4 g6 3. ♘c3 d5
— R ┘ 4. ♘f3

D 9

1. d4 ♘f6 2. c4 g6 3. ♘c3 d5 4. ♘f3

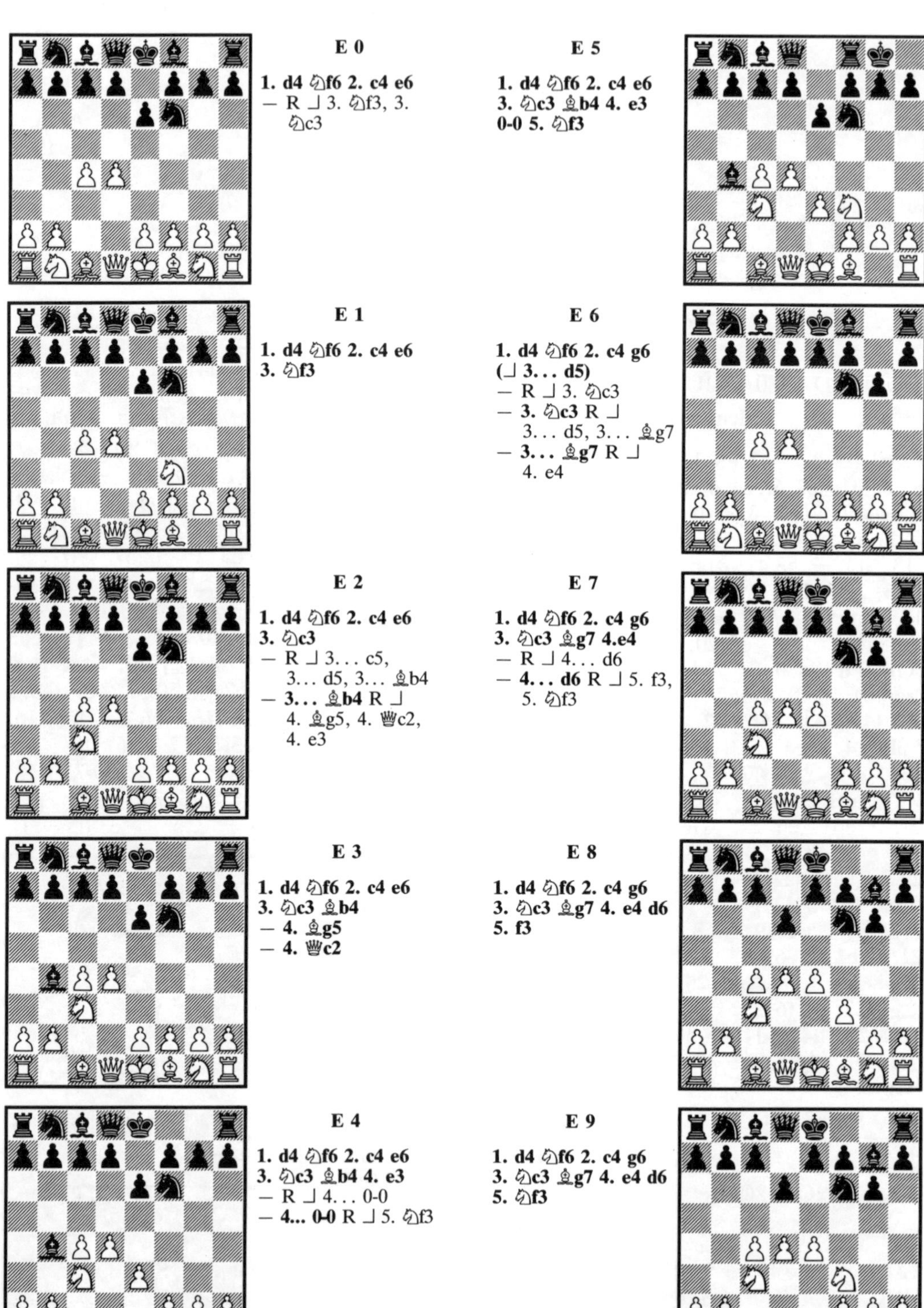

E 0

1. d4 ♘f6 2. c4 e6
— R ┘ 3. ♘f3, 3. ♘c3

E 1

1. d4 ♘f6 2. c4 e6 3. ♘f3

E 2

1. d4 ♘f6 2. c4 e6 3. ♘c3
— R ┘ 3. . . c5, 3… d5, 3. . . ♗b4
— **3. . . ♗b4** R ┘ 4. ♗g5, 4. ♕c2, 4. e3

E 3

1. d4 ♘f6 2. c4 e6 3. ♘c3 ♗b4
— **4. ♗g5**
— **4. ♕c2**

E 4

1. d4 ♘f6 2. c4 e6 3. ♘c3 ♗b4 4. e3
— R ┘ 4. . . 0-0
— **4... 0-0** R ┘ 5. ♘f3

E 5

1. d4 ♘f6 2. c4 e6 3. ♘c3 ♗b4 4. e3 0-0 5. ♘f3

E 6

1. d4 ♘f6 2. c4 g6 (┘ 3. . . d5)
— R ┘ 3. ♘c3
— **3. ♘c3** R ┘ 3. . . d5, 3. . . ♗g7
— **3. . . ♗g7** R ┘ 4. e4

E 7

1. d4 ♘f6 2. c4 g6 3. ♘c3 ♗g7 4.e4
— R ┘ 4. . . d6
— **4. . . d6** R ┘ 5. f3, 5. ♘f3

E 8

1. d4 ♘f6 2. c4 g6 3. ♘c3 ♗g7 4. e4 d6 5. f3

E 9

1. d4 ♘f6 2. c4 g6 3. ♘c3 ♗g7 4. e4 d6 5. ♘f3

A

1.* A 07

GUFEL'D 2480 – JU. HODGSON 2565
Calcutta 1993

1. g3 d5 2. ♗g2 e5 3. d3 g6 4. ♘f3 ♗g7 5. 0–0 ♘e7 6. e4 0–0 7. ♘bd2 h6 8. c3 ♘bc6 9. ♖e1 ♗e6 N [9... ♖e8 10. ed5 ♘d5 11. ♘c4 a5 12. a4 ♗f5 13. ♘h4 N (13. h3 – 53/4) ♗e6 14. ♗d2 ♕d7 15. ♘f3 ♗f5 16. ♕b3!? ♖ad8 (16... ♗d3?! 17. ♘fe5!) 17. ♖ad1? ♗d3! 18. ♘ce5?! ♘e5 19. ♘e5 ♖e5 20. ♖e5 ♗e5 21. ♗h6 (Gufel'd 2480 – Adams 2630, Hastings (rapid) 1993) ♘b6∓; 17. ♗f1=] **10. ♕c2 a5 11. b3± g5!? 12. ♗a3 ♖e8 13. ed5 ♘d5 14. ♘c4 ♘c3! 15. ♘ce5** [15. ♕c3 e4 16. ♘fe5 ♗c4 17. ♕c4 ♘e5 (17... ♗e5?! 18. ♖ad1 ed3 19. ♖d3 ♕f6 20. ♖f3! ♕e6 21. ♕e6 ♖e6 22. ♖fe3±) 18. ♕e4 ♘d3 19. ♕e8 ♕e8 20. ♖e8 ♖e8 21. ♖d1 ♘b4 22. ♗b7 ♘a2 23. ♖d7±] **♘b5 16. ♗b2 ♘b4 17. ♕d2 g4!?= 18. ♘g4?** [18. ♘h4 ♕g5∞] **♗g4 19. ♖e8 ♕e8 20. ♗g7 ♔g7 21. ♖e1 ♗e6! 22. ♘e5 c6!∓ 23. ♘g4?! ♗g4 24. ♖e8 ♖e8 25. h3⊕ ♗f5! 26. g4 ♗g6 27. f4 f6 28. f5?** [28. g5!?; 28. h4!?] **♗f7 29. h4 ♘d4–+ 30. g5 ♘d5 31. ♕f2 ♘e2 32. ♔h2 hg5 33. hg5 ♖h8 0 : 1 [Gufel'd]**

2.* A 08

KAJDANOV 2620 – A. ZAPATA 2580
New York 1993

1. e4 c5 2. ♘f3 e6 3. d3 d5 4. ♘bd2 ♘c6 [RR 4... ♘f6 5. g3 b6 6. ♗g2 ♘c6 7. 0–0 ♗e7 8. ♖e1 ♗b7 9. c3 ♕c7 10. e5 (10. ♕e2 – 33/10) ♘d7 11. ♘f1!? N (11. ♕e2 g5! 12. g4 h5 13. h3 hg4 14. hg4 0-0-0 △ ♖dg8∓; 11. d4) ♘ce5?! 12. ♘e5 ♘e5 13. ♗f4 ♗d6 14. ♗e5 ♗e5 15. ♕h5 *a)* 15... ♗f6? 16. ♖e6 ♔f8 17. ♖f6! gf6 18. ♕h6 ♔e7 (18... ♔g8 19. ♘e3 △ ♘g4+–) 19. ♖e1 ♔d7 20. ♕f6+– Nadirhanov 2450 – Saltaev 2470, Taškent 1993; *b)* 15... ♗d6 16. ♖e6 ♔f8 17. ♖e2± △ 17... d4 18. cd4 cd4 19. ♗b7 ♕b7 20. ♖c1 ♖c8 21. ♕d5!±; ⌓ 11... 0-0-0 Nadirhanov] **5. g3 g6 6. ♗g2 ♗g7 7. 0–0 ♘ge7 8. ♖e1 b6 9. c3 a5 10. a4 ♗a6 11. ed5 ♘d5** [11... ed5 12. ♘f1±] **12. ♘c4 0–0 13. h4!? N** [13. ♕e2 – 50/3] **♕c7** [13... h6!?] **14. h5 ♖ad8 15. ♕e2 ♖fe8 16. hg6 hg6 17. ♘g5 e5!?** [17... f6? 18. ♘e6 ♕d7 19. ♗h3 △ ♕f1+–; 17... ♗b7!?] **18. ♕e4 ♗b7 19. ♕h4 ♘f6 20. ♘e4 ♘h7!** [20... ♘e4 21. de4 △ ♗g5, ♘e3-d5+–]

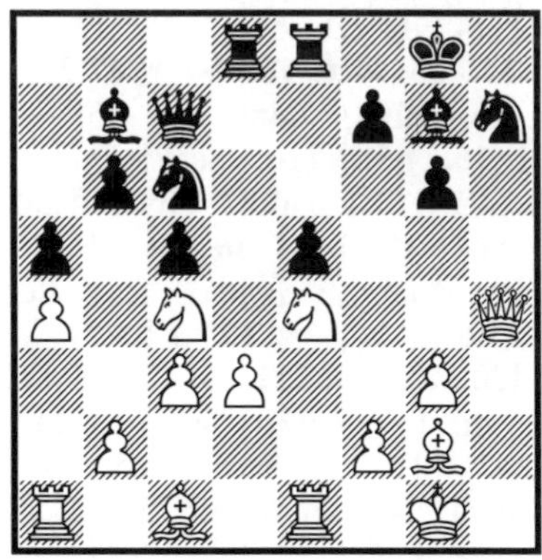

21. g4!! [△ ♖e3-h3; 21. ♖e3 f5! 22. ♘g5 ♘g5 23. ♕g5 ♔f7 △ ♗f6, ♖h8] **♖d3 22. ♗f1 ♖d7** [22... ♖dd8 23. ♖e3 ♕e7 24. g5 ♗c8 25. ♘b6 ♗e6 26. ♖e1! △ ♗e3± ×c5] **23. ♖e3 ♘d8?** [23... g5! (D. Gurevich) 24. ♘g5 (24. ♕h5?! ♘d8) ♘g5

25. ♕g5 ♖d1? 26. ♖d3 ♖d8?! 27. ♖d1 ♖d1 28. ♘e3 ♖e1 29. ♘f5 f6 30. ♕g6 △ ♗h6+−; 25... ♘d8!?; 25... e4!?∞] **24. ♖h3+− ♗e4 25. ♕h7 ♔f8 26. ♗h6 f6 27. ♖e1** [27. ♕h8?? ♔f7 28. ♕g7 ♔e6+−] **♕b7 28. g5! fg5 29. ♕h8**
1 : 0 **[Kajdanov]**

3.** **A 11**

ANIĆ 2415 – SKEMBRIS 2560
Cannes 1993

1. ♘f3 ♘f6 2. c4 c6 3. g3 d5 4. b3 [RR 4. ♗g2 dc4 5. ♕c2 b5 6. a4 N (6. b3 – 14/40) ♗b7 7. b3 cb3 8. ♕b3 a6 9. ♗a3 ♘bd7 10. 0–0 e6 11. ♗f8 ♔f8 12. ♖c1 ♕b6 13. ♘a3 g6 14. ♕b2 ♔g7 15. ♘c4 bc4 16. ♕b6 ♘b6 17. ♖ab1 ♘fd7 18. a5=∞ V. Salov 2660 – Anand 2710, Linares 1993] **g6 5. ♗b2 ♗g7 6. ♗g2 0–0 7. 0–0 e6!? N** [7... a5 8. ♘a3!?⩲; 7... ♘bd7 8. d3 (8. cd5!?) ♖e8 9. ♘bd2 (9. ♘c3 e5 10. cd5 cd5 11. ♖c1 a6!? 12. ♘a4 e4⇆) e5 10. cd5 ♘d5 11. e4!? N (11. ♘c4 ♕e7=) ♘5b6 12. a4 ♘c5 13. a5!⩲ Nalbandian 2405 – Papaioannou 2335, Sas van Gent 1992] **8. d3 ♘bd7 9. ♕c2** [9. cd5 ed5∞] **♖e8 10. ♘bd2** [10. ♘c3!?] **e5 11. cd5 ♘d5!?** [×♕c2; 11... cd5 12. e4⩲] **12. e4** [12. ♘c4 ♕e7=; 12. a3!? ♕e7 13. e4 ♘c7 14. d4 ed4∞] **♘b4!? 13. ♕c3 c5** [×d4] **14. a3 ♘c6 15. b4 ♕e7!?∞** [15... b6 (△ 16. ♘b3 ♘d4⇆) 16. b5!?→; 15... ♘b6!?] **16. b5!?** [16. bc5?! ♘c5∓ ×a4, d4; 16. ♘c4!?∞] **♘d8!?** [16... ♘d4?! 17. ♘d4⩲ ×c4] **17. ♘c4 b6 18. a4** [△ a5→] **a5!⇆ 19. ♕a3** [△ ♖ad1, ♕a1 ×e5; 19. ba6?! ♗a6 △ ♘c6→; 19. ♗h3!?] **♖b8 20. ♖ad1** [20. ♗h3 f6!?] **f6! 21. ♘e1!?** [△ ♘c2-e3 ×d5] **♘f7 22. ♘c2 ♘f8 23. ♘2e3 ♗e6 24. f4!?** [△ ♕a1 ×e5; 24. ♕a1 ♘d6⇆ ×c4; 24. ♘d5 ♗d5 25. ed5 ♘d6∞] **♗c4!?** [24... ♘d6?! 25. fe5±] **25. ♘c4** [×b6; 25. dc4!? (×d5) ♖bd8!? (△ ♘e6, ♖d4∞; 25... ♘e6? 26. ♘d5 ♕b7 27. f5±) 26. ♘d5 ♕b7 △ ♘d6, ♘e6⇆] **♘e6∞ 26. ♗h3** [26. ♘e3!?∞; 26. f5!?∞] **ef4 27. gf4** [27. ♗e6 ♕e6 28. ♖f4 (28. gf4 f5⇆) ♘g5→] **f5!→ 28. ef5** [28. e5?! ♖ed8∓ ×d3, f4, ♔g1; 28. ♗g7 ♔g7!? 29. ♕b2 ♘d4 30. ef5 ♕h4=∞] **♘d4! 29. fg6 hg6 30. ♖d2?!** [30. ♖de1? ♘f3−+; 30. ♗d4 ♗d4 31. ♔h1 ♕h4→; 30. ♔h1 ♕h4=∞] **♕h4∓ 31. ♗g2??⊕** [31. ♔g2∓] **♘e2−+ 32. ♖e2** [32. ♔h1 ♘g3] **♖e2 33. ♗g7 ♕g4! 34. ♖f2** [34. ♘e3 ♖e3 35. ♕b2 ♖e2] **♖f2 35. ♔f2 ♕f4 36. ♔g1 ♔g7 37. ♗e4** [37. ♕b2 ♕d4] **♘g5 38. ♕b2 ♕f6?!⊕** [38... ♔h6 △ ♖f8−+ ×♔g1] **39. ♕f6 ♔f6 40. ♔f2 ♘f7 41. ♔g3 ♘e5 42. ♘e3** [42. ♘e5 ♔e5 △ 43. ♗g6? ♖g8−+] **g5 43. h3 ♔e6 44. ♗d5** [44. ♘d5 ♘d3−+] **♔d6 45. ♗e4 ♖f8!⊙ 46. ♗f5 ♖d8! 47. ♗e4 ♔e6** [×d3, d4] **48. ♗f5 ♔f7! 49. ♗e4 ♖d4** **0 : 1**
[Skembris]

4. !N **A 12**

K. SPRAGGETT 2565
– DORFMAN 2580
Cannes 1993

1. ♘f3 d5 2. g3 c6 3. b3 ♗g4 4. ♗g2 ♘d7 5. ♗b2 ♘gf6 6. 0–0 e6 [6... ♗f3!? 7. ♗f3 e5] **7. c4 ♗d6 8. ♘a3 0–0 9. ♘c2 ♗f3! N** [9... ♖e8 10. d3 – 54/8] **10. ♗f3** [10. ef3? dc4 11. bc4 e5∓] **♘e5 11. ♗e5** [11. ♗g2 dc4 12. f4 ♗c5 13. e3 cb3 (13... ♘d3 14. ♗f6 ♕f6 15. bc4±) 14. fe5 bc2 15. ♕c2 ♘d7 16. d4=∞] **♗e5 12. d4 ♗d6 13. ♕d3 ♖e8?!** [13... ♕c7 △ e5 K. Spraggett] **14. ♖fd1 e5 15. de5 ♗e5 16. ♖ac1 dc4 17. ♕c4 ♕e7** [17... ♕b6 △ ♖ad8] **18. b4 a6** [18... ♖ad8 19. b5 cb5 20. ♕b5 b6 21. ♘b4±] **19. a4 g6 20. ♘e3** [20. b5?! cb5 21. ab5 ♖ac8 22. ♕b3 ab5 23. ♕b5 ♖c5∓; 20. ♘d4!?] **♘d7!** [△ ♗b2, ♘e5] **21. ♕b3 ♘b6!⊕** [21... ♗g7? 22. ♘c4 ♘e5 23. ♘e5 ♗e5 24. b5±□] **22. ♖d3** [22. ♘c4 ♕e6=] **♖ad8 23. ♖cd1 ♖d3 24. ♖d3 ♖d8 25. ♖d8 ♕d8 26. b5 ab5 27. ab5 ♕c7 28. bc6 bc6 29. ♘g4 ♗d4!** [29... ♗g7 30. ♕e3 h5 31. ♕e8 ♗f8 32. ♘e3±] **30. ♘h6** [30. e3 ♗g7] **♔g7 31. e3 ♗e5 32. ♘g4** [32. ♘f7? ♕f7] **♘d7 33. ♘e5 ♘e5 34. ♕c3 c5** [34... ♔g8] **35. ♗d5 ♔g8 36. e4 ♘d7** [37. f4!? ♘b6 38. ♕f6 ♘d5 39. ed5 c4 40. d6 ♕c5=] **1/2 : 1/2**
[Dorfman]

5.* **A 12**

JA. NESTEROV 2445 – NENAŠEV 2565

Biškek (zt) 1993

1. ♘f3 ♘f6 2. g3 d5 3. ♗g2 c6 4. 0–0 ♗g4 5. b3 ♘bd7 6. ♗b2 e6 7. d3 ♗d6 8. c4 0–0 9. ♘a3 [RR 9. ♘bd2 ♕e7 (9... e5!? 10. cd5 cd5 11. e4 ♖e8=) 10. a3 a5 11. cd5!? N (11. h3 — 20/27) ed5 (11... cd5!? 12. ♘d4 ♕d8 13. ♘2f3 ♕b6 14. ♖c1 e5 15. h3!?∞; 13. h3!? △ ♘2f3 ×f5) 12. h3 ♗h5 (12... ♗f3 13. ♘f3 ♖fe8 14. e3±) 13. ♘d4 ♗g6!? (13... ♖fe8 14. ♘f5 ♕e6 15. ♘d6 ♗e2? 16. ♘e8!□ ♗d1 17. ♘f6 ♘f6 18. ♖ad1±; 15... ♕d6 △ c5, d4⩲) 14. ♘2f3 (14. e4 ♘c5!) ♖fe8 (14... ♘e5 15. ♘h4 △ 15... ♕d7? 16. f4) 15. ♘h4 ♕d8 *a)* 16. ♘df5?! ♗f8 17. ♕c2 ♗f5!□ 18. ♘f5 g6! 19. ♘d4 ♗g7 20. e3 ♘e5 21. ♖ad1 ♕b6 22. ♘e2 (Nalbandian 2405 – Borovikov, Sas van Gent 1992) h5 △ h4∓; *b)* 16. ♕c2 c5?! 17. ♘b5 ♗e5 18. ♗e5 ♖e5 19. ♘g6 hg6 20. d4±; 16... ♕b6 △ ♗e5∞ Nalbandian] **♖e8 10. ♘c2 dc4!? N** [10... a5 — 54/8] **11. bc4** [11. dc4 ♕c7 12. ♘e3 ♗f3 13. ♗f3 ♗e5=] **e5 12. ♘e3** [12. ♘d2!?] **♗f3 13. ♗f3 ♗c5 14. ♘g4?!** [14. ♗g2?! ♗e3 15. fe3 ♘g4 16. ♕d2 ♕b6 17. ♗c1 e4∓; 14. ♕d2 e4!? 15. de4 (15. ♗e4 ♘e4 16. de4 ♘e5 17. ♕c3 ♗e3 18. fe3∓) ♘e5 16. ♕d8 (16. ♕c3 ♗e3 17. fe3∓) ♖ad8 17. ♘f5 g6 18. ♘h4 ♗d4 19. ♖ab1 b6 20. ♖fc1 ♗b2 21. ♖b2 ♖d4 22. ♖bc2 ♘ed7∓] **♗d4 15. ♖b1 ♗b2 16. ♖b2 ♘c5** [16... ♘g4!? 17. ♗g4 ♘f6 18. ♗f3 ♕c7∓] **17. ♖d2 ♘g4 18. ♗g4 ♕d4?!** [18... ♕g5 19. ♗f3 ♖ad8 20. e3 ♖d6 21. ♕c2 ♖ed8 22. ♖fd1 ♕f5 23. ♗e2∓] **19. e3 ♕c3 20. ♕c1 ♕c1 21. ♖c1 ♖ad8 22. ♖cd1 ♖d6 23. ♔f1** [23. d4!?] **♔f8** [23... g6!?] **24. ♔e2** [24. d4!?] **g6 25. ♗f3 f5 26. ♗g2?!** [⌓ 26. d4] **♔f7?!** [26... e4 27. d4 (27. de4 ♖d2 28. ♖d2 fe4∓) ♘a4 28. ♔e1 c5∓] **27. d4 ed4 28. ♖d4 ♖d4 29. ♖d4= ♔e7 30. f4 ♖d8** [30... ♖c8!? △ b5] **31. ♖d8 ♔d8 32. ♗f3 h5** [△ 33. h3 ♔e7 34. g4 h4 ×h3; 32... ♔e7 33. g4 ♔d6 34. gf5 gf5 35. ♔d2=] **33. ♔d2 ♔e7 34. ♔c3 ♔d6 35. ♔d4 b6** [35... b5?? 36. cb5 cb5 37. ♗d5+–; 35... ♘e6 36. ♔c3 ♔c5 37. e4 ♘d4 38. ef5! ♘f5 39. ♗e4=] **36. e4⊕ ♘e4⊕ 37. ♗e4 fe4 38. h3 h4 39. g4** [39. gh4?? ♔e6 40. ♔e4 ♔f6–+] **♔e6 40. ♔e4 a6 41. ♔d4 c5**
1/2 : 1/2 **[Nenašev]**

6.* **!N** **A 13**

O. RENET 2535 –
VAN DER WIEL 2555

Bruxelles (zt) 1993

1. c4 e6 2. ♘c3 ♗b4 3. ♕b3 [RR 3. e4 c5 4. f4!? N (4. ♘b5 — 33/13) d6 5. ♘f3 ♘f6 6. ♗d3 0–0 7. 0–0 ♘c6 8. b3 ♗c3 9. dc3 ♘e8 10. f5 ef5 11. ef5 ♘e5 12. ♗c2±○⊞ Kamsky 2655 – Zarnicki 2470, Buenos Aires 1993] **♘c6** [3... c5? 4. ♘b5! △ ♕g3→; 3... a5; 3... ♕e7] **4. a3** [⌓ 4. ♘f3] **♘d4! N** [4... ♗e7; 4... ♗c3 — 56/(9)] **5. ♕a4** [5. ♕d1 △ 5... ♗c3 6. bc3 ♘c6 7. d4] **♗c3 6. dc3 ♘c6 7. e4!?** [7. ♘f3; 7. g3] **♕h4!↑ 8. ♗d3** [8. ♕c2? ♘f6 9. ♗d3 ♘e5 ×e4] **♘e5 9. ♗c2 ♘f6** [9... ♕g4 10. g3 (△ ♗f4) ♘f3 11. ♘f3 ♕f3 12. 0–0⩲] **10. c5!?** [10. g3 ♕h5!; 10. ♕a5 ♘fg4 11. g3 ♕f6 12. f4 b6 13. ♕a4 ♗b7!? 14. h3 ♕g6 15. hg4 ♗e4 16. ♖h2 ♘g4$\overline{\overline{\infty}}$] **♕g4** [10... 0–0 11. ♕d4] **11. ♔f1?!** [11. g3 ♘f3 12. ♘f3 ♕f3 13. 0–0 ♕h5! 14. ♕d4 b6 15. cb6 ab6 16. f3 d6 17. ♗e3=] **♕h5! 12. ♘h3?** [△ 12... ♘g6?! 13. ♗g5; ⌓ 12. ♘e2 ♘c6 13. b4 0–0∓; ⌓ 12. f3 △ ♗e3] **♘c6!∓ 13. b4?!** [13. ♗e3? ♘g4; 13. ♕c4?! b6; ⌓ 13. ♗g5 h6 14. ♗f6 gf6∓] **♕e5 14. ♕b3** [⌓ 14. ♗f4 ♕c3 15. ♖d1] **♘e4 15. f4** [15. ♗f4 ♕f4 16. ♘f4 ♘d2–+] **♕c3 16. ♕c3 ♘c3 17. ♗b2 ♘d5 18. ♗g7?** [18. ♔f2] **♖g8** [19. ♗b2 ♘e3 20. ♔f2 ♘c2 21. ♖ad1! b5! (21... ♘2b4 22. ab4 ♘b4 23. ♘g5↑; 21... b6 22. b5 ♘a5 23. ♖c1) 22. ♘g5 ♗b7–+]
0 : 1 **[van der Wiel]**

7. **A 13**

M. MAKAROV 2510 –
G. GEORGADZE 2525

Podol'sk 1992

1. c4 e6 2. ♘f3 d5 3. b3 ♗e7!? 4. ♗b2 ♗f6 5. d4 [5. ♕c2 ♗b2 6. ♕b2 ♘f6=]

♘**e7!? N** [5... c5!?; RR 5... dc4 6. bc4 c5 △ 7. e4?! cd4 8. e5? ♗e5 9. ♘e5 ♕a5 10. ♘d2 ♕e5 11. ♗e2 ♘c6∓ G. Georgadze] **6.** ♘**bd2 0–0** [6... c5? 7. e4±] **7. e4 g6 8.** ♗**e2** [8. ♕c2!?] ♗**g7 9. 0–0** [9. e5 c5 (RR 9... f6?! 10. ef6 ♗f6 11. 0–0 ♘bc6⩲ G. Georgadze) 10. dc5 ♘ec6∞] **c5 10. e5** [10. ♖b1 cd4 11. ♗d4 ♗d4 12. ♘d4 ♕b6=; 10. ♖c1!? cd4 11. ♗d4 ♗d4 12. ♘d4±] **cd4 11.** ♘**d4** [RR 11. ♗d4 ♘bc6 12. ♗b2 d4 13. ♘e4 ♘e5 14. ♘d4 ♘7c6 15. ♘c6 ♘c6= G. Georgadze] ♗**e5 12.** ♘**e6** ♗**h2 13.** ♔**h2** ♗**e6 14.** ♘**f3** ♘**bc6!** [14... dc4 15. ♕c1 ♘bc6 16. ♖h1!=/∞→»] **15.** ♖**h1 f6! 16.** ♔**g1** ♖**f7 17.** ♕**c2 dc4 18.** ♖**d1** ♕**b6?!** [⌓ 18... ♕c7] **19. bc4** [19. ♖d6 (G. Georgadze) cb3 20. ♕c1 ♗d5 (20... ♘f5 21. ♖e6 ♘cd4 22. ♘d4 ♘d4 23. ♗d4 ♕e6 24. ♗c4 ♖c8 25. ab3!+–) 21. ♖f6 ♖f6 (21... ba2 22. ♖f7 ♗f7 23. ♕c3 ♔f8 24. ♖h7±) 22. ♗f6 ♘f5! △ ♘cd4∓; 19. ♗c4 ♘b4! 20. ♕e2 ♗c4 21. ♕c4 ♖c8∞] ♖**d8 20.** ♖**d8** ♕**d8 21.** ♕**c3** ♘**f5** [21... ♕a5 22. ♕a5 ♘a5 23. ♘d2 △ ♗c3, ♘e4=/∞] **22.** ♔**h2** ♕**a5 23.** ♖**d1** ♕**c3 24.** ♗**c3** ♔**f8?!** [24... h5!? △ b6∓] **25.** ♖**d2!** [25. g4? ♘h6 26. g5 fg5 27. ♘g5 ♖f2] **h5** [25... b6 26. g4 △ g5=/∞] **26. c5** ♘**fe7 27.** ♘**d4**□ ♘**d4 28.** ♗**d4** ♔**g7** [28... ♗d5 29. c6! ♗c6 30. ♗a7] **29.** ♗**f3** ♗**d5 30.** ♗**f6** ♖**f6 31.** ♗**d5** ♘**d5 32.** ♖**d5** ♖**f2 33. a4** ♖**f5 34.** ♖**d7** ♖**f7 35.** ♖**d5** ♖**f5⊕ 36.** ♖**d7** ♖**f7 37.** ♖**d5** ♔**f6 38.** ♔**g3** ♔**e6 39.** ♖**d6** ♔**f5 40. a5 a6 41. c6 bc6 42.** ♖**c6** ♖**f6 43.** ♖**c5** ♔**e4 44.** ♔**h4** ♔**d4 45.** ♖**c2** ♖**f4 46.** ♔**g3** ♖**g4 47.** ♔**f3** ♖**g5 48.** ♖**c6** ♖**a5 49.** ♖**g6** ♖**f5 50.** ♔**e2 a5 51. g4!= hg4 52.** ♖**g4** ♔**c3 53.** ♖**g8!** ♖**d5 54.** ♖**c8** ♔**b3 55.** ♖**b8 1/2 : 1/2 [M. Makarov]**

8. **A 13**

B. GEL'FAND 2690 – ŠIROV 2670

Linares 1993

1. c4 e6 2. ♘**f3 d5 3. g3 c6 4. b3!? a5!? N** [4... b5 – 17/36; 4... ♘f6] **5.** ♗**b2 a4 6.** ♗**g2** [6. ba4 ♘d7=/∞] **a3!? 7.** ♗**c3 b5?** [7... ♘f6 △ b5∞] **8. c5!±** ♘**f6 9. b4** [⌓ 9. d4 ♘e4 10. ♗b4±] ♘**e4!? 10. 0–0?!** [10. ♕b3!±] ♘**c3 11.** ♘**c3?** [11. dc3 g5!? 12. e4! (12. ♕b3 g4 13. ♘fd2 h5!∞) ♗g7 13. ed5 ed5□ 14. ♖e1 ♔f8±] **d4!∞ 12.** ♘**e4** [12. ♘b1!? ×a3] **f5! 13.** ♘**eg5** ♗**e7 14. h4!** ♗**f6!**

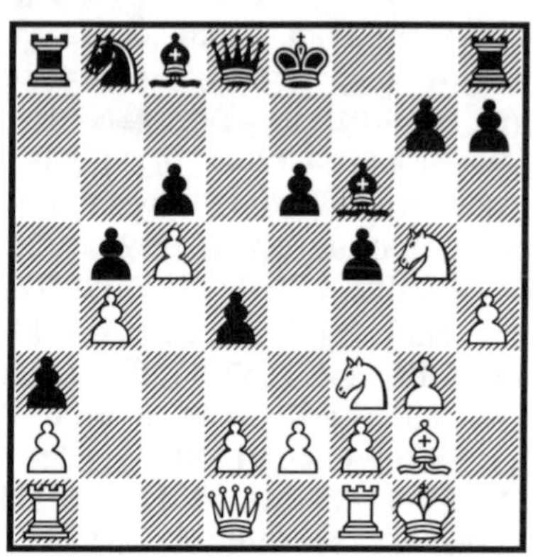

15. ♕**b3?!** [15. e3! h6 16. ♘h3 de3 17. de3 (17. fe3 g5!∞) ♗a1 18. ♕a1 0–0 19. ♘f4=/∞] ♕**d5 16.** ♕**b1?!** [16. ♕d3?! h6 17. ♘h7 (17. ♘h3 e5∓; 17. ♘e1 ♕d7 18. ♘gf3 ♖a4! 19. ♘c2 e5∓) ♗e7! (17... ♖h7? 18. ♘g5 hg5 19. ♗d5 ed5 20. hg5 ♗g5 21. ♔g2±) 18. ♘d4 ♕d7∓; 16. ♕c2! h6 17. ♘h3 e5 18. d3∓⇆] **h6 17.** ♘**h3 e5 18. e3** [18. d3 ♖a4∓] **de3!** [18... d3? 19. ♘d4! e4 20. ♘f4 ♕f7 21. h5!!± △ f3] **19. de3** [⌓ 19. fe3 e4 20. ♘f4 ♕d7 21. ♘d4 ♗d4 22. ed4 ♕d4∓] ♖**a4!∓** [×b4, ♘h3] **20.** ♘**d4** [20. ♖d1 ♕c4] ♕**d7 21.** ♘**c2 0–0 22. e4?!** [22. ♖d1 ♕f7 23. f4!?∓] **f4 23.** ♕**b3** ♕**f7 24.** ♕**f7** ♖**f7 25.** ♖**fd1 f3! 26.** ♗**f1 g5–+ 27.** ♖**d3** [27. ♔h2 g4 28. ♘g1 h5 ×♘g1, ♔h2] **g4 28.** ♔**h2** ♖**d7! 29.** ♖**ad1** [29. ♖a3 ♖a3 30. ♘a3 ♖d2] ♖**d3 30.** ♖**d3** ♗**e6** [×a2] **31.** ♖**d6** ♔**f7 32.** ♗**b5 cb5 33.** ♖**b6** ♘**a6 34.** ♖**b5** ♗**a2 35. c6** ♗**b1 36.** ♖**b7** ♔**e6 37.** ♘**a3** ♖**a3 38. b5** ♗**e4 39.** ♖**a7 gh3 40. c7⊕** [40... ♔d7]
0 : 1 **[Širov]**

9.* **A 13**

M. MAKAROV 2510
– SVEŠNIKOV 2525

Podol'sk 1992

1. c4 e6 2. g3 d5 3. ♗**g2** ♘**f6 4.** ♘**f3 dc4 5.** ♕**a4** ♘**bd7 6.** ♕**c4 c5 7. d3** ♗**d6** [RR

7... a6 8. ♕b3 ♖a7 (8... ♗d6 9. a4 △ a5) 9. ♘bd2!? N (9. 0–0 — 46/12; 9. a4 △ ♘a3-c4±) b6 *a)* 10. ♘c4 b5! 11. ♘ce5 *a1)* 11... ♗b7?! 12. ♘d7 (12. ♘f7?! ♔f7 13. ♘g5 ♔e8 14. ♗b7 ♖b7 15. ♕e6 ♕e7∓ △ 16. ♕a6 ♘b8) ♘d7 13. 0–0 ♗e7 14. a4 ♗d5 15. ♕c3! ♗f6 16. ♕c2 ba4 17. ♖a4 0–0 18. ♘d2 ♕a8 19. ♗e4! ♖b7 20. ♘c4 ♖b4 (20... ♗e7±) 21. ♗d5 ed5 (Anastasian 2470 – Svešnikov 2555, Rostov na Donu (open) 1993) 22. ♖b4! cb4 23. ♘a5!±; *a2)* 11... ♘e5! 12. ♘e5 ♗b7 13. ♗b7 ♖b7 14. a4 ♗d6 15. ♘c4 ♗c7=; *b)* 10. a4! ♗b7 11. ♘c4 ♗e7 12. ♗f4± Svešnikov] **8. a4 0–0 9. 0–0 b6!? N** [9... ♘b6 — 49/9] **10. ♘g5!? ♘e5□** [10... ♖b8? 11. ♘e6+–] **11. ♕c2 ♘d5!?** [11... ♖b8 12. f4 ♘g6 13. e4∞] **12. d4 ♘g6 13. ♘c3 ♗e7! 14. h4 cd4 15. ♘d5 ed5 16. ♘f3!** [16. ♘h7? ♔h7 17. h5 ♗g4 18. hg6 fg6∓] **♗f6 17. ♖d1 ♗g4 18. ♘d4 ♖c8 19. ♕b3 ♖c4 20. ♘f3! [△ ♗g5] h6 21. ♗e3 ♕e7 22. ♗d4** [22. ♖d5 ♖e4⇆] **♗d4 23. ♘d4 ♕e5 24. ♕d3 ♖fc8⇆ 25. a5?!** [25. b3=] **♘f8 26. ab6 ab6 27. ♕d2 ♘e6 28. ♘f3□ ♗f3 29. ♗f3 ♖d4** [29... ♘d4 30. ♖a3=] **30. ♕e3!□ ♕e3 31. fe3 ♖d1 32. ♖d1 ♖c2 33. b3 ♖b2 34. ♔f2 ♖b3 35. ♗d5 ♖b2 36. ♗e6 fe6 37. ♖d7 ♔f8 38. ♔f3 b5 39. ♖b7 b4?!** [⌓ 39... ♖b4=] **40. ♔f4 ♔g8 41. g4 ♖e2 42. ♖b4 ♔f7 43. ♖b7 ♔f6 44. g5 hg5 45. hg5 ♔g6 46. ♖e7 ♖f2 47. ♔e5 ♖f5 48. ♔e6 ♖g5 49. e4 ♖a5 50. ♖d7 ♖a6 51. ♖d6 ♖d6 52. ♔d6** [52... ♔f7=] **1/2 : 1/2**
[M. Makarov]

10. !N A 15

POLUGAEVSKIJ 2640
– I. GUREVICH 2510

Hastings 1992/93

1. ♘f3 ♘f6 2. c4 g6 3. b4 ♗g7 4. ♗b2 0–0 5. e3 d6 6. ♗e2 e5 7. ♘c3?! e4 8. ♘d4 c5 9. bc5 dc5 10. ♘b3 ♕e7! 11. 0–0 ♖d8! N ∓ [11... ♘c6] **12. f3 ♗f5 13. g4!?** [13. ♘e4? ♘e4 14. ♗g7 ♘d2–+; 13. fe4 ♘e4 14. ♘d5 ♖d5 15. ♗g7 ♖d8! (15... ♘d2? 16. cd5 ♕e3 17. ♔h1 ♘f1 18. ♗b2±) 16. ♗h6 (16. ♗b2 ♘d2–+) ♘c3–+] **ef3 14. gf5 fe2 15. ♕e2 ♘c6 16. ♖ad1 ♖ac8?** [16... ♖d7! (△ ♖e8 ×e3, d3) 17. d3 ♖ad8 18. e4 ♘b4 19. ♖f3 gf5! 20. ♖g3 f4∓] **17. d3 ♘e5?** [17... a6 18. e4 b5 19. cb5 ♘d4 20. ♕g2 ab5∞] **18. e4!± a6 19. ♔h1 b5 20. ♘d5** [20. cb5?! ab5 (20... c4!?) 21. ♘b5 ♘fg4∞] **♘d5 21. ed5 ♖e8 22. ♗e5** [22. ♖de1 (△ f6) ♕h4 23. d6 ♘g4 24. d7!; 22... ♕d7!∞] **♗e5 23. ♕f2** [23. ♖de1 ♕h4 24. f6 h5∞] **♗c3 24. ♖c1 b4 25. ♖c2 ♕c7** [△ a5-a4] **26. ♖e2 ♖e2 27. ♕e2 a5 28. ♘d2 ♗d2 29. ♕d2 ♖e8 30. f6! ♕d6 31. d4?** [31. ♖f2 (△ ♕h6) a4 32. ♕h6 ♕f8 33. ♕f4 h6 34. ♕c7 ♖c8 35. ♕b7 ♖b8 36. ♕c6 b3 37. ab3 ab3 38. ♖b2 ♕d8±] **cd4 32. ♕h6** [32. ♕d4 ♖e2∓] **♕f8 33. ♕f4** [33. ♕f8 ♔f8 34. ♖d1 ♖e4∓] **♖e2! 34. ♕d4 ♕d6 35. ♖f2** [35. ♕f4? ♕f4 36. ♖f4 ♖a2 △ b3–+; 35. ♖f4? g5–+] **♖f2 36. ♕f2 [♕ 4/l] ♕e5!∓ 37. ♕d2?⊕** [37. ♕b6 ♕a1 38. ♔g2 ♕a2 39. ♔g3 ♕b3 40. ♔f2 ♕c2 41. ♔g3 ♕d3! (41... ♕c3 42. ♔g2 h5 43. ♕d8 ♔h7 44. ♕e7 ♔h6 45. ♕f7 ♔g5 46. h4) 42. ♔g2 ♕e2 43. ♔g3 ♕e5 44. ♔g2 ♕g5 45. ♔f3 ♕f5 *a)* 46. ♔e3? ♕h3 47. ♔e4 h5 48. ♕d8 ♔h7 49. ♕e7 ♔h6 50. ♕f7 (50. d6 b3) b3∓; *b)* 46. ♔g3 h5 47. ♕d8 ♔h7 48. ♕e7 ♕g4 49. ♔f2 ♕h4 50. ♔g2 ♔h6!?∓] **♕f6 38. ♔g2 ♕c3?** [38... ♔f8! 39. c5 ♔e8∓] **39. ♕e2 ♕d4 40. ♕e8?** [40. ♕e7 ♕b2 41. ♔f3 ♕a3 42. ♔f4 ♕c1 43. ♔g3 ♕g1 44. ♔f3=] **♔g7 41. ♕a4 ♕c4 42. ♕a5 h5!–+ 43. ♕a8 ♕e2 44. ♔g1 h4 0 : 1 [I. Gurevich]**

11. A 15

DENG KONGLIANG 2430
– YE JIANGCHUAN 2540

Beijing (zt) 1993

1. b3 ♘f6 2. ♗b2 g6 3. g3 ♗g7 4. ♗g2 0–0 5. c4 d6 6. ♘f3 e5 7. 0–0 ♖e8!? N [7... c6; 7... ♘c6] **8. ♘c3 c6 9. e4 d5?!** [9... ♘bd7 10. d4 — E 68; 9... ♘a6!? Ye Jiangchuan] **10. ed5 cd5** [10... e4? 11. ♘e1 cd5 12. ♘d5 ♘d5 13. ♗g7 ♔g7 14. cd5 ♕d5 15. d3±] **11. d4!** [11. ♘d5??

♘d5 12. cd5 e4 13. ♘d4 ♕b6−+; 11. cd5 e4 12. ♘d4 (△ 12... ♘d5? 13. ♘d5 ♕d5 14. d3! ♖d8 15. ♖c1! ♘a6 16. ♖c4±) ♗g4!] **ed4** [11... e4 12. ♘e5 ♘c6 13. cd5 ♘e5 14. de5 ♖e5 15. ♘e4 ♖e4 16. ♗f6± Ye Jiangchuan] **12. ♘d5 ♘d5 13. cd5 ♕d5 14. ♗d4?!** [14. ♖e1! ♖d8 (14... ♖e1 15. ♕e1±) 15. ♘d4 ♕c5 (15... ♕d7 16. ♖c1 ♘a6 17. ♕e2 ♗d4 18. ♖cd1 ♗f2 19. ♔h1!+−) 16. ♘e6!±] **♘c6! 15. ♗g7 ♕d1 16. ♖fd1 ♔g7 17. ♘d4± ♗g4!□ 18. ♗c6** [18. f3 ♘d4 19. ♖d4 ♗e6 20. f4 ♖e7=] **bc6 19. f3** [19. ♖dc1 ♖ad8 20. ♘c6 ♖d2=] **♗d7 20. ♖ac1 ♖e5! 21. ♘c6?!** [21. ♔f2!? ♖c8 22. ♖d2±] **♗c6 22. ♖c6 ♖e2 23. ♖c7 ♖a2 24. ♖dd7 ♖f8 25. ♖a7 ♖b2! 26. ♖ab7 ♔g8 1/2 : 1/2 [Deng Kongliang]**

12. A 17

RIBLI 2620 − ROZENTALIS 2595

Deutschland 1993

1. ♘f3 ♘f6 2. c4 e6 3. g3 b6 4. ♗g2 ♗b7 5. ♘c3 ♗b4 6. d3 0−0 7. e4 d5 8. e5 ♘fd7 [8... d4 9. a3!±] **9. cd5 ♗d5 10. 0−0 ♗c3 11. bc3 ♘c6!? N** [11... c5 − 50/11] **12. d4 f6 13. ♕c2! fe5** [13... ♕e7!?] **14. ♘g5 ♘f6 15. ♘e6 ♗e6 16. ♗c6 ed4! 17. ♖d1! ♗d7?!** [17... ♖b8? 18. ♗a3! ♖f7 19. ♖d4±; 17... ♗d5! 18. ♖d4 ♗c6! 19. ♖d8 ♖ad8 20. ♗g5 h6 21. ♗f6 ♖f6 22. ♖d1 ♖e8 23. f4 ♖fe6 24. ♔f2 ♖e3 25. ♖d3 ♖e2 26. ♕e2 ♖e2 27. ♔e2 ♗b5=] **18. ♗a8 ♕a8 19. cd4 ♘d5** [19... ♗h3 20. ♕c4 ♔h8 21. d5±] **20. ♖e1 ♔h8 21. ♖e5 ♗c6?!** [21... ♘b4 22. ♕e2 ♗h3 23. f3 ♘c2 24. ♕c2 ♕f3 25. ♗f4 ♖f4 26. ♖e8 ♖f8 27. ♕e2+−; 21... c6!?±] **22. ♗a3 ♖f7 23. ♖c1** [23. ♖ae1!?] **♗d7 24. ♖ce1 c6 25. ♕e2 ♕g8** [25... h6 26. ♕h5±] **26. ♕a6! h6** [26... ♘c7 27. ♕a7 ♘b5 28. ♕a4+−] **27. ♕a7 ♔h7 28. ♕a4 ♕c8** [28... ♕d8 29. ♕c2+−] **29. ♗d6 ♖f6 30. ♗e7 ♖f3⊕ 31. ♖c1 ♕e8 32. ♕c2 ♔g8 33. a3 ♕f7** [RR 33... ♘e7 34. ♖ce1 ♖f7 35. ♕b3 (△ ♖e7) ♔f8□ 36. ♕b6 △ ♕c5+−⊙] **34. ♗b4 b5 35. ♖ce1 ♔h8 36. ♖1e2 ♔g8 37. ♕d1 ♗g4** [37... ♔h8 38. ♖e7 ♘e7 39. ♖e7 ♕f5 40. ♖d7 ♖f2 41. ♖d8 ♔h7 42. ♖f8+−] **38. ♖e8 ♔h7 39. ♕c2 ♗f5 40. ♕c6 ♗d7 41. ♕c2 ♗f5 42. ♕a2! ♗d3 43. ♖2e5 ♗c4 44. ♕b1! ♖d3 45. ♕e1 ♘f6** [45... ♕f3 46. ♖f8 ♕g4 47. ♕e4+−] **46. ♖8e7 ♕g6 47. ♖e3 ♘d5** [47... ♖d4 48. ♗c3+−] **48. ♖d3 ♗d3 49. ♖e5 ♘f4 50. ♕e3 ♘h3 51. ♔g2 ♘g5 52. h4 ♘f7** [52... ♗e4 53. ♔f1 ♗d3 54. ♔g1+−] **53. ♖e7 1 : 0 [Ribli]**

13. A 17

KRAMNIK 2685 − ANAND 2710

Amsterdam 1993

1. ♘f3 ♘f6 2. c4 e6 3. ♘c3 ♗b4 4. g3 0−0 5. ♗g2 b6?! 6. ♕b3!? N [6. ♘e5 − 47/20] **a5 7. ♘e5!? c6** [7... ♖a7 8. ♘b5 ♗b7!? (8... ♖a6 9. a3 ♗e7 10. d4±) 9. ♗f3!? (9. ♘a7 ♗g2 10. ♖g1 ♗b7 11. ♘b5±) ♗f3 10. ♕f3 ♖a6 11. a3 (11. ♕b7 ♘e8) ♗e7 12. d4 c6 13. ♘c3±] **8. a3** [8. 0−0±] **♗c3 9. ♕c3 ♗b7** [9... ♕c7 10. d4 d6 11. ♘d3 ♗a6 12. b3±] **10. d4 d6** [10... ♕c7!? 11. ♗g5 (11. c5!?) d6! (11... c5 12. d5! ed5 13. ♗f6 d4 14. ♕d2 gf6 15. ♘g4+−) 12. ♗f6 gf6 13. ♘g4 ♘d7 14. c5!±] **11. ♘d3 ♕c8 12. c5!± bc5 13. dc5 d5 14. ♗f4 ♘bd7** [⌓ 14... ♗a6] **15. ♗d6 ♖e8 16. 0−0 ♗a6 17. ♖fe1 ♕b7** [17... ♘e4 18. ♗e4 de4 19. ♘e5 ♘e5 (19... ♘f6 20. ♕a5! ♗e2 21. ♕d2 ♗h5 22. b4+−) 20. ♕e5 f5 21. ♕c3±] **18. ♘e5!** [18. a4 ♘e4!□⇆] **a4 19. ♖ad1** [19. e4 ♘e4 20. ♗e4 de4 21. ♘d7 ♕d7 22. ♖e4 ♗b5 (△ 23. ♖g4? e5) 23. ♖ae1± ×♗b5] **♘e5□ 20. ♗e5 ♘g4! 21. ♗g7!** [21. ♗d6 f5±] **e5**

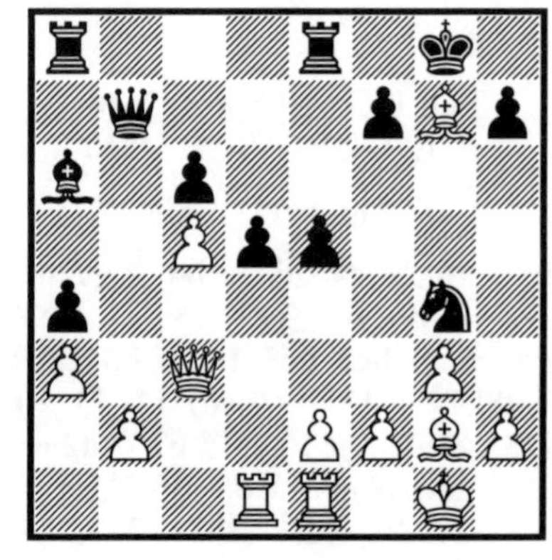

22. ♗f3! [22. h3 ♘f2; 22. ♕f3 f5] **f5!** [22... ♔g7 23. ♗g4+−; 22... ♘h2 23. ♗e5+−; 22... ♘f2 23. ♗f6!! ♖e6 (23... ♘d1 24. ♕d2+−; 23... ♘h3 24. ♔g2+−) 24. ♔f2 ♖f6 25. ♕e5+−] **23. ♗g4 d4 24. ♕c1** [24. ♕c2!? fg4 25. ♗e5 ♖e5 26. ♖d4∞̄] **fg4 25. ♗f6 ♕f7 26. ♕g5 ♕g6 27. ♕g6 hg6 28. f4! ef4 29. gf4** [29. ♖d4 f3□ (29... ♖e2 30. ♖e2 ♗e2 31. gf4+−; 29... fg3 30. ♖a4) 30. e4! (Anand) ♔f7 31. e5 ♗c8 32. ♖b4!?+−] **♔f7 30. ♗e5 ♖ad8 31. ♔f2 g5!** [31... d3 32. ed3 ♖d3 33. ♖d3 ♗d3 34. ♔g3 ♗f5 35. ♖d1+−] **32. ♔g3** [32. e3 d3!] **gf4** [32... ♖d5 33. e4!+− Anand] **33. ♔f4 ♔g6!?** [33... ♖d5 34. ♗d4 ♖e2 35. ♖e2 ♗e2 36. ♖d2 ♗f3 37. h3+−] **34. ♗d6?** [34. ♖d2+−] **♖e3!!⇆ 35. ♖d4 ♖de8 36. ♖c1!** [36. ♔g4?! ♗e2 37. ♖e2□ ♖e2 38. ♖a4 ♖b2∓] **♔h5!?** [36... ♗e2 37. ♖c3; 36... ♖e2] **37. ♖c3⊕** [37. ♖a4!? ♗e2 38. ♔f5] **♖e2= 38. h3 ♗c8 39. hg4 ♗g4 40. ♔g3**
1/2 : 1/2 **[Kramnik]**

14. !N A 17

TIMMAN 2635 − AN. KARPOV 2725

Linares 1993

1. ♘f3 ♘f6 2. c4 e6 3. ♘c3 ♗b4 4. g3 b6 5. ♗g2 ♗b7 6. 0−0 0−0 7. ♕c2 ♖e8?! [⌓ 7... d5] **8. ♖d1! N ±** [8. b3 − 52/(19)] **d6 9. d4** [9. ♘a4?! d5=] **♗c3 10. ♕c3 ♘bd7 11. b3 a6 12. ♗b2** [12. ♗a3 ♕e7 △ c5] **b5 13. ♖ac1 ♘b6** [△ 14... bc4 15. bc4 ♘a4=] **14. ♗a3! ♗e4 15. ♗f1** [△ ♘d2] **bc4 16. bc4 ♗c6 17. ♕a5?!** [⌓ 17. ♘d2] **♗f3! 18. ef3 d5 19. cd5** [19. c5 ♘c4! 20. ♗c4 dc4 21. ♖c4 ♘d5∞̄] **♘fd5** [19... ♘bd5? 20. ♖c6] **20. f4 ♕d7** [20... ♕f6 21. ♕e1! △ ♕e5± An. Karpov] **21. ♖d2 ♘f6 22. ♗g2 ♘bd5 23. ♖b2 h5 24. ♗f3 ♖ec8 25. ♖b7 ♕d8 26. ♔g2 h4 27. ♕a4!** [27. ♖c6 ♘b6 28. ♗c5 ♘fd5] **a5** [27... ♖cb8?! 28. ♖cb1 ♖b7 29. ♖b7 ♖b8 (29... ♕c8 30. ♕c6 ♖b8 31. ♖a7!) 30. ♕a6 ♖a8 31. ♕d3 ♕d7 32. ♖b2] **28. ♖c5!?** [28. ♕c6!?] **♘d7!** [△ 29. ♖a5 ♘7b6] **29. ♖c2 ♘7b6** [29... ♘7f6±] **30. ♕b5 ♕f6?⊕** [30... ♖cb8 31. ♖b8 ♖b8 32. ♗c5 ♕f6 33. ♕a5 ♕f5 34. ♕d2⩲] **31. ♕d3!** [△ 31... ♕f4 32. ♖b6! h3 33. ♔g1 ♕f3□ 34. ♕f3 cb6 35. ♕d3+−] **♖d8** [⌓ 31... ♖cb8±] **32. ♕e4 ♘d7?! 33. f5+− hg3 34. hg3 ♘f8 35. ♖c6! ♘b4⊕** [36. ♖cc7 ♖d4 37. ♗b2+−; 35... ♕f5 36. ♕f5 ef5 37. ♗f8 ♔f8 38. ♗d5 ♖d5 39. ♖cc7+−]
1 : 0 **[Timman]**

15. A 17

LOBRON 2620 − AN. KARPOV 2725

Dortmund 1993

1. ♘f3 ♘f6 2. c4 e6 3. ♘c3 ♗b4 4. g3 b6 5. ♗g2 ♗b7 6. 0−0 0−0 7. ♕c2 ♕e7!? N [7... ♗c3 8. ♕c3⩲; 8. bc3!? △ d3, e4, ♘h4, f4] **8. b3** [8. d3 d5] **♗c3 9. ♕c3 c5 10. ♗b2 d5** [10... d6 11. d4±] **11. cd5** [11. d4 dc4 12. ♕c4 ♗d5] **♗d5 12. d3** [12. d4 ♘bd7] **♖d8= 13. ♖fc1 ♘a6** [13... ♘bd7 14. a3 △ b4] **14. a3 ♗b7 15. ♖ab1 ♖ac8 16. ♕e1** [16. ♕e5 ♘e8! △ f6, e5] **♘e8 17. ♖c2** [17. ♗c3 ♘ec7 18. b4 ♘b5 19. bc5 ♘c3=] **♘ec7** [17... ♘d6!?] **18. ♖bc1 ♘b5 19. ♕f1 ♗d5** [19... f6 20. e3!? △ d4] **20. ♘d2□ ♖c7 21. ♗d5 ed5 22. e3** [22. e4 d4∞] **d4 23. ed4 ♘d4 24. ♗d4 cd4** [24... ♖d4? 25. ♘f3 ♖dd7 26. d4±] **25. ♖c7 ♘c7 26. ♘f3 h6 27. ♕h3?!** [27. ♖c4 ♘e6 28. a4=] **♘e6 28. b4 a5 29. ♕f5** [29. ♘e5? ♘g5 30. ♕f5 ♕e5!−+; 29. ba5 ♕a3∓] **ab4 30. ab4 ♕b4 31. ♘e5 ♕e7! 32. ♘c6** [32. ♖c6 ♖b8 33. ♘f7 ♕f7 34. ♕e6 ♕e6 35. ♖e6 b5∓] **♕c7 33. ♖c4 ♖d6! 34. ♕e4** [34. ♘d4 ♘d4−+; 34. ♘e5 ♘c5!] **b5 35. ♖c2 ♕b7 36. ♘b4 ♕e4 37. de4 d3** [37... ♘g5−+] **38. ♖d2 ♘c5 39. f3 ♖d4 40. ♘d5 b4 41. ♔f2 g5** [41... b3 42. ♔e3 ♖c4 43. ♘f4 ♖c3!−+] **42. ♔e3 ♖c4 43. ♖d3□ ♘d3 44. ♔d3 ♖c1 45. ♘b4 ♖h1 46. h4 gh4** [46... ♖h3 47. hg5 hg5 48. ♔e3 ♖g3∓] **47. gh4 ♖h4 48. ♘d5 ♖h2 49. ♔e3 ♖g2 50. ♘e7 ♔h7 51. e5 ♖a2 52. f4 ♖a7 53. ♘f5 ♖a6 54. ♘d4? ♖a3 55. ♔e4 ♖a4 56. f5** [56. ♔e3 ♔g6 57. ♔e4 ♖d4!−+] **♔g7 57. ♔e3 h5 58. ♘f3 h4 59. ♔f2 ♖f4 60. f6 ♔g6**
0 : 1 **[An. Karpov]**

16. **A 17**

VAGANIAN 2615 – K. BISCHOFF 2505

Deutschland 1993

1. ♘f3 ♘f6 2. c4 e6 3. ♘c3 ♗b4 4. ♕c2 0–0 5. g3 b6 6. ♗g2 ♗b7 7. 0–0 c5 8. d3 N [8. ♖d1 – 26/22] **♗c3** [8... ♘c6 9. ♘e4!? d5!? (9... ♘e4 10. de4 △ ♗f4±) 10. ♘f6 ♕f6 11. ♗g5 ♕g6 12. ♗f4⩲] **9. bc3** [9. ♕c3 d5 10. cd5 ♘d5=] **♘c6 10. e4 h6 11. ♘h4!⩲** [△ f4] **g5 12. ♘f3 ♘h7 13. d4! ♘a5** [⌓ 13... d6 14. ♗e3 ♘a5 15. ♘d2 f5] **14. ♘e5! d6 15. ♘g4± ♔g7 16. f4 ♘c4 17. fg5 hg5** [17... ♘g5 18. h4+–]

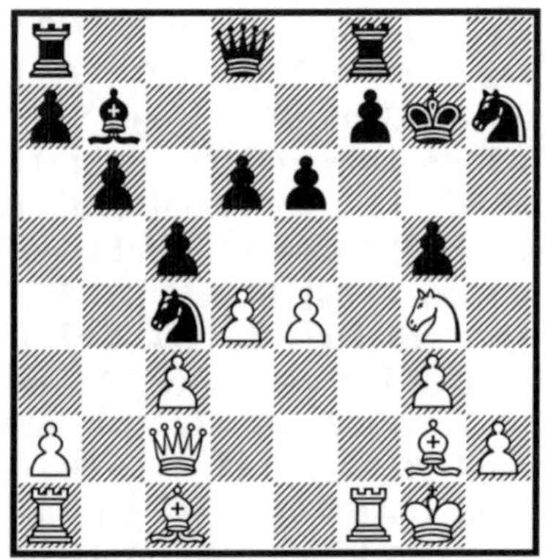

18. ♘f6! ♖h8□ 19. ♕e2 [19. ♘h7 ♖h7 20. e5 ♕d7 21. ♗b7 ♕b7 22. ♗g5 ♔g8 23. ♕e2±] **b5□ 20. ♗g5 ♘g5 21. ♕g4 ♖h6** [21... ♕f6 22. ♖f6 ♔f6 23. e5+–] **22. ♕g5 ♖g6 23. ♘h5 ♔g8 24. ♕f4 ♕e7 25. dc5** [25. ♘f6 ♖f6!? (25... ♔g7 26. ♕h4 ♖h8 27. ♘h5 ♔f8□ 28. ♘f4!! ♖gh6 29. ♘g6+–) 26. ♕f6 ♕f6 27. ♖f6 cd4 28. cd4 ♘e3⇆] **dc5 26. ♖ad1 e5 27. ♘f6 ♔g7 28. ♕h4 ♕f6** [28... ♖f6 29. ♕g5+–] **29. ♖f6 ♖f6 30. ♗f1! ♖h8 31. ♕g5 ♖g6 32. ♕e7** [32... ♘e3 33. ♕e5+–]

1 : 0 **[Vaganian]**

17. ** !N **A 18**

LAUTIER 2645 – JUSUPOV 2645

München 1993

1. c4 ♘f6 2. ♘c3 e6 3. e4 d5 4. e5 d4 5. ef6 dc3 6. bc3 ♕f6 7. d4 e5 8. ♘f3 ed4 9. ♗g5 ♕e6 10. ♗e2 f6 11. ♘d4 ♕f7 [11... ♕e4? 12. ♘b5 ♘a6 13. 0–0 △ 13... fg5 14. ♗h5 g6 15. ♖e1+– Ribli] **12. ♗f4 ♗c5!? N** [12... c6?! 13. ♗g4! N (13. 0–0 – 32/(24)) ♘a6 14. 0–0 ♗e7 15. ♗c8 ♖c8 16. ♘f5 0–0 17. ♘e7 ♕e7 18. ♗d6+– O. Renet 2530 – van Gisbergen 2350, Groningen (open) 1992] **13. 0–0 0–0 14. ♕c2** [14. ♘b3 ♘a6 15. ♘c5 ♘c5 16. ♗e3!? Štohl; RR 14. ♘b5!? ♘a6 15. ♕d5 c6 16. ♕f7 ♖f7 17. ♘d6 ♖e7 18. ♖fe1 g5 (Reinderman 2415 – Hauchard 2450, Bruxelles (zt) 1993) 19. ♘c8 ♖c8 20. ♗g4 ♖ce8 21. ♗d2⩲] **♘a6 15. ♖ab1?!** [15. ♗d3 g6 (△ 16... ♗d4 17. cd4 ♘b4) 16. ♖ab1 ♖d8=; 15. ♘b5!?; 15. ♖ad1!?] **♖d8 16. ♖fd1 c6 17. ♖d3** [17. ♘c6?? ♖d1 18. ♖d1 bc6 19. ♖d8 ♗f8 20. ♗d6 ♗f5–+; 20... ♗b7!?–+] **♗f8= 18. ♖g3** [18. ♘c6?? ♖d3 19. ♗d3 bc6 20. ♗h7 ♔h8 21. ♗g6 ♕c4–+; ⌓ 18. ♖e3=] **♘c5 19. ♖d1 ♖e8** [19... ♗e6!? Lautier] **20. ♘b3 ♗e6 21. ♖d4?** [21. ♗e3! ♗c4 (21... ♘d7∞) 22. ♗c4 ♕c4 23. ♘c5 ♗c5 24. ♗c5 ♕c5 25. ♕b3 ♔f8 26. ♕b7 ♕e7=] **♗f5!∓ 22. ♕f5 ♖e2 23. ♗d2!** [23. ♖e3? ♖a2] **♖ae8 24. ♖e3 ♖e5** [24... ♕g6 25. ♕g6 hg6 26. ♔f1 ♖2e3 27. ♗e3 b6 28. ♖d1=] **25. ♕g4** [25. ♕f3 ♖2e3 26. ♗e3 ♕g6↑] **♖2e3 26. ♗e3 ♘e6 27. ♖d3 f5** [27... b6∓] **28. ♕d1 f4** [28... b6!? △ 29. f4? ♖e4 30. ♘d2 ♖e3 31. ♖e3 ♗c5] **29. ♗a7 ♘g5** [29... ♕e8 30. ♔f1∞; 29... b5 30. ♗b8!] **30. ♗b8?!** [30. ♗d4=∞] **♖e8?** [30... ♖e6! △ 31... ♕e8 32. ♖d8 ♕e7 33. ♔f1 f3→ △ 34... ♖e1! 35. ♕e1 fg2–+] **31. ♖d8! f3 32. ♖e8 ♕e8 33. ♗f4 ♘e6** [33... ♕e2? 34. ♕e2 fe2 35. ♗d2 ♘e4 36. ♗e1 ♗c5 (△ 37. ♘d4? ♘c3! 38. ♗c3 ♗d4, △ 37. ♘c1? ♘f2! 38. ♘e2 ♘g4 39. ♔h1 ♘e5∓) 37. g4!± △ ♔g2-f3 ×e2] **34. ♗e3** [34. ♕f3?? ♘f4–+] **fg2 35. ♕g4!± ♕f7 36. ♔g2 h5 37. ♕e4 ♗d6 38. h3 g6 39. ♕f3** [39. ♘a5!?] **♗c7 40. ♘d2 ♘g7** [40... ♕f3⩲] **41. ♕e4! ♕e6 42. ♕e6** [42. ♕b1!? ♘f5 43. ♕b7 ♘h4⇆] **♘e6 43. ♔f3 ♗e5!? 44. ♘e4 ♔f7 45. ♔e2 ♔e7 46. ♔d3 ♗c7 47. ♘d2** [47. a4!?] **♔f6 48. ♘f3 ♗e5?!** [48... ♔f5 49. ♘h4 ♔f6 50. ♔e4 ♘g5 51. ♗g5 ♔g5 52. ♘f3⩲] **49. a4**

g5 [49... ♔f5 50. ♘d4 ♔f6 51. ♘b3±] **50. ♗d4±** [50... ♗d4 51. cd4 ♘f4 52. ♔e3 ♘h3 53. ♘d2! ♘f4 54. ♘e4 *a)* 54... ♔g6 55. ♘d6 h4 (55... b6 56. c5±) 56. ♔f3±; *b)* 54... ♔f5 55. ♘d6 ♔g4 56. ♘b7 h4 57. ♘d6 h3 58. ♘e4 h2 59. ♘g3 ♘h5 60. ♘h1 ♔h3 61. a5 ♔g2 62. a6 ♔h1 63. a7 ♔g1 64. a8♕ h1♕ 65. ♕a1 ♔h2 66. ♕h1 ♔h1 67. ♔e4=; 56. f3!±] **1/2 : 1/2** **[Jusupov]**

18. **A 20**

SERPER 2590 — CH. LUTZ 2550
Dortmund 1993

1. c4 e5 2. g3 ♘f6 3. ♗g2 c6 4. d4 ed4 5. ♕d4 d5 6. ♘f3 ♗e7 7. cd5 cd5 8. 0—0 ♘c6 9. ♕a4 0—0 10. ♗e3 ♘e4 11. ♘c3! ♘c3 12. bc3 ♘a5!? N [12... ♕a5 — 27/44] **13. ♘e5! ♗e6** [13... ♗f6 14. ♖ad1! ♗e6□ — 13... ♗e6] **14. ♖ad1 ♗f6 15. ♘d3** [15. ♗d5!? ♗d5 16. ♘d7! (16. ♕b5? ♗c6 17. ♘c6 bc6!—+; 16. c4 ♘c4! 17. ♘c4 ♗c6∓) *a)* 16... b5 17. ♘f6 (17. ♕b5? ♗c4!) ♕f6 (17... gf6?? 18. ♕g4 ♔h8 19. ♕h5!+—) 18. ♕a5 ♗c4 19. ♖d2 ♖fc8!±; *b)* 16... ♗c6 17. ♘f6 ♕f6 18. ♕a5 ♕e6!? △ ♕e4$\overline{\overline{\infty}}$; *c)* 16... ♗c4 17. ♘f8 ♕f8 18. ♕a5 ♗e2 19. ♖d7 ♗f1 20. ♔f1 b6 21. ♕d5 (△ ♖f7!) ♖d8!=] **♘c4** [15... ♗c3?! 16. ♘f4±] **16. ♗d4 b6 17. ♕b3 ♗d4 18. cd4±** [×d5] **♖c8 19. ♘f4 ♕d6 20. ♖fe1 a6 21. ♕f3! ♖fd8 22. ♕h5!** [△ e4] **f5 23. ♕g5?!** [23. ♗h3±] **♕d7 24. ♗h3 ♖f8?** [24... ♘d6! (△ ♘f7) 25. ♘e6 (25. ♘d3!?) ♕e6 26. ♖c1⩲] **25. e4!+— de4 26. d5??** [26. ♖e4+—] **♘e5!□ 27. ♖e3?** [27. de6! ♕d1 28. ♖d1 ♘f3 29. ♔g2 ♘g5 30. e7 ♖fe8 31. ♗f5 ♖c5 (31... ♖c7 32. ♘e6! ♘e6 33. ♗e6 ♔h8 34. ♗f7 ♖ce7 35. ♗e8 ♖e8 36. ♖d6 ♖b8 37. ♖e6=) 32. ♘d5 ♔f7 (32... ♖d5? 33. ♖d5 ♖e7 34. ♗c8!±) 33. h4! ♘e6 34. ♗e4 (△ ♖d3-f3) ♘c7 35. ♘c7 ♖c7 36. ♖d6=] **♕a4!—+** [27... ♘f3? 28. ♖f3 ef3 29. ♘e6+—] **28. ♖de1 ♗d7 29. ♘e6 ♗e6 30. de6 ♕b4 31. ♗g2 ♖ce8 32. ♗e4?⊕ ♕e4! 33. ♕h5 ♕g4 34. ♕e8 ♖e8 35. ♖e5 ♕c4 36. a3 g6 37. ♖5e3 ♔g7 0 : 1** **[Serper]**

19. **A 21**

LAUTIER 2645 — KRAMNIK 2685
Cannes (m/1) 1993

1. c4 e5 2. ♘c3 ♗b4 3. ♘d5 ♗c5 4. ♘f3 e4?! N [⌓ 4... c6 5. ♘c3⩲ — 39/(28)]

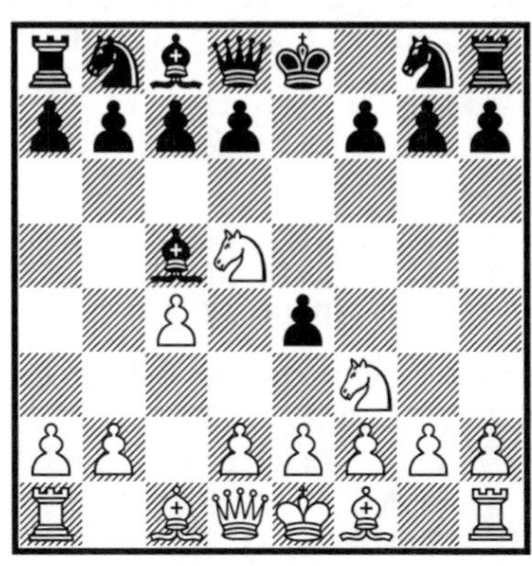

5. ♘g5! e3! [5... f5 6. d4±; 5... c6 6. ♘e4 cd5 7. ♘c5 dc4 8. ♕a4±] **6. d4** [6. de3? c6 7. ♘e4 cd5 8. ♘c5 ♕a5; 6. fe3? c6 7. ♘e4 ♕h4] **ef2 7. ♔f2 ♗e7 8. ♘e7 ♕e7 9. e4± d6** [9... ♘c6!?] **10. ♗d3 ♘c6** [10... c5?! 11. dc5 dc5 12. e5! ♘c6 13. ♖e1±↑] **11. ♗c2 ♘f6** [11... ♕f6 12. ♘f3 ♗g4 13. ♗e3±] **12. ♖e1?!** [12. h3!± △ ♖e1, ♘f3] **♗g4! 13. ♕d3** [13. ♘f3 ♗f3 14. gf3 ♘h5⇆; 13. ♕d2!⩲] **♘d7!** [13... ♘b4 14. ♗a4 ♗d7 15. ♕b3±] **14. ♗a4** [14. ♗d2? ♕f6∓ △ 15. ♔g3? ♕d4] **h6** [14... ♕f6 15. ♔g3 ♗h5±] **15. e5!?** [15. ♘f3? ♗f3 16. gf3 ♕h4∓; 15. ♕g3? ♕f6∓] **de5 16. d5 ♘d4!?** [16... ♘c5 17. ♕g3 hg5 18. dc6 0—0 19. cb7 ♖ad8 20. ♗c2↑; 16... ♘b4!?∞] **17. ♕e4** [17. ♕g3 ♕f6! 18. ♘f3 (18. ♔g1? ♘e2) ♗f3 19. ♕e5 ♕e5 20. ♖e5 ♔d8 21. ♗d7 ♔d7 22. gf3∓] **♗e2!□ 18. ♘h3** [18. ♘f3 ♗f3 19. gf3 (19. ♕e5∓) c6! 20. dc6 bc6∓ △ 21. ♗e3 ♘c5! 22. ♗c6 ♔f8 23. ♕d5 ♖d8; 18. ♗e3 f5! 19. ♕h4 0-0-0!↑; 19. ♕b1!?∞] **b5!** [18... 0—0 19. ♗d7 ♕d7 20. ♖e2 ♘e2 21. ♕e2 c6 22. dc6⩲] **19. ♗b5 ♘b5 20. ♕e2** [20. d6 ♕f6 21. ♔e2 (21. ♔g1 0—0) ♘d4 22. ♔d1 0—0∓→] **♘d4 21. ♕d1 ♕h4! 22. ♔f1** [22. ♔g1? ♘c2! 23. g3 ♕c4∓] **0—0 23. ♗e3 ♘f5 24. ♕c2** [⌓ 24. b3] **♘e3 25. ♖e3 f5∓ 26. ♔g1 ♖ae8⊕ 27. ♘f2 e4 28. ♕c3 ♘f6 29.**

g3?!⊕ [⌓ 29. ♖h3 ♕f4 30. ♖e1] **♕h5 30. ♖f1 ♘d7!∓ 31. ♔g2 ♘e5 32. h3** [32. ♖h1!?] **f4! 33. gf4?** [33. ♖e4□ fg3 34. ♕g3 ♖f3 35. ♕h4∓] **♖f4−+ 34. ♖e4? ♕g6 35. ♕g3 ♖f2 36. ♖f2 ♕e4 37. ♔h2 ♘c4 38. ♕c7 ♕d5 39. ♕a7 ♕d6 40. ♔g2 ♘e3 41. ♔h1 ♕d5 42. ♔h2 ♘d1 43. ♖g2 ♕d6 44. ♔h1 ♖e1 45. ♖g1 ♕d5**
0 : 1 **[Kramnik]**

20. **A 21**

V. SALOV 2660 − KRAMNIK 2685
Linares 1993

1. c4 e5 2. ♘c3 ♗b4 3. ♘d5 ♗d6 N 4. d4! c6 [4... ♘c6 5. ♘f3 e4 6. ♘g5 ♘f6 (6... f5 7. c5!) 7. a3!] **5. de5 ♗e5 6. ♘f3 d6 7. ♘e5 de5 8. ♘c3 ♕d1 9. ♘d1± ♗e6?** [9... a5! 10. ♘c3 ♘f6 11. b3 ♘a6±] **10. b3 a5 11. ♗b2! f6 12. ♘c3 ♘a6 13. 0-0-0 ♘h6 14. h3 ♘f7 15. e3 0−0** [15... ♔e7!? △ 16. ♗a3 ♘b4 17. ♘a4 ♘d6!] **16. ♗e2 ♘b4 17. f4!± b5! 18. g4** [18. cb5? cb5 19. ♘b5 ♖fc8] **ef4** [18... bc4 19. f5 ♗c8 20. ♗c4 ♗a6 21. a3 ♗c4 22. bc4 ♘a6 23. ♘e4 ♖fd8 24. ♗c3±] **19. ef4 bc4 20. bc4 f5 21. a3 ♘a6 22. ♘a4 ♖ab8 23. ♖hg1 fg4 24. hg4 ♖fe8 25. ♖d2 ♘d8 26. f5** [26. ♖g3!? ♘b7 27. ♗e5 ♖bd8 28. ♖e3!±] **♗f7 27. g5 ♘b7 28. g6 hg6 29. fg6 ♗e6 30. ♖g5 ♖bd8 31. ♖d8 ♖d8 32. ♖e5 ♖e8 33. ♔d2** [33. ♗g4!? ♘c7 (33... ♘ac5? 34. ♘c5 ♘c5 35. ♔c2! ♗d7 36. ♗d7 ♖e5 37. ♗e5 ♘d7 38. ♗d6 ♘f8 39. ♔b3+−) 34. ♗f3±] **♘d6 34. ♗d4 ♘c7 35. ♔c3 ♗f5! 36. ♗d3 ♗d3** [⌓ 36... ♘e4] **37. ♔d3 ♖d8?⊕** [37... ♘e6□] **38. ♘c5+− ♘a8 39. ♘e4 ♘e4 40. ♔e4 ♘c7** [41. ♗b6] **1 : 0** **[V. Salov]**

21.* **A 21**

LJUBOJEVIĆ 2605 − V. SALOV 2660
Linares 1993

1. c4 f5 2. ♘c3 ♘f6 3. g3 e5 4. ♗g2 g6?! [RR 4... ♗b4 5. ♕c2 0−0!? N (5... ♘c6; 5... d6) 6. ♕f5 ♘c6 7. ♕c2 ♕e8 8. d3 d6 9. a3 ♗c5 10. e3 ♗f5 11. h3 ♕g6 12. ♘e4 ♘e4 13. de4 ♗e6 14. ♘f3 a5 15. ♗d2 a4 16. ♖c1 ♕f6 17. ♕d3 ♖f7 18. ♕e2 ♖af8∞̄ B. Larsen 2540 − Zarnicki 2470, Buenos Aires 1993] **5. d4! ed4 6. ♕d4 ♘c6 7. ♕h4 N** [⌓ 7. ♕d2±] **♗g7 8. ♗h6 0−0 9. ♘h3** [9. ♘f3!?] **♘e5 10. ♗g7 ♔g7 11. ♕d4 d6 12. b3 c6 13. 0−0 ♘f7 14. ♖ad1 ♕b6 15. ♕d2±** [△ ♘g5] **♕a5 16. ♔h1?! ♗e6 17. ♕b2 ♖ae8 18. ♖d3 ♗c8 19. ♕d2** [△ ♘g5] **h6= 20. ♕b2 ♖e7 21. ♘f4 ♖fe8 22. ♔g1 ♖e5 23. ♖d4?! ♕b6 24. ♖d2 a5 25. ♖fd1 ♕c7 26. ♖d4 ♔h7 27. h4 g5 28. hg5 hg5 29. ♘d3 ♖5e6 30. ♘e1 ♘e4!?** [30... ♕e7 31. ♕c2 ♔g7=] **31. ♘e4 fe4 32. ♕c2 ♕e7 33. ♗e4 ♖e4 34. f3 ♗f5 35. fe4 ♗e4∞̄ 36. ♕d2?!** [36. ♕c3 c5 37. ♖4d2 ♕e6∞̄] **♕e5?!** [36... c5 37. ♖d6 ♕e5! 38. ♖d3□ (38. ♔f2? ♕f5 39. ♘f3 g4 40. ♖h1 ♔g8−+) ♗d3 39. ♕d3 ♔g7∓] **37. ♕e3 ♖e6??⊕** [37... c5 38. ♖4d2 ♕f5∞̄] **38. ♘d3! ♕f5 39. ♖f1 ♕f1□** [39... ♕g6 40. ♖f7+−] **40. ♔f1 ♗g2 41. ♔f2 ♖e3 42. ♔e3 c5 43. ♖e4! ♗e4 44. ♔e4** [♘♗ 2/j] **♔g6 45. ♔d5+− ♔f5 46. ♘f2 ♔f6 47. e4 ♔e7 48. ♘d3** [48. ♘g4+−] **♔f6 49. a4 ♔e7 50. e5 g4 51. ed6 ♘d6 52. ♘c5 ♘f5 53. ♘e4 ♘e3 54. ♔e5 ♘c2 55. ♘d6 b6 56. ♘f5 ♔d7 57. ♘d4 ♘e1** [57... ♘d4 58. ♔d4 ♔d6 59. ♔c3 ♔c5 60. b4!+−] **58. ♔f4 ♔d6 59. ♔g4 ♔c5 60. ♘f3 ♘d3 61. ♔f5 ♘f2 62. ♘e5!** [62. g4? ♘g4 63. ♔g4 ♔b4=; 62. ♔f4?? ♘h1!! 63. g4 ♘f2=] **♔b4 63. ♘d7 ♔b3 64. ♘b6 ♔b4 65. g4 ♘h1 66. ♔f4 ♘f2 67. g5 ♘h3 68. ♔f5** **1 : 0** **[V. Salov]**

22. **A 21**

D. RAJKOVIĆ 2450 − KIROSKI 2290
Star Dojran 1993

1. ♘f3 d6 2. g3 e5 3. ♗g2 g6 4. c4 ♗g7 5. ♘c3 f5 6. 0−0 ♘f6 7. b4!? N [7. d3 − 31/49] **0−0 8. ♖b1 e4?!** [⌓ 8... ♘h5 △ f4, g5] **9. ♘d4 ♘c6 10. ♘c6** [10. ♘c2 ♗e6 11. d3 ed3 12. ed3 ♖b8 13. b5 ♘e7 14. ♘e3±] **bc6 11. d3!** [11. d4 d5 12. b5 dc4 13. bc6 ♘d5!∞] **d5 12. b5 ♗b7** [12... d4 13. ♘a4 cb5 14. cb5 ♗e6 15. ♕c2 ♕d5 16. ♗g5! ♕a2 17. ♖b2 ♕d5 18. ♗f6 ♗f6 19. de4±] **13. ♗a3** [13. bc6 ♗c6 14. cd5

♘d5 15. ♘d5 ♕d5! 16. de4 fe4 17. ♕c2 ♕e6 18. ♗e3 ♗d5 △ c6±] **♖f7** [13... ♖e8!?] **14. ♘a4** [14. bc6 ♗c6 15. cd5 ♘d5 16. ♘d5 ♕d5! 17. de4 fe4 18. ♕c2±] **♘d7** [14... cb5 15. ♘c5 ♕c8 (△ 16. ♘b7 ♕b7 17. ♖b5 ♕c6±) 16. cb5!±] **15. ♕c2 cb5 16. ♖b5 ♗c6 17. ♖a5!± ♘b6 18. ♘c5 ♕e8** [18... dc4 19. de4±] **19. cd5 ♗d5 20. de4 ♘c4 21. ed5!** [21. ♖a4 ♘a3 22. ♖a3 fe4 23. ♗e4±] **♘a5 22. ♘e6+− ♗e5** [22... ♖c8 23. ♘g7 ♖g7 24. ♗b2] **23. f4 ♗d6 24. ♗b2 ♖b8 25. ♗a1!** [△ ♕c3] **♗b4 26. ♔h1** [△ ♕b2; ⌓ 26. a3!] **h6 27. e4** [27. ♕b2 ♔h7] **♕b5 28. ef5 gf5 29. ♕d1! ♕c4 30. ♕h5 1 : 0**
[D. Rajković]

23. !N A 21**

LAUTIER 2645 – KRAMNIK 2685
Cannes (m/3) 1993

1. c4 e5 2. ♘c3 d6 3. d4 ed4 4. ♕d4 ♘c6 [RR 4... ♘f6 5. ♗g5!? N (5. g3 – 55/19) ♘c6 6. ♕d2 ♗e6 7. e4 h6 8. ♗e3 ♘e5 9. b3 ♘eg4 10. ♗d4 c5 11. ♗f6 ♘f6 12. ♘ge2 g6 13. g3 ♗g7 14. ♗g2 0–0 15. ♖d1 a6?! 16. ♕d6 ♕a5 17. ♕d2 b5 18. ♘d5 ♕d2 19. ♖d2± Lautier 2580 – Romero Holmes 2470, Pamplona 1992/93; ⌓ 15... ♘e8] **5. ♕d2 ♘f6 6. b3 a5! 7. ♗b2** [RR 7. e4 a4 8. ♖b1 ab3 9. ab3 g6 10. ♗d3!? N (10. g3 – 24/41) ♗g7 11. ♘ge2 ♘b4 12. 0–0 0–0 13. ♘f4 ♖e8 14. ♖d1 ♘d3 15. ♕d3 ♘e4! 16. ♘e4 ♖e4 17. ♕e4 ♗f5 18. ♕b7 ♗b1 19. ♘d5 ♖b8! (19... ♗c2 20. ♖e1 ♖b8 21. ♕c6 ♗b3 22. h3±) 20. ♕a7 (20. ♕c7 ♕c7 21. ♘c7 ♗c2 22. ♖e1 ♗b3=) ♖b3 21. ♖e1 h6 (An. Karpov 2725 – Epišin 2620, Dos Hermanas 1993) 22. ♘c7 ♕d7 (22... ♔h7? 23. ♘d5) 23. ♕a8 ♔h7 24. ♘e8 ♗h8 25. ♗f4±] **a4 8. ♖d1** [8. ♘a4? d5 9. c5 (9. cd5 ♘e4 10. ♕e3 ♖a4! 11. ba4 ♗b4 12. ♔d1 ♕d5–+) ♘e4 10. ♕c1 ♖a4 11. ba4 ♗c5∓] **ab3 9. ab3 g6 10. e4 ♗g7 11. ♗d3 ♘d4! N** [11... ♗e6 12. ♘ge2 0–0 13. 0–0 ♘d7 14. ♘d5±; 11... 0–0 12. ♘ge2 ♘d7 13. ♘d5 ♖a2 14. ♘ec3±] **12. ♗c2 ♘c2 13. ♕c2 0–0 14. ♘ge2 ♘h5** [14... ♖e8 15. 0–0 ♘e4? 16. ♘e4 ♗b2 17. ♘d6!±] **15. 0–0 f5 16. c5 fe4 17. ♘e4** [17. cd6 e3! 18. fe3 (18. dc7 ef2 19. ♖f2 ♕c7 20. ♖f8 ♔f8=) ♖f1 19. ♔f1 (19. ♖f1 ♕d6 20. ♘b5 ♕c6=) cd6 20. ♘b5 (20. ♘e4 ♗b2 21. ♕b2 ♕f8 22. ♔g1 ♕e7!) ♗b2 21. ♕b2 ♕b6 *a)* 22. ♘d6 ♕e3 23. ♘c4 ♕e7 24. ♘b6 ♖a6! 25. ♘c8 (25. ♘d5 ♕f8 26. ♔g1 ♗e6=) ♕f8 26. ♔g1 ♕c8=; *b)* 22. ♖d6 ♕b5 23. ♖d8 ♔f7 24. ♕h8 ♕f5 (24... ♗g4?? 25. ♕f8 ♔e6 26. ♖d6 ♔e5 27. ♕e7 ♔f5 28. e4#) 25. ♔e1 ♕b1 26. ♔f2 ♕f5=; 17. ♕e4 ♖e8 *a)* 18. ♕f3?! ♗e5 19. cd6 cd6 20. ♘a4 (20. ♖d2 ♕h4 21. g3 ♕b4!∓) ♗b2 21. ♘b2 ♖a2 22. ♖d2 ♕g5∓; *b)* 18. ♕d5 ♗e6 19. ♕b7 ♖b8 20. ♕c6 ♖b3=] **d5?!** [17... ♗b2 18. ♕b2 ♕e7! 19. cd6 ♕e4 20. d7 ♕e7! 21. dc8♕ ♖ac8=] **18. ♗g7 ♘g7 19. c6! ♗f5 20. ♘2g3** [20. cb7 ♖b8 21. ♘2g3 ♗e4 22. ♘e4 ♖b7 23. ♘c5 (23. ♕c6 ♖b6! 24. ♕d5 ♕d5 25. ♖d5 ♖b3=) ♖b6=] **♗e4 21. ♘e4 ♖b8! 22. ♖d3 bc6 23. ♕c6 ♖b6 24. ♕c3 ♖e6 25. ♘c5 ♖ee8** [25... ♖e2 26. b4 ♘e6 27. ♘e6 ♖e6 28. b5 ♕d6=] **26. b4 c6** [26... ♘e6=] **27. ♘b3! ♕d6 28. ♘d4 ♖f6 29. ♖e3 ♖ef8** [29... ♖e3!? 30. fe3 ♖f1 31. ♔f1 ♕h2 32. ♕c6 (32. ♘c6 ♘f5) ♕h1 33. ♔f2 ♕h4 34. ♔e2 ♕g4 35. ♔d2 ♕g2 36. ♔c3 ♕e4=] **30. ♖e2 ♘f5 31. ♘b3 ♘h6?!** [31... ♖e6 32. ♖e6 (32. ♖fe1 ♖fe8=) ♕e6 33. ♖e1 ♕f6=] **32. h3 ♘f7 33. ♘c5** [△ ♘d7] **♘g5 34. ♖fe1** [34. h4 ♘e6=] **♖6f7?** [34... ♘e4? 35. ♖e4! de4 36. ♘e4+–; 34... ♖f4! 35. ♕g3 (35. ♖e7 ♕f6 36. ♕f6 ♖4f6? 37. ♘d7; 36... ♖8f6=) ♘e4 36. ♘e4 de4 37. ♖e4 ♖e4 38. ♖e4 ♕g3 39. fg3=] **35. h4 ♘e4 36. ♘e4 de4 37. ♕c4 ♕d5 38. ♖c1!± ♖f6?!** [38... e3 39. ♕d5 (39. fe3? ♖f1 40. ♔h2 ♖c1 41. ♕c1 ♕d6) ef2 40. ♖f2 cd5 41. ♖f7 ♖f7 42. b5 ♖b7 43. ♖b1 ♖b6 (43... ♔f7 44. ♔f2 ♔e6 45. ♔e3 ♔e5 46. b6±) 44. ♔f2 ♔f7 45. ♔e3 ♔e6 46. ♔d4 ♔d6±] **39. ♕e4 ♕e4 40. ♖e4 ♖f2 41. ♖c6 ♖f1 42. ♔h2 ♖8f4** [42... ♖b8 43. ♖c7 ♖b1 44. ♖ee7 ♖1b4 45. ♖g7 ♔h8 46. ♖h7 ♔g8 47. ♖cg7 ♔f8 48. ♖g6+–] **43. ♖cc4 ♖e4 44. ♖e4 ♔f7** [44... ♖b1 45. g4! h6 46. g5 hg5 47. hg5 ♖b3 48. ♔g2 ♔f7 49. ♔f2 ♖b2 50. ♔e3 ♖g2 51. ♖e5+–; 44... h5 45. b5 ♖b1 46. ♖e5

♔f7 47. ♖g5+−] **45. ♔g3** [45. g4 ♔f6! 46. ♔g3 ♖h1! 47. ♔f3 (47. g5? ♔f5 48. ♖e7 ♖b1 49. ♖f7 ♔e5 50. ♖h7 ♖b3 51. ♔g2 ♖b4=) ♖h4? 48. g5 ♔g5 49. ♖h4 ♔h4 50. b5+−; 47... h5⇆] **♖b1 46. ♔f4 h5** [46... ♔f6 47. g4 ♖f1 48. ♔e3 ♖b1 (48... ♖h1 49. ♔d4 h5 50. ♔c5 hg4 51. ♖g4 ♔f5 52. ♖c4+−) 49. ♔d3 h5 50. ♔c4+−] **47. ♔g5!** [47. ♔e5?! ♖g1 48. ♔d6 (48. b5? ♖b1; 48. ♖e2 ♖b1) ♖g2 49. ♖f4 ♔g7 50. b5 ♖b2 51. ♔c5 g5! 52. hg5 ♔g6 53. b6 ♔g5 54. ♖b4 ♖c2 55. ♔d6 ♖c8 56. b7 ♖b8 57. ♔c7 ♖f8 58. b8♕ ♖b8 59. ♖b8 h4 60. ♔d6 ♔g4 61. ♔e5 h3 62. ♔e4 h2 63. ♖h8 ♔g3 64. ♔e3 ♔g2=] **♖b2** [47... ♖g1 48. ♖e2 (△ ♖b2) ♖b1 49. ♖f2 ♔g7 50. ♖f6 ♖b4 51. ♖g6 ♔f7 52. ♔h5+−] **48. g3! ♖b3 49. g4 ♖d3** [⌓ 49... hg4 50. ♖g4 ♖d3 51. ♖f4 ♔g7 52. ♖c4 ♖d5 (52... ♖g3 53. ♔f4 ♖g1 54. ♔e5+−) 53. ♔f4 ♔f6 54. ♔e4 ♖h5 55. ♔d3 ♔e6 (55... g5 56. hg5 ♖g5 57. ♖e4+−) 56. ♖d4+−] **50. ♔h6! hg4 51. ♖f4! ♔e7 52. ♖g4 ♖d6 53. ♔g7** [53. ♖g6? ♖d4 54. h5 ♖b4 55. ♔g7 ♖f4!] **♖b6 54. ♖e4 ♔d8 55. ♔f7** [55... ♔c7 56. ♖g4 ♔d7 57. ♖g6 ♖b4 58. h5 ♖e4 (58... ♖f4 59. ♔g7? ♔e7!; 59. ♖f6+−) 59. ♖f6! ♖e7 60. ♔g6+−] **1 : 0** **[Lautier]**

24.* !N **A 21**

LPUTIAN 2610 − MINASIAN 2545

Protvino (zt) 1993

1. d4 d6 2. c4 e5 3. ♘f3 e4 4. ♘g5 f5 5. ♘h3 [RR 5. f3 ♗e7 6. ♘h3 ♘f6 7. ♘c3 0−0 8. ♘f2 ♘c6! N (8... c6 9. fe4 ♘e4 10. ♘fe4 fe4 − 55/21) 9. e3 (9. fe4 fe4 10. ♘fe4 ♘e4 11. ♘e4 ♗f5! 12. ♘c3□ ♗f6∓) ef3 10. gf3 *a)* 10... ♘h5?! 11. f4 g6 (Pieterse 2390 − Nogueiras 2570, Tilburg (Interpolis) 1992) 12. ♗g2 △ 0−0±; *b)* 10... f4! 11. e4 ♘h5∓ Nogueiras, Hernández Ruíz] **♗e7 6. ♘c3 c6 7. g3 ♘f6 8. ♗g5** [8. ♗g2 − 56/28, 29] **♘g4!? N** [8... 0−0; 8... ♘a6] **9. ♗e7 ♕e7 10. e3 g5?** [10... 0−0∞] **11. ♕d2 ♘a6** [11... 0−0 12. 0-0-0 △ ♖e1, f3±] **12. 0-0-0 ♗d7?!** [12... ♘c7 13. d5 c5 14. ♘g1 ♘e5 15. ♗e2 △ f4±] **13. c5! dc5** [13... d5 14. ♗a6 ba6 15. ♕e2 ♗c8 16. ♘g1±] **14. ♗a6 ba6 15. ♘a4 ♗e6** [15... c4? 16. ♘c5 h6 17. ♕c3±] **16. ♘c5 ♗d5 17. ♔b1 ♖b8 18. ♖c1 0−0 19. ♘g1 ♖b5** [19... f4 20. gf4 gf4 21. ♘h3! fe3 22. fe3 ♕h4 23. ♘f4! ♖f4 24. ef4 e3 25. ♕e1 ♕f2 26. ♕f2 ef2 27. ♖hf1 ♗g2 28. ♖f2!±] **20. h3 ♘e5 21. de5 ♖c5 22. ♖c5 ♕c5 23. ♘e2 ♕e7?** [23... ♗c4! 24. ♖c1 ♗d3 25. ♔a1 ♕e5 26. ♖c6 ♗e2 27. ♕e2±] **24. ♕c3 ♖e8 25. ♖c1 ♕e5 26. ♘d4 ♖c8 27. ♕c5 ♖c7 28. b3 f4□ 29. gf4 gf4 30. ♕a5 fe3 31. fe3 ♕h2⊕ 32. ♘f5** [32. ♖c2 ♕g1 33. ♔b2 ♖f7] **h5 33. ♕b4 c5 34. ♕b8 ♔h7 35. ♕f8 ♕g2 36. ♕d6** **1 : 0** **[Lputian]**

25. **A 23**

KLINGER 2480 − ĆIRIĆ 2385

Österreich 1992

1. c4 e5 2. g3 c6 3. ♘f3 d6 4. ♗g2 ♘f6 5. ♘c3 ♗e7 6. 0−0 0−0 [6... a5!? 7. a3 0−0 8. ♖b1 ♗e6 9. d3 h6 10. b4 ab4 11. ab4 ♘bd7 12. b5 d5!=] **7. b4!? N** [7. ♕c2 − 15/46; 7. d3 − 39/35; 7. d4 ♘bd7 − A 54] **e4?!** [⌓ 7... ♗e6] **8. ♘d4 d5 9. cd5 cd5 10. b5!± ♗c5! 11. ♘b3 ♗b4** [11... ♗e7 12. d3±] **12. ♗b2 ♗f5 13. ♘d4 ♗g6 14. ♕b3 ♕d6 15. d3 ♘bd7 16. de4 de4 17. ♖fd1 ♕e7 18. ♗h3 ♗c5! 19. ♖ac1 ♘b6 20. ♘a4?** [⌓ 20. a4] **♘a4 21. ♕a4 ♕e5!= 22. e3 ♕h5 23. ♗g2 ♖fc8 24. h3 ♘d7 25. ♘b3** [⌓ 25. ♕b3] **♘b6 26. ♕a5 ♗f8 27. g4 ♕g5 28. ♖c8 ♖c8 29. ♕a7 ♘c4** [×b5] **30. ♕b7 ♘b2 31. ♕c8 ♘d1 32. b6 ♕f6?⊕** [32... ♘f2! 33. b7□ (33. ♔f2? ♕f6 34. ♔g1 ♕b6 35. ♕c3 h5∓) ♕e3 34. ♔h2 (34. ♔f1? ♘d3−+) ♕f4 35. ♔g1 ♕e3=] **33. ♕c2 ♘c3 34. b7 ♕e5 35. ♘d4 ♕c7 36. ♕b3 ♗d6 37. ♘c6!! ♘e2 38. ♔f1** **1 : 0** **[Ćirić]**

26.* **A 24**

A. ROTŠTEJN 2465 − DYDYŠKO 2490

Minsk 1993

1. c4 g6 2. g3 ♗g7 3. ♗g2 ♘f6 4. ♘f3 0−0 5. 0−0 d6 6. ♘c3 e5 7. d3 ♖e8 8.

♖b1 [RR 8. ♘d2 c6 9. ♖b1 *a)* 9... d5!? 10. cd5 (10. b4!? △ b5∞) cd5 11. ♕b3 d4! (11... ♘c6!? 12. ♘d5 ♘d4 13. ♘f6 ♗f6 14. ♕d1 ♗g4⩱ Itkis) 12. ♗b7 ♗b7 (12... ♗e6!? 13. ♕c2 dc3 14. ♗a8 cd2 15. ♗d2∞) 13. ♕b7 dc3 14. ♕a8 cd2 15. ♗d2 ♕d7!⩱; *b)* 9... ♗e6!? N 10. b4 d5 11. b5 ♘bd7 12. ♗a3?! ♘b6 13. bc6 (13. ♘b3?! dc4 14. ♘c5 ♕c8!∓) bc6 14. c5 (14. ♕c2!? △ ♖fc1) ♘bd7 15. ♕a4 (O. Foişor 2450 – Golod 2410, Olăneşti 1992) ♕c7!∓; 12. a4!? △ ♗a3∞ Golod] **h6!? N** [8... ♘c6 9. ♗g5±; 8... e4 9. de4 ♘e4 10. ♘e4 ♖e4 11. c5±; 8... c6 – 18/58] **9. b4 ♗e6 10. ♗b2 ♘c6 11. b5 ♘e7 12. e4?!** [12. ♘d2 d5?! 13. cd5 ♘fd5 14. ♘de4±; 12... ♕c8!?] **♘d7⇆ 13. ♘h4 ♘c5!** [13... g5 14. ♘f5! ♘f5 15. ef5 ♗f5 16. g4 ♗g6 17. ♗b7 ♘c5! 18. ♗e4!±] **14. ♘d5?** [14. f4 ef4 15. gf4 f5∞] **♘d5! 15. cd5** [15. ed5 ♗d7∓ △ g5, f5↑] **♗d7 16. ♗c3 a6∓ 17. a4 ab5 18. ab5 ♖a3 19. ♗b4! ♖a7** [19... ♖d3 20. ♕c2 ♖d4 21. ♘f3 ♗b5 22. ♗c5 ♗f1 23. ♗f1 dc5 24. ♘d4=] **20. ♗c3?!** [⌓ 20. ♘f3 △ 20... ♕a8 21. ♗c5 dc5 22. ♘d2 ×c4] **♕a8 21. f4 ♖a3! 22. ♕d2**

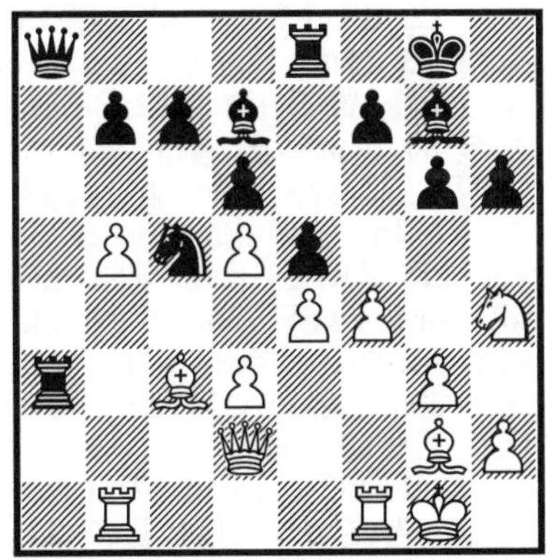

22... ♖c3! 23. ♕c3 ef4 24. ♕d2 fg3 25. hg3 ♕a3! 26. ♕f2 [26. ♖fd1 ♗g4! 27. ♗f3 (27. ♘f3 ♘e4!) ♗f3 28. ♘f3 ♘e4!∓] **♖e7 27. d4 ♕c3! 28. e5** [28. ♖bd1 ♘d3 29. ♕f3 ♕d4 30. ♔h1 ♗b5–+] **♘d3 29. ♕e3 de5 30. ♗e4 ♘f4!!–+ 31. ♕c3 ♘e2 32. ♔h2 ♘c3 33. d6 cd6 34. ♗b7 ♗b5 35. ♖b5 ♘b5 36. ♗d5 ♘c3 37. ♗b3 ♖b7 0 : 1** [Dydyško]

27.* !N** **A 25**

CVETKOVIĆ 2500 – A. KOVAČEVIĆ 2405

Aranđelovac 1993

1. c4 e5 2. ♘c3 ♘c6 [RR 2... d6 3. g3 f5 4. ♗g2 ♘f6 5. d3 ♘c6 6. e3 ♗e7 7. ♘ge2 0–0 8. 0–0 ♕e8 *a)* 9. b3?! ♗d8 10. ♗b2 ♕h5 11. ♕d2 (11. f4? ♘g4) f4 12. ef4 ♗h3⩱; *b)* 9. f4 – 26/32; *c)* 9. ♗d2! N ♘d8 10. ♕c2 ♗d7 11. ♖ae1 ♗c6?! 12. e4 ♕h5 13. ♘d5 ♗d5 14. cd5 c5 15. dc6 bc6 16. ef5 ♕f5 17. ♘d4± M. Pavlović 2455 – Kontić 2400, Podgorica 1993; ⌓ 11... c6 △ ♘f7, ♗d8 M. Pavlović] **3. g3 g6 4. ♗g2 ♗g7 5. e3 d6 6. ♘ge2 ♘ge7** [RR 6... h5 7. d4 h4 8. d5 ♘ce7 9. e4 f5 10. ♗g5 h3 (10... ♗h6 11. gh4±; 10... ♗f6 11. gh4±; 10... ♘h6 11. ♗h4 ♘f7 12. ♗e7±) *a)* 11. ♗f3 N ♗f6 12. ♗f6 (12. ♗e3 ♘h6∞) ♘f6 13. ♕d2 ♔f8! 14. 0–0 (14. 0-0-0 a6! △ b5⇆) ♘eg8! 15. ♘c1 ♘h6 16. ♘d3 ♔g7 17. ♗h1 ♘f7 18. ♖ae1 ♗d7 19. f4 ♕e7 20. c5!? ♖ae8 21. fe5 de5 (21... ♘e5?! 22. ♘e5 de5 23. b4± ×g5) 22. b4 b6! 23. ♖e2 ♖hf8 24. ♖fe1 (∞ 1/2 : 1/2 I. Sokolov 2625 – A. Chernin 2600, Debrecen 1992) ♘g4 25. ♖f1 ♘f6; *b)* 11. ♗f1! ♘f6 (11... ♗f6 12. ♗e3 ♘h6 13. ♗h3 f4 14. ♗c8 fe3 15. ♗e6+–; 11... ♗h6 12. ♗e7 ♕e7 13. ♗h3±) 12. ♕d2! (12. ef5 – 39/41) ♘e4 (12... fe4 13. ♗f6! ♗f6 14. ♘e4± ×g6, h3) 13. ♘e4 fe4 14. ♘c3 ♗f5 15. ♗e2 ♕d7 16. ♖g1 △ g4± A. Chernin] **7. d3** [RR 7. 0–0 h5 8. ♘d5?! (8. d4 – 34/35) h4 9. ♘ec3 ♘d5! N (9... hg3) 10. ♘d5 ♗e6 11. d3 ♕d7 12. ♗d2 ♘d8 13. ♕f3 f5 14. e4 c6 15. ♘c3 ♘f7 16. ♕e2 hg3 17. fg3□ f4!? 18. gf4 ef4 19. ♗f4 ♗d4 *a)* 20. ♗e3 ♗e5 21. d4 (21. ♗f4 g5!) ♗h2 22. ♔f2 ♗g4 23. ♗f3 ♗g3! 24. ♔g3□ ♖h3 25. ♔g2 ♗f3 26. ♕f3□ ♖f3 27. ♖f3 ♕g4 28. ♖g3 ♕e6∓ M. Pavlović 2450 – A. Chernin 2600, München 1992/93; *b)* 20. ♔h1 g5 21. ♗g3 ♗e5⩱→⟫ A. Chernin] **♗g4!? 8. h3! ♗e6 9. ♘d5 0–0** [9... ♕d7!?] **10. ♗d2 N** [10. 0–0 – 40/41; 10. b3!? (△ ♗b2) e4 11. ♖b1±; 10. ♖b1!? △ b4±] **♕d7 11. ♗c3** [11. ♖b1; 11. ♖c1!?] **♘c8** [△ ♘d8, c6; 11... f5] **12. b3** [×c4] **♘d8 13. d4! f5** [13... c6 14. de5 (14. ♘b4 ed4! 15. ♗d4 ♗d4 16. ♘d4±) de5 (14... cd5 15. cd5⩲) 15. ♘b4± ×♘c8, ♘d8] **14. 0–0 c6** [14... e4 15. ♘df4 ♗f7 16. d5⩲] **15. de5 de5** [15... cd5?! 16. cd5 ♗f7 (16... de5?! 17. de6 ♕e7□±) 17. e6 ♘e6 18. de6 ♗e6±] **16. ♘b4 ♕c7** [16... ♕d1?! 17. ♖ad1 △ ♘d3 ×e5, c5] **17. ♘d3 b6?!** [⌓ 17... e4] **18. ♕d2** [△ ♖ad1, ♕b2 ×e5] **e4 19. ♘df4 ♗f7 20. ♗g7 ♔g7 21. h4± ♘b7** [21... ♕e5 22. ♖ad1 △ ♕d7±; 22. ♕d7!?] **22. g4 ♘e7** [△ 23. gf5 ♘f5!] **23. ♕c3 ♔g8 24. ♘g3 ♘d6** [24... fg4 25. ♘e4+– ×f6] **25. h5** [25. ♖ad1!±→ △ 25... fg4? 26. ♖d6 ♕d6 27. ♘e4+–] **fg4□ 26. hg6?!** [26. ♖ad1!±→] **♘g6 27. ♘fh5 ♘e8 28. ♗e4** [28. ♘e4 ♕e5!] **♕e5 29. ♕d4** [⌓ 29. ♕e5 ♘e5 30. ♖ad1±] **♕d4 30. ed4 ♘e7 31. ♖ae1 ♗h5 32. ♘h5 ♖f7 33. ♖e3 ♖d8 34. ♖fe1 ♔f8!= 35. ♗g2** [35. ♘g3 ♘f6 (35... ♖d4 36. ♗c6⩲) 36. ♗g2 (△ 36... ♖d4? 37. ♖e7+–) h5!⇆] **♖d4 36. ♗c6 ♘g7 37. ♘g7 ♖g7 38. ♗g2 ♖d2 39. ♖3e2 ♖e2 40. ♖e2** [♖ 9/i] **♘f5?!** [40... g3!?=] **41. ♖e5 ♖f7 42. ♗d5 ♖f6 43. ♗e4** [43. ♗e6 ♘h4!= △ 44. ♗g4?? ♖g6 45. f3 ♘f3–+] **♘d4 44. ♔g2** [44. ♖d5? ♘e2!–+] **h6 45. ♖d5** [45. ♗d5!?⩲] **♘e2 46. ♖d7 a5** [△ ♘c3] **47. a3 h5** [△ h4⇆] **48. ♖d2 ♘f4 49. ♔g3 ♔e7 50. b4 ab4 51. ab4⩲ ♖d6?! 52. ♖a2?** [52. ♖d6 ♘e2 53. ♔h4 ♔d6 54. ♗g6! (54. ♔h5? g3=) ♘f4 55. ♗h5 ♘d3 56. ♔g3 ♘b4 57. ♗g4 △ ♗e2±] **♘d3= 53. b5 ♖d4 54. ♗d5 ♔d6 55. ♔h4 ♔c5 56. ♖a7 ♘e5** [56... ♘f2] **57. ♖h7 ♘c4 58. ♗c4** [58. ♗c6 ♘e5 59. ♖h5 ♔d6=] **♔c4 59. ♖h5 ♖f4 60. ♔g3 ♖f3 61. ♔g2 1/2 : 1/2 [Cvetković]**

28. A 27

M. SOROKIN 2550 – OBUHOV 2465

Beloreščensk 1992

1. c4 e5 2. ♘c3 ♘c6 3. ♘f3 g6 4. d4 ed4 5. ♘d4 ♗g7 6. ♘c6 bc6 7. g3 ♘e7 8. ♗g2 0–0 9. c5!? N [9. ♗g5?! h6 10. ♗c6 ♖b8; 9. 0–0 – 26/45] **♘f5!** [△ ♘d4-e6⇆] **10. 0–0 ♘d4 11. ♗e3 ♘e6 12. ♖c1 a5! 13. ♕a4!?** [13. ♕d2 ♕e7 14. ♘a4 ♗a6 15. ♖fd1 ♖fd8∞] **♕e7 14. ♖fd1 ♗a6 15. ♖d2 ♖fb8 16. ♕d1 ♗c8 17. ♘a4 ♖b4!⇆ 18. b3 f5! 19. ♖d3 ♖ab8** [19... f4 20. ♗d2 ♖d4 21. ♖d4 ♘d4 22. e3±] **20. ♕d2 ♕f7 21. f4 ♗f6!** [21... ♘f8 22. ♗d4!±] **22. ♖d1 ♘f8** [△ ♗a6] **23. ♗d4 ♗a6! 24. ♗f6 ♗d3 25. ♗c3** [25. ♗b2? ♗e4 26. ♕c3 ♕e7–+] **♗e4 26. ♗b4 ♖b4∓ 27. ♗f1?!** [⌓ 27. ♗e4 ♖e4 28. ♔f2] **♕e7 28. e3 ♗d5 29. ♗g2 ♗g2 30. ♔g2 h5!? 31. h4 ♔f7** [△ ♔e8-d8-c8, ♘h7-f6 ×e3, e4, g4] **32. ♔f2 ♔e8** [×d7] **33. ♕c3 ♔d8 34. ♖d4** [34. ♕h8! ♕f7?! 35. ♘b2! △ ♘d3-e5; 34... ♖e4!?] **♖b5! 35. e4?⊕ fe4 36. ♕e3 ♖b4!–+ 37. ♖b4 ab4 38. ♕d4 ♕e6 39. ♕e5** [39. ♕b4 e3 40. ♔e2 ♕g4 41. ♔e3 ♕g3] **♕d5 40. ♕f6 ♔e8 0 : 1 [Obuhov]**

29. !N A 28**

A. CHERNIN 2600 –
ZSU. POLGÁR 2560

Budapest (zt) 1993

1. c4 e5 2. ♘c3 ♘f6 3. ♘f3 ♘c6 4. e3 ♗b4 [RR 4... ♗e7 5. a3 a5!? N (5... 0–0 – 36/29) 6. ♕c2 0–0 7. ♗d3 g6 (7... h6!?) 8. b3 (8. ♘d5 a4!?) d5! 9. cd5 ♘d5 10. ♘d5 ♕d5 11. ♗b2 (11. ♗e4!? ♕d6 12. ♗b2) ♕d6 (11... ♗e6!? 12. ♗e4 ♕b3 13. ♕b3 ♗b3 14. ♗c6 bc6 15. ♘e5 ♗f6=) 12. ♗e4 (12. h4!?) ♖a6! 13. h4 (△ 13... h5 14. ♗d3 ♖b6 15. ♘g5↑) ♗e6? 14. h5 f5 (14... ♖b6 15. hg6 hg6 16. ♗g6 ♗b3 17. ♗h7 ♔g7 18. ♕f5→⟫) 15. ♗d3 ♖b6 16. hg6 hg6 17. ♗c4 ♗f6 (17... ♔g7? 18. ♘e5! ♘e5 19. f4 ♗f6 20. fe5 ♗e5 21. ♗e6 ♕e6 22. ♕c7+–) 18. g4! (18. 0-0-0 e4⇆) e4! (Krasenkov 2560 – Biolek 2420, Katowice 1993) 19. ♗f6! ♖f6 (19... ef3 20. gf5±) 20. ♘g5 ♘e5 (20... ♘d8 21. ♘e6 ♘e6 22. gf5 gf5 23. ♔e2±; 20... ♗d5 21. ♔e2±) 21. ♘e6! (21. ♗e6 ♖e6 22. ♘e6 ♖c6!) ♘c4 (21... ♖e6 22. ♗e6 ♕e6 23. ♕c7+–) 22. gf5 gf5 (22... ♘e5 23. ♕e4 ♖f5 24. ♘d4±) 23. ♘d4 ♘e5 (23... ♘a3? 24. ♕a2 ♘b5 25. b4+–) 24. ♔e2±→; 13... ♖d8! △ f5∞ Krasenkov] **5. ♕c2 ♗c3 6. ♕c3 ♕e7 7. d3** [RR 7. ♗e2 d5!? N (7... 0–0 – 34/37) 8. cd5 ♘d5 9. ♕b3 ♘b6 10. 0–0 (10. d3!? 0–0 11. 0–0 ♗f5∞) e4 11. ♘e1 0–0 12. d3 ♗e6 13. ♕c2 ♘b4 14. ♕b1 ♗f5! 15. ♗d2! (15. a3 ed3 16. ♘d3 ♘4d5 17. ♕c2

♖ad8∓) ♘d3!? 16. ♘d3 ♕d7!? 17. ♘f4 ♕d2 18. ♖d1 ♕a5 19. g4 ♗d7 20. ♕e4 ♗c6 (Cerisier 2285 – Jakovič 2510, Cappelle la Grande 1993) 21. ♕f5!? ♕b4!? (21... ♕f5 22. gf5 ♖fe8=) 22. ♖d4 ♕e7∞ Jakovič] **d5 8. cd5 ♘d5 9. ♕c2 0–0 10. a3 a5 11. b3** [11. ♗e2 a4=] **♗g4 12. ♗e2 ♖ad8 13. 0–0 f5 14. h3 ♗h5 15. ♗b2** [15. ♘e5? ♕e5 16. ♗h5 ♕a1? 17. ♗b2 ♕a2 18. ♖a1 ♕a1 19. ♗a1±; 16... f4!∓]

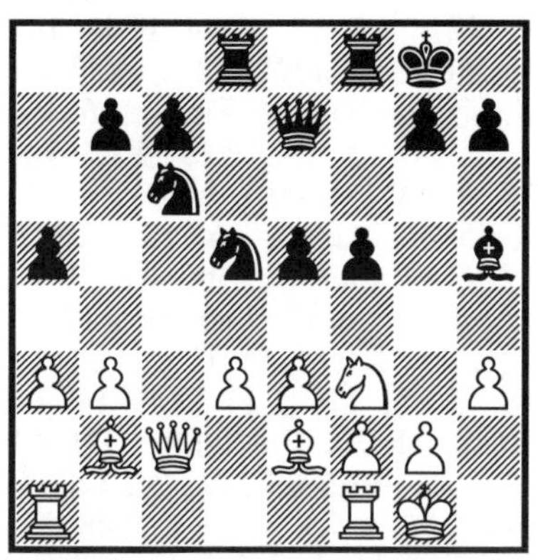

15... e4! N [15... ♔h8?! – 28/43] **16. de4 fe4 17. ♘e5** [17. ♘e1 ♗e2? 18. ♕e2=; 17... ♗g6∓] **♗e2 18. ♘c6 bc6 19. ♕e2 ♖d6! 20. ♖ac1?** [20. f4!? ef3 21. ♖f3 ♖f3 22. ♕f3 ♕e3 23. ♕e3 ♘e3 24. ♗e5∞; 20. ♗d4! ♖g6 21. f4 ef3 22. ♖f3 ♖f3 23. ♕f3 ♖e6=] **♖g6∓ 21. ♗d4** [21. ♔h1 ♖f3! 22. gf3 ♕e6 23. ♔h2 ♖h6–+]

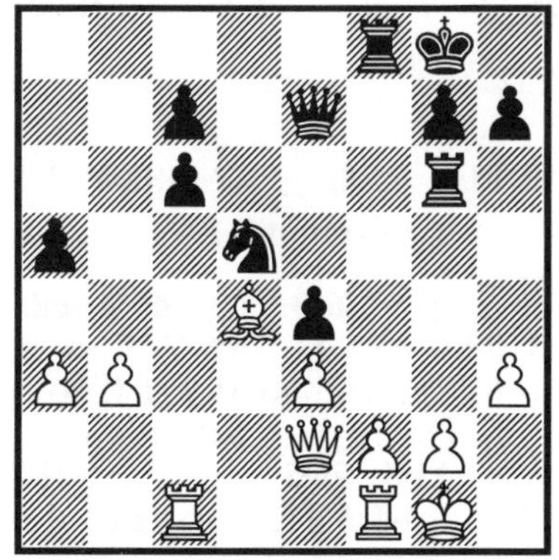

21... ♖f3! 22. g3 [22. ♕a6 ♖g2? 23. ♔g2 ♕g5 24. ♔h2 ♕f5 25. ♔g1 ♖h3 26. ♗e5!=; 22... ♕d7!–+] **♕h4 23. ♔h2 ♖gg3! 24. fg3 ♕g3** [24... ♖g3?? 25. ♖f8! ♔f8 26. ♕f2+–] **25. ♔h1 ♕h3 26. ♔g1 ♖g3 27. ♔f2 ♕h4! 28. ♖h1** [28. ♔e1 ♖e3 29. ♔d2 ♖e2 30. ♔e2 ♕g4 31. ♔d2 ♕g3–+] **♖h3 0 : 1 [Zsu. Polgár]**

30.* A 28

LJUBOJEVIĆ 2605 –
AN. KARPOV 2725
Linares 1993

1. c4 e5 2. ♘c3 ♘f6 3. ♘f3 ♘c6 4. e3 ♗b4 5. ♕c2 0–0 6. ♘d5 ♖e8 7. ♗d3 g6 [7... h6?! 8. a3 ♗f8 9. ♘f6 ♕f6 10. ♗h7 ♔h8 11. ♗e4± △ 11... d6 12. b4; 12. b3] **8. ♘f6** [8. h4?! ♗f8 9. h5 ♘d5 10. hg6 ♘db4! 11. gf7 ♔f7 12. ♖h7 ♔g8!–+; RR 8. a3 ♗f8 9. ♖b1 N (9. ♘f6; 9. 0–0 – 46/(28)) ♗g7 10. b4 d6 11. b5 ♘d4 12. ♘f6 ♕f6 13. ♘d4 ed4 14. 0–0 ♕h4 15. ♗b2 ♗d7 16. g3 ♕h5 17. ♗d4 ♗h3 18. ♖fe1 ♕f3 19. ♗f1 ♗f1 20. ♖f1 ♗d4 21. ed4 ♕a3= Ljubojević 2605 – Anand 2710, Monaco 1993] **♕f6 9. a3 ♗f8 10. ♗e4 d6 11. b3 N** [11. b4 – 23/(56)] **♘d8!** [11... ♘e7 12. ♗b2 ♗f5 13. d4!±] **12. ♗b2 ♕e7!∓ 13. ♖c1 c6** [△ f5, e4] **14. ♕b1 ♗g7 15. 0–0 ♗d7** [15... ♗g4!? (△ f5, ♗f3∓) 16. h3 ♗d7] **16. b4 f5 17. ♗c2 ♘f7 18. ♘e1 c5!∓ 19. ♗c3 b6 20. ♕b2** [△ f4, ♘f3] **♘g5 21. f3** [21. f4 ef4 22. ♗g7 ♕g7 23. ♕g7 ♔g7 24. ef4 (24. ♖f4 ♗c6∓) ♘e6∓] **♗c6 22. ♗b3 ♘e6 23. ♘c2** [△ d4] **♕h4 24. ♘e1** [24. ♖ce1!? △ ♖e2] **♖e7** [24... ♘d4 25. ♖f2□] **25. ♕c2 ♖f8 26. ♕d3 ♖d8** [△ e4] **27. ♕c2** [27. ♕e2 ♘d4 28. ♕d1□ ♖de8 29. ed4 ed4 30. ♗b2 ♗e5] **♗f6** [27... ♘d4 28. ed4 ed4 29. ♘d3 dc3 30. dc3∓] **28. ♖d1**

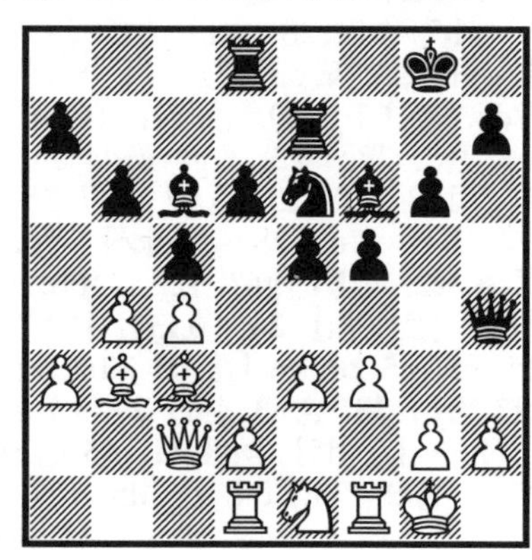

28... ♘d4! 29. ed4 ed4 30. ♖f2 [30. ♗b2 ♖e2 (30... ♗e5!? 31. f4 ♗f4 32. ♖f4 ♕f4 33. d3 ♖de8 34. ♕f2 ♕f2 35. ♔f2 ♖e2−+) 31. ♘d3 ♖de8 32. ♖f2 ♖f2 33. ♘f2 ♖e2 34. ♖f1 ♗e5−+; 30. ♗a1 ♗e5 31. f4 ♗f4 32. ♖f4 ♕f4 33. d3 ♖de8 34. ♕f2 ♕g4 35. ♘f3 ♖e2 36. ♕g3 ♗f3 37. gf3 ♖e1−+] **dc3 31. dc3 ♗g5 32. g3 ♕h5! 33. f4 ♖de8 34. ♘g2** [34. fg5 ♖e1 35. ♖f1 ♕f3−+] **♖e2 35. ♖d2 ♖e1!−+ 36. ♖f1** [36. ♘e1 ♖e1 37. ♖f1 ♕f3 38. ♖e1 ♕h1 39. ♔f2 ♕g2 40. ♔e3 ♕f3#] **♖f1 37. ♔f1 ♕h2 38. ♖d5 ♗d5 39. cd5 ♕g3 40. fg5 ♕f3** [41. ♕f2 ♕d3 42. ♔g1 ♕b1] **0 : 1**
[An. Karpov]

31. **A 29**

KAMSKY 2655 – CÁMPORA 2550

Buenos Aires 1993

1. c4 e5 2. ♘c3 ♘f6 3. ♘f3 ♘c6 4. g3 ♘d4 5. ♗g2 ♘f3 6. ♗f3 ♗b4 7. d4!? e4 8. ♗g2 0–0 N [8... ♗c3 — 53/39] **9. 0–0 ♗c3 10. bc3 ♖e8 11. ♗g5!? h6** [11... d6? 12. ♕b1±] **12. ♗f6 ♕f6 13. f3 ef3?!** [13... e3 14. f4 d6 15. f5! ♖e7! (15... ♖b8? 16. ♕a4!±) 16. ♕d3±] **14. ♗f3 ♕g5?!** [14... ♕e7!?] **15. ♗d5 ♖e7 16. ♕d3↑ c6 17. ♖f5 ♕g4** [17... ♕g6?? 18. ♖f7+−] **18. ♗f3 ♕g6! 19. ♗h5 ♕h7□** [19... ♕d6? 20. c5 ♕c7 21. ♖af1 f6 22. ♖f6 gf6 23. ♕g6 ♖g7 24. ♕e8 ♔h7 25. ♖f6 △ ♗g6+−] **20. ♖e5!** [20. ♗f7?! ♖f7 21. ♖af1 ♖f6!! (21... ♖f5? 22. ♖f5 g6□ 23. ♖e5! ♕f7 24. ♕e3! ♕f6□ 25. ♕h6 ♔f7□ 26. ♖e3 d5 27. ♕h7 ♔f8 28. ♖f3 ♗f5 29. g4±) 22. ♖f6 gf6 23. ♕e3 ♕g6 24. ♕e7 ♕f7 25. ♕d6 ♕e6∓; 20. ♖f7!? (Cámpora) ♕d3 21. ♖e7 ♕c3 22. ♗g6 ♕d4 23. ♔g2 ♕f6 24. ♖e8 ♕f8 25. ♗h7 ♔f7 26. ♖f8 ♔f8 27. ♖f1 ♔e7 28. ♗g6∞] **♕d3 21. ed3 ♖e6 22. ♖b1 g6?** [22... b6!?] **23. ♖e6! de6** [♖ 9/k] **24. ♗f3±** [×b7, c6] **♔f8 25. c5! a5 26. c4** [△ d5 ×b7,f7] **♖a7 27. ♔f2 ♔e7 28. ♔e3 ♗d7 29. a3 ♗e8?! 30. ♖b6!+−** [△ d5] **♔d8 31. d5 ♔c7 32. d6** [32... ♔c8 33. d4 △ d5 ×c6, e6]
1 : 0 **[Kamsky]**

32. **A 29**

SEIRAWAN 2605 – I. GUREVICH 2510

USA (ch) 1992

1. ♘f3 ♘f6 2. c4 g6 3. ♘c3 d5 4. cd5 ♘d5 5. d3!? ♗g7 6. ♗d2 ♘c6 7. g3 e5 8. ♗g2 ♘de7 [△ ×d4] **9. ♖b1 N** [9. 0–0 — 17/27] **0–0** [9... a5! 10. a3 0–0 11. b4 ab4 12. ab4= ⇔a] **10. b4 ♘d4 11. 0–0 c6** [11... ♗g4 12. ♘d4 ed4 13. ♘a4±] **12. b5!** [△ 12... c5 13. ♘a4 ♕d6 14. ♘d4 cd4 15. ♗b4±] **♘f3?!** [12... ♗d7 13. ♘d4 ed4 14. ♘a4 cb5 15. ♘c5 ♗c6 16. ♘b7 ♕c7 17. ♗c6±] **13. ♗f3 ♗h3 14. ♖e1 ♕d7 15. ♕a4!±** [△ 16. bc6 ♘c6 17. ♖b7] **f5?** [△ e5-e4; ×♗h3, e6; 15... c5 16. b6! ♕a4 17. ♘a4 ab6 18. ♘b6 ♖a2 19. ♗e3± ×b7, c5; 15... a6 16. bc6 ♘c6 17. ♖b6±] **16. ♗g5!+−** [×c6] **f4** [16... e4 17. de4 ♗c3 18. ♕b3] **17. ♗e7 ♕e7 18. bc6 bc6 19. ♗c6 ♖ac8 20. ♘e4!** [△ ×f2] **♖b8 21. ♖b5 ♖b5 22. ♕b5 h5 23. ♖b1 h4 24. ♕b7** [24. gh4!? ♕h4 25. f3+−] **♕d8 25. ♕a7** [△ ♖b7] **hg3 26. hg3 fg3 27. fg3 ♗g4 28. ♖b7 ♗h6 29. ♔g2! ♗e6** [29... ♗e2 30. ♖d7 ♗f3 31. ♔h2 ♕c8 32. ♗d5 ♔h8 33. ♖h7#] **30. ♖e7 ♗f7** [30... ♗f5 31. ♕b7 △ ♗d5] **31. ♖d7 ♕c8 32. ♘f6** [32. ♖f7 ♕c6] **♔h8** [32... ♔g7 33. ♗d5 ♔f6 34. ♖f7 ♔g5 35. ♕e7 ♔h5 36. ♕h4#] **33. ♖f7 ♕c6 34. ♔h2 ♕f6 35. ♖f6 ♖f6 36. ♕b8 ♔h7 37. ♕e5 ♗g7 38. ♕e4 ♖f5 39. a4 ♖e5 40. ♕g4** **1 : 0** **[Seirawan]**

33. **A 29**

SERPER 2590 – KAMSKY 2655

Dortmund 1993

1. c4 e5 2. g3 ♘f6 3. ♗g2 d5 4. cd5 ♘d5 5. ♘c3 ♘b6 6. ♘f3 ♘c6 7. 0–0 ♗e7 8. ♖b1! 0–0 [8... a5?! ×b5] **9. b4! a6 N** [9... ♗b4? 10. ♘e5!; 9... ♗f5 10. b5! ♗b1? 11. bc6 △ ♗b7, ♘e5+−; 9... e4!?] **10. a4 ♗f5** [10... ♗b4?! 11. ♘e5 ♗c3 12. ♘c6 bc6 13. dc3 ♕d1 14. ♖d1 ♘a4 15. ♗a3!±; 15. ♖b3!?±] **11. b5! ab5 12. ♖b5?!** [12. ab5! △ 12... ♗b1? 13. bc6+−] **f6! 13. d3** [13. d4!? ed4! (13... ♘d4?! 14. ♘d4 ed4 15. ♖f5 dc3 16. ♕b3 ♔h8 17. ♕c3 ♘a4 18. ♕c2± △ 19. ♗b7, 19. ♖h5) *a)* 14.

♘d5?! ♘d5 (14… ♘a4? 15. ♘e7 ♘e7 16. ♘d4±; 14… ♗e6!?) 15. ♘d4 ♘c3! (15… ♘d4 16. ♖d5 ♘e2 17. ♕e2 ♗d7 18. ♖fd1 ♗d6 19. ♗f4=) 16. ♕b3 ♔h8 17. ♘c6 bc6 18. ♖f5 ♘e2 19. ♔h1 ♘d4–+; *b)* 14. a5?! dc3 (14… ♖a5?! 15. ♘d4 ♖b5 16. ♘cb5 ♘d4 17. ♘d4 ♗c8 18. ♕b3 ♔h8 19. ♖d1±) 15. ♕b3 ♘d5!! 16. ♘h4 (16. ♖d5 ♗e6!) ♘d4! 17. ♕d5 ♕d5 18. ♗d5 ♔h8 19. ♘f5 (19. ♖b7 ♗h3!) ♘b5 20. ♘e7 c6 △ ♖a5∓; *c)* 14. ♖f5 dc3 15. ♕b3 ♔h8 16. ♕c3 ♖a4 17. ♕c2 (△ ♖h5) ♖c4∓] **♗e6 14. ♗d2 ♘d4 15. ♖b1 c5! 16. ♘e4!** [△ a5; 16. a5? ♖a5 17. ♘d4 cd4 18. ♘b5 ♖a2 19. ♗b7 ♘d5∓ ×♗b7, ♘b5] **♖a7** [16… ♖a4?? 17. ♖b6] **17. a5 ♘d7 18. ♗c3** [△ ♘d2-c4] **♘c6 19. ♖b5 ♕c7 20. ♕b1?** [⌓ 20. ♕a1] **♖b8 21. ♕a1 b6** [21… ♖ba8 22. ♕b2] **22. ab6 ♖b6 23. ♕b1 ♘d4 24. ♘d4 cd4 25. ♗d2 ♖b5 26. ♕b5 ♕b6 27. ♕b6 ♘b6 28. ♖c1 ♔f7 29. h4 ♘d5 30. ♗f3** [30. ♘c5?! ♖a2 31. ♘e6 ♔e6 32. ♗d5 (32. ♖d1? ♘c3; 32. ♖c6 ♗d6 △ 33. ♗c1? ♘c3!) ♔d5 33. ♖d1∓] **♖c7 31. ♖c7⊕ ♘c7 32. ♔f1 h6 33. g4 ♘d5 34. e3! de3 35. fe3 ♘b4 36. ♔e2 ♗c8?** [36… g6=] **37. h5!± ♗a6 38. ♘f2 ♗b5 39. ♗e4 ♘a6?** [39… ♔f8±] **40. ♗d5 ♔e8 41. ♗c4! ♗c4** [41… ♘c7 42. ♗a5] **42. dc4±** [♙c, ×g7; ♘♗ 9/c] **♔d7 43. ♘e4 ♘c7 44. ♔d3 ♘e6 45. ♔c2 ♔c6 46. ♔b3 ♗d8 47. ♘g3 ♗b6 48. ♘f5 ♘c5 49. ♔c2 ♘e6 50. ♗b4 e4** [50… ♗a7!? △ 51. ♔b3 ♗b6 52. ♔a4 ♗a7 53. ♘e7 ♔d7 54. ♘d5 ♔c6 55. ♔a5 ♗c5!; 50… ♗a7 51. ♔d3! △ 51… ♗b6? 52. ♘e7 ♔d7 53. ♘d5 △ ♔e4+–] **51. ♘g3 ♗e3?** [⌓ 51… ♘g5 52. ♘f5 ♘e6 53. ♔c3! △ ♘d4] **52. ♘e4 ♗f4 53. ♔d3 ♗c7 54. ♗d2! ♘d8 55. ♗c3! ♘f7 56. ♘d2 ♘g5 57. ♗d4! ♘f7 58. ♘f3 ♗g3 59. ♗b2 ♗f2** [△ 60. ♗a3 ♗c5!] **60. ♗c1!+–⊕** [△ ♗f4, ♔e4-f5-g6+–; 60… ♗g3□ 61. ♗a3! ♗d6 62. ♘d4 ♔d7 63. ♗d6 ♔d6 (63… ♘d6 64. c5 ♘f7 65. ♔e4+–) 64. ♘f5 ♔c5 (64… ♔e5 65. ♔e3!+–) 65. ♘g7! (65. ♔e4!? ♘e5 66. ♔f4 ♘c4 67. ♘g7 ♔d6 68. ♘f5 ♔e6 69. ♘h6±) ♘e5 66. ♔e4 ♘g4 (66… ♔c4 67. ♔f5 ♔d5 68. ♘e8!+–; 66… ♘c4 67. ♘e8!+–) 67. ♘f5! ♔c4 68. ♔f4 ♘e5 69. ♘h6 ♔d5 70. ♔f5 ♔d6 71. ♘g8!+–]

1 : 0 **[Serper]**

34.* **!N** **A 29**

HERTNECK 2575 – M. GUREVICH 2610

Deutschland 1993

1. c4 e5 2. ♘c3 ♘f6 3. ♘f3 ♘c6 4. g3 d5 5. cd5 ♘d5 6. ♗g2 ♘b6 7. d3 ♗e7 8. a3 [RR 8. ♗e3 0–0 9. ♖c1 ♖e8 10. 0–0 ♗f8 11. ♘e4 ♗e6?! N (11… ♘d4) 12. ♘c5 ♗c5 13. ♖c5 ♗d5 14. ♘d2 ♗g2 15. ♔g2 ♘b4?! 16. ♘e4 ♘4d5 17. ♗g5 f6 18. ♗d2 c6 19. ♕b3± R. Hübner 2620 – Hertneck 2575, München 1993; ⌓ 15… ♘d4 Hertneck] **0–0 9. b4 ♗e6 10. ♖b1 f6 11. 0–0 ♘d4 12. ♗b2 ♘f3 13. ♗f3 c6 14. ♕c2 a5! N** [14… ♕d7 15. ♖fd1 ♖fd8 16. ♘e4! △ d4; 14… ♕e8 – 50/(33)] **15. b5 cb5 16. ♘b5** [16. ♗b7?! ♖b8 17. ♗c6 b4 18. ab4 ab4↑] **♖c8 17. ♗c3** [17. ♕d2 ♘c4!] **♘d5 18. ♕b2 ♘c3 19. ♘c3 ♕d7** [19… b6!?] **20. ♕a1?!** [20. ♗b7!? ♖b8 21. ♖fc1! △ ♘e4; 20… ♖c7!?∞] **♖c7 21. ♖b6!?** [△ ♖e6] **♗f7 22. ♖fb1 ♖b8 23. ♘b5 ♖c2!? 24. ♘c3 ♖c8 25. ♖b7 ♕d8 26. ♘d5□** [26. ♘e4 ♖a2–+] **♗d5** [26… ♗c5 27. ♖f7!? ♔f7 28. ♖b7 ♔g8 29. ♔g2∞] **27. ♗d5 ♕d5 28. ♖e7 ♔f8?!** [28… ♖a2? 29. ♕c3+–; 28… ♕c5!? 29. ♖eb7 ♖e2 30. ♖f1□∓] **29. ♖eb7 ♖e2** [29… ♖a2? 30. ♖b8!] **30. ♖b8 ♖b8 31. ♖b8 ♔f7 32. ♕b1= ♖d2 33. ♕b7**

1/2 : 1/2 **[M. Gurevich]**

35.* **A 29**

LAUTIER 2645 – B. GEL'FAND 2690

München 1993

1. c4 ♘f6 2. ♘c3 e5 3. ♘f3 ♘c6 4. g3 d5 5. cd5 ♘d5 6. ♗g2 ♘b6 7. 0–0 ♗e7 8. a3 0–0 [RR 8… a5 9. d3 0–0 10. ♗e3 ♗e6 11. ♖c1 ♕d7!? N (11… ♘d5 – 33/40; 11… f5) 12. d4 ed4 13. ♘d4 ♘d4 14. ♕d4 ♕d4 15. ♗d4 c5 16. ♗e3 ♘c4 17. ♘a4 ♘e3 18. fe3 c4 19. ♗b7 ♖a7 20. ♗f3 ♗g5 21. ♔f2 ♖e8=∞ Seirawan 2595 – Zsu. Polgár 2560, Monaco 1993] **9. b4 ♖e8 10. ♖b1 ♗f8 11. d3 ♘d4 12. ♘e1!? N** [12. ♘d2 – 55/38] **c6 13. e3 ♘e6?!** [⌓ 13… ♘b5] **14. ♘f3 ♘c7** [14… f6!?] **15. ♕c2 ♘bd5?!** [15… f6!?±; 15… ♗f5!? △

16. ♘e4 ♗e4 17. de4 ♕c8⇆] **16. ♘e2! ♗g4 17. ♗b2** [17. h3!?] **♕f6 18. d4! ed4** [18... e4 19. ♘e5 ♗f3 20. ♗f3 ef3 21. ♘f4 ♘f4 22. gf4±] **19. ♘fd4 ♕g6 20. e4 ♖ad8?!** [20... ♘b5! 21. f3 (△ 21... ♘e3 22. ♕d3 ♘f1 23. fg4+−; 21. ♘b5 cb5 22. ♕d3 ♖ad8!) ♗d7±] **21. ♖be1 ♘b6** [21... ♘b5 22. ♘b5 cb5 23. ♘d4±] **22. f4** [22. ♘f4!?] **♗e2 23. ♖e2** [23. f5 ♕h5 24. ♖e2 f6!?±] **♘b5** [23... f6!?±] **24. ♘f3** [24. ♘b5 cb5 ×c4] **c5?!** [24... f6!?] **25. bc5** [25. a4 ♘d4] **♖c8 26. ♕b3! ♗c5 27. ♔h1 ♘d6 28. e5** [28. ♘e5 ♕e6 29. ♕e6 fe6±] **♘f5** [28... ♘dc4 29. ♘g5±] **29. ♘g5 h6**

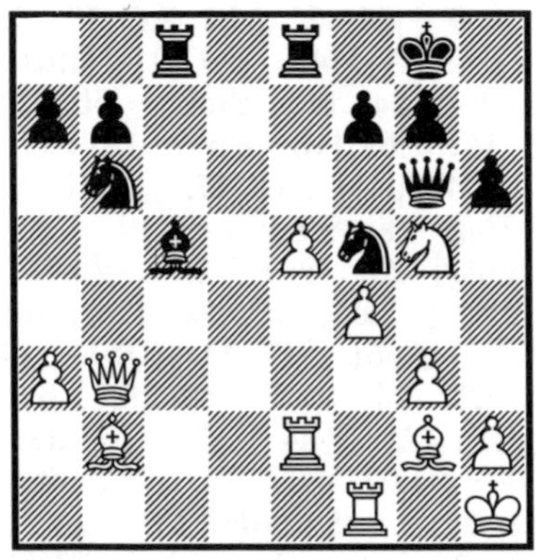

30. g4! [30. ♘e4 ♗d4 31. ♘d6 ♖c3! (31... ♘d6 32. ♗d4) 32. ♕f7 (32. ♗c3?? ♘g3−+; 32. ♕c3? ♗c3 33. ♘e8 ♘g3!−+) ♕f7 33. ♘f7 ♔f7 34. ♗c3 ♗c3±; 30. ♗e4!?] **hg5 31. gf5 ♕f5 32. fg5 ♕e6 33. ♕f3** [33. ♕e6!? fe6 34. ♗b7 ♖c7 (34... ♖b8 35. ♗c6 △ ♗b5) 35. ♗a6±] **♖c7⊕ 34. ♖e4** [34. ♗h3!? ♕c6 (34... ♕d5 35. e6+−) 35. ♖e4±] **♘c4 35. ♗c3 b5 36. ♖h4** [36. ♗h3! *a)* 36... ♕d5 37. e6 fe6 38. ♕h5! (38. ♖e6!?) ♘d6 (38... ♕e4 39. ♗g2) 39. ♕e8!+−; *b)* 36... ♕c6 37. e6 fe6 (37... ♘d6 38. ef7 ♖f7 39. ♖e8 ♕e8 40. ♕d5+−) 38. ♕h5! ♘e3 (38... ♘d6 39. g6+−) 39. ♗g2! ♘f1 40. ♖f4+−] **♘e3 37. ♕h5** [37. ♖e1 ♘g2∓; 37. ♗h3 ♕d5∓] **♔f8 38. ♖f3??** [38. ♗h3? ♕c6 (38... ♕d5 39. ♖f3∞) 39. ♖f3 ♖d8−+; 38. ♕h8 ♔e7 39. ♕g7 ♘f1 40. ♖h6!+−] **♖d8−+ 39. ♖e3 ♗e3 40. ♗b4 ♗c5** [40... ♔e8 41. ♕h8 ♔d7 42. ♗h3∓] **41. ♗a5 ♕b3!** [42. ♖f4 ♖d1 43. ♖f1 ♖f1 44. ♗f1 ♕d5 45. ♗g2 ♕d4] **0 : 1** **[B. Gel'fand]**

36. !N **A 29**

LOBRON 2620 − BAREEV 2670

München 1993

1. c4 e5 2. g3 ♘f6 3. ♗g2 d5 4. cd5 ♘d5 5. ♘c3 ♘b6 6. ♘f3 ♘c6 7. 0−0 ♗e7 8. a3 0−0 9. b4 ♗e6 10. d3 f6?! 11. ♗b2 a5! N [11... ♕e8 − 31/59; 11... ♕d7 − 47/(43)] **12. b5 ♘a7 13. ♘d2 ♖b8** [13... c6 14. bc6 ♘c6 15. ♖b1±] **14. ♖b1?!** [14. ♘b3!⩲] **♕d7 15. a4?!** [15. ♗c1!?] **c6 16. bc6 ♘c6= 17. ♘b5 ♗b4 18. ♗c3 ♕e7! 19. ♔h1?** [19. ♖e1; 19. ♖c1] **♖fd8 20. ♖c1** [20. f4? ♘d5−+] **♖a8!? 21. ♔g1 ♗f7 22. ♘e4?** [22. ♖e1!∓] **f5 23. ♘d2** [23. ♗b4 ab4 24. ♘c5 e4 25. ♕c2 ♘a4 26. de4 ♘c5 27. ♕c5 ♕c5 28. ♖c5 ♖a5−+ ×♘b5] **h6?** [23... e4! 24. de4 fe4 25. ♗e4 ♖d2 26. ♗h7 ♔h7 27. ♕d2 ♖d8−+] **24. ♕c2 ♗c3 25. ♘c3 ♘d4 26. ♕b1 ♕b4 27. ♔h1!□⊕** [27. e3 ♘a4!−+; 27. ♖fe1 ♖ac8−+] **♘a4 28. ♘a4 ♕a4 29. e3?** [29. ♕b7!∞] **♘b3 30. ♘b3 ♕b3 31. ♕a1?** [31. ♗b7 ♖ab8? 32. ♕b3 ♗b3 33. ♗a6=; 31... ♖a7!∓] **♕d3 32. ♕e5** [32. ♖fd1 ♕b3−+] **♗d5!−+ 33. ♕a1 a4 34. ♖c7 ♖d7 35. ♖fc1 ♖ad8 36. h3 b5 37. ♕e5 ♗g2 38. ♔g2 ♕e4 39. ♕e4 fe4 40. ♖7c5 0 : 1** **[Bareev]**

37. **A 29**

CH. LUTZ 2550 − HERTNECK 2575

Deutschland 1993

1. c4 e5 2. ♘c3 ♘f6 3. ♘f3 ♘c6 4. g3 d5 5. cd5 ♘d5 6. ♗g2 ♘b6 7. 0−0 ♗e7 8. a3 0−0 9. b4 ♗e6 10. d3 a5 11. b5 ♘d4 12. ♘d2 a4 13. ♗b7 ♖a5 14. ♖b1! [14. ♗c6 ♘c6 15. bc6 ♕a8∓; 14. ♗g2 ♘b5↑《] **♕d7 15. ♘f3 N** [15. ♘c4 − 36/(37)] **♗b3** [15... ♘b5!? 16. ♘e5 ♘c3 17. ♘d7 ♘d1 18. ♘f8 ♗b3 (18... ♘c3? 19. ♘e6 ♘b1 20. ♘c7 ♘a3 21. ♗e3! ♖a7 22. ♘d5 ♖b7 23. ♘b6 ♘c2 24. ♘a4 ♘e3 25. fe3+−) 19. ♗d2 ♖a7 20. ♗f3! ♔f8 21. e3 ♘f2 22. ♔f2 ♗a3±] **16. ♕e1?!** [16. ♘e5 ♕e6 17. ♖b3 ab3 18. ♘c6 ♘c6 19. ♗c6 ♗a3∞; 16. ♕d2! ♖a7□ (16... ♕e6 17. ♗a6!?±) 17. ♗c6 (17. ♗e4 f5! 18. ♘e5!? ♕d6 19. ♘c6 fe4 20. ♘a7 ed3$\overline{\overline{\infty}}$)

♘c6 18. bc6 ♕c6 19. ♘e5 ♕e6=/∞] **♖b5!?** [⌓ 16... ♕e6 △ 17. ♘d4 ed4 18. ♘d5 ♘d5 19. ♕a5 ♘c3 20. ♖a1 ♕e2!=/∞] **17. ♘d4 ed4 18. ♘b5 ♕b5=/∞ 19. ♗f3 c5 20. ♕d2 ♖d8** [20... g5!?] **21. ♕f4 c4 22. dc4 ♘c4 23. ♗e4 ♕h5** [23... ♘a3? 24. ♗a3 ♗a3 25. ♕h4+−; 23... ♕c5] **24. ♕c7 ♕c5 25. ♕c5 ♗c5 26. ♖a1 ♗b6! 27. ♗d3 ♗a5 28. ♖b1 ♖c8 29. ♗c4!? ♖c4** [29... ♗c4? 30. ♗b2 ♗e2 31. ♖fc1 ♗c3 32. ♗c3 dc3 33. ♖c3+−] **30. ♗f4** [30. ♗b2 f5 31. ♖fc1 ♗c3 32. e3 ♗a2! 33. ♗c3 ♗b1 34. ed4 ♗e4=] **f6** [30... f5? 31. ♖fc1 ♗c3 32. ♗e5 ♔f7 33. ♗d4 ♗d4 34. ♖c4 ♗c4 35. ♖b4+−] **31. ♖fc1 ♗c3 32. g4!** [32. ♗d6 ♔f7 33. ♗b4 ♔e6 34. e3 ♗a2!=] **♔f7 33. ♗g3 ♔e6 34. f3!** [△ ♗e1, e3] **♔d5 35. ♔f1** [35. ♗e1 ♗e1 36. ♖e1 ♖c2 37. ♖bc1 ♔c4=/∞ ×a3] **g6 36. ♗e1 f5 37. gf5 gf5 38. e3 ♖c6?!** [38... ♗e1∞] **39. ed4 ♗c4 40. ♔g2 ♗d4 41. ♗g3 ♗e3!** [△ f4, ♖g6] **42. ♖d1 ♔c5 43. ♖b8** [43. ♗b8 ♖g6 44. ♔h3 (44. ♔h1? ♗e2 45. ♗a7 ♔c4−+) ♖h6=] **f4 44. ♗e1 ♖g6** [44... ♗d5? 45. ♗f2 ♖g6 46. ♔f1 ♗c4? 47. ♔e1 ♖g2 48. ♖d2!+−; 44... ♗e2? 45. ♗b4 ♔c4 46. ♖d6±] **45. ♔h3 ♗e6 46. ♔h4 ♖h6 47. ♔g5 ♖h2 48. ♔f6! ♖h6 49. ♔e5 ♗h3 50. ♖e8?** [50. ♖d5 ♔c6 51. ♔e4 ♖e6 52. ♖e5 ♖d6 53. ♗c3 ♗f1? 54. ♖c8 ♔d7 55. ♖ee8±; 53... ♗e6±] **♖h5 51. ♔f6 ♖f5 52. ♔g7 ♖d5=** [×f3] **53. ♗b4 ♔c6 54. ♖d5 1/2 : 1/2**
[Hertneck]

38. A 29

M. GUREVICH 2610 − ADAMS 2630

München 1993

1. c4 ♘f6 2. ♘c3 e5 3. ♘f3 ♘c6 4. g3 ♗b4 5. ♘d5 e4 6. ♘h4 d6 7. ♘b4 ♘b4 8. a3 ♘c6 9. d3 [9. ♗g2? g5−+] **ed3 N** [9... 0−0] **10. ♕d3 0−0 11. ♗g2 ♖e8 12. 0−0 ♗g4 13. e4 ♘d7!?** [△ ♕f6⇆] **14. ♗d2 ♘c5 15. ♕c3 ♗e2!?** [15... ♘e4? 16. ♗e4 ♖e4 17. f3 ♘d4 18. ♕d3+−] **16. ♖fe1 ♘e4 17. ♗e4 ♖e4 18. f3 ♖c4** [18... ♖e6 19. ♔f2 ♕e8 20. ♘f5 f6 21. ♘e3+−] **19. ♕e3 ♖h4 20. gh4 ♗c4∞ 21. ♕f4!?** [△ ♗c3, ♔h1↑] **d5?** [21... ♗e6 22. ♗c3 ♘e7!∞ △ 23... ♘d5, 23... ♘f5] **22. ♗c3 ♗b3** [△ d4; 22... d4 23. ♖ad1±] **23. ♖e2! d4 24. ♖d2 ♗d5 25. ♗d4± ♘d4 26. ♕d4 c6 27. ♖e1 h5 28. ♔f2 ♕d7 29. ♕e5 ♕h3 30. ♕g3 ♕f5 31. ♖e5 ♕f6 32. ♖h5 ♖e8 33. ♖g5 ♕h6** [△ f6] **34. ♕f4 ♕e6 35. ♖g1 f6 36. h5?⊕ ♔f7 37. ♖c2 ♕e5!? 38. ♕e5 ♖e5 39. h6 gh6 40. ♖e2?!** [40. ♖g4 ♖f5 41. ♖c3±] **♖h5 41. ♖h1 ♖h3 42. ♖e3 a5 43. ♔g2 ♖h4± 44. ♖d1 b5 45. ♔g3 ♖c4 46. ♖c3 ♖a4 47. ♖d2 ♔g6** [47... b4? 48. ♖e3 ba3 49. ♖a3±] **48. ♖c5 ♔f7 49. ♖c1 ♔g6 50. ♖dd1 ♔f5 51. ♖d3 ♔g6 52. ♖d2 ♔f7 53. h3 ♔g6 54. ♖c3 ♔g5 55. ♖cd3 ♖f4?! 56. ♖c2 h5 57. ♖c5 h4 58. ♔f2 f5? 59. b3 ♔f6 60. ♖c1?⊕** [60. ♖dd5! cd5 61. ♖d5 ♔e6 (61... a4 62. ♔e3 ♔g5 63. ♖d8 ab3 64. ♖g8 ♔f6 65. ♔f4 b2 66. ♖g1+−) 62. ♖d8!+− △ ♔e3] **♔e5 61. ♖e1 ♔f6 62. ♖e8 ♗e4 63. ♖e3 ♗d5 64. ♖a8 ♖d4 65. ♔e2 a4 66. ba4 ba4 67. ♖c3 ♔g5 68. ♖h8 ♖f4 69. ♔f2 ♔f6 70. ♖e8 ♔g5 71. ♖e1 ♔f6 72. ♖f1!** [△ ♔e3] **♔e5** [72... ♗c4 73. ♔e3 ♔e5 74. ♖f2±] **73. ♔e3 ♗c4 74. ♖f2 ♖d4** [74... ♗d5 75. ♖c5+− △ 75... ♖d4 76. f4] **75. ♖fc2 ♔d5** [75... f4 76. ♔f2 ♗d5 77. ♔e1!+− △ ♖c2-g2-g4] **76. ♔f2 ♔c5 77. ♔e3 ♔d5 78. ♖c1 ♔c5 79. ♔f2 ♖d2 80. ♔e3 ♖d4 81. ♖3c2 ♔d5 82. ♔f2 ♔c5 83. ♖b1!** [△ 84. ♖b4, 84. ♖b8] **♔d5 84. ♖b8 c5□** [84... ♔c5 85. ♖b4 ♔d5 86. ♖a4+−] **85. ♖a8!** [85. ♖d8 ♔e5 86. ♖d4 ♔d4⇆] **♖d3□** [85... ♗b3 86. ♖d8+−] **86. ♖d8 ♔c6 87. ♖d3+− ♗d3 88. ♖d2 c4 89. ♔e3 ♔c5** [△ f4] **90. f4 ♗f1 91. ♖d1 ♗h3 92. ♖h1 ♗g2 93. ♖h4 c3□ 94. ♖h8!** [94. ♔d3 c2! 95. ♔c2 ♔d4 96. ♔d2 ♔c4⇆] **♔c4 95. ♖b8! c2 96. ♔d2 c1♕ 97. ♔c1 ♔d3 98. ♖b5 ♗e4 99. ♖a5 ♔e3 100. ♖a4 ♔f4 101. ♔d2 ♔e5 102. ♖b4 ♔d6 103. a4 ♔c7 104. a5 ♗b7 105. ♔e3 ♗a6 106. ♔f4 ♗c8 107. ♔e5 1 : 0**
[M. Gurevich]

39. A 29

SERPER 2590 − LOBRON 2620

Dortmund 1993

1. c4 ♘f6 2. ♘c3 e5 3. ♘f3 ♘c6 4. g3 ♗b4 5. ♘d5 ♗c5 6. ♗g2 0−0 7. 0−0 d6

8. e3 ♗b6!? N [8... a5 — 34/40; 8... ♗g4 — 34/41; 8... a6 — 38/39; 8... ♖e8 — 52/41] **9. d4 ♗g4** [9... ed4? 10. ♘b6 ab6 11. ♘d4±] **10. h3!?** [10. ♘b6 ab6 11. d5?! e4! 12. dc6 bc6∓] **♗f3 11. ♕f3□** [11. ♗f3? ed4 12. ♘b6 ab6 13. ed4 d5!∓ ×d4] **ed4 12. ♘b6 ab6 13. ed4 ♘d4 14. ♕d3!** [14. ♕b7? ♖a4∓] **♘c6 15. b3 ♖e8 16. ♗b2=∞⧉ ♕e7 17. ♗c3** [△ ♖fe1±] **♕e2□ 18. ♕f5 ♕h5□** [18... ♕e6?! 19. ♕f4! △ ♖fe1±] **19. ♕f4** [19. ♕h5!? ♘h5 20. ♖fe1=∞] **♖e6 20. h4 ♖ae8** [20... h6!?] **21. ♗h3! ♖e4 22. ♕g5 h6□ 23. ♕h5 ♘h5 24. ♖fe1** [24. ♗d7!? ♖d8 (24... ♖8e7?? 25. ♗f5 ♖e2 26. ♗g4 ♖c2 27. ♗e1! ♘f6 28. ♗d1 ♖b2 29. ♗c3+−) 25. ♗f5 ♖e7 26. ♖fe1=∞] **♖e1 25. ♖e1 ♖e1 26. ♗e1±** [⧉, ×b7; ♘♗ 9/d] **♘f6 27. ♗c8 ♘d8 28. ♗c3** [28. f3?! d5!] **♘e4 29. ♗b2 ♘c5 30. ♗f5!** [30. ♔f1?! ♘d3! 31. ♗a3 (31. ♗c3 ♘c1 32. ♗d2 ♘a2 △ c5) c5! △ ♘b4] **♘de6 31. f4 h5 32. ♔f2?⊕** [32. ♗c2! △ 32... g6?! 33. f5!± ×»] **g6 33. ♗c2 f5!∓ 34. b4 ♘d7 35. ♗d1 ♔f7 36. ♗f3 ♘d8 37. a4 ♔e7 38. ♔e3 ♘f6 39. ♗a3?! ♔e6 40. ♗b2 ♘g4⊕ 41. ♔d3 ♘f6 42. ♔e3 c6 43. ♗d4 ♘d7□** [43... c5? 44. ♗f6 ♔f6 45. b5=] **44. ♗c3 ♔e7 45. ♗d2 ♘f6 46. ♔d3?!** [⌓ 46. ♗c3] **♔e6 47. ♗e3 c5! 48. ♗d2** [48. a5 ba5 49. ba5 (△ ♗b7!) ♘e4!∓] **♘e4! 49. ♗e4 fe4 50. ♔e4** [♘♗ 5/d] **♘c6∓ 51. bc5?!** [⌓ 51. b5] **bc5 52. ♗c3 ♘e7 53. ♗e1 ♘f5 54. ♗f2 ♘h6 55. ♗e1 ♘g4 56. ♗c3 ♘f2!?⊕** [56... ♘f6? 57. ♗f6! ♔f6 58. ♔d5 ♔e7 59. ♔e4! ♔e6 60. a5 ♔f6 61. ♔e3 ♔f5 62. ♔f3 ♔e6 63. ♔e4= △ 63... d5? 64. cd5 ♔d6 65. f5! gf5 66. ♔f5 ♔d5 67. g4!] **57. ♔f3** [57. ♔e3?? ♘d1] **♘g4 58. ♔e4 ♘h6 59. ♗e1 ♘g8 60. ♗c3 ♘e7** [60... ♘f6? 61. ♗f6!= — 56... ♘f6?] **61. ♗e1 d5 62. cd5 ♘d5 63. ♔d3! ♔d6 64. ♔c4 ♔c6 65. ♔d3! ♘e7 66. ♔e4 ♔d6 67. ♗f2?!** [⌓ 67. ♔f3 △ g4] **♘f5 68. g4?** [68. ♗e1? ♔e6 △ ♘d6−+; 68. ♔f3∓] **hg4 69. h5 g3 70. ♗g1 ♔e6??** [70... gh5?? 71. ♔f5 c4 72. ♔e4! c3 73. ♔f3; 70... c4! 71. hg6 ♔e6 72. g7 ♔f7! 73. ♔f5 c3−+] **71. h6!□** [71. hg6?? c4−+] **♘h6 72. ♗c5 ♘f5 73. ♔f3= ♔d5 74. ♗b6 ♔c6 75. ♗g1 ♔d5 76. ♗b6 ♔c4 77. ♗d8 ♔b4 78. a5 ♔c4 79. ♗c7 ♔d3 80. ♗b6 ♔d2 81. ♗c5 ♔e1 82. ♔g2 ♔e2 83. ♗b6 ♔d3 84. ♔f3 1/2 : 1/2** [Serper]

40. A 29

LAUTIER 2645 — AN. KARPOV 2725

Dortmund 1993

1. c4 ♘f6 2. ♘c3 e5 3. ♘f3 ♘c6 4. g3 ♗b4 5. ♘d5 e4 6. ♘h4 0—0 7. ♗g2 ♖e8 8. 0—0 d6 N [8... ♗f8 — 14/60; 8... ♗c5 — 46/(33)] **9. d3!? ed3 10. ♕d3 ♘e5 11. ♕c2 ♘d5 12. cd5 ♗c5 13. b3!** [13. ♗d2?! ♗g4 14. ♗c3 ♕d7=] **♕e7** [13... ♗g4?! 14. h3 ♗h5 15. ♗b2 ♕g5 16. ♔h2±; 13... ♘g4 14. ♗b2 ♕g5 15. e4 ♗d7 △ ♗b5⇆; 15. ♖ad1± △ ♗d4; 13... ♘g6 14. ♘f3! ♘e5 15. ♘e5 ♖e5 16. ♗b2 ♖e8 17. e4±] **14. ♗b2 a5 15. a3** [15. ♖ae1 a4!⇆] **♘g6 16. ♘g6** [16. ♕c3 ♕e5=] **hg6 17. e4 g5?!** [17... c6? 18. ♕c3 f6 19. dc6 bc6 20. b4+−; 17... ♗d7 18. ♖fe1 (18. ♖ae1? ♗b5) f6 (18... c6?! 19. e5 cd5 20. ♗d5±) 19. ♕c4 ♕f7 20. ♗d4 ♗d4 21. ♕d4±] **18. ♖ae1 f6 19. ♔h1 g4** [19... c6 20. f4 (20. dc6 bc6 21. b4? ab4 22. ab4 ♗b4 23. ♕b3 d5 24. ♖c1 ♗a6∓) cd5 21. e5 fe5 22. fe5→] **20. f4 gf3 21. ♖f3 ♗d7?!** [21... ♗g4 22. ♖f4 ♕d7 23. ♕c4 (△ e5) ♖e5!? (23... b5 24. ♕d3±) 24. ♗e5 fe5 25. ♖ff1 ♗a3=; 24. ♖ef1±] **22. ♖f4 ♖f8** [△ g5] **23. ♖ef1** [△ ♖h4] **♗e3!** [23... c6? 24. ♖h4 (△ e5) g5 25. ♖h6+−; 23... ♗b5? 24. ♗h3!? (24. ♖1f3±) ♗f1 25. ♗e6±→] **24. ♖4f3 ♗b6** [24... ♗h6?! 25. ♕c7 ♖fc8 26. ♕b6 ♖c5 (26... ♖c2 27. ♖3f2±) 27. ♖c3±] **25. g4!** [25. ♕d3 (△ ♖f4) ♕e8! △ ♗b5] **♖ae8?** [25... ♗b5!□ 26. ♖e1 ♗e8! (△ ♗g6; 26... ♗d7? 27. ♖h3 g5 28. ♖f1 ♖f7 29. ♖h6 ♖af8 30. ♕d2 ♗g4 31. ♕g5+−) 27. g5 fg5 28. ♖f8 ♕f8 29. e5±] **26. ♖h3!** [△ e5] **♗g4 27. ♖g3 ♗h5** [27... ♗d7 28. ♕d2 (△ ♕h6; 28. ♖g6 ♔h7! 29. e5 de5 30. ♖gf6 ♔h8) ♔h7 29. ♕f4 g5 30. ♕f3 ♔g6 31. ♕d3 ♔h6 32. ♗h3! ♗h3 33. ♖h3 ♔g7 34. e5+−] **28. ♕d2!** [28. ♖f5? ♕f7! (△ ♗g6) 29. ♖f6 ♕f6 30. ♗f6 ♖f6=∞] **g6** [28... ♔h7 29. ♕f4 ♕f7 30. ♕h4! △ ♖f5] **29. ♖f5 ♕h7** [29... ♔h7 30. ♕f4! gf5 31. ♕f5 ♔h8 32. ♕h5 ♕h7

33. ♗f6+−] **30. ♗f6 ♖f7 31. ♕g5 c6** [31... ♔f8 32. ♖f4 c6 33. ♗h3 cd5 34. ♕d5+−] **32. e5** [⌓ 32. dc6 bc6 33. e5 d5 (33... de5 34. ♗c6 ♖c8 35. ♗d5+−) 34. ♕h5?? ♕h5 35. ♖h5 ♖f6! 36. ef6? ♖e1 37. ♗f1 ♖f1 38. ♔g2 ♖g1−+; 34. ♖f4+− △ ♖h4] **de5 33. dc6 ♔f8** [⌓ 33... e4 34. cb7 ♗c7 (34... ♖b7 35. ♕h5+−) 35. ♗e5! ♖f5 (35... ♗e5 36. ♖e5+−) 36. ♕f5 ♗e5 (36... ♖e5 37. ♕c8+−) 37. ♕e5+−] **34. ♖e5 ♖e5 35. ♕e5 ♗c7 36. ♕e6! ♗g4** [36... ♗g3 37. ♕c8#] **37. ♕g4 ♖f6 38. ♕c8 1 : 0** **[Lautier]**

41. A 30

GRANDA ZUÑIGA 2590 − SEIRAWAN 2595

Buenos Aires 1993

1. ♘f3 ♘f6 2. c4 c5 3. ♘c3 e6 4. g3 b6 5. ♗g2 ♗b7 6. 0−0 ♘c6 7. e4 e5 8. d3 g6 N [8... ♗e7 − 29/78]

9. ♘e5!? [9. ♘h4 ♘h5 10. ♗f3 (10. f4 ♘f4) ♗e7 11. ♗h5 ♗h4 12. ♗e2 ♗f6 13. ♗h6 ♗g5] **♘e5 10. f4 ♘c6** [10... ♗d6 11. fe5 ♗e5 12. ♗h6±] **11. e5 ♘g8!** [11... ♘h5 12. g4 ♘g7 13. f5 △ ♘e4] **12. f5 ♘h6?** [12... ♘a5? 13. ♗b7 ♘b7 14. ♕f3+−; 12... ♕b8 13. ♗f4 g5 14. ♗g5 (14. e6!?) ♘e5 15. ♘d5→; 12... gf5 13. ♕h5! ♘ge7 14. ♗g5 ♗g7 15. ♖f5!? (15. ♗f6) 0−0 16. ♖af1→; 12... ♖b8! (△ 13... ♘e5, 13... ♘d4 Illescas Córdoba) 13. e6 (13. ♗f4 gf5! 14. e6 de6 15. ♗b8 ♕b8−+) de6 14. fe6 f5 15. ♖f5 ♕d4 16. ♖f2∞; 14... f6∞] **13. ♘e4! ♘f5 14. ♘f6 ♔e7 15. ♘d5 ♔e8 16. ♘f6 ♔e7 17. g4!?** [17. ♖f5 gf5 18. ♗g5 ♕b8 19. ♕h5 ♔d8 20. ♕f7 ♗e7] **♘fd4 18. ♕e1! ♕b8** [18... ♗g7 19. ♕f2 ♔f8 20. ♗g5 ♕c8 21. ♘h7 ♔g8 22. ♕f7 ♔h7 23. ♗e4 ♘e5−+; 21. ♘h5! ♘e5 22. ♘g7 ♘ef3!; 21. ♖ae1!? △ ♘h5] **19. ♘d5 ♔d8 20. ♗g5 ♔c8 21. ♖f7 ♘e6!** [21... ♘e5? 22. ♖f8 ♖f8 23. ♘e7 ♔c7 24. ♕e5; 21... ♕e5 22. ♗f6 ♘e2 23. ♔h1 ♕e6 24. ♗h8 ♕f7 25. ♕e2] **22. ♗f6 ♘cd8 23. ♖e7!** [23. ♗h8? ♘f7 24. ♗f6 ♗c6 △ ♔b7−+; 23. ♘e7? ♗e7 24. ♖e7 ♗g2 25. ♗h8 ♗b7 △ ♕c7-c6−+] **♖g8??** [23... ♗e7 24. ♘e7 ♔c7 25. ♗h8 ♗g2 26. ♔g2 ♘c6 27. ♘d5 ♔b7 28. ♗f6±; 23... ♗d5 24. cd5 ♗e7 25. ♗h8 ♘d4 (△ d6) 26. d6 ♗g5 27. h4 ♗f4 28. ♕e4 ♘8c6 29. ♖f1 ♔b7 30. ♗f6 ♗d2∞ △ ♔a6, ♕g8; 25... ♘f4!?] **24. ♖e8! ♗c6 25. ♗d8! ♘d8 26. ♘f6 ♖h8 27. ♗c6** [27. e6!] **dc6 28. ♕e4 ♕c7** [28... ♔b7 29. ♘d7] **29. e6 ♗g7?!** [29... ♕d6 30. e7+−; 30. ♖f1+−; 29... ♗e7 30. ♖h8 ♗f6 31. ♖f1! ♗e7 32. ♖h7 a5 33. ♕g6+−] **30. e7+− ♖e8** [30... ♗f6 31. ed8♕! ♗d8 32. ♖h8] **31. ♘e8 ♗d4 32. ♔h1** [32. ♕d4? ♕e7] **♕d7 33. ♘d6 ♕d6 34. e8♕ a5 35. ♖f1 ♖a7 36. ♖f8 ♖d7 37. ♕4e6 ♕e6 38. ♕e6 ♔c7 39. ♕e2 ♗g7 40. ♖f2 ♗d4?** [40... ♘f7 △ ♘e5] **41. ♖f3 ♘f7 42. ♖f4 ♘d6 43. ♔g2 ♘c8 44. b3 ♖e7 45. ♖e4 ♖f7 46. ♕e1 ♖d7 47. ♕g3 ♔b7 48. h3 ♖f7 49. h4 ♖d7 50. ♖e6 ♗c3 51. ♕f3 ♘d6 52. ♕f8 ♘c8 53. ♖e8 ♖c7 54. ♖d8 ♗g7 55. ♕e8 ♗f6 56. ♖c8 1 : 0** **[Seirawan]**

42. A 30

ILLESCAS CÓRDOBA 2615 − SEIRAWAN 2595

Buenos Aires 1993

1. ♘f3 ♘f6 2. c4 c5 3. ♘c3 e6 4. g3 b6 5. ♗g2 ♗b7 6. 0−0 d6 7. d4 cd4 8. ♕d4 a6 9. ♗g5 ♘bd7 10. ♘d2 ♗g2 11. ♔g2 ♖c8?! N [11... ♗e7 − 40/(46)] **12. ♘ce4! ♖c6 13. ♗f6** [13. b4!] **gf6** [13... ♘f6 14. ♘f6 ♕f6 15. ♕e4 ♔d7 16. b4→] **14. b4 ♗e7!** [14... b5 15. a4 bc4 16. b5 ♖c7 17.

♘d6 ♗d6 18. ♕d6±] **15. b5 ab5 16. cb5 ♖c2 17. ♘d6 ♗d6 18. ♕d6 ♘e5 19. ♕d8 ♔d8 20. ♖fd1 ♔e7=∞ 21. ♔f1** [21. f4 ♘g4 22. ♘f1 f5!=∞] **♖b2?!** [21... ♖a8 22. a4 ♘c4 23. ♘c4 ♖c4 24. ♖dc1 ♖aa4∓; 23. ♘f3!⩲; 21... ♖d8! 22. ♔e1 ♘g4! 23. ♘b3□ ♖d1 24. ♔d1 ♖b2 25. ♘d4 ♔d6 26. a3 ♘e5!=∞] **22. a4 ♖c8 23. ♔e1⩲ ♘d7** [23... ♖cc2 24. ♖ac1 ♖c1 (24... ♘c4 25. ♖c2 ♖c2 26. ♘c4 ♖c4 27. ♖a1±) 25. ♖c1 ♖a2 26. ♘c4! ♘d7 (26... ♖a4 27. ♘e5! fe5 28. ♖c6±) 27. ♖d1! e5 (27... ♖c2 28. ♖d4±; 27... ♔e8 28. ♖d4±) 28. ♖d6±; 28. e4!±] **24. ♘f3!** [△ ♘d4] **♖cc2?** [24... e5 25. ♖d2 ♖b4 26. ♘h4! ♖a8 27. ♖ad1 ♘c5 28. ♖d6±; 24... ♘c5 25. ♘d4 ♖a8 (25... ♘b3 26. ♘b3 ♖b3 27. ♖ac1±) 26. a5! ba5 27. ♖ac1 ♘b3 28. ♘b3 ♖b3 29. ♖c7 ♔e8 30. ♖dd7 ♖b1 31. ♔d2 ♖d8 32. ♖d8 ♔d8 33. ♖f7±; 24... ♖c4! 25. ♘d4 ♘c5 26. a5⩲] **25. ♘d4 ♖c4 26. a5! ba5 27. ♘c6 ♔e8 28. ♖a5 ♔f8 29. ♖d7 ♖cc2 30. ♔d1 ♖e2 31. ♘d4!+−** [31. ♖a8 ♔g7 32. ♖ad8 ♖f2 33. ♖d2 ♖fd2 34. ♖d2 ♖b5⩲] **♖f2 32. ♔c1 e5** [32... ♔g7 33. ♖aa7] **33. ♘e6 ♔e8 34. ♖c7 1 : 0**
[Illescas Córdoba]

43. A 30

TOLSTIH 2345 – GIPSLIS 2490

Katowice 1993

1. ♘f3 ♘f6 2. c4 c5 3. ♘c3 e6 4. g3 b6 5. ♗g2 ♗b7 6. 0–0 ♗e7 7. ♖e1 d6 8. e4 a6 9. d4 cd4 10. ♘d4 ♕c7 11. ♗e3 ♘bd7 12. f4 0–0 13. ♖c1 ♖fe8 14. g4 ♘c5 15. ♗f2 g6 16. b4 ♖ad8 N [16... ♘cd7 – 48/34] **17. ♕e2** [17. ♕f3 ♘ce4! (17... ♘cd7? 18. ♘d5 ed5 19. cd5 ♕b8 20. ♘c6 ♕a8 21. e5±) 18. ♘e4 ♘e4 19. ♖e4 ♗e4 (19... f5? 20. gf5 △ 20... ef5? 21. ♖e7+−) 20. ♕e4 d5 21. ♕e3 dc4 22. a3 ♗d6 23. ♘e2 b5∓; 17. bc5 dc5 18. ♘e6 fe6 19. ♕f3 ♗d6 20. ♗e3 ♗c6 21. a4 ♕b7 22. g5 ♘h5 23. ♕g4∞; 17. g5 ♘h5 18. ♕f3 ♘d7 19. ♘d5 ed5 20. cd5 ♕b8 21. ♘c6 ♕a8 22. ♗h3 f6 (22... ♘g7 23. ♗d4 ♗f8 24. ♖e2 △ ♖ec2, ♘d8, ♖c7) 23. ♗d4∞; 17. f5 ♗f8 18. fe6 fe6 19. g5 ♘h5 20. bc5 dc5 21. ♘e6 ♖e6 22. ♘d5 *a)* 22... ♕b8 23. ♗f3 ♘f4 24. ♗g3 ♗d6 25. e5±; *b)* 22... ♕d6 23. ♗f3! (23. e5?! ♖e5 24. ♖e5 ♕e5 25. ♘f6 ♘f6 26. ♕d8 ♗g2 27. ♕f6 ♕f6 28. gf6 ♗c6∓) ♖e5 24. ♗h5 ♖g5 25. ♗g4 h5 26. ♗g3 ♖g4 27. ♕g4 hg4 28. ♗d6±; *c)* 22... ♕f7!?∞] **♘cd7 18. ♘d5!?** [18. ♗f3 e5∞; 18. e5!? de5 19. fe5 ♘g4 20. ♕g4 ♘e5 21. ♕e2 (21. ♕g3 ♗g2 22. ♔g2 ♕b7 △ ♘c4) ♗g2 22. ♔g2 ♘c4 23. ♘e4 b5 24. ♕f3 ♔g7∞] **ed5 19. cd5 ♕b8 20. ♘c6 ♕a8 21. ♕f3** [21. e5 de5 22. fe5 *a)* 22... ♗d6 23. ♗d4 ♘d5 24. ♗d5 ♘e5 (24... ♘b8 25. ♕c4+−) 25. ♗e5 ♗e5 26. ♗f7 ♔f7 27. ♘e5 ♔g8 28. ♖c7 ♕b8 29. ♖ec1∞; 25. ♕f2!± △ 25... ♗f8 26. ♖e5 ♖d5 27. ♖d5+−; *b)* 22... ♗f8 23. ♗d4 (23. ♕f3? ♘d5 24. ♕d5 ♘e5−+) ♘d5 (23... ♖c8 24. ♕f3 ♘d5 25. ♕d5 ♘b8 26. e6+−) 24. ♗d5 ♘e5 25. ♘d8 ♗d5 26. ♗e5 ♕d8=∞] **♗f8 22. ♘d8 ♕d8 23. g5 ♘h5 24. ♗h3 b5** [24... f6 25. ♗e6 ♔h8 26. h4 ♘g7 27. ♗d7 ♕d7 28. ♗d4∞] **25. ♖c2 ♘b6 26. ♗g4 ♘g7 27. ♗b6 ♕b6 28. ♕f2 ♕d8□ 29. ♕d4 ♘f5 30. ♕f2 ♘g7 31. ♕d4 ♘f5 1/2 : 1/2**
[Tolstih]

44. A 30

WOJTKIEWICZ 2580 – FTÁČNIK 2535

Budapest (zt - play off) 1993

1. ♘f3 ♘f6 2. c4 c5 3. ♘c3 e6 4. g3 b6 5. ♗g2 ♗b7 6. 0–0 ♗e7 7. d4 cd4 8. ♕d4 d6 9. ♖d1 a6 10. ♘g5 ♗g2 11. ♔g2 ♘c6 12. ♕f4 0–0 13. ♘ce4 ♘e8 [13... ♘e4?! 14. ♘e4 ♘e5 15. b3 △ ♗a3 ×d6] **14. b3 ♖a7** [14... b5!? 15. cb5 ab5 16. ♘f3 f5 17. ♘c3 ♘c7 18. ♗b2 b4 19. ♘a4 ♘d5 20. ♕d2 ♗f6 21. ♖ac1 ♖c8=; ⌓ 16. ♗b2∞] **15. ♗b2 b5!? N** [15... ♖d7 – 45/(32)] **16. ♘f3** [16. cb5?! ab5 △ d5, ♕a8↑] **♕a8** [16... bc4?! 17. bc4⩲ ×d6, ⇔b] **17. ♖ac1 h6** [△ f5, e5-e4↑⊞] **18. ♘ed2** [18. ♘c3 ♘e5!?⇆ △ ♗g5] **♖d7 19. ♔g1 ♕b7 20. ♕e4** [20. ♗a3!? ♘f6 (20... ♗f6?! 21. ♘e4 b4 22. ♘f6 ♘f6 23. ♗b2±) 21. ♘e4 ♘e4 22. ♕e4 ♖c8=] **bc4 21. ♕c4□** [21. ♘c4? d5 22. ♕d3 ♘b4 23. ♕d2 ♘a2∓] **♖c7 22. ♕d3** [22. ♕a4!?

d5 (22... ♘f6 23. ♗f6 ♗f6 24. ♘e4) 23. ♘e5↑] **d5 23. ♕b1** [23. ♘e5 ♗f6 24. ♘df3 (24. ♘c6 ♗b2 25. ♘a5 ♖c1 26. ♘b7 ♖d1 27. ♔g2 ♗c1 28. ♕c2 ♖d2 29. ♕c1 ♖e2∓) ♘b4 (24... ♘d6 25. ♘c6 ♗b2 26. ♘a5 ♕b6 27. ♖c7 ♕c7 28. ♕a6) 25. ♕b1∞; 23. e4!? ♘b4 24. ♕b1 (24. ♖c7 ♘c7 25. ♕d4 ♗f6 26. e5 ♗e7∞) ♖c1 25. ♖c1 ♘f6 26. ed5 ed5 27. a3 ♘c6 28. ♕d3 ♖d8∞] **♘f6 24. e4 ♕b6** [24... ♖d8 △ 25. ed5 ♖d5=] **25. ed5 ed5** [25... ♘g4? 26. dc6! (26. ♖f1 ed5 27. ♕f5 ♘f6 28. ♗f6 ♗f6 29. ♕d5 ♘b4) ♕f2 27. ♔h1 ♘e3 28. ♖g1+−; 25... ♘d5 26. ♘c4↑] **26. ♕f5 ♖d8 27. ♘e5 ♗c5 28. ♘dc4?** [28. ♘c6 ♖c6 29. ♔g2 ♖e6↑; 28. ♔g2 ♘d4 29. ♕d3 ♘e6 30. f4∞; 28. ♘d3 ♘d4 (28... ♗d4 29. ♘f3 ♗b2 30. ♘b2 ♘e4 31. ♘d3 ♖d6∞) 29. ♗d4 ♗d4∞] **dc4 29. ♘c4 ♖d1** [29... ♕a7 30. ♖d8 ♘d8 31. ♗f6 gf6 32. ♕f6 ♘e6 33. ♖d1∓] **30. ♖d1 ♕a7 31. ♗f6 gf6 32. ♕f6** [32. ♖e1 ♘e5 (32... ♖e7? 33. ♕c8 ♔h7 34. ♕f5 ♔g7 35. ♕g4=; 32... ♘e7 33. ♕f6 ♗d4 34. ♕f4∓) 33. ♘e5 (33. ♕f6 ♗f2 34. ♕f2 ♘f3 35. ♔g2 ♕f2 36. ♔f2 ♘e1 37. ♔e1 ♖d7−+) fe5 34. ♖e5 ♕b6∓] **♗f8! 33. ♘e3 ♗g7 34. ♕d6 ♘d4 35. ♕d8 ♔h7 36. ♕d5 ♕b7?!** [36... ♕c5∓] **37. ♖d4 ♗d4 38. ♕d4** [♕ 9/b] **♖c1 39. ♘f1** [39. ♘d1 ♕f3−+] **♕f3** [△ ♕e2−+] **40. ♕d7 ♖c2 41. ♘d2 ♖c1** [41... ♕d1? 42. ♔g2 △ ♕f7=] **42. ♘f1 ♖a1 43. a4** [43. ♕d2 ♕d1! 44. ♕d1 ♖d1 45. ♔g2 ♖a1 46. a4 ♖b1 47. ♘d2 ♖b2 48. ♘e4 ♖b3 49. ♘c5 ♖b6−+] **♖d1 44. ♕a7 a5! 45. ♕e7** [45. ♕a5? ♕d3 46. ♕b5 ♖f1−+] **♔g6!** [45... ♕b3?! 46. ♕e4 ♔g7 47. ♕g4⇆] **46. h4** [46. ♕e8 ♕d3 47. ♕g8 ♔f6 48. ♕h8 ♔e7 49. ♕e5 ♔d7 50. ♕b5 ♕b5 51. ab5 ♖b1−+] **♖c1** [46... ♔h5 47. ♕c5 ♔g4 48. ♔h2! △ 48... ♖f1 49. ♕c4 ♔h5 50. ♕f1; ⌓ 46... ♕d3 47. h5 ♔g7 48. ♕e5 ♔h7−+] **47. ♕d6 ♔h5 48. ♕d7 ♖d1 49. ♕c8 ♕d3 50. ♕h3 ♔g6 51. ♕g2 ♔g7** [51... ♕b3 52. ♕e4] **52. g4 ♕b3 53. ♔h2 ♕a4−+ 54. ♘g3 ♕f4 55. ♔h3 ♖d3 56. ♕g1** [56. ♕f1 ♖g3] **♕f3 57. ♕a1 ♔g8 58. ♕a5?** [58. ♕e1 ♖d1 59. ♕e8 ♔h7 60. ♕e4 ♕e4 61. ♘e4 a4] **♕h1#**

0 : 1 **[Ftáčnik]**

45.* **A 30**

M. SOROKIN 2490 − S. KISELËV 2510

Sankt-Peterburg (zt) 1993

1. ♘f3 ♘f6 2. c4 b6 3. g3 ♗b7 4. ♗g2 c5 5. ♘c3 g6 6. 0–0 ♗g7 7. d4 cd4 8. ♕d4 ♘c6 9. ♕f4 ♖c8 10. ♗d2!? N [10. ♖b1 − 54/(37)] **d6** [10... d5 11. ♖ad1 0–0 12. ♕h4 dc4 13. ♗h6 ♕e8 14. ♘g5 ♘h5 15. ♗g7 ♔g7 16. ♕c4 ♘f6 17. ♕b5 ♘a5 1/2 : 1/2 M. Sorokin 2570 − Savon 2440, Ljubljana 1992] **11. ♖ad1** [11. ♗h3 ♖b8] **♘b8 12. b3 ♘bd7 13. e4 a6 14. ♖fe1** [14. e5? ♘h5 △ de5] **0–0 15. ♕h4** [15. e5? ♘h5 16. ♕h4 de5 17. ♗g5 (17. ♘e5 ♗g2 18. ♘d7 ♗f3! 19. ♘f8 ♗d1 20. ♖d1 ♗c3−+) f6 18. ♘e5 (18. ♗h3 ♖c7) fg5 19. ♕g5 ♗e5 20. ♗b7 ♗c3 21. ♗c8 ♗e1−+] **♖c5 16. ♘d5 e6□ 17. ♘f6** [17. ♘c3!?] **♗f6 18. ♕f4 e5 19. ♕e3 ♖c6 20. h4?!** [20. ♗b4 ♕b8 21. ♘d2 △ ♘b1-c3, △ ♘f1, ♕e2, ♘e3; 21. ♖d2 △ ♖ed1↑ ⇔d] **♘c5 21. ♗c1** [⌓ 21. ♗b4] **b5 22. cb5** [22. b4 ♘e6 23. c5 ♕b8 24. cd6 ♖d6 25. ♗b2 ♖fd8 26. ♖d6 ♕d6∓] **ab5 23. ♗a3 ♕c7∓** [23... ♕a8? 24. ♗c5 dc5 25. ♖d5 ×c5, e5] **24. ♘d2 ♖a8 25. ♘b1 ♘e6 26. ♖c1 ♘d4 27. ♖c6 ♗c6 28. ♕d2 ♕b7! 29. ♗b4** [29. ♗d6? ♖d8−+] **d5 30. ♘c3 de4 31. ♘e4 ♗g7 32. f4?⊕** [32. ♗c5! ♖d8 (32... f5? 33. ♗d4! ed4 34. ♘c5) 33. ♗d4! ♖d4 34. ♕c2 ♗d5 *a)* 35. ♘c5 ♕c6 36. ♗d5 ♖d5! (36... ♕d5 37. ♘e4∓) 37. b4 ♗f8 38. ♖c1 ♖d4 39. a3 ♕d5∓; *b)* 35. ♘d6 ♕d7 36. ♗d5 ♖d5 37. ♘e4∓] **ef4 33. gf4 ♕d7∓** [×f4, h4] **34. ♗c3 ♖d8 35. ♗a5 ♖c8 36. ♔f1 b4!−+** [△ ♗b5, ♕a7, ♖c2] **37. ♖c1 ♕g4 38. ♗b6 ♗b5 39. ♔f2 ♖c1 40. ♗d4** [40. ♕c1 ♕e2 41. ♔g3 ♕e4 42. ♕c8 ♕e8−+] **♗d4 41. ♕d4 ♖c2**

0 : 1 **[S. Kiselëv, Gagarin]**

46.* **!N** **A 31**

AN. KARPOV 2725 − ADAMS 2630

Dos Hermanas 1993

1. ♘f3 ♘f6 2. c4 c5 3. ♘c3 b6 4. d4 cd4 5. ♘d4 ♗b7 6. f3 [RR 6. ♗g5 e6 7. ♘db5 d6 8. ♗f4 e5 9. ♗g5 a6 10. ♗f6 gf6 11. ♘a3 *a)* 11... d5 12. cd5 (12. ♘d5?

– 11/40) b5 13. ♘c2!± △ 13... b4? 14. ♘b4 ♗b4 15. ♕a4+–; *b)* 11... b5 N 12. ♘c2! (12. cb5? d5 13. e3 ♗c5!⩱↑ V. Atlas) bc4 13. e4! (×d5, f5) ♕a5 14. ♗c4 ♗e4 (Hardiscay 2360 – V. Atlas 2470, Österreich 1993) 15. 0–0± Hardicsay] **e6** [6... d5 7. cd5 ♘d5 8. ♘d5 ♕d5 9. e4±] **7. e4 ♘c6 8. ♗e3** [8. ♗g5!?; 8. ♗f4!?] **♗c5 9. ♕d2** [9. ♘c6 ♗c6 10. ♗c5 bc5 11. ♕d6 ♕e7 12. e5 ♕d6 13. ed6∞] **0–0 10. 0-0-0** [10. ♘c6 ♗c6 11. ♗c5 bc5 12. ♕d6 ♕b6 13. 0-0-0 ♖ab8 14. ♖d2 ♖fd8 15. e5 ♘e8 △ d6⇆] **♕b8! N** [10... d5 11. ♘c6 ♗c6 (11... ♗e3 12. ♕e3 ♗c6 13. e5±) 12. ♗c5 bc5 13. ed5 ed5 14. cd5±; 10... ♕e7 – 40/55] **11. ♗e2 ♖d8 12. ♗f4! ♕c8** [12... e5?! 13. ♘c6 ♗c6 (13... dc6 14. ♕d8 ♕d8 15. ♖d8 ♖d8 16. ♗e5) 14. ♗g5±] **13. ♘c6 ♗c6** [13... dc6 14. ♕d8 ♕d8 15. ♖d8 ♖d8 16. e5 ♘h5 (16... ♘e8±) 17. ♗d2 g6 18. g4 ♘g7 19. ♗g5 ♖d7 20. ♘e4±] **14. e5 ♘e8 15. ♗g5 f6 16. ef6 ♘f6 17. ♗d3 ♗e7 18. ♔b1 a6 19. ♖he1! ♕b7** [19... b5 20. ♘d5! ♘d5 21. cd5 ♗g5 22. ♕g5 ♗d5 23. ♗h7 ♔h7 24. ♖d5± △ 24... ed5? 25. ♖e7 ♖g8 26. ♕h5#] **20. ♗c2** [△ ♕d3] **b5**

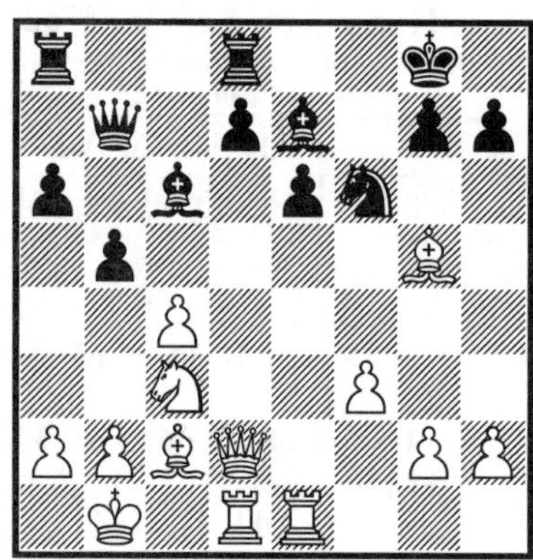

21. ♘d5! ♗d5 [21... ♘d5? 22. cd5 ♗g5 23. dc6 ♗d2 24. cb7+–] **22. cd5 ♘d5** [22... ♕d5? 23. ♕d5 ♘d5 24. ♖d5+–] **23. ♗e4! ♗g5□** [23... ♗b4? 24. ♕b4; 23... ♖e8 24. ♗e7 ♖e7 25. ♗d5+–] **24. ♕g5** [△ ♖d5+–] **♕b6 25. ♗d5 ed5 26. ♖e7!± ♕g6** [26... g6? 27. ♕e5+–; 26... ♕f6 27. ♕f6 gf6 28. ♖d5 ♖a7 29. ♖d6+–] **27. ♕g6 hg6 28. ♖d5 ♖a7 29. ♖d6 ♔h7 30. ♖e4 ♖c7** [30... a5 31. ♔c2±] **31. ♖a6 d5 32. ♖h4 ♔g8 33. ♖d4 ♔f7 34. ♖f4 ♔g8 35. ♖d4 ♔f7 36. ♖b6 ♖c4 37. ♖d2+– b4** [37... d4 38. ♖b5 d3 39. ♖b3 ♖cd4 40. g3 g5 41. h3] **38. b3 ♖f4 39. ♔c2 g5 40. h3 ♖d7 41. ♔d1 1 : 0** **[An. Karpov]**

47. **A 34**

KRAMNIK 2685 – N. SHORT 2655

Amsterdam 1993

1. ♘f3 ♘f6 2. c4 g6 3. ♘c3 d5 4. cd5 ♘d5 5. g3 ♗g7 6. ♗g2 0–0 7. 0–0 c5 8. ♕a4!? N [8. d4 – 47/544, D 75; 8. ♘d5 – 52/61, A 38; 8. ♘g5 – 41/45] **♘b6** [8... ♘c6 9. ♕c4 ♘c3 10. dc3±; 8... e6 9. ♕c4⩲] **9. ♕h4 e6** [9... ♘c6 10. d3 △ ♗h6±] **10. ♕d8 ♖d8 11. d3 h6?** [11... ♘c6 12. ♘e4 ♘a4 13. ♗g5 f5! 14. ♘c3 ♘c3 15. bc3 ♖e8 16. ♖fc1⩲; 11... ♘d5! (Anand) 12. ♗g5 f6 13. ♗d2 ♘c6 (13... b6? 14. d4±) 14. ♖fc1 b6=] **12. ♗e3 ♘a6 13. ♖ac1!±** [13. ♖fc1 ♘d5 14. ♘d5 ed5= △ 15. d4?! ♗g4] **♗d7** [13... c4!? 14. d4! (14. ♗b6 ab6 15. dc4 ♘c5⩱) ♘b4 (14... ♘d5 15. ♘d2±) 15. ♘e5±] **14. ♘d2 ♖ab8 15. ♘b3!** [15. ♘de4 c4! 16. ♗b6 (16. dc4 ♘c4 17. ♗a7 ♖a8 18. b3 ♖a7 19. bc4 ♘b4=) ab6 17. dc4 ♗c6⩲] **♖dc8 16. ♘a5 ♗c6** [16... ♖c7 17. ♗f4! e5 18. ♗e3 f5 19. b3± △ a4] **17. ♘c6 bc6 18. b3?!** [18. ♗f4 e5 19. ♗e3 c4!? (19... f5 20. b3±) 20. ♗b6 ab6 (20... ♖b6 21. ♘a4) 21. dc4 f5±] **♘d5 19. ♗d2 ♘ab4 20. ♘a4** [20. ♘e4 ♘a2 21. ♖c2 ♘ab4 22. ♖c5 f5! 23. ♘d6 ♗f8!] **♘a2 21. ♖c2 ♘db4** [21... ♘ab4 22. ♖c5 ♘a6 23. ♖a5±] **22. ♖c5 ♖b5 23. ♖c4 ♘d5 24. ♖b1 a5 25. d4** [25. ♗f3!⩲ △ ♔g2] **♖cb8 26. e4** [26. ♘c5!?] **♘e7 27. ♖a1 ♘b4 28. ♘c3 ♘c2?⊕** [28... ♖5b7 29. ♖a5 ♘d3!=] **29. ♖a2 ♘d4 30. ♘b5 cb5 31. ♖c7 ♘ec6 32. f4!+– e5 33. ♗e3 ♖d8 34. ♗f1 ♖d6 35. ♗d4 ♘d4 36. ♖a5 ef4 37. ♖a8 ♔h7 38. ♖f7 fg3 39. hg3 ♖f6 40. ♖f6 ♗f6 41. b4 h5 42. ♖b8 ♗e5 43. ♖b7 ♔h6 44. ♔g2 ♔g5 45. ♗b5 h4 46. gh4 ♔h4 47. ♗e8 ♔g5 48. ♖b6 ♗c7 49. ♖g6 ♔f4 50. b5 ♔e4 51. b6 1 : 0** **[Kramnik]**

48. **A 34**

MOROZEVIČ 2440 – MOSKALENKO 2555
Alusta 1993

1. c4 c5 2. ♘f3 ♘f6 3. ♘c3 d5 4. cd5 ♘d5 5. d4 cd4 6. ♕d4 ♘c3 7. ♕c3 ♘c6 8. e4 e6 9. a3 [9. ♗d2!? f6 (△ ♗b4=) 10. a3!? ♗d6 11. ♖d1⩲] **♗d7** [9... ♕a5?! 10. b4!± △ 10... ♘b4? 11. ♗d2+−] **10. ♗e2 ♖c8 N** [10... ♕f6? – 6/88] **11. 0–0 ♘a5!** [11... ♘b4? 12. ♕b3 ♘c2 13. ♖b1± ×♘c2] **12. ♕e5** [12. ♕d3 ♗a4 △ ♘b3=] **♘b3 13. ♖b1 ♕f6** [13... ♕c7 14. ♕c7 ♖c7 15. ♗f4 ♖c8 16. ♖fd1 *a)* 16... ♗e7? 17. ♖d7 ♔d7 18. ♗b5±; *b)* 16... ♘c5 17. ♘e5±; *c)* 16... f6 17. e5 △ 17... f5?! 18. ♖d7 ♔d7 19. ♗b5 *c1)* 19... ♔e7 20. ♖d1 ♖c7 21. ♗g5 ♔f7 22. ♗d8 ♖c1 23. ♘g5 ♔g8 (23... ♔g6 24. ♗e8) 24. ♖c1 ♘c1 25. ♗c4+−; *c2)* 19... ♔c7 20. ♘g5±; *d)* 16... a6⩲; 13... ♖c2 14. ♗b5⩲; 13... ♖c5 14. ♕g3 △ ♗e3⩲; 13... ♘c1 14. ♖bc1⩲; 13... f6 14. ♕g3⩲ △ 14... ♖c2 15. ♗d3 ♘c1 16. ♖fc1 ♖c1 17. ♖c1±, △ 14... ♕c7 15. ♗f4 e5 16. ♘e5! fe5 17. ♗e5±] **14. ♕g3 ♕g6?!** [14... ♘c5 15. ♘e5 (15. e5 ♕g6 16. ♕g6 hg6 17. ♗e3 ♗e7=) ♗a4 16. ♕c3!? (16. b3 ♘e4 17. ♕e3 ♕e5 18. ♗b2 ♗c5!; 16. f3 ♗d6∓) ♗d6 17. ♘c4 (17. f4? 0–0 18. ♗e3 ♘e4 19. ♕d4 ♗c2!−+) ♕c3 (17... ♗e7 18. e5 ♕g6 19. ♗e3±) 18. ♘d6 ♔d7□ 19. bc3 ♔d6 20. ♗e3 b6 21. ♖b4 ♗c6 22. f3±; 14... ♘c1 15. ♖bc1 ♖c1 16. ♖c1 ♕b2 17. ♕b8 ♔e7 18. ♖e1!? (18. ♖d1 ♕e2 19. ♕d6 ♔f6=) g6! 19. e5 ♕b6! △ ♗g7∞] **15. ♕f4! ♗c5** [15... ♕f6 16. ♕e3! (×a7, ♘b3) ♘c1 17. ♖fc1 ♖c1 18. ♕c1 (△ ♕c7) ♗d6 19. e5! ♗e5 20. ♕c5 ♗b8 21. ♗b5± △ 21... ♕e7? 22. ♕c8+−] **16. ♗e3?!** [16. ♘e5 ♕f6 17. ♕g3! (17. ♘d7 ♕f4 18. ♗f4 ♔d7=) *a)* 17... ♘c1 18. ♖bc1 ♗f2 19. ♕f2 ♖c1 20. ♕f6! (20. ♖c1 ♕e5 21. ♕a7 ♕b2!∓) gf6 21. ♖c1 fe5 22. ♖c7! (22. ♗b5? ♗c6! 23. ♗c6 bc6 24. ♖c6 ♔d7 25. ♖a6 ♖a8=) ♔e7 23. ♖b7+−; *b)* 17... ♘d4 18. ♗d1 ♗d6 19. ♘d7 ♔d7 20. f4±; *c)* 17... ♗a4 18. ♗g5±] **♕f6** [16... 0–0? 17. ♘e5+−; 16... ♗e3 17. fe3±] **17. ♕g3 ♕g6** [17... ♗e3 18. fe3 0–0 19. ♘d2 ♘d2 20. ♖f6 ♘e4 21. ♕h4 ♘f6 22. ♗d3⩲ △ ♖f1] **18. ♕f4 ♕f6 19. ♕g3 ♕g6 20. ♕h4!? ♗c6** [20... ♗e3 21. fe3↑; 20... ♗e7 21. ♕f4± △ 21... ♕f6 22. ♕f6 ♗f6 23. ♗a7] **21. ♗c5 ♘c5 22. ♖bc1!? ♘d7?!** [22... ♗e4? 23. b4+−; 22... ♕e4! 23. ♖c5 ♕e2 24. ♘d4 *a)* 24... ♕b2? 25. ♘f5! ♕f6 (25... 0–0 26. ♘e7 ♔h8 27. ♕h7! ♔h7 28. ♖h5#; 25... ef5 26. ♖e1 ♔f8 27. ♕e7 ♔g8 28. ♖c6 ♖f8□ 29. ♕f8! ♔f8 30. ♖c8#) 26. ♘d6 ♔d7 27. ♕b4±; *b)* 24... ♕d2! 25. ♘b5 (25. ♘f5? ef5−+) 0–0 26. ♘a7 ♖a8 27. ♘c6 bc6=] **23. ♘d4 ♕f6!? 24. ♕f6 gf6** [24... ♘f6 25. ♗b5±] **25. ♘c6** [25. ♘b5 ♖d8!⩲] **bc6 26. ♖c2 ♔e7 27. ♖fc1 ♘b8 28. b4 ♖c7 29. f3** [29. g3!? ♖hc8 30. ♔g2 ♔d6 31. ♔h3! ♔e7 (31... c5 32. bc5 ♖c5 33. ♖c5 ♖c5 34. ♖c5 ♔c5 35. ♔h4+−) 32. ♔h4 ♔f8 33. ♔h5 ♔g7 34. a4±; 29. f4±] **♖hc8 30. ♔f2 ♔d6 31. ♖c5** [31. ♔g3 △ ♔h4±] **♘d7 32. ♖h5 ♖h8 33. ♔e3?!** [33. f4 c5 34. ♗b5 cb4! 35. e5 fe5 36. fe5 ♘e5 37. ♖c7 ♔c7 38. ♖e5 ba3∞; 33. ♖h6!? △ 33... c5 34. ♗b5 cb4 35. ♖c7 ♔c7 36. ab4±] **c5 34. bc5 ♘c5 35. f4** [35. ♖c3 e5!? △ ♘e6-d4⇆] **♖b8! 36. ♖c3 ♖b3 37. ♖b3 ♘b3 38. ♖h7 ♖c3 39. ♔f2 ♘c5⊕** [⌓ 39... ♘d2=] **40. ♗f3 ♔e7 41. ♖h8 ♖a3** [⌓ 41... ♘d3 42. ♔g3 ♘e1=] **42. h4 ♘d3 43. ♔g1!? ♘f4 44. ♖a8** [44. h5 ♘h3 (44... ♖d3 45. ♔h2!⩲ △ 45... ♖d8 46. ♖d8 ♔d8 47. g3 ♘d3 48. h6 ♘e5 49. ♗h5+−) 45. ♔h2 ♘g5 46. h6 ♘f3 47. gf3 ♖a2 48. ♔g3 ♖a1=] **1/2 : 1/2**
[Morozevič, Jurkov]

49. **A 34**

PSAKHIS 2575 – TUKMAKOV 2605
Rostov na Donu 1993

1. c4 c5 2. ♘c3 ♘f6 3. g3 d5 4. cd5 ♘d5 5. ♗g2 ♘c7 6. ♕b3 ♘c6 7. ♗c6 bc6 8. ♕a4 ♕d7 9. ♘f3 f6 10. d3 e5 11. ♗e3 ♘e6 12. 0–0 ♖b8 13. ♖ab1 h5?! N [13... ♗e7 – 31/83] **14. ♘e4 ♘d4** [14... h4?! 15. ♘h4] **15. ♗d4 cd4 16. ♖fc1 ♖b5!** [16... ♖b6 17. ♘c5; 17. b4!?⩲] **17. ♖c2 a5□** [17... ♗e7 18. ♖bc1±] **18. ♖bc1 ♗b7 19. ♘h4! ♖h6!?** [19... ♔f7?! 20. ♕b5! cb5 21. ♖c7 ♔e6 22. ♖d7 (22.

♘g6!?) ♔d7 23. ♘g6 ♗e4! (23... ♖g8? 24. ♘f8 ♖f8 25. ♘c5 ♔c8 26. ♘e6+−) 24. de4 (24. ♘h8? ♗f5) ♖g8 25. ♔g2!? (25. ♘f8 ♖f8 26. ♖c5 ♖b8=) ♗d6 26. ♔h3±] **20. b3** [20. ♘f5? ♕f5? 21. ♖c6 ♗c6 22. ♖c6 ♖b4 23. ♖c8+−; 20... ♖b4!−+; 20. ♘c5?! ♗c5 21. ♖c5 ♖b2∞] **♕d5** [20... g5!? 21. ♘f5 ♖g6! (21... ♕f5 22. ♖c6+−) 22. a3 (22. h3? ♖b4!) ♔f7 23. ♕b5 cb5 24. ♖c7 ♔e6 25. ♖d7 ♔d7∞; 21. ♘f3!?⩲] **21. ♕c4!± ♔d7 22. ♕d5 ♖d5** [22... cd5 23. ♘c5±] **23. ♘c5 ♗c5 24. ♖c5 ♖h8 25. ♘f3 ♖b8** [25... a4 26. b4!?] **26. ♘d2 ♗a8 27. ♖5c4! ♔c7 28. ♘e4 ♖b4 29. ♔g2!** [×h5] **f5?!⊕ 30. ♘g5 ♔d6 31. f4! ef4** [31... c5 32. ♔f2] **32. gf4 c5 33. ♔f2 ♖b7 34. ♘e4!+− fe4 35. de4 ♖f7** [35... ♖c7 36. ed5 ♗d5 37. ♖4c2] **36. ed5 ♖f4 37. ♔e1 ♖g4** [37... ♗d5 38. ♖c5 ♖h4 39. ♖a5 ♖h2 40. ♖a6 ♔e5 41. ♖c5 ♔e4 42. ♔d2] **38. ♖c5 ♗d5 39. ♖a5 ♖g1 40. ♔d2 ♖g2 1 : 0**
[Psakhis]

50. **A 34**

ILLESCAS CÓRDOBA 2615
− KAMSKY 2655

Buenos Aires 1993

1. ♘f3 ♘f6 2. c4 c5 3. ♘c3 d5 4. cd5 ♘d5 5. g3 ♘c6 6. ♗g2 ♘c7 7. 0−0 e6 8. d3 ♗e7 9. ♗e3 0−0 10. d4 cd4 11. ♘d4 ♘a5 N [11... ♘b4 − 13/63] **12. ♕a4! ♘d5** [12... e5 13. ♕a5 ed4 14. ♗d4 ♕d4 15. ♕c7±] **13. ♘d5 ed5 14. ♗d2! ♘c4 15. ♗c3** [×d4] **♗e6?** [15... ♘b6] **16. ♘e6 fe6 17. b3 ♘d6 18. ♕g4 ♘f5 19. e4 de4 20. ♕e4** [20. ♗e4!?] **♕b6! 21. ♕b7 ♖ac8 22. ♖ac1!± ♗a3 23. ♗b2 ♖c1 24. ♗c1 ♗c5 25. ♕b6 ab6 26. ♖d1! b5** [△ b4] **27. a4 ♘d4 28. ♗e3 ♘e2?!** [28... ♘b3 29. ♗c5 ♘c5 30. ab5 ♖b8 31. ♗c6±] **29. ♔h1 ♗e3 30. fe3 ba4 31. ba4 ♘c3 32. ♖a1 ♖f7 33. a5 ♖a7 34. a6 ♔f7 35. ♗b7 ♘b5 36. ♔g2+− ♔e7⊕ 37. ♖c1** [⌓ 37. ♔f3 ♘d6 38. ♖b1 e5 39. ♔g4 ♔d7 40. ♖d1 ♔c7 41. ♖d6 ♔d6 42. ♔f5] **♔d6 38. ♖c6** [38. ♔f3!] **♔d7 39. ♖c8** [39. ♔f3! ♘d6 40. ♖d6 ♔d6 41. ♔e4] **♘c7 40. ♖h8??** [40. ♖g8!□ g6 (40... ♔d6 41. ♖g7 ♘a6 42. ♖h7 ♘c5 43. ♗e4+−) 41. ♖g7 ♔d6 42. ♖c7 ♔c7 43. ♔f3+−] **h6 41. ♖h7 ♔d6! 42. ♔f3 ♔e5! 43. ♖g7 ♘a6 44. ♖h7 ♘c5 45. ♗e4 ♖h7 46. ♗h7± ♘d7 47. g4 ♔f6 48. h4 ♘b6 49. ♗d3 ♘d5 50. ♗e4 ♘b6 51. ♔f4 e5 52. ♔f3 ♘c4 53. ♗d5 ♘d6 54. ♗b3 ♘b7 55. ♔e2 ♘d6 56. ♔d3 ♔g7 57. ♗c2 h5! 58. g5 ♘f5= 59. ♔e4 ♘h4 60. ♔e5 ♘g2 61. ♔e4 h4 62. ♗b1 h3 63. ♔f3 ♘h4 64. ♔g3 h2 65. ♗e4 ♘f5 66. ♔f4 ♘d6 67. ♗h1 ♔g6 68. ♗g2 ♘f7 69. ♗e4 ♔h5 70. ♗f3 1/2 : 1/2**
[Illescas Córdoba]

51.* **A 35**

SKEMBRIS 2560 − GIFFARD 2370

Cannes 1993

1. c4 c5 2. ♘f3 ♘c6 3. ♘c3 g6 4. d4 cd4 5. ♘d4 ♗g7 6. e3 ♘f6 [6... ♘d4 7. ed4 ♘h6 8. ♗d3!?⩲] **7. ♗e2** [7. ♘c2 ♕a5!? N (7... d6 − 17/68) 8. ♗d2 ♕e5 9. ♗e2 d5∞ Tibenský 2410 − Gljanec 2370, České Budejovice 1992] **0−0 8. ♘c2 d6 9. 0−0 ♘d7!? N** [9... a6 − 9/558] **10. ♗d2! a5** [10... ♘c5 11. b4±] **11. ♖b1 ♘c5 12. f3 f5** [12... ♗f5!? 13. e4 ♗e6 △ f5⇆; 13. ♗e1!?⩲] **13. b3 ♗e6** [13... g5!?] **14. ♗e1 ♔h8 15. ♘d5 ♗d5!? 16. cd5** [16. ♕d5 ♘b4!?⇆] **♘b4! 17. a3!** [17. ♗b4?! ab4 18. ♘b4 ♕b6 19. ♕d2 f4∓] **♘c2 18. ♕c2 ♕b6!?** [18... ♖c8 19. ♗c3!?± ×♔h8] **19. ♗f2!** [19. ♗c3?! ♘e6!∓ ×e3] **♖fc8?!** [19... ♖ac8 20. ♖fc1±⊞] **20. e4!** [20. ♖fc1?! ♕d8∞] **♕d8□** [20... fe4? 21. b4±] **21. ef5 ♘a4!? 22. ♕d3** [22. ♗c4 b5=∞] **♘c3 23. ♖be1** [23. fg6 ♘b1⇆ ⇔c] **g5□ 24. ♗d1!± ♗f6** [24... ♖c5? 25. ♗c5 dc5 26. f6! ♗f6 27. ♗c2+−; 24... ♗e5 (△ ♕g8 ×d5) 25. ♗d4 ♘d5 26. f4! gf4 27. ♗f3±; 27. ♕e4±] **25. ♖e6 b5 26. ♖fe1 b4 27. a4 ♕f8** [27... ♖c5 28. ♗c5 dc5 29. d6 ♗d4 30. ♔f1 ed6 31. f6 (△ ♗c2+−) ♘d1 32. ♖e7 ♕g8 33. ♖g7+−] **28. ♗d4 ♖c7** [28... ♕g7 29. ♖e7! ♗d4 30. ♔f1; 28... ♘d5 29. ♗f6 ♘f6 30. ♖e7± ×d6, ♔h8] **29. ♗f6 ef6 30. ♕d4 ♖f7** [30... ♖c5? 31. ♖f6 ♕g7 32. ♖e7! ♖d5 33. ♖f8+−; 30... ♔g7 31. f4±] **31. f4! ♕h6□** [31... gf4?? 32. ♗h5+−; 31... ♘d1 32. fg5!? ♘c3 33. g6→] **32. ♖d6 gf4 33. ♖de6?!** [33. ♗f3±] **♘d1** [33... ♕g5 34. ♗f3 △ d6+−] **34.**

♕d1 [×f3] **♖g8 35. ♖e8** [35. d6 ♕h3→] **♖g7 36. ♖g8 ♖g8 37. d6 ♕g5?!⊕** [37... f3! 38. ♕f3 ♕d2 39. ♖d1? ♖g2 40. ♔f1 ♖f2 41. ♔g1 ♖g2=; 39. ♖e6!?±] **38. ♕c2! f3 39. d7 ♕f4** [39... ♕g2?? 40. ♕g2 ♖g2 41. ♔f1+–; 39... ♕g4 40. ♕f2! ♕f5 41. ♖d1+–] **40. ♖d1! ♕e3** [40... ♖g2?? 41. ♕g2+–; 40... ♖d8 41. ♕f2 ♕f5 42. ♕f3 ♕f3 43. gf3 ♔g7 44. ♔f2 ♔f7 45. ♔e3 ♔e7 46. ♔e4 ♖d7 47. ♖d7 ♔d7 48. ♔d5+–; 40... fg2!? 41. ♕f2! (41. d8♕? ♕e3 42. ♕f2 ♕f2 43. ♔f2 g1♕ 44. ♖g1 ♖d8) ♕c7 (41... ♕f2 42. ♔f2 h5 43. ♔g1!+–) 42. ♕d4 ♕d8 43. ♖e1 △ ♖e2+– ×g2] **41. ♕f2!±** [41. ♔h1 ♕e2!∞̄; 41. ♔f1 ♖d8± ×b3, ♔f1] **♖g2 42. ♔h1 ♕f2□** [42... ♖f2 43. d8♕ ♔g7 44. ♖d7 ♔h6 45. ♕f6 ♔h5 46. ♖h7 ♔g4 47. ♖h4#] **43. d8♕ ♔g7 44. ♖d7 ♔h6 45. ♕f6 ♖g6□** [45... ♔h5 46. ♖h7 ♔g4 47. h3 ♔f4 (47... ♔g3 48. ♕g5#) 48. ♖h4 ♔e3 49. ♕d4 ♔e2 50. ♖e4 ♔f1 51. ♕d1+–] **46. ♖h7! ♔h7 47. ♕g6!** [47. fg6? ♔h6 48. g7 ♔h7 49. ♕g5 ♔g8∞̄] **♔h8 48. ♕g3!** [△ f6+–; 48. ♕g1?! ♕b2!∞̄] **♕b2□** [48... ♕e2 49. f6+–; 48... ♕f1 49. ♕g1 ♕a6□ (×f6) 50. ♕d4 ♔h7 51. ♕h4 ♔g7 52. ♕g4 △ ♕f3+–] **49. ♕f3 ♕a1 50. ♔g2 ♕b2?!** [50... ♔g7±] **51. ♔h3 ♕c3** [51... ♔g7 52. ♕g2+–] **52. ♕g3! ♕c2 53. ♕e5 ♔h7 54. ♕e7 ♔h6 55. ♕f6 ♔h7 56. ♕g6 ♔h8 57. ♕h6 ♔g8 58. ♕e6 ♔h8** [⌓ 58... ♔g7] **59. f6+– ♕d3 60. ♔h4 ♕h7 61. ♔g4** [61. ♔g5 ♕h6] **♕g6 62. ♔f4 ♕h6 63. ♔e4** [△ ♔d5-c6-b6; 63... ♕h2 64. ♕e8 ♔h7 65. ♕f7 ♔h6 66. ♕g7 ♔h5 67. ♕h7] **1 : 0** **[Skembris]**

52. !N** **A 40**

SKEMBRIS 2560 – WARD 2430

Gausdal 1993

1. d4 e6 2. c4 ♗b4 3. ♗d2 a5 4. g3!? [4. ♘f3 d6 5. ♘c3 f5 6. g3 ♘f6 7. ♗g2 0–0 N (7... ♗c3?! – 55/59) 8. 0–0 ♕e7 9. ♕c2 ♘bd7 10. ♖ac1 ♖b8 11. a3 ♗c3 12. ♗c3 b6 13. b4 ab4 14. ab4 b5!? 15. ♘d2 bc4 16. ♘c4 ♗b7 17. f3 ♘d5∞ 18. ♗d2 1/2 : 1/2 Razuvaev 2525 – Ward 2430, Bern 1993] **d6 5. ♗g2! N** [5. ♘f3 – 53/(61)] **e5** [5... ♘c6!?] **6. de5 de5 7. ♘c3 ♘f6** [7... ♘c6 8. ♗c6!? bc6 9. ♕a4± △ 0-0-0] **8. ♘f3 ♘c6** [8... e4? 9. ♘g5± ×e4] **9. 0–0 h6** [9... 0–0 10. ♕c2 ♗g4 11. ♖ad1 ♕e7 12. ♘d5 ♘d5 13. cd5 ♗f3 14. dc6 ♗g2 15. ♔g2 bc6 16. ♕c6 ♕d6 17. ♕d6 cd6 18. ♗e3 ♖fc8 19. a3 ♗c5 20. ♗c5± Elsness 2260 – Ward 2430, Gausdal 1993; 9... ♗e6!?] **10. ♕c2 ♗e6** [10... 0–0 11. ♖ad1± ⇔d, ×d5; 10... ♘d4 11. ♘d4 ed4 12. ♘d5 ♗d2 13. ♕d2 c6 14. ♘f6 ♕f6 15. ♖ad1 c5 16. e3±] **11. ♖ad1** [△ ♗h6] **♕c8?!** [11... ♗c3?? 12. ♗c3+–⊞ ×e5; 11... ♕e7!?] **12. ♘d5!± ♘d5** [12... ♗d5 13. cd5 ♘d5 14. ♘e5 ♘e5 15. ♕e4!? 0–0 16. ♕e5±; 12... ♗f5±] **13. cd5 ♗d5□** [13... ♗f5?? 14. ♕a4+–] **14. ♗b4 ♘b4** [14... ♗f3 15. ♗f3 ♘b4 (15... ab4 16. ♗c6±) 16. ♕c5± ×e5, ♔e8] **15. ♕c5!→ e4** [15... b6 16. ♕b5 c6□ 17. ♕b6 0–0 18. a3±; 15... ♗a2 16. ♕e5 ♔f8 17. ♘d4→] **16. ♘d4** [△ ♘b5] **b6□** [16... ♗a2?? 17. ♘f5+–] **17. ♕b5 c6** [17... ♕d7 18. ♕d7 ♔d7 19. ♘f5 c6 20. a3 ♘a6 21. ♗e4±] **18. ♕b6 ♘a2?!** [18... 0–0 19. a3 ♘a6 20. ♕a5±; 18... ♕d8!? 19. ♕d8 ♖d8 20. a3 ♘a6 21. f3! ef3 (21... e3 22. ♘f5 0–0 23. ♘e3±) 22. ♗f3± ×c6] **19. ♕c5** [△ ♘b5+–] **♘b4 20. ♗e4!± ♗e4 21. ♕e5 ♔f8 22. ♕e4 ♕e8?!** [22... h5±] **23. ♕f5!** [×a5] **h5** [23... g6 24. ♕f6 ♔g8±] **24. ♖a1 a4 25. ♖fc1 ♔g8** [25... ♖h6 26. ♕c5 ♕e7 27. ♕e7 ♔e7 28. ♘f5+–] **26. ♖c4 ♕e7 27. ♕f3!+–** [×c6, f5] **g6 28. ♘c6 ♘c6 29. ♕c6 ♔g7 30. ♖e4 ♕g5** [30... ♖hc8 31. ♕a8+–; 30... ♕f6 31. ♕f6 ♔f6 32. ♖aa4+–] **31. ♕c3 f6 32. h4 ♕f5** [32... ♕b5 33. ♖e7+–] **33. ♖ea4 ♖a4 34. ♖a4 ♖d8** [34... ♖c8 35. ♖a7+–] **35. ♖a7 ♔h8 36. ♕e3!** [36. ♕c7?? ♖d1 37. ♔g2 ♕e4–+] **g5 37. ♔g2 ♕d5 38. f3⊕** **1 : 0** **[Skembris]**

53. **A 40**

ZSU. POLGÁR 2560 – SPEELMAN 2595

Nederland 1993

1. d4 e6 2. c4 ♗b4 3. ♘c3 b6 4. e4 ♗b7 5. d5!? ♕e7 [5... ♗c3 – 25/117] **6. ♗e2?!**

[6. ♘e2 ♘f6 (6... ed5 7. ed5 ♘f6∞) 7. f3 ed5 8. cd5 c6 9. dc6 ♘c6?! 10. a3 ♗c3 11. ♘c3 d5?! 12. ♘d5! (12. ♗g5 de4 13. ♘e4 ♖d8) ♘d5 13. ♕d5 ♖d8 (13... 0–0 14. ♗g5) 14. ♕g5! f6 15. ♕h5! g6 16. ♕h6 ♘d4 17. ♔f2±; 10... ♗d6=; 9... dc6=; 6. ♗e3!?] **♘f6 7. f3 N** [7. ♕d4 ed5 8. ed5 ♕e4; 7. ♗g5!? h6 8. ♗h4 (8. ♗f6 ♕f6 9. ♖c1) ♗c3 (8... ed5 9. ed5 0–0 10. ♘f3 ♖e8 11. ♔f1∞; 8... g5 9. ♗g3 ♘e4 10. ♕d4 ♘f6 11. ♗e5 c5!□; 11. 0-0-0∞) 9. bc3 ♕a3 10. ♕d4 (10. f3 ♕c3 11. ♔f1=) ♘e4 11. ♕g7 ♕c3? 12. ♕c3 ♘c3 13. ♗f6 ♘e2 14. ♗h8 ♘g1 (14... ♘f4) 15. ♖g1 d6±; 11... ♖f8∞] **ed5 8. cd5 c6 9. dc6 ♘c6 10. ♘h3 d5! 11. ed5 0-0-0 12. ♗g5** [12. 0–0 ♗c3 *a)* 13. bc3 ♖d5 14. ♕c2 (14. ♕e1 ♖e5 15. ♘f4 g5–+) ♕c5 15. ♘f2 ♘d4–+; *b)* 13. dc6 ♖d1 14. cb7 ♔b7 15. ♗d1 ♗d4 16. ♔h1∓] **♖he8!** [12... ♕c5!?] **13. ♗f6** [13. ♘f4 ♕e5 14. ♗f6 ♕f6!?; 14... gf6!] **gf6!** [13... ♕f6 14. 0–0 ♗c3 15. bc3 ♕c3 16. ♘f2 ♕e5! (×♖a1) 17. ♗c4 (17. dc6!? ♖d1 18. cb7 ♔b7 19. ♖ad1 ♕e2 20. ♖d7 ♔a6 21. ♖f7 ♕a2!?; 21... ♖e7–+) ♘a5∓] **14. ♘f4** [14. ♔f1 ♗c3 15. bc3 ♖d5 16. ♕d5 ♕e2 17. ♔g1 ♕e3!? 18. ♔f1 (18. ♘f2 ♕e1!) ♕e2! 19. ♔g1 ♘e5 20. ♕d6 ♘f3 21. gf3 ♕f3] **♕e5 15. ♕d2** [15. ♕c1 *a)* 15... ♘d4 16. 0–0 ♔b8 (16... ♗c3 17. ♗d3!!) 17. ♗d3 ♗c5 18. ♔h1 ♗d6 19. g3 ♕e3!?∞; *b)* 15... ♖d5! 16. 0–0 ♖c5 (16... ♗c5 17. ♔h1 ♗e3 18. ♘fd5) 17. ♘d3 ♕d4 18. ♔h1 ♗c3 (18... ♖c3 19. bc3 ♗c3–+) 19. ♘c5 ♗b2 20. ♘b3 ♕e5–+] **♗c3!** [15... ♘d4 16. 0-0-0!] **16. bc3 ♘b4 17. ♔f2?** [17. 0-0-0 ♘d5 18. ♘d5 ♖d5 19. ♗d3 ♖ed8 20. f4 (20. ♖he1 ♖d3 21. ♖e5 ♖d2; 20. ♕e2 ♖d3 21. ♕d3 ♖d3 22. ♖d3) ♕d6 21. ♔c2 (21. ♗f5 ♔c7 22. ♕c2 ♕f4 23. ♔b2 ♖d1 24. ♖d1 ♖d1 25. ♕d1 ♕f5) ♖d3 (21... ♕a3–+) 22. ♕d3 ♕d3 23. ♖d3 ♗e4 24. ♖hd1 b5!–+; 17. ♖c1 ♘d5 (17... ♕f4?? 18. cb4) 18. ♘d3 ♕e7 19. ♔f2 (19. c4 ♘f4!; 19. g3 ♘f4 20. gf4 ♗f3 21. 0–0 ♗e2–+) ♘f4! 20. ♖he1 ♕c5! (20... ♘d3 21. ♗d3 ♕c5 22. ♔f1 ♖e1 23. ♖e1 ♕d5 24. ♖d1) *a)* 21. ♔f1 ♖e2 22. ♕f4 (22. ♖e2 ♘d3) ♖e1 23. ♘e1 ♗a6 24. c4 ♖d4–+; *b)* 21. ♘c5 ♖d2 22. ♘e4 ♗e4 23. fe4 (23. ♔e3 ♖e2) ♖e4 (23... ♖e2 24. ♖e2 ♘d3 25. ♔e3 ♘c1 26. ♖c2) 24. ♔f3 ♖de2 25. ♖e2 ♖e2! (25... ♘e2?! 26. ♖c2! f5 27. ♖e2 ♖e2 28. ♔e2 ♔d7∞) 26. ♔f4 ♖g2–+; 17. ♖d1 ♘d5 18. ♘d3 *a)* 18... ♕c7 19. c4! (19. ♔f2 ♘c3 20. ♖c1 ♖e2 21. ♕e2 ♘e2 22. ♖c7 ♔c7 23. ♔e2 ♗a6–+) ♘e3 20. ♖c1 ♖d3!? 21. ♕d3 ♘g2 22. ♔f2 ♕c5 (22... ♘f4 23. ♕f5 ♔b8 24. ♖he1) 23. ♔g2 ♖g8 24. ♔f1 ♕g5 25. ♔f2!□ ♕g2 26. ♔e3 ♖e8 27. ♔d2 ♖d8; *b)* 18... ♕e2!? 19. ♕e2 ♖e2 20. ♔e2 ♘c3 21. ♔e3 ♘d1 22. ♖d1∓] **♘d5 18. ♘d3 ♘c3!** [19. ♗f1 ♕d4 20. ♔g3 ♖e3 21. ♔h3 ♔b8; 19. ♕c3 ♕c3 20. ♖hc1 ♖e2 21. ♔e2 ♖d3; 19. ♖he1 ♕d4 (19... ♕e2) 20. ♔f1 ♖e2 21. ♖e2 ♘e2 22. ♔e2 ♗a6–+] **0 : 1** **[Speelman]**

54. **A 40**

ROHDE-JENSEN – TYŠKOVEC

corr. 1987/91

1. d4 ♘f6 2. c4 e6 3. ♘c3 b6?! 4. e4 ♗b7 5. ♗d3 ♗b4 6. ♕c2 N [6. f3 – 8/71] **c5 7. d5 d6 8. f4?!** [8. ♘f3 △ 0–0⩲] **ed5 9. cd5 0–0 10. ♘e2 ♘bd7 11. 0–0 ♘g4!? 12. h3** [12. e5? ♕h4! 13. h3 c4! 14. ♗c4 ♗c5 15. ♔h1 ♘f2 16. ♔h2 de5 17. fe5 ♘e5–+] **c4! 13. ♗c4 ♖c8 14. ♗d3 ♕h4! 15. ♘d4 ♗c5 16. ♕a4 f5! 17. hg4 ♘f6 18. ♗e2 fg4 19. ♗e3 ♖ce8 20. ♖fe1** [20. ♘f5? ♗e3 21. ♘e3 g3–+] **♘e4 21. ♗b5!?**

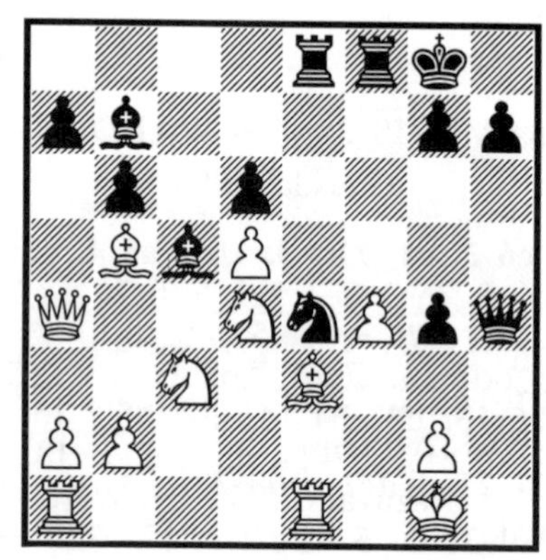

21... ♖e5!!–+ 22. ♘e4 [22. fe5 g3 23. ♘f3 ♖f3 24. gf3 ♕h2 25. ♔f1 ♘d2 26. ♗d2 ♕f2#] **♖e4 23. ♘f5!** [23. ♗f2 ♖e1 24. ♖e1 g3] **♖e3 24. ♘e3?!** [24. ♘h4 ♖e1 25. ♔h2 ♖a1 26. ♗c6 ♗f2 27. ♗b7 g3 28. ♔h3 h5; 24. ♖e3 ♖f5 25. ♕e4 ♕g3! 26. ♕e6 ♖f7 27. ♕e8 ♖f8 28. ♕e6 ♔h8] **g3 25. ♕e4** [25. ♗d7 ♖f4] **♗c8! 26. ♗d3 ♗f5 27. ♕f5 ♖f5 28. ♗f5 ♕f4 29. ♗e6 ♔f8 30. ♖f1 ♗e3 31. ♔h1 ♗f2 32. ♖ac1 ♕h4 33. ♗h3 g5 34. ♖c8 ♔f7 35. ♖fc1 g4 36. ♖1c4 h5 37. ♖4c7 ♔f6 38. ♖e8 ♗d4! 39. ♖e6 ♔f5 40. ♖f7 ♗f6**
0 : 1 **[Tyškovec]**

55. **A 40**

ALBURT 2535 – VIGORITO

New York 1993

1. d4 g6 2. c4 ♗g7 3. ♘c3 c5 4. d5 ♗c3!? 5. bc3 f5! 6. h3 N [△ 6... ♘f6 7. ♗h6; 6. g4!? fg4 7. h3 g3!=; 6. ♘f3 – 56/58] **d6 7. ♘f3 ♕a5 8. ♕c2 ♘f6 9. ♗h6! ♘bd7 10. e3 ♘b6 11. ♗d3 ♗d7 12. 0–0 ♕a4 13. ♕b3 ♘e4 14. ♗e4!± fe4 15. ♘d2 0-0-0 16. f3 ef3 17. ♖f3 ♕a6! 18. ♖f7** [18. ♖f4±] **♗a4 19. ♕b2** [19. ♕a3 ♗b5! 20. ♕a6 ♗a6±] **♘c4 20. ♘c4 ♕c4 21. ♖b1! ♕d5** [21... ♖d7 22. ♖f4 ♕d5?? 23. c4 ♕g8 24. ♗g7+–] **22. ♖e7 ♗c6?** [22... ♗d7!□ 23. c4∞] **23. c4 ♕d3**

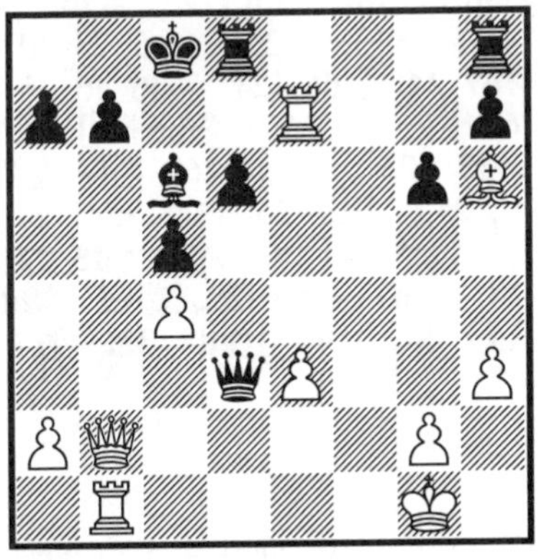

24. ♕b7!!+– [24. ♖b7? ♕b1±] **♗b7 25. ♖bb7 ♖d7□ 26. ♖ed7 ♕f5** [26... ♕d1 27. ♔h2 ♕h5 28. ♗g7 ♖f8! 29. ♗f8! ♕e5 30. g3] **27. ♖dc7 ♔d8 28. ♖f7** **1 : 0**
[Alburt]

56.* **A 40**

M. PAVLOVIĆ 2455 – VAULIN 2515

Podgorica 1993

1. c4 c5 2. ♘f3 g6 3. d4 ♗g7 4. e4 ♕a5 5. ♗d2 ♕b6 6. ♗c3 ♘c6 N [6... ♘f6 – 19/304] **7. dc5** [RR 7. d5 ♘d4 8. ♘a3 (8. e5 ♘f3 9. ♕f3 ♘h6=) e5□ 9. de6 de6 10. ♘b5?! e5 11. b4 ♗g4! 12. bc5 ♕c5 13. ♘bd4 ed4! (13... 0-0-0? 14. ♕a4 ed4 15. ♗b4 ♕c6 16. ♕c6 bc6 17. ♘d2± M. Makarov 2515 – Vaulin 2515, Podgorica 1993) 14. ♗d4 ♕b4 15. ♕d2 ♕d2 16. ♔d2 0-0-0∞⇆; 10. e5± Vaulin, M. Makarov] **♗c3 8. ♘c3 ♕b2** [8... ♕c5 9. ♘d5!±] **9. ♘d5 ♔f8?!** [9... ♘f6 10. ♗d3 0–0 11. 0–0±] **10. ♗e2 ♕a3** [RR 10... e6!? Vaulin, M. Makarov] **11. 0–0 ♕c5 12. ♕d2 ♔g7** [12... d6!?] **13. ♖ab1!** [△ 13... d6 14. ♕c3 △ ♖b5+–] **♕a5 14. ♕b2 f6** [14... ♘f6 15. ♖fd1±] **15. e5 fe5?** [15... ♕d8□ 16. ♖fe1→] **16. ♘e5 ♘f6 17. ♗f3± ♕c5! 18. ♖fe1 ♕d4 19. ♘c7! ♕b2 20. ♖b2 ♘e5!□** [20... ♖b8 21. ♗c6+–] **21. ♖e5! ♖b8 22. ♖e7 ♔h6□** [22... ♔f8 23. ♖be2] **23. ♖f7!+– ♘e8 24. ♘e8 ♖e8 25. h4 b6 26. g4 g5 27. ♖b5 ♔g6 28. ♖bf5 gh4 29. ♗d5! d6 30. ♖5f6 ♔g5 31. f4 ♔g4 32. ♖g7** **1 : 0**
[M. Pavlović]

57. **A 41**

ILLESCAS CÓRDOBA 2615 – SPANGENBERG 2505

Buenos Aires 1993

1. ♘f3 d6 2. d4 ♗g4 3. c4 ♗f3 4. ef3 c6 N [4... g6 – 44/46] **5. ♘c3 ♘f6** [△ d5] **6. d5!? g6 7. ♗d3 ♗g7 8. 0–0 0–0 9. ♖e1 a6 10. f4** [10. ♗f1±] **b5! 11. ♕f3** [11. dc6 bc4 12. ♗c4 e6!=] **b4 12. ♘e4 cd5 13. ♘f6 ♗f6 14. ♕d5 ♘d7= 15. f5 ♘e5 16. fg6 hg6 17. ♗f1 ♖c8** [△ e6, ♘c4] **18. ♗d2** [⌓ 18. ♕e4] **a5 19. ♕e4 ♘d7 20. ♖ab1 ♘c5 21. ♕f3 ♘a4!? 22. a3!** [22. b3 ♘c3] **♖b8** [22... ♘b2 23. ab4 ♘c4 24. ♗c4 ♖c4 25. ba5±] **23. ab4 ab4 24. g3** [△ h4-h5] **♕a5!?** [24... ♕d7 25. b3 ♘c3 26. ♖a1=] **25. ♖a1!? ♕a8** [25... ♗b2! 26. ♖a2 (△ ♕b3) *a)* 26... ♗f6? 27. ♕d1 ♖a8

28. ♗g2 ♖a7 29. ♗c6+−; *b)* 26... ♗c3? 27. ♕d1 ♖a8 (27... ♗d2 28. ♕d2 ♖a8 29. ♖ea1±) 28. ♗g2 ♗d2 (28... ♖a6 29. ♗b7 ♖a7 30. ♗c6±) 29. ♗a8! (29. ♕d2 b3! 30. ♗a8 ♕d2 31. ♖d2 ♖a8 32. ♖a1 ♖b8!=) ♗e1 30. ♖a4±; *c)* 26... ♗d4! 27. ♕d1 ♕f5! 28. ♗b4 (28. ♗h6 b3 29. ♕d4 e5∓) ♖b4 29. ♕d4 ♕d7!=] **26. ♕g4** [26. ♕a8 ♖a8 27. ♗g2 ♗b2 28. ♗a8 ♗a1=] **♗b2⊕ 27. ♗g2** [⌓ 27. ♖a2 ♗g7! 28. ♗g2 ♕a7± − 27. ♗g2] **♕a7** [27... ♕a6? 28. ♗d5 ♗a1 (28... e6 29. ♖e6!+−) 29. ♕g6 ♔h8 30. ♕h5 ♔g8 31. ♖a1+−] **28. ♖a2** [28. ♗d5 ♗a1? 29. ♖a1 (29. ♕g6 ♗g7 30. ♗h6 ♕d4!−+) e6 30. ♗c6 b3 31. ♖a4 ♕c5 32. ♗e4±; 28... e6!∞] **b3?** [28... ♗g7 29. ♗c6 (29. ♗d5? b3) ♕c5! 30. ♗a4 b3 31. ♖aa1!? (31. ♗b3 ♖b3 32. ♖e7 d5=) ♗a1 32. ♖a1±; 28... ♗d4!∞ 29. ♖a4 ♗f2 30. ♔f1 ♕a4 31. ♔f2] **29. ♖b2! ♘b2 30. ♗d5! e6 31. ♖e6!+− fe6 32. ♕e6 ♔h7 33. ♕h3 ♔g7 34. ♗h6** [34. ♕h6!] **♔h8 35. ♗e3 ♔g7 1 : 0**
[Illescas Córdoba]

58.* !N **A 41**

FTÁČNIK 2535 − ERMENKOV 2505
Budapest (zt) 1993

1. d4 d6 2. ♘f3 g6 3. c4 ♗g7 4. ♘c3 e5 5. ♗g5 [RR 5. g3 ♘c6 6. de5 N (6. d5 − 18/37) ♘e5 7. ♘e5 ♗e5 8. ♗g2 ♘e7 9. 0−0 c6 10. ♕d3 ♗e6 11. ♘e4 d5 12. cd5 ♗d5 13. ♗f4 ♗e4 14. ♕e4 ♗f4 15. ♕f4±↑⟳ Milos 2560 − Seirawan 2595, Buenos Aires 1993] **f6 6. ♗d2! N** [6. ♗h4?! g5 7. ♗g3 f5 8. h3 e4 9. ♘d2 ♗d4 10. ♘de4 ♗g7 11. ♘d2 f4∞] **♘c6** [6... f5 7. ♗g5 ♕d7 8. de5 (8. e3 h6 9. ♗h4 g5 10. ♗g3 f4−+) de5 9. e4±; 6... ed4! 7. ♘d4 f5 8. ♗f4 (8. e3 ♘e7 9. ♗e2 ♘bc6=) ♘f6 9. g3∞] **7. d5 ♘ce7** [7... ♘d4 8. ♘d4 ed4 9. ♘b5 f5 10. ♗g5 ♕g5 11. ♘c7 ♔d8 12. ♘a8±] **8. e4 ♘h6** [8... f5!? 9. ♗d3 ♘f6 10. 0−0 0−0 11. ♘g5 h6 12. ♘e6 ♗e6 13. de6 f4 14. g3∞] **9. h4 ♗g4** [9... f5 10. h5 ♘f7 11. ♗d3 f4 12. hg6 hg6 13. ♖h8 ♗h8 14. ♕c2 ♗g4 15. 0-0-0±; 11. ♗e2 △ 11... f4 12. g3!] **10. ♗e2 c5** [10... ♘f7? 11. ♘e5! ♗e2 (11... ♘e5 12. ♗g4+−) 12. ♕a4+−; 10... f5? 11. ♘g5±; 10... 0−0!? 11. ♕c1 (11. ♕b3 b6 12. ♗h6 ♗h6 13. ♘g5 ♕c8!) ♘f7 12. ♘g5 ♕c8 13. ♘f7 ♖f7 14. f3 ♗d7 15. h5→] **11. ♕c1 ♘f7** [11... ♗f3 12. ♗f3 ♘f7 13. ♗g4 f5 14. ♗h3±] **12. ♘g5! fg5** [12... ♗e2? 13. ♘e6+−; 12... ♗d7? 13. ♘e6 ♗e6 14. de6+−; 12... ♘g5 13. ♗g4 ♘f7 14. ♗e6±] **13. ♗g4 gh4 14. ♗e6!** [14. ♖h4? ♘d5 15. ♘d5 ♕h4 16. ♘c7 ♔d8−+] **♗f6** [14... h6 *a)* 15. ♖h4 ♘d5 16. ♘d5 ♕h4 17. ♕c2 (17. ♘c7 ♔e7) ♕h1? 18. ♔e2 ♕a1 19. ♕a4 ♔f8 20. ♕d7; 17... 0−0!; *b)* 15. ♕d1 ♘g5! 16. ♗g5 hg5 17. ♖h3 ♕a5 (17... ♗f6 18. ♖f3 ♖f8 19. ♕a4+−) 18. ♕b3±; *c)* 15. ♖b1! g5 16. b4 cb4 17. ♖b4 b6 18. ♕d1 ♘g6 19. ♕h5 ♕f6 20. ♘b5 ♔e7 21. ♖b3±→] **15. ♖h3 h5?** [15... g5 16. ♗f7 (16. ♖f3 ♘g8 17. ♗f7 ♔f7 18. ♗g5±) ♔f7 17. ♗g5 ♘d5 18. ♖f3 ♔e8 19. ♗f6 ♘f6 20. ♕h6±; 15... ♘g8 16. ♖f3] **16. ♖f3 ♘g8 17. ♖b1 ♘gh6** [17... ♘g5 18. ♖f6 ♕f6 19. ♗g5+−; 17... ♘fh6 18. b4 cb4 19. ♘b5 a6 20. ♘d6 ♕d6 21. ♗h6+−] **18. b4 cb4** [18... b6 19. bc5 dc5 20. d6! ♘d6 21. ♘d5 ♗g7 22. ♗g5 ♕b8 23. ♘f6 ♗f6 24. ♗f6+−] **19. ♘b5!** [19. ♖b4 b6] **♗e7** [19... a6 20. ♗h6 ♘h6 (20... ab5 21. ♗f7 ♔f7 22. ♗g5+−) 21. ♘d6 ♕d6 22. ♖f6+−] **20. c5 dc5** [20... a6 21. c6+−; 20... ♕a5 21. cd6 ♕b5 22. d7+−] **21. ♗h6 ♘h6 22. d6! ♗d6** [22... ♗f6 23. ♘c7 ♔f8 24. ♘a8+−; 22... ♗g5 23. d7] **23. ♖d3 ♕e7 24. ♘d6** [24. ♖d6 a6 25. ♗b3 ♔f8 26. ♖g6 ab5 27. ♕h6+−] **♔f8 25. ♕c4 ♔g7** [25... ♕c7 26. ♘f7 ♘f7 27. ♖d7+−; 25... ♖d8 26. ♘c8 ♕c7 27. ♖d8 ♕d8 28. ♕c5+−] **26. ♘f5! ♘f5 27. ♖d7 ♕d7 28. ♗d7 ♘d4 29. ♕c5 ♔h6 30. ♕e5 ♘c2 31. ♔f1 ♖hd8 32. ♕f4 ♔g7 33. ♕c7 1 : 0** **[Ftáčnik]**

59. **A 43**

JAGUPOV 2400 − BLOH
Rossija (ch) 1992

1. e4 c5 2. ♘f3 g6 3. d4 ♗g7 4. d5 ♘f6 5. ♘c3 0−0 6. ♗e2 b5 7. e5 ♘g4 8. ♗f4 b4 9. ♘e4 d6 10. ed6 ed6 [10... ♗b2 11.

♖b1 (11. h3?! ♘f6□ 12. ♖b1 ♘e4 13. ♖b2 ♘c3 14. ♕d2 ed6∓) ♗g7 12. 0–0↑] **11. 0–0 ♘f6!** [11... ♗b2 12. ♖b1 ♗g7 (12... ♗e5? 13. ♘e5 de5 14. ♗g5) 13. ♘d6↑] **12. ♘fd2 N** [12. ♘d6 – 37/(65); 12. ♗g5 ♖e8 13. ♘fd2 (13. ♗d3?! c4 14. ♗f6 ♗f6 15. ♘f6 ♕f6 16. ♗c4 ♕b2∓) ♗f5 14. ♘g3 ♗c8 15. ♘de4 (15. ♘ge4=) h6 16. ♘f6 ♗f6 17. ♗h6 ♗b2 18. ♖b1 ♗d4 19. ♔h1∞] **♗a6□ 13. ♗g5** [13. ♗a6 ♘a6 14. ♕f3 (14. ♗g5 ♘c7 △ ♘cd5) ♘e4 (14... ♘d5?! 15. ♗d6 ♖e8 16. ♘c4±) 15. ♘e4 ♗b2 16. ♗d6 *a)* 16... ♗a1 17. ♗f8 ♔f8 18. ♖a1 ♕d5? 19. ♖d1 ♕b7 (19... ♕c6 20. ♖d6 ♕b7 21. ♖a6 ♕a6 22. ♘g5+–) 20. ♕f4+–→; *b)* 16... ♖e8 17. ♖ab1 ♗d4 18. ♗f4 ♘c7 19. ♘d6 ♖f8 (19... ♖e7? 20. ♘f5!) 20. ♖fe1∞] **♗e2** [13... h6?! 14. ♗a6 ♘a6 15. ♘f6 ♗f6 16. ♗h6 ♗b2 17. ♗f8 ♗a1 18. ♕a1 ♕f8 19. ♘e4±] **14. ♕e2 h6 15. ♘f6 ♗f6 16. ♗h6 ♖e8** [16... ♗b2? 17. ♗f8 ♗a1 18. ♗e7+–] **17. ♘e4! ♗b2 18. ♖ae1 ♘d7□ 19. ♕f3 f5** [19... ♘e5?? 20. ♘f6 ♔h8 21. ♕h3+–; 19... ♕c7 20. ♗f4 ♗e5 21. h4↑; 19... ♗e5 20. ♗g5 f6 (20... ♕c7 21. h4↑) 21. ♗f4 ♕e7 22. h4↑] **20. ♕g3** [20. ♘d6? ♖e1 21. ♖e1 ♘e5 22. ♕b3 ♗c3–+; 20. ♗g5 ♕c7 21. ♘g3 ♘e5 22. ♕d1∞; 20. ♘g5! ♘e5 21. ♕g3 ♕f6 22. ♘e6 ♘f7 23. ♗d2! (×c3) ♗e5 24. f4 ♗d4 25. ♔h1±] **♖e4□** [20... fe4? 21. ♕g6 ♔h8 22. ♗g5 △ ♖e3-h3+–] **21. ♕g6 ♔h8 22. ♕f5 ♖e1 23. ♖e1 ♘f8!** [23... ♕f6 24. ♕h5 ♔g8 25. ♖e6+–; 23... ♗e5 24. ♖e3 ♘f6 (24... ♘f8? 25. ♖e5) 25. ♗g5 ♔g7 26. ♖h3+–] **24. ♗g5 ♕d7 25. ♗f6 ♗f6 26. ♕f6 ♕g7 27. ♕d6 ♖e8! 28. ♖f1 ♘d7** [28... ♕d4!?∓] **29. ♕a6⊕ ♘b6** [30. ♕b5∞]

1/2 : 1/2 **[Jagupov]**

60.** **A 43**

YERMOLINSKY 2615 – ALBURT 2535

New York 1993

1. d4 ♘f6 [RR 1... e6 2. c4 c5 3. d5 ed5 4. cd5 d6 5. ♘c3 ♗e7!? 6. e4 a6 (6... ♗f6!? N 7. h3 ♘e7 8. ♘f3 0–0 9. ♗d3 ♘g6 10. 0–0 ♘a6 11. ♖e1 ♘c7 12. a4 a6 13. ♘d2 b6 14. ♘c4 ♖b8 15. f4!± Meulders 2385 – Vanderwaeren 2315, Belgique (ch) 1992; 6... ♘f6 – A 65) 7. a4 ♗f6!? N 8. ♗d3 ♘e7 9. h3 ♘g6 10. ♘f3 0–0 11. 0–0 b6 12. ♗e3 ♘d7 13. ♘d2 ♖e8 14. ♕c2 ♖b8 15. f4 b5! 16. ab5 ♗c3 17. bc3 ab5 18. c4 ♘b6!∓ 19. ♖ae1 (19. cb5 ♘d5∓) bc4 20. ♘c4 ♗a6! 21. ♘b6 (21. ♘a5 ♘d5! 22. ♘c6 ♗d3 23. ♕d3 ♘b4! 24. ♘b4 ♖b4–+) ♗d3 22. ♕d3 ♕b6 23. ♖b1 c4!! *a)* 24. ♗b6 cd3 25. ♗c7 ♖b1 26. ♖b1 ♘f4 27. ♔f2 g5! (Karp – Meulders 2330, Bruxelles (zt) 1993) 28. ♗d6 ♖e4 29. ♗f4 gf4! 30. ♖d1 (30. ♖b8 ♔g7 31. d6 ♖d4–+) ♖d4–+; *b)* 24. ♖b6 cd3 25. ♖b8 (25. ♖d6 ♖e4) ♖b8 26. ♖d1 ♖e8 27. ♖d3 ♖e4∓; *c)* 24. ♕d2 ♕b1 25. ♖b1 ♖b1 26. ♔f2 ♖c8! △ c3∓ Meulders] **2. ♘f3 c5 3. d5 e6 4. ♘c3 b5!? 5. de6 fe6 6. ♘b5 ♕a5 N** [6... d5 – 37/65] **7. ♘c3 d5 8. ♗d2 ♕b6** [8... ♕d8!] **9. e4! d4 10. ♘a4 ♕c6 11. e5 ♘e4?** [11... ♕a4?! 12. ef6→; 11... ♘g4⩱; 11... ♘fd7] **12. b3± ♗e7 13. ♗d3! ♗b7 14. 0–0 0–0 15. ♖e1 ♘d2 16. ♕d2 ♕d7** [16... ♖f3 17. ♗e4+–] **17. ♘g5 h6 18. ♘e4 ♕c6 19. c3 ♘d7 20. cd4?** [20. f4±] **cd4⩱ 21. f4** [21. ♖ac1? ♗g5] **♗a3!** [⇔c] **22. ♖f1 ♖f7 23. ♖f3** [⌓ 23. ♘b2 △ ♘c4] **♖c8 24. ♕e2 ♖cf8 25. ♖af1 ♗c1∓ 26. g3 ♗e3** [26... g5! △ 27... ♗e3, 27... g4, 27... gf4] **27. ♔g2 g5 28. ♔h3!□ ♖f5** [28... ♔h8!? △ gf4] **29. fg5??** [29. ♘b2] **♘e5 30. ♖f5 ef5 31. ♘f6 ♖f6 32. gf6** [32. ♗b5 hg5!–+] **♘d3** [33. ♖f5 ♕e4] **0 : 1** **[Alburt]**

61. **A 45**

NORWOOD 2525 – TIVJAKOV 2595

Calcutta 1993

1. d4 ♘f6 2. c3 e6 3. ♗g5 c5 4. e3 ♗e7!? [4... b6] **5. ♘d2** [5. ♗f6!? ♗f6 6. dc5 ♕c7 (6... ♕a5!? 7. b4 ♕c7⩱ △ a5, b6; 6... ♕e7 7. ♘d2 ♕c5 – 6... ♕c7) 7. ♕d6! (7. b4 a5; 7. ♘d2 ♕c5 8. ♘e4 ♕e5= △ 9. ♘d6 ♔e7∓) ♕d6□ 8. cd6 ♗e5□ 9. ♘a3! ♗d6 10. ♘b5 ♔e7□ (10... ♗e5 11. ♘f3 a6□ 12. ♘e5 ab5 13. ♗b5+–) 11. ♖d1 ♗e5□ 12. f4 (12. ♘f3 ♘c6 13. ♘e5 ♘e5 14. ♘d6 f6 △ ♘f7=) a6□ 13. fe5 ab5 14. a3 ♘c6 15. ♘f3 ♖a5∞ ×e5, b5; 5... gf6!?∞⊞, ⚇f] **d5!? 6. ♗d3** [6. ♗f6 ♗f6 7. dc5 ♕c7 8. ♘b3 (8.

♗b5 ♗d7) 0–0 (△ ♘d7) 9. ♗b5!? a6 10. ♗a4 ♗d7!? 11. ♗d7 ♘d7=] **♘bd7!? 7. f4!? N** [7. ♘gf3 – D 03] **h6** [7... ♕b6!?] **8. ♗f6** [8. ♗h4 g5!?∞; 8... ♕b6∞ △ 9. ♕c2 ♘g4] **gf6!** [8... ♘f6 9. ♘gf3±; 8... ♗f6 9. ♘gf3± △ g4, h4, g5↑»⊞ ×e5, ♗c8] **9. ♘gf3 f5! 10. ♕e2?** [10. 0–0?! c4∓○, ⊞, ↑«; 10. c4∞] **c4 11. ♗c2 b5 12. 0–0 a5** [12... h5!?] **13. ♔h1** [13. ♘e5!?∓] **♗a6?!** [13... h5∓○, ⊞, ↑«] **14. ♘e5 ♘e5 15. fe5** [15. de5!? (△ ♘f3-d4) h5□∓] **h5□ 16. ♖f3** [△ 17. ♖h3 h4 18. g4] **h4□** [16... ♖g8? 17. ♖g3! ♖h8 (17... ♖g3 18. hg3 ×h5) 18. ♖h3 h4 19. g4↑] **17. g4** [17. ♖h3 ♖g8] **hg3□ 18. ♖g3 ♕c7** [18... ♕d7!? △ 0-0-0] **19. ♖ag1 0-0-0 20. ♘f3** [20. ♖g7!? ♗f8 21. ♖g8 ♗h6! 22. ♖h8 (22. ♖d8?! ♕d8 23. ♕h5 ♕f8) ♖h8 23. ♕h5 ♔d8! 24. ♘f3 ♔e8 25. ♘g5 ♕e7∓ △ ♗c8-d7, ♕f8, b4↑] **♗f8!?** [△ ♗h6, ♕e7, b4] **21. ♘g5 ♕e7** [21... ♗h6!?] **22. ♕f3?!** [×«; 22. ♘h3 △ ♘f4-h5-f6∓] **♗h6 23. ♘h3 b4∓ 24. ♗b1** [24. ♘f4 bc3 25. bc3 ♕a3∓ ×a2, c3] **bc3 25. bc3 ♔c7!** [△ ♖b8-b2; 25... ♕a3? 26. ♗f5 ef5?! 27. ♕f5→] **26. ♘f4 ♕a3** [26... ♖b8!?∓] **27. ♕f2** [△ 27... ♕c3 28. e4; 27. ♘e2 ♖b8∓] **♖b8 28. ♗f5!? ♗f4 29. ♕f4 ef5 30. ♖g7** [30. e6 ♕d6–+; 30. ♕f5 ♕e7!?–+ △ ♖b2] **♖b2! 31. ♖f7** [31. e6 ♕d6! 32. ♖f7 ♔c6–+] **♔b6 32. h4 ♕c3** [32... ♔b5 △ ♔a4–+] **33. e6** [33. a4 ♗b7□ 34. e6 ♔a7–+; 34... ♔a6–+] **♔b5!** [33... ♕e3? 34. ♕d6 (34. ♕e3 ♖h4–+) ♔b5 35. a4! ♔a4 36. ♖a1 ♔b3 37. ♖a3+–] **34. a4⊕** [34. e7 ♕e3! 35. a4 ♔b4! (35... ♔a4? 36. ♖a1+–) 36. ♕d6 ♔b3 37. ♕b6 (37. ♖g3 ♖h4–+) ♔a2–+] **♔a4 35. e7 ♕a3!** [35... ♕e3? 36. ♖a1+–] **36. ♖f5?! ♕e7 37. ♖f6 ♗b5 38. ♖a1 ♔b4 39. ♕g5 ♕e4 40. ♔g1 ♖h4 0 : 1**
[Tivjakov]

62. **A 45**

JE. PIKET 2590 – OLLS 2585
Wijk aan Zee (open) 1993

1. d4 ♘f6 2. ♗g5 e6 3. e4 d6 N [3... h6 – 53/70] **4. ♘c3** [4. ♗d3!? △ ♘f3, ♘bd2] **♗e7 5. ♘f3 0–0 6. ♕d2** [6. ♗e2 △ 0–0] **♘c6! 7. ♗b5 ♗d7 8. 0-0-0 a6 9. ♗c6 ♗c6 10. ♖he1 h6 11. ♗f6** [11. ♗h4?! ♘e4 12. ♖e4 ♗h4 13. d5 ♗g5 14. ♘g5 ed5] **♗f6 12. d5 ed5 13. ♘d5 ♖e8= 14. g4?!** [14. c3] **a5 15. ♕f4 ♖e6 16. h4?!** [16. ♔b1] **♗d5 17. ♖d5 c6!** [17... ♗h4? 18. ♖h1↑] **18. ♖d3 ♕b6 19. ♖b3 ♕f2 20. ♖b7 ♖ae8!** [△ 21... d5, 21... ♕e1!?] **21. ♔d1!**

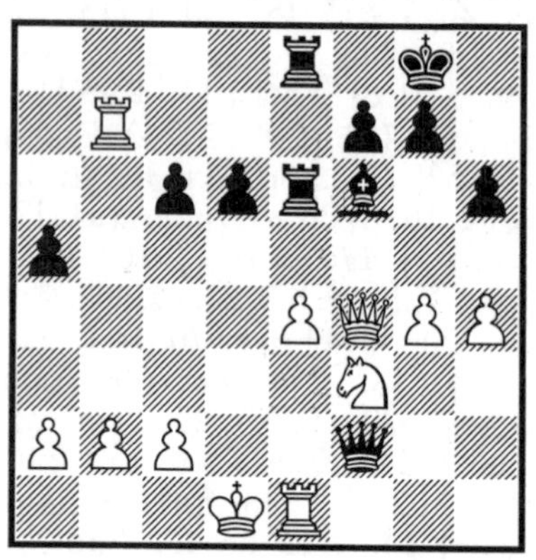

21... ♖e5! [△ ♖d5; 21... ♖6e7 22. ♖e7 ♖e7 23. ♕f5∞] **22. ♕e3□** [22. ♖f7 ♖d5 (22... ♕e1 23. ♘e1 ♖e4 24. ♖f6∞) 23. ♔c1 ♖c5] **♕e3 23. ♖e3 ♖e4 24. ♖e4 ♖e4** [♖ 9/i] **25. g5 hg5?** [25... ♗e5!∓] **26. hg5 ♗e7** [26... ♗e5? 27. g6] **27. ♖a7 a4 28. g6! fg6 29. ♘d2 ♖e6 30. ♖a4 g5 31. ♖g4 d5 32. c4!** [32. a4 c5∓] **♔f7 33. cd5?⊕** [33. a4! dc4 34. ♖c4∞̅] **cd5 34. a4 ♖b6 35. ♔c2** [35. b3 ♖b4 36. ♖g2 g4∓] **♖b4∓ 36. ♖b4 ♗b4** [♘♗ 4/b] **37. ♘f1** [37. ♘b3 ♔e6 38. a5 (38. ♘d4 ♔d7 39. ♔d3 g4 40. ♘c2 ♗c5 41. b4 g3 42. ♔e2) ♔d7 39. a6 ♔c6 40. ♔d3 ♔b6 41. ♔d4 g4 42. ♔d5 g3 43. ♘c1 g2 44. ♘e2 ♔a6 45. ♔e6 ♗c5 46. ♔f7 ♗d4–+] **♔e6 38. ♔d3 g4 39. ♘e3 g3 40. ♔e2 d4 41. ♘g2 ♔d5 42. ♔f3 d3–+ 43. ♘f4** [43. ♔g3 d2 44. ♔f2 d1♘] **♔c4 44. ♘d3 ♔d3 45. ♔g3 ♔c4 46. ♔f4 ♔b3 0 : 1 [Je. Piket]**

63.* **A 45**

YULDASHEV 2410 –
ZAGREBEL'NYJ 2490
Uzbekistan 1993

1. d4 ♘f6 2. ♗g5 ♘e4 3. ♗h4 [RR 3. h4 d5 4. ♘d2 ♘g5 5. hg5 c5 N (5... ♗f5 – 43/56) 6. dc5 (6. e3 ♘c6 7. ♘gf3 cd4 8.

ed4 ♕b6↑) e5 7. ♘b3 ♘c6 8. e3 ♗e6 *a)* 9. f4 ♕c7 10. ♕d2 0-0-0 11. fe5□ d4!!→ (×♔e1) 12. ♘d4□ ♗c5 13. ♖h4!□ *a1)* 13... ♕e5!? 14. ♘gf3 ♗d4!! 15. ♘e5□ (15. ♖d4 ♕g3–+) ♗e5 16. ♕f2 ♗b2 17. ♖d1 ♗c3 18. ♔e2 ♘e5⩱→; *a2)* 13... ♘e5 14. ♘e6 (14. 0-0-0 ♗a2∓) fe6 15. ♕c3 ♔b8!∓ M. Hansen 2305 – Istrăţescu 2470, Cappelle la Grande 1993; *b)* 9. ♘f3 e4 10. ♘fd4 ♕g5∓ Istrăţescu] **d5 4. f3 ♘d6 5. ♘c3 ♘f5 6. ♗f2 c5 7. dc5 d4 8. e4!? N** [8. ♘e4 – 31/101] **dc3** [8... de3!? 9. ♕d8 ♔d8 10. 0-0-0 ♘d7 11. ♗e1 e5 12. ♘e4 ♔c7 13. g4 ♘d4 14. ♗g3 ♘e6 15. ♘d6 f6 16. b4∞ △ 16... a5?! 17. ♗c4 ♘f4? 18. ♘f7 ♖g8 19. ♘e5! fe5 20. ♗g8 ab4 21. ♗f4 ef4 22. ♘h3+–] **9. ♕d8 ♔d8 10. 0-0-0 ♔e8** [10... ♘d7!?] **11. b4!** [11. ef5?! cb2 12. ♔b2 ♗f5 13. ♘e2 ♘c6 14. ♘c3 ♖c8 15. ♗b5 g5!? 16. ♖he1 ♗g7∓] **♘h6** [11... a5?! 12. b5] **12. ♘e2 e6 13. ♘c3 ♗e7 14. ♘b5 ♘a6 15. a3⩱ f5! 16. ef5** [16. e5!? ♗g5 17. ♔b1 ♘f7 18. ♘d6 ♔e7∞] **♘f5 17. ♗c4 ♗g5 18. ♔b1 ♗e3! 19. ♗e1! ♗f4 20. ♗f2 ♘c7?** [⌓ 20... ♗e3 21. ♗e1 ♗f4 22. ♗d2!? (22. ♗f2=) ♗d2 23. ♖d2 ♔e7 (23... ♘e3? 24. ♘d6 ♔e7 25. ♗a6 ba6 26. ♖e1+–) 24. ♖e1↑] **21. g3?** [21. ♖he1 ♘b5 22. ♗b5 ♔e7 23. g3! ♗c7 24. g4 ♘h6 25. ♗h4 ♔f7 26. ♗d7 e5 27. f4! ♘g4 28. h3 ♘f6 29. fe5+–] **a6!□ 22. ♘d6!?** [22. ♘c7 ♗c7 23. ♖he1 ♔f7 24. g4 ♘e7 25. ♗g3 ♗g3 26. hg3 ♘c6 27. ♖d6 ♘d8 28. f4∞] **♗d6 23. cd6 ♘b5 24. ♔b2□ ♘fd6** [24... ♘bd6 25. ♗b3 △ g4⩱] **25. ♗b3 ♘f7** [25... ♔e7!? 26. a4 ♘c7 27. ♗c5 ♖d8 28. ♖d3 △ ♖hd1⩱] **26. a4 ♘a7?** [26... ♘bd6 27. ♗c5 ♔e7 28. ♖d3 ♖d8 29. ♖hd1 b5 30. ab5 ab5 31. f4 △ f5∞] **27. ♖he1 ♔e7 28. ♗c5 ♔f6 29. ♖e4!→ e5** [29... g5 30. f4!] **30. f4! ♖e8 31. fe5 ♔g6** [31... ♘e5?! 32. ♖f1+–] **32. ♖f1?!⊕** [32. c3! (△ ♗c2) ♗f5 33. ♖f4+–] **♘g5 33. ♗e3! ♗f5?⊕** [33... ♘e4?? 34. ♗f7#; 33... ♗h3!] **34. ♖ef4 ♗h3 35. c3!+– h5□** [35... ♗f1 36. ♗c2+–] **36. ♗c2 ♔h6 37. ♖f7!** [△ 38. ♖1f6 gf6 39. ♖h7#] **♖h8** [37... ♗f1 38. h4+–; 37... ♖e6 38. ♖1f6 ♖f6 39. ef6 g6 40. ♖g7+–] **38. ♗g5** [38... ♔g5 39. ♖g7 ♔h6 40. ♖g6 ♔h7 41. ♖f7#] **1 : 0**
[Serper]

64.* A 45**

VLADO KOVAČEVIĆ 2485
– SMIRIN 2590
Zagreb (zt) 1993

1. d4 ♘f6 2. ♗g5 ♘e4 3. ♗f4 c5 [RR 3... d5 4. ♘d2 ♗f5 5. e3 e6 6. ♗d3 ♗d6 N (6... ♘d2 – 55/75) 7. ♗e4 de4 8. ♘e2 ♘c6 9. ♘c4 ♗g4 10. c3 0–0 11. d5 ed5 12. ♘d6 cd6 13. ♕d5 ♕b6 14. b3 ♗e2 15. ♔e2 ♕a6 16. c4 ♖ad8∞ Lputian 2610 – Winants 2520, Wijk aan Zee (open) 1993] **4. f3 ♕a5** [RR 4... ♘f6 5. d5 ♕b6 6. e4 N (6. ♗c1 – 38/72) ♕b2 7. ♘d2 ♕c3 8. ♗d3 (8. ♖b1!? d6 9. ♗b5 ♘bd7 10. ♘e2 ♕a5 11. 0–0⩱) d6 9. ♘e2 ♕a5 10. 0–0 g6 *a)* 11. e5 de5 12. ♗e5 ♘bd7 13. ♗c3 ♕c7 14. ♗b5 ♗g7 15. ♗d7 ♕d7 16. ♘e4 0–0 (A. Gol'din 2555 – Aseev 2515, Sankt-Peterburg (zt) 1993) 17. ♗f6 ef6!? (17... ♗f6 18. ♘f6 ef6 19. ♕d2⩱) 18. ♘c5 ♕c7∓; *b)* 11. ♘c4 ♕c7? 12. ♘c3 ♗g7 13. e5→; 13. ♘b5!?→; 11... ♕d8□∞ Aseev] **5. c3 ♘f6 6. ♘d2 cd4 7. ♘b3 ♕b6** [RR 7... ♕f5!? N 8. ♗b8! dc3!?∞ McCamon – C. Thomson 2325, London 1992] **8. ♕d4 ♘c6 N** [8... ♕d4 – 56/68] **9. ♕b6 ab6 10. a3?! d5 11. ♗c7?** [11. ♘d4! e5!? (11... ♗d7 12. ♘b5; 11... ♘d4=) 12. ♘c6 ef4 13. ♘d4 ♗d6 14. ♔f2 0–0 15. g3 (15. e3? fe3 16. ♔e3 ♖e8 17. ♔f2 ♗f4) ♘h5! 16. gf4 ♘f4 17. e3 ♘e6∓] **e5! 12. ♗b6 d4! 13. cd4 ♗e6 14. ♘c5** [14. de5? ♘d7–+; 14. d5 ♘d5 15. ♗c5 (15. ♗f2? ♘db4!–+) ♘a5! 16. ♘a5 ♗c5 17. ♘b7 ♗d4! 18. ♘d6 ♔e7 19. ♘c4 ♖hc8 20. e4 ♘b4 21. ♖c1 ♗b2!–+] **♘d5 15. ♘e6 fe6 16. ♗c5 ♘d4! 17. ♗d4** [17. ♗f8 ♔f8 18. ♖c1 (18. ♔f2 e4!) ♘e3 19. ♔f2 ♘dc2 20. ♘h3 h6! 21. ♔g3 ♖a4!⊙ △ 22. ♘f2? ♘f5 23. ♔h3 ♖h4#] **ed4 18. ♖c1** [18. g3? ♗b4 19. ♔f2 ♗d2] **♗d6 19. e4?!** [19. ♘h3? ♔e7 20. ♘f2 ♗f4 21. ♖b1 ♖hc8–+; 19. g3 ♔e7 20. f4 ♖hc8 21. ♖c8 ♖c8 22. ♔d2 ♘e3 23. ♘f3∓] **de3 20. ♗c4 ♗e5 21. ♗d5** [21. ♖c2 ♖c8] **ed5 22. ♖c2 ♔d7–+ 23. ♘e2 ♖hc8 24. ♔d1 ♖c6! 25. f4 ♗f6 26. ♖c6 bc6 27. ♔c2 ♔d6 28. ♖d1 c5 29. ♖d3 d4** [30. ♖d1□ ♔d5 31. ♘c3 ♔c6 32. ♘e2 ♖d8 33. b3 ♖a8! 34. a4

♖b8 35. ♖d3 (35. ♖b1 c4 36. bc4 d3) c4! 36. bc4 ♔c5] **0 : 1** **[Smirin]**

65.** **A 46**

S. KISELËV 2510 – CO. IONESCU 2475

Bucureşti 1993

1. d4 ♘f6 2. ♘f3 b5!? [RR 2... e6 3. ♗g5 c5 4. e3 h6 5. ♗h4 b6 6. c3 ♗e7 7. ♘bd2 0–0 N (7... ♗b7 — 50/74, A 47) 8. e4 cd4 9. cd4 d5 10. ♗f6 ♗f6 11. e5 ♗e7 12. ♗b5 ♗a6 13. a4 ♗b7= Jusupov 2645 – Beljavskij 2610, Linares 1993] **3. ♕d3!?** [3. g3 ♗b7 4. ♗g2 e6 5. 0–0 c5 6. ♘a3 ♕b6 7. c4 N (7. dc5 — 55/(76)) b4 8. ♘c2 ♘a6! 9. ♗g5 cd4! (9... ♗e7 10. d5! ed5 11. cd5 ♘d5 12. e4↑) 10. ♘cd4 ♗e7 11. ♘b3 0–0 12. ♖c1 ♖ac8 13. ♕d4 (13. ♗e3 ♘c5=) ♕d4 14. ♘fd4 ♗g2 15. ♔g2 ♘c5 16. ♖fd1 a6= Itkis 2435 – Co. Ionescu 2475, Bucureşti 1993] **a6 N** [3... b4] **4. ♗g5 e6 5. e4 ♗e7 6. ♘bd2 ♗b7 7. ♗e2 h6! 8. ♗f6 ♗f6 9. a4! b4 10. c4 bc3 11. bc3 d5! 12. 0–0 0–0 13. ♖fb1 ♖a7 14. ed5 ♗d5 15. ♘e4± ♘d7 16. ♘fd2** [16. a5!?] **♗e7 17. ♗f3 c5! 18. ♘c4 cd4 19. cd4 ♖c7 20. ♘ed2! ♘f6 21. a5?!** [21. ♘b6! ♗f3 22. ♘f3 a5 23. ♖b5±] **♗c4! 22. ♘c4 ♗c5 23. ♖d1 ♖d7 24. ♘e5 ♖d4 25. ♕a6 ♘e4!∓ 26. ♘c6?!** [26. ♕e2? ♘f2!; 26. ♖dc1 ♗d6 *a)* 27. ♘c6 ♗h2 28. ♔f1 (28. ♔h2 ♕h4 29. ♔g1 ♕f2 30. ♔h2 ♘c5–+) ♘d2 29. ♔e2 ♕d6–+; *b)* 27. ♘g4 h5 28. ♗e4 hg4∓; 26. ♘d3! ♘c3 27. ♘c5 ♘d1 28. ♕b7=∞] **♖d1 27. ♖d1 ♕h4 28. ♗e4□ ♗f2! 29. ♔f1 ♗e3∓ 30. ♔e2!? ♕e4 31. ♘e7 ♔h8 32. ♕c6! ♕g4 33. ♕f3** [⌓ 33. ♔e3 ♕g5 34. ♔e2 ♕e7 35. a6] **♕c4 34. ♖d3 ♗c5!–+ 35. ♘c6 f6 36. g3 ♖c8 37. ♔d2 ♕a2** [37... ♖c6–+] **38. ♔e1 ♕a4 39. ♖c3 ♖c6** **0 : 1** **[Co. Ionescu]**

66.* **A 48**

MALANJUK 2600 – L. RAVI 2415

Calcutta 1993

1. d4 ♘f6 2. ♘f3 g6 3. ♗g5 ♗g7 4. ♘bd2 [RR 4. c3 c5!? N (4... d5 — D 03) 5. dc5 ♘a6! (5... ♕c7 6. ♕d4 △ e4±) 6. ♕d4 ♘c7! 7. ♘bd2 ♘e6 8. ♕c4 (8. ♕b4!?) b6 9. cb6 ♕b6 10. ♕b3 ♕c7 *a)* 11. ♗h4!? ♖b8 12. ♕c2 ♕b7! (12... ♕b6 13. ♘c4 ♕c5 14. e3 0–0 15. ♗d3 ♗b7 16. ♘cd2 ♕b6 17. ♘c4 ♕c7=∞ M. Sorokin 2490 – Sakaev 2555, Sankt-Peterburg (zt) 1993) 13. ♖b1 d5! (13... ♘c5 14. ♗f6! ♗f6 15. e4) 14. ♗g3 ♘c5! 15. ♗b8 ♗f5 16. ♕c1 ♕b8∓; *b)* 11. e3 ♖b8 12. ♕c2 ♘g5 13. ♘g5 0–0=∞; *c)* 11. ♕c4 ♕b8!? (11... ♕b6 12. ♕b3=) 12. ♕b3 ♗b7∞ Sakaev] **0–0 5. c3 d6 6. e4 c5 7. dc5 dc5 8. ♕c2 N ♘c6 9. ♗e2 ♗e6 10. 0–0 h6?!** [10... ♕c7!?] **11. ♗e3 b6 12. h3± ♕c7** [⌓ 12... ♘e8] **13. ♘h2! ♘d7** [⌓ 13... ♘e8] **14. f4±↑ f5□ 15. ♗d3!** [△ ♘hf3-h4] **♘a5□ 16. ♘hf3 c4 17. ♗e2** [×d4] **fe4 18. ♘e4 ♗f7 19. ♖ad1 ♖ad8 20. ♔h1 ♘b7□** [20... ♘c6 21. ♕a4; 20... ♘f6 21. ♘e5; 20... e5 21. ♘d6] **21. ♘d4** [△ f5] **♘dc5** [21... ♘bc5 22. ♗f3] **22. f5 ♗d5** [22... g5 23. ♗f3±] **23. ♘c5 ♘c5** [23... bc5 24. ♘b5 ♗g2 25. ♔g2 ♕c6 26. ♖f3 ♕b5 27. ♖d8 ♖d8 28. f6 ef6 29. ♕g6+–] **24. ♗f3 ♗f3** [24... g5?! 25. ♗d5 ♖d5 26. ♕e2 ♗d4 27. ♗d4 ♖df5 28. ♖f5 ♖f5 29. ♕c4+–] **25. ♖f3 e5** [25... g5 26. ♕e2+–] **26. fe6 ♖f3 27. ♘f3 ♖d1 28. ♕d1 ♘e6 29. ♕d5 ♔f7 30. ♗d4!+– ♔e7 31. ♗g7 ♘g7 32. ♘e5 ♔f6 33. ♘g4 ♔e7 34. ♕e4 ♘e6⊕ 35. ♕g6 ♕f4 36. ♕h6 ♕f1 37. ♔h2 ♘f4 38. ♕f6 ♔e8 39. ♕c6 ♔f8 40. ♘e3 ♕f2 41. ♘f5** **1 : 0** **[Malanjuk]**

67.* **A 48**

NISHIMURA 2325 – MOHD

Jakarta (zt) 1993

1. d4 ♘f6 2. ♘f3 g6 3. ♗g5 ♗g7 4. ♘bd2 0–0 5. e4 d6 [5... c5 6. d5 N (6. e5 — 48/(86)) d6 7. ♗e2 b5 8. a4!? b4 9. 0–0 h6 10. ♗h4 ♘h5 11. ♘c4 ♘f4 12. ♖e1 ♘e2 13. ♕e2 ♗a6 14. e5!? de5 15. ♘fe5 *a)* 15... ♕d5? 16. ♖ad1 (Nishimura 2325 – R. Rodríguez 2415, Jakarta (zt) 1993) ♕e5 17. ♘e5 ♗e2 18. ♖e2=∞ ×e7; *b)* 15... ♗e5 16. ♕e5 ♗c4 17. ♗e7 ♕d5 18. ♗f8 ♕e5 19. ♖e5 ♔f8 20. ♖d1! ♘a6□ 21. b3 ♗e6 22. ♖d6 ♘c7 23. ♖c5 ♘e8 24. ♖a6=] **6. c3 c5 7. dc5 dc5 8. ♗c4 ♘c6 9. 0–0 ♕c7** [⌓ 9... ♘a5] **10. ♕e2**

♘d7?! N [10... h6; 10... ♘a5] **11. h3 ♘de5 12. ♘e5 ♘e5 13. ♗b3 b5!? 14. ♗d5!** [14. ♕b5? a5 △ ♗a6∞̄] **♖b8 15. f4 e6** [15... ♘c6 16. e5±] **16. fe5 ed5 17. ed5 ♗e5 18. ♖ae1 f6** [18... ♖e8? 19. ♗f4+−] **19. ♗h6 ♖e8** [19... ♖f7 20. ♘f3±] **20. ♘e4** [20. ♖f6? ♗g4!] **♗f5**

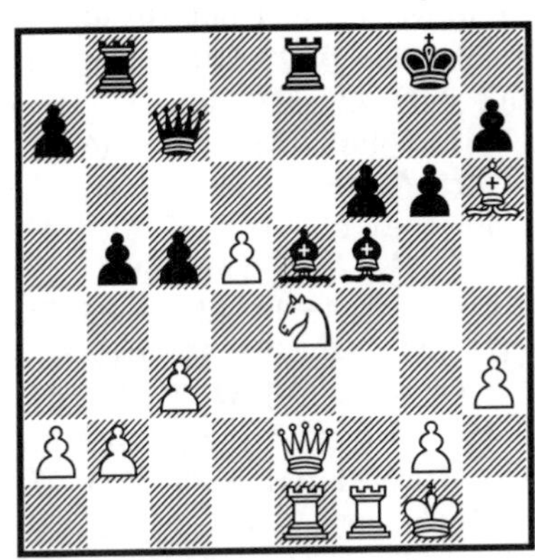

21. ♘f6! ♗f6 22. ♕e8 ♖e8 23. ♖e8 ♔f7 24. ♖f8 ♔e7 25. ♖e1 ♗e5 26. ♗g7! ♕d6 27. ♖a8!? [27. ♖e5 ♕e5 28. ♗e5 ♔f8 29. ♗d6+−⊥] **♔f7 28. ♖a7 ♗d7 29. ♗e5** [29. ♖e5 ♔g7 30. ♖e6! ♕d5 31. ♖e7 △ ♖ed7+−] **♕d5 30. c4!+− bc4 31. ♖a3 ♗c6 32. ♖f3 ♔e7 33. ♖f2 ♔d7 34. ♗c3 ♔c7 35. ♖e7 ♔b6 36. ♖e5 ♕d1 37. ♔h2 h6⊕** [37... ♕d6 38. ♖fe2 △ ♗e1-f2+−] **38. ♖e6 ♕d3 39. ♖ff6** **1 : 0**
[Nishimura]

68. !N **A 49**

GARCÍA-PALERMO 2475
– ŠTOHL 2540

Bad Wörishofen 1993

1. ♘f3 d6 2. g3 g6 3. ♗g2 ♗g7 4. d4 ♘f6 5. 0–0 0–0 6. ♖e1 ♘c6!? 7. d5! N [7. e4 — 22/110] **♘b4** [7... ♘e5 8. ♘e5 de5 9. c4 △ ♘c3, c5⊞] **8. c4** [⌓ 8. e4!? e6 (8... c6? 9. a3 ♘a6 10. dc6 bc6 11. e5± ×c6) 9. c4⩲○] **♗f5! 9. ♘a3** [9. e4? ♗e4 10. ♖e4 ♘e4 11. ♕e1 ♘c2∓; 9. ♘d4 ♗b1 (9... ♗e4!? 10. ♘c3 ♗g2 11. ♔g2 c5∞) 10. ♖b1 ♘a2 11. ♗d2 a5 12. ♕b3 ♘b4 13. ♗b4 ab4 14. ♕b4 ♘d7=] **c6 10. ♘d4** [10. e4? ♗e4 11. ♖e4 ♘e4 12. ♕e1 ♘d3 13. ♕e4 ♘c1 14. ♕c2□ (14. ♖c1 ♗b2−+) ♕b6−+] **♗d7 11. ♗d2** [11. e4?! ♕b6! (△ ♘fd5) 12. ♗e3 ♘g4 13. ♘c6 ♘e3 14. ♘e7 ♔h8 15. ♖e3 ♖fe8−+] **c5** [11... a5 12. dc6 ♗c6!? (12... bc6 13. ♗c3± △ ♕d2, b3, ♖ad1⊞) 13. ♘c6 (13. ♗c3 ♗g2 14. ♔g2 ♘e4↑) bc6∞; ⌓ 11... ♕b6!? *a)* 12. ♗b4 ♕b4 13. dc6 bc6 14. ♗c6 (14. ♘c6 ♗c6 15. ♗c6 ♖ac8∓ △ ♕b2) ♗c6 15. ♘c6 ♕b7! (15... ♕b2 16. ♘e7 ♔h8 17. ♘b5±) 16. ♕a4□ ♘e4! (16... ♖fc8 17. ♘b4 △ ♘d3) 17. ♕b5 (17. ♖ab1 ♖fc8 18. ♘b4 ♘d2∓) ♕c7 18. ♖ab1 ♖fc8 19. ♘b4 ♖ab8 20. ♘d5 (20. ♕a4 ♘c5−+) ♖b5 21. ♘c7 ♖b2↑; *b)* 12. dc6□ ♘c6 13. ♗c3 ♖fc8⇆] **12. ♗b4!** [12. ♘dc2 ♘c2 13. ♘c2 b5⇆; 12. ♘db5!? △ ♗c3, e4⊞] **cb4 13. ♘ac2± ♕b6 14. ♕d2 a5 15. ♖ad1?!** [15. b3 e5 16. de6 fe6⇆; 15. ♖ac1!? ♕c5 16. b3 b5 17. ♘b5 ♗b5 18. cb5 ♘d7 19. ♕e3!±; 15... ♗e8!?⩲ △ ♘d7-c5] **♕c5 16. b3 b5!= 17. ♘b5□** [17. cb5? ♘d5 18. ♘c6 ♗c6 19. bc6 ♘c3∓ △ d5] **♗b5 18. cb5 ♘d7!** [△ ♗c3; 18... ♕b5? 19. ♘d4 ♕b7 20. ♘c6±] **19. ♘d4□** [19. ♕d3 ♖fb8∓] **♗d4 20. ♕d4 ♕d4** [20... ♕b5?! 21. e4 △ f4, e5, h4-h5→] **21. ♖d4 ♖fb8 22. e4** [22. ♖c4 ♘c5 23. ♖c5 dc5 24. d6 ed6 25. ♗a8 ♖a8 26. ♖d1 ♖d8 27. b6 ♔f8∓; 22. ♖c1!? ♘c5 23. ♖c5 dc5 24. ♖c4 ♖c8 (24... ♖b5 25. d6 ♖a7 26. ♗c6 ♖b8 27. d7 ♖c7 28. ♖c5 ♖d8 29. ♖c4=) 25. d6 ed6 (25... ♖a7 26. de7 ♖e7 27. e3 △ ♗c6, △ b6-b7=) 26. ♗a8 ♖a8 27. a4! ba3 28. ♖a4=] **♖b5 23. ♗h3!** [23. ♗f1?! ♖c5∓] **♘c5** [23... ♘e5 24. ♖e3 △f4+−] **24. ♗f1 ♖b7 25. ♗c4 a4** [25... ♘d7 26. f4 ♖c7 27. ♗b5!=] **26. e5 ab3 27. ♗b3!=⇆** [×b4; 27. ab3 ♖a3 28. ed6□ ed6 29. ♖e3 ♔f8∓ ×b3, d5] **♖a3 28. ed6 ed6 29. ♖e3 ♔f8 30. h4 ♖a8** [30... h5 31. f3 △ g4↑] **31. g4 h6 32. g5 hg5** [33. hg5 ♖e8 34. ♖e8 ♔e8 35. f4 f6=]
1/2 : 1/2 **[Štohl]**

69. **A 49**

RIVAS PASTOR 2515
– HALIFMAN 2630

Dos Hermanas 1993

1. d4 ♘f6 2. ♘f3 g6 3. g3 ♗g7 4. ♗g2 0–0 5. 0–0 d6 6. ♖e1 ♘bd7 7. e4 e5 8.

a4 N [8. ♘c3 – 38/151, B 07] ♖e8 9. de5?! de5 10. ♘a3?! [10. ♘c3 c6=] b6! 11. ♗e3 [11. b3] ♗b7 12. ♘d2 h5∓ 13. f3 [13. h3 ♕e7∓] ♕e7 14. ♕e2 ♘c5 15. a5 ♘e6 16. a6?! [16. ab6 ab6 17. c3] ♗c8 17. c3 h4! 18. ♘c2 ♘h5 19. ♘f1 [19. ♕f2 c5∓] c5 20. ♖ed1 ♘ef4! 21. gf4 [21. ♕d2 ♗e6 22. gf4 ♖ad8∓; 21. ♗f4 ef4 22. g4 ♘f6∓] ef4 22. ♗c1 [22. ♗f2 h3∓] h3 23. ♗h1 ♗e6!=/∞ [×♗h1; 23... ♕g5 24. ♘g3 ♘g3 25. hg3 ♕g3 26. ♔f1∞] 24. ♘d2 ♖ad8 25. ♔f1 ♖d7 26. ♖e1 ♖ed8 27. e5 [27. ♖a3 b5!∓] ♖d5 28. ♖a4 ♖d2! 29. ♗d2 ♗b3∓ 30. ♖a3 ♗c2 31. c4 ♗f5 32. ♗c1?! [32. ♗c3 ♗d3; 32. b4!? ♖e8∓] ♖e8 33. b4 cb4 34. ♖b3 ♕c5–+ 35. ♗d2 ♖e5 36. ♗b4 ♕c7 37. ♕d1 ♕c4 38. ♔g1 ♖d5 0 : 1 [Halifman]

70. **A 49**

V. SALOV 2660 – B. GEL'FAND 2690

Linares 1993

1. d4 ♘f6 2. ♘f3 g6 3. g3 ♗g7 4. ♗g2 0–0 5. 0–0 d6 6. a4 ♘a6 7. ♘c3 c5 8. h3 N [8. e4 – 53/(74); 8. a5 – 53/(74)] cd4 9. ♘d4 ♘c5 10. ♗e3 [10. e4!?] ♗d7 11. a5 [11. b4?! ♘e6 12. ♘b3 (12. ♗b7 ♘d4 13. ♗d4 ♗h3∓) ♗c6∓] ♕c8 12. ♔h2 d5!? 13. ♘f3 [13. ♘b3 ♘b3 14. cb3 e6=] e6 14. ♗d4 ♖d8 15. ♘e5 ♕c7?! [⌓ 15... ♗e8 △ 16. ♘g4 ♘g4 17. hg4 e5! 18. ♗c5 ♕c5 19. ♘d5 (19. ♗d5 e4) e4∓] 16. f4? [16. ♘g4! ♘g4 17. hg4⩲] ♗e8 17. e3 ♘fe4! 18. ♕e1 [18. ♘e4 ♘e4 △ f6, e5=] ♘d6 [△ ♘f5] 19. ♘g4 ♘d7 20. ♗g7 ♔g7 21. ♕d2 [21. e4!? d4 (21... h5 22. ♘f2 d4 23. ♘e2 ♕c2 24. ♘d4 ♕b2 25. ♖d1=/∞) *a)* 22. e5 ♘c4 23. a6! ba6 (23... dc3 24. ab7 ♖ab8 25. ♕c3±) 24. ♗a8 dc3 25. ♕c3±; 22... ♘f5!∞; *b)* 22. ♘e2 ♕c2 23. ♘d4 ♕b2 24. ♖d1=/∞] h5 22. ♘f2?! [⌓ 22. ♕d4 f6 23. ♘f2=] ♔g8 23. e4? [23. ♘e2 ♘c4 24. ♕c3∓] ♘c4 24. ♕d4 ♕c5!∓ 25. ♕c5 ♘c5 26. ed5 ♘e3 27. ♖fc1 ♘g2 [27... ed5!?∓] 28. ♔g2 ed5 29. ♘a2! d4 30. ♘b4 ♖ac8 31. ♖d1?⊕ [31. ♖e1 ♗b5 (31... ♘a4 32. ♘fd3 ♗b5 33. ♖e7) 32. ♖e5⇆] ♘a4 32. ♘fd3 ♗b5 33. ♖d2 ♖e8 34. ♔f2 ♔g7 35. ♖e1 [35. ♘e5 ♘b2 36. ♖d4 f6 37. ♘ed3 ♘d3 38. cd3 ♖c3∓] ♖e1 36. ♔e1 [36. ♘e1 ♘b2 37. ♖d4 ♘c4∓] ♗d7 37. h4 [37. ♘f2 ♘b2 38. ♖d4 ♗b5 39. ♘e4 (39. ♘d1 ♖c4 40. ♖c4 ♘c4 41. ♘c3 ♗d7 42. a6 ba6 43. ♘a6 ♗h3 44. ♘b5 ♗c8–+) ♖c4 40. ♖c4 ♘c4∓] ♗f5 38. ♔f2? [⌓ 38. b3! ♘c3 39. ♘e5 ♖e8 40. ♔f1 f6 41. ♘f3⇆] b6! 39. ab6 [39. a6 ♘c5∓] ♘b6 40. ♖e2? [40. b3 a5 41. ♘a6 (41. ♘a2 ♗d3 42. cd3 ♘d5∓) ♘d7!∓; 40. ♘e5 a5 41. ♘bd3 (41. ♘bc6 f6 42. ♘e7 fe5 43. ♘c8 ♘c4!–+) f6 42. ♘f3 ♘c4 43. ♖e2∓; 40. ♘e1 a5 41. ♘a2 ♘c4 42. ♖d4 ♘b2∓] a5 41. ♘a6 [41. ♘a2 ♗g4–+] ♘d5?? [41... ♗g4–+] 42. ♘ac5 ♘e3 43. b3 ♗g4?! [43... ♘c2?? 44. ♖c2 ♗d3 45. ♘e6+–; 43... ♖c7!∓] 44. ♖d2 ♗d1 [44... ♖c7∓] 45. ♘b7 ♗c2 [45... ♖c2 46. ♖c2 ♗c2 47. ♘dc5=] 46. ♘a5 ♖c3 47. ♘e5 f6 48. ♘ec6 ♘g4 49. ♔e1! ♗e4 [49... ♖e3 50. ♖e2 d3 51. ♖e3 ♘e3 52. ♘d4 ♘f1 53. ♘c4 ♘g3 54. ♘d2!=] 50. ♘d4 ♖g3 51. ♖e2!= f5? [51... ♗d5] 52. ♘e6 ♔f6 53. ♘g5 ♖g1 54. ♔d2 ♖h1? [54... ♖a1=] 55. b4! ♗d5 [55... ♖h4 56. b5±] 56. ♘h7 ♔f7 57. ♘g5 ♔f6 58. ♘h7?⊕ [58. ♔c3!±] ♔f7 59. ♘g5 ♔f6 60. ♘h7 1/2 : 1/2 [B. Gel'fand, Huzman]

71. !N **A 54**

LPUTIAN 2610 – EPIŠIN 2620

Rostov na Donu 1993

1. d4 d6 2. c4 e5 3. ♘f3 e4 4. ♘g1 h6?! 5. ♘c3 ♘f6 6. e3! N [6. g3 c6 7. d5 ♗f5 8. ♗g2 ♘bd7=; 6. ♗f4] c6 7. ♘ge2 ♗f5 [7... d5 8. ♘f4±] 8. ♘g3 ♗g6 9. f3 d5 [9... ef3 10. gf3 △ e4±] 10. cd5 [⌓ 10. ♕b3 ♕b6 11. cd5 ♕b3 12. ab3 cd5 13. ♘b5 ♔d7 14. ♖a7 ♖a7 15. ♘a7 ♘c6 16. ♘c6 bc6=/∞] ef3! 11. gf3 [11. dc6 fg2 12. cb7 gh1♕ 13. ♘h1 ♘bd7 14. ba8♕ ♕a8∞] cd5 12. ♗d3! [12. ♕b3 ♕d7 13. ♗b5 ♘c6 14. e4 a6!∓] ♗d3 13. ♕d3 ♘c6 14. ♗d2 ♖c8 15. 0–0 [15. 0-0-0!? g6 (15... ♘b4? 16. ♕b5 ♕d7 17. ♔b1 ♕b5 18. ♘b5 a6 19. ♘c3 △ e4±) 16. ♔b1 ♗g7 17. f4 0–0 18. f5 ♘e7 19. ♖hf1 ♖c6∞] g6 16. e4 de4□ 17. fe4 [17. ♘ge4 ♗g7 18. d5 ♘e4! (18... 0–0 19. ♘f6 ♗f6

20. ♗h6 ♖e8 21. ♘e4±) 19. ♕e4 ♘e7 20. ♖ae1 ♔f8 △ ♘f5, ♗f6, ♔g7∞] **♗c5□ 18. ♔h1** [18. ♗e3 ♘g4−+] **♗d4 19. ♖ad1?** [19. ♕f3? ♘e5!! 20. ♕f6 ♕f6 21. ♖f6 ♘c4∓] **♘g4! 20. ♕e2 ♕h4 21. ♖f4?!⊕** [21. ♗e1 ♗e5!∓] **h5 22. ♘b5 0–0!–+ 23. ♘d4 ♘d4 24. ♕g2 ♖c2 25. e5 ♘e6 26. ♖b4 a5 27. ♖e4 ♖d8 28. h3 ♖d3 0 : 1** **[Epišin]**

72. **A 55**

JUSUPOV 2645 – L. CHRISTIANSEN 2620
Deutschland 1993

1. d4 ♘f6 2. c4 d6 3. ♘c3 ♘bd7 4. ♘f3 c6 5. e4 e5 6. ♗e2 ♗e7 7. 0–0 0–0 8. ♕c2 a6 9. ♖d1 ♕c7 10. ♗g5 ♖e8 11. ♖ac1 [11. ♖d2] **b6** [11... h6; 11... ♘f8!?] **12. ♗h4!? N** [12. b4 – 42/72] **♗b7**

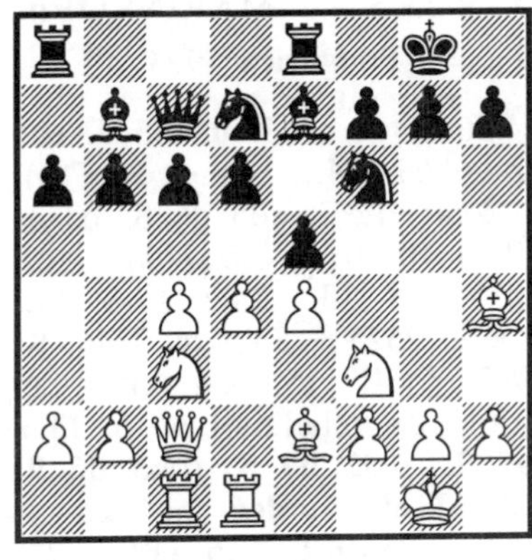

13. c5!? ed4 [13... bc5 14. de5± ×c5, c6; 13... dc5!? 14. de5 ♘e5 (14... ♘g4 15. e6 fe6 16. ♗g3=∞) *a)* 15. ♗g3 *a1)* 15... ♘fd7 16. ♘a4 ♗f6 17. ♖d7; *a2)* 15... ♗d6 16. ♖d6 ♕d6 17. ♘e5 ♖e5 18. f4 (18. ♘a4 ♘e4 19. ♗e5 ♕e5 20. ♘b6±) ♖ee8 19. e5 ♕d4 20. ♗f2 ♕f4 21. ef6± △ ♘a4; *a3)* 15... ♘fg4!?; *b)* 15. ♘e5 ♕e5 16. ♘a4 b5 (16... ♘e4 17. ♗e7 ♖e7 18. ♘b6 ♖ae8 19. ♗d3; 18. ♗d3!?; 16... ♗d8 17. ♗f3↑) 17. ♗f6 ♕f6 18. ♘c5 ♗c5 19. ♕c5=∞] **14. cb6± ♕b6 15. ♘d4 ♗f8** [15... c5?! 16. ♘f5±] **16. ♘f5 d5! 17. ♗f3 g6 18. ♘e3 ♖ac8!** [18... d4 19. ♘c4 ♕a7 (19... ♕b4? 20. ♖d4 c5 21. a3+–) 20. e5! ♘d5 21. ♘e4 (21. ♘d5 cd5 22. ♘d6±) ♘e5 22. ♘e5 ♖e5 23. ♘f6 ♘f6 24. ♗f6±] **19. ed5 cd5 20. ♕b3!** [20. ♘ed5 ♘d5 21. ♗d5 ♗d5 22. ♖d5 ♘e5=∞; 20. ♗f6 ♘f6 21. ♘ed5 ♗d5 22. ♗d5 ♘g4=∞ △ ♘f2] **♕b3 21. ab3 ♗h6 22. ♘cd5 ♖c1 23. ♘f6 ♘f6 24. ♖c1 ♗f3** [24... ♖e3? 25. fe3 ♗e3 26. ♔f1 ♗c1 27. ♗b7+–] **25. ♗f6 ♗e3?** [25... ♗e2±] **26. fe3±** [♖ 9/j] **♗e2 27. ♔f2 ♗b5 28. g4! h6 29. h4 ♗d7 30. g5 h5 31. ♖c7 ♗b5 32. ♗e7 ♗d3 33. ♔f3 ♗f5 34. e4 ♗e6 35. b4 ♖c8 36. ♖b7 ♗c4 37. ♔f4 ♗b5 38. ♖a7 ♔g7 39. b3 ♗f1 40. e5 ♔g8 41. ♔e4** [41. e6?! fe6 42. ♔e5 ♗d3±] **♗e2 42. ♔d4 ♗f1 43. ♗d6!** [△ ♗c7, ♔c5-b6 ×a6] **♗b5 44. ♗c7 ♔f8 45. ♔c5 ♔e7 46. ♔d5!?** [△ ♗d6; 46. ♔b6 ♔e6 47. ♗d6±] **♗d7?!** [⌓ 46... ♔f8 47. ♔d6±] **47. ♗d6 ♔d8 48. ♗c5!+–** [×a6, f7] **♖c6 49. ♖a8 ♔c7 50. ♗d6** [50... ♔b7 51. ♖b8 ♔a7 52. ♖d8] **1 : 0** **[Jusupov]**

73.*** **A 55**

ČEHOV 2535 – J. HICKL 2540
Deutschland 1992

1. d4 ♘f6 2. c4 d6 3. ♘c3 ♘bd7 4. ♘f3 c6 5. e4 e5 6. ♗e2 ♗e7 7. 0–0 0–0 8. d5!? a6 9. ♗e3 cd5 N [9... c5 – 32/(118)] **10. cd5 ♘g4** [10... b5 11. ♘d2 ♘b6 12. a4 b4 13. a5±; RR 12... ba4 13. ♘a4⩲ Piskov] **11. ♗d2** [RR 11. ♗c1 b5 *a)* 12. ♘d2 ♘gf6 13. b4 ♘b6 14. a4 ba4 15. ♘a4 ♘a4 16. ♕a4 ♗d7 17. ♕b3 1/2 : 1/2 Ribli 2620 – J. Hickl 2540, Deutschland 1993; *b)* 12. h3 ♘gf6 13. a3 ♘b6 14. ♗e3 ♕c7 (14... ♗d7?! 15. ♘e5) 15. ♖c1 ♕b8 16. ♘d2 ♗d7 17. b3 ♖c8 18. ♕c2 (18. ♖c2 ♗d8 19. ♕a1 a5 20. ♖fc1 b4∞ Malanjuk) ♕b7 19. ♕a2 ♗d8 20. ♖c2 ♗e8 21. ♖fc1 ♘bd7 22. a4 ♗b6 23. ♗b6 ♕b6 24. ab5 ab5 25. ♕b1± Malanjuk 2600 – J. Hickl 2540, Calcutta 1993] **b5 12. ♘e1!** [Kramnik; RR 12. b4 ♘b6 13. a4 ba4 14. ♘a4 ♘f6 15. ♘c3! ♕c7 16. ♕b3 ♕b7 17. ♖a5 ♘e8 18. b5!± Piskov 2520 – V. Ikonnikov 2485, Douai 1993; 14... f5∞ Malanjuk] **♘gf6 13. ♘c2** [13. ♘d3?! ♘c5! 14. f3 ♘d3 15. ♗d3 ♘d7=] **♘c5** [13... ♘b6 14. ♘b4 ♗d7 15. ♗e3⩲] **14. f3 ♗d7** [14... b4 15. ♘b4 ♕b6 16. ♘c6 ♘ce4 17.

♔h1+−] **15. b4 ♘a4 16. ♘a4 ba4 17. ♘a3!± ♕b8?!** [17... ♘h5!? 18. g3±] **18. ♔h1 ♖c8** [18... ♘e8 19. ♗d3 ♘c7 20. ♗c2 ♘b5 21. ♗a4] **19. ♖b1?** [19. ♗d3! △ ♗c2±] **♘e8! 20. b5** [20. ♗d3 ♘c7 21. ♗c2 ♘b5 22. ♗a4 ♘c3! (22... ♘a3 23. ♗d7 ♘b1 24. ♕b1!±) 23. ♗c3 ♗a4 24. ♕a4 ♖c3=∞] **ab5 21. ♗b5** [21. ♘b5 ♕b6⇆] **♕c7 22. ♖c1** [22. ♕e2 ♗b5 23. ♘b5 ♕c4] **♕b7?!** [22... ♕a7! 23. ♕e2 ♗b5 24. ♘b5 ♕a6=] **23. ♕e2 ♗b5 24. ♕b5 ♖c1 25. ♖c1 ♕b5 26. ♘b5 ♖b8 27. ♘a3 f5□ 28. ♖b1 ♖b1 29. ♘b1 fe4 30. fe4** [♘♗ 9/c] **♘f6 31. ♘c3 ♗d8?!** [31... h6!?±] **32. ♗g5! ♘d5□** [32... ♗a5? 33. ♗f6 ♗c3 34. ♗h4 ♔f7 35. ♔g1 ♔e8 36. ♔f2 ♔d7 37. ♔e3 ♔c7 38. ♔d3 ♗a5 39. ♔c4+−] **33. ♘d5?** [33. ed5 ♗g5 34. ♘a4 ♔f7 (34... ♗d2 35. ♘b2 △ ♘c4±) 35. ♘c3±] **♗g5=** [♘♗ 4/c] **34. ♔g1 ♔f7 35. ♔f2 ♗c1 36. ♔e2 ♗b2 37. ♔d3 a3 38. ♔c4 ♗d4 39. ♔b5** [39. ♔d3 ♔g6 40. ♔e2=] **♔g6! 40. ♔c6 ♗c5 41. ♘c7! ♗g1 42. h3 ♔h5 43. ♘e8 ♔h4 44. ♘g7 ♔g3 45. ♔d6** [45... ♗d4 46. ♔d5 ♔g2 47. ♘f5 ♗b2 48. h4 ♔f3 49. h5 ♔e2 50. ♘d6 ♔d3 51. ♘c4 ♔c2 52. ♘a3=]
1/2 : 1/2 **[Čehov]**

74. **A 56**

KAJDANOV 2620 − EHLVEST 2625
Pleasantville 1993

1. d4 ♘f6 2. c4 c5 3. d5 e5 4. ♘c3 d6 5. e4 ♗e7 6. ♗d3 0−0 7. h3 ♘a6 8. ♘f3 ♘c7 9. ♗e3 N [9. g4 − 46/96] **♗d7 10. ♘h2 a6 11. a4 b5! 12. 0−0** [12. cb5 ab5 13. ab5 ♖a1 14. ♕a1 ♕b8=] **bc4 13. ♗c4 ♖b8 14. b3 ♘fe8 15. ♕d2 ♘a8 16. f4** [16. a5?! ♘ac7 △ ♘b5; 16. ♗a6 ♖b3 17. a5±] **ef4 17. ♗f4 ♕a5 18. ♘f3 ♘b6 19. ♗e2 ♗f6 20. e5** [20. ♖ac1 c4 21. bc4 ♘c4 22. ♗c4 ♕c5 23. ♔h1 ♕c4 24. e5 de5 25. ♗e5±] **de5 21. ♘e5 ♖d8 22. ♖ac1 ♘d6 23. ♕d3 ♖fe8 24. ♘d7 ♖d7 25. ♗g4** [25. ♗d6? ♖d6 26. ♘e4 ♗d4!] **♖dd8 26. ♕f3 ♕b4 27. a5 ♘a8** [27... ♘bc8 28. ♔h1! ♗e5 29. ♗e5 ♖e5 30. ♘a4 c4 31. ♗c8±] **28. ♘a4 c4?!⊕** [28... ♘b5 *a)* 29. ♖c4? ♘d4 30. ♕d1 ♕b3 31. ♖c5 ♕d1 32. ♖d1 (32. ♗d1 ♗e7) ♖e4!∓; *b)* 29. ♘c5!! ♗d4 30. ♔h1 ♗c5 31. ♖c4! ♘d4 (31... ♕a3 32. ♗c1+−) 32. ♖b4 ♘f3 33. ♖c4! ♘d4 34. ♖c5 ♘b3 35. ♖c3! ♘a5 36. d6+−] **29. ♗d6 ♖d6 30. ♖c4 ♕a5 31. ♘c5!+− ♘c7** [31... ♘b6 32. ♘b7] **32. ♘e4 ♕b6 33. ♕f2 ♘d5 34. ♘d6 ♕d6 35. ♖d1 ♕e5 36. ♗f3?⊕** [36. ♖c5+−] **♘c3 37. ♖c1 ♘b5 38. ♖e4??** [38. ♗c6+−] **♕e4! 39. ♗e4 ♗d4 40. ♗d3 g6 41. ♗b5 ♗f2 42. ♔f2 ab5 43. ♖c5= b4 44. ♖c4 ♖b8 45. g4 ♔g7 46. ♔g3 g5 47. ♖d4** [47. h4? ♖d8!] **h6 48. ♖c4 ♖b6 49. ♖d4 ♔g6 50. h4 ♖b5 51. hg5 ♔g5 52. ♖c4 f6 53. ♖d4 h5 54. gh5 ♔h5 55. ♔f4 ♔g6 56. ♔g4 ♖g5 57. ♔f3 ♖b5 58. ♔g4 ♖b8 59. ♔f4 ♔f7 60. ♔f3 ♔e6 61. ♖c4 f5 62. ♔f2** **1/2 : 1/2** **[Kajdanov]**

75.* **!N** **A 57**

F. LEVIN 2505 − I. MARINKOVIĆ 2445
Podgorica 1993

1. d4 ♘f6 2. c4 c5 3. d5 b5 4. cb5 [RR 4. ♘d2 e6!? N (4... bc4 − 56/(78)) 5. e4 bc4 6. ♗c4 ed5 7. ed5 d6 8. b3 ♗e7 9. ♘gf3 0−0 10. 0−0 ♘bd7 11. ♖e1 ♘b6 12. ♘f1 ♖e8 13. ♗b2 ♖b8 14. ♗c3 (Grószpéter 2525 − Ščipkov 2345, Kecskemét 1993) ♘c4!? 15. bc4 ♗f5= Ščipkov; 7... ♗d6!? Zagrebel'nyj] **a6 5. f3 ab5 6. e4 ♕a5 7. ♗d2 b4 8. ♘a3 d6 9. ♘c4 ♕c7 10. a3 e6 11. de6 ♗e6 12. ♗f4! N** [12. ab4 − 53/76] **♖a6** [12... ♗c4 13. ♗c4±] **13. ab4** [13. e5?! de5 14. ♗e5 (14. ♘e5 ♖b6?! 15. ♘c4!±; 15. ♕a4±; 14... c4!∓) ♕a7 15. ♘d6 ♗d6 16. ♗d6 c4 17. ♗b4 ♘c6=∞↑] **♖a1 14. ♕a1 cb4 15. ♕a4** [15. ♕a5!? ♕a5 16. ♘a5 ♗e7 17. ♘e2 0−0 18. ♘d4 ♖c8 19. ♘e6 fe6 20. ♗d3±] **♘c6 16. e5! ♗c4** [16... de5 17. ♗e5 (17. ♘e5? ♗d6!) ♕d7 18. ♘b6 ♕b7 19. ♗b5 ♕b6 20. ♗c6 ♗d7 (20... ♘d7 21. ♘e2± △ 21... ♗c5 22. ♗g7 ♖g8 23. ♗d7 ♗d7 24. ♕a8 ♕d8 25. ♕e4+−) 21. ♗d7 ♘d7 22. ♘e2±] **17. ef6 ♗f1 18. ♔f1 gf6 19. ♘e2 ♕b6 20. g3** [20. ♘d4 ♕d4 21. ♕c6 ♔e7 22. g3 f5 23. ♔g2 ♔f6∞] **♗e7 21. ♘d4 ♔d7□ 22. ♗e3 ♖c8 23. ♔g2=∞→ ♕a5 24. ♕b3 ♘d4?** [⌓ 24... ♘e5] **25.**

♗d4 ♔e8 [25... ♕f5? 26. ♕a4] **26. ♖e1 ♕f5 27. ♖e2** [27. ♕b4?! ♖c2 28. ♗f2 ♔f8!∞] **♔f8 28. ♕e3 ♖c7 29. g4! ♕g6** [29... ♕g5 30. ♕e4±→] **30. ♗b6 ♖b7 31. ♗d8! ♗d8 32. ♕e8 ♔g7 33. ♕d8+− ♕d3 34. ♖e8 ♕c2 35. ♔g3 1 : 0**
[F. Levin]

76. !N **A 57**

HJARTARSON 2625
– HERTNECK 2575
München 1993

1. d4 ♘f6 2. c4 c5 3. d5 b5 4. cb5 a6 5. f3 ab5 6. e4 ♕a5 7. ♗d2 b4 8. ♘a3 d6 9. ♘c4 ♕a7! N [Bukal] **10. a4 ♘bd7** [10... g6 11. a5 ♘fd7 12. f4 ♗g7 13. ♘f3±] **11. a5 ♗a6 12. ♕a4 ♖b8?!** [⌓ 12... g6 13. ♘b6 ♗f1 *a)* 14. ♘a8?! ♗g2 15. ♕c6 ♔d8 16. a6 ♗h1 17. ♖a5 ♗g7 (17... ♘b8 18. ♕b6 ♕b6 19. ♘b6 ♘a6 20. ♖a6 ♔c7 21. ♘c4∞) 18. ♖b5 ♘b8!∓ (18... c4 19. ♔f1) 19. ♖b8 ♕b8 20. ♘b6 e6 21. ♗g5 ♕c7; *b)* 14. ♔f1 ♖b8∓] **13. ♗g5** [13. ♕c6 ♗b7! 14. ♕a4 ♗a6] **♔d8□** [13... g6 14. ♘d6+−; 13... ♗b5 14. ♘d6+−] **14. ♕c2 g6 15. b3?** [×c3; 15. f4 b3!⇆; ⌓ 15. ♗d3 ♗g7 16. ♘e2 ♘e8∞] **♗g7 16. ♖a2 ♘e8!∓** [16... h6? 17. ♗c1 △ 17... ♘e8 18. ♗b2] **17. ♘h3?!** [17. ♗d3 ♘e5 18. ♘e2 ♘c7 19. 0–0 ♘c4 20. ♗c4 ♗c4 21. ♕c4 ♕a6∓ ×a5] **h6** [17... ♘c7 18. ♘d6 f6 19. ♘f7 ♔e8 20. ♘h8 fg5 21. ♘g6 hg6 22. ♘g5∞; 17... ♘e5 18. ♘e5 ♗e5 19. ♗a6 ♕a6∓] **18. ♗c1 ♗c3! 19. ♗d2 ♗d4 20. ♗d3** [20. ♗e3? ♗c4 21. ♗d4 ♗b3−+] **♘c7 21. ♘f4 ♘e5 22. ♘e5?** [22. ♘e2 ♘d3 23. ♕d3 ♗g7∓] **♗e5∓ 23. ♘e2** [23. ♗a6 ♕a6 24. ♘d3 ♗d4] **♗d3 24. ♕d3 ♖b5 25. f4 ♗g7 26. h4 ♖a5 27. ♖a5 ♕a5 28. ♔f2 h5 29. ♖c1 ♕b5 30. ♕f3 ♔c8 31. f5 ♔b7?** [31... gf5! 32. ♕f5 e6 33. ♕g5 ♗e5∓] **32. ♗g5 gf5?** [32... ♕d7∓] **33. ef5** [33. ♕f5 e6! 34. ♕f3 ed5 35. ed5 ♕d7] **♗e5 34. ♖c4?** [34. ♗e7! f6 35. ♘f4 ♗d4 36. ♔g3 ♖g8 37. ♘g6 ♕d7 38. ♗f8 ♗e5 39. ♔f2∞] **f6−+ 35. ♗e3 ♔c8** [△ ♕b7] **36. ♖c2 ♕d3 37. ♖a2 ♕b3 38. ♘c1 ♕c4 0 : 1**
[Hertneck]

77. **A 57**

B. GEL'FAND 2690 – ADAMS 2630
München 1993

1. d4 ♘f6 2. c4 c5 3. d5 b5 4. cb5 a6 5. f3 ab5 6. e4 ♕a5 7. ♗d2 b4 8. ♘a3 d6 9. ♘c4 ♕a7!? 10. a3 N g6 11. ♗d3 ♗g7 12. ♘e2 0–0 13. 0–0 ba3 14. ♖a3 ♕b7 15. ♘c3 ♘a6!? [15... ♖a3 16. ba3±] **16. ♕a1** [16. ♘a5 ♕b6! △ 17. ♘a4 ♕c7 18. ♘c6 ♘b8=] **♘d7!?** [16... ♖b8 17. ♖b1 ♘b4! 18. ♖a7 ♘d3! 19. ♖b7 ♖b7∞̅; 17. ♗e2!±] **17. f4** [17. ♘a5!? ♕b6 18. ♘a4 ♕c7 19. ♘c6 ♘b4! 20. ♘e7 (20. ♘b4 cb4 21. ♗b4 ♘e5∞̅) ♔h8 21. ♘c8 ♘d3!? (21... ♖fc8 22. ♗b1!?) 22. ♖d3 ♖fc8∞̅] **♘b6! 18. ♘a5 ♕c7 19. ♘c6 c4 20. ♗e2 ♗b7 21. ♗e3** [21. ♘b5 ♕d7 22. ♗e3 ♘c5∓] **♗c6!** [21... ♘c5 22. ♗c5 dc5 23. ♘a5 f5 24. e5±] **22. ♖a6** [22. dc6 ♘b4]

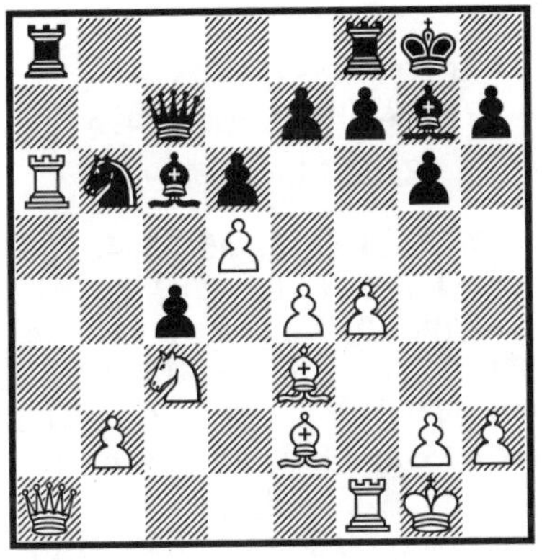

22... ♗d7!! [22... ♗b7 23. ♗b6 ♕b6 24. ♖b6 ♗d4 25. ♔h1 ♖a1 26. ♖b7+−] **23. ♗b6** [23. ♔h1!? ♖a6 (23... ♘a4?! 24. ♖a4 ♗a4 25. ♘a4 ♕a5 26. ♗d1±) 24. ♕a6 ♖b8=] **♕b6** [23... ♕b7? 24. ♗c4] **24. ♖b6 ♗d4 25. ♔h1 ♖a1 26. ♖a1 ♗b6 27. ♗c4** [27... ♖c8 28. b3 ♗d4 29. ♖c1 ♖a8 30. g3 ♗h3∞̅] **1/2 : 1/2**
[B. Gel'fand]

78. **A 57**

M. GUREVICH 2610 – HERTNECK 2575
München 1993

1. d4 ♘f6 2. c4 c5 3. d5 b5 4. cb5 a6 5. f3 ab5 6. e4 ♕a5 7. ♗d2 b4 8. ♘a3 g6

N 9. ♘c4 ♕c7 10. a3 ba3 [10... e6 11. ♗g5 ♗g7 12. de6 fe6 13. ♕d6!?↑] **11. ♖a3 ♖a3 12. ba3 d6 13. ♕a4! ♘fd7** [13... ♗d7? 14. ♕a8 ♗g7 15. ♗a5 ♕c8 16. ♘b6+−; ⌓ 13... ♘bd7] **14. ♗c3 f6 15. ♗d3 ♗h6 16. ♘e2 0–0 17. 0–0 f5?!** [17... ♘e5 18. ♗e5 fe5 19. ♖b1±; 17... ♗a6 18. ♖b1 ♘b6 19. ♗a5! ♘a4 20. ♗c7±] **18. ef5 gf5 19. ♕c2→ ♘e5** [19... ♗a6 20. ♗f5 ♖f5 21. ♕f5 ♗c4 22. ♕e6 ♔f8 23. ♕h6 ♔e8 24. ♘f4+−] **20. ♘e5 de5 21. ♘g3 ♗e3** [21... e4 22. ♗c4 ♕d6 23. fe4±] **22. ♔h1 f4 23. ♗h7 ♔h8 24. ♕g6!+−** [△ ♕h6] **e6** [24... fg3 25. ♕h5 ♗g4□ 26. ♗e5 ♖f6 27. fg4+−] **25. ♘h5!** [25... ♗d4 26. ♗d4 ed4 27. ♕h6+−; 25. ♕h5 ♕h7 26. ♕e5 ♔g8 27. ♕g5 ♔f7 28. ♘e4 ed5 29. ♕d5↑] **1 : 0**
[M. Gurevich]

79. **A 57**

PÉTURSSON 2560 – D. GUREVICH 2495

Saint-Martin 1993

1. d4 ♘f6 2. c4 c5 3. d5 b5 4. cb5 a6 5. f3 e6 6. e4 ed5 7. e5 ♕e7 8. ♕e2 ♘g8 9. ♘h3 ♕d8 10. ♘f4 ♗b7 11. ♘c3 ♘e7 12. ♔f2!? N [12. ♘h5 – 51/68; 12. ♗d2!? △ 0-0-0] **c4?!** [12... ♕b6 13. ♕d1 d4 14. ♘a4 ♕c7 15. b6!± △ 15... ♕e5 16. ♘d3; 12... g6 13. ♕d3 (13. ba6 ♘a6 14. ♘b5 ♘f5 15. ♘d6 ♗d6 16. ed6 ♔f8; 13... ♗c6!?) *a)* 13... ♗g7 14. ♘cd5 ♘d5 15. ♘d5 ab5 16. ♘f6! ♗f6 17. ef6 0–0 (17... ♕f6 18. ♕e3 ♕e7 19. ♗b5±) 18. ♕b5 ♕c7 19. ♗e3±; *b)* 13... c4! 14. ♕d1 ab5 15. ♘cd5 ♘d5 16. ♘d5 ♗g7∞] **13. ♗e3 ♘f5 14. ♘fd5 ♗d5 15. ♘d5 ♘e3 16. ♕e3 ab5 17. ♘f6! gf6 18. ef6 ♗e7 19. fe7 ♕c7** [19... ♕e7 20. ♖e1! (20. ♕d4 0–0 21. ♖e1 ♕g5∞) ♕e3 21. ♖e3 ♔d8 22. ♖e5! c3 23. ♖b5±] **20. b3!?** [20. ♗e2 ♕a7 21. ♕a7 ♖a7 22. a4 ba4 23. ♗c4 ♔e7±; 21. a4±] **d5 21. a4 ♘c6?!** [21... ♕a7 22. ♕a7 ♖a7 23. ♗e2 ba4 24. bc4 dc4 25. ♗c4 ♔e7 26. ♖he1 ♔f6 27. ♗b5 a3 28. ♖e3±] **22. ♗e2!±** [22. ♖e1 ♘b4?!] **d4** [22... ba4 23. bc4 dc4 24. ♗c4] **23. ♕e4 f5 24. ♕e6!** [24. ♕f5 d3 25. ab5 ♕b6 26. ♔g3 ♕b8 27. ♔h3 ♘e7∞] **d3 25. ab5 ♕b6 26. ♕e3** [26. ♔g3 ♕b8 27. ♔h3 ♘e7∞] **♕e3 27. ♔e3 ♖a1 28. ♖a1 de2 29. bc6 cb3 30. ♔e2 ♔e7 31. ♖a7 ♔d6⊕ 32. ♖b7 ♔c6** [32... ♖e8 33. ♔f2 ♔c6 34. ♖b3 △ ♖e3+−] **33. ♖b3 ♔d6 34. ♔e3 ♖e8 35. ♔f4 ♖e2 36. ♖d3!+− ♔c5 37. g3 ♖h2 38. ♔f5 h5 39. f4 ♔c4 40. ♖d8 ♖g2 41. ♖h8** [41. ♔g5!] **♖g3 42. ♖h5 ♔d5 43. ♔f6 ♔e4 44. f5 ♖a3 45. ♖h1 ♖a2 46. ♖b1 ♖a3 47. ♖b4 ♔d5 48. ♔f7 1 : 0**
[Pétursson]

80. **A 57**

A. CHERNIN 2600 – BELLÓN LÓPEZ 2415

Benidorm 1993

1. d4 ♘f6 2. c4 c5 3. d5 b5 4. cb5 a6 5. f3 g6 6. e4 ♗g7 7. ♘a3! [7. e5 ♘g8 8. f4 d6∞] **0–0 8. ♘e2 e6?! 9. ♘c3 ed5 N** [9... d6 – 49/(84)] **10. ♘d5 ab5 11. ♘b5 ♗a6** [11... ♗b7!?] **12. ♗g5!** [12. ♘dc3 d5! 13. ed5 ♖e8 14. ♔f2 c4; 12. ♘bc3] **♗b5□ 13. ♗b5 ♕a5 14. b4** [14. ♕d2?? ♘d5–+] **♕b5 15. ♗f6 ♖a3?** [15... ♘c6 16. ♗g7 ♔g7 17. a4 ♕c4 18. ♖c1 ♕a2 19. ♖c2 ♕a4 20. bc5±] **16. ♕c1!+− ♖a6□** [16... cb4 17. ♕h6!!+−] **17. ♗g7** [17. a4+−] **♔g7 18. ♕b2 f6 19. ♘c7 ♕d3 20. ♘a6 ♕e3 21. ♕e2 ♕c3 22. ♔f2 ♕d4 23. ♕e3 ♕b2 24. ♕e2 ♕d4 25. ♔g3 ♘a6** [25... ♕e5 26. f4 ♕c3 27. ♕f3] **26. ♖ad1** [26. ♕a6+−] **♕e5 27. ♔f2 ♘b4□ 28. ♖d7 ♔h8 29. ♖hd1 ♕h2 30. ♕d2** [△ ♕d6] **♕e5 31. ♕h6 1 : 0**
[A. Chernin]

81. **A 57**

BAREEV 2670 – ADAMS 2630

München 1993

1. d4 ♘f6 2. c4 c5 3. d5 b5 4. cb5 a6 5. f3 g6 6. e4 d6 7. a4 ♗g7 8. ♘a3 N [8. a5 – 22/138] **0–0 9. ♘e2 ab5** [9... e6 10. de6 ♗e6 11. ♘f4] **10. ♘b5 ♘e8?!** [⌓ 10... ♘a6] **11. ♘ec3 ♘c7 12. ♗g5 ♘ba6 13. ♗c4 ♖b8 14. 0–0 h6 15. ♗e3 ♗d7**

16. ♕d3 ♔h7 [16... ♘b5 17. ab5 ♘c7 18. ♖a7±] **17. f4 f5** [⌓ 17... ♘b5 18. ab5 ♘c7 19. ♖a7±] **18. e5+– de5 19. fe5 ♗e5 20. ♖ae1** [20. ♗h6! ♗h2 21. ♔h2 ♔h6 22. ♕e3 ♔g7 23. ♕e5 ♖f6 24. ♖ae1+–] **♘b4 21. ♕d2 ♗b5 22. ♘b5** [22. ab5 ♕d6] **♘b5 23. ab5 ♕d6□ 24. ♗h6 ♖fd8□** [24... ♗h2 25. ♔h1 △ ♖e6, △ ♖f3-h3] **25. ♔h1** [25. ♗f4 ♗f4 26. ♖f4 (26. ♕f4 ♕f4 27. ♖e7 ♔h6 28. ♖f4 ♘d5⩲) e5! 27. ♖h4 ♔g7 28. ♕h6 ♔f6±; ⌓ 25. ♖f3 ♘d5 26. ♖h3 (26. ♗d5 ♕d5 27. ♕d5 ♖d5 28. ♖e5 ♖e5 29. ♗f4 ♖e1 30. ♔f2 e5) ♗d4 27. ♗e3+–] **♖b7□** [25... ♘d5 26. ♗d5 ♕d5 27. ♕d5 ♖d5 28. ♖e5 ♖e5 29. ♗f4+–] **26. ♖f3 ♘d5 27. ♖h3 ♔g8 28. ♗g5** [28. ♖he3 ♔h7! (28... ♗f6 29. ♖e6 ♕d7 30. ♖f6 ef6 31. ♗d5 ♕d5 32. ♖e8+–) 29. ♖e5 ♘b6±] **♔f8 29. ♕f2 ♖dd7?** [⌓ 29... ♘b6] **30. ♕h4 ♗g7 31. ♗h6⊕** [31. ♕h7+–] **♕f6 32. ♗g7 ♕g7 33. b3 ♘f6 34. ♖he3 ♖d4 35. ♕h3 ♘g4** [35... ♘e4? 36. ♖e4] **36. ♖3e2 e5 37. ♕g3 e4 38. h3** [⌓ 38. ♖a2±→] **♘e5 39. ♕f4** [⌓ 39. ♖a2] **♘c4 40. bc4 ♔g8** [40... ♖c4 41. ♖a2→] **41. ♖a2 ♔h7 42. g4?** [⌓ 42. ♕h4 ♕h6 43. ♕f6 ♕g7=] **♕h6 43. ♕h6 ♔h6 44. gf5 gf5 45. ♖g1 e3 46. ♖a6 ♔h7 47. ♖e6 f4 48. b6** [48. ♖e5 ♖g7–+] **♖c4 49. ♖c6 ♖e4 50. ♖c7?** [⌓ 50. ♖c5 ♖b6 51. ♖h5 ♖h6 52. ♖h6 ♔h6 53. ♔g2] **♖e7 51. ♖e7 ♖e7–+ 52. ♖b1 f3 53. ♔g1** [53. b7 e2 54. b8♕ f2–+] **♖g7 54. ♔f1 ♖g2 0 : 1** **[Adams]**

82.* !N **A 57**

KÖRHOLZ 2295 – LÉKÓ 2465

Budapest 1993

1. d4 ♘f6 2. c4 c5 3. d5 b5 4. cb5 a6 5. ♘c3 ab5 6. e4 b4 7. ♘b5 d6 8. ♗f4 g5! 9. ♗g5 ♘e4 10. ♗f4 ♗g7! N [10... ♕a5 – 47/100] **11. ♕e2 ♘f6 12. ♘d6** [12. ♗d6 ♘d5 13. ♖d1 0–0!∓] **♔f8 13. ♘c8 ♕c8 14. d6 ed6 15. ♗d6 ♔g8 16. ♕f3** [16. ♘f3 ♕f5 17. ♕e5 ♕e5 18. ♗e5 ♘bd7 19. ♗f6 ♖e8! 20. ♗e5 ♘e5∓ F. Németh – Lékó 2460, Gyula 1992] **♘c6! 17. ♘e2** [17. ♗c5 ♘e5 18. ♕e3 ♘d5 19. ♕c1 ♕e6 20. ♗e3 ♘g4–+] **♕e8! 18. ♗c5 ♘e4 19. ♗e3 b3! 20. ♘c1!□** [20. a3 ♘b4!–+] **♘d4!** [20... ♘b4?! 21. ♗d3!] **21. ♗d4 ♗d4 22. ♗e2** [22. ♘b3 ♗f2–+] **♗b2 23. ♕g4 ♔f8 24. ♘b3 ♗c3 25. ♔f1 ♗a1 26. ♘a1 ♖a2 27. ♘b3⊕ ♖b2** [27... ♖g8–+] **28. ♗d3□ ♖f2?** [28... ♘f2!! 29. ♕d4 ♘d3 30. ♕h8 ♔e7–+] **29. ♔g1 ♖b2** [29... ♖g8 30. ♕e4 ♖gg2 31. ♕g2 ♕e1 32. ♗f1 ♖g2 33. ♔g2 ♕e4 34. ♔g1 ♕e3 35. ♔g2 ♕b3 36. ♗e2=] **30. ♕e4 ♖b3 31. ♔f2?!** [31. ♕e8 ♔e8 32. ♗f1! ♖b2! 33. h3 ♖g8! 34. ♔h2 f5! 35. ♖g1 f4 36. ♗c4 ♖g5–+] **♖b2 32. ♔f3 ♕d8! 33. ♖e1 ♖g8 34. ♗f1 ♕f6 35. ♔e3 ♕c3 0 : 1** **[Adorján, Lékó]**

83.* **A 57**

V. MIKHALEVSKI 2305 – PALATNIK 2515

Netanya 1993

1. d4 ♘f6 2. c4 c5 3. d5 b5 4. cb5 a6 5. b6 e6 [RR 5... a5 6. ♘c3 ♗a6 7. e4 N (7. ♘f3 – 56/(78)) ♗f1 8. ♔f1 d6 9. b7! ♖a7 10. f4 e6□ (10... ♘bd7 11. e5±) 11. de6 fe6 12. ♘f3 ♕d7! (12... ♖b7 13. e5 de5 14. ♕d8 ♔d8 15. ♘e5± ×a5, c5, e6) 13. ♕e2 ♖b7 (13... ♕b7 14. ♘g5 ♕d7 15. f5±) 14. e5 de5 15. ♘e5 ♕c8 16. ♘e4 ♗e7 17. ♘f6 ♗f6 18. ♘c4 ♗e7 19. ♗d2 (19. ♘a5?! ♖a7 20. ♘c4 0–0 △ ♘c6$\overline{\overline{\infty}}$) ♘c6 (Brenninkmeijer 2475 – Kajdanov 2620, New York 1993) 20. g3! △ ♔g2, ♕e4, ♖he1, ♖ac1⩲; 9... ♖a6!? Kajdanov] **6. ♘c3 ♘d5 7. ♘d5 ed5 8. ♕d5 ♘c6 9. ♘f3 ♖b8 10. e4 ♗e7 11. ♗c4 0–0 12. 0–0 ♖b6 13. b3!? d6?! N** [×♖b6; 13... ♘a5 14. ♗f4 (14. ♗e2 – 56/78) ♗b7 15. ♕d3 ♘c4 16. bc4± ×d7, ⇔b; 13... ♗b7 14. ♕h5!? ♘b4! 15. ♘e5 ♕e8 (15... g6? 16. ♘f7! gh5 17. ♘d8 d5 18. ♘b7 dc4 19. ♘a5+–) 16. ♕g4!? ♖d6! (16... d6 17. ♘d7 ♗c8 18. ♗b2 g6 19. ♕f4!+–; 16... ♗f6 17. ♘d7±) 17. ♗b2 ♗f6∞ △ 18. ♘f7? ♖f7 19. ♗f7 ♕f7 20. e5 ♗e5 21. ♗e5 ♖g6–+] **14. ♗b2 ♗g4 15. ♖ad1!±** [×d6] **♘b4 16. ♕d2** [△ ♕f4] **♗f3** [16... ♗f6 17. e5! de5 18. ♕d8 ♖d8 (18... ♗d8 19. ♗f7!) 19. ♖d8 ♗d8 20. ♘e5±] **17.**

gf3 ♗g5 [17... ♗f6 18. e5 de5 19. ♕d8 ♖d8 20. ♖d8 ♗d8 21. ♖d1 △ ♖d7±] **18. f4 ♗h6** [△ ♕h4] **19. ♔h1! ♔h8** [19... ♕h4 20. ♖g1 g6? 21. ♕c3+−] **20. ♖g1 ♕h4 21. f3!+−** [21. a3!? f6 22. f3!+−] **♘a2 22. ♖g4! ♕d8□** [22... ♕e7 23. ♕a5!+−] **23. ♕g2** [×g7, ⇔d] **f6□ 24. e5!** [⁄⁄a1-h8] **fe5** [24... f5 25. ♖g3+−] **25. fe5 ♘b4 26. ed6 ♖d6 27. ♖d6 ♕d6 28. ♖g7 ♕d1 29. ♕g1** **1 : 0**
[J. Kagan, V. Mikhalevski]

84. **A 58**

HULAK 2540 – B. ALTERMAN 2600
Zagreb (zt) 1993

1. d4 ♘f6 2. c4 c5 3. d5 b5 4. cb5 a6 5. ba6 g6 6. g3 d6 7. ♗g2 ♗g7 8. ♘c3 0–0 9. ♘f3 ♘a6 10. 0–0 ♕b6 11. ♖e1 N [11. ♘d2 – 31/674] **♘g4! 12. h3 ♘e5 13. ♘d2** [13. ♘e5 ♗e5 14. ♗h6 ♕b2!] **♘c7 14. f4 ♘d7 15. a4 ♗a6 16. ♔h2 ♖ab8!?** [16... ♖fb8] **17. ♖a3** [17. ♕c2 ♖b7 △ ♖fb8=∞] **c4! 18. ♕c2 ♘c5 19. ♘d1 ♕b4!=∞ 20. ♘e3 ♘b3 21. ♘ec4 ♗c4?** [21... ♘d4! 22. ♕c3!□ (22. ♕d3? ♗c4 23. ♕c4 ♕c4 24. ♘c4 ♘c2∓) ♕c5! (22... ♗c4 23. ♘c4 ♘c2 24. ♕c2 ♕e1±) 23. e4 ♘db5! 24. ♕a5! ♘a3 25. ♕c5 dc5 26. ba3! ♗c3!∓] **22. ♕c4! ♘c1 23. ♖c1 ♕d2 24. ♖c2!** [24. ♕c7? ♗b2 25. ♖c2 ♕c2∓] **♕e1 25. ♕c7 ♗d4?!** [25... ♖b2±] **26. h4 ♗c5?** [26... ♖b2] **27. ♖ac3!** [27. ♖c5!? dc5 28. ♕e7 △ h5-h6] **♕a1** [27... ♖b2 28. ♖c5+−] **28. ♖c5!± dc5 29. ♕e7 ♖fe8 30. ♕c5 ♖b2 31. ♕c6 ♖eb8 32. ♗f3! ♖c2 33. ♕c2⊕ ♔g7?!** [33... ♕d4±] **34. ♕c7! ♖b1 35. d6 ♕d4 36. d7 ♖d1 37. a5+− ♔h6 38. d8♕** **1 : 0** **[B. Alterman]**

85. **A 58**

ILINČIĆ 2470 – D. SEKULIĆ 2410
Jugoslavija 1993

1. d4 ♘f6 2. c4 c5 3. d5 b5 4. cb5 a6 5. ba6 ♗a6 6. ♘c3 d6 7. ♘f3 g6 8. g3 ♗g7 9. ♗g2 0–0 10. 0–0 ♘bd7 11. ♕c2 ♖a7 12. h3 ♕a8 13. ♖d1 ♗c4!? [13... ♖b8 14. e4 ♘e8 15. ♖b1 △ b3±] **14. e4 N** [14. b3 ♗d5 15. ♘d5 ♘d5 16. ♗b2 ♘b4∓; 14. a3 – 44/73] **♗a2** [14... ♖b8 15. ♕b1! ♘e8 16. ♘d2 ♗a6 17. ♕c2 ♘e5 18. ♗f1±]

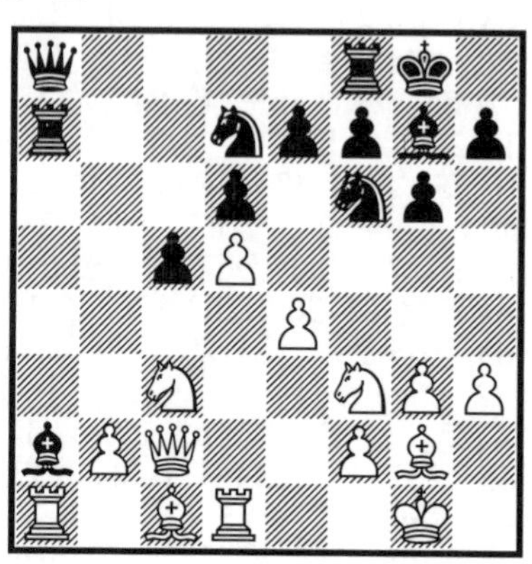

15. e5! [15. ♖a2 ♖a2 16. ♘a2 ♕a2 △ ♖b8∓] **de5** [15... ♘e5 16. ♘e5 de5 17. d6 e4 18. de7 ♖e8 19. ♖d8+−; 15... ♘e8 16. e6 ♘b6 17. ef7 ♖f7 18. ♖a2 ♖a2 19. ♘a2 ♕a2 20. ♘g5 ♖f6 21. h4 △ ♗h3±] **16. d6! ♗b3** [16... ed6 17. ♘e5 d5 18. ♘d7 ♘d7 19. ♖a2 ♖a2 20. ♗d5+−; 16... e4 17. de7 ♖e8 18. ♘g5 ♖e7 19. ♖a2 ♖a2 20. ♘a2 ♕a2 21. ♘e4 ♘e4 22. ♗e4 ♗d4 23. ♗g5±] **17. ♖a7** [17. ♕b3 ♖a1 18. de7 ♖b8! 19. ♕c4 ♕a6−+] **♗c2** [17... ♕b8 18. ♕b3! (18. ♕d2 ♕a7 19. de7 ♖e8 20. ♖e1 ♖e7∓) ♕b3 19. de7 ♖e8 20. ♖dd7 ♘d7 21. ♖d7 ♗f6 22. ♗g5±] **18. ♖a8 ♖a8 19. ♘e1!!** [19. ♖d2 ♗b3 20. ♘e5 (20. de7 ♖e8−+) ♖a1 21. ♘d7 ♖c1 22. ♔h2 ed6!∓] **♗d1 20. ♗a8 ♗b3** [20... ed6 21. ♘d1 d5 22. b3+−] **21. de7 ♘e8** [21... ♘b8 22. ♘d3! ♘e8 23. ♘c5 ♗c2 24. b4±] **22. ♗c6 ♗e6 23. ♘e4 ♗f6** [23... f5 24. ♘g5+−; 23... f6 24. ♘c5! ♘c5 25. ♗e8 ♘d7 26. ♗g6+−; 23... h6 24. ♗e3 f5 25. ♘c5 ♘c5 26. ♗e8+−] **24. ♗g5! ♗g5** [24... ♔g7 25. ♘f6 ♘df6 26. ♗f6+−] **25. ♘g5 ♘df6 26. ♘e4! ♘e4** [26... ♔g7 27. ♘f6+−; 26... ♘d7 27. ♘d3+−] **27. ♗e8 ♘d6 28. ♗c6 f6 29. e8♕ ♘e8 30. ♗e8 ♗h3 31. ♘d3! c4 32. ♘c5 ♗g4 33. ♗b5 c3 34. bc3 ♗f3 35. ♗f1 f5 36. ♘d7 e4 37. c4 ♗d1 38. c5 ♔f7 39. c6 ♔e7 40. ♘f8 ♔d6 41. ♗b5** **1 : 0** **[Ilinčić]**

86. **A 59**

WESSMAN 2435 – TH. ERNST 2540
Avesta 1993

1. d4 ♘f6 2. c4 c5 3. d5 b5 4. cb5 a6 5. ba6 ♗a6 6. ♘c3 g6 7. e4 ♗f1 8. ♔f1 d6 9. g3 ♗g7 10. ♔g2 0–0 11. ♘f3 ♘bd7 12. h3 ♘b6 13. ♖e1 ♕d7 14. a4 ♖fb8 N [14... ♕b7 – 42/(83)] **15. ♖a2 ♘e8 16. e5 ♘c7 17. ♗f4** [17. b3 de5 18. ♘e5 ♕d6!∓] **♘a6 18. b3** [18. ed6 ed6 19. ♘e4 ♘b4 20. ♖a1 ♘a4=] **♘b4 19. ♖ae2** [19. ♖d2 ♕b7∞̅ △ ♖d8, de5] **♕b7!** [19... ♕f5? 20. ♖e4±] **20. ♘b5** [20. ♕d2? ♘6d5 21. ♘d5 ♘d5∓; 20. ♘e4 de5 21. ♘c5 ♕c8 22. ♗e3 ♘6d5∓] **de5** [20... ♘6d5!? 21. ed6 ♘f4 22. gf4 e6 23. ♖d2! (23. ♘c7 ♖a7 24. ♕d2 ♘c6 25. ♘b5 ♘d4 26. ♘bd4 cd4∞̅) ♘d5 24. ♖d5! ♕d5 25. ♕d5 ed5 26. ♘c7 ♖a7 27. d7 ♖c7! (27... ♖f8? 28. ♖e8 ♗f6 29. ♘d5 ♗d8 30. ♘e5 f6 31. ♘e7! ♗e7 32. ♖e7 fe5 33. fe5±) 28. ♖e8 ♗f8 29. ♘e5 ♖d7! 30. ♘d7 ♖e8 31. ♘f6 ♔g7 32. ♘e8 ♔h6 33. ♘c7 c4 34. bc4 dc4 35. ♘d5 ♗c5 36. a5 ♗d4 37. a6 ♔h5 38. ♔g3=] **21. ♗e5 ♗e5 22. ♘e5 ♘6d5** [22... ♕d5? 23. ♕d5 ♘6d5 24. ♖c1± ×c5] **23. ♔h2 ♖d8 24. ♖d2 e6 25. ♕f3 ♕e7 26. ♖ed1 ♖ac8 27. h4 h5 28. ♘c3** [28. ♖c1 ♔g7 29. ♖c4? f6 30. ♘d3 ♘b6∓] **♔g7 29. ♘e4 ♖f8 30. ♖c1 ♖c7 31. ♘d3** [31... ♖fc8=] **1/2 : 1/2**
[Th. Ernst]

87. **A 60**

ULYBIN 2565 – ASEEV 2515
Sankt-Peterburg (zt) 1993

1. d4 ♘f6 2. c4 e6 3. g3 c5 4. d5 ed5 5. cd5 b5 6. ♗g2 ♗b7 7. e4 d6 8. ♘f3 N [8. ♘e2] **♗e7** [8... ♘e4 9. 0–0 (9. ♕e2 ♕e7 10. ♕b5? ♗c6!) ♘f6 10. ♕e2 ♗e7 11. ♕b5 ♕d7 12. ♘c3 ♘d5 13. ♘d4! (13. ♘h4? ♗c6!∓) cd4 14. ♕d7 ♘d7 (14... ♔d7 15. ♘d5 ♘c6 16. ♖e1 ♖he8 17. ♗d2↑) 15. ♘d5 ♗d5 16. ♗d5 ♖b8 17. b3∞̅] **9. 0–0 0–0 10. ♘h4 ♖e8** [10... g6? 11. e5 de5? 12. d6+–] **11. ♖e1 ♘bd7 12. a4** [12. b3? ♘d5! 13. ed5 (13. ♘f5 ♗f8! 14. ed5 ♕f6–+) ♗f6–+; 12. ♘f5 ♗f8 13. ♗f4 ♘e5] **b4?!** [12... a6!? 13. b3 c4 14. bc4 bc4] **13. b3 ♗f8 14. ♗b2 a5 15. ♘d2 ♗a6 16. ♘f5 g6 17. ♘e3 ♗g7 18. ♕c2!?** [18. ♘ec4?! ♗c4 19. ♘c4 ♘b6 20. ♘d6 (20. ♘b6 ♕b6 21. e5?! ♘d7 22. e6 ♗b2 23. ed7 ♖e1 24. ♕e1 ♗a1 25. ♕e8 ♖e8 26. de8♕ ♔g7∓) ♕d6 21. e5 ♕d8 22. ef6 ♖e1 23. ♕e1 ♗f6 24. ♗f6 ♕f6∓] **♘b6 19. ♖ad1 ♘fd7 20. ♗g7 ♔g7 21. f4± ♕f6?!** [21... ♔g8; 21... ♖c8] **22. e5! de5 23. ♘e4 ♕d8** [23... ♕e7 24. d6 ♕d8 25. fe5 ♖e5 (25... ♘e5 26. ♕c5) 26. ♘g4 ♖f5 27. ♕b2 f6 28. ♘ef6 ♘f6 29. ♖e7+–] **24. f5 ♕c7?⊕** [24... f6 25. h4!→ (△ fg6, h5) ♖h8 26. ♘c5+–; 24... ♖c8 25. ♘d6 ♘f6 26. ♘c8 ♕c8 27. d6 e4 28. ♕b2+–; 24... ♖b8! (△ c4) 25. ♔h1! (25. ♗f1 c4 26. bc4 b3⇆) c4 26. ♘c4 ♗c4 27. bc4 b3 28. ♕b3 ♘d5 29. ♕f3±] **25. d6 ♕d8 26. f6 ♔g8** [26... ♘f6 27. ♘f6 ♕f6 28. ♗a8 ♖a8 29. ♕c5+–] **27. ♘g4 ♖c8** [27... h5 28. ♘h6 ♔f8 29. ♘g5+–] **28. ♕d2 ♔h8** [28... ♖e6 29. ♘h6 ♔f8 30. ♘f7 ♔f7 31. ♘g5 ♔f6 32. ♖f1+–] **29. ♕h6 ♖g8 30. ♘g5** **1 : 0**
[Ulybin, Lysenko]

88.* **A 61**

MI. CEJTLIN 2485 – SHAUGHNESSY
Hastings (open) 1992/93

1. d4 ♘f6 2. ♘f3 e6 3. c4 c5 4. d5 ed5 5. cd5 d6 6. ♘c3 g6 7. ♗g5 [RR 7. h3 a6 8. a4 ♕e7 9. g3!? N (9. ♘d2 – 52/87; 9. ♖a3!? △ e4 Co. Ionescu) ♗g7 10. ♗g2 ♘e4! 11. ♘e4 ♕e4 12. 0–0 0–0 13. ♘d2 ♕e7 14. ♘c4 ♘d7 15. ♗f4 ♘e5 16. ♘b6!? (16. ♘e5 ♗e5 17. ♗e5 ♕e5 18. ♕d2 ♗d7= Atalik) ♖b8 17. ♕d2 ♕c7!? 18. a5 ♗d7 19. ♖ac1 ♗b5 20. ♖fe1 ♘d7 21. ♘d7 ♕d7 22. ♗h6 ♗h6 23. ♕h6 f5 24. e4 ♖be8= Atalik 2510 – Co. Ionescu 2480, Mangalia 1992; 10. ♘d2!?⩲ Co. Ionescu, Atalik] **h6 8. ♗h4 g5 9. ♗g3 ♘h5 10. e3 ♘g3 11. hg3 ♗g7 12. ♗b5!? N** [12. ♕c2 – 48/(105)] **♗d7** [12... ♘d7] **13. a4 0–0 14. ♕d3!** [14. ♕c2] **f5 15. ♘d2 a6 16. ♗d7 ♘d7 17. f4⩲ ♕e7 18. a5 ♘f6 19. fg5! ♘g4!** [19... hg5? 20. ♕f5] **20. gh6 ♗h6 21. ♖a4! ♖f6** [21... ♘e3?

22. ♖h6 ♘g4 23. ♖e6+−; 21... ♗e3 22. ♖g4! *a)* 22... fg4? 23. ♕g6 ♕g7 24. ♕e6 ♖f7 (24... ♕f7 25. ♕g4+−) 25. ♕e3+−; *b)* 22... ♗g5 23. ♔d1 fg4 24. ♕g6 ♕g7 25. ♕e6 ♖f7 26. ♘de4±] **22. ♖g4! fg4 23. ♘ce4 ♖g6 24. ♘c4** [24. ♖h4!?] **♔g7 25. ♕c3 ♔g8 26. ♕d3 ♔g7 27. ♕c3 ♔g8 1/2 : 1/2** **[Mi. Cejtlin]**

89. **A 64**

MARIN 2515 – SAX 2570

Odorheiu Secuiesc 1993

1. d4 ♘f6 2. c4 e6 3. g3 c5 4. d5 ed5 5. cd5 d6 6. ♘c3 g6 7. ♘f3 ♗g7 8. ♗g2 0–0 9. 0–0 ♖e8 10. ♘d2 a6 11. a4 ♘bd7 12. ♘c4 [12. h3 ♘h5 13. ♔h2 f5 14. f4 (14. ♘c4?! – 40/105) ♘df6∞] **♘e5 13. ♘a3 ♘h5 14. ♖b1!? N** [14. e3?! – 29/139] **♗f5!?** [14... f5 15. b4 cb4 16. ♖b4 ♕a5 17. ♕b3±] **15. e4 ♗d7** [15... ♗g4 16. f3 ♗d7 17. g4 ♘f6 18. h3 (18. b4 ♘fg4 19. fg4 ♘g4 20. ♘e2 cb4 21. ♖b4 ♕a5 22. ♖c4 b5∞) c4 19. ♗e3±] **16. b4 cb4 17. ♖b4 ♕a5 18. ♘a2** [18. ♕b3? ♘d3∓; 18. ♖b3 ♖ac8 19. ♗d2 ♗a4∓] **b5 19. ♗e3! ♖ac8** [19... ba4?? 20. ♗b6; 19... ♕d8!? 20. ♗d4 a5! 21. ♖b5 ♗b5 22. ab5∓] **20. ♗d4 f5 21. f4** [21. ef5 ♗f5 22. ♗e5 ♗e5 23. g4 ♖c3! 24. gf5 ♖a3 25. fg6 hg6 26. ♕g4 ♖a2 27. ♕g6 ♘g7 28. ♖h4 ♖a4∓] **♘g4 22. h3 ♗d4 23. ♕d4 ♘g3 24. ♖e1 fe4** [24... ♘h6? 25. e5 △ e6±] **25. hg4 ♗g4 26. ♕f2 ♘f5 27. ♖be4 ♖e4 28. ♖e4 ba4∞ 29. ♘b4** [29. ♘c4 ♕b5 30. ♘c3 ♕b3] **♖c3?** [29... ♖c1 30. ♔h2 ♕d8 31. ♘c6 ♕f8 32. ♖e1 ♕h6 33. ♔g1 ♖e1 34. ♕e1 ♕f4∓] **30. ♘c6 ♖c1 31. ♔h2 ♕c3 32. ♘e7! ♘e7 33. ♖e7 ♕f6** [33... ♕a3?? 34. ♕a7+−] **34. ♖e4 g5! 35. ♔g3 ♗f5 36. ♖e3 ♕g6** [36... ♖c3] **37. fg5 ♕g5 38. ♔h2 ♕h5 39. ♗h3** [39. ♔g3 ♖c7 40. ♕f4; 39... ♕g5=] **♗h3 40. ♖h3 ♖h1 41. ♔h1 ♕h3 42. ♕h2 ♕a3** [42... ♕f1 43. ♕g1 ♕g1 44. ♔g1 ♔f7 45. ♘c4 ♔e7 46. ♔f2 ♔d8 47. ♔e3 ♔c7 48. ♔f4 a3 49. ♘a3 ♔b6 50. ♔f5 ♔c5 51. ♔e6 h5 52. ♘b1! h4 53. ♘c3 h3 54. ♘e4 ♔b4 55. ♔d6=] **43. ♕g3 1/2 : 1/2** **[Sax]**

90.** !N **A 65**

CO. IONESCU 2475 –
A. ARDELEANU 2355

Bucureşti 1993

1. d4 ♘f6 2. c4 g6 3. ♘c3 ♗g7 4. e4 d6 5. f3 0–0 6. ♗g5 c5 7. d5 e6 8. ♕d2 ed5 9. cd5 a6 10. a4 h6 [10... ♖e8 11. ♗e2 *a)* 11... ♘bd7 12. ♘h3 h6 13. ♗e3 ♘e5 N (13... ♔h7 – 34/117) 14. ♘f2 h5 15. 0–0 ♘h7 16. h3! f5 17. f4 (17. ef5 ♗f5 18. g4? ♗d3!∓) ♘f7 18. ef5 ♗f5 19. g4! hg4 20. hg4 ♘h6!? (20... ♗d7 21. g5± ×♘h7, ♘f7) 21. g5! (21. gf5?! ♘f5 22. ♘ce4 ♖e4! 23. ♘e4 ♘e3=∞; 21. ♖ae1 ♖e3! 22. ♕e3 ♘g4 23. ♗g4 ♗g4 24. ♕e7! ♗d4 25. ♔g2 ♗f5=∞⊞ Co. Ionescu 2480 – A. Ardeleanu 2335, România (ch) 1992) ♗h3!? (21... ♘f7 22. ♗d3±) 22. gh6 ♕h4 23. ♘ce4! ♘f6 24. ♗f3±; *b)* 11... ♕e7!? 12. ♗d1 ♘bd7 13. ♘ge2 ♘e5 14. b3 ♖b8∞; *c)* RR 11... ♕a5 12. ♖a3 ♘bd7 13. ♘h3 ♘e5! N (13... c4?! – 38/(99)) 14. ♘f2 ♕b4! 15. 0–0 (15. a5 ♗d7) ♘c4 16. ♗c4 ♕c4 17. ♕f4!? ♘h5! 18. ♕h4! (18. ♕d6 ♕b4 19. ♘d3 ♕d4 20. ♘f2 ♕b4=) h6! 19. ♗h6 (19. ♗e7 ♕b4!) ♗h6 20. g4 ♗e3! 21. gh5 ♔g7 22. hg6 fg6 23. ♕g3! ♖f8! 24. ♕d6 (24. ♘d1? ♗f4 25. ♕g2 ♖h8∓ Šiškin – Ju. Cimmerman 2410, Katowice 1993) ♗f4! 25. e5! ♖f5 26. ♘ce4 ♗e5 27. ♕c5 ♗h2! 28. ♔g2 ♕c5 29. ♘c5 ♖d5 30. ♔h2 ♖c5= Ju. Cimmerman] **11. ♗e3 ♘h7 12. ♗d3!? N** [12. ♘ge2 – 40/109] **♘d7 13. ♘h3 ♘e5 14. ♘f2 ♘d3** [14... f5! 15. ♗e2 g5 16. ef5 ♗f5=] **15. ♘d3 ♗d7 16. 0–0 h5 17. ♖ab1 b5 18. ab5 ab5?!** [18... ♗b5!=] **19. b4 c4** [⌓ 19... ♖a3 20. ♖fc1 c4] **20. ♘f4! ♖a3 21. ♘fe2 ♕c7 22. ♗d4! ♗d4 23. ♘d4± ♕b6 24. ♔h1 ♖fa8 25. f4 ♘f6 26. e5?** [26. f5! ♘g4 (26... ♔g7? 27. fg6 fg6 28. ♘e6! ♗e6 29. de6+−) 27. fg6 fg6 28. h3 ♘e5 29. ♘e6!→] **♖c3! 27. ♕c3 ♘d5** [28. ♕f3 ♕d4 29. ♖bd1 ♕b2! (29... ♗g4!? 30. ♕d5 ♕d5 31. ♖d5 de5±) 30. ♕d5 ♖a2 31. ed6 h4!=∞] **1/2 : 1/2** **[Co. Ionescu]**

91. **A 65**

YERMOLINSKY 2615 – SHERZER 2460
USA (ch) 1992

1. d4 ♘f6 2. c4 g6 3. ♘c3 ♗g7 4. e4 d6 5. h3 0–0 6. ♗g5 c5 7. d5 e6 8. ♗d3 ed5 9. cd5 h6 10. ♗e3 ♖e8 N [10... ♘a6 – 55/92] **11. ♘ge2 ♘bd7 12. ♘g3 a6 13. a4 ♘e5 14. ♗e2** [14. 0–0 ♘d3=] **♘h7! 15. 0–0 ♕h4↑ 16. ♘h1** [16. ♕e1 △ 16... f5 17. f4 ♘f7 18. ♗d3∞] **♘g5?!** [16... f5∓] **17. f4□ ♘h3** [17... ♗h3? 18. g3! ♘gf3□ 19. ♗f3 ♘f3 20. ♕f3 ♕e7 21. ♖fe1+–] **18. gh3 ♕h3 19. ♕d2** [19. ♗f3 ♘g4] **♘g4 20. ♗g4 ♕g4 21. ♕g2** [21. ♔f2?! ♗f6 22. ♘g3 ♗h4 23. ♖g1 f5→ Browne; 21... f5!?] **♕g2** [21... ♗c3 22. ♕g4 ♗g4 23. bc3 (23. ♘f2? ♗b2 24. ♘g4 ♖e4!–+) ♖e4 24. ♔f2 ♖ae8 25. ♖fe1∞] **22. ♔g2 ♗c3 23. bc3 ♖e4 24. ♔f2 b6!?** [24... ♖b8 25. a5 b5 26. ab6 ♖b6 27. ♖fb1 ♖b7! 28. ♘g3 ♖c4 29. ♗d2±] **25. ♘g3 ♖c4 26. ♖h1?** [26. ♖fb1 ♖b8 *a)* 27. ♖h1? ♔g7 (27... h5? 28. ♘h5 gh5 29. ♖h5 ♔g7 30. ♖g1 ♔f6 31. ♖g8±) 28. ♖ag1 ♗g4! 29. f5 h5∓; *b)* 27. ♖b3! ♗d7 28. a5 b5 29. ♘f1!±] **h5?** [26... ♔g7] **27. ♘h5! gh5 28. ♖h5 ♔g7** [28... ♗b7? 29. f5! ♔f8 (29... ♔g7 30. ♖h6!+–) 30. ♖e1!+– △ 31. f6, 31. ♗h6] **29. f5??⊕** [29. ♖g1 ♔f6 30. ♖h6 ♔e7 31. ♖e1! ♔d7 (31... ♖e4 32. ♗c5! ♖e1 33. ♗d6±) 32. ♖h7 ♔c7 33. ♖f7 ♗d7 34. ♖g1± △ ♖gg7, f5] **♔f6! 30. ♔e2?** [30. ♗g5? ♔e5 (30... ♔g7? 31. ♗e7+–; 30... ♔f5 31. ♗e7 ♔e4□ 32. ♖e1 ♔d3 33. ♖e3 ♔c2∓) 31. ♖e1 ♔d5 (31... ♖e4? 32. ♗f4!) 32. ♖d1 ♔e5 33. ♖e1 ♖e4! 34. ♗f4 ♔f4 35. ♖h4 ♔f5 36. ♖he4 ♗e6–+; 30. ♖h6 ♔e5 31. ♖e1! ♗f5! (31... ♖e4 32. ♔f3 ♗f5 33. ♗f4=) 32. ♗c5 ♔d5 33. ♗b4 ♗e6∓] **♗b7 31. ♔d3 ♖g4 32. c4 b5–+ 33. ♖e1** [33. ab5 ab5 34. ♖a8 bc4] **bc4 34. ♔c3 ♗d5 35. ♖h6 ♔f5 36. ♖d6 ♗e6 37. ♗c5 ♖b8 38. ♗b6 ♖g3 39. ♔c2 ♖h8 40. ♖e2 ♖hh3 41. a5 ♖c3 42. ♔b2 ♖b3 43. ♔c2 c3 44. ♖f2 ♔g5 45. ♖d1 ♖a3 46. ♖g1 ♔h5 47. ♖gf1 ♗b3 48. ♔b1 c2 49. ♔c1 ♖a1 50. ♔b2 ♖d1 0 : 1** **[Yermolinsky]**

92.* **A 65**

A. CHERNIN 2600 – A. SZNAPIK 2440
Budapest (zt) 1993

1. c4 ♘f6 2. ♘c3 g6 3. d4 ♗g7 4. e4 d6 5. h3 0–0 6. ♗g5 c5 7. d5 e6 8. ♗d3 ed5 9. cd5 h6 10. ♗e3 b5 N 11. ♘b5 [11. ♗b5 ♘e4 12. ♘e4 ♕a5 13. ♘c3 ♗c3 14. bc3 ♕b5 15. ♕e2=] **♖e8** [RR 11... ♘a6 12. ♘e2 ♖b8 13. 0–0± Gulko 2610 – Sherzer 2460, USA (ch) 1992] **12. ♘c3 ♘e4 13. ♘e4 f5 14. ♘e2!** [14. ♘c5 dc5 15. ♘e2⩲; 14... f4∞] **fe4 15. ♗c2 ♗a6** [15... ♕a5 16. ♗d2±; 15... ♗b2 16. ♖b1 ♕a5 17. ♗d2 ♕a2 18. ♗h6=∞] **16. 0–0 ♘d7 17. ♖e1!** [17. ♖b1 ♘e5 18. ♗e4 ♘c4] **♗b2** [17... ♘e5 18. ♘f4 ♘c4 19. ♘g6±→] **18. ♖b1 ♗g7** [18... ♗e2!?] **19. ♘f4 ♘f8□ 20. ♗d2 ♗d4** [20... ♗d3 21. ♘d3 ed3 22. ♗d3→; 20... c4 21. ♖e3! △ ♗c3, ♖g3, ♕g4] **21. ♗e4 ♕f6** [21... ♕h4 22. ♕f3 △ ♘e6±] **22. ♖b3!** [22. ♕g4 g5 23. h4 (23. ♕g3 ♗e5) ♗f2 (23... ♗c8 24. ♕h5) 24. ♔f2 ♕d4 25. ♔g3 ♖e4 26. hg5 h5 27. ♕h5 ♖ae8∞] **g5□**

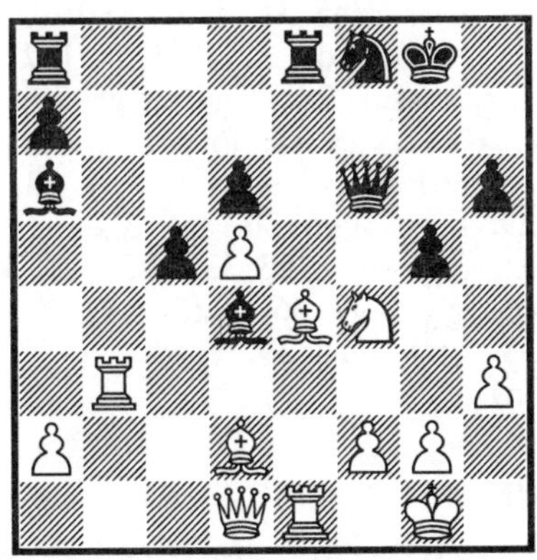

23. ♖f3! gf4 24. ♖f4 ♕e7⊕ [24... ♕e5! 25. ♕g4! ♔h8□ (25... ♕g7 26. ♕h4 △ 26... ♗c8 27. ♗h7) 26. ♖f5 ♕g7 (26... ♕e7 27. ♕h5 ♗c8 28. ♕h6 ♘h7 29. ♖h5) 27. ♕h5 ♘g6 (27... ♖e5 28. ♗h6 ♕h7 29. ♖f8 ♖f8 30. ♗g7) 28. ♗h6 ♕h7 29. ♖g5 ♘f4 30. ♗g7+–] **25. ♕h5! ♗g7 26. ♖g4 ♗c8** [26... ♕e5 27. ♗h7 ♔h7 (27... ♘h7 28. ♖e5 ♖e5 29. ♕h6 ♖e7 30. ♗c3+–) 28. ♖e5 ♖e5 29. ♕f7 ♖g5 30. ♗g5 hg5 31. ♖g5] **27. ♖g3 ♕f7** [27...

♔h8 28. ♗h6 ♗h6 29. ♕h6 ♘h7 30. ♗h7 ♕e1 31. ♔h2] **28. ♗h7 ♘h7 29. ♖e8 ♘f8 30. ♗c3 1 : 0 [A. Chernin]**

93. !N A 65

NIKITIN 2420 – HAUSRATH 2260

Dortmund (open) 1993

1. d4 ♘f6 2. c4 g6 3. ♘c3 ♗g7 4. e4 d6 5. ♗g5 0–0 6. ♕d2 c5 7. d5 e6 8. ♗d3 ed5 9. cd5 a6 10. a4 ♕a5 11. ♖a3 [11. ♘ge2 b5 12. 0–0 b4 13. ♘d1 c4∓] **♖e8** [11... ♘bd7 12. ♘f3 ♖e8 13. 0–0 c4 14. ♗c2 ♘c5 15. ♖e1 ♕b4∞] **12. ♘ge2 ♘bd7 13. ♘g3! N ♘e5 14. ♗e2± h5?!** [14... ♕b4!?] **15. f4 ♘ed7 16. 0–0 ♘h7 17. ♗h4± ♗h6 18. ♕c2 ♖b8 19. ♔h1 ♕c7 20. ♗h5! gh5 21. ♘h5 ♘df8 22. f5! f6! 23. ♘e2** [23. ♘f6 ♘f6 24. ♗f6 ♘d7 25. ♗h4 ♘e5 26. ♘e2 ♔f7 △ ♖g8∞] **♕f7 24. ♖g3 ♔h8 25. ♘ef4 ♗g5 26. e5!** [26. ♘g6 ♔g8! (26... ♘g6 27. fg6 ♕g6 28. ♘f6! ♕f6 29. ♖f6 ♗h4 30. ♖d6 ♗g3 31. hg3±) 27. ♗g5 fg5∞] **♗h4** [26... fe5 27. ♗g5 ef4 28. ♕c3! ♖e5 29. ♗f4 ♕f5 (29... ♘d7 30. ♖g7 ♕h5 31. ♖d7!+–) 30. ♗e5 ♕e5 31. ♕f3 ♗d7 32. ♕f7+–] **27. e6! ♕e7** [27... ♕c7 28. ♖g4! ♗g5 29. ♖g5! fg5 30. ♕c3 ♔g8 31. f6→ ♖e7 32. ♘g6! ♘g6 33. fe7 ♕e7 34. ♖f7+–] **28. ♖h3 ♗g5 29. ♘g6 ♘g6 30. fg6 ♗e6 31. de6 ♕e6 32. ♘g3+– ♕h3 33. gh3 ♘f8 34. h4 ♗h4 35. g7 ♔g7 36. ♘f5 ♔f7 37. ♘d6 ♔e7 38. ♘e8 ♖e8 39. ♕e4 1 : 0 [Nikitin]**

94.* !N A 67

J. IVANOV 2410 – PRIEHODA 2420

Orange 1992

1. d4 ♘f6 2. c4 e6 3. ♘c3 c5 4. d5 ed5 5. cd5 d6 6. e4 g6 7. f4 ♗g7 8. ♗b5 ♘fd7 [RR 8... ♘bd7?! 9. e5 de5 10. fe5 ♘h5 11. e6 ♕h4 12. g3 ♘g3 13. hg3 ♕h1 14. ♗e3 ♗c3 15. bc3 ♕e4 16. ♕f3 ♕f3 17. ♘f3 fe6 18. de6 0–0 19. ♗h6!! N (19. ed7?! – 44/(91)) *a)* 19... ♖f3 20. ♖d1! ♖c3 (20... ♖g3 21. ♗c4! ♔h8 22. e7+–; 20... ♖f5 21. ♗c4! ♖e5 22. ♔f2 ♔h8 23. ed7 ♗d7 24. ♖d7 ♖g8 25. ♗g7!+–; 20... ♘f8 21. e7 ♗d7 22. ef8♕ ♖af8 23. ♗c4 ♔h8 24. ♖d7+–) 21. ed7 ♗d7 22. ♖d7 a6 (22... c4 23. ♖g7! ♔h8 24. ♖b7+–) *a1)* 23. ♖g7? ♔h8 (O. Kalinin 2420 – Konev, corr. 1991/92) 24. ♖b7 ab5 25. ♗g7 ♔g8 26. ♗c3 b4 27. ♗e5±; *a2)* 23. ♗f1! ♖f8 (23... b5 24. ♗g2+–) 24. ♖g7 ♔h8 25. ♖b7+–; *b)* 19... ♖e8 20. 0-0-0 ♘f6 (20... ♖e6 21. ♗c4 ♘b6 22. ♘g5!+–) 21. ♗e8 ♗e6 22. ♗a4 ♗a2 23. ♘e5!± △ c4, ♖d6 O. Kalinin, Hnydiuk] **9. ♗e2 0–0 10. ♘f3 ♖e8 11. 0–0** [11. ♕c2!?; 11. ♘d2!?] **♘a6** [11... ♗c3? 12. bc3 ♖e4 13. ♘g5 ♖e8 14. f5⩱↑] **12. ♔h1! N** [12. ♘d2 ♘c7 – 55/93] **♘c7** [12... ♘b6!? △ c4, ♘c5] **13. a4 b6 14. f5!** [14. e5? de5 15. d6 ♘e6 16. fe5 ♗b7∓] **♗a6** [14... ♘e5? 15. ♗g5 f6 (15... ♕d7 16. f6) 16. ♘e5 ♖e5 (16... fg5 17. ♘c6+–; 16... de5 17. d6!±) 17. ♗f4 ♖e8 18. fg6 hg6 19. ♕e1 △ ♕g3±] **15. ♗a6 ♘a6 16. ♘g5** [16. ♗f4!?; 16. ♗g5!?; 16. ♖a3!?] **♗f6** [16... ♘e5 17. fg6 hg6 18. ♕e1 △ ♕h4±] **17. fg6** [17. ♕g4 ♘e5 18. ♕h4 h5] **hg6 18. ♕g4 ♖e5□ 19. h4** [19. ♘f3? ♖h5] **♘b4! 20. ♖f3!** [20. ♗f4 ♘d3 21. ♗e5 ♘7e5⩱] **c4 21. ♗d2!** [21. ♗e3 ♘c2] **♘d3 22. ♖af1** [△ ♖g3, h5±↑] **♖g5!□ 23. ♗g5 ♘3e5 24. ♕g3 ♗g5** [24... ♘f3? 25. ♕f3 ♔g7 26. h5! (26. e5 ♗g5 27. ♕f7 ♔h8 28. hg5 ♘e5±) ♗g5 27. ♕f7 ♔h8 28. hg6 ♕g8 (28... ♕e7 29. g7+–) 29. ♕d7 ♕g6 30. ♖f3±] **25. hg5 ♘f3 26. gf3!** [△ f4, e5, ♘e4 ×f6] **♕e7 27. f4 ♖e8** [27... f6!? 28. gf6 ♕f6±] **28. ♖e1?** [28. ♖f2! ♘c5 29. ♕h4+–] **♘c5** [28... f6!?] **29. ♖e2** [29. e5!? ♘d3 30. ♖e2 de5 31. fe5 ♘e5 32. ♘e4!+–; 29... ♕d7!?] **a6?** [29... f6□] **30. ♕h4!+– ♕f8 31. f5!** [△ f6] **♕g7 32. ♖h2 gf5 33. ef5 ♕e5 34. ♖e2 ♕e2 35. ♘e2 ♖e2 36. g6 fg6 37. fg6 1 : 0 [J. Ivanov]**

95. A 67

MOSKALENKO 2555 – MAGERRAMOV 2565

Rostov na Donu (open) 1993

1. d4 ♘f6 2. c4 e6 3. ♘c3 c5 4. d5 ed5 5. cd5 d6 6. e4 g6 7. f4 ♗g7 8. ♗b5

♘fd7 9. ♗e2 0–0 10. ♘f3 ♘a6 11. 0–0 ♘c7 12. a4 ♖e8 N [12... a6] **13. ♕c2** [13. ♗d2 ♗c3!? 14. ♗c3 ♘f6!∞] **♘f6** [13... a6 14. ♗d2!? ♖b8 15. ♗e1! b5 16. e5 de5 17. ♗h4↑] **14. ♗d2 ♗g4 15. ♖ae1 ♘a6** [15... a6 16. h3 ♗f3 17. ♗f3 b5 18. e5!±] **16. ♗c4 ♘b4 17. ♕b3 ♗f3 18. ♖f3 ♘g4 19. g3!± f5 20. h3 fe4 21. ♘e4 ♘h6 22. g4 ♘f7 23. ♔g2 ♗d4 24. ♗c3+– ♕h4 25. ♗d4! ♕e1 26. ♘f6 ♔h8 27. ♗c3 ♖e2 28. ♗e2 ♕e2 29. ♖f2 ♕e7** [29... ♕e3 30. g5 ♕d3 31. ♖d2 ♕f5 32. ♕c4] **30. ♕c4 1 : 0 [Moskalenko]**

96.* !N **A 70**

SAPIS 2420 – MORCHAT 2240

corr. 1992/93

1. d4 ♘f6 2. c4 c5 3. d5 e6 4. ♘c3 ed5 5. cd5 d6 6. e4 g6 7. ♘f3 ♗g7 8. h3 0–0 9. ♗d3 b5 10. ♘b5 ♖e8 11. ♘d2 [11. ♘c3 ♘e4 12. ♘e4 f5 13. ♗g5 ♕d7 14. ♘d2 fe4! N (Szczepaniak – Sapis 2420, corr. 1992/93; 14... ♗a6 – 55/(97)) 15. ♘e4 c4! 16. ♗c2 ♕f5 17. ♕e2 ♘d7⩱] **♘d5 12. ♘c4 ♘b4 13. ♗e2 N** [13. ♗b1 – 51/77] **♗a6 14. ♘bd6 ♖e6 15. ♗f4** [15. 0–0? ♖d6–+] **♘d7** [15... ♘8c6?? 16. a3+–; 15... ♗f8 16. e5 ♗d6 17. ♘d6 ♗e2 18. ♕e2 ♕d6 19. ed6 ♘d3 20. ♔d2 ♖e2 21. ♔d3!±] **16. 0–0 ♘e5 17. ♗e5 ♗e5 18. a3 ♗b2!?** [18... ♘c6? 19. ♘e5 ♖d6 20. ♘c6 ♖d1 21. ♘d8 ♖a1 22. ♖a1 ♗e2 23. ♘c6±; 18... ♖d6! 19. ♘d6 ♕d6 20. ab4 ♕d1 21. ♖fd1 ♗e2 22. ♖d2 ♗b5 23. bc5 a6=] **19. ♖b1** [19. ♘b2 ♖d6 20. ab4 ♖d1 21. ♖fd1 ♕f6 22. ♗a6 ♕b2 23. bc5 ♖e8 24. c6 ♖e7!=] **♘a2??** [19... ♗e5 20. ab4 ♗d6 21. b5 ♗c8□ (21... ♗b7 22. ♗g4 ♖e4 23. ♘d6 ♖d4 24. ♘b7) 22. e5 ♗c7 23. ♕d8 ♗d8 24. ♖fd1⩲] **20. ♖b2 ♘c3 21. ♕b3 ♘e2 22. ♖e2 ♖b8** [22... ♖d6 23. ♘d6 ♕d6 24. ♖d1+–] **23. ♕a2+– ♖d6 24. ♘d6 ♕d6** [24... ♗e2 25. ♕f7 ♔h8 26. ♕d5] **25. ♖d2 ♕f4 26. ♖fd1 ♕e4 27. ♖d8 ♖d8 28. ♖d8 ♔g7 29. ♕b2 ♔h6 30. ♕c1 ♔g7 31. ♕c5 1 : 0 [Sapis]**

97.** **A 70**

A. CHERNIN 2600 – MARIN 2515

Budapest (zt) 1993

1. d4 ♘f6 2. c4 c5 3. d5 d6 4. ♘c3 g6 5. e4 ♗g7 6. h3 0–0 7. ♗d3 e6 8. ♗g5 ed5 9. cd5 ♖e8 10. ♘f3 c4 [RR 10... h6 11. ♗e3 ♗d7!? 12. 0–0!? (12. a4 ♘a6 13. 0–0 ♘b4 14. ♗b1 b6 15. ♗f4 ♘h5∞) b5 13. ♘b5 ♘e4 14. ♘d2!? a6 15. ♘c3 (15. ♘a3 ♘f6 16. ♘ac4 ♗b5=) ♘c3 16. bc3 ♗c3! 17. ♗h6!? (17. ♘e4 ♖e4! 18. ♗e4 ♗a1 19. ♕a1 ♔h7∞) ♕h4 18. ♖c1 ♗d4 19. ♗e3 ♖e3! (19... ♗h3?! 20. ♗d4 ♕d4 21. ♘e4! ♗f5 22. ♖c4 ♕e5 23. g4!± J. Ivanov 2420 – Zontah 2455, Beograd 1993; 19... ♗e3!? 20. fe3 ♖e3∞) 20. fe3 ♗e3 21. ♔h2 ♗f4 22. ♔g1 ♗e3= J. Ivanov] **11. ♗c2 b5 12. a3 a5?! N** [12... ♘a6 – 56/89; 12... a6; 12... h6 13. ♗e3 ♘a6 △ b4; RR 12... ♗d7 N 13. 0–0 a5 14. ♘d4 ♕b6 (14... ♘a6 15. ♘db5 ♗b5 16. ♘b5 ♕b6 17. ♘c3 ♕b2 18. ♗d2!± Rogozenko 2480 – Marin 2515, Odorheiu Secuiecs 1993) 15. ♗e3 ♕b7 16. a4 ba4! (16... b4 17. ♘cb5 ♘e4 18. ♗e4 ♖e4 19. ♘d6 ♕d5 20. ♘4b5! ♕d1 21. ♖ad1±) 17. ♕d2 ♘a6 18. f3 ♘c5 △ ♘b3∞ Rogozenko] **13. ♘b5! ♕b6** [13... ♘e4 14. ♗d8 ♘c3 15. ♔f1 ♘d1 16. ♗h4 ♘b2 17. ♘c7+–; 13... h6 14. ♗f6 ♗f6 15. ♘c3±] **14. ♕d4!** [14. 0–0 ♕b5 15. ♗f6 ♗f6 16. ♗a4 ♕b2 17. ♖b1±; 14... ♘e4∞] **♕b5** [14... ♕d4 15. ♘fd4 ♘e4 16. ♗e3± △ ♘c7, 0-0-0] **15. ♗f6 ♗f6 16. ♕f6 ♘d7** [16... ♕d5 17. 0–0±] **17. ♕d4!** [17. ♕c3 ♘c5 (17... ♕d5 18. 0–0±) 18. ♘d2 ♖b8 19. ♖b1 ♘d3⩱] **c3□ 18. bc3** [18. ♗a4! (Marin) cb2 19. ♖b1! (19. ♗b5 ♖e4! 20. ♔d2 ♖d4 21. ♘d4 ba1♕ 22. ♖a1 ♘c5=) ♕a6 (19... ♕c5 20. ♕c5 dc5 21. e5±) 20. ♖b2 △ ♗b5±] **♕b2 19. ♔d2□ ♘c5□ 20. ♕c5! dc5** [20... ♖e4 21. ♕c7 ♗f5 22. ♖ae1 ♖ae8 (22... ♕c2 23. ♔c2 ♖e1 24. ♔d2 ♖h1 25. ♘g5 △ g4±) 23. ♖e4 ♖e4 24. ♖c1+–] **21. ♖hb1 ♖b8?** [21... ♕a1 22. ♖a1 ♗a6! 23. ♗d3! c4 24. ♗c2± f5?! 25. ef5 ♗b7 26. fg6 hg6 27. ♗g6±] **22. ♖b2 ♖b2 23. ♔c1 ♖b8 24. c4± ♗a6 25.**

♗d3 ♔g7 [25... ♖b3 26. ♔c2 ♖eb8 27. ♘d2 ♖b2 28. ♔c3] **26. ♔c2 f6 27. ♔c3 ♖e7 28. ♗c2 ♗c8 29. ♘d2 f5 30. ♘b3!**+– **fe4 31. ♘c5 e3 32. d6 ♖e8** [32... ♖e5 33. d7; 32... ♖f7 33. fe3] **33. d7** [33. ♗a4! ♖d8 34. d7 △ ♘e6 Marin] **♗d7 34. ♘d7 ef2 35. ♖f1□ ♖b7 36. ♘c5 ♖f7 37. ♘e4 ♖f4 38. ♔d4 ♖f7 39. c5 ♖d7 40. ♔c3 ♖de7 41. ♖f2! ♖e4 42. ♗e4 ♖e4 43. ♖c2 ♔f7 44. c6** [44... ♔e7 45. c7 ♔d7 46. c8♕ ♔c8 47. ♔d3] **1 : 0**
[A. Chernin]

98. !N **A 70**

EPIŠIN 2620 – IZETA 2505
Dos Hermanas 1993

1. d4 ♘f6 2. c4 e6 3. ♘f3 c5 4. d5 d6 5. ♘c3 ed5 6. cd5 g6 7. e4 ♗g7 8. h3 0–0 9. ♗d3 ♖e8 10. 0–0 ♗d7?! 11. ♖e1! N [11. ♗f4 – 56/88] **b5□ 12. a3** [12. ♘b5 ♘e4 13. ♘a3 ♘f6 14. ♖e8 ♗e8 15. ♘c4 ♘a6 △ ♘c7=] **c4** [12... b4? 13. ab4 cb4 14. ♘a2±; 12... ♘a6 13. a4 b4 14. ♘b5 △ ♘d2-c4±] **13. ♗c2 ♘a6 14. ♗e3 ♕c7 15. ♕d2?!** [15. ♗d4 ♘c5 16. e5 de5 17. ♗e5 ♕b6 18. ♕d4±] **♘c5 16. ♗d4 a5 17. e5** [17. ♕g5 ♘h5∞] **de5 18. ♗e5 ♕d8□** [18... ♕b6 19. ♕d4 (△ ♘e4) ♖a6 20. d6±] **19. ♕d4** [19. d6 *a)* 19... b4? 20. ♘d5 b3 21. ♘e7 ♔f8 (21... ♔h8 22. ♘g5+–) 22. ♗f6 ♗f6 23. ♕h6 ♗g7 24. ♕h7+–; *b)* 19... ♗c6! 20. ♘d4 ♕d7⇆] **♖c8□ 20. ♘e4! ♘ce4 21. ♗e4 c3?!** [21... ♘h5 22. d6±; 21... b4 22. ab4 ab4 23. ♖ac1! (23. ♖a6 ♘h5⇆) ♗b5 24. d6 ♘e4 25. ♖e4 ♗h6 26. ♖d1±] **22. ♗d3□ cb2 23. ♖ab1!** [23. ♕b2 ♖c5!=] **♖e5?**⊕ [23... ♘h5] **24. ♘e5 ♗e6 25. d6! ♘d5** [25... ♘d7 26. f4+–] **26. ♖b2 ♕d6 27. ♖b5 a4 28. g3 ♖d8** [⌓ 28... h5] **29. ♗c4 h5 30. ♖a5 ♔h7 31. ♗d5 ♗d5 32. ♖d1!**+– **♕c7** [32... ♗e5 33. ♕d5 ♗g3 34. ♕d6] **33. ♖d5 ♗e5 34. ♕e4 ♖d5 35. ♖d5 ♗g3 36. ♖h5 ♔g7 37. ♕d4 f6 38. ♖d5 ♕c1 39. ♔g2 ♗e5 40. ♖d7 ♔f8 41. ♖d8** [41... ♔g7 42. ♕d7 ♔h6 43. ♖h8 ♔g5 44. ♕g4#] **1 : 0** **[Epišin]**

99. !N** **A 70**

P. WELLS 2455 – TOCKIJ 2390
Harkány 1992

1. d4 ♘f6 2. c4 e6 3. ♘f3 c5 4. d5 ed5 5. cd5 d6 6. ♘c3 g6 7. h3 ♗g7 8. e4 0–0 9. ♗d3 ♖e8 10. 0–0 c4 11. ♗c4 ♘e4 12. ♘e4 ♖e4 13. ♗g5 ♗f6 14. ♗d3 [14. ♕c2 N ♖e8 15. ♗f6 ♕f6 16. ♖fe1 ♖d8 17. ♘d2 ♗f5 18. ♗d3 ♗d3 19. ♕d3 ♘d7 20. b4 a5! (20... ♖e8? 21. ♘e4 ♕f4 22. ♕d4 ♕e5 23. ♕e5 ♖e5 24. ♘d6 ♖d5 25. ♘b7± Ionov 2510 – Tockij 2390, Rossija (ch) 1992) 21. ♘e4 ♕f4 22. ♕b5 ab4 23. ♕b7 ♖ab8 24. ♕c7 ♘f6=] **♖e8 15. ♕a4! N** [15. ♕d2 – 52/(95)] **♗g5** [15... ♘d7 16. ♕h4 *a)* 16... a6 17. ♖fe1 ♖e1 18. ♖e1 b5 19. ♖e4 ♗b7 20. ♖f4 ♔g7 21. ♕h6 ♔g8 22. ♖f6 ♘f6 23. ♘d4! ♕f8 (23... ♕e7? 24. ♘f5 ♕e1 25. ♗f1 ♘h5 26. ♘e7 ♔h8 27. g4 f6 28. ♘g6 ♔g8 29. ♗e3+–) 24. ♕f8 ♔f8 25. ♗f6 ♗d5 26. b3 ♖c8 27. ♘e2±; *b)* RR 16... ♗g5 17. ♘g5 *b1)* 17... ♘f6 18. f4! ♔g7 19. f5 h6 20. ♘f7! (20. ♘f3 ♖e3 21. ♖ad1± Ravelo Gil 2325 – Riverón, La Habana 1993) ♔f7 21. ♕h6 g5 (21... gf5 22. ♗f5 ♗f5 23. ♖f5 ♖h8 24. ♕f4 ♖g8 25. ♖f1 ♖g6 26. h4 ♕h8 27. ♕d6+–) 22. ♕g6 ♔f8 23. ♖ae1! ♖e5 24. ♖e5 de5 25. d6! ♕d6 (25... b5 26. ♗c2 a5 27. ♗b3 ♖a7 28. ♕h6 ♖g7 29. ♕h8 ♘g8 30. f6+–) 26. ♗c4! ♕e7 (26... ♕c5 27. ♔h2 ♕c4 28. ♕f6 ♕f7 29. ♕h8 ♕g8 30. ♕e5+–) 27. ♖d1 ♗d7 28. ♖d6!+–; *b2)* 17... ♘f8 18. f4! f6 (18... ♖e3 19. f5 ♖d3 20. fg6 fg6 21. ♖f8 ♔f8 22. ♕h6+–; 18... ♗f5 19. ♗f5 gf5 20. ♖f3 ♕f6 21. ♖g3 ♔h8 22. ♕h6! ♕g6 23. ♕g6 fg6 24. ♘f7 ♔g8 25. ♘d6 ♖ed8 26. ♘f5+–) 19. ♘e4 ♔g7 20. f5! ♗f5 21. ♖f5! gf5 22. ♕g3 ♔h8 23. ♘d6 ♖e7 24. ♘f5 ♖f7 25. d6± Ravelo Gil, Becerra] **16. ♘g5 ♖e5 17. f4 ♖d5 18. ♖ae1** [18. ♗c4? b5 19. ♗d5 ba4 20. ♗a8 ♘c6∓; 18. ♕b3!? ♕b6□ (18... ♖g5? 19. fg5 ♗e6 20. ♗c4! d5 21. ♖ad1+–) 19. ♕b6 ab6 20. ♗c4 ♖c5 21. ♗f7 ♔g7 22. ♗b3 d5 23. ♖fe1! ♘c6 24. ♖e8 h6 25. ♘f3±] **♘c6 19. ♕b3 ♖g5 20. fg5 ♗e6**

21. ♕b7 [21. ♖e6?! fe6 22. ♕e6 ♔h8 23. ♖f7 ♕g5 24. ♕d6 ♖d8 25. ♖f8 ♔g7=] **♘e5 22. ♗e4 ♖b8 23. ♕a7 ♖b2 24. ♕d4?!** [24. ♖f2!? ♖f2 25. ♕f2 ♕g5 26. a4! d5 27. ♗c2 ♗h3 28. ♖e5 ♕e5 29. gh3±] **♘c4 25. ♖f6 ♖d2?** [25... ♕a5! (△ ♖d2) 26. ♖b1 ♖b1 27. ♗b1 ♕g5$\overline{\overline{\infty}}$] **26. ♕a7 ♘e5**

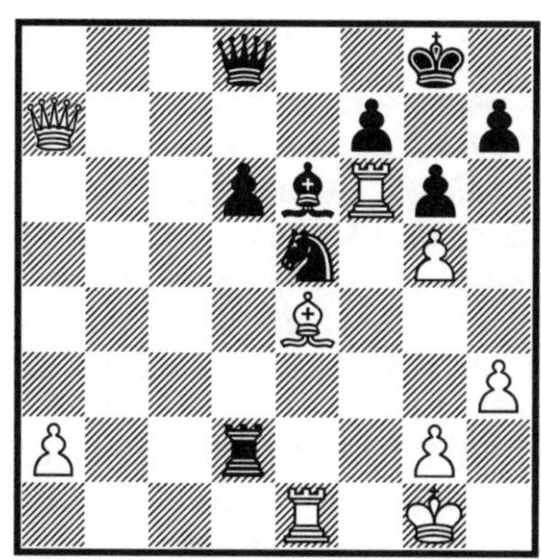

27. ♖e6!+– fe6 28. ♖b1 ♘d7 29. ♗c6 ♘f8 30. ♖f1! ♔h8 31. ♕f7 ♖c2 32. ♗e8 1 : 0 **[Tockij]**

100. !N **A 70**

KRASENKOV 2560 – KÁROLY HONFI 2350

Passau 1993

1. d4 ♘f6 2. c4 g6 3. ♘c3 ♗g7 4. e4 d6 5. ♘f3 0–0 6. h3 c5 7. d5 e6 8. ♗d3 ed5 9. cd5 ♖e8 10. 0–0 c4 11. ♗c2 ♗d7 12. ♗f4 ♕b6 13. ♖b1 ♘a6 14. a3! N [14. e5 – 56/88] **♘c5 15. ♖e1 ♖ac8?!** [15... ♖e7!? △ ♖ae8] **16. ♕d2 a5?! 17. e5! de5 18. ♘e5± ♘b3?!** [18... ♕a6 19. ♘d7 △ a4±] **19. ♗b3 ♕b3** [19... cb3!?] **20. ♘d7 ♘d7 21. d6! ♖e6** [21... ♖e1 22. ♖e1 ♗c3 23. bc3 ♕a3 24. ♖e7+–] **22. ♘d5 ♖c5 23. ♘c7! ♖e1 24. ♖e1 ♗e5?!** [24... ♕b2? 25. ♖e8+–; 24... c3? 25. bc3 ♕c3 26. ♖e8 ♗f8 27. ♕c3 ♖c3 28. ♖d8+–; 24... h5±] **25. ♗e5 ♖e5 26. ♖e5 ♘e5 27. d7 ♘d7 28. ♕d7 ♕b2 29. ♕d8 ♔g7 30. ♘e8 ♔f8 31. ♘f6 ♔g7 32. ♕g8 ♔h6 33. ♘g4 ♔g5 34. g3 ♕d4 35. ♕f7 1 : 0** **[Krasenkov]**

101.* **A 70**

BROWNE 2525 – DE FIRMIAN 2560

Reno 1993

1. d4 ♘f6 2. c4 e6 3. ♘f3 c5 4. d5 ed5 5. cd5 d6 6. ♘c3 g6 7. e4 ♗g7 8. h3 0–0 9. ♗d3 a6 10. a4 [RR 10. 0–0 b5 11. ♗f4 ♖e8 12. ♖e1 ♖a7 N (12... ♕b6 – 47/(121)) 13. a3 ♖ae7 14. ♕c2 ♘h5 15. ♗g5 ♗f6 16. ♗f6 ♘f6 17. b4 ♘bd7 18. ♕d2 ♔g7 19. ♖ac1 ♕b6 20. ♕b2 ♔g8 21. ♗b1 ♗b7 22. ♕d2 ♔g7= I. Ibragimov 2540 – Pigusov 2575, Sankt-Peterburg (zt) 1993] **♘bd7 11. 0–0 ♕e7 12. ♖e1 h6?! 13. ♗f4 ♘h7** [13... ♘h5 14. ♗h2 ♘e5 (14... g5? 15. e5! de5 16. d6 ♕e6 17. ♘g5 hg5 18. ♕h5+–) 15. ♗e2 ♘f6 (15... ♘f3? 16. ♗f3±) 16. ♘e5±; 13... g5!? 14. ♗h2! (14. ♗g3 ♘h5 15. ♗h2 ♘f4∞) g4 15. hg4 (15. ♘h4!? ♘e5 16. hg4±) ♘g4 16. ♗g3 ♘de5 17. ♗e2 (17. ♘e5? ♗e5 18. ♗e5 ♕e5 19. g3 ♕h5∞) f5 18. ef5 ♗f5 19. ♘h4!±] **14. ♕d2 g5 15. ♗g3 ♖d8 N** [15... ♘e5 16. ♗e2 (16. ♘e5 – 49/106) *a)* 16... f5 17. ef5 ♖f5 (17... ♗f5 18. ♘e5 ♗e5 19. ♗c4 ♔h8 20. ♗e5 de5 21. d6 ♕e8 22. ♕d5+–) 18. ♘e5 ♗e5 19. ♗d3±; *b)* 16... ♘f3 17. ♗f3 ♗e5 18. ♗e5 ♕e5 19. ♖a3!?±] **16. a5** [16. ♖ad1?! ♘hf8 17. e5 ♘e5 18. ♘e5 de5 19. d6±; 16... ♘e5!; 16. e5!? ♘e5 (16... de5 17. d6!) 17. ♘e5 de5 18. ♖ad1] **♘hf8 17. ♘a4 ♘g6 18. ♖a3! ♘de5 19. ♘e5 ♗e5** [19... ♘e5 20. ♘b6 ♖b8 (20... ♘d3? 21. ♖d3 ♖b8 22. e5 de5 23. d6 △ d7+–) 21. b4±] **20. ♗e5 ♕e5 21. ♘b6 ♖b8 22. b4** [22. ♘c4!? ♕e7 (22... ♕d4?! 23. ♕c3! ♕c3 24. bc3 △ 24... ♔f8 25. ♖b3 ♔e7 26. ♖eb1±) 23. ♖b3 ♗d7 24. e5 ♘e5 25. ♘e5 de5 26. ♖b6 ♔g7 27. ♕c3 f6 28. d6 ♕f7 29. ♗e4!±] **cb4 23. ♕b4 ♕f6 24. ♕c3** [24. ♖c3 ♗d7 25. ♖c7 ♗c8±] **♕e7 25. ♗f1** [25. ♗b1!? △ 25... ♔h7 26. e5!; 25. ♕d4 ♗d7 (25... f5 26. ♖c3 f4 27. ♖ec1 ♗d7 28. ♖c7±) 26. ♖c3 ♗c8 27. ♖ec1 ♘f4 28. ♗f1±] **♗d7 26. ♖aa1** [26. ♖c1 ♘e5 27. ♕c7? ♖bc8 28. ♘c8 ♖c8 29. ♕c8 ♗c8 30. ♖c8 ♔g7 31. ♖b3 ♕d7! 32. ♖b8 ♕a4 33. ♖8b7 ♕e4 34. ♗a6 ♕e1∓; 26. ♕a1

h5!? 27. ♖c3 ♗e8 28. ♕c1±] **♘e5 27. ♖ac1 ♕f6 28. ♕g3 ♗e8** [28... h5 29. h4 g4 30. f4 ♘g6 31. ♖c7 ♗e8 32. e5! de5 (32... ♕f4 33. ♕f4 ♘f4 34. e6 fe6 35. de6 ♗b5 36. ♗b5 ab5 37. e7 ♖e8 38. ♖e4 ♘g6 39. ♘d7+−) 33. fe5 ♕h4 34. ♕h4 ♘h4 35. d6 ♗b5 36. ♗b5 ab5 37. e6 fe6 38. ♖e6 ♖e8 39. ♖e8 ♖e8 40. ♖c8 ♔f7 41. d7+−] **29. ♖c7** [29. h4!?] **♔g7 30. ♖ec1 ♗d7 31. ♘c4** [31. ♗e2!? ♗e8 (31... ♕f4 32. ♕f4 gf4 33. ♗h5!±) 32. h4±] **♘c4** [31... ♗e8? 32. ♘e5 ♕e5 33. ♕e5 de5 34. ♖b1 ♖d7 35. ♖d7 ♗d7 36. ♗a6+−; 31... ♗b5? 32. ♘e5 ♕e5 (32... ♗f1 33. ♘g4+−) 33. ♕e5 de5 34. ♗b5+−] **32. ♗c4** [32. ♖1c4 ♗b5 33. ♖c3 ♗f1 34. ♖f3 (34. ♔f1? ♕d4!) ♕a1 35. ♖ff7 ♔g8 36. ♖g7 ♕g7 37. ♖g7 ♔g7 38. ♔f1±] **♗e8** [32... b5?! 33. ab6 ♖b6 34. ♕e3 ♕b2 35. ♖a7 (35. ♗d3?! ♖b3 36. ♖b1? ♕b1!) ♗b5 36. ♗b5 ♖b5! (36... ♕b5 37. ♖cc7 ♖f8 38. ♕f3+−) 37. ♖cc7 ♖f8 38. ♖a6 ♖b3 39. ♕e1±] **33. ♕e3 ♖dc8 34. ♕b6** [34. ♗f1 ♖c7 35. ♖c7 ♕a1 36. ♕a7 ♖d8 △ 37. ♕b6? ♗b5−+] **♖c7 35. ♕c7 ♕d8!⊕ 36. ♕d8 ♖d8** [♖ 9/k] **37. ♖b1 ♖d7?!** [37... ♖c8 38. ♗f1 ♖c5! 39. ♖b7 ♖a5 40. g3! ♔f6 (40... ♗b5!?) 41. f4 gf4 42. gf4 ♖a4 43. ♗g2 ♗b5 44. ♖b6 ♔e7 45. ♔h2 ♗d3 46. e5 ♖f4=] **38. g3 ♔f6 39. f4 gf4 40. gf4 ♖c7 41. ♗f1! ♔e7?** [41... ♗b5! 42. ♗b5 ab5 43. ♖b5 ♖c4 44. ♖b7 ♖e4 45. ♖d7 ♖f4 46. ♖d6 ♔e5 47. ♖h6 ♔d5±] **42. ♖b6** [42. ♔f2 ♗d7! 43. ♔e3 ♗c8! (43... ♗h3? 44. ♗h3 ♖c3 45. ♔d4 ♖h3 46. ♖b7 ♔e8 47. ♖b6+−) 44. ♔d4 ♖c5 (44... ♖c2 45. ♗d3 ♖a2±) 45. e5 ♖a5 46. ed6 ♔d6 47. ♖b6±] **f6** [42... ♖c5 43. ♖b7 ♗d7 44. h4 f5 (44... ♔d8 45. ♖b6+−) 45. ef5 ♖d5 46. f6 ♔d8 47. f7 ♖f5 48. ♖d7 ♔d7 49. ♗h3+−] **43. e5 fe5 44. fe5 ♖c5 45. ♖b7 ♔f8?** [45... ♔d8! 46. ed6 (46. ♖b8 ♔d7 47. e6?! ♔e7 48. ♖b7 ♔f6 49. ♖b6 ♖a5 50. ♖d6 ♔e7=) ♖a5 47. ♖b8?! ♔d7 48. ♖b6 ♖d5 49. ♗a6 ♖d1 50. ♔f2 ♔e6 51. ♗c4 ♔e5=; 47. ♖b6±] **46. ed6 ♖d5 47. ♗a6 ♖d6** [47... ♖a5 48. ♖b8! ♖d5 49. ♖d8! ♖d1 50. ♔f2 ♔f7 51. ♗c4 ♔f8 52. ♗b5+−] **48. ♗f1!+− ♗c6 49. ♖c7 ♖g6 50. ♔f2 ♖f6 51. ♔e1 ♖e6⊕ 52. ♔d2 ♗h1 53. a6 ♔e8 54. a7 ♔d8 55. ♖h7 ♖d6 56. ♔e3 ♔c8 57. ♗d3 ♖e6 58. ♔f4 ♖d6 59. ♗f5 ♔d8 60. ♗e4 1 : 0 [Browne]**

102. !N **A 75**

EHLVEST 2625 – MINASIAN 2545
New York 1993

1. d4 ♘f6 2. ♘f3 c5 3. d5 g6 4. c4 d6 5. ♘c3 ♗g7 6. e4 0–0 7. ♗e2 e6 8. 0–0 ed5 9. cd5 a6 10. a4 ♗g4 11. ♗f4 ♗f3 12. ♗f3 ♕e7 13. ♖e1 ♘bd7 14. a5 ♘e8 15. ♘a4! N [15. ♕d2 – 38/121, 122] **♘c7 16. ♗g4!** [×b6] **♘e5 17. ♘b6 ♖ad8 18. ♗h3 ♘a8** [18... ♘b5 19. ♗d2! △ f4±] **19. ♗e5! ♗e5 20. ♘c4± ♗d4 21. ♕d2?** [21. g3!±] **♕h4!=** [×♗h3] **22. ♖e2 ♖fe8 23. ♖ae1?!** [23. ♕e1 △ ♔h1, f3±] **♘c7 24. ♔h1 ♗g7⇆ 25. f3 ♘b5 26. ♖b1 ♘d4 27. ♖f2□** [27. ♕e1 ♘f3!∓] **♗h6 28. ♕e1⊕ f5 29. ♖f1 ♕h5** [29... ♕e1 30. ♖fe1 ♘c2=] **30. ♕f2 fe4 31. fe4 ♖f8 32. ♕e1 ♖f1 33. ♕f1 ♖f8 34. ♕d3 ♕h4 35. b4!?** [35. ♗e6!? △ ♖f1±] **♕f2 36. bc5 ♘e2 37. g3□ ♖f3?⊕** [37... ♗c1! 38. ♖c1 ♘c1 39. ♗e6 ♔g7 40. ♕c3 ♖f6 41. ♕c1 ♕f3]

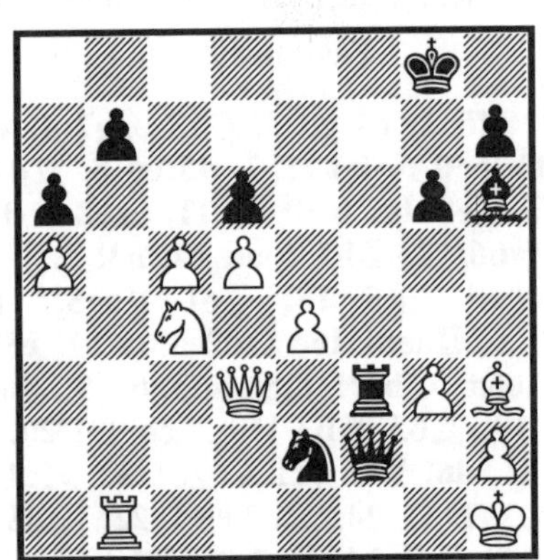

38. ♖f1!□ ♖g3 [38... ♕f1 39. ♗f1 ♖d3 40. ♗e2 ♖b3□ 41. cd6±⊥] **39. ♕d1□** [⇗d1-h5] **♕c5** [39... ♖g1 40. ♖g1 ♕f3 41. ♗g2 ♘g3 42. hg3 ♕h5 43. ♕h5+−] **40. ♗e6 ♔h8 41. ♕e2+− ♖c3 42. ♘b6 ♕d4 43. ♖d1 ♖c1 44. ♖c1 ♗c1 45. ♔g2 ♗e3 46. ♕f3 ♕d2 47. ♔h3?** [47. ♔g3+−] **♗f4**

48. ♕g2 ♕e3 49. ♔h4 ♔g7?⊕ [49... ♗e5!−+] **50. ♘c4+− ♕e1 51. ♔g4 ♗c1 52. ♕f3 1 : 0** **[Ehlvest]**

103. A 80

SEIRAWAN 2605 – D. GUREVICH 2490

USA (ch) 1992

1. d4 f5 2. ♗g5 h6!? 3. ♗h4 g5 4. e3 [4. ♗g3 f4? 5. e3 e5!?±] **♘f6 5. ♗g3 d6! 6. h4!?** [6. c4 ♗g7 7. ♘c3 0–0 8. ♗d3 ♘c6 △ e5∞] **g4 N** [6... ♖g8 – 55/101] **7. h5** [×f4, g6] **♗e6! 8. ♘e2** [8. ♗d3? ♕d7! △ ♗f7] **♗f7 9. ♘f4 ♘c6 10. ♗b5** [10. d5? ♘e5 11. c4 c6 12. ♘c3 ♗g7∓] **a6!?** [10... ♗g7!? 11. ♕d3 e6 12. ♕b3 ♕d7 13. c4!?∞] **11. ♗a4 ♗g7 12. ♗b3 d5! 13. ♘c3?!** [13. ♘d2 ♘a5 14. c3 ♘b3 15. ♕b3 b5!? 16. a4 c6 △ 0–0, ♕e8∞] **e6 14. ♕d2?!** [14. f3 △ ♕d3, 0-0-0, e4] **♕d7** [△ 0-0-0] **15. f3** [⌓ 15. 0-0-0] **♖g8! 16. 0-0-0 ♗h8 17. ♗h4 ♕d6!?** [17... ♘h5? 18. e4↑; 17... 0-0-0 18. ♘d3±] **18. ♘d3** [18. e4 ♘d4!] **gf3** [18... 0-0-0 19. f4 △ ♘e5±] **19. gf3 0-0-0 20. f4 ♖df8 21. ♗f6 ♗f6 22. ♘e5 ♗e5??** [22... ♗e8 △ ♗d8∓] **23. fe5±** [×f4] **♕e7 24. ♘e2 ♖g2?** [24... ♖g4! 25. ♘f4 ♖fg8 △ ♖8g5±] **25. ♕e1 ♕g5?!** [25... ♖fg8□] **26. ♘f4 ♖g3 27. c4!±** [×e6] **dc4 28. ♗c4 ♖e8 29. ♔b1 ♔b8 30. ♕c3** [30. ♖g1! ♖g1 31. ♕g1 △ ♕h1, ♖d1-g1+−] **♘d8□ 31. ♖c1 ♖e7!** [△ ♗e8-c6] **32. a3**⊕ [△ 32... ♗e8 33. ♕b3 ×a6, e6] **♖d7**⊕ [32... ♕g8! △ ♗e8] **33. ♗b3 ♕g4?** [33... ♕e7; 33... ♕g8] **34. ♗a4! c6** [34... ♖e7 35. ♕b4 ♕g5 36. ♖c3↑] **35. ♗d1 ♕g5?! 36. ♗e2?** [36. ♖h2 △ b4, ♖b2+−] **♗e8 37. ♔a2** [△ ♕b3, ♖c3; 37. ♕b3? ♕f4] **♖g7 38. ♕b3 ♔a7 39. ♗c4?** [39. ♖c3] **♗d7 40. ♖c3! ♕e7 41. ♘g6 ♕e8 42. ♕b4!± ♘f7 43. ♖b3 b5 44. ♗e2 ♘g5 45. ♕e1! ♘e4 46. ♗d3 ♖g4 47. ♗e4 ♖e4 48. ♕b4+− ♕d8 49. ♖c1 ♔b7 50. ♖bc3 ♖f7 51. ♘f4** [×♖e4] **♔b8 52. ♕d6 ♕c7 53. ♕c7 ♔c7 54. ♖g1 ♖e7 55. ♖g6 ♗e8 56. ♖h6 ♔d7 57. b4 ♖g7 58. ♔b2 ♗f7 59. ♖f6 ♖f4 60. ef4 ♗h5 61. ♖h3 ♗e2 62. ♖fh6 1 : 0** **[Seirawan]**

104.* A 80

SKEMBRIS 2560 – TISDALL 2425

Gausdal 1993

1. d4 f5 2. ♗g5 g6 3. c3!? [3. ♘c3 ♗g7 4. e4 fe4 5. ♘e4 d5 6. ♘c5 b6!? 7. ♘b3 ♘f6 8. ♗b5 N (8. ♘f3 – 51/81) c6 9. ♗e2 ♘e4 10. ♗h4 0–0 11. ♘f3 c5 12. c3 ♘c6 13. 0–0 ♕d6∞⇆ S. Guliev 2470 – Glek 2520, Staré Město 1992] **♗g7** [3... ♘h6!? △ ♘f7 Jansa] **4. h4 N** [4. ♘d2; 4. ♕d3!?] **h6** [4... c6!?] **5. ♗c1** [△ ♕d3-g3 ×g6] **♘c6! 6. e4!?∞** [6. ♕d3 e5→] **fe4!** [6... d6?! 7. ef5 ♗f5 8. g4!± ×g6] **7. ♕g4** [7. f3!?] **d5! 8. ♕g6 ♔f8** [△ 9... ♕d6, 9... e5] **9. f3!?** [9. ♘e2 e5∓; 9. ♗f4 e5⇆] **♕d6?!** [9... e5!∞] **10. ♕d6□ cd6** [10... ed6 11. ♗f4 △ ♘d2±] **11. fe4 de4 12. ♘h3** [12. ♘e2!?] **e5!? 13. de5 ♘e5** [13... de5 14. ♘f2±; 13... ♗h3!?] **14. ♘f4 ♘f6 15. ♘a3!± ♗f5 16. ♘c4** [16. ♘b5 ♔e7 17. ♘d4±] **♔e7 17. ♗e3?** [△ 0-0-0; 17. ♘e3!?± Tisdall] **♖hc8⇆ 18. ♘e5 de5 19. ♘e2 ♘d5 20. ♗c1 e3!?** [20... ♘f4 21. ♘f4 ef4 22. ♗f4 ♖c3 23. ♗h6!] **21. ♘g3 ♗h7 22. ♔e2?!** [22. ♗e2 ♘f4 23. ♗f3!? Tisdall] **e4!∓ 23. ♘h5** [23. ♗e3? ♗c3! 24. ♗h6 (24. bc3 ♘e3 25. ♔e3 ♖c3−+ ×♘g3) ♗b2∓] **♗e5 24. ♗e3 ♗g6?**⊕ [24... ♗f5 25. ♔d2=∞; 24... ♘e3 25. ♔e3 ♖f8! 26. ♗e2 ♗c7!∓ ×♔e3, ♙e] **25. g4 ♘e3 26. ♔e3 ♖f8 27. ♗g2!±** [27. ♗e2? ♗c7∓] **♗c7 28. ♖hf1 ♗b6 29. ♔e2** [△ ♘f4±] **♗h5 30. gh5 e3! 31. ♗f3!** [31. ♗b7?! ♖ad8!→ ×d2, f2] **♖f4?!** [31... ♖ad8! 32. ♖ad1±] **32. ♗b7± ♖af8 33. ♖f4 ♖f4 34. ♗f3 ♖h4 35. ♖h1 ♖f4?!** [35... ♖h1±] **36. b4!** [×♗b6] **♔d8 37. ♖g1 ♖h4 38. ♖g6 ♖h2 39. ♖g2 ♖h4?**⊕ [39... ♖g2□] **40. ♔d3+−** [△ a3, c4-c5, ♖g6 ×e3, h6] **1 : 0** **[Skembris]**

105. A 81

SMYSLOV 2530 – OLLS 2585

Rostov na Donu 1993

1. d4 f5 2. g3 ♘f6 3. ♗g2 g6 4. ♘h3 ♗g7 5. ♘f4 c6 6. h4 [△ h5] **d6 N** [6... 0–0 – 56/(97)] **7. ♘c3 e5** [7... ♕a5 8. ♗d2 ♕b6 9. d5 ♕b2 10. ♖b1 ♕a3 11.

dc6 bc6 12. ♘b5!] **8. de5 de5 9. ♕d8 ♔d8 10. ♘d3 ♘bd7** [10... e4 11. ♘f4 ♔e7 12. f3 ef3 13. ef3±] **11. e4!± ♖e8 12. ♗g5 h6 13. ♗d2 ♘b6 14. 0-0-0 ♔c7** [14... ♘c4 15. ♘e5 ♘e5 16. ♗h6] **15. b3 fe4 16. ♘e4 ♘e4 17. ♗e4 ♗f5 18. ♖de1 ♖ad8 19. ♗c3 ♘d7 20. ♖e2 ♖e7 21. h5 ♗e4 22. ♖e4 gh5** [22... g5 23. f4 gf4 24. gf4 ♖de8 25. ♖he1 ♔d6 26. fe5 ♗e5 27. ♘e5 ♘e5 28. ♗d2 ♖e6 29. ♗f4+−] **23. ♖h5 ♖de8 24. ♖h1 ♗f6 25. ♔d1 ♗g5 26. ♔e2 ♔d6 27. ♖d1 ♔e6** [⌓ 27... ♔c7] **28. f4 ♔f5** [28... ♗f6 29. fe5 ♔f5 30. ♖f1 ♔g6 (30... ♔e4 31. ef6 ♖f7 32. ♘b4 △ ♖f4#) 31. ♖f3 ♗e5 32. ♘e5 ♘e5 33. ♖fe3 ♔f5 34. g4+−]

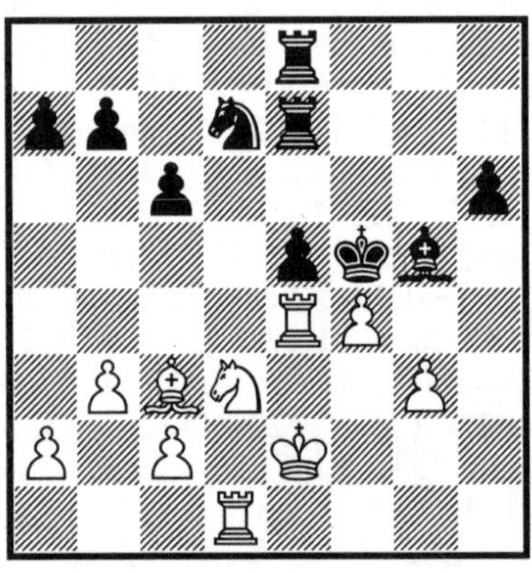

29. g4! ♔e4 30. ♘f2 ♔f4 31. ♖g1! [31... e4 32. ♘h3#; 31. ♗d2 ♔g3 32. ♖g1 ♔h4!=] **1 : 0** **[Smyslov]**

106. A 81

LAUTIER 2645 – BAREEV 2670
München 1993

1. ♘f3 f5 2. d4 ♘f6 3. g3 g6 4. ♗g2 ♗g7 5. 0–0 0–0 6. b3 d6 7. ♗b2 ♘g4 N [7... ♕e8 – 53/93] **8. ♘bd2 ♘c6 9. ♘c4 d5 10. ♘cd2 e5** [10... b6 11. c4 e6∞] **11. h3 e4 12. hg4 ef3 13. ♘f3 fg4 14. ♘e5± ♘e5 15. de5 c6 16. f4 gf3 17. ef3 g5** [17... h5 △ ♗f5±] **18. ♕d2!** [18. f4 gf4 19. gf4 ♕h4∞] **♗e6 19. ♖ae1 ♖f7** [19... ♕e7±] **20. ♗a3!** [20. ♗c1 h6 21. f4±] **h5?!** [20... ♔h8!?] **21. ♕d3** [21. ♗c1 g4 22. fg4 ♖f1 23. ♗f1±] **h4** [21... ♗f5 22. ♕e3±] **22. ♕g6?!** [22. g4!? ♕b6 23. ♖f2 ♕a6□ 24. ♕a6 ba6 25. ♗c1±] **♗f5 23. ♕h5 hg3** [23... ♗e5! 24. ♖e5 (24. ♕f7 ♔f7 25. ♖e5 △ ♖fe1=∞) ♖h7 25. g4 ♖h5 26. gh5=∞] **24. ♗h3! ♕e8! 25. ♔g2** [25. e6 ♖f6!] **♗h3** [25... ♕e6 26. ♖h1±] **26. ♕h3 ♖f4 27. ♕g3 ♕g6 28. ♗c1** [28. e6!] **♖f5 29. ♖f2!** [29. e6 ♖e8 30. e7 △ ♗a3±] **♖e8= 30. f4** [30. ♖fe2 ♖ee5 31. ♖e5 ♖e5 32. ♖e5 ♕c2=] **♖e6 31. ♖ef1?⊕** [31. fg5 ♖ee5 32. ♖e5 ♗e5 33. ♕d3=] **gf4 32. ♗f4 ♕e8?** [32... ♖f4 33. ♖f4 ♕g3 34. ♔g3 ♗e5∓ 35. c4!] **33. ♕h3?** [33. ♕d3! ♖g6 34. ♔h2=] **♖h5−+ 34. ♕d3 ♖g6 35. ♗g3 ♖hg5 36. ♖f3 ♗e5 37. ♖e1 ♕b8 38. ♖ee3 ♗g3 39. ♖g3 ♖g3 40. ♖g3 ♕g3 41. ♕g3 ♔f7 42. ♔f3 ♖g3 43. ♔g3 ♔f6 44. ♔f4 c5 45. ♔e3** [45. c4 d4 46. b4 (46. ♔e4 ♔g5 47. b4 b6) cb4 47. ♔e4 d3 48. ♔d3 ♔e5] **♔e5 46. ♔d3 b5 47. ♔e3 b4 48. ♔d3 ♔f4 0 : 1 [Bareev]**

107. A 85

S. KISELËV 2510 – AGREST 2460
Sankt-Peterburg (zt) 1993

1. d4 f5 2. c4 ♘f6 3. ♘c3 e6 4. e3 b6 5. ♗d3 ♗b7 6. f3 ♘h5 N [6... ♗e7; 6... g6; 6... c5; 6... ♗b4] **7. ♘h3** [7. ♘ge2?! ♗d6! 8. 0–0 ♕h4 9. g3 ♘g3 10. hg3 ♗g3 11. ♘g3 ♕g3 12. ♔h1 0–0!→] **♕h4?!** [⌓ 7... g6] **8. ♘f2 ♘c6 9. g3 ♕e7 10. a3?!** [10. g4!? fg4 (10... ♘f6!? 11. gf5 ef5 12. ♗f5 g6 13. ♗b1□ ♗g7=∞) 11. fg4 ♘f6 12. g5 ♘g8 13. ♕h5 ♔d8 △ ♕e8∞] **♘f6 11. f4** [11. 0–0 g5!→] **g6 12. 0–0 ♗g7 13. ♗e2 ♘d8 14. b3** [⌓ 14. b4] **0–0 15. ♗b2 ♘f7 16. ♗f3 d5! 17. ♘d3 ♘e4 18. c5!□ ♗a6!** [18... bc5? 19. ♗e4 cd4!∓; 19. ♘e4!!±] **19. cb6** [19. b4 bc5 20. bc5 ♖ab8!∓] **ab6∓ 20. ♖c1 c5 21. ♘b1□ ♖fc8 22. ♗e2 ♖c7?!** [22... g5!∓↑⟫] **23. ♘f2 cd4?! 24. ♖c7** [24. ♗a6 de3!] **♕c7 25. ed4□ ♗e2 26. ♕e2 ♖c8** [△ ♕c2∓] **27. ♘d3!□∞ ♕a7** [27... ♕c2 28. ♕c2 ♖c2 29. ♖c1! △ 29... ♖b2? 30. ♖c8] **28. ♖c1 ♖c1 29. ♘c1 b5 30. ♕d3!** [30. ♕e3 e5 31. fe5 ♗h6!∓] **e5 31. fe5 ♗e5** [31... ♘e5? 32. ♕b5 ×d5] **32. ♘e2 ♘fd6 33. ♘bc3 ♘c3 34. ♕c3 ♕b6 35. ♗c1 ♗f6 36. ♕c5⊕** [36. a4!?] **♕c5 37. dc5 ♘c8 38. b4** [♘♗ 9/c] **♔f7 39. ♔f2 ♘e7 40. ♔e3 ♘c6 41. ♘f4 d4! 42. ♔d3 g5! 43.**

♘**d5**□ ♗**d8 44. a4 ba4 45. b5** ♔**e6 46.** ♘**b6** ♘**a7 47.** ♔**c4 f4! 48. gf4 gf4 49.** ♘**d5** [49. ♗f4 a3 50. ♗c1 a2 51. ♗b2 d3 52. ♘d5 ♘b5 53. ♘f4 ♔f5 54. ♘d3=] **f3 50.** ♘**f4** ♔**d7 51.** ♘**d3** ♔**c8! 52.** ♗**b2** ♗**f6 53.** ♘**f2?!** [53. c6 ♔c7 54. ♔c5 ♗e7 55. ♔c4 ♗f6 56. ♔c5=] ♗**h4 54.** ♘**e4**□ [54. ♗d4 ♗f2 55. ♗f2 ♘b5!∓] **f2 55.** ♘**d2** ♗**g5 56.** ♘**f1** ♘**b5!?** [56... d3 57. b6 d2 58. ba7 ♔b7 59. c6!□ ♔a7 60. ♘d2 ♗d2 61. ♗d4=] **57.** ♔**b5 d3 58.** ♗**d4!** [58. ♗c3 a3 59. ♔b4 (59. ♔c4 d2−+) a2 60. ♔b3 d2 61. ♔c2 ♔d7 △ ♔c6−+⊙] **a3 59.** ♔**c4**□ [59. ♗f2 ♗f6 60. ♘d2 a2 61. ♘b3 d2−+] **d2 60.** ♘**d2** ♗**d2 61.** ♗**f2**
1/2 : 1/2 **[Agrest]**

108. **A 85**

SAVČENKO 2535 – P. TREGUBOV 2445

Rostov na Donu (open) 1993

1. d4 d5 2. c4 c6 3. ♘**f3 e6 4. e3** ♗**d6 5.** ♘**c3 f5 6.** ♘**e5** ♘**f6 7. f4 N** [7. ♗e2] **0–0 8.** ♗**e2 b6** [8... ♘bd7 9. 0–0 ♘e4 10. ♘e4 fe4 11. ♗d2±] **9. 0–0** ♗**b7 10. cd5!? ed5** [10... cd5 11. ♗d2 ♘c6 12. ♕a4±] **11.** ♗**d2 c5 12.** ♕**a4 a6 13.** ♕**c2±** ♘**e4 14.** ♘**e4 fe4 15.** ♗**g4** ♔**h8 16. dc5 bc5 17.** ♕**b3** ♖**a7** [17... ♕e7 18. ♗c3 (18. ♕b6!?) ♘c6? 19. ♘d7 ♗c8 20. ♘f8 ♗g4 21. ♕d5 ♖c8 22. h3+−] **18.** ♗**c3** ♗**a8 19.** ♖**ad1±** ♘**c6** [19... ♖e7 20. h3! ♘c6? 21. ♕d5 ♘e5 22. ♕d6+−] **20.** ♗**e6!** ♗**e5?** [20... d4!? 21. ♘f7! (21. ♘c6 ♗c6 22. ed4 e3=∞) ♖af7 22. ♗f7 dc3 23. bc3 ♕f6 24. ♗d5 ♘e7 25. ♗a8 ♖a8 26. ♕b7 ♖b8 27. ♕e4±] **21. fe5** ♖**f1 22.** ♖**f1+− d4 23.** ♕**b6** ♕**e7 24. ed4 cd4 25.** ♗**b4!** ♕**e6 26.** ♖**f8** ♕**g8 27.** ♖**g8** ♔**g8 28. e6 a5 29.** ♗**c5 d3 30.** ♕**b3** **1 : 0**
[Savčenko]

109. **A 85**

LIMA 2445 – GIARDELLI 2425

Brasilia (zt) 1993

1. d4 d5 2. c4 e6 3. ♘**c3 f5 4.** ♘**f3 c6 5.** ♗**f4** ♘**f6 6. e3** ♗**e7 7.** ♗**d3 0–0 8.** ♕**c2** [△ cd5 ×f5] ♘**e4 9. g4!?** ♘**a6 N** [9... fg4 10. ♗e4 de4 11. ♘e5± ×e4, g4; 9... ♕a5 – 50/(103)] **10. a3** ♕**a5 11.** ♔**e2!** ♘**c3** [11... ♘c7? 12. b4+−; 11... fg4 12. ♘e5±] **12. bc3** ♘**c7 13. c5!±** [×♘c7] ♘**e8 14.** ♖**hg1** ♔**h8** [14... ♘f6 15. gf5 ef5 16. ♗f5 ♗f5 17. ♕f5 ♘e4 18. ♕e6+−] **15.** ♖**g2** ♘**f6 16.** ♖**ag1!** [⇔g] ♘**e4** [16... ♘g4 17. h3 ♘f6 18. ♖g7+−; 16... g6 17. ♗e5! ♔g8□ 18. gf5+−; 16... fg4 17. ♘e5→] **17. gf5 ef5 18.** ♖**g7** ♗**f6** [18... ♘c3 19. ♕c3! ♕c3 20. ♖e7 △ ♗e5] **19.** ♗**e5** ♗**e6** [19... ♘c3 20. ♕c3! ♕c3 21. ♗f6 △ 22. ♖f7#, 22. ♖g8#] **20.** ♖**e7** ♗**g8 21.** ♖**gg7 b6 22.** ♕**b2?!** [△ 22... bc5 23. ♕b7+−] ♘**c3?** [22... ♕c3!] **23.** ♔**f1** ♘**e4 24.** ♘**g5!** ♗**e5** [24... ♗e7 25. ♖h7#; 24... ♘g5 25. ♖g5 ×f5, h7, ⇗b1-h7] **25. de5+−** ♕**c5 26.** ♘**e6!** ♕**a5 27.** ♘**f8** ♖**f8 28.** ♗**e4** [28... fe4 29. ♖h7 ♗h7 30. e6] **1 : 0**
[Lima]

110.* **A 85**

AGREST 2460 – ULYBIN 2565

Sankt-Peterburg (zt) 1993

1. d4 e6 2. c4 f5 3. ♘**f3** ♘**f6 4.** ♘**c3** ♗**b4 5.** ♗**g5** [RR 5. ♕b3 a5 6. g3 b6 7. ♗g2 ♗b7 8. 0–0 0–0 9. ♗g5 ♘a6!? N (9... ♗c3 – 56/99) 10. ♖ad1 ♗c3! 11. ♗f6 (11. ♕c3 ♘e4!) ♕f6 12. ♕c3 d6 *a)* 13. e3 ♖fd8 14. ♖d2 e5! 15. de5 de5 *a1)* 16. ♖fd1 ♖d2 17. ♕d2 (17. ♖d2 ♖e8∓) e4! 18. ♘e1 (18. ♘d4 ♖d8) ♘c5 19. ♕d4 ♕e7 20. b3 ♖e8∓ Š. Gross 2325 – Glek 2545, Cuxhaven 1993; *a2)* 16. ♖d8 ♖d8 17. ♕e5 (17. ♘e5? ♗g2 18. ♔g2 ♘c5 △ ♘e4∓) ♕e5 18. ♘e5 ♗g2 19. ♔g2 ♖d2=∞↑; *b)* ⌓ 13. ♖d2 ♗e4= Glek] **0–0 6.** ♖**c1 d6 7. g3 b6 N** [7... ♘bd7 – 52/104] **8.** ♗**g2** ♗**b7 9. 0–0** ♗**c3 10.** ♖**c3** ♘**bd7 11. d5! e5** [11... ed5 12. ♘h4 (12. ♘d4!?) ♕e8 13. ♗f6 ♘f6 (13... ♖f6 14. ♗d5 ♗d5 15. ♕d5 △ ♘f5) 14. cd5 ♕d7 15. ♕d3 △ ♖fc1±; 11... ♘c5 12. ♘d4 (△ b4) ed5 (12... a5 13. de6 ♗g2 14. ♔g2 h6 15. ♘f5!±) 13. cd5 h6 14. ♗f6 ♕f6 15. b4 (15. ♘b5!?) ♘e4 16. ♖c7 ♗d5 17. f3 ♘g5 18. e4! fe4 19. fe4 ♕e5 20. ed5 (20. ♖f8 ♖f8 21. ed5 ♕e3 22. ♔h1 ♘e4 23. ♖c2 ♘f2 24. ♖f2 ♖f2∞) ♕e3 21. ♔h1 ♖f1 22. ♗f1 ♘e4 23. ♖g7 ♔g7 (23...

♔h8 24. ♖f7+−) 24. ♘f5 ♔f6 25. ♘e3 ♘f2 26. ♔g1! ♘d1 27. ♘d1 ♔e5 28. ♘e3±] **12. ♘h4 g6** [12... h6 13. ♗f6 (13. ♗c1 ♘e4 14. ♖e3! ♘g5 15. f4 ♘h7 16. ♕e1±; 13. ♗h6!? gh6 14. ♘f5=∞→) ♖f6□ 14. ♗h3 f4 △ ♘f8∞; 14. f4!±↑] **13. e4 fe4 14. f3!?** [14. ♗e4 ♘e4!? 15. ♗d8 ♘c3 16. ♕c2 ♖ad8=∞] **e3□ 15. ♖e3** [15. ♗e3!?] **♘d5** [15... ♔g7 16. ♖ee1 h6 17. ♗c1±↑≫] **16. ♗d8** [16. ♕d5! ♗d5 17. ♗d8 *a)* 17... ♗c4 18. ♗c7 ♗f1 (18... g5 19. ♖fe1 d5 20. ♗h3) 19. ♗f1±; *b)* 17... ♖ad8 18. cd5 g5 19. ♖c1 gh4 (19... ♘c5 20. b4 △ 20... ♘a6? 21. ♗f1+−) 20. ♖c7 hg3 21. hg3 a5 (21... ♘f6 22. ♗h3!±) 22. ♖b3!±] **♘e3 17. ♕d3 ♘g2 18. ♘g6! ♘c5** [18... hg6 19. ♕g6 ♔h8 20. ♗g5+−; 18... ♖fd8 19. ♘e7 ♔h8 20. ♔g2 ♘c5 21. ♕e3 △ ♕h6±→] **19. ♘e7 ♔h8 20. ♕d2 ♖ad8 21. ♔g2** [21. ♕h6!? ♖f7□ 22. ♔g2±] **♖f6 22. ♘d5 ♖f7 23. ♕h6 ♖g8 24. ♔g1! ♖g6 25. ♕d2 ♘e6 26. f4! ef4 27. ♘f4 ♖gf6 28. ♕c3 ♔g8□ 29. ♖e1! ♘f4 30. ♖e8 ♖f8 31. ♖f8 ♖f8 32. gf4** [♕ 5/h] **a5□ 33. ♕e3?⊕** [33. c5!! dc5 (33... bc5 34. ♕b3+−) 34. ♕e5! △ f5-f6+−] **♖f7 34. ♕e6?** [34. ♕e8! ♔g7 (34... ♖f8 35. ♕e7 ♖f7 36. ♕d8 ♔g7 37. f5!) 35. f5! △ 35... ♖f5 36. ♕b8+−] **♗c6 35. ♕c8 ♔g7 36. h4 ♗e4± 37. ♕g4 ♔f6 38. ♔f2 ♗f5 39. ♕g5 ♔e6 40. ♕d8 ♗b1 41. ♕c8 ♔f6 42. a3 ♔g7 43. ♕g4** [43. ♔e3 ♗f5 44. ♕d8 h6!?] **♔f8 44. ♕g5 ♗f5 45. ♔e3 ♔e8 46. ♕g8 ♔e7 47. ♕g5 ♔d7 48. ♔d4 ♗e6 49. ♕h6 ♔e7 50. ♔c3 ♔d7 51. ♔d3 ♗f5 52. ♔d4 ♗e6 53. b3 ♔e7 54. ♕g5 ♔d7 55. ♕b5 ♔d8 56. ♕g5 ♔d7 57. ♔e3 ♖f5 58. ♕g7 ♖f7 59. ♕g5 ♖f5 60. ♕h6 ♖f7 61. ♔d3 ♗f5 62. ♔d2 ♗e6 63. ♕h5 ♔e7 64. ♔e3 ♗f5□** [64... ♔d7? 65. f5!+−] **65. ♔d4 ♗e6 66. ♔e4 ♔d7 67. ♔f3 ♔e7 68. ♕g5 ♔d7 69. ♔e4 ♖e7 70. ♔f3 ♖f7 71. ♔g3 ♖f5 72. ♕g7 ♖f7 73. ♕d4 ♔e7 74. ♕h8 ♔d7 75. h5 ♔e7 76. ♕g8 ♗f5□** [76... ♔d7 77. f5+−] **77. ♕a8 ♔d7 78. ♕g8⊕ ♔e7 79. ♕a8 ♔d7 80. ♕d5 ♗e6 81. ♕b5 ♔d8 82. ♕c6** [82... ♖f5 83. ♕e4 ♔d7□ (83... ♔e7 84. c5! bc5 85. ♕c6 ♔d8 86. ♕a8±) 84. ♔h4 ♖f7 *a)* 85. ♔g5 ♖g7 86. ♔h6 ♖f7 87. ♕d4 ♔e7 88. ♕e3 ♔d7 89. ♕d2 ♔e7 90. ♕d4 (△ 90... ♔d7 91. c5!) ♖f6! 91. ♔g5 (91. ♔h7?? ♔f7−+) ♖f7; *b)* 85. b4!? ab4 86. ab4 △ b5, ♕c6, c5±]

1/2 : 1/2 **[Agrest]**

111. **A 86**

LAUTIER 2645 − M. GUREVICH 2610

München 1993

1. c4 f5 2. g3 ♘f6 3. ♗g2 g6 4. d4 ♗g7 5. ♘c3 0−0 6. ♘h3 e6!? [△ d6, e5 ×♘h3] **7. b3 d6 8. 0−0 c6** [8... e5 9. de5 de5 10. ♗a3 ♖e8 11. ♕d8 ♖d8 12. ♘d5±] **9. ♕c2 e5 N** [9... a5] **10. de5 de5 11. ♗a3 ♖e8 12. ♖ad1 ♘bd7** [12... ♕a5?! 13. ♗d6 △ b4↑≪] **13. ♗d6** [13. e4 f4!? 14. gf4 ♘h5 15. fe5 ♕h4 16. f4 ♘e5⇆] **♘g4?!** [△ ♕f6, e4; 13... e4!? 14. f3 ♕b6 15. ♔h1 ♘c5⇆] **14. e4! f4?!** [⌓ 14... ♕f6] **15. gf4 ♕h4 16. ♖d3!** [△ ♖g3] **ef4 17. ♗f4 ♘c5 18. ♖g3** [△ ♗g5; 18. ♗g5 ♕h5 19. ♘e2 (△ ♘g3) ♘f2!∓] **♘e6 19. ♗d2 ♘f6!?** [△ ♘h5, ♗e5 ×f4] **20. ♘e2! ♘h5 21. ♖d3 ♘c5** [21... ♗e5 22. f4±] **22. ♗g5 ♕g4 23. f3 ♕e6 24. ♖d2± a5!** [△ a4⇆≪] **25. ♖fd1?** [25. ♗e3 ♕e7 26. ♘hf4±] **♕f7!** [△ ♗h3] **26. ♖f1** [26. ♘f2 ♘e6 27. ♗e3 ♘ef4⇆] **a4 27. b4?! ♘a6 28. a3 ♗e6 29. ♗e3 h6** [29... ♗c4? 30. ♘g5+−] **30. c5 ♘c7 31. f4?** [31. ♘hf4 ♘f4 32. ♘f4 ♗b3 33. ♕c1 ♘b5 34. ♘e2 ♗c4 35. ♖f2 ♔h7⇆] **♘b5 32. ♕c1** [32. f5 ♗b3 33. ♕c1 (33. fg6? ♕f1 34. ♔f1 ♗c2 35. ♖c2 ♘a3−+) g5⇆] **♗h3 33. ♗h3 ♖e4∓ 34. ♖d3 ♖ae8 35. ♗g2 ♖4e7 36. ♔h1 ♕f5 37. ♕d2 ♔h7 38. ♖f2** [38. ♘g3?! ♕d3! (38... ♘g3 39. hg3 ♖e3?! 40. ♖e3 ♗d4 41. ♖e8 ♕h5 42. ♗h3 ♕h3 43. ♕h2 ♕f1; 41. ♖fe1∞) 39. ♕d3 ♖e3 40. ♕d2 ♖g3 41. hg3 ♘g3 42. ♔h2 ♘f1 43. ♗f1 ♘d4∓]

(diagram)

38... **♕d3! 39. ♕d3 ♖e3 40. ♕d2** [40. ♕c2 ♘f6!? (40... ♖e2 41. ♖e2 ♘d4 42. ♖e8 ♘c2 43. ♖e7⇆) 41. ♘g3 ♖a3∓] **♘f6!?** [40... ♘a3 41. f5 g5 42. f6 ♘f6 43. ♘g3⇆] **41. ♗f1 ♘a3?!** [41... ♖a3 42. ♘g3 ♖a1 43. ♔g2 a3 44. ♗d3 (44. ♗c4 ♘c7∓ △ ♘cd5) a2∓] **42. ♘g3 ♖e1 43. ♔g2 ♘g4**

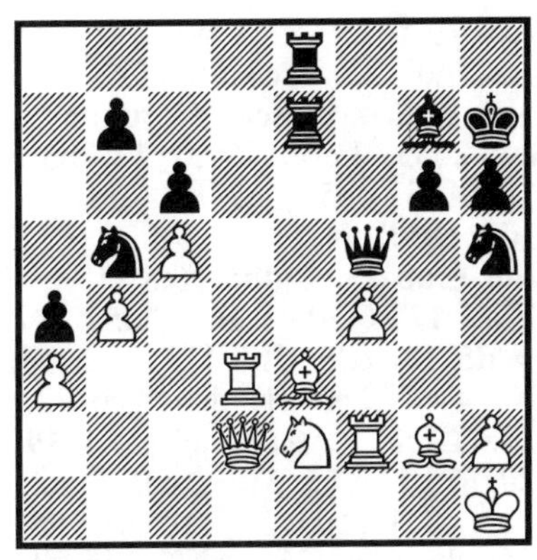

44. ♗e2! [44. ♖e2 ♘e3 45. ♔h3 ♖d1 46. ♕a2 ♘ac4∓] **♘f2 45. ♕e1 ♘g4 46. ♕d2 ♘e3 47. ♔f2 ♘d5 48. ♕d1!** [48. f5 ♘b1 49. fg6 ♔h8 50. ♕d3 ♘bc3∓] **♘f4 49. ♕a4 ♘b1 50. ♕d1 ♘c3 51. ♕d7 ♖e2** [51... ♖f8 52. ♗f3 h5 53. ♕b7⇆] **52. ♘e2 ♘fe2** [♕ 6/e] **53. b5?⊕** [53. ♕b7 ♘d4∓] **♘d4 54. bc6** [54. b6 ♘e4 55. ♔g2 ♘c5 56. ♕e7 ♘de6−+] **bc6−+ 55. ♔g2 ♘d5 56. h4 h5 57. ♔h3 ♘f4 58. ♔h2 ♘fe6 59. ♕e7 ♔h6 60. ♔h1 ♗f8 61. ♕f6 ♗g7 62. ♕e7 ♘f8!** [△ ♘de6, ♗d4-c5] **63. ♕e3 ♔h7 64. ♕e8 ♔g8 65. ♔g2 ♗f6 66. ♔h3 ♘de6 67. ♕c6 ♗d4 68. ♕d5 ♗c5 69. ♕b7 ♗d4 70. ♕d5 ♔h7 71. ♕f3 ♗g7 72. ♕f7 ♘d4 73. ♔g2 ♘fe6 74. ♔h3 ♘c5** [△ ♘d3-e5, ♘f5 ×h4] **75. ♕e7 ♘d3 76. ♕e3 ♘e6! 77. ♔g3 ♘e5 78. ♕b6 ♘f8 79. ♕d6 ♘f7 80. ♕e7 ♗e5 81. ♔h3 ♔g7 82. ♔g2 ♘h7 83. ♔h3 ♘f6 84. ♕e6 ♘g8** [△ ♘gh6-f5, ♗f6-h4] **0 : 1**

[M. Gurevich]

112. A 87

M. VUKIĆ 2500 − KONTIĆ 2400

Cetinje 1993

1. ♘f3 f5 2. g3 ♘f6 3. ♗g2 g6 4. 0−0 ♗g7 5. c4 0−0 6. d4 d6 7. d5 ♕e8 8. ♘c3 ♘a6 9. ♘d4 ♗d7 10. e4!? fe4 11. ♘e4 ♘e4 12. ♗e4 c5 13. dc6 bc6 14. ♖e1!? N ± [14. ♗e3?! c5!; 14. ♖b1 − 39/(144)] **♘c5** [14... ♕f7? 15. ♘c6 ♕f2 16. ♔h1 ♗g4 17. ♗e3!±] **15. ♗g2 a5 16. ♗e3 ♖b8 17. ♖b1 e5?!** [17... a4!?] **18. ♘c2 ♗f5?!** [18... ♕e7!? 19. ♗c5 dc5 20. ♘e3±] **19. ♕d6! ♘d3** [19... ♗c2 20. ♕c5 ♗b1 21. ♖b1 e4 22. ♕a3 a4 23. ♕a4 ♗b2 24. c5!±] **20. ♖e2□** [20. ♗c6? ♖d8!−+] **♘b2** [20... ♘b4? 21. ♘b4 ♗b1 22. ♘c6+−] **21. ♗c6 ♕c8 22. ♗d5 ♔h8 23. ♕a3!± ♗d3 24. ♖ee1!** [24. ♖d2? e4 △ ♘c4∓] **e4 25. ♗d4!!+− ♗d4** [25... ♕f5 26. ♖b2+−] **26. ♘d4 ♗b1** [26... ♘c4 27. ♕c3 ♘e5 28. ♘c6 ♕f5 29. ♖b2 ♖be8 30. f4! ef3 31. ♖f2!+−] **27. ♘e6! ♘a4** [27... ♖f3 28. ♖e3! ♘d1 29. ♕e7 ♕g8 30. ♖f3+−] **28. ♕e7 ♕e6 29. ♕e6 ♖be8 30. ♕d7 ♘c3 31. ♗f7 ♖d8 32. ♕e7 e3** [32... ♔g7 33. ♗e8 △ ♕d8] **33. ♕e5#**

1 : 0 **[M. Vukić]**

113. A 87**

JUSUPOV 2645 − BAREEV 2670

München 1993

1. d4 f5 2. ♘f3 ♘f6 3. c4 g6 4. g3 ♗g7 5. ♗g2 0−0 6. 0−0 d6 7. ♘c3 ♕e8 [RR 7... e6 8. ♗g5!? N (8. b3 − 54/(88)) h6! 9. ♗f6 ♕f6 10. e4 ♘c6?! 11. ef5 gf5 12. d5 ♘b4 13. a3 ♘a6 14. ♖c1 e5 15. b4 ♗d7 16. ♘h4! (×f5) ♖ae8 17. ♗h3 (17. ♘b5!?) ♖e7 18. ♕c2! (18. ♕h5 ♔h7) ♕f7 19. ♖cd1± Dorfman 2580 − Meulders 2330, Bruxelles (zt) 1993; 10... e5!? Meulders] **8. d5 a5 9. ♗e3** [RR 9. ♘d4 ♘a6 10. e4 fe4 11. ♘e4 ♘e4 12. ♗e4 ♗h3 13. ♖e1 ♘c5 14. ♗h1 ♕a4 N (14... ♕f7 − 56/(103)) 15. b3 ♕b4 16. ♗e3 (16. ♗b2? ♘a4; 16. ♖b1? ♘d3; 16. ♖e7!? ♗f6 17. ♖e3 a4!?⇆; 16... ♕c3!?) a4 17. a3 ♕c3 18. ♖c1 (18. b4 ♘b3 19. ♘b3 ab3 20. ♖c1 ♕b2=) ♕b2 19. b4 ♘b3 20. ♖b1 ♕c3 21. ♘b3 ab3 22. ♕b3? ♖a3!∓ Komarov 2530 − Piskov 2520, Douai 1993; 22. ♖c1= Piskov] **h6 10. h4!? N** [10. ♕d2 g5!?; 10. ♘b5 − 54/89] **♘a6 11. ♕d2 ♔h7 12. ♖ae1 e5!** [12... c5 13. ♗f4 △ e4; 12... ♘c5 13. ♗c5; 12... c6 13. ♗d4; 12... ♗d7 13. ♗d4 c5 14. ♗f6 △ e4] **13. de6 ♗e6 14. ♘d4?!** [14. b3!∞] **♗c4 15. ♗b7!** [15. b3 ♗g8 16. ♗b7 c5 17. ♘db5 d5!! 18. ♗a8 (18. ♗a6 d4! 19. ♘c7 de3 20. ♕e3 ♕e3 21. fe3 ♘g4∓) ♕a8 △ d4⩱] **♖b8 16. ♗c6 ♕c8 17. ♗f3 ♘b4! 18. a3 ♘bd5 19. ♘d5 ♗d5** [19... ♘d5 20.

♖c1!?] **20. ♘c6?** [20. ♕a5 c5 21. ♘b5 ♕c6 22. a4 ♗f3 23. ef3 ♘d5∓; 20. b4 ♗f3 21. ef3 ab4 22. ab4 c5∓]

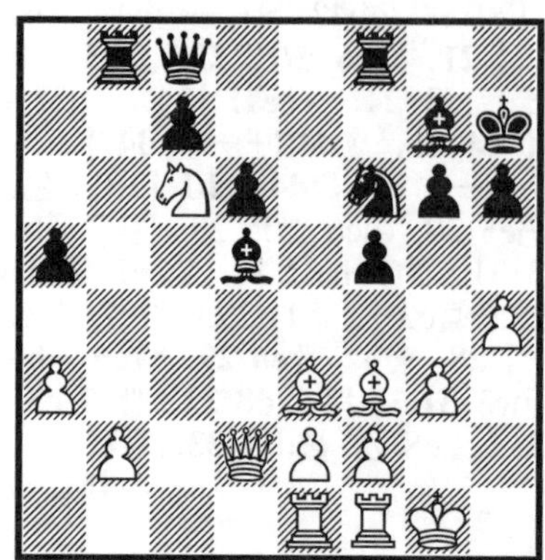

20... f4!!∓ 21. ♘e7 [21. ♗f4 ♕h3 22. ♘b8 ♘g4−+; 21. ♗d5 fe3 22. fe3 ♕h3 23. ♗g2 ♕g3 24. ♘b8 ♖b8 25. ♖f3 ♕h4 26. ♖ef1 ♘g4 27. ♖h3 ♕e7! 28. ♕a5 ♖b2∓; 28... h5! △ ♗h6∓] **fe3 22. ♕e3 ♕b7 23. ♘d5 ♘d5 24. ♕d3⊕ c6 25. h5 ♔h8 26. ♕g6 ♖f6 27. ♕d3 ♘b6! 28. b4! ab4 29. ab4 ♘d7 30. ♕c2 d5** [30... ♘e5 31. ♗g2 ♕b4? 32. ♖b1] **31. ♗g2!** [△ e4] **♘e5!** [31... ♕b4 32. e4 d4 33. f4∓ ×♗g7] **32. b5** [32. e4 d4 33. f4 ♘g4 34. e5 ♖ff8 35. ♕c6 ♕b4 △ ♘e3, d3-d2−+] **cb5 33. ♖d1 ♖d8 34. ♕b3 ♖fd6−+ 35. ♕b4** [35. ♖b1 ♘c4 36. ♕b5 ♖b6] **♕b6 36. ♖d2** [36. ♖b1 ♘c6 37. ♕b5 ♕b5 38. ♖b5 ♘d4 39. ♖b7 ♘e2 40. ♔h2 d4] **♘c6 37. ♕g4 b4 38. ♖fd1 ♘e5 39. ♕h4 b3 40. ♖d5 b2 41. ♖d6 ♖d6 42. ♖b1 ♖f6! 43. e3 ♘f3** [43... ♘d3−+] **44. ♗f3 ♖f3 45. ♕e4 ♖f8 46. ♕c2 ♕f6 47. ♔f1** [47. ♔g2 ♕c3 48. ♕e4 ♕d2] **♕e5 48. g4 ♕e3 49. ♖b2 ♕h3 50. ♔e1 ♕g4 0 : 1** **[Bareev]**

114.* A 88

JE. PIKET 2625 − M. GUREVICH 2625

Groningen 1992

1. ♘f3 f5 2. g3 ♘f6 3. ♗g2 g6 4. 0−0 ♗g7 5. c4 d6 6. d4 0−0 7. ♘c3 ♕e8 8. d5 ♘a6 9. ♖b1 ♗d7 10. b4 c6 11. dc6 bc6 [RR 11... ♗c6 12. ♕b3 N (12. b5 − 56/104) ♘e4 13. ♗b2 ♘c3 14. ♗c3 ♗c3 15. ♕c3 ♖c8 16. ♖bc1 ♖f6 17. a3 ♔g7 18. ♖fe1 ♘b8 19. c5 ♗e4 20. ♕e3 dc5 21. ♖c5 ♖c5 22. ♕c5 a6 23. ♘e5 ♗g2 24. ♔g2 ♘d7 25. ♕c3 ♘e5 26. ♕e5 ♕c6 27. ♔g1 ♕d6= Illescas Córdoba 2615 − Topalov 2635, León 1993] **12. b5 ♘c5?!** [12... cb5 13. cb5 ♘c5 14. ♘d4 ♘fe4∞] **13. ♘d4 cb5?! N** [13... ♘fe4 − 53/103] **14. ♗a8 ♕a8 15. ♘db5 ♖c8** [15... a6 16. ♘c7 ♕a7 17. ♘3d5!] **16. ♘d5± ♘d5 17. ♕d5 ♕d5 18. cd5 ♖b8** [18... a6 19. ♘a7 ♖c7 20. ♘c6 ♗c6 21. dc6 ♖c6 22. ♗g5! ♔f7 23. ♖fc1 △ ♗e3, a4-a5±] **19. ♘a3 ♖b1 20. ♘b1 ♗b5 21. ♗e3! ♘a6!** [21... ♗e2? 22. ♖e1 ♗d3 23. ♗c5 dc5 24. ♖e7 ♗b1 25. d6 ♗f6 (25... ♗f8 26. ♖b7) 26. ♖a7 ♗e4 27. ♖c7+−] **22. ♗a7** [22. ♖c1!? △ 22... ♗e2 23. ♖c8 ♔f7 24. ♖a8 ♘c7 25. ♖a7 ♘d5 26. a4] **♗e2 23. ♖e1 ♗c4?** [23... ♗d3!□ 24. ♘d2 ♔f7 25. ♘f3 h6 26. ♗d4 ♗f8 27. a4 ♗c4 (27... ♗e4 28. ♖e4 fe4 29. ♘d2) 28. ♖b1±] **24. ♖e7 ♗a2 25. ♖b7!± ♗e5** [25... ♗d5 26. ♖b6 ♗e4 27. ♘d2 (27. ♖a6?! ♗b1 28. ♖d6 ♗a2) ♘c5 28. ♖d6 ♘b7?! 29. ♘e4+−] **26. f4 ♗a1 27. ♗e3 ♗d5 28. ♖b6 ♘c7 29. ♖d6 ♗f7** [29... ♗g7 30. ♖d8 ♗f8 31. ♖d7 ♗e4 32. ♘c3+−] **30. ♗d4+− ♗d4 31. ♖d4 ♘e6 32. ♖b4 h6 33. ♘d2 g5 34. ♘f3 ♔g7 35. ♘d4 1 : 0** **[Je. Piket]**

115.** A 88

I. FARAGÓ 2510 − JAGUPOV 2415

Passau 1993

1. d4 f5 2. c4 ♘f6 3. ♘c3 g6 4. g3 ♗g7 5. ♗g2 d6 6. ♘f3 0−0 7. 0−0 c6 8. d5 e5 9. de6 [RR 9. e4!? cd5 10. cd5 ♘a6 11. ef5 ♗f5 12. ♘g5 ♘c5 N (12... ♕e7 − 52/111) 13. b4!? ♘d3 14. ♘e6 ♗e6 15. de6 e4!□ (15... ♘c1?! 16. ♖c1±) 16. ♗g5! d5 17. ♕b3 (Magerramov 2565 − Renner 2385, Bad Wörishofen 1993) ♕b6!□ 18. e7 ♘f2!! 19. ef8♕ ♖f8 20. ♘e4!! (20. h3? ♘h3 21. ♔h2□ ♘g5 22. ♘d5 ♘g4! 23. ♔h1 ♘f2 24. ♔g1 ♕d4∞) ♘2e4 21. ♗e3±; 14... ♕b6!?∞ Magerramov] **♗e6 10. b3 ♘a6 11. ♘g5** [11. ♗f4 ♘h5 12. ♗d2 ♕e7 N (12... ♘c5 − 40/134) 13. ♖c1 f4 14. ♘a4 d5 15. cd5 ♗d5 16. ♗c3 ♖ad8 17. ♕c2 ♗e4 18. ♕b2 c5 19. ♗g7 ♘g7 20. ♖fd1 ♖de8 21. ♕c3

♗c6! 22. ♖d2 ♘e6∞ Juferov 2415 – Jagupov 2415, Minsk 1993] **♗c8 12. ♗b2 ♕e7 13. ♕c2 h6!? N** [13... ♘c5 – 49/137] **14. ♘f3 ♗e6 15. ♖ad1 ♖ad8 16. ♗a3 ♘c5** [16... ♗f7!? *a)* 17. ♖fe1 (△ e4) ♘c5 (17... ♘e4?! 18. ♘e4 fe4 19. ♘h4 ♖fe8 20. f3 ♗f6 21. fe4 ♗h4 22. gh4 ♘c5 23. ♕c3± ⇗a1-h8) 18. ♗c5 dc5 19. ♖d8 ♖d8 20. e4 ♘e4 21. ♘e4 fe4 22. ♖e4 (22. ♘d2 ♗d4) ♕d6=; *b)* 17. e4 ♘e4 (17... fe4 18. ♖fe1) 18. ♘e4 ♕e4 (18... fe4 19. ♖fe1 ♘c5 20. ♘d2) 19. ♕e4 (19. ♕d2 ♕e7 20. ♕a5 c5∓) fe4 20. ♘d2 d5 21. ♗f8 ♖f8=∞] **17. ♘h4 ♗f7 18. ♗c5 dc5 19. ♖d8 ♖d8 20. e4 f4□** [20... fe4?! 21. ♘e4 ♖e8 (21... ♘e4 22. ♗e4 g5 23. ♘f5±) 22. ♖e1↑] **21. ♘e2** [21. gf4? ♘h5] **♘h5 22. ♗f3 ♕g5!□ 23. ♗h5 fg3 24. hg3 ♕h5∞ 25. ♖d1 ♖d1 26. ♕d1 ♗f6 27. ♘g2□ ♕f3 28. ♕c2□ g5** [28... ♗d4? 29. ♘d4 cd4 30. ♘e1±; 28... h5 29. ♘e1 ♕g4 30. ♕d3 h4 31. f3 ♕e6 32. g4±] **29. ♘e1 ♕g4 30. ♕d3 ♗g6 31. f3 ♕e6 32. ♘c2 ♕e5** [32... g4? 33. ♘f4 ♕e5 34. ♔f2! ♗h7 35. ♕d7 ♕b2? 36. ♕e8 ♔g7 37. ♘e6#] **33. ♘e3** [33. ♔g2 g4!; 33. ♔f2 ♕b2 34. ♘e3 ♗d4!] **♕a1 34. ♔f2 ♗d4□** [34... ♕a2? 35. ♕d6! ♕b2 36. ♘g4+–] **35. ♕d2! h5⊕ 36. ♘d4 ♕d4** [36... cd4? 37. ♘f5+–] **37. ♔e2** [37. ♕d4 cd4 38. ♘f1 c5 39. ♘d2 ♔g7 40. f4 ♔f6=] **1/2 : 1/2 [Jagupov]**

116. A 88

ČUČELOV 2500 – KINDERMANN 2495

Cuxhaven 1993

1. d4 f5 2. g3 ♘f6 3. ♗g2 g6 4. ♘f3 ♗g7 5. 0–0 0–0 6. c4 d6 7. ♘c3 c6 8. d5 e5 9. de6 ♗e6 10. b3 ♘a6 11. ♗b2 ♕e7 12. ♘g5 ♘c5 13. ♘e6 N [13. ♕d2 – 32/(145)] **♘e6!?** [13... ♕e6] **14. e3 ♖ad8 15. ♕c2 ♖fe8 16. ♖ad1 h5!?** [△ h4, hg3, ♘g4; 16... ♘c5; 16... a5] **17. e4!?** [17. h4 ♘g4 18. ♘e2 ♗b2 19. ♕b2 g5 20. hg5 ♕g5 21. ♘d4! (Čučelov) ♘d4 22. ♕d4 h4 23. gh4 (23. ♕f4 ♕f4 24. gf4 ♔f7=) ♕h4 24. ♕f4 ♕f6 25. ♗h3 (25. e4 ♖e7! △ ♖g7→) ♘h6 △ ♔h8∞] **f4 18. e5 de5 19. ♕g6 ♕f7 20. ♕f7** [20. ♕b1!?] **♔f7 21. ♘e4 ♘e4 22. ♗e4 ♘g5= 23. ♗f5!?** [23. f3 h4! 24. ♔g2 hg3 25. hg3 fg3 26. ♔g3 ♘e4 27. fe4 ♔e6=] **♘f3!** [23... h4?! 24. ♗c1!] **24. ♔g2** [24. ♔h1 ♘d2 25. ♖fe1 ♘f3=] **♘d2 25. ♖fe1 f3 26. ♔g1** [26. ♔h3 e4 27. ♗g7 (27. ♗c1?! e3!) ♔g7 28. ♗e4 ♘e4 (28... ♖e4? 29. ♖e4 ♘e4 30. ♖d8 ♘f2 31. ♔h4 ♘g4 32. ♖d4+–) 29. ♖e4 ♖d1 30. ♖e8 ♖d2=] **e4 27. ♗c1 ♔f6!□** [27... ♗h6? 28. ♗d2 ♗d2 29. ♖e4 ♗b4 30. ♖f1±] **28. ♗h7□ ♗h6 29. ♗e4□** [29. ♗d2? ♗d2 30. ♖e4 ♖h8–+] **♘e4!** [29... ♖e4? 30. ♖e4 ♘e4 31. ♖d8 ♗c1 32. ♖f8±] **30. ♖d8** [30. ♗h6? ♘c3!] **♖d8 31. ♗h6 ♘c3=∞** [♖ 9/i] **32. h3** [△ ♖e3] **♘e2 33. ♔h2 ♔f5 34. ♖b1!** [△ b4, ♖b3] **b5! 35. cb5 cb5 36. ♖b2** [36. b4 ♖d3] **♖d1 37. ♗e3 ♖g1 38. ♖d2** [38... ♖g2 39. ♔h1 ♔e4?! (△ ♘g3–+) 40. b4□ a6 41. a3□ (41. h4? ♔f5 △ ♔g4-h3) ♖g3!? 42. fg3 ♔e3 43. ♖c2! ♘g3 44. ♔h2! (44. ♔g1? ♘e4 45. ♔f1 ♘d2–+) ♘e4 45. ♖c8! ♔e2 46. ♖f8 h4 47. ♖f4 ♔e3 48. ♖f8=] **1/2 : 1/2 [Kindermann]**

117.* A 90

VOJSKA 2305 – VAÏSSER 2570

Cappelle la Grande 1993

1. d4 f5 2. g3 ♘f6 3. ♗g2 e6 4. c4 [RR 4. ♘f3 c6 5. 0–0 d5 6. ♘bd2 ♘bd7 7. b3 ♗d6 8. ♗b2 ♕e7 9. c4 b6 10. ♘e5 ♗b7 11. ♖c1 ♖c8 N (11... 0–0?! – 48/144) 12. ♘df3 0–0 13. cd5 ed5 14. ♘d3 ♘e4 15. ♘fe5 ♖fd8 (×f5) 16. f3 ♘g5 17. e3 ♗e5! 18. de5 c5∞ Zajac 2350 – Prudnikova 2335, Debrecen 1992; ⌓ 15... c5 Prudnikova] **c6 5. ♘h3 d5 6. 0–0 ♗d6 7. ♗f4 ♗e7 8. ♘c3 0–0 9. ♕c2 dc4!? N** [9... h6 – 49/143] **10. ♖ad1 ♘bd7 11. ♗c1** [⌓ 11. f3 △ e4] **♘b6 12. e4 ♗b4! 13. f3** [13. ef5?! ♗c3! (13... ef5 14. d5! cd5 15. ♘d5!) 14. ♕c3 ef5 15. ♘f4 ♘fd5∓] **♕e7 14. a3 ♗a5 15. ♔h1** [⌓ 15. ♗f4] **fe4 16. fe4 e5 17. de5 ♕e5 18. ♘g5 h6** [18... ♗c3?! 19. bc3 ♗g4 20. ♖d4 h6 21. ♗f4 ♕e8 22. e5 hg5 23. ef6 gf4 24. ♖df4! ♕h5 25. f7! ♔h8 26. h3+–; 18... ♗g4!? 19. ♗f4! ♗d1 20. ♖d1 ♕e8 21. e5! h6 22. ef6 hg5 23. fg7 ♔g7 24. ♗g5=∞↑] **19. ♗f4 ♕e8 20. ♗d6! hg5 21. ♗f8 ♔f8 22. e5! ♕e5 23. ♖de1 ♗c3!□** [23... ♕c7 24.

♕h7; 23... ♕d6 24. ♘e4!→] **24. bc3! ♕d6 25. ♕g6 ♗g4 26. ♖f6! gf6 27. ♕h6 ♔g8 28. ♕g6 1/2 : 1/2 [Vojska]**

118.** **!N** **A 90**

ČEHOV 2480 – JUSUPOV 2645

Deutschland 1993

1. d4 e6 2. c4 f5 3. ♘f3 ♘f6 4. g3 d5 5. ♗g2 c6 6. 0–0 ♗d6 7. ♕c2 [RR 7. b3 ♕e7 8. ♗b2 0–0 9. ♕c1 b5?! 10. ♗a3!? N (10. ♘e5 – 51/(96)) b4 11. ♗b2 a5 12. a3! ♘a6 13. ab4 ♘b4 14. ♘c3 ♘e4 15. ♘a4! (×a5) ♗b7 16. ♘e5 c5!? (16... ♗c7 17. ♘d3!± △ ♘dc5) 17. dc5 (17. f3?! cd4 18. ♗d4 ♘c5⇆) ♘c5 18. ♘c5 ♗c5 19. cd5 ♖fc8 (19... ed5 20. ♕d2± ×d5; 19... ♗d5 20. ♗d5 ed5 21. ♕d2± ×a5, d5 Magerramov, S. Guliev) 20. ♕d2 ♘d5± S. Guliev 2485 – Moskalenko 2555, Nikolaev (zt) 1993] **0–0 8. ♘c3!? ♘e4! N** [8... ♗d7 9. ♗g5 ♗e8 10. ♘e5 h6 11. ♗f6 ♕f6 12. cd5 cd5 13. ♘d5!+–; 9... h6 – 50/116] **9. ♖b1 ♗d7** [RR 9... a5!? 10. a3 ♕e7 11. b4 ab4 12. ab4 ♗d7 13. c5 ♗c7 14. ♗f4 ♗f4 15. gf4± Grabuzova 2220 – Zajceva 2300, Orël 1993] **10. b4 ♗e8** [10... a6 11. c5 ♗c7 12. ♘a4 ♗e8 13. ♗f4 ♗f4 14. gf4 ♘d7 15. ♘e5±] **11. b5 ♘d7** [11... ♘c3 12. ♕c3 cb5 13. cb5 ♘d7 14. ♗a3 ♖c8 15. ♕e3±] **12. bc6 bc6 13. ♘e4!?** [13. cd5 cd5 14. ♘b5 ♖c8 15. ♕b3 ♗b8∞] **fe4** [13... de4 14. ♘g5 ♖f6 15. c5 ♗c7 16. ♕c4 ♘f8 17. f4!±] **14. ♘g5 ♖f6 15. c5 ♗c7 16. f4!± h6 17. ♘h3 ♗h5 18. ♗e3** [18. ♖b2!? ♖b8 19. e3 △ ♖f2, ♕a4±] **♕c8! 19. ♖b2 ♕a6 20. ♖fb1 ♖ff8 21. ♗f1?!** [21. ♖b7!? ♖fc8 22. ♗f1 ♖ab8 23. ♕b2±] **♖ab8 22. ♗c1** [22. ♘f2!?] **♖b2 23. ♖b2 ♖b8 24. e3 ♕c8 25. ♘f2 ♘f6 26. ♗d2 ♖b2 27. ♕b2 ♗d8 28. ♕a3 ♕c7** [28... ♕b7 29. ♕b4] **29. ♗a6 ♗f3 30. ♕b3 ♘d7 31. ♕b7 ♘b8= 32. ♕c7 ♗c7 33. ♗c8?!** [33. ♗f1=] **♔f7 34. ♔f1 ♔e7 35. ♗c3** [35... ♗h5 36. f5]
1/2 : 1/2 **[Čehov]**

119. **A 99**

D. RAJKOVIĆ 2450 – POLULJAHOV 2515

Star Dojran 1993

1. d4 e6 2. c4 f5 3. ♘f3 ♘f6 4. g3 ♗e7 5. ♗g2 0–0 6. 0–0 d6 7. ♘c3 a5 8. b3 ♕e8 9. ♗a3 ♘a6 10. ♖e1 c6 N [10... ♘b4; 10... ♗d7] **11. ♘a4** [11. e4? fe4 12. ♘e4 ♘e4 13. ♖e4 d5–+] **♘d7 12. ♗b2** [12. e4 b5! (12... fe4? 13. ♖e4 b5 14. cb5 cb5 15. ♖e6 ♘f6 16. ♖e2! ba4 17. ♗d6 ♖a7 18. ♕e1 ♘d5 19. ♕a5+–) 13. ef5 ba4 14. fe6 ♘f6 15. ba4 ♖b8∓] **b5 13. cb5 cb5 14. ♘c3 b4 15. ♘a4 ♗b7 16. ♖c1 ♕b8!= 17. ♕d2 ♗d5 18. ♘g5 ♗g2** [18... ♕b7 19. ♗d5 ♕d5 20. ♕e3 ♗g5 21. ♕g5 h6 22. ♕d2∞] **19. ♔g2 ♗g5 20. ♕g5 ♘f6! 21. ♕f4 ♕b7 22. ♔g1 ♖ad8 23. ♕f3 ♘d5 24. e3□** [24. ♖c2 f4 25. ♕e4 ♖f6∓] **♘b8 25. ♕g2! ♘d7 26. e4 fe4 27. ♖e4 ♖f6 28. ♖ce1 ♘f8 29. ♖4e2 ♕f7** [△ 30... ♘f4 31. gf4 ♖g6–+] **30. ♗c1 ♖c8 31. ♕e4 ♘g6?!** [×e6, d6, a5] **32. ♗g5 ♖f5 33. ♗d2 ♖e8 34. ♘b2 ♘c3?⊕** [34... ♘f8! 35. ♘c4 ♖d8□∞ 36. ♘a5? ♘f6–+] **35. ♗c3 bc3 36. ♘a4± ♖f3 37. ♔g2?⊕** [37. ♖c2! d5 38. ♕e2± ×e6, c3] **♖f8∞ 38. ♖f1□ e5 39. de5** [39. ♘b6 ed4 40. ♕d4 ♕b7 41. ♔g1 (41. ♕d5 ♕d5 42. ♘d5 ♖d3∓) ♘e5 42. ♕d5 ♕d5 43. ♘d5=] **♘e5 40. ♘b6 ♕h5** [40... h6 41. ♘c4 ♘c4 42. bc4 ♖f5 43. ♖c2 ♖c5 44. ♖c3 d5=] **41. ♕d5 ♕f7** [41... ♔h8 42. ♕d6 ♘g6! 43. ♘d7 ♖g3 44. hg3 ♘f4! 45. gf4 ♕g4=] **42. ♕f7** [42. ♕d6? ♖g3! 43. hg3 ♕f3 44. ♔g1 ♕e2∓] **♖3f7 43. ♘d5 ♖c8 44. ♖c2 ♖c5 45. ♖d1 ♘g4 46. ♘f4□** [46. h3? ♖f2 47. ♖f2 ♘f2 48. ♔f2 ♖d5! 49. ♖d5 c2–+] **g5 47. h3 ♘f2 48. ♔f2 gf4 49. g4=** [♖ 9/q] **d5 50. ♖d3 ♖fc7 51. ♔f3 ♔f7 52. ♖d4 ♔e6 53. ♖f4 ♖b5 54. ♔e3 ♖b4 55. ♖f5 a4 56. ba4 ♖a4 57. ♔d3 ♖a3 58. ♖f8 ♔e5 59. ♖e8 ♔f4 60. ♖d8 ♔e5**
1/2 : 1/2 **[D. Rajković]**

B

120.* !N **B 01**

SUĖTIN 2410 – BEZGODOV 2345
Alusta (open) 1993

1. e4 d5 2. ed5 ♘f6 3. d4 ♘d5 4. c4 [RR 4. ♘f3 g6 5. g3! N ♗g7 6. ♗g2 0–0 7. 0–0 c5 (7... ♘b6 8. ♕e2!) 8. dc5 ♘a6 9. ♕e2! ♕c7 10. c4 ♘f6 11. ♗f4 ♕c5 12. ♘c3 (Vatnikov 2445 – Ri. Bauer 2245, USA 1992) ♗e6 13. b3 ♖ad8 14. ♖ad1⩲ Vatnikov] **♘b6 5. ♘f3 g6 6. ♘c3 ♗g7 7. h3 c5 8. ♗e3 N** [8. d5 – 45/(121)] **cd4 9. ♗d4 0–0 10. ♗g7 ♔g7 11. ♕d4! ♕d4** [11... f6?! 12. 0-0-0 ♕e8 13. c5!±] **12. ♘d4 e5** [12... ♗d7 13. c5!; 12... ♘c6 13. ♘c6 bc6 14. 0-0-0⩲] **13. ♘db5 ♘c6 14. 0-0-0⩲ ♖b8** [14... a6 15. ♘c7 ♖b8 (15... ♖a7 16. ♖d6! ♖d8 17. c5! ♘d7 18. b4±) 16. ♖d6 (△ ♘a6) ♖d8 17. c5 ♖d6 (17... ♘d7 18. b4) 18. ♘e8 ♔f8 19. ♘d6 ♘d7 20. ♘a4±] **15. ♘d5! ♗f5 16. ♘b6 ab6 17. ♗e2** [17. b3⩲] **♖a8 18. a3 ♖fc8 19. g4** [19. b4? ♘b4! 20. ab4 ♖a2∓] **♗e6 20. b3 ♔f8 21. ♔b2 ♔e7 22. ♗f3 ♖d8 23. ♖he1** [23. ♗d5!] **f5?!** [23... ♖d1 24. ♗d1 (24. ♖d1 ♖d8) ♖d8 25. ♔c3⩲] **24. ♗d5! ♖ac8 25. gf5 gf5 26. ♖g1± e4!?** [26... ♖g8 27. ♖g8 (27. ♘c3±) ♖g8 28. ♗e6 ♔e6 29. ♖d6 ♔e7 30. ♖h6±] **27. ♖g7?** [27. f3!! ♘e5 (27... ef3 28. ♖ge1+–) 28. fe4 fe4 29. ♗e4+–] **♔f6 28. ♖b7 ♗d5 29. cd5 ♘e5 30. ♖b6 ♔g5= 31. ♘d6** [31. a4 ♘d3 32. ♔a3 ♘f2 33. ♖g1 ♔f4 34. ♖c6] **♖c7 32. ♘b5 ♖cc8** [32... ♖c5 33. ♘d4!±] **33. ♘d6 ♖c7 1/2 : 1/2 [Suėtin]**

121.** !N **B 01**

ZAJCEV 2450 – GIPSLIS 2490
Minsk 1993

1. e4 d5 2. ed5 ♘f6 3. d4 ♘d5 4. c4 ♘b6 5. ♘f3 ♗g4 6. ♘bd2 N [RR 6. ♗e2 *a)* 6... ♘c6 7. d5 ♗f3 8. gf3 ♘e5 9. f4 ♘ed7 10. ♘c3 (10. f5 g6 11. ♗e3 ♘f6! 12. ♘c3 ♗g7 13. ♗f3 ♕d7 14. ♕d3 ♕f5 15. ♕f5 gf5 16. ♖g1 ♖g8 17. c5 ♘bd7 18. d6!∞) ♘f6 11. ♗e3 g6! N (11... c6 – 55/(114)) 12. ♕c2 c6 13. dc6 bc6 14. ♖d1 ♕c7 15. f5 ♗g7 16. b3 ♘bd7!? 17. ♗f3∞ Kirilovs 2360 – Gipslis 2490, Katowice 1993; 13. 0-0-0!?; 12... ♗g7!? Gipslis; *b)* 6... e6 7. 0–0 ♘c6 8. ♗e3 (8. ♘c3 – 55/(114)) ♗f3 9. ♗f3 ♘c4 10. ♕b3 ♘b6 11. d5 ed5 12. ♗b6 ab6 13. ♗d5 ♕f6 14. ♘c3 ♗e7 15. ♘e4 ♕f5 N (15... ♕g6 – 26/151) 16. ♘g3 ♕f6 17. ♘e4 1/2 : 1/2 L. Pantaleoni – T. Peters, corr. 1993] **e6 7. c5 ♘6d7□** [7... ♘d5 8. ♕b3 b6 (8... ♕c8 9. ♘e5±) 9. ♘e5±] **8. ♕b3** [8. b4 ♘c6∞] **b6!?** [8... ♕c8? 9. h3 ♗h5 10. g3 ♗e7 11. ♗g2±↑] **9. h3 ♗f3** [9... ♗h5?! 10. g4 ♗g6 11. ♗g2±↑] **10. ♘f3** [10. ♕f3 c6 11. b4 ♘f6∞] **♗e7** [10... bc5 11. ♗g5 f6□ 12. ♕e6 ♕e7 13. ♕e7 ♗e7 14. ♗f4⩲] **11. g3!?** [11. ♗d3 0–0 12. c6 ♘f6; 11. a4!? bc5 12. ♕b7 ♘b6 13. a5 ♕d5!] **0–0 12. ♗g2 bc5 13. 0–0** [13. ♘e5? cd4!↑] **♘c6! 14. dc5 ♘c5?!** [14... ♖b8! (Gipslis) △ 15. ♕a4 ♘c5 16. ♕c6 ♖b6] **15. ♕c4!⩲ ♕d3□** [15... ♕d5? 16. ♘d2!±] **16. ♘d2** [16. ♕d3?! ♘d3 17. ♘e1 ♘db4 △ ♘d5] **♘d4** [16... ♕d6? 17. b4±] **17. ♗a8 ♖a8 18. b3□** [18. ♕d3 ♘d3 19. ♘b3 ♘e2 20. ♔g2 ♘ec1 21. ♘c1 ♘b2=∞] **♗f6 19. ♖b1**

♘e2 20. ♔g2 ♘c3 21. ♖b2 ♕d5 22. ♘f3 ♘5e4 23. ♖c2! c5 24. ♗b2?! [24. ♗d2! ♘d2 25. ♖d2 ♕b7 26. ♖d3± ♘d5 27. ♕c5 ♖c8 28. ♕a5] **♕c4! 25. bc4 ♘a2!=∞ 26. ♗f6 ♘b4 27. ♖c3 gf6 28. ♖a3 ♘d6 29. ♖a5 ♘c4 30. ♖c5 ♘b6 31. ♖a1 ♘6d5 32. ♘d4 ♔g7 33. ♖a4** [33. ♘b5 a6 34. ♘c7↑] **a6 34. ♖b5 ♘d3 35. ♖b7??⊕ ♘c5 36. ♘e6 ♘e6 37. ♖g4 ♔f8 38. ♖h4 ♔g7?!** [38... ♘c5 39. ♖h7; 38... h5!?∓] **39. ♖g4 ♔f8 40. ♖h4 ♔g8?! 41. ♖g4 1/2 : 1/2**
[Zajcev]

122.* **B 01**

ROZENTALIS 2595 — HALIFMAN 2630
Deutschland 1993

1. e4 d5 2. ed5 ♕d5 3. ♘c3 ♕a5 4. g3 ♘f6 5. ♗g2 c6 [5... ♗g4 N 6. ♘ge2 ♘c6 7. h3 ♗h5 8. d3 e5 9. 0–0 0-0-0 10. a3 ♘d4 11. g4 ♗g6 12. f4!± Rozentalis 2590 — Milos 2555, Tilburg (Interpolis) 1992] **6. ♘f3 ♗g4 N** [6... ♗f5 7. 0–0 e6 8. d3 ♗e7 9. h3 h6±] **7. 0–0 e6 8. h3 ♗f3** [8... ♗h5] **9. ♕f3 ♗e7 10. a3!? 0–0 11. ♖b1 ♕c7 12. b4 a6 13. d3 ♘bd7 14. ♗f4 ♗d6 15. ♗d2 a5 16. ♕e2!± ♗e7?** [16... ♖fe8] **17. f4 ♖fe8 18. g4 ♗f8 19. ♕f3** [⌓ 19. ♕f2] **g6 20. ♔h1?** [20. f5!] **ab4 21. ab4 ♗g7 22. b5 ♖ac8?** [22... ♘d5 23. ♘e4 f5!=] **23. bc6 bc6 24. ♘e2!± ♕d6 25. ♘g3 ♕d5?⊕ 26. ♕f2 ♕d6 27. f5 ef5 28. gf5 c5 29. ♗f4! ♘e5** [29... ♕d4 30. ♗b7] **30. ♗g5 ♘ed7 31. ♖b7 ♕d4 32. ♘e4 ♘e4 33. ♗e4 ♕f2 34. ♖f2 ♘e5 35. ♗d5 ♖b8 36. ♖a7 ♔h8** [⌓ 36... gf5] **37. f6 ♗f8 38. ♗f7 ♘f7 39. ♖f7 h6 40. ♗d2 ♖e6 41. ♗c3+– c4 42. dc4 ♖e3 43. ♗d4 ♖h3 44. ♔g2 ♖h5 45. ♖c7 ♖g5 46. ♔f1 ♖g4 47. c3 ♖b1 48. ♔e2 ♖g3 49. ♖f3** [49. c5? ♖b2=] **♖g2 50. ♔d3 ♖d1 51. ♔e4 ♖e1 52. ♖e3 ♖f1 53. c5 1 : 0**
[Rozentalis]

123.* **B 04**

PSAKHIS 2575 — VAGANIAN 2615
Rostov na Donu 1993

1. e4 ♘f6 2. e5 ♘d5 3. d4 d6 4. ♘f3 de5 5. ♘e5 g6 6. ♗c4 ♗e6 [RR 6... c6 7. 0–0 ♗g7 8. ♖e1 0–0 9. ♗b3 ♗e6 10. ♘d2 ♘d7 11. ♘ef3 ♘c7 12. c3 c5 13. ♗c2!? N (13. ♗e6 — 55/119) cd4 14. ♘d4 ♗d5 15. ♘f1 e5 16. ♘f3 ♔h8 17. b3?! f5∞↑⊞ Wang Zili 2515 — Deng Kongliang 2430, Beijing (zt) 1993; 17. ♘e3!? ♗e6 18. ♕d6!? Wang Zili; 17. ♗b3!? Deng Kongliang] **7. ♗b3** [7. ♘c3 ♗g7 8. ♕f3 c6 9. 0–0 0–0 10. ♘e4 ♘c7! 11. ♗e6 ♘e6 12. c3 ♕d5∞] **♗g7 8. 0–0 0–0 9. ♘f3!? N** [9. ♕e2 — 4/138] **♗g4 10. ♘bd2 a5** [10... ♗d4?? 11. h3!+–] **11. a3 c6 12. h3 ♗f3 13. ♘f3± e6 14. ♗g5 ♘e7 15. ♕d2 ♘d7 16. ♖fe1 ♖e8!?** [16... ♘f6 17. ♕f4! ♘fd5 18. ♕h4↑] **17. h4** [17. ♕f4 ♕b8!] **♘f6 18. c3 ♕b6 19. ♗a2 ♘f5 20. h5! c5!** [20... ♘h5? 21. g4 h6 22. gf5 hg5 23. fe6] **21. h6 ♗h8 22. ♕f4 cd4** [22... ♘h5!? 23. ♕h2!? (23. ♕d2 ♘f6!=) ♕b2 24. g4 ♕c3 25. gf5 ♕f3 (25... ef5 26. ♕c7) 26. fe6 fe6 27. ♖e6 (27. ♗e6? ♖e6 28. ♖e6 ♕g4–+) ♕g4 28. ♕g2 ♕g2 29. ♔g2 ♖e6 30. ♗e6 ♔f8 31. ♖b1=∞] **23. g4 ♘g4** [23... dc3 24. gf5 cb2 25. fe6!] **24. ♕g4 dc3 25. bc3 ♗c3 26. ♖ab1 ♕c5 27. ♖e2** [27. ♖ec1?! ♕a3] **b5** [27... ♕a3? 28. ♖b3 ♕c5 29. ♖c2+–] **28. ♕f4!?** [△ ♘e5] **♖a6?! 29. a4! b4** [29... ba4 30. ♕a4↑] **30. ♖d1 ♖d6□ 31. ♖d6 ♕d6 32. ♕d6 ♘d6 33. ♔g2 ♘b7 34. ♗e3 ♖c8 35. ♘g5!** [△ ♘e6] **♘c5 36. ♗c5 ♖c5 37. ♘e4 ♖c8 38. ♘c3 ♖c3** [♖ **8/g6**; 38... bc3 39. ♖c2 ♔f8 40. ♔f3 ♔e7 41. ♔e3 ♔f6 42. ♔d4±] **39. ♖e5 ♔f8** [39... ♖a3 40. ♖a5] **40. ♖a5 b3 41. ♗b1 ♖c1 42. ♗e4 f5** [42... ♖c4 43. ♔f3; 42... b2 43. ♖b5 (43. ♖a8 ♔e7 44. ♖h8 ♖e1) ♖c4 44. ♔f3 ♖a4 45. ♖b2 f5 46. ♗b1 ♖h4 47. ♖b8 ♔f7 48. ♖b7 ♔f6 (48... ♔g8? 49. ♗a2 ♖h6 50. ♗e6 ♔f8 51. ♔f4+–) 49. ♖h7 e5!? (49... ♔g5 50. ♖e7 ♔f6 51. ♖e8 ♖h6 52. ♗a2+–) 50. ♔g3! (50. ♖h8 ♔g5 51. h7 ♔f6 52. ♗a2 ♔g7 53. ♖e8 e4 54. ♔g3 ♖h7) ♖h5 (50... ♔g5 51. ♖e7+–; 50... g5 51. ♖h8) 51. ♖h8 e4!? 52. ♗a2 ♔g5 53. h7 ♔f6 (53... ♔h6 54. ♗f7! ♖g5 55. ♔f4 ♖g4 56. ♔e5 ♔g7 57. ♖a8 ♔h7 58. ♔f6+–) 54. ♖f8 ♔g7 55. ♖f7 ♔h8 56. ♔f4 ♖h2 (56... ♖h7 57. ♖h7 ♔h7 58. ♔g5+–) 57. ♔g5 ♖f2 58. ♗d5! ♖g2 (58... e3? 59. ♔g6+–) 59. ♔h6 ♖h2 60. ♔g6 ♖g2 61. ♔f6 ♖h2 62. ♖f8 ♔h7 63. ♗g8 ♔h6 64.

♗f7+−] **43. ♖a8 ♔e7** [43... ♔f7 44. ♖a7 ♔g8 45. ♗d3 (45. ♖g7 ♔f8 46. ♖h7 fe4 47. ♖b7 ♔g8 48. ♖b3 ♖a1 49. ♖b4 ♔h7=) b2 (45... ♖c3 46. ♗f1) 46. ♖b7 ♖a1 (46... ♖d1 47. ♗c2+−) 47. ♖b2 ♖a4 48. ♖b8 ♔f7 49. ♖b7 ♔f6 (49... ♔g8 50. ♖g7) 50. ♖h7 ♖h4 51. ♖h8+−] **44. ♖a7 ♔f6 45. ♖h7! fe4 46. ♖b7 e3!?** [46... ♖c4 47. ♖b3 ♖a4 48. ♖h3+−] **47. fe3 ♖c4 48. a5! ♖g4** [48... ♖h4 49. a6 ♖h6 50. a7 ♖h8 51. ♖b8 b2 52. ♖h8 b1♕ 53. a8♕ ♕c2 (53... ♕b2 54. ♔h3+−) 54. ♔g3 ♕c7 55. ♔h3+−] **49. ♔f3 ♖h4 50. a6 ♖h6 51. a7 ♖h8 52. ♖b8 b2 53. ♖b2** [53. ♖h8 b1♕ 54. a8♕ ♕f1] **♖a8 54. ♖a2+− ♔g5 55. ♖a4!** [55. ♔e4? ♔g4 56. ♔e5 ♔f3 57. e4 g5 58. ♖a3 ♔f2 59. ♔e6 g4 60. e5 g3=] **♔f6** [55... ♔f5 56. ♖a5 e5 57. e4 ♔f6 58. ♔g4] **56. ♖a5 ♔e7 57. ♔f4 ♔d6 58. ♔g5 ♔c6 59. ♔g6**
1 : 0 [Psakhis]

124.* **B 06**

V. MILOV 2410 − ANNE SEGAL 2180
Israel 1993

1. d4 g6 2. e4 ♗g7 3. ♘c3 c6 4. ♗c4 d6 [4... d5 5. ed5 b5 6. ♗b3 b4 7. ♘ce2 cd5 8. a3 N (8. ♘f3 − 32/(164)) ba3 9. ♖a3 ♘f6 10. ♘f3 0−0 11. 0−0 ♘c6 12. ♘e5 ♗b7 (V. Milov 2340 − Gofshtein 2550, Israel (ch) 1992) 13. ♘f4±] **5. ♕f3 e6 6. ♘ge2 ♘f6 7. ♗g5 ♘bd7 8. 0−0 0−0 9. ♗b3 ♕a5!? N** [9... ♕e7 − 53/116] **10. ♗h4 e5 11. ♖ad1 ed4 12. ♘d4 ♘e5 13. ♕e2** [13. ♕f4!? ♘h5 14. ♕d2 △ 14... c5 15. ♘de2 c4 16. ♗a4 a6 17. ♕d6! (17. ♗e7 b5 18. ♗f8 ♗f8 19. ♕d5 ♖b8 △ ♗b7) b5 18. b4 cb3 19. ♗d8 ♘c4 20. ♗a5 ♘d6 21. ♗b3±] **b6!?** [△ ♗a6, c5-c4]

(diagram)

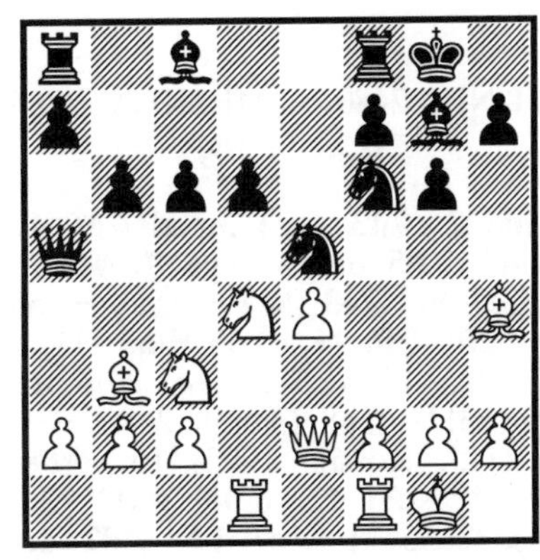

14. f4! ♗a6 15. fe5! [15. ♕d2? ♗f1 16. fe5 de5∓] **♗e2** [15... de5 16. ♘c6 ♕c3 17. ♘e7 ♔h8 18. ♕f2! ♘e4 19. bc3 ♘f2 20. ♖f2+−] **16. ef6 ♗f1** [16... ♗d1 17. fg7 ♔g7 18. ♗f6] **17. fg7 ♔g7 18. ♖f1 ♖ae8?!** [18... ♕c5? 19. ♗f6 ♔g8 20. ♘a4 △ ♘c6+−; 18... ♖ac8?! 19. ♗f6 ♔g8 20. h3 △ ♖f3±; 18... ♕e5 19. ♗f6 ♕f6 20. ♖f6 ♔f6 21. ♘c6± ×d5] **19. ♗f6 ♔g8 20. ♘c6 ♕c5 21. ♘d4 ♖e5 22. ♖d1 h6 23. h3± ♖fe8 24. ♔h1 ♖h5 25. ♖f1 ♕c8 26. ♖f3 ♖f8 27. ♘d5 ♖d5 28. ♗d5 ♕c7 29. ♘f5 ♔h7 30. ♘e3 ♕d7 31. ♗c3 h5 32. ♖f6+− b5 33. ♘f1 ♕c7 34. ♘d2 b4 35. ♗b4 ♕c2 36. ♗c3 g5 37. ♗b3 ♕d3 38. ♘f3 ♖g8 39. ♗f7 ♖g7 40. ♗h5 ♕e4 41. ♗g4 ♕e3 42. ♖f8 ♔h6 43. ♗f5 ♕c1 44. ♔h2 1 : 0** [V. Milov]

125. **B 06**

V. DIMITROV 2445 − NIJBOER 2485
Debrecen 1992

1. e4 d6 2. d4 g6 3. ♘c3 ♗g7 4. ♗e3 a6 5. ♕d2 b5 6. f3 c6 7. h4 N [7. ♘ge2 − 25/168] **♘f6 8. ♗h6 ♗h6 9. ♕h6 ♕a5 10. ♘e2 ♘bd7 11. ♘c1 c5 12. ♘b3 ♕c7 13. ♕e3 cd4 14. ♕d4 ♕b6** [14... ♗b7?! 15. a4 e5 16. ♕b4 ba4 17. ♕a4±] **15. ♕d2 ♗b7 16. 0-0-0 ♘c5 17. ♘c5 ♕c5 18. ♗d3 0-0-0 19. ♔b1 ♔b8 20. ♕h6 ♖c8 21. ♖he1 ♘d7 22. f4 e5 23. g3 ♕f2?!** [23... ♕b6] **24. ♕g5 ♖he8** [24... f6? 25. ♕g4 f5 26. ef5? ♗f3∓; 26. ♕g5±] **25. ♖f1 ♕b6 26. f5 ♖c3! 27. bc3 ♘c5 28. fg6 fg6 29. ♖f7 ♘a4 30. ♖df1 ♕c5 31. ♔c1** [31. ♖f8? ♕a3 32. ♖e8 ♔a7−+] **♕a3 32. ♔d1 ♘c3 33. ♔e1 d5 34. ♖d7?** [34. ♖h7 ♕b4 35. ♖ff7 ♘e4 36. ♔f1 ♘g5 37. ♖b7=] **de4 35. ♖ff7 ♗c8 36. ♕e3 ♗d7 37. ♖d7 ♔c8 38. ♕a7 ♕c1 39. ♔f2 ♘d1! 40. ♔e1 ♘c3 41. ♔f2 ♘d1 42. ♔e1 ♘b2** [43. ♔f2 ♘d3 44. cd3 ♖f8 45. ♖f7 ♕c2 46. ♔g1 ♕b1 47. ♔h2 ♕a2 48. ♔h3 ♕e6 49. ♔g2 ♖f7−+] **0 : 1** [Nijboer]

126.* **B 07**

TUNIK 2480 – MEŠKOV 2285

Rossija 1992

1. d4 d6 2. ♘f3 ♗g4 3. e4 ♘f6 4. ♘c3 e6 5. h3 ♗h5 6. g4 ♗g6 7. ♕e2 c6 8. ♗g5 ♗e7 9. ♕e3 N [9. ♗f6 – 55/124] **d5 10. ♗f6 ♗f6 11. ♗d3 ♕a5** [11... ♘a6 12. a3 ♘c5 13. dc5 d4 14. ♕f4 dc3 15. b4 (15. b3!?) ♕b8 (Tunik 2480 – Vorotnikov 2445, Rossija 1992) 16. ♕b8 ♖b8 17. ♔e2± ×c3] **12. 0-0-0 ♘d7 13. ♔b1** [13. ♘d2? c5!∓] **♗e7 14. ♘d2 de4 15. ♗e4! ♘f6 16. ♘c4 ♕c7 17. ♘e5 ♗e4 18. ♘e4 ♘e4 19. ♕e4± 0–0 20. h4?** [20. f3! △ h4, g5→] **f5!⇆ 21. ♕e2 fg4 22. ♘g4 ♕d6 23. h5 ♖f4** [23... h6? 24. ♘e5± ×g6] **24. h6 g6 25. ♖he1 ♗g5 26. ♖d3 ♖e8 27. a3! ♕f8** [27... ♖d4? 28. ♖d4 ♕d4 29. ♖d1+–] **28. ♖e3 ♖d4** [28... ♖g4? 29. ♖e6!+–] **29. ♖e6 ♖ed8 30. ♖e4 ♖d2 31. ♕c4 ♖2d5 32. f4 ♗h6 33. f5!∞̄** [33. ♘e3 ♔h8∞; 33. ♖e8 ♖e8 34. ♖e8 ♕e8 35. ♘f6 ♔f7 36. ♘e8 ♔e8∞] **♗g5!** [33... gf5 34. ♘h6 ♕h6 35. ♖e7→] **34. fg6 hg6 35. ♘e5 ♔g7 36. ♘d3 ♕f7?!** [36... ♖f5 △ ♖dd5, ♖f1∞] **37. ♖g4 ♖f5 38. ♕b4 ♖dd5?⊕** [38... a5 39. ♕b6∞̄] **39. ♖g5! ♖g5 40. ♖e7 1 : 0** **[Tunik]**

127. **B 07**

A. GOL'DIN 2555 – EPIŠIN 2620

New York 1993

1. d4 d6 2. ♘f3 ♗g4 3. e4 ♘f6 4. ♘c3 e6 5. h3 ♗h5 6. ♕e2 c6 [6... ♘bd7 7. g4 ♗g6 8. h4 h6 9. h5 ♗h7 10. g5 hg5 11. ♗g5 ♗e7 12. h6 gh6 13. ♖h6 ♘g4 14. ♗e7 ♕e7 15. ♖h4 ♘gf6 16. e5 de5 17. de5 ♘d5 18. ♘d5 ed5 19. 0-0-0±] **7. g4 ♗g6 8. h4 h5** [8... h6!? 9. h5 ♗h7 10. g5 hg5 11. ♗g5 ♕b6 12. 0-0-0 ♘bd7∞] **9. g5 ♘fd7 10. ♗h3** [10. ♗e3!? d5 (10... b5 11. a3 ♘b6 12. d5!→) 11. ♘d2 ♗b4 12. ♗g2 ♕a5 13. 0–0 ♗c3 14. bc3 ♕c3 15. f4!∞̄] **♗e7 11. ♘d2 N** [11. ♗e3 – 53/119] **d5** [11... e5 12. de5 de5 (12... ♘e5 13. f4±) 13. ♘f1! △ ♘g3±] **12. f4 de4 13. ♘de4 ♘b6 14. ♗e3 ♘d5 15. 0–0 ♘e3 16. ♕e3 ♘a6!** [16... 0–0 17. ♖ad1 △ ♕e2, ♘g3±; 16... ♘d7 17. f5! ♗f5 (17... ef5 18. ♘d6 ♔f8 19. ♗f5±) 18. ♗f5 ef5 19. ♘d6 ♔f8 20. ♘f5 g6 21. ♘e7 ♕e7 22. ♕e7 ♔e7 23. ♖ae1 ♔f8 24. ♘e4±] **17. f5?** [17. ♖ad1 ♘b4 (17... ♕b6 18. f5! ef5 19. ♘d6±; 17... ♗e4 18. ♘e4 g6 19. c4→) 18. ♖d2 ♘d5 19. ♘d5 ♕d5 (19... cd5 20. ♘g3±) 20. ♘g3 △ f5±] **ef5 18. ♗f5 0–0!= 19. ♗g6 fg6 20. ♖f8 ♗f8 21. ♖f1 ♕d7 22. ♘e2 ♖e8 23. ♘2g3 ♔h8?!** [23... ♘b4 24. c3 ♘d5 25. ♕f3 b5=] **24. c3 ♘c7 25. ♕f3 ♔g8 26. ♕f6! ♕e6□ 27. ♕e6 ♘e6± 28. ♔g2** [28. ♖f3! △ ♔f2-e2-d3] **♗e7 29. ♖f3 ♖d8 30. ♘e2 ♖d5 31. ♘d2?!⊕** [31. ♘f4 ♘f4 32. ♖f4 ♖f5 33. ♖f3!±] **♗d6! 32. ♘c4 ♗c7 33. ♔f2 b5!? 34. ♘e3 ♖d8 35. ♔e1?!** [35. ♘g2! a5 (35... c5? 36. ♘gf4 ♘f4 37. ♘f4 cd4 38. ♘e6±) 36. ♘gf4 ♘f8] **c5! 36. d5** [36. ♘c2 ♗b6 37. ♖d3 ♔f7=] **♘f8 37. ♘f4 ♖e8 38. ♔d2 ♖e4 39. ♘eg2 c4** [40. b3 ♗d6 41. ♖f2 ♔h7 42. bc4 bc4 43. ♘e2=] **1/2 : 1/2** **[A. Gol'din]**

128. **B 07**

SMIRIN 2590 – HUZMAN 2510

Wijk aan Zee (open) 1993

1. e4 d6 2. d4 ♘f6 3. ♗d3 e5 4. c3 d5 [4... ♘c6 – 56/129, 130] **5. de5 ♘e4 6. ♘f3 ♘c6 7. ♘bd2 N** [7. 0–0 – 38/147] **♗g4 8. 0–0 ♘d2** [8... ♘c5!?] **9. ♗d2 ♗e7 10. ♖e1 0–0 11. ♕c2 ♗f3 12. gf3 g6 13. f4 ♗c5 14. ♕d1! f6** [14... ♕h4 15. ♕f3±⊡] **15. b4** [15. e6? f5] **♗b6 16. c4! dc4** [16... fe5? 17. c5] **17. ♗c4 ♔g7 18. b5 ♘d4 19. a4!** [△ ♗b4, a5, △ ♖a3] **♘f5** [19... ♗c5!?] **20. ♗b4 fe5□ 21. ♗f8 ♕f8 22. ♖e5 ♘d6 23. ♕e2□ ♕f4 24. ♖e7 ♔h6 25. ♗d3 ♖f8**

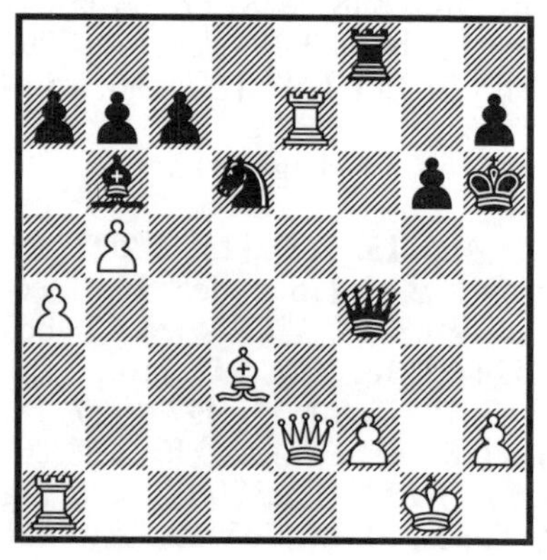

26. ♔h1! ♕g5 [26... ♕f2? 27. ♖h7! ♔h7 28. ♕h5; 26... ♗f2 27. ♖f1] **27. f3 ♘f5?** [27... ♖f4! 28. a5 ♗d4 29. ♖f1 ♖h4±⇆] **28. ♗f5 ♖f5 29. ♖f1± a6 30. ba6 ba6 31. ♖e4 a5 32. ♕e1! ♕f6?!** [32... ♖f4 33. ♕d2!+−] **33. ♕d2 ♕g5** [33... ♔g7 34. ♕d7 ♔h6 35. ♖e7 ♖f3 36. ♖h7 ♔g5 37. h4+−] **34. ♖h4+− ♔g7 35. ♕d7 ♖f7 36. ♖h7 ♔h7 37. ♕f7 ♔h6 38. ♕f8 ♔h7 39. ♖e1 ♗c5 40. ♕f7 ♔h6 41. ♕c7 ♕d2 42. ♕g3 ♕c2 43. ♕f4 ♔g7 44. ♖c1 ♕e2 45. ♕e4 ♗e3 46. ♖c7 1 : 0 [Smirin]**

129. **B 07**

HERTNECK 2575 – ADAMS 2630

München 1993

1. d4 d6 2. e4 ♘f6 3. ♗d3 e5 4. d5!? N ♘bd7! [△ c6, ♘c5] **5. ♘e2!?** [5. f3] **c6 6. c4 ♘c5 7. ♘bc3 ♘d3 8. ♕d3 ♗e7= 9. ♖b1?!** [9. 0–0] **0–0 10. b4** [⌓ 10. 0–0] **cd5 11. cd5 ♘h5! 12. 0–0** [12. ♘g3 ♘f4 (12... ♘g3 13. hg3 f5!?) 13. ♗f4 ef4 14. ♘ge2∞] **f5 13. f3** [13. ef5 ♗f5 14. ♘e4∓] **f4 14. ♗d2** [⌓ 14. g4 (Hertneck) fg3 (14... ♘f6!?) 15. hg3 ♗g5∓] **♕b6!** [14... ♗h4 15. ♗e1 ♕b6 16. ♗f2] **15. ♔h1 ♗h4 16. a4** [16. ♗e1!?] **♖f6 17. a5 ♕d8 18. ♘d1!□ ♖h6 19. ♔g1 ♖g6 20. ♘f2 ♗d7!?** [20... ♕g5 21. g4 ♘f6 22. ♔h1 h5 23. ♘h3 ♕h6 24. g5 ♗g5 25. ♘g5 ♖g5∓] **21. ♖bc1** [21. b5 ♖c8] **a6** [△ ♗b5] **22. ♗e1** [⌓ 22. ♕b3] **♕g5−+ 23. ♘g4 ♗e1 24. ♖ce1□ ♗g4 25. fg4 ♕g4 26. ♕f3 ♘f6!** [×e4] **27. ♕g4 ♖g4 28. h3** [28. ♘c3 ♖c8 29. ♖c1 ♖c4] **♖g6 29. ♖f3 ♖c8 30. ♖c3** [30. ♘c3 ♖g3!] **♖c3 31. ♘c3 ♖g3 32. ♖c1 ♖e3 33. b5 ab5 34. ♘b5 ♘e4 35. ♔f1 h5 36. ♖c7 ♘g3 37. ♔f2 ♖e2 38. ♔f3 g5 39. ♘d6 e4** [40. ♘e4 ♖e3 41. ♔f2 ♘e4 42. ♔f1 g4] **0 : 1 [Adams]**

130.** **B 07**

SAX 2570 – V. NEVEDNIČIJ 2495

Odorheiu Secuiesc 1993

1. e4 d6 2. d4 ♘f6 3. ♘c3 e5 [RR 3... ♘bd7 4. f4 e5 5. ♘f3 ed4 (5... c6 – 56/131, 132) 6. ♕d4 c6 *a)* 7. e5 N de5 8. fe5 ♗c5 9. ♕h4 ♕e7 10. ♗f4 ♗b4 11. 0-0-0 ♗c3 12. ef6 ♗f6 13. ♕g3 0–0 14. ♗c4 ♕b4 15. ♗b3 ♘c5 16. ♗d6 ♗f5 17. ♗f8 ♖f8 18. ♖hf1 ♘b3 19. ab3 ♗c2 1/2 : 1/2 Judasin 2610 – Rivas Pastor 2515, Dos Hermanas 1993; *b)* 7. ♗e3 d5 8. ed5!? N (8. e5 ♘g4 9. ♗g1) ♗c5 9. ♕d3 ♕e7 10. ♘d4 ♘b6 11. dc6 0–0 12. 0-0-0 bc6 13. ♗g1 ♕c7 14. g3 ♖d8?? 15. ♘db5 1 : 0 J. Polgár 2595 – Rivas Pastor 2515, Dos Hermanas 1993; 11... bc6] **4. ♘ge2 N** [4. de5 – 54/(112)] **c6 5. f3 h5!? 6. a4 a5 7. ♗e3 ♗e7 8. ♕d2 ♘a6** [8... ♘bd7 9. ♘g3 ♘f8 10. 0-0-0±] **9. ♘c1 ♘b4 10. ♘b3 ♗e6 11. 0-0-0 ♕b8** [11... ♗b3 12. cb3 ed4 13. ♗d4 d5 14. ♔b1 de4 15. fe4±] **12. de5 de5 13. ♘c5 ♕c8 14. ♕f2 h4 15. b3** [△ ♘e6, ♗c4] **♘h7 16. g3 ♘f8 17. ♗e2 ♗f6 18. ♖hg1 ♖b8 19. ♖d2 ♕c7** [19... b6 20. ♘e6 ♘e6 21. ♗b6 ♘d4 22. ♗d4 ed4 23. ♘b1±] **20. ♖gd1 b6 21. ♘e6 ♘e6 22. ♗c4 ♘d4 23. f4 ♘dc2** [23... ♘bc2 24. fe5 ♗e5 25. ♗d4 ♘d4 26. ♖d4 ♗d4 27. ♕d4 0–0 28. e5±] **24. ♖d7! ♕d7 25. ♖d7 ♔d7 26. fe5 ♘e3 27. ef6 ♘c4 28. ♕f5** [28. fg7?? ♘d3] **♔c7 29. fg7 ♘d6 30. gh8♕ ♖h8 31. ♕f6 ♖e8 32. ♕h4 ♘d3 33. ♔c2 ♘c5 34. ♕h7** [△ h4-h5] **b5 35. ab5 cb5 36. ♘d5 ♔c6 37. ♘f6 ♖e6 38. ♕h8 b4 39. ♕a8 ♔c7 40. ♕a5 ♔b7?⊕ 41. ♕c5 1 : 0 [Sax]**

131.* **B 07**

GAŽÍK 2425 – A. CHERNIN 2600

Budapest (zt) 1993

1. e4 d6 2. d4 ♘f6 3. ♘c3 g6 4. ♗e3 [RR 4. ♗g5 h6 5. ♗e3 ♘g4 6. ♗c1 N (6. ♗f4) e5 (6... ♗g7 7. f3 ♘f6 8. ♗e3± △ ♕d2) 7. f3 ed4 (7... ♘f6 8. ♗e3 ♘c6 9. ♘ge2±) 8. ♕d4 ♘f6 (8... ♘e5 9. f4!? c5 10. ♗b5 ♗d7 11. ♗d7 ♕d7 12. ♕d5±) 9. ♗e3 ♗g7 10. ♕d2 0–0 11. 0-0-0 ♔h7 (Gruzman 2260 – Gavrilov 2370, corr. 1991/93) 12. ♘ge2 ♘bd7 13. ♘f4 ♘e5 14. h4 ♘e8!? 15. ♗e2 c6 16. g4 b5± Gavrilov] **c6 5. ♕d2 b5 6. f3 ♘bd7 7. g4 ♘b6!? 8. b3 N** [8. g5; 8. h4; 8. ♗d3; 8. 0-0-0] **♗b7** [8... a5!?] **9. h4 h5 10. g5 ♘fd7 11. f4 ♗g7 12. f5!?** [12. ♗g2 △ ♘h3, 0–0] **0–0 13. ♗h3?!** [13. ♗g2∞] **c5!** [13... b4

14. ♘d1 c5 15. ♘f2] **14. fg6 fg6 15. ♘ge2 b4 16. ♘d5□ ♘d5 17. ♗e6 ♔h7 18. ed5 ♘b6 19. c4** [19. ♘f4 ♖f4! 20. ♗f4 ♗d5 21. ♗d5□ ♘d5∓] **bc3 20. ♘c3 ♗c8!∓ 21. 0-0-0 ♗e6 22. de6 ♕c8** [22... ♕c7!?] **23. dc5** [23. d5 ♕a6] **dc5 24. ♖he1** [24. ♖hf1! (△ ♖f7) ♕e6 25. ♗c5∓] **♖f5–+ 25. ♗g1 ♕a6 26. ♖e4 ♖af8 27. ♔b1 ♕b7 28. ♖e2** [28. ♖de1 ♖f3 29. ♖1e3 ♗c3 30. ♕c3 ♕e4] **♘c4 29. ♕d7** [29. ♕c1 ♕b4] **♘a3 30. ♔c1 ♕b4 31. ♘a4** [31. ♘d5 ♖d5] **c4 32. ♖e4** [32. ♗d4 cb3! 33. ♗g7 ba2 34. ♗b2 a1♕ 35. ♗a1 ♕b1 36. ♔d2 ♕c2 37. ♔e3 ♖f3 38. ♔d4 ♕c4 39. ♔e5 ♖8f5#] **♖f3 33. ♗c5 ♖c3 34. ♔d2 ♖c2 35. ♔e3 ♕b8** [35... ♖ff2] **36. ♖d6⊕ ♖cf2 37. ♖e5 ♘c2 38. ♔e4 ♖8f4 39. ♔d5 ♕a8 40. ♖c6 ♖d2 41. ♗d4 ♖fd4 0 : 1**
[A. Chernin]

132. B 08**

SAVON 2420 – ČERNIŠOV 2485

Podol'sk 1992

1. e4 d6 2. d4 g6 3. ♘f3 ♗g7 4. ♗e2 ♘f6 5. ♘c3 c6 6. 0–0 0–0 7. ♖e1 [RR 7. a4 a5 8. ♗f4 ♘a6 9. ♕d2 N (9. h3 – 27/180) ♗g4 10. ♗h6 ♗f3 11. ♗f3 *a)* 11... e5 12. ♖fd1 ♘b4?! 13. ♖ac1 ♕e7 14. ♗g5 ♖fe8 15. d5! cd5 16. ♗f6 ♗f6 17. ♘d5 ♘d5 18. ♕d5 ♗g5 19. ♖b1 ♕d7 20. ♗e2± P. Blatný 2515 – Danschczyk 2290, Deutschland 1992; *b)* 11... ♗h6 12. ♕h6 e5 13. ♖fd1 ♕e7 14. ♕e3 ♖fd8 15. ♘e2 ♖d7 16. c3 ♖ad8 17. ♖d2? d5! 18. de5 ♕e5 19. ed5 ♕e3 20. fe3 ♘d5 21. ♗d5! ♖d5 22. ♖d5 ♖d5 23. ♘d4 ♘c5∓ P. Blatný 2505 – Kaliničev 2480, Deutschland 1993; 17. ♘g3= Kaliničev] **♘bd7 8. ♗f4 ♕c7 9. e5 ♘h5 10. ♗g5 de5 11. ♗e7 ♖e8 12. d5 ♕b6!? N** [12... ♖e7 – 55/134] **13. dc6** [13. ♗a3 e4!?∞] **bc6 14. ♗a3 e4! 15. ♗c4** [15. ♘g5?! ♗c3 (15... ♘hf6? 16. ♘f7!+–) 16. bc3 ♕a5 17. ♗c1 ♘hf6∞; 15... e3!∓] **♘hf6 16. ♘g5 ♘e5 17. ♘ce4 ♗g4! 18. ♘f6** [18. ♗e2?! ♖ad8 19. ♕c1 ♘e4 20. ♘e4 ♗e2 21. ♖e2 ♘c4∓] **♗f6 19. ♕d6 ♗g5** [19... c5?! 20. ♘e4 ♗g7 21. ♗d5 ♖ad8 22. ♕b6 ab6 23. ♗b3±] **20. ♖e5 ♖ed8! 21. ♕c5 ♗f6 22. ♖ee1** [22. ♕b6?! ab6 23. ♖e3 (23. ♖ee1 ♖a3 24. ba3 ♗a1 25. ♖a1 ♗f5 26. ♗b3 ♖d2=∞) b5 24. ♗f1 (24. ♗b3 ♖a3–+) ♖d2 25. c3 ♖ad8=∞] **♕c5 23. ♗c5 ♗b2 24. ♖ab1 ♗d4!= 1/2 : 1/2**
[Černišov, Raeckij]

133. B 08

MORÓVIĆ FERNÁNDEZ 2570 – NOGUEIRAS 2570

Las Palmas 1992

1. e4 d6 2. d4 g6 3. ♘f3 ♗g7 4. ♗e2 ♘f6 5. ♘c3 0–0 6. 0–0 c6 7. ♗f4 ♘bd7 8. ♖e1 ♕a5 9. ♘d2 ♕c7 10. d5 ♘b6 N [10... a6 11. a4 c5 (11... b6 12. dc6 ♕c6 13. ♗f3) 12. a5 b6 13. ab6 ♘b6 14. ♘b3 ♘fd7 15. ♘a5 ♘e5 16. ♗g3 △ f4±; 11... ♖b8 – 48/188] **11. ♗f3 cd5** [11... ♘fd7!? 12. a4 a5 13. ♕e2 (13. ♗g5 ♘e5 14. ♗e2 f5∞) ♘e5∞] **12. ed5 ♖e8 13. a4 ♗d7 14. ♗e3 ♘c4 15. ♘c4 ♕c4 16. ♗d4 h5?! 17. b3 ♕c7 18. ♘e4** [⌓ 18. ♘b5 ♗b5 (18... ♕a5 19. c4±) 19. ab5 ♖ec8 (19... ♕d7 20. ♕d3 △ ♖a4±) 20. ♖e2 (△ 21. ♖a7 ♖a7 22. b6!+–) b6 21. ♖a4±] **♘e4 19. ♗e4 e5! 20. de6 ♖e6 21. ♗g7 ♔g7 22. ♕d4 ♔g8 23. ♗d5 ♖e5** [23... ♖e1 24. ♖e1 ♕c2 25. ♕f6 ♖f8 26. h3±] **24. f4 ♖e1 25. ♖e1 ♖e8 26. ♖e8 ♗e8 27. ♕e4 ♔f8□ 28. ♗b7 ♗d7 29. ♔f1 ♗f5 30. ♕c6 ♕c6 31. ♗c6 ♗c2 32. b4 ♔e7 33. a5 h4 34. ♔e2 ♔d8 35. ♔e3 ♗b3 36. ♔d4 ♗e6= 37. b5 ♔c7 38. ♗d5 ♔b8 39. ♔c4 ♔c7 40. ♔d4 ♔d7 41. ♗c6 ♔c7 42. ♗d5 ♔c8 43. ♔e4 ♔c7 44. ♗e6 fe6 45. ♔f3 d5 46. ♔g4 ♔d6 47. ♔h4 ♔c5 48. g4 ♔b5 49. ♔g3 ♔c4 1/2 : 1/2**
[Nogueiras, Hernández Ruíz]

134. B 08

MILES 2595 – NOGUEIRAS 2570

Tilburg (Interpolis) 1992

1. d4 d6 2. e4 ♘f6 3. ♘c3 g6 4. ♘f3 ♗g7 5. ♗e2 0–0 6. 0–0 c6 7. ♖e1 ♘bd7 8. a4 e5 9. ♗e3!? N [9. ♗f1 – 9/134] **♖e8** [9... ♘g4 10. ♗g5 f6 11. ♗c1 △ 12. h3 ♘h6 13. ♗e3±] **10. ♗c4!? ♕e7 11. d5! h6** [11... c5 12. ♘d2 h6 (12... ♖f8 13.

♖b1 ♘e8 14. b4 f5 15. f3 f4 16. ♗f2±) 13. ♖b1 ♘h7 14. ♗d3 ♖f8 15. ♘c4 *a)* 15... f5 16. ♘b5 (16. ef5 gf5 17. ♕d2 ♕f6 18. f3 a6 △ 19. b4 e4) f4 17. ♗d2 ♖f6 18. b4±; *b)* 15... a6 16. ♕d2 h5 17. ♗h6 (17. ♕d1!? h4 18. h3 f5 19. f3 ♘df6 20. b4±) f5 18. ♗g7 ♔g7 19. f4±] **12. a5 a6 13. ♘d2 ♘f8 14. h3 ♗d7 15. ♖a3! ♖ed8 16. ♖b3 cd5 17. ♘d5 ♘d5 18. ♗d5 ♗c6 19. ♘c4 ♘e6 20. ♘b6** [20. ♗b6 ♖dc8 (20... ♖d7 21. ♗c6 bc6 22. ♖d3±) 21. ♘e3 ♘d4 22. ♖d3 ♗b5 23. ♖d2 △ c3±] **♖ab8 21. ♕e2** [21. ♖c3!? ♗d5 22. ♘d5 ♕f8 23. ♗b6 ♖dc8 24. ♖e2 ♖c6 25. ♖d2 ♖bc8 26. ♖c6 ♖c6 27. c3±; 21... ♗b5] **♘d4!□ 22. ♗d4 ed4 23. ♗c6?** [23. ♕c4 ♗b5 (23... ♗d5 24. ♕d5 ♕e6 25. ♖b4±) 24. ♖b5! ab5 25. ♕b5=∞] **bc6 24. ♕c4** [24. ♕a6 d5 25. ♕d3 ♖e8 26. f3 f5∓] **♕b7 25. f4 ♖e8 26. ♘a4**

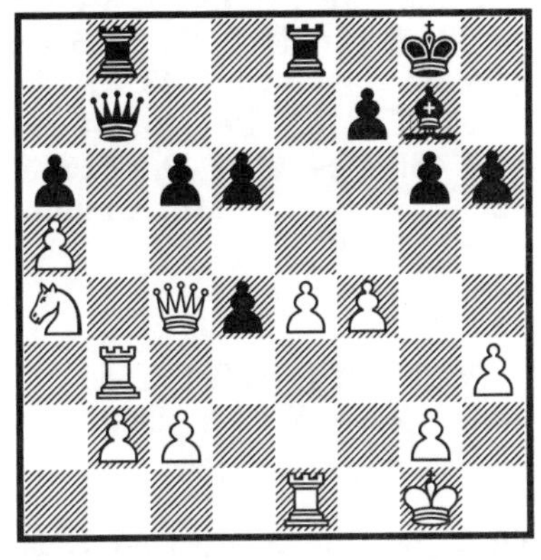

26... d5! 27. ♕c5 ♕c7 28. ♖b8? [28. e5 ♖b3 29. cb3 g5!∓] **♖b8 29. ed5 ♕f4 30. dc6 d3!−+ 31. c3 d2 32. ♖d1 ♖e8! 33. ♕f2□ ♕a4 34. ♕d2 ♕c6 35. ♕d6⊕ ♕b5 36. ♕b6 ♕b6 37. ab6 ♖b8 38. ♖d6 ♗f8 39. ♖c6 ♖b6** **0 : 1**

[Nogueiras, Hernández Ruíz]

135. **B 08**

KUCZYŃSKI 2525 – A. CHERNIN 2600

Budapest (zt) 1993

1. e4 d6 2. d4 ♘f6 3. ♘c3 g6 4. ♘f3 ♗g7 5. ♗e2 0–0 6. 0–0 ♗g4 7. ♗e3 ♘c6 8. ♕d2 e5 9. d5 ♘e7 10. ♖ad1 ♗d7 11. ♘e1 b5 12. a3 a5 13. ♘d3 ♕b8 14. f3 c6 15. dc6 ♗c6 16. b4 N [16. ♗h6 – 40/(148); 16. ♘f2 ♖d8 △ d5] **d5 17. ♗c5 ♖e8 18. ♘f2?!** [18. ♗e7 ♖e7 19. ed5 ♘d5 20. ♘d5 ♗d5 21. ba5 ♕a7 22. ♔h1 ♕a5 23. ♕a5 ♖a5 24. ♘b4 ♗b7 25. ♖d8 ♗f8=; 18. ba5!?∞] **ab4!** [18... d4 19. ♘a2 ab4 20. ♘b4±] **19. ab4 d4 20. ♘b1 ♖a2** [20... ♘d7 *a)* 21. ♗e7 ♖e7 22. c3 ♘b6 23. cd4 ed4 24. ♕g5 ♕e5 25. ♕e5 ♗e5 26. ♘d3 ♗g7∓; *b)* 21. c3 ♘c5 22. bc5 ♗d7 23. cd4 ed4 24. ♘d3 (24. f4 ♗e6 25. e5 ♖a2 26. ♕e1 ♘f5∓) ♘c6 △ ♗e6-c4, ♖a2∓; *c)* 21. ♘d3 ♘c5 22. ♘c5 – 20... ♖a2] **21. ♘d3 ♘d7 22. ♘c1 ♖b2 23. ♘d3 ♖a2 24. ♘c1 ♖a8 25. ♘b3 ♘c5 26. ♘c5** [26. bc5 ♗d7] **♘c8 27. ♘b3** [27. ♗d3 ♘d6 28. ♕e2 ♘c4] **♕b6 28. ♔h1 ♘d6 29. ♘a5 ♖ec8 30. c3** [⌓ 30. ♗d3 △ ♕e2] **♗d7 31. cd4 ed4 32. ♖c1 ♗e6** [32... ♘b7!?∓] **33. ♘a3 ♖c3 34. ♘b1 ♖cc8 35. ♘a3 ♖c3 36. ♖c3** [36. ♘b1 ♘c4! 37. ♘c4 ♖c4 38. ♗c4 bc4−+] **dc3 37. ♕f4⊕ ♘b7 38. ♘b5** [38. ♘b7 ♖a3 39. ♘c5 c2 40. ♘e6 ♕e6−+] **♘a5 39. ♘c7** [39. ba5 ♕a5 40. ♘c7 ♗e5] **♖c8 40. ♘e6 ♕e6 41. ba5 c2−+ 42. ♗d3** [42. a6 ♗b2 43. a7 c1♕ 44. ♖c1 ♗c1] **♗b2** **0 : 1**

[A. Chernin]

136. **B 09**

BOLOGAN 2520 – NUNN 2580

Deutschland 1993

1. e4 d6 2. d4 ♘f6 3. ♘c3 g6 4. f4 ♗g7 5. ♘f3 c5 6. ♗b5 ♗d7 7. ♗d7 ♘bd7 8. d5!? N [8. e5 – 50/144] **0–0** [8... b5?! 9. e5 de5 10. fe5 ♘g4 11. e6↑] **9. a4** [9. 0–0 b5 10. e5 de5 11. fe5 ♘g4 12. e6 b4!?∞] **a6** [△ b5] **10. a5!? ♕c7** [△ e6] **11. ♕e2 e6 12. de6 fe6 13. 0–0** [13. ♘g5 ♖ae8 14. ♕c4? d5 15. ed5 ed5−+] **♖ae8 14. ♗d2 ♔h8?** [14... ♘b8! (△ ♘c6 ×a5, d4) 15. e5 de5 16. ♘e5 ♘c6=] **15. ♘g5!** [△ ♖f3-h3] **h6 16. ♘f3 ♔h7 17. ♖ad1?** [17. ♘h4! (△ ♕d3 ×g6) ♖f7 18. ♕d3 ♘f8±] **e5!** [△ ♕a5; 17... ♕a5? 18. e5 de5 19. fe5 △ ♘e4-d6↑] **18. ♕c4?!** [18. fe5 ♘e5 19. ♘e5 ♖e5 20. ♗f4 ♖e6∓] **♕a5 19. fe5 de5** [19... ♘e5 20. ♘e5 ♖e5 21. ♗f4 △ ♗d6±] **20. ♘d5 ♕b5 21. ♕b5 ab5 22. ♘c7 ♖e7 23. ♘b5!** [23. ♖fe1? b4!∓] **♘e4**

24. ♖fe1 ♘ef6!? [⌓ 24... ♘d2 25. ♘d2 ♘f6 26. ♘e4 ♘e4 27. ♖e4∓] **25. ♗c3 e4 26. ♘d2 e3 27. ♘c4 ♘g4 28. ♗g7?** [28. h3!∞] **♔g7 29. h3** [29. ♖e2 ♖f2 30. ♖de1 ♘de5!∓ △ 31. ♘e3 ♖e2 32. ♖e2 ♘c6!−+] **e2 30. ♖d2** [30. ♖e2 ♖e2 31. ♖d7 ♖f7 32. ♖f7 ♔f7 33. hg4 ♖c2∓ 34. ♘cd6 ♔f6 35. ♘b7 ♖b2 △ ♔g5]

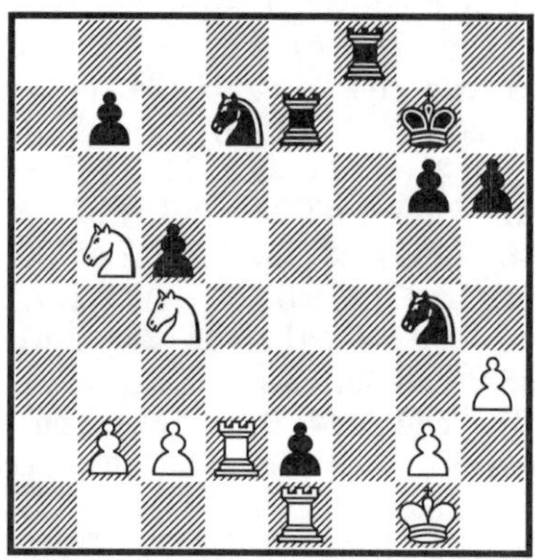

30... ♘b6!!∓ [30... ♖f1? 31. ♖f1 e1♕ 32. ♖d7! ♕f1□ 33. ♔f1 ♘h2 34. ♔g1 ♖d7 35. ♔h2±] **31. ♖de2!** [31. ♘b6 ♖f1 32. ♖f1 e1♕ (△ ♕e3) 33. ♖d3□ ♕a5 34. ♘d5 ♖e1!] **♖e2 32. ♖e2 ♘c4 33. hg4 ♘b2 34. ♘d6 b6 35. ♖e7?⊕** [35. g3!∓] **♔f6 36. ♖b7 ♘a4 37. ♘c4 ♔g5! 38. ♘b6 ♘b6 39. ♖b6 ♖f4!−+ 40. ♖d6 ♖c4 41. ♖d2 ♔g4 42. ♔f2 ♖c3 43. ♔g1 h5 44. ♔h2 g5 45. ♖e2 ♔h4 46. ♖e4 g4 47. ♖e2 g3 48. ♔g1 ♔g4 49. ♔f1 ♖c4** [50. ♖d2 h4 51. ♖e2 ♖f4 52. ♔g1 ♖d4 53. ♖e1 h3 54. gh3 ♔h3 55. ♖c1 c4 56. c3 ♖d2 57. ♔h1 ♖d3 58. ♔g1 ♖e3 59. ♔h1 g2 60. ♔g1 ♔g3 61. ♖a1 ♖f3 △ ♖f1] **0 : 1**
[Nunn]

137. **B 09**

KORNEEV 2490 –
JU. CIMMERMAN 2410

Katowice 1993

1. e4 d6 2. d4 ♘f6 3. ♘c3 g6 4. f4 ♗g7 5. ♘f3 c5 6. ♗b5 ♗d7 7. e5 ♘g4 8. e6 ♗b5 9. ef7 ♔d7 10. ♘b5 ♕a5 11. ♘c3 cd4 12. ♘d4 ♗d4 13. ♕d4 ♘c6 14. ♕c4 ♕b6 15. ♕e2 h5 16. h3 ♘h6 17. ♗d2 ♘f5 18. 0-0-0 ♘g3 19. ♕d3 ♘h1 20. ♖h1 ♖af8! 21. ♖e1! [21. ♕g6!?] **♖f7 22. ♕g6 ♖f6!? 23. ♕g7** [23. ♖e7?! ♘e7 24. ♕f6 *a)* 24... ♖g8?! 25. f5! ♖g2 26. ♕e6 ♔d8 27. f6 ♘g6 28. ♗e3! (28. f7? ♕g1 29. ♘d1 ♕d4∓) ♕c6 29. ♕g8$\overline{\overline{\infty}}$; *b)* 24... ♖h7! (△ ♕g1) 25. ♕g5 ♕c5 26. ♕c5 dc5∓⊥] **♕d8□ 24. ♘d5 ♖e6 25. ♖e6 ♔e6 26. f5!□ ♔d5!□** [26... ♔d7 27. ♗c3 ♖f8 28. f6± △ 28... ♕e8 29. fe7+−] **27. ♕f7 ♔c5 28. ♗e3 ♘d4□** [28... ♔b5? 29. ♕d5 ♔a6 30. ♕c4 ♔a5 31. a4! a6 32. ♕d5 b5 33. ♕c6 ♕c8 34. ♕b6 ♔b4 35. ♕d4 ♕c4 36. ♗d2 ♔a4 37. b3+−] **29. b4! ♔c6 30. ♗d4** [♕ 9/c] **♕g8!** [30... ♖g8 31. ♕c4 ♔d7 32. ♗a7 ♕c8 33. ♕e6 ♔c7 34. ♕e4±] **31. ♕e7** [31. b5?! ♔b5 32. ♕e7 ♖h7 33. ♕d6 b6!∓] **♕e8! 32. ♕h4□** [32. b5?? ♔d5 33. ♕f6 ♕e1 34. ♔b2 ♕b4−+] **♖g8 33. ♗c3 ♕e2** [33... ♖g2? 34. ♕c4 ♔d7 35. ♕b5!+−] **34. g3 b5 35. ♔b2 ♕f3 36. ♕e7! ♕f5 37. g4 hg4 38. hg4 ♖g4 39. ♕a7= ♕c8 40. ♕e3 ♖c4 41. ♕f3 ♔b6 42. ♗d4 ♔c7 43. ♗c3! ♕e6 44. a3 ♖e4 45. ♕h5 ♕c4 46. a4! ba4 47. ♕a5 ♔b7 48. ♕a4 ♕c6 49. ♕c6 ♔c6**
1/2 : 1/2 **[Ju. Cimmerman]**

138. **B 09**

VAN DER WIEL 2555
– VAN WELY 2560

Ter Apel 1993

1. e4 d6 2. d4 ♘f6 3. ♘c3 g6 4. f4 ♗g7 5. ♘f3 c5 6. ♗b5 ♗d7 7. e5 ♘g4 8. h3 cd4 9. ♕d4 ♘h6 10. g4 0–0?! [10... ♗b5 11. ♘b5 ♕a5 12. ♘c3 ♘c6 13. ♕e4⩲; 11... 0–0] **11. ♗d7!** [11. ♗e3?! ♗b5 12. ♘b5 ♕a5 13. ♘c3 ♘c6↑] **♕d7 N** [11... ♘d7 – 16/144] **12. ♗e3 de5 13. ♕d7** [13. fe5 ♕d4 14. ♘d4 ♗e5! 15. ♗h6 ♗d4 16. ♗f8 ♗c3 17. bc3 ♔f8 18. 0-0-0 ♔e8⩲] **♘d7 14. fe5 f5! 15. ef6** [15. g5?! ♘f7 16. e6 ♗c3 17. bc3 ♘fe5∓] **♖f6** [15... ♗f6 16. ♘d4⩲; 15... ef6 16. 0-0-0↑] **16. ♘g5** [16. ♘d4!?] **♘f7 17. 0-0-0 ♘b6 18. ♘ge4 ♖c6** [18... ♖e6] **19. ♗b6! ♖b6?!** [19... ab6 20. ♘d5 ♖e8±; 20... ♔f8!?] **20. ♖d7↑** [20. ♘d5!? ♖b2 (20... ♗b2? 21. ♔b1 ♖e6 22. ♘c5+−) 21. ♘ef6 ef6 22. ♔b2 f5 23. ♔b3 fg4 24. hg4+− Halifman] **♔f8?!**

[20... ♘d6 21. ♘d6 ed6 22. ♖e1±] **21. ♘d5!→ ♖b2□** [21... ♖e6 22. ♘c7+−] **22. ♖f1 ♖a2** [22... ♖c8 23. ♖f7! ♔f7 24. ♘g5 ♔f8 25. ♘e6 ♔g8□ 26. ♘e7 ♔f7 27. ♘c8 ♔e6 28. ♖g7+−] **23. ♖f3!+− ♖a1** [23... ♖c8 24. ♖e7; 24. c3] **24. ♔d2 ♖a5□ 25. ♘g5** [25. ♘c7? ♖c8 26. ♘e6 ♔e8 27. ♖b7 ♗e5∞; 25. ♘e7? ♔e8! 26. ♖b7 ♖d8⇆] **♗f6!** [25... ♖d5 26. ♖d5 ♗f6 27. ♘h7 ♔g7 28. ♘f6 ef6 29. ♖d7] **26. ♘f7□⊕** [26. ♘f6? ♘g5!] **♖d5** [26... ♔f7? 27. ♖f6] **27. ♖d5 ♔f7** [♖ 9/o] **28. g5 ♔e6 29. c4! ♗g7 30. ♖e3 ♔f7 31. ♖d7 ♖e8 32. ♖e4** [×d4] **h6 33. h4 hg5 34. hg5 ♔f8 35. ♖b7 ♖d8 36. ♔e3 a5 37. c5 ♗c3 38. c6 ♖c8 39. ♖c4 ♗e5 40. ♔e4 ♗g3 41. ♔d5 ♖d8 42. ♖d7** [42. ♔e6?? ♖d6#] **1 : 0**
[van der Wiel]

139. **B 09**

DOLMATOV 2615 − SMIRIN 2590

Rostov na Donu 1993

1. e4 d6 2. d4 ♘f6 3. ♘c3 g6 4. f4 ♗g7 5. ♘f3 0−0 6. ♗d3 ♘a6 7. 0−0 c5 8. d5 ♗g4 9. ♗c4 ♘c7 10. h3 ♗f3 11. ♕f3 e6 12. de6 fe6 13. ♗e3 ♕e7?! N [13... ♘d7 14. ♖ad1 ♕e7 15. ♕e2⩲; 13... b6 − 49/(184)] **14. e5! de5 15. ♕b7 ♖fb8□** [15... ♖ab8? 16. ♕c6 ♖b6 17. ♕c5±] **16. ♕f3** [16. ♕c6?! ♖b6 △ 17. ♕c5?? ♕c5 18. ♗c5 ♖c6∓] **♖b2** [16... ♖b4?! 17. b3!±] **17. ♘e4!** [17. ♘a4? e4 18. ♕e2 ♖bb8→] **♘e4□** [17... ♘d7 18. f5 gf5 19. ♕f5±] **18. ♕e4 ef4 19. ♗f4 ♖e8** [19... ♖d8!? 20. ♗c7 ♕c7 21. ♕e6 ♔h8 22. ♖ae1 ♖bb8 23. ♖f7→] **20. ♗b3 ♖b3□ 21. ab3 ♗a1 22. ♖a1∞̅ ♘b5!? 23. ♗e3!?** [23. ♗e5?! ♘d6 △ ♘f7⩲] **♖c8** [23... ♘d4 24. ♗d4 cd4 25. ♕d4±] **24. ♖a6 ♘d6 25. ♕e5 ♘f7 26. ♕e6** [26. ♖e6?! ♘e5 27. ♖e7 ♘c6 28. ♖b7 ♘d4⩲] **♕e6 27. ♖e6** [♖ 9/i] **a5 28. ♗d2!** [28. ♖a6? c4 29. ♖a5 cb3 30. cb3 ♖b8! 31. ♖a3⩲] **♖a8** [28... c4 29. ♗a5 cb3 30. cb3±] **29. ♖c6 a4 30. ba4 ♖a4 31. ♖c5 ♘d6 32. ♖c6 ♘c4 33. ♗g5!** [33. ♗h6? ♔f7] **♔f7 34. ♔f2 ♔e8 35. ♖c7 ♘d6 36. ♔e2 ♖c4 37. ♖c4 ♘c4** [♘♗ 4/b] **38. ♔d3 ♘e5 39. ♔d4 ♘c6 40. ♔c5 ♔d7 41. ♗f6!+− ♘a7 42. ♔d5 ♘c8 43. ♗g5 ♘b6 44. ♔e5 ♘c4 45. ♔f6 ♘a3 46. ♔g7** [46... ♔e6 47. ♔h7 ♔f5 48. ♔h6 ♘c2 49. g4] **1 : 0** **[Dolmatov]**

140.** **!N** **B 09**

J. POLGÁR 2595 − FTÁČNIK 2535

Budapest (zt - play off) 1993

1. e4 d6 2. d4 ♘f6 3. ♘c3 g6 4. f4 ♗g7 5. ♘f3 0−0 6. ♗d3 ♘c6 7. 0−0 [RR 7. e5 de5 8. fe5 ♘h5 9. ♘e2!? N (9. ♗e2 − 27/(187)) ♗g4 (9... f6?! 10. ♗c4 ♔h8 11. e6 ♘a5 12. ♕d3 ♘c4 13. ♕c4 f5 14. ♘g5±) 10. c3 *a)* 10... f6 11. ♕b3 ♔h8 12. ♕b7 (12. ef6 ♖f6!? 13. ♗g5 ♖d6∞) ♘e5 (12... ♗f3!? 13. gf3 ♘e5 14. ♗e4 ♖b8 15. ♕a7 f5 16. de5 fe4 17. f4 ♕d3 18. ♕e3 ♕e3 19. ♗e3 ♖b2 20. a4 ♖a8±) 13. ♗e4 ♖b8 14. ♕a7 ♗f3 15. ♗f3 ♘d3 16. ♔d2 ♘b2 17. g4!? (17. ♔c2 ♕d7!□ 18. g4 ♕b5 19. ♗b2 ♕b2 20. ♔d3 ♗h6∓ Najdoskij − Gavrilov 2415, Moskva 1992) ♗h6 18. ♔c2 ♗c1 19. ♖hc1 ♘g7 20. ♖ab1 ♘c4 21. ♖b8 ♕b8 22. ♕b8 ♖b8 23. ♔d3⩲; *b)* 10... ♔h8!? 11. 0−0 f6 12. ef6 ♗f6∞ △ e5 Gavrilov] **e5 8. fe5 de5 9. d5 ♘d4 10. ♘e5 ♘e4 11. ♗e4 ♗e5 12. ♗f4 ♗f4?!** [12... ♗g7!? N 13. ♕d2 ♘f5 14. ♘b5 ♘d6 15. ♘d6 cd6= Zsó. Polgár 2415 − Arduman 2390, Budapest 1993] **13. ♖f4 ♘f5 14. ♗f5 ♗f5 15. ♕d4 ♗c2 16. ♖e1! N** [16. ♖af1 − 52/145] **f5?** [16... ♗f5 17. g4 ♗c8 18. d6 ♕d6 19. ♘d5 f5 20. gf5 ♗f5 21. ♘e7 ♔f7 22. ♘f5; RR 17... ♗d7!? △ 18. ♘e4 f5∞ Ftáčnik; 16... g5! 17. ♖f6 ♗g6∞̅; RR 16... h5!?∞ Ftáčnik] **17. ♕c4?!** [17. ♖c1!] **♔h8** [17... ♔g7 18. ♖f2 ♗e4 19. ♘e4 fe4 20. ♖f8] **18. ♖c1** [18. ♖f2 ♗e4 19. ♘e4 fe4 20. ♖f8 ♕f8 21. ♕c7 ♕f6!] **♗e4 19. ♘e4 fe4 20. ♕d4 ♔g8 21. ♖f8 ♕f8 22. ♖c7+− e3** [22... ♖e8 23. d6 e3 24. ♕d5 ♔h8 25. ♖f7; 22... ♖d8 23. h3] **23. ♕e3 ♖e8 24. ♕f2 ♕f2 25. ♔f2** [♖ 6/e] **♖d8 26. ♖b7 ♖d5 27. ♔e3 a5 28. a4 ♖d1 29. h4?!** [29. ♖b5! ♖b1 (RR 29... ♖g1 30. ♖a5 ♖g2 31. ♖b5 ♖h2 32. a5 ♖h1 33. b4 ♖a1 34. ♖b6 g5 35. a6+− Ftáčnik) 30. ♔d4 (RR 30. g4 ♔g7 31. ♔d3+− Ftáčnik) ♖g1 31. ♖a5 ♖g2 32. b4+−] **♖e1 30. ♔f3?!** [30.

♔d4 ♖g1 31. b4 ab4 (31... ♖a1 32. b5 ♖a4 33. ♔c5+−) 32. a5 ♖d1 (32... ♖a1 33. ♖b5 △ ♔c5-b6+−) 33. ♔c4 ♖c1 34. ♔b3 ♖b1 35. ♔a2+−] **♖f1 31. ♔g3** [31. ♔g4!?] **♖d1 32. ♖b5** [32. b3!? △ ♔f4] **♖d3 33. ♔f2 h5⊕** [33... ♔f7!? 34. ♔e2 (34. ♖a5 ♖d2 35. ♔g3 ♖b2 36. ♖a7 ♔f6 37. ♖h7 ♖b3 38. ♔h2 ♖b4! 39. a5 ♖a4) ♖g3 35. ♔f2 ♖d3 (35... ♖g4 36. b3 ♖h4 37. ♖a5 ♖b4 38. ♖b5+−) 36. g4 △ h5, ♔e2-d2-c2+−] **34. ♔e2** [RR 34. ♖a5 ♖d2 35. ♔f3 ♖b2 36. ♖a7+− Ftáčnik] **♖g3 35. ♔f1 ♖g4 36. b3** [36. ♖a5 ♖b4] **♖g3 37. ♔f2 ♖c3 38. ♖a5 ♖b3** [♖ 6/b] **39. ♖a7** [39. ♖g5!] **♖b4** [RR 39... ♖b2 40. ♔f3 ♖b3 41. ♔f4 ♖b4 42. ♔g5 ♖g4 43. ♔h6 ♖g2 44. a5! (44. ♖g7 ♔f8 45. ♖g6 ♖g4!! 46. ♖g4 hg4 47. a5 g3 48. a6 g2 49. a7 g1♕ 50. a8♕=) ♔f8 45. a6 ♖a2 46. ♖a8 ♔f7 47. a7 ♖a6 48. ♖h8+− Ftáčnik] **40. g3 ♖b3 41. a5 ♖a3 42. a6 ♔f8 43. ♔e2 ♔e8 44. ♔d2 ♔d8 45. ♖a8 ♔c7 46. a7 ♔b6 47. ♖g8 ♖a7 48. ♖g6** [♖ 5/a] **♔c5 49. ♔e3** [49. ♖g5?! ♔d4 50. ♖h5 ♖a2 51. ♔e1 ♔e3 52. ♖e5 ♔f3 53. ♖g5 ♔e3 54. ♔d1 ♔d3 55. ♔c1 ♔c3 56. ♔b1 ♖h2] **♖h7 50. ♔e4 ♖h8 51. ♔e5 ♔c4 52. ♖g5** [52. ♔f6 ♔d4 53. ♔g7 ♖a8] **♔d3 53. ♔f4** [53. ♔f6 ♔e4 54. ♔g7 ♖a8 55. ♔g6 ♖h8 56. ♖h5 ♖g8] **♔d4** [53... ♖f8 54. ♖f5 ♖h8 55. ♖d5 ♔e2 56. g4 hg4 57. h5! ♖g8 58. ♔g3 ♔e3 59. h6 ♔e4 60. h7 ♖h8 61. ♖h5+−] **54. ♖f5 ♖h7 55. ♖f8 ♔d5 56. ♔f5 ♖g7 57. ♖d8 ♔c6 58. ♔f4 ♖g4 59. ♔f3 ♖g7 60. ♖h8 ♖f7** [61. ♔e4 ♖g7 62. ♔f4 ♖f7 63. ♔e5 ♖g7 64. ♖h6 ♔d7 65. ♔f4 ♖f7 66. ♔g5 ♖g7 67. ♖g6 ♖h7 68. ♖g8 △ ♔g6+−]
1 : 0 **[J. Polgár]**

141. **B 10**

NIJBOER 2485 − MILES 2595

Groningen 1992

1. e4 c6 2. c4 e5 3. ♘f3 ♕a5?! 4. ♗e2 ♘f6 5. ♘c3 ♗b4 6. 0−0 0−0 [6... ♗c3 7. dc3 ♘e4 8. ♗d3 ♘f6 9. ♘e5 0−0 10. ♗f4±] **7. d3 d5** [7... ♗c3 8. bc3 ♕c3 9. ♗d2 ♕b2 10. ♖b1 ♕a2 11. ♗c3 (△ ♖a1) ♕a6 12. ♗e5→; 7... d6 8. ♗d2 △ a3±⊡] **8. cd5 N** [8. ed5 − 54/126] **♗c3 9. bc3 cd5 10. ♘e5 de4** [10... ♕c3 11. ♗f4 de4 12. de4 ♘e4 13. ♖c1±→] **11. ♘c4 ♕c7 12. ♗g5 ♘d5 13. ♖c1 ed3 14. ♕d3?** [14. ♗d3 h6 (14... ♗e6 15. ♕h5 g6 16. ♕h6→) 15. ♗h4 △ ♗g3] **♘f4 15. ♗f4 ♕f4 16. ♕d6 ♕g5?** [16... ♕d6 17. ♘d6 ♘c6 18. ♗f3 ♘a5=] **17. f4 ♕h4 18. ♘e5 ♕f6 19. ♖cd1 ♕d6 20. ♖d6 ♘c6! 21. ♘c6 bc6 22. ♖c6 ♖b8 23. ♖c7?!** [23. ♗c4 ♖b2 24. ♖e1! ♗e6 (24... ♗b7 25. ♖c7 ♖g2 26. ♔f1+− △ ♖f7) 25. ♖e2 ♖e2 26. ♗e2 ♗a2 27. ♖a6 ♗e6 28. ♖a7±] **♖b2 24. ♗c4 ♗e6! 25. ♗e6 fe6 26. ♖d1!** [26. ♖a7? ♖d8] **♖f4 27. h3 ♖b5! 28. ♖a7 h5 29. ♖d8 ♔h7 30. ♖dd7 ♖g5 31. ♖d2 ♖f3= 32. ♖a5 ♖a5 33. gf3 ♖c5 34. ♖c2 ♔g6 35. ♔f2 ♔f5 36. c4 ♔f4 37. h4 e5 38. a3 e4 39. fe4 ♔e4 40. ♖c1 g5**
1/2 : 1/2 **[Nijboer]**

142.*** **!N** **B 10**

LERNER 2530 − DREEV 2560

Rostov na Donu (open) 1993

1. c4 c6 2. e4 d5 3. cd5 cd5 4. ed5 ♘f6 5. ♗b5 ♘bd7 6. ♘c3 a6 7. ♕a4 ♖b8 8. ♗d7 ♕d7! N [8... ♗d7 − 48/201] **9. ♕d7** [9. ♕f4 ♖a8!=; RR 9. ♕b3 b5 10. ♘f3 ♗b7 11. ♘e5 ♕d6 12. d4 ♗d5 13. ♘d5 ♕d5 14. 0−0 e6 15. ♗g5 ♖a8 16. ♖fc1 ♗d6= Romero Holmes 2455 − Judasin 2610, León 1993] **♗d7 10. d3!?** [RR 10. ♘f3 ♖d8 11. b3 ♗f5 12. ♗b2 ♘d5 13. ♘d5 ♖d5 14. ♖c1 f6 15. 0−0 ♔d7 16. d4 ♗d3 17. ♖fe1 e6 18. ♖e3 ♗b5 19. ♘d2 ♗d6 20. ♘e4 ♗f4 21. ♘c5 ♖c5= Fernández García 2475 − Magem Badals 2510, Dos Hermanas 1993; 10. d4 b5 11. a3 ♗c8 12. ♗f4 ♖a8 13. ♗e5 ♗b7 14. ♗f6 ef6 15. ♘ge2 ♔d7 16. 0−0 ♗e7 17. ♖ac1 ♖hc8$\overline{\overline{\infty}}$ Magem Badals 2510 − Adams 2630, Dos Hermanas 1993] **♗f5 11. ♗g5 ♖d8!** [11... ♗d3 12. 0-0-0↑] **12. ♗f6 ef6 13. 0-0-0 ♗c5 14. d4?!** [14. ♖d2!∞] **♗d6 15. ♘ge2 ♖c8 16. ♔d2 ♔d7 17. ♖c1 ♖c4!∓** [△ ♖hc8, b5-b4] **18. h3?** [18. f3] **♖e8!∓ 19. g3□** [19. g4 ♗f4! 20. ♘f4 ♖d4−+] **h5 20. h4** [20. f4 h4! 21. g4 ♗f4−+; 20. b3 ♖c7 △ ♗a3] **♗g4 21. a3**

b5 [△ b4] **22. ♔d3 g5! 23. ♖ce1** [23. ♖he1 gh4 24. gh4 ♗f5 25. ♔d2 ♗f4!−+] **♗f5 24. ♔d2 b4 25. ab4 ♖b4 26. ♔c1 ♖eb8 27. ♘d1 ♗g6!−+ 28. hg5⊕ fg5 29. ♘ec3 ♖d4 30. ♘e3 a5 31. ♘c2** [31. ♖d1 ♖db4 32. ♖d2 a4 △ 33... a3 34. ba3 ♖b1] **♖c4 32. ♖e3 a4 33. ♖d1** [△ ♖d4] **♗c5 34. ♖f3** [34. ♖e2 a3] **g4 35. ♖e3 ♖b3!⊕ 0 : 1** **[Dreev]**

143.* !N **B 12**

YERMOLINSKY 2615
– SEIRAWAN 2605

USA (ch) 1992

1. e4 c6 2. d4 d5 3. e5 [RR 3. f3 e6 4. ♘c3 ♗b4 5. ♘e2!? de4 6. fe4 e5 7. a3 ♗a5 8. ♗e3 N (8. ♕d3) ♘f6 9. ♕d3 ♘bd7 10. 0-0-0 0–0 11. d5 ♘g4 12. ♗g1 ♗b6! 13. ♕g3 ♘gf6 14. ♔b1!? ♗g1 15. ♘g1! (15. ♖g1 ♕b6) cd5 16. ed5 ♖e8 17. ♘f3 e4 18. ♘d4 ♘e5 19. ♗b5 ♗d7 20. ♘c6?! bc6 21. dc6 ♘c6 22. ♗c6 ♖b8 23. ♗d7 ♘d7 24. ♖d4 ♕b6 25. ♖b4 (Smagin 2520 – Brunner 2455, Dortmund (open) 1993) ♕c6=; 20. ♖he1!±; ⌓ 17... a6; 10... ed4!? Smagin] **♗f5 4. ♘f3 e6 5. ♗e2 c5 6. 0–0 ♘c6 7. c3 cd4 8. cd4 ♘ge7 9. a3 ♗e4 10. ♘bd2 ♘f5 11. b4 a5! N** [11... ♕b6 – 54/133] **12. ba5** [12. b5? ♘cd4 13. ♘d4 ♘d4 14. ♘e4 de4 15. ♗e3 ♘e2 16. ♕e2 ♕d3 17. ♕b2$\overline{\overline{\infty}}$; ⌓ 15... ♗c5∓; 12. g4!? ♘fd4 (12... ♗f3? 13. ♘f3 ♘h4 14. ♘h4 ♕h4 15. b5 ♘b8 16. ♗f4± △ ♗g3, f4-f5) 13. ♘d4 ♘d4 14. ♘e4 *a)* 14... ♘e2 15. ♕e2 de4 16. ♕e4 ♕d5 (Seirawan; 16... ab4 17. ♗e3 ba3 18. ♕b7∞) 17. ♕d5 ed5 18. ♗e3 h5! 19. g5 ♗e7∞; *b)* 14... de4 15. ♕a4 (15. ♗e3 ♘c6! 16. ♕a4 ab4 17. ♕b5 ♖b8∓) ♔e7! 16. ♖a2 (16. ♖d1? ♘e2 17. ♔f1 ♕c8 18. ♗e3 f6∓) *b1)* 16... ♕d5 17. ♗e3! ♕e5 (17... ♕a2 18. ♗d4 ♕e2 19. ♗c5 ♔d8 20. ♖d1 ♕d1 21. ♕d1 ♔c7 22. ♗d6 ♗d6 23. ♕d6 ♔c8 24. b5!+−) 18. ♗d4 ♕d4 19. ♖d1 ♕e5 20. ♕d7 ♔f6 21. f4! ef3 22. ♗f3→; *b2)* 16... b5! 17. ♕d1 (17. ♗b5? ♕d5−+) ♘e2 18. ♕e2 ♕d3 19. ba5 f5!=] **♕a5 13. g4?** [13. ♗b2] **♘fd4 14. ♘d4 ♘d4 15. ♘e4 ♘e2 16. ♕e2 de4 17. ♕e4 ♗c5! 18. ♕b7** [18. ♖b1 ♕a4∓] **0–0 19. ♕e4 ♕c3** [19... ♕a4 20. ♕e2] **20. ♖a2 ♕b3!∓ 21. ♖b2!** [21. ♕c2 ♕d5] **♕a4** [21... ♕a3 22. ♖c2 ♕a7 23. ♗f4 △ ♔g2, h3=; ⌓ 21... ♖a4 22. ♖b3 ♖e4 23. h3 ♖e5 24. ♗d2∓] **22. ♖e2 ♗a3 23. ♕a4 ♖a4 24. ♗a3 ♖a3 1/2 : 1/2** **[Yermolinsky]**

144. **B 12**

ŠIROV 2670 – LOBRON 2620

München 1993

1. e4 c6 2. d4 d5 3. e5 ♗f5 4. h4 h5 5. c4 e6 6. ♘c3 dc4 7. ♗c4 ♘d7 8. ♗g5 ♗e7 9. ♕d2 ♘b6 10. ♗b3 a5 N [10... ♕d7 – 44/156] **11. a3 a4 12. ♗a2 ♗g5 13. hg5 ♘e7 14. ♘ge2 ♘ed5** [14... ♘bd5 15. f3!±] **15. ♘g3 ♗g6?!** [15... ♘c3!? 16. ♘f5 (16. bc3 ♗g6=) ♘a2 17. ♘d6 ♔f8 18. ♕f4! (18. ♖a2? ♘c8; 18. g6 fg6 19. ♕f4 ♔g8 20. ♕f7 ♔h7 21. ♖h5 gh5 22. ♕h5 ♔g8 23. ♕f7 ♔h7=) *a)* 18... ♕e7? 19. g6! f5 (19... f6 20. ♕g4!±) 20. ♕f3! h4 21. g4! ♔g8 (21... ♘c8 22. gf5 ♘d6 23. f6!) 22. ♘f7!; *b)* 18... ♕d7! 19. g6 f5 20. ef6! (20. ♕f3? ♘c4! 21. ♘c4 ♕d4 22. ♕e2 ♘c3!−+) ♘d5 21. fg7 ♔g7 22. ♕e5 ♔g6! (22... ♘f6? 23. ♘f7!+− △ 23... ♖hf8 24. ♕g5) 23. ♖h3! h4! (23... ♕e7 24. ♖g3 ♔h6 25. ♖g5!+−; 23... ♖ag8 24. ♖g3 ♔h6 25. ♔e2!+− △ 26. ♕h5 ♔h5 27. ♖h1#) 24. ♕e4 *b1)* 24... ♔g5 25. f4! ♔f6 (25... ♘f4 26. ♕e5 ♔g4 27. ♘e4! ♘g2 28. ♔f2+−) 26. ♕e5 ♔e7 27. ♘f5 ♔f7 28. ♕g7+−; *b2)* 24... ♔g7 25. ♕g4 ♔f8 26. ♖f3? ♔e7 27. ♖f7 ♔d6 28. ♖d7 ♔d7 29. ♖a2 ♖ag8⇆; 26. ♘c4!±→] **16. ♘ge4 ♘c8 17. g4?** [17. ♘c5 ♘c3! 18. bc3 b6 19. ♘d3 c5∞; 17. ♗d5! cd5 18. ♘c5 b6 19. ♘5a4±] **♘c3 18. ♘c3 ♔d7! 19. 0-0-0 ♔c7?** [19... ♘e7∓] **20. ♗b1!± ♘e7** [⌓ 20... ♗b1 21. ♔b1 hg4] **21. ♗g6 fg6 22. ♕c2! hg4 23. ♖h8 ♕h8 24. ♘a4 ♘d5** [24... b6? 25. ♘b6+−; 24... ♕h5 25. ♘c5! ♕g5 26. ♖d2 ♕f5 27. ♕b3 b6 28. ♘e6+−] **25. ♘c5 ♕e8 26. ♕e2 b6 27. ♘e4 ♕f7 28. ♕g4 ♕f5?** [28... ♖h8 29. ♘d6 ♕f4 30. ♕f4 ♘f4 31. ♔d2±] **29.**

♕e2 ♖h8 30. ♘d6! ♕g5 31. ♔b1 ♕h5 32. ♕c2 ♖a8 33. ♖c1 ♘e7 34. ♕b3 ♕g4 35. f3! ♕h3 36. ♕b4! ♕h4?⊕ [36... ♘d5 37. ♘e8! ♔b7 (37... ♖e8 38. ♕d6+−) 38. ♕d6 ♖c8 39. ♕d7 ♔b8 40. ♘d6 ♖c7 41. ♕e8 ♔a7 42. ♖c6+−; 36... ♘c8 37. ♖c3! △ ♖b3+−] **37. ♘c4 ♘c8 38. d5** [38. ♘b6 ♘b6 39. ♖c6 ♔c6 40. d5+−] **c5** [38... ed5 39. ♘b6+−] **39. ♘b6 1 : 0**
[Širov]

145. B 13**

ALEXA. IVANOV 2545
– SEIRAWAN 2605
USA (ch) 1992

1. e4 c6 2. d4 d5 3. ed5 cd5 4. c4 ♘f6 5. ♘c3 ♘c6 6. ♘f3 [RR 6. ♗g5 *a)* 6... dc4 7. d5 ♘e5 8. ♕d4 h6 9. ♕e5 N (9. ♗f4 – 54/139) hg5 10. ♗c4 a6 11. 0-0-0 ♕d6 12. ♘f3 g4 13. ♖he1 ♕e5 14. ♘e5 ♖h2 15. d6 e6 16. ♘e4 ♘e4 17. ♖e4 f6 18. d7 ♗d7 19. ♘d7 e5 20. ♘e5 fe5 21. ♖e5 ♗e7 22. ♖de1+− J. Polgár 2595 – Seirawan 2595, Monaco 1993; *b)* 6... ♕a5 7. a3!? N (7. ♗d2 – 45/(148)) dc4 8. d5 ♘e5 9. ♕d4 ♘d3 10. ♗d3 cd3 11. ♘f3 ♗f5 12. 0–0 ♖d8 13. ♘h4 ♗d7 14. ♖fe1 ♕b6 15. ♕d3 ♗c6 16. ♗f6 gf6 17. ♕f3 ♗d7 18. ♘e4 ♗g7 19. d6+− Lanka 2545 – Fridman 2380, Vilnius (zt) 1993] **♗g4 7. cd5 ♘d5 8. ♕b3 ♗f3 9. gf3 e6 10. ♕b7 ♘d4 11. ♗b5 ♘b5 12. ♕c6 ♔e7 13. ♕b5 ♕d7 14. ♘d5 ♕d5 15. ♕d5 ed5 16. 0–0 ♔e6 17. ♖e1 ♔f5 18. ♗e3 ♗e7 19. ♖ad1 N** [19. ♖ac1 – 6/231] **♖hd8 20. ♖d4 g5!= 21. ♖ed1 ♔e6 22. ♖e1 ♔f5 23. ♖ed1 ♔e6 24. ♖e1 ♗c5** [24... ♔f5] **25. ♗g5** [25. ♖a4?! ♗e3 26. ♖e3 ♔f5 27. ♖e7 d4] **♔f5 26. ♗d8** [26. ♖g4?! f6 (26... h5!?) 27. ♗d2 ♖g8!? △ h5$\overline{\overline{\infty}}$] **♗d4 27. ♖d1 ♖d8** [27... ♗f2?! 28. ♔f2 ♖d8 29. ♖d4 ♔e5 30. ♔e3 △ f4, ♖a4±; 27... ♗b2!? 28. ♖d5 ♔e6 29. ♖b5!? (29. ♖d3 ♖c8∓) ♗e5 (29... ♗d4 30. ♗c7=) 30. ♗a5 ♖g8 31. ♔f1 (31. ♔h1 ♗d4!?) ♗h2 32. ♖b7=] **28. ♖d4 ♔e5 29. ♖a4 d4 30. ♔f1 ♖d7 31. ♔e2 ♔f4 32. ♔d3 ♔f3 33. ♖d4 ♖e7?!** [33... ♖d4 34. ♔d4 *a)* 34... ♔f2? 35. a4! (35. b4? f5 36. ♔e5 ♔e3!=) f5 36. ♔e5 ♔g2 37. b4 ♔h2 38. b5 ♔g3 39. ♔f5 h5 40. a5 h4 41. b6 ab6 42. ab6 h3 43. b7 h2 44. b8♕ ♔g2 45. ♔g4+−; *b)* 34... h5! *b1)* 35. h4 ♔f2 36. b4 ♔g3 37. b5 (37. ♔e5? ♔g4!) f5 38. a4 f4 39. a5 f3 40. b6 ab6 41. ab6 f2 42. b7 f1♕ 43. b8♕ ♔h4 44. ♔e3=; *b2)* 35. b4 h4 36. b5 ♔g2 37. a4 ♔h2 38. a5 h3 39. b6 ab6 40. ab6 ♔g1 41. b7 h2 42. b8♕ h1♕=; 33... ♖b7!? 34. b4 (34. ♖d5!? ♔f2 35. ♖h5 f6 36. ♖f5=) f5 35. a4 f4 (35... ♖f7 36. ♔d2 ♔f2 37. ♖f4 ♔g2 38. ♔e3) 36. ♔d2! (36. b5? ♖f7 37. ♖b4 ♔f2 38. a5 f3 39. b6 ab6 40. ab6 ♔g2 41. b7 f2 42. b8♕ f1♕) ♖f7 (36... ♖e7 37. b5 ♖e2 38. ♔c3 ♖f2 39. ♖d7) 37. ♔e1 ♔g2 38. ♖e4 h5 39. h4=] **34. ♖d5!?** [34. b4 f5 35. a4 f4 36. ♔d2∞] **♔f2 35. ♖h5 f6 36. b4!** [36. ♖f5 ♔g2=] **♔g2?** [36... ♖f7 37. ♔e4; 36... ♔f3! 37. ♖f5 ♔g2 38. ♖f6 ♔h2 39. a4 ♔g3 40. ♖h6 ♔g4=] **37. a4 f5 38. ♖f5 ♔h2 39. a5 ♔g3 40. a6! ♔g4 41. ♖f8** [41. ♖b5? ♖e6!=] **h5 42. ♖b8+− ♖e6** [42... h4 43. ♖b7; 42... ♔g5 43. ♖b7 ♔f6 44. b5 h4 45. ♖e7 ♔e7 46. b6 h3 47. ba7; 42... ♖d7 43. ♔c4 ♖c7 (43... ♔f5 44. ♖b7 ♔e6 45. b5 h4 46. ♖d7 ♔d7 47. b6 h3 48. ba7) 44. ♔b5] **43. b5 ♖d6 44. ♔e4 ♖e6 45. ♔d4 ♖d6 46. ♔e5 ♖g6 47. b6 ♔h3** [47... h4 48. b7] **48. ba7 1 : 0**
[Alexa. Ivanov]

146. B 14

KUCZYŃSKI 2525 – SAPIS 2420
Polska (ch) 1993

1. e4 c6 2. d4 d5 3. ed5 cd5 4. c4 ♘f6 5. ♘c3 g6 6. ♕b3 ♗g7 7. cd5 0–0 8. ♗e2 ♘bd7 9. ♗f3 ♘b6 10. ♗g5 a5 11. ♘ge2 a4 12. ♕b5 ♗d7 13. ♕b4 ♗f5 14. 0–0 ♕d6!? N [14... ♗d3] **15. ♕d6 ed6 16. ♘g3 ♗d3 17. ♖fd1** [17. ♖fe1 h6 18. ♗f4 ♖fd8 19. ♖e7 ♗a6 △ g5] **♗c4 18. ♘ge4 ♘e4 19. ♘e4 ♘c8! 20. ♘d2** [20. ♘f6 ♔h8 (20... ♗f6 21. ♗f6 ♖a5 △ ♗d5=) 21. ♘d7 ♖g8!] **♗b5 21. ♘b1 h6 22. ♗e3 f5 23. g3 g5 24. ♘a3 ♗a6 25. ♖ac1 f4 26. gf4 gf4 27. ♗d2 ♗d4 28. ♗c3**

♗c3 29. ♖c3 ♘e7 30. ♗g4 ♘g6 31. ♘c2 [⌓ 31. f3 ♘e5 32. ♗e6 ♔h8 33. ♔f2±] ♘e5 32. ♗e6 ♔h8 33. ♘d4 f3 34. h3 [34. ♘f5 ♖f6 35. ♘d6 ♖g6? 36. ♔h1 ♗e2 37. ♖d2 ♖ag8 38. ♗g8 ♘g4 39. ♘e4+−; 35... ♖d8⇆] ♖f6 35. ♔h2 ♖af8 36. ♖g1 [36. ♖c8 ♖c8 37. ♗c8 ♘d3⇆] ♖f4! 37. ♘c2 ♘d3 38. ♖c7 ♖c4 [38... ♘f2 39. ♖gg7 ♗d3 40. ♘e3 ♗e4 41. ♘f5 ♗f5 42. ♗f5 ♖8f5 43. ♖h7 ♔g8 44. ♖cg7 ♔f8 45. ♖b7 ♖f7 46. ♖b8 ♔e7 47. ♖b7=] 39. ♖e7 ♖c2 40. ♖gg7 ♖f2 41. ♔h1 ♖f1 42. ♔h2 ♖f2 43. ♔h1 ♖f1 1/2 : 1/2 [Sapis]

147. **B 14**

L. CHRISTIANSEN 2620
− SCHWARTZMAN 2455

Wijk aan Zee (open) 1993

1. c4 c6 2. e4 d5 3. ed5 cd5 4. d4 ♘f6 5. ♘c3 e6 6. ♘f3 ♗b4 7. cd5 ♘d5 8. ♕b3 ♘c6 9. ♗d3 ♕b6 10. ♗d2 ♗a5 11. 0−0 ♕b3 12. ab3 ♗b6 13. ♘d5!? N [13. ♗c4 − 55/150] **ed5 14. ♗c3 0−0 15. b4 ♖e8 16. ♖fe1 ♗d7 17. b5 ♘e7 18. ♗b4 ♗f5! 19. ♗e2?!** [19. ♗f1 ♗e4!; 19. ♗f5 ♘f5 20. ♗c5 h5=] **♘g6 20. g3 ♖ac8 21. ♗c5 ♗g4** [21... ♗c5 22. dc5 ♖c5 23. ♘d4±; 22... ♗g4!?] **22. ♗b6 ab6 23. ♔g2 ♖e4 24. h3 ♗h5!** [24... ♗f3 25. ♗f3 ♖d4⩱] **25. ♗f1 ♗f3 26. ♔f3 ♖d4 27. ♖a7 ♖b8 28. h4! ♔f8 29. h5 ♘e7 30. ♖c1?!** [30. ♗h3⩱] **♘c8 31. ♖a3 ♘d6 32. ♖c7** [△ ♖d7] **♖d8 33. ♖d3 ♖c4! 34. ♖c3□ ♖b4** [34... ♖c7 35. ♖c7 ♔e8 36. ♔f4 ♖c8 37. ♖c8 ♘c8 38. ♔e5 ♔e7 39. ♔d5 ♘d6=] **35. ♖e3 ♖b2 36. ♖ee7 ♖a2 37. g4** [37. ♖ed7 ♖aa8=] **♖a3 38. ♔g2 ♖a4 39. f3 ♖f4 40. ♗d3 h6 41. ♔g3 ♖f6 42. ♖e5 d4 43. f4 ♖e8** [43... ♖e6? 44. ♖e6 fe6 45. ♔f3±] **44. ♖d7 ♖fe6 45. ♖e6** [45. ♔f2 ♖f6 46. ♔g3 ♖fe6=] **♖e6** [♖ 9/i] **46. f5 ♖f6?!** [46... ♖e3 47. ♔f4 ♖d3 48. ♖d6 ♖b3 49. ♖b6 d3 50. ♔e3 ♔e7 51. ♖b7 ♔f6=] **47. ♖d8 ♔e7 48. ♖b8↑ ♘e8! 49. ♖b7 ♔d8 50. ♔f4 ♘c7!□ 51. ♔e5** [51. ♖b8 ♔d7 52. ♖g8 ♔e7 53. ♖g7? ♔f8 54. ♖h7 ♔g8 55. g5 ♘d5 56. ♔e5 hg5−+] **♔d7 52. ♗c4**

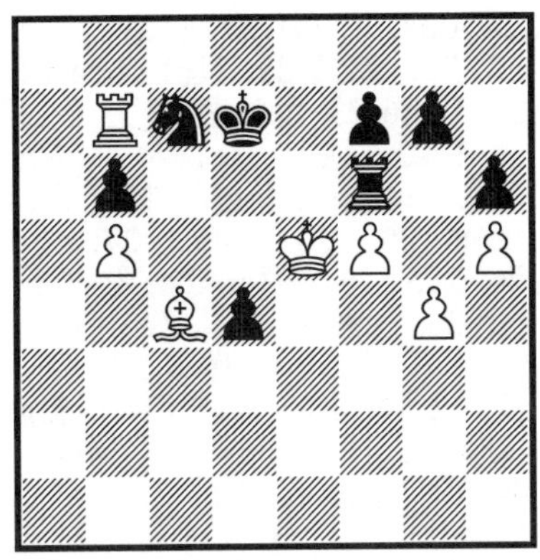

52... d3!□ [52... ♖d6 53. ♗f7 d3 54. ♗e6!+−] **53. ♗d3 ♖d6 54. ♔e4 ♔c8 55. ♖a7 f6!** [55... ♘d5?? 56. ♔e5+−] **56. ♖a1 ♖d5 57. ♖c1 ♖e5 58. ♔f3 ♖c5 59. ♖a1** [59. ♖c5?? bc5 60. b6 ♘a8 61. ♗a6 ♔b8 62. b7 ♘c7−+] **♖d5** [59... ♘b5? 60. ♗b5 ♖b5 61. ♖a7±] **60. ♗f1 ♔d7 61. ♖a7** [△ ♖b7-b8-g8] **♔c8 62. ♖a3 ♔d7 1/2 : 1/2** **[Schwartzman]**

148.* **!N** **B 14**

POLULJAHOV 2460 − P. WELLS 2455

Balatonberény 1992

1. e4 c6 2. c4 d5 3. ed5 ♘f6 4. ♘c3 cd5 5. d4 e6 6. ♘f3 ♗b4 7. cd5 ed5 8. ♗d3 0−0 9. 0−0 ♗g4?! 10. ♕b3! N [10. ♗g5 ♗c3 11. bc3 ♘bd7 12. ♕d2 ♗f3 13. gf3 ♖e8 N (13... ♖c8 − 47/190) 14. ♖ab1 ♕c7 15. ♖fc1 b6 16. ♗a6 ♘h5 17. c4 1/2 : 1/2 Belikov 2460 − Haritonov 2505, Podol'sk 1992] **♗c3** [10... ♘c6 11. ♘e5 *a)* 11... ♗d6?! 12. ♘g4 ♘g4 13. h3 ♘f6 14. ♕b7 (14. ♗e3±) ♘d4 15. ♗g5±; *b)* 11... ♗c3 12. bc3±] **11. bc3** [11. ♕b7?? ♗a5 12. ♕a8 ♗f3 13. gf3 ♕d7 △ ♘c6−+] **♗f3 12. gf3** [12. ♕b7?! ♗g2! 13. ♔g2 ♘bd7∞] **♕c7 13. ♔h1 ♘bd7 14. ♖g1± ♔h8 15. ♖b1 ♖ac8 16. ♗d2 ♘b6** [⌓ 16... b6] **17. ♖g5?!** [17. a4! ♘c4 (17... ♖b8 18. ♖g5!?±) 18. ♗c4 ♕c4 19. ♕c4 ♖c4 20. a5! ♖a4 (20... ♖c7 21. ♖b3 ♖e8 22. ♖gb1 ♖ee7 23. ♗f4 ♖cd7 24. ♗b8! a6 25. ♗a7! ♖c7 26. ♗b6! △ ♗c5+−) 21. ♖b7!? ♖a5 22. c4; 21. ♖b5!±] **♖fe8 18. a4 ♖e7□ 19. ♕b4!** [△ a5] **♖ce8 20. ♖f5!** [20. ♖bg1?! g6] **♕c8** [20... ♘c4!?

21. ♗c4 dc4 22. ♖c5? ♕d7 △ ♕h3→; 22. ♔g2; 22. ♖g1] **21. ♖g1 ♘c4 22. ♗g5** [22. ♗h6? gh6 23. ♖f6 ♕h3 △ ♖e1] **♖e6** [22... ♖e1 23. ♖e1! ♖e1 24. ♔g2±] **23. ♗f6! ♖f6 24. ♖f6 gf6 25. ♗c4 dc4** [25... ♕c4 26. ♕b7 ♕c3 27. ♕d5+−] **26. ♕d6 ♕f5** [26... ♖e6 27. ♕g3 ♕f8 28. ♕c7+−; 26... ♕d8 27. ♕c5! (27. ♕d8 ♖d8 28. ♖e1 ♖d5!⇆) ♕c8 28. ♕a7 ♕c6 29. ♖g3+−] **27. ♕g3 ♕g5** [27... ♕g6? 28. ♕f4] **28. ♕c7! ♕d5 29. ♕f4!** [29... ♕d8 30. d5! b5 (30... ♖e5 31. d6! △ 31... ♖d5 32. h4!+−, △ 31... ♖e6 32. d7!+−) 31. d6 ♖g8 (31... ♖e6 32. d7) 32. ♖d1 △ d7+−] **1 : 0** **[Poluljahov]**

149. **B 15**

HECTOR 2470 – PÉTURSSON 2560
Århus 1993

1. e4 g6 2. d4 ♗g7 3. ♘c3 c6 4. f4 d5 5. e5 h5 6. ♗e3 ♘h6 7. ♘ge2!? N [7. ♘f3 – 41/138] **♗g4** [7... ♘f5!? 8. ♗f2 e6 △ b6, ♗a6] **8. ♕d2 ♘d7** [8... ♗e2 9. ♗e2±] **9. ♘c1 h4 10. h3 ♗h5!?** [△ ♘f5, e6, ♗f8; 10... ♗e6 11. ♗d3 ♘f5 12. ♗f2 f6∞] **11. ♗d3 e6 12. 0–0 ♗f8 13. ♘b3 ♗e7 14. a4 b6?!** [14... a5=] **15. ♘a2! ♘f5 16. ♗f5** [16. c4] **gf5 17. ♖ac1 ♖c8** [17... c5?! 18. c4] **18. c4 0–0 19. ♖c2** [19. a5 ♘b8 (19... dc4 20. ♖c4 b5? 21. ♖c2 ♘b8 22. ♘b4±) 20. cd5 cd5=; 19. cd5 cd5 20. ♖c8 ♕c8 21. ♖c1 ♕a6! 22. ♘b4!? (22. ♖c7 ♕a4 23. ♘c3 ♕b3 24. ♖d7 ♕b4 25. ♖a7 ♖c8=) ♕a4 23. ♘c6∞̄] **dc4! 20. ♖c4 a5! 21. ♖fc1 ♘b8 22. ♕f2** [△ d5] **♕d5! 23. ♘d2 ♘a6! 24. ♘c3 ♕d8! 25. d5?** [25. ♘f3 ♘b4∓ 26. ♘g5 ♘d3! 27. ♕h4 ♗g6 28. ♖b1 ♗g5 29. fg5 f4! 30. ♗f4 b5 31. ab5 cb5 32. ♖c8 ♕d4 33. ♔h1 ♖c8∓; 25. ♘a2 ♕d7 (25... c5?! 26. ♘b3±) 26. ♘f3 ♗f3 27. ♕f3 c5 28. dc5 ♘c5 29. ♖d1 ♕a7 30. ♘c3⩲; 25... ♕d5!=] **ed5** [25... cd5? 26. ♘d5 ♖c4 27. ♘e7 ♕e7 28. ♖c4+−] **26. ♗b6 ♕d7** [26... dc4? 27. ♗d8 ♗c5 28. ♗h4 ♗f2 29. ♗f2± ×a5, c4, f5] **27. ♖d4 ♖b8 28. ♗a5 ♖b2∓** [28... ♗c5 29. ♔h2 ♖b2 30. ♕h4∞] **29. ♔h2** [29. ♘d1 ♗d1 30. ♖d1 ♘c5∓] **♘c5! 30. ♘d1 ♖a2!?** [×a4; 30... ♗d1! 31. ♖d1 ♘b3 (31... ♘e6 32. ♖d3 c5∓) 32. ♗c3 ♖c2 33. ♖d3 ♘c5 34. ♖f3 ♘e4 35. ♘e4 (35. ♕d4 ♗c5−+) ♖f2 36. ♘f2 c5−+] **31. ♘c3 ♖d2 32. ♖d2 ♘b3 33. g4□ ♗g6 34. ♘e2 ♘a5** [34... ♘c1 35. ♘c1 ♖a8∓] **35. gf5 ♕f5 36. ♘d4 ♕h5 37. f5 c5! 38. fg6 fg6! 39. ♕g2 cd4 40. ♕d5 ♔h8 41. ♕a5 ♗g5−+ 42. ♖e1 ♗f4 43. ♔g1 ♕f3 44. ♖g2 ♕h3 45. ♕c5 ♗e3 46. ♖e3 ♕e3 47. ♔h2 ♖b8** [47... ♖f3! 48. ♕c8 ♔g7 49. ♕d7 ♔h6 50. ♖g6 ♔g6 51. ♕g4 ♔f7 52. ♕d7 ♔f8 53. ♕c8 ♔g7 54. ♕d7 ♔h6 55. ♕e6 ♔g5 56. ♕e7 ♔f5−+] **48. ♕c2 ♕e5 49. ♔h3 g5 50. ♕g6! ♖b3 51. ♔g4 ♖g3 52. ♖g3 ♕f4! 53. ♔h5 hg3 54. ♕h6 ♔g8 55. ♕g6 ♔f8 56. ♕c6 d3! 57. ♕c8 ♔e7 58. ♕c5 ♔f7 59. ♕a7 ♔f6 60. ♕b6 ♔e5 61. ♕b5 ♔e4 62. a5 ♕f3 63. ♔g5 d2** **0 : 1** **[Pétursson]**

150. **B 15**

BALINOV 2270 – SRIENZ
Österreich 1992

1. e4 c6 2. ♘c3 d5 3. d4 g6 4. h3 ♗g7 5. ♘f3 ♘f6 6. e5 ♘e4 7. ♘e4 de4 8. ♘g5 c5 9. e6 ♗e6 10. ♘e6 fe6 11. ♗c4 N [11. dc5 – 18/(192)] **♕b6** [11... ♕a5 12. c3 (12. ♗d2!?) cd4 13. 0–0 dc3 (13... d3 14. ♖e1 ♕f5 15. ♕b3) 14. ♗e6 cb2 15. ♖b1 bc1♕ 16. ♖c1 ♘c6 17. ♕d7 ♔f8 18. ♕b7 ♖d8 19. ♕c6 ♗f6 20. ♕e4 ♔g7 21. ♗b3±; 11... ♕d4 12. ♕e2∞̄⊞; 12. ♗e6!?] **12. 0–0! cd4 13. ♕g4 ♘d7! 14. ♕e4 ♖c8 15. ♕e2 e5** [15... ♘c5 16. b4 d3 17. cd3 ♗a1 18. bc5 ♕c6 19. d4! a6 20. ♗e3 ♗c3 21. ♖c1 ♗a5 22. ♕g4 ♔f7 23. ♕f4 ♔e8 24. ♕e5 ♔f7 25. ♗h6 ♖hg8 26. d5+−] **16. b3!?** [16. c3!] **e6 17. a4 0–0 18. a5 ♕d6 19. ♗a3 ♘c5 20. ♖ad1∞̄⊞ ♔h8 21. h4 ♖f5 22. ♖d3! ♕d8 23. ♗c5! ♖c5 24. ♗e6 ♖h5 25. g3± ♖a5 26. ♕e4! ♖c5 27. ♗g4 ♖h6 28. ♖a1! g5 29. ♖a7 ♖b6 30. hg5 ♖c2 31. ♗f5 ♖c1 32. ♔g2 h6 33. ♖b7 ♖b7 34. ♕b7 hg5 35. g4 ♖c3□ 36. ♖d1 ♖c7□ 37. ♕f3 ♕f6 38. ♕a8 ♗f8 39. ♖h1 ♔g8 40. ♕d5 ♖f7 41. f3** [41. ♖c1 ♔g7□ 42. ♖c6 ♕e7 43. ♖g6 ♔h8 44. ♗e6 ♖g7 45. ♕e5 △ ♖h6#] **e4□ 42. ♕e4** [42... d3 43. ♗e6

♕b2 44. ♔g3! ♗d6 45. f4! ♗f4 46. ♔f3+−] **1 : 0** **[Balinov]**

151. **B 17**

KAMSKY 2655 – AN. KARPOV 2725
Dortmund 1993

1. e4 c6 2. d4 d5 3. ♘d2 de4 4. ♘e4 ♘d7 5. ♘g5 ♘gf6 6. ♗d3 e6 7. ♘1f3 ♗d6 8. ♕e2 h6 9. ♘e4 ♘e4 10. ♕e4 ♘f6 11. ♕h4 [11. ♕e2 – 56/(154)]

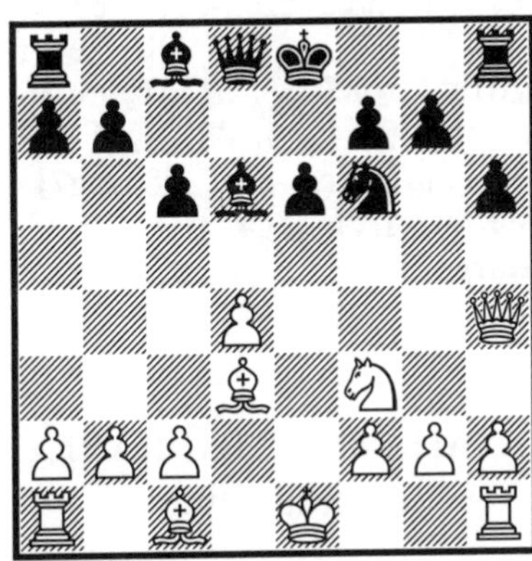

11... ♔e7!? N 12. ♘e5 [12. 0–0 g5 13. ♕h3 g4−+; 12. ♘d2 g5 13. ♕h3 e5] **♗e5 13. de5 ♕a5 14. c3 ♕e5 15. ♗e3=∞ b6** [15... c5 16. 0-0-0 g5 17. ♕g3! △ 17... ♕g3 18. hg3 △ 19. ♗c5, 19. ♗g5] **16. 0-0-0 g5 17. ♕a4** [17. ♕h3 c5 18. ♖he1∞] **c5 18. ♖he1 ♗d7 19. ♕a3 ♖hd8 20. g3** [20. ♗d4 ♕f4∓; 20. f4 gf4 21. ♗d4 *a)* 21... ♕d5 *a1)* 22. ♖e5 ♕d6 (22... ♕g2 23. ♖c5 bc5 24. ♕c5 ♔e8 25. ♗f6+−) 23. ♖c5 ♔e8; *a2)* 22. ♗f6 ♔f6 23. ♗e4+−; *b)* 21... ♕c7 22. ♗e5 ♕c6 23. ♗f6 (23. ♗f4!? △ 23... ♕a4? 24. ♗d6! ♔e8 25. ♖e6!! fe6 26. ♗g6#) ♔f6 24. ♗e4 ♕a4±; *c)* 21... ♕g5 22. ♖e5 ♕h4!⇆] **♕c7 21. ♗d4** [21. f4 ♘g4⇆] **♗e8! 22. ♔b1** [22. ♗e5 ♕c6 23. ♗f6 ♔f6 24. ♗e4 ♖d1 25. ♔d1 ♖d8−+] **♖d5** [22... ♗c6!? 23. ♗e5 ♕d7 24. ♗c2 ♕b7∓] **23. f4! ♖ad8** [23... gf4 24. gf4 ♕f4? 25. ♖f1+−] **24. ♗c2!** [24. ♗e5 ♕c6! (24... ♕d7 25. ♗c2 △ c4) 25. c4 ♖5d7 26. ♕c3 ♘g4 27. fg5 hg5 28. ♖f1 ♖d4!∓] **♖5d6 25. ♗f6 ♔f6 26. fg5 hg5 27. ♖d6 ♖d6** [27... ♕d6∓ 28. ♕a7] **28. c4□ ♔e7 29. ♕e3 f6 30. h4 gh4 31. gh4 ♕d7** [31... ♕d8!?] **32. ♕h6 e5?!** [32... ♖d2! 33. ♕g7 (33. ♖f1 ♕d4! △ 34. ♖f6 ♖d1−+) ♗f7 34. h5 (34. ♗g6? ♖d1 35. ♔c2 ♕d2 36. ♔b3 ♕b4−+) ♕d4∓] **33. h5 ♕g4** [33... ♖d2!?] **34. ♕h7 ♔d8** [34... ♗f7 35. ♗g6 ♕c4 36. b3 ♕e6 37. ♖g1; 35... ♖d1=] **35. h6 ♖d2 36. ♕f5 ♕f5 37. ♗f5** [♖ 9/k] **♗d7 38. ♗g6?** [38. ♔c1! ♖d4 39. ♗d7! ♖c4 (39... ♖d7 40. ♖d1+−) 40. ♔b1 ♖h4 (40... ♔d7 41. ♖h1+−) 41. ♖d1±] **♖h2 39. h7 ♔e7 40. ♗d3 ♗e6 41. ♖g1 f5 42. ♖g7 ♔f6 43. ♖a7 e4 44. ♗e2 f4 45. b3 f3 46. ♗d1 ♗f5 47. ♔c1 ♗h7 48. ♖b7 ♔e5 49. ♖b6 ♖a2 0 : 1** **[An. Karpov]**

152. **B 17**

HALIFMAN 2630 – EPIŠIN 2620
Dos Hermanas 1993

1. e4 c6 2. d4 d5 3. ♘d2 de4 4. ♘e4 ♘d7 5. ♘g5 ♘gf6 6. ♗d3 e6 7. ♘1f3 ♗d6 8. ♕e2 h6 9. ♘e4 ♘e4 10. ♕e4 ♕c7 11. ♗d2 [11. ♕g4 – 54/143] **b6 12. ♕g4 ♔f8?! 13. 0-0-0 N** [13. ♕e4?!] **♗b7 14. ♖he1 ♖d8** [14... c5 15. ♗c3±] **15. ♔b1** [15. ♖e6? fe6 16. ♘h4 ♘f6 17. ♕e6 ♕f7!−+; 15. c4 c5 16. ♗c3?! ♘f6 17. ♕h4 ♗f3 18. gf3 ♗f4] **♘f6 16. ♕h4** [16. ♕h3 ♗f4!] **♔e7 17. ♘e5 c5 18. f4** [18. ♘g4 cd4 19. ♘f6 gf6 20. ♕d4 ♗c5! 21. ♕h4 ♖d4 22. f4 ♗b4!=; 18. ♗c3 g5 19. ♕h3 ♗e5 20. de5 ♘e4!∞] **cd4 19. g4?!** [19. ♕g3 ♔f8∞; 19. ♖e2!↑] **g5 20. ♕f2** [20. fg5 hg5 21. ♕g3 (21. ♕g5 ♖dg8∓) ♖hg8∓] **♖hg8** [20... ♗e5 21. fe5 ♘g4 22. ♗b4 ♔e8 23. ♕f1=∞] **21. h3 a5?!** [21... ♘d5!∓] **22. ♖e2 ♘d5 23. ♖de1** [23. ♘f7!? ♔f7 24. fg5 ♔e7 25. gh6∞] **♘e3 24. ♗e3 de3 25. ♕e3** [25. ♖e3? ♗c5 26. fg5 ♕e5!−+] **♕c5∞⊕** **1/2 : 1/2** **[Halifman]**

153. !N **B 17**

SIÓN CASTRO 2390
– AN. KARPOV 2725
León 1993

1. e4 c6 2. d4 d5 3. ♘d2 de4 4. ♘e4 ♘d7 5. ♘g5 ♘gf6 6. ♗d3 e6 7. ♘1f3 ♗d6 8.

♕e2 h6 9. ♘e4 ♘e4 10. ♕e4 ♕c7 11. ♗d2 b6 12. ♕g4 g5! N 13. ♕h3 ♖g8! 14. g4 [14. ♕h6 ♗f8 15. ♕h7 ♘f6! 16. ♕h3 g4 17. ♕h4 gf3 18. ♕f6 fg2∓; RR 19. ♖g1 ♕h2 20. 0-0-0=; 14. ♗h7 ♖h8 15. ♗d3= Halifman] **♗b7 15. 0-0-0** [15. ♕h6 c5 16. ♘g5 ♖g5! (16... ♗h1 17. ♘e6!) 17. ♗g5 ♗h1 18. 0-0-0 c4∓] **0-0-0 16. ♖he1 ♗f4** [16... c5 17. ♗e4 ♗e4 18. ♖e4 ♘f6 19. ♖ee1 c4 20. ♘e5 ♘d5!?] **17. ♔b1** [17. ♕h6 ♗d2 18. ♘d2 (18. ♖d2 ♕f4 19. ♕h3 c5∓) ♕f4 19. ♖e4 ♕f6! 20. ♕h3 c5∓] **♖h8** [17... c5!? 18. ♗e4 ♗e4 19. ♖e4 ♗d2 20. ♖d2 ♘f6 △ ♕f4] **18. ♗c3** [18. ♗f4 ♕f4 19. ♕g3 ♕g3 20. hg3 c5∓] **♔b8 19. d5 cd5 20. ♗h8 ♖h8 21. ♘d4 a6** [21... ♘c5 22. ♕h5 △ h4⇆] **22. ♘e6** [22. ♕f1 ♘c5∓] **fe6 23. ♖e6 ♘e5! 24. ♗f5 ♘c4 25. ♖h6 ♖h6 26. ♕h6 ♕e5 27. ♕f8 ♔a7 28. ♕b4 ♘d2!−+ 29. ♔a1 ♕e2 30. ♖g1 ♕f2 31. ♖d1 ♕e2 32. ♖g1 ♕h2 33. ♖d1 ♕e2 34. ♖h1 a5 35. ♕c3** [35. ♕f8□ ♘c4 △ 36... ♕e5, 36... ♗e5] **d4**

0 : 1 **[An. Karpov]**

154.** **B 17**

IZETA 2505 – AN. KARPOV 2725

Dos Hermanas 1993

1. e4 c6 2. d4 d5 3. ♘d2 de4 4. ♘e4 ♘d7 5. ♗c4 ♘gf6 6. ♘g5 e6 7. ♕e2 ♘b6 8. ♗d3 [RR 8. ♗b3 h6 9. ♘5f3 c5 10. ♗f4 ♘bd5 11. ♗e5 ♕a5 12. ♘d2 cd4 13. ♘f3 ♗e7 14. ♘d4 0–0 15. 0–0 ♗d7 *a)* 16. ♖fe1 N ♖fc8 17. a3 b5 18. c3 ♕b6 19. ♗c2 ♗d6 20. ♗f6!? ♘f6 21. ♘e4! ♗e7 22. ♖ad1 ♖d8 23. ♖d3⩲→⟫ Ja. Nesterov 2445 – Švedčikov 2405, Kazahstan 1993; 17... ♗a4!= Švedčikov; *b)* 16. c4 N ♘b4 17. ♘4f3 ♘c6 18. ♗c3 ♕f5 19. a3 ♖fd8 20. ♖fd1 ♗e8= Anand 2710 – An. Karpov 2725, Monaco 1993; *c)* 16. a3 – 16/156] **h6 9. ♘5f3 c5 10. dc5 ♗c5 11. ♘e5 ♘bd7 12. ♘gf3 ♕c7 13. 0–0 0–0 14. ♖e1 ♗d6 15. ♘c4?!** [15. ♗f4 – 34/178] **♗e7 16. ♘ce5 N** [16. c3 b6; 16. ♘fe5 ♘c5 17. ♗f4 ♘d3 18. ♕d3 ♘h5; 16. ♘d4 – 56/154] **♘c5 17. ♗c4** [17. ♗f4 ♘h5=] **a6 18. a3** [18. ♗f4 ♘h5 19. ♗e3 b5=] **b5 19. ♗a2 ♗b7 20. ♗e3 ♘ce4 21. ♗d4** [21. c4 b4∓] **♖ad8 22. c3 ♗c5** [22... ♗d5 23. c4 bc4 24. ♗c4=; 23. ♗b1!?] **23. ♘d3** [23. ♗c5 ♕c5∓] **♗d4 24. ♘d4 ♖d6** [24... ♘c3?! 25. bc3 ♕c3 26. ♘e6] **25. ♖ac1** [25. f3!? ♘c3?! 26. bc3 ♕c3 27. ♘e6! fe6 28. ♗e6 ♔h8 29. ♘e5!; 25... ♘c5] **♖fd8 26. f3 ♘c5 27. ♘e5 ♗d5 28. b3** [28. ♗d5 ♘d5∓] **♕b6 29. ♔h1 ♘cd7 30. ♗b1 ♘e5 31. ♕e5 ♗b7∓ 32. ♕e2 ♕c5! 33. b4 ♕g5 34. ♕f2** [34. ♕e3 ♕e3 35. ♖e3 ♘d5 36. ♖ee1 ♘c3 37. ♘e6 ♖e6 38. ♖e6 fe6 39. ♖c3 ♖d1#] **♘h5 35. ♖cd1 e5 36. ♕c2 g6 37. ♘b3 ♕h4!−+ 38. ♔g1** [38. ♘c5 ♖d2! 39. ♘b7 ♖c2 40. ♖d8 ♔g7] **e4 39. fe4 ♗e4 40. ♕c1 ♕g4** **0 : 1**

[An. Karpov]

155. **B 18**

PRASAD 2480 – TH. RAVI 2370

Calcutta 1993

1. e4 c6 2. d4 d5 3. ♘d2 de4 4. ♘e4 ♗f5 5. ♘g3 ♗g6 6. h4 h6 7. f4 e6 8. ♘f3 ♘d7 9. h5 ♗h7 10. ♗d3 ♗d3 11. ♕d3 ♕c7 12. ♗d2 ♘gf6 13. ♘e5 c5 N [13... ♗d6 – 5/170] **14. 0-0-0 cd4 15. ♕d4 ♗c5 16. ♕c4 ♗b6** [16... ♘e5 17. fe5 ♘d7 (17... ♕e5 18. ♕b5) 18. ♘e4±; 16... 0–0 17. ♘d7 ♘d7 18. ♘e4⩲] **17. ♕e2 ♖c8** [⌓ 17... 0–0] **18. ♗b4! ♘e5** [18... ♘d5? 19. ♖d5+−; 18... ♘c5 19. ♕b5±; 18... ♗c5 19. ♗c5 ♘c5 (19... ♕c5 20. ♘f5! 0–0 21. ♘h6+−) 20. ♕b5 ♔e7⩲; 18... ♗e3 19. ♔b1 ♗f4 20. ♘d7] **19. fe5 ♘d5□ 20. ♖d5! ed5 21. ♘f5±→ ♗c5□ 22. ♘d6 ♔f8** [22... ♔d7 23. ♕g4 ♔c6 24. ♗c5 ♔c5 25. ♖h3!+−] **23. ♗c5 ♕c5 24. ♘c8 ♕c8 25. ♖d1 ♕c6** [25... ♕e6 26. c4+−] **26. ♕f3 ♔e7 27. ♖d5+−** [♕ 9/e] **♖c8 28. c3 b5 29. ♕e4 a5 30. ♕d4 b4 31. ♔d2! bc3 32. bc3 ♖b8 33. ♔e3 ♖c8 34. ♔f2! ♖b8** [34... ♕c3 35. ♖d7 ♔e6 (35... ♔e8 36. ♖d8) 36. ♕d5] **35. ♔g3! ♖b2 36. c4 ♖a2⊕ 37. ♕a7 ♔e8 38. ♕b8 ♔e7 39. ♕d8 ♔e6 40. ♖d6**

1 : 0 **[Prasad]**

156.* **B 19**

J. BENJAMIN 2570 – SEIRAWAN 2605
USA (ch) 1992

1. e4 c6 2. d4 d5 3. ♘c3 de4 4. ♘e4 ♗f5 5. ♘g3 ♗g6 6. h4 h6 7. ♘f3 ♘d7 8. h5 ♗h7 9. ♗d3 ♗d3 10. ♕d3 ♘gf6 11. ♗f4 ♕a5 [RR 11... e6 12. 0-0-0 ♗e7 13. c4 b5 14. c5 a5 N (14... 0–0 – 50/165) 15. ♘f1 a4 16. ♘e3 ♕a5 17. g4 0-0-0 18. ♔b1 ♔b7 19. ♕c2 ♖he8 20. ♖dg1 a3∞ Ivančuk 2710 – Kortchnoi 2605, Monaco 1993] **12. ♗d2 ♕c7 13. 0-0-0 e6 14. ♕e2 c5** [14... ♗e7?! 15. ♘e5±] **15. ♖he1!? N** [15. ♔b1 – 56/(155)] **♗d6?!** [15... cd4 16. ♘d4 ♗c5 17. ♘e6□ (17. ♘b3 0–0 18. ♘c5 ♕c5∓ ×h5) fe6 18. ♕e6 ♔f8 19. ♘f5=∞] **16. dc5 ♗g3?!** [16... ♗c5 17. ♗c3!? 0–0 18. ♘e5 ♘d5!? 19. ♘d7 ♕d7 20. ♕g4↑] **17. fg3 ♕g3** [17... 0–0 18. ♗f4 ♕c5 (18... ♕a5) 19. ♗d6 ♕h5 20. ♗f8 ♖f8 21. ♘e5±] **18. ♗e3 0–0**

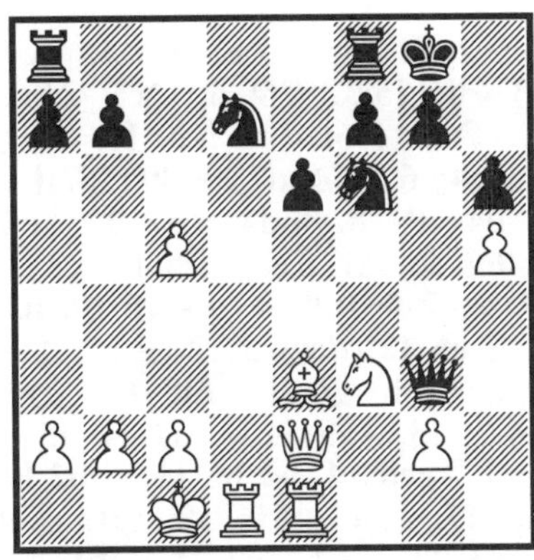

19. ♖d4! ♖fc8 [19... ♕c7 *a)* 20. ♗f4 ♕c5 (20... ♕a5 21. ♔b1) 21. ♗d6 ♕h5 22. ♗f8 ♖f8 23. ♘e5±; *b)* 20. g4! ♘c5 21. g5!±↑] **20. ♗f4 ♕g4 21. ♗h6 ♕h5** [21... ♕f5 22. ♗g5 △ g4+–] **22. ♗g5 ♖c5 23. ♖h4!±** [23. ♗f6? ♘f6 24. ♖h4 ♕d5 25. ♖eh1 ♔f8∞] **♖g5□ 24. ♖eh1! ♕h4 25. ♖h4 ♖c5 26. g4?!** [26. ♖c4! ♖ac8 27. ♖c5 ♖c5 28. b4!±] **♖ac8 27. c3 ♘f8!± 28. g5?** [28. ♘e5! ♖e5 29. ♕e5 ♘g6 30. ♕g3 ♘h4 31. ♕h4 ♖c4 32. ♕f2 ♖g4? 33. ♕a7 g5 34. ♕b7 ♔g7 35. b3 ♖e4 36. a4 g4±; 32... b6⩲] **♘6h7 29. ♘e5?** [29. ♖g4 ♘g6=] **♘g5 30. ♕h5?! ♘fh7** [△ f6∓] **31. ♘f7 ♘f6∓ 32. ♕g5□** [32. ♘h6 ♔h7 33. ♕e2 gh6–+] **♖g5 33. ♘g5** [♖ 9/h] **e5?⊕** [33... ♖e8! 34. ♖a4 a6 35. ♖b4 ♖e7 36. ♖b6 (36. ♖c4 g6) e5 37. c4 e4∓] **34. ♖a4!∓ a6 35. ♖b4 b5 36. a4 ♖c5 37. ab5 ab5 38. ♘e6 ♖c6 39. ♘g5 ♖c5 40. ♘e6 ♖c6 41. ♘g5 ♖b6 42. c4! ♘d7** [42... ♖c6 43. b3!] **43. ♖b5!** [43. cb5? ♔f8∓] **♖b5 44. cb5=** [♘♗ 2/i] **♔f8 45. ♔d2 ♔e7 46. ♔e3 ♔f6 47. ♘e4 ♔e6 48. ♘c3 g5 49. ♘e4 g4 50. b3 ♘b6 51. ♘g3 ♘d5** [51... ♔d5 52. ♘h5 △ ♘f6] **52. ♔d3 ♘f6** [△ ♔d5∓] **53. ♔c4 ♘d7 54. b4 ♔d6 55. ♘e4 ♔e6 56. ♘g3 1/2 : 1/2** **[Seirawan]**

157.** **!N** **B 20**

NADIRHANOV 2450 – SERPER 2590
Taškent 1993

1. e4 c5 2. g3 d5 [2... ♘c6 3. ♗g2 g6 4. d3 ♗g7 5. f4 e6 6. ♘f3 ♘ge7 7. 0–0 d6 8. c3 0–0 9. ♗e3 b6 10. ♘a3!? N (10. ♗f2 – 54/(148)) ♗a6 11. ♗f2 ♕d7 12. ♖e1 ♖ac8 13. ♕d2 f5 14. ef5 gf5 15. d4 c4 16. ♘g5 ♘d8 17. ♖e2 d5 18. ♖ae1± Nadirhanov 2445 – Zagrebel'nyj 2440, Taškent 1992; 13... e5!?] **3. ed5 ♕d5 4. ♘f3 ♗g4 5. ♗g2 ♕e6** [5... ♘c6 6. h3 ♕e4?! 7. ♔f1 ♗d7 8. ♘c3 ♕b4 9. d3 e6 10. ♘d2!±] **6. ♔f1 ♘c6** [6... ♗h3 7. b4! cb4 8. a3 g6 9. ♗b2 ♘f6 10. ♘g5 ♗g2 11. ♔g2 ♕c6 12. ♕f3 ba3 13. ♖a3 ♗g7 14. ♖e1 ♕f3 15. ♖f3±] **7. h3 ♗h5 8. ♘c3 ♕d7?!** [8... ♘f6! 9. d3 ♕d7 10. ♗e3 N (10. a4 – 50/169) e6 11. g4 ♗g6 12. d4!∞ Nadirhanov 2445 – V. Loginov 2540, Taškent 1992] **9. ♘e5! N** [9. d3 – 54/148] **♗d1** [9... ♕f5!? 10. ♘g4!±] **10. ♘d7 ♗c2 11. ♘c5 0-0-0□ 12. b4!⩲** [×↗h1-a8] **e6!** [12... a6?! 13. ♘a6?! ♘d4! (13... ♗d3 14. ♔g1 ♗a6 15. b5⩲) 14. ♘c5 b6∓; 13. a4! △ 14. b5, 14. ♘b7±] **13. ♘b7** [13. b5? ♘a5] **♔b7 14. b5 ♘e7** [14... ♗d3? 15. ♔g1 ♗b5 16. ♘b5±⊡ ×♔b7] **15. ♗a3 ♘d5!□ 16. bc6 ♔c6 17. ♘d5 ed5 18. ♗f8?!** [⌓ 18. ♗b2 ♗d3 19. ♔g1 f6 20. ♖c1 ♔d6 21. ♗a3?! ♔e6; 21. ♔h2!↻] **♗d3 19. ♔g1 ♖hf8 20. ♖c1 ♔d6 21. ♖c3 ♗e4 22. ♗e4 de4 23. d3 1/2 : 1/2** **[Serper, Nadirhanov]**

158. **B 21**

S. KISELËV 2510 – ULYBIN 2565
Sankt-Peterburg (zt) 1993

1. e4 e6 2. f4 c5 3. ♘f3 ♘f6 4. d3 [4. e5 ♘d5 5. d3 d6 6. ♗e2; 6. g3!?] **♘c6 5. g3 d5 6. e5 ♘d7 7. ♗g2 ♗e7 8. 0–0** [8. c4!? ♘b6 9. b3 (9. ♕e2) dc4 10. dc4 ♕d1 11. ♔d1⩲⊥○ ×♘b6] **b5** [8... 0–0 9. c4 ♘b6 10. b3 dc4 11. dc4⩲○] **9. c4** [9. ♗e3; 9. c3 △ d4] **bc4 10. dc4 ♘b6□ 11. cd5 ed5 12. ♘c3 0–0?! N** [12... ♗a6 13. ♖f2 ♘b4 14. ♘e1⩲; 12... d4 13. ♘g5 (13. ♘e4 0–0∞) ♗d7 (13... ♗b7 14. e6!; 13... ♗g5 14. ♗c6 ♗d7 15. ♗a8 ♕a8 16. fg5 dc3 17. ♕d6!±) 14. ♘ce4↑; 12... ♗e6 – 13/331] **13. ♘e1!** [×d5] **♗a6 14. ♖f2 d4 15. ♗c6 dc3 16. ♕c2!** [16. ♕d8 ♖ad8 17. bc3 ♖d1 18. ♗b2 ♖a1 19. ♗a1 ♘c4⩱ △ ♖d8-d1, ×♗a1, ♘e1] **cb2 17. ♗b2 ♖b8 18. ♗e4±↑» h6 19. f5 f6□ 20. ♖d1 ♕c7 21. ♘f3** [△ ♘h4-g6] **♗b5!⊕** [△ 22... ♗a4, 22... ♗e8 ×g6] **22. ♖c1** [×c5] **♗a4 23. ♕e2 ♗d7 24. ♘h4 ♗e8 25. e6 c4! 26. ♗d4** [△ ♕e3] **♗c5** [26... ♖d8!? 27. ♕e3 ♖d4 28. ♕d4 ♗c5 29. ♕d2±]

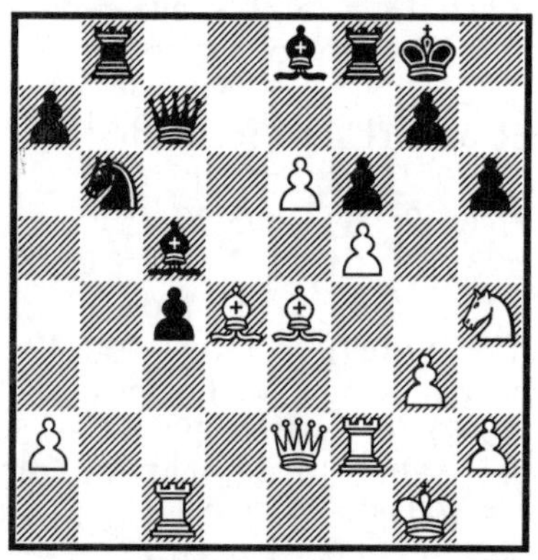

27. ♖c4! [27. ♕e3 ♗d4 28. ♕d4 ♖d8 29. ♕c3±] **♘c4 28. ♕c4 ♖c8** [28... ♗d6 29. ♕c7 ♗c7 30. ♗a7 ♖b4 31. ♗d5+–] **29. ♖c2⊕** [⌓ 29. ♕c5 ♕c5 30. ♗c5 ♖c5 31. e7 ♖f7 32. ♘g6 ♔h7 33. ♗c2 ♖c7 (33... ♖e5 34. ♘e5 fe5 35. f6+–) 34. ♖e2 △ ♗a4+–] **♗d4** [29... ♕a5 30. ♗c5 ♖c5 (30... ♗b5 31. ♕b4) 31. ♕c5 ♕e1 32. ♔g2 ♕e4 33. ♔f2!+–] **30. ♕d4 ♖d8** [30... ♕b8 31. ♖c8 ♕c8 32. e7 ♖f7 33. ♘g6+–] **31. ♖c7?!** [31. ♕b4! ♖d1 32. ♔g2 ♕e5 (32... ♕b6 33. ♕b6 ab6 34. e7 ♖f7 35. ♘g6+–) 33. e7 (33. ♖c8 ♕b5!∞) ♖f7 34. ♘g6+–] **♖d4 32. ♗c2** [32. e7 ♖e4 (32... ♖f7 33. ♗c2) 33. ef8♕ ♔f8 34. ♖a7±⊥] **♗a4 33. ♘f3 ♖g4 34. ♗d3?!** [34. h3 ♖g3 35. ♔f2 ♗c2 (35... ♖f3? 36. ♔f3 ♗c2 37. ♖c2±) 36. ♔g3 ♗f5 37. ♘d4 ♗e4 38. ♖a7±] **♖d8 35. ♗c4 ♔h7 36. ♔f2** [36. e7 ♖b8] **♖e4 37. ♗e2 a5 38. ♖a7** [38. ♖c5 ♗d1 39. ♗d1 ♖d1 40. ♖a5 ♖c1 (×♔f2) 41. ♘h4 h5! (×g4) 42. ♘g6 ♖c2 43. ♔f3 ♖ce2 44. ♖a8 ♖4e3=] **♖d5 39. ♖c7 ♗b5 40. ♗b5 ♖b5 41. ♘h4 ♖h4** [42. gh4 ♖f5 43. ♔g3 ♖e5 44. e7 ♔g6 45. ♖a7 h5 46. ♔f3=; 41... ♖a4?! 42. ♖c8 △ e7, ♘g6] **1/2 : 1/2**
[S. Kiselëv]

159. **B 21**

ERMENKOV 2505 – ADORJÁN 2545
Budapest (zt) 1993

1. e4 c5 2. f4 d5 3. ♘c3 de4 4. ♘e4 ♕c7 5. ♘f3 ♘f6 [5... ♕f4 6. ♘c5 ♘f6 7. d4 ♕c7 8. ♘e5⩲] **6. ♘f6?! N** [6. d3 ♘c6!? 7. g3 ♗g4; 6... ♘bd7 – 40/(167)] **ef6 7. g3** [7. d4 cd4 8. ♘d4 ♗e7 9. ♗e2 0–0 10. 0–0 ♖d8 11. ♗e3 ♘c6 12. c3 ♗c5∓] **♗e7 8. ♗g2 0–0 9. 0–0 ♘c6 10. b3 ♗g4 11. h3 ♗e6 12. d3** [⌓ 12. ♗b2 ♖fd8 13. ♕e2 ♖ac8 14. ♔h2] **♖fd8 13. ♗e3** [13. ♗b2 c4!?; 13... a5 △ 14. a4 c4! 15. bc4?? ♕b6–+] **♖ac8 14. a4 b6 15. ♔h2 h6! 16. ♕e2 f5 17. ♖ae1 ♗f6 18. ♕f2 ♖e8 19. ♘d2 ♗c3 20. ♖e2 ♖e7 21. ♘b1 ♗f6 22. ♖ee1 ♖ce8∓ 23. ♗d2 ♕d7 24. ♘a3** [24. ♘c3? ♘b4 25. ♖c1 ♗c3 26. ♗c3 ♘a2–+] **♘d4 25. ♗e3 ♗d5 26. ♗d5 ♕d5 27. ♘c4 ♖e6 28. ♗d4 ♗d4 29. ♕d2 ♕c6 30. h4 a6!** [30... ♗c3 31. ♖e6 ♖e6 32. ♕g2 ♕e8 33. ♖f2 ♗d4 34. ♖d2 ♖e1 35. ♕f3∓] **31. ♖e6 ♕e6 32. ♕g2 b5 33. ab5 ab5 34. ♘e5** [34. ♘d2 ♕e2 35. ♘f3 ♕g2 36. ♔g2 ♖e2 37. ♔h3 ♗c3∓] **♗e5 35. fe5** [35. ♖e1 ♕d6 (35... f6!? 36. ♕b7 ♕f7?! 37. ♕b5 ♖b8 38. ♕c5 ♗c7 39. ♖e7 ♗b6 40. ♕d6 ♕f8 41. ♕e6 ♔h8 42. b4∞; 36... b4–+) 36. fe5 ♖e5 37. ♖e5 ♕e5–+] **♕e5 36. ♖f2 b4 37. ♕f3 g6 38. ♕f4 ♔g7**

39. ♕e5 ♖e5 40. ♔g2 g5 41. hg5 hg5 42. ♖d2 ♔g6 43. ♔f3 g4 [43... f4 44. gf4 ♖f5–+] **44. ♔f4** [44. ♔f2 ♔g5–+] **♖e1 45. ♖h2 f6 46. ♖f2 ♖g1 47. c3 bc3 48. ♖c2 ♖f1 49. ♔e3 ♖f3 50. ♔e2 ♖g3 51. ♖c3 f4 52. ♖c5 ♖g2 53. ♔f1 ♖b2 54. ♖b5 f3 55. ♖b8 ♔g5 0 : 1**
[Adorján, Gy. Fehér]

160.* !N **B 22**

DOLMATOV 2615 – LAUTIER 2645

Dortmund 1993

1. e4 c5 2. c3 [RR 2. ♘f3 ♘c6 3. c3 e5 4. ♗c4 ♕c7 5. 0–0! N (5. d3 — 56/157) *a)* 5... ♘f6 6. ♘g5 ♘d8 7. f4! h6 (7... ef4 8. e5!±) 8. ♘f3! ef4 9. e5 ♘h5 10. ♘a3 △ d4±; *b)* 5... ♗e7 6. ♘g5! *b1)* 6... ♗g5 7. ♕h5 d5!□ (7... ♗e7? 8. ♕f7 ♔d8 9. ♕g7+–) 8. ed5 (8. ♕g5? f6!–+) ♗f4! (8... h6?! 9. dc6 ♘f6 10. ♕e2 bc6 11. d3 △ 11... ♘d5?! 12. f4!) 9. dc6 ♘f6 10. ♕e2 0–0 11. cb7 ♗b7 12. d3 e4! 13. ♗f4 ♕f4 14. de4 ♘e4 15. ♕e3! (15. f3?! ♘d6!∞) ♕e3 16. fe3 ♖ad8 (16... ♘d6!?) 17. ♘a3 ♘d2 (17... ♖d2 18. ♖ad1! ♖b2 19. ♖f7!!+–) 18. ♖f2 ♘c4 19. ♘c4 ♗a6 20. ♘d2 ♖d3 21. ♘b3! ♖c8 22. ♖e1 ♗c4 23. ♖d2± Smagin 2520 – Brendel 2355, Dortmund (open) 1993; ⌓ 18... ♘e4; *b2)* 6... ♘d8 7. d3⩲ Smagin] **e6 3. ♘f3 d5 4. ed5 ed5 5. d4 c4?! 6. b3 cb3 7. ab3 ♗d6** **N** [7... ♘f6 — 32/(204)] **8. ♗d3 ♘e7 9. 0–0 ♗g4?!** [9... 0–0!? 10. b4!?⩲] **10. ♖e1 ♘bc6** [10... 0–0? 11. ♗h7 ♔h7 12. ♘g5+–] **11. ♘bd2 ♕d7?** [△ 0–0; 11... ♕c7 12. ♘f1 h6 13. ♘e3 ♗e6 (13... ♗h2? 14. ♔h1 ♗f3 15. ♕f3±) 14. c4→] **12. ♕c2 ♖c8 13. ♕b1 h6 14. b4!± b6** [14... a6 15. h3 ♗e6 16. ♘b3±] **15. b5 ♘a5 16. ♘e5 ♗e5 17. ♖e5 0–0?** [17... ♖c3□ 18. ♗a3 ♗e6 19. ♗b4 ♖c7 20. ♗e7 ♕e7 21. f4=∞→] **18. ♗a3 ♖fe8 19. ♗b4 ♘c4 20. ♘c4 dc4 21. ♗h7 ♔h8 22. ♗e4 f6** [22... ♗e6 23. ♗e7 ♖e7 24. ♕b4+–] **23. ♖e7 ♖e7 24. ♗c6 ♕e6 25. ♗e7 ♕e7 26. ♕e1+– ♕f7 27. d5 ♗f5 28. ♕e2 ♗d3 29. ♕e6 ♖c7 30. ♕f7 ♖f7 31. d6 ♗f5 32. ♖e1 ♔h7 33. ♖e7 ♖f8 34. ♗e8 1 : 0**
[Dolmatov]

161. **B 22**

V. SALOV 2660 – KASPAROV 2805

Linares 1993

1. e4 c5 2. c3 e6 3. d4 d5 4. ed5 ed5 5. ♘f3 ♘c6 6. ♗e2?! ♗d6 [6... cd4!? 7. ♘d4 ♘f6 8. 0–0 ♗d6 9. ♗g5 (9. ♗b5 0–0! 10. ♘c6 bc6 11. ♗c6 ♗h2!) h6 10. ♗h4 0–0 11. ♗f3 g5 (11... ♗e6!?) 12. ♗g3 ♗g3 13. hg3 ♕b6⇆] **7. dc5 ♗c5 8. 0–0 ♘ge7 9. ♘bd2 0–0 10. ♘b3 ♗b6 11. ♗g5?!** [11. ♘bd4!? ♘f5=] **h6 N** ∓ [11... f6 12. ♗h4!? (12. ♗f4 — 27/(335)) g5?! 13. ♗g3 f5 14. ♘g5 f4 15. ♗d3! (15. ♗h4? ♘g6–+) ♘g6 16. ♕h5 (16. ♗g6? ♕g5–+) ♕c7 17. ♗g6 (17. ♗h4? ♘ce5∓) hg6 18. ♕g6 ♕g7 19. ♕g7 ♔g7 20. ♗h4±] **12. ♗e7** [12. ♗h4? g5 13. ♗g3 f5∓] **♕e7 13. ♖e1 ♗e6 14. a4 a5!** [14... a6 15. a5 ♗a7 (15... ♗c7 16. ♘fd4 ♕f6 17. ♘c6 bc6 18. ♘c5 ♗c8 19. g3∞) 16. ♘bd4=] **15. ♕d3 ♖ad8 16. ♕b5?!** [16. ♗d1!? ♕c7 17. ♗c2 g6∞] **♕c7 17. ♘bd4?!** [17. g3!?] **♗g4 18. ♗f1** [18. ♖ad1 ♖fe8∓] **g6 19. g3** [19. h3 ♗f3 (19... ♗d7!?) 20. ♘f3∓] **h5 20. ♕d3 ♖fe8 21. ♗g2 ♔g7 22. ♔f1!** [22. ♖ad1 ♗d4!? 23. cd4 ♘b4 24. ♕b3 ♖e1 25. ♖e1 ♕c4 26. ♕c4 dc4 27. ♘e5 ♖d4 28. ♗b7 ♘d3∓] **♕d6** [22... ♕d7?! 23. ♕b5∞] **23. ♕b5 ♘d4 24. ♘d4 ♖e1 25. ♖e1 h4! 26. ♕d3 ♕f6! 27. ♔g1 h3!∓ 28. ♗f1 ♖c8 29. ♕d2 ♗d7! 30. ♘b5 ♖d8 31. ♘d4 ♖c8⊕ 32. ♘b5 ♖h8 33. ♖e2 ♗g4 34. ♖e1 ♗d7 35. ♖e2 d4?** [35... ♗c6 36. b3 d4 37. ♘d4 ♖d8∓; 35... ♖h5!?∓ 36. ♕d3? ♗g4! 37. ♖d2 ♖e5!–+ 38. ♕b1 ♕e7; 35... g5!?∓ 36. ♕d5 ♗c6 37. ♕d3 ♖d8 38. ♘d4 ♗d4 39. cd4 ♖d4 40. ♕c3 ♖d1?! 41. ♖e5!∞; 40... ♖d5!] **36. ♘d4 ♗a4 37. ♖e4! ♗d7 38. ♕e3 ♗c6 39. ♖f4 ♗d4** [39... ♕d6!? 40. ♘f5 (40. ♗c4 ♗d5) gf5 41. ♕b6 ♖e8 42. ♖d4 ♕h6 43. ♖h4 (43. ♕a5? ♕c1 44. ♕f5 ♕f1! 45. ♔f1 ♗g2) ♕c1 44. ♕d4 f6 *a)* 45. ♖h3?! ♗b5 46. c4 ♖e1 47. cb5 (47. ♕d3 ♕c4–+) ♖f1 48. ♔g2 *a1)* 48... ♖d1?! 49. ♕h4 (49. ♕c3 ♖g1 50. ♔f3 ♕c3 51. bc3 ♖c1–+) ♖g1 50. ♔f3 ♕d1 51. ♔f4 ♕d4 52. ♔f5 ♕e5 53. ♔g4 ♕e4 54. f4 ♕e2 55. ♔f5 ♕d3 56. ♔g4 ♕d1

57. ♔f5 ♕d7−+; *a2)* 48... ♖g1 49. ♔f3 ♕d1 50. ♕d1 ♖d1 51. ♖h4 ♖d3 52. ♔g2 ♖b3 53. ♖d4 ♖b5 54. ♖d2∓; *b)* 45. ♕c4!= ♗g2 46. ♖h7!] **40. ♕d4 ♕d4 41. ♖d4 ♖e8** [41... a4!=] **42. f4 a4 43. ♖d2 ♖e1 44. ♔f2 ♖c1 45. ♗h3 a3 46. ba3 ♖c3 47. ♗g2** [47. ♖a2 ♗d5 48. ♖a1 ♖c2 49. ♔g1 b5 50. ♗f1 ♗c4=] **♖a3**
1/2 : 1/2 **[Kasparov]**

162.* **B 22**

LAUTIER 2645 − SERPER 2590

Dortmund 1993

1. e4 c5 2. c3 d5 3. ed5 ♕d5 4. d4 ♘f6 5. ♘f3 [RR 5. ♗e3 N ♘g4 6. ♘a3 ♘e3 7. fe3 e6 8. ♘f3 ♗e7 9. ♘b5 ♘a6 10. ♗d3 0−0 11. a4⩲ van Mil 2435 − József Horváth 2535, Budapest 1993] **♘c6 6. ♗e3 ♘g4! 7. ♗d3!? N** [7. ♗g5 h6 8. ♗h4 g5 9. ♗g3 ♗g7∞; 9... f5! − 51/143] **♘e3 8. fe3 e6 9. 0−0 ♗e7 10. ♕c2 ♕h5! 11. ♘bd2 0−0** [△ b6, ♗b7∓] **12. ♗e4!? ♗d7 13. ♘c4 ♖ad8 14. ♘fe5?!** [⌓ 14. ♖f2 △ ♖af1] **♘e5 15. ♘e5 ♗c8!** [15... ♗d6? 16. ♖f3! △ ♖h3±] **16. ♖f3 f5! 17. ♗d3 ♗d6 18. ♖h3 ♕e8** [18... ♕g5!?] **19. ♘c4 ♗c7!∓** [⌂, ×♖h3] **20. a4** [20. dc5? e5 △ e4, f4−+] **b6!?** [△ ♗b7; 20... e5 21. de5 ♗e5 22. ♖f1 g6 23. ♘e5 ♕e5∓] **21. dc5 bc5??** [21... e5! 22. cb6 ab6 23. ♘a3!? e4 24. ♗c4 ♔h8 25. ♘b5 ♗b8 △ f4−+→] **22. e4!□ ♕d7?!** [22... ♕c6∞] **23. ♖e1 ♗b7 24. ef5 ef5 25. ♘e5! ♗e5□ 26. ♖e5 ♕c6?** [26... ♕d6!=] **27. ♖g3!±** [×f5; 27. ♗f5?? ♖d1!−+] **♕d6□ 28. ♖e1!** [28. ♖ge3? ♗e4!∓; 28. ♕b3?! ♗d5?? 29. ♖d5!; 28... ♔h8!] **♔h8?⊕** [⌓ 28... ♗c8] **29. ♗f5 ♕d2 30. ♕d2** [30. ♖ge3!? ♗g2!□ (30... ♕c2? 31. ♗c2 ♖d2 32. ♖3e2+−) 31. ♕d2 ♖d2 32. ♖e8 ♖g8! Lautier; 30. ♖f1 g6!] **♖d2 31. b4?⊕** [31. ♖e7! ♖d1? 32. ♔f2 ♖f5 33. ♔e2+−; 31... ♖b2? 32. ♖eg7!+−; 31... ♗c8!? 32. ♖d3!□ ♖b2 33. ♖f7!+−; 31... ♗c6!□±] **cb4 32. cb4 ♖d4?** [32... h6] **33. ♖g4 ♖d2 34. ♖f1?** [34. ♗e4? ♖e8 35. ♖f1 h5!; 34. h3!?±] **♖fd8?!** [⌓ 34... ♖e8] **35. ♗e4 h5! 36. ♖h4 ♗e4 37. ♖e4 ♖a2 38. ♖e5** [38. b5? ♖dd2] **♖a4 39. ♖h5 ♔g8 40. b5 a6!= 41. ba6** [41. b6 ♖b4] **♖a6 42. ♖g5 ♖dd6 43. h3 ♖f6 44. ♖f6 ♖f6 45. ♔h2** **1/2 : 1/2**
[Serper]

163.* **!N** **B 22**

HARLOV 2580 − ISTRĂŢESCU 2470

Metz 1993

1. e4 c5 2. c3 d5 3. ed5 ♕d5 4. d4 ♘f6 5. ♘f3 e6 6. ♗e2 ♘c6 [RR 6... cd4?! 7. ♘d4! N (7. cd4 − 48/(217)) a6 (7... ♕g2 8. ♗f3 ♕h3 9. ♘b5 ♘a6 10. ♗f4⩲) 8. ♗f3 ♕d6 9. ♕e2 ♕c7 10. ♘d2 ♗d7 11. ♘c4 ♘c6 12. ♘f5! b5 13. ♘ce3 ♖d8 14. 0−0! ♘e5 15. ♖e1! (Kveinys 2545 − Wojtkiewicz 2530, Polska 1992) ef5 16. ♘c2 ♗d6 17. ♗f4⩲ Kveinys] **7. 0−0 ♗e7 8. c4 ♕d8 9. dc5 ♕d1 10. ♖d1 ♗c5** [10... ♘e4 − 52/159] **11. ♘c3 0−0 12. ♗f4 b6 13. a3 ♗b7 14. b4 ♗e7 15. ♘b5 ♖ad8 16. ♗c7! N** [16. ♘e5] **♖d1 17. ♖d1 ♖c8 18. ♗d6 ♔f8 19. ♗e7 ♔e7 20. ♘d6 ♖b8** [20... ♖c7 21. ♘g5! ♘d8 22. ♘b5+−] **21. b5!⩲** [21. ♖c1 ♘d7=] **♘d8 22. ♘e5 ♗d5!!** [22... ♗a8 23. f4±] **23. ♘f5 ef5 24. cd5 ♔d6 25. ♘c4** [25. ♘c6 ♖a8! △ ♘b7-c5=; 25. f4!?±] **♔c5 26. d6** [△ ♘b2!-a4#] **♔b5□** [26... ♘d5 27. ♘e5 ♔d6 28. f4±] **27. ♘b6! ♔c5□ 28. ♘c8!?** [28. ♘a4 ♔c6 29. ♗f3 ♘e4 30. ♘c3 ♖b3 31. ♘e4 fe4 32. ♗e4 ♔d7=] **a5 29. ♖c1 ♔d4 30. ♖c4 ♔d5 31. ♘e7 ♔e6! 32. g3 g6 33. ♖d4 ♖b6 34. ♗c4 ♔d7 35. ♘d5 ♘d5 36. ♖d5 ♘b7= 37. ♖d1 ♖d6 38. ♖b1 ♘c5 39. ♗f7 ♘e4 40. ♗g8 ♘f6 41. ♗h7 ♘h7 42. ♖b7 ♔e6 43. ♖h7 ♖d1 44. ♔g2 ♖a1 45. g4 fg4 46. ♔g3 ♖a3 47. ♔g4 ♔f6 48. ♖a7 ♖a1 49. h4**
1/2 : 1/2 **[Harlov]**

164. **!N** **B 23**

K. THOMPSON − RHINE

corr. 1992

1. e4 c5 2. ♘c3 ♘c6 3. f4 g6 4. ♘f3 ♗g7 5. ♗c4 e6 6. f5 ♘ge7 7. fe6 fe6 8. d3 d5 9. ♗b3 b5! 10. ed5 ed5 11. 0−0!? [11. ♘b5?! ♕a5 12. ♘c3 c4! (12... d4 − 49/(198)) 13. dc4 d4−+] **♗c3! N** [11... c4?! − 55/162] **12. bc3 c4 13. ♘g5 ♗f5 14.**

dc4 dc4 15. ♕e2 cb3 16. ab3 ♕d5! [16... 0–0 17. ♘e6 ♗e6 18. ♕e6 ♔g7 19. ♗b2!± Ju. Hodgson, Day] **17. ♗a3 b4 18. cb4!?** [18. ♗b4 ♘b4 19. cb4 ♕d4 20. ♔h1 ♕b4 21. ♖fe1 0–0! 22. ♕e7 ♕e7 23. ♖e7 ♗c2= Silman; 19... h6!?] **♘d4 19. ♕f2 ♘c2!□** [19... h6? 20. c4! ♕d7□ (20... ♕d6? 21. b5; 20... ♕e5? 21. ♖fe1 ♘e2□ 22. ♔h1?? ♕h2!–+; 22. ♕e2!+–) 21. ♖ad1 hg5 (21... ♖d8 22. ♗b2+–) 22. ♖d4 ♕c7 23. g4! ♗e6 24. ♖e1 ♗f7 25. b5+–; ⌓ 23... 0–0+–; 19... ♗c2? 20. ♕f6±; 19... 0–0? 20. ♕h4 h5 21. ♖ad1±; 19... 0-0-0? 20. c4! ♕d7 (20... ♕g8? 21. b5+–) 21. ♘f7±] **20. ♗b2!□** [20. g4? ♗d3! (20... ♗g4 21. ♕c2 ♕g5 22. ♕g2!=∞) 21. ♘f7 ♖f8! (21... 0–0?? 22. ♘h6 ♔g7 23. ♗b2+–) 22. ♘d6 ♔d7!–+] **0–0** [⌓ 20... ♘a1 21. ♗h8 ♘b3 22. ♖e1 (22. ♘h7!? 0-0-0!?) 0-0-0!? 23. ♖e7 ♖h8 24. ♕a7 ♕d4 25. ♕d4 ♘d4 26. ♘h7∓⊥]

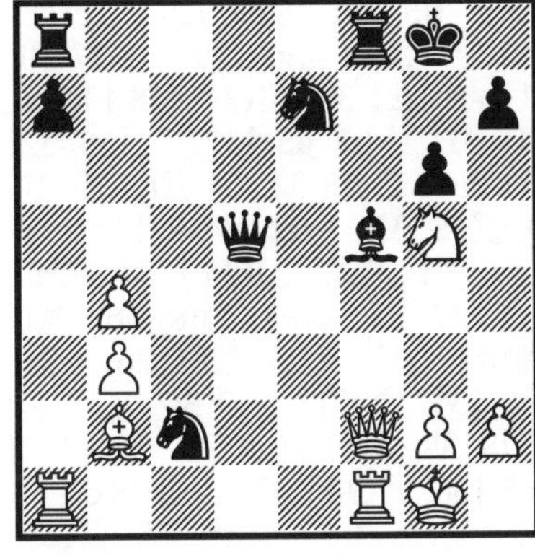

21. ♘h7?! [21. g4?! ♗g4 22. ♕h4 (22. ♕c2? ♕g5–+) h5! 23. ♘h7 g5!! (23... ♔h7?? 24. ♕e7 ♔h6 25. ♗g7+–) 24. ♘g5 (24. ♕g3 ♔h7 25. ♕c3 ♘d4–+) ♘g6! 25. ♕g3 ♕g5–+; 21. ♕h4?! h5 22. ♕g3 (22. ♘h7? ♔h7 23. ♕e7 ♖f7–+; 22. g4?! ♗g4–+ – 21. g4; 22. h3 ♕b3 23. ♖ab1 ♕b4 24. ♖f4 ♕c5 25. ♔h1 ♘e3 26. ♗d4 ♕c2 27. ♖g1 ♘7d5 28. ♖f2 ♕c4 29. ♖d2 ♗d3–+ △ 30... ♖f4, 30... ♘f5) ♘d4! 23. ♔h1 (23. ♕c7? ♗d7! 24. ♖ad1 ♘e2 25. ♔h1 ♗c6!! 26. ♘f3 ♖f3!! 27. gf3 ♕f3! 28. ♖f3 ♗f3#) ♗g4 24. h4 (24. ♕c7 ♗d7!; 24. ♕e3 ♘ec6 △ ♖fe8) ♕b3 25. ♕c7 ♘dc6–+; 21. ♖a7!? ♖a7 (21... ♗d3?? 22. ♘f7!! ♘f5 23. ♕f5+–) 22. ♕a7 ♕d7!? 23. ♕d7?! ♗d7 24. ♖f8 ♔f8 25. ♘h7 ♔f7!∓⊥; 23. ♕f2∞] **♔h7□** [21... ♗h3?? 22. ♕f8!+–; 21... ♘a1? 22. ♕h4 ♔f7 23. ♕f6 ♔e8 24. ♕f8 ♔d7 25. ♘f6 ♔d6 26. ♕e7 ♔e7 27. ♘d5 ♔d6 28. ♘e3+–⊥] **22. ♖a5?** [⌓ 22. ♕h4! ♔g8 23. ♖ae1!! (23. ♕e7? ♖f7 24. ♕h4 ♖h7–+) ♘e1□ 24. ♖e1 (△ ♕h8-g7-e7#) ♗e6!!□ (24... ♕d6? 25. ♖e7±) 25. ♕e7 (25. ♕h8? ♔f7 26. ♕g7 ♔e8–+) ♖f7!□ (25... ♗f7? 26. ♕f6) 26. ♕e6 ♕e6 27. ♖e6 ♔h7 28. ♖e3 (△ ♖h3+–) ♔h6!∓⊥ ×b3, b4] **♕d3!!–+** [22... ♕b3 23. ♕h4 ♔g8 24. ♕h8 ♔f7 25. ♕g7 ♔e8 26. ♖e5 ♕f7 (26... ♖f7?? 27. ♕g8!+–) 27. ♕h6 ♕g8 (27... ♖d8 28. g4!?) 28. ♗c1 ♖f7 29. ♗g5 ♖d8 30. ♕h4 ♖d7 31. ♕c4 (△ ♖e7!) ♕g7∞] **23. ♕h4** [23. g4? ♕e3!; 23. ♖e5! ♘d5! (23... ♗e6?? 24. ♕h4 ♔g8 25. ♕h8!! ♔h8 26. ♖h5 ♔g8 27. ♖h8#; 23... ♘c6 24. ♕h4 ♔g8 25. ♖ef5! ♖f5 26. ♕h8 ♔f7 27. ♕g7 △ ♕g6) *a)* 24. ♕h4 ♔g8 25. ♖ef5 ♖f5 26. ♕h8 ♔f7 27. ♕g7 (27. ♖f5 gf5! 28. ♕a8 ♕e3) ♔e6! 28. ♕g6 ♘f6; *b)* 24. ♖e2 g5! 25. ♖d2 ♕e3! 26. ♖d5 (26. ♖c2 ♗d3!! 27. ♕e3 ♖f1#) ♗d3!! 27. ♖d7 ♔g6! 28. ♖d6 ♔h5! 29. ♖f6 ♖f6 30. ♗f6 ♗f1; *c)* 24. g4! ♘ce3! (24... ♗g4?? 25. ♕h4 ♔g8 26. ♕h8!!+–) 25. ♖c1 (△ 26. ♖c7! ♘c7 27. ♖e7+–; 25. gf5 ♕f1 26. ♕f1 ♘f1 27. ♖d5 ♖f5! 28. ♖f5 gf5 29. ♔f1 ♖b8–+) ♖ac8! (25... ♗d7?? 26. ♕h4 ♔g8 27. ♕h8!! ♔h8 28. ♖d5! ♔g8 29. ♖d3=⊥) 26. ♖c8 ♕d1] **♔g8 24. ♕h8** [24. ♕e7? ♕f1! 25. ♔f1 ♗d3 26. ♔g1 ♖f1#; 24. h3 ♘e3 25. ♖f2 ♘3d5! 26. g4 ♕e4 27. ♕h8 ♔f7 28. ♕g7 ♔e8 (△ ♕e1–+) 29. gf5 gf5 (△ ♖g8) 30. ♖g2 ♔d7–+] **♔f7 25. ♕g7 ♔e8 26. ♖e5??** [⌓ 26. ♗f6 ♕e3 27. ♔h1 ♗d3! 28. ♖g1 ♖g8 29. ♕h7 g5! 30. ♕h6 (30. ♕h5 ♗g6) ♘c6!–+] **♕f1!! 27. ♔f1 ♗d3 28. ♔g1 ♖f1# 0 : 1** **[Rhine]**

165. **B 27**

VYDESLAVER 2285 – FLASH

Beer-Sheva 1993

1. e4 c5 2. ♘f3 g6 3. d4 cd4 4. ♕d4 ♘f6 5. ♘c3 N [5. ♗b5 – 42/169] **♘c6 6. ♕a4**

d6 [6... ♕c7 7. ♘d5 ♘d5 8. ed5 ♘e5 9. ♗f4 ♗g7 (9... ♘f3 10. gf3 ♕b6 11. ♗e3± △ 0-0-0, d6) 10. 0-0-0 0–0 11. d6 ed6 12. ♕b4±] **7. e5 ♘g4** [7... de5 8. ♘e5 ♗g7 (8... ♕c7 9. ♗f4 ♘h5 10. ♘b5 ♕b8 11. ♘c6 ♕f4 12. ♕f4 ♘f4 13. ♖d1 ♘e6 14. ♘c7+–) 9. ♗b5±] **8. ♗f4 ♗g7** [8... de5 9. ♘e5 ♘e5 10. ♗e5±; 8... ♕b6 9. 0-0-0 ♘f2 10. ♘d5 ♕d8 11. ed6→] **9. ed6 ♕b6** [9... 0–0 10. ♗g3 △ 0-0-0±; 9... ed6 10. ♕e4!±] **10. 0-0-0! ♘f2 11. ♖e1 ♘h1 12. ♖e7 ♔f8 13. ♗c4** [13. ♘g5!? ♗e6 14. ♖e6! fe6 15. ♘e6 ♔g8 16. ♕c4 ♘e5!! 17. ♕d5 (17. ♗e5? ♕e3) ♕c6 18. ♕b3 ♕b6=] **♗e6□ 14. ♗e6 fe6 15. ♗g5!** [△ ♕f4+–] **♕b4?!** [15... ♕c5 16. ♖b7! (△ ♖c7) ♕d6 17. ♘e4 ♕d5 18. ♕a3! ♔g8 19. ♘f6 ♗f6 20. ♗f6+– △ ♖g7#; 15... ♘e7 16. ♕d7 (16. ♗e7 ♔g8 17. ♕e4 h6!∞) ♘f5 17. ♗e7! ♘e7 18. de7! (18. ♕e7 ♔g8 19. ♕e6=) ♔g8 19. ♘g5!! (△ e8♕) ♗f8!□ 20. e8♕ ♕e3 21. ♔b1 ♕e1 22. ♘d1 ♕d1 23. ♕d1 ♖e8 24. ♕h1±] **16. ♕b4 ♘b4 17. ♖b7 ♘c6 18. ♖c7! ♘d8** [18... ♘d4 19. ♖g7 ♘f3 20. ♗h6±] **19. ♘e4⊙ ♘f7 20. ♗e7 ♔e8 21. ♘f6 ♗f6 22. ♗f6 ♖d8□ 23. ♗d8! ♘d8 24. ♘g5 ♘f2 25. ♖e7 ♔f8 26. ♘h7 ♖h7 27. ♖h7** [♖ 8/a] **♘f7 28. d7 ♘d8 29. ♖h4 g5 30. ♖a4 e5 31. ♔d2 e4 32. ♔e2 ♘g4 33. ♖e4 ♘f6 34. ♖e5 g4 35. h3?!** [35. ♖a5 △ ♖a7+–] **gh3 36. gh3 ♘d7 37. ♖f5 ♔e7 38. h4 ♘c6 39. c3 ♔e6 40. ♖f4 ♘f6 41. b4 ♘d5 42. ♖c4 ♘e5 43. ♖c5 ♔d6 44. a3 ♘g6 45. c4 ♘f6 46. h5! ♘h5 47. ♖g5+– ♘hf4 48. ♔e3 ♔e6 49. ♔e4 ♔d6 50. ♖g4 ♘e5 51. c5 1 : 0**
[Vydeslaver, Faerman]

166.*** !N **B 29**

MINERVA – AZEVEDO

corr. 1989/92

1. e4 c5 2. ♘f3 ♘f6 3. e5 [3. ♘c3 ♘c6 4. e5 ♘g4 5. ♕e2 ♕c7 6. ♘b5 N (6. ♘d5 – 34/(199)) ♕b8 7. d4 a6 8. ♘d6 ed6 9. ed6 ♔d8 10. dc5 b6 11. h3 ♘h6 12. ♗h6 f6 13. ♗f4 bc5 14. ♘g5!+– ♘e5 15. ♗e5 fg5 16. ♗g7! Wegener 2310 – Troyke 2340, Deutschland 1992] **♘d5 4. ♘c3 e6 5. ♘d5** [5. ♗c4 N ♘b6 6. ♗e2 d5 7. ed6 ♗d6 8. 0–0 ♘c6 9. ♘e4± Topalov 2520 – Alvarez de T., Sevilla 1992] **ed5 6. d4 ♘c6 7. dc5 ♗c5 8. ♕d5 ♕b6** [RR 8... d6! 9. ed6 ♕b6 10. ♕e4 ♗e6 11. ♗c4 ♗f2! N (11... ♕b4 – 49/200) 12. ♔e2 0–0 13. ♗e6 ♖ae8! 14. ♘g5 ♖e6! 15. ♘e6 ♖e8 16. ♖f1□ ♖e6 17. ♕e6 ♘d4 18. ♔f2 ♘e6 19. ♗e3 ♕d6 20. ♔g1!= Hachian 2465 – Mnacakanian 2405, Armenia 1992] **9. ♗c4 ♗f2 10. ♔e2 0–0 11. ♖f1 ♗c5 12. ♘g5 ♘d4 13. ♔d1 ♘e6 14. ♘e4 d6 15. ed6 ♖d8 16. ♕f5 ♗d6 17. ♘d6 ♕d6 18. ♗d3 ♘f8 19. ♕f7 ♔h8 20. ♕f4 ♕e7 21. ♕g5 ♕e8 22. ♗d2!? N** [22. ♗e3 – 39/195] **♗e6□ 23. ♗c3 ♘g6 24. ♔d2 ♖d5 25. ♕g3 ♕d7 26. ♖ae1± ♗f5 27. ♖f3** [27. ♖e3 ♖d8 28. ♖ff3 ♗g4 29. ♖f2±] **♗d3?!** [27... ♖d8] **28. cd3!± b5 29. ♖fe3** [29. ♖ef1!? ♖d8 30. ♗a5! △ ♖f7] **♖g8** [29... ♕f7 30. ♔c1 ♖c8 31. ♔b1±] **30. ♔c1 ♕d8** [30... ♖f5!? △ ♘f4] **31. ♔b1 a5** [31... ♖g5 32. ♕f2 ♖f8 33. ♕d2 ♖gf5 34. d4 ♖f2 35. ♖3e2±] **32. a3 ♖g5 33. ♕f2 ♕d6** [33... ♕b6?? 34. ♗g7+–; 33... ♖f8!±] **34. ♕f7! b4?** [34... ♖g2? 35. ♖e8 ♘f8 36. ♖f1!+–; 34... ♕f8!? 35. ♕f8 ♖f8 36. g3±] **35. ♖e8!+–** [35. ♗g7!? ♖g7 36. ♖e8 ♘f8 37. ♕f8 ♕f8 38. ♖f8 ♖g8 39. ♖g8+–] **♘f8 36. ♗e5** [36... ♕d3 37. ♔a1 ♕d7 38. ♖f8 ♕f7 39. ♖f7; 36... ♖e5 37. ♖1e5 ♕d3 38. ♔a1] **1 : 0** **[Minerva]**

167. **B 30**

M. MAKAROV 2515 – DAMLJANOVIĆ 2550

Podgorica 1993

1. e4 c5 2. ♘c3 ♘c6 3. ♘f3 e6 4. ♗b5 ♘d4 5. 0–0 a6 6. ♗d3 ♘f3 N [6... ♘c6 – 33/(217)] **7. ♕f3 d6 8. ♘d1!?** [8. ♘e2 ♘f6=] **♘e7** [8... ♘f6 9. ♘e3 △ c3, ♗c2, d4±; 8... g6 9. b4!? ♗g7 10. ♖b1±] **9. b3□** [9. c3 ♘c6 △ g6, ♗g7=] **♗d7** [9... ♘g6 10. ♗b2 e5 11. ♗c4±] **10. ♗b2 ♘g6 11. ♕g3 e5**

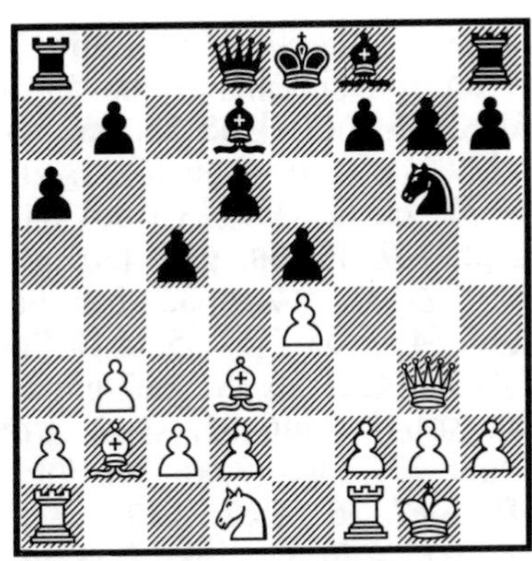

12. f4!□ [12. ♘e3 ♘f4 13. ♘d5 g5!∞ Damljanović] **ef4 13. ♖f4 ♘f4 14. ♕f4 ♗e6** [14... g5 15. ♕f3 ♖g8 16. ♗c4! ♗e6 17. ♘e3 ♗g7 18. ♖f1! ♕d7 19. ♘d5 ♗d5 20. ♗d5 0-0-0 21. ♗g7 ♖g7 22. ♕f6=∞] **15. ♘e3 ♗e7** [15... g5 16. ♕f3 ♖g8 17. ♘f5 ♗f5 18. ♕f5 ♗g7 19. ♖f1 ♕e7 20. ♗c4 ♗b2 21. ♗f7 ♔f8? 22. ♕h7+−; 15... ♕d7 16. ♘d5 ♗d5 17. ed5=∞] **16. ♗g7 ♗g5 17. ♕f3 ♖g8 18. ♗c3 ♗e3 19. ♕e3 ♕h4 20. ♖f1 0-0-0** [20... ♖c8!?] **21. ♗f6 ♕g4 22. ♕f3 ♖d7 23. ♕g4 ♗g4 24. ♖f4 h5?** [24... ♗e6±] **25. ♔f2 d5 26. e5 b5 27. h3 c4?⊕** [27... ♗e6 28. ♗e2±] **28. ♗h7 1 : 0** **[M. Makarov]**

168.* **B 30**

AKOPIAN 2615 – SVEŠNIKOV 2555

Rostov na Donu (open) 1993

1. e4 c5 2. ♘f3 ♘c6 3. ♗b5 e6 4. 0–0 [RR 4. ♗c6 bc6 5. 0–0 d5 6. d3 ♘f6 N (6... ♘e7 – 16/304) 7. e5 ♘d7 8. c4 h6!? 9. ♖e1 g5 10. ♘c3 ♗g7 11. h3 0–0 12. ♗d2 f5 13. ef6 ♖f6 14. ♕e2 ♕f8 15. ♘h2 ♗b7 16. ♘g4 ♖g6 17. ♖ac1 ♖e8 18. b3 ♗d4 19. ♘a4 h5!? 20. ♘h2 g4 21. hg4 hg4 22. ♗e3 ♗g7! 23. ♘g4 d4 24. ♗d2 ♕f5 25. f3 ♖f8=∞ Adams 2630 – J. Polgár 2595, Dos Hermanas 1993; 14. ♘a4!?] **♘ge7 5. b3 ♘d4 6. ♘d4 cd4 7. c3 a6 8. ♗d3 ♘c6 9. cd4 ♘d4 N** [9... d5 – 55/173] **10. ♗b2** [10. ♘c3!? ♗c5 11. ♘a4! ♗a7 12. ♗a3; 10... ♗d6!?] **♗c5 11. ♘c3 d6** [11... 0–0 12. e5!?] **12. ♘e2 ♘e2** [12... ♕f6 13. ♔h1!; 12... ♕b6 13. ♘f4±] **13. ♗e2 0–0** [13... e5 14. d4 ed4 15. ♗d4 0–0 16. ♖c1⩲] **14. d4 ♗a7 15. ♗a3** [15. ♖c1!? *a)* 15... d5 16. ♗f3!±; *b)* 15... ♗d7 16. ♗a3 ♗c6 (16... ♕b6 17. e5) 17. e5 ♗b8 18. ♗f3 ♗f3 19. ♕f3 ♕d7 20. d5!±; *c)* 15... ♖e8! 16. ♗a3 – 15. ♗a3] **♖e8□ 16. ♖c1 d5! 17. ed5** [17. e5 ♕a5 *a)* 18. ♗c5 ♗c5 19. ♖c5 ♕a2 20. ♖c7 ♖d8 21. ♗d3 ♗d7! (21... ♖d7? 22. ♕c1!) 22. ♖b7 ♖ab8=; *b)* 18. ♗d6!? ♗b8! (18... ♕a2 19. ♗d3↑; 18... ♗d7 19. ♖c7↑) 19. ♗b8 ♖b8 △ ♗d7] **ed5 18. ♗c5 ♗b8 19. ♗f3 ♗f4! 20. ♖c2 ♗f5 21. ♖e2 ♖e2 22. ♕e2 ♗e6!= 23. g3 ♗g5 24. ♖e1 ♗f6?!** [24... ♕d7] **25. ♗g4! ♗g4** [25... b6 26. ♗e6 bc5 27. ♗d5!] **26. ♕g4 g6 27. h4 ♔g7?** [27... b6! 28. ♗a3 ♕c8 29. ♕f3 ♕f5 30. ♕f5 gf5=] **28. h5 ♕c8 29. ♕f4 g5?** [29... ♕f5 30. h6! ♔g8 31. ♕c7; 29... gh5□ 30. ♗e7 ♕c6; 30. ♕f3!] **30. ♕f3 ♕d7** [30... ♕c6 31. ♗e7! h6 (31... ♗d4 32. ♗g5±) 32. ♗f6 ♕f6 33. ♕d5 ♖d8 34. ♕b7±] **31. h6 ♔g6 32. g4!+− ♗d8** [32... ♖g8 33. ♕h3 ♗d8 34. ♖e5 △ ♖f5+−] **33. ♕h3 ♔f6** [33... f5 34. ♕h5 ♔f6 35. ♗f8+−] **34. ♖e5** [34. ♗f8] **b6** [34... ♗c7 35. ♖f5] **35. ♕h5 1 : 0** **[Akopian]**

169. !N **B 32**

TH. ERNST 2540 –
E. MORTENSEN 2445

Sverige – Danmark 1993

1. e4 c5 2. ♘f3 ♘c6 3. d4 cd4 4. ♘d4 ♕c7 5. ♘b5 ♕b8 6. c4 ♘f6 7. ♘5c3 b6! 8. ♗e3! N [8. ♗e2 – 51/(151)] **♗b7** [8... e6 9. f4 ♗b4 10. a3] **9. ♘d2 e6 10. f4□** [10. ♗e2 ♗c5!∓] **h5** [10... ♗b4 11. e5 ♘e5 12. fe5 ♕e5 13. ♕e2 ♗c3 14. bc3 ♕c3 15. ♖b1 0–0∞] **11. ♗e2 h4 12. 0–0 d6** [12... e5 13. ♘d5 ♗c5 14. ♗c5 bc5 15. fe5 ♕e5 16. ♘f3±] **13. a3 ♗e7 14. b4±○ ♕d8** [△ d5] **15. ♗f3 ♘d7 16. ♖c1 g5?!** [×e5] **17. f5!± ♘de5 18. ♗h5** [18. fe6 fe6 19. ♗h5 ♔d7 20. c5 bc5 21. bc5 g4±] **g4** [18... ♔d7 19. ♘d5!→ ed5 20. cd5 ♘b8 21. ♕a4] **19. ♗g4 ♗g5 20. ♗g5 ♕g5 21. ♗h3 ♘d4** [21... ♕e3 22. ♔h1 ♘d3 23. fe6 ♘f2 24. ♖f2 ♕f2 25. ♘d5±]

22. fe6 fe6 23. ♘b3 [23. ♘b5 ♔e7=∞] **♘b3 24. ♕b3 ♘g4** [24... ♕e3 25. ♔h1 *a)* 25... ♗e4 26. ♖ce1! ♕h3 (26... ♕d3 27. c5 ♗d5 28. ♕b2+−) 27. ♖e4 ♕d3 28. ♖d1 0−0 29. ♔g1 ♘f3 30. gf3 ♕f3 31. ♕c2+−; *b)* 25... ♘d3 26. ♕a4 ♔e7 (26... ♔d8 27. ♖c2 ♔e7!? 28. ♘d5! ♗d5 29. cd5+−) 27. ♖f7!! (Cu. Hansen) ♔f7 28. ♕d7 ♔f6 29. ♖f1 ♘f2 30. ♔g1!+−] **25. ♘b5 ♔e7 26. c5! dc5 27. bc5 ♖af8!** [27... bc5 28. ♗g4 ♕g4 29. ♕c3] **28. ♗g4 ♕g4 29. c6 ♖f1 30. ♖f1 ♗c6** [30... ♖g8 31. ♕b4 ♔e8 32. ♘d6 ♔d8 33. ♘b7] **31. ♕b4 ♔e8** [31... ♔d8 32. ♕d6 ♗d7 33. ♕b8] **32. ♕c3+− ♗b5 33. ♕h8 ♔e7 34. ♕f8 ♔d7 35. ♖f7 ♔c6 36. ♕c8 1 : 0 [Th. Ernst]**

170. **B 32**

LJUBOJEVIĆ 2605 − IVANČUK 2710
Linares 1993

1. e4 c5 2. ♘f3 ♘c6 3. d4 cd4 4. ♘d4 e5 5. ♘b5 d6 6. c4 ♗e7 7. ♘1c3 a6 8. ♘a3 ♗e6 9. ♘c2 ♖c8 10. ♗d2!? N [10. ♘d5 − 50/(180)] **♗g5** [10... h6!? 11. ♘d5 (11. ♗e2 ♗g5=) ♘f6!? (11... ♗g5 12. ♗c3±) 12. ♗d3 ♘d7; 10... ♘f6!? 11. ♗d3 ♘d7 12. 0−0 ♘c5 (12... 0−0 13. ♖e1! ♘c5 14. ♗f1±) 13. ♗e3 (13. ♗e2 ♘d4!?⇆) ♗g5 (13... ♘d3 14. ♕d3 ♘d4 15. b3 ♘c2 16. ♕c2±; 15. ♘a3!?) 14. ♗e2 0−0 (14... ♗e3 15. fe3 △ b4) 15. b4 ♘d7∞] **11. ♗g5 ♕g5 12. ♕d2! h6?!** [⌓ 12... ♕d2 13. ♔d2 g6 △ f5] **13. ♖d1 ♕d2** [13... ♖d8!?] **14. ♔d2± ♘f6 15. f3 ♔e7?!** [15... 0−0 16. ♗d3 (16. b3 ♖fd8 △ ♘d7) ♘d7±] **16. ♗d3 ♖c7 17. ♖c1** [17. ♘d5!? ♗d5 18. cd5 ♘b8 19. ♘e3 g6 20. ♖c1 ♖hc8 21. ♘c4 ♘fd7 (21... ♘bd7 22. b4±; 21... b5 22. ♘a5 ♖c1 23. ♖c1 ♖c1 24. ♔c1 ♔d8 25. a4!? ba4 26. ♗e2±; 25. b4±) 22. b4 b5 23. ♘a5 ♖c1 24. ♖c1 ♖c1 25. ♔c1 ♘b6 26. ♗c2±] **♖hc8 18. ♘d5 ♗d5 19. cd5 ♘b8 20. ♘e3 ♖c1** [20... g6± − 17. ♘d5!?] **21. ♘f5 ♔d8 22. ♖c1 ♖c1 23. ♔c1** [♘♗ 9/b] **♘e8 24. g4!± ♘d7 25. b4 ♔c7** [25... ♘df6 26. b5 a5 27. b6] **26. a4?!** [26. h4! ♘df6 27. ♔d2 h5 28. g5 ♘h7 29. ♔e3 f6 30. f4±] **♘df6 27. a5** [27. h4 h5 28. g5 ♘h7 29. b5 a5 30. b6 ♔b6 31. ♗b5 ♘c7=] **h5 28. g5 ♘h7 29. h4 f6?** [29... g6! 30. ♘h6 f6 31. gf6 (31. f4?! ef4 32. e5 fg5 33. ♗g6 de5 34. ♗e8 ♘f6 △ gh4) ♘ef6] **30. gf6?** [30. g6! ♘f8 31. b5+− △ 31... ♘g6 32. ba6 ba6 33. ♗a6 ♔b8 34. ♗b5 ♘c7 35. ♗f1 ♘e8 36. ♔d2 ♘f4 37. ♔c3 g6 38. ♘e7 g5 39. ♘f5 ♘g6 40. ♔b4] **♘hf6 31. ♔d2 ♔d8 32. ♔e3 ♘g8! 33. ♘g3 ♘ef6 34. ♘f5 ♘e8 35. ♗f1 ♘e7 36. ♘e7 ♔e7= 37. ♗h3 ♔d8 38. ♗f5 ♘f6 39. ♔d3 ♘g8 40. ♗g6 ♘f6 41. ♔e3 ♔e7 42. ♔f2 ♔d8 43. ♔g3 ♔c7 44. f4 b5 45. ♔f3 ♔d7 46. ♗f7 ♔c7 47. ♗e6 ♔b8 1/2 : 1/2 [Ivančuk]**

171. **B 32**

KOTRONIAS 2530 − NIKOLAIDIS 2380
Athens 1993

1. e4 c5 2. ♘f3 ♘c6 3. d4 cd4 4. ♘d4 e5 5. ♘b5 d6 6. ♘1c3 a6 7. ♘a3 b5 8. ♘d5 ♘ge7?! 9. c4 ♘d4 10. ♗e3 ♘d5 11. cd5 ♗e7 12. ♗d3 0−0 [12... ♕a5 13. ♕d2±] **13. 0−0 ♗d7 N** [13... f5 − 46/(207)] **14. ♕d2 ♖c8** [14... ♕b8!? △ ♗d8-b6] **15. f4 ♕b6** [15... ♕c7 16. f5±] **16. ♘c2 ♗f6 17. fe5?** [17. ♘d4 ed4 18. ♗f2 △ ♖ae1±] **de5 18. ♘d4 ed4 19. ♗f4 ♖ce8!□±** [19... ♖fe8? 20. ♕f2!!+− ×f7] **20. ♖ac1 ♗e5 21. b4 ♕d6 22. ♗e5 ♖e5 23. ♕f4 f6 24. a3 h6!** [△ f5] **25. ♕f2?! ♖h5 26. g3 ♖g5 27. ♕f4 ♖e5= 28. ♖c2 a5** [28... f5!? 29. ef5 ♗f5? 30. ♖e2+−; 29... ♖d5] **29. ba5 ♕a3 30. ♕d2 f5!** [30... ♖a8!? Kotronias] **31. ♖a2 ♕c3 32. ef5 ♖e3??** [32... b4? 33. a6 b3 34. ♖b2+−; 32... ♗f5! 33. ♕c3 dc3 34. ♖af2 ♗d3! 35. ♖f8 ♔h7 36. ♖c1! (36. d6? ♗f1 37. d7 ♖d5 38. d8♕ ♖d8 39. ♖d8 c2 40. ♖c8 ♗c4−+) b4 37. ♖f4 ♖d5 38. ♖b4 c2 △ 39. ♖a4 ♗b5! 40. ♖aa1 ♖d2 41. a6 ♗a6 42. ♖a6 ♖d1 43. ♔g2 ♖c1 44. ♖c6=] **33. ♕c3 dc3 34. ♗c2 b4 35. d6 ♗b5 36. ♖f4!** [36. ♗b3? ♔h7 37. ♖f4 c2! 38. ♗c2 b3 Kotronias] **♖e1□ 37. ♔g2 ♖e2 38. ♔f3 ♖c2 39. ♖c2 ♗d3 40. ♖c1 b3 41. ♖c3 b2 42. ♖b4 b1♕ 43. ♖b1 ♗b1** [43... ♖f5 44. ♔e3 ♗b1 45. d7+−]

44. g4+− ♖d8 45. ♖c6 ♖e8 46. ♖b6! ♗e4 47. ♔f4 ♗h1 48. ♖b1! ♗d5 49. ♖d1 ♗c6 50. ♖c1 ♖e4 51. ♔g3 ♗b5 52. ♖c5 ♗a4 53. ♖c8 ♔f7 54. a6 ♖e8 55. ♖e8 ♔e8 56. ♔f4 ♔d7 57. a7 ♗c6 58. ♔e5 ♗f3 59. h4 ♗c6 60. g5 hg5 61. hg5 ♗f3 62. g6 1 : 0 [Andrianov, Nikolaidis]

172. B 33

VOULDIS 2280 − GRIVAS 2495

Greece (ch) 1993

1. e4 c5 2. ♘f3 ♘c6 3. d4 cd4 4. ♘d4 ♕b6 5. ♘b3 ♘f6 6. ♘c3 e6 7. ♗e3 ♕c7 8. f4 ♗b4 9. ♗d3 ♗c3!? 10. bc3 d6 11. 0−0 e5 12. ♔h1!? N [12. f5 − 46/(208)] **h6** [12... ♘g4 13. ♗g1 ef4 14. ♖f4 ♘ge5 15. ♘d4 0−0 16. ♘f5→ △ 16... ♘g6 17. ♖f3 ♘ce5 18. ♖g3 ♕c3 19. ♗d4 ♕c7 20. ♕h5] **13. ♕e1 b6 14. fe5 de5 15. ♕g3 ♔f8!** [15... ♘g4 16. ♗c1] **16. ♘d4! ♘h5?** [16... ♘e7! 17. ♘f3 (17. ♘f5? ♘f5 18. ef5 ♕c3) ♘g6 18. ♘h4! ♘h4 (18... ♘e7? 19. ♗d4 ♘c6 20. ♗b5) 19. ♕h4 *a)* 19... ♘g4? 20. ♗c4!! *a1)* 20... f6 21. ♗d5 ♖b8 (21... ♘e3 22. ♖f6!+−) 22. ♗c1!? (22. ♗d2 △ h3 ×♘g4) ♕c3 23. ♖b1→; *a2)* 20... g5 21. ♗g5 ♕c4 22. ♗e7 ♔e8 (22... ♔g7? 23. h3→ △ 23... ♕e4 24. ♗f6!+−; 22... ♔g8!? 23. h3 ♕e4 24. ♖ae1 ♕g6 25. hg4 ♕g4 26. ♕f6±→ △ 26... ♖h7? 27. ♕c6!) 23. ♖ad1! *a21)* 23... ♗a6 24. ♗b4 ♕c7 (24... ♕e6 25. ♖d6 ♕c8 26. ♖h6!+−) 25. ♕g4 ♗f1 26. ♕g7! ♗g2 27. ♔g2+−; *a22)* 23... ♗d7 24. ♗b4 f6 (24... ♕e6 25. ♖d6 ♕e7 26. ♕e7 ♔e7 27. ♖h6 △ ♖h8-a8+−) 25. ♖f6!+−; *a23)* 23... ♗e6 24. ♗d6 f6 25. h3±; *b)* 19... ♘e8! (△ ♗e6, f6) 20. a4!∞ ♗e6 (20... ♕c3? 21. a5! ba5 22. ♕d8!) 21. ♕e1 ♔g8 22. ♖a3! △ a5, ♕a1] **17. ♕g6! ed4 18. cd4 ♘f6 19. ♖f6! gf6 20. ♕f6 ♖g8** [20... ♔g8 21. ♖f1! ♕e7! 22. ♕c6 ♗b7 23. ♕c4 ♖c8 24. ♕b3 ♖h7 25. d5 ♖g7 26. ♗d4±→] **21. ♗f4 ♕d7 22. ♗d6 ♔e8** [22... ♘e7 23. ♗c4 ♖g7 24. ♖f1!+− (24. ♗f7 ♕d6) ♕e8 25. ♗f7! ♕f7 26. ♕e7] **23. ♗b5 ♗b7 24. d5 ♖c8** [24... ♕d8 25. dc6! ♕f6 26. c7!+−] **25. ♖d1! a6 26. dc6 ♗c6 27. ♖d5! 1 : 0 [Andrianov, Vouldis]**

173. B 33

NADANIAN 2285 − PALEVIČ

corr. 1992/93

1. e4 c5 2. ♘f3 ♘c6 3. d4 cd4 4. ♘d4 ♕b6 5. ♘b3 ♘f6 6. ♘c3 e6 7. ♗d3 a6 8. ♗e3 ♕c7 9. 0−0 ♗e7 10. f4 d6 11. ♕f3 0−0 12. ♖ae1 b5 13. e5! ♘d7 N [13... de5 14. fe5 ♘d7 (14... ♘e5? − 54/(166)) 15. ♗f4! (15. ♕h3?! g6 16. ♗h6 ♖d8!∞) ♗b7 16. ♕g3±; 13... ♘e8!?±] **14. ed6** [14. ♕h3!?] **♕d6** [14... ♗d6? 15. ♗b5!] **15. ♘a5!?** [15. ♘d4; 15. ♘e4! ♕c7 16. ♕h5 g6 17. ♕h6→] **♘a5** [15... ♘db8? 16. ♗e4 ♗d7 17. ♖d1 ♕c7 18. ♖d7+−] **16. ♕a8 ♗b7□** [16... ♘c6? 17. ♗e4+−; 16... b4?! 17. ♘e4 (17. ♕e4? f5) ♕c7 18. ♕a7 ♗b7 19. ♗f2! ♕c6 (19... f5? 20. ♘d2 ♕c6 21. ♘f3 ♘c5 22. ♖e5! ♖a8 23. ♖c5 ♖a7 24. ♖c6 ♘c6 25. ♗a7 ♘a7 26. ♗c4+−) 20. ♕e3! ♘c5 (20... f5 21. ♕h3!) 21. ♕h3 ♘d3 22. cd3±] **17. ♕a7** [17. ♘b5? ♕c6!−+] **b4!□ 18. ♖d1!□** [18. ♘b5? ♕c6 19. ♖f2 ♖a8 20. ♘d4 ♕d5−+; 18. ♘e4? ♕c6 (△ f5) 19. ♖e2 f5 20. ♘g5 ♖a8 21. ♕d4 ♗c5−+] **♕c7!□** [18... bc3? 19. ♗h7 ♔h7 20. ♖d6 ♗d6 21. ♕d4! ♗c5 22. ♕d3 ♔g8 23. ♗c5 ♘c5 24. ♕c3+−; 18... ♕c6? 19. ♗e4 ♕c7 20. ♗b7 ♘b7 (20... bc3 21. ♗f3+−) 21. ♘a4 ♕c6 22. b3+−] **19. ♗a6!□ ♖a8** [19... bc3!? 20. ♗b7 ♘b7 21. b3±; 21. bc3!?] **20. ♘b5!□ ♕c2!□** [△ ♕g2#; 20... ♕c6? 21. ♗b7+−; 20... ♕d8? 21. ♕d4 ♗c5 (21... ♗a6 22. ♕d7 ♕d7 23. ♖d7 ♗b5 24. ♖e7 ♗f1 25. ♔f1+−) 22. ♕c5! ♘c5 23. ♖d8 ♖d8 24. ♗b7 ♘cb7 (24... ♘ab7 25. c3+−) 25. b3 ♖c8 26. c3! bc3 27. ♖c1+−] **21. ♖d2!?** [21. ♗b7 ♖a7 22. ♗a7 (22. ♘a7? ♗c5 23. ♖d7 ♗e3 24. ♔h1 ♘b7 25. ♖b7 h5∓) ♘b7 23. ♖d7 ♗c5 24. ♗c5 ♕c5 25. ♘d4 f6= Palevič] **♖a7** [21... ♕d2? 22. ♕a8+−; 21... ♕f5!?; 21... ♕g6!?] **22. ♖c2 ♖a6 23. ♖d1** [23. ♖c7?! ♗c6 24. ♖c8 (24. ♘a7 ♗d6 25. ♖c8 ♘f8∓) ♗f8! (24... ♘f8? 25. ♘c7 ♗b7 26. ♖e8+−) 25. ♘c7 ♗b7 26. ♖d8 ♖d6∓] **♘f6** [23... ♘f8!?] **24. ♖c7 ♗f8!∞** [△ 25. ♖d8 ♘e4; 24... ♔f8? 25. ♖e7!+−]

1/2 : 1/2 [Nadanian]

174. **B 33**

AKOPIAN 2615 – JAKOVIČ 2510
Rostov na Donu (open) 1993

1. e4 c5 2. ♘f3 ♘c6 3. d4 cd4 4. ♘d4 ♘f6 5. ♘c3 e5 6. ♘f5 d5 7. ed5 ♗f5 8. dc6 bc6 9. ♕f3 ♕d7 10. ♗g5 e4 11. ♕e2 ♗e7! 12. ♖d1 N [12. ♗f6 – 48/229] **♕e6 13. ♕c4 ♖b8!** [13... 0–0 14. ♕e6 ♗e6 15. ♘e4 ♘e4 16. ♗e7 ♖fe8 17. f3! ♖e7 18. fe4 ♗d5 19. ♗d3 ♗e4 20. ♔f2±] **14. ♕e6?!** [14. b3 ♗b4 15. ♕e6 ♗e6 16. ♗d2=] **fe6! 15. b3□** [15. ♘a4? e3∓] **♘d5 16. ♗e7 ♔e7 17. ♘a4!** [17. ♘d5 ed5∓⊥; 17... cd5∓⊥] **e3!** [17... ♘b4 18. c3! ♘c2 19. ♔d2 e3 *a)* 20. fe3 ♖hd8 21. ♔c1 ♖d1 22. ♔d1 ♖d8! (22... ♘e3 23. ♔d2) 23. ♔c1 ♘e3∓; *b)* 20. ♔c1!? ♖hd8 (20... ef2 21. ♖d2) 21. ♗e2!∞] **18. c4!** [18. ♗d3? ef2 19. ♔f2 ♖hf8! 20. ♔g3 ♘e3 21. ♖d2 ♗d3 22. cd3 ♖b5∓→] **ef2 19. ♔f2 ♘b4 20. ♗e2!** [20. ♘c5 ♖hd8! 21. ♗e2 ♘a2 22. ♖a1 ♖d2 23. ♖hd1 ♖e2 24. ♔e2 ♘c3 25. ♔e1 ♘d1; 20. ♘c3 ♖hf8 21. ♔g3 ♘a2!→] **♘a2 21. ♖a1** [21. ♘c5 ♖hd8 – 20. ♘c5] **♘b4** [21... ♖hf8 22. ♗f3 ♘b4 23. ♘c5 a6 24. ♖hd1 (24. ♘a6? ♘d3) e5 25. ♔g3=∞] **22. ♘c5 a6 23. ♖hd1!** [23. ♘a6 ♘a6 24. ♖a6 ♖b3 25. ♖c6 ♖b2! 26. ♔e3 ♖a8] **♖hd8 24. ♖d8 ♖d8** [24... ♔d8 25. g4] **25. ♖a4** [25... ♘c2?! 26. g4! ♗g6 27. ♖a6 ♖d2 28. ♖a7 ♔f6 29. h4 ♘d4 30. ♘d7 ♔e7 31. ♔e3; 25... ♖b8=]

1/2 : 1/2 **[Jakovič]**

175.**** **!N** **B 33**

DVOJRIS 2565 – N. NIKČEVIĆ 2395
Paris 1993

1. e4 c5 2. ♘f3 ♘c6 3. d4 cd4 4. ♘d4 ♘f6 5. ♘c3 e5 6. ♘db5 d6 7. ♗g5 a6 8. ♘a3 b5 9. ♗f6 [RR 9. ♘d5 *a)* 9... ♗e7 10. ♗f6 ♗f6 11. ♘b1!? 0–0 12. a4 b4 13. ♘d2 ♗g5! N (13... ♗e6 – 55/193) *a1)* 14. ♘f3?! ♗h6 15. ♗c4 a5 16. ♕d3 ♘e7! 17. ♘e3 (17. ♖d1 ♘d5 18. ♗d5 ♗a6 19. ♗c4 ♗c4 20. ♕c4 ♖c8∓ ×♘f3) ♗e3 18. fe3 (Barua 2530 – Koshi 2420, Isfahan (zt) 1993; 18. ♕e3?! d5 19. ed5 ♘d5 20. ♕e4 ♗b7 21. ♖d1 ♘c3 22. ♖d8 ♘e4 23. ♖a8 ♖a8 24. ♘e5?! ♘d6!∓; 24. 0–0∓) ♕c7 △ ♗b7, ♖ad8∓; *a2)* 14. ♘c4!? ♖b8 15. a5 ♖b5! *a21)* 16. ♘cb6?! ♖c5!∓ (16... ♖a5?! 17. ♖a5 ♘a5 18. h4! ♗f6 19. ♘c8 ♕c8 20. ♘b4±) 17. h4 ♗h6 18. ♘c8 ♕c8 19. ♕d3?! ♔h8 20. ♕a6 ♘d4 21. ♘b4 ♖c2!–+; 19. ♗d3; *a22)* 16. ♘db6 ♗e6 *a221)* 17. ♕d6?! ♘d4 18. ♗d3 b3! 19. cb3□ ♖b3 20. ♕d8 (20. ♗b1 ♕f6∓ 21. ♕e5 ♘f3!) ♖d8 21. ♗b1 (21. ♖d1 ♗g4) ♖b4! 22. ♗d3 ♘b3 23. ♖d1 ♖d3 24. ♖d3 ♖c4∓; *a222)* 17. ♘d6 ♖a5 18. ♖a5 ♘a5 19. ♘d5∞ Koshi; *b)* 9... ♕a5 10. c3!? N (10. ♗d2 – 56/(177)) *b1)* 10... ♘d5 11. ed5 *b11)* 11... ♘e7 12. ♘c2 h6 (12... f6!? Savko) 13. ♗d2!± Blodštejn 2340 – Savko, Vilnius 1993; *b12)* 11... ♘b8 12. ♘c2 △ a4⩲; *b2)* 10... ♘e4 *b21)* 11. b4!? ♕a3 12. ♗c1 ♕a4 (12... ♘c3 13. ♕d2! ♘e4 14. ♕c2+–) 13. ♕a4 (13. ♕d3 ♖b8□∞) ba4 14. ♘c7 ♔d8 15. ♘a8 ♘c3=∞; *b22)* 11. ♕f3 ♘g5 (11... f5 12. b4! ♕a3 13. ♗c1 ♕a4 14. ♘c7+–) 12. ♘f6 ♔d8 13. ♕c6 ♖b8 (13... ♖a7 14. ♕e8 ♔c7 15. ♘d5 ♔b8 16. ♘c2! △ ♘cb4-c6, a4+–) 14. 0-0-0!=∞→ Blodštejn] **gf6 10. ♘d5 ♗g7** [RR 10... ♗e6 11. c3 ♗g7 12. ♘c2 ♗d5 13. ♕d5 ♘e7 14. ♕d3! N (14. ♕d2 – 55/(195)) f5? 15. ef5 d5 16. g4! 0–0 (16... h5? 17. g5+–; 16... ♕d7 17. ♗g2±; 17. ♗h3! P. Thipsay) 17. ♗g2 ♕b6 18. 0–0 ♖ad8 19. ♖ad1 ♗h6 20. ♕f3!± P. Thipsay 2465 – Saravanan 2400, India (ch) 1993] **11. ♗d3** [RR 11. c4 f5 12. cb5 ♘d4 13. ♗d3 0–0 14. ♘c2 fe4! N (14... ♘c2 – 55/196) 15. ♗e4 ♖b8 16. 0–0 (16. ♘d4 ed4 17. ♕h5? f5 18. ♗f3 ♖b5∓; 17. 0–0 ♖b5 – 16. 0–0) ♖b5 (16... ab5?! 17. ♘d4 ed4 18. ♖c1±) 17. ♘d4 ed4 18. ♖c1 (18. a4!? ♖b2 19. ♖c1 ♕h4!? 20. ♕d3∞; 19... ♗e6! △ 20. ♕h5 h6! △ ♕g5) ♗b7 19. ♕f3 ♕g5 20. a4!□ ♖b2 (20... ♖d5 21. ♖c7! ♗a8 22. ♖a7 ♗c6 23. ♖a6 ♗b7 24. ♖a7= I. Herrera) 21. ♖c7 ♗d5 22. ♗d5 ♕f6 23. ♕d3 ♖b6= I. Herrera 2355 – A. Díaz 2285, La Habana 1993; 11. c3 f5 12. ef5 ♗f5 13. ♘c2 0–0 14. ♘ce3 ♗g6!? 15. h4! h6 *a)* 16. h5 ♗h7 17. ♗d3 f5 18. g4 e4 19. ♗e2 (19. ♗c2 fg4 20. ♘g4 ♕g5∓○) f4 20. ♘f4 ♖f4 21. ♕d5 ♔h8 22. ♕c6 ♕f8!=∞; *b)* 16. g4 ♘e7! (16... e4 – 24/370) 17. ♗d3 (17. ♗g2 ♖a7!? 18.

♕d2 f5∞) ♘d5 18. ♘d5 e4 19. ♗c2 ♖b8! (△ b4) 20. ♕d2 b4⇆ Čeluškina, Jocić] **♘e7 12. ♘e7 ♕e7 13. c4 f5 14. 0–0 0–0 15. ♕h5 ♖b8** [△ 16... d5 17. cd5 fe4 18. ♗e4 f5→] **16. ef5 e4 17. ♖ae1 ♗b7 18. ♕g4 ♔h8! N** [18... ♖fe8 — 51/157] **19. ♗e4 ♖fe8** [19... ♗b2?! 20. ♘c2 bc4 21. ♗b7 ♕b7 22. ♕c4±] **20. ♖e3?!** [20. ♗b7? ♕e1; 20. ♗d3?! ♕e1 21. ♖e1 ♖e1 22. ♗f1 ♗b2∓; 20. f3!? ♗b2 21. ♘c2 (21. ♗b7 ♕b7 22. ♘c2 b4↑) ♗c3∞̄] **♗e4 21. ♖fe1**

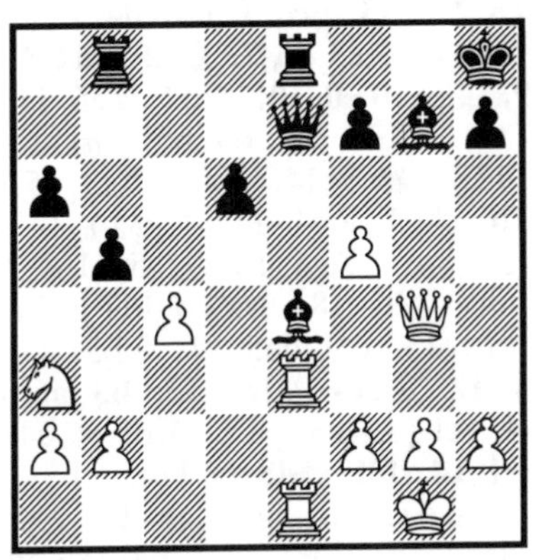

21... ♕f6!□ [21... ♗b2? 22. ♖e4±; 21... d5?! 22. cd5 ♕b4 23. ♘c2! (23. ♖e4?? ♕e1) ♕b2 24. ♖e4 ♖e4 25. ♕e4±; 21... b4?! 22. ♖e4? ba3! 23. ♖e7 ♖e7∓; 22. ♘c2!] **22. ♖e4 ♖e4 23. ♕e4 ♕b2 24. ♕d3** [24. ♘c2 b4?! 25. ♕d3!; 24... bc4!∓ △ 25. ♕c4? ♗c3–+] **♕c3!∓ 25. ♕c3 ♗c3 26. ♖b1 b4 27. ♔f1?** [27. ♘c2 a5∓] **♖c8 28. ♖b3** [28. ♘c2 ♖c4 29. ♔e2 (29. ♘e3 ♖d4–+; 29. a3 ba3! 30. ♘a3 ♖a4–+) a5–+] **d5–+ 29. cd5 ba3 30. ♖a3 a5 31. d6 ♗b4 32. ♖d3 ♖d8!** [32... ♔g7?? 33. a3 ♗c5 34. ♖c3+–] **33. d7 ♔g7 34. a3 ♗f8 35. ♖d5 a4 36. ♖d4 ♔f6 37. ♖a4 ♖d7 38. g4⊕ ♖d2 39. h4 ♗c5 40. ♖a6 ♔e5 41. ♖h6 ♗f2!** [42. ♖h7 ♔f4 43. ♖f7 ♔f3] **0 : 1** **[N. Nikčević]**

176.* **!N** **B 33**

TIMOŠENKO 2515 – GAGARIN 2450

Bucureşti 1993

1. e4 c5 2. ♘f3 ♘c6 3. d4 cd4 4. ♘d4 ♘f6 5. ♘c3 e5 6. ♘db5 d6 7. ♗g5 a6 8. ♘a3 b5 9. ♗f6 gf6 10. ♘d5 ♗g7 11. ♗d3 ♘e7 12. ♘e7 ♕e7 13. 0–0 0–0 14. c4 f5 15. ♕e2 ♗b7 16. ♖ad1 [16. f3 N fe4! *a)* 17. fe4 f5! 18. ♖ad1 (18. ♖f5 ♖f5 19. ef5 e4 △ 20. ♖e1 d5∓; 18. ef5 e4 △ 19. ♖ae1 d5∓) *a1)* 18... fe4? 19. ♗e4! (19. ♖f8? ♖f8 20. ♗e4 ♗e4 21. ♕e4 ♕a7 22. ♔h1 ♕f2∓) ♖f1 (19... d5 20. cd5 ♖f1 21. ♕f1 △ ♕d3, ♘c2±) 20. ♖f1 ♖c8 (20... d5 21. cd5 ♕c5 22. ♕f2+–) 21. ♖d1 bc4 22. ♘c4 d5 23. ♗d5 ♗d5 24. ♖d5 ♕a7 25. ♘e3!±; *a2)* 18... ♔h8 19. ♔h1 ♖ad8 20. cb5 fe4 21. ♖f8 ♕f8 22. ♗e4 ♗e4 (22... d5?! 23. ♖f1 △ ♗f5, ♕h5→) 23. ♕e4 d5 24. ♕e2 ab5 25. ♘b5 d4 (△ ♕b4) 26. ♘a3 ♕f5 27. ♘c4 e4∓ Mojseev 2460 – V. Ikonnikov 2505, Rossija 1992; *a3)* 18... ♖ad8 — 16. ♖ad1; *b)* 17. ♗e4 d5 (17... bc4 18. ♗b7 ♕b7 19. ♘c4 d5 20. ♘e3∞) 18. ♗d5 (18. cd5 ♗d5 — 18. ♗d5) ♗d5 19. cd5 ♕c5 20. ♔h1 ♕d5=] **♖ad8! N** [16... ♖fd8?! — 55/(195)] **17. f3 fe4 18. fe4** [18. ♗e4 d5=] **f5 19. ♘c2 bc4?!** [19... fe4! *a)* 20. ♗e4? ♖f1 21. ♖f1 (21. ♔f1 bc4∓) bc4 22. ♗b7 ♕b7 23. ♕c4 d5∓; *b)* 20. ♖f8 ♖f8 21. ♗e4 ♗e4 22. ♕e4 ♕a7 23. ♘e3 (23. ♔h1 ♕f2 24. h3 bc4 25. ♕c4 ♔h8 △ e4, ♗e5∓→; 23. ♕e3 ♕c7!∓) ♗h6 24. ♖e1 ♕f7! 25. ♕d5□ ♗e3 26. ♖e3 bc4∓] **20. ♗c4 d5 21. ed5 ♕c5** [21... ♔h8 22. ♔h1 ♖d6?! 23. ♘d4±; 22... ♕c5 — 21... ♕c5] **22. ♔h1 ♔h8∞̄** [22... ♗d5?? 23. ♖d5+–] **23. ♘e3** [23. b4!? ♕d6∞̄; 23... ♕b6∞̄] **f4 24. ♘g4 ♗d5 25. ♘e5** [25. ♗d5 ♖d5 26. ♘f2 (26. ♖d5 ♕d5 27. ♕a6? f3–+→) ♖fd8 △ ♕e3∓⊞] **♗g2 26. ♔g2!** [26... ♕e5 27. ♕e5 ♗e5 28. ♖d8 (28. ♗a6 ♖d1 29. ♖d1 f3 △ ♗b2∓) ♖d8 29. ♗a6 ♖d2=⊥■; 26. ♕g2? ♖d1 27. ♖d1 ♕e5 △ f3∓ ×b2] **1/2 : 1/2** **[S. Kiselëv, Gagarin]**

177. **B 36**

DOLMATOV 2615 – TIVJAKOV 2595

Rostov na Donu 1993

1. e4 c5 2. ♘f3 ♘c6 3. d4 cd4 4. ♘d4 g6 5. c4 ♘f6 6. ♘c3 d6 7. ♗e2 ♘d4 8. ♕d4 ♗g7 9. ♗g5 0–0 10. ♕e3 ♗e6 11. 0–0 ♕b6 12. b3!? ♕e3 [12... ♖fc8!?] **13. ♗e3**

♘d7 [13... ♘g4 14. ♗d2 ♗e5 15. ♗g4 (15. h3 ♘f6=) ♗c3 16. ♗c3 ♗g4=■; 15. g3; 13... ♖fc8] **14. ♖ac1 ♖fc8!** [14... ♘c5 15. ♘d5! ♗d5 16. ed5 a5 17. ♖c2!±○⊡] **15. ♘d5 N** [15. ♖c2 – 23/355; 15. f4 ♘c5 16. ♘d5 (16. ♗f3 ♘d3 17. ♖c2 ♘b4; 16. f5 ♗d7 17. ♘d5 ♔f8∞; 16... ♗c3!?) ♔f8!?] **♔f8** [15... ♗d5 16. ed5 ♗b2 17. ♖b1! △ 17... ♗a3 18. b4 a5□ 19. ba5 ×b7; 16... a5!? △ 17. ♖c2 b5⇆; 16. cd5±⊡ △ 16... ♗b2 17. ♖c8 ♖c8 18. ♗g4± ×a7, ♘d7, △ 16... ♘c5 17. ♗g4 ♖c7 18. b4±] **16. f4 a5** [16... ♘c5 17. f5 ♗d7!?; 17. ♗f3!?; 16... ♗d5 17. ed5 ♗b2∞ △ 18. ♖b1 ♗a3 19. b4 a5 20. ba5 ♗c5; 17... a5!?⇆; 17. cd5±⊡ △ 17... ♗b2 18. ♖c8 ♖c8 19. ♗g4 ♔e8 20. ♗a7 ♖a8 21. ♖f2!±; 16... ♗b2!?∞ △ 17. ♖b1 ♗d5 18. cd5 (18. ed5 ♗a3 19. b4 a5 20. ba5 ♗c5) ♗a3 19. b4 ♖c2!?] **17. f5** [17. ♗f3 ♗b2 △ ♗a3; 17. ♖c2 ♗d5!? 18. ed5 b5↑《] **♗d5 18. ed5 ♗b2!** [18... ♗f6 19. fg6 hg6 20. ♗g4 ♖c7 21. ♗d7 ♖d7 22. a4!±↑》 ×a5; 18... ♗e5 19. g4±↑》; 19. h4!?; 18... ♘c5 19. g4↑》 △ 19... a4 20. b4] **19. ♖c2** [19. ♗h6 (×d4) ♔g8 △ ♗d4, △ ♗a3, a4⇆; 19... ♗g7!?; 19. ♖cd1 ♔g7!?; 19... ♗a3; 19. ♖b1 ♗a3⇆] **♗a3! 20. ♗h6** [20. ♗g4 ♖c7 (20... ♘e5?! 21. ♗h6! △ fg6, ×♖c8) 21. fg6 hg6 22. ♗d7 ♖d7=] **♔g8** [20... ♔e8?!] **21. h4** [21. ♗g4 ♗c5 22. ♔h1 ♖c7 23. fg6 hg6 24. ♗d7 ♖d7 25. a4!±; 21... ♖c7!=; 21. g4 a4⇆; 21... b5!?∞] **♘f6** [×h5] **22. h5** [22. g4 b5⇆; 22... a4↑》; 22... ♘d5∞] **gh5 23. ♖c3 ♔h8 24. ♖h3 b5!?** [24... a4 25. ♗h5 ♘h5 26. ♖h5 ab3 27. ab3 ♗b2=; 27... ♗c5!? △ ♖a2, ♖g8⇆] **25. ♗h5** [25. cb5?! ♖c2 26. ♗h5 (26. ♗f3 ♗c5 △ ♖a2) ♖g8 27. ♗f3□ ♗c5! 28. ♔h1 ♖a2∓ △ 29... ♘g4, 29... ♖b2] **♘h5** [25... bc4?! 26. ♗f7 △ ♖g3] **26. ♖h5 bc4 27. bc4** [27. f6 c3!? (27... ef6 28. ♖f6 c3 ♙c) 28. fe7 (28. ♖g5 c2 29. ♗g7 ♔g8 30. ♗h6=) c2 *a)* 29. ♖f7 c1♕ 30. ♗c1 ♖c1 31. ♔h2 ♔g8 32. ♖hf5 (32. ♖hh7 ♗b2!∓; 32. ♖fh7 ♗b2!∓) ♖cc8!□∓; *b)* 29. ♖hf5 c1♕ 30. e8♕ ♖e8 31. ♗c1=; *c)* 29. ♗c1=] **♗b2!?** [27... ♖c4 28. f6 ef6 29. ♖f6⩱↑] **28. ♖h4!?** [28. ♖f4 ♖ab8!? 29. ♖fh4 ♗f6 30. ♗g5 ♗g5 31. ♖g5 ♖g8∓; 28... ♗f6] **♗f6** [28... ♖ab8 29. ♗g5!? f6 30. ♗d2∞] **29. ♖e4 ♖ab8 30. g4□ ♖b4 31. g5 ♗g5** [32. ♗g5 ♖g8 33. ♖g4 (33. f6!?) f6 (33... h6 34. f6!) 34. ♗f6 (34. ♖e1!?) ef6 35. ♖g8 (35. ♖ff4∓) ♔g8∓; 31... ♗e5!? 32. f6 (32. ♖c1∓) ef6 33. gf6 ♖bc4∓] **1/2 : 1/2** **[Tivjakov]**

178. **B 36**

ŠIROV 2670 – PANNO 2495

Buenos Aires 1993

1. e4 c5 2. ♘f3 ♘c6 3. d4 cd4 4. ♘d4 g6 5. c4 ♘f6 6. ♘c3 d6 7. ♗e2 ♘d4 8. ♕d4 ♗g7 9. ♗g5 0–0 10. ♕d2 ♗e6 11. 0–0 ♕a5 [11... ♖c8 12. b3 b5!? *a)* 13. cb5 ♖c3! (13... ♕a5 14. ♖ac1 ♖c3 15. ♕c3 ♕c3 16. ♖c3 ♘e4 17. ♖g3±) 14. ♕c3 ♘e4 15. ♕e3 ♘g5 16. ♕g5 (16. ♖ac1? h6 17. h4 ♘h7 18. ♕a7 ♘f6∓) ♗a1 17. ♖a1=; *b)* 13. e5! de5 14. ♘b5 ♕d2 15. ♗d2±] **12. ♖ac1 ♖fc8 13. b3 a6** [13... b5? 14. cb5 ♖c3? 15. ♖c3 ♘e4? 16. ♖c8+–] **14. f4! ♕d8 N** [14... b5 15. f5 *a)* 15... ♗d7? 16. fg6 hg6 17. e5! ♘g4 (17... de5? 18. ♗f6; 17... b4 18. ef6 bc3 19. ♖c3+–; 17... ♘e8 18. ♘d5 ♕d2 19. ♗d2+–; 17... ♘h7 18. ♗e7 ♗e5 19. ♗d6+–) 18. ♕f4! ♘e5 19. ♘d5 ♖e8 20. ♘e7 (20. ♗e7!?) ♖e7 21. ♗e7 ♕a2 22. ♖f2 ♕b3 23. ♗d6+–; *b)* 15... gf5 16. ef5 ♗d7 17. ♔h1±; *c)* 15... b4 – 24/339] **15. ♖cd1!±** [△ 15... b5 16. f5 ♗d7 17. e5] **♔h8 16. f5 gf5 17. ef5 ♗d7 18. ♘d5?!** [⌓ 18. ♗f6 ♗f6 19. ♘d5 ♗e5 20. ♕h6! ♕f8 (20... f6 21. ♖d3±) 21. ♕f8 (21. ♕h4 ♕g7!⇆ △ 22. ♘b6?! ♗c6 23. ♗f3 ♗f3 24. ♖f3 ♖g8) ♖f8 22. ♘e7±] **♘d5 19. ♕d5 ♕b6! 20. ♔h1 f6 21. ♗d2! ♖c5?!** [⌓ 21... ♗c6 22. ♕e6 ♕c5 23. ♗f3± ×♗g7] **22. ♕d3 ♖e5?! 23. ♗c3 ♖e3 24. ♕d2 ♗c6!? 25. ♗d4 ♕d4 26. ♕d4 ♖e2 27. ♖f2 ♖e4?!** [27... ♖e5 28. ♕c3 △ ♖e1+–] **28. ♕c3 ♖g8 29. ♖e1+– ♖e5 30. h3?!** [⌓ 30. ♔g1 ♗h6 31. ♔f1+–] **♗h6⇆ 31. ♖e5 de5!** [31... fe5 32. c5+–] **32. ♕b4! ♖g7** [32... ♗e3 33. ♖e2 ♖g3 34. ♔h2 ♗f4 35. ♔g1 ♖d3 (35... ♗e3 36. ♖e3+–) 36. ♕e7+–] **33. ♕b6 ♔g8 34. b4! ♖g3 35. b5 ab5** [35... ♗e4 36. ♖e2 ♗f5 37. ♕b7 ab5 38. cb5+–] **36.**

cb5 ♗e4 37. ♖e2! ♗d3 [37... ♖h3 38. ♔g1 ♖h4 39. ♕d8 ♔f7 40. ♖e4! ♖e4 41. ♕d5+–] **38. ♖e5⊕** [38... fe5 39. ♕e6 ♔h8 40. ♕h6+–] **1 : 0** **[Širov]**

179. **B 36**

ILLESCAS CÓRDOBA 2615
– LÉKÓ 2465
León 1993

1. c4 c5 2. ♘f3 g6 3. d4 cd4 4. ♘d4 ♘c6 5. e4 ♘f6 6. ♘c3 d6 7. ♗e2 ♘d4 8. ♕d4 ♗g7 9. 0–0 0–0 10. ♕e3 ♗d7 11. ♖d1 ♕b6!? N [11... a6 – 13/379] **12. ♕b6 ab6 13. ♗e3 ♗c6 14. f3 ♘d7 15. ♖dc1?!** [15. ♗d4±] **♘c5 16. ♖c2 ♖fc8= 17. ♘d5 ♗d5 18. cd5 ♖a3!?** [18... ♘a4 19. ♖ac1 ♖c2 20. ♖c2 ♗b2! (△ ♗a3-c5; 20... ♘b2 21. ♖c7±) 21. ♖c7 ♗f6 (21... ♗a3!?) 22. ♖b7 ♘c5 23. ♖b6 ♖a2=] **19. ♗f2** [19. ba3 ♗a1=] **♖ca8 20. ♗c4 b5! 21. ♖ac1 ♖3a4! 22. ♗b5 ♖a2?** [22... ♖b4!= 23. ♗c4 b5 24. ♗b3 ♘b3=] **23. b4! ♖c2 24. ♖c2 ♘a6** [24... ♖a1 25. ♗f1 ♘b3 26. ♖c8 ♗f8 27. ♗e3±] **25. ♗e1!±** [×♘a6] **♗d4 26. ♔f1 h5 27. ♗d7! ♔g7 28. ♖c8 ♖b8** [28... ♘b8 29. ♗h3 (29. ♗e8±) ♖a1 30. b5! ♖b1 31. ♔e2 ♗a7 32. b6 ♖b6 33. ♗c3 f6 34. ♗d4+–] **29. ♔e2 ♗g1 30. ♗c3 f6 31. h4 ♔h6 32. ♖b8 ♘b8 33. ♗c8 b6 34. ♗d2 ♔g7 35. ♗e3 ♗e3 36. ♔e3 ♔f7 37. g4⊕ ♔e8 38. gh5 gh5 39. ♔d4+–** [×♘b8] **b5 40. f4 ♔f7 41. ♗b7** [△ ♗c6] **♔f8 42. f5!** [42. ♗c6? e5!] **♔f7 43. ♗c6 ♘a6 44. ♗b5** [44... ♘b4 45. ♔c3 ♘a2 46. ♔b3 ♘c1 47. ♔b2] **1 : 0**
[Illescas Córdoba]

180. **B 36**

ĖJNGORN 2575 – KRASENKOV 2560
Metz 1993

1. ♘f3 c5 2. c4 g6 3. d4 cd4 4. ♘d4 ♘c6 5. e4 ♘f6 6. ♘c3 d6 7. ♗e2 ♘d4 8. ♕d4 ♗g7 9. 0–0 0–0 10. ♕e3 ♗e6 11. ♖b1!? N [11. ♗d2 – 28/350] **a6** [11... ♕b6!? 12. ♕g3!? △ ♔h1, f4↑»] **12. a4! ♘d7 13. ♘d5 ♘c5** [13... ♖e8±] **14. b3 ♖e8 15. ♗a3! ♖c8 16. ♖fd1 a5** [16... ♗d5!?±] **17. f4! ♗d5** [17... f5?! 18. e5!] **18. ♖d5** [18. cd5!±⊡↑«⊞] **♕b6 19. e5 ♗f8! 20. ♖bd1** [20. e6?! fe6 21. ♗g4? ed5 22. ♗e6 ♔h8 23. ♗b2 ♗g7 24. ♗g7 ♔g7 25. ♕c3 d4! 26. ♕d4 ♔h6] **♖ed8?** [20... e6! 21. ♖d6 ♗d6 22. ♖d6 (22. ed6 ♖ed8) ♕c7 23. ♗f3 b6∞]

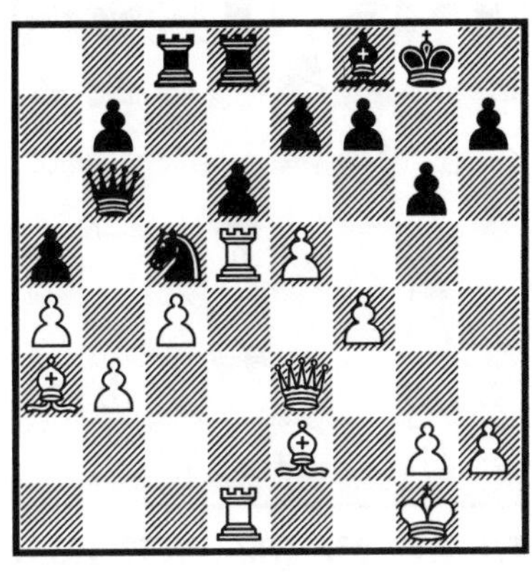

21. e6! fe6 [21... f5 22. ♔h1 △ g4→] **22. ♗g4!! ed5 23. ♗e6 ♘e6** [23... ♔h8 24. ♗b2 ♗g7 25. ♗g7 ♔g7 26. ♕d4 ♔h6 27. ♖d3! ♘d3 28. ♕b6+–] **24. ♕b6 dc4 25. ♕e3?!** [25. ♕b7±; 25. ♕a5±] **♘g7 26. ♗b2?!** [26. bc4 ♖c4 27. ♕b3] **d5 27. bc4** [27. g3±] **♖c4 28. ♗g7 ♔g7 29. ♕e5 ♔f7 30. f5** [30. ♖d5? ♗g7] **♖d6!= 31. ♖f1 ♔g8 32. f6 ef6 33. ♖f6 ♖c1** [33... ♖cc6!? 34. ♖f1!?] **34. ♔f2 ♖cc6 35. ♖d6 ♖d6 36. ♔e2 b6 37. ♔d3 d4 38. ♕e8 h5 39. h3 ♔g7 40. g4 hg4 41. hg4 ♔g8**
1/2 : 1/2 **[Krasenkov]**

181. **B 40**

KIR. GEORGIEV 2660
– J. POLGÁR 2595
Budapest (zt) 1993

1. e4 c5 2. ♘f3 e6 3. d4 cd4 4. ♘d4 ♕b6 5. ♘b3 ♕c7 6. g3 N [6. c4 – 56/189] **♘c6 7. ♗g2 ♘f6 8. ♗f4?!** [8. 0–0 △ ♘c3, a4] **d6 9. ♘a3?! a6 10. 0–0** [10. ♘c4 ♘e5 11. ♘e5 de5 12. ♗e3 ♗e7=] **♗e7 11. c4 0–0 12. ♖c1** [12. c5 e5 13. cd6 ♗d6 14. ♘c4 ♖d8=] **e5** [⌓ 12... ♘e5 △ b6, ♗b7] **13. ♗e3 ♗e6** [⌓ 13... ♖b8 △ b5 J. Polgár] **14. h3 b5 15. f4!** [15. cb5?! ab5 16. ♘b5 ♕d7! (△ 17... ♖a2,

17... ♗h3) 17. a4 ♗h3 18. ♗h3 ♕h3 19. ♖c6 ♘g4 20. ♖e1 ♕h2 21. ♔f1 ♕h1 22. ♔e2 ♕e4=∞] **b4** [15... ♘b4!? 16. cb5 ♕b8 17. f5 ♗d7∞] **16. ♘b1 a5 17. f5 ♗c8 18. g4 ♘d7?** [18... h6] **19. g5 ♖e8 20. f6 ♗f8□ 21. fg7 ♗g7**

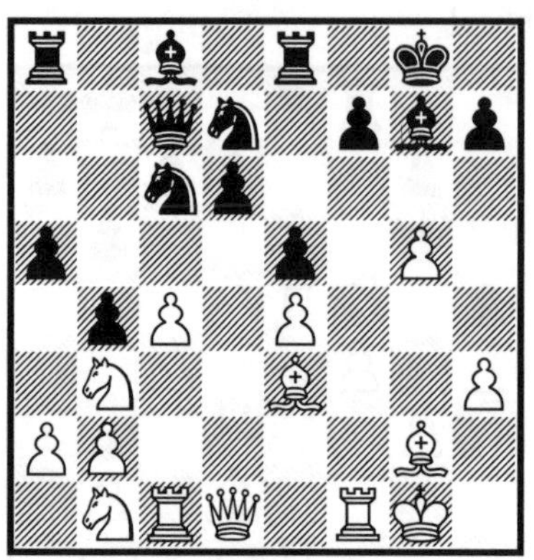

22. ♖f7! ♔f7 23. ♕h5 ♔e7? [23... ♔g8 24. ♕e8 ♘f8 (△ ♗b7, ♘d4=∞) 25. c5 ♗b7∞] **24. ♕h7 ♔d8 25. ♕g7 a4 26. ♘3d2± ♘d4** [26... ♘c5? 27. ♕f6 ♕e7 28. ♗c5 ♕f6 29. ♗b6+−] **27. g6?!** [27. ♖f1] **♘e6** [⌓ 27... ♘e2 △ ♘f4] **28. ♕h6 ♗a6 29. ♖f1 ♔c8 30. g7 ♔b7 31. ♖f7! ♖ad8 32. g8♕ ♖g8 33. ♕e6+− ♔b8 34. ♔h2 ♗c8 35. ♘f3 ♘f8 36. ♖c7 ♗e6 37. ♖c6 ♘h7 38. ♘bd2⊕** [38. ♘e5] **♖g7 39. ♖b6 ♔c7 40. c5 ♘f6 41. cd6 ♖d6 42. ♖b4 a3 43. ♘e5 ♘h5 44. ba3 ♗a2 45. ♖b2 ♗e6 46. ♖c2 ♔b7 47. ♘ec4 1 : 0**
[Kir. Georgiev]

182. B 42

PSAKHIS 2575 – ORATOVSKIJ 2335
Tel-Aviv 1993

1. e4 c5 2. ♘f3 e6 3. d4 cd4 4. ♘d4 a6 5. ♗d3 g6 6. c4 ♗g7 7. ♘b3 [7. ♗e3 d5!?] **♘e7** [7... d6?! 8. ♘c3 ♘c6 9. ♗f4 b6 10. ♗e2 ♘e5 11. ♕d2±] **8. 0–0** [8. ♘c3!? 0–0 9. ♗e2 ♘bc6 10. ♗f4⩲] **0–0 9. ♘c3 ♘bc6 10. ♗e2** [10. ♗g5!? h6 11. ♗h4] **f5!? N** [10... b6 11. ♗g5!? (11. ♗f4 – 30/327) h6 12. ♗e3 f5 13. ♕d2 ♔h7 14. f3!?⩲] **11. c5** [11. ♗f4 fe4 12. ♗d6 e3! 13. fe3 ♖f1 14. ♗f1 ♘f5] **b6!?** [11... fe4 12. ♘e4] **12. cb6 ♕b6 13. ♗e3 ♕d8** [13... ♕c7 14. ♗c5] **14. ♕d2 fe4 15. ♘e4 d5 16. ♘ec5 ♘f5 17. ♗g5 ♕d6** [17... ♕b6 18. ♖ac1] **18. ♖ac1 h6 19. ♗f4 ♕e7?** [19... e5 20. ♗e3 (20. ♗f3 ♘ce7!; 20. ♗g3 h5! 21. ♗f3 ♘ce7∓) d4 (20... ♘e3?! 21. fe3±) 21. ♘e4□ ♕d7 (21... de3 22. ♕d6 ♘d6 23. ♘d6±) 22. ♕c2 (22. ♘bc5? ♕e8−+) de3 23. ♕c6 ♕c6 24. ♖c6 ♗b7 25. ♖c4 ♘d4! 26. ♘d4 ed4 27. ♘c5 ♗d5 28. ♖c2 (28. ♖a4 ♖fc8!? 29. b4 a5) ef2 (28... ♗a2? 29. b3 ef2 30. ♔h1!) 29. ♖f2 ♖f2 30. ♔f2 ♗a2!? 31. b3 ♗b1; 31. ♗a6=] **20. h3!** [20. ♘a6?! ♘fd4!↑; 20. ♘a4!? g5! 21. ♘b6 gf4 22. ♘a8 (22. ♖c6 ♗b7) ♗b7∞] **♘e5 21. ♖fe1 g5** [21... ♕h4 22. ♗f1 ♘c4 23. ♗c4 dc4 24. ♖c4 g5! 25. g3□ ♕h3 26. ♗c7∞; 24. ♘a5!±] **22. ♗h2 ♘d6** [22... ♕f7 23. ♗h5!? ♕h5 24. ♗e5±] **23. ♘a5!± ♘df7 24. ♗h5 ♕f6 25. ♖c3! ♘g6!□ 26. ♖f3** [26. ♘c6 ♘f4] **♘f4 27. ♗f4 gf4 28. ♕f4** [28. ♖f4 ♕g5] **♘g5** [28... ♕f4 29. ♖f4 e5 (29... ♗b2 30. ♘e6 ♗e6 31. ♖e6+−) 30. ♖f7 ♖f7 31. ♗f7 ♔f7 32. ♘c6 e4 33. ♖d1 ♗e6 34. ♘d4+−] **29. ♕f6 ♗f6 30. ♖g3 ♔h8** [30... ♗d4 31. ♘d3 ♔h8 32. ♘c6+−] **31. ♘c6! ♗b2 32. h4 ♘h7** [32... ♘e4 33. ♘e4 de4 34. ♖e4 ♗b7 35. ♖e6+−] **33. ♘e7! ♘f6 34. ♘e6?** [34. ♘g6 ♔g7 35. ♘f8 ♔f8 36. ♗g6+−] **♘h5! 35. ♘g6 ♔g8 36. ♘gf8 ♘g3 37. fg3 ♔f7?⊕** [37... d4! 38. ♘c7 (38. ♘g6 d3 39. ♘gf4 d2 40. ♖d1 ♗c3 41. ♘d5 ♗a5!∓) ♖a7 (38... d3 39. ♘a8 ♗g4 40. ♘g6 d2 41. ♖f1 ♗e2 42. ♖f8 ♔g7 43. ♖d8±; 41. ♔f1!?±) 39. ♖e8 *a)* 39... ♖c7? 40. ♘e6 ♔f7 41. ♘c7+−; *b)* 39... ♗g4 40. ♘d7 ♔g7 (40... ♔f7 41. ♘e5) 41. ♖e7; *c)* 39... d3! 40. ♖c8 (40. ♔f2 ♗g4) ♗d4! (40... d2 41. ♖d8) 41. ♔f1 (41. ♔h2 d2) ♖b7 42. ♘fe6 (42. ♔e1? ♗e3−+) ♔f7 43. ♘d4 ♖b1 44. ♔f2 d2 45. ♘d5 *c1)* 45... d1♕ 46. ♖c7 ♔g6□ (46... ♔e8 47. ♘f6+−; 46... ♔f8 47. ♘e6 ♔g8 48. ♘f6+−) 47. h5!? (47. ♖c6 ♔f7 48. ♖c7=) ♔h5! (47... ♔g5? 48. ♖g7+−) 48. g4!? ♔g6! (48... ♕g4? 49. ♘f6; 48... ♔h4 49. ♘f3 ♔g4 50. ♘e3+−; 48... ♔g5 49. ♖g7) 49. ♖c6 ♔f7 50. ♖c7=; *c2)* 45... ♖f1!? 46. ♔f1 d1♕ 47. ♔f2 ♕d4 48. ♘e3 ♕d2 (48... ♕b2? 49. ♖c2±) 49. ♔f3 ♕a2 50. ♖c7 ♔e8 (50... ♔g6 51. ♖c6 ♔h7=)

51. g4!∞] **38. ♖f1 ♗f6** [38... ♔e7 39. ♘c7+−] **39. ♘c7 ♖b8** [39... ♖a7 40. ♘d5 ♔f8 41. ♖f6 ♔g7 42. ♖c6+−] **40. ♘h7! ♖b6 41. ♘d5 1 : 0** **[Psakhis]**

183. **B 42**

NIJBOER 2505 – SMIRIN 2590
Wijk aan Zee (open) 1993

1. e4 c5 2. ♘f3 e6 3. d4 cd4 4. ♘d4 a6 5. ♗d3 ♘f6 6. 0–0 ♕c7 7. ♕e2 d6 8. c4 g6 9. ♘c3 ♗g7 10. ♘f3 0–0 11. ♗f4 ♘bd7 12. ♖fd1 ♘h5 N [12... ♘g4 – 47/(225)] **13. ♗e3 b6?!** [13... ♘e5 14. ♘e5 de5⩲] **14. ♕d2! ♖e8 15. ♗e2 ♗f8 16. ♗h6 ♗e7 17. ♗g5 ♗f8** [17... ♗g5? 18. ♘g5+−; 17... ♘hf6 18. ♕f4 ♗b7 19. ♕h4 △ 20. e5 de5 21. ♖d7 ♘d7 22. ♗e7±; 17... f6 18. ♗e3±] **18. ♖ac1 ♖b8** [18... ♗b7 19. e5! ♘e5 20. ♘e5 de5 21. ♗h5 gh5 22. ♗f6 h6 23. ♕d3 ♕c6 24. ♕g3 ♔h7 25. ♖e1!±] **19. a3** [△ b4] **f6 20. ♗h4! ♗b7 21. ♘d4 ♘g7 22. f4 ♖bc8**

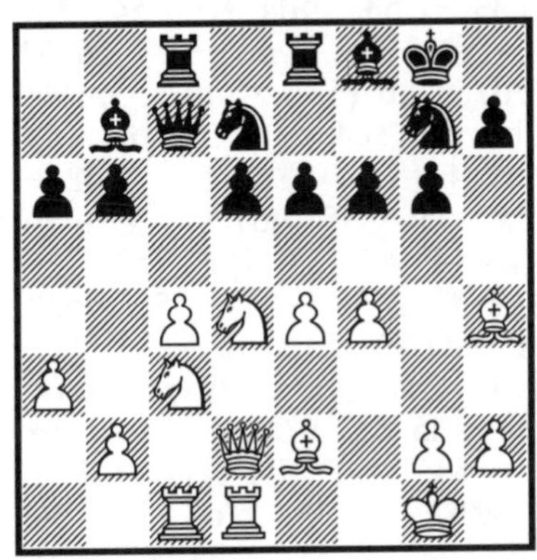

23. f5! ♘c5 [23... gf5 24. ef5 e5 25. ♘e6 ♘e6 26. fe6 ♖e6 27. ♘d5 ♕c5 28. ♗f2 ♕a5 29. b4 ♕a3 30. ♗g4+−; 23... ef5 24. ef5 g5 25. ♗g3± ×d5, e6; 23... e5 24. ♘e6 ♘e6 25. fe6 ♖e6 26. ♘d5 ♕c5 27. ♗f2 ♕a5 28. ♕a5 ba5 29. ♗g4 ♔f7 30. ♗e6 ♔e6±] **24. fg6! hg6 25. ♗f6 e5 26. ♘f3 ♘h5** [26... ♕f7 27. ♕h6! ♕f6 28. ♘g5+−] **27. ♘d5 ♗d5 28. ♕d5 ♕f7 29. ♗g5 ♕d5 30. ed5 ♗g7 31. b4 ♘a4 32. ♘d2 e4 33. ♗g4! e3 34. ♗e3+− ♖e3 35. ♗c8 ♘c3 36. ♖e1 ♗d4 37. ♔f1 ♖d3 38. ♘f3 ♗e3 39. ♖e3 ♖e3 40. ♗a6 ♘a2 41. ♖a1 ♖a3 42. ♗b5 ♘f4 43. c5 bc5 44. bc5 ♖a5 45. ♗c4 ♖c5 46. ♗a2 ♖a5 47. ♘e1 ♔g7 48. ♘c2 1 : 0** **[Nijboer]**

184. **B 42**

ANAND 2710 – LJUBOJEVIĆ 2605
Linares 1993

1. e4 c5 2. ♘f3 e6 3. d4 cd4 4. ♘d4 a6 5. ♗d3 ♕c7 6. 0–0 ♘f6 7. ♕e2 ♗d6 8. ♔h1 N [8. f4!? ♗c5 9. c3 ♘c6 10. ♗e3 d5 (10... d6 11. ♘d2) 11. e5 ♘d7 12. ♘d2±; 8. h3 – 2/332] **♘c6 9. c3** [9. ♘c6! dc6! (9... bc6 10. f4 e5 11. ♘d2⩲) 10. f4 e5 11. f5⩲] **♘e5 10. f4 ♘d3 11. ♕d3 ♗e7 12. c4** [12. e5 ♘d5 13. c4 ♘b4∞] **d6 13. ♘c3 0–0 14. b3 ♘d7 15. f5?!** [15. ♗b2!⩲] **♗f6** [15... ♘c5! 16. ♕g3 ♗f6 17. ♗e3 ♗e5⇆] **16. fe6 ♘e5** [16... ♘c5 17. ef7 ♖f7 18. ♕e3±] **17. ♕g3!** [17. ef7 ♖f7 18. ♕g3 (18. ♕e3? ♘g4−+) ♘c4! △ 19. ♘d5? ♗d4] **fe6 18. ♗g5 ♗g5 19. ♖f8 ♔f8 20. ♕g5 h6 21. ♖f1 ♔g8 22. ♕h4?** [22. ♕g3=] **b6?** [22... b5!∓] **23. ♘ce2 ♖a7 24. ♘f4 ♕e7 25. ♕e1 ♗d7 26. ♕b4 ♖b7 27. ♔g1 ♔h7 28. ♖d1 ♕f6 29. ♕d2 ♗c8 30. ♘h5 ♕h4 31. ♘g3 ♖f7 32. ♕e2 ♗b7?! 33. ♘e6 ♘g4 34. h3! ♘f2** [34... ♕g3! 35. hg4 ♗c8∓; 35. ♕g4=] **35. ♘f5 ♘h3?** [35... ♕e4! 36. ♕e4 ♗e4 37. ♘d6 ♘d1 38. ♘f7 ♗b1!=∞] **36. gh3 ♖f5 37. ef5+− ♕g3 38. ♔f1 ♗f3 39. ♕c2 ♕h3 40. ♔e1 ♕h1 41. ♔d2 ♗d1 42. ♕d1 ♕e4 43. ♕g1 ♕e5 44. ♕g6 1 : 0** **[Anand]**

185. **B 42**

R. HÜBNER 2620 – CH. LUTZ 2550
Deutschland 1993

1. e4 c5 2. ♘f3 e6 3. d4 cd4 4. ♘d4 a6 5. ♗d3 ♘f6 6. 0–0 ♕c7 7. ♔h1 d6 [⌓ 7... d5 8. ed5 ♘d5 9. ♗e4 (9. f4 g6) ♘f6 10. ♗f3 ♗e7=] **8. f4 ♘bd7 9. c4 g6?! N** [9... ♗e7 10. ♘c3 0–0 11. ♗e3 b6 12. ♖c1±; 9... ♘c5 – 38/(213); 9... b6 – 38/213] **10. f5 e5** [10... gf5 11. ef5 e5 12. ♘e6±] **11. ♘c2** [△ ♘e3 ×d5, f5; 11. ♘b3?! ♗e7 12. ♘c3 ♘b6 △ gf5∞; 11.

♘e6?! fe6 12. fe6 ♗g7 13. ed7 ♗d7 14. ♘c3 0–0 △ ♗e6=] **gf5** [11... ♗e7 12. ♘e3 △ ♘c3, g4] **12. ♖f5 ♗e7 13. ♘c3** [13. ♗g5 ♖g8 *a)* 14. ♘c3 ♘b6 15. ♖f6 (15. ♗f6 ♗f5 16. ♗e7 ♗g4–+) ♖g5 16. ♖f2 ♗e6∓; *b)* 14. ♕f1 ♘c5 15. ♗f6 (15. ♖f6 ♖g5 16. ♖h6 ♗e6∞) ♗f5 16. ♗e7 ♗e4 17. ♗e4 ♘e4 18. ♗h4 ♖g4$\overline{\overline{\infty}}$; *c)* 14. ♕f3 ♘c5 15. ♖f6 ♖g5 16. ♖h6 (16. ♖f7? ♘d3) ♗e6 17. ♘c3 0-0-0∞; *d)* 14. ♗h4 ♖g6 15. ♘c3 ♘b6∞] **♘c5** [13... ♘b6 14. ♖f1 △ 14... ♘c4? 15. ♖f6 ♗f6 16. ♘d5+–] **14. ♖f1 ♗g4□** [14... ♖g8 15. ♘e3 ♗e6 16. ♘cd5 ♗d5 17. ed5+–] **15. ♗e2** [15. ♕d2!? Ch. Lutz] **♗e6 16. ♘d5 ♕d8□** [16... ♗d5 17. ed5+– ×f5; 16... ♘d5 17. ed5 ♗d7 18. ♗h6 △ ♗h5+–] **17. ♗e3** [△ b4] **♘fe4** [17... ♘ce4 18. ♗b6+–; 17... ♗d5 18. ed5+–] **18. ♗g4** [△ b4] **h5!** [18... ♘f6 19. ♗e6 ♘e6 (19... fe6 20. ♘f6 ♗f6 21. ♕h5 ♔d7 22. ♗c5+–) 20. ♗b6+–; 18... ♖g8 19. ♗e6 ♘e6 (19... fe6 20. ♕h5 ♔d7 21. ♘e7 ♖g7 22. b4 ♘a4 23. ♘f5 ♘f6 24. ♕h3+–) 20. ♕f3 ♘4g5 21. ♕f5 △ h4±; 18... ♗d5 19. ♕d5 ♘f6 20. ♕f3 e4 21. ♕h3±] **19. ♗h5 ♗d5?⊕** [19... ♗f8 20. ♗c5 (20. ♕f3 ♕h4∞) dc5 (20... ♘c5 21. ♘f6 ♔e7 22. ♘e3+–) 21. ♕f3 ♕h4 *a)* 22. g4? 0-0-0 23. ♕e4 ♖h5; *b)* 22. ♘c7 ♔d7 (22... ♔d8 23. ♘e6 fe6 24. g4+–) 23. ♘e6 (23. ♘a8 ♖h5 24. h3 ♔c8∞) ♖h5 24. ♕f7 ♗e7 25. h3 ♘g3 26. ♔h2 ♘f1 27. ♖f1 ♔c6∞; *c)* 22. ♗f7 ♔d8 23. h3 ♘g3 24. ♔h2 ♘f1 (24... ♗h3 25. ♕g3+–) 25. ♖f1+–; 19... ♘f6 20. ♗f3 ♘d5 21. ♗d5 ♕d7 △ 22... 0-0-0, 22... ♗d5∞] **20. ♕d5 ♘g3 21. hg3** [21. ♔g1?! ♖h5 (21... ♘h5 22. ♕f7 ♔d7 23. ♗c5+–; 21... ♘f1 22. ♕f7 ♔d7 23. ♗c5 ♘h2 △ 24. ♔h2 ♖h5 25. ♕h5 ♕h8=) 22. ♕f7 (22. hg3 – 21. hg3) ♔d7 23. ♗c5 (23. hg3 ♕h8 △ ♖f8) ♕h8∞] **♖h5 22. ♔g1 ♘e6** [22... ♖h7 23. ♗c5 dc5 24. ♕b7+–] **23. ♕b7** [23. ♕f3? ♖h7 24. ♕f5 ♖g7 25. ♗h6 ♕b6 26. ♖f2 ♖g3 27. ♕f7 ♔d7∞] **♖b8 24. ♕f3 ♖h7 25. b3** [25. ♕f5 ♖g7 26. ♗h6 ♕b6 27. ♖f2 ♖g3 28. ♕f7 ♔d7∞] **♗g5 26. ♗a7?!** [26. ♖ad1 ♗e3 27. ♘e3 ♕b6 28. ♖f2] **♖a8** [26... ♖c8!?] **27. ♗f2 a5 28. ♖ad1 ♖c8 29. ♘a3** [29. ♕e4!? ♖h6 (29... ♖g7 30. ♘a3 △ ♘b5; 29... ♖h8 30. ♘a3) 30. ♘e3 ♗e3 31. ♗e3 ♖g6 32. ♖f3] **♔e7 30. ♕d3 ♕h8** [30... ♖h6 31. ♘b5+–] **31. ♕d6 ♔f6 32. ♗e3?** [32. ♗c5 ♔g6 (32... ♔g7 33. ♕e5 f6 34. ♖d7+–) 33. ♕d3 ♔h6 (33... ♔g7 34. ♖f7 ♔f7 35. ♕f5+–) 34. ♗e3 f6 35. ♗g5 ♘g5 36. ♕f5+–] **♔g6 33. ♕d3** [33. ♗g5 ♔g5 34. ♕d2 ♔g6 35. ♕d3 ♔g7 36. ♕f5 ♖h1 37. ♔f2 ♖h5∞] **♔g7 34. ♗g5 ♘g5 35. ♕f5 ♖h1 36. ♔f2 ♖f1 37. ♖f1 f6 38. ♔e2?!** [38. ♘c2 ♕f8 (38... ♖d8 39. ♘e3 ♖d2 40. ♔g1) 39. ♘e3 ♖d8 40. ♔g1+–] **♕f8 39. ♘c2 ♖d8 40. ♘e3 ♘h7 41. ♖h1** [41. ♘d5 ♕a3∞] **♘g5 42. ♘d5 ♖d6 43. ♖h5** [△ ♘f6] **♕d8 44. ♔f1 ♖d5 45. cd5 ♕d5 46. ♕c2?** [46. ♖g5 fg5 47. ♕g5 ♔f7 48. ♕f5 ♔e7 49. g4+–] **♕d4 47. ♖h4 e4 48. ♖f4 ♔g6 49. ♔e2 ♕e5** [49... ♕g1 50. ♖f2 ♕a1 (50... ♕h2 51. ♕c3) 51. ♖f1 ♕e5 52. ♖f4 ♕d4 53. ♕d2] **50. ♔e3** [50. ♕d2 ♘e6 (50... f5 51. g4) 51. ♖g4 ♘g5∞] **♔g7 51. ♕d2?** [51. g4 ♔h6 (51... ♘e6 52. ♖e4 ♕g3 53. ♔d2 ♕g2 54. ♔c1+–) 52. ♖e4 ♕g3 (52... ♘e4 53. ♕e4 ♕c3 54. ♔f4 ♕d2 55. ♕e3+–) 53. ♔d4 ♕d6 54. ♔c3 ♕c5 55. ♖c4 ♕e5 56. ♔d2+–] **♘e6 52. ♖g4** [52. ♕d7 ♔h6 (52... ♔f8? 53. ♕c8 ♔f7 54. ♕b7 △ ♕e4+–) 53. ♖e4 (53. ♖h4 ♔g5) ♕e4 (53... ♕g3 54. ♔d2+–) 54. ♔e4 ♘c5 55. ♔f5 ♘d7 56. ♔e6 ♘c5 57. ♔f6 ♘e4=] **♔f8 53. ♔e2** [53. ♖e4 ♕g3 54. ♔e2 ♕g2 55. ♔e3 (55. ♔d3? ♘c5) ♕g3=] **♘d4?⊕** [53... f5 54. ♖f4□∞] **54. ♔f2** [54. ♔f1 ♔f7∞ △ 55. ♕f4 ♕b5] **♘f5** [54... f5 55. ♕h6+–; 54... ♕c5 55. ♕h6+–; 54... ♔f7 55. ♕f4 ♕c5 56. ♕e4 f5 57. ♕b7+–] **55. ♕d8 ♔f7 56. ♕d7 ♔f8** [56... ♘e7 57. ♖h4 ♕c5 58. ♔e2 ♕c2 59. ♕d2 ♕b1 60. ♖f4+–] **57. ♕c8 ♔f7 58. ♕b7 ♔f8 59. ♕a8 ♔f7 60. ♕e4 ♕c5 61. ♔e2 1 : 0 [R. Hübner]**

186. B 42

DOLMATOV 2615 – CH. LUTZ 2550

Deutschland 1993

1. e4 c5 2. ♘f3 e6 3. d4 cd4 4. ♘d4 a6 5. ♗d3 ♘f6 6. 0–0 ♕c7 7. ♔h1 d6 8. f4 ♗e7 9. c4 N [9. ♘d2 – 26/348] **b6 10. ♕e2 ♗b7 11. b3 ♘bd7** [11... ♘c6!?] **12.**

♘d2 0–0 [12... b5!? 13. cb5 ♕c3 14. ba6 ♗a6 15. ♗a6 ♕a1 16. ♘2f3=∞] **13. ♗b2 ♖fe8 14. ♖ae1 e5?!** [14... g6!? △ 15. e5 ♘h5 16. f5 de5 17. fe6 fe6 18. ♘e6 ♕d6] **15. fe5 de5 16. ♘f5 ♗f8 17. ♕e3 ♘c5 18. ♗b1 ♘fd7 19. ♕g3 ♔h8?!** [19... f6!? 20. b4 ♘a4!; 20. a3 △ b4] **20. ♖f4 ♘e6** [20... ef4?? 21. ♗g7 ♔g8 22. ♘h6#] **21. ♖h4** [21. ♖g4!?] **♗b4 22. ♖d1 ♖ad8 23. ♘f3?!** [23. ♘f1! △ ♘e3-d5→] **f6 24. ♖f1 b5?!** [24... ♘df8 25. ♘e3∞] **25. a3 ♗d6 26. cb5 ab5**

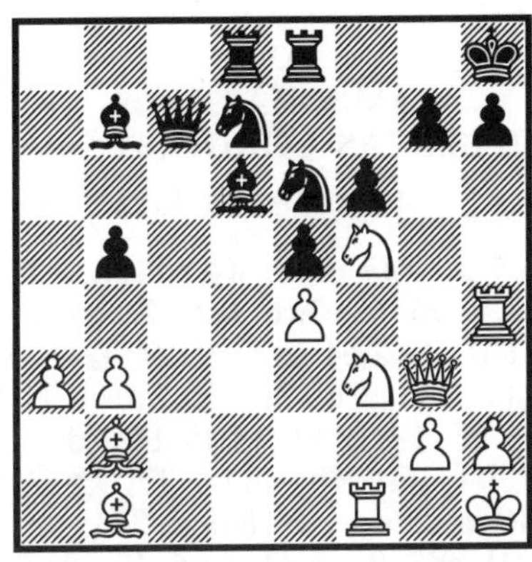

27. ♘3d4! ed4□ 28. e5! [28. ♘d6 ♘e5□ 29. ♘e8 ♖e8 30. ♖d1∞] **♘e5□** [28... ♗e5 29. ♖h7 ♔h7 30. ♘e7+−] **29. ♖h7 ♔h7?** [29... ♔g8!□ 30. ♘h6 ♔f8 31. ♖f6 ♔e7 32. ♖g7 (32. ♕g6 ♔d7□ 33. ♕f5 ♔c8!∓) ♔f6 33. ♖c7 ♗c7 34. ♕h4 ♔g7 35. ♘f5 ♔f7∞] **30. ♘e7 g6** [30... d3 31. ♕h4#] **31. ♕h4** [31. ♗g6? ♔g7∓] **♔g7 32. ♕f6 ♔h6 33. ♕h4 ♔g7 34. ♕f6 ♔h6 35. ♘g6!+− ♗g2 36. ♔g2 ♘g4 37. ♕h4 ♔g7 38. ♕g4 ♘g5 39. ♕d4 ♗e5 40. ♕e5 ♖e5 41. ♗e5 1 : 0 [Dolmatov]**

187. B 42

V. NEVEDNIČIJ 2495 – CO. IONESCU 2475

București 1993

1. e4 c5 2. ♘f3 e6 3. d4 cd4 4. ♘d4 a6 5. ♗d3 ♘f6 6. 0–0 ♕c7 7. ♕e2 d6 8. c4 ♗e7 9. ♘c3 0–0 10. ♗e3 b6 N [10... ♘bd7 – 7/316] **11. ♖ac1 ♗b7 12. f4 ♖e8 13. f5 ♗d8?!** [13... ♗f8 14. fe6 fe6 15. g4!↑] **14. fe6 fe6**

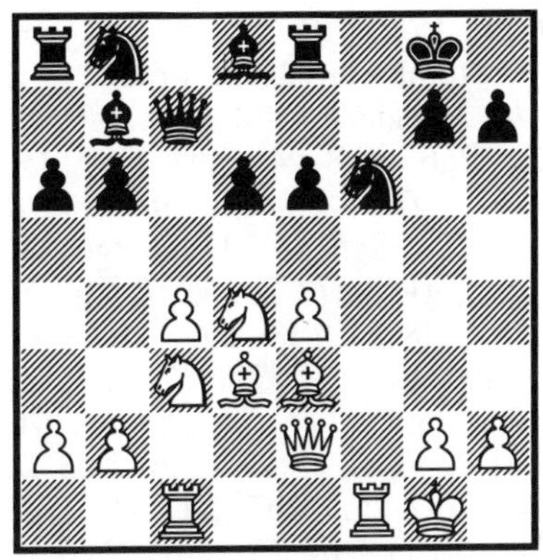

15. e5! de5 16. ♖f6!! gf6 [16... ed4? 17. ♗h7 ♔h8 18. ♕h5 gf6 19. ♗f5 ♔g8 20. ♕e8 ♔g7 21. ♗h6! ♔h6 22. ♕g6#; 16... ♗f6 17. ♗h7 ♔f8 (17... ♔h7? 18. ♕h5 ♔g8 19. ♕e8 ♔h7 20. ♘e6 ♕c6 21. ♘f8 ♔g8 22. ♘d7 ♔h7 23. ♕h5 ♔g8 24. ♘f6+−) 18. ♘f3±→] **17. ♘e6!** [17. ♕h5!? ed4! 18. ♕e8 ♔g7 19. ♗d4 ♕c6!∞] **♕f7** [17... ♖e6 18. ♕g4 ♔f7 19. ♘d5 (19. ♗h7!?) ♕d7 20. ♗h7 ♗d5 21. cd5 ♖e8 22. ♗f5 ♕d5 23. ♗e4 ♕a2 24. ♗a8±] **18. ♘d8 ♖d8 19. ♗b6 ♖f8** [19... ♖d3!?±] **20. ♘e4!** [×d6] **♘d7 21. ♗e3 ♕e6 22. c5 ♔h8 23. ♘d6 e4** [23... ♗d5 24. ♗f5±] **24. ♗c4 ♗d5 25. ♗d5 ♕d5 26. ♕c4! ♕c6** [26... ♕c4 27. ♖c4+−] **27. ♗h6 ♘e5 28. ♕e6!⊕ ♖ae8 29. ♕f5 ♘d3 30. ♗f8 ♖f8 31. ♖c4+− ♘b2 32. ♕e4 ♕c7 33. ♖c2 ♖b8 34. ♕f4 ♕e7 35. ♘e4 ♖b4 36. ♕f6 ♕f6 37. ♘f6 ♘d3 38. h3 ♖b1 39. ♔h2 1 : 0 [V. Nevedničij]**

188.* !N B 42

JAKOVIČ 2510 – EMMS 2450

Cappelle la Grande 1993

1. e4 c5 2. ♘f3 e6 3. d4 cd4 4. ♘d4 a6 5. ♗d3 ♗c5 6. ♘b3 ♗a7 7. ♘c3 ♘c6 8. ♕e2 d6 9. ♗e3 ♘f6 10. 0-0-0 b5 11. f4 b4 12. ♘a4 e5 13. ♗a7 [13. f5 ♗d7 14. ♗a7 ♘a7] **♖a7 14. f5 0–0** [14... ♗d7 15. ♕f2!] **15. g4 ♗d7 16. g5 ♘e8 17. ♕e3** [RR 17. ♖hg1!? N ♘b8!□ (17... ♘e7 18. ♕e3 ♖b7 19. ♗a6 ♖b8 20. ♘ac5 ♕b6 21. ♗c4 ♗c6 22. g6→) 18. ♕h5 ♗a4 19. ♖g3 ♗b5 (19... ♘d7 20. ♗c4) 20. ♖h3 h6 *a)* 21. f6?? ♘f6 22. gf6 ♕f6–+ Prié 2470 – Stefánsson 2495, France – Ísland 1993; *b)* 21. gh6? ♘f6! (21... g6? 22. fg6 fg6 23. ♕g6 ♔h8 24. ♖g1 ♖h7 25. ♕g7 ♘g7 26. hg7 ♔g8 27. gf8♕ ♔f8 28. ♖h7+–) 22. ♕g5 g6 23. fg6 fg6 24. ♕g6 ♔h8 25. ♖g1 ♘h7? 26. ♕g7 ♖g7 27. hg7 ♔g8 28. gf8♕ ♔f8 29. ♖h7+–; 25... ♖e8!∓; *c)* 21. ♖g1! ♕b6 (21... f6 22. gh6 ♖ff7 23. hg7 ♖g7 24. ♕h8 ♔f7 25. ♖g7+–) 22. ♖g2 f6 23. gh6 ♗d3 24. cd3 (24. hg7 ♖g7 25. ♕h7 ♔f7 26. ♖g7 ♘g7 27. ♕g6 ♔e7) ♖c7 25. ♔b1 ♘c6 26. hg7 ♖g7 27. ♕h7 ♔f7 28. ♖g7 ♘g7 29. ♕g6 ♔g8 30. ♕h7= Stefánsson] **♖b7 18. ♗a6 ♖b8 19. ♗c4! N** [19. ♔b1 – 54/182] **♔h8** [19... g6 20. fg6 hg6 21. h4 ♘d4 22. h5 ♗a4 23. hg6 △ ♖h8+–; 19... ♘d4 20. g6 ♘f6 21. gf7 ♔h8 22. ♘d4 ed4 23. ♖d4 ♗a4 24. e5+–] **20. ♕d2!⊕** [△ ♘ac5] **♘a5 21. ♘a5 ♕a5 22. b3 ♖c8** [22... ♗a4 23. ba4 ♕a4 24. ♖hg1 ♖b6 25. ♖g3 ♘c7 26. ♖h3+–→] **23. ♕d5! ♕a7 24. ♔b1 ♕e3 25. ♖he1 ♕g5 26. ♘b6 ♗c6** [26... ♖c5 27. ♕c5! dc5 28. ♘d7+–] **27. ♕a5 ♕d8 28. ♗d5 ♗d5** [28... ♘f6 29. ♕b4] **29. ♖d5 ♖c6 30. ♘c4 ♕h4** [30... ♘f6 31. ♕d8 ♖d8 32. ♘e5!+–] **31. ♕b4 ♕h2 32. ♖c1 ♔g8 33. ♘d6 ♖d6 34. ♖d6 ♘d6 35. ♕d6 h5 36. a4 h4 37. a5 h3 38. a6 ♕f4 39. ♕d5 h2 40. a7 ♕c1 41. ♔c1 h1♕ 42. ♔b2 g5 43. fg6 ♔g7 44. a8♕ ♖a8 45. ♕f7 1 : 0** [Jakovič]

189. **B 45**

RAŠÍK 2405 – J. GDAŃSKI 2480

Budapest (zt) 1993

1. e4 c5 2. ♘f3 e6 3. d4 cd4 4. ♘d4 ♘f6 5. ♘c3 ♘c6 6. ♗f4 d6 7. ♘c6 bc6 8. e5 ♘d5 9. ♘d5 cd5 10. ♗d3 ♗e7 11. ♕g4 de5 N [11... ♔f8 – 26/398] **12. ♕g7!?** [12. ♗e5 ♗f6 13. ♗f6 ♕f6 14. ♗b5 ♔f8 △ g6=] **♗f6 13. ♗b5 ♔e7□ 14. ♗g5 ♗g5 15. ♕g5 ♔d6∞ 16. ♕d2** [16. ♕d8 ♖d8∓] **♕b6 17. c4 ♗b7 18. ♖c1 ♖ac8 19. b4?!** [19. 0–0 ♖hg8∞] **♕d4 20. c5 ♔c7** [20... ♔e7? 21. ♕g5 ♔f8 22. 0–0 △ c6↑] **21. ♕d4 ed4 22. ♖d1 a5!** [22... e5 23. f4 f6 24. 0–0 ♖hf8 25. ♖fe1±] **23. a3?!** [23. ba5!? ♗c6! (23... ♔b8 24. ♖d4 ♖c5 25. a4) 24. ♗c6 (24. ♗e2 ♖b8) ♔c6 25. ♖d4 ♖a8∓] **♖b8** [23... ab4 24. ab4 ♖b8 25. ♖a1!] **24. ♖d4 e5 25. ♖d2** [25. ♖g4? ♗c8–+] **ab4 26. ab4 ♗a8∓ 27. ♗e2 ♖b4 28. 0–0 ♗c6 29. f4⊕ e4 30. ♖fd1 ♖a8 31. ♗h5 f5 32. ♔f2 ♖a3 33. ♔e1 ♗a4 34. ♖d5 ♗d1 35. ♗d1 ♖b2 36. ♖f5 ♖g2 37. ♖g5 ♖h2 38. ♖g1 ♖a1 39. f5 e3 0 : 1** **[J. Gdański]**

190.* **B 45**

CÁMPORA 2550 – ILLESCAS CÓRDOBA 2615

Buenos Aires 1993

1. e4 c5 2. ♘f3 e6 3. d4 cd4 4. ♘d4 ♘f6 5. ♘c3 ♘c6 6. ♘c6 bc6 7. e5 ♘d5 8. ♘d5 [RR 8. ♘e4 ♕c7 9. f4 ♕a5 10. c3 ♗e7 11. ♗d3 ♕b6 12. ♕e2 0–0 N (12... ♗b7 – 56/(198)) 13. c4 f5 14. cd5 fe4 15. ♕e4 ♕b4 16. ♕b4 ♗b4 17. ♔e2 ed5= de la Riva 2365 – F. Braga 2435, Zaragoza 1993] **cd5 9. ♗d3 ♗a6 10. 0–0 ♗d3 11. ♕d3 ♕c7 12. ♖e1** [12. ♗f4?! ♖c8 13. c3 f5∓] **♖c8 13. c3** [13. ♗d2!? △ 13... ♕c2? 14. ♖ac1! ♕d3 15. ♖c8 ♔e7 16. ♗b4 d6 17. ♖ec1 △ ♖1c7#] **g6 N** [13... d6? 14. ♕d5!; 13... ♕b6 – 26/(401)] **14. ♗e3 ♗g7 15. ♗d4 0–0 16. ♕a6 ♖a8 17. ♖ac1 ♖fc8 18. g3 ♕c4?!** [18... ♕c6=] **19. ♕c4 ♖c4** [19... dc4 20. b4±] **20. ♔f1± ♖c6 21. ♔e2 ♗f8 22. ♔d3 ♗c5 23. ♖c2 ♖ac8 24. ♖ec1** [△ c4] **d6! 25. f4 ♔f8 26. b4** [26. c4 ♗d4 27. ♔d4 dc4 28. ♖c4 ♖c4 29. ♖c4 ♖c4 30. ♔c4 d5=] **♗b6 27. a4 de5! 28. fe5 ♖b8!□⊕** [28... ♔e7? 29. a5 ♗d4 30. cd4+–] **29. c4?** [29. a5?! ♗d4 30. cd4 ♖c2 31. ♖c2 ♖b4∓] **♗d4 30. b5 ♗e5!□ 31. bc6 ♖b3! 32. ♔e2** [32. ♖c3? ♗c3! △ 33. c7 ♗e5 34. ♔c2 ♖b2!–+] **d4∓ 33. ♖d1 ♔e7 34. ♖d3 ♖b4 35. g4 h6 36. h4 g5! 37. hg5 hg5 38. c5 ♔d8 39. ♖h3 ♔c7 40. ♖h7 ♔c6 41. ♖f7 ♖a4 42. ♖e7 ♖a3! 43. ♖e6** [⌓ 43. ♖d2∓] **♔d5 44. ♖e5 ♔e5–+ 45. ♔d2 ♖c3 46. ♖a2 ♖c5 47. ♖a7 ♔f4 48. ♔d3 ♖d5 49. ♖a1 ♔g4 50. ♔e4 ♖d8 51. ♖g1 ♔h5 0 : 1** **[Illescas Córdoba]**

191. **** !N **B 47**

ULYBIN 2565 – P. TREGUBOV 2445

Sankt-Peterburg (zt) 1993

1. e4 c5 2. ♘f3 e6 3. d4 cd4 4. ♘d4 ♘c6 5. ♘c3 ♕c7 6. f4 [RR 6. ♗e2 a6 7. 0–0 ♘f6 8. ♔h1 ♘d4 9. ♕d4 ♗c5 *a)* 10. ♗f4!? N ♗d4 (10... d6 11. ♕d3±) 11. ♗c7 ♗c3 12. bc3 ♘e4 13. c4 d5 14. cd5 ♘c3! 15. ♗f3 ♘d5 16. ♗g3 b5 17. a4 b4 18. a5 ♗b7 19. ♖ab1 ♖c8 20. ♖fc1 (△ c4) ♗c6 21. ♗d5 ♗d5?! 22. ♖b4 0–0 23. c4 ♖fd8 24. h4± Velimirović 2510 – Matulović 2460, Aranđelovac 1993; 21... ed5=; 15... ♗d7= Matulović; *b)* 10. ♕d3 h5 11. f4 ♘g4 12. e5 ♘f2 13. ♖f2 ♗f2 14. ♘e4 ♗c5 *b1)* 15. ♕c4!? N b6 16. b4 d5 17. ed6 ♗d6 18. ♗b2! ♗b7! (18... ♕c4?? 19. ♘d6+–; 18... 0–0?? 19. ♕d4+–; 18... f6? 19. ♘d6 ♕d6 20. ♖d1 ♕b8 21. f5!+–→) 19. ♗g7 ♖g8 20. ♘f6 ♔e7 21. ♘g8 ♖g8 22. ♕d4 ♗g2! (22... ♗f4 23. ♕f6 ♔e8 24. ♗h5 ♗d5 25. ♖d1+–; 22... e5 23. fe5 ♗e5 24. ♕e5 ♕e5 25. ♗e5 ♖g2 26. ♗a6! ♗a8 27. h4 ♖e2 28. ♔g1 ♖e5 29. ♗d3+–⊥ Zafirovski) 23. ♔g2 e5 24. ♕e4 ♖g7 25. ♔h1 f5 26. ♕d5 ♕c2 27. fe5 ♕e2 28. ed6 ♔f6 29. d7 ♖d7 30. ♕d7 ♕f3 1/2 : 1/2 Z. Marković 2320 – Zafirovski 2300, Jugoslavija 1992; *b2)* 15. ♗e3! N ♗e3 (15... ♗e7 16. ♘d6! ♗d6 17. ed6 ♕a5 18. ♗f3 ♖b8 19. ♗a7 ♖a8 20. ♗d4 0–0 21. c4! ♖b8 22. c5 b6 23. ♗h5 bc5 24. ♗c3 ♕b5 25. ♕g3 f6 26. ♗g6 1 : 0 Tockij 2405 – Landa 2450, Rossija 1992) 16. ♘d6 ♔f8 17. ♕e3±↑ Tockij; *b3)* 15. ♕c3 – 53/(180)] **a6 7. ♘f3 ♗c5 8. ♗d3 b5 9. ♕e2 ♘d4 10. ♘d4 ♗d4 11. ♗d2 ♗b7 N** [11... b4 – 55/(213)] **12. e5!** [12. 0-0-0 b4 13. ♘b1 (13. ♘a4 ♗c6) a5=] **f5!** [12... d5? 13. ♗b5! ab5 14. ♘b5 ♕b6 15. ♘d4 ♕b2 (15... ♕d4 16. ♕b5+–) 16. ♕b5+–; 12... ♗c3? 13. ♗c3 ♘e7 14. ♗b4±; 12... ♘e7 13. ♘e4±; 12... ♖c8 13. ♕g4±] **13. ♘d1!?** [13. ♕h5 g6 14. ♕g5 ♕c6!∓ ×g2; RR 13. a4 b4 14. ♘d1 ♕c6 15. ♔f1? ♗c5 16. ♗e3 ♘e7 17. ♕f2 ♖c8 18. ♗c5 ♕c5 19. ♘e3 ♕d4 20. ♖d1 ♘d5 21. ♘d5 ♕d5 22. h4 ♖c4! 23. ♖d2 ♖d4 24. ♖h3 0–0 25. b3 ♖c8∓ Tolnai 2495 – József Horváth 2505, Magyarország (ch) 1992; 15. ♗e3] **♕c6!** [13... ♘e7?! 14. ♗e3 ♗b2 15. ♘b2 ♕c3 16. ♕d2 ♕b2 17. 0–0 ♖c8□ (17... 0–0? 18. ♗c5 △ ♖fb1+–) 18. a4±↑] **14. ♗e3□ ♕g2 15. ♕g2 ♗g2 16. ♖g1 ♗e3 17. ♘e3 ♗c6 18. ♖g7 ♘e7!∓** [×f4] **19. ♖g1□** [19. 0-0-0 ♘g6–+] **♘g6 20. ♖f1 ♔e7?!** [20... ♔f7! 21. 0-0-0 ♖hd8 (△ d6) 22. ♗e2 ♔e7! △ d6∓] **21. 0-0-0 ♖hd8** [21... ♖ad8 22. a4⇆] **22. c3!** [22... d6 *a)* 23. ed6?! ♖d6 24. ♘c2 ♖ad8 25. ♗e2 (25. ♘d4? ♖d4 26. cd4 ♖d4∓) ♗e4∓; *b)* 23. ♗f5!? ef5 (23... de5?! 24. ♗g6 △ 24... ef4? 25. ♗h5! fe3 26. ♖f7+–) 24. ♘f5 *b1)* 24... ♔f8 25. ♘d6 ♗g2 (25... ♖a7? 26. e6 ♔e7 27. ♘f5 ♔e8 28. ♘d4 △ f5+–; 25... ♗d7 26. e6±) 26. ♖f2 ♗h3 27. ♖d3±; *b2)* 24... ♔d7 25. ♖d6 ♔c7 26. ♖d8 ♖d8 27. ♘d4! △ e6, f5±; 22. c4?! d6] **1/2 : 1/2**

[P. Tregubov]

192. **B 48**

MA. TSEITLIN 2460 – FAERMAN

Israel 1993

1. e4 c5 2. ♘f3 e6 3. ♘c3 a6 4. d4 cd4 5. ♘d4 ♕c7 6. ♗d3 ♘c6 7. ♗e3 ♘f6 8. 0–0 ♗e7 9. f4 ♗c5 10. ♘f5 [10. ♗e2?! ♕b6 11. ♘a4 ♗d4! 12. ♘b6 ♗e3 13. ♔h1 ♗b6∓] **♘e7!? N** [10... ♗e3 – 6/472] **11. ♘g7! ♔f8 12. ♗c5 ♕c5 13. ♔h1 ♔g7 14. e5 ♘e8!?** [14... ♘fd5? 15. ♘e4 ♕c7□ 16. f5! ♘f5 (16... ef5 17. ♘d6 ♘e3 18. ♕h5 ♘g6 19. ♕g5+–) 17. ♖f5! ef5 18. ♘d6 h5□ (18... ♘e7 19. ♕h5 ♘g6 20. ♕g5 ♖f8 21. ♕f6 ♔g8 22. ♘f5 ♕e5 23. ♘h6#) 19. ♕f3 ♘e7 20. ♗f5!+–→] **15. ♘e4 ♕c7□ 16. ♕h5 ♘g6□ 17. ♖f3! d5** [17... ♔g8 18. ♕h6 ♕d8 (18... f5 19. ef6 d5 20. ♖g3! de4 21. ♗e4 ♘f6 22. ♗g6+–) 19. ♘g5 f5! 20. ef6 ♕f6 21. ♖e1!±→; 17... ♕d8 18. ♖h3 ♔g8 (18... h6 19. ♖g3→) 19. ♘g5 ♘g7 20. ♕h6 ♘f5 21. ♗f5 ef5 22. ♘h7±] **18. ♘g5 ♔g8?!** [18... h6 19. ♘f7 ♕f7 20. ♖g3+–; 18... f6 19. ♘h7 f5 (19... ♕f7 20. ♖g3 ♖h7 21. ♕g6! ♕g6 22. ♗g6±) 20. ♖h3 ♕f7

21. g4!±; 18... f5!?] **19. ♕h6! ♘g7** [19... f6? 20. ♗g6+−; 19... f5!? 20. g4! *a)* 20... fg4 21. ♗g6! hg6 22. ♕g6 ♘g7 23. ♖g3 ♕e7□ 24. ♖g4 ♕e8 25. ♕f6 ♕f8□ (25... ♕h5 26. ♖h4+−; 25... ♖h2 26. ♔h2 ♕h5 27. ♘h3 ♕g4 28. ♖g1+−) 26. ♖ag1! ♕f6 27. ef6 ♘f5 28. ♘f3! ♔f7 29. ♖g6! △ ♘e5+−; *b)* 20... ♕g7 21. ♕h5 h6 (21... fg4 22. ♕g4 ♘c7 23. ♖g1±→) 22. ♘e6 ♗e6 23. gf5±→] **20. ♖h3!+− ♗d7⊕** [20... ♘f4 21. ♘h7 ♘h3 22. ♘f6] **21. ♘h7 ♗e8 22. ♗g6 fg6 23. ♘f6 1 : 0**
[Judasin, Ma. Tseitlin]

193. **B 53**

KAMSKY 2655 – LAUTIER 2645
Dortmund 1993

1. e4 c5 2. ♘f3 d6 3. d4 cd4 4. ♕d4 a6 5. ♗g5 ♘c6 6. ♕d2 ♘f6!? N [6... h6 – 35/(251)] **7. ♗d3 e6 8. c4!? h6 9. ♗f4 d5! 10. ed5 ed5 11. 0–0 ♗e7 12. ♘c3 ♗g4?** [12... ♗e6!? 13. cd5 ♘d5 14. ♗e4 ♘f4 15. ♕f4 0–0 16. ♗c6 bc6 17. ♘d4 ♗d7 18. ♖ad1 ♕b6 19. b3±; 12... dc4!? 13. ♗c4 ♕d2 14. ♘d2 0–0 15. ♘de4 ♘e4 16. ♘e4 ♗f5 17. ♘d6 ♗d6 18. ♗d6 ♖fd8±] **13. cd5 ♗f3?!** [13... ♘d5!? 14. ♗e4 ♘f4 15. ♕f4 ♗e6 16. ♖ad1 ♕b8 17. ♕b8 ♖b8 18. ♗c6 bc6 19. b3 △ ♘d4± ×c6] **14. dc6** [14. d6!? ♗d6 15. ♕e3 ♕e7 16. ♗d6 ♕e3 17. fe3 ♗h5⇆] **♗c6 15. ♖ad1± 0–0**

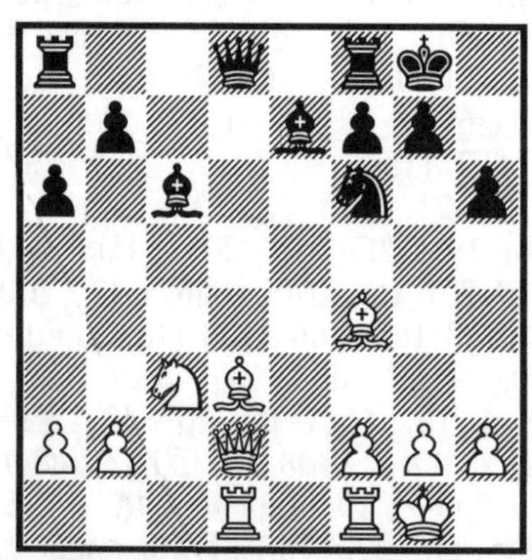

16. ♗h6! gh6 17. ♕h6 ♖e8 [17... ♕b6!? 18. ♖fe1 ♕f2 19. ♔f2 ♘g4 20. ♔f1 ♘h6 21. ♖e7±] **18. ♗c4!+−** [18. ♗f5 ♕a5! △ 19. ♕g5 ♔f8 20. ♖d3 ♘g8∓] **♗d7 19. ♖d4! ♗f8 20. ♕g6 ♗g7 21. ♕f7 ♔h8 22. ♖h4 ♘h7 23. ♖h7! ♔h7 24. ♕h5 ♗h6 25. ♗d3 ♔g8 26. ♕h6 1 : 0**
[Kamsky]

194.* **B 54**

ŠIROV 2670 – V. SALOV 2660
Linares 1993

1. e4 c5 2. ♘f3 ♘c6 [RR 2... d6 3. d4 cd4 4. ♘d4 ♘f6 5. f3 e5 6. ♘b3 ♗e7 7. c4 0–0 8. ♘c3 a5!? N (8... ♗e6) 9. ♗e3 a4 10. ♘d2 ♕a5 11. a3 ♗d7 12. ♗e2 ♘a6 13. 0–0 ♘c5 14. ♔h1 ♖fc8∞ P. Wolff 2590 – Browne 2515, USA (ch) 1992] **3. d4 cd4 4. ♘d4 e6 5. ♘c3 d6 6. g4 a6 7. ♗e3 ♘ge7 8. ♘b3 b5 N** [8... ♘g6 – 53/184] **9. ♕e2 ♘a5!** [9... ♘e5 10. ♘d2! △ f4] **10. 0-0-0 ♘c4 11. f4 ♕c7 12. ♖d4** [12. ♔b1!? △ ♗c1] **♗b7 13. ♖c4!? bc4 14. ♕c4 ♕c4 15. ♗c4 ♘c6!** [15... d5 16. ♘a5! dc4 (16... 0-0-0 17. ♘b7 ♔b7 18. ed5 ♘d5 19. ♘d5 ed5 20. ♖d1$\overline{\infty}$) 17. ♘b7 ♘c6 18. ♖d1 ♖b8 19. ♘d6 ♗d6 20. ♖d6 ♖c8 21. ♘a4$\overline{\infty}$] **16. f5!□ ♘e5 17. ♘a5?** [17. ♗e2□ ♗e7 18. ♘a5 ♗c8! 19. ♘a4 ♗d8 20. ♘b6 ♗b6 21. ♗b6 h5!∓] **♘c4 18. ♘c4 ♖c8 19. ♘a5 ♖c3! 20. bc3 ♗e4 21. ♖f1** [21. ♖e1 ef5−+] **h5! 22. fe6 fe6 23. g5 ♗e7 24. c4 ♖f8! 25. ♖f8 ♗f8 26. ♔d2** [⌓ 26. c5∓] **♔d7!−+ 27. ♘b3 e5 28. ♘c1 ♔e6 29. ♘e2 h4 30. ♘c3 ♗c6 31. ♔d3 ♗e7 32. ♘d5 ♗d5 33. cd5 ♔d5 34. c4 ♔e6 35. ♔e4 h3 36. a4 ♗d8!** [36... g6? 37. a5!] **37. g6 ♗h4** [△ ♗g3] **38. ♗g1 ♗e1 39. ♔f3 ♔f5 40. ♔e2 ♗b4 0 : 1**
[V. Salov]

195. !N** **B 56**

CH. BAUER 2505 – DORFMAN 2580
France 1993

1. e4 c5 2. ♘f3 d6 3. d4 cd4 4. ♘d4 ♘f6 5. ♘c3 ♘c6 6. ♗e3 [RR 6. f4 e5 7. ♘c6 N (7. ♘f3 – 44/228, 229) bc6 8. fe5 ♘g4 9. ♗e2 ♘e5 10. 0–0 ♗e7 11. ♔h1 0–0

12. ♗f4 ♗e6 13. ♕d2 ♖e8 14. ♖ad1 ♗f8 15. b3 ♕c7 16. ♘a4 ♖ad8 17. ♘b2 f6 1/2 : 1/2 V. Spasov 2535 – V. Nevedničij 2455, Debrecen 1992] **♘g4** [RR 6... e5 7. ♘f3 ♗e7 8. ♗c4 ♗e6 9. ♗b3 0–0 10. 0–0 ♘a5 11. ♕e2 ♕c8!? N (11... a6 – 53/(185)) *a)* 12. ♘d2?! ♕c6∓; *b)* 12. ♖ad1 *b1)* 12... ♘c4?! 13. ♗c1± Vlad 2405 – V. Nevedničij 2495, Bucureşti 1993; *b2)* 12... ♗c4 13. ♗c4 ♕c4 14. ♕d2!? (14. ♕e1?! ♕c6 ×♖f1) ♘c6!? (14... ♖fc8 15. ♗g5 ♕c6 16. ♗f6 ♘c4 17. ♗e7 ♘d2 18. ♖d2±) 15. b3 ♕b4∞; *b3)* 12... ♘b3! 13. ab3 h6=; *c)* 12. ♖fd1! (V. Nevedničij) *c1)* 12... ♗g4?! 13. ♘d5! (13. h3 ♗h5 △ 14. g4? ♘g4) ♘d5 14. ♗d5± △ 14... ♗f3 15. ♕f3 ♕c2 16. ♖ac1 ♕b2 17. ♖c7 ♗f6□ (17... ♖ae8? 18. ♗g5! ♗g5 19. ♖f7) 18. g4→ ×♘a5, f7; *c2)* 12... ♘b3 13. ab3 a6 14. ♗g5±; *c3)* 12... ♘g4 13. ♘d5±; *c4)* 12... ♗c4 13. ♗c4 (13. ♕e1 b5!?) *c41)* 13... ♘c4 14. ♗c1 ♕c6 15. b3 ♘a5 (15... ♘a3 16. ♗b2; 15... ♘b6 16. ♗b2 △ a4-a5 ×d5) 16. ♗b2 b5!? 17. ♕b5 ♕b5 18. ♘b5 ♘e4 19. ♘c7 △ ♘d5, c4±; *c42)* 13... ♕c4 14. ♕e1 ♕c6! (14... ♖fc8 15. ♗g5±; 14... h6 15. b3! ♕c6 16. ♘d5 ♘d5 17. ♖d5±) 15. b3! b6!? 16. ♗g5⩲; *c5)* 12... ♘c4!? 13. ♗c1 (△ ♘g5) h6 14. ♘h4!?∞ Vlad] **7. ♗b5 ♘e3 8. fe3 ♗d7 9. ♗c6 bc6 10. 0–0 e5! N ∓** [10... ♕b6 – 42/218] **11. ♕f3** [11. ♘f5 ♗e6 △ g6∓] **f6 12. ♘de2 ♗e7 13. ♘a4 ♕a5 14. b3 ♗e6 15. ♘g3** [15. c4? ♗c4∓] **g6 16. ♖ac1 d5!** [16... 0–0 17. c4] **17. ed5 ♕d5!** [17... cd5 18. c4 0–0 19. cd5 ♗d5 20. ♕g4∞] **18. ♕e2** [18. ♘e4 f5∓] **0–0 19. c4 ♕a5 20. ♕f3 ♖ac8** [20... ♕c7 21. ♘e4] **21. ♖fd1 f5 22. ♘e2 ♗a3! 23. ♖c2** [23. ♖b1 ♗c4 24. bc4 ♕a4 25. ♖d7 ♖fd8∓] **♖fd8∓ 24. ♘ec3 ♖d1 25. ♕d1 ♖d8 26. ♖d2 ♖d2 27. ♕d2 ♔f7 28. ♔f2 ♔e8 29. g3 ♕d8 30. ♕e2 h5 31. ♘d1** [⌓ 31. c5 ♕a5 32. ♘b1 ♗c5 33. ♕c2 ♗e7 34. ♕c6 ♔f7∓] **♗b4 32. ♘db2 e4 33. ♘d1 ♕d2 34. ♕d2 ♗d2 35. ♔e2** [35. ♘ac3 ♔e7 36. ♔e2 ♗c1 37. ♘b1 g5∓] **♗b4 36. ♘f2 g5!** [36... ♔e7 37. ♘h3] **37. ♘b2** [37. ♘h3 ♗e7 △ f4] **♔e7 38. ♘bd1 ♔f6 39. ♘b2 ♔g6⊕** [39... ♔e5? 40. ♘bd3] **40. ♘a4 ♔f6 41. ♘b2 ♗d6 42. ♘bd1 h4–+ 43. ♘h1** [43. gh4 g4; 43. ♘c3 ♔g6 44. ♘h1 ♗e5] **♗f7 44. ♘df2 ♗h5 0 : 1 [Dorfman]**

196.* **B 57**

IVANČUK 2710 – KRAMNIK 2685

Linares 1993

1. e4 c5 2. ♘f3 ♘c6 3. d4 cd4 4. ♘d4 ♘f6 5. ♘c3 d6 6. ♗c4 ♕b6 7. ♘b3 [RR 7. ♘de2 e6 8. 0–0 ♗e7 9. a3 0–0 10. ♗a2 ♘e5 11. ♔h1!? N (11. h3 – 9/351) ♘ed7!? (11... ♕a6?! 12. f4 ♘c4 13. ♕d3±; 11... ♗d7?! 12. f4 ♘eg4 13. ♕d4±) 12. ♘g3 ♕c6 13. f4 ♘c5 14. e5 (14. ♕f3!? ♗d7 15. f5 ♔h8 16. ♗g5 ♖ae8 17. ♖ae1 ♘a4!) de5 15. fe5 ♘fe4 *a)* 16. ♕g4?! (1/2 : 1/2 A. Sokolov 2555 – Ruban 2595, Sankt-Peterburg (zt) 1993) ♘g3 (16... ♘c3? 17. ♗h6) 17. ♕g3 ♘e4 18. ♘e4 (18. ♕g4 ♘c3 19. ♗h6 g6 20. ♗f8 ♗f8 21. ♕f4 ♕c7 22. bc3 b6=∞) ♕e4 19. ♗h6 ♕g6=; *b)* 16. ♘ce4 ♘e4 17. ♘h5 f5 18. ef6 ♘f6 19. ♘g3±; 10... a6!? △ ♕c7, b5, ♘a5-c4 Ruban] **e6 8. ♗f4 ♘e5 9. ♗e2 N** [9. ♗b5] **a6** [9... ♗e7?! 10. ♗e3 ♕c7 11. ♘b5! ♕b8 12. f4 ♘g6 13. ♘c3±] **10. ♗g3** [10. 0–0 ♗e7 11. ♗e3 ♕c7=] **h5!** [10... ♕c7 11. f4 ♘c4 12. e5! de5 (12... ♘b2? 13. ♕d4) 13. fe5 ♘e5 14. ♕d4 ♘fd7 15. 0-0-0±↑] **11. h3** [11. f4? ♘eg4; 11. f3 ♕c7 12. ♕d4 h4 13. ♗f2 b5∞ △ 14. a4?! ♘c6! 15. ♕d2 b4 16. ♘d1 d5↑] **♕c7 12. f4** [12. a4 ♗d7 13. ♕d4 ♖c8=; 12. ♕d4 b5 13. a4 ♘c6 14. ♕e3 ♘b4 15. ♗d3 ba4 16. ♖a4 ♖b8=] **♘c4= 13. ♗c4** [13. e5? de5 14. fe5 ♘e5 △ 15. ♕d4? ♘f3–+; 13. ♕d4 b5 14. e5 (14. a4 e5!) de5 15. fe5 ♗b7 16. 0–0 ♖d8 17. ♕f2 ♘e4 18. ♘e4 ♗e4∓] **♕c4 14. ♕f3 h4! 15. ♗h2** [15. ♗f2 b5! 16. e5 (16. 0-0-0 ♕c7∓) ♘d5 17. ♘d5 ♕d5 18. ♕d5 ed5 19. 0-0-0 (19. ed6 ♗d6 ×f4) de5 20. fe5 ♗f5!∓] **♗d7 16. 0-0-0 ♖c8 17. ♖he1 b5!** [17... ♗e7=] **18. ♕f2?** [18. a3] **♕c7!∓ 19. e5** [19. a3 a5] **b4 20. ♖d3!?** [20. ef6 bc3 21. f5 cb2 22. ♔b1 e5 23. fg7 ♗g7∓] **de5 21. fe5 bc3 22. ♖c3** [22. ef6 ♕h2 23. ♖d7!? ♕g3! 24. ♕g3 hg3 25. ♖a7 cb2 26. ♔b2 gf6 27. ♖a6 f5∓]

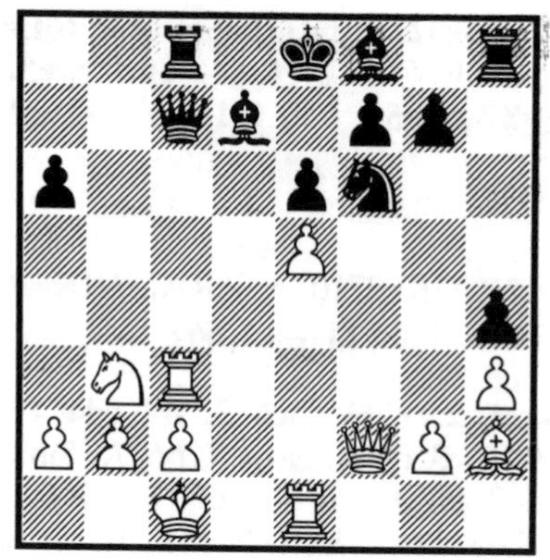

22... ♕c3 [⌓ 22... ♕b8 23. ♖c8 ♗c8 24. ♖f1! ♖h7! 25. ♕f4 ♗e7!? 26. ef6 ♕f4 27. ♗f4 gf6∓ Ivančuk] **23. bc3 ♗a3 24. ♔d2?⊕** [24. ♔b1! ♘d5 25. ♗f4!∓ Anand] **♘d5 25. ♖e4 ♖c3 26. ♖g4 0–0! 27. ♕h4 ♖fc8 28. ♘d4 ♗b4 29. ♔e2 ♗b5!–+ 30. ♘b5** [30. ♔f2 ♖c2! 31. ♘c2 ♖c2 32. ♔f3 (32. ♔g1 ♖c1 33. ♔f2 ♗e1) ♗e2! 33. ♔e4 ♖c4#] **♖c2 31. ♔f3 ab5 32. ♖b4 ♘b4 33. ♕b4 ♖8c3 0 : 1 [Kramnik]**

197.* **B 57**

RUBLEVSKIJ 2515 – S. KISELËV 2510
Sankt-Peterburg (zt) 1993

1. e4 c5 2. ♘f3 ♘c6 3. d4 cd4 4. ♘d4 ♘f6 5. ♘c3 d6 6. ♗c4 ♕b6 7. ♘b3 e6 8. 0–0 ♗e7 9. ♗g5 0–0 10. ♔h1 N [10. ♗f6 ♗f6 11. ♕d6 ♖d8 12. ♕g3 ♗e5 N (12... ♕b4 – 45/(229)) 13. ♕h3 ♗d7 (13... a5) 14. ♖ad1 (14. ♔h1!?) a5 15. a4 ♘b4 16. ♖d2 ♗f4 17. ♖dd1 ♘c2 18. ♗b5 ♗b5 19. ♘b5 ♗e5∞ Rublevskij 2515 – A. Gol'din 2555, Sankt-Peterburg (zt) 1993] **♖d8** [10... a6 11. ♗d3 (11. ♕e2 ♕c7 12. f4 h6 13. ♗h4 ♘e4 14. ♗e7 ♘c3 15. ♗d6 ♕d6 16. bc3 b5∓) ♕c7 12. ♕e2 b5 13. f4 b4 14. ♘d1 a5 15. ♘e3 ♗b7∞] **11. ♗d3** [11. ♕e1 h6 12. ♗h4 (12. ♗e3 ♕c7 △ d5) ♘e5 13. ♗d3 ♘g6 14. ♗g3 e5 △ ♗e6=; 11. ♕e2!? ♘e4?! 12. ♗e7 ♘e7 13. ♕e4 d5 14. ♗d5 ♘d5 15. ♘d5 ♖d5 (15... ed5 16. ♕d4±) 16. ♖fd1 ♕d6 (16... ♗d7 17. ♖d5 ed5 18. ♕d5 ♗c6 19. ♕d4!±) 17. ♖d5±; 11... a6!?; 11... ♗d7!?] **d5 12. ed5 ♘d5 13. ♘d5** [13. ♗e7 ♘ce7 △ ♗d7-c6] **♖d5 14. ♗e7 ♘e7 15. ♕g4?!** [15. ♕f3 ♗d7 16. ♗e4 ♖g5 17. h4 (17. ♗b7? ♖b8 18. ♗e4 f5) ♖b5 18. ♖ad1 (18. a4 ♖b4 19. a5 ♕b5 ×h4) ♗e8∞] **♗d7!∓ 16. ♕h3** [16. ♗h7? ♔h7 17. ♕h4 ♔g6! 18. ♕e7 ♖h8 △ 19... ♖dh5 20. h3 ♗c6 21. ♔g1 ♖h3! 22. gh3 ♖h3–+→] **g6** [16... h6 17. c4 ♖e5 18. ♕h4! (18. c5?! ♕b4□∞) ♘c6 (18... ♘f5 19. ♕f4± ×♖e5) 19. ♖ad1±] **17. ♗e4 ♖h5 18. ♕g3 ♗c6 19. ♗c6 ♕c6 20. c3 ♖d8 21. ♖ae1 ♖hd5 22. ♘d4 ♕b6 23. b3 ♕a6!** [×a2, ♖f1] **24. ♕h4 ♘c6?** [24... ♘f5! 25. ♘f5 ef5∓ ⇔d] **25. ♘f3! ♖h5 26. ♕f4 ♖f5 27. ♕h6 ♖h5⊕ 28. ♕f4 ♖f5 29. ♕h6 ♕a5 30. b4 ♖h5 31. ♕f4 ♖f5** [31... ♕a2 32. g4! ♖hd5 33. ♘g5 ♖5d7 34. ♘e4∞] **32. ♕h6 ♖h5 33. ♕f4 ♖f5 34. ♕h6 ♖h5 1/2 : 1/2 [S. Kiselëv, Gagarin]**

198.* **B 58**

SMIRIN 2555 – LERNER 2530
Moskva (open) 1992

1. e4 c5 2. ♘f3 d6 3. d4 cd4 4. ♘d4 ♘f6 5. ♘c3 ♘c6 6. ♗e2 e5 7. ♘f3 h6 8. 0–0 ♗e7 9. ♖e1 0–0 10. h3 ♗e6 11. ♗f1 ♘b8 12. a4 ♘bd7 13. a5 a6 14. b3 N [14. ♘d5 – 56/207, 208] **♖c8 15. ♗b2 ♖e8 16. ♘d5 ♘d5 17. ed5 ♗f5 18. c4 e4 19. ♘d2** [19. ♘d4?! ♗g6 △ ♘e5 ×d3] **♗f6** [19... ♗g5 20. b4 e3 21. ♘f3 ♗f6 22. ♗f6 ef2 23. ♔f2 ♕f6 24. ♕d4 ♘e5∞ Smirin 2590 – A. Greenfeld 2560, Israel 1993] **20. ♕c1 ♗g6** [20... ♘c5 21. b4 ♘d3 22. ♗d3 ♗b2 23. ♕b2 ed3 24. ♕d4±; 20... ♗g5 21. ♕c3 (21. ♗d4!? ♘e5 22. ♗e3) ♗f6=] **21. ♗f6 ♕f6 22. b4 ♕h4 23. ♕c3 f5 24. c5!? dc5 25. b5 ♖a8!?** [25... ab5 26. ♗b5 ♖ed8 27. a6! (27. ♘c4 ♕f6) ba6 28. ♖a6 ♘f6 29. d6$\overline{\overline{\infty}}$] **26. ba6 ba6 27. d6 ♗f7** [27... ♕f6 28. ♕f6! ♘f6 29. ♘c4] **28. ♖ab1 ♖a7 29. ♖b2** [29. ♗c4!?] **♔h7! 30. ♗c4 ♗c4?!** [30... ♘e5 31. ♗e2! (31. ♗f7 ♖f7 △ 32. ♕c5? ♘d3) ♘d7=] **31. ♘c4 f4?** [31... ♕f6 32. ♕f6 ♘f6 33. ♖eb1±] **32. ♖e4! ♖e4 33. ♕c2 f3** [33... ♘f6 34. ♘d2] **34. gf3 ♕h3 35. ♕e4 ♔g8 36. ♕d5 ♔h7 37. ♕e4 ♔g8 38. ♘e3! ♕h5 39. f4! ♕h4**

[39... ♕f7 40. ♘d5] **40. ♖b7 ♖b7 41. ♕b7+− ♕d8 42. ♕a6 ♘f6 43. ♕c4 ♔h8 44. ♕c5 ♕e8 45. ♔f1 ♕a8 46. ♔g1 ♕f3** [46... ♕e8 47. f5] **47. a6 ♘e4 48. ♕c8 ♔h7 49. ♕c2 g6 50. a7 ♘g3 51. fg3**
1 : 0 **[Smirin]**

199. **B 59**

LJUBOJEVIĆ 2605 – ŠIROV 2670

Linares 1993

1. e4 c5 2. ♘f3 d6 3. d4 cd4 4. ♘d4 ♘f6 5. ♘c3 ♘c6 6. ♗e2 e5 7. ♘b3 ♗e7 8. ♗g5 0–0 N [8... ♘e4] **9. ♗f6 ♗f6 10. ♘d5 ♗g5 11. a4 ♘e7 12. ♗c4 ♔h8!** [△ 13... ♗e6, 13... f5] **13. ♘e7 ♕e7 14. ♗d5 f5 15. ef5!** [15. 0–0 fe4 16. ♗e4 ♗e6 17. ♗d5 ♖ac8! 18. c3 ♕f7∓ ×♘b3] **♗f5 16. 0–0 e4!? 17. ♖e1** [17. ♘d4 ♗g6!? (17... e3 18. ♘f5 ♖f5 19. fe3=) 18. ♘e6 ♖f5 19. ♖e1!∞] **e3 18. fe3 ♗e3 19. ♔h1 ♕e5!?** [19... ♖ae8 20. ♘d4 ♗c8 21. ♘f3!∞] **20. ♗b7 ♖ab8!** [20... ♖ae8?! 21. c3!] **21. ♗f3!** [21. ♕d5?! ♗c2 22. ♕e5 de5 23. ♖e3 ♖b7 24. ♘c5 ♖b2 25. ♖e5 h6! 26. ♖e2 ♗b1! 27. ♖e1 ♗g6∓; 25... ♗g6∓] **♕f4! 22. a5!?** [22. g3?! ♕h6→; 22. ♕e2 ♖be8→] **♕h6 23. ♖e2! ♗f4 24. g4?** [24. ♕g1 ♗c2 25. ♖c2 ♖b3 26. a6!∓] **♗c8 25. ♖g2** [25. ♘d4 ♖b2∓] **♗e5 26. ♖a4** [⌓ 26. ♘d2 ♖b2 27. ♘c4 ♖b4 28. ♘e5 de5∓] **♕e3 27. ♘d2** [27. ♗d5 ♗a6 28. ♘d2 (28. ♖e4 ♕h3−+) ♖b2−+] **♖b2 28. ♖e4 ♕c3 29. ♖c4 ♕a5−+ 30. ♘b3 ♕a2 31. ♘d2 ♗e6 32. ♖c7 ♕a5 33. ♖b7 ♖a2 34. ♘b3 ♕c3⊕ 0 : 1** **[Širov]**

200. !N **B 65**

KAMSKY 2655 – ANAND 2710

Linares 1993

1. e4 c5 2. ♘f3 d6 3. d4 cd4 4. ♘d4 ♘f6 5. ♘c3 ♘c6 6. ♗g5 e6 7. ♕d2 ♗e7 8. 0-0-0 0–0 9. f4 ♘d4 10. ♕d4 ♕a5 11. ♗c4 ♗d7 12. e5 de5 13. fe5 ♗c6 14. ♗d2 ♘d7 15. ♘d5 ♕d8 16. ♘e7 ♕e7 17. ♖he1 ♖fd8 18. ♕g4 ♘f8 19. ♗f1 ♕c5! N [19... ♕c7 – 56/214] **20. ♗c3 ♘g6** [20... ♖d5!?] **21. ♕g5 ♖d5 22. ♖d5 ♗d5 23. a3 ♖c8** [23... a6!] **24. ♕e3 ♕c6 25. g3** [25. ♕a7 ♗g2 26. ♗g2 ♕g2∓; 26. ♗d3!∞] **a6 26. ♗e2 ♘e7 27. ♕g5 ♕c7 28. ♗d3 h6 29. ♕h4 b5 30. ♗b4 ♘f5 31. ♕f4 ♗c4! 32. ♗c4** [32. ♗f5 ef5 33. ♕f5 ♗e6 34. ♕f2 a5=] **bc4 33. ♖f1 ♕a7 34. ♗d2 ♕c7 35. ♗c3 ♕c5 36. g4 ♕e3 37. ♗d2 ♕f4 38. ♖f4 ♘e7 39. ♖d4 ♘d5 40. h4?! ♖c6 41. ♔b1 ♔h7** [△ 42... ♔g6 43. h5 ♔h7⇆] **42. h5?×》 f6 43. ♖e4 fe5 44. ♖e5 ♘f6 45. g5 hg5 46. ♗g5** [46. ♖g5 ♘e4∓] **♘h5 47. b3 ♘f6 48. bc4 ♘d7 49. ♖a5 ♔g6 50. ♗e3 ♔f6 51. c5 e5!∓** [×♖a5] **52. ♖a4 ♔f5 53. ♖b4 g5 54. a4** [54. ♖b6 ♘b6 55. cb6 ♖c8 56. c4 ♔e6−+] **g4 55. a5** [△ ♖b6] **♖c8! 56. ♔c1** [56. ♖b6 ♘b6! 57. ab6 ♔e6 58. c6 ♔d6 59. b7 ♖g8 60. ♗a7 ♔c7−+] **♘f6 57. ♖b7 ♘d5 58. ♗f2 ♔e4 59. ♖b3 ♖f8 60. ♗h4 ♖f3 61. c6?** [61. ♖b7∓] **♖b3 62. cb3 ♔f3−+ 63. ♗d8 e4** [63... g3 64. c7 ♘c7 65. ♗c7 g2 (65... e4 66. ♔d2) 66. ♗b6 ♔e2 67. ♔c2 e4 68. ♗g1 ♔f1 69. ♗e3 g1♕] **64. ♗b6** [64. c7 ♘c7 65. ♗c7 e3 66. ♔d1 ♔f2 67. ♗b6 g3 68. ♔c2 ♔e2!] **e3 65. c7 ♘c7 66. ♗c7 g3 67. ♔d1 g2 68. ♗h2 ♔f2 0 : 1** **[Anand]**

201.* !N **B 66**

YANG XIAN 2415 –
D. JOHANSEN 2500

Jakarta (zt) 1993

1. e4 c5 2. ♘f3 ♘c6 3. d4 cd4 4. ♘d4 ♘f6 5. ♘c3 d6 6. ♗g5 e6 7. ♕d2 a6 8. 0-0-0 h6 9. ♗f4 ♗d7 10. ♘c6 ♗c6 11. f3 d5 12. ♕e1 ♗b4 13. a3 ♗a5 14. e5 ♗c7 15. ♗d2 ♘d7 16. f4 ♘c5 17. ♗e3 ♕e7 18. ♘e2?! N [18. ♕f2! N ♘a4 19. ♘a4 ♗a4 20. ♗d3 0-0-0 21. ♗c5! ♕d7 22. ♗d4± △ g4, f5 Canfell 2300 – I. Rogers 2575, Queensland 1993; 18... b6!?±; 18. ♔b1 – 51/(195)] **♗b5!= 19. ♘d4 ♗f1 20. ♖f1 ♘e4 21. ♕e2 0–0!** [21... 0-0-0±] **22. ♕g4 ♔h7 23. ♕h3 ♖ac8 24. g4 ♗b6 25. ♔b1?!** [25. f5!? ef5 26. ♖f5∞] **♖c4 26. g5 ♖fc8 27. gh6 g6 28. f5!?** [28. ♕g2∓] **ef5 29. ♘f5! ♕e6! 30. ♗b6 ♘c3!! 31. bc3** [31. ♔a1 ♘d1−+] **♕b6 32. ♔c1** [32. ♔a1 ♖c3 33. ♖d3 ♖c2 (33... ♕a5 34.

♘d4) 34. ♖b3 (34. ♖b1 ♕f2) ♖c1 (34... ♕e6 35. ♕g3!±) 35. ♖c1 ♖c1 36. ♔b2 ♕g1 37. ♕d3 ♖c7! 38. ♘d4 ♕h2 39. ♔b1 ♕e5∓] **♖c3 33. ♘e3 ♖8c7!** [△ 34... d4, 34... ♕b3] **34. ♖f3** [34. e6□ fe6 35. ♖f3∓] **d4 35. e6 f5!−+ 36. ♕h4** [36. e7 de3] **♕b3! 37. ♖d2 de3 38. ♖e3 ♖c2 39. ♔d1 ♖d2 40. ♔d2 ♖c2** **0 : 1**
[D. Johansen, I. Rogers]

202.* !N** **B 66**

DE LA VILLA GARCÍA 2440 – HUZMAN 2510

San Sebastian 1993

1. e4 c5 2. ♘f3 d6 3. d4 cd4 4. ♘d4 ♘f6 5. ♘c3 ♘c6 6. ♗g5 e6 7. ♕d2 a6 8. 0-0-0 h6 9. ♗f4 ♗d7 10. ♘c6 ♗c6 11. f3 d5 12. ♕e1 ♗b4 13. a3 ♗a5 14. ♗d2 d4 [RR 14... ♕e7 15. e5 ♘d7 16. ♔b1 ♗b6 17. f4 h5 18. h4 N (18. ♗e3 – 56/(218); 18. g3 – 56/218) ♗c5 19. ♖h3 b5 20. ♘a2 ♗b7 21. ♘c1 g6 22. ♘d3± Mališauskas 2570 – Lanka 2545, Vilnius (zt) 1993; 14... ♖c8 15. ♕g3 N (15. ♔b1 – 56/220) ♗c7 16. e5 ♘d7 17. f4 0–0 18. ♗d3 ♘c5 19. ♗e3 ♘d3 20. ♖d3 f6 21. ♖e1 1/2 : 1/2 Adams 2630 – Širov 2670, München 1993] **15. e5 ♕c7 16. ♘b1! N** [16. ef6 dc3 17. ♗c3 ♕f4 N (17... ♗c3 – 55/(226)) 18. ♗d2 ♗d2 19. ♕d2 ♕d2 20. ♖d2 gf6= de la Villa García 2475 – Kramnik 2625, Pamplona 1992/93] **♗a4** [16... ♗d2 17. ♘d2! (17. ♖d2 ♘d7 18. f4 ♘c5 △ 19. ♖d4? ♗g2!) ♘d7 (17... ♘d5 18. ♘c4) 18. ♘c4 0–0 19. ♖d4±]

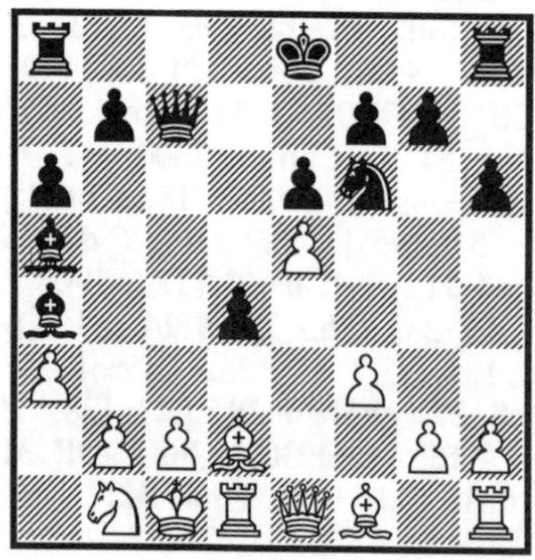

17. b3!! [17. ♗d3 ♗d2! (17... ♖c8 18. b3!+−) 18. ♖d2 (18. ♘d2 ♗c2−+) ♘d7=] **♗b3** [17... ♖c8 18. ♗d3 ♗b3 (18... ♗d2 19. ♖d2+−) 19. ♔b2 ♗d2 20. ♖d2+−] **18. ♗d3 ♗d2 19. ♔d2 ♗c2!** [19... ♕a5 20. ♔c1+−] **20. ♗c2** [20. ♖c1!? ♘d5! (20... ♘d7 21. ♖c2 ♕e5 22. ♕e5 ♘e5 23. ♖e1+−) 21. ♖c2 (21. ♗c2? ♕a5 22. ♔e2 d3! 23. ♔d3 ♕b5 24. ♔d2 ♖d8−+) ♕a5! 22. ♔c1 (22. ♔e2 ♘f4; 22. ♔d1 ♕b6) ♕b6 23. ♕e4 (23. ♘d2 0–0 24. ♕e4 g6) ♘e3±] **♘d7!** [20... ♘d5 21. ♕e4±] **21. ♖c1 ♘c5** [21... ♘e5 22. ♗a4 ♘c6 23. ♗c6 bc6 24. ♕e4+−] **22. ♔e2!** [22. f4 d3 23. ♗d1 ♖d8∞; 22. ♕f2 ♕e5 23. f4 ♕d6∞] **d3!** [22... ♕e5 23. ♔f2 ♕d6 24. ♕b4±] **23. ♗d3 ♕e5 24. ♗e4 ♘e4** [24... f5 25. ♕c3!+−] **25. fe4 ♕e4 26. ♔f2 ♕f4 27. ♔e2 ♕e4 28. ♔f2 ♕f4 29. ♔g1± 0–0 30. g3 ♕f5 31. ♕f2 ♕d5 32. ♖c5** [32. h3 ♖ac8 33. ♔h2 ♖c1 34. ♖c1 ♖d8 35. ♖c7±] **♕d3 33. ♔g2?!** [33. ♕c2 ♕c2 34. ♖c2 ♖ac8 35. ♖b2 b5 36. ♔f2±] **♖ac8 34. ♖hc1 ♖c5 35. ♕c5 ♖d8 36. ♕f2 b5 37. ♖c7?!** [37. h4; 37. h3] **♕d5= 38. ♕f3?!** [38. ♔h3 ♕h5 39. ♔g2=] **♕f3 39. ♔f3 ♖d1 40. ♘c3 ♖a1 41. ♔e4 ♖a3 42. ♔d4 b4 43. ♘e4 ♖a2 44. h4 a5 45. ♖b7 ♖b2 46. ♔c4∓ ♖c2 47. ♔d4** [47. ♔b5? b3 48. ♔a5 b2 49. h5 f5 50. ♘d6 ♖c5 51. ♔a4 ♖c6−+; 47. ♔b3? ♖e2∓] **♖g2 48. ♖b5!= ♔h7** [48... f5 49. ♘c5 ♖g3 (49... ♔f7 50. ♖b7 ♔f6 51. ♘d7 ♔g6 52. ♘e5 ♔h5 53. ♖g7) 50. ♘e6 ♖g4 51. ♔e5 ♖h4 52. ♖b8 ♔h7 53. ♘f8=] **1/2 : 1/2**
[de la Villa García]

203. !N **B 66**

TIVJAKOV 2595 – TUKMAKOV 2605

Rostov na Donu 1993

1. e4 c5 2. ♘f3 d6 3. d4 cd4 4. ♘d4 ♘f6 5. ♘c3 ♘c6 6. ♗g5 e6 7. ♕d2 a6 8. 0-0-0 h6 9. ♗f4 ♗d7 10. ♘c6 ♗c6 11. f3 d5 12. ♕e1 ♗b4 13. a3 ♗a5 14. ♗d2 d4 15. e5 ♕c7 16. ♘e2! N ♗d2 17. ♕d2 ♕e5 18. ♘d4 ♗d7 [18... ♗d5 19. c4; 18... 0–0!?] **19. ♗c4!± 0–0** [19... 0-0-0 20. ♕b4!± △ ♖d2, ♖hd1↑; 19... ♖c8 20.

♗b3±] **20. ♗b3** [20. h4!?] **♕c7!?** [20... b5 21. g4 a5 22. h4↑; 22. f4 △ g5; 22. ♖hg1↑»] **21. h4!?** [21. g4 e5 22. ♘f5 ♗f5 23. gf5 ♖ad8 24. ♕e3 ♖d1 25. ♖d1 ♖e8!?∞; 24. ♕g2!?↑», ⇔g] **♖ad8** [21... e5 22. ♘e2↑ ↗a2-g8 ×e5] **22. ♕e3** [22. g4 e5 23. g5 (23. ♘e2 ♗g4) ♘h5] **♖fe8** [22... e5 23. ♘e2⩲ △ 24. g4, 24. ♘c3] **23. ♘e2** [23. g4 e5 24. ♘e2 e4] **♗c6?!** [23... ♗b5 24. ♘c3 ♗c4 25. ♗c4 ♕c4 26. g4⩲] **24. g4 ♘d5** [24... ♗d5!?] **25. ♗d5 ♖d5** [25... ed5?! 26. ♕f2! (△ ♘d4) d4 27. ♘d4 ♕f4 28. ♔b1±; 25... ♗d5 26. g5→] **26. ♖d5 ♗d5□ 27. g5±→» hg5** [27... h5 28. ♘f4 ×h5, ♗d5; 27... ♖c8 28. c3±] **28. hg5 e5 29. ♘c3?!** [29. ♕f2!± (Tukmakov) △ 29... e4 30. ♕h4 ♔f8 31. ♘c3+−, △ 29... ♕c4 30. ♖h4 △ ♕h2+−] **♗c6** [29... ♕c6 30. ♖f1±; 30. ♖h3!?] **30. ♘e4 ♖e6?!** [30... ♗e4 31. ♕e4→; 30... ♕e7 31. ♔b1 ♗e4 32. ♕e4 ♕g5 33. ♕b7 ♕g6±; 31. g6!?] **31. ♖d1! ♕e7?** [31... ♗e4 32. ♕e4 ♕e7 33. ♔b1!? ♕g5 34. ♕b7±] **32. ♘c5 ♖d6** [32... ♖g6 33. f4+− ×e5] **33. ♖e1 ♕d8** [33... f6 34. f4!?+−; 33... ♖d5 34. ♘d3 e4 35. f4+−] **34. ♘d3+− ♖g6?! 35. ♘e5 ♖g5 36. ♘f7! ♔f7 37. ♕e6 ♔f8 38. ♖h1 1 : 0**
[Tivjakov]

204.* !N B 66

ANAND 2710 – ŠIROV 2670

Linares 1993

1. e4 c5 2. ♘f3 d6 3. d4 cd4 4. ♘d4 ♘f6 5. ♘c3 ♘c6 6. ♗g5 e6 7. ♕d2 a6 8. 0-0-0 h6 9. ♗e3 ♕c7 10. f3 ♖b8 11. g4 ♘e5 [11... ♘d4 – 26/414] **12. h4 b5 13. ♕g2 ♗b7! N** [13... b4?! 14. ♘b1 ♗b7 (14... ♘c4? 15. ♗c4 ♕c4 16. b3 ♕c7 17. g5 ♘d7 18. g6± Anand 2690 – Širov 2710, Paris 1992) 15. ♘d2⩲] **14. g5** [14. ♗e2!?] **hg5 15. hg5 ♖h1 16. ♕h1 ♘fd7 17. f4** [17. g6!? ♘g6 18. f4=∞] **♘c4 18. g6** [18. ♗c4 ♕c4 19. g6?! b4!∓] **♘e3 19. gf7 ♔f7 20. ♕h5?** [20. ♕h3 ♘c5 21. ♕e3 b4 22. ♘b1 ♗e4 23. ♘d2 ♗d5⩱] **♔e7** [20... ♔g8? 21. ♗h3 ♘c5 22. ♖h1! (△ ♘e6+−) ♗c8! (22... ♕f7 23. ♗e6 ♕e6 24. ♘e6 ♘e6 25. ♕h3+−; 22... ♕e7 23. b4 ♗c8 24. bc5 dc5 25. ♘c6 ♕f7 26. ♗e6 ♕e6 27. ♕h8 ♔f7 28. ♘d8+−) 23. ♘f3! (△ 24. ♘g5 g6 25. ♗e6 ♗e6 26.♕h8#) ♘e4 (23... g6 24. ♕g6 ♕g7 25. ♕e8! b4 26. ♘e2+− △ ♖g1) 24. ♗e6! (24. ♘g5? ♘g5 25. fg5 ♕c5!) ♗e6 25. ♕h7 ♔f7 26. ♕e4±→] **21. ♕h3 e5!∓ 22. fe5 de5 23. ♘db5!** [23. ♕e6 ♔d8 24. ♕f7 ed4 25. ♖d4 ♗d5!−+; 23. ♕e3 ed4 24. ♖d4 ♖e8! (24... ♘e5 25. ♘d5 ♗d5 26. ♖d5=∞) 25. ♗h3 ♘e5−+; 23. ♘e6 ♕b6 24. ♖d7 ♔d7 25. ♘f8 (25. ♘c5 ♔c6 26. ♕d7 ♔c5−+) ♔e7 (25... ♔e8 26. ♘d7 ♗c8−+ Anand) 26. ♘d7 ♕h6! 27. ♘b8 ♘f1 28. ♕h6 gh6−+ ×♘b8] **ab5 24. ♕e3 b4 25. ♘b5!** [25. ♘d5 ♗d5 26. ed5 ♕d6−+] **♕c5 26. ♕g5 ♘f6 27. ♘d6! ♕d6□ 28. ♖d6 ♔d6 29. ♕d2 ♔c7 30. ♕h2!?** [30. ♕g5 ♖e8 31. ♗b5 ♗c6−+] **♗d6** [30... ♖e8 31. ♗b5 ♗c6 32. ♕e2!∓] **31. ♕g1 ♗e4** [31... ♘e4!? 32. ♕g7 ♔b6∓] **32. ♕g7 ♘d7 33. ♗h3??** [33. ♗g2∓ △ 33... ♗f5 34. ♕f7!⇆] **♗c6−+ 34. ♗g4 ♖f8 35. ♕h7 ♖f1 36. ♔d2 ♗c5 37. ♕h5 ♗d4?!** [37... ♖h1 38. ♕f7 ♖h2 39. ♔d1 ♗d4 40. ♗d7 ♗d7 41. ♕c4 ♗c6 △ 42. ♕b4? ♗f3 43. ♔e1 ♖h1 44. ♔d2 ♖d1#] **38. c3 ♘f6 39. ♕f7 ♔b6 40. ♕b3 ♘e4 41. ♔c2 ♖f2 42. ♔d1 ♗c5??** [42... ♗c3?? 43. bc3 ♗a4 44. ♕a4 ♘c3 45. ♔e1 ♘a4 46. ♔f2=; 42... ♖d2 43. ♔c1 ♗c5 44. a3 (44. cb4 ♗d4−+) ♖g2!−+] **43. ♗e2!∞ ♖f4 44. a3 ♖f6! 45. cb4! ♗d4 46. a4!** [46. ♕g8 ♔a7!∓] **♖d6 47. ♔c1 ♗d5 48. ♕d3 ♖c6?!** [48... ♔c7!∓] **49. ♔b1 ♖c4 50. ♗f3 ♘d2 51. ♕d2 ♗f3 52. ♕h6 ♔b7 53. ♕h7 ♖c7 54. ♕d3!= ♗c6 55. b5 ♗d5 56. ♕g6 ♖f7 57. a5 ♖f2 58. ♕h7 ♗f7 59. ♕e4 ♔b8 60. ♕c6 ♖b2 61. ♔c1 ♖f2 62. a6 ♗e3 63. ♔d1 ♗h5 64. ♔e1** [64... ♖e2 65. ♔f1 ♖f2=] **1/2 : 1/2** **[Širov]**

205. B 66

ŠIROV 2670 – CH. LUTZ 2550

München 1993

1. e4 c5 2. ♘f3 d6 3. d4 cd4 4. ♘d4 ♘f6 5. ♘c3 ♘c6 6. ♗g5 e6 7. ♕d2 a6 8. 0-0-0 h6 9. ♗e3 ♗e7 10. f3 ♘d4 11. ♗d4 e5 12. ♗e3 ♗e6 13. g4 [13. h4 ♕a5 14. ♔b1

♖c8 15. ♘d5 ♕d2 16. ♘f6 gf6 17. ♖d2 f5=] **♕a5 14. a3** [14. ♔b1 ♖c8 △ 15. h4? ♖c3 16. ♕c3 ♕a2 17. ♔c1 d5∓] **b5!?** [14... ♖c8 *a)* 15. h4? ♖c3 16. ♕c3 ♕c3 17. bc3 d5∓; *b)* 15. ♘d5 ♕d2 16. ♖d2 ♘d5! 17. ed5 ♗d7 (△ ♗g5∓) 18. h4 f5!∓; *c)* 15. ♗d3! d5 (15... ♖c3 16. ♕c3 ♕c3 17. bc3 d5 18. g5! ♗a3 19. ♔b1∞; 15... b5 16. ♔b1!∞) 16. ♘d5 ♕d2 17. ♖d2 ♘d5 18. ed5 ♗d5 19. ♗b5! ♗c6 20. ♗c6 ♖c6=] **15. h4 N** [15. ♔b1 – 55/227] **b4 16. ♘d5** [16. ab4? ♕a1 17. ♘b1 ♖c8! (17... ♗a2? 18. ♕c3∞) 18. ♗d3 (18. c3 d5 19. g5 d4 20. gf6 dc3 21. bc3 ♗b4–+) d5! 19. g5 d4 20. gf6 gf6!–+] **♗d5 17. ed5 ♖b8 18. ♔b1** [18. ♗c4? ♕c7] **♗d8?** [18... ♕a4 19. b3 ♕a3 20. ♗c4!=/∞ △ g5; 18... ♘d7! 19. ♗d3! ♕a4 (19... ♘c5?! 20. ♗c5 ♕c5 21. a4!⩲; 19... ♕d5 20. ab4 ♕f3 21. g5!=/∞ △ 21... hg5 22. ♖hf1 ♕g4 23. hg5 ♕b4 24. c3→) 20. b3 (20. ab4?! ♖b4 21. c3 ♖b7 22. ♕c2 ♕a5 △ 0–0, ♖fb8→) ♕a3 21. g5=/∞] **19. ab4 ♖b4** [19... ♕b4 20. ♕b4 ♖b4 21. ♗a6⩲] **20. ♕c3! 0–0** [20... ♖a4 21. ♕a5 ♖a5 22. ♗c4!± ×♖a5; 20... ♖b8 21. ♕a5 ♗a5 22. ♗a6⩲] **21. ♗d2!** [21. g5? ♘d5 22. ♖d5 ♕d5 23. ♕b4 ♕f3–+] **♖a4!?** [21... ♘d5 22. ♕d3⩲] **22. b4!±** [×♖a4; 22. ♕a5? ♗a5 23. b3 ♖b8; 22. b3 ♕c3 23. ♗c3 ♖f4 24. ♗e2 a5⇆ Ch. Lutz] **♕c7** [22... ♕d5 23. ♕b3 ♕c6 24. b5+–] **23. ♔b2!** [23. ♕c7 ♗c7 24. ♔b2 ♖b8! 25. ♔b3 ♖a5! △ 26. c4 ♘d7!⇆; 23. ♕b3 ♕d7 24. ♗h3 ♕e8⩲] **♘d5?** [23... ♕d7? 24. ♕c6+–; 23... a5!? 24. ♕c7 ♗c7 25. ♔b3 ♖b4 26. ♗b4 ab4 27. ♗b5±; 23... ♕b7! 24. ♕b3 ♕d7 25. ♗h3 ♕e8 26. ♖a1! ♖a1 27. ♖a1± ×a6] **24. ♕c7 ♗c7 25. ♔b3 ♘b6 26. ♗e3!+– a5□ 27. c3! ab4 28. ♗b6 1 : 0 [Širov]**

206.* B 66

EHLVEST 2635 – SERPER 2575

Moskva (open) 1992

1. e4 c5 2. ♘f3 d6 3. d4 cd4 4. ♘d4 ♘f6 5. ♘c3 ♘c6 6. ♗g5 e6 7. ♕d2 a6 8. 0-0-0 h6 9. ♗e3 ♗e7 10. f3 ♘d4 11. ♗d4 b5 12. ♔b1 e5 N [RR 12... ♖b8 13. ♕f2!? N (13. g4 – 56/222) ♕c7 14. g4 ♗d7 15. h4 b4 16. ♘e2 e5 17. ♗e3 ♖c8 18. ♘g3 ♗g4 19. ♗b6 ♕c2 20. ♕c2 ♖c2 21. fg4 ♖c6 22. ♗a7 ♘g4 23. ♗h3± B. Ivanović 2470 – M. Makarov 2515, Podgorica 1993] **13. ♗e3 ♗e6 14. g4 ♕a5** [14... ♖c8 15. ♘d5!⩲] **15. ♕f2 ♖b8 16. ♘d5 ♗d5** [16... ♘d5 17. ed5 ♗d7 18. ♖g1±] **17. ed5 ♗d8 18. ♕e2! ♖b7** [18... 0–0 19. h4±] **19. h4±○ ♕c7 20. ♕g2! ♕e7?!** [20... h5!?±] **21. ♗c1 ♘d7 22. ♖e1 ♗b6 23. f4 ♖c7 24. ♖h3! 0–0 25. h5↑ ♕f6 26. ♗d3** [△ ♕e4] **♕d8 27. g5+– hg5 28. fg5 ♘c5 29. ♗f5 e4 30. ♖f1 ♖e7 31. g6 e3 32. h6 1 : 0 [Ehlvest]**

207. B 66

BOLOGAN 2520 – TUKMAKOV 2605

Nikolaev (zt) 1993

1. e4 c5 2. ♘f3 d6 3. d4 cd4 4. ♘d4 ♘f6 5. ♘c3 ♘c6 6. ♗g5 e6 7. ♕d2 a6 8. 0-0-0 h6 9. ♗e3 ♘d4 10. ♗d4 b5 11. f3 ♗e7 12. ♔b1 ♗b7 13. ♗f6 gf6 14. ♗d3 ♕c7 N [14... ♕b6 – 43/255] **15. ♘e2! d5** [15... 0-0-0 16. c4!] **16. ed5 ♗d5 17. ♘f4 ♗b7** [17... 0-0-0 18. ♘d5 ♖d5 19. g3! h5 20. ♕e2 ♖hd8 21. f4! △ f5±] **18. ♗e4⩲ ♗e4 19. fe4 ♖d8 20. ♕f2 ♖d1 21. ♖d1 ♖g8 22. ♘h5?!** [22. ♕f3 ♗d6! 23. ♘h5 (23. e5 fe5 24. ♕a8 ♕b8) ♗e5 24. g4 ♖g6 25. h3⩲; 22. h3!? ♗d6 23. ♘d3 ♗e5 24. g4⩲] **♖g5! 23. ♕f3** [23. ♘f6 ♗f6 24. ♕f6 ♖g2=] **♖c5?** [23... ♕h2 24. e5 (24. ♕c3 ♕b8) ♕g2 25. ♘f6 ♗f6 26. ♕f6 ♕d2!□ (26... ♕d5 27. ♔c1!+–) 27. ♕f3 ♕g2 (27... ♖g3 28. ♕a8 ♔e7 29. ♕a7+–) 28. ♕f6=] **24. e5!± f5□** [24... fe5?? 25. ♘g7+–; 24... ♖c2 25. ef6+–; 24... ♖e5 25. ♕a8 ♗d8 26. ♘f6 ♔e7 27. ♕f3 ♖f5 28. ♕f5 ef5 29. ♘d5+–] **25. g4! f4** [25... ♖e5 26. gf5→] **26. ♕e4** [26. ♕a8! ♕c8 27. ♕e4+–] **♖e5 27. ♘g7 ♔f8 28. ♕h7 ♗d6□ 29. ♕h8 ♔e7 30. ♕e8 ♔f6 31. ♘h5 ♔g5** [31... ♖h5 32. ♕h8 ♔e7 33. gh5+–] **32. ♕g8 ♔h4 33. ♕h7!+– ♖e2 34. ♘g7 ♔h3!? 35. ♘e8??⊕** [35. ♕d3 ♖e3 36. ♕f1 △ ♘e8+–] **♕c6 36. ♕h6?? ♔g2–+⊕ 1 : 0 [Bologan]**

208. **B 66**

DOLMATOV 2615 – TUKMAKOV 2605
Rostov na Donu 1993

1. e4 c5 2. ♘f3 d6 3. d4 cd4 4. ♘d4 ♘f6 5. ♘c3 ♘c6 6. ♗g5 e6 7. ♕d2 a6 8. 0-0-0 h6 9. ♗e3 ♗e7 10. f3 ♘d4 11. ♗d4 b5 12. ♔b1 ♗b7 13. g4 ♕c7 14. ♕f2 N [14. h4 – 30/393; 14. a3!?] **b4 15. ♘a4 e5 16. ♗e3** [16. ♗b6 ♕c6 17. b3 d5] **d5 17. ♘b6 de4!?** [17... ♖d8 18. ♘d5 ♘d5 19. ed5 ♖d5 (19... ♗d5 20. ♗b6) 20. ♗d3∞] **18. ♘a8 ♗a8 19. ♗g2** [19. ♗e2!?] **0–0 20. h4 ♕c6!?** [20... ef3 21. ♗f3 e4 22. ♗e2∞] **21. ♖h3** [21. g5? ef3 22. gf6 fg2 23. fe7 gh1♕ 24. ef8♕ ♔f8–+; 21. fe4 ♘g4 22. ♕e2 ♘e3 23. ♕e3 ♗c5 △ ♗d4] **♖c8?!** [21... ef3 22. ♗f3 e4 23. ♗e2 ♖c8∞] **22. ♕e2! ♘d5** [22... ef3 23. ♖f3! e4 (23... ♘g4 24. ♖g3) 24. ♖f5!] **23. fe4 ♘e3 24. ♖e3 ♗h4 25. ♖ed3 ♕b5** [25... a5!?] **26. ♖3d2 ♕e2 27. ♖e2 ♗g5?!** [27... ♗c6 28. ♖ed2 ♔f8∞] **28. ♖ee1** [△ ♗f1] **♗h4 29. ♖e3 ♗c6 30. ♗f1 ♗g5 31. ♖ee1 a5 32. ♗c4± ♖c7 33. ♗d5 ♗d7 34. ♖g1 ♔f8 35. ♖d3 ♗e7⊕ 36. ♖f3 f6 37. c3** [37. g5 h5!∞] **♗c5 38. ♖g2 ♔e7 39. ♖fg3 ♗a4 40. ♖h2 ♗d6 41. ♖h1 ♗d7 42. ♖c1 ♖a7 43. ♔c2 ♖a6 44. ♔d3 ♖b6 45. ♖g2 ♖b8 46. ♔e3 ♗c5 47. ♔f3 ♗d6 48. ♗b3 ♖b6 49. ♖d2 ♗c6 50. ♖cd1 ♗e8 51. ♗g8!?** [51. cb4!? ab4] **bc3!?** [51... h5 52. c4 hg4 53. ♔g4 ♗d7 54. ♔f3 △ 55. c5, 55. ♖d5] **52. bc3 h5 53. ♖h1 hg4 54. ♔g4 ♗d7 55. ♔f3 ♖c6!? 56. c4 ♗e6 57. ♗e6 ♔e6 58. ♖c1 ♗c5⊕** [58... a4!? 59. ♖g2 ♖c7] **59. ♖d8 f5!? 60. ♖e8 ♔f6** [△ g6] **61. ef5** [61. ♖a8!?] **♔f5 62. ♖e1 ♗d6** [62... ♗d4 63. ♖f8 ♔e6 64. ♖c1 △ ♔e4±] **63. ♖e4 a4!?** [63... ♖c7] **64. ♖g8 g5 65. ♖g7** [65. ♖g4 ♗e7] **♗c5!□ 66. ♖f7** [66. ♖g4 ♗e3! △ ♗f4] **♔e6 67. ♖g7 ♔f5** **1/2 : 1/2**
[Tukmakov]

209.* **B 66**

N. SHORT 2655 – KRAMNIK 2685
Amsterdam 1993

1. e4 c5 2. ♘f3 ♘c6 3. d4 cd4 4. ♘d4 ♘f6 5. ♘c3 d6 6. ♗g5 e6 7. ♕d2 a6 8. 0-0-0 h6 9. ♗e3 ♗d7 10. f4 b5 [RR 10... ♕c7 11. h3 ♘d4 N (11... b5 12. ♗b5 ab5 13. ♘db5 ♕b8 14. ♘d6 ♗d6 15. ♕d6 ♕d6 16. ♖d6 ♘a5∞; 16... ♘e7 – 45/240) 12. ♕d4 (12. ♗d4) ♖c8! 13. g4 d5 (13... ♘e4?? 14. ♕e4 ♗c6 15. ♘d5+–) 14. ♖h2 de4 15. ♘e4 (15. ♖hd2!? ♗c6∞) ♘e4 16. ♕e4 ♗c6 17. ♕d4 ♖d8 18. ♕d8 ♕d8 19. ♖d8 ♔d8 20. ♖d2 ♔c7 21. a3 (21. ♗d4 f6 22. ♗c4 ♗d6∓ △ 23. ♗b6?? ♔b6 24. ♖d6 ♔c5–+) a5 22. ♗d4 f6 23. c4 b6 24. ♔c2 ♗c5 25. ♗c5 bc5 26. ♗g2 g5∓ Murrey 2530 – Dorfman 2580, France 1993; 20. ♗g2= Dorfman] **11. ♗d3 ♗e7 12. ♔b1 0–0 13. ♖hf1 N** [13. ♖he1 – 52/204] **♘g4!? 14. ♘c6 ♗c6 15. ♗g1 ♘f6! 16. e5** [16. ♕e3 ♕c7 17. g4!? ♘g4? 18. ♕g3→; 17... ♕b7! △ 18. g5 b4!] **de5 17. fe5 ♘d7** [17... ♘d5?! 18. ♘e4 ♘b4 19. ♘f6 ♔h8 20. ♕e2!± △ 20... gf6 21. ♕h5] **18. ♗d4 ♗c5! 19. ♗e4 ♕c7 20. ♗c6 ♕c6 21. ♖f4! ♕c7?!** [21... ♖ac8 △ 22. ♗c5 ♘c5 23. ♖g4 ♔h8=] **22. ♗c5 ♘c5 23. ♕d6 ♖ac8** [23... ♕d6!? 24. ♖d6 ♖fd8] **24. ♕c7 ♖c7 25. ♖fd4± ♖b8?!** [25... ♖fc8 26. ♖1d2 ♔f8 27. a4!?±] **26. b4! ♘b7 27. ♘e4 ♔f8 28. ♔b2** [28. ♖1d3 ♔e7 29. ♖g3!?] **♔e7 29. a3 ♖d8 30. ♖d8 ♘d8 31. ♘c5 a5 32. c4!± ab4 33. ab4 bc4** [33... ♘c6 34. cb5 ♘b4 35. ♘a6!+–] **34. ♔c3 ♘c6 35. ♖e1 ♘a7 36. ♔c4 ♔d8 37. ♖d1** [⌓ 37. b5 ♘c8 38. ♖a1 ♘b6 39. ♔d4 △ ♖a6] **♔e7 38. b5 ♘c8 39. ♔b4 ♘b6 40. ♖d6 ♘d5 41. ♖d5** [41... ed5 42. b6 ♖c8 43. b7 ♖b8 *a)* 44. ♔c3? f6! (44... ♔d8 45. ♔d4 ♔c7 46. ♘a6 ♔b7 47. ♘b8 ♔b8 48. ♔d5 ♔c7 49. e6 ♔d8!= Kasparov) 45. ♔d4 fe5 46. ♔e5 d4! △ 47... ♔d4 48. ♔d6; *b)* 44. ♔b5 ♖b7 (44... d4 45. ♔c4! ♖d8 46. ♔d3+–) 45. ♘b7 ♔e6 46. ♔b4! ♔e5 47. ♔c3 ♔e4 48. ♔d2±]
1 : 0 **[N. Short]**

210. **B 66**

ANAND 2710 – KRAMNIK 2685
Amsterdam 1993

1. e4 c5 2. ♘f3 ♘c6 3. d4 cd4 4. ♘d4 ♘f6 5. ♘c3 d6 6. ♗g5 e6 7. ♕d2 a6 8.

0-0-0 h6 9. ♗e3 ♗d7 10. f3 b5 11. ♔b1 ♘e5 N [11... ♕c7? 12. ♗b5!±; 11... ♗e7 – 22/(445)] **12. ♗d3 ♕c7** [12... b4!? 13. ♘ce2 d5 Anand] **13. g4** [13. ♖he1 ♖c8∞] **b4 14. ♘ce2 d5 15. ♗f4!** [15. ♘g3 ♘c4 16. ♕e2 (16. ♗c4 dc4∓) ♘e3 17. ♕e3∓] **de4** [15... ♗d6?! 16. ed5 ♘d5 17. ♗e5 ♗e5 18. ♗e4±] **16. ♗e4 ♘e4** [16... ♖c8 17. ♗e5 ♕e5 18. ♗b7 ♖c7 19. ♗a6±] **17. fe4 ♖c8?** [17... 0-0-0?? 18. ♗e5 ♕e5 19. ♘c6+–; 17... f6!∞] **18. b3!±** [18. ♖hf1? ♘c4] **f6** [18... ♗d6 19. ♘f5! ef5 20. ♕d6 ♕d6 21. ♖d6 ♘g4 22. ef5± Anand] **19. h4 ♕b7 20. ♗e5 fe5 21. ♘f3 ♗c6** [21... ♗b5? 22. ♘e5 ♕e4 23. ♘f4+–] **22. ♘g3 ♗c5!** [22... ♕c7? 23. g5+–→] **23. g5** [23. ♘e5 0–0 24. ♘d7 (24. ♘c6 ♕c6 25. ♖hf1 ♖f1 26. ♖f1 ♗d6=∞) ♗d7 25. ♕d7 ♕d7 26. ♖d7 ♖f3! 27. ♘h5 ♗f8=∞] **0–0□ 24. ♘e5** [24. ♕e2 ♕c7!? 25. gh6 gh6∞] **♗f2!□** [24... ♗e4 25. ♘e4 ♕e4 26. ♖he1+–; 24... ♖f2 25. ♕e1] **25. ♘c6?** [25. ♕d6! ♗g3 (25... ♖fe8 26. gh6! ♗g3 27. ♖hg1! ♗e5 28. ♕e5±→) 26. ♕e6 ♔h7 27. g6 ♔h8 28. ♘f7 ♖f7 29. gf7 ♗e4 30. ♖hf1! ♗c2 (30... ♖f8 31. ♕e8+–) 31. ♔b2 ♗d1 32. f8♕ ♖f8 33. ♖f8 ♔h7 34. ♕f5 g6 35. ♖f7 ♔h8 36. ♕f6+–; 29... ♖f8!?±] **♕c6 26. ♘f5** [26. ♘h5 ♕e4! (26... ♗e3? 27. ♕d3 ♖f2 28. g6!? ♕c2 29. ♕c2 ♖fc2 30. ♖hf1 ♖2c5 31. ♘g3±; 28. ♖hf1) 27. gh6 ♗e3 28. ♖he1 (28. ♕e2 ♖f2) ♗d2 29. ♖e4 ♗h6↑ ×♘h5] **ef5 27. ♕f2 fe4=**

1/2 : 1/2 **[Kramnik]**

211.** **B 67**

ALEXA. IVANOV 2525 – WAITZKIN 2345

New York 1993

1. e4 c5 2. ♘f3 ♘c6 3. d4 cd4 4. ♘d4 ♘f6 5. ♘c3 d6 6. ♗g5 e6 7. ♕d2 a6 8. 0-0-0 ♗d7 9. f4 ♕c7 [RR 9... b5 10. ♗f6 gf6 11. ♘c6 ♗c6 12. ♕e1 *a)* 12... b4 13. ♘d5 a5 14. ♖d4 f5 15. ♖c4 N (15. ef5 – 53/(197)) ♗d5 16. ed5 ♕f6 17. de6 fe6 18. ♖c7 ♔d8 (18... ♗g7? 19. ♖g7!) 19. ♖b7!? (19. ♖c6 ♗g7 20. ♖d6 ♔e7 21. ♕e5 ♕e5 22. fe5 ♗e5=) ♔c8! 20. ♖b5 (20. ♖b6? ♔c7) ♗g7 21. c3 bc3 (Zontah 2455 – Poluljahov 2515, Beograd 1993; 21... ♖a7? 22. ♕f2 ♖c7 23. ♕b6! bc3 24. ♗c4!! △ ♖d1→) 22. ♗c4! ♖e8 (22... d5? 23. ♕e3) 23. ♕e3∞ Poluljahov; *b)* 12... ♕e7 13. ♗d3 h5!? N (13... ♗g7 – 42/(232)) 14. ♔b1 h4 15. ♖f1 ♗b7 (15... 0-0-0 16. a4±) 16. f5 0-0-0 (16... e5 17. ♗e2 ♖c8 18. ♘d5⩲) 17. ♕f2 *b1)* 17... ♗g7? 18. ♕a7 ♕c7 19. a4 b4 20. ♗a6 bc3 21. ♖f3 ♗a6 22. ♕a6 ♔d7 23. ♖c3 ♕b8 24. ♖b3 ♕c8 25. ♖d6 ♔e7 (25... ♔e8 26. ♖bd3!) 26. ♖b7+–; *b2)* 17... ♔b8 18. ♗b5!? (18. fe6 fe6 19. ♕f6 ♖h6 20. ♕e7 ♗e7 21. ♖f7 ♗f6=∞) ab5 (18... d5? 19. ♗d3± Hába 2485 – Hausner 2480, Deutschland 1993) 19. ♘b5 d5 (19... ♕d7 20. ♕a7 ♔c8 21. ♕b6!+–) 20. ♕a7 ♔c8 21. ♕b6 (21. ♖f3 ♗c6 22. ♖c3 ♕b7∞) ♖d6□ 22. ♕c5 ♖c6 23. ♘a7 ♔c7∞ Hába] **10. ♗f6 gf6 11. ♔b1 N** [11. ♗e2 – 36/339] **0-0-0 12. ♘b3 h5 13. ♗e2 ♘a5?!** [13... ♗e7; 13... ♔b8!?] **14. ♖hf1 ♔b8 15. ♖f3 ♗e7 16. ♖h3 h4 17. ♕e1 ♘b3 18. ab3 f5! 19. ef5 d5=∞ 20. ♗d3** [△ ♘d5] **♗f6** [20... ♗b4 21. ♕f2] **21. fe6 fe6 22. f5! ♖de8?!** [22... ♕c6! 23. ♗e2 d4 (23... ♖c8 24. ♕d2 d4 25. ♗f3 ♕c7 26. ♘e4 ♗e5 27. f6 ♗f4 28. ♕d4 ♕c2 29. ♔a2±) 24. ♗f3 ♕b6 25. ♘e4 ef5 26. ♘f6 ♕f6∓] **23. ♕f2 ♖hf8** [23... ♖ef8 24. ♖e1! (24. ♖f3 ♗c3 25. bc3 e5 26. ♗e2 e4 27. ♖f4 ♕e5) ♗c3 25. bc3 ♕c3 26. ♗b5! (26. ♗a6 ♖f5) ♕c7 27. ♗d7 ♕d7 (27... ♖f5 28. ♕d4) 28. fe6 ♖f2 29. ed7 ♖d8⩲] **24. fe6 ♗e6** [24... ♗c3? 25. ed7 ♕d7 26. ♕h4±] **25. ♖f3 ♗e7 26. ♖e1 ♖f3 27. gf3?!** [27. ♕f3 ♖f8 28. ♕e3 (28. ♘d5 ♕h2) ♖f6 29. ♕e5 (29. ♘d5?! ♗d5 30. ♕e7 ♕e7 31. ♖e7 ♗g2 32. ♗e4 h3 33. ♖b7 ♔c8 ×h2) ♕e5 30. ♖e5 ♗d6 31. ♖h5 ♗h2 32. ♖h4 ♗g3 33. ♖h8 ♔c7⩲; 27... ♕c6] **♗f7 28. f4 ♖g8 29. ♗f5 ♗f6 30. ♕f3?! ♕a5! 31. ♖f1!□ d4 32. ♕d3□ ♖g2** [32... dc3 33. ♕d6; 32... ♖e8 33. ♘d1 ♖e1 34. ♖e1 ♕e1 35. ♔c1] **33. ♗h3 ♖h2 34. ♘e4 ♗e7 35. f5 ♕e5 36. f6 ♗b4 37. ♖f5?! ♖h1! 38. ♔a2 ♕e8! 39. ♕d4??⊕** [39. c4 dc3 40. ♖d5 ♗d5 41. ♕d5 c2 42. f7

♕h8 43. ♘d6 ♖a1; 39. ♗f1□ ♕a4 40. ♔b1 ♕d7∓] **♕a4#** **0 : 1**
[Waitzkin, Kajdanov]

212.* **B 69**

TIVJAKOV 2595 – SAKAEV 2555
Sankt-Peterburg (zt) 1993

1. e4 c5 2. ♘f3 d6 3. d4 cd4 4. ♘d4 ♘f6 5. ♘c3 ♘c6 6. ♗g5 e6 7. ♕d2 a6 8. 0-0-0 ♗d7 9. f4 ♗e7 10. ♘f3 b5 11. ♗f6 gf6 12. f5 [RR 12. ♔b1 ♕b6 13. ♗d3 b4 14. ♘e2 a5 15. f5 a4 16. ♘f4 ♕c5 17. ♘h5!? N (17. ♗e2 – 49/(246)) a3! 18. ♕h6 (18. b3 ♘e5) ab2 19. ♘f6 ♔d8□ 20. ♕g7! (20. ♘g5? b3!–+) ♗f6 (20... ♖f8 21. ♘h7!) 21. ♕f6 ♔c7 22. ♕b2 ♖hg8 23. g3 ♖a3 24. ♘d2 (△ ♘c4) ♘e5 25. ♘b3 (Luther 2490 – Tukmakov 2535, Lenk 1992) ♕c3! (25... ♕a7 26. c3!? ♖a8 27. cb4 ♖a2 28. ♕c3 △ ♘a5; 26. ♗e2! △ ♖d6 Luther) 26. ♕c3 bc3$\overline{\overline{\infty}}$ Tukmakov] **♕b6 13. g3 b4 14. fe6 fe6 15. ♘e2 ♕f2 16. ♘h4 a5 N** [16... ♘e5] **17. ♘f4** [17. ♗h3 a4 18. ♖hf1 ♕c5 (18... ♕h2? 19. ♗g2! △ ♖h1+–) 19. ♔b1∞] **♕d2 18. ♖d2 ♔f7 19. ♗h3 ♖ab8** [⌓ 19... ♘e5] **20. ♖f1 ♘e5** [20... ♖b5? 21. ♘d5!] **21. ♘f3 ♘f3 22. ♖f3 h5** [⌓ 22... ♖hg8∓] **23. ♗f1 ♖bc8 24. h4!** [×h5] **♖c5 25. ♘d3 ♖c7 26. ♗h3 ♗c8** [26... ♖b8 △ ♖b5] **27. ♖e2 ♗d8 28. ♘f4 ♖c5 29. a3 ba3 30. ♖a3 ♖e8 31. ♖b3 ♗c7 32. ♖f2 ♖g8 33. ♗f1 ♖e5 34. ♗g2 a4! 35. ♖a3 ♔e7! 36. ♖a4 ♖g3 37. ♖a7 ♔d8 38. ♘e2 ♖g6 39. ♘d4 ♗d7 40. c3 ♖a5! 41. ♖a5 ♗a5 42. ♗f3 ♗b6 43. ♖d2** [43. ♖g2!∓] **♔e7 44. ♔c2 ♖g3! 45. ♖g2!** [45. ♗h5 ♗a4! 46. b3 (46. ♘b3 ♖h3) ♗d4∓] **♖h3 46. ♖g7 ♔d8 47. ♗h5 ♖h4 48. ♗f3** [48. ♗g4 ♗d4 49. cd4 f5 50. ef5 ef5 51. ♗f3 ♖d4∓] **e5! 49. ♘f5** [49. ♘e2 f5∓] **♖f4 50. ♗g2 ♗f5** [50... d5?! 51. ♖g8 ♔c7 52. ♘e7! ♖f2 53. ♔b1!; 50... ♖f2!? 51. ♔d3 d5! 52. ♖g8 ♔c7 53. ♖g7 ♖g2! 54. ♖g2 de4–+; 51. ♔b1!] **51. ef5 e4?** [51... ♖f5∓] **52. ♔d1 d5 53. ♖b7! ♖f2?** [53... ♗g1! 54. ♖b5 ♖f5 55. c4 (55. ♗e4? ♖f1 56. ♔e2 ♖f2–+) ♔e7∓] **1/2 : 1/2**
[Sakaev]

213. **B 70**

J. BENJAMIN 2585 – KALIKSHTEYN
New York 1993

1. e4 c5 2. ♘f3 d6 3. d4 cd4 4. ♘d4 ♘f6 5. ♘c3 g6 6. g3 ♘c6 7. ♗g2 ♘d4 8. ♕d4 ♗g7 9. 0–0 0–0 10. ♕d3 N [10. h3 – 54/203] **♗e6 11. ♘d5 ♘d5 12. ed5 ♗f5 13. ♕e2± b5 14. c3 ♖b8 15. ♗e3 ♕c7 16. ♕d2 ♖fc8 17. ♖fe1 b4!? 18. cb4 ♕c2 19. ♖ac1 ♕d2** [19... ♕b2 20. ♖c8 ♗c8 21. ♕b2 ♗b2 22. ♗d2 (22. ♗a7 ♖b7!=) ♗f6 23. ♖c1±] **20. ♗d2 ♗b2 21. ♖c6** [21. ♖c8 ♖c8 22. ♖e7 ♗c1! 23. ♗e1 ♗g5 24. ♖e2 ♗d3 25. ♖b2 ♖c1–+] **♔f8** [21... ♗d7? 22. ♖c8 ♖c8 23. ♖e7] **22. a4 ♗d7 23. b5 ♗c6 24. dc6$\overline{\overline{\infty}}$ ♗d4 25. ♗h3 f5?!** [25... ♖c7 26. ♗d7 *a)* 26... a6? 27. ♖e4 e5 (27... ♗c5 28. ♗h6 ♔g8 29. ♖e7) 28. ♖d4 ed4 29. ♗a5 ♖d7 30. cd7 ♔e7 31. d8♕ ♖d8 32. ♗d8 ♔d8 33. ba6 ♔c7 34. ♔f1+–; *b)* 26... ♖d7 27. cd7 ♖d8 28. ♗h6 ♗g7 29. ♗g7 ♔g7 30. ♖e7 ♔f6 31. ♖e8 ♖d7±; *c)* 26... e5 27. ♗a5 ♗b6 28. ♗b4 ♖d7 29. cd7 ♔e7 30. ♖e5 ♔d7 31. ♖d5 ♗c7±; 25... e6 26. ♖d1 ♗c5$\overline{\overline{\infty}}$] **26. g4 a6 27. gf5 ab5 28. ab5± ♖c7** [28... ♖b5 29. f6! ♖c7 (29... ♖c6 30. fe7 ♔e8 31. ♗d7+–) 30. fe7 ♖e7 31. ♖e7 ♔e7 32. c7+–] **29. ♖e4 ♗c5 30. fg6 hg6** [30... ♖b5 31. ♗h6 ♔g8 32. ♗e6 ♔h8 33. g7#] **31. ♗e6 ♔g7□** [31... ♖b5 32. ♗h6 ♔e8 33. ♖f4+–] **32. ♗a5! ♗b6 33. ♗c3 ♔h6 34. ♖h4 ♔g5 35. ♖g4 ♔h6 36. ♔g2** [△ f4] **g5 37. ♗d2+– ♖f8 38. ♗g5 ♔h7 39. f4 ♖a8 40. ♖h4 ♔g7 41. ♖g4 ♔h7 42. f5 ♖ca7 43. f6! ef6** [43... ♖a2 44. ♗a2 ♖a2 45. ♔h3] **44. ♗f5 ♔g7 45. ♗e3**
1 : 0 **[J. Benjamin]**

214. **B 70**

KOVALЁV 2580 – BANGIEV 2400
Deutschland 1992/93

1. e4 c5 2. ♘f3 d6 3. d4 cd4 4. ♘d4 ♘f6 5. ♘c3 a6 6. a4 g6 7. ♗e2 ♗g7 8. 0–0 0–0 9. ♗e3 ♘c6 10. f4 ♗d7 11. ♔h1 N [11. ♘b3 – 25/515] **♖c8?!** [11... ♘d4!? 12. ♗d4 ♗c6 13. ♗d3 (13. ♕d3 b5!?) b5!?=; 13. ♗f3!?] **12. ♘b3 ♗e6 13. f5!?** [13. a5 ♗b3 14. cb3 ♘a5 15. e5!?] **♗d7!?**

[13... ♗b3 14. cb3 ♘a5!? (14... ♘d7 15. ♗c4) 15. e5!? (15. g4 ♘d7) ♘e8 (15... de5 16. ♕d8 ♖fd8 17. ♗b6 ♘b3 18. ♖a3±) 16. b4 ♘c4 17. ♗c4 ♖c4 18. ♕b3 ♖c8 19. e6±] **14. ♕e1?!** [14. a5!? ♘e5 15. ♗b6 ♕e8 16. g4!?] **♘e5 15. a5 ♘c4! 16. ♗c4** [16. ♗c1!?] **♖c4 17. ♕e2 ♗b5?!** [17... ♕c8! 18. ♗d4 ♖c3 19. ♗c3 ♗b5=] **18. ♘b5 ab5 19. ♗d4! ♘d7 20. c3 ♗d4 21. ♘d4** [21. cd4?! ♕c7] **♘f6 22. g4!?** [22. ♖a3!? ♕d7 23. ♖b3 ♖a8!? 24. ♖a1 (24. ♖b5 ♖c5!?) ♖c5 25. ♖b4 (25. ♘b5 gf5; 25. fg6 hg6 26. ♘b5 ♘e4!) ♖e5] **♕d7 23. g5 ♘h5 24. ♖f3!? ♖c5 25. ♖af1 ♖e5 26. ♕f2?!** [26. ♖e3] **♕e8?!** [26... ♖e4! 27. fg6 hg6 28. ♖f7 ♖f4! 29. ♖f4 ♖f4 30. ♕e2 ♖f1 31. ♕f1 ♕g4 32. ♕b5 ♕d1 33. ♔g2 ♕d2=] **27. ♖e3** [△ b4] **♖c5 28. b4 ♖c4** [28... ♖c8 29. ♕e2 ♖c4 30. e5 d5 31. f6±] **29. ♖f3!?** [△ 30. fg6 hg6 31. ♘e6] **♘g7** [29... ♖c8 30. ♕e2 ♖c4 31. fg6 hg6 32. ♘e6 fe6 33. ♖f8 ♕f8 34. ♖f8 ♔f8 35. ♕f2 △ ♕b6±] **30. ♕h4 ♕c8** [30... ♘h5 31. fg6 hg6 32. ♘e6±]

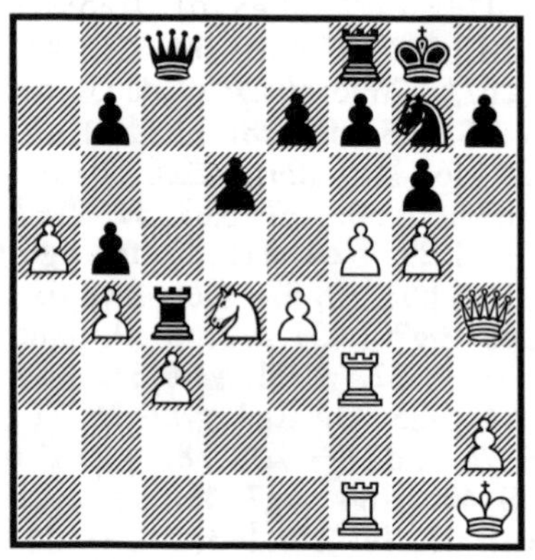

31. ♕h6! ♖c3 32. f6 ef6 33. gf6 ♘h5 34. ♘f5! [34. ♖c3? ♕c3 35. ♖c1 ♕d4 36. ♕f8!+−; 35... ♕h3!] **♖f3 35. ♘e7 ♔h8 36. ♘c8 ♖f1 37. ♔g2 ♖c8 38. ♔f1+− ♘f6 39. ♕g5! ♘e4 40. ♕b5 ♖c1 41. ♔g2 ♖c2 42. ♔f3 f5 43. ♕b7 1 : 0**
[Bangiev]

215. !N **B 70**

ZAGREBEL'NYJ 2440 – SERPER 2575
Taškent 1992

1. e4 c5 2. ♘f3 d6 3. d4 cd4 4. ♘d4 ♘f6 5. ♘c3 g6 6. ♗e2 ♗g7 7. 0–0 ♘c6 8. ♘b3 0–0 9. ♖e1 a6 10. ♗f1 b5 11. ♘d5 ♘d7! N [11... ♘d5 – 55/232] **12. c3** [△ ♗g5; 12. a4!? b4 13. a5!± ×a6; 12... ♖b8!?] **e6 13. ♘e3 ♘b6** [13... ♘c5!?] **14. f4** [14. ♘g4?! h5!] **♗b7 15. ♘g4 ♘c4 16. ♘d2 ♕b6 17. ♔h1 ♘d2 18. ♗d2 f5! 19. ♗e3 ♕c7 20. ♘f2** [20. ef5? gf5 21. ♘f2 ♖f6 △ ♖g6, ♘e7-d5∓] **e5! 21. ef5 ♖f5 22. ♘d3?** [22. ♗d3! ♖f7 (22... ef4? 23. ♗f5 fe3 24. ♗e6+−) 23. ♘h3 △ ♘g5∞; 22. ♘h3!?] **♖af8 23. fe5□ ♘e5 24. ♘e5 ♗e5∓ 25. ♕g4 ♕e7** [25... ♗c8!? (△ ♖f1) 26. ♕e2 (26. ♕e4 ♗h2!) ♗h2 27. ♔h2 ♖h5 28. ♔g1 d5 29. g3 (29. g4 ♗g4!) ♕g3 30. ♕g2 ♖f1!−+] **26. h3 ♖f3! 27. ♗h6□** [27. ♗d4? ♖8f4−+; 27. ♗g5? ♕g5! 28. ♕g5 ♖h3 29. ♔g1 ♗h2 30. ♔h1 ♗g3 31. ♔g1 ♗f2#] **♖8f5 28. ♔g1 ♕f6??** [28... ♖f2 29. ♖e2 ♖e2 30. ♕e2 (30. ♗e2 ♖h5! △ ♖h4−+ ×♕g4) ♕h4 △ ♕g3−+] **29. gf3 ♗f3 30. ♖e5!□ ♕e5?!** [30... de5 (△ ♕b6) 31. ♕g3□ g5!∞] **31. ♕h4 g5 32. ♕e1 ♗e4 33. ♗g2 ♗g2** [⌓ 33... d5] **34. ♔g2 ♖f6 35. ♕e5 de5 36. ♗g5 ♖g6 37. h4 h6 38. ♔f3 hg5 39. ♖g1 ♖f6 40. ♔e3 ♔f7 41. ♖g5+− ♖f4 42. ♖e5** [42. h5 ♖h4! △ ♖h2] **♖h4 43. ♔d3 ♔f6 44. ♖e4 ♖h1** [44... ♖h2 45. ♖e2 ♖h4 46. b3 △ c4] **45. a4! ♔f5 46. ab5 ♖d1** [46... ab5 47. ♖b4 ♖d1 48. ♔c2 ♖d5 49. ♔b3 △ ♖d4, ♔b4] **47. ♔c2 ♔e4 48. ♔d1 ab5 49. ♔c2 ♔d5 50. ♔d3 ♔c5 51. b3 ♔d5 52. b4 ♔e5 53. c4 ♔d6 54. cb5** [54. c5 ♔d5 55. ♔e3 ♔e5 56. ♔f3 ♔f5 57. ♔g3] **♔c7 55. ♔d4** [55. ♔c4?? ♔b6=] **♔b6 56. ♔c4 ♔c7 57. ♔c5 ♔b7 58. b6 ♔a6 59. b7! ♔a7 60. b8♕ 1 : 0**
[Serper]

216.* **B 76**

JANSA 2520 – M. JIROVSKÝ 2430
Česko 1993

1. e4 c5 2. ♘f3 d6 3. d4 cd4 4. ♘d4 ♘f6 5. ♘c3 g6 6. ♗e3 ♘c6 7. f3 ♗g7 8. ♕d2 0–0 9. 0-0-0 [RR 9. g4 ♘d7 10. h4 ♘b6 N (10... ♘de5 – 15/406) 11. h5 ♘d4 12. ♗d4 ♗d4 13. ♕d4 g5 14. 0-0-0 f6 15. h6 ♔h8 16. e5 fe5 17. ♕e3 ♗e6 18. ♕g5 ♖g8 19. ♕e3 ♕f8 20. ♗d3 ♕f7∞ Akopian 2615 – Kortchnoi 2605, Wijk aan Zee (open) 1993] **♘d4 10. ♗d4 ♗e6 11. ♔b1 ♕c7 12. g4 ♖fc8 13. h4 ♕a5 14. a3 ♖ab8 15. ♘e2 ♕d2** [15… ♕a4!? 16. g5 (16. h5? ♗h6) ♘d7? 17. h5±; 16… ♘h5∞] **16. ♖d2 a6 17. ♘f4 ♘d7 18. ♗g7 ♔g7 19. ♗h3 ♖c5** [19… h6 20. ♘e6 fe6 21. g5 ♘f8±] **20. g5 ♗h3 21. ♖h3 h6 N** [21… ♖h8?! – 54/209; 21… h5 22. ♘d5 ♖e8 23. f4±] **22. ♘d5 hg5** [22… e6? 23. gh6 ♔h6 24. ♘b4 ×d6] **23. hg5 e6 24. b4□ ♖c6 25. ♘e3 ♖h8 26. ♖h8 ♔h8 27. ♔a2!±** [△ ♔b3, c4±⊞; 27. ♔b2? ♘e5 28. f4 ♘c4=] **b5!** [27… ♘e5?! 28. f4 ♘c4 29. ♖h2 ♔g7 30. ♘g4 ♖c8 31. ♔b3 b5 32. a4±; 27… ♔g7?! 28. ♔b3±] **28. ♔b3 ♘b6 29. ♘g4 ♔g7 30. ♘f6 ♔f8□ 31. ♖h2 ♔e7 32. ♖h8 ♖c8 33. ♖c8 ♘c8** [♘♗ 2/j] **34. a4!?** [34. c4 ♘b6=] **♘b6 35. ab5 ab5 36. ♔c3 ♘c4 37. ♘g4 e5!? 38. ♔d3 ♘b2 39. ♔e2 ♔d7 40. ♘e3 ♔c6 41. ♘g4** [△ ♘h6] **♔d7 42. ♘f6 ♔c6 43. ♘d5 ♔d7 44. ♔d2 ♔c6 45. ♘e3 ♘c4!?** [45… ♔d7? 46. ♔c3 ♘a4 47. ♔b3 ♘b6 48. c4 ♔c6 (48… bc4 49. ♘c4±) 49. cb5 ♔b5 50. ♘g4! ♘c4 51. ♔c3 △ ♘h6+–; 45… ♘a4 46. c4 ♘b6 47. ♔c3⩲] **46. ♘c4** [46. ♔d3 ♘b2 (46… ♘e3? 47. ♔e3 △ ♔d3, c4+–; 46… ♘b6 47. c4 bc4 48. ♘c4 ♘d7 49. ♘a5 ♔b5 50. ♘b7 ♔b4 51. ♘d6 f6 52. gf6 ♘f6 53. ♘f7 ♘d7=) 47. ♔c3 ♘a4 48. ♔b3 ♘b6 49. c4 bc4 50. ♘c4 ♘d7 51. ♘a5 ♔b6! (51… ♔b5? 52. ♘b7+– ♔c6 53. ♘d8; 51… ♔c7?! 52. ♔c4 f6 53. ♔d5! fg5 54. ♔e6±) 52. ♔c4 ♘f8! 53. ♔d5 ♘e6 54. ♘c4 ♔c7 55. ♘d6 ♘g5=] **bc4 47. f4!?** [47. ♔e3!? ♔b5 48. c3 ♔c6 49. f4 ♔b5 50. f5 ♔b6 51. ♔d2 ♔b5 52. ♔c2 ♔b6 53. ♔b2 ♔c6 54. ♔a3 ♔b5 55. f6 *a)* 55… ♔b6? 56. ♔a4 d5 (56… ♔c6 57. b5+–) 57. ♔a3! de4 (57… d4 58. cd4 ed4 59. e5+–) 58. ♔b2 ♔c6 59. ♔c2 ♔b6 60. ♔d2 ♔c6 61. ♔e3 ♔d5 62. b5 ♔c5 63. ♔e4 ♔b5 64. ♔d5! e4 65. ♔e4 ♔c5 (65… ♔a4 66. ♔d5+–) 66. ♔e5+–; *b)* 55… ♔c6! 56. ♔a4 ♔b6 57. b5 (57. ♔a3=) d5! 58. ♔b4 (58. ed5? e4 59. d6 e3 60. d7 ♔c7–+) de4 59. ♔c4 ♔a5□ (59… ♔b7? 60. ♔b3+–) 60. ♔c5□ e3 61. b6 ♔a6!? 62. ♔c6 e2 63. b7 e1♕ 64. b8♕ ♕c3 65. ♔d6 ♕a3 66. ♔d7 ♕h3=] **♔b6?** [47… ♔b5? 48. fe5 de5 49. ♔c3+–⊙; 47… ef4! 48. c3 d5□ 49. ed5 (49. e5?? d4–+) ♔d5 50. ♔e2 ♔e5 51. b5 (51. ♔f3 f6 52. gf6 ♔f6 53. ♔f4 ♔e6=) ♔d6 52. ♔f3 ♔c5 53. ♔f4 ♔b5 54. ♔e5 ♔c5! 55. ♔f6 ♔d5 56. ♔f7 ♔e4 57. ♔g6 ♔d3=] **48. f5+– ♔c6 49. ♔c3 d5** [49… ♔b5 50. f6⊙] **50. ed5 ♔d5 51. fg6** [51… fg6 52. b5 ♔c5 53. b6]

1 : 0 [Jansa]

217.* **B 76**

A. SOKOLOV 2555 – TIVJAKOV 2595
Sankt-Peterburg (zt) 1993

1. e4 c5 2. ♘f3 d6 3. d4 cd4 4. ♘d4 ♘f6 5. ♘c3 g6 6. ♗e3 ♗g7 7. f3 ♘c6 8. ♕d2 0–0 9. 0-0-0 d5 10. ed5 ♘d5 11. ♘c6 bc6 12. ♗d4 e5 [RR 12… ♗d4 13. ♕d4 ♕b6 14. ♘a4 ♕a5 15. b3 ♗f5 N (15… ♖b8) 16. g4 ♗e6 (16… ♗c2?! 17. ♖d2!) 17. ♕e5! (17. ♕d2!?) ♕b4 18. c4 ♕a3 (18… ♘b6 19. ♕c5±) 19. ♔b1 ♖ab8!? (19… ♘b4 20. ♕b2±; 19… ♘b6 20. ♕c5 ♕c5 21. ♘c5± I. Herrera) 20. cd5 ♗d5 21. ♘b2! ♗f3 22. ♗c4 ♗h1 23. ♖h1± I. Herrera 2355 – Alb. Hernández 2330, La Habana 1993] **13. ♗c5 ♗e6 14. ♘e4 ♖e8 15. h4 h6 16. g4 ♘f4 17. ♕c3 ♗d5 18. g5 ♘e6 N** [18… h5 – 48/(296)] **19. gh6!? ♗h6 20. ♗e3 ♗g7** [⌓ 20… ♘f4 21. h5 gh5 22. ♔b1∞] **21. h5 f5** [21… g5 22. h6 ♗f6 23. ♗h3 ♘d4 24. ♘f6 ♕f6 25. ♖d4! ed4 26. h7+–] **22. hg6 ♕e7** [22… ♕b8 23. ♕d2 fe4 24. ♕h2 ef3 25. ♕h7 ♔f8 26. ♖h5 e4 27. ♖f5 ♔e7 28. ♖f7 △ ♖g7+–] **23. ♘g3 f4** [23… e4 24. ♘f5 ♗c3 25. ♘e7 ♖e7 26. bc3 ef3 27. ♗d3±] **24. ♘f5 ♕g5 25. ♘g7 fe3 26. ♖h5 ♕f4** [26… ♕g6 27. ♘e8 ♗f3 28. ♗d3+–] **27. ♘e6 ♖e6 28. ♗e2 ♖ae8 29. ♖dh1 ♖g6 30. ♕d3 ♖g7 31. ♖5h4 ♕g5 32. ♖g4** [32. b3!] **♕g4 33. fg4 ♗h1 34. ♕e3 ♗d5 35. b3 ♖ee7 36. ♔b2 e4 37. a4 ♗e6 38. ♕c5 ♗d7 39. g5 e3 40. ♕a7 ♖g5 41. a5 ♖g2 42. ♗c4 ♔f8 43. ♕d4 ♗e6 44. ♕h8** [44. ♕e3 ♖c2 45. ♔c2 ♗f5 46. ♔d2 ♖e3 47. ♔e3 ♔e7 48. a6 ♗c8 49. a7 ♗b7 50. ♔d4 ♔d6 51. b4 ♗a8 52. ♗a6+–] **♗g8** [44… ♔f7 45. ♕h5 ♔g8 46. ♕h3+–] **45.**

♕h6 ♖gg7 46. ♕f6 ♖gf7 47. ♕c6 ♗h7 [47... e2 48. ♕c8 ♖e8 49. ♕c5 ♔g7 50. ♕g5 ♔f8 51. ♕h6 ♖g7 52. ♕d6 △ ♗e2+−] **48. ♕h6 ♖g7 49. ♕f6 ♔e8 50. ♗b5 ♔d8 51. ♕d6 1 : 0**
[A. Sokolov]

218. B 77

APICELLA 2495 – MOLDOVAN 2435
Bucureşti 1993

1. e4 c5 2. ♘f3 ♘c6 3. d4 cd4 4. ♘d4 g6 5. ♘c3 ♗g7 6. ♗e3 ♘f6 7. ♗c4 0–0 8. ♗b3 d6 9. f3 ♗d7 10. ♕d2 ♘d4 11. ♗d4 b5 12. h4 a5 13. h5 a4 14. ♗f6 ef6 15. ♗d5 ♖c8 16. hg6 N [16. a3?! – 19/399] **hg6**

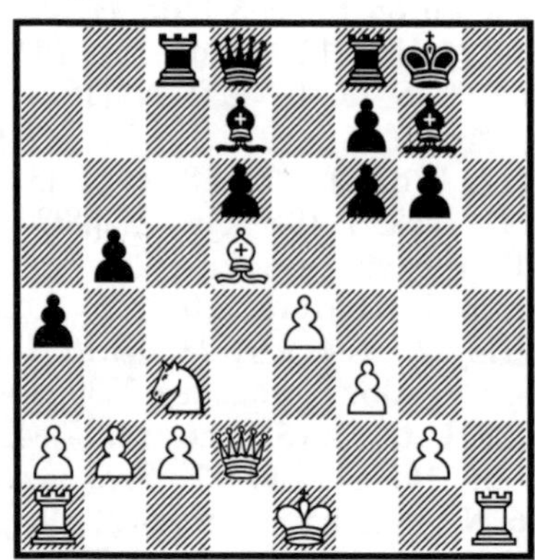

17. ♖h6! b4 [17... g5 18. ♖h5 △ g4] **18. ♖g6 ♔h7!** [18... bc3?? 19. ♕h6+−] **19. ♖g7 ♔g7 20. ♘e2=/∞ ♕b6 21. ♘d4 ♖h8 22. 0-0-0 ♖h2?** [22... ♖h6 23. g4 ♖ch8 24. g5 fg5 25. ♕g5 ♔f8 26. ♕f4∞] **23. ♕f2± ♔h8** [23... ♖ch8? 24. ♘f5+−] **24. ♗f7 ♕c5 25. ♗d5 a3 26. ♕g3 ♖h6** [26... ♖h7!? 27. ♕f4 ♔g7 *a)* 28. g4?? ♕d4!! 29. ♖d4 ♖h1 30. ♔d2 (30. ♖d1 ♖d1 31. ♔d1 ab2−+) ab2 31. g5 ♖c2−+; *b)* 28. ♗e6 b3□ 29. ♗b3 (29. ♘f5? ♕f5! 30. ♕f5 ♖c2=) ♕g5±] **27. ♕f4 ♔g7 28. g4** [28. ♗e6 b3] **b3□** [28... ♕d4? 29. ♕h6+−] **29. ♗b3 ♕g5 30. ♕g5 fg5 31. ba3± ♖h2 32. ♔b2 ♔f6 33. a4 ♖c5 34. ♔a3 ♖h8 35. ♘e2?!** [35. ♔b4! ♖b8 36. ♘b5 ♔e7 37. c4±] **♔e7 36. ♖d3 ♖hc8 37. ♔b2 ♗e6 38. ♘d4 ♗d7 39. ♖d2 ♖h8 40. ♔a3?** [40. c4± △ ♘b5] **♖a8! 41. ♖h2** [41. ♘f5 ♗f5 42. gf5 ♖c3∞] **♗a4! 42. ♘f5 ♔f6 43. e5 ♔e5 44. ♖e2 ♔f4** [44... ♔f6? 45. ♖e6 ♔f7 46. ♘d6 ♔f8 47. ♗a4+−] **45. ♖e4 ♔f3 46. ♖a4 ♖a4 47. ♔a4 ♔g4 48. ♘d6=** [♖ 8/b3] **♔f4 49. ♔b4 ♖c6 50. ♘b5 ♔e5 51. ♘c3** [51. c4 g4 52. ♗d1 g3 53. ♗f3 ♖f6 54. ♗d5 ♖f2 55. a4 g2 56. ♗g2 ♖g2] **g4 52. ♘e2 ♖g6 53. a4 g3 54. a5 ♔d6 55. ♔b5 ♔c7 56. ♗d5 g2 57. a6 ♔b8 58. ♗g2** [58. ♘g1 ♖h6 59. ♗g2 (59. c4 ♔a7) ♖g6] **♖g2 59. ♘d4 ♖g1 60. ♔b6 ♖c1 61. a7 1/2 : 1/2 [Apicella]**

219.* !N B 77

TOLNAI 2495 – LÉKÓ 2460
Magyarország (ch) 1992

1. e4 c5 2. ♘f3 ♘c6 3. d4 cd4 4. ♘d4 g6 5. ♘c3 ♗g7 6. ♗e3 ♘f6 7. ♗c4 0–0 8. ♗b3 d6 9. f3 ♗d7 10. ♕d2 ♘d4 11. ♗d4 b5 12. h4 a5 13. h5? [13. a4 ba4 14. ♘a4 e5 15. ♗e3 ♗e6 16. ♘b6 ♖b8 17. ♘c4 ♗c4! (17... d5 18. ♘a5 d4 19. ♗g5 ♗b3 20. ♘b3 ♕b6 – 16/410; 20... d3!?; 19. ♗f2!?) 18. ♗c4 ♖b2 19. ♗b3 d5! 20. ed5 e4 21. ♗d4 ♖b3 22. cb3 ef3∓ △ 23. gf3 ♕d5 24. 0–0 ♘e4!−+; 16. 0-0-0∞ – 16/409] **e5 14. ♗e3 a4 15. ♗d5 b4 16. ♘e2 ♘d5 17. ♕d5 ♗e6 18. ♕d2 d5! N** [18... ♕b8? N 19. ♗h6 ♗h6 20. ♕h6 ♖a7 21. f4! ef4 22. ♘f4 ♕c8 23. 0–0 ♗c4 24. ♖f2 ♕g4 25. a3 b3? 26. cb3 ♗b3 27. ♖af1 ♖a5 28. hg6 hg6 29. ♘g6 1 : 0 Tolnai 2495 – J. Stojnov 2320, Budapest 1992; 18... b3] **19. hg6** [19. ♗c5 de4! 20. ♗f8 ♕f8 21. hg6 hg6 22. fe4 ♕c5=/∞ △ ♗f6, ♖d8] **fg6** [19... hg6 *a)* 20. ♗h6 de4 21. ♕e3 ef3 22. ♗g7 ♔g7 23. ♕h6 (23. ♕e5 f6 24. ♕e6 ♖e8) ♔f6 24. ♘g3 ♕d4−+; *b)* 20. ♕b4 ♖b8 21. ♕a3 ♕a5∓; *c)* 20. ed5 ♕d5 21. ♕b4 e4! 22. fe4 (22. ♘c3 ♕c4) ♕e5 23. c3 (23. ♗h6 ♕b2) ♖fb8∓; *d)* 20. ♗c5 de4 21. ♗f8 ♕f8=/∞ – 19. ♗c5] **20. ♗c5** [20. ♕b4 ♖b8 21. ♕a3 ♕a5!∓] **♖f7 21. ♗b4 ♖d7! 22. ed5 ♖d5 23. ♕e3 ♗f5 24. 0–0** [24. ♖c1 ♗c2 25. ♘c3 ♖d4 26. ♖c2 (26. ♗c5 ♗f5!) ♖b4 27. ♘e4 ♖ab8 28. 0–0 (28. ♕e2 ♕d4)

♖b2∓] **♖b8! 25. a3** [×b3; 25. ♗c3? ♗f8–+] **♗c2 26. ♕f2 ♖c8 27. ♖fe1 e4! 28. ♗c3 ♗c3 29. ♘c3 ♖d2 30. ♖e2 ♖e2 31. ♘e2 ef3?** [31... ♕d2! 32. fe4 (32. ♘c3 e3) ♖f8 33. ♕e1 ♕e3 34. ♔h2 ♖f2 35. ♘g3 ♕f3 36. ♕g1 ♕f4–+] **32. ♘d4! ♗e4 33. ♖e1 ♗d5 34. ♘f3 ♕f6 35. ♘d4?⊕** [35. ♕d4 ♕d4 36. ♘d4 ♖b8∓] **♕g5 36. ♘f3 ♕f5 37. ♘d4 ♕g4 38. ♘f3?** [38. ♖e2 ♗g2] **♖f8–+ 39. ♖e3 ♗f3 40. ♖f3 ♖f3 41. ♕f3 ♕f3 42. gf3 ♔f7 0 : 1**
[Adorján, Lékó]

220.** **B 78**

GUDJEV – NESIS

corr. 1993

1. e4 c5 2. ♘f3 d6 3. d4 cd4 4. ♘d4 ♘f6 5. ♘c3 g6 6. f3 ♗g7 7. ♗e3 0–0 8. ♕d2 ♘c6 9. ♗c4 ♗d7 10. 0-0-0 [RR 10. h4 h5 11. 0-0-0 ♘e5 12. ♗b3 ♖c8 13. ♗g5 ♖c5 14. ♔b1 b5 15. g4 a5 16. gh5 a4 17. h6 ♗h8 18. h7!? N (18. ♗d5 – 55/237) ♘h7 19. ♗d5 ♘g5 20. hg5 ♗g7 21. ♖h4 e6 22. ♖dh1 ♖e8 23. ♖h7 ♔f8 24. f4 ♘g4 25. f5 ed5 26. ♕f4 ♖c3 27. fg6 ♘e5 28. gf7 ♘f7 29. ♖g7! ♔g7 30. ♖h7! 1 : 0 I. Almasi 2385 – Videki 2415, Kecskemét 1993] **♖c8 11. ♗b3 ♘e5 12. h4 ♘c4 13. ♗c4 ♖c4 14. h5 ♘h5 15. g4 ♘f6 16. ♘d5 e6** [16... ♘d5 17. ed5 ♗e5!? N (17... ♕b6 – 53/(209)) 18. f4? ♗d4 19. ♗d4 ♗g4∓ Gonschier – Mielke, corr. 1992; 18. ♖dg1!] **17. ♘f6** [17. ♘c3 ♕c7 18. ♘db5 ♗b5 19. ♘b5 ♕c6 20. ♘d6 ♖a4 21. ♔b1 ♖d8 22. ♕h2 h5 23. e5 ♘d5 24. ♘e4 ♖c8 25. ♗c5 ♖c4∓] **♕f6 18. ♕h2 ♖fc8 19. ♕h7 ♔f8 20. ♔b1 d5 N** [20... e5 – 44/256] **21. ed5 e5 22. ♗h6!** [22. ♘b3 e4 23. ♗d4 ♖d4 24. ♘d4 ef3 25. ♕h3 ♖c4 26. c3 ♕f4 27. ♕f1!?∞] **♗h6 23. ♕h6 ♕g7** [23... ♔g8 24. ♘f5!±] **24. ♕h8 ♕h8 25. ♖h8 ♔e7 26. ♖c8 ♖c8!** [26... ♗c8 27. ♘b5!] **27. ♘b3 ♔d6** [△ f5] **28. ♘d2!? ♔d5! 29. ♘e4 ♔e6 30. ♖d6** [30. ♘g5 ♔e7 31. ♘f7 ♗a4! 32. b3 ♔f7 33. ba4 ♔e6 △ ♖c4=] **♔e7 31. ♖d5 ♔e6 32. ♖d6** [32. ♖a5] **♔e7 33. ♖d5 ♔e6**
1/2 : 1/2 **[Nesis]**

221.* **!N** **B 80**

KASPAROV 2805 – KAMSKY 2655

Linares 1993

1. e4 c5 2. ♘f3 e6 3. d4 cd4 4. ♘d4 ♘f6 5. ♘c3 d6 6. ♗e3 [RR 6. g3 ♘c6 7. ♗g2 ♗d7 8. 0–0 a6 9. ♗e3 ♕c7 10. a4 ♘e5 11. h3 ♗e7 12. ♘de2! N (12. ♕e2 – 40/(265)) *a)* 12... ♖c8 13. b3 0–0 14. a5 ♗c6 15. f4 ♘ed7 16. ♘d4 (16. g4!?±) e5 17. ♘f5 ♖fe8 18. ♘e7 ♖e7 19. f5 ♘c5 20. ♗g5 ♘fe4!□ 21. ♘e4 ♘e4 22. ♗e7 ♕e7 (1/2 : 1/2 Matulović 2460 – Cvetković 2500, Aranđelovac 1993) 23. ♕e1 ♘f6 (23... d5 24. ♗e4 de4 25. ♕e3±) 24. ♗c6 ♖c6 25. c4 △ ♖d1±; *b)* 12... ♘c4 13. ♗c1⩲ △ b3 Matulović] **a6 7. f3 ♘bd7 8. g4 h6 9. ♖g1! N** [9. h4?! ♘e5 10. ♖g1 ♕b6 11. ♕c1 d5!∓; 10. ♗e2 – 48/(302)] **♕b6** [9... ♘e5?! 10. f4! ♘eg4 11. ♖g4 ♘g4 12. ♕g4 e5 13. ♘f5 g6 14. 0-0-0 gf5 15. ef5; 9... g5! 10. h4±] **10. a3 ♘e5 11. ♗f2! ♕c7** [11... ♗d7? 12. ♘e6 ♕b2 13. ♘c7 ♔d8 14. ♗d4 ♖c8 (14... ♘f3 15. ♕f3 ♕a1 16. ♔d2 ♖c8 17. ♗f6 gf6 18. ♕f6 ♔c7 19. ♘d5+–) 15. ♖a2 ♘f3 16. ♕f3 ♕c1 17. ♔e2 ♔c7 (17... ♖c7 18. ♗f6) 18. ♗e3+–; 11... d5?! 12. ed5 ed5 (12... ♗c5 13. ♘a4 ♕a5 14. c3 ♗d4 15. ♗d4 ♕d5 16. ♘b6 ♕f3 17. ♘a8 ♕e4 18. ♕e2 ♘f3 19. ♔d1+–) 13. ♕e2!] **12. f4 ♘c4?!** [12... ♘g6!?] **13. ♗c4 ♕c4 14. ♕f3 e5?** [14... b5□ *a)* 15. g5 hg5 16. fg5 ♘d7 (16... ♘h5 17. g6↑) 17. g6 ♘e5 (17... fg6 18. b3!+–) 18. gf7 ♘f7 19. 0-0-0; *b)* 15. e5!? ♘d5 16. ♘e4!? (16. ♘d5?! ♕d5 17. ♕d5 ed5±) de5 17. fe5 b4!⇆ 18. g5 *b1)* 18... ba3 19. ♖a3! *b11)* 19... g6? 20. ♖c3! ♘c3 (20... ♗b4? 21. ♘d6+–) 21. ♘f6 ♔d8 22. bc3; *b12)* 19... ♖b8 20. gh6 ♖h6 (20... ♖b2 21. hg7 ♖b1 22. ♔d2 ♗b4 23. c3+–) 21. ♖g7! f5 22. ♘d6 (22. ef6∞) ♗d6 23. ed6 ♖b2 24. ♕g3 ♘f6! (24... ♖b1 25. ♔d2 ♕b4 26. ♔e2 ♕c4 27. ♖d3+–) 25. ♖g8 ♔d7 (25... ♘g8 26. ♕g8 ♔d7 27. ♕g7 ♔d6 28. ♗g3 ♔c5 29. ♕c7 ♔d4 30. ♕e5#) 26. ♕g7 ♔d6 27. ♗g3 ♔d5 28. ♖d8 ♔e4 29. ♕h6! ♖b1 30. ♔d2+–; *b2)* 18... hg5! 19. ♖g5 g6!?

(19... ba3 20. ♖g7!) 20. 0-0-0! (20. ♘f6 ♘f6 21. ♕a8 ♘d5!⇆) ba3 21. b3 ♕b4 22. c3 a2 23. ♔b2 ♕a3 24. ♔a1 ♖b8 25. c4+−] **15. ♘f5 ♗f5 16. gf5 d5 17. fe5 ♘e4 18. ♖g4+− h5 19. ♖h4** [19. ♖f4!+−] **♗c5** [19... ♗e7? 20. ♘e4 de4 21. ♕e4; 19... ♖c8 20. ♘e4 (20. ♖d1? ♗c5 21. ♗c5? ♘g5!) de4 21. ♖e4 ♕c2 22. e6 ♕b2 *a)* 23. ♗d4 ♖c1 (23... ♕h2 24. ef7 ♔f7 25. ♕b3+−) 24. ♖c1 ♕c1 25. ♔f2 ♗c5 26. ef7 ♔f8! 27. ♖e8 ♔f7 28. ♕b7 ♔e8 29. ♕c8 ♔f7 30. ♕c7 ♔e8=; *b)* 23. ♖d1! *b1)* 23... ♕a3 24. ef7 ♔f7 25. ♖d7 ♔g8 26. ♖g7 ♔g7 27. ♕g2+−; *b2)* 23... ♕c3 24. ♕c3 ♖c3 25. ef7 ♔f7 26. ♖d7 ♔g8 27. ♖e8 ♔h7 (27... ♖f3 28. ♗c5 ♖f5 29. ♗f8 ♖f8 30. ♖f8 ♔f8 31. ♖d8) 28. ♖dd8 ♖a3 29. ♖f8 ♖f8 30. ♖f8+−; *b3)* 23... ♖c1 *b31)* 24. ♖c4!? ♕e5 (24... ♖c4 25. ef7 ♔f7 26. ♕d5 ♔f6 27. ♕e6 ♔g5 28. ♗e3 ♔g4 29. ♕g6 ♔f3 30. ♕g3 ♔e4 31. ♕f4#) 25. ♔f1 ♖d1 (25... ♖c4 26. ♕b7 ♕c7 27. ef7 ♔e7 28. ♗h4 ♔f7 29. ♖d7+−) 26. ♕d1 fe6 27. ♖c8 ♔f7 28. ♕d7 ♔g8 29. ♕e6 ♕e6 30. fe6 ♔h7 31. ♗h4 ♗a3 32. ♖h8 ♔h8 33. e7 ♗e7 34. ♗e7; *b32)* 24. ♕d3! ♖d1 25. ♔d1 fe6 26. fe6 ♕a1 27. ♔e2 ♕b2 28. ♔f1 ♕b5 29. ♕b5? ab5 30. e7 ♗e7 31. ♗c5 0−0!!; 29. ♖c4+−] **20. 0-0-0!** [20. ♘e4? de4 21. ♕e4 ♗f2 22. ♔f2 ♕c5] **♗f2 21. ♘e4 de4 22. ♕f2 ♖c8** [22... ♕a2 23. c3+−; 22... ♖d8 23. ♖d8 (23. ♖e1!?) ♔d8 24. ♕g2!+−; 22... 0−0 23. ♖h5 ♖fd8 24. ♖g1 ♕a2 25. ♖g7! ♔g7 26. f6+−] **23. ♔b1 ♖d8 24. ♖d8 ♔d8 25. ♖h3!+− ♕d5 26. ♖c3 ♔d7 27. ♕b6 ♖d8** [27... ♖c8 28. e6] **28. ♖c5 ♕d1 29. ♔a2 ♔e8 30. ♕b7 ♕g4** [30... ♕d4 31. e6!] **31. e6 fe6 32. ♖e5 ♕g5 33. h4 ♕h4 34. ♖e6 ♔f8 35. f6 1 : 0 [Kasparov]**

222.** **!N** **B 81**

ŠMUTER 2440 − OBUHOV 2465
Rossija 1993

1. e4 c5 2. ♘f3 d6 3. d4 cd4 4. ♘d4 ♘f6 5. ♘c3 e6 6. g4 e5 [RR 6... a6 7. h3 d5 8. ♗g2 ♘e4 N (8... e5?! − 50/(252)) 9. ♘e4 de4 10. c3!? e5 11. ♘c2 ♕d1 12. ♔d1 *a)* 12... ♘d7 13. ♘e3 ♘c5 14. ♘d5 ♗d6 (14... ♖b8 15. b4! ♘a4 16. ♔c2 f5 17. gf5 ♗f5 18. ♔b3 b5 19. ♗e3 ♖c8 20. ♖ac1 ♗e6 21. ♖hd1 ♔f7 22. c4± Daniel Popescu 2305 − Badea 2385, Herculane 1993; 15... ♘e6±) 15. ♘b6 ♖b8 16. ♔c2 0−0 17. ♗e3 △ ♖ad1±; *b)* 12... ♘c6!? 13. ♗e4 ♗e6 14. ♘e3 0-0-0 15. ♔c2 ♘e7 16. ♗d2 g6 17. g5 ♘f5∞ Daniel Popescu] **7. ♗b5 ♗d7 8. ♗d7 ♕d7 9. ♘f5 h5 10. gh5** [RR 10. f3 hg4 11. fg4 g6 12. ♘e3 ♖h3 13. 0−0 (13. ♕e2) ♗e7 14. ♘ed5 ♘g4!∞ 15. ♘e7 ♔e7 16. ♘d5 ♔f8 17. ♖f7 ♔f7 18. ♕f1 ♘f2!□ 19. ♕f2 ♔g7= 20. ♕f6 ♔h7 21. ♕g5 ♔g7; 10. ♗g5 ♘h7 11. ♗d2 hg4 12. ♕g4 g6 13. ♘e3 ♕g4 14. ♘g4 ♘c6 △ 15. ♘d5 ♖c8 16. c3 ♔d7 △ f5, ♔e6 D. Kosić] **♘h5 11. ♗h6!! N** [V. Neverov; RR 11. ♘d5 g6 12. ♘g3 ♗e7 *a)* 13. ♗e3?! ♘f6! N (×♘g3, h2; 13... ♘a6 − 46/(290)) 14. ♘f6 ♗f6 15. ♕f3 (15. ♕e2) ♕e6 16. 0-0-0 ♘c6 17. a3 0-0-0∓ M. Pavlović 2455 − D. Kosić 2455, Jugoslavija 1993; *b)* 13. ♘h5 ♖h5 14. ♗e3 ♘c6 15. ♕e2⩲; 14... ♘a6!? △ ♘c7 D. Kosić] **♘c6** [11... g6 12. ♗f8 gf5 13. ♗d6 ♘c6 14. ♗c5±] **12. ♕h5 g6 13. ♕g5 gf5 14. ♗f8 ♘d4** [14... ♔f8 15. 0-0-0 ♕e6 16. ef5 ♕h6 17. h4 ♘d4 18. f6+−; 15... ♘d4 − 14... ♘d4] **15. 0-0-0 ♔f8 16. ♖hg1 ♕e6□**

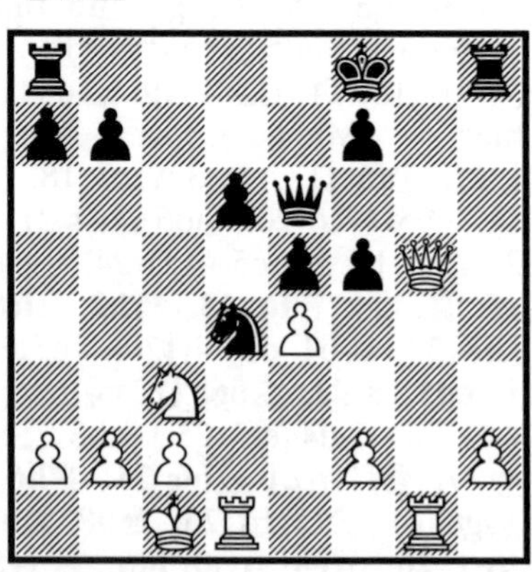

17. ♖d4! ed4 18. ♕g7 ♔e7 19. ♘d5 ♔d7 20. ♕d4→ ♖hc8 [20... fe4 21. ♕a4 ♔c8 (21... ♔d8 22. ♕a5 b6 23. ♘b6) 22. ♕c4 ♔d8 23. ♕c7 ♔e8 24. ♕b7 ♖c8 25. ♘c7 ♖c7 26. ♕c7 ♕a2 27. ♖g4!+−; 20... ♕e5 21. ♕b4 ♖ab8 22. f4 ♕e6 23. ♕a4+−;

20... ♕h6 21. f4 fe4 (21... ♕h2 22. e5! ♖h6 23. e6!!) 22. ♕e4 ♕e6 23. ♕a4 ♔d8 24. ♕a5 b6 25. ♕c3+−; 20... b5 21. ♕d3 ♖ab8 22. ef5 ♕h6 23. f4 ♕h2 24. ♖e1 ♕f2 (24... ♕h4 25. ♕c3 ♖bc8 26. ♘f6 ♔d8 27. ♕a5 ♖c7 28. ♘d5) 25. ♕c3 ♕c5 26. ♖e7 ♔c6 27. ♖c7 ♔d5 28. ♕f3+−; 20... ♖ac8 21. ♖d1! (21. ♕a7? ♖c2 22. ♔b1 ♖c7!) fe4 22. ♕a7 ♖h2 23. ♕b7 ♔d8 24. ♕b6 ♔d7 25. ♕a7 ♔d8 26. ♕a5 ♔e8 27. ♘c7 ♖c7 28. ♕c7+−] **21. ♕b4!** [21. ♕a4? ♖c6 22. ♘b6 ab6 23. ♕a8 ♕e4] **♖ab8 22. ♕a4 ♖c6 23. ♕a7 ♕h6 24. ♔b1 ♕h8 25. ♘b4! ♖c7** [25... ♖c4 26. ♘a6 ♖bc8 27. ♕b7 ♔e8 (27... ♖4c7 28. ♕b5!+−) 28. ♘b4!→] **26. e5! ♖a8** [26... b6 27. e6! fe6 (27... ♔c8 28. ♕a6 ♖bb7 29. ♘c6!) 28. ♕b8 ♕b8 29. ♖g7 ♔c8 30. ♖g8 ♔b7 31. ♖b8 ♔b8 32. ♘a6+−; 26... ♖g8 27. ♕a4 ♔d8 28. ♕a8 ♖c8 29. ♕a5 ♔e8 (29... ♔d7 30. ♖d1) 30. ♖e1+−] **27. e6! ♔e6** [27... fe6 28. ♕a8 ♕a8 29. ♖g7+−] **28. ♕b6!+− ♖c5 29. ♘d3 ♕d4 30. ♕b7! ♖h8 31. ♘c5**
1 : 0 **[Šmuter]**

223.* !N B 81

OCHOA DE ECHAGÜEN 2415 – VEINGOLD 2475

Zaragoza 1993

1. e4 c5 2. ♘f3 e6 3. d4 cd4 4. ♘d4 ♘f6 5. ♘c3 d6 6. ♗e3 ♗e7 7. g4 h6 [7... d5 8. ♗b5 ♔f8 9. ed5 (9. e5!?) ♘d5 10. ♘d5 ♕d5 11. ♕f3±; RR 7... h5!? N 8. gh5 ♖h5 9. ♗g2 ♗d7 10. ♕e2 ♘c6 11. 0-0-0 a6 12. f4 ♕c7 13. ♗f3 ♖h7 14. ♘b3 ♔f8 15. h4 ♗e8 16. h5 b5 17. a3± Magem Badals 2510 – Epišin 2620, Dos Hermanas 1993; ⌓ 8... ♘h5; 7... ♘c6 – 42/269] **8. ♕e2! N** [8. ♖g1 – 42/261] **♘c6 9. 0-0-0 ♗d7** [9... ♘d4 10. ♗d4 e5 11. ♗e5 ♗g4 12. f3±] **10. ♖g1** [△ h4, g5, ♘db5; 10. ♘db5!?] **g5?** [10... a6 11. h4±] **11. ♘db5! ♕b8 12. ♕d2± ♘e5 13. ♗e2 ♗b5 14. ♗b5 ♔f8** [14... ♘ed7 15. e5!+−; 14... ♘fd7±] **15. ♗e2** [△ f4] **♘g6 16. h4! ♘h4 17. f4 ♘e8 18. f5 ♕c8 19. ♗d4 ♖h7 20. ♖g3! a6 21. ♘a4!+− ♗d8 22. ♖c3! ♗a5** [22... ♕d7 23. ♘c5 ♕e7 24. f6!] **23. ♘b6! ♗c3□ 24. ♗c3 ♕d8 25. ♘a8 ♕a8 26. ♗b4** [△ e5] **ef5⊕ 27. e5 ♕d8 28. ed6 ♕d7 29. gf5 ♘f5 30. ♗g4 ♔g8 31. ♖f1 ♘eg7 32. ♗f5 ♘f5 33. ♖f5⊕ 1 : 0**
[Ochoa de Echagüen]

224. B 81

STEFÁNSSON 2495 – V. GUREVICH 2425

Cappelle la Grande 1993

1. e4 c5 2. ♘f3 d6 3. d4 cd4 4. ♘d4 ♘f6 5. ♘c3 a6 6. ♗e3 e6 7. g4 h6 8. h3 N [8. ♗g2 – 56/243] **b5 9. a3 ♗b7 10. ♗g2 ♘bd7 11. ♘de2 ♗e7** [11... ♘e5 12. b3 g5!?∞] **12. f4 ♕c7 13. 0–0 ♘b6 14. b3 0-0-0?!** [14... 0–0] **15. ♕e1 d5 16. e5 ♘fd7 17. a4! b4 18. a5 ♗c5 19. ♘d1 ♘a8 20. ♗c5** [20. c3 bc3 21. ♖c1? ♗e3 22. ♘e3 ♕a5! 23. ♖c3 ♘c7∓] **♕c5 21. ♕f2!** [21. ♔h1 g5∞] **♔b8 22. ♕c5 ♘c5 23. ♘d4±** [×b4] **♘c7 24. ♘b2 ♘b5** [24... ♖hf8 25. ♘a4 ♘e4 26. ♘b6 (△ ♖a4) ♘c5 27. f5] **25. ♘b5 ab5 26. f5 ♖c8 27. fe6 fe6 28. ♖f7** [28. ♖f4? ♘a6 29. ♖c1 ♖c3 30. ♘d3 ♖hc8 31. ♘b4 ♖b3⇆] **♘a6 29. ♖c1 g5** [29... ♖c3 30. ♖g7 ♖hc8 31. h4! ♖b3 32. cb3 ♖c1 33. ♔h2 ♖c2 34. g5 hg5 35. h5+−] **30. ♗f1 ♗c6 31. ♗d3 ♘c5 32. ♖cf1 ♘d7 33. ♖e1⊕ ♘c5 34. ♖ef1 h5** [34... ♘d7 35. ♖e7 ♘e5 (35... ♖ce8 36. ♖e8 ♖e8 37. ♗g6) 36. ♖e6 ♖ce8 37. ♖ff6±] **35. ♗h7 hg4 36. hg4 d4** [36... ♘d7! 37. ♘d3! ♘f8 38. ♘b4 ♘h7 *a)* 39. ♖g7!? *a1)* 39... ♗e8 40. ♘a6 ♔a8 41. ♘c7 ♔b8 (41... ♖c7 42. ♖c7 ♗g6 43. ♖g7 ♗c2 44. ♖ff7+−) 42. ♘e8 ♖ce8 43. ♖ff7+−; *a2)* 39... ♘f8 40. ♘c6! ♖c6 41. ♖ff7 *a21)* 41... ♖c2 42. a6+−; *a22)* 41... ♖a6 42. b4+−; *a23)* 41... b4 42. ♖e7 (△ a6) ♖c2 43. a6+−; *a24)* 41... ♘g6 42. ♖g6 ♖c2 43. ♖gg7 d4 (43... ♖c1 44. ♔f2 ♖c2 45. ♔e3 ♖h3 46. ♔d4+−) 44. a6 d3 (44... ♖c1 45. ♔f2 ♖c2 46. ♔f3 ♖h3 47. ♔e4 ♖e2 48. ♔d4 ♖d2 49. ♔c5+−) 45. ♖b7 ♔c8 46. a7 ♖c1 47. ♔g2 ♖c2 48. ♔g3+−; *a25)* 41... d4!□ 42. ♖e7 ♘g6 43. ♖g6 ♖c2 44. ♖gg7 d3 45. ♖b7 ♔c8 46.

♖a7 ♔d8 47. ♖gd7 ♔c8 48. ♖d3±; *b)* 39. ♘a6 ♔a8 40. ♘c7 ♔b8 41. ♘e6 ♗e8 42. ♖g7 ♖c2 43. a6] **37. ♖g7 ♖c7 38. ♖c7 ♔c7 39. ♖f7 ♔b8 40. ♖g7 ♗f3 41. ♘d3+− ♘a6** [41... ♘d3 42. cd3 ♗g4 43. ♗e4] **42. ♘f2 ♘c5 43. ♗d3 ♘d3** [43... ♗c6 44. ♖g5 ♘d3 45. ♘d3 ♖h1 46. ♔f2 ♖h2 47. ♔e1 ♖c2 48. ♘b4 ♖c3 49. ♖g8 ♔c7 50. ♘c6 ♖c6 51. ♖g7 ♔d8 52. g5] **44. ♘d3 ♗g4 45. ♘b4 ♗f3 46. ♖g5 ♖c8 47. ♖g6 ♗e4 48. ♖e6 ♗c2 49. ♘c6**
1 : 0 **[Stefánsson]**

225.* **B 81**

KUPREJČIK 2560 – ŠIPOV 2490

Passau 1993

1. e4 c5 2. ♘f3 d6 3. d4 cd4 4. ♘d4 ♘f6 5. ♘c3 e6 6. g4 h6 7. ♗g2 [RR 7. h4 a6 8. ♗g2 ♘c6 9. g5 hg5 10. hg5 ♖h1 11. ♗h1 ♘d7 12. f4 ♕b6 13. ♘de2 g6 14. b3 ♖b8 15. ♗b2 ♕c7 16. ♕d2 b5 17. 0-0-0 N (17. ♗g2 – 54/219) ♘b6 18. ♖e1!? (18. a3 ♗d7 19. ♗g2 b4 20. ab4 ♘b4= Kir. Georgiev 2660 – Şubă 2520, Budapest (zt) 1993) b4 19. ♘d1 △ ♘e3-g4± Stoica] **♘c6 8. h3 a6 9. ♘b3 g5!? N** [9... ♗e7 – 41/(242)] **10. f4 gf4 11. ♗f4 ♘e5** [11... ♕c7!? △ ♘e5⇆] **12. ♗e5!?** [12. ♕e2 △ 0-0-0∞] **de5 13. ♕d8 ♔d8 14. 0-0-0 ♘d7!** [14... ♗d7 15. ♖hf1 ♗e7 16. ♖d3 (△ ♖df3) ♖g8□ 17. ♘a4 ♔c7 18. ♖c3 ♗c6 19. ♘a5 h5 20. ♗f3±] **15. ♖d3** [15. ♖hf1 ♔e8=] **b5** [15... b6!? 16. ♘a4! ♔c7 17. ♖f1 ♖h7 18. ♖df3 f6 19. ♖c3 ♔b7∞] **16. a4! b4 17. ♘d1 h5! 18. gh5 ♖h5** [18... a5!⇆] **19. ♔b1** [19. ♘e3 ♗h6=] **♔e8** [19... a5!?] **20. ♘e3 ♖a7** [20... ♘c5 21. ♘c5 ♗c5 22. ♘g4 ♔e7 23. ♖hd1 ♗d4 24. c3! bc3 25. bc3 ♗c5 26. ♖d8↑; 25... ♗b6!∞] **21. ♘g4 ♗e7 22. c3!⩲ ♖h8** [22... f5!? 23. ♘e3□ ♘f6 24. cb4!⩲] **23. ♖hd1!** [23. cb4? ♗b4 24. ♖c1 ♔e7=] **a5 24. cb4 ab4** [24... ♗b4? 25. ♘e5!] **25. ♖c1 ♗a6 26. ♖dd1 ♗e2 27. ♖c8 ♗d8 28. ♘f6 ♔e7 29. ♖d7 ♖d7 30. ♘d7 ♔d7 31. ♖c2 ♗h5□ 32. a5 ♗g5?** [32... ♖g8!⩲ Krasenkov] **33. ♖c4± ♗e3 34. ♗f1** [34. ♖b4?? ♖g8 35. ♗f1 ♖g1−+] **f5?!⊕ 35. ♖b4 f4 36. a6 f3 37. ♘a5 ♗d4 38. ♖b7 ♔d6 39. ♘c4 ♔c6 40. b4 ♗g6**

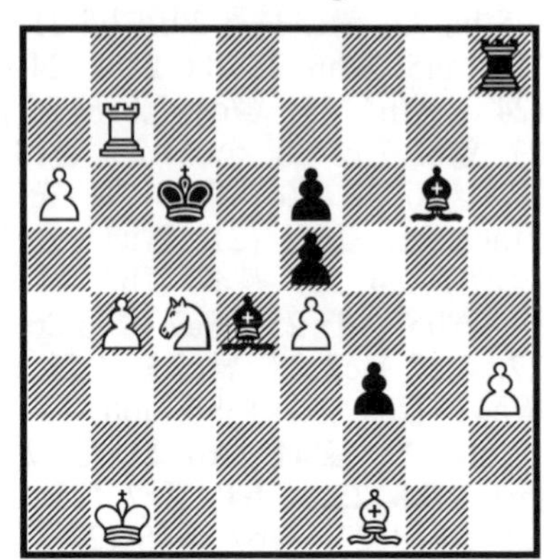

41. ♘e5! **1 : 0** **[Šipov]**

226. !N **B 81**

LANDENBERGUE 2385 – MAGERRAMOV 2565

Bad Wörishofen 1993

1. e4 c5 2. ♘f3 d6 3. d4 cd4 4. ♘d4 ♘f6 5. ♘c3 a6 6. ♗e3 e6 7. g4 ♘c6 8. g5 ♘d7 9. h4 ♗e7 10. ♕h5 0–0 11. 0-0-0 ♖e8 12. f4 ♗f8 13. ♗d3! N ± [13. ♗c4 – 49/260] **g6** [13... ♘d4 14. ♗d4 e5 15. ♗c4! g6 16. ♗f7±→; 13... ♘c5 14. ♘c6 ♘d3 15. ♖d3 bc6 16. e5! △ ♘e4-f6±→] **14. ♕f3 ♘d4?!** [14... ♗g7 15. ♘de2±] **15. ♗d4 e5 16. ♗e3 ef4 17. ♗f4?!** [17. ♕f4!± △ 17... ♘e5 18. ♘d5 ♗g7 19. ♗b6+−] **♘e5 18. ♕g3 ♗g7± 19. ♗e2 ♗e6 20. h5** [20. ♔b1!? △ ♘d5±] **♖c8 21. hg6 hg6 22. ♖h4 ♕a5⇆ 23. ♖dh1 ♖c3! 24. bc3?** [24. ♕c3 ♕c3 25. bc3 ♗a2=] **♖c8↑ 25. c4!□ ♘c4 26. ♕h2 ♕a3 27. ♔d1 ♕b2!** [27... ♕c3?? 28. ♖h8!+−] **28. ♗d3** [28. ♗c4 ♖c4 29. ♖h8 ♗h8 30. ♕h7 ♔f8 31. ♗d6 ♔e8 32. ♕h8 ♕h8 33. ♖h8 ♔d7∓] **♔f8! 29. ♖h7** [29. ♗c4 ♖c4 30. ♗d6 ♔e8∓→; 29. ♗d6 ♘d6 30. ♕d6 ♔g8⩱↑] **♗g4 30. ♔e1 ♘e5!−+ 31. ♗e5 ♗e5 32. ♕h6** [32. ♖f7 ♔e8!! (32... ♔f7? 33. ♕h7 ♔e6 34. ♗c4!! ♖c4 35. ♕g8 ♔d7 36. ♖h7+−) 33. ♕h7 ♕c1 34. ♔f2 ♖c2] **♔e8 33. ♔f2 ♖c2** **0 : 1**
[Magerramov]

227. **B 81**

GLEK 2545 – VOLKE 2460
Cuxhaven 1993

1. e4 c5 2. ♘f3 e6 3. d4 cd4 4. ♘d4 ♘f6 5. ♘c3 d6 6. g4 ♗e7 7. g5 ♘fd7 8. h4 0–0 9. ♗e3 ♘b6!? N [9... ♘c6 – 56/245] **10. ♕e2** [10. f4 d5 11. e5 ♗b4∞; 10. a3!?] **d5 11. 0-0-0!?** [11. ed5 ♘d5=] **e5?!** [11... ♗b4! 12. ♘db5 a6 13. a3 ab5 14. ♕b5 ♗c3 15. ♗b6∞] **12. ♘f3 ♗g4 13. ed5!** [13. ♗b6 ab6 14. ♖d5 ♕c7$\overline{\overline{\infty}}$; 13. ♘d5 ♘d5 14. ♖d5 ♕c7 △ ♘c6, ♗e6$\overline{\overline{\infty}}$] **♗b4 14. ♘e4 ♕c8** [△ ♕f5] **15. ♗g2 ♖d8** [15... ♘c4 16. ♕d3 b5 17. h5! △ h6, g6±→] **16. ♕b5! ♘a6 17. a3 ♗f8 18. d6!± ♘c4** [18... ♕c4 19. ♘c3! ♕b5 20. ♘b5 e4 21. ♘e5!±] **19. ♘e5! ♘e3 20. fe3 ♗d1 21. ♖d1 ♕e6 22. g6!+– hg6 23. ♘g5** [△ ♗d5] **1 : 0** **[Glek]**

228. **B 82**

ŠABALOV 2575 – EHLVEST 2625
New York 1993

1. e4 c5 2. ♘f3 e6 3. d4 cd4 4. ♘d4 ♘f6 5. ♘c3 d6 6. f4 ♗e7 7. ♗d3 ♘c6 8. ♘f3 0–0 9. a3!? ♘d7 10. 0–0 b6 11. b4 N [11. ♕e2 ♗b7 – 4/533] **♗b7 12. ♗b2 ♖c8 13. ♕e1± a5!? 14. ♘b5 e5** [14... ab4 15. ab4 d5 16. c3! de4 17. ♗e4 ♘f6 18. ♖d1 ♕e8 19. ♗d3±] **15. ♖d1! ab4 16. ab4 ef4 17. ♗e2 ♘cb8 18. c4 ♗e4 19. ♘d6 ♗d6 20. ♖d6 ♕e7 21. ♕c3$\overline{\overline{\infty}}$ f6 22. ♖fd1 ♖fe8** [22... g5? 23. ♘g5! fg5 24. ♕h8 ♔f7 25. ♗h5+–] **23. ♕d2 ♗a8** [23... ♗c2!?] **24. ♗f1 ♘e5** [24... ♕e3 25. ♕f2$\overline{\overline{\infty}}$] **25. ♕f4 ♗f3 26. gf3 ♘bc6 27. b5 ♘g6 28. ♕e4 ♕e4 29. fe4 ♘ce5 30. ♗h3 ♖a8?!** [30... ♘c4! 31. ♗c8 ♘d6 32. ♗d7 ♖d8 33. ♖d6 ♘f8 34. ♖b6 (34. ♗e6 ♘e6 35. ♖e6 ♖d1 36. ♔f2 ♖d2=) ♖d7=] **31. ♗e6 ♔h8?** [31... ♖e6 32. ♖e6 ♘c4±] **32. ♖a1! ♖ab8 33. ♖a7 ♘f3 34. ♔f1 ♘g5** [34... ♘h2? 35. ♔g2] **35. ♗f5 ♘h4** [35... ♘e4 36. ♖dd7!+–] **36. ♖dd7 ♘f5 37. ef5 ♖bd8** [37... ♖g8 38. ♖e7 h6 39. h4 ♘h7 40. ♗d4+–] **38. c5!+– bc5 39. b6 ♖b8 40. ♖ab7 ♖a8** [40... ♖b7 41. ♖b7 ♘e4 42. ♖d7 c4 43. ♗a3 c3 44. b7 c2 45. ♖c7] **41. ♖g7 ♘e4 42. ♖h7 ♔g8 43. ♖bg7 ♔f8 44. b7 ♖a2** [44... ♖ab8 45. ♗c1 ♘g5 46. ♗g5 fg5 47. f6] **45. ♖g2!** **1 : 0** **[Byrne, Mednis]**

229.* **B 82**

J. POLGÁR 2595 – FTÁČNIK 2535
Budapest (zt) 1993

1. e4 c5 2. ♘f3 d6 3. d4 cd4 4. ♘d4 ♘f6 5. ♘c3 a6 [RR 5... ♘c6 6. ♗c4 ♕b6 7. ♘b3 e6 8. 0–0 ♗e7 9. ♗e3 ♕c7 10. ♗d3 a6 11. f4 b5 12. ♕f3 ♗b7 13. ♕h3 ♘b4 14. a3 ♘d3 15. cd3 e5 16. ♖ac1 ♕d8 17. ♘d2!? N (17. g4? – 11/326; 17. d4 ♘e4 18. ♘e4 ♗e4 19. de5 0–0 20. ♖fd1±) 0–0 18. d4 ef4 (18... ed4?! 19. ♗d4 ♖e8 20. ♖ce1 ♕d7 21. f5 a5 22. ♖e3 b4 23. ♘e2 ♖ac8 24. ♖g3 ♔f8 25. ♘f4 ba3 26. ♘e6!+– A. Frolov 2530 – Šmuter 2440, Nikolaev (zt) 1993; ⌓ 19... a5) 19. ♗f4 d5± A. Frolov] **6. f4 e6 7. ♗d3 b5 8. ♕f3 ♗b7 9. ♗e3 ♘bd7 10. a3** [10. 0-0-0 b4 11. ♘ce2 ♘c5⇆] **g6** [10... ♘c5 11. g4; 10... e5 11. ♘f5 g6 12. ♘g3 ♗g7∞] **11. 0-0-0 N** [11. 0–0] **♕c7** [11... e5 12. ♘db5!? ab5 13. ♗b5→] **12. g4 ♘c5** [12... e5 13. fe5 de5 14. ♘db5 ab5 15. ♗b5 ♗c6 16. ♗c4→] **13. ♔b1 ♗e7** [13... d5 14. ♘db5 ab5 15. ♗b5 ♔e7 16. ♗d4→; 13... ♘d3 14. cd3 ♗e7 15. ♖c1±] **14. ♖he1 0-0-0?** [14... e5 15. fe5 de5 16. ♘db5 ab5 17. ♗b5 ♔f8 18. ♗h6 ♔g8 19. g5→; 14... d5!? 15. ♘db5!? (J. Polgár; 15. e5 ♘fe4∞) ab5 16. ♗b5 ♔f8 17. ed5 ♘d5 18. ♘d5 ♗d5 19. ♕h3↑] **15. g5 ♘e8** [15... ♘fd7 16. b4 ♘a4 (16... ♘d3 17. cd3 ♘b8 18. ♘cb5 ab5 19. ♘b5 ♕d7 20. ♘a7 ♔c7 21. ♖c1 ♘c6 22. b5 ♖b8 23. ♔a2+–) 17. ♘a4 ba4 18. ♕e2 e5 19. ♗a6!? (19. ♘f3±) ed4 20. ♖d4 ♔b8 21. ♗b7 ♕b7 22. ♖d5→; 15... ♘h5 16. b4 ♘d3 (16... ♘d7 17. ♘cb5 ab5 18. ♘b5 ♕b8 19. ♘a7 ♔c7 20. ♗e2 ♖de8 21. ♗d4+–) 17. cd3 ♔b8 18. ♖c1 ♕d7 19. ♗g1±] **16. b4! ♘d3** [16... ♘d7 17. ♘cb5 ab5 18. ♘b5 ♕b8 19. ♘a7 ♔c7 20. ♗b5 e5 21. ♗f2 ♕a8 22. ♕c3 ♔b8 23. ♘c6 ♗c6 24. ♗c6 ♕a6 25. b5 ♕a4 26. fe5+−; 16... ♘a4 17. ♘a4 ba4 18. ♕e2 e5 19. ♘f3±] **17. cd3 ♔b8 18. ♖c1 ♕d7 19. ♗g1 ♖c8 20. ♕f2 ♗a8** [20... ♗c6 21. ♘a4! ba4 22. ♘c6 ♖c6 23. ♖c6 ♕c6 24. ♕a7 ♔c8 25. ♖c1+−; 20... ♖c7 21. ♘b3 d5 22. ♕a7 ♔c8 23. ♘a5+−]

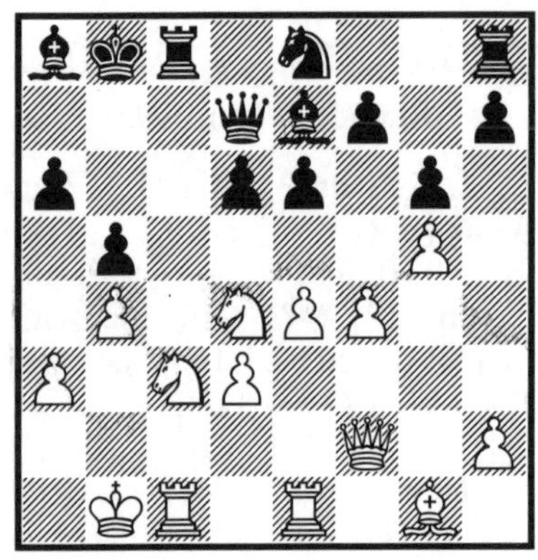

21. a4! ba4 [21... ♘c7 22. ♘c6!+−; 21... e5 22. ♘b3 ba4 23. ♘a5 ♗d8 24. ♘d5+−] **22. b5!+− ab5** [22... e5 23. ba6 ed4 24. ♕b2 ♗b7 25. ♗d4; 22... ♕b7 23. ♔a1; 22... ♗b7 23. ♘a4 ♖c1 24. ♖c1 ab5 25. ♘b6 ♕d8 26. ♘e6 fe6 27. ♘d7] **23. ♘db5 a3** [23... ♕b7 24. ♕b2 a3 25. ♕b3 ♖c6 26. ♗a7 ♔c8 27. ♗d4] **24. ♘a3** [24. ♕b6 ♕b7 25. ♕a5 ♖c6 26. ♗a7 ♔c8 27. ♘a4] **♖c7 25. ♕b2 ♖b7 26. ♘cb5 ♖f8 27. ♗a7! ♖a7 28. ♘a7 ♔a7 29. ♘b5 ♔b8** [29... ♔a6 30. ♕a3 ♔b6 31. ♖e2 d5 32. ♕a8 ♘d6 33. ♖c6 ♕c6 34. ♕a7 ♔b5 35. ♖b2#] **30. ♘d4 ♗b7** [30... ♔a7 31. ♕a3 ♔b8 32. ♕b4] **31. ♘c6 ♔c8 32. ♘e5** [32. ♘e7 ♔d8 33. ♘c6 ♗c6 34. ♕b6] **♕c7 33. ♖c7 ♘c7 34. ♘c4** [34. ♘d7 ♔d7 35. ♕b7] **♗a6** [34... ♗c6 35. ♖c1] **35. ♘b6 ♔d8 36. ♖c1 d5** [36... ♗d3 37. ♔a1 ♗e4 38. ♕c3] **37. ♕c2 ♗d6 38. ♕c6 ♗d3 39. ♔a1 1 : 0** **[Ftáčnik]**

230. **B 82**

KOTRONIAS 2550 − VAN WELY 2525

München (open) 1992/93

1. e4 c5 2. ♘f3 d6 3. d4 cd4 4. ♘d4 ♘f6 5. ♘c3 a6 6. ♗e3 e6 7. f4 b5 8. ♕f3 ♗b7 9. ♗d3 b4 10. ♘ce2 h5!? N [10... ♘bd7] **11. c3 e5?!** [11... ♘bd7∞ 12. cb4? e5∓; 12. ♘b3] **12. ♘b3 d5 13. 0-0-0↑ ♘bd7 14. ed5 ♗d5 15. ♕h3 e4 16. ♗c2 a5 17. ♖d5!□ ♘d5 18. ♖d1 ♘5f6** [18... ♘e3? 19. ♕e3 ♗e7 20. ♗e4 ♖c8 21. ♗f5 ♖c7 22. ♘c5!+−; 18... ♘7f6! 19. ♘c5!? (19. c4?! a4! 20. ♘a1 b3! 21. ab3 a3→) ♗c5 20. ♗c5 (20. ♗a4 ♔f8 21. ♗c5 ♔g8∓) ♕d7□ 21. ♕d7 ♔d7 22. c4 ♖hc8! (22... ♔c6? 23. ♗d4 △ ♗f6, ♗e4±) 23. ♗d4 ♖c4 24. ♗f6 ♔e6! (24... ♖ac8 25. ♖d5? ♔e6−+; 25. ♗c3!) 25. ♗h4!±] **19. ♘c5! ♗c5 20. ♗c5± ♕c7?** [20... ♘c5! 21. ♖d8 ♖d8 22. ♕f5! ♘d3 (22... ♘fd7? 23. ♗e4 g6 24. ♕d5+−) 23. ♗d3 ed3 24. ♕e5!+− △ 24... ♔f8 25. ♕a5, △ 24... ♔d7 25. ♘d4; 22... ♘cd7!?±] **21. ♗d6+− ♕c4 22. ♘d4! bc3** [22... ♕a2?? 23. ♗b3] **23. ♗b3 cb2 24. ♔b2!** [⇔c] **♕a6 25. ♘e6! ♖a7** [25... fe6 26. ♕e6 ♔d8 27. ♕e7 ♔c8 28. ♖c1 ♔b7 29. ♗d5] **26. ♘g5!** [26. ♘g7? ♔d8⇆] **♖b7** [26... ♖f8 27. ♘f7] **27. ♔a1 ♖b3 28. ♕b3 1 : 0** **[Kotronias]**

231. !N **B 82**

HJARTARSON 2625 − FAHNENSCHMIDT 2365

Deutschland 1993

1. e4 c5 2. ♘f3 d6 3. d4 cd4 4. ♘d4 ♘f6 5. ♘c3 a6 6. f4 e6 7. ♕f3 ♕b6 8. a3 ♗e7 9. ♗d3 ♘c6 10. ♘b3 ♕c7 11. g4! N [11. ♗d2 − 46/305] **h6** [11... b5 12. g5 ♘d7 13. h4→] **12. h4 h5!?** [12... b5 13. g5 ♘d7 14. ♗e3 (14. g6!? fg6 15. e5∞̄) ♗b7 15. 0-0-0⩲] **13. g5 ♘g4 14. ♗e2! b5 15. ♕g2 b4 16. ab4 ♘b4 17. ♗g4 hg4 18. ♖h2 ♖b8□ 19. ♕g4 ♘c2 20. ♖c2 ♖b3 21. h5⩲ ♗b7** [21... e5 22. ♕e2±] **22. ♕e2 ♕d7 23. ♗e3 e5 24. 0-0-0 ef4** [24... ♕h3!? *a)* 25. g6!? 0−0 (25... ♕h5? 26. ♕c4+−) 26. ♗d2± △ ♕c4; *b)* 25. fe5 de5 26. h6 0−0 27. g6! fg6 (27... gh6 28. ♖g1±) 28. ♕c4 ♔h7 29. ♕b3 ♕e3 30. ♖cd2±] **25. ♗f4 ♕e6 26. h6± gh6 27. gh6 ♖b4 28. ♖cd2 d5?** [28... ♖h6 29.

♗h6 ♕h6 30. ♔b1 ♗f6 31. ♘d5±] **29. ed5 ♕e2 30. ♖e2!** [30. ♘e2? ♔d7=∞] **♔d7 31. d6 ♗f8 32. ♖e7!+– ♔d8** [32... ♗e7 33. de7 ♔e6 (33... ♔c8 34. ♗g5; 33... ♔c6 34. ♖d8) 34. ♖d8 ♖f4 35. ♖h8 ♔e7 36. h7 ♖h4 37. ♖b8] **33. ♗e5 ♗h6 34. ♔b1 ♖f8 35. ♗f6 ♖f4 36. ♖b7 ♖f6 37. d7 ♗f4□ 38. ♘d5 ♖d6 39. ♖b8 1 : 0 [Hjartarson]**

232. B 83

KAMSKY 2655 – B. LARSEN 2540

Buenos Aires 1993

1. e4 c5 2. ♘f3 e6 3. d4 cd4 4. ♘d4 ♘c6 5. ♘c3 d6 6. ♗e2 ♘f6 7. 0–0 ♗e7 8. ♗e3 0–0 9. f4 ♗d7 10. ♕d3?! N [10. ♘b3 – 56/256] **a6 11. ♖ad1 ♖c8 12. a3 ♕c7 13. ♘b3!?** [13. g4!? ♘d4 14. ♗d4 e5 15. fe5 (15. g5?! ed4 16. gf6 ♗f6 17. ♘d5 ♕c2∓; 15. ♗e3!? ♗g4 16. ♗g4 ♘g4 17. ♘d5 ♕d8 18. ♗b6 ♕e8 19. ♕g3 ♘f6 20. fe5 ♘d5 21. ed5 de5 22. d6 ♕c6 23. ♗e3 ♗d6∓) de5 16. g5 ed4 17. gf6 ♗f6 18. ♘d5 ♕c2 19. ♘f6 gf6 20. ♕d4!? ♕e2 21. ♖f2 ♕h5 22. ♕d7∞] **♖fd8 14. ♔h1 b5 15. ♗f3** [△ ♕e2-f2, g4↑] **b4?! 16. ab4 ♘b4 17. ♕d2± d5!? 18. e5** [18. ♕f2? de4 19. ♗b6 ♕b7 20. ♗d8 ef3! 21. ♗e7 fg2 22. ♕g2 ♗c6∓] **♘e4 19. ♗e4 de4 20. ♕f2** [×b6, c5, e4] **♗b5!? 21. ♖d8!?** [21. ♗b6?! ♖d1 22. ♖d1 ♕c6∓; 21. ♘b5 ab5 22. ♗b6 e3 23. ♕e3 ♖d1 24. ♖d1 ♕c2 25. ♖c1 ♕c1! 26. ♘c1 ♘d5 27. ♕e1 ♘b6= △ ♘d5-b4] **♕d8** [21... ♖d8 22. ♖e1 △ ♗b6±] **22. ♖d1 ♕e8 23. ♗c5** [23. ♘d4!? ♗c6 24. f5!? ♗f8∞] **♗c5 24. ♘c5 e3 25. ♕e3 ♘c2 26. ♕f2 ♘b4 27. ♘3e4± ♖b8 28. ♕g3⊕ ♔h8?** [28... ♕e7⇆ 29. ♘d6 △ f5↑] **29. ♘d6 ♕e7 30. f5!+– ♖f8⊕ 31. h3!?** [31. f6 gf6 32. ef6 ♕f6 33. ♘b5 ab5 34. ♘d7 ♖d8!∞; 31. ♖d4! ♘c6 32. ♖g4 ef5 33. ♖g7 f4 34. ♘f7 ♕f7 35. ♖f7 fg3 36. ♖f8+–] **♘c6?** [31... ♗c6] **32. f6+– gf6 33. ef6 ♕f6 34. ♘d7 ♕g7 35. ♕g7 ♔g7 36. ♘f8 ♔f8 37. ♘b5 ab5 38. ♖d6 1 : 0 [Kamsky]**

233.* B 83

J. POLGÁR 2595 – SAX 2570

Budapest (zt) 1993

1. e4 c5 2. ♘f3 e6 3. d4 cd4 4. ♘d4 ♘f6 5. ♘c3 d6 6. ♗e2 ♘c6 7. 0–0 ♗e7 8. ♗e3 ♗d7 9. f4 [RR 9. ♘db5 ♕b8 10. ♗f4!? N (10. a4 – 55/251) ♘e5 11. ♗g5 a6 12. ♗f6 gf6 13. ♘d4 b5 (13... ♕a7?! 14. ♔h1 ♖c8 15. ♕d2 ♕b6?! 16. ♘b3 h5 17. a4 h4 18. h3!⩲ Fedorowicz 2560 – I. Ivanov 2510, USA (ch) 1992; 15... b5) 14. f4 *a)* 14... b4 15. fe5 de5 (15... bc3 16. ef6 cb2 17. ♖b1±) 16. ♘e6 fe6 17. ♗h5 ♔d8 18. ♘e2↑; *b)* 14... ♘c6 15. ♘c6 ♗c6 16. ♗d3 ♕b6 17. ♔h1 ♕c5⇆; 16. a3!? P. Wolff] **0–0 10. ♔h1 ♘d4 11. ♗d4 ♗c6 12. ♗d3 ♘d7 13. ♕f3 N** [13. ♕g4 – 50/(263)] **a6?!** [13... ♗f6 14. ♗f6 ♘f6 (14... ♕f6 15. ♕h3 h6 16. ♖ae1 ♘c5 17. ♖e3⩲) 15. ♕h3 e5 16. f5 h6 17. g4 ♘h7 18. ♕g3=] **14. ♕g3 e5** [14... ♗f6 15. e5 de5 16. fe5 ♗g5 17. ♘e4±] **15. fe5 ♗h4 16. ♕h3 ♘e5 17. ♗e5 de5 18. ♗c4 ♕e7 19. a4** [19. ♘d5 ♗d5 20. ♗d5 ♖ab8 21. ♕b3 ♗f6 22. ♖f3 ♔h8 23. ♖af1⩲] **♗g5 20. ♘d5 ♕c5 21. ♗b3 ♔h8** [21... ♖ac8 22. ♖f7] **22. ♕h5 f6 23. ♖ad1** [23. ♘c7 ♗e8 24. ♘e6! ♗h5 25. ♘c5±; 23... ♗e4!∞] **♖ad8** [23... ♗d5 24. ♖d5 ♕b4=] **24. ♖d3 ♗d5 25. ♖d5 ♖d5 26. ♗d5 g6** [26... ♕c2?? 27. ♕g5+–] **27. ♕e2 ♕c7 28. ♕d3 a5 29. c3 b6 30. b4** [30. g3 △ h4, b4±] **♖c8 31. ba5 ba5 32. c4 ♖b8 33. ♕g3 ♔g7 34. ♕f2 ♕b6 35. c5 ♕b2 36. ♕f3** [36. ♕b2 ♖b2 37. c6 ♗e3 △ ♗b6=] **♕c2⊕ 37. c6** [37... ♖b2=] **1/2 : 1/2 [Sax]**

234. !N B 83

DOLMATOV 2615 – RAZUVAEV 2525

Rostov na Donu 1993

1. e4 c5 2. ♘f3 d6 3. d4 cd4 4. ♘d4 ♘f6 5. ♘c3 e6 6. ♗e2 ♗e7 7. 0–0 0–0 8. f4 ♘c6 9. ♗e3 ♗d7 10. ♘b3 a6 11. a4 ♘a5 12. e5 ♘e8 13. ♘a5 ♕a5 14. ♘e4 [14. ♗d4!?] **♕c7 15. a5 d5** [15... ♗c6 16. ♗b6 ♕d7 17. ♗f3 ♖c8 18. ♖f2 ♗e4 19. ♗e4 f5 20. ♗f3 d5 21. b3±] **16. ♘d2! N** ± [16. ♘g3 — 27/434] **g6** [16... ♗c5!? 17. ♗c5 ♕c5 18. ♔h1 f6 19. ♘f3±] **17. ♘b3 ♘g7 18. ♗b6 ♕c8 19. ♖f3?!** [19. c3±] **f6! 20. ef6 ♗f6 21. ♘d4** [21. c3 ♘f5=] **♕e8 22. ♕d2 e5 23. fe5 ♕e5 24. ♗d3 ♗g4 25. ♖e3** [25. ♖ff1? ♗g5∓] **♕d6?!** [25... ♕g5 26. ♖ae1 ♕h6!⇆] **26. ♖ee1 ♗e5 27. g3** [27. h3? ♗h2 28. ♔h1 ♘h5∓] **♗h3** [27... ♘f5=] **28. ♗f1! ♗f1 29. ♖f1 ♘h5 30. ♕d3 ♘f6 31. ♘b3! ♘e4 32. c3 ♕e6 33. ♖fd1?** [33. ♖ad1 ♖f1 34. ♖f1 ♖f8±] **♘g5! 34. ♕d5?** [34. ♖f1 d4! △ ♕d5∓; 34. ♘c5□ ♗d4 35. cd4 ♘h3 36. ♔g2 ♖f2 37. ♔h1 ♕g4 *a)* 38. ♕e3 ♖e2∓; *b)* 38. ♖f1 ♘f4 (38... ♖af8!?) 39. ♖f2 (39. ♕d1 ♖h2–+) ♘d3 40. ♘d3 ♕e4∓; *c)* 38. ♖d2 ♘f4 (38... ♖af8!?) 39. ♕e3?! ♖d2 40. ♕f4 (40. ♕d2 ♕f3 41. ♔g1 ♘h3#) ♕e2–+; 39. ♖f2∓]

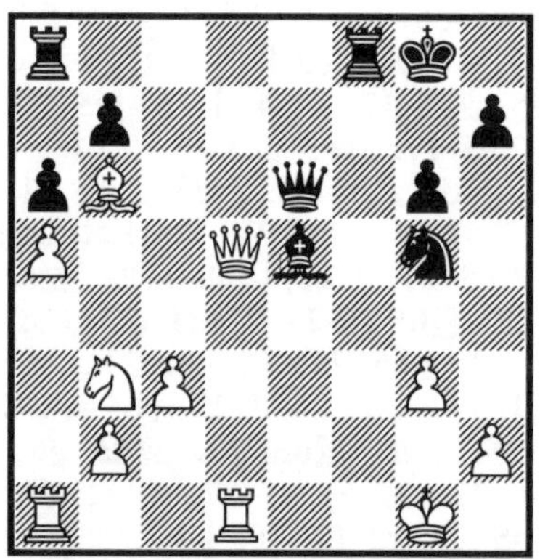

34... ♗d4!! 35. ♖d4 ♘f3 36. ♔g2 ♘d4 37. ♕e6 [37. ♕d4 ♕b3∓] **♘e6∓ 38. ♖d1 ♖ae8 39. h4 h5 40. ♖d2 ♖f7 41. ♘d4 ♖d7 42. ♖f2 ♖de7!** [△ 43... ♘d4 44. cd4 ♖e2∓] **43. ♘e2** [43. ♘f3 ♘f8 44. ♘d4 ♘d7∓] **♖f7! 44. ♘f4□ ♘f4∓ 45. gf4** [♖ 9/o] **♖e4 46. ♔g3 ♖d7 47. ♗d4 ♖d5 48. b4 ♔f7 49. ♔f3 ♖e1 50. ♖g2 ♖f5 51. ♖d2 ♖d5 52. ♖g2 ♖h1 53. ♔g3 ♖d7 54. ♖e2 ♖e7 55. ♖d2 ♖d7** [55... ♖ee1!? △ ♖d1] **56. ♖e2 ♖d1** [△ ♖d3] **57. f5!□ gf5 58. ♖e5 ♖f1 59. ♔g2 ♖f4 60. ♔g3 ♖g4 61. ♔h3 ♔g6 62. ♖e6 ♔h7 63. ♖f6 f4 64. ♖f5 ♖g3 65. ♔h2 ♖e7 66. ♖f4 ♖d3! 67. ♖f2 ♔g8 68. ♔g2 ♖e4 69. ♗f6** [69. ♖f5 ♖h4 70. ♖g5 ♔f8∓] **♖ee3!–+ 70. c4 ♖g3 71. ♔f1 ♖gf3! 72. b5 ♔f7 73. ba6 ba6 74. ♗d4 ♖f2 75. ♗f2 ♖c3 76. c5 ♔e6 77. ♔e2 ♔d5 78. ♗e1 ♖a3 0 : 1**
[Razuvaev]

235.* **B 84**

V. NEVEDNIČIJ 2495
— TIMOŠENKO 2515
Bucureşti 1993

1. e4 c5 2. ♘f3 d6 3. d4 cd4 4. ♘d4 ♘f6 5. ♘c3 a6 6. ♗e3 e6 7. ♗e2 ♕c7 8. g4 h6 [8... b5 9. g5 ♘fd7 10. a3 ♗b7 11. ♕d2 N (11. h4 — 54/(227)) ♘c5 12. f3 ♘c6 13. ♘c6! ♗c6 14. ♕d4± V. Nevedničij 2495 — Itkis 2435, Moldova 1993] **9. ♕d2 b5 10. a3 ♗b7 11. f3 ♘bd7 N** [11... ♘c6 — 54/227] **12. 0-0-0 d5** [12... 0-0-0? 13. ♘db5!+–] **13. ed5 ♘d5 14. ♘d5 ♗d5 15. ♖he1!± ♗c5?!** [15... g6?! 16. f4!±; 15... ♖c8 16. ♔b1±] **16. ♗b5! ab5** [16... 0–0 17. ♗d7 ♕d7 18. ♘f5 ♕c7 19. ♗c5 ♕c5 20. ♕d4!±; 16... ♗d4 17. ♗d7 ♕d7 18. ♕d4±] **17. ♘b5 ♕c6?** [17... ♕b6! 18. ♗c5 ♘c5 19. ♕d5 0–0 20. ♕c4 ♖fb8 21. b4! ♖a4! 22. bc5 ♕b5 23. ♕b5 ♖b5 24. ♖d8 ♔h7 25. ♖d3±] **18. ♗c5 ♔d8 19. ♗e7!! ♔e7** [19... ♔e8 20. ♗b4+–] **20. ♕d5+– ♖hc8 21. ♕c6 ♖c6 22. ♘d4 ♖c7 23. ♖e3 g6 24. ♘e2 ♘f6 25. ♘f4 ♖ac8 26. c3 ♖c5 27. ♘d3 ♖a5 28. ♘b4 ♘d7 29. ♔c2 h5 30. h3 h4? 31. f4 ♖a7 32. f5 gf5 33. gf5 ♘c5 34. ♖d4 1 : 0**
[V. Nevedničij]

236. !N **B 84**

BOLOGAN 2520 — I. NOVIKOV 2540
New York 1993

1. e4 c5 2. ♘f3 d6 3. d4 cd4 4. ♘d4 ♘f6 5. ♘c3 a6 6. ♗e3 e6 7. ♗e2 ♗e7 8. f4 ♕c7 9. 0–0 0–0 10. g4 d5 11. e5 [11. ed5] **♘e4 12. ♘e4 de4 13. g5! N ♘c6 14. c3** [14. ♘c6 ♕c6 15. c3 ♗c5 16. ♗c5 ♕c5 17. ♕d4±] **♗c5 15. ♕c2 b5!□ 16. ♕e4 ♗b7 17. ♗f3 ♖ad8** [17... ♘d4 18. ♕b7 ♘e2 19. ♔f2; 17... ♘a5 18. ♕d3] **18. ♖ad1 ♗a8 19. ♕c2± ♕a7 20. ♕f2 ♘d4 21. ♗d4 ♗d4 22. ♖d4 ♗f3 23. ♖d8 ♕f2 24. ♔f2 ♖d8 25. ♔f3 ♖d3 26. ♔e4?** [26.

♔e2 ♖h3 27. ♖f2 △ ♔d2-c2-b3, a4±] **♖d2 27. a4** [27. b4 ♖a2 28. ♔d4 f6!⇆] **♖b2 28. ab5 ab5 29. ♖a1 h6 30. h4** [30. g6!? fg6 31. ♖a8 ♔h7!? (31... ♔f7?! 32. ♖a7 ♔f8 33. ♔d4 △ ♔c5-d6±) 32. ♔d4 g5!∞] **♖e2 31. ♔d4 ♖f2 32. ♔c5!?** [32. ♔e4=] **♖f4 33. ♔b5 ♖e4 34. c4 hg5 35. hg5 ♖e5 36. c5 ♖g5 37. ♔b6 ♖g2 38. ♖a8 ♔h7 39. c6 ♖b2 40. ♔a7 ♖c2 41. ♔b7 g5 42. c7 g4 43. ♖a6 g3 44. ♖a3! ♖b2 45. ♔a7 ♖c2 46. ♔b7 1/2 : 1/2** **[Bologan]**

237.** **B 85**

KLOVANS 2440 — DYDYŠKO 2490

Katowice 1993

1. e4 c5 2. ♘f3 d6 3. d4 cd4 4. ♘d4 ♘f6 5. ♘c3 a6 6. ♗e3 e6 7. ♗e2 ♗e7 8. f4 0—0 9. 0—0 ♕c7 10. a4 ♘c6 11. ♔h1 [RR 11. ♕e1 ♘d4 12. ♗d4 e5 13. ♗e3 ef4 14. ♗f4 ♗e6 15. ♕g3 ♘d7 16. ♗h6 ♕c5 17. ♔h1 ♕e5 18. ♗f4 ♕c5 19. ♗e3 ♕e5 20. ♗f4 ♕c5 21. ♘d5 ♗d5 22. ed5!? N (22. ♗h6 — 46/319) ♕c2 23. ♗d3 ♕b2 24. ♕h3 ♘f6 25. ♖ab1 ♕d4 26. ♖b7 ♖ae8 27. ♗g5 h6 28. ♖e7 hg5 29. ♖f6 ♕a1 30. ♖f1+— V. Spasov 2520 — Istrăţescu 2470, Budapest (zt) 1993] **♖e8 12. ♘b3** [RR 12. ♗f3 ♖b8 13. ♕d2 ♗d7 14. ♘b3 b6 15. ♕f2 N (15. g4 — 52/(231)) ♘b4 16. ♘d4 e5 17. ♘f5 ♗f5 18. ef5 e4 19. ♘e4 ♕c2 20. ♖fc1 ♕f2 21. ♘f2 d5 22. ♗d2 a5 23. g3 ♗c5 24. ♗b4 ♗b4 25. ♔g2 h5 26. ♖c2 b5 1/2 : 1/2 Ivančuk 2710 — Kasparov 2805, Linares 1993] **b6** [12... ♘a5?! 13. e5 de5 14. fe5 ♘d7 (14... ♕e5? 15. ♗f4+—) 15. ♗d3→] **13. ♕e1 ♗b7!?** [13... ♖b8 14. ♕f2 ♘a5 15. ♘d2!±] **14. ♕f2 ♘d7 15. ♖ad1 ♘b4 N** [15... ♖ac8 — 37/261] **16. ♗g4!? ♖ac8 17. ♖d2** [17. f5!? e5!? (17... ♗f6 18. fe6 fe6 19. ♘d4 ♘c5 20. ♕g3↑) 18. ♗f3 ♕b8 △ ♖c4⇆] **♗a8 18. ♖fd1 ♘f6 19. ♗f3 ♖b8 20. ♕g3!** [20. g4?! d5!] **♗f8** [20... d5 21. ♗d4!] **21. ♘d4 ♖bc8!** [21... d5?! 22. e5 ♘e4 23. ♗e4 de4 24. f5↑] **22. f5!? e5 23. ♘de2?** [23. ♗g5!∞ △ 23... ed4 24. ♗f6 dc3 25. ♗g7! f6 (25... ♗g7? 26. f6+—) 26. ♗f6+—] **d5! 24. ♗g5** [24. ed5? e4 25. d6 ♗d6—+] **♘e4?** [24... de4! 25. ♗f6 ef3 26. gf3 (26. ♗g7 fg2 27. ♔g1 ♕c5 28. ♘d4 f6—+) e4!∓] **25. ♗e4 de4 26. ♗f6! ♔h8!** [26... ♕c6? 27. ♖d6!+—; 26... g6?! 27. ♕h4→] **27. ♖d7**

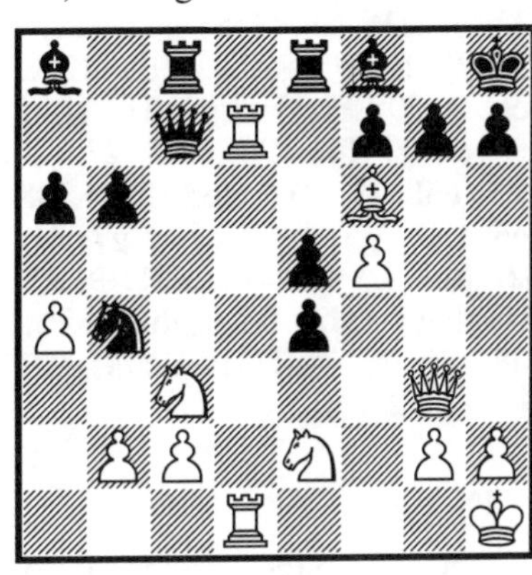

27... gf6! 28. ♖c7 ♖c7 29. ♕h4 ♗e7=/∞ **30. ♘e4 ♖g8!** [30... ♖c4?! 31. ♘2g3 ♖g8 (31... ♘c2? 32. b3! ♖b4 33. ♖d7+—) 32. ♖d7↑] **31. c3** [31. ♘f6? ♖g7 ×g2] **♘d5 32. ♘2g3 ♘f4 33. ♖f1?⊕ ♖c4 34. ♖f4** [34. ♖e1 ♘d3 35. ♖e2 ♖g3! △ ♗e4∓] **ef4 35. ♕f4 ♖g3! 36. hg3** [36. ♕g3 ♖e4 37. ♕b8 ♔g7 38. ♕g3 (38. h3 ♗c6—+) ♔h6—+] **♗e4** [♕ 6/f3] **37. ♔h2 ♗d5—+ 38. ♕b8 ♔g7 39. ♕b6 ♖a4 40. ♕c7 ♖e4 41. ♕a5 ♗c4 42. ♕c7 ♗f1 43. ♔g1 ♗d3 44. ♕d7 ♗c5 45. ♔h2 ♗e2** [△ ♗g4] **46. ♕c6 ♖e5 47. g4 ♗f2 48. g5 fg5 49. g4 ♗g4 50. ♕a6 ♖e2 51. f6 ♔h6 52. ♕a8 ♗c5 53. ♔g3 ♗h5 54. ♕d5 ♗e3** **0 : 1** **[Dydyško]**

238. !N **B 85**

ŠIROV 2670 — IVANČUK 2710

Linares 1993

1. e4 c5 2. ♘f3 e6 3. d4 cd4 4. ♘d4 ♘c6 5. ♘c3 ♕c7 6. ♗e2 a6 7. 0—0 ♘f6 8. ♗e3 ♗e7 9. f4 d6 10. ♕e1 0—0 11. ♕g3 ♘d4 12. ♗d4 b5 13. a3 ♗b7 14. ♖ae1 ♗c6 15. ♔h1 ♕b7 16. ♗d3 b4 17. ab4 ♕b4 18. ♘e2 ♕b7 19. e5 ♘h5 20. ♕h3 g6 21. ♘g3 de5 22. ♗e5 ♘g3 23. hg3 ♗b5! N [23... ♖ac8 — 55/(257)] **24. c4** [24. ♕h6 f6 25. ♗g6 hg6 26. ♕g6 ♔h8=] **♗c6 25. g4 ♖ad8!** [25... ♖fd8? 26. ♖e3! f6 27. ♗c3± △ 27... ♗c5 28. ♖e6

♖d3 29. ♕d3 ♗g2 30. ♔h2 ♗f1 31. ♕f1 ×f6] **26. ♖e2** [26. ♖e3 f6 27. ♗c3 e5! (Ivančuk; 27... ♗c5?! 28. ♖e6 ♖d3 29. ♕d3 ♗g2 30. ♔h2 ♗f1 31. ♕f1⩲ △ 31... ♕d7 32. ♕e2) 28. fe5 ♗c5 29. ♖ee1 (29. ♖e2?! fe5→ ×g2) ♖d3 (29... fe5 30. ♗e5∞) 30. ♕d3 ♗g2 31. ♔h2 ♗f1 32. ♖f1 fe5=] **f6!** [26... f5 27. ♗c2!±] **27. ♗c3 e5! 28. fe5 fe5 29. ♖f8 ♗f8 30. ♖e5** [30. g5 ♕f7!∞] **♗g7 31. ♖e3 ♗c3 32. bc3** [△ g5⇆] **♖d3!?⊕ 33. ♖d3 ♗g2 34. ♕g2 ♕b1 35. ♔h2** [35... ♕d3 36. ♕a8 (36. c5 ♔f7! Ivančuk) ♔g7 37. ♕a6=] **1/2 : 1/2** **[Širov]**

239.** !N B 86

ISTRĂŢESCU 2470 – ŠTOHL 2540

Budapest (zt) 1993

1. e4 c5 2. ♘f3 d6 3. d4 cd4 4. ♘d4 ♘f6 5. ♘c3 e6 6. ♗c4 ♗e7 7. ♗e3 0–0 8. ♗b3 ♘a6 9. f4 ♘c5 10. ♕f3 a5 [RR 10... a6 11. 0–0 (11. g4?! – 14/447) ♕c7 12. g4!? N (12. f5 b5 13. fe6 fe6 14. ♘f5 ♘b3 15. ♘e7 ♕e7 16. ab3 ♗b7 17. ♗g5=) b5 13. g5 ♘fe4 14. ♘e4 ♗b7 15. ♘c5!! dc5 (15... ♗f3 16. ♘ce6! ♕b7□ 17. ♖f3 fe6 18. ♘e6!∞̅→ Istrăţescu, Stoica) 16. ♘e6! ♕c8!□ 17. ♗d5 ♗d5 18. ♕d5 ♕e6 19. ♕e6 fe6 20. a4⩲ 1/2 : 1/2 Istrăţescu 2450 – Cebalo 2500, Debrecen 1992] **11. 0-0-0 a4 12. ♗c4 a3 13. ♘db5** [13. e5 de5 14. ♘c6 ab2 15. ♔b1 ♕c7 16. ♘e7 ♕e7 17. fe5 ♘fd7∞; RR 13. b3!? N *a)* 13... ♕a5 14. ♘db5 ♗d7 15. e5 *a1)* 15... ♗c6 16. ef6! ♗f3 17. fe7 ♗d1 18. ef8♕ ♖f8 19. ♖d1 ♖d8 20. f5 d5 21. ♗e2 ♘e4 (21... ♖c8!? 22. fe6 fe6 23. ♔b1!?±) 22. ♘e4 de4 23. ♖d8 ♕d8 24. fe6 fe6 25. g3! ♕f6 26. ♘d4⩲ Istrăţescu 2450 – Şubă 2525, România (ch) 1992; *a2)* 15... de5!? 16. fe5 ♘d5∞; *b)* 13... ♘fe4!? 14. ♘e4 ♘e4 15. ♕e4 d5 16. ♕f3 (16. ♕d3 dc4 17. ♕c4 ♗d7=) dc4 17. ♘e6 ♗e6 18. ♖d8 ♖fd8∞̅ Istrăţescu, Stoica] **ab2 14. ♔b1 ♕a5 15. e5** [15. ♗c5 dc5 16. e5 ♘d7↑ △ ♘b6, ♗d7] **de5 16. fe5 ♘fd7 17. ♕g3 ♔h8! N** [17... ♘b6?! – 54/(236)] **18. ♖hf1?!** [18. ♗g5=] **♘b6 19. ♗c5□** [19. ♗g5 ♗g5 20. ♕g5 ♗d7! (20... ♘c4 21. ♖f7! ♖g8 22. ♖g7 ♖g7 23. ♖d8 ♕d8 24. ♕d8 ♖g8 25. ♕f6 ♖g7 26. ♕f8 ♖g8 27. ♕c5±) 21. ♘d6 ♘c4 22. ♘f7 ♖f7 23. ♖f7 ♘a3 24. ♔b2 ♘c4–+] **♗c5 20. ♗b3 ♗d7 21. ♘d6 ♗d6□ 22. ♖d6 ♗c6** [22... ♗a4? 23. ♖b6±; 22... ♘a4! 23. ♘d1!? (23. ♖d7 ♘c3 24. ♔b2 ♖fc8→ △ 25. ♖df7 ♕a3 26. ♔a1 ♕a2!–+; 23. ♘a4 ♗a4∓; 23. ♗a4 ♗a4 24. ♖d4 ♗c2 25. ♔c2 ♖fc8 26. ♖f3 b5!→) ♘c5∓] **23. ♖d4 ♘d7 24. ♖e1□** [24. ♖h4 ♕e5 25. ♕h3 h6 26. ♖h5 (26. ♖h6 gh6 27. ♕h6 ♔g8 28. ♖f4 ♕g7–+) ♕d4 27. ♖h4 ♗g2! (27... ♕e5 28. ♖h5=) 28. ♖h6□ gh6 29. ♕h6 ♔g8–+] **♘c5 25. ♖h4⊕** [25... ♖fd8 26. ♕h3 h6! *a)* 27. ♖h6 gh6 28. ♕h6 ♔g8 29. ♖e3 ♘e4! (29... ♗e4 30. ♖h3→) 30. ♖h3 ♘d2 31. ♔b2 ♕a3–+; *b)* 27. ♖f1 ♘b3 28. cb3 ♖d7∓ △ 29. ♖h6? gh6 30. ♕h6 ♔g8 31. ♖f4 ♖d1!–+] **1/2 : 1/2** **[Štohl]**

240.* B 86

WAITZKIN 2345 – WOJTKIEWICZ 2580

New York 1993

1. e4 c5 2. ♘f3 d6 3. d4 cd4 4. ♘d4 ♘f6 5. ♘c3 a6 6. ♗c4 e6 7. ♗b3 ♗e7 8. g4 d5 N [⌓ 8... h6 9. ♗e3 ♘c6 10. ♖g1 ♕a5 N (10... ♘a5 – 43/(306)) 11. ♕d2 ♘e5 12. f3 b5?! (Kelleher – Kajdanov 2555, USA 1992) 13. h4±; 12... g5!? Kajdanov; 8... ♘c6 – 44/290] **9. ed5 ♘d5 10. ♘d5 ed5 11. ♘f5 ♗f5 12. gf5 d4 13. ♕g4** [13. ♕h5!? 0–0 14. ♗d2 (14. ♖g1!?) ♘d7 15. 0-0-0±] **♗f6** [13... 0–0? 14. ♗h6 ♗f6 15. ♖g1+–] **14. ♗f4** [14. ♗d2!?] **♕e7?** [14... ♕a5 *a)* 15. c3?! dc3? 16. ♗f7 ♔f7 17. ♕h5 ♔e7 18. ♕e2 ♗e5 (18... ♔d8 19. 0-0-0 ♘d7 20. ♖d7 ♔d7 21. ♕e6 ♔d8 22. ♖d1+–) 19. ♗e5 cb2 20. ♗c3! ♔f7 (20... ♔f8 21. ♕b2+–) 21. ♕c4 ♔e7 22. ♗b4 (22. ♕e6 ♔f8 23. ♕c8 ♔e7 24. ♕b7 ♘d7 25. ♕b2+–) ♔f6 23. ♕e6+–; 15... 0–0!; *b)* 15. ♗d2 ♕e5 16. ♔f1 ♕b5 17. ♔g2 0–0∞] **15. ♔f1 0–0 16. ♖g1 ♔h8 17. ♖e1** [17. ♖g3] **♕d7 18. ♖g3** [18. ♗g5 ♗g5 19. ♕g5 f6 20. ♕h5 ♘c6 21. ♖e4 (△ 22. ♕h7, 22. ♖h4) h6 22. ♖eg4

♘e5 23. ♖g7 ♕g7 24. ♖g7 ♔g7 25. f4+–] **♘c6** [18... g6 19. ♗g5 ♗g5 20. ♕g5 ♕f5 21. ♕f5 gf5 22. ♖e7 ♘c6 23. ♖b7±] **19. ♖h3 g5□** [19... g6? 20. ♖h7! ♔h7 21. fg6+–] **20. ♗g5+– ♗g5 21. ♕g5 f6 22. ♕h5 ♖ad8 23. ♖e4 ♕c7 24. ♖eh4 ♖d7 25. ♕h6 ♖g7 26. ♖g3 ♕e7 27. ♖e4 ♘e5 28. f4 ♖g3 29. hg3 ♘g4 30. ♖e7 ♘h6 31. ♗e6 ♖d8 32. ♔e2 b5 33. ♖a7 ♘g4 34. ♖a6 ♘e3 35. ♔d3 h5 36. ♖a7 ♘f1 37. ♖f7 ♘g3 38. ♖f6 ♔h7 39. ♖g6 ♘h1** [39... h4 40. ♖g4] **40. ♖g2 1 : 0** **[Waitzkin]**

241. **B 86**

BALINOV 2300 – H. NAGEL 2280

Österreich 1993

1. e4 c5 2. ♘f3 d6 3. d4 cd4 4. ♘d4 ♘f6 5. ♘c3 a6 6. ♗c4 e6 7. ♗b3 ♘bd7 8. ♗g5 ♘c5 9. ♕e2 ♗e7 10. f4 h6 11. ♗f6 ♗f6 12. 0-0-0 ♕c7 13. ♔b1 b5?! N [13... ♗d7 – 53/224] **14. ♘db5 ab5 15. ♘b5 ♕a5 16. ♘d6 ♔e7** [16... ♔f8!?] **17. ♘c4! ♕a7 18. e5 ♗h4** [18... ♘b3 19. ef6 gf6 20. cb3 ♕a2 21. ♔c2 ♗a6 (21... ♖b8 22. ♕e3 ♕a6 23. ♕c5+–) 22. ♖a1 ♗c4 23. bc4 ♕a1 24. ♖a1 ♖a1±] **19. g3 ♗b7** [19... ♗a6 20. ♕e3!] **20. ♖he1** [20. ♖hf1!?] **♗e4** [20... ♘b3 21. cb3 ♕a2 22. ♔c2±; 20... g5 21. a3 gf4 22. gh4 ♗e4 23. ♘d6 ♗h7 24. ♕f3 △ ♕f4→] **21. ♕e3 ♖hb8 22. ♘a3! ♕a5 23. gh4+– ♖b7 24. ♖d4!? ♘b3 25. ab3 ♖b3 26. ♕b3 ♕e1 27. ♔a2 f6** [27... ♗d5? 28. ♖d5 ed5 29. ♕b7] **28. ♕g3** [28. ♖d6!+–] **♕g3 29. hg3** [♖ 9/i] **♗c2 30. ♖c4± ♗a4 31. ♖c7 ♗d7 32. ♔b3 fe5 33. fe5 ♖b8 34. ♔c3 ♖f8 35. ♔d4 ♖f1 36. ♘c4 ♔d8 37. ♖a7 g5 38. hg5 hg5 39. ♘b6 ♗c6 40. ♔c5+– ♗e4 41. ♔d6 ♖b1 42. ♖g7 ♔e8 43. ♔e6 ♔f8 44. ♖g5 1 : 0** **[Balinov]**

242.***** **B 86**

FILIPENKO 2395 – AKOPIAN 2615

Rostov na Donu (open) 1993

1. e4 c5 2. ♘f3 d6 3. d4 cd4 4. ♘d4 ♘f6 5. ♘c3 a6 6. ♗c4 e6 7. ♗b3 ♘bd7 8. f4 ♘c5 9. ♕f3 [RR 9. e5 *a)* 9... ♘fd7!? 10. ed6 ♘f6 11. ♗e3 ♗d6 12. ♕f3 0–0 N (12... ♗d7 13. 0-0-0 ♕c7 14. g4 ♘b3 15. ab3 0-0-0 16. g5 ♘d5! 17. ♘d5 ed5 18. ♔b1 ♖he8∞) 13. 0-0-0 ♘b3 14. ♘b3 ♕c7 15. ♖d6 ♕d6 16. ♗c5 ♕c7 17. ♗f8 ♔f8 18. ♖d1 ♗d7= Morozevič 2385 – Muhutdinov 2425, Moskva 1992; *b)* 9... de5 10. fe5 ♘fd7 11. ♗f4 *b1)* 11... ♘b6 N 12. ♕d2 ♗e7 13. 0-0-0 0–0 14. h4 ♗d7 15. ♕e2±↑ Jagupov 2400 – Tataev 2310, Moskva 1992; *b2)* 11... b5 *b21)* 12. ♕e2 ♗b7 13. 0–0 N (13. 0-0-0 ♕a5 14. ♖hf1 ♘b3 15. ♘b3 ♕c7 16. ♘d4 ♘c5 17. a3 ♗e7 18. ♕g4 0–0=) b4 14. ♘a4 ♘b3 15. ab3 ♘c5 16. ♖ad1 ♘a4 17. ba4 ♗c5 18. ♗e3? ♕c7!∓ Zapolskis 2420 – Šlekys 2340, Marijampole 1992; 18. ♔h1!∞; *b22)* 12. ♕g4!? N ♘f6! (12... ♘b6?! 13. 0-0-0! ♗d7 14. ♖hf1 h5?! 15. ♕f3 ♖c8 16. ♔b1 ♘c4 17. ♗c4 bc4 18. ♗g5! 1 : 0 Zapolskis 2420 – Tataev 2310, Staré Město 1992) 13. ef6 ♕d4∞ Zapolskis; *b3)* 11... g5!? N 12. ♘e6 (12. ♗g3 h5 13. h3 ♕c7 14. ♕e2 b5 △ ♗b7∞) ♘e6 13. ♗e6 gf4 14. ♗f7 (14. ♕h5 ♘e5! 15. ♕e5 ♗e6 16. ♕h8 f3∓) ♔f7 15. ♕h5 ♔g7 (15... ♔g8 16. ♕g4 ♗g7 17. ♕e6 ♔f8 18. ♕f5 ♘f6 19. ♕f4∞̄) 16. ♕g4 ♔h6 17. h4□ (17. 0-0-0 ♕g5–+; 17. 0–0 ♘e5 18. ♕f4 ♕g5–+) ♘e5 (17... ♗e7!?) 18. ♕f4 ♔g7 (18... ♔g6 19. h5) 19. ♕e5 ♕f6 20. ♕g3 ♕g6 21. ♕e5 ♕f6 (21... ♔g8 22. 0-0-0∞̄ A. Sokolov) 22. ♕g3 ♕g6 1/2 : 1/2 A. Sokolov 2605 – R. Har-Zvi 2425, Biel (open) 1992; *b4)* 11... ♘b3 – 51/235] **♗e7 10. g4 d5 11. e5 N** [11. ed5 ed5 (11... ♘b3 – 20/466) 12. f5 ♘fe4!∞] **♘fe4 12. 0–0 ♕c7! 13. ♘ce2** [13. ♘d5? ed5 14. ♗d5 ♕d7!–+; 13. ♘e4?! de4 △ b5; 13. ♗e3?! ♘c3 14. bc3 ♗d7] **♗d7** [13... b5!?] **14. c3?** [14. c4!∞] **♘b3 15. ab3 f6!∓** [15... 0–0?! 16. g5!] **16. ef6** [16. f5 0–0!∓] **♗f6 17. ♗e3 0–0 18. ♕g2 e5 19. fe5 ♗e5 20. ♖ad1** [20. c4? ♘f6!] **♖ae8 21. ♖f8 ♖f8 22. h3** [22. ♖f1? ♗h2] **h5!∓** [22... ♕c8?! 23. c4!; 22... b5?! 23. ♖f1] **23. c4** [23. ♘f5 ♗f5 24. gf5 ♖f5 25. ♖d5 ♗h2–+; 23. gh5 ♕c8 24. h6 ♗h3 25. ♕g6 ♕g4 26. ♕g4 ♗g4 27. hg7 ♖f7!–+; 23. ♖f1∓] **hg4 24. cd5** [24. hg4 ♘f6! 25. g5 ♘g4 26. ♕d5 ♔h8 27. ♕h1 ♗h2! 28. ♔g2 ♘e3#] **♘f6 25. ♘e6 ♕c2!–+ 26. ♖c1** [26. ♖d2

♕b1 27. ♕f1 ♗h2 28. ♔g2 gh3; 26. ♘c3 ♕g2 27. ♔g2 gh3 28. ♔h3 ♘d5!] **♕b3 27. ♗d4** [27. ♗c5 ♖c8] **♗d4 28. ♘2d4** [28. ♘6d4 ♕e3 29. ♕f2 ♕f2 30. ♔f2 ♘d5 31. ♔g3 gh3] **♕e3 29. ♔h2 ♕c1**
0 : 1 **[Akopian]**

243.** **B 86**

WINANTS 2520 – L. CHRISTIANSEN 2620
Wijk aan Zee (open) 1993

1. e4 c5 2. ♘f3 d6 3. d4 cd4 4. ♘d4 ♘f6 5. ♘c3 a6 6. ♗c4 e6 7. ♗b3 ♘bd7 8. f4 ♘c5 9. f5 ♗e7 10. ♕f3 0–0 11. ♗e3 ♗d7?! [11... e5 12. ♘de2 ♘b3 13. ab3 b5 *a)* RR 14. ♖d1 *a1)* 14... ♗b7 15. 0–0 N (15. ♘g3 – 48/(342)) ♖c8 16. ♖d2 b4 (16... ♕a5 17. ♘g3) 17. ♘d5 ♘d5 18. ed5 ♗g5 19. ♘g3 ♗e3 20. ♕e3 ♕a5 21. f6!? ♕c5□ 22. ♕c5 ♖c5 23. fg7 ♔g7 24. ♘f5 ♔h8 25. ♘e3 (Golubev 2490 – G. Ginsburg 2395, Ukrajina (ch) 1992) ♔g7±; ⌓ 17... ♗d5; *a2)* 14... b4!? 15. ♘d5 ♘d5 16. ♖d5 (16. ed5∞) ♗b7 17. ♖d2 ♗h4!? 18. g3 ♗e7∞ △ ♕c7-c6; *a3)* 14... ♕a5!? Golubev; *b)* 14. g4!? N b4 15. ♘a4 ♗b7 16. ♘g3 d5 17. 0-0-0 *b1)* 17... d4 18. ♗d2 (18. g5? ♘e4! 19. ♘e4 ♕d5–+) ♖c8 19. ♔b1 (19. g5? ♕c7 20. ♕d3 ♘e4! 21. ♘e4 ♕c2! 22. ♕c2 ♖c2 23. ♔c2 ♗e4 24. ♔c1 ♖c8–+ Ftáčnik) ♘d7 *b11)* 20. g5? ♗g5 21. ♗b4 ♖e8 22. ♖hg1?! ♗e3 23. ♖g2 ♕h4!∓ Winants 2505 – Ftáčnik 2535, Tilburg (Interpolis) 1992; *b12)* 20. h4?! ♗c6 21. g5 ♗a4 22. ba4 ♘b6 23. f6 (23. b3 ♖c3→) ♘a4!? (23... ♗c5 24. fg7 ♔g7 25. ♘h5 ♔h8 26. ♘f6) 24. fe7 ♕e7∞̄ △ ♘c3; *b13)* 20. ♖hg1! ♗c6 (20... h6 21. g5→) 21. g5 ♗a4 22. f6! ♗c6 23. ♘f5!! ♗c5 (23... ♗f6 24. gf6 ♘f6 25. ♖g7 ♔h8 26. ♕g3 △ ♖h7) 24. fg7 ♖e8 25. ♖g3+– △ ♖h3, ♕h5; *b2)* 17... de4 18. ♕e2 ♕a5 19. g5 ♘d5 20. f6!±→; *b3)* 17... ♘e4!? 18. ♘e4 de4 19. ♕h3 ♕c7 20. g5∞̄→; 16... ♕c7!?] **12. g4 ♕a5 N** [12... e5 13. ♘de2± ♘fe4? 14. ♘e4 ♘e4 15. ♕e4 ♗c6 16. ♗d5 ♕a5 17. ♘c3+–; 12... b5 13. g5 ♘e8 14. ♖g1 b4 15. ♘ce2 (15. ♘d5?! – 48/342) ♘b3 16. ab3 d5 17. ed5±] **13. 0-0-0 e5 14. ♘de2 ♘b3 15. cb3 ♗c6** [△ 16... ♘e4 (⇆⊞) 17. ♘e4 d5, 17... ♕a2] **16. ♘g3 ♖fd8** [16... ♘e4 17. ♘ge4 d5 18. ♖d5 ♗d5 19. ♘d5+–] **17. g5 ♘e4□** [17... ♘d7 18. f6+–→] **18. ♘ge4 ♖ac8** [△ ♕a2; 18... d5 19. f6? ♗b4∞; 19. g6!+–] **19. ♔b1 d5 20. g6 de4 21. ♕h3 ♗f6 22. ♕h7 ♔f8 23. a3 ♗d5 24. ♖d5 ♖c3** **1 : 0**
[Winants]

244. **B 87**

VELIMIROVIĆ 2510 – VAULIN 2515
Beograd 1993

1. e4 c5 2. ♘f3 d6 3. d4 cd4 4. ♘d4 ♘f6 5. ♘c3 a6 6. ♗c4 e6 7. ♗b3 b5 8. ♗e3 ♗b7 9. f4 ♘bd7 10. 0–0 ♖c8 11. ♕e2 b4 12. e5!? N [12. ♘a4 – 45/(284)] **de5** [12... bc3 13. ef6 ♘f6±] **13. fe5 ♘e5 14. ♖ad1 ♘ed7?** [14... ♕c7?! 15. ♗a4 (15. ♗f4 ♗d6 16. ♘db5 ab5 17. ♘b5 ♕b6 18. ♗e3 ♗c5) ♘ed7 16. ♖f6 gf6 17. ♘e6 fe6 18. ♖d7 ♕d7 19. ♗d7 (19. ♕h5!? ♔e7 20. ♗d7 ♔d7 21. ♘a4↑) ♔d7 20. ♘a4 △ ♘b6↑; 14... bc3!? 15. ♘e6 fe6 16. ♖d8 ♖d8 17. ♗f4 (17. ♗b6 ♗d6) ♗c5 18. ♔h1 0–0 19. ♕e5 (19. ♗e5 ♖d2; 19. ♗e6 ♔h8 20. ♕e5 ♘e4⇆) ♗d5∞] **15. ♘a4!?** [15. ♘e6!? fe6 16. ♗e6 (Velimirović) bc3 *a)* 17. ♗d7 ♕d7 18. ♖d7 (18. ♗c5 ♔d8 19. ♗b6 ♖c7 20. ♕e5 ♘d5; 18... ♕e7!?) ♔d7 19. ♖d1 ♘d5 △ 20. bc3 ♔c7∞; *b)* 17. ♗g5!? ♗e7 18. ♖d7 ♕d7 (18... ♘d7? 19. ♕h5 g6 20. ♗f7 ♔f8 21. ♕h6#) 19. ♗d7 ♔d7 20. ♖d1 ♔e8 21. ♖e1 ♖c7 (21... ♘e4!? 22. ♗e7 ♔e7 23. ♕g4∞) 22. ♕e5 ♔d8!? (22... ♘d5 23. ♕g7 ♖f8 24. bc3↑) 23. ♖d1 ♖d7 (23... ♔c8 24. ♗f4) 24. ♕b8 ♗c8 25. ♕b6 ♔e8 26. ♖d7 ♔d7 27. bc3∞] **♕a5 16. ♘e6 fe6 17. ♗d4** [17. ♗e6 ♕e5!? (17... ♗e7) 18. ♖d7 ♘d7 19. ♗f7 ♔d8 20. ♗b6 ♖c7] **e5 18. ♘b6 ♗c5 19. ♘d7 ♘d7 20. ♖f7 ♗d4 21. ♖d4 ♗c6 22. ♖d1 ♖f8 23. ♖g7∞̄ ♔d8** [23... ♕c5 24. ♔h1 ♔d8 25. ♗e6 ♖c7 26. h3 △ 27. ♕g4, 27. ♕a6∞̄] **24. ♗e6 ♖c7 25. ♕e3! h6⊕ 26. ♖d6?⊕** [26. h3!?] **♕b5 27. h3?** [27. ♖d1] **♕f1 28. ♔h2 ♕f4 29. ♕f4 ♖f4 30. ♗g4 ♗b5 31.**

♖h6 [⌓ 31. ♖g8 ♔e7 32. ♖h6∓] **♖c2 32. ♖d6 ♖d4−+ 33. ♖d4 ed4 34. h4 ♗c6 35. ♗f5 ♖f2 36. ♗d3 ♘e5 37. ♗a6⊕ 0 : 1** **[Vaulin, M. Makarov]**

245. **B 87**

GOLUBEV 2490 – ZAGORSKIS 2440
Karvina 1992/93

1. e4 c5 2. ♘f3 d6 3. d4 cd4 4. ♘d4 ♘f6 5. ♘c3 a6 6. ♗c4 e6 7. ♗b3 b5 8. 0–0 ♗b7 9. ♖e1 ♘bd7 10. ♗g5 h6 11. ♗f6 ♕f6 N [11... ♘f6 – 48/(343)] **12. a4 b4 13. ♘a2 ♘c5 14. ♘b4 a5** [14... ♘e4 15. f3 ♘c5 16. ♘d5!?↑] **15. ♘bc6!** [15. ♘a2 ♘e4 16. ♕e2 0-0-0 17. ♕c4 ♔b8 18. ♖e4; ⌓ 17... ♘c5] **e5** [15... ♔d7 16. e5!?±; 15... ♖a6 16. ♗d5!?±; 15... ♘b3 16. cb3 e5 17. ♖c1!? ed4 18. e5→] **16. ♗d5** [16. ♘b5!? ♗c6 17. ♘c7 ♔d7 18. ♘a8; 16. ♗c4 ed4 17. ♗b5 ♔d7!!; 17. e5!?; 16. ♖a3] **ed4□ 17. e5** [17. ♖a3!$\overline{\infty}$↑ d3!? (17... ♖c8 18. ♖f3 ♗c6?! 19. ♖f6 gf6 20. ♕f3!) 18. cd3] **de5 18. ♖e5 ♔d7** [⌓ 18... ♘e6 19. ♕d4 ♖a6!! (Stripunskij; 19... ♗d6? 20. ♗e6; 19... ♗e7? 20. ♕b6) 20. ♖d1!? (20. ♘b8?! ♖d6; 20. ♖ae1 ♖c6; 20. ♕c4 ♗d6!; 20. ♕d3 ♗c5!; 20. ♕e4 ♗d6) ♖c6! 21. ♗c6 (21. ♗e6 ♗d6 22. ♗f7 ♔d7!?∓) ♗c6 22. ♕c3 *a)* 22... ♗d7 23. ♕d3! (23. ♕a5?! ♗e7! △ 24. ♖d7 ♔d7 25. ♕b5 ♔c8, △ 24. ♕a8 ♘d8) ♕e7 24. ♖a5 △ 24... ♗c6?? 25. ♖a8+−; *b)* 22... ♗b7!? 23. ♕a5 (23. ♕c7 ♗e7!) ♗e7 24. ♕b5 ♔f8 25. ♖f5 ♘c7! (25... ♕g6 26. ♕b7 ♕f5 27. ♕c8) 26. ♕b7 ♕f5 27. ♕c7∞; RR 26. ♖f6 ♘b5 27. ♖b6 ♘d6 28. c4+− R. Bakić] **19. ♕g4 ♔c7 20. ♖f5! ♕g6!** [20... h5 21. ♕f3!; 20... ♕d6 21. ♘d4!? △ ♘b5; 20... ♗c8 21. ♕f4 ♕d6 22. ♖f7±→] **21. ♕f4** [21. ♖f7! ♕f7 22. ♗f7 ♗c6 23. ♕d4] **♕d6! 22. ♖f7 ♔b6! 23. ♖b7!□ ♘b7 24. ♕d4$\overline{\infty}$ ♕c5 25. ♕d3 ♗d6** [25... ♖e8?! 26. b4!; 25... ♔c7!? 26. ♖a3! ♖e8 27. g3!?∞] **26. ♕b3 ♔c7 27. ♘d4! ♕b4□ 28. ♘b5 ♔b6 29. ♗b7 ♕b3 30. cb3 ♖ad8** [30... ♗h2 31. ♔h2 ♔b7 32. ♖e1] **31. ♗f3 ♗e5?⊕** [31... ♗c5! 32. ♘a3!] **32. ♘a3!± ♗c7?! 33. ♖c1 ♗f4?! 34. ♖c6 ♔a7 35. ♘b5 ♔b8 36. ♖b6 ♔c8 37. ♗g4 1 : 0** **[Golubev]**

246. !N **B 87**

ADAMS 2630 – SADLER 2540
Dublin (zt) 1993

1. e4 c5 2. ♘f3 d6 3. d4 cd4 4. ♘d4 ♘f6 5. ♘c3 a6 6. ♗c4 e6 7. ♗b3 b5 8. 0–0 ♗b7 9. ♖e1 ♘bd7 10. ♗g5 ♕b6 11. a4 b4 12. ♘d5 ed5 13. ed5 ♘e5 [13... ♔d8 14. a5 ♕c7 15. c3→] **14. a5** [14. f4 – 32/332] **♕c5 15. ♗e3! N** [15. f4 0-0-0 16. fe5 de5 17. ♖e5 ♗d6 18. ♖f5±] **♕c8** [15... ♗e7 16. ♘c6 ♕b5 17. ♘e5 de5 18. ♗a4+−; 15... ♘d5 16. ♗a4 ♔d8 17. ♘e6+−; 15... ♗d5 16. ♗a4 ♘fd7 17. ♘e6 ♕c8 (17... ♕c4 18. b3) 18. ♘f8] **16. ♗a4 ♔e7!?** [16... ♘fd7 17. f4 *a)* 17... ♘g6 18. ♘f5 ♗e7 (18... ♔d8 19. ♗b6+−) 19. ♗d4 ♔d8 20. ♖e7 ♘e7 21. ♘d6+−; *b)* 17... ♗d5 18. fe5 de5 19. ♗f4 ♗c5 20. ♖e5 ♗e6 21. ♔h1 ♗d4 22. ♕d4 0–0 23. ♖e6 fe6 24. ♗d7 ♖f4 25. ♕f4 ♕d7 26. ♕b4±] **17. f4 ♘d5 18. fe5 de5 19. ♕h5 f6 20. ♗f2!** [△ ♖ad1, ♗g3; 20. ♘f5 ♔e6] **g6** [20... ♔d6 21. ♕f7; 20... ♘f4 21. ♖e5] **21. ♖e5+− ♔f7** [21... ♔d6 22. ♗g3 gh5 23. ♖e6 ♔c5 24. ♘b3 ♔c4 25. ♖e4#; 21... fe5 22. ♕e5 ♔f7 23. ♕h8 ♕g4 24. ♕h7 ♗g7 25. ♖f1] **22. ♕f3 ♘c7 23. ♕b3 ♔g7 24. ♘f5! gf5 25. ♕g3 ♔f7 26. ♗b3 ♘d5 27. ♖d5 1 : 0** **[Adams]**

247. !N** **B 87**

KASPAROV 2805 – B. GEL'FAND 2690
Linares 1993

1. e4 c5 2. ♘f3 d6 3. d4 cd4 4. ♘d4 ♘f6 5. ♘c3 a6 6. ♗c4 e6 7. ♗b3 b5 8. 0–0 ♗e7 9. ♕f3 ♕c7 10. ♕g3 0–0 11. ♗h6 ♘e8 12. ♖ad1 ♗d7 13. ♘f3! N [13. a3!?; RR 13. f4 b4 N (13... ♘c6 – 48/343) 14. ♘ce2 ♔h8 15. ♗g5 ♘c6 16. f5 ♘d4 17. ♘d4 ♘f6 18. ♕h4 ♖ae8 19. fe6 fe6 20. ♗e6 ♗d8 21. ♕h3 ♖e6 22. ♘e6 ♕b6 23. ♔h1 ♖e8 1/2 : 1/2 I. Almasi 2385 – Vaulin 2515, Kecskemét 1993] **b4?!** [13... ♘c6!?; RR 14. ♘e2 a5 15. c3 a4 16. ♗c2 e5 17. ♘d2 ♗e6 18. ♗b1 ♔h8 19. ♗e3 ♘f6 20. f4 ♘h5 21. ♕f3 ♘f4 22. ♘f4 ef4

23. ♕f4 a3 24. b3 ♗f6 25. ♘f3 ♘e5 26. ♗d4 ♗b3 27. ab3 a2 28. ♗a2 ♖a2 29. ♘h4 ♕c8 30. ♘f5 ♕e6∞ Ashley 2365 – J. Árnason 2535, Saint-Martin 1993] **14. ♘e2 a5 15. ♘f4! ♔h8 16. ♗g5 ♘f6** [16... ♗g5? 17. ♘g5+–] **17. ♕h4! ♗b5?** [17... a4 18. ♘h5 ab3 19. ♘f6! (19. ♗f6? ♗f6 20. ♘f6 h6 21. ab3∞) *a)* 19... h6 20. ♗h6 ♗f6 21. ♘g5 ♗g5 (21... ♔g8 22. ♗g7!) 22. ♗g7 ♔g7 23. ♕g5 ♔h7 24. ♖d3 e5 25. ♖g3+–; *b)* 19... ♗f6 20. ♗f6 *b1)* 20... ♖a5? 21. ♘g5 ♖g5 22. ♕g5 ♖g8 (22... gf6 23. ♕f6 ♔g8 24. ♖d3) 23. ♖d3+– △ 23... bc2 24. ♖g3; *b2)* 20... bc2? 21. ♘g5 h6 22. ♕h6+–; *b3)* 20... gf6 21. ♕f6 ♔g8 22. ♘g5! ♗b5 (22... ♗c8 23. ♖d3 ♖d8 24. ♕h6) 23. ♕h6 f6 24. ♕f8 ♔f8 25. ♘e6 ♔e7 26. ♘c7+–; 17... ♘c6!?] **18. ♘d4!+– ♗e8** [18... ♗f1 19. ♘de6! fe6 20. ♗e6 g6 (20... h6 21. ♗h6) 21. ♘g6 ♔g7 22. ♕h6#]

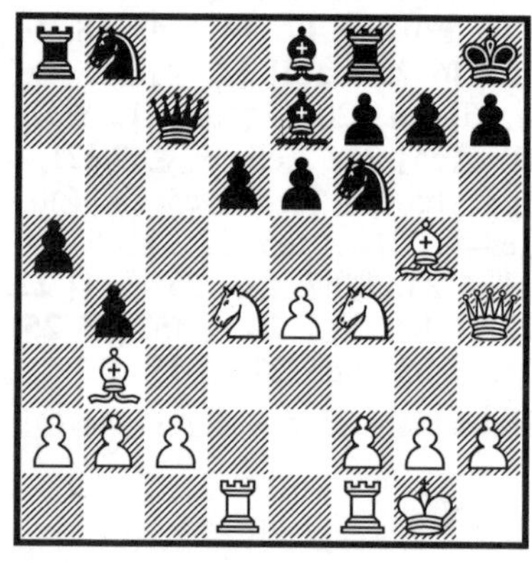

19. ♘de6! fe6 20. ♘e6 ♕a7 21. e5! de5 22. ♘f8 ♗f8 23. ♗f6 gf6 24. ♖d8 ♘d7 25. ♕g4! [25... ♗g7 26. ♕e6] **1 : 0**
[Kasparov]

248. **B 87**

KIR. GEORGIEV 2660
– FTÁČNIK 2535

Budapest (zt) 1993

1. e4 c5 2. ♘f3 d6 3. d4 cd4 4. ♘d4 ♘f6 5. ♘c3 a6 6. ♗c4 e6 7. 0–0 b5 8. ♗b3 ♗e7 9. ♕f3 ♕b6 10. ♗e3 ♕b7 11. ♕g3 ♘c6 12. ♖ad1 0–0 13. ♘c6 ♕c6 14. ♗h6 ♘e8 15. ♖fe1 ♗b7 16. a3!? [16. ♖d3=] **♔h8** [16... ♖d8!?] **17. ♗g5 ♗g5 18. ♕g5 ♘f6 19. ♖d3 ♖ad8 20. ♕d2 ♕b6 N** [⌂ 20... ♖d7 – 47/311] **21. ♖d1! ♘e4** [21... ♗e4 22. ♖d6 ♖d6 23. ♕d6 ♕d6 24. ♖d6 ♗b7 25. ♖b6±] **22. ♘e4 ♗e4 23. ♖d6 ♖d6 24. ♕d6 ♕d6 25. ♖d6±** **[♖ 9/k]** **a5** [25... ♖a8 26. f3 ♗f5 27. ♔f2 g5 28. ♔e3 ♔g7 29. ♔d4±] **26. f3 ♗g6** [26... ♗f5!? (△ g5, ♔g7) 27. g4 ♗g6 △ h5] **27. a4! ba4 28. ♗a4 h5 29. c4 ♖c8 30. b3! ♗c2 31. ♖d2 ♗f5 32. h4 f6 33. ♔f2 g5 34. hg5 fg5 35. ♖d7 h4 36. ♖a7 ♖c5 37. ♖b7 g4 38. fg4 ♗g4 39. ♖b5!+– ♖f5 40. ♔e3 ♔g7 41. c5 h3 42. gh3 ♖f3 43. ♔d4 ♗h3 44. c6 ♔f6 45. ♖a5 ♖f1 46. b4 ♖b1 47. b5 e5 48. ♔c5 e4 49. b6 e3 50. ♗b5 ♖c1 51. ♔d6 ♗g2 52. ♖a2 1 : 0**
[Kir. Georgiev]

249. **B 88**

A. MIHAL'ČIŠIN 2515
– SALTAEV 2465

Groningen (open) 1992

1. e4 c5 2. ♘f3 e6 3. d4 cd4 4. ♘d4 ♘c6 5. ♘c3 d6 6. ♗e3 ♘f6 7. ♗c4 a6 [RR 7... ♗e7 8. ♗b3 0–0 9. f4 ♘d4 10. ♗d4 b5 11. e5 de5 12. fe5 ♘d7 13. ♕g4 ♗c5 14. 0-0-0 ♗d4 15. ♕d4 ♕g5 16. ♔b1 ♖b8!?⇆ Razuvaev; 16... ♕e5] **8. ♗b3 ♗d7!? 9. f4** [9. f3 b5 10. g4; 9. a4!?] **b5 10. f5 N** [10. 0–0 – 56/265; 10. ♕f3 ♘d4 11. ♗d4 ♗c6 12. 0-0-0 b4 13. ♘d5 ed5 14. ed5 ♗b5 15. ♖he1 ♗e7 16. g4∞̅] **♘d4** [10... b4 11. fe6 fe6 12. ♘ce2±] **11. ♕d4** [11. ♗d4 ♗e7 12. ♕f3 0–0 13. g4→] **♗e7 12. fe6** [12. g4!? 0–0 13. ♖g1 △ g5, f6→] **♗e6** [12... fe6 13. e5! de5 14. ♕e5±] **13. 0-0-0 0–0 14. ♗e6** [14. ♗f4!? ♘g4 15. ♘d5 ♗g5 16. ♖df1⩲] **fe6 15. e5 de5 16. ♕e5± ♕c8 17. ♗d4 ♖f7! 18. ♖he1 b4 19. ♘e4** [19. ♘a4 ♕c6 20. ♘b6 ♖e8 21. ♕e6 ♗d6!∞̅] **♕c6** [19... ♘e4 20. ♕e4 ♗f6 21. ♗f6 ♖f6 22. ♕b4 ♖f2 23. ♖d2±] **20. ♘f6 ♖f6 21. ♕e4** [21. ♕e2! ♖g6 22. g3 ♗g5 23. ♔b1 ♖e8 24. ♗e5±] **♕e4 22. ♖e4 ♖g6 23. g3 ♖c8 24. ♗e5** [24. ♗e3!? △ ♖d7] **♖c6 25. ♖d7 ♔f8 26. ♖b7** [26. ♔d2 △ ♔d3, ♖c4±] **♖g5 27. ♖f4** [27. g4 h5 28. h3 hg4 29. hg4⩲] **♔e8**

[27... ♖f5 28. ♖f5 ef5 29. ♗g7+−] **28. ♖b8 ♗d8□ 29. ♖d4?** [29. ♖e4! a5 30. c4!? bc3 31. ♗c3±] **♖e5 30. ♖bd8 ♔e7 31. ♖8d7 ♔f6 32. ♖b4** [32. ♔d1!? a5 33. ♖f4 ♖f5 34. ♖f5 ef5 35. ♖d5±] **♖e2 33. c3** [33. ♖d2 ♖e1 34. ♖d1 ♖e2 35. ♖f1 ♔e5⩱] **♖h2 34. ♖f4 ♔g6 35. ♖g4 ♔f6 36. ♖f4⊕ ♔g6 37. ♖g4 ♔f6 38. ♖gg7 ♖h1 39. ♔d2 ♖h2 40. ♔c1 ♖h1 41. ♔d2 ♖h2 1/2 : 1/2** **[A. Mihal'čišin]**

250. **B 90**

RAŠÍK 2405 – FTÁČNIK 2535

Budapest (zt) 1993

1. e4 c5 2. ♘f3 d6 3. d4 cd4 4. ♘d4 ♘f6 5. ♘c3 a6 6. ♗e3 ♘g4 7. ♗g5 h6 8. ♗h4 g5 9. ♘f5 ♘f6!? N [9... e6 – 56/272] **10. ♗g3 ♘e4 11. ♕d4?!** [11. ♘e4 ♗f5 12. ♕d4 e5!? (12... ♖g8 13. 0-0-0 ♘c6 14. ♕e3 ♗e4 15. ♕e4 e6 16. ♕h7⇆) 13. ♕d5 (13. ♗e5? ♕a5 14. b4 ♕e5−+) ♘c6 14. 0-0-0 ♗e6 15. ♘d6 ♗d6 16. ♕d6 ♕a5 17. ♕a3 ♕a3 18. ba3∓] **♘f6** [11... ♘g3 12. hg3 e5 13. ♕e4∞] **12. ♗d3 ♘c6 13. ♕e3** [13. ♕a4? ♗f5 14. ♗f5 b5 15. ♕a3 e6 16. ♗d3 d5−+] **♗f5 14. ♗f5 ♕a5 15. ♕f3** [15. ♗d3 ♘d5 16. ♕d2 ♘c3 17. ♕c3 ♕c3 18. bc3 ♗g7−+; 15. ♕d3 e6 16. ♗e4 d5 17. ♗f3 g4 18. ♗e2 d4−+] **h5!?** [15... d5 16. 0–0 ♘d4 17. ♕d3 ♘f5 18. ♕f5 ♗g7 19. ♖fe1 e6 20. ♖e6 fe6 21. ♕e6 ♔d8 22. ♗e5→; 15... ♗g7 16. 0–0 ♘d4 17. ♕b7 0–0 18. ♗d3 ♖fb8 19. ♕e7 ♖b2 20. ♘d1 ♖a2 21. ♖a2 ♕a2 22. ♕d6∞; 16... 0–0∓] **16. 0–0** [16. ♗d3 g4 17. ♕e2 (17. ♕f5 ♕f5 18. ♗f5 e6 19. ♗d3 ♘b4∓) ♘d5 (17... ♘d4 18. ♕e3 e5 19. 0–0 ♗h6 20. ♕e1∓) 18. 0–0 ♘c3 19. bc3 0-0-0∓] **h4 17. ♗d6 ed6 18. ♗c8** [18. ♖fe1 ♗e7 19. ♗c8 *a)* 19... 0–0!? 20. ♗b7 ♘d4 (20... ♘e5 21. ♖e5 ♕e5 22. ♗a8) 21. ♕d3 ♘e6 22. ♗a8 (22. ♖e6 fe6 23. ♕g6 ♔h8 24. ♕h6 ♘h7 25. ♗a8 ♖a8 26. ♕e6 ♗f6−+) ♖a8∓; *b)* 19... ♖c8 20. ♕f6 ♖g8 21. ♕d6 (21. ♖ad1 ♘e5 22. ♕f5 ♖c5∓) ♖d8∓] **♖c8** [18... ♖h6?! 19. ♖fe1 ♔d8 20. ♗b7 ♘d4 21. ♕d3 ♖b8 22. ♗a6∞] **19. ♕f6** [19. ♖fe1 ♘e5 (19... ♗e7 20. ♕f6 ♖g8) 20. ♕f6 ♖h6 – 19. ♕f6] **♖h6** [⌓ 19... ♖g8 20. ♖fe1 ♗e7] **20. ♖fe1 ♘e5□** [20... ♘e7? 21. ♖e7 ♗e7 22. ♕h6] **21. ♕g5 ♕d8 22. ♕f5 ♕d7** [22... ♖e6 23. f4 ♕b6 24. ♔h1 ♕b2 25. ♘d5 ♕c2∓; 25. ♘e4!∞] **23. ♕f4** [23. ♕g5 ♕c6 24. ♘e4 ♖g6 25. ♕f5 ♗e7∓] **♔d8** [23... h3 24. ♖ad1 ♖g6 25. g3 ♗g7∓] **24. ♘d5?!** [24. ♖ad1 ♖c4 25. ♕g5 f6 (25... ♕e7? 26. ♖e5) 26. ♕g8 ♕f7 27. ♖d6 ♔c7 28. ♕f7 ♘f7∓ △ 29. ♖f6 ♖f6 30. ♘d5 ♔c6 31. ♘f6 ♖c2−+; 24. ♕g5 ♕e7 25. ♕f5 (25. ♕g8 ♖g6 26. ♕h8 ♘f3−+) ♖e6∓] **♕g4 25. ♕e3 ♖g6 26. ♘f4** [26. ♕b6 ♔e8 27. ♘e3 ♕e4−+] **♘f3 27. ♔h1** [27. ♔f1 ♘h2 28. ♔g1 ♘f3 29. ♔f1 ♘e1−+] **♘e1−+ 28. ♖e1 ♖e6** [28... ♖g7 29. ♕b6 ♖c7] **29. ♘e6 fe6 30. ♕b3 ♖c7 31. h3 ♕c4 32. ♕f3 ♗e7 33. b3 ♕c3** [33... ♕c2 34. ♖e6 ♕a2 35. ♕f7 ♕a1 36. ♔h2 ♕h8 37. ♖g6 ♗f8] **34. ♖e3 ♕a1 35. ♔h2 ♕f6 36. ♕g4** [36. ♕f6 ♗f6 37. ♖e6 ♗e5 38. ♔g1 ♖c2] **e5** [36... ♔d7; 36... ♖c2] **37. ♖f3 ♕h8** [37... ♕g5? 38. ♖f8] **38. c4** [38. ♖f7 ♗f6] **♖d7 39. ♕e6** [39. ♖f7 ♔c7 40. ♕e6 ♕d8] **♔c7 40. ♖d3 ♕d8 41. b4 ♗g5 42. c5 ♗f4 43. g3 dc5** [44. ♖d7 ♕d7 45. ♕d7 ♔d7 46. gf4 c4] **0 : 1** **[Ftáčnik]**

251. **B 90**

J. BENJAMIN 2585 – KAJDANOV 2620

Pleasantville 1993

1. e4 c5 2. ♘f3 d6 3. d4 cd4 4. ♘d4 ♘f6 5. ♘c3 a6 6. ♗e3 ♘g4 7. ♗g5 h6 8. ♗h4 g5 9. ♗e2 ♗g7 [9... ♘e3 10. fe3 gh4 11. 0–0 ×f7] **10. ♗g3 h5 11. ♗g4 ♗g4** [11... hg4 12. 0–0 ♘c6 13. ♘f5 ♗f5 14. ef5 ♗c3 15. bc3 f6 16. ♖b1±] **12. f3 ♗e6?! N** [12... ♗d7 – 56/(273)] **13. ♕d2 g4 14. ♘e6 fe6 15. fg4 hg4 16. e5!** [16. ♕g5?! ♗h6 17. ♕g4 ♕b6∓] **♘c6 17. ed6 ed6 18. 0–0?!** [×↗a7-g1, h2; 18. ♘e4?! d5 19. ♘d6 ♔d7 20. ♘f7 ♕b6 21. ♘h8 ♕b2⩱; 18. ♗d6 ♕f6; 18. ♕d6 ♕d6 19. ♗d6 0-0-0 20. 0-0-0 ♗c3 21. bc3 e5±; 18. 0-0-0! ♗h6 19. ♗f4 ♕f6 20. ♗h6 ♕h6 21. ♕h6 ♖h6 22. ♖d6 ♔e7 23. ♖hd1 ♘e5 (23... ♖d8 24. ♖d8 ♘d8 25. ♖d4) 24. ♖b6 ♖b8 25. ♘d5+−] **♕b6 19. ♗f2 ♕c7 20. ♕g5**

♗e5⇆ **21. ♗g3 ♕h7** [21... ♗g3 22. ♕g6 ♔d8 23. hg3 ♕b6 24. ♖f2 ♖f8 25. ♖f1 ♔d7 26. ♕g7 ♘e7 27. ♘e4±; 21... ♕b6! 22. ♖f2 ♕b2! (22... ♗d4 23. ♘e4↑) 23. ♕g6 ♔d8 24. ♗e5 ♕a1 (24... ♘e5 25. ♕f6 ♔c7 26. ♕g7 ♔c6 27. ♖b1 ♕c3 28. ♕b7 ♔c5 29. ♕b6 ♔d5 30. ♖d1 ♔e4 31. ♕d6 ♖ad8 32. ♖e2 ♔f5 33. ♖e5 ♕e5 34. ♖f1+−) 25. ♖f1 ♕f1 26. ♔f1 ♘e5 27. ♕e6 ♔c7=] **22. ♕g4± ♗g3** [22... 0-0-0 23. ♕e6 ♔b8 24. ♕f5] **23. ♕g3 0-0-0 24. ♖ae1 e5 25. ♘e4 d5 26. ♘g5 ♕c2 27. ♖f2 ♕a4 28. ♘f7 ♖dg8** [28... ♖hg8 *a)* 29. ♕h3 ♖d7 *a1)* 30. ♖c1? ♕d4 31. ♕e6 ♖f8! 32. ♖c6 (32. ♕e5 ♕b6−+) bc6 33. ♕c6 ♖c7 34. ♕a8 ♔d7 35. ♘e5 ♔e6−+; *a2)* 30. ♕e6 ♕g4 31. ♕g4 ♖g4 32. ♘e5; *b)* 29. ♕c3 ♖df8 30. ♖ef1 ♔c7 31. ♘e5 ♖f2 32. ♖f2 ♕d1 33. ♖f1 ♕e2 34. ♖f7 ♔d6 35. ♖f6 ♔e7 (35... ♔c7 36. ♖c6 bc6 37. ♕c6 ♔b8 38. ♘d7 ♔a7 39. ♕c7 ♔a8 40. ♘b6#) 36. ♘c6 bc6 37. ♖f2+−] **29. ♕f3 ♖f8 30. ♕d5 ♕b4 31. ♖ef1 ♘d4 32. ♘d6 ♔c7 33. ♖f7 ♖f7 34. ♖f7 ♔d8 35. ♘b5 1 : 0** **[J. Benjamin]**

252. !N B 90

DE LA VILLA GARCÍA 2440 – JU. HODGSON 2565

Zaragoza 1993

1. e4 c5 2. ♘f3 d6 3. d4 cd4 4. ♘d4 ♘f6 5. ♘c3 a6 6. ♗e3 ♘g4 7. ♗g5 [7. ♗c1 ♘c6 8. f3 ♕b6∓] **h6 8. ♗h4 g5 9. ♗g3 ♗g7 10. ♗e2 h5 11. h4 gh4 12. ♖h4! N** [12. ♗h4 – 50/275] **♘c6 13. ♘b3 ♗e6 14. ♕d2 ♕b6 15. ♘d5 ♗d5 16. ed5 ♘ce5 17. 0-0-0 ♗h6** [17... ♗f6 18. ♖hh1 h4 19. ♗f4 ♕f2 (19... ♘f2 20. ♗e3+−) 20. ♗e5 ♗e5 21. ♖df1 ♕g3 22. ♖h3+−; 17... ♘g6 18. ♖h3 h4 19. ♗g4 hg3 20. ♖h8 ♗h8 21. f4!± ♕f2 22. ♕f2 gf2 23. g3] **18. f4 ♕e3! 19. ♕e3** [19. ♗g4? ♕g3−+; 19. ♖h3 ♘g6∓] **♘e3 20. fe5!** [20. ♖dh1 ♖c8! (20... ♘g2 21. ♖h5 ♘f4 22. ♖h6 ♘e2 23. ♔d2 ♖h6 24. ♖h6 ♘g3 25. ♖h8 ♔d7 26. ♖a8±) 21. ♖h5 (21. c3 ♘g2∓) ♖c2 22. ♔b1 ♖e2 23. fe5 (23. ♖h6 ♖h6 24. ♖h6 ♘d3−+) ♖g2 24. ♗f4 ♗f4! 25. ♖h8 ♔d7 26. ed6 ♗e5∓] **♘f5 21. ♔b1 ♘g3**

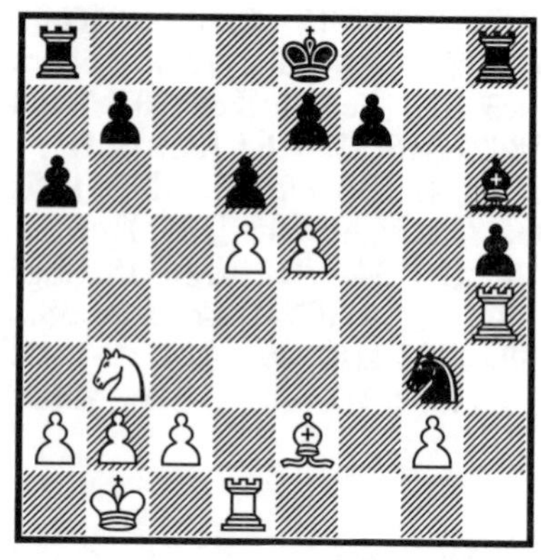

22. ed6! [22. ♗h5 ♗g5 23. ♖g4; 22... de5∓] **♗g5** [22... ♘e2 23. ♖e4 ♘f4 24. ♖e7 (24. de7!?) ♔f8 25. g3 ♘g6 26. ♖b7±; 22... ed6 23. ♗f3±] **23. ♖b4 ♘e2 24. de7!** [24. ♖b7 0-0-0∓] **♗e7 25. ♖b7** [25. d6? 0-0-0 26. ♖e1 ♘c3∓] **♗d6?!** [25... ♖g8 26. d6 ♗f8 27. c4∞; 26. c4!] **26. c4!±** [26. ♖e1 0-0-0∓] **♖g8!?** [26... 0-0-0 27. ♖a7 ♖hg8 28. c5 ♗c5 29. d6±] **27. c5 ♖b8 28. ♖b8** [28. ♖a7? ♗c5 29. ♘c5 ♘c3 30. ♔c1 ♘d1 31. ♘d7 ♖c8 32. ♔d1 ♖g2−+; 28. ♘a5! ♖b7 29. ♘b7 ♗e5 30. d6+−] **♗b8 29. d6!+−** [29. ♖e1 ♖g2 30. ♘d4 ♗g3! 31. ♖e2 ♖e2 32. ♘e2 h4∓ 33. b4 ♗e1] **♖g6! 30. ♘a5** [30. d7 ♔d8 31. ♘a5 ♗c7 32. ♘b7 ♔e7 33. d8♕ ♗d8 34. ♘d8 ♖g2∞] **♗d6! 31. cd6** [♖ 9/h] **♔d7 32. ♘c4 f6 33. ♘b6 ♔d8 34. a4?!** [34. ♖h1 ♖g5 (34... f5 35. ♘c4) 35. a4] **♖g2 35. ♔c2?** [35. ♖d5 ♖g5 36. ♖d2±] **h4 36. ♔b3** [36. ♔d3∞] **h3 37. ♖d5?** [37. ♖f1!∞] **♖g5 38. ♖d2 h2−+ 39. ♖e2 h1♕ 40. ♖c2 ♕d1 0 : 1** **[de la Villa García]**

253. B 90

BRUNNER 2490 – BANGIEV 2400

Deutschland 1992

1. e4 c5 2. ♘f3 d6 3. d4 cd4 4. ♘d4 ♘f6 5. ♘c3 a6 6. ♗e3 e5 7. ♘b3 ♗e7 8. f4 N ♕c7 9. ♕d2 b5 10. 0-0-0 ♗b7 11. ♘d5 [11. fe5 de5 12. ♘d5!? ♗d5 (12... ♘d5 13. ed5 ♗d6 14. ♕a5!? ♘d7 15. ♕c7 ♗c7 16. ♘c5 ♘c5 17. ♗c5 ♖d8 18. d6 ♗b8 19. ♗e2±) 13. ed5 *a)* 13... ♘e4!? 14. ♕a5!? (14. d6?! ♘d6 15. ♕d5 ♘c6) ♕a5

15. ♘a5±; *b)* 13... ♗d6 14. ♕e2!? 0–0 15. g4 ♘bd7 16. ♗g2∞] **♘d5 12. ed5 ♘d7** [△ ♘f6] **13. ♘a5 0–0 14. ♘b7 ♕b7 15. f5!?** [△ g4-g5→»; 15. ♔b1 ♗f6 (△ ef4, ♗e5) 16. f5 e4!?∞] **♖fc8** [15... e4!? 16. g4 ♘e5 (16... ♗f6!? 17. g5 ♗e5 18. ♗g2 ♖fe8∞) 17. g5 ♖fe8 18. h4 ♖ac8∞] **16. g4 b4** [△ b3] **17. ♔b1 ♘c5 18. g5!?** [18. ♗c5 ♖c5 19. g5 ♖ac8 20. ♗d3 ♗d8!? 21. ♗e4 ♖c4∞] **♘a4?!** [18... ♘e4!? 19. ♕c1□ ♖ab8!? 20. ♔a1 (20. ♗d3 ♘c3! 21. bc3 bc3 22. ♔a1 ♕b4! △ ♕a4, ♖b2∓) b3 21. ab3 ♕b4!? 22. ♗g2 (22. ♗d3 a5!?) a5 23. ♖he1 (23. c3 ♕b3 24. ♗e4 ♕a4∓) a4 24. c3 ♕b3 25. ♗e4 a3↑] **19. ♔a1 ♕c7?!** [19... ♘c3?! 20. bc3 bc3 21. ♕c1 ♖ab8 22. ♕a3!±; 19... ♖ab8!? 20. f6 (20. ♗d3 ♘c3! 21. bc3 bc3 22. ♕c1 ♕b4! △ ♕a4, ♖b2∓) ♗f8 21. ♗h3 ♖c3!? △ 22. bc3 bc3 23. ♕c1 ♕b2–+; 21. h4!?∞; 19... ♗d8!? 20. f6 ♗a5∞] **20. f6** [20. ♕b4 ♕d7 (20... ♕c2 21. ♗d3±) 21. ♕d2 ♖ab8∞] **♗d8?!** [20... ♗f8 21. ♗d3 (21. ♕b4 ♕d7∞) ♕a5 22. h4 ♖ab8 23. h5↑] **21. ♗d3 ♕a5** [21... g6 22. ♕f2 ♕a5 23. ♕h4±] **22. fg7! ♖ab8** [22... ♘c3 23. bc3 bc3 24. ♕g2+–; 22... ♔g7 23. ♕g2+–] **23. ♕g2! ♔g7?** [23... ♘c3! 24. bc3 b3! 25. cb3 ♖b3! (25... ♕c3 26. ♕b2±) 26. ♖c1 (26. ♗d2 ♖cc3! 27. ♕e4 ♕a2! 28. ♔a2 ♖a3 29. ♔b1 ♖ab3=) ♖cc3!∞] **24. ♕h3!+–** [24. ♕e4? ♘c3! 25. ♕h7 ♔f8 26. bc3 (26. a3 ba3 27. b3 ♘d1–+) b3!! 27. ♕h8 (27. cb3 ♕c3 28. ♔b1 ♖b3 29. ab3 ♕b3 30. ♔a1 ♕a3 31. ♔b1 ♖b8–+) ♔e7 28. ♕f6 ♔e8 29. ♕h8 ♔d7 30. ♗f5 ♔c7 31. cb3 ♕c3 32. ♔b1 ♖b3!∓] **♔f8** [24... ♘c3 25. ♕h6] **25. ♖hf1! f6** [25... ♘c3 26. ♖f7!] **26. gf6 ♘c3 27. ♗h6 1 : 0** [Bangiev]

254. !N **B 90**

V. DAMJANOVIĆ 2320 – VAULIN 2515

Beograd 1993

1. e4 c5 2. ♘f3 d6 3. d4 cd4 4. ♘d4 ♘f6 5. ♘c3 a6 6. ♗e3 e5 7. ♘b3 ♗e7 8. f3 0–0 9. ♕d2 ♗e6 10. 0-0-0 ♘bd7 11. g4 b5 12. g5 b4! N [12... ♘h5 – 48/(356)] **13. ♘e2!?** [13. ♘a4 ♘h5=] **♘e8?!** [13... ♘h5!? 14. ♘g3 ♘f4 15. h4 a5 16. ♔b1 a4 17. ♘d4 ed4 18. ♗f4 ♘e5 19. ♗e2 ♕c7 20. ♘f5 (20. ♕d4 ♗a2 21. ♔a2 b3 22. ♔a1 a3 23. ♖d2 ♕a5 24. ♔b1 ab2 25. ♕b2 bc2–+) ♗f5 21. ef5 ♖fc8 22. ♖c1 a3 23. b3 ♕c3∞] **14. h4 a5 15. ♔b1 ♘c7** [△ d5] **16. f4 a4 17. ♘bc1 b3 18. cb3 ab3 19. f5!? ba2 20. ♔a1 ♗c4 21. ♘g3 ♗f1 22. ♖df1** [22. ♖hf1!?±] **d5□ 23. f6 ♗c5 24. fg7?!** [24. ♘f5!? g6 25. ♘h6 ♔h8 26. h5 △ ♘f7, hg6→] **♔g7 25. ♘f5 ♔h8 26. ed5 ♗e3 27. ♘e3 ♘b5 28. ♘f5 ♕b6 29. h5 ♖fc8! 30. d6** [30. g6 fg6 31. hg6 ♕g6 32. ♖h6 ♘d4!! △ ♖c1] **♘a3!∓ 31. ♖h2 ♘c2** [31... ♕b5!?∓] **32. ♕c2 ♖c2 33. ♖c2 e4?** [33... ♕b5!? △ 34. ♖cf2 ♘c5 35. g6 ♕c4 (△ ♕c1) 36. ♖f3 ♕c2] **34. g6 fg6 35. hg6 ♘e5 36. g7 ♔g8 37. ♖c7 ♕b2??⊕** [37... ♘f7 38. ♘e7 ♔g7 39. ♖f7 ♔f7 40. ♘d5 ♕c7 41. dc7 ♖c8=] **38. ♔b2 a1♕ 39. ♔c2 ♕a4 40. ♘b3+– ♘g4 41. d7** [41. ♘h6!? ♘h6 42. d7 ♖d8 43. ♖f8 ♔g7 44. ♖d8 ♘f7 45. ♖e8 ♔g6 46. ♖g8 ♔h5 47. ♖f8] **♖d8 42. ♖a1 ♕b5 43. ♖a8! ♕d3 44. ♔b2 ♕e2 45. ♖c2 ♕c2 46. ♔c2 ♘e3 47. ♔c1 ♖a8 48. ♘e7 ♔g7 49. ♘c8 ♖c8 50. dc8♕ 1 : 0**
[Vaulin, M. Makarov]

255.** **B 90**

TIVJAKOV 2595 – SAHU 2390

Calcutta 1993

1. e4 c5 2. ♘f3 d6 3. d4 cd4 4. ♘d4 ♘f6 5. ♘c3 a6 6. ♗e3 e5 7. ♘b3 ♗e6 8. ♕d2 [RR 8. f4 ef4 9. ♗f4 ♘c6 10. ♕d2 d5 N (10... ♗e7 – 52/(241)) 11. ed5 ♘d5 12. ♘d5 ♕d5 13. ♕d5 ♗d5 14. 0-0-0 0-0-0 15. ♗d3 g6 16. ♖d2 ♗d6 17. ♗d6 ♖d6 18. ♗e4 ♖hd8 19. ♖hd1 ♘b4 20. ♖d4 f5 21. ♗d5 ♖d5 22. a3 ♖d4 23. ♘d4 ♘d5= Szalánczy 2365 – V. Loginov 2505, Kecskemét 1993] **♗e7 9. f3 0–0** [RR 9... ♘bd7 10. g4 h6 11. 0-0-0 b5 12. ♔b1 ♘b6 13. ♗b6 ♕b6 14. h4 b4 15. ♘d5 ♗d5 N (15... ♘d5 – 31/(309)) 16. ed5 a5 17. ♗h3 a4 18. ♘c1 ♖a5 19. g5 ♘d5 20. ♘e2 ♖c5 21. ♔a1 ♕c6 22. ♗f5 1/2 : 1/2 Lanka 2545 – Piesina 2395, Vilnius (zt) 1993] **10.**

0-0-0 b5 11. g4 b4 12. ♘d5! ♗d5 13. ed5 a5 14. ♔b1 a4 N [14... ♘bd7 — 56/(272)] **15. ♘c1 ♕a5 16. g5 ♘h5?!** [16... ♘fd7±; 16... ♘e8±] **17. ♗h3! ♖e8?!** [17... g6 18. ♗g4 ♘g7 19. h4±→»] **18. ♗g4 ♘f4 19. ♗f4 ef4 20. ♖he1+−** [20. ♕f4 ♗f8 21. h4! g6 22. h5 ♗g7 23. hg6 hg6 (23... fg6 24. ♗e6+−; 24. ♖h7+−) 24. ♖h7!+− (△ 25. ♖g7 ♔g7 26. ♕f6 ♔g8 27. ♖h1) ♔h7 25. ♕f7 △ ♖h1#] **♕b5** [20... ♘a6 21. ♗d7; 20... ♕d8 21. ♕b4 ♗g5 (21... ♘a6 22. ♕f4) 22. ♕d6; 20... a3 21. b3!?; 20... g6 21. ♖e4] **21. ♕f4 ♘a6 22. ♗f5 g6** [22... ♘c5 23. ♗h7 ♔h7 24. ♕f7 ♗g5 25. ♕f5 ♔h6 26. f4 △ ♖g1; 26. h4 △ h5] **23. ♗d3 ♕d7 24. ♗a6 ♖a6 25. ♖e4 ♗d8 26. ♕g4! ♖e7 27. ♖b4 ♕e8 28. ♘d3 ♖a8 29. h4 a3 30. b3 ♗a5 31. ♖c4 ♕b5 32. ♖c8 ♖c8 33. ♕c8 ♖e8 34. ♕c6 ♕b8 35. ♕a4 ♗c3 36. ♕a3 ♖e3 37. f4 ♕e8 38. b4 ♕c8 39. b5 ♗d4 40. ♕b4 ♖e2 41. ♕b3 ♕g4 42. a4 ♖e4 43. ♖c1 ♗b6 44. a5 ♗a5 45. ♘f2 1 : 0 [Tivjakov]**

256.* **B 90**

NUNN 2580 — KUCZYŃSKI 2525
Deutschland 1993

1. e4 c5 2. ♘f3 d6 3. d4 cd4 4. ♘d4 ♘f6 5. ♘c3 a6 6. ♗e3 e5 7. ♘f3 ♕c7 8. a4 ♗e7 [RR 8... h6 9. a5 ♗e6 10. ♘d5 ♗d5 11. ed5 ♘bd7 12. ♗e2 ♗e7 N (12... g6 — 47/315) 13. c4 0−0 14. b4 ♘h7 15. ♖c1 f5 16. c5 f4 17. cd6 ♕d6 18. ♗c5 ♘c5 19. bc5 ♕c7 20. d6 ♕a5 21. ♕d2 ♕d2 22. ♔d2 ♗f6 23. ♗c4 ♔h8 24. ♗d5 ♖ab8 25. ♖b1 b5 26. c6 1 : 0 Liang Jinrong 2505 — Sitanggang 2385, Baguio City 1993] **9. a5 0−0 10. ♗e2 ♘c6 11. ♗b6 ♕d7 12. ♘d2 d5 13. ed5 ♘d5 14. ♘d5 ♕d5 15. 0−0 ♗e6 16. ♘c4!? N** [16. ♗f3 — 42/(299); 16. c3] **♕e4!?** [16... ♕d1 17. ♖fd1±; 16... ♗d8 17. ♕d5 ♗d5 18. ♖fd1 ♗c4 19. ♗c4 ♗b6 20. ab6 ♖fd8 21. ♗d5! ♖dc8 22. ♗e4! △ ♖d7±; 16... ♕b5!? 17. b3 e4⩲] **17. ♖a4** [△ ♗f3; 17. ♘e3!?; 17. b3!⩲] **♘b4!?** [17... ♘d4 18. ♗d4⩲] **18. ♘e3** [18. b3!? ♕c2 (18... ♘c2? 19. ♗d3+−) 19. ♕c2 ♘c2 20. ♗f3 ♗d7 (20... ♖ab8 21. ♗c7±) 21. ♖a2 ♘b4 22. ♖d2 ♗c6 23. ♘e5±] **♕c6 19. c3** [19. b3 ♘c2?! 20. ♘c2 ♗b3 21. ♘d4! ♕a4 22. ♘b3⩲; 19... ♖ac8∞] **♘d5 20. ♗f3** [20. ♖c4? ♘e3 21. ♖c6 ♘d1 22. ♖e6 fe6 23. ♖d1∓] **♘e3 21. fe3 ♕b5 22. ♖a1?** [22. ♗b7! ♖ab8 (22... ♗b3 23. ♖b4! ♕b4 24. cb4 ♗d1 25. ♖d1 ♗b4 26. ♗a8 ♖a8±) 23. ♗e4 *a)* 23... ♗b3?! 24. ♖b4 ♕b4 (24... ♗d1 25. ♖b5 ab5 26. ♖d1±; 24... ♕b6 25. ♖b6 ♗d1 26. ♖d1 ♗c5 27. ♖b8 ♗e3 28. ♔f1 ♖b8 29. b4±) 25. ♗h7! ♔h8□ 26. ♕h5? ♕h4; 26. ♗c2!± △ 26... ♗c2 27. ♕h5+−; *b)* 23... ♕b2! 24. ♕d3 ♕b3! (24... f5 25. ♗d5±) 25. ♗h7 (25. ♗c6!? △ ♖b1) ♔h8 26. ♖aa1 ♗c4 (26... g6 27. ♗g6±) 27. ♕f5 ♗f1 28. ♖f1 ♖b6 29. ab6 ♕b6=] **♖ab8∓ 23. b4 ♖fc8 24. ♖c1** [△ 25. ♗a7 ♖a8 26. ♗b6=] **♗d8** [24... ♗c4 25. ♖f2 ♗d3 (△ e4) 26. ♗g4∞; 24... f5!? 25. e4!∞] **25. ♗a7 ♖a8 26. ♗c5 ♗c4** [26... ♗a5 27. c4! (27. ♗d5 ♕d7∓) ♗c4 28. ♖c4 ♕c4 29. ♗d5 ♕h4 (29... ♕c3!? 30. ♖f7 ♔h8 31. ♕g4 ♖g8 32. ♗e4∞) *a)* 30. ♖f7? ♔h8 31. ♗b7 (31. ♗e7? ♕h6 32. ba5 ♕e3 △ ♖c1−+) ♗b4 32. ♗b4 ♕b4 33. ♗a8 ♖a8 34. ♖a7 ♖f8! 35. ♖a6 ♕c3∓; *b)* 30. ♕f3! ♔h8 (30... ♗b4 31. g3!∞) 31. ♗b7∞]

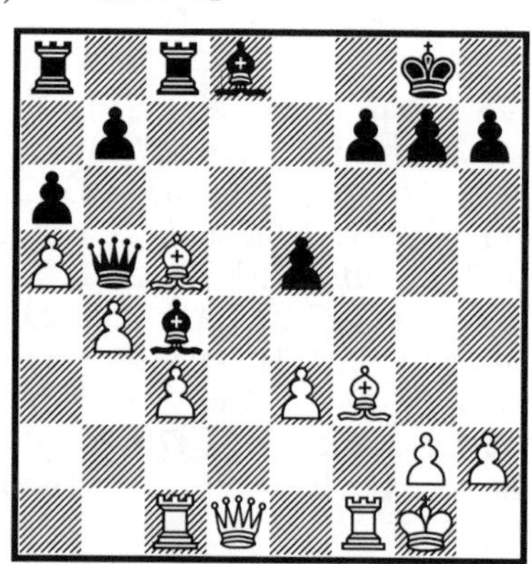

27. ♗d5!! [27. ♖f2? ♗a5 28. ♗d5 ♖c5! 29. bc5 ♖d8 30. e4 (30. ♖d2 ♕c5−+) ♕c5 31. ♕h5 ♗d5 32. ed5 ♕d5∓] **♗f1 28. ♕f3 ♗f6!** [28... ♕d7 29. ♖f1 ♖c7 30. ♖d1=/∞] **29. ♖f1 e4?⊕** [29... ♖c7 30. c4 ♕d7 31. ♗b6±; 29... ♖c5! 30. bc5 ♕c5 (30... ♖c8 31. ♕g4±) 31. ♗f7 ♔h8 32. ♕b7 ♖f8! 33. ♗d5 ♕e3 34. ♔h1 ♕d3=] **30. ♕h5?** [30. ♗e4? ♖c5 31. bc5 ♕c5

32. ♗b7 ♖e8=; 30. ♕f5! (△ ♗e4) ♖c5□ 31. bc5 ♕a5 32. ♗b7 (32. ♗e4 ♕c3 33. ♕h7 ♔f8 34. ♕h8 ♔e7 35. ♕a8 ♕e3 36. ♔h1 ♕e4±) ♖e8 33. ♗e4 ♕c3 34. ♗d3±; 32. c4!±] **g6!□ 31. ♕h6** [31. ♗f7 ♔g7 (31... ♔f7? 32. ♕h7 ♔e6 33. ♕g6 ♖f8 34. ♕f5+−) 32. ♕d5∞] **♖c5!** [31... ♗g7? 32. ♖f7! ♗h6 33. ♖d7 ♔h8 34. ♗d4+−; 31... ♕d3? 32. ♗f7! ♔f7 33. ♕h7 ♔e6 34. ♕g6 ♕d8 (34... ♖f8 35. ♕f5+−; 34... ♕c3 35. ♗d4+−) 35. ♗d4+−; 31... ♕d7? 32. c4↑] **32. bc5 ♕c5 33. c4** [33. ♗f7 ♔f7 34. ♕h7 ♔e6 35. ♕h3 ♔e5 36. ♕g3=] **♕e7= 34. ♕f4 ♗g5 35. ♕g3** [35. ♕f7 ♕f7 36. ♖f7 ♗e3 37. ♔f1 ♖f8=] **♖f8 36. ♖b1 ♕f6 37. ♗b7 ♗h4 38. ♕g4** [38. ♕f4=] **♗f2** [38... ♕f2 39. ♔h1 f5 40. ♕f4 ♕f4 41. ef4=] **39. ♔h1 ♗e3 40. ♕e4 ♗d2 41. ♕f3 1/2 : 1/2** [Nunn]

257. !N **B 90**

DE LA VILLA GARCÍA 2440 – AT. KOLEV 2510

Zaragoza 1993

1. e4 c5 2. ♘f3 d6 3. d4 cd4 4. ♘d4 ♘f6 5. ♘c3 a6 6. ♗e3 e5 7. ♘f3 ♕c7 8. a4 ♗e7 9. a5 0–0 10. ♗e2 ♕c6 11. ♕d3 h6 12. 0–0 ♗e6 13. ♖fd1 ♘g4?! 14. ♗b6! N [14. ♘d5 – 53/232] **♘d7 15. ♘d5 ♗d5 16. ed5 ♕c8 17. ♘d4! ♘b6 18. ♘f5 ♕d8 19. ♕g3!** [19. ab6 ♘f6 20. ♕g3 g6 21. ♘h6 ♔h7 22. ♕e3 ♘d7∓] **♘d7** [19... ♘c8 20. ♕g4 ♗g5 21. h4 g6 22. hg5 gf5 23. ♕f5 ♕g5 24. ♕d7 ♕e7 25. ♕h3±] **20. ♕g4 g6 21. ♘h6 ♔h7** [21... ♔h8?! 22. ♖d3 ♘f6 23. ♖h3+−] **22. ♘f5 ♖h8** [22... gf5 23. ♕f5 ♔g7 24. ♕g4 ♔f6 (24... ♔h7 25. ♖d3+−) 25. ♖a3 e4 26. ♕f4+−] **23. ♖d3 ♔g8 24. ♖h3** [24. ♖b3!?; 24. ♖aa3!?] **♖h3 25. ♘e7 ♕e7 26. ♕h3± ♔g7 27. c4 ♖h8 28. ♕c3 ♕h4 29. h3 ♘f6 30. ♕e3 ♘e4 31. b4 f5 32. c5?!** [32. ♖c1!] **♘f6! 33. ♕b3 ♘e4 34. ♕e3 ♘f6 35. cd6 ♕b4 36. ♗f1!** [36. ♕e5? ♖e8 37. ♕e8 ♘e8 38. d7 ♕e7 39. de8♕ ♕e8 40. ♗f3=] **♖e8!?** [36... ♕d6 37. ♕a7±] **37. ♕a7 ♖d8 38. ♗a6 ♖d7 39. ♗f1 ♕d6 40. ♖d1 e4** [40... ♘d5 41. ♗c4 ♕c6 42. ♗d5 ♖d5 43. ♖d5 ♕d5 44. a6+−] **41. ♗b5 ♖c7?!** [41... ♖f7!] **42. ♕b6! ♕b6 43. ab6 ♖c5** [43... ♖c2 44. d6+−] **44. ♗c6!+− ♔f7** [44... bc6 45. b7 ♘d7 46. dc6 ♘b8 47. ♖d7] **45. ♗b7 ♘d7** [45... ♖b5 46. d6 ♔e6 47. d7 ♘d7 48. ♗c8] **46. ♖b1 ♔e7 47. h4 ♔d6 48. ♗c6 ♘b8 49. g3 ♖c3 50. b7 e3 51. ♖e1 ♖b3 52. ♖e3 ♖b1 53. ♔g2 ♘c6 54. dc6 ♔c6 55. ♖e6 ♔d5 56. ♖e7 ♔d6 57. ♖g7 ♔e5 58. ♔f3 ♖b3 59. ♔e2 f4 60. ♔d2 ♔e4 61. ♔c2 ♖b5 62. ♖f7 fg3 63. fg3 ♔d4 64. ♖d7 ♔c5 65. ♔c3 ♔c6 66. ♔c4 1 : 0**
[de la Villa García]

258. **B 92**

EHLVEST 2625 – I. GUREVICH 2515

Saint-Martin 1993

1. e4 c5 2. ♘f3 d6 3. d4 cd4 4. ♘d4 ♘f6 5. ♘c3 a6 6. ♗e2 e5 7. ♘b3 ♗e7 8. 0–0 0–0 9. ♔h1 ♘c6?! 10. f4 ef4 [10... b5!?] **11. ♗f4 ♗e6 12. ♕e1** [12. ♘d4!? ♘d4 13. ♕d4 △ ♖ad1±] **♘e8□ N** [12... d5?! 13. ♖d1±; 12... ♘e5 – 30/478] **13. ♘d5!± ♗g5 14. ♗g3 ♘e5?!** [14... ♗d5 15. ed5 ♘e5 16. c4!±] **15. ♖d1!** [×d5] **♗d5 16. ♖d5 ♘f6 17. ♖d1 ♕c7 18. ♖f5! ♗h6** [18... ♗e3 19. ♖f6 gf6 20. ♗e5 de5 21. ♕g3 ♗g5 22. h4 ♕c2 23. hg5±; 18... h6 19. h4!] **19. ♖f6! gf6 20. ♘d4**$\overline{\overline{\infty}}$ **♖fe8 21. ♘f5 ♗f8 22. c3 ♕c6 23. ♖d4!** [△ ♗d1-b3] **b5 24. ♗d1 ♖e6 25. ♗b3± ♘c4 26. ♗h4 ♖ae8 27. ♗c4 bc4 28. h3 ♕c5 29. ♕g3 ♔h8 30. ♕g4 ♕c7 31. ♗g3⊕ ♖d8 32. ♔h2 ♕b7?!** [32... ♖de8±] **33. ♖c4 ♖de8** [33... ♕b2 34. ♖c7+−] **34. ♖b4 ♕a8 35. ♗h4 d5 36. ♖d4! ♕b8** [36... de4 37. ♖d7+−] **37. ♗g3 ♕b2 38. ed5+− ♖e2 39. ♗h4 ♕b8 40. d6 ♖2e6 41. ♗g3 ♕b6 42. ♕h5 ♕c5 43. ♖h4 h6 44. d7 ♖d8 45. ♕g4 ♔h7 46. ♕f4 ♔g6 47. ♖h6 1 : 0** **[Ehlvest]**

259.* **B 92**

CEŠKOVSKIJ 2540 – NASYBULLIN 2345

Kazahstan 1993

1. e4 c5 2. ♘f3 d6 3. d4 ♘f6 4. ♘c3 cd4 5. ♘d4 a6 6. ♗e2 e5 7. ♘b3 ♗e7 8. 0–0

0–0 9. ♔h1 ♘bd7 N [9... b5 – 50/(280)] **10. f3!? ♘b6** [10... ♕c7 11. a4 h6 12. ♘d2 ♖d8 13. ♘c4 ♘b6 14. ♘e3 ♗e6 15. a5 ♘c8± Ceškovskij 2540 – Pigusov 2575, Sankt-Peterburg (zt) 1993] **11. a4 d5 12. a5 d4 13. ♘b1** [13. ab6 dc3 14. ♕d8 ♗d8 15. bc3 ♗b6 16. ♗a3 ♖d8 17. c4⩲] **♘bd7 14. c3 dc3** [14... ♘c5!? 15. cd4 ♘b3 16. ♕b3 ed4∞] **15. ♘c3 ♘c5 16. ♘c5!? ♕d1 17. ♖d1 ♗c5 18. ♘a4! ♗d4 19. ♘b6 ♖b8□ 20. ♗d2!± ♗e6** [20... ♗b2 21. ♖ab1 *a)* 21... ♗d4 22. ♗b4 ♖e8 23. ♗d6 ♗b6!□ 24. ♗b8 (24. ♖b6⩲) ♗a5 25. ♖dc1! (×e5) ♘d7□ 26. ♗c7±; *b)* 21... ♗a3 22. ♗c3; 22. ♘c4] **21. ♗b4 ♖fd8 22. ♗e7 ♗b6** [22... ♗b3 23. ♖d3 ♗c2 24. ♖d2 ♗b2 25. ♗d8 ♗a1 26. ♗f6+–] **23. ab6 ♖d1 24. ♖d1 ♘e8?!** [24... ♖c8] **25. g3! f6 26. f4 ♔f7 27. ♗b4 ef4 28. gf4 g6□ 29. ♗f3!?** [29. f5 gf5□ 30. ♗h5 *a)* 30... ♔g7 31. ♖g1 ♔h8 (31... ♔h6 32. ♗f3 f4 33. ♗f8+–) 32. ♗e7 ♘g7□ 33. ♗f6 ♖g8 34. ♗f3+–; *b)* 30... ♔g8□ 31. ♖g1 ♘g7 32. ♗e7 ♗f7□ 33. ♗f6 ♗g6!□ 34. ♗g6 hg6 35. ♗g7 ♔g7 36. ef5 ♖f8!=] **♘g7 30. ♗c3! ♖e8 31. e5 f5 32. ♗b4! ♗c8 33. ♗d5 ♘e6 34. ♖c1 ♔g7 35. ♖c4 ♗d7⊕ 36. ♗d6 ♗b5 37. ♖c3+– ♘f4 38. ♗b7 ♘d3 39. ♖d3! ♗d3 40. ♔g1 a5 41. ♗c6 1 : 0**
[Ceškovskij]

260. **B 92**

GAŽÍK 2425 – ZAGREBEL'NYJ 2440
Magyarország 1992

1. e4 c5 2. ♘f3 d6 3. d4 cd4 4. ♘d4 ♘f6 5. ♘c3 a6 6. ♗e2 e5 7. ♘b3 ♗e7 8. ♗e3 ♗e6 9. ♕d2 0–0 10. 0–0 ♘bd7 11. a4 ♖c8 12. ♖fd1 ♘b6! 13. a5 ♘c4 14. ♗c4 ♖c4 15. f3 ♕c8 16. ♖ac1 N [16. ♗b6 – 36/(335)] **h6 17. ♕d3** [17. ♘d5?! ♘d5 18. ed5 ♗f5∓] **♖b4 18. ♘a2!? ♖c4 19. ♘c3 ♖d8!?** [19... ♖b4=] **20. ♗b6 ♖d7 21. ♘d5 ♗d5 22. ed5 ♗d8 23. ♗e3 ♖e7 24. ♘d2 ♖b4 25. c3!?** [25. c4 b6! (25... ♗a5?! 26. c5! dc5 27. d6±) 26. ab6 ♕b7∓] **♖b2! 26. ♘c4 e4! 27. fe4□** [27. ♘d6? ed3 28. ♘c8 ♖e3–+]

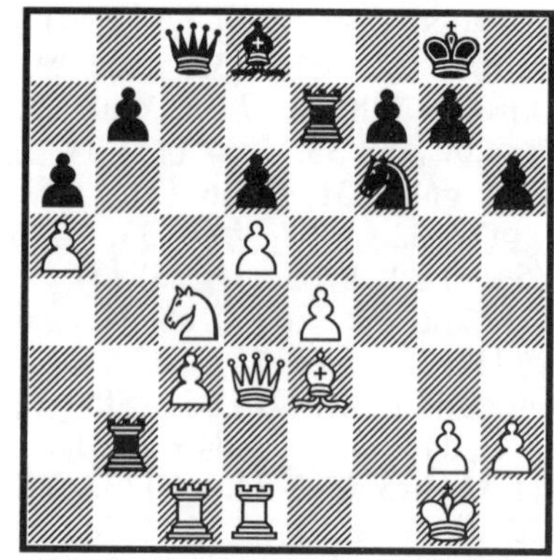

27... ♖g2!! 28. ♔g2 ♕g4 29. ♔f1 [29. ♔h1 ♕f3 30. ♔g1 ♖e4 31. ♗f2 ♕d3 32. ♖d3 ♖c4∓] **♖e4 30. ♖c2!** [30. ♗d4? ♖f4 31. ♔e1 ♘e4 △ ♗h4–+; 30. ♘d2 ♕h3 31. ♔e2 ♕h2 32. ♔f1 ♕h3 33. ♔e2 ♕g2 34. ♔e1 ♘g4 35. ♘e4 ♗h4–+] **♖c4 31. ♗d4 ♕e4!** [31... ♘d5? 32. ♖e1+–] **32. ♖g2 ♕d3 33. ♖d3 ♖a4 34. ♖b2!** [34. ♗b6?! ♗b6 35. ab6 ♖a1 36. ♔e2 ♖b1∓] **♘d5 35. ♗e5?⊕** [35. ♗g7? ♘f4 36. ♖d4 (36. ♖g3 ♘h5!–+) ♖a1 37. ♔f2 ♘e6–+; 35. ♖b7□ ♘f4! 36. ♖f3 ♖a1 37. ♔f2 ♗g5!∓] **de5 36. ♖d5 ♗a5 37. ♖b7 ♖f4 38. ♔e2 ♗c3–+ 39. ♖a7 a5 40. ♖c7 ♗d4 41. ♖a5 g5 0 : 1 [Zagrebel'nyj]**

261.** **B 92**

JANSA 2520 – M. RÖDER 2405
Bad Wörishofen 1993

1. e4 c5 2. ♘f3 d6 3. d4 cd4 4. ♘d4 ♘f6 5. ♘c3 a6 6. ♗e2 e5 7. ♘b3 ♗e7 8. 0–0 0–0 9. ♗e3 ♗e6 10. ♕d2 ♘bd7 11. a4 ♖c8 12. a5 ♕c7 13. ♖fd1 ♘c5 [13... ♖fe8 14. h3 h6 15. ♕e1 ♗f8?! N (15... ♕c6 – 46/334) 16. ♖d2 ♕b8 17. ♖a4! ♖c6 18. ♕d1! (△ ♘d5±; 18. ♘d5? ♘e4! 19. ♖e4 ♗d5 20. ♖d5 ♘f6∓) ♖c3!? 19. bc3 ♖c8± Jansa 2520 – A. Bach 2345, Bad Wörishofen 1993; RR 13... h6 N 14. f3 ♖fe8! 15. ♘c1 ♗f8! (15... ♘h7?! 16. ♘d3 △ ♘b4-d5) 16. ♔h1 (16. ♘d3?! d5∓; 16. ♕e1?! ♕c6! △ d5∓) ♖ed8! (16... ♕c6? 17. ♘1a2± ×d5) 17. ♗f2 (17. ♗f1?! d5! 18. ed5 ♘d5∓ ×♖d1 P. Thipsay) ♖e8 18. ♗f1 ♖ed8 (△ d5) 19. ♗e2 1/2 : 1/2 P.

Thipsay 2465 – Ju. Hodgson 2565, Calcutta 1993] **14. ♘c5 dc5 15. ♗f3!? N** [15. ♕e1 – 54/245] **c4** [⌓ 15... ♖fd8 16. ♕e2 ♖d1 17. ♕d1 ♖d8 18. ♕e2 c4 (18... ♕c6 19. ♗g5!? △ ♗f6, ♗g4±) 19. ♘a4 ♘d7 20. ♗g4!; 19... h6!?] **16. ♘a4! ♖fe8?!** [16... ♖fd8?! 17. ♕c3 ♖d1 18. ♖d1↑ ×c4, e5; 16... h6⩲] **17. ♘b6 ♖cd8 18. ♕c3 ♖d1 19. ♖d1±** [△ b3] **♖d8?** [19... ♗d6 20. ♗g5! △ 20... ♘d7? 21. ♘d7 ♗d7 22. ♕d2 ♖e6 23. ♗g4 ♖g6 24. ♗f5+–; 19... ♘d7 20. ♘d7 ♗d7 21. ♗b6 ♕c6 22. ♕e5 ♗f6 23. ♕c7 ♕c7 24. ♗c7±; 20. ♘d5±; 19... ♗c5 20. ♗c5 ♕c5 21. b3±] **20. ♘d5! ♘d5** [20... ♗d5 21. ♗b6+–] **21. ed5 ♕d6□ 22. ♗b6 ♖d7 23. g4!+–** [23. ♕c4±] **♗g4 24. ♗g4 ♕g6 25. ♕g3 f5 26. ♗e2 ♕f6 27. d6 ♖d6 28. ♗c4 ♔h8 29. ♖d6 ♗d6 30. h4 e4 31. ♕g5 1 : 0 [Jansa]**

262.** **B 93**

KINDERMANN 2495 – AV. BYHOVSKIJ 2520

Cuxhaven 1993

1. e4 c5 2. ♘f3 d6 3. d4 cd4 4. ♘d4 ♘f6 5. ♘c3 a6 6. f4 ♘bd7 [RR 6... g6 7. e5 de5 8. fe5 ♘g4 9. e6 f5 10. ♗c4 ♗g7 11. ♘d5 N (11. ♘ce2 – 10/536) ♘c6 12. ♗f4 ♘d4 13. ♘c7 ♔f8 14. ♘a8 b5 15. ♗e2 ♕d5 16. 0–0 ♗b7 17. ♗f3 ♘f3 18. gf3 ♗d4 19. ♔g2 ♗a8–+ Minasian 2545 – Anastasian 2470, Protvino (zt) 1993; 6... e5 7. ♘f3 ♘bd7 8. a4 ♗e7 9. ♗d3 0–0 10. 0–0 ef4 11. ♔h1 ♘e5 12. ♗f4 ♕c7 13. ♕d2 ♗e6 14. ♘d4 ♖fe8!? N (14... ♖ac8 – 45/297) 15. ♗e5 de5 16. ♘e6 fe6 17. ♕e2 ♖ad8 18. ♘d1 ♗c5 19. ♘e3 ♖f8 20. ♘g4?! ♘d7! 21. ♗c4?! ♕c6 22. ♗b3?! h5!∓ ×♗b3, a4, e4 Sherzer 2465 – Wojtkiewicz 2580, Pleasantville 1993; 20. ♘c4!= △ a5, c3, b4 Byrne, Mednis] **7. ♗e2 g6 8. 0–0 ♗g7 9. ♔h1 0–0 10. ♗f3!? ♖e8!? 11. ♘b3 ♕c7** [△ ♘b6-c4] **12. ♕e2 N** [12. a4 – 55/264] **e6** [12... ♘b6?! 13. e5 de5 14. fe5 ♘fd7 15. e6; 12... e5 13. ♕f2 △ ♕h4] **13. a4 ♖b8** [13... ♘b6 14. a5 ♘c4 15. ♖a4! b5 (15... d5? 16. ed5 ed5 17. ♘d5+–) 16. ab6 ♘b6 17. ♖a1 ♖b8 – 13... ♖b8] **14. a5 b5 15. ab6 ♘b6 16. ♘a5 d5?** [16... e5!? 17. ♕f2 △ ♕h4∞; 16... ♘fd7 △ ♘c5, ♗d7∞] **17. e5 ♘fd7 18. ♗e3 ♗f8 19. ♗d4** [19. ♕f2 (△ ♘e2) ♗b4 20. ♘d1; 19. ♘d1 △ ♘f2-g4→] **♗c5** [19... ♘c5 20. ♕f2 ♗d7 21. b3±] **20. ♕f2** [20. ♕d2 ♗b4 21. ♘b5!] **♗d4 21. ♕d4 ♘c5** [21... ♕c5 22. ♘e2 ♕d4 23. ♘d4 ♘c5 24. b3! ♗d7 25. ♗e2 ♖a8 26. ♘ac6!± △ ♖a5, ♘b4 ×a6] **22. b4?** [22. ♘d1 △ ♘e3±] **♘cd7?** [22... ♘b7! △ 23. ♘b3 ♘d8!∞] **23. ♘d1± ♘c4 24. c3 ♘db6 25. ♘b3 ♖a8 26. ♘f2 ♗d7⊕ 27. ♘g4 ♖ec8 28. ♕f2 ♗b5 29. ♕h4+– ♘d7 30. ♘h6 ♔g7 31. ♘f7 ♘e3** [31... ♔f7 32. ♕h7 ♔f8 (32... ♔e8 33. ♕g6 ♔d8 34. ♕g5 ♔e8 35. ♗h5) 33. ♘d4 ♕b6 34. ♗g4 ♖c6 35. ♕h8; 35. ♕g6] **32. ♘d4 ♕b6 33. ♘d6 ♖e8** [33... ♗f1 34. ♘e6 ♔g8 35. ♕e7] **34. ♖fe1 1 : 0 [Kindermann]**

263. **B 96**

YERMOLINSKY 2615 – BROWNE 2515

USA (ch) 1992

1. e4 c5 2. ♘f3 d6 3. d4 cd4 4. ♘d4 ♘f6 5. ♘c3 a6 6. ♗g5 e6 7. f4 ♘c6 8. ♘c6 bc6 9. e5 h6 10. ♗h4 g5 11. fg5 ♘d5 12. ♘d5?! ed5 [12... cd5 13. ♕g4⩲ – 48/(366)] **13. ♕e2 N** [13. ed6 ♕d6 (13... hg5) 14. ♕e2 ♗e7 – 53/237] **hg5 14. ♗g3 ♕a5!? 15. ♕d2** [15. ♔d1?! Browne; 15. c3 ♖h6! ×♔e1] **♕d2 16. ♔d2 ♗e6!= 17. ♗d3 ♔d7 18. ♖ae1 ♗g7 19. h3!** [19. ed6? ♗b2∓; 19. b3 de5 20. ♗e5 ♗e5 21. ♖e5 g4!∓ ×h2] **de5 20. ♗e5 ♗e5 21. ♖e5 ♖hg8** [21... g4 22. h4] **22. g3 ♔d6 23. ♖ee1 ♖h8 24. h4 gh4 25. gh4 ♖h6 26. ♖ef1 ♔e5 27. ♖e1 ♔d6 28. ♖ef1 ♔e5= 29. h5 a5 30. ♗e2 ♖b8! 31. b3 ♖b4 32. a4!?** [×a5] **♖d4 33. ♔c3 c5 34. ♗f3 ♖f4 35. ♔d2 d4 36. ♗e2 ♖e4?** [36... ♖f1 37. ♖f1 f5=] **37. ♖hg1 ♖h8⊕** [37... c4? 38. ♖g5 f5 39. ♗c4; 37... ♖f4!? 38. ♖f4 ♔f4 39. ♖g8 f5 40. ♖a8 ♗f7 41. ♖a5 ♗h5⇆] **38. ♖g5 ♔d6** [38... f5? 39. ♗d3 ♖f4 40. ♖e1] **39. ♖h1⩲ ♖e5 40. ♖g7 ♔e7** [⌓ 40... ♖h6] **41. h6 ♔f8 42.**

♖g3 ♖h7? [42... ♗d5 43. ♖h2 ♗e4] **43. ♗d3 f5 44. ♖g6+− ♖h8** [44... ♔e7 45. ♖hg1 ♔d6 46. ♗c4! △ ♖e1] **45. h7 ♔e7 46. ♖hh6 ♗f7** [46... ♔f7 47. ♖e6; 46... ♖e3 47. ♖g7 ♔d6 48. ♗c4] **47. ♖a6 ♖e6 48. ♗f5 ♖h6 49. ♖h6 c4 50. bc4 ♗c4 51. ♗d3 ♗e6** [52. ♖h4] **1 : 0**
[Yermolinsky]

264. **B 96**

KAMSKY 2655 – B. GEL'FAND 2690
Linares 1993

1. e4 c5 2. ♘f3 d6 3. d4 cd4 4. ♘d4 ♘f6 5. ♘c3 a6 6. ♗g5 e6 7. f4 ♘bd7 8. ♕f3 ♕c7 9. 0-0-0 b5 10. e5 ♗b7 11. ♕h3 de5 12. ♘e6 fe6 13. ♕e6 ♗e7 14. ♘b5 ab5 15. ♗b5 ♗e4 16. ♖d2 ♔f8 17. ♗c4 ♗g6 18. ♗f6 ♘f6 19. fe5 ♗b4 20. ♖f2 ♗f7 21. ♕f7 ♕f7 22. ♗f7 ♔f7 23. a3 ♗e7 N [⌓ 23... ♗c5 24. ♖f3 ♗d4 (24... ♖he8 – 39/332) 25. ef6 gf6!?∓] **24. ef6 ♗f6** [⇔e] **25. c3 h5 26. ♖d1?!** [26. ♖e2!? h4 27. h3 ♖h5 28. ♖d1=] **h4 27. h3 ♖he8⩱ 28. ♖d7 ♔g6 29. ♔d1** [△ ♖e2] **♖ab8 30. ♖dd2 ♖b6! 31. ♖fe2** [⌓ 31. ♖de2] **♖eb8** [×b2] **32. ♖f2 ♗g5 33. ♖de2 ♖8b7!⊙ 34. a4 ♗f6 35. ♔c1 ♖a6 36. ♖e4 ♖ba7 37. b3 ♗c3 38. ♖g4 ♔h5 39. ♖f5 ♔h6 40. ♖h4 ♔g6 41. ♖c5 ♗f6 42. ♖g4 ♔h6 43. ♔c2!** [43. ♖e4 ♖d6 44. ♔c2 ♖ad7 45. ♖e2 ♖d1→] **♖e6** [43... ♖d7 44. a5 ♖e6 45. b4 ♖e3 – 43... ♖e6] **44. a5** [⌓ 44. ♔d3] **♖e3 45. b4 ♖a3?!** [45... ♖d7 46. b5! ♖a3 47. b6⇆; 45... ♖ae7! 46. a6! ♖a3 47. ♖a5 ♖e2 48. ♔d1 ♖a5 49. ♔e2 ♖a6∓] **46. ♖e4 ♖d7** [46... ♖a2?! 47. ♔b3 ♖g2 48. ♔a4⇆] **47. g4!** [△ h4] **♗g5 48. ♖e6** [48. ♔b2? ♖h3 (48... ♖dd3?! 49. ♖e6 g6 50. h4) 49. b5 ♖d2 50. ♖c2 ♗f6 51. ♔c1 ♖d5!−+; 48. h4!? ♖d2 49. ♔b1 ♗e3□ 50. ♖c2 ♖d1 51. ♔b2 ♖ad3 52. ♖e2!! △ ♔c2; 50... ♖dd3!∓] **g6 49. ♔b2!** [49. h4 ♖d2 50. ♔b1 ♗f4−+] **♖h3 50. ♖c3 ♖h4 51. a6** [51. ♖cc6! ♖g4 52. ♖g6 ♔h5 53. ♖gd6=] **♖g4 52. ♔b3?!** [52. ♖cc6!?; 52. b5!?] **♖dd4 53. ♖h3** [53. ♖b6 ♗e7; 53. ♖cc6 ♖b4 54. ♔c3 ♖bf4 55. ♖g6 ♔h5∓] **♔g7 54. ♖b6 ♗e7 55. a7** [55. b5 ♖a4∓] **♖b4 56. ♔c2 ♖a4 57. ♖b7 ♖ge4 58. ♖c3 ♔f6 59. ♖c8** [59. ♖f3!? ♔e6 60. ♖c3∓] **♖e2 60. ♔d3 ♖ea2−+ 61. ♖c6 ♔f7 62. ♖cc7 ♖4a3 63. ♔c4?!** [63. ♔d4 ♖d2 64. ♔e5 ♖e2 65. ♔d5 g5 66. ♖c8 ♖d2 67. ♔e5 ♖da2 68. ♖cc7 ♖e2 69. ♔d4 (69. ♔f5 ♖a4; 69. ♔d5 ♖a4) g4] **♖c2 64. ♔b5 ♖b3 65. ♔a4 ♖a3 66. ♔b5 ♖b2 67. ♔c6 ♖a6 68. ♔d5 ♖b7** [⌓ 68... ♖a5 69. ♔c4 (69. ♔c6 ♖c5 70. ♔d7 ♖d2 71. ♔c8 ♖d8#) ♖b7 70. ♖b7 g5] **69. ♖b7 ♖a5! 70. ♔c6 ♔e6 71. ♖c7** [71. ♔b6 ♗d8 72. ♔c6 ♗f6 73. ♖d7 ♗e5 74. ♔b6 ♖a7] **♗c5! 72. a8♕ ♖a8 73. ♔c5 ♖d8 74. ♖h7 g5 75. ♔c4 ♔f5 76. ♖f7 ♔e4 77. ♖e7 ♔f4 78. ♖f7 ♔g3 79. ♔c3 g4 80. ♖g7 ♔f3** **0 : 1**
[B. Gel'fand, Huzman]

265.* !N **B 97**

STOLZ 2325 – A. PETROSIAN 2490
Deutschland 1993

1. e4 c5 2. ♘f3 d6 3. d4 cd4 4. ♘d4 ♘f6 5. ♘c3 a6 6. ♗g5 e6 7. f4 ♕b6 8. ♘b3 ♗e7 9. ♕f3 ♘bd7 10. 0-0-0 ♕c7 11. ♗d3 [RR 11. g4 h6 12. ♗h4 (12. ♗f6 – 34/347) g5 13. fg5! ♘e5 14. ♕g3 ♘fg4 15. gh6 ♗h4 (15... ♖h6 16. ♗e7 ♕e7 17. h4!⩲) 16. ♕h4 ♖h6 17. ♕g3 ♗d7 18. ♗e2 ♖g6 19. h4! N ± 0-0-0 20. h5 ♖gg8 21. ♖h4! (21. ♕f4 d5!) ♘f6 22. ♕f4! ♘h7 23. ♕f2 ♔b8 24. ♖h3 (24. ♖g1!? ♘g5 25. ♕e3 f6 26. ♖f1↑) ♗c6 25. ♖g3 ♕e7 26. ♖g8 ♖g8 27. ♘a5 ♕c7 28. ♘c4! ♘c4 29. ♗c4 ♖g5 30. ♗e2 ♕e7 31. ♕d4 ♔c7 32. ♖f1 ♖e5 (Nikitin 2420 – A. Petrosian 2490, Dortmund (open) 1993) 33. ♕f2! f5 34. ef5 ♖f5 35. ♕h2 ♕g5 36. ♔b1 ♖f1 37. ♗f1 △ ♗d3± Nikitin] **b5 12. ♖he1 b4 13. ♘e2 N** [13. ♗f6 – 49/(297)] **♗b7 14. ♔b1!?** [14. g4 ♘c5 15. ♘c5 dc5 16. ♗f6 ♗f6 17. ♗c4 g5!] **♘c5?! 15. ♘c5 dc5 16. ♗f6! ♗f6 17. ♗c4⩲ 0–0 18. g4?** [18. ♕e3⩲] **g5! 19. ♕e3** [19. h4 gf4 20. ♘f4 ♕e5 21. ♘d3 ♕d4!] **♖ad8!** [19... gf4?! 20. ♘f4 △ 20... ♗g5? 21. ♘e6!] **20. fg5 ♗g7∞** [×e5] **21. ♕g3 ♗e5 22. ♕g2 ♖d1 23. ♖d1 ♖d8 24. ♖f1?** [24. ♖d3 ♖d3 25. cd3 ♗h2∓] **♗h2∓ 25. ♕f3 ♗e5 26. ♘c1**

♗g7! [△ ♕e5] **27. ♕b3⊕** [27. ♘d3 ♖d4!] **♕e7 28. ♘d3 ♕g5−+ 29. e5 ♕g4 30. a3 ♖d4 31. ♘c5 ♖c4 32. ♘b7 ♗e5 33. ♘d8 ♖f4 34. ♖f4 ♕f4 35. ab4 h5 36. ♘c6 ♗f6 37. ♔a2 h4 38. ♕d3 ♕g3 39. ♕a6 h3 40. b5 0 : 1** **[A. Petrosian]**

266. **B 99**

ŠABALOV 2575 − HELLERS 2565

New York 1993

1. e4 c5 2. ♘f3 d6 3. d4 cd4 4. ♘d4 ♘f6 5. ♘c3 a6 6. ♗g5 e6 7. f4 ♗e7 8. ♕f3 ♕c7 9. 0-0-0 ♘bd7 10. ♗f6 ♘f6 11. g4 b5 12. g5 ♘d7 13. f5 ♗g5 14. ♔b1 ♘e5 15. ♕h5 ♕e7 16. fe6?! N [16. ♘e6 − 36/355] **g6 17. ef7 ♔f7 18. ♕e2 ♗g4! 19. ♕f2 ♕f6 20. ♕f6 ♗f6 21. ♗e2 ♗c8!**∓⊡ **22. ♖hf1 ♔g7 23. ♘d5 ♗d8 24. ♖f4 ♖a7 25. h4?** [25. ♖g1∓] **h5!**∓ [×h4] **26. ♖df1 ♖f7! 27. ♖f7 ♘f7 28. a4?!** [28. ♖h1∓] **♗h4! 29. ab5 ab5 30. ♗b5 ♗g3! 31. ♘c7 ♘g5 32. ♖g1 h4 33. ♘e2 ♘f3 34. ♖d1 ♗e5 35. ♘e8 ♔h7 36. c4 h3 37. ♘d6 ♗e6!−+** [37... ♗d6?! 38. ♖d6 h2 39. ♘g3∓] **38. c5 h2 39. ♖h1** [39. ♘c4 ♗c4 40. ♗c4 ♘d2] **♔g7 40. ♘e8 ♔f8 41. ♘c1 ♗h3 42. ♘d3 ♗g2 43. ♖h2 ♗h2 0 : 1** **[Byrne, Mednis]**

C

267.* **C 00**

GUFEL'D 2480 – TIVJAKOV 2595
Calcutta 1993

1. g3 ♘f6 2. ♗g2 e6 3. e4 d5 4. e5 N [4. ♘c3 – 22/(215)] **♘fd7 5. d4 c5 6. c3 ♕a5!?** [RR 6... ♘c6 7. ♘e2 h5 8. h4 ♘b6 9. 0–0 ♗e7 10. ♘d2 cd4 11. cd4 g5 12. hg5 ♗g5 13. ♘f3 ♗e7 14. ♗h3 h4 15. g4 ♗d7 16. ♔h1± Damljanović 2550 – Abramović 2475, Podgorica 1993] **7. ♘d2 ♘c6 8. ♘e2 b5 9. 0–0** [9. f4!?] **♕b6 10. ♘f3 ♗a6 11. ♖e1 b4= 12. ♗e3 ♗e7 13. dc5** [13. h4 △ ♗g5] **♗c5** [13... ♘c5? 14. cb4±] **14. ♘ed4 0–0 15. cb4!? ♘b4□ 16. ♕a4** [16. ♗f1] **♕b7 17. ♖ed1** [17. ♗f1] **♘b6** [17... ♘d3? 18. ♗f1; 17... ♖fc8 18. b3!?] **18. ♕a5!?** [18. ♕b3=] **♘c4** [18... ♗d4] **19. ♕c5 ♖fc8 20. ♘e6 fe6** [20... ♖c5?! 21. ♘c5±] **21. ♕d4 ♘e3!** [21... ♘c2 22. ♕g4±] **22. ♕e3** [22. fe3 ♘c2 23. ♕g4 ♖e8∓] **♘c2 23. ♕g5** [23. ♕f4 ♖c4] **♘a1** [23... ♗e2 24. ♖ac1! (24. ♘d4? ♘d4 25. ♖d4 ♕b2–+) ♗d1 25. ♖d1∞] **24. ♘d4! ♖e8 25. ♘e6! ♖e6 26. ♗d5 ♕d7 27. ♗f3!!± ♕e8□ 28. ♗a8 ♖e5 29. ♖d8□** [29. ♕c1? ♘c2!! 30. ♕c2 ♖e1 31. ♖e1 (31. ♔g2 ♗f1–+) ♕e1 32. ♔g2 ♕f1 33. ♔f3 ♕h1–+] **♖g5 30. ♖e8 ♔f7 31. ♖e3!** [31. ♖d8?! ♔e7? 32. ♖d1 ♘c2 33. ♗e4 ♘b4 34. a3 ♖e5 35. f3±; 31... ♖e5!] **♖a5!** [31... ♗c4 32. ♖c3±] **32. ♗e4?⊕** [32. b4! ♖b5 (32... ♖a4? 33. ♗d5 ♔f6 34. ♖e6 ♔f5 35. ♖e1±) 33. a3 ♗b7!? 34. ♗b7 ♖b7 35. ♖c3∞] **♗c4∓ 33. a3?!** [33. b3] **♘b3 34. ♖f3** [34. ♗h7 g6] **♔g8 35. ♖c3 ♘d2 36. ♗a8 ♖e5 37. f4?** [37. ♔g2] **♖e1∓ 38. ♔f2 ♖e2 39. ♔g1 ♗e6 40. ♗g2 ♘e4 41. ♖c1 ♘f6 42. b4 ♖a2 43. h3 ♖a3 44. g4 h6 45. b5 ♗d5 46. ♗f1 ♖a4 47. ♖c8 ♔h7 48. ♗d3 ♗e4 49. ♗c4 ♖a3 50. ♔h2⊕ ♗b7 51. ♖c7?!** [51. ♖b8; 51. ♖d8∓] **♗d5!–+ 52. ♗f1 ♘e4 53. ♖d7 ♘g3! 54. ♗g2 ♗g2 55. ♔g2 ♘e2 56. f5 ♘f4 57. ♔f1 ♖h3 58. f6 ♖f3 59. ♔g1 ♘e2 60. ♔g2 ♖f6 61. ♖a7 ♖b6 0 : 1**
[Gufel'd]

268. **C 01**

SMYSLOV 2530 – VAGANIAN 2615
Rostov na Donu 1993

1. e4 e6 2. d4 d5 3. ♘c3 ♗b4 4. ed5 ed5 5. ♘f3 ♘e7 6. ♗d3 ♗g4 7. h3 N [7. 0–0] **♗h5 8. a3** [8. 0–0 *a)* 8... c6 9. ♖e1 ♘d7 10. ♗f4 ♘f8 11. a3 ♗c3 (11... ♗d6? 12. ♘d5!+–) 12. bc3 ♘e6 13. ♗d2 ♕d6 14. c4±; *b)* 8... ♘bc6 9. a3 ♗d6] **♗d6 9. ♘b5 ♘bc6 10. ♗e3 a6 11. ♘d6 ♕d6 12. ♕d2?!** [12. g4!? ♗g6 13. ♕d2 △ 0-0-0] **♗f3 13. gf3 ♕f6!** [×f3, d4] **14. 0-0-0 h6 15. ♖hg1 0-0-0 16. c3?!** [16. ♖g4! ♘f5 17. ♗f5 ♕f5 18. ♖g7=] **♘a5 17. ♕e2□ ♘f5 18. b4□ ♘c6 19. ♗f5?!** [⌓ 19. ♔b2∓] **♕f5 20. ♖g7 ♘a7!∓ 21. c4** [21. a4 ♔b8! △ ♘c8-b6-c4∓] **dc4 22. ♕c4** [22. d5 ♘b5 23. ♕c4 ♘a3? 24. ♕g4±; 23... ♕e5!?; 22... ♕e5!∓] **♖d5! 23. ♖dg1 ♘b5 24. ♖g8 ♖g8 25. ♖g8 ♔d7** [25... ♖d8?! 26. ♖d8 ♔d8 27. ♕c5=] **26. ♔b2 ♘d6 27. ♕e2 b5 28. f4?** [28. ♖a8 ♘c4 29. ♔c1 ♕e6 △ 30... ♖d4, 30... ♖g5∓; 28. ♖g4!?] **♘c4 29. ♔c1** [29. ♔a2 ♕e4–+] **♕h3–+ 30. ♕g4 ♕g4 31. ♖g4 ♘a3 32. ♖g8 ♘c4 33. ♖a8 h5 34. ♖a6 ♖d6** [34... ♘b6 35. ♔d2 h4 36. ♔e2 h3 37. ♔f1] **35. ♖a8 ♖h6 36. f5□ ♘e3 37. fe3 h4 38. ♖a2 ♔e7!** [△ 39. e4 ♔f6] **39. ♔d1 ♔f6 40. ♔e1 h3 41. ♖h2 ♔f5 42. ♔f1 ♔e4 43. ♔g1 ♔e3 44.**

d5 ♔d3 45. ♖f2 ♔c4 46. ♖f7 ♔b4 47. ♖c7 ♖d6 0 : 1 **[Vaganian]**

269.* !N C 02

SVEŠNIKOV 2555 – MOSKALENKO 2555

Rostov na Donu (open) 1993

1. e4 e6 2. d4 d5 3. e5 c5 4. c3 ♘c6 5. ♘f3 ♘h6!? 6. dc5 ♗c5 7. b4 ♗b6 [RR 7... ♗e7 8. ♗d3 ♘g4 9. ♗f4 f6 10. b5 ♘ce5 11. ♘e5 ♘e5 12. ♗e5 fe5 13. ♕h5 ♔f8 14. ♕e5 ♗f6 15. ♕g3 e5∓ Sax] **8. b5! N** [RR 8. ♗h6 gh6 9. b5 ♘e7 10. ♗d3 ♘g6 11. 0–0 0–0 N (11... f6? – 55/(271); 11... ♕c7 – 55/(271)) 12. ♕a4?! ♗d7 13. h4 (13. ♕g4 f5! 14. ♕g3 ♔h8 15. h4 ♗c7∓) f5 (13... h5!?; 13... f6!?) 14. h5 ♘h8 15. ♘bd2 ♘f7 16. c4!? ♘g5 17. cd5 ed5 18. ♖ae1 (△ 18... ♘e4? 19. ♕b3) ♔h8!? (△ ♘e4; 18... ♘e6!?∓ △ 19. ♘b3 a6!) 19. ♘g5 ♕g5 20. ♘f3 (Gallagher 2500 – Glek 2545, Douai 1993) ♕g4! 21. ♕g4□ fg4 22. e6 ♗e8 23. ♘h4 g3 24. ♖e5 gf2 25. ♔h1 ♖c8 △ ♖c3∓; 12. ♖e1!?; 12. a4!? Glek] **♘e7 9. ♗d3 ♘g6 10. 0–0 0–0 11. ♗h6 gh6 12. a4!?** [12. ♘bd2 ♕c7] **f6 13. ♗g6!? hg6 14. ♕d3 ♔g7 15. ♘bd2 ♗d7 16. c4 fe5! 17. cd5** [17. ♘e5 ♗e8 18. ♖ad1 ♖c8∞] **ed5 18. ♕d5 ♗f5 19. ♕e5** [19. ♕b7? ♖f7] **♕f6**=∞⧉ **20. ♖fe1 ♕e5 21. ♖e5 ♖ae8** [21... ♗d8!?] **22. ♖e8 ♖e8 23. a5 ♗d8! 24. ♘c4 ♗f6 25. ♖d1 ♖d8 26. ♖d8 ♗d8** [♘♗ 9/d] **27. ♘d4 ♗d7 28. f4!? ♗e7 29. ♘e5 ♗c8 30. ♔f2 ♗b4! 31. ♘c4 ♗c5 32. ♔e3 ♗d7 33. b6 ab6 34. ♘b6 ♗c6 35. g3** [35. ♔d3 ♗b6!] **♗g2 36. ♔d3 ♗b4 37. ♘b3 ♔f6 38. ♔c4 ♗e1 39. g4** [39. ♘d5 ♔f7=] **h5! 40. ♘d7 ♔e6 41. ♘dc5 ♔d6 42. ♘d3=** [42. gh5 gh5!∓] **♗d5 43. ♔d4 ♗h4 44. ♘bc5 hg4 45. ♘e4 ♗e4 46. ♔e4 g3 1/2 : 1/2** **[Moskalenko]**

270. C 02

SAX 2570 – M. GUREVICH 2610

Deutschland 1993

1. e4 e6 2. d4 d5 3. e5 c5 4. c3 ♘c6 5. ♘f3 ♘h6!? 6. ♗d3 [6. ♗h6 gh6 7. ♗e2 ♕b6 8. ♕d2 ♗g7 9. 0–0 ♗d7 10. ♘a3 0–0 11. ♘c2 f6! 12. ♗d3 c4!∞] **cd4 7. cd4 ♘f5 8. ♗f5 ef5 9. ♘c3** [9. 0–0!? ♗e7 10. ♘c3 g5 11. ♘e1 f4 12. h4 h6 13. ♕h5 ♘d4 14. hg5 ♗g5 15. ♕d1 ♘c6 16. ♕d5±] **♗e6 10. ♘e2 ♕b6 N** [10... ♗e7 – 43/(315)] **11. ♘f4 h6 12. h4 g6 13. ♔f1** [13. 0–0 ♗e7 14. g3 a5 15. ♔g2 a4 16. ♖b1±] **♗e7 14. g3 0-0-0 15. ♔g2 ♔b8** [15... g5 16. ♘e6 fe6 17. hg5 hg5 18. ♖h8 ♖h8 19. ♗g5 ♗g5 20. ♘g5 ♘d4 21. ♕d2±] **16. ♖b1 ♗c8** [16... g5 17. hg5 hg5 18. ♖h8 ♖h8 19. ♘e6 fe6 20. ♗g5 ♗g5 21. ♘g5 ♘d4 22. ♕d2 ♖g8 23. b4⩲] **17. e6!?** [17. b4? ♖hg8 18. ♘d3 g5 19. hg5 hg5 20. ♘c5 f4!∓] **♗e6 18. ♘e6 fe6 19. ♖e1 e5!** [19... ♘a5 20. ♘e5±] **20. ♘e5 ♘e5 21. ♗f4 ♗f6 22. de5** [22... g5 23. ♕b3! ♕b3 24. ef6! gf4 25. ab3! ♖hf8 26. ♖e6 ♖d7⩲] **1/2 : 1/2** **[Sax]**

271.** !N C 02

JAGUPOV 2415 – DREEV 2560

Rostov na Donu (open) 1993

1. e4 e6 2. d4 d5 3. e5 c5 4. c3 ♘c6 5. ♘f3 ♗d7 6. ♗e2 [RR 6. ♗d3 cd4 7. cd4 ♕b6 8. 0–0 ♘d4 9. ♘d4 ♕d4 10. ♘c3 (10. ♕e2 ♘e7 11. ♘c3 ♘c6 12. ♘b5 ♕e5 13. ♕e5 ♘e5 14. ♘c7 ♔d8 15. ♘a8 ♘d3∓) a6 11. ♕e2 ♘e7 12. ♔h1 ♘c6 13. f4 ♘b4 14. ♖d1 ♗c5! N (14... ♘d3 – 54/(252)) 15. ♗a6 (15. ♗b5? ♕f2 16. ♗d7 ♔d7 17. ♕g4 ♘d3! 18. h3 h5 19. ♕g7 ♖ag8 20. ♕f7 ♔d8–+; 15. ♗h7 ♕f2 16. ♕f2 ♗f2 17. ♗b1 f6!?; 17... g5!?∞) ♕f2 16. ♕f2 ♗f2 (Organdžijev 2230 – Draško 2485, Skopje 1992) 17. ♗e2 (17. ♗b5!?) 0–0 (17... ♔e7 18. f5!) 18. ♗d2 (△ ♘e4) ♘c2 (18... ♖fc8 19. ♖dc1) 19. ♖ab1 ♘e3 20. ♖dc1 ♖fc8∞ Draško] **♘ge7 7. ♘a3 cd4 8. cd4 ♘f5 9. ♘c2 ♘b4 10. 0–0 ♘c2 11. ♕c2 h5!?** [11... ♕b6 12. ♕d3 ♖c8!? N (12... a6 – 52/(252); 12... ♗e7 – 52/(252)) 13. ♗d2 ♗b4! (Filipenko; 13... ♗e7?! 14. g4!±) *a)* 14. ♗f4?! a6! 15. a4 (15. ♕b3 ♗a5!) ♘e7!? (15... 0–0!?) 16. h4 ♗a5 17. ♖fc1 ♖c1 18. ♗c1 h6 (1/2 : 1/2 Svešnikov 2555 – Dreev 2560, Rostov na Donu (open) 1993) 19.

b3 0–0 20. ♗b2=; *b)* △ 14. ♗b4 ♕b4 15. a3 ♕b6] **12. ♗d2 ♗e7 13. ♗d3 ♕b6 14. ♗f5 ♖c8! N** [14... ef5 – 56/(285)] **15. ♕b3 ef5 16. ♕d5** [16. ♕b6!? ab6 17. ♖fc1=] **♗e6**$\overline{\overline{\infty}}$ **17. ♕a5 ♕a5 18. ♗a5 b6** [18... ♗d5] **19. ♗d2 ♗d5 20. ♖fc1 ♔d7 21. ♘e1 a5! 22. ♘c2** [22. ♘d3 g5 23. h4 ♗e4!] **g5 23. ♘e3 ♔e6 24. a3 f4?!** [24... h4$\overline{\overline{\infty}}$] **25. ♘d5 ♔d5 26. h4 g4 27. ♗f4 ♗h4 28. a4!**± **♗e7 29. g3 ♔d4! 30. ♖d1 ♔e4 31. ♖d7 ♖he8 32. ♖e1 ♔f5 33. ♗e3?!** [33. e6!? f6 △ 34. ♗d6 ♗d6 35. ♖d6 ♖b8=] **♖c6 34. ♖b7 ♗b4= 35. ♖d1 ♖e7 36. ♖b6 ♖b6 37. ♗b6 [♖ 9/k] ♖e5 38. ♗e3 ♔e6 39. ♖d8 ♖d5 40. ♖h8 ♗e7** [40... ♗c5=] **41. ♔f1 ♖e5?! 42. ♗d2**$\pm$ **♖d5 43. ♗c3** [43. ♔e2 ♖e5 44. ♔d3 ♖d5=] **♗d8 44. ♔e2 ♔e7 45. ♖h6 ♖f5 46. ♗d4 ♖d5 47. ♔d3** [47. ♔e3 f5□ △ 48. ♔d3 ♖d6 49. ♖h7 ♔e6 50. ♔c4 ♖d4! 51. ♔d4 ♗b6]

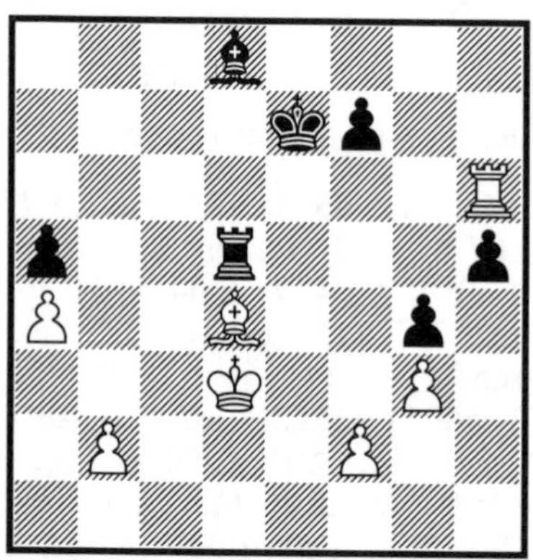

47... ♖d6!!= 48. ♖d6 [48. ♖h5 ♗b6 49. ♖e5!□ ♔d7 50. ♖e4 f5 51. ♖f4 ♔e6 52. ♔c4□ ♗c7! *a)* 53. ♗c5 ♖d2; *b)* 53. ♗c3 ♖c6 54. ♔b5 ♖b6 55. ♔c5 ♖b8 56. ♖d4 (56. ♖c4? ♗b6) ♗b6 57. ♔c4 ♗d4 58. ♔d4=; *c)* 53. ♗e3 ♖c6 54. ♔b5 ♗f4! (54... ♖c2 55. ♖c4 ♖b2 56. ♔c6 ♗d8±) 55. ♔c6 ♗e3 56. fe3 ♔e5 57. ♔b5 ♔e4=] **♔d6 [♘♗ 7/k] 49. ♔e4 ♔e6 50. ♗c5 ♗c7 51. b4 f5 52. ♔d4 f4 53. ba5 ♗a5 54. ♔e4 f3 55. ♗e3 ♗d8 56. ♗d2 ♗b6 57. ♗e1 ♔d6 58. a5 ♗a7 59. a6 ♔c6 60. ♔f5 ♔d5 61. ♔g5 ♔e4 62. ♔h5 ♔f5!** [62... ♔d3? 63. ♔g4 ♔e2 64. ♔f4+–] **63. ♔h6 ♔f6 1/2 : 1/2**
[Dreev]

272.* !N C 05

ISTRĂŢESCU 2470 – APICELLA 2495
Bucureşti 1993

1. e4 e6 2. d4 d5 3. ♘d2 ♘f6 4. e5 ♘fd7 5. f4 c5 6. c3 ♘c6 7. ♘df3 ♕b6 8. h4 cd4 9. cd4 a5! N [RR 9... ♗b4 10. ♔f2 f6 11. ♗e3 ♗e7 12. ♕d2 ♕a5!? N (12... 0–0 – 54/254) 13. ♗d3 ♘b6 14. ♕a5 ♘a5 15. b3±○ ♘c6 16. h5! ♗d7 17. h6 g6□ 18. ef6 ♗f6 19. ♘e5 ♘b4 20. ♗e2 ♘c8!□ 21. ♘gf3 ♘d6 22. ♖hc1! ♘c6 (22... ♘e4 23. ♔e1 ♘g3 24. ♖c7 ♘e2 25. ♘d7 ♗d8□ 26. ♖b7 ♘c2 27. ♔e2 ♘a1 28. ♔d3+–) 23. g4! ♖c8 24. ♔g2 ♘f7□ (Istrăţescu 2470 – Topalov 2635, Budapest (zt) 1993) 25. ♘d7 ♔d7 26. ♘e5 ♘fe5 27. fe5 ♗e7 28. a3!± Istrăţescu] **10. h5 a4 11. h6 g6 12. g4?!** [12. ♘e2 a3 13. b3∞] **a3 13. ba3** [13. b3? ♗b4 14. ♔f2 ♗c3∓] **♗a3∓ 14. ♘e2 f6 15. ef6** [15. ♗h3] **♘f6 16. ♗h3 ♘e4 17. 0–0 0–0 18. ♕b3! ♕a6** [18... ♗b4 19. a3 ♗c5 20. ♕b6 ♗b6 21. ♗e3∞] **19. ♗a3 ♕a3 20. ♖fb1 ♗d7 21. g5** [21. ♕a3 ♖a3 22. ♖b7 ♖f3 23. ♗g2 ♖e3 24. ♖d7 ♖e2∓] **b5! 22. ♕a3 ♖a3 23. ♗g4 ♘c3** [23... b4 24. ♖b3 ♖fa8 25. ♖a3 ♖a3 26. ♘c1 ♘c3∓] **24. ♘c3 ♖c3 25. ♖c1 b4** [25... ♖c1? 26. ♖c1 ♖f4 27. ♗e6! ♗e6 28. ♖c6=] **26. ♖c3 bc3 27. ♔g2 ♖f4 28. ♔g3 ♖e4?** [28... ♖g4!! 29. ♔g4 e5 30. ♔g3 e4 31. ♘e1 (31. ♘e5 ♘e5 32. de5 d4 33. ♔f4 ♗c6 34. a4 c2 35. a5 e3 36. a6 ♔f7∓) ♘d4∓] **29. ♖c1 ♘d4 30. ♘d4 ♖d4 [♖ 9/k;** 30... ♖g4 31. ♔g4 e5 32. ♔f3 ed4 33. ♔e2 ♗b5 34. ♔d1 ♗a4 35. ♔e2=] **31. ♖c3 ♔f7 32. ♖b3 ♖c4** [32... ♖a4? 33. ♖b8 ♖a2 34. ♖h8 ♔e7 35. ♖h7 ♔d6 36. ♖h8+–] **33. a4** [33. ♖b8! ♗c8 34. a4∞] **d4 34. a5 ♔e7 35. a6 ♖a4 36. ♖b8 d3 37. a7** [37. ♖h8? ♖g4! 38. ♔g4 d2–+] **♖a7 38. ♖h8 d2 39. ♖h7 ♔d6 40. ♖g7 ♖a4⊕ 41. ♗e2 ♖e4! 42. ♗d1□** [42. ♔f2? ♗a4! (△ ♖e2; 42... ♗b5?? 43. ♗b5+–) 43. ♗f3 ♖f4–+; 42. ♔f3? ♗b5! 43. ♗d1 ♖e1∓] **♖e1 43. h7 ♖d1 44. h8♕ ♖g1 45. ♔h2!□** [45. ♔f2? d1♕ 46. ♕b8 ♔c6 47. ♕a8 ♔b6 48. ♕b8 ♔c5 49. ♕a7 ♔b4 50. ♕b7 (50. ♕b6 ♗b5–+) ♔a3 (50... ♗b5? 51. ♕e4 ♗c4 52. ♖b7 ♔a5 53. ♖a7

♗a6 54. ♕e5 ♔b6 55. ♕c7 ♔b5 56. ♕b8 ♔c5 57. ♕e5 ♔b4 58. ♕b8=) 51. ♕a7 ♔b2 52. ♕b6 ♔a2 53. ♕a6 ♗a4 54. ♕c4 ♗b3 55. ♖a7 ♔b2–+] **♖h1** [46. ♔h1 d1♕ 47. ♔h2 ♕e2 48. ♔g3 ♕e3 49. ♔h2 ♕f2 50. ♔h3 ♕e3 51. ♔h2 ♕f4 52. ♔h3 e5 53. ♖d7 ♔d7 54. ♕g7=; 45... d1♕ 46. ♕b8 ♔c6 47. ♕a8 ♔b6 48. ♖g8! ♖h1 49. ♕h1 ♕h5 50. ♔g1 ♕g5 51. ♕g2 ♕c1 52. ♕f1=] **1/2 : 1/2** **[Apicella]**

273.* !N C 06

RUBLEVSKIJ 2515 – ULYBIN 2565

Sankt-Peterburg (zt) 1993

1. e4 e6 2. d4 d5 3. ♘d2 ♘f6 4. e5 ♘fd7 5. ♗d3 c5 6. c3 ♘c6 7. ♘e2 cd4 8. cd4 f6 9. ef6 ♘f6 10. 0–0 ♗d6 11. ♘f3 0–0 [RR 11... ♕c7 12. ♗g5 0–0 13. ♘g3 ♗d7 N (13... ♔h8 – 39/355) 14. ♖c1 ♕b6 15. ♗f6!? *a)* 15... gf6 16. ♕d2 ♖f7□ 17. ♘h5 ♕d8! 18. ♕h6 ♗e7□ (A. Frolov 2530 – Borovikov 2385, Nikolaev (zt) 1993) 19. h3!⩲ ×h6, f6; *b)* 15... ♖f6 16. ♗h7 ♔h7 17. ♘g5 ♔g8 18. ♕h5 ♗e8! (18... ♕d4 19. ♕h7 ♔f8 20. ♕h8 ♔e7 21. ♕a8±) 19. ♕h7 ♔f8 20. ♕h8 ♔e7 21. ♕g7 ♗f7 22. ♘f7 ♖f7 23. ♘f5 ef5 24. ♖fe1 ♗e5 25. ♖e5 ♘e5 26. ♕e5 ♔d7 27. ♕d5 ♔e8= 28. ♕e5 ♔d7 29. ♖c5 ♖d8! A. Frolov] **12. ♗f4 ♗f4 13. ♘f4 ♘e4 14. ♘h5 g6 15. ♘g3 ♘g3 16. hg3 ♕b6 17. ♕a4 a6 18. ♖ab1 ♗d7 19. ♗e2 ♘e5! N** [19... e5 20. de5 ♘e5 21. ♕d1 ♘f3 22. ♗f3 d4 23. ♕d2±; 19... ♖f6 – 52/(258)] **20. ♕d1 ♘f3 21. gf3** [21. ♗f3 ♖ac8 22. ♕d2 ♖c4 23. ♖fd1 ♖fc8 24. ♖bc1 ♖c1 25. ♖c1 ♖c1 26. ♕c1 ♕d4 27. ♕c7 ♗c6 28. ♕e7 e5 29. ♕e6 ♔g7 30. ♕e7=] **♖ac8 22. ♕d2 ♗b5 23. ♖fc1 ♖fe8!** [23... ♗e2 24. ♕e2 ♖c6 25. ♖c6 ♕c6 26. ♕e3 ♖c8 27. ♖e1±] **24. ♗d1!?** [24. ♗b5 ♕b5 25. ♕e3 ♖c1 26. ♖c1 e5!? 27. de5 ♕b2=; 24. ♕e3 ♖c1 25. ♖c1 ♗e2 26. ♕e2 ♕d4 27. ♖c7 e5 28. ♖b7 e4=; 24. ♕b4 ♖c6□ 25. ♖c6 (25. ♗b5 ♕b5 26. ♕b5 ab5 27. ♖c6 bc6 28. ♖c1 ♖c8 △ ♔f7-e7-d6=) ♕c6 26. ♗b5 ♕b5 27. ♕b5 (27. ♕c3 ♕c4; 27. ♕e1 ♕c4; 27. ♕d2 e5; 27. ♕d6 ♕e2! 28. ♖c1 ♖f8 29. f4 g5 30. ♕e5 ♕e5 31. fe5 g4 32. ♖c7 ♖f7 33. ♖c8 ♖f8=) ab5 28. ♖c1 ♖a8 29. a3 ♖a4 30. ♖c7 b4=] **♖c4!? 25. ♖c4 dc4 26. b3 ♗c6** [26... ♖d8? 27. bc4 ♖d4 28. ♕e2!+–] **27. ♖c1 ♖d8!** [27... cb3 28. ♗b3 ♕d8 (28... ♗f3? 29. ♕e3! △ ♕e5, ♖c7+–) 29. ♕e3 ♕d6±] **28. ♖c4** [28. ♕e3 ♕d4 29. ♕e6 ♔f8 30. ♕c4 (30. bc4 ♖e8–+) ♕c4 31. bc4 ♖d2∓] **e5 29. b4! ♗d5!** [29... ed4 30. ♗b3 ♔g7 31. ♕f4 △ ♕e5±; 29... ♖d4 30. ♗b3! ♖c4□ (30... ♔g7? 31. ♕e3 ♔f6 32. f4+–) 31. ♗c4 ♔g7 32. ♕d6 ♕d4 33. ♕e7 ♔h6 34. ♕f8 ♔g5 35. ♗e6!↑] **30. ♖c5 ed4 31. a3** [31. ♕d4? ♗f7 32. ♕a1 ♕b4∓; 31. ♖d5 ♖d5 32. ♗b3 ♕e6 33. ♕c1! ♔g7! (33... ♔h8 34. ♕c7!) 34. ♕c4 ♕e1 35. ♔g2 ♖d7 36. ♕g8 ♔h6 37. ♕f8 ♖g7 38. ♕f4 g5 39. ♕f6 ♖g6 40. ♕f8 ♖g7=] **♗e6** [31... ♗f7?! 32. f4 △ f5] **32. f4 ♖d5** [32... ♖d7 33. ♗f3 ♕d6 34. ♗e4 d3? 35. ♖c3±] **33. ♕e1** [33. ♖c1 ♖d7 34. ♗f3 d3! 35. ♖c3 ♕d4; 33. f5 ♖f5 34. ♕d4 ♖c5 35. bc5 ♕c6=] **♖c5 34. bc5 ♕c6 35. ♗f3** [35... ♕d7? 36. ♗b7; 35... ♗d5 36. ♗d5 ♕d5 37. ♕e8 ♔g7 38. ♕e7=] **1/2 : 1/2** **[Ulybin, Lysenko]**

274. C 07

ADAMS 2630 – LEVITT 2460

Dublin (zt) 1993

1. e4 e6 2. d4 d5 3. ♘d2 c5 4. ♘gf3!? cd4 5. ♘d4 ♘f6 6. ed5 N [6. ♗b5 ♗d7 7. e5 ♗b5 8. ef6 ♗d7∓] **♕d5!?** [6... ♘d5∞] **7. ♘b5 ♕d8** [⌓ 7... ♘a6 8. ♘c4 ♕d1 9. ♔d1 ♗c5] **8. ♘c4 ♘d5 9. ♘e3 ♘c7?!** [9... a6 10. ♘d5 ed5 11. ♘d4⩲] **10. ♗d2** [10. ♕d8 ♔d8 11. ♘c7 ♔c7 12. ♘c4 f6 13. ♗f4 e5 14. ♗g3 ♗e6 15. f4 ♗c4 16. ♗c4 ♘c6±] **♘b5 11. ♗b5 ♗d7 12. ♗d7 ♕d7** [12... ♘d7 13. ♗c3±] **13. ♕g4 ♘c6 14. 0-0-0 ♕d4□** [14... 0-0-0 15. ♗a5] **15. ♕e2 ♕a4** [15... ♗a3? 16. c3+–] **16. ♔b1 ♗e7 17. ♗c3 0–0 18. ♖d7 ♘b4?** [18... b6±] **19. ♕g4 g6 20. ♕d4!?** [20. ♖e7 ♕a2 21. ♔c1 ♖fd8 22. b3+–] **♕a2 21. ♔c1 f6 22. ♗b4 ♗b4 23. c3!** [23. ♕b4? ♖ad8 24. ♖d8 ♕a1 25. ♔d2 ♖d8 26. ♔e2 ♕h1∓] **♕a1** [23... ♗a5 24. ♘g4; 23... ♗c3 24. bc3 ♕a1 25. ♔c2 ♕h1 26. ♕h4] **24. ♔c2 ♕h1 25.**

♕b4! [25. ♘g4 ♗c3 26. bc3 ♕e1=] **♖ad8** [25... ♖ae8 26. ♕h4 ♖f7 27. ♖d1+−] **26. ♖d8 ♖d8 27. ♕e7** [27... ♖f8 28. ♘g4+−] **1 : 0** **[Adams]**

275. **C 07**

SVIDLER 2490 − DREEV 2560
Rostov na Donu (open) 1993

1. e4 e6 2. d4 d5 3. ♘d2 c5 4. ♘gf3 cd4 5. ♘d4?! ♘f6 6. e5 ♘fd7 7. ♘2f3 ♘c6 8. ♘c6 N [8. ♗f4 ♕b6; 8. ♗b5 − 52/(260)] **bc6 9. ♗d3 ♗a6!= 10. 0−0 ♗d3 11. ♕d3 ♗e7 12. c4** [12. b3 0−0 13. ♗b2=] **0−0 13. ♕c2 a5 14. ♖d1 a4 15. ♗f4** [15. ♗e3 ♕b8!∓] **♘b6 16. b3** [△ 17. c5 ♘d7 18. b4] **c5!∓ 17. ♖ac1 h6** [17... ♕b8? 18. ♗g5] **18. ♗e3 ♕b8 19. h4?** [19. cd5 ♘d5 20. ♗c5? ♖c8; ⌓ 19. ♖d3∓] **♕b7!∓ 20. h5 ♖fd8 21. ♖d3? d4!** [×h5] **22. ♗d2 ♕e4 23. ♖e1 ♕f5 24. ♘h2 ab3 25. ♕b3** [25. ab3 ♖a2 26. ♕a2 ♕d3 27. ♘f3 (27. ♕a5 ♘d7) ♕f5∓; 25... ♕h5] **♖db8 26. ♖g3 ♘a4 27. ♘g4** [27. ♕d1 ♘b2−+] **♖b3!?** [27... ♗g5!?−+] **28. ♘h6 ♔f8 29. ♘f5 ♖g3 30. ♘g3 ♘b2 31. ♖b1 ♘c4 32. ♗f4 ♘a5! 33. ♘e4 c4 34. ♔f1 ♔e8! 35. g4** [35. ♔e2 ♘c6] **c3 36. ♔e2 ♘c6 37. ♔d3 ♖a4!−+** [△ ♘b4] **38. a3 ♗a3 39. ♖b6 ♘b4 40. ♔e2 d3 41. ♔f3 ♘d5 42. ♖b8 ♔d7** **0 : 1** **[Dreev]**

276.**** !N **C 07**

TIVJAKOV 2595 − DEGERMAN 2460
Gausdal 1993

1. e4 e6 2. d4 d5 3. ♘d2 c5 4. ed5 ♕d5 5. ♘gf3 cd4 6. ♗c4 ♕d6 7. 0−0 ♘f6 8. ♘b3 ♘c6 9. ♘bd4 ♘d4 10. ♘d4 a6 [10... ♗d7 *a)* RR 11. c3 ♕c7 12. ♕e2 ♗d6 13. ♘b5 ♗b5 14. ♗b5 ♔e7 15. g3 h6 N (15... a6 − 55/278) 16. ♗e3 ♖hd8 17. ♗d4 ♖ac8 18. a4 a6 19. ♗d3 ♔f8 (△ e5) 20. ♗f6 (20. a5 ♘d7 △ e5) gf6 21. ♕h5 ♔g7 22. ♕g4 ♔f8 23. ♕h4 ♔e7 24. ♕h6 (24. ♗e4 ♖h8 25. ♗g2 a5 △ b6, ♕c4=) ♗c5! (Brajović 2295 − Miljanić 2395, Jugoslavija 1992) 25. ♕d2 (25. ♗e4 ♖h8 26. ♕d2 ♖cd8!!→) ♖d5=∞ Miljanić; *b)* 11. b3! *b1)* 11... ♕c7?! 12. ♘b5! N (12. ♕e2 ♗d6 13. h3 0−0 14. ♗b2 a6=) ♕e5□ 13. ♕e1! (13. ♖e1?! ♕a1 14. ♘c7 ♔d8 15. ♘a8∓; 13. ♕e2 ♕e2=) ♕e1 (13... ♕a1 14. ♘c7 ♔d8 15. ♘a8 ♗d6□ 16. ♕a5 ♔e7 17. ♕a7±; 17. ♗a3±) 14. ♖e1 ♗b5□ 15. ♗b5±⊡ Tivjakov 2535 − Keitlinghaus 2445, Groningen (open) 1991; *b2)* 11... ♗e7 12. a4! N (12. ♗b2 − 41/(327)) a6 (12... 0−0 13. ♗a3; 12... ♕c7 13. ♘b5; 12... ♕b8 ×♖a8) 13. ♖e1 (13. ♗a3 ♕c7 14. ♗e7 ♔e7 △ ♖hd8, ♔f8±; 13. ♗b2!?±) *b21)* 13... ♖d8 14. ♗b2 (14. ♗a3 ♕c7 15. ♗e7 ♔e7±) ♗c8 (14... 0−0 15. ♗a3; 14... ♕c7 ⇔e, ×♗e7) 15. ♕e2!? ♕c5 (15... 0−0 16. ♘f5±; 15... ♕c7!? △ 0−0±) 16. ♘f3 0−0 17. ♘e5±↑⊞, » Tivjakov 2585 − Holmov 2485, Moskva (open) 1992; *b22)* 13... ♕c7 14. ♕f3 (14. ♗b2!? 0−0 15. ♘f5; 14... 0-0-0!?±) *b221)* 14... 0-0-0 15. ♘f5!? (15. ♗f4 ♗d6 16. ♗d6 ♕d6 17. ♖ad1⩲; 15. ♗e3!? △ ♘b5; 15. ♗g5; 15. ♗b2) ♗b4 (15... ♗c6 16. ♕g3±) 16. ♗f4 ♕c6 17. ♕c3!!±; *b222)* 14... 0−0 15. ♘f5!? (15. ♗f4 ♗d6 16. ♗d6 ♕d6 17. ♖ad1⩲; 15. ♗b2!?) ♗d8□ (15... ef5 16. ♖e7; 15... ♗c6 16. ♕g3; 15... ♖fe8 16. ♘e7 ♖e7 17. ♗g5; 15... ♗b4 16. ♘h6! ♔h8 17. ♗b2± △ 17... ♗e1 18. ♕f6+−) 16. ♘g7!? (16. ♗f4 ♕c6 17. ♕c6 ♗c6 18. ♘d4±⊥) ♔g7□ (16... ♗c6? 17. ♕h3 ♔g7 18. ♕h6 ♔g8 19. ♗b2 ♕e7 20. ♖ad1+−) 17. ♗b2 ♖g8□ (Tivjakov 2575 − U. Andersson 2605, Haninge 1992; 17... ♗c6 18. ♕g4 ♔h8 19. ♕h4 ♕e7 20. ♖ad1+−; 20. ♗d3+−; 17... ♗e7 18. ♕g4 ♔h8 19. ♕h4 △ ♗d3+−) 18. ♖e4! ♗c6 (18... ♔f8 19. ♗f6 ♗c6± − 18... ♗c6) 19. ♗f6 ♔f8! (19... ♗f6 20. ♖g4 ♔f8 21. ♖g8 ♔g8 22. ♕f6+−) 20. ♖ae1 (20. ♗d8 ♖d8 △ 21... ♖d4, 21... f5; 20. ♗d3!?) ♖g6 (20... ♗e4 21. ♖e4±↑) 21. ♗d8 ♖d8 22. g3 ♗e4 23. ♖e4±↑] **11. b3!? ♗d7** [11... ♕c7!? 12. ♗b2 (12. ♕f3!?) ♗d6 13. ♘f3!? (13. h3 0−0 14. ♕f3!?∞; 14. ♗d3!?) b5 (13... 0−0 14. ♗f6 gf6 15. ♕d4±; 14. ♖e1!?) 14. ♗d3 ♗b7 N (14... 0−0 − 32/(280)) 15. ♖e1 0−0 (15... ♗f3? 16. ♕f3 ♗h2 17. ♔h1+− ×♖a8, ♗h2) 16. ♘e5 ♖ad8!? 17. ♕e2 ♘d5! 18. ♕g4 f5 19. ♕h4 ♘b4 20. ♖e2! ♘d3 21. ♘d3 ♗e4! 22. ♖ae1!? ♖fe8= Tivjakov 2595 − Psakhis 2575, Ro-

stov na Donu 1993] **12. ♗b2 ♕c7 13. ♕e2 0-0-0** [13... ♗d6? N 14. ♘f5! 0-0-0?! 15. ♘g7! *a)* 15... ♘d5 16. ♗d5 ed5 17. ♕h5 ♖hg8 18. ♖ad1!?+− Tivjakov 2595 − Smyslov 2530, Rostov na Donu 1993; *b)* 15... ♗h2 16. ♔h1 ♘d5 (16... ♕f4 17. ♘h5+−; 16... ♘e8 17. ♘e6+−) 17. ♗d5 ed5 18. g3+−; 14... ♗f8±; 14... ♖g8±] **14. ♘f3!** [14. a4!?] **♗c6 N** [14... h5?! − 34/368; ⌓ 14... ♗d6 15. ♘e5 ♗e8] **15. ♘e5± ♔b8** [15... ♗d6? 16. ♘f7+−; 15... ♗e4? 16. ♘f7 ♕f7 17. ♗f6+−; 15... ♗d5 16. ♗d5!? (16. ♗d3 △ c4) ♘d5 17. c4 ♘f6 18. c5!?±↑⟪ ×♗f8; 15... ♘d5 16. ♗d5!? ♗d5 (16... ed5 17. c4↑) 17. c4 ♗c6 18. c5!? △ b4, a4, b5±→⟪, ⟳; 15... ♗e8] **16. ♕e3!** [△ ♗d4-b6] **♘d5** [16... h5 17. h3 △ ♗d4; 16... ♗d6 17. ♗d4 ♖c8□±; 16... ♗d5 17. ♗d4 ♖c8 (17... ♗c4 18. ♗b6+−) 18. ♗b6 ♕e7± ×♗f8; 16... ♖c8!?±] **17. ♗d5 ♗d5?** [17... ♖d5 18. c4 ♗c5 (18... ♖d8+− − 17... ♗d5) 19. ♕g3 △ 20. ♘f7, 20. ♕g7; 17... ed5□ 18. c4!? *a)* 18... ♗d6 19. c5+−; *b)* 18... dc4 19. ♘c4 (△ ♗e5) f6 20. ♗d4 (△ ♗b6, △ ♗a7, ♘b6) ♖e8 (20... ♕e7 21. ♕g3+−) 21. ♗b6! ♕f7 (21... ♕c8 22. ♕g3; 21... ♕d7 22. ♕g3) 22. ♕g3 ♔a8 (22... ♔c8 23. ♗a7+−) 23. ♗e3+−; *c)* 18... f6□ 19. ♘c6 (19. cd5 ♗d5 20. ♖ac1 ♕e7 21. ♖fd1!+− △ 21... fe5 22. ♗e5 ♔a8 23. ♖d5; 19... ♖d5!± △ 20. ♘c6 ♕c6 21. ♖ac1 ♕d7) ♕c6 20. ♖ad1± △ 20... ♗c5 21. ♕g3 ♗d6 22. cd5!? ♕c2 23. ♕c3 ♖c8 24. ♕d2±; 22. ♕g7!?±] **18. c4+− ♗c5?** [18... ♗c6 *a)* 19. ♗d4 ♖c8 (19... ♖e8 20. ♘c6; 19... ♕e7 20. ♘c6; 20. ♖ad1) 20. ♘c6 ♕c6 (20... bc6 21. ♗e5 ♗d6 22. ♗d6 ♕d6 23. ♕b6) 21. ♕f4 △ ♕f7; *b)* 19. ♖ad1!? ♖d1 (19... ♖e8 20. ♘c6; 19... ♖c8 20. ♘c6 ♕c6 21. ♕f4; 19... ♗d6 20. c5) 20. ♖d1 f6 (20... ♗e8 21. ♗d4 △ ♗b6) 21. ♘c6 ♕c6 22. ♖d8 ♔c7 (△ 23. ♕d2? ♗b4) 23. ♕d3] **19. ♕g3 f6** [19... ♗e4 20. ♘f7] **20. cd5** [20. ♘f7] **♗d6** [20... fe5 21. ♖ac1] **21. ♖ac1 ♕e7** [21... ♗e5 22. ♖c7 ♗g3 23. ♖g7] **22. de6 ♕e6** [22... fe5 23. ♖cd1! ♕e6 (23... ♔a8 24. ♗e5; 23... ♗c7 24. ♗e5) 24. ♖d6 ♖d6 25. ♗e5] **23. ♕g4** **1 : 0**
[Tivjakov]

277. **C 07**

RELANGE 2295 −
O. DANIELIAN 2440
Cannes 1993

1. e4 e6 2. d4 d5 3. ♘d2 c5 4. ed5 ♕d5 5. ♘gf3 cd4 6. ♗c4 ♕d6 7. 0−0 ♘f6 8. ♘b3 ♘c6 9. ♘bd4 ♘d4 10. ♘d4 a6 11. ♖e1 ♗d7 12. ♗g5 0-0-0 [12... ♕c5? 13. ♗e6! (13. ♗f6?! ♕c4!∓) fe6 14. ♗f6 gf6 15. ♘e6 ♗e6 16. ♖e6 *a)* 16... ♔f7 17. ♕d7 *a1)* 17... ♔g8 18. ♖e3 ♗d6 19. ♖d1+−; *a2)* 17... ♗e7 18. ♖ae1 ♖ae8 (18... ♖he8 19. ♕d3!+−) 19. ♕b7+−; *a3)* 17... ♔g6 18. ♕b7±; *b)* 16... ♗e7 17. b4! ♕b4 (17... ♕f5 18. ♕e2+−) 18. ♕h5 ♔f8 19. ♖ae1 ♖e8 20. g3±] **13. ♗b3 ♕c7 14. ♕f3 ♗d6 15. h3 ♕c5 16. ♕e3** [16. ♗f6?! gf6 17. ♕f6 ♖hg8 18. ♖ad1 ♖g6 19. ♕f7 ♕g5 20. g4 ♖f8 21. ♕h7 ♕f4→] **♕c7 17. ♕f3 ♗h2 N** [17... ♕c5= − 55/279] **18. ♔h1 ♗e5 19. ♕e3 ♗d6** [19... ♗d4?! 20. ♕d4 ♗c6 21. ♕a7 ♖d7±] **20. ♕f3 ♕c5** [20... ♗e5=] **21. ♗f6!? gf6 22. ♕f6 ♖hg8 23. ♖ad1 ♖g6 24. ♕f7 ♕g5 25. ♖g1 ♖f8 26. ♕h7** [26. ♘e6? ♖e6!] **♖f2** [26... ♖h6? 27. ♕d3 ♕f4 28. ♕g3! (28. ♘f3? ♗c6! 29. ♕d6 ♖h3 30. gh3 ♕f3 31. ♔h2 ♕f2−+) ♕e4 29. ♕e3!± ♖f2? 30. ♕h6!; 26... ♕f4!? *a)* 27. g3 ♕e4 (27... ♗c6? 28. ♘c6 ♕f3 29. ♔h2 ♕f2 30. ♖g2 ♗g3 31. ♔h1+−) 28. f3 (28. ♖g2? ♖f2) ♖f3 29. ♕g6 ♕g6 30. ♘f3∞; *b)* 27. ♘f3 ♖h6 28. ♕g7 (28. ♕d3? ♗c6 29. ♕d6 ♖h3 30. gh3 ♕f3 31. ♔h2 ♕f2−+) *b1)* 28... ♖h3? 29. gh3 ♕f3 (29... ♗c6 30. ♗e6 ♔b8 31. ♗d5!+−) 30. ♕g2 ♗c6 31. ♗e6 ♔c7 32. ♗d5+−; *b2)* 28... ♗c6! 29. ♖d6! ♖h3 30. gh3 ♗f3 (30... ♕f3? 31. ♖g2+−) 31. ♖g2 ♗g2 32. ♕g2 ♕d6 33. ♕g3!∞] **27. ♘b5?** [27. ♘e6?! ♖g2! 28. ♕h8 ♖g8 29. ♕g8 ♕g8 30. ♖g2 ♗c6 31. ♘f4 ♗g2 32. ♘g2 ♕g3 33. ♗e6 ♔c7 34. ♖d6 ♔d6∓; 27. ♘f3! *a)* 27... ♖f3? 28. ♖d6! (28. gf3? ♕f4 29. ♕h8 ♔c7 30. ♕c3 ♗c6 31. ♖d6! ♖g1 32. ♔g1 ♕g3 33. ♔f1 ♕h3 34. ♔e2 ♕g2 35. ♔e1 ♕g3±) ♗c6 29. ♗e6 ♔b8 30. ♕h8 ♔c7 31. ♖c6 ♔c6 32. ♗g4±; *b)* 27... ♖g2! 28. ♕g6! (28. ♕d7? ♔d7 29. ♖d6 ♔d6 30. ♘g5 ♖g1 31. ♔g1 ♖g5∓) ♕g6

29. ♖g2 ♕h5 30. ♖d6 ♕f3 31. ♖d3 ♕f1 32. ♔h2 ♗c6 33. ♗e6 (33. ♖gd2 e5↑) ♔c7 34. ♗d5 (34. ♖gd2? ♕h1 35. ♔g3 ♕e1) ♗d5 35. ♖d5 ♕f4 36. ♔g1 ♕e3=] **♖g2?** [27... ♗b5! 28. ♖d6 ♖g2 29. ♗e6 *a)* 29... ♔b8 30. ♕h8 ♔c7 31. ♕c8 ♔d6 32. ♖d1 ♔e7 33. ♕c7 ♔e6 34. ♖d6 ♔f5 35. ♖d5 (35. ♕c5 ♔f4 36. ♖d4 ♔f3 37. ♕c3 ♔f2 38. ♖d2 ♗e2 39. ♕d4 ♕e3−+) ♔e4 36. ♖g5 ♖2g5−+; *b)* 29... ♖e6! 30. ♖g2 ♖e1 31. ♔h2 ♕f4 32. ♖g3 ♖e2−+] **28. ♘d6 ♔b8** [28... ♔c7? 29. ♕d7! ♔d7 30. ♘e4+−] **29. ♕g6** [29. ♕h8? ♔c7 (29... ♖g8? 30. ♕g8 ♕g8 31. ♖g2 ♗c6 32. ♗d5!+−) 30. ♕c3 ♗c6−+] **♕g6 30. ♖g2 ♗c6 31. ♖d2** [31. ♗d5? ♕h5!−+] **♕g3! 32. ♘c4⊕** [32. ♘f7!? ♕f4 33. ♘d8=] **b5⊕ 33. ♘a3** [33. ♘a5 ♗g2 34. ♖g2 ♕e1 35. ♔h2 ♕a5 (35... ♕e5 36. ♖g3 ♕e2 37. ♔h1 ♕e1 38. ♖g1 ♕e4=) 36. ♗e6 ♕c7 37. ♔h1 ♕e5=] **♕h3 34. ♔g1 ♗g2 35. ♖g2 ♕e3 36. ♔h2?!** [36. ♖f2 ♕c1 37. ♔g2 ♕b2 38. ♘b5 ab5 39. ♗e6=] **♕h6! 37. ♔g3 ♕g7 38. ♔f3 ♕b2 39. ♘b5 ab5 40. ♖g8** [40. ♖e2!?] **♔c7∓**

1/2 : 1/2 **[Vaïsser, Relange]**

278.** **C 09**

DOLMATOV 2615 − LOBRON 2620

Dortmund 1993

1. e4 c5 [RR 1... e6 2. d4 d5 3. ♘d2 c5 4. ed5 ed5 5. ♘gf3 ♘c6 6. ♗e2 ♘f6 7. 0−0 ♗d6 N (7... cd4 − 53/265) 8. dc5 ♗c5 9. ♘b3 ♗b6! 10. c3!? *a)* 10... h6!? 11. ♕d3! (△ ♗e3) 0−0 (11... ♘e4 12. ♗e3±) 12. ♗e3 ♗e3 (12... ♗c7 13. ♖ad1±; 12... ♖e8!? 13. ♗b6 ♕b6±; 12... ♗g4!?) 13. ♕e3 ♖e8 14. ♕d2! (14. ♕d3 ♗f5∞) ♘e4 15. ♕c2 ♗f5 16. ♘bd4 (16. ♗d3!? ♖c8 17. a3± △ ♘bd4, ♖fe1-e3, ♖ae1) *a1)* 16... ♘d4 17. ♘d4 ♘g3 (17... ♗g6±) 18. ♕d1!! ♘e2 (18... ♘f1? 19. ♘f5 ♕g5 20. ♘d4! ♘d2 21. h4! ♕f4 22. g3+−) 19. ♘e2± ×♗f5; *a2)* 16... ♘g3 17. ♘f5 (17. ♕d1 ♘e2 18. ♘e2 ♗g4∞) ♘e2□ 18. ♔h1±; *a3)* 16... ♗g6 (Tivjakov 2595 − Vaganian 2615, Rostov na Donu 1993) 17. ♗d3 ♖c8 18. a3!±; *b)* 10... 0−0 11. ♘fd4!? (11. ♗g5 ♖e8∞ 12. ♗h4!? Tivjakov) ♖e8 12. ♗f4 ♘e4 13. ♕c2 ♕f6 14. ♗e3 ♗c7 15. ♗f3 ♗d7 16. ♖ad1 ♘e5 17. ♕e2 ♖ad8∞ Tivjakov 2575 − Brynell 2410, Haninge 1992] **2. ♘f3 e6 3. c3 d5 4. ed5 ed5 5. d4 ♘c6 6. ♗b5 ♗d6 7. dc5 ♗c5 8. 0−0 ♘ge7 9. ♘bd2 0−0 10. ♘b3 ♗b6 11. ♖e1 N** [11. ♘bd4 − 23/220] **♘f5?!** [11... ♗g4!? 12. ♗e3 ♖e8±] **12. ♗d3 h6 13. ♗c2!? a5** [13... ♗e6 14. ♕d3 ♕f6 15. g4 ♕g6 16. h3 h5 17. ♘g5±; 13... d4 14. ♗f5 (14. c4 ♘b4 15. ♗b1→) ♗f5 15. ♘fd4 ♘d4 16. ♘d4 ♗d4 17. cd4±] **14. ♕d3!** [14. a4?! d4!⇆] **a4 15. ♘bd4 g6!□** [15... ♘cd4?! 16. ♘d4 ♗d4 17. cd4 ♕h4 (17... ♕b6 18. g4 ♕g6 19. ♕d1! h5 20. h3±) 18. ♖e5±] **16. ♘f5 ♗f5 17. ♕d1 ♗c2 18. ♕c2 ♔g7 19. ♗f4** [19. ♕d2!? ♖h8 20. ♖b1 △ b3, ♗b2; 19. ♗e3!?] **♕f6 20. ♕d2 g5 21. ♗e3 d4!?** [21... ♗e3 22. ♖e3 ♘a5 23. ♘e5±→] **22. ♗d4 ♘d4 23. ♘d4 ♖fd8 24. ♖ad1 ♖a5 25. ♖e3 ♖ad5?!** [25... ♗d4!? 26. cd4 ♖ad5 27. ♖d3±] **26. ♖d3 ♗d4 27. ♖d4! ♖d4 28. cd4** [♕ 9/e] **♖d5 29. h3 b5 30. b3 ab3 31. ab3 h5 32. ♕d3 h4 33. ♕e4 ♕d6 34. ♖d3 b4**

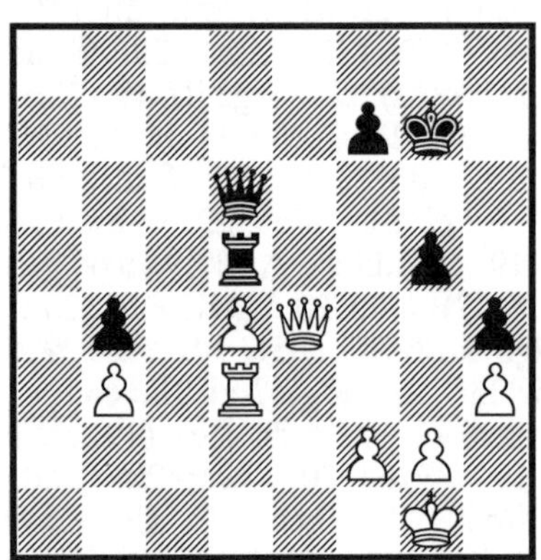

35. g3! hg3 36. ♖g3± ♔f8 [36... ♖d4 37. ♖g5 ♔h6 38. ♕f5 ♖d1 39. ♔g2 ♕c6 40. ♔g3 ♕d6 (40... ♖g1 41. ♔h4; 40... ♕c3 41. ♔h2 ♕c7 42. ♖g3→) 41. ♔h4 ♖d4 42. ♖g4 ♕d8 43. ♔g3 ♕d6 44. f4→] **37. ♖d3?** [37. h4! f5 (37... gh4 38. ♕h4 ♖d4 39. ♕h8 ♔e7 40. ♖e3+−; 37... ♖d4 38. ♕a8+−) 38. ♖f3!+−] **♕d8 38. ♔g2 ♔g7 39. ♕g4 ♔f8 40. ♖g3 ♕f6 41. h4 ♖f5 42. ♔h3 ♕e6?** [42... gh4!□ 43. ♕g8 ♔e7 44. ♖e3 ♔d6=] **43. hg5 ♖f2 44. ♕e6 fe6 45. ♔g4 ♖d2?!** [45... ♔g7□ 46. ♖f3 ♖c2

47. ♔f4 ♔g6 48. ♔e5 ♖c3±] **46. ♔f4 ♖d4 47. ♔e5 ♖h4 48. ♔e6+− ♔g7 49. ♔f5 ♖h8 50. ♖g4 ♖b8 51. g6 ♖f8 52. ♔e6 ♖f3 53. ♖b4 ♔g6 54. ♖b8 ♖e3 55. ♔d6 ♔f7 56. b4 ♖d3 57. ♔c6 ♔e7 58. b5 ♖d6 59. ♔b7 ♖d7 60. ♔a6 ♖d6 61. b6 ♔d7 62. ♔b7 ♖h6 63. ♖a8 ♖h7 64. ♖c8 1 : 0** **[Dolmatov]**

279.* !N **C 10**

GLEK 2545 − BUDNIKOV 2520

Douai 1993

1. e4 e6 2. d4 d5 3. ♘c3 de4 [3... a6 4. ♗d3 ♘c6 (4... c5?! − 48/(388)) 5. ♘f3 ♘b4 6. 0−0! N (6. ♗e2 ♘f6 7. e5 ♘e4∞) *a)* 6... ♘f6 7. e5 (7. ♗g5 de4±) ♘d7 8. ♘g5! (8. ♗g5 f6∞) ♘d3 9. cd3 ♗e7 (9... h6 10. ♘e6! fe6 11. ♕h5 ♔e7 12. ♗g5 hg5 13. ♕h8 △ f4→) 10. ♕h5 g6 11. ♕h6 ♗f8 12. ♕h3 ♗g7 (12... ♗e7 13. f4±) 13. b3! (13. ♘e6 fe6 14. ♕e6 ♔f8 15. ♕d5 c6∞; 13. f4±) ♕e7 14. a4 (Glek 2545 − Lëgky 2510, Douai 1993) ♘f8 15. ♗a3 ♕d7 16. ♖fc1 △ ♖c2, ♖ac1±; *b)* ⌓ 6... de4 7. ♘e4 (7. ♗e4 ♘f6 8. ♗g5±) ♘d3 8. ♕d3 ♗e7 9. ♗f4!? (9. ♘e5±; 9. ♗g5!?) ♘f6 10. ♘f6 ♗f6 11. ♕c3±; 7... ♗e7⩲] **4. ♘e4 ♗d7 5. c4 ♗c6 6. ♘c3 ♘f6 7. ♘ge2!? N** [7. ♘f3 − 56/299] **♗e7 8. ♘f4 0−0 9. ♗e2 ♗d6** [9... b6 10. 0−0 △ ♗f3⩲] **10. 0−0 e5 11. ♘fd5 ♗d5 12. cd5 ed4 13. ♕d4 ♘c6 14. ♕d1 ♘e7 15. ♗f3 a6** [15... ♘g6 16. g3⩲] **16. ♗g5** [16. g3⩲] **♘g6 17. ♕b3** [17. ♘e4 ♗e7 18. d6 cd6 19. ♘f6 ♗f6 20. ♗f6 ♕f6 21. ♗b7 ♖ab8∞] **h6 18. ♗f6 ♕f6 19. ♘e4 ♕e5 20. g3 ♖ab8 21. ♖fe1** [21. ♖ad1!? ♖fe8 22. ♗g2 △ f4⩲] **♕d4 22. ♘d6** [22. ♖ad1 ♕b4∞] **cd6 23. ♖e4 ♕c5 24. ♖c4 ♕a5 25. ♕c3 ♕b6 26. ♖c7?!** [26. ♖b4⩲] **♘e5!↑ 27. ♔g2□=** [27. ♗e2? ♘c6!↑; 27. ♖c1? ♘f3 28. ♕f3 ♕b2 29. ♖e1 ♖bc8] **♖be8 28. ♖c1 ♘f3 29. ♔f3** [29. ♕f3!? ♕b2 30. ♖1c4 △ ♖f4⩱] **♖e5 30. ♔g2! ♖d5 31. ♕f3! ♖b5** [31... ♖d2 32. ♖f7; 32. ♖c8!→] **32. ♖f7!** [32. ♖c8? ♖c5∓] **♖f7 33. ♖c8 ♔h7 34. ♕f7 ♕d4 35. ♕g8 ♔g6 36. ♕e8 ♔h7 37. ♕g8 ♔g6 38. ♕e6 1/2 : 1/2** **[Glek]**

280. **C 10**

ANAND 2710 − AN. KARPOV 2725

Linares 1993

1. e4 e6 2. d4 d5 3. ♘c3 de4 4. ♘e4 ♗d7 5. ♘f3 ♗c6 6. ♘eg5 ♗d6 N [6... ♘d7 − 36/(373)] **7. ♗d3 h6 8. ♘e4 ♗e4 9. ♗e4 c6 10. ♕e2 ♘f6 11. ♗d3 ♘bd7 12. ♗d2?!** [12. 0−0 0−0 13. ♖e1 ♖e8 14. ♘e5±] **♕c7 13. 0−0** [13. 0-0-0 ♗f4=] **0−0 14. c4 ♖fe8** [14... e5!? 15. c5 e4! 16. ♗e4 ♖fe8 (16... ♗c5!?) 17. cd6 ♕d6 18. ♘e5 ♘e4! 19. ♕e4 ♘e5 20. ♗f4 ♕g6!=] **15. c5 ♗f4 16. ♗f4 ♕f4 17. ♖fe1 ♖ad8 18. ♖ac1 ♘d5 19. g3 ♕c7 20. a3 b6 21. ♗c4 ♘5f6** [21... bc5 22. ♗d5 cd5 23. dc5±] **22. ♗a2 ♖b8 23. cb6! ♕b6 24. ♖c2 a5 25. ♖ec1 ♖b7 26. ♗c4! ♘d5 27. ♕e1!** [×a5] **♖d8 28. ♘d2 ♘5f6** [28... ♘e7! (×c6) 29. ♗f1 ♖a8!] **29. ♗f1 ♖a7 30. ♘c4 ♕c7 31. ♗g2± ♘b8 32. ♕e5 ♘d5 33. ♕c7?** [33. h4! △ ♗f3, ♔g2] **♘c7 34. ♘e5 ♘b5!= 35. ♘c6** [35. d5 ♘d4!∓] **♘c6 36. ♖c6 ♖d4 37. h4 g6 38. ♖b6 1/2 : 1/2** **[Anand]**

281. **C 10**

A. ZAPATA 2530 −
GARCÍA-PALERMO 2440

Bucaramanga 1992

1. e4 e6 2. d4 d5 3. ♘d2 de4 4. ♘e4 ♗d7 5. ♘f3 ♗c6 6. ♗d3 ♘d7 7. 0−0 ♘gf6 8. ♕e2 ♗e7 N [8... ♘e4] **9. ♘g3 ♗f3 10. ♕f3 c6 11. ♖e1 0−0 12. c3!?** [12. c4 ♕b6⇆] **♕b6 13. a4!○《 a5 14. ♘f5! ef5** [14... ♖fe8 15. ♘e7 ♖e7 16. ♖e2!? △ 17. ♗f4, 17. ♗g5] **15. ♖e7 ♖ae8 16. ♖e8 ♖e8 17. ♕d1±** [⊞, 8; 17. ♕f5?? ♖e1 18. ♗f1 ♕a6−+] **g6 18. b3 ♘d5 19. ♗d2 ♘7f6 20. ♕c2** [△ 20... ♘e4 21. ♖e1±] **♕d8 21. ♖e1± ♖e1 22. ♗e1 ♕e7 23. ♕d1!** [23. ♕c1?! ♘f4! 24. ♗f1 ♘e2±] **♘e4 24. ♕c1** [△ f3, c4] **b6 25. c4 ♘b4 26. ♗b1 c5 27. f3 cd4?⊕** [27... ♘f6 28. d5!? △ ♗c3, ♔f2, △ 29. ♗f5 gf5 30. ♗h4; 27... ♘d6 28. ♗f2±; 28. ♗c3!?] **28. fe4 fe4 29. ♕f4 f5 30. ♕b8?** [30. g4!+−] **♔f7 31. ♕b6 ♕g5!** [△ ♕c1] **32. ♕c7** [32. ♕a5? ♕e3 33. ♔f1 ♕f4=] **♔e8 33. ♕e5**

♔f7 34. ♕d4 ♕c1 35. ♔f2!? ♕b1 [♕ 8/f] **36. ♗c3 ♕c2?** [36... ♕b3! (△ ♘d3⇆) 37. h3!?] **37. ♔g3 ♕b3 38. ♔f4! ♘d3 39. ♔g5 ♕a4 40. ♕d5 ♔e8 41. ♗f6! ♕b4 42. ♕d8 ♔f7 43. ♕d7 ♔f8 44. ♔h6!** [△ ♗g7; 44... ♕d2 45. ♔h7] **1 : 0**
[A. Zapata, Henao]

282. **C 10**

GOLUBEV 2495 – EPIŠIN 2620
Genève 1993

1. e4 e6 2. d4 d5 3. ♘c3 de4 4. ♘e4 ♗d7 5. ♘f3 ♗c6 6. ♗d3 ♘d7 7. 0–0 ♘gf6 8. ♘eg5 ♗d6 9. ♖e1 h6 10. ♘h3 b6 N [10... ♗f3 – 55/282] **11. ♘e5 ♗b7 12. ♗b5 0–0 13. ♗c6± ♖b8!? 14. ♗b7** [14. ♕f3? ♗e5 △ 15. de5 ♘e5!] **♖b7 15. ♕f3 ♕c8** [15... ♕a8 16. ♘c6 ♘b8 17. ♘b8 ♖bb8; 16. ♕g3] **16. ♕g3!?** [△ →»; 16. ♘c6!○ ♘b8? 17. ♘b8 △ ♗h6] **♔h7□ 17. ♕h4 c5!** [17... ♗e5? 18. de5 ♘g8 19. a4!?± △ ♖a3] **18. ♗h6** [18. ♘d7 ♕d7?! 19. dc5; 18... ♘d7?! 19. ♘g5! △ ♘e4; 18... ♖d7!=] **gh6 19. ♘g5** [19. ♖e3?!] **♔g7□ 20. ♖e3 cd4??** [20... ♗e5 21. de5 ♘g8 22. ♖ae1!=∞ △ 22... ♔h8 23. ♖f3; 20... ♘g8!! (Epišin) *a)* 21. ♖ae1? ♘e5!; *b)* 21. ♘gf7? ♗e5; *c)* 21. ♘ef7? ♖f7∓; *d)* 21. ♘e4 ♗e5! 22. de5 ♘e5; *e)* 21. ♖g3 ♘e5 (21... ♗e5 22. de5 ♔h8 23. f4!; 22... ♘e5∞) 22. ♘e4 ♘g6 23. ♘d6∓; *f)* 21. ♕g3 ♗e5 22. de5 ♔h8 23. ♖f3?! ♘e5? 24. ♕e5 f6 25. ♕e4; 23... ♕e8!; 23. ♕f3!∞] **21. ♖g3 ♗e5 22. ♘e6 ♔h8 23. ♕h6 ♘h7 24. ♖h3! ♕c2 25. ♘f8+– ♔g8** [25... ♗g7 26. ♕h7 ♕h7 27. ♘h7] **26. ♘h7 ♖c7?⊕ 27. ♘f6** **1 : 0**
[Golubev]

283. **C 10**

GOLUBEV 2495 – ŠER 2500
Genève 1993

1. e4 e6 2. d4 d5 3. ♘c3 de4 4. ♘e4 ♗d7 5. ♘f3 ♗c6 6. ♗d3 ♘d7 7. 0–0 ♘gf6 8. ♘eg5 h6 N 9. ♘e6! fe6 10. ♗g6 ♔e7 11. c4!? [11. b3∞ ♗f3!? △ 12. ♗a3 c5 13. dc5 ♗d1 14. c6 ♘c5 15. ♗c5 ♕d6 16. ♗d6 ♔d6 17. cb7 ♖b8; 11... ♘b6; 11. ♖e1=∞ △ 11... ♘b6 12. ♘e5 ♕d5 13. f3 ♖d8 14. c3] **♗f3** [11... ♗e4 12. ♗e4 ♘e4 13. ♖e1=∞] **12. ♕f3 ♘b6!? 13. ♖e1! ♘c4**

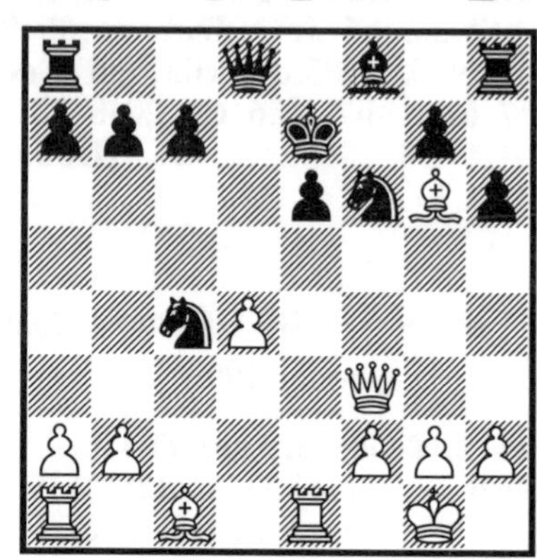

14. ♖e6! [14. ♗f5 ♕d5] **♔e6 15. ♕e2→ ♘e3** [15... ♔d6? 16. ♗f4; 15... ♔d7 16. ♗f5; 15... ♔d5 16. ♗f7; 15... ♘e5 16. ♕e5; 16. de5!?→ △ 16... ♘d5 17. ♕f3] **16. ♕e3 ♔d6 17. ♕g3!?** [17. ♕e5 ♔c6 18. ♗f4 △ 18... ♕e7 19. d5 ♔b6 20. ♗e3 ♔a6 21. ♗d3 b5 22. ♕c3→] **♔c6 18. ♕c3 ♔b6** [18... ♔d7!? 19. ♕h3 ♔e7!? (△ 20. ♗g5 ♕d7; 19... ♔c6 20. ♗f4→ b5!?) 20. ♕e3!? △ 20... ♔d6 21. ♕e5] **19. ♕b3 ♔c6□ 20. ♗f4!± b5?** [20... ♕d4 21. ♖c1 ♗c5 22. ♗e3+–; 20... ♕d5 21. ♖c1 ♔d7 22. ♕h3! ♔e7□ 23. ♗c7! ♕e6 24. ♕a3 ♔d7 25. ♕a4+– △ 25... ♔e7 26. ♕b4 ♔d7 27. ♕b5 ♔e7 28. ♕b7 ♕d5 29. ♗d8 ♔d8 30. ♕c7#; 20... ♗d6 21. ♖c1 ♔d7 22. ♗d6! ♔d6 23. ♕a3! ♔d7 24. ♗f5 ♔e8 25. ♖e1 ♔f7 26. ♗e6+–; 20... b6□ 21. ♕f3! ♕d5 (21... ♘d5 22. ♗e4!?+–) 22. ♕c3! ♗c5□ 23. dc5±→] **21. ♖c1 ♔b6 22. a4!+– ♕d5** [22... c6 23. ♖c6 ♔c6 24. ♕b5#; 22... a6 23. a5 ♔b7 24. ♕f3; 22... b4 23. ♕c4 ♕d7 24. a5] **23. ♗c7 ♔b7** [23... ♔a6 24. ab5 ♔b7 25. ♕d5 ♘d5 26. ♗e4] **24. ♗e4!** **1 : 0**
[Golubev]

284. **C 10**

ŠIROV 2670 – R. HÜBNER 2620
München 1993

1. e4 e6 2. d4 d5 3. ♘c3 de4 4. ♘e4 ♗d7 5. ♘f3 ♗c6 6. ♗d3 ♘d7 7. 0–0 ♘gf6 8.

♘g3 ♗e7 9. b3 0–0 10. ♗b2 ♗f3 N [10... a5 – 55/281] **11. ♕f3 c6 12. c4 ♖e8 13. ♖fe1** [13. ♖ad1±] **♘f8** [13... ♕c7 14. ♖ac1!? △ d5] **14. h4!?** [⌓ 14. ♖ad1 ♘g6 15. ♘e4±] **♕c7 15. ♖ac1 ♘g6!** [15... ♖ad8?! 16. d5! cd5 17. cd5 ♕d7 18. d6! *a)* 18... ♗d6? 19. ♗f6 gf6 20. ♘h5 ♗e5 (20... ♗e7 21. ♖ed1+–) 21. ♖e5+–; *b)* 18... ♕d6 19. ♗b5 ♘8d7 20. ♖ed1! (20. ♕b7±) ♕b6 21. ♗f6 ♕b5 22. ♗e7 ♖e7 23. ♖c7!±] **16. h5** [16. ♗g6 hg6 17. d5 ed5 18. cd5 ♖ac8± R. Hübner] **♘h4 17. ♕e3 ♗d6!** [17... h6? 18. d5 ed5 19. ♗f6 gf6 20. cd5+–] **18. ♘e4 ♗f4!** [18... ♗h2 19. ♔h1 ♗f4 20. ♘f6 gf6 21. ♕e4 f5 22. ♕e2 ♗c1 23. ♗c1! (23. ♖c1? ♕f4) ♖ad8 24. ♗g5 ♖d4 25. g3±] **19. ♘f6 gf6 20. ♕e4! f5 21. ♕e2** [×♘h4] **♗c1 22. ♖c1** [22. ♗c1!? ♖ad8 23. ♗g5 ♖d4 24. g3 ♖ed8! 25. ♗b1 ♖d2! 26. ♕e3! (26. ♗d2 ♖d2 27. ♕e3 f4!∞) f4! 27. ♗f4 ♕a5 28. gh4 ♖d1 29. ♔f1 ♖e1 30. ♕e1 ♕h5 31. ♗c2 ♕h4 32. ♕e4±] **f6!** [22... ♕f4 23. g3 ♕g5 24. ♔f1±] **23. g3** [23. ♕e3 ♕g7∞] **♔f7! 24. gh4 ♕f4 25. ♖e1 ♖g8!** [25... ♕h4? 26. ♕f3±] **26. ♔f1 ♖ae8 27. ♕e3 ♕h4 28. ♔e2!** [28. ♕f3?! ♖g4→] **♕h5 29. ♔d2 ♖g2! 30. ♖e2 ♕g5 31. f4 ♖e2** [31... ♕g3!? 32. ♕g3 ♖g3 33. ♖h2±] **32. ♗e2 ♕g2 33. ♕f3! ♕f3!** [33... ♖g8 34. ♕h5! ♕g6 (34... ♔g7 35. ♕h4!±) 35. ♕h3!±] **34. ♗f3±** [♖ 8/c] **♔g6?!** [⌓ 34... ♔e7 35. ♔e3 ♔d6±] **35. ♔e3 ♖d8** [35... h5 36. ♔f2 ♖g8 37. ♔g3 ♔h6 38. ♔h4 △ d5±] **36. ♗c3 ♔f7 37. a4! ♔e7 38. a5± ♔d7?!** [38... a6 39. b4!± △ b5; 38... ♔d6!? 39. d5 e5±] **39. d5! ed5 40. cd5 cd5** [40... ♖f8 41. dc6 bc6 42. ♔d4 ♖b8 43. ♔c4 ♖f8 44. ♔c5+–] **41. ♗f6 ♖f8 42. ♗h4!+– ♔c6 43. ♔d4 ♔b5 44. ♗d5 ♔a5 45. ♗b7 ♖b8 46. ♗d5 h5 47. ♗e6 ♔a6 48. ♗c4 ♔b6 49. ♔e5 a5 50. ♔f5 ♔c5 51. ♔e5 1 : 0** [Širov]

285.** **C 10**

CEŠKOVSKIJ 2540 – HOLMOV 2460

Akmola 1993

1. e4 e6 2. d4 d5 3. ♘c3 de4 4. ♘e4 ♘d7 5. ♘f3 [RR 5. ♗d3 ♘gf6 6. ♕e2! ♗e7 7. ♘f3 0–0 8. 0–0 b6 (8... ♘e4 9. ♕e4 ♘f6 10. ♕h4±) 9. ♗f4 N (9. ♘f6) ♗b7 10. ♖ad1 *a)* 10... ♕c8 11. c4! ♘e4 12. ♗e4 ♗d6 13. ♗e5! (13. ♗h7 ♔h7 14. ♘g5 ♔g8 15. ♕d3 f5 16. ♕h3 ♘f6 17. ♗e5 ♕d7 18. c5 bc5 19. dc5∞) ♗e5 14. de5 ♖d8 15. ♘g5 ♗e4 16. ♕e4 ♘f8 17. ♕f3! ♖d1 18. ♕f7 ♔h8 19. ♖d1 h6 20. ♘e4 ♕a6 21. ♘f6! 1 : 0 Kveinys 2545 – Luther 2435, Ostrava 1992; *b)* 10... ♘e4 11. ♗e4 ♗e4 12. ♕e4 ♘f6 13. ♕c6± Kveinys] **♘gf6 6. ♘f6 ♘f6 7. ♗d3** [7. ♗g5 c5 8. dc5 ♕d1 N (8... ♕a5) 9. ♖d1 ♗c5 10. ♗b5 ♔e7 11. ♘e5 h6 12. ♗e3?! ♗e3 13. fe3 a6 14. ♗e2 ♗d7 15. ♗f3 ♖ab8 16. 0–0 ♖hc8 17. ♖d2 ♖c5 18. ♘d3 ♖c7∓ Holmov 2485 – Puškov 2430, Orel 1992] **c5 8. 0–0 cd4 9. ♘d4 ♗e7 N** [9... ♗c5 – 36/373] **10. c3 0–0 11. ♖e1 a6 12. ♗g5 ♖e8 13. ♗h4?!** [13. ♕f3! ♕d5!? 14. ♕e3!? ♘g4 15. ♕h3 ♗g5 16. ♗h7 ♔f8 17. ♗e4! (17. ♕g4 g6 18. ♖ad1 ♗f6 19. ♗g6 fg6 20. ♕g6 ♕g5!∓) ♘f2! 18. ♕h8! (18. ♔f2 ♕c5! 19. b4 ♕b6∞) ♔e7 19. ♕e8! ♔e8 20. ♗d5 ♘d3 21. ♖e4 ♘b2 22. ♗b3±] **♗d7 14. ♗c2 b5** [14... ♕b6 15. ♘f5! ef5 16. ♗f6±; 14... g6 15. ♕f3 ♘d5 16. ♗e7 ♕e7 17. ♗e4±] **15. a4! ba4 16. ♗a4 ♘d5 17. ♗e7 ♘e7 18. ♗c2 ♕b6 19. ♕d3 ♘g6?!** [⌓ 19... g6!?] **20. h4 e5** [20... ♖ed8!? 21. h5 ♘f8 △ 22. h6? gh6! 23. ♕h3 ♔g7∓] **21. ♘f3** [21. ♘f5 ♗f5 22. ♕f5 ♕b2 23. h5 ♘f8 24. ♖ab1! ♕a3! (24... ♕c3? 25. ♖b7!! ♕e1 26. ♔h2 f6 27. ♕g4+– Ceškovskij) 25. ♖b7 ♖e7 26. ♖e7 ♕e7 27. ♖e5 ♕a3=] **♗b5! 22. c4 ♗c6 23. ♘e5** [23. h5 e4! 24. ♕d4! ♕b7! 25. hg6 ef3 26. gh7 ♔h8∞] **♖e5 24. ♖e5 ♘e5 25. ♕h7 ♔f8 26. ♕h8** [26. ♖e1 f6!∓] **♔e7 27. ♕g7 ♕b2! 28. ♖e1 ♔e6 29. ♕h6!** [29. h5 ♖e8! 30. h6 ♔d7 31. ♗f5 ♔c7 △ 32. h7? ♘f3!–+] **f6 30. f4** [30. ♕h7 ♕d4! 31. ♖d1 (31. ♗f5 ♔d6 32. c5 ♔c5 33. ♕e7 ♔b6 34. ♖b1 ♗b5 35. ♕f6 ♘c6∓) ♕g4 32. ♗f5 ♕f5 33. ♖d6 ♔d6 34. ♕f5 ♔e7 35. h5 a5 36. h6 a4 37. h7 a3∞] **♕c2! 31. ♖e5 ♔f7 32. ♕h5 ♔f8** [32... ♕g6? 33. ♖e7!; 32... ♔g8 33. ♕g4 ♔f8 34. ♖e6 ♗e8 35. ♖f6 ♗f7 36. f5!=] **33. ♕h8 ♔f7 1/2 : 1/2 [Holmov]**

286. **C 11**

SAX 2570 – GLEK 2545
Deutschland 1993

1. e4 e6 2. d4 d5 3. ♘c3 ♘f6 4. e5 ♘fd7 5. ♘ce2 c5 6. c3 cd4 7. cd4 f6 8. ♘f4! ♗b4 9. ♗d2 ♗d2 [9... ♕e7 10. ♗b4 ♕b4 11. ♕d2±] **10. ♕d2 ♕e7 11. ef6 ♘f6 12. ♗d3 ♘c6 N** [12... e5 – 13/321] **13. ♘ge2 0–0** [13... ♕b4 14. ♕b4 ♘b4 15. a3 ♘c6 16. f3 g5 17. ♘h3 g4 18. fg4 ♘g4 19. 0–0 e5 20. ♗b5±] **14. 0–0 ♗d7 15. a3 ♕d6 16. ♖ad1 ♖f7 17. ♗b1 ♖e8 18. f3 ♖fe7 19. ♘d3 e5 20. de5 ♘e5 21. ♘e5 ♖e5 22. ♘d4 ♕b6 23. ♕b4** [23. ♔h1? ♗b5=; 23. ♕f2 ♗a4 24. ♖d2 ♖e3±] **♕b4 24. ab4 ♖c8 25. ♗a2 ♔f8 26. ♖c1 ♖c1 27. ♖c1 ♔e7 28. ♖c7?!** [28. ♔f2 △ g4±] **♖e1 29. ♔f2 ♖a1 30. ♗b3 ♔d8! 31. ♖c2** [31. ♖b7? ♔c8] **♖a6 32. g4 h6 33. h4 g5 34. hg5 hg5 35. ♖e2** [35. ♖d2] **♖b6 36. ♘c2 a5 37. ♖e5?** [37. ♔g3] **ab4?⊕ 38. ♖g5 1 : 0** **[Sax]**

287.* !N** **C 11**

ŠIROV 2670 – M. GUREVICH 2610
München 1993

1. e4 e6 2. d4 d5 3. ♘c3 ♘f6 4. e5 ♘fd7 5. ♘ce2 c5 6. c3 ♘c6 7. f4 ♕b6 8. ♘f3 ♗e7 [RR 8... f6 9. g3 cd4 10. ♘ed4 fe5 11. fe5 ♘d4 12. cd4 ♗b4 13. ♔f2 0–0 14. ♔g2 ♗e7 15. ♗d3 ♖f7 N (15... ♘b8? – 7/194) 16. h4 ♘f8 17. ♘g5 ♗g5 18. hg5 g6 19. ♖h4 ♗d7 20. b3 ♖c8 21. a4 ♖c3 22. ♖b1 ♕d8 23. ♕d2 ♕c8 24. ♗a3 ♗a4 25. ♗f8 ♗b5 26. ♗g6 1/2 : 1/2 Psakhis 2575 – G. Dizdar 2490, Zagreb (zt) 1993] **9. a3 f6 10. b4 cd4 11. cd4** [RR 11. ♘ed4 ♘d4 12. cd4 0–0 13. ♗d3 fe5 14. fe5 ♖f3 15. gf3 ♗h4 16. ♔e2 ♘e5 17. ♗f4 ♘d3 18. ♕d3 ♗d7 19. ♕e3± Sax] **0–0 12. ♖b1 N** [RR 12. ♕d3 ♕c7! N (12... a6) 13. ♕c2? b5∓ Sax 2570 – Luther 2465, Deutschland 1993] **a5!?** [12... fe5 13. de5 a5! 14. b5 ♗c5!∞ Širov 2710 – Ceškovskij 2510, Moskva (rapid) 1992; 13. fe5!?; 12... ♘a5!?] **13. b5 a4!? 14. ♘c3?** [14. ef6 ♘f6 15. ♘c3 ♘d8 16. ♗d3 ♘f7∞] **♘ce5! 15. fe5 fe5→ 16. ♗d3!** [16. de5 ♘e5 17. ♗e2 ♘f3 18. ♗f3 ♗d7∓; 16. ♗e3 e4 17. ♘d2 ♗a3∓] **e4?** [16... ed4! 17. ♘d4 ♘e5! 18. ♗e2! (18. ♗h7? ♔h7! 19. ♕h5 ♔g8 20. ♕e5 ♗f6–+; 18. ♗e3? ♕a5! 19. ♕d2 ♘d3 20. ♕d3 e5–+) ♗d7 19. ♕d2∓] **17. ♘e4 de4 18. ♗e4∞ e5!** [18... ♘f6 19. ♗c2±] **19. 0–0 ♘f6** [19... ed4 20. ♗d5 ♔h8 21. ♗b2∞] **20. ♗g5! ♘e4?** [20... ed4 21. ♕d3 h6 22. ♗f6 ♕f6 (22... ♗f6? 23. ♗h7 ♔h8 24. ♘h4!+–) 23. ♖be1=∞] **21. ♗e7 ♖f7** [21... ♖f4 22. ♕d3!± △ 22... ed4 23. ♘g5!+–] **22. ♕d3! ♗f5!** [22... ♖e7 23. ♕e4±] **23. ♘e5 ♖e7 24. ♖f5 ♖d8! 25. ♖bf1!** [25. ♕e4?? ♖d4–+] **g6!** [25... ♘d6? 26. ♖h5!; 25... ♘f6 26. ♕c4 ♕e6 27. ♕a4+–] **26. ♕c4 ♕e6 27. ♕e6** [27. d5? ♕b6 28. ♔h1 ♘d6–+] **♖e6 28. ♖f7!!±** [28. ♖5f4 ♖d4 29. ♘g4 g5!∞] **♘d2?** [28... ♘d6 29. ♖c7 ♘b5 30. ♖b7 ♘d4 31. ♘f7 ♘e2 (31... ♖c8 32. ♘h6 ♔h8 33. h4!!±) 32. ♔h1 ♖c8 33. g3!?±] **29. ♖1f4 g5 30. ♖4f5 ♘e4 31. ♖b7 ♖d4 32. h3!+– ♖d5⊕ 33. ♖b8 ♔g7 34. ♖f7 ♔h6 35. ♘g4 ♔g6 36. ♖c7! ♖d1 37. ♔h2 ♖b1? 38. ♖g8 ♔f5 39. ♖f7 ♘f6 40. ♖gf8 h5 41. ♘f6 1 : 0** **[Širov]**

288. **C 11**

ANAND 2710 – BAREEV 2670
Linares 1993

1. e4 e6 2. d4 d5 3. ♘c3 ♘f6 4. e5 ♘fd7 5. f4 c5 6. ♘f3 a6 7. ♗e3 b5 8. ♕d2 ♗e7 N [8... ♗b7 – 56/304] **9. ♗d3 g6?! 10. 0–0 ♗b7 11. ♘d1!** [△ c3] **cd4 12. ♘d4 ♘c5 13. b4 ♘a4** [13... ♘d3 14. cd3 ♘c6 15. a3 a5 16. ♖b1±; 13... ♘e4 14. ♕e1±] **14. c3 ♘b6 15. ♗f2 ♕c7 16. ♘b2 ♘c4 17. ♕e2 ♘c6?** [17... ♘a3! 18. ♖ac1 ♘d7 19. ♘b3 ♘b6 20. ♘a5 ♘bc4±⇆] **18. a4± ♘d4 19. ♗d4 ♗c6 20. ab5 ab5 21. ♖a8!** [21. ♘c4 dc4 22. ♗e4? 0–0] **♗a8 22. ♘c4 bc4** [22... dc4 23. ♗e4 0–0 24. ♖a1+–] **23. ♗c2 ♗c6 24. ♕e3 0–0 25. f5 ef5 26. ♗f5 ♕d8 27. ♗g4! ♗g5 28. ♕e2 h5** [28... ♗d7 29. e6+–; 28... ♖e8 29. e6 f6 30. g3±] **29. ♗h5!+– gh5 30. ♕h5 ♗e8** [30... f6 31. ♕g6; 30... ♕e7

31. h4! ♗h4 32. ♖f4] **31. ♖f6!** [31... ♗c1 32. e6 fe6 33. ♖g6] **1 : 0**
[Anand]

289. C 11

SMIRIN 2590 – LPUTIAN 2610
Rostov na Donu 1993

1. e4 e6 2. d4 d5 3. ♘c3 ♘f6 4. e5 ♘fd7 5. f4 c5 6. ♘f3 ♘c6 7. ♗e3 a6 8. ♕d2 cd4 9. ♘d4 ♗c5 10. 0-0-0 0–0 11. h4 ♘d4 12. ♗d4 b5 13. h5 b4 14. ♘e2!? N [14. ♘a4 – 55/286] **a5 15. ♗c5** [15. ♕e3 ♕b6 16. ♗c5 ♕c5] **♘c5 16. ♕e3 ♕b6** [16... ♘e4 17. ♘g3±] **17. f5!?** [17. ♔b1 a4 18. ♘d4] **a4 18. ♔b1 b3 19. cb3 ab3 20. a3 ef5 21. ♖d5 ♖a5?!** [21... f4? 22. ♕c5 ♗f5 23. ♔a1 ♖a3 24. ♕a3 ♕c6 25. ♘c3+–; ⌓ 21... ♘a4 *a)* 22. ♘d4 ♗e6 23. ♖b5 (23. ♖d6 ♕c5) ♕a7! △ 24... ♘b2, 24... ♖fd8; *b)* 22. ♕b6 ♘b6 23. ♖d4 ♗e6 24. ♘f4 ♖fd8 25. ♘e6 fe6 26. ♖d6! ♖d6 27. ed6 ♖d8 28. ♗e2 ♖d6 29. ♖d1!∞⊥] **22. ♘f4□** [22. h6? f4–+] **h6□** [22... ♗b7 23. h6 ♗d5 (23... g6 24. ♗c4!±) 24. ♘d5 ♕e6 25. ♘f6!] **23. ♗d3** [23. ♗c4 ♗b7 △ 24. ♖d6? ♗e4 25. ♕e4 (25. ♔a1 ♖a3) ♕d6–+] **♗e6 24. ♖d6 ♕b7!** [24... ♕a7 25. ♘e6 fe6 26. ♗c4±] **25. ♖c1** [25. ♖d1±] **♖c8** [25... ♘d3 26. ♖d3 (26. ♘d3? ♕g2) ♕b5! 27. ♘e6 fe6 28. ♖b3 ♕e5 29. g3=] **26. ♕d4 ♘d3?** [26... ♔h7□∞] **27. ♖c8 ♗c8**

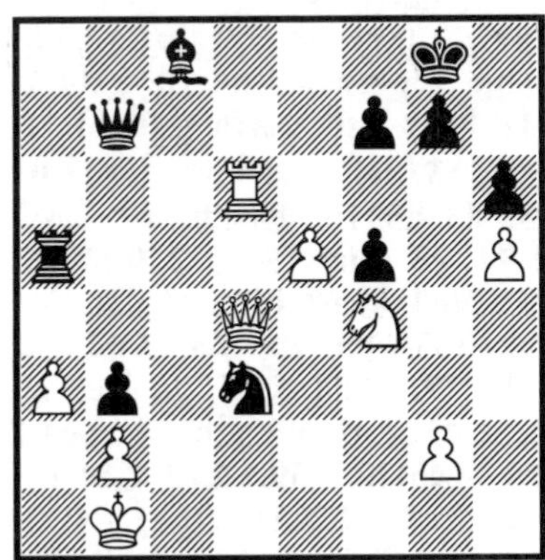

28. ♘g6!! ♔h7 [28... fg6 29. hg6 ♔f8 30. ♖d8 ♔e7 31. ♕d6#] **29. ♘f8 ♔g8 30. ♖d8 g5 31. ♕d6 1 : 0** **[Smirin]**

290. C 11

TISCHBIEREK 2495 – KNAAK 2515
Deutschland 1993

1. e4 e6 2. d4 d5 3. ♘c3 ♘f6 4. e5 ♘fd7 5. f4 c5 6. ♘f3 ♘c6 7. ♗e3 cd4 8. ♘d4 ♗c5 9. ♕d2 0–0 10. 0-0-0 ♘d4 11. ♗d4 a6 12. h4 b5 13. ♖h3 ♗b7!? N [13... b4 – 55/(286)] **14. h5 b4 15. ♘a4** [15. ♘e2 a5∞] **♗d4 16. ♕d4 ♕a5 17. b3 ♗c6 18. ♘b2** [18. ♖g3?! ♗a4 19. f5!? ♔h8!∓] **♖fc8!** [18... ♕a2 19. ♘d3!↑] **19. f5** [19. ♔b1!? ♗b5 20. ♗d3∞] **♕c7! 20. ♕b4 ♘e5 21. h6?!** [21. fe6 fe6 22. ♖c3=] **ef5! 22. hg7 ♗d7! 23. ♖d2?** [23. c4□ ♗e6 24. ♖c3 a5 25. ♕a3∓] **f4 24. ♖h6** [24. ♖h5 ♗g4 25. ♖g5 h6–+] **♗f5–+ 25. ♗a6** [25. ♖a6 ♗c2] **♗c2! 26. ♗c8 ♗e4□ 27. ♔d1 ♖c8 28. ♔e2 f3! 29. gf3 ♘f3 0 : 1**
[Knaak]

291. C 11

NIJBOER 2485 – M. GUREVICH 2625
Groningen 1992

1. e4 e6 2. d4 d5 3. ♘c3 ♘f6 4. e5 ♘fd7 5. f4 c5 6. ♘f3 ♘c6 7. ♗e3 cd4 8. ♘d4 ♗c5 9. ♕d2 ♘d4 10. ♗d4 ♗d4 11. ♕d4 ♕b6 12. ♕b6 ♘b6 13. ♗d3 ♔e7 14. 0-0-0 N [14. ♘b5 – 50/(312)] **♗d7 15. ♖hf1** [△ 15... g5 16. f5; 15. ♖he1 g5 16. fg5 ♖hg8 17. h4 h6 18. g4 hg5 19. h5∞] **♗c6 16. ♘e2 f6!?** [16... g6 △ h5±] **17. ef6 gf6 18. ♘d4 ♔d6** [18... e5? 19. fe5 fe5 20. ♖de1 e4 21. c4 ♖ac8 22. ♔b1 ♘c4 23. ♗c4 dc4 24. ♘c6 ♖c6 25. ♖e4±] **19. ♖de1 ♖ae8 20. g4! ♖hg8 21. h3 h6** [21... ♖g7? 22. ♖e6 ♖e6 23. ♘f5+–] **22. ♖f3 ♗d7 23. ♗b5 ♖e7 24. ♗d7 ♔d7?** [24... ♘d7 25. a4 (25. ♖c3 a6?? 26. ♖e6 ♖e6 27. ♘f5#; 25... ♘c5∞) ♘c5 (25... a6 26. ♖b3 ♘c5 27. ♖b6 ♔c7 28. a5 ♖ge8 29. b4 ♘e4 30. c4→) 26. ♘b5 ♔d7 27. ♘c3 d4 28. ♘e4 ♘e4 29. ♖e4 e5 30. fe5 fe5 31. c3±] **25. ♖fe3 ♖ge8 26. b3 a6 27. ♔b2 ♔d6 28. ♖d1!± ♔c7 29. a4 ♘c8** [29... ♔d6 30. a5 ♘d7 31. c4 ♘c5 32. cd5+–] **30. f5 ef5** [30... e5 31. ♘e6 ♔d6

32. ♖ed3 d4 33. c3+−] **31. ♖c3 ♔b8 32. ♘f5 ♖h7 33. ♖d5 h5 34. ♖cd3! hg4 35. hg4 ♖h2 36. ♖d8 ♖he2 37. ♖3d7 ♖d8 38. ♖d8 ♔c7 39. ♖f8⊕** [39... ♖e4 40. ♖c8+−; 39... ♖g2 40. ♘e3 ♖g1 41. ♘d5+−; 39... ♖e6 40. ♘g7 ♖e4 41. ♘e8+−] **1 : 0** **[Nijboer]**

292. **C 14**

HJARTARSON 2625 − BRICARD 2460
Ísland − France 1993

1. e4 e6 2. d4 d5 3. ♘c3 ♘f6 4. ♗g5 ♗e7 5. e5 ♘fd7 6. ♗e7 ♕e7 7. f4 a6 8. ♕g4 0−0 N [8... g6; 8... f5] **9. ♗d3** [9. f5!? *a)* 9... ef5 10. ♘d5 ♕d8 (10... fg4 11. ♘e7 ♔h8 12. ♗d3 c5 13. h3 g3 14. c3 ♘c6 15. ♘c6 bc6 16. ♘e2±) 11. ♕f3 c5 12. c3 cd4 13. cd4 ♘c6 14. 0-0-0±; *b)* 9... f6! 10. fe6 ♘b6 11. ef6 ♖f6 12. 0-0-0 ♗e6 13. ♕h4∞] **c5?!** [9... f5!? 10. ef6 ♕f6 (10... ♘f6? 11. ♕h4±) *a)* 11. ♘ce2 e5! (11... c5 12. c3 ♘c6 13. ♘f3±) 12. de5 ♘e5 13. ♗h7 ♔h7 14. ♕h5 ♔g8 15. ♕e5 ♕e5 16. fe5 ♗g4$\overline{\overline{\infty}}$; *b)* 11. ♘f3 c5 12. ♘g5∞] **10. f5!?** [10. ♘f3 f5! 11. ef6 ♕f6 12. ♘g5∞] **cd4□** [10... f6? 11. fe6 ♘b6 12. dc5+−; 10... ef5? 11. ♘d5±] **11. f6 ♘f6 12. ♕h4! h6 13. ef6** [13. ♘a4 ♘bd7□ 14. ef6 ♕f6 15. ♕f6 gf6 − 13. ef6] **♕f6 14. ♕f6 gf6 15. ♘a4 ♘d7 16. b3 b5 17. ♘b2 e5 18. ♘e2!± ♘c5** [18... e4 19. ♘d4 ed3 20. ♘d3 ♖e8 21. ♔d2 ♘e5 22. ♖hf1 ♘d3 23. cd3±] **19. 0−0 ♘d3** [19... e4 20. ♖f6 ed3 21. ♘d3 ♘d3 22. cd3±] **20. ♘d3 ♔g7** [20... f5!? 21. ♘e5 ♖e8 22. ♘f7! ♔f7 23. ♘d4 ♔f6 24. ♖f3±] **21. ♘g3 ♔g6□ 22. ♖f2 ♖b8?!** [22... a5 23. ♖af1 ♖a6 24. h4±] **23. ♖af1 ♖b6 24. h4** [24. ♖f6? ♖f6 25. ♘e5 ♔g5 26. h4 ♔h4 27. ♖f6 ♖e8! (27... ♔g3 28. ♖f3 ♔h4 29. ♘g6 fg6 30. ♖f8 ♗f5 31. ♖d8 ♗e4 32. ♔f2± b4) 28. ♘f7 ♔g3 29. ♖g6 ♔f4 30. ♖f6=] **♖e8□** [24... a5? 25. ♖f6 ♖f6 26. ♘e5 ♔g7 27. ♘h5+−] **25. ♘f5 a5 26. ♖f3 ♗f5 27. ♖f5 b4?** [27... h5! 28. ♖5f3±] **28. g4± ♖g8 29. ♔h2** [29. g5? hg5 30. hg5 ♔h5∞] **♖c6 30. ♖1f2 ♖gc8 31. ♔g3 ♖8c7 32. ♖f1!+−** [32. g5? hg5 33. hg5 e4 34. gf6 (34. ♖f6? ♖f6 35. ♖f6 ♔g5 36. ♖d6=) ed3 35. ♔g4? ♖c2 36. ♖g5 ♔h7 37. ♖g7 ♔h6 38. ♖f3 ♖h2∓] **♖c8** [32... ♔g7 33. g5] **33. g5 hg5 34. hg5 e4 35. gf6!** [35... ed3 36. ♔g4 ♔h7□ 37. ♖h5 ♔g8 38. ♖fh1 ♖f6 39. ♖h8 ♔g7 40. ♖c8] **1 : 0**
[Hjartarson]

293.* **C 15**

HEYKEN 2375 − KINDERMANN 2495
Dortmund (open) 1993

1. e4 e6 2. d4 d5 3. ♘c3 ♗b4 4. ♘e2 ♘c6!? N [RR 4... de4 5. a3 ♗e7 6. ♘e4 ♘f6 7. ♕d3 ♘c6 8. ♗f4 0−0 9. 0-0-0 e5!? N (9... b6 − 38/(402)) *a)* 10. de5?! ♕d3 11. cd3 ♘h5 12. d4 ♘f4 13. ♘f4 ♖d8 *a1)* 14. ♘e2?! ♗f5 15. ♘4g3 ♗e6 16. f4 ♖d7 17. f5 ♗b3 18. ♖d3 ♗c4 19. ♖c3 ♗g5 20. ♔b1 *a11)* 20... ♗e2 21. ♗e2 ♖d4 22. ♖d1 ♖d1 23. ♗d1 (S. Biró 2305 − Bogdanov 2405, Budapest 1993) ♗f4 24. e6 fe6 25. fe6∞; *a12)* 20... ♗d5! 21. h4 ♗d2 22. ♖d3 ♗e1∓; *a2)* 14. ♗c4 ♖d4 15. ♖d4 ♘d4 16. ♘d5 ♗d8=; *b)* 10. ♗e5 ♘e5 11. de5 ♕d3 12. cd3 ♘g4!? (12... ♘e4 13. de4 ♗c5 14. f3 c6) 13. d4 f5 14. ef6 gf6 15. f3 f5 16. fg4 fe4∞ Ėjngorn, Bogdanov] **5. a3 ♗a5 6. e5 f6 7. b4?!** [⌓ 7. f4 (△ g3, ♗g2) fe5 8. de5 d4?! 9. b4; ⌓ 8... ♘h6] **♗b6 8. b5 ♘a5 9. ♘f4 fe5!∓ 10. ♕h5** [10. de5 ♕g5!→ Heyken] **g6 11. ♕e5** [11. ♘g6 ♘f6 12. ♕h3 (12. ♕h4 ♗d4) ♖g8 13. ♘e5 ♗d4 14. ♗f4 ♕d6∓] **♕f6∓** [×d4, c4] **12. ♕f6 ♘f6 13. ♗e3 c6 14. ♘a4 ♗c7 15. ♘c5 e5 16. ♘fd3 ed4 17. ♗d4 0−0 18. ♘b4!? b6 19. ♘cd3** [19. ♘b3 ♘b3 20. cb3 c5 21. ♗f6 cb4∓] **♗b7 20. bc6 ♖ae8 21. ♗e2 ♘c6 22. ♘c6 ♗c6 23. f3 ♗a4 24. c3 ♗d6 25. ♔d2 ♘d7! 26. ♗d1 ♗b5 27. a4?** [⌓ 27. g3 ♘c5 28. ♘c5 bc5 29. ♗e3 ♗c4 30. ♖b1∓] **♗c4 28. g3 ♘c5 29. ♘c5 bc5 30. ♗e3 ♖b8∓ 31. f4 ♖fe8 32. ♗c2 ♖b2 33. ♖he1 d4! 34. cd4 cd4 35. ♗d4** [35. ♗f2 ♖e1 △ d3] **♗b4 36. ♔c1** [36. ♗c3 ♖d8] **♖c2 37. ♔c2 ♗e1 38. ♗e5 ♗b4 39. ♖d1 ♗e6 40. ♔b2 ♖c8** **0 : 1** **[Kindermann]**

294. **C 18**

KAMSKY 2655 – JUSUPOV 2645
Linares 1993

1. e4 e6 2. d4 d5 3. ♘c3 ♗b4 4. e5 ♘e7 5. a3 ♗c3 6. bc3 c5 7. ♕g4 0–0 8. ♗d3 ♘bc6 9. ♕h5 ♘g6 10. ♘f3 ♕c7 11. ♗e3!? N [11. ♘g5 – 54/(275)] **c4 12. ♗g6 fg6 13. ♕g4** [△ h4-h5↑] **♕f7!** [△ ♕f5 ×c2, e4] **14. h4** [14. ♔d2!? △ 14... ♕f5 15. ♕g3] **♕f5 15. ♕f5 ♖f5 16. ♔e2** [16. ♘g5!? △ 16... h6 17. g4 ♖f8 18. ♘h3 ♗d7 19. ♔e2! ♖f7?! 20. ♘f4 ♘e7 (20... ♔h7 21. h5 g5 22. ♘h3± △ 23. f4, 23. ♗g5) 21. h5 g5 22. ♘g6!∞↑] **h6 17. g4 ♖f7 18. ♖ag1 ♗d7 19. ♘e1** [19. h5!? g5 20. ♘g5 hg5 21. ♗g5 ♖af8 22. f4 ♘e7 23. ♔e3 (△ h6) ♔h7 24. h6 g6 25. ♗f6 △ g5∓] **♖af8 20. f4 ♖f4?!** [20... ♗e8?! 21. ♘g2 (21. h5? gh5 22. ♖h5 ♖f4) ♖c7⇆] **21. ♗f4 ♖f4 22. ♖g3! ♘d8 23. ♘g2 ♖f8 24. ♔e3 ♗a4 25. ♖c1?!** [25. ♘e1 △ ♖f3, ♔d2±] **g5 26. hg5 hg5 27. ♖h3 ♘f7 28. ♖h5!?** [×g5] **♖c8 29. ♘e1 ♖c6 30. ♖b1 ♖c7 31. ♔d2 ♗e8 32. ♘f3 ♖e7⊕** [32... ♘h6? 33. ♖g5 g6 34. ♘h4 △ ♖f1-f6+–] **33. ♖bh1 ♖c7! 34. ♖h7 ♖c6 35. ♖1h5!?** [△ 36. ♘g5 ♘g5 37. ♖h8 △ ♖g5] **♖c8!□ 36. ♔e3 a5 37. ♖h1** [37. ♘g5? ♘g5 38. ♖h8 ♔f7 39. ♖g5 g6! 40. ♖h7 ♔g8 41. ♖b7 ♗f7 △ ♔g7=] **a4 38. ♖7h2 b5 39. ♖f2 ♖c7 40. ♖h5 ♖e7 41. ♖f1 ♖b7 42. ♔f2! ♖b6?!** [⌓ 42... ♖c7] **43. ♔g3 ♖a6 44. ♖g5!± ♘g5 45. ♘g5 ♗g6 46. ♖f2 ♖b6 47. ♔h4!** [△ ♘h3-f4] **♖a6 48. ♘h3 ♗e4?** [48... ♔h7!? 49. ♖f8! (49. ♔g5?! ♗e4 50. ♘f4⇆; 49. ♘f4!? ♗e4 50. ♘h5 ♖b6 51. ♖h2) ♗c2 50. ♘g5 ♔g6 51. ♖e8 b4 52. cb4 c3 53. ♖e6 ♖e6 54. ♘e6 ♗e4 55. ♘f4 △ ♘e2] **49. ♔h5! ♖a7□ 50. ♘g5 ♖e7 51. ♘e4 de4 52. ♔g6 e3 53. ♖e2 ♖f7 54. ♖e3 ♖f2 55. ♖e1!+– ♖c2 56. ♖b1 ♖c3 57. ♖b5 ♔f8 58. ♖b4 ♖a3 59. ♖c4 ♖a1 60. g5 a3 61. ♖a4 a2 62. ♖a7 ♔e8 63. ♔g7 ♔d8 64. g6 ♔e8 65. ♖a6 ♔e7 66. ♖a8! ♔d7 67. ♔g8 ♔e7 68. ♖a7 ♔e8 69. g7 ♖h1!□ 70. ♖a2 ♔e7 71. ♖a7 ♔e8 72. ♖a5 ♔e7 73. d5 ed5 74. ♖d5 ♖h2 75. ♖a5 ♖h1 76. ♖a7 ♔e8 77. e6 ♖h2 78. ♖f7 ♖h1 79. e7 ♖h2 80. ♖f8 ♔e7 81. ♖f3 ♔e8 82. ♖e3 ♔d7 83. ♖e4 1 : 0** **[Kamsky]**

295.* **C 18**

HERTNECK 2575 – UHLMANN 2500
Deutschland 1993

1. e4 e6 2. d4 d5 3. ♘c3 ♗b4 4. e5 ♘e7 5. a3 ♗c3 6. bc3 c5 7. ♕g4 0–0 8. ♗d3 ♘bc6 9. ♗g5!? ♕a5 10. ♘e2 cd4 N [10... ♕a4 – 54/275; 10... ♘g6!?] **11. f4 dc3** [11... ♘f5 12. 0–0 ♔h8 13. ♕h5 f6 14. ♗f5 (14. ef6 g6!?) ef5 15. ef6 gf6 16. ♕h6 (16. ♗f6 ♖f6 17. ♕e8 ♔g7 18. ♘g3 ♖f8 19. ♘h5 ♔g8 20. ♘f6 ♔g7=; 16. ♗h6 ♖g8 17. ♕f7 ♕d8 18. ♘d4 ♕e7 19. ♕d5 ♘d4 20. ♕d4 ♗e6 21. ♗g5 ♖g6∞) ♕d8= Luther 2465 – Hertneck 2575, Deutschland 1993] **12. 0–0 ♘g6! 13. ♕h5** [13. h4? f5 14. ef6 e5 15. ♗f5 ♕b6 16. ♔h2 ♗f5 17. ♕f5 ♘ce7∓; 13. ♖f3 ♘ce5!? 14. fe5 ♘e5 15. ♗h7 ♔h7 16. ♕h5 ♔g8 17. ♗f6! (V. Atlas; 17. ♖g3? f5! 18. ♗h6 ♕c5 19. ♔h1 ♘g4–+; 17. ♖h3? f6∓) ♘f3 18. gf3 gf6 19. ♔h1 ♕c5=] **♕c5** [13... ♕c7? 14. ♖f3 f5 (14... h6 15. ♗h6 gh6 16. ♕h6 ♘ce7 17. ♘g3+–) 15. ef6 gf6 16. ♗h6±] **14. ♔h1 ♘ce7 15. ♖f3** [15. ♗f6?! gf6 16. ef6 ♖e8 (16... ♖d8!?) 17. ♖f3 e5 18. ♕h6 (18. fe5 ♘c6; 18. f5 ♘f5 19. ♗f5 ♗f5 20. ♖c3 ♕d6 21. ♕f5 e4∓) ♘f5 19. ♗f5 ♕f8 20. ♕f8 ♘f8 21. ♗c8 ♖ac8 22. fe5 ♖e5∓] **f6 16. ef6** [16. ♖h3? fg5 17. ♕h7 ♔f7 18. fg5 ♘f5 19. ♗f5 (19. g4 ♖h8 20. gf5 ef5 21. ♕g6 ♔g6 22. ♖h8 ♕f2∓) ef5 20. ♖h6 ♘e5 21. ♖f6 ♔e8 22. ♕g7 ♘g4!∓] **gf6 17. ♖h3 ♖f7 18. ♗f6! ♖f6** [18... e5? 19. ♗g6 ♘g6 20. ♕g6!+–] **19. ♕h7 ♔f8 20. ♖g3 ♕f2□**

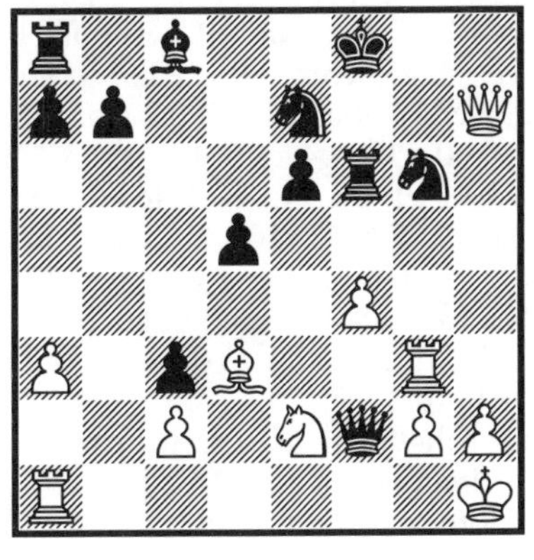

21. h4!? [21. ♘c3? ♕f4! (21... ♕d4 22. ♖d1!) 22. ♖f3 (22. ♗g6? ♕f1−+) ♕e5 23. ♖af1 (23. ♖f6 ♕f6 24. ♖f1 ♘f4∓) ♘f5 24. g4 ♘gh4∓; 21. ♕h6 ♔f7 22. ♕h7=] **♔e8** [21... ♘f4? 22. ♕h8+−; 21... ♖f4? 22. ♘f4 (22. ♗g6 ♘g6 23. ♘f4!+−) ♕g3 23. ♘g6 ♘g6 24. ♗g6 ♕f4 25. ♗d3+−; 21... ♘f5? 22. ♗f5 ef5 23. h5 ♘e7 24. ♕g7 ♔e8 25. ♕f6 ♕e2 26. h6+−; 21... ♖f7?! 22. ♕h6 ♔e8 23. ♖g6! ♘g6 24. ♗g6 ♔e7 (24... ♕e2 25. ♕g7±) 25. ♕g5! ♔f8 26. ♘g3!? ♖f4 27. ♖f1 ♕f1 28. ♘f1 ♖f1 29. ♔h2±] **22. ♗g6** [22. ♖g6 ♖f7!?] **♘g6** [22... ♖g6 23. ♖g6 ♕e2? 24. ♖g7+−] **23. ♖g6 ♖g6** [23... ♖f7? 24. ♕h5!; 23... ♖f8 24. ♖g7 ♕e2? 25. ♖c7+−] **24. ♕g6 ♔d7** [24... ♔f8 25. ♕f6 ♔g8 26. ♘d4±] **25. ♕g7 ♔d6** [25... ♔e8 26. ♘c3 ♕h4 (26... ♕f4 27. ♘d5! ♕h4 28. ♔g1 ed5 29. ♖f1+−) 27. ♔g1±] **26. ♕e5 ♔e7 27. ♘c3!** [27. h5] **♕h4 28. ♔g1 ♗d7** [28... ♔f8 29. f5 ef5 30. ♘d5 ♗d7 31. ♕d6 ♔g8 32. ♘f6+−] **29. ♕g7!+−** [29. ♘d5 ♔f7 30. ♘e3 ♖h8 31. ♖d1 ♗c6=∞] **♔d6** [29... ♔d8 30. ♕g8! ♗e8 (30... ♔c7 31. ♕a8 ♕f6 32. ♖b1) 31. ♕e6 ♕f4 32. ♖d1! d4 33. ♘e2 ♕f8 34. ♘d4 ♕c5 35. ♕e3! ♕b6 36. c4] **30. ♘e4! de4** [30... ♔c7 31. ♘c5; 30... ♔c6 31. ♕c3 ♔b6 32. ♖b1] **31. ♖d1 ♔c5 32. ♕d4! 1 : 0** **[Hertneck]**

296.* **C 18**

JUNEEV 2370 – SE. IVANOV 2500

Rossija 1993

1. e4 e6 2. d4 d5 3. ♘c3 ♗b4 4. e5 c5 5. a3 ♗c3 6. bc3 ♘e7 7. ♕g4 0−0 8. ♗d3 cd4!? N 9. ♕h5 [9. ♘f3 f5 10. ef6 ♖f6 11. ♗g5 e5∞; 9. ♗g5!? ♕c7 10. ♘e2; 9. cd4 ♘bc6 10. ♕h5 ♘f5 11. ♘f3 f6 12. 0−0 (12. g4? g6 13. ♕h3 ♘fd4∓) ♗d7 13. ♖b1 b6 14. ♖e1 fe5?! 15. ♘e5! ♘e5 (15... ♘cd4? 16. c3 ♘c6 17. ♘c6 ♗c6 18. ♖e6+−) 16. ♖e5 ♖c8 17. ♗d2 ♕f6 18. c3 ♗e8 19. ♕e2 ♗g6 20. f3! (20. ♖e1?! ♘d4! 21. cd4 ♗d3 22. ♕d3 ♕f2 23. ♔h1 ♖c2!!∓; 20. ♖e6 ♘d4! 21. cd4 ♗d3=) ♘h4? 21. ♖e1± Morozevič 2385 − Se. Ivanov 2470, Rossija (ch) 1992; 20... ♘d6; ⌓ 14... ♗e8 △ ♗g6⇆] **♘f5** [9... h6 10. ♗h6!?; 9... ♘g6] **10. ♘f3** [10. g4 ♕h4] **f6 11. g4 fe5! 12. ♘e5** [12. gf5 e4 13. ♖g1 (13. ♘g5 h6) ♖f5 14. ♕g4 ♕c7∓] **♕c7 13. cd4** [13. ♗f4!? ♘c6 14. gf5 (14. cd4 ♘e5 15. ♗e5 ♕c3 16. ♔e2 g6 17. ♕g5 ♘d4∓) ♘e5 15. 0−0 ♕f7□ 16. ♕f7 ♘f7 17. fe6 ♗e6 18. cd4 ♘d8=] **♕c3 14. ♔d1** [14. ♔e2 ♘d4 15. ♔d1; 14... ♕d4] **♕a1 15. gf5 ef5** [15... ♕d4? 16. fe6; 16. f6→] **16. ♖g1 ♕d4 17. ♖g7!** [17. ♗h6 ♕e5 18. ♗g7 ♕g7 19. ♖g7 ♔g7 20. ♕g5 ♔h8 21. ♕e7 ♘d7−+] **♔g7 18. ♕g5** [18. ♗h6 ♔h8 19. ♘f7 (19. ♗f8 ♕e5 20. ♕f7 ♘c6 △ ♗e6−+) ♔g8!? (19... ♖f7 20. ♕f7 ♕g4 21. ♗e2 ♕g1 22. ♔d2 ♘d7∞) 20. ♗f8 ♔f8−+; 18. ♕h6 ♔g8 19. ♕g5=] **♔h8 19. ♘f7!** [19. ♕h6 ♘d7 20. ♘g6 ♔g8 21. ♘e7 ♔f7 22. ♘f5 ♕g4−+] **♖f7 20. ♕d8 ♔g7 21. ♕g5 1/2 : 1/2** **[Se. Ivanov]**

297. **C 18**

J. POLGÁR 2595 – J. GDAŃSKI 2480

Budapest (zt - play off) 1993

1. e4 e6 2. d4 d5 3. ♘c3 ♗b4 4. e5 ♘e7 5. a3 ♗c3 6. bc3 c5 7. ♕g4 ♕c7 8. ♗d3 c4 9. ♗e2 0−0 10. ♘f3 [10. f4!?] **♘bc6 11. ♗g5 N** [11. 0−0] **♕a5 12. ♔d2 f5 13. ♕h3** [13. ef6 e5; 13. ♕h5 ♗d7 △ ♗e8; 13. ♕g3 f4! △ ♘f5; 13. ♕h4!?] **♗d7 14. a4 ♘c8?** [14... f4!] **15. ♕g3 ♔h8** [15... ♘b6 16. ♗f6 ♖f7 17. ♘g5] **16. h4 ♘b6 17. h5 ♘a4** [17... f4 18. ♕g4 ♘a4 19. ♖a4 ♕a4 20. h6 g6 21. ♗f6]

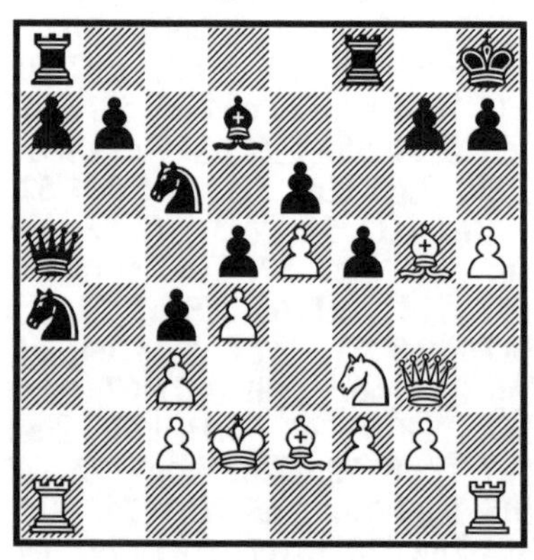

18. ♖a4! ♕a4 19. h6 g6 20. ♗f6 ♖f6□ [20... ♔g8 21. ♕g6! hg6 22. h7 ♔f7

23. h8♕ ♖h8 24. ♘g5 ♔e8 25. ♖h8#] **21. ef6 ♔g8** [21... ♖f8 22. ♕d6; 21... ♕a3 22. ♕c7] **22. ♕c7 ♘b4** [22... ♘d8 23. ♘e5] **23. cb4 ♕b4 24. ♔e3 g5** [24... ♕c3 25. ♔f4] **25. ♘g5** [25... ♕c3 26. ♗d3+−] **1 : 0** **[J. Polgár]**

298. **C 18**

VÖKLER 2335 – ĖJNGORN 2575

Cuxhaven 1993

1. e4 e6 2. d4 d5 3. ♘c3 ♗b4 4. e5 ♘e7 5. a3 ♗c3 6. bc3 c5 7. ♕g4 ♕c7 8. ♕g7 ♖g8 9. ♕h7 cd4 10. ♘e2 ♘bc6 11. f4 dc3 12. ♕d3 d4 13. ♘g3 ♗d7 14. ♗e2 N [14. ♖b1 – 56/317] **♘f5 15. ♘e4?!** [15. ♖b1; 15. 0–0] **♖g2 16. ♗f3** [16. ♘f6 ♔e7 17. ♗f3 (17. ♕f5? ef5 18. ♘d5 ♔d8∓) ♖g6 △ ♘e5] **♖g6 17. ♖b1 ♘e5 18. fe5 ♕e5 19. ♔d1 ♗c6 20. ♖e1** [20. ♘g5!? ♖d8 21. ♖e1] **♕h2?** [20... ♖d8! *a)* 21. ♘d6 ♕d6 22. ♕f5 d3 23. ♗c6 ♕c6−+; *b)* 21. ♗g5 ♗e4 22. ♗e4 (22. ♖e4 ♕h2 23. ♗d8 ♖g1 24. ♖e1 ♘e3 25. ♕e3 de3 26. ♗e2 ♖e1 27. ♔e1 ♕g1−+; 22. ♗d8 ♘e3 23. ♖e3 ♖g1−+) ♖g5! 23. ♗c6 bc6 24. ♖e5 ♘e3 25. ♔e2 ♖e5−+; *c)* 21. ♘g5 ♘e3?? 22. ♗e3 de3 23. ♕d8+−; 21... ♕f6∓] **21. ♘g5 ♘e3?!** [21... ♗f3 22. ♘f3 (22. ♕f3 d3) ♕h5] **22. ♗e3 de3 23. ♗c6 bc6 24. ♘f3** [24. ♘f7!? ♕d2 25. ♕d2 cd2 (25... ed2 26. ♖f1) 26. ♘d6! (26. ♖f1 ♖g2−+) ♔d7 27. ♖b7 ♔d6 28. ♖e3∓] **♕g2** [24... e2 25. ♖e2 (25. ♕e2 ♕d6 26. ♕d3 ♕a3∞; 26... ♕c5∞) ♕h3 (25... ♕f4? 26. ♕e3? ♖d8 27. ♔c1 ♕f3−+; 26. ♖b4!) 26. ♖h2! (26. ♔c1? ♕f3−+; 26. ♕c3 ♖g1−+) ♖g1 27. ♔e2! (27. ♘g1 ♕h2) ♖g2 28. ♖g2 ♕g2 29. ♔e3±; 24... ♕h3 25. ♕e4 (25. ♕e3 ♖d8 26. ♔c1 ♖g3) e2 26. ♔e2! ♖g2 27. ♔d3±; 24... ♕f4 25. ♕e3 ♕d6 26. ♔e2 (26. ♕d3 ♕c5∞) ♖g2 27. ♔f1 ♖c2 (27... ♕g3 28. ♖e2±) 28. ♖bd1 ♕g3 29. ♖e2∞; 24... ♕h5 25. ♕e4 e2 (25... ♖d8 26. ♔c1 △ 26... e2? 27. ♕c6 ♔f8 28. ♕c3) 26. ♔e2 (26. ♕e2 ♖d8 27. ♔c1 ♖g3) ♖g2 27. ♔d3? ♖d8 28. ♔c3 ♕c5−+; 27. ♔e3∞; 24... ♕g3!? 25. ♕e3 (25. ♕e4 ♕d6) ♖d8 26. ♔e2 (26. ♔c1 ♖f6 27. ♖f1 ♕h3) ♕g2 27. ♕f2 ♕g4∞] **25. ♕e2 ♖d8 26. ♔c1 ♖d2 27. ♕g2 ♖gg2 28. ♖e3 ♖c2 29. ♔d1 ♔e7 30. ♖b3** **1/2 : 1/2** **[Ėjngorn, Bogdanov]**

299. !N **C 24**

KASPAROV 2805 – BAREEV 2670

Linares 1993

1. e4 e5 2. ♗c4 ♘f6 3. d3 c6 4. ♘f3 d5 5. ♗b3 a5! N [5... ♘bd7 – 23/233; 5... ♗d6 – 20/260; 5... ♗b4 – 41/356] **6. ♘c3** [6. a3 a4 7. ♗a2 ♗d6 8. ♘c3 ♗e6 9. ♘g5∞ ×♗a2; 6. a4 ♗d6 (6... ♗b4!? 7. c3 ♗d6∞) 7. ♘c3 d4 8. ♘e2 ♘a6⇆] **♗b4** [6... d4 7. ♘e5 dc3 8. ♘f7] **7. a3 ♗c3 8. bc3 ♘bd7** [8... ♗g4?! 9. ed5 ♘d5 10. h3 ♘c3 11. ♗f7!; 8... ♕c7!?] **9. ed5 ♘d5!** [9... cd5 10. 0–0 0–0 11. ♖e1 e4 (11... ♕c7? 12. ♘e5! ♘e5 13. ♗f4; 11... a4 12. ♗a2 ♖e8 13. ♗g5→) 12. ♘d4 ♘c5 13. ♗g5 ♗e6 14. ♗a2 h6 15. ♗h4] **10. 0–0 0–0** [10... a4? 11. ♗d5 cd5 12. ♘e5]

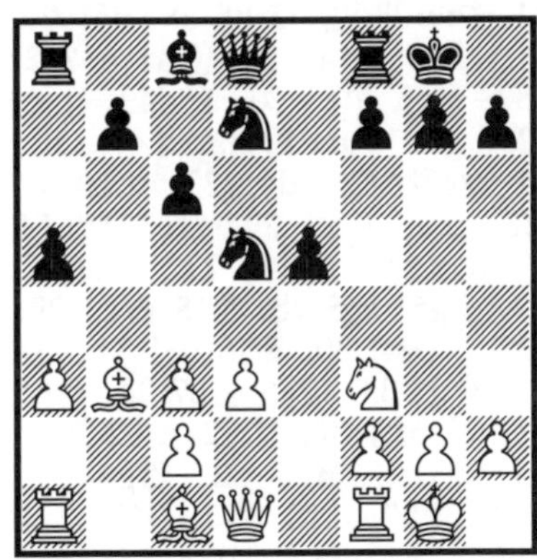

11. ♖e1! ♖e8 [11... ♘c3 12. ♕d2 ♘b5 13. ♗b2 ♘c5 14. ♗a2 e4 15. ♘g5! *a)* 15... ♘a4 16. ♘f7 (16. ♗e5) ♖f7 17. ♕f4 ♕f8 (17... ♘d6 18. ♗f7 ♘f7 19. ♕e4+−) 18. ♖e4 ♗e6 (18... ♘c5 19. ♕f7+−) 19. ♗e6 ♘b2 20. ♕e5+−; *b)* 15... ed3 *b1)* 16. a4?! ♘d6 (16... ♘d4? 17. ♘f7 ♖f7 18. ♗d4 ♘e6 19. ♕d3 ♘d4 20. ♕d4+−) 17. ♖e5 ♘e6!∞ 18. ♘h7!? △ 18... ♔h7 19. ♖h5 ♔g8 (19... ♔g6? 20. ♗g7!+−) 20. ♕d3 f5 21. ♕g3 ♕e7 22. ♕g6 ♖f6 23. ♕h7 ♔f7 24. ♖e1 ♖g6 25. ♗a3!+−; *b2)* 16. ♖e5! ♘e6 17. ♘h7! ♖e8! (17... ♔h7 18. ♖h5 ♔g8 19. ♗e6 fe6 20. ♖h8!

♔f7 21. ♕f4 ♔e7 22. ♕g5 ♔d7 23. ♕g7+−) 18. ♘g5! (18. ♖ae1? ♔h7 19. ♖h5 ♔g6 20. ♗g7 ♘f4! 21. ♗f7! ♔g7 22. ♖e8 ♕f6∓; 18. ♖h5? ♘bd4 △ 19. ♕d3? ♘f4!) dc2 19. ♕c2 ♘g5 20. ♖d1 ♗d7 21. ♖e8 ♕e8 22. ♕g6+−] **12. c4!** [12. ♗d2 f6!∞] **♘e7** [12... ♘c7? 13. ♗b2 f6 14. c5 ♔h8 15. d4; 12... a4!? 13. cd5 ab3 14. dc6 bc2 15. ♕c2 bc6 16. ♗b2!] **13. ♘g5! h6 14. ♘e4 a4** [14... ♘f5 15. c5 ♕e7 16. ♗b2 ♘c5 17. ♘c5 ♕c5 18. ♕h5 ♗e6 19. ♗e6 fe6 20. ♖ac1] **15. ♗a2 c5 16. ♘d6 ♖f8 17. c3! ♘g6 18. ♗b1!** [18. d4?! ♖a6!∞] **♘f6 19. ♘c8 ♕c8 20. ♕f3** [20. ♗c2!? ♕c6 21. ♖b1] **♖e8 21. ♗c2** [21. g3!? e4 22. de4 ♘e5 23. ♕e2 ♕g4!⩲] **♘h4! 22. ♕g3?** [22. ♕e2 ♕c6 23. f3 g5!? (23... ♘h5?! 24. ♕e4 ♕f6 25. d4!↑) 24. ♖f1!⩲] **g5! 23. d4** [23. ♗g5?? ♘f5−+; 23. f3!? ♘h5 24. ♕g4 ♘f4!∞ △ 25. ♗f4 ef4 26. ♕c8 ♖ac8 27. ♗a4 ♖e1 28. ♖e1 ♖a8 29. ♖e8 ♖e8 30. ♗e8 ♔f8=] **♘f5! 24. ♕h3?** [24. ♗f5 ♕f5 25. de5 ♖ad8→ △ 26. ♗g5? ♘h5!; 24. ♕f3 e4 25. ♕d1 cd4 26. cd4 ♕c4 27. ♗b2 b5 28. d5! ♘d5 29. ♖c1=/∞ △ 29... ♕a2 30. ♗a1 e3? 31. fe3 ♘fe3 32. ♖e3 ♘e3 33. ♕d4+−] **e4! 25. f3□** [25. g3? ♘d4!] **ef3?** [⌓ 25... cd4! 26. fe4 ♕c5! 27. cd4 (27. ♔h1 d3!−+) ♕d4 28. ♗e3 ♘e3 29. ♕e3 ♕c4∓] **26. ♖e8** [26. ♗g5? ♘d4! 27. ♕h6 f2!−+] **♕e8 27. ♗g5! hg5 28. ♕f5 ♕e3 29. ♔h1 fg2?!** [29... cd4! 30. ♕f6 d3! 31. ♗d3 fg2 32. ♔g2 ♕d3 33. ♕g5 ♔h7 34. ♕h5 ♔g7 35. ♖g1 ♖a6⩲] **30. ♔g2 ♕e2 31. ♔g1! ♘g4?** [⌓ 31... ♕g4 32. ♕g4 ♘g4 33. ♖e1] **32. ♕h7 ♔f8 33. ♖f1!+− f6 34. ♗g6** [34... ♕e6 35. h3!] **1 : 0**
[Kasparov]

300. **C 41**

DORFMAN 2580 − V. IKONNIKOV 2485
Cannes 1993

1. d4 ♘f6 2. ♘f3 d6 3. ♘c3 ♘bd7 4. e4 e5 5. g3 ♗e7 [5... b6? 6. ♗b5] **6. ♗g2 c6 7. a4 0−0 8. 0−0 N** [8. a5?! ♕c7 − 16/200; 8... ♖b8 △ b5] **♖e8 9. ♖e1 ♗f8 10. h3** [10. ♗e3!? (△ ♘d2) ♘g4 11. ♗g5 f6 (11... ♗e7? 12. ♗c1 ♗f8 13. h3 ♘gf6 14. ♗e3) 12. ♗c1 g6 13. h3 ♘h6 14. ♗e3 ♘f7] **a5 11. ♗e3** [△ ♘d2-c4] **ed4 12. ♗d4** [12. ♘d4?! ♘c5] **♕c7** [12... b6? 13. e5 de5 14. ♘e5 ♘e5 15. ♗e5 ♕d1 16. ♖ad1±] **13. ♘d2 b6** [13... ♘c5 14. f4 △ ♗c5] **14. f4** [14. g4? h6; 14. ♘c4?! ♗a6 15. b3 ♗c4 16. bc4 g6] **♗b7** [14... ♗a6 15. ♘f3 △ ♗f2, ♘d4] **15. ♕f3** [15. ♘e2 d5 16. e5 c5⇆; 15. ♘c4 ♗a6⇆] **♖ab8 16. ♕f2 ♗a8** [16... ♗a6 17. ♘f3 △ e5] **17. ♘c4! ♘e4** [17... b5 18. ab5 cb5 19. ♘a5 b4 20. ♘d5 ♘d5 21. ed5 △ ♘c6±; 17... d5 18. ed5 cd5 19. ♘e3±; 17... g6!?] **18. ♖e4 ♖e4 19. ♘e4 c5** [19... d5 20. ♘b6!±] **20. ♗c3 d5 21. ♘g5** [21. ♘ed2 d4 (21... dc4 22. ♗a8 ♖a8 23. ♘c4±) 22. ♗a5 ba5 23. ♗a8 ♖a8 24. ♕f3⩲; 24. ♖e1±] **h6** [21... dc4? 22. ♗a8 ♖a8 23. ♕f3 △ ♕h5+−] **22. ♘f7** [22. ♘e3 d4 23. ♗a8 dc3 24. ♗d5 hg5 25. fg5 ♘e5 26. bc3 c4! △ ♗c5] **♔f7** [22... dc4? 23. ♗a8 ♖a8 24. ♕f3 △ ♕d5±] **23. ♗e5** [23. ♘e5? ♔g8] **♘e5 24. ♘e5 ♔g8 25. c4** [25. ♖d1? c4] **♗d6** [25... dc4 26. ♗a8 ♖a8 27. ♕e2±; 25... d4 26. ♗a8 ♖a8 27. ♕f3±] **26. cd5 ♗e5 27. fe5 ♕e5 28. ♖e1 ♕d6?** [28... ♕d4 29. ♕d4 cd4 30. ♖d1 b5 *a)* 31. ab5 ♖b5=; *b)* 31. ♖d4 ba4 32. ♖a4 ♖b2 33. ♖a5 ♗b7=; *c)* 31. b3!? △ 31... ba4 32. ba4 ♖b4 33. d6 ♗g2 34. d7 ♖b8 35. ♖d4 ♖d8 36. ♔g2+−] **29. ♖e6 ♕d7 30. ♕f4!+−** [30. ♕f5? ♖e8=] **♖f8 31. ♕e4** [31. ♕e5? ♕a4 △ ♕d4] **♕f7** [31... ♖f6 32. ♖f6 gf6 33. ♕g6 ♕g7 34. ♕g7 ♔g7 35. d6; 31... ♖d8 32. ♖e7] **32. ♖b6 ♖d8 33. ♕e5 ♗b7** [33... ♗d5 34. ♖b8!] **34. ♖e6 ♗c8 35. ♖e7 ♕f6** [35... ♕f8 36. d6; 35... ♕g6 36. ♗e4 ♕g5 37. ♖e8] **36. ♕f6 gf6 37. ♖c7 ♗d7 38. b3 ♔f8 39. ♗f1 ♔e8 40. ♖c5 ♖b8 41. ♗c4 ♖a8 42. d6** [42... ♗h3 43. ♖h5] **1 : 0** **[Dorfman]**

301.* **C 41**

JUDASIN 2610 − ADAMS 2630
Dos Hermanas 1993

1. e4 e5 2. ♘f3 d6 3. ♗c4 ♗e7 4. d4 ed4 [RR 4... ♘d7 5. ♘c3 ♘gf6 6. 0−0 0−0 7. ♖e1 c6 8. a4 b6 9. ♗g5!? N (9. ♕e2 − 55/298) a6 10. ♗f6 ♗f6 11. d5 c5 (11... ♗b7 12. dc6 ♗c6 − 43/385) 12. ♘b1! g6

(12... ♕c7 13. c3 ♖b8 14. ♕e2 ♕b7 15. ♘a3⩲; 12... ♗g5!?) 13. ♘bd2 ♗g7 14. c3 f5 15. b4 (Harlov 2580 – A. N. Pančenko 2460, Rostov na Donu (open) 1993) g5! 16. ♘b3 f4 17. ♘fd2∞ Harlov] **5. ♘d4 ♘f6 6. ♘c3 0–0 7. 0–0 a6!? N** [7... ♘e4 – 6/303] **8. a4 ♘e4!** [8... ♘c6 9. ♖e1⩲] **9. ♘e4 d5 10. ♗d3 de4 11. ♗e4 ♗f6** [11... ♘d7 12. c3 △ ♗c2, ♕d3, ♗h6⩲↑] **12. ♗e3** [12. c3 ♗d4 △ ♘c6=] **♘d7!** [12... c5? 13. ♘b3 ♗b2 14. ♖b1→《] **13. c3** [↑《, ⊞] **♖e8** [△ 14... ♘e5, 14... ♘c5] **14. ♕c2 g6 15. ♖fe1!?** [15. ♖ad1!? △ 15... ♕e7 16. ♖fe1! ♕f8 17. h3⩲↻] **♗g7! 16. ♖ad1 c5!** [16... ♕h4 17. g3!±; 16... c6 17. ♗f4↑] **17. ♘e2!?** [17. ♘f3 ♕c7 △ ♘f6, c4, ♗f5⇆; 17. ♘b3 ♕c7⩲ △ c4!?, ♘f6, ♗f5⇆] **♕c7!** [17... ♕e7 18. ♘g3 △ ♗f3, ♘e4→ ×c5, d6, f6] **18. ♘f4** [18. ♗f4!? ♘e5!? 19. ♗g3 △ ♘f4⩲↑] **♘f6□ 19. ♘d5** [19. ♗f3?! ♗f5 (19... ♗g4 20. ♕e2 ♗f3=; 19... ♘g4=) 20. ♕b3 ♖e7=] **♘d5 20. ♖d5** [20. ♗d5 ♗f5 21. ♕b3 ♖e7 (21... ♗e4 22. ♗c5!) 22. ♗g5 ♖d7!?⩲ △ 23. ♗f7? ♖f7 24. ♖e7 c4!; 20... ♗e6!=] **b6! 21. ♖dd1** [21. ♖c5? bc5 22. ♗a8 ♗f5–+] **♖b8** [21... ♗b7 22. ♗b7 ♕b7 23. a5⩲] **22. h3 ♗e6⩲ 23. ♗d5** [↑×《] **♗f5** [⌓ 23... ♗d5 24. ♖d5 ♖bd8⩲] **24. ♕e2! b5** [24... a5 25. ♕c4 △ b4↑] **25. ab5 ab5 26. ♕f3!** [△ 27. ♗f4, 27. g4↑] **♖b6!** [26... ♗e6? 27. ♗f4 ♗d5 28. ♗c7 ♗f3 29. ♗b8+–; 26... ♖bd8 27. ♗g5!±] **27. b4!** [27. ♗f4 ♖e1 28. ♖e1 ♕d7 △ ♗e6=] **♗f8□** [27... ♗c3? 28. ♗f4 ♖e1 (28... ♗e5 29. ♕e3!+–) 29. ♖e1 ♕d7 30. ♕c3 ♕d5 31. ♖e8#] **28. bc5** [28. g4?! ♗e6=; 28. ♗f4?! ♖e1 29. ♖e1 ♕d7 30. ♗e3 ♖d6] **♗c5 29. ♗f7!** [29. g4 ♗e6=] **♔f7□ 30. ♕d5 ♗e6□ 31. ♕c5 ♕c5 32. ♗c5⩲⊥ ♖c6⊕** [⇆ ×c3, △ b4] **33. ♗b4⊕ ♖c7!** [×⇔a7-h7] **34. ♖d4** [→♔] **♗d7! 35. ♖ed1** [35. ♖e3!? △ 35... ♖e3 36. fe3 δe; 35. ♖f4!? ♔g7 36. ♖e8 ♗e8 37. ♗f8 ♔g8 38. ♗h6 ♗f7⩲; 38... ♖f7⩲] **♗e6!** [△ ♖c4] **36. ♖1d3** [36. g4 h5 37. ♖f4 ♔g7 38. ♗d6 ♖c4!⩲] **h5! 37. ♖f3 ♔g7 38. ♖e3 ♗f7 39. ♖e8** [39. ♔f1!?] **♗e8 40. f3 ♗f7 41. ♔f2 ♗c4 42. g4 hg4 43. hg4** [43. fg4 g5⩲] **♖f7?** [43... g5 44. ♗d6 ♖c6 45. ♗e5 ♔g6 46. ♖d7 ♖e6⩲] **44. ♔g3?** [44. f4! △ ♔g3-h4-g5±] **g5⩲ 45. ♗d6 ♗e2 46. f4 gf4 47. ♗f4 ♔h7 48. ♖d2 ♖e7 49. g5 ♖e6 50. ♖d8 ♔g6⩲ 1/2 : 1/2**
[Judasin]

302.* !N C 42**

DVOJRIS 2570 –
SCHWARTZMAN 2340
Groningen (open) 1992

1. e4 e5 2. ♘f3 ♘f6 3. ♘e5 [RR 3. ♗c4 ♘e4 4. ♘c3 ♘c3 5. dc3 f6 6. ♘h4 g6 7. f4 ♕e7 8. f5 c6!? N (8... ♕g7 – 55/(300)) 9. fg6 d5 10. ♕h5 ♔d8□ 11. 0–0 ♕g7 (11... ♕c5? 12. ♔h1 ♕c4 13. ♖f6 ♗e7 14. ♗g5 ♘d7 15. g7 ♖g8 16. ♕f7+–) 12. ♖f6! hg6 (12... ♗e7 13. ♖f7 hg6 14. ♖g7 gh5 15. ♘g6 ♗f6 16. ♖f7 ♖g8 17. ♖f6 ♘d7 18. ♖e6±) 13. ♕e5 ♗c5 (13... ♖h4? 14. ♗g5+–) 14. ♔h1 ♘d7 15. ♖f8! ♕f8 (15... ♗f8 16. ♗g5+–) 16. ♗g5 ♗e7 17. ♗e7 (I. Kuznecov – Dement'ev, Rossija 1992) ♔e8! 18. ♕d4 c5 (18... ♖h4? 19. ♗h4+–) 19. ♕d5 ♕e7 20. ♘g6 ♖h2 21. ♔h2 ♕h7 22. ♔g1 ♕g6∞ I. Kuznecov] **d6 4. ♘f3** [RR 4. ♘c4 ♘e4 5. d4 d5 6. ♘e3 ♕f6 7. ♕e2 ♗e6 8. c3 c6! N (8... ♘c6 – 50/330) 9. g3 ♘d7 10. ♗g2 ♕g6 11. ♘d2 f5 12. 0–0 ♗d6 13. ♘f5 ♕f5 14. ♘e4 de4 15. ♗e4 ♕f6 16. d5 cd5 17. ♗d5 ♗e5 18. ♗b7 ♖b8 19. ♗g2 0–0 20. ♗e3 ♘b6 21. ♖fe1 ♗c4∓ Jansa 2455 – Forintos 2465, Münster 1992] **♘e4 5. d4** [RR 5. d3 ♘f6 6. d4 ♗e7 7. ♗d3 ♗g4 8. 0–0 0–0 9. ♖e1 c5!? N (9... ♘c6) 10. h3 (10. dc5 dc5 11. ♗g5 ♘c6 12. h3 ♗h5 13. ♘bd2 ♖e8=) ♗h5 11. dc5 (11. d5!? ♘bd7 12. ♘c3 ♘e5 13. ♗e2 ♗f3 14. ♗f3 ♘e8!? 15. ♗e2 f5∞) dc5 12. g4 ♗g6 13. ♗g6 hg6 14. ♕d8 ♗d8 15. ♗f4 ♗a5! (15... ♘bd7? 16. g5 △ ♗d6+–) 16. c3 ♖d8 17. ♘bd2 ♘c6 18. ♘e4 (18. ♘c4!? ♘d5 19. ♗d6 b5 20. ♘a5 ♖d6 21. ♘b7 ♖f6 22. ♘e5 ♘e5 23. ♖e5 ♘f4⇆ Raeckij) ♘e4 19. ♖e4 ♖d5= Dolmatov 2610 – Raeckij 2460, Podol'sk 1992] **d5 6. ♗d3 ♘c6 7. 0–0 ♗g4 8. c4 ♘f6 9. cd5 ♗f3 10. ♕f3 ♕d5 11. ♕d5!? N** [11. ♕e2 – 44/376] **♘d5 12. ♘c3 0-0-0 13. ♗c4 ♘ce7** [⌓ 13... ♘f6 14. ♗f7 ♘d4⩲] **14. ♗d2 ♘c3 15. bc3**

♘d5 16. ♖fe1± c6 17. ♗b3 ♗a3 18. c4 ♘f6 19. ♗c3 ♖he8 20. f3?! [⌓ 20. ♗c2] **♖e1 21. ♖e1 ♖e8 22. ♖d1?!** [⌓ 22. ♖e8] **♖e3** [22... ♘h5!? △ ♘f4⇆] **23. ♗e1 ♘e8 24. ♔f2 ♖e7 25. ♗c3 ♘d6 26. ♖e1 ♖e1 27. ♔e1 f6 28. ♔d2 ♔d7 29. ♔d3 ♔e7?** [29... c5! (Dvojris) 30. f4 b6 31. ♗d1±]

30. c5! [×♗a3] **♘b5 31. ♗d2 b6 32. ♗g8! bc5 33. dc5 ♗c5** [33... h6 34. ♔c4±] **34. ♗h7 ♘d6 35. h4** [△ h5, g4-g5] **♗f2 36. h5 ♗g3 37. ♗e3 a6 38. ♔d4 ♘b7□ 39. ♔c4 ♔d6 40. ♗d2!** [×⫽a3-f8] **♘d8 41. ♗b4 ♔e5 42. ♗g8!** [×♘d8] **♗f4 43. ♔d3 ♘b7 44. ♗f8 ♗h6 45. g3!** [△ f4 ×♗h6] **♔f5 46. ♗c4! a5 47. a4 ♗c1□** [47... ♘d8 48. ♗d6 ♘b7 (48... ♗c1 49. g4 ♔g5 50. ♗e7 ♘b7 51. ♗a6+−) 49. g4 (49. ♗e7 ♗c1 50. f4+−) ♔g5 50. ♗e7+−] **48. ♗g7 ♘c5 49. ♔c2 ♗e3 50. ♗f7!+− ♘e6 51. h6 ♘g5 52. ♗g8 ♔g6 53. f4 1 : 0**
[Schwartzman]

303. C 42

KAMSKY 2655 − BAREEV 2670
Linares 1993

1. e4 e5 2. ♘f3 ♘f6 3. ♘e5 d6 4. ♘f3 ♘e4 5. d4 d5 6. ♗d3 ♗d6 7. 0−0 0−0 8. c4 c6 9. ♘c3 ♘c3 10. bc3 dc4 11. ♗c4 ♗g4 12. ♕d3 ♘d7 13. ♘g5 ♘f6 14. h3 ♗h5 15. f4 h6 16. ♘f3 N [16. g4 − 48/416] **♗f3 17. ♖f3 ♖e8 18. ♗e3** [△ ♖af1, g4-g5↑≫] **♗c7!= 19. ♖af1 ♕d6 20. ♗f2 ♖e4 21. ♗h4 ♖ae8 22. ♗f6 ♕f6 23. ♔h1 ♖e1 24. a4 h5 25. g3! a6** [25... ♖8e4 26. ♔g2 ♕e7=] **26. ♔g2 b5 27. ab5 cb5 28. ♗d5 ♖f1** [28... g6 29. h4=] **29. ♖f1 h4? 30. gh4 ♕h4 31. ♕f5 ♕e7?** [31... ♖e2 32. ♔f3! (32. ♔h1 ♕f6!∓) ♖e7 33. ♖g1? ♗f4 34. ♕c8 (34. ♕f4 ♕h5−+) ♔h7 35. ♗e4 g6 36. ♖g4 ♕h3 37. ♔f4 ♖e4 38. ♔e4 f5 39. ♔e5 fg4∓; 33. ♗b3!±] **32. ♖f3?** [32. ♖e1! ♕f8 (32... ♕e1 33. ♕f7+−) 33. ♕f7! ♕f7 34. ♖e8+−] **♖d8 33. ♗b3 ♖d6= 34. ♕c8** [34. ♖e3 ♕d7□ (34... ♕e3 35. ♕f7 ♔h7 36. ♕g8 ♔h6 37. ♕h8 ♔g6 38. f5! ♔f5 39. ♗c2+−) 35. ♕f7 ♕f7 36. ♖e8 ♔h7 37. ♗f7 ♖f6=] **♕d8 35. ♕f5 ♖f6 36. ♕e4 g6 37. f5 ♕d6 38. ♔f1 ♕h2 39. ♕g4 ♕b2** [39... ♔g7=] **40. ♗d5 ♕c1 41. ♔g2 ♕c2** [42. ♖f2 ♕c3 43. fg6 ♖f2 44. ♔f2 ♕d2=] **1/2 : 1/2**
[Bareev]

304.* C 42

IVANČUK 2710 − BAREEV 2670
Linares 1993

1. e4 e5 2. ♘f3 ♘f6 3. ♘e5 d6 4. ♘f3 ♘e4 5. d4 d5 6. ♗d3 ♗d6 7. 0−0 0−0 8. c4 c6 9. cd5 cd5 10. ♘c3 ♘c3 11. bc3 ♗g4 [11... ♘c6!? 12. ♘g5 g6 13. ♕f3; 12. ♖b1!?] **12. ♖b1 b6** [RR 12... ♘d7 13. h3 ♗h5 14. ♖b5 ♘b6 15. c4 ♗f3 16. ♕f3 dc4 17. ♗c2 ♕d7 18. a4 ♖ab8 19. ♗g5 ♘c8!? N (19... ♗c7 − 50/332) 20. ♕h5 (20. ♗f6 ♘e7) f5 21. ♕e2 ♘b6 22. ♖fb1 ♖be8 23. ♕f1 (23. ♕f3!? ♕e6 24. ♔f1 f4 25. a5 ♘c8 26. ♖b7 h6 27. d5 ♕e5 28. ♗h4 ♗c5±) ♕c6 24. ♗d1 (24. ♗f5? ♘d5 25. ♗g4 ♘c3∓) ♖e4 (24... ♗b8!? 25. a5 ♕g6 26. ab6 a6=) 25. ♗f3 (25. ♗c2 1/2 : 1/2 Wahls 2540 − Hába 2485, Deutschland 1993) ♘a4 26. ♗e4 fe4 27. ♖a5 ♗b8 28. ♖b7 ♕b7 29. ♕c4± Hába] **13. ♖b5 ♗c7 14. h3** [14. ♖e1!? a6 15. ♖b1 ♘d7 16. ♗a3 (16. ♗g5 ♘f6!=) ♖e8 17. ♗h7 ♔h7 18. ♖e8 ♕e8 19. ♘g5 ♔g6! 20. ♕g4 ♘f6 21. ♕h4 ♕e2 22. ♖f1! ♗h2?! 23. ♕h2 ♔g5 24. ♗e7!! ♕e7 25. f4 ♔f5 26. ♕h3 ♔g6 27. ♕h4! ♕e3 28. ♔h1! (28. ♔h2? ♔f5! 29. ♕g5 ♔e6 30. f5 ♔d7 31. ♕e3 ♘g4−+) ♘h5 29. ♕g5 ♔h7 30. ♕h5 ♔g8 31. ♕d5±; 22... ♖e8!∞] **a6 15. hg4 ab5 16. ♕c2 g6 17. ♗b5!? N** [17. ♗h6 − 54/281] **♕d6?** [17...

♘d7 18. ♗h6 (18. g5!?) ♖e8 (18... ♘f6 19. ♗f8 ♔f8 20. ♖e1!±) 19. ♗g5! (19. ♗c6 ♖a5 20. ♕b3 ♖e2! 21. ♗d5 ♘e5!∞; 19. c4 ♖c8!∞; 19. ♕b3 ♖e6! 20. c4!? ♘f6 21. cd5 ♖e7∞) f6 (19... ♕c8 20. ♕b3!±) 20. ♗d2!± △ 21. ♕b3, △ 21. ♗c6 ♖a5 22. c4!; 17... ♕c8! 18. ♗h6 (18. ♕b3 ♕b7 19. ♗h6 ♖c8 20. ♖e1 ♗d6∞; 18. ♖e1 ♘d7! 19. ♖e7 ♘f6 20. ♗h6 ♗d6 21. ♗f8 ♔f8=) ♖d8 19. ♗g5 ♖d6 *a)* 20. c4 ♘c6?! 21. ♗f4 ♘a5 (21... ♘a7 22. ♗d6 ♗d6⩲) 22. ♗d6 ♗d6 23. ♖e1 ♕c7!⩲; 20... ♘d7!?∞ △ 21. cd5 ♗d8!; *b)* 20. ♘e5 ♖a7! (20... f6? 21. ♘g6+−) 21. f4 ♗d8!∞] **18. g3!** [△ ♗f4, ♔g2, ♖h1; 18. ♗h6 ♖c8 19. ♘e5 f6∞] **♖a7** [18... ♘d7 19. ♗f4 ♕f6 20. ♗d7 ♗f4 21. gf4 ♕f4 22. ♘e5±; 18... ♘c6 19. ♔g2 △ ♖h1; 18... ♕e6!? 19. g5 ♘c6 (19... ♕e4? 20. ♕e4 de4 21. ♘d2±) 20. ♖e1 ♕d7 21. c4!↑] **19. ♖e1 ♘d7?** [19... ♘c6□] **20. g5! ♖d8 21. a4 ♘b8** [21... ♘f8 22. ♕b3+−] **22. ♘h2!+− ♕f8 23. ♘g4 ♗d6 24. ♔g2 ♔h8 25. ♖h1 ♕g7 26. ♘f6 h5 27. ♕d1 1 : 0** **[Ivančuk]**

305. **C 42**

L. BO HANSEN 2545 – DANIELSEN 2445

Valby 1993

1. e4 e5 2. ♘f3 ♘f6 3. ♘e5 d6 4. ♘f3 ♘e4 5. d4 d5 6. ♗d3 ♗d6 7. 0–0 0–0 8. c4 c6 9. cd5 cd5 10. ♘c3 ♘c3 11. bc3 ♗g4 12. ♖b1 b6 13. ♖b5 ♗c7 14. h3 a6 15. hg4 ab5 16. ♕c2 g6 17. ♗b5 ♕d6 18. g3 ♘c6!? N 19. ♔g2 ♖fe8? [19... f5!? 20. gf5 (20. g5?! f4!⇆ ×♔g2) ♖f5 *a)* 21. ♘g5?! ♖af8 22. f4 ♘a7 (22... ♖g5 23. ♗c6 ♕c6 24. fg5 ♖f1 25. ♔f1 ♗g3 26. ♔g2=) 23. ♗d3 ♖g5 24. fg5 ♕g3 25. ♔h1 ♖f1 26. ♗f1 △ ♕g2∞; *b)* 21. ♘h4! ♖f7 22. f4=∞] **20. ♖h1! ♖e4 21. ♕d2! ♖g4 22. ♗c6!?** [22. ♕h6! ♖g3 *a)* 23. fg3? ♕g3 24. ♔f1 ♕f3 25. ♔g1 ♖a2! 26. ♕h7 ♔f8 27. ♕h8 ♔e7 28. ♗g5 ♔d7 29. ♕h3 (29. ♗c6 ♔c6 30. ♕e8 ♔b7−+) ♕h3 30. ♖h3 ♖b2−+; *b)* 23. ♔f1! ♖f3 24. ♕h7 ♔f8 25. ♕h8 ♔e7 26. ♗g5! *b1)* 26... f6 27. ♖h7 ♔e6 28. ♕a8 *b11)* 28... ♖f2 29. ♔e1! (E. P. Hansen) ♘e7! (29... fg5 30. ♕g8 ♔f5 31. ♖f7 ♔g4 32. ♖f2+−) 30. ♕f8! ♖f3 31. ♗h4! ♖e3 (31... g5 32. ♗e2!) 32. ♔d1 ♔f5 (32... g5 33. ♗g5!) 33. ♗f2! ♖f3 (33... ♖e6 34. ♗d3 ♔g4 35. ♕h6+−→) 34. ♖e7 ♖f2 35. ♗d3 ♔g5 36. ♕f7! f5 37. ♖e6+−; *b12)* 28... fg5 29. ♕c8 (29. ♕g8 ♔f5 30. ♖f7 ♔e4 31. ♕e8 ♘e5 32. de5 ♕c5□ 33. ♖f3 ♔f3 34. ♗e2 ♔f4 35. e6 ♗d6 36. ♕g6 ♗e7±) ♔f6 30. ♖c7 ♖f2 (30... ♘d8 31. ♖d7) 31. ♔f2 ♕h2 32. ♔e1 ♕g3 33. ♔d2 ♕f4 34. ♔d1! (E. P. Hansen) ♕f3 35. ♗e2 ♕h1 36. ♔d2+−; *b2)* 26... ♔d7 27. ♕a8 (△ ♖h8) ♖f2 (27... ♖c3 28. ♖h8+−→) 28. ♔f2 ♕g3 29. ♔e2 ♕g2 (29... ♕g4 30. ♔d2 ♕g5 31. ♔d1!+−) 30. ♔d3 ♕e4 31. ♔d2 ♕g2 32. ♔c1! ♕h1 33. ♔b2 ♕h2 (33... ♕g2 34. ♔b3 ♕g5 35. ♕c6 ♔c8□ 36. ♕a8 ♗b8 37. ♗a6+−) 34. ♔b3 ♕d6 35. ♕b7!⊙ f6 (35... ♕e6 36. ♗f4+−; 35... f5 36. ♗h6! f4 37. ♗g7! △ ♗e5+−) 36. ♗f4! ♕f4 37. ♕c6 ♔c8 (37... ♔e7 38. ♕e8 ♔d6 39. ♕d7#) 38. ♕e8 ♗d8 (38... ♔b7 39. ♗c6+−) 39. ♕d7+−] **♕c6?** [22... ♖g3!□ 23. ♔f1! (23. fg3 ♕g3 24. ♔f1 ♕f3 25. ♔g1□ ♕g3 26. ♕g2 ♕e1=) ♕c6 24. fg3 ♕c4 25. ♕e2□ ♕e2 26. ♔e2 ♖a2 27. ♔d3 ♗g3 28. ♗g5!±⊥] **23. ♕h6 ♖a2** [23... ♖e8 24. ♕h7 ♔f8 25. ♗a3 ♗d6 26. ♘e5! ♖e5 27. ♕h8 ♔e7 28. ♕e5 ♔d7 29. ♕d6 ♕d6 30. ♗d6 ♔d6 31. f3 ♖g5 32. g4+−; 23... ♖d8 24. ♕h7 ♔f8 25. ♖e1 ♖e4 26. ♘g5+−] **24. ♕h7 ♔f8 25. ♕h8 ♔e7 26. ♗g5!+− ♖g5** [26... f6 27. ♖h7; 26... ♔d7 27. ♘e5! ♗e5 28. ♕d8 ♔e6 29. ♕e7 ♔f5 30. ♕e5#; 26... ♔d6 27. ♕f6 ♔d7 28. ♘e5 ♗e5 29. ♕d8] **27. ♖e1 ♖e5** [27... ♗e5 28. ♘g5] **28. ♘e5 ♕c3 29. ♘d3! ♔d6 30. ♕f8** [30... ♔d7 31. ♕e8 ♔d6 32. ♕e7 ♔c6 33. ♖c1 ♖c2 34. ♖c2 ♕c2 35. ♘b4] **1 : 0** **[L. Bo Hansen]**

306. !N **C 42**

ANAND 2710 – JUSUPOV 2645

Linares 1993

1. e4 e5 2. ♘f3 ♘f6 3. ♘e5 d6 4. ♘f3 ♘e4 5. d4 d5 6. ♗d3 ♘c6 7. 0–0 ♗e7

8. ♖e1 ♗g4 9. c3 f5 10. ♕b3 0–0 11. ♘bd2 ♘a5 [11... ♔h8 – 55/302] **12. ♕a4 ♘c6 13. ♗b5 ♘d2** [13... ♖f6 14. ♗c6 ♖c6 15. ♘e5 ♖a6 16. ♕c2 ♗h5 17. f3±] **14. ♘d2 ♕d6** [14... ♘b8?! 15. h3! ♗h5 16. ♗e2±] **15. ♘b3?!** [15. ♘f1!? f4 16. f3∞; 15. f3 ♗h4!? (15... ♗h5!?∞) 16. ♖e2 ♗h5 17. ♘f1 f4!∞]

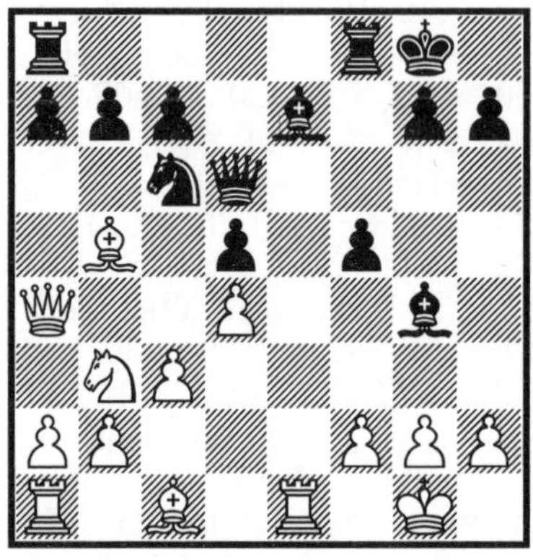

15... ♗h4! N [15... f4 16. f3 (16. ♘c5 ♕g6? 17. ♗d3 ♗f5 18. ♗f5 ♖f5 19. f3=; 16... ♗h4! – 15... ♗h4!) ♗h4 17. ♖e2∞] **16. ♖f1!** [16. g3? f4! 17. gh4 ♕g6–+; 16. ♘c5? *a)* 16... f4!? 17. ♘b7 ♕g6 18. ♗d3 (18. ♗c6 ♗f3–+) ♕d3 19. ♕c6 ♖ae8! 20. ♕e8 (20. ♗f4 ♗f2! 21. ♔f2 ♕d2–+) ♖e8 21. ♖e8 ♔f7 22. ♖e1 ♕c2 23. g3 (23. ♖f1 ♗e2–+) fg3 24. hg3 ♗g3!∓ △ 25. fg3? ♗f3–+; *b)* 16... ♗f2! 17. ♔f2 ♕h2 (△ f4-f3→) 18. ♗c6 (18. ♘e6 f4 19. ♘f4 ♖f4 20. ♗f4 ♖f8→) bc6 (18... f4!? 19. ♗d5 ♔h8→) 19. ♕c6 (19. ♘e6 f4→) f4 20. ♕d5 ♔h8→] **f4** [16... ♕g6!? 17. ♗f4 ♗h3 18. g3! (18. ♗g3? f4 19. gh3 fg3 20. hg3 ♗g3 21. fg3 ♕g3 22. ♔h1 ♕h3 23. ♔g1 ♕g3 24. ♔h1 ♖ae8 25. ♗c6 ♕h3 26. ♔g1 ♕g4 27. ♔h1 ♕h5 28. ♔g1 ♕g5 29. ♔h1 ♖f1 30. ♖f1 ♖e2–+; 24... ♖f3–+) ♗g5 19. ♗g5 ♗f1 20. ♗f1! (20. ♖f1 ♕g5 21. ♗c6 bc6 22. ♕c6 f4∓) ♕g5 21. ♘c5∓] **17. f3 ♗f5 18. ♘c5 ♕g6** [18... ♖ae8?! 19. ♘b7 ♕g6 20. ♗f4 ♗h3 21. ♗g3 ♗g3 22. hg3 ♕g3 23. ♕c2±] **19. ♕d1!□** [19. ♗c6? ♗h3–+; 19. ♗f4? ♗c2–+] **♗h3** [19... ♖ae8 20. ♗f4 (20. ♗d3 ♗d3 21. ♘d3 ♗g5∓; 20. ♘d3 ♗d3 21. ♗d3 ♕h5 22. ♗d2 ♗g3 23. h3∞) ♗h3 21. ♗g3 ♗g3 22. hg3 ♕g3 23. ♕d2=] **20. ♕d2 ♖ae8 21. ♘d3!** [△ ♔h1, ×f4; 21. ♗d3 ♗f5∓] **a6!** [21... ♖e3? 22. ♔h1! ♖d3? 23. ♗d3 ♗g2 24. ♔g1!+–] **22. ♗c6 bc6 23. ♘e5** [23. ♔h1?? ♗g2–+] **♖e5!** [23... ♕g5? 24. ♔h1 △ 24... ♖e5 25. de5 ♗e6 26. g3+–] **24. de5 ♗e6!?** [△ 25... ♖f5, 25... c5] **25. ♕d4 ♗h3 26. ♕d2 ♗e6**=/∞ **27. ♕d4**

1/2 : 1/2 **[Jusupov]**

307. **C 42**

A. ZAPATA 2530 – LIMA 2440

Bogotá 1992

1. e4 e5 2. ♘f3 ♘f6 3. ♘e5 d6 4. ♘f3 ♘e4 5. d4 d5 6. ♗d3 ♘c6 7. 0–0 ♗e7 8. ♖e1 ♗g4 9. c4 ♘f6 10. cd5 ♘d5 11. ♘c3 0–0 12. ♘d5!? N [12. h3!? ♗e6 13. a3 (13. ♕c2 – 52/304; 13. ♘e4!?) ♗f6? 14. ♘e4 ♗f5 15. ♕b3!±; ⌓ 13... ♖e8] **♕d5 13. ♗e4 ♕d6 14. ♗c6 bc6 15. ♖e4!?** [15. h3!?] **♗e6 16. ♗g5 ♗g5** [16... f6 17. ♕e1±] **17. ♘g5 ♗d5 18. ♖e3 ♕f4** [18... ♖ae8 19. ♕e2!? ♖e3 20. ♕e3 (×c6, c7, a7 ⇔c) ♕f6 21. ♘e4 ♕e7 22. ♘c5 ♖e8 23. ♖e1 ♕e3 24. fe3±; RR 18... h6! 19. ♘e4 ♗e4 20. ♖e4 ♖ab8=] **19. ♖e5! ♖ab8** [19... f6?? 20. g3+–; 19... h6 20. g3 ♕f6 21. ♘e4±] **20. g3 ♕f6 21. b3 ♖fd8** [△ c5 ×d4] **22. ♕e2 h6 23. ♘e4 ♕g6 24. ♘c5 ♔h7** [△ ♖b4; 24... ♖b4? 25. ♖e8 ♖e8 26. ♕e8 ♔h7 27. ♘d7] **25. ♖e1 ♖b4 26. ♕d2 a5 27. ♘a6 ♖b7 28. ♕e2!** [×f3, g4, △ h4-h5; 28. ♕a5? ♖a8–+] **c5** [28... a4 29. ba4±; 29. b4±] **29. ♘c5 ♖b4 30. ♖d1 ♗a8 31. d5!± ♕d6⊕ 32. ♕c2 ♕g6** [32... ♔g8 33. ♖de1±; 32... ♔h8 33. ♕e2 △ ♘e4±] **33. ♕g6 ♔g6 34. ♘a6 ♖b7 35. ♖c1?!** [⌓ 35. ♖e7 c6 36. ♖b7 ♗b7 37. ♘c5 ♗c8 38. d6+–] **f6 36. ♖ee1?!⊕** [⌓ 36. ♖e7 ♖d5 37. ♘c7 ♖d8? 38. ♖g7!+–] **♖d5 37. ♘c7** [37. ♖e8 ♖a7 △ 38. ♘c7?? ♖c7!–+] **♖d8 38. ♘e6?! ♖d2 39. ♘c7 ♖a7 40. ♘a8 ♖a8 41. a4 ♖a7 42. ♖e3 ♖b2 43. ♖c5± h5?!** [43... ♖b7 44. ♖b5 (44. h4!?) ♖b5 45. ab5 *a)* 45... ♖c2 46. b4 ab4 (46... a4 47. ♖a3) 47. ♖b3; *b)* 45... ♖d2! 46. b4 a4 47. ♖a3 ♖d5 48. ♖a4 ♖b5±] **44. ♖b5 ♔h6?! 45. ♖e8 ♖d7 46. ♖h8 ♔g6 47. ♖hh5+– ♖d3 48. ♖hf5 ♔f7 49. ♔g2** [△ ♖f3] **♖db3 50. ♖b3 ♖b3 51. ♖a5 g5 52. h4! gh4 53. gh4 ♖a3 54.**

f3 ♔g6 55. ♔g3 ♖a1 56. ♔f4 ♖h1 57. h5 ♔h6 58. ♔e4 ♖c1 59. f4 ♖c6 60. ♔d5 ♖c1 61. ♔e6 ♖c6 62. ♔d5 ♖c1 63. ♔e4 ♖c6 64. ♔f3 ♖c1 65. ♖b5 ♖c4 66. a5 ♖a4 67. ♔g4 ♖a1 68. ♔f5 ♖a4 69. ♔f6 ♖f4 1 : 0 [A. Zapata, Henao]

308. C 42

N. SHORT 2665 – ANAND 2710
Amsterdam 1993

1. e4 e5 2. ♘f3 ♘f6 3. ♘e5 d6 4. ♘f3 ♘e4 5. d4 d5 6. ♗d3 ♘c6 7. 0–0 ♗e7 8. c4 ♘b4 9. ♗e2 ♗e6 10. ♘c3 0–0 11. ♗e3 ♗f5 12. ♘e5!? N [12. ♕b3 – 48/(418); 12. ♖c1 – 48/418] **♗f6?** [12... ♘c3 13. bc3 ♘c2 14. ♖c1 (14. ♗g4!? Je. Piket) ♘e3 15. fe3 ♗e4∞; 12... f6!?] **13. g4! ♗e6 14. f4± ♘c3 15. bc3 ♘c6**

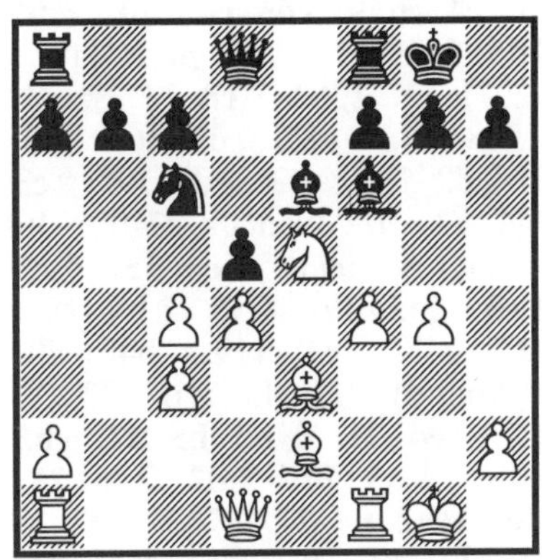

16. ♗f3! [16. f5 ♗c8 17. ♘f3! ♖e8 18. ♗f4 ♖e4 19. ♕d2±; 16. ♖b1 dc4 (16... ♖b8? 17. f5) 17. ♖b7±] **♗e5□ 17. de5 d4!?** [17... dc4 18. f5±] **18. cd4 ♗c4 19. d5!** [19. ♖f2? ♗d5∞] **♘e7 20. ♗c5! ♗f1 21. ♔f1 ♕d7 22. ♕b3! b6 23. ♗a3 ♖ae8 24. ♖d1** [⌓ 24. ♖e1 △ 24... c5 25. dc6 ♘c6 26. ♖d1 ♘d4 27. ♗f8 ♖f8 28. ♕c4 ♖d8 29. ♔f2! △ ♔e3+–] **♘g6! 25. e6 ♕d8 26. f5 ♘e5 27. ♗e2 ♕h4 28. ♕g3** [28. h3!? (Anand) h5] **♕g3 29. hg3 fe6 30. ♗f8 ♔f8** [♖ 9/i] **31. de6 ♔e7 32. g5** [32. ♖d5? ♔f6] **c6 33. g4** [⌓ 33. ♖d4 ♖f8 34. g4] **g6□ 34. ♖d4 gf5 35. gf5 ♖f8 36. ♖f4 b5 37. ♔e1!+–** [△ ♔d2-e3-e4; 37. ♔f2? ♘g6!] **h6 38. gh6 ♖h8** [38... ♔f6 39. ♖e4! ♔f5 40. e7 ♖e8 41. h7!! ♔e4 42. ♗h5] **39. ♖e4 ♔f6 40. e7 ♔f5 41. ♖e5 1 : 0 [N. Short]**

309.* C 42

ADAMS 2630 – JUSUPOV 2645
München 1993

1. e4 e5 2. ♘f3 ♘f6 3. ♘e5 d6 4. ♘f3 ♘e4 5. d4 d5 6. ♗d3 ♘c6 7. 0–0 ♗e7 8. c4 ♘b4 9. ♗e2 ♗e6 10. ♘c3 0–0 11. ♗e3 f5 12. a3 ♘c3 13. bc3 ♘c6 14. ♖b1 f4? [RR 14... ♖b8 15. ♕a4 (15. cd5 ♗d5 16. ♗f4 ♗d6∞) f4 16. ♗c1 ♔h8 17. ♖e1 a6 18. ♗d3 ♗g4!? N (18... dc4 19. ♗h7± – 44/376) 19. cd5 ♗f3 20. gf3 ♕d5 21. ♗e4 ♕h5! 22. ♔h1 ♗d6 23. ♖g1 b5 24. ♕d1 ♘e7 25. ♕f1 ♘d5 26. ♕g2 g6∞ J. Benjamin 2555 – Zarnicki 2385, Manila (ol) 1992] **15. ♗c1 ♖b8 16. cd5 N** [16. ♖e1 – 49/(365)] **♗d5 17. ♖e1 ♔h8** [17... ♗f6 (△ 18. c4 ♗e4) 18. ♗f4 ♗d4 19. ♗c7 ♕c7 20. ♘d4±] **18. ♗d3 ♕d7?!** [18... ♗f6 (△ 19. ♗f4 ♗d4 20. ♘d4 ♖f4∞) 19. ♗c2!±] **19. c4! ♗f3 20. ♕f3 ♘d4** [20... ♕d4 21. ♕h3 h6 22. ♗b2 ♕d6 23. ♖e6+–] **21. ♕e4 ♘f5** [21... ♕f5 22. ♕d4+–; 21... g6 22. ♕e7 ♖be8 23. ♕b4+–] **22. ♖b5 c5** [22... g6 23. ♖f5 ♖f5 24. ♕e7 ♕e7 25. ♖e7 ♖d8 26. ♗e2+–] **23. ♗f4 ♖bd8** [23... ♗d6 24. ♕d5 ♕c7 25. ♗d6 ♘d6 26. ♖c5 ♕d8 27. ♕d4+–] **24. ♗c2 b6 25. g4!** [25. ♖bb1±] **♖de8□ 26. ♖d1** [26. gf5 ♗f6] **♗d6 27. ♕d3!?** [27. ♖d6 ♕c8 28. ♕d3 ♖e1 29. ♔g2+–] **g5□ 28. ♕c3!** [28. ♗d6? ♘d6 29. ♕d6 ♖e1 30. ♔g2 ♕g4 31. ♕g3 ♖f2 32. ♔f2 ♕e2#] **♘d4 29. ♖d4 ♕g4 30. ♔h1 ♖e1 31. ♕e1 ♕f3 32. ♔g1 gf4 33. ♖e4!+–** [33. ♕e4? ♖g8 34. ♔f1 ♕h3 35. ♔e2 f3] **♖g8 34. ♔f1 ♕h1 35. ♔e2 ♖g1 36. ♕c3 ♔g8 37. ♖e8 ♔f7 38. ♗e4 ♕h2 39. ♖a8 ♖g3 40. ♖a7 ♔e6 41. ♗d5 1 : 0 [Adams]**

310. C 43

TIMMAN 2635 – MURREY 2530
France 1993

1. e4 e5 2. ♘f3 ♘f6 3. d4 ♘e4 4. ♗d3

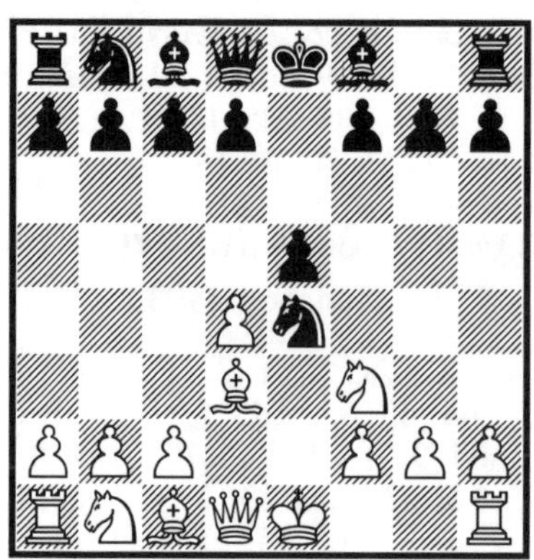

4... ♘c6!? N 5. ♗e4 [5. d5 ♘c5! 6. ♗e2 (6. ♗c4 e4!) e4!; 5. 0–0 d5 6. c4 ♘d4!=] **d5 6. ♗g5 ♕d7** [6... f6 7. ♘e5! ♘e5 (7... de4 8. ♕h5 g6 9. ♘g6 hg6 10. ♕g6+–) 8. de5 de4 9. ♕d8 ♔d8 10. ef6±; 6... ♕d6!? 7. de5 ♕b4 8. ♘c3 de4 9. a3 ♕a5 10. ♘d2 (10. b4? ♗b4 11. ab4 ♕b4∓) ♕e5 11. ♘de4 f5? 12. ♕h5 g6 13. ♕h4±; 11... ♗e7!±; 6... ♗e7!? 7. ♗e7 ♘e7 8. ♗d5 (8. ♗h7 e4 9. ♗e4 de4 10. ♘e5 ♗e6↑) ♕d5 9. de5±] **7. ♗d3** [7. ♗d5 ♕d5 8. ♘c3 ♗b4=; 7. ♘e5 ♘e5 8. de5 de4 9. 0–0 h6 10. ♗h4 g5 11. ♗g3 ♗g7; 9... ♗e7=] **e4 8. 0–0 f6 9. ♖e1! ♗e7** [9... ♔f7 10. ♗e4! (10. ♗f4? ef3 11. ♕f3 ♘d4 12. ♕h5 ♔g8∓) de4 11. ♖e4 fg5 12. ♘g5 ♔g8 13. ♕e2+–; 9... fg5! 10. c4 ♗b4 *a)* 11. cd5 ♗e1 12. ♕e1! (12. dc6? ♕e6! 13. ♗b5 ♗f2 14. ♔f2 0–0) ♘e7 13. ♗e4 g4 14. ♘e5 ♕d6 15. ♘a3!=∞ Murey; *b)* 11. ♘c3 ♗c3 12. bc3 0–0 13. cd5 ef3 14. dc6 ♕g4 (14... ♕c6 15. ♕b3 ♔h8 16. ♗e4±) 15. g3 bc6 16. ♕b3 ♔h8 17. ♖e7±] **10. ♗f4 ed3 11. ♕d3 0–0 12. ♘c3 ♗b4** [12... ♘d8 13. ♗c7!; 12... ♗d8!?] **13. ♖e2 ♘e7** [13... a6 14. a3 ♗a5 15. ♖ae1; 13... ♕f7!?= △ 14. ♕b5 ♖d8, △ 14. ♘b5 ♗a5 R. Hübner] **14. ♕b5 ♘g6 15. ♕d5** [15. ♕d7?! ♗d7 16. ♘d5 ♘f4 17. ♘f4 ♗d6=∞⊞] **♖f7 16. ♗d2 ♗c3 17. ♕d7 ♗d7 18. ♗c3 ♘f4 19. ♖e3** [19. ♖ee1?! ♗c6 20. ♗d2 ♘h3] **♘d5 20. ♖ee1 ♗f5** [20... b5? 21. ♗a5! △ b3, c4; 20... a5! 21. ♗d2 b5] **21. ♖ac1 ♘c3** [21... a5 22. ♗d2 b5 23. c4 bc4 24. ♖c4±] **22. bc3 ♖d8 23. c4 ♗g4 24. c3 ♗f3 25. gf3 ♔f8 26. ♖b1 b6 27. ♖e4 f5 28. ♖e5 ♖d6 29. ♖be1 g5 30. ♖e8 ♔g7 31. ♖1e6 ♖e6 32. ♖e6 ♖f6 33. ♖e7 ♖f7 34. ♖e5 ♔f6 35. c5 ♖f8!?** [35... ♖e7? 36. ♖e7 ♔e7 37. cb6+–] **36. ♔f1 ♖b8 37. ♔e2 b5** [37... bc5 38. ♖c5 ♖b2 39. ♔f1+–] **38. ♔d3 b4 39. ♖e1 bc3 40. ♔c3 c6 41. d5** [41. a3!?] **cd5 42. ♔d4 ♖b2 43. c6 ♖c2!** [43... ♖a2 44. ♖c1+–] **44. ♔d5 ♖d2 45. ♔c5 ♖c2 46. ♔d6 ♖d2 47. ♔c7 ♖a2 48. ♖c1 ♔e7 49. ♔c8 ♖f2 50. c7 ♖b2 51. ♖c5 h6 52. h3 f4 53. ♖e5 ♔f6 54. ♖a5 1 : 0**
[Timman]

311.* **C 43**

TIMMAN 2635 – JUSUPOV 2645
Linares 1993

1. e4 e5 2. ♘f3 ♘f6 3. d4 ♘e4 4. ♗d3 d5 5. ♘e5 ♘d7 6. ♘d7 ♗d7 7. 0–0 ♗d6 8. c4 c6 9. cd5 cd5 10. ♕h5 0–0 11. ♕d5 ♗c6 12. ♕h5 g6 N [12... ♗c7 – 51/297] **13. ♕h3 ♖c8 14. ♗e4!?** [14. ♗h6 ♖e8 15. ♘d2 ♗d7 16. ♕f3 ♕h4 17. g3 ♘d2 18. ♗d2 ♕d4 19. ♗c3 ♕g4 20. ♕g4 1/2 : 1/2 Ivančuk 2710 – Jusupov 2645, Linares 1993] **♗e4 15. ♘c3 ♖e8 16. ♗e3 ♗f5 17. ♕f3 ♗b8 18. ♖fe1 b5!□ 19. g4!? ♖c3?** [19... b4□ 20. ♘d5 ♖e4! (Anand) 21. gf5 ♕d5 22. ♖ec1±] **20. bc3 ♗e4 21. ♕h3 h5 22. gh5 ♖e6 23. f3+– ♗d5 24. ♗d2 ♖c6 25. ♖e2 ♗e6 26. ♕g2 b4 27. ♕g5 ♕d7 28. hg6 bc3 29. gf7 ♔f7 30. ♕h5 ♔e7 31. ♗g5 ♔f8 32. ♗h6 ♔e7 33. ♕g5 ♔d6 34. ♕f4 ♔d5 35. ♕e4 ♔d6 36. ♗f4 ♔e7 37. ♗b8 1 : 0 [Timman]**

312.* !N **C 43**

ANAND 2710 – IVANČUK 2710
Linares 1993

1. e4 e5 2. ♘f3 ♘f6 3. d4 ♘e4 4. ♗d3 d5 5. ♘e5 ♘d7 6. ♘d7 ♗d7 7. 0–0 ♕h4 8. c4 0-0-0 9. c5 g5 [RR 9... g6 10. ♘c3 ♗g7 11. g3 ♕f6 12. ♗e3! N (12. ♘e4 – 55/(303)) ♘g5 13. f4 ♘h3 14. ♔g2 ♖he8 15. ♕d2± Lékó 2465 – S. Faragó 2340, Magyarország 1993] **10. ♘c3 ♗g7 11. g3 ♕h3 12. ♘e4 de4 13. ♗e4 ♗b5 14. ♗g2!**

[14. ♗g5 – 50/(334)] **♕f5 15. ♗e3! N** [15. ♕b3] **♗f1 16. ♗f1!**=∞⊟ [△ ♕a4, ♖d3; 16. ♔f1?! ×♔f1] **♖he8** [16... ♗d4 17. ♗d4 ♕e4 18. ♗h8 ♖d1 19. ♖d1; 16... ♕d7 17. ♕b3 ♖he8 18. ♖d1] **17. ♕a4 ♔b8** [17... ♖e3 18. fe3 ♕e4 (18... ♕f3 19. ♖e1) 19. ♕b3! (19. ♖e1 ♗d4) ♖e8 (19... ♖d4 20. ♗g2±) 20. ♖e1 ♗d4 21. ♗g2 ♗e3 22. ♔h1+–] **18. ♖d1 c6** [18... ♖e3?! 19. fe3 ♕f3 20. ♖d3±] **19. ♖d3** [19. ♗g2 ♖e7! 20. d5 cd5 21. c6 d4∞] **♕e4 20. ♖a3 a6 21. ♗d3** [21. ♗a6 ♖d4! 22. ♗d4 ♗d4 23. ♗f1 ♗c5⇆] **♕g4?** [×c6; 21... ♕d5! (×c6) *a)* 22. ♖b3?! ♗d4 23. ♗d4 (23. ♖b7? ♔b7 24. ♕a6 ♔b8 25. ♕b6 ♔c8 26. ♕a7 ♖d7 27. ♕a8 ♔c7 28. ♕e8 ♗e3–+; 23. ♗a6 ♖e7! 24. ♖d3 ♖e4 25. ♖b3 ♖d7) ♖e1 (23... ♕d4 24. ♖b7 ♔b7 25. ♕a6 ♔b8 26. ♕b6 ♔a8 27. ♕c6 ♔b8=) 24. ♗f1 ♕d4 25. ♖b7 (25. ♕c6? ♖f1 26. ♔f1 ♕d1 27. ♔g2 ♕b3) ♔b7 26. ♕a6 ♔c7 (26... ♔b8 27. ♕b6) 27. ♕a5 ♔b8 28. ♕e1 ♕c5∓; *b)* 22. ♗c4 ♕e4!=; *c)* 22. ♗a6 ♗d4 23. ♗b7 (23. ♗c4 ♕c5∓) ♗c5!□ 24. ♖b3 (24. ♗c6 ♕d1 25. ♔g2 ♕a4 26. ♖a4 ♖e3 27. fe3 ♖d2 28. ♔h3 ♖b2=) ♕d1 25. ♔g2 ♖e3! 26. ♕a8 (26. fe3?? ♖d2 27. ♔h3 ♕h5) ♔c7 27. ♕a5 ♔b8 (27... ♔d7 28. fe3 ♕e2=) 28. ♖e3 ♕d5! 29. ♖f3 g4–+; 28. ♕a8=] **22. ♖b3! ♗d4?** [22... ♖e7 23. ♖b4±; 22... ♖d7 23. ♗a6 (23. ♖b4? ♖e3 24. fe3 ♕f3∓; 23. ♕c6 ♕d1 24. ♔g2 ♕b3 25. ♕d7) ♗d4 24. ♕c6!] **23. ♖b7! ♔b7 24. ♕a6 ♔b8 25. ♕b6 ♔a8 26. ♕c6 ♔b8 27. ♕b6 ♔a8 28. ♗b5!** [28... ♖c8 29. ♗c6 ♖c6 30. ♕c6 ♔a7 31. ♕e8 ♕d1 32. ♔g2 ♗e3 33. ♕e3+–] **1 : 0**

[Anand]

313. **C 43**

LÉKÓ 2465 – JÓZSEF HORVÁTH 2535

Budapest 1993

1. e4 e5 2. ♘f3 ♘f6 3. d4 ♘e4 4. ♗d3 d5 5. ♘e5 ♘d7 6. ♘d7 ♗d7 7. 0–0 ♕h4 8. c4 ♘f6!? N 9. ♕e2 ♗e7 10. cd5 [10. ♖e1? 0–0 11. ♕e7 ♖ae8 12. ♕b4 ♘g4–+] **♘d5?** [10... ♕d4! 11. ♘c3 ♘d5 12. ♘d5 ♕d5 13. ♖e1 ♕e6 14. ♗f4 ♕e2 15. ♖e2 ♗e6 16. ♗c7=] **11. ♗e4!± ♗c6** [11... c6 12. ♗d5 cd5 13. ♖e1± △ 13... 0–0? 14. ♕e7 ♖ae8 15. ♕b4+–; 11... ♗e6 12. ♕b5 c6 13. ♕b7 0–0 14. ♘d2±] **12. ♘c3?!** [12. ♕f3!] **0-0-0?** [12... ♘c3 13. ♗c6 bc6 14. bc3 0–0±] **13. ♕f3! ♘c3** [13... ♘b4 14. d5+–] **14. ♗c6 ♘e2** [14... bc6 15. bc3 ♕f6 16. ♕d3 ♔b7 17. ♖b1 ♔a8 18. ♗g5!+–] **15. ♕e2 bc6 16. ♗e3 ♖d6 17. ♖ac1 ♖g6 18. g3!** [△ ♖c6!] **♕e4 19. ♕a6 ♔d7 20. d5! cd5 21. ♕b5 ♔c8 22. ♗a7+– ♗d6?** [22... ♗d8 23. ♖fd1 ♖d6 24. ♗c5 ♖e6 25. ♗e3+–] **23. ♕b8 ♔d7 24. ♕h8** **1 : 0**

[Adorján, Lékó]

314. !N **C 43**

A. ZAPATA 2530 – ZARNICKI 2450

São Paulo 1992

1. e4 e5 2. ♘f3 ♘f6 3. d4 ♘e4 4. ♗d3 d5 5. ♘e5 ♗d6 6. 0–0 0–0 7. c4 ♗e5 8. de5 ♘c6 9. cd5 ♕d5 10. ♕c2 ♘b4 11. ♗e4 ♘c2 12. ♗d5 ♗f5 13. g4 ♗g4 14. ♗f4 ♘a1 15. ♗e4 f5 16. ♗d5 ♔h8 17. ♖c1 c6 18. ♗g2 ♖fd8 19. ♘d2 ♖d2? [19... h6 – 54/285] **20. ♗d2 ♖d8 21. ♗c3 ♖d1 22. ♖d1 ♗d1**

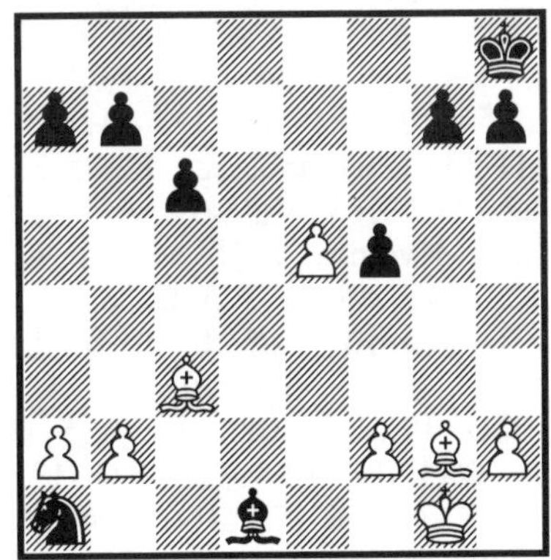

23. ♗f1!! N +– [△ ♗c4-f7; 23. f4? – 51/(297)] **♗f3** [23... ♘c2? 24. ♗c4 b5 (24... ♗h5 25. ♗d3 ♘a1 26. b4) 25. ♗b3 (25. ♗f7?! ♗f3 △ ♗d5) b4 (25... g6? 26. e6) 26. ♗d2 △ e6; 23... b5 24. ♗g2 c5 25. b4!; 23... ♔g8 24. ♗c4 ♔f8 25. b4

(25. ♗b4!? ♔e8 26. ♗g8 h6 27. ♗h7 △ ♗g6) ♘c2 26. ♗b3; 23... g6 24. ♗c4 ♔g7□ (24... b5? 25. e6+−) 25. b4!? (25. ♗e6 △ ♗c8, e6) ♘c2 26. ♗b3] **24. ♗d3!** [△ b4] **♗e4□ 25. ♗c4** [△ e6] **♗d5** [25... b5? 26. e6] **26. ♗d5! cd5 27. ♔f1** [△ ♔e2-d3 ×♘a1] **d4** [27... ♘c2 28. ♔e2 d4 29. ♗d2 △ ♔d3; 27... a5 28. ♔e2 (28. ♗a5?! ♘c2 29. ♗c3 d4 30. ♗d2⇆) ♘c2 29. ♔d3 ♘b4 30. ♗b4 ab4 31. ♔d4] **28. ♗d4 ♘c2 29. ♗c3! b5 30. e6 ♔g8 31. ♔e2 b4 32. ♗e5** [△ ♔d2] **b3 33. ab3 ♘b4** [33... ♔f8 34. ♔d2 ♘b4 35. ♗d6] **34. ♗d6 ♘c6 35. ♔d3** **1 : 0**
[A. Zapata, Henao]

315.* !N** **C 45**

BALINOV 2270 – REICHMANN 2305
Österreich 1992

1. e4 e5 2. ♘f3 ♘c6 3. d4 ed4 4. ♘d4 ♕f6 [RR 4... ♘f6 5. ♘c6 bc6 6. e5 ♘e4 7. ♕f3 ♘g5 8. ♕g3 ♘e6 9. ♗d3 d6!? N (9... d5) 10. 0–0 g6 11. ♘c3 de5 12. ♕e5 ♗g7 13. ♕e4 0–0 14. ♕c6 ♖b8 15. ♕a4 a6 16. ♗e3 ♖b2 17. ♕a3 ♖b8 18. ♖ad1 ♕h4 19. ♘d5 ♗b7 20. ♗a6 ♗a6 21. ♕a6 ♖a8 22. ♕c6 ♕a4 23. ♘e7 1/2 : 1/2 Kamsky 2655 – Kortchnoi 2605, Buenos Aires 1993] **5. ♗e3 ♗c5 6. c3 ♘ge7 7. ♗c4** [RR 7. ♘c2 ♗e3 8. ♘e3 ♕e5 9. ♕f3 f5! N (9... 0–0) 10. ♘f5 (10. ♘d2 fe4 11. ♕e4□ d5=; 10. ef5 d5 11. g4?! d4! 12. cd4 ♘d4 13. ♕d1 h5=∞; ⌓ 11. ♗e2) ♖f8 11. ♕e2 (11. ♕e3? ♘f5 12. ef5 ♕e3 13. fe3 ♖f5∓ Kveinys 2555 – Jandemirov 2465, Katowice 1993) ♘f5 12. ef5 ♖f5 13. ♘d2= Jandemirov] **b6 8. 0–0 ♗b7 9. ♘b5! N** [9. b4 – 53/(299); 9. f4 – 56/(341)] **♖c8** [9... 0-0-0!? 10. ♗c5 bc5 *a)* RR 11. ♕a4 d5! 12. ♗e2 de4 13. ♘a7 ♘a7 14. ♕a7 ♕b6 15. ♕b6 cb6= P. Tregubov 2445 – R. Ščerbakov 2570, Sankt-Peterburg (zt) 1993; *b)* 11. ♗d5! (△ c4) a6 12. ♘5a3 ♘d5 13. ed5 ♘e7 14. c4 ♕b2 15. ♘c2=∞ △ ♕d2, ♘c3] **10. b4! ♗b4 11. cb4 ♕a1 12. ♘a7 ♖d8?!** [12... ♘a7?? 13. ♗d4+−; ⌓ 12... ♕f6 13. ♘c8 ♗c8 (13... ♘c8 14. ♗d5!) 14. ♕d2±⊡, ⊞] **13. ♘c6 dc6** [13... ♘c6? 14. b5 △ ♗d4+−] **14. ♗f7! ♔f7 15. ♕b3 ♔e8 16. ♘c3 ♕f1 17. ♔f1± ♖f8 18. a4** [⌓ 18. ♕c4] **♖f7 19. ♕c4 h6 20. h3! ♔f8 21. ♔g1! ♖a8 22. ♔h2 ♘g6 23. a5** [×b6] **♘e5⊕ 24. ♕d4 ♘d7 25. e5 c5?** [25... ♖e8 26. f4± △ ♕c4, a6, e6] **26. bc5 bc5** [26... ♘c5 27. ab6 cb6 28. ♕d6 ♔g8 29. ♕b6+−] **27. ♕c4 ♘e5 28. ♕c5 ♖e7 29. ♕b4!** [△ ♗c5, ×♗b7] **♘d7 30. ♕b7 ♖a5 31. ♘d5** **1 : 0**
[Balinov]

316.* **C 45**

ASHLEY 2365 – KAJDANOV 2620
New York 1993

1. e4 e5 2. ♘f3 ♘c6 3. d4 ed4 4. ♘d4 ♗c5 5. ♗e3 ♕f6 6. c3 ♘ge7 7. ♗c4 ♘e5 8. ♗e2 ♕g6 9. 0–0 d6 10. f3 0–0 11. ♔h1 [RR 11. ♘d2 f5!? N (11... d5 – 53/300) 12. ef5 (12. ♘f5? ♗f5 13. ♗c5 ♗h3; 12. f4 ♘g4 13. ♗g4 ♕g4 14. ♕g4 fg4=; 12... ♘5c6!?; 12. ♔h1!? f4 13. ♗g1) ♗f5 (12... ♘f5? 13. ♘f5 ♗f5 14. ♗c5 dc5 15. ♕b3 ♔h8 16. ♕b7 ♖ab8 17. ♕c7±) 13. ♘f5 (13. ♕b3 ♔h8 △ 14. ♕b7? ♖ab8 15. ♕a6 ♘d5 16. ♗f2 ♗h3−+) ♘f5 14. ♗c5 dc5 15. ♘c4 (15. ♕b3? ♔h8 16. ♕b7 ♖ad8 17. ♘e4 ♘e3 18. ♖f2 ♘f3∓→⟫) ♘c4 16. ♗c4 ♔h8 17. ♗d3 ♖ad8 (17... c4 18. ♗f5 ♕f5 19. ♕d4⩲) 18. ♕c2 c4 (Žurov 2350 – Vul' 2340, Moskva (open) 1992) 19. ♗e4⩲ Vul'] **d5 12. ♘d2 de4 13. fe4 ♘g4!? N** [13... ♗b6 – 54/293; 13... ♗g4 – 55/(307)] **14. ♗f4 ♗d6 15. ♘c4!** [15. ♗d6?? ♘e3−+] **♗f4 16. ♖f4 ♘f6 17. e5?!** [17. ♘f3!? △ 17... ♘e4? 18. ♘fe5+−] **♘fd5 18. ♖h4 f5!= 19. ef6 ♕f6 20. ♖e4 c5!?** [20... c6=] **21. ♘f3 ♗f5 22. ♖e5 ♘f4!? 23. ♘e3!** [23. ♖c5 ♖ad8 24. ♕f1 (24. ♕e1 ♗d3!) ♘c6=∞ ×♖c5] **♖ad8 24. ♗c4 ♔h8 25. ♕e1! ♗c8 26. ♖d1** [26. ♖c5? ♘g2! 27. ♘g2 ♕f3∓ △ 28. ♕e7? ♖d1−+] **♖d1 27. ♕d1 ♘c6?!** [27... b6!?] **28. ♘d5** [28. ♖c5? ♕e7!−+] **♕d6 29. ♖e1 ♗g4?** [29... ♗e6=] **30. ♘f4 ♕f4** [30... ♕d1 31. ♖d1 ♖f4 32. ♗d5⩲] **31. ♕d5 h6 32. ♘h4 ♕f6 33. ♕c5!± ♖d8 34.**

g3?! [34. ♘f3±] **♗h3 35. ♕h5?!** [⌓ 35. ♔g1] **♘e7!! 36. ♕f3** [36. ♖e7 ♕c6 37. ♔g1 ♕b6=] **♖d2! 37. ♕f6 gf6 38. ♔g1 ♘c6 39. ♘g6 ♔g7 40. ♘f4 ♗g4 41. ♗e2 ♗c8! 42. ♖d1?** [42. b4=] **♖b2**∓ **43. ♖d6?**⊕ [43. a4∓] **♘e5 44. ♘h5 ♔f7 45. ♖f6 ♔e7 46. ♖f2 ♖a2**−+ [♂a] **47. ♘f6 a5 48. ♘g8?! ♔d6 49. ♘h6 a4 50. ♗d1 ♖f2** [51. ♔f2 a3 52. ♗b3 ♗e6] **0 : 1**
[Kajdanov]

317. !N C 46

ISTRĂŢESCU 2470
– HAUCHARD 2450

Bucureşti 1993

1. e4 e5 2. ♘f3 ♘c6 3. ♘c3 ♗c5 4. ♘e5 ♘e5 5. d4 ♗d6 6. de5 ♗e5 7. ♗d3 ♕h4 8. ♗e3! N [8. g3 — 55/309] **♘f6 9. g3 ♕g4** [9... ♕h3 10. ♕d2± △ 10... ♘g4?! 11. ♗f4 ♗d4? 12. 0-0-0! ♘f2 13. ♘b5+−] **10. ♕g4 ♗c3** [10... ♘g4 11. ♗d2 ♗d4 12. f3 ♘f2 13. ♘b5! ♘d3□ 14. cd3 ♗b6 15. ♖c1 ♔d8 16. ♔e2±] **11. bc3 ♘g4 12. ♗d4 0–0 13. f3 ♘f6 14. e5 ♘d5 15. ♔f2± d6 16. ed6 cd6 17. ♖ab1 ♘b6□ 18. ♗b6 ab6 19. ♖b6 ♖a2** [19... ♖d8 20. ♖a1±] **20. ♖d6 ♖b2 21. ♖a1 g6 22. ♔e3** [△ ♔d2-c1, ×♖b2] **♗e6 23. ♔d2 ♖c8□ 24. ♔c1 ♖a2 25. ♖a2 ♗a2 26. ♗e4! ♗e6 27. ♗b7 ♖c3 28. ♔d2 ♖a3?**⊕ [⌓ 28... ♖c5 29. ♗e4±] **29. ♖a6+− ♖a6 30. ♗a6 ♔f8 31. ♔e3 ♔e7 32. ♔d4 ♔d6 33. c3 f6 34. ♗d3 ♗f7 35. c4 h6 36. c5 ♔e7 37. f4 ♗e8 38. ♔d5 g5 39. ♗f5 1 : 0**
[Istrăţescu]

318. !N C 47**

NADIRHANOV 2450 – NENAŠEV 2565

Biškek (zt) 1993

1. e4 e5 2. ♘f3 ♘c6 3. ♘c3 ♘f6 4. d4 ♗b4 5. ♘e5 ♕e7 [5... ♘e4 6. ♕g4 ♘c3 7. ♕g7 ♖f8 8. a3 ♗a5 9. ♘c6 dc6 10. ♕e5 ♕e7 11. ♕e7 ♔e7 12. ♗d2 ♗f5 13. bc3! N (13. ♗c3; 13. ♗d3) ♗c2 14. c4 ♗d2 15. ♔d2 ♗g6 16. h4! h6 17. ♖h3 ♖ad8 18. ♔c3± Nadirhanov 2450 – Safin 2455, Biškek (zt) 1993; RR 5... 0–0 6. ♕d3 ♖e8 7. ♗d2 ♘d4!? N (7... d5 8. ♘c6 bc6 9. e5 c5 10. 0-0-0 ♘g4 11. ♗e1 ♕g5 12. ♔b1 ♖b8 13. f4!±) 8. ♕d4□ (8. ♘f7?! ♘c2!) c5 9. ♕d3! (9. ♕d6? ♖e6 10. ♘f7 ♕e8!−+; 9. ♕c4 d5! 10. ed5 ♖e5 11. ♗e2 ♘d5 12. 0-0-0 ♗e6!∓) ♖e5 10. 0-0-0 d5□ (10... ♗c3 11. ♗c3±; 10... d6 11. f3!±) *a)* 11. ♘d5! ♘d5 (11... ♘e4? 12. ♘b4+−; 11... ♗d2 12. ♕d2! ♘d5 13. ed5 ♕d6 14. ♗e2!±) 12. ♗b4 cb4 13. ed5 ♗f5 14. ♕b3 ♖c8 (14... ♕g5 15. ♔b1 ♖c8 16. ♗d3! ♗d3 17. ♖d3 ♕g2 18. ♖hd1 ♕f2 19. d6!±) 15. ♗d3 ♖d5 (15... ♕d5 16. ♗f5 ♕b3 17. ♗h7 ♔h7 18. ab3 ♖e2 19. ♖d2±) 16. ♗f5 ♕g5= Nogueiras, Estévez; *b)* 11. ed5 ♗g4 12. ♕g3 (12. f3 ♗f5 13. ♕c4 ♘d5∓ △ 14. f4? ♘b6!−+) ♖d5! 13. ♘d5 ♕d5 14. ♕b3!□ ♕b3 15. ab3 ♗d1 16. ♔d1□ (16. ♗b4? ♗c2!) ♖d8 17. ♗d3 ♘g4! 18. ♗e3 ♘e3 19. fe3= Estévez 2330 – Espinosa 2315, La Habana 1992] **6. ♕d3! ♘e5 7. de5 ♕e5 8. ♗d2 0–0 9. 0-0-0 d6 10. ♔b1! N** [10. f4 — 3/246] **♗d7 11. f3** [11. f4! ♕e7 12. ♕g3 ♗c6 13. ♗d3 ♗e4 14. ♖he1!±] **♖ad8 12. ♗e1! ♖fe8 13. ♗g3 ♕a5 14. ♘d5 ♘d5 15. ♕d5 ♕d5 16. ♖d5± ♗e6? 17. ♖b5! ♗c5 18. ♖b7 ♗b6 19. ♗b5 ♖f8 20. a4± f5 21. a5 ♗a5 22. ef5?!** [22. ♖a7 ♗b6 23. ♖a4±] **♖f5! 23. ♗d3 ♖h5 24. ♖a7 ♖b8 25. ♗e1 ♗b6 26. ♖a4 ♖g5 27. g3** [27. ♗g3!?] **♖f8 28. f4 ♗d5!** [28... ♖h5 29. ♗e4±] **29. ♗e4 ♖e8!** [29... ♖h5 30. g4! ♖h3 31. ♗g3+−] **30. fg5?** [30. ♗d5 ♖d5 31. ♗c3 ♖e2±] **♗e4 31. ♖e4 ♖e4 32. ♗c3 ♔f7 33. ♖e1?! ♖e1 34. ♗e1 ♔g6**∓ **35. ♗c3 ♗g1 36. ♗a5! c6 37. ♗c7 ♗h2 38. ♗d6 ♔g5 39. b4 ♔g4 40. c4 h5 41. b5 cb5 42. cb5 h4 43. b6 ♗g3** [♘♗ 7/e] **44. ♗c7!□ ♗f2 45. b7 ♗a7 46. ♔c2 ♔f3 47. ♔d3 h3 48. ♔c4!!= ♔g2 49. ♔b5 h2 50. ♔a6 h1♕ 51. ♔a7 1/2 : 1/2**
[Nadirhanov, Galahov]

319.* !N C 48

LJUBOJEVIĆ 2605 – BELJAVSKIJ 2610

Linares 1993

1. e4 e5 2. ♘f3 ♘c6 3. ♗b5 ♘f6 4. 0–0 ♗c5 5. ♘c3 0–0 6. ♘e5 ♖e8 7. ♘f3 ♘e4

8. d4 [8. ♘e4!? ♖e4 9. c3 d5 10. d4 ♗d6 11. ♗d3 ♗g4 12. h3 ♗h5 13. g4 ♗g6 14. ♘g5 ♖e7 15. f4↑] **♘c3 9. bc3 ♗f8! N** [9... ♗e7 – 53/(305)] **10. ♘g5** [RR 10. c4!? h6?! 11. ♗f4 a6 12. ♗a4 ♘a5? 13. ♘e5 ♕f6 14. ♗g3 c6 15. ♕d2± Kamsky 2655 – Winants 2505, Tilburg (Interpolis) 1992; ⌓ 10... b6 △ ♗b7] **h6 11. ♘h3 d6** [11... d5? 12. ♕f3 ♗e6 13. ♘f4!±] **12. ♕f3 ♗d7 13. ♖b1** [△ ♗c4] **♖b8= 14. ♕g3?!** [△ 14... ♕f6 15. ♘f4]

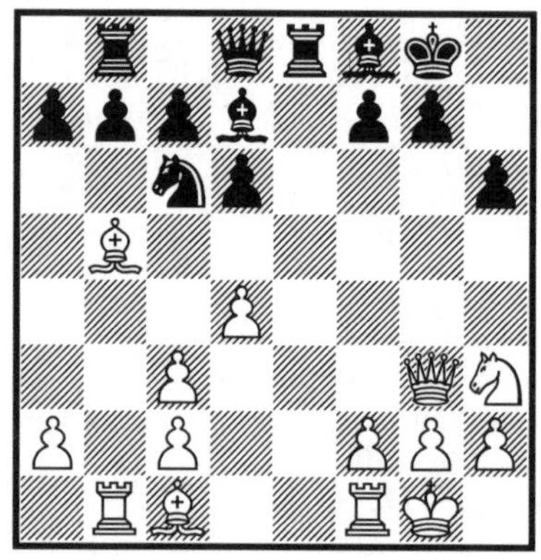

14... ♘e7! 15. ♗d7 ♕d7 16. ♗h6 ♕a4! [△ ♘f5; 16... ♘f5? 17. ♕g4±] **17. ♗c1?! ♕a2 18. ♖b5 ♕c2** [RR 18... c5!? 19. dc5 ♕c2 20. cd6 ♘f5 21. ♕f3 ♘d6 22. ♖h5 ♕e4⇆ M. Gurevich] **19. ♖h5 ♘f5** [19... g6 20. ♘f4 ♗g7 21. ♖h3 ♕f5 22. ♕f3 b5 23. g4 ♕f6 24. ♕g3 b4 25. g5 ♕f5∓] **20. ♕g5 g6 21. ♘f4 ♗g7?** [21... ♗e7 22. ♕g4 ♘g7 23. ♖h3 ♕f5 24. ♕f3 ♗g5 25. ♘g6 ♕g6 26. ♖g3 f6 27. h4 ♘f5 28. h5 (28. ♕d5 ♔g7 29. h5 ♘g3 30. hg6 ♘e2 31. ♔h2 ♖h8#) ♕h7 29. ♗g5 ♘g3 30. ♕d5 ♕f7 31. ♕f7 ♔f7 32. fg3 ♔e6 33. ♖f6 ♔d5 34. h6 b5 35. g4 a5–+] **22. ♖h3→⟫ c6?** [RR 22... ♕e4! △ 23. g4 ♕e7 24. ♘d5 (24. ♘g6 ♕g5 25. ♗g5 fg6 26. gf5 gf5∓) ♕g5 25. ♗g5 c6∓ M. Gurevich] **23. g4 ♘e7 24. ♕h4 f6** [RR 24... ♔f8 25. ♘e6! fe6 26. ♗h6→; 24... ♘d5 25. ♕h7 ♔f8 26. ♘h5→; 24... ♕e4 25. f3 ♕c2 26. ♕h7 ♔f8 27. ♘e6 fe6 28. ♗h6 ♗h6 29. ♕h6↑ M. Gurevich] **25. ♕h7 ♔f7 26. ♘h5!+– ♖g8 27. ♗h6 ♕e2 28. ♗g7 ♕g4 29. ♖g3 ♕h5 30. ♗h6 ♔e6 31. ♖e1**

1 : 0 **[Beljavskij]**

320. **C 48**

HJARTARSON 2625
– J.-R. KOCH 2450
Ísland – France 1993

1. e4 e5 2. ♘f3 ♘f6 3. ♘c3 ♘c6 4. ♗b5 ♘d4 5. ♗a4 ♗c5 6. ♘e5 0–0 7. ♘d3 ♗b6 8. e5 ♘e8 9. ♘d5 ♕g5 10. ♘e3 d6 11. ed6 ♘d6 12. 0–0 ♘4f5 N [12... ♘6f5? – 51/305] **13. ♘e1 ♘e3 14. fe3 ♗g4 15. ♘f3 ♕e7!?** [15... ♕h5 16. ♕e1 c6 △ ♖ae8∞ R. Hübner] **16. ♔h1** [16. ♕e1!? c6 17. ♕h4 (17. h3 ♗d7 18. ♕h4 f6∞̄) ♕h4 18. ♘h4⩲] **f5 17. d3!** [17. ♕e1 f4! 18. ef4 ♕e1 19. ♖e1 (19. ♘e1? ♗e2–+) ♖f4 20. ♗b3 ♔h8∞̄ △ 21. d3?? ♖f3–+, △ 21. ♘e5 ♖af8; 17. d4 c6 18. ♕d3 ♗c7 19. ♗b3 ♔h8 20. ♘e5 ♗h5∞̄ ✕e4] **♗e3 18. ♗e3 ♕e3 19. ♕e1 ♕e1** [19... f4?! 20. ♕c3 ♗f3□ 21. ♖f3 ♕e7 22. ♖af1±] **20. ♖ae1 ♗f3□ 21. ♖f3 c6 22. ♗b3 ♔h8 23. ♖fe3 ♖ae8 24. h4!±** [24. ♔g1 ♖e3 25. ♖e3 ♖e8 26. ♔f2 g6 27. ♖e8 ♘e8 28. ♔e3 ♔g7 29. ♔d4 ♔f6=] **♖e3 25. ♖e3 ♖e8** [25... g6? 26. ♖e7±] **26. ♖e8 ♘e8 27. h5! h6?!** [27... g5? 28. hg6 hg6 29. ♗f7+–; 27... ♘f6 28. ♗f7 ♘g4 29. b4 ♘h6 30. ♗e6 g6 31. d4 ♘g4 32. h6! (32. ♗c8 ♘e3⇆) ♘h6 (32... ♘e3 33. c4 ♘c2 34. d5 cd5 35. cd5±) 33. ♗c8±] **28. ♔g1 g5?!** [28... ♔h7 29. ♗f7 ♘d6 30. ♗g6 ♔g8 31. ♔f2 ♔f8 32. ♔e3 ♔e7 33. ♔f4±] **29. hg6 ♔g7 30. ♗f7+– ♘d6 31. ♔f2 ♘f7 32. gf7 ♔f7 33. ♔g3 ♔g6 34. ♔f4 ♔f6 35. d4?!** [35. a4! ♔e6 (35... b5 36. ab5 cb5 37. b4 ♔e6 38. c4+–) 36. b4 b6 37. d4 ♔f6 (37... a5 38. ba5 ba5 39. c4+–) 38. c4 ♔e6 39. b5+–] **b5 36. c3 a5 37. b3 a4 38. c4 ♔e6 39. ♔g3!** [39. ba4?? bc4 40. a5 ♔d7–+] **bc4?!** [39... ♔f6 40. ♔h4 ♔g6 41. c5! (41. cb5? cb5 42. b4 a3 43. g3 ♔f6 44. ♔h5 ♔e6 45. ♔h6 ♔d5 46. ♔g5 ♔d4 47. ♔f5 ♔c3 48. g4 ♔b2=; 41. g3? ab3! 42. ab3 b4=) ♔f6 (41... a3 42. d5+–; 41... ab3 42. ab3 ♔f6 43. ♔h5+–) 42. ba4 ba4 43. ♔h5 ♔e6 44. ♔h6 ♔d5 45. ♔g5 ♔d4 46. ♔f5+–] **40. bc4 a3 41. ♔f4 ♔f6 42. d5+– cd5 43. cd5 ♔e7 44. ♔f5 ♔d6 45. ♔e4 h5 46. g3 ♔d7 47. ♔d4 ♔d6 48. ♔c4 ♔d7**

49. ♔c5 ♔c7 50. d6 ♔d7 51. ♔d5 ♔d8 52. ♔c6 ♔c8 53. ♔b5 ♔d7 54. ♔c5 1 : 0 **[Hjartarson]**

321.* **C 49**

ISTRĂŢESCU 2470 – TIMOŠENKO 2515

Bucureşti 1993

1. e4 e5 2. ♘c3 ♘c6 3. ♘f3 ♘f6 4. ♗b5 ♗b4 5. 0–0 0–0 6. d3 [RR 6. ♗c6 dc6 7. ♘e5 ♗c3!? N (7... ♖e8 – 54/(304)) 8. dc3 ♕d1 9. ♖d1 ♘e4 10. ♗f4 ♗f5 11. ♘c4 ♖fc8 12. ♘e3 ♗e6 13. f3 ♘f6 14. c4 ♘h5 15. ♗e5 f6 16. ♗c3 ♘f4 17. ♖e1 ♖e8 18. g3 ♘g6 19. ♔g2 h5 20. b3 ♔f7 21. ♖e2 ♖ad8 22. ♖ae1 ♗c8 1/2 : 1/2 Miles 2595 – Jusupov 2640, Groningen 1992] **d6 7. ♗g5 ♗c3 8. bc3 h6 9. ♗h4 ♕e7 10. ♖e1 ♘b8!? N** [10... ♗d7 – 15/234; 10... ♘d8 – 54/304] **11. d4 c6 12. ♗d3** [12. ♗c4!? Timošenko] **♖e8 13. h3 ♘bd7 14. ♕d2 ♘f8 15. g4 ♘g6** [15... g5 16. ♘g5!? (16. ♗g3 ♘g6 △ ♘f4=) hg5 17. ♕g5 ♘g6 18. f4! ♘h7□ 19. ♕e7 ♘e7 20. f5⩱→] **16. ♗g3 ♘h7 17. ♔g2 ♕f6!** [17... ♘g5?! 18. ♘h4! ♘h4 19. ♗h4 ♕f6 20. ♕e3 c5 21. d5±] **18. ♕e3 ♘g5 19. ♘g5 hg5 20. ♖h1** [△ f3, ♖h2, ♖ah1, h4] **♘f4 21. ♔f1 ♗e6 22. f3 ♖ad8 23. ♔f2** [23. h4? gh4 24. ♖h4 g5! 25. ♖h2 ♗g4!∓] **d5! 24. h4!?∞ ed4 25. cd4 de4?!** [25... ♘d3 26. cd3 de4 27. de4 ♕d4 28. ♕d4 ♖d4 29. hg5 ♖d2 30. ♔e3 ♖a2 31. ♖a2 ♗a2 32. ♖a1 ♗c4 33. ♖a7 ♗a6 34. ♗d6=] **26. ♗e4 ♕d4 27. ♕d4 ♖d4 28. hg5± ♘g6 29. ♖hd1 ♖ed8 30. ♖d4 ♖d4 31. a4! ♖d7⊕ 32. a5 a6 33. ♖a3!± ♘e7** [33... ♘f8 34. ♖d3 ♖d3 35. ♗d3 ♘d7 36. ♗d6±] **34. ♖d3 ♖d3 35. ♗d3 ♔f8 36. ♔e3 ♔e8 37. ♔d4 ♔d7 38. c4 ♘c8 39. ♔c5 ♔e7 40. ♗e5 g6 41. ♗b8!** [×♘c8] **♔d7 42. ♔d4** [△ ♔e5, ♗e2, f4-f5+–] **♘d6 43. ♗d6!+– ♔d6 44. c5 ♔e7 45. ♔e5 ♗d5 46. f4 ♗f3 47. f5 gf5 48. gf5 ♗d5 49. f6 ♔d7 50. ♗f5 ♔c7 51. g6 fg6 52. ♗g6 ♔d7 53. ♗f5 ♔e8 54. ♗c8 ♗c4 55. ♗b7 ♔d7 56. ♔f5 ♗d3 57. ♔g5 ♔e6 58. ♗a6! ♗a6 59. ♔g6 ♗c4 60. a6! 1 : 0** **[Istrăţescu]**

322. **C 49**

ŠIROV 2670 – JUSUPOV 2645

München 1993

1. e4 e5 2. ♘f3 ♘f6 3. ♘c3 ♘c6 4. ♗b5 ♗b4 5. 0–0 0–0 6. d3 d6 7. ♗g5 ♗c3 8. bc3 ♕e7 9. ♖e1 ♘d8 10. d4 ♗g4 11. h3 ♗f3 [11... ♗h5 12. ♗h4! △ 12... ♘e6? 13. g4 ♗g6 14. ♘e5±] **12. ♕f3 ♘e6!? N** [12... h6±] **13. ♗h4!?** [13. ♗e3 c5!? 14. de5 de5=] **♖ad8** [13... ed4 14. e5! de5 15. ♖e5 dc3 16. ♖ae1!⩱; 13... ♘f4!? 14. a4 ♘g6 15. ♗g5 h6 16. ♗c1±] **14. ♖ad1 ♘f4** [△ ♕e6] **15. ♗g5!?** [15. ♗c4 ♘g6 16. ♗g5 h6 17. ♗c1 ♖fe8=] **♘e6** [15... ♘g6? 16. h4! h6 17. h5 hg5 18. hg6±] **16. h4!?** [16. ♗c1 c5=] **h6?!** [16... ♘g5! 17. hg5 ♘d7 18. ♕g3 c6 (Ka. Müller) 19. ♗f1 (19. ♗c4 ♘b6 △ 20. ♗b3?! c5!) f6 (19... g6!?∞) 20. g6 h6∞] **17. ♗c1** [17. ♗e3±] **♔h8?!** [17... ♘d7 18. g3±] **18. g3 ♘d7 19. ♕h5** [19. ♕g4!? c5! (19... ♘f6?! 20. ♕f5±; 19... c6 20. ♗f1 △ 20... d5? 21. de5 ♘e5 22. ♕h5) 20. d5 ♘c7 21. ♗f1±] **c6** [19... c5? 20. de5 de5 (20... ♘e5 21. f4±) 21. ♗d7 ♖d7 22. ♕e5±] **20. ♗f1 ♕f6 21. ♗e3 ♔g8 22. ♗h3?** [22. ♕g4! (△ f4) d5 23. f4 ef4 24. e5 ♕g6 25. ♕g6 fg6 26. ♗h3 ♖de8 27. gf4! ♘b6 28. ♖f1±] **♘b6 23. ♖d3?! ♘c4 24. ♖f1 ♖fe8 25. f4 ♘e3!** [25... ed4 26. f5!→] **26. fe5 ♕g6 27. ♕g6 fg6 28. ♖e3 de5 29. ♖d1?!** [29. ♗e6 ♖e6 30. ♖d1=] **♘c5!∓ 30. ♗g2 ♘a4?⊕** [30... ♖d6! 31. d5∓] **31. ♖b1!∞ b5** [⌓ 31... ♘b6=] **32. d5! a6?!** [32... ♘b6 33. dc6 a6=] **33. c4!± ♖d6 34. ♖a3 ♖c8** [34... ♘c5!? 35. dc6 bc4±] **35. ♗h3 ♖cd8 36. ♖a4! ba4 37. c5 ♖f6 38. c4! ♔f8 39. ♖b6 cd5?** [39... ♖f3! 40. dc6 ♖g3 41. ♔h2 ♖h3 42. ♔h3 ♖c8 43. ♖a6 ♔e7±] **40. ed5 ♖f3 41. c6 ♖g3 42. ♔h2 ♖c3 43. c7 ♖e8 44. ♖b8 ♖c4 45. d6 1 : 0** **[Širov]**

323.** **C 54**

B. GEL'FAND 2690 – ŠIROV 2670

München 1993

1. e4 e5 2. ♘f3 ♘c6 3. ♗c4 ♘f6 4. d3 ♗c5 5. c3 0–0 [RR 5... a6 6. 0–0 ♗a7

7. ♘bd2 d6 8. ♗b3 ♘e7 9. ♖e1 ♘g6 10. ♘f1 c6 11. h3 ♕c7 12. d4 0–0 13. ♘g3 ♗e6 14. ♗c2?! h6 15. ♗e3 ♖ad8!? N (15... ♖fe8 – 46/409) 16. ♕c1 ♖fe8 17. b3 ♗c8! (△ d5=) 18. c4 ed4 19. ♗d4 ♗d4 20. ♘d4 d5 21. cd5 1/2 : 1/2 P. Wolff 2580 – I. Sokolov 2640, Wijk aan Zee (open) 1993; 14. ♗e6 △ ♗e3±; 14. ♗g5± I. Sokolov; 5... d6 6. ♗b3 a6 7. ♘bd2 (7. h3!? ♗e6 8. ♘bd2 0–0 9. ♕e2 ♗a7 10. g4!?) 0–0 8. 0–0 ♗a7 9. h3 ♘e7 10. ♖e1 ♘g6 11. ♘f1 ♔h8!? N (11... ♘h5 – 47/(394)) 12. ♘g3 c6 13. ♕e2?! ♗e6 14. ♗d2 ♕c7 15. ♖ad1 ♖ae8 16. ♗c1 h6 17. ♘h2 d5 18. ♘h5 ♕e7! 19. ♘f6 ♕f6 20. ♘g4 ♕h4 (A. Kofidis 2360 – Skembris 2565, Greece (ch) 1993) 21. ed5∓; ⌓ 13. d4 Skembris] **6. b4 ♗b6 7. a4 a6 8. 0–0 d5!? N** [8... h6 – 54/309; 8... d6] **9. ed5 ♘d5 10. ♕b3 ♘f6** [10... ♘f4? 11. ♗f4 ef4 12. a5 ♗a7 13. d4±; 10... ♗e6 11. ♘g5 h6 12. ♘e6 fe6 *a)* 13. ♘d2? ♖f2 14. ♖f2 ♗f2 15. ♔f2 ♕h4 16. ♔e2 (16. ♔g1? ♕e1 17. ♘f1 ♖f8 18. d4 ♕f2 19. ♔h1 ♕f1–+) ♕g4→; *b)* 13. ♖a2 ♖f7 14. ♔h1!? △ f3, ♘d2-e4±] **11. ♘g5 ♕e8 12. ♘d2** [12. ♗e3!? ♗e3 13. fe3 h6 14. ♘e4 ♘e4 (14... ♘g4 15. ♖f3 △ h3) 15. de4±] **h6 13. ♘ge4 ♘h5** [13... ♘e4 14. de4 ♔h8 15. ♗d3 (15. ♕c2!?) ♗e6 16. ♕c2 ♖d8 17. ♘c4±] **14. a5** [14. ♗a3 ♘f4 (14... ♔h8 15. b5 ♘a5 16. ♕d1!±) 15. b5 ♘a5 16. ♕c2 (16. ♕b4 ♘g6 17. ♕b2 ♘e7 18. ♕b4 ♘g6=) ♘c4 17. dc4!? (17. ♘c4 f5 18. ♗f8 fe4=/∞) f5! 18. ♗f8 fe4 19. ♗b4 (19. c5 ♗a5 20. ♘c4 ♗c3∓) ♗h3! 20. g3 ♕h5 21. c5 ♗g2! 22. cb6 ♗f3 (22... ♕h3? 23. f3! ♘e2 24. ♔f2) 23. ♘f3 ♕f3 24. gf4 ♕g4=] **♗a7 15. b5 ab5 16. ♕b5 ♗b6!?** [16... ♔h8?! 17. ♗a3 ♖g8 18. ♗c5 ♘f4 19. ♗e3!?±; 16... ♔h7 17. ♗a3 ♖h8 △ 18... f5, 18... ♘f4∞ Širov] **17. ab6!** [17. ♘d6 ♗f2 18. ♖f2 cd6 19. ♘e4 ♕d8∓] **♖a1 18. ♘b3** [18. bc7 ♘f4 19. ♘b3 ♘e2 20. ♔h1 ♖b1!∓] **♖c1** [18... ♖a6 19. bc7 ♕e7 20. ♕c5!±; 18... ♖b1 19. bc7 ♕e7 20. ♕b6 ♘f4 21. ♗f4 ♖f1 22. ♔f1 ef4 23. ♘bc5=/∞] **19. ♖c1 ♘f4** [19... ♕d8!? 20. ♘a5 (20. d4?! cb6 21. de5 ♕e7 △ 22. e6 ♗e6!; 20. bc7 ♕c7=) ♘f4 21. ♖b1 cb6 22. ♘c6 bc6 23. ♕b6 ♗e6!=] **20. ♖b1 ♔h7?** [20... ♕d8 21. ♘bc5 ♔h8 (△ 22. bc7 ♕c7 23. ♘b7?? ♗b7 24. ♕b7 ♖b8–+) 22. bc7 ♕c7 23. ♕b6 (23. g3? ♘h3 24. ♔g2 f5 25. ♘d2±; 23... f5!∓) ♕e7 24. ♖e1∞; 20... ♔h8] **21. bc7 f5 22. ♘g3 h5 23. d4! ed4** [23... h4 24. ♘e2 ♘g2 25. ♔g2 ♕g6 (25... f4 26. f3 ♕g6 27. ♔f2+–) 26. ♔f1 f4 27. ♗d3!+–] **24. ♘d4 h4 25. ♘ge2 ♘e2 26. ♗e2 ♖f7 27. ♗f3 ♖c7?** [27... ♖e7! 28. ♔f1! (28. ♗c6 bc6 29. ♘c6 ♖e1 30. ♖e1 ♕e1 31. ♕f1 ♕c3=) ♕d7! 29. ♗c6 (29. ♘c6 bc6 30. ♗c6 ♕c7⇆) bc6 30. ♕c5! (30. ♕c6 ♕c6 31. ♘c6 ♗a6 32. ♔g1 ♖c7=) ♕c7 31. ♘f3±] **28. ♘f5+– ♗f5 29. ♕f5 ♕g6 30. ♕e4 ♕e4 31. ♗e4** [♖ 9/i] **g6 32. f3 ♔h6 33. ♔f2 ♘e5 34. ♖b5** [34. ♔e3!? ♖d7 35. ♖b4 △ ♖d4] **♘c4 35. ♖b7 ♖c5 36. ♖b4** [36. ♖d7 ♖a5⇆] **h3 37. gh3??** [37. g4 ♘d2 38. ♖d4 ♘e4 39. ♖e4 ♖c3 40. ♔g3+–] **♘d2!** [37... ♘d6 38. ♗b1 ♖c3 39. ♖b6+–] **38. ♗d3** [38. ♔e3 ♘e4 39. fe4 ♖c3=] **♖c3 39. ♖d4 ♖c6= 40. ♔e3 ♘b3 41. ♖d5 ♘c5 42. ♗b5 ♖e6 43. ♔f2** [43. ♔d4!?] **♘b7 44. h4 ♘d6 45. ♗d7 ♖f6 46. ♗g4 ♘e8 47. h5 g5 48. ♖d8 ♘d6 49. ♔e3** [49. ♖h8!? ♔g7 50. ♖a8 ♔h6 51. ♖a5 ♘e8 52. ♔g3 △ h4] **♘f5 50. ♔e4 ♘h4 51. ♔e5 ♖f4 52. ♖d3 ♔g7 53. ♖a3 ♔h6 54. ♖a6 1/2 : 1/2**
[B. Gel'fand]

324. C 54

MEN – SHERZER 2460

USA (ch) 1992

1. e4 e5 2. ♘f3 ♘c6 3. ♗c4 ♗c5 4. d3 ♘f6 5. 0–0 d6 6. c3 ♗g4?! [⌓ 6... 0–0 △ ♗e6] **7. ♗b3 N** [7. ♕b3 – 3/249; 7. b4; 7. h3 ♗h5] **♕d7 8. ♘bd2 0-0-0 9. ♗c2** [△ b4] **d5 10. b4 ♗b6 11. ♕e2?!** [11. a4 a5! 12. ♗a3!? (12. b5 ♘e7 13. h3 ♗h3!? 14. ♘e5 ♕e6 15. d4 ♗g4) ab4 13. cb4→⟪; 11. ♗b2 de4 12. de4 ♘h5!? 13. a4 a5 14. b5!? ♘e7 15. ♘c4 ♕d1 16. ♗d1±] **♖he8 12. ♖e1** [△ 13. h3 ♗h3 14. gh3 ♕h3 15. ♕f1] **♘h5** [12... d4? 13. b5 ♘e7 14. c4 (14. ♘c4!?) ♘g6 (14... ♗a5 15. ♘e5) 15. ♘b3 ♘h5 16. ♗d1 ♘hf4 17. ♕f1→⟪] **13. ed5** [⌓ 13. ♕f1 ♘f4 14. a4 a5 15. b5 ♘b8 ×♘b8] **♘f4 14. ♕e4**

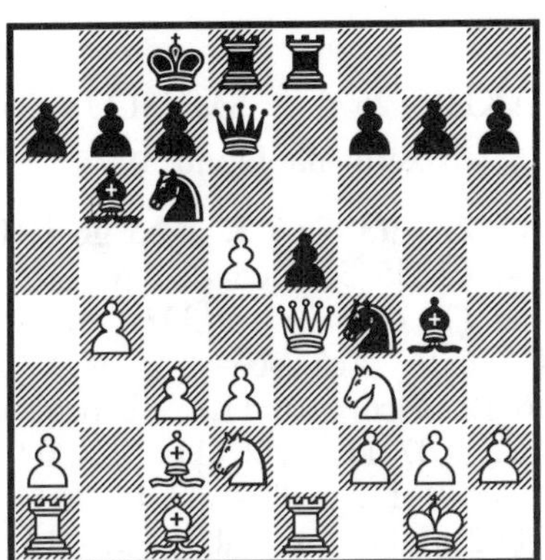

14... ♘d4!! 15. cd4 [15. ♘d4?? ed4−+; 15. ♘e5?? ♖e5 16. ♕e5 ♘c2 17. ♕f4 ♘e1−+] **f5 16. ♘e5?** [16. ♕e3 ♘d5 (16... ♗d4 17. ♘d4 ed4 18. ♕f4 ♖e1 19. ♘f1 △ 19... ♗e2? 20. ♗b2±) 17. ♕g5 (17. ♕e2? ♗d4 18. ♖b1 ♘c3) h6 18. ♕h4 g5 19. ♕h6 ♖h8 20. ♕g5!? ♖dg8 21. ♘e5 ♖g5 22. ♘d7 ♔d7=∞ Sherzer] **fe4 17. ♘d7 ♗d4!** [17... ed3? 18. ♘b6 ab6 19. ♖e8 ♖e8 20. ♘f3!? (20. ♘f1) ♘e2 21. ♔f1 dc2 22. ♘e5±] **18. ♘e4 ♘e2! 19. ♔f1 ♗a1 20. ♗g5 ♘d4! 21. ♗d8** [21. ♗a4 ♗d7 22. ♗d7 ♖d7 23. ♘d6 cd6!−+] **♘c2 22. ♖c1 ♗d7! 23. ♗h4 ♗a4⊕ 24. d6!** [△ d7] **♗b2! 25. ♖b1 ♗d4 26. b5! c6!** [26... ♘a3? 27. ♖b4 ♗b5 28. ♖d4 ♖e4?? (28... ♘c2 29. d7) 29. d7+−] **27. bc6 ♗c6 28. ♖c1 ♘b4?? 29. ♖c4 ♘d3 30. d7?** [30. ♖d4 ♘e5 (30... ♖e4? 31. d7+−) 31. f3±] **♔d7 31. ♖d4 ♔c7 32. f3?** [32. ♗g3 ♔b6 (△ 33. ♘d6? ♖e1#) 33. f3±] **♗e4 33. fe4 ♘e5 34. ♔e2 ♔c6 35. ♗g3 b5! 36. ♖d5 ♘c4 37. ♔d3 ♖f8 38. a4!? a6 39. ab5?** [⌓ 39. ♔d4 ♖f1 40. ♖c5 ♔b6 41. ♗c7 ♔b7 42. ab5] **ab5 40. ♔d4 ♖f1 41. ♖c5 ♔b6 42. ♗c7 ♔a6 43. ♖c6?** [⌓ 43. ♔d5] **♔b7 44. ♖c5 ♖d1 45. ♔c3 ♔a6 46. ♖c6?** [⌓ 46. ♗f4] **♔b7 47. ♖c5 ♘d2!!−+ 48. ♔c2 ♘e4 49. ♔d1?** [49. ♖b5 ♔c7 50. ♖e5 (50. ♔d1? ♘c3) ♖d4 51. ♖e7 ♔d6 52. ♖g7 ♘f6!] **♘c5 50. ♗e5 g6 51. ♗c3 ♔c6 52. ♔e2 ♔d5 53. ♔e3 ♘e6 54. ♔f3??** [⌓ 54. ♗d2] **♔c4 55. ♗a5 ♔d3! 56. ♗e1 ♘c7 57. ♔f4!** [57. ♔g4 h6 △ ♘d5] **♘d5 58. ♔g5 ♘c3 0 : 1**
[Seirawan]

325. C 54

DJURHUUS 2485 − SKEMBRIS 2565

Gausdal 1993

1. e4 e5 2. ♗c4 ♘f6 3. d3 ♗c5 4. ♘f3 0−0 5. 0−0 [5. ♘e5 d5→] **d6 6. h3 ♘c6 7. c3 ♗b6 8. ♗b3 ♘e7 9. ♘bd2** [△ ♘c4 ×♗b6] **c6 10. ♖e1 ♘g6 11. d4 N** [11. ♘f1 − 53/311] **♕e7 12. ♗c2** [△ ♘f1 ×e4] **♗e6∞ 13. ♘f1 ♖fe8 14. ♘g3 ♖ad8!?** [14... h6 15. ♗e3 ♖ad8 16. ♕c1=] **15. ♘f5** [15. ♗e3 d5!?] **♕f8!** [15... ♗f5? 16. ef5±] **16. ♗g5** [16. ♗e3=] **♔h8!⇆ 17. ♘h2?!** [17. ♗f6 gf6⇆ △ d5; 17. ♕c1!?] **d5! 18. ed5** [18. ♗f6 gf6 19. ♘g4 ♗f5 20. ef5 ♘f4→» △ 21. ♘f6? ♕g7; 18. de5 ♘e4!?∞; 18. ♘g4 ♘g4! 19. ♗d8 (19. hg4 f6∓) ♘f2! 20. ♔f2 ♖d8=∞↑ ×♔f2, ⇔d] **♖d5∓ 19. ♗f6** [19. ♘e3 ♖d7∓] **gf6 20. ♘g4 ♗f5 21. ♗f5 ♕g7** [△ ♘f4→»] **22. ♗g6 hg6! 23. ♕f3 ♖e6 24. ♘e3!?** [24. de5 fe5∓ ×f2, ⇔d] **♖b5 25. ♘c4 ed4 26. ♘b6** [26. ♖e6 fe6∓] **ab6?!** [26... ♖b6∓] **27. cd4 ♖b2 28. d5! cd5 29. ♖e6?!** [29. ♕d5! ♖e5 30. ♖e5 (30. ♕b7 ♕f8∓ △ ♕c5, ♔g7) fe5 31. ♖e1! (31. ♕b7 ♕f6∓ △ ♔g7 ×a2, f2) ♕f6□ (31... f6? 32. ♖c1→) 32. ♕e5=] **fe6 30. ♖c1 ♖b4!∓** [△ ♖c4 ×h4; 30... ♕d7? 31. ♕f4+−] **31. ♖c8 ♔h7 32. ♕a3!?** [32. ♕c3 ♖c4∓] **♕e7** [△ ♖b1−+; 32... ♕d7 (△ 33. ♕b4 ♕c8 34. ♕e7=) 33. ♕a8→] **33. ♕a8?!⊕** [33. ♔h2!?∓] **♔h6!!∓ 34. ♕b8** [34. ♖h8∓] **e5** [×g3] **35. ♖c7?⊕** [35. ♖h8!? ♔g5 36. ♕g8! (△ 36... ♖b1? 37. ♔h2→ ×h4) ♕c5!∓] **♖b1 36. ♔h2 ♕b4** [△ ♕f4−+] **37. g3** [37. ♕h8 ♔g5 38. g3−+ − 37. g3] **♕e4 38. ♕h8 ♔g5 39. h4** [39. ♕h4 ♕h4 40. gh4 ♔h4−+] **♔g4 40. ♕c8 f5 41. ♖c1 ♕f3!−+** [42. ♖b1 ♕f2 43. ♔h1 ♔h3] **0 : 1** **[Skembris]**

326.* !N **C 55**

B. GEL'FAND 2690 − BAREEV 2670

München 1993

1. e4 e5 2. ♗c4 ♘f6 3. d3 ♘c6 4. ♘f3 h6 [RR 4... ♗e7 5. 0−0 0−0 6. ♗b3 d5

7. ed5 ♘d5 8. h3! N (8. ♖e1 — 53/(313)) ♖e8 (8... f5?! 9. ♘c3 ♗e6 10. ♖e1 ♗f6 11. ♗g5! △ 11... ♗g5 12. ♘g5 ♕g5 13. ♘d5 ♖ac8 14. f4±; 8... ♔h8 9. ♖e1 f6 10. d4 ed4 11. ♘d4 ♘d4 12. ♕d4 ♘b6 13. ♕d8 ♗d8 14. ♘c3⩲; 8... ♗f6 9. ♖e1 △ ♘bd2-c4±) 9. ♖e1 ♗b4!? (9... ♗f8 10. d4 e4 11. ♘g5 ♗f5 12. ♘f7 ♔f7 13. ♕h5 g6 14. ♕h7 ♗g7 15. ♗h6 ♖g8 16. ♘c3±) 10. c3 ♗f8 11. d4! e4□ 12. ♘e5! (12. ♘g5 ♗f5!∞) ♗f5 (12... f6 13. ♘c6 bc6 14. ♘d2 f5 15. ♘c4±; 12... f5 13. ♗f4 ♗e6 14. ♘c6 bc6 15. ♗e5 △ ♘d2, f3⩲) *a)* 13. ♘f7? ♔f7 14. ♕h5 g6□ 15. ♕h7 ♗g7 16. ♗h6 ♖g8 17. c4 ♘f6 18. c5 ♔e7!−+; *b)* 13. ♘c6?! bc6 14. ♘d2 ♕h4 15. ♘f1 (P. Stratil 2255 – Novik 2430, Bratislava 1992) ♖ad8 16. ♘g3 ♗g6 17. ♕g4∞; *c)* 13. ♘g4!? △ ♘e3⩲ Novik] **5. 0–0 d6 6. c3 g5!? N** [6... g6 — 53/313] **7. ♘bd2** [7. h4!?] **♗g7 8. ♗b3 0–0** [8... ♘e7!?] **9. ♘c4 ♗e6 10. ♖e1 ♖e8?!** [10... b5 *a)* 11. ♘e3 d5 12. ♕c2 (12. a4?! de4 13. ♗e6 fe6 14. ab5?! ef3 15. bc6 fg2∓ ×f4, ⟫) ♕d7=; *b)* 11. ♘a3 a6 12. d4 ♗b3 13. ab3 ed4 14. ♘d4 ♘d4 15. cd4⩲] **11. h4 g4** [11... gh4?! 12. ♘h4 △ 12... ♘e4? 13. ♖e4 d5 14. ♖g4! dc4 15. ♗c4 ♗g4 16. ♕g4±→] **12. ♘h2 h5** [12... ♕d7 13. ♘e3 h5 14. ♘hf1 ×f5] **13. ♗g5! ♕d7** [13... d5 14. ed5 ♗d5 15. ♘f1±] **14. ♘f1 d5?!** [14... ♘h7 15. ♕d2! (15. ♘g3 ♘g5 16. hg5 h4 17. ♘h5 ♕e7⇆) f6 16. ♗h6± △ ♘g3 ×h5, f5] **15. ♘cd2!** [15. ed5? ♘d5 16. ♘g3 f6 17. ♗d2 ♕f7∞] **d4** [15... ♘h7 16. ♘g3 ♘g5 (16... f6 17. ♗e3 d4 18. cd4! ed4 19. ♗f4+−) 17. hg5 h4 18. ed5 ♗d5 19. ♘h5 ♗b3 20. ♕b3± △ ♘e4] **16. ♘g3 dc3** [16... ♘h7 17. ♘h5 f6 18. cd4!+−] **17. bc3 ♕d3 18. ♗f6 ♗f6 19. ♘h5 ♗h8** [19... ♗h4!? 20. ♗e6 ♖e6 21. ♕g4 ♖g6 22. ♕h4 ♕d2 23. ♖e3 ♕d8 24. ♕h2!±→⟫] **20. ♖e3 ♕d7 21. ♗e6 ♕e6 22. ♖g3 ♖ad8 23. ♕e2!+−** [23. ♖g4? ♔f8 (△ ♖d2) 24. ♖g3 ♕d7] **♔f8 24. ♘f1! ♔e7 25. ♖g4 ♖g8** [⌓ 25... ♔d7 △ ♔c8] **26. ♖g8 ♖g8 27. ♖b1! ♘d8 28. ♘hg3 ♔d7 29. ♘e3 ♗g7 30. ♖d1 ♔c8 31. ♕g4 1 : 0** **[B. Gel'fand]**

327.* !N **C 60**

PSAKHIS 2575 – SMYSLOV 2530
Rostov na Donu 1993

1. e4 e5 2. ♘f3 ♘c6 3. ♗b5 g6 [RR 3... ♘ge7 4. c3 d5 5. ♘e5 de4 6. ♕e2 ♕d5 7. f4! N (7. ♘c6 — 55/(322)) ef3 8. ♘f3 (8. gf3 a6 9. ♗c6 bc6=) ♕e6 9. d4 (9. ♘e5 f6 10. ♘c6 ♘c6 11. ♗c6 bc6=) ♕e2 10. ♔e2 ♗d7 11. ♔f2 (11. ♗f4 0-0-0) f6 (11... ♘e5?! 12. ♗d7 ♘d7 13. ♗f4 Vul') 12. ♘bd2 0-0-0 13. ♘b3 ♘d5 14. ♗d2 ♘b6 15. ♖ad1⩲○ Arbakov 2430 – Vul' 2360, Rossija 1993] **4. d4 ed4 5. ♗g5 ♗e7 6. ♗e7 ♕e7 7. ♗c6 dc6 8. ♕d4 ♘f6 9. ♘c3 ♗g4 10. ♘d2 0–0 N** [10... c5 — 55/322] **11. h3** [11. f3!? ♗e6 12. 0-0-0 ♖fd8 13. ♕f2⩲] **♗e6 12. 0-0-0 ♖fd8 13. ♕e3 b5! 14. f4 ♘d7** [14... b4 15. ♘a4 ♗a2 16. ♕c5! (16. b3 ♘d5!) ♕c5 17. ♘c5 ♗e6 18. ♘a6⩲] **15. ♘f3 b4 16. ♘a4 ♘b6?!** [16... ♗c4!? 17. e5 (17. b3 ♗b5 18. ♘b2 a5⇆; 17. ♘d4 ♗b5 18. b3 ♗a4 19. ba4 ♕c5) ♗b5 18. ♖d7!? (18. ♕b3 ♘b6) ♕d7 (18... ♖d7 19. ♘c5 ♖d5 20. ♘e4 ♖e8 21. ♖e1!≂) 19. ♘c5 ♕d5 20. b3≂] **17. ♖d8** [17. ♘c5?! ♗a2! 18. b3 ♘d5!] **♖d8 18. ♘e5! ♘a4** [18... ♖d6 19. ♘c5+−] **19. ♘c6 ♕e8 20. ♘d8 ♕d8 21. ♕a7 ♘b6 22. ♖d1 ♕e7 23. ♕a5!± ♘c4 24. ♕a8 ♔g7 25. ♕d8 ♕c5 26. ♕d4 ♕d4 27. ♖d4 c5 28. ♖d3 h5!□** [28... ♔f6 29. g4+−] **29. b3** [29. f5 gf5 30. ef5 ♗f5 31. ♖d5 ♔g6 32. ♖c5 ♘e3] **♘b6 30. ♖d6 ♘d7 31. ♔d2 ♔f8 32. ♔e3** [32. c3?! ♘f6!; 32. ♔d3 ♔e7 33. ♖c6 g5!? 34. ♔e3 f6; 32. h4!?] **♔e7 33. ♖c6 h4 34. ♔f2** [34. ♔f3 f5!?] **♘f6 35. ♔e3** [35. ♔f3!? ♘d7 36. g4 hg3 37. ♔g3 ♘f6 38. ♔f3 ♘d7 39. h4±] **♘d7 36. ♖c8?! f5! 37. ♖h8** [37. e5? ♘e5] **♘f6** [37... fe4 38. ♖h4±] **38. ♖h4 ♘e4 39. ♖h8** [39. g4 ♔f8!? 40. ♖h7 ♗f7] **♘c3 40. ♖a8 ♗d5 41. ♖a7 ♔e6** [41... ♔f6!? 42. ♖a6 ♔g7] **42. ♖a6 ♔f7 43. g3 ♗g2 44. h4 ♗h3** [44... ♔g7!?] **45. a4! ba3 46. ♖a3 ♗g4 47. ♖a7 ♔e6 48. ♖a6 ♔f7 49. ♖c6 ♘e4 50. c3! ♘c3 51. ♖c5 ♘e4 52. ♖c6 ♗d1 53. b4 ♗a4 54. ♖a6** [54. ♖c7 ♔e6 55. g4 ♘f6!=] **♗b5 55. ♖b6?** [55. ♖a7

♔e6 56. g4! ♘c3 (56… ♘f6 57. gf5 gf5 58. ♔d4 ♘d5 59. ♖a5 ♗c6 60. b5+−) 57. h5! (57. ♔d4? ♘e2 58. ♔c5 fg4 59. ♔b5 g3 60. ♖a1 g2 61. ♔a6 g1♕ 62. ♖g1 ♘g1 63. b5 ♘f3 64. b6 ♘d4 65. b7 ♘c6 66. ♔b6 ♘b8=) gh5 58. gh5 ♘d5 59. ♔d4 ♘f4 60. h6 ♘g6 61. h7 ♔f6 62. ♖b7+−] **♗d7 56. ♔d4 ♘g3 57. b5 ♗b5! 58. ♖b5 ♔g7= 59. ♔e5 ♘h5 60. ♖b4 ♔h7 61. ♔e6 ♔g7 62. ♖a4 ♘g3 63. ♖a8 ♘h5 64. ♔e5 ♘g3 1/2 : 1/2 [Psakhis]**

328. !N C 65

A. ZAPATA 2530 – W. ARENCIBIA 2535

Linares 1992

1. e4 e5 2. ♘f3 ♘c6 3. ♗b5 ♘f6 4. d4 ed4 5. 0–0 a6 6. ♗c6 dc6 7. e5 ♘e4 8. ♖e1! N [8. ♕e2 – 23/258] **♘c5 9. ♗g5! ♕d5 10. ♘d4± ♘e6 11. ♘e6 ♗e6** [11… ♕d1? 12. ♘c7] **12. ♕h5!** [△ ♘c3⟳] **♕c4** [12… ♗c5? 13. ♘c3 ♕d4 (13… ♕c4? 14. ♖e4) 14. ♘e4 ♗b6 (14… 0–0 15. ♖ad1 ♕c4 16. b3+−) 15. ♖ad1 ♕b2 16. ♗f6! gf6 17. ♘f6 ♔e7 18. ♕g5 ♔f8 19. ♘h5+−] **13. ♘c3 ♕g4 14. ♕g4 ♗g4 15. ♘e4± h6** [15… ♗e7 16. ♘d6!] **16. ♗h4 ♔d7 17. f4 ♖e8 18. ♗f2 ♔c8 19. h3** [19. ♗c5!?] **♗e6** [19… ♗f5 20. g4] **20. ♗c5 ♗c5 21. ♘c5 h5 22. ♖ad1 ♗f5 23. ♖e2 ♖d8 24. ♖d8 ♖d8** [♖ 9/i] **25. ♔f2 ♖d4!?** [25… b6!? (△ 26. ♘a6? c5 27. b4 ♔b7 28. b5 ♖d4−+ △ ♗d7) 26. ♘e4±] **26. ♔e3 ♖c4 27. ♘d3 b6** [27… ♗d3 28. cd3±] **28. ♘e1** [△ ♔f3, g4] **h4 29. b3 ♖e4 30. ♔f3 ♖d4** [30… ♖e2 31. ♔e2 c5 32. ♔d2 (△ ♘f3) ♗e4 33. ♔e3 ♗f5 34. a3 ♔d7 35. c3 (△ ♘f3) ♗e6 36. c4 (36. b4 cb4 37. cb4 ♗d5) b5 37. ♘f3 bc4 38. bc4 ♗c4 39. ♘h4±] **31. c3 ♖d1 32. ♔e3!?** [△ ♘f3 ×h5; 32. ♔f2 ♗d3 33. ♖e3 ♖d2 34. ♔g1 ♗e2⇆] **c5 33. ♘f3 ♖d3 34. ♔f2 ♖c3 35. ♘h4 ♗d3 36. ♖d2 c4 37. bc4 ♗c4 38. ♘f5 g6 39. ♘e3 ♗e6 40. g4** [△ h4-h5, f5] **♖c5** [40… ♖a3 41. h4 ♖a2 42. ♖a2 ♗a2 43. h5+−] **41. h4 ♖c1 42. f5+− gf5 43. gf5 ♗d7 44. ♔g3 ♖e1** [44… ♖h1 45. ♖h2 ♖h2 46. ♔h2 ♔d8 47. h5 ♔e8 48. h6 ♔f8 49. ♔g3 ♔g8 (49… c5 50. ♔f4 b5 51. ♔g5 c4 52. ♔f6 ♔g8 53. h7!) 50. ♔f4 ♔h7 51. ♔g5 c5 52. ♘d5 c4 53. ♘f6 ♔h8 54. e6 fe6 55. ♘d7 c3 56. ♔g6! c2 57. ♘e5 c1♕ 58. ♘f7 ♔g8 59. h7 ♔f8 60. h8♕ ♔e7 61. ♕d8#] **45. ♔f4 ♖h1 46. ♔g5 ♖h3 47. ♘g4 c5 48. h5 c4 49. h6 c3 50. ♖c2 ♔b7** [50… ♗a4 51. ♖c3! ♖c3 52. h7 ♖h3 53. ♘h6] **51. ♘f6** [51. ♖c3? ♖c3 52. h7 ♖c8] **♖g3 52. ♔f4 1 : 0 [A. Zapata, Henao]**

329. C 65

TIMMAN 2635 – BELJAVSKIJ 2610

Linares 1993

1. e4 e5 2. ♘f3 ♘c6 3. ♗b5 ♘f6 4. 0–0 ♗c5 5. ♘e5 ♘e5 6. d4 a6 7. de5?! N [⌓ 7. ♗a4 – C 78; 7. ♗e2 – 49/(379)] **ab5 8. ef6 ♕f6 9. ♘c3 c6□ 10. ♕d3 0–0 11. ♗e3 ♗e3 12. ♕e3 ♖e8** [⌓ 12… b4 13. e5 (13. ♘d1 ♖e8=) ♕f5 14. ♕e4! d6 15. ♕b4 de5 16. ♘e4 ♗e6=] **13. ♕c5! d6 14. ♕b4 ♕f4!** [△ d5] **15. a3?** [15. ♖ad1 d5 16. ♖fe1 ♗g4 17. f3 ♗h5=]

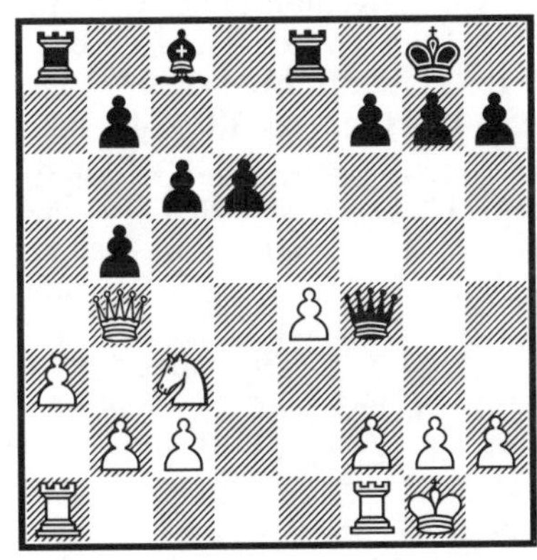

15… ♖e6!∓ 16. ♖ad1 ♖h6 17. g3 ♕f3 18. ♖d3 ♕h5 19. h4 g5 20. ♖d6? [20. f3∓] **♗h3!−+ 21. e5□** [21. ♖h6 ♕f3] **♖d6 22. ed6 ♕f3 23. ♕e4 ♕e4 24. ♘e4 ♗f1 25. ♔f1 gh4 26. gh4** [26. g4 ♖d8 27. ♔g2 ♔g7 28. f4 h5 29. g5 ♔g6] **♖d8 27. ♔e2 f5 28. ♘g3 ♖d6 29. ♘f5 ♖f6 30. ♘g3 ♖f4 31. h5 ♔f7 32. ♔e3 ♖h4 33. ♔f3 ♔f6 34. ♔e3 ♔g5 35. ♔f3 ♖f4 36. ♔e3 ♔g4 37. ♔e2 ♖f3 0 : 1 [Beljavskij]**

330.** C 67

SMIRIN 2555 – Y. ZILBERMAN 2490

Israel (ch) 1992

1. e4 e5 2. ♘f3 ♘c6 3. ♗b5 ♘f6 4. 0–0 ♘e4 5. d4 ♘d6 6. ♗c6 dc6 7. de5 ♘f5 8. ♕d8 ♔d8 9. ♘c3 [RR 9. ♖d1 ♔e8 10. ♘c3 ♗e6 11. h3 ♗b4 12. ♗d2 a5 13. a3!? N (13. ♘e2 – 52/329) ♗c3 14. ♗c3 c5 15. g4 ♘e7 16. ♔g2 (16. ♘g5? ♗d5) h5 17. ♔g3 ♖a6!? (Alexa. Ivanov 2545 – Sherzer 2460, USA (ch) 1992) 18. ♖d2!? hg4 19. hg4 b5 (19... ♘d5 20. ♖ad1 c6 21. a4 ♔e7 22. ♘g5± △ ♘e4) 20. ♘g5 (20. ♖ad1 ♘c6 21. b3 b4 22. ♗b2±) ♗d5 (△ 21. ♖ad1? b4) 21. b3⩲ P. Wolff] **h6** [9... ♗e6 10. ♘g5 ♗c4 11. ♖d1 ♔c8 12. b3 ♗b4 13. ♗b2 ♗c3 14. ♗c3 ♗d5 15. f3!⩲] **10. h3 ♔e8 11. ♘e2!? N** [11. b3 – 54/316; RR 11. ♖e1 N ♗b4 12. ♗d2 ♗e6 13. ♘e4 ♗d2 14. ♘ed2 ♖d8 15. ♖e4 c5 16. ♖a4 a6 17. ♖a5 c4 18. ♖e1 ♘e7 19. ♖e4 ♘c6 20. ♖a3 a5 21. ♘c4 ♗d5 22. ♖g4 ♗e6 23. ♖e4 ♗d5 1/2 : 1/2 Ljubojević 2605 – Zsu. Polgár 2560, Monaco 1993] **♗e6 12. ♘f4 ♗d5 13. ♘d5 cd5 14. g4 ♘e7 15. ♘d4! a6?** [15... c5? 16. ♘b5; 15... ♘c6 16. ♘c6 bc6 17. ♗e3 c5⩲; 15... ♘g6!? 16. f4 ♗c5] **16. f4± h5?!** [×g5; ⌓ 16... c5] **17. ♔g2 c5 18. ♘f3 d4 19. f5 ♘c6** [19... ♘d5 20. ♗d2] **20. ♗d2 ♖d8 21. ♖ae1** [△ ♘g5, e6] **hg4 22. hg4 ♖d5 23. c4! dc3** [23... ♖d8 24. ♘g5+–] **24. ♗c3 ♘b4?!** [⌓ 24... b5] **25. e6! ♘a2** [25... f6 26. ♗b4 cb4 27. ♖d1+–] **26. e7! ♘c3** [26... ♗e7 27. ♗g7 ♖g8 28. f6] **27. ef8♕ ♔f8 28. bc3 ♖h6 29. ♘e5** [△ ♘g6!] **♖hd6 30. g5** [△ ♘g6] **b5** [30... ♔g8 31. ♘d7! ♖d2 32. ♔g3 ♖6d3 33. ♔f4 ♖d7 34. ♖e8 ♔h7 35. ♖h1] **31. ♘g6!? ♖g6 32. fg6 ♖g5 33. ♔f3 ♖g6 34. ♖h1 ♖f6 35. ♔e4 g6 36. ♖ef1 ♖d6 37. ♖d1 ♖e6 38. ♔d5 c4 39. ♖de1 ♖f6 40. ♖hf1 1 : 0** **[Smirin]**

331.** C 67

VELIMIROVIĆ 2510 – M. KNEŽEVIĆ 2415

Beograd 1993

1. e4 e5 2. ♘f3 ♘c6 3. ♗b5 ♘f6 4. 0–0 ♘e4 5. d4 ♗e7 6. ♕e2 ♘d6 7. ♗c6 bc6 8. de5 ♘b7 9. ♘c3 0–0 10. ♖e1 ♘c5 11. ♘d4 [11. ♗e3 ♘e6 12. ♖ad1 ♖b8 13. ♘a4!? N (13. b3 – 44/397) f6!? 14. b3 a6 15. ♕d3 ♕e8 16. ef6 ♗f6 17. ♘c5 d6 18. ♘e6 (18. ♘a6!? ♖a8 19. ♘b4 c5 20. ♘d5 ♖a2±) ♗e6 19. ♗d4 (19. ♕a6?! ♗d5) ♕f7 20. ♖d2 (20. ♕a6 ♗d5!) ♗d5! 21. c4 ♗f3 22. ♕f3 ♖be8 23. ♖e8 ♖e8 24. ♗e3 ♗g5± Soloženkin 2465 – M. Knežević 2400, Moskva 1992; RR 11. ♗f4 ♘e6 12. ♗g3 ♖b8 (12... d5?! 13. ed6 cd6 14. ♖ad1±) 13. b3 f5 14. ef6 ♗f6 15. ♘e5 ♗e5 16. ♕e5 d6 17. ♕a5!? N (17. ♕e4) a6 18. ♖ad1 ♔h8 19. ♘e4 ♖b5 20. ♕c3 (△ 20... ♕e8? 21. ♗d6!) ♕d7?! 21. ♘d6! cd6 22. ♖d6 (E. Geller 2525 – P. Benkö 2420, Bad Wörishofen 1992) ♕e8!? 23. ♖c6 ♗d7⩲; ⌓ 20... ♗d7⩲ P. Benkö] **♘e6 12. ♗e3 ♖b8 13. ♖ab1 N** [13. ♘e6] **♘d4 14. ♗d4 c5 15. ♗e3 d5 16. ed6 ♗d6 17. ♕h5** [17. ♘e4!?] **♖b4! 18. h3 ♗b7 19. a3** [19. ♗c5? ♖h4 20. ♕f5 g6–+] **♖h4 20. ♕g5 ♗e7 21. ♕f5 g6 22. ♕e5 ♗d6 23. ♗g5 ♕d7!** [23... ♗e5 24. ♗d8 ♗c3±] **24. ♖bd1?** [24. ♕e3!? ♖d4∞] **f6!** [24... ♗g2?! 25. ♕g3!] **25. ♕d6!** [25. ♗f6? ♗e5 26. ♖d7 ♗f6 27. ♖c7 ♖f7–+] **cd6 26. ♗h4 ♖e8** [26... d5? 27. ♘d5 ♗d5 28. c4 ♕a4 29. b3 ♕b3 30. cd5] **27. ♖e8 ♕e8 28. ♖d6?** [28. ♗g3!?] **g5 29. ♗g3 f5 30. f3 ♕e3 31. ♗f2 ♕c1 32. ♖d1 ♕b2 33. ♘a4 ♕c2 34. ♖d8 ♔f7 35. ♘c5 ♗c6 36. ♖h8 ♕d1 37. ♔h2 ♕d6 38. ♔h1 ♕d1⊕ 39. ♗g1 ♗f3!–+ 40. ♖h7** [40. gf3 ♕f3 41. ♔h2 f4] **♔g6 41. ♖d7 ♗d5 42. ♘e6 ♗g2 43. ♔h2** [43. ♔g2 ♕e2 △ ♕e6] **♗d5 0 : 1** **[M. Knežević]**

332.** C 68

ROZENTALIS 2595 – V. MIKHALEVSKI 2305

Netanya 1993

1. e4 e5 2. ♘f3 ♘c6 3. ♗b5 a6 4. ♗c6 dc6 5. 0–0 ♕d6 6. ♘a3 b5 7. c3 c5 8. ♘c2 ♘e7 9. d4 [RR 9. a4!? N ♖b8 (9... ♗b7?! 10. ab5 ab5 11. ♖a8 ♗a8 12. ♕e2; 11. ♘a3!?) 10. ab5 ab5 11. d4 cd4 12. cd4 ed4 13. ♘cd4 c5 14. ♘b5!? (14. ♘b3 ♘c6 15. ♗e3 ♕d1 16. ♖fd1 c4=) ♕d1

15. ♘c7 ♔d8 16. ♖d1 ♔c7 17. ♗f4 ♔b7 18. ♗b8 (18. ♖a3?! ♘c6 19. ♘e5!? ♘e5 20. ♖b3 ♔c6 21. ♖b8 ♗d6; 18. ♖a5?! ♖a8 19. ♖c5 ♘g6) ♔b8 19. ♘e5 f6 (19... ♗e6?! 20. ♘d7!) 20. ♘f7!? (20. ♘d7 ♗d7 21. ♖d7 ♘c8=) ♖g8 21. ♖d8 ♔b7! (△ ♗e6, ♘c6; 21... ♔c7? 22. ♖a7; 21... ♘c6? 22. ♖e8 ♔c7 23. ♖a8 ♘b8 24. ♘d6; 24. ♘d8) 22. ♘d6 ♔c7 23. ♖a7! (1/2 : 1/2 Relange 2295 – Geenen 2320, Bruxelles (zt) 1993) ♔d8 24. ♘f7 ♔e8 25. ♘d6=; 22. ♖ad1!? Geenen] **cd4 10. cd4 ed4 11. ♘fd4 c5 12. ♘b3 ♕d1 13. ♖d1 ♘c6 14. ♘e3 N** [14. ♗e3 c4 15. ♘c5 f5 16. ♖d5 fe4 17. a4 b4 18. ♖c1 ♗e7 19. ♘e1 0–0 20. ♖c4 ♖f5 21. ♖d1 ♗c5 22. ♖c5 ♖c5 23. ♗c5 ♗g4 24. f3 ef3 25. ♘f3 b3 26. ♖d3 1/2 : 1/2 R. Hübner 2615 – Kamsky 2655, Manila (ol) 1992] **♗e6** [14... c4? 15. ♘d5 ♖a7 16. ♗e3 cb3 (16... ♖d7 17. ♘c5 ♗c5 18. ♗c5 ♘e5 19. ♗d4 △ ♘b6±; 16... ♖b7 17. a4! cb3 18. ab5 ab5 19. ♖a8 ♖b8 20. ♘c7 ♔e7 21. ♖b8 ♘b8 22. ♗c5 ♔f6 23. ♖d8 ♘a6□ 24. ♗f8 ♘c7 25. ♖c8 ♔e6 26. ♖c7 ♖f8 27. ♖c3±) 17. ♗a7 ♘a7 18. ♘c7 ♔e7 19. ab3 △ ♘a6±] **15. ♘d5 0-0-0 16. a4!?** [16. ♗e3 c4 17. ♘c5 ♗c5 18. ♗c5 ♔b7 19. a4 ♖d7∞] **ba4!□** [16... ♔b7? 17. ab5 ab5 18. ♗e3 c4 19. ♘a5+–; 16... c4?! 17. ab5 ab5 18. ♖a6 ♗d5 19. ♖d5! ♖d5 20. ♖c6!±] **17. ♖a4 ♘b4 18. ♖a5** [18. ♗e3!? ♘d5 19. ed5 ♖d5 (19... ♗d5?! 20. ♖a6!±) 20. ♖da1 ♖d3=] **♘d5** [18... c4! *a)* 19. ♘b6 ♔c7 20. ♖d8 ♔d8 (△ ♔c7!) 21. ♘d2? ♘d3 22. ♖a1 ♗c5∓; *b)* 19. ♘c5 ♘d5 20. ed5 (20. ♘e6 fe6 21. ed5 ♔b7∓) ♖d5 21. ♖d5 ♗d5 22. ♘a6 ♗c6!∓] **19. ed5 c4!** [19... ♖d5 20. ♖d5 ♗d5 21. ♘c5 ♗c4 22. ♗e3±] **20. ♗f4!?** [20. ♘a1? ♔b7! 21. ♗e3 ♗e7∓; 20. ♖a6 ♔b7! 21. ♗g5! ♖d5 (21... ♖d7? 22. ♖aa1!) 22. ♖d5 ♗d5 23. ♖a5!□ ♗c6! (△ ♗b4) 24. ♘c5! ♗c5 (24... ♔b6?? 25. ♗d8!#; 24... ♔c7 25. ♗e3!) 25. ♖c5=] **cb3⊕** [⌓ 20... ♗d5 21. ♖ad5 ♖d5 22. ♖d5 cb3 23. ♖d3=] **21. ♖c1 ♔b7 22. de6 fe6 23. ♖g5!** [△ ♖g3 ×g7, b3] **♖d4! 24. ♗e5 ♖d5 25. f4 ♖g8** [⌓ 25... a5 △ 26. ♖g3 a4] **26. ♖g3 ♖b5?!** [26... ♗c5! 27. ♔f1 g5!∞] **27. ♔f1 g6?** [27... ♗c5□ 28. ♖cc3±] **28. ♖c7+– ♔b6 29. ♖c8 ♔b7 30. ♖gc3 ♖d5 31. ♖3c7 ♔b6 32. ♖b8 ♔a5 33. ♗c3 1 : 0** **[V. Mikhalevski, J. Kagan]**

333.** !N **C 69**

MALIŠAUSKAS 2570 – JANDEMIROV 2465

Katowice 1993

1. e4 e5 2. ♘f3 ♘c6 3. ♗b5 a6 4. ♗c6 dc6 5. 0–0 f6 6. d4 ed4 7. ♘d4 c5 8. ♘b3 ♕d1 9. ♖d1 ♗g4 10. f3 ♗e6 11. ♗e3 [RR 11. ♗f4 c4 12. ♘d4 0-0-0 13. ♘c3 ♗f7 14. a4! N (14. ♘f5) ♗c5 15. ♗e3 ♘e7 16. ♘f5! ♗e3 (16... ♘f5 17. ♗c5±) 17. ♘e3 b6 (17... ♖d1 18. ♖d1 ♖d8 19. ♖d8 ♔d8 20. ♔f2⩲→») 18. ♔f2 c6 19. g4 ♔c7 20. h4 ♖d1 21. ♖d1 b5 22. h5 ♖b8 23. ♖a1± Nadanian 2380 – Seredenko 2335, corr. 1992; 14... ♘e7!? Nadanian] **b6 12. a4 c4!? N** [12... ♘e7 – 26/275; 12... ♔f7 – 47/409; RR 12... a5 N 13. ♘c3 c6 14. ♘c1 g6 15. ♘1e2 ♘h6 16. ♗h6 ♗h6 17. ♖d6 ♗d7 18. ♖ad1 ♖d8 19. ♖f6 ♔e7 20. ♖fd6 ♗e3 21. ♔f1 ♗d4 22. ♖6d4 cd4 23. ♘d4± Moróvić Fernández 2570 – Topalov 2635, León 1993] **13. ♘d4 0-0-0 14. ♘c3 ♗f7 15. a5 b5 16. ♘db5!?** [16. ♘c6 ♖d6! 17. ♘b5 (17. ♖d6 ♗d6 △ 18. ♘b5? ab5 19. a6 ♘e7 20. a7 ♔b7–+) ♖c6 18. ♘a7 ♔b7 19. ♖d8 ♗e7 20. ♘c6 ♔c6 21. ♖a8 ♔b7 22. ♖a7 ♔b8 23. ♖a6 ♗d6∓; 16. ♔f2!?∞] **♖d1 17. ♖d1 ab5 18. ♘b5 ♗e7□** [18... ♗e8 19. ♘a7 ♔b7 20. ♖d8+–; 18... ♘e7 19. a6 ♘c6 20. a7 ♔b7 21. ♖d7+–; 18... ♗b4 19. a6 ♘e7 20. a7 ♔b7 21. ♖d7+–] **19. a6** [19. ♘a7 ♔b7 20. ♖d7 ♗e8 21. a6 ♔a6 22. ♖c7 ♗d6 23. ♖g7 ♘e7∓ ×♘a7] **♗e8 20. a7 ♗c6 21. ♖a1 ♗a8 22. ♖a4 ♔d7** [22... c6!?] **23. ♖c4 ♗d6** [23... c6!? 24. ♖d4 ♔c8 25. ♖c4 ♘h6 (25... ♔d7=) 26. ♘d4 ♔d7 27. ♗h6 gh6 28. ♘f5∞] **24. ♘d6** [24. ♗b6!? cb6 25. ♖d4 (25. ♘d6 ♘e7!∓) ♘e7□ (25... ♔c6? 26. ♖d6 ♔b5 27. ♖d8 ♗b7 28. c4 ♔a6 29. a8♕ ♗a8 30. ♖a8 ♔b7 31. ♖f8 ♔c6 32. b4+–) 26. ♖d6 ♔c8 27. ♖b6 ♘c6 28. ♔f2 ♖d8 29. ♔e2∞] **cd6 25. ♖d4 ♘e7 26. ♗f4 ♘c6** [26... ♘c8!?] **27. ♖d6 ♔e7**

28. ♖d2 [[28... ♖d8?! 29. ♖d8 ♔d8 30. ♗e3 ♔c8 31. ♔f1 ♔b7 32. ♔e2 ♘a7 33. ♗a7 ♔a7 34. ♔d3 ♔b6 35. ♔d4±; 28... ♘a7!? 29. ♗e3 ♘c6 30. ♗c5 ♔f7 31. ♖d7 ♔g6 32. b4 ♖c8∞] **1/2 : 1/2** **[Jandemirov]**

334. **C 69**

WAITZKIN 2345 – I. GUREVICH 2515

New York 1993

1. e4 e5 2. ♘f3 ♘c6 3. ♗b5 a6 4. ♗c6 dc6 5. 0–0 f6 6. d4 ♗g4 7. c3 ♗d6 8. ♘bd2 ♘h6 9. ♘c4?! N [9. h3 – 3/275; 9. ♕b3 – 45/(379)] **♘f7 10. ♘e3 ♗e6 11. c4?** [×d4; 11. ♖e1 0–0 12. ♘f5 ♗f5 13. ef5 ♕d7∓] **c5!∓ 12. de5** [12. d5 ♗d7 13. ♘f5 ♗f8∓] **fe5 13. ♕c2 0–0 14. b3** [14. ♘f5 ♕f6! 15. ♘d6 ♘d6 16. ♘d2 (16. b3? ♗g4 17. ♘d2 ♗e2–+) ♕g6 17. ♔h1 ♖f4 18. f3 ♖af8→] **♕f6 15. ♗b2 ♖ae8 16. ♗c3 ♘d8! 17. ♘e1!? ♕g6 18. f3 ♘c6 19. ♖f2 ♖f7?!** [◠ 19... ♖f6! 20. ♘d5 ♖f7] **20. ♘f1 ♖ef8 21. ♔h1 ♕h5 22. ♘d3 b5! 23. cb5?!** [23. ♗b2 bc4 24. bc4 ♘d4 25. ♕c1 ♘f3! 26. gf3 ♖f3 27. ♕d2 ♗h3! 28. ♘g3! ♖f2 29. ♕f2 ♖f2 30. ♘h5 ♖d2 31. ♗e5 ♖d3 32. ♗d6 ♖d6∓] **ab5 24. a4 ba4 25. ba4 c4 26. ♘e1 ♗c5 27. a5!? ♕h4! 28. g3□** [28. ♖e2 ♘d4–+; 28. ♖d2 ♘d4 29. ♕a2 ♘b3–+] **♕h5** [×f3] **29. a6 ♘d4 30. ♗d4 ♗d4** [30... ed4? 31. ♖a5!∞] **31. ♖a3 ♗c5! 32. ♖a1 ♗f2 33. ♕f2 ♗g4 34. a7 ♖f3** [34... ♗f3? 35. ♘f3 ♖f3 36. ♕e2 △ 36... ♖f1? 37. ♕f1! ♖f1 38. ♖f1 ♕e8 39. ♖b1+–] **35. ♘f3 ♗f3 36. ♔g1 ♗e4 37. ♕e3 ♗a8 38. ♖b1 ♕f7! 39. ♖d1 c5 0 : 1** **[I. Gurevich]**

335.* **C 70**

GOFSHTEIN 2560 –
S. AGDESTEIN 2630

Cappelle la Grande 1993

1. e4 e5 2. ♘f3 ♘c6 3. ♗b5 a6 4. ♗a4 b5 5. ♗b3 ♘a5 6. 0–0 d6 [RR 6... ♗b7!? N 7. ♘e5 ♘b3 8. ab3 ♘f6 (8... d5?! 9. ♕h5!±) 9. d3 d5 10. ed5 ♕d5 11. ♕f3 (11. ♘f3 0-0-0!?=∞) ♗d6 12. ♕d5 ♘d5 13. ♖e1 0–0 14. ♗d2 ♖fe8 15. ♘f3 ♖e1 16. ♘e1 ♖e8 17. ♘c3 ♘b4 18. ♔f1 (Suėtin 2410 – Pirožkov, Rossija 1993) f5!=∞ Suėtin] **7. d4 f6 8. ♕e2 N** [8. ♘c3 – 55/332; 8. ♗g8 – 55/333] **♘e7 9. ♖d1 ♘g6 10. c4 c6 11. h3?!** [11. ♗d2!?±] **♗e7 12. ♗d2 ♘b3 13. ab3 ♗d7 14. ♘a3 0–0 15. ♘c2 f5∞ 16. ♘b4!** [16. de5? fe4; 16. ef5 e4 17. ♘h2 ♗f5 18. ♘b4 ♕b6∞] **ed4** [16... a5 17. ef5 (17. cb5? ab4 18. bc6 fe4! 19. ♕e4 ♗f5∓) ♖f5 18. ♘c2] **17. ♘d4 c5 18. ♘dc6 ♕e8** [18... ♕b6 19. ♘e7 ♘e7 20. ♗g5!] **19. ♘e7 ♘e7 20. ♘a6!? ♕g6** [20... ♕c8 21. cb5 ♕b7 22. ♖a5! fe4 23. b4±] **21. ♗f4 fe4 22. ♖d6 ♗e6 23. ♖ad1! ♖ac8⊕** [23... ♖f4 24. ♘c7; 23... ♖a6 24. ♖a6 ♖f4 25. ♖d8 ♔f7 26. cb5±; 23... ♘f5 24. ♖e6 ♕e6 25. ♘c7±] **24. ♘c7 ♖c7 25. ♖e6 ♕e6 26. ♗c7 ♘f5?** [26... b4±; ◠ 26... bc4] **27. cb5+– ♕b3 28. ♖c1 ♘d4 29. ♕c4 ♖f7** [29... ♕c4 30. ♖c4 ♘b5 31. ♗e5+–; 31. ♗b6+–] **30. b6 ♕b2 31. ♖f1 h6 32. ♕d5 ♘e2 33. ♔h2 ♘c3 34. ♕c4 ♘b5 35. ♖d1 g5 36. ♖d8 ♔g7 37. ♕e6 ♘c7 38. bc7 ♕f2 39. ♕e5 ♔g6 40. ♕e4 1 : 0** **[Gofshtein]**

336. !N **C 70**

ANAND 2710 – TIMMAN 2635

Linares 1993

1. e4 e5 2. ♘f3 ♘c6 3. ♗b5 a6 4. ♗a4 b5 5. ♗b3 ♘a5 6. 0–0 d6 7. d4 ♘b3 8. ab3 f6 9. ♘c3 ♗b7 10. ♘h4 ♕d7 11. ♘d5! N [11. f4?! – 55/332] **♕f7** [11... ♘e7 12. ♕h5!±; 11... g6 12. c4 ♗g7 13. f4!±] **12. c4 c6 13. ♘e3?!** [13. ♘c3! b4 (13... ♘e7 14. f4!±) 14. ♘e2±] **♘e7 14. d5** [14. f4 ef4 15. ♖f4 ♘g6!∞] **cd5! 15. cd5** [15. ed5 f5! △ g5∓] **g6!∞ 16. ♗d2 f5!** [16... ♗g7 17. ♗b4 ♖d8 18. ♖c1 ♖d7 19. ♕g4!±] **17. ♖c1 ♖c8!** [17... f4 18. ♖c7±] **18. ♖c8 ♗c8 19. ef5 gf5 20. ♗b4 f4□** [20... ♕f6 21. ♕h5±] **21. ♗d6□ fe3 22. fe3 ♕g7 23. ♕c2 ♗d7 24. ♕c7 ♕g5?** [24... ♕h6!? (△ 25. ♕b8 ♘c8 26. ♗f8 ♕e3!) 25. ♗c5!=∞ △ 25... ♕h4 26. ♕b8 ♗c8 27. ♗e7; 24... ♖g8! (×g2) 25. ♕b8

♘c8 26. ♖c1 ♗d6 (26... ♕g4 27. ♗f8 ♖f8 28. ♕e5±) 27. ♖c8 ♔f7! 28. ♕b7! ♕g4! (28... ♔e7? 29. ♘f5+−; 28... ♔f6 29. ♖g8 ♕g8 30. ♕d7+−) 29. h3! ♕d1 30. ♔f2 ♕d2 31. ♔f1=] **25. ♘f3! ♕e3 26. ♔h1 ♗g7** [26... ♘c8 27. ♘e5+−; 26... ♕d3 27. ♖e1+−] **27. ♖e1+− ♕f4 28. ♗e7 ♔e7 29. ♘e5 1 : 0 [Anand]**

337. !N C 78

BECERRA RIVERA 2445
– ALE. MORENO 2350

Pinar del Rio 1993

1. e4 e5 2. ♘f3 ♘c6 3. ♗b5 a6 4. ♗a4 ♘f6 5. 0–0 b5 6. ♗b3 ♗b7 7. c3 h6 8. d4 d6 9. ♘bd2 g6 10. ♗c2 ♗g7 11. ♘b3! N [11. b3] **0–0** [11... ed4? 12. cd4 ♘b4 13. ♗b1! ♘e4? 14. ♕e1!+−; 13... a5!?] **12. de5!** [×a5, c5] **♘e5 13. ♘e5 de5 14. ♕e2 ♘h5!? 15. ♖d1 ♕e7 16. ♗e3 ♘f4 17. ♕f1! f5!? 18. ♗f4!!±** [18. ♗c5? ♕g5! 19. ♗f8 ♖f8!=∞↑⟫ △ 20. ♘c5 fe4! △ ♘h3-f2−+] **ef4 19. ef5 f3 20. g3 gf5** [20... ♖f5!?] **21. ♖e1! ♕f7** [21... ♗e4 22. ♘d2!±] **22. ♖ad1±** [△ 23. ♘c5 ♗d5 24. ♖d5!+−] **♗d5!? 23. ♘d4!** [×f5] **♗a2** [23... ♗d4 24. ♖d4 ♗a2 25. ♖e5!+−] **24. ♘f5 ♖fe8** [24... ♗e6 25. ♘e7!+−] **25. ♕d3!** [×f3, ↑↗b1-h7] **♖e1** [25... ♖ad8? 26. ♘e7!+−] **26. ♖e1 ♕f6 27. ♘h4?!** [27. ♘e7! ♔f8 (27... ♔f7 28. b3 c6 29. ♘d5!+−) 28. ♘g6! ♔g8□ 29. b3! (×♗a2) c6 (29... ♖d8 30. ♘e7!+−; 29... ♕d6 30. ♕d6 cd6 31. ♖a1+−) 30. ♘e7 ♔f8 (30... ♔f7 31. ♘d5!+−) 31. ♕h7!+−] **♖d8 28. ♕h7 ♔f7 29. ♘f5 ♖h8⊕** [⌓ 29... ♖g8 30. ♖e7 ♔f8 31. ♖c7 ♗e6 32. ♖g7 ♖g7 33. ♕g7 ♕g7 34. ♘g7 ♔g7 35. ♗e4+−] **30. ♖e7! 1 : 0**
[Jó. Hernández, Elizart Cardenas]

338.* C 78

LAUK 2410 – SEPP 2390

Vilnius (zt) 1993

1. e4 e5 2. ♘f3 ♘c6 3. ♗b5 a6 4. ♗a4 ♘f6 5. 0–0 b5 6. ♗b3 ♗b7 7. c3 ♘e4 8. d4 ♘a5 9. ♘e5 ♘b3 10. ♕b3 ♘d6 11. c4 [RR 11. ♖e1!? N ♗e7 12. ♘d2 (12. ♗f4 0–0 13. a4!?±) 0–0 13. a4 (13. ♘f1? ♘f5=) ♖b8 (13... ♗g5 14. ♘f1 ♗c1 15. ♖ac1±) 14. ab5 ab5 15. ♘f1 ♖a8 16. ♗f4 (16. ♖a8!? ♗a8 17. ♘g3±) ♗g5 17. ♖a8 (17. ♗g5 ♕g5 18. ♘e3 △ 18... ♘f5? 19. ♕b5±) ♗a8 (Tilak 2315 – A. Kuz'min 2545, Doha 1992) 18. ♗g3⩲ A. Kuz'min] **♕f6!? N** [11... bc4? – 47/(415); 11... f6!? A. Mihal'čišin] **12. ♘c3** [12. c5 ♘f5 13. ♗g5 ♘d4 14. ♗f6 ♘b3 15. ♖e1 gf6 16. ♘g6 ♗e7 17. ♘e7 ♘a1 18. ♘g6 ♔d8 19. ♘h8 ♗d5 20. ♘c3 ♘c2 21. ♖e2 ♘b4 22. ♘d5 ♘d5 23. ♘f7 ♔c8=; 13... ♕e6!?] **♕e6! 13. ♘d5** [13. ♖e1 bc4 14. ♕d1 0-0-0∞] **0-0-0! 14. ♘f4 ♕e8! 15. c5 ♘f5 16. ♗e3 f6! 17. ♘f7 g5 18. ♘d8 ♔d8 19. ♘d3 ♘h4!?** [19... ♗g2?! 20. ♔g2 ♕e4 21. f3 (21. ♔g1 ♕g4=) ♘e3 22. ♔h1 ♕d4 23. ♖fe1±; 19... ♘e3 20. fe3 ♕e3 21. ♘f2 ♕d4 22. ♖ad1 ♕c4∞] **20. ♗g5!?** [20. ♘e1 ♗g2! 21. ♗g5! (21. ♘g2? ♘f3 22. ♔h1 ♕h5 23. h4 ♕g4−+) ♗f1 22. ♗h4 ♗c4 23. ♕f3 ♖g8 24. ♗g3 ♕e6∞] **fg5 21. ♖fe1** [⌓ 21. ♘e5 ♔c8 22. ♘f7 ♖g8 23. ♖fe1 ♗e7 24. ♘d6 cd6 25. cd6∞] **♗e7 22. ♘e5 ♖f8 23. c6?** [23. d5? ♖f2!! (23... ♗c5 24. ♘c6 dc6 25. ♖e8 ♔e8 26. dc6 ♗f2 27. ♔h1 ♗c8 28. ♖f1 ♗c5 29. ♖e1 ♗e7 30. ♕e3 △ 30... ♖f7? 31. ♕a7 ♔d8 32. ♖d1 ♗d6 33. ♖d6+−) 24. ♔f2 ♗c5 25. ♔f1 (25. ♔g3 ♗d6!−+→) ♕f8 26. ♘f3 (26. ♔e2 ♕f2 27. ♔d1 ♘g2−+→) g4 27. ♖e4 ♘f3 28. gf3 ♗d5 29. ♕d5 ♕f3 30. ♔e1 ♗b4−+; 23. a4! d6! 24. cd6 (24. ab5? de5 25. c6 ♗c6 26. bc6 ♕c6 27. f3 ed4∓) ♗d6 25. ab5 ab5∞] **dc6∓⊕ 24. ♖ac1⊕ ♖f6 25. ♕c3 ♕f8 26. ♖e2 ♘g6! 27. ♘g6** [27. ♕h3 ♗c8 28. ♕e3 (28. ♕h7 ♘f4 △ ♗f5−+) ♘f4 29. ♖ec2 ♗b7 30. ♘c6 ♗c6 31. ♖c6 ♖c6 32. ♖c6 ♕f5∓] **♖g6 28. ♖ce1 ♖g7! 29. ♖e6 ♗c8 30. ♖6e4** [30. ♖c6 ♗b4] **♗d7 31. ♕b3 ♗d6 32. a4 ♖e7 33. ♖e7 ♗e7 34. ab5 ab5 35. ♕a2 ♗c8 36. ♕a8 ♕f6 37. d5 ♗c5 38. ♖e2 ♕d6** [38... ♕d4!?] **39. ♕c6 ♕c6 40. dc6 ♗d6−+ 41. f3 b4 42. g3 ♗a6 43. ♖c2 ♗d3 44. ♖d2 ♗g6 45. ♔f2 ♔e7 46. ♖e2 ♔f6 47. ♔e1 ♗f7**
0 : 1 [Lauk, Sepp]

339. !N **C 78**

KRUSZYŃSKI 2385 – KIŠNËV 2510
Deutschland 1993

1. e4 e5 2. ♘f3 ♘c6 3. ♗b5 a6 4. ♗a4 ♘f6 5. 0–0 b5 6. ♗b3 ♗b7 7. ♖e1 ♗c5 8. c3 d6 9. d4 ♗b6 10. ♗e3 0–0 11. ♘bd2 h6 12. h3 ed4 13. cd4 ♘b4 14. ♕b1 c5 15. a3 ♘c6 16. d5! N [16. e5 – 40/408] **♘e7 17. ♗c2!? ♘d7** [17... ♘g6!?] **18. ♗f4 c4!** [18... ♗c7±] **19. ♘f1** [19. ♗d6 ♗f2 20. ♔f2 ♕b6 21. ♔f1 ♕d6 22. e5 ♕b6 (22... ♕d5? 23. ♗e4) 23. d6 ♘d5 24. ♗e4∞; 19. ♗h2!?] **f5 20. ef5 ♘d5 21. ♗g3 ♘5f6 22. ♕d1 ♗f3!** [22... d5? 23. ♘d4±] **23. ♕f3 d5∞ 24. ♖e6** [24. ♗d6?! ♖e8 25. ♖e6 ♘c5] **♖a7** [24... ♖f7!?] **25. ♖ae1?** [25. ♗d6 ♖f7 26. ♘e3!? d4 27. ♘d5 d3 28. ♗d1∞] **♘c5 26. ♖6e5** [26. ♖d6 ♖d7∓] **♗c7 27. ♖e7 ♗b8!∓ 28. ♖a7 ♗a7 29. ♗h4 d4 30. ♘d2 d3 31. ♗d1 ♕d4 32. ♖e7!? ♕h4 33. ♖a7 ♕d4 34. ♕g3** [34. ♕e3 ♕b2∓] **♘cd7!?** [34... ♘fe4 35. ♕f4] **35. ♕e3⊕ ♕b2 36. ♕e6 ♔h8 37. ♘f3 ♕a1 38. ♘h4 ♖e8 39. ♕f7 ♕d1 40. ♔h2 ♕e2–+ 41. ♘g6 ♔h7 42. ♖d7 ♘d7 43. ♕d7 ♖g8!** [43... d2? 44. f6! ♖g8 (44... ♔g6 45. ♕g7 ♔f5 46. f7∞) 45. ♘f8=] **44. ♕f7 ♕e8 45. ♕d5 ♕d8 46. ♕e4 ♖e8 47. ♘e5 ♖e5 48. ♕e5 d2 49. ♕e4 ♕d3 50. ♕e6 ♕d8 51. ♕e4 d1♕ 52. f6 g6 53. ♕b7 ♕1d7** **0 : 1** [Kišnëv]

340. !N **C 78**

DUTREEUW 2425 – KIŠNËV 2510
Belgique 1993

1. e4 e5 2. ♘f3 ♘c6 3. ♗b5 a6 4. ♗a4 ♘f6 5. 0–0 b5 6. ♗b3 ♗b7 7. ♖e1 ♗c5 8. c3 d6 9. d4 ♗b6 10. ♗g5 h6 11. ♗h4 g5 12. ♗g3 0–0 13. a4 ed4! N [13... ♘a5 – 30/269; 13... ♖e8 – 26/283] **14. cd4 ♖e8!** [14... g4?! 15. d5! (15. ♘h4? ♘d4) gf3 16. dc6 ♗c6 17. ♕f3↑] **15. e5!?** [15. ab5!?] **de5 16. ♘e5?!** [16. de5! ♕d1 17. ♖d1 ♘e4!? 18. ab5!? (18. ♖d7? ♘d8 △ ♘c5∓; 18. ♗d5 ♘g3 19. hg3 ♖ab8 △ ♘e5∓) ab5 19. ♖a8 ♗a8 20. ♘a3!? (20. ♖d7 ♘d8 21. e6 ♘e6 22. ♗e6 fe6 23. ♗c7? ♗c6–+; 23. ♗e5∓) ♘a5 21. ♗d5 ♗d5 22. ♖d5 c6 23. ♖d7 h5!↑]

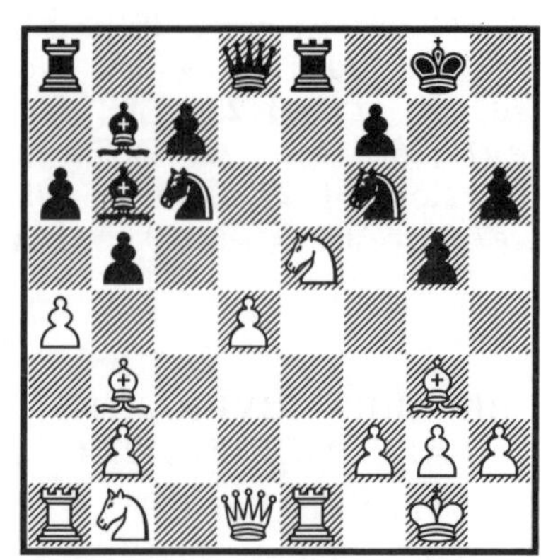

16... ♕d4!! 17. ♗f7 [17. ♕d4 ♗d4! 18. ♗f7 ♔f8! 19. ♗e8 ♘e5! 20. ab5 ♖e8! (△ ♘f3) 21. ♗e5 ab5! 22. ♘c3 ♗e5 23. ♘b5 ♘d5∓] **♔f8!□ 18. ♗e8** [18. ♘c6 ♖e1 19. ♕e1 ♗c6∓] **♘e5! 19. ♗h5?!** [19. a5! ♗a7 20. ♗h5 ♘d3 21. ♖e3 ♘b2 22. ♕d4 ♗d4 23. ♗f3! ♗f3 24. ♖f3 c5∓] **♘d3!** [19... g4? 20. ♕c1 ×h6] **20. ♖e3** [20. ♖e6 ♘h5 21. ♕h5 ♘f4! 22. ♕h6 ♔f7 23. ♖e1 (23. ♘c3 ♘e6 24. ♖d1 ♖h8–+) ♘e2 24. ♔h1 ♖h8 25. ♕g5 ♕e4 26. ♕f4□ (26. f3 ♕f3–+) ♕f4 27. ♗f4 ♘f4 28. f3 ♘g2! 29. ♔g2 ♖g8–+] **♘b2! 21. ♕e2** [⌓ 21. ♕d4 ♗d4 22. ♗f3! ♗f3 23. ♖f3 ♘a4–+] **♘c4 22. ♖aa3⊕ ♘a3–+ 23. ♘a3** [23. ♗e5 ♕b4] **♘h5 24. ♗e5 ♕d5 25. ♖f3 ♔g8 26. ♗a1 ♖d8** **0 : 1** [Kišnëv]

341.* **C 80**

KINDERMANN 2495 –
A. MIHAL'ČIŠIN 2520
Dortmund (open) 1993

1. e4 e5 2. ♘f3 ♘c6 3. ♗b5 a6 4. ♗a4 ♘f6 5. 0–0 ♘e4 6. d4 b5 7. ♗b3 d5 8. de5 ♗e6 9. ♘bd2 ♘c5 10. c3 d4 11. ♗e6 [RR 11. ♘g5 ♕g5 12. ♕f3 ♔d7 13. ♗d5 ♗d5 14. ♕d5 ♗d6 15. ♘c4 ♕g6 16. ed6 ♕e6!? N (16... ♘d3?! – 30/271) 17. ♕c5 ♕c4 (17... bc4? 18. dc7 ♔c7 19. ♗f4 ♔b7 20. cd4±) 18. ♕c4 (18. ♕f5 ♕e6 19. ♕e6 fe6=; 18. ♕g5 dc3 19. dc7! ♔c7 20. ♕g7∞) bc4 19. dc7 (19. cd4 ♘d4 20. dc7 ♔c7 21. ♗d2 – 19... dc7) ♔c7 (19... d3?

20. ♗f4 △ b3±; 19... dc3 20. bc3 ♔c7 21. ♗f4±) 20. cd4 (20. ♗f4!? △ ♖fd1) ♘d4 21. ♗d2 ♖ac8 22. ♖fd1 ♔c6 23. ♔f1 ♖hd8 24. ♗a5 (24. ♖ac1 ♔b5 25. ♗c3 ♘e6 △ f6, a5-a4⇆) ♖d5! 25. ♗c3 (Pujols – H. González, La Habana 1993) ♖cd8∞⇆ Pujols, Pérez Cruz] **♘e6 12. cd4 ♘cd4 13. a4 ♗e7 14. ♘d4 ♘d4 15. ab5 ♘b5** [15... ab5 16. ♖a8 ♕a8 17. f4 △ f5→] **16. ♕c2!? N** [16. ♘e4 0–0 – 49/393] **0–0** [16... ♘d4?! 17. ♕c4 0–0 18. ♘e4 △ ♗e3±] **17. ♘f3** [17. ♘e4 ♕d5 18. ♗f4 c5! △ ♘d4∞] **♘d4!** [17... ♕d7 18. ♖d1 ♕e6 19. ♗g5±; 17... c5 18. ♖d1 ♕b6 19. ♕e4 △ ♗e3±] **18. ♘d4** [18. ♕e4 ♘f3 19. ♕f3 ♕d4! (×b2, e5) 20. ♕g3 ♔h8∞] **♕d4 19. ♕c7 ♗b4!** [19... ♖fe8 20. ♕c6! △ ♖a6±] **20. e6** [20. ♕c6 ♖fc8! 21. ♕b7 a5∓; 20. ♕c2 ♕e5 21. ♗e3 ♖ac8 22. ♕b3 a5∓] **fe6** [20... ♗d6 21. ef7 ♖f7 22. ♕c2 ♖af8 23. ♗e3 ♕h4 24. g3±] **21. ♕c6! ♕d6** [21... ♗d6 22. ♗e3 (22. ♖a6? ♖ac8 23. ♕a4 ♕f2!–+) ♕e5 23. g3 a5 24. ♖ad1±] **22. ♕e4** [22. ♕d6 ♗d6 23. ♗e3 ♗e5 24. ♖a2 ♖fb8∓] **♗c5!** [22... a5 23. ♗e3 ♕d5 24. ♕d5 ed5 25. ♖fd1 ♖fd8 26. ♗d4±] **23. ♗e3 ♗e3 24. ♕e3 ♖ab8 1/2 : 1/2**
[A. Mihal'čišin]

342. C 82

A. SZNAPIK 2440 – MARIN 2515
Budapest (zt) 1993

1. e4 e5 2. ♘f3 ♘c6 3. ♗b5 a6 4. ♗a4 ♘f6 5. 0–0 ♘e4 6. d4 b5 7. ♗b3 d5 8. de5 ♗e6 9. ♘bd2 ♘c5 10. c3 ♗e7 11. ♗c2 ♗g4 12. ♖e1 0–0 13. h3 ♗h5 14. ♘f1 ♖e8 15. ♘g3 N [15. g4 – 51/333] **♗g6 16. ♗e3 ♕d7 17. ♗g6 hg6?!** [×♔g8; 17... fg6 18. ♗c5!? ♗c5 19. ♘e4 ♗e7 20. ♘eg5 ♗g5 21. ♘g5 ♘d8=] **18. ♕c2 ♘e6** [18... ♗f8 19. ♗c5 ♗c5 20. ♖ad1 ♗b6 21. ♕d2 ♖ad8 22. ♕f4 ♕e7 23. ♖e2 ♕f8 24. ♖de1 △ ♘g5±] **19. ♖ad1 ♘a5 20. h4!→⟫ ♘c4 21. ♗c1 c5 22. h5 gh5** [22... g5 23. ♕f5] **23. ♘h5 ♖ad8** [⌓ 23... ♘f8] **24. b3 ♘b6 25. ♕f5 ♕c6** [25... ♘f8 26. e6 fe6 (26... ♘e6 27. ♘e5+–) 27. ♕g4+–]

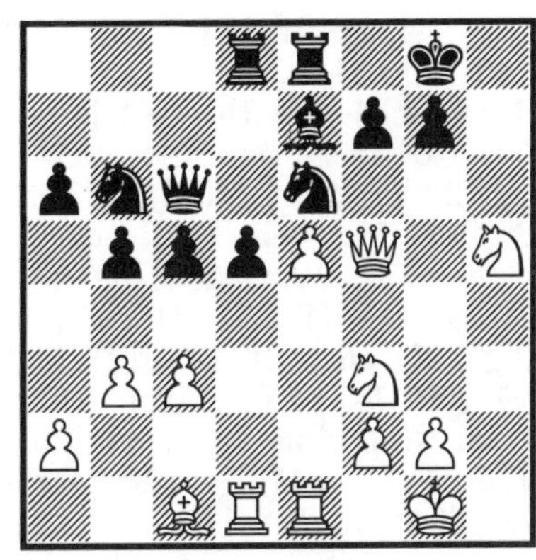

26. ♘f6! ♗f6 [26... gf6 27. ef6 ♗f8 28. ♘e5 ♕c7 29. ♕g4 ♔h8 30. ♖d3+–] **27. ef6 g6 28. ♘e5!** [28. ♕g4 ♘d7 29. ♕h4 ♘ef8 30. ♗g5 ♘h7] **gf5 29. ♘c6 ♔h7** [29... ♖d7 (△ 30. ♘e7 ♖de7 31. fe7 ♖e7⩲) 30. ♖e3+–] **30. ♘e7** [30. ♘d8 ♖d8 △ ♔g6⩲] **♖d7 31. ♖d3 ♖de7 32. ♖h3 ♔g8** [32... ♔g6?? 33. ♖h6#] **33. fe7?!** [33. ♖g3 ♔h7 34. f3!! △ ♔f2, ♖h1# Zsu. Polgár] **♔g7** [33... ♖e7 34. ♗g5 ♖e8 35. ♗f6] **34. ♗h6 ♔f6 35. ♗e3** [35. ♗f8 ♘d7 △ ♘ef8] **♘c8 36. b4 cb4** [36... c4 37. ♗d4 ♔e7 38. ♖e5+–] **37. ♗d4 ♔e7 38. cb4 ♔d7 39. ♗c5 ♘d6 40. ♗d6 ♔d6 41. ♖h5 f4 42. ♖f5 ♖e7 43. ♖c1??** [43. ♖d1 d4 44. ♖c1+– A. Sznapik] **♘d4–+ 44. ♖f6 ♔e5 45. ♖cc6 ♘c6 46. ♖c6 ♖e6 47. ♖c5 ♔d6** [△ ♖e4-c4] **48. a4 ♖e1 49. ♔h2 ba4 50. ♖a5 ♖a1 51. ♖a6 ♔c7 52. ♖a5 d4 53. ♖d5 ♖d1 54. ♖a5 ♖a1 55. ♖d5 a3 56. ♖d4 a2 57. ♖d2 ♔b6** [57... ♖h1–+] **58. g3?!** [58. ♖e2 ♔b5 59. ♖c2 (59. ♖b2 ♖h1 60. ♔h1 a1♕ 61. ♔h2 ♕b2) ♔b4] **f3 59. b5 ♖h1 0 : 1**
[Marin]

343. C 82

KUCZYŃSKI 2525 – MARIN 2515
Budapest (zt) 1993

1. e4 e5 2. ♘f3 ♘c6 3. ♗b5 a6 4. ♗a4 ♘f6 5. 0–0 ♘e4 6. d4 b5 7. ♗b3 d5 8. de5 ♗e6 9. ♘bd2 ♘c5 10. c3 ♗e7 11. ♗c2 ♗g4 12. ♖e1 0–0 13. ♘b3 ♘e4 [13... ♖e8 14. h3 ♘b3 15. ♕d3 g6 16. ♗b3 ♗e6 17. ♘d4±] **14. ♗f4** [14. ♗e4 de4 15. ♕d8 ♖ad8 16. ♖e4 ♖d1 17. ♘e1

(17. ♖e1?? ♗f3) ♖fd8∓] **♖e8!? N** [14... f5 15. ef6 ♘f6 (15... ♖f6? 16. ♗c7!) 16. ♕d3±] **15. ♗e4 de4 16. ♖e4** [16. ♕d8? ♗d8! 17. ♖e4 f5 △ ♗f3, g5, ♘e5∓] **♕d1** [16... ♕c8!? 17. ♕d5 ♘d8] **17. ♖d1 ♗f3 18. gf3 ♖ad8 19. ♖ee1** [19. ♘d4 ♗c5 △ ♗d4, ♘b4-d5$\overline{\overline{\infty}}$; 19. ♖d8 ♖d8 20. ♘d4 ♘d4 21. ♖d4 ♖d4 22. cd4 c6=] **g5 20. ♗g3 ♔g7 21. e6 ♖d1 22. ♖d1 f5** [⇆»] **23. ♗c7 ♔f6 24. f4** [24. ♖e1 ♗f8± ×f2, f3] **g4 25. ♖e1 ♗f8 26. ♘d4** [26. ♗e5 ♔e6⩲] **♘d4 27. cd4 ♖e6 28. ♗e5 ♔f7 29. ♖c1 ♖h6 30. ♖c8** [30. ♖c7 ♔e6 31. ♖c8 (31. ♖c6 ♔d5 32. ♖h6 ♗h6=) ♔f7□ 32. ♖a8 ♖c6 △ h5-h4] **♖h3 31. ♖a8 h5 32. ♖a6 ♗e7$\overline{\overline{\infty}}$** [↑», ×♗e5] **33. ♖h6 h4 34. ♖h7** [34. d5? ♖d3 35. d6?? ♖d1 36. ♔g2 h3 37. ♔g3 ♖g1#] **♔e8 35. ♖h8 ♔f7 36. ♖h7 ♔e8 37. ♔f1** [37. b3 b4; 37. a3 ♖b3; 37. ♖h5 ♖d3 38. ♔f1 ♖d2$\overline{\overline{\infty}}$] **♖h2 38. d5 ♖h1 39. ♔e2 h3 40. d6 ♗d8 41. ♗c3 ♖b1 42. b3 ♗b6 43. d7** [43. a4 ♖b3 44. a5 ♗d8 45. ♔d2 b4 46. d7 ♔f8 47. ♗g7 ♔f7 (47... ♔g8 48. ♖h8 ♔g7 49. ♖d8+−) 48. a6 ♔g6 (48... ♖a3? 49. ♗b2+−; 48... h2 49. a7+−) 49. ♖h8 (49. a7 ♖a3) h2] **♔f8 44. ♗g7 ♔g8 45. ♗d4 ♔h7 46. ♗b6 h2 47. d8♕ h1♕ 48. ♕e7 ♔h6 49. ♕g5 ♔h7 50. ♕f5 ♔h6 51. ♕f6 1/2 : 1/2** **[Marin]**

344.* !N C 82

HAMARAT — PALMO
corr. 1990/92

1. e4 e5 2. ♘f3 ♘c6 3. ♗b5 a6 4. ♗a4 ♘f6 5. 0–0 ♘e4 6. d4 b5 7. ♗b3 d5 8. de5 ♗e6 9. ♘bd2 ♘c5 10. c3 ♗e7 11. ♗c2 ♗g4 12. ♖e1 ♕d7 13. ♘b3 [RR 13. ♘f1 ♖d8 14. ♘e3 ♗h5 15. b4 ♘e6 16. g4 ♗g6 17. ♘f5 0–0 18. a4 d4!? N (18... ♖fe8 — 46/(436)) 19. ab5 ab5 20. ♗e4 ♖fe8 21. ♕d3! (×b5) ♘b8 (21... ♘b4!?) *a)* 22. ♗d2 c5 (22... dc3 23. ♕d7 △ ♗c3±) 23. cd4 ♘d4 (23... cd4 24. ♖a5; 23... c4 24. ♕b1 ♘c7 25. ♖a7 ♘c6 26. ♖b7+−) 24. ♘3d4 ♗f5 (24... cd4 25. ♖a5±) 25. ♘f5 (25. gf5 ♕d4 26. ♕d4 ♖d4∞) ♕d3 26. ♗d3 ♖d3 27. ♘e7 ♖e7 28. ♖a8 ♖e8 29. ♗f4 (Hába 2485 — Marin 2515, Budapest (zt) 1993) ♔f8 30. bc5 ♘c6 31. ♖a6 (31. ♖e8 ♔e8$\overline{\overline{\infty}}$) ♖e6$\overline{\overline{\infty}}$; *b)* 22. cd4! ♗b4 (22... ♘d4 23. ♘3d4 ♗f5 24. ♘f5 ♕d3 25. ♗d3 ♖d3 26. ♘e7 ♖e7 27. ♖a8 ♖e8 28. ♗e3± Hába) 23. ♖d1 c6 (23... c5? 24. d5 c4 25. ♕b1 ♗c3 26. ♗b2 ♗b2 27. ♕b2 ♘c5 28. ♗c2± △ e6) 24. ♗e3 ♗f8± Marin] **♘e6 14. h3 ♗h5 15. ♗f5 ♘cd8 16. ♗e3 a5 17. ♗c5** [17. ♘c5 ♗c5?! 18. ♗c5 g6 19. ♗e6 ♘e6 20. ♗e3 ♗f3 21. ♕f3 c5 22. ♖ad1 ♖d8 23. ♗h6 d4 24. ♕f6 ♖g8 25. cd4 cd4 26. ♗d2 b4 27. a3 ba3 28. ba3 ♕a7 29. ♖b1±; ⌓ 17... ♕c6 — 45/386] **a4 18. ♗e7 ♕e7 19. ♘bd4! N** [19. ♘bd2 — 26/290] **♘d4 20. cd4 ♘e6 21. g4!±** [21. ♖c1 ♗f3 22. ♕f3 ♘d4 23. ♕d5 ♖d8 24. ♕e4 ♘f5 25. ♕f5 0–0 26. e6 fe6 27. ♕b5 ♖d2 28. ♖e2 ♕d6 29. ♖ce1 ♖e2 30. ♕e2 ♖f6 31. ♕e4⩲] **♗g6 22. ♖c1 0–0 23. ♕d2 ♖a6 24. ♖c2 ♖b8** [24... ♗f5 25. gf5 ♘d8 26. ♖ec1! (26. f6? gf6 27. ♕h6 ♖e6!) c6 27. f6 gf6 28. ♕h6 fe5 29. ♔h1 f6 30. ♖g1 ♔h8 31. de5 c5 (31... fe5 32. ♘e5+−) 32. ♖c5 fe5 33. ♕a6 ♕c5 34. ♕h6 ♕e7 35. ♘e5+−] **25. ♖ec1 ♖bb6 26. h4 h5 27. ♗g6 fg6 28. ♘g5! ♕e8** [28... ♘g5 29. ♕g5 ♕g5 30. hg5 c6 31. f4 hg4 (31... ♔f7 32. gh5 gh5 33. f5 g6 34. e6 ♔e7 35. fg6 ♔e6 36. ♖f1 ♖a8 37. ♖f6 ♔d7 38. ♖f7 ♔d6 39. ♖cf2+−) 32. ♔g2 ♔f7 33. ♔g3 ♔e6 34. ♔g4 b4 35. ♖c5⊙ ♔f7 36. f5 gf5 37. ♔f5 g6 38. ♔g4!⊙ b3 39. a3 ♔f8 40. ♖f1 ♔g8 41. ♖f6 ♔g7 42. ♖c1+−; 28... hg4 29. ♘e6 ♖e6 (29... ♕e6 30. ♖c7 ♖c6 31. ♕g5! ♖c7 32. ♖c7 ♖c6 33. ♖b7+−) 30. ♖c7 ♕h4 31. ♕f4 ♔h7 32. ♕f8 ♕h6 33. ♖c8 g5 34. ♖1c5+−; 28... c6 29. ♘e6 ♕e6 30. ♕g5+−] **29. ♘e6 ♕e6 30. ♕g5 hg4 31. ♖c7 ♖c6 32. ♔g2!+− ♖c1 33. ♖c1 ♖a8 34. ♖c7 ♖f8 35. h5!** [35... ♔h7 36. ♖b7] **1 : 0** **[Hamarat]**

345.* C 86

TIVJAKOV 2585 — ZAJCEV 2445
Podol'sk 1992

1. e4 e5 2. ♘f3 ♘c6 3. ♗b5 a6 4. ♗a4 ♘f6 5. ♕e2 ♗e7 6. c3 d6 7. 0–0 0–0 8. ♖d1 ♕e8!? N [8... ♖e8 9. d3 — 24/276;

9. d4⩲; 8... ♗d7 9. ♗c2 △ d4⩲; 9. ♗b3!?; 8... b5 9. ♗c2± △ 10. a4, 10. d4; 8... ♗g4 N 9. h3 ♗h5 (9... ♗f3 10. ♕f3⩲⊡) 10. d3 b5 11. ♗c2⩲ △ ♘bd2-f1-g3, ♘h4, ♘hf5‖↑ Tivjakov 2595 – Sharma 2260, Calcutta 1993] **9. ♗c2** [9. d4? ♘d4 10. ♖d4 b5] **♗d8!** [⇔e, △ ♘e7-g6↑⟫, ×f4] **10. d3** [10. d4 ed4 11. cd4 ♘b4 12. ♘c3 ♘c2=] **♘e7 11. ♘bd2** [11. d4 ♘g6↑⟫, ↻] **♘g6?** [11... ♘h5!∞ △ 12... ♘f4, 12... f5] **12. g3! ♗g4** [12... ♘h5? 13. ♘e1; 12... ♘d7 13. d4±] **13. ♘c4!□ ♘h5?!** [△ f5] **14. h3!±** [14. ♘e3? ♘hf4–+; 14. d4? ed4 15. cd4 d5 16. ♘e3 ♘hf4–+] **♗h3** [⌓ 14... ♗e6; 14... ♗d7] **15. ♘g5 ♗g5 16. ♗g5 ♘f6 17. ♗f6 gf6 18. ♕h5** [→⟫, ↑⊞] **♗e6** [18... ♕e6 19. ♘e3 △ ♔h2; 18... ♕d7 19. ♘e3 △ d4, ♔h2, d5] **19. ♔g2** [△ ♖h1; 19. ♘e3±↑] **♕c6** [19... ♔g7 20. ♖h1 ♖h8 21. ♘e3 △ f4+–] **20. ♘e3!** [20. ♖h1 ♖fd8 21. ♕h7 ♔f8 △ ♔e7⩲] **♖fd8** [20... ♖fe8; 20... d5!?] **21. d4! ed4** [21... d5? 22. c4+–; 22. ♗b3+–; 21... ♕b6±; 21... ♕b5!?] **22. cd4 ♕b5** [22... d5? 23. ♗b3 de4 24. d5 ♕b5 25. ♖h1+–; 22... ♕b6!?±] **23. d5 ♗d7 24. b3! ♖e8** [△ 25. f4 ♕c5] **25. ♗d3 ♕b4!?** [→ ×e4] **26. ♖ac1! ♖e4 27. ♖h1!** [27. ♘c2?! ♖g4!□ (△ ♘f4) 28. ♗g6 hg6; 27. a3?! ♕d4 28. ♖c4 ♕e5; 27. ♗e4?! ♕e4 28. ♔g1 ♘e5⇆] **♕d4!** [27... ♖e3 28. ♕h7 ♔f8 29. ♗g6 fg6 30. ♕h8 △ ♖h7#; 27... ♖ae8 28. ♖c4! ♖c4 29. ♕h7 ♔f8 30. ♗g6 fg6 31. ♕d7+–; 27... ♔f8 28. ♘c2+–] **28. ♖c7!** [28. ♕h7? ♔f8 29. ♖c7 ♖e3! ×d5] **♖e3** [⌓ 28... ♕d3 29. ♕h7 ♔f8 30. ♘f5!! ♖h4 (30... ♔e8 31. ♕g8 ♘f8 32. ♕f8 ♔f8 33. ♖h8#) 31. ♕g7 ♔e8 32. ♕g8 ♘f8 33. ♘h4+–] **29. ♗g6** [29... fg6 30. ♕h7 ♔f8 31. ♕h8 △ ♖h7#; 29... ♔f8 30. ♖d7 fg6 31. ♕h6 ♔e8 32. ♕e3 ♕e3 33. fe3 ♔d7 34. ♖h7 △ ♖h8-a8+–] **1 : 0** **[Tivjakov]**

346. !N **C 86**

JUDASIN 2610 – HALIFMAN 2630
Dos Hermanas 1993

1. e4 e5 2. ♘f3 ♘c6 3. ♗b5 a6 4. ♗a4 ♘f6 5. 0–0 ♗e7 6. ♕e2 b5 7. ♗b3 0–0 8. c3 d6 9. h3 ♘a5 10. ♗c2 c5 11. d4 ♕c7 12. ♖d1 [12. d5?! – 27/300] **♗d7! N** [12... ♗e6 13. d5 ♗d7 14. b3⩲↑ ×♘a5] **13. de5□** [13. d5 ♘c4=; 13. ♗g5 cd4 14. cd4 ♖ac8 15. ♗d3 ♘c6! △ ♘b4↑] **de5 14. ♘bd2 ♖fd8 15. ♘f1 ♗e6!** [⇆⇔d, ×a2, c4] **16. ♖d8 ♖d8 17. ♘g3! g6 18. ♗g5! ♘c4** [18... ♔g7!? (△ h6) 19. ♕e3!? ♘c4 20. ♕c1∞] **19. ♗b3!** [×♗e6] **♘e8! 20. ♘f1!** [20. ♗e7∓] **f6** [20... ♗g5? 21. ♘g5±] **21. ♗h6!** [△ ♘e3] **♗f7! 22. ♘3h2!** [△ h4-h5] **♘cd6** [22... ♘ed6!?] **23. ♘g4** [23. ♗f7 ♘f7 △ c4, ♖d3↑⊞] **c4 24. ♗c2 ♗e6! 25. ♖e1** [△ ♗c1] **♘f7** [25... g5 26. ♘fe3 △ ♕f3, h4±] **26. ♗c1 ♕c6** [26... b4?! 27. cb4 ♗b4 28. ♖d1± ×a6, f6] **27. h4!?** [△ h5 ×♔g8] **b4!** [⇆⟪; 27... h5 28. ♘ge3 △ g4→] **28. ♘d2** [28. h5 b3!] **a5!** [→⟪] **29. h5 a4** [△ 30... a3, 30... b3] **30. hg6 hg6 31. cb4□ ♗b4 32. ♘e3 c3⊕ 33. bc3 ♕c3 34. a3** [34. ♗a4 ♖d2 35. ♗d2 ♕d2 36. ♕d2 ♗d2 37. ♖e2 ♗e3∞] **♗a5** [34... ♗a3? 35. ♘b1; 34... ♗f8 35. ♗a4] **35. ♖d1⊕** [35. ♗a4 ♖d2 36. ♗d2 ♕d2 37. ♕d2 ♗d2∞] **♗b3! 36. ♗b3** [36. ♘b3! ab3 37. ♗d3⩲↑] **ab3 37. ♕b5** [37. ♕c4!?∞] **♘ed6!□ 38. ♕a4** [38. ♕b3 ♘e4 39. ♘d5! ♘d2 40. ♕c3 ♗c3 41. ♘c3 ♘b3⩲; 41... ♘c4!?⩲] **♖b8! 39. ♘dc4** [39. ♘d5 ♕c2 40. ♘e3 ♕c3=] **♘c4 40. ♘c4 ♕c2?!** [40... ♗b4!! 41. ♕c6!? (41. ♗d2? ♕c4 42. ♗b4 b2! 43. ♖b1 ♕c1 44. ♕d1 ♕d1 45. ♖d1 ♖c8 46. ♗d2 ♖d8–+; 41. ♘e3 ♗c5∓; 41. ♕a6!?) ♕c2! 42. ♖f1∞] **41. ♘e3 ♕c3?!** [41... ♕c5 42. ♗b2±↑ ×d5, f6, g6] **42. ♗d2! ♕d4** [42... ♕d2 43. ♖d2 ♗d2 44. ♕a7 ♖b5 (44... ♖d8 45. ♕b6+–) 45. ♕d7 ♖b8 46. ♘c4 ♗c3 47. ♕c7! (47. ♘d6 b2 48. ♕f7 ♔h8∞) ♖b5 48. ♘d6+–] **43. ♗b4! b2** [43... ♕e4! 44. ♕b3! (44. ♕a5 b2!∞) ♗b4 (44... ♕b7 45. ♕e6! △ ♕f6, ♖d7+–→; 44... ♖b7 45. ♘d5±) 45. ♖d7! ♖f8 46. ab4±] **44. ♖d4+– ed4 45. ♕b3 de3 46. fe3!** [46. ♕b2 e2!? 47. ♕e2 ♗b4±; 46... ef2] **♗b4 47. ab4** [♕ 5/e] **♔f8!** [△ ♔e7, ♘e5-d7] **48. ♕b2 ♔e7 49. ♕c3 ♘e5 50. ♕c5 ♔e6 51. ♔f1 ♘d7 52. ♕c4 ♔e7 53. ♔e2 ♖b6** [△ ♖d6 ×♔e2] **54. ♔d2 ♔d6 55. b5 ♔e7 56. ♔c3 ♖e6 57. ♔b4 ♖e5 58. ♔a5 ♖e6 59. ♕b4** [△ ♕b1-h1-h7] **♖d6 60. ♕a3** [60. e5? ♘e5 61. b6?? ♘c6] **♘e5 61. ♕a2** [△ 62. ♕g8, 62. b6] **♖d2!□ 62. ♕b3** [△

b6] **♖d3□ 63. ♕c2! ♖d2!□ 64. ♕c5** [△ b6] **♖d6□ 65. ♕c1!** [△ b6; 65. b6?? ♘d7] **♘d7□ 66. ♕h1! g5 67. ♕h7 ♔e6** [67... ♔d8 68. ♕g8 ♔c7 69. ♕f7 △ e5, b6] **68. ♕g8 ♔e7 69. e5! ♘e5** [69... fe5 70. ♕g5] **70. b6 ♖d7** [70... ♖d1 71. ♕h7] **71. ♕c8 ♖d2 72. ♕c3! ♖d5** [72... ♖g2 73. b7 △ b8♕] **73. ♔a4 ♖d8 74. b7 ♘d7 75. ♔b5 ♖h8 76. ♔c6 ♘b8 77. ♔c7 ♘a6 78. ♔b6 ♘b8 79. ♕c7 ♔e6 80. ♕c8 1 : 0**
[Judasin]

347.* !N C 88**

HOLMOV 2460 – KOSTYRA 2365

Katowice 1993

1. e4 e5 2. ♘f3 ♘c6 3. ♗b5 a6 4. ♗a4 ♘f6 5. 0–0 ♗e7 6. ♖e1 b5 7. ♗b3 0–0 [RR 7... d6 8. a4 b4 9. d4 0–0 10. de5 ♘e5 11. ♘bd2 a5 N (11... ♗b7 – 43/427; 11... ♘f3) 12. ♘e5 de5 13. ♘c4! ♕d1 14. ♖d1 *a)* 14... ♗e6?! 15. f3 (Ulybin 2570 – Zajcev 2445, Podol'sk 1992) ♗c4! 16. ♗c4 ♗c5 17. ♔f1 h6±; *b)* 14... ♘e4!? 15. ♘e5 ♗c5 16. ♘d3! (16. ♗e3 ♗e3 17. fe3 ♘d6 18. ♗d5 ♖a6=) ♗b7 (16... ♗g4 17. ♖e1 ♖ae8 18. ♗e3 ♗e3 19. ♖e3 ♘d6 20. ♖ae1±; 16... ♖d8 17. ♗f4 ♗g4 18. ♖e1 ♖d3 19. ♖e4 ♖d4 20. ♖ae1±) 17. ♘c5 ♘c5 18. ♗c4 ♖ad8 19. ♖d8 ♖d8 20. ♗g5 (20. ♗e3?! ♘a4 21. ♖a4 ♖d1 22. ♗f1 ♗a6=) ♖d4 21. ♗e2 b3 22. cb3 ♘b3 23. ♖d1± Ulybin, Lysenko] **8. a4** [RR 8. d4 ♘d4 9. ♘d4 ed4 10. e5 ♘e8 *a)* 11. ♕d4 ♗b7 12. c4 N (12. c3 d6=) bc4 13. ♕c4 d5 14. ed6 ♘d6 15. ♕g4 ♗f6 16. ♘c3 ♘b5 17. ♘b5 ab5 18. ♗f4 c5 (18... ♗b2? 19. ♖ad1 ♕c8 20. ♕c8 ♖ac8 21. ♖d7) 19. ♖ad1 ♕c8 20. ♕c8 ♖ac8 21. ♗d6 ♖fd8 22. ♗c5 ♖d1 23. ♗d1 ♗b2 24. ♗b3 g6= J. Polgár 2575 – Nunn 2595, Hastings 1992/93; *b)* 11. c3 dc3 12. ♘c3 d6 13. ♘d5 ♗e6 14. ♕f3 ♖c8 15. ♗f4 ♗g5 16. ♖ad1 (16. ♗g3 c6) ♔h8 (16... ♗f4? 17. ♘f4 ♗b3 18. ♕b3 ♔h8 19. e6!) 17. ♗c2!? N (17. ♗g3 – 43/(426)) f5? 18. ♕h5! h6 (18... ♗f4 19. ♘f4 ♗f7 20. ♕f5 g6 21. ♕h3+–) 19. ♗g5 ♕g5 20. ♕g5 hg5 21. ♘e7+– I. Gurevich 2510 – Nunn 2595, Hastings 1992/93; ⌓ 17... g6] **♗b7 9. d3 ♖e8 10. ♘c3 b4 11. ♘d5 ♘a5 12. ♘e7** [12. ♗a2 – 48/457] **♕e7 13. ♗a2 d5! N** [13... ♖ab8?! 14. ♗g5 h6 15. ♗h4 c5 16. ♘d2 △ f4-f5±] **14. ♗g5 h6** [14... de4!? 15. de4 h6!=] **15. ♗f6 ♕f6 16. ed5** [16. ♗d5? ♗d5 17. ed5 ♕d6 18. ♕d2 ♖ab8 19. ♖e4 f5 20. ♖h4 e4! 21. de4 fe4 22. ♘e1 ♕f6!∓] **♖ad8?!** [16... b3! 17. cb3 (17. ♗b3 ♘b3 18. cb3 ♗d5 19. ♖e3 ♖ab8$\overline{\infty}$) ♗d5 18. b4 ♗a2 19. ba5 (19. ♖a2?! ♘c6 20. ♕b3 ♖eb8 21. ♖e4 ♕d6∓) ♗d5 20. b4 ♖ab8 21. ♖b1 e4! 22. de4 ♗e4 23. ♖b3 ♗f3 24. ♖e8 ♖e8 25. ♖f3 ♕d4!=] **17. ♕d2!± ♕d6 18. c4 c6** [18... c5!?] **19. d4 e4** [19... ed4 20. ♖e8 ♖e8 21. ♘d4 cd5 22. cd5 ♗d5 23. ♘f5 ♕e5 24. ♘h6! (24. ♕d5?? ♕e1!) gh6 25. ♗d5±] **20. c5 ♕b8 21. ♕b4?!** [21. d6! ef3 22. ♕b4 ♕c8 (22... ♗a8 23. ♕a5 ♕b2 24. ♕c7 ♕a2 25. ♕d8!+–) 23. gf3 ♕h3 24. ♕a5 ♕f3 25. ♕c3 ♕g4 26. ♔f1 ♗c8 27. ♖e3+–] **cd5!** [21... ef3? 22. d6!+–] **22. ♕a5!** [22. ♘e5?! ♘c6 23. ♘c6 ♗c6 24. ♕c3 (24. ♕b8 ♖b8$\overline{\infty}$) a5! 25. ♕a5 ♕b2 26. ♕b6! ♕b6 27. cb6 ♗a4 28. ♗d5 ♖d5 29. ♖a4 ♖b5 30. f3±] **ef3 23. ♖e8 ♖e8 24. ♖e1** [24. gf3?! ♖e6! (24... ♕f4?! 25. ♖e1! ♖e1 26. ♕e1 ♕f3 27. ♕e8 ♔h7 28. ♗b1 g6 29. ♗c2!+–) 25. ♖e1 ♖g6 26. ♔f1 ♗c6! (26... ♕h2? 27. ♕d8! ♔h7 28. ♗b1 ♕h3 29. ♔e2 f5 30. ♕d7+–) 27. ♗b1 ♖f6 28. ♖e3 g6!$\overline{\infty}$] **fg2 25. ♔g2 ♗c6 26. ♖e8 ♕e8 27. ♗b1! ♕e7** [27... ♗a4 28. ♕a6 ♗b5 29. ♕a3 ♕e2 30. ♕a8 ♗e8 31. h3!+–] **28. ♕a6 ♕g5 29. ♔f3□ ♕h5 30. ♔e3 ♕g5** [30... ♕h3 31. ♔d2!] **31. ♔d3 ♗d7** [31... ♕f5 32. ♔c3 ♕b1 33. ♕c6 ♕c1 34. ♔b3 ♕c4 35. ♔a3 ♕d4 36. ♕b5!+–] **32. ♔c3 ♕c1 33. ♗c2 ♗f5 34. ♕e2 1 : 0**
[Holmov]

348. C 89

ANAND 2710 – N. SHORT 2665

Amsterdam 1993

1. e4 e5 2. ♘f3 ♘c6 3. ♗b5 a6 4. ♗a4 ♘f6 5. 0–0 ♗e7 6. ♖e1 b5 7. ♗b3 0–0 8. c3 d5 9. ed5 ♘d5 10. ♘e5 ♘e5 11. ♖e5 ♗b7 12. d4 ♗f6 13. ♖e1 c5?! N [13... ♖e8 – 49/402] **14. dc5 ♖e8 15.**

♘a3! [15. ♗e3? ♘e3 16. fe3 ♗g5∓; 15. ♖e8 ♕e8 16. ♗d5 ♗d5 17. ♗e3 ♕e4 18. ♕f1 ♕c2 19. ♕c1 ♕g6 20. ♕f1=; 15. ♘d2 ♘f4 16. ♘f3 ♘g2! 17. ♔g2 (17. ♕d8 ♘e1! 18. ♗f7!□ ♔f7 19. ♕d7 ♖e7 20. ♕e7 ♗e7 21. ♘e1 ♗c5∞̄) ♖e1 18. ♕e1 ♕d7 19. h3□ ♗f3 20. ♔f3 ♕h3 21. ♔e2 ♕h5! 22. ♔f1□ (22. f3? ♖e8 23. ♗e3 ♗g5−+; 22. ♔d3? ♖d8 23. ♔c2 ♕f5−+) ♕h1=] **♕c7?!** [⌓ 15... ♕d7±] **16. ♖e8! ♖e8 17. ♗d5 ♖d8 18. ♗f4!** [18. ♗f7?! ♕f7→] **♕f4 19. ♕f3?** [19. ♗b7! ♖d1 20. ♖d1+− △ 20... h5 21. g3 ♕g4 22. ♖e1 △ c6, ♗a6] **♕f3 20. ♗f3 ♗f3 21. gf3 b4! 22. ♘c2** [22. ♘c4] **bc3 23. bc3** [23. b4?! ♖d2 24. ♘e3 (24. c6? ♖d6) ♔f8!∞] **♖c8 24. ♖b1 h6± 25. c4 ♖c5 26. ♘e3 ♗d4** [26... ♗g5] **27. ♖c1 ♗e3 28. fe3 ♔f8 29. ♔f2 ♔e7 30. f4 g5 31. ♔f3 gf4?!** [⌓ 31... f5 △ 32. ♔e2 gf4 33. ef4 ♖a5 34. ♖c2 ♖a3] **32. ♔f4 ♔e6 33. ♔e4?!** [33. ♖c2!] **♖h5! 34. ♖c2 ♖h4 35. ♔d3 f5 36. ♖f2 ♔e5 37. ♖c2 ♔d6 38. ♖g2 ♖h3 39. ♖f2 ♔e5 40. c5 ♔e6 41. ♖c2 ♔d7 42. ♔d4** [⌓ 42. c6 ♔c7 43. ♔d4±] **♔c6 43. ♖e2 h5 44. ♖c2 ♖h4 45. ♔e5 ♖e4 46. ♔f5 ♖e3 47. ♔g5 ♖e5** [47... ♖h3? 48. ♔g6 ♖h4 49. ♔h6! ♖h3 50. ♔g5⊙] **48. ♔h4 a5 49. h3 ♖d5** **1/2 : 1/2**
[N. Short]

349.** !N **C 89**

BADŽARANI 2260 − MALININ
corr. 1991/93

1. e4 e5 2. ♘f3 ♘c6 3. ♗b5 a6 4. ♗a4 ♘f6 5. 0−0 ♗e7 6. ♖e1 b5 7. ♗b3 0−0 8. c3 d5 9. ed5 ♘d5 10. ♘e5 ♘e5 11. ♖e5 c6 12. d4 [RR 12. ♖e1 ♗d6 13. d3 ♗f5 14. ♕f3 ♖e8 15. ♖e8 ♕e8 16. ♘d2 ♕e1 17. ♘f1 ♗g6 18. g3! N (18. h3± − 49/404) ♖e8 19. ♗d1 ♕e6 20. ♗d2 ♕h3 (Dolmatov 2615 − Kamsky 2655, Dortmund 1993) 21. ♕g4! (21. ♗c2!? ♗h5 22. ♕g2 ♕f5 23. ♘e3 ♘e3 24. fe3± Smagin) ♕g4 22. ♗g4 ♘f6 (22... ♗d3 23. ♗d7 ♖e2 24. ♗c6 ♗c5 25. ♗d5 ♖f2 26. ♗e3 ♖f1 27. ♖f1 ♗e3 28. ♖f2 ♔f8 29. ♔g2 ♗f2 30. ♔f2 ♔e7 31. ♔e3 ♗g6 32. ♔d4 ♔d6 33. b4!+−) 23. ♗f3± Dolmatov] **♗d6 13. ♖e1 ♕h4 14. g3 ♕h3 15. ♗e3 ♗g4 16. ♕d3 ♖ae8 17. ♘d2 ♖e6** [RR 17... ♕h5 18. a4!? N (18. ♘f1 − 52/346) ♗f5 19. ♗d1! ♕d1 20. ♕f5 ♘e3 21. ♕d3! ♕c2□ 22. ♖e3 ♕b2 23. ♖b1 ♕a2 24. ab5 ab5 25. ♘e4 ♗e7 26. ♖be1 ♖d8 27. ♕f1 f5 28. ♖1e2! ♕f7 (28... ♕d5!? 29. ♘c5 ♗c5 30. ♖e5 ♕f7 31. ♖c5 b4=) 29. ♘d2 (R. Leyva 2275 − Pupo 2395, Holguin (m/2) 1992) ♗f6!? 30. ♕h3 g6 31. ♘f3 b4∞ Pupo] **18. a4 b4 19. ♕f1** [19. cb4? ♗b4; 19. c4 ♗f4!] **♕h5 20. c4 ♘e3 21. ♖e3 N** [21. fe3 c5!∞̄] **♖h6 22. ♕g2** [22. h4? g5!] **c5!∞̄ 23. dc5!□** [23. d5? ♗e5 △ ♗d4∓] **♗c5 24. ♖d3** [△ ♖d5] **♗h3 25. ♕f3** [25. ♕d5? ♗f5−+] **♕e5?** [25... ♗g4□ 26. ♕g2 (26. ♕h1? ♕f5 27. ♘e4 ♗e2−+) ♗h3 27. ♕f3=] **26. ♖d5!± ♕b2?** [26... ♕c7 27. ♘e4 ♗e7±] **27. ♖b1 ♖e8 28. ♕d1!** [28. ♖b2?? ♖e1] **♗f2□ 29. ♔f2 ♖f6 30. ♔g1 ♕c3** [△ ♕e3]

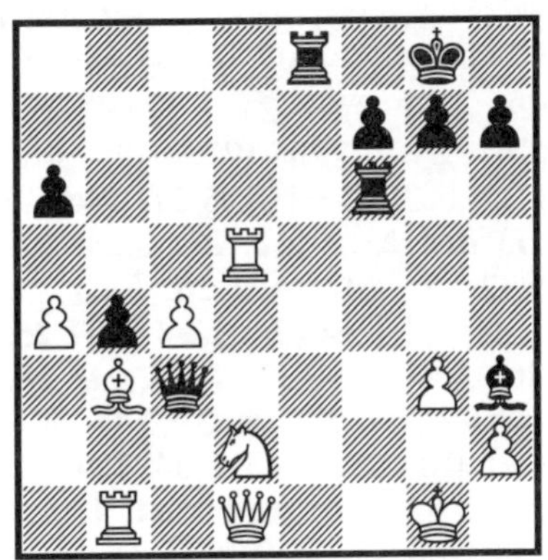

31. ♕e2!!+− ♔f8 [31... ♖e2? 32. ♖d8; 31... ♖fe6 32. ♘e4 ×♕c3] **32. ♘e4! ♖e4□** [×♕c3] **33. ♕e4 ♖e6 34. ♕d3!! ♖e1 35. ♔f2** [35. ♖e1?? ♕e1−+] **♕d3 36. ♖e1!!** [36. ♖d3?? ♖b1∓] **1 : 0**
[Magerramov, Badžarani]

350. **C 90**

ABRAMOVIĆ 2475 −
A. MIHAL'ČIŠIN 2520
Lviv 1993

1. e4 e5 2. ♘f3 ♘c6 3. ♗c4 ♘f6 4. d3 ♗e7 5. 0−0 0−0 6. ♖e1 d6 7. c3 ♘a5 8.

♗b5 a6 9. ♗a4 c5! [9... b5?! 10. b4!? ♘c6 11. ♗b3 a5 12. ♗d2±] **10. ♘bd2 b5 11. ♗c2 ♖e8** [11... ♘c6!? 12. ♘f1 d5!?⇆] **12. ♘f1 h6** [12... ♘c6 13. ♘g3 (13. ♗g5 — 43/434) g6 14. h3 ♗f8 15. ♘h2! ♗g7 16. ♕f3?! ♗e6 17. ♘g4 ♘g4 18. hg4 ♕h4 19. g5 ♗g4 20. ♕e3 f5!⇆; 16. f4!⩲] **13. ♘g3!? N** [13. ♘e3 — 8/260; 13. d4 — 56/(381)] **♗f8** [13... ♘c6!?] **14. d4! cd4** [14... ed4 15. cd4 ♗b7 16. d5 ♘c4 17. b3 ♘e5 18. ♘e5 de5 19. ♗b2±] **15. cd4 ♘c6** [15... ♗g4 16. d5 ♖c8 17. ♗d3 △ a4±] **16. h3?** [16. d5 ♘b4 17. ♗b1 a5 18. a3 ♘a6 19. b4!±] **ed4! 17. ♘d4 ♘d4** [17... ♗d7!?; 17... ♗b7!?] **18. ♕d4 ♕c7** [18... g6!?; 18... ♗b7!? △ ♖c8] **19. ♗b3 d5?!** [19... ♗e6!⇆] **20. ♗d2?** [20. ♗h6? ♗c5 21. ♕c3 ♕b6! (21... b4 22. ♕f3 gh6 23. ♕f6 ♕g3 24. ♗d5∞) 22. ♗g7 ♗f2 23. ♔h1 ♗d4!∓; 20. ♗d5 ♘d5 21. ♕d5 ♗b7 22. ♕b3 ♗d6=/∞; 20. e5! ♗c5 21. ♕c3! (21. ♕f4? ♗d6!∓) d4 22. ef6! dc3 (22... ♗b7!? 23. ♕d2 d3!? △ ♕c6) 23. ♖e8 ♔h7 24. fg7 ♔g7 (24... ♕g3? 25. g8♕ ♕g8 26. ♗c2! ♔h8 27. ♖g8 ♔g8 28. bc3±) 25. bc3!?=/∞→] **♗c5 21. ♕c3 ♕b6!∓ 22. ♕f3 de4 23. ♘e4** [23. ♖e4 ♗f2! 24. ♕f2 ♕f2 25. ♔f2 ♘e4 26. ♘e4 ♖e4 27. ♗d5 ♖d4−+] **♖e4! 24. ♖e4 ♗b7 25. ♗c2 ♘e4 26. ♗e4 ♗e4 27. ♕e4 ♗f2 28. ♔f1** [28. ♔h1 ♖d8 29. ♗c3 ♗d4 30. ♗d4 ♕d4−+] **♖d8 29. ♗c3 ♗d4!** [29... ♗g3!? 30. ♕f3 ♖d3] **30. ♗d4 ♖d4!** [30... ♕d4 31. ♕d4 ♖d4 32. ♔e2 f5∓] **31. ♕e8 ♔h7 32. ♕f7 ♖d6!!−+ 33. ♕f5 ♔g8 34. ♕c8** [34. ♔e2 ♖e6 35. ♔d3 ♕e3] **♔f7 35. g4 ♖f6 36. ♔g2 ♖f2 37. ♔g3** [37. ♔h1 ♕d6! 38. ♕b7 ♔f6!] **♕e3 38. ♔h4 g5 39. ♔h5 ♕h3# 0 : 1** **[A. Mihal'čišin]**

351. **C 91**

NIJBOER 2505 — I. SOKOLOV 2640

Wijk aan Zee (open) 1993

1. e4 e5 2. ♘f3 ♘c6 3. ♗b5 a6 4. ♗a4 ♘f6 5. 0−0 ♗e7 6. ♖e1 b5 7. ♗b3 0−0 8. d4 d6 9. c3 ♗g4 10. d5 ♘a5 11. ♗c2 c6 12. h3 ♗c8 13. dc6 ♕c7 14. ♘bd2 ♕c6 15. ♘f1 ♘b7 N [15... ♖d8 — 56/382] **16. ♘g3 ♘c5 17. ♘h2 ♗e6** [17... ♖e8; 17... g6] **18. ♘f5 ♗f5 19. ef5 e4?!** [⌓ 19... ♘cd7 △ d5, ♗c5] **20. ♗e3 d5 21. ♗d4 ♘cd7 22. ♘f1 a5 23. ♘e3 a4 24. g4 h6 25. f4 ef3 26. ♕f3 ♗c5 27. h4 ♖fe8 28. g5 ♘e5?** [28... hg5 29. hg5 ♘e4 30. ♘d5! ♗d4 31. ♔g2! ♕d5 32. ♗e4 ♖e4 33. ♕e4 (33. ♖e4? ♘e5 34. ♕f4 ♖e8 35. cd4 ♘d3−+) ♕e4 34. ♖e4±] **29. ♕g2 hg5 30. hg5 ♘fg4 31. ♘g4 ♗d4 32. cd4 ♘g4 33. ♗d3! ♖e3 34. ♖e3** [34. ♗f1? ♖ae8] **♘e3 35. ♕h3⊕ ♖e8 36. f6 gf6 37. ♕h6?!** [37. ♕h7 ♔f8 38. ♗b5! ♕b5 39. gf6+−] **♘g4?!** [37... ♕c7! 38. ♔h1! f5 39. g6 f6 (39... fg6 40. ♕g6 ♔f8 41. ♖g1 ♔e7 42. ♕g5 ♔d7 43. ♗b5+−) 40. ♖e1 ♕g7 (40... f4 41. g7 ♕g7 42. ♖g1+−) 41. ♕f4 ♕h8! 42. ♔g1 ♕h3 43. ♗f1 ♕g4 44. ♕g4 fg4 45. ♔f2 ♖e4 46. ♖e3 ♖d4 47. ♗b5 ♖b4 48. ♗c6 ♖b2 49. ♖e2 g3 50. ♔f3+−] **38. ♕h7?** [38. ♗h7 ♔h8 39. ♕h5 ♔g7 40. ♗f5 ♘e3 41. ♕h6 ♔g8 42. ♗h7 ♔h8 43. ♗g6 ♔g8 44. ♕h7 ♔f8 45. ♕f7#] **♔f8 39. ♕h8 ♔e7 40. ♖e1 ♔d8 41. ♕e8 ♕e8 42. ♖e8 ♔e8 43. ♗b5 ♔d8 44. ♗e2 ♘e3 45. gf6 a3?** [45... ♔d7 46. ♔f2 ♘c2 47. ♗b5 ♔e6 48. ♗a4 ♘d4=] **46. ba3 ♔d7 47. a4! ♘c2 48. a5 ♘d4 49. a6 ♔c6 50. ♗h5 ♔b6 51. ♗f7 ♘f3 52. ♔g2 ♘e5 53. ♗d5 ♔a6 54. f7 ♘d7 55. ♗e6 ♘f8 56. ♗f5 ♔b6 57. ♔g3 ♔c6 58. ♔f4 ♔d6 59. a4 1 : 0** **[Nijboer]**

352.* **C 92**

N. SHORT 2665 — JE. PIKET 2590

Amsterdam 1993

1. e4 e5 2. ♘f3 ♘c6 3. ♗b5 a6 4. ♗a4 ♘f6 5. 0−0 ♗e7 6. ♖e1 b5 7. ♗b3 d6 8. c3 0−0 9. h3 ♗e6 [RR 9... ♘d7 10. d4 ♗f6 11. a4 ♗b7 12. ♘a3 ed4 13. cd4 ♖e8 14. ♕d2 ♖e7 15. ♖b1!? N (15. ♗c2 — 53/(346)) ba4 (15... b4? 16. ♘c4) 16. ♗a4 ♘b6 17. ♗c2 (17. ♗c6!? ♗c6 18. d5 ♗b7 19. ♕c2) a5 18. ♕c3 ♘b4 19. ♗g5 ♘c2 (19... ♗g5 20. ♘g5 ♕e8 21. ♗b3 h6 22.

♘f7 ♖f7 23. ♗f7 ♕f7 24. ♖e3±) 20. ♕c2 ♖e4! 21. ♖e4 (21. ♗f6 ♖e1 22. ♘e1 gf6∞) ♗e4 22. ♕e4 ♗g5 (R. Mainka 2550 – Xie Jun 2480, Baden-Baden II 1992) 23. ♕c6 △ ♘b5=∞ Xie Jun] **10. d4 ♗b3 11. ab3 ed4 12. cd4 ♘b4 13. ♘c3 c5 14. ♗f4 ♖e8!?** [14... c4 – 48/(468); 14... ♕b6 15. ♖e2 ♖ad8 16. ♖d2 ♖fe8∞] **15. ♖e2 N** [15. d5] **♕b6 16. e5?!** [16. ♖d2 ♖ad8] **de5 17. de5 ♖ed8□** [17... ♖ad8 18. ef6 (18. ♖d2!?) ♖d1 19. ♖d1 gf6 20. ♗d6+–] **18. ♖d2 ♘e8 19. ♕e2 ♘c7 20. ♕e4** [20. ♖ad1; 20. ♘e4] **♘e6 21. ♗e3 ♖d2 22. ♘d2 ♖d8 23. ♘f3** [23. f4 ♘d4 24. f5 ♕c6∓] **♘d4** [23... ♕c7!] **24. ♖d1 ♘f3!** [24... f5? 25. ef6 ♗f6 26. ♘g5!; 24... ♘b3 25. ♖d8 (25. ♕b4? cb4 26. ♗b6 bc3–+) ♗d8 (25... ♕d8 26. e6!) 26. ♕a8 h6 27. e6 fe6 28. ♘e5=∞; 27. ♘d5!] **25. ♕f3 ♖d1 26. ♕d1** [26. ♘d1] **♕e6 27. f4** [27. ♗f4 h6∓] **f6 28. ♘e4! fe5 29. ♕h5 g6 30. ♕e5 ♕e5 31. fe5 ♘d3 32. e6** [32. ♔f1 ♔f7 33. ♔e2 c4∓] **♘b2** [32... c4 33. bc4 bc4 34. ♗d4; 32... ♔f8 33. ♔f1; 32... a5 33. ♘c3 b4 34. ♘d5?! ♔f8 35. ♔f1 (35. ♗h6 ♔e8 36. ♗g7 ♘c1) ♘b2 36. ♘e7 ♔e7 37. ♗c5 ♔e6 38. ♗b6 a4; 34. ♘a4! △ ♔f1-e2=] **33. ♗c5 ♗c5 34. ♘c5 a5 35. ♘b7!= a4 36. ♘d6 ♔f8 37. ♘b5 ab3 38. ♘d4 ♔e7 39. ♘b3** **1/2 : 1/2**
[Je. Piket]

353. **C 92**

MATULOVIĆ 2460 – ILINČIĆ 2470

Aranđelovac 1993

1. e4 e5 2. ♘f3 ♘c6 3. ♗b5 a6 4. ♗a4 ♘f6 5. 0–0 ♗e7 6. ♖e1 b5 7. ♗b3 d6 8. c3 0–0 9. h3 ♗b7 10. d3 h6 11. ♘bd2 ♖e8 12. ♘f1 ♗f8 13. ♘g3 ♘a5 14. ♗c2 g6 N [14... c5; 14... d5 – 32/443] **15. d4 ♗g7 16. b3 ed4** [16... c5 17. d5±] **17. cd4 c5 18. ♗b2 ♘d7 19. ♕d2** [19. ♖b1!? △ d5] **♘c6 20. ♖ad1 ♕e7** [20... ♕a5!?] **21. ♗b1 ♖ad8 22. d5 ♘ce5 23. ♘h2 ♘b6** [△ ♘ec4] **24. ♖e2 h5?!** [⌓ 24... ♕g5] **25. ♕c1! ♘ed7** [25... h4 26. ♘gf1± △ f4] **26. ♗g7 ♔g7 27. ♖e3** [△ ♘h5!] **♘f6?!** [27... ♖h8 28. f4±]

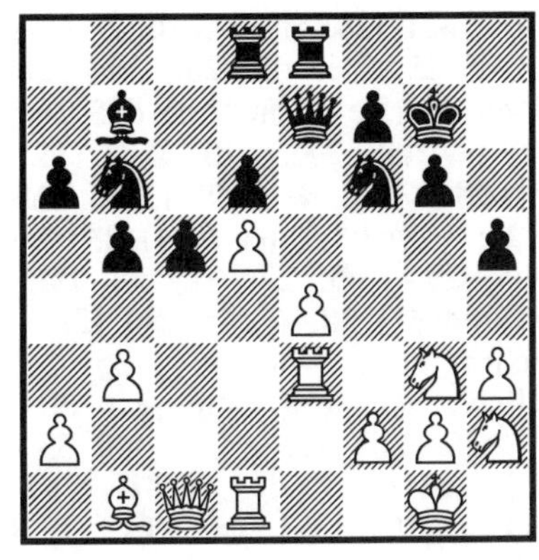

28. e5! de5 [28... ♘fd5 29. ♘f5! gf5 30. ♖g3+–] **29. ♘f5! gf5 30. ♖g3 ♘g4□ 31. ♗f5 ♖h8 32. hg4?!⊕** [32. d6! ♖d6 33. ♖d6 ♕d6 34. hg4 h4 35. ♕g5 ♔f8 36. ♖d3 ♗d5 37. ♗e4±] **h4 33. ♖c3 ♘d5?!⊕** [33... c4!=] **34. ♖c5 ♘f4 35. ♖e1!+– ♖d5 36. ♖c7 ♕g5 37. ♘f3** [37. ♖b7?? ♘e2–+] **♕d8 38. ♖b7 ♘e2 39. ♖e2 ♖d1 40. ♖e1 ♖c1 41. ♖c1** **1 : 0**
[Matulović]

354.* **C 92**

MAGEM BADALS 2510 – AN. KARPOV 2725

Dos Hermanas 1993

1. e4 e5 2. ♘f3 ♘c6 3. ♗b5 a6 4. ♗a4 ♘f6 5. 0–0 ♗e7 6. ♖e1 b5 7. ♗b3 d6 8. c3 0–0 9. h3 ♗b7 10. d4 ♖e8 11. ♘g5 ♖f8 12. ♘f3 ♖e8 13. ♘bd2 ♗f8 14. ♗c2 [RR 14. a4 h6 15. ♗c2 g6!? N (15... ed4) 16. d5 ♘b8 17. b3 c6 18. c4 bc4 19. bc4 a5 20. ♖b1 ♕c7 21. ♘b3 ♗a6 22. ♗d3 ♘bd7 23. ♗d2 cd5 24. ♗a5 ♕a7 25. cd5 ♗d3 26. ♕d3 ♘c5 27. ♘c5 ♕a5 28. ♘b3 ♕a4= Ivančuk 2710 – Ljubojević 2605, Monaco 1993] **g6 15. d5 ♘b8 16. b3 c6 17. c4 ♕c7 18. ♘f1 ♘bd7 19. ♗e3 ♘c5!? N** [19... ♖ec8!? 20. ♖c1 ♕a5 (20... ♕d8 – 27/(315)) 21. ♗b1 cd5⇆] **20. ♘g3** [20. ♗c5 dc5 21. ♗d3 ♗h6!?⇆] **a5** [20... bc4 21. bc4 (21. ♗c5?! cb3) ♘fd7 △ a5, ♗a6] **21. ♕d2** [21. ♗c5 dc5 22. ♗d3 cd5 23. cd5 c4!?∞⇆] **♘fd7 22. cb5?!** [22. ♖ac1 bc4 23. bc4 ♗a6∓; 22. dc6 ♗c6 23. cb5 ♗b5∞] **cd5!** [22... cb5? 23. a3!⩲] **23. ed5**

♘**f6 24.** ♖**ac1** [24. ♗h6 ♗d5!?∓] ♘**d5!**∓ [24... ♗d5 25. ♗c5 dc5 26. ♘e4 ♗e4 27. ♗e4 ♘e4 28. ♖e4] **25.** ♗**c5 dc5 26.** ♗**d3** [26. ♗e4 ♖ad8 27. ♗d5 ♖d5 28. ♕c3 f5∓] ♖**ad8 27.** ♗**c4** ♗**g7!** [27... ♘f4 28. ♕c3!; 27... ♔g7 (△ f6, ♘f4) 28. ♕g5 △ 29. ♘h5, 29. ♘f5; 27... f5 28. b6! ♕g7 29. ♕a5 e4∞̄↑] **28.** ♘**e4** ♘**f6!** [28... ♘f4 29. ♕e3⇆; 28... ♔h8 29. ♗d5 ♖d5 30. ♕e3⇆] **29.** ♕**c2** [29. ♘f6 ♗f6 30. ♕e3 e4 31. ♘g5 ♗d4 32. ♗f7 ♔h8! 33. ♕e2 ♖f8−+] ♘**e4 30.** ♖**e4** ♗**e4 31.** ♕**e4** ♗**h6 32.** ♖**e1** ♔**g7!−+ 33. g4** ♗**f4** **0 : 1** **[An. Karpov]**

355. **C 93**

ŠABALOV 2575 − A. GOL'DIN 2555
Pleasantville 1993

1. e4 e5 2. ♘**f3** ♘**c6 3.** ♗**b5 a6 4.** ♗**a4** ♘**f6 5. 0−0** ♗**e7 6.** ♖**e1 b5 7.** ♗**b3 d6 8. c3 0−0 9. h3** ♖**e8 10. d4 h6 11. a3** ♗**f8 12.** ♘**bd2** ♗**b7** [12... a5!? △ a4, ♘a5] **13.** ♗**a2** ♕**d7!? N** [13... ♘a7; 13... ♘b8 − 40/(438)] **14. b4 a5!** [14... d5?! 15. ♘e5 ♘e5 16. de5 ♖e5 17. f4 ♖ee8 (17... ♖e7 18. e5 ♘e4 19. ♘e4 de4 20. ♕d7 ♖d7 21. e6! ♖d3 22. ef7 ♔h8 23. ♗b1 ♖c3 24. ♗e4±) 18. e5 ♘h7 19. ♘f3±; 14... ed4!? 15. cd4 d5 16. e5 ♘e4 17. ♕b3 (17. ♘e4? de4 18. ♖e4 ♘b4! △ 19. ♖g4 ♘a2 20. ♗h6 ♘c3 21. ♕d2 ♖e6−+) ♘d8! 18. ♗b2∞] **15. d5** ♘**e7 16. c4** [16. ♘b3 ab4 17. cb4 c6 18. dc6 ♘c6 19. ♗b2 ♕c7 △ ♕b6=] **ab4 17. cb5** [17. ab4? ♖a4! 18. c5 ♖ea8 19. ♕c2 (19. ♕b3? ♘ed5!−+; 19. c6? ♗c6 20. dc6 ♘c6 21. ♕b3 ♘b4−+) c6∓] ♕**b5 18.** ♖**b1 c5= 19.** ♗**c4** ♕**a5 20. ab4 cb4 21.** ♕**b3** ♖**eb8 22.** ♕**b4** ♕**b4 23.** ♖**b4** ♘**d7!** [△ f5] **24. g4□** ♘**g6!?** [24... g6 25. ♘f1 f5 26. gf5 gf5 27. ♘g3 fe4 28. ♘e4 ♗d5 (28... ♘d5?? 29. ♖b7 ♖b7 30. ♗d5+−) 29. ♖b8 ♖b8 30. ♘d6 ♗g7 31. ♗d5 ♘d5 32. ♘f5 ♖f8!=] **25.** ♘**f1** ♗**c8 26.** ♖**b8** ♖**b8 27.** ♗**e3** ♘**f4 28.** ♔**h2□** [28. ♗f4? ef4 29. e5 de5 30. ♘e5 ♘e5 31. ♖e5 ♗d7 32. ♘d2 ♖b4∓] ♗**e7 29.** ♘**g3** [29. ♔g3 ♘g6=] **g6 30.** ♖**c1?!** [30. ♘e2=] ♘**f6!∓ 31.** ♗**f1** ♗**d7 32.** ♖**c7** ♗**d8 33.** ♖**a7** ♗**b6 34.** ♖**a6□** [34. ♗b6 ♖b6∓] ♗**g4!?** [34... ♗c7? 35. ♘e5 ♗c8 36. ♖c6+−] **35.** ♗**b6** [35. ♖b6 ♖b6 36. ♗b6 ♗f3 37. ♗c7 ♘e4 38. ♘e4 ♗e4 39. ♗d6 f6−+; 35. hg4 ♘g4 *a)* 36. ♔g1 ♘e3 37. fe3 (37. ♖b6 ♖b6 38. fe3 ♖b3−+) ♗e3 38. ♔h1 ♖b1 39. ♖d6 ♗f2−+; *b)* 36. ♔h1! ♘f2!? 37. ♗f2 ♗f2 38. ♘e2 ♘e2 39. ♗e2 ♖b2! 40. ♗c4 ♗c5∓] ♗**f3 36.** ♗**c7!** ♖**b2?⊕** [36... ♖c8 37. ♗d6 ♘e4 38. ♗e5 ♘d5 39. ♘e4 ♗e4∓] **37.** ♗**d6** ♖**f2?!** [37... ♗g2 38. ♗e5 ♖f2 39. ♗g2! ♖g2 40. ♔h1 ♖g3 41. ♗f4 ♖f3 42. ♖f6 ♔g7 43. ♔g2+−; 37... ♘d7 38. ♖a8! (38. ♖a7 ♗g2! 39. ♖d7 ♖f2 40. ♗g2 ♖g2 41. ♔h1 ♖g3 42. ♗e5 g5=) ♔h7 39. ♖a7 ♗g2 40. ♖d7 ♖f2 41. ♖f7 ♔g8 42. ♖f4 ef4 43. ♗g2+−] **38.** ♔**g1** ♘**e4 39.** ♗**e5+−** ♖**f1 40.** ♘**f1 g5 41. d6** ♘**c5 42.** ♗**f4! gf4 43.** ♘**d2** ♗**e2 44.** ♖**a7** ♔**f8 45.** ♖**c7** **1 : 0** **[A. Gol'din]**

356. **C 93**

HELLERS 2565 − A. GOL'DIN 2555
Pleasantville 1993

1. e4 e5 2. ♘**f3** ♘**c6 3.** ♗**b5 a6 4.** ♗**a4** ♘**f6 5. 0−0** ♗**e7 6.** ♖**e1 b5 7.** ♗**b3 d6 8. c3 0−0 9. h3** ♖**e8 10. d4 h6 11.** ♘**bd2** ♗**f8 12.** ♘**f1** ♗**d7 13.** ♘**g3** ♘**a5 14.** ♗**c2** ♘**c4 15. b3** ♘**b6 16.** ♗**e3** [16. a4 ba4 17. ba4 a5 18. ♗b3 c5] **c5!?** [16... a5 17. ♕d2 a4∞] **17.** ♘**d2!? N** [17. ♕d2 − 6/371; 17. dc5 dc5 18. ♕e2 ♕c7 19. ♘h2 a5 20. ♘g4 ♘g4 21. hg4 a4 22. ♘f5 ab3 23. ab3 ♕c6=; 17. d5 a5 △ a4⇆] **cd4 18. cd4** ♖**c8 19.** ♖**c1** [19. f4? ef4 20. ♗f4 ♘bd5! 21. ed5 ♖e1 22. ♕e1 ♖c2∓] ♘**a8!?** [19... ♖c3 20. ♘b1! ♖c8 21. f4↑; 19... g6!? 20. f4 ♖c3! △ 21. ♘b1 ♖e3!∓; 20. ♗b1!?] **20.** ♘**f3** ♕**a5 21. a4** ♕**d8!=** [21... ♘b6? 22. ♗d2 b4 23. ♗d3±] **22. d5 ba4 23. ba4** ♘**b6 24.** ♘**d2?** [24. ♗b3 ♖c1 25. ♗c1 ♕c7=] ♘**a4! 25.** ♗**a4** ♖**c1 26.** ♕**c1** ♗**a4∓ 27.** ♕**a3** ♗**b5 28.** ♘**e2** ♕**d7 29.** ♘**c3** ♗**d3 30. f3** ♖**b8 31.** ♘**d1** ♗**b5 32.** ♘**c3** ♗**d3 33.** ♘**d1** ♗**b5⊕ 34.** ♘**c3** ♗**e7 35.** ♖**b1** ♘**h5! 36.** ♘**c4** ♘**f4 37.** ♘**a5** [37. ♘b6 ♕c7 38. ♘b5 ab5 39. ♖b5 ♘e2 40. ♔h2 (40. ♔f1 ♘d4 41. ♗d4 ed4 42. ♕b2 ♗d8! 43. ♘a4 ♕c4−+) ♘d4 41. ♗d4 ed4 42. ♘a8 (42. ♕b3 ♕c3−+) ♕d8 43. ♖b8 (43. ♖a5 d3−+) ♕b8 44. ♕a6 d3 45. ♘b6 d2−+] **♗g5 38. ♗f2 ♖a8! 39. ♔h2 ♗d8 40. ♗e3 ♗g5 41. ♗f2 ♗d8 42. ♗e3 ♕c7 43. ♘c6□ ♗c6 44. dc6 ♕c6 45. ♗f4 ef4 46. ♘d5 ♕c5!** [46... a5 47. ♘f4 (47. ♖c1 ♕d7 48. ♘f4 ♗g5! 49. g3 a4∓) ♕c5 48. ♕a4 ♕e5 49. g3] **47. ♕b2□ ♗h4** [47... ♖c8 48. ♕b7! △ ♕d7, ♖b7⇆] **48. ♘f4 ♕e5! 49. ♕e5** [49. g3 ♗g3 50. ♔g3 ♕g5−+; 49. ♕d2 ♗g5 50. g3 a5−+] **de5 50. ♘d3 ♗f6!** [50... f6?! 51. g3 ♗g5 52. f4 ef4 53. gf4 ♗h4 54. ♔g2∓] **51. ♔g1 a5 52. ♔f1 a4−+ 53. ♔e2 a3 54. ♖a1 ♗e7! 55. ♘e5?** [55. ♔d2 h5 56. ♔c2 h4 57. ♖a2 ♗d6 △ ♔h7-g6-g5, g6, f5−+] **♗f6 56. f4 ♗e5 57. fe5 ♔f8 58. e6 fe6 59. ♔d3 ♔e7 60. e5 ♔d7 0 : 1** [A. Gol'din]

357. **C 95**

R. MAINKA 2515 − NIKITIN 2420

Dortmund (open) 1993

1. e4 e5 2. ♘f3 ♘c6 3. ♗b5 a6 4. ♗a4 ♘f6 5. 0−0 ♗e7 6. ♖e1 b5 7. ♗b3 d6 8. c3 0−0 9. h3 ♘b8 10. d4 ♘bd7 11. ♘bd2 ♗b7 12. ♗c2 ♖e8 13. a4 ♗f8 14. ♗d3 b4 15. ♕c2 d5!? N [15... a5 16. d5±; 16. cb4 − 45/(418)] **16. de5! ♘e5 17. ♘e5 ♖e5 18. ♘f3 ♖e4** [18... ♖e8 19. e5 ♘e4 20. c4 ♗c5 21. ♗e3 ♗e3 22. ♖e3 f5 23. ef6 ♘f6 24. ♘g5 ♖e3 25. ♗h7 ♔f8 26. fe3 ♕e7 27. ♖e1 dc4 28. ♕c4 ♗d5 29. ♕f4±] **19. ♗e4 de4 20. ♖d1?!** [20. ♘h2!? △ ♘f1] **♕e8 21. ♘d4 ♕e5 22. ♘e2 ♘d5** [22... g5 23. ♕d2 h6 24. ♕d4 ♕f5 25. ♘g3 ♕g6 26. cb4 ♗d6±; 22... ♘h5!? 23. g4 ♘f6 24. ♗f4 ♕e6 25. ♘d4 ♕c8 26. cb4 ♘d5$\bar{\bar{\infty}}$] **23. c4 ♗d6! 24. g3** [24. cd5? ♕h2 25. ♔f1 ♕h1 26. ♘g1 a5!! △ ♗a6→] **♘f6 25. ♗f4 ♕h5 26. ♗d6 e3! 27. ♘f4! ♕f3 28. ♔h2 cd6** [28... g5 29. ♕e2 gf4 30. ♕f3 ♗f3 31. ♗f4 ♗d1 32. ♖d1 ef2 33. ♔g2 ♘e4 34. ♗c7∞] **29. fe3 ♕e3 30. ♖e1 ♕c5 31. ♖e7 ♗c6?!** [31... b3! 32. ♕d2 ♗c6∞] **32. ♕e2 ♖f8** [32... b3; 32... ♖d8] **33. b3 a5 34. ♖d1 ♖d8?⊕** [34... g5! 35. ♘g2 ♘d7 36. ♘e3 ♘e5 37. ♖f1 ♘g6 38. ♖c7 ♗f3 39. ♖c5 ♗e2 40. ♖g5 ♗f1 (40... ♖e8?! 41. ♘d5! ♗f1 42. ♘f6 ♔f8 43. ♘e8 ♔e8 44. ♖a5±) 41. ♘f1 ♖e8 42. ♖a5 ♖e2 43. ♔h1 ♘e5 44. ♖d5 ♖e1 45. ♔g2 ♖e2 46. ♔g1 ♘f3 47. ♔h1 ♖f2 48. ♖d1 ♖b2 49. ♖d3 ♖f2 50. ♖d1 ♖b2=] **35. ♘d3?** [35. ♘d5 ♘d5 36. ♖d5!±] **♕g5 36. ♘f4 h5 37. ♕e3 ♕f5 38. ♖e1 ♕c2 39. ♖e2 ♕b1 40. ♖e1 ♕c2 41. ♖e2 ♕b1 42. ♕g1! ♕f5 43. ♕b6 ♖c8 44. ♖c7 ♖c7 45. ♕c7 ♗f3 46. ♖f2 ♗d1 47. ♕d6 ♗b3 48. ♕d4! ♕e4?** [48... ♘e4! 49. ♖e2 ♘g5∞] **49. ♕d8 ♔h7 50. ♕a5 ♗c4 51. ♕b4 h4?** [51... g5 52. ♘g2 ♔g6 53. ♕b2 ♘d5 54. a5 h4 55. gh4 gh4 56. ♕h8!±] **52. gh4 ♕e3 53. ♕d2!+− ♕c5 54. ♕c2 ♔g8 55. ♖d2 ♔f8 56. ♕b2 ♕c7 57. ♕b4 ♔g8 58. ♕d6 ♕a7 59. ♕e5 ♕b6 60. a5 ♕b1 61. ♖b2 ♕f1 62. ♘h5 ♗e6 63. ♘f6 gf6 64. ♕g3 ♔f8 65. ♕d6! ♔g7 66. ♖g2 1 : 0** [Nikitin]

358. **C 95**

TH. ERNST 2540 − ORNSTEIN 2440

Avesta 1993

1. e4 e5 2. ♘f3 ♘c6 3. ♗b5 a6 4. ♗a4 ♘f6 5. 0−0 ♗e7 6. ♖e1 b5 7. ♗b3 0−0 8. c3 d6 9. h3 ♘b8 10. d4 ♘bd7 11. ♘bd2 ♗b7 12. ♗c2 ♖e8 13. ♘f1 ♗f8 14. ♘g3 g6 15. a4 c5 16. d5 c4 17. ♗g5 h6 18. ♗e3 ♗g7 19. ♖f1 ♘c5 20. ♕d2 h5 N [20... ♔h7 − 39/434] **21. ♗g5 ♕b6 22. ♗h6** [△ 23. ♗g7 ♔g7 24. ♘f5!] **♗h8 23. ♔h1 ba4! 24. ♖a2** [24. ♘h4? ♘b3! 25. ♗b3 ab3∓] **a5 25. ♘h4 a3 26. ba3 ♗a6?! 27. f4 ♘b3 28. ♕d1 ef4** [28... ♗g7 29. ♗g7 ♔g7 30. f5±; 28... ♕e3 29. ♖f3 △ 29... ♕c1? 30. ♗b3+−] **29. ♗f4 ♘d7?** [29... ♖a7 30. ♕f3±] **30. ♘h5!+− ♕d8 31. ♘g6?!** [31. ♕g4! ♘f6 32. ♘f6 ♕f6 33. ♖f3] **fg6 32. ♕g4 ♘f8 33. e5 ♕d7! 34. e6 ♕h7 35. ♘g3 ♗b7 36. ♘f5 ♗c3!** [36... ♗d5? 37. ♘h6 ♔g7 38. ♗e5 de5 39. ♖f7+−; 36... ♕h5? 37. ♘h6 ♔g7 38. ♗g5+−] **37. ♘h6 ♔h8 38. ♗e3! ♗d5** [38... ♖e7? 39. ♕c4] **39. ♖f7 ♗g7?** [39... ♖e6! 40. ♖h7 *a)* 40... ♔h7 41. ♕h5 *a1)* 41... ♗e4? 42. ♗e4 ♖e4 43. ♕d5 ♖e3 44. ♕a8+−; *a2)* 41... ♗b7 42. ♕h4 d5 43. ♗b3 ♗f6 (43... cb3 44. ♖f2+−) 44. ♗g5 cb3 45. ♘g4+−; *a3)* 41... ♗c6 42.

♕h4 d5 43. ♘f5 ♔g8 44. ♘e7 ♔f7 45. ♘c6 ♖c6 46. ♗d1± △ ♖f2, ♗f3; *a4)* 41… ♖e5 42. ♕h4 ♔g7 43. ♘g4 ♖e6 44. ♕h6 ♔g8 45. ♕g5±; *a5)* 41… ♖e3! 42. ♕d5 ♖e1 43. ♔h2 ♗e5 44. g3 ♖a7 (44… ♖e8 45. ♘g4 ♘c1 46. ♕f7 ♔h8 47. ♘h6+−) 45. ♕c4 ♘c1 46. ♕h4 ♔g7 47. ♘g4 ♘a2 48. ♕h6 ♔f7 49. ♕d2 ♖c1 (49… ♖f1 50. ♔g2) 50. ♗b3 ♔e8 51. ♕a2→; *b)* 40… ♘h7 41. ♘f7 ♔g7 42. ♗f5 ♖ae8! (42… ♖f6 43. ♗e4 ♗e6 44. ♕h4 d5 45. ♕h6 ♔g8 46. ♗g6 ♖f7 47. ♗h7 ♖h7 48. ♕e6+−) 43. ♖f2 ♖f6 (43… ♖e3 44. ♕g6 ♔f8 45. ♕h7 ♗f7 46. ♗g6 ♖e1 47. ♔h2 ♗e5 48. g3 ♗g3 49. ♔g2+−) 44. ♗g6!! (44. ♗h6?! ♔f7 45. ♗g6 ♔e7 46. ♗e8 ♔e8 47. ♕c8 ♔e7 48. ♖e2 ♗e5 49. ♖e5 de5 50. ♕c7 ♔e6 51. ♕h7 ♖f1 52. ♔h2 ♖f2=) ♖e3 (44… ♖g6 45. ♗h6+−) 45. ♗h7 ♔f7 46. ♖f6 ♗f6 47. ♗g8 ♔e7 48. ♗d5±] **40. e7+− ♗f7** [40… ♖e7 41. ♖e7 c3 42. ♗b3 ♗b3 43. ♖g7! ♕g7 44. ♗d4 ♗a2 45. ♘f5] **41. ♘f7 ♔g8 42. ef8♕** [42. ♕c4 ♕h5 43. ♘h6] **♗f8** [42… ♖f8 43. ♗g6 ♕g6 44. ♕g6 ♖f7 45. ♗h6] **43. ♗g6 ♕g7 44. ♘h6 ♔h8 45. ♘f5** [45… ♕d7 46. ♕h4 ♔g8 47. ♕c4 d5 48. ♕b3] **1 : 0** **[Th. Ernst]**

359. **C 96**

HALIFMAN 2630 − GSCHNITZER 2475
Deutschland 1992/93

1. e4 e5 2. ♘f3 ♘c6 3. ♗b5 a6 4. ♗a4 ♘f6 5. 0−0 ♗e7 6. ♖e1 b5 7. ♗b3 d6 8. c3 0−0 9. h3 ♘a5 10. ♗c2 c5 11. d4 ♘d7 12. ♘bd2 cd4 13. cd4 ♘c6 14. ♘b3 ♗f6 15. d5 ♘a5 [15… ♘e7 16. a4!] **16. ♘bd2!?** [16. ♘a5 ♕a5 17. ♘d2±] **♘b6 17. ♘f1 ♗d7 18. b3 ♘b7 19. ♘g3 N** [19. ♗e3 − 25/350] **g6 20. ♗h6** [20. ♗e3!?±] **♗g7 21. ♗g7 ♔g7 22. b4 a5 23. a3 ♕c7! 24. ♕d2** [24. ♗d3 ab4 25. ab4 ♕c3!] **♖fc8 25. ♖ac1 ♕d8?** [25… ♘c4 26. ♕g5 ♕d8! 27. ♘h5 ♔h8 28. ♘f6 ♔g7=] **26. ♗d3 ♘c4** [26… ab4 27. ab4 ♖c1 28. ♖c1 ♖c8 29. ♘e2!±] **27. ♗c4 bc4 28. ♖c3** [28. ♕e3 ab4 29. ab4 ♖a4] **ab4 29. ab4 ♖a4 30. ♖b1 ♕b6** [30… h6 31. ♕e3!±]

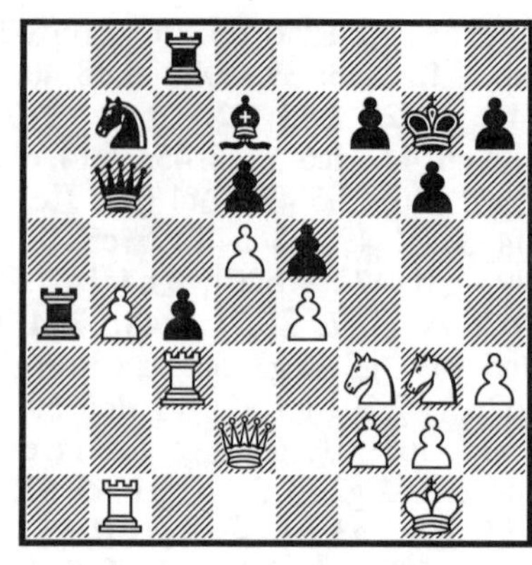

31. ♕g5! [31. ♕b2 ♖ca8!∞] **♖b4** [31… ♕d8 32. ♕e3!±] **32. ♖b4 ♕b4 33. ♖e3!** [33. ♖c1 c3 34. ♘h5 ♔f8 35. ♕f6 gh5 36. ♘g5 ♘d8] **♔f8** [33… c3 34. ♘h5 ♔f8 35. ♕f6! gh5 (35… c2 36. ♘g5 c1♕ 37. ♔h2+−; 35… h6 36. ♘h4+−) 36. ♘g5 ♘d8 (36… ♔e8 37. ♕f7 ♔d8 38. ♘e6 ♗e6 39. de6+−) 37. ♘h7 ♔g8 38. ♕h6+−; 33… ♘d8 34. ♕e7!+−] **34. ♕f6 ♘d8 35. ♘g5 c3 36. ♘h7 ♔g8 37. ♘h5!+− gh5 38. ♕h6 f6 39. ♕g6 ♔h8 40. ♘f6** **1 : 0** **[Halifman]**

360.* !N **C 99**

ANAND 2710 − JE. PIKET 2590
Amsterdam 1993

1. e4 e5 2. ♘f3 ♘c6 3. ♗b5 a6 4. ♗a4 ♘f6 5. 0−0 ♗e7 6. ♖e1 b5 7. ♗b3 d6 8. c3 0−0 9. h3 ♘a5 10. ♗c2 c5 11. d4 ♕c7 12. ♘bd2 cd4 13. cd4 ♗d7 [RR 13… ♗b7 14. ♘f1 ♖ac8 15. ♗b1 d5 16. ed5 ed4 17. ♗g5! ♖fe8 18. ♕d3! N (18. ♕d4) g6 19. ♖e7 ♕e7 20. ♕d4 ♖c4 21. ♕f6 ♕f6 22. ♗f6 ♖c1! 23. d6 ♗c6 24. b4! (24. ♗e7 ♘c4 25. ♗e4 ♖a1 26. ♗c6 ♘d6! 27. ♗e8 ♘e8 28. a3 ♖a2= Th. Ernst) ♘b7 25. ♗e4□ ♖f1 26. ♔f1 ♖e4 27. ♘e5 ♖d4 28. ♘c6 ♖d6 29. ♘e7 ♔f8 30. ♗h4 ♖d4 31. ♗g5+− Th. Ernst 2540 − E. Hedman 2225, Avesta 1993] **14. ♘f1 ♖ac8 15. ♘e3 ♘c6 16. d5 ♘b4 17. ♗b1 a5 18. a3 ♘a6 19. b4 ♖a8 20. ♗d2 ♖fc8 21. ♗d3 ab4 22. ab4 ♕b7 23. ♘h2 ♘c7 24. ♘hf1?! N** [24. ♕e2 g6 − 42/454; 24. ♘c2!] **♖a1 25. ♕a1 ♘h5! 26. ♘c2?** [26. ♗e2! ♘f4 27.

♗g4] **f5!∓ 27. ef5** [27. ♘fe3 fe4 28. ♗e4 ♘f6 29. ♗f3 e4; 27. ♘ce3!? fe4 28. ♗e4 ♘f6∓] **♘d5** [27... ♕d5!? 28. ♗e4 ♕f7 Kramnik] **28. ♘fe3 ♔h8 29. ♗f1 ♘hf6 30. ♖d1 ♘b6 31. ♘a3 ♖a8 32. ♕b2 ♗c6 33. ♖c1 d5** [33... ♗f8!? Je. Piket] **34. ♗b5 ♗b5 35. ♘b5 d4 36. ♖c7 ♕a6?** [36... ♕b8!! 37. ♖e7 de3 38. ♗e3 ♘c4 39. ♕c1 ♘e3! (39... ♕b5 40. ♗h6!) 40. ♕e3 ♕b5∓] **37. ♖e7 ♕b5** [37... de3! 38. ♗e3 ♕b5 (38... ♘c4? 39. ♘c7) 39. ♖e5=] **38. ♘g4 ♘c4!** [38... ♘g4 39. hg4 ♘c4 40. ♕c1±] **39. ♗h6!** [39. ♕c1 ♘d5∞] **♘g4 40. ♗g7 ♔g8 41. ♕c1 ♕b4??** [41... ♘ge3 42. fe3 ♘e3 43. ♗h6±; 41... d3! 42. ♗h6□ d2 43. ♗d2 ♘d2 44. hg4 ♕b4 45. ♖e5±] **42. ♗f6!+− ♔f8 43. hg4 ♕d2 44. ♕d2 ♘d2 45. ♖d7 ♖a5 46. f3 ♘c4 47. g5 ♖a1 48. ♔h2 ♖a6 49. ♖c7** [⌓ 49. g4!+−] **♘e3 50. ♗g7** [50. ♗e5 d3 51. ♗c3 ♘d5 (51... d2 52. ♗d2 ♘f1 53. ♔h3 ♘d2 54. ♖h7+−) 52. ♖h7 ♘c3 53. ♖d7!+−] **♔g8 51. ♗e5 d3 52. ♗c3 d2 53. ♗d2 ♘f1 54. ♔h3 ♘d2 55. f6! ♖a1 56. ♔g4! ♖g1 57. ♔g3** [×♖g1] **♖h1 58. ♔f4 ♖h4 59. ♔f5 ♖a4 60. ♖g7 ♔f8** [60... ♔h8 61. ♖d7] **61. ♖h7**

1 : 0 **[Anand]**

D

361. **D 02**

NOGUEIRAS 2570 – FERNÁNDEZ GARCÍA 2470

Las Palmas 1992

1. d4 ♘f6 2. ♘f3 g6 3. g3 ♗g7 4. ♗g2 0–0 5. 0–0 d5 6. ♗f4 ♘a6 N [6... c6 – 56/394; 6... ♘h5!? Vlado Kovačević] **7. ♘bd2 c5 8. c3 b6 9. ♕b3 ♗b7 10. a4 ♖c8?!** [10... ♘h5 11. ♗e3 c4 12. ♕b5 ♘c7 13. ♕b4 ♘a6 14. ♕a3 ♖c8=] **11. a5 c4 12. ♕b5 ♘c7 13. ♗c7 ♕c7 14. ab6 ab6 15. e4!?**± **♗c6 16. ♕b4 de4 17. ♘e5 ♗d5 18. ♖fc1 ♖fd8 19. ♕b5!** [△ ♖a4] **♘e8 20. ♗e4 e6 21. ♗d5 ♖d5** [21... ed5 22. ♖a6±] **22. ♕a6! ♘d6 23. ♘g4 ♖b5 24. ♖a2 ♕b7 25. ♕b7 ♘b7 26. ♘e3 ♘a5?!**⊕ [26... ♘d6 27. f4 f6] **27. f4 f6 28. ♘e4 ♖d8 29. ♖c2!** [△ ♖a4] **e5 30. fe5 fe5 31. d5+– h5 32. ♖a4 ♔h8 33. d6 ♗f8 34. ♘c4 ♘c4 35. ♖c4 ♗d6 36. ♖c6 ♖d5 37. ♖b6 1 : 0**
[Nogueiras, Hernández Ruíz]

362. **D 03**

MALANJUK 2600 – BELJAVSKIJ 2610

Jugoslavija 1993

1. d4 ♘f6 2. ♘f3 e6 3. ♗g5 ♗e7 4. ♘bd2 d5 5. e3 c5 6. c3 ♕b6 [6... ♘c6 – 51/376] **7. ♖b1!?** [7. ♕b3] **♗d7!? N** [7... ♘c6 8. ♗d3 0–0 (8... ♗d7) 9. a3⩲] **8. ♘e5 cd4!** [8... ♗b5?! 9. c4! *a)* 9... dc4 10. ♘dc4 ♗c4 (10... ♕a6 11. dc5 ♗c5 12. ♘d6 ♗d6 13. ♗b5 ♕b5 14. ♕d6 ♕d5!=; 12. a3! △ 13. ♗f6 gf6 14. ♘f7±) 11. ♕a4! ♘c6 12. ♗c4 cd4 13. 0–0! ♕b4 14. ♗b5±; *b)* 9... ♗a6 10. ♕a4 ♘c6 11. dc5 ♗c5 12. ♗f6 gf6 13. cd5 ♗f1 14. ♖f1 ed5 (14... fe5 15. dc6 bc6 16. ♘c4 ♕c7 17. b4 ♗b6□ 18. ♘b6 ♕b6 19. ♖c1 ♖c8 20. ♖c5±) 15. ♘c6 bc6 16. ♔e2 0–0 17. ♖fc1±] **9. cd4** [9. ed4 ♗b5=; 9. ♘d7!? ♘fd7! 10. ♗e7 de3 11. ♗a3 ed2 12. ♕d2∞] **♗b5 10. ♗b5 ♕b5 11. ♕e2! ♕e2 12. ♔e2 ♘fd7! 13. ♗e7 ♔e7 14. ♘d3⩲ ♘c6** [14... ♖c8 15. ♖hc1 ♘a6! △ ♘c7-e8-d6] **15. ♖hc1 f6?! 16. b4 ♖hc8 17. ♘b3 ♘b6?** [17... ♘d8⩲] **18. ♘a5!± ♘d8□ 19. ♘c5 ♖ab8** [19... ♖c7? 20. ♘cb7+–] **20. ♔d3 ♘a8?** [20... ♘d7 21. ♘cb7+–; 20... ♖c7□ *a)* 21. ♖c2 ♘f7 22. ♖bc1 ♘d6 23. ♘cb7! (23. ♘a6 ♖c2 24. ♖c2 ♖c8 25. ♘c5 ♘bc4! 26. ♘cb7 ♘b7 27. ♘b7 ♖b8 28. ♘a5 ♘a5 29. ba5 ♔d7=) ♖cb7 24. ♘c6 ♔f8□ (24... ♔e8 25. ♘b8 ♖b8 26. ♖c7+–) 25. ♘b8 ♖b8 26. ♖c7 ♘b5; *b)* 21. ♖c3! ♘f7 22. ♖bc1 ♘d6 23. ♘a6! ♖c3 24. ♖c3 ♖c8 25. ♘c5 ♘bc4 26. ♘cb7 ♘b7 27. ♘b7 ♖b8 28. ♘a5 ♘a5 29. ba5 ♔d7 30. ♖b3! ♖b3 31. ab3 ♔c6 32. b4 ♔b5 33. ♔c3 ♔a4 34. g4!+–] **21. ♘cb7! ♘b7** [21... ♖c1 22. ♖c1 ♖b7 23. ♘b7 ♘b7 24. ♖c8+–] **22. ♖c8 ♖c8 23. ♘b7** [♖ 9/h] **♘b6 24. ♘c5 e5 25. f3** [25. de5 fe5 26. f4 ♖f8! 27. g3 g5⇆] **♔d6 26. e4! de4 27. ♘e4 ♔d5 28. de5 ♔e5 29. ♖e1!+– ♖d8 30. ♔c3 ♖c8 31. ♔b3 f5 32. ♘c5** [32. ♘g5 ♔d6 (32... ♔f6 33. h4!) 33. a4] **♔f6 33. a4! ♖c7 34. a5 ♘c8 35. ♔a4! ♘e7 36. ♔b5 ♔f7 37. f4 h6 38. ♖d1 ♔e8 39. ♖d6 ♖c8 40. ♔a6 1 : 0 [Malanjuk]**

363.** **D 03**

CIFUENTES PARADA 2480 – SMIRIN 2590

Wijk aan Zee (open) 1993

1. d4 ♘f6 2. ♘f3 g6 3. ♗g5 ♗g7 4. ♘bd2 0–0 5. c3 d5 6. e3 ♘bd7 [RR 6... b6 7.

a4 N (7. ♗e2 – 46/(478)) c5 8. ♗d3 ♗a6 9. ♗a6 ♘a6 10. 0–0 ♕c7 11. ♕e2 ♕b7 12. h3 ♖fe8 13. ♘e5! ♘e4 (13... ♖ac8!?) 14. ♘e4 de4 15. ♗f4 ♖ac8 (Malanjuk 2600 – Gufel'd 2480, Calcutta 1993) 16. ♖fd1! ♖ed8 17. f3± Malanjuk] **7. ♗e2 ♖e8 8. b4** [RR 8. 0–0 e5 9. h3 N c5 10. ♗b5 ♕b6 11. ♕a4 a6 12. ♗f6 ♕b5 13. ♕b5 ab5 14. ♗e5 ♘e5 15. ♘e5 ♗e5 16. de5 ♖e5 17. b4 cb4 18. cb4 ♖e6 19. ♘b3 ♖ea6 20. ♖fc1 ♗f5 21. g4 ♗e6 22. ♘c5 ♖c6 23. ♘b7 ♖c1 24. ♖c1 ♖a4 25. ♘c5 ♖b4 26. ♘e6 fe6= J. Benjamin 2585 – Hellers 2565, Pleasantville 1993] **h6 N** [8... e5 – 53/353] **9. ♗h4 g5!? 10. ♗g3 ♘h5 11. ♘b3?!** [11. ♗e5! g4 12. ♘g1 ♘e5 (12... ♗e5 13. ♗g4 ♘hf6 14. de5 ♘e5 15. ♗e2±) 13. de5 f5 14. f4∞; RR 14. h3!] **♘g3 12. hg3 e5 13. ♖c1** [△ 13. ♘c5] **c6?!** [13... e4 14. ♘fd2 f5 15. c4 c6 16. ♘c5 ♘f6↑] **14. ♘c5! e4 15. ♘d2 f5 16. ♘d7 ♗d7 17. c4 f4! 18. cd5?** [18. ♗g4! fe3 19. fe3 ♕c7 20. ♖h3∞] **fe3 19. fe3 ♕b8! 20. 0–0□ ♕g3 21. ♕b3** [21. ♖c3? ♗d4!] **cd5 22. ♕d5** [22. ♘e4? ♖e4 23. ♕d5 ♖e6 24. ♖f3 (24. ♕d7 ♕e3–+) ♕d6 25. ♕b7 ♖b8 26. ♕a7 ♖e3! 27. ♖e3 ♗d4 28. ♗c4 ♔h8 29. ♕a3 ♕f4 30. ♖e1 ♖e8–+] **♔h8!** [22... ♗e6 23. ♕e4 ♗a2 24. ♖f3!∞] **23. ♕b3?!** [23. ♕d7? ♕e3 24. ♔h1 ♕e2 25. ♖c7 ♖g8 26. ♖f6 ♕h5 27. ♔g1 ♖ad8; 23. ♖c3□ ♗c6 (23... ♗h3?! 24. ♖f2 ♖ad8 25. ♕b7 ♗d4? 26. ♘f1+–) 24. ♕f5 ♖f8 (24... ♗d4? 25. ed4 ♕c3 26. ♕f6) 25. ♕g4 ♖f1 26. ♘f1 ♕g4 27. ♗g4 ♗f8 28. a3 a5!∓] **♗a4! 24. ♕c3** [24. ♕a3 ♗d4 25. ♘c4 ♗b5! 26. ed4 ♕a3 27. ♘a3 ♗e2 28. ♖f7 e3 29. ♖cc7 ♗d3–+]

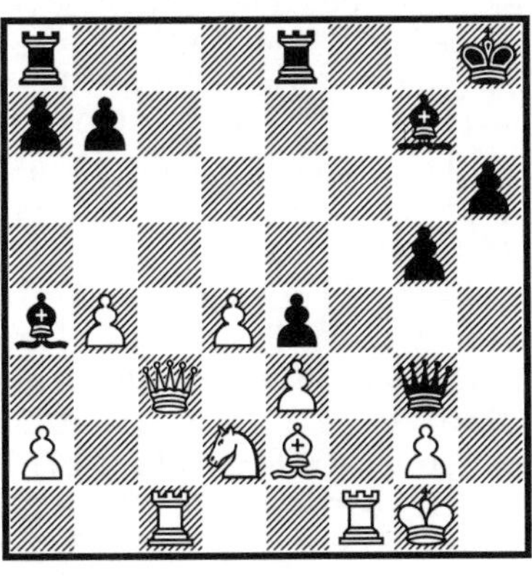

24... ♖ac8! 25. ♕c8 ♕e3 26. ♔h1 ♕e2! [26... ♖c8? 27. ♖c8 ♔h7 28. ♗g4!⇆ △ ♗f5#] **27. ♕c3 ♕h5 28. ♕h3** [28. ♔g1 ♖d8–+] **♕h3 29. gh3 ♗d4 30. ♘b3 ♗g7–+ 31. ♔g2 e3 32. ♖fe1⊕ ♗c6 33. ♔g1 ♗e5! 34. ♖c2** [34. ♖e3 ♗h2 35. ♔f2 ♖e3 36. ♔e3 ♗f4] **♗g3 35. ♖ee2 ♗f3 36. ♘d4 ♗e2 37. ♘e2 ♗d6 38. ♖c4 ♔g7 39. ♖d4 ♖e6 40. ♔f1 h5 41. ♘c3 ♗e5 42. ♖d7 ♔g6 43. ♘d5 ♖d6 44. ♖d6 ♗d6 45. ♔e2 ♗f4 46. h4 ♔f5 47. hg5 ♗g5 48. a4 ♔g4 49. ♘c3 h4 50. ♔f1 h3 0 : 1 [Smirin]**

364.* D 10

HERTNECK 2575 – ŠIROV 2670
München 1993

1. d4 d5 2. c4 c6 3. ♘c3 ♘f6 4. cd5 cd5 5. ♗f4 ♘c6 6. e3 a6 7. ♗d3 [RR 7. ♗e2 N ♗f5 8. g4 ♗g6 9. ♕b3 e6 10. ♕b7 ♘a5 11. ♕c7 ♕c7 12. ♗c7 ♗b4 13. ♘f3 ♘c4 14. ♗c4 dc4 15. ♘d2 ♗d3 16. g5 ♗c3 17. bc3 ♘d5 18. ♗g3 1/2 : 1/2 Azmajparašvili 2655 – Akopian 2615, Wijk aan Zee (open) 1993] **♗g4 8. ♘ge2 e6 9. 0–0 ♗e7 10. a3 0–0 11. b4 N** [11. ♖c1 – 54/(352)] **♖c8?!** [11... b5 12. f3±] **12. ♘a4 a5?!** [12... b5 13. ♘c5 ♕b6] **13. b5±↑≪ ♘b8 14. f3 ♗h5** [14... ♗f5? 15. ♗f5 ef5 16. ♕d3±] **15. ♕b3** [15. b6!? ×a5] **♗d6** [15... b6!? (Ka. Müller) 16. ♗b8!? (16. ♖fc1 ♖c1 17. ♖c1 ♗d6 18. ♗d6 ♕d6 19. ♘f4±) ♖b8 17. ♖fc1 △ ♖c6±] **16. ♖fc1 ♕e7 17. ♘b6! ♖ce8?!** [17... ♖c1? 18. ♖c1 ♗a3 19. ♖c7 ♕b4 20. ♕b4 ab4 21. ♖b7+–; 17... ♖c7 18. ♖c3 (18. ♕a4? ♗f4 19. ♘f4 ♕d8 20. ♖c7 ♕c7 21. ♕a5 ♘bd7 22. ♘c4 b6–+) ♕d8! 19. ♘a4!±] **18. ♕c3 e5 19. de5** [19. ♗g5? ♕d8! (19... e4? 20. ♘d5 ♘d5 21. ♗e7 ♘c3 22. ♗d6+–) 20. ♗f6 ♕b6!∞] **♗e5 20. ♗e5 ♕e5 21. ♕e5 ♖e5 22. ♔f2** [22. ♖c7!? ♖e3 23. ♘f4 g5! 24. ♘h5 ♘h5 25. ♗f1] **♖fe8** [22... ♖e6 23. ♘c8!±] **23. ♖c7!** [×♘b8; 23. ♖c3 ♔f8] **♖e3 24. ♘f4 ♗g6?** [24... g5 *a)* 25. ♘fd5!? ♘d5 26. ♘d5 ♖d3 27. ♘f6 ♔f8 28. ♘e8 ♔e8 29. ♖b7 ♘d7 30. ♖b1!? (30. b6 ♗g6⇆) ♗g6 31. ♖b2 ♖a3 32. b6 ♘c5 33. ♖b8 ♔d7 34. b7 ♘d3 35. ♔g3 ♘b2 36. ♖d8 ♔d8

37. b8♕ ♔d7 38. ♕b5 ♔d6 39. ♕b2±; *b)* 25. ♘h5 ♘h5 26. ♗f1 ♘f4 27. ♖ac1! (27. ♖b7 ♖c3!⇆) d4 (27... ♖a3 28. ♖c8 ♖a2 29. ♔g3±) 28. ♖b7±] **25. ♖d1! ♖3e7** [25... d4 26. ♖b7 ♗d3 27. ♘d3 ♖e2 28. ♔f1±] **26. ♖e7 ♖e7 27. ♗g6 fg6 28. ♘fd5 ♖e8** [28... ♘d5 29. ♖d5 ♔f7 30. ♖d8 ♖e8 31. ♖e8 ♔e8 32. ♘c4 a4 33. ♘b6±] **29. ♘f6 gf6 [♖ 9/h] 30. a4 ♔f8 31. ♘c4??** [31. ♖c1 ♔f7 32. ♘c4!+−] **♖c8!⇆ 32. ♘a5** [32. ♖d4 ♘d7 33. ♘a5 ♘c5 34. ♖c4 ♖a8 35. ♖c5 ♖a5 36. ♖c4±] **b6 33. ♘b3** [33. ♘b7 ♔e7] **♔e7 34. ♖e1!?** [34. ♖a1 ♖c2] **♔d6 35. ♘d2 ♖c2?!** [35... f5! 36. ♖a1±] **36. ♔e3!** [36. ♖e2 ♔d5 37. ♘e4 ♖e2 38. ♔e2 ♘d7 39. ♔d3 f5∞] **♖a2 37. ♘e4 ♔e6!** [37... ♔e7? 38. ♘c3! (38. ♔d4 ♖a4 39. ♔d5 ♖a5 40. ♘c3 ♔d7 41. ♖e6) ♖g2 39. ♘d5 ♔d6 40. ♖d1! ♖h2 41. ♘f6 ♔e6 42. ♖d8±; 37... ♔c7? 38. ♘f6 ♖g2 39. ♘d5] **38. ♔d3! ♖g2 39. ♘d2 ♔d7** [39... ♔d5 40. ♘c4! ♖h2 41. ♖e7+−; 39... ♔f7 40. ♘c4 ♘d7 41. ♘d6 ♔g8 42. ♖e8 ♘f8 43. a5+−] **40. ♘c4 ♔c7 41. ♖e7 ♘d7 42. ♖h7 ♔d8?** [42... ♖a2 43. ♘b6 ♔b6 44. ♖d7 ♖a4 45. ♖d6 ♔b5 46. ♖f6 ♔c5 47. ♖g6 ♔d5 48. ♔e3±] **43. ♔d4+− ♖f2 44. ♔d5 ♖f3 45. ♔c6 ♘e5 46. ♘e5 fe5 47. ♖h8! ♔e7 48. ♔b6 e4 49. ♖h4** [49. ♖c8] **♖f6 50. ♔a7□** [50. ♔c7? e3 51. b6 e2 52. ♖e4 ♖e6 53. ♖e2 ♖e2 54. b7 ♖c2 55. ♔b6 ♖b2 56. ♔a7 ♖a2!=] **e3 51. b6 e2** [51... ♖e6 52. b7 e2 53. b8♕ e1♕ 54. ♖h7 ♔f6 55. ♕f4#] **52. ♖e4 ♖e6 53. ♖e2 ♖e2 54. a5!** [54. b7?? ♖a2=] **♖h2 55. b7**
1 : 0 **[Hertneck]**

365.* **D 12**

PANNO 2495 –
ILLESCAS CÓRDOBA 2615
Buenos Aires 1993

1. d4 d5 2. c4 c6 3. ♘f3 ♘f6 4. e3 ♗f5 5. ♗d3 ♗d3 6. ♕d3 e6 7. ♘c3 ♘bd7 8. 0–0 ♗b4 [8... ♗e7 9. e4 de4 10. ♘e4 0–0 11. ♖d1 ♘e4 12. ♕e4 ♘f6 13. ♕e2 ♕c7 14. ♗g5 N (14. g3) ♖fe8 15. ♘e5 ♘d7 16. ♗e7 ♖e7 17. ♖d3 ♖d8 18. ♖ad1 ♘e5 19. ♕e5 ♖ed7 20. ♕c7 ♖c7= G. Flear 2505 – Illescas Córdoba 2600, France 1992] **9. ♗d2 a5!** [9... 0–0?? 10. ♘d5+−; 9... ♗c3 – 47/457] **10. a3 N** [10. b3] **♗e7 11. ♖fd1 0–0 12. e4 de4 13. ♘e4 ♘e4 14. ♕e4 ♘f6 15. ♕e2 ♕b6!** [△ ♕a6] **16. b4?** [16. ♗e3! ♕a6 17. a4=] **ab4 17. ab4 ♕c7 18. g3 ♖fd8! 19. ♗c3** [19. ♗f4 ♕d7 20. ♘e5 ♕e8 21. ♕b2 b5∓] **♗f8** [19... b5!? 20. ♖a8! (20. ♘e5 ♘d7∓) ♖a8 21. d5! cd5 22. ♗f6 ♗f6 23. cd5 ♕c4! 24. ♕c4 bc4 25. de6 fe6 26. ♖d6!∓] **20. h4** [⌓ 20. ♘e5] **h6** [20... ♘d7 21. ♘g5! h6 22. ♘e4∞] **21. ♘e5 ♘d7 22. ♘g4** [22. ♕f3 ♘e5 23. de5 ♖a1 24. ♖a1 ♕d7∓] **b5! 23. c5** [23. ♖a8 ♖a8 24. cb5 cb5 25. ♕b5 ♕c3 26. ♕d7 ♕f3 27. ♘e3 ♗b4!∓] **h5 24. ♘e5 ♘f6 25. ♕f3 ♘d5∓ 26. ♗d2 g6 27. ♗f4** [27. ♗g5 ♖dc8 28. g4 ♗g7 29. gh5 ♗e5 30. de5 ♕e5∓] **♕b7 28. ♗g5 ♘b4??** [28... ♖dc8! 29. g4 ♗g7 30. gh5 f6!∓ 31. ♘g6 fg5 32. ♖a8 ♖a8 33. hg5 ♕f7] **29. ♗d8 ♖d8 30. ♕c3!+− ♘d5 31. ♕a5 ♖c8 32. ♕a7 ♕c7 33. ♕c7 ♖c7 34. ♖a6 ♘b4 35. ♖a8⊕ ♔g7 36. ♖da1 ♘c2 37. ♖1a7 ♖a7 38. ♖a7 ♘d4 39. ♖f7 ♔g8 40. ♖c7 ♗c5 41. ♘c6 ♘f3? 42. ♔g2 ♘e1 43. ♔f1 ♘d3 44. ♘e5 ♘e5 45. ♖c5 ♘f7? 46. ♖c6** **1 : 0**
[Illescas Córdoba]

366.* !N **D 13**

L. VALDÉS 2300 – OTERO 2365
Cuba 1993

1. d4 d5 2. c4 c6 3. ♘f3 ♘f6 4. cd5 cd5 5. ♘c3 ♘c6 6. ♗f4 e6 7. e3 ♗e7 8. ♗d3 a6 9. 0–0 b5 10. ♖c1 ♕b6 11. a4! N [11. ♘e5 ♗b7 12. ♗g3 0–0 N (12... ♖c8) 13. ♕e2 ♘e5 14. de5 (14. ♗e5 ♘e4) ♘e4! 15. ♗e4 de4 16. ♕g4 ♖ad8 17. ♘e4 ♗e4 18. ♕e4 ♖d2=∞ ×♗g3 1/2 : 1/2 L. Valdés 2300 – Otero 2365, Cuba 1993] **b4 12. ♘b5 0–0** [12... ab5 13. ♖c6!] **13. a5! ♕b7** [13... ♕a5 14. ♘c7; 13... ♘a5 14. ♗c7 ♕b7 15. ♘d6 ♗d6 16. ♗d6=∞↑] **14. ♘e5!±** [14. ♘d6] **♘e5 15. ♗e5 ♕d7 16. ♕e2!** [16. ♖c7 ♕d8 17. ♘a7±] **ab5 17. ♗b5 ♕a7 18. ♖c7 ♕a5 19. ♖e7 ♕d8** [19... ♗a6 20. ♗a6 ♕a6 21. ♕f3! ♘e4 22. ♕g4 g6 23. ♕f4→] **20. ♖c7?⊕** [20. ♗f6! gf6 21. ♕g4 ♔h8 22. ♕h4 ♔g7 23. f4! ♕e7 24. ♖f3 ♖g8□ 25. ♖g3 ♔h8 26.

♗d3 ♖g6 27. ♖h3+−] **♘d7 21. ♗g3?** [21. ♗d6+−] **♘b8! 22. ♖fc1 ♘a6 23. ♖7c6 ♗b7 24. ♗a6 ♗c6 25. ♖c6 ♕a5 26. h3 ♕a4 27. ♖b6 ♕a5 28. ♖c6 ♕a4**
1/2 : 1/2 **[L. Valdés]**

367.** **D 15**

A. GOL'DIN 2555 − BOLOGAN 2520
New York 1993

1. d4 d5 2. c4 c6 3. ♘f3 ♘f6 4. ♘c3 a6 5. g3!? N [RR 5. ♘e5?! ♘bd7 6. g3 e6 N (6... dc4 − 56/416) 7. ♗g2 ♘e5 8. de5 ♘d7 9. cd5 ed5 10. f4 (10. e4 d4! 11. ♕d4 ♗c5 12. ♕d1 ♘e5=) ♗c5 11. e4 d4 12. ♘b1 (12. ♘a4? ♗b4 13. ♗d2 ♗d2 14. ♕d2 b5−+; 12. ♘e2!?) ♕a5!? (12... 0−0 △ ♗a7, c5, b5, c4⇆) 13. ♗d2 *a)* 13... ♕b5? 14. ♕c2 0−0 (14... d3 15. ♕c3 0−0 16. ♘a3⩲) 15. a4 ♕b6 16. ♘a3 ♕a7 17. b4! (Komarov 2530 − Kirov 2505, France 1993; 17. ♘c4 b5!?∞) ♗e7 18. ♘c4 (18. a5 b5!∞) b5 19. ♘a5⩲; *b)* 13... ♕b6 14. ♕b3 0−0 15. ♘a3 ♕b3 16. ab3 b5=; 14. ♘a3!? Komarov; 5. c5 ♘bd7 6. ♗f4 ♘h5 7. e3 N (7. ♗d2 − 54/358) ♘f4 8. ef4 ♕c7 9. ♕d2 g6 10. ♗d3 ♗g7 11. 0−0 e6 (11... 0−0 12. f5!?) 12. h4 0−0 13. ♖fe1 (13. h5? ♗h6 14. g3 e5 15. ♘e5 ♘e5 16. de5 ♕e5 17. hg6 hg6 18. fe5 ♗d2∓ Moskalenko 2555 − Rogozenko 2480, Nikolaev (zt) 1993) f6? 14. ♕e3 (14. ♖e6 ♘c5) ♖e8 15. h5±; 13... b6∞; ⌓ 9. g3 Rogozenko] **b5** [5... dc4 6. a4 c5 (6... b5? 7. ab5 cb5 8. ♘b5 ♗b7 9. ♘c3 ♗f3 10. ef3±) 7. d5 e6 8. e4 ed5 9. ed5 ♗e7 10. ♗g2 0−0 11. 0−0 ♗g4 12. h3 ♗f3 (12... ♗h5 13. g4 ♗g6 14. ♘e5±) 13. ♕f3 ♘bd7 14. ♗f4=/∞] **6. c5!**±○ **g6 7. ♗g2 ♗g7 8. 0−0 0−0 9. ♘e5 ♗e6** [9... ♘g4 10. f4 ♘e5 11. de5! ♘d7 (11... f6? 12. ef6 ♗f6 13. ♘d5+−) *a)* 12. e4 ♘c5 13. ed5 b4! 14. ♘e2 cd5 (14... ♗g4 15. ♗e3) 15. ♕d5 ♕d5 16. ♗d5 ♖b8 17. ♗e3⩲; *b)* 12. ♗e3!? e6 (12... f6 13. ♗d5+−) 13. ♗f2 △ e4⩲] **10. h3 ♕c8 11. ♔h2 ♘e4!? 12. ♘e4 de4 13. ♗e4□ ♖d8** [13... ♗h3 14. ♖h1 ♖d8 15. f4 f6 16. ♘f3 e5 17. fe5 fe5 18. ♘g5 ♗e6 19. ♘e6 ♕e6 20. ♗c2 ♔h8∞; 18. ♗g5!] **14. f4 ♗h3 15. ♖f2 ♗e6** [15... f6 16. ♘f3 e5 17. fe5 fe5 18. ♗g5±] **16. e3 f5 17. ♗f3 ♗d5 18. a4!**± **♕e6 19. ♕h1!?** [19. ♗d2 ♗e5 20. fe5 ♗b3 21. ♕h1 ba4 22. ♗a5=/∞] **♗e5 20. fe5 ♗f3 21. ♕f3 ♘d7 22. ♗d2 ♘f8 23. ♗c3 ♖db8 24. ab5?!** [24. e4! fe4 25. ♕e4 b4 26. ♗d2 a5 27. ♗h6 ♖d8 28. ♖af1±↑] **ab5 25. ♖a8 ♖a8 26. e4! fe4 27. ♕e4 ♖d8 28. ♗d2 ♘d7?** [28... ♕d5!□ 29. ♕f4 ♘d7! (29... ♘e6 30. ♕f7 ♔h8 31. ♗h6 ♕d7 32. ♗g7! ♘g7 33. ♕f8 ♖f8 34. ♖f8#) 30. ♕h4 ♖f8 31. ♖f8 ♘f8 32. ♕e7 ♕d4 33. ♗h6 ♕f2□ 34. ♔h3 ♕f1 35. ♔h2 ♕f2=] **29. ♗h6!**± **♖a8** [29... ♘f6?? 30. ef6+−] **30. ♕h4 ♖a1 31. ♕f4 ♖a8 32. ♕f3! ♖d8** [32... ♕d5 33. ♕d5 cd5 34. c6+−] **33. ♔g2 ♖c8 34. b3 ♖a8 35. ♔h2 ♖c8 36. ♔g1 ♖a8 37. ♔g2⊙ ♖c8 38. ♖a2! ♘f8** [38... ♕f5 39. ♕f5 gf5 40. ♖a7 ♖d8 41. ♖c7 ♘b8 42. ♖e7+−] **39. ♖a7 ♘d7 40. ♔h2!!⊙ ♘f8 41. ♖c7+− ♖d8 42. ♖c6 ♕f7** [42... ♕d7 43. d5 ♕d5 44. ♕d5 ♖d5 45. ♖c8] **43. ♕f7 ♔f7 44. ♗f8 ♔f8 45. ♖b6 ♖d4 46. ♖b5 ♔f7 47. b4 ♖c4 48. ♖b6 h5 49. c6 ♔e6 50. b5 ♔e5 51. ♖b8 ♖c2 52. ♔g1 ♔f5** [52... ♔d6 53. b6 ♖c6 54. ♖d8] **53. ♖f8 ♔g4 54. b6 ♖c1 55. ♔f2 ♖c2 56. ♔e3 ♖c3 57. ♔d2 ♖c6 58. b7 ♖b6 59. b8♕ ♖b8 60. ♖b8 ♔g3 61. ♖g8 h4 62. ♖g6 ♔f3 63. ♖h6 ♔g3 64. ♔e3 h3 65. ♖g6**
1 : 0 **[A. Gol'din]**

368.* **D 15**

SEIRAWAN 2595 − ŠIROV 2670
Buenos Aires 1993

1. d4 d5 2. c4 c6 3. ♘c3 ♘f6 4. e3 a6 5. ♘f3 [5. a4!?] **b5 6. cd5 cd5 7. ♘e5** [RR 7. ♗d2 e6 8. ♗d3 ♗d6 N (8... ♘bd7 − 54/359) 9. 0−0 ♘bd7 10. ♘e2 ♘e4 11. a4 b4 12. a5 0−0 13. ♘g3 (13. ♕a4?! ♘d2 14. ♘d2 ♘f6 △ e5, ♗d7) ♘d2 (13... ♘g3 14. hg3⩲) 14. ♘d2 f5! (14... ♘f6? 15. ♘b3± ×a6, c5, ♗c8) 15. ♕e2 (15. f4? g5↑) ♕h4?! 16. f4 (16. ♖ac1 ♗b7 17. f4⩲) ♘f6 17. ♘f3 ♕h6 18. ♘h1! (△ ♘f2, ♔h1, ♖g1, g4→) g6 19. ♘f2 ♕g7 20. ♔h1 (⊕ 1/2 : 1/2 A. Chernin 2600 − Rogozenko 2480, Odorheiu Secuiesc 1993) h6 (20...

♘e4 21. ♖g1 △ 21... h5 22. ♘h3±) 21. ♖g1 g5 22. fg5! hg5 23. g4 f4 24. e4 de4 25. ♘e4 ♘e4 26. ♗e4↑; 15... ♘f6∞; 15... g5!? Rogozenko] **♘bd7 8. f4 e6 9. ♗d3 ♗b7 10. 0–0 ♗d6 11. ♗d2 N** [11. ♕f3 – 40/458] **0–0 12. ♗e1 ♘e4!?** [12... ♘b6!? 13. ♗h4 ♗e7=] **13. ♕b1!? ♘df6** [13... f5 14. a4! (Seirawan) b4 (14... ♘c3? 15. bc3±; 14... ba4 15. ♘d7! ♕d7 16. ♘a4⩲ △ 17. ♘b6, 17. b4 ×c5; RR 15... ♘c3) 15. ♘e4 fe4 (15... de4? 16. ♗c4 ♗d5 17. ♗d5 ed5 18. ♕a2± Seirawan) 16. ♗e2 (16. ♘d7 ♕d7 17. ♗e2 a5=) ♘e5 17. fe5 ♖f1 18. ♗f1 ♗e7=] **14. ♗h4!? ♖c8** [14... ♘d2? 15. ♕c2! (15. ♗h7?? ♘h7–+) ♘f1 16. ♗h7 ♘h7 (16... ♔h8? 17. ♖f1± △ 17... g6 18. ♗g6! fg6 19. ♕g6 ♕e7 20. ♕h6! ♔g8 21. ♖f3+–) 17. ♗d8 ♘e3 18. ♕f2!⩲ △ 18... ♘g2? 19. ♗b6+–; 14... ♗e7 15. ♗f6 ♘f6 16. a4!? b4 17. ♘d1 △ ♘f2∞; 15... gf6!?; 14... ♕a5!? △ 15. ♖c1 ♖fc8!] **15. ♖c1** [15. ♗e4! de4 16. ♘g4 ♗e7□ 17. ♘f6 ♗f6 18. ♗f6 ♕f6 19. ♘e4 ♕g6 20. ♘g3! (20. ♘g5 ♖c2 21. ♖f2 ♖fc8≅ △ 22. f5 ♖f2 23. fg6 ♖g2 24. ♔f1 ♖g5) ♖c2! (20... ♕b1 21. ♖ab1 ♖c2 22. ♖f2 ♖fc8 23. ♖e1!⩲) 21. ♖f2 ♖fc8!! 22. f5! ♖f2! 23. fg6 ♖g2 24. ♔f1 fg6 25. e4 ♖cc2 26. ♕e1 h5! 27. ♖c1 ♖b2 28. ♖b1! (28. h4 g5! △ 29. ♖c7 gh4 30. ♘h5 h3!) ♖a2 29. ♖a1=] **♕a5** [15... ♗e7!? 16. ♗f6 ♘f6 (16... gf6 17. ♘g4 f5 18. ♘e5=) 17. b4! ♕d6 18. a3 ♖c7 19. ♖a2 ♖fc8 20. ♖ac2=] **16. ♗e4** [16. a4!? b4 (16... ba4 17. ♗f6 ♘f6 18. ♖a4 ♕b6 19. ♕a2 ♖a8 20. ♘d1∞ △ ♖a1, ♘f2) 17. ♘e4 ♖c1 18. ♕c1 ♘e4 19. ♗e4 de4 20. ♘c4 ♕d5 21. b3 ♖c8 22. ♖a2 ♖c6 23. ♖c2 f6=] **♘e4 17. ♘e4 de4 18. ♘d7 ♕d2!?** [18... ♖fe8 19. ♘c5 ♗d5 20. b4 ♕b6=] **19. ♘f8 ♕e3 20. ♗f2 ♕f4 21. g3?!⊕** [21. ♖c8! ♕h2 22. ♔f1 ♗c8 23. ♕e4! ♗f8 24. ♖c1 ♗d7 25. ♕b7 ♕h1! 26. ♗g1 ♕h6! 27. ♖c7 ♗e8! 28. ♖c8 ♕d2! 29. ♖e8 ♕d1 30. ♔f2 ♕d4=] **♖c1 22. ♕c1 ♕f5! 23. ♗e3** [23. ♘e6? e3!! 24. ♕e3 ♕d5 25. ♔f1 ♕h1 26. ♗g1 (26. ♔e2 ♕a1–+) ♕g2 27. ♔e1 ♗b4 28. ♔d1 ♗f3 29. ♔c1 ♗d2! 30. ♕d2 ♕f1 31. ♔c2 ♗e4 32. ♔b3 ♕c4 33. ♔a3 ♕a4#] **♗f8!∓** [23... ♔f8? 24. ♗f4!=] **24. ♕c7 ♕f3 25. ♕f4 ♕e2 26. ♕f2 ♕d3!** [26... ♕c4?! 27. ♖c1! ♕a2? 28. ♖c7] **27. ♕d2** [27. ♖c1!? ♗d5 28. ♕d2! f6! (28... ♗a2 29. ♕d3 ed3 30. ♖a1=) 29. b3 a5!∓] **♕c4 28. b3 ♕d5 29. ♖c1 ♗d6 30. ♕a5 h6 31. ♕d8 ♔h7 32. ♕d7??** [32. ♔g2∓] **♗f4 0 : 1** [Širov]

369.* **D 15**

DLUGY 2550 – BOLOGAN 2520
New York 1993

1. d4 d5 2. c4 c6 3. ♘c3 ♘f6 4. e3 a6 5. ♘f3 b5 6. b3 ♗g4 7. h3 ♗f3 8. ♕f3 [RR 8. gf3 ♘bd7 9. f4 e6 10. c5 ♘g8 N (10... g6 – 56/420) 11. ♗b2 ♘e7 12. a4 (Bareev 2670 – Širov 2670, München 1993) g6= Širov] **e5!? N** [8... bc4 – 56/419] **9. de5 ♗b4 10. ♗d2 ♗c3 11. ♗c3 ♘e4 12. ♗b4 bc4 13. bc4** [13. ♕g4!?] **♕b6 14. a3 a5 15. cd5!□ cd5** [15... ab4 16. ♕e4 ♖a3 17. ♖b1] **16. ♗d2!** [16. ♗c4 ♕c6] **♕b2** [16... ♘d2?! 17. ♕d5 ♘f1 18. ♕a8 0–0 19. ♕e4 ♘d2! 20. ♕c2!□ (20. ♔d2 ♕b2 21. ♔d3 ♖d8–+) ♘b3 21. ♖b1 a4 22. 0–0 ♘a6 23. ♕c4 ♘ac5 24. ♖fd1∞] **17. ♖d1 ♘c6 18. a4?!** [18. ♗d3 ♘e5 19. ♕e2 0–0 20. 0–0 ♕a3 21. ♗e4 de4 22. ♕b5! △ ♖a1=] **0–0 19. ♗d3 ♘e5 20. ♕e2 ♕a2 21. ♗e4** [21. 0–0 ♘d2 22. ♖d2 ♕a4∓] **de4 22. ♗c3?!** [22. 0–0 ♕a4∓] **♘d3 23. ♔f1** [⌓ 23. ♖d3 ♕e2 24. ♔e2 ed3 25. ♔d3 ♖fb8∓] **♕a4 24. ♖a1 ♕c4 25. ♗d4 a4–+ 26. ♔g1 f5 27. ♔h2 ♕c7 28. g3 ♖fc8 29. ♖a3?! ♕c2 30. ♖a2 ♕e2 31. ♖e2 a3 32. g4!? fg4 33. hg4 ♘c1** [33... ♖c1 34. ♖c1 ♘c1 35. ♖c2 ♘b3 36. ♗e5 a2 37. ♖c7 g6! 38. ♖g7 ♔f8 39. ♖h7 a1♕ 40. ♗a1 ♖a1 41. ♔g3 g5!] **34. ♖ee1 ♘b3 35. ♖e2 ♖c1 36. ♖c1 ♘c1** [♖ 9/i] **37. ♖c2 ♘b3 38. ♗e5 ♖a7?** [38... a2 – 33... ♖c1] **39. ♖a2 ♘c1 40. ♖a1 ♘d3 41. ♗d4 ♖a4∓ 42. ♖a2! ♔f7 43. ♔g3 g6 44. ♖c2 ♔e6 45. ♖c7 a2 46. ♗a1 ♔d5⊕ 47. ♖h7 ♘c5 48. ♔f4 ♘b3 49. ♖h1 ♘a1 50. ♖a1** [♖ 7/h] **♖a6 51. g5 ♖a4 52. ♖d1 ♔e6 53. ♖a1 ♔d6! 54. ♖d1 ♔e7! 55. ♖a1 ♔e6–+⊙ 56. ♔g4 ♔e5 57. f4 ef3 58. ♔f3 ♔f5 59. ♔e2 ♔g5 60. ♔d3 ♔f5 0 : 1** [Bologan]

370. **D 15**

P. NIKOLIĆ 2630 – TUKMAKOV 2605

Wijk aan Zee (open) 1993

1. d4 d5 2. c4 c6 3. ♘f3 ♘f6 4. ♘c3 dc4 5. e3 b5 6. a4 b4 7. ♘b1 e6 8. ♗c4 c5 9. 0–0 ♗b7 10. ♘e5!? N [10. ♘bd2] **♘bd7 11. ♘d2 ♗e7** [11... ♗d6?! 12. ♗b5 *a)* 12... a6 13. ♘dc4 ♗e5 (13... ♗c7 14. ♗c6) 14. ♗d7 △ de5; *b)* 12... 0–0 13. ♘dc4 ♗e7 14. ♘c6; 14. ♗c6!?; 14. a5!?] **12. ♘d7** [12. ♗b5?! a6] **♘d7** [12... ♕d7 13. ♘b3∞] **13. a5 ♖c8** [13... cd4!?] **14. ♘b3 0–0 15. ♕e2 cd4 16. ♘d4 ♕c7 17. ♗b5?!** [17. b3 ♗d6 18. h3 ♘e5 19. ♗b5∞] **♗d6 18. h3 ♘c5 19. ♗d2 a6 20. ♗c4 ♘e4 21. ♖fc1 ♘d2 22. ♕d2 ♕e7! 23. ♕e2?** [23. ♗e2! △ ♗f3=] **♕g5! 24. f4 ♕g3 25. ♕f2 ♕g6!∓** [25... ♕f2 26. ♔f2=] **26. ♗f1** [26. ♗e2 ♗c5! P. Nikolić] **e5!** [26... ♗c5!?] **27. fe5 ♗e5 28. ♖c8 ♖c8 29. ♖d1 ♕d6!** [△ g6] **30. b3 g6 31. ♗c4 ♖c7 32. ♖d2 ♕e7 33. ♘e2 ♔g7** [33... ♖c5? 34. ♕f7; 34. ♗f7] **34. ♘f4 ♖c5 35. ♘d5 ♗d5⊕** [36. ♖d5□ ♖c4! (B. Gel'fand) 37. bc4 b3 38. c5 ♕b7! (38... b2 39. ♕c2) 39. ♖d1 (39. c6? ♕c6 40. ♖e5 ♕c1 41. ♔h2 ♕c7 42. ♕b2 f6 43. ♕b3 ♕e5 △ ♕a5–+) *a)* 39... ♕e4 40. ♕f3! (40. ♖d7? ♕b1 41. ♕f1 ♗h2 42. ♔f2 ♕f5–+) ♕c4 41. ♕d5; *b)* 39... ♕b5 40. ♖f1 f6 41. ♖d1; 40... ♕c4∓; 35... ♕e8!? 36. ♘b4!□ ♗c3 37. ♗f7 (37. ♖d6? ♖f5) ♕e7 (37... ♕e4? 38. ♗g6! hg6 39. ♖d7 ♔h6 40. ♕f8+–) 38. ♘d5 ♗d5 39. ♗d5 (39. ♖d5 ♖c7∓; 39... ♖c6!?∓) ♗d2 40. ♕d2∓] **1/2 : 1/2** **[Tukmakov]**

371.* **!N** **D 16**

TUKMAKOV 2605 – OLLS 2585

Rostov na Donu 1993

1. d4 d5 2. c4 c6 3. ♘f3 ♘f6 4. ♘c3 dc4 5. a4 ♗g4 6. ♘e5 ♗h5 7. g3 [RR 7. h3 ♘a6 8. g4 ♗g6 9. e3 ♘b4 10. ♗c4 ♘d7 11. ♘g6 hg6 12. a5 N (12. ♕f3 – 56/423) e6 13. ♗d2 ♗e7 14. ♔f1 g5 15. ♘e2 b5 16. ab6 ♘b6 17. ♗b3 a5 18. ♘g3 c5 19. dc5 ♗c5 20. ♗c3 0–0 21. ♘e4 ♗e7 22. ♕d4 ♕d4 23. ♗d4 ♖fb8= Ch. Lutz 2550 – Lautier 2645, München 1993] **e6 8. ♗g2 ♗b4 9. ♘c4 ♘d5 10. ♕d3 ♗e7 11. 0–0 0–0 12. e4 ♘b4 13. ♕d2 ♘8a6 14. b3 ♕c7 15. ♘e2! N** [15. e5 – 56/(423)] **♖ad8** [15... f6 16. ♘f4 ♗f7 17. ♗h3 e5 18. ♘e6; 15... ♗e2±] **16. ♘f4 ♗g6 17. h4!** [17. ♗b2 e5 18. ♘g6 hg6 19. d5±; 17... ♗g5!] **b5** [17... ♗f6 18. ♗b2 e5 19. ♘g6 hg6 20. d5±] **18. ab5** [18. ♘e3!? e5 19. ♘g6 hg6 20. d5 cd5 21. ed5 ♕b6!? 22. ♗b2 ♘c6] **cb5 19. ♘e3 ♕b7** [19... ♖d4 20. ♕d4 ♗f6 21. ♕d1 ♗a1 22. h5; 19... e5 20. ♘fd5; 19... ♗f6 20. ♗b2] **20. ♘g6 hg6 21. ♗b2 ♘c7** [21... ♕b6] **22. ♗c3! ♘ba6 23. b4± ♕b6 24. ♖fd1 f5!? 25. d5! fe4** [25... f4 26. gf4 ♖f4 27. ♘c4] **26. ♗e4 ed5 27. ♗d5! ♔h7 28. ♕b2 ♗f6 29. ♗e4 ♖de8 30. ♗f6 ♖f6** [30... ♖e4 31. ♖d7 ♖e3 32. ♗d4!+–] **31. ♖d4! ♔h8 32. ♖ad1 ♕e6 33. ♗b1 ♖ef8 34. ♘g4 ♖f3 35. ♖d7+– ♘e8 36. ♘e5 ♖3f6 37. ♗a2 ♕b6 38. ♘f7 ♔h7 39. ♘g5 ♔h8 40. ♘f7 ♔h7 41. ♕d2!** [△ 42. ♕h6! gh6 43. ♘g5 ♔h8 44. ♖h7#] **♔g8□ 42. ♖e1?** [42. ♖b7!] **♘b4□ 43. ♖e8 ♖e8 44. ♘d6 ♔f8 45. ♘e8 ♔e8 46. ♖g7 ♕d6□ 47. ♕e3 ♔d8 48. ♖a7??** [48. ♕a7+–] **♘c6 49. ♖g7 ♘d4 50. ♕e4 ♘c6 51. ♕e3 ♘d4 52. ♕e4 ♘c6 53. ♖b7?!** [53. ♕d5] **♖f5 54. ♗f7?⊕ ♘e5?** [54... ♔c8! 55. ♖b6□ (55. ♗g6 ♖e5) ♔c7 56. ♗g6 ♖f6! (56... ♖e5 57. ♖c6) 57. ♖b5 ♖g6] **55. ♗b3 ♘f3 56. ♔g2 ♘d2?** [56... ♘e1 57. ♔f1□ (57. ♕e1 ♕c6) ♘d3 58. ♖f7!] **57. ♕e6! ♕e6 58. ♗e6 ♖e5 59. ♗f7 ♖e7 60. ♖e7 ♔e7 61. ♗g6 b4 62. g4 ♔f6?** [62... b3] **63. h5! ♔g5 64. ♔g3 b3** [64... ♘f1 65. ♔h3 ♘d2 66. f4] **65. f4 ♔h6 66. g5 ♔g7 67. ♗d3 b2 68. h6 ♔g8 69. g6 b1♕ 70. ♗b1 ♘b1 71. f5 ♘c3 72. ♔f4 ♘d5 73. ♔g5 ♘c7 74. h7** **1 : 0** **[Tukmakov]**

372.* **D 17**

KOHLWEYER 2420 – TUKMAKOV 2605

Bern 1993

1. ♘f3 d5 2. d4 c6 3. c4 ♘f6 4. ♘c3 dc4 5. a4 ♗f5 6. ♘e5 e6 7. g3 ♗b4 8. ♗g2 ♗e4 9. f3 ♗g6 10. e4 c5 11. dc5 N [11. ♗e3 cd4 12. ♕d4 ♕d4 13. ♗d4 ♘c6 14.

♘c6 bc6 15. 0-0-0 N (15. ♗f1 — 44/(446)) 0-0-0 16. ♗a7 ♘d7 17. ♗d4 e5 18. ♗e3 ♘c5 19. ♖d8 1/2 : 1/2 Tukmakov 2605 – L. Bo Hansen 2545, Wijk aan Zee (open) 1993; 17. ♗e3!?; 16. ♗f1!?] **♕d1** [11... ♕a5?! 12. ♕d4 ♘c6 13. ♘c6 bc6 14. ♗e3 ♘d7 15. ♕g7 0-0-0∞; 11... ♘c6!?] **12. ♔d1 ♘c6! 13. ♘c6 bc6 14. ♗e3** [14. ♗f1 0-0-0 *a)* 15. ♔c2 ♗c3! 16. ♔c3 (16. bc3? ♘e4!) ♖d1 17. ♗g2 ♖hd8 18. ♗f4 ♖1d3 19. ♔c2 ♘d5!; *b)* 15. ♔e1 ♘d7 16. ♗c4 ♘c5 17. ♗e3 ♘d3 18. ♔e2 ♘b2∞] **♘d7 15. ♔e2** [15. ♗f1 0-0-0 16. ♔c2 ♘e5] **♗c5** [15... ♘c5? 16. ♘a2] **16. ♖hd1 ♖b8!** [16... ♗e3?! 17. ♔e3 ♘c5 18. ♗f1! ♖b8 19. ♗c4 ♖b2 20. ♖ab1 ♖b1 21. ♖b1 ♔e7 22. ♔d4 ♘d7 23. ♖b7±] **17. ♖d7!** [17. ♖d2 ♗e3 18. ♔e3 ♘c5 19. ♖ad1 ♔e7 20. ♗f1 ♖b4∓] **♗e3 18. ♖c7 ♗d4 19. ♖a2! f5!** [19... 0–0 20. ♖c6 f5 21. ♖c4 e5 22. ♘d5 fe4 23. ♘e7 ♔h8 24. ♘g6 hg6 25. b4!; 19... h5!? 20. ♖c6 h4 21. ♖c4 ♗g1 22. gh4 ♗h2∞] **20. ♖c6 fe4** [20... 0–0 — 19... 0–0] **21. ♖c4** [21. ♘b5 ♗g1! 22. ♖e6 ♔f7 23. ♖a6 ef3 24. ♗f3 ♖hd8! 25. ♘a7 ♗b1–+; 21. ♖e6 ♔f7 22. ♖a6 ef3 23. ♗f3 ♖he8 24. ♔f1 ♗d3 25. ♔g2 ♖e1; 21. ♘e4 0–0 22. ♖c4 e5 △ ♗f7] **e5!?** [21... ef3!? 22. ♗f3 e5 23. ♗c6 (23. ♗d5!? ♖f8 24. ♘e4) ♔e7 24. ♗e4!] **22. fe4** [22. ♘b5 0–0 23. ♘d4 ♗f7; 22. ♘e4 0–0 23. ♘d6 ♖b6] **0–0 23. ♗f3□ ♖b3** [23... ♗f7! 24. ♘d5 ♖b3 25. ♗g4 h5 26. ♗h3 ♗d5 27. ed5 ♖f2 28. ♔e1 ♖h2 29. ♗e6 ♔h7–+] **24. ♖c7** [24. ♗g4 ♗f7 25. ♘d5 — 23... ♗f7; 24. ♖c6 ♗e8! 25. ♖c7 ♗f7] **♗f7 25. ♗g4** [25. ♖c6 ♗g1!] **♗b6! 26. ♖f7□ ♔f7 27. ♔d3 ♗d4 28. ♔c2 ♖fb8 29. ♗e2 ♖3b4 30. ♘b5 ♖c8 31. ♔d2 ♖d8 32. ♔c2 ♖c8 33. ♔d2 ♔e7** [34. ♘d4 ed4 (34... ♖d4 35. ♗d3 ♖cd8 36. ♖a3 ♖e4) 35. ♗d1 ♔d6 36. b3 ♔e5–+] **0 : 1** **[Tukmakov]**

373. **D 17**

HERTNECK 2575 – HÁBA 2485

Deutschland 1993

1. d4 d5 2. c4 c6 3. ♘f3 ♘f6 4. ♘c3 dc4 5. a4 ♗f5 6. ♘e5 e6 7. f3 ♗b4 8. e4 ♗e4 9. fe4 ♘e4 10. ♗d2 ♕d4 11. ♘e4 ♕e4 12. ♕e2 ♗d2 13. ♔d2 ♕d5 14. ♔c3 0–0 15. ♕e3 [15. ♘c4 b5 16. ♘e5 f6∞] **b5 16. ♗e2?! N** [16. ab5 — 54/363] **f6!** [16... ♘d7? 17. ♘d7 ♕d7 18. ♕c5 △ 18... ♕d5 19. ♕d5 ed5 20. ab5 cb5 21. ♗f3 ♖fd8 22. ♖hd1±] **17. ♘f3** [17. ♘c4!? bc4 18. ♗c4 ♕a5! (18... ♕e5 19. ♕e5 fe5 20. ♖he1±) 19. b4 ♕c7 20. ♕e6 ♔h8 21. ♖hd1 a6 △ ♖a7, ♘d7∞; RR 17. ab5?! *a)* 17... ♕e5 18. ♕e5 fe5 19. ♗c4 (19. b6 ♘d7 20. ba7 ♘b6 21. ♖a6 ♘d5 22. ♔c4 ♖f2∓) cb5 20. ♗e6 ♔h8 21. ♗d5 ♘c6∓; *b)* 17... fe5 18. ♖hd1 ♕g2∓ Hába] **♘d7** [17... e5? 18. ♖hd1 ♕f7 19. ♕e4!±; RR 18... ♕e6!? Hába] **18. ♖hd1 ♘b6!∓ 19. ab5** [19. a5? b4 20. ♔c2 ♕f5 21. ♔c1 ♘d5; RR 19. g4!? f5 20. ♔c2 ♕e4 21. ♕e4 fe4 22. ♘d4 Hába] **cb5** [19... ♕b5 20. ♕e6 ♔h8 21. ♗c4 ♘a4 22. ♖a4 ♕a4 23. ♖d7=∞] **20. ♕b6□** [20. ♘e1 ♕c6 21. ♗f3 ♘d5 22. ♗d5 ed5 23. ♖a7 b4 24. ♔c2 ♖fe8∓] **ab6 21. ♖d5 ed5 22. ♖a8 ♖a8** [♖ 8/b5] **23. ♘d4 ♖e8** [23... ♔f7 24. ♗f3 b4 25. ♔b4 ♖a5 26. ♔c3! ♖c5 27. ♘c2 ♔e6 28. ♔d4=∞; 23... ♖a5 24. ♗f3 ♔f8 25. ♘c6=∞] **24. ♗f3 ♖e3 25. ♔c2** [25. ♔b4? ♖d3 26. ♘b5 ♖b3∓; RR 26... ♔f7 27. ♘c7 ♖b3 28. ♔a4 d4 29. ♘b5 ♖b2 30. ♘d4 c3–+ Hába] **♖d3?** [25... ♖f3! 26. gf3 b4 (26... ♔f7? 27. ♔c3) 27. ♘c6 ♔f7 (27... b3? 28. ♔c3 ♔f7 29. ♔d4 ♔e6 30. ♘b4 b5 31. ♘d5 ♔f5 32. ♘c7±) 28. ♘b4 d4 (28... ♔e6 29. ♔c3 ♔e5 30. ♘c6∞) 29. ♘d5 b5 30. ♘c7 b4 31. ♘d5 b3 32. ♔d2 ♔e6 33. ♘b6 c3 34. bc3 b2 35. ♔c2 dc3 36. ♘a4 ♔e5 37. ♘c3 ♔f4 38. ♔b2 ♔f3∓; RR 25... ♔f8 26. ♘b5 (26. ♗d5 ♖d3 27. ♘e6 ♔e7 28. ♘f4 ♔d6 29. ♗f3 ♖e3∓) ♖d3 — 25... ♖d3 Hába] **26. ♘b5 ♔f8!** [26... ♔f7 27. ♘c7 ♖f3 28. gf3 d4 29. ♘b5 d3 30. ♔c3 ♔e6 31. ♘a3±; 26... ♔h8 27. ♘c7 d4 28. ♗e2 ♖e3 29. ♗c4±] **27. ♘c7 f5** [27... d4? 28. ♗e2; 27... b5 28. ♘d5 f5 — 27... f5] **28. ♘d5± b5 29. ♘c7 b4 30. ♗e2** [RR 30. ♗d5 b3 31. ♔c1 c3∓ Hába] **b3⊕** [30... ♖d6 31. ♗c4 ♖c6 32. ♘e6 ♔e7 33. ♔b3±] **31. ♔c1 ♖d6 32. ♘b5 ♖g6 33. ♗f3** [33. ♗f1!?] **♖h6?** [33... ♖b6 △ g5-g4, ♖h6; RR 33... ♖a6 Hába] **34. h3 ♖b6** [RR ⌓ 34... ♖a6 35. ♗d5 (35. ♔d2 g5 36. ♔c3 ♖a1 37. ♔c4 g4) g5 36. ♗c4 ♖c6 37. ♘a3 g4 Hába] **35.**

♘**d4?!** [35. ♘a3 c3 36. bc3 b2 37. ♔c2 ♔e7 38. ♗e2 △ ♘b5±] **g6?** [35... ♖a6! 36. ♘f5 ♖a1 37. ♔d2 ♖b1 38. ♘e3! ♖b2 39. ♔c3⩲] **36. ♔d2±** [×c4, b3] **♖a6 37. ♔c3 ♖a2 38. ♗d5 ♖a1 39. ♔c4 ♔e7 40. ♘b3 ♖b1 41. ♔c3 g5** [41... ♔d6 42. ♗f3 ♔e5 43. ♘d4! △ 43... ♔f4? 44. ♘e6 ♔g3 45. ♘f8±; RR 43... g5!? 44. b4 ♖c1 45. ♔d3 ♖a1 46. ♘c6 ♔d6 Hába] **42. ♘d2 ♖d1?!** [42... ♖c1; RR 43. ♔d3 g4 44. hg4 fg4 45. b4 ♔d6 46. ♗e4 h5 47. b5 h4 48. b6 ♖c8 49. ♘c4 Hába] **43. b4 g4** [43... ♔d6 44. ♘c4!±; RR ⌓ 43... h5 44. b5 g4 45. b6 ♔d8 Hába] **44. hg4 fg4 45. b5 h5** [45... ♔d6 46. b6 h5 47. ♔c2! △ ♘e4±] **46. b6 ♔d8!**

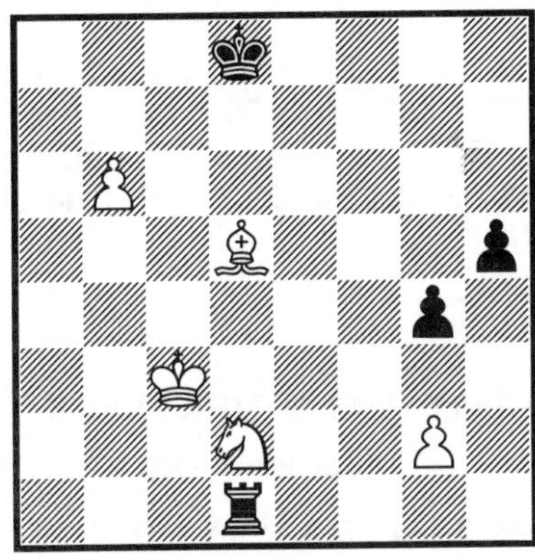

47. g3!+− [RR 47. ♗e4 h4 48. ♘b3 h3 49. b7 ♔c7 50. gh3 gh3 51. ♘c5 ♖d6= Hába] **♖a1** [47... ♖c1 48. ♔d3 (48. ♔d4 ♖d1 49. ♔e3 ♖e1 50. ♔f2±) ♖g1 49. ♘e4 h4 50. ♘c5!; 47... ♖g1 48. ♘e4 h4 49. gh4 g3 *a)* 50. b7 ♔c7 51. ♘c5 ♖c1 *a1)* 52. ♔d4? ♖d1 53. ♘d3 (53. ♔e5?? ♖d5−+) ♖d2=; *a2)* 52. ♔b4 ♖b1 53. ♔a4!±; *b)* 50. ♘c5!? g2 51. b7 ♖c1 52. ♔d3 ♖d1 53. ♔e2 (53. ♔e4? ♖b1) ♖e1 54. ♔f3 g1♕ (54... g1♘ 55. ♔g2 ♖b1 56. ♗e4) 55. b8♕ ♔e7 56. ♕c7 ♔f6 57. ♘d7 ♔g6 58. ♕c6! ♔h7 59. ♘f8 ♔g7 60. ♕c3! ♔f8 61. ♕f6 ♔e8 62. ♗c6#] **48. ♘b3** [△ ♘c5] **♖a6** [RR 48... ♖g1 49. b7 ♖g3 50. ♔d4 ♖b3 51. ♗b3 ♔c7 52. ♗d5 h4 53. ♔e3 Hába] **49. b7 ♔c7 50. ♘c5 ♖d6** [50... ♖b6 51. b8♕] **51. ♔c4** [51. ♔d4?? h4 52. gh4 g3 53. ♘e6 ♖e6−+] **♔b8** [51... h4 52. gh4 g3 (52... ♖d5 53. ♔d5 g3 54. ♘e6 ♔b7 55. ♘f4) 53. ♗g2] **52. ♘e6 ♖a6** [52... ♖d7 53. ♔d4! ♔a7 (53... ♖h7 54. ♘c5 ♔a7 55. ♘a6 ♖b7 56. ♗b7 ♔b7 57. ♘c5) 54. ♘c5 ♖d8 55. ♔e5 h4 (55... ♔b6 56. b8♕) 56. gh4 ♖d5 (56... g3 57. ♗g2) 57. ♔d5 g3 58. ♔c6] **53. ♔c5 ♖a3 54. ♔d6** **1 : 0**
[Hertneck]

374. !N **D 17**

KRAMNIK 2685 − HÁBA 2485
Deutschland 1993

1. d4 d5 2. ♘f3 ♘f6 3. c4 c6 4. ♘c3 dc4 5. a4 ♗f5 6. ♘e5 e6 7. f3 ♗b4 8. e4 ♗e4 9. fe4 ♘e4 10. ♗d2 ♕d4 11. ♘e4 ♕e4 12. ♕e2 ♗d2 13. ♔d2 ♕d5 14. ♔c2 ♘a6 15. ♘c4 0−0?! 16. ♕e5 ♖fd8 17. ♗e2 f6 18. ♕d5 cd5 19. ♘a5± ♖dc8 20. ♔b1 ♘b4? [20... ♘c5±] **21. ♘b7 ♖ab8 22. ♘a5! N +−** [B. Gel'fand; 22. ♘d6?∞ − 51/(389)] **♖c2** [22... ♘c2 23. ♗a6 (23. ♖a2? ♘d4 △ ♖c5) ♖c5 24. ♘b7 ♖c6 25. ♗b5 ♖c7 26. ♖c1 ♖bc8 27. ♘d6 ♘a3 28. ♔a2 ♖c1 29. ♘c8] **23. ♖e1 ♖d2!? 24. ♖a3!** [24. ♘b3? ♘d3! 25. ♗d3 ♖d3⇆] **♘c2** [24... ♖b2 25. ♔b2 ♘d3 26. ♔c3 ♘e1 27. g3] **25. ♔c1 ♖e2** [25... ♘a3 26. ♔d2 ♖b2 27. ♔c3; 25... ♘e1 26. ♔d2 ♘g2 27. ♖b3! ♖b3 (27... ♖c8 28. ♖c3 ♖b8 29. b3 △ ♖c7) 28. ♘b3 e5 29. ♘a5 ♘f4 30. ♘c6 ♔f7 31. ♘a7] **26. ♖e2 ♘a3 27. ba3 ♖b6** [27... e5 28. ♘c6 ♖c8 29. ♖c2 ♖c7 30. a5] **28. ♖c2 ♖a6 29. ♖c5 ♔f7** [29... d4 30. ♘c4!? ♖a4 31. ♖c6 d3 32. ♔b2 d2 33. ♘d2] **30. ♔b2 ♔e7 31. ♔c3 ♔d7 32. ♖b5 g5 33. ♔b4 h5 34. ♖b7 ♔c8** [34... ♔d6 35. ♔b5] **35. ♖f7** [35... e5 36. ♔b5 ♖b6 37. ♔c5] **1 : 0**
[Kramnik]

375. **D 17**

KRAMNIK 2685 − LAUTIER 2645
Cannes (m/6) 1993

1. d4 d5 2. ♘f3 ♘f6 3. c4 c6 4. ♘c3 dc4 5. a4 ♗f5 6. ♘e5 e6 7. f3 ♗b4 8. e4 ♗e4 9. fe4 ♘e4 10. ♗d2 ♕d4 11. ♘e4 ♕e4 12. ♕e2 ♗d2 13. ♔d2 ♕d5 14. ♔c2 ♘a6 15. ♘c4 0-0-0 16. ♕e5 f6 17. ♕e3 ♔b8 18. ♗e2 ♕g2 19. ♖hg1 ♕h2 20. ♖g7 ♘b4 21. ♔b3 ♘d5 22. ♕f3 h5 N [22... ♘f4? 23. ♖b7 ♔b7 24. ♘a5 ♔b8 25. ♘c6 (25. ♕c6? ♕g2 26. ♗f3 ♖d3 27.

♔a2 ♕f3–+) ♔c7 26. ♘d8 ♖d8 27. ♕c3! *a)* 27... ♔b8 28. ♕f6 ♖c8 29. ♕e5 ♖c7 30. ♖c1 ♘e2 (30... ♕g3 31. ♖c3+–) 31. ♕h2 ♘c1 32. ♔a3 ♔b7 33. ♕d6+–; *b)* 27... ♔d6 28. ♗f3! ♖b8 (28... ♔e7 29. ♖h1+–) 29. ♔a2 ♕f2 30. ♕c6 ♔e5 31. ♕e4+–; 22... ♕f4 – 52/377] **23. ♖f1** [23. ♘a5?! ♔a8 24. ♖b7 ♖b8 25. ♗a6 (25. ♖b8 ♖b8 26. ♔c2 ♘b4→) ♕c7 26. ♖b8 ♖b8 27. ♗b7 ♖b7 28. ♘b7 ♕b7 29. ♔c2 ♕b4∓; 23. ♖ag1!?] **♖c8?!** [23... ♖hg8!?] **24. ♔a2 ♖c7 25. ♖fg1 ♕f4 26. ♕f4 ♘f4 27. ♖c7 ♔c7 28. ♖g7 ♔b8 29. ♗f3± ♘d5 30. ♘d6 b6 31. ♘f7 ♖e8 32. ♗h5 ♖e7 33. ♖g8 ♔c7 34. ♖a8 ♔b7 35. ♖f8 ♔c7 36. ♗e2 f5?!** [36... a6!? △ b5] **37. ♔b3 a5 38. ♗a6 ♘b4 39. ♗e2 ♘d5 40. ♗c4 ♘b4 41. ♔c3 e5 42. ♘g5! f4 43. b3⊙ ♔d6 44. ♖f6 ♔d7 45. ♖f5** [△ ♘f7] **♘d5 46. ♔d3 ♘e3** [46... e4 47. ♔d2 f3 48. ♗d5 e3 49. ♔e1 f2 50. ♔e2 cd5 51. ♖d5 ♔c6 52. ♖f5+–] **47. ♖f6 ♖g7 48. ♘f3 ♘g4! 49. ♖f8 ♔d6** [49... ♘f2!? 50. ♔e2 ♘g4 51. ♖b8 ♔c7 52. ♖e8 ♔d7 53. ♖e6 ♖e7] **50. ♔e4 ♖e7 51. ♘e1 ♘f2 52. ♔f3 ♘d1 53. ♖f6 ♔c5?!** [53... ♔c7] **54. ♘d3 ♔d4 55. ♖d6 ♔c3 56. ♖c6± ♘e3** [56... e4 57. ♔e2 ed3 58. ♔d1 ♖g7 59. ♗b5! ♔b3 60. ♔d2+–] **57. ♔e4 ♘c4 58. bc4+– f3 59. ♘e5 ♔d2 60. ♖b6 f2 61. ♖b2 ♔e1 62. c5! f1♕ 63. ♖b1 ♔e2 64. ♖f1 ♔f1 65. c6 ♔e2 66. ♔d5 ♔d2 67. ♔d6 ♖e8 68. c7 ♔c3 69. ♘d7 ♔b3 70. ♘b6 ♖h8 71. ♔c6 ♖g8 72. ♔b5**
1 : 0 **[Kramnik]**

376.* **D 17**

BAREEV 2670 – HERTNECK 2575
München 1993

1. d4 ♘f6 2. ♘f3 d5 3. c4 c6 4. ♘c3 dc4 5. a4 ♗f5 6. ♘e5 e6 7. f3 ♗b4 8. ♗g5 h6 9. ♗h4 c5 10. dc5 ♕a5! 11. ♕d4 ♘c6 N [11... ♗c5 – 46/497] **12. ♘c6 bc6 13. e4 ♗g6** [13... ♗c5!? 14. ♕c4 ♗g6∞] **14. ♗f2!** [14. ♗f6 ♗c5 15. ♕e5 gf6 16. ♕f6 0–0 △ 17. ♗c4 ♕b4 18. ♗e6 ♔h7 19. ♗f5 ♗d4 20. ♗g6 fg6 21. ♕c6 ♕b2 22. ♕d7 ♗g7–+; 14. 0-0-0 ♗c5 15. ♕c4 0–0→] **0–0 15. ♗e2 ♖fd8** [15... ♘d7 16. 0–0] **16. ♕c4 ♘d7 17. 0–0** [17. ♖d1 ♘c5 18. 0–0±; 17... ♘e5!= van Wely 2525 – Tukmakov 2570, Helsinki 1992] **♗c5 18. ♖ab1!? ♗f2 19. ♖f2 c5?** [19... ♘e5 20. ♕a6 ♕b4! △ 21. f4 ♗e4 22. ♘e4 ♕e4 23. ♖c1 ♘d3 24. ♗d3 ♖d3 25. ♕c6 ♖d1 26. ♖f1 ♖f1 27. ♔f1 ♕f4 28. ♔g1∓] **20. ♖d1 ♘b6 21. ♖d8!** [21. ♕b5 ♖d1 22. ♗d1 ♕b5 23. ♘b5 (23. ab5 a6=) ♖d8 24. ♗c2 a5=] **♖d8 22. ♕b5±** [×c5, ♗g6] **♕b5** [22... ♕b4!? 23. a5 ♘c8 △ 24. ♘a4 ♖d1] **23. ♗b5 a5 24. ♖c2 c4!** [24... ♖d4 25. ♘e2 ♖b4 26. b3! ♖b3 27. ♖c5 ♖b4 28. ♘c3±] **25. ♔f2?!** [25. ♘e2 e5 (25... ♖c8? 26. ♖d2) 26. ♗c4 ♘a4 27. ♗b3 ♖d1□ (27... ♘b6 28. ♖c6+–) 28. ♔f2 ♖a1± ×♗g6] **f6= 26. ♔e3** [26. ♘e2 ♗e8 27. ♗c4 ♘c4 28. ♖c4 ♖b8 29. ♖c5 ♖b2 30. ♖a5 ♖a2 31. ♖a8 ♔f7=] **♔f8 27. ♘b1** [27. ♖d2 ♖d2 28. ♔d2 ♗e8□ 29. ♔c2 ♔e7 30. ♗e8 ♔e8 31. ♘b5 ♔d7=] **♗e8 28. ♘d2 ♖d3 29. ♔e2 ♖d4 30. b3**
1/2 : 1/2 **[Hertneck]**

377.* **D 17**

JUSUPOV 2645 – HERTNECK 2575
München 1993

1. d4 d5 2. c4 c6 3. ♘f3 ♘f6 4. ♘c3 dc4 5. a4 ♗f5 6. ♘e5 e6 7. f3 ♗b4 8. ♗g5 h6 9. ♗h4 c5 10. dc5 ♕d1 11. ♔d1 ♘bd7 12. ♘d7 0-0-0 13. e4 ♖d7 14. ♔c2 ♗h7 15. ♗c4 ♗c5 N [15... a5 16. c6!?±; 15... ♖hd8 16. ♖ad1; 16. a5!?; 16. ♔b3!?] **16. a5** [16. ♔b3 a5!?] **g5 17. ♗g3 ♘h5?!** [17... ♖hd8 18. ♔b3 (18. ♘a4 ♗d6) ♘h5 19. ♘a4 ♘g3 20. hg3 ♗f8= Jusupov 2640 – Bareev 2670, Paris 1992; 19. ♗e5!?±]

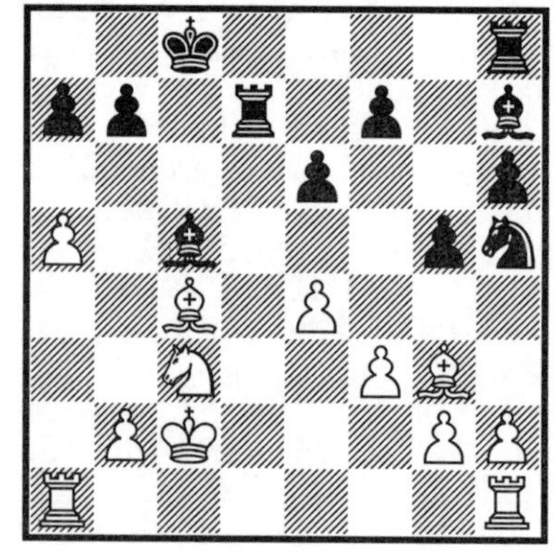

18. ♗b5! ♖e7 [18... ♖dd8 19. ♔b3 (19. ♘a4 ♘g3 20. hg3 ♗f8±) ♘g3 20. hg3 ♗f8 21. a6!?±] **19. ♗e5 f6** [19... ♖d8 20. ♖a4 (20. h4!± Hertneck) ♗d6 21. ♖c4 ♖c7 22. ♗d6 ♖d6 23. ♖c7 ♔c7 24. ♗e8±] **20. ♘a4± fe5□** [20... ♗b4? 21. ♘b6 ab6 22. ab6+−] **21. ♘c5 ♘f4** [21... ♖c7 22. b4±; ⌓ 21... a6±] **22. ♖hc1! ♘g2?** [22... a6 23. ♗f1±] **23. ♔b3→** [△ ♘a6] **♖c7** [23... ♔b8 24. ♘d7 ♔a8 25. ♖c7+−] **24. a6 b6□** [24... ba6 25. ♗a6 (25. ♘a6 ♖c1 26. ♖c1 ♔b7 27. ♖c7 ♔b6 28. ♔b4+−) ♔b8 26. ♗f1+− Hertneck] **25. ♘d7!** [25. ♘e6 ♖c1 26. ♖c1 ♔b8 27. ♖c7 ♗g8 28. ♖b7 ♔a8 29. ♗c4 ♗e6 30. ♗e6 ♘f4 31. ♗d5 ♖c8±] **g4** [25... ♘h4 26. ♘b6! ♔d8 (26... ab6 27. a7+−) 27. ♖c7 ♔c7 28. ♖c1!! ♔d6 (28... ♔b6 29. ♔b4+− △ ♖c6) 29. ♘c8+−] **26. ♘e5+−** [26. ♘b6 ♔d8 27. ♖c7 ♔c7 28. ♖c1 ♔d6 29. ♘c8 ♖c8 30. ♖c8 gf3±] **♖f8** [26... gf3 27. ♖c7 ♔c7 28. ♖c1 ♔d6 29. ♘f7; 26... ♖g8 27. ♖c7 (27. ♘c6 △ 28. ♘e7, 28. ♘a7) ♔c7 28. ♖c1 ♔d6 29. ♘g4] **27. ♖c7! ♔c7 28. ♖d1!** [28... ♖d8 29. ♖c1] **1 : 0**
[Jusupov]

378. !N **D 18**

RAZUVAEV 2525 – SCHWARTZMAN 2455
Dortmund (open) 1993

1. d4 d5 2. c4 c6 3. ♘f3 ♘f6 4. ♘c3 dc4 5. a4 ♗f5 6. e3 e6 7. ♗c4 ♗b4 8. 0–0 ♘bd7 9. ♕e2 ♗g6 10. e4 ♗c3 11. bc3 ♘e4 12. ♗a3 ♕c7 13. ♖fc1 0-0-0 14. a5 ♖he8 15. a6 [15. ♘h4 – 55/382] **b6 16. ♘h4** [16. ♕a2!? ♘d6 17. ♗f1∞̄] **♘d6 17. ♗b3 e5 18. ♘g6 hg6** [18... fg6!?] **19. ♕g4! N** [×f7, g6] **♔b8** [19... c5 (Nikitin) 20. dc5 bc5 21. ♗a4 ♖e7 22. ♖cb1∞̄] **20. ♗d6! ♕d6 21. ♗f7 ♖e7 22. ♕g6± ♕c7** [22... ♕g6 23. ♗g6 ♘f8 24. ♗h5 △ ♗f3±] **23. ♗c4 ♘f6! 24. de5 ♖e5** [24... ♕e5!?] **25. ♖d1 ♖de8 26. h3 ♘e4?!** [26... ♘d5 27. ♗d5±] **27. ♖e1!± ♖8e7?** [27... ♘c3 28. ♕e8+−; 27... ♘d6! 28. ♖e5 ♖e5 29. ♗f1±] **28. ♖e3?** [28. f4!+−] **♘f6!** [28... ♘f2 29. ♖f3+−] **29. ♖e5 ♕e5 30. ♕c2 ♕f4 31. ♗f1 ♖d7 32. ♖d1 ♖d1 33. ♕d1 ♔c7 34. g3 ♕e5 35. c4 ♘d7 36. ♗g2 ♕f6** [36... ♘c5 37. ♕f3 ♕e6 38. ♕f8+−] **37. ♕e2** [37. h4!?] **♘c5 38. ♕e8 ♘a6 39. h4!** [39. ♕a8? ♕a1 40. ♔h2 ♘b8=] **♕a1** [39... ♘b8 40. ♗h3+−; 39... ♘c5 40. ♗h3±] **40. ♔h2 ♕f6 41. ♕a8 ♘c5 42. ♕a7 ♘b7 43. ♕a2 ♘c5 44. ♕e2 ♘d7 45. ♗h3 ♘c5 46. f4 ♔d6 47. ♕d2 ♔c7 48. ♗g4 ♕e7 49. h5 ♘b7 50. ♕c2** [△ ♕f5-c8] **♕f6 51. ♔h3 ♘d6** [51... ♘c5 52. ♕e2 △ ♕e8] **52. c5 bc5 53. ♕c5 ♕a1 54. ♗f3 ♕f1 55. ♔g4 ♕a6 56. ♔g5 ♕a8 57. ♕e5 ♕f8 58. g4 ♔d7 59. ♔h4 ♕f7 60. ♔g3 ♘b5 61. g5+− ♘d6 62. ♗g4 ♔c7 63. g6 ♕f8 64. h6 gh6 65. g7 ♕f7 66. ♗e6 ♕g6 67. ♔h4 1 : 0** **[Razuvaev]**

379. !N **D 18**

KASPAROV 2805 – ANAND 2710
Linares 1993

1. d4 d5 2. c4 c6 3. ♘f3 ♘f6 4. ♘c3 dc4 5. a4 ♗f5 6. e3 e6 7. ♗c4 ♗b4 8. 0–0 ♘bd7 9. ♘h4 ♗g6 10. h3!? 0–0?! [10... a5!?] **11. ♘g6 hg6 12. ♕c2 ♖c8 13. ♖d1 ♕b6! N** [13... ♕e7 – 49/448] **14. e4 c5?!** [14... e5!? 15. ♗e3 (15. de5 ♘e5 16. ♗e3 ♕a5∞) ed4 16. ♗d4 ♗c5 (16... ♕a5 17. ♘a2 ♗e7 18. b4!) 17. ♗f6 ♘f6 18. e5] **15. d5 ♘e5 16. ♗e2!** [16. a5 ♗a5 17. ♘a4 ♕c7 18. de6 ♘c4∞] **ed5** [16... c4 17. ♗f4] **17. ♘d5 ♘d5 18. ♖d5 ♘c6 19. ♗c4 ♘d4** [19... ♘a5 20. ♗f4; 20. b3!?] **20. ♕d3 ♖cd8 21. ♗e3** [21. ♗g5!? ♖d5 22. ♗d5 ♗a5!] **♖d5 22. ♗d5 ♖d8 23. ♕c4 ♖d7 24. ♖c1** [24. ♖d1 ♕a6 25. ♕a6 (25. ♖d4? cd4 26. ♕c8 ♔h7 27. ♕d7 de3 28. ♕f7 e2 29. f4 e1♕ 30. ♔h2 ♔h6 31. ♕g8 ♕h1 32. ♔h1 ♕f1=) ba6 26. ♗d4 cd4 27. ♖d4; 26. h4!] **♕f6** [24... ♗a5 25. b3 ♕b4 26. ♗d4] **25. ♖d1 ♘e6 26. ♕b3 a5** [26... b6 27. g3→] **27. ♖d3!** [△ 28. ♗e6 ♖d3 29. ♗f7!] **♘f4?!** [27... ♔f8] **28. e5! ♕f5** [28... ♕e5 29. ♗f7+−] **29. ♗f4 ♕f4 30. e6+− ♖d8** [30... ♖e7 31. ef7 ♔f8 32. g3! (32. ♗e6 ♕c1 33. ♖d1 ♕d1 34. ♕d1 ♖e6⇆) c4 (32... ♕c1 33. ♔h2; 32... ♕f5 33. ♗e4! ♕f7 34. ♖d8 ♖e8 35. ♕f7 ♔f7 36. ♗g6) 33. ♕c4 ♕c4 34. ♗c4]

31. e7! ♖e8 32. ♖f3 ♕c1 33. ♔h2 ♖e7 [33... c4 34. ♗f7 ♔h8 35. ♗e8 (35. ♕b4 ab4 36. ♗g6) cb3 36. ♖f8 ♔h7 37. ♗g6 ♔h6 38. ♖h8 ♔g5! 39. h4 ♔f6 40. e8♕ ♕f4 41. ♔h3] **34. ♗f7 ♔h7 35. ♗g6?!** [35. ♕d3! ♕g5 36. ♕d8] **♔h6!** [35... ♔g6 36. ♕d3 ♔h6 (36... ♔h5 37. ♕h7) 37. ♕d6] **36. ♕d5?!** [36. ♗c2! ♖e2!? (36... ♖e1 37. h4! ♖h1 38. ♔g3 c4 39. ♕c4 ♗d6 40. ♔g4 ♖h4 41. ♔h4 ♕h1 42. ♖h3 ♕g2 43. ♕e6) 37. ♕f7 ♕c2 38. ♖g3 g6□ (38... g5 39. h4) 39. ♕f8 ♔h7 40. ♖f3] **♕g5 37. ♗f5 g6 38. h4 ♕f6 39. ♗d3 ♕e5 40. ♕e5 ♖e5** [♖ 9/j] **41. ♖f6** [41. ♖f7; 41. b3!] **c4! 42. ♗c4** [42. ♖g6 ♔h7 (42... ♔h5 43. ♔h3 cd3 44. ♖f6) 43. ♗b1 ♖e1 (43... ♔h8 44. ♖g4 ♖e2) 44. ♗f5] **♗e7! 43. ♖b6 ♗c5!** [43... ♖e4 44. ♖g6!] **44. ♖f6 ♖e4!** [44... ♖f5 45. ♖f5 gf5 46. f4! ♔g6 47. g3 ♔f6 48. ♔g2 b6 49. ♔f3 ♗d4 50. b3 ♗c5 51. h5 ♗f8 52. ♗d3 ♔e6 53. ♗f5! ♔f5 54. g4] **45. ♗d3** [45. ♖g6?? ♔g6 46. ♗d3 ♗f2 47. ♗e4 ♔f6 48. ♔h3 b6 49. g4 ♔e5=] **♖g4!** [45... ♖h4 46. ♔g3 ♖d4 47. ♖g6 ♔h5 48. ♗f5 ♖a4 49. f4] **46. ♔h3 ♗e7! 47. ♖e6!** [47. ♔g4⇆] **♖h4 48. ♔g3 ♖d4 49. ♖g6 ♔h5 50. ♗f5 ♗d6 51. ♔f3 ♗c5! 52. g4 ♔h4 53. ♖h6 ♔g5 54. ♖g6 ♔h4 55. ♗e4 ♖d6!? 56. ♖g7!** [56. ♖d6 ♗d6 57. ♗b7⇆] **♖f6 57. ♗f5 ♖b6 58. ♖h7 ♔g5 59. ♖h5 ♔f6 60. ♗d3 ♗d4 61. g5 ♔g7** [61... ♔e6 62. ♖h6 ♔e5 63. ♖b6 ♗b6 64. ♔g3] **62. ♖h7 ♔f8 63. ♗c4 ♖b2 64. ♖f7 ♔e8 65. g6!** [65... ♖f2 66. ♔e4] **1 : 0** **[Kasparov]**

380. !N D 18

JE. PIKET 2590 – ANAND 2710

Amsterdam 1993

1. d4 d5 2. c4 c6 3. ♘c3 ♘f6 4. ♘f3 dc4 5. a4 ♗f5 6. e3 e6 7. ♗c4 ♗b4 8. 0–0 ♘bd7 9. ♘h4 ♗g6 10. h3 ♗h5! N 11. ♕b3 [11. g4!? ♘d5 (11... ♘g4 12. hg4 ♕h4 13. gh5 ♗d6 14. ♖e1) 12. ♘g2 ♗g6 13. ♘a2 ♗e7 14. f3 h5∞] **a5 12. f4?! 0–0!** [12... ♘d5 13. ♘f3 ♗f3 14. ♖f3 f5 15. e4⩲] **13. ♘f3?!** [13. g4! ♘g4 (13... ♗g6?±) 14. hg4 ♕h4 15. gh5 ♕g3=] **♘b6 14. ♗e2 c5! 15. ♘a2?** [15. dc5 ♗c5!∓; 15. ♖d1 ♕e7!∓] **♖c8 16. ♘b4** [16. ♖d1?? c4 17. ♕c2 ♗g6–+] **cb4∓ 17. ♗d2 ♘e4?!** [17... ♕d5! 18. ♕d5□ (18. ♕d3 ♘c4–+; 18. ♗d1 ♘c4∓) ♘bd5 19. ♖fc1 ♘e4 ×e3] **18. g4 ♗g6 19. ♖fc1 ♕d5 20. ♗d1 ♘c4** [20... f6!] **21. ♗e1 ♘ed6 22. ♗e2** [22. ♘e5 ♗e4 23. ♘c4 (23. ♗c2 ♘e5 24. ♕d5 ed5 25. de5 ♘c4∓) ♖c4! (23... ♗h1 24. e4 ♕e4 25. ♘e3+–) 24. ♖c4 ♗h1!! (Je. Piket; 24... ♘c4 25. ♗e2) 25. e4 ♕e4 26. ♖c2 ♕e1 27. ♔h2 ♗d5–+] **♖c7??** [22... ♗e4 23. ♘g5 ♗h1 24. e4 ♗e4 25. ♗c4±; 23... f5!∞; 22... f6!∓ △ 23. ♘d2 ♘d2 24. ♕d5 ed5 25. ♗d2 ♗c2!∓] **23. ♘e5 ♖fc8 24. ♘c4??** [24. f5! ef5 25. ♘c4 ♘c4 26. ♖c4 ♖c4 27. ♖c1 ♖c1 28. ♕d5 fg4! (28... f4 29. ef4 ♖e1 30. ♔f2 ♖b1 31. f5 ♖b2 32. ♔f3!±; 28... ♖e1 29. ♔f2 ♖e2 30. ♔e2 fg4 31. hg4 h6±) 29. ♗g4 ♖e8 30. ♔f2 ♖c2 *a)* 31. ♔g3 h5! (31... ♖e3 32. ♔f4 ♖e4) 32. ♗f3 ♖e3; *b)* 31. ♔g1=; *c)* 31. ♔f3 ♗e4 32. ♕e4 ♖e4 33. ♔e4 ♖b2∞] **♗e4!–+ 25. ♘a5** [25. ♗f2 ♘c4; 25. ♗g3 ♘c4 26. f5 ♖c6] **♖c1 26. ♖c1 ♖c1 27. ♕b4 g5! 28. fg5 ♕g5 29. ♔f1 ♕e3** [29... ♕h4; 29... ♕f6! 30. ♔g1 ♕h4] **30. ♕d6 ♖c2** **0 : 1** **[Anand]**

381.* !N D 20**

M. GUREVICH 2610 – R. HÜBNER 2620

München 1993

1. d4 d5 2. c4 dc4 3. e4 ♘f6 [RR 3... ♘c6 4. ♘f3 ♗g4 5. d5 ♘e5 6. ♕d4 ♘f3 7. gf3 ♗f3 8. ♗c4 e5! N (8... a6 – 55/(384)) *a)* 9. ♕e5 ♕e7 10. ♗b5 ♔d8□ (10... c6 11. dc6 0-0-0 12. ♕f5+–) 11. ♕e7 ♗e7 12. ♖g1 ♗e4∓; *b)* 9. ♕c3 ♕f6□ 10. ♖g1 (10. ♗b5 c6 11. dc6 0-0-0–+) ♗e4 11. ♗g5 (11. ♘d2 ♗f5 12. ♗b5 ♔d8!∓ D. Rajković) ♕d6 12. ♘d2 ♗f5 13. ♗b5 ♗d7 14. ♘c4 ♕b4 15. ♗d7 ♔d7 16. ♘e5 ♔e8∓ D. Rajković 2450 – Ž. Đukić 2410, Cetinje 1993] **4. e5 ♘d5 5. ♗c4 ♘b6 6. ♗d3** [RR 6. ♗b3 ♘c6 7. ♘e2 ♗f5 8. ♘bc3 e6 9. a3 ♗e7 10. 0–0 0–0 11. ♗a2 *a)* 11... ♕d7 12. ♗e3 ♖fd8 13. ♕c1 N (13. h3 – 56/430) ♗f8 14.

♖d1 ♘e7 15. ♘g3 ♗g6 16. ♘ce4 ♘bd5 17. ♘c5 ♕c8 18. ♗b1 ♘f5 19. ♗g5 ♖e8 20. ♕c4 ♘g3 21. hg3 ♗c5 22. dc5 h6 23. ♗f4 ♗b1 24. ♖ab1 ♖d8 25. ♖d4 ♘e7= Ruban 2595 – Jakovič 2510, Sankt-Peterburg (zt) 1993; *b)* 11... h6 N 12. ♗e3 ♗g5 13. f4 ♗h4 14. h3 ♕d7 15. ♕d2 ♘a5 16. b3 ♗e7 17. ♖ad1 ♗a3 18. g4 ♗h7 19. ♘b1 ♕e7 20. ♘a3 ♕a3 21. f5 ♘b3 22. ♗b3 ♕b3 23. ♖b1 ♕a3 24. ♖a1 ♕b3 25. ♖ab1= Ruzele 2500 – Žuravlovs 2485, Vilnius (zt) 1993] **♘c6 7. ♗e3 ♗e6 8. ♘c3 ♘b4 9. ♗e4 ♘4d5 N** [9... c6 – 39/(467)] **10. ♘f3 ♕d7** [10... ♘c4? 11. ♕e2 c6 12. 0–0±] **11. ♘g5!? g6** [11... ♗f5!? 12. ♘d5 ♘d5 13. ♕b3 ♗e4 14. ♘e4 (14. ♕b7? ♘e3 15. ♘e4 ♕d5–+) 0-0-0 15. 0–0⩲] **12. ♘e6 ♕e6 13. 0–0 f5!? 14. ♗f3 ♘e3 15. fe3 ♗h6 16. ♕e2** [16. e4?! ♗e3 17. ♔h1 0-0-0 18. ♘d5 ♘d5 (18... fe4? 19. ♗g4+–) 19. ed5 ♕b6⇆] **c6 17. b3 ♕d7!** [△ ♘d5=; 17... ♘d5 18. ♗d5 cd5 19. ♕b5 ♕c6 20. ♕c6 bc6 21. ♔f2 △ ♘a4±] **18. ♘a4! ♘a4** [18... ♘d5 19. ♘c5 ♕c8 (19... ♗e3? 20. ♔h1 ♕c8 21. ♗d5 ♗d4 22. ♗e6+–) 20. ♗d5 cd5 21. ♖ac1±] **19. ba4 e6 20. ♖fd1 0–0 21. ♖ac1±⊞ ♖f7 22. ♖c3 ♖d8 23. e4 fe4 24. ♗e4 ♗f8 25. h4!** [△ h5→⟫] **♗b4 26. ♖cd3** [26. ♖g3!? ♗c5 27. h5 ♗d4 28. ♔h1 ♕e7 (28... g5!? 29. ♖g5 ♔h8 30. h6→) 29. hg6 ♖g7 (29... hg6 30. ♗g6 ♖g7 31. ♕h5→) 30. ♕h5→] **♖df8 27. h5 g5 28. h6 ♗a5 29. ♕g4 ♕e7 30. g3!** [△ ♔g2-h3] **♗d8** [30... ♖f2 31. ♖f3 ♖2f3 (31... ♖a2 32. ♖f8 ♔f8 33. ♖f1→) 32. ♗f3 ♗d8 33. ♔g2 ♕f7 34. ♗e4±] **31. ♖f3 ♖f3 32. ♗f3 ♕f7 33. ♔g2** [33. ♗e4 ♕f2 34. ♔h1 ♕e3 (34... ♔h8!?∞) 35. ♕e6 ♔h8 36. ♕g4 ♖f2⇆] **♕f5** [33... ♕g6? 34. ♗e4 ♕h6 35. ♖h1+–] **34. ♕f5 ef5** [♖ 9/j; 34... ♖f5 35. ♗g4±] **35. ♗h5!** [35. d5 g4 36. ♗e2 cd5 37. ♖d5 ♔f7 38. ♖d7 ♔e6 39. ♖h7 ♔e5 40. ♖b7 ♗b6=] **♗e7□** [35... g4 36. d5 cd5 37. ♖d5 ♗g5 38. e6+–; 35... ♗c7 36. e6 ♗d6 37. d5 ♖d8 (37... c5 38. ♖e1 ♗e7 39. d6 ♗d6 40. e7+–) 38. dc6 ♔f8 (38... bc6 39. ♖d6 ♖d6 40. e7 ♖e6 41. e8♕ ♖e8 42. ♗e8+–) 39. cb7±] **36. d5 cd5 37. ♖c1!** [37. ♖d5 ♖d8=] **♖d8□** [37... ♗d8 38. e6±] **38. ♖c7 ♔f8 39. ♔f3!** [△ ♔e2-d3] **d4 40. ♔e2 d3 41. ♔d1± a5 42. ♖b7 g4 43. e6 ♖d6 44. ♖b5** [44. ♗g6? hg6 45. h7 ♔g7 46. ♖e7 ♔h8 47. ♔d2 f4–+] **♗f6** [44... ♖e6? 45. ♖b8 ♗d8 46. ♖d8 ♔e7 47. ♖e8+–] **45. ♖f5 ♖e6 46. ♖a5 ♗d8?!** [46... ♗c3 47. ♖a8 ♔e7 48. ♖e8 ♔f6 49. ♖e6 ♔e6 50. ♗g4 ♔f6 51. ♗d7 ♔g5 52. ♗b5 d2 53. ♗e2 ♔h6 54. ♔c2+–; 46... ♔e7 47. ♖a7 ♔d8 48. ♗g4 ♖e3 49. ♖d7 ♔e8 50. ♗f5 ♖e5=; 47. ♔d2!?±] **47. ♖f5 ♗f6** [47... ♔e7 48. ♖f7 ♔d6 49. ♗g4+–] **48. ♔d2 ♔e7 49. ♔d3 ♖d6 50. ♔c4 ♖d2 51. ♖a5!** [51. ♗g4? ♖d4] **♖g2 52. ♖a7 ♔d6 53. ♖a6 ♔e7 54. ♗g4 ♖g3 55. ♖e6 ♔f7 56. ♖e4± ♔g6** [56... ♖a3 57. ♔b4 ♖a2 58. ♗e6+–] **57. ♔b4!** [57. a5?! ♖a3 58. ♔b5 ♖a2 59. a6±] **♗c3 58. ♔b5 ♖g2 59. ♗e6 ♔h6 60. ♔b6! ♖d2** [60... ♖g5? 61. ♖h4 ♔g6 62. ♖g4+–] **61. a5 ♗d4 62. ♔b7** [62. ♖d4! ♖d4 63. ♗b3 ♔g5 64. a6 h5 65. a7 ♖d8 66. ♗d5+–] **♗f2 63. a6 ♖d6 64. ♗c4 ♖d7 65. ♔c6 ♖g7 66. ♖f4 ♗g1 67. ♖f6! ♔g5** [67... ♔h5 68. ♗f7 ♔g5 69. ♖f1+– △ ♔b7, a7] **68. ♖f7 ♖g6 69. ♔b7 ♖b6 70. ♔c7 ♖b4 71. ♖g7+– ♔f4 72. ♖g1 ♖c4 73. ♔b6 ♖e4** [73... ♖a4 74. ♖h1 ♖a2 75. ♖h7; 73... h5 74. a7 ♖a4 75. ♖a1! h4 76. a3 h3 77. ♔b7 h2 78. a8♕] **74. ♖c1** [74. a7?? ♖e6=] **♖a4 75. ♖h1 ♖a2 76. ♖h7 ♔e5**

1 : 0 **[M. Gurevich]**

382. **D 20**

ŠIROV 2670 – KRAMNIK 2685

Linares 1993

1. d4 d5 2. c4 dc4 3. e4 c5 4. d5 ♘f6 5. ♘c3 b5 6. ♗f4 ♕a5 N [6... a6 – 45/450] **7. ♗d2! b4** [7... e5!? 8. de6 (8. f4? ♘bd7 9. ♘f3 ♗d6 △ 10. a4 b4 11. ♘b5 ♗b8 12. ♗c4 a6∓) fe6 9. e5 ♘fd7 10. ♘f3=∞; 7... ♕d8!?] **8. e5 bc3** [8... ♘fd7 9. e6!→] **9. ♗c3 ♕a6** [9... ♕c7 10. ef6 (10. d6 ed6 11. ef6 gf6∞) ef6 11. ♗c4 ♗d6 12. ♕e2!⩲] **10. ef6 ef6 11. b3 ♗e7 12. ♗c4** [12. ♘f3!? (△ ♘d2) ♕d6 (12... ♗g4 13. h3±) 13. bc4!?⩲] **♕d6 13. ♘e2!? 0–0 14. 0–0 f5 15. ♖e1! ♘d7** [15... ♗f6? 16. ♗f6 ♕f6 17. d6±] **16. ♘g3 g6□** [△ ♗f6=]

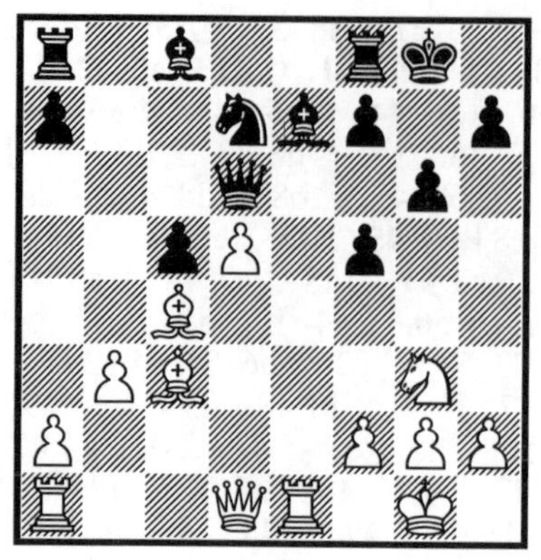

17. ♖e7! ♕e7 18. d6?! [18. ♕d2! ♕d6 (18... ♕h4?! 19. ♗b5!± △ 19... ♖e8 20. ♖e1) *a)* 19. ♖e1!? ♘b6 20. ♕h6 f6 21. ♖e7! ♕e7 22. d6 ♕f7! (22... ♕e6?! 23. ♘h5! gh5 24. ♗e6 ♗e6 25. ♗f6±) 23. ♗f7 ♖f7=; *b)* 19. b4!? ♖e8! 20. bc5 ♕c5 (20... ♘c5? 21. ♕d4 f6 22. ♗b4) 21. ♗b3 (△ ♘f5) f4! (21... ♘b6 22. ♘h5!) 22. ♗b4 ♕b6 23. ♕f4 ♕f6 24. ♕c1!=∞] **♕h4 19. ♕d5 ♖b8 20. ♘f5?** [20. ♖e1 ♗b7□ 21. ♘f5 (21. ♕d3? ♖be8 22. ♖e8 ♖e8 23. ♘f5 ♕g5!∓) ♗d5 (21... gf5? 22. ♕f5+−) 22. ♘e7 ♕e7 23. de7 ♗c4 24. ef8♕ ♘f8 25. bc4=] **gf5 21. ♖e1** [21. ♕f5 ♕h6?! 22. ♖e1 ♕g6 23. ♕g6 hg6 24. ♖e4 g5 25. ♖g4=∞; 21... ♖b6!∓] **♕g4!** [21... ♘f6? 22. ♕e5 ♕f2 23. ♔f2 ♘g4±; 22. ♕c5!±] **22. f3 ♕g6 23. ♖e7 ♗b7 24. ♕d3 ♘b6 25. ♗a1 ♘c4 26. ♕c3□ f6 27. ♕c4 ♔h8?!** [27... ♖f7! 28. d7 ♗c6 29. ♕e6 ♔g7! (29... ♖d8? 30. ♖e8 ♖e8 31. ♕e8 ♔g7 32. ♕f7!; 29... ♗d7 30. ♖d7∓) 30. ♖f7 ♕f7 31. ♕c6 ♖d8∓ △ ♕e7, ♔f7] **28. ♔f2 ♕h6?!** [28... f4!? 29. ♕f4 ♕c2 30. ♖e2 ♕g6 31. ♖e7=] **29. ♗c3 ♕g6?!** [29... ♕h2 30. d7=∞ △ 30... ♕d6? 31. ♖e6 ♕d5 (31... ♕d7? 32. ♖f6+−) 32. ♖f6! ♖f6 (32... ♔g8? 33. ♕h4!+−) 33. ♗f6 (33. ♕h4 ♕d6!=) ♔g8 34. ♕f4! ♕d7 35. ♕b8 ♔f7 36. ♗c3±] **30. d7 ♖bd8** [30... ♗c6 31. ♕c5±] **31. ♕c5** [31. ♗a5 ♖a8!⇆] **♖g8** [31... f4 32. ♗a5! ♖d7 (32... ♖g8 33. ♗d8 ♕g2 34. ♔e1 ♗f3 35. ♖e8+−) 33. ♖d7 ♖g8 34. ♖b7 ♕g2 35. ♔e1+−] **32. g3 f4 33. g4 ♖df8 34. ♕d4?** [34. ♕f5! ♕h6 35. ♕h5! ♕h5 36. gh5+− △ d8♕] **♕h6 35. h3 ♗a6?⊕** [35... ♗c6 36. ♔g2! (36. d8♕? ♕h4) ♗d7 37. ♖d7+−; 35... ♕h4 36. ♔e2 ♗c6! 37. ♔d2! (37. d8♕? ♗b5 38. ♔d2? ♖d8−+) ♗d7 38. ♖d7±] **36. ♔g2+− ♕h4 37. ♕f4⊕** [△ 38. d8♕ ♖d8 39. ♗f6]

1 : 0 **[Širov]**

383.* **D 20**

B. GEL'FAND 2690 − ANAND 2710

Linares 1993

1. d4 d5 2. c4 dc4 3. e4 c5 4. d5 ♘f6 5. ♘c3 b5 6. ♗f4 ♕a5 7. e5 N ♘e4 8. ♘e2 ♘a6! 9. f3 [9. a3 ♗b7 10. f3 ♘c3 11. ♘c3 ♘c7!∓ ×d5] **♘b4!** [9... ♘c3 10. ♘c3 ♗f5 11. g4 ♗g6 12. a4 ♘b4 13. ♔f2 ♗d3 14. ab5 ♕b6 15. ♗e3 g6 (Beljavskij 2610 − Anand 2710, Linares 1993) 16. ♕a4! *a)* 16... ♗g7 17. ♕b4! cb4 18. ♗b6 bc3 19. bc3 ♗e5 20. ♖a7 ♖a7 21. ♗a7 ♗c3 22. ♗d3 cd3 23. ♔e3 d2 24. b6 ♔d7 25. b7 ♗e5 26. ♔d2 ♗b8 27. ♗e3 ♖d8 (27... ♔d6 28. ♖c1±) 28. ♖b1±; *b)* 16... ♗f1 17. ♖hf1 ♗g7 (17... ♘d3 18. ♔g2 ♘e5 19. ♘e4± ×c5) 18. ♕b4 cb4 19. ♗b6 bc3 20. bc3 ♖b8 21. ♗d4 ♖b5 22. ♖a7 ♖d5 23. ♖b1± Beljavskij] **10. fe4 ♘d3 11. ♔d2**

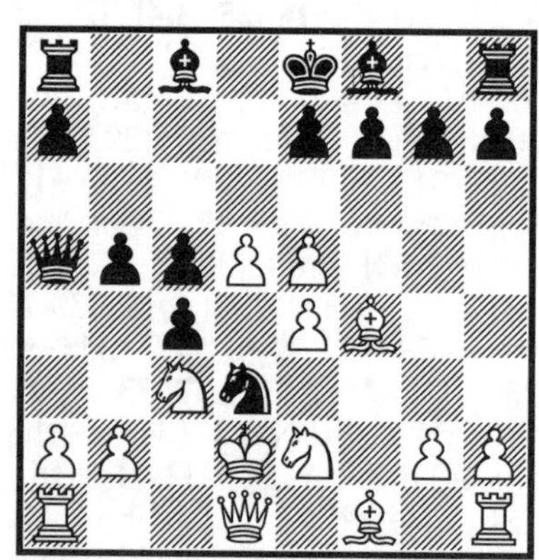

11... g6!!=∞ [11... ♘f2?! 12. ♕e1 ♘h1⩲] **12. b3?!** [12. a4? b4 13. ♘b5 (13. ♘b1−+) a6−+; 12. d6 ed6 13. a4 ♘f4! (B. Gel'fand) 14. ♘f4 ♗h6 15. g3 de5∓; 12. ♔c2 ♗g7 13. ♔b1 0−0 △ ♖b8, b4→; 12... b4∓; 12. ♔e3! ♗g7] **♗g7∓ 13. bc4 ♘f4 14. ♘f4** [14. cb5!? ♗e5 15. ♕b3 ♘e2 16. ♗e2 0−0∓] **♗e5 15. ♘e2 b4 16. ♕a4□ ♕a4 17. ♘a4 ♗a1 18. ♘c5 0−0!**

[18... f5? 19. ♘f4! △ ♘e6⇆] **19. ♘d3 a5 20. g3 ♗g7 21. ♗g2 ♗a6!−+** [×a2, c4, ♘d3, ♔d2] **22. c5 ♖ac8 23. c6 ♖fd8!** [△ 24... ♗d3 25. ♔d3 ♖c6] **24. ♖c1 ♗h6 25. ♘ef4** [25. ♘df4 e5] **♗d3 26. ♔d3 e5 27. ♔c4** [27. ♗h3 f5] **ef4 28. ♖e1 fg3** [28... f6 29. ♖f1! g5 30. h4] **29. e5** [29. hg3 f6 △ ♗f8-d6] **♗f4 30. hg3 ♗g3 31. ♖e3 ♗f4!** [31... ♗h2 32. d6] **32. ♖e4 ♗h2 33. ♗h3 ♖c7 34. ♖e2 ♗g3 35. ♖e3 ♗f4!** [35... ♗f2?! 36. ♖e2 ♗a7] **36. ♖e4 g5 37. ♔c5 ♖e7 38. ♔d4** [38. d6 ♖e5 39. ♖e5 ♗e5 40. ♗d7!□ h5 41. c7 ♖f8 42. ♔d5 (42. ♗e8 ♗d6) ♗d6! (42... ♗f4? 43. ♗e8) 43. ♔d6 g4 44. ♔e7 ♖a8!] **f6! 39. d6 ♗e5 40. ♖e5 ♖d6 0 : 1** **[Anand]**

384. !N D 20

BELJAVSKIJ 2610 – KAMSKY 2655

Linares 1993

1. d4 d5 2. c4 dc4 3. e4 c5 4. d5 ♘f6 5. ♘c3 b5 6. ♗f4 ♕a5 7. a4! N ♘e4□ [7... b4? 8. ♘b5 ♘a6 9. ♗c4 ♘e4 10. ♕e2+−] **8. ♘e2** [8. ab5 ♘c3 9. ♖a5 ♘d1 10. ♔d1 ♘d7 11. ♗c4 ♘b6 12. b3 ♗b7 13. ♘f3 ♗d5 14. ♗d5 ♘d5 15. ♗e5 f6 16. ♗g3 e5 17. ♔c2 ♗e7 18. ♖ha1 ♔f7 19. ♖a7 ♖a7 20. ♖a7 ♖b8 21. ♔d3 ♔e6∓] **♘d6□ 9. ab5 ♕b6 10. ♗d6** [10. ♘g3!?] **ed6** [10... ♕d6 11. ♘g3 g6 12. ♗c4 ♗g7 13. 0–0 0–0 14. ♘ge4⩲] **11. ♘g3 ♗e7 12. ♗c4 0–0 13. 0–0 ♗f6!□ 14. ♕c2!⩲ a6!? 15. ♗d3** [15. ♘ce4!? ♕d8 16. f4↑] **g6 16. ♘ge4 ♗g7 17. ♘d2 ♗b7** [17... ♘d7 18. ♘c4 ♕b8 (18... ♕c7 19. ♘e4 ♗e5 20. ba6±) 19. ♘a5 ♘b6!□ 20. ♘c6 ♕c7 21. ♕b3±] **18. ♘c4 ♕c7 19. b6! ♕d8 20. ♖fd1!±** [20. ♘e4!? ♗e5 21. ♘e5 de5 22. ♘c5 (22. ♕c5?! ♘d7 23. ♕c7 ♗d5) ♕b6⩲] **♘d7 21. ♘d6 ♕b6 22. ♘c4 ♕d8 23. ♘a5 ♕b6 24. ♗e4?⊕** [24. ♘b7!?] **f5⇆ 25. ♘c4 ♕f6 26. ♗f3 ♖ab8!? 27. ♘a4 g5↑ 28. h3 ♕h6 29. ♖e1 ♕h4!?⊕ 30. ♘e3?** [30. ♖e7□ g4 31. ♖d7 gf3 32. ♖g7!?∞] **♘e5 31. ♗e2 ♗c8!** [⇔b, ×b2, h3, f5] **32. ♘c5?** [32. ♘c4□∓] **f4 33. ♘g4 ♗g4 34. ♗g4 ♘g4 35. hg4 ♖b2 0 : 1** **[Kamsky]**

385. D 20

VYŽMANAVIN 2620 – I. IBRAGIMOV 2540

Sankt-Peterburg (zt) 1993

1. d4 d5 2. c4 dc4 3. e4 c5 4. d5 e6 5. ♘c3 ed5 6. ♘d5 ♘f6 7. ♗c4 ♘d5 8. ♗d5 ♗e7 9. ♘f3 0–0 10. 0–0 ♘a6 N [10... ♕b6 – 45/451; 10... ♘d7; 10... ♘c6] **11. ♕e2** [11. ♗d2 ♘c7 12. ♗b3 ♗e6=; 11. b3 ♘c7 12. ♗b2 ♘d5 13. ed5 ♗d6∞] **♕b6!?** [11... ♘c7 12. ♗c4 ♗e6 13. ♗e3 ♕c8 14. ♖ac1⩲ ♗c4 15. ♕c4 b6 16. ♖fd1] **12. ♘e5□ ♘c7 13. ♗f4** [13. ♘c4 ♕a6 14. ♗f4∞; 13. ♗c4 ♗f6!? 14. ♘g4 ♗g4 15. ♕g4 ♗d4; 14... ♗d4!?] **♕f6 14. ♗g3 ♘d5 15. ed5 ♗d6 16. ♖fe1⩲ ♗f5 17. ♕b5 b6 18. ♖e3!? a6 19. ♕e2 ♖ae8 20. ♖e1 b5 21. ♘c6?!** [21. b3!? △ h3] **♖e3 22. ♕e3 ♗d7!** [22... ♗g6? 23. ♗d6 ♕d6 24. ♕e8!+−; 22... ♗g3 23. hg3] **23. ♘e5 ♗c8⊕ 24. b3 h6 25. h3 ♕f5** [25... ♖e8? 26. ♘g4] **26. ♕d2 ♔h7** [26... ♖e8!] **27. ♘c6 ♗g3 28. fg3 ♗b7 29. ♘e7 ♕g5?** [29... ♕f6 30. ♕f4 ♕f4 31. gf4 ♖e8 32. d6] **30. ♕c2 g6 31. ♔h2± ♖d8** [31... ♗d5 32. h4 ♕h5 33. ♕c5 ♖d8 (33... ♗e6 34. ♘d5) 34. ♕c7 △ ♖e5] **32. ♕c5 ♕d2 33. ♖e5⊕** [33... f6 34. ♕c7; 33... ♖d7 34. ♘c6 ♔g7 35. ♖e8; 34. ♘g8!?] **1 : 0** **[Vyžmanavin, B. Arhangel'skij]**

386. !N D 20

BELJAVSKIJ 2610 – MATULOVIĆ 2460

Jugoslavija 1993

1. d4 d5 2. c4 dc4 3. e4 e5 4. ♘f3 ed4 5. ♗c4 ♗b4 6. ♘bd2 ♘c6 7. 0–0 ♘f6 8. e5 ♘d5 9. ♘b3 ♘b6 10. ♗b5 ♕d5 11. ♗c6 [11. ♘bd4 – 54/(378)] **♕c6 12. ♗d2! N** [×c7; RR 12. ♘bd4 ♕d5 13. ♕c2 ♗g4 14. ♖d1 0-0-0 15. ♗g5 ♖d7=] **♗e7** [RR 12... ♗d2 13. ♕d2⩲ Matulović] **13. ♖c1 ♕g6 14. ♖c7 ♘d5** [14... ♗h3 15. ♘e1; RR ⌓ 14... d3 15. ♘e1 ♘d5 16. ♖c4 ♗f5 17. ♖d4 (17. ♘d4 0–0=) ♖d8= Matulović] **15. ♖c4 d3 16. ♖d4 ♗e6** [RR 16...

♗h3 17. ♘e1 ♖d8 18. ♖d3±; ⌓ 16... ♘b6 17. ♗b4 (17. ♘e1 ♗f5) ♗h3 18. ♘e1 ♗b4 19. ♖b4 ♖d8 20. ♖d4 ♖d4 21. ♘d4 0–0 22. ♕d3 ♕d3 23. ♘d3 ♖d8 24. gh3 ♖d4= Matulović] **17. ♘e1 0–0 18. ♘d3 ♖ad8?!** [18... ♖ac8 19. ♕f3 ♖fd8 20. h3 ♖c2 21. ♖c1±; RR 18... ♖fd8 Matulović] **19. ♘dc5 ♘b6 20. ♘e6 ♕e6 21. ♗b4± ♘d7** [21... ♖d4 22. ♘d4 ♕e5 23. ♖e1+–; 21... ♕e5 22. ♖e1 ♕d4 23. ♘d4 ♗b4 24. ♖e4 ♗c5 25. b4 ♗b4 26. ♕b3 ♗c5 27. ♘f5±] **22. ♗d6 ♘e5?!** [22... ♗d6 23. ♖d6±] **23. ♘c5 ♕f6 24. ♗e5 ♕e5 25. ♘d7+– ♗c5⊕ 26. ♘e5 ♗d4 27. ♘d3 ♗b2 28. ♕b3 ♗d4 1 : 0**
[Beljavskij]

387.* D 20

AGREST 2460 – RUBLEVSKIJ 2515

Sankt-Peterburg (zt) 1993

1. d4 d5 2. c4 dc4 3. e4 e5 4. ♘f3 ed4 5. ♗c4 ♗b4 6. ♗d2 ♗d2 7. ♘bd2 ♕f6 8. 0–0 ♘e7 N [8... ♘c6 – 54/378, 380] **9. ♘b3!?** [RR 9. e5 ♕g6 10. ♘d4 ♘bc6 11. ♘2f3 0–0 12. e6 fe6 13. ♘b5 ♔h8 14. ♘c7 ♖b8 15. ♕e2 ♘d5 16. ♘d5 ed5 17. ♗d5 ♗g4 18. ♕e4 ♕h5 19. ♕c4 ♘a5∞̄ Širov 2670 – Spangenberg 2505, Buenos Aires 1993] **♘bc6 10. ♘fd4** [10. ♘bd4!?] **0–0 11. ♕f3 ♕g6?!** [11... ♕f3 12. ♘f3 ♗g4 13. ♖fc1!⩲] **12. ♕f4!** [×c7] **♗h3 13. ♕g3 ♘d4** [13... ♕g3 14. hg3±] **14. ♘d4 ♖ad8□** [14... ♕e4 15. ♖ad1!+–] **15. ♕g6** [15. ♘f3!? ♕g3□ (15... ♕e4 16. ♗f7!+–) 16. hg3 ♗d7 17. ♖fd1! △ 17... ♗c6 18. ♘g5!±; ⌓ 16... ♗e6] **♘g6 16. ♖fd1 ♘e5! 17. ♗e2?!** [17. ♗b3±↑] **♗d7 18. ♖ac1 ♘c6□ 19. ♘b5 ♗e6□ 20. b3 ♖d1 21. ♖d1 ♖c8 22. f4 f6!□** [22... a6 23. f5 ab5 24. fe6 fe6 25. ♗b5 ♘e5 26. ♗d7!±] **23. ♔f2** [23. f5 ♗f7 24. ♖d7 a6!□ 25. ♖c7 ♖c7 26. ♘c7 ♘b4 27. a3 ♘c2=] **♔f8 24. ♔e3 ♔e7 25. ♖c1 a6 26. ♘c3** [△ ♘a4-c5±] **♘b8!□ 27. ♘a4 ♘d7 28. ♔d4 a5 29. ♗b5?!⊕** [29. g4 △ h4, g5↑] **c6 30. ♗e2 ♖d8 31. ♔e3** [31... ♔d6 △ b5⇆] **1/2 : 1/2** **[Agrest]**

388. D 24

DREEV 2560 –
GALJAMOVA-IVANČUK 2445

Rostov na Donu (open) 1993

1. d4 d5 2. ♘f3 ♘f6 3. c4 dc4 4. ♘c3 a6 5. e4 b5 6. e5 ♘d5 7. a4 ♗b7 8. e6 f6 9. ♗e2 ♘c3 10. bc3 g6 11. h4!? N [11. 0–0] **♕d5 12. h5 ♖g8** [12... g5 13. 0–0 ♕e6 14. ♖e1 ♕d5 15. ♘h4!∞̄↑] **13. hg6 hg6 14. ♘h4 ♕e6?!** [14... g5!∞] **15. 0–0 ♘d7** [15... ♕e4 16. ♗f3 ♕h4 17. ♗b7 ♖h8 18. f3±] **16. ♖e1 0-0-0 17. ab5 ab5 18. ♗g4 ♕f7 19. ♗e6** [19. ♖a7 e5!] **♕h7 20. ♗g8 ♕g8 21. ♕g4 ♔b8?!** [21... g5 22. f4!±] **22. ♖b1!+– ♕d5 23. ♘g6 e5 24. de5 ♗c5⊕ 25. ♖d1 ♕g8 26. ♖b5 ♗b6 27. ♗f4 ♗c6 28. ♖b2 fe5 29. ♘e5 ♘e5 30. ♖d8 ♕d8 31. ♗e5 ♔b7 32. ♗d4⊕ ♕d5 33. f3 ♔a6 34. ♖d2 ♕b5 35. ♕c8 ♗b7 36. ♖a2 ♗a5 37. ♕e6 c6 38. ♖a1 ♕b3 39. ♕f5 ♕b5 40. ♕c5 ♕c5 41. ♗c5 ♔b5 42. ♗d4 1 : 0** **[Dreev]**

389. D 26

GAVRILOV 2415 – SE. IVANOV 2470

Rossija (ch) 1992

1. d4 ♘f6 2. c4 e6 3. ♘f3 d5 4. ♘c3 dc4 5. e3 a6 6. ♗c4 b5 7. ♗d3 ♘bd7?! N [7... ♗b7 8. ♕e2 (8. ♕c2 – 33/508) ♘bd7 9. e4 c5 10. d5 (10. e5!?) ed5 11. e5!? (11. ed5 ♕e7) ♘g8 12. ♘g5!?∞̄] **8. a4!?** [8. e4!? c5] **b4 9. ♘e4 ♗b7 10. ♘f6 ♘f6** [10... ♕f6?! 11. e4 c5 12. ♗g5 ♕g6 13. d5!?±] **11. 0–0 c5 12. dc5** [12. ♕e2?! cd4 13. ♘d4 ♗d6!?∓] **♗c5 13. ♕e2 ♕d5!?** [13... 0–0 14. e4⩲; 13... ♘e4!? 14. ♖d1 ♕c7 (14... ♕f6 15. ♗b5!±) 15. ♘d2 ♘d2 16. ♗d2 0–0 17. ♖ac1±] **14. ♖d1 ♕h5** [14... ♔e7? 15. ♗a6 ♗a6 16. ♖d5 ♗e2 17. ♖c5±] **15. h3** [15. e4?! ♘g4; 15. b3 ♘d5∞ ×c3] **♖d8?!** [15... 0–0 16. e4 ♖fd8 17. ♗f4±; 15... ♘e4 16. ♘d4!? ♕e2 17. ♗e2± (△ ♘b3) ♗d5 18. a5] **16. b3! e5?!** [16... 0–0 17. ♗b2 a5 18. ♖ac1±] **17. ♗b2! e4 18. ♗b5!** [18. ♗a6? ♖d1 19. ♖d1 ♗a6 20. ♕a6 0–0! 21. ♗f6 ef3∓] **♔e7** [18... ab5? 19. ♕b5 ♘d7 20. ♘e5 ♗c8 21. ♖d7!? ♗d7 22. ♕c5 ♖c8 23.

♕d6+−→; 21. ♖ac1+−] **19. ♘e5** [19. ♘d4 ♗d4! (19... ♕e2 20. ♘f5! ♔e6 21. ♘g7+−) 20. ♗d4 ♖d4 21. ♖d4 ab5 22. ♕d2 ♕c5∞] **♕e2** [19... ab5? 20. ♘c6+−; 19... ♖d1 20. ♖d1 △ 20... ab5? 21. ♖d7 ♔e6 22. ♕b5+−] **20. ♗e2± ♖d1** [20... a5 21. ♘c4; 20... ♘d5 21. ♖ac1; 20... ♔e6 21. ♗c4 ♗d5 22. ♘f7! ♔f7 23. ♗f6 ♗c4 (23... ♔f6 24. ♗d5 ♔e5 25. ♗b7 a5 26. ♖dc1+− △ ♖c4) 24. ♗d8 ♗b3 25. ♖d2± △ ♖c1] **21. ♖d1 ♔e6?!** [21... ♗d5 22. ♗d4!? (22. ♖c1!? ♔d6 23. ♗a6 ♗b3 24. ♘c4 ♗c4 25. ♗c4±⊡) ♗d4 23. ♖d4 a5 (23... ♗b3 24. ♖b4±) 24. ♗c4 ♗c4 25. ♖c4± △ ♘c6] **22. ♗c4 ♗d5 23. ♗d5 ♘d5 24. ♘f7! ♘c3** [24... ♘e3 25. ♘d8 ♔e7 26. ♘c6+−] **25. ♗c3** [25. ♘g5 ♔e5 (25... ♔f5 26. ♗c3+− △ ♖d5) 26. ♖c1 ♔f5 27. ♗c3 bc3 28. ♖c3 ♗e7 29. h4 (29. ♘f7? ♖f8) h6 30. ♘h3±] **bc3** [25... ♔f7 26. ♖d7+− △ ♗g7] **26. ♘h8 ♗a3 27. ♘f7!+− c2** [27... ♔f7 28. ♖d7 △ ♖c7] **28. ♘d8 ♔f6 29. ♖e1 c1♕ 30. ♖c1 ♗c1 31. ♘c6 ♗b2 32. ♔f1⊕** [32. b4 ♔e6 33. b5 ♔d6 34. ♘d4 ab5 35. ab5] **♔e6 33. ♔e2 ♔d6 34. ♘b4 a5 35. ♘c2 ♗c3 36. ♘d4 ♔d5 37. ♘f5 g6 38. ♘g3 h5 39. f3 ef3 40. ♔f3** [40. gf3!?] **♗e5 41. ♘e2 g5 42. g4 hg4 43. hg4 ♗b2 44. ♘g3! ♔c5 45. ♘f5 ♔d5** [45... ♔b4 46. ♘d4 △ ♔e4] **46. ♔e2 ♗f6** [46... ♔e4 47. ♘g3 △ ♔d3] **47. ♔d3 ♔c5** [47... ♗d8 48. ♘d4 ♗f6 49. ♘f3 ♗d8 50. ♘d2 ♔c5 51. e4 ♔b4 (51... ♗c7 52. ♘c4 ♗d8 53. ♔c3) 52. e5 ♔c5 53. ♘c4 ♔d5 (53... ♗c7 54. e6 ♗d8 55. ♔e4) 54. ♔c3 ♗c7 55. b4 ab4 56. ♔b4] **48. ♔e4 ♔b4 49. ♘d4 ♔c3 50. ♔f5 ♗d8 51. ♘c6 ♗b6 52. e4 ♔b3 53. e5 ♔a4 54. e6 ♗c5 55. ♘a5 ♔a5 56. ♔f6 1 : 0** **[Gavrilov]**

390. **D 28**

KOŽUL 2550 − PSAKHIS 2575

Zagreb (zt) 1993

1. d4 d5 2. c4 dc4 3. ♘f3 ♘f6 4. e3 e6 5. ♗c4 c5 6. 0−0 a6 7. ♕e2 b5 8. ♗d3 cd4 9. ed4 ♘c6 10. a4 ba4 11. ♖a4 ♘b4 12. ♗b5 [12. ♗c4 ♗e7 13. ♗d2 (13. ♘c3 0−0 14. ♖d1 ♗b7=; 13. ♗g5 − 42/497) ♘fd5 14. ♘e5 0−0 15. ♖a3 f6∞] **♗d7 13. ♗d7 ♕d7 14. ♘c3 ♗e7 15. ♗g5 0−0? N** [15... ♕b7] **16. ♗f6 gf6 17. ♖a5!! ♔h8** [17... f5 18. d5!; 17... ♕c7 18. ♖h5] **18. ♖h5 ♖g8 19. ♖e1!** [19. d5 ed5 20. ♖d1 ♕e6±] **♖g7 20. d5 ♘d5!? 21. ♘d5 ed5 22. g3!±** [22. ♕e7? ♕g4!] **♗b4 23. ♖d1 ♕e6 24. ♕d3 ♖d8 25. ♕b3!** [25. ♖d5?! ♖d5 26. ♕d5 ♕d5 27. ♖d5 ♖g6±] **a5 26. ♖d4! ♕e2 27. ♔g2 ♖c8 28. ♕d5 ♕b2** [28... ♖c2? 29. ♕d8] **29. ♕f5+− ♕c3 30. ♖dh4 ♕c2 31. ♕f6 ♔g8 32. ♘d4! ♕g6 33. ♕f3 ♕a6 34. ♘f5 ♖c1 35. ♔h3 ♖g1⊕ 36. ♖e4** [36. ♘g7 ♕f1 37. ♔g4 ♕c4 38. ♕f4 ♕e2 39. f3] **♕c8 37. ♖g4 ♗f8** [37... ♖g6 38. ♘h6] **38. ♖g7 ♗g7 39. ♕g4 ♕c3 40. ♖g5 1 : 0** **[Psakhis]**

391. !N **D 29**

VAGANIAN 2615 − GARCÍA-PALERMO 2440

Reggio Emilia 1992/93

1. d4 d5 2. c4 dc4 3. ♘f3 a6 4. e3 e6 5. ♗c4 c5 6. 0−0 ♘f6 7. ♕e2 b5 8. ♗b3 ♗b7 9. ♖d1 ♘bd7 10. ♘c3 ♕b6 11. d5 [11. e4 cd4 12. ♘d4 ♗c5 13. ♗e3 ♘e4? 14. ♘e4 ♗e4 15. ♖ac1!±; 13... 0−0; 13... ♘e5!?] **♘d5 12. ♘d5 ♗d5 13. ♗d5 ed5 14. ♖d5 ♕b7 15. e4 ♗e7 16. ♗g5 f6 17. ♖ad1 ♘b6** [17... fg5 18. ♖d7 ♕d7 19. ♖d7 ♔d7 20. ♘g5 ♗g5 21. ♕g4±; 20. ♕d2! △ ♘g5-e6±] **18. ♗f4 ♘d5 19. ed5 0−0 20. d6** [20. ♕e6 ♖f7 21. d6 ♗f8!] **♗d8 21. d7 ♗c7 22. ♕e6 ♖f7**

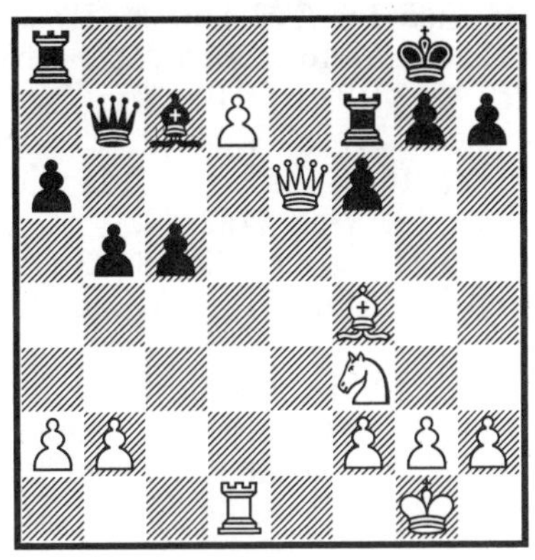

23. b4!! N ± [23. ♗e3 ♕b6 24. ♕d5 (24. ♕e4 − 29/(409)) ♖d8 25. ♗c5 ♖d7 26.

♕f7 ♖f7 27. ♗b6 ♗b6 28. ♖d6 ♖b7=] **c4** [23... ♖d8 24. ♗e3! (24. bc5 ♗f4 25. c6∞) ♕b6 25. ♕e8 ♖f8 26. ♕e4!+−; 23... cb4 24. ♖c1! (△ ♖c8; 24. ♗e3!?) ♗d8 25. ♕e8 (25. ♖c8? ♕d7−+) ♖f8 26. ♗d6+−] **24. ♗e3 c3 25. ♘e1** [⌓ 25. ♗c5 ♖d8□ (25... c2 26. d8♕+−) 26. ♕e8 ♖f8 27. ♗f8 ♕c6 28. ♕e7! ♖f8 29. d8♕ ♗d8 30. ♖d8 ♖d8 31. ♕d8 ♔f7 32. ♕d1 c2 33. ♕c1 ♕c4 34. a3? ♕e2−+; 34. ♘e1±] **♖d8 26. ♗c5 g6 27. ♘c2 ♔g7 28. ♗e7 ♕b6 29. ♕e4!± ♗h2** [29... f5!? 30. ♕h4! h6 31. ♗d8 ♗d8 32. ♕g3!± △ ♖d6 ×g6] **30. ♔f1** [30. ♔h2? ♕c7 31. g3 ♖d7=] **♗e5 31. ♗d8 ♕d8 32. ♕c6 f5 33. ♕c8 ♗f6** [33... ♖f8 34. ♕a6 ♕h4 35. ♕b5 ♕h1 36. ♔e2 ♕h5 37. ♔e1! ♕h1 38. ♕f1 ♕h4 39. ♖d3 ♗c7 (39... ♕c4 40. d8♕) 40. ♔d1] **34. ♘d4! ♕b6 35. ♘e6 ♔h6** [35... ♕e6? 36. d8♕+−] **36. ♖d3 ♗h4 37. ♖e3! c2 38. d8♕!** [38... ♗d8 39. ♖h3] **1 : 0** **[Vaganian]**

392. **D 30**

KORTCHNOI 2605 – JE. PIKET 2590
Nijmegen (m/1) 1993

1. d4 d5 2. c4 e6 3. ♘f3 c5 4. cd5 ed5 5. ♗g5 ♗e7 6. ♗e7 ♕e7 7. ♘c3 ♘f6 8. dc5 ♕c5 9. e3 ♘c6 [9... 0–0 10. ♕d4] **10. ♗e2 0–0 11. 0–0 ♖d8 12. ♖c1** [12. ♘a4!?] **♕b4 13. ♘a4 ♗g4 14. ♖c5** [14. a3 ♕e7 (14... ♕d6 15. h3) 15. ♖e1 ♘e4 △ 16. h3 ♗f3 17. ♗f3 ♕h4 18. ♖f1 ♘e5 19. ♖c2 ♘g5 20. ♗d5 ♕a4 21. f4∞] **♗f3 15. ♗f3 ♘e5 16. ♗e2** [16. ♗d5!? *a)* 16... ♘e4? 17. a3; *b)* 16... ♕c5!? 17. ♘c5 ♖d5 18. ♕c2 ♖c8 19. b4 (19. ♕f5 ♘ed7) b6 20. f4 ♘ed7 21. e4 ♖d4 22. e5 ♘e8 23. ♖d1!±; *c)* 16... ♘d5 17. ♖d5 ♖d5 18. ♕d5 ♕a4 19. ♕e5 ♕a2 20. ♖c1 ♖d8=] **b6 17. ♖c1** [17. ♖b5 ♕h4 18. a3 (△ ♖b4) ♘c6!] **d4** [17... b5?! 18. ♘c3 a6 19. ♕d4 ♕d4 20. ed4 ♘c4 21. b3 ♘d2 22. ♖fd1 ♘de4 23. f3±; 21... ♘d6] **18. a3 ♕d6 19. ed4 ♕d4 20. ♕d4 ♖d4 21. ♗b5! ♖ad8** [21... a6? 22. ♘b6 ♖b8 23. ♗a6 ♖d6 24. ♘c4+−] **22. ♘c3 ♔f8** [22... ♖d2 23. ♖cd1 ♘e4 24. ♖d2 ♘d2 25. ♖d1 ♔f8 26. f3 ♔e7 27. ♔f2 ♘ec4∓; 23. ♖fe1 ♘d3=; 23. ♖fd1!?] **23. ♖c2 g6 24. ♖e1 ♘d3 25. ♖d1 ♘c5 26. ♖d4 ♖d4 27. f3 a5 28. ♔f2 ♘d5 29. ♘d5 ♖d5 30. ♗e2 ♔e7 31. ♔e3 ♖e5 32. ♔f2** [32. ♔d4 ♖h5 33. h3 ♘e6] **♖d5 33. ♔e3** [33. ♗c4 ♖d6 34. ♔e3 △ b4±; 33... ♖d1! △ 34. ♔e2 ♖h1 35. h3 ♖b1=] **1/2 : 1/2** **[Je. Piket]**

393. **D 30**

CVETKOVIĆ 2500 – M. MAKAROV 2515
Aranđelovac 1993

1. c4 e6 2. ♘f3 d5 3. d4 c6 4. ♕c2 ♘f6 5. g3 dc4 6. ♕c4 b5 7. ♕c2 ♗b7 8. ♗g2 ♘bd7 9. ♘c3 c5 N [9... a6 – 43/(603)] **10. 0–0** [10. ♘b5? ♕a5 11. ♘c3 cd4 12. ♕a4 ♗b4−+] **♕b6** [10... b4 11. ♘a4!? ♗e4 12. ♕c4 ♗d5 13. ♕a6±; 10... a6!?] **11. ♗e3! ♘g4**

12. dc5! ♘e3 13. cb6 ♘c2 14. ♖ac1 a6 [14... ♘b4?! 15. ♘b5±; 14... ♘b6 *a)* 15. ♘b5 ♖c8 (15... ♘b4 16. ♘c7±) 16. ♘a7 ♖c7∞⇆; 16... ♖c5!?∞⇆; *b)* 15. ♖c2 a6 16. ♘e5 ♗g2 17. ♔g2±] **15. ♘e5! ♘e5** [15... ♗g2 16. ♘d7 ♗b7 (16... ♗f1?! 17. b7 ♖d8 18. b8♕ ♖b8 19. ♘b8±) 17. ♘f8 (17. ♖c2?! ♔d7 18. ♘b5 ab5 19. ♖c7 ♔d6! 20. ♖b7 ♔c6∓) *a)* 17... ♘d4 18. ♖fd1 e5 (18... ♘c6 19. ♘e4±) 19. ♘d7! ♔d7 20. e3±; *b)* 17... ♘b4 18. a3 ♘d5 (18... ♘c6 19. ♘e4±) 19. ♘e4±] **16. ♗b7 ♖b8 17. ♗a6 ♘d4** [17... ♖b6? 18. ♗b5] **18. b7 ♘d7** [18... ♗b4!? (△ ♗c3, ♘e2) 19. ♔g2!] **19. ♖fd1 ♘c5** [19... e5!?] **20. ♖d4 ♘a6 21. ♘b5 ♖b7 22. ♖c8 ♔e7 23. a4!** [23. ♘d6 *a)* 23... ♖b2 24. ♖e8 ♔d7! (24... ♔f6 25. ♖f4 ♔g6 26. ♘f7 ♖g8 27.

♘e5+−) 25. ♖a8 (25. ♖f8? ♖b1−+) *a1)* 25... ♘c7 26. ♘c4 ♔c6 (26... ♔e7 27. ♖a7+−) 27. ♘a5 ♔c5 28. ♖c4 ♔d6 29. ♖d8 ♔e7 30. ♘c6 ♔f6 31. ♖f4+−; *a2)* 25... ♗d6 26. ♖a6±; *b)* 23... ♖c7 24. ♖e8 ♔f6 (24... ♔d7 25. ♖a8 ♗d6 26. ♖h8±) 25. ♖f4 ♔g6 26. ♘f7 ♖f7 27. ♖e6 ♖f6 28. ♖ff6 gf6 29. ♖a6⩲; *c)* 23... ♖a7 24. ♖e8 ♔d7 (24... ♔f6 25. ♖f4 ♔g6 26. ♘f7 ♖f7 27. ♖e6 − 23... ♖c7) 25. ♖f8 ♖f8 26. ♘b5 ♔c6 27. ♘a7 ♔b6 28. ♖d7 ♘c5 29. ♖e7 ♖a8 30. b4 ♘a4 31. ♘c6 ♔c6 32. ♖f7⩲; *d)* 23... e5!∞] **f5** [23... g6 24. ♖dd8 f5 (24... ♖d7? 25. ♖e8) 25. ♖e8 ♔f7 26. ♘d6 ♗d6 27. ♖h8±] **24. b4** [24. ♖dd8 ♖d7] **g6 25. ♖a8 ♘b8** [25... ♗g7 26. ♖a6 ♗d4 27. ♘d4±; 25... ♘c7 26. ♘c7 ♖c7 27. ♖dd8±] **26. ♖c4 ♗g7 27. ♘a7! ♖d8 28. a5 ♖d4 29. ♖c8! ♖db4 30. ♖cb8 ♖b8 31. ♘c6 ♔d6 32. ♘b8 ♖b5** [32... ♖a4 33. ♖a7±; 32... ♗d4 33. e3!?±] **33. a6** [33. e3!?±] **♗d4 34. a7 ♖b7?** [34... ♖a5? 35. ♘a6+−; 34... ♗a7! 35. ♖a7 ♖b8 36. ♖h7 ♔e5 37. ♖f7 g5 38. h3±] **35. ♘c6 ♗a7 36. ♘a7 ♔d7 37. ♖h8 ♔d6 38. ♘c8 ♔e5 39. ♔g2 ♖b8 40. ♖g8 g5 41. ♘e7 ♖b7 42. ♘c6 ♔d5 43. ♘a5** [43... ♖b5 44. ♖d8 ♔c5 45. ♖c8]

1 : 0 **[Cvetković]**

394. **D 30**

B. MAKSIMOVIĆ 2325
− B. IVANOVIĆ 2470
Cetinje 1993

1. d4 d5 2. ♘f3 ♘f6 3. c4 c6 4. e3 e6 5. ♗d3 ♗e7 6. 0−0 0−0 7. b3 ♘bd7 8. ♘bd2 c5 9. ♗b2 b6 10. ♕e2 ♗b7 11. ♖fd1 cd4 N [11... ♖c8 − 10/624] **12. ed4** [12. ♘d4 ♘c5 (12... ♘e5? 13. ♘e6) 13. ♗c2 dc4 14. ♘c4 ♕d5∞] **♘h5** [12... ♖e8 △ ♗f8, g6] **13. ♕e3! g6 14. ♖ac1 ♖c8 15. g3** [△ ♗f1-g2] **♖e8 16. ♗f1 ♘g7?!** [16... ♗f8] **17. g4!⩲** [×♘g7] **h5 18. h3 ♗f8 19. ♗g2 ♖c7 20. ♕f4 ♕b8 21. ♘e5 ♘e5 22. de5 hg4?! 23. hg4** [⇔h] **♖d8 24. ♘f3!** [△ ♘g5, ♕h2] **dc4** [⌓ 24... ♗e7] **25. ♘g5 ♖d1 26. ♖d1 ♗g2 27. ♔g2** [27. ♕h2 ♘h5] **♕b7 28. ♔g1! ♖d7 29. ♖c1 ♖d3 30. ♕c4!±** [30. ♕h2 ♗c5 △ 31. ♕h7 ♔f8 32. ♕h8 ♔e7 33. ♕g7 ♖g3−+] **♕d7** [30... ♕d5 31. ♕d5 △ ♖c8+−] **31. ♘e4 ♘e8 32. ♔g2 ♗e7? 33. ♘d6+− ♖d2 34. ♕f4 ♖d6 35. ed6 ♗d6 36. ♕c4 ♗c5 37. b4 ♗f8 38. a3 ♗g7 39. ♗g7 ♔g7 40. ♕c3 ♘f6? 41. ♕e5!** [41. g5? ♕d5] **1 : 0** **[B. Maksimović]**

395. **D 30**

HENKIN 2575 − ĖJNGORN 2575
Metz 1993

1. d4 e6 2. ♘f3 c5 3. e3 ♘f6 4. c4 d5 5. cd5 ed5 6. ♗b5 ♘c6 7. 0−0 ♗d6 8. ♕c2!? N [8. dc5] **♕b6 9. dc5!** [9. ♗c6 ♕c6! 10. dc5 ♕c5!=] **♗c5** [9... ♕c5?! 10. ♕c5 ♗c5 11. b3±; 9... ♗h2 10. ♘h2 ♕b5 11. ♘a3! ♕a6 12. ♗d2 0−0 13. ♗c3±] **10. ♗c6 ♕c6!** [10... bc6 11. ♘c3± ×♕b6, ♗c5, c6] **11. b3 0−0 12. ♗b2** [12. ♗a3 ♗a3 13. ♕c6 bc6 14. ♘a3 a5! 15. ♖fc1 ♗d7 16. ♘e5 ♖fc8 17. ♘d3 ♗f5! 18. ♘c5 ♘e4=; 13. ♘a3!?⩲] **♗g4** [12... ♘e4!? 13. ♘e5! (13. ♘bd2 ♗f5 14. ♘e4 ♗e4 15. ♕e2 ♖ac8=) ♕d6 14. ♘d3⩲] **13. ♘e5 ♕d6 14. ♘d3! ♖fc8□** [14... b6? 15. b4!+−; 14... ♖ac8?! 15. ♘c5 ♖c5 16. ♕d3 △ ♗a3±] **15. ♘c5 b6?!** [15... ♕c5 16. ♕c5 ♖c5 17. ♗d4! ♖c2 18. ♘c3! ♗e6□ 19. ♖ac1±; 15... ♖c5 16. ♕d3 ♕e6 17. ♕d4 ♖ac8 18. ♘c3⩲] **16. h3!** [16. f3?! ♗e6! 17. ♗f6 gf6∞] **♗h5□** [16... bc5? 17. ♗f6 ♕f6 18. hg4 ♕a1 19. ♘c3+−; 16... ♗e6 17. ♗f6 gf6 18. ♕b2!±; 16... ♗d7 17. ♗f6 gf6 (17... ♕f6 18. ♘d7! ♕a1 19. ♕d2±) 18. ♘e4! de4 19. ♕e4±] **17. ♕f5 bc5□** [17... ♖c5? 18. ♗a3+−; 17... ♗g6? 18. ♘b7!+−] **18. ♗f6 ♕f6 19. ♕f6 gf6 20. ♘c3± ♖d8** [20... d4?! 21. ♘e4! (21. ♘d5 ♔g7 22. f4 ♖d8! 23. e4 f5!∞) ♖c6 (21... ♔g7 22. f4!+− ×♗h5) 22. ♖ac1 ♖ac8 (22... ♖e8 23. ♘g3! ♗g6 24. ed4+−; 22... ♗e2 23. ♖fe1 d3 24. ♘d2 △ ♖c4, ♖ec1+−) 23. ed4 cd4 24. ♘f6!+−] **21. ♖fc1!** [21. ♖ac1 ♖ac8 22. e4 d4 23. ♘d5 ♖d5! 24. ed5 ♗e2 25. ♖fe1 d3 26. ♖e2 de2 27. f3 ♖d8! 28. ♔f2 ♖d5 29. ♔e2±; 21... ♔g7!? △ 22. ♘a4 c4!, △ 22. g4 ♗g6 23. ♖fd1 d4 24. ♘a4 de3 25. fe3 ♖d1 26. ♖d1 c4!=; 21. e4 d4 22. ♘d5 ♗g6! (22... ♔g7? 23. g4! ♗g6 24. f3+− ×♗g6) 23. f3 (23. ♖fe1 ♔g7! △ 24. g4?! ♗e4!; 23. ♘f6 ♔g7 24. e5 d3!∞̄) f5! 24. ♘e7 ♔f8! 25. ♘f5 ♗f5 26.

ef5±] ♗g6!? [21... ♖ac8?! 22. e4! d4 23. ♘d5 ♔g7□ 24. g4! ♗g6 25. f3+− ×♗g6] **22. ♘a4?!⊕** [22. ♘b5! d4 (22... ♖dc8 23. ♖d1!+−) 23. ♖c5 de3 24. fe3 ♖d2 (24... ♖d3 25. ♖e1+−) 25. ♘c3! ♖e8 26. ♖d1! ♖b2 (26... ♖c2 27. ♘d5!+−) 27. ♘d5! ♔g7 28. ♖a5!+−] **d4 23. ♘c5 de3 24. fe3 ♖d2 25. ♖f1!□** [△ 26. ♖f2, 26, ♖f6; 25. ♖c3? ♖ad8! △ ♖b2, ♖dd2⩱] **♖c8** [⌓ 25... ♖e8! 26. ♖f6 (26. ♖f2 ♖d5 27. ♖c1 ♖e3 28. ♖f6 ♖e2 29. ♖f2□ ♖f2 30. ♔f2 ♖d2=; 26. ♖f3 ♖e5!⩱↑) ♖e3 27. ♖f2 ♖f2 (27... ♖d5?! 28. ♖c1±) 28. ♔f2 ♖c3 29. ♘d7 (29. b4?! a5 30. a3 ♖c4!=) ♖c2 30. ♔f3 ♗f5⩱↑] **26. b4 ♖b2?** [26... a5!□ 27. a3 (27. ♘b3? ♖b2 △ 28... ♖cc2, 28... ab4) ab4 28. ab4 ♖b2! 29. ♖f4 ♖d8! (29... ♖e8? 30. ♖a3 △ ♖b3+−; 29... ♖b8?! 30. ♘d7 ♖8b4 31. ♘f6 ♔g7 32. ♖b4 ♖b4 33. ♖f1±) 30. ♖af1□ ♖dd2 31. ♖1f2 ♖f2 32. ♖f2 ♖b4 33. ♖f6 ♔g7 34. ♖f4!⩲] **27. a3 a5 28. ♖f2!+− ♖f2 29. ♔f2 ab4 30. ab4 ♖b8 31. ♖a4!** [31. ♘d7 ♖b4 32. ♘f6 ♔g7 33. ♖a6± ×♗g6, ♔g7] **♔g7** [31... ♗c2? 32. ♖a2 △ ♖b2; 31... f5 32. ♔e2 f6 33. ♘d7 ♖d8 34. ♖a7!] **32. ♔e2 h5 33. ♔d2 h4 34. ♔c3 ♖c8** [34... ♖e8 35. b5! ♖e3 36. ♔d4 ♖e2 37. b6 △ b7, ♖a8] **35. ♖a2⊕ ♗e4 36. ♔c4!** [36. ♔d4?! ♗c6! △ ♗b5] **f5 37. b5 ♔f6 38. ♔b4 ♗d5 39. ♖d2 ♖d8** [39... ♔e5? 40. ♘d7 △ ♖d5; 39... ♗a8 40. b6] **40. b6 ♖d6 41. b7** [41. ♖d5?! ♖d5 42. b7 ♖d8 43. ♘d7 ♔g5 44. b8♕ ♖b8 45. ♘b8 f4] **♖b6 42. ♔c3!** [42. ♔a5 ♖b7 43. ♖d5 ♖b2] **1 : 0**
[Henkin]

396.*** !N **D 31**

HERTNECK 2575 − LAUTIER 2645
München 1993

1. d4 d5 2. c4 e6 3. ♘c3 ♗b4 [RR 3... c6 4. e4 de4 5. ♘e4 ♗b4 6. ♗d2 ♕d4 7. ♗b4 ♕e4 8. ♘e2 ♘a6 9. ♗c3 *a)* 9... ♘e7 10. ♗g7 ♘b4 11. ♗h8! N (11. ♕d6) e5 12. ♕d6! (12. f3? ♘c2 △ ♕e3−+) ♘c2 13. ♔d2 ♗f5 *a1)* 14. ♘g3?! ♕f4 15. ♔c3 ♘d5! (15... ♘a1 16. ♕d2 ♕d2 17. ♔d2 0-0-0 18. ♔c3 ♖h8 19. ♘f5 ♘f5 20. ♗d3±) 16. cd5 ♕d4 17. ♔b3 ♘a1 18. ♔a3 ♘c2 19. ♔b3 ♘a1 1/2 : 1/2 Gómez Esteban 2410 − Illescas Córdoba 2615, Lisboa (zt) 1993; *a2)* 14. ♖d1! ♖d8 15. ♕d8 ♔d8 16. ♔c1 ♔e8 17. ♘c3 ♕f4 18. ♖d2±; 16. ♘g3!?; *b)* 9... f6!? 10. ♕d6 ♘e7 (10... e5 11. 0-0-0 ♗f5 12. ♘d4!!→) 11. 0-0-0⩱ Illescas Córdoba] **4. cd5** [RR 4. ♘f3 c5 5. cd5 ed5 6. ♗g5 ♘e7 7. dc5!? N (7. e3) ♘bc6 8. e3 ♕a5 9. ♖c1 ♕a2 10. ♕d2 ♕a5 11. ♗e7 ♘e7 12. ♗b5 ♘c6 13. 0−0 0−0 14. ♕d3 ♘e7 15. ♖a1 ♗f5 16. ♕d4 ♗c3 17. ♖a5 ♗d4 18. ♘d4 a6 19. ♖fa1 ♖ad8 20. ♗e2± L. Christiansen 2620 − Kortchnoi 2605, Monaco 1993] **ed5 5. ♗f4 N** [5. ♘f3 − 39/479] **♘f6 6. e3 c5 7. ♗d3** [7. ♗b5 ♗d7 8. ♗d7 ♕d7 9. dc5 ♗c3 10. bc3 0−0 11. ♘e2 ♖c8⩱ Hertneck 2560 − Lautier 2580, Tilburg (Interpolis) 1992; 7. dc5] **♘c6 8. ♘ge2 cd4 9. ed4 ♗g4?!** [9... 0−0 10. 0−0 ♖e8 11. a3±] **10. f3 ♗e6** [10... ♗h5 11. 0−0 △ ♗g5 ×d5] **11. 0−0 0−0 12. a3 ♗e7?!** [12... ♗d6 13. ♗d6 ♕d6 14. b4± ×♗e6] **13. b4 ♘e8!? 14. ♘a4 ♗f6 15. ♔h1** [15. ♘c5] **♘d6 16. ♘c5 ♗c8** [16... b6!? 17. ♘e6 fe6 18. ♕c2 (18. ♗h7? ♔h7 19. ♕c2 ♘f5! 20. ♕c6 ♘d4 21. ♘d4 ♗d4 22. ♗c7∞; 18. ♖c1±) ♘d4 19. ♗h7 ♔h8 20. ♘d4 ♗d4 21. ♗d6 ♕d6 22. ♖ad1 e5 23. ♗d3⩲] **17. ♖c1** [17. ♕b3? ♘f5! 18. ♗f5 (18. ♘b7? ♘cd4! 19. ♘d8 ♘b3 20. ♖ab1 ♘bd4∓) ♗f5 19. ♘b7 ♕b6 20. ♘d6∞] **b6** [17... ♖e8 18. ♘c3!] **18. ♕a4!** [18. ♘e6? ♗e6 19. ♖c6 ♘c4∞; 18. ♘a6 ♗b7 19. ♗h7 (19. ♕b3 ♖e8 20. ♕d5 ♘b4!⇆) ♔h7 20. ♖c6 ♗c6 21. ♕c2 ♔g8 22. ♕c6 ♘c4 23. ♘c7 ♖c8∞; 18. ♘b3 ♗b7 19. b5 ♘e7 20. ♕c2 ♖c8!∞] **♘b8!** [18... ♘d4? 19. ♘d4 ♗d4 20. ♕c6±; 18... ♘e7?! 19. ♘a6 △ ♘c7]

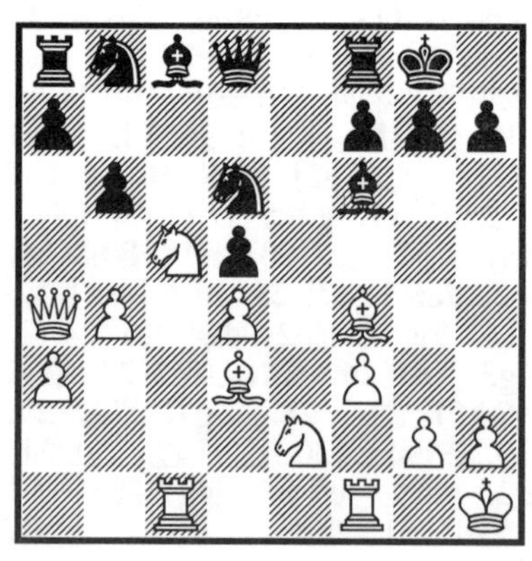

19. ♖fd1!? [△ ♘c3; 19. ♘a6? ♘a6 20. ♗a6 ♗a6 21. ♕a6 ♘c4∓; 19. ♗d6?! ♕d6 20. ♘e4 de4 21. ♗e4 ♗d7 22. b5 ♖e8□ 23. ♖fe1 ♖e4 24. fe4∞; 19. ♘b3 ♘c4!? 20. ♗c4 dc4 21. ♖c4 ♕d5⩱; 19. ♕c2!? bc5 20. dc5 ♘e8 21. ♗h7 ♔h8 22. ♗d3⩱; 19. ♘e4!? de4 20. fe4⩱] **bc5 20. dc5 ♘f5 21. c6⩱ ♕e7!** [21... ♕e8 22. b5 △ 22... ♗e6? 23. g4 ♘h4 24. g5±] **22. ♕b5** [22. c7? ♘d7 23. ♗f5 ♘b6!∓; 22. ♖e1 ♗e6∞; 22. b5∞] **♘c6?!** [22... ♗a6? 23. ♕d5 ♗d3 24. c7±; 22... ♗e6! 23. ♕b7 (23. c7 ♘d7 24. ♗f5 ♗f5 25. ♕d5 ♘b6 26. ♕f5 ♕e2∓) ♘c6 24. ♕c6 ♖fc8∞] **23. ♕c6 ♗e6** [23... ♗b7 24. ♕b5] **24. ♗a6** [24. ♗f5 ♖ac8! (24... ♗f5? 25. ♘g3±) 25. ♗c7 (25. ♕b5 ♗f5 26. ♕d5 ♕e2 27. ♕f5 ♖c1 28. ♖c1 ♗b2∞) ♗f5 26. ♘f4 ♗e6 27. ♘d5 ♗d5 28. ♖d5 ♗b2 29. ♖d7 ♕e3∞] **♖ad8∞ 25. ♖c2??** [25. ♖d2] **♗d7!∓ 26. ♕c5** [26. ♕b7 ♗a4 27. ♖c7 ♕e6 28. ♖d2 g5! 29. ♗g3 ♖b8 30. ♕a7 ♖a8−+] **♗a4 27. ♖cd2 ♗d1 28. ♖d1 ♕e6?!⊕** [28... ♖fe8 29. ♗b5 ♘d4!∓] **29. ♗d3 a6?!** [29... ♗e7!] **30. ♗c7 ♖c8??** [30... ♘e3! 31. ♘f4 ♕c8! 32. ♖c1 (32. ♗d8? ♕c5 33. bc5 ♘d1 34. ♗f6 ♘f2 35. ♔g1 ♘d3−+) ♖d7 33. ♕e3 (33. ♕c6? ♕c7! 34. ♕c7 ♖c7 35. ♖c7 ♗e5−+) ♖c7 34. ♖c7 ♕c7 35. ♘d5 ♕d6∓; 30... ♗e7! 31. ♗f5 ♕f5! (31... ♕e2? 32. ♕g1∞) 32. ♕e7 ♖de8 33. ♕d6 ♖e2 34. ♕a6 ♖g2!−+; ⌓ 31. ♕a5] **31. ♘f4± ♕d7 32. ♘d5 ♖c7□ 33. ♘c7 ♖d8?!** [33... ♖c8 34. ♕f5 ♕f5 35. ♗f5 ♖c7 36. ♔g1±] **34. ♘a6±** [34. g4 ♕a4□ △ 35. ♕c2? ♕c2 36. ♗c2 ♘e3!∓] **♕a4 35. ♖e1!** [35. ♕c2 ♕a3 36. ♗f5 (36. b5? ♘e3 37. ♗h7 ♔h8 38. ♖d8 ♗d8 39. ♕b1 g6∓) ♖d1 37. ♕d1 ♕a6±] **g6□** [35... ♖d3?? 36. ♕c2!+−] **36. ♗f5⊕** [36. b5?? ♕h4∓; 36. ♕b5! ♕a3 37. ♗f5 gf5 38. ♘c5±] **♕a6 37. ♗e4** [37. b5?? ♕a5−+] **♕a3 38. ♖b1?** [38. ♗d5±] **♖d2!↑ 39. ♕c1 ♕a2 40. f4 ♖d4 41. ♗f3?** [41. ♕c2=] **♖f4!∓ 42. ♗d5! ♕f2 43. g3 ♖f5** [43... ♖d4 44. ♕f1 ♕c2!?] **44. ♗e4?** [44. ♗g2 △ 45. ♕c8 ♔g7 46. ♖f1] **♕e2! 45. ♗g2□** [45. ♕c2?? ♖f1−+; 45. ♕e1?? ♖f1!−+] **h5** [45... ♖f2 46. ♕c6∞] **46. ♕e1 ♕a2** [46... ♕b5!? 47. ♕e4 h4 48. gh4 ♖h5] **47. ♕e4 ♔g7 48. ♖f1= ♖f1 1/2 : 1/2** **[Hertneck]**

397. **D 31**

SAFIN 2455 − NENAŠEV 2565

Biškek (zt) 1993

1. d4 d5 2. c4 e6 3. ♘c3 ♗b4 4. cd5 ed5 5. ♗f4 ♘f6 6. e3 ♘e4 N 7. ♕c2 [7. ♖c1!] **c5 8. ♗d3 cd4 9. ed4** [9. ♗e4?! dc3 10. bc3 ♕f6! 11. ♖c1 ♗a3! 12. ♕a4 ♘c6 13. ♕a3 de4∓] **♗f5** [9... 0−0?! 10. f3] **10. ♘e2** [10. ♗b8 ♗c3 11. bc3 ♖b8 12. ♘e2 (12. f3? ♕h4) ♕d7=] **0−0** [10... ♘c6 11. 0−0 ♘c3 12. ♗f5 ♘e2 13. ♕e2 ♗e7 (13... ♕e7 14. ♕d3 g6 15. a3±) 14. ♖fd1±] **11. 0−0** [11. f3 ♘c3 12. bc3 ♗d3 13. ♕d3 ♗e7 14. ♗b8 ♖b8 15. 0−0 ♗d6∓] **♖e8** [11... ♘c3 12. bc3 ♗d3 13. ♕d3 ♗e7 14. ♕b5 ♕d7 15. ♖ab1±] **12. ♘b5 ♘a6□ 13. a3** [13. f3 ♘d6 14. ♗f5 ♘f5 15. ♕f5 ♖e2 16. ♕d3 ♖e8 (16... ♖b2? 17. ♗c1) 17. a3 ♗f8 18. ♘c3 ♕d7=] **♗f8 14. f3** [14. ♖fe1!?] **♘d6 15. ♘ec3** [15. ♗f5; 15. ♘d6=] **♘b5 16. ♘b5** [16. ♗f5? ♘d4 17. ♗h7 ♔h8 18. ♕d3 ♕h4−+] **♖c8 17. ♕b1 ♗d3 18. ♕d3 ♕b6 19. ♖ac1 ♘b8 20. ♗c7?** [20. ♖c8? ♖c8 21. ♕f5 ♖e8 22. ♕d5 a6∓; 20. ♘c7 ♖ed8 21. ♘d5 ♕b2 22. ♖c8 ♖c8 23. ♖b1 ♕a3 (23... ♕a2 24. ♖b7 △ 24... ♖c2? 25. ♘e3+−) 24. ♕a3 (24. ♕f5 ♖d8 25. ♖b7 ♕a1 26. ♔f2 ♕d4 27. ♘e3 ♘d7∓) ♗a3 25. ♖a1! ♗f8 (25... ♗b2? 26. ♘e7 ♔f8 27. ♘c8 ♗a1 28. ♗b8 ♗d4 29. ♔f1) 26. ♖a7 ♘c6 27. ♖b7 ♘d4=] **♕h6 21. g3** [21. ♘a7? ♖c7 22. ♖c7 ♗d6−+] **♘c6** [21... a6? 22. ♘a7±] **22. ♗f4 ♕f6 23. ♖cd1 a6 24. ♘c3 ♖ed8** [24... ♘d4? 25. ♘d5=] **25. ♔h1⊕ h6 26. ♘a4?!** [26. ♖fe1 ♘a5 △ ♘c4∓] **♘a5 27. b4? ♘c4 28. ♕b3 b6 29. ♘c3 b5 30. ♖d3 ♕c6 31. ♘d1 a5 32. ba5 ♖a8−+ 33. ♗d2 ♘d2 34. ♖d2 ♖a5 35. ♘b2 ♖a3 36. ♕d1 ♗b4 37. ♖d3 ♗c3 38. ♕c1 b4 39. ♘d1 ♕c4 40. ♕c2 ♖a2 41. ♕b1 ♖a1 42. ♕c2 ♖da8 0 : 1** **[Nenašev]**

398. **D 31**

KASPAROV 2805 − JUSUPOV 2645

Linares 1993

1. d4 d5 2. c4 e6 3. ♘c3 ♗e7 4. cd5 ed5 5. ♗f4 ♘f6 6. e3 ♗f5 7. ♘ge2 0−0 8.

♘**g3 N** [8. ♖c1 — 44/477] ♗**e6** [8... ♗g6?! 9. h4 h6 10. h5 ♗h7 11. ♗d3 ×f5] **9. ♗d3 c5 10. dc5** [10. ♘f5 ♗f5 11. ♗f5 cd4 12. ed4 ♘c6∞ ×d4] ♗**c5 11. 0–0** ♘**c6 12.** ♖**c1** ♗**d6** [12... d4!? 13. ♘b5 ♗b6 14. e4∞] **13.** ♘**h5!** ♗**e7!** [13... ♘h5? 14. ♗d6 ♕d6 15. ♕h5 g6 16. ♕h4 ♕e5 17. ♗b5! △ 17... d4? 18. ♘e4 ♕b5 19. ♖c5 ♕b2 20. ♘f6 ♔g7 21. ♘h5!+–] **14.** ♘**b5!**□ [14. ♗g5 d4!=] ♘**h5?!** [14... a6!? 15. ♘d4 (15. ♘f6 ♗f6 16. ♘d6 ♕d7∞) ♘d4 16. ed4 ♖c8 17. ♖c8 ♕c8 18. ♗e5?! ♗g4!; 18. ♖e1±; 14... ♖c8!?] **15.** ♕**h5 g6 16.** ♕**f3** ♖**c8?!** [16... a6 17. ♘d4±] **17.** ♖**fd1** ♕**d7** [17... a6 18. ♘c3!] **18. h3** [18. ♕g3!?] ♖**fd8 19.** ♕**g3** [19. ♗f1] ♘**b4 20.** ♘**c3** [20. ♗f1?! ♘a2 21. ♖a1 a6! △ 22. ♘a7 ♖a8] ♘**d3 21.** ♖**d3** ♗**f5** [21... b5? 22. a3! a5 23. ♖cd1! b4 24. ab4 ab4 25. ♘d5! ♗d5 26. e4+–] **22.** ♖**d2** [22. e4? ♗e4 23. ♘e4 ♖c1 24. ♗c1 ♕e6! 25. ♘c3 ♕e1 26. ♔h2 ♕c1 27. ♘d5 ♕c5=] ♕**e6 23.** ♖**cd1 h5 24. h4?!** [24. ♘d5 ♖d5 25. ♖d5 h4 26. ♕f3 ♗e4 27. ♖e5!] ♖**c5 25. f3** ♕**c6 26. e4?** [26. ♗e5!] ♖**c3!** [26... ♗e6? 27. ♗g5+–] **27. bc3** ♕**b6 28.** ♔**h2 de4 29.** ♖**d8** [29. ♗c7 ♖d2 30. ♗b6 ♖d1 31. ♗d4 f6∞ △ 32. fe4 ♗e4 33. ♕c7 ♔f8 34. ♕f4 f5 35. ♕h6 ♔e8 36. ♕g6 ♔d7⇆] ♗**d8 30.** ♗**e3?!** [30. ♖d6?! ♕a5 31. fe4 ♗e4 32. ♕e3 ♗c6□ 33. ♕d4 ♗c7=; 30. fe4 ♗e4 31. ♕e3 ♗c6 32. ♕b6! (32. ♕e5 ♔h7∞) ♗b6 33. ♗e5] ♕**a5 31.** ♕**b8** ♕**c7 32.** ♕**c7** ♗**c7 33.** ♔**g1 ef3 34. gf3** [34. ♗a7∞] **b6 35.** ♔**f2** [35. ♖d4!? ♔f8 36. ♖a4! a5! (36... ♗b8? 37. ♗b6 ab6 38. ♖a8) 37. ♗f4 ♗d8 38. ♗g5 ♗d7 39. ♖c4∞] ♔**f8 36.** ♖**d4** ♔**e7?!** [36... ♔e8!±] **37.** ♗**f4** ♗**f4 38.** ♖**f4** [♖ 2/j] ♔**d6 39.** ♔**e3** ♔**c5 40.** ♖**d4** ♗**e6 41. a3 a5 42.** ♔**e4 b5** [42... f6 43. f4 ♗f5 44. ♔e3 b5 45. ♔d2 a4 46. ♔c1!+–] **43.** ♔**e5 a4 44. f4** ♔**c6 45.** ♔**f6** ♔**c5 46.** ♖**b4** ♗**c4!**□ [46... ♔c6? 47. f5! ♗f5 48. c4+–] **47.** ♔**e7** ♗**e6 48.** ♖**e4** ♔**d5 49.** ♖**d4** [49. ♖e5?! ♔c4 50. ♔d6 ♔b3 51. ♖b5 ♔a3 52. ♔c5 ♗b3 53. ♖a5 ♗d1!□ 54. ♔b5 ♔b3 (54... ♔b2? 55. ♔b4+–) 55. ♖a4 ♔c3=] ♔**c6 50.** ♔**d8** ♗**f5 51.** ♔**e8** ♗**e6 52.** ♔**f8** ♔**c5 53.** ♔**g7** ♔**c6 54.** ♔**g8** ♔**c5 55.** ♔**f8** ♔**c6 56.** ♔**g7** ♔**c5 57.** ♔**h8** ♔**c6 58.** ♔**h7** ♔**c5 59.** ♔**h6** ♗**f5 60.** ♔**g5** ♗**e6 61.** ♔**f6** ♔**c6 62. f5** ♗**f5 63.** ♔**f7** ♔**c5 64.** ♔**f6** ♗**c2 65.** ♔**e7** ♗**f5 66.** ♔**d8** ♔**c6 67.** ♖**f4** ♔**d6 68.** ♖**b4** ♔**c5 69.** ♔**c7** ♗**d3 70.** ♖**d4** ♗**e2 71.** ♔**b7** ♗**f1 72.** ♔**a7** ♗**e2 73.** ♖**e4** ♗**d3** [73... ♗c4?? 74. ♔a6!+– b4 75. ♖c4 ♔c4 76. cb4 g5 77. hg5 h4 78. g6 h3 79. g7 h2 80. g8♕] **74.** ♖**b4** ♗**c4 75.** ♔**a6** ♔**d5 76.** ♔**a5** ♔**e5** [76... ♔c5 77. ♖b1 ♗d3 78. ♖b2!+–⊙] **77.** ♖**b1 g5?** [77... ♔f4 78. ♖g1 ♗d3 79. ♔b4 ♔f3 80. c4!? (80. ♔c5 ♔f2 81. ♖g5 ♔f3) ♗c4! (80... bc4? 81. ♔a4 ♔e3 82. ♔b4 ♔d2 83. ♖g2 ♗e2 84. a4! c3 85. ♖e2 ♔e2 86. ♔c3 g5 87. hg5 h4 88. g6 h3 89. g7 h2 90. g8♕ h1♕ 91. ♕g4! ♔f2 92. ♕f4 ♔e2 93. ♕d2+–) 81. ♖g6 ♔f4 82. ♖g5 ♗e2 83. ♔c5 ♗g4 84. ♔d4 ♔g3 85. ♔e3 ♔h4 86. ♔f4 ♗d7! (86... ♔h3 87. ♖b5 ♔g2) 87. ♖c5 ♗e8! 88. ♖c3! ♗f7 89. ♖c2 ♔h3 90. ♖c5 *a)* 90... h4? 91. ♖b5 ♔g2 92. ♖b2 ♔g1 (92... ♔f1 93. ♖h2 ♔e1 94. ♔e3+–) 93. ♔g4 ♔f1 94. ♔h4 ♔e1 95. ♔g4 ♔d1 96. ♔f4 ♗b3 97. ♔e3 ♔c1 98. ♖h2 ♗c2 99. ♔d4 ♔b2 100. ♔c4?? ♔a3 101. ♖c2=; 100. ♖g2!+–; *b)* 90... ♗c4! 91. ♖h5 ♔g2 92. ♔e3 ♔f1 93. ♖g5 ♗e2 94. ♔d2 ♗c4 95. ♖f5 ♔g1! 96. ♔e3 ♔g2=] **78. hg5** [♖ 2/h] ♔**f5 79.** ♖**g1** ♔**g6 80.** ♔**b4 h4 81.** ♔**c5 h3 82.** ♔**d4!** [82. ♖h1? ♗e6 83. ♔b5 ♔g5 84. ♔a4 ♔g4 85. ♔b5 ♗d5! 86. ♖h3 ♔h3 87. c4 ♗a8 88. c5 ♔g4 89. c6 ♔f5 90. c7 ♗b7 91. ♔b6 ♗c8 92. a4 ♔e6 93. a5 ♔d7=] ♗**e6**□ [82... ♔f5 83. ♖g3+–; 82... ♔h5 83. g6 ♔h4 84. g7 h2 85. g8♕!+–] **83.** ♔**e5** ♗**d7 84.** ♔**f4** ♗**c6 85.** ♔**g3** ♔**g5 86.** ♖**d1** [86. ♔h3? ♔f4 87. ♖g4 ♔e3 88. c4 ♗d7 89. cb5?? ♔f3!–+; 86. ♖e1? ♔f5! (86... h2? 87. ♔h2 ♔f4 88. ♔g1 ♔f3 89. ♖e5+–) 87. ♔h3 ♔f4 88. ♔h2 ♗e4 89. ♔g1 ♔f3=; 86. ♖f1! ♗d7 87. ♖f8! ♗e6 88. ♖b8 ♗c4 89. ♖e8!+– △ 89... ♗f1 90. ♖e1] **h2!** [86... ♔f5 87. ♖d4 ♗g2 88. ♖b4+–] **87.** ♔**h2** ♔**f4 88. c4!** [88. ♔g1? ♔e3 89. ♔f1 ♗e4 90. ♖d8 ♗d3 91. ♔e1 ♗c4!=] **bc4 89.** ♖**d4** ♔**e5 90.** ♖**c4+–** [♖ 2/g1] ♔**d5 91.** ♖**b4** ♔**c5 92.** ♔**g3** ♗**b5 93.** ♔**f4** ♔**b6 94.** ♔**e3** ♔**a5** [94... ♔c5 95. ♔d2 ♗e8 96. ♔c3 ♗b5 97. ♖g4 ♗c6 98. ♖c4! ♔d5

(98... ♔b5 99. ♔d4) 99. ♔b4 ♗d7 100. ♖c5 ♔d6 101. ♖a5 ♗e8 102. ♔c3 ♔c7 103. ♔d4 ♔b6 (103... ♔d6 104. ♖a6 ♗c6 105. ♔c4 ♔c7 106. ♔c5) 104. ♖c5!] **95. ♔d4 ♗e2 96. ♖b1 ♗h5 97. ♖e1 ♗f7 98. ♔c5 ♗b3 99. ♖e8 ♔a6 100. ♔c6 ♔a7 101. ♔b5** [101. ♖c8; 101. ♖d8] **♔b7 102. ♖e7??** [102. ♖d8! ♔c7 103. ♖d3 ♔b7 104. ♖c3 ♗d1 105. ♔a5 ♗b3 106. ♖c1 ♔a7 107. ♖c7 ♔b8 108. ♔b6 ♗a2 (108... ♗d1 109. ♖d7) 109. ♖h7 ♔c8 110. ♖h4 ♗b3 111. ♖d4+−] **♔c8 103. ♔c6 ♔d8 104. ♖d7 ♔e8!= 105. ♔c7 ♗c2 106. ♖d2 ♗b3 107. ♖e2 ♔f7 108. ♔d6 ♗c4 109. ♖e7 ♔f8 110. ♖e4 ♗b3 111. ♔d7 ♔f7 112. ♖f4 ♔g6 113. ♔d6 ♔g5 114. ♔e5 ♔g6 115. ♖f3 ♔g7 116. ♖f6 ♗c4 117. ♔f5 ♗b3 118. ♔g5 ♗c2** **1/2 : 1/2**
[Kasparov]

399. **D 32**

BAREEV 2670 − LJUBOJEVIĆ 2605
Linares 1993

1. d4 d5 2. c4 e6 3. ♘c3 c5 4. cd5 cd4 5. ♕a4 b5 N [5... ♗d7 − 50/(423)] **6. ♕d4 ♘c6** [6... b4? 7. ♘b5 a6 (7... ed5 8. ♕d5+−) 8. de6+−] **7. ♕d2 ed5 8. ♕d5 ♗d7 9. ♕e4?** [9. ♗g5 ♘f6 10. ♗f6 ♕f6 11. e3±] **♗e7 10. ♗g5 h6 11. ♗e7 ♘ge7=∞ 12. e3 ♗f5 13. ♕f4 a6** [13... g5! 14. ♕g3 a6] **14. ♘f3** [14. g4!] **g5!** [14... ♕a5 15. ♘d4! △ 15... ♘d4 16. ♕d4 ♖d8 17. b4 ♕a3 18. ♘b5 ab5 19. ♗b5 ♗d7 20. ♖d1+−] **15. ♕g3 ♕a5 16. ♗e2 b4!** [16... ♕b4 17. 0-0-0! (17. 0−0 ♕b2 △ b4) ♕a5 18. ♘e5!±] **17. ♘d1□ ♗e6! 18. ♘d4□ ♘d4 19. ed4 ♘f5** [19... ♖d8 20. ♕e5=] **20. ♕e5 ♕e5 21. de5 ♔e7= 22. ♗d3! ♖hd8** [22... ♘d4=∞] **23. ♗f5 ♗f5 24. ♘e3 ♔e6** [24... ♗d3!?] **25. 0−0 ♔e5?** [25... ♖d2 26. ♖fc1!±; 25... ♗d3 26. ♖fd1 ♖ac8 27. a3 b3=] **26. f4± gf4 27. ♘c4 ♔f6** [27... ♔d4 28. ♖f4 ♗e4 29. ♖e1 f5 30. ♘e3 ♔e5 31. g3 ♔f6 32. ♖ef1±] **28. ♖f4 ♔g5 29. ♖af1 ♗d3** [29... ♗e6 30. ♘e5 f5 31. ♘f7!±] **30. h4 ♔h5 31. ♖1f3 f5** [31... ♗c4□] **32. ♘e5 ♗e4 33. ♔h2! ♖g8 34. ♔h3 ♗f3 35. ♖f5 ♖g5 36. hg5** **1 : 0** **[Bareev]**

400. **D 34**

KORTCHNOI 2605 − JE. PIKET 2590
Nijmegen (m/3) 1993

1. d4 d5 2. c4 e6 3. ♘f3 c5 4. cd5 ed5 5. g3 ♘c6 6. ♗g2 ♘f6 7. 0−0 ♗e7 8. ♘c3 0−0 9. ♗g5 ♗e6 10. dc5 ♗c5 11. ♖c1 ♗b6 12. b3 d4 [12... ♘b4 13. a3 d4 14. ♘e4 ♘a2 15. ♗f6 gf6 16. ♕d2 ♘c1 17. ♕h6 ♘e2 18. ♔h1 ♔h8 19. ♘f6 ♗f5 20. ♘g5+−; 12... h6 13. ♗f6 ♕f6 14. ♘d5 ♗d5 15. ♕d5 ♕b2 16. ♕d2 ♕a3 (16... ♕d2 17. ♘d2 ♘d4) 17. e3 ♖ad8 18. ♕e2; 12... ♖c8 13. ♗f6 ♕f6 14. ♘d5 ♗d5 15. ♕d5 ♕b2 16. ♕d2 ♕d2 17. ♘d2 ♘d4 18. ♗f3⩲; 12... ♖e8 13. e3 ♘b4 14. a3 ♘c6 15. b4] **13. ♘e4 ♕e7 14. ♘h4 N** [14. ♘f6] **♔h8** [14... ♘e5!?] **15. ♗f6 gf6 16. ♕d2 ♘e5□** [16... f5? 17. ♕h6 fe4 18. ♗e4 f5 19. ♘g6+−] **17. ♕h6** [17. ♕f4 ♘g6 18. ♕f6 ♕f6 19. ♘f6 ♘h4 20. gh4 ♗d8=∞] **♘g6 18. ♕h5!** [×f5] **♖ad8 19. ♘f5 ♗f5 20. ♕f5 ♔g7 21. a4! ♕e5** [21... ♕e6 22. ♕e6 fe6 23. b4 f5 24. a5±] **22. ♕f3** [22. ♕e5 fe5 (22... ♘e5 23. b4 a5) 23. b4 d3] **♖fe8 23. b4 f5 24. ♘g5** [24. ♘c5!? ♗c5 25. ♖c5 ♕e2 26. ♕e2 ♖e2 27. ♗b7 △ ♗f3; 26. ♕b7] **♖d7** [24... h6 25. ♘f7 (25. ♘h3 ♖d7⩲) ♔f7 26. a5 ♗c7 27. ♖c5 (27. ♕b7 ♖e7 28. ♖c5 ♗d6!=∞ Kortchnoi) ♕e7 28. ♕f5 ♔g7 29. h4!↑] **25. ♕h5 h6** [⌓ 25... ♕e2 26. ♕h7 ♔f6 27. ♕h6 (27. ♗f3 ♕d2; 27. ♗b7 ♔g5) ♖h8 (27... d3? 28. ♘h7 △ ♕g5, ♘f6+−) 28. ♘h7 ♖h7 29. ♕h7 d3=∞ △ 30. a5 d2 31. ab6 dc1♕ 32. ♖c1 ♖d1 33. ♖d1 ♕d1 34. ♗f1 ab6 35. h4!±; 30... ♗d4! △ 31. a6 d2] **26. ♘f3 ♕e6 27. a5 ♗d8 28. ♖c2 ♗f6?⊕** [28... d3□ 29. ed3 ♖d3 30. ♖fc1⩲] **29. ♘e1± ♖de7 30. ♘d3 b6 31. ♗h3 ♕b3** [31... ♕d5 32. ♖fc1⊙] **32. ♖fc1 ♕d5 33. ♖c7** [33. ♗f5? ♖e5∓; 33. ♗g2 ♕e6 34. ♗f3⊙] **♗g5** [⌓ 33... ♖c7 34. ♖c7 ♖e7] **34. f4!+− ♖c7 35. ♖c7 ♗d8 36. ♖a7 ba5 37. ♗f5 ♘e7 38. ♕g4 ♔h8 39. ♗d7 ♖g8 40. ♕h3 ♔h7 41. ba5 ♕e4 42. ♕h5 ♕e3 43. ♔f1** **1 : 0**
[Je. Piket]

401. **D 34**

AN. KARPOV 2725 – ILLESCAS CÓRDOBA 2615

León 1993

1. c4 c5 2. ♘f3 ♘f6 3. ♘c3 e6 4. g3 d5 5. cd5 ed5 6. d4 ♘c6 7. ♗g2 ♗e7 8. 0–0 0–0 9. ♗g5 cd4 10. ♘d4 h6 11. ♗e3 ♖e8 12. ♖c1 ♗f8 13. a3 N [13. ♘c6 – 56/(442)] **♗g4 14. h3 ♗e6** [14... ♗h5?! 15. ♘b3; 15. ♘c2] **15. ♘c6!? bc6 16. ♗d4! ♗d7!?** [16... ♘d7 17. e4 c5 18. ed5 cd4 19. de6+–; 16... c5 17. ♗f6 ♕f6 18. ♘d5 ♕b2 19. ♕a4±; 16... ♘e4 17. ♘e4 de4 18. ♗c5 ♗c5 19. ♖c5 ♗d5 20. b4±] **17. ♕d3 ♘h7 18. ♗e3!** [18. ♘a4 ♘g5 19. ♔h2 ♘e4⇆] **♗d6** [18... ♘g5 19. ♗g5 ♕g5 20. e4±; 18... ♘f6 19. ♖fd1±] **19. ♖fd1 ♗e6** [19... ♘f8 20. ♘d5 cd5 21. ♕d5 ♗e5 22. ♕a8 ♕a8 23. ♗a8 ♖a8 24. ♗d4 ♗d4 25. ♖d4 ♗h3 26. g4 h5□ 27. gh5±] **20. b4! ♘f8** [20... ♕d7 21. b5±; 20... a5 21. b5! ♗a3 22. bc6 ♗c1 23. ♖c1±] **21. ♘a4 ♘g6 22. ♕c3! ♗d7 23. ♘c5 ♗c5 24. ♗c5!± ♖e2 25. ♗e3! ♕e7 26. ♗f1 ♖e3 27. ♕e3 ♕e3 28. fe3 ♖e8 29. ♔f2 ♘e5 30. ♖c5 ♖e7 31. e4 ♗e6 32. b5 cb5 33. ed5 ♗d7 34. d6 ♖e6 35. ♗b5 ♖f6 36. ♔g2 1 : 0**
[An. Karpov]

402.** **!N** **D 35**

EPIŠIN 2620 – ĖJNGORN 2575

Bern 1993

1. d4 ♘f6 2. c4 e6 3. ♘f3 d5 4. ♘c3 ♘bd7 [RR 4... ♗e7 5. cd5 ed5 6. ♗f4 0–0 7. e3 ♗f5 8. ♕b3 ♘c6 *a)* 9. a3 a6!? N (9... ♖b8 – 52/395) 10. ♕b7 ♘a5 11. ♕c7 ♕c7 12. ♗c7 ♘b3 13. ♖d1 ♗c2 14. ♗e2 ♗a3!∓ Illescas Córdoba 2615 – Milos 2560, Buenos Aires 1993; *b)* 9. ♖c1 N ♘a5 10. ♕a4 c6 11. ♗e2 ♘h5? 12. ♗c7 ♕c7 13. ♘d5 ♕d8 14. ♘e7 ♕e7 15. ♕a5 g6 16. ♘e5± Thorsteins 2480 – Marciano 2430, Ísland – France 1993] **5. cd5 ed5 6. ♗f4 ♘b6 7. ♕c2 g6 8. h3! N** [8. e3 – 46/(526)] **♗f5 9. ♕b3 c6 10. e3 ♗g7 11. ♗e2 ♗e4** [11... 0–0 12. 0–0 a5 13. a4 ♖a7 14. ♘e5 ♘c8 15. g4 ♗e6 16. ♕c2 ♘d6 17. ♗d3±] **12. 0–0 ♗f3 13. ♗f3 0–0 14. a4 a5 15. ♘e2!** [△ ♘c1-d3] **♖a7 16. ♘c1 ♘e4 17. ♖d1** [17. ♗e4 de4 18. ♗g5 ♕g5 (18... ♕c7 19. ♘e2 ♘d5 20. ♘c3±) 19. ♕b6 ♖fa8 20. ♘e2 ♕e7 21. ♘c3 ♖a6=] **♘d7?** [17... ♖e8 18. ♘d3 ♘c4 19. ♕c2 △ b3±] **18. ♗e4! de4 19. ♘e2 ♖e8 20. ♘c3 ♕e7 21. ♖ac1 ♘f6** [21... ♕b4 22. ♕c2 ♘f6 23. ♗e5±] **22. d5± ♕b4 23. ♕a2 ♖aa8** [23... cd5 24. ♘d5 ♘d5 25. ♖d5 ♕b2 26. ♕b2 ♗b2 27. ♖c7+–] **24. ♖d4! ♕b6 25. dc6 bc6 26. ♖d6! ♖ed8!** [26... ♖ad8 27. ♘b5! ♖d6 28. ♘d6 ♖f8 29. ♗e5+–; 26... ♕b7 27. ♖cd1±] **27. ♖cd1 ♖d6 28. ♖d6 ♖d8 29. ♖d8 ♕d8 30. ♕c4 ♘d5 31. ♕c6** [31. ♘d5 ♕d5 32. ♕d5 cd5 33. ♗c7 ♗b2 34. ♗a5 ♔f8=] **♘f4 32. ef4 f5?** [32... ♗c3 33. bc3 f5 34. ♕c4 ♔g7 35. ♕e2!±] **33. ♘d5!+– ♗b2 34. g4 ♔h8 35. ♕e6 ♕g8 36. ♕d7 fg4 37. hg4 ♕f8 38. ♔g2 h5 39. g5! ♗g7 40. ♕e6 ♔h7 41. ♘e7 ♕e8 42. f5 gf5 43. ♕f5 ♔h8 44. ♕e4 1 : 0 [Epišin]**

403.** **D 35**

SKOMOROHIN 2445 – SE. IVANOV 2500

Katowice 1993

1. d4 d5 2. c4 e6 3. ♘c3 ♘f6 4. cd5 ed5 5. ♗g5 c6 [RR 5... ♘bd7 6. e3 ♗e7 7. ♗d3 0–0 8. ♕c2 b6 N (8... ♖e8 – 48/534) 9. ♘ge2 ♗b7 10. 0–0 c5 11. dc5 bc5 12. ♖fd1 (Y. Zilberman 2510 – V. Mikhalevski 2305, Haifa 1993) h6 *a)* 13. ♗f6 ♘f6 14. e4 (14. ♗c4? ♗d6! △ 15. ♕b3? ♖b8–+) d4 15. ♘a4 ♖c8 16. b3 (△ ♘b2-c4) ♘g4! 17. h3 (17. ♘b2? ♗d6 18. h3 ♕h4 19. hg4 ♕h2 20. ♔f1 ♕h1 21. ♘g1 ♗h2 22. ♔e2 ♕g2 23. ♘f3 ♕g4→) ♘e5∓; *b)* 13. ♗h4 ♕a5 14. ♗f5 ♘b6∞ J. Kagan, V. Mikhalevski] **6. e3 ♕b6 7. ♕c2** [7. ♗d3 N ♕b2 8. ♘ge2 ♗e7 9. 0–0 0–0 10. e4 de4 11. ♘e4 ♘bd7 12. ♘2g3=∞ R. Ščerbakov 2530 – Se. Ivanov 2470, Podol'sk 1992] **♘e4 8. ♗h4 N** [8. ♘e4?! de4 9. ♕e4 ♗e6 10. 0-0-0□ ♕a5

11. ♘f3 ♕a2 12. d5 cd5 13. ♗c4 ♕a1 14. ♔c2 ♘c6!∓; 8. ♗f4 — 48/(525)] **♘a6** [8... ♗f5 9. ♗d3 ♘a6] **9. ♘e4** [9. ♗a6 ♕a6 10. ♘e4 de4 11. ♕e4 ♗e6 12. ♘e2 ♗b4 13. ♘c3 0–0 14. f3 ♖fe8=∞; 9. a3 ♗f5 10. ♗d3 ♕a5 11. ♖c1 ♘c3 12. ♕c3 ♕c3 13. ♖c3 ♗d3 14. ♖d3 ♗d6=; 11. ♖a2!?] **♘b4** [9... de4 10. ♕e4 ♗e6 11. 0-0-0 ♘b4 12. ♗c4±] **10. ♕b1** [10. ♘f6? gf6 11. ♕b3 (11. ♕b1 ♕a5↑) ♗f5 12. ♖c1 ♕a5∓] **de4 11. ♕e4 ♗e6 12. ♘h3?!** [12. ♘e2 ♕a5 13. ♘c3 g5! 14. ♗g3 ♗e7 (△ ♗f5) 15. ♕b1 (15. ♗d3 ♗d5 16. ♕f5 ♘d3 17. ♕d3 ♗g2) ♘d5↑; 12. ♗c4 *a)* 12... ♘c2 13. ♔d1! (13. ♕c2 ♕b4 14. ♕c3 ♗c4 15. ♕b4 ♗b4 16. ♔d1 ♗f1! 17. ♘e2 ♗g2 18. ♖g1 ♗e4 19. ♖g7 ♗g6 20. ♗f6∞) ♘a1 (13... ♕b2 14. ♖c1!+–) 14. ♗e6 f6 15. ♔c1±; *b)* 12... ♘d5 13. 0-0-0 ♕b4! 14. ♕d3 (14. ♕c2 ♘e3; 14. ♗b3 a5; 14. ♗d5 cd5 15. ♕d3 g6 16. f3 ♗h6 17. ♔b1 0–0=∞) ♘f4 (14... ♘e3!? 15. ♗e6 ♘d1 16. ♗b3 ♗e7∞) 15. ef4 ♕c4 16. ♕c4 ♗c4 17. ♖e1 ♔d7 18. ♘f3 f6=; 12. ♘f3!? ♘d5 (12... ♕a5 13. ♘d2 g5! 14. ♗g3 ♗e7↑; 13. ♗c4!) 13. ♕c2 (13. 0-0-0 ♕a5) ♕a5 14. ♘d2 c5∞] **♘a2!** [12... ♕a5 13. ♗c4!; 12... ♘d5 13. 0-0-0 ♕a5∞] **13. ♗d3□** [13. ♖a2? ♕b4 14. ♔d1 (14. ♔e2 ♕c4–+) ♕b3–+; 13. ♗e2? ♕b2 14. ♖b1 ♕e2! 15. ♔e2 ♘c3 16. ♔f3 ♘e4 17. ♔e4 ♗d5 18. ♔d3 ♗g2–+] **♕b4 14. ♔e2** [14. ♔f1 ♕b2 15. ♖b1 ♕d2 (△ ♘c3) 16. ♖b7?? ♕d1#] **♕b2 15. ♔f3 ♗e7!** [15... ♘c3 16. ♕e5∞] **16. ♖hb1 ♕d2 17. ♖b7** [17. ♘f4 ♗h4 18. ♘e6 ♕f2 19. ♔g4 ♘c3∓; 17. ♖d1 ♕d1! 18. ♖d1 ♗d5 19. ♗e7 ♗e4 20. ♗e4 ♘c3∓] **♗d5 18. ♕d5** [18. ♗e7 ♕d3!; 18. ♖e7 ♔f8 19. ♖f7 ♔f7 20. ♗c4 ♗c4 21. ♘g5 ♔g8–+] **cd5 19. ♗b5 ♔f8 20. ♗e7 ♔g8∓** [×♔f3] **21. ♘f4** [21. ♘g5 (△ ♘f7) ♕c2!; 21. ♗c6!?] **h5 22. ♗d3?** [22. ♘d5 ♖h6∓; 22... ♔h7∓] **♘c1!–+ 23. ♖aa7** [23. ♗b4 ♕d1 24. ♗e2 ♕c2] **♘d3 24. ♖a8 ♔h7 25. ♖h8 ♔h8 26. ♘d3** [26. ♘e2 ♘e1; 26. ♗h4 ♕d1; 26. ♖b8 ♔h7 27. ♘d5 ♕d1 28. ♔e4 ♘f2 29. ♔e5 ♕g4] **♕d1 27. ♔f4 ♕g4 28. ♔e5 ♕e6** [29. ♔f4 ♕e4 30. ♔g5 ♕g4#]

0 : 1 **[Se. Ivanov]**

404.* **D 36**

BELJAVSKIJ 2610 – IVANČUK 2710

Linares 1993

1. d4 ♘f6 2. c4 e6 3. ♘f3 d5 4. ♘c3 ♘bd7 5. cd5 ed5 6. ♗g5 ♗e7 7. e3 c6 [RR 7... ♘f8 8. ♕c2 ♘e6 9. h4 c6 10. ♗d3 h6 11. ♗f6 ♗f6 12. 0-0-0 h5!? N (12... ♘c7) 13. ♔b1 ♕a5?! 14. ♘d2 ♗d7 15. ♖c1 ♕d8! *a)* 16. ♘b3 (△ ♘a4-c5) b5!∞; *b)* 16. f4 ♘c7 17. ♘f3 ♗g4 18. ♘e5 ♗e5 19. fe5 ♕e7 20. ♘a4?! ♘e6 21. g3 0–0! 22. ♖hf1 f6∓ Podgaec 2450 – Smagin 2520, Dortmund (open) 1993; 20. ♖cf1=; 13... ♗d7!? Smagin] **8. ♕c2 0–0 9. ♗d3 ♖e8 10. h3 ♘f8 11. ♗f4 ♗e6 12. 0–0 ♘6d7 13. ♖ab1 ♘b6 N** [13... f6 – 50/431] **14. b4 ♗d6 15. ♗d6 ♕d6 16. a4 a6 17. ♘d2 ♖e7 18. ♘b3! ♖c7** [18... ♕b4 19. ♘c5 ♕a5 20. ♖b3 △ ♖fb1± ×b7] **19. ♘c5 ♘bd7 20. f4± f6 21. f5 ♗f7 22. ♕f2?** [22. a5±○] **a5 23. ♘d7 ♖d7 24. ba5 ♖a5 25. ♖b6 ♕a3 26. ♖fb1! ♖a8 27. ♖6b3 ♕e7= 28. ♕f4 ♖e8 29. ♔f2 g5 30. ♕f3 h5 31. a5 h4?** [31... ♕d8 32. ♖b7 ♖b7 33. ♖b7 ♕a5=] **32. ♘a4± ♕d8 33. ♘c5 ♖de7 34. ♘b7 ♕c7 35. ♗f1 ♔g7⊕** [⌓ 35... ♕h2±] **36. ♔g1 ♔h6 37. a6 ♗h5 38. ♕f2 ♘d7 39. ♖c1** **1 : 0**
[Beljavskij]

405.* **D 36**

B. GEL'FAND 2690 – IVANČUK 2710

Linares 1993

1. d4 ♘f6 2. c4 e6 3. ♘f3 d5 4. ♘c3 ♘bd7 5. cd5 ed5 6. ♗g5 ♗e7 7. e3 0–0 8. ♗d3 ♖e8 9. ♕c2 ♘f8 10. 0–0 c6 11. h3 g6 [RR 11... ♗e6 12. ♖ab1 a5 N (12... ♘6d7 – 50/431) 13. a3 ♘6d7 14. ♗e7 (14. ♗f4!?) ♕e7 15. b4 ab4 16. ab4 ♖ec8! 17. ♖fc1 g6 18. ♘d2 ♘f6 19. ♘a4 ♘8d7 20. ♘c5 b6 (20... ♘c5? 21. bc5⩲) *a)* 21. ♘a6 ♘e4!; *b)* 21. ♘d7 ♘d7 22. ♕b2 c5 23. bc5 (23. dc5 bc5 24. b5 ♘b6=) bc5 24. dc5 ♖c5 25. ♖c5 ♕c5 26. ♖c1 ♕a3= Nogueiras, Hernández Ruíz; *c)* 21. ♘e6 ♕e6 22. ♖a1 ♖a1 23. ♖a1 ♕d6 24. ♕c3 c5 25. bc5 bc5 26. dc5 ♕c5 27. ♕c5 ♖c5

28. ♘f3 ♖c8 29. ♖d1 1/2 : 1/2 Franco 2505 – Nogueiras 2570, Las Palmas 1992] **12. ♖ab1 ♘e6 13. ♗h6 ♘g7 14. b4 a6 15. a4** [⌓ 15. ♘a4 ♗f5 16. ♗g7 (16. ♘c5 b6!? 17. ♘a4 ♗d3 18. ♕d3 b5∞) ♗d3 17. ♕d3 ♔g7 18. ♘c5 ♖b8 19. a4 ♗d6 20. b5 ab5 21. ab5 ♘e4 22. ♖fc1±] **♗f5 16. ♘e5?! N** [16. ♗g7 – 53/390; 16. b5 ab5 (16... cb5?! 17. ab5 a5 18. ♗f5 ♘f5 19. ♗g5±) 17. ab5 ♖a3 18. ♖a1 ♗d3 19. ♕d3 ♕a5 20. ♖a3 ♕a3 21. ♘e5 △ 21... ♘e4 22. ♘e4 ♕d3 23. ♘f6! ♗f6 24. ♘d3±] **♖c8= 17. ♗g7 ♗d3 18. ♘d3 ♔g7 19. ♖b3 ♗d6 20. b5?** [20. ♕b2 ♔g8 21. b5 ab5 (21... cb5?! 22. ab5 a5 23. b6) 22. ab5 c5=] **cb5! 21. ab5 a5 22. ♕b2 b6∓ 23. ♘a4 ♖c4 24. ♖a1 ♘e4 25. f3 ♘g3 26. ♘e5 ♗e5 27. de5 ♕c7 28. ♔h2 ♘f5 29. f4 ♖c2 30. ♖c3 ♖c3 31. ♕c3 ♕c3 32. ♘c3 ♘e3–+ 33. ♘a4 d4 34. ♖a3** [34. ♘b6 d3 35. ♖a2 d2] **♘c4 35. ♖d3 ♖d8 36. ♔g3 ♖d5 37. ♔f2 g5 38. g3 ♔g6 0 : 1** **[Ivančuk]**

406. **D 37**

D. BLAGOJEVIĆ 2510 – CVETKOVIĆ 2500

Jugoslavija 1993

1. d4 ♘f6 2. c4 e6 3. ♘f3 d5 4. ♘c3 ♘bd7 5. ♗f4 dc4 6. e3 ♘b6 7. ♗c4 ♘c4 8. ♕a4 ♗d7 9. ♕c4 ♗d6 10. ♗g5 N [10. ♘e5 ♘h5!∞; 10. ♗d6 – 56/(449)] **h6 11. ♗f6** [11. ♗h4!?] **♕f6 12. 0–0 0–0 13. e4 ♕d8 14. ♖fd1○ a6 15. a4** [15. d5?! e5∓⊞; 15. e5!? ♗e7 16. d5∞] **♖e8 16. h3 ♕b8** [△ 17... b5 18. ab5 ab5 19. ♖a8 bc4 20. ♖b8 ♖b8∓⊞] **17. ♕d3 b5 18. ab5 ♗b5** [18... ab5 19. ♖a8 ♕a8 20. ♘b5 ♗b5 21. ♕b5 ♖b8 22. ♕e2 ♕a2=; 20. e5!±] **19. ♕c2** [19. ♘b5 ♕b5=] **♕b7 20. ♖ac1 ♗c6!? 21. ♘d2 ♗f4?!** [21... ♖ed8] **22. ♘cb1?!** [22. ♘e2! ♗d2 23. ♕c6 ♕c6 24. ♖c6 ♗a5±] **♗b5 23. g3 ♗d2** [23... ♗g5!?; 23... ♗d6!?] **24. ♖d2 ♖ad8 25. f3 c6 26. ♘c3 ♖d7 27. ♘a4 ♗a4 28. ♕a4 ♕b5 29. ♕b5** [29. b3?? ♕g5–+] **cb5 30. ♔f2!** [30. ♖c6?! ♖ed8∓] **a5⊕ 31. ♔e3⊕ a4 32. ♖c6 ♖b8 33. ♖a6** [33. ♖dc2 ♖a7=; 33... ♖bd8=] **♖c7 34. d5 ed5 35. ♖d5?!** [35. ed5=] **♖c2** [35... ♖c4!?] **36. ♖d2 ♖c4 37. ♖a5 ♖b4∓ 38. e5 ♖e8** [38... g5!?] **39. f4 ♖b3** [39... f6!? 40. ♖a7!⇆ ⇔a7-h7] **40. ♔f2 g5 41. ♔g2 gf4 42. gf4 ♔g7 43. ♖a7 ♖e6!** [43... ♔g6?! 44. ♔h2 △ ♖g2 ×f7] **44. ♖dd7!** [44. ♔h2 ♖f3] **♖c6! 45. ♖f7** [45. f5? (△ ♖f7) ♖b2! 46. ♔f3 (46. ♔g3? ♖c3 47. ♔h4 ♖b4 48. ♔h5 ♖h3#) ♖c3 47. ♔e4 ♖b4 48. ♔d5 ♖d3 49. ♔c5 ♖d7 50. ♖d7 ♖f4–+] **♔g6 46. ♖ac7 ♖c7 47. ♖c7 ♖b2** [♖ 7/j] **48. ♔f3 a3** [48... ♖b3! (Vujačić) *a)* 49. ♔g4 h5 50. ♔h4 a3–+ ×f5; *b)* 49. ♔f2 a3 50. ♖c6 ♔f5 51. ♖f6 ♔e4 52. e6 ♖b2 53. ♔g3 ♔d5! 54. e7 ♖e2 55. ♖f5 (55. ♖a6 b4 56. ♖a7 ♖e7–+; 55. ♖b6 ♔c5 56. ♖b7 b4 57. f5 a2 58. ♖a7 b3 59. f6 b2 60. f7 b1♕–+→) ♔c6 56. ♖f6 (56. ♖e5 ♖e5 57. fe5 ♔d7–+) ♔d7 (56... ♔b7 57. ♖f7 ♔b6 58. ♖f6 ♔a5 59. ♖f7 ♔b4!–+) 57. ♖b6 a2 58. ♖b7 ♔e8 59. ♖a7 b4 60. f5 (60. ♔f3 b3–+) b3 61. f6 ♔f7–+; *c)* 49. ♔e4 ♖b4 50. ♔d5 a3 (50... ♖f4 51. e6!=∞) 51. ♖c6 ♔g7 (51... ♔h5 52. e6!=) 52. f5 a2 53. ♖c7 ♔f8 54. ♔e6 ♖c4! 55. ♖a7 ♖a4–+] **49. ♖c6 ♔f7** [49... ♔h5 50. e6! ♔g6 51. f5! (51. e7? ♔f7 52. ♖e6 ♔e8 53. f5 ♖b1! 54. ♔f2 a2 55. f6 ♖f1!–+) ♔f6 52. ♖a6 a2 53. ♖a7 b4 54. h4! ♖c2 (54... ♖b3? 55. ♔f4 ♖a3 56. ♖f7#) 55. ♔e4 (55. ♖f7!? ♔e5 56. e7 ♖c8 57. ♖f8 a1♕ 58. ♖c8=) ♖e2 (55... ♖c4? 56. ♔d5–+) 56. ♔f3 ♖e1 57. ♖a2 ♔f5 58. ♖b2=] **50. ♖a6 a2 51. f5 b4** [△ ♖b3-a3] **52. ♖a7 ♔e8 53. ♖a8 ♔e7 54. ♖a7** [54. f6? ♔f7 55. ♖a7 ♔g6–+] **♔e8** [54... ♔d8? 55. f6! ♖b3 56. ♔e4 ♖a3 57. f7 ♖a7 58. f8♕ ♔c7 59. ♕e7+–] **55. ♖a8 ♔e7** [55... ♔d7 56. ♖a7 ♔c6? 57. e6! ♖b3 58. ♔f4 ♖a3 59. e7 ♖a7 60. e8♕+–; 56... ♔e8=] **56. ♖a7 ♔e8 1/2 : 1/2** **[Cvetković]**

407.** **D 37**

DORFMAN 2580 – IVKOV 2505

France 1993

1. d4 ♘f6 2. ♘f3 d5 3. c4 e6 4. ♘c3 ♗e7 5. ♗f4 0–0 6. e3 c6 [RR 6... b6 7. cd5 ♘d5 8. ♘d5 ♕d5 9. ♗d3 c5 N (9...

♗b4?! 10. ♔e2±; 9... ♗a6) 10. ♕c2 ♗b7 (10... cd4 11. ♗h7 ♔h8 12. ♗e4 ♕a5 13. ♘d2 e5!; 11. 0–0!) 11. 0–0?! (11. ♗h7 ♔h8 12. ♗d3 cd4 13. 0–0 – 11. 0–0) cd4?! (11... ♘a6∞) 12. ♗h7 ♔h8 13. ♗d3 (13. ♖ad1!?) de3 14. fe3 ♘a6 15. ♖ad1! ♘b4 (15... ♘c5 16. ♗g6!) 16. ♕c7 ♗f6 17. ♗b1! ♕c6 18. ♕c6 ♘c6 (18... ♗c6? 19. ♗d6+– Dreev) 19. ♖d7± Dreev 2560 – Doroškevič 2425, Rostov na Donu (open) 1993] **7. ♗d3 ♘bd7 8. 0–0** [RR 8. ♘e5 N ♘e5 9. ♗e5 dc4 (9... b6⩲) 10. ♗c4 b6 11. 0–0 ♗b7 12. ♕e2 (12. e4?! ♘d7 13. ♗g3 b5 14. ♗d3 b4 15. ♘e2 c5⇆) ♗d6 (12... c5?! 13. ♖fd1 cd4 14. ♗d4±; 12... ♘d5 13. e4) 13. ♖ad1 ♘d5 (13... ♕e7?! 14. f4 △ f5↑) 14. ♘e4 ♗e7 15. ♕g4 ♘f6 16. ♕g3!? (P. Tregubov 2445 – Pigusov 2575, Sankt-Peterburg (zt) 1993) g6 17. ♗f6 ♗f6 18. ♘d6 ♖b8 19. ♖c1 ♗e7 20. ♘b7 ♖b7 21. ♕f3 ♖c7 22. ♖c2± △ 22... c5 23. d5; 17. ♘c3!? △ e4 P. Tregubov] **♘h5 9. ♕c2 N** [9. c5 ♘f4 10. ef4 b6 11. b4 bc5 12. bc5 ♕a5 △ ♗a6; 9. ♗e5 – 51/410] **♘f4 10. ef4 dc4** [10... g6] **11. ♗c4 ♘b6** [11... c5 12. ♖ad1 cd4 13. ♘d4 △ ♗e6] **12. ♗d3 g6 13. a3 ♘d5 14. g3 ♗d7** [14... ♘c3 15. bc3 △ ♗e4, ♘e5, h4±] **15. ♘e4± ♖c8 16. ♖ac1 b6 17. ♕e2 ♖c7 18. ♘e5 ♗e8 19. ♖c2 f6 20. ♘f3 ♗f7 21. ♖fc1 ♕a8 22. h4 h6** [22... ♖e8 23. h5 gh5 24. ♘h4 f5 25. ♘g5 ♗g5 26. fg5±] **23. ♕e1** [△ ♗f1-h3, ♖e2; 23. h5!? g5 24. fg5 hg5 25. ♘eg5 fg5 26. ♕e4 ♘f6 27. ♕e5↑; 23... gh5! △ 24. ♘h4 f5] **♖d8 24. ♗f1 ♔g7 25. ♗h3 ♖e8 26. ♖e2 c5 27. dc5 bc5 28. ♘fd2** [28. ♘ed2 ♗f8] **f5 29. ♘c3 ♗f6 30. ♘c4** [30. ♘a4!?] **♘c3 31. bc3 ♖d8 32. ♘e5 ♗e5 33. ♖e5± ♕f3?!⊕** [33... c4 34. ♗g2 ♕c8 35. ♖a5±] **34. ♗g2** [34. ♖f5 ef5 35. ♕e5 ♔g8 36. ♕c7 ♖d1 37. ♖d1 ♕d1 38. ♔h2 ♕f3 39. ♗g2±] **♕d3 35. ♖e6 ♕d7 36. ♖e5?⊕** [36. ♕e5 ♔g8 37. ♖a6 ♖e8 38. ♕f6±] **♕d2!± 37. h5 ♕e1 38. ♖ce1 gh5 39. ♖f5 ♖d3 40. ♖c1 ♗g6 41. ♖e5 ♗f7 42. ♗f1 ♖d2 43. c4 h4! 44. gh4?!** [44. ♗e2±] **♖d4 45. ♔h2 ♖f4 46. ♔g3 ♖d4= 47. f4 ♖c6 48. h5 ♖f6 49. ♖c5 ♖ff4 50. ♗e2 ♖fe4 51. ♔f3 ♖f4 52. ♔e3 ♖fe4 53. ♔f3 ♖f4 1/2 : 1/2** **[Dorfman]**

408.* !N **D 37**

SLUKIN – KIBALNIČENKO

Rossija 1992

1. ♘f3 ♘f6 2. c4 e6 3. d4 d5 4. ♘c3 ♗e7 5. ♗f4 0–0 6. e3 c5 7. dc5 ♗c5 8. cd5 ed5 [RR 8... ♘d5 9. ♘d5 ed5 10. a3 ♘c6 11. ♗d3 ♗b6 12. 0–0 ♗g4 13. h3 ♗h5 14. b4 ♖e8 15. ♖c1 d4 16. g4 ♗g6 17. ♗g6 hg6 18. b5 de3 19. bc6 e2 20. ♕d8 ef1♕ 21. ♔f1 ♖ad8 22. cb7 f6?? 23. ♖b1! (△ a4, ♖b5, a5) g5 24. ♗g3 *a)* 24... ♖b8 25. ♗b8 ♖b8 26. a4 ♔f7 27. ♖b5 △ a5+–; *b)* 24... ♖d3 25. ♔g2 (25. ♘e1 ♖g3) ♖a3 26. ♖e1! ♖f8 (26... ♖d8 27. ♖c1+–) 27. ♗d6 ♖b3 28. ♗f8 ♗c7 (28... ♗a5 29. ♗b4!+–) 29. ♖e7! ♗d6 30. ♖e8+–; *c)* 24... ♖d7 25. b8♕ ♖b8 26. ♗b8 ♖d3 27. ♔e2 ♖a3 28. ♖b2+– Lima 2445 – Milos 2560, Brasilia (zt) 1993; 22... a6; 22... a5 Lima] **9. ♖c1 ♘c6 10. a3 d4! N** [10... a6 – 6/605] **11. ♘a4?!** [11. ♘e2 de3! 12. ♕d8 (12. ♖c5 ef2–+) ef2 13. ♔d2 ♖d8–+; 11. ♘b5 ♕a5 *a)* 12. b4 ♘b4 13. ab4 (13. ♗c7? ♘d3; 13. ♖c5? ♘d3) ♗b4 14. ♘d2 ♘e4 15. ed4 ♖e8 16. ♘c7 ♘d2 17. ♘e8 ♘b3 18. ♔e2 ♘c1 19. ♕c1 ♗g4 20. f3 ♖e8 21. ♗e3∓; *b)* 12. ♕d2!? ♕d2 13. ♘d2 de3 14. ♖c5 ed2 15. ♗d2 ♘e4; 11. ed4 ♘d4 12. ♘d4 ♕d4 13. ♕d4 ♗d4 14. ♘b5 ♗b2!? 15. ♖c2 ♘d5 16. ♖b2 (16. ♗d6 ♖e8 17. ♔d1 ♗f6 18. ♗c4 ♗e6!? 19. ♗d5 ♗d5 20. ♘c7 ♗g2) ♘f4 17. ♘c7 ♖b8 18. ♘a6 ♖e8 19. ♔d2 ♖d8 20. ♔c1 ♖a8 21. ♘c7 ♖b8 22. ♘a6=; RR 15... ♖e8!; 14. ♗e2] **♕a5 12. b4 ♘b4 13. ♘d2□** [13. ♘c5? ♘d3; 13. ♖c5? ♘d3; 13. ab4 ♗b4 14. ♔e2 (14. ♘d2 ♗d2) d3!? 15. ♔d3 ♕b5] **de3** [13... ♘a6 14. ♗a6!? (14. ♘c5 ♘c5 15. ♗d6 ♘fe4 16. ♗f8 de3 17. fe3 – 13... de3) ♗a3] **14. fe3** [14. ♖c5 ed2 15. ♗d2 ♖e8 16. ♗e2 ♘d3 17. ♔f1 ♕d8∓; 14. ♘c5!? ed2 15. ♗d2 ♕a3 16. ♖c3 ♖e8 17. ♗e2 ♕a2∓] **♘a6 15. ♗a6** [15. ♘c5 ♘c5 16. ♗d6 ♘fe4 17. ♗f8 ♔f8 18. ♗e2 (18. ♗c4 ♗g4; 18. ♖c2 ♘b3) ♗e6!? 19. ♖c5 ♘c5∓] **♗a3! 16. ♖a1 ♕a6 17. ♖a3 b5 18. 0–0 ba4∓** [18... ♗d7?! 19. ♕e2] **19. ♖a4 ♕c6 20. ♖c4 ♕e6 21. ♕a4 ♗d7 22. ♕a5 ♕b6 23. ♕a3 ♗b5 24. ♖b1 ♗c4 25. ♖b6 ab6 26. ♕b4 ♖a1 27. ♔f2 ♖a2**

28. ♔f3 ♗e6 29. e4 ♗g4 30. ♔g3 ♗e6⊕ 31. ♗e3 b5 32. h3 [32. ♕b5? ♖d2] **♖d8 33. ♔f4 h6 34. h4 ♘g4 35. ♘f3 ♘e3 36. ♔e3 ♗c4 37. ♘e5 ♖g2 38. ♘c4 bc4 39. ♕c4 ♖g4 40. ♕c6⊕ 0 : 1**
[Kibalničenko, Zinov]

409. **D 37**

KIŠNËV 2510 – BARSOV 2440
Zwolle 1993

1. d4 ♘f6 2. c4 e6 3. ♘f3 d5 4. ♘c3 ♗e7 5. ♗f4 0–0 6. e3 c5 7. dc5 ♗c5 8. ♕c2 ♘c6 9. a3 ♕a5 10. 0-0-0 ♗d7 11. g4 ♖fc8 12. ♔b1 b5 13. cb5 ♘e7 14. ♗e5!? N [14. ♘d2 – 51/415] **♘g4 15. ♗g7 ♘e3!?** [15... ♔g7 16. ♖g1 f5 17. h3 h5 18. hg4 hg4 19. ♘e5 ♗e8 20. ♘g4!?→] **16. fe3 ♔g7 17. h4!** [17. ♖g1? ♘g6 18. h4 ♗e3∓] **♗e3 18. ♖d3** [18. ♕g2!? ♔f8 19. ♘g5 ♖c3!?∞] **♕b6!** [18... ♗f4? 19. ♖g1 ♔f8 20. ♕g2 ♗b5 21. ♕g7 ♔e8 22. ♖d5! ♘d5 23. ♗b5 ♔e7 24. ♘d5] **19. ♕g2 ♔f8 20. ♘e5?!** [20. ♘g5! ♗g5 21. hg5 e5 (21... d4 22. ♘e4 ♗b5 23. ♖h7 ♗d3 24. ♗d3→) 22. ♘d5 ♘d5 23. ♕d5 ♗f5 24. ♕e5 ♕f2! 25. ♕h8 ♔e7 26. ♕f6=; 22. ♖f3!?; 22. ♖h7!?] **♗e8 21. ♘g4 ♖c3!** [21... ♘f5? 22. ♘f6 △ ♕g8, ♘cd5±] **22. ♖c3** [22. bc3?! ♗b5 23. ♖e3 ♗d3! (23... ♗f1? 24. ♕b2 ♕c7 25. ♘f6!±) 24. ♔c1 ♕b1 25. ♔d2 ♗f5→] **♗d4∓ 23. ♖f3 f5⊕ 24. h5 ♗b5 25. ♗b5 ♕b5 26. ♕d2 ♗g7** [26... ♘c6!?] **27. ♖e1 ♖b8 28. ♘e5 ♖b7 29. ♘d3 ♘c6? 30. h6! ♗h8 31. ♖e6 ♘d4 32. ♕c3!⊕ ♔f7** [32... ♘e6? 33. ♕h8±] **33. ♖fe3?** [33. ♖ee3! ♗f6 34. ♕c8±] **f4! 34. ♘f4?** [34. ♖e8 ♗f6 35. ♕c8] **♕f1 35. ♔a2 ♕f4 36. ♕c8 ♖b2!–+ 37. ♔b2 ♘e6 38. ♕h8 ♕e3 39. ♕h7 ♔f6 40. ♕h8 ♔g6 41. h7 ♕b6 42. ♔a2 ♕f2 43. ♔b3 ♘d4** [44. ♔c3 ♕c2! 45. ♔d4 ♕b2] **0 : 1**
[Kišnëv]

410. **D 37**

B. GEL'FAND 2690 – JUSUPOV 2645
Linares 1993

1. ♘f3 d5 2. c4 e6 3. d4 ♘f6 4. ♘c3 ♗e7 5. ♗f4 0–0 6. e3 c5 7. dc5 ♗c5 8. ♕c2 ♘c6 9. a3 ♕a5 10. 0-0-0 ♗e7 11. g4 dc4 12. ♗c4 e5 13. g5 ef4 14. gf6 ♗f6 15. ♘d5 ♘e7 16. ♘f6 gf6 17. ♖hg1 [17. ♘d4 ♕e5 (17... ♗d7 18. ♘b3 ♕a4 19. ♖hg1 ♔h8 20. ♕c3∞; 17... ♗f5 18. ♘f5 ♕f5∞) 18. ♔b1 fe3 (18... b5? 19. ♗d3±) 19. fe3 ♔h8] **♔h8 18. ♕e4 ♘g6 19. ♕d4 ♕b6 20. ♕b6 ab6 21. ♖d6 ♗h3!? N** [21... fe3 – 53/394] **22. ♔b1** [22. ♗d5!? ♖ac8 23. ♔b1 ♖fd8 24. ♖d8 ♖d8 25. ♗b7 fe3 26. fe3=] **♗f5!** [22... fe3?! 23. fe3 ♖ae8 24. ♖f6 ♖e3±] **23. ♔a1** [23. ♗d3 ♗d3 24. ♖d3 ♖fd8∓] **♗e4 24. ♘d4!** [24. ♘d2 ♗c6 25. ♖f6 b5∓ △ b4] **♘e5 25. ♗b5!?** [25. ♗b3 ♖g8∓] **fe3** [25... f3 26. ♖f6 ♖g8 27. ♖g3 ♖ac8 28. b4∞] **26. fe3 ♖g8∓ 27. ♖f1 ♖g6 28. ♖df6** [28. ♖b6? f5∓] **♖f6 29. ♖f6 ♖g8 30. ♗f1 ♖g6 31. ♖f4 ♖g4 32. ♘b5 f5 33. ♘d6 ♖f4 34. ef4 ♘g6?** [34... ♘g4∓] **35. ♗h3 ♘h4 36. b4± ♘f3 37. ♘f5 ♘h2 38. ♘d6 ♗f3 39. ♔b2 h5 40. ♔c3 ♘g4 41. ♔d4 ♔g7 42. ♘f5 ♔f6 43. ♘h4 ♗c6 44. ♗f1 ♔e6 45. ♗c4 ♔f6 46. ♗d3 ♔e6 47. ♗f5 ♔d6** [47... ♔f6? 48. ♗g6] **48. ♗g6 ♘f6 49. ♘f5 ♔d7 50. ♔e5 ♘g4! 51. ♔d4 ♘f6 52. ♗f7 ♔c7 53. ♔e5 ♘g4 54. ♔d4** [54. ♔e6?? ♗d7–+] **♘f6= 55. ♔e5 1/2 : 1/2** **[Jusupov]**

411.* **D 38**

DOHOJAN 2510 – LUTHER 2465
Bad Godesberg 1993

1. d4 ♘f6 2. c4 e6 3. ♘f3 d5 4. ♘c3 ♗b4 5. cd5 ed5 6. ♗g5 [RR 6. ♕a4 ♘c6 7. ♗g5 h6 8. ♗f6 ♕f6 9. e3 0–0 10. ♗e2 ♖d8 11. 0–0 a6 (11... ♗g4? 12. ♘e5 ♗e2 13. ♘e2 ♘e5 14. ♕b4±) 12. ♖ac1 ♗f8 N (12... ♗e6? – 16/517) 13. ♕d1 (△ ♘a4 ×c5) ♕d6 14. ♘e1 ♘e7 15. ♘d3 b6 16. b4 ♗d7 17. ♕b3 (17. a4!?) ♗b5 18. ♘b2 ♗e2 19. ♘e2 ♘c6 (19... ♘f5?! 20. ♘d3± Malanjuk 2600 – Močalov 2445, Katowice 1993) 20. ♘d3□ (20. a3 a5) ♘b4 21. ♘b4 ♕b4 22. ♕b4 ♗b4 23. ♖c7± Malanjuk] **♘bd7 7. ♖c1 h6 8. ♗f6 ♗c3 9. bc3 ♘f6 10. e3 0–0 11. c4!? N** [11. ♗d3 – 55/417] **♗g4** [11... c5 12. dc5 ♕a5 13. ♕d2 ♕c5 14. cd5 ♕d5 15. ♕d5 ♘d5 16. ♘d4 b6 17. ♗b5±] **12. c5** [12. cd5!? ♕d5 13. ♗c4 ♗f3 14. gf3±] **♘e4** [12... ♗f3 13. gf3 (13.

♕f3 c6∓) c6∞] **13. ♗e2 b5!? 14. ♘e5! ♗e2 15. ♕e2 b4** [15... a6!?] **16. ♘c6 ♕g5 17. ♕f3 a5?** [17... f5!? 18. ♘b4 f4 19. 0–0 a5!? (19... ♘d2 20. ♕d5 ♕d5 21. ♘d5 ♘f1 22. ♖f1 fe3 23. fe3 ♖f1 24. ♔f1 ♖f8 25. ♔e2 ♖f7 26. c6±) 20. ♘c6 ♘d2 21. ♕d5 ♕d5 22. ♘e7 ♔h7 23. ♘d5 ♘f1 24. ♖f1±] **18. h4 ♕f6 19. ♕f6 ♘f6 20. f3 ♖fe8 21. ♘e5** [21. ♔d2? ♘d7] **♖e7 22. c6!±** [×d5, ♘f6] **♔f8 23. ♖c5 ♖ee8 24. g4!?** [24. ♔d2 ♔e7 25. g4 ♔e6] **g5 25. ♖b5?** [25. ♔d2! △ ♔d3, ♖b5, e4±] **♔g7! 26. ♖b7** [26. ♔d2!?] **♖ec8 27. hg5 hg5 28. a3⊕** [28. ♔e2 ♘g8! (28... ♘e8 29. ♖b5) 29. ♖h5 f6 30. ♘d7 ♖a6 31. ♘c5 ♖c6 32. ♖a7±] **ba3** [28... ♘e8 29. ab4 ♘d6 30. ♔f2 a4 31. b5 ♖h8 (31... ♖a5 32. b6) 32. ♖h8 ♔h8 33. b6 cb6 34. ♖b6 a3 35. c7 ♔g7 36. ♖b1! (36. ♖d6 a2 37. c8♕ a1♕ 38. ♖g6 ♔h7!=) a2 37. ♖a1±; 30... ab4!?] **29. ♔e2 ♖h8** [29... ♘e8!? 30. ♖b5] **30. ♖a1 ♖h2 31. ♔d3 ♘e8 32. ♖a3 f6⊕ 33. ♘d7 ♖f2** [33... ♔g6 34. ♖b5] **34. ♘b6 ♖a6 35. ♘d5 ♖c6 36. ♖a5 ♖cc2** [36... ♖f3 37. ♘e7! (37. ♘c7 ♖c7 38. ♖c7 ♘c7 39. ♖a7 ♖g3 40. ♖c7 ♔g6 41. d5 ♖g4 42. d6 ♖g1) ♖e6 (37... ♖c1 38. ♘f5 ♔g6 39. ♖a8±) 38. ♘f5 ♔g6 39. ♖a8± △ 39... ♘d6 40. ♖g8 ♔f7 41. ♘h6, △ 39... ♖h3 40. ♖bb8 ♖h8 (40... ♔f7 41. ♖d8 ♖h7 42. d5 ♖e5 43. d6! cd6 44. ♖e8!; 40... ♘g7 41. ♖g8 ♖h7 42. d5 ♖e5 43. e4) 41. d5+–] **37. ♖a6! ♔g6?** [37... ♔f7□ 38. ♔e4 ♖c1±] **38. ♘e7 ♔f7 39. ♘f5 ♖c1 40. ♔e4 ♖cf1 41. d5 1 : 0**
[Dohojan]

412.** !N D 38

KRAMNIK 2685 – SERPER 2590
Dortmund 1993

1. d4 d5 2. ♘f3 e6 3. c4 ♘f6 4. ♘c3 ♗b4 5. ♗g5 ♘bd7 6. cd5 ed5 7. ♕c2! N h6 [RR 7... c5 8. dc5 ♘c5 9. e3 0–0 10. ♗d3 h6 11. ♗h4 ♗e6 12. 0–0 ♖c8 13. ♘d4 g5 14. ♗g3 ♗c3 15. ♕c3 ♘fe4 16. ♗e4 de4 17. ♘e6 fe6 18. ♕a3 a6 19. ♖ac1 ♕d5 20. h4 ♘d3 21. ♖c3 ♖c3 22. bc3 ♖f7∞ Gofshtein 2560 – Vlado Kovačević 2485, Zagreb (zt) 1993] **8. ♗h4 c5 9. e3 ♕a5?!** [RR 9... c4 10. ♗e2 ♕a5 11. 0–0 ♗c3 12. bc3 ♘e4 13. ♖fc1 ♘b6 14. a4 ♗f5 15. ♕b2 0–0 16. ♗d1± Kramnik 2685 – Lautier 2645, Cannes (m/2) 1993] **10. ♗d3 0–0 11. 0–0 c4** [11... b6 12. ♘d5!? ♘d5 13. a3±] **12. ♗f5± ♖e8** [12... g6 13. ♗d7 ♘d7 14. e4 ♗c3 (14... de4 15. ♘e4±) 15. bc3 de4 16. ♘d2!?↑; 13. ♗g6!?] **13. ♘d2 ♗e7 14. ♖ae1 ♘b6** [⌓ 14... ♘f8 15. ♗c8 ♖ac8 16. ♕f5 g6□ (16... ♖ed8 17. e4 g6 18. ♕e5!+–) 17. ♕f3 ♘8d7⩲; 15. f4!? △ 15... g6 16. ♗c8 ♖ac8 17. f5 (17. ♗f6!? ♗f6 18. ♘f3) g5 18. ♗g3±] **15. a3!?** [15. f3 ♗f5 16. ♕f5 ♕b4 17. ♕c2 ♕d6 18. ♔h1±] **♗e6** [15... ♘e4!□ 16. ♗e4 ♗h4 17. ♗h7 ♔h8 18. ♗f5 ♗f6±] **16. ♗e6 fe6 17. ♗f6! ♗f6 18. f4!+–→ ♘d7** [18... ♘c8 19. g4! ♘d6 20. ♕g6 ♕d8 (20... ♘f7 21. g5) 21. ♘f3 ♘f7 22. ♖e2 △ ♖g2] **19. ♘f3 ♕c7** [19... ♘f8 20. e4! g6 21. e5 ♗g7 22. ♘h4!? ♔f7 23. g4 ♕b6 24. ♕f2]

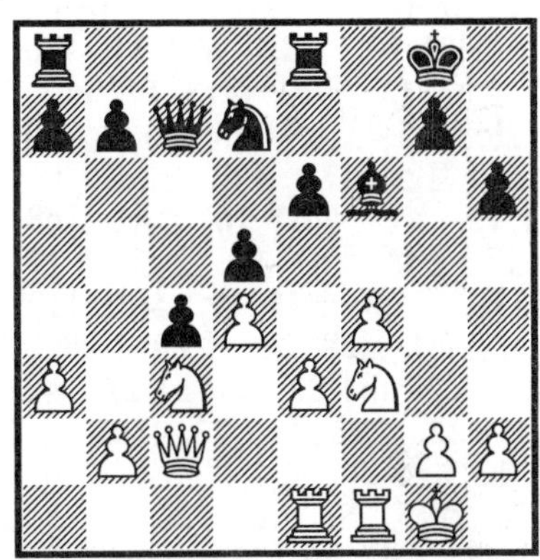

20. g4! ♘f8 21. g5! [21. h4 g6 22. g5 ♗g7] **hg5 22. fg5 ♗e7 23. e4 de4 24. ♕e4 ♖ad8 25. ♖e2** [25. ♕g4] **a6 26. ♕g4 ♕a5** [26... b5 27. ♘e4 △ ♘f6] **27. ♘e5!** [27... ♖d4 28. ♕h5] **1 : 0** **[Kramnik]**

413.* !N D 38

AN. KARPOV 2725 – LAUTIER 2645
France 1993

1. d4 d5 2. c4 e6 3. ♘c3 ♗b4 4. ♘f3 ♘f6 5. ♗g5 ♘bd7 6. cd5 ed5 7. e3 c5 8. dc5!? N [RR 8. ♗d3 c4 9. ♗f5 ♕a5 10. ♕c2 0–0 11. 0–0 ♖e8 12. ♘d2 g6 13. ♗d7 ♘d7 14. f3 ♘b6 15. ♗f4 ♗c3 16. bc3

♕a4 *a)* 17. ♕b1 ♕a3 18. ♕c2 (18. ♖c1 ♘a4 19. ♕c2 b5 20. ♖ab1 ♗d7 △ 21. ♖b4? a5 22. ♘b1 ♕c1 23. ♕c1 ab4 24. cb4 ♗f5∓) ♗d7 (18... ♕a4=) 19. e4 ♘a4 20. ♖fc1 b5↑; *b)* 17. ♕c1 ♗f5 18. ♖e1 (18. e4 de4 19. fe4 ♗e4 20. ♘e4 ♖e4 21. ♗e5 ♘d7!∓) ♗d3! N (18... ♕c6 — 55/419) 19. h4 ♖e6 20. ♘f1 ♕d7!? *b1)* 21. ♘g3?! (△ ♘h1-f2) ♕e7 22. ♗g5 f6 23. ♗f4 ♘d7 24. ♘h1 g5 25. hg5 fg5 26. ♗g3 ♖e8 27. ♗f2 g4∓↑; *b2)* 21. g4 ♘a4!? (21... h5 22. gh5 gh5 23. ♘g3∞; 21... f5 22. g5 ♘a4 23. ♘g3 ♖b6 24. ♖d1 ♖b2 25. ♖d2 ♕b5 26. ♖b2 ♕b2 27. ♕b2 ♘b2 28. a4= S. Kiselëv 2530 — G. Georgadze 2525, Podol'sk 1992) 22. ♘g3 ♖b6 23. ♖d1 ♕e7 (23... h5 24. gh5 ♕h3 25. ♖d2∞) 24. ♗g5 f6 25. ♗f4 ♖b2 26. ♖d2 ♖d2 27. ♕d2 ♕a3 28. ♖c1 ♖e8∓ G. Georgadze] **♕a5 9. ♘d2 ♘e4!?** [9... ♗c3 10. bc3 ♕c3 11. ♖c1 ♕a5 12. ♗f6 ♘f6 13. ♕c2 0–0 14. ♗d3± △ 0–0, ♘b3; 10... ♕c5!?] **10. ♘de4 de4 11. ♕d4 0–0 12. a3 ♗c3 13. ♕c3 ♕c3 14. bc3 ♘c5!?** [14... ♖e8 15. ♗b5 (15. c6 bc6=) ♖e5! 16. ♖d1 ♖g5 17. ♗d7 ♗d7 18. ♖d7 ♖c5=] **15. ♗e7 ♘b3 16. ♖d1 ♖e8** [16... ♗g4? 17. ♗f8 ♗d1 18. ♗g7±] **17. ♗b5 ♗g4□ 18. ♗e8 ♗d1 19. ♔d1** [19. ♗d7 ♗c2= △ f6] **♖e8 20. ♗b4 ♖c8□** [20... a5? 21. ♔c2! ab4 22. ab4±] **21. ♔c2 ♘c5** [△ ♘d3] **22. ♗c5 ♖c5 23. ♖d1 g6 24. g4 h5 25. h3 hg4 26. hg4 ♖g5** [⌓ 26... ♖a5 27. ♔b3 ♖b5 28. ♔c4 (28. ♔a2 ♖c5=) ♖b2=] **27. ♖d7 b6** [27... ♖g4?! 28. ♖b7 ♖g2 29. c4! ♖f2 30. ♔c3↑] **28. ♖a7 ♖g4 29. ♔d2** [29. ♖d7!? ♖g2 30. ♖d2 ♔f8 31. c4 ♔e7 32. a4 ♖g1 33. ♔b2 f5 34. c5 bc5 35. a5 c4=] **♖g2 30. ♔e2 ♖g1 31. ♖a4 ♖c1 32. c4 ♖c2 33. ♔f1 ♖a2 34. ♔g2 ♔g7 35. ♔g3 f5 36. ♖a6 ♔h6 37. ♖b6 1/2 : 1/2** **[Lautier]**

414. **D 40**

GLUZMAN 2440 — I. ROGERS 2575

Canberra 1993

1. e4 c6 2. d4 d5 3. ed5 cd5 4. c4 ♘f6 5. ♘c3 e6 6. ♘f3 ♘c6 7. ♗d3 dc4 8. ♗c4 ♗e7 9. 0–0 0–0 10. ♗b3 b6 N [10... a6 — 12/199] **11. a3 ♗a6!= 12. ♖e1 ♖c8 13. ♗g5 h6!?** [13... ♘d5=] **14. ♗f4 ♘a5 15. ♗c2 ♘c4 16. ♕c1 ♗b7** [16... ♘d5!?] **17. ♗h6! ♘d5!** [17... gh6 18. ♕h6→; 17... ♗f3 18. ♗g7! ♔g7 19. ♕g5 ♔h8 20. ♕h6 ♔g8 21. gf3→; 17... ♘h5!?⩲] **18. ♘e5!?** [18. ♗g5 ♘c3 19. bc3 ♗f3 20. ♗e7 ♕e7 21. gf3 ♕f6 22. ♗e4 g6 23. ♕h6!=; 22... ♖c7! △ ♖fc8, g6, ♔g7∓; 18. ♘d5 ♗d5 19. ♗e3 ♗f3 20. gf3 ♗d6=∞; 18. ♗d2 ♘c3 19. bc3 (19. ♗c3!?) ♗f3 20. gf3 ♗d6=∞; 18. ♖e4!! ♘c3 19. ♖g4 (19. ♗g7 ♘e2!!–+) ♘e2 20. ♔f1 ♘c1 (20... f5 21. ♖g7 ♔h8 22. ♔e2∞) 21. ♖g7 ♔h8 22. ♖h7=] **♘b2! 19. ♕b2□** [19. ♘g4 ♖c3 20. ♗g7 ♗g5–+; 19. ♘e4!? ♕c7! (19... gh6 20. ♕b2∞) *a)* 20. ♖e2 ♗a6 21. ♘g4!? (21. ♖d2 ♘c4! 22. ♘c4 ♗c4 23. ♗e3 ♗b3–+) ♗e2 22. ♗g7 ♕f4! (22... ♗g4? 23. ♘f6!!+–) 23. ♘ef6 ♗f6 24. ♘f6 ♔g7–+; *b)* 20. ♕b2 ♕c2∓] **♘c3 20. ♗e3 ♕d5 21. f3 ♕b5∓ 22. ♕b5 ♘b5 23. ♗d3 ♘c3** [23... ♘a3!? 24. ♗c1 ♘c2 25. ♗c2 ♖c2 26. ♖a7 ♗b4 27. ♖d1 ♗d5 28. ♘d7 ♖fc8 29. ♗f4∓ ×b6] **24. ♖ec1 ♘d5 25. ♗d2 ♖c1 26. ♗c1 ♖d8 27. ♗b2 f6 28. ♘g4 ♔f7 29. ♖e1 ♗d6** [29... ♖c8!?] **30. ♗c4! ♖c8 31. ♗b3 ♗f4 32. ♖d1 g5?!** [32... ♘e3? 33. ♗e6! ♔e6 34. ♖e1=; 32... b5!?∓] **33. g3 ♗d6 34. ♖e1 b5?! 35. ♘h6= ♔e7 36. ♘f5 ♔d7 37. ♘g7! a5 38. ♘e6 a4 39. ♘c5??⊕** [39. ♗d5 ♗d5 40. ♘c5 ♗c5 41. dc5 ♖c5 42. ♗f6 ♗f3 43. ♖e5=] **♖c5! 40. dc5 ♗c5 41. ♔f1 ab3 42. h4 gh4 43. gh4 ♘f4! 44. ♗c1 b4!** [45. ♖d1 ♔e6 46. a4 ♗a6 47. ♔e1 ♘g2 48. ♔d2 ♗e3#; 45. ♗f4 ba3–+] **0 : 1**
[I. Rogers]

415. **D 41**

ADORJÁN 2545 — I. FARAGÓ 2510

Magyarország 1993

1. ♘f3 d5 2. d4 e6 3. c4 ♘f6 4. ♘c3 c5 5. cd5 ♘d5 6. e4 ♘c3 7. bc3 cd4 8. cd4 ♘c6 9. ♗c4 b5 10. ♗e2 ♗b4 11. ♗d2 ♕a5 12. d5 ed5 13. ed5 ♘e7 14. 0–0 ♗d2 15. ♘d2 0–0 16. ♘b3 ♕d8 [16... ♕b6?! 17. d6 ♘c6 18. d7! ♗b7 19. ♕d6±] **17. ♗f3 ♘f5 18. ♕d3 N** [18. ♖c1 — 40/519]

♘d6 [18... ♖b8 (△ 19. ♗e4 g6) 19. ♖fd1 △ d6±; 18... ♕f6 19. d6 ♖b8 20. d7 ♗b7 21. ♗b7 ♖b7 22. ♖ad1 ♖bb8 23. ♕d5±] **19. ♘d4 ♗d7** [19... ♕f6 20. ♖ac1 ♗d7 21. ♖c7±] **20. a4!** [20. ♘e6 fe6 21. de6 ♖f3 22. ♕d6 ♖f6=] **a6** [20... ba4 21. ♘c6±; 20... b4 21. ♘c6±] **21. ♘e6! fe6 22. de6 ♖c8** [22... ♖f3 23. ♕f3 ♗e6 24. ♖fd1 ♖b8 25. ab5 ab5 26. ♖a6 ♖b6 27. ♖a8 ♗c8 (27... ♖b8 28. ♖b8 ♕b8 29. ♕f4+–; 29. ♕c6+–) 28. ♕d5 ♔h8 29. ♕c5!+–] **23. ♕d6** [23. ed7 ♕d7 24. ab5 ab5 25. ♕d4! (25. ♖fd1 ♖f6 26. ♖a6 ♖d8 27. ♗c6 ♕c7 28. ♗b5 ♘f7 29. ♕e2 ♖d1 30. ♕d1 ♖a6 31. ♗a6⩲) ♕d8!□±] **♗c6 24. ♕e5** [24. ♕b4!? ♕g5 25. ♗c6 (25. h4!? ♕f4 26. ♕f4 ♖f4 27. ♖fc1 ♖c4) ♖c6 *a)* 26. ♖fe1 ♖f2! (26... ♖e8 27. ♕e4!±) *a1)* 27. ♔f2 ♖c2 28. ♔f3 (28. ♖e2? ♕f6–+) ♕g2 29. ♔e3 ♕f2 30. ♔d3 ♖b2! 31. ♕b2 (31. e7 ♕c2 32. ♔e3 ♕f2=) ♕b2 32. e7 ♕b3=; *a2)* 27. ♕e4! ♖cc2 28. ♕a8 ♖f8 29. ♕e4 ♖ff2=; *b)* 26. ♖ae1 ♖e8 27. f4 ♕c5 28. ♕c5 ♖c5 29. ab5 ab5 30. f5 h5! 31. ♖e4 (31. h3 b4 32. g4 hg4 33. hg4 ♖c4=) ♖c4! 32. ♖fe1 (32. ♖c4 bc4 33. h3 h4 △ 34. ♔f2 g6! 35. ♖c1 gf5 36. ♖c4 ♖e6 37. ♖h4 ♔g7=) ♔f8 33. h3 ♔e7 34. g4 hg4 35. hg4 g6 36. fg6 ♔f6=] **♕e7** [24... ♕f6 25. ♕f6 gf6 (25... ♖f6? 26. ♖fc1 ♖e6 27. ♗g4+–; 27. ♗d5+–) 26. ♗h5! ♖c7 27. ♖ac1 ♖fc8 28. ♖fe1! △ 28... ♔f8 29. ♖c6!+–] **25. ♗c6?** [25. ♗g4!?; 25. ♗e2! *a)* 25... ♖f6 26. ab5 *a1)* 26... ♗b5 27. ♗b5 ab5 28. ♖fe1 △ 28... b4 29. ♖ad1 ♕a7 (29... ♖c6 30. ♖d7 ♕e6 31. ♖d8 ♔f7 32. ♕h5+–) 30. e7 ♕f2 (30... ♖f2 31. ♔h1+–) 31. ♔h1 ♖e8 32. ♕b5 ♔f7 33. ♕h5!+–; *a2)* 26... ab5 27. ♖fe1±; *b)* 25... ba4 26. ♗a6 ♖a8 27. ♗c4 a3 28. ♖fd1 (△ ♖d7) ♔h8 29. ♕d6! (29. ♖d6 ♗e8) ♕d6 30. ♖d6 ♗e4 31. f3 ♗f5 32. g4 ♗g6 33. ♗d5±] **♖c6 26. ab5 ♕e6** [26... ♖e6 27. ♕d5 ♖d8! 28. ♕b3 ab5 29. ♖a6 ♖dd6 30. ♖d6 ♕d6 31. ♖e1 ♔f7 32. ♖e6 ♕e6 33. ♕b5 ♕e1 34. ♕f1 ♕d2±] **27. ♕e6 ♖e6 28. ♖a6 ♖e2 29. ♖a7** [29. ♖c1!? *a)* 29... ♖ff2? 30. ♖a8 ♔f7 (30... ♖f8 31. ♖f8 ♔f8 32. ♖b1+–) 31. ♖c7 ♔g6 32. ♖a6 ♖f6 (32... ♔h5 33. ♖g7+–) 33. ♖f6 ♔f6 34. b6 ♖b2 35. b7+–; *b)* 29... ♖b2! 30. f3 (30. ♖a7 ♖ff2 31. ♖c8 ♖f8=) ♖d8! (30... ♖b5 31. ♖c7 ♖g5 32. ♖aa7±) 31. b6 (31. ♖a7 h6 32. h3 ♖dd2=) ♖dd2?? 32. ♖c8 ♔f7 33. ♖c7 ♔g6 34. b7 ♔h5 35. ♖c5+–; 31... h6! △ ♖dd2=] **♖b2 30. f3 ♖f7 31. ♖f7 ♔f7 32. ♖c1 ♖b5 33. ♖c7 ♔g6** **1/2 : 1/2**
[Adorján, Gy. Fehér]

416.** **D 41**

HALIFMAN 2630 – AN. KARPOV 2725
Dos Hermanas 1993

1. ♘f3 ♘f6 2. c4 c5 3. ♘c3 d5 [RR 3... e6 4. g3 ♘c6 5. ♗g2 d5 6. cd5 ♘d5 7. 0–0 ♗e7 8. d4 0–0 9. ♘d5 ed5 10. ♗e3 c4 11. b3 cb3 12. ♕b3!? N (12. ab3) ♘a5 13. ♕b1 b6 14. ♘e5 f6 15. ♘d3 ♗e6 16. ♗d2 ♘c4 17. ♗b4 ♗d6 18. ♖c1 ♖c8 19. e3 g5 20. h4 (M. Pavlović 2455 – M. Makarov 2515, Podgorica 1993) gh4 21. gh4 ♔h8∞; 19. h4!⩲ M. Pavlović] **4. cd5 ♘d5 5. d4 e6 6. e4 ♘c3 7. bc3 cd4 8. cd4 ♘c6 9. ♗c4 ♗b4 10. ♗d2 ♗d2 11. ♕d2 0–0 12. 0–0 b6 13. ♖ad1 ♘a5 14. ♗d3 ♗b7 15. ♕f4 N** [RR 15. d5 N ed5 16. e5 d4! 17. ♘g5 (17. ♘d4 ♕d5! 18. ♘f3? ♕c5!; 18. ♕g5! Seirawan) h6 18. ♘h7 ♕h4! 19. ♘f8 ♗g2 20. ♔g2 ♕g4 1/2 : 1/2 Kamsky 2655 – Seirawan 2595, Buenos Aires 1993; 15. ♖fe1 – 8/485] **♕f6** [15... ♕e7 16. d5↑; 15... f6 16. d5 e5 17. ♕g3 ♕d6∞; 16. ♖c1!?⩲] **16. ♕g3 ♕e7** [16... ♕g6 17. ♕h4 ♕f6 18. ♕h3 ♕h6!? 19. ♕h6 gh6 20. ♘e5!? ♖fd8 21. ♗b1 ♖d6 22. ♖d2 ♖ad8 23. ♖fd1⩲] **17. d5 ♖ad8** [17... ed5 18. ed5±]

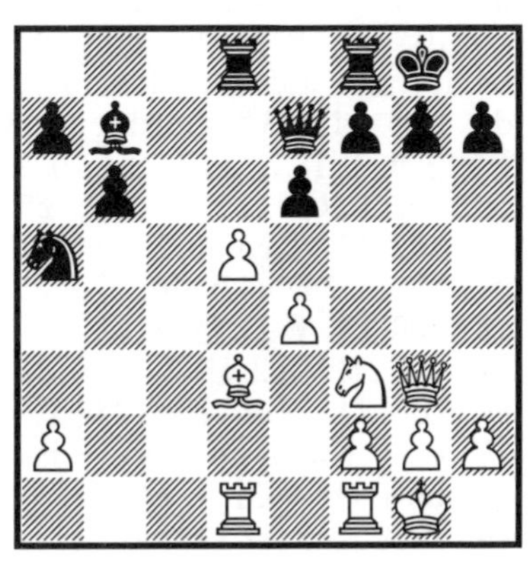

18. e5!? [18. ♖fe1!?] **♗d5** [18... ♖d5 19. ♗h7 ♔h7 20. ♘g5 ♔g8 21. ♕h4+−] **19. ♗h7! ♔h7 20. ♖d5!** [20. ♘g5 ♔g8 (△ 21. ♕h4? ♗e4!−+) 21. ♖d5] **♖d5!** [20... f6 21. ef6 ♕f6 22. ♖h5±; 20... g6 21. ♖d8 ♖d8 22. h4±] **21. ♘g5 ♔g8 22. ♕h4 ♕g5 23. ♕g5 ♘c6!** [23... f6? 24. ♕g4 ♖e5 25. f4 ♖e4 26. ♖c1+−; 23... ♘c4 24. f4 ♘e3 25. ♖e1 ♘f5∞] **24. f4** [24. ♖c1=] **♘d4 25. h4?** [25. g4 ♖c8 26. f5 ♖e5; 25. g3! ♖c8 26. ♕g4∞] **♖c8∓ 26. ♕g4 ♘f5 27. ♖e1 ♖c4! 28. h5 ♖dd4 29. ♕f3 ♖f4 30. ♕a8 ♔h7 31. ♕a7 ♖g4! 32. ♕f7 ♖c2 33. ♕b7 ♘h4 34. ♔f1 ♘g2** [34... ♖f4! 35. ♔g1 ♖a2!−+ △ 36. ♕b6 ♖g2 37. ♔h1 ♖f3] **35. ♖e4! ♖g5 36. ♕e7 ♖f5 37. ♔g1 ♘f4 38. ♖f4! ♖f4 39. ♕e6= ♖cc4 40. ♕g6 ♔h8 41. ♕e8 ♔h7 42. ♕g6 ♔h8 43. ♕e8** [43. ♕b6 ♖f5]
1/2 : 1/2 **[Halifman]**

417.** **D 43**

BAREEV 2670 − ŠIROV 2670
Linares 1993

1. d4 d5 2. c4 c6 3. ♘f3 ♘f6 4. ♘c3 e6 5. ♕b3!? dc4 6. ♕c4 b5 7. ♕d3 ♗e7? N [RR 7... a6 8. ♗g5!? N (8. e4 − 39/(514); 8. a4!?) c5 9. a4 *a)* 9... ba4? 10. ♗f6! gf6 (10... ♕f6 11. d5±) 11. d5 ed5?! 12. ♕d5 ♖a7 13. ♕e4 ♗e6 14. e3!? ♕b6 15. ♘d5 (15. ♕a4 ♖d7) ♕a5 (15... ♕b2 16. ♖b1+−) 16. ♘d2 ♗e7 17. ♘e7 (17. ♖a4!? ♗d5 18. ♖a5 ♗e4 19. ♘e4±) ♖d7 18. ♘d5 ♖d5 19. ♕a4 ♕a4 20. ♖a4± Gofshtein 2560 − Zvjagincev 2445, Cappelle la Grande 1993; ⌓ 11... ♗g7±; *b)* 9... ♘c6 10. dc5 ♕d3 11. ed3 ♗c5 12. ab5 ♘b4 13. ♖c1 ab5 14. d4±; *c)* 9... cd4 10. ♘d4 ♗c5 11. e3⩲ Gofshtein] **8. a3!** [△ e4-e5±] **0−0** [8... a6 9. e4 *a)* 9... c5 10. dc5±; *b)* RR 9... ♗b7 10. e5 ♘d5 11. ♘e4 ♘d7 12. ♗g5 f6 13. ef6 gf6 14. ♗h6 c5 15. ♗e2± c4?! 16. ♘fd2! ♕b6 17. ♗h5 ♔d8 18. ♕g3 ♕d4 19. ♗f7 ♘e5 20. ♗e6 ♘d3 21. ♔e2 ♕b2 22. ♘d6 ♘3f4 23. ♗f4 ♗d6 24. ♗d6 ♖e8 25. ♖he1 c3 26. ♗c7! 1 : 0 Kumaran 2385 − P. Wells 2485, Dublin (zt) 1993] **9. e4 c5?!** [⌓ 9... a6±] **10. dc5 ♗c5 11. ♕b5?!** [11. ♕d8 ♖d8 12. ♗b5 ♗b7 13. ♗g5 ♘c6 (13... h6 14. ♗f6 gf6±) 14. ♔e2!! (Kotronias; 14. 0−0 ♘d4∞; 14. e5 ♘d4! 15. ♘d4 ♗d4 16. ef6 ♗c3 17. bc3 ♖d5⩲) ♘d4 (14... ♖ab8 15. ♖hd1±) 15. ♘d4 ♗d4 16. f3±] **♕c7!⯹ 12. ♗g5! ♘bd7 13. ♕a4?** [13. ♖c1! ♖b8 14. ♕e2 ♖b3!?⯹] **♗f2!! 14. ♔f2 ♘c5 15. ♕d4?** [15. ♕c4 ♗a6→; 15. ♕c2! ♘ce4 16. ♕e4 ♘e4 17. ♘e4 ♕b6 18. ♗e3 ♕b2 19. ♗e2∓] **♘g4 16. ♔g1** [16. ♔e1 ♘b3 17. ♕c4 (17. ♘b5 ♕c2−+) ♕b6−+] **♘b3 17. ♘b5 ♕b8 18. ♕d6** [18. ♕d1 ♘a1 19. ♕a1 ♕b6 20. ♘fd4 e5 21. h3 ♘f6−+] **♘a1−+ 19. h3 ♘f6 20. ♗d3 ♘b3! 21. e5 ♘d5 22. ♗c4** [22. ♗h7 ♔h7 23. ♕f8 ♕b5 24. ♕f7 ♕d7! 25. ♕h5 ♔g8] **h6! 23. ♗h4 ♘e3 24. ♗d3 ♕d6??** [24... ♘c1−+] **25. ed6 ♗a6 26. ♗e7 ♖fb8?** [26... ♘c5!∓] **27. ♘c7 ♗d3 28. ♘a8 ♘f5** [28... ♘c5 29. b4] **29. ♘c7 ♗e4 30. ♔f2 ♘c5 31. b4 ♘d3 32. ♔e2 ♘f4 33. ♔d2!? ♘g2?!⊕** [33... f6!∓] **34. ♘e5 f6 35. ♖e1??⊕** [35. ♘d7 ♖c8 36. ♘c5 ♗c6∓; 35. ♘a6! ♖c8 (35... ♖b5? 36. ♘c5!; 35... ♖a8 36. ♘c7=) 36. ♖c1 ♖c1 37. ♔c1 ♘d6 38. ♗d6 fe5 39. ♗e5=] **♘e1 36. ♘d7 ♘f3 37. ♔c3 ♖c8** **0 : 1**
[Širov]

418. **D 43**

AN. KARPOV 2725 −
B. GEL'FAND 2690
Linares 1993

1. d4 ♘f6 2. c4 e6 3. ♘f3 d5 4. ♘c3 dc4 5. ♕a4 c6 6. ♕c4 b5 7. ♕d3 ♗b7 8. e4 [8. ♗g5!?] **b4** [8... ♘bd7?! 9. e5 ♘d5 10. ♘d5±] **9. ♘a4** [9. ♘e2!? △ ♘g3] **♘bd7** [9... ♗a6 10. ♕c2 ♗f1 11. ♔f1⩲] **10. ♗g5 N** [10. ♗e2 − 40/(521)] **♕a5 11. b3 c5 12. ♗f6 gf6□** [12... ♘f6? 13. ♕b5 ♕b5 14. ♗b5 ♔d8 15. ♘e5± ♔e7 16. ♘c5 ♗e4 17. ♘e4 ♘e4 18. ♗c6+−] **13. ♗e2** [13. ♖c1 ♗h6 14. ♖c2 (14. ♖c5!? ♘c5 15. ♘c5⯹) 0−0 15. ♘c5 ♘c5 16. dc5 ♖fd8⯹; 13. d5!?] **0-0-0 14. 0−0 ♔b8** [14... cd4 15. ♕d4 ♔b8 16. ♕e3 ♘e5 17. ♘d4±; 14... ♘b6 15. ♘c5 ♗c5 16. ♖fc1±] **15. d5!** [15. ♕e3 h5⇆] **♘b6** [15... f5?!

16. ♘g5!±; 15... ♘e5 16. ♘e5 fe5 17. ♕g3±] **16. ♘b6 ♕b6** [16... ab6 17. ♕e3±] **17. ♖ad1 ♗h6** [17... f5 *a)* 18. ef5 ed5 (18... ♖d5 19. ♕e3± ♖f5 20. ♘e5) 19. ♘e5 ♕f6 20. ♘g4 ♕c3 21. ♕b5↑; *b)* 18. ♘g5 fe4 19. ♕e4 (19. ♕h3 ed5 20. ♘f7 ♗d6 21. ♘h8 ♖h8$\overline{\infty}$) ed5 20. ♕f5 ♗d6 21. ♗f3±; 17... ed5 18. ed5 ♖d5 19. ♕d5!? ♗d5 20. ♖d5 ♗e7 21. ♗c4 ♖d8 22. ♖h5±] **18. ♕c4 ♖d6 19. de6 ♖e6** [19... fe6 20. e5±]

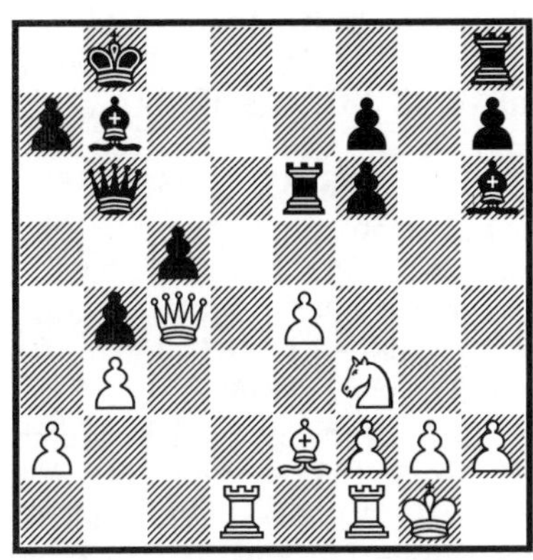

20. ♖d5! [20. ♗d3 ♖g8 △ f5⇆] **♖he8** [20... ♗d5 21. ed5 ♖e7 22. ♖d1±] **21. ♗d3 ♖d8! 22. ♖d1** [22. ♖d8 ♕d8 23. ♕c2 f5⇆] **♖ed6 23. ♗e2 ♗d5 24. ed5 ♕b7 25. ♕h4 ♗f8** [25... ♖d5? 26. ♖d5 ♕d5 27. ♕h6 ♕d1 28. ♗f1+−; 25... ♗g5 26. ♕g3 ♕c7 27. ♗c4±] **26. ♗c4 ♖d5** [26... h6 27. ♕e4 ♕d7 28. ♕d3 △ ♘h4-f5] **27. ♗d5 ♖d5 28. ♖e1 ♖d8 29. ♕f6** [29. ♕h7 ♕d5 △ c4] **♕c7 30. g3** [30. ♘g5? ♗e7] **♗d6** [30... h6 31. ♘e5±] **31. ♘g5 ♖d7 32. ♖e8** [32. ♘h7 c4⇆] **♔b7 33. ♘e4 ♗e7 34. ♕f5 ♕c6 35. ♔g2 ♖c7 36. ♖h8 ♕g6** [36... c4 37. bc4 ♕c4 38. ♖h7+−] **37. ♕d5 ♕c6 38. ♕c6 ♔c6 39. ♖h7 ♔d5 40. ♘d2 ♗f6 41. ♘c4 ♔d4 42. ♖h6 ♖c6 43. g4 ♖e6 44. h4 ♔d5 45. g5 1 : 0** **[An. Karpov]**

419.* !N D 43

ŠTOHL 2540 – KUCZYŃSKI 2525

Budapest (zt) 1993

1. d4 d5 2. c4 c6 3. ♘c3 ♘f6 4. ♘f3 e6 5. ♗g5 h6 6. ♗f6 ♕f6 7. ♕b3 a5 8. e4 de4 [RR 8... a4!? 9. ♘a4!? N (9. ♕c2 – 46/558) de4 10. ♘b6!? (10. ♘e5 ♘d7=) ef3!? (10... ♖a5 11. ♘e5 ♕d8 12. 0-0-0 ♗d6 13. ♔b1 ♗c7 14. c5 ♗b6 15. cb6 0–0 16. ♗c4!± ♘d7 17. ♘d7 ♗d7 18. ♖he1 ♖f5 19. ♖e4! ♖f2 20. ♖g4 ♕f6 21. ♕g3 e5 22. ♖g7+− Miles 2565 – Speelman 2595, Dublin (zt) 1993) 11. ♘a8 ♕d4$\overline{\infty}$ Miles] **9. ♘e4 ♗b4 10. ♔d1** [10. ♕b4 ab4 11. ♘f6 gf6 12. c5 ♘d7⇆ △ b6] **♕f4 11. ♗d3** [11. ♕e3 ♕e3 12. fe3 ♗e7 13. c5 ♘d7∞⊞ △ 14... b6, 14... e5⇆] **♗e7 12. ♘e5 h5□** [12... 0–0 13. g3 ♕f5 14. ♘d6 ♕f2 15. ♘c8 ♖c8 16. ♕b7+−] **13. g3 ♕h6 14. ♕b6! N** [△ ♕c7; 14. c5 – 28/577] **f6!?** [14... ♘a6? 15. ♘c6+−; 14... h4 15. ♕c7 ♘a6 16. ♘d6! ♔f8 17. ♕b6+− △ 17... ♗d6?? 18. ♕d8#; 14... 0–0 15. ♕c7 ♖e8 (15... ♗f6 16. ♘f7+−) *a)* 16. ♘f7 ♔f7 17. ♘d6 ♔f8 18. ♘e8 (18. ♘c8 ♘a6∓) ♘a6∓ △ 19. ♕a5? ♗b4−+; *b)* 16. ♘d6 ♘a6 17. ♘ef7 ♘c7∓; *c)* 16. c5! (△ ♘f7) ♘d7!? (16... ♘a6 17. ♗a6+−) 17. ♘d7 ♗d8 18. ♕d6 ♗e7 19. ♘b6! ♗d6 20. ♘d6 ♗d7 21. ♘d7!? ♖ed8 22. ♘b6±; 21. ♘e8±; 14... ♘d7 15. ♘d7 ♔d7□ 16. d5!→ ×♔d7] **15. ♘g6□** [15. ♕c7? ♘a6 16. ♘d6 ♔f8−+] **♘d7 16. ♕b3□** [16. ♕c7? ♕g6! 17. ♘d6 ♗d6 18. ♗g6 ♔e7−+] **a4 17. ♕c3□** [17. ♕c2 f5 18. ♘e7 fe4 19. ♘c8 ed3−+] **f5□** [17... ♖g8 18. ♘e7 ♔e7 19. ♕b4+−→] **18. ♘e7 fe4 19. ♘c8 ♖c8** [19... ed3 20. ♘d6 ♔e7 21. ♘e4+−] **20. ♗e4 ♘f6** [20... 0–0!? 21. ♔e2±] **21. ♗f3?!** [21. ♗c2 0–0 22. ♔e2 b5!?$\overline{\infty}$ △ bc4, ♘d5, ×♔e2; ⌓ 21. ♗g2! 0–0 22. ♔e2 *a)* 22... e5?! 23. de5 ♘g4 24. f4±; *b)* 22... ♖ce8 23. ♖he1! (23. f4 c5!? 24. dc5 e5!$\overline{\infty}$) ♘g4 24. f3 e5! 25. de5 (25. d5?! ♘h2 26. ♖h1 e4→) ♖e5 (25... ♘e5 26. ♔f1 ♕f6 27. ♖e3±) 26. ♔f1 ♘e3 27. ♔g1 ♖fe8 28. ♖e2± △ ♖ae1; *c)* 22... h4 23. f4⩲ △ ♗f3, ♕e3; *d)* 22... ♖cd8 23. ♖hd1⩲] **0–0 22. ♔e2** [22. ♕e3 ♕g6$\overline{\infty}$ 23. ♕e6? ♔h7∓] **e5!** [22... ♘g4!? 23. h3 (23. ♗g4?! hg4↑) ♖f3! *a)* 24. ♔f3 ♕f6! 25. ♔e2 ♕f2 26. ♔d1 ♘e3 27. ♔c1 ♖d8!$\overline{\infty}$ (△ ♖d4) 28. ♖e1? ♘c2!∓; *b)* 24. ♕f3 ♖f8 25. hg4 (25. ♕c3 ♖f2 26. ♔e1 ♘f6! 27. ♕c1 ♕c1 28. ♖c1 ♖b2∓; 25. ♕f8 ♔f8 26. hg4 ♕g6⇆) ♖f3 26. ♔f3 hg4 (26... ♕g6!?∞) 27. ♔g2 ♕g6=] **23. de5 ♘g4** [△ 24... ♘e5, 24... ♖f3] **24.**

♗**g4**□ **hg4**∞ **25. ♖ad1 ♖ce8 26. ♖d3!** [26. ♖d2 ♖f5 27. ♔d1 ♖fe5 28. ♔c2 ♖e2∞] **♖f5 27. ♖e3 ♖ef8 28. ♖f1**□ [28. ♕e1?! ♕e6→] **♕h2 29. ♕e1**□ [29. ♔d1 ♖f2 30. ♖f2 ♖f2→ 31. e6? ♖b2] **♕h6?!**⊕ [29... ♕g2! 30. e6 ♖f3 31. e7!□ (31. ♖f3 ♕f3 32. ♔d2 ♖d8 33. ♔c1 ♕d3! 34. e7 ♕c4 35. ♔b1 ♖e8∓ △♔f7,♖e7) ♖e3 32. ♔e3 ♖e8 33. ♔d2 ♖e7 (33... ♔f7 34. ♖g1 ♕f3 35. ♕e3 ♕f6 36. ♕f4!=) 34. ♕e7 ♕f1=] **30. ♔d1! ♖f3** [30... ♕e6!? 31. ♕e2 ♖f3⇆] **31. ♖f3 gf3?** [31... ♖f3! (♕ **9/e**) 32. e6 ♕g6! (32... ♔f8 33. ♕e4±) 33. ♔c1 ♖f6! 34. e7 ♖e6 35. ♕b4 ♕g5=] **32. ♕e3?**⊕ [32. ♕d2! ♕e6 33. ♕d4±] **♕e6?** [32... ♕e3! 33. fe3 g5 (33... ♖f5 34. ♔d2 g5 35. g4 ♖e5 36. ♔d3!±) 34. g4□ ♖f7 35. ♖f2 ♔f8 36. ♔d2 ♔e7 37. ♔d3 ♔e6 38. ♔e4 c5! 39. ♖f3 ♖f3 40. ♔f3 ♔e5 41. ♔f2 ♔e4 42. ♔e2 ♔e5 43. ♔d3 ♔d6 44. ♔e4 ♔e6=] **33. ♕e4± b5 34. ♔c2!** [34. cb5 cb5⇆] **bc4 35. ♖d1** [35. ♔c3!?±] **♖e8** [35... ♖f5 36. ♖d8 ♔f7 37. ♖d6! ♕e5 38. ♕c6! (38. ♕c4 ♔e7 39. ♖c6 ♕e2=) ♕c5□ 39. ♖d7 ♔g8 40. ♖d8 ♔h7 41. ♕c5 ♖c5 42. ♖f8+−; 35... c3 36. ♕a4! (36. ♔c3 ♕a2 37. ♕c4 ♕c4 38. ♔c4 ♖b8=; 36. b3 ab3 37. ab3 ♖b8=) ♕e5 (36... cb2 37. ♕b3+−⊥) 37. ♕c4±→] **36. ♕f3 ♕e5 37. ♕c6+−** [△ 38... ♕c4, 38... ♕a4] **♕f5 38. ♔c1 ♕g5?** [38... ♖c8 39. ♕d5 ♕d5 40. ♖d5 c3 41. b3+−] **39. f4 ♕e7 40. ♕c4 ♔f8 41. ♖h1 ♕e3 42. ♔b1 1 : 0** [Štohl]

420. **D 43**

JUSUPOV 2645 − M. GUREVICH 2610
München 1993

1. d4 d5 2. c4 c6 3. ♘f3 ♘f6 4. ♘c3 e6 5. ♗g5 h6 6. ♗f6 ♕f6 7. e3 ♘d7 8. ♗d3 dc4 9. ♗c4 ♗d6 10. 0−0 ♕e7 11. ♘e4 ♗c7 12. ♖c1 0−0 13. ♕c2 ♖d8 14. ♖fd1 a5 15. ♗b3 ♘f8 16. a3 ♗d7 17. ♘c5 ♖ab8 N [17... ♖a7 − 56/470] **18. e4!**±○ **♗c8** [△ b6; 18... ♗e8 19. e5 ♗b6 20. ♘e4±] **19. ♘d3!? ♘g6** [19... ♗d7 20. e5± △ ♘f4] **20. e5 ♘h4?!** [20... ♗d7] **21. ♘de1!± ♘f3** [21... ♘g6!?] **22. ♘f3 ♗d7 23. ♕e4** [23. ♘d2 (△ ♘e4) c5!⇆ (△ ♗c6) 24. ♘e4 ♗c6 25. ♘c5 ♗b6∞] **c5!?** [23... ♗e8 24. h4± △ h5, ♗c2] **24. ♖c5** [24. dc5? ♗c6 25. ♕e3 ♗f3 26. gf3 ♕g5=; 24. d5 ed5 25. ♗d5 b5∞] **♗c6** [24... ♗b6 25. ♖c3±] **25. ♕f4 ♗f3!?** **26. gf3!** [26. ♕f3? ♖d4!=] **b5** [26... ♗b6 27. ♖c3±] **27. ♔h1** [△ ♖g1→] **♗b6!? 28. ♖b5 ♗a7!** [28... ♗d4?! 29. ♕d4!! ♖d4 30. ♖b8 ♔h7 31. ♖d4+−] **29. ♖b8** [29. a4?! ♖b5 30. ab5 ♕b4] **♖b8 30. ♗c4!?** [30. ♖d3 a4 31. ♗a4 ♖b2⇆] **♖b2 31. d5 ed5 32. ♖d5 ♗f2!?** [32... ♖f2 33. ♖a5 ♖b2 34. ♕f7 ♕f7 35. ♗f7 ♔f7 36. ♖a7±] **33. ♖a5 ♕d8** [33... ♗a7 34. ♕f7±] **34. ♗f7** [34. ♕f7? ♔h8 35. ♖d5 ♖b1 36. ♔g2 ♕g5→] **♔h8 35. ♗d5?!** [35. ♕a4?! (△ ♖a8) ♖b1 36. ♔g2 ♕g5 37. ♔h3 ♕f5; 35. ♖d5! ♕c8 36. ♗g6+−] **♗e3!!** [35... ♖b8? 36. e6! ♗e3 37. ♕b8+−] **36. ♕a4!!** [36. ♕f5? ♖b8!−+] **♖b1!** [36... ♖b8 37. ♖a8+−] **37. ♔g2 ♕g5?**⊕ [⌓ 37... ♖b8 △ 38. ♖a8 ♕g5 39. ♔h3 ♕e5±] **38. ♔h3+− ♕e5** [38... ♕h5 39. ♕h4+−; 38... ♕f5 39. ♕g4+−] **39. ♖a8?**⊕ **♖b8 40. ♖b8 ♕b8±** [♕ **8/h**] **41. ♕c2! ♗f4 42. a4 ♗c7 43. ♕g6 ♕c8** [43... ♗h2 44. ♗e4 ♔g8 45. a5±] **44. ♗e6 ♕a8 45. ♕f7 ♕d8 46. ♗f5 ♕a8 47. ♔g4!?** [47. ♗e4 ♕c8 48. ♔g2 ♕d8] **♗h2 48. ♕g6 ♔g8 49. ♗e6 ♔h8 50. a5 ♕b8 51. ♔h3 ♗c7 52. ♗f5 ♔g8 53. ♗e6 ♔h8 54. a6 ♗b6 55. ♗f5 ♔g8 56. ♕e6 ♔h8** [56... ♔f8?? 57. ♗g6+−] **57. ♕g6 ♔g8 58. ♗e4 ♕c8 59. ♔g2 ♕d8** [△ ♕g5] **60. ♕e6 ♔h8 61. ♔h3 ♕b8 62. ♕f5 ♔g8** [62... ♕g8!?] **63. f4** [63. ♕d7 ♔h8 64. f4 ♗a7 65. ♗d3 ♗b6 66. ♕f5 ♕g8!±] **♕d8! 64. ♔g3 ♗a7 65. ♗b1?!** [65. ♗c2 ♕b6!]

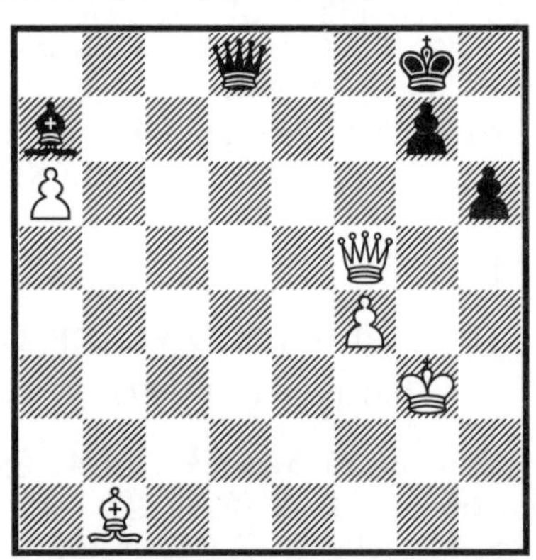

65... ♗f2!! [65... ♗b6 66. ♗c2 ♗a7 67. ♔g4 ♕b6 68. ♔h5 ♕c5 69. ♗b3 ♔h8 70. ♗d5 ♗b6 71. ♕e6 ♕f8±] **66. ♔g2** [66. ♔f2 ♕d2 67. ♔f3 ♕d1 68. ♔e3 ♕e1 69. ♔d4 ♕b4 70. ♔d5 ♕b5=] **♕d2 67. ♕e6 ♔f8 68. ♔f3** [68. ♗g6 ♗a7 69. ♔f3? ♕f2 70. ♔g4 ♕g2 71. ♔f5?? ♕h3 72. ♔e5 ♗b8 73. ♔d5 ♕b3−+; 68. ♗a2 ♕f4] **♗g1! 69. ♕f5** [69. ♗a2 ♕f2 70. ♔g4 h5! 71. ♔h5 ♕h2=] **♔e7 70. ♕e5 ♔d8 71. ♕b8 ♔e7 72. ♕c7 ♔f8 73. ♕c8 ♔e7 74. ♕b7 ♔d8 75. ♗e4⩲ ♕f2** [75... g5!?; 75... ♕d1] **76. ♔g4 ♕a7 77. ♕b3!± ♗d4** [77... ♕a6 78. ♕d1+−] **78. ♗f5 ♔c7 79. ♕d5** [79. ♕b5!?±] **♗f6 80. ♕d7 ♔b6 81. ♕d6 ♔a5!** [81... ♔b5? 82. ♗d7 ♔c4 (82... ♔a5 83. ♕a3 ♔b6 84. ♕e3 ♔a6 85. ♗c8+−) 83. ♕c6 *a)* 83... ♔b4 84. ♕b7+−; *b)* 83... ♔d3 84. ♗f5 ♔e3 (84... ♔d4 85. ♕d7+−) 85. ♕e4 ♔d2 86. ♕c2 ♔e1 (86... ♔e3 87. ♕d3 ♔f2 88. ♕d2+−) 87. ♔f3+−; *c)* 83... ♔d4 84. ♗e6 (△ ♕d7) ♔e3 (84... h5 85. ♔f3+−; 84... ♕b8 85. ♕b7 ♕d6 86. ♕d7+−; 84... ♗e7 85. ♕c4 ♔e3 86. ♕c1+−) 85. ♕c1 ♔d3 (85... ♔f2 86. ♕d2 ♔g1 87. ♔f3 ♕a8 88. ♗d5+−; 85... ♔e4 86. ♕b1! ♔e3 87. ♕g1+−) 86. ♗c4 ♔e4 87. ♕h1 ♔d4 88. ♕g1+−] **82. ♕a3** [82. ♗d3 ♗e7!?] **♔b5** [82... ♔b6?? 83. ♕e3+−] **83. ♗d3** [83. ♕b3!? ♔a5!? (83... ♔c6?! 84. ♗e4! ♔c7! 85. ♕c4 ♔b6! 86. ♕c6 ♔a5 87. ♗d3 ♕b6±; 83... ♔c5 84. ♕b7 ♕b6 85. ♗e4 ♕e6 △ 86. ♔g3 g5 87. a7 gf4 88. ♔h2 ♕a2) 84. ♕a3] **♔c6** [83... ♔b6!? 84. ♕d6 ♔a5±] **84. ♕c1! ♔d6** [84... ♔d7 85. ♗b5 ♔d8 86. ♕c6 ♕g1 87. ♔f5 (87. ♔h5!?) ♕b1 88. ♔e6 ♕b3 89. ♗c4 ♕e3 90. ♔f7 ♕e7 91. ♔g6 ♗d4 92. ♕a8 ♔c7 93. ♕b7 ♔d8 94. ♕b8 ♔d7 95. ♗b5 ♔e6 96. ♕c8 ♔d6 97. ♕c6#; 84... ♔d5 85. ♗b5] **85. ♗b5** [△ ♕c6-b7] **♗d4?!** [85... ♕a8? 86. ♕a3! ♔e6 (86... ♔c7 87. ♕c5+−) 87. ♕e3 ♔f7 88. ♕e8+−; 85... ♕b6 86. ♕a3 ♔c7 87. a7 ♕e6! (87... ♕g1 88. ♔f5 ♕b1 89. ♗d3+−; 87... h5 88. ♔h3 ♕e6 89. ♔h2+−) 88. ♔g3 ♕e1 89. ♔g2! ♕e4 90. ♔h3 ♕e6 (90... ♕h1 91. ♔g4+−) 91. ♔h2; 85... h5 86. ♔f5 ♕b6 87. ♕c4 ♗d4 (87... ♔e7 88. ♕d5! g6 89. ♔g6 ♕g1 90. ♔h6 ♕g7 91. ♔h5+−) 88. a7 g6 (88... ♕a7 89. ♕c6 ♔e7 90. ♕e6 ♔d8 91. ♕d6 ♔c8 92. ♗a6+−) 89. ♔e4 ♕b7 90. ♔d4 ♕a7 91. ♔d3 ♕a3 92. ♔e4 ♕a8 93. ♔e3+−; 85... ♔e7!? 86. ♕a3 ♔f7 87. ♗c4 ♔e8 88. ♕d6±; 86... ♔e6±] **86. ♕c6 ♔e7 87. f5! ♕b6** [87... ♗f2 88. ♕e6 ♔d8 89. ♕g8 ♔c7 90. ♕g7 ♔b6 91. ♕a7 ♔a7 92. ♔h5 ♗e3 93. ♔g6+−; 87... ♗c5!? 88. ♕d5 (88. ♕e6 ♔d8 89. ♕g8 ♔c7 90. ♕g7 ♔b6 91. f6 ♗d4! 92. ♕e7 ♗c5) ♕b6 89. ♕d7 ♔f6 90. a7 h5 91. ♔h5 g6 92. ♔g4! ♕a7 93. ♕e6 ♔g7 94. f6 ♔h6 (94... ♔h7 95. ♗d7+−) 95. ♕e5 ♕a2 (95... ♔h7 96. ♕h2 ♔g8 97. ♗c4+−; 95... ♗g1 96. ♕g5+−) 96. ♕f4 ♔h7 97. ♕c7+−] **88. ♕d7 ♔f6 89. ♗c4+−** [89. a7 h5 90. ♔h5 (90. ♔f3? ♗g1) g6 91. ♔h6! ♗e3 92. ♔h7 ♕a7 93. ♕a7 ♗a7 94. fg6+−] **h5 90. ♔h5 ♔e5 91. ♔g4! ♕d6** [91... ♔e4 92. ♕e6+−] **92. ♕g7 ♔e4 93. ♕b7 ♔e5 94. ♕h1 ♕c5 95. ♕h2 ♔f6 96. ♕h6 ♔e7 97. ♕e6 ♔d8 98. ♕d5 1 : 0** **[Jusupov]**

421. **D 43**

LOBRON 2620 − M. GUREVICH 2610
München 1993

1. d4 d5 2. c4 c6 3. ♘c3 ♘f6 4. ♘f3 e6 5. ♗g5 h6 6. ♗f6 ♕f6 7. e3 ♘d7 8. ♗d3 ♕d8 9. ♕c2!? N [△ 0-0-0; 9. 0−0 − 48/(570)] **♗e7 10. cd5 ed5 11. 0-0-0 ♘f6** [11... b5 12. e4!? b4 13. ♘a4±; 11... 0−0 12. g4↑] **12. h3!?** [12. ♘e5 ♘g4 13. ♘g4 ♗g4 14. f3 ♗e6 15. e4 0−0⇆] **♗d6 13. ♘e5 ♕e7 14. f4 ♗e6!?** [△ 0-0-0; 14... 0−0 15. g4↑] **15. ♔b1 0-0-0 16. ♖c1** [16. ♘b5 ♔b8 17. ♘d6 ♖d6∞ △ ♖c8, ♘e8, f6⇆] **♔b8 17. g4 ♖c8 18. ♘a4 ♖c7 19. ♖h2 ♖hc8!** [△ c5⇆≪] **20. ♕d1** [20. ♕b3?! c5 21. ♘c5 ♗c5 22. dc5 d4⇆; 20. ♘c5 ♗c5 21. ♕c5 ♕c5 22. ♖c5 ♘d7=] **c5! 21. ♘c5 ♗c5 22. dc5 ♖c5 23. ♖hc2 ♘d7 24. ♘f3 ♖c2 25. ♗c2!?** [25. ♖c2 ♖c2 26. ♕c2 ♘c5=] **♘b6 26. ♕d4 f6 27. ♗d3 ♖c1 28. ♔c1 ♕d6 29. ♘d2!?** [△ ♘b1-c3] **♘c8!?** [△ ♘e7-c6] **30. ♔d1 ♗d7** [30... ♘e7?! 31. ♘e4! ♕c7 32. ♘c3⩲] **31. a3 h5!? 32. ♗e2** [32. gh5 ♗h3⇆] **hg4 33. hg4 b6!?** [△ ♕c5=] **34. ♗f3 ♗c6 35. ♘b1**

[35. b4! ♔c7 36. ♘b1 ♘e7 37. ♘c3±] **♕c5!= 36. ♕c5?!** [36. ♘c3 ♕d4 37. ed4 ♘e7=] **bc5** [♘♗ 9/c] **37. b4 cb4 38. ab4 ♘e7! 39. ♘d2** [39. ♘c3 d4 40. ♗c6 ♘c6 41. ed4 ♘b4∓; 39. ♔d2 d4 40. ♗c6 ♘c6 41. b5 de3 42. ♔e3 ♘e7=] **♔c7!?** [39... d4=] **40. ♔c2 ♔d6 41. ♔c3 g5!? 42. fg5** [⌓ 42. f5=] **fg5∓ 43. ♘b3** [43. ♔d4 ♗d7∓ △ ♘c6-e5] **♘g6 44. ♗e2!** [44. ♘c5? d4 45. ♔d4 ♗f3−+; 44. ♘d4 ♗d7 45. ♗e2 ♘e5∓] **♘e5 45. ♘d4** [45. ♘c5!? ♗d7 46. ♘d7 ♘d7 (46... ♔d7 47. e4 ♔d6 48. ed5 ♔d5 49. ♔b3= △ ♔a4) 47. ♗d3=] **♗d7 46. ♘f3?! ♘f3!** [46... ♗g4 47. ♘e5 ♗e2 48. ♘f7 ♔e7 49. ♘g5 ♗g4 50. ♔d4 ♔f6 51. ♘h7 ♔g6 52. ♔d5 ♔h7 53. b5=] **47. ♗f3 ♔e5∓** [♘♗ 7/k] **48. ♔d3 ♗b5 49. ♔d2** [49. ♔c3 ♗a6 50. ♔d2□] **d4 50. ♗b7** [50. ♗d1 ♔e4 51. ♗c2 d3 52. ♗b3 ♗d7 53. ♗c4 ♗g4 54. ♗d3 ♔f3∓] **♗e8!** [△ ♗g6-e4] **51. ♗f3 ♗g6 52. ♗b7 ♗e4 53. ♗c8 ♗c6 54. ♗a6** [54. ♔d3 ♗b5 55. ♔d2 ♔d5−+] **♗d7 55. ♗e2 ♔d5!−+⊙ 56. ♗f3** [56. ♔d3 ♗b5 57. ♔d2 ♗e2 58. ♔e2 ♔e4−+] **♔c4 57. ♗e2 ♔b4 58. ed4 a5 59. ♔c2 ♗c6 60. ♔b2 ♗d5 61. ♗d3** [61... a4 62. ♔c2 a3 63. ♗f5 ♗b3 64. ♔b1 ♔c3−+] **0 : 1**
[M. Gurevich]

422.* **D 44**

BELJAVSKIJ 2610 − KRAMNIK 2685
Linares 1993

1. d4 d5 2. c4 c6 3. ♘f3 ♘f6 4. ♘c3 e6 5. ♗g5 dc4 6. e4 b5 7. e5 h6 8. ♗h4 g5 9. ♘g5 hg5 10. ♗g5 ♘bd7 11. g3 ♖g8!? 12. h4 [RR 12. ♗h4?! ♗b7 N (12... ♕a5?! − 55/(423)) 13. ♗g2 ♕c7 14. ef6 0-0-0 15. ♕f3 (15. 0−0 ♘e5∞; 15. ♕h5!?∞) b4! (15... c5 16. ♕b7 ♕b7 17. ♗b7 ♔b7 18. ♘b5 cd4 19. ♘d4 ♘e5 20. ♘c2±) 16. ♘e2 (16. ♘e4 c5∓; 16. ♘a4 c5 17. ♕b7 ♕b7 18. ♗b7 ♔b7 19. 0-0-0 ♔c6∞̄) ♘b6! (16... c5?! 17. ♕b7 ♕b7 18. ♗b7 ♔b7 19. 0-0-0±) *a)* 17. 0−0 c5 18. ♕b7 ♕b7 19. ♗b7 ♔b7 20. ♖fd1 ♘a4 (20... ♔c6!? △ a5∓) 21. ♖ab1 ♔c6 22. ♔f1 ♖d5 (22... c3? 23. bc3 ♘c3 24. ♘c3 bc3 25. ♖bc1 cd4 26. ♖c3±) 23. ♖dc1 ♔b5?! 24. b3! cb3 (24... ♘b6? 25. bc4 ♘c4 26. ♘c3+−) 25. ab3 ♘b6 26. ♖a1 a5 27. dc5 ♗c5 28. ♘f4 (Magerramov 2565 − Savčenko 2535, Rostov na Donu (open) 1993) ♖f5∓; 23... ♘b6∓; *b)* 17. 0-0-0 ♘d5 △ c5∞̄ Savčenko] **♖g5 13. hg5 ♘d5 14. g6 fg6 15. ♕g4 ♕e7 16. ♗g2!? N** [16. ♕g6 − 47/(517)] **♕f7!** [16... ♘7b6] **17. ♗e4 ♘e7 18. 0-0-0?!** [⌓ 18. ♘b5 cb5 19. ♗a8 ♘b6 20. ♗e4 ♘bd5∞] **♗a6!** [18... ♘b6?! 19. ♗c2! △ ♘e4; 18... ♗b7 19. ♘b5 cb5 20. ♗b7 ♖b8 21. ♗e4↑] **19. ♘e2 ♗g7! 20. ♘f4 ♘f8∓ 21. ♘h3 0-0-0** [21... ♘d5? 22. ♘g5 ♕e7 23. ♗g6!! ♘g6 24. ♘e6±→; 21... c3!? 22. bc3 ♘d5; 21... ♗h6!?; 21... ♗b7!?] **22. ♘g5 ♕e8! 23. ♕f3** [23. ♘e6? ♕d7] **♘f5 24. ♕a3!** [24. ♗c6 ♕e7 25. ♕f4 (25. ♘e4 ♘d4 26. ♘d6 ♖d6 27. ed6 ♕g5 28. ♕e3 ♕e3 29. fe3 ♘c6−+) ♗h6 26. ♖h6 ♘h6 27. ♘e4 ♔c7!?∓] **♗b7** [24... ♔b7?! 25. ♗g2!] **25. ♕a7 ♕e7 26. ♘f3 c5! 27. ♗b7 ♕b7 28. ♕b7** [28. ♕c5 ♔b8∓] **♔b7 29. dc5 ♖c8 30. b4** [30. g4 ♘h6!] **cb3 31. ab3 ♖c5 32. ♔b2 ♘e7 33. ♖c1 ♖d5 34. ♖hd1** [34. ♖c2 ♔b6 35. ♖hc1 ♘d7 36. ♖c7 ♖e5! 37. ♔b1 ♖d5∓] **♖d1 35. ♖d1 ♘c6 36. ♔c2 ♔b6 37. ♘d4?⊕** [37. ♔d3!∓ △ 37... ♘d7 38. ♔e4! ♘c5 39. ♔f4] **♗e5** [37... ♘e5? 38. ♘e6!] **38. ♘c6 ♔c6 39. ♖d8 ♗d6 40. ♖a8 g5−+ 41. ♖a6 ♔d5 42. ♖a5 ♔c5 43. ♖a7 e5! 44. ♔d3 ♘e6** [44... ♔d5 45. ♖a5! △ 45... e4?! 46. ♔c3 ♔c5 47. b4 ♔c6 48. ♖a8] **45. ♔e4□ ♘d4 46. ♖g7 ♘b3 47. ♖g5 ♔c4 48. ♖g6** [48. f4 ♘c5 49. ♔f3 ef4 50. gf4 ♗f4! 51. ♖g4 ♘d3−+] **♘c5 49. ♔f5 ♔d5 50. ♖h6 b4 51. ♖h1 ♘d3! 52. f3** [52. g4 b3 53. g5 e4! 54. g6 ♗e5 55. ♖b1 b2−+] **b3 53. g4 b2** [△ ♘c1] **54. ♖b1 ♔d4! 55. g5 ♔c3 56. ♔e6** [56. g6 ♗f8−+; 56. ♔f6 ♘f4 57. g6 ♘g6−+] **♗b8! 57. ♔d7** [57. g6 ♘f4 58. ♔f7 ♘g6−+] **♘f4 58. ♖h1 ♔c2 59. ♖h2 ♔b3** [60. ♖h8 ♗a7] **0 : 1**
[Kramnik]

423.* **D 44**

LOBRON 2620 − KRAMNIK 2685
Dortmund 1993

1. d4 d5 2. c4 c6 3. ♘f3 ♘f6 4. ♘c3 e6 5. ♗g5 dc4 6. e4 b5 7. e5 h6 8. ♗h4 g5

9. ♘g5 hg5 10. ♗g5 ♘bd7 11. ef6 ♗b7 12. g3 c5 13. d5 ♘f6 [RR 13... ♘b6 14. de6 ♗h1 15. e7 ♕d7 16. ♕d7 ♘d7 N (16... ♔d7 – 44/(511)) 17. ♘b5 ♗e7 18. fe7 f6 19. ♗e3! ♔e7 20. h4 ♗f3! 21. ♗c4 ♖hc8 22. ♖c1 ♘e5 23. ♘a3 ♖ab8 24. b3 ♖b4 25. ♗f1 (Ionov 2500 – R. Ščerbakov 2570, Rostov na Donu (open) 1993) ♗g4 26. ♔d2! ♘f3 27. ♔c3±; 24... ♘c4!?; ⌓ 23. b3 △ ♗f1± Ionov] **14. de6!? N** [14. ♗c4!? – 47/519] **♗g7!** [14... ♕d1 15. ♖d1 ♗h1 16. ♗f6 ♖h6 17. ♘b5!± △ 17... ♖f6 18. ♘c7 ♔e7 19. ♖d7#] **15. ♖g1 ♕b6 16. ♕e2!** [16. ef7 ♔f7 17. ♗g2 ♖h2 18. ♗b7 ♕b7∓; 16. ♗f6 ♕e6 17. ♕e2 ♗f6 18. ♘b5 ♕e2 19. ♗e2 ♗b2 20. ♖b1 c3∓] **♕e6□** [16... fe6? 17. 0-0-0 ♖h2 18. ♘b5! ♘e4 19. ♘d6!+–] **17. ♘b5 ♕e2 18. ♗e2 ♘e4! 19. 0-0-0** [19. ♘c7 ♔f8 20. ♗f4 (20. ♘a8 ♘g5∓) ♖d8⇆; ⌓ 19. ♗f4∞] **♘g5 20. ♘d6 ♔f8 21. ♘b7 ♖h2∓ 22. ♖gf1 ♗d4** [22... ♖b8 23. ♖d7↑] **23. ♗c4?!** [23. ♘d6 ♖f2 24. ♖f2 ♗f2 25. ♗c4 ♗g3 26. ♘f7! ♗f4 27. ♔c2 ♘f7 28. ♖f1=] **♖b8 24. ♗d5** [24. ♘d6 ♗b2 25. ♔c2 ♗d4∓] **♗f2 25. ♖d3 ♗d4 26. ♖b3 ♔g7 27. ♔b1** [27. ♖d1!? △ ♖d2] **♖d2 28. ♔c1 ♖h2 29. ♔b1 ♔g6 30. a4** [30. g4!?] **f5!** [△ ♘e4] **31. ♖e1□ ♔h5!? 32. ♖f1⊕ ♖e8 33. ♘a5** [33. ♘d6? ♖d8; 33. ♖f5 ♔g6 △ 34. ♖f1 ♖ee2↑] **♖e5 34. ♗f3** [34. ♗c6] **♘f3 35. ♖ff3 ♖e1 36. ♔a2 ♖ee2 37. ♘c4□ ♖c2 38. ♘e3 ♖b2 39. ♖b2 ♖b2 40. ♔a3= ♖e2 41. ♘f5**
1/2 : 1/2 **[Kramnik]**

424. **D 44**

JUSUPOV 2645 – ŠIROV 2670

Linares 1993

1. d4 d5 2. c4 c6 3. ♘f3 ♘f6 4. ♘c3 e6 5. ♗g5 dc4 6. e4 b5 7. e5 h6 8. ♗h4 g5 9. ♘g5 hg5 10. ♗g5 ♘bd7 11. ef6 ♗b7 12. g3 c5 13. d5 ♗h6 14. ♗h6 ♖h6 15. ♕d2 ♕f6 16. 0-0-0!?± [16. ♘e4 ♕f3 17. ♘d6 ♔e7 18. ♖g1 (18. ♘b7 ♖h5∞) ♕d5 (18... ♗d5) 19. ♕h6 ♕d6$\overline{\overline{\infty}}$; 16. ♗g2 – 39/524] **♗d5 N** [16... 0-0-0? 17. ♘e4±] **17. ♘d5 ed5 18. ♗g2** [18. ♕d5 ♖d8 19. f4±] **♘b6 19. ♕e3?** [19. ♗d5 0-0-0 (19... ♖c8 20. ♗b7 ♖c7 21. ♗a6±) 20. ♗b7 ♔c7 21. ♕d8 ♕d8 22. ♖d8 ♔d8 23. ♗a6±] **♔f8 20. ♕c5** [20. ♗d5? ♘a4!↑] **♔g8 21. ♕d4** [21. ♗d5? ♖h5–+] **♖e8∓ 22. ♗d5 ♕d4 23. ♖d4 ♖e2** [23... ♖d8?? 24. ♗f7] **24. ♗e4! c3!?** [24... ♖f2 25. ♖d2=] **25. bc3 ♘a4 26. ♗c2!? ♘c3 27. ♖d2 ♘a2 28. ♔d1 ♘c3 29. ♔c1 ♖he6!?** [29... ♖e5 30. ♔b2 b4∞] **30. ♗d3 ♖2e5 31. ♔b2 b4 32. ♖a1 a5 33. ♗c2 ♖a6 34. f4** [34. ♖d4!?] **♖e3 35. ♖d4!** [△ ♖b4] **♖e2** [35... a4 36. ♖b4 a3 37. ♖a3 ♘d1 (37... ♖a3? 38. ♖b8) 38. ♗d1=] **36. ♖b4 ♖c6! 37. ♖a5! ♘d1 38. ♔c1 ♖cc2 39. ♔d1= ♖ed2 40. ♔e1 ♖h2 41. ♔d1 ♖cg2 42. ♖e4** **1/2 : 1/2** **[Jusupov]**

425.* **!N** **D 45**

MICHAELSEN 2405 – KNAAK 2525

Deutschland 1992

1. d4 e6 2. c4 d5 3. ♘f3 c6 4. e3 ♘f6 5. ♘c3 ♘bd7 6. ♕c2 ♗d6 7. g4 dc4 [RR 7... ♗b4!? N 8. ♗d2 a5 (8... ♕e7!?) 9. g5 (9. ♗d3 dc4) ♗c3 10. ♗c3 ♘e4 11. ♖g1 ♕e7 12. ♗d3 ♘c3 13. ♕c3 ♕b4! 14. ♔e2 ♕c3 15. bc3 (Krasenkov 2560 – Pekárek 2440, Deutschland 1993) b6! △ ♗a6= Krasenkov] **8. ♗c4 b5 9. ♗e2 ♗b7! N** [9... b4 – 56/(476)] **10. g5 ♘d5 11. ♘e4 ♗e7 12. ♗d2 ♖c8! 13. ♖c1?!** [13. ♘c5?! ♘c5 14. dc5 ♗g5 15. ♘g5 ♕g5 16. 0-0-0 e5∓; 13. ♖g1!? ⁄⁄h1-a8 ×g5] **c5! 14. dc5 ♘c5 15. ♘c5** [15. ♗b5 ♘d7! (15... ♔f8!?) 16. ♕a4 ♖c1 17. ♗c1 0–0! 18. ♕a7 (18. ♗d7?! ♘b6∓) ♕c7 19. 0–0 ♘c5! 20. ♘c5 ♗c5 21. ♕a4 ♘b4 22. ♗e2 (22. ♘d4?! ♕e5 23. f4 ♕e4∓) ♖a8 23. ♕d1 ♖a2∓ ⁄⁄a8-h1] **♖c5 16. ♕b3 ♖c1 17. ♗c1 0–0∓ 18. ♖g1** [18. ♕b5?! ♕a8∓] **♕c7 19. ♗d2 ♘b4 20. a3** [20. ♗b4 ♕c1 21. ♗d1 ♗b4 22. ♕b4 ♗f3 23. ♕d2 ♕a1∓] **♗d5 21. ♕c3 ♘c6 22. ♖g4 e5 23. h4 ♖c8 24. b4 ♕b8** [24... ♕b7∓] **25. ♕b2 ♗e6 26. ♖g3** [26. ♖g1!?] **♗d6 27. ♖g2 e4∓ 28. ♘d4 ♗e5 29. ♘c6 ♖c6 30. ♕b1 ♗d5 31. h5 a6 32. ♖g4 ♕c8 33. ♔f1** [33. ♖e4!? ♗e4 34. ♕e4 ♖c1! 35. ♗d1! (35. ♗c1 ♕c1 36. ♗d1 ♗c3 37. ♔f1 ♕d1 38. ♔g2 ♕d8–+) ♗c3∓]

♖c2−+ 34. ♕d1 ♕c6 [34... ♗c4!] **35. ♔g2 ♖a2 36. ♗e1 ♖a1 37. ♕d2 ♖a2 38. ♕d1 ♕e6 39. ♖h4 ♖a1 40. ♕d2 ♖a2 41. ♕d1 f5! 42. gf6 ♗f6 43. ♖f4 ♖a3 44. ♗g4 ♕c6 45. ♗f5 ♖a1 46. ♕d2 ♕c4 47. ♖g4 ♕d3! 48. h6 ♖d1 0 : 1 [Knaak]**

426. D 45

KRASENKOV 2560 − DOHOJAN 2510
Deutschland 1993

1. c4 e6 2. ♘f3 d5 3. d4 ♘f6 4. ♘c3 c6 5. e3 ♘bd7 6. ♕c2 ♗d6 7. g4 dc4 8. ♗c4 e5!? N 9. g5 [9. ♘g5 0−0∓] **♘d5! 10. ♗d2!** [10. ♘e4 ♗b4 11. ♗d2 ♕e7∞; 10. ♗d5 cd5 11. ♘d5 0−0∞] **ed4** [10... ♘b4? 11. ♕b3 ed4 12. ♘e4!] **11. ♘d5 cd5 12. ♗d5 de3 13. fe3?!** [13. ♕e4 ♕e7 14. ♕e7 ♔e7 15. ♗e3 ♘b6 16. ♗e4 ♖e8 17. 0-0-0 ♘c4 18. ♗d4 ♔f8∞; 13. ♗c3!? ef2 14. ♔f2 (14. ♕f2 ♕e7 15. ♔f1 ♘b6∞) 0−0 15. ♖ad1 (15. g6 hg6 16. ♕g6 ♘e5↑) ♕c7! (×c2) 16. ♖he1 ♘b6 (16... ♗h2 17. ♔g2!) 17. ♗e4 g6∞] **♘b6** [13... ♘e5 14. ♘e5 ♗e5 15. ♕e4↑] **14. ♗b3 ♗e6?!** [14... ♕e7 15. ♘d4 (15. 0−0 0−0∓) 0−0 16. 0-0-0 ♕g5!?] **15. ♗e6 fe6 16. ♕b3** [16. ♕e4 ♕e7 17. ♘d4 0−0 18. ♕e6 ♕e6 19. ♘e6 ♖fe8 20. ♘d4 ♗f4∓] **♕e7 17. ♘d4 ♕g5** [17... ♘d5!? 18. e4 ♘c7 19. ♖c1 0−0 20. ♘f5 ♕d7 △ 21. ♘d6 ♕d6 22. ♗b4 ♕f4] **18. ♕e6 ♕e7 19. ♖f1!** [19. ♗c3 ♘a4∓] **♖f8! 20. ♔e2= ♖f1⊕ 21. ♖f1 ♕e6 22. ♘e6 g6 23. e4⊕** [23. ♘g5 ♗h2 24. ♘h7 ♗e5; 23. h4 ♔d7 24. ♘g5 h6!?; 23... ♖c8!] **♔d7 24. ♘g5 h6 25. ♘f3 ♖e8 26. ♗h6 ♖e4 27. ♔d3 1/2 : 1/2 [Dohojan]**

427.* !N D 45

ŠIROV 2670 − BANGIEV 2395
Hamburg 1993

1. d4 d5 2. c4 c6 3. ♘c3 ♘f6 4. ♘f3 e6 5. e3 ♘bd7 6. ♕c2 ♗d6 7. g4!? ♘g4 8. ♖g1 ♘h6 [RR 8... ♕f6 N 9. ♖g4 ♕f3 10. ♖g7 ♘f6 11. ♖g1 ♘e4 12. ♘e4 ♕e4 13. ♕e4 de4 14. ♗g2 f5 15. f3 h5 16. ♗h1 ef3 17. ♗f3 h4 18. h3 ♗d7 19. ♗d2± Fedorowicz 2535 − Vučić 2385, New York 1993] **9. ♗d2! N** [9. e4 — 55/425] **♕e7** [△ f5; 9... ♘f5 10. 0-0-0 ♘f6 11. e4 de4 12. ♘e4 0−0 13. ♗c3±] **10. e4 de4 11. ♘e4 ♘f5 12. 0-0-0 ♘f6?!** [12... b5!?±] **13. ♘f6 ♕f6** [13... gf6 14. ♗d3 (×♘f5) ♔d8 15. ♗f5 ef5 16. ♖ge1 ♕c7 17. d5 cd5 18. ♗c3+−] **14. ♗g5 ♕g6 15. c5 ♗c7** [15... h6 16. ♗d2 ♕h5 17. ♕e4 ♗c7 18. ♗e2+−; 15... ♗h2 16. ♖g2 ♗c7 17. ♘e5 ♕h5 18. ♕e4! △ 19. ♗e2 ♕h3 20. ♗g4+−] **16. ♘e5 ♕h5** [16... ♗e5 17. de5 f6 (17... 0−0 18. ♗e2!+− △ h4-h5) 18. ef6 gf6 19. ♕c3! 0−0 (19... e5 20. ♗c4!+− △ 21. ♕e5 fe5 22. ♖d8#) 20. h4! h6 21. ♗h6 ♕g1 22. ♗f8+−]

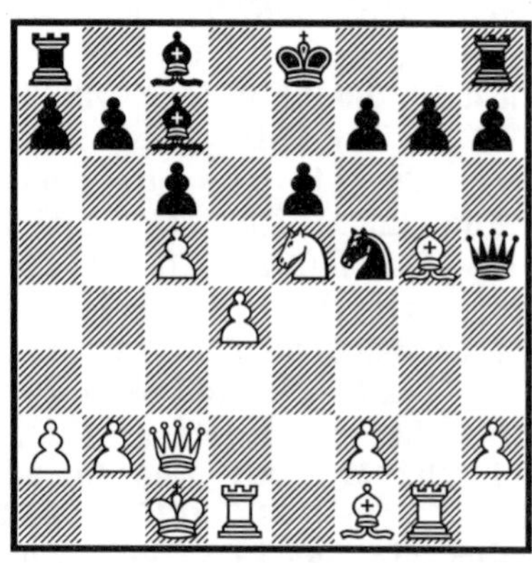

17. h4! [17. ♗e2 ♕h2 18. ♘f3 (18. ♘g4 ♗f4 19. ♔b1 ♕g1! 20. ♖g1 ♗g5±) ♕f2 19. ♖df1 ♘d4!± Bangiev] **♗d8□** [17... ♘h4? 18. ♗e2+−] **18. ♕e4! 0−0** [18... ♗g5 19. hg5 ♕h4 (19... ♕h2 20. ♗g2+−) 20. ♕f3!+−] **19. ♗e2 ♗g5 20. hg5 ♕h4 21. f4 ♖d8?!** [21... ♘g3 22. ♖g3! ♕g3 23. ♖h1 *a)* 23... h6 24. gh6 f5 25. ♕f3 ♕f3 26. h7 ♔h8 27. ♘g6#; *b)* 23... g6 24. ♘g4 h5 (24... f5 25. gf6+−) 25. ♘f6 ♔h8 26. ♘h5+−; *c)* 23... f5 24. gf6 ♖f6 25. ♕h7 ♔f8 26. ♕h8 ♔e7 27. ♖h7 ♕f4 (27... ♕e3 28. ♔b1 ♕e4 29. ♔a1+−) 28. ♔c2 ♕e4 29. ♔b3 ♕e3 (29... ♕d5 30. ♔a3+−) 30. ♗d3 ♖f7 31. ♕g8+−; 21... f6! 22. gf6 ♕f6 23. ♘g4 ♕e7 24. ♗d3! ♗d7 (24... ♔h8 25. ♖h1!+−→) 25. ♘h6 ♔h8 26. ♘f5 ♖f5 27. ♕h1!±] **22. ♖h1 ♘g3** [22... ♕g3 23. ♖d3 ♕f2 24. ♘g4+−; 22... ♕f2 23. ♘g4 ♕g3 24. ♖d3+−] **23. ♖h4 ♘e4 24. ♗d3! ♘g3** [24... ♖d4? 25.

♗e4+−; 24... ♘f2 25. ♗h7 ♔f8 26. ♖d2+−; 24... f5 25. ♗e4 fe4 26. ♖dh1+−] **25. ♖h7! ♘e2** [25... ♖d4 26. ♖h3 ♘f5 27. ♖dh1 ♔f8 28. ♗f5 ef5 29. ♖h8 ♔e7 30. ♖e1 ♖e4□ 31. ♖d1! f6 (31... ♖f4 32. ♖dd8 ♖f1 33. ♔d2+−) 32. gf6 gf6 (32... ♔f6 33. ♖f8 ♔e6 34. ♖d6 ♔e7 35. ♘g6#) 33. ♖h7 ♔e8 34. ♖g1+−] **26. ♔b1! ♘d4** [26... ♘f4 27. ♖dh1!? (27. ♗e4+−) ♔f8 28. ♖f1 ♖d4 29. ♖h4 ♖d3 (29... ♘d3 30. ♖h8 ♔e7 31. ♖f7#) 30. ♖ff4! ♖d1 31. ♔c2+−] **27. g6!+− fg6 28. ♗g6 ♖d5 29. ♖dh1 ♔f8 30. ♖h8 ♔e7 31. ♖e8 ♔f6 32. ♖f8**
1 : 0 **[Širov]**

428.** **D 45**

M. GUREVICH 2610 − JUSUPOV 2645
Deutschland 1993

1. c4 e6 2. d4 d5 3. ♘c3 c6 4. e3 ♘f6 5. ♘f3 [RR 5. ♕c2 ♘bd7 6. ♗d2 a6? 7. ♘f3 dc4 8. a4 ♖b8 9. ♗c4 b5 10. ♗d3 ♗b7 11. 0−0 ♗e7 12. ♘e4 ♘e4 13. ♗e4 c5 14. ab5 ab5 15. ♖a7 ♕b6 16. ♖b7 ♖b7 17. dc5 ♕c5 18. ♕c5 ♘c5 19. ♗b7 ♘b7 20. ♖c1 ♗d6 21. ♘d4 ♔d7 22. ♘b5± Kortchnoi 2605 − Je. Piket 2590, Nijmegen (m/5) 1993] **♘bd7 6. ♕c2 ♗d6 7. ♗e2 0−0 8. 0−0 ♖e8 9. ♖d1 ♕e7 10. h3 b6 11. e4 ♘e4 12. ♘e4 de4 13. ♕e4 ♘f6!? N** [RR 13... ♗b7 14. ♗f4 ♗f4 N (14... ♖ad8 − 55/430) 15. ♕f4 c5 16. ♕c7 ♖ab8 17. dc5 ♘c5 18. ♕e7 ♖e7 19. ♖ac1 ♖c7 20. ♘d4 a6 21. f3 ♔f8= Cosma 2365 − Kir. Georgiev 2660, Budapest (zt) 1993] **14. ♕h4** [14. ♕c6 ♗d7 15. ♕b7 ♖eb8 16. ♕a6 ♘e8! 17. c5 bc5 18. dc5 ♗c5∞] **♗b7 15. ♗f4** [15. ♗d3 c5 16. ♗g5 h6⇆ 17. ♗h6? gh6 18. ♕h6 ♘e4!−+] **♖ad8 16. ♗d6 ♖d6** [⌓ 16... ♕d6] **17. ♕g5! h6** [17... ♖ed8 18. c5±] **18. ♕e3 c5 19. dc5 ♖d1 20. ♖d1 ♗f3 21. ♗f3 bc5 22. ♕e5± ♖c8 23. ♕d6 ♔f8 24. b3 ♕d6 25. ♖d6** [♖ 9/i] **♖c7 26. ♔f1 ♔e7 27. ♖a6 ♘d7 28. ♔e2** [△ ♔d2-c3, a3, b4] **♘e5 29. ♗a8 g5!? 30. g3 ♖d7 31. ♗c6 ♖c7 32. ♗a8 ♖d7 33. ♖a5 ♖c7 34. ♔e3 f5 35. f4 ♘d7 36. ♖a6 ♘b6 37. ♗f3 ♔f6 38. ♖a5?! e5 39. ♗d5 gf4?!** [39... h5!? (△ h4) 40. h4 ef4 41. gf4 gh4⇆] **40. gf4 ♖g7⊕ 41. ♖c5!** [41. fe5 ♔e5 42. ♖c5 f4 43. ♔f2 ♘d5 44. ♖d5 ♔e4⇆] **♖g3 42. ♔f2 ef4 43. ♖c6** [43. ♗f3 ♘d7⇆] **♔e5 44. ♗f7!±** [×♘b6] **♖g7** [44... ♘d7? 45. ♖e6 ♔d4 46. ♖d6+−] **45. ♖e6 ♔d4 46. ♗g6 ♘d7 47. ♗f5 ♘e5 48. ♖d6 ♔c3 49. ♖e6 ♔d4 50. ♖d6 ♔c3 51. ♖d5** [51. ♖h6? ♖g3⇆] **♖e7 52. c5 ♔b4 53. ♖d4 ♔c5 54. ♖f4 ♖f7 55. ♔e3 ♖g7 56. ♖a4 ♔b5 57. ♖h4 ♖e7 58. ♔f4 ♘f7 59. ♗g6 ♘d8 60. ♖h6 a5 61. ♗d3 ♔b4 62. ♗c4 ♘b7 63. ♖b6 ♔a3 64. ♖b5 ♔a2 65. ♗d5 ♘d6 66. ♖a5 ♔b2 67. ♖a6 ♘b5 68. ♖g6 ♘c3 69. ♗e6 ♘e2 70. ♔e5 ♔c3 71. ♖g4 ♖h7 72. ♖c4 ♔d2 73. b4 ♔d3 74. ♖g4! ♔c3** [74... ♖h3 75. ♗c4 ♔d2 76. ♗e2 ♔e2 77. ♔d6+−] **75. b5 ♖h5 76. ♗f5 ♖h3 77. b6 ♖h6 78. b7 ♖b6 79. ♗e4 ♘c1! 80. ♖g3** [80. ♖g8? ♘d3 81. ♔f5 ♖b5 82. ♔f6 ♘c5=] **♔d2!** [80... ♔b4 81. ♖g8 ♘d3 82. ♔d4+−]

81. ♔f5! [81. ♖g8 ♘d3 82. ♔d4 ♖b4=] **♖b5** [81... ♘b3 82. ♖d3 ♔e2 83. ♖d8+−] **82. ♔f6 ♘b3 83. ♖g5! ♖b6 84. ♔f7 ♘d4 85. ♗h1!+−** [△ ♖g8; 85. ♖g8? ♘f5!] **♖b1** [85... ♘b5 86. ♖d5 ♔c3 87. ♖d8+−] **86. ♖g8 ♖f1 87. ♔e8 ♖b1 88. ♔d7** **1 : 0** **[M. Gurevich]**

429. **!N** **D 45**

M. GUREVICH 2610 − BAREEV 2670
München 1993

1. d4 d5 2. c4 c6 3. ♘c3 ♘f6 4. e3 e6 5. ♘f3 ♘bd7 6. ♕c2 ♗d6 7. ♗e2 0−0 8. 0−0 ♕e7 9. e4 de4 10. ♘e4 ♘e4 11. ♕e4

e5 12. ♗g5 ♘f6! N = [Ivančuk; 12... f6? – 54/(431)] **13. ♗f6** [13. ♕h4 h6 14. ♗h6 gh6 15. de5 ♗e5 16. ♖ae1=/∞] **gf6 14. de5** [14. c5? ed4] **fe5 15. c5 ♗c5** [15... ♗c7=] **16. ♗c4 ♔g7!?** [16... ♗e6!] **17. ♘e5 f6 18. ♗d3 ♖h8 19. ♘c4!** [19. ♘f3 ♕e4 20. ♗e4 f5 21. ♗c2 ♔f6∓] **♕e4 20. ♗e4 ♖d8 21. ♖ac1! f5! 22. ♗f3 ♔f6 23. a3!** [△ b4, ♘a5] **a5 24. ♘a5!** [24. ♖c2 a4∓] **♖a5 25. b4 ♗f2 26. ♖f2 ♖a3 27. b5** [27... cb5 28. ♖b2 ♖a5 29. ♖c7=] **1/2 : 1/2** **[Bareev]**

430.** !N **D 45**

LPUTIAN 2610 – ANASTASIAN 2470

Protvino (zt) 1993

1. d4 d5 2. c4 c6 3. ♘c3 ♘f6 4. e3 e6 5. ♘f3 ♘bd7 6. ♕c2 ♗d6 7. b3 0–0 8. ♗e2 e5 [RR 8... dc4 9. bc4 e5 10. 0–0 ♖e8 11. ♖d1 *a)* 11... ♕e7 12. ♖b1 b6!? N (12... e4 – 56/485) 13. a4 e4 14. ♘d2 ♘f8 15. a5 ♘g6 16. ♘f1 ♘h4 17. ♘g3 ba5 18. c5 ♗c7 19. ♕a4 ♗d7=/∞ K. Bischoff 2505 – Schlemermeyer 2335, Deutschland 1993; *b)* 11... ed4! N 12. ed4 ♘f8 13. ♘e5?! ♕e7 14. ♗f4 ♘e6 15. ♕d2 ♘f4 16. ♕f4 c5 17. ♘b5 cd4 18. ♘d6 ♕d6 19. ♘d3 ♕f4 20. ♘f4 g5 21. ♘h5 ♘h5 22. ♗h5 ♖d8 23. ♖ab1 ♗e6 24. ♖b7 ♗c4 25. a3 d3∓ Zsu. Polgár 2560 – Ioseliani 2460, Monaco (m/7) 1993; 13. h3!?] **9. cd5 cd5 10. ♘b5 ♗b4 11. ♗d2 ♗d2 12. ♘d2 e4 13. 0–0 N** [13. a4 ♘e8 △ ♕g5; 13. ♖c1 – 32/518] **a6** [13... ♘e8 14. ♖fc1 ♕g5 15. ♘c7 ♘c7 16. ♕c7 ♘f6⩲] **14. ♘c3 ♘b6** [14... ♘b8 15. b4 ♘c6 16. ♖fb1±] **15. a4 ♗e6** [15... ♗g4 16. a5 ♘c8 17. b4⩲] **16. a5 ♘c8 17. b4 ♘e7 18. ♘b3** [18. ♘a4±] **♘f5 19. ♖fb1?** [19. b5 ♘h4 20. ba6 ba6 21. ♘c5 ♕c8 22. ♖fc1⩲ △ 22... ♗h3? 23. ♘d5! ♗g2 24. ♘f6 gf6 25. ♘e4±] **♘h4 20. ♘c5 ♘d7 21. ♕d1 ♕g5 22. g3 ♘f6 23. b5** [23. ♘e6 fe6 24. h3 h5 △ ♘f3↑] **♗h3 24. ba6 ba6 25. ♖b6 ♕f5 26. ♖f6 gf6 27. ♖b1?⊕** [27. ♘b1 △ ♘d2∞] **♔h8 28. ♖b6 ♖g8 29. ♘b7?** [29. ♘b1] **♖ac8! 30. ♘c5** [30. ♘d6 ♘f3 31. ♗f3 ♕f3 32. ♕f3 ef3 33. ♘c8 ♖c8 34. ♖b3∓] **♗g4 31. ♗g4 ♖g4 32. ♕f1 ♘f3 33. ♔h1 ♖cg8⊕ 34. ♘e2 ♘d2?** [34... ♖4g6 35. ♘g1 ♘h2! 36. ♔h2 ♖g3–+] **35. ♕g2 ♘c4 36. ♖b7** [36. ♖a6 ♖b8 37. h3 ♖b1 38. ♔h2 ♘d2 39. hg4 ♕g4!–+] **♕f3 37. ♕f3 ef3 38. ♘f4** [38. ♘c3! ♘a5 39. ♖f7] **♘a5 39. ♖f7 ♘c4 40. h3 ♖4g7 41. ♖f6 a5 42. ♘d5 ♖a8 43. ♘a4 ♖b7 44. ♖f3± ♘b2 45. ♘c5 ♖g7 46. e4 a4 47. ♖a3 ♘c4 48. ♖a2?⊕** [48. ♖a4+–] **a3 49. ♘b4** [49. ♔g2! ♖b8 50. ♘d3 ♖b3 51. ♘5f4 ♖b2 52. ♖a1⩲] **♖b8 50. ♘ca6 ♖gb7!** [50... ♖b6 51. ♖c2±] **51. ♘b8 ♖b4 52. ♘c6 ♖b2 53. ♖a1 a2 54. ♔g2 ♘e3 55. ♔f3 ♘c2 56. ♖a2 ♖a2 57. d5 ♖a4 58. ♔f4 ♔g7** [58... ♘b4] **59. d6 ♘b4 60. ♘b4 ♖b4 61. ♔f5 ♔f7 62. e5 ♖b3 63. e6 ♔e8 64. ♔e4 1/2 : 1/2** **[Lputian]**

431.*** !N **D 46**

B. GEL'FAND 2690
– LJUBOJEVIĆ 2605

Linares 1993

1. d4 d5 2. c4 c6 3. ♘f3 ♘f6 4. ♘c3 e6 5. e3 ♘bd7 6. ♗d3 [RR 6. ♕c2 ♗d6 7. ♗e2 0–0 8. 0–0 dc4 9. ♗c4 *a)* 9... e5 10. ♗b3 ♕e7 *a1)* 11. h3 a6 12. ♗d2 N (12. a4 – 52/423) c5 13. ♘g5 cd4 14. ed4 ed4 15. ♘d5 ♕d8 16. ♗f4 ♗f4 17. ♘f4 ♘e5 18. ♖fe1 ♕d6 19. ♘d5 g6 20. ♘f6 ♕f6 21. ♕c5 ♕g5 22. ♖e5 ♗f5 23. ♕d4 ♖ad8 24. ♕b4 b5⩲ M. Makarov 2515 – Mi. Lazić 2450, Podgorica 1993; *a2)* 11. ♖e1! N *a21)* 11... ♖e8 12. ♘g5 ♖f8 13. ♗d2 h6 14. ♘ge4 ♘e4 15. ♘e4 ♗b8 (15... ♗c7 16. d5) 16. f4!+– ed4 17. ed4 ♘f6 (17... ♘b6 18. ♘g5; 17... ♕d8 18. ♗b4 ×f7) 18. ♗b4! ♕b4 19. ♘f6 gf6 20. ♕g6 ♔h8 21. ♕h6 ♔g8 22. ♕g6 ♔h8 23. ♕f6 ♔g8 24. ♖e3 1 : 0 Miles 2565 – Summerscale 2345, Dublin (zt) 1993; *a22)* 11... e4 12. ♘d2! (12. ♘g5 ♗h2 13. ♔h2 ♘g4 14. ♔g1 ♕g5 15. ♕e4 ♕h4 16. ♕f4 ♘df6 △ ♘h5) ♖e8 13. f3 ef3 14. ♘f3± △ e4-e5, △ ♘g5 ×f7; *a23)* 11... ed4 12. ed4± Miles; *b)* 9... ♕e7 10. a3 e5 11. h3 ♗b8 12. ♗a2 h6 13. ♘h4 ♖d8 14. ♘f5 ♕e8 15. ♗d2 ♘f8 16. ♖ad1 ♕d7! N (16... ed4 – 56/(486)) 17. ♘g3 (17. g4 ed4 18. ♘d4? ♘g4–+; 18. ed4; 17. de5 ♕f5 18. ♕f5 ♗f5 19. ef6 ♗c2∓) ed4 18.

ed4 *b1)* 18... ♗g3 19. fg3 ♕d4 20. ♔h2 ♕d3 21. ♕c1 (21. ♕d3 ♖d3 22. ♗h6 ♖d1 23. ♘d1=) ♕g6 22. ♗b1 ♕h5 23. ♖f6 gf6 24. ♘e4→; *b2)* 18... ♕c7! 19. ♘ce2 ♗e6 20. ♗f4 ♕b6 21. ♗e6 (1/2 : 1/2 L. Portisch 2580 – A. Chernin 2600, Budapest (zt) 1993) ♘e6 22. ♗e5! (22. ♗e3 ♘d5∓; 22. ♗b8 ♖ab8∓) ♘d7 (22... ♗e5 23. de5 ♘d7 24. ♕c3 ♕c5 25. ♕c5 ♘dc5 26. f4=) 23. ♗b8 ♖ab8 24. d5 cd5 25. ♖d5= A. Chernin] **♗e7 7. 0–0 0–0 8. ♕e2 b6 9. e4 de4 10. ♘e4 c5 N** [10... ♗b7 – 45/(503)] **11. ♘f6 ♘f6 12. ♖d1!** [12. dc5 bc5=] **cd4** [12... ♕c7!?± ⇗b8-h2] **13. ♗f4! ♗c5?** [⌓ 13... ♗b7 14. ♘d4 (14. ♗e5 ♗f3! 15. ♕f3 ♗c5) ♕c8 15. ♘f5±; 14... ♕e8!±] **14. ♗e5 ♗b7 15. ♘d4 ♘d7 16. ♘b3!** [16. ♗h7? ♔h7 17. ♕h5 ♔g8 18. ♗g7 ♔g7 19. ♖d3 (19. ♕g4 ♔f6 20. ♕h4 ♔g6–+) ♖g8∓] **♕g5** [16... ♗e7 17. ♗h7 ♔h7 18. ♕d3±] **17. ♗g3 ♖ad8 18. ♘c5 ♘c5 19. ♗c2±⊞ f5!? 20. f3 f4 21. ♗f2 e5** [21... a5 22. a3! a4 23. ♖d8 ♖d8 24. ♖d1 ♖e8 25. ♖d6 e5 26. ♗c5+–] **22. b4! ♘d7** [22... e4 23. bc5 ef3 24. ♕e6 ♔h8 25. ♕h3+–; 22... ♘e6 23. c5 ♘d4 24. ♗d4 ed4 25. c6!+–] **23. c5 bc5 24. bc5 ♔h8** [24... ♘f6 25. c6+–] **25. h4!+– ♕h5** [25... ♕e7 26. ♕b5 ♘b8 27. ♖d8 ♖d8 28. ♖b1 ♖d7 29. ♗e4+–] **26. ♕b5 ♗f3** [26... ♗c8 27. c6 ♘f6 28. ♖d8 ♖d8 29. c7+–] **27. gf3 ♕f3 28. ♕d3 ♕g4 29. ♔h2 e4 30. ♕e4 ♘f6 31. ♕g2 ♕e2 32. ♖d8 ♖d8 33. ♖g1 g6 34. ♗e1! ♕c4** [34... ♕e3 35. ♖f1+–] **35. ♖f1 ♖e8 36. ♗b3 ♕c5 37. ♕b2 ♔g7** [37... ♖e5 38. ♖f4 ♕e7 39. ♖f6! ♕f6 (39... ♖e2 40. ♖f2!) 40. ♗g3 ♖f5 41. ♕f6 ♖f6 42. ♗e5+–] **38. ♗c3 f3 39. ♗f6 ♔h6 40. ♕d2 ♔h5 41. ♕d5 ♕d5 42. ♗d5 ♖e2 43. ♔g3**

1 : 0 **[B. Gel'fand, Huzman]**

432. **D 46**

KRASENKOV 2560 – ČERNIKOV 2400

Katowice 1993

1. d4 d5 2. c4 c6 3. ♘c3 ♘f6 4. e3 e6 5. ♘f3 ♗d6 6. ♗d3 ♘bd7 7. e4 de4 8. ♘e4 ♘e4 9. ♗e4 0–0 10. 0–0 h6 11. ♗c2 e5 12. ♕d3 f5 13. c5 ♗c7 14. de5 ♘e5 15. ♕b3 ♔h8 16. ♖e1! ♘f3 [16... ♖e8!? 17. ♗f4 ♗e6 18. ♕c3 ♘f3 19. ♕f3± ×f5; 16... ♕f6!?] **17. ♕f3 ♕f6** [17... f4 (Černikov) 18. ♕h5!? ♕g5 19. ♕g5 hg5 20. ♗d2±] **18. ♗f4 ♗f4 19. ♕f4 ♕b2 20. ♗b3 ♗d7 N** [20... b6 – 51/433] **21. ♕c7?!** [21. ♖ad1! *a)* 21... ♖ae8 22. ♕d6 ♕c3 (22... ♖e1 23. ♖e1 ♖d8 24. ♖d1+–; 22... ♗c8 23. ♖e8 ♖e8 24. ♗f7+–) 23. ♔f1!+–; *b)* 21... ♗e8 22. ♖d6 ♖f6 23. h4±] **♗e8 22. ♖ab1** [22. ♖ad1 ♗h5 △ ♖ae8⇆; 22. ♕b7 ♗f7 23. ♕c6 ♗b3 24. ab3 (24. ♖eb1 ♕d4 25. ab3 ♖fc8=) ♕b3±] **♕f6 23. ♖e6** [23. ♕b7 ♗f7 24. ♗f7 ♕f7 25. ♕c6 ♕a2±] **♕g5** [23... ♕d8 24. ♕b7±; 23... ♕d4 24. ♕b7 ♗f7 25. ♖c6±] **24. ♖e7** [24. ♕b7 ♗f7 25. ♖c6 ♖ab8 26. ♕a6! (26. ♕a7?? ♗d5–+) ♗d5? 27. ♖g6!; 26... f4!∞⇆»] **♗h5 25. f4** [25. h4!?] **♕g6** [25... ♕f6 26. ♕d6 (△ ♖e6) ♕d6 27. cd6±⊥] **26. ♔h1** [26. ♕b7? ♗f3; 26. ♖e6 ♖f6 27. ♕b7 ♖e6 28. ♕a8 ♖e8 29. ♕a7 ♗f3] **♖ad8** [26... ♖ab8!?] **27. ♗f7□ ♕f7!** [27... ♕g4? 28. h3 ♖d1 29. ♔h2 ♕h4 30. ♗h5 ♖b1 31. ♖g7 ♕f6 32. ♖g6 ♖f7 33. ♕c8 ♖f8 34. ♕d7 ♖d8 (34... ♖f7 35. ♕e8+–) 35. ♕c7 ♕f8 36. ♕e5 ♔h7 37. ♖f6+–] **28. ♖f7 ♗f7 29. h3** [29. a4 ♖d2! △ ♗d5∞] **♗a2 30. ♖b7 ♖g8 31. ♖a7 ♗d5 32. ♔g1⊕ ♖b8⊕** [32... ♖df8!?] **33. ♖a3 ♖b1 34. ♔h2 ♖b2 35. ♖g3 ♗e4 36. h4 ♔h7 37. h5 ♖bb8 38. ♖g6 ♖bf8 39. ♕e7** [39. ♖c6 ♗c6 40. ♕c6 ♖c8! 41. ♕g6 (41. ♕d6 ♖gf8=) ♔h8 42. ♕f5 ♖c6 △ ♖gc8=] **♗d5 40. g4!?** [40. ♖g7 ♖g7 41. ♕f8 ♖g2 42. ♔h3 ♗e4=] **fg4?!⊕** [40... ♖f7 41. ♕e5 fg4 △ ♖gf8=] **41. ♖g7 ♖g7 42. ♕f8 g3 43. ♔g1**

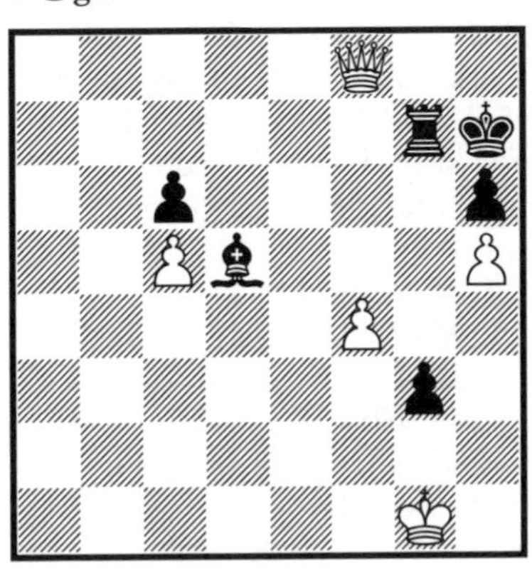

43... g2! [♕ 5/h] **44. ♕f5 ♔g8 45. ♕f6 ♖g3** [45... ♔h7 46. f5 ♖g5 47. ♕e7 ♖g7 48. ♕d6 ♔g8 49. ♕h6 ♖a7 50. ♕g6 ♔h8 51. ♕f6 ♔g8 52. h6 ♔h7 △ ♖f7=; 48... ♖g5!? △ 49. f6?! ♖h5 50. ♕e7 ♔g6 51. ♕g7 ♔f5 52. f7 ♖h1 53. ♔f2 ♖f1 54. ♔e2 ♔e6∓] **46. ♕h6 ♖e3?!** [46... ♖g7=] **47. ♕g6 ♔f8?** [47... ♔h8! 48. ♔f2 ♖a3 △ ♖a7=] **48. ♕b1?** [48. ♔f2! ♖e6 (48... ♖e7 49. h6; 48... ♖a3 49. h6; 48... ♖f3 49. ♔g2) 49. ♕g5+−] **♔e7?** [48... ♔g7! 49. ♔h2 (49. ♕g6 ♔h8!=) ♖e7 50. ♕g6 ♔h8 51. ♕f6 ♖g7 52. ♔g1 ♔h7=] **49. h6 ♖h3** [49... ♔f6 50. ♕a1+−] **50. ♕h7 ♔d8 51. ♕h8 ♔c7 52. ♕g7 ♔d8 53. h7 ♖h1 54. ♔f2 g1♕□ 55. ♕g1 ♖h7 56. f5+−⊥ ♖f7 57. ♕g5 ♔d7 58. ♔g3 ♖f8 59. ♔f4 ♗e6 60. ♕g6!?** [60. ♔e5] **♗d5** [60... ♗f5 61. ♕g7! (61. ♕f5?? ♔e7!=) ♔e8 62. ♔e5 ♖f7 (62... ♗c8 63. ♔d6 ♖f7 64. ♕e5+−) 63. ♕f7 ♔f7 64. ♔f5+−] **61. ♕d6 ♔e8 62. f6 ♖f7 63. ♕b8 ♔d7 64. ♔e5⊙ 1 : 0**
[Krasenkov]

433.* **D 47**

PIESINA 2395 – RUZELE 2500
Lietuva (ch) 1993

1. c4 e6 2. ♘c3 d5 3. d4 c6 4. e3 ♘f6 5. ♘f3 ♘bd7 6. ♗d3 dc4 7. ♗c4 b5 8. ♗e2 ♗b7 [RR 8... a6 9. e4 b4 10. e5 bc3 11. ef6 ♘f6 12. bc3 ♗d6 13. ♘d2 0–0 14. ♗f3 ♕c7 N (14... ♗d7) 15. ♘c4 ♗e7 16. ♗g5 ♘d5 17. ♗e7 ♕e7 18. ♕d2 ♖b8 19. 0–0 c5 20. ♗d5 ed5 21. ♖fe1 ♗e6 22. ♘e5 ♖fc8= Ehlvest 2625 – Lesiège 2505, New York 1993] **9. 0–0 a6 10. e4 c5 11. e5 ♘d5 12. a4 b4 13. ♘e4 cd4** [13... h6?! 14. ♘fd2 ♘f4 15. ♗f3 ♗d5 16. ♘b3 ♘g6 17. ♘bc5 ♘c5 18. ♘c5 ♗c5 19. dc5 ♗f3 20. ♕f3 ♘e5 21. ♕e4±; 13... ♗e7?! 14. ♗g5] **14. ♕d4 N** [14. ♗g5 – 55/438, 439] **♕b6 15. ♕d3** [15. ♕d1 ♕c7=] **h6** [15... ♕c7 16. ♕d4 ♕b6=] **16. ♗d2 ♗e7** [16... a5 17. ♕b5 ♕b5 18. ♗b5 ♘c7 19. ♗d3±] **17. a5 ♕a7 18. ♖fc1 0–0 19. ♖c4 ♖fc8 20. ♖ac1 ♖c4 21. ♖c4 ♖d8!** [21... ♖c8 22. ♖c8 ♗c8 23. ♘d6 ♗d6 24. ed6 ♕c5 25. ♕c4± ×b4; 21... ♕b8 22. ♕d4 ♕d8 23. ♘g3 (23. ♘d6 ♗d6 24. ed6 ♕a5 25. ♗b4 ♘b4 26. ♖b4 ♗d5∓) ♕a5 24. ♕g4! (24. ♘h5?! ♘f8 25. ♕g4 ♘g6 26. h4 ♗f8∞) ♘f8 25. ♗h6 ♘g6 26. ♗d3±→] **22. ♘g3 ♘f8** [22... ♗f8 23. ♖g4→] **23. ♕c2! ♕b8** [23... ♘g6 24. ♗d3] **24. ♗h6 gh6?** [24... ♘g6□ 25. ♖g4 (25. ♗d2 ♘e5 26. ♘e5 ♕e5∞) ♕c8! (△ gh6) 26. ♖c4 ♕b8 27. ♖g4 ♕c8=] **25. ♖g4+− ♔h8 26. ♕d2 ♔h7 27. ♗d3 ♘g6 28. h4! ♖g8** [28... ♗f8 29. h5 ♘e7 30. ♕f4!+−] **29. h5 ♕e8?! 30. hg6 fg6 31. ♘h4 ♗h4** [31... ♗g5 32. ♖g5] **32. ♖h4 ♕f8 33. ♘e4 h5 34. ♘g5 ♔h8 35. ♘e6 1 : 0**
[Ruzele]

434.** **D 47**

VYŽMANAVIN 2620 – ILLESCAS CÓRDOBA 2615
León 1993

1. d4 d5 2. c4 c6 3. e3 ♘f6 4. ♘c3 e6 5. ♘f3 ♘bd7 6. ♗d3 dc4 7. ♗c4 b5 8. ♗d3 ♗b7 9. a3 a6 [9... b4 10. ♘e4 ♘e4 N (10... a5 – 56/500) 11. ♗e4 ♕c7! *a)* 12. ♕c2!? ba3 13. ba3 h6 14. ♗d2 ♗d6 15. ♗b4 0–0 16. ♗d6 (16. ♘d2!?) ♕d6 17. ♘d2 (17. 0–0 f5 18. ♗d3 c5) ♖ab8 18. 0–0 c5 19. ♗b7 (1/2 : 1/2 Vyžmanavin 2620 – Moróvić Fernández 2570, León 1993) ♖b7 20. ♘e4 ♕d5 21. dc5 ♘c5 22. ♘c5 ♖c7=; *b)* RR 12. 0–0 ba3 13. ba3 ♗d6 14. ♖b1 0–0 15. ♕c2 h6 16. ♗d2 ♖ab8 17. ♗b4 c5 18. dc5 ♗e4 19. ♕e4 ♘c5 20. ♕g4 ♘d3 21. ♗d6 ♕d6 22. ♕a4 ♕c5= B. Gel'fand 2690 – Bareev 2670, Linares 1993] **10. b4 a5 11. ♖b1 ab4 12. ab4 ♗d6 N** [12... ♘d5 – 56/(500)] **13. 0–0 0–0 14. ♕c2!? h6** [14... ♕e7 15. ♗d2 ♗b4 16. e4=∞] **15. ♗d2 ♕e7 16. e4 e5 17. ♘e2** [△ ♘g3] **ed4 18. ♘ed4 ♘e5□ 19. ♘e5** [19. ♘f5 ♘f3 20. gf3 ♕e6 (20... ♕c7 21. ♔h1! ♗h2 22. ♖g1!→) 21. ♔h1 ♘h5 22. ♖g1 ♔h8∞] **♕e5** [19... ♗e5 20. ♘f5 △ f4] **20. ♘f3 ♕h5 21. ♗c3 ♘g4 22. h3 ♘e5 23. ♗e5!** [23. ♘e5 ♗e5 24. ♗e2 ♕g5 △ ♕f6] **♗e5 24. ♕c5 f6□ 25. ♗c2 ♕e8 26. ♖fd1 ♗c7** [26... ♗b8!? (△ ♗a7)

27. ♗b3 ♔h8 28. ♖d7 ♗a7 29. ♕e7±] **27. ♘d4 ♔h8 28. ♗b3± ♕e5** [28... ♕e4 29. ♖e1 ♕f4 30. g3 △ ♖e7] **29. ♕e5 ♗e5 30. ♘e6 ♖f7 31. f4! ♗c3 32. ♘c5 ♖e7 33. ♗e6⊙ g5⊕ 34. ♖d3 ♖a3□** [34... ♖a1 35. ♖a1 ♗a1 36. ♖d8 ♔g7 37. ♔f1+− △ ♖b8] **35. ♖d8 ♔g7 36. ♗f5 ♔f7 37. ♔h1 gf4 38. ♖h8 ♗a8 39. ♖d1 1 : 0**
[Vyžmanavin, B. Arhangel'skij]

435. **D 47**

M. GUREVICH 2610 — KRAMNIK 2685

Deutschland 1993

1. d4 d5 2. c4 c6 3. ♘c3 ♘f6 4. e3 e6 5. ♘f3 ♘bd7 6. ♗d3 dc4 7. ♗c4 b5 8. ♗d3 ♗b7 9. e4 b4 10. ♘a4 c5 11. e5 ♘d5 12. 0–0 cd4 13. ♖e1 a6 14. ♘d4 ♕b8?! N [14... g6 — 19/(531)] **15. ♕h5 g6 16. ♕h3 ♘e5 17. ♗e4** [△ ♘e6; 17. ♘e6!? ♗c8 18. ♗g6! (18. ♗f5!?↑) fg6 19. f4 ♕a7!? 20. ♔h1 ♕f2⇆] **♕d6 18. a3!? ♗g7 19. ab4 ♕b4 20. ♘c2 ♕e7!? 21. b3 0–0 22. ♗a3 ♕c7 23. ♗f8 ♖f8∞̅ 24. ♗d5** [24. ♕g3 f5!?↑] **♗d5 25. ♘b4 ♗b7 26. ♖ac1 ♕a5 27. ♘d3 ♘d3 28. ♕d3 ♗d5 29. ♖ed1** [29. ♘c5!? ♗h6 (29... ♖a8!⇆) 30. ♘d7! ♗c1 31. ♖c1 ♖d8 32. ♘f6→] **♕b4 30. ♘c5 a5 31. h3 h5 32. ♕e2 ♕f4 33. ♕e1?⊕** [33. ♕e3 ♕f5∞̅] **♗b2!** [33... ♗e5 34. g3 ♕f3 35. ♖d5 ♕d5 36. ♘d7 ♕d7 37. ♕e5=] **34. ♖c2 ♗e5 35. ♖d5□** [35. g3 ♕f3 36. ♖d5 ♕d5 37. ♘d7?? ♕d7 38. ♕e5 ♕d1−+] **ed5 36. ♘d7!?** [36. g3 ♕f5∓] **♕h2 37. ♔f1 ♕h1** [37... ♖e8? 38. ♘f6+−] **38. ♔e2 ♕g2!** [38... ♕e1 39. ♔e1 ♖e8 40. ♔d2!= △ ♔d3] **39. ♘f8** [39. ♘e5 ♖e8 40. ♔d1 ♕h3→] **♔f8** [♕ 9/c] **40. ♔d1 ♗f6?** [40... ♕f3 41. ♕e2 ♕f5!∓] **41. ♕e3!=** [△ ♔e2, ♕d3→] **♕f1 42. ♔d2 ♔g7** [42... d4 43. ♕h6⇆] **43. ♖c1 ♕b5 44. ♖c2!** [△ ♕d3] **d4 45. ♕d3 ♕e5 46. ♔d1 h4?! 47. ♖c6 ♕d5 48. ♖b6 ♕c5 49. ♖b5 ♕a7 50. ♔e2 ♕a8 51. ♖c5 ♕a7 52. ♖d5 a4 53. ba4 ♕a4 54. ♔f1 ♕c6 55. ♕e4 ♕c1 56. ♔g2 ♕c7 57. ♖b5 ♕d6 58. ♖d5 ♕c7 59. ♖b5 ♕d6 60. ♕d5 ♕f4 61. ♕f3 ♕d6 62. ♕e4 ♕c7 63. ♖d5 ♔f8 1/2 : 1/2 [M. Gurevich]**

436. **D 47**

KAJDANOV 2620 — ŠABALOV 2575

New York 1993

1. c4 c6 2. ♘f3 d5 3. e3 ♘f6 4. ♘c3 e6 5. d4 ♘bd7 6. ♗d3 dc4 7. ♗c4 b5 8. ♗d3 ♗b7 9. e4 b4 10. ♘a4 c5 11. e5 ♘d5 12. 0–0 cd4 13. ♖e1 ♗e7 14. ♘d4 ♕a5 15. ♗d2 ♖d8 N [15... 0–0 — 20/584] **16. a3 ♘5b6 17. ♗b5 ♘a4 18. ♗b4!± ♗b4 19. ab4 ♕b6 20. ♗d7!** [20. ♕a4? ♕d4 21. ♖ad1 ♕g4 22. ♗d7 ♔e7∓] **♖d7 21. ♕a4 ♔e7?** [21... ♗g2 22. ♔g2 ♕d4 23. h3!! ♕d5 24. ♔g1 ♕b7 25. ♖ed1±] **22. ♘b3 ♗c6 23. ♕a3 ♗d5 24. ♘c5 ♖c7 25. ♕g3 ♔f8 26. ♕h4?!** [26. ♕g5 ♖e7 27. ♖ec1 ♕b8 28. ♘a6 ♕d8 29. ♖c7 h6 30. ♕e7 ♕e7 31. ♖c8! ♕e8 32. ♖e8 ♔e8 33. ♘c7+−] **♔e8 27. ♖ec1 h6 28. ♘a4 ♖c1 29. ♖c1 ♕b7 30. f3?** [30. ♕d4 ♗g2 31. ♕c5 △ ♕c8+−] **g5 31. ♕d4 ♔f8 32. ♘c5 ♕b5 33. ♘e4 ♔g7 34. ♘d6 ♕b6** [34... ♕e2 35. ♕a7 ♖f8 36. ♕d4 ♖d8 37. ♕c3 ♖a8 38. ♕c7 ♕e3 39. ♔h1 ♖a7 40. ♘e8 ♔f8 41. ♕d6 ♔g8 42. ♘f6 ♔g7 43. ♕f8!! ♔g6 (43... ♔f8 44. ♖c8+−) 44. ♕g8 ♔f5 45. ♕h7 ♔f4 46. ♘h5 ♔e5 47. ♕g7 ♔d6 48. ♕f8 ♔e5 49. ♕b8 ♔f5 50. g4 ♔g6 51. ♕g8#] **35. ♕b6 ab6 36. ♖c7 ♖f8 37. ♔f2+− ♔g6 38. ♖c8 ♖c8 39. ♘c8 ♔f5 40. ♘d6** [40. ♘b6+−] **♔e5 41. ♘f7 ♔d4 42. ♘h6 e5 43. ♘f5 ♔d3 44. ♘e3 ♗e6 45. g3 e4 46. f4 gf4 47. gf4 b5 48. h4 ♗f7 49. ♘g4 ♔d2 50. f5 ♗h5 51. ♘e3 ♔d3 52. f6 ♗g6 53. ♘f1 ♔d4 54. ♘g3 e3 55. ♔e2 ♗d3 56. ♔f3 1 : 0**
[Kajdanov]

437. !N** **D 47**

JE. PIKET 2590 — KRAMNIK 2685

Amsterdam 1993

1. d4 d5 2. c4 c6 3. ♘c3 ♘f6 4. ♘f3 e6 5. e3 ♘bd7 6. ♗d3 dc4 7. ♗c4 b5 8. ♗d3 ♗b7 9. e4 b4 10. ♘a4 c5 11. e5 ♘d5 12. 0–0 cd4 13. ♖e1 g6 14. ♗g5 ♕a5 15. ♘d4 a6 16. ♖c1 ♗g7 17. ♘c6 ♗c6 18. ♖c6 0–0 19. ♗c4! N [19. ♖e4] **h6** [19... ♗e5 20. ♘c5 (20. ♖e5? ♘e5 21. ♖c5 ♘c4) ♘c5 21. ♖e5 ♘d7 22. ♖e1

♖fc8 (22... ♘5b6!?) 23. ♗d5 ♕d5 24. ♕d5 ed5 25. ♖d6 ♘c5 26. ♖d5 ♘e6 27. ♗f6± Je. Piket 2590 – M. Gurevich 2610, Belgique 1993; 19... ♘5b6 20. ♘b6 ♘b6 21. ♗b3 ♖fc8 (21... ♖ac8 22. ♕d6) 22. ♖c8 ♖c8 23. ♕d4 (23. h4!? △ 23... ♗e5 24. ♗d8) ♕b5 24. h4 ♘d7 25. ♗f6 ♗f8 26. ♖d1 ♘f6 27. ef6 a5 28. ♕d7 ♕d7 29. ♖d7 h5 30. f3 ♖c5 31. g4 hg4 1/2 : 1/2 Je. Piket 2625 – Anand 2690, Dortmund 1992] **20. ♗d5** [20. ♗d2 ♘e5 21. ♖c5 ♕c5 22. ♘c5 ♘c4∓; 20. ♗h4 ♘5b6=; 20... b3!?] **♕d5 21. ♕d5 ed5 22. ♗f6**

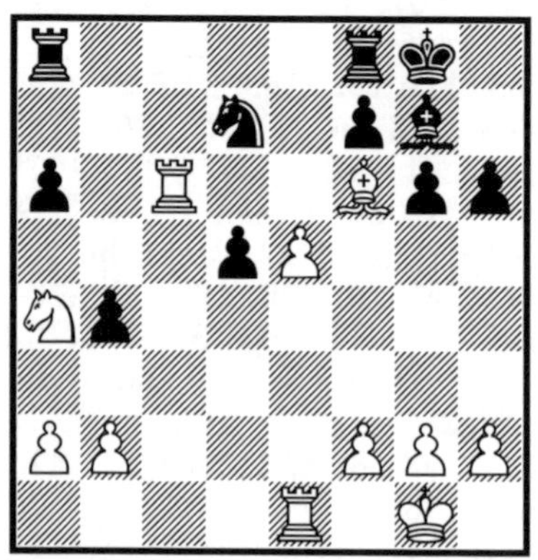

22... ♘e5!! [22... ♗f6 23. ef6 ♖ae8 24. ♔f1 ♖e1 25. ♔e1 ♖e8 26. ♔d1 ♖e6 27. ♖c8 ♔h7 28. ♖c7±] **23. ♗e5□** [23. ♖e5 ♖ac8 24. ♗g7 ♖c6 25. ♗h6 g5 26. ♗g5 f6 27. ♖d5 fg5 28. ♖g5 ♔h7 29. f3 ♖d8∓] **♖ae8 24. f4 f6 25. ♘b6** [25. ♗c3=] **fe5 26. ♘d5 ef4** [26... ♔h7 27. ♖c7] **27. ♖e8 ♖e8 28. ♖g6 ♔h7 29. ♖a6 ♖e2 30. ♔f1 ♖b2 31. ♘f4** [31... ♗d4 32. ♘d3 ♖d2 33. ♘b4 ♖f2=] **1/2 : 1/2**
[Je. Piket]

438. !N **D 49**

B. ALTERMAN 2600 – ROGIĆ 2280
Zagreb (zt) 1993

1. d4 d5 2. c4 c6 3. ♘c3 ♘f6 4. e3 e6 5. ♘f3 ♘bd7 6. ♗d3 dc4 7. ♗c4 b5 8. ♗d3 a6 9. e4 c5 10. e5 cd4 11. ♘b5 ♘g4 12. ♕a4 ♗b7 13. ♘bd4 ♕b6 14. 0–0 ♗c5 15. h3 ♗f3 16. hg4 ♗b7 17. ♘f3 h5 18. ♗d2 ♗f3! N [18... h4] **19. gf3 hg4 20. fg4** [20. ♕g4 ♕b2 △ ♕e5∓] **♕b2! 21. ♖ad1** [21. ♗f4 ♗f2!–+] **♔e7!!∓** [△ ♘e5, ♖h3] **22. ♔g2** [22. ♗f4 ♘e5 23. ♗e4 ♖ad8∓ △ 24. ♕a5 ♗f2 25. ♖f2 ♖d1 26. ♔g2 ♘d7–+] **♘e5 23. ♗g5⊕** [23. ♗f4∓] **f6 24. ♗f4 ♖h4 25. ♗e5 ♕e5 26. ♖h1 ♖ah8??** [26... ♕d5 27. ♗e4 ♖g4 28. ♔f3 ♕f5!∓] **27. ♗h7!!+–** [27. ♖h4? ♖h4–+] **♖4h7** [27... ♖h1 28. ♕d7 ♔f8 29. ♕d8 ♔f7 30. ♖d7+–] **28. ♖h7 ♖g8 29. ♕d7?** [29. ♖g7! ♖g7 30. ♖d7 ♔f8 31. ♖d8 ♔f7 32. ♕e8#] **♔f8 30. ♕b7± ♗d6 31. ♖h5 ♕f4 32. ♕f3 ♕b4 33. ♖hh1 ♔f7 34. ♖b1 ♕c5 35. ♖hc1 ♕e5 36. ♖b7 ♔g6 37. ♕d3 f5 38. gf5 ♔f6 39. fe6?** [39. ♕f3+–] **♕h2 40. ♔f1 ♕h1 41. ♔e2 ♕c1??** [41... ♕b7 42. ♕d6 ♕e4 43. ♔d2 ♕e6 44. ♕f4 ♔e7 45. ♖c7 ♔d8] **42. ♖f7** **1 : 0**
[B. Alterman]

439. **D 49**

BAREEV 2670 – JUSUPOV 2645
Linares 1993

1. d4 d5 2. c4 c6 3. ♘c3 ♘f6 4. e3 e6 5. ♘f3 ♘bd7 6. ♗d3 dc4 7. ♗c4 b5 8. ♗d3 a6 9. e4 c5 10. e5 cd4 11. ♘b5 ♘e5 12. ♘e5 ab5 13. ♗b5 ♗d7 14. ♘d7 ♕a5 15. ♗d2 ♕b5 16. ♘f8 ♔f8 17. b3 [△ a4; 17. ♕e2 ♕e2?! 18. ♔e2 ♔e7 19. a4±] **♘d5!?** [△ 18. a4 ♕d3 19. ♗b4?? ♘b4–+] **18. a4 ♕d3 19. ♕e2** [19. ♕f3 ♕f3 20. gf3 ♔e7 21. ♔e2 ♖hb8 22. ♖hb1 ♘b4⇆] **♕b3** [19... ♕e2?! 20. ♔e2 ♔e7 21. b4±] **20. 0–0 ♕c2 N** [20... ♘c3 – 51/(438)] **21. ♖fc1 d3 22. ♕e1** [22. ♖c2 de2 23. ♗e1=] **♕b2 23. ♖c4?!** [⌓ 23. a5] **♖b8! 24. a5 ♔e7 25. a6 ♖b5?!** [25... ♖b6!? 26. ♖a5 ♖b5 27. ♗c1 d2 (27... ♕b3 28. ♗a3 ♔d7) 28. ♕d2 (28. ♗d2 ♖a5 29. ♗a5 ♖a8) ♕d2 29. ♗d2 ♖a5 30. ♗a5 ♖a8 31. ♖c6 ♔d7; 25... ♖hd8!? △ ♖d7; 25... ♖hc8! 26. ♖c8 (26. a7?? ♖c4–+) ♖c8 27. a7 (27. ♖b1 ♕a2 28. ♖b7 ♖c7 29. ♕c1 ♖b7 30. ab7 ♕b3) ♖a8 (×a7) 28. ♖b1 (28. ♖a6∓) ♕d4 29. ♖b7 ♔d6! (29... ♔f6 30. ♕d1 ♔g6 31. h4∞) 30. ♖f7 (30. ♕b1 ♖a7 31. ♖a7 ♕a7 32. ♕d3∓) ♖a7∓] **26. ♖cc1!** [△ ♖cb1; 26. a7 ♖a8∓] **♕d4 27. ♖cb1 ♖b1 28. ♕b1** [28. ♖b1 ♖a8 29. ♖b7 ♔f6 30. ♕d1 g5∞; 30... ♔g6∞; 29... ♔d6!∓] **♖b8! 29. ♕c1 ♖a8?!** [29... ♖b2? *a)* 30. a7? ♖d2! 31. ♕f1 (31. ♔h1 ♕f2

32. ♕g1 ♕g1 33. ♔g1 ♘b6−+) ♖f2 32. ♕f2 ♕a1 33. ♕f1 ♕a7−+; *b)* 30. ♗e3! *b1)* 30... ♘e3 31. fe3 *b11)* 31... ♖g2 32. ♔g2 ♕g4 33. ♔f2+−; *b12)* 31... ♕f6 32. ♕c7 ♔e8 (32... ♔f8 33. ♕c5 ♔e8 34. ♕c6+−) 33. ♕c6 ♔e7 34. a7+−; *b13)* 31... d2 32. ♕c7 ♕d7 33. ♕d7 ♔d7 34. a7 ♖c2 (34... d1♕ 35. ♖d1+−; 34... ♖a2 35. ♖a2 d1♕ 36. ♔f2+−) 35. a8♕ ♖c1 36. ♔f2 d1♕ 37. ♕b7 ♔d6 38. ♕b8 ♔e7 (38... ♔d5 39. ♕d8+−; 38... ♔c6 39. ♕c8+−; 38... ♔d7 39. ♖a7 ♔c6 40. ♖c7 ♔d5 41. ♖d7+−) 39. ♖a7 ♔f6 40. ♕f4+−; *b2)* 30... d2 31. ♗d4 dc1♕ 32. ♖c1 ♖a2 33. a7 ♔d7 34. ♖a1! (34. ♖b1 ♘c7±; 34. f3 ♘c7±) ♖a1 35. ♗a1 ♘c7 36. ♗g7+−; 29... ♔f6! 30. ♖a5 h6±] **30. ♖a5! ♖a7?** [30... ♔f6!? 31. ♕a3 (△ ♖a4 ×d3) ♘f4 △ 32. ♗f4 ♕f4 33. ♕d3 ♕c1 34. ♕f1 ♕f1 35. ♔f1 ♔e7=] **31. ♕a3 ♔f6 32. ♖a4± ♕b6 33. ♕d3 g6 34. ♗h6! ♕b2 35. h4 ♔e7 36. g3 ♕c3 37. ♕b5** [△ ♕b8] **♕c7 38. ♕b2** [△ ♕h8 ×f8] **♖a8 39. a7?!** [×a7; 39. ♗g5 f6 40. ♗f4 ♕c6 (40... ♘f4 41. ♖f4 e5 42. ♖b4+−) 41. ♕b7+−] **f6** [39... ♖a7?? 40. ♕a3+−] **40. ♗f4** [40. ♗d2±] **♘f4 41. ♖f4** [♕ 9/f] **e5 42. ♖a4 ♔f7 43. ♕d2 ♔g7 44. ♕e3 ♕b7** [44... h5? 45. ♖a6 ♕b7 46. ♕a3 (×f6, g6) ♕f7 47. ♔h2 ♕b7 48. ♕d6 ♕f7 49. ♕b8 ♕d5 50. ♖d6 ♕f3 51. ♕c7 ♔h6 52. ♕c1 (52. ♔g1 △ ♖d7+−) ♔g7 53. ♖d7+−] **45. ♕c5 ♖d8 46. ♖a1 ♖a8 47. ♔h2 ♔g8 48. g4!? ♕e4?!** [48... ♔h8!?±] **49. ♖a4! ♕b7** [49... ♕a4? 50. ♕d5+−] **50. g5?!** [50. ♖a3!±] **fg5 51. hg5 h6!! 52. gh6** [52. ♕e5 ♖a7=] **♔h7± 53. ♖a3 ♕f7 54. ♕e3 ♕b7 55. ♔g3 ♕c7 56. ♖a6 ♕f7 57. ♔h2 ♕b7 58. ♖a5 ♕c7 59. ♖a6 ♕b7 60. ♕d3 ♕f7 61. ♕e3 1/2 : 1/2 [Jusupov]**

440. D 52

KRAMNIK 2685 − KAMSKY 2655

Linares 1993

1. d4 d5 2. ♘f3 ♘f6 3. c4 c6 4. ♘c3 e6 5. ♗g5 ♘bd7 6. e3 ♕a5 7. ♘d2 ♗b4 8. ♕c2 e5!? N [8... ♘e4 − 55/447; 8... dc4 − 55/448] **9. ♘b3** [9. ♗f6 ♘f6 10. de5 ♘e4 11. ♘de4 de4 12. 0-0-0 ♗c3! 13. ♕c3 ♕a2∞] **♕c7** [9... ♕b6!?] **10. ♗e2 dc4** [10... ♘e4!? 11. ♗h4 ed4 12. ♘d4! (12. ed4 0−0 13. 0−0 ♕f4!=) ♕a5 (12... ♘c3 13. bc3±) 13. 0−0! *a)* 13... ♘c3 14. bc3 ♗d6 (14... ♗c3? 15. ♘b3 ♕b4 16. a3+−) 15. ♘f5±; *b)* 13... ♗c3 14. cd5! cd5 (14... ♗d4? 15. ♕e4 ♗e5 16. dc6 bc6 17. f4±) 15. bc3 ♕c3 16. ♕d1∞̅] **11. ♗c4 0−0 12. 0−0± ♗d6 13. h3 ♖e8?** [13... h6?! 14. ♗h4 (14. ♗h6? ♘b6 15. ♕g6 ♘e8) ♘b6 15. ♗d3 (15. ♗f6!? ♘c4) ed4 16. ♘d4± △ 16... g5?! 17. ♗g3 ♗g3 18. fg3 ♕g3 19. ♖f6 ♕e3 20. ♕f2 ♕d3 21. ♖h6+−; 13... a6± △ b5, ♗b7] **14. ♖ad1± ed4** [⌓ 14... a6] **15. ♘d4 ♗e5 16. f4! ♗d4**

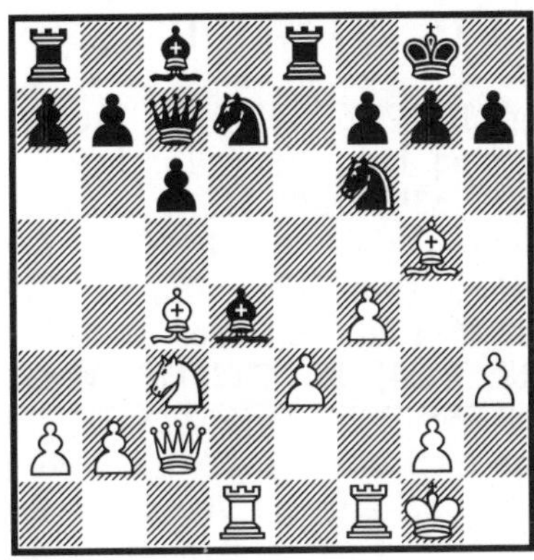

17. ♖d4! [17. ed4 ♘b6 18. ♗b3 ♕d6 19. f5±] **♖e3 18. ♖fd1 ♘f8** [18... ♖e7 19. ♘b5! ♕b6 20. ♘d6+−; 18... a6 19. ♖d7!! ♘d7 (19... ♗d7 20. ♗f6 gf6 21. ♗f7! ♔f7 22. ♘d5+−) 20. ♗f7! ♔f7 21. ♘d5 ♕a5 (21... ♖e2 22. ♕e2! cd5 23. ♕e7 ♔g8 24. ♕e6+−) 22. ♘e3±] **19. f5 ♕e5** [19... ♖e7 20. ♗f6 gf6 21. ♕f2 ♗d7 22. ♖g4 ♔h8 23. ♕h4 ♕e5 24. ♕h6 ♕e3 25. ♕e3 ♖e3 26. ♗f7 h5 27. ♖g8 ♔h7 28. ♖d7+−] **20. ♗e3 ♕e3 21. ♕f2! ♕f2 22. ♔f2 ♗f5 23. ♖d8 ♖d8 24. ♖d8+− b5 25. ♗e2 a5 26. ♗f3 ♗d7 27. ♖a8 g5 28. ♖a6 ♘e6 29. ♗c6 ♗c6 30. ♖c6 b4 31. ♘e2 a4 32. ♖c4 ♘d5 33. g3 ♔f8 34. ♘d4 ♘ec7 35. ♘c6 b3 36. ab3 ab3 37. ♘b4 ♔e7 38. ♘d5 ♘d5 39. ♖d4 ♔e6 40. ♖d3 h5 41. ♖b3 f5 42. ♖b8 f4 43. ♖h8 fg3 44. ♔g3 ♘f6 45. b4 ♔d5 46. ♖h6 ♘e4 47. ♔g2 h4 48. ♔f3 ♘d2 49. ♔g4 ♘e4 50. b5 ♘f2 51. ♔f5 1 : 0 [Kramnik]**

441. **D 52**

CH. LUTZ 2550 – M. GUREVICH 2610
München 1993

1. d4 d5 2. c4 c6 3. ♘f3 ♘f6 4. ♘c3 e6 5. ♗g5 ♘bd7 6. e3 ♕a5 7. ♘d2 ♗b4 8. ♕c2 e5 9. de5!? N ♘e4 [9... ♘g4 10. cd5 cd5 11. ♖c1 ♘ge5 12. a3±; 9... ♗c3!? 10. ♕c3 ♕c3 11. bc3 ♘e5 12. ♗f6 gf6 13. cd5 cd5=] **10. ♘de4 de4 11. 0-0-0! f6!?** [11... ♗c3 12. ♕c3 ♕c3 13. bc3 0–0 14. ♖d4±] **12. ef6!** [12. ♗f4 ♗c3 13. ♕c3 ♕c3 14. bc3 ♘e5⇆] **♕g5** [12... ♗c3? 13. bc3 ♕g5 14. ♕e4 ♕e5 (14... ♔f7 15. ♕e7+–; 14... ♔d8 15. ♕e7 ♔c7 16. fg7+–) 15. f7! ♔f8□ 16. ♕e5 ♘e5 17. ♖d8+–] **13. ♘e4 ♕e5?** [13... ♕a5□ 14. a3! (14. fg7 ♖g8 15. a3 ♗e7⇆) ♗f8 15. fg7 ♗g7 16. ♘d6 ♔e7□ 17. ♕e4 ♕e5∞] **14. f4 ♕a5** [14... ♕e6 15. fg7 ♖g8 16. c5→] **15. a3!± ♗f8** [15... ♗a3 16. fg7 ♖g8 17. ba3 ♕a3 18. ♔b1±] **16. fg7 ♗g7 17. ♘d6+– ♔d8** [17... ♔f8 18. ♘c8 ♖c8 19. ♖d7 ♕e1 20. ♖d1 ♕e3 21. ♔b1; 17... ♔e7 18. ♕e4] **18. ♘f7** [18. ♕d3! ♔c7 19. ♘c8 ♘c5□ 20. ♕d6 ♔c8 21. g3] **♔c7 19. ♘h8 ♘c5 20. ♘f7!** [△ ♘e5; 20. ♕h7? ♘b3 21. ♔c2 ♗f5–+; 20. ♗d3? ♗e6 21. ♗h7 ♖h8 △ ♘a4→] **♗f5 21. ♗d3 ♘d3 22. ♖d3 ♖f8⊕ 23. ♘d6 ♗d3 24. ♕d3 ♕h5 25. ♖d1 ♗h8 26. ♘e4 ♕f5 27. ♕d6 ♔c8 28. ♕e7 1 : 0 [M. Gurevich]**

442.*** **D 56**

R. HÜBNER 2620 – JUSUPOV 2645
München 1993

1. d4 d5 [RR 1... ♘f6 2. c4 e6 3. ♘c3 d5 4. ♗g5 ♗e7 5. e3 h6 6. ♗h4 0–0 7. ♖c1 ♘bd7 8. ♘f3 c6 9. ♗d3 dc4 10. ♗c4 ♘d5 11. ♗e7 ♕e7 12. 0–0 ♘c3 13. ♖c3 e5 14. ♗b3 *a)* 14... ed4 15. ed4 ♘f6 16. ♖e1 ♕d6 (16... ♗e6 17. ♗e6 △ ♘e5±) 17. ♘e5 ♘d5 18. ♖g3 ♗e6 (18... ♗f5 – 48/574) 19. ♕h5 ♔h8 20. ♖f3→; *b)* 14... ♖e8 15. ♕c2!? N (15. d5 – 48/(574)) ed4 (15... e4?! 16. ♘d2 ♘f6 17. ♖c5± Vyžmanavin 2620 – Klovans 2440, Bern 1993) 16. ♘d4! (16. ed4 ♘f6 17. ♖e3 ♕d6 18. ♖e8 ♘e8 19. ♖e1 ♘c7 △ ♗e6=; 17... ♕d8) ♘f6 17. f3 (△ e4±) c5 18. ♖c5 ♕e3 19. ♕f2± Vyžmanavin, B. Arhangel'skij] **2. c4 e6 3. ♘c3 ♗e7 4. ♘f3 ♘f6 5. ♗g5 h6 6. ♗h4 0–0 7. e3 ♘e4 8. ♗e7 ♕e7 9. ♕c2 ♘c3 10. ♕c3 dc4 11. ♗c4 b6 12. 0–0** [RR 12. d5 N ed5 13. ♗d5 c6 14. ♗c4 ♗b7 15. ♘e5 b5 16. ♗b3 ♕c7 17. a4 ♘d7 18. ♘g6 ♖fe8 19. ab5 ♖ac8 20. 0–0 c5 21. ♘f4 c4 22. ♗c2± Lobron 2620 – Jusupov 2645, München 1993] **♗b7 13. ♗e2 c5** [RR 13... ♖c8 14. b4 ♘d7 15. ♖fd1 N (15. ♖fc1 – 56/514) ♘f6= Ch. Lutz 2550 – Jusupov 2645, München 1993] **14. dc5 ♖c8 15. b4** [15. ♘d4 – 48/573] **bc5 16. b5 a6 17. ♘d2 N** [17. ♖fd1; ◠ 17. a4 ab5 18. ab5 ♘d7 19. ♘d2±] **ab5 18. ♗b5 ♗g2 19. ♔g2 ♕b7 20. ♔h3 ♕b5 21. ♖g1 e5** [◠ 21... g6 22. ♘c4 (22. ♘e4 ♕b4) ♘d7 (22... ♕b4? 23. ♕c2; 22... ♖a6 23. ♘e5 △ 24. ♘g6, 24. ♘g4) 23. ♘d6 ♕c6 24. ♘c8 ♖c8 25. ♔g3 c4$\overline{\overline{\infty}}$] **22. ♖g7□** [22. ♕e5? ♕d7 23. ♖g4 f6–+] **♔g7 23. ♕e5 ♔f8 24. ♕h8 ♔e7 25. ♕c8 ♖a4!** [25... ♕d7 26. ♕d7 ♘d7 27. a4±] **26. ♖b1** [26. ♖c1 ♘d7→] **♕d7 27. ♕d7 ♘d7** [♖ 9/h] **28. ♖b2 f5** [28... ♘e5 29. f4 (29. ♔g2 ♘d3 30. ♖c2? ♘e1; 29. ♔g3 ♖g4 30. ♔h3 ♖a4) ♘d3 30. ♖c2 ♔e6 31. ♔g3 (31. ♖c3 ♘f2 32. ♔g3 ♖a2) ♔d5=] **29. ♔g2?!** [29. f4 ♘f6 30. ♔g3 ♘g4 31. ♘f1±; 29... ♖a3 △ 30. ♘c4 ♖c3; 29. ♔g3 ♖g4 30. ♔f3 ♘e5 31. ♔e2 ♖h4 32. ♘f1±] **f4 30. ef4 ♖f4 31. ♖b3 ♖d4 32. ♖e3 ♔d6 33. ♘b3** [33. ♘e4 ♔d5 34. ♘c3 ♔c4] **♖d1** [33... ♖a4? 34. ♖d3 ♔c6 35. ♖d7+–; 33... ♖d5 34. ♘a5 ♘b6 35. ♖b3 ♔c7 36. ♖b5] **34. ♖h3 c4 35. ♘a5** [35. ♖h6 ♔d5 36. ♖h5 ♔e4 37. ♖h4 ♔d5 38. ♘a5 ♘e5 (38... c3 39. ♖c4 ♖d3 40. h4∞) 39. ♖h5 ♔d4 40. f4 (40. h4 ♖a1; 40. ♔g3 ♖d3) ♘d3=] **♔c5 36. ♖h5 ♖d5** [36... ♔b4? 37. a3 ♔c3 38. ♖h6±] **37. ♖d5 ♔d5** [♘♗ 2/d] **38. ♔f3 ♘e5 39. ♔e2 ♘d3 40. ♔e3 ♘b4 41. a4 ♘d3 42. ♘b7 ♘e5 43. h3 c3 44. a5** [44. f4 c2 45. ♔d2 ♘d3 46. ♔c2 ♘f4] **♔c6=** [44... ♔c4? 45. a6 ♔b3 (45... c2 46. ♔d2 ♔b3 47. ♘c5 ♔b2 48. ♘a4 ♔b1 49. ♘c3 ♔b2 50. ♘e2+–) 46. ♘c5 ♔b2 47. ♘a4 ♔b3 48. ♘c3 ♔c3 49. a7 ♘c4 50. ♔e4 ♘b6

51. f4+−; 44... c2?! 45. ♔d2 ♘d3 46. ♔c2 ♘f2 47. a6 ♔c6 48. ♘c5 ♔b6 49. h4] **45. a6 ♔b6 46. ♘c5 ♔c5 47. a7 ♘c4 48. ♔d3 ♘b6 49. ♔c3 ♔c6 50. ♔d4 ♔b7 51. ♔e5 ♔a7 52. ♔f5 ♔b7 53. ♔g6 ♔c6 54. ♔h6 ♔d6 55. h4 ♔e6 56. ♔g7 ♘d5 57. h5 ♘e7 58. f4 ♘f5 59. ♔g6 ♘e7 1/2 : 1/2** **[R. Hübner]**

443.*** **D 58**

EPIŠIN 2620 — VAGANIAN 2615
Rostov na Donu 1993

1. d4 ♘f6 2. c4 e6 3. ♘f3 d5 4. ♘c3 ♗e7 5. ♗g5 h6 6. ♗h4 0—0 7. e3 b6 8. ♗e2 [RR 8. ♖b1 ♘e4 N (8... ♘bd7 — 52/440) 9. ♗e7 ♕e7 10. cd5 ♘c3 11. bc3 ed5 12. c4 dc4 13. ♗c4 ♗b7 14. ♘e5 ♘c6 15. ♘g6 ♕g5 16. ♘f8 ♕g2 17. ♕h5! ♘d8 18. ♔e2 ♔f8 19. ♖hg1 ♕e4 20. ♗d3 ♕e6 21. ♖bc1± Ju. Hodgson 2565 — Parker 2350, Dublin (zt) 1993] **♗b7 9. ♗f6 ♗f6 10. cd5 ed5 11. b4 c6 12. 0—0 ♖e8 13. ♕b3 a5 14. ba5 ♖a5 15. ♖fe1** [RR 15. a4 ♘d7 16. ♖fe1 ♗a6 17. ♖ac1 N (17. ♗a6 — 56/(516)) ♗e2 18. ♖e2 c5 19. ♘d5 cd4 20. ♘f6 ♕f6 21. ♘d4 ♘c5 22. ♕d1 ♖ea8 23. h3 ♖a4 24. ♖b1 ♖a2 25. ♖a2 ♖a2 26. ♕f3 ♕f3 27. ♘f3 ♘e4 1/2 : 1/2 Ch. Lutz 2550 — Lobron 2620, München 1993; 15. ♖ab1 N ♘d7 16. ♖fd1 ♗a6 17. ♗a6 ♖a6 18. a4 ♖a5 19. ♖dc1 ♖e6 20. ♖c2 ♕a8 21. ♖bc1 g6 22. ♘e1 ♔g7 23. ♘d3 ♗g5 24. ♘b4 h5 25. h3 h4∞ van Wely 2560 — Tisdall 2425, Gausdal 1993] **♘d7 16. e4?** [16. ♖ab1; 16. ♖ad1 △ e4] **c5∓ 17. ♘d5 cd4 N** [17... ♗d5 — 56/516] **18. ♗c4! ♘c5 19. ♕b6** [19. ♘f6 ♕f6 20. ♕b2 ♖e4 21. ♖e4 ♗e4 22. ♕d4 ♕d4! 23. ♘d4 ♖a4 24. ♖c1 ♘d3 25. ♗d3 ♗d3∓] **♕b6 20. ♘b6 ♖e4 21. ♘d5! ♗d5** [21... ♗d8 22. ♘e5!∞] **22. ♗d5 ♖e1 23. ♖e1!** [23. ♘e1? ♘a4 24. ♗b3 ♘b2! △ d3∓] **♔f8 24. ♗b3!!= ♖b5** [24... ♘a4 25. ♗a4 ♖a4 26. ♖e2=] **25. ♔f1 d3** [25... ♘b3 26. ♖b1=] **26. ♖d1 ♖b4! 27. ♖c1!** [27. ♘e1 ♖d4 28. ♘f3 ♖d8 △ ♗c3∓] **♘b3 28. ab3 ♖b3 29. ♖d1 ♗g5 30. ♘e1 d2 31. ♘f3 1/2 : 1/2** **[Epišin]**

444. **D 58**

ŠIROV 2670 — BELJAVSKIJ 2610
Linares 1993

1. d4 ♘f6 2. c4 e6 3. ♘f3 d5 4. ♘c3 ♗e7 5. ♗g5 h6 6. ♗h4 0—0 7. e3 b6 8. ♗d3 ♗b7 9. 0—0 ♘bd7 10. cd5 ♘d5 11. ♗e7 ♕e7 12. ♖e1?! c5 13. e4?! [13. ♘d5=] **♘f4 14. d5 ed5 15. ed5 ♕d6 16. ♗c4 ♘f6 N** [16... a6 — 30/544] **17. ♘b5 ♕d8 18. d6 ♘e4!∓ 19. d7 ♕f6 20. ♖e3 ♖ad8 21. ♕e1 a6?** [21... ♖d7 22. ♖e4 ♘h3! 23. ♔f1□ ♗e4 24. ♕e4 ♕b2 (×f2) 25. gh3 ♕a1 26. ♔g2 a6 27. ♘a3 b5 28. ♗b3 (28. ♗d3 ♖d3 29. ♕d3 ♕a2−+) ♖d6 29. ♘c2 ♕b1 △ c4−+] **22. ♖e4 ab5 23. ♖f4!** [23. ♗b5? ♘h3! 24. ♔f1□ ♗e4 25. ♕e4 ♕b2 26. gh3 ♕b5−+] **♕f4 24. ♗b5 ♗f3 25. gf3 ♕f3 26. ♖d1∞̅ ♕g4 27. ♔h1 f5 28. ♖d6 ♔h8 29. ♕e3** [29. ♕e5!?] **♔h7 30. a4 ♖f7 31. f3** [⌓ 31. h3=] **♕h4 32. ♕e6?!⊕** [32. ♕e8] **♖f6 33. ♕e7?!** [33. ♕e5] **♕f4! 34. ♖f6 ♕c1 35. ♔g2 ♕b2 36. ♔h3 ♕f6∓ 37. ♕e8 h5 38. ♔g2 ♔h6 39. ♔f1 h4 40. h3 c4 41. ♔e2** [41. ♗c4 ♕a1 42. ♔e2 ♕b2 43. ♔d3 ♕b1 44. ♔e2 (44. ♔d2 ♕b4 45. ♔e3 ♕c5 46. ♔d3 ♕d6−+) ♕c2 45. ♔e3 ♕c1 46. ♔d4 ♕d1 47. ♗d3 ♕a4 48. ♔e5 ♕d7−+] **g5! 42. ♔d1 g4 43. fg4 fg4 44. hg4 h3 45. ♔c2 ♔g7 46. ♗c6 h2 47. ♗e4 ♕g5!⊙ 48. ♔c3** [48. ♗c6 ♕g6−+; 48. ♕e6 ♖h8−+; 48. ♔b1 c3 49. ♔c2 ♕d2 50. ♔b3 ♕d7 51. ♕g6 ♔f8−+] **♕a5 49. ♔d4 ♕c5 50. ♔c3 ♕a3−+ 51. ♔d4 ♕d6 52. ♔c4 ♖d7 0 : 1** **[Beljavskij]**

445. **D 63**

NENAŠEV 2565 — PEREGUDOV 2495
Akmola 1993

1. d4 ♘f6 2. c4 e6 3. ♘c3 d5 4. ♗g5 ♗e7 5. e3 0—0 6. ♘f3 ♘bd7 7. ♖c1 dc4 8. ♗c4 c5 9. 0—0 a6 [9... cd4 10. ed4±] **10. ♗e2 N** [10. dc5!? ♘c5 (10... ♗c5 11. ♘e4 ♗e7 12. ♘d6) 11. ♘d4±; 10. a4 — 46/594] **cd4** [10... b5 11. dc5 ♘c5 12. ♘d4 ♗b7 13. ♗f3±] **11. ♘d4 ♕b6 12. ♕c2** [12. ♕b3!?] **♖e8 13. ♖fd1 ♘f8 14. ♘f3 ♘8d7** [14... ♗d7 15. ♘e5±] **15. ♘d2 ♕a5 16. ♗h4** [16. ♗f4 b5 17. a4 e5 18. ♗g3 b4∞] **b5 17. a4 ba4** [17... b4 18. ♘ce4±]

18. ♘c4 ♕b4 19. ♖d4! ♗c5 [19... ♕b3 20. ♕b1 △ ♘a5, ♖a4] **20. ♖f4 ♕b8** [20... ♕b3 21. ♘a4 ♕c2 22. ♖c2 ♘d5? 23. ♘c5 ♘f4 24. ef4 ♘c5 25. ♘d6+–] **21. ♘a4 ♗e7** [21... ♘d5? 22. ♖f7! ♔f7 23. ♕h7+–] **22. ♘a5?** [22. ♗g3 e5 23. ♖f5 ♗f8 24. ♗f3±] **♘e5 23. ♘c5 ♕c7?⊕** [23... ♗c5 24. ♕c5 ♕b2 25. ♗f6 (25. ♖f6? ♘d7) gf6 26. ♖c2 ♕b1 27. ♗f1$\overline{\infty}$] **24. ♖a4 ♘fd7 25. ♗e7 ♖e7 26. f4 ♘c5 27. fe5** [27. ♕c5 ♕c5 28. ♖c5 ♘g6 29. ♖b4 (29. ♗f3?! ♖b8 30. ♘c6 ♖c7) ♗d7±] **♘a4 28. ♕c7 ♖c7 29. ♖c7 ♘b6□ 30. e4 ♔f8 31. ♔f2 ♖b8 32. b3 ♗d7 33. ♔e3 ♔e8 34. ♔d4 ♖c8 35. ♖c8 ♗c8 36. ♔c5 ♘d7 37. ♔d6 f6?** [37... ♘f8 38. b4 △ ♘b3-c5+–] **38. ♔c7 1 : 0 [Nenašev]**

446. D 64

VYŽMANAVIN 2620 – F. BRAGA 2435

Benidorm 1993

1. d4 ♘f6 2. c4 e6 3. ♘c3 d5 4. ♗g5 ♘bd7 5. e3 ♗e7 6. ♘f3 0–0 7. ♖c1 a6 8. ♕c2 c6 9. a4 ♖e8 [9... ♕a5!?] **10. ♗d3 dc4 11. ♗c4 ♘d5** [11... b5 12. ♗d3 ♗b7∞] **12. ♗e7 N** [12. ♗f4] **♕e7 13. 0–0 ♘b4 14. ♕b3 a5 15. e4⩲ b6 16. e5 ♗b7 17. ♘e4 c5 18. ♘d6 ♖eb8** [18... ♗f3 19. ♕f3 ♖ed8 20. ♕g3 cd4 21. f4→] **19. ♗b5** [19. ♕e3!? ♗f3 20. ♕f3 cd4 21. ♕g3 △ f4-f5] **♗d5 20. ♕e3 ♘c6! 21. ♗c6□ ♗c6 22. ♘d2 cd4** [22... ♗a4 23. f4$\overline{\infty}$] **23. ♕d4 ♘c5 24. ♖c3 ♗a4 25. ♘2e4!** [25. ♖c5 bc5 26. ♕a4 ♖b2 27. ♘2c4 ♖b4 28. ♕c6 ♖ab8 29. ♘a5 ♖b1 30. g3⩲] **♗c6?** [25... ♘e4 26. ♕e4 ♗e8 27. ♖fc1 f5! 28. ♕f4$\overline{\infty}$]

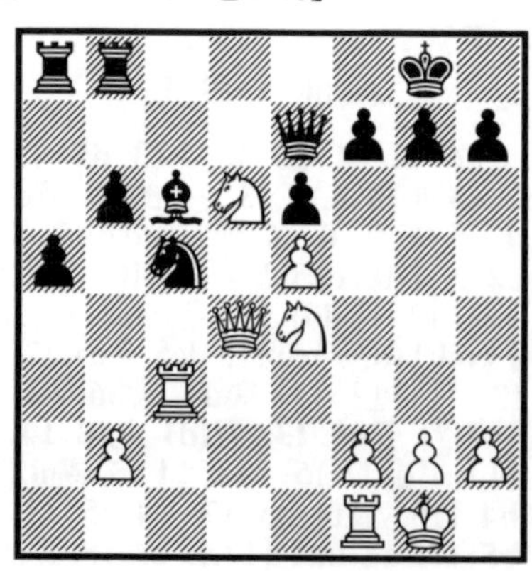

26. ♘f6 ♔h8 [26... gf6 27. ♖g3 ♔h8 28. ef6] **27. ♖h3 gf6** [27... h6 28. ♕f4 ♕f8 29. ♘f7] **28. ♕h4 1 : 0**
[Vyžmanavin, B. Arhangel'skij]

447. D 76

RIBLI 2620 – ROGOZENKO 2480

Odorheiu Secuiesc 1993

1. ♘f3 ♘f6 2. c4 g6 3. g3 ♗g7 4. ♗g2 d5 5. cd5 ♘d5 6. ♘c3 0–0 7. 0–0 ♘c6 8. d4 ♘b6 9. d5 ♘a5 10. ♕c2 c6 11. dc6 ♘c6 12. ♖d1 ♗f5 13. e4 ♗d7 14. ♘d5!? N [14. ♗f4 – 52/448] **♘d5 15. ed5 ♘a5 16. ♕e2?!** [16. ♗g5! h6 17. ♗f4 ♖c8 18. ♕e2 ♘c4 19. b3! ♗a1 20. ♖a1 ♘d6 21. ♗h6$\overline{\infty}$] **♗a4! 17. ♖d4!** [17. ♖d2? ♖c8∓] **♗d4 18. ♘d4 e5?** [18... ♕b6 19. ♗e3 ♕b4 20. b3 ♗d7 21. ♘c2 ♕b5 22. ♕d2$\overline{\infty}$; 18... ♕d6!? 19. b3 ♗d7 20. ♗f4 ♕b4 21. ♖d1$\overline{\infty}$] **19. ♕e5 ♖e8**

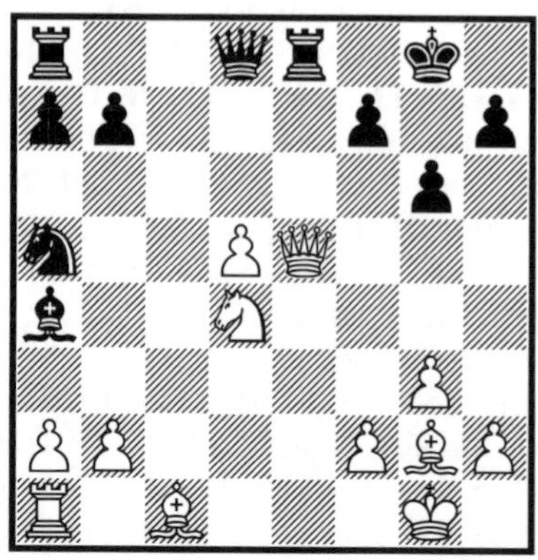

20. ♘e6! fe6 [20... f6 21. ♕f4? ♖e6 22. de6 ♕d1 23. ♗f1 ♗b5–+; 21. ♕e4!±] **21. b3! ♖e7** [21... ♕b8 22. d6 ♘c6 23. ♗c6 ♗c6 24. ♗b2+–] **22. ♗b2 ♕f8 23. d6 ♕g7** [23... ♖d7 24. ♕e6 ♖f7 25. ♗d5 ♖e8 26. ♕f6+–] **24. ♕e2! e5** [24... ♗b5 25. ♕d2+–] **25. de7 ♗c6 26. ♗h3 ♕e7 27. b4 ♕b4 28. ♕e5 1 : 0 [Ribli]**

448. D 77

R. HÜBNER 2620 – SCHMITTDIEL 2450

Deutschland 1993

1. c4 e6 2. ♘f3 ♘f6 3. g3 d5 4. ♗g2 ♘bd7 5. 0–0 g6?! [5... ♗e7; 5... dc4 –

28/33, A 13] **6. d4 ♗g7 7. ♕c2 0–0 8. ♗f4 c6?!** [×d6; 8... b6 9. cd5 ♘d5 10. ♗g5±; 8... ♘h5 9. ♗g5 f6 10. ♗d2 f5 △ ♘df6] **9. ♘bd2 ♕e7** [9... ♘h5 10. ♗d6±] **10. e4** [10. c5 ♘e8 11. e4 f6 △ 12... g5, 12... ♕f7±] **h6** [⌓ 10... ♘h5 11. ♗g5 f6 12. ♗e3 f5] **11. c5** [11. ♖fe1?! ♘h5 12. ed5 (12. ♗e3 ♘df6) cd5 13. cd5 ♘f4 14. gf4 ♘f6=/∞] **♘e8 12. ♖fe1** [12. e5 g5 13. ♗e3 f5 14. ef6 ♘ef6 △ 15... ♘g4, 15... e5⩲] **g5□ 13. ♗e3 de4** [13... f5 14. ef5 ♖f5 15. h4± △ 15... g4 16. ♘h2 h5 17. f3] **14. ♘e4 f5 15. ♘c3 ♘c7 16. ♖ad1 ♕f7 17. ♗c1 g4** [17... ♘d5 18. ♗g5] **18. ♘h4** [18. ♘e5?! ♘e5 19. de5 ♘d5⩲] **e5 19. de5 ♘c5?** [19... ♘e5 20. ♗f4 (20. ♗h6 ♗h6 21. ♖e5 ♗g7 22. ♖e2 ♗e6=/∞) ♖e8 21. ♖e2± △ 21... ♔h7 22. ♖de1 ♘g6 23. ♘g6 ♔g6 24. ♗c7 ♖e2 25. ♘e2 ♕c7 26. ♘f4 ♔h7 27. h3] **20. b3+–** [×f5] **♖e8 21. ♗a3 ♗f8** [21... ♘5a6 22. ♗d6; 21... ♘7a6 22. b4 ♘e4 (22... ♘d7 23. b5) 23. ♘e4 fe4 24. ♗e4] **22. ♗c5 ♗c5 23. ♘e4 fe4** [23... ♗e7 24. ♘d6 ♗d6 25. ed6 ♖e1 26. ♖e1 ♘d5 27. ♗d5 ♕d5 28. ♖e8 ♔f7 29. ♖e7 ♔f8 30. ♕c3 ♕d1 31. ♔g2 ♕d5 32. f3] **24. ♕c5 ♘e6 25. ♕d6 ♖f8** [25... ♘g5 26. ♕h6] **26. ♖d2 ♖d8 27. ♕d8 ♘d8 28. ♖d8 ♔g7 29. ♗e4 ♕c7 30. ♖e8** [30... ♕d7 31. ♘f5; 30... ♔f7 31. ♗g6; 30... ♕a5 31. ♖e2; 30. ♖d6 ♕a5∞] **1 : 0** **[R. Hübner]**

449.*** **D 77**

KONOPKA 2380 – LAGUNOV 2450
Deutschland 1993

1. ♘f3 g6 2. d4 ♘f6 3. g3 ♗g7 4. ♗g2 0–0 5. 0–0 d5 6. c4 dc4 7. ♘a3 c3 8. bc3 c5 9. e3 [RR 9. ♘e5 ♘bd7 *a)* 10. ♘d7 ♘d7 11. ♖b1 cd4 N (11... ♘b6) 12. cd4 ♘b6 13. ♗e3 (13. e3 ♖b8) ♗e6∞ Nadanian 2285 – Aronian, Armenia 1993; 13... ♘d5!?; 10... ♕d7!?; *b)* 10. ♖b1!? N ♘e5 11. de5 ♘g4 12. ♕d8 (12. f4 ♕a5∞ Hachian, Aronian) ♖d8 13. f4 ♖b8 14. h3 ♘h6 15. ♘c4 ♘f5 16. g4 ♘g3 17. ♖f2 h5 18. ♔h2 h4 19. ♗e3 b6 20. ♘a5 ♗d7 21. ♘c6 ♗c6 22. ♗c6 f6∞ Nadanian 2285 – Hachian 2415, Armenia 1993] **♘c6 10. ♕e2 ♗f5 11. ♗b2 e5 12. ♖fd1 N** [12. ♘e5 ♘e5 13. de5 ♗d3 14. ♕d1!? (14. ♕e1 ♘g4 15. ♖d1 ♕b6 16. ♖d3 ♕b2∓) ♗f1 15. ef6 ♕d1 16. ♖d1 ♗g2 17. fg7 ♖fd8 18. ♖d8 ♖d8 19. ♔g2 ♖d2 20. ♘c4 ♖c2 21. a4 b6 22. ♔f1! a6 23. ♔e1 b5 24. ab5 ab5 25. ♔d1 ♖f2 26. ♘d2 c4 27. ♗a3 ♔g7 28. h4∞⊥; RR 12. ♘c4 e4 N (12... ed4 – 56/(523)) 13. ♘fe5 ♘e5 14. ♘e5 h5 15. ♗a3?! b6 16. h3 ♕c8 17. ♔h2 ♕c7 18. ♖ac1 ♖ac8 19. ♔g1 ♖fe8! 20. c4 (20. g4 hg4 21. hg4 ♖e5!∓) cd4 21. ed4 ♘d7! 22. g4 (22. ♘d7 ♕d7∓ ×d4, h3) hg4 23. ♘g4 (23. hg4 ♗e6∓) ♗g4 24. ♕g4 ♗d4∓ Abramović 2475 – D. Paunović 2450, Jugoslavija 1993; 15. c4∞; 15. h3!? D. Paunović] **e4!** [12... ed4 13. cd4 cd4 14. ♘d4 ♘d4 15. ♗d4 ♕e7 16. ♕b2±] **13. ♘e5** [13. ♘d2 ♗g4 14. f3 ef3 15. ♘f3 ♖e8∓] **♘e5** [13... ♖e8 14. ♘ac4±] **14. de5 ♘d7** [△ ♕e7, ♘e5∓] **15. g4!? ♗e6 16. ♗e4 ♕h4! 17. f4□ ♗g4 18. ♗f3 ♗f3 19. ♕f3 ♘b6!∓** [×♘a3, ♗b2] **20. c4** [20. ♕b7?! ♘a4 21. ♕g2 (21. ♖ab1? ♖ab8 22. ♕g2 ♘b2 23. ♖b2 ♖b2 24. ♕b2 ♕g4–+; 21. ♕b3? ♖ab8 22. ♕a4 ♖b2 23. ♘c2 ♗e5–+) f6!↑] **f6 21. ef6 ♗f6 22. ♖ab1 ♖ad8** [22... ♖ae8!? 23. ♗f6 ♖f6 24. ♖d3 ♖fe6 25. ♖c1∓] **23. ♖d8! ♖d8 24. ♗f6 ♕f6 25. ♖d1! ♖e8?!** [25... ♖f8! 26. ♘b5! ♘c4 27. ♘a7 ♕e6 28. ♖e1∓] **26. e4!= ♖f8** [26... ♕e6?! 27. e5! ♘c4 28. ♘c4 ♕c4 29. ♖d7±] **27. ♘b5! ♕f4** [27... ♘c4?! 28. ♕b3! ♕f7 29. ♘a7⇆] **28. ♕f4 ♖f4 29. ♘d6 ♔f8 30. ♖e1! ♔e7** [⌓ 30... ♘d7] **31. ♘b7 ♘d7 32. ♖d1!** [32... ♖e4?? 33. ♖d7+–; 32... ♖f6 33. ♖d5 ♖b6 34. ♘c5 ♖b1 35. ♔g2 ♖b2 36. ♔g3 ♘b6=] **1/2 : 1/2** **[Lagunov]**

450. **D 78**

WOJTKIEWICZ 2580
– J. BENJAMIN 2585
Pleasantville 1993

1. ♘f3 ♘f6 2. c4 g6 3. g3 ♗g7 4. ♗g2 c6 5. d4 d5 6. ♕b3 0–0 7. ♘c3 dc4 8. ♕c4 ♗f5 9. 0–0 ♘bd7 10. e3 [10. ♕b3 ♕b6 11. ♖e1 ♘e4 12. ♘h4 ♘c3 13. ♘f5!±; 10... ♘b6] **♘b6 N** [10... ♘e4] **11. ♕e2 ♘e4 12. ♖d1 ♘c3 13. bc3 ♘a4= 14.**

♗d2 ♗e4 [14... ♘b2?! 15. e4 ♘d1 16. ef5 ♘b2 17. ♖b1 ♘a4 18. ♖b7±] **15. ♗e1** [15. ♘e1=] **♕c7 16. ♗f1 h6 17. ♖ac1** [17. ♘d2 ♘c3 18. ♕c4 ♘d1 19. ♘e4 ♘e3 20. fe3∞] **c5 18. c4 b6 19. ♘d2 ♗b7 20. ♘b1** [⌓ 20. ♘b3 cd4 21. ed4 e6 22. d5∞] **cd4 21. ed4 ♖ac8 22. ♘c3?! ♘c3 23. ♗c3 e6∓ 24. ♗b2 ♖fe8 25. ♗g2?! ♗g2 26. ♔g2 ♕b7 27. f3** [⌓ 27. ♕f3] **♕a6 28. ♖d3 ♖c7∓ 29. ♖a3 ♕b7 30. ♖b3?! ♖d8 31. ♖d3 ♕a6 32. ♔h3?⊕ ♕c8!−+ 33. ♖dd1 e5 34. ♔g2 ed4 35. ♕d3 ♖e7 36. ♖e1 ♖e3 37. ♕d2 h5 38. ♖cd1 ♖e1 39. ♖e1 ♕c4 40. ♖e7 ♕a2 0 : 1 [J. Benjamin]**

451. D 85

ALBURT 2535 − J. BENJAMIN 2585
New York 1993

1. d4 ♘f6 2. c4 g6 3. ♘c3 d5 4. cd5 ♘d5 5. ♗d2 ♗g7 6. e4 ♘b6 7. ♗e3 0−0 8. a4?! N [×b4; 8. h3 − 56/529] **a5 9. ♗e2 ♘c6 10. d5 ♘b4 11. ♖c1** [⌓ 11. ♘f3] **f5 12. ♘b5? c6 13. dc6 ♕d1 14. ♔d1 ♘a4∓ 15. ♗c4 ♔h8 16. ♘c7 f4! 17. ♘a8** [17. ♗d2 ♗g4 18. f3 ♖ac8−+] **fe3 18. ♘f3□ ♗b2 19. ♗b3?!** [19. ♔e2 ♗c1 20. ♖c1 bc6∓] **♘c3 20. ♖c3 ♗c3 21. c7 b5!−+ 22. ♔e2 a4 23. ♗d5 ef2?⊕** [23... e6−+; 23... ♘d5 24. ed5 a3−+] **24. ♘b6 e6 25. ♖c1** [25. ♗a8 a3 26. ♖d1 a2 27. ♖d8 f1♕ 28. ♔f1 a1♕−+] **ed5 26. ed5** [26. ♖c3 de4 27. ♘d2 ♘a6! (Byrne) 28. h3 b4 29. ♖c6 ♘c7 30. ♖c7 ♗a6 31. ♔e3 f1♕ 32. ♘f1 ♗f1−+] **♗b2 27. ♖d1 a3 28. d6 ♘c6 29. d7 ♗d7 30. ♖d7 a2 31. ♖d1 ♘e7 0 : 1 [J. Benjamin]**

452.* D 85

EHLVEST 2625 − J. BENJAMIN 2585
Pleasantville 1993

1. d4 ♘f6 2. c4 g6 3. ♘c3 d5 4. cd5 ♘d5 5. e4 ♘c3 6. bc3 ♗g7 7. ♗b5 ♗d7 8. ♗e2 c5 9. ♘f3 cd4 [RR 9... ♗g4!? N 10. ♖b1 cd4 11. cd4 ♗f3 12. ♗f3 (12. gf3 0−0!∞) ♕d4! (12... ♗d4 13. ♖b7±) 13. ♕d4 ♗d4 14. ♖b7 ♘d7! (14... ♘c6 15. ♖c7±) 15. ♗a3 ♗b6 16. e5 ♖c8 17. 0−0 ♘c5 18. ♖c1 (18. ♗c5 ♗c5 19. ♗c6 ♔f8=) ♔f8!= (△ e6, ♔g7; 18... 0−0 19. ♖e7 ♖fd8 20. ♗g4 ♖c6 21. ♗d7 ♖c7 22. ♖e8 ♖e8 23. ♗e8±) 19. h4 (19. ♖c4 e6 20. ♖f4; 19... h5! △ 20... e6 21. ♖f4 ♖h7=) h5 20. ♖d7 ♘d7 21. ♖c8 ♔g7 22. ♖h8 ♔h8 23. ♗e7 ♔g7 24. ♗d6 (1/2 : 1/2 Kajdanov 2620 − Kudrin 2575, Reno 1993) ♗d4 △ ♘e5-g4= Kajdanov] **10. cd4 ♗c6 11. ♕d3 f5 12. ef5 ♕a5 13. ♗d2 ♕f5 14. ♕f5 gf5 15. 0−0 N** [15. ♖c1 − 56/(531)] **♗d5!** [15... ♘d7 16. ♖fe1±] **16. ♘e5! ♗e5** [16... ♘c6 17. ♗h5 ♔f8 18. ♖fe1 ♘d4 19. ♖ad1$\bar{\bar{\infty}}$] **17. de5 ♖g8 18. f3 ♘c6 19. ♗c3⩲ 0-0-0 20. a4?!** [×b3; 20. ♖fc1 f4 21. ♔f2 ♖g5 22. ♗f1 ♔b8 23. ♖e1±] **♗e6** [20... e6!?] **21. ♖fb1 ♘d4 22. ♗d1 ♖d7 23. ♖b2 ♖gd8 24. ♗a5 b6?!** [24... ♖f8] **25. ♗e1 f4 26. a5 b5 27. a6!↑ ♗c4 28. ♗a5 ♖f8 29. ♖c1 ♘c6 30. ♗c3 ♖fd8 31. ♗c2 e6 32. ♔f2** [32. h4! △ ♔h2±] **♖d2 33. ♔g1□ h6?⊕** [33... ♖e2] **34. h4** [34. ♗d2! ♖d2 35. ♖cb1 △ ♗e4±] **♖e2 35. ♗e4 ♖b2 36. ♗b2 ♘d4 37. ♔h2 ♘e2 38. ♖c2 ♖d1 39. h5 ♘g3 40. ♗b7 ♔d7 41. ♖c1 ♖d3** [41... ♖c1 42. ♗c1 ♘h5 43. ♗a3 △ ♗c5±] **42. ♔h3 ♔c7 43. ♗c3 ♖d7 44. ♗a5 ♔b8 45. ♗b4! ♔c7 46. ♗c5 ♘e2 47. ♖e1 ♖g7 48. ♖d1!+− ♖g5 49. ♗e7! ♖g3 50. ♔h2 ♔b6 51. ♗b4 ♗d5⊕ 52. ♗d5 ed5 53. ♖d2! ♘c1 54. ♖d5 ♔a6 55. e6 1 : 0 [Ehlvest]**

453.* D 85**

GOFSHTEIN 2560 −
V. MIKHALEVSKI 2305
Netanya 1993

1. d4 ♘f6 2. c4 g6 3. ♘c3 d5 4. cd5 ♘d5 5. e4 ♘c3 6. bc3 ♗g7 7. ♗b5 c6 8. ♗a4 0−0 9. ♘e2 c5 [RR 9... e5 10. 0−0 ♘d7 11. ♗b3!? N (11. ♗e3 − 56/(533)) ♕e7 12. ♕c2 ♖e8 13. f3 ♘b6 14. a4 ♗e6 15. a5 ♗b3 (15... ♘c4 16. ♕a2 ♘d6 17. ♗a3±; 16. ♖a4; 16. f4) 16. ♕b3 ♘c8 *a)* 17. ♗a3 ♕c7 18. ♗c5 (18. ♔h1?! b5! 19. ab6 ab6= Vyžmanavin 2620 − Sánchez Almeyra 2415, Zaragoza 1993) ♖b8 19. ♖fb1 b6 20. ab6 ab6 21. ♖a6± Vyžmanavin, B. Arhangel'skij; *b)* 17. ♗e3 ♕c7 18. ♘g3 ♖d8 19. de5 ♗e5 20. f4 ♗g7 21. e5

♖b8 22. ♘e4 b6 23. ab6 ab6 24. c4± S. Kiselëv 2510 – Rogozenko 2480, Bucureşti 1993; 9... ♗e6 N 10. h4 ♗c4 11. ♗b3 ♗b3 12. ♕b3 ♕b6 13. h5 e5 14. hg6 1/2 : 1/2 Kramnik 2685 – Kamsky 2655, Dortmund 1993] **10. 0–0 ♕a5!? N** [10... ♘c6 – 54/(459)] **11. d5** [11. ♗g5!? ♗d7 *a)* 12. ♗d7 ♘d7 13. dc5 ♘c5 14. ♗e7 ♖fe8 15. ♗c5 ♕c5 16. ♕c2 ♕c4 17. f3 f5∓; 16. ♕b3!?; *b)* 12. ♗c2 cd4 13. ♗e7 ♖e8 14. ♗b4 ♕b6 15. ♘d4 ♘c6 16. ♘c6 ♗c6 △ a5∓; *c)* 12. ♗b3 c4 (12... cd4 13. ♗e7 ♖e8 14. ♗b4 ♕b6 15. ♘d4 ♗d4 16. ♕d4 ♕d4 17. cd4 ♘c6±) 13. ♗e7 cb3 14. ab3±] **e6 12. ♖b1?!** [12. ♗g5 b5 13. ♗b3 (13. ♗c2 ♖e8∞) c4 14. ♗c2 ♘a6∞] **ed5 13. ed5 ♘d7! 14. ♗g5** [14. d6? ♘b6 15. d7 (15. ♖b6 ab6 16. d7 ♕a4 17. d8♕ ♖d8 18. ♕d8 ♗f8–+) ♘a4 16. ♖b5 ♕b5□ 17. d8♕ ♗g4∓; 14. ♖b5?! ♕a6 15. c4 ♕d6 (15... ♘b6? 16. ♗b3+–) 16. ♗f4 ♘e5 17. ♘c3 b6∓; 14. ♗d7 ♗d7 15. ♖b7 ♗b5!⩱; 14. c4! ♘b6 15. ♗b3 ♗f5 16. ♗d2 ♕a6 17. ♖c1 ♗b2∞] **♘b6 15. ♗c2 c4!∓** [15... ♕a2 16. ♗b3 ♕a5 17. c4 (17. ♖a1? ♕b5 18. ♗e7 ♖e8 19. c4 ♕b4–+) ♗f5 18. ♗c2 ♗c2 19. ♕c2 ♖fe8 20. ♘g3⩱ ♂d, ×♕a5] **16. ♗e7** [16. ♗e4? ♖e8!] **♖e8 17. d6 ♗d7 18. ♗e4 ♖ab8 19. ♕d2?!** [19. ♕c2] **♗f8!** [19... ♘c8 20. ♖b7 ♖b7 21. ♗b7 ♘e7 22. de7 ♖e7 23. ♘d4 ♗d4!? 24. ♕d4 ♕a2 25. ♕d6 ♕e2□ 26. ♗a6!⩱] **20. ♗f8 ♖e4!∓** [×c3, d6] **21. ♘g3!?** [21. ♗h6 ♕d5∓; 21. ♗e7 ♕d5∓] **♖e6 22. ♗h6** [22. ♗e7 ♘d5 23. ♕g5 h6! 24. ♕h6 ♕c3–+] **♕d5! 23. ♕f4 ♕e5?!⊕** [23... ♕d6?? 24. ♕d6 ♖d6 25. ♗f4+–; 23... ♖d6? 24. ♘e4+–; 23... ♗c6! 24. f3□ ♕c5 25. ♔h1 ♘d7 (25... ♘d5? 26. ♘e4!) 26. ♘e4 ♗e4 27. fe4 f6∓] **24. ♕h4?!⊕** [24. ♕e5 ♖e5 25. ♗e3 ♗c6∓] **♕c3 25. ♖bd1** [25. ♘e4 ♕d4!] **♗c6 26. ♖d4?!** [26. ♗e3 ♘d7 27. ♖c1 (27. ♗d4 ♕a5 28. ♕h6 f6–+) ♕a5∓] **♕c2 27. ♗g5 ♘d7 28. ♖c4 ♕a2 29. ♖f4 ♕d5 30. f3 f5** [⌓ 30... ♕d6–+] **31. ♗e7 ♗b5!–+ 32. ♖b1** [32. ♕g5?! ♗f1 33. ♘f5 ♔h8!] **♕d3 33. ♖fb4 ♕e3 34. ♔h1 ♕e1 35. ♘f1 ♕h4 36. ♖h4 ♗f1 37. ♖f1 ♖c8 38. ♖a4 a6 39. h4** [△ ♖b1] **♖c6 40. g4** [40. ♖b1 b5] **♖e5 41. ♔g2 a5 42. ♔g3 ♔f7 43. h5 gh5 44. ♔h4 hg4 45. fg4 ♖cc5 46. ♖b1 b6 47. ♗d8 ♖b5 48. ♖f1 ♔e6 49. g5 ♖b3 50. ♖h1 ♖ee3 51. ♔h5 ♘e5! 0 : 1** [J. Kagan, V. Mikhalevski]

454. ***** !N **D 85**

FTÁČNIK 2535 – ADORJÁN 2545
Budapest (zt) 1993

1. d4 ♘f6 2. c4 g6 3. ♘c3 d5 4. cd5 ♘d5 5. e4 ♘c3 6. bc3 ♗g7 7. ♗b5 c6 8. ♗a4 b5 9. ♗b3 b4 10. ♕f3 [RR 10. ♗e3 bc3 11. ♖c1 0–0 12. ♖c3 (12. ♘e2 ♗a6 13. f4 ♘d7 △ ♘f6∞) ♗a6 13. ♘e2 ♘d7! N (13... ♕a5 – 51/456) 14. 0–0 (14. e5 ♕a5 15. ♕d2 c5 16. f4 cd4 17. ♘d4 ♘e5! 18. fe5 ♕e5 19. ♗c4 ♗c4 20. ♖c4 ♕d5⩱) c5 15. ♗c4 cd4 16. ♗d4 (16. ♘d4?! ♖c8 17. ♕c2 ♕a5∓ A. Mihal'čišin) ♗c4 17. ♖c4 ♘b6 18. ♖c2 ♖c8= Kišnëv 2510 – A. Mihal'čišin 2520, Lublin 1993] **0–0 11. ♘e2 bc3 12. ♕c3 N** [12. 0–0 – 56/537, 538; 12. h4 h5 N (12... c5?! – 56/(537)) *a)* 13. ♗g5 ♗b7 14. ♕c3 ♘a6 15. ♖d1 c5 16. 0–0 cd4 17. ♘d4 ♕b6 18. ♗d5 (18. ♕e3 e6∓) ♗d5 19. ed5 ♘b4 20. ♕d2 ♘d5 21. ♘f5 ♖fd8 (21... gf5? 22. ♕d5 e6 23. ♕f3±; 21... e6? 22. ♘g7 ♔g7 23. ♗h6±) *a1)* 22. ♘g7 ♔g7 23. ♕e2 *a11)* 23... ♖d7? 24. ♕e5 f6 25. ♖d5! fe5 26. ♖d7 ♖e8 27. ♖c1 ♔f7 28. ♖cc7 ♕b4 (28... a5 29. ♗e7 ♕c7!? 30. ♖c7 ♖e7 31. ♖c5 e4 32. ♔f1 e3 33. f3 ♖d7 34. ♖c2 ♖d3=) 29. ♖a7 ♕e1 30. ♔h2 ♕f2 31. ♖e7 1/2 : 1/2 Kállai 2450 – Adorján 2545, Magyarország 1993; *a12)* 23... ♖d6 24. ♗e7 ♖e6 (24... ♖e8?? 25. ♕e5+–) 25. ♕f3=; *a13)* 23... ♕d6! (Kállai; △ ♖d7, f6) 24. ♖fe1 (24. ♖d3 ♖d7 25. ♗e7 ♖e7 26. ♖d5 ♖e2 27. ♖d6 ♖a2 28. g3 ♖b8∓) ♖d7 25. ♕f3 f6? 26. ♖d5 ♕d5 27. ♖e7 ♔g8 28. ♖d7 ♕f3 29. gf3 fg5 30. hg5 ♖f8 31. ♖a7 ♖f5=; 25... ♖e8∓ △ 26. ♗e7? ♖de7 27. ♖e7 ♖e7 28. ♕d5 ♖e1–+; *a2)* 22. ♗e7 *a21)* 22... gf5? 23. ♗d8 ♖d8 24. ♕g5 ♘f6 (24... ♕f6? 25. ♖d2+–) 25. ♕f5±; *a22)* 22... ♘e7 23. ♘e7 ♔f8 24. ♘d5 ♕c5 25. ♕g5 ♖ab8 26. ♘f6!; *b)* RR 13. ♕c3 ♗b7 14. e5 ♘a6 15. ♘f4 e6 16. ♖h3 c5 17. dc5 ♕c7 18. ♗b2 ♘c5 19. ♔f1 ♕b6 20. ♔g1 ♖fd8 21. ♕e3 ♘e4 22. ♕b6 ab6 23. ♖d3 ♘c5

24. ♖d8 ♖d8 25. ♖d1 ♖d1 26. ♗d1 ♘d7 27. ♘d3 ♗e4 28. ♗a4 ♗d3 1/2 : 1/2 Grószpéter 2525 – Fogarasi 2395, Kecskemét 1993] **♗b7 13. ♗g5** [13. ♕b4 ♕b6 14. ♗a3 ♕b4 15. ♗b4 c5 16. ♗c5 ♗e4 17. 0–0!=; RR 13. ♖b1!? c5□ 14. ♗f7 ♖f7 15. ♖b7 cd4 *a)* 16. ♕c4?! ♘d7 17. ♗a3 (17. 0–0 ♖c8 △ ♘c5∓) *a1)* 17... ♘e5 18. ♕b3 ♕a5 19. ♗b4 ♕a6 20. ♖e7 ♖b8 (20... ♘d3?! 21. ♔d2 ♗h6 22. f4) 21. ♖f7 ♘f7 (21... ♖b4?! 22. ♖f8!) 22. a3 ♗f8 23. ♕d1 ♗b4 24. ab4 ♕c4 (1/2 : 1/2 Čehov 2480 – Lingnau 2415, Deutschland 1993; 24... ♖b4 25. 0–0 d3 26. ♘c3 ♕c4 27. ♕d2 △ ♖c1⇆) 25. ♕d4 ♕d4 26. ♘d4 ♖b4 27. ♘f3 ♖e4 28. ♔d2=; *a2)* 17... ♘b6!? 18. ♕e6 ♖c8!↑; *b)* 16. ♕c7!? ♕c7 (16... ♘a6 17. ♕d8 ♖d8 18. ♖a7) 17. ♖c7 e5 (17... ♘a6 18. ♖c4±) 18. ♖c8 ♖f8 19. ♖f8 ♗f8 20. f4⇆ Čehov] **♘a6!** [13... ♘d7? 14. ♕b4! ♗a6 15. ♗e7 c5 16. ♗d8 cb4 17. ♗g5 ♘c5 18. ♗d5 ♖ac8 19. ♗e3 ♘e6 20. ♖d1 ♖c2 21. ♖d2 ♖fc8 22. e5 ♖d2 23. ♔d2 ♘d4? 24. ♘d4 ♖d8 25. ♗e4 ♗e5 26. ♗d3 1 : 0 Kramnik 2685 – József Horváth 2535, Österreich 1993] **14. e5?** [14. ♖d1 c5 15. 0–0 cd4 16. ♘d4 ♕b6 17. ♕e3∞] **c5 15. d5** [15. dc5 ♖c8∓; 15... ♕c7∓] **♘b4 16. ♖d1?** [16. a3? ♗e5–+; 16. 0–0 ♘d5 17. ♕c5 ♕b6 18. ♕b6 ab6 19. ♘f4=; 16... ♕c7!∓] **♕c7 17. f4 ♖ad8 18. d6** [18. ♖c1 ♖c8 19. ♖d1 ♖fd8∓] **♖d6 19. ♖d6 ed6 20. a3 ♘d5 21. ♕d3**

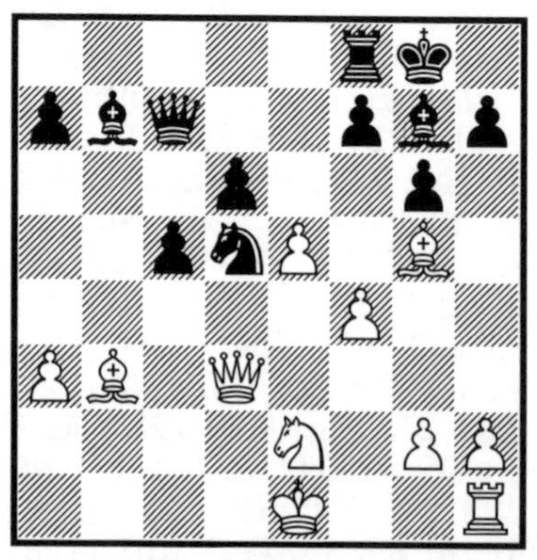

21... c4! 22. ♗c4 de5 23. ♗d5 ♕a5 24. ♔f2 ♗d5 25. fe5 f6 26. ♗d2 [26. ef6 ♗f6 27. ♗f6 (27. ♗f4 ♗h4–+) ♖f6 28. ♔g3 ♕c7 29. ♔h3 ♕d7 30. ♔g3 ♕d6 31. ♔h3 ♕e6 32. ♔g3 ♕e5 33. ♔h3 ♕h5 34. ♔g3 ♕g5 35. ♔h3 ♗e6–+] **fe5 27. ♔e1 ♕c5** [27... ♕d8–+] **28. ♗e3 ♕c6 29. ♗a7 ♗g2 30. ♖g1 ♗f3** [30... ♗d5 △ ♗c4–+] **31. ♖f1 ♖f7** [31... e4–+] **32. ♗e3 ♗f8 33. ♕b3 ♗d5 34. ♕b8 ♖f1 35. ♔f1 ♗c4??** [35... ♕f6–+] **36. ♕e5 ♕f3** [36... ♗d6! 37. ♕f6 ♕h1 38. ♗g1 ♕e4 39. ♕d8 ♔f7 40. ♕d7 ♗e7 41. ♕d2 ♗a3 42. ♕e3! ♕g4∓] **37. ♗f2 ♗a3 38. ♕e3 ♕h5 39. ♗g3 ♕f5 40. ♗f2 ♕g4 41. ♕e8 ♗f8 42. ♔e1 ♕f5 43. ♗d4 ♕g4 44. ♕e5 ♕e6 45. ♕e6 ♗e6 46. ♗e5 ♗e7 47. ♔f2 ♔f7 48. ♔g3 ♗b4 49. ♘d4 ♗d7 50. ♔f4 ♗d2 51. ♔g3 ♗c8 52. ♘f3 ♗e3 53. ♗f4 ♗b6 54. ♘g5 ♔g8 55. ♘e4 ♗d4 56. ♗d2 ♗b7 57. ♗c3 ♗b6 58. ♘f6 ♔f7 59. ♘h7 ♗c7 60. ♔h3 ♔e6 1/2 : 1/2**
[Adorján, Gy. Fehér]

455.* !N D 85

DREEV 2560 – B. ALTERMAN 2600

Rostov na Donu (open) 1993

1. d4 ♘f6 2. c4 g6 3. ♘c3 d5 4. cd5 ♘d5 5. e4 ♘c3 6. bc3 ♗g7 7. ♗b5 c6 8. ♗a4 b5 9. ♗b3 b4 10. ♕f3 0–0 11. ♘e2 a5! N [V. Neverov] **12. 0–0** [12. h4 a4 13. ♗c4 ♗a6 14. ♗a6 ♘a6 15. h5 ♕d7!∞] **♗a6 13. ♖d1 a4 14. ♗c2 b3! 15. ab3?** [15. ♗d3∞ A. Šnejder 2540 – V. Neverov 2550, Ukrajina 1993] **ab3 16. ♗d3 ♕b6!∓ 17. ♗g5?!** [17. ♗b2 ♘d7∓] **♗d3 18. ♕d3** [18. ♖a8 ♗c2 19. ♖aa1 b2!–+] **♖a1 19. ♖a1 ♘d7!∓ 20. ♗e7 b2 21. ♖b1** [21. ♖f1 ♖a8 22. ♗b4 ♖a1 23. ♕c2 ♕a6! 24. ♕b2 ♖a2] **♖a8! 22. ♕d1 ♕b5! 23. ♘f4 ♕a4!–+** [23... ♘b6 24. ♘d3 ♘c4 25. g3∓] **24. ♘d3 ♕d1 25. ♖d1 ♖a2** [△ ♗h6-c1] **26. g4 ♘b6 27. g5** [27. ♔g2 ♘c4 △ ♘e3] **♘a4** [⌓ 27... ♗f8!] **28. ♗b4 ♗f8 29. ♗a5⊕ ♗a3 30. ♔g2** [30. d5 cd5 31. ed5 ♖a1 32. ♘b2 ♗b2 33. ♖a1 ♗a1 34. d6 ♘c5 35. ♗b4 ♘d7 36. ♔g2 ♔f8 37. ♔f3 ♔e8] **♖a1 31. ♘b2 ♗b2 32. ♖d3 ♘c5! 33. ♖d2 ♖a5 34. ♖b2 ♘e4 35. h4 ♘c3 36. ♖c2 ♖a3 0 : 1**
[B. Alterman, A. Vaisman]

456. **D 85**

A. MARIĆ 2390 – ČIBURDANIDZE 2505
Shanghai (ct) 1992

1. d4 ♘f6 2. c4 g6 3. ♘c3 d5 4. cd5 ♘d5 5. e4 ♘c3 6. bc3 ♗g7 7. ♗a3 0–0 8. ♘f3 b6 9. ♗c4 ♗b7 10. ♕e2!? N [10. ♕d3] **c5 11. 0–0 ♘c6 12. ♖ad1** [12. ♖fd1!?] **♕c7 13. ♗b2** [13. e5 ♘a5 14. ♗d3 ♗f3 (14... e6 15. ♘g5) 15. ♕f3 e6=; 13. ♗a6 ♖fd8 14. ♗b7 ♕b7 15. dc5 ♗c3 16. e5 ♘d4 17. ♘d4 ♗d4 18. c6 ♕c6 19. ♗e7 ♖e8!=] **♘a5 14. ♗d3 e6 15. ♘d2 ♖fd8 16. ♖c1 ♕d7 17. ♘f3 ♖ac8 18. ♗b5 ♗c6 19. ♗a6 ♗b7 20. ♗b5 ♕c7** [20... ♗c6=] **21. ♕e3 a6 22. ♗d3 ♕d7 23. ♕e2 b5** [23... ♕a4!?] **24. ♖fd1 cd4 25. cd4 ♖c1 26. ♗c1 ♖c8 27. ♗f4 ♕e7 28. h4 ♘c6 29. ♗b1 ♕b4 30. ♗e3 ♖d8 31. e5 ♘e7 32. ♗g5 ♖c8 33. ♗e7 ♕e7 34. ♗e4 ♖c4 35. ♕e3 h6 36. g3 ♕c7** [36... ♗d5!? 37. h5 g5 38. ♗d5 (38. ♘d2 ♖a4) ed5±] **37. h5 ♖c3 38. ♕e2 g5 39. ♘d2 ♖a3** [39... ♗d5 40. ♗d5 ed5 41. ♘b3 ♕c4 42. ♕e1!±] **40. ♗b7 ♕b7 41. ♘e4 ♕d5 42. ♖d2 b4 43. ♔h2 a5?** [43... b3 44. ab3 ♖b3 45. ♖c2 ♖b8 46. ♕e3±]

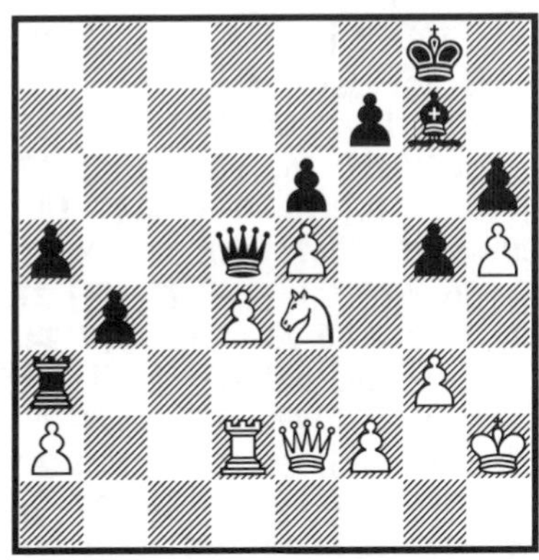

44. ♖c2! ♔h7 [44... ♕d4 45. ♖c8 *a)* 45... ♔h7 46. ♕c2 ♕d3 (46... ♖d3 47. ♘c5+–) 47. ♕c7 ♕f3 (47... ♕e4 48. ♕f7) 48. ♘f6+–; *b)* 45... ♗f8 46. ♘f6 ♔g7 47. ♕c2 ♖d3 (47... ♕d3 48. ♖f8!+–) 48. ♔g2!⊙ a4 49. ♖c7 *b1)* 49... ♕d8 50. ♕a4 △ ♕a7; *b2)* 49... b3 50. ab3 ab3 (50... a3 51. ♖c4 ♕d8 52. ♖c3 a2 53. ♖d3 ♕a8 54. ♖f3+–) 51. ♕b1 *b21)* 51... ♗b4 52. ♖c8 ♗f8 53. ♖c1!! (△ ♖d1) ♗c5 54. ♖c5+–; *b22)* 51... b2 52. ♖c8 g4 53. ♕c2+–; *b3)* 49... a3 50. ♖c4 ♕d8 51. ♔h2 b3 52. ab3 a2 53. ♕a2 ♖d2 54. ♕a7 ♗e7 55. ♖c7 ♖f2 56. ♕f2 ♕c7 57. ♘e8+–] **45. ♖c8!+– ♗e5** [45... ♖a2 46. ♕d3; 45... ♕a2 46. ♘f6 ♗f6 47. ♕e4 ♔g7 48. ef6 ♔f6 49. ♕e5 ♔e7 50. ♖c7; 45... ♕d4 46. ♕c2 ♕d3 47. ♕c7 ♕f3 48. ♘f6] **46. de5 ♕e5 47. ♖c5** [47. ♕d2! △ ♕d8] **♕d4 48. ♖c7 ♔g7 49. ♖c4 ♕a1 50. ♕d2 ♕e5 51. ♕d8 1 : 0**
[A. Marić]

457. **D 85**

SAVČENKO 2535 – TUKMAKOV 2605
Bern 1993

1. d4 ♘f6 2. c4 g6 3. ♘c3 d5 4. cd5 ♘d5 5. e4 ♘c3 6. bc3 ♗g7 7. ♗e3 c5 8. ♕d2 ♕a5 9. ♖b1 b6 10. ♗b5 ♗d7 11. ♗e2 ♘c6 12. ♘f3 0–0 13. ♖c1 ♗g4!? N [13... cd4 – 56/(541)] **14. d5 ♗f3 15. gf3 ♖ad8! 16. f4 e6 17. d6?!** [17. c4∞] **♕a4!** [17... e5 18. f5 ♕a4 19. ♕d5 (△ ♗d1) ♘e7? 20. de7] **18. f3** [18. e5 f6! (18... ♘e5? 19. fe5 ♗e5 20. ♗g5! ♖d6 21. ♕e3 f6 22. f4!±) 19. ♗g4 fe5 20. ♗e6 ♔h8 21. ♗b3 ♕b5 22. c4 ♕b4∓; 19... f5!?] **♘a5! 19. h4 h5!** [19... ♘c4 20. ♗c4 ♕c4 21. h5] **20. ♔f2 ♘c4 21. ♗c4 ♕c4 22. d7** [22. ♖hd1 ♖d7 (△ e5) 23. e5 f6∓] **f5! 23. ♖hg1 ♔h7 24. ♖cd1 ♖f7?!** [24... ♗c3! 25. ♕d6 *a)* 25... ♕a2 26. ♔g3 ♖f7 27. ♕c7! (27. e5 ♖fd7 28. ♕d7 ♖d7 29. ♖d7 ♔h6 △ ♕e2∓) ♗f6 28. ♖d6; *b)* 25... ♗f6! 26. ♔g3 fe4–+] **25. ♕d6 ♖fd7?** [25... fe4! 26. ♕c7 ♗f6–+] **26. ♕d7 ♖d7 27. ♖d7 ♕a2 28. ♖d2 ♕a4 29. e5** [△ ♖gd1, ♖d7⩱] **♗e5!? 30. fe5 f4 31. ♗c5□ bc5** [♕ 6/b] **32. ♖b1 g5! 33. ♖b7 ♔g6 34. ♖e7 ♕b3 35. hg5 ♔g5 36. ♖f7 ♕c3 37. ♖e2 h4?** [37... a5!∓] **38. ♖g7 ♔h6 39. ♖g8?!** [39. ♖g4!] **a5?** [39... c4] **40. ♖h8 ♔g6 41. ♖h4 ♕d4 42. ♔g2 c4 43. ♔h3 ♔f5** [43... c3 44. ♖g2 ♔f7 45. ♖h7 ♔f8 46. ♖h8] **44. ♖h6** [44. ♖h5 ♔g6 45. ♖h4] **♔g5! 45. ♖f6** [45. ♖e6? ♕d7 46. ♖g2 ♔f5–+] **♔h5 46. ♖f8** [46. ♖e4 ♕g1=] **♕d1 47. ♖h8 ♔g6 48. ♖g2 ♔f7 49. ♖h7 ♔f8 50. ♖h8 ♔f7 51. ♖h7 ♔f8**

52. ♔g4?? [52. ♖h8=] **♕d3! 53. ♖h8 ♔e7!** [53... ♔f7 54. ♔h4 c3 55. ♖h6 c2 56. ♖f6 ♔e8∓] **54. ♔h4 ♔d7 55. ♖g7 ♔c6 56. ♖e8 ♕f3 57. ♖e6 ♔d5 58. ♖a6 ♕h1 59. ♔g5 f3 60. ♖a5 ♔e4 61. e6 f2 62. e7 ♕h8 63. ♖g6 f1♕ 64. ♖e6 ♔d4 65. e8♕ ♕g2 66. ♔f5 ♕gh3 67. ♔g5 ♕8h4 68. ♔g6 ♕3g4 69. ♔f7 ♕h7**
0 : 1 **[Tukmakov]**

458.* **D 85**

ONIŠČUK 2420 – A. MIHAL'ČIŠIN 2520
Dortmund (open) 1993

1. d4 ♘f6 2. c4 g6 3. ♘c3 d5 4. cd5 ♘d5 5. e4 ♘c3 6. bc3 ♗g7 7. ♗e3 c5 8. ♕d2 ♕a5 [8... 0–0 9. ♘f3 ♗g4 10. ♘g5 cd4 11. cd4 ♘c6 12. h3 ♗d7 13. ♘f3 ♖c8 14. ♖b1 ♘a5 15. ♗e2 ♗e6 16. 0–0 ♗c4 17. d5 N (17. ♖fd1 – 52/459) b6 18. ♖bd1 ♕d6 19. ♗d4 ♖fd8= Iz. Jelen 2425 – A. Mihal'čišin 2530, Bled 1992] **9. ♖b1 b6 10. ♗b5 ♗d7 11. ♗e2** [11. a4!?] **♘c6 12. ♘f3 0–0 13. ♖c1** [13. ♖b5 ♕a4 14. dc5 ♖ad8!∞] **♗g4 14. d5 ♗f3** [14... ♖ad8 △ e6] **15. ♗f3 N ♖ad8 16. 0–0** [16. h4 e6 17. h5 ed5 18. ed5 ♘e7! △ ♘f5∓; 16. ♗h6 ♗h6 17. ♕h6 ♘e5 18. ♗e2 f6!?∓] **e6** [16... e5!? △ ♘e7-c8-d6∞] **17. ♖fd1** [17. c4 ♘b4! △ ♕a2∓] **♘e5** [17... c4!? 18. dc6!? (18. ♗e2 ed5 19. ed5 ♘e5 △ ♘d3∓) ♖d2 19. ♖d2 ♗c3 20. ♖dc2 ♗e5 21. ♖c4 ♗c7 22. ♖d4 △ ♖d7$\overline{\overline{\infty}}$; 19... ♗e5!?] **18. c4!** [18. ♗e2 ed5 19. ed5 c4 △ ♘d3] **♕d2** [18... ♕a4!? 19. ♗e2 ed5 20. ed5 ♖fe8 △ f5, ♘f7-d6∓] **19. ♖d2?!** [19. ♗d2 ed5 20. ed5 ♘d3 21. ♖c2 ♖fe8∓; 19... ♘d3!?] **f5!** [19... h6!? 20. ♗e2 g5∞] **20. ♗g5** [20. ef5 ♘f3! 21. gf3 ed5! 22. fg6 (22. cd5 ♖f5∓) hg6 23. cd5 ♖f3∓; 20. de6 ♖d2 21. ♗d2 ♘f3 22. gf3 fe4 23. fe4 ♖e8 24. f3 ♖e6∓] **♗f6 21. h4** [21. ♗h6 ♖fe8 22. ef5 ♘f3 23. gf3 gf5∓] **♗g5** [21... ♔g7!? △ h6∓] **22. hg5 ♘f7** [22... ♖fe8!? 23. ♖dd1 ♔f7∓] **23. ef5 ef5** [23... gf5 24. ♖e2 e5 25. ♗h5 e4 26. ♗f7 ♔f7 27. f3∞] **24. a4! ♘g5** [24... a5? 25. ♖b1 ♖d6 26. ♖db2 ♖b8 27. ♖b5! △ ♖c5±] **25. a5 ♖d6 26. ♖b1 h5?** [26... ♔f7! 27. ♖db2 ♔f6 28. ab6 ab6 29. ♖b6 ♘f3 30. gf3 ♖b6 31. ♖b6 ♔e5 32. ♖b1 (32. ♖b7 ♔d4 33. ♖h7 ♔c4 34. d6 ♖d8 35. d7 ♔d3! △ c4–+) ♔d4 33. ♖c1 f4! 34. ♔g2 g5 35. ♔h3 h5 36. ♖c2 ♖a8 37. ♖c1 ♖a2 38. ♔g2 ♖d2!∓] **27. ♖e2! ♔g7** [27... ♔f7 28. ♖be1! ♖d7 29. ♖b1 ♖b8 30. ♖eb2 ♖d6 31. ♖b5! △ ♖c5∞] **28. ♖e7 ♖f7 29. ♖e8 ♖f8** [29... h4 30. ♖b8 ♖ff6 31. ♖b7 ♖f7 32. ♖b8!=] **30. ♖e7 ♖f7 31. ♖e8 ♖f8 32. ♖e7 ♖f7**
1/2 : 1/2 **[A. Mihal'čišin]**

459. !N **D 85**

EPIŠIN 2620 – I. GUREVICH 2515
New York 1993

1. d4 ♘f6 2. c4 g6 3. ♘c3 d5 4. cd5 ♘d5 5. e4 ♘c3 6. bc3 ♗g7 7. ♗e3 c5 8. ♕d2 ♕a5 9. ♖b1 b6 10. ♗b5 ♗d7 11. ♗e2 0–0 12. ♖c1 ♖d8! N 13. d5 [13. ♘f3 *a)* 13... ♗g4 *a1)* 14. h3? ♗f3 15. ♗f3 ♘c6 16. d5 (16. e5 ♕b5! 17. ♗c6□ ♕c6 18. f4 f5!?∓) e6 17. c4 (17. 0–0 ed5 18. ed5 ♘e5 19. ♗e2 c4∓) ♘b4!∓; *a2)* 14. 0–0! cd4 15. cd4 ♕d2 16. ♗d2± △ 16... ♗d4? 17. ♘d4 ♗e2 18. ♘e2 ♖d2 19. ♖c8 ♔g7 20. ♘f4; *b)* 13... ♗b5! 14. 0–0 cd4 15. ♗b5 ♕b5 16. cd4 ♘c6 17. d5 ♘a5=] **♕a4! 14. ♗d3?!** [14. c4 ♘a6! △ 15. ♗h6 ♘b4∓, △ 15. ♗d1 ♕a3 16. ♘e2 ♘b4; 14. f3!? ♗b5 15. ♗b5 ♕b5 16. ♘e2 e6=] **e6 15. ♘e2 ed5 16. ed5 ♗g4! 17. ♘f4 ♗c8!** [×c4, ♘f4] **18. 0–0 ♘d7 19. ♗c2? ♕a2 20. ♘h5 ♘f6?!** [20... ♗h8 21. ♗g5 ♖e8 22. d6 ♗b7 23. ♗e7 ♕c4∓] **21. ♘g7 ♖d5 22. ♕e2 ♗a6 23. ♕f3 ♔g7 24. ♖fe1 ♖e8!** [×♖e1] **25. h4!** [△ ♗g5] **♗c8! 26. c4** [26. ♗g5 ♖e1 27. ♖e1 ♘g8 28. ♗b1 ♕c4 29. ♖e8 ♗f5; 26. ♗b1 ♕c4 27. ♗h6 ♔h6 28. ♕f6 ♖dd8!∓] **♖d6 27. h5** [27. ♗b1 ♕a5] **♖de6 28. h6 ♔g8 29. ♖e2 ♕a3 30. ♖ce1 ♕c3! 31. ♗a4 ♗d7 32. ♗d7 ♘d7 33. ♕b7 ♘f8! 34. ♕a7 ♕c4 35. ♕a1 f6 36. ♖d2?!** [36. ♖a2!?] **♕h4! 37. g3?** [37. ♕a7 ♖8e7 38. ♕b8 ♖e3; 37. ♕a2 g5] **♕h6–+ 38. ♖d8 ♕g7 39. ♖ed1 g5 40. ♕a8 ♕f7 41. ♕b8 ♖d8 42. ♖d8 ♔g7 43. ♕c8 ♖e7 44. ♖d6 ♖d7 45. ♖b6 ♖d1 46. ♔g2 ♕h5** **0 : 1**
[I. Gurevich]

460.* D 85

AN. KARPOV 2725 – FERNÁNDEZ GARCÍA 2475

Dos Hermanas 1993

1. d4 ♘f6 2. c4 g6 3. ♘c3 d5 4. cd5 ♘d5 5. e4 ♘c3 6. bc3 ♗g7 7. ♗e3 c5 8. ♕d2 0–0 9. ♘f3 ♕a5 10. ♖c1 b6 [RR 10... e6 11. ♗h6 ♖d8 N (11... ♘c6 – 50/484) 12. h4 cd4 13. ♗g7 ♔g7 14. cd4 ♘c6 15. ♕a5 ♘a5 16. ♔d2 ♗d7 17. ♗d3 ♖ac8 18. h5 gh5 19. ♖b1 b6 20. ♖h5 h6 21. ♖bh1 ♖h8 22. ♘e5 ♗e8 23. ♖5h3 ♘c6 24. ♖c1 ♘e7 25. ♖c8 ♘c8 26. ♖h1± H. Ólafsson 2515 – J. Benjamin 2585, Saint-Martin 1993] **11. d5** [11. h4!?] **♗g4 N** [11... ♗a6 12. c4±; 11... e6] **12. ♘g5! ♘a6** [12... h6 13. h3 ♗d7 14. ♘f3±] **13. h3** [13. f4 △ f5, h3∞] **♗d7 14. ♗e2** [14. h4!?] **♖ad8 15. 0–0 e6 16. ♗f4** [16. ♗a6 ♕a6 17. c4 ed5 18. cd5 ♗b5⇆; 18. ed5⩲] **♗a4 17. ♖fe1** [17. ♕e3 ed5 (17... h6 18. ♘f3 ed5 19. ed5 ♖fe8 20. ♕d3 c4!? 21. ♕c4 b5⇆; 20. ♕d2⩲) 18. ed5 ♖d5 19. ♗c4 ♖f5 20. g4=∞↑] **ed5** [17... b5 18. ♕e3 ed5 19. ed5 ♘c7 (19... ♖d5 20. ♗f3!±) 20. ♕c5 ♘d5 21. ♗d6 ♗c3 22. ♗f8 ♗e1 (22... ♗b4 23. ♕d4; 22... ♖f8 23. ♕d5 ♗e1 24. ♖c8!+–) 23. ♗d6 ♕d2 (23... ♘b6 24. ♕c7 ♘d7 25. ♗e7+–) 24. ♘e4 ♕e2 25. ♕d5±] **18. ed5 b5 19. d6± h6 20. ♘e4 ♔h7** [20... g5 21. ♗g5!? hg5 22. ♕g5 f6 23. ♕d5 ♔h8 24. ♕h5 ♔g8 25. ♗g4+–; 22... f5=∞; 22. ♘g5 △ 23. ♕d3, 23. ♗h5, 23. ♕d5] **21. h4 ♕b6 22. ♗d3 c4** [22... f5 23. ♘g3 ♖d6 24. ♖e7! (24. ♗d6 ♕d6 25. ♕e2±) c4 25. ♖g7 ♔g7 26. ♗h6±] **23. ♗b1 ♘c5 24. h5 ♘d3** [24... ♘e4 25. ♖e4+–] **25. ♗d3 cd3 26. ♕d3 ♕c6 27. ♕h3!** [27... ♕d5 28. ♘f6! ♗f6 29. hg6 fg6 30. ♕h6 ♔g8 31. ♕g6 ♗g7 32. ♖e7 ♖f7 33. ♖ce1 b4 34. ♗e5+–] **1 : 0**
[An. Karpov]

461.*** !N** D 85

PÉTURSSON 2560 – KOUATLY 2505

Ísland – France 1993

1. d4 ♘f6 2. c4 g6 3. ♘c3 d5 4. cd5 ♘d5 5. e4 ♘c3 6. bc3 ♗g7 7. ♘f3 c5 8. ♖b1 [RR 8. ♗b5 ♘d7 9. 0–0 0–0 10. ♗g5 a6!? N (10... h6 – 31/508) 11. ♗d3 *a)* 11... ♕e8 (△ e5) 12. e5! b5 13. a4 *a1)* 13... b4 14. cb4 cd4 (14... cb4 15. a5 ♗b7 16. ♖b1±) 15. ♗e4 ♖b8 16. ♕d4±; *a2)* 13... ♖b8 14. ab5 ab5 15. ♖e1!? (15. ♖a7?! ♗b7!?∞ △ 16. ♗b5? ♗f3 17. ♗d7 ♗d1 18. ♗e8 ♗e2 19. ♖e1 ♖fe8–+) cd4 16. cd4 ♘b6 (16... e6 17. ♖a7 ♗b7 18. ♗b5 ♗f3 19. ♗d7 ♗d1 20. ♗e8±) 17. ♕b3!± M. Gurevich 2610 – D. Roos 2410, France 1993; *b)* 11... b5!? 12. a4 ♗b7 13. ab5 ab5 14. ♖b1 b4∞ M. Gurevich; 8. ♗e2 ♘c6 9. d5 ♗c3 10. ♗d2 ♗a1 11. ♕a1 ♘d4 12. ♘d4 cd4 13. ♕d4 f6 14. 0–0 0–0 15. ♗c4 N (15. e5 – 50/(487)) ♗d7 16. ♖b1 b5 17. ♗b3 a5 18. a3 ♖c8 19. h4 a4 20. ♗d1 e5 21. ♕e3 ♖f7 22. ♗e2 ♕e8 23. ♖b2 ♖g7 1/2 : 1/2 García Ilundain 2475 – Tukmakov 2605, Zaragoza 1993] **0–0** [RR 8... a6 9. ♗e2 ♕a5 10. 0–0 ♕a2 11. ♗g5 ♕a5 12. ♕c1 ♘d7 13. ♖d1 N (13. e5 – 54/467) ♘f6 (13... ♕c7 14. ♗f4 e5 15. de5 ♘e5 16. ♖d5↑) 14. ♖a1 (14. e5 ♘e4 △ ♘c3) ♕c7! (14... ♕b6 15. e5 ♘e4 16. ♗e3 ×♘e4) 15. e5 (15. ♗f4 ♕b6 16. dc5!? ♕c5 17. ♗e3=∞) ♘e4 16. ♗f4 (16. d5 ♘g5 17. ♕g5 0–0 18. d6 ed6 19. ed6 ♕c6∓; 16. ♗b5!?) cd4 (16... 0–0? 17. ♗d3± ×♘e4) 17. ♖d4 (17. cd4!? ♘c3 18. ♗f1 ♘d5 19. ♗b5! ♔f8 20. ♕d2=∞ ×♔f8) ♘c3! (17... ♘c5 18. e6→) 18. ♗f1 ♗e6 *a)* 19. ♘g5!? (△ 20. ♘e6 fe6 21. ♖c4) ♘d5 20. ♗b5 ♔f8 21. ♗c4 ♗e5! (21... ♖d8 22. ♗d5 ♕c1 23. ♖c1 ♗d5 24. ♖d5!+–; 21... ♘f4 22. ♕f4 ♗c4 23. ♖c4+–) 22. ♗d5 ♕c1 23. ♖c1 ♗d4 24. ♗e6 fe6 25. ♘e6 ♔f7 26. ♘d4∞; *b)* 19. ♗h6 0–0 *b1)* 20. ♖h4!? ♖fc8! 21. ♕g5 f6! (21... ♗h8 22. ♗f8! ♔f8 23. ♖h7 ♗g7 24. ♖e1=∞ △ ♕h4→) 22. ♕g3 ♗h6 23. ♖h6 ♔g7∞; *b2)* 20. ♗g7 ♔g7 21. ♖h4 h5 (Se. Ivanov 2500 – Bešukov 2435, Katowice 1993) 22. ♕g5 f6 23. ♕g3 fe5 24. ♘e5 ♖f6 25. ♖e1=∞↑ Se. Ivanov] **9. ♗e2 ♕a5** [RR 9... b6 10. 0–0 ♗b7 11. ♕d3 ♗a6 12. ♕e3 ♕c8 13. ♖d1!? N (13. d5) ♗e2 14. ♕e2 ♕a6 15. ♔f1!? cd4!? (15... ♖c8? 16. dc5!± Stangl 2505 – Brunner 2455, Altensteig 1992) 16. cd4 ♖c8∞ A. Mihal'čišin; 9... cd4 10. cd4 ♕a5 11. ♗d2 ♕a2 12. 0–0 a5 13. ♖e1 ♘c6!? N (13... ♗g4 – 50/491) 14. ♗c3!?

a) 14... ♗e6 15. ♖a1 ♕b3 16. ♕d2 △ ♖eb1; *b)* 14... ♕a3 15. ♕d2 ♗g4 (Ziegler 2335 – Ju. Zezjul'kin 2415, Hisinger 1993) 16. ♕e3!? (16. ♖b7 ♖fd8 17. ♖a1 ♕d6 18. d5 ♗f3 19. ♗f3 ♘e5 20. ♗e2 ♖ac8! 21. ♗b2 ♘c4 22. ♗c4 ♖c4 23. ♗g7 ♔g7 24. ♖a5 ♖e4) ♘b4!? 17. ♖a1 ♕b3 18. ♘d2 ♕e6 19. ♗c4 (19. d5 ♘d5! 20. ed5 ♕e3 21. fe3 ♗c3∓) ♕d7 20. ♖ec1⩱; 18. ♖eb1!?; *c)* 14... ♖d8!? 15. ♖a1 (15. ♕d3 ♘b4 16. ♗b4 ab4 17. ♖b4 ♖a3 18. ♕c4 ♕c4 19. ♗c4 e6∓⊡) ♕e6 *c1)* 16. d5? ♗c3 17. de6 ♖d1 18. ef7 ♔f7 19. ♖ed1 ♗a1 20. ♖a1∓; *c2)* 16. ♕d3 ♕d6 17. d5 (17. ♖ed1 ♗g4∓; 17. ♖a4 ♗d7∓) ♘b4 18. ♕d2 ♗c3 19. ♕c3 ♗g4∓; *c3)* 16. ♗b5 ♘d4? 17. ♘d4 (17. ♗d4? ♗d4 18. ♘d4 ♕b6 19. ♖a4 e5–+) ♕b6 18. e5 ♖d4 19. ♕d4 ♕b5 20. ♕d8 ♗f8 21. ♖a5+–; 16... ♕d6!?∞ Ju. Zezjul'kin] **10. 0–0 ♕a2 11. ♗g5 cd4 12. cd4 ♖e8 13. d5! N** [13. ♗b5 – 45/(551)] **b6** [13... ♘d7; 13... a6] **14. e5 ♗a6 15. ♖e1 ♘d7 16. ♗a6** [16. ♖a1!? ♗e2 17. ♖e2 ♕c4 18. ♖c1 ♕b5 19. e6⩱] **♕a6 17. e6 fe6 18. ♖e6 ♗f6** [18... ♘c5 *a)* 19. ♖e7 ♖e7 20. ♗e7 ♕d3! 21. ♕d3 ♘d3 22. ♖d1 ♘c5 23. d6 ♖c8!∞; *b)* 19. ♕e1 ♕d3! (19... ♘e6? 20. ♕e6 ♔h8 21. ♘e5→) 20. ♖d1 ♗c3 (20... ♕c3!? 21. ♗d2 ♕c4 22. ♖e7 ♖e7 23. ♕e7 ♕d5? 24. ♕g7+–; 23... ♕b3!) 21. ♖d3 ♗e1 22. ♘e1 ♘e6 23. de6 a5∞; *c)* 19. ♖e3! ♕b7 20. ♘e5⩱] **19. d6 ♕c4 20. ♕e1 ♘c5 21. ♖e3 ♗g5?** [21... ♕f7 22. de7 h6 23. ♗f6 ♕f6 24. ♕d2] **22. ♘g5 e5** [22... e6? 23. ♘h7! ♔h7 24. ♖h3 ♔g8 25. ♕e5+–] **23. ♖e5 ♖e5 24. ♕e5 h6**

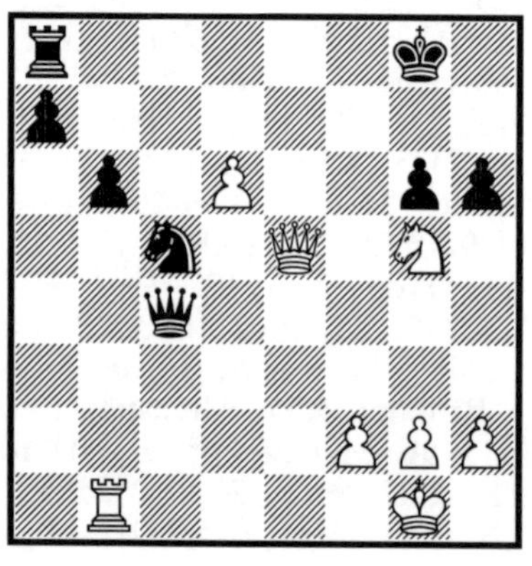

25. ♕f6! [25. ♘f3 ♕e4 26. ♕a1!± Chabanon; 25... ♕f7⩲] **hg5 26. ♕g6 ♔f8 27. ♕h6 ♔g8 28. ♕g5 ♔h8⊕ 29. ♕h5** [29. ♕h6! ♔g8 30. ♖e1 ♕g4 (30... ♖f8 31. ♖e7+–; 30... ♕d4 31. h3!; 30... ♕c3 31. ♕g5 ♔h8 32. ♕h5 ♔g8 33. ♕d5 ♔g7 34. ♖e7+–) 31. h3! ♕g7 32. ♕h5! ♖f8 33. ♖e5!+–] **♔g8 30. ♖e1?!** [30. ♕g5 ♔h8 31. ♕h6 – 29. ♕h6+–] **♘e6! 31. h4?⊕** [31. d7! ♘g7! (31... ♖f8 32. h4 ♘g7 33. ♕g5 ♕d4 34. ♖e7 ♕f2 35. ♔h2 ♕d4 36. h5 ♔h8 37. h6+–; 31... ♔g7 32. ♕e8 ♘d8 33. ♕e5+–) 32. ♕g5 (32. ♖e8 ♘e8 33. de8♕ ♖e8 34. ♕e8 ♔g7±) ♕d4 33. ♕e7! ♖f8 34. ♔h1! a5 35. h3 a4 (35... ♕d2 36. ♖e3!+–) 36. ♖e4!+–] **♘g7 32. ♕g5 ♕c5!∓ 33. ♕h6 ♖f8 34. ♖e3 ♕f5! 35. ♖e2 ♕f6 36. ♕d2 ♖d8 37. ♕d5 ♕f7 38. ♕c6 ♕d7 39. ♕d5 ♕f7** [39... ♔h7!] **40. ♕c6 ♕d7 41. ♕c4! ♕f7 42. ♕c6 1/2 : 1/2** **[Pétursson]**

462. **D 87**

KRASENKOV 2560 –
JANDEMIROV 2465
Katowice 1993

1. d4 ♘f6 2. c4 g6 3. ♘c3 d5 4. cd5 ♘d5 5. e4 ♘c3 6. bc3 ♗g7 7. ♗c4 0–0 8. ♘e2 ♘c6 9. ♗e3 ♘a5 10. ♗d3 c5 11. ♖c1 b6 [11... e5 – 55/464] **12. ♕d2 ♗b7** [12... e5!?] **13. h4 N** [13. 0–0] **cd4 14. cd4 ♖c8 15. ♗h6** [15. h5 ♖c1 16. ♕c1 ♕c8 17. ♕d2 ♘c4] **♗h6 16. ♕h6 ♖c1 17. ♕c1 e5 18. h5!** [18. d5] **♕f6?!** [18... ed4 19. ♕h6 ♕e7 20. e5! ♗g2 21. hg6! fg6 22. ♖h2 ♗f3 23. ♗g6 ♕b4 24. ♔f1 ♗e2 25. ♔e2 ♕b5 26. ♗d3 ♕e5 27. ♔f1+–; 18... ♕e7! 19. ♕h6 g5 20. 0–0± △ 20... ♖d8 21. ♘g3 ♗c8 22. ♖c1] **19. ♕h6 ♖c8** [19... ♕g7 20. hg6 △ de5±; 19... ed4 20. hg6 ♕g6 21. ♕f4±→] **20. hg6 hg6 21. f4!** [21. ♕h7 ♔f8 22. ♕h8 ♔e7±] **ed4?!** [21... ef4 22. e5 ♕g7 23. ♕f4 ♗g2?! 24. ♖g1 △ ♘g3→ ×f6, g6; 23... ♘c6±↑»] **22. e5 ♕g7 23. ♕g5** [×g6] **♗d5** [23... ♘c6 24. ♖h6 ♘b4 25. ♗g6 d3 26. ♘g3!+–] **24. ♖h6 ♘c6** [24... ♔f8 25. ♗g6!+–→] **25. ♗g6 ♘e7** [25... ♔f8 26. ♖h7!; 25... d3 26. ♘c3!+–] **26. ♗h7 ♔f8**

27. ♕h4 ♕g2 [27... ♖c6 28. ♖h5! (28. ♖d6 ♖d6 29. ed6 ♘c6 30. d7 f6 31. ♘d4 ♕e7∞) ♕g2 29. ♗d3! (29. ♗f5? ♕h1!) ♔e8 30. f5 △ ♕d4+−→] **28. ♗f5! d3□** [28... ♗c4 29. ♖h8 ♘g8 30. ♕h6 ♔e8 31. ♖g8 ♕g8 32. ♗c8; 28... ♖c1 29. ♘c1 ♕g1 30. ♔d2 ♕e3 31. ♔c2 ♕c3 32. ♔b1 ♕b4 33. ♘b3+−] **29. ♗d3** [29. ♖h8!? ♘g8 30. ♗d3] **♔e8! 30. ♕f6! ♖c5** [30... ♘g8 31. ♖h8; 30... ♖c6 31. ♗b5+−; 30... ♗e6 31. f5+−] **31. ♕d6 ♗b7 32. ♗b5! ♖b5 33. ♖h8 ♘g8 34. ♖g8! ♕g8 35. ♕b8 ♔e7 36. ♕g8 1 : 0 [Krasenkov]**

463. D 87

P. LUKÁCS 2480 – FOGARASI 2395

Budapest 1993

1. d4 ♘f6 2. c4 g6 3. ♘c3 d5 4. cd5 ♘d5 5. e4 ♘c3 6. bc3 ♗g7 7. ♗c4 0–0 8. ♘e2 c5 9. ♗e3 ♘c6 10. ♖c1 e6 11. 0–0 ♕a5 12. f4 b5!? N [12... cd4 – 54/(473)] **13. ♗b3!** [13. ♗d3?! ♖d8! 14. f5 cd4! (14... ef5 15. ef5 cd4 16. cd4 ♘d4 17. ♘d4 ♗d4 18. ♗d4 ♖d4 19. fg6 △ ♕f3+−) 15. cd4 ♘d4 *a)* 16. ♘d4? ♗d4 17. ♗d4 ♖d4 18. ♕f3 (18. fg6 hg6 19. ♕f3 ♖d7−+) ♕b6! 19. ♔h1 ef5 20. ef5 ♗b7−+; *b)* 16. f6 ♘e2 17. ♕e2 ♗f8 18. ♗b5=] **c4!** [13... f5? 14. d5! ♖d8 (14... c4 15. dc6+−) 15. ♗c5+−; 13... ♖d8?! 14. f5! ef5 15. ♗g5! (15. ef5 ♗f5 16. ♖f5 gf5 17. ♘g3 cd4? 18. ♘f5!+−; 17... ♘e7!∞) ♖d6 (15... ♖e8 16. ♗d5!±) 16. ef5 ♗f5 17. ♘g3±] **14. ♗c2 f5!?** [14... ♘e7! 15. f5!? (15. g4 f5 16. ♘g3? ♕c3!∓; 16. ♕e1!∞) ef5 16. ♗g5 f6 (16... ♖e8 17. ♗e7 ♖e7 18. ef5±) 17. ♗f4⩱] **15. d5!** [15. ♗b1 △ g4, ♘g3⩲] **♖d8□ 16. d6!** [16. ♘d4!? ♘d4 17. ♗d4 ♗d4 18. ♕d4 ♕b6!⇆] **♗b7** [16... ♘e7?? 17. de7!+−; 16... fe4 17. ♗e4 ♗b7 18. ♗c5 b4!⇆; 18. ♕d2!±] **17. e5!** [17. ♕d2!? b4!⇆] **♘e5!?** [17... ♘e7 18. ♘d4! ♘d5 (18... ♕c3 19. ♕e1! ♕e1 20. ♖fe1+−) 19. ♗d2 ♖e8 20. ♖b1! a6 21. a4!±] **18. fe5 ♗e5 19. ♗d4!?** [19. ♕e1! ♖d6 (19... ♗d6 20. ♘f4±) 20. ♗d4±] **♗d6** [19... ♖d6?! 20. ♕e1! ♗d4 21. ♘d4 △ ♗f5!] **20. ♕d2 ♕c7!** [20... e5? 21. ♗f5! gf5 (21... ed4 22. ♗e6+−) 22. ♕g5 ♔h8 23. ♕f6 ♔g8 24. ♖f5+−] **21. ♕g5! ♗h2!** [21... e5? 22. ♗f5! ed4 23. ♗e6 ♔h8 24. ♖f7+−] **22. ♔h1 ♗e5** [22... e5? 23. ♗f2] **23. ♕e3 ♕c6** [23... ♗d4 24. ♕e6 ♕f7 25. ♕f7 ♔f7 26. ♘d4±] **24. ♖f2 ♗c7 25. ♗f6 ♖f8** [25... ♖e8 26. ♖d1! △ ♕h6+−; 25... ♗b6 26. ♘d4±] **26. ♘d4 ♕d5 27. ♗f5?** [27. ♘e6! ♗b6 (27... ♖f6? 28. ♘c7+−; 27... ♖ae8 28. ♕h6!±) 28. ♕h6!±] **♖f6!** [27... ef5? 28. ♘f5! △ 29... ♖ae8? 29. ♘h6#] **28. ♗e6 ♖e6 29. ♕e6** [29. ♘e6? ♕h5 30. ♔g1 ♕h2 31. ♔f1 ♖e8−+] **♕e6 30. ♘e6 ♗g3!** [31. ♖e2∓] **1/2 : 1/2 [P. Lukács]**

464. D 87

ŠIROV 2670 – KAMSKY 2655

Linares 1993

1. d4 ♘f6 2. c4 g6 3. ♘c3 d5 4. cd5 ♘d5 5. e4 ♘c3 6. bc3 ♗g7 7. ♗c4 c5 8. ♘e2 ♘c6 9. ♗e3 0–0 10. ♖c1 cd4 11. cd4 ♕a5 12. ♔f1 ♗d7 13. h4 ♖fc8 14. h5 ♘d8 15. f4!? N ♗b5 [15... ♗a4 16. ♕d3 b5 17. ♗d5 ♖c1 18. ♗c1 ♖c8 19. hg6 hg6 20. f5→; 15... e6!? 16. ♔f2 ♖c7∞] **16. ♗b5 ♕b5 17. ♔f2 e6!** [17... ♖c1 18. ♕c1 ♘c6 19. ♕b1⩲] **18. g4!** [18. ♕b3 ♕b3 19. ab3 ♘c6=; 18. hg6 hg6 19. ♕d2 ♖c1 20. ♖c1 ♘c6 △ ♖d8=] **♖c1 19. ♕c1 ♘c6 20. ♕b1** [20. f5 ♘b4!⇆] **♕b1** [20... ♕a6?! 21. f5→] **21. ♖b1 b6 22. f5!** [22. ♖c1 ♖c8 23. d5 ed5 24. ed5 ♘e7 25. ♖c8 ♘c8=] **♘e7?** [22... ef5 23. gf5 gf5 24. h6! ♗f6! (24... ♗f8 25. ♖c1! ♘e7□ 26. ♖g1 ♔h8 27. d5 f6 28. ♗d4 ♘g8 29. e5±) 25. e5 ♗h4 26. ♔f3±; 22... ♖d8 23. e5 ♗f8!⩲] **23. h6! ♗f8□ 24. fe6!** [24. ♖c1 ef5 (24... ♖c8? 25. f6! ♖c1 26. fe7+−) 25. gf5 f6! (25... gf5? 26. ♖g1± – 22... ef5) 26. fg6 hg6 27. ♖c7⩲] **fe6 25. ♘f4 ♔f7** [25... ♗h6 26. ♘e6±; 25... e5 26. de5 ♗h6 27. ♘d5!±] **26. ♘h3!** [26. ♔e2?! ♗h6 27. ♖h1 ♗g7! (27... ♗f4? 28. ♖h7 ♔g8 29. ♖e7 ♗e3 30. ♔e3+−) 28. ♖h7 e5! (28... ♔g8? 29. ♖g7 ♔g7 30. ♘e6±) 29. de5 ♔g8=] **♔g8□ 27. ♘f4⊕ ♔f7 28. ♘h3 ♔g8 29. ♘g5! e5□ 30. d5 ♘c8!?** [30... ♗h6 31. ♘e6! (31. ♖h1?! ♗g5 32. ♗g5

♘c8⇆) ♗e3 32. ♔e3 ♘c8□ 33. ♖c1 ♘d6 34. ♖c6 ♘f7 35. ♔d3!± △ 36. d6 ♘d8 37. ♘d8 ♖d8 38. ♔c4+−] **31. ♖c1 ♘d6** [31... ♗h6 32. ♘e6±] **32. ♖c7! ♖c8** [32... ♘e8 33. ♖b7! ♘d6 34. ♖d7+−; 32... ♗h6 33. ♘h7! ♘e4 34. ♔f3 ♘d2 35. ♗d2 ♗d2 36. ♔e4! ♗b4 37. ♘f6 ♔f8 38. ♔e5 ♖d8 39. ♖a7+−] **33. ♖d7 ♖c3 34. ♘h7 ♘e4 35. ♔e2** [35. ♔f3? ♗c5] **♗b4** [35... ♘g3 36. ♔d1+−] **36. ♖a7 b5 37. g5! ♘g3 38. ♔d1 ♘e4 39. ♔e2 ♘g3 40. ♔d1 ♘e4 41. ♗b6!+− ♖f3** [41... ♖d3 42. ♔e2 ♖d5 43. ♔e3!] **42. ♗d8! ♖f1 43. ♔c2 ♖f2 44. ♔b3 ♗c5 45. ♘f6 ♘f6 46. ♖g7 ♔f8 47. gf6 ♖f3 48. ♔c2 ♖f2 49. ♔d1 ♖f1 50. ♔e2 ♖f2 51. ♔e1 ♖a2 52. ♗e7 ♗e7 53. fe7 ♔e8 54. d6 1 : 0** [Širov]

465. !N D 87

MARIN 2515 — ŠTOHL 2540
Budapest (zt) 1993

1. d4 ♘f6 2. c4 g6 3. ♘c3 d5 4. cd5 ♘d5 5. e4 ♘c3 6. bc3 ♗g7 7. ♗c4 0–0 8. ♘e2 c5 9. ♗e3 ♘c6 10. ♖c1 cd4 11. cd4 ♕a5 12. ♔f1 ♗d7 13. h4 ♖fc8 14. h5 ♘d8 15. f3 ♗a4 16. ♗b3! N [16. ♕d3?! — 56/548; 16. ♕e1 ♕e1 17. ♔e1 b5!?; 17... ♘c6↑ △ 18... ♘a5, 18... ♘b4, 18... ♖d8] **♗b3** [16... ♖c1!? 17. ♕c1 ♗b3 18. ab3 ♕b5 19. ♕c4!? ♕c4 (19... ♕d7 20. h6! ♗f8 21. d5 ♖c8 22. ♕d4± ×♘d8, g7) 20. bc4 ♖c8!? (20... b6 21. ♔f2±⊞) 21. c5 (21. d5 b6) e5∞ △ 22. d5 ♗f8 23. hg6 fg6 (23... hg6? 24. ♗g5→) 24. d6 ♘e6∓; 24. c6!?=] **17. ♕b3 ♕a6** [17... ♖c1 18. ♗c1 ♖c8 19. ♔f2 ♕a6 20. ♗e3⩲] **18. ♔f2** [18. ♖c8! ♖c8 19. ♔f2⊞ (×♘d8) ♘c6 20. ♖c1↑] **♘c6! 19. h6?!** [19. a4 ♘a5 (19... e6 20. ♕b5 ♕b5 21. ab5 ♘b4 22. ♖c8 ♖c8 23. ♖a1 a6 24. ba6 ba6 25. ♖a4⩲) 20. ♕b5 ♕b5 21. ab5 ♘c4⇆] **♗f8 20. a4** [20. ♗d2? ♘a5 21. ♕a4; 20... ♕e2!∓] **e6=** [20... e5!? 21. d5 ♘b4 22. ♖hd1 ♖c1 23. ♘c1 ♖c8 24. ♘d3!±; 22... ♗d6!∞] **21. ♕b5 ♘b4** [21... ♕b5 22. ab5 ♘b4 23. ♖c8 ♖c8 24. ♖a1±] **22. ♖c8** [⌓ 22. ♕a6 ba6 23. ♖hd1↑; 22... ♘a6=] **♖c8 23. ♗d2** [23. ♕a6 ba6!? △ ♖c2 ×a4] **♕b5** [23... ♘d3 24. ♔e3 ♕b5 25. ab5 ♘b2⇆] **24. ab5 ♘c2! 25. ♖c1** [⌓ 25. ♖b1!?∞] **♖c4!∓** [×b5] **26. g4 f6?!** [26... ♘a3! 27. b6 (27. ♖c4 ♘c4 28. ♗f4 f6∓ ×b5, h6) ab6 28. g5⩱; 27... a6!↑ ×b6] **27. g5 fg5 28. ♗g5** [⇆ ×e6] **♘a3 29. ♖c4 ♘c4** [♘♗ 9/c] **30. ♘f4 ♔f7 31. ♔e2** [31. d5!? ed5 (31... e5 32. ♘d3⇆) 32. ♘d5 ♘d6 33. b6 ab6 34. ♘f6 (34. ♘b6?! ♔e6 △ ♘f7) ♗h6 35. ♘h7 ♗g7 36. ♗d2=] **♘a3 32. b6 ab6 33. d5 ed5 34. e5?⊕** [34. ♘d5= △ ♘f6] **♘b5! 35. ♘d5** [35. e6 ♔e8 36. ♘d5 ♘d4 37. ♔f2 ♘e6 38. ♘f6 ♔f7 39. ♘h7 ♘g5 40. ♘g5 ♔g8 41. h7 ♔h8−+ △ ♗e7] **♘d4 36. ♔f2 ♔e6?⊕** [36... ♘e6! 37. f4 (37. ♗e3 g5 38. ♘f6 ♔g6−+) ♘g5 38. fg5 ♔e6 39. ♘f6 ♗e7 (39... ♔e5? 40. ♘d7=) 40. ♘h7 ♔e5 41. ♔e3 b5 42. ♔d3 b4 43. ♔c4 ♔e6 44. ♔b3 ♔f7 45. ♔c4 b6 46. ♔b3 (46. ♔d3 ♔g8 47. ♘f6 ♗f6 48. gf6 b3 49. ♔c3 g5 50. ♔b3 g4−+) ♔g8 47. ♘f6 ♗f6 48. gf6 g5 49. ♔c4 b3!□ (49... g4 50. ♔d5=) 50. ♔b3 g4−+] **37. ♘f6 ♘f5** [37... ♔e5? 38. ♘h7↑] **38. ♘h7 ♗h6 39. ♗h6 ♘h6 40. ♘f8 ♔f5** [40... ♔e5!? 41. ♘g6 ♔d4 42. ♔e2 ♔c3 43. ♘e7=] **41. e6! ♘g8** [41... ♔f6 42. e7=] **42. ♔e3 g5** [42... ♘e7 43. ♔d4 ♔f4 44. ♔c4 ♔f3 45. ♘g6! ♘g6 46. ♔b5=] **43. ♔d4** [43. ♘h7? ♘f6! 44. e7 ♘d5−+] **♔f4 44. ♘h7□= ♔f3**
1/2 : 1/2 [Štohl]

466. !N D 87

BARKHAGEN 2405
— I. SOKOLOV 2625
Malmö 1992

1. d4 ♘f6 2. c4 g6 3. ♘c3 d5 4. cd5 ♘d5 5. e4 ♘c3 6. bc3 ♗g7 7. ♗c4 0–0 8. ♗e3 c5 9. ♘e2 ♘c6 10. 0–0 ♗g4 11. f3 ♗d7 12. ♕d2 ♕a5! N [12... ♖c8 — 46/(622)] **13. ♖fd1 ♖ac8 14. ♖ab1 b6** [14... cd4 15. cd4 ♕d2 16. ♖d2 ♘a5=] **15. ♗b5** [15. dc5?! ♘e5] **♖fd8 16. ♕b2** [16. dc5?! bc5 △ 17. ♗c5?? a6 18. ♗e7 ♘e7 19. ♗d7 ♖c7] **♗e8 17. ♕b3** [△ 18. d5 ♘e5 19. ♗e8 ♖e8 20. c4] **a6!∓ 18. ♗c6 ♗c6 19. ♕b6 ♕a2 20. ♘f4** [20. ♖d2 *a)* 20... ♕c4 21. ♕c5 ♕c5 22. dc5 ♖d2 23. ♗d2 ♗b5 24. ♘d4=; *b)* 20... ♕a4!∓↑ △ 21. d5? ♗b5 22. ♗c5? ♗e2 23. ♖e2 ♕c4 24.

♗e7 ♖d7−+, △ 21. dc5? ♖d2 22. ♗d2 ♗b5 23. ♘f4 ♕c2−+] **♗a4! 21. ♖dc1** [21. ♖d2?! ♕a3] **cd4 22. cd4 ♕a3!∓ 23. ♔f2 ♗b5! 24. ♘d5 e6 25. ♘c3** [25. ♘c7? ♕a2! 26. ♔g1 ♖b8 27. ♕c5 ♗f1!−+] **♗d3 26. ♖a1 ♕e7 27. ♘a4 ♗b5! 28. ♘c3** [28. ♘c5 ♖b8 29. ♕a5 ♗d4 30. ♗d4 ♖d4 31. ♘a6 ♗a6 32. ♕a6 ♖d2 33. ♔g1 ♕g5 34. ♕f1 (34. ♖c8 ♔g7) ♖bb2−+] **♗c4** [28... ♖c6! 29. ♕a5 (29. ♘d5?? ♕h4−+) ♗c4 30. d5 ed5 31. ♘d5 (31. ed5 ♖cc8) *a)* 31... ♕h4 32. ♔g1 ♗a1 33. g3! (33. ♗f2? ♗d4!) ♖d5! 34. ed5 ♕e7 35. ♔f2 ♗d5 (35... ♗b2 36. ♖c2) 36. ♖c6 ♗c6 37. ♕a1∓; *b)* 31... ♗d5 32. ed5 ♖e8! *b1)* 33. ♕a3 *b11)* 33... ♕a3? 34. ♖a3 ♖e3?? 35. dc6 ♖a3 36. c7+−; *b12)* 33... ♕h4?! 34. ♔f1! (34. ♔g1? ♖e3! 35. dc6 ♖a3 36. c7 ♕d4 37. ♔h1 ♖a1 38. c8♕ ♗f8−+) ♖c1 35. ♖c1 ♕h2 36. d6∞̄; *b13)* 33... ♖d6! 34. ♖ab1 ♕h4 35. ♔g1 ♖d5 36. ♗f2 ♗d4∓; *b2)* 33. ♕d2 ♖d6 34. ♗c5 (34. ♖ab1? ♖d5!−+) ♕h4 35. ♔g1 ♖d5! 36. ♕d5 ♗a1 37. ♗f2 ♕f6∓ △ 38. ♖c6? ♖d8!−+] **29. ♔g1?** [29. ♘a4 ♗b5 30. ♘c3 ♖c6! — 28... ♖c6] **♖b8−+ 30. ♕c6 ♗d4 31. ♗d4 ♖d4 32. f4 ♗d3! 33. ♖a4 ♗b5!** **0 : 1** **[I. Sokolov]**

467. !N **D 94**

A. CHERNIN 2600 − HÁBA 2485

Budapest (zt) 1993

1. c4 c6 2. d4 d5 3. ♘c3 ♘f6 4. e3 g6 5. ♘f3 ♗g7 6. ♗e2 0−0 7. 0−0 ♗g4 8. cd5 cd5 9. ♕b3 b6 10. h3 ♗f3 11. ♗f3 e6 12. ♗d2 ♘c6 13. ♕a4 ♘a5 14. b3 a6 15. ♘e2 ♘b7 16. ♕c6 ♘d6! N [16... ♖a7 — 56/558] **17. ♗b4 ♘fe8 18. ♖fc1 ♗f6 19. ♕c2 ♗e7 20. ♗e1 ♘f5 21. g3** [21. ♘f4!?] **♗a3 22. ♖cb1 a5 23. ♘f4** [23. e4?! ♖c8 24. ♗c3 de4 25. ♕e4 ♘f6∓] **♘ed6 24. ♘d3 ♖c8 25. ♕e2 ♘b5 26. b4 ♘c3 27. ♗c3 ♖c3 28. ba5 ba5 29. ♕d2** [29. ♖b7 ♘d6=] **♕c7 30. ♘c5** [30. ♖b7 ♖c2 31. ♖c7 ♖d2 32. ♘c5 ♗c5 33. ♖c5 ♖b8=] **♗b4** [30... ♘d4 31. ♕c3 ♘f3 32. ♔g2 ♗b4 33. ♖b4□ ab4 34. ♕b4±] **31. ♘a6 ♕c4 32. ♘b4 ab4 33. ♕e2 ♖b8 34. ♖b2 ♘d6 35. ♖ab1** [35. a4 b3=] **♕e2 36. ♗e2 ♖a3 37. ♖b4** [37. ♖c1?! ♘e4 38. ♗f3 ♘c3∓] **♖b4 38. ♖b4 ♖a2 39. ♗d3 ♔f8** [39... ♖a3 40. ♖b6=] **40. ♔f1 ♖d2 41. ♖b3 h5** **1/2 : 1/2** **[Hába]**

468. **D 94**

ŠTOHL 2540 − HÁBA 2485

Budapest (zt) 1993

1. c4 c6 2. ♘c3 d5 3. d4 ♘f6 4. e3 g6 5. ♘f3 ♗g7 6. ♗e2 0−0 7. 0−0 ♗g4 8. cd5 cd5 9. ♕b3 b6 10. h3 ♗f3 [10... ♗c8 11. ♘e5±] **11. ♗f3 e6 12. ♗d2 ♘c6 13. ♗e2 a6 14. ♖fc1 ♘a5 15. ♕b4 ♘d7 16. b3!? N** [16. ♘a4 — 48/632] **♖e8 17. ♘a4** [△ ♘b6] **♘b7□ 18. ♕c3!** [18. ♖c6?! ♗f8 19. ♕c3 b5 20. ♘b2 (20. ♖c7 ♖a7 21. ♘b2 ♗d6 22. ♖c6 ♘b8∓) ♗a3⇆] **b5□ 19. ♕c7** [19. ♘b2 ♖c8=; 19. ♕c6 ♖a7!? (19... ♘a5 20. ♗a5 ♕a5 21. ♕d7 ba4 22. ♖c7 ♖f8 23. ba4±) 20. ♘b2□ (20. ♘c3? ♘b8−+) e5!⇆] **♖b8** [19... ♕c7 20. ♖c7±; 19... ba4 20. ♕b7 ♖b8 21. ♕a6 ab3 22. ab3 ♖b3 23. ♗b5± △ ♕a4] **20. ♘b2** [20. ♕d8 ♖bd8 21. ♖c7 (21. ♘b2 e5 — 20. ♘b2) ♘d6 22. ♘b2 e5=] **e5 21. ♕d8 ♖bd8 22. de5 ♗e5 23. ♖ab1±⊞** [23. ♖c2 d4 24. ♖ac1 ♘dc5!?⇆ △ d3] **♘bc5 24. ♘d3** [24. ♗b4 ♖c8 25. ♖d1 ♘e4! △ 26. ♖d5? ♘df6 27. ♖dd1 ♖c2−+] **♘d3 25. ♗d3 ♖c8□ 26. ♗b4** [26. ♖c8 ♖c8 27. ♖c1 ♖c1 28. ♗c1 ♘c5 29. ♗c2 b4=; 26. ♗e2!? ♘c5 27. f3 (△ ♖c2, ♖bc1) d4 28. ed4 ♗d4 29. ♔f1⩲] **d4 27. ed4** [27. e4 ♗f4 28. ♖c8 ♖c8 29. g3 ♘e5⇆; 27. a4 de3 28. fe3 ♗g3!? 29. ab5 ab5 30. ♗b5 ♖c1 31. ♖c1 ♖b8 32. ♗d7 ♖b4=] **♗d4 28. a4 ♘c5!** [28... ba4 29. ba4 ♖c1 30. ♖c1 ♖b8 31. ♖c4! ♘e5 32. ♖d4 ♘d3 33. ♗c3±] **29. ♗c5 ♖c5 30. ab5** [30. ♖c5 ♗c5 31. ab5 ♖d8!=] **ab5 31. ♖c5 ♗c5 32. ♗b5 ♖d8 33. b4** [33. ♖b2 ♗b4 △ ♖d2=] **♗b6 34. ♗e2** [34. ♖b2 ♖d1 35. ♗f1 (35. ♔h2 ♗d4 36. ♖e2 ♖b1=) ♗d4 36. ♖c2 ♖b1=] **♖d2 35. ♔f1 h5!= 36. g3 ♔g7 37. b5 ♔h6** [37... ♖c2=] **38. ♖c1 ♖b2 39. ♖c6 ♗d4 40. ♖d6 ♗c5 41. ♖f6** [41. ♖c6 ♗d4 42. ♖c7 ♔g7 △ ♖b1=] **♔g7 42. ♖c6 ♗d4 43. ♖d6 ♗c5 44. ♖d5**

♗b6 45. f4!? h4! [45... ♖b1 46. ♔g2 ♖b2 47. ♔f3 ♖b3 48. ♗d3±] **46. gh4** [46. g4 ♖b1=] **♖b4 47. f5 ♖f4 48. ♔e1 ♖f5 49. ♖f5 1/2 : 1/2** **[Štohl]**

469. **D 94**

SPEELMAN 2595 – JU. HODGSON 2565

Dublin (zt) 1993

1. ♘f3 ♘f6 2. c4 c6 3. ♘c3 d5 4. e3 g6 5. d4 ♗g7 6. ♗e2 0–0 7. 0–0 dc4 8. ♗c4 ♗g4 9. ♗e2!? N [9. h3 — 56/(557)] **♘bd7 10. e4 ♗f3 11. ♗f3 e5 12. d5** [12. de5 ♘e5 13. ♗e2 ♕e7 14. ♕c2 ♖fe8] **cd5 13. ♘d5** [13. ed5] **♘c5!** [13... ♘b6 14. ♘f6 ♕f6 15. ♕b3 ♕c6 16. ♗e3 ♘c4 17. ♖fc1 b5=; 15. b3] **14. ♗e3!?** [14. ♗g5 ♘e6=] **♘e6** [14... ♘ce4 15. ♘f6 (15. ♗e4!? ♘e4 16. ♕b3) ♘f6 16. ♗c5 (16. ♕b3!? e4 17. ♗e2 b6∞) ♖e8 17. ♗b7 ♕d1 18. ♖fd1 ♖ab8 19. ♗c6 ♖ec8 20. ♗a7 ♖b2 21. ♖dc1 ♖c7 22. ♗e3 ♘g4 23. ♗d5 ♖c1 24. ♗c1 (24. ♖c1 ♘e3 25. fe3 ♗h6) ♖f2 25. ♖b1 (25. ♗f3? e4 26. ♗g4 ♗d4!–+) ♗f8!∞; 22... e4] **15. ♘f6 ♗f6 16. ♕b3 ♕e7** [16... ♗g5 17. ♕b7!? (17. ♗g4 ♗e3 18. ♗e6 ♗d4 19. ♗d5=; 17... ♘d4) ♗e3 18. fe3 ♕d2 (18... ♕d3 19. ♕b3 ♕b3 20. ab3 ♖fb8) 19. ♕b3 ♖ab8 (19... ♘c5 20. ♕c3 ♕c3 21. bc3) 20. ♖f2 ♕f2 21. ♔f2 ♖b3 22. ab3 ♖b8 23. ♖a7 ♖b3 24. ♖a2 ♘c5 25. ♔e2 ♖b4 (25... ♘d3 26. ♖a3!) 26. ♔d2±] **17. ♗g4! ♘f4** [17... ♘d4 18. ♗d4 ed4 19. ♕d3⩲ △ ♗d1-b3-d5, f4, e5 ×d4] **18. ♖ac1 b6 19. g3 h5 20. ♗d1 ♘e6 21. ♕b5** [21. h4=] **♖ad8?** [21... ♗g5! 22. ♕e5 (22. ♗g5 ♕g5 23. ♗b3 ♘d4 24. ♕d3) ♗e3 23. fe3 ♖ae8! 24. ♗b3 (24. ♗a4 ♘c5!) ♘c5 25. ♕e7 ♖e7 26. ♗d5 ♘e4 27. ♗e4!? ♖e4 28. ♖c7 ♖e3 29. ♖a7; 28... a5] **22. ♗b3 ♘d4 23. ♗d4 ♖d4 24. ♗d5 ♗g5 25. ♖cd1!?** [25. ♖c6 ♔g7; 25. ♖c4] **♖d1 26. ♖d1 ♖c8 27. ♗b3 ♖c1?** [27... ♖c5 28. ♕d7 ♖c1!=; 28. ♕a4!?; 27... ♖c7] **28. ♖c1 ♗c1 29. ♕c6!± ♗b2 30. ♕g6 ♔f8 31. ♕h6 ♔g8 32. h4!** [32. ♕h5 ♕f6 ×f2] **♗d4 33. a4 a6** [33... ♗c5] **34. ♔g2 b5?⊕** [34... ♗c5 35. ♗d5 (35. ♗c4) ♕d6 (35... a5) 36. ♕g5 (36. ♕h5 ♕f6 37. ♕e2 b5) ♔f8 37. ♕f5 ♕e7 38. ♗c4 (38. ♕c8 ♔g7 39. ♕a6 ♕f6 40. ♕e2) b5 39. ab5 ab5 40. ♗f7! (40. ♗b5 ♔g7 41. ♕h5 ♕f6 42. ♕e2±) ♕f7 41. ♕c8 ♔g7 42. ♕c5+–; 38... a5±] **35. a5+– ♕a7 36. ♕h5 ♗f2 37. ♕f7! ♕f7 38. ♗f7 ♔f7 39. ♔f2** [△ g4, h5, ♔e2-d3-c3-b4-c5-d5 ×e5]
1 : 0 **[Speelman]**

470. **D 94**

B. GEL'FAND 2690 – HERTNECK 2575

München 1993

1. d4 d5 2. c4 c6 3. ♘c3 ♘f6 4. e3 g6 5. ♘f3 ♗g7 6. ♗d3 0–0 7. h3 ♘a6 N [7... ♘bd7 — 56/560] **8. 0–0 ♗f5** [8... ♘b4 9. ♗e2±] **9. ♗f5 gf5 10. b3 ♘e4 11. ♗b2± e6 12. ♘e2 ♔h8 13. ♘f4 ♘c7 14. ♕e2** [14. ♘e5?! ♗e5 15. de5 dc4 16. bc4 ♘d2!] **♖g8 15. ♘h5 f6** [15... ♘e8!?] **16. ♘d2 ♕e7** [16... ♕e8 17. ♖ad1±] **17. f4** [△ 18. ♘e4 fe4 19. f5; 17. ♘e4 fe4 18. f4 ef3!? 19. ♕f3 f5] **♘d2 18. ♕d2 ♗h6 19. ♔h2 ♖g6 20. a4** [20. ♖f3!? ♖ag8 21. ♖g1 △ ♘g3] **♖ag8 21. ♖f2 ♗f8 22. c5 ♕e8 23. ♕e2 ♗e7 24. ♖g1 ♕b8** [24... ♖g4 25. hg4 ♖g4 26. ♖f3 ♕h5 27. ♖h3 Hertneck] **25. ♕c2 ♘a6 26. ♗c3 b6 27. b4 ♘c7 28. ♕d3 b5 29. ♖a2± ba4** [29... a6 30. ♗e1±] **30. ♖a4 a6 31. ♗e1 ♕f8 32. ♖a2 ♗d8 33. ♕f1** [33. ♘g3 ♕g7 34. ♘f1±] **♕f7 34. ♘g3 ♕g7 35. ♘e2** [△ ♘c1-b3-a5, △ ♘c1-d3, b5, ♘b4] **♖f8 36. ♕f3 ♔g8 37. ♘c1 e5? 38. ♕h5?!** [38. ♘e2+–] **ef4 39. ef4 ♕d7 40. ♘e2 ♖e8 41. ♘g3 ♘e6 42. ♕f5 ♗c7 43. ♖f1 ♕c8 44. ♘h5 ♔f7?** [44... ♘d4 45. ♘f6 ♔f7 46. ♕c8 ♖c8 47. ♘g4+–; 44... ♖g5! 45. ♘f6 ♔f7 46. ♕h7 ♔f6 47. ♗h4 ♖h8 48. ♗g5 ♘g5 49. ♕d3 ♕f5 50. ♕f5 ♔f5 *a)* 51. g3 ♘e6 (51... ♘h3 52. ♔g2 ♔g4 53. ♖h1+–) 52. ♖a6 ♘d4∞; *b)* 51. ♖a6 ♗f4 52. ♔g1 ♔e4 (52... ♘e4 53. ♖c6+–) 53. ♖c6 ♗e3 54. ♔h2 ♔d4±] **45. ♗c3+– ♕b7 46. ♖e2 ♕c8 47. ♖fe1 ♖h6 48. ♔h1 ♗d8 49. ♗d2 ♖e7 50. g4 ♕d7 51. ♖e6 ♖e6 52. ♖e6 1 : 0** **[B. Gel'fand]**

471. D 99

IVANČUK 2710 – TIMMAN 2635
Linares 1993

1. d4 ♘f6 2. c4 g6 3. ♘c3 d5 4. ♘f3 ♗g7 5. ♕b3 dc4 6. ♕c4 0–0 7. e4 ♗g4 8. ♗e3 ♘fd7 9. ♕b3 ♘b6 10. ♖d1 ♘c6 11. d5 ♘e5 12. ♗e2 ♘f3 13. gf3 ♗h5 14. ♖g1 ♕c8 15. ♖g3 c6 16. a4 ♕c7 17. ♕a3!? N [17. a5 ♘d7 (17... ♘c8) 18. ♕a3 ♘e5 19. ♗d4 ♖fd8!? 20. f4 ♗e2 21. ♘e2 ♘c4 22. ♕c3 ♗d4 23. ♘d4 ♘d6∞; 17. ♖c1 ♖fc8! 18. a5 ♘d7 19. a6 ba6 20. ♗a6 ♘e5!∞] **f5!?** [17... cd5 18. ♘d5 ♘d5 19. ♖d5 ♔h8!⩲; 18. ♗b6!?] **18. dc6!** [18. a5? ♘d5! 19. ed5 f4∓] **bc6** [18... f4? 19. ♗b6 △ ♘d5] **19. a5 ♘c8□** [19... ♘d5 20. ed5 f4 21. dc6!±] **20. ♕c5!?** [20. ♗d4 ♗d4 21. ♖d4 ♖b8∞; 20. ef5 ♘d6!? 21. fg6 hg6$\overline{\overline{\infty}}$; 20... ♖f5∞] **fe4!** [20... f4? 21. ♘d5 ♕e5 22. ♗f4 ♖f4 23. ♕c6] **21. ♘b5!** [21. ♘e4 ♖f5 22. ♕c4 ♔h8∓] **♕a5 22. b4 ♕a4**

(diagram)

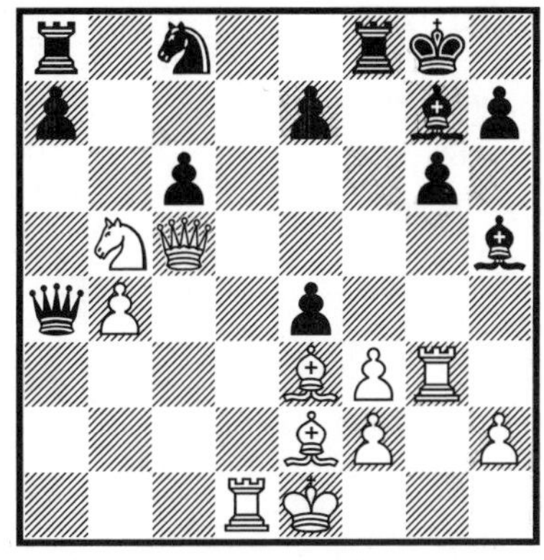

23. ♗d4! [23. ♘c7? ♘d6! 24. ♘a8 ♖a8∓] **♗f3?!** [23... cb5 24. ♗b5 ♕d1 25. ♔d1 ♖d8 26. ♗c4 ♔f8 27. ♗d5 ♘b6 28. ♗g7 ♔g7 29. ♕e7 ♔h6 30. ♕g5 ♔g7 31. ♕e5 ♔h6 32. ♕f4 ♔g7 33. ♕c7 ♔h6 34. ♕c1 ♔g7 35. ♕c3 ♔h6 36. ♕d2 ♔g7 37. ♖g5 (37. ♗a8 ♗f3!=; 37. ♕c3=) ♗f3 38. ♔c1∞] **24. ♗g7 ♗e2?** [24... ♔g7! 25. ♕c3 ♖f6 26. ♖a1 cb5 (26... ♕a1 27. ♕a1 cb5$\overline{\overline{\infty}}$) 27. ♖a4 ba4$\overline{\overline{\infty}}$] **25. ♘c3! ♕c2?** [25... ♕a6 26. ♗f8 ♗d1 27. ♕e5 ♔f8 28. ♕h8 ♔f7 29. ♘d1→] **26. ♗f8 ♗d1 27. ♗h6!+– ♘d6 28. ♕e5 ♘f5 29. ♕e6⊕ ♔h8 30. ♕e5 ♔g8 31. ♕f5! ♕c3 32. ♖c3 gf5 33. ♔d1 a5 34. ♖c5 a4** [⌓ 34... ab4 35. ♖f5 e6] **35. ♖a5 ♖d8 36. ♗d2 f4 37. ♔c2 a3 38. ♗f4 1 : 0**
[Ivančuk]

E

472.* E 04**

PÉTURSSON 2560 –
ZSÓ. POLGÁR 2415

Århus 1993

1. d4 d5 2. c4 e6 3. ♘f3 ♘f6 4. g3 dc4 5. ♗g2 ♗d7 [RR 5... ♘c6 6. ♕a4 ♗b4 7. ♗d2 ♘d5 8. ♗b4 ♘b4 9. ♘e5 N (9. 0–0 – 53/(479)) 0–0 10. ♗c6 ♘c6 11. ♘c6 bc6 12. ♕c4 ♖b8! 13. 0–0 ♖b2 14. ♘c3 ♕d6 15. ♖ab1 ♖b6 16. ♖fc1 ♖d8 17. e3 e5 18. de5 ♕e5∓ Stajčić 2270 – Luther 2465, Kecskemét 1993] **6. ♘e5 ♗c6** [RR 6... ♘c6 N 7. ♘c4 ♗b4 8. ♘c3 ♘d5 *a)* 9. 0–0 ♘c3 (9... ♗c3 10. bc3 ♘c3 11. ♕d3 ♘d4 12. ♖e1±) 10. bc3 ♗c3 11. ♖b1=/∞; *b)* 9. ♕d3 ♕f6 10. e3 ♕g6 11. ♗e4 ♕h5 12. a3 (12. 0–0±) ♗c3 13. bc3 ♘f6 14. ♗g2 0–0 15. h3!? (15. 0–0 e5) ♖ad8 16. g4 ♕b5 17. a4 ♕a6 18. ♕e2 ♘a5 (18... ♘d5 19. ♗d2 ♘b6±) 19. ♘e5! (19. ♘a5 ♕a5 20. ♗d2 ♗c6=) ♘b3 20. ♕a6 ba6 21. ♘d7 ♖d7 (21... ♘a1 22. ♘f8 ♔f8 23. ♗a3 ♔g8 24. ♔d2± Razuvaev) 22. ♖b1 ♘c1 23. ♖c1 ♖b8 24. ♔d2± Razuvaev 2525 – Klovans 2440, Bern 1993] **7. ♘c6 ♘c6 8. 0–0 ♕d7 9. e3 ♖b8 10. ♕e2 b5 11. b3 cb3 12. ab3 ♖b6 13. ♖d1** [RR 13. ♗b2 ♗b4 N *a)* 14. ♖d1 a6 (14... 0–0 15. d5 ed5 16. ♗f6 gf6 17. ♖d5 △ ♖b5) 15. d5!? (15. e4 0–0 16. d5 ed5 17. e5 ♖e8!) ed5 16. ♗f6 gf6 17. ♖d5 (17. ♗d5 0–0) ♕e6 18. ♘d2 *a1)* 18... ♘e7 19. ♖d3!? (19. ♖h5 0–0∞) 0–0 20. ♖c1=/∞; *a2)* 18... ♔e7!? 19. ♖d1 ♖d8 20. ♕h5! ♖bb8□ 21. ♘e4! ♖d5 (21... ♘e5 22. ♘f6! ♔f6 23. ♕h4 △ ♕b4) 22. ♖d5 ♖d8 23. ♖f5! (23. ♘c5 ♗c5 24. ♖c5 ♘e5! 25. ♖c7 ♖d7∓) ♖d1! (23... ♕b3? 24. ♗f3!+–→ Tukmakov 2605 – Sánchez Guirado 2335, Benidorm 1993) 24. ♕d1 ♕f5 25. g4 ♕e6 26. ♘g3=/∞; *b)* 14. ♗c6 ♕c6 15. ♖a7 0–0 16. ♖c1 ♕d5 17. ♕c2 (17. ♖ac7 ♕b3=) c5 18. dc5 ♖c6± Tukmakov] **a6 14. ♘c3 ♗e7 15. ♗b2** [15. d5?! ed5 16. ♘d5 ♘d5 17. ♖d5 (17. ♗d5 ♗f6!∓) ♕e6∓] **♘b4 16. e4 0–0 17. ♗h3 N** [17. h4 – 52/(491); 17. d5!? e5; 17. f4!?] **♕e8?!** [17... c6 18. ♘a2 ♘a2 19. ♖a2=/∞⊞ ×a6; 18. ♗c1!? △ ♗e3] **18. ♘a2 ♘d7 19. ♗c3 ♘a2 20. ♖a2 c5?** [20... c6? 21. d5! △ 21... cd5 22. ed5 ed5? 23. ♖e1!+–; 22... ♘b8±] **21. d5 ed5 22. ed5 ♘f6 23. ♗a5 ♖d6**

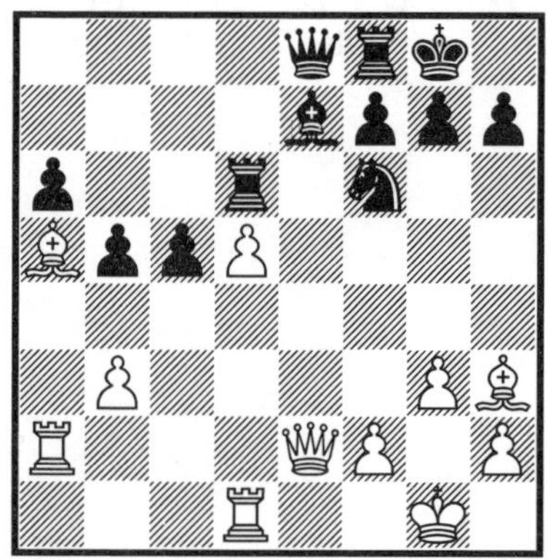

24. ♖e1!! ♘d5 [24... ♕b8 25. ♕e7 ♖e8 26. ♗c7!+–; 24... ♗d8 25. ♕f3 ♗e7 26. ♗c7! ♖d5 27. ♖ae2+–] **25. ♖d2 b4** [25... ♕a8 26. ♕e5! (△ ♖ed1+–; 26. ♕f3? ♗d8; 26. ♗g2? ♗d8 27. ♗d8 ♕d8!; 26. ♖ed1? ♗g5!; 26. ♖d5 ♕d5 27. ♕e7±) ♖e8 27. ♖ed1 ♗f8 28. ♕f5 g6 29. ♕f3 ♖e5 30. ♗g2 ♖f5 31. ♕e4 ♖e6 32. ♕c2 ♖d6 33. ♖d5! ♖fd5 34. ♖d5 ♖d5 35. ♕e2 (△ ♕f3+–) c4 36. bc4 bc4 37. ♕f3 c3

38. ♗c3 ♕c8 (38... ♕c6 39. ♗d2+−) 39. ♕f6+−; 25... ♕c6 26. ♗g2! ♗f6 (26... ♗d8 27. ♗d8 ♖dd8 28. ♕d1+−) 27. ♖d5! ♖d5 28. ♕f3 ♗d8 29. ♗c3+−] **26. ♕f3 ♕c6 27. ♗g2 ♖e6 28. ♕d1!** [28. ♖ed1? ♕b5; 28. ♖dd1 ♗d8 29. ♗d8 ♖d8 30. ♖e3! (30. ♖e2? ♖de8! 31. ♖ed2 ♘e7) c4 (30... ♖ed6 31. ♖ed3 △ 31... ♘e7? 32. ♖d6 ♖d6 33. ♖d6 ♕d6 34. ♕a8+−) 31. bc4 ♕c4 32. ♖ed3±] **♕b5** [28... ♖e1 29. ♕e1 ♕e6 30. ♖e2 ♕d6 31. ♗d5 (31. ♖e5 ♘f4±) ♕d5 32. ♖e7 ♕b3 33. ♗b6 ♕c4 34. ♖e5+−] **29. ♗d5 ♕a5 30. ♗e6 fe6 31. ♖d7! ♗f6 32. ♕d6!+− e5 33. ♖c7 ♕a2 34. ♕e6 ♔h8 35. ♖c8 ♗d8 36. ♕f7! 1 : 0** **[Pétursson]**

473. E 04

TUKMAKOV 2605 − LPUTIAN 2610

Rostov na Donu 1993

1. d4 ♘f6 2. c4 e6 3. ♘f3 d5 4. g3 dc4 5. ♗g2 a6 6. ♘e5 ♗b4 7. ♘c3 ♘d5 8. ♗d2 b5 9. a4 ♗c3 [9... ♗b7!?; 9... f6!?] **10. bc3 f6 N** [10... ♗b7] **11. e4 ♘e7 12. ♘g4 ♗b7 13. ♕b1 c6 14. ♘e3 ♕c8 15. 0−0 0−0 16. ♗c1 ♖e8 17. ♗a3 ♘d7 18. ♗h3!?** [18. ♖d1!?] **♘f8 19. ♗c5 ♕c7 20. ♕b4 ♖ad8 21. ♖fd1! ♗c8 22. ♗g2! ♘eg6?!** [22... ♗b7] **23. f4! ♘e7** [23... e5!? 24. fe5 fe5 25. d5] **24. ab5! cb5 25. d5 ed5 26. ed5 ♕b7 27. ♕a3! ♕d7 28. ♗b6** [28. d6!? ♘c6 29. ♘d5∞] **♕d6!□ 29. ♗c5 ♕d7 30. ♗b6 ♕d6 31. ♕d6! ♖d6 32. ♗c7! ♖d7** [32... ♖ed8 33. ♗d8 ♖d8 34. d6+−] **33. d6 ♘eg6** [33... ♖c7 34. dc7 ♘e6 35. ♘d5 ♔f8 (35... ♔f7 36. ♖e1+−) 36. ♘e7 ♔e7 (36... ♖e7 37. ♖d8 ♖e8 38. ♖e8 ♔e8 39. ♖e1+−) 37. ♖e1+−] **34. ♘d5 ♘e6 35. f5** [35. ♘b6 ♖c7] **♘c7 36. ♘c7 ♖ed8 37. fg6** [37. ♗d5 ♔h8 38. ♗e6 ♖d6 39. ♖d6 ♖d6 40. ♗c8+−] **♖d6 38. ♖d6 ♖d6 39. ♗d5?!⊕** [39. ♘d5+−] **♔h8 40. ♖e1 ♗d7 41. gh7 ♔h7 42. ♗e4?** [42. ♔f2±] **f5 43. ♗b1 ♔h6∞ 44. ♔f2 g6 45. ♔e2 ♔g5 46. ♖d1 ♖d1 47. ♔d1 a5 48. ♘d5 ♗c6 49. ♘e3 ♔f6** [49... f4? 50. h4] **50. h4 ♔e5 51. ♔e2 ♗e4!= 52. ♗e4 ♔e4 53. ♘c2 f4 54. g4 b4 55. cb4 ab4 56. ♘b4 f3 57. ♔f2 ♔f4 1/2 : 1/2** **[Tukmakov]**

474.** E 05

M. VUKIĆ 2500 − CVETKOVIĆ 2500

Jugoslavija 1993

1. ♘f3 d5 2. g3 ♘f6 3. ♗g2 e6 4. 0−0 ♗e7 5. c4 0−0 6. d4 dc4 7. ♕c2 [7. ♘bd2 b5 8. a4 N (8. ♘e5) c6 9. ♘e5! ♘d5 10. e4 ♘f6 (10... ♘b6!?; 10... ♘b4!?) 11. d5 ♕c7! 12. ♘c6 ♘c6 13. dc6 ♕c6 14. ab5 ♕b5 15. e5 (15. ♕a4?! ♕a4 16. ♖a4 ♗d7∓) ♘d5 16. ♕g4 ♗a6 17. ♘e4 ♔h8 (17... ♖fd8!?) 18. ♘c3 ♘c3! 19. ♗a8 ♖a8 20. bc3 ♗b7∞ V. Kostić 2320 − Cvetković 2500, Jugoslavija 1993; RR 7. ♘e5 ♘c6 8. ♘c6 bc6 9. e3 N (9. ♘a3 — 49/573) ♗a6 10. ♗c6 ♖b8 11. ♘c3 ♘d5 12. ♘d5 ed5 13. ♕f3 ♗b7 14. ♗b7 ♖b7 15. b3 cb3 16. ab3± Seirawan 2605 − Ivančuk 2720, Tilburg (Interpolis) 1992] **a6 8. a4 ♗d7 9. ♖d1 ♗c6 10. ♘c3 ♗b4 11. ♗g5 ♗c3 12. ♗f6 ♕f6 13. bc3!** [13. ♕c3] **♘d7** [13... b5 14. ab5 ab5 15. ♘e5! ♗g2 16. ♔g2 ♖a1 17. ♖a1±↑; 14. ♘e5!?; 13... ♕e7!?] **14. ♕a2! ♘b6** [14... b5? 15. ♘e5] **15. a5 ♘d5 16. ♖dc1!** [16. ♕c4? ♗b5∓ ×e2, c3] **b5 N** [16... ♗b5 17. e4 ♘e7 18. e5 ♕h6 19. ♘d2 c5 20. dc5! ♖ac8 21. ♘e4±] **17. ♘e5 ♗e8** [⌓ 17... ♗b7 18. ♘d7 ♕e7 19. ♘f8 ♖f8±] **18. e4 ♘e7 19. ♘c4!± ♕g5** [19... bc4? 20. e5+−; 19... ♖b8!?] **20. ♘e5 ♘g6 21. f4 ♕d8 22. ♘d3 ♘e7 23. ♕a3 ♘c8 24. ♕c5 c6** [24... ♕d6 25. e5 ♕c5 26. ♘c5 c6□±; 24... ♘d6 25. e5 ♘c4 26. ♗a8 ♕a8 27. ♘b4 ♘e3 28. ♖a2±] **25. c4 ♘d6 26. cb5 ♘b5 27. ♖c4 f6 28. h4 ♖a7 29. ♘b4 e5?⊕ 30. de5 fe5 31. ♕e5 ♕d2 32. ♕c5 ♗f7 33. ♖cc1** [33. ♖c2 ♕d4! 34. ♕d4 ♘d4⇆] **♖d7?** [33... ♘d4!?] **34. ♘c6 ♖d3 35. ♖c2 ♕e3 36. ♕e3 ♖e3 1 : 0** **[Cvetković]**

475. E 05

HULAK 2540 − PSAKHIS 2575

Zagreb (zt) 1993

1. d4 e6 2. g3 ♘f6 3. ♘f3 d5 4. ♗g2 ♗e7 5. 0−0 0−0 6. c4 dc4 7. ♕c2 a6 8. a4 ♗d7 9. ♕c4 ♗c6 10. ♗f4 ♘d5 11. ♘c3 ♘f4 12. gf4 a5!? N [12... ♘d7 — 27/508] **13. ♖fd1 ♗d5!?** [13... ♘a6 14. d5!

ed5 15. ♘d5↑] **14. ♕b5** [14. ♘d5 ed5 15. ♕b5 ♘a6 16. ♕b7 ♘b4=] **♘a6 15. e4 ♗c6 16. ♕c4** [16. ♕e2!? ♘b4 17. ♘e5 ♗e8∞] **♘b4 17. ♘e5 ♗e8 18. d5** [18. f5 ef5 19. ef5 ♖b8] **ed5 19. ♘d5 ♘d5 20. ♖d5 ♗d6 21. ♘f3** [21. ♕d3 ♕e7 22. ♘c4 ♗b4; 21. ♘d3!? ♗c6 22. ♖d4] **♗c6 22. ♖d3 ♕c8 23. e5 ♗e7∞ 24. ♘e1** [24. ♘d4 ♗g2 25. ♔g2 ♕g4 *a)* 26. ♖g3 ♕f4 27. ♕c7 (27. ♖g7?? ♔g7 28. ♘e6 fe6−+) ♗h4 △ 28. ♘e6 ♕e4; *b)* 26. ♔h1 ♕f4 27. ♕c7 ♗b4] **♖a6! 25. ♗h3 ♕e8 26. ♘c2?!** [26. f5!?] **b5! 27. ♕c3** [27. ♕d4!?] **♗e4 28. ab5 ♕b5 29. ♖e3** [29. ♖g3 ♖c6] **♖g6!** [29... ♖c6 30. ♘d4 ♖c3 31. ♘b5 ♖e3 32. fe3] **30. ♖g3 ♖c6 31. ♘d4□ ♖c3 32. ♘b5 ♖c2! 33. ♘c3 ♗a8∓ 34. ♗g2?! ♗h4!−+ 35. ♖d3 ♗f2** [35... ♗g2 36. ♔g2 ♗f2 37. ♔f3] **36. ♔f1 ♗b6 37. ♗a8 ♖a8⊕ 0 : 1** **[Psakhis]**

476. **E 06**

LAUTIER 2645 – KRAMNIK 2685

Cannes (m/5) 1993

1. c4 e6 2. g3 d5 3. ♗g2 ♘f6 4. ♘f3 ♗e7 5. 0–0 0–0 6. b3 a5 7. ♘c3 c6 8. d4 [8. ♗b2 – 42/14, A 14] **b6 9. ♗b2** [9. ♗f4!?] **♗a6 10. ♘d2 ♖a7 N** [10... b5] **11. ♕c2** [11. e4 ♖d7 (11... dc4 12. ♘c4 ♖d7 13. ♘e2 c5 14. ♘e5 ♖d6 15. ♘c4 ♖d7 16. ♘e5=) 12. e5 ♘e8 13. ♘e2 dc4 14. bc4 c5 (14... ♘c7?! 15. ♕c2!? c5 16. ♘f3±) 15. d5 ed5 16. cd5 ♖d5 17. ♗d5 ♕d5 18. ♘f4 ♕c6 19. ♖e1 ♗b7 20. ♘e4∞] **♖d7 12. e3 c5 13. ♖fd1 cd4 14. ed4 ♘c6 15. ♘b5 ♘b4 16. ♕b1 ♗b7 17. a3 ♘a6 18. ♕d3** [18. ♘f3 dc4 19. ♘e5 (19. bc4 ♕a8 20. ♕d3 e5∓) ♗g2 20. ♔g2 c3! 21. ♗c3∓] **♕a8 19. ♕e2 ♘c7 20. a4 ♖c8 21. ♖ac1** [21. ♖dc1] **♘b5 22. ab5** [22. cb5 ♖dc7 23. ♘b1 ♕b8 24. ♖c7 ♕c7 25. ♘c3 △ ♖c1] **♖dc7 23. ♖c2 ♘e8 24. ♖dc1 h6 25. f4?! dc4 26. ♗b7 ♕b7 27. bc4 ♘d6∓ 28. ♕d3 a4 29. ♔f2?!** [29. ♗a3!?] **♗f6 30. ♘f3 ♖d8 31. ♔g1** [31. ♘e5!?] **♘f5 32. c5?⊕** [32. ♖d2] **bc5 33. ♖c5 ♖cd7∓ 34. ♖1c4 ♗e7 35. ♖e5 ♗d6 36. ♖a4 ♗e5 37. ♘e5 ♖d5 38. ♖b4** [⌓ 38. ♘c6] **♘e7−+ 39. ♕b3 ♖b8 40. ♗a3 ♖bd8 41. b6 ♘f5 42. ♕a4 ♖d4 43. ♖d4 ♘d4 44. ♕a7 ♕a7 45. ba7 f6 46. ♘g6 ♖a8 0 : 1** **[Kramnik]**

477. **E 06**

D. RAJKOVIĆ 2450 – ČOLOVIĆ 2305

Cetinje 1993

1. d4 d5 2. c4 e6 3. ♘f3 c6 4. ♘bd2 ♘f6 5. g3 ♘bd7 6. ♗g2 ♗e7 7. 0–0 0–0 8. ♕c2 b5 9. c5 a5 10. e4 ♘e4 11. ♘e4 de4 12. ♕e4 ♘f6 N [12... ♖a6?! – 44/613] **13. ♕c2** [13. ♕c6 ♗d7 14. ♕b7 ♖b8=] **♘d5 14. ♗d2 b4 15. ♖fe1 ♗a6 16. ♘e5 ♕c7 17. ♗e4** [17. a3 ba3 18. ♖a3 ♗b5 19. b3± ×a5, c6; 17... ♗b5!] **g6?!** [17... h6 18. a3 ba3 19. ♖a3 ♗b5 20. b3!± ×a5, c6] **18. h4 ♗f6 19. ♗f3 ♗g7 20. h5 ♗b5 21. ♕e4 ♖fd8** [21... ♖fe8 22. hg6 hg6 23. ♕h4 △ ♔g2, ♖h1→] **22. hg6 hg6 23. ♔g2 ♘e7 24. ♗f4!** [24. ♘f7 ♖d4! 25. ♕e6 ♗c4−+] **♕c8 25. ♖ad1 ♖a7 26. ♖h1 ♘f5 27. g4 ♘e7 28. ♗h6!+− ♘d5** [28... ♗h8 29. ♗g5! △ ♖h8, ♗f6] **29. g5 ♕b8** [29... ♗h8 30. ♕h4 ♘e7 31. ♗f8! ♔f8 (31... ♗e5 32. ♗e7 ♖e7 33. de5) 32. ♕h8 ♘g8 33. ♖h7] **30. ♗g7 ♔g7 31. ♖h7! ♔h7 32. ♕h4 ♔g7** [32... ♔g8 33. ♗d5 ♖d5 34. ♖h1 ♔f8 35. ♕h8 ♔e7 36. ♕f6 ♔e8 37. ♖h8#] **33. ♕h6 ♔g8 34. ♗d5 ♗e2 35. ♖h1 ♗h5 36. ♘g4 1 : 0** **[D. Rajković]**

478. **E 08**

MARIN 2515 – GAGARIN 2450

Bucureşti 1993

1. d4 ♘f6 2. c4 e6 3. g3 ♗b4 4. ♗d2 ♗e7 5. ♗g2 d5 6. ♘f3 0–0 7. 0–0 c6 8. ♗f4 ♘bd7 9. ♕c2 b6 10. ♖d1 ♗b7 11. ♘c3 ♖c8 N [11... dc4 12. ♘d2±; 11... ♘h5 – 40/614] **12. b3** [△ e4; 12. e4?! dc4!∓] **♘h5 13. ♗c1 f5 14. ♗b2 ♗d6 15. e3** [△ ♘e2-f4-d3 ×e5] **♕e7 16. ♘e2 ♘hf6 17. ♘f4 ♘e4 18. ♘d3 ♘df6** [18... g5 19. ♘fe5 ♗e5 20. de5 g4 21. ♘f4⩲ ⊡] **19. ♘fe5 ♖fd8?!** [19... c5! 20. ♕e2] **20. f3 ♘g5 21. c5± ♗b8 22. a4** [△ a5-a6 ×♗b7]

♘**d7** 23. **a5** ♗**a6**□ [23... bc5 24. a6+−] 24. ♘**d7** ♗**d3** 25. ♕**d3** ♖**d7** 26. **cb6 ab6** 27. ♕**a6** ♖**b7** 28. **ab6** [28. ♗a3? ♕c7 29. ♗d6 ♕d7∞] ♗**d6** 29. ♖**dc1** [×c6] ♕**d7** 30. ♗**c3** ♖**cb8** 31. ♗**a5** [△ ♖c3, ♖ac1, b4-b5] ♗**b4!?** 32. ♗**b4** ♖**b6** 33. ♕**a4** [33. ♕b6!? ♖b6 34. ♗c5 ♖b3 35. ♖a8 ♔f7 36. h4 ♘f3 37. ♗f3=∞ △ 37... ♖e3? 38. ♖a7+−] ♖**b4** 34. ♕**c6** ♕**e7** [34... ♕c6 35. ♖c6 ♖b3 36. h4 ♘f7 37. ♖e6+−] 35. ♖**a6** ♖**b3** 36. **h4** ♘**f7** 37. ♕**e6** ♖**e3** 38. ♖**c8** ♖**c8** 39. ♕**c8** ♕**d8**□ [39... ♕e8 40. ♕f5+−; 39... ♕f8 40. ♖a8+−] 40. ♕**d8** [40. ♕f5?! g6⇆ ×♗g2] ♘**d8** [♖ 9/i] 41. ♖**a8** ♖**e8** 42. **f4** ♔**f7** 43. ♗**d5** ♔**e7** 44. ♔**f2** ♔**d6** 45. ♗**f3?!** [45. ♗c4+−] ♔**e7** 46. ♖**a5** ♔**f6** [46... ♘e6? 47. ♖e5+−] 47. ♗**d5** ♔**e7** 48. ♗**f3** ♔**f6** 49. ♗**d5** ♔**e7** 50. ♖**a6** ♔**f8** [50... ♔d7 51. ♗c4!? (51. h5 h6 52. ♖g6 ♖e7±) ♖e7 52. ♗g8 h6 (52... ♘c6 53. d5 ♘d4 54. ♖a7 ♔d6 55. ♖e7 ♔e7 56. ♔e3 ♘c2 57. ♔d2 △ ♗h7) 53. ♗h7+−] 51. ♖**a8** ♔**e7** 52. ♗**c4!+−** ♔**d6** 53. ♖**a6** ♔**e7** 54. ♖**a7** ♔**f8** 55. ♖**d7** ♘**e6** 56. **h5** ♘**d8** 57. **h6!** [57. d5 ♘f7 58. d6 ♘h6⇆] **gh6** 58. **d5** ♔**g8** [58... ♘f7 59. d6 ♘h8 60. ♖h7 ♘g6 61. ♗f7] 59. **d6** ♔**h8** 60. ♖**e7** ♖**f8** 61. ♗**d5** **1 : 0** **[Marin]**

479. **E 11**

TUNIK 2465 – N. VLASSOV 2385
Minsk 1993

1. d4 ♘**f6** **2. c4** ♘**c6** **3.** ♘**f3 e6** **4. g3** ♗**b4** **5.** ♘**bd2 a5** N [5... d5] **6.** ♗**g2 d6** **7. 0−0 e5** [7... 0−0? 8. ♘b1! △ a3] **8. a3** [8. ♘b1!?] ♗**d2** **9.** ♕**d2** ♗**g4!** [9... 0−0 10. b3⩲] **10. de5** [10. d5 ♗f3 11. ef3 ♘d4 12. ♕d3 a4 13. f4! ♘b3 14. fe5 ♘a1?! 15. ef6 ♕f6 16. ♖e1↑; 14... de5!=] **de5** **11.** ♕**e3** [11. ♕g5? e4!] **0−0!** [11... ♕e7 12. b3⩲] **12.** ♘**e5** [12. b3? a4 13. b4 e4 14. ♘g5 (14. ♘d2 ♘d4∓) ♕d4!↑] ♘**e5** **13.** ♕**e5** ♖**e8** **14.** ♕**b5** [14. ♕c3 ♗e2 15. ♖e1 ♕d3=] ♗**e2** **15.** ♖**e1** ♘**g4!** **16.** ♕**b7** ♘**f2**□ **17.** ♕**d5** [17. ♕a8 ♘h3 18. ♔h1 ♘f2=; 17. ♖e2 ♕d1 (17... ♖e2? 18. ♕a8) 18. ♗f1 ♘h3 19. ♔g2 ♖e2 20. ♗e2 ♕e2 21. ♔h3 ♕h5 22. ♔g2 ♕e2=] ♘**d3** **18.** ♗**g5!** [18. ♖e2? ♖e2 19. ♕a8 ♖e1−+] ♕**d5** **19.** ♗**d5** ♖**ab8** [19... ♘e1 20. ♗a8 ♖a8 (20... ♗f3?! 21. ♖e1! ♖e1 22. ♔f2 ♗a8 23. ♔e1±⊥ ×a5, c7) 21. ♖e1 ♗c4 22. ♖c1=] **20.** ♖**eb1** ♖**b2** [20... ♖b3? 21. ♗d2!±; 20... ♘b2? 21. ♗c6 ♖e6 22. ♗b5 ♘d3 23. c5! ♖f8 24. ♖a2±] **21.** ♖**b2** ♘**b2** **22.** ♖**c1** ♘**d3** **23.** ♖**b1** ♘**e5** **24.** ♗**f4** ♗**c4** **25.** ♗**e5** ♗**d5** **26.** ♗**c7 a4** **27.** ♖**b8!=**
1/2 : 1/2 **[N. Vlassov, Šipov]**

480. **E 11**

EPIŠIN 2620 – G. KUZ'MIN 2525
Moskva (open) 1992

1. d4 ♘**f6** **2. c4 e6** **3.** ♘**f3** ♗**b4** **4.** ♘**bd2 b6** **5. a3** ♗**d2** **6.** ♗**d2 d6!?** **7.** ♗**g5 h6** **8.** ♗**h4** ♘**bd7** **9. e3 g5** N [9... ♗b7 – 56/571] **10.** ♗**g3** ♘**e4** **11. d5 e5** **12.** ♗**d3** ♘**df6** **13.** ♕**c2** ♘**c5** [13... ♗f5? 14. ♘e5! de5 15. ♗e5 ♗g6 16. f3 ♕e7 17. ♗d4±] **14.** ♗**e2 a5** [14... ♘ce4!? 15. ♗d3 ♘c5 16. ♘d2 ♘d3 17. ♕d3 ♘h5 18. f4! ♘g3 19. hg3 ♕e7 20. 0-0-0 ♗d7 21. f5 0-0-0 22. g4 f6 23. ♘f1⩲] **15.** ♘**d2** ♕**e7?** [15... a4 16. f4±] **16. b3** [△ ♖c1, b4±] ♗**d7** **17.** ♖**c1** ♔**f8?!** [17... h5 18. h4 g4±] **18. b4** ♘**b7** **19.** ♕**b2! ab4** **20. ab4 c5** **21. 0−0** **h5?!** [21... ♗g4! 22. f3 ♗h5±] **22. f4!** **ef4**□ **23. ef4 h4**

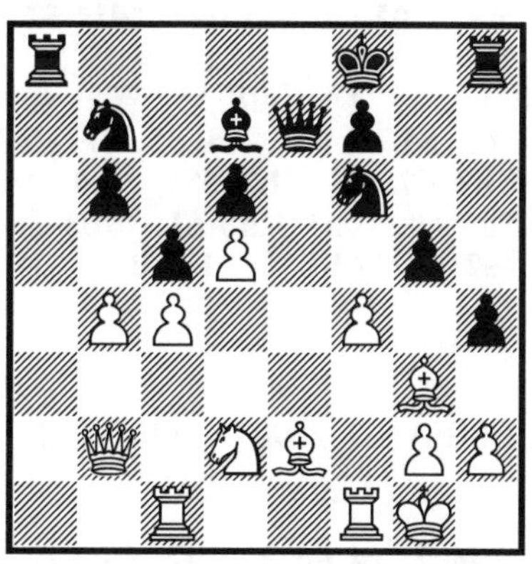

24. ♖**ce1!!+− hg3** **25.** ♗**d1!** ♕**d8** **26. fg5** ♖**g8** **27.** ♖**f6** ♖**g5** **28.** ♘**e4** ♖**e5** **29.** ♖**ef1** ♗**e8** **30.** ♘**d6** ♕**f6**□ **31.** ♖**f6** ♖**e1** **32.** ♖**f1** **gh2** **33.** ♔**h2** ♖**f1** **34.** ♕**h8** ♔**e7** **35.** ♕**e5** ♔**f8** **36.** ♗**e2! f6** **37.** ♕**e6** ♖**f2** **38.** ♘**f5**
1 : 0 **[Epišin]**

481. !N **E 11**

EPIŠIN 2620 – KOSTEN 2505
Genève 1993

1. d4 e6 2. c4 ♘f6 3. ♘f3 ♗b4 4. ♘bd2 b6 5. a3 ♗d2 6. ♗d2 ♗b7 7. ♗g5 d6 8. e3 ♘bd7 9. ♕c2 ♕e7 10. ♖d1 ♗e4! N [10... h6 11. ♗h4 ♗e4 – 55/(492)] **11. ♕a4** [11. ♕c3 ♗f3! 12. gf3 ♘e4 13. fe4 ♕g5=] **0–0 12. ♗h4 a6 13. ♗d3 ♗d3 14. ♖d3 e5 15. ♖d1 ed4 16. ♖d4 ♘e5 17. 0–0 ♘f3 18. gf3 ♕e6 19. ♗g3! a5 20. ♖fd1 ♕e8 21. ♕c2 a4?!** [⌓ 21... ♘h5] **22. e4 ♘d7?!** [22... ♘h5 23. ♖d5 ♘g3 24. hg3⩲] **23. f4 f6** [23... ♘c5! 24. f5 (24. e5 de5 25. fe5 f5! 26. ef6 ♖f6 27. ♗c7 ♕f7=∞) ♘d7!⩲] **24. ♖d5 ♖f7 25. f3 ♖e7 26. ♔h1 ♘c5 27. ♖g1 ♕f7 28. ♗e1!** [△ ♗c3±] **♖d8 29. ♗c3 c6 30. ♖d2** [30. ♖f5? ♕c4 31. ♖f6 d5∞] **d5 31. ed5 cd5 32. ♕f5! ♖ed7□ 33. ♗f6** [33. ♕f6? d4=] **g6** [33... ♖f8 34. ♖g7 ♕g7 35. ♖g2±] **34. ♖dg2!! dc4□ 35. ♖g6 hg6 36. ♖g6 ♔f8 37. ♖h6 ♖d1 38. ♔g2 ♖8d2 39. ♔h3 ♕e6 40. ♗g7 ♔g7 41. ♖e6 ♘e6 42. ♕e6** [♕ 6/b] **♖h1 43. ♕e5 ♔h7 44. ♕c7 ♔h8 45. f5 ♖hh2** [45... ♖dh2 46. ♔g3 ♖h3 47. ♔f4 ♖h4 48. ♔e5 ♖e1 49. ♔f6 ♖h6 50. ♔g5 ♖eh1 51. ♕b8 ♔g7 52. ♕a7 ♔g8 53. ♕a4+–] **46. ♔g3 ♖b2 47. f6 ♖bg2 48. ♔f4 ♖g8□ 49. ♕e7!!+– ♖h4 50. ♔e3 ♖h1 51. ♔d4 ♖d1 52. ♔c4 ♖dd8** [52... ♖c8 53. ♔b5 ♖d5 54. ♔a6] **53. f4!** [△ 54. f7 ♖gf8 55. ♕f6 ♔h7 56. f5+–] **b5 54. ♔b5 ♖c8 55. f7 ♖gf8 56. ♕f6 ♔h7 57. f5 ♖b8 58. ♔a4 ♖a8 59. ♔b3 ♖a3 60. ♔a3 ♖a8 61. ♔b3 ♖a3 62. ♔c2 ♖a2 63. ♔b1 1 : 0 [Epišin]**

482. **E 11**

B. GEL'FAND 2690 – TIMMAN 2635
Linares 1993

1. d4 ♘f6 2. c4 e6 3. ♘f3 ♗b4 4. ♘bd2 d5 5. ♕a4 ♘c6 6. a3 ♗d2 7. ♗d2 0–0 8. e3 ♘e4 9. ♖d1 ♕f6 10. ♗d3 ♕g6 N [10... ♘d6 – 39/608] **11. 0–0 ♘c5! 12. ♕c6!** [12. dc5 ♕d3 13. ♗a5 ♕c4 14. ♕c4 dc4 15. ♗c7 f6! 16. ♖c1 (16. ♘d4 ♖f7! 17. ♗g3 ♘d4 18. ♖d4 ♗d7=) ♖f7 17. ♗d6 ♘a5 18. ♘d2 ♗d7=] **♘d3 13. ♕c7 ♘b2** [13... dc4 14. ♘e5 ♘e5 15. de5±] **14. ♗b4 ♖e8 15. ♘e5 ♕f6 16. cd5!** [16. ♖c1 ♘c4 17. ♘c4 dc4 18. ♖c4 b6=] **♘d1** [16... ed5? 17. ♖b1 ♘a4 18. ♕a5 ♘b6 19. ♗c5±] **17. d6 ♘b2 18. d7 ♗d7** [18... ♖d8 19. dc8♕ (19. ♗e7? ♖d7!) ♖ac8 20. ♕b7±] **19. ♕d7 ♖ac8 20. ♕b7 a5! 21. ♗a5 ♘c4 22. ♘c4 ♖c4 23. ♗b4 ♖cc8! 24. ♕b5 h6** [⌓ 24... ♕g6 25. ♗c5±] **25. a4?** [25. ♕d3±] **♖b8 26. ♕c4 ♕f5?** [26... ♖ec8 27. ♗c5 ♕d8!=] **27. ♗c5 ♖b1 28. a5 ♖eb8 29. ♗b6 ♕b5 30. ♕b5 ♖b5** [♖ 9/o] **31. ♖a1?!** [31. g3!±] **♖a8 32. ♖c1?** [32. ♖d1! △ 32... e5 33. d5±] **e5! 33. g3** [⌓ 33. ♔f1 ed4 34. ed4 ♖ba5 35. ♗a5 ♖a5 36. ♖c8 ♔h7 37. ♔e2±] **ed4 34. ed4 ♖ba5 35. ♗a5 ♖a5** [♖ 6/f] **36. ♔g2 ♔f8 37. ♖e1?!** [37. ♖c3!?±] **♖a4 38. ♖d1 ♖a3! 39. g4 ♔e7 40. ♖e1 ♔d6 41. h4 ♖d3 42. ♖e4 g5! 43. h5 ♔d5 44. ♖e5 ♔d6 45. ♖e4 ♔d5 46. ♖e8 ♖d4 47. ♔g3 ♖f4 48. ♖a8 ♖f6 49. ♖a7 ♔e5 50. f3 ♖f4 51. ♖a6 ♖f6 52. ♖a5 ♔e6 53. ♖a7 ♔e5 54. ♔f2 ♖f4 55. ♔e3 1/2 : 1/2 [B. Gel'fand, Huzman]**

483. **E 11**

AN. KARPOV 2725 – SERPER 2590
Dortmund 1993

1. d4 ♘f6 2. c4 e6 3. ♘f3 ♗b4 4. ♗d2 ♗d2 5. ♕d2 d5 6. g3 ♘bd7 7. ♗g2 c6 8. ♕c2 0–0 9. ♘bd2 b6 10. e4!? N [10. 0–0 – 55/(493)] **de4 11. ♘e4 ♘e4 12. ♕e4 ♗b7 13. 0–0 ♖b8** [13... ♕c7 14. ♘e5±] **14. ♕e3** [14. ♕f4 ♕f6 15. ♕c7 c5 (15... ♖fd8 16. ♘e5 ♘e5 17. de5 ♕g5 18. f4±; 15... ♕d8 16. ♕d6 c5 17. ♖fd1±) 16. ♕d7 ♖fd8 17. ♕c7 ♗f3 18. ♗f3 ♕f3 19. dc5 ♖bc8 20. ♕a7 bc5=∞] **c5 15. dc5** [15. ♖fd1!?] **♘c5 16. ♖fd1 ♕c7 17. b4 ♘d7 18. ♖d4 ♘f6** [18... e5 19. ♖d2⩲] **19. ♕e5!± ♕e7** [19... ♕e5 20. ♘e5 ♗g2 21. ♔g2±] **20. a3 ♖bc8 21. ♖ad1 ♖c7** [21... ♖fd8 22. ♖d8 ♖d8 23. ♖d8 ♕d8 24. ♘d4±] **22. ♘h4 ♖fc8?** [22... ♗g2 23. ♘g2 ♖fc8 24. ♘e3±] **23. ♘f5!± ef5 24. ♕e7 ♖e7 25. ♗b7 ♖f8 26. ♗a6! g6 27. c5 bc5 28. bc5 ♖c7 29. ♖c1 ♖e8 30. c6! ♔g7**

[30... ♖e6 31. ♖d8 ♔g7 32. ♖c8 ♖ee7; 31. ♗b7!? △ ♖a4] **31. ♔f1 ♖e5 32. ♗b7 ♖a5** [32... g5!?] **33. ♖cd1! ♖e5** [33... ♖a3 34. ♖d7 ♘d7 35. cd7+−] **34. ♖d7! ♖e7 35. ♖c7 ♖c7 36. ♖d8+− ♖e7 37. f3 g5 38. ♖a8** [38. ♖c8? ♘d5] **g4 39. fg4 fg4 40. ♖a7 ♘d5 41. ♖a4 ♘e3 42. ♔g1 ♔f6 43. ♖f4 1 : 0 [An. Karpov]**

484. E 11

TUKMAKOV 2605 – SMYSLOV 2530

Rostov na Donu 1993

1. d4 ♘f6 2. c4 e6 3. ♘f3 ♗b4 4. ♗d2 a5 5. g3 d5 6. ♗g2 dc4 7. ♕c2 ♘c6 [7... ♕d5] **8. ♕c4 ♕d5 9. ♕d3 0–0 10. ♘c3 ♕h5 11. a3 ♗c3 N** [11... ♗e7 – 36/591] **12. ♗c3 b6** [12... ♖d8] **13. 0–0 ♗a6 14. ♕c2 ♘e7 15. ♖fe1** [15. b4!?] **c5 16. ♕b3 ♘ed5 17. e4 ♘c3 18. bc3 cd4 19. cd4 ♕b5 20. ♕e3!± ♕a4 21. ♘e5 ♖ad8 22. d5! ed5 23. ♕b6 ♗b5□ 24. ed5 ♘d5 25. ♕c5 ♘f6 26. ♖ab1 ♗d7□** [26... ♗d3 27. ♗c6 ♕d4 28. ♘d3 ♕d3 29. ♕a5] **27. ♗c6 ♗c6 28. ♘c6 ♖a8 29. ♖b7 h6 30. ♔g2 ♔h8** [△ ♖ac8] **31. ♘e5 ♔g8 32. ♕c4!? ♕c4 33. ♘c4 a4! 34. ♖ee7 ♘d5 35. ♖ed7 ♘f6 36. ♖e7 ♘d5 37. ♖ed7 ♘f6 38. ♖d4 ♖fb8 39. ♖b8 ♖b8** [♖ 9/h] **40. ♘e3** [40. ♘e5!? ♖b5!?] **♖a8 41. ♔f3** [41. ♘c4 ♖b8; 41. ♘d1 ♘e8 42. ♘b2 ♘c7] **♔f8 42. ♔e2 ♘e8 43. ♔d3 ♘c7 44. ♖b4 ♔e7 45. ♔c4 ♔d7 46. ♘d1 ♘e8 47. ♘b2!** [47. ♘c3 ♘d6 48. ♔d3 ♔c6 49. ♘a4 ♘b5] **♘d6 48. ♔c3 f5** [48... ♖c8 49. ♔d3 ♖a8 50. ♘a4 △ ♔c3-b3; 48... ♔c6 49. ♘a4 ♘b5 50. ♔b3] **49. ♘a4 ♔c6 50. ♔b3 ♘e4 51. ♖b6 ♔d5 52. ♖b5 ♔c6** [52... ♔d4? 53. ♘b6 ♖d8 54. ♖f5+−] **53. ♖b6 ♔d5 54. ♖b5 ♔c6 55. ♖f5 ♖b8 56. ♔c2 ♖a8 57. ♔b3 ♖b8 58. ♔a2 ♖d8 59. f3 ♖d2 60. ♔b3 ♖d3 61. ♔b2** [61. ♔c4 ♖f3!□ 62. ♖f3 ♘d2 63. ♔b4 ♘f3 64. h4 h5 △ g5; 61. ♔b4 ♘d2 (61... ♖d4 62. ♔a5 ♘d2 63. ♖c5 ♔d6 64. ♖c3) 62. ♖c5 ♔d6 63. ♖c3 ♖c3 64. ♘c3 ♘f3] **♘d2 62. ♖c5** [62. ♔c2 ♖a3 63. ♔d2 ♖a4 64. ♖f7 ♖a2 65. ♔e3 ♖h2 66. ♖g7 (66. ♔f4 ♔d6 67. ♔f5 ♖h5) ♔d6 67. ♔f4 ♔e6 68. ♖g6 ♔f7] **♔d6 63. f4 ♘f1** [63... ♖d4 64. ♖c2] **64. ♖c3 ♖d2 65. ♔b3 ♖h2 66. ♘c5 ♖g2 67. ♔c4 g5 68. fg5?** [68. ♘e4! ♔c6 (68... ♔e6 69. fg5 hg5 70. ♘g5 ♔f5 71. ♖f3 ♔g5 72. ♖f1 ♖g3 73. a4+−) 69. f5±] **hg5 69. ♖d3 ♔c6 70. ♘e4 g4 71. ♔d4⊕ ♔b5 72. ♖b3 ♔a5** [72... ♔a4? 73. ♘c5 ♔a5 74. a4] **73. ♔c5?!** [73. ♔e5! ♖e2 74. ♖d3 ♔b5 75. ♔f4; 74... ♖e3!?] **♖c2 74. ♔d5 ♖e2! 75. ♘c5 ♘d2! 76. ♖b8** [76. ♖b2 ♘e4!] **♘f3 77. a4 ♖d2 78. ♔e4** [78. ♔e6 ♘d4] **♖d4 79. ♔e3 ♖b4 80. ♖a8 ♔b6 81. ♘d3 ♖c4 82. a5 ♔b5⊕ 1/2 : 1/2 [Tukmakov]**

485. E 11

S. KISELËV 2510 –

V. NEVEDNIČIJ 2495

Bucureşti 1993

1. d4 ♘f6 2. c4 ♘c6 3. ♘f3 e6 4. g3 ♗b4 5. ♗d2 ♕e7 6. ♘c3 0–0 7. ♗g2 d6 8. 0–0 a5 9. ♕c2 N [9. ♖c1 – 29/486] **e5 10. de5 ♘e5** [10... de5 11. ♘d5 ♘d5 12. cd5 ♘d4 13. ♘d4±; 11. ♗g5!?±] **11. ♘d5** [11. ♗g5!? ♗c3 (11... c6 12. ♘e4±) 12. ♕c3 h6 13. ♗f6 ♘f3 (13... ♕f6 14. ♘d4±) 14. ♗f3 ♕f6 15. ♕f6 gf6 16. c5±⊥] **♘d5 12. cd5 ♗f5! 13. ♕f5** [13. ♕d1 (△ ♘d4) ♘f3 14. ♗f3 ♗e4 15. ♗b4 ♗f3 16. ef3 ab4 17. ♕d2±] **♘f3 14. ♗f3 ♗d2 15. a3±** [×c7; 15. e3 ♗b4 △ ♗c5] **♗g5** [15... a4 16. ♕c2± ×a4] **16. b3** [16. e3!?] **♖a6!?** [△ 17... c5 18. dc6 bc6 △ d5] **17. ♕d3 ♖b6** [△ c5] **18. ♖fd1 g6?!** [18... ♖d8!? △ c5] **19. ♖ab1 ♕d7** [19... ♖d8 20. b4!?] **20. e3 ♗f6 21. ♕c2** [△ ♗e2 ×♖b6] **♖a6 22. ♖dc1 ♖c8** [△ c6] **23. ♕c4** [△ ♗g4] **h5 24. ♖c2 ♗e5** [24... b5 25. ♕d3 △ b4 ×c6, b5] **25. ♔g2 ♔g7 26. h3 ♖aa8** [△ b5-b4, ♗c3] **27. b4** [△ b5-b6; ⌓ 27. ♖bc1] **ab4 28. ab4 ♖a4 29. ♖bc1** [△ ♕b3, ♖c4] **♖ca8!? 30. ♕c7 ♕c7?!** [⌓ 30... ♕b5 31. ♖b1 ♖b4 32. ♖b4 ♕b4 33. ♕d7 △ ♖c7±] **31. ♖c7 ♖b4 32. ♖d7 ♖f8 33. ♖cc7 b5 34. g4!± h4** [34... hg4 35. ♗g4 (△ ♗e6) ♔f6 36. f4+−] **35. g5** [△ ♗g4-e6] **♖b2** [△ ♗g3] **36. ♗d1** [△ ♗c2] **♖d2?!** [36... b4 37. ♔f1 (△ f4) ♖b1 38. ♔e2 ♖b2 (38... b3 39. ♖b7 b2 40. ♗c2 ♖h1 41. f4 ♗c3 42.

♖d6± △ 43. ♖g6, 43. ♖c6) 39. ♖c2 ♖c2 40. ♗c2 △ f4± ×d6] **37. ♗b3 ♖b2 38. ♗c2 b4 39. ♔f1 b3 40. ♗e4 ♖a2 41. f4** [41. ♖b7!? b2 42. f4±] **♖a4 42. ♗d3 ♗f4□ 43. ef4 ♖f4 44. ♔e2 ♖e8 45. ♔d2 ♖e5** [45... ♖f2 46. ♔c3 ♖e3 47. ♔d4! (47. ♖d6?! ♖c2 48. ♔d4 ♖d3 49. ♔d3 ♖c7 50. ♖b6±) ♖h3 48. ♖d6 ♖d2 49. ♖g6 ♔h7□ (49... ♔f8 50. ♖c8 ♔e7 51. d6 △ ♖c7, ♖g8#; 49... ♔h8 50. ♖c8 ♔h7 51. ♖h6 △ ♖h7#) 50. ♖h6 ♔g7 51. ♖h7 ♔f8 52. ♖hf7 ♔g8 53. ♖g7 ♔f8 54. ♖cf7 ♔e8 55. g6!+− ♖hd3 56. ♔c4 ♖d4 57. ♔c3 ♖4d3 (57... ♖2d3 58. ♔b2 △ ♔a3) 58. ♔b4 ♖d4 59. ♔a3 ♖a2 60. ♔b3+−] **46. ♖d6 ♖g5 47. ♖c4!+− ♖g2 48. ♔c3 ♖f3 49. ♖b6** [♙d] **♖c2 50. ♔d4** [50. ♔b3?? ♖d2] **♖d2 51. ♖b3 ♖h3 52. d6 ♔f6 53. d7 ♔e7 54. ♖c7** [△ ♖a7, d8♕, ♖b8#] **g5 55. ♖a7 ♖hd3 56. ♖d3 ♖d3 57. ♔d3 h3 58. d8♕ 1 : 0**
[S. Kiselëv, Gagarin]

486.* !N **E 11**

JE. PIKET 2590 − KORTCHNOI 2605
Nijmegen (m/4) 1993

1. d4 ♘f6 2. c4 e6 3. ♘f3 ♗b4 4. ♗d2 ♕e7 5. g3 ♘c6 6. ♘c3 d5 7. ♗g2 [RR 7. a3 ♗c3 8. ♗c3 ♘e4 9. ♕b3! N (9. ♕c2 − 44/(626)) 0−0!? 10. ♗g2 (10. cd5 ed5 11. ♕d5 ♖e8 12. ♕c4 ♗g4 13. ♗g2 ♖ad8=∞ △ 14. e3? ♘f2! 15. 0−0□ ♘h3∓) ♖d8 11. 0−0 a5 12. e3 b6 13. ♖fc1 *a)* 13... ♗b7 14. ♗e1 a4?! (×a4) 15. ♕c2 ♘d6?! 16. ♘d2 ♕f6?! 17. ♕d1! ♘f5 18. cd5 ed5 19. ♘b1!!± Kajdanov 2620 − A. Gol'din 2555, Pleasantville 1993; 15... ♕e8!?; ⌓ 14... ♘f6; *b)* 13... ♗a6!? 14. cd5 (14. ♗f1?! ♕f6 15. ♔g2 dc4 16. ♗c4 ♗b7!∓) ed5 15. ♗e1 ♗c4 16. ♖c4! dc4 17. ♕c4⩲ Byrne, Mednis] **0−0 8. a3 ♗c3 9. ♗c3 ♘e4 10. ♖c1 N** [10. ♕c2] **♖d8 11. ♕c2 a5** [11... ♘d6!? 12. c5 ♘e4 13. b4 ♘c3 14. ♕c3 e5 15. ♘e5 ♘e5 16. de5 d4 17. ♕d3 ♕e5 18. e4⩲] **12. 0−0 ♗d7 13. ♖fe1 ♗e8 14. cd5 ed5 15. ♘d2! f5□ 16. e3 ♗g6 17. ♕b3 ♕d6 18. ♘f3?** [18. f4! a4 (18... ♘d2 19. ♗d2 △ ♖c5, ♖ec1±) 19. ♕c2⩲] **a4 19. ♕b5 ♕d7 20. ♘h4 ♗f7 21. ♗b4?** [21. ♘f3∞]

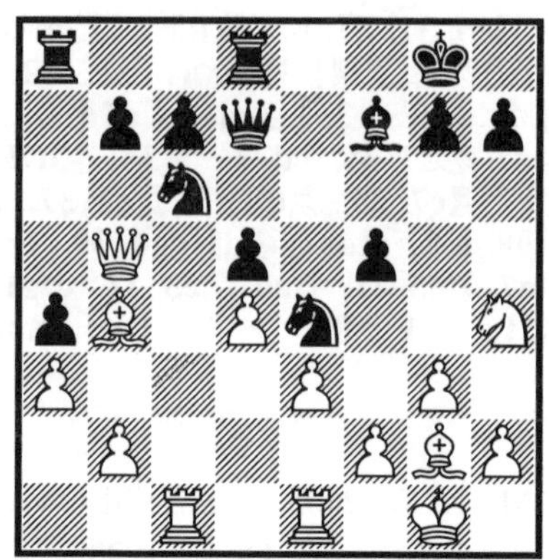

21... ♖a6! 22. f3 ♘b4 23. ♕d7 [23. ♕b4 ♖b6] **♖d7 24. ab4 ♘d6 25. ♗h3 ♗e6?** [25... g6! 26. e4 ♖e7 27. ef5 ♖e1 28. ♖e1 ♖b6−+] **26. e4 de4 27. d5!□ ♗d5 28. ♘f5 ♘f5 29. ♗f5 ♗e6 30. b5 ♖b6 31. ♗e6 ♖e6 32. ♖e4 ♖e4 33. fe4 ♖d2 34. ♖c4??** [34. ♖c7 ♖b2 35. ♖c8 ♔f7 36. ♖a8=] **♖b2 35. ♖a4 ♖b5−+** [♖ 6/h] **36. ♖d4 ♔f8 37. ♖d7 ♖c5 38. ♔f2 ♖c3 39. e5 b5 40. e6 b4 41. ♖f7 ♔e8 42. ♖g7 b3 43. ♔e2 ♖c6 44. ♔d3 b2 45. ♖g8 ♔e7 46. ♖b8 ♖b6 47. ♖b6 cb6 48. ♔c2 ♔e6 0 : 1** **[Je. Piket]**

487. **E 11**

SKEMBRIS 2565 − TIVJAKOV 2595
Gausdal 1993

1. d4 ♘f6 2. c4 e6 3. g3 d5 4. ♘f3 ♗b4!? 5. ♗d2 ♗e7 6. ♗g2 c6!? [△ 7. 0−0 dc4∞] **7. ♕c2 b6!?** [7... 0−0; 7... ♘bd7] **8. 0−0 ♗b7** [8... ♘bd7!? △ ♗a6] **9. ♖d1** [9. ♘e5 ♘fd7; 9... ♘bd7!? △ 10. cd5 cd5 11. ♘c6 ♕c7; 9. ♗f4; 9. b3] **0−0** [9... ♘bd7!?=] **10. ♘e5 N** [10. ♗f4 − 47/598, E 06; 10. b3 ♘bd7!? △ c5=] **♘fd7** [10... ♘bd7?! 11. cd5 cd5 (11... ♘e5 12. de5 ♘d5 13. e4±) 12. ♘c6±] **11. ♘d3** [11. ♘d7 ♘d7 12. cd5 (12. e4=) cd5 13. ♘c3=] **♘a6!?** [11... ♗f6 12. ♗b4 (12. e3 ♘a6) ♖e8 13. e3 △ 13... ♘a6 14. ♗d6⩲; 11... a5!? △ 12... a4, 12... ♘a6] **12. a3** [12. e4 de4 13. ♗e4 ♘f6 ×♗e4, d4; 12. cd5 cd5 13. ♘c3=; 12... ed5!? △ ♘c7-e6, △ ♗f6, c5↑⊞; 12. b3 ⤢a1-h8; 12. ♗e1!? △ ♘d2=; 12. ♗e3!? △ ♘d2, ♖ac1=] **♖c8** [12... c5?! 13. cd5! ed5 (13... cd4? 14.

d6+−; 13... ♗d5 14. ♗d5 ed5 ×d5) 14. ♘c3±↑⊞ ×d5; 14. ♘f4!?; 12... ♗f6!? △ 13... c5, 13... ♕e7, 13... ♖c8] **13. ♗e3** [13. b4? ♗f6 △ c5∓; 13. ♗e1 ×♗e1; 13. cd5 cd5 14. ♘c3=; 13... ed5! △ ♗f6, c5, △ ♘c7-e6∓↑] **♗f6** [13... c5 14. dc5□ *a)* 14... bc5 15. ♘f4 ♘b6 (15... ♘f6 16. ♘c3 △ ♕b3) 16. cd5 ed5 17. ♘c3 ♘c7 18. ♕b3 (→×d5) c4 19. ♕a2 △ ♗b6, ♘d5; 15. cd5 △ ♘f4, ♘c3↑⊞, →×d5; *b)* 14... ♘ac5 15. cd5! (15. ♘c5?! ♗c5 16. ♗c5 ♖c5∓) ed5=; *c)* 14... ♘dc5 15. cd5! (15. ♘c5 ♗c5!∓) ed5 △ ♘e4=] **14. ♘d2** [14. b4? c5] **♕e7** [14... c5 15. dc5□ *a)* 15... bc5 16. ♘f4↑⊞, →×c5, d5, △ 16... ♘b6 17. cd5 ed5 18. ♘e4 ♗e7 (18... ♗e5 19. ♘d3; 19. ♘c5) 19. ♘c3; *b)* 15... ♘ac5 16. cd5 (16. ♘c5 ♘c5 − 15... ♘dc5) ♘d3 17. ♕d3 ♗b2∞; *c)* 15... ♘dc5 16. ♘c5 (16. cd5 ♘d3!? 17. ♕d3 ♗b2; 16... ed5; 16... ♗d5) ♘c5 17. cd5□ ♗d5 (17... ed5 18. ♘f3 △ 18... ♘e4 19. ♕b3; 19. ♕b1∞) 18. ♗d5 ♕d5 (△ 19. ♘c4 ♕e4!∓⊥) 19. ♖ac1!=] **15. ♖ac1 c5!?** [15... ♖fd8 16. b4=] **16. dc5□ bc5!?** [16... ♘dc5 17. ♘c5 ♘c5 18. cd5 ed5=] **17. ♘b3** [17. ♘f4 ♘b6∓ △ d4⊞; 17. b4!?∞⇆《] **♘b6! 18. ♘a5?!** [18. cd5 c4□ 19. d6□ ♕d7□ 20. ♗b7□ cb3□ (20... cd3 21. ♕d3 ♕b7 22. ♘a5+−; 20... ♕b7 21. ♘a5 cd3 22. ♕d3+−) *a)* 21. ♕b3 ♕b7∓; *b)* 21. ♕c8 ♖c8 22. ♖c8 (22. ♗c8 ♘c8∓; 22. ♗a6 ♖c1∓) ♘c8 23. ♗a6 ♘d6∓; *c)* 21. ♗c8□ bc2□ 22. ♗d7 cd1♕ 23. ♖d1 ♘d7 24. ♗a7∞] **♗a8!∓ 19. cd5?!** [19. ♗d2∓ △ 19... d4 20. b4⇆《] **ed5∓ 20. ♗c5** [20. ♘c5 d4−+; 20. ♗h3 d4! 21. ♗c8 ♖c8−+→⊞, ↗h1-a8] **♘c5 21. ♘c5 ♘c4!** [21... ♗b2 22. ♕b2 ♖c5 23. ♖c5 ♕c5∓] **22. ♘d3** [22. b4 ♘a5 23. ba5 ♖c7!! 24. ♗d5 ♖fc8−+ △ 25. ♗a8 ♖c5; 22. ♘cb3 ♘a5 23. ♕c8 ♘b3−+; 22. ♘ab3 ♗b2−+; 22. ♘a4 ♘b2 (22... ♘b6 23. ♘c5□; 22... ♗g5 23. e3 ♘e3 24. ♕c8 ♘d1−+; 23. f4□∞ △ 23... ♘e3 24. ♕c8 ♘d1 25. ♕c5□) 23. ♕c8 ♘d1∓ △ 24. ♕c2 ♘f2! (Skembris) 25. ♔f2 ♗d4 26. ♔e1 (26. ♔f1 ♕e3−+) ♕e3−+] **♘b2 23. ♕c8 ♘d1−+** [×a3, e2, ♘a5, c3] **24. ♘c6⊕** [24. e3 ♕a3 25. ♕c2 ♘e3; 24. ♕c2 ♘c3 25. e3 ♕a3 26. ♘b3] **♕e2 25. ♕f5 ♘c3 26. ♘ce5 ♕d2 27. ♖e1?!** [27. ♖f1 ♕g5! 28. ♕g5 ♗g5] **♗e5 28. ♖e5 ♘e2 29. ♖e2** [29. ♔f1 ♘d4] **♕e2 30. h4** [30. ♗d5 g6] **g6 0 : 1** **[Tivjakov]**

488.* **E 11**

RAZUVAEV 2525 − RO. MANDL 2390
Dortmund (open) 1993

1. d4 ♘f6 2. c4 e6 3. ♘f3 ♗b4 4. ♗d2 c5 5. ♗b4 [RR 5. g3 ♗d2 6. ♘bd2 cd4 7. ♘d4 ♕b6 *a)* 8. ♘2b3 d5 9. c5 ♕b4= △ 10. ♕d2 ♕d2 11. ♘d2 ♗d7; *b)* 8. ♘4b3 ♕c6 9. e4 (9. f3 0−0 10. ♖c1 a6 △ b6, ♗b7, d6=) ♘e4 10. ♘d4 (10. ♗g2 ♘c3!) *b1)* 10... ♘f2 11. ♔f2 (11. ♘c6 ♘d1 12. ♘b8 ♘e3−+) ♕h1 12. ♘4f3! g5 (12... d5 13. ♕c2 △ ♖e1, ♗g2+−) 13. ♘e4=∞→; *b2)* 10... ♘c3 11. ♘c6 ♘d1 12. ♘b8 ♘b2 13. a4 d5! 14. cd5 ed5 15. ♖a2 ♘c4 16. ♘a6! ba6 17. ♘c4 dc4 18. ♗c4=; *c)* 8. ♘b5!? N a6 (8... ♕c6 9. e4! △ 9... ♘e4? 10. ♗g2±) 9. ♘c3 ♕c6 (9... ♕b2 10. ♘a4 △ ♗g2, ♖b1, c5=∞↑《) 10. e4 d6 (10... 0−0 11. ♗g2 b5 12. 0−0 ♗b7; 11. ♖c1) 11. ♗g2 0−0 (11... b5? 12. cb5 ab5 13. ♖c1 ♕b7 14. ♘b5+−) 12. 0−0 ♕c7 13. ♔h1!? (13. ♖c1!?) ♘c6 (13... b6 14. g4 △ f4↑) 14. ♖c1 ♗d7 15. f4 (15. g4 ♖fc8 16. g5 ♘e8±) ♖ac8 16. g4! h6 17. ♘b3! (Judasin 2610 − Izeta 2515, Dos Hermanas 1993) ♘e7! △ ♘g6⩲⇆ Judasin] **cb4 6. g3 0−0 7. ♗g2 d6 8. ♘bd2 ♖e8 9. ♘f1 ♕a5 N** [9... a5 − 52/(504)] **10. ♘3d2** [10. ♘e3!? b3 11. ♕d2 ♕d2 12. ♘d2 ba2 13. ♖a2 ♘c6 14. ♗c6!⩲] **e5 11. ♘b3 ♕c7 12. ♘e3 a5 13. de5 de5 14. 0−0 a4 15. ♘d2 ♘c6 16. ♘d5 ♕d8** [16... ♘d5 17. cd5 ♘d4 18. e3±] **17. ♘e4 ♘e4 18. ♗e4 ♗g4!** [18... f5 19. ♗g2 e4 20. ♕d2±] **19. ♖e1 ♘d4 20. ♕d3 f5 21. ♗g2** [△ 22. h3 ♗h5 23. e3±] **b3 22. h3** [22. ab3 ♘b3 23. ♖ad1 ♘c5⩲] **♗h5 23. ab3 ♘b3** [23... ab3 24. ♖a8 ♕a8 25. e3 (25. ♘c7? ♕a5!) ♘c2 26. ♖f1 ♕a2 27. ♕f5 ♗g6 28. ♘e7 ♖e7 29. ♗d5+−] **24. ♖ad1 e4** [⌓ 24... ♗g6 25. ♕c3 ♕a5 26. ♕a5 ♖a5 27. ♘c7 ♖c8 28. ♗d5±] **25. ♕e3 ♕a5** [25... ♖a6 26. ♘f4±] **26. ♕g5 ♗g6 27. ♘e7 ♔f7** [27... ♔h8 28. ♘g6±; 28.

h4±] **28. ♘g6 hg6 29. ♖d7 ♔f8** [29... ♔g8 30. ♕g6+−] **30. ♖ed1** [30. ♕g6 ♕e1 31. ♔h2 ♖e7∞] **♖a6?** [30... ♘c5□ 31. ♖7d6±] **31. ♕h4 ♔g8 32. ♖g7!**
1 : 0 **[Razuvaev]**

489. !N **E 12**

KRAMNIK 2685 − TIMMAN 2635
Linares 1993

1. d4 ♘f6 2. c4 e6 3. ♘f3 b6 4. a3 c5 5. d5 ♗a6 6. ♕c2 ed5 7. cd5 g6 8. ♘c3 ♗g7 9. g3 0−0 10. ♗g2 d6 11. 0−0 ♘bd7 12. ♖e1 ♖e8 13. ♗f4?! [13. h3] **♕e7 14. e4?!** [14. h3] **♘g4∓ 15. ♗g5!□ N** [15. ♖ad1 − 30/593] **f6 16. ♗f4 ♘ge5 17. ♘e5 ♘e5 18. ♖ad1 ♕d7 19. b3 ♖e7?!** [⌓ 19... ♖ac8∓] **20. ♗c1 c4 21. bc4 ♖c8 22. ♕b1!∞ ♖c4** [⌓ 22... ♘c4] **23. ♘a2 ♖c5** [⌓ 23... ♖c8] **24. ♘b4 ♗b5 25. ♗e3 ♖c8 26. ♗d4± ♖ee8 27. f4 ♘c4 28. ♕a1 ♖f8 29. ♖c1 ♘a5 30. ♖c8 ♕c8 31. ♕b2 ♘c4 32. ♕c3 ♘a5 33. ♖c1 ♕c3 34. ♖c3 ♗c4!□ 35. ♗h3** [35. ♘c6 ♘c6 36. dc6 ♗e6±] **b5** [△ 36. ♗a7 f5] **36. a4! ♘b3!□ 37. ♗e6?** [37. ♗a7 △ 37... f5 38. e5±, △ 37... ♘d2 38. ab5 ♗b5 39. ♗g2] **♔h8 38. ♗a7 ♘d2 39. ab5 ♗b5 40. ♖c7± ♖a8?** [⌓ 40... ♘e4] **41. ♖b7 ♗c4 42. ♖c7 ♗b5 43. g4!?** [43. ♘c6 △ ♘b8±] **g5□ 44. ♘c6 gf4 45. ♘d4?!** [45. ♘b8! ♗f8□±] **♗d3 46. ♗f5 ♗e4 47. ♘e6 ♗f5 48. gf5 ♗h6 49. ♔f2 ♔g8 50. h4 ♘c4!□= 51. ♖c4 ♖a7 52. ♖c8 ♔f7 53. ♘d8 ♔g7 54. ♘e6 ♔f7 55. ♘d8 ♔g7 56. ♖c7 ♖c7 57. ♘e6 ♔f7 58. ♘c7 f3?!** [⌓ 58... ♗g5!!= Ljubojević] **59. ♔f3 ♗d2** [♘♗ 5/d] **60. ♔e2 ♗f4 61. ♘e6 ♗c1 62. h5 ♔e7 63. ♔d3 ♗h6 64. ♔c4 ♗e3 65. ♔b5 ♔d7 66. ♔a6** [⌓ 66. ♔a5 ♔c8 67. ♔a6 ♗f2 68. ♘f8 h6 69. ♘g6 ♗e3 70. ♘h4 ♔c7 71. ♘f3 ♗f2 72. ♘h2 ♗e3 73. ♘g4 ♗g5 74. ♔a7⊙ ♗f4 75. ♘f6 ♔d8= Kramnik] **♔c8 67. ♘f8 ♗h6!= 68. ♘e6 ♗e3 69. ♘f8 ♗h6 70. ♘h7 ♗g7 71. ♔b5 ♔d8□ 72. h6 ♗h6 73. ♘f6 ♗f4 74. ♔c4 ♔e7 75. ♘e4 ♔f7 76. ♔d3 ♔g7 77. ♔e2 ♔h6 78. ♔f3 ♗h2 79. ♔g4 ♗e5⊙ 80. ♘d2 ♗d4 81. ♘e4 ♗e5 82. ♘d6** **1/2 : 1/2**
[Timman]

490. **E 12**

ŠIROV 2670 − AN. KARPOV 2725
Linares 1993

1. d4 ♘f6 2. c4 e6 3. ♘f3 b6 4. a3 ♗a6 5. ♕b3 d5 6. cd5 ♕d5!? N [6... ed5 − 47/(612)] **7. ♕c2** [7. ♕d5 ed5 (7... ♘d5 8. e4 ♗f1 9. ♖f1 ♘f6 10. ♘c3±) 8. ♗f4 c6=] **c5 8. ♘c3 ♕d7!** [8... ♕b7 9. dc5 ♗c5 10. g3±] **9. dc5** [9. ♘e5 ♕d4 10. e3 ♕e5 11. ♗a6 ♘a6 12. ♕a4 ♘d7 13. ♕a6 ♗e7∓; 9. ♗g5 cd4 10. ♘e5 (10. ♖d1 ♘c6=) ♕b7 11. ♕a4 (11. ♗f6 gf6 12. ♕a4 b5 13. ♕d4 fe5−+) ♘fd7!] **♗c5 10. g3 ♗b7 11. ♗g2 ♘c6** [11... 0−0 12. 0−0 ♖c8 13. ♖d1 ♕e8=] **12. 0−0 ♘d4 13. ♘d4 ♗g2 14. ♔g2** [14. ♘e6? ♗f1 15. ♘g7 ♔f8 16. ♗h6 ♗f2!] **♗d4 15. ♖d1 ♕c6 16. f3 ♗e5** [16... ♗c3 17. ♗d2 ♖c8 (17... ♘d5?! 18. e4 ♕b5 19. ed5 ♕e2 20. ♔h3!) 18. ♗c3 ♘d5 19. ♖d3±] **17. ♗g5 0−0 18. ♖ac1 ♖ad8 19. ♖d8 ♖d8 20. ♘e4 ♕c2 21. ♖c2 ♘d5! 22. ♘f2 f6 23. ♗d2 ♖d7 24. ♖c8 ♔f7 25. ♘d3 ♗d6 26. ♔f2 ♘e7 27. ♖c2** [27. ♖a8 ♘c6 △ ♖d8]
1/2 : 1/2 **[An. Karpov]**

491. **E 12**

BAREEV 2670 − BELJAVSKIJ 2610
Linares 1993

1. d4 ♘f6 2. c4 e6 3. ♘f3 b6 4. a3 ♗a6 5. ♕c2 ♗b7 6. ♘c3 c5 7. dc5 bc5 8. ♗f4 ♗f3!? 9. gf3 ♘c6 10. e3 [10. ♗g2 ♘h5 11. ♗d2 ♘d4 12. ♕d3 ♖b8∞] **♘h5 N** [10... ♗e7] **11. ♗g3 ♘g3 12. hg3 ♖b8= 13. f4 g6** [13... ♕b6 14. ♘a4 ♕a5 15. ♔e2∞] **14. ♗g2 ♘a5 15. ♘e4! ♗g7 16. ♘d6 ♔e7 17. ♖d1 ♖b2** [17... ♗b2 18. ♔f1∞̄; 17... ♕b6 18. ♕a4 ♕b2 19. 0−0 △ ♘f7∞̄] **18. ♕a4 ♗c3 19. ♔f1 ♗d2** [19... f5 20. ♘f7 ♔f7 21. ♖d7 ♔f6 22. ♖d8 ♖d8 23. ♗f3 (23. ♖h7? ♖b1 24. ♔e2 ♖d2 25. ♔f3 ♖bb2−+) h5 (23... ♖dd2? 24. ♕e8) 24. ♔g2 ♖dd2 25. ♖f1 ♔e7 26. ♔g1=] **20. ♘e4 ♘b3 21. ♕a7 ♕a5 22. ♕b7 ♕a4?** [22... f5 23. ♘g5 ♕c3 24. ♗c6 ♕d3 25. ♔g2 ♕d6 26. ♗b5 h5 (26... h6

27. ♕a7) 27. a4 ♖b8 28. ♕a7∞] **23. ♔g1** [23. ♖d2? ♖b1−+] **♕c6** [23... ♕c4? 24. ♖d2 ♕c1 25. ♔h2 ♘d2 26. ♕c7+−] **24. ♕c6 dc6 25. ♖h6!± ♗a5 26. g4 ♖a2 27. f5!** [27. g5!? ♖a3 28. ♖d3 (28. ♘f6 ♘d2) ♖d8] **ef5 28. gf5 ♘d2 29. ♘d2 ♗d2** [29... ♖d2 30. ♖d2 ♗d2 31. fg6 fg6 32. ♗c6±] **30. fg6 fg6 31. ♗c6 ♔f6 32. ♔h1?** [32. a4 ♔g7 33. ♖h4±] **♗c3 33. ♖d6 ♔g7 34. ♖h2 ♖a3 35. ♖d7 ♔f6 36. ♗d5** [36. ♖hh7⩲] **♖a1** [36... h5 37. ♖g2 (37. ♖d6 ♔g7 38. ♖g2 ♖a1=) g5 38. ♖d6 ♔f5=] **37. ♔g2 h5 38. ♖h3 h4?⊕** [38... ♖a6! 39. ♖g3 (39. ♖f7 ♔g5=) g5=] **39. ♖f7 ♔e5** [39... ♔g5 40. f4 ♔h5 41. ♗f3+−] **40. f4 ♔d6 41. e4+− ♖a2 42. ♔f1 ♗e5** [42... ♖a1 43. ♔e2 ♖a2 44. ♔f3 △ e5+−] **43. fe5 ♔e5 44. ♖f2! ♖a1 45. ♔g2 ♖h5 46. ♔h2 ♖g5 47. ♖h4 ♖gg1 48. ♖g2 1 : 0** **[Bareev]**

Long-range exchange sacrifice

492.* !N **E 12**

CH. LUTZ 2550 − AN. KARPOV 2725

Dortmund 1993

1. d4 ♘f6 2. c4 e6 3. ♘f3 b6 4. a3 ♗a6 5. ♕c2 ♗b7 6. ♘c3 c5 7. e4 cd4 8. ♘d4 ♘c6 [RR 8... ♗c5 9. ♘b3 ♘c6 10. ♗f4 d6!? N (10... ♗e7 − 56/581) 11. ♖d1 e5 12. ♗g5 (12. ♗g3) h6 13. ♗h4 (13. ♘c5 bc5 14. ♘b5? hg5 15. ♘d6 ♔f8 16. ♘b7 ♕b6∓) g5 14. ♗g3 *a)* 14... ♕e7?! 15. ♘d5!? ♘d5 16. cd5 ♘d4 17. ♘d4 ♗d4 (Gofshtein 2560 − Kosashvili 2490, Israel 1993) 18. ♖d4! ed4 19. ♕a4=∞; *b)* 14... ♘d4!? 15. ♘d4 ♗d4⇆; *c)* 14... 0−0∞ Gofshtein] **9. ♘c6 ♗c6 10. ♗f4 ♘h5 11. ♗e3 ♕b8! N** [11... ♗c5 − 45/(632)] **12. g3 f5 13. 0-0-0 ♘f6 14. ♗d3 ♕b7 15. f3** [15. ♘d5 fe4 16. ♗e4 ed5 17. cd5 ♘d5∓] **fe4** [15... ♗e7 16. ♖hf1 fe4 17. ♘e4⩲] **16. ♘e4 ♘e4** [16... ♗e4!? 17. fe4 ♘g4⇆] **17. fe4** [17. ♗e4 ♗e4 18. fe4 (18. ♕e4? ♕e4 19. fe4 ♖c8∓) ♗e7 19. ♖hf1 ♖f8∞] **♗d6** [17... e5 18. ♖hf1 d6∞] **18. ♖hf1 ♗e5 19. ♗f4 ♕b8** [19... ♕c7 20. ♕c3! d6 21. ♗e5±] **20. ♕e2 0−0 21. ♕h5**

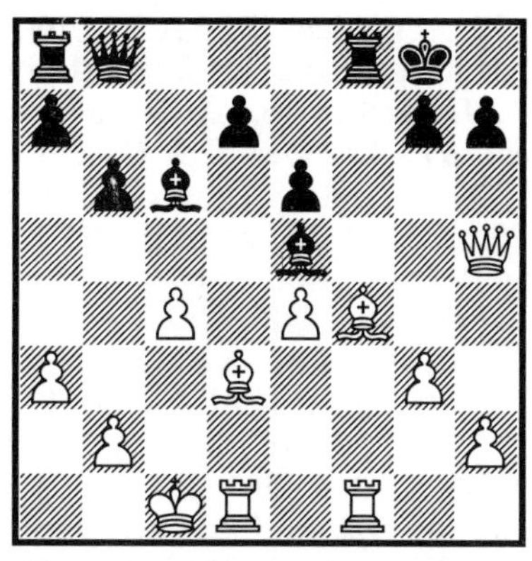

21... ♖f4! 22. gf4 ♗f4 23. ♔b1 ♕e5 24. ♕e5 ♗e5 25. h3 a5 26. b3 d6! 27. ♖d2 ♗e8 28. ♔c2 ♗g6 29. ♖df2 ♖c8! 30. ♔d1 ♗d4 31. ♖a2 ♖c5 32. ♖g2 [32. b4 ♖g5∓] **♖h5 33. ♖f3 ♗e8 34. ♔c2 g6 35. ♗e2 ♖e5 36. ♗d3 ♔g7 37. ♖g4 g5 38. ♖f1** [38. h4 ♗h5 39. ♖fg3 ♗g4 40. ♖g4 h5 (40... ♗e3 41. hg5 ♗g5∓) 41. ♖g5 ♖g5 42. hg5 h4∓; 38. ♖fg3!?] **♗c5 39. ♔b2** [39. a4] **♗g6** [39... ♗h5 40. ♖g2 ♗g6 41. ♖e2] **40. h4 gh4 41. ♖h4 ♖g5** [41... d5!−+] **42. ♖h2 ♖g3 43. ♗c2 ♗d4 44. ♔c1 a4 45. ba4 ♖a3 46. ♔d2 ♖g3 47. ♗d3 ♖g5 48. ♖fh1 ♗e5 49. ♖h3 ♗d4** [49... ♖g2 50. ♔d1 ♖a2 51. ♗c2∓] **50. ♖3h2 ♖g3 51. ♖f1 ♗f6 52. ♖b1 ♗g5 53. ♔c2 ♗e3 54. ♖a1 ♗g1 55. ♖d2 ♔f6! 56. a5 ba5 57. ♖a5 ♗c5 58. ♖a1 ♔e5 59. ♖f1 ♗g1** [△ h5-h4-h3] **60. ♖dd1 ♗e3 61. ♖f8 ♖g2 62. ♔b3 ♖h2! 63. ♗b1 ♗h5 64. ♖e1 ♗f2 65. ♖f1 ♗c5 66. ♖e1 ♗e2 67. ♗a2 ♖h3 68. ♔b2 ♗a3 69. ♔a1 ♗d3 70. ♗b1 ♗b4! 71. ♖c1 ♗d2 72. ♖d1 ♗c3 73. ♔a2 ♗c4 74. ♔a3 ♗e2 0 : 1 [An. Karpov]**

493. !N **E 12**

KRAMNIK 2685 − CH. LUTZ 2550

Dortmund 1993

1. d4 ♘f6 2. c4 e6 3. ♘f3 b6 4. a3 ♗a6 5. ♕c2 ♗b7 6. ♘c3 c5 7. e4 cd4 8. ♘d4 ♘c6 9. ♘c6 ♗c6 10. ♗f4 ♘h5 11. ♗e3 ♕b8 12. 0-0-0! N ♗d6 [12... ♗c5 13. ♗c5 bc5 14. g3±] **13. g3 ♗e5 14. ♗d3 ♕b7** [14... ♘f6 15. f4! ♗c3 16. ♕c3 ♕b7 (16...

♗e4 17. ♗e4 ♘e4 18. ♕g7±; 16... 0–0 17. ♗d4±) 17. ♖he1] **15. ♖he1 ♘f6 16. f4!** [16. f3 ♖c8∞; 16. ♗d2 ♘g4 17. ♖e2 ♗d4!∞] **♗c3 17. ♕c3 ♖c8** [17... 0–0 18. ♗d4±; 17... ♗e4 18. ♗e4 ♕e4 19. ♗b6 ♕c6 20. ♗d4±] **18. e5?** [18. b3 b5!□∞; 18. ♗d4! ♘e4 (18... ♗e4 19. ♗f6 ♗d3 20. ♖d3 gf6 21. ♕f6 ♖c4 22. ♔b1 ♖f8 23. f5±→) 19. ♗e4 ♗e4 20. ♗g7 ♖g8 21. ♗f6! d5 22. ♖d4±] **♘d5∞ 19. ♕d4** [19. ♕c2 ♘e3 20. ♖e3 b5∞ △ 21. c5 b4!] **♗a4□** [19... ♘e3 20. ♖e3 b5 21. c5±] **20. ♖d2 b5** [20... ♘e3 21. ♕e3 ♗b3 (21... b5 22. c5 ♕d5 23. b4!±) 22. ♔b1 ♗c4 23. ♗e4!?∞̅] **21. ♔b1** [21. c5 ♗b3! 22. ♔b1 a5∞ △ b4; 21. ♕a7 ♕a7 22. ♗a7 bc4 23. ♗e4 c3 24. ♖d4 ♗b3=] **bc4** [21... ♘e3? 22. ♖e3 bc4 (22... ♗b3?? 23. ♗e4) 23. ♗c4 0–0 24. ♗e6±] **22. ♗c4 ♗b3 23. ♗d5 ♗d5 24. ♕b4** [24. ♕a7?? ♕b3] **♕b4** [24... ♕c7?! 25. ♖d5! ed5 26. ♖c1 ♕b8 27. ♖c8 ♕c8 28. ♗a7↑] **25. ab4 a6= 26. ♗c5 ♔d8 27. ♗b6 ♔e7 28. ♗c5 ♔d8 29. f5 ♔c7 30. fe6 fe6 31. ♖f2 ♔c6 32. ♖f7 1/2 : 1/2 [Kramnik]**

494.* **E 12**

POLULJAHOV 2515 — SAVON 2415

Rossija 1993

1. d4 ♘f6 2. ♘f3 b6 3. c4 e6 4. ♘c3 ♗b7 5. a3 ♘e4 6. ♘e4 ♗e4 7. ♘d2 ♗b7 8. e4 ♕f6 9. e5 ♕d8 10. ♘f3 d6 N [10... d5 — 35/601] **11. ♗f4 ♘d7 12. ♕c2! ♗e7 13. ♖d1** [13. 0-0-0!?] **g5?!** [13... 0–0?! 14. h4! h6? 15. ♘g5! hg5 (15... g6 16. ♘e6) 16. hg5 g6 17. ♖d3! ♗g5 (17... ♖e8 18. ♖dh3 ♘f8 19. ♖h8 ♔g7 20. ♕c3 △ ♕h3+–) 18. ♖dh3 f5 19. ef6 ♕f6 20. ♗g5 ♕g5 21. ♖g3 ♕f5 22. ♗d3 ♕a5 23. ♔f1→; ⌓ 14... ♗f3; 13... d5 14. h4! h6 15. cd5 (15. ♖h3!?) ♗d5 16. ♗c4 c6 17. ♗d5?! cd5 18. ♖c1 b5!= Poluljahov 2515 — Gorbatov 2385, Katowice 1993; ⌓ 17. ♖h3] **14. ♗g3 d5** [14... h5 15. h4 (15. h3 d5) g4 (15... ♗f3 16. gf3 gh4 17. ♗h2±) 16. ♘g5 (16. ♘d2!? △ 16... d5 17. cd5 ♗d5 18. ♘e4) de5 (16... ♗g5 17. hg5 de5 18. g6!) 17. ♗e5!±] **15. h4 g4 16. ♘g5! ♘f8** [△ h6; 16... h6 17. ♘e6 fe6 18. ♕g6 ♔f8 19. ♗f4±; 16... dc4 17. ♗c4 ♗g2 18. ♖h2 ♗g5 19. ♖g2 ♗h4 20. d5±] **17. cd5 ♕d5 18. ♗c4!** [18. ♕c7?? h6 19. ♗b5 ♕b5 20. ♕b7 ♕d5!–+] **♕g2** [18... ♕d7 19. ♘e4±; 18... ♕a5 19. b4 ♕a3 20. ♗b5 ♘d7 21. 0–0∞̅↑] **19. ♖h2 ♕c6 20. d5?** [20. ♕b3! ♕d7 21. ♗b5 c6 (21... ♗c6 22. d5!! ♗b5 23. de6 ♘e6 24. ♖d7 ♗d7 25. f4!± △ 25... ♗g5 26. hg5 ♘d4 27. ♕d5 ♘f3 28. ♔f2 c6 29. ♕d6 ♘h2 30. f5!+–) 22. d5!! *a)* 22... cb5 23. de6 ♕d1 24. ♕d1+–; *b)* 22... ed5 23. ♖d5 ♕c8 24. ♖d6! ♘e6 (24... ♗d6 25. ♕f7 ♔d8 26. ed6+–→; 24... ♗g5 25. ♗c4!+–→; 24... ♕f5 25. ♖c6 ♘d7 26. ♖c7+–) 25. ♖e6! fe6 26. ♗c4±→; *c)* 22... ♕c8 23. de6! ♘e6 (23... ♗g5 24. ef7 ♔e7 25. ♗e2 ♗h6 26. ♖d6 ♗g7 27. h5+–) 24. ♗c4±↑] **ed5 21. ♖d5** [21. ♗d5?? ♗b4!] **♗a6!□ 22. ♖d4 ♗c4 23. ♖c4 ♕d5 24. ♖c7 ♗g5 25. hg5 ♘e6** [26. ♖c8 ♖c8 27. ♕c8 ♔e7! 28. ♕h8 ♕e4=] **1/2 : 1/2 [Poluljahov]**

495.** **E 12**

KRAMNIK 2625 — EHLVEST 2635

Moskva (open) 1992

1. d4 e6 2. c4 b6 3. ♘c3 ♗b7 4. a3 d5 5. cd5 ed5 6. ♘f3 ♘f6 7. ♕a4 [RR 7. g3 ♗e7 8. ♕a4 c6 9. ♗g2 0–0 10. ♗f4 ♘h5 11. ♗b8 ♕b8 12. ♘e5 N (12. 0–0 — 49/587) ♕e8 13. 0–0 ♗d6 14. f4 (14. ♘d3!? △ b4⩲) ♘f6 15. ♕b3 ♖d8 16. ♖ad1 ♕e7 17. ♕a4?! b5!∞ Serebrjanik; 17. e4!⩲ Serebrjanik 2425 — Y. Grünfeld 2510, Israel 1992] **c6 8. ♗g5 ♗e7 9. e3 0–0 10. ♗d3 ♘bd7** [RR 10... ♘e4 11. ♗e4 ♗g5 12. ♘g5 ♕g5 13. ♗f3 ♘a6 14. 0–0 ♘c7 N (14... ♖fd8 — 40/649) 15. ♖ac1 ♖fd8 16. g3 ♘e6 17. ♗g2 ♕e7 18. ♖fd1 h6 19. b4 a5 20. b5 c5 21. dc5 ♘c5 22. ♕c2 ♘e4 23. ♕b2 ♖d6= Bareev 2670 — R. Hübner 2620, München 1993] **11. ♖d1 c5 12. ♘e5 h6** [12... ♘e5 13. de5 ♘h5 14. h4!±] **13. ♗f4** [13. ♗h4 ♘e5 14. de5 ♘h5∞] **a6 14. ♗b1** [14. ♘c6 ♕e8 15. 0–0 b5 16. ♘e7 ♕e7 17. ♕c2 c4∞] **♖e8 15. 0–0 N** [15. ♘d7 ♕d7 (15... ♘d7 — 47/(624)) 16. ♕d7 ♘d7 17. dc5 d4 18. ♖d4 ♘c5 19.

0–0 ♘e6=∞] **b5 16. ♕c2 c4 17. f3 ♘f8**∞ **18. ♘e2!?** [18. e4 ♕b6 △ ♖ad8∞] **♘6d7 19. ♘d7** [19. ♘g3 ♘e5! 20. ♗e5 (20. de5 g5!) ♗g5∞] **♕d7 20. e4 b4?!** [20... a5! △ b4⇆] **21. ab4 ♗b4 22. ♘g3 a5! 23. e5 ♗c6 24. ♘h5 ♖a6! 25. ♕f2 ♗b5** [×♖f1] **26. e6!? ♖ee6! 27. ♗f5 ♕e7 28. ♗e6 ♖e6 29. ♕g3 ♖g6** [30. ♕f2 ♘e6 31. ♗d2 ♗d2 32. ♕d2 c3 33. ♕c3 ♗f1=] **1/2 : 1/2 [Ehlvest]**

496. E 12

BAREEV 2670 – V. SALOV 2660
Linares 1993

1. d4 ♘f6 2. c4 e6 3. ♘f3 b6 4. ♘c3 ♗b7 5. a3 d5 6. ♕c2 ♗e7 7. cd5 ♘d5 8. ♗d2 ♘d7 9. e4 ♘c3 10. ♗c3 0–0 11. ♖d1 c5!? N [11... ♕c8 – 50/535] **12. ♗b5** [12. dc5 ♕c8 13. cb6 ab6 14. ♘d2 (14. ♗e2 ♘c5 15. ♘d2 ♘a4=∞) ♗f6 15. ♖c1 ♗c3 16. ♕c3 ♘c5↑] **♕c8 13. d5** [13. ♗d7 ♕d7 14. dc5 ♕b5=∞] **ed5 14. ed5 ♗a6 15. a4** [15. ♕a4!?] **♗b5 16. ab5 a6 17. 0–0 ab5 18. ♕e2 b4 19. ♗g7?** [19. ♗b4 ♗f6 20. ♗c3 ♕a6=] **♖e8 20. ♗h6** [20. ♘e5 ♘e5 21. ♗e5 ♗d6 22. f4 f6–+] **♗g5 21. ♕e8□ ♕e8 22. ♗g5 f6 23. ♗f4 ♕f7∓ 24. ♖fe1 ♖e8 25. d6 c4 26. ♘d4!** [26. ♖e8 ♕e8 27. ♖e1 ♕a8–+] **c3 27. bc3 bc3 28. ♘f5 ♖e1 29. ♖e1 ♕h5 30. ♘h6 ♔f8 31. h3!□** [31. g4 ♕d5–+] **c2?** [31... ♘e5! 32. ♘g4 ♕f5! (32... ♘g4?? 33. d7+–) 33. ♗e5 fe5 34. ♘e5 c2 35. d7 ♔e7–+] **32. ♘g4 ♘e5 33. ♗e5 fe5** [♕ 5/e] **34. ♖c1 ♕f5?** [34... ♕g6 35. d7 ♕d3 36. ♖c2 ♕d7∓] **35. ♘e3 ♕d3 36. ♖c2 ♕d6 37. ♖c8! ♔f7 38. ♖h8! ♕g6** [38... ♕d3!?] **39. ♖b8 ♕b1 40. ♔h2 b5 41. ♘c4!⇆ ♕b4** [41... ♔e6!? 42. ♖b6 ♔d5 43. ♘a3 ♕a2∓] **42. ♘e5** [♕ 5/f] **♔e6 43. ♖e8 ♔d5 44. ♘f3 ♕d6 45. g3 b4 46. ♘d2 ♔c6 47. ♘b3 ♕d1 48. ♖e3 h5 49. ♔g2 ♕d5 50. ♔g1 ♔b5 51. h4= ♔a4 52. ♔h2 ♕b5 53. ♔g1 ♕c6 54. ♔h2 ♕d5 55. ♖d3!** [55. ♔g1?? ♕b3–+] **♕f5 56. ♔g1 ♕g4 57. ♘c5 ♔b5 58. ♘b3 ♕g8 59. ♖f3 ♕d5 60. ♖f5??⊕ ♕f5** [61. ♘d4 ♔c5 62. ♘f5 b3–+] **0 : 1 [V. Salov]**

497. E 12

ŠIROV 2670 – M. GUREVICH 2610
France 1993

1. d4 ♘f6 2. c4 e6 3. ♘f3 b6 4. a3 ♗b7 5. ♘c3 d5 6. cd5 ♘d5 7. e3 g6 8. ♘d5 ♕d5!? 9. ♕c2 ♘d7 10. ♗c4!? N [10. ♕c7 – 37/(569)] **♕c6!? 11. ♕e2** [11. 0–0 b5 12. ♗d3 ♕c2 13. ♗c2 c5⇆] **♗g7 12. ♗d2 0–0 13. 0–0** [13. ♗b4 ♖fd8 14. 0–0 ♕e4!?⇆ △ c5] **♕d6 14. ♖fd1 c5 15. ♗c3** [15. dc5 ♘c5 16. ♗c3 ♕e7 17. ♗g7 ♔g7 18. b4 ♘e4 19. ♕b2 ♕f6 20. ♕f6 (20. ♘e5 ♖fd8⇆) ♘f6=] **♖fd8** [15... ♗f3?! 16. ♕f3 cd4 17. ♗b4?! ♘c5 18. ed4 ♗d4∓ 19. ♖d4? ♕d4 20. ♗c3 ♕h4 21. g3 ♕g5–+; 17. ♗d4±] **16. dc5!? ♕c5 17. ♗b4!?** [△ ♗e7; 17. ♗g7 ♔g7 18. b4 ♕e7=] **♗f3!?** [17... ♕c7 18. ♗d6 ♗f3? 19. ♗c7 ♗e2 20. ♗e2+–] **18. ♕f3** [18. gf3 ♕g5 19. ♔h1 ♘c5∓] **♕c7!=** [18... ♕c4? 19. ♖d7±; 18... ♘e5? 19. ♕a8 ♖a8 20. ♗c5 ♘c4 21. ♗d4±] **19. ♕e2** [19. ♗d6? ♕c4 20. ♗e7 ♘e5–+; 19. ♗e7? ♘e5–+] **♘c5 20. ♖dc1?! ♕e5 21. ♗c3?!** [21. ♗c5 bc5=] **♕f5 22. ♗g7 ♔g7 23. b4 ♘e4** [△ ♖d2] **24. ♖c2** [24. ♗d3 ♕f2 25. ♕f2 ♘f2∓] **♖d6 25. f3 ♘f6∓** [×♔h1, a3, b4] **26. ♖d2 ♖ad8** [26... ♖d2!? 27. ♕d2 ♖c8∓ Širov] **27. ♖d6 ♖d6 28. ♖d1 ♖d1 29. ♕d1 ♕e5 30. ♕d4!** [30. ♕d3 ♕b2∓] **♕d4 31. ed4** [♘♗ 5/d] **♔f8 32. ♔f2 ♔e7 33. ♔e3 ♔d6** [33... ♘e8!? △ ♘d6, g5↑≫] **34. g3 h6 35. ♗b5 ♘d5 36. ♔d3 ♘c7 37. ♗a4 g5 38. ♔c4 a6?! 39. ♔d3 b5 40. ♗d1 ♘d5 41. ♗b3 ♘e7 42. ♗c2 ♘d5 43. ♗b3 ♘e7 44. ♗c2 h5 45. ♔d2 f5 46. ♗d1!? ♔d5 47. ♔c3 ♔d6 48. ♔d2 ♘d5 49. ♗b3 ♘f6 50. ♗d1 ♔d5 51. ♔d3 ♔d6 52. ♔d2 g4 53. ♔e3 ♘d5 54. ♔d2 ♘b6 55. ♗e2 ♔d5 56. ♔c3 ♘a4 57. ♔d3 ♘b2 58. ♔c3 ♘a4 59. ♔d3 ♘b6 60. ♔c3 ♔d6 61. ♔d2 ♔c6 62. ♔c3 ♘c8 63. ♗d1 ♘d6 64. ♗e2 ♘f7 65. ♔d3 ♔d5 66. fg4 hg4 67. ♗f1!?=** [△ ♗g2⇆] **♔c6 68. ♔e3 ♘d6 69. ♗g2 ♔c7 70. ♗f1 ♘e4 71. ♔d3 ♔d7 72. ♔e3 ♘c3 73. ♔d3 ♘e4** [73... ♘b1 74. ♔c2 ♘a3 75. ♔b3 ♘c4 76. ♗c4 bc4 77. ♔c4 ♔c6 78. ♔c3=] **74. ♔e3 ♔e7 75. ♔d3 ♘d6 76. ♔e3 ♘c8 77. h4 gh3 78. ♗h3 ♘b6 79. g4 ♘d5** [79... fg4 80. ♗g4 ♘c4

81. ♔d3 ♔d6 82. ♗f3=] **80. ♔f3 fg4 81. ♗g4 ♔d6 82. ♔e2 ♘b6 83. ♗f3 ♘c4 84. ♔d3!?=** [84. ♗b7 ♔c7 85. ♗a6 ♘d6 86. a4 ba4∓] **♔c7 85. ♗g4 ♔d7 86. ♔c3 ♔e7 87. a4** [87. ♗f3? ♘a3 88. ♗b7 ♘c4 89. ♗a6 ♘d6−+] **♘e3 88. ab5 ab5** [88... ♘g4 89. ba6 ♘e3 90. a7 ♘d5 91. ♔c4 ♔d6 (91... ♘c7? 92. b5 ♘a8 93. ♔c5+−) 92. a8♘ ♔c6 93. b5 ♔b7 94. ♔c5 ♔a8 95. ♔d6 ♘f4 96. ♔e5=] **89. ♗e2 ♘d5 90. ♔d2 e5 91. de5 ♔e6 92. ♗b5 ♔e5**
1/2 : 1/2 **[M. Gurevich]**

498.* **E 12**

KRAMNIK 2685 − CH. LUTZ 2550
Deutschland 1993

1. d4 ♘f6 2. c4 e6 3. ♘f3 b6 4. a3 ♗b7 5. ♘c3 d5 6. cd5 ♘d5 7. e3 g6 8. ♘d5 ed5 9. b4 [9. ♗b5 c6 10. ♗d3 ♗g7 11. e4 de4 12. ♗e4 0−0 N (12... ♗a6 − 55/502) 13. 0−0 ♘d7 14. ♗g5 ♕c7! 15. ♖c1 ♖fe8 16. ♖e1 c5= Kramnik 2685 − Anand 2710, Linares 1993] **♗g7 10. ♗e2 0−0 11. 0−0 N** [11. ♕b3 − 39/(637)] **c6 12. a4 a6** [12... ♘d7 13. a5!?] **13. ♗b2 ♘d7 14. ♕b3 b5 15. a5 ♖e8** [⌓ 15... ♕e7 16. ♖ac1 f5 17. g3 ♔h8] **16. ♖ac1 ♖e6 17. ♖c2 ♕e7 18. ♘e1± ♖e8 19. ♘d3 ♔h8 20. ♖fc1 f5 21. ♗f3 ♕d6?!** [21... ♘f6!? 22. ♘e5 ♖c8 △ ♘e4, ♕e8, ♘d6-c4] **22. g3 g5?!** [×f5; ⌓ 22... ♖8e7 △ ♖e8] **23. ♕c3!±** [△ ♕d2-d1, ♗g2] **♖6e7 24. ♕d2 ♖f8 25. ♗g2 g4?⊕** [25... h5 26. f4! g4 27. ♘e5 ♘e5 28. de5 ♕e6 29. ♕d4± △ ♕b6, ♗d4] **26. h3! ♗f6?** [⌓ 26... gh3±] **27. hg4 fg4 28. ♕d1!+− ♖g7** [28... ♖g8 29. ♖e2 ♖ge8 30. ♖e1+−] **29. e4 de4 30. ♗e4 ♘b8** [30... ♗d4 31. ♘f4 ♖f4 32. gf4+−] **31. ♘f4→ ♖d8** [31... ♖g5 32. ♖c5!? ♖c5 33. ♖c5+−] **32. ♘h5 ♗d4 33. ♖d2 ♗f2 34. ♖f2 ♕d1 35. ♖d1 ♖d1 36. ♔g2** **1 : 0** **[Kramnik]**

499. **E 12**

KAMSKY 2655 − IVANČUK 2710
Linares 1993

1. d4 ♘f6 2. c4 e6 3. ♘f3 b6 4. ♘c3 ♗b4 5. ♗g5 ♗b7 6. e3 ♗c3 7. bc3 d6 8. ♘d2 ♘bd7 9. f3 ♕e7 10. e4 N [10. ♗e2 − 50/538] **h6 11. ♗e3?!** [11. ♗h4] **e5 12. ♗d3**

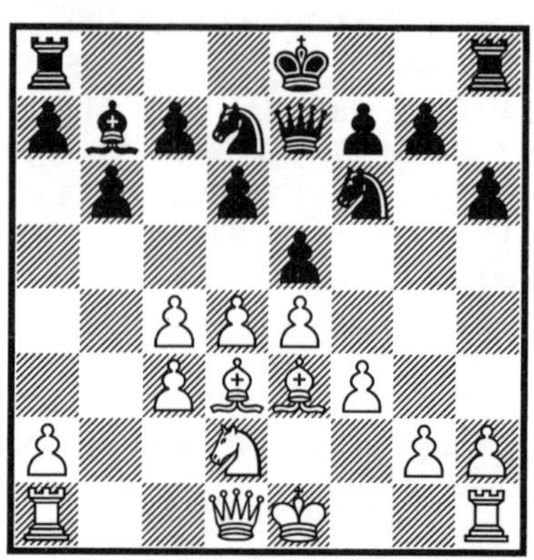

12... d5!∞ 13. 0−0 [13. cd5?! ♘d5!∓; 13. ♕c2 de4 14. ♘e4 ♘e4 15. ♗e4 ed4 16. ♗d4 0−0!] **de4 14. fe4 ed4 15. cd4 ♘e4!? 16. ♘e4** [16. ♗f4 0−0! 17. ♗c7 ♘dc5 18. ♘e4 ♘d3 19. ♕d3 ♕c7=] **♗e4 17. ♖e1!?** [17. ♗g5!? ♕g5 18. ♗e4 ♖d8 △ 0−0∓] **f5□** [17... 0−0? 18. ♗h6±; 17... 0-0-0? 18. ♗e4 ♕e4 19. ♗g5 △ ♗d8±; 17... ♘f6!? 18. ♗e4 ♘e4 19. ♕g4↑] **18. ♗e4 fe4 19. ♕g4!?** [19. ♖f1!? ♘f6 20. ♖f6!?∞] **♘f6 20. ♕g3 ♖d8! 21. d5?!** [21. ♖ad1!? △ ♗f4∞] **♖d7 22. ♖ac1 ♕a3!∓ 23. ♗d4□ ♕g3 24. hg3 ♖e7 25. ♖c3** [25. ♗f6!?] **♔f7 26. ♖a3 a5 27. d6 cd6 28. ♗b6 ♖c8! 29. ♖a4?!** [29. ♖c1 d5 30. ♖a5 dc4 31. ♔f2∓⇆] **h5!?⊕ 30. ♗e3 ♖ec7 31. ♖c1 ♔e6 32. ♗f4** [×a5, d6, e4] **♖c5! 33. ♗e3 ♖5c6 34. ♗f4 g6 35. ♖d1⊕ ♖b6!−+ 36. ♖a5 ♖c4 37. ♖g5 ♔f7?** [37... ♖c2! 38. ♖g6 ♔f7 39. ♖h6 ♖bb2! 40. ♗g5 (40. ♔h1 ♘g4−+) ♖g2 41. ♔h1 ♖h2 42. ♔g1 ♖bg2 43. ♔f1 ♘g4 44. ♖hd6 ♖g3 △ ♖h1, ♖g2#] **38. ♗d6∓ e3 39. ♗f4 e2 40. ♖e1 ♖c2 41. a4 ♘g4 42. a5⇆ ♖bb2 43. ♖d5** [43. a6? ♖a2 44. ♖g4 hg4 45. ♔f2 ♖a6 46. ♖e2 ♖aa2! (46... ♖e2?! 47. ♔e2∓) 47. ♖c2 ♖c2 48. ♔f1 ♔e6 △ ♔d5-e4-d3, ♖e2-e6, ♔c2-d1, ♖f6 (△ g5), ♔e2, ♖a6-a1, ♔f1, ♖a2 ×g2] **♖a2 44. ♖b5 ♔e6 45. ♖g5 ♔d7** [△ ♔c8-b7-a6 ×a5] **46. ♖d5! ♔c8 47. ♖g5** [△ 47... ♔b7?! 48. ♖g6 ♖a5 49. ♖b1=] **♖a3** [△ ♖d3-d1] **48. ♖d5 ♖a4 49. ♖b1! ♖b4⊕ 50. ♖e1 ♔b7?! 51. ♖d7! ♔a8** [51... ♔a6 52. ♖d6 ♔b5 53. ♖g6∞]

52. ♖d6!? ♖b5 53. ♖a6 ♔b7 54. ♖g6∞ **♖a2 55. ♖d6!** [△ ♗d2] **♖ab2?! 56. a6!**⩲ **♔a7 57. ♖e6** [△ ♗e3] **♖b6? 58. ♗e3**+− **♘e3 59. ♖e3 ♖a6 60. ♖3e2 ♖e2 61. ♖e2 ♔b8 62. ♖c2** [×h5, ♔b8] **♖a1 63. ♔h2 ♖e1 64. ♖c5 1 : 0 [Kamsky]**

500.* **E 13**

KAMSKY 2655 – TIMMAN 2635

Linares 1993

1. d4 ♘f6 2. ♘f3 e6 3. c4 b6 4. ♘c3 ♗b4 5. ♗g5 ♗b7 6. e3 h6 7. ♗h4 ♗c3 [RR 7... g5 8. ♗g3 ♘e4 9. ♕c2 ♗c3 10. bc3 d6 11. ♗d3 f5 12. d5 ♘c5 13. h4 g4 14. ♘d4 ♕f6 15. 0–0 ♘ba6 16. ♘e6 ♘e6 17. ♗f5 ♘g7 18. ♗g6 ♔d7 19. f3 ♖af8 20. fg4 ♕e7 21. e4 ♘c5 N (21... ♔c8 – 45/653) 22. ♕e2 ♔c8 23. e5 ♗a6 24. e6 c6 25. ♖f8 ♖f8 26. ♖f1 ♖f1 27. ♕f1 ♔d8 28. ♕f4 ♗b7 29. ♕h6 cd5 30. ♗d6 ♕d6 31. ♕h8 ♔c7 32. ♕g7 ♔d8 33. ♕h8 1/2 : 1/2 Ivančuk 2710 – Anand 2710, Monaco 1993] **8. bc3 d6 9. ♘d2 ♘bd7 10. f3 ♕e7 11. ♕a4 e5 12. e4 0–0 13. ♗d3 c5 N** [13... ♕e8 – 55/504] **14. 0–0!? cd4 15. cd4 ed4 16. ♕d1!?** [△ ♘b3; 16. ♖ad1!? ♖fc8 17. ♘b3 ♘c5 18. ♕a3∞] **♘e5!** [×c4] **17. ♘b3 ♗a6 18. ♘d4 ♖ac8** [18... ♗c4?! 19. ♘f5] **19. ♖c1** [⌓ 19. ♖e1!? ♗c4 (19... ♘d3?! 20. ♕d3 ♗c4 21. ♘f5!±) 20. ♗c2↑⊞] **♗c4 20. ♘f5 ♕e6 21. ♗c4 ♖c4 22. ♕d6 ♕d6 23. ♘d6**⩲ **♖a4! 24. ♗f6?!** [24. ♗g3!?; 24. f4!?] **gf6 25. ♖c2 ♖d8 26. ♘f5 ♔h7**= **27. h4?! h5 28. ♖ff2 ♘c4! 29. ♔h2 b5 30. ♖c3!** [△ ♘e3] **♖a3 31. ♖a3 ♘a3** [♖ 9/h] **32. ♘e3 ♖d3?**⊕ [32... ♖d4=] **33. ♘d5**± **♔h6 34. ♘f6 a5 35. ♔g3 b4 36. ♘d5 ♘b5 37. ♔f4 ♘c3 38. ♔e5 ♘d5 39. ed5 ♔g7** [△ ♔f8-e7] **40. ♖e2 ♔f8 41. ♔d6! a4 42. ♖e4 ♖d2 43. ♖b4 a3 44. ♖b3!** [44. ♔e5!? (△ ♔f6) ♔g7 45. d6 ♖a2 46. d7 ♖d2 47. ♖d4 ♖d4 48. ♔d4 a2 49. d8♕ a1♕⇆] **♖a2 45. g3 ♖a1 46. ♖c3! a2 47. ♖c2** [△ ♔c6, d6] **♖f1?! 48. ♖a2 ♖f3 49. ♖c2**+− **♖g3 50. ♔c7** [50... ♖a3 51. d6 ♖a7 52. ♔b6 ♖d7 53. ♖c8 ♔g7 54. ♔c6]
1 : 0 [Kamsky]

501.** **E 14**

A. MIHAL'ČIŠIN 2515 – VAN DER WERF 2395

Groningen (open) 1992

1. d4 ♘f6 2. ♘f3 e6 3. c4 b6 4. e3 ♗b7 5. ♗d3 ♗b4 6. ♘bd2 c5 7. a3 [7. dc5!? ♗c5 8. a3 a5 9. 0–0 0–0 10. b3 ♕e7 11. ♗b2 ♘c6∞] **♗d2 8. ♗d2 d6 9. ♗c3!?** [9. dc5 bc5 10. ♗c3 *a)* 10... a5? 11. ♕c2 ♘bd7 12. 0–0 ♕c7 N (12... 0–0 – 54/503) 13. ♘g5! ♘e5 14. ♖ad1 h6 15. ♘e4 ♘e4 16. ♗e4 ♗e4 17. ♕e4 0–0 18. ♖d2! f5 19. ♕h4± A. Mihal'čišin 2520 – Draško 2495, Jugoslavija 1991; *b)* 10... ♘bd7 N 11. ♕c2 ♕e7 12. 0–0 0–0 13. ♘g5 h6 14. ♘h7 ♖fd8 15. ♘f6 ♘f6 16. ♖ad1 a5! 17. b3 ♗c6 18. f4 d5!∞ A. Mihal'čišin 2520 – King 2505, Eeklo 1991] **♘bd7 10. 0–0 ♕c7?! N** [⌓ 10... ♕e7 △ e5 ×e4; 10... 0–0 – 47/632] **11. b4! 0–0 12. ♖c1** [12. ♘d2!?; 12. ♕e2!?] **♖fe8 13. ♘d2 ♖ac8 14. f3!?** [14. ♕e2 △ 14... d5 15. dc5 bc5 16. ♗f6 ♘f6 17. cd5+−] **d5** [14... a6!? △ ♗c6, b5] **15. ♕e2!** [15. dc5 bc5 16. ♗f6 ♘f6 17. cd5 ♕e5=/∞] **e5!?** [15... dc4 16. ♘c4 cd4 17. ♗d4 b5!? 18. ♘a5 ♕c1 19. ♖c1 ♖c1 20. ♔f2±; 15... cd4 16. ♗d4 e5 17. ♗b2 e4 18. fe4 de4 19. ♗b1±] **16. dc5 bc5 17. cd5** [17. ♘b3 d4 18. ♗b2 ♕d6 19. b5 e4∓] **cb4** [17... ♘d5 18. ♗a1 ♕b8 19. b5 △ ♘c4±] **18. ♗b2** [18. d6 ♕b6! 19. ♗b4 a5 20. ♗c3 ♘d5 21. ♘c4 ♖c4!? 22. ♗c4 ♘e3=/∞] **♕a5** [18... ♕b6 19. ♘c4±] **19. ♘c4**± [19. e4!? ba3 20. ♗a1=/∞; 19. ab4 ♕b4 20. ♖b1!? ♗d5 21. ♗e5 ♕e7 22. ♗d4⩲] **♕d5 20. ab4 ♗a6!?** [20... e4!? 21. fe4 ♘e4 22. ♖cd1!?±⊞] **21. ♘e5! ♖c1 22. ♖c1 ♗d3 23. ♘d3 a5 24. ba5** [24. e4 a4!⇆] **♕a5 25. e4 ♕g5 26. ♕f2 h6 27. h4 ♕h5 28. ♖c7?** [⌓ 28. e5 ♘d5 29. ♕d4+−] **♕b5! 29. ♕d4 ♘f8 30. ♕c4 ♕c4 31. ♖c4 ♘6d7 32. ♔f2** [32. h5!] **h5** [32... ♘g6!? 33. h5 ♘ge5 34. ♘e5 ♘e5 35. ♖d4±] **33. ♘f4 g6 34. ♘d5 ♘e6 35. ♔e3** [35. g4!?; 35. f4!?] **♖b8 36. ♗c3 ♔f8 37. g4** [37. f4!? f5 38. ef5 gf5 39. ♔f3 ♔f7 40. ♘e3 ♔g6 41. ♖c6 ♖b6⇆] **hg4 38. fg4**

♔g8 39. ♖c6 ♔h7 40. ♖a6 ♘ef8 41. ♖a7 [41. ♖a1!? ♔g8 42. h5! gh5 43. ♘e7 ♔h7 44. ♖h1+−] **♔g8 42. ♔f3 ♖e8 43. h5!?** [43. g5!? △ ♘e3-g4-h6+−] **gh5 44. gh5 ♖e6 45. ♔f4** [45. ♖a8 ♔h7 46. ♗b4 ♔g7 47. ♘e3 ♘e5 48. ♔g3 ♘fd7 49. ♘f5 ♔h7 50. ♗c3 ♖c6 51. ♗d4 △ ♔f4+−] **♖h6 46. ♖a8! ♔h7** [46... ♖h5 47. ♘f6 ♘f6 48. ♗f6 △ ♗e7+−] **47. ♔g4** [47. ♘f6 ♘f6 48. ♖f8 ♔g7! 49. ♖d8 ♖h5 50. ♖d6 ♖h4 51. ♔f5 ♖h5=] **♖e6 48. ♔f5 ♖h6 49. ♔g4 ♖e6 50. ♔g5 ♔g8** [50... ♖e4? 51. ♖f8+−] **51. ♔f5! ♖h6** [51... ♔h7 52. ♘f6 ♘f6 53. ♗f6+−; 51... ♘b6 52. ♖b8 ♘d5 53. ed5 ♖d6 54. ♔e4 △ ♗b4+−] **52. ♘f6+− ♘f6 53. ♗f6 ♖h5 54. ♔f4 ♖h1 55. ♗e7 ♖f1 56. ♔e3 ♖e1 57. ♔f3 ♖f1 58. ♔e2 1 : 0**
[A. Mihal'čišin]

502. **E 15**

EPIŠIN 2630 — TIVJAKOV 2585

Moskva (open) 1992

1. d4 ♘f6 2. c4 e6 3. ♘f3 b6 4. g3 ♗b4 5. ♗d2 ♗e7 6. ♘c3 c6 N [⌓ 6... ♗b7 — 56/610] **7. e4 d5 8. ♗d3 de4 9. ♘e4 ♗b7 10. ♕e2 ♘bd7 11. 0-0-0 0—0 12. ♖he1 c5 13. ♗c3! ♘e4 14. ♗e4 ♗e4 15. ♕e4 ♘f6?!** [15... ♗f6 16. ♘e5! ♗e5 (16... cd4 17. ♗d4±) 17. de5 △ ♖d6, ♖ed1±] **16. ♕b7! ♖e8!□ 17. dc5 ♕c8 18. c6!** [18. ♕c8 ♖ec8 19. b4 a5 20. a3 ab4 21. ab4 bc5 22. b5 ♘g4! 23. ♖e2 ♖a4±] **♕b7 19. cb7 ♖ab8 20. ♗f6 ♗f6 21. ♖d7 ♖e7 22. ♘e5!± ♖d7 23. ♘d7 ♖b7 24. ♘f6 gf6** [♖ 7/g] **25. ♔c2 ♔f8 26. ♖d1 ♖c7 27. ♔c3 ♔e7 28. b4 e5 29. a4 f5 30. c5!+− bc5** [30... a5? 31. ♖d5+−] **31. b5** [♖ **6/f**] **c4 32. a5 f6 33. ♖d2 h5 34. h4?!** [34. b6 ab6 35. ab6 ♖b7 36. ♖b2 ♔d6 37. ♔c4 ♔c6 38. ♖b5!+−] **♔e6 35. ♖d8?** [35. b6+−] **♖c5 36. ♖b8 ♔d5 37. a6 ♖c7 38. ♖b7 ♖c5= 39. ♖d7 ♔e4 40. ♖a7 ♖b5 41. ♖f7 ♖a5 42. ♖f6 ♖a4 43. ♖e6 ♔f3 44. ♖e5 ♔f2 45. ♖f5 ♔g3 46. ♖h5 ♖a6 47. ♖h8 ♔g4 48. h5 ♔g5 49. h6 ♖h6 1/2 : 1/2** **[Epišin]**

503.**** !N** **E 15**

MOLLOV 2400 — SKEMBRIS 2565

Cannes 1993

1. d4 ♘f6 2. c4 e6 3. ♘f3 b6 4. g3 ♗b4 5. ♗d2 a5 6. ♗g2 ♗a6 7. ♕c2 [7. b3 0—0 8. 0—0 ♗b7 9. ♘c3 ♘e4 N (9... d6 — 44/659) 10. ♘e4 ♗e4 11. ♘e5 ♗g2 12. ♔g2 ♘c6!?∞ Vyžmanavin 2590 — L. Christiansen 2595, Manila (ol) 1992; 7. ♕b3 N c5 8. 0—0 0—0 9. dc5 ♗c5 10. ♘c3 ♘c6 11. ♖fd1 d6 12. ♗g5 h6 13. ♗f6 ♕f6 14. ♘e4 ♕e7∞ Ruzele 2340 — J. Benjamin 2555, Manila (ol) 1992; 7. ♗b4 ab4 8. ♘e5 c6 9. ♕b3 ♕e7 N (9... 0—0) 10. a3 0—0 11. ♕b4 d6 12. ♘c6 ♘c6 13. ♗c6 ♖ac8 14. ♗b5 ♗b7 15. 0—0± I. Faragó 2510 — Motwani 2500, Gent 1992] **c5 8. 0—0 ♖a7 9. dc5 N** [9. ♗f4 cd4 10. ♘d4 0—0 11. ♘c3 *a)* 11... d6 12. ♘db5 ♖d7 13. b3 h6 14. ♖fd1± Magerramov 2565 — Kahiani 2360, Helsinki 1992; *b)* 11... ♗c3! N 12. ♕c3 d6 13. ♘c2 ♖c7 14. ♘a3 ♘d5!? 15. ♕d2 ♘f4 16. ♕f4 ♖d7! 17. ♖ac1 ♕c7 18. ♖fd1 ♕c5 (△ ♘c6∓) 19. ♕d4 ♖fd8∓ Velikov 2425 — Skembris 2565, Cannes 1993; 9. ♖d1!? N 0—0 10. ♗f4 cd4 11. ♘d4 ♕c8?! 12. ♘a3! ♗a3□ 13. ba3 ♖e8 (13... ♕c4?! 14. ♕b2±) 14. ♗d6 e5 15. ♘f5 ♕c4 (Skembris 2565 — Kohlweyer 2420, Gausdal 1993) 16. ♕d2!→ ♕g4 17. ♘e7 ♔h8 18. ♗e5!±; 11... ♖e8!?] **♗c5 10. ♗f4 0—0 11. ♘bd2** [11. ♖d1!?] **d5 12. ♘e5** [12. cd5?! ♘d5∓] **♘h5! 13. cd5 ♘f4 14. gf4 ed5□ 15. ♘b3 ♖c7! 16. ♕d2!?** [16. ♘c5 bc5∓ ×f4, e2, ♔g1; 16. ♕d1 ♕f6∓] **♗b4 17. ♕d1** [×d4] **♕f6!? 18. a3 ♗d6!?→ 19. ♕d5 ♗e2 20. ♖fe1** [20. ♖fc1!?] **♗a6** [△ ♗b7] **21. ♖ad1 ♗e7⇆ 22. ♘g4?!** [22. ♕d2!? ♖d8?? 23. ♘g4+−; 22... h5!⇆ ×g4] **♕b2!** [22... ♕f4!?∞̄] **23. ♗e4!?** [23. ♘d4 ♖d7∓] **♗b7!∓** [23... ♗c4 24. ♗h7 ♔h7 25. ♕h5 ♔g8 26. ♘d4→ △ ♖e7, ♘f6] **24. ♗h7□ ♔h7 25. ♕h5 ♔g8 26. ♖d3?** [26. ♘d4!? ♖d8! (26... ♗c5?? 27. ♘f6 gf6 28. ♕g4 ♔h7 29. ♖e3+−; 26... ♖d7?! 27. ♖e7! △ ♘f6) *a)* 27. ♘f5 ♖d1 28. ♘gh6 (28. ♖d1? ♗f8−+) gh6 29. ♘h6

♔g7 30. ♘f5 (30. ♕f7 ♔h6−+) ♔f8! (30... ♔g8 31. ♘h6=) 31. ♕h6 (31. ♖d1 ♕f6−+) ♔g8! 32. ♘e7 (32. ♖d1 ♕f6−+) ♖e7 33. ♕g5 ♕g7−+; *b)* 27. ♖d3!? (△ ♖h3) ♖c1! (27... ♖c3 28. ♘f5→) 28. ♘h6∓ △ ♖g3] **♖c3! 27. ♘d4 g6!−+** [27... ♖d3 28. ♘f5→] **28. ♕e5** [28. ♘h6 ♔h7 29. ♕h3 ♖d3 30. ♕d3 ♔h6 31. ♘f5 gf5 32. ♕h3 ♔g6 33. ♕g3 ♔h5 34. ♕h3 ♗h4 35. ♕f5 ♔h6−+] **♖d3 29. ♘h6** [29. ♕e7 ♕d4−+] **♔h7 30. ♕e7** [30. ♘hf5!? ♖g8! 31. ♘e7 ♕d4 32. ♕g5 ♕c5! 33. f5 (33. ♕h4 ♕h5−+) ♕f5!−+] **♕d4 31. ♕f8** [31. ♘f7 ♖f7 32. ♕f7 ♕g7−+] **♖d1** [32. ♕f7 ♔h6 33. ♕f8 ♔h5−+] **0 : 1** **[Skembris]**

504. **E 15**

MAGERRAMOV 2565 – KOHLWEYER 2420

Bad Wörishofen 1993

1. d4 ♘f6 2. c4 e6 3. ♘f3 b6 4. g3 ♗b4 5. ♗d2 a5 6. ♗g2 0–0 7. 0–0 ♗a6 8. ♕c2 c5 9. ♗f4 cd4 10. ♘d4 d5 N [10... ♖a7 11. ♘c3 – 57/(503)] **11. cd5 ♘d5 12. ♖d1 ♘d7 13. ♗d5!± ed5 14. a3 ♗c5 15. ♘c3 ♗b7 16. ♕f5?!** [⌓ 16. ♘f3! ♖c8 (16... ♘f6 17. ♗g5 ♖c8 18. ♕f5±) 17. ♕f5 g6 18. ♕h3 ♖e8 19. e4!±] **g6 17. ♕h3 ♖e8** [17... ♗d4!? 18. ♖d4 ♘c5 19. ♗h6 ♖e8 20. ♖ad1 ♘e6∞⇆] **18. ♘f3 ♘f8 19. ♗e5 ♘e6 20. ♕h6!± ♗f8 21. ♕d2 ♘g5** [21... ♘c5 22. ♕f4! △ ♕f6±] **22. ♕g5 ♕g5 23. ♘g5 ♖e5 24. ♘f3 ♖ee8 25. ♘d4±⊥ ♗g7 26. e3 ♖ed8 27. ♘a4 ♖d6 28. ♖ac1 ♖c8 29. ♖c8** [29. f3!?] **♗c8 30. ♘b5 ♖d8! 31. ♘d4!±** [31. ♘b6?! ♗g4 32. ♖d5 ♖b8⩱] **♖d6 32. f3 ♗d7 33. ♘c3 h5 34. ♔f2 ♔f8 35. ♔e2 ♗c8 36. b4 ab4 37. ab4 ♗a6 38. b5 ♗b7 39. ♖a1 ♗f6 40. ♔d3 ♖d7!** [40... ♔e7? 41. ♖a7 ♖d7 42. ♖b7+−] **41. ♘a4 ♗d8 42. ♖c1 ♗c7 43. ♘c6± f6 44. f4 ♔f7 45. ♔d4 ♔e6 46. h3 ♖h7 47. ♘c3! ♖d7□ 48. g4 hg4 49. hg4 ♗d6?** [⌓ 49... ♖h7□ 50. ♘d5 ♖d7 51. f5 gf5 52. gf5 ♔f5 53. ♘e7 ♔e6 54. ♖c7 ♖c7 55. ♘c7 ♔e7 56. ♘d5 ♔d6□ 57. ♘f6!±] **50. ♘a4 ♗c7 51. ♖h1!± ♖g7 52. ♘c3 ♖d7 53. ♖h6 ♖g7** [53... ♗c6 54. bc6 ♖d6 55. ♖g6+−] **54. ♘d5+− ♖d7 55. f5! 1 : 0** **[Magerramov]**

505. **E 15**

EHLVEST 2635 – PSAKHIS 2575

Tilburg (Interpolis) 1992

1. d4 ♘f6 2. ♘f3 e6 3. c4 b6 4. g3 ♗a6 5. ♘bd2 d5 6. cd5 ed5 7. ♗g2 ♗e7 8. 0–0 0–0 9. ♘e5 ♗b7 N [9... c5 – 46/721] **10. ♘df3 c5 11. b3** [11. ♗f4!?] **♘bd7** [11... ♘a6 12. ♗b2 △ e3, ♕e2, ♖fc1±] **12. ♗b2 ♖e8 13. ♖c1 ♘e4 14. ♖c2!?** [14. ♘d7 ♕d7 15. dc5 bc5 16. ♘e5 △ ♘d3±] **♘e5 15. ♘e5 ♗d6 16. ♘d3 ♖c8= 17. ♕c1** [17. dc5 bc5 18. ♕e1 ♕e7⇆] **c4** [17... ♕e7=] **18. ♘e5! b5 19. ♗e4 de4 20. bc4 ♗e5 21. de5 bc4**

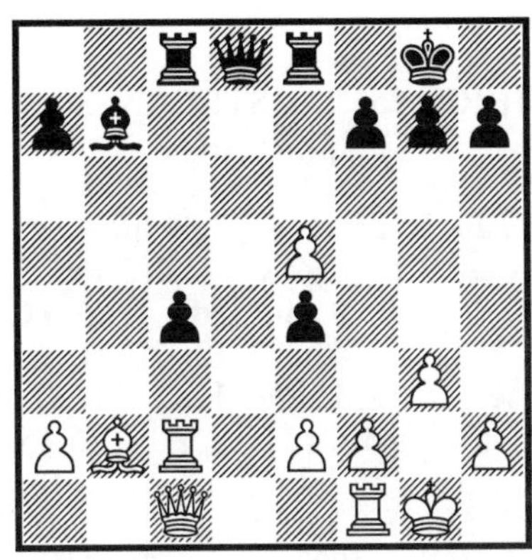

22. ♗c3!!± ♕e7 23. ♕e3 ♕c5 24. ♗d4 ♕a5 25. ♖b1 ♗a8 26. ♗c3 ♕c5 27. ♕c5 [27. ♕c1!? △ ♖cb2⩲] **♖c5 28. ♖cb2 h6 29. a4 ♖d8 30. a5** [30. ♖b8! ♖cc8 31. ♖c8 ♖c8 32. a5±] **♖cd5!⇆ 31. ♔g2 ♔h7 32. g4 ♗c6 33. ♔g3 ♖d1⊕** [33... ♖d3!? 34. ed3 ♖d3 35. ♔g2 ♖c3 36. ♖b7!=] **34. ♔f4?** [34. ♖d1 ♖d1 35. h3=] **♔g6⊕** [34... ♖1d3!!−+] **35. ♖d1 ♖d1 36. ♖b4± ♖c1** [36... ♗d5□] **37. ♖c4 ♗b5 38. ♖c7 a6 39. e6!+− f6 40. h4 ♗e2 41. h5 ♔h7 42. e7 ♗b5 43. ♔f5 ♖c2 44. ♔e6 ♖f2 45. ♖d7! ♗c4 46. ♖d5 ♖c2 47. e8♕ ♖c3 48. ♕g6 ♔h8 49. ♕e4 1 : 0** **[Ehlvest]**

506. **E 15**

OLLS 2585 – RAZUVAEV 2525

Rostov na Donu (open) 1993

1. d4 ♘f6 2. c4 e6 3. ♘f3 b6 4. g3 ♗a6 5. ♘bd2 d5!? 6. cd5 ed5 7. ♗g2 ♗e7 8. 0–0 0–0 9. ♘e5 ♗b7 10. ♘df3 c5 11. dc5 N bc5 12. ♗f4 ♘a6 [12... ♘bd7 13. ♘d7 ♕d7 14. ♕c2±] **13. ♖c1 h6!? 14. ♘d2 ♖b8! 15. ♘d3** [15. e4? g5 16. ♗e3 d4–+] **♗d6 16. b3?!** [⌓ 16. e3!?=] **♗f4 17. ♘f4 d4** [×e2] **18. ♗b7 ♖b7 19. ♘d3** [19. ♘c4!?] **♕d5∓ 20. ♖c4 ♖e7 21. ♖a4?! ♕b7 22. ♕c1 ♘d5!∓** [22... ♖e2 23. ♘f4∞] **23. ♕c4 ♘c3 24. e4□** [24. ♕a6?? ♘e2#] **♘a4 25. ♕a4 ♖c8 26. ♖c1 ♘b4?** [⌓ 26... ♖ec7 △ ♘b4∓] **27. ♘c5 ♕b6 28. ♖c4 a5 29. ♘d7 ♕b7 30. ♕b5!!** [30... ♕b5 31. ♖c8 ♔h7 32. ♘f8=]
1/2 : 1/2 **[Razuvaev]**

507.*** **E 15**

SKEMBRIS 2565 – STEFÁNSSON 2495

Gausdal 1993

1. d4 ♘f6 2. c4 e6 3. ♘f3 b6 4. g3 ♗a6 5. ♕a4 ♗b7 6. ♗g2 c5 7. dc5 bc5 8. 0–0 ♗e7 9. ♘c3 0–0 10. ♖d1 ♕b6 11. ♗f4 ♘a6!? N [11... ♕b2?? 12. ♖ab1 ♕c3 13. ♖b7 ♘c6 14. ♗d2+–; 11... ♘h5?! N 12. ♗e3 f5 13. ♕a3 d6 14. ♗g5! ♘f6 15. ♖d2 h6 16. ♗f6 ♗f6 17. ♖ad1 ♖d8 18. ♕b3 ♕a6 19. ♖d6+– Grivas 2465 – Mi. Lazić 2450, Iraklion 1992; 11... ♕b4?! N 12. ♕b4 cb4 13. ♘b5 ♘a6 14. ♗d6 ♗d6 15. ♘d6 ♗c6 16. ♘e5 ♗g2 17. ♔g2 ♘c5 18. f3± Skembris 2520 – I. Csom 2540, Iraklion 1992; 11... d6 12. ♖d2 h6 13. ♕c2 N (13. ♖ad1 – 52/521) e5 14. ♗e3 ♘c6 15. ♘h4 ♘d4 16. ♗d4 cd4 17. ♘f5 ♖fe8 18. ♘e4∞ Rajiv 2230 – Prasad 2480, Calcutta 1993; 11... ♘c6 12. ♕b5 ♖fd8!?] **12. ♖d2 ♖fd8** [12... d5!?] **13. ♘e5!? ♗g2** [13... d5 14. ♕b5!?±] **14. ♔g2 ♖ac8** [△ d6; 14... d6? 15. ♘c6±] **15. ♖ad1 d6** [15... ♕b7!? 16. ♘f3 d5 17. cd5 ed5 18. ♕b5±] **16. ♘f3!? h6** [△ e5; 16... e5 17. ♗g5± ×d5] **17. ♕b5!± ♖c6?** [17... ♕b5 18. cb5+– ×d6; 17... ♖b8!?± Stefánsson] **18. ♘a4! ♕c7□** [18... ♘c7 19. ♕b6! ab6 20. ♘e5+–]

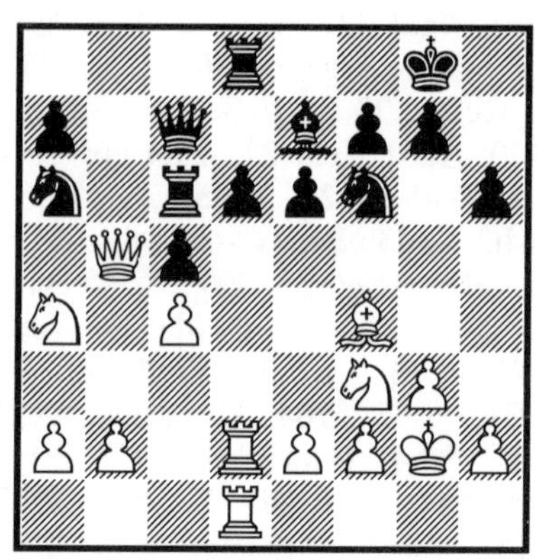

19. ♘e5!!± ♘b4 [19... de5 20. ♖d8 ♗d8 21. ♗e5±] **20. ♘c6 ♘c6?** [⌓ 20... ♕c6+–] **21. ♘c5! g5** [21... e5 22. ♘a6+–; 21... ♖b8 22. ♘a6+–] **22. ♗d6!+–** [22. ♘a6 ♕c8 23. ♗d6 ♘e4±→] **♗d6□** [22... ♖d6 23. ♖d6 ♗d6 24. ♘a6+– ×♘c6, ♗d6] **23. ♘a6** **1 : 0**
[Skembris]

508.** **E 15**

AN. KARPOV 2725 – JUDASIN 2610

Dos Hermanas 1993

1. d4 ♘f6 2. c4 e6 3. ♘f3 b6 4. g3 ♗a6 5. b3 d5 [RR 5... ♗b7 6. ♗g2 ♗b4 7. ♗d2 a5 8. 0–0 0–0 9. ♘c3 d6 10. ♕c2 ♘bd7 11. ♖ad1 N (11. ♖fe1 – 54/514) ♗c3 12. ♗c3 ♗e4 13. ♕b2?! c6! 14. ♖fe1 b5 15. ♗f1 ♘b6 16. ♘d2□ (Epišin 2620 – J. Benjamin 2585, New York 1993) b4 17. ♘e4 ♘e4 18. ♗d2 d5! 19. c5 ♘d2 20. ♕d2 ♘d7=; ⌓ 13. ♕c1 Epišin] **6. ♗g2 ♗b4 7. ♗d2 ♗d6 8. cd5 N** [8. ♘c3 – 7/515] **ed5 9. ♘c3 0–0 10. 0–0** [RR 10. ♗g5 ♗b4! 11. ♖c1 ♘bd7! 12. 0–0 (12. ♘e5? ♘e5! 13. de5 d4!∓→ Judasin) ♖e8 13. ♖e1 ♗b7!= Epišin 2620 – Judasin 2610, Dos Hermanas 1993] **♘bd7 11. ♖e1** [11. ♘h4 c6 12. ♘f5 ♗b8 13. ♖e1±] **c5** [11... ♖e8 12. ♘h4 c6 13. ♘f5 ♗f8 14. e4±] **12. ♗e3 ♗b7** [12... ♖e8 13. dc5 ♗c5 14. ♗d4±] **13. ♘h4 ♘g4** [13... g6?! 14. dc5 ♗c5 15. ♗g5±; 13... ♖e8 14. ♘f5

♗f8 15. dc5 ♘c5 16. ♗d4±] **14. ♘d5 ♗d5** [14... ♘e3 15. ♘e3 ♗g2 16. ♔g2 cd4 17. ♘ef5 ♗e5 (17... ♗b4 18. ♕d4+–) 18. ♘d4 ♘c5 19. ♘hf3±] **15. ♗d5 ♘e3 16. fe3 ♖c8 17. ♕d3 ♘f6** [17... ♕g5 *a)* 18. ♗f3 ♘f6 19. ♘f5 (19. ♘g2 ♖fe8=∞) ♖cd8⇆; *b)* 18. ♗c4 g6 19. ♖f1±] **18. ♗c4! g6□ 19. ♖f1** [19. ♘g6 hg6 20. ♕g6 ♔h8 21. ♕h6 ♘h7 22. ♗d3 f5 23. ♖f1=∞] **♔g7 20. ♖f3 ♘g4 21. h3** [21. ♖af1!? f5 (21... ♘h2 22. ♔h2 ♕h4 23. ♔g2+–) 22. e4 cd4 (22... ♘h2?! 23. e5 ♘f3 24. ♘f3 ♗e7 25. d5±) 23. ef5 ♘e5⇆] **♘h6 22. ♘g2 ♘f5** [22... ♕g5 23. ♕e4 (△ ♕h4±; 23. ♖af1 ♗g3 24. e4 ♗b8 25. e3±) ♘f5 (23... ♗g3? 24. h4+–) 24. g4 ♘h4 (24... ♖ce8 25. ♕d5+–) 25. ♘h4±] **23. ♖af1** [23. ♖f5!? gf5 24. ♘h4 ♔h8 25. ♘f5±] **b5! 24. ♗d5 ♕g5** [24... ♘g3 25. ♖f7 ♖f7 26. ♖f7 ♔h6 27. ♕d2! ♕g5 28. h4!+–; 24... c4 25. bc4 bc4 26. ♕c3±] **25. dc5! ♗c5** [25... ♖c5 26. b4 ♖c7 27. ♗e4+–] **26. h4 ♕e7 27. ♖f5± gf5 28. ♖f5 f6 29. ♔h2 ♗d6** [29... b4 30. ♘f4+–] **30. ♕b5+– ♔h8** [30... ♖c2 31. a4] **31. ♕d3 ♕c7 32. ♘f4 ♖ce8 33. ♔g2 ♖e7 34. ♗f3 ♖g7 35. g4 ♗f4 36. ef4 ♖d8 37. ♕c4 ♕e7 38. ♕c3 ♖d6 39. ♖c5 ♖d8 40. ♖c6 ♖d6 41. ♖c4 ♖d8 42. ♖c6 ♖d6 43. ♖c5 ♖d8 44. b4 ♖dg8 45. ♔f2 ♕d6 46. ♖f5 ♖f8 47. ♕c5 ♕d8 48. ♖d5 ♕b8 49. ♕d4 ♕c8 50. b5 ♖g4 51. ♗g4 ♕g4 52. f5 ♕h3 53. ♔e1 ♖f7 54. ♔d2 ♕g3 55. a4 ♔g7 56. ♖d7 1 : 0** **[An. Karpov]**

509. **E 15**

TUKMAKOV 2605 –
WOJTKIEWICZ 2580

Bern 1993

1. d4 ♘f6 2. c4 e6 3. ♘f3 b6 4. g3 ♗a6 5. b3 d5 6. ♗g2 ♘bd7 7. 0–0 ♗d6 8. ♘c3!? [8. cd5] **0–0** [8... dc4!? 9. bc4 ♗c4∞] **9. ♘d2 N** [9. ♗b2 – 54/(507)] **♗b7** [9... c5!? 10. cd5 ed5 (10... cd4 11. ♘ce4) 11. ♘d5 ♘d5 12. ♗d5 cd4 13. ♘f3±] **10. ♗b2** [10. e4?! ♗b4!] **c5 11. cd5** [11. dc5!? ♘c5 12. cd5 ♘d5 13. ♘d5 ♗d5 14. ♗d5 ed5 15. ♘f3 ♗e7±] **ed5** [11... cd4 12. ♘ce4; 11... ♘d5 12. ♘d5 ed5 (12... ♗d5 13. e4 ♗b7 14. ♘c4 △ d5±) 13. ♘c4] **12. dc5** [12. ♘c4 ♗e7 13. ♘e3 cd4 14. ♕d4 ♗c5 △ d4] **♘c5□** [12... bc5? 13. ♘c4] **13. ♘f3 ♖e8 14. ♘b5! ♗e7** [14... ♗f8? 15. ♗f6; 14... ♗b8 15. ♖c1] **15. ♖c1 a6?!** [×b6; ⌓ 15... ♕d7±] **16. ♘bd4 ♘fe4 17. b4! ♘e6 18. ♕b3 ♘d4 19. ♗d4 ♗f6 20. ♖c2 ♘d6?!** [20... h6] **21. ♖d1 h6 22. e3 ♘c4?** [⌓ 22... ♘e4] **23. ♘e1!** [△ ♗f6, ♘d3-f4] **b5 24. ♕c3!** [24. ♘d3 ♗d4 25. ed4±] **♗d4 25. ♕d4 a5 26. ♘d3 ab4 27. ♘b4 ♖a4 28. ♕c5! ♕b6□ 29. ♖c4 ♕c5 30. ♖c5 ♖b4 31. ♖c7 ♗a8 32. ♗d5 ♗d5 33. ♖d5 ♖a4 34. ♖b5 ♖a2** [♖ 9/q] **35. ♖bb7 ♖f8 36. g4! ♖a4 37. h3 h5?** [37... g6 △ ♔g7] **38. g5** [△ g6] **g6 39. ♔g2 ♖aa8 40. ♖c6 ♖ab8 41. ♖bc7 ♖b5 42. h4 ♖b4 43. f3!** [43. ♔h3 ♖e4!] **♖fb8** [43... ♖h4 44. e4 (△ ♖c1, ♔g3) ♖a8 45. ♖c8 ♖c8 46. ♖c8 ♔g7 47. ♖c1 f6 48. ♖c7] **44. ♖f6 ♖8b7 45. ♖ff7 ♖c7 46. ♖c7 ♖h4** [♖ 6/c] **47. e4 ♔f8 48. ♖c8 ♔g7 49. ♖c7 ♔f8 50. ♖c1 ♖f4 51. ♖c8 ♔g7 52. ♖c7 ♔g8 53. ♖c6 ♔g7 54. ♖c7 ♔g8 55. ♔g3 ♖f8 56. f4 ♖e8** [56... ♖a8 57. f5 ♖a4 58. f6 ♖e4 59. ♖g7 ♔f8 60. ♖g6 ♖g4 61. ♔f3!+–] **57. ♖c4 ♖f8 58. ♖c5 ♖e8 59. ♔f3 ♖a8 60. f5 ♖a3 61. ♔f4 h4 62. ♖c8 ♔g7 63. f6 ♔f7 64. ♖c7 ♔f8 65. ♖g7 1 : 0** **[Tukmakov]**

510. **E 15**

D. RAJKOVIĆ 2450
– BELJAVSKIJ 2610

Jugoslavija 1993

1. d4 ♘f6 2. c4 e6 3. ♘f3 b6 4. g3 ♗a6 5. b3 d5 6. ♗g2 dc4 7. ♘e5 ♗b4 8. ♔f1 c6 9. ♘c4!? N [9. ♘c6 – 32/600] **0–0 10. ♗b2 ♕c7 11. ♘bd2 ♘bd7 12. ♖c1 ♖ac8 13. ♗f3** [13. a3 ♗e7 14. ♗f3 ♖fd8 15. ♔g2∞] **♖fd8 14. ♔g2** [14. a3 ♗d2 15. ♕d2 ♗c4 16. bc4 ♘e5 17. ♗g2 c5 18. d5∞] **c5 15. a3** [15. ♘b1!? b5! (15... ♗c4 16. ♖c4 ♘e5 17. ♖c2 ♘f3 18. ef3 e5 19. a3 ♗a5 20. b4 ♗b4 21. ab4 ed4∞) 16. a3 (16. ♘e3 ♕b8!∓) bc4 17. ab4 cb4 18. bc4 ♗c4∓] **♗d2 16. ♕d2?** [⌓ 16. ♘d2 ♕d6!

17. e3 (17. dc5?! ♘c5 18. ♗f6 gf6 19. ♘e4 ♕e7!∓) cd4 18. ed4∞] **♗c4! 17. bc4** [17. ♖c4 ♘e5 18. ♖c2 ♘f3 19. ef3 e5!∓] **♘e5 18. d5□ ed5 19. ♗e5** [19. ♗d5 ♘c4−+] **♕e5 20. cd5 ♖d7∓** [20... ♖d6 21. ♖hd1 ♖cd8 22. ♕c3! ♕f5 23. ♕d3∞] **21. ♕c2! h5** [21... ♘d5 22. ♗g4+−] **22. e4 g5 23. ♖he1 g4 24. ♗e2□ ♖e7** [24... ♕e4 25. ♕e4 ♘e4 26. ♗a6+−] **25. f3 ♔g7 26. ♕d2 ♖h8** [26... ♖g8∞] **27. ♖cd1 gf3 28. ♗f3 ♘e8?** [⌓ 28... b5 29. ♕f4 c4∓] **29. d6! ♖d7 30. ♕f4 f6** [30... ♕f4 31. gf4 ♖d6 32. e5±] **31. ♖d5 ♕f4 32. gf4 ♖d6 33. ♖ed1!± ♖d5 34. ♖d5 [♖ 9/i] ♔f8?** [34... ♖h7! 35. ♗h5 ♘c7 36. ♖d7 ♔h6±] **35. ♗h5 ♖h7 36. ♗g4?±** [36. ♗g6! ♖g7□ 37. f5 ♔e7 38. h4 ♘d6 39. ♔f3 ♘f7 40. ♔f4 a6 41. a4+−] **♖c7! 37. ♔f3⊕ ♔e7 38. e5 fe5 39. fe5 c4 40. ♔e2 ♘g7 41. ♔d2 ♘e6 42. ♔c3 ♘f4 43. ♖d4 ♘g6 44. ♖d6 ♘f4 45. h4 ♖c5 46. ♖d7** [46. h5 ♘d5! 47. ♔d2 c3 48. ♔c1 ♘e3 49. ♖d7 ♔e8 50. h6 ♘g4 51. h7 ♔d7∓] **♔e8 47. ♖a7 ♘d5 48. ♔d2** [48. ♔d4 c3 49. ♗f5 ♘c7] **c3 49. ♔c1 ♘e3= 50. ♗d7 ♔d8 51. e6 ♖e5 52. ♖a8 ♔e7 53. ♖e8 ♔d6 54. ♖c8 ♘d5 55. ♖c6 ♔e7 56. ♔c2 ♖h5 57. ♔b3 ♖h4 58. ♖c3 ♘c3 59. ♔c3 ♔d6 60. a4 ♖e4 61. ♔d3 ♖f4 62. ♔c3 1/2 : 1/2** **[D. Rajković]**

511.** **E 15**

A. CHERNIN 2600 — VEINGOLD 2475

Sevilla 1993

1. d4 ♘f6 2. c4 e6 3. ♘f3 b6 4. g3 ♗a6 5. b3 ♗b4 6. ♗d2 ♗e7 7. ♗g2 c6 8. 0–0 d5 9. ♘e5 ♘bd7 10. ♘d7 ♘d7 11. ♗c3 0–0 12. ♘d2 ♖c8 13. e4 [13. ♖e1 *a)* 13... c5!? 14. cd5 cd4 N (14... ed5 — 47/639) 15. ♗d4 ed5 *a1)* 16. a3 ♘c5 17. ♗b2 ♗f6! 18. ♗f6 ♕f6 19. b4 (19. ♗d5 ♖fd8=∞) ♘e6 20. e3 (20. ♗d5 ♖fd8 21. e4 ♘c7=) ♖fd8= A. Chernin 2600 — Titz 2345, München 1992/93; *a2)* 16. ♗h3! ♖c7 17. a3 ♘c5 18. ♘f1 △ ♘e3±; *b)* 13... f5!? 14. ♖c1 N (14. f3 — 42/698) ♕e8 (14... ♘f6 15. ♗h3 ♘e4 16. ♘e4 de4 17. f3±) 15. ♗b2 ♕f7 16. e3 g5!? 17. ♖c2 g4! (×f3) 18. ♕c1 ♘f6 19. ♗a3 ♘e4= A. Chernin 2600 — Pogorelov 2400, Sevilla 1993; 17. ♘b1!? △ ♗a3±] **c5 14. ed5 ed5 15. dc5 dc4 16. c6 cb3 17. ♖e1 ♗b5 18. ab3 ♗c6 19. ♗c6 ♖c6 20. ♖a7 ♗f6 21. ♘c4!? N** [21. ♘e4 — 54/519] **♗c3** [21... ♖c4? 22. bc4 ♗c3 23. ♖e3+−] **22. ♖d7 ♕f6 23. ♖e4!?** [23. ♖e3 ♖e6 24. ♖f3 ♖e1 25. ♕e1 ♕f3=] **♖e6 24. ♖f4 ♕g6?** [24... ♕f4 25. gf4 ♖e1 26. ♕e1 ♗e1 27. ♘b6±] **25. ♖df7!+− ♕f7** [25... ♖fe8 26. ♕d5 ♗f6 27. ♖d7] **26. ♖f7 ♖f7** [26... ♔f7 27. ♕d7 ♔f6 (27... ♖e7 28. ♘d6 ♔f6 29. ♕f5#) 28. ♕d3 △ ♕h7] **27. ♕d8 ♖f8 28. ♕d5 ♖f6** [28... ♖e8 29. ♘d6 ♖e7 30. ♕a8] **29. ♘d6** [⌓ 29. ♘b6 ♗e1 (29... ♗b4 30. ♘d7 ♖h6 31. f4 △ f5+−) 30. ♘d7 ♗f2 31. ♔g2+−] **♗b4 30. ♘e4 ♔h8 31. ♘f6 ♖f6 32. ♔g2 h6 33. ♕d8 ♔h7 34. ♕d3 ♔g8 35. f4 ♗f8 36. ♔f3 g6 37. b4 ♔g7 38. b5 ♗d6 39. ♕c3 1 : 0** **[A. Chernin]**

512.* **E 15**

HALIFMAN 2630 — VAN DER WIEL 2555

Ter Apel 1993

1. d4 ♘f6 2. c4 e6 3. ♘f3 b6 4. g3 ♗a6 5. b3 ♗b4 6. ♗d2 ♗e7 7. ♗g2 c6 8. ♗c3 d5 9. ♘e5 [RR 9. ♘bd2 ♘bd7 10. 0–0 0–0 11. ♖e1 c5 12. e4 dc4 13. bc4 cd4 14. ♘d4 ♘e5 15. ♘e6 fe6 16. ♗e5 ♗c5 17. ♖f1 ♕d3 18. ♗f6 ♖f6 19. ♘b3 ♕d1 N (19... ♖d8 — 42/(693)) 20. ♖ad1 ♖c8 21. ♘c5 ♖c5 22. ♖d7 ♖f7 23. ♖d8 ♖f8 24. ♖fd1 ♗c4 25. ♖8d7 ♖f7= V. Salov 2660 — Timman 2635, Linares 1993] **♘fd7 10. ♘d7 ♘d7 11. ♘d2 0–0 12. 0–0 ♖c8 13. e4 c5 14. ed5 ed5 15. dc5 dc4 16. c6 cb3 17. ♖e1 ♗b5 18. ab3 ♗c6 19. ♗c6 ♖c6 20. ♖a7 ♗f6 21. ♘c4!? ♗c3 22. ♖d7 ♕c8 N** [22... ♕a8 23. ♖e3 ♗f6 24. ♕d5±] **23. ♖e3 ♗f6** [23... b5?! 24. ♖c3 bc4 25. ♕d5 ♖c5 26. ♕d4±] **24. ♕d5 b5 25. ♘a3 b4** [25... ♖a6?! 26. ♘b5 ♖a1 27. ♔g2 ♕c1 28. ♖e8!±] **26. ♘c4 h6 27. ♔g2 ♖c7?** [27... ♖c5 28. ♕b7 ♕b7 29. ♖b7 ♗c3±]

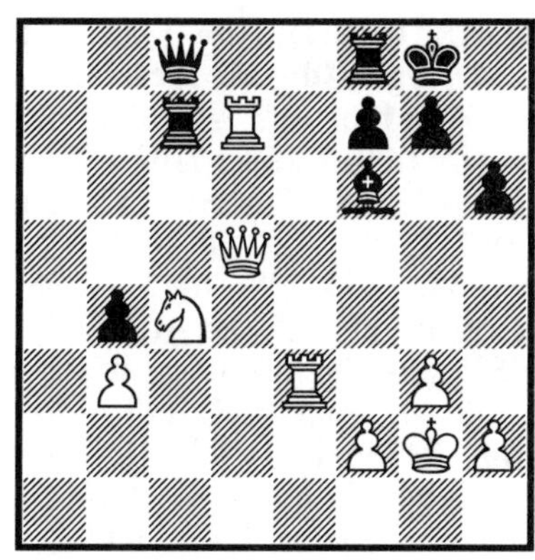

28. ♘b6!± ♖d7 [28... ♕b8 29. ♖c7 ♕c7 30. ♘d7±] **29. ♘d7 ♖e8** [29... ♕a8 30. ♕a8 ♖a8 31. ♘f6 gf6 32. ♖e4 ♖b8 33. ♖f4±; 29... ♗g5 30. ♖f3 ♕d8 31. h4!±] **30. ♘f6 gf6 31. ♖f3 ♕a6 32. ♖f4! ♖e1?!** [32... ♖e5 33. ♖g4 ♖g5 34. ♕e4±] **33. ♖g4 ♔f8 34. ♕c5 ♖e7 35. ♖e4!+− ♕b7 36. ♕e7 ♕e7 37. ♖e7 ♔e7 38. ♔f3 f5** [38... ♔d6 39. ♔e4 ♔c5 40. g4+−] **39. ♔e3 ♔e6 40. ♔d4 f4 41. gf4 ♔f5 42. ♔c4 1 : 0 [Halifman]**

513. E 15

AN. KARPOV 2725 – BELJAVSKIJ 2610

Linares 1993

1. d4 ♘f6 2. c4 e6 3. ♘f3 b6 4. g3 ♗a6 5. b3 ♗b4 6. ♗d2 ♗e7 7. ♗g2 c6 8. ♗c3 d5 9. ♘e5 ♘fd7 10. ♘d7 ♘d7 11. ♘d2 0–0 12. 0–0 ♖c8 13. e4 c5 14. ed5 ed5 15. dc5 dc4 16. c6 cb3 17. ♖e1 ♗b5 18. ab3 ♗c6 19. ♗c6 ♖c6 20. ♖a7 ♗f6 [20... ♖c3?! 21. ♘b1! ♖c7 22. ♖c7 ♕c7 23. ♖e7±] **21. ♘c4!? ♘c5 N 22. ♕d8 ♖d8** [22... ♗d8 23. ♗b4 ♘d3 24. ♗f8 ♘e1 25. ♗b4 ♘f3 26. ♔g2 ♘d4 27. ♖a8 ♘e6 28. ♗e7+−] **23. ♗f6 ♖f6** [23... gf6 24. ♖ee7±] **24. b4!± ♘e6** [24... ♘d3? 25. ♖d7!+−; 24... ♘a4!?; 24... b5] **25. ♘b6 ♘g5 26. ♖d7! ♘f3 27. ♔f1** [27. ♔h1? ♖f8 28. ♘d5 ♖h6−+] **♖b8** [27... ♖f8 28. ♘d5 ♖h6 29. ♖d1! ♘h2 (29... g5 30. ♘e7 ♔h8 31. ♖d8+−) 30. ♔g2 ♘g4 31. ♘e7 ♔h8 32. ♖d8+−] **28. ♖ed1 ♔f8 29. ♘d5 ♖e6 30. ♘c7!± ♖h6** [30... ♖e4? 31. ♖d8 ♖d8 32. ♖d8 ♔e7 33. ♖e8 ♔d7 34. ♖e4 ♘d2 35. ♔e2 ♘e4 36. ♘b5; 31. b5!?] **31. h4** [31. ♔g2 ♘e5 32. ♖d8 ♖d8 33. ♖d8 ♔e7 34. ♖e8 ♔d6 35. ♘b5 ♔d5 36. ♘c3±] **g5** [31... ♘e5 32. ♖d8 (32. ♖7d5 ♖c6! 33. ♖e5 ♖c7 34. ♖b1±) ♖d8 33. ♖d8 ♔e7 34. ♖e8±] **32. hg5** [32. ♖d8 ♖d8 33. ♖d8 ♔e7 34. ♖d3 g4 (34... ♘e5 35. ♖e3 ♔d6 36. hg5+−) 35. ♘d5 ♔e6 36. ♘e3 f5 37. ♖d6! ♔d6 38. ♘f5+−] **♘g5** [32... ♖h1 33. ♔g2 ♖d1 34. ♖d1 ♘g5 35. ♖d5+−] **33. ♖1d5!+− ♘e4 34. ♖d8 ♖d8 35. ♖d8 ♔g7** [35... ♔e7 36. ♖e8 ♔d7 37. ♖e4 ♔c7 38. ♖f4] **36. ♘e8 ♔g6** [36... ♔f8 37. ♘f6 ♔e7 38. ♖e8 ♔f6 39. ♖e4] **37. ♔g2 f6 38. ♖d7 ♖h5 39. ♖g7 ♔h6 40. ♖e7 f5** [40... ♖e5 41. ♘f6 ♖e7 42. ♘g8] **41. ♖e6 ♔g5** [42. f4 ♔g4 43. ♖e4 fe4 44. ♘f6] **1 : 0 [An. Karpov]**

514. E 15

FTÁČNIK 2535 – SAX 2570

Budapest (zt) 1993

1. d4 ♘f6 2. c4 e6 3. ♘f3 b6 4. g3 ♗a6 5. b3 ♗b4 6. ♗d2 ♗e7 7. ♗g2 c6 8. 0–0 d5 9. ♘e5 ♘fd7 10. ♘d7 ♘d7 11. ♗c3 0–0 12. ♘d2 ♖c8 13. e4 c5 14. ed5 ed5 15. dc5 dc4 16. c6 cb3 17. ♖e1 ♗b5 18. ab3 a5 19. ♖c1! [19. ♗g7!? ♔g7 20. ♕g4 *a)* 20... ♗g5!? 21. ♘f3! (21. cd7 ♗d7 22. ♕e2 ♖c2; 21. h4 h5 22. ♕g5 ♕g5 23. hg5 ♗c6=) ♖c6 (21... h6 22. ♘g5 hg5 23. cd7 ♗d7 24. ♕d4±) 22. ♘g5 ♖g6 23. h4 h6 24. ♕d4 ♕f6 25. ♕f6 ♖f6 26. ♘e4±; *b)* 20... ♔h8 21. cd7 ♗d7 (21... ♖c7 22. ♘f3! ♕d7 23. ♕f4 ♕d6 24. ♘e5 f6? 25. ♘g6! hg6 26. ♕h6 ♔g8 27. ♕g6 ♔h8 28. ♖ad1! ♕c5 29. ♕h6 ♔g8 30. ♗d5+−) 22. ♕e4! ♗b4! (22... ♖e8?! 23. ♖ad1 ♗g5 24. ♕d4 ♗f6 25. ♕f4 ♖e1 26. ♖e1 ♗g5 27. ♕f7! ♗d2 28. ♖e8!! ♕e8 29. ♕f6 ♔g8 30. ♗d5+−) 23. ♕f4! f6 24. ♖ed1± △ 25. ♘c4, 25. ♘e4] **♘c5!? N** [19... ♗c6 – 53/513] **20. ♕g4! ♗f6** [20... g6 *a)* 21. ♘c4 f5 22. ♕e2 ♗f6 23. ♖cd1 ♕c7 (23... ♗c3 24. ♖d8 ♖fd8 25. ♖d1±) 24. ♗f6 ♖f6 25. ♕b2±; *b)* 21. ♖cd1! f5 22. ♖e7!! ♕e7 (22... ♖f7 23.

♖e8! ♕e8 24. ♕d4 ♔f8 25. ♕h8 ♔e7 26. ♖e1 ♘e6 27. ♖e6 ♔e6 28. ♕e5#; 22... fg4 23. ♖g7 ♔h8 24. ♖g6+−) 23. ♗d5 ♘e6 24. ♕d4 ♖c6 25. ♕h8 ♔f7 26. ♕h7 ♔e8 27. ♕g6 ♕f7 28. ♕f7 ♔f7 29. ♗c6 ♗c6 30. ♘c4±] **21. ♗f6 ♕f6 22. ♘e4! ♕d4!?** [22... ♘e4 23. ♕e4± △ 23... ♖c7 24. ♕e5] **23. ♖ed1 ♗d3** [23... ♘d3 24. ♕f5! *a)* 24... ♗c6 25. ♘g5 (25. ♖d3 ♗e4!! 26. ♗e4 ♖c1 27. ♔g2 g6) g6 26. ♕d3+−; *b)* 24... ♗a6 25. ♖c3+−; *c)* 24... ♕b4 25. ♘f6! gf6 26. ♗e4 ♖fd8 (26... ♖fe8 27. ♕h7 ♔f8 28. ♗d3 ♖c6 29. ♕h6 ♔e7 30. ♖e1+−) 27. ♕h7 ♔f8 28. ♗d3 ♗c6 29. ♗c4+−; *d)* 24... ♘c1 25. ♖d4 ♘e2 26. ♔h1 ♘d4 27. ♘f6! (27. ♕e5 ♖c6⇆) gf6 28. ♕g4 ♔h8 29. ♕d4 ♖c6□ (29... ♔g7 30. ♕g4 ♔h8 31. ♕f5+−) 30. ♗c6 ♗c6 31. ♔g1 ♔g7 32. ♕b6±] **24. ♖c5!□** [24. ♖c4 ♕b2 25. ♘c5 ♗c4 (25... ♗e2? 26. ♕d4) 26. ♘d7 (26. ♕c4 bc5 27. ♕c5∞) ♗b3∞] **bc5 25. ♕d7 ♖fd8** [25... ♖c6!? *a)* 26. ♕c6 ♗e4 27. ♖d4 ♗c6 28. ♖c4=; *b)* 26. ♖d3 ♕d7 27. ♖d7 c4 28. bc4 (28. ♘d2 c3! 29. ♗c6 c2−+) ♖c4±; *c)* 26. ♕d4! cd4 27. ♖d3±] **26. ♕d4 cd4** [26... ♖d4 27. ♘c5 ♖cd8 28. c7 ♖c8 29. ♖d3 ♖d3 30. ♘d3 ♖c7 31. ♗d5±] **27. ♖d3 ♖c6 28. ♗f1 ♔f8** [28... ♖b6 29. ♖f3 (29. ♗e2 ♖db8 30. ♗d1) ♖b4 30. ♗c4 ♖d7 31. ♘c5 ♖e7 32. ♖d3±; 28... ♖c1 29. ♔g2 h6 (29... ♖a1 30. ♖f3 a4 31. ♗c4 a3 32. ♖f7 ♔h8 33. ♖a7±) 30. ♗e2±; 28... h6 29. ♖d1 (29. ♘d2 ♖c3 30. ♘c4 ♖d5=) ♖b8! 30. ♘d2 (30. ♗c4 a4! 31. ♗d5 ♖a6 32. ba4 ♖a4=) ♖b4 31. ♘f3 ♖b3 (31... ♖d6 32. ♘e5 ♖b3 33. ♘f7!±) 32. ♘d4 ♖d6 33. ♘b3 ♖d1 34. ♘a5±] **29. ♘g5!? ♔e7** [29... ♖c3! 30. ♘h7?! ♔e7 31. ♘g5 ♖d3 32. ♗d3 ♖c8 33. ♘e4 f5! 34. ♘d2 ♖c1 35. ♗f1 d3⇆; 30. ♘f3±] **30. ♖d1 h6** [30... ♖c3 31. ♗c4 a4 32. ♖e1 ♔f8 33. ♗f7 ab3 34. ♗b3! (34. ♘e6 ♔f7 35. ♘d8 ♔f6 36. ♖e6 ♔f5∞) ♖b3 35. ♘e6 ♔e7 36. ♘d4+−] **31. ♘f3 ♖c3?** [31... ♖cd6 32. ♘e5±; 31... d3! 32. ♘d2 (32. ♗d3 ♖c3 33. ♘e5 ♔f6 34. ♘g4 ♔e7 35. ♘e5=) ♖c3 33. ♔g2 a4 34. ba4 ♖a3 35. ♘c4 ♖a4 36. ♘e5±] **32. ♘d4 ♔f6 33. ♖d2** [33. ♗e2 ♖c5 34. ♗f3 a4 35. ba4 ♖c4 36. ♘c2 ♖d1 37. ♗d1 ♖a4] **♖d6** [33... ♖c5 34. ♘f3±] **34. ♔g2 ♖d5 35. ♗c4** [35. ♘f3!?] **♖d8 36. ♘e2** [36. ♘f3 ♖d2 37. ♘d2 ♖c2 38. ♘e4 ♔e7 39. ♘c5±] **♖d2** [36... ♖g3? 37. ♘g3 ♖d2 38. ♘e4+−] **37. ♘c3** [♖8/b4] **♔e7** [37... ♖c2 38. ♘d5 ♔e5 39. ♘e3+−] **38. ♔f3** [38. h4!? △ 38... h5 39. ♘d5 ♔f8 40. ♘f4 g6 41. ♘d3+−] **f6 39. ♘d5?!** [39. h4 h5 40. ♘d5 ♔d6 41. ♘f4] **♔d6 40. ♘e3 ♔c5!** [40... ♔e5 41. h4 h5 42. ♗f7+−] **41. h4** [41. ♘f5? a4!] **h5** [41... ♔b4 42. h5 a4 43. ba4 ♔a4 44. ♘f5 ♖d7 45. ♔e4+−] **42. ♗f7 ♖d7 43. ♗e8** [43. ♗h5 ♖b7 44. ♔e4 ♖b3∞] **♖b7** [43... ♖d3 44. ♗a4 ♔d4 45. ♔f4±] **44. ♗a4 g5!?** [44... ♔b4 45. ♘d5 ♔a3 46. ♘f4 ♖b3 47. ♗b3 ♔b3 48. ♔e2 a4 49. ♔d3 a3 50. ♘e2 ♔b2 51. ♘c3 g6∞; 45. ♘c4±] **45. hg5** [45. ♔e4 gh4 46. gh4 ♖b4 47. ♘c4 (47. ♔f5 ♖h4) ♖a4 48. ba4 ♔c4 49. ♔f5 ♔b4 50. ♔f6 ♔a4 51. f4 ♔b3=] **fg5 46. ♘c4 ♖f7** [46... ♔b4 47. ♘e5 ♔c3 48. ♘c6+−] **47. ♔g2 ♔b4 48. ♘e5 ♖f5 49. f4! gf4 50. gf4** [50. ♘d3 ♔c3 51. ♘f4 h4 52. ♘e2 ♔d3] **♔c3 51. ♔f3** [51. ♔g3 ♖f8 (51... ♔d4 52. ♗d7 ♖f6 53. ♘f3 ♔e3 54. ♘h4±) 52. ♘f3 ♖g8 53. ♘g5 ♔d4⩲] **♖f8** [51... ♔d4 52. ♗d7 ♖f8 53. ♘c6 ♔c5 54. ♘a5 ♔b4 55. ♘c6 ♔b3 56. f5+−] **52. ♔e3!?** [52. ♔e4 h4 53. f5 (53. ♘g6 h3! 54. ♘f8 h2) h3 54. ♘f3 ♖h8 55. ♘h2 ♖g8 56. f6 ♖g6! (56... ♖g2 57. f7 ♖f2 58. ♘f3) 57. ♔e5 ♖g2 58. f7 ♖f2 59. ♔e6 ♖e2 60. ♔d7 ♖f2] **♖f6!** [52... h4 53. ♘g6 h3 54. ♘f8 h2 55. ♗c6+−] **53. ♔e4** [53. ♘c6 h4 54. ♘a5 h3] **h4 54. f5 h3 55. ♘g4 ♖h6** [55... ♖f8 56. ♔f4 (56. ♔e5 ♖g8 57. f6 ♖g4 58. f7 ♖g5 59. ♔e6 ♖g6=) ♔b4 57. ♘h2 ♖g8 58. f6 ♖g6 59. ♔e5 ♖g2=] **56. ♘h2** [56. ♘h6 h2] **♖d6 57. ♔f4 ♖d2 58. ♔g3 ♖g2?** [58... ♖d5? 59. f6 ♖f5 60. ♘g4+−; 58... ♖d3! 59. ♔g4 ♖d4 60. ♔h3 ♖f4 61. ♗d7 ♔b3 62. ♔g3 ♖f5 63. ♗f5 a4 64. ♘f3 a3 65. ♘d2 ♔b2 66. ♘c4 ♔b3 67. ♗e6 a2=] **59. ♔h3 ♖f2 60. ♗d7 ♔b3 61. ♘g4 ♖f1** [61... ♖f5 62. ♗f5 a4 63. ♗e6 ♔b2 64. ♘e3 a3 65. ♘c4 ♔b3 66. ♘b6 ♔b2 67. ♘a4 ♔b1 68. ♘c3+−; 61... ♖d2 62. ♗e6 ♔b4! (62... ♔b2 63. ♘e5! ♔c3 64. f6 ♖f2 65. f7 a4 66. ♔g3 ♖f6 67. ♘g4 ♖f7 68. ♗f7 a3 69.

♘e5 ♔b2 70. ♘d3 ♔c2 71. ♘b4+−; 62... ♔c3 63. f6 ♖d8 64. f7 a4 65. ♘e5 a3 66. ♘c6 ♖a8 67. ♔g3+− − 61... ♖f1) *a)* 63. ♘e5 ♔c5 64. ♘g6 (64. f6 ♔d6 65. f7 ♖f2 66. ♔g3 ♖f7=) ♔d6; *b)* 63. f6 ♖d8 64. f7 ♔c5 65. ♔h4 ♔d6 66. ♗a2 ♔e7 67. ♔g5 (67. ♘e5 ♔f8 68. ♘g6 ♔g7) ♖d2 68. ♔g6! *b1)* 68... ♖a2 69. ♔g7+−; *b2)* 68... ♔f8 69. ♘e5 ♖f2 70. ♗e6 ♔e7 (70... a4 71. ♗f5 ♖f5 72. ♔f5 ♔g7 73. ♔e6 a3 74. ♔e7+−) 71. ♗f5 a4 (71... ♖g2 72. ♘g4 ♔f8 73. ♔f6 a4 74. ♘e5+−) 72. ♘c6 ♔f8 73. ♘d4! ♔e7 (73... ♖f5 74. ♘f5 a3 75. ♘d4 a2 76. ♘e6+−) 74. ♔g7 ♖g2 75. ♗g6 ♖f2 76. ♘f5+−; *b3)* 68... ♖g2 69. ♗e6 ♖g1 (69... ♖g3 70. ♔g7 ♖f3 71. ♘e5 ♖f2 72. ♗a2 a4 73. ♘g6+−) 70. ♔g7 ♖f1 71. ♗c4 ♖f5 72. ♘e5 ♔d6 73. ♘g6 ♔c5 74. ♗e6 ♖f2 75. f8♕ ♖f8 76. ♘f8 a4 77. ♘d7 ♔b4 78. ♘e5 a3 79. ♘d3 ♔c3 80. ♘c1+−] **62. ♔g2 ♖d1 63. ♗e6 ♔c3** [63... ♔b2 64. ♘e3 ♖d2 65. ♔f3+−] **64. f6 ♖d8 65. ♘e5 a4 66. f7 a3 67. ♘c6 ♖a8 68. ♔g3 ♔b2 69. ♘b4** [69... ♔c3 70. ♘a2 ♔d4 71. ♔f4 ♔c5 72. ♔e5 ♖b8 73. ♔f6 ♔d6 74. ♗c4 ♖a8 75. ♔g7 ♔e7 76. ♘c3+−] **1 : 0**
[Ftáčnik]

515. **E 15**

R. HÜBNER 2620 − HJARTARSON 2625

München 1993

1. d4 ♘f6 2. ♘f3 e6 3. g3 b6 4. ♗g2 ♗b7 5. 0−0 c5 6. dc5 ♗c5 7. c4 ♗e7 [7... 0−0 8. ♘c3 d5!?] **8. ♘c3 d6?!** [8... a6!? 9. ♗f4 0−0] **9. ♗f4 0−0** [9... a6!? 10. ♕d2 (10. ♕d3? e5 △ e4; 10. ♕c2 0−0 11. ♖fd1 ♕c7=) 0−0 11. ♖fd1 ♕c8 12. ♖ac1±] **10. ♘b5 ♘e8 11. ♕c2** [11. ♕d3 ♘a6 12. ♘g5 ♗g5 13. ♗b7 ♘c5 14. ♗g5 ♕g5 (14... ♕d7 15. ♗a8+−; 14... ♕b8 15. ♕f3 ♕b7 16. ♕b7 ♘b7 17. ♗e7+−) 15. ♕f3 ♘b7 (15... ♖b8 16. ♗c6 a6 17. ♗e8±; 15... ♖d8 16. b4±) 16. ♕b7 ♘f6 17. ♖fd1 (17. ♘d6 ♕d2; 17. ♘a7 ♖fb8∞) d5 18. ♘c7 ♖ab8 19. ♕a7 dc4∞] **♘c6□ 12. ♖fd1 a6 13. ♘c3 ♖c8** [13... ♘f6 14. ♕d2] **14. ♕d2** [14. b3 b5 15. cb5 (15. c5 d5 16. e4 ♗c5 17. ed5 ♘b4) ab5 16. ♘b5 ♘a7 17. ♕d3 ♗a6 18. a4 ♕d7∞] **♘b8 15. b3 ♘d7 16. ♖ac1 h6** [16... ♕c7!?] **17. ♘e1** [17. e4 ♕c7 18. ♕e1 ♘e5 (18... ♘ef6 19. e5 ♘e5 20. ♘e5 ♗g2 21. ♘g6) 19. ♘d4 ♘f6=] **♗g2 18. ♔g2 ♕c7 19. f3** [19. ♘e4 ♘df6 20. ♘f6 ♘f6= 21. ♗d6? ♕c6 △ ♖fd8] **♕b7** [△ b5; 19... ♘e5 20. ♗e5 de5 21. ♕d7±] **20. ♘e4 ♘c5 21. ♘c5** [21. ♘d6? ♘d6 22. ♗d6 ♖fd8 23. ♕f4 ♗g5−+] **♖c5** [21... bc5 22. ♕a5 △ ♖d3, ♖cd1±] **22. ♘d3 ♖c8** [22... ♖c6!?] **23. ♘f2 ♖d8** [23... ♘f6 24. ♗d6 ♖fd8 25. ♕f4 (25. ♕b4? a5 26. ♕a3 ♖d6 27. ♖d6 ♕c7 28. ♖cd1 ♘e8−+) g5 *a)* 26. ♗e7 gf4 (26... ♖d1 27. ♕f6 ♖c1 28. ♘g4+−) 27. ♗d8±; *b)* 26. ♕e5 ♖d6 27. ♖d6 ♕c7 28. ♖cd1 ♘e8 29. ♖e6+−; 23... b5 24. ♘e4 bc4 25. bc4±] **24. ♘e4 f5** [24... d5 25. cd5 ♖d5 26. ♕c2 ♘f6 (26... ♖d1? 27. ♕d1 ♘f6 28. ♖c7 ♕d5 29. ♘f6 ♗f6 30. ♕d5 ed5 31. ♖c6+−) 27. ♘f6 ♗f6 28. ♖d5 ♕d5 29. ♕c6 ♕b5 30. ♖c2±] **25. ♘c3 ♘f6 26. ♕d3 ♘g4?!** [26... ♘d7?! 27. e4 ♘c5 28. ♕e2 fe4 29. ♘e4 ♘e4 30. ♕e4 ♕e4 31. fe4 ♔f7 (31... ♗g5 32. ♗g5 hg5 33. ♖c2 ♔f7 34. ♔h3 △ ♔g4±) 32. ♖c2±; 26... ♖d7 27. e4 fe4 28. ♘e4 d5 29. ♘f6 ♗f6 30. ♖e1±; 26... d5!? 27. cd5 (27. ♗e5 d4 28. ♘b1 ♘g4) ♗a3 28. ♖b1 ♘d5 29. ♘d5 ♖d5 30. ♕e3 ♕c6 31. ♖d5 ed5 (31... ♕d5 32. ♕b6) 32. b4 ♖e8 33. ♕a3 (33. ♕d3 ♕c4) ♖e2 34. ♔h3 (34. ♔g1 ♕c2−+) ♕g6 35. g4 fg4 36. fg4 ♕b1] **27. e4** [27. h3 ♘e5 28. ♕e3 ♗f6=] **fe4?!** [27... ♘e5 28. ♕e3 (28. ♕e2 ♗g5 Hjartarson) ♘g6 (28... ♘f7 29. ef5 e5 30. ♘d5 ♖d7 31. f6) 29. ef5 ♘f4 30. gf4 ef5 31. ♘d5+−; 27... g5 28. fg4 fe4 (28... gf4 29. gf5 ♖f5 30. ♘d5 f3 31. ♔h1 ♖f7 32. ♘f4±) 29. ♕e4 (29. ♘e4 gf4 30. ♔g1 d5) ♕e4 30. ♘e4 gf4 31. ♖d3 d5 32. cd5 ed5 33. ♘c3 fg3 34. ♔g3 d4 35. ♘e4±] **28. ♘e4** [28. ♕e4 ♕e4 29. ♘e4 ♖f4 30. gf4 ♘e3=] **g5** [28... ♘f6 29. ♖e1±; ⌓ 28... ♘e5 29. ♗e5 (29. ♕c3 ♘f7) de5 30. ♕c3 ♕c7 △ 31. b4 ♖d4] **29. h3 gf4?** [29... ♘f6 30. ♘d6+−; 29... ♘e5 30. ♗e5 de5 31. ♕c3 ♕c7±] **30. hg4 fg3** [30... d5 31. ♘c3 ♗g5 (31... ♗f6 32. gf4+−) 32.

cd5+−; 30... ♔g7 31. ♖h1 d5 32. cd5 ♕d5 33. ♕c3 ♕d4 34. ♕d4 ♖d4 35. ♖c7 ♖f7 36. gf4+−] **31. ♖h1?** [⌓ 31. ♘c5 ♕f3□ 32. ♕f3 ♖f3 33. ♘e6 ♖f2 34. ♔g3 ♖a2 35. ♘d8 ♗d8 36. ♔f3 ♗e7 (36... ♖b2 37. ♖b1+−) 37. ♔e4+−] **d5 32. ♘g3 ♗f6** [⌓ 32... ♗g5 33. ♕g6 ♕g7 34. ♕e6 ♕f7 (34... ♔h8 35. ♖c2+− ×f5) 35. ♕f7 ♔f7 36. ♖c2] **33. ♖h6+− dc4 34. ♕g6 ♗g7** [34... ♕g7 35. ♘h5 ♖d2 36. ♔h3+−] **35. ♘e4 ♖f4** [35... ♖f7 36. ♖ch1 ♔f8 37. ♖h8 ♔e7 (37... ♗h8 38. ♖h8 ♔e7 39. ♕g5+−) 38. ♕g5 ♗f6 39. ♕f6 (39. ♘f6+−) ♖f6 40. ♖1h7 ♖f7 41. ♖f7 ♔f7 42. ♖h7+−] **36. ♖ch1 1 : 0 [R. Hübner]**

516.** **E 16**

BAREEV 2670 − HJARTARSON 2625

München 1993

1. d4 ♘f6 2. c4 e6 3. ♘f3 ♗b4 4. ♘bd2 [RR 4. ♗d2 *a)* 4... a5 5. g3 b6 6. ♗g2 ♗b7 7. 0−0 0−0 8. ♗f4 ♗e7 9. ♘c3 ♘e4 10. ♕c2 ♘c3 11. bc3 ♖a7 N (11... f5 − 48/(696)) 12. e4 d6 13. ♖fe1 ♘d7 14. ♖ad1 ♕e8 (Je. Piket 2590 − Kortchnoi 2605, Nijmegen (m/8) 1993) 15. a4± Kortchnoi; *b)* 4... c5 5. ♗b4 cb4 6. g3 b6 7. ♗g2 ♗b7 8. 0−0 0−0 9. a3 ba3 10. ♖a3 d5 N (10... ♘c6 − 37/(597)) 11. ♘e5 ♕e7 12. cd5 ♘d5 13. ♘c3 ♘c3 14. ♖c3 ♗g2 15. ♔g2 ♕b7 16. ♔g1 ♘d7= Kállai 2450 − U. Andersson 2625, France 1993] **b6 5. a3 ♗d2 6. ♗d2 ♗b7 7. g3 d6 8. ♗g2 ♘bd7 9. 0−0 a5!? N** [9... 0−0 − 54/521] **10. b4 ab4 11. ab4 0−0 12. b5! ♖a1 13. ♕a1 ♕a8 14. ♗b4± ♗e4 15. ♖c1** [△ ♕c3, ♗f1, ♘d2] **h6** [15... ♕a1 16. ♖a1 ♖a8 17. ♖a8 ♗a8 18. ♗f1±] **16. ♕c3 e5! 17. d5 ♕b7 18. ♖a1 ♖a8 19. ♖a3 ♘c5 20. ♗h3 ♗h7** [20... g5? 21. ♘e5! de5 22. ♕e5+−] **21. ♘h4 ♘ce4 22. ♕a1 ♖a3 23. ♕a3 ♘g5 24. ♗f5 ♕b8** [24... ♗f5!? 25. ♘f5 ♔h7] **25. f3 ♔h8 26. ♔g2** [△ g4] **♗f5 27. ♘f5 ♕c8 28. g4 h5!? 29. h4 ♘gh7 30. ♕a6 ♕d8** [30... ♕d7 31. ♕a8 ♘g8 32. ♕c6 ♘gf6 33. ♕d7 ♘d7 34. gh5±] **31. g5 ♘d7 32. ♘g3 f6** [32... g6 33. e3 △ f4±] **33. gf6 ♘hf6** [33... ♕f6? 34. ♕c8] **34. ♗d2 e4 35. ♗g5 ef3 36. ef3 ♘e5 37. ♕a2** [37. ♘h5 ♕f8 38. ♗f6 gf6 39. ♕b7±; 37... ♕g8!=] **♕f8 38. ♕e2 g6 39. f4 ♘eg4 40. ♕e6 ♔h7** [40... ♔g7 41. f5 ♕f7±] **41. f5 ♕g7 42. ♔f3! ♘g8** [42... ♘e5 43. ♔f4 ♘d3 44. ♔e3 ♘e5 45. ♔e2±] **43. ♘e2! gf5 44. ♕f5 ♔h8** [44... ♕g6 45. ♕g6 ♔g6 46. ♗d8 ♘e5 47. ♔e4±] **45. ♗f4!** [45. ♗d8? ♘8h6!; 45. ♗c1 ♘e5 46. ♔f2 ♕f6] **♕h7 46. ♕h7 ♔h7 47. ♗g5! ♘e5?!** [47... ♔g6 48. ♗d8!±; 47... ♘8f6!? 48. ♘f4 △ ♘e6±] **48. ♔e4 ♘c4 49. ♔f5!+− ♘h6 50. ♔e6 ♔g7 51. ♗f6** [51. ♗d8!] **♔g8** [51... ♔f8 52. ♗d8 ♘f7 53. ♗c7 ♔e8 54. ♘c3 ♘d8 (54... ♔f8 55. ♘e4 ♘a3 56. ♘d6+−) 55. ♗d8 ♔d8 56. ♔f6+−] **52. ♗d8 ♔f8 53. ♗c7 ♘f7 54. ♘c3** [54. ♘d4!] **♔e8** [54... ♔g7 55. ♘e2 △ ♘d4+−] **55. ♘e4 ♘a3 56. ♘d6!** [56. ♗d6? ♘d6!] **♘d6 57. ♗d6 ♘b5 58. ♗e5 ♘a7 59. ♗f6! ♘c8 60. d6 ♘d6 61. ♔d6 1 : 0 [Bareev]**

517.* !N **E 17**

AN. KARPOV 2725 − IVANČUK 2710

Linares 1993

1. d4 ♘f6 2. c4 e6 3. ♘f3 b6 4. g3 ♗b7 5. ♗g2 ♗e7 6. ♘c3 0−0 7. d5 [RR 7. ♕c2 c5! 8. d5 ed5 9. ♘g5 h6 10. ♘d5 ♗d5 11. cd5 hg5! N (11... d6) 12. d6 ♘c6 13. de7 ♕e7 14. ♗g5 (14. ♗c6 dc6 15. ♗g5=) d5! 15. e3 (15. ♗d5? ♘b4; 15. ♗f6 ♕f6 16. ♗d5 ♘b4 17. ♕b3 ♘d5 18. ♕d5 ♕b2; 15. ♖d1 ♘d4!? 16. ♕d2 ♖ad8 17. e3 ♘e6 18. ♗f6 ♕f6=; 15... ♖ad8!? △ ♘d4-e6=) ♕e6 (△ ♘e4) 16. ♗f6 ♕f6 17. 0−0 ♖ad8!? 18. ♖fd1 ♖d6 19. ♖d2 (19. ♗d5? ♘b4 20. ♕b3 ♖d5 21. ♖d5 ♘d5 22. ♕d5 ♖d8∓ △ 23... ♕b2, 23... ♖d2) ♖fd8 20. ♖ad1 ♕e5= Balašov 2545 − Tivjakov 2595, Sankt-Peterburg (zt) 1993; 20... ♕e6!? Tivjakov] **♗b4 8. ♗d2 ♗c3 N** [8... c6 − 43/685] **9. ♗c3 ed5 10. ♘h4 ♘e4 11. cd5 ♘c3 12. bc3 d6 13. 0−0 ♘d7 14. e4 ♘c5** [14... ♕f6 15. ♕d4 ♖fe8 (15... c6 16. dc6 ♗c6 17. ♖ad1±) 16. f4 c6 17. e5 de5 18. fe5±] **15. ♕d4 ♗a6** [15... ♗c8 16. f4 △ e5±] **16. ♖fe1 ♕d7 17. f4 f6 18. ♘f3!± ♖ae8** [18... ♕a4 19.

e5 fe5 20. fe5 de5 21. ♘e5±] **19. e5** [19. ♖e3 ♕b5 △ ♕b2] **de5 20. fe5 fe5 21. ♘e5 ♕d6 22. ♖e3 ♗b5** [22... ♕f6 23. h4 ♕f2 24. ♔h2 ♘d3 25. ♖d3 ♖e5!; 25. ♘g4!] **23. ♖ae1 ♘d7 24. ♘c6 ♖e3 25. ♖e3 ♘f6 26. g4!** [26. h3 ♗c6 27. dc6 ♕d4 28. cd4 ♔f7] **♗c6 27. dc6 ♕d4 28. cd4** **[♖ 9/i]** **♖e8** [28... ♘g4 29. ♖e7 ♖c8 30. ♗d5+−; 28... h6 29. d5 ♖d8 30. ♖e7 ♘d5? 31. ♖d7+−] **29. ♖a3 ♘g4** [29... a5 30. g5 ♘e4 31. ♖e3 ♘d6 32. ♗d5±] **30. ♖a7?!** [30. ♗d5! ♔f8 31. ♖a7 ♘f6 *a)* 32. ♗b3 ♖e7 33. d5 (33. ♖a8 ♖e8) ♘e8 34. ♖a8 g6; *b)* 32. ♗g2 ♖e7 33. d5 ♘e8 34. ♗h3 ♘d6 35. a4± △ 36. ♗d7, 36. ♗e6] **♖e1! 31. ♗f1 ♖c1 32. ♖c7 ♔f8! 33. ♖c8** [33. d5 ♘e3!] **♔e7 34. c7 ♔d6!** [34... ♔d7 35. ♖g8 ♘e3 36. c8♕ ♖c8 37. ♗h3+−] **35. ♖h8 ♔c7 36. ♖h7 ♔d6 37. ♖g7 ♘h2 38. ♔h2 ♖f1 39. ♔g2 ♖a1 40. ♔f3 ♖a2 41. ♔e4 ♖e2 42. ♔d3 ♖e8**
1/2 : 1/2 **[An. Karpov]**

518.* **E 17**

IVANČUK 2710 − V. SALOV 2660
Linares 1993

1. d4 ♘f6 2. c4 e6 3. ♘f3 b6 4. g3 ♗b7 5. ♗g2 ♗e7 6. ♘c3 ♘e4 7. ♗d2 f5 8. d5 ♗f6 [RR 8... 0−0 9. ♘d4 N (9. ♕c2 − 54/522) ♗f6 10. e3 *a)* 10... ♗d4 11. ed4 ed5 (11... ♘c3 12. bc3 ed5 13. cd5 ♕e7 14. ♗e3±) 12. cd5 ♘d2 13. ♕d2 ♖e8 14. ♔f1 △ ♗f3, ♔g2, h4, ♕f4±; *b)* 10... ♘d2 11. ♕d2⩲; *c)* 10... ♘d6! 11. b3□ (11. ♕b3 ♘a6↑) c5! *c1)* 12. dc6 ♘c6 13. ♘c6 (13. ♘de2 ♘e5) ♗c6 14. 0−0 ♕c7 15. ♖c1 ♕b7 16. ♗c6 (16. f3 b5↑) dc6∓ A. Chernin 2600 − Z. Almasi 2470, Magyarország (ch) 1992; *c2)* 12. ♘de2 ed5 13. cd5 b5 14. ♖c1 a5 △ ♘a6∓; *c3)* 12. ♘db5 ♘b5 13. cb5 a6!! (13... e5 14. 0−0±) 14. ba6□ (14. 0−0 ab5∓) ♗a6 15. de6 ♘c6!∞̄→ A. Chernin] **9. ♕c2 ♘d6 10. ♗f4 ♕e7** [10... 0−0 11. 0−0 ♘a6 12. ♖fd1 ♘c5 13. ♖ac1⩲] **11. ♗d6 cd6 12. 0−0 N** [12. ♖d1] **0−0 13. ♖fd1** [13. e3!? △ 14. ♘d4 ♗d4 15. ed4] **g6** [13... ♖c8 14. ♘d4 ♖c4? 15. de6 ♗g2 16. ♘f5±] **14. ♘d4 e5 15. ♘db5 ♖c8 16. e4 f4 17. ♕b3** [⌓ 17. ♗f1] **♘a6 18. ♕a3 ♖c5 19. ♗f1 ♘c7 20. ♖ac1** [20. ♘d6?! ♕d6? 21. b4 ♖a5 22. ♕b3 ♖a6 23. c5+−; 20... ♖a5!] **fg3 21. hg3 ♗g5 22. ♖c2 ♘b5 23. cb5 h5 24. ♗d3 ♔g7?!** [24... h4! △ 25. b4 ♖cc8 26. ♘e2 hg3 27. fg3 ♖f8⇆; 27. ♘g3∞] **25. b4 ♖c7 26. ♘e2 ♖c2 27. ♗c2 a6 28. ♔g2 ab5 29. ♕b3 h4 30. ♘g1 hg3 31. fg3 ♕f8 32. ♘f3 ♗h6 33. ♕b2 ♕c8 34. ♗b3** [⌓ 34. a3] **♕c7 35. ♘g1** [35. ♘h4 (△ ♕e2-g4) ♕d8 (35... ♗g5 36. ♖f1 ♗h4? 37. ♕f2!+−) 36. ♕e2 ♕g5∞] **♖c8?!** [35... ♗e3!? 36. ♘e2 ♖f8 37. ♖f1 ♖f1 38. ♔f1 ♕d8 39. ♔g2 ♕f6 40. ♘c3 (△ 40... ♗d4?! 41. ♕d2±) ♕g5!] **36. ♘e2 ♕d8 37. ♕b1 ♕g5 38. ♕d3 ♖f8 39. ♖f1 ♕d2 40. ♕d2 ♗d2 41. ♖f8 ♔f8** **[♘♗ 9/e]** **42. a3 ♔e7 43. ♔f3 ♔f6 44. ♔g4 ♔g7 45. ♗c2 ♔f6 46. ♗d3 ♗a6 47. ♘g1! ♗c1 48. a4 ba4** [48... ♗d2 49. ab5 ♗c8 50. ♘h3 ♗b4 (50... ♗e3 51. ♔f3 ♗d4 52. ♘f2 ♗f2 53. ♔f2 ♔g5 54. ♔f3 ♔h5 55. ♗f1 ♔g5 56. ♗g2! ♔h5 57. ♗h3 ♔g5 58. ♗g4 ♔f6 59. ♔g2 ♔g5 60. ♔h3+−⊙) 51. ♘f2 ♗c5 52. ♘d1 (△ ♘b2-c4) ♗d4 53. ♗f1 ♗b7 54. ♗h3 ♗c8 55. ♔h4 ♗g1 56. ♘b2 ♗d4 57. ♘c4 ♗c5 58. ♗g4+−⊙] **49. ♗a6** **[♘♗ 8/g]** **a3 50. ♗c4 b5 51. ♗b3 ♗d2 52. ♘f3 ♗b4 53. ♔h3 ♔e7 54. ♔g2 ♔d8 55. ♔f1 ♔c7 56. ♔e2 ♔b6 57. ♔d3 ♗c5 58. ♔c3 ♗f2 59. g4 ♔c5 60. ♗a2 ♗g3 61. ♔b3 b4 62. ♔a4?!** [62. ♗b1 ♗f4 63. g5 ♗e3 64. ♗d3 ♗f4 65. ♗f1 ♔b6 (65... ♗e3 66. ♗h3 a2 67. ♔a2 ♔c4 68. ♗f1 ♔c3 69. ♔b1 ♗f4 70. ♗b5 b3 71. ♗e2 ♗e3 72. ♗f1 ♗f4 73. ♗b5 ♗e3 74. ♗d7 ♔d3 75. ♗f5 gf5 76. ef5 e4 77. f6+−) 66. ♗h3 ♔c7 67. ♘h4 ♗g5 68. ♘g6 ♔b6 69. ♗d7 ♔c5 70. ♘f8+−] **♗f4 63. ♗b3?** [63. g5!] **g5!= 64. ♔a5 ♗e3 65. ♔a6 ♗f4 66. ♔b7 ♗e3 67. ♔c7 ♗f4 68. ♔d7 ♗e3 69. ♔c7 ♗f4 70. ♔b7 ♔b5 71. ♘g1 ♔c5 72. ♘e2 ♗d2 73. ♔a7 ♗c3 74. ♔a8 ♗e1 75. ♔b8 ♗c3 76. ♔a7 ♗d2 77. ♔b7 ♗c3 78. ♔c8 ♗d2 79. ♔d8 ♗e3 80. ♔e7 ♗d2 81. ♔e6 ♗e3 82. ♗a2 ♗d2** [82... ♗f4!] **83. ♘g3 ♔d4 84. ♘f5 ♔c3?** [84... ♔e4! 85. ♘d6 ♔f4 86. ♘b5 (86. ♘c4 e4!) e4 87. d6 e3 88. ♘d4 b3! 89. ♗b3 ♔g4=] **85. ♘d6+− b3 86. ♘b5 ♔b4**

87. ♗b3 ♔b3 88. ♘a3 ♔a3 89. d6 ♔b3 90. ♔f6 ♔c4 91. d7 ♗a5 92. ♔g5 ♔c5 93. ♔h6 1 : 0 [Ivančuk]

519.* E 17

B. GEL'FAND 2690 – HJARTARSON 2625

München 1993

1. d4 ♘f6 2. c4 e6 3. ♘f3 b6 4. g3 ♗b7 5. ♗g2 ♗e7 6. ♘c3 ♘e4 7. ♗d2 f5?! 8. d5 ♗f6 9. ♕c2 ♘d6 10. ♗f4 ♕e7 11. ♗d6 ♕d6 12. 0–0 ♘a6 13. e4 N [13. de6 de6 14. ♖fd1 ♕c5 15. ♕a4 c6 16. ♖ac1±; 13. ♖ad1 – 46/(729)] **♗c3 14. ♕c3 fe4** [RR 14... 0-0-0? 15. ♖fd1 (15. ♖ad1!?) fe4 16. ♘g5 ed5 *a)* 17. cd5!? e3! 18. ♕e3 (18. ♘f7 ef2 19. ♔h1 ♕e7∞) ♖de8 19. ♕d4 ♕f6 20. ♕f6 gf6 21. ♘e4 ♖hf8 (21... f5 22. ♘c3 ♘c5 23. b4 ♘e4 24. ♗e4 fe4 25. ♖d4 e3 26. f4±) 22. ♖ac1 ♔d8 23. ♖d4 ♖e5 24. ♘c3 ♖fe8 25. ♗e4! f5 26. ♗b1 c5! 27. dc6 ♗c6 28. ♔f1 ♘c7! (Huzman 2510 – Kosashvili 2490, Israel 1993) 29. ♖f4!± ×d7, f5, h7; *b)* 17. ♘f7! ♕e7 18. ♘d8 d4! 19. ♖d4 ♖d8 20. ♖e1±; 14... 0–0! 15. e5 (15. ♖ad1!?) ♕c5 16. de6 de6 17. a3⩲ Huzman] **15. ♘g5** [15. ♕g7? 0-0-0=] **ed5 16. cd5 0–0** [16... ♕f6?! 17. ♕f6 gf6 18. ♘e4 0–0 19. d6 ♗e4 20. ♗e4 c6 21. ♗f5±] **17. ♘e4± ♕b4 18. ♖fd1 ♖ae8 19. ♖d4 ♕c3 20. ♘c3 c5 21. dc6?** [21. ♖a4 ♖a8□ 22. ♘b5 ♖f6 23. ♖e1±] **dc6 22. ♖d6 ♘b8 23. ♖ad1 ♖e7 24. f4 c5 25. ♗b7 ♖b7± 26. ♔f2 g5! 27. ♘d5 ♖bf7 28. ♔g2** [28. ♔f3!?⩲] **gf4 29. ♘f4 ♘a6 30. ♖1d5⊙** [30. a3⩲] **♘c7= 31. ♖g5 ♔h8 32. ♖h6 ♖d8 33. ♘g6 ♔g8 34. ♘e7?** [34. ♘e5 ♖g7 35. ♖g7 ♔g7 36. ♖c6=] **♔f8 35. ♘f5 ♖d2 36. ♔h3 ♖b2∓ 37. ♖gh5 ♖a2 38. ♖h7 ♖h7 39. ♖h7 ♘e6 40. ♔g4 c4 41. ♖h8 ♔f7 42. ♘d6 ♔e7** [42... ♔g7!? 43. ♖c8 ♘c5∓ △ 44. ♘c4 ♖a4–+] **43. ♘e4 ♘c5 44. ♘c5 bc5** [♖ 6/d] **45. ♔f3 c3 46. ♔e3 ♖d2! 47. ♖h7 ♔d6 48. ♖a7 c4?** [48... ♖d1 49. ♖a2□ ♔d5 50. ♔e2 ♖d4! 51. h4 ♔c4 52. h5 ♔b3 53. ♖a5 ♖d5–+] **49. ♖a8!= ♔c5 50. ♖c8 ♔b4 51. ♖b8 ♔a3 52. ♖a8 ♔b2 53. ♖b8 ♔c1 54. ♖c8 ♖h2 55. ♖c4 c2 56. g4 ♔b2 57. ♔f4 ♔b3 58. ♖c7 ♖h1 59. ♔f5 c1♕ 60. ♖c1 ♖c1 61. g5 ♔c4 1/2 : 1/2** [Hjartarson]

520. E 18

RAZUVAEV 2525 – TIVJAKOV 2595

Rostov na Donu 1993

1. d4 ♘f6 2. c4 e6 3. ♘f3 b6 4. g3 ♗e7 5. ♗g2 ♗b7 6. ♘c3 0–0!? 7. d5?! ♗b4! 8. ♗d2□ ♘a6! 9. 0–0 ♘c5 10. ♘e1 N [10. ♘h4 – 56/(611)] **♖e8!** [↑⊞, →×d5] **11. ♘c2** [11. a3 ♗c3 12. ♗c3 ed5 △ ♘ce4→ ×d5; 11. de6∓] **♗c3 12. ♗c3 ed5 13. cd5** [13. ♗d5 ♘d5 14. cd5 ⇗h1-a8] **♘ce4! 14. ♘e3** [14. ♘b4? a5; 14. ♗d4 ♘d5 15. f3 ♘g5∓; 14. ♗f6 ♕f6∓→ ×b2, d5, e2] **♘c3 15. bc3**

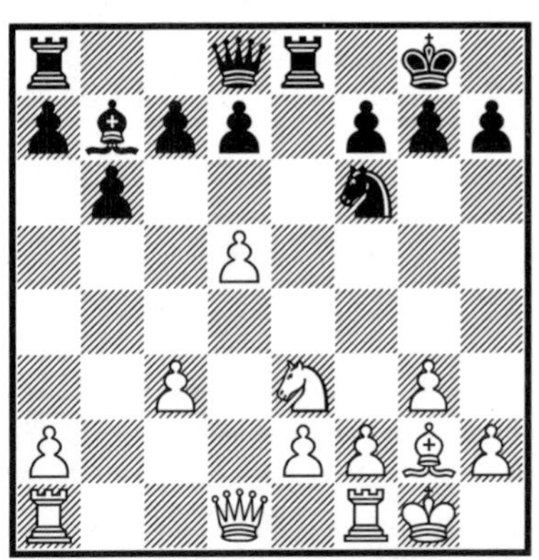

15... ♖e3!!∓ 16. fe3 d6 17. ♕d4 ♘d7 [17... ♕e7 18. ♖f6!?] **18. ♖f4** [18. a4 a5 ×a4] **♕e7** [18... ♘c5?! 19. ♖af1 f6 20. ♗e4 △ ♖h4↑⟫; 18... ♘e5∓] **19. ♖af1 ♘e5** [19... ♖f8] **20. ♗e4 ♖f8 21. ♗d3 ♗c8!? 22. ♕e4 g6 23. ♖f6** [23. ♔g2; 23. ♕d4] **♔g7 24. c4?!** [×♗d3; 24. ♕h4∓; 24. ♖6f4∓] **♗d7** [24... ♕f6 25. ♖f6 ♔f6 26. c5 bc5 (26... dc5? 27. ♕f4) 27. ♕a4⇆] **25. h4?** [×⟫; ⌓ 25. ♕h4; 25. ♖6f4∓] **♕f6 26. ♖f6 ♔f6∓⊥ 27. ♕d4 ♖e8! 28. ♔f2 ♔g7 29. ♔e1 f6 30. ♔d2 ♘g4 31. e4** [31. ♗c2 ♖e5!? (31... ♘e3 32. ♕e3 ♖e3 33. ♔e3∓⊥) 32. ♗d3 ♗f5!? 33. e4 (33. ♗f5 gf5 34. ♕f4 h5 △ ♔g6, ♖e4–+) ♗d7∓] **♘e5** [31... ♖e5!? △ ♔f8-e7, ♗e8, g5, ♗g6, gh4, ♖h5→ ×⟫] **32. ♕c3 ♖e7** [△ ♗e8, ♘d7-c5, ♖e5, g5,

♗g6∓→ ×e4, △ ♘f7, ♖e5, ♔f8-e7, ♘d8-b7-c5, ♗e8, g5, ♗g6∓→ ×e4] **33. ♕a3 a5 34. ♕b2 ♘f7!** [34... ♗e8?! 35. c5!⇆] **35. ♗c2 ♖e5 36. ♕a3 ♔f8 37. ♗a4 ♗g4 38. ♕d3** [38. ♗c2] **♔e7 39. c5?** [39. ♗c2∓] **dc5 40. ♕b5 ♘d6 41. ♕c6 ♔d8 42. ♗c2 ♗c8** [△ ♗b7] **43. ♕a8** [43. ♗d3 ♗b7 44. ♕a4 c4−+; 43. ♕a4!?] **g5 44. ♕c6** [44. hg5 ♖g5 ×g3; 44... fg5−+ △ h5 ♁h; 44. h5 g4 △ ♖h5; 44... h6 △ g4−+] **gh4 45. gh4 ♖h5 46. e5** [46. ♕a4 ♖h4 47. ♕b3 (47. ♕a3 ♘c4) ♖h3 *a)* 48. ♗d3 c4 49. ♕b2 (49. ♕c3 ♘e4) ♘e4 50. ♗e4 c3; *b)* 48. ♕b1 ♘c4 49. ♔c1 ♖h1 50. ♗d1 ♘e3; *c)* 48. e3 ♗a6 49. ♕c3 ♘c4 50. ♔c1 ♖h1 51. ♗d1 ♘e5−+] **fe5 47. ♕a4 e4** [47... c4−+] **48. ♕b3 ♗b7** [48... c4 △ ♖d5−+] **49. ♕c3 ♗d5 50. ♕f6 ♔d7 51. a4! ♔c6?!** [51... ♖f5 △ ♖f7−+] **52. ♕e7!** [×e4, h7] **♔b7 53. ♔c3 ♗c6 54. ♔b2 c4 55. ♔c3 ♘c8!** [△ ♖c5, ♘e7-d5 ♁c] **56. ♕f6 ♖c5 57. ♕h6 ♘e7 58. ♕h7 ♘d5 59. ♔d4** [59. ♔d2 e3 60. ♔c1 ♘f4 61. ♗d1 c3−+; 59... c3−+ △ ♘f4; 59. ♔b2 c3 60. ♔b1 ♘b4−+ △ 61. h5 ♖g5] **c3 60. ♗e4 ♘b4 61. ♗g6** [61. ♗c2 ♘c2 62. ♕c2 ♗a4] **♗a4** [61... c2−+] **62. h5 c2 63. ♗c2 ♗c2 64. ♕f7** [64. e4 ♘c6 65. ♔e3 ♖c4!? 66. h6 ♗e4 67. ♕e4 ♖e4 68. ♔e4 ♘e7 69. h7 ♘g6 70. ♔f5 ♘h8 71. ♔f6 a4 72. ♔g7 a3 73. ♔h8 a2−+; 64... a4−+] **a4 65. h6 a3 0 : 1**
[Tivjakov]

521.* **E 18**

AN. KARPOV 2725 − V. SALOV 2660
Linares 1993

1. d4 ♘f6 2. c4 e6 3. ♘f3 b6 4. g3 ♗b7 5. ♗g2 ♗e7 6. ♘c3 ♘e4 7. ♗d2 ♗f6 8. 0−0 0−0 9. ♖c1 c5 10. d5 ed5 11. cd5 ♘d2 12. ♘d2 d6 13. ♘de4 ♗e7 14. f4! ♘d7 [RR 14... ♗c8 15. ♔h1!? N (15. e3 − 45/(673)) *a)* 15... ♘d7!? 16. g4 ♘f6 17. ♘f6 ♗f6 18. g5 ♗e7 (18... ♗c3 19. ♖c3 f6 20. ♖g3→) 19. ♘e4 △ ♖c3, h4→; *b)* 15... ♖e8 16. ♗f3 a6 17. a4 *b1)* 17... ♗f8 18. g4 h6 19. ♖g1 ♕h4 20. ♕d2 *b11)* 20... f5 21. gf5 ♗f5 22. ♘g3 ♗g4 23. ♗e4 ♘d7 24. ♗g6 ♘f6! (24... ♖e7? 25. ♘ce4+−) 25. ♗e8 ♖e8 26. ♖cf1 ♕h3 27. f5 (27. e4 h5∞) b5 (27... h5 28. ♖f4 h4? 29. ♘ge4+−) 28. ab5 ab5 29. ♖f4 ♖e5 30. ♘ce4 (Savčenko 2535 − Timošenko 2515, Nikolaev (zt) 1993) ♘e4 31. ♘e4 ♗f5 32. ♘f6 ♔h8 33. ♖g3 ♕g3 34. hg3 gf6±; *b12)* 20... ♖a7 21. g5 ♗f5 (21... ♖ae7 22. ♘f6+−; 21... hg5 22. ♖g5 △ ♖h5+−) 22. gh6 ♕h6 23. ♖g5±; *b2)* 17... ♘d7 18. g4 ♘f6 19. ♘f2 (19. g5 ♘e4 20. ♘e4↑) h6 20. e4↑ Savčenko] **15. g4 a6 16. a4 ♖e8 N** [16... ♘f6 17. ♘f2 h6 18. h4 g5 19. hg5 hg5 20. e3±; 16... b5 − 53/517] **17. g5 ♗f8 18. ♔h1!± b5!?** [18... g6 19. ♗h3±; 18... ♖b8 19. b3±] **19. ab5 ab5 20. ♘b5 ♕b6** [20... ♘b6 21. ♘bc3 ♘c4 22. ♕d3 ♗a6 (22... ♘b2? 23. ♕b5+−) 23. ♕g3 △ f5, g6] **21. ♘bc3** [21. ♘a3 ♗a6!⇆] **♕b4** [21... ♗a6 22. ♖f3 △ ♖h3, ♕e1-h4] **22. ♕d3 ♘b6 23. ♕g3! ♔h8** [23... ♘d5 24. ♘d5 ♗d5 25. ♘f6 gf6 26. gf6 ♔h8 27. ♗d5+−] **24. ♖cd1 ♘c4** [24... ♘a4 25. ♖b1!?; 24... ♗c8 25. f5 ♖e5 26. g6 ♗f5 27. ♘g5!] **25. b3!** [25. f5 ♘e5!] **♘b6 26. g6!** [26. f5 ♖a3 27. g6 f6!] **fg6** [26... hg6 27. ♕h4 ♔g8 28. ♘g5+−; 26... f6 27. gh7 △ ♘f6] **27. f5 gf5 28. ♖f5 ♘d7 29. ♖df1** [29. ♘d6 ♗d6 30. ♕d6 ♘f8 (30... ♕c3 31. ♕d7 ♗a6 32. ♖df1 ♖g8 33. d6 ♗e2) 31. ♕g3 ♘g6 (31... ♖a3 32. ♘e4!) 32. e4] **♘e5 30. ♖5f4** [30. ♘g5 ♕g4 31. ♖e5?! ♕g3 32. ♖e8 ♕g2! 33. ♔g2 ♖e8] **♕b6** [30... ♘g6 31. ♖g4 ♗c8 32. ♖g6 hg6 33. ♕g6 △ ♘g5+−] **31. ♘g5 ♘g6** [31... ♗e7 32. ♘f7 ♘f7 33. ♖f7 ♗f8 34. ♗e4 ♔g8 35. ♗h7 ♔h7 36. ♖g1+−] **32. ♘f7 ♔g8 33. ♕g6!+−** [33... hg6 34. ♖h4] **1 : 0**
[An. Karpov]

522. **E 18**

GAUSEL 2485 − TIVJAKOV 2595
Gausdal 1993

1. ♘f3 ♘f6 2. c4 b6 3. g3 e6 4. ♗g2 ♗e7 5. 0−0 ♗b7 6. ♘c3 0−0 7. d4 ♘e4 8. ♗d2 f5! 9. d5 ♗f6 10. ♖c1 ♘a6!? 11. ♗e1!? ♘ac5!? 12. ♘d4 ♕e7 [12... a5 13. ♘e4!? (13. b3 − 55/525) *a)* 13... ♘e4 14. de6 de6 (14... ♗d4 15. ♕d4 de6 16.

♕e3!?±⊡; 14... c5 15. ♘f5 de6 16. ♕d8 ♖ad8 17. ♘e3± △ 17... ♗b2 18. ♖b1 ×b6) 15. ♘e6 ♕d1 16. ♖d1 ♖f7 17. b3±; 17. ♖b1!?±; *b)* 13... fe4 14. ♘b3!? *b1)* 14... ♗b2? 15. ♘c5 ♗c1 (15... bc5 16. ♖b1+− ×♗b2, ♗b7) 16. ♘b7+−; *b2)* 14... ed5? 15. ♘c5 bc5 16. cd5± ×c5, e4, ⇔b; *b3)* 14... ♘b3□ 15. ♕b3 (15. ab3 ♗b2 16. ♖b1 △ ♗e4∞) a4!□∞] **13. ♘b3 N** [13. ♘e4 − 52/(535); 13. b4] **a5!**∓ [13... ♘b3=; 13... ♘c3=] **14. ♘c5** [14. ♘e4 ♘e4∓ △ a4 ×b2, d5; 14. de6!? de6 (14... ♕e6!?) 15. ♘c5 ♘c5 (15... ♕c5!? △ 16. ♘e4 ♗e4 17. ♗e4 fe4) 16. ♗b7 ♘b7∓; 14. e3!?] **♘c5 15. ♕c2** [15. de6 ♗g2 16. ♔g2 de6∓; 16... ♕e6!?; 15. e3!?] **d6!?** [15... ♖ae8 16. de6 (16. e3 d6) ♕e6 (16... ♗g2?! 17. ed7!; 16... de6 17. ♗b7=) 17. ♗b7 ♘b7 18. e3∓] **16. e4?!** [16. e3 ♖ae8!?∓; 16. de6 ♗g2 17. ♔g2 ♗c3! (17... ♕e6 18. ♘d5∞ ×c7) 18. ♗c3 (18. ♕c3 ♕e6∓) ♕e6∓↑⊞, »] **f4!** [16... ed5 17. ♘d5 (17. ed5∞) ♗d5 18. ed5∞; 16... ♗c3 17. ♗c3 fe4 (17... ed5 18. ed5∞ ×♗b7; 17... f4!?∓) 18. ♗e4 ed5!? (18... ♘e4 19. ♕e4∞) 19. ♗d5 (19. ♗h7 ♔h8∓) ♗d5 20. cd5∓ ×d5] **17. gf4** [17. ♘e2 f3!? 18. ♗f3 ♗g5∓ ×♗f3, ♖c1; 17. f3∓; 17. ♗d2∓] **♗c3! 18. ♗c3 ♖f4 19. ♗d2 ♖g4!**∓ [↑», ⊞, ⇔g, ⁄⁄a8-h1; 19... e5 20. ♗f4 ef4∞̄; 19... ♖af8 20. ♗f4 ♖f4∞̄; 19... ♖f7 20. f4∞] **20. ♖ce1** [20. f3 ♖g6 21. ♔h1 (21. de6 ♕e6∓ △ 22... ♘e4 23. fe4 ♖g2−+) ed5 22. cd5 (22. ed5 c6−+→», ⁄⁄a8-h1, ×f3) c6 23. dc6 ♗c6∓; 20. f4 ed5 21. ed5 c6∓→] **ed5** [20... c6?! 21. de6 ♕e6∓] **21. ed5** [21. cd5 ♗a6!? (21... c6∓) 22. f3 ♖g6 △ 23. ♖f2 ♘d3−+] **♕h4! 22. f4** [22. ♖e3!? ♖c4 23. ♗c3 (△ ♖h3) ♖g4 24. ♖g3 ♖f8∓] **c6 23. ♖e2** [23. ♖e3 cd5 24. ♗e1 ♕f6!?∓] **cd5 24. ♗e1 ♕f6** [24... ♕h5!? △ 25. ♗g3 d4 26. ♗b7 d3 27. ♗d5 ♔h8−+] **25. ♗g3 ♕d4** [25... d4?! 26. ♗b7 ♘b7 (26... d3 27. ♗d5! ♔h8 28. ♕d1 de2 29. ♕e2 ♖g3 30. hg3=) 27. ♕e4∓] **26. ♔h1 ♕c4** [26... dc4?! 27. ♗b7 ♘b7 28. ♖d1! ♕c5 29. ♕e4∞̄] **27. b3** [27. ♕d2 ♘e4−+; 27. ♕d1 d4!? 28. ♗b7 ♘b7−+ △ 29. ♖e7 ♕d5 30. ♔g1 h5] **♕c2 28. ♖c2 ♖e8!?** [28... d4 29. ♗b7 ♘b7 30. ♖c6∓; 30. ♖d2; 30. ♖d1!?; 28... h5 29. ♗f3 d4 30. ♗b7 ♘b7 31. ♖d2∓; 31. ♖c6∓; 28... ♖f8!?] **29. ♖d1** [29. ♗f3 d4 30. ♗b7 ♘b7−+ △ ♘c5-e4, d3] **♘e4 30. ♖c7 ♗a8 31. ♖a7** [31. ♗e4 de4 32. ♖d6 e3 33. ♔g1 e2−+] **♔f8⊕** [31... ♘g3 32. hg3 ♖g3?? 33. ♖a8+−; 31... ♔h8!?] **32. ♖c1** [32. ♗f3 ♘g3 33. ♔g2 (33. hg3 ♖g3−+) ♖f4−+] **h5!?** [32... ♘g3 33. hg3 ♖g3−+] **33. b4** [33. ♗h3 ♘g3 34. hg3 ♖g3 35. ♗c8 d4! 36. ♖a8 ♖c3−+; 33. ♗f3 ♘g3 34. hg3 ♖g3−+; 33. ♖cc7 ♘g3!? 34. hg3 ♖g3−+] **ab4** [33... h4!?−+] **34. ♖cc7 h4!?** [34... ♘g3 35. hg3 ♖g3−+] **35. ♗h3□ ♘g3 36. hg3 ♖g3 37. ♗c8 d4 38. ♖a8 d3** [38... ♖c3 39. ♖aa7!=] **39. ♖c6⊕** [39. ♖d7 ♖g6!−+; 39. ♖c1 d2 40. ♖d1 (40. ♖f1 ♖c3−+) ♖e1 41. ♔h2 ♖e2 42. ♔h1 ♔e7−+ △ ♖e1] **d2 40. ♖d6 ♖c3 41. ♖d2 ♖ec8 42. ♖c8 ♖c8 43. ♖d4 b5! 44. ♖b4** [44. f5 ♖c4 45. ♖d5 ♔f7 46. ♖b5 ♔f6 47. ♔h2 ♔g5−+] **♖c4 45. ♖b5 ♖f4−+ 46. ♔h2 ♔f7 47. ♔h3 ♔f6 48. ♖a5 g5 49. ♖a6 ♔f5 50. ♖a5 ♔g6 51. ♖a8 ♖f3 52. ♔g2 ♖c3 53. ♖b8 ♔h5 54. ♖b2 h3 55. ♔h2 ♔h4 56. ♔h1 ♖c1 0 : 1 [Tivjakov]**

523. **E 19**

EPIŠIN 2620 − TIVJAKOV 2595

Rostov na Donu 1993

1. d4 ♘f6 2. c4 e6 3. ♘f3 b6 4. g3 ♗b7 5. ♗g2 ♗e7 6. ♘c3 0−0 7. 0−0 ♘e4 8. ♕c2 ♘c3 9. ♕c3 c5 10. ♖d1 d6 11. b3 ♗f6 12. ♗b2 ♘d7!? 13. ♖d2!? ♕e7 N [13... ♕c7 − 37/(602)] **14. ♖ad1 ♖fd8** [14... ♖ad8] **15. ♕c2 ♖ac8** [△ d5; 15... a6!? 16. dc5!? dc5 17. ♘e5!? *a)* 17... ♘e5 *a1)* 18. ♗b7 ♖d2 19. ♕d2 ♘c4! (19... ♕b7 20. ♗e5±) 20. ♗f6 gf6□ 21. ♕d7 (21. bc4 ♕b7) ♕d7 22. ♖d7 ♘e5!=; *a2)* 18. ♖d8 ♖d8 19. ♖d8 ♕d8 20. ♗b7 a5⩲; *b)* 17... ♗g2 *b1)* 18. ♖d7 ♖d7 19. ♘d7 (19. ♖d7 ♕e8 △ ♗e5) ♗b2 *b11)* 20. ♘b6? ♗d4! (20... ♗f6 21. f3! △ 21... ♖b8 22. ♘d7) 21. e3 (21. ♔g2 ♕b7; 21. ♘a8 ♗a8) ♗f6 22. e4 ♕b7! 23. ♘a8 ♗e4−+; *b12)* 20. ♔g2 *b121)* 20... ♗d4 21. ♕e4! ×b6, ♖a8; *b122)* 20... ♗f6 21. ♕e4 ♖d8 22. ♕c6!?⩲; 21. ♘f6!?; *b123)* 20... ♖d8!□ △ 21. ♘b6 ♖d1 22. ♕d1 ♕b7 △ ♕b6;

b13) 20. ♕b2 ♗c6 (20... ♖d8 21. ♕d2+−; 20... ♗h3 21. f3 ×b6, ♗h3) 21. ♘b6 ♕c7 (21... ♖b8 22. ♘a4 ♗a4 23. ♕e5±) 22. ♘a4 ♗a4 23. ba4±; *b2)* 18. ♘d7 ♗b2 19. ♕b2 (19. ♔g2 ♗d4! △ 20. ♘b6 ♕b7) ♗c6□ 20. ♘b6 ♕c7□ 21. ♘a4 ♗a4 22. ba4±] **16. e4** [16. dc5 dc5 17. ♘e5!? ♘e5 (17... ♗g2? 18. ♖d3 △ ♖a7) *a)* 18. ♗b7 ♖d2! (18... ♕b7 19. ♗e5±) 19. ♕d2 ♘c4! 20. ♗f6 (20. ♕d7 ♖c7!∓) gf6□ 21. ♕d7 ♖c7!□∓; *b)* 18. ♖d8 ♖d8 19. ♖d8 ♕d8 20. ♗b7=⊥; 16. ♕b1=] **cd4 17. ♘d4 a6** [17... ♘c5? 18. ♘b5 (×a7, d6) ♗b2 (18... ♗e4? 19. ♗f6+−) 19. ♕b2 ♘e4 (19... ♗e4 20. ♘d6) 20. ♗e4 ♗e4 21. ♘d6 ×♗e4, ♖c8] **18. ♘e2!?** [→×d6] **♗b2 19. ♕b2 ♘c5 20. ♘c3 ♗c6!** [△ 21. b4 ♘a4] **21. ♖d4!?** [△ ♕d2; 21. ♕a3 a5; 21. ♖e2 ♕c7!?=] **e5!?** [21... b5 22. cb5 ab5 ×b5, d6; 21... ♕c7 22. ♕d2 ♘b7±; 21... a5!?] **22. ♖4d2** [22. ♘d5 ♕b7 23. ♖4d2 a5; 23... b5; 23... ♖b8!?∞ △ ♘e6-d4; 22... ♕a7!?] **a5** [22... ♘e6?! 23. ♗h3 △ ♗e6, ♕a3, ×a6, d6; 22... ♖b8!?∞ △ ♘e6-d4] **23. ♘d5** [23. ♕a3=] **♗d5!?** [23... ♕b7∞; 23... ♕a7!?] **24. ♖d5** [24. cd5?! b5 △ b4↑«, ×♗g2; 24. ed5?! ×♗g2] **f6!?** [24... ♖c6? (△ ♘e6-d4) 25. ♕e5!!±; 24... ♖c7? 25. ♕e5!!; 24... ♘e6 25. ♗h3□ ♖c5 26. ♗e6 fe6 27. ♖5d3± △ ♕d2, f4↑⊞, →×d6; 24... ♖b8 25. ♕d2 ♘b7□± ×d6, ♘b7; 24... g6!?] **25. ♕e2** [25. ♗h3 ♖c6 26. ♕e2 — 25. ♕e2] **♖c6 26. ♗h3** [×e6] **g6!? 27. ♕e3 ♔g7 28. ♔g2** [28. a3 a4!? 29. b4 ♘b3 △ ♘d4∞] **♖b8!?** [△ b5; 28... ♕c7; 28... ♕b7] **29. a3!?** [△ 29... a4 30. b4 ♘b3 31. b5 ♖c4 32. ♖d6] **♘a6! 30. ♕d2 ♖d8** [30... ♘c5!? 31. ♖d6 ♖d6 32. ♕d6 ♕d6 33. ♖d6 ♘b3±⊥] **31. ♔g1** [×♗h3] **a4** [31... ♘c7 32. ♖d3 a4 33. ba4 ♘a6!? △ ♘c5=∞; 33. b4 — 31... a4; 31... ♘c5∞] **32. b4** [32. ba4 ♘c5!?∓ ×a4, e4, ♗h3] **♘c7 33. ♗f1?!** [⌓ 33. ♖d3 ♖c4 (33... b5? 34. c5; 33... ♕f7!?) 34. ♖d6 ♖d4 (34... ♖d6 35. ♕d6 ♕d6 36. ♖d6 ♘b5⇆) 35. ♖d4□ ♖d4 (35... ed4!?) 36. ♕c2 ♖d1 37. ♕d1 b5±; 36... b5±; 36... ♘b5!?⇆] **♘d5 34. ♕d5** [34. cd5 △ ♗b5=∞] **♖cc8** [34... ♕d7 35. c5! △ ♗b5; 34... ♖dc8 35. b5 △ ♕d6; 34... ♖c7 35. ♕b5 ×a4, b6; 34... ♕c7 ×♖c6; 34... ♕b7!?] **35. ♕b5⊕** [35. ♗h3=∞] **♕b7** [×e4; 35... ♕c7!?] **36. ♗h3** [36. ♕a4 (△ 36... ♕e4 37. ♕a7 △ ♕b6) ♕c6!? 37. ♕c2 (37. ♕c6 ♖c6∓⊥) ♖a8∓; 37... b5!?] **♖c7** [△ ♕c6] **37. ♗e6 ♕c6⊕ 38. ♖d5□** [38. ♕c6 ♖c6 39. ♗d5 ♖c7∓⊥] **♕c4** [38... ♕b5 39. ♖b5 ♖b8 40. ♗d5=; 38... ♔f8 39. ♕c6 ♖c6 40. ♖b5 ♖b8 41. ♗d5 ♖c7=] **39. ♕b6 ♕c1 40. ♔g2 ♕c2!? 41. ♖c5** [41. ♖d6?? ♖d6 42. ♕d6 ♕e4 43. ♔h3 ♖c3−+; 41. ♔h3∞] **♖c5 42. ♕d8??** [42. bc5□ ♕e4□ 43. ♔h3□ (43. f3 ×») ♖e8□ *a)* 44. ♕d6 ♕d4! *a1)* 45. ♕d7 ♕d7 46. ♗d7 ♔f7 (46... ♖a8 47. c6 ♖a7−+) 47. ♗e8 (47. c6 ♔e7!−+) ♔e8 48. ♔g4 ♔d7 △ ♔c6-c5−+; *a2)* 45. ♕c7 ♔h6 46. ♕d7 (46. ♗d7 ♖e7 47. c6 ♕f2−+ △ ♔g5, ♕f1#) ♖a8 (46... ♕d7!? 47. ♗d7 ♖a8−+) 47. ♕b7 (47. ♕d4 ed4 48. c6 d3 49. c7 d2−+; 47. c6 ♖a7!?−+) ♖a5 48. c6 ♕f2 49. c7 e4−+; *b)* 44. cd6 ♖e6 45. ♕c7 ♔h6 46. d7 ♖e7∓; *c)* 44. ♕c7 ♔h6 45. ♗d7□ (45. ♕d7 ♖e6−+; 45. ♕d6 ♕d4 46. ♕d7 — 44. ♕d6) dc5! 46. ♗e8 ♕f5 47. ♔g2 ♕e4=; *d)* 44. ♗d7 dc5□ 45. ♗e8 ♕f5 46. ♔g2 ♕e4 47. ♔g1 (47. f3 ♕e2) ♕e1 48. ♔g2 ♕e4 49. ♔f1 ♕h1!? 50. ♔e2 ♕e4 51. ♔d2 (51. ♔d1 ♕d3 52. ♔c1 ♕a3; 52. ♔e1=) ♕d4 52. ♔c1 (52. ♔c2 ♕f2=) ♕c3 53. ♔b1 ♕d3 54. ♔a2 (54. ♔b2 ♕d2=) ♕c4 55. ♔b2 (55. ♔a1 ♕c1=) ♕d4 56. ♔c2 ♕c4=] **♕e4 43. ♔h3** [43. f3 ♖c2−+] **♖c3!−+** [△ ♖f3-f2] **44. ♕d6** [44. ♕e7 ♔h6 45. ♕f6 ♖f3; 44. ♕g8 ♔h6 45. ♕f8 ♔g5; 44. b5 ♖f3! 45. b6 (45. ♕b6 ♔h6!? △ ♕d4) ♖f2] **♖f3! 45. ♕c5** [45. ♕c7 ♔h6 46. ♕c1 ♕f4 — 45. ♕c5; 45. ♕d7 ♔h6 46. ♕d2 (46. ♗d5 ♕d4) ♕f4] **♕d4 46. ♕c7 ♔h6 47. ♕c1 ♕f4** [47... ♔h5!] **48. ♕c5 ♕d4 49. ♕c1 ♔h5! 50. b5 f5!** [50... ♕f2 51. ♗g4#; 50... ♖f2 51. g4] **51. ♕c7 h6 52. ♗f7 ♖f2** [53. ♗g6 ♔g6 54. ♕c6 ♔g5] **0 : 1** **[Tivjakov]**

524.* **E 20**

JE. PIKET 2590 − KORTCHNOI 2605

Nijmegen (m/2) 1993

1. d4 ♘f6 2. c4 e6 3. ♘c3 ♗b4 4. ♘f3 c5 5. g3 0−0 [RR 5... ♘e4 6. ♕d3 d5 7.

dc5 ♕f6 8. cd5 ♘c3 N (8... ed5 9. ♗g2!?; 9. ♗d2 — 53/(520)) 9. a3 ♘d5 10. ab4 ♘b4 11. ♕b3 ♘8c6 12. ♗d2 a5 13. ♗g2 e5 14. ♗b4! ♘b4 *a)* 15. ♕a4!? ♔e7 (15... ♗d7? 16. ♕b4; 15... ♕c6 16. ♘e5; 15... ♘c6 16. ♘e5) 16. 0–0⩲ △ ♖fd1; *b)* 15. 0–0 0–0 *b1)* 16. ♕c3!? ♘c6 (16... ♖e8 17. ♖fd1±) 17. e3⩲ △ ♘d2-c4; 17. ♖fd1⩲; *b2)* 16. ♖fd1 *b21)* 16... ♕e7?! 17. ♕c3 f6 (17... e4 18. ♕e5!) 18. ♖d6± L. Valdés 2300 – J. C. González 2460, Cuba 1993; *b22)* 16... ♗e6 17. ♕c3 ♘c6⩲ L. Valdés] **6. ♗g2 cd4 7. ♘d4 d5 8. cd5 ♘d5 9. ♗d2 ♗c3 10. bc3 e5** [10... ♕e7] **11. ♘b5 ♘c6 12. 0–0 N** [12. ♗c1 ♗e6 13. ♗a3 ♕a5 14. ♗f8 (14. ♗d5 ♖fd8) ♕b5 15. ♗a3 (15. ♗b4 a5 16. e4 ♘db4 17. cb4 ♘d4–+) ♘c3=/∞; 12. c4 — 55/526] **♗e6 13. ♗c1 a6 14. c4 ♘b6** [14... ♘f4 15. gf4 ab5 16. cb5 ♕d1 17. ♖d1 ♘d4 18. e3⩲] **15. ♘d6 ♘c4 16. ♘b7 ♕b6** [16... ♕c8!? 17. ♘c5 ♗h3 18. ♗h3 ♕h3 19. ♕d5 ♘6a5 20. ♘b7⩲] **17. ♕b3 ♕d4** [17... ♕c7 18. ♘c5 ♘d4 19. ♘e6 fe6 20. ♕d3 ♖ad8 21. ♕e4 ♖f5 22. e3 ♘e2 23. ♔h1±] **18. ♗a3 ♘a3** [18... ♘d2 19. ♕d1 (19. ♕c2 ♘f1 20. ♖f1 ♘b4) ♘f1 20. ♗c6 ♘d2 21. ♗c5 ♕b2 22. ♗f8 ♖f8 23. ♘c5 ♖c8 24. ♘d3 ♕d4 25. ♗b7 ♖c2 26. ♗a6 e4 27. ♕c2 ♕a1 28. ♘c1; 25... ♖b8 △ 26. ♗a6 ♖b6] **19. ♕a3 ♕b4 20. ♕b4 ♘b4 21. ♘c5 ♗d5 22. a3 ♗g2 23. ♔g2 ♘d5 24. ♖fc1 ♖fd8 25. ♖ab1 h6 26. a4** [26. ♖b7 ♖dc8 27. ♘b3 (27. ♘d3 e4) ♖cb8] **♘f6 27. ♖d1** [27... ♖dc8 28. ♘d7 ♘d7 29. ♖d7 ♖c4 30. ♖bb7 ♖f8; 27. ♖b6 ♖d2 28. ♖a6 ♖a6 29. ♘a6 ♖e2 30. ♘b4 ♖b2 31. ♖c4 e4 △ ♘g4∞; 27... ♖dc8!?]
1/2 : 1/2 **[Je. Piket]**

525.* !N **E 20**

V. MILOV 2410 – OREN 2295

Israel 1993

1. d4 ♘f6 2. c4 e6 3. ♘c3 ♗b4 4. f3 c5 [RR 4... d5 5. a3 ♗e7 6. e4 0–0 *a)* 7. cd5 ed5 8. e5 ♘e8 9. f4 c5 10. ♘f3 (10. dc5 ♗c5 11. ♘d5 ♗e6=/∞) cd4 11. ♘d4 ♘c6 12. ♗e3 ♘c7 △ ♘e6∞; *b)* 7. e5 ♘fd7 8. cd5 N (8. c5 — 13/605) ♘b6 9. de6 ♗e6 10. ♗e3 ♘c6! (10... ♕d7 11. f4 ♖d8 12. ♘f3 c5 13. ♗b5±) 11. f4 ♘a5=/∞ 12. ♘f3 *b1)* 12... ♘bc4?! 13. ♗c4 ♗c4 (13... ♘c4 14. ♕e2±) 14. ♔f2±; *b2)* 12... c5?! 13. dc5 ♘bc4 14. ♗c4 ♘c4 15. ♕e2 △ b4±; *b3)* 12... ♗b3! *b31)* 13. ♕d2 *b311)* 13... ♘bc4 14. ♗c4 ♘c4 (14... ♗c4 15. ♖d1±) 15. ♕e2± △ 15... c5? 16. d5 ♘e3 17. ♕e3 ♗d5 18. ♖d1+–; *b312)* 13... c5! 14. dc5 ♘bc4 15. ♗c4 ♘c4 16. ♕e2 ♕a5!=/∞; *b32)* 13. ♕d3 ♘bc4 14. ♕e4!? (14. ♖b1 f6!?=/∞) ♘b2 15. ♖b1 ♘bc4 16. ♗d3 g6 17. ♖b3!? (17. ♗c1 ♘a3 18. ♖a1 ♘3c4∞) ♘e3 18. ♖b1 ♘g2 19. ♔f1 ♘h4 20. ♘h4 ♗h4 (1/2 : 1/2 Marin 2505 – Stoica 2435, România (ch) 1992) 21. f5 c5!? 22. d5 c4 23. ♗c2 ♘b3 24. ♗b3 cb3 25. ♖b3 ♖c8∞ Stoica] **5. d5 ♘h5 6. ♘h3 ♕h4 7. ♘f2 ♕c4 8. e4 ♗c3 9. bc3 ♕c3 10. ♗d2 ♕d4 11. ♕c1 ed5 12. ♗c3 ♕a4 13. ♕g5 d4 14. ♕c5! N** [14. ♗d2 — 48/(705)] **♕c6□** [14... ♘c6 15. ♗d2 ♘f6 16. ♗b5 b6 17. ♕c6+–; 14... dc3 15. ♕c8 ♔e7 16. ♕c5! △ ♕h5+–] **15. ♕d4 0–0 16. ♖b1!± ♕g6** [16... d6? 17. ♖b5+–; 16... a6? 17. g4 ♘f6 18. ♖b6+–] **17. ♖b5 ♘c6 18. ♕d2 d5□** [18... d6 19. ♖g5 ♕h6 20. ♖g7+–; 18... f5 19. g4! fg4 20. ♕d5+–] **19. ♖d5 h6 20. ♗d3!** [△ 21. g4 ♘f6 22. e5] **f5?!** [20... ♗e6 21. g4 ♘f6 22. ♘h3! ♖ad8 23. ♘f4 ♕h7 24. e5 ♘d5 25. ♗h7 ♔h7 26. 0–0±; 24. 0–0!±] **21. 0–0** [△ 22. ef5 ♗f5 23. ♗f5 ♖f5 24. ♖f5 ♕f5 25. g4 ♕g6 26. ♕d5] **f4** [21... ♘e7 22. ♖e5] **22. ♖d6 ♕f7 23. ♗c2! ♔h7** [23... ♕a2 24. e5+–] **24. ♘g4 ♗e6 25. e5 ♔h8 26. ♕d3 ♗f5 27. ♘h6!+– ♗d3 28. ♘f7 ♖f7 29. ♗d3 ♖c7 30. ♖d1** [30. ♗g6 ♘e7 ×♗c3] **♘e7 31. ♗b4 ♘c6 32. ♗g6! ♖g8 33. ♗e1**
1 : 0 **[V. Milov]**

526. **E 21**

SEIRAWAN 2595 – ZARNICKI 2470

Buenos Aires 1993

1. d4 ♘f6 2. c4 e6 3. ♘f3 b6 4. ♘c3 ♗b4 5. ♕b3 c5 6. a3 ♗a5 7. ♗g5 ♘c6 8. 0-0-0 ♗c3 9. d5 ♗e5 N [9... ed5? — 50/564] **10. dc6 ♕c7? 11. g3! ♗d6** [11... ♕c6 12.

♘e5 ♕h1 13. ♘f3 ♗b7 14. ♗h3 ♗f3 15. ♖h1 ♗h1 16. f3 △ ♕d1+−] **12. ♗g2 dc6**

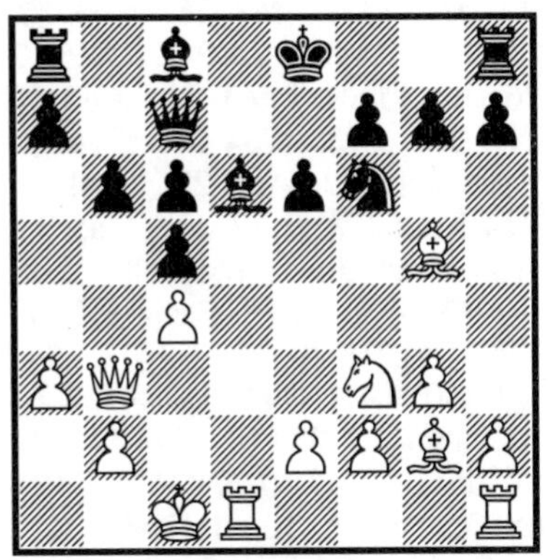

13. ♖d6! ♕d6 14. ♖d1 ♕c7? [14... ♘d5 15. e4!±] **15. ♗f4 ♕b7 16. ♘e5 ♗d7 17. ♖d7+− ♘d7 18. ♗c6 ♕a6 19. ♘d7 ♕c8 20. ♗a4** [20. ♘b8!] **♔e7 21. ♕d3 f6 22. ♕d6 ♔f7 23. ♘e5 fe5 24. ♗d7 ♕d8 25. ♕e6 ♔f8 26. ♗e5 g6 27. ♗f6 1 : 0**
[Seirawan]

527. E 29

JUSUPOV 2645 − V. SALOV 2660
Linares 1993

1. d4 ♘f6 2. c4 e6 3. ♘c3 ♗b4 4. e3 c5 5. ♗d3 ♘c6 6. a3 ♗c3 7. bc3 b6 8. ♘e2 0−0 9. e4 ♘e8 10. 0−0 ♗a6 11. f4 f5 12. ♘g3 g6 13. ♗e3 d6 N [13... ♘d6 − 48/713] **14. d5 ♘e7 15. ef5 gf5** [15... ef5 16. ♗f2 ♘f6 17. h3± ×♘e7] **16. ♘h5 ♘f6 17. de6 ♗b7?** [17... d5!?; 17... ♕e8!?] **18. ♗f2! ♘h5** [18... ♕e8 19. ♘f6 ♖f6 20. ♗h4 ♖e6 21. ♖e1!±] **19. ♕h5 ♕e8 20. ♕g5** [20. ♕h3↑] **♕g6 21. ♗h4 ♖ae8 22. g4** [22. ♖ae1!? △ 22... ♗c8? 23. ♖e3 h6 24. ♕e7!] **♗c8 23. ♖ae1 h6□ 24. ♕g6 ♘g6 25. ♗g3 ♖e6 26. ♖e6 ♗e6 27. ♖e1 ♗d7 28. ♗c2?** [28. h4! h5□ 29. gh5 ♘h8 30. h6 (30. ♖e7 ♖f7 31. ♖d7 ♖d7 32. ♗f5∞) ♖f7 (30... ♖f6 31. h7) 31. h5±] **♔f7 29. gf5 ♘e7 30. f6 ♘f5 31. ♗f5 ♗f5 32. ♗h4 ♖e8 33. ♖e7 ♖e7 34. fe7 ♗e6 35. ♔f2 ♗c4 36. ♔e3 b5 37. f5 ♗d5** [⌓ 37... ♔e8 38. f6 ♗f7 39. ♗g3 ♔d7∓] **38. f6 ♗c6 39. ♗g3 ♔e6 40. f7!= ♔e7 41. ♗d6 1/2 : 1/2** **[V. Salov]**

528. E 29

JUSUPOV 2645 − AN. KARPOV 2725
Linares 1993

1. d4 ♘f6 2. c4 e6 3. ♘c3 ♗b4 4. e3 c5 5. ♗d3 ♘c6 6. a3 ♗c3 7. bc3 0−0 8. ♘e2 b6 9. e4 ♘e8 10. 0−0 ♗a6 11. f4 f5 12. ♘g3 g6 13. ♗e3 cd4 14. cd4 d5!? N 15. cd5 [15. ♕a4? ♘a5; 15. ef5 ef5∞ (15... gf5!?) 16. cd5 ♗d3 17. ♕d3 ♕d5] **♗d3 16. ♕d3 fe4 17. ♕e4** [17. ♘e4!?] **♕d5 18. ♕d5 ed5 19. ♖ac1** [19. f5 ♘d6 20. ♗h6 ♖f7∓] **♖c8** [19... ♘e7?! 20. f5!? (20. ♗d2 △ ♗b4) ♘f5 21. ♘f5 ♖f5 22. ♖f5 gf5 23. ♖c6$\overline{\overline{\infty}}$] **20. f5 ♘d6 21. fg6** [21. ♗h6 ♖f7 22. f6 ♖d7! △ ♔f7] **hg6 22. ♖f8 ♔f8 23. h4! ♘c4** [23... ♔e7 24. h5 gh5 25. ♘h5 ♘f5 26. ♗g5⇆] **24. ♗g5 ♘d4 25. h5?!** [25. ♖f1 ♔e8 26. ♖e1 ♔d7 27. ♖e7 ♔c6 28. ♖g7!?] **gh5 26. ♖f1 ♔e8 27. ♘h5 ♘a3** [27... ♔d7 28. ♖d1 ♘e6 29. ♘f6 ♔c6 30. ♘d5 ♘g5 31. ♘e7 ♔b7 32. ♘c8 ♔c8 33. ♖c1 b5 34. a4 a6 35. ab5 ab5 36. ♖b1=] **28. ♘g7 ♔d7 29. ♖f7 ♔c6 30. ♖a7 ♘ac2! 31. ♗f6 b5 32. g4 b4 33. ♖a2 b3 34. ♖b2 ♔c5 35. ♘f5 ♖g8! 36. ♘d4 ♖g4 37. ♔f2 ♘d4 38. ♗d4 ♔d4 39. ♖b3 ♖e4 40. ♖a3 ♖e8 0 : 1**
[An. Karpov]

529. E 31**

ROGOZENKO 2480 − SAX 2570
Odorheiu Secuiesc 1993

1. d4 ♘f6 2. c4 e6 3. ♘c3 ♗b4 4. ♗g5 h6 5. ♗h4 c5 6. d5 d6 7. e3 ♗c3 8. bc3 e5 [RR 8... ♕e7 9. ♘f3 ♘bd7 10. ♘d2 0−0 11. ♗e2 ♘e5 12. ♘e4 g5 13. ♘f6 ♕f6 14. ♗g3 ♘c4 15. 0−0 ♘e5 N (15... ed5 − 53/528) 16. f4 ♘d7 17. fg5 ♕g5 18. ♗d6 ♖e8 19. de6 ♕e3 20. ♔h1 ♖e6 21. ♗c4 ♖f6 22. ♕h5 ♕g5 23. ♗f7 ♔g7 24. ♗e7 ♖f1 25. ♖f1 ♕h5 26. ♗h5 a5 27. ♗e2 b6 28. ♗f3 ♖a7 29. ♗d5 ♗b7 30. ♗e6 ♗c6 31. h4+− Rogozenko 2480 − Timošenko 2515, Bucureşti 1993] **9. f3** [RR 9. ♗d3 e4 10. ♗c2 ♘bd7 11. ♘e2 0−0 12. ♕b1 ♕e7 13. a4 N (13. 0−0) ♘e5! 14. ♗f6 ♕f6 15. ♗e4 ♘c4 16. ♕a2

(16. ♕d1 ♕h4 17. ♘g3 f5 18. ♗d3 ♘e5 19. ♗e2 f4 20. ef4 ♖f4 21. 0–0 ♗d7 22. a5 ♖e8∓) ♘e5 17. 0–0 b6 18. ♖ad1 (18. c4 ♕h4 19. f3 f5 20. g3 ♕e7 21. ♗c2 ♘d3∓ Sax) ♕h4 19. f3 ♗a6 20. ♖fe1 ♗c4 21. ♕b1 ♖ab8∓ Bangiev 2395 – Sax 2570, Deutschland 1993] **g5 10. ♗g3 e4 11. h4 g4 12. h5 ef3 13. gf3 ♕e7 14. ♗h4 ♕e5 N** [14... ♕e3? – 51/545] **15. ♕d2 ♘h5 16. 0-0-0=/∞** [×♔e8, ♘h5] **gf3?** [16... ♗f5 17. e4 ♗d7 (×f4) 18. ♗e2 ♘f4 19. ♗g3!? ♘d3 (19... ♘e2? 20. ♘e2 ♕e7 21. ♖h6+–) 20. ♗d3 ♕g3 21. ♖h6 ♖h6 22. ♕h6 ♕e5∞; 21. f4!?=/∞] **17. ♘f3 ♕e4 18. ♕f2** [18. ♗e2? ♗f5 △ ♘d7] **♗g4 19. ♗e2 f5** [19... ♘d7 20. ♘d2 ♕g6 21. ♗g4 ♕g4 22. ♖dg1+–] **20. ♘d2!** [20. ♖df1 0–0!! 21. ♘d2 ♕e8 22. ♖hg1 ♘d7 23. ♗g4 fg4 24. ♖g4 ♔h7∞] **♕e5 21. ♗g4 ♕c3 22. ♔b1 ♕d3 23. ♔b2 fg4 24. ♖hf1+– ♕g6 25. ♘e4! ♘a6 26. ♕f5! ♕f5 27. ♖f5** [27... ♘g7 28. ♘d6 ♔d7 29. ♖f7 ♔d6 30. ♗g3#] **1 : 0** **[Rogozenko]**

530.* **E 32**

S. GULIEV 2485 – TUKMAKOV 2605

Nikolaev (zt) 1993

1. d4 ♘f6 2. c4 e6 3. ♘c3 ♗b4 4. ♕c2 0–0 [RR 4... b6 5. a3 ♗c3 6. ♕c3 ♗b7 7. b3 0–0 8. ♗b2 d6 N (8... ♘e4 – 55/541) 9. f3 c5 10. dc5 bc5 11. e3 ♘c6 12. ♘h3 ♕e7 13. ♖c1 a5 14. ♗e2 ♖fb8 15. ♘f2 e5 16. 0–0 ♗c8 17. f4 ♖a6 18. fe5 ♘e5 19. ♘d3 ♘e4 20. ♕c2 ♘g6 21. ♘f4 ♗b7 22. ♗d3 ♖b6∞ Ehlvest 2625 – Adianto 2490, Saint-Martin 1993] **5. a3 ♗c3 6. ♕c3 b6 7. ♘f3 c5!? 8. dc5!?** [8. ♗g5 cd4; 8... ♗b7 – 56/623] **bc5 9. b4!? N** [9. ♗g5 – 51/551] **♘e4!?** [9... d5!?] **10. ♕c2 f5 11. e3 ♘c6!? 12. b5 ♘e7 13. ♗e2 ♗b7** [13... ♖f6?! 14. ♗b2 ♖g6 15. g3; 13... ♘g6 14. h4!?] **14. 0–0 ♘g6 15. ♘e1** [15. a4!?] **♕h4 16. f3 ♘g5 17. ♘d3** [17. g3 ♕h5∞] **d6 18. ♘f4 e5 19. ♘d5 ♗d5 20. cd5 f4 21. ♗d3** [21. e4 ♖f6∞] **e4!** [21... ♖f6 22. ef4! ♘f4 (22... ef4 23. ♗b2) 23. g3 ♘fh3 24. ♔g2 ♕h5 25. ♗f5!±] **22. ♗e4** [22. fe4? f3∓] **♘e4 23. fe4** [23. ♕e4 ♖ae8 24. ♕d3 *a)* 24... ♘e5?! 25. ♕b3 (25. ♕c3 fe3 26. ♗e3 ♕c4!=/∞) c4!? (25... fe3 26. ♗e3 ♕c4 27. ♖fb1) 26. ♕c3 g5∞; *b)* 24... ♖e5! 25. ef4 ♖h5 26. h3 ♕g3→] **fe3 24. ♗e3 ♖f1 25. ♖f1 ♖e8 26. ♗f2! ♕e4 27. ♕e4 ♖e4 28. ♖e1!?** [28. ♗g3!? ♘e5 29. ♖f4! ♖f4 30. ♗f4 ♘c4 31. a4 ♔f7 32. a5! ♘a5 33. ♗d6 ♘b3! (33... c4 34. ♗e5!) 34. ♗b8 ♘d4 35. ♗a7 ♘b5 36. ♗c5 ♘c3=] **♖e1** [28... ♖a4?! 29. ♗g3!] **29. ♗e1** [♘♗ 5/e] **♔f7 30. ♗g3** [30. a4!] **♔e7 31. ♔f2?** [31. a4! ♔d7 32. a5 ♘e7 33. b6 ab6 34. ab6 ♘f5 (34... ♘d5 35. b7 ♔c7 36. ♗d6=) 35. ♗f4 h5 36. g3 △ h3=] **♘e5! 32. ♗e5?** [32. a4 ♘c4 △ ♘b6∓] **de5**

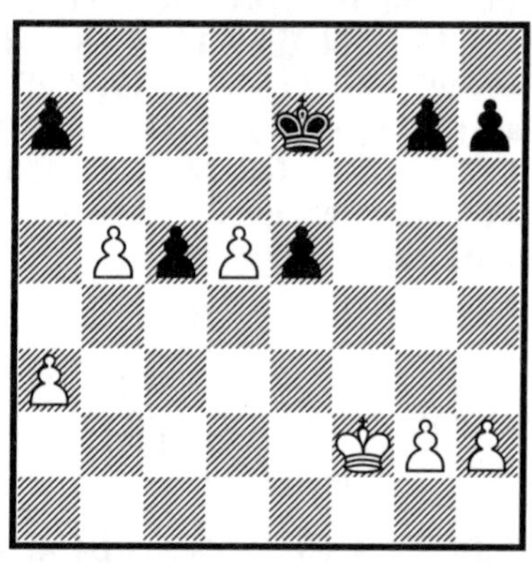

33. ♔e3 [RR 33. a4! ♔d6 34. a5 c4 (34... ♔d5 35. a6+–) 35. a6! (35. b6? a6!=) ♔c5 36. d6 ♔d6 37. b6+– S. Guliev, Magerramov] **♔d6 34. ♔e4 c4 35. a4 c3 36. ♔d3 ♔d5** **0 : 1** **[Tukmakov]**

531. **E 32**

BAREEV 2670 – AN. KARPOV 2725

Linares 1993

1. d4 ♘f6 2. c4 e6 3. ♘c3 ♗b4 4. ♕c2 0–0 5. a3 ♗c3 6. ♕c3 b6 7. ♘f3 ♗b7 8. e3 d6 9. b3 ♘bd7 10. ♗b2 ♘e4 11. ♕c2 f5 12. ♗d3 ♘df6 [12... ♕e8 – 53/534] **13. 0–0 ♕e7 N 14. ♘d2 ♘d2 15. ♕d2 ♘e4?!** [15... c5=] **16. ♕e2 c5 17. f3 ♘f6** [17... ♘g5!?] **18. b4 ♖ac8 19. ♖ab1 ♖c7 20. ♖fd1± ♘h5?** [20... ♖fc8±] **21. dc5 bc5 22. bc5 ♖c5** [22... dc5 23. ♗e5±] **23. ♗d4 ♖cc8** [23... ♖a5 24. ♕d2] **24. ♗a7**

♘f6 [24... ♗f3? 25. ♕f3+−; 24... ♖a8 25. ♗d4 ♖a3 26. ♕b2+−] **25. ♗b6± ♗a6** [25... ♘d7 26. e4!?] **26. ♗a5 ♖c6 27. ♗b4 ♖fc8 28. h3!? ♕a7 29. ♔h1 h6 30. ♕e1 d5** [30... ♗c4 31. ♗c4 ♖c4 32. ♗d6! (32. ♖d6 ♘d5∞) ♘d5 33. ♖d3±] **31. cd5 ♘d5 32. ♗a6 ♖a6** [32... ♕a6? 33. e4+−] **33. e4 ♘e3 34. ♖dc1 ♘c2 35. ♕d2 ♖ac6 36. ef5 ef5 37. ♕d5?** [37. ♗a5! (△ a4, ♖b5) ♘a3 (37... ♕a6 38. a4 ♖d6 39. ♕f4±) 38. ♖c6 ♖c6 39. ♕d5 ♔h7 (39... ♔h8 40. ♕c6 ♘b1 41. ♕c8+−) 40. ♕c6 ♘b1 41. ♗b4±] **♕f7!** [37... ♔h8? 38. ♕f5 ♘b4 39. ♕c8+−] **38. ♖d1?** [38. ♕f7 ♔f7 39. ♖d1±] **♕d5 39. ♖d5 ♘e3 40. ♖d4! ♖c1 41. ♖c1 ♖c1 42. ♔h2 ♖c2 43. ♔g3 g5** [44. f4 ♘f1 (44... g4 45. hg4 fg4 46. ♖d8 ♔f7 47. f5=) 45. ♔f3 ♘h2 46. ♔g3 (46. ♔e3 ♖g2∓) ♘f1=; 43... ♘g2? 44. ♖d2; 43... ♖g2 44. ♔f4] **1/2 : 1/2**
[Bareev]

532. E 32

KRAMNIK 2625 − ASEEV 2550
Moskva (open) 1992

1. ♘f3 ♘f6 2. c4 e6 3. ♘c3 ♗b4 4. ♕c2 0−0 5. a3 ♗c3 6. ♕c3 c5 7. e3 b6 8. b4 ♕e7?! 9. ♗e2 d6 10. d4 cd4 11. ed4 ♘bd7 12. 0−0 ♗b7 13. ♖e1 ♖fc8 14. ♕b3± ♘f8 15. ♗f1 ♕d8 16. ♗b2 ♘g6 17. ♖ad1 ♘d7 18. g3 ♖c7 19. d5 e5⇆ 20. h4?! h6 21. ♘d2 ♘f6 22. ♗g2 ♖b8 [22... ♗c8 23. f4↑] **23. ♘e4 ♘e4 24. ♗e4 ♗c8 25. ♕d3 ♘f8 26. ♖d2 ♗g4!? 27. f3 ♗h5 28. f4 ef4 29. ♕d4 f6 30. gf4 ♘g6?!** [30... ♗g6!? 31. f5 ♗h5 △ ♘d7-e5⇆] **31. ♗g6?** [31. ♖g2 ♘h4 (31... ♘f4 32. ♖g3→ △ 32... ♘e2 33. ♖e2 ♗e2 34. ♕e3 △ 35. ♕h6, 35. ♕e2+−) 32. ♖g3∞↑ ×♘h4] **♗g6 32. ♖g2 ♔h7∓ 33. f5□ ♗f5 34. ♕f4 ♕d7⊕ 35. ♖ge2 ♗d3 36. ♖e6 ♖c4 37. ♕f3?** [37. ♕g3 ♗g6!? (37... ♗f5 38. ♖e7 ♖g4 39. ♕g4 ♗g4 40. ♖d7 ♗d7 41. ♖e7=) 38. ♗f6 ♖g8!?∓] **♗c2 38. ♗f6 ♖f8 39. ♕e2** [39. ♖e7 ♕g4−+] **b5 40. ♗e7 ♖ff4** [41. ♖c1 ♗f5∓; 41... ♕c8!?−+]
0 : 1 **[Aseev]**

533. E 32

KASPAROV 2805 − TIMMAN 2635
Linares 1993

1. d4 ♘f6 2. c4 e6 3. ♘c3 ♗b4 4. ♕c2 0−0 5. a3 ♗c3 6. ♕c3 b6 7. ♗g5 ♗b7 8. f3 d5? [8... h6!] **9. e3 ♘bd7** [9... ♖e8!?] **10. cd5! ed5** [10... ♘d5 11. ♗d8 ♘c3 12. ♗c7 ♘d5 13. ♗f4] **11. ♗d3 ♖e8 N** [11... c5 − 46/(754)] **12. ♘e2 h6 13. ♗h4! c5** [13... ♖e3? 14. ♗f6! ♘f6 15. ♗h7; 13... ♘e4? 14. ♗d8 ♘c3 15. ♗c7 ♖e3 (15... ♘a4 16. b3+−) 16. ♔d2+−] **14. 0−0 ♖c8 15. ♕d2** [15. ♗b5!? ♗c6 16. ♗a6 ♖b8 17. b4 (17. ♗g3 b5) c4 18. b5 ♗b7 19. ♗g3 ♗a6 20. ♗b8 ♗b5±] **♕e7 16. ♗f2 ♗c6** [16... cd4 17. ♘d4 ♘e5 18. ♗f5 ♘c4 19. ♕e2 ♖c7 20. ♖fe1; 17. ed4! △ 17... ♘e4 18. fe4 de4 19. ♗b5 e3 20. ♕e3 ♕e3 21. ♗e3 ♖e3 22. ♗d7 ♖e2 (22... ♖d8? 23. ♗g4) 23. ♗c8 ♖g2 24. ♔h1 ♗a8 25. d5 ♗d5 26. ♖fd1 ♗f3 (26... ♖g5 27. ♖d5 ♖d5+−) 27. ♖d3 ♗c6 28. ♖c3 ♗a8 29. h4!+−] **17. ♘c3!** [17. ♘g3 ♕f8 18. ♘f5 ♖e6!] **♘f8 18. ♖fe1 ♘e6 19. ♗h4 ♘g5 20. ♗f5 ♗d7** [20... ♖cd8 21. ♖ad1] **21. ♗c2 ♗c6 22. ♖ad1 ♕e6 23. ♕f2 ♖cd8 24. h3** [△ 25. ♗g5 hg5 26. ♕g3] **♘gh7 25. dc5** [25. ♗b3!?] **bc5 26. e4! de4** [26... d4 27. e5! dc3 28. ♖d8 ♖d8 29. ef6 ♖d2 (29... ♕c4 30. fg7 ♖d2 31. ♗h7! ♔h7 32. g8♕ ♔g8 33. ♕g3 ♔h7 34. ♗f6+−) 30. ♗h7 ♔h7 31. ♕g3 ♕e1 32. ♕e1 cb2 33. ♕b1 g6 34. ♗e1 ♖e2 35. ♗c3+−] **27. ♖d8 ♖d8 28. ♕c5** [28. ♘e4? ♗e4 29. ♗e4 ♘e4∞ △ 30. ♗d8 ♘f2 31. ♖e6 ♘h3!] **♘g5!** [28... ♖d2 29. ♘e4+−; 28... ♖c8 29. ♕a7] **29. ♗g5 hg5 30. ♕g5 ♕c4** [30... ♖b8 31. b4+−] **31. fe4** [31. ♘e4 ♕d4! (31... ♗e4 32. ♗e4 ♕d4 33. ♕e3 ♕b2 34. ♕a7+−) 32. ♕e3 ♕b2 33. ♘f6 ♕f6 34. ♕a7 ♕c3 35. ♖c1 g6 36. ♕f7 ♔f7 37. ♗g6] **♕d4 32. ♕e3 ♕e3 33. ♖e3 ♖d2 34. ♖e2 ♖e2 35. ♘e2 ♘e4 36. ♗e4** [36. ♘d4!?] **♗e4** [**♘♗ 4/h**] **37. ♔f2 ♔f8 38. g3 ♔e7 39. ♔e3 ♗c6 40. h4 ♗d7 41. ♔f4 ♔d6 42. g4** [42. ♘d4!] **f6 43. h5?!** [43. ♘d4! g5!? 44. hg5 fg5 45. ♔g5 ♔e5 46. ♘f5 a5 47. b4 ab4 48. ab4 ♗e8 (48... ♔e4 49. ♔f6 ♔f4 50.

g5! ♗f5 51. b5+−) 49. ♘e3 ♗d7 50. ♘c2 ♔e4 51. ♘a3 ♔f3 52. ♘c4 ♔e4 (52... ♗g4 53. ♘e5 ♔e4 54. ♘g4 ♔d4 55. ♘e3!+−) 53. ♘d6 ♔e5 54. ♘f5 ♗a4 55. ♘e3 ♔e4 56. ♘c4 ♔d4 57. ♘a3 ♔c3 58. b5 ♔b4 59. b6 ♗c6 60. ♔f6 ♔c5 61. g5 ♔b6 62. g6 ♔c5 63. ♘c2 ♗e4 64. g7 ♗h7 65. ♘e3 ♔d6 66. ♘g4 ♔d7 67. ♔f7 ♔d6 68. ♘f6 ♗c2 69. ♔f8 ♗b3 70. ♘g4+−] **♔e7 44. ♘d4 ♔f7 45. b4 ♗a4** [45... g6 46. hg6 ♔g6 47. b5+−] **46. ♘f5 g6** [46... a6 47. ♘d6 ♔e6 48. ♘e4 ♗b5 49. a4 ♗f1 50. ♘c3 ♔d6 51. b5 ab5 52. ab5 ♔c5 53. ♘e4 ♔b5 54. ♘g3+−] **47. ♘d6 ♔g7 48. ♘c8 a6 49. ♘d6 ♗d1?** [49... ♔h6 50. ♘e4 gh5 (50... g5 51. ♔g3 ♔g7 52. ♘d6+−) 51. gh5 ♔h5 52. ♘f6 ♔g6 53. ♔e5 ♔f7 54. ♘d5+−; 49... ♗d7 50. ♘e4 f5 51. ♘c5 ♗c8 52. h6 ♔h6 53. g5 ♔g7 54. a4+−; 49... ♗c6!? 50. ♘e4 *a)* 50... f5 51. h6! ♔h6 *a1)* 52. g5 ♔g7 53. ♘c5 ♗b5 54. a4 ♗e2! (54... ♗c6 55. ♔e5 ♔f7 56. ♔d6+−; 54... ♗e8 55. ♔e5 ♔f7 56. a5 ♗b5 57. ♘e6 ♗f1 58. ♘c7 ♔e7 59. b5 ab5 60. a6 ♗g2 61. ♘d5+−) 55. ♘d7 ♗d1 56. b5 ♗a4 57. b6 ♗c6 58. ♘e5 ♗a8 59. ♘c4 ♔f7 60. ♔e5 f4 61. ♔f4 ♔e6 62. ♘a5 ♔d5 63. b7 ♗b7 64. ♘b7 ♔d4 65. ♔f3 ♔e5 66. ♘d8!+− a5 67. ♔e3 a4 68. ♔d3; *a2)* 52. gf5! gf5 53. ♔f5+−; *b)* 50... g5 51. ♔f3 ♔h6 (51... ♔f7 52. ♔e3 ♗d7 53. ♘d6!+−) 52. ♔e3 f5 53. gf5 ♔h5 54. ♘d6 ♔h6 55. ♘f7 ♔h5 56. ♘e5+−] **50. ♘e8! ♔f7 51. ♘f6! ♔f6 52. g5 ♔f7 53. h6 1 : 0** **[Kasparov]**

534. **E 39**

KORTCHNOI 2575 – TIVJAKOV 2585

Tilburg (Interpolis) 1992

1. d4 ♘f6 2. c4 e6 3. ♘c3 ♗b4 4. ♕c2 c5 5. dc5 0–0 6. a3 ♗c5 7. ♘f3 ♘c6 8. ♗g5 b6 9. ♖d1 ♗e7 N [9... ♗b7 – 48/(751)] **10. e3±** [10. e4!?] **♗b7 11. ♗e2 d6 12. ♖d2 ♕b8 13. 0–0 h6 14. ♗h4 ♖d8 15. ♖fd1 ♘a5** [15... a6? 16. ♕b3 ♕c7 17. ♘a4 ♘d7 18. ♗e7 ♘e7 19. ♖d6 b5 20. ♖d7±; 15... ♘e5 16. ♘e5 de5 17. ♖d8 ♗d8 18. ♗f3±] **16. b4 ♘c6** [16... ♗f3 17. gf3 ♘c6 18. c5±] **17. ♗g3 ♘h5** [17... a5 18. ♕b1±] **18. ♘g5! hg5** [18... ♘f6 19. ♘ge4±] **19. ♗h5 ♘e5?** [19... a5 20. b5 ♘a7 21. ♘a4±; 20. ♕b1±] **20. ♗e5!** [20. c5!?] **de5 21. ♖d8 ♗d8 22. ♖d7± ♗c6 23. ♗f7** [⌓ 23. ♖f7 *a)* 23... ♗e8 24. ♕g6 ♗f6 (24... ♗f7 25. ♕f7 ♔h8 26. ♕e8 ♔h7 27. ♗g6 ♔h6 28. ♗e4+−) 25. ♘e4+−; *b)* 23... e4 24. b5 ♗e8 25. ♖g7 ♔g7 26. ♗e8 ♕e5□ 27. ♗c6 ♖c8 28. g3 ♗f6 29. ♘e4 ♕a1 30. ♔g2 ♕a3 31. ♗d7 △ ♗e6±] **♔f8 24. ♗h5** [24. ♕h7?! ♗d7 25. ♕g8 ♔e7 26. ♕g7 ♗c6∓] **♗d7 25. ♕g6 ♔g8** [25... ♔e7 26. ♘e4+−] **26. ♕f7 ♔h8 27. ♗f3! ♗e7 28. ♗a8 ♕e8 29. ♕e8** [29. ♕f3 g4 30. ♕e4 a5±; 29... ♕c8!?] **♗e8** [♘♗ 9/e] **30. ♗e4± a5?** [30... ♔g8 △ ♔f8‖《] **31. b5 ♔g8** [31... ♗a3 32. ♘a4+−] **32. ♘a4** [⌓ 32. g4 △ ♔f1-e2-d2-c2] **♗d8 33. g4 ♔f8 34. ♔f1 ♔e7 35. ♘b2** [35. ♔e2 △ ♔d2-c2-b3, △ ♘b2] **♔d6 36. ♘d3 ♗c7 37. a4?** [37. ♔e2 △ ♔d2-c2-b3-a4, ♘c1-b3, c5+−] **♗d8 38. ♔e2 ♗c7 39. ♔d2 ♗f7 40. h3?! ♗e8 41. ♔c3 ♗f7 42. c5 bc5 43. ♘b2 c4! 44. ♔c4 ♗d8 45. ♘d3 ♗b6 46. ♘e1 ♗d8 47. ♘f3 ♗e8 48. ♔b3 ♗f7 49. ♘d2 ♔c5 50. ♘c4 ♗c7 51. ♗c6 ♗g6 52. e4 ♗f7 53. f3 ♗g6 54. ♗d7 ♗f7 55. ♗c8 ♗g8 56. ♗b7 ♗f7 57. ♗a6!⊙ ♗g8 58. ♗c8 ♗f7 59. ♗d7 ♗d8 60. ♘e5 ♗g8 61. ♗e8 ♔d6** [61... ♗c7 62. ♘d7 ♔d6 63. b6+−] **62. ♘c4 ♔e7?** [62... ♔c5 63. ♔c3 ♗c7 (63... e5 64. ♘d2 △ ♗c6-d5+−) 64. ♗g6 (△ e5) e5 65. ♘d2 △ ♗e8-c6-d5+−] **63. ♗c6 e5 64. ♗d5 1 : 0** **[Kortchnoi]**

535. **E 42**

LAURENC – JEŽEK

corr. 1991/92

1. d4 ♘f6 2. c4 e6 3. ♘c3 ♗b4 4. e3 c5 5. ♘e2 cd4 6. ed4 d5 7. c5 ♘e4 8. ♗d2 ♘c6 9. ♘e4 de4 10. ♗b4 ♘b4 11. ♕a4 ♘c6 12. ♖d1 0–0 13. ♘c3 e3 14. fe3 ♕g5 15. ♔f2 ♗d7 16. d5!? N [16. ♕c2 – 46/764] **ed5 17. ♖d5 ♘e5 18. ♕f4 ♘g4 19. ♔g3 ♕g6 20. ♖g5** [20. ♖d7? ♘e5∓] **♕c2 21. ♗b5!** [21. ♖g4 ♗g4 22. ♕g4 ♖fe8=∞]

♗b5 [21... ♗e6 22. ♖g4±; 21... h6 22. ♗d7 hg5 23. ♕g4 ♕b2 24. ♕d4 ♖ad8 25. ♖b1±] **22. ♘b5** [22. ♕g4 ♗c6 23. ♖g7 ♔h8∞] **f5** [22... ♘h6 23. ♕f6 g6 24. ♘c7 ♖ad8 25. ♘d5 ♖fe8 26. ♖f1 ♕c5 (26... ♕e2 27. ♖f2 ♕d3 28. ♘e7 ♔f8 29. ♖e5+−) 27. ♕d8! ♖d8 28. ♘f6+−; 22... ♕b2 23. ♘c7±] **23. ♘d4 ♕d2** [23... ♕b2 24. ♘f5 ♘f6 25. ♖g7 ♔h8 26. ♔h3±] **24. ♘f5 ♖f5!□ 25. ♕f5 ♘e3 26. ♕e6 ♔h8 27. ♕e4 ♖f8** [27... ♘g2? 28. ♖d5+−] **28. h4!** [28. ♖e5? ♕f2 29. ♔h3 ♘g2! 30. ♖e8 ♘f4 31. ♔g4 h5 32. ♔g5 ♘h3 33. ♔h5 ♕f7−+] **h6 29. ♖e5** [29. ♖g6? ♕f2 30. ♔h3 ♖f4−+] **♕f2 30. ♔h2!** [30. ♔h3? ♘g2! 31. ♕g2 (31. ♖e8 ♘f4 32. ♔g4 h5 33. ♔g5 ♕g3#) ♖f3 32. ♔h2 ♕h4 33. ♔g1 ♕d4−+] **♘f1** [30... ♘g2 31. ♕e2!+−] **31. ♖f1 ♕f1 32. ♖e7 ♖f4 33. ♖e8 ♖f8 34. b4 ♖e8 35. ♕e8 ♔h7 36. ♕e4 ♔h8 37. ♕b7** [♕ 4/g; 37. a4 (△ b5, c6+−) a6! (37... ♕c1 38. ♕d4±; 37... ♕f2 38. ♕c4±) 38. ♕b7 ♕c4!] **♕c4! 38. ♕b8 ♔h7 39. ♕g3 a5!** [39... ♕b4 40. c6] **40. ba5 ♕c5 41. a6 ♕d4! 42. h5 ♔h8 43. a3 ♔g8** [⌓ 43... ♔h7] **44. ♕b3 ♔h8 45. ♕b8 ♔h7 46. ♕b4! ♕e5 47. ♔g1 ♕h5 48. ♕e4 ♔h8 49. ♕d4! ♕e8 50. a7 ♔h7 51. a4! ♕c6 52. a5 h5** [52... ♕e8 53. ♔f2! (△ ♕d5) ♕f7 54. ♔e3+−] **53. ♔h1** [53. ♔f2] **♕e8 54. ♕f4!** [△ ♔h2, ♕b8] **g6 55. a6 ♔g7 56. ♔g1 ♕d8 57. ♔h2!+− g5 58. ♕e4! ♕d6** [58... ♕c7 59. g3 ♕a7 60. ♕b7] **59. g3 h4 60. a8♕ ♕g3 61. ♔h1 ♕h3 62. ♔g1 ♕g3 63. ♕g2 ♕e1 64. ♕f1**
1 : 0 **[Franzen, Laurenc]**

536. **E 42**

IVANČUK 2720 − SEIRAWAN 2605
Tilburg (Interpolis) 1992

1. d4 ♘f6 2. c4 e6 3. ♘c3 ♗b4 4. e3 c5 5. ♘e2 cd4 6. ed4 d5 7. c5 ♘e4 8. ♗d2 ♘d2 9. ♕d2 a5 10. a3 ♗c3 11. ♘c3 ♗d7 12. ♗d3 a4 13. 0−0 ♘c6 N [13... 0−0 − 26/648] **14. ♖ae1??** [14. ♗c2 ♘e7 15. ♖ae1 △ ♖e3±] **♘d4!□** [14... ♘e7? 15. ♖e3±] **15. ♘d5 ♗c6 16. ♘b6**

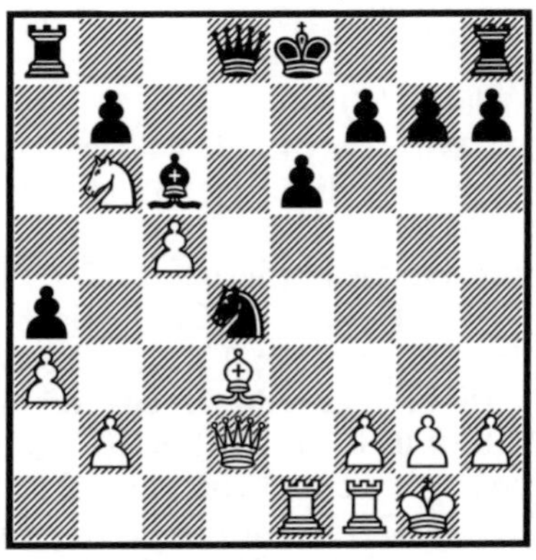

16... ♖a5!∓ 17. ♖d1! [17. ♕a5?? ♘f3 18. ♔h1 ♕h4 19. h3 ♕f4−+] **♖c5** [△ ♘f3] **18. ♗e4! ♕b6** [18... ♗e4 19. ♕d4 ♕d4 20. ♖d4 ♗c6 21. ♘a4 ♖c2∓] **19. ♕d4 0−0 20. ♖c1!** [20. ♗c6? ♕c6−+] **♖b5 21. ♕a4! ♗e4 22. ♕e4 ♖b2 23. ♖b1 ♖c8?** [23... ♖d8 24. ♖b2 ♕b2 25. ♕b1 ♕a3 26. ♕b7 ♕c5∓] **24. g3 g6 25. a4! ♕b3?!** [25... ♖c7] **26. ♖b2 ♕b2 27. ♕b1! ♖c2 28. ♕b2 ♖b2 29. a5! g5 30. ♖a1 ♔g7∓ 31. a6 ba6 32. ♖a6** [♖ 6/e] **g4?!** [32... ♖b4! △ h5-h4 Ivančuk] **33. ♖a4 h5 34. h3 gh3 35. ♖h4 ♖b1 36. ♔h2 ♖f1 37. ♖f4! e5 38. ♖f3 ♔g6 39. ♔h3 e4 40. ♖e3 f5 41. ♔g2 ♖d1 42. ♖a3** [42. f3?? ♖d3 43. ♖d3 ed3 44. ♔f2 f4−+] **h4 43. gh4 ♔h5 44. ♖a5 ♔g4 45. h5 ♖d6 46. f3!= ef3 47. ♔f2 ♖d2 48. ♔e1□ ♖h2 49. ♖a8! ♖h5 50. ♔f2 ♖h2 51. ♔f1 ♔f4 52. ♖b8 ♖d2 53. ♖a8 ♖b2 54. ♖c8 f2 55. ♖c3 ♔e4 56. ♖a3 ♖d2 57. ♖b3 ♖d3 58. ♖d3 ♔d3 59. ♔f2 ♔e4 60. ♔e2 f4 61. ♔f2 f3 62. ♔f1** **1/2 : 1/2** **[Seirawan]**

537.*** **!N** **E 48**

AV. BYHOVSKIJ 2490 − TUNIK 2480
Rossija 1992

1. d4 ♘f6 2. c4 e6 3. ♘c3 ♗b4 4. e3 c5 [RR 4... 0−0 5. ♗d3 d5 6. ♘e2 dc4 7. ♗c4 e5 8. 0−0 ed4 9. ♘d4 ♘bd7!? N (9... a6) *a)* 10. ♕b3!? ♗d6 11. ♘f5 ♘c5 12. ♕c2 ♗e5 13. ♖d1 ♕e8 14. ♘d5!? ♘d5 15. ♗d5 (15. ♖d5?! b6 △ ♗b7) ♗f5 16. ♕f5 ♖d8= Yuldashev 2410 − Serper 2590, Taškent 1993; *b)* 10. a3 *b1)* 10...

♗e7? 11. ♗f7!! ♖f7 (11... ♔f7 12. ♕b3 △ ♘e6→) 12. ♘e6 ♕e8 13. ♘c7+−; *b2)* 10... ♗d6!?; *b3)* 10... ♗c3 11. bc3 ♘e5 12. ♗e2 ♕e7 13. c4 (13. a4?! c5 14. ♗a3 b6 △ ♗b7, ♖ad8∓ ×♗a3) c5 14. ♘b5 ♖d8 (14... a6?! 15. ♕d6!) 15. ♕c2 a6 16. ♘c3 ♗e6 17. ♘e4? (Serper 2575 – V. Loginov 2540, Taškent 1992) ♗c4! 18. ♗c4 ♘c4 19. ♘f6 ♕f6−+; 17. ♘a4 Serper] **5. ♗d3 ♘c6 6. ♘e2 cd4 7. ed4 d5 8. cd5 ♘d5 9. 0–0 0–0 10. a3** [RR 10. ♗c2 ♗e7 11. ♕d3 g6 12. a3 b6 13. ♗h6 ♖e8 14. ♖ad1 ♗b7 15. ♖fe1 ♖c8 16. ♕g3! N (16. ♗a4 – 52/(576)) ♘c3 (16... ♗f6? 17. ♘e4±; 16... ♗d6 17. ♕h3±↑) 17. bc3 ♗f6! (17... ♗a3?! 18. h4 ♗d6 19. ♕h3→) 18. ♘f4 ♘d4! *a)* 19. ♗b1? e5 20. cd4 ef4 21. ♖e8 ♕e8 22. ♗f4 ♕e2∓; *b)* 19. ♗a4 ♘f5!! (19... b5?! 20. ♗b5 ♘b5 21. ♖d8 ♖ed8 22. ♗g5 ♗g5 23. ♕g5 ♘c3 24. ♘h5 ♘d5 25. h4±↑) 20. ♖d8 ♖ed8 21. ♕h3 ♖c3 22. f3 (22. g3? ♘d4) ♖a3 23. ♗c2 (23. ♗b5 ♘d4) ♗d4 24. ♔h1 ♗f2⩱↑; *c)* 19. ♘h5!? ♖c3□ (19... ♗h8 20. ♖d4!+−; 19... ♗h4 20. ♕g4+−) 20. ♕c3 gh5! 21. ♕d3 ♘c2 22. ♕c2 ♗d5⩱; *d)* 19. ♗g6 hg6 20. cd4 (1/2 : 1/2 Ščipkov 2345 – Siklosi 2390, Kecskemét 1993) ♔h7! 21. ♕h3 ♗h4 22. d5! ♔h6 (22... e5? 23. ♖e4!+−) 23. de6 ♕f6 24. g3∞ Ščipkov] **♘c3 11. bc3 ♗d6 12. ♘g3 f5! N** [×♘g3; 12... ♗g3 – 53/557; 12... b6 13. ♘e4⩲] **13. f4** [13. ♕f3 ♔h8 △ e5; 13. ♕c2 ♕h4 △ e5] **♗d7 14. ♗e3 ♘e7 15. c4 b5! 16. d5** [16. cb5 ♘d5⩱] **ed5 17. cb5 ♗c7!** [×d4] **18. ♘e2 ♗b6 19. ♘d4 ♔h8!** [△ ♘g8-f6] **20. ♔h1** [20. ♕b3 ♘g8! △ 21. ♕d5 ♘f6 22. ♕f3 ♘g4→] **♖c8?** [20... ♘g8! △ 21. ♖c1 ♕e7!] **21. ♕b3 ♘g8 22. ♖ad1** [22. ♕d5 ♘f6 (22... ♖c3 23. ♘e2!) 23. ♕b3 (×c3) ♘g4 24. ♗g1 ♕f6 (24... ♘h2 25. ♗h2 ♗d4 26. ♖ac1 ♕f6∞) 25. ♕b4 ♗c5 26. ♕a4 a6 27. h3 ab5 28. ♗b5 ♗b5 29. ♕b5 ♗d4 30. ♗d4 ♕d4 31. hg4 fg4 32. ♕e5∞] **♘f6 23. ♘f5 ♘g4 24. ♗b6 ♕b6 25. h3 ♘f2 26. ♖f2 ♕f2 27. ♘d6** [27. ♕d5? ♗f5 28. ♗f5 ♖c5−+] **♖c5 28. f5** [28. ♘b7 ♗h3! 29. gh3 (29. ♗f1 ♗g4) ♕f3 30. ♔h2 ♕f4 31. ♔h1 ♕f3 32. ♔h2 ♕f2 33. ♔h1 ♖f3−+] **♕f4** [29. ♘b7 ♖c1−+] **0 : 1** **[Tunik]**

538. **E 53**

AGREST 2460 – LANDA 2455
Sankt-Peterburg (zt) 1993

1. d4 d5 2. c4 e6 3. ♘f3 ♘f6 4. ♘c3 ♗b4 5. e3 0–0 6. ♗d3 c5 7. cd5 cd4 [7... ed5 8. ♘e5 (8. 0–0; 8. a3) ♘c6 9. a3!?] **8. ed4 ♕d5?! N** [8... ♘d5; 8... ed5 – 47/190, B 14] **9. 0–0 ♗c3 10. bc3 b6 11. c4 ♕h5 12. ♖e1 ♘bd7** [12... ♗b7 13. ♖e5 (13. d5!?) ♗f3 (13... ♕g4 14. ♗e2! ×♕g4) 14. gf3 ♕h3 15. ♗f1 ♕h4 16. ♗g5 ♕h5 17. ♗f6 ♕g6 18. ♗g5 ♘d7 (18... f6 19. ♖e6±; 18... h6 19. h4±) 19. h4 ♘e5 (19... h6 20. h5±) 20. de5 h6 (20... f6 21. ♗d3) 21. ♗d3 ♕h5 22. ♗f4 ♕h4 23. ♗g3±] **13. ♗e2 ♕a5** [13... ♗b7 14. ♘e5 ♕h4 15. g3 ♕h3 16. ♗f1 ♕f5 17. g4 ♘e5□ 18. gf5 ♘f3 19. ♕f3 ♗f3 20. fe6±] **14. ♗d2 ♕a3 15. ♖b1! a5□** [15... ♕a2? 16. ♖a1 ♕b2 17. ♕a4 △ ♖eb1+−; 15... ♖d8 16. ♗b4 ♕a6 17. ♕c2±] **16. ♗c1 ♕d6** [16... ♕a2? 17. ♗d3 △ ♖e2+−] **17. ♖b3 ♕c7 18. ♗d3 ♗b7 19. ♘e5** [△ f4±] **♘e5 20. de5 ♕c6□** [20... ♘d7 21. ♗h7+−] **21. ♗f1!** [△ ♖h3; 21. f3?! ♘d7∞] **♖fd8 22. ♕c2 ♘d7** [22... ♘e4 23. ♖h3 h6 (23... g6 24. f3 ♘c5 25. ♗g5 △ ♗f6, ♕c1-h6) 24. ♖he3! ♘c5 (24... ♘g5 25. h4 ♘h7 26. ♖g3 ♔h8 27. ♗d3 ♘f8 28. ♗h6 gh6 29. ♕c1) 25. ♖g3 ♔h8 (25... ♔f8 26. ♕h7) 26. ♗h6! gh6 27. ♕c1 ♔h7 28. ♖h3+−] **23. ♗g5 ♖dc8 24. ♖h3→ ♘f8 25. ♕d1! ♗a6** [25... ♖c7 26. ♕g4 ♖d7 27. ♖g3! △ h4-h5+−] **26. ♕g4 ♘g6** [26... ♗c4 27. ♖c1 b5 28. ♗d3 ♕c5 (28... ♕d7 29. ♗h7 ♘h7 30. ♗f6+−) 29. ♗f6 ♘g6 30. ♕h5 h6 31. ♗g6+−] **27. ♗d3 ♗b7** [27... ♗c4 28. ♕h5+−] **28. ♗e4 ♕c7 29. ♕h5 h6 30. ♗h6!+− gh6** [30... ♗e4 31. ♗g5! △ ♕h7-h8] **31. ♗g6 fg6 32. ♖g3** [32. ♕g6] **♔f8 33. ♕g6 ♕f7 34. ♕h6 ♔e8 35. ♖g7 1 : 0** **[Agrest]**

539. !N **E 54**

ĖJNGORN 2575 – LANDENBERGUE 2385
Bern 1993

1. d4 ♘f6 2. ♘f3 e6 3. c4 d5 4. ♘c3 ♗b4 5. e3 0–0 6. ♗e2 c5 7. 0–0 cd4 8. ed4

dc4 9. ♗g5 ♘bd7 10. ♗c4 ♗c3 11. bc3 ♕c7 12. ♗d3 ♕c3 13. ♖e1! N [13. ♖c1 – 51/569] **b6 14. ♘e5 ♗b7 15. ♖e3** [15. ♖c1 ♕a5 16. ♖c7 ♕d5 17. f3 (17. ♕f3 ♕a5!; 17. ♗e4 ♘e4 18. ♖d7 ♘f2 19. ♖d5 ♘d1 20. ♖d7 ♗c8 21. ♖c7 f6! 22. ♖d1 fe5 23. de5 ♗a6!=) ♘e5 18. de5□ ♖fd8 (18... ♘g4 19. ♗b1! ♘e5 20. ♕d5 ♗d5 21. ♖e5 f6 22. ♖d5 ed5 23. ♗d2±) 19. ♗f6 (19. ♗c2 ♖d7!; 19. ef6 ♕g5 20. ♖b7 ♕f6! 21. ♔h1 ♕c3) gf6 20. ef6∞; 15. ♘d7!? ♘d7 16. ♗b5! ♕c7□ (16... ♘f6 17. ♗f6 gf6 18. ♖e3; 16... ♕a5 17. a4; 16... h6 17. ♗h6; 16... ♗c6 17. ♖c1 ♕c1 18. ♗c1 ♗b5 19. d5±) 17. ♕g4 f5□ (17... ♔h8 18. ♖ac1 ♕d6 19. ♗f4 ♕d5 20. ♗d7 ♕d7 21. ♖c7 ♕d5 22. ♗e5+–; 17... ♖fc8 18. ♗h6 g6 19. ♖e6± △ 19... fe6? 20. ♕e6 ♔h8 21. ♕f7) 18. ♕g3! ♕g3 19. hg3 ♘f6 20. ♖e6⩲] **♕a5 16. ♖b1 a6?! 17. ♘d7± ♘d7 18. ♕h5 g6□** [18... f5 19. ♖h3; 18... h6 19. ♖b5! (19. ♖g3? ♖fc8 20. ♕h6=) ab5 20. ♗h6+–] **19. ♕h6 f5** [19... ♕d5 20. ♗e4 ♕e4 21. ♖e4 ♗e4 22. ♖b6!+–] **20. ♖e6 ♕d5 21. ♖g6 hg6 22. ♕g6 ♔h8 23. ♕h6 ♔g8 24. ♕g6 ♔h8 25. ♕h6 ♔g8 26. ♗c4!! ♕c4 27. ♕g6 ♔h8 28. ♕h6 ♔g8 29. ♕g6 ♔h8 30. ♖b3 ♕b3□ 31. ♕h6 ♔g8 32. ♕g6 ♔h8 33. ♕h6?⊕** [33. ab3 ♖ac8!□ 34. ♕e6! ♗c6 35. h4±] **♔g8 34. ♕g6 1/2 : 1/2**
[Ėjngorn, Bogdanov]

540. E 54

SPEELMAN 2595 – KUMARAN 2385
Dublin (zt) 1993

1. e4 c6 2. d4 d5 3. ed5 cd5 4. c4 ♘f6 5. ♘c3 e6 6. ♘f3 ♗b4 7. ♗d3 dc4 8. ♗c4 0–0 9. 0–0 b6 10. ♗g5 ♗b7 11. ♖c1 ♗c3 12. bc3 ♘bd7 13. ♗d3 ♕c7 14. ♖e1 ♖fe8 15. ♗h4 ♖ac8 16. ♗g3 ♕c6 17. c4 [17. ♗f1 ♕d5!? (17... ♘e4) 18. c4 ♕a5!?; 18... ♕h5!?] **♖cd8 N** [17... ♘f8 – 28/656] **18. ♗f1 ♕c8 19. ♗h4 ♕a8?** [19... ♕b8! 20. ♘e5 ♘e5 21. ♖e5 ♕e5 22. de5 ♖d1 23. ♖d1 ♘e4 24. f3 ♘c5 25. ♗e7 (25. ♗f2 ♔f8!) ♗c6!□ 26. ♗c5 bc5 27. ♖d6 ♖c8 28. ♔f2 (28. f4 ♔f8 29. g3 ♔e7 30. ♗g2 ♗g2 31. ♔g2 ♖b8 32. ♖a6 ♖b4=) ♔f8 29. ♔e3 ♔e7 30. ♗d3 h6 (30... f5!? 31. g4) 31. ♗e4 (31. g4!?) ♗e4 32. ♔e4 ♖c7±; 32... f5!?] **20. ♘e5 ♘e5 21. ♖e5 ♗e4 22. ♗f6 gf6 23. ♕g4 ♗g6** [23... ♔f8 24. ♕e4 fe5 25. ♕e5±] **24. ♖ee1 e5!? 25. de5 fe5 26. h4! ♕c8 27. ♕g3 ♕f5 28. c5 bc5 29. ♖c5 ♕f4!?** [29... f6 30. ♖c7 ♔h8 31. ♕e3] **30. ♖ce5** [30. ♕f4 ef4 31. ♖e8 ♖e8 32. h5 ♗b1 33. ♗c4 ♖e7□ 34. ♖g5 (34. f3; 34. h6!? ♔f8!□) ♔f8 35. f3] **♖e5 31. ♖e5 ♕g3** [31... ♕c1!? *a)* 32. h5 ♖d1 33. ♖e8 ♔g7 34. ♕e5 *a1)* 34... f6 35. ♖e7 ♗f7 (35... ♔h6 36. ♕f6 ♖f1 37. ♔h2 ♖h1 38. ♔g3) 36. ♕e2!+–; *a2)* 34... ♔h6! 35. hg6 ♖f1 36. ♔h2 *a21)* 36... ♖h1 37. ♔g3 fg6 (37... ♖h5 38. gf7! ♖g5 39. ♔h2+–) 38. ♖e7 (38. f4 ♖h5 39. ♕f6 ♕a3 40. ♔g4 ♖f5 41. ♕h4 ♖h5) ♕g5 39. ♕g5 ♔g5 40. ♖a7; 40. f4!?; *a22)* 36... fg6! *a221)* 37. ♖e7 ♖f2! (37... ♖h1 38. ♔g3 – 36... ♖h1) 38. ♕g7 ♔g5 39. ♖e5 ♔g4 (39... ♖f5 40. ♕e7 ♔g4) 40. ♕d7 ♖f5 41. ♖f5 gf5 42. ♕a7=; *a222)* 37. ♔g3 ♕d2 38. ♕e3 ♕e3 39. ♖e3 ♖d1 40. ♖a3 ♖d7 41. ♖a6; *b)* 32. ♕e3 ♖d1! (32... ♕e3 33. ♖e3±) 33. ♕c1 (33. ♕e2!?) ♖c1 34. ♖d5 (34. ♖e3 f6 35. f3 ♗f7 36. ♔f2 ♖c2=) f6 (34... f5 35. f3 ♗f7 36. ♖d8 ♔g7 37. ♖d7 ♔f6 38. ♔f2 f4 39. ♗d3!) 35. f3 ♗f7 36. ♖d8 ♔g7 37. ♖d7 ♔g8 38. ♔f2 ♖c2 39. ♔g3 △ 39... ♖a2?? 40. ♖f7] **32. fg3± ♗d3 33. ♖a5 ♗f1 34. ♔f1** [♖ 6/e] **♖d7 35. ♔e2 ♔g7 36. g4! ♖b7?!** [36... h6 37. g5 h5!? 38. ♖a6 ♖c7 39. g3 (39. ♔d3) ♖c3 40. ♔f2 ♖c2 41. ♔f3 ♖c3 42. ♔g2 ♖c2 43. ♔h3 ♖c7 44. ♖h6 ♖c2 45. ♖h5 ♖a2 46. ♖h6; 36... ♖c7!] **37. g5 f6** [37... ♔g6 38. ♔f3 ♔h5 39. ♔g3] **38. gf6 ♔f6 39. ♔f3 ♖c7 40. ♔g4 ♔g7?⊕** [40... ♖g7 41. ♖g5! ♖b7 42. ♔h5+–; 40... ♔g6 41. ♖a6 ♔g7] **41. ♔h5!+– h6 42. g4 ♖b7 43. a4 ♖c7 44. ♖a6 ♖c5 45. g5 hg5 46. ♖a7** [46... ♔f6 47. ♖a6 ♔g7 48. hg5]
1 : 0 [Speelman]

541. E 58**

JUSUPOV 2645 – HJARTARSON 2625
München 1993

1. d4 ♘f6 2. c4 e6 3. ♘c3 ♗b4 4. e3 0–0 5. ♗d3 d5 6. ♘f3 c5 7. 0–0 ♘c6 8.

a3 ♗c3 9. bc3 ♕c7 10. cd5 ed5 11. a4 ♖e8 [11... c4 12. ♗c2 N (12. ♗b1) ♗g4 13. ♕e1 ♗f3 14. gf3 ♕d7 15. ♕e2 (15. ♔g2!?) ♖fe8 16. ♔h1 ♕h3 17. ♖g1 ♘h5∞ Azmajparašvili 2610 – Vaganian 2590, Manila (ol) 1992] **12. ♗a3 c4 13. ♗c2 ♗g4 14. ♕e1 ♗h5 15. ♘h4 ♖e6?! N** [RR 15... ♘g4 16. g3 ♗g6 17. ♗d1 ♕d7 18. ♘g6 hg6 19. ♖a2 f5?! 20. ♖e2 ♘f6 21. f3 ♖e6? 22. ♗c2 ♖ae8 23. g4! fg4 24. ♗g6 gf3 25. ♖f3! ♘e4 26. ♗e8 ♖e8 27. ♖g2 ♘d8 28. ♕h4 ♘e6 29. ♕h5 b6 30. ♖g4 ♘d8 31. ♖h4 1 : 0 Kortchnoi 2605 – Illescas Córdoba 2615, Buenos Aires 1993] **16. f3! ♖ae8**

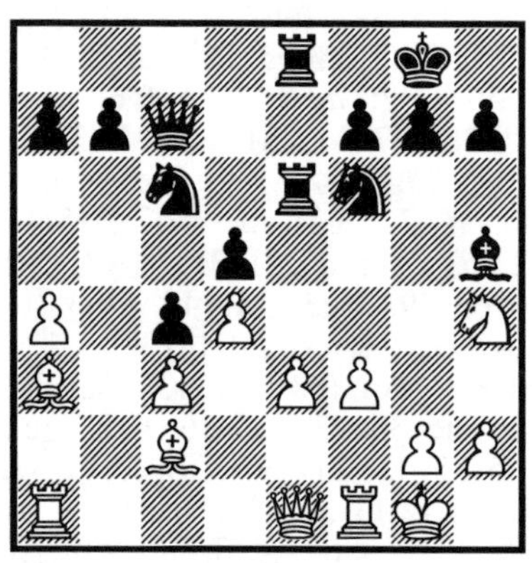

17. e4! de4 18. fe4 ♘g4! [18... ♘e4? 19. d5 ♕b6 20. ♔h1 ♖f6 21. ♗e4 ♖f1 22. ♕f1 ♖e4 23. dc6 ♖h4 24. ♕e1 g5 25. ♕e5+–; 18... ♖e4?! 19. ♗e4 ♖e4 20. ♕g3+–] **19. g3** [19. e5? ♘ce5 20. de5 ♖e5 21. ♕g3 ♕b6 22. ♔h1 ♖e2∓ △ ♘f2; 19. ♘f3 ♗g6! 20. d5 ♘ce5 21. de6 ♘f3 22. ♖f3 ♕h2 23. ♔f1 ♕h1 24. ♔e2 ♕g2=/∞] **♘f6 20. ♖b1!?** [20. e5 ♘e5 21. de5 ♖e5=/∞] **♘e4 21. d5 ♖e5 22. dc6 ♘g5** [22... ♕c6? 23. ♗e4 ♖e4 24. ♕f2+–] **23. cb7!** [23. ♕d2 ♕c6! 24. ♕g2 ♕g2! 25. ♘g2 (25. ♔g2 ♖e2 26. ♖f2 ♖f2 27. ♔f2 ♖e2∓) ♘f3 26. ♖f3 (26. ♔h1 ♘d2∓) ♗f3 27. ♖f1±] **♖e2?** [23... ♘h3? 24. ♔g2 ×♘h3; 23... ♖e1 24. ♖fe1=/∞ ♖b8□ *a)* 25. ♘f5?! ♘f3 (25... ♔h8∞) 26. ♔f2 ♘e1 27. ♗d6 ♕d7 28. ♗e4 ♗f3 29. ♗f3 ♘f3 30. ♗b8 ♕d2 31. ♔f3 ♕d3∓; *b)* 25. ♖b5?! ♘f3 26. ♘f3 ♗f3 27. ♗e4 (27. ♖e7 ♕d8∓) ♗e4 28. ♖e4 h6⩱; *c)* 25. ♗f5 ♘e6 26. ♗e4 ♘c5 27. ♗d5↑; *d)* 25. ♖e7 ♕c6 26. ♗f5↑] **24. ♗f5±** [△ ♗c8; 24. ♕e2? ♗e2 25. ♖fe1 ♕c6 △ ♘h3] **g6** [⌓ 24... ♘f3 25. ♘f3 ♗f3 26. ♕e2 ♗e2 27. ♗c8 ♗f1 (27... ♖c8 28. ♗d6+–) 28. b8♕ (28. ♔f1 ♕e5 29. b8♕ ♕e2=) ♕b8 29. ♖b8 ♗h3 30. ♗h3 ♖b8 31. ♗b4± ×c4] **25. ♕c1!+– h6 26. ♕f4 ♕c6 27. ♕d6** [27. b8♕ gf5 28. ♕f5] **♘f3 28. ♖f3** [28. ♘f3? ♗f3] **1 : 0** **[Jusupov]**

542. **E 60**

R. HÜBNER 2620 – ADAMS 2630
München 1993

1. d4 ♘f6 2. ♘f3 g6 3. c4 ♗g7 4. g3 0–0 5. ♗g2 d6 6. 0–0 c6 7. b3 ♕a5 8. ♗b2 N [8. ♕d2 – 47/(697)] **♕h5 9. ♘bd2 ♗h3** [9... ♗g4!? △ ♘bd7, e5] **10. e4 ♘a6 11. ♖e1** [11. ♘h4!? ♗g4 (11... ♕d1 12. ♖fd1±; 11... ♗g2 12. ♔g2±) 12. f3 ♗d7 13. f4±] **♘g4?!** [11... ♘b4?! 12. ♗c3 ♘d3 13. ♖e2±; 11... ♘d7!? 12. ♘h4 ♕d1 13. ♖ed1 ♗g2 14. ♘g2 c5=] **12. ♘h4 ♗g2 13. ♔g2 e5** [13... c5 14. h3 ♘h6 (14... ♘f6 15. ♘df3 cd4 16. e5+–) 15. ♕h5 gh5 16. ♘df3±; 13... ♘b4 14. h3 ♘f6 15. ♘df3±] **14. h3 ♘f6 15. ♘hf3** [15. ♘df3 ♖fe8 16. de5 (16. d5 cd5 17. cd5 ♘c5 ×e4; 16. g4 ♘g4 17. hg4 ♕g4 18. ♔f1 ed4∞) de5 17. g4 ♘g4 18. hg4 ♕g4 19. ♔f1 ♖ad8 20. ♕e2 ♘c5∞] **♖fe8** [15... ♘d7? 16. g4 ♕h6 17. g5 ♕h5 18. ♘f1+–; 15... ed4 16. e5 de5 17. ♖e5 ♕h6 18. ♗d4 △ ♗e3] **16. d5** [16. g4 ♘g4 17. hg4 ♕g4 18. ♔h1 ed4∞; 16. de5 de5 17. g4 ♘g4 18. hg4 ♕g4 19. ♔h1 ♖ad8 20. ♕e2 ♘b4∞] **♘c5 17. ♕b1 ♗f8 18. ♗c1 ♕h6 19. b4 ♘cd7** [19... ♘a4 20. ♕b3 ♘b6 (20... b5 21. dc6+–) 21. a4±] **20. ♘b3 ♕g7 21. ♘a5 c5 22. a3** [22. ♘b7 ♖ab8 23. ♘a5 cb4 △ ♘c5∞] **♖ab8 23. ♗e3 ♖ec8 24. ♕d3?** [24. ♖a2 *a)* 24... ♗e7 25. bc5 dc5 (25... ♘c5 26. ♗c5 ♖c5 27. ♘c6+–) 26. ♖b2 △ 26... ♘b6 27. ♘e5+–; *b)* 24... ♘e8 25. ♖b2 ♘b6 26. ♖c1 △ ♘e1-d3±] **♗e7 25. ♖ab1 ♗d8 26. ♘b3 ♗b6 27. ♘fd2 ♕f8 28. ♖b2 ♕d8?!** [28... ♘e8!? △ f5] **29. ♖eb1?!** [29. b5 △ g4, ♘f1-g3; 29. ♗g5!?; 29. ♗h6!?] **cb4 30. ab4 ♗e3 31. ♕e3 b6** [31... ♕b6 32.

♕b6 ab6 33. ♖a2±] **32. ♖a2** [32. ♖a1 ♖b7 33. b5 ♘c5 34. ♘c1 (△ ♘a2-b4-c6) ♖a8 35. ♘a2 a5] **♖c7 33. ♖ba1 ♖bb7 34. ♘c1** [34. ♖a3!? △ b5, ♘c1-a2-b4-c6] **b5! 35. cb5 ♖b5 36. ♘d3 ♘b6 37. ♖a7 ♘c4 38. ♘c4 ♖c4 39. ♖c1** [39. ♖a8 ♖b8 40. ♕a7 ♖a8 41. ♕a8 ♖c8 △ ♘e4∞; 39. f3 ♖c2 40. ♔g1 (40. ♘f2 ♖b4) ♘h5∞; 39. ♕g5 ♔g7∞] **♖e4** [39... ♖c1 40. ♕c1 ♘e4 41. ♕c4 ♕b8 42. ♖a5 ♖a5 43. ba5+−] **40. ♕f3 ♔g7□** [40... ♖d4 41. ♖cc7 *a)* 41... e4 42. ♕f4 ed3 (42... ♖d3 43. ♖f7 △ ♕h6+−) 43. ♕d4 ♖d5 44. ♕c4 d2 45. ♖c8 ♕c8 46. ♕c8 ♔g7 47. ♕e6+−; *b)* 41... ♖bd5 42. ♖f7 ♖d3 43. ♕f6 ♕f6 44. ♖f6 △ ♖ff7±] **41. ♖cc7 ♕f8 42. ♖c6** [42. ♘c5 dc5 43. ♖c6 ♕d8 44. bc5 ♖e1 45. ♖d6 ♕d6 (45... ♖bb1 46. ♖d8 e4 47. ♖f7 ♔f7 48. ♖f8 ♔f8 49. ♕f6 ♔g8 50. h4+−; 45... e4 46. ♕c3 ♖bb1 47. ♕e1 ♕d6 48. ♕b1±) 46. cd6 e4 47. ♕c3 ♖bb1 48. ♕e1 (48. g4 ♖g1 49. ♔h2 g5) ♖e1 49. d7 ♘d7 50. ♖d7 ♔f6∓] **♕d8** [42... ♖d5? 43. ♘c5+−] **43. ♖cc7** [43. ♘c5 dc5 44. ♖aa6 ♖eb4 45. ♖f6 ♖b7∓] **♕f8 44. ♖c6 ♕d8 45. ♖cc7 1/2 : 1/2 [R. Hübner]**

543. !N E 61

SMYSLOV 2530 – EPIŠIN 2620

Rostov na Donu 1993

1. d4 ♘f6 2. c4 g6 3. ♘c3 ♗g7 4. ♗g5 0–0 5. e3 c5 6. ♘f3 d6 7. ♗e2 cd4 8. ed4 [⌓ 8. ♘d4=] **h6! N** [8... ♗g4 – 17/116] **9. ♗f4** [9. ♗h4?! ♘h5 10. 0–0 f5!↑] **♗f5 10. 0–0 ♘e4 11. ♘e4 ♗e4 12. ♕d2 g5 13. ♗e3 e6!∓** [13... f5 14. d5 ♗f3 15. ♗f3 ♘d7 16. ♗d4 ♗d4 17. ♕d4 ♘e5 18. ♖fe1 △ ♖e3, ♖ae1, △ ♖e5±] **14. ♘e1** [14. d5 ed5 15. cd5 ♘d7 16. ♗d4 ♘f6 ×d5] **♘c6 15. f3 ♗g6 16. d5 ed5 17. cd5 ♘e7 18. ♖d1 ♖c8! 19. ♗f2** [19. ♗a7? ♖a8 20. ♗d4 ♗d4 21. ♕d4 ♘f5∓] **a6 20. ♗d3 ♗d3 21. ♕d3 ♕a5 22. ♕b3 ♕b5! 23. ♕b5 ab5 24. ♖d2 b4?** [24... ♖fe8! 25. g3 b4∓] **25. ♗d4! ♖fe8 26. ♗g7** [26. ♔f2 ♗d4 27. ♖d4 ♖c5 28. ♖b4 ♘d5 29. ♖b7 ♘e3↑] **♔g7 27. ♘c2?** [27. ♔f2 ♖c5 28. ♘c2 ♘d5 29. ♖fd1 ♖e5 30. ♘e1=] **♘d5 28. g3?!** [28. ♘d4] **♖e5 29. ♘d4 ♘e3 30. ♖b1** [30. ♖e1 ♘c4 31. ♖de2 (31. ♖e5 de5−+) ♔f6∓] **♖d5 31. b3!□ ♔f6?** [31... f5! 32. ♔f2 (32. f4 gf4 33. gf4 ♖e8∓) f4∓] **32. ♖e1 ♖c3 33. ♔f2 ♘f5 34. ♖ed1 ♘d4 35. ♖d4 ♖c2 36. ♔g1 ♖d4 37. ♖d4 ♔e5 38. ♖b4 ♖a2 39. ♖b7 f5 40. ♖e7 ♔d4 41. ♖e6?!** [41. ♖e1 d5 42. ♖d1 ♔e5 43. ♖e1 ♔d6 44. ♖d1 ♖b2 45. ♖d3 f4 46. gf4 gf4 47. h4 ♔e5 △ d4, ♖e2-e3∓] **d5 42. ♖h6 ♔e3 43. ♖f6** [43. h4 ♔f3 44. hg5 ♔g3 45. ♔f1 f4−+] **d4−+ 44. ♖f5 d3 45. ♖e5 ♔f3 46. ♖f5 ♔e3 47. ♖e5 ♔d4 48. ♖e8 d2 49. ♖d8 ♔e3 50. ♖e8 ♔f3** [51. ♖f8 ♔g4 52. ♖f1 ♖c2] **0 : 1 [Epišin]**

544.* E 62

TUKMAKOV 2605 – OVSEEVIČ

Nikolaev (zt) 1993

1. d4 ♘f6 2. c4 g6 3. ♘f3 ♗g7 4. g3 0–0 5. ♗g2 d6 6. 0–0 c6 7. ♘c3 ♗f5 8. b3 [RR 8. ♕b3 ♕b6 9. ♖e1 ♘a6 N (9... ♘fd7 – 48/(764)) 10. e4 ♗g4 11. ♗e3 ♘d7 12. ♕c2 c5 13. d5 ♗f3 14. ♗f3 ♗d4 15. ♗g2 e6 1/2 : 1/2 Wojtkiewicz 2580 – Kir. Georgiev 2660, Budapest (zt) 1993] **♘e4 9. ♗b2 ♘c3 10. ♗c3 ♗e4 11. ♕d2 ♘d7 12. ♕e3 d5 13. ♗h3 ♗f3 14. ♕f3 e6 15. ♕d3 N** [15. ♖fd1 – 44/708] **♕e7** [15... f5!?] **16. ♖fd1 ♖fd8** [16... f5] **17. e3 ♘b6** [△ ♘c8-d6] **18. a4 ♖ab8 19. ♖a2 ♘c8 20. ♗a5!? ♖e8** [20... b6 21. ♗e1 c5 22. cd5 ♖d5 (22... ed5 23. ♗c3) 23. ♗g2 △ d5] **21. ♗e1 ♘d6 22. ♗g2 ♖ed8** [22... f5!?] **23. c5 ♘e8 24. b4 e5 25. b5 ♘c7 26. ♖b2 ♘e6 27. ♗c3 ed4 28. ed4 ♖e8** [28... ♕c7? 29. b6] **29. a5** [29. ♖db1 ♖bd8 30. bc6 bc6 31. ♖b7 ♖d7!?; 31... ♕f6!?] **♘c7 30. b6 ♘e6** [30... ♘b5 31. ♖b5 cb5 32. ba7 ♖a8 33. ♕b5±; 30... ab6 31. ♖b6±] **31. ba7 ♖a8 32. ♖db1 ♖a7 33. ♖b6** [33. a6 ba6 34. ♖b6 ♕c7] **♖ea8 34. ♗f1 ♕d7** [34... ♕c7] **35. ♕d2 ♗f6** [35... ♘d8 36. ♕b2 △ 37. a6 ba6 38. ♗a5] **36. ♗h3! ♗d8 37. ♗e6! fe6 38. ♖6b3 ♕f7** [38... ♗a5? 39. ♗a5 ♖a5 40. ♖b7 △ ♕h6±] **39. h4 ♕d7 40. ♕e2 ♕f7 41. ♗d2 ♗f6**

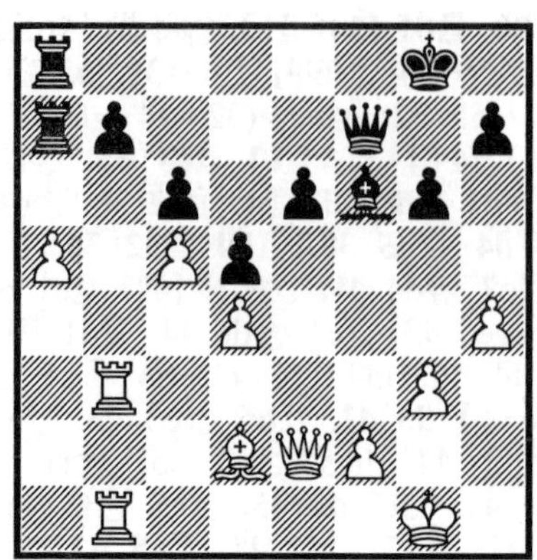

42. a6!! ♖a6 [42... ♗d4 *a)* 43. ab7 ♖b8 44. ♗f4 e5 (44... ♖bb7 45. ♖b7 ♖b7 46. ♖b7 ♕b7 47. ♕e6 ♔g7 48. h5!) 45. ♗e5 ♗e5 46. ♕e5 ♖bb7=; *b)* 43. ♖b7 ♖b7 44. ♖b7±] **43. ♖b7 ♖a1! 44. ♖f7 ♖b1 45. ♔g2 ♔f7 46. ♕f3 ♔e7** [46... ♔g7 47. ♗h6! ♔h6 48. ♕f6+−] **47. ♕f4!** [47. ♗g5 ♗g5 48. hg5 ♖f8!] **♖a7 48. ♕d6 ♔f7 49. ♗g5!** [49. ♕c6 ♗d4] **♗g5** [49... ♗d4?? 50. ♕f4] **50. hg5 ♖e7 51. ♕c6** [♕6/b] **♖b4** [51... ♖b8 52. ♕d6 △ g4, f4-f5] **52. ♕a8! ♖d4** [52... ♔g7 53. c6 ♖c4 54. ♕d8 ♖f7 55. ♕d6 ♖c2 56. ♕e6 ♖ff2 57. ♔h3+−] **53. ♕h8 ♖c4 54. ♕h7 ♔e8** [54... ♔f8 55. ♕h8 ♔f7 56. ♕f6] **55. ♕g6 ♔d7 56. ♕f6 ♖c5 57. g6 ♖c8 58. f4 ♖ee8 59. g4+− ♖cd8 60. f5 ef5 61. gf5 ♔c7 62. g7! d4 63. ♕f7 ♔b8** [63... ♔b6 64. f6 d3 65. ♕e8! ♖e8 66. f7] **64. f6**
1 : 0 **[Tukmakov]**

545.* **E 62**

VUČIĆ 2385 – J. BENJAMIN 2585
Saint-Martin 1993

1. d4 ♘f6 2. ♘f3 g6 3. g3 ♗g7 4. ♗g2 0–0 5. 0–0 d6 6. c4 c6 7. ♘c3 ♕b6!? 8. h3 ♕a6 9. ♕b3 [9. b3 b5 10. ♘d2 bc4 11. ♘c4 ♗e6 12. ♘e3 ♘bd7 13. ♗b2 ♖ac8 N (13... ♖fc8) 14. ♕d2 ♘b6 15. ♖fd1 ♖fd8 1/2 : 1/2 Adianto 2490 – J. Benjamin 2585, New York 1993] **♘bd7 10. ♗e3 N** [10. e4 – 40/724] **♘b6 11. ♘d2 d5 12. c5 ♘bd7** [12... ♘c4 13. ♘c4 dc4 14. ♕c2 ♗f5 15. ♕c1±] **13. ♕a4 ♕a4 14. ♘a4 e5 15. ♘c3?** [15. ♘f3 ♘e4 16. de5 ♘e5 17. ♘e5 ♗e5 18. ♖fd1=] **♘g4! 16. ♘d5□** [16. hg4 ed4 17. ♘d5 de3∓] **♘e3 17. ♘e7 ♔h8 18. fe3 ed4 19. ♘e4! f5 20. ♘d6 ♘c5 21. ♘ec8 de3!?** [21... ♖ac8 22. ♘c8 ♖c8 23. ♖ac1 ♘e6 24. e4 f4 25. gf4 ♗h6 26. f5 ♗c1 27. fe6=] **22. ♖ac1 ♘e6 23. ♘e7 ♗f6** [23... ♘d4 24. ♔h2 (24. ♗f3 ♗f6) ♗e5 25. ♘b7 ♘e2 26. ♖c6 ♘g3 27. ♖e1∞] **24. ♘ef5** [24. ♘b7! ♗e7 25. ♖fd1! ♗f6 26. ♖c4 ♗e5 27. ♘c5 ♘c5 28. ♖c5 ♗g3∓] **gf5 25. ♘f5 ♖ad8∓ 26. ♔h1 ♗b2 27. ♖b1 ♖d2 28. ♘e3 ♖f1 29. ♗f1 b5 30. ♖d1 ♖d1 31. ♘d1 ♗e5 32. ♗g2⊕ c5 33. g4 ♘f4 34. e3** [⌓ 34. ♗c6] **♘g2 35. ♔g2 c4−+ 36. e4 b4 37. ♘e3 b3 38. ab3 cb3 39. ♘c4 a5 40. ♔f3 a4 41. ♔e2 b2 42. ♘b2** [42. ♘a3 ♗d6 43. ♘b1 a3] **♗b2** [42... a3] **43. ♔d3 ♔g7 44. ♔c4 ♔f6** **0 : 1**
[J. Benjamin]

546.** **E 62**

AN. KARPOV 2725 – J. POLGÁR 2595
Dos Hermanas 1993

1. ♘f3 ♘f6 2. c4 g6 3. g3 ♗g7 4. ♗g2 0–0 5. 0–0 d6 6. d4 ♘c6 7. ♘c3 e5 8. d5 [RR 8. de5 ♘e5 9. ♘e5 de5 10. ♕d8 ♖d8 11. ♗g5 ♖d4 12. ♘d5 ♘d5 13. cd5 e4 14. ♖fd1 ♗f5 15. ♖d4 ♗d4 16. ♖c1 ♗e5 N (16... f6 – 1/428) 17. f3 ef3 18. ♗f3 ♖c8 19. ♗f4 1/2 : 1/2 Adorján 2545 – J. Polgár 2595, Budapest (zt) 1993] **♘e7 9. b4 N** [9. c5 – 55/567] **♘d7** [9... a5?! 10. ba5 ♖a5 11. ♘d2± Ivančuk 2720 – J. Polgár 2550, Roquebrune 1992] **10. ♖b1 a5 11. a3 h6** [11... f5 12. ♘g5!? △ ♘e6] **12. e4 f5 13. ef5 gf5 14. ♘h4⩲ e4** [14... ♘f6 15. ♗d2 ♕e8 16. ♘b5±] **15. ♕b3!** [15. ♕c2 ♘e5 16. ♘e2 ab4 17. ab4 c6 △ b5!?⇆] **♘e5 16. f3 ef3** [16... ♘d3 17. fe4 ♗d4 18. ♔h1 ♘f2 (18... fe4 19. ♘e4 ♖f1 20. ♗f1 ♘c1 21. ♖c1 ♘f5 22. ♘f3±) 19. ♖f2 ♗f2 20. ♗h6±] **17. ♘f3 ♘d3?** [17... ♘7g6 18. ♘e2±] **18. ♗d2 ab4 19. ab4 ♘g6** [19... f4 20. ♘e4!±] **20. ♘e2 ♘de5** [20... ♘ge5 21. ♘e5 (21. ♘fd4!?) ♘e5 22. ♘f4±] **21. ♘fd4 ♕f6 22. c5 ♖f7 23. ♔h1** [23. ♗c3 ♕g5; 23. ♘e6 dc5 24. bc5 ♗e6 25. de6 ♖e7 26. ♗b7 ♖d8; 23. c6!? △ b5, ♔h1, ♘f4] **dc5 24. bc5 ♕a6!?**

25. c6! [25. d6 cd6 26. cd6 ♘c4 27. ♗b4 ♗d7; 25. ♗c3 ♕c4□ 26. ♕c4 ♘c4 27. ♖a1 ♖a1 28. ♖a1 ♘e3 29. ♖a8 ♖f8 30. d6 cd6 31. cd6 ♘g2 32. ♔g2 ♗d7±] **bc6 26. dc6 ♘e7□** [26... ♔h7 27. ♗c3! (27. ♘b5 ♕a2⇆) ♕d3 (27... ♕c4 28. ♕c4 ♘c4 29. ♗d5+−) 28. ♘f4 ♘f4 29. gf4+−] **27. ♗f4! ♕c4□** [27... ♕a2 28. ♕a2 ♖a2 29. ♘c3 ♖a6 30. ♘cb5+−] **28. ♕c4 ♘c4 29. ♖fc1?!** [29. ♖b7! ♘c6 30. ♗c6 ♗b7 31. ♗b7 ♖a5 32. ♗c8!] **♘e5** [29... ♘d6 30. ♗d6 cd6 31. ♘b5 ♗e5 32. ♘f4±] **30. ♖b3** [30. ♘b5 ♘d3 31. ♖c2! (31. ♖d1 ♘f2) ♘f4 32. ♘f4 ♖b8 33. ♖cc1! ♗e5 34. ♘d3 ♗d6 35. ♘d6±] **♖a4 31. ♘b5 ♘5c6 32. ♖c6 ♘c6 33. ♗c6 ♗e6 34. ♖e3 ♗c4 35. ♘a3! ♖a6** [35... ♖a3 36. ♖a3 ♗e2 (36... ♖e7 37. ♘c3 ♖e1 38. ♔g2 ♗d4 39. ♗d5+−) 37. ♗d5±] **36. ♘c4 ♖c6 37. ♘e5 ♗e5 38. ♖e5 ♖c4** [38... ♔h7 39. ♘d4+−] **39. ♗h6 ♖e4 40. ♖e4 fe4 41. ♗f4** [41. ♘c3 e3! 42. ♔g2 (42. ♗f4 ♖d7! 43. ♔g1 ♖d2!⇆) ♖f2 43. ♔h3 (43. ♔g1 ♖f3!) ♖c2] **c5 42. ♘c3 c4** [42... ♖e7 43. ♔g2 e3 44. ♘e2+−] **43. ♘e4 ♖a7 44. ♘c3 ♖b7 45. ♔g1 ♖b2** [45... ♖b3 46. ♗e5 ♔f7 47. ♔f2 ♔e6 48. ♗d4+−] **46. h4 ♔f7** [46... ♖c2 47. ♗e5 ♔f7 48. h5+−] **47. h5 ♔e6 48. h6 ♔f6 49. ♘e4 ♔g6 50. ♔f1 ♖h2 51. ♔e1 1 : 0** **[An. Karpov]**

547. E 62

A. MIHAL'ČIŠIN 2515 – D. JAĆIMOVIĆ 2400

Prilep 1992

1. d4 ♘f6 2. c4 g6 3. ♘f3 ♗g7 4. g3 0–0 5. ♗g2 d6 6. 0–0 ♘c6 7. ♘c3 ♗g4 8. ♗e3 ♘d7 N [8... ♕d7!? 9. ♖e1 (9. d5; 9. ♕a4) ♖ad8 △ e5] **9. ♕d2** [9. d5 ♘ce5 (9... ♗f3 10. ef3 ♘ce5 11. ♕e2 ♘b6 12. ♗b6 ab6 13. f4±) 10. ♘e5 ♘e5 11. ♗d4 c5 12. dc6 ♘c6? 13. ♗g7 ♔g7 14. ♗c6+−; 12... bc6] **♖e8** [9... e5 10. d5 (10. de5!? ♘de5 11. ♘e5 ♘e5 12. b3±) ♘e7 (10... ♗f3 11. ef3 ♘d4 12. f4±) 11. ♗h6±] **10. b3! e5 11. de5** [11. d5 ♘e7 12. h3 ♗f3 13. ef3 ♘f5 14. h4 △ ♗h3±] **♘de5 12. ♖ad1** [12. ♘g5!? △ ♘ge4, ♗g5] **♖c8 13. ♘d5 ♗e6** [13... ♕d7 14. ♘g5 △ ♘e4 ×f6] **14. ♘d4** [14. ♘g5!] **♕d7 15. ♘f4** [15. ♘e6 fe6 16. ♘c3 ♘g4 17. ♗g5 h6 18. ♗e3±] **♘g4 16. ♘de6 fe6 17. ♗h3 ♘e3 18. ♕e3 ♗e5 19. ♘d3** [19. c5 ♗f4 20. ♕f4 d5∞] **♕g7 20. b4** [20. c5!? d5 21. b4 a6 22. a4±] **a6 21. a4 ♔h8 22. c5** [22. b5 ♘a5 23. ♕c1 ♘b3∞] **♗d4 23. ♕c1 g5!? 24. ♕b1** [24. ♗g2! d5 25. e4±] **♗c3 25. cd6 cd6 26. e3 ♘e5 27. ♘e5 ♗e5 28. b5 a5 29. ♖c1 g4 30. ♗g2 d5 31. ♕d3** [31. ♖c2 ♖c4!∞] **♗b2 32. ♖c2 ♖c2 33. ♕c2 ♕c3 34. ♕e2 ♖g8 35. h3 h5 36. hg4 hg4 37. ♖d1⊕ ♕f6 38. ♕c2 ♕c3 39. ♕e2 ♕f6 40. e4! ♗d4 41. ed5 ♖f8 42. ♖d2??** [42. ♖f1±; 42. ♕g4!±] **e5?** [42... ♗f2! 43. ♕f2 ♕a1∓] **43. ♕g4± ♗f2 44. ♔h2 ♗c5 45. ♗e4 ♖g8** [45... ♕h6 46. ♕h3 ♕h3 47. ♔h3+−] **46. ♕h3 ♔g7 47. ♕d7 ♕f7 48. ♕f7 ♔f7 49. d6 ♖h8 50. ♔g2 ♔e6 51. ♗b7 ♗d4 52. ♗e4 ♖b8** [52... ♔d6 53. b6+−] **53. ♖c2 ♖b6 54. ♖c6!+− ♖c6 55. ♗c6 ♔d6 56. ♔f3 ♗b6 57. ♔e4 ♔c5 58. g4 ♔d6 59. g5 ♗d8 60. ♔f5 ♗e7 61. g6 1 : 0** **[A. Mihal'čišin]**

548. E 62

A. GOL'DIN 2555 – WOJTKIEWICZ 2580

Pleasantville 1993

1. d4 ♘f6 2. c4 g6 3. g3 ♗g7 4. ♗g2 0–0 5. ♘c3 d6 6. ♘f3 ♘c6 7. 0–0 ♗f5 8. ♘e1 ♘a5 9. e4 N [9. b3 – 55/568] **♗g4 10. f3 ♗d7 11. ♕e2!?** [11. b3 c5 12. ♘c2 cd4 13. ♘d4 ♘c6 14. ♗e3±] **♘c6** [11... c5 12. dc5 dc5 13. e5! ♘e8 14. f4 ♘c6 (14... ♗e6 15. b3 ♕d4 16. ♕e3 f6 17. ♘f3 ♕e3 18. ♗e3±) 15. ♘c2 ♘d4 16. ♘d4 cd4 17. ♘e4 f6 18. ♗d2! fe5 19. fe5 ♖f1 20. ♖f1 ♗c6 (20... ♗e5 21. ♘c5±) 21. ♕f2→] **12. ♘c2** [12. d5 ♘d4 13. ♕f2 c5 14. ♗e3 e5!∞] **e5 13. de5 ♘e5!** [13... de5 14. ♗e3 ♘e7 (14... ♕c8 15. ♖fd1 ♗h3 16. ♘d5±) 15. ♖fd1 c6 16. ♕f2! b6 17. c5 b5 18. a4±] **14. ♗e3** [⌓ 14. ♗g5 h6 15. ♗e3] **♗e6 15. b3± c5!? 16. ♕d2 ♕a5 17. ♘b5!** [17. ♘d5 ♕d2 18. ♗d2 (18. ♘f6 ♗f6 19. ♗d2 ♘c6 20. ♖ad1 ♘d4 21. ♘d4 ♗d4 22. ♔h1 b5 23. cb5 ♖ab8=)

♘d5 19. cd5 ♗d7=] **♕d2 18. ♗d2 ♘e8** [18... a6? 19. ♘d6 ♖fd8 20. ♗c3 ♖d6 (20... ♘h5 21. ♘b7±) 21. ♗e5 ♖d2 22. ♘e3±] **19. ♘c3 a6 20. a4! ♘c6 21. ♖ad1 ♘c7** [21... ♘d4 22. ♘d4 ♗d4 (22... cd4 23. ♘d5 ♗d5 24. ed5±) 23. ♔h1 b5 (23... f5 24. ♘e2 ♗g7 25. ♘f4±; 23... ♘c7 24. ♘e2 ♗g7 25. ♗a5±) 24. ab5 ♗c3 25. ♗c3 ab5 26. f4! (26. cb5 ♗b3 27. ♖b1 c4 28. f4∞) bc4 (26... ♖a3 27. f5 ♗c4 28. bc4 ♖c3 29. cb5⩲) 27. f5 ♗c8 28. bc4 ♗a6 29. ♖a1⩲] **22. ♘d5! ♗d5 23. cd5 ♘d4 24. ♘d4 ♗d4 25. ♔h1 b5?** [25... b6 26. ♖fe1⩲] **26. ♗a5!± ♖ac8 27. f4 f5** [27... ♘a8 28. e5! de5 29. fe5 ♗e5 30. d6+−] **28. e5 ♖fd8 29. ♖fe1 ♖d7** [29... de5 30. ♗c7! ♖c7 31. fe5+−] **30. e6 ♖e7 31. ♖d4??⊕** [31. ♖e2 △ ♖c2, b4±] **cd4 32. ♖c1 ba4 33. ba4 ♖b8!−+ 34. ♗f3** [34. ♗c7 ♖c8; 34. ♖c7 ♖c7 35. ♗c7 ♖b1 36. ♗f1 ♖f1 37. ♔g2 ♖a1 38. ♗d6 d3 39. ♗b4 d2] **♘e8 35. ♖d1 ♖eb7 36. ♖d4 ♖b1 37. ♔g2 ♖8b2 38. ♗d2 ♖a2 39. ♔f2 ♖ba1 40. a5 ♖a4 41. ♖a4 ♖a4 42. ♗e2 ♘f6 43. ♗e1 ♘e4 44. ♔f1 ♘c5 45. ♗c3 ♔f8 46. ♔g2 ♔e7 47. ♔f1 h5 48. h3 ♖a3 49. ♗e1 ♘d3 50. g4 ♘e1 51. ♔e1 hg4 52. hg4 ♖a5 0 : 1 [A. Gol'din]**

549.* **E 62**

VAULIN 2515 − GUFEL'D 2480
Alusta (open) 1993

1. c4 g6 2. d4 ♘f6 3. ♘f3 ♗g7 4. g3 0−0 5. ♗g2 d6 6. 0−0 ♘c6 7. ♘c3 ♗f5 8. d5 ♘a5 9. ♘d4 ♗d7 10. ♕d3 c5 11. ♘c2 N [11. dc6 bc6!?; 11. ♘b3 − 4/786] **a6 12. b3 b5!?** [RR 12... ♖b8 13. ♗d2 b5 14. ♖ab1 e6! (14... ♕c7?! 15. e4±○ M. Makarov 2515 − Poluljahov 2515, Beograd 1993) 15. de6 ♗e6 16. cb5 (16. ♘e3∞) ab5 (16... c4?! 17. bc4 ♗c4 18. ♕f3 ab5 19. ♘b4⩲) 17. b4 (17. ♘b5 d5!∞̄) ♘c4∞ Poluljahov] **13. ♖b1** [13. cb5 ab5 14. ♘b5 ♘g4 15. ♘c3 c4! 16. bc4 ♘e5 17. ♕d1 ♘ec4∞; RR 16... ♘c4!∞̄ Poluljahov] **♖b8 14. ♗d2 e6! 15. de6 ♗e6 16. ♘e3 ♖e8= 17. ♖fd1 bc4** [17... ♘g4!? 18. ♘g4 ♗g4 19. h3 ♗f5 20. e4 ♗e6 △ ♘c6-d4=] **18. bc4 ♖b1 19. ♖b1**

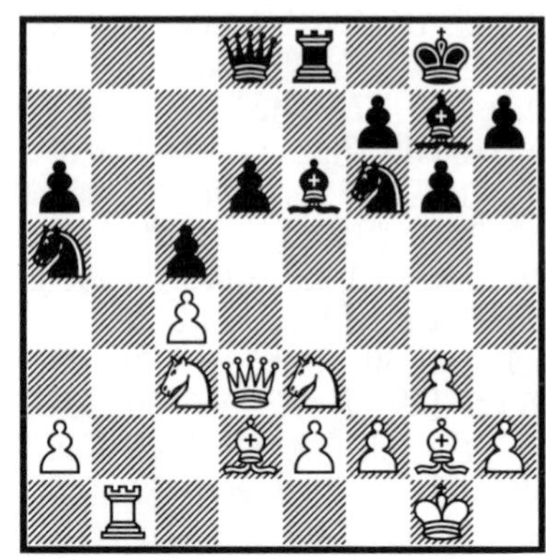

19... ♘c4!? 20. ♘c4 d5 21. ♗g5!□ dc4 22. ♕d8 ♖d8 23. ♘e4 ♘e4 [23... c3!! 24. ♘f6 ♗f6 25. ♗f6 c2 26. ♖f1 ♖d1 27. ♗g5 ♗a2= Vaulin] **24. ♗d8 ♘c3 25. ♖b8 h5 26. ♗f6 ♔h7 27. ♗c3** [27. ♗g7 ♔g7 28. ♖b2 ♘b5 29. e3 c3 30. ♖c2 ♗f5 31. e4 ♘d4] **♗c3 28. ♗e4 ♗f5??** [28... ♗b4⩲] **29. ♗f5 gf5 [♖ 2/l] 30. ♖d8□+− ♗b2 31. ♖d5! ♗a3 32. ♖d2 c3 33. ♖c2 ♗b2 34. f3 ♔g6 35. ♔f2 ♔f6 36. ♔e3 ♔e5 37. ♔d3 ♔d5 38. e4 fe4 39. fe4 ♔e5 40. ♖f2 c4 41. ♔c4 ♔e4 42. ♔b3 1 : 0 [Gufel'd]**

550. **E 63**

RIBLI 2620 − V. NEVEDNIČIJ 2495
Odorheiu Secuiesc 1993

1. ♘f3 g6 2. d4 ♗g7 3. c4 d6 4. ♘c3 ♘f6 5. g3 0−0 6. ♗g2 ♘c6 7. 0−0 a6 8. b3 ♖b8 9. ♘d5 ♘h5 10. ♗b2 e6 11. ♘f4!? N [11. ♘c3 − 47/(702)] **♘f4 12. gf4 b5** [12... ♕e7!? △ e5] **13. ♖c1 ♗b7 14. ♕c2** [14. ♕d2!?] **bc4 15. ♕c4 ♘b4! 16. ♕b4** [16. a3 ♘d5 (16... ♘a2!?∞) 17. e3 ♕d7 18. b4 ♖fc8=] **♗f3 17. ♕d2** [17. ♕c4 ♗g2 18. ♔g2 ♕h4 19. ♕c7 ♕f4∓] **♗g2 18. ♔g2 ♖b5⩱ 19. ♖c3! ♖h5 20. ♖g3 ♕h4 21. h3 c5 22. dc5! ♖d5?!** [22... ♗b2 23. ♕b2 ♖c5⩱] **23. ♖d3 ♖d3 24. ed3 ♗b2 25. ♕b2 dc5?** [25... ♕f4 26. c6 ♕g5 27. ♔h2 ♕f4=] **26. ♖c1!⩲ ♖d8 27. ♖c5 ♕f4** [27... ♖d3 28. ♖c8 ♖d8 29. ♕c3±] **28. ♕c3 ♕d6! 29. ♖c8** [29. ♖a5 ♕b6!] **♖c8 30. ♕c8 ♔g7 31. ♕c4 g5! 32. b4 f5 33. a4 h5 34. a5 g4 35. hg4 hg4 36. b5 ab5 37. ♕b5 f4!= 38. ♕b7** [38. ♕g5 ♔f7 39. ♕g4 ♕d5 △ ♕a5] **♔f6 39. ♕e4 f3**

40. ♔g1 ♕c7! 41. ♕g4 ♕a5 42. ♕f3 ♔e7 43. ♕b7 ♔f6 44. ♕e4 ♕g5 45. ♔h2 ♕h5 46. ♔g3 ♕g5 47. ♔f3 1/2 : 1/2 [V. Nevedničij]

551. E 63

ASEEV 2515 – ŠEVELEVIČ

Rossija 1993

1. d4 ♘f6 2. c4 g6 3. g3 ♗g7 4. ♗g2 0–0 5. ♘c3 d6 6. ♘f3 ♘c6 7. 0–0 a6 8. h3 ♗d7 9. e4 e5 10. ♗e3 [10. d5 – 53/(568)] **b5 N** [10... ♕c8 11. ♔h2 ed4 12. ♘d4 ♘e5 13. ♕e2!? c5 14. ♘f3!? ♘f3 (14... ♖e8 15. ♘d2 b5 16. cb5 ab5 17. f4 ♘c4 18. ♘c4 bc4 19. ♕c4 ♖b8 20. ♖f2 ♖b4 21. ♕d3 ♕b8 22. ♖d1 ♖b2 23. ♕d6 ♖f2 24. ♗f2 ♕b2 25. ♗e1 ♗e6 26. e5+–) 15. ♕f3±] **11. de5** [11. d5!? ♘a5 12. ♘d2!? (12. cb5 ab5 13. ♘d2 b4 14. ♘e2 ♗b5∞) bc4 13. ♕e2 ♘h5!? (13... ♘e8?! 14. ♘c4 ♘c4 15. ♕c4 f5 16. ef5 gf5 17. f4±) 14. b4 cb3 15. ab3±; 13... ♕b8!?⇆] **♘e5 12. ♘e5 de5 13. ♕c2 c6 14. ♖fd1 ♕c8 15. ♔h2 ♗e6 16. ♗f1!** [16. cb5 cb5=] **♖d8 17. a4! b4** [17... bc4? 18. a5± △ ♘a4] **18. ♘a2 b3** [18... a5?! 19. ♖d8 ♕d8 20. ♘c1 △ ♘b3± ×a5] **19. ♕b3 ♘e4 20. ♖d8 ♕d8 21. ♖d1 ♕c7** [21... ♕f6? 22. ♗g2! ♘g5 23. ♗g5±; 21... ♕c8!?] **22. ♕b6** [22. ♗g2! *a)* 22... ♖b8 23. ♘b4! △ ♘a6+–; *b)* 22... ♘d6 23. ♗b6 ♕b8 24. ♗c6 ♘c4 25. ♗a8! ♘b6 (25... ♕b6 26. ♕b6 ♘b6 27. ♖d8 ♗f8 28. ♘c3+–) 26. ♗d5! ♗d5 27. ♖d5+–; *c)* 22... f5□ 23. ♗e4 fe4 24. ♕c2±] **♕b6 23. ♗b6 ♗f8 24. a5± ♖c8 25. ♘c1 ♘d6?** [25... f6] **26. b3 ♘b7 27. ♘d3⊕ e4 28. ♘f4 ♗b4** [28... ♖e8 29. ♘e6 ♖e6 30. c5 ♘c5 31. ♖d8+– △ 31... ♘b3 32. ♗c4] **29. ♘e6 fe6 30. c5 ♗c5** [30... ♗a5 31. ♗a6 ♗b6 32. cb6 ♖b8 33. b4+–] **31. ♗a6 ♖b8 32. b4 ♗b4 33. ♖b1 c5 34. ♗b7 ♖b7 35. ♗c5 ♖f7 36. ♖b4 1 : 0 [Aseev]**

552. E 64

P. NIKOLIĆ 2625 – SMIRIN 2555

Tilburg (Interpolis) 1992

1. d4 ♘f6 2. c4 g6 3. ♘f3 ♗g7 4. g3 c5 5. d5 0–0 6. ♗g2 d6 7. 0–0 ♘a6 8. ♘c3 ♘c7 9. e4 ♗g4 10. h3 ♗f3 11. ♕f3 ♘d7 N [11... a6 – 37/(643)] **12. ♗g5 ♖b8 13. ♕e2 ♕e8!? 14. a4 e6 15. ♗e3** [15. de6 ♘e6 16. ♗e3 ♘e5∞] **ed5 16. cd5** [16. ed5!?⩲] **a6 17. a5 b5 18. ab6 ♖b6 19. ♖a2 ♖b4?!** [19... ♕b8⇆ ⇔b] **20. ♗d2! ♕b8 21. ♘d1 ♖b3 22. ♗c3 ♗c3 23. bc3 ♕b6 24. ♕c2 c4 25. ♘e3 ♘e5 26. ♖fa1! ♖b8 27. ♕d2** [△ ♕d4] **♖b1 28. ♔h2 ♖a1 29. ♖a1 ♕b3?** [29... ♕c5 30. ♕d4; ⌓ 29... ♕b2 30. ♕b2 ♖b2 31. f4 ♘f3 32. ♔h1 ♘d2±] **30. f4 ♘d3 31. e5! de5 32. fe5 ♘e5 33. d6 ♘e6 34. ♘d5** [△ ♕h6] **♕b2 35. ♕e3!** [35. ♕h6?? ♘f3] **♘d7□** [35... ♕a1 36. ♕e5+–] **36. ♖f1 ♕c2 37. ♖f2 ♕d3 38. ♕h6 ♖f8□ 39. ♖d2 ♕b1 40. ♖e2 a5** [40... ♕d3 41. ♖e4! ♕d5? 42. ♖h4] **41. ♖e4!** [△ 42. ♘e7 ♔h8 43. ♘g6 fg6 44. ♖e6] **♘g7□ 42. ♖c4+– ♕e1!? 43. ♖c7 ♘h5** [43... ♘f5 44. ♕f4] **44. ♖d7 ♕g3 45. ♔g1 ♖b8** [45... ♕e1 46. ♗f1 ♕g3 47. ♔h1 ♕f3 48. ♗g2] **46. ♕c1 a4 47. ♖a7 ♕d6 48. ♖a4 ♘g3 49. ♖a2 ♘f5 50. ♕f4 ♕c5 51. ♔h2 ♖b1 52. ♖f2 ♖d1 53. ♕b8 ♔g7 54. ♕e5 ♔h6 55. ♖f5 1 : 0 [Smirin]**

553.* E 64

COSMA 2365 – J. GDAŃSKI 2480

Budapest (zt) 1993

1. d4 ♘f6 2. c4 c5 3. d5 g6 4. ♘c3 d6 5. g3 ♗g7 6. ♗g2 0–0 7. ♘f3 ♘a6 8. 0–0 ♘c7 9. a4 ♖b8 10. e4 ♗g4 11. h3 ♗f3 12. ♗f3 e6 [12... b6 13. ♗g5 N (13. ♖b1 e6 14. ♗f4 ed5 15. ed5 a6 16. ♕d3 ♕d7 17. b4 cb4 18. ♖b4 a5 19. ♖bb1 ♖fe8 20. ♔g2 ♘a6 21. ♘b5 ♘c5∞) a6 14. ♗e2 e5!? 15. ♔g2 ♕e8 16. ♕c2 ♔h8 17. ♗d2 ♘g8 18. f4 ef4 19. gf4 f5 20. ♖ae1 ♕d7± Ftáčnik 2535 – J. Gdański 2480, Budapest (zt) 1993] **13. ♗f4 ed5 14. ed5 a6** [14... b6? 15. ♘b5±] **15. a5 ♘ce8 N** [15... b5] **16. ♖a3** [⌓ 16. ♕d2⩲] **♘d7 17. ♕d2 ♗e5! 18. ♗h6 ♘g7∞ 19. ♗e4 ♖e8 20. ♗c2 ♗d4 21. ♔g2 ♘e5 22. b3** [△ f4±] **♘f3!?** [22... ♕f6 23. f4 ♘g4 24. hg4 (24. ♗g5? ♗c3 25. ♗f6 ♘e3!) ♗c3 25. ♕d3 ♕d4 26. f5±] **23. ♔f3□ ♕f6 24. ♕f4 ♗c3 25. ♕f6 ♗f6 26. ♗d2! ♗d4 27. b4 ♘h5**

28. bc5 [28. ♖b3±] ♗c5⇆ 29. ♖b3 ♘f6 30. ♖fb1 ♖e7 31. ♗g5 ♔g7 32. g4 h6 33. ♗h4 g5 34. ♗g3 h5 35. ♗d3 ♔f8⊕ 36. gh5 ♘h5 37. ♗h2 ♔g7 38. ♖b6!? ♘f4□= 39. ♗f4 gf4 40. ♖g1 ♔f6 41. ♖bb1 ♖h8 42. ♗f1 b6 43. ab6 ♖b7 44. ♖g4 ♖b6 45. ♖f4 ♔g7 46. ♖g4 ♔f6 47. ♖f4 ♔g7 1/2 : 1/2 [J. Gdański]

554. E 67

GUFEL'D 2480 – GOLUBEV 2495

Alusta (open) 1993

1. g3 e5 2. ♗g2 d6 3. c4 ♘f6 4. ♘c3 g6 5. ♘f3 ♗g7 6. 0–0 0–0 7. d4 ♘bd7 8. ♕c2 ed4 9. ♘d4 ♘b6 10. ♖d1 ♘c4 11. ♘cb5 a6 12. ♕c4 ab5 13. ♘b5 ♘e8 14. ♕c2! [14. ♗f4] ♗d7 N [14... c6? 15. ♘d6 ♘d6 16. ♗f4+−; RR 14... ♗f5 15. e4 ♗g4 16. ♖d3; 16. f3!?±; 14... ♕e7!? △ 15. ♗f4 g5 16. ♗e3 c6⇆ Golubev] 15. ♘c3 c6 [RR 15... ♗c6 16. e4± Golubev] 16. e4 b5!? [16... f5?! 17. ♗f4 ♕e7 18. ♖e1±] 17. b4!□ [△ ♗b2, ♖d2, ♖ad1±] ♗g4 [17... c5 18. ♗b2 cb4 (18... c4) 19. ♘d5±; RR 17... ♗e6! 18. ♗b2± Golubev] 18. ♖d2 d5! 19. ed5! [19. h3 ♗e6 20. ♗b2 ♘c7±] ♘d6! 20. dc6 ♕f6 21. ♗b2 [21. ♖b1 ♗f5 22. ♘e4 ♘e4 23. ♗e4 ♗e4 24. ♕e4 ♖fe8 25. ♕c2 ♕f3±] ♘c4 22. ♘a4□± [22. ♘d1?? ♗d1] ♘b2 [22... ♕f5 23. ♗g7 ♔g7 24. ♕c3 ♔g8 25. ♖d5+−] 23. ♘b2 ♗f5 [23... ♖ad8 24. ♖d8 ♖d8 25. ♖b1] 24. ♕b3 [24. ♕c5!?] ♕c3! 25. ♖ad1 ♕b3 26. ab3 ♗c3 27. ♖e2 ♖a2 [27... ♗b4±; 27... ♗g4 28. f3 ♗e6 29. ♖e6! fe6 30. ♘d3±]

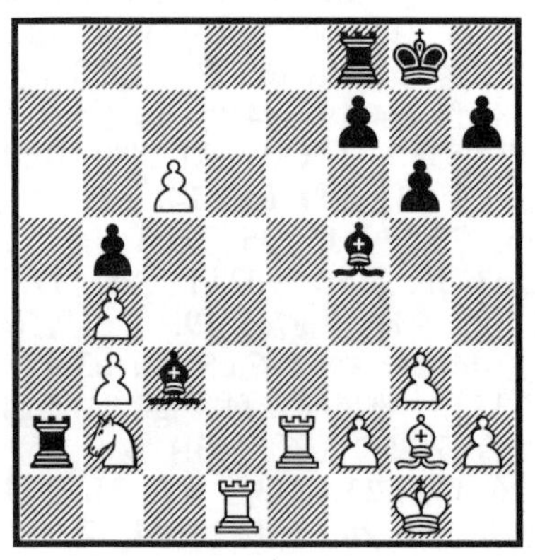

28. ♘a4! ba4 [28... ♖e2 29. ♘c3 ♖b2 30. ♗d5+−] 29. ♖a2 ab3 30. ♖a3! ♗c2 31. ♖b3!+− ♗b3 32. ♖d3 ♗b4 33. ♖b3 ♗d6 [33... ♗a5!?] 34. ♖b7 ♖c8 35. ♖d7 ♗e5 36. f4 ♗c7 37. ♗d5 ♗b6 38. ♔f1 ♖c7 39. ♗f7 ♔f8 40. ♖c7 ♗c7 41. ♗d5 h6 42. h4 g5 43. hg5 hg5 44. fg5 ♗g3 45. g6 1 : 0 [Gufel'd]

555.* E 69

ŠIROV 2670 – KASPAROV 2805

Linares 1993

1. d4 ♘f6 2. c4 g6 3. g3 ♗g7 4. ♗g2 0–0 5. ♘c3 d6 6. ♘f3 ♘bd7 7. 0–0 e5 8. h3 c6 9. e4 ♕b6 10. c5 dc5 11. de5 ♘e8 12. e6!? N fe6 13. ♘g5 ♘e5! [13... ♘c7 14. f4 ♗d4 15. ♔h2 e5 16. f5 ♘f6 17. g4!±; 13... e5!? 14. ♕e2 ♕a6 15. ♕a6 ba6∞ ×♗g7] 14. f4 ♘f7! [14... h6 15. fe5 ♖f1 16. ♕f1 hg5 17. ♗g5 ♕b2 18. ♖d1!± Možný 2425 – Mich. Ankerst 2360, München 1992] 15. ♘f7 ♗d4! 16. ♔h2 ♖f7 17. e5 ♘c7 18. ♘e4 ♘d5 19. a4!⩱ a5 [19... ♕d8 20. a5! ♖b8 21. ♕c2 b6 22. ab6 ab6 23. ♖a3] 20. ♖a3 ♕c7?! [20... ♕d8 21. h4⩱; 21. g4!? △ 22. ♖g3⩱, 22. ♖af3⩱] 21. ♘d6! ♖f8 [21... ♖g7? 22. ♘e8; 21... ♖d7!? (△ ♖d6!) 22. ♗d5! cd5 23. ♘b5! (23. ♘e8 ♕d8 24. ♘f6 ♔g7 25. ♘d7 ♗d7⩱) ♕d8! (23... ♕b6 24. ♖d3! ♖f7 25. b3 ♗d7 26. ♘d4 cd4 27. ♗b2±) 24. ♘d4 cd4 25. ♕d4 b6±] 22. h4→ b6 23. h5 ♕g7 24. hg6 hg6 25. ♗e4!? [25. ♕g4!? ♗d7 26. ♗e4? ♗e5; 26. ♗f3! △ ♔g2, ♖h1→] ♗a6! 26. ♖e1 [26. ♖h1? ♗e5 27. fe5 ♖f2 28. ♔g1 (28. ♔h3 ♕h8 29. ♔g4 ♕e5−+; 28. ♗g2 ♕e5−+) ♖af8! 29. ♖f3 ♖8f3 30. ♗f3 ♖f1 31. ♕f1 ♗f1 32. ♔f1 ♕e5 33. ♘e4 ♕d4! 34. ♔g2 ♕a4∓] ♘e7! 27. ♔g2 ♖ad8! [△ ♗e5; 27... ♘f5 28. ♗f5 ♖f5 (28... gf5 29. g4!±; 28... ef5 29. g4!±) 29. ♗e3!±] 28. ♖b3 [28. ♕g4?! ♘f5∓; 28. ♕b3 c4! 29. ♘c4 ♗c5∞] ♗e5! [28... c4? 29. ♕d4 cb3 30. ♕b6+−] 29. fe5 ♕e5 30. ♕g4 [30. ♗f4? ♖f4 31. gf4 ♕f4−+] ♖d6 31. ♗f4?! [31. ♗g6 *a)* 31... ♕e1? 32. ♗d3! ♔f7 33. ♕h5 ♔g7 (33... ♔f6 34. ♗g5 ♔e5 35. ♗d2 ♔d4 36. ♕h4+−) 34. ♗h6 ♔g8 35. ♕g5

♔f7 36. ♕g7 ♔e8 37. ♕f8 ♔d7 38. ♗a6 ♖d1 (38... ♕e4 39. ♕f3) 39. ♖d3 ♖d3 40. ♗d3+−; *b)* 31... ♕g7! 32. ♖e6 *b1)* 32... ♖d4? 33. ♕g5! ♗f1 34. ♔h2+− Kasparov; *b2)* 32... ♘g6!? 33. ♖d6 ♘f4 34. ♕f4 ♖f4 35. ♗f4 ♗c4 36. ♖b6 ♗d5 37. ♔f1 (37. ♔h3 ♕h7 38. ♔g4 ♕g7=) ♕g4! 38. ♖b8 ♔f7 39. ♖b7 ♔e8 40. ♔e1 ♕f3!=; *b3)* 32... ♖e6! 33. ♕e6 ♔h8 34. ♕h3 (34. ♗e4? ♖f6!) ♔g8 35. ♕e6=] **♖f4 32. gf4 ♖d2!** [32... ♕d4?! 33. ♕h4! ♔f7 34. ♖b6±] **33. ♔g3 ♕f6** [33... ♕d4! 34. ♕e6 ♔f8 35. ♖be3 (35. ♖f3? ♕h8!∓) ♗c8 36. ♕e5 ♕e5 37. fe5 ♖b2 38. ♖d3! (38. e6 ♗e6 39. ♗g6 ♖b3!∓) ♗f5 39. e6! *a)* 39... ♖b4? 40. ♖d8 ♔g7 41. ♗f5 ♘f5 42. ♔g2 ♘e7 (42... ♔f6 43. e7 ♘e7 44. ♖d6 ♔f7 45. ♖d7+−) 43. ♖e8! ♔f6 44. ♖f8 ♔g5 45. ♖f7 ♖g4 46. ♔f3 ♘f5 47. e7+−; *b)* 39... ♗e6 40. ♗g6 ♗d5 41. ♗e4! ♖b3 (41... c4 42. ♖f3 ♔g7 43. ♗d5 ♘d5 44. ♖e6 c5 45. ♖d6 ♖d2 46. ♔h4!=) 42. ♖b3 ♗b3 43. ♖b1 c4 (43... ♗d5 44. ♗c2! ♔e8 45. ♔f4 △ ♗f5) 44. ♔f4! b5 45. ab5 cb5 46. ♔e5 a4 47. ♔d4 a3 48. ♔c5=] **34. ♖b6 ♗d3! 35. ♖b8 ♔f7 36. ♕h3** [36. ♖h1 ♕g7! (36... ♗e4 37. ♖h7 ♕g7 38. ♖g7 ♔g7 39. ♕e6 ♘f5 40. ♔h3 ♖d3 41. ♔h2 ♖d2 42. ♔g1? ♖g2 43. ♔f1 ♘g3 44. ♔e1 ♖e2 45. ♔d1 ♗c2−+; 42. ♔h3=) 37. ♗d3 ♖d3 38. ♔g2 ♖d2! 39. ♔f1 (39. ♔f3 ♖b2 40. ♖b2 ♕c3!!∓) ♖d4!→ ×a4, △ 40... ♕f6, 40... e5] **♗e4 37. ♕h7 ♕g7 38. ♕g7 ♔g7 39. ♖e4 ♘f5 40. ♔f3 ♔f6= 41. ♖c4 ♖d5 42. ♖f8!? ♔e7 43. ♖a8 ♘d6 44. ♖c3** [44. ♖c2 c4 △ 45. ♖h2 ♘f5! 46. ♖h7 ♔d6] **c4 45. ♖a6 ♖c5 46. b3 ♔f6 47. bc4** [47... ♘c4 48. ♔e4 ♘d6 49. ♔d3 ♖d5 50. ♔c2 ♘f5! 51. ♖d3 ♖c5 52. ♖c3=] **1/2 : 1/2** **[Širov]**

556.* **E 69**

A. GOL'DIN 2555 − SHERZER 2465

Pleasantville 1993

1. d4 ♘f6 2. c4 g6 3. g3 ♗g7 4. ♗g2 0−0 5. ♘c3 d6 6. ♘f3 ♘bd7 7. 0−0 e5 8. e4 c6 9. h3 ♕b6 10. c5 dc5 11. de5 ♘e8 12. e6!? fe6 13. ♘g5 ♘e5 14. f4 c4 N 15. ♔h2 ♘d3 [RR 15... h6 16. ♘f3 ♘f3 17. ♖f3 e5 18. ♕e2 ♗e6 19. ♗e3 ♕a5 20. f5 1/2 : 1/2 Dorfman 2580 − O. Renet 2535, Bruxelles (zt) 1993] **16. e5!=∞ ♘c7?** [16... ♘b2!? 17. ♕e2 ♘d3 *a)* 18. ♗e4?! *a1)* 18... ♘c7? 19. ♘h7! ♔h7 20. ♕h5 ♔g8 21. ♗g6 ♖f5 (21... ♖d8 22. f5 ef5 23. ♕h7 ♔f8 24. ♗f5 ♘f2 25. ♗h6+−) 22. ♕h7 ♔f8 23. g4 ♖f7 24. ♗f7 ♔f7 25. f5+−; *a2)* 18... ♕d4! 19. ♗d2 ♘c7 20. ♘h7 ♔h7 21. ♕h5 ♔g8 22. ♗g6 ♖f5 23. ♕h7 ♔f8 24. g4 ♘f4!□ (24... ♘e5 25. fe5 ♕d2 26. ♔h1 ♕c3 27. gf5+−; 24... ♖f7 25. ♗f7 ♔f7 26. ♘e4→) 25. ♗f4 ♖f4 26. ♖ad1□ (26. ♘e2 ♖f2! 27. ♔h1 ♕e3−+; 26. ♘e4 ♕e5! 27. ♖f4 ♕f4 28. ♔g2 ♗a1−+) ♕e5! (26... ♖f2? 27. ♔h1 ♕f4 28. ♖d8 ♔e7 29. ♕h4 ♗f6 30. ef6 ♕f6 31. ♕f2 ♕f2 32. ♖f2 ♔d8 33. ♖f8 ♔e7 34. ♖f7 ♔d8□ 35. g5±) 27. ♔g2 ♘d5 28. ♘d5 ed5 29. ♖f4 ♕f4 30. ♖f1 ♕f1 31. ♔f1 ♗e6=∞; *b)* 18. ♖b1!? ♕d4 19. ♘ce4 △ ♗e3=∞] **17. ♘ce4 ♘d5 18. ♘d6! ♘b2□ 19. ♕c2 c3 20. ♘c8 ♖ac8?!** [20... ♖fc8 21. ♘e6 ♘c4 (21... ♕b4 22. ♖b1 ♕e7 23. ♘g7 ♕g7 24. ♗b2±) 22. ♖b1 ♕a6 23. ♘c5! ♕a5 24. ♘b7±] **21. ♘e6 ♖fe8 22. ♘g7 ♔g7 23. ♖b1!± ♘e3?** [23... ♕c7] **24. ♗e3 ♕e3 25. ♖f3!+− ♕d2 26. ♕c3 ♕c3 27. ♖c3 ♘a4 28. ♖b7 ♔h6 29. g4** **1 : 0** **[A. Gol'din]**

557.* **!N** **E 69**

JUSUPOV 2645 − LJUBOJEVIĆ 2605

Linares 1993

1. d4 ♘f6 2. c4 g6 3. ♘f3 ♗g7 4. g3 0−0 5. ♗g2 d6 6. 0−0 ♘bd7 7. ♘c3 e5 8. h3 c6 9. e4 ♕b6 10. c5 dc5 11. de5 ♘e8 12. ♘a4 ♕b5 [12... ♕a6 − 55/575] **13. ♗g5 ♘c7 14. ♗e7 ♖e8 15. ♗d6 ♘e6** [15... ♘a6 16. b3 △ 16... ♘e5 17. ♘e5 ♗e5 18. ♗e5 ♖e5 19. ♕d8] **16. b3! N** [16. ♖e1 c4 N (16... ♕a5) 17. ♖e3 ♘e5 18. ♘e5 ♗e5 19. ♘c3 ♗c3 20. ♖c3 ♘g5∓ Wojtkiewicz 2530 − Blees 2415, Komotini 1992] **♕a6** [16... a5 17. ♘b2 ♕a6 18. a4 b6 19. ♘c4 ♕a7 20. ♘fd2± △ f4; 16...

c4 17. ♘c3 (17. bc4 ♕c4 18. ♖e1) ♕a5 18. b4±] **17. ♕c2?!** [17. ♘b2! b5 18. a4 ♕b6 19. a5 ♕d8 20. ♘d3↑] **b6 18. ♘b2** [18. ♖fd1] **♕b7** [18... ♘e5 19. ♗e5 ♗e5 20. ♘e5 ♘d4 21. ♕d2 ♖e5 22. ♘c4=∞] **19. ♘d3** [19. a4!? a5 20. ♘c4] **a5! 20. h4 ♕a7 21. ♖fd1 ♗a6 22. ♗h3 ♘ef8** [22... ♖ad8 23. ♗e6 ♖e6 24. ♘f4 ♖ee8 25. e6↑] **23. ♕c3** [△ ♘f4] **♗d3 24. ♖d3 a4 25. ♖ad1 ab3 26. ab3 ♕a5! 27. ♕a5 ba5!** [27... ♖a5? 28. ♗f8 ♘f8 29. ♖d8±] **28. ♗f8 ♘f8 29. ♖c1 a4 30. ba4 ♖a4 31. ♖c5 ♖e4= 32. ♖c6** [32. ♖e3!? ♖e3 33. fe3 ♖a8 (33... ♗h6 34. ♔f2 f6 35. ♖c6 fe5±) 34. ♖c6 ♖a3 35. ♔f2 ♗h6] **♗e5 33. ♖c8 ♖c8 34. ♗c8 ♗f6 1/2 : 1/2**
[Jusupov]

558. **E 69**

PRUDNIKOVA 2430 – UMANSKAJA 2340

Beograd 1993

1. ♘f3 g6 2. c4 ♗g7 3. d4 ♘f6 4. g3 0–0 5. ♗g2 d6 6. 0–0 ♘bd7 7. ♘c3 e5 8. e4 c6 9. b3 ed4 10. ♘d4 ♘c5 11. h3 ♖e8 12. ♖e1 ♘fd7 13. ♗e3 a5 14. ♖b1 ♘e5 15. ♖e2 ♕e7 16. ♖d2 h5!? N [16... a4] **17. ♘de2** [17. f4!? ♘ed7 18. ♗f2 ♘f6 19. ♕c2 ♘h7!? 20. ♖e1 g5 △ 21. ♘f5 ♗f5 22. ef5 ♕f6⇆] **♗h3□ 18. ♗h3** [18. f4? ♗g2 19. fe5 ♗f3 20. ed6 ♕d7 21. ♗c5 ♗c3∓; 18. ♖d6?! ♗g2 19. ♗c5 ♗f3 20. ♖c6 ♕d7 21. ♕d7 ♘d7∓; 18. ♗c5!? dc5 19. ♗h3 ♘f3 20. ♔g2 ♘d2 21. ♕d2 ♖ad8∞] **♘f3 19. ♔f1 ♘d2** [19... ♘e4!? 20. ♘e4 ♕e4 21. ♖d3 ♘h2=] **20. ♕d2 ♘e4** [20... ♗c3!? 21. ♕c3□ (21. ♘c3 ♘e4 22. ♕d3 ♘c3 △ ♕e4∓) ♘e4! (21... ♕e4? 22. ♖d1 ♕h1 23. ♘g1 △ ♗g2) 22. ♕d3 h4∞] **21. ♘e4 ♕e4 22. ♖d1 a4! 23. ♗g2** [23. ♕d6 ab3 24. ab3 ♖a2 25. ♗g2 ♕g4∞] **♕g4 24. ♕d6 ab3 25. ab3 ♖a1** [25... ♖a2!?] **26. ♖a1 ♗a1 27. ♘f4!** [27. ♕c7? ♕f5 28. ♕b7 ♕b1∓] **♗e5 28. ♕d2 ♖a8 29. ♔g1 h4 30. ♗h3 ♕f3 31. ♗g2 ♕g4** [31... ♖a1 32. ♔h2 hg3 33. fg3 ♕d1! 34. b4∞] **32. ♗h3 ♕f3 1/2 : 1/2**
[Umanskaja]

559.* **E 69**

V. SALOV 2660 – KAMSKY 2655

Linares 1993

1. d4 ♘f6 2. c4 g6 3. ♘f3 ♗g7 4. g3 0–0 5. ♗g2 d6 6. 0–0 ♘bd7 7. ♘c3 e5 8. e4 c6 9. b3 ♖e8 10. h3 ed4 11. ♘d4 ♘c5 12. ♖e1 a5 13. ♗f4 ♘h5 [RR 13... a4 14. ♖b1 N (14. b4 – 55/(577)) ab3 15. ab3 h6 16. ♕c2 ♖a3 17. ♖bd1± Abramović 2475 – Zontah 2455, Podgorica 1993] **14. ♗e3 ♗d7 15. ♕c2 ♕c7 N** [15... ♕c8 – 55/577] **16. ♖ad1 ♖ad8 17. ♗g5! f6** [17... ♘f6? 18. ♘db5! cb5 19. ♗f6 ♗f6 20. ♘d5+–] **18. ♗e3!±** [18. ♗c1 f5!⇆] **♗f8 19. g4 ♘g7 20. f4** [△ f5] **f5□ 21. ef5 gf5 22. gf5 ♗c8** [22... ♘h5!?] **23. ♘e6?** [23. f6 ♘h5 24. ♘d5! *a)* 24... ♕f7 25. ♘f3! h6 (25... cd5 26. ♘g5+–) 26. ♘e7! ♗e7 27. fe7+–; *b)* 24... cd5 25. ♗d5 ♔h8 26. ♘b5 ♕d7 27. ♗d4 ♖e1 (27... ♘f4 28. ♖e7!!+–) 28. ♖e1 ♕h3! (28... ♘f4 29. ♖e7+–) 29. f7 ♘g7 *b1)* 30. ♖e8 ♕g4! (30... ♕d7 31. ♗g7 ♔g7 32. ♕g2+–) 31. ♕g2 ♕d1 32. ♔f2! ♘d3! (32... ♕d2 33. ♔g3 ♕d3 34. ♔h2+–; 32... ♕c2 33. ♖e2 ♘d3 34. ♔e3 ♕b1 35. ♗e4+–) 33. ♔e3 ♘e5!=; *b2)* 30. ♗g7! ♔g7 (30... ♗g7? 31. ♖e8 ♗f8 32. ♕b2+–) 31. ♕b2 ♔g6 32. ♖e8→] **♘ge6 24. fe6 ♖e6! 25. ♕f2! ♗g7** [25... ♖de8? 26. f5! ♖e5 27. ♗d4! ♖e1 28. ♖e1 ♖e1 29. ♕e1 ♗f5 30. ♕g3+–] **26. f5** [26. ♗d4? ♖e1 27. ♕e1 (27. ♖e1 ♘d3) ♗d4 28. ♖d4 ♕g7∓] **♖f8!** [26... ♗c3? 27. fe6 ♗e1 28. ♖e1 ♘e6 29. ♗b6+–] **27. fe6! ♖f2 28. ♗c5! dc5?** [28... ♖g2 29. ♔g2 ♗e5! 30. ♖d3!∞] **29. e7 ♖f8□** [29... ♕g3 30. e8♕ (30. ♖d8 ♗f8) ♗f8 31. ♕e4 ♗h3 32. ♖e2 ♗g2 33. ♕e6 ♔h8 34. ♕e5 ♕e5 35. ♖e5 ♖c2 36. ♖e8+–] **30. ef8♕ ♔f8 31. ♘e4?** [31. ♖d3!±] **♗d4 32. ♔h1 ♕e5! 33. ♖f1** [33... ♔e7 34. ♖fe1 ♔f8=] **1/2 : 1/2**
[V. Salov]

560.* **E 70**

MARIN 2515 – V. SPASOV 2520

Budapest (zt) 1993

1. d4 ♘f6 2. c4 g6 3. ♘c3 ♗g7 4. e4 d6 5. ♗d3 [RR 5. ♘ge2 0–0 6. ♘g3 c6 7.

♗e2 a6 8. 0–0 b5 9. e5 ♘fd7 N (9... ♘e8 – 40/741) 10. f4 bc4 11. ♗c4 d5 12. ♗e2 e6 13. ♗e3 a5 14. ♘a4 ♗a6 15. ♖c1 ♕c7 16. ♖c3 ♖c8 17. ♕c2 ♗e2 18. ♘e2 ♘b6 19. ♖c1 ♘a4 20. ♕a4 ♖a6 21. ♖1c2 ♗f8 22. ♘c1 ♘d7 23. ♘d3 ♕b7 24. ♖c1 1/2 : 1/2 I. Novikov 2540 – Wojtkiewicz 2580, New York 1993] **0–0 6. ♘ge2 ♘c6 7. 0–0 ♘d7 8. ♗e3 e5 9. d5 ♘d4 10. ♘b5 ♘e2 11. ♗e2** [11. ♕e2 f5 12. ef5 gf5 13. f4 e4 14. ♗b1□ a6 15. ♘d4 ♘f6⇆] **♘c5 N** [11... a5 – 53/582; 11... f5 – 53/(582)] **12. f3** [12. ♕c2?! f5 13. ef5 ♗f5 14. ♕d2?! ♘e4 △ a6] **a5 13. ♕c2** [13. ♕d2?! f5 14. ef5 gf5 15. f4?! ♘e4 16. ♕c2 ef4 17. ♗f4 c6] **f5 14. ef5 ♗f5** [14... gf5 15. f4±] **15. ♕d2 b6 16. ♖ae1?!** [16. ♖ac1! ♖f7 17. b3 ♕f8 18. ♗d1 (△ ♗c2 ×e4, △ a3, b4) ♘d3? 19. g4 ♘c1 20. gf5 ♘b3 21. ab3 gf5 22. f4±] **♖f7 17. b3 ♕f8 18. g4!?** [18. ♗d1 ♘d3! (18... ♗d3 19. ♗c5 ♗f1 20. ♗f2+–) 19. g4 ♘e1 20. gf5 ♘f3 21. ♗f3 gf5∞] **♗c8 19. ♔g2 ♗b7** [△ c6⇆ ⇗a8-h1] **20. ♘c3** [20. h4 (V. Spasov) c6 21. ♘c3 e4 22. f4 ♗c3 23. ♕c3 cd5 24. cd5 ♗d5 25. ♔g3=∞⧉, ⇗a1-h8] **♕e7 21. ♗d1** [21. h4!?] **♖af8 22. ♗c2 ♗c8 23. ♘e4 ♘e4 24. ♗e4 ♗f6∞ 25. ♖c1 ♗h4 26. a3 ♕f6 27. b4 ab4 28. ab4 h5 29. h3** [29. gh5?! ♗f5∓] **hg4 30. fg4** [30. hg4 ♗f5!] **♕e7** [30... ♕f1 31. ♖f1 ♖f1 32. ♗g6±] **31. ♕d3 ♔g7= 32. ♗g6?!⊕** [32. ♖f7 ♕f7 33. ♖f1 ♕f1 34. ♕f1 ♖f1 35. ♔f1 ♗a6 36. ♗d3 e4; 36. b5=] **♖f1 33. ♖f1 ♖f1 34. ♔f1 ♕f6 35. ♗f5 ♗f5 36. gf5 ♗g5 37. ♗f2 ♕h6∓** [×h3, f5] **38. c5 bc5 39. bc5 ♔f6 40. c6 ♗h4 41. ♗e3 ♗g5** [41... ♕h5 42. ♗b6; 41... ♕h7 42. ♔e2 ♕f5 43. ♕f5 ♔f5 44. ♔d3 e4 45. ♔d4=] **42. ♗f2 ♗h4**
1/2 : 1/2 **[Marin]**

561. !N **E 70**

ILLESCAS CÓRDOBA 2615 – ROMERO HOLMES 2455

León 1993

1. d4 ♘f6 2. c4 g6 3. ♘c3 ♗g7 4. e4 d6 5. ♗d3 0–0 6. ♘ge2 ♘c6 7. 0–0 ♘d7 8. ♗e3 e5 9. d5 ♘d4 10. ♘b5?! ♘b5! N 11. cb5 f5 12. f3 [12. ef5 gf5 13. f4 e4 14. ♗c4 ♗b2 15. ♖b1 ♗g7 16. ♘d4 ♘f6∓] **f4 13. ♗f2 ♘f6 14. ♖c1 g5∓ 15. ♖c3 g4 16. ♔h1** [16. ♕c2 gf3 17. gf3 ♗h3→] **♘e8?** [16... h5! (△ ♘e8) 17. ♗h4 ♕d7! 18. ♕c2 ♘e8 19. ♖c1 ♗f6 20. ♗f6! ♖f6 21. ♖c7 ♘c7 22. ♕c7 ♕c7 23. ♖c7 ♖f7 24. ♖c3!∓] **17. fg4!** [17. ♕c2? h5∓] **♗g4 18. ♕e1 f3** [18... ♕g5 19. ♘g1±] **19. ♘g1** [19. ♘g3? ♕h4 20. ♘f5 fg2 21. ♔g2 ♕h3 22. ♔g1 ♗f3–+] **fg2 20. ♔g2 ♕d7?!** [20... ♕g5 21. ♔h1 ♕g6∞] **21. ♗h4± ♖f1 22. ♗f1 ♗h6 23. ♗e2 ♘g7 24. ♖g3 ♗e2 25. ♕e2 ♖f8 26. ♘h3 ♔h8 27. a4 ♕e8 28. ♖f3 ♗f4?** [28... ♖g8±] **29. ♘f4 ef4 30. ♗e1! ♖f6 31. ♗c3 ♖g6 32. ♔f1 ♔g8⊕ 33. ♖f4+– c6 34. dc6 bc6 35. ♕c4 ♕e6 36. ♕e6 ♘e6 37. bc6 ♖g5 38. ♖f6⊕** **1 : 0** **[Illescas Córdoba]**

562. **E 71**

A. CHERNIN 2600 – UHLMANN 2500

Österreich 1993

1. d4 ♘f6 2. c4 g6 3. ♘c3 ♗g7 4. e4 d6 5. h3 0–0 6. ♗g5 ♘c6!? N [6... ♘a6 – 55/583; 6... c5 – 55/584] **7. ♘f3** [7. ♘ge2!? △ g3, ♗g2] **h6 8. ♗e3 e5 9. d5 ♘e7** [9... ♘d4?! 10. ♘d4 ed4 11. ♗d4 ♖e8 12. ♗d3±] **10. ♕c1** [10. g4!? h5!? 11. ♘h2] **♔h7 11. ♗d3 c6!** [11... ♘h5 12. g4 ♘f4 13. ♗f4 ef4 14. ♕f4±] **12. 0–0 b5?!** [12... cd5 13. cd5 ♘fg8 △ f5∞] **13. dc6 bc4?!** [13... b4 14. ♘d5 ♘c6 15. a3 b3 16. ♕c3 ♖b8 17. ♘b4!±] **14. ♗c4 ♘c6 15. ♖d1± ♗b7** [⌓ 15... ♗e6] **16. ♗c5 ♘d4** [16... ♘e8 17. ♘b5 dc5!? 18. ♖d8 ♖d8±] **17. ♘d4 ed4 18. ♗d4 ♖c8** [18... ♘e4 19. ♘e4 ♗e4 20. ♕e3±] **19. ♗d3 d5** [19... ♘e4 20. ♗e4 ♗e4 21. ♗g7 ♔g7 22. ♕e3 ♗a8 23. ♕a7 ♖c5 △ ♖g5; 22. ♕f4+–] **20. e5 ♘e4 21. ♗e4** [21. ♕e3+–] **de4 22. ♗c5 ♖c5 23. ♖d8 ♖d8 24. ♕e3 ♖c7 25. ♘e4 ♗e5** [⌓ 25... ♗e4 26. ♕e4 ♖d2] **26. ♘g5 hg5 27. ♕e5 ♖dd7 28. ♕g5 ♖d5 29. ♕f4 ♖cd7 30. ♖c1 ♖d4 31. ♕b8 a6 32. ♖c7 ♖c7 33. ♕c7 ♗d5 34. a3 ♗e6 35. b4 ♖d3 36. a4 ♖b3 37. ♕b6 ♗c4 38. b5** [38... ab5 39. a5]
1 : 0 **[A. Chernin]**

563. !N **E 73**

SAPIS 2445 – KULCZEWSKI

corr. 1992/93

1. d4 ♘f6 2. c4 g6 3. ♘c3 ♗g7 4. e4 d6 5. ♗e2 0–0 6. ♗g5 ♘bd7 7. ♕d2 a6 8. ♘f3 ♖b8 9. 0–0 b5 10. cb5 ab5 11. e5 de5 12. de5 b4 13. ef6 ef6 14. ♗e3 bc3 15. bc3! N [15. ♕c3 – 44/(722)] **c5** [⌓ 15... ♘e5 16. ♕d8 ♖d8 17. ♘d4 c5 18. ♘b3 c4 19. ♘d4⩲] **16. a4 ♕a5 17. ♗b5! f5?!** [17... ♖d8 18. c4± ×c5] **18. ♗d7 ♖d8** [18... ♗c3 19. ♕d6 ♗d7 20. ♕d7 ♗a1 21. ♖a1+–] **19. ♕d6! ♗d7** [19... ♖a8 20. ♘e5+–; 19... ♖b7 20. ♗c8 ♖d6 21. ♗b7] **20. ♗g5 ♗e6** [20... f6 21. ♗f6 ♗f6 22. ♕f6+–] **21. ♗d8 ♖d8 22. ♕e7± ♗c3?!** [22... h6!? 23. ♖ac1±] **23. ♖ad1 ♖d1□** [23... ♖a8 24. ♘g5 ♗c4 25. ♖d7 ♖f8 26. ♘h7+–] **24. ♖d1 ♕a4 25. ♖d8 ♔g7 26. ♕f8 ♔f6 27. h4+– h5** [27... c4 28. ♖e8 ♕a1 (28... f4 29. ♕h8 ♔f5 30. ♕c3 ♕e8 31. ♕e5 ♔g4 32. ♕g5#) 29. ♔h2 ♗e5 30. g3] **28. ♖a8!** [28. ♕c5? ♕b4!] **♕d1 29. ♔h2 ♗e5** [29... ♕d3 30. ♖a7 f4 31. ♕e7 ♔g7 32. ♕e6] **30. ♘e5** [30... ♔e5 31. ♕c5 ♕d532. ♕c3 ♔d6 33. ♕b4] **1 : 0** **[Sapis]**

564. !N **E 74**

UHLMANN 2500 – WAHLS 2525

Erfurt 1993

1. c4 g6 2. e4 ♗g7 3. d4 d6 4. ♘c3 ♘f6 5. ♗e2 0–0 6. ♗g5 h6 7. ♗e3 ♘bd7?! 8. ♕d2 c5 9. d5 ♔h7 [9... h5 10. f3 ♘e5 11. h3 △ f4±] **10. ♘f3! N** [10. h3 – 56/(661)] **♘g4 11. ♘g5 hg5 12. ♗g4 ♘e5** [12... f5? 13. ef5 gf5 14. ♕c2 ♘e5 15. ♗e2±] **13. ♗e2** [13. ♗c8? ♘c4 14. ♕e2 ♘e3∓] **g4 14. f4!** [14. h3!? gh3 15. f4 ♘g4 16. ♖h3 ♔g8 17. ♗g4 ♗g4 18. ♖h4 f5!∞; 14. 0–0!? △ a3, b4±] **gf3 15. gf3 ♗h3** [15... a6 16. h4 b5 17. h5→⟫; 15... f5 16. 0-0-0] **16. ♖g1 ♖h8** [16... ♕d7? 17. ♖g3 △ f4+–] **17. f4 ♘d7 18. 0-0-0 ♕a5 19. ♖g3** [19. f5!? gf5 20. ♗d3!±] **♔g8 20. ♖dg1** [20. ♗d3! a6 21. e5 de5 22. f5!±→⟫] **a6** [20... ♗c3 21. bc3 a6 22. f5 b5 23. ♗h6! △ ♖h3+–] **21. ♗d3 b5 22. e5! de5** [22... bc4? 23. ♗e4 de5 24. f5 ♖b8 25. fg6 f5 26. ♖h3 ♖h3 27. ♗f5+–] **23. f5 ♘b6** [23... bc4? 24. fg6 f5 25. ♖h3! cd3 (25... ♖h3 26. ♗f5+–) 26. ♖h8 ♔h8 (26... ♗h8 27. g7+–) 27. ♕g2! f4 (27... e4 28. ♕h3 ♔g8 29. ♕h7 ♔f8 30. ♗h6 ♗h6 31. ♕h6 ♔e8 32. g7 ♘f6 33. ♕f6+–) 28. ♕h3 ♔g8 29. ♕e6 ♔h8 30. ♖g4 ♗f6 31. g7 ♗g7 32. ♖h4+–; 23... ♖f8 24. d6! e6 (24... ed6 25. fg6 f5 26. ♗f1!+–) 25. fe6 ♗e6 26. ♗g6! fg6 27. ♖g6 ♖h7 28. ♗h6! ♖f7 29. ♕g5+–]

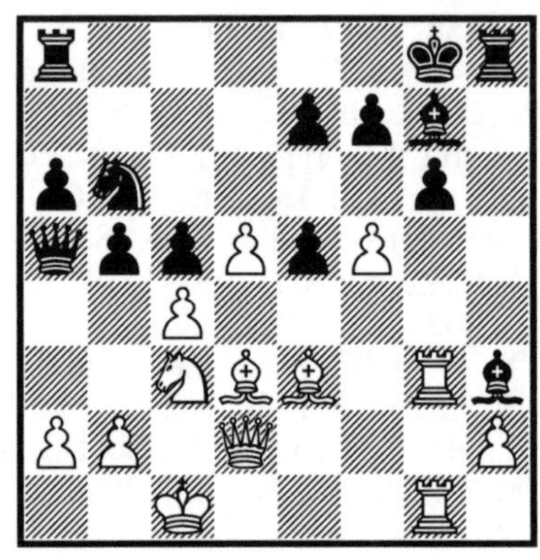

24. d6!! [24. fg6?! f5 25. ♖h3 ♖h3 26. ♗f5 ♘c4∞] **ed6** [24... bc4 25. fg6 f5 26. ♗c4! ♘c4 27. ♕d5+–] **25. f6! ♗f6 26. ♗g6!! ♖d8** [26... fg6 27. ♕d6! ♔f7 (27... ♘d7 28. ♖h3! ♖h3 29. ♕e6 ♔f8 30. ♕h3+–) 28. ♖g6 ♘d7 29. ♘d5 ♗e6 30. ♖f6 ♘f6 31. ♕e7#; 26... ♘c4 27. ♗d3 ♔f8 28. ♗c4 bc4 29. ♕d6 ♗e7 30. ♗h6! ♔e8 31. ♖g8+–] **27. ♕f2! ♘d7 28. ♗f5 ♔f8 29. ♗d7** **1 : 0** **[Uhlmann]**

565. **E 74**

L. VALDÉS 2300 – ALDAMA 2470

Cuba 1993

1. d4 ♘f6 2. c4 g6 3. ♘c3 ♗g7 4. e4 d6 5. ♗e2 0–0 6. ♗g5 h6 7. ♗e3 c5 8. d5 e6 9. ♘f3 ed5 10. ed5 ♖e8 11. 0–0 ♖e3!? N [11... ♘bd7 – 10/809] **12. fe3 ♘g4 13. ♕d2 ♕e7 14. ♗d3 ♘d7 15. ♖ae1 a6** [15... ♘de5=∞; 15... h5=∞] **16. a4 h5 17. a5 ♖b8 18. ♘d1 b6 19. ab6 ♖b6=∞ 20. ♕a5 ♖b4 21. ♕c7 ♕f8** [△ ♘de5∓] **22. b3!** [22. ♗g6 fg6 23. ♘e5 ♕e8 24. ♘g6 ♔h7∓; 22. ♘g5 ♖b7 23. ♕a5 ♘de5∓]

♖b7! [22... ♖b3 23. ♗g6! ♖b7 (23... fg6 24. ♘d2) 24. ♗f7! ♔h8 25. ♕c6 ♘de5 26. ♘e5 ♘e5 27. ♗h5! (27. ♕e8 ♖f7) ♕f1 28. ♖f1 ♘c6 29. dc6 ♖c7 (29... ♖b6 30. ♗e8 △ ♗d7) 30. ♗f3 a5 31. ♖f2+−; 22... ♘de5 23. ♗c2±] **23. ♕a5 ♖b3! 24. ♗g6! fg6 25. ♘d2⊕ ♕e7 26. ♘b3 ♘de5=∞⇆** [26... ♕h4 27. h3 ♘de5 (△ ♕g3) 28. ♘d2 △ 28... ♕g3? 29. hg4 ♘g4 30. ♘f3+−] **27. ♕d2** [27. ♘d2 ♘d3 28. ♖e2 ♘c1⇆] **♘c4⊕ 28. ♕e2 ♘ge5 29. ♘d2** [29. ♘f2 a5 △ ♗a6↑; 29. ♖f4 ♗g4! 30. ♕c2 (30. ♕f1 ♗d1) ♘a3 31. ♕a2 (31. ♕d2 ♘ac4) ♘d3⇆] **♘b6** [29... ♗g4!?] **30. ♘f3 ♘d5 31. ♕a2 ♗e6 32. ♕a6 ♔h7** [32... ♘b4↑] **33. ♕e2 ♗g4 34. ♕d2 ♘f3 35. gf3 ♗e6 36. ♖f2 c4 37. ♖g2 ♕f7 38. ♕e2 ♗h6 39. f4 ♕a7!↑ 40. ♘f2 ♗f5 41. ♕f3 ♘c3** [△ d5∓] **42. e4 ♘e4! 43. ♖e4 ♗e4 44. ♕e4 ♕a1 45. ♘d1 ♕d1 46. ♔f2 ♕d2 47. ♔f3 1/2 : 1/2 [L. Valdés]**

566.* E 75

KAJDANOV 2620 − SHERZER 2465

Pleasantville 1993

1. d4 ♘f6 2. c4 g6 3. ♘c3 ♗g7 4. e4 d6 5. ♗e2 0−0 6. ♗g5 c5 7. d5 e6 8. ♕d2 ed5 9. ed5 ♕b6 [RR 9... ♖e8 10. ♘f3 ♗g4 11. 0−0 ♘bd7 12. h3 ♗f3 13. ♗f3 a6 14. a4 ♕b6 15. ♕c2 h5 N (15... ♖e7) 16. ♗d2 ♘h7 17. ♖fe1 ♗d4 18. ♖e8 ♖e8 19. ♖e1 1/2 : 1/2 F. Levin 2505 − Damljanović 2550, Podgorica 1993] **10. ♘f3 ♗f5 11. ♘h4 ♗g4?! N** [11... ♘e4 − 42/777] **12. f3 ♗c8 13. 0-0-0! ♘bd7?!** [13... ♖e8 14. ♗h6 ♗h8 15. g4 ♘bd7 16. ♖de1! (16. ♘g2?! a6 17. h4 ♘e5 18. h5 ♕b4 19. hg6 fg6 20. ♘e3 b5∞) a6 (16... ♕b4? 17. ♘b5; 16... ♘e5 17. h3! ♕b4 18. g5 △ f4+−) 17. f4 ♘f8 18. g5 ♘e4 19. ♘e4 ♖e4 20. ♗d3 ♖e1 21. ♖e1 ♗d7 22. f5 ♗d4 23. f6! (△ ♘f3) ♗g4 24. ♗f8 ♖f8 25. ♖e4±] **14. ♗h6 a6 15. g4 ♘e8 16. ♗g7 ♘g7 17. ♘g2 f5** [17... ♘e5 18. h4 ♕b4 19. h5±] **18. h4 fg4 19. fg4 ♘e5** [19... ♖f2 20. ♘e3 △ ♘e4] **20. h5! ♖f2 21. hg6 ♘c4** [21... ♖g2 22. ♕h6 hg6 23. ♕h8 ♔f7 24. ♖h7+−] **22. gh7 ♔h8 23. ♘h4!+− ♘h5** [23... ♔h7 24. ♗d3] **24. ♘g6 ♔h7 25. ♖h5 ♔g8 26. ♘a4 ♘d2 27. ♘b6 ♖e2 28. ♘a8 1 : 0 [Kajdanov]**

567. !N E 76**

INK’OV 2450 − J. IVANOV 2385

B”lgarija 1992

1. d4 ♘f6 2. c4 g6 3. ♘c3 ♗g7 4. e4 d6 5. f4 0−0 6. ♘f3 ♘a6 [RR 6... c5 7. d5 b5 8. cb5 a6 9. a4 ♕a5 10. ♗d2 ♕b4 11. ♕c2 ab5! N (11... c4 − 32/(684)) 12. ♗b5 ♗a6 13. e5 de5 14. fe5 ♘g4 15. ♘d1 (15. ♘e4?! ♘e3!∓ Kekhcher − V. Lőwy 2285, Netanya 1993) ♗b5 16. ♗b4 cb4 17. ♕e4 (17. ab5 ♖a1 18. 0−0 ♘d7 19. e6 fe6 20. de6 ♘de5∓→) ♗d7 18. e6 ♘f6=∞ V. Lőwy] **7. ♗e2 e5 8. de5** [8. fe5 de5 9. d5 c6 10. 0−0 N (10. ♗g5 − 48/777) cd5 11. cd5 ♘e8 (11... ♕b6?! 12. ♔h1 ♘g4 13. ♕e1 ♘e3? 14. ♘a4!+−) 12. ♗e3 ♘d6 13. ♘d2!? ♘c7 14. ♗c5 ♘ce8 15. ♘b5 ♘b5! 16. ♗b5 ♘d6 17. ♗d3 ♗f6! 18. ♘c4 ♗e7 19. ♘e5 ♘e4!= Badžakov − J. Ivanov 2385, Albena 1992] **de5 9. ♕d8 ♖d8 10. ♘e5 ♘c5 11. ♗f3 ♗e6 12. ♘d5 ♘fd7 13. ♘d7** [13. ♘c7? ♘e5! 14. fe5 ♗e5 15. ♘a8 ♘d3∓; 15. ♘e6!?; 14... ♘d3!?∓; 14... ♗c4!∓] **♖d7 14. 0−0 N** [14. ♔e2] **c6 15. ♘e3** [15. ♖b1 ♘e4!∓] **♗d4! 16. ♔h1□ ♘d3!? 17. f5! ♘c1 18. fe6 fe6 19. ♗g4! ♖e8□ 20. ♖d1!** [20. ♘c2?! ♘d3 21. ♘d4 ♖d4 22. ♖ad1 c5 (△ ♘e5∓) 23. ♖f6? ♖e4! 24. ♗f3 ♘f2−+; 20. ♘d5?! cd5 21. ed5 ♘d3 22. ♗e6 ♖e6 23. de6 ♖e7∓; 20. ♖ac1 ♗e3=] **♗b2□ 21. ♖d7!?** [21. ♖ac1 ♗c1 22. ♖c1 (22. ♖d7 ♗e3=) ♖d3 23. ♖e1 ♔f7 △ ♔e7=] **♗a1 22. c5!** [△ ♘c4-d6; 22. ♖d1 ♗b2 23. c5 (23. ♖d2 ♗a3) ♘a2 24. ♖d2 ♗c1; 22. ♖b7 ♗d4=] **♗f6!** [△ ♖e7] **23. ♘c4 ♖e7 24. ♖e7** [24. ♖d8 ♔g7 25. e5! ♗g5 26. g3 h5! (26... ♘a2 27. h4 ♗c1 28. ♘d6 h5 29. ♗e2 ♗b2 30. ♘e8 ♖e8!? 31. ♖e8 ♗e5∞) 27. h4! (27. ♗h3? ♘a2 28. ♘d6 ♘c3 29. ♘e8 ♔h6 30. ♘f6 ♗f6 31. ef6 ♖f7∓) ♗h4! 28. gh4 hg4 29. ♘d6 ♘d3 30. ♘e8 ♔f7 31. ♘d6=] **♗e7 25. ♗e6 ♔f8= 26. ♘a5 ♘d3**

27. ♘b7 [27... ♘f2 28. ♔g1 ♘e4 29. ♗d7 ♘c5] **1/2 : 1/2** **[J. Ivanov]**

568. **E 77**

BANGIEV 2395 – M. MUŠE 2490

Deutschland 1993

1. d4 ♘f6 2. c4 g6 3. ♘c3 ♗g7 4. e4 d6 5. f4 0–0 6. ♘f3 ♗g4 7. ♗e2 ♘c6 8. d5 ♗f3 N [8... ♘b8] **9. ♗f3 ♘a5!?** [9... ♘b8 10. 0–0 c6 11. ♗e3±] **10. ♕e2 c6 11. e5** [11. b4? cd5 12. ba5 de4∓] **de5** [11... ♘e8 12. b4 de5 13. ♗d2±] **12. fe5 ♘d7 13. ♗f4 ♕b8 14. 0–0! ♗e5 15. ♗e5 ♕e5** [15... ♘e5!? 16. ♖ae1 ♘ac4 (16... ♘ec4? 17. b4) 17. b3 ♘f3 18. ♕f3 (18. ♖f3 ♘d6! 19. ♕e7 ♖e8 20. ♕h4 ♖e1 21. ♕e1 ♕f8∓) ♘d6 19. ♖e7 ♘f5∓; 16. b3!?∞] **16. ♖ae1!? ♕d4** [16... ♕e2 17. ♖e2 ♖fe8 18. b4 ♘c4 19. dc6 bc6 20. ♗c6 ♖ad8 21. ♖d1±] **17. ♔h1 ♘f6** [17... ♕c4 18. ♕c4 ♘c4 19. dc6⩲; 17... ♘c4 18. dc6⩲; 17... e6 18. de6⩲] **18. ♖d1! ♕c5 19. a3! ♖ad8** [19... ♘c4? 20. b4!±; 19... ♘b3!? 20. ♕c2 ♘d4 21. ♕f2 ♘b3 22. ♕c5 (22. ♕c2 ♘d4=) ♘c5 23. b4±] **20. b4! ♕c4 21. ♕e1! ♘d5** [21... ♘b3? 22. ♗e2+–] **22. ♘d5 cd5 23. ba5 e6 24. ♖c1! ♕a6?! 25. ♖c7 ♖c8?! 26. ♗e2 ♕d6 27. ♖b7± d4 28. ♕f2 d3 29. ♗d1 ♖c5** [29... ♖c7 30. ♕a7±] **30. ♖f7 ♖f5 31. ♖f8 ♕f8 32. ♗f3 ♖a5** [32... ♕a3 33. ♕a7] **33. ♕e1 ♕f5 34. ♗g4** [34. g4 ♕e5 35. ♕e5 ♖e5 36. ♖d1+–] **d2 35. ♕d1 ♕d3** [35... ♕d5 36. ♕e2] **36. ♗e6 ♔g7 37. h3 ♖c5 38. ♕a1 ♔h6 39. ♗g4 ♕e3 40. ♕f6 ♖c1 41. ♕f8 ♔g5 42. ♗d1 a6 43. h4 ♔h4 44. ♕f6 1 : 0** **[Bangiev]**

569. **E 80**

JUSUPOV 2640 – NIJBOER 2485

Groningen 1992

1. d4 ♘f6 2. c4 g6 3. ♘c3 ♗g7 4. e4 d6 5. f3 e5 6. de5 de5 7. ♕d8 ♔d8 8. ♗e3 ♗e6 9. 0-0-0 ♘fd7 10. g3 [10. b3 ♘c6 11. ♘ge2±; 10... c6 △ ♘a6=] **♘c6 11. ♗h3 ♘d4 12. f4 c5 13. ♗e6** [13. ♘d5 ♘b6!] **fe6 14. ♘ge2 ♗h6!** [14... ♔e7? 15. fe5 ♘e2 16. ♘e2 ♗e5 17. ♗g5 ♔e8 18. ♖hf1±] **15. ♔b1 ♔e7 16. ♘c1 a6 17. ♘b3 b5! 18. ♖he1** [18. cb5 ab5 19. ♗d4 ed4 20. ♘b5 ♖hb8 21. ♘a3 e5! 22. ♖hf1 ♖a3 23. ba3 c4 24. fe5 ♗e3!∓] **♖hc8 19. fe5** [19. cb5 ab5 20. ♗d4 ed4 21. ♘b5 ♖cb8 22. ♘a3 e5 23. fe5 ♘e5→] **♗e3 20. ♖e3 ♘b3 21. ab3 ♖ab8 22. cb5?** [22. ♘d5 ed5 23. ed5 bc4 (23... ♖b6 24. e6 ♘f6 25. ♖f1 ♖f8 26. ♖ef3 h6=) 24. e6 ♖b3 25. d6 ♔d8 26. ed7 ♖e3 27. dc8♕ ♔c8 28. ♖d5 ♔d7 29. ♖c5 ♔d6 30. ♖c4=] **ab5 23. g4 ♖f8! 24. ♖h3 ♖f7 25. g5 ♘e5 26. ♖c1 ♘f3! 27. ♖d1** [27. ♖g3 ♘d2 28. ♔c2 ♖f2–+] **♘g5 28. ♖hd3 ♖b7 29. e5 ♖f5 30. h4 ♘f7 31. ♘e4 ♖e5 32. ♘g3 c4 33. bc4 bc4 34. ♖d4 c3?!** [34... ♖eb5 35. ♖c4 ♖b2 36. ♔c1 ♖b1 37. ♔c2 ♖7b2 38. ♔c3 ♖b3 39. ♔c2 ♖d1 40. ♔b3 ♖d3 41. ♖c3 ♖c3 42. ♔c3–+] **35. b4 ♖eb5 36. ♔c2 ♖b4 37. ♖b4 ♖b4 38. h5 ♖g4 39. ♖d3 gh5 40. ♘h5 e5 41. ♖c3 ♔e6 42. ♔d1 ♘d6 43. ♘g3 ♖d4 44. ♔e2 ♘e4 45. ♖a3 ♘g3 46. ♖g3** [♖ 4/e] **h5 47. ♖g5 ♖e4 48. ♔f3 ♖f4 49. ♔e3 ♖f5 50. ♖g8 ♔f7 51. ♖a8 ♔f6 52. ♔e4 ♖f4 53. ♔e3 ♔f5 54. ♖h8 ♔g4 55. ♖g8 ♔h4 56. ♖e8 ♖f5 57. ♖a8 ♔g4 58. ♔e4 ♖g5 59. ♖a1 h4 60. ♖g1 ♔h5 61. ♖h1 ♖g2! 62. ♔f5 ♖e2 63. ♖g1 ♖f2 64. ♔e4 h3 65. ♔e3 ♖f4 66. ♖g8 ♔h4 0 : 1** **[Nijboer]**

570. !N **E 80**

VYŽMANAVIN 2620 – DAMLJANOVIĆ 2550

Zaragoza 1993

1. d4 ♘f6 2. c4 g6 3. ♘c3 ♗g7 4. e4 d6 5. f3 e5 6. d5 ♘h5 7. ♗e3 f5 8. ♕d2 ♕h4 9. ♗f2 ♕f4?! [9... ♕e7!?] **10. ♕f4 ef4** [10... ♘f4±] **11. ef5! N ±** [11. ♘b5 – 55/589] **♗f5** [11... ♗c3!?] **12. ♘ge2 0–0 13. 0-0-0 ♘a6 14. ♘d4 ♗d7 15. ♗d3 ♘c5 16. ♗c2 a5 17. ♖he1 ♖f7** [17... ♖ae8 18. ♘cb5 ♘a6 19. ♘e6 ♗e6 20. de6 ♖e7±] **18. ♖e2 ♖c8 19. ♘cb5 ♗f6 20. ♗e1 b6 21. ♗f2 ♘g7 22. ♖de1 ♔f8 23. b3 ♗d4 24. ♘d4 ♘f5 25. ♔d2 ♘d4 26.**

♗**d4 b5**⊕ [26... g5 27. h4 h6 (27... g4 28. h5± △ h6, ♗g7) 28. hg5 hg5 29. ♖h1; 26... ♗f5 27. ♗f5 ♖f5 28. ♗c5 bc5 29. ♖e7 ♖f7 30. ♖f7 ♔f7 31. h4 h6 32. h5 △ ♖e6±] **27. h4!**± [×f4] **c6** [27... bc4 28. bc4 c6] **28. dc6** ♗**c6 29. h5 gh5 30.** ♖**h1 bc4 31. bc4** ♗**d7 32.** ♖**h5** ♘**e6 33.** ♗**c3** ♖**c5** [33... a4 34. ♗h7 ♖c4 35. ♗g6+−] **34.** ♖**c5** ♘**c5** [34... dc5 35. ♖e5!] **35.** ♗**a5** ♗**e6 36.** ♔**c3**+− ♔**e7 37.** ♗**b4** ♔**d7 38.** ♔**d4** ♔**c6 39.** ♗**a4!** ♔**b6 40.** ♗**b5** ♗**d7 41.** ♗**d7** ♖**d7 42.** ♔**d5** ♖**g7 43.** ♗**c5 dc5 44.** ♖**b2** ♔**c7 45.** ♔**c5 h5 46.** ♔**d4** ♖**e7 47.** ♖**b5** ♖**e2 48.** ♖**h5** ♖**g2 49.** ♖**f5** ♖**a2 50.** ♖**f4** ♔**d6 51. c5** ♔**d7 52.** ♔**d5** ♖**d2 53.** ♖**d4** ♖**f2 54. f4**
1 : 0 **[Vyžmanavin, B. Arhangel'skij]**

571.* **E 81**

PSAKHIS 2575 − R. HAR-ZVI 2485
Zagreb (zt) 1993

1. d4 ♘**f6 2. c4 g6 3.** ♘**c3** ♗**g7 4. e4 d6 5. f3 0−0 6.** ♘**ge2 c6** [RR 6... ♘bd7 7. ♗g5 a6 8. ♘c1 N (8. ♕d2 − 51/588) c6 9. a4 a5 10. ♘b3 e5 11. d5 ♕b6 12. ♖a3 h6 13. ♗h4 ♖e8 14. ♗f2 c5 15. g3 ♕d8 16. ♗d3 b6 17. ♘d2 ♘f8 18. ♘f1 ♖a7 19. ♘e3±○ Kortchnoi 2605 − Je. Piket 2590, Nijmegen (m/7) 1993] **7.** ♗**g5 a6 8.** ♕**d2 b5 9. h4 N** [9. cb5 − 6/767; 9. ♗h6 e5 10. ♗g7 ♔g7 11. ♘g3 ♗e6 12. d5 cd5 13. cd5 ♗d7=] ♘**bd7** [9... h5!? 10. ♘g3 ♘bd7 11. 0-0-0 c5∞] **10. g4** [10. h5!? ♘b6 (10... ♘h5? 11. g4 ♘hf6 12. ♗h6±) 11. ♘g3∞] **b4** [10... ♘b6 11. ♘g3 ♘c4 12. ♗c4 bc4 13. h5→; 10... c5 11. cb5] **11.** ♘**d1 c5 12. h5** [12. d5 ♘e5 13. ♘g1□ ♗g4!?∞] **cd4 13.** ♘**d4** ♕**b6** [13... ♘e5 14. ♘f2! ♕b6 15. ♗e2±] **14.** ♗**e3**□ ♘**e5 15.** ♗**e2**□ [15. ♘f2?? ♕d4−+] ♗**g4!?** [15... ♘eg4 16. fg4 ♘e4 17. ♕c2] **16. fg4** ♘**e4 17.** ♕**c2** ♕**b7** [17... ♘g3? 18. ♘f5 ♕b7 19. ♘g3+−] **18.** ♘**f2!** ♘**g3** [18... ♘f2 19. ♔f2±] **19.** ♖**g1** ♘**e2 20.** ♕**e2 d5** [20... ♖ac8 21. ♖c1 d5 22. c5 ♘c4 23. ♖c4! dc4 24. ♕c4±] **21. c5!** [21. cd5?! ♕d5$\overline{\overline{\infty}}$] ♘**c4 22. b3 e5** [22... ♘a3!?±; 22... ♘e3 23. ♕e3 e5 24. ♘f5!]

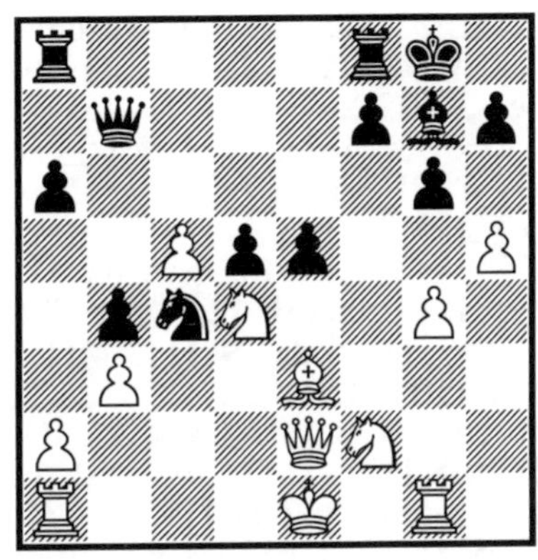

23. ♘**f5!** ♘**e3** [23... gf5 24. gf5] **24.** ♕**e3 d4** [24... gf5 25. gf5 ♔h8 (25... f6 26. h6; 25... h6 26. f6) 26. ♖g7! ♔g7 27. ♕g5 ♔h8 28. ♕f6 ♔g8 29. h6+−; 24... ♗h8 25. ♘h6 ♔g7 26. ♕e5 f6 27. ♘f5! ♔g8 28. ♕e6+−] **25.** ♕**g3!** [25. ♕e4!? ♕e4 26. ♘e4 gf5 27. gf5 ♔h8□ 28. f6 ♗h6 29. ♔e2±] **e4** [25... ♖ae8 26. ♘d6] **26.** ♘**g7** ♔**g7 27.** ♕**e5 f6 28. h6!** ♔**h8** [28... ♔h6 29. g5 ♔g7 30. gf6 ♖f6 31. ♘g4+−] **29.** ♕**d4 e3** [29... ♖ad8 30. ♕e3] **30.** ♘**e4** ♖**ad8 31.** ♘**d6** ♕**f3 32.** ♕**b2** [32. ♘f7? ♔g8!] ♕**h3 33. 0-0-0!** [33... ♕h6 34. ♘f7 ♖f7 35. ♖d8 ♔g7 36. g5+−] **1 : 0**
[Psakhis]

572.** **E 81**

NENAŠEV 2565 − KAŽGALEEV
Akmola 1993

1. d4 ♘**f6 2. c4 g6 3.** ♘**c3** ♗**g7 4. e4 0−0 5.** ♗**e3 d6 6. f3 c5 7. dc5** [RR 7. ♘ge2 ♘c6 8. ♕d2 cd4 9. ♘d4 ♘d4 10. ♗d4 ♗e6 11. ♗e2 ♕a5 12. ♖b1 ♖fc8 13. b3 a6 N (13... ♘d7 − 52/610) *a)* 14. a4 ♕b4! 15. ♘d5 (15. 0−0 b5 16. ♖fd1 bc4 17. bc4 ♕a5∓) ♕d2 16. ♔d2 ♘d5 (16... ♗d5 17. ed5 a5!? 18. ♗e3 ♘d7 19. ♖be1 ♘c5 20. ♗d1= Hába 2485 − Glek 2545, Deutschland 1993) 17. ♗g7 ♘f4! 18. ♗h6 ♘e2 19. ♔e2 b5↑; *b)* 14. 0−0 b5∞ Glek] **dc5 8.** ♕**d8** ♖**d8 9.** ♗**c5** ♘**c6 10.** ♗**a3 a5 11.** ♖**d1** ♖**d1** [RR 11... ♗e6 12. ♘d5 ♘b4 13. ♘e7 ♔h8 14. ♘d5 N (14. ♖d8 − 56/669) *a)* 14... b5 15. ♗b4 ab4 16. ♘b4 ♖d1 (16... bc4 17. ♘e2±) 17. ♔d1 ♗f8 18. ♘c2 ♖a2 19. ♔c1 ♘d7 (19... bc4

20. ♘e2±) *a1)* 20. ♔b1 (Rogozenko 2480 – Golubev 2495, Nikolaev (zt) 1993) ♖a6! 21. ♘e2 ♖d6 22. ♘ed4 (22. ♘c3 ♖d2 23. cb5 ♗g7=∞) ♗c4 23. ♗c4 bc4 △ ♗g7=∞; *a2)* 20. ♘e2! ♗g7 (20... ♘c5 21. ♔b1) 21. ♘c3 ♗c3 22. bc3 △ ♔b1±; *b)* ⌓ 14... ♘c2 15. ♔f2 ♘a3 16. ba3 b5 17. ♘h3 ♖ac8!=∞ Rogozenko] **12. ♔d1 ♘b4 13. ♘ge2 ♗e6 14. ♘d5 N** [14. ♘f4 – 43/(733)] **♗d5** [14... ♘fd5!? 15. cd5 ♗d7 △ e6] **15. cd5 e6 16. ♗b4 ab4 17. de6 ♖a2 18. ef7 ♔f8** [18... ♔f7? 19. ♔c2 ♘d7 20. ♘c3 △ ♗c4±] **19. ♘f4** [19. b3? ♘d7 20. ♘g3 ♘c5 21. ♗c4 b5∓] **♖b2** [19... b3!?] **20. ♔c1 ♖a2** [20... ♖b3 21. ♘e6 ♔f7 22. ♘g7 ♔g7 23. ♗b5±; 20... ♖f2!? 21. ♘d3 ♗h6 22. ♔b1 ♖d2 23. ♘b4 ♘d7∞] **21. ♔b1 ♖d2** [21... b3 22. ♗c4 ♘d5? 23. ♘e6 ♔e7 (23... ♔f7 24. ♘g7) 24. f8♕ ♗f8 25. ♗d5] **22. ♗c4 ♘d7 23. ♔c1 ♖d6?!** [23... ♗c3 24. ♖d1 ♖d1 25. ♔d1±] **24. ♔c2 ♗h6 25. ♘d3** [25. ♘d5; 25. g3±] **♖c6 26. ♔b3 b5 27. ♗b5 ♖c3 28. ♔a4** [28. ♔b4? ♗d2] **♘b6⊕** [28... ♖d3 29. ♗d3 ♘c5 30. ♔b4 ♘d3 31. ♔c4 ♘e5 32. ♔d5 ♘f7 33. ♖b1±] **29. ♔a5 ♘c8 30. ♖d1 ♔f7 31. ♘e5** [31. ♔b4 ♖c2 32. g3 ♗f8 33. ♔b3 ♖h2] **♔e6 32. ♘c4 ♘e7 33. ♔b4⊕** [33. ♖d6 ♔f7 34. ♘e5 ♔g7 35. ♖d7 b3!] **♖c2 34. ♖d6 ♔f7 35. ♘e5 ♔g7 36. ♖d7 ♔f8 37. g3 ♖h2 38. f4** [38. ♖d8 ♔g7 39. ♖e8 ♗g5 40. f4 ♗f6 41. ♘d3 ♖g2 42. e5 ♖g3 43. ef6 ♔f6±] **♖b2 39. ♔a4 ♖a2 40. ♔b4 ♖b2 41. ♔a4 ♖a2 42. ♔b3 ♖g2 43. ♖d8** [43. ♖d3!? ♔g7 44. ♗c4 △ ♔b4-c5] **♔g7 44. ♖d3 ♖g1?** [44... ♖g3 45. ♖g3 ♗f4 46. ♘g6 hg6±] **45. ♔c2 ♖g3 46. ♖g3 ♗f4 47. ♘g6 hg6** [♖ 9/e] **48. ♖a3+– g5 49. ♖a7 ♔f6 50. ♖a6 ♔g7 51. ♗e8 ♘g8 52. ♖g6 ♔f8 53. ♖e6 ♔g7 54. e5 ♘h6 55. ♗h5 ♘f5 56. ♔d3 ♘g3 57. ♗g4 ♘f1 58. ♔e4 ♘d2 59. ♔d5 ♘f1 60. ♗e2 ♘e3 61. ♔e4 ♔f7 1 : 0**
[Nenašev]

573. **E 81**

VAN DER STERREN 2490 – VAN WELY 2560

Bruxelles (zt) 1993

1. d4 ♘f6 2. c4 g6 3. ♘c3 ♗g7 4. e4 d6 5. f3 0–0 6. ♗e3 ♘bd7 7. ♕d2 c5 8. d5 ♘e5 9. ♗g5 a6 10. f4 ♘ed7 11. ♘f3 b5 12. cb5 ♕a5 13. e5 de5 14. fe5 ♘g4 15. ♗e7 ♖e8 16. d6 ♗h6 17. ♘g5 ♘ge5 18. ♗e2 c4 19. 0–0 [19. ba6? ♘d3 20. ♗d3 ♗g5–+] **ab5 20. ♕d4 N** [20. ♗f3 ♘f3 21. ♖f3 ♘e5 22. ♖e3 ♘d3 – 56/671; 22... ♘g4! △ ♗f5] **♗b7□ 21. ♕h4?!** [21. ♘f7 ♘f7 22. ♖f7 ♔f7 23. ♘b5! ♗e3 24. ♕e3 ♕b5 25. ♖f1 ♔g7 26. ♕e6 ♕d5 27. ♖f7 ♔g8 28. ♖f8=; 21. h4!?] **♗g5 22. ♕g5 b4 23. ♘d1 c3 24. bc3 bc3 25. ♘e3??** [25. ♖c1□ ♖e7 26. ♕e7 ♕d5 △ ♖a2=∞] **♖e7! 26. ♕e7** [26. de7 ♘f3 △ ♕g5–+] **♕c5 27. ♔f2□ ♖a4!–+** [△ 28... ♖e4, 28... ♖f4] **28. ♕e8 ♔g7 0 : 1**
[van Wely]

574. **E 81**

AN. KARPOV 2725 – TOPALOV 2635

León 1993

1. d4 ♘f6 2. c4 g6 3. ♘c3 ♗g7 4. e4 d6 5. f3 0–0 6. ♗e3 a6 7. ♕d2 ♘bd7 8. ♘h3!? [8. 0-0-0!? c6 9. e5 ♘e8 10. f4] **c6 9. ♘f2 b5 N** [9... e5 – 51/592] **10. b3** [10. ♖c1!? bc4 11. ♗c4 d5 12. ♗e2±] **e5 11. d5 cd5** [11... b4?! 12. dc6 bc3 13. ♕d6 ♘e8 14. ♕d3] **12. ♘d5** [12. cd5 ♘h5 13. ♘d3 f5⇆] **♘d5 13. ♕d5 ♕a5** [13... ♘b6 14. ♕c6 ♖b8 15. ♖d1±] **14. ♕d2 ♕d2 15. ♔d2** [15. ♗d2 bc4 16. ♗c4 ♘b6 17. ♗d3±] **♖b8** [15... f5 16. ♔c2 ♖b8 17. ♖d1±] **16. ♖d1** [16. cb5 ab5 17. ♖c1 f5 18. ♖c7±; 17... d5!⇆; 16. ♖c1 ♘c5!?] **bc4 17. ♗c4 ♘b6 18. ♗d3** [18. ♗b6 ♖b6 19. ♔e2±] **♗e6 19. ♖c1 d5 20. ♔e2 a5 21. ♗b5** [21. ♖c6 d4□ 22. ♗d2 a4 23. ♗a5 ♘d7 (23... ab3?! 24. ab3 ♘d7 25. b4±) 24. b4 ♗a2⇆] **♖fd8** [21... d4 22. ♗d2 a4 23. ba4 ♗a2 24. ♘d3±] **22. h3** [△ ♘d3] **♗f8 23. ♘d3** [23. ♗g5!? ♖dc8 (23... ♖d6?! 24. ♘d3 ♘d7 25. ♗c6±) 24. ♖c8 ♘c8!?∞] **f6** [23... ♗a3 24. ♖c6 ♗d7 25. ♘e5!] **24. ♘c5** [24. ♖hd1!?] **♗c5 25. ♖c5 de4 26. fe4 ♘d7 27. ♖c6!?** [27. ♗d7 ♗d7 28. ♖a5 ♗c6⇆] **♖b5** [27... ♗b3 28. a4!±] **28. ♖e6 ♘c5 29. ♖e7□** [29. ♖f6 ♘e4 30. ♖f3 ♘c3] **♘e4 30. ♖c1± ♘g3 31. ♔f2 ♘f5 32. ♖a7 h5** [32... ♘e3 33. ♔e3 ♖bd5 34. ♖cc7 ♖d2 (34... ♖d3 35. ♔f2 ♖d2

36. ♔g3+−) 35. ♖g7 ♔h8 36. ♖h7 ♔g8 37. ♖ag7 ♔f8 38. ♖g6±] **33. ♖c6! ♖f8 34. ♗c5?!** [34. ♖cc7! h4□ 35. ♗d2±] **♘d4□** [34... ♖f7? 35. ♖c8 ♔g7 36. ♗f8+−] **35. ♗d4 ed4 36. ♖cc7 ♖f5 37. ♔g1** [37. ♔e2 ♖e8 38. ♔d3 ♖g5=] **♖d8 38. ♖g7 ♔h8 39. ♖h7 ♔g8 40. ♖ag7 ♔f8 41. ♖g6 ♖d6 42. ♖gg7 ♖fd5 43. ♖c7 ♔g8 44. ♖hg7 ♔h8** [44... ♔f8 45. ♖cf7 ♔e8 46. ♖h7!±] **45. ♖ge7 ♖d8 46. ♖e2 d3 47. ♖d2 ♖f5 48. ♖c3 ♖fd5 49. ♔f2 ♔h7 50. ♔e1 ♖e8 51. ♔d1 ♖e3 52. ♖f2 ♖g3 53. ♖c6 ♖dg5 54. ♖cf6 ♖g2 55. ♔d2 ♖5g3 56. h4 ♖g4 57. ♔d3 ♖f2 58. ♖f2 ♖h4 59. ♖f7 ♔g6 60. ♖a7 ♖h1** [60... ♖g4?! 61. ♖a6 ♔g5 62. ♖a5] **61. ♖a5 [♖ 5/h] h4 62. ♔e2** [62. ♖c5 h3 63. ♖c2 ♔g5 64. ♔c4 ♔g4 65. a4 ♔g3=] **h3 63. ♔f2 ♖c1= 64. ♔g3 ♖c3 65. ♔h2 ♔f6 66. b4 ♔e6 67. a4 ♔d6 68. b5 ♔c7 69. ♖a7 ♔b6 70. ♖h7 ♖a3 71. ♖h6 ♔b7 72. ♖h4 ♔a7 1/2 : 1/2 [An. Karpov]**

575.** E 83

DYDYŠKO 2490 – HAIT 2410

Katowice 1993

1. d4 ♘f6 2. c4 g6 3. ♘c3 ♗g7 4. e4 d6 5. f3 0–0 6. ♗e3 ♘c6 7. ♘ge2 a6 8. ♕c2!? N ♗d7 9. ♖d1 ♘e8 [9... ♖b8 10. ♘c1 e5 11. de5 de5 12. ♘b3 b6!? (12... ♕c8 13. ♗e2 ♗e6 14. 0–0 ♘d7 15. ♘d5 ♖e8? 16. c5!± Dydyško 2490 – Kruppa 2475, Minsk 1993; 15... b6) 13. c5 b5±; ⌓ 11... ♘e5; 9... b5!? 10. ♘c1 bc4 11. ♗c4 ♘b4!? (11... e5 12. de5 ♘e5 13. ♗b3±) 12. ♕d2 d5 13. ed5 ♗f5 14. 0–0 ♘bd5 15. ♗g5± Dydyško 2490 – R. Kempinski 2340, Katowice 1993] **10. g3** [10. ♘c1 e5] **e5 11. ♗g2** [11. d5 ♘e7 △ f5⇆] **ed4 12. ♘d4 ♘e5 13. b3 c5 14. ♘de2 b5 15. f4 ♘g4 16. ♗c1 bc4 17. bc4 ♗e6 18. ♕d3 ♖b8 19. h3?!** [19. 0–0! △ 19... ♖b4 20. ♘d5 ♗d5 21. ♕d5±] **♘gf6 20. f5** [20. g4!?] **♗c8! 21. e5!? ♗f5?** [21... ♘d7!∞ Hait] **22. ef6! ♗d3 23. fg7 ♘g7 24. ♖d3 ♕f6 25. ♗d5!±** [25. ♖f1 ♕e6∞] **♘e6 26. ♖f3 ♕e5 27. 0–0 ♘d4?! 28. ♘d4 cd4** [28... ♕d4 29. ♔h1 ♔h8 30. ♘e4 △ ♗d2+−] **29. ♘e4 ♖b1 30. ♗f4+− ♖f1 31. ♔f1 ♕g7 32. ♗d6 ♕h6 33. ♔g2 ♕c1 34. ♗e5! d3 35. ♖d3 ♖d8 36. ♖f3 ♖d5 37. ♘f6 ♔f8 38. cd5 ♔e7 39. ♖f2 ♕e1 40. d6 ♔e6 41. d7 ♕a5 42. ♗c3 ♕c7 43. ♖e2 1 : 0 [Dydyško]**

576. !N E 86

AN. KARPOV 2725 – KASPAROV 2805

Linares 1993

1. d4 ♘f6 2. c4 g6 3. ♘c3 ♗g7 4. e4 d6 5. f3 0–0 6. ♗e3 e5 7. ♘ge2 ♘bd7 8. ♕d2 c6 9. ♖d1 a6 10. de5 [10. d5 cd5 11. ♘d5!±; 10... c5!⇆] **♘e5! N** [10... de5? – 51/(597)] **11. b3 b5! 12. cb5** [12. c5? d5 13. ed5 b4!∓; 12. ♕d6 ♕d6 13. ♖d6 bc4∓] **ab5 13. ♕d6 ♘fd7 14. f4?!** [14. ♘d4?? ♖a6!−+; 14. ♗g1 b4 15. ♘a4 ♖a4 16. ba4 ♕a5 17. ♗d4 c5↑; 14. ♕d2!? b4 15. ♘a4 ♖a4 16. ba4 ♘c4 17. ♕c1 ♘e3 18. ♕e3 ♕a5=∞; 15. ♘b1!?; 14. a4!? ba4 15. ♘a4 ♖a4 16. ba4 ♘c4 17. ♕d3 ♘b2 18. ♕c2 ♘d1 19. ♕d1 ♕a5 20. ♔f2 ♘e5! (20... ♖d8 21. ♕c2 ♘b6 22. ♕c6 ♘a4 23. ♘f4; 20... ♘c5 21. ♘d4 ♖d8 22. ♘c6 ♖d1 23. ♘a5 ♘a4 24. ♖g1 ♗c3 25. ♗b5!) 21. ♘f4 f5 22. ef5 ♗f5] **b4! 15. ♘b1?** [15. ♕b4? c5! 16. ♗c5 ♘c5 17. ♖d8 ♘ed3−+; 15. ♘a4 ♖a4! 16. ba4 ♘c4 17. ♕d3 ♘b2 (17... ♘e3!? 18. ♕e3 ♕a5↑) 18. ♕c2 ♘d1 19. ♕d1 ♕a5∓; 15. fe5! bc3 16. ♘c3 (16. e6 fe6 17. ♕e6 ♔h8−+) *a)* 16... ♕a5!? 17. ♕c6 (17. ♗d2 ♘e5↑ 18. ♘a4; 17. b4 ♕a3 18. ♗d4 ♖e8) ♘e5 (17... ♗b7∞) 18. ♕c5∞; *b)* 16... ♗e5 17. ♕c6!□ (17. ♕d2 ♗c3 18. ♕c3 ♕h4∓) ♗c3 (17... ♕a5 18. ♗d2!; 17... ♕h4 18. ♔d2! ♖b8∞; 17... ♗b7!? 18. ♕b7 ♗c3 19. ♔f2 ♖a2 20. ♔g1 ♘c5 21. ♖d8 ♘b7 22. ♖f8 ♔f8=) 18. ♕c3 ♕h4 19. ♔d2! (19. g3 ♕e4 20. ♖g1 ♖a2∓; 19. ♗f2 ♕e4 20. ♕e3 ♖e8 21. ♕e4 ♖e4 22. ♗e2 ♗a6! 23. ♖d2 ♖ae8 24. 0–0 ♗e2 25. ♖d7 ♗f1 26. ♔f1 ♖e2∓) *b1)* 19... ♘f6 20. ♔c1 ♘e4 21. ♕e5 ♗f5 22. g3 (22. ♗d4 f6 23. ♗c4 ♔h8 24. ♕e7 ♕g5!−+) ♕g4 23. ♗d4 (23. ♗c4 ♖fe8 24. ♕f4 ♖a2 25. ♕g4 ♗g4) f6 24. ♗c4 ♔h8 25. ♕f4 ♕f4 26. gf4 ♖a2∞; *b2)* 19... ♖a2 20. ♔c1 *b21)* 20... ♕e4? 21. ♗h6

♘e5 22. ♗f8? ♗f5 23. ♗d3 ♕e3 (23... ♕d3? 24. ♖d3 ♘d3 25. ♔b1 ♘b4=) 24. ♔b1 ♖g2 25. ♗h6 ♗d3 26. ♖d3 ♕d3 27. ♕d3 ♘d3 28. ♖d1 ♖h2!−+; 22. ♗d3!; *b22)* 20... ♘f6! 21. ♔b1 ♘e4 22. ♕e5 ♖a3∞; 21... ♖a8!∓] **♘g4 16. ♗d4** [16. ♗g1!? ♖a2 17. h3 ♕h4 18. g3 ♖e2 19. ♔e2 (19. ♗e2 ♕g3 20. ♔f1 ♗a6 21. ♗a6 ♕f3 22. ♔e1 ♕h1−+) ♕g3 *a)* 20. ♖d3 *a1)* 20... ♗a6 21. hg4 (21. ♕d7 ♘f6 22. ♕d4 ♘h5 23. ♕e3 ♖d8−+) ♘f6 22. ♘d2 ♘d5 23. ♘c4 ♗c4 24. bc4 ♘c3 (24... ♘f4 25. ♔d2 ♕g4) 25. ♖c3□ (25. ♔d2 ♘e4 26. ♔c2 ♕e1) ♗c3 26. ♗e3 ♖a8 27. ♔d3? ♕f3!−+; *a2)* 20... ♕h4! 21. ♗g2 ♘ge5 22. fe5 ♘e5 23. ♘d2 (23. ♖d2 ♕g3!) ♗a6 24. ♘c4 ♗c4 25. bc4 ♘d3 26. ♕d3 ♖a8−+; *b)* 20. ♕d3 ♕f4 21. hg4 ♘e5 22. ♕e3 ♕g4!? (22... ♗g4 23. ♔e1 ♘f3 24. ♔f2 ♕e3 25. ♔e3 ♘g1∓) 23. ♔e1 (23. ♔f2 f5!) ♘f3 24. ♔f2 ♘g1 25. ♖d2 ♗f6! (25... f5? 26. ♖g1 fe4 27. ♔e1) 26. ♖g1 ♗h4 27. ♖g3 ♗g3 28. ♕g3 ♕e4∓; *c)* 20. hg4 ♘f6 *c1)* 21. ♕d3 ♗g4 22. ♔d2 ♘e4 (22... ♕f4 23. ♗e3 ♘e4 24. ♔c1 ♕f3↑) 23. ♕e4 (23. ♔c1 ♗d1) ♖d8 24. ♗d3 ♗d1 25. ♔d1 ♖d3 26. ♔c2 ♖b3∓ 27. ♕e8 ♗f8 28. ♖h7 ♕d3 29. ♔c1 ♖b1#; *c2)* 21. ♗f2 ♗g4 (21... ♕g4 22. ♔e1 ♘e4) 22. ♔e1 ♕f3 23. ♖h2 ♘e4∓] **♗d4 17. ♕d4** [17. ♘d4 ♖a2 18. ♖d2 (18. ♘c6 ♕h4 19. g3 ♘h2!! 20. ♕d3 ♕f6 21. ♘b4 ♘e5!−+) ♖a1 19. ♗d3 ♕b6 20. 0−0 ♘c5 (20... ♖d8 21. ♗c4 ♘de5 22. fe5 ♖d6 23. ed6 ♘e5∓) 21. ♗c2 (21. ♕c6 ♕c6 22. ♘c6 ♘d3 23. ♘e7 ♔g7 24. ♘c8 ♘e3) ♗a6 22. ♖e1 (22. ♖fd1 ♘e6) ♖d8−+] **♖a2 18. h3** [18. ♕b4 ♘e3 19. ♖d2 ♘c2−+] **c5 19. ♕g1** [19. ♕d3 ♗a6 20. ♕f3 (20. ♕d7 ♕h4 21. g3 ♖e2 22. ♗e2 ♕g3 23. ♔d2 ♕e3 24. ♔c2 ♕e2−+) ♘de5 21. fe5 ♘e5 22. ♕e3! (22. ♖d8 ♘f3 23. gf3 ♖d8−+ 24. ♘c1 ♖c2) ♘d3 23. ♖d3 *a)* 23... ♗d3 24. ♘d2 (24. ♘c1 ♗f1 25. ♘a2 ♗g2 26. ♖h2 ♕h4!−+) ♖e8 25. ♘g3; *b)* 23... ♕d3 24. ♕d3 ♗d3 25. ♘c1! (25. ♘d2 ♖d8 26. ♘c1 ♖d2!) ♗b1 26. ♘a2 ♗a2 27. ♗c4 ♗b1 28. e5 ♗f5 29. ♔d2 ♖e8 30. ♖e1 h5−+] **♘gf6 20. e5 ♘e4 21. h4?!** [21. ♕e3 ♗b7 22. ♘d2 (22. ♘c1? ♕h4; 22. h4 ♕e7 △ ♖e8, ♘e5) ♘d2 23. ♖d2 ♖d2 24. ♕d2 ♘b6! (24... ♕h4 25. g3 ♕e7 26. ♖g1 ♖a8; 24... ♕e7!∓) 25. ♕d8 ♖d8 26. ♘c1 ♘d5 27. ♘d3 ♘e3−+] **c4! 22. ♘c1** [22. bc4? ♕a5 23. ♕e3 b3 24. ♘ec3 (24. ♘d2? ♘dc5) ♘dc5 25. ♗e2 ♖c2; 22. ♕e3!? c3 23. ♕e4 c2! 24. ♖d2 (24. ♖c1 ♘c5−+) ♘c5! 25. ♖d8 ♘e4]

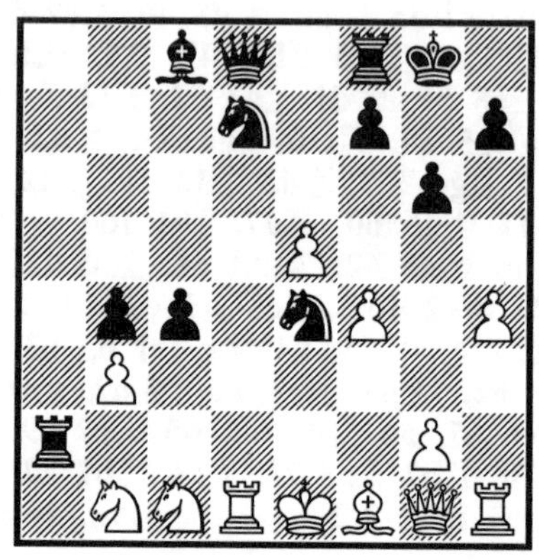

22... c3!! 23. ♘a2 c2 24. ♕d4 [24. ♖c1 ♘e5! 25. ♖c2 (25. fe5? cb1♕ 26. ♖b1 ♕d2#; 25. ♕e3?! cb1♕ 26. ♖b1 ♘g4−+) ♗g4 26. ♖d2 (26. ♗e2 ♘d3 27. ♗d3 ♕d3−+; 26. ♘d2 ♘d3 27. ♗d3 ♕d3 28. ♘e4 ♕e4 29. ♔d2 ♕f4−+) ♘d2 27. ♘d2 (27. fe5 ♘e4 28. ♗e2 ♗e2 29. ♔e2 ♘g3 30. ♔f3 ♘h1−+) ♖e8 28. fe5 ♖e5 29. ♔f2 ♕d2 30. ♔g3 ♖e3 31. ♔h2 ♖h3#] **cd1♕ 25. ♔d1** [25. ♕d1 ♘g3 26. ♖h3 ♘f1 27. ♔f1 (27. ♕d4 ♘e5!) ♘c5 28. ♕d8 ♖d8 29. ♖e3 ♖d1 30. ♖e1 ♗a6 31. ♔f2 ♘d3−+] **♘dc5! 26. ♕d8 ♖d8 27. ♔c2** [27. ♔e1 ♗g4 28. ♗e2 ♗e2 29. ♔e2 ♘g3; 27. ♔c1 ♘f2 28. ♖g1 ♖d1 29. ♔b2 ♘cd3] **♘f2** [28. ♖g1 ♗f5 29. ♔b2 ♘d1 30. ♔a1 (30. ♔c1 ♘b3#) ♘b3#]
0 : 1 **[Kasparov]**

577. **E 86**

PANNO 2495 − B. LARSEN 2540

Buenos Aires 1993

1. d4 ♘f6 2. c4 g6 3. ♘c3 ♗g7 4. e4 d6 5. f3 0−0 6. ♗e3 e5 7. ♘ge2 ♘bd7 8. ♕d2 c6 9. d5 ♘b6?! N 10. ♘g3 [10. b3?! cd5 11. cd5 ♘h5 △ f5] **cd5 11. cd5 ♗d7**

[11... ♘e8 12. ♗d3 f5 13. ♘ge2] **12. ♖c1 ♖c8 13. b3 ♘e8 14. ♗d3 f5 15. ♘ge2 ♘f6 16. 0–0 f4?!** [16... fe4 17. ♘e4!⩲] **17. ♗f2 g5 18. ♘b5 ♗b5□ 19. ♗b5** [△ ♕a5] **a6 20. ♗d3?** [20. ♕a5!] **♘a8!** [×a5, b6, c7] **21. ♖c8 ♕c8 22. ♕b4 ♕d7 23. ♖c1 g4∓↑ 24. ♔h1 ♔h8** [⌓ 24... h5 △ ♘h7-g5] **25. ♘g1 ♖g8 26. ♗h4 h5 27. ♖c2 ♘h7 28. ♕e1 ♗f6 29. a4?!⊕** [29. ♗f6 ♘f6 30. ♕h4 △ g3, ♖g2 Najdorf] **♘g5 30. ♗e2 ♗d8 31. ♗g5** [31. a5?! ♘c7 △ ♘b5∓] **♗g5 32. ♕c1 ♔h7 33. ♕d1 ♗d8 34. ♕e1** [34. fg4!? hg4 35. h3∞] **g3 35. h3 ♗b6∓** [×♔h1] **36. a5 ♗e3 37. ♕b4 ♔g7!** [×d6] **38. ♗d3 ♔f7 39. ♘e2 ♔e7 40. ♖c4 ♖c8 41. ♕c3 ♖c4 42. ♗c4 h4?** [42... ♔d8 △ 43. ♘g3? ♗d4–+] **43. ♘c1 ♕c7 44. ♘d3 ♔d8** [44... b5!? 45. ab6 ♕b6] **45. ♕b4 ♔c8 46. ♘e1 ♕c5?!** [46... ♗c5! △ ♘b8-a7] **47. ♕c5 ♗c5** [47... dc5!? 48. ♘d3 ♗d4 49. d6 ♔d7 50. ♗d5 ♔d6 51. ♗b7 ♘c7 △ ♗c3–+ ×a5] **48. ♘c2 ♘c7 49. ♗e2 ♔b8 50. b4 ♗f2 51. ♘a3! ♔a7** [51... ♗e1 52. ♘c2 △ ♔g1] **52. b5 ab5 53. ♘b5= ♘b5 54. ♗b5 ♗e1 55. a6 ba6 56. ♗a6 ♔a6**

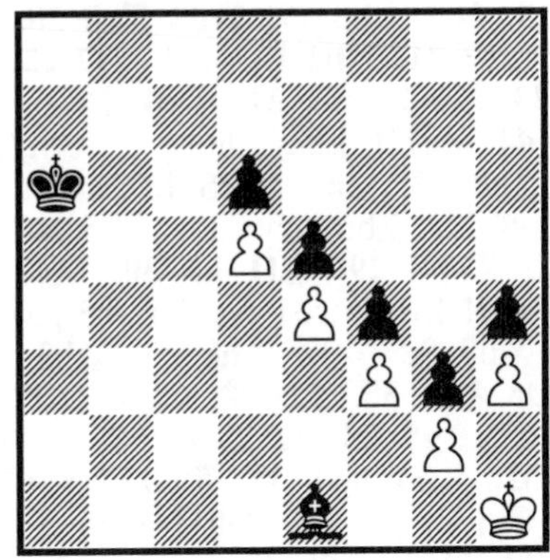

57. ♔g1 1/2 : 1/2 [Panno]

578. ** !N **E 86**

ŠIROV 2670 – KAMSKY 2655

Buenos Aires 1993

1. d4 ♘f6 2. c4 g6 3. ♘c3 ♗g7 4. e4 d6 5. f3 0–0 6. ♗e3 e5 7. ♘ge2 c6 8. ♕d2 ♘bd7 9. d5 cd5 10. ♘d5 ♘d5 11. ♕d5 ♘b6 12. ♕b5 ♗h6 13. ♗f2 ♗e6 [RR 13... ♗d7 N 14. ♕b4 ♘a4 15. ♘c3 ♘c3 16. ♕c3 *a)* 16... b5 17. ♖d1 bc4 18. ♗c4 ♖c8 19. b3 1/2 : 1/2 Kramnik 2685 – Dolmatov 2615, Dortmund 1993; *b)* 16... ♗e6 17. ♗d3 ♕c7 1/2 : 1/2 van der Sterren 2490 – O. Renet 2535, Bruxelles (zt) 1993] **14. ♘c3 ♕c7 15. b3** [15. ♘d5 ♘d5 16. cd5 ♗d7∓] **♘d7! N** [×♕b5; 15... ♘c8] **16. ♖d1** [16. ♘d5 ♗d5 17. ♕d5 ♘c5∓] **a6** [16... ♘c5 17. ♕b4 a6 – 16... a6] **17. ♕b4 ♘c5 18. ♗e2** [18. ♘d5 ♗d5 19. ♖d5 b5!→ △ 20. ♗e2?! a5!∓] **f5?!** [18... b5! 19. ♘d5 (19. cb5? a5 20. ♕a3 ♘b3! 21. ♕b2 ♘d4!∓) ♗d5 20. cd5 f5 21. ef5 ♖f5 22. 0–0 ♖c8=] **19. 0–0⩲ ♖f7** [19... fe4 20. ♘e4⩲] **20. ef5! gf5?!** [20... ♗f5 21. ♘d5 ♕c6⩲] **21. ♘d5 ♕c6** [21... ♗d5 22. ♖d5±] **22. f4!± a5 23. ♕e1!?** [23. ♕a3!? (△ fe5 ×♘c5) ♘e4 24. fe5 ♗d5! 25. ♖d5! (25. cd5 ♕c3!∞̄ △ 26. e6 ♖g7 27. ♔h1 ♕c2!) ♘f2 26. ♖f2! ♗e3 27. ed6!±] **♗g7!** [23... ♘e4 24. fe5! de5 25. ♗f3! ♘f2 26. ♘f6! ♖f6 27. ♗c6 ♘d1 28. ♕e5! ♖af8 29. ♗d5! ♗e3 30. ♔h1 ♘f2 31. ♖f2 ♗f2 32. ♗e6±] **24. fe5?** [24. ♗f3! e4 25. ♗h5 ♖d7 26. ♗d4±; 26. ♗h4±] **de5 25. ♗h5 ♖d7 26. ♕e3 ♘e4 27. ♗h4 ♗d5?!** [27... ♗f8! 28. ♔h1 ♗c5∞ △ 29. ♕e4? fe4 30. ♘f6 ♔h8 31. ♘d7 ♗d7 32. ♖f7 ♗e8–+] **28. cd5 ♖d5 29. ♖f5?!** [29. ♖d5 ♕d5 30. ♖f5 ♕d4! 31. ♕d4 ed4 32. ♗f3 ♘c3 (32... ♖e8 33. ♖a5±) 33. ♗b7 ♖a7! (33... ♖b8 34. ♗d5± △ 34... ♘d5? 35. ♖d5 a4 36. ♖d8+–) 34. ♗d5 ♘d5 35. ♖d5 a4!⩲] **♖d1 30. ♗d1 ♘c3∞ 31. ♗h5 ♖c8** [31... ♘a2!?] **32. ♗f7 ♔h8 33. ♖e5 ♘a2 34. ♗c4** [34. ♖a5 ♘c3∞̄] **a4 35. ♖e7 ab3 36. ♗b3** [36. ♖g7 ♕c4 37. ♗f6? ♕c1 38. ♕c1 (38. ♔f2? ♖c2 39. ♔f3 ♕f1–+) ♖c1 39. ♔f2 ♖c6! 40. ♗e5 ♖c5! 41. ♗d4 ♖d5! 42. ♖d7 ♖d4 43. ♖d4 b2 44. ♖d8 ♔g7 45. ♖d7 ♔f6 46. ♖b7 ♘c3! 47. ♖b6 ♔g5–+; 37. ♖b7=] **♕c1 37. ♕c1 ♘c1 38. ♗e6 ♖f8= 39. g4 ♘e2 40. ♔h1 b5 41. ♖b7 ♘d4 42. ♗d5 h6 43. ♗e7 ♖c8 44. ♗e4 ♗e5 45. ♔g2 ♖a8 46. h4 ♖a2 47. ♔f1 ♘e2! 48. ♖b8!** [48... ♗b8 49. ♗f6 ♔g8 50. ♗d5] **1/2 : 1/2 [Širov]**

579.*** **E 86**

B. ALTERMAN 2600 – CVITAN 2575
Zagreb (zt) 1993

1. d4 ♘f6 2. c4 g6 3. ♘c3 ♗g7 4. e4 d6 5. f3 0–0 6. ♗e3 e5 7. ♘ge2 c6 8. ♕d2 ♘bd7 9. 0-0-0 a6 10. ♔b1 [RR 10. ♗h6 ♗h6 11. ♕h6 b5 12. h4 ♕a5 13. h5 b4 14. ♘b1 ♕a2 15. ♘g3 ♘b6 16. c5 ♘c4 17. ♖d2 ♘a5 N (17... ♘d2 — 51/597) 18. cd6 ♘b3 19. ♔c2 ♘a1 20. ♔c1 ♘b3 21. ♔c2 ♘a1 22. ♔c1 1/2 : 1/2 Beljavskij 2610 – Kasparov 2805, Linares 1993] **b5 11. ♘c1 ed4 12. ♗d4 ♖e8** [RR 12... ♖b8 N 13. ♘b3 (13. c5!? b4 14. ♘3e2 Vaïsser) bc4 14. ♗c4 a5 15. a3 1/2 : 1/2 Kramnik 2685 – Lautier 2645, Cannes (m/4) 1993; 12... b4 N 13. ♘a4 c5 14. ♗f6 ♗f6 15. ♕d6 ♗e7 16. ♕g3 ♗h4 17. ♕h3 ♗e7 18. ♕g3 ♗h4 19. ♕h3 1/2 : 1/2 Kramnik 2685 – Kasparov 2805, Linares 1993] **13. ♘b3 ♗f8 14. h4 N** [14. c5 — 56/676] **h5** [14... b4 15. ♘e2 c5 16. ♗e3∞] **15. ♕f4** [15. g4!?] **b4 16. ♘a4 c5 17. ♗f6 ♕f6** [17... ♘f6 18. ♘ac5±] **18. ♕f6 ♘f6 19. ♘b6 ♖b8 20. ♘c8 ♖bc8 21. g3!± ♖c7 22. ♗h3 ♔g7 23. ♖h2 ♖a7 24. ♘a5!?** [24. ♖hd2 a5 25. ♘c1 a4 26. ♘e2±] **♘d7 25. ♗d7 ♖d7 26. ♘b3 ♖de7 27. ♖d5! ♖e5 28. ♖e5 ♖e5 29. ♘d2 f5 30. ♔c2 ♔f7 31. ♖e2 ♗h6 32. f4?!** [32. ♔d3! ♔e7 (32... ♗d2 33. ♖d2 fe4 34. fe4 g5 35. ♖f2 ♔e7 36. ♖f5!±) 33. ♘f1 a5!? 34. b3 ♖e6! 35. ef5 (35. ♘e3 fe4 36. fe4 ♗e3 37. ♔e3 ♖f6=) ♖e2 36. f6! (36. ♔e2 gf5 37. ♘e3 ♗e3 38. ♔e3 ♔e6 39. ♔f4 d5!□ 40. cd5 ♔d5 41. g4 fg4 42. fg4 hg4 43. h5 ♔e6!=) ♔f6 37. ♔e2 ♔e6 38. ♔d3 d5 39. cd5 ♔d5 40. f4±] **♖e7= 33. ♔d3 ♔e8 34. ♘f3⊕ ♔d7 35. b3 ♗g7 36. ♖e1 ♗c3 37. ♖e2 ♗f6 38. ♖e1 1/2 : 1/2 [B. Alterman]**

580. **E 88**

STEFÁNSSON 2495 – O. RENET 2535
Ísland – France 1993

1. d4 ♘f6 2. c4 g6 3. ♘c3 ♗g7 4. e4 d6 5. f3 0–0 6. ♗e3 e5 7. d5 c6 8. ♗d3 cd5 9. cd5 ♘h5 10. ♘ge2 f5 11. ef5 gf5 12. 0–0 ♘d7 13. ♖c1 a6?! 14. ♔h1 ♕e8 N [14... ♘df6 — 21/558] **15. b4** [15. ♗b1!] **♔h8 16. ♗b1** [△ g4] **♘df6** [16... b5 17. g4 fg4 18. fg4 ♖f1 19. ♕f1 ♘hf6 20. g5 ♘g4 21. ♗g1±] **17. ♘a4!± f4 18. ♘b6 ♖b8 19. ♗g1** [19. ♗f2?! e4!] **♗d7** [19... e4 20. ♘c8 ♖c8 21. ♖c8 ♕c8 22. ♗e4 ♘e4 23. fe4 ♕c4 24. ♘d4+–] **20. a4 ♖f7 21. ♖c4 ♗h6** [21... ♗a4 22. ♘a4 b5 23. ♖c6] **22. ♕c2 ♕g8 23. ♖c1 ♗e8** [◯ 23... e4 24. ♘d7 ♖d7 25. ♖c8±] **24. ♖c8 ♖c8 25. ♕c8 ♗f8 26. ♕h3+– ♘g7 27. ♖c8 ♗d7?⊕ 28. ♘d7 ♖d7 29. ♗h7! ♘h7 30. ♕d7 ♕d5 31. ♘c3 ♕d3 32. ♘e4 d5 33. ♘f6 1 : 0 [Stefánsson]**

581. **E 88**

MARIN 2515 – GAŽÍK 2425
Budapest (zt) 1993

1. d4 ♘f6 2. c4 g6 3. ♘c3 ♗g7 4. e4 d6 5. ♗d3 0–0 6. ♘ge2 e5 7. d5 ♘a6 8. 0–0 c6 9. f3 cd5 10. cd5 ♘c5 11. ♗c2 a5 12. ♗e3 ♘e8 13. ♖b1 ♗d7 14. a3 f5 [14... a4!? 15. ♗c5 dc5 16. ♗a4 ♘d6] **15. ef5 N** [15. b4] **gf5 16. b4 ab4 17. ab4 ♘a6 18. f4± ♔h8 19. ♕d2 ♖c8 20. ♗d3** [×c4] **♕e7 21. ♖b3** [×♘c3] **♕f7 22. ♘g3 e4□ 23. ♗e2 ♘f6 24. ♖d1** [×d5] **♖g8 25. ♗d4 ♘c7?!** [25... h6!? △ ♔h7] **26. ♖a3! ♖a8 27. ♖a5 ♖gc8** [27... ♖a5 28. ba5 ♖a8 29. ♗b6 ♘a6 30. ♗b5 ×f5] **28. ♖da1○ ♖ab8 29. ♘f1 h5 30. ♘e3 ♖g8 31. ♖1a3?!** [31. ♘cd1 (△ ♘f2-h3-g5) ♘g4 (31... ♔h7 32. ♘f2 ♗h6 33. ♘h3 ♘cd5 34. ♘d5 ♘d5 35. ♗c4 ♗e6 36. ♗d5 ♗d5 37. ♘g5 ♗g5 38. fg5± △ 38... f4? 39. ♗f6) 32. ♘g4 hg4 33. ♘e3±] **♔h7 32. ♘cd1?⊕** [32. g3; 32. ♔h1] **♗h6 33. ♖c3 ♖bc8 34. ♘c4 ♘fd5 35. ♘d6 ♕g6–+ 36. ♗h5 ♕d6 37. ♗f7 ♘c3 38. ♗g8 ♖g8 39. ♗c3 ♗f4 40. ♕e1 ♗h2 41. ♔f1 ♕d3 0 : 1 [Marin]**

582.* **E 89**

AN. KARPOV 2725 – KAMSKY 2655
Linares 1993

1. d4 ♘f6 2. c4 g6 3. ♘c3 ♗g7 4. e4 d6 5. f3 0–0 6. ♗e3 e5 7. ♘ge2 c6 8. ♕d2

♘bd7 9. d5 cd5 10. cd5 a6 11. g4 [11. ♘g3 h5!?; 11... b5 – 16/654; RR 11. ♘c1 ♘h5 12. ♘b3 f5 13. ef5 N (13. 0-0-0) gf5 14. ♗e2 b5 15. a3 ♕h4 (15... b4?! 16. ab4 ♕h4 17. ♗f2 ♕b4 18. ♘a5 ♘f4 19. ♖a4! ♕b8□ 20. ♘c6±; 18. ♘b5!± △ 18... ♕b3? 19. ♖a3!+–) 16. ♗f2 ♕f6!? 17. g3 ♗h6 18. ♕d1 ♕d8!? (×a5) 19. 0–0 ♘hf6 20. ♕d3?! e4! 21. fe4 ♘e5 22. ♕d4 *a)* 22... fe4? 23. ♗e3! ♗g7 24. ♘e4± Švedčikov 2405 – Asanov 2405, Kazahstan 1993; *b)* 22... f4!? 23. gf4 ♗f4∞; *c)* 22... ♘fg4!→ Asanov; 20. ♔h1!? △ ♗g1, f4 Švedčikov] **b5 12. ♘g3 ♘c5 13. b4 ♘a4** [13... ♘cd7 14. a4±] **14. ♘a4 ba4 15. b5!? N** [15. ♖b1; 15. ♗e2 ♗d7 16. 0–0 ♕b8 △ ♘e8-c7-b5-d4±] **♗g4!?** [15... ab5 16. ♗b5 ♗d7 17. ♗d7 ♘d7 18. 0–0±] **16. fg4 ♘g4 17. ♗g5** [17. b6 f5 18. ef5 gf5 19. b7 f4⇆; 17. ♖g1!? △ 17... f5 18. ef5 gf5 19. ♘f5] **f6 18. h3** [18. ♗e2 fg5 19. ♗g4 ab5⇆] **fg5 19. hg4 ♖f3! 20. ♘e2** [20. ♖g1 ♕b6 21. ♖g2!? ♖af8 22. ♖c1 ♖e3! 23. ♔d1 ♖g3 24. ♖g3 ♖f1 25. ♔c2 ♖f2–+; 22. 0-0-0; 20. ♖h3 ♕b6 21. ba6 ♖af8!⇆] **ab5** [20... ♕b6 21. ♖c1 (21. ba6 ♕f2 22. ♔d1 ♕f1 23. ♖f1 ♖f1 24. ♔c2 ♖a1∞) ab5 22. ♖c6↑] **21. ♗g2 ♖f8 22. ♘c1?** [22. ♖f1!± ♕b6 23. ♖f3 ♖f3 24. ♗f3 ♖f8 25. ♕d3] **♕c8! 23. ♖b1** [23. ♗h3 ♖f4–+] **♕g4 24. ♖h3** [24. ♘d3 ♕g3 25. ♔d1 g4∓] **♖ac8 25. ♕e2 ♕d7** [25... ♕e2 26. ♘e2 ♖c2 27. ♖c3 ♖a2 28. ♗h3 g4 29. ♗g4 ♗h6 30. ♖c8 ♖c8 31. ♗c8 b4!–+; 27. ♖a3!?] **26. ♖g3 g4 27. ♕g4 ♕a7 28. ♘e2□ ♕f2 29. ♔d1 ♗h6 30. ♖f3 ♖f3 31. ♕c8 ♖f8 32. ♕h3 ♔g7 33. ♖b5 ♖f7 34. ♖b8?!** [34. ♕g3!? ♕g3 35. ♘g3 ♖f2 36. ♗h3 ♖f3 37. ♖b7=] **♗g5** [34... ♖c7!? 35. ♖c8 ♖b7 36. ♖g8 ♔g8 37. ♕c8 ♗f8] **35. a3 ♖c7 36. ♖b1 h5 37. ♕f3 ♖f7 38. ♕h3 ♗h4 39. ♔d2 ♖c7 40. ♕f3 ♕c5 41. ♕d3 ♗g5 42. ♔e1 ♖f7 43. ♔d1 ♕f2 44. ♕h3 h4 45. ♖b8 ♖c7 46. ♖c8 ♖f7** [46... ♖b7 47. ♖g8 ♔g8 48. ♕c8 ♗d8! 49. ♕b7 ♕g2 50. ♕a8 ♕g5–+] **47. ♖c6 ♖b7 48. ♕f3 ♕f3?** [48... ♖b1! 49. ♔c2 ♖f1! 50. ♕g4 ♖c1 51. ♔b2 ♖e1 52. ♕g5 ♖e2 53. ♔b1 ♕g1 54. ♖c1 ♕b6–+] **49. ♗f3 h3 50. ♔c2 h2 51. ♘g3 ♖f7 52. ♖c3 ♗h4 53. ♘h1 ♗e1 54. ♖d3 ♖c7 55. ♔b2 ♖b7 56. ♔c2 ♖c7 57. ♔b2 ♖c4** [57... ♖b7 58. ♔c1 ♖c7 59. ♔d1±] **58. ♗g2 ♗a5 59. ♘f2!± ♗b6 60. ♘g4 ♗g1 61. ♖h3 ♖c8** [61... ♗c5!? 62. ♘h2 ♖d4 63. ♔c2 (63. ♘f1 ♖d1∞) ♖c4 64. ♖c3 ♖c3 65. ♔c3 (♘♗ **8/g**) ♔h6! (65... ♗a3? 66. ♘g4+–) 66. ♗f3 ♔g5 67. ♗d1 ♔f4 68. ♔d3 ♗a3 (68... g5 69. ♘g4 ♗a3 70. ♘f6!+–) 69. ♗a4 ♗c5 70. ♗d1 ♗b6 71. ♘g4 ♗d8 72. ♘h6 ♗h4 73. ♗e2 ♗e7 74. ♘f7 ♗f8 75. ♘d8±] **62. ♘h2 ♗h2** [62... ♖b8?! 63. ♔c2 ♖c8 64. ♔d2 ♗d4 65. ♗f3 ♖c3 66. ♗g4 ♖h3 67. ♗h3 (♘♗ **8/g**) ♗c5 68. ♘g4 ♗a3 69. ♔c3 ♗c5 70. ♗f1 a3 71. ♗b5 ♔f7 72. ♔b3 ♔e7 73. ♘h2 ♔f7 (73... ♔f6 74. ♗e8) 74. ♘f3 ♗b4 75. ♗c4 ♗c5 76. ♘g5 ♔f6 77. ♘e6+–; 62... ♗d4 63. ♔b1 ♖b8 64. ♔c1 ♖b2 65. ♗f3! (65. ♗f1 ♖a2 66. ♗b5 ♖a1 67. ♔c2 ♖a2 68. ♔d1 ♖a1 69. ♔e2 ♖a2 70. ♔f1 ♖a1 71. ♔g2 ♖a2 72. ♔h1 ♖a1 73. ♘f1 ♖b1 74. ♗e2 ♖e1 75. ♗d3 ♗c5) ♖a2 66. ♗d1 ♖a1 67. ♔d2 ♖a2 68. ♗c2 *a)* 68... ♗c5 69. ♖c3 ♗a3 70. ♖c4; *b)* 68... ♔f6 69. ♘g4 ♔g5 70. ♘e3 ♖a3 (70... ♔f4 71. ♘c4 g5 72. ♖h6 g4 73. ♖d6 g3 74. ♖g6 ♔f3 75. d6+–) 71. ♖g3 ♔h5 (71... ♔f4 72. ♖g4 ♔f3 73. ♗d1 ♔f2 74. ♖g2#) 72. ♗d1 ♔h4 73. ♘f5; *c)* 68... ♗b2 69. ♗a4 ♗a3 70. ♔c3 ♗c5 71. ♗d7!? (71. ♗c2±) ♔f6 72. ♘f3 ♖e2 73. ♗e6 ♖e4 74. ♖h7 ♖e3 75. ♔d2 g5 76. ♘h2 ♖a3 77. ♘g4 ♔g6 78. ♖h8 ♖f3 (78... e4 79. ♖g8 ♔h5 80. ♘f6 ♔h4 81. ♖h8+–) 79. ♖c8 ♗b4 80. ♔e2 ♖f4 81. ♔d3 (△ ♖c4) ♔h5 82. ♔e3 ♗c5 83. ♖c5 dc5 84. d6 ♖d4 85. ♘f6 ♔g6 86. ♘d5 ♖h4 (86... ♖a4 87. d7 ♖a8 88. ♘e7 ♔f6 89. ♘c8+–) 87. d7 ♖h8 88. ♘e7 ♔f6 89. ♘g8+–] **63. ♖h2 ♖f8 64. ♗h3 ♖b8 65. ♔c3 ♖b3 66. ♔c4 ♖a3 67. ♔b5 ♖e3 68. ♔c6 ♖e4 69. ♖a2 ♖e3 70. ♗g2 a3 71. ♔d6 ♔f6 72. ♖f2 ♔g5 73. ♔e6 ♖b3 74. d6 ♖b2 75. ♖b2 ab2 76. ♗e4 ♔f4 77. ♔d5 1 : 0** **[An. Karpov]**

583. !N **E 89**

AN. KARPOV 2725 – DOLMATOV 2615

Dortmund 1993

1. d4 ♘f6 2. c4 g6 3. ♘c3 ♗g7 4. e4 d6 5. f3 0–0 6. ♗e3 e5 7. ♘ge2 c6 8. ♕d2

♘bd7 9. d5 cd5 10. cd5 a6 11. g4 h5 12. g5 ♘h7 [12... ♘e8 13. h4⩲] **13. ♖g1! N** [13. h4 f6 14. gf6 (14. ♗g2∞) ♗f6 (14... ♖f6 – 34/725) 15. ♗f2∞] **f6 14. gf6 ♕f6** [14... ♖f6∞] **15. 0-0-0 ♖f7?!** [15... ♕f3 16. ♖g6 ♖f6? 17. ♗g2+–; 15... b5] **16. ♔b1 b5 17. ♘c1± ♘df8** [17... b4 18. ♘a4 ♕f3 19. ♖g6 ♕e4 (19... ♖f6? 20. ♗g2+–) 20. ♗d3 ♕d5 21. ♖d6±] **18. ♗e2 ♗d7 19. a3 ♕d8** [19... ♖b8 20. ♘3a2! ♕d8 21. ♘b3±] **20. ♘1a2** [20. b4?!; 20. ♘b3 ♗f6 21. ♘a2 a5] **♕b8 21. ♘b4 ♕b7 22. ♖c1** [22. ♘c6 ♗c6 23. dc6 ♕c6 24. ♕d6 ♕d6 25. ♖d6 ♖f6⩲] **♗e8 23. ♘ca2 ♖c8** [23... ♖c7 24. ♘c6±] **24. ♖c8 ♕c8 25. ♖c1 ♕a8** [25... ♕h3 26. ♘a6 ♕h2 27. ♘c7 ♗d7 28. ♘c3+–] **26. ♘c6 ♗f6 27. ♕a5 ♗g5 28. ♗g5 ♘g5 29. ♘ab4 ♘f3 30. ♗f3 ♖f3 31. ♘e7! ♔f7 32. ♘c8 ♗d7 33. ♘d6 ♔g8 34. ♘c6!+– ♖f6 35. ♕c7 ♗c6 36. ♖c6 1 : 0**
[An. Karpov]

584.* E 90

MI. CEJTLIN 2485 – ZAJCEV 2450

Bucureşti 1993

1. d4 ♘f6 2. c4 g6 3. ♘c3 ♗g7 4. e4 d6 5. ♘f3 0–0 6. ♗e3 ♘c6 [RR 6... e5 7. de5 de5 8. ♕d8 ♖d8 9. ♘d5 ♘a6 10. 0-0-0 ♗g4 11. ♗g5 N (11. h3 – 38/792) ♖d6 12. h3 ♗f3 13. gf3 h6!? (13... ♖e6) 14. ♘f6 ♗f6 15. ♗h6 ♖d1 16. ♔d1 ♘c5 17. h4 ♖d8 18. ♔c2 ♘e6 19. ♗e3 ♘d4 20. ♗d4 ♖d4 21. h5 g5 22. b3 ♔h7 23. ♗h3 ♔h6 24. ♗c8 b6 25. ♔c3 a5 26. a3 c5 27. b4 ab4 28. ab4 cb4 29. ♔b4 (Cifuentes Parada 2480 – Geenen 2320, Belgique 1993) ♗e7 △ ♗c5= Geenen] **7. d5 N** [7. h3 – 2/633] **♘b4 8. ♗e2** [8. ♕b3 a5 9. a3 ♘a6; 8. a3 ♘a6 9. ♖c1 ♘c5] **e6 9. 0–0** [9. de6 ♗e6 10. ♘d4 ♗d7±] **♖e8** [9... ed5 10. cd5±] **10. de6 ♗e6** [10... fe6 11. e5±] **11. ♕b3!?** [11. ♘d4!? ♗d7 12. f3 d5!? 13. a3 (13. cd5 ♘bd5! 14. ♘d5 ♘d5) c5! (13... de4? 14. ab4 ef3 15. ♖f3±) 14. ab4 cd4 15. ♗d4 de4∞] **a5 12. a3 ♘c6 13. ♕b7 ♗d7 14. ♘d5!⩲** [14. ♘b5 ♘e4 15. ♕c7 (15. ♘c7? ♖b8–+) ♗b2∞] **♖c8 15. ♖ad1?!** [15. ♖ac1! ♘e4 16. b4±] **♘e4 16. b4** [16. c5? dc5 17. ♘b6 ♘d6 18. ♖d6 cd6 19. ♕d7 (19. ♘d7 ♖c7–+) ♕b6–+] **ab4 17. ab4 ♘e7!!** [△ 18... ♘d5, 18... ♘c3] **18. ♘g5! ♘c3!** [18... ♘d5 19. ♕d5 (19. ♘e4 ♘e3∓) ♘c3 20. ♕f7 ♔h8∞] **19. ♘c3** [19. ♘e7 ♖e7] **♗c6! 20. ♕a6 ♖a8 21. ♗a7 ♗c3 22. c5!** [△ ♘f7, ♕c4] **♗f6 23. cd6 cd6 24. h4 ♕d7 25. b5 ♖a7** [25... ♗g2 26. ♔g2 ♖a7 27. ♕d6] **26. bc6 ♘c6 27. ♕c4 ♘d4∓ 28. ♖d4! ♗d4 29. ♗f3!** [29. ♕d4 ♖e2 30. ♘e4 ♖e4! 31. ♕e4 ♖a4 △ ♖h4–+] **♗f6 30. ♘f7 ♔g7 31. ♘g5 ♖c7 32. ♕d3 d5 33. ♖d1⊕ d4 34. g3** [△ ♘e4] **♗g5 35. hg5 ♖d8 36. ♔g2 ♕f5 37. ♕d2 ♖c2 38. ♕b4 ♕d7 39. ♖e1 ♖c7 40. ♕b6?!** [40. ♖e5! ♕d6 41. ♕a5] **♕d6 41. ♕b3 ♖e7 42. ♖d1 ♕e5 43. ♕b6 ♖d6 44. ♕b4 d3 45. ♖e1! ♕e1 46. ♕d6** [♕ 9/c] **♕e5 47. ♕d3 ♕g5 48. ♕d8 ♕f6 49. ♕d2 ♖f7 50. ♕e3 h5 51. ♕e4 ♖d7 52. ♕a4 ♖d4 53. ♕e8 ♖d8 54. ♕e4 ♖f8 55. ♕e3 ♖f7 56. ♕e4 ♖e7 57. ♕c4 ♖d7 58. ♕a4 ♖d4 59. ♕e8 h4 60. gh4 ♖h4 61. ♕d7 ♔h6** [61... ♕f7 62. ♕f7=] **62. ♕d2 ♖f4** [62... ♕g5 63. ♕g5=] **63. ♕e3 ♕g5 64. ♔f1 ♕f6 65. ♔g2 ♕g5 66. ♔f1 ♖f6 67. ♕g5 ♔g5** [♖ 2/g1] **68. ♔g2 ♔h4 69. ♗e2** [69. ♗b7=] **g5 70. ♗f3 ♖f4 71. ♗e2 g4 72. ♗b5 ♖f6 73. ♗e2 ♖d6 74. ♗b5 ♖d2 75. ♔g1 ♖d1** [75... g3 76. fg3 ♔g3 77. ♗c6=] **76. ♔g2 ♖d6 77. ♗c4??** [77. ♔h2!=] **♖d2–+ 78. ♔g1 g3 79. fg3 ♔g3 80. ♔f1 ♔f3 81. ♔e1 ♔e3 82. ♔f1 ♖f2 83. ♔g1** [83. ♔e1 ♖c2] **♔f3 0 : 1**
[Mi. Cejtlin]

585. E 90

CVETKOVIĆ 2500 – ZONTAH 2455

Aranđelovac 1993

1. c4 ♘f6 2. ♘c3 g6 3. e4 d6 4. d4 ♗g7 5. ♘f3 0–0 6. h3 e5 7. de5 de5 8. ♕d8 ♖d8 9. ♗g5 [9. ♘d5 ♖d7!? 10. ♘f6 ♗f6 11. c5 ♘a6!? (11... ♘c6 12. ♗b5 ♖d8 13. ♗c6 bc6 14. 0–0±) 12. ♗a6 ba6 13. ♗e3 ♗b7 14. ♘d2 ♖ad8 15. ♔e2 ♗c6 16. ♖hd1 ♗b5 17. ♔e1 c6=] **♖e8 10. ♘d5 ♘d5 11. cd5 c6 12. ♗c4 cd5 13. ♗d5 ♘d7** [△ ♘f6; 13... ♘c6] **14. ♘d2 ♘c5 N** [14...

♘b6 15. ♗b3 ♗e6 16. ♔e2! (16. ♗e3! ♗f8 17. ♔e2 ♗d7 18. a4 ♖ac8 19. a5 ♗b5 20. ♔f3 ♘c4 21. ♘c4 ♗c4 22. ♗a4 ♖e6 23. ♖hc1 ♖f6 24. ♔g3 ♖d6 25. ♗a7 ♗h6 26. ♗e3±) ♗b3 17. ab3 a6 18. ♗e3 ♘d7 19. ♘c4 ♗f8 20. ♖hd1 ♘c5 21. ♗c5 ♗c5 22. ♖d7 b6 23. b4±] **15. ♘c4!** [15. ♗e3!? ♘d3 16. ♔e2 ♘f4 (16... ♘b2? 17. a4 △ ♖hb1+−) 17. ♗f4 ef4 18. ♖ac1∞] **♗f8□** [15... ♘d3? 16. ♔d2! ♘f4 (16... ♘f2? 17. ♖hf1+−) 17. ♘d6!±] **16. 0–0** [16. ♔e2!?] **♗e6 17. ♗e6 ♘e6 18. ♗f6± ♘c5 19. f3 ♘d7 20. ♗h4 b5! 21. ♘e3 ♗c5 22. ♗f2 ♘b6 23. ♘g4** [△ ♘f6] **♗f2 24. ♖f2 ♔g7 25. ♖c1** [25. ♖d2!? ⇔d] **h5 26. ♘e3 ♖ac8** [26... h4?! 27. ♖c7±; 27. ♖c5±] **27. ♖fc2** [27. ♖c8!? ♖c8 28. ♖d2 ⇔d] **♖c2** [27... h4?! 28. ♖c7 ♘c4 29. ♘d5!±] **28. ♖c2 ♖c8 29. ♖c8** [29. ♖d2!? ⇔d] **♘c8** [♘♗ 2/j] **30. ♔f2 ♘d6** [30... ♔f6?! 31. ♘d5 ♔g5 (31... ♔e6? 32. ♘c7) 32. g3 (△ h4) h4 33. f4±; 30... h4 31. ♘g4 f6 32. ♔e3 ♔f7 △ ♔e6, f5=; 31. ♔e2±] **31. ♔e2 f5 32. ef5 gf5 33. g4 ♔f6 34. ♔d3 ♔g5 35. b3 e4 36. fe4 fg4 37. hg4 hg4** [37... h4?! 38. e5] **38. e5 ♘f5 39. e6 ♘e7** [39... g3? 40. ♘f5 ♔f5 (40... g2 41. ♘d4!±) 41. e7 g2 42. e8♕ g1♕ 43. ♕e4! ♔f6 (43... ♔g5 44. ♕e3+−) 44. ♕d4+−] **40. ♔d4** [40. ♔e4 ♔f6 41. ♘g4 ♔e6=] **♔f6 41. ♘g4 ♔e6 42. ♔c5 ♘d5! 43. a3** [43. ♘f2 ♘c3 44. a3 ♘b1=] **a6!** [43... ♘c3 44. ♘e3! △ ♘c2] **44. ♔c6 ♘e7 45. ♔b6 ♘f5 46. b4** [46. ♔a6 ♘d4 47. b4 ♘c2=; 47... ♔d5=] **♘d6 47. ♔a6 ♘c4 48. ♔b5 ♘a3 49. ♔c5 ♔d7 50. ♘f6**
1/2 : 1/2 **[Cvetković]**

586.* **E 90**

KRASENKOV 2560 – KUPREJČIK 2560
Passau 1993

1. d4 ♘f6 2. c4 g6 3. ♘c3 ♗g7 4. e4 d6 5. ♘f3 0–0 6. h3 e5 7. d5 a5 [RR 7... ♘h5 8. ♘h2 ♕e8 9. ♗e2 ♘f4 10. ♗f3 f5 11. g3 ♘h3 12. ♗g2 fe4 13. ♗e3 ♕e7 N (13... ♗f5 – 22/720) 14. ♕d2 h6 15. ♘e4 ♘g5 16. ♘g5 hg5 17. ♗g5 ♕f7 18. g4?! ♘d7 19. ♖c1 ♘f6 20. ♕e2 ♗d7 21. ♖c3 c6 22. ♖f3? e4 23. ♖b3 (23. ♖f4 cd5 24. ♗f6 ♗f6 25. g5 ♗c3−+) cd5 24. ♖b7 ♖fb8 25. ♖b8 ♖b8 26. cd5 ♕d5 27. ♗f6 ♕a5! (M. Grünberg 2205 – Szuhanek 2235, Călimăneşti 1993) 28. ♕d2 ♕d2 29. ♔d2 ♗f6∓; 18. ♘f1 Szuhanek] **8. ♗g5 ♘a6 9. ♘d2 N** [9. ♗d3 – 51/602; 9. g4 – 51/603] **♕e8 10. ♗e2 ♗d7 11. h4 c6?!** [11... h6 12. ♗e3 h5] **12. h5 cd5?! 13. ♗f6 ♗f6 14. ♘d5 ♗g5?!** [14... ♕d8 15. ♗g4!±; 14... ♗g7±] **15. ♘b6! ♖d8 16. ♘f3 ♗e7** [16... ♗f6 17. ♕d6±] **17. ♕d2 ♘c5 18. ♘d5!** [18. ♕h6 f6; 18. hg6 fg6] **♘e4!□ 19. ♕h6?** [19. ♕e3! f5!□ 20. hg6 ♗f6! 21. gh7 ♔h8 22. ♖h6!! (△ ♗d3) ♗c6! (22... ♗g7? 23. ♘h4 f4 24. ♕e4 ♗h6 25. ♘g6 ♔g7 26. ♘f8 ♕f8 27. ♗d3+−; 22... ♗e6 23. ♘c7 ♕f7 24. ♘e6 ♕e6 25. g4!+−) 23. ♗d3?! ♗d5 24. cd5 ♘c5 25. ♗f5 e4!∞; 23. 0-0-0±]

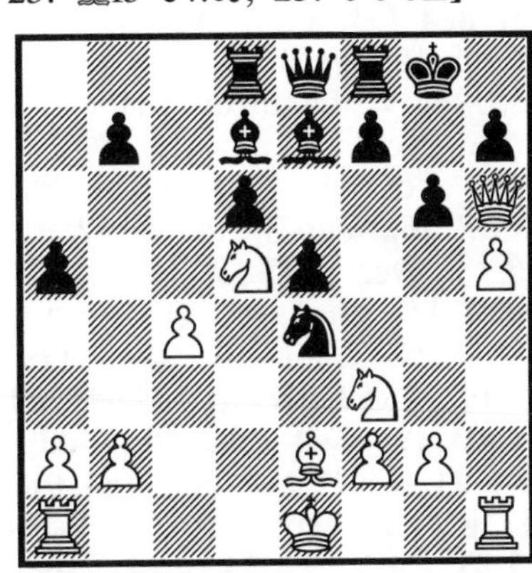

19... g5!! 20. ♗d3! [20. ♘c7? f5! 21. ♘e8 ♖fe8 △ ♗f8∓] **f5** [20... ♗f5? 21. g4 f6 22. gf5 ♘c5 23. ♗c2+− △ 23... ♖f7 24. ♘g5 fg5 25. f6] **21. ♗e4 fe4 22. ♘g5 ♗g5 23. ♕g5 ♔h8 24. ♘e7! ♖f7! 25. ♘g6 ♔g8 26. ♖d1! ♗e6!** [26... ♗c8? 27. ♘e7 ♔f8 28. ♘c8 ♖c8 29. ♖d6; 26... ♗c6? 27. ♘e5 ♖g7 28. ♕f6] **27. ♘f4!** [27. ♘e5? ♖g7 28. ♕f6 ♕e7! 29. ♕e7 ♖e7 ×♘e5] **♖g7 28. ♕d8 ♕d8 29. ♘e6 ♕b6 30. ♘g7 ♔g7** [30... e3?! 31. h6!] **31. 0–0 e3!** [31... ♕b2 32. ♖d6→] **32. fe3 ♕e3 33. ♖f2 ♕b6± 34. ♖d3** [34. ♖d5!? △ c5 Kuprejčik] **♔h6 35. ♖f3 ♕d4 36. b3 ♔h5** [36... e4!?] **37. ♔h2** [△ ♖h3, ♖g3, ♖ff3, ♖g8, ♖h3#] **h6!□** [37... e4? 38. ♖h3 ♔g6 39. ♖g3 ♔h5 40. ♖f5 ♔h6 41. ♖f4 ♔h5 42. ♔h3+−] **38. ♖g3??** [38. ♖h3 ♔g6! 39.

♖g3 ♔h7 40. ♖f7 ♔h8 41. ♖h3 ♕d2!=] **♕f2 0 : 1** **[Krasenkov]**

587.** **E 90**

J. IVANOV 2410 – KALANTARIAN

Val Thorens 1992

1. ♘f3 ♘f6 2. c4 g6 3. ♘c3 ♗g7 4. e4 d6 5. d4 0–0 6. h3 e5 7. d5 ♘a6 8. ♗e3 ♘h5 9. ♘h2 [RR 9. a3 f5 10. b4 ♔h8 N (10... ♘b8 – 50/(634)) 11. ♖c1 c5! 12. dc6 bc6 13. ♗e2 fe4 14. ♘e4 d5 15. cd5 cd5 16. ♗g5 ♕d7 17. ♗a6 (17. ♘c5?! ♘c5 18. ♖c5 ♗b7 19. 0–0 ♖ac8 20. ♖a5 ♗a8∓ G. Flear 2510 – Cvitan 2575, Bern 1993) ♗a6 18. ♘c5 ♕b5 19. ♘a6 ♕a6 20. ♕d5 ♖ac8∞] **♕e8 10. ♗e2 f5 11. ♗h5 N** [11. 0–0 – 51/(602)] **gh5 12. g4!? hg4 13. hg4 fe4!** [13... f4 14. ♗d2 ♗f6 15. f3 ♘c5 16. ♔e2! a5 17. ♗e1± Andonov 2360 – V. Dimitrov 2445, B"lgarija 1992] **14. ♕c2** [14. ♘e4!? ♕g6 15. f3 ♘c5! 16. ♗c5 dc5 17. ♕e2±] **♕g6 15. ♕e4 ♘c5! 16. ♕g6□** [16. ♗c5?! dc5 17. f3 ♗h6 18. ♔e2 ♗d7 19. ♘f1 ♗f4∓] **hg6 17. ♔e2!?** [△ ♖ag1, g5, ♘g4→; 17. ♗c5 dc5 18. ♘e4 ♗h6! 19. ♔e2 (19. g5? ♗f5∓; 19. ♘c5? ♖f4∓) ♗f4=] **e4! 18. ♖ag1 ♘d3 19. ♘e4 ♘b2 20. ♘d2□** [20. g5? ♘c4 21. ♘g4 ♗g4 22. ♖g4 ♘e3–+] **b5! 21. g5!** [21. cb5? ♗d7–+] **bc4 22. ♘g4 c3 23. ♘e4 ♗a6 24. ♔e1 ♖fb8** [24... ♘d3 25. ♔d1 c2 26. ♔c2 ♘b4 27. ♔d2 ♘d5 28. ♘gf6→; 25... ♘b2=] **25. ♘gf6** [25. ♘ef6? ♔f7 26. ♖h7 ♘d3 27. ♔d1 ♖b1? 28. ♔c2 ♖g1 29. ♘h6 ♔f8 30. ♘d7±→; 27... ♖b2–+] **♔f7 26. ♘c3 ♘d3 27. ♔f1?** [27. ♔d1!?] **♖b4** [27... ♘f4 28. ♔e1 ♘h5∓] **28. ♖h7! ♘f4 29. ♔e1 ♖ab8 30. ♖gh1 ♘h5 31. ♖h3!** [△ ♖f3] **♖h8!= 32. ♖h8 ♗h8 33. ♗a7 ♗c8 1/2 : 1/2** **[J. Ivanov]**

588. **E 90**

DAMLJANOVIĆ 2550 – FRANCO 2505

Zaragoza 1993

1. d4 ♘f6 2. c4 c5 3. d5 d6 4. ♘c3 g6 5. e4 ♗g7 6. ♘f3 0–0 7. h3 ♘a6 8. ♗d3 ♘c7 9. 0–0 e5 10. ♗g5 N [10. de6 ♘e6 11. ♖e1 ♘d7 12. ♗f1 ♘e5=; 10. ♗d2 – 20/(690)] **h6 11. ♗d2** [11. ♗h4?! ♕e8] **a6** [⌓ 11... ♘h5; 11... ♘h7] **12. a4 ♘h5 13. ♖e1! ♘f4 14. ♗f4** [14. ♗f1!? f5 15. ef5 ♗f5 (15... gf5 16. ♗f4 ef4 17. ♕d2±) 16. ♗f4 ef4 17. ♗d3±; 14... g5!?] **ef4 15. a5** [15. e5 de5 16. ♘e5 ♘e8! △ ♘d6∞] **♖e8 16. ♗c2 ♗e5 17. ♕d2 ♕f6 18. ♘a4± g5 19. ♖a3 h5 20. ♘e5 ♖e5 21. ♘b6 ♖b8 22. ♗d1** [22. h4 ♘e8! (22... g4 23. g3 △ b4±) 23. hg5 ♕g5 △ ♘f6∞] **♕e7!** [22... ♕g6 23. ♖b3] **23. g3!!** [23. ♗h5 f5∞] **fg3□** [23... ♖e4 24. ♖e4 ♕e4 25. gf4 ♕f4 (25... gf4 26. ♗h5 △ ♖f3) 26. ♕f4 gf4 27. ♗c2! (×♗c8) ♔f8 28. ♖b3 ×b7] **24. ♖g3 h4 25. ♘c8** [25. ♖b3!?] **♖c8 26. ♖g4 ♖e8** [26... ♘e8 27. f4 ♖e4 28. ♖e4 ♕e4 29. fg5] **27. ♗c2?⊕** [27. ♔h1 ♔h7 (27... ♔f8 28. ♗a4 ♖b8 29. ♖eg1+–; 27... ♔h8 28. ♖h4+–) 28. f4 gf4 (28... ♖e4 29. ♗c2+–) 29. ♕f4+–] **♔h7 28. ♔h1 ♖g8 29. ♖eg1 ♖g6 30. f4 gf4 31. ♕f4 ♘e8 32. ♖h4+– ♔g8 33. ♕h6 ♖g1 34. ♔g1 ♖g5 35. ♔f2 ♕f6 36. ♕f6 ♘f6** [♖ 9/i] **37. ♗d1** [37. ♗a4] **♔g7 38. b3 ♖e5 39. ♔e3 ♖e8 40. ♖f4 ♘d7 41. ♖f2 ♘e5 42. h4 ♖b8 43. h5 b5 44. ab6 ♖b6 45. ♖a2 ♔h6 46. ♔d2 ♔g5 47. ♔c3 ♔h6 48. ♗e2 ♔g5 49. ♖a1 ♔f4** [49... ♔h6 50. ♖a4 △ b4] **50. h6 ♔e4 51. ♗d1 ♘g6 52. ♗c2 ♔e5 53. ♖e1 ♔f6 54. ♖e8 1 : 0** **[Damljanović]**

589. **E 90**

M. GRÜNBERG 2205 – SZUHANEK 2235

Timişoara 1993

1. ♘f3 ♘f6 2. c4 g6 3. ♘c3 ♗g7 4. e4 d6 5. d4 0–0 6. h3 c5 7. d5 a6 8. a4 e6 9. ♗d3 ed5 10. ed5 ♖e8 11. ♔f1!? N [11. ♗e3 – 45/738] **♘bd7 12. ♗g5 ♘e5 13. ♘e5 ♖e5 14. ♗f4 ♖e8 15. g4!± ♕c7 16. ♕d2 ♘d7 17. ♗h6 ♗h8 18. ♔g2 b6 19. f4 ♗b7 20. h4?!** [20. ♖he1] **♘f6 21. ♔f3!** [21. ♔g3? ♕d7 22. f5 b5 23. ab5 ab5 24. ♘b5 ♗d5! 25. cd5 c4∓] **♖e7 22. ♗g5 ♖ae8 23. h5 ♕d7 24. f5 b5 25. ab5 ab5**

26. hg6 [26. ♘b5 ♘e4 27. ♗e4 ♖e4] **fg6 27. ♗f6 ♗f6 28. ♘e4 ♗d4 29. f6⊕** [29. fg6 ♖e4! 30. gh7 ♔h8 31. ♗e4 ♖e4 32. ♔e4 ♕g4 33. ♕f4 ♕e2 34. ♔f5 ♗c8 35. ♔g6 ♕e8−+]

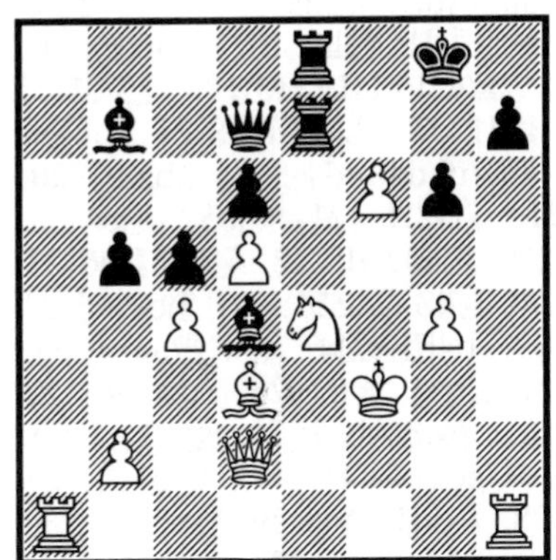

29... ♖e4! 30. ♗e4 ♖e4 31. f7! [31. ♔e4 ♕g4 32. ♔d3 ♕f5 33. ♔e2 ♕e4−+] **♔f8□ 32. ♕h6 ♗g7 33. ♕g7! ♔g7 34. ♖h7 ♔h7 35. f8♘ ♔h6−+** [35... ♔g7? 36. ♘d7 ♖c4 37. ♘b6 △ ♖a7] **36. ♘d7 ♖c4 37. ♘f6 g5 38. ♖a7 ♔g6!** [38... ♖f4 39. ♔g3 ♖f6 40. ♖b7 b4 41. ♖d7] **39. ♖b7 ♔f6 40. ♖b5 ♖f4 41. ♔g3 ♖b4 42. ♖a5 ♖b3 43. ♔f2 ♖b2 44. ♔e3 ♔e5 45. ♖a8 c4 46. ♖g8 ♖b3 47. ♔e2 ♔d4 48. ♖g5 c3 0 : 1** **[Szuhanek]**

590. **E 90**

EPIŠIN 2620 − GHEORGHIU 2475

Genève 1993

1. d4 ♘f6 2. c4 c5 3. d5 d6 4. ♘c3 g6 5. e4 ♗g7 6. ♘f3 0−0 7. h3 e6 8. ♗d3 ♘a6 9. ♗g5 ♘c7 N [9... ed5 − 50/637] **10. a4 ♕e7?! 11. 0−0 h6 12. ♗h4 e5** [12... g5 13. ♗g3 ♘h5 14. ♗h2 ♘f4 15. ♗f4 gf4 16. e5! ed5 17. cd5 ♗e5 18. ♘e5 ♕e5 19. ♖e1±] **13. a5 ♕e8 14. ♗c2! ♘d7 15. g4!± ♗f6 16. ♗g3 ♔g7 17. ♕d2 ♕e7** [⌓ 17... ♕d8] **18. ♔g2 ♖h8 19. h4 ♕d8 20. ♘d1! b5 21. ab6 ♘b6 22. ♘e3 ♘a6 23. ♖h1 ♘b4 24. ♗d1 ♗d7 25. ♗e2 a5** [⌓ 25... ♗e7±] **26. g5! hg5 27. hg5 ♗e7** [27... ♗g5? 28. ♘g5 ♕g5 29. ♘f5 ♔f6 30. ♕g5 ♔g5 31. ♘d6+−]

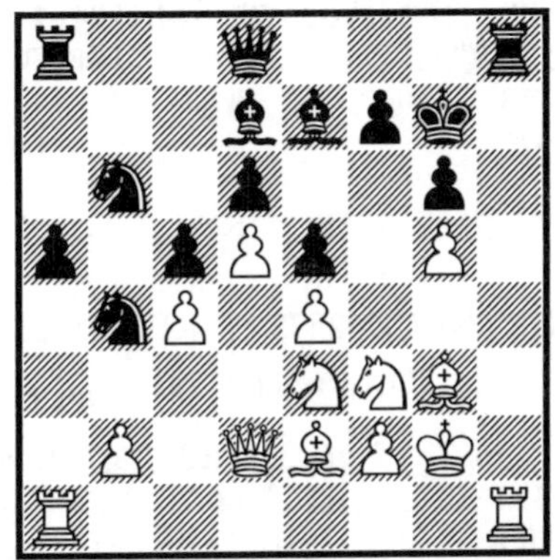

28. ♘e5! de5 29. ♗e5 f6 30. ♗c3! ♘a4□ 31. ♖a4! ♖h1 32. ♔h1 ♗a4 33. ♘g4+− ♕h8 34. ♔g1 ♔f8 35. gf6 ♗d6 36. e5 ♗c7 37. ♕e3! ♘a6 38. e6 ♗d6 39. e7 1 : 0 **[Epišin]**

591. **E 90**

ZSU. POLGÁR 2560 − MARIN 2515

Budapest (zt) 1993

1. d4 ♘f6 2. c4 c5 3. d5 d6 4. ♘c3 g6 5. e4 ♗g7 6. ♗d3 0−0 7. h3 e6 8. ♘f3 ♘a6 9. ♗g5 h6 10. ♗e3 ♘c7 11. ♕d2 ♔h7 12. e5?! de5 13. ♗c5 ♖e8 14. d6 ♘a6 15. ♗e3 ♘d7 16. h4 f5 17. h5 f4 18. ♗g6 ♔g8 19. ♘h4?! [19. ♗e8∞] **fe3 20. ♕e3 ♖f8 21. ♘e4** [21. ♕e4 (△ ♗h7, ♘g6) ♘f6 22. ♕e5 ♕b6 (△ ♕f2) 23. 0−0 ♘g4!? 24. ♕e4 ♖f2 25. ♗h7 ♔f8 26. ♘g6 ♔e8; 21. ♕d3 e4 22. ♕e4 (22. ♘e4 ♘e5) ♘f6] **♘ac5!∓ 22. 0-0-0 ♕b6 23. ♖h3 ♖f4 24. ♘c3 ♖d4** [24... ♖f2?! 25. ♕f2!? ♘b3 26. ab3 ♕f2 27. ♘e4$\overline{\overline{\infty}}$; 24... ♖c4] **25. ♗c2 ♖d1 26. ♘d1 e4** [26... ♕d6 27. b4!?] **27. ♕f4** [27. ♖g3 ♕d6 28. ♕h6 ♕g3−+] **♘e5 28. ♔b1 ♕d6** [28... ♘ed3! 29. ♗d3 ♘d3 30. ♕e4 ♘b2 31. ♖b3 ♘d1!−+] **29. ♖g3 ♘f7 30. ♕e3 ♗d7** [30... ♘g5 31. ♖g5!?] **31. ♖g6 ♕e5 32. g4 ♖d8** [△ ♗a4] **33. ♘c3 ♗c6 34. g5 hg5 35. h6 ♘h6 36. ♘f3** [36. ♖g5 ♘f5−+] **♕f4** [⌓ 36... ♕f5 37. ♖g5 ♕f3 38. ♖g7 ♔g7 39. ♕g5 ♔h7−+] **37. ♕c5 ♕f3??⊕** [37... ef3 38. ♕e7 ♘f7−+] **38. ♖g7 ♔g7 39. ♕g5 ♔f7 40. ♕d8 ♕f2 41. b4 ♕f1 42. ♔b2 ♕c4 43. ♕c7 ♔g6 44. ♗e4 ♘f5 45. a3!= ♕d4 46. ♗c6 bc6 47. ♕c6 ♕d2 48. ♔b1**

♕e1 49. ♔b2 ♕d2 50. ♔b1 ♕e1 [50... ♘d4 51. ♕e4 ♔g5 52. ♕e5 ♔g4 53. ♕e4 ♔h3 (53... ♔g3? 54. ♕d4) 54. ♕h1]
1/2 : 1/2 **[Marin]**

592.* !N **E 91**

HERTNECK 2575 – REICH 2375
Österreich 1993

1. d4 ♘f6 2. c4 g6 3. ♘c3 ♗g7 4. e4 d6 5. ♘f3 0–0 6. ♗e2 ♗g4 7. ♗e3 ♘fd7 8. ♕d2 [RR 8. 0–0 ♘c6 9. d5 ♗f3 10. ♗f3 ♘a5 11. ♗e2 ♗c3 12. bc3 e5 13. de6 fe6 14. ♗h6! N (14. f4 – 15/624) ♖f7 15. f4 *a)* 15... ♘b6? 16. ♗g4! ♕e8 17. ♕f3 ♘d7 (17... ♘c6 18. ♕h3 ♘d8 19. ♗g5 h5!? 20. ♗e2□±) 18. ♕h3 ♘c5 19. f5!± Sbarra – L. Pantaleoni, corr. 1992; *b)* 15... ♘f6 16. e5 ♘e4 17. ♕d4 ♕h4? 18. ♕e4 ♕h6 19. ♗g4±; 17... d5!?; 17... ♘c5! L. Pantaleoni] **e5 9. 0-0-0 N** [9. d5] **♘c6** [9... ed4 10. ♗d4 ♗d4 11. ♘d4 ♗e2 12. ♘de2⩲; 9... ♗f3 10. ♗f3 ed4 (10... ♘c6 11. de5 ♘ce5 12. ♗e2⩲) 11. ♗d4 ♗d4 12. ♕d4 ♘e5! 13. ♗e2! ♕g5 14. ♕d2 ♕g2 15. f4=∞] **10. d5 ♗f3 11. dc6!** [11. gf3? ♘d4 12. ♗d4 ed4 13. ♘b5 ♕h4 14. ♔b1 a6! 15. ♘d4 ♕f2∓; 11. ♗f3? ♘d4 12. ♗d4 ed4 13. ♘b5 ♘e5 14. ♗e2 c5 15. dc6 ♘c6∞] **♗e2 12. cb7 ♖b8?!** [12... ♗d1 13. ba8♕ ♕a8 14. ♖d1 ♖b8 (14... f5? 15. ♕d5! ♕d5 16. ♘d5±) 15. ♕d5 (15. ♕c2!? △ 16. ♖d5, 16. ♖d3) ♕b7 16. ♕b7 ♖b7 17. b3⩲] **13. ♕e2** [13. ♘e2 ♖b7 14. c5! ♘f6□ 15. f3 ♕b8 16. cd6 cd6 17. ♘c3 ♖c8 18. ♔b1⩲] **♖b7 14. c5! ♖b4!?** [14... dc5 *a)* 15. ♕a6!? ♖b4 (15... ♖b6 16. ♕a7 ♖d6 17. ♘b5±) 16. ♕a7 (16. ♕c6? ♖d4=∞) ♖d4 17. ♔b1!; 16... ♖e8 △ 17. ♗c5? ♕g5 18. ♗e3 ♕g2 19. ♕c7 ♘f6=∞; *b)* 15. ♗c5 ♖e8 (15... ♕g5 16. ♗e3 ♕g2? 17. h3+–) 16. ♕a6? ♘c5 17. ♖d8 ♖d8 18. ♕c6 ♘d3 19. ♔b1 ♖b2 20. ♔a1 ♖db8!∞ △ ♘b4-c2; 16. ♗e3±] **15. cd6** [15. ♕a6] **cd6 16. ♕a6?!** [16. ♖d6 ♕c7 17. ♖hd1 ♘c5 18. ♗c5 ♕c5 19. ♖1d5±] **♘b6** [16... ♕b8? 17. ♕d6 ♖b2 18. ♕b8+–] **17. a3** [17. ♕a5? ♖b2∓; 17. ♕a7 ♘c4 18. b3 ♕c8! (△ ♖b7) 19. ♖d3 ♖b7 20. ♕a4 ♘e3 21. fe3 ♖c7 22. ♔b2 d5? 23. ♘d5 ♖c2 24. ♔b1±; 22... ♕g4=∞] **♖d4□ 18. ♔b1!** [18. ♕a7? ♘c4 19. ♗d4 ed4 20. ♘d5 ♕g5=∞; 18. ♗d4?! ed4 △ ♕g5-g2=∞] **♕a8!** [18... ♖d1? 19. ♖d1± ×a7, d6; 18... ♕h4 19. g3! ♕g4 (19... ♖d1 20. ♖d1 ♕h2 21. ♖d6±) 20. ♗d4 ed4 21. ♕e2!±] **19. f3** [19. ♖he1!?] **♖b8!** [19... ♖d1? 20. ♖d1 ♘c8 21. ♘b5±; 19... ♖c8? 20. ♗d4 ed4 21. ♘b5±] **20. ♗d4 ed4 21. ♘a2!?** [21. ♘b5? ♘c4 22. ♖c1 d5=∞; 21. ♘a4? d5 22. ♘b6 ♖b6 23. ♕d3 ♕b7 24. ♖d2 ♖b3=∞; 21. ♘e2 d5 22. ♘d4 ♘c4 23. b4□ ♖b6 24. ♕a4 ♘e3 (24... a5? 25. ♖he1 ♕b7 26. ed5 ab4 27. ♖e8 ♗f8 28. ♕a8! ba3 29. ♔a1±) 25. ♖d3 ♘g2 26. ed5 ♘f4 (26... ♕d5=∞) 27. ♖e1 ♖b8! 28. ♖dd1 ♘d5 29. ♕c6! a5! 30. ♕a8 ♖a8 31. ♘b5 ♘c3 32. ♘c3 ♗c3 33. ♖e4 ab4 34. ab4 ♖b8=] **d5 22. ♖he1 ♘c4** [22... de4? 23. ♖e4 ♘d5 24. ♖dd4 (24. ♖ed4?! ♘e3) ♗d4 25. ♖d4±] **23. ♘b4 ♖b6?** [23... ♘e3? 24. ♘d5±; 23... d3! 24. ed5 ♘b2 *a)* 25. ♕c6 ♘d1 26. ♖d1 ♖b7! 27. ♖e1 ♔f8□ 28. ♕c5 ♔g8 29. ♔a2? d2 30. ♖d1 a5 31. ♘d3 ♕b8↑ 32. ♕c2; 29. ♕c6=; *b)* 25. d6 ♘d1 26. ♖d1 ♕d5! 27. ♕c8 (27. ♕d3? ♕e5!→) ♗f8 28. ♕b8 ♕b3 29. ♔c1 ♕c3= V. Atlas] **24. ♕a4 d3** [24... a5? 25. ed5 ♖b8 26. ♘d3 ♘e3 (26... ♕d5 27. ♖e8±) 27. ♕c6 ♘d1 28. ♖d1±] **25. ed5 ♔f8□** [25... ♖b8? 26. ♕c6±] **26. ♕d7** [26. ♘d3 ♘b2 27. ♘b2 ♖b2 28. ♔c1 ♕c8! 29. ♕c6 ♕b8→] **♗b2!** [26... ♗f6? 27. ♖d3 a5 (27... ♘e5 28. ♖e5 ♗e5 29. d6±) 28. ♕c7 ab4 29. ♕c4+–; 26... ♘b2? 27. ♖c1+–; 26... ♖b7? 27. ♕c6 ♘b2 28. ♖c1! ♗d4 29. ♖e4!! d2 30. ♕c8 ♕c8 31. ♖c8 ♔g7 32. ♖d4 d1♕ 33. ♖d1 ♘d1 34. ♔c2±] **27. ♖e7! ♗d4?** [27... ♘e5□ *a)* 28. ♕c7 ♗a3 29. ♕e5 f6! (29... ♖b4? 30. ♔a2 ♗b2 31. ♖f7 ♔f7 32. ♕e6+–) 30. ♖h7! ♔g8 31. ♕e7 ♖b4 32. ♔a1□ ♗b2 (32... ♖b1 33. ♖b1 ♗e7 34. ♖e7∞) 33. ♔b1 ♗a3=; *b)* 28. ♕a7 ♕a7 29. ♖a7 ♗a3! 30. ♖a3 ♖b4 31. ♔c1 (31. ♔a2 ♔e7!=∞) ♖d4! 32. ♔d2 ♖d5 33. ♔e3 ♘c4 34. ♔e4 ♖d8!= △ f5, d2 V. Atlas] **28. ♖f7 ♔g8 29. ♖e7!** [29... ♖b8 30. ♕e6 ♔h8 31. ♕f7+–] **1 : 0** **[Hertneck]**

593. E 92

V. SEGAL – J. WEST 2205
USA 1993

1. d4 ♘f6 2. ♘f3 g6 3. c4 ♗g7 4. ♘c3 0–0 5. e4 d6 6. ♗e2 e5 7. ♗e3 ♕e7 8. de5 de5 9. ♘d5 ♕d8 10. ♗c5 ♘e4 11. ♗e7 ♕d7 12. ♗f8 ♔f8 13. ♕d3 f5 [13... ♘c5 14. ♕e3 ♕d6 15. ♖d1±] **14. ♕a3 N** [14. ♖d1 – 56/683] **♔g8 15. ♕e7 ♘a6** [15... c6 16. ♘e5 ♕e7 17. ♘e7 ♔f8 18. ♘c8 ♗e5 19. f3 ♘c5 20. 0-0-0 ♘ba6 21. ♖d8 ♔g7 22. ♖hd1±] **16. ♖d1 ♕e7** [16... c6? 17. ♕d7 ♗d7 18. ♘c7!] **17. ♘e7 ♔f8 18. ♘c8 ♖c8 19. 0–0± ♘ac5 20. ♖fe1 ♘a4 21. ♘d2 ♘d2 22. ♖d2 e4 23. ♖b1 ♔e7 24. ♗d1 ♘c5 25. ♗c2 a5 26. ♖d5 b6 27. b3 c6** [27... ♘e6 28. ♖e1 (△ f3) ♘d4 29. ♗e4!±] **28. ♖dd1 ♘e6** [△ ♘d4] **29. b4!± ♘d4?** [29... ab4 30. ♖b4 ♗d4 31. ♔f1±] **30. ba5!+– ♘c2** [30... ba5 31. ♖b7] **31. ab6 ♘d4 32. ♔f1 ♖b8 33. a4 ♘e6 34. a5 ♘c5 35. ♖d2! ♗c3** [⌓ 35... ♖b7] **36. ♖a2 ♘a6 37. ♔e2⊕** [⌓ 37. b7 △ ♖b6+–] **♖b7 38. g3 ♗d4 39. h4 h5 40. f3 e3 41. ♔d3 c5 42. g4! hg4 43. fg4 fg4 44. ♖g2 ♔f7 45. ♖g4 ♖e7 46. ♖f1 ♔g7 47. ♔e2 ♗c3 48. h5 ♘b8 49. ♖g6 ♔h7 50. ♖f8 ♘d7 51. a6! ♘f8 52. a7 ♘g6 53. hg6 ♔g6 54. a8♕ ♗d4 55. b7 ♖f7 56. ♕g8 1 : 0 [V. Segal]**

594. E 92

TIMMAN 2635 – LJUBOJEVIĆ 2605
Linares 1993

1. d4 ♘f6 2. ♘f3 g6 3. c4 ♗g7 4. ♘c3 0–0 5. e4 d6 6. ♗e2 e5 7. ♗e3 ed4 8. ♘d4 ♖e8 9. f3 c6 10. ♕d2 d5 11. ed5 cd5 12. 0–0 ♘bd7 N [12... ♘c6 – 54/596] **13. ♖ad1 ♘b6 14. c5 ♘c4 15. ♗c4 dc4 16. ♕f2!± ♕e7 17. ♖fe1 a6?** [17... ♗d7□ 18. ♘db5±] **18. ♗h6 ♕f8** [18... ♕e1 19. ♖e1 ♖e1 20. ♕e1 ♗h6 21. ♕e7+–] **19. ♗g7 ♔g7 20. ♖e8 ♕e8 21. ♘de2!+– ♗e6** [21... ♕e5 22. ♖d8] **22. ♕d4 ♕d7 23. ♕e5 ♕e7 24. ♘e4 ♖e8 25. ♘2c3 h5 26. h4⊙ ♗f5 27. ♕e7 ♖e7 28. ♘f6 1 : 0 [Timman]**

595. E 92

NENAŠEV 2565 – KANCLER 2445
Biškek (zt) 1993

1. d4 d6 2. ♘f3 g6 3. c4 ♗g7 4. ♘c3 ♘f6 5. e4 0–0 6. ♗e2 e5 7. d5 a5 8. ♗g5 h6 9. ♗h4 ♘a6 10. ♘d2 ♕e8 11. 0–0 ♘h7 12. a3 ♗d7 13. ♘b5 h5 14. f3 ♗h6 15. ♕c2 ♕b8 N [15... f5 – 56/688] **16. ♖ab1 c6** [16... a4 17. b4 ab3 18. ♘b3±] **17. ♘c3 ♗g5 18. ♗f2 c5 19. ♘b3 b6** [19... a4 20. ♘c1 ♘c7 21. b4 ab3 22. ♕b3 △ a4] **20. ♘c1 h4 21. ♘d3 ♘f6 22. b4 ab4 23. ab4 ♕d8** [23... cb4? 24. ♘b4 ♘c5 25. ♘c6±] **24. ♖b2!? ♘h5 25. bc5 bc5 26. ♖a1 ♘f4 27. ♘f4 ♗f4** [27... ♘b4!? 28. ♖a8 ♕a8 29. ♕d1 ♗f4 (29... ef4? 30. e5+–) 30. ♗h4 ♗e3 31. ♗f2 ♗d4=∞] **28. ♕b1 ♗c8?** [28... ♘b4! 29. ♖a8 ♕a8 30. ♗h4 ♗e3 31. ♗f2 ♗d4=∞] **29. ♖a3! h3?!** [29... ♗g5 △ ♗e7] **30. g3 ♗g5 31. ♗f1 ♔g7⊕ 32. ♕a1 ♔g8 33. ♖ba2 ♕b6 34. ♘a4?!** [34. ♘b5 △ ♗h3] **♕c7 35. ♘b2 ♕b6 36. ♘d3** [36. ♘a4! △ ♘c3-b5] **f6 37. f4 ♗h6 38. ♕d1** [38. f5 gf5 39. ♗h3 fe4 40. ♗c8 ♖fc8 41. ♖a6 ♖a6 42. ♖a6 ♕b3 43. ♘b2 ♖b8=∞] **♗g7** [38... f5!?±] **39. ♗e3 ♖b8 40. ♖b2 ♕c7 41. ♖b8 ♕b8** [41... ♘b8 42. ♘f2±] **42. f5 gf5 43. ef5 ♘b4 44. ♗h3 ♘d3 45. ♕d3 ♕b4 46. ♖b3 ♕e1 47. ♗f1 ♗a6 48. ♕c2 ♗c8 49. g4 ♗d7** [49... ♕h4 50. h3 ♗h6 51. ♕f2] **50. ♗f2 ♕a5 51. ♕b2 ♗h6 52. ♖b6 ♗c1 53. ♕b1 ♗f4 54. ♖d6 ♗a4 55. ♕b6 ♕d2 56. ♖f6 ♖f6** [56... ♗h2 57. ♔g2 ♖f6 58. ♕f6 ♗c2 59. ♕h4 ♗f4 60. ♕d8 ♔f7 61. ♕c7 ♔g8 62. ♕c5+–] **57. ♕f6 ♗e3 58. ♕h4 ♗d4 59. ♗d4 cd4 60. ♕d8 ♔f7 61. ♕c7 ♔g8 62. ♕e5 d3 63. f6 1 : 0 [Nenašev]**

596. E 92

D. GUREVICH 2490 –
YERMOLINSKY 2615
USA (ch) 1992

1. ♘f3 ♘f6 2. c4 g6 3. ♘c3 ♗g7 4. e4 d6 5. d4 0–0 6. ♗e2 e5 7. d5 a5 8. ♗g5 h6 9. ♗h4 ♘a6 10. ♘d2 ♕e8 11. a3 ♗d7 12. b3 ♘h7 13. 0–0 h5 14. f3 ♗h6 15.

♖a2 ♗e3 16. ♔h1 ♔g7?! N [16... f5 17. ef5 gf5 18. f4 (18. ♕b1 – 45/(747)) ef4 19. ♗h5 ♕e5] **17. ♕b1! f5 18. ef5 gf5 19. b4⩲** [×a6] **♕g6 20. ♘d1 ♕h6** [⌓ 20... ♗g5] **21. ♘b3± ab4 22. ♘e3 ♕e3 23. ♗f2 ♕g5** [23... ♕f4 24. g3] **24. ab4 ♘b4□ 25. ♖a8 ♖a8 26. ♘d4?** [26. ♘c1! c5 (26... ♖a4 27. ♗d1; 26... ♕d2 27. ♖d1) 27. dc6 ♘c6 28. ♕b7 ♕d8 29. f4] **ed4 27. ♗d4 ♔f7 28. f4 ♕h6 29. ♕b4 b6⩲ 30. ♗b2 ♘f6⊕ 31. ♕c3 ♘e4 32. ♕d4** [32. ♗h5? ♕h5 33. ♕g7 ♔e8 34. ♕g8 ♔e7 35. ♕a8 ♕e2–+] **h4 33. ♔g1 ♖a2!** [△ ♕f6] **34. ♖a1 ♖a1 35. ♗a1 ♔e7! 36. ♕e3 ♔d8 37. ♗f3 ♔c8!= 38. ♗d4** [38. ♗e4 fe4 39. ♕e4 ♕h5 40. ♗f6 h3=∞] **♔b7 39. h3 ♕g6 40. ♕e1 ♕h6 41. ♕e3** [41. ♗e4? ♕f4] **♕g6 42. ♗d1 ♕h7 43. ♗b2 ♕g6 44. ♗c2 c5!** [△ 45... ♕g3 D. Gurevich, 45... b5] **45. dc6 ♗c6 46. ♗d3□ ♘c5 47. ♕e7** [47. ♗f1 ♗e4=] **♔a6 48. ♗f1 ♕g3 49. ♗f6?** [49. ♕d6 ♕e3 50. ♔h2 ♕g3 51. ♔g1=] **♘e4 50. ♗h4?** [50. ♗d4 ♘d2! 51. c5 b5 52. ♗b5□ ♔b5 53. ♕e2 ♘c4 54. cd6 ♕f4–+; 50. c5 b5 51. ♕c7 ♕e3 52. ♔h2 ♕f4 53. ♔g1 ♕f2 54. ♔h2 ♕c5 55. ♗h4 ♗d5∓] **♕e3 51. ♔h2 ♕f4 52. ♔g1 ♕e3 53. ♔h2 ♘g3!–+ 54. ♗e2** [54. ♗d3 ♕d3 55. ♗g3 ♕d2] **♕e7 55. ♗e7 ♘e2 56. ♗d6 ♔b7 57. ♗e5 f4 58. h4 ♗e8 59. ♔h3 ♗h5 60. ♗f6 ♔c6 61. ♗e5 ♔c5 62. ♗c7 f3! 63. gf3 ♗f3 64. ♗d8 ♗h5 65. ♔g2 ♘f4 66. ♔f2 ♘e6 0 : 1 [Yermolinsky]**

597. !N E 93

D. GUREVICH 2495 – GOLUBEV 2490

Genève 1993

1. d4 ♘f6 2. c4 g6 3. ♘c3 ♗g7 4. e4 d6 5. ♗e2 0–0 6. ♘f3 e5 7. d5 ♘bd7 8. ♗e3 ♘c5 9. ♘d2 a5 10. a3! N [10. 0–0 – 49/(740); 10. g4!?] **♘e8** [10... ♗d7 11. b4⩲↑《] **11. 0–0** [11. b4 ab4 12. ab4 ♖a1 13. ♕a1 ♘a6 △ 14. ♕a3 f5 15. f3 ♗h6] **f5 12. f3 a4! 13. b4!** [13. ♗c5 dc5 14. ♘a4 ♗h6!=∞] **ab3 14. ♘b3 ♘b3 15. ♕b3 b6 16. a4⩲ f4 17. ♗d2** [17. ♗f2 g5] **h5 18. a5 ba5 19. ♘d1!** [19. ♘b5 g5⇆》] **a4** [19... ♘f6 20. ♗a5; 19... g5 20. ♘f2 ♘f6 21. h3 ♘d7; 21. ♗a5!] **20. ♖a4 ♖a4 21. ♕a4 g5 22. ♘f2 ♘f6 23. h3± ♗d7 24. ♕a3 ♕a8 25. ♕a5!? ♕a5 26. ♗a5 ♖c8 27. ♖d1** [27. c5?! dc5 △ 28. ♘d3 ♗b5, △ 28. ♗c4 ♘e8] **c5 28. dc6 ♖c6 29. ♘d3! ♖c4!?** [29... ♗e6 30. ♘b4; 29... ♖a6 30. ♗d8 ♖a2 31. ♗f1; 30. ♗c7 △ 30... ♘e8 31. ♗d8 ♗f6 32. ♘b4+–] **30. ♘e5 ♖c5 31. ♘d7 ♖a5 32. ♗c4! ♔h8** [32... d5 33. ♗d5!] **33. ♖d6 ♘d7 34. ♖d7** [♖ 9/j] **♗e5 35. ♗e6 ♖c5 36. ♗f5!? ♖c1?!⊕** [36... ♔g8] **37. ♔f2 ♖c2 38. ♔f1 ♖c1 39. ♔e2 ♖c2 40. ♔d3 ♖g2 41. ♔c4** [41. ♖e7!±] **♗b2! 42. ♖h7!? ♔g8 43. ♖h5 ♗f6 44. ♖h6** [44. ♔d5 ♔f7] **♔f7 45. ♖h7 ♗g7 46. e5 ♖b2!** [46... ♖a2? 47. e6 ♔f6 48. e7 ♔e7 49. ♖g7 ♔f6 50. ♗b1+–] **47. e6** [47. ♔c5!? ♖a2] **♔f6 48. ♗e4 ♖b8 49. ♔d5?!** [49. h4! gh4 50. ♗c6!] **♖d8 50. ♔c6 ♗f8!= 51. ♖d7 ♗e7 52. ♖d8** [52. ♔c7 ♖h8] **1/2 : 1/2 [Golubev]**

598. E 93

NENAŠEV 2565 – JURTAEV 2540

Biškek (zt) 1993

1. d4 ♘f6 2. c4 g6 3. ♘c3 ♗g7 4. e4 d6 5. ♘f3 0–0 6. ♗e2 e5 7. d5 ♘bd7 8. ♗g5 h6 9. ♗h4 ♖e8!? N [9... g5 – 46/814] **10. ♘d2** [10. 0–0!? ♘f8 11. ♘e1 g5 12. ♗g3 ♘g6 13. ♘c2±] **♘f8 11. f3 c5 12. a3 b6 13. b4** [13. ♗f2 ♘h5 △ f5; 13. 0–0; 13. ♘f1]

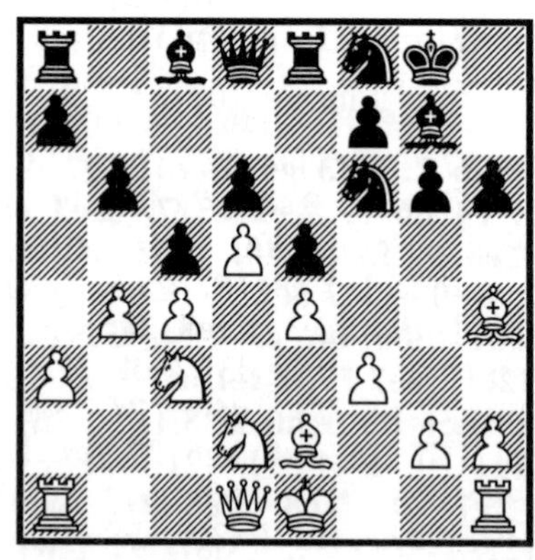

13... ♘d5!? 14. ♗d8 ♘c3 15. ♕c2 ♘e2 16. ♔e2 ♘e6 17. ♔f2 ♖d8 18. ♖he1?! [18. ♘f1±] **♘d4 19. ♕d3 ♗e6** [19... f5!?

20. ♘f1 f4] **20. ♘f1 b5 21. ♘e3** [21. cb5? c4∓] **bc4 22. ♘c4 cb4?** [22... d5! 23. ed5 ♖d5 24. ♖ad1∞] **23. ab4 ♖ab8** [23... d5? 24. ed5 ♖d5 25. ♘b6] **24. ♘e3 ♖b4 25. ♖eb1! ♖db8 26. ♖b4 ♖b4 27. ♖b1!** [27. ♖a7 ♖b2 28. ♔f1 ♖b3 29. ♕d2 h5⩱] **♖a4?!** [27... a5 28. ♘d5 ♗d5 29. ed5±] **28. ♕c3 h5** [⌓ 28... ♖a6 29. ♖b2±] **29. ♖a1 ♘b5 30. ♕b2+− ♖a1 31. ♕a1 ♗f8 32. ♕a6 ♘d4 33. ♕a7 ♘b3 34. ♕a8 ♘c5 35. g3 ♘d3 36. ♔e2 ♘c1 37. ♔d2 ♘b3 38. ♔e1 ♘c5 39. ♔e2 ♔g7 40. ♕d8** [40. f4? ef4 41. gf4 ♘d7±] **♘b7** [40... ♘d7!?] **41. ♕e8 ♘c5 42. ♘d5! ♘d7** [42... ♗d5 43. ed5 △ ♔e3, g4] **43. ♘c7 ♗c4 44. ♔f2 ♘f6 45. ♕c6** [45. ♕a4 ♗e6 (45... d5 46. ♕c6; 45... ♗d3 46. ♕b3) 46. ♘e6 fe6 47. ♕a7 ♔g8 48. ♕c7 g5 49. ♔g2 g4 50. h3] **♗b3 46. ♕b5 ♗d1** [46... ♗a2 47. ♕a4 ♗e6 − 45. ♕a4] **47. ♕c4 ♗e7 48. ♘b5 d5** [48... ♘e8 49. ♕a2 ♗d8 50. ♘c3] **49. ed5 ♗d8 50. ♘c3 ♗c2 51. ♕e2**
1 : 0 **[Nenašev]**

599. **E 94**

B. MAKSIMOVIĆ 2325
− DAMLJANOVIĆ 2550
Cetinje 1993

1. d4 ♘f6 2. c4 g6 3. ♘c3 ♗g7 4. e4 d6 5. ♘f3 0−0 6. ♗e2 c6 7. 0−0 e5 8. de5 de5 9. ♕d8 ♖d8 10. ♘e5 ♘a6 N [10... ♘e4 11. ♘e4 ♗e5 12. ♗g5 ♖e8 13. ♗f3 ♗f5!? (13... ♗e6 − 47/(732)) 14. ♘f6 ♗f6 15. ♗f6 ♘d7] **11. ♘d3!± ♖e8** [11... ♗e6 12. ♘f4] **12. e5** [12. f3] **♘d7 13. f4 f6 14. ♘e4 fe5 15. ♘d6** [15. f5] **♖e7 16. ♗g4! e4 17. ♘c8** [17. ♘e5 ♘e5! 18. ♗c8 (18. ♘c8 ♖c8 19. ♗c8?! ♘c4⩱; 19. fe5∞) ♘c4 19. ♗b7 ♖b7 20. ♘c4 (20. ♘b7? ♖b8∓) ♗d4!∞] **♖c8 18. ♘e5 ♘ac5** [⌓ 18... ♘e5] **19. ♗e3 ♖ce8 20. ♘d7** [20. ♖ad1 ♘e5! 21. fe5 ♘d3] **♘d7 21. ♖ad1! ♘f6 22. ♗e2 b6 23. ♖d6 c5 24. f5!± ♖d7 25. ♖c6 ♖f7 26. fg6 hg6 27. a4** [△ a5 ×《] **♔h7 28. a5** [28. b3! △ a5] **ba5 29. ♖c5 ♖b7□ 30. ♖b5?!** [30. ♖a5! ♖b2 31. ♖e1± △ ♖a7] **♖b5 31. cb5 ♘d5 32. ♗a7 ♖e7!± 33. ♗f2** [33. ♗c5 ♖c7!] **♗b2 34. ♗c4 e3! 35. ♗d5 ef2 36. ♔f2** [♖ 9/j] **♗d4 37. ♔g3 ♖e3 38. ♔g4 ♖e5 39. ♗c6 ♔h6 40. ♖f8 ♖c5 41. ♖a8 ♖c4 42. ♔f3 a4 43. ♖a6 ♔g7 44. ♗e4 g5□ 45. b6** [45. ♖g6] **♗e5 46. h3** [46. g3! g4 47. ♔g4 ♖e4 48. ♔f5 ♖e2 49. ♖a4 (△ ♖e4) ♗d6□ 50. ♖d4 ♗c5!=; 47. ♔e3!±] **g4! 47. hg4 ♖c3 48. ♔e2 a3 49. b7 ♖b3 50. g5 ♖b2 51. ♔f3 a2 52. ♗d5 ♖b7 53. ♖a2 ♖d7 54. ♗e4 ♖f7 55. ♔e2 ♗f4** **1/2 : 1/2**
[B. Maksimović]

600.* **!N** **E 94**

KIŠNËV 2510 − DIETRICH 2295
Dortmund (open) 1993

1. d4 ♘f6 2. c4 g6 3. ♘c3 ♗g7 4. e4 d6 5. ♗e2 0−0 6. ♘f3 e5 7. 0−0 ed4 8. ♘d4 ♖e8 9. f3 ♘h5 [RR 9... ♘c6 10. ♗e3 ♘h5!? N (10... ♘d4 − 18/661) 11. ♖c1 (11. ♘d5 ♘d4 12. ♗d4 ♗h6 △ c6∞; 11. g4 ♘d4 12. ♗d4 ♘f4=; 11. f4 ♘f6 12. ♗f3 ♘g4! 13. ♗g4 ♗g4 14. ♕d2 ♘a5! 15. b3 c5 16. ♘db5 a6 17. ♘d6 ♗c3 18. ♕c3 ♕d6 19. ♕a5 b6 20. ♕d2 ♕d2 21. ♗d2 ♖ad8 22. ♗c3 ♖e4=; 11. c5 ♘d4 12. ♗d4 dc5 13. ♗c5 ♘f4=; 11. ♕d2 f5 12. ♘c6 bc6 13. ef5 ♕h4! 14. ♖ad1 ♗f5 15. g4 ♗c3 16. ♕c3 ♕e7 17. ♗h6 ♕e2 18. gh5 ♕e5=) f5 12. c5! (12. ♘d5!? ♘d4 13. ♗d4 ♗h6 14. ♖c2 c6⇆) ♘d4 13. ♗d4 dc5 14. ♗c5 (14. ♗g7 ♔g7∞) ♘f4 15. ♗c4 ♗e6 16. ♘d5 (16. ♗e6 ♘e6 17. ♗e3 ♗c3! 18. ♖c3 fe4 19. fe4 ♕d1 20. ♖d1 ♖ad8 21. ♖cd3 ♖d3 22. ♖d3 ♔f8= Morozevič, Jurkov) ♘d5 17. ed5 ♗f7∞ Zločevskij 2455 − Morozevič 2440, Alusta 1993] **10. g4 ♘f6 11. ♗e3 h5 12. g5 ♘h7 13. f4** [13. h4!?] **♗h3! N** [13... a6 − 51/613] **14. ♖e1** [14. ♖f2!?] **♘a6?!** [14... ♘c6! 15. ♕d2 f6∞] **15. ♗f3** [15. ♗h5? gh5 16. ♕h5 ♗d7∓ △ 17. f5? ♗d4] **♘c5 16. ♖c1** [△ ♖c2-d2] **♘e6 17. ♘e6** [17. ♖c2? ♗d4 18. ♗d4 ♘f4−+] **♗e6 18. c5!?** [18. b3±] **dc5 19. e5!** [19. ♗c5 ♘g5! 20. fg5 ♕g5 21. ♔h1 ♕c5 22. ♘d5 ♕a5 23. ♘c7 ♖ad8−+] **b6!?** [19... c6 20. ♘e4⩱] **20. ♗c6!** [20. ♗a8? ♕a8→] **♕c8 21. ♘d5 ♗d5□ 22. ♕d5 ♖d8 23. ♕f3 ♖b8 24. ♖ed1 ♕f5 25. ♗e4 ♕g4?** [25... ♕e6 26.

♗d5 ♕f5! (26... ♕e7 27. b4! cb4 28. ♖c6 ♘f8 29. f5 gf5 30. g6±) 27. b4 ♗f8! 28. bc5 ♗c5 29. ♗c5 bc5 30. ♖c5 ♘f8 31. ♖c7 ♘e6∞] **26. ♕g4 hg4 27. ♔f2± ♘f8 28. ♔g3 ♘e6 29. ♔g4 ♔f8** [29... ♘d4 30. ♗d4] **30. h4 ♖d1⊕ 31. ♖d1 ♖d8 32. ♖d8 ♘d8** [♘♗ 9/e] **33. h5 gh5 34. ♔h5 a5 35. ♗f2! ♘e6 36. ♗g3 ♘d4 37. f5 ♔e8 38. f6 ♗f8 39. ♗f2 ♘e2** [39... a4 40. ♗d4 cd4 41. e6 fe6 42. g6 △ ♗c6+−] **40. ♗c6 ♔d8 41. ♗e3+− c4 42. ♗d5 1 : 0**
[Kišnëv]

601.* E 94

HJARTARSON 2625 – APICELLA 2495
Ísland – France 1993

1. d4 ♘f6 2. c4 g6 3. ♘c3 ♗g7 4. e4 d6 5. ♘f3 0–0 6. ♗e2 e5 7. 0–0 ♘a6 8. ♗e3 ♘g4 9. ♗g5 ♕e8 10. de5 de5 11. h3 h6 12. ♗d2 ♘f6 13. ♗e3 c6 14. a3 [14. b4?! ♘b4! 15. ♗c5 ♘a6 16. ♗f8 ♗f8∞̅] **♕e7 N** [14... ♘d7 – 48/(804)] **15. b4 ♘h5** [RR 15... ♘c7 16. c5 ♖d8 17. ♕c1 ♔h7 18. ♘d2⩲ Apicella] **16. c5 ♖d8** [16... ♘c7!? 17. ♕d6 ♖e8 18. ♖fd1⩲] **17. ♕c1 ♘f4 18. ♗f4 ef4 19. e5!** [19. ♗a6 ba6 20. e5 ♖d3!= Hauchard 2450 – Apicella 2495, Bucureşti 1993] **g5** [19... ♗e5 20. ♗a6 ♗c3 21. ♕c3 ba6 22. ♖fe1 ♗e6 23. ♕e5! ♖d5 (23... g5 24. ♘d4 ♖d5 25. ♘c6 ♕d7 26. ♘e7! ♕e7 27. ♕d5+−) 24. ♕f4 g5 25. ♕c4 a5 26. ♘d4±] **20. ♗a6** [20. ♘e4? ♗e5 21. ♗a6 ♗a1 22. ♕a1 ♕e4 23. ♕f6 ♖f8∓; RR 20. ♖e1! △ ♘e4-d6 Apicella] **ba6 21. ♘e4!** [21. ♖e1 ♗f5! 22. ♘e4 ♗e4 23. ♖e4 f5!∞] **♗e5** [21... ♗f5 22. ♘d6 ♗g6 23. ♖e1±] **22. ♖e1 ♗g7□** [22... ♗a1? 23. ♕a1 ♕f8□ (23... ♗e6 24. ♘f6 ♔f8 25. ♘d5+−) 24. ♘f6 ♔h8 25. ♘e5!+−] **23. ♖a2** [23. ♘eg5? ♕f6 24. ♘e4 ♕a1] **♗e6 24. ♖ae2∞̅ ♕c7** [24... ♕f8 25. ♕c2! ♗d5 26. ♘d6±; RR 24... a5!∞ Apicella] **25. ♕c2!** [25. ♘d6? ♖d6 26. cd6 ♕d6∞] **♖d5** [25... a5? 26. ♘eg5! hg5 27. ♘g5 ♗d5 28. ♖e7+−] **26. ♘d6 a5** [26... ♖d6 27. cd6 ♕d6 28. ♖e6! fe6 29. ♕g6 ♕e7 30. ♖e6 ♕f7 31. ♕e4±; RR 26... ♕d7∞ Apicella]

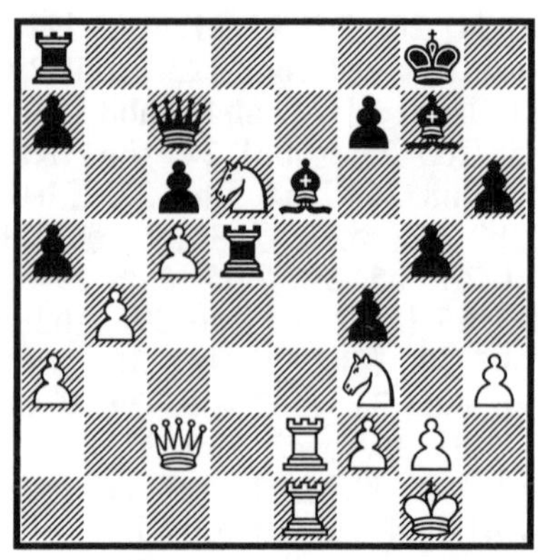

27. ♖e6! fe6 28. ♖e6 ab4 29. ab4 a5 30. ♕e4± ab4 [30... ♗f8 31. ♖g6 ♗g7 32. ♕e6 ♔h7 33. ♘f5+−] **31. ♖e7 ♕e7?!** [31... ♖a1? 32. ♔h2 ♖dd1 33. ♖e8! ♗f8 34. ♕g6 ♕g7 35. ♖f8 ♔f8 36. ♕e8#; 31... ♕a5□ 32. ♘e8! ♕a1□ (32... ♖a7 33. ♘f6 ♔f8 34. ♕e6!+−; 32... ♖e8 33. ♕e6! ♔h7 34. ♖e8 ♕a1 35. ♔h2 ♕f6 36. ♕g8 ♔g6 37. ♖e6 ♖c5 38. ♘d4+−) 33. ♔h2 ♖a7□ 34. ♕e6 ♔h8 (34... ♔h7 35. ♖g7 ♖g7 36. ♘f6+−) 35. ♖g7 ♖g7 36. ♕h6 ♔g8 (36... ♖h7 37. ♕f8#) 37. ♘f6 ♔f7 38. ♘d5 cd5 39. ♘g5 ♖g5 40. ♕g5+−] **32. ♕e7 b3 33. ♕f7!** [33. ♘e8? ♖e8 34. ♕e8 ♔h7 35. ♔f1□ b2 36. ♕e4 ♔h8 37. ♔e2 ♖c5 38. ♕g6 ♖c1 39. ♘d2 c5=] **♔h8 34. ♘f5 ♖f5?** [34... ♖g8□ 35. ♘e7 ♖gd8□ 36. ♘g5!! (36. ♘d5? ♖d5=) ♖g5 (36... b2 37. ♘g6#) 37. ♕b3 ♖c5 38. ♘g6 ♔h7 39. ♘f4 ♖c1 40. ♔h2 ♗e5 41. g3+− ♗f4? 42. ♕f7 ♔h8 43. ♕f6 ♔h7 44. ♕d8] **35. ♕f5+− b2 36. ♘d2 ♖d8 37. ♘b1 ♖d1 38. ♔h2 ♖f1 39. ♕c8 ♔h7 40. ♕c6 ♖f2 41. ♕e4 ♔h8 42. c6 1 : 0**
[Hjartarson]

602. E 94

M. GUREVICH 2610 –
HJARTARSON 2625
München 1993

1. d4 ♘f6 2. c4 g6 3. ♘c3 ♗g7 4. e4 d6 5. ♘f3 0–0 6. ♗e2 e5 7. 0–0 ♘a6 8. ♗e3 ♘g4 9. ♗g5 ♕e8 10. de5 de5 11. h3 h6 12. ♗d2 ♘f6 13. ♗e3 c6 14. c5!? N ♕e7 15. ♗a6 ba6 16. ♕a4!? ♕c7 [16...

♖b8 17. ♕c6 ♖b2 18. ♖ab1 ♗b7 (18... ♖c2 19. ♘d5±) 19. ♕d6 ♕d6 20. cd6 ♖b1 21. ♖b1±] **17. ♖fd1 ♖b8 18. ♕c2!?** [18. b3 a5⇆ △ ♖b4] **♗e6** [18... ♘e8!? △ f5⇆»] **19. ♖d6 ♘e8 20. ♖ad1!** [20. ♖d2 f5⇆; 20. ♖e6!? fe6 21. ♘d2 △ ♘c4→«] **♘d6 21. cd6 ♕a5** [21... ♕b7 22. b3 ♖fd8 23. ♘a4↑] **22. b3** [△ ♘a4-c5] **♖fd8** [22... c5 23. ♘d5! ♔h7 (23... ♖fd8 24. ♘e7 ♔h7 25. ♘c6±) 24. ♘c7±] **23. ♘a4 ♗f8 24. ♗a7!?** [24. ♘c5!? ♖d6 25. ♖d6 ♗d6 26. ♘e6 fe6 27. ♕c4↑] **♖b7 25. ♗c5 f6 26. ♘d2!±** [△ ♘c4; 26. b4? ♖b4! (26... ♕b5? 27. ♘c3 ♕c4 28. ♘d2+−) 27. ♗b4 ♕b4 28. ♘c5 ♕c4!⇆] **♕b5** [26... ♗d6? 27. ♘c4±] **27. ♘c4** [△ ♗a3, ♘c5] **♗c4** [27... a5 28. ♗a3 ♖bd7 29. ♘c5±] **28. bc4 ♕a5 29. a3!** [△ ♗b4, ♘c5] **♖db8** [29... ♖dd7 30. ♗b4 ♕d8 31. ♘c5 ♖b4 32. ♘d7+−] **30. ♗b4 ♖b4** [30... ♕d8 31. ♘c5 (31. c5±) ♖a7 32. ♕a4±] **31. ab4 ♖b4 32. ♘b2 c5!?** [32... ♕a2 33. d7 ♗e7 34. d8♕ ♗d8 35. ♖d8 ♔f7 36. ♕d3+−; 32... ♗d6 33. ♖d6 ♕a1 34. ♘d1+−] **33. d7!** [33. ♕d2? ♕d8 34. ♕d5 ♔h8 35. ♘d3 ♖b6⇆] **♗e7** [⌓ 33... ♕d8 34. ♕d2 ♔g7 (34... ♖b6 35. ♕d5 ♔g7 36. ♘a4! ♖d6 37. ♕d6 ♗d6 38. ♖d6 ♔f7 39. ♘c5+−) 35. f4!↑ ef4 36. ♘d3 ♖c4 37. ♘f4 ♖e4 38. g3± △ ♕d5] **34. ♕d2 ♗d8?⊕** [34... ♔g7 *a)* 35. d8♕? ♕d8! (35... ♗d8 36. ♕d7 ♔f8 37. ♕h7 ♖b2 38. ♖d7+−) 36. ♕d8 ♗d8 37. ♖d7 ♗e7 38. ♘d1 ♔f7 39. ♘e3 ♔e6 40. ♖a7 ♖a4∞; *b)* 35. f4!→ ♕c7 (35... ef4 36. ♘d3 ♖a4 37. ♕a5 ♖a5 38. ♘f4+−) 36. fe5 fe5 (36... ♕e5 37. d8♕ ♗d8 38. ♕d8+−) 37. ♖f1!± △ ♕d5] **35. ♕d5 ♔h8 36. ♘d3 1 : 0 [M. Gurevich]**

603.* !N E 94

CVETKOVIĆ 2500 − ILINČIĆ 2470
Aranđelovac 1993

1. c4 ♘f6 2. ♘c3 g6 3. e4 d6 4. d4 ♗g7 5. ♘f3 0−0 6. ♗e2 e5 7. 0−0 ♘a6 8. ♖e1 ♕e8 [RR 8... c6 9. ♗f1 ♗g4 10. ♗e3 ♗f3 11. ♕f3 ♘g4 12. ♕g4 ed4 13. ♗g5 f6 14. ♕e6 N (14. ♗d2 − 53/(622)) ♖f7 15. ♗f4 dc3 16. ♗d6 cb2 17. ♖ab1 ♘c7 18. ♗c7 ♕c7 19. c5 ♔h8 20. ♖b2 ♖e7 21. ♕c4 b5 22. cb6 ab6 23. ♖c2 f5 24. ♕c6 ♕c6 25. ♖c6 ♗d4 26. ♖c4 1/2 : 1/2 Sosonko 2535 − Nijboer 2505, Bruxelles (zt) 1993] **9. de5 de5 10. b3 ♘d7 11. ♗a3 ♘dc5 12. b4! N** [12. ♕c2] **♘e6 13. b5 ♘ac5 14. ♘g5! b6 15. ♘e6 fe6** [15... ♗e6 16. ♘d5±] **16. ♘a4 ♕e7** [16... ♘a4 17. ♕a4 (17. ♗f8? ♘c3!∓) ♖f7 (17... ♖f4 18. c5!±) 18. c5! (△ c6+−) bc5 19. ♗c5±] **17. ♘c5 bc5 18. ♕c1!** [⫽c1-h6] **♖d8 19. ♕e3±** [×c5] **♗f8 20. ♗b2** [×e5] **♗g7 21. a4 ♗b7 22. a5○ ♖ab8 23. ♗c3 ♖d7 24. ♖ad1 ♖bd8 25. ♖d7 ♖d7 26. ♖d1 ♖d1 27. ♗d1 h5?! 28. g4! hg4** [28... h4 29. g5+− ×h4] **29. ♗g4 ♗c8 30. ♔g2 ♕h4 31. ♕g3 ♕f6** [31... ♕g3 32. fg3+− △ ♙h] **32. h4 ♔h7 33. ♗f3 ♗b7 34. ♗b2 ♔g8 35. ♗c1 ♔h7 36. ♕g5 ♕g5** [36... ♕f8 37. ♗b2 ♕d6 38. h5+−→] **37. ♗g5** [♘♗ 9/f] **♗f8 38. ♗d8 ♗d6 39. ♔g3 a6 40. ba6 ♗a6 41. ♗e2+− ♗b7 42. f3 ♔g7 43. ♔g4 ♔f7 44. ♔g5 ♔g7 45. ♗f6 ♔f7 46. ♗d3 ♗a6 47. f4 c6 48. ♗e5! ♗e7** [48... ♗e5 49. fe5 ♔g7 50. ♗e2 ♗b7 51. ♗g4! (51. ♗d1 ♗a6 52. ♗b3 ♗c8! 53. ♗a4 ♗b7) ♗c8 (51... ♔f7 52. ♔h6 ♗a6 53. ♗e2 ♗c8 54. ♗d1 ♗a6 55. ♗b3 ♗c8 56. ♗a4 ♗b7 57. ♔h7+−) 52. ♗e6! (52. ♗h3⊙ ♔f7 53. ♔h6+−) ♗e6 53. a6 ♗c8 54. a7 ♗b7 55. e6+−] **49. ♔g4 ♗d8 50. ♗c3 ♗c8 51. f5 ef5 52. ef5 ♗e7 53. ♔f4 gf5 54. h5 ♗a6 55. ♔f5 ♗c8 56. ♔f4 ♗f8 57. ♗g6 1 : 0 [Cvetković]**

604. !N E 94

EPIŠIN 2620 − SMIRIN 2590
Rostov na Donu 1993

1. d4 ♘f6 2. c4 g6 3. ♘c3 ♗g7 4. e4 d6 5. ♘f3 0−0 6. ♗e2 e5 7. 0−0 ♘a6 8. ♖e1 ♕e8 9. ♗g5! N [9. ♗f1 − 52/(641)] **h6** [9... c6 10. d5 c5 11. ♘d2±; 9... ed4 10. ♕d4 ♕e7 11. ♘d5 ♘d5 12. cd5±] **10. ♗f6 ♗f6 11. c5! ♘b4!□** [11... ♘b8 12. ♘b5 ♕e7 13. ♖c1±] **12. de5! de5 13. ♕b3 ♘c6 14. ♘d5 ♗d8 15. h3!** [15. ♖ad1 ♗g4 16. ♕b7 ♖b8∞] **♘d4□ 16. ♘d4 ed4 17. ♗g4!** [17. ♗c4 c6! 18. ♘f4 b5! 19.

cb6 ab6 20. ♕g3 (20. ♘g6 b5) ♔h7 21. e5 ♗c7±] **♗g4 18. hg4** [18. ♕b7? ♗g5! 19. hg4 c6∓] **b6 19. ♘f4 ♔h7 20. e5 ♗g5** [20... bc5 21. e6 ♗g5 22. ♘d3±] **21. ♘d5?** [21. ♘d3 ♕e6 (21... bc5 22. e6±) 22. ♕e6 fe6 23. ♖e4! ♖ad8 24. ♖d1±] **♖d8! 22. cb6 ab6 23. ♖ad1?** [23. ♘c7 ♕c6 24. ♘b5 d3 25. ♘d6±] **c5□ 24. f4!** [24. ♘b6?? ♖b8 25. a4 c4−+] **♕c6?!** [24... ♕e6 25. ♘b6! ♕b3 26. ab3 ♗f4 27. ♘c4=] **25. ♘b4 cb4 26. fg5 hg5 27. e6 fe6 28. ♖e6 ♕d7!□ 29. ♖b6 ♕g4 30. ♖b4 ♕h4!!= 31. ♕h3□ ♕h3 32. gh3 ♖f4 33. ♖b3 ♔h6 34. ♖bd3 g4 35. hg4 ♔g5 36. a4 ♖g4 37. ♔f2 ♖h8 38. ♖d4 1/2 : 1/2** **[Epišin]**

605. **E 95**

S. T. JOVANOVIĆ 2370 – ILINČIĆ 2470

Aranđelovac 1993

1. d4 ♘f6 2. c4 g6 3. ♘c3 ♗g7 4. e4 d6 5. ♘f3 0–0 6. ♗e2 e5 7. 0–0 ♘a6 8. ♖e1 ed4 9. ♘d4 ♘c5 10. ♗f1 a5 11. ♘db5 ♗d7 12. ♗g5 N [12. ♗f4] **h6 13. ♗h4 ♗c6 14. ♕c2?!** [14. f3 ♕d7 15. ♕d2 △ ♖ad1±] **g5 15. ♗g3 ♘fe4! 16. ♘e4 ♘e4** [16... ♗e4 17. ♖e4 f5 18. ♖e2 f4 19. ♖ae1 △ ♖e7±] **17. ♖e4 f5 18. ♖e6 f4 19. ♖ae1** [19. ♕g6 fg3 20. hg3 ♖f6 21. ♖f6 ♕f6 22. ♕f6 ♗f6 23. ♘c7 ♖c8∓] **fg3 20. hg3 ♖f7** [20... ♖e8 21. ♖e8 ♗e8 22. ♖e8! ♕e8 23. ♘c7±] **21. ♗d3 ♗d7** [21... ♕f8 22. ♗g6 ♖f6 23. ♘c7+−] **22. ♖6e3** [22. ♖g6 ♖f6 23. ♖f6 ♗f6 △ ♗e5∓] **♗e5 23. c5** [23. ♘c3 ♔g7 24. ♘e4 ♕f8∓] **♔g7 24. cd6** [24. ♕e2 ♗b5 25. ♗b5 ♗d4 26. ♖e8 ♖f2 27. ♕h5 ♖e2 28. ♔h2 ♖e1 29. ♖d8 ♖d8 30. ♗d3 ♗g1! 31. ♔h3 ♖e6 32. ♕g4 ♖e5 (32... ♖f6 33. ♕e4 ♔f8 34. ♕h7 dc5 35. ♗c4±) 33. ♕h5 ♖e6 34. ♕g4=] **cd6 25. ♕e2 ♕b6! 26. a4?** [26. ♖e5 de5 27. ♕e5 *a)* 27... ♔g8 28. ♘d6 ♕f2 (28... ♖g7 29. ♗c4 ♔h8 30. ♕f6+−) 29. ♔h2 ♖g7 30. ♗c4 ♔h7 31. ♖f1+−; *b)* 27... ♕f6 28. ♘d6 ♕e5 29. ♖e5 ♗c6 30. ♘f7±; *c)* 27... ♖f6 28. ♕e7 (28. ♕e4 ♖h8=) ♖f7 29. ♕e5 (29. ♕e4 ♕f2 30. ♔h2 ♕f5 31. ♕d4 ♕f6−+) ♖f6 30. ♕e7=] **♖af8 27. ♕h5 ♖f6** [27... ♗f5 28. ♗f5 ♖f5 29. ♖f3 ♖f3 (29... ♗g3 30. ♖e7 ♔f6 31. ♖f5 ♔e7 32. ♖f8 ♔f8 33. ♕h6 ♔e8 34. ♕h5 ♔f8 35. ♕f3 ♗f4 36. g3 ♕c6 37. ♕c6 bc6 38. gf4 cb5 39. fg5+−) 30. gf3 ♗g3 31. ♖e7 ♔f6 32. ♖e2! ♔g7 33. ♖e7=] **28. ♖f3 ♗c6 29. ♗e4**

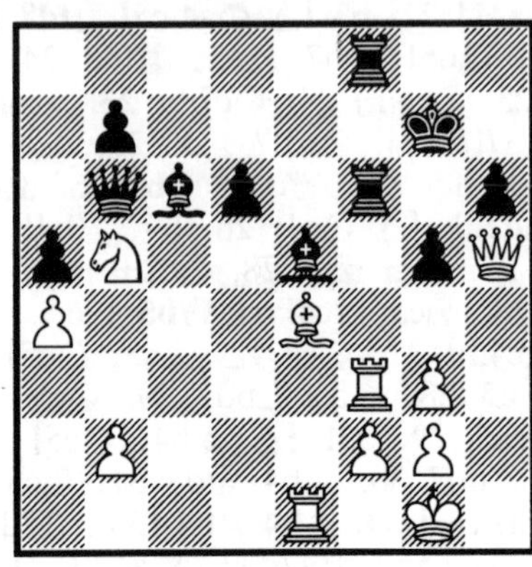

29... ♗g3! 30. ♖g3 [30. ♗c6 ♖f3 31. ♖e7 ♖3f7−+] **♕f2 31. ♔h2 ♕e1 32. ♖g5 ♔h8 33. ♗g6** [33. ♖g6 ♖g6 34. ♕g6 ♕h4 35. ♔g1 ♗e4−+] **♖g6 34. ♖g6 ♕e5 35. ♕e5 de5 36. ♖h6** [36. ♔g1 ♔h7 37. ♖e6 ♖e8−+] **♔g7 37. ♖e6 ♖f2 38. ♖e5 ♔f6 39. ♖c5 ♖g2 40. ♔h3 ♖b2 41. ♔g3** [⌓ 41. ♘c3 ♗d7 42. ♔g3 b6 43. ♘d5 ♔e6 44. ♘b6 ♖b6 45. ♖a5 ♖b3] **♗b5?** [41... ♗d7 △ b6∓] **42. ab5 a4 43. ♔f4?** [43. ♖c4! a3 44. ♖a4 a2 45. ♔f3 ♔e5 46. ♔e3 ♔d5 47. ♔d3 ♔c5 48. ♔c3 ♔b5 49. ♖a8 ♖h2 50. ♔b3=] **a3 44. ♖c3 a2 45. ♖a3 ♖b4 0 : 1** **[Ilinčić]**

606.* !N **E 95**

CVETKOVIĆ 2500 – J. IVANOV 2420

Aranđelovac 1993

1. c4 g6 2. e4 ♗g7 3. d4 d6 4. ♘c3 ♘f6 5. ♘f3 0–0 6. ♗e2 ♘bd7 7. 0–0 e5 8. ♖e1 c6 9. d5 [RR 9. ♗f1 ed4 10. ♘d4 ♖e8 11. ♖b1 ♘g4! N (11... a5 – 32/705, E 96) 12. ♕g4 ♗d4 13. ♕g3 ♘f6! 14. ♕d3 ♗e5 15. f4? ♗c3 16. bc3 ♘e4 17. ♗a3 ♗f5 18. ♖b2 ♕a5! 19. ♗b4 ♕b6 20. ♕e3 c5 21. ♗a3 ♕a6 22. ♖b3 ♘f6 23. ♕d2 ♖e1 24. ♕e1 ♖e8 25. ♕h4 ♘g4 26. h3 ♘e3 27. g4 ♘f1 28. gf5 ♘d2

0 : 1 Sellos 2425 – Akopian 2615, Cannes 1993; 15. g3= Akopian] **♘c5 10. ♗g5! N** [10. ♗f1 a5 – E 96] **a5** [10... h6 11. ♗f6 ♗f6 12. b4 ♘a6 13. dc6 bc6 14. b5 cb5 15. cb5 ♘c5 16. ♗c4± ×d5; 10... cd5! 11. cd5 h6 12. ♗f6□ ♗f6 13. b4±] **11. ♘d2!** [11. ♗f1 – E 96] **h6 12. ♗e3 ♘fd7 13. ♘b3 ♘b3 14. ♕b3± c5** [△ f5] **15. ♘b5! ♘f6** [15... ♕b6 16. ♕c2 △ a3, b4 ×♕b6] **16. ♕c2 ♔h7 17. a3 ♘e8 18. b4 b6 19. bc5 bc5 20. ♖ab1 ♗f6 21. ♖b3 ♗g5 22. ♗g5 ♕g5** [22... hg5!?] **23. ♖eb1± ♕e7 24. ♘c3 ♘f6 25. ♖b8 ♗a6 26. ♖a8! ♖a8 27. ♕a4 ♖a7□ 28. ♕c6 ♗b7 29. ♕b6 ♗a6 30. ♕b8! ♔g7 31. ♖b6 ♘e8 32. g3 ♔f8 33. ♘b5 ♖b7 34. ♖b7 ♗b7** [34... ♕b7 35. ♕e8? ♔e8 36. ♘d6 ♔e7 37. ♘b7 ♗b7=; 35. ♕d8+–] **35. ♕a7+– f5 36. ef5 gf5 37. ♗h5! ♘f6 38. ♕b8 ♔g7 39. ♘d6 1 : 0** **[Cvetković]**

607. E 97

OLLS 2585 – SMIRIN 2590

Rostov na Donu 1993

1. d4 ♘f6 2. c4 g6 3. ♘c3 ♗g7 4. e4 d6 5. ♘f3 0–0 6. ♗e2 e5 7. 0–0 ♘c6 8. ♗e3 ♖e8 9. de5 de5 10. c5 ♗g4 11. ♗b5 ♕c8 12. h3 ♗h5 N [12... ♖d8 – 54/609] **13. ♗c6 bc6 14. ♗g5 ♖b8 15. ♖b1** [15. ♗f6 ♗f6 16. g4 ♖d8 17. ♕e2 ♗g4 18. hg4 ♕g4 19. ♔h2 ♕f4 20. ♔g2 ♖b2! 21. ♕b2 ♕g4=; 15. b3!?] **♗f3 16. ♕f3 ♘d7 17. b4** [17. ♗e3 ♘f8 △ ♘e6-d4=] **a5 18. b5!?** [18. a3 ab4 19. ab4 ♘f8=] **♘c5** [18... cb5? 19. c6 ♘c5 20. ♘d5↑] **19. bc6 ♘e6 20. ♕e3!** [20. ♗e3 ♖b1 21. ♖b1 ♕a6 ×c6] **f6 21. ♗h6** [21. ♗h4 ♖b1 22. ♖b1 g5 23. ♗g3 ♕a6∓] **♖b1 22. ♖b1 ♕a6 23. ♘d5 ♕c6 24. ♖c1 ♕b7!** [24... ♕d6 25. ♗g7 ♔g7 26. ♕a7±] **25. ♗g7 ♔g7 26. ♕f3 ♖f8 27. ♕g4 f5!□** [27... ♖e8? 28. ♘c7+–] **28. ♕g3 ♕b2 29. ♖c4?** [29. ♖c6 ♕b1 30. ♔h2 ♕e4 31. ♖e6 ♕d5 32. ♖e5 (32. ♕e5 ♕e5 33. ♖e5 ♖c8 34. ♖c5! ♔f6 35. ♔g3=) ♕a2 33. ♖e7 ♖f7 34. ♕e5 ♔h6 35. ♕f4 g5 36. ♕c7 ♖e7 37. ♕e7= ×♔h6] **c5!–+ 30. ♖a4 f4 31. ♕g4 ♘d4 32. ♖a5 ♖f7! 33. ♖c5** [33. ♕d1 f3 34. g3 ♘e2 35. ♔h2 ♘c3 36. ♕e1 ♘e4] **♕a1 34. ♔h2 h5!** [35. ♕g5 ♘e2] **0 : 1** **[Smirin]**

608.** E 97

FTÁČNIK 2535 – WOJTKIEWICZ 2580

Budapest (zt) 1993

1. d4 ♘f6 2. c4 g6 3. ♘c3 ♗g7 4. e4 d6 5. ♗e2 0–0 6. ♘f3 e5 7. 0–0 ♘c6 8. d5 ♘e7 9. ♗g5 ♘h5 10. ♘e1 ♘f4 11. ♘d3 ♘e2 [11... f5 12. f3 ♘d3 13. ♗d3 ♗f6 14. ♗e3 f4 15. ♗f2 g5∞] **12. ♕e2 h6** [12... c5 13. ♖ab1 h6 14. ♗d2 b6 15. f4±; 12... f6 13. ♗e3 f5 14. f3 f4 15. ♗f2 g5⇆] **13. ♗d2** [13. ♗e3 N f5 14. f3 f4 15. ♗f2 g5 16. c5 ♘g6⇆ Bonin 2405 – Sherzer 2460, Chicago 1992] **c6?! N** [RR 13... g5 14. g4 N (14. h4? – 56/695) ♘g6 15. f3 ♘f4 16. ♘f4 ef4 17. ♘d1 c6 18. ♗c3 cd5 19. ♗g7 ♔g7 20. cd5 ♗d7 21. ♘f2 ♖c8 22. ♕d2 ♕b6 23. ♖fe1 ♖c5 24. ♔g2 ♖fc8 25. ♖ac1 ♖c1 26. ♖c1 ♖c1 27. ♕c1 ♕d4 28. ♕c3 ♕c3 29. bc3 ♗b5= Olls 2585 – Dolmatov 2615, Rostov na Donu 1993] **14. ♖ac1** [14. f4!? ef4 15. ♗f4 cd5 16. cd5 f5 △ 17. e5 g5 18. ed6 ♘g6 19. ♗e3 ♖e8∞] **f5 15. f3 cd5?!** [15... f4!? 16. c5 *a)* 16... cd5 17. ed5 ♘f5! (17... dc5 18. ♘e5) 18. cd6 ♘d4 19. ♕e1 ♗f5 20. ♘f2 ♕d6 21. ♘fe4∞; *b)* 16... dc5 17. ♘c5 b6 (17... cd5 18. ed5 b6 19. ♘e6 ♗e6 20. de6 △ ♘b5) 18. ♕c4!? (18. ♘e6 ♗e6 19. de6 ♕d6∓) ♔h8 (18... bc5 19. d6 ♔h7 20. de7 ♕e7 21. ♘a4 ♗e6 22. ♕c5∞) 19. ♘d3∞; 16. g4!∞; 15... g5 16. ♘f2 (16. dc6 bc6 17. c5 ♗a6! 18. ♖fd1 d5∓) ♘g6 17. g3∞] **16. cd5 g5?** [16... ♗d7! 17. ♘f2 a6] **17. ♘b5! ♗d7** [17... ♕b6 18. ♘f2 ♗d7 19. a4] **18. ♘f2** [18. ♘c7?! ♖c8 19. ♘e6 ♗e6 20. de6 d5∓; 18. ♘d6 ♕b6 19. ♕e3 ♕d6 20. ♗b4 ♕f6 21. ♖c7 ♖fd8 22. ♘c5 ♗b5 23. ♖c1↑] **♕b6** [18... ♖f6 19. ♖c2±] **19. a4 ♘g6** [19... a6 20. ♘c7 (20. ♗e3 ♗b5 21. ab5 ♕b5 22. ♕b5 ab5 23. ♖c7 ♖f7 24. ♖b7? ♘d5! 25. ♖f7 ♘e3 26. ♖b7 ♘f1 27. ♔f1=; 24. ♖fc1!±) ♖ac8 21. ♗e3 ♕a5 22. b3± △ 22... ♖c7 23. b4; 19... f4 20. ♘c7 ♖ac8 21. a5 ♕b2 22. ♖b1 ♕a2

23. ♖b7±] **20. ♕e3!** [20. ♗e3?! ♗b5! 21. ab5 ♘f4 22. ♗f4 ef4∓] **♘f4 21. ♖fe1** [21. ♕b6 ♘e2 22. ♔h1 ab6 23. ♖c7 ♗b5 24. ab5 ♖a2 (24... ♖f7 25. ♖f7 ♔f7 26. ef5±) 25. ♗b4 ♖b2 26. ♗d6 ♖f7 (26... ♖a8? 27. ♖g7 ♔g7 28. ♗e5+−) 27. ♗e7±] **fe4 22. fe4 ♗b5** [22... ♕e3 23. ♗e3 ♗b5 24. ab5±] **23. ♕b6 ab6 24. ab5 ♖fc8** [24... ♖a2 25. ♗c3 ♖fa8 26. g3 ♘g6 27. ♘d3±] **25. ♖c8 ♖c8 26. ♗c3 ♖c5?!** [26... ♔f7 27. g3 ♘h5 28. ♖a1±] **27. g3 ♘g6 28. ♗b4** [28. ♖a1!? ♖b5? 29. b4+−] **♖b5** [28... ♖c2 29. ♗c3 ♘e7 30. ♘d3 ♔f7 31. ♘b4+−] **29. ♘d3+− ♗f8 30. ♖c1 ♘h8** [30... ♔f7 31. ♖c7 ♔e8 32. ♗c3 ♖b3 33. ♘c1 ♖b5 34. b4] **31. ♖c8 ♘f7** [31... ♔g7 32. ♗c3] **32. g4!** [32. ♗c3 g4 33. b4 ♘g5⇆] **♔g7** [32... h5 33. h3 hg4 34. hg4 ♔g7 35. ♔f2 ♘h6 36. ♔f3] **33. ♗c3 h5 34. b4 ♘h6 35. ♘b2!** [△ ♘c4-a3]

1 : 0 **[Ftáčnik]**

609.* **E 97**

RUZELE 2500 – LAPIENIS 2280
Lietuva (ch) 1993

1. d4 ♘f6 2. c4 g6 3. ♘c3 ♗g7 4. e4 d6 5. ♗e2 0–0 6. ♘f3 e5 7. 0–0 ♘c6 8. d5 ♘e7 9. b4 ♘h5 [9... a5 10. ♗a3 ab4 11. ♗b4 b6 12. a4 ♘e8 13. ♕b3 N (13. ♘b5 – 55/(627)) ♖b8 *a)* 14. ♕a3 f5 (14... c5 15. dc6 ♘c6 16. ♖fd1 ♘b4 17. ♕b4 f5 18. c5±) 15. a5 c5 16. dc6 ♘c6 17. ab6 fe4 (17... ♘b4 18. ♕b4 ♕b6 19. ♕b6 ♖b6 20. ♘d5 ♖b2 21. ♘e7 ♔h8 22. ♘c8 ♖e2 23. ♘g5 fe4 24. ♖a7±) 18. ♘e4 ♗f5 (18... ♘b4 19. ♕b4 ♕b6 20. ♕b6 ♖b6 21. ♘fd2!⩲ Ruzele 2500 – Mališauskas 2570, Vilnius (zt) 1993) 19. ♗d6 ♘d6 (19... ♗e4 20. ♗b8 ♕b8 21. c5±) 20. ♘d6 e4 21. ♘f5 ♗a1 (21... ♖f5 22. ♖ad1 ♕b6 23. ♘h4 △ g3±) 22. ♘h6 ♔g7 23. ♕a1 ♔h6 24. ♘e5 ♘e5 25. ♕e5 ♕b6 26. ♕e4=; *b)* 14. ♘b5!? f5 15. ♘d2 *b1)* 15... ♗h6 16. ef5 ♘f5 (16... gf5 17. a5±) 17. ♘e4⩲; *b2)* 15... ♘f6 16. a5 ba5 (16... ♘e4 17. ♘e4 fe4 18. ab6 ♖b6 19. c5±; 16... fe4 17. ab6 ♖b6 18. c5 ♖b7 19. ♖a8±) 17. ♗a5 ♘e4 18. ♘e4 fe4 19. ♕a2 ♖b7 20. c5∞ Ruzele, Zagorskis] **10. ♘d2 ♘f4 11. a4 f5 12. ♗f3 g5 13. ef5 ♘f5 14. g3 ♘h3 15. ♔g2 ♕d7 16. ♗e4!? N** [16. ♘b3 – 20/721] **♘f2□ 17. ♔f2 ♘g3 18. ♔g1 ♘f1 19. ♘f1 ♕h3** [19... a5 20. ba5 h6 21. ♕h5; 19... h6!?] **20. ♘g3 ♗g4 21. ♕d3 ♖f4** [21... h6!?] **22. ♖a2! ♖af8 23. ♖c2□ ♗f3?!** [23... ♖f3? 24. ♗f3 ♖f3 25. ♕d2 ♖g3 26. hg3 ♕g3 27. ♕g2 ♕e1 28. ♕f1 ♕g3 29. ♖g2+−; 23... h6!?] **24. ♗f4 ef4□** [24... ♗e4 25. ♘ce4 gf4 26. ♘g5 ♕h4 27. ♘3e4±; 24... gf4 25. ♘f1±] **25. ♘f1□** [25. ♗f5? g4 26. ♕f3 fg3−+] **♕g4 26. ♔f2 ♕g2 27. ♔e1 ♗e4 28. ♘e4 ♕g1** [28... f3 29. ♖f2 △ 29... g4 30. ♘g5; 28... ♕g4 29. h3 ♕f5 30. ♖f2±] **29. h3 h5?!** [29... h6!?] **30. ♖f2 ♖e8⊕** [30... g4 31. ♘g5; ⌓ 30... ♗e5] **31. ♖e2 ♖e5 32. ♕f3+− ♕d4 33. ♘ed2 ♕a1 34. ♔f2 ♕d4 35. ♔g2 g4?! 36. hg4 hg4** [36... ♖g5 37. ♘h2] **37. ♕g4 f3 38. ♕f3 ♖g5 39. ♘g3 ♗e5 40. ♘e4 ♖g7 41. ♖c2 ♕a1 42. ♖f2 ♕c1 43. ♕f8 ♔h7 44. ♖f5** **1 : 0** **[Ruzele]**

610. !N **E 97**

KIŠNËV 2510 – HAUSRATH 2260
Dortmund (open) 1993

1. d4 ♘f6 2. c4 g6 3. ♘c3 ♗g7 4. e4 d6 5. ♗e2 0–0 6. ♘f3 e5 7. 0–0 ♘c6 8. d5 ♘e7 9. ♘d2 c5 10. ♖b1 ♘e8 11. b4 b6 12. bc5 bc5 13. ♘b3 f5 14. ♗g5 ♗f6 15. ♗d2 ♔h8 16. ♘b5! N [16. ♔h1 – 56/699] **♘g8** [16... fe4 17. ♗a5 ♕d7 18. ♘d2 ♕f5 19. ♘c3 e3 20. fe3 ♕g5 21. e4±; 21. ♖f3!?] **17. ♘a5 ♗d7** [17... fe4?! 18. ♘c6 ♕d7 19. ♘c3 ♕f5 20. g4 ♕d7 21. ♘e4±] **18. ♗f3!** [18. ♘c6?! ♗c6 19. dc6 ♘e7] **♕c8** [△ f4] **19. h3! ♗d8 20. ef5 ♗f5** [20... gf5 21. ♘c6 e4 22. ♗h5 ♗c6 23. dc6 ♕c6 24. ♗e8 ♖e8 25. ♘d6 ♖f8 26. ♖b7!±] **21. ♖b3 ♗h4 22. ♘c6 a6 23. ♘c3± ♘e7 24. ♗h6 ♖f7 25. ♘e4 ♗e4 26. ♗e4 ♘f6 27. ♘e7 ♖e7 28. ♗f3 ♖b8 29. ♗d2** [29. g3 ♘g8] **♘g8 30. ♗g4 ♕e8 31. ♕b1 ♖b3 32. ♕b3 ♘f6 33. ♗f3 ♘g8⊕ 34. ♗e3 ♗f6 35. ♕b6+− e4 36. ♗g4 ♕a4 37. ♕d6 ♕c4 38. ♗e6 ♕c3 39. ♕b8 ♖g7 40. ♗h6** **1 : 0** **[Kišnëv]**

611. **E 97**

M. GUREVICH 2610 – B. GEL'FAND 2690
München 1993

1. d4 ♘f6 2. c4 g6 3. ♘c3 ♗g7 4. e4 d6 5. ♘f3 0–0 6. ♗e2 e5 7. 0–0 ♘c6 8. d5 ♘e7 9. ♘d2 a5 10. a3 ♗d7 11. b3 ♘e8 12. ♖b1 f5 13. b4 ab4 14. ab4 ♘f6 15. c5!? N [15. f3 – 56/705] **♔h8** [15... dc5 16. bc5 fe4 17. ♘de4 ♘e4 18. ♘e4 ♗f5 19. ♕c2 ♘d5 20. ♖b7±; 18... ♗a4!?] **16. f3 ♘h5 17. ♘c4 ♘f4 18. ♗e3 ♘c8** [△ ♕g5] **19. ♔h1! g5 20. ♘a5 ♕e8!** [20... b6 21. ♘c6 ♕f6 22. ♘b5 ♖f7 23. ♘c7 ♗c6 24. ♘a8 ♗a8 25. c6±] **21. ♘b7 ♖a3 22. c6!** [22. ♗d2 ♖c3! 23. ♗c3 ♘e2 24. ♕e2 ♗b5 25. ♕d1 (25. ♕d2? ♗f1 26. ♖f1 ♕b5–+) ♗f1 26. ♕f1 fe4⇆] **♖c3** [22... ♗c6 23. dc6 ♖c3 (23... ♕c6 24. ♗f4 ef4 25. ♘b5 ♖a2 26. ♘a5+–) 24. ♗d2 ♘e2 (24... ♖c6 25. ♗b5±) 25. ♕e2 ♖c6 26. ♘a5 ♖b6 27. ♗g5±] **23. cd7 ♕d7 24. ♗d2 ♖a3 25. ♘a5 g4!? 26. ♗c1** [26. ♗f4!? ef4 27. ef5 gf3 28. ♗f3 ♕f5 29. ♖c1±] **♘e2 27. ♕e2 gf3 28. gf3 ♖a4 29. ♗g5!** [29. ♘c4?! ♕b5⇆] **h6** [29... ♘e7 30. ♘c4! ♘g6 31. ♘e3 ♘f4 32. ♕d2±] **30. ♗e3 ♘e7 31. ♖g1 f4 32. ♗f2± ♗f6 33. ♖b3 ♖b8 34. ♖gb1 ♕h3 35. ♘c4** [35. ♕f1? ♕f1 36. ♖f1 ♖a5–+] **♖g8 36. ♕f1** [36. ♖g1?? ♖a1 37. ♗e1 ♖g1 38. ♔g1 ♗h4–+] **♕h5 37. ♕e2** [37. b5!± △ b6] **♕h3 38. ♕f1 ♕h5 39. ♕e2?⊕ ♕h3** **1/2 : 1/2**
[M. Gurevich]

612. **E 97**

DOHOJAN 2510 – UHLMANN 2500
Deutschland 1993

1. d4 ♘f6 2. c4 g6 3. ♘c3 ♗g7 4. e4 d6 5. ♗e2 0–0 6. ♘f3 e5 7. 0–0 ♘c6 8. d5 ♘e7 9. ♘d2 a5 10. a3 ♗d7 11. b3 c5 12. ♖b1 ♘e8 [12... ♗h6] **13. b4 b6 14. bc5** [14. ♕b3!? ♘c8 15. bc5] **dc5** [14... bc5 15. ♕b3± ×b6, d6] **15. ♕b3 N** [15. ♘f3 – 47/741] **♘c8 16. ♗b2!↑⊞ ♘ed6 17. ♖be1 ♖e8** [17... f5 18. ef5 gf5 19. ♘d1 ♘e7?! 20. ♗h5] **18. ♕c2!?** [18. ♘d1 ♗h6! 19. ♘e3 f5 20. ef5 gf5 21. ♗h5±; 19... f6!±] **♘e7?!** [△ f5, g5, ♘g6; ⌓ 18... ♗h6 19. ♗d3 f6 (19... f5 20. f4↑) 20. ♘e2±] **19. ♘d1 ♕b8** [19... f5 20. f4±] **20. f4 ef4** [20... f6 21. fe5 fe5 22. ♘f2±] **21. ♗g7 ♔g7 22. ♕b2** [×b6] **f6** [22... ♔g8 23. e5 △ ♘e4] **23. ♖f4 ♘g8** [23... ♘df5 24. ♖f2 ♘d4 25. ♘f3±] **24. ♖ef1** [△ ♖f6] **♕d8□ 25. ♘e3** [△ 26. ♘g4, 26. ♗g4] **h5** [25... g5 26. ♖4f3 ♘e4 27. ♘e4 ♖e4 28. ♗d3± ♖e8 (28... ♖e5 29. ♖f6; 28... ♖d4 29. ♗f5) 29. ♕b1↑] **26. h4!±** [△ g4] **♘f7!□** [26... ♖b8 27. g4 hg4 (27... b5 28. g5 bc4 29. gf6) 28. ♗g4] **27. g4 hg4 28. ♗g4** [28. ♘g4! ♗g4 29. ♗g4 ♘e5 30. ♕c3±] **♘e5 29. ♗d7 ♕d7□** [29... ♘d3 30. ♕b5; 29... ♘d7 30. ♘g4] **30. ♕b6 ♕h3?!** [30... ♖ab8!? 31. ♕c5!? (31. ♕a5 ♕h3 32. ♕c5 ♖b2 33. ♕d4 ♖a2=∞) ♘d3 32. ♕a5 ♘f4 33. ♖f4 ♕d6∞] **31. ♕c5** [31. ♕b3 a4! 32. ♕c3 (32. ♘f5 ♕f5!) ♕g3=] **♘d3 32. ♕c7⊕** [32. ♖1f3! ♘c5 (32... ♕f3 33. ♕c7; 32... ♕d7 33. ♕d4 ♘f4 34. ♖f4) 33. ♖h3 ♖ab8 34. h5 ♖b2 35. ♖f2±] **♖e7 33. ♖4f3 ♕f1! 34. ♘ef1 ♖c7 35. ♖d3 ♘h6!⊕ 36. ♘e3** [36. ♖c3!? ♖ac8 37. ♘e3] **♘f7 37. ♖c3 ♖ac8** [37... ♖h8!?] **38. ♔f2?** [38. ♘c2! ♘e5 39. ♘d4 ♖c4!? (39... ♔f7 40. ♘b5; 39... ♘c4 40. d6) 40. ♘c4 ♖c4 41. ♖c4 ♘c4 42. ♘e6 ♔f7 43. a4±] **♘e5 39. ♖b3 a4 40. ♖b6∞** **1/2 : 1/2**
[Dohojan]

613.* **!N** **E 97**

HALIFMAN 2630 – NIJBOER 2505
Ter Apel 1993

1. d4 ♘f6 2. ♘f3 g6 3. c4 ♗g7 4. ♘c3 0–0 5. e4 d6 6. ♗e2 e5 7. 0–0 ♘c6 8. d5 ♘e7 9. ♘d2 a5 10. a3 ♘d7 11. ♖b1 f5 12. b4 ♘f6?! 13. c5! [13. f3 c6!?] **ab4 14. ab4 ♔h8** [14... ♗h6 15. ♗f3?! – 27/685; 15. f3± △ 15... dc5?! 16. bc5 ♗e3 17. ♔h1 ♗c5 18. ♘c4→] **15. f3 ♘h5 16. ♘c4 ♘g8** [16... ♘f4 N 17. ♗e3 (17. b5!? dc5 18. b6=∞) g5 18. b5 dc5 19. b6 c6!∞ Halifman 2635 – Dolmatov 2610, Moskva (rapid) 1992; 19. ♗c5!±] **17. b5! N** [17.

g3 – 49/746] **b6** [17... dc5 18. b6±] **18. cd6 cd6 19. ♗e3 ♖b8 20. ♘a4 ♗h6** [20... ♘gf6 21. ♗b6 ♕e7 22. ♘a5±] **21. ♗b6!** [21. ♕d2 ♗e3 22. ♕e3 ♘f4∞; 21. ♗f2 ♘f4 22. ♗b6 ♕g5] **♖b6□ 22. ♘ab6 ♗e3 23. ♘e3 ♕b6 24. ♖b3 f4 25. ♕c1 ♗d7 26. ♔h1 fe3** [26... ♕d8 27. ♖e1! (27. ♘c4? ♘g3–+) fe3 28. ♕e3 ♘f4 29. ♗f1+–] **27. ♕e3 ♕e3** [27... ♕d8 28. g3+–] **28. ♖e3+– ♘f4 29. ♖b1**
1 : 0 **[Halifman]**

614. **E 97**

EPIŠIN 2620 – WOJTKIEWICZ 2580
Bern 1993

1. d4 ♘f6 2. c4 g6 3. ♘c3 ♗g7 4. e4 d6 5. ♘f3 0–0 6. ♗e2 e5 7. 0–0 ♘c6 8. d5 ♘e7 9. ♘d2 a5 10. ♖b1 ♘d7 11. a3 f5 12. b4 ♔h8 13. ♕c2 ♘f6 14. f3 ♘h5 15. c5 ab4 16. ab4 ♘f4 17. ♘c4 g5 18. ♗e3 ♘eg6 19. b5 N [△ b6; 19. cd6 – 55/(638)] **♘h4 20. g3 ♘h3** [20... ♘e2?! 21. ♕e2 f4 22. ♗d2 △ b6±] **21. ♔h1 f4 22. ♗d2 g4** [22... fg3?! 23. hg3 g4 24. fg4 ♘f2 (24... ♖f2 25. ♖f2 ♘f2 26. ♔g1 ♘h3 27. ♔h2 ♘f2 28. ♗e1+–) 25. ♔g1 ♘g4 26. b6±] **23. gh4 g3 24. ♗e1 ♕h4 25. ♗d1!** [⇔a2-h2] **♖f6** [25... ♖g8!? 26. ♖b2 ♕d8 27. hg3 fg3 28. ♗g3 ♗h6 29. ♘e5 de5 30. ♗e5 ♗g7 31. ♗h2±] **26. ♖b2 ♖g6**

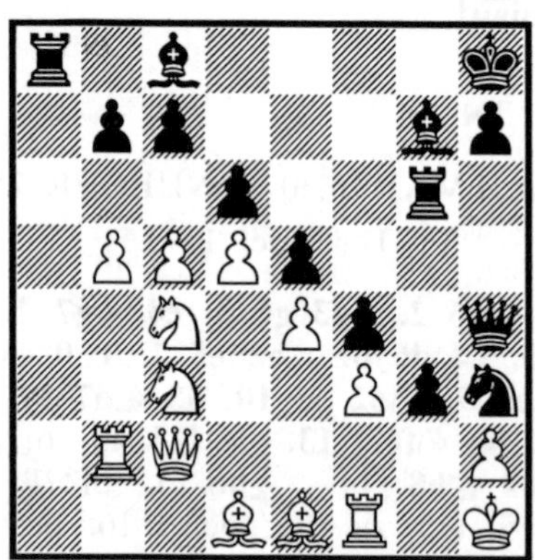

27. ♕e2!! [27. b6?? ♘f2 28. ♖f2 g2 29. ♔g1 ♕h2!–+] **♕h5 28. b6!! dc5⊕** [28... g2 29. ♕g2 ♖g2 30. ♖g2 ♘g5 31. bc7 ♗h3 32. ♖fg1 ♘f3 33. cd6+–] **29. bc7 b5 30. ♘b5+– ♗a6 31. ♘bd6 ♖f6 32. ♕g2 ♖d6 33. ♘d6 ♗f1 34. ♕f1**
1 : 0 **[Epišin]**

615. **E 97**

LPUTIAN 2610 – DOLMATOV 2615
Rostov na Donu 1993

1. d4 ♘f6 2. c4 g6 3. ♘c3 ♗g7 4. e4 d6 5. ♘f3 0–0 6. ♗e2 e5 7. 0–0 ♘c6 8. d5 ♘e7 9. ♘d2 a5 10. a3 ♘d7 11. ♖b1 f5 12. b4 ♔h8 13. ♕c2 ♘f6 14. f3 ab4 15. ab4 c6!? N [15... g5 – 55/639] **16. ♔h1** [16. ♘b3 f4∞] **f4 17. dc6?!** [17. ♖d1!? cd5 18. cd5 ♗d7] **♘c6 18. ♘b5 ♕e7** [18... ♗e6?! 19. ♕d3] **19. ♖d1 ♗e6 20. ♘f1?!** [20. ♖b3!? ♖fd8 21. ♘b1 ♘h5!∞] **♖fd8 21. ♗d2 g5 22. ♗e1 ♗f8!** [22... g4? 23. ♗h4±] **23. ♗f2 ♕g7** [23... ♖ac8!?] **24. g4?** [24. ♖d2 △ ♕d1⇆] **h5 25. h3 ♕h7!∓ 26. ♔g1□** [26. ♔g2 d5 27. cd5 (27. ♘c7? de4–+) ♘d5∓] **♖d7** [26... d5!? 27. ♘c7 (27. cd5 ♘d5∓) ♘b4 28. ♖b4 ♕c7 29. ♖b6∞] **27. ♘h2 hg4 28. hg4 ♕h3** [28... ♕h6!? 29. ♔g2 ♖h7 30. ♖h1 ♖c8→] **29. ♗f1 ♕h6 30. ♗e1 ♗e7 31. ♖b2 ♔g7 32. ♕g2 ♖c8! 33. ♗e2** [33. ♖bd2 ♖cd8∓] **♘d8! 34. ♕f1 ♘f7 35. ♗c3?** [35. ♗f2 ♖dd8! △ ♖h8∓] **♗d8!–+ 36. ♖bd2 ♗b6 37. ♔h1 ♗g4 38. ♘d6** [38. fg4 ♘e4] **♖d6 39. ♖d6 ♖h8** [40. ♕g2□ ♗h3] **0 : 1**
[Dolmatov]

616. **E 97**

LJUBOJEVIĆ 2605 – KASPAROV 2805
Linares 1993

1. d4 ♘f6 2. c4 g6 3. ♘c3 ♗g7 4. e4 d6 5. ♗e2 0–0 6. ♘f3 e5 7. 0–0 ♘c6 8. d5 ♘e7 9. ♘d2 a5 10. ♖b1 ♘d7 11. a3 f5 12. b4 ♔h8 13. f3 f4 14. ♘b3?! [14. ♕c2 – 53/639] **ab4 15. ab4 g5 16. ♗d2? N** [16. g4□; 16. c5 – 45/(758)] **♘g6 17. ♖a1 ♖a1 18. ♕a1 ♘f6∓ 19. ♕a7** [19. g4 fg3 20. hg3 ♘h5 21. ♔g2 ♘gf4! 22. gf4 gf4 23. ♖h1 ♕g5 24. ♔f2 ♕g3 25. ♔f1 ♗h3–+] **g4 20. fg4** [20. ♘a5 g3 21. ♘b7 ♕e7 22. h3 ♗h3 23. gh3 ♕d7–+] **♘g4 21. h3** [21. ♗g4 ♗g4 22. ♕b7 ♘h4–+]

♘h6 22. ♗e1 ♖g8 23. ♘d2 ♗f6! 24. ♔h1? [24. ♘f3!□ ♗h4! (24... ♗h3? 25. gh3 ♘h4 26. ♔h1 ♕d7 27. ♘g1) 25. ♗f2! ♘f7!∓ (25... ♗h3? 26. gh3 ♕d7 27. ♗h4 ♘h4 28. ♔f2∞) 26. ♖a1 ♘g5 27. ♔f1 ♗f2 28. ♕f2 ♘f3 29. ♗f3 ♘h4] **♗h4!−+ 25. ♘f3 ♗e1 26. ♘e1** [26. ♖e1 ♘h4 27. ♖g1 ♘f3 28. ♗f3 ♕h4] **♘h4 27. ♖f2 ♕g5 28. ♘f3 ♘f3 29. ♗f3 ♗h3 0 : 1**
[Kasparov]

617. !N E 97

EPIŠIN 2620 − DOLMATOV 2615
Rostov na Donu 1993

1. d4 ♘f6 2. c4 g6 3. ♘c3 ♗g7 4. e4 d6 5. ♘f3 0−0 6. ♗e2 e5 7. 0−0 ♘c6 8. d5 ♘e7 9. ♘d2 a5 10. ♖b1 ♘d7 11. a3 f5 12. b4 ♔h8 13. f3 f4 14. c5 ab4 15. ab4 dc5 16. bc5 ♘c5 17. ♘c4 b6 18. ♘b5 ♗a6□ 19. ♗a3 [19. ♘c7 ♗c4! (19... ♕c7 20. d6 ♕d8 21. de7 ♕e7 22. ♘b6 △ ♘d5⩲) 20. ♗c4 ♕c7 21. d6 ♕d8 22. de7 ♕e7 23. ♗d5 (23. ♖b6?? ♕a7−+) ♖ab8$\overline{\overline{\infty}}$] **c6! N** [19... ♘c8 20. ♗c5 bc5 21. ♘a5 ♗b5 22. ♖b5 ♘d6 23. ♖c5 △ ♘b3, ♖c6, ♘c5±; 21... ♘d6 − 52/(654)] **20. dc6 ♘c6 21. ♕d8 ♖fd8 22. ♘b6 ♗b5 23. ♗b5 ♖a3 24. ♗c6± ♖c3! 25. ♘d5 ♖c2 26. ♘b4! ♖c3 27. ♗d5 ♗f6! 28. ♘c6 ♖d6! 29. ♖fc1** [29. ♖b8 ♔g7 30. ♖a1 h5=] **♖c1 30. ♖c1 ♘e6!** [30... ♘a4 31. ♔f1 ♘b6 32. ♖c5±] **31. ♗e6** [31. ♔f2 ♘d4 32. ♘d4 ed4 33. g3 ♗g5!=] **♖e6** [♖ 9/i] **32. ♔f1 ♔g7 33. ♘b4 ♖b6!** [33... h5 34. ♖c7 ♔h6 35. ♖c6!±] **34. ♘d5 ♖a6 35. ♖c7 ♔h6?** [35... ♔g8!⩲] **36. g3** [36. ♘f6? ♖f6 37. ♖e7 ♖a6=] **♖a1 37. ♔g2 ♖a2 38. ♔h3 ♗g5 39. ♖c3 ♖f2 40. ♖b3 ♔h5 41. ♘b6 ♗f6□ 42. ♘d5 ♗g5 43. ♘c7!!** [△ ♘e6] **fg3** [43... ♗f6 44. ♘e8! ♗h8 45. ♖b7 ♔h6 46. ♘d6 ♗f6 47. ♔g4+−; 43... ♗h6 44. ♘e8! ♗g5 (44... ♔g5 45. ♖b5+−) 45. ♘g7 ♔h6 46. ♘e6±] **44. hg3 ♗c1!! 45. ♘d5?** [45. ♘e6 ♖b2 46. ♖c3 ♖b6!! 47. ♘f8 ♗h6□ 48. ♘d7 (48. ♘h7? ♗g7=) ♖e6 49. ♖c5 (49. f4 ♗f4!□ 50. gf4 ef4=) ♗g7 50. f4 ♔h6 51. f5 gf5 52. ef5 ♖e7=] **♔g5= 46. ♘b4 ♖b2 47. ♖b2 ♗b2 48. ♘d5 1/2 : 1/2**
[Epišin]

618. !N E 97

EPIŠIN 2620 − DOLMATOV 2615
Rossija 1992

1. d4 ♘f6 2. c4 g6 3. ♘c3 ♗g7 4. e4 d6 5. ♗e2 e5 6. ♘f3 0−0 7. 0−0 ♘c6 8. d5 ♘e7 9. ♘d2 a5 10. ♖b1 ♘d7 11. a3 f5 12. b4 ♔h8 13. f3 ♘g8 14. ♕c2 ♘gf6 15. ♘b5 ab4 16. ab4 ♘h5 17. g3 ♘df6 18. c5 ♗d7 19. ♖b3 ♗h6 20. ♖c3 ♘g7! N [△ ♘ge8; 20... ♗f4 − 54/621] **21. ♖d1!** [△ ♗b2] **♘ge8 22. ♗b2 fe4?!** [22... ♖f7!∞] **23. ♘e4 ♘e4 24. ♕e4 ♗f5 25. ♕c4 ♗g7 26. ♕b3!** [△ ♖c4, ♘c3, ♗c1-e3±] **♔g8 27. ♖c4 ♖f7 28. ♘c3** [28. ♗c1! ♘f6 29. ♗e3 ♕f8 (29... e4 30. f4 ♘g4 31. ♗d4±) 30. cd6 cd6 31. ♘c7 △ ♘e6±] **♘f6 29. ♗c1 ♕f8! 30. ♗e3?** [30. cd6 cd6 31. ♘b5 ♘e8 (31... ♗d7 32. ♖c7 ♗b5 33. ♖f7 ♕f7 34. ♗b5±) 32. ♗e3 ♗h6 33. ♗f2 △ ♘c3, b5-b6, ♘b5⩲] **♗h6 31. ♗f2 ♗d7?** [31... e4! 32. fe4 ♘e4 33. ♖e4 ♗e4 34. ♘e4 ♖e8 35. ♕d3 ♖e4 36. ♕e4 ♖f2=] **32. b5± ♘g4 33. ♘e4! ♘f2 34. ♔f2 b6** [34... dc5 35. ♖c5 ♗f5 36. d6 ♗e4 37. ♖c7+−] **35. cd6 cd6 36. ♖c6!+− ♗c6 37. dc6 ♔h8 38. ♖d6 ♗c1 39. ♕c3 ♗a3 40. ♖e6 ♕g7 41. ♔g2! ♖e7 42. ♗c4 ♖aa7 43. h4 ♖e6 44. ♗e6 ♗f8 45. ♗b3! h6 46. ♕c4 g5 47. hg5 hg5 48. ♕e6 g4 49. fg4 1 : 0** **[Epišin]**

619. E 97

M. GUREVICH 2610
− DOLMATOV 2615
Deutschland 1993

1. d4 ♘f6 2. c4 g6 3. ♘c3 ♗g7 4. e4 d6 5. ♘f3 0−0 6. ♗e2 e5 7. 0−0 ♘c6 8. d5 ♘e7 9. ♘d2 a5 10. a3 ♘d7 11. ♖b1 f5 12. b4 ♔h8 13. f3 ♘g8 14. ♕c2 ♘gf6 15. ♗d3 f4 16. ♘b5 ♘e8!? 17. ♗e2!? [17. c5 dc5 18. bc5 c6 19. dc6 bc6 20. ♘d6 ♘c5∞] **b6** [17... g5?! 18. c5 dc5 19. bc5 c6 20. dc6 bc6 21. ♘d6↑] **18. c5!? N** [18. ♗b2 − 56/708] **bc5 19. bc5 ♘c5 20. a4!? h5 21. ♗a3 ♘a6 22. ♖fc1 ♗d7 23. ♘c3!** [△ ♗b5-d7, ×b7, c6, c7] **g5 24. ♗b5 g4 25. ♗d7 ♕d7 26. ♘b5 gf3 27. ♘f3** [27. gf3?! ♕h3 28. ♔h1 ♘f6 29. ♖g1 ♘g4!?⇆]

♗f6 28. ♕c6 ♕c6?! [28... ♕g4!? 29. ♕a8 ♖g8 30. ♘e1 f3 31. ♖c2 ♗h4⇆; 28... ♕c8!? △ ♖g8, ♕g4⇆] **29. dc6!** [△ ♘c3-d5, ♖b5↑《] **♘g7** [29... ♗d8? 30. ♘e5] **30. ♘c3 ♘e6 31. ♘d5 ♖f7 32. ♖b5 ♘ac5 33. ♗c5** [33. ♘f6 ♖f6 34. ♘e5 ♘d4!⇆] **♘c5** [33... dc5 (△ ♘d4) 34. ♔f1!? ♖a6 35. ♘d2±] **34. ♘f6 ♖f6 35. ♘e5!± ♖g8** [35... ♖e6 36. ♘d7 ♘d7 37. cd7 c5 38. ♖cb1+−; 35... ♖e8 36. ♘d7±] **36. ♘f3 ♖e6 37. ♖c4 ♖gg6?** [37... ♘e4 38. ♖h5 ♔g7 39. ♖a5±; 37... ♖ge8!? 38. e5 ♘d3 39. ♘g5! (39. ed6?? ♖e1 40. ♘e1 ♖e1#) ♖g6 (39... ♘e5 40. ♘e6 ♘c4 41. ♘c7 ♖c8 42. ♖h5±) 40. e6 ♘e5 41. h4±] **38. ♖a5 ♘e4 39. ♖h5 ♔g8 40. ♖f5 ♖e8 41. a5!+−** [41. ♖f4 d5 42. ♖c2 ♖a8±] **♘c5 42. ♖cf4 ♖b8 43. h3 ♘d3 44. ♖e4 ♘b4** [44... ♖b1 45. ♔h2 ♘f2 46. ♖e8 ♔g7 47. ♘g5+−] **45. ♖e7 ♖g7 46. ♖g7 ♔g7 47. ♘d4 ♔g6 48. ♖b5 ♘c6 49. ♖b8** [49. a6!] **♘b8 50. ♔f2 ♔f6** [50... c5 51. ♘b5 d5 52. ♘c7 d4 53. a6] **51. h4 d5 52. g4 c5 53. g5 ♔e5 54. h5! 1 : 0** **[M. Gurevich]**

620. E 97

A. CHERNIN 2600 − ISTRĂŢESCU 2470

Odorheiu Secuiesc 1993

1. d4 ♘f6 2. c4 g6 3. ♘c3 ♗g7 4. e4 d6 5. ♘f3 0−0 6. ♗e2 e5 7. 0−0 ♘c6 8. d5 ♘e7 9. ♘d2 a5 10. a3 ♘d7 11. ♖b1 f5 12. b4 ♔h8 13. f3 ♘g8 14. ♕c2 ♘gf6 15. ♗d3 f4 16. ♗e2! g5 17. ♘b5 b6 18. ♗b2 ♘e8 19. g4! h5 20. h3 ♖f6 N [20... ♖f7 − 55/646] **21. ♘b3!** [21. ♔g2 M. Gurevich] **a4 22. ♘c1 ♖h6 23. ♘d3 hg4 24. hg4 ♘f8** [24... ♖h3 25. ♖f2 △ ♖h2±] **25. ♔g2 ♘g6 26. ♖h1 ♘h4 27. ♔f2!** [△ ♖bg1; 27. ♔f1 ♗d7 △ ♕f6-g6-h7, ♘g6⇆ ⇔h] **♗d7 28. ♘c3 ♘f6 29. ♖bg1 ♕g8 30. ♔f1 ♕h7 31. ♘f2± ♗f8 32. ♕d1 ♔g7 33. ♘b5 ♘e8 34. ♗d3** [34. ♔e1? ♘g2 △ ♘e3] **♗e7 35. ♔e2 ♖c8 36. ♘a7 ♖a8 37. ♘b5 ♖c8 38. ♕a4** [38. ♘c3] **♘f6 39. ♕d1 ♖h8** [39... ♘f3 40. ♔f3 ♘g4 41. ♘g4 ♖h3 42. ♖h3 ♕h3 43. ♔f2 ♗g4 44. ♖g4 ♕e3 45. ♔g2 ♖h8 46. ♕e2 ♕h3 47. ♔f2 ♕h1 48. ♕f1 ♖h2 49. ♖g2+−] **40. ♔d2** [40. ♘c7? ♘f3!→] **♗d8 41. ♔c1+− ♔f8 42. ♗e2 ♘g6 43. a4** [⌓ 43. ♖h6 ♕h6 44. ♖h1] **♕e7 44. ♗a3** [⌓ 44. ♖h6] **♖h2 45. ♕e1 c6! 46. dc6 ♗c6 47. ♘c3 b5! 48. cb5 ♗b6 49. ♖h2 ♖h2 50. ♘fd1!± ♗a8! 51. ♖h1 ♖h1 52. ♕h1 ♘h4 53. a5 ♗d4 54. ♗c4!** [54. ♕e1 d5!∞] **♕c7 55. ♕f1 d5 56. ed5 ♘d5 57. b6 ♕c8 58. ♗a6! ♕d7?** [58... ♕d8 59. b7 ♗b7 60. ♗b7±] **59. ♕b5+− ♗c6 60. ♕c6 1 : 0**
[A. Chernin]

621. E 97

A. CHERNIN 2600 − MARIN 2515

Odorheiu Secuiesc 1993

1. d4 ♘f6 2. ♘f3 g6 3. c4 ♗g7 4. ♘c3 0−0 5. e4 d6 6. ♗e2 e5 7. 0−0 ♘c6 8. d5 ♘e7 9. ♘d2 a5 10. a3 ♘d7 11. ♖b1 f5 12. b4 ♔h8 13. f3 ♘g8 14. ♕c2 ♘gf6 15. ♗d3 f4 16. ♗e2! h5 N [16... ♘e8!?] **17. c5! dc5** [17... ab4] **18. bc5 ♘c5 19. ♘b5 b6** [19... ♘a6!?] **20. a4 g5?!** [20... ♖e8 △ ♗f8] **21. ♗a3 g4** [21... ♘a6!? 22. ♗f8 ♗f8=/∞] **22. ♗c5 bc5 23. ♕c5± ♘h7** [23... ♖f7 24. ♖fc1±] **24. ♘c7 g3 25. ♖fc1 ♕h4** [25... gh2 26. ♔h1+−] **26. ♘f1** [26. ♘a8 ♕h2 27. ♔f1 ♘g5! △ 28. ♕g1? ♘h3!−+] **♘g5 27. ♘a8 ♗h3** [27... ♘h3 28. ♔h1 ♘f2 29. ♕f2! gf2 30. ♘b6 ♗b7 31. ♘d7+−] **28. ♖b7 ♖g8** [28... ♗g2 29. ♔g2 ♕h3 30. ♔g1 gh2 31. ♔h1] **29. hg3!+− fg3 30. ♖g7 ♖g7 31. ♕f8 ♔h7 32. ♖c7 ♖c7 33. ♘c7 ♗g2 34. ♕f5 ♔h6 35. ♔g2 1 : 0** **[A. Chernin]**

622. E 98**

FTÁČNIK 2535 − WOJTKIEWICZ 2580

Budapest (zt - play off) 1993

1. d4 ♘f6 2. c4 g6 3. ♘c3 ♗g7 4. e4 d6 5. ♘f3 0−0 6. ♗e2 e5 7. 0−0 ♘c6 8. d5 ♘e7 9. ♘e1 ♘e8 10. ♗e3 f5 11. f3 f4 12. ♗f2 h5 13. a4 g5 14. a5 N ♖f6 15. c5 ♖g6 [15... dc5 16. ♗c5 ♘d6 17. ♘b5 a6 18. ♘d6 cd6 19. ♗b6 ♕e8 20. ♖c1±] **16. cd6** [16. ♘b5 a6 17. cd6 ab5 18. de7 ♕e7 19. ♗b5 g4⇆] **♘d6!** [16... cd6 17. ♘b5 a6 18. ♗b6 ♕d7 19. ♕b3 g4 20. ♖c1 ♗f8 21. ♘c7 ♘c7 22. ♖c7± R. Odendahl 2295 − Kuprejčik 2555, Deutschland 1992] **17.**

♘b5 g4 18. ♘d6 cd6 [18... ♕d6 19. ♖c1 g3 20. ♗c5 ♕f6 21. ♔h1∞ ×c7] **19. ♗h4 ♕f8** [19... g3?! 20. hg3 fg3 21. f4!±; 19... ♔f7 20. fg4 ♗g4 (20... hg4 21. g3 △ 21... f3 22. ♗f3! gf3 23. ♕f3+−) 21. h3 ♗e2 22. ♕e2±; 19... gf3 20. ♗f3 ♗g4 21. ♘d3 ♕d7 22. ♕a4± D. Becker − Kuprejčik 2560, Eupen 1993] **20. ♕a4! ♗f6 21. ♗f6 ♖f6** [21... ♕f6 22. ♕e8 ♔h7 23. ♖c1 g3 24. ♖c7 ♖g7 25. ♕h5 ♔g8 26. hg3±] **22. ♖c1 ♘g6** [22... g3 23. ♖c7 ♕d8 24. ♕c2↑] **23. a6** [23. ♖c7 ♕d8 24. ♕c2 ♖f7 25. ♖f7 ♔f7 26. b4 ♗d7∞; 23. ♗b5 △ 23... ♘h4 24. ♗d7 gf3 25. ♘f3 ♕g7? 26. ♖c8 ♖c8 27. ♘h4+−] **♖f7** [23... ba6 24. ♗a6 (24. ♕c6 ♖b8 25. ♕c7 ♖a8=) ♗a6 25. ♕a6 ♕d8∞] **24. ♗b5 ♕d8!** [24... ba6 25. ♗a6 ♗a6 26. ♕a6 ♕e7∞] **25. ab7** [25. ♗e8 ♖g7 26. ab7 ♗b7 27. ♗g6 ♖g6∓] **♗b7** [25... ♖b7 26. ♗c6 ♕b6 27. ♔h1 ♖c7 28. ♘d3 ♖b8 29. ♕a3! ×d6] **26. ♗c6 ♕b6 27. ♔h1 ♗a6** [27... ♕b2? 28. ♘d3 ♕e2 29. ♗b7 ♖b7 30. ♕c6 ♖ab8 31. ♕d6→] **28. ♖g1** [28. ♗a8 ♗f1 29. ♕e8 ♘f8 30. ♕c8 ♕b2 31. fg4 ♗a6 32. ♕c2 ♕b5∓] **♖c8** [28... ♖c7 29. ♖c2!? (29. ♗a8 ♖c1 30. ♕e8 ♘f8 31. ♕h5? ♕g1 32. ♔g1 ♖e1 33. ♔f2 ♖f1#) ♖ac8] **29. ♖c2 ♖g7 30. ♗d7?** [30. ♕a3 ♖d8∞; 30. b4! ♘e7 (30... ♘h4 31. b5 ♗b7 32. fg4∞) 31. b5 (31. ♕a5 ♕a5 32. ba5 ♖b8 33. ♗d7∞) ♗b7 32. ♕a3∞] **♖c2 31. ♘c2** [31. ♗e6 ♔h7 32. ♕c2 ♖c7∓] **♗e2?** [31... gf3! 32. ♗e6 ♔h7 33. gf3 ♕f2 34. ♘e1 ♘h4−+] **32. ♘e1** [32. fg4 hg4 33. ♗e6⇆] **♔h7?** [32... gf3 33. gf3 (33. ♘f3 ♗f3 34. gf3 ♕f2 35. ♗e6 ♔h7 36. ♕a3 ♘h4−+) ♕f2 34. ♗e6 ♔h7 35. ♗f5 ♗f3 36. ♘f3 ♕f3 37. ♖g2 ♔h6−+] **33. ♗f5 ♔h6** [33... gf3 34. gf3 ♗b5 (34... ♕f2 35. ♕e8 ♗f3 36. ♘f3 ♕f3 37. ♖g2 ♕f1=) 35. ♕c2∞] **34. ♕e8 ♕f2 35. fg4 ♗g4?** [35... hg4 36. ♗g6 ♖g6 37. ♕h8 ♔g5 38. ♕d8 ♖f6 39. ♕g8=] **36. ♗g6 ♖g6** [36... ♗d7 37. ♕f8 ♔g6 38. ♕d6±] **37. ♕h8 ♔g5 38. ♕d8** [38. h3! ♗e2 (38... ♖h6 39. ♘f3 ♗f3 40. ♕d8 ♖f6 41. gf3+−) 39. ♘f3 ♗f3 40. gf3 ♔h4 41. ♖g6 ♕f3 42. ♖g2+−] **♔h6** [38... ♖f6 39. ♘f3 ♔g6 40. ♕g8 ♔h6 41. ♕g5+−] **39. ♕h8 ♔g5 40. ♘f3?** [40. h3!+−] **♗f3 41. gf3 ♔h4 42. ♕d8??⊕** [42. ♖g6 ♕f1 43. ♖g1 ♕f3=] **♔h3 43. ♕d7 ♔h4?** [43... ♖g4! 44. fg4 ♕h2#] **44. ♕e7?? ♔h3 45. ♕d7 ♔h4?** [45... ♖g4!−+] **46. ♖g6 ♕f1 47. ♖g1 ♕f3 1/2 : 1/2** **[Ftáčnik]**

623.*** !N **E 98**

KORTCHNOI 2605 − ŠIROV 2670

Buenos Aires 1993

1. c4 ♘f6 2. ♘c3 g6 3. e4 d6 4. d4 ♗g7 5. ♗e2 0−0 6. ♘f3 e5 7. 0−0 ♘c6 8. d5 ♘e7 9. ♘e1 ♘e8 10. ♗e3 f5 11. f3 f4 12. ♗f2 h5 13. c5 g5 14. a4 ♘g6 15. a5 ♗h6 16. ♘b5! N [16. b4?!; RR 16... ♔h7 17. cd6 cd6 18. ♘b5 *a)* 18... a6 N 19. ♘a3 ♘f6 20. ♖c1 g4 21. ♗b6 ♕e8 22. ♖c7± Züger 2415 − Gallagher 2500, Schweiz 1993; *b)* 18... g4 19. fg4 hg4 20. ♗g4 ♗g4 21. ♕g4 ♘f6 22. ♕f5 N (22. ♕f3 − 56/710) f3 23. ♘f3 ♘d5 24. ♗h4 ♖f5 25. ♗d8 ♖f4∞ Züger 2415 − Cvitan 2575, Bern 1993; 16. ♔h1 N ♔h7 17. cd6 cd6 18. ♘b5 a6 19. ♘c3 ♘f6 20. ♘a4 g4 21. ♘b6 ♖b8 22. ♘c8 ♕c8± Kožul 2550 − Cvitan 2575, Zagreb (zt) 1993] **a6 17. ♘a3 ♔h8 18. ♘c4 ♖g8 19. ♖a3 ♘f6 20. cd6 cd6 21. ♘b6?** [21. ♕b3! ♕e7 (21... g4 22. ♕b6±) 22. ♕b4 ♖d8 23. ♘b6 ♖b8 24. h3!±] **♖b8 22. ♖c3** [22. ♕c2!? g4 23. fg4 hg4∞ Širov] **g4 23. fg4** [23. ♔h1 g3↑] **♘e4! 24. ♖c8 ♖c8 25. ♘c8 ♕c8 26. ♗b6!? ♘e7 27. gh5 ♘f6∓ 28. b3 ♘ed5 29. ♗c4 ♕c6 30. ♖f2 ♖c8?** [30... ♖f8! 31. ♗d5 ♘d5 32. ♖c2 ♕b5 33. ♘f3 (33. ♕g4? ♘e3−+; 33. ♕d3 ♕d3 34. ♘d3 e4∓) ♕b3 34. ♖d2 ♕d1 35. ♖d1 ♘b6 36. ♖d6 ♗g7 37. ab6∓] **31. ♗d5 ♘d5 32. ♖c2 ♘c3 33. ♕g4± ♗f8** [33... ♕e8 34. ♕h3±] **34. ♘d3 ♕e8 35. ♘b4!** [△ ♘d5] **d5 36. ♘d5 ♗c5 37. ♗c5 ♖c5** [37... ♘d5 38. ♗f8!+−] **38. h6 ♕f8 39. ♖c3**
1 : 0 **[Kortchnoi]**

624. **E 98**

V. NEVEROV 2550 −
V. NEVEDNIČIJ 2495

Nikolaev (zt) 1993

1. d4 ♘f6 2. c4 g6 3. ♘c3 ♗g7 4. e4 0−0 5. ♘f3 d6 6. ♗e2 e5 7. 0−0 ♘c6 8. d5

♘e7 9. ♘e1 ♘d7 10. ♘d3 f5 11. ♗d2 fe4 12. ♘e4 ♘f5 13. ♗c3 a5!? N [13... ♘f6 — 43/758] **14. g4!?** [14. c5?! ♘f6!=; 14. g3!±] **♕h4** [14... ♘d4?! 15. ♗d4 ed4 16. f4±] **15. ♘e1** [15. ♗e1 ♘d4 16. f3 (16. f4? ♕e7∓) ♕e7=] **♘d4□ 16. ♘g2** [16. ♗d4!? ed4 17. f4∞] **♕e7 17. f3 b5! 18. cb5?!** [18. b3! a4! 19. cb5 ab3 20. ab3 ♖a1 21. ♗a1 ♘b6 22. ♗c4 ♗b7 (22... ♗d7∞) 23. ♘e3∞] **♘b6 19. a4!? ♗b7** [19... ♘e2!? 20. ♕e2 ♘d5 21. ♕d2! ♘b6 (21... ♘f4!?∞) 22. ♘e3 ♗h6 (22... ♗b7 23. ♗a5 d5 24. ♗b6 de4∞) 23. ♘d5 ♘d5 24. ♕h6∞] **20. ♘e3 ♔h8 21. ♖c1?!** [21. b4! ab4 22. ♗b4 ♘d5 23. ♘d5 ♗d5 24. a5∞] **♗d5! 22. ♘d5 ♘d5 23. ♗d2 ♘f4 24. ♗f4 ♖f4 25. ♗c4 ♖af8 26. ♖c3 d5!** [26... h5 27. gh5 gh5 28. ♔h1! ♕h4 29. ♗d5!∞] **27. ♗d5 ♖d8 28. ♗c4** [⌓ 28. ♗a2 ♘f3 29. ♕f3 ♖f3 30. ♖cf3 ♕h4 31. h3 ♗h6∓] **♘f3 29. ♕f3 ♖f3 30. ♖cf3 ♖d4! 31. ♗d3 ♕d8 32. ♘f2⊕ ♗h6?!⊕** [32... ♖a4] **33. b3 ♗f4 34. ♗c4 ♕d6 35. ♖e1 ♔g7 36. ♖e2 ♕d8 37. ♔g2 ♕g5 38. h3 h5 39. ♘e4 ♖e4! 40. ♖e4 hg4 41. ♖d3?** [41. hg4∓] **gh3 42. ♔f1 ♕g2**

0 : 1 **[V. Nevedničij]**

625. **E 99**

NIKOLAIDIS 2380 — KR. GEORGIEV 2525

Athens 1993

1. ♘f3 ♘f6 2. c4 g6 3. ♘c3 ♗g7 4. e4 d6 5. d4 0–0 6. ♗e2 e5 7. 0–0 ♘c6 8. d5 ♘e7 9. ♘e1 ♘d7 10. f3 f5 11. g4 h6!? [△ fg4, g5, ♘g6] **12. h4 N** [12. ♘d3 — 5/679] **♘f6 13. ♘g2 c6 14. ♗e3 cd5?!** [14... ♕d7!? △ 15. ef5 gf5 16. g5 hg5 17. hg5 f4 18. gf6 ♖f6→] **15. cd5 ♕d7 16. ef5!?** [16. ♗b5 ♕c7 17. ♗e2=] **gf5 17. g5 hg5 18. ♗b5!□** [18. hg5 f4→] **♕d8 19. hg5 ♘h5 20. f4 ♘f4 21. ♗f4!** [21. ♘f4? ef4 22. ♗f4 ♗c3! 23. bc3 ♕b6 24. ♖f2 ♕b5; 21. ♖f4?! ef4 22. ♘f4 ♗e5∓] **ef4 22. ♘f4 a6!** [22... ♗c3? 23. bc3 ♕b6 24. ♖f2 ♕b5 25. ♕h5 △ g6, ♖h2→] **23. ♕h5!□** [23. ♗a4? ♕b6 △ 24. ♖f2 ♗d4, △ 24. ♔h1 ♕b2] **ab5 24. ♖ae1=∞** [24. g6!? ♘g6 25. ♘g6 △ ♖ae1=∞] **♗d7** [24... b4?! 25. g6 (25. ♘b5!?) ♘g6 26. ♘g6 ♖e8 27. ♘b5 (△ 27... ♕b6 28. ♔h2 ♕b5 29. ♘e7+–) ♗d7 28. ♖e8 ♕e8 29. ♕g5→] **25. g6 ♘g6** [25... ♖f6 26. ♕h7 ♔f8 27. ♘e4 △ 27... fe4? 28. ♘h5+–] **26. ♘g6 ♖e8** [26... ♖f7 27. ♘e4!±] **27. ♖e8 ♕e8** [27... ♗e8 28. ♕f5↑] **28. ♕g5 ♔h7** [28... ♔f7 29. ♘b5; 28... ♗d4!? 29. ♔g2 ♔f7 30. ♖h1! ♕g8 31. ♖h6∞↑] **29. ♘e7 ♗h6 30. ♕h4** [30. ♕f6? ♕h5] **♕h8!** [30... ♕f7? 31. ♘e4!→] **31. ♖f2?!** [31. ♔h1?! (△ ♘e4) ♕e5!; 31. ♘f5!∞] **♖f8?!⊕** [31... ♖e8! 32. ♘f5□∞] **32. ♘e4! ♕g7 33. ♔h1** [33. ♖g2? ♕d4–+] **♕e5?** [33... ♕g4? 34. ♘f6! ♖f6 35. ♕g4! fg4 36. ♖f6+–; 33... fe4! 34. ♕e4 ♗f5 35. ♖f5 ♖f5 36. ♕f5⩲]

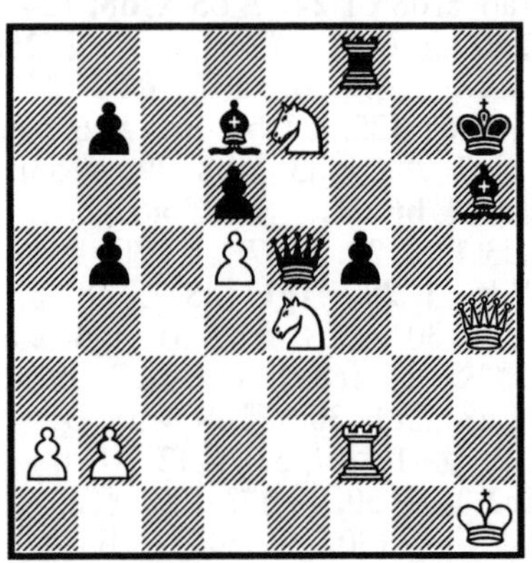

34. ♘g5 ♔g7 35. ♖g2!+– ♗g5 [35... ♕e7 36. ♘e6 ♔f7 37. ♕h5] **36. ♕g5!□** [36. ♖g5? ♔f7 △ ♔e8] **♔f7 37. ♘g6!** [37. ♕h5? ♔e7 38. ♖e2 ♖f6±] **♕e1 38. ♔h2 ♖g8 39. ♕h5!** [39. ♕h6?! ♔e8! 40. ♕h7! ♖g6 41. ♕g6 ♔d8±] **♔f6 40. ♕h6 ♖e8 41. ♘f4** **1 : 0**

[Andrianov, Nikolaidis]

626. **E 99**

P. LUKÁCS 2480 — V. LOGINOV 2505

Budapest 1993

1. d4 ♘f6 2. c4 g6 3. ♘c3 ♗g7 4. e4 d6 5. ♘f3 0–0 6. ♗e2 e5 7. 0–0 ♘c6 8. d5 ♘e7 9. ♘e1 ♘d7 10. f3 f5 11. g4 ♘f6 12. ♘d3 c6 13. ♗e3 ♔h8 14. h3 b5 15. ♘b4 ♗b7 N [15... cd5 — 39/755; 15... bc4 — 39/756] **16. dc6 ♘c6 17. ♘c6 ♗c6 18. cb5** [18. ♘b5!? *a)* 18... ♗b5 19. cb5 d5 (19...

f4 20. ♗f2 d5 21. ed5±) 20. g5 ♘d7 (20... ♘h5 21. ♕d5) 21. ♕d5 f4 22. ♗f2 ♕g5 23. ♔h1±; *b)* 18... fe4! 19. ♕d6 ♗b5 20. ♕d8 ♖fd8 21. cb5 ef3! (21... ♘d5 22. ♗g5!) 22. ♗f3 e4! (22... ♘d5 23. ♗g5±) 23. ♗g2 (23. ♗e2 ♘d5=/∞) ♘d5=/∞] **♗b7 19. ♗c4!** [19. ♕a4 d5 20. ed5 ♘d5 21. ♘d5 (21. ♖ad1?! ♘c3 22. bc3 ♕h4!) ♕d5 22. ♖ad1 ♕e6=/∞] **fe4** [19... ♖c8 20. ♗e6±; 19... h5 20. ♗g5±] **20. fe4 ♕c8!?** [20... ♘e4?! 21. ♖f8 ♗f8 (21... ♕f8 22. ♘e4 ♗e4 23. ♗d5±) 22. ♘e4 ♗e4 23. ♗d5 ♗d5 24. ♕d5±; 20... ♕d7 21. ♗d5! ♘d5 (21... ♗d5 22. ed5 h5 23. ♗g5! △ 23... hg4 24. ♗f6 ♗f6 25. ♕g4) 22. ed5 ♖f1 23. ♕f1 ♖f8 24. ♕d3±] **21. ♗b3!** [21. ♗d5 ♘d5 22. ed5 ♕c4!⇆ V. Loginov; 21. b3 ♘e4 22. ♘e4 (22. ♖f8 ♗f8 23. ♘e4 ♗e4 24. ♗d5? ♕c3!∓) ♖f1 (22... ♗e4 23. ♕d6+−) 23. ♗f1 ♗e4 24. ♖c1 (24. ♕d6? ♕c3!) ♕b7∞; 21. ♕b3!? ♖e8 (21... ♘e4 22. ♘e4 ♗e4 23. ♗d5±; 21... h5 22. ♗e6!±) 22. ♖f2! (22. ♗f7? ♘g4!) h5 23. ♗g5] **♕d7 22. ♗c2!?** [22. ♗d5±] **h5** [22... d5 23. ed5 ♘d5 (23... e4 24. ♕d2±) 24. ♗e4!±] **23. ♕e1! d5** [23... hg4 24. ♕h4 ♘h7 25. ♕g4±] **24. ed5 e4** [24... ♘d5 25. ♖f8 ♖f8 26. ♖d1±] **25. ♕h4! ♘d5 26. gh5 g5** [26... ♗f6 27. ♖f6! ♘f6 28. hg6+−; 26... ♗c3 27. bc3 ♘e3 28. hg6 ♔g8 29. ♗b3 *a)* 29... ♗d5 30. ♗d5 ♘d5 31. ♖f8! ♖f8 32. ♖d1 ♖f5 (32... e3 33. ♖d5) 33. c4 e3 34. ♖d5 ♖d5 35. ♕h7!+−; *b)* 29... ♘d5 30. ♖f8! ♖f8 31. ♖d1 ♖f3 (31... e3 32. ♖d5+−) 32. c4 ♕e7 (32... e3 33. cd5 e2 34. d6!+−) 33. ♕h7+−] **27. ♕e4 ♘f6 28. ♕f5 ♕f5** [28... ♕c7 29. ♕g5 ♖g8 30. ♗g6!+−] **29. ♖f5 ♖fe8 30. h6! ♖e3 31. hg7 ♔g7 32. ♖g5 ♔h8 33. ♖f1 ♘e4 34. ♘e4 ♗e4 35. ♗e4 ♖e4 36. ♖f6 ♔h7 37. ♖a6 ♖e2 38. ♖g2 1 : 0** **[P. Lukács]**

627. **E 99**

ROGOZENKO 2480 –
V. NEVEDNIČIJ 2495

Odorheiu Secuiesc 1993

1. d4 d6 2. c4 g6 3. ♘c3 ♗g7 4. ♘f3 ♘f6 5. e4 0–0 6. ♗e2 e5 7. 0–0 ♘c6 8. d5 ♘e7 9. ♘e1 ♘d7 10. ♗e3 f5 11. f3 ♖f7 N 12. a4 [12. ♖c1 ♕f8 △ ♗h6] **a5 13. ♘d3 b6** [13... ♕f8 14. c5 ♗h6 15. ♗f2; 14. ♕d2!?] **14. b4 f4 15. ♗f2 ab4 16. ♘b4 g5** [⌓ 16... h5 17. ♘d3!? g5 18. ♗e1 ♘f6 19. ♘f2 △ ♘b5, a5∞] **17. g4! fg3** [17... h5 18. h3⩲] **18. hg3 ♘g6 19. ♗e3** [19. ♕c2!? h5! (△ ♘d1-e3; 19... ♘f4? 20. gf4 gf4 21. ♔h2 ♕g5 22. ♖g1 ♕h5 23. ♔g2+−) 20. ♘d1 h4 21. g4 ♘f4 22. ♔h2 ♕f6 23. ♗e1∞] **♘f4!? 20. ♗d3!** [20. gf4? gf4→; 20. ♗d2?! ♘e2 21. ♘e2 (△ g4, ♘g3) g4! 22. fg4 ♘f6↑; 21. ♕e2∞] **♘h3** [20... ♘c5? 21. gf4 gf4 22. ♗c5 bc5 23. ♘c6 ♕h4 24. ♖f2 △ ♖h2+−] **21. ♔g2 ♘f6** [21... ♘c5! 22. ♘c6 ♕f6⩲] **22. ♘c6 ♕f8 23. ♗e2± h5 24. ♕d2 h4 25. ♖h1!** [25. ♗g5?!; 25. g4 ♘f4 26. ♗f4 ef4 27. e5; ⌓ 26... gf4±] **♘h5 26. ♖h3 ♗h3 27. ♔h3 ♖f3** [27... ♘g3 28. ♔g2! ♘e2 29. ♕e2 h3 30. ♔g3 △ ♖h1+−] **28. ♘e7!+− ♔h7 29. ♘f5 ♖f5 30. ef5 ♕f5 31. ♗g4** [31. g4? ♘f4 32. ♗f4 ♕f4 33. ♕f4 ef4 34. ♖c1 ♗c3 35. ♖c3 ♖a4] **♕g6 32. ♗h5 ♕h5 33. g4 ♕g6 34. ♖f1 e4 35. ♖f5 ♖f8 36. ♖f8 ♗f8 37. ♗g5 1 : 0**
[Rogozenko]

628. !N **E 99**

SAVČENKO 2535 – A. FEDOROV 2490

Nikolaev (zt) 1993

1. d4 ♘f6 2. c4 g6 3. ♘c3 ♗g7 4. e4 d6 5. ♘f3 0–0 6. ♗e2 e5 7. 0–0 ♘c6 8. d5 ♘e7 9. ♘e1 ♘d7 10. ♗e3 f5 11. f3 f4 12. ♗f2 g5 13. g4 fg3! N [13... h5 – 55/(651)] **14. hg3 ♘g6 15. ♕d2** [15. ♘g2 ♘f6 16. ♕d2 ♘h5⇆ △ 17. f4? ♘g3 18. ♗g3 ef4 19. ♗e1 ♘e5∓; 16. ♘e3!?] **h5 16. ♘g2 a5 17. ♘a4** [17. ♘e3 ♘c5 18. ♕c2 △ ♘f5∞; 17. ♗e3 ♗h6 △ 18... h4 19. g4 ♘f4∞] **b6 18. a3** [18. ♘e3!? ♘c5 19. ♘c5 bc5 20. ♕c2 h4 21. g4 ♘f4 22. ♔h2 a4 23. ♗e1 △ ♗c3, ♘f5∞] **h4** [18... ♘c5!? 19. ♘c5 bc5 20. b4 ab4 21. ab4 ♖a1 22. ♖a1 cb4 23. ♕b4 g4 (23... h4 24. g4 ♘f4 25. ♘f4 ef4 26. ♖a8±) 24. fg4 ♗g4 25. ♗g4 hg4 26. ♘e3∞] **19. g4 ♘f4 20. ♔h2 ♘f6 21. ♘e3⩲ ♗d7 22. ♘c3 a4 23. ♖fb1**

♖a5 24. b4 ab3 25. ♖b3 ♕e7 [25... ♕a8!? 26. ♘b5! ♕b7 27. ♗d1 (27. ♘d6 cd6 28. ♕a5 ba5 29. ♖b7 ♘e2∞) ♖fa8 28. ♗e1 △ ♕c2, ♖c3, a4, ♖ca3±] **26. ♘b5 ♘e8 27. ♗d1± ♕f7 28. ♖a2 ♗f6 29. a4 ♗d8⊕ 30. ♗e1 ♘f6 31. ♕c2 ♖a8 32. ♖ba3 ♘g6 33. ♔h1 ♔h8 34. a5 ♗b5 35. cb5 ba5 36. ♗a5 ♖b8 37. ♕c4 ♘d7 38. ♗d2 ♘c5 39. ♖a7 ♗f6 40. ♘f5 ♕d7 41. ♗e2+− ♖fc8 42. ♗e3 ♗e7** [⌓ 42... ♘b7 43. ♕c6!? ♕c6 44. bc6 ♘c5 45. ♗c5 dc5 46. ♖b7+−] **43. ♗c5 dc5 44. ♖2a6** [44... ♗d6 45. ♖d6; 44... ♔h7 45. d6 ♗d8 46. b6] **1 : 0** **[Savčenko]**

629.* **E 99**

SAVČENKO 2535 — A. FROLOV 2530

Nikolaev (zt) 1993

1. d4 ♘f6 2. c4 g6 3. ♘c3 ♗g7 4. e4 d6 5. ♘f3 0–0 6. ♗e2 e5 7. 0–0 ♘c6 8. d5 ♘e7 9. ♘e1 ♘d7 10. ♗e3 f5 11. f3 f4 12. ♗f2 g5 13. a4 h5 14. ♘b5 [14. a5 N a6 15. ♘d3 ♘f6 16. c5 g4 17. cd6 cd6 18. ♘a4 ♘g6 19. ♘b6 ♖b8 20. ♘c8!? (20. ♖c1 gf3 21. ♗f3 ♗g4∞) ♖c8! 21. fg4 ♘e4 22. gh5 ♘h4 23. ♗g4 ♖c4! 24. ♗e6 ♔h8 25. h6 ♗f6 26. ♕g4 ♘f2 27. ♘f2 e4 28. ♘h3 f3 29. gf3 ♖c2 30. ♕e4 ♖g8 31. ♗g4 ♕c7=∞ 32. ♔h1□ ♕c5! (32... ♗e5?! 33. ♖f2 ♖c4 34. ♕e2 ♕c5 35. ♖d1 ♗d4 36. h7 ♖f8 37. ♕e7 ♘g6 38. ♕g5 ♘e5? 39. ♗e6 1 : 0 Maksimenko 2435 — A. Frolov 2530, Nikolaev (zt) 1993) 33. ♕e6□ ♗e5 34. f4 ♖g6 35. ♕e8 ♖g8=] **a5 N** [14... ♘f6 — 44/754] **15. ♘d3 b6 16. b4 ab4 17. ♗e1 ♘f6 18. ♗b4 g4 19. a5 ba5 20. ♖a5 ♖b8 21. ♖a7 g3! 22. ♘c7** [22. ♗a5 ♘ed5 23. ed5 ♘d5] **♘e4!? 23. fe4 ♘c6□ 24. dc6 ♕h4 25. hg3□ fg3 26. ♖f8 ♗f8 27. ♗f3□ ♗g4□ 28. ♘f4** [28. ♘e1 ♖b4 29. ♖a2□ ♕h2 30. ♔f1 ♕h1 31. ♔e2 ♗f3∞; ⌓ 28. ♘d5±] **♕h2□ 29. ♔f1 ♖b4 30. ♕d5?** [30. ♗g4 ♖b1 31. ♗e6 ♔h8 32. ♕b1 ♕h1 33. ♔e2 ♕b1±] **♔h8□ 31. ♘g6 ♔g7 32. ♘e8 ♔h6 33. ♕d2⊕** [33. ♖h7 ♔g5 34. ♕d2 ♔g6 35. ♖h6 ♗h6 36. ♕d6 ♔f7−+] **♔g6 34. ♕b4 ♕h1 35. ♔e2 ♕g2 36. ♔d3 ♕f3 37. ♔c2 ♕e4 38. ♔b3 ♕e3 39. ♕c3 ♕a7 40. ♕d3 ♔g5 0 : 1** **[A. Frolov]**

630.* **E 99**

HAUSNER 2480 — DOLMATOV 2615

Deutschland 1993

1. c4 ♘f6 2. d4 g6 3. ♘c3 ♗g7 4. e4 d6 5. ♗e2 0–0 6. ♘f3 e5 7. 0–0 ♘c6 8. d5 ♘e7 9. ♘e1 ♘d7 10. ♗e3 f5 11. f3 f4 12. ♗f2 g5 13. a4 ♘g6 14. a5 h5 [RR 14... ♖f7 15. c5 ♘c5 16. ♗c5 dc5 17. a6 N (17. ♗c4 — 56/712) b6 18. ♗c4 ♔h8 19. d6 ♖f8 20. ♕d5 ♗d7 21. dc7 ♕c7 22. ♕b7 (22. ♘b5!?) ♕b7 (22... ♖fc8?! 23. ♘c2 ♗c6 24. ♕c7 ♖c7 25. ♖fd1 ♗f6 26. ♖d6! ♔g7 27. ♗d5 ♗d5 28. ♘d5 ♖f7 29. ♘a3± Soloženkin 2480 — M. Kamiński 2395, Cappelle la Grande 1993) 23. ab7 ♖ab8 24. ♖a7 ♗c6 25. ♗d5 ♘e7 26. ♘c2 ♘d5 27. ed5 ♗b7 (27... ♖b7 28. ♖fa1=∞) 28. ♘a3=∞ Soloženkin, Ševelëv] **15. b4** [15. ♘b5 ♘f6 16. ♘a7 ♗d7!? (16... g4 17. ♘c8 g3 18. hg3 fg3 19. ♗g3 h4=∞→) 17. c5 (17. a6 — 56/(712)) ♖a7 18. c6 ♕a8∞] **♘f6 16. h3** [16. c5? g4 17. cd6 g3 18. hg3 fg3 19. ♗g3 cd6→] **♖f7 17. c5 ♗f8 18. c6 ♖h7!? N 19. b5?** [△ b6; 19. cb7!? ♗b7 20. a6 ♗c8 21. ♗b5 ♘e7⇆; 19. ♘b5!? bc6!□ 20. ♘a7 g4 △ 21. ♘c8? g3] **b6!□ 20. ab6 cb6 21. ♖a3** [21. ♖a6!? ♖b8 22. ♕a4 ♕e7 23. ♘d3 g4 24. ♖a1 ♗a6 25. ba6 gh3 26. gh3 ♘e8 27. ♘b5 ♖a8! △ ♘c7∓] **♕c7!∓** [△ 22... g4 23. hg4 hg4 24. fg4 ♕g7→] **22. ♘d3 g4 23. hg4 hg4 24. fg4 ♕g7 25. ♗b6 ♕h6 26. ♘e1 ♕h2** [26... ♗e7!? 27. ♖a7 ♖a7 28. ♗a7 ♕h2 29. ♔f2 ♘e4 30. ♘e4 ♗h4 31. ♔f3 ♗g4 32. ♔g4 ♗e1 33. ♘f6 ♔f7−+] **27. ♔f2 ♕g3 28. ♔g1 ♘g4 29. ♗g4 ♗g4 30. ♕d2** [30. ♘f3 ♘h4−+] **♕h2 31. ♔f2 ♕h4 32. ♔g1 ♗e7 33. ♘f3 ♕h1 34. ♔f2 ♗h4 35. ♘h4 ♕h4 36. ♔g1 ♕h2 37. ♔f2 ♘h4 38. ♖g1** [38. ♘e2□ ♘g2 39. ♖g1 f3−+] **♘f3 39. ♕c1 ♕g3 40. ♔e2 ♘g1 41. ♔d2 ♕g2 42. ♔d3 ♗e2 43. ♔c2 ♗b5 44. ♔b3 ♘e2 0 : 1** **[Dolmatov]**

registar • индекс • index • register • registre • registro • registro • register • 棋譜索引 • الفهرس

C

D

E

F

G

H

I

J

K

L

M

N

O

P

R

S

T

U

V

W

X

Y

Z

komentatori • комментаторы • commentators • kommentatoren • commentateurs • comentaristas • commentatori • kommentatorer •
棋譜解説 • المعلقون

kombinacije • комбинации • combinations • kombinationen • combinaisons • combinaciones • combinazioni • kombinationer • 手筋 • التضحيات

I Kombinacije sa matnim napadom
Комбинации на мат
Combinations with mating attack
Mattkombinationen
Combinaisons avec attaque de mat
Combinaciones con ataque mate
Combinazioni con attacco di matto
Mattkombinationer
攻撃の手筋
خطة لاماتة الشاه

II Kombinacije za postizanje remija
Комбинации на ничью
Combinations to reach the draw
Remiskombinationen
Combinaisons pour faire nulle
Combinaciones para la obtencion de tablas
Combinazioni di patta
Remikombinationer
引分の手筋
خطة التوصل الى تعادل

III Kombinacije za postizanje materijalnog preimućstva
Комбинации для достижения материального перевеса
Combinations leading to material advantage
Kombinationen zwecks Materialgewinn
Combinaisons pour obtenir avantage matériel
Combinaciones para la obtencion de ventaja material
Combinazioni con guadagno materiale
Kombinationer som leder fill materiel fördel
駒得の手筋
خطة تحقيق أفضلية مادية

IV Sve ostale kombinacije
Все остальные комбинации
All the other combinations
Weitere Kombinationstypen
Autres combinaisons
Todas las demas combinaciones
Altre combinazioni
Alla övriga kombinationer
その他の手筋
سائر الخطط الاخرى

1. HENKIN 2575 – AFEK 2370
Netanya 1993

I

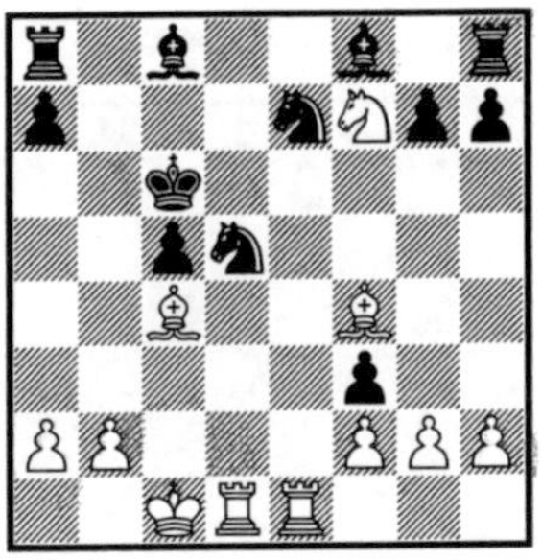

1. ? +–

2. PELAEZ 2240 – DE DEVITTIS 2335
La Habana 1993

I

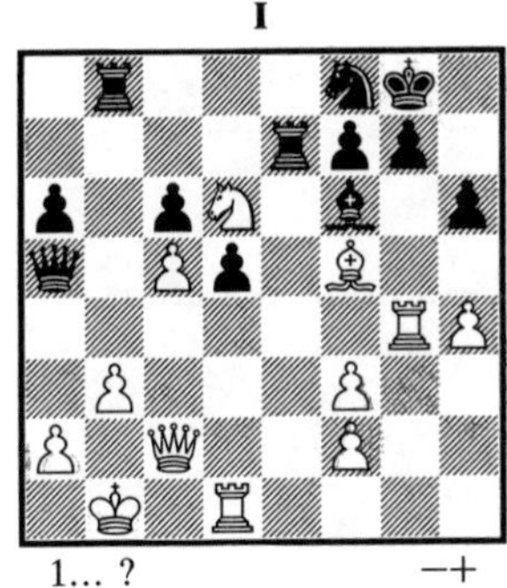

1... ? –+

3. G. KUZ'MIN 2525 – AKOPIAN 2615
Rostov na Donu (open) 1993

I

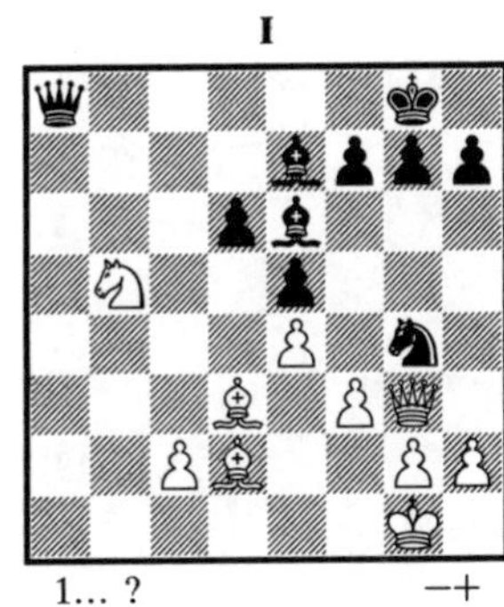

1... ? –+

4. MA. TSEITLIN 2460 – MOTSEASHVILI
Israel 1992

I

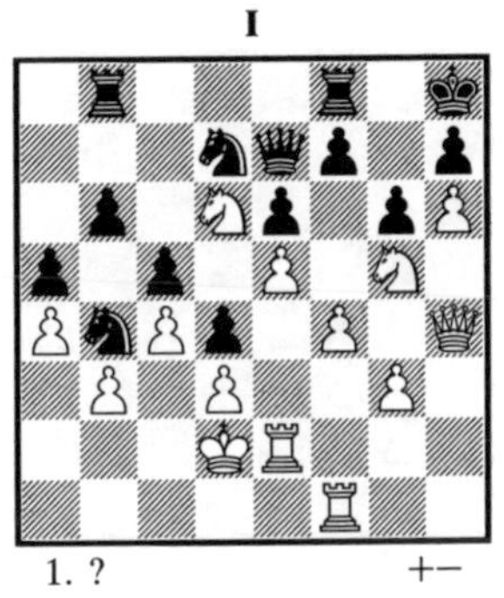

1. ? +–

5. LUGO 2415 – ELIZART CARDENAS 2265
La Habana 1992

I

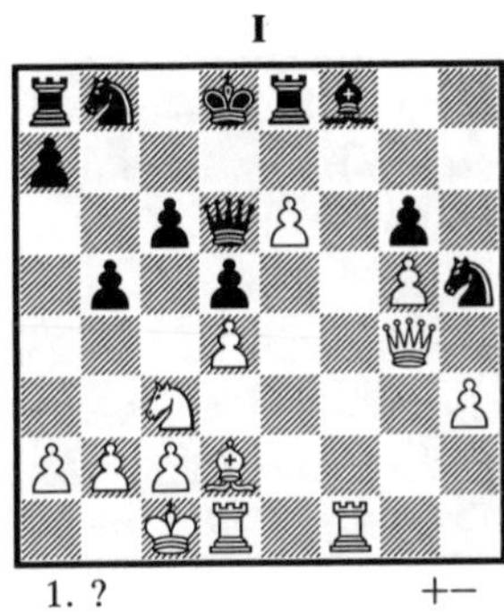

1. ? +–

6. MĂRTINUŞ – MATEI
Călimăneşti 1992/93

I

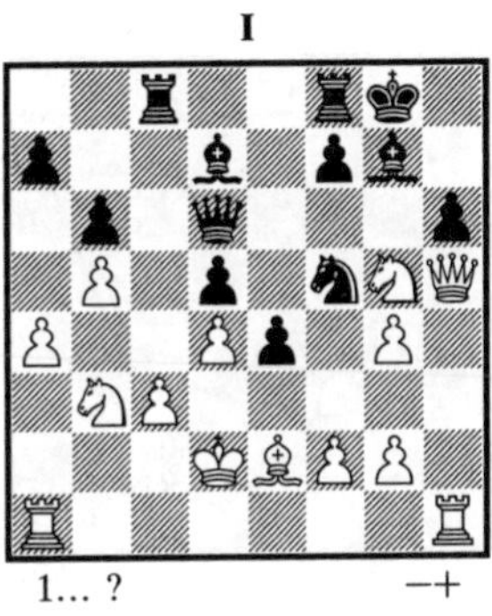

1... ? –+

7. NADANIAN 2285 – MARTIROSIAN
Armenia 1993

I

1. ? +–

8. PASCUAL PÉREZ – CRUZ-LIMA 2280
Cuba 1993

I

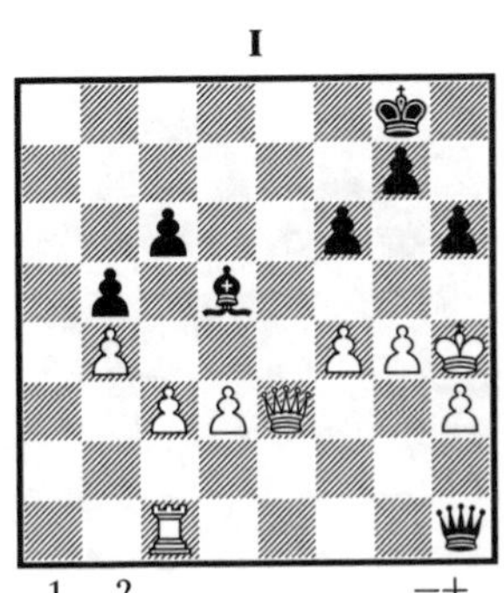

1... ? –+

9. KOMLIAKOV 2435 – GADJILU 2365
Nikolaev (zt) 1993

I

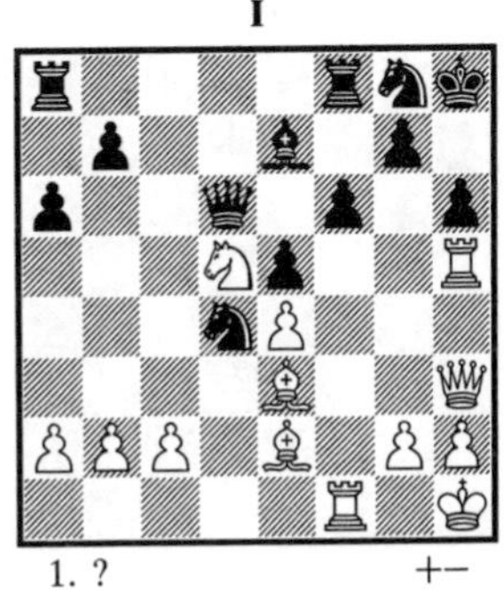

1. ? +–

10. M. KAMIŃSKI 2395 – STEFÁNSSON 2495

Cappelle la Grande 1993

II

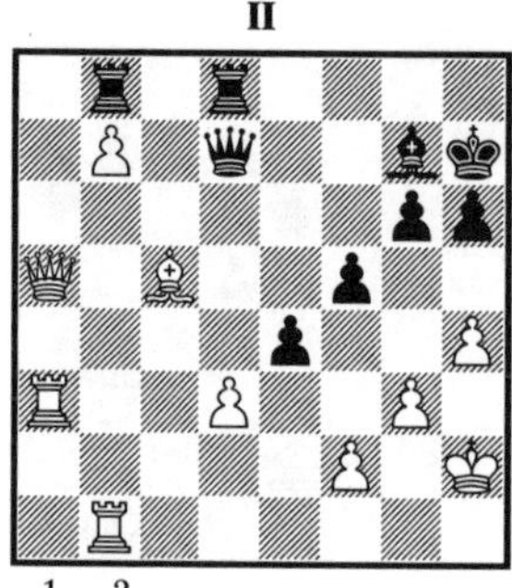

1... ? =

11. ANDRÉS 2320 – LEBREDO 2290

La Habana 1993

II

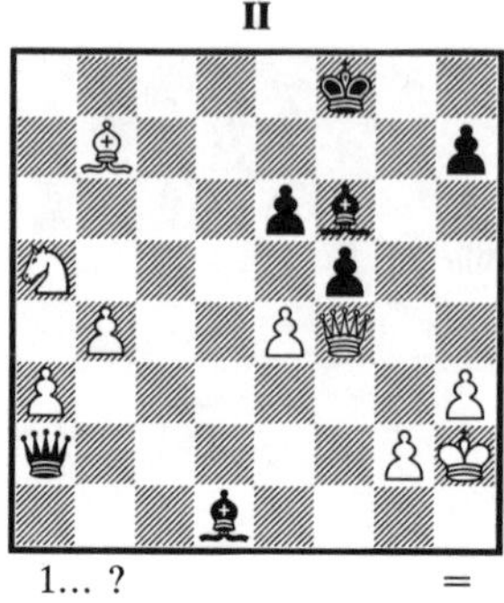

1... ? =

12. NISHIMURA 2325 – HSU LI YANG 2370

Jakarta (zt) 1993

III

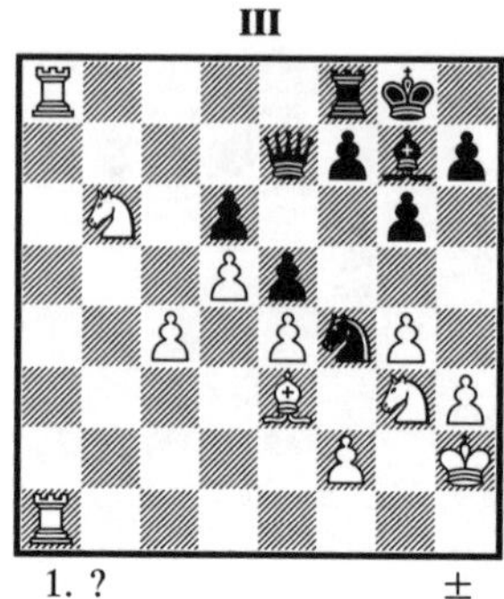

1. ? ±

13. ISTRĂŢESCU 2450 – BOGDAN 2280

România (ch) 1992

III

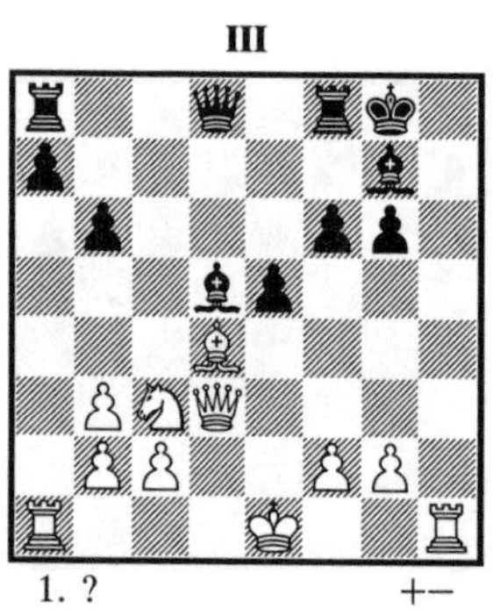

1. ? +–

14. LANGIER 2305 – LIMA 2440

São Paulo 1992

III

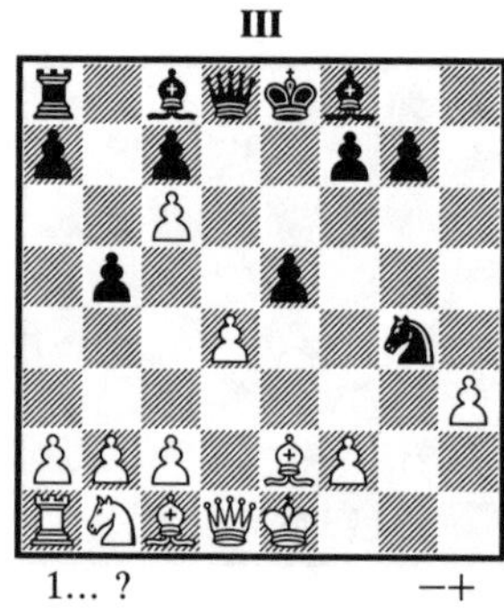

1... ? –+

15. MEŠJERINA – UMANSKAJA 2340

Rossija 1992

III

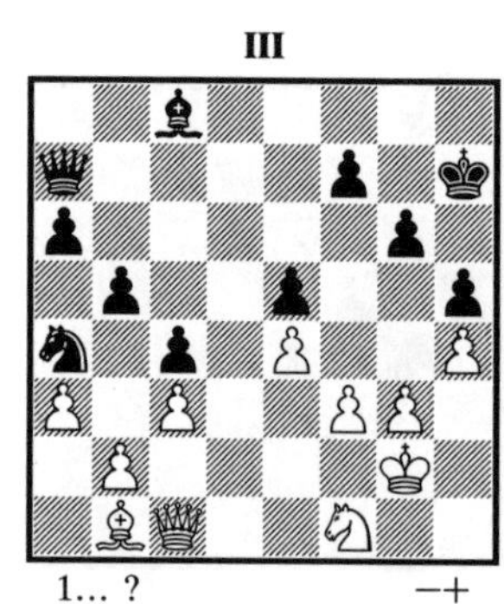

1... ? –+

16. SHANTARAM 2255 – PRASAD 2480

Bangalore 1992

III

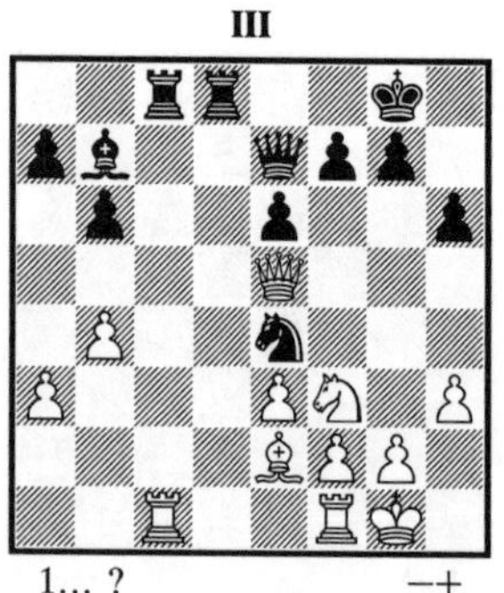

1... ? –+

17. STRIKOVIĆ 2465 – MARCOS

España 1993

III

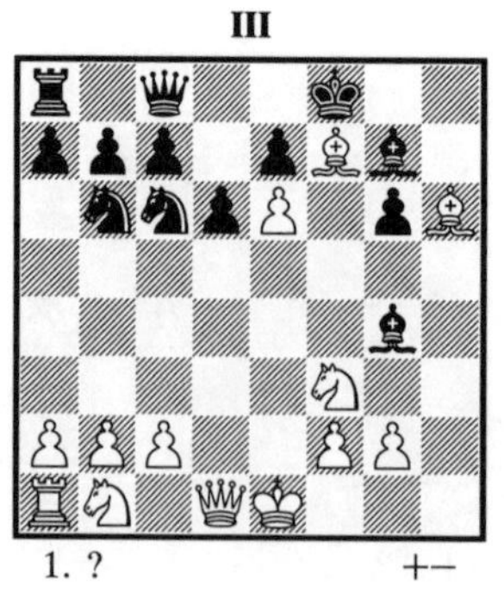

1. ? +–

18. McCAMON – CARLIER 2355

Cappelle la Grande 1993

III

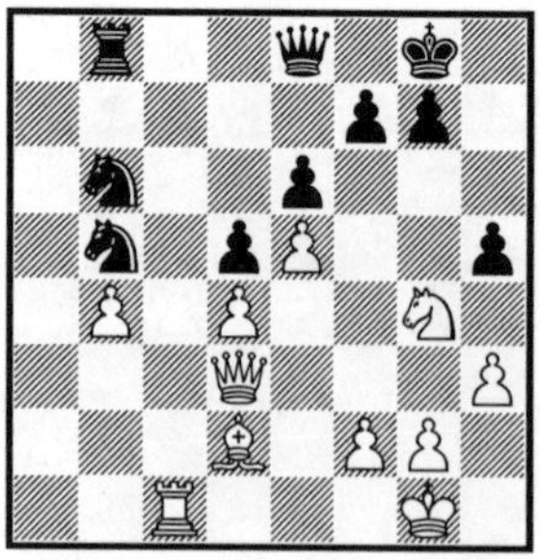

1. ? +–

19. NIKOLAIDIS 2380 – GRIVAS 2495
Athens 1993

III

1. ? +–

20. N. VLASSOV 2385 – TH. MARTIN 2235
Passau 1993

III

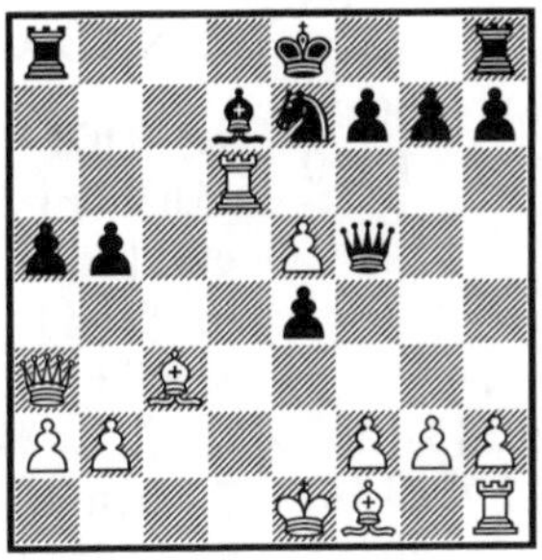

1. ? +–

21. CORONA – STRIKOVIĆ 2465
España 1993

III

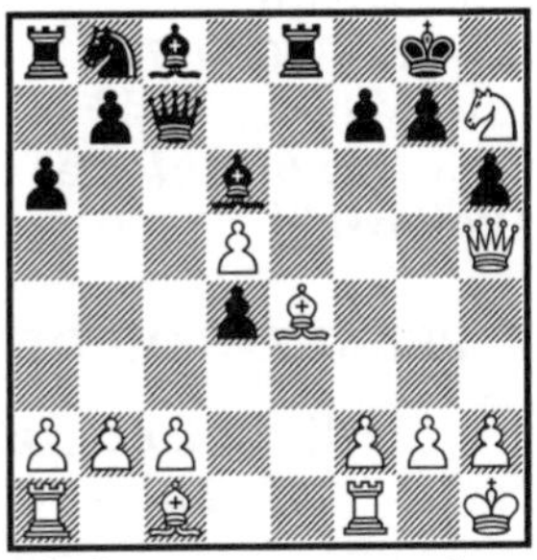

1. ? +–

22. ČELUŠKINA 2380 – PRUDNIKOVA 2420
Beograd 1993

III

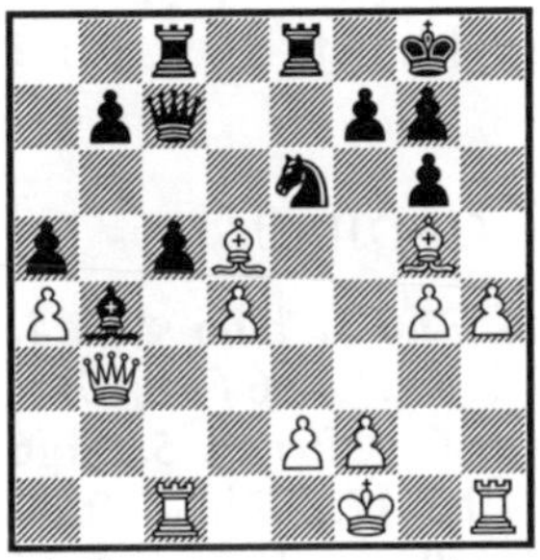

1. ? +–

23. G. ORLOV 2495 – LESKI 2430
Reno 1993

IV

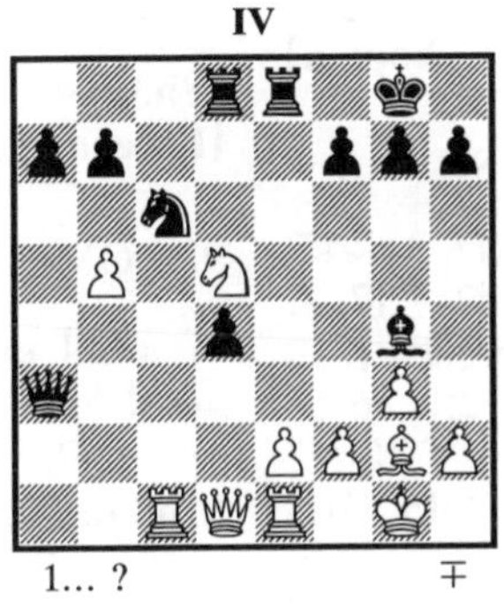

1... ? ∓

24. FAHNENSCHMIDT 2360 – ŠTOHL 2540
Deutschland 1993

IV

1. ? +–

25. EGIN 2395 – SERPER 2590
Uzbekistan 1993

IV

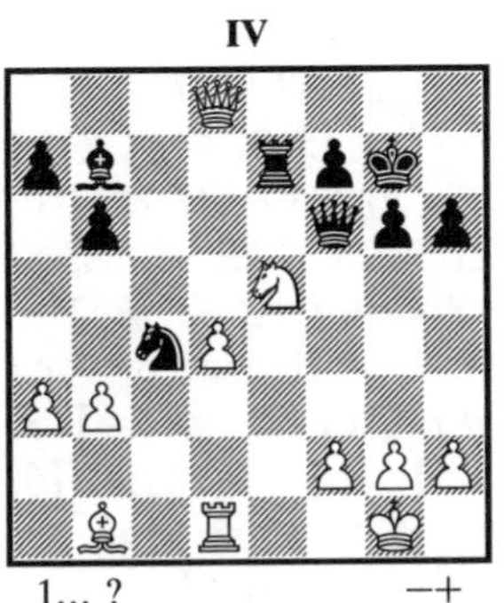

1... ? –+

26. G. M. TODOROVIĆ 2445 – TOŠIĆ 2440
Aranđelovac 1993

IV

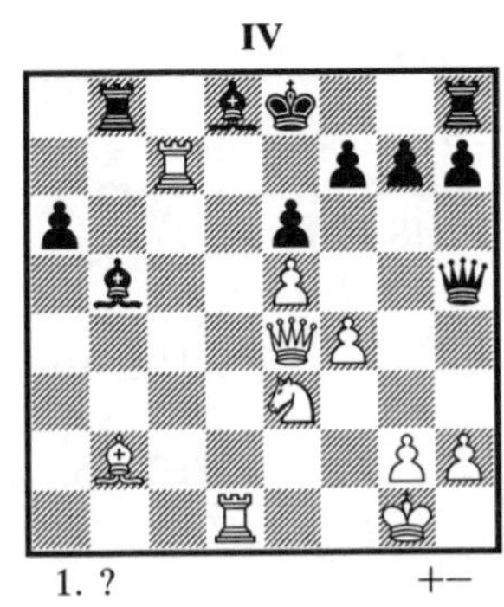

1. ? +–

27. RABIEGA 2420 – G. GEORGADZE 2540
Cuxhaven 1993

IV

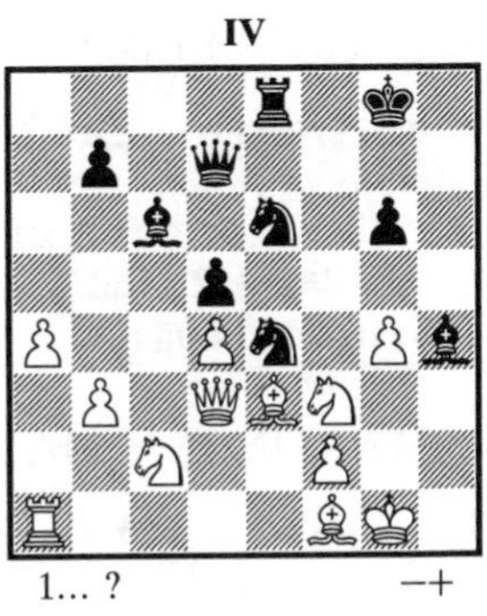

1... ? –+

1. HENKIN – AFEK

1. ♖e7! ♘e7 [1... ♘f4 2. ♖d6#; 1... ♗e7 2. ♗d5 ♔b6 3. ♘h8 ♗b7 4. ♗b7 ♔b7 5. ♖d7 ♔b6 6. ♖e7 fg2 7. ♖e1+–] **2. ♘d8 ♔b6 3. ♖d6 ♔c7** [3... ♔a5 4. ♗d2 ♔a4 5. ♗b3 ♔b5 6. a4#] **4. ♖d3!** [4... ♔b6 5. ♖b3 ♔a5 6. ♗c7 ♔a4 7. ♗b5#] **1 : 0 [Postovskij]**

2. PELAEZ – DE DEVITTIS

1... ♖e2!! 2. ♕e2 ♖b3! 3. ♔c1 [3. ab3 ♕a1 4. ♔c2 ♕b2 5. ♔d3 ♕c3#] **♕c3** [4. ♕c2 ♖b1! 5. ♔b1 ♕a1#] **0 : 1 [Nogueiras, Hernández Ruíz]**

3. G. KUZ'MIN – AKOPIAN

1... ♗g5!! 2. fg4 [2. ♗g5 ♕a1 3. ♗f1 ♗c4–+; 2. ♕e1 ♗d2 3. ♕d2 ♕a1 4. ♗f1 ♗c4–+; 2. ♗c3 ♗e3–+; 2. ♗e1 ♗f4 3. ♕h4 g5 △ ♕a1–+] **♗d2 3. ♔f1 ♗g4!! 0 : 1 [Akopian]**

4. MA. TSEITLIN – MOTSEASHVILI

1. f5! gf5 [1... ef5? 2. ♘gf7 ♖f7 3. ♘f7 ♕f7 4. e6+–; 1... ♘e5 2. ♘gf7 ♖f7 3. ♘f7 ♕f7 4. ♖e5+–] **2. ♕h5! ♔g8□** [2... ♘e5 3. ♖e5 ♕d6 4. ♕f7!+–; 2... f6 3. ef6! ♘f6 (3... ♕d6 4. ♕f7!+–) 4. ♘gf7 ♖f7 5. ♕f7!+–] **3. ♖f5! ef5 4. ♘f5 ♕d8** [4... ♕e8 5. ♕g4! ♘e5 (5... ♔h8 6. ♘e6 ♖g8 7. ♕g7!+–) 6. ♖e5 ♕e5 7. ♘e6 ♔h8 8. ♕g7 ♕g7 9. hg7 ♔g8 10. ♘h6#; 10. ♘e7#] **5. ♘e6 ♔h8** [5... fe6 6. ♕g4 ♔f7 7. ♕g7 ♔e8 8. ♘d6#] **6. ♕g4! ♖g8 7. ♕g7!** [7... ♖g7 8. hg7 ♔g8 9. ♘h6#] **1 : 0 [Judasin, Ma. Tseitlin]**

5. LUGO – ELIZART CARDENAS

1. e7! ♕e7 [1... ♗e7 2. ♘b5!+–; 1... ♖e7 2. ♖f8+–; 1... ♔e7 2. ♖de1 ♔d8 3. ♘b5!+–; 1... ♔c7 2. ef8♕ ♖f8 3. ♖f8 ♕f8 4. ♕e6!+–] **2. ♘d5!** [△ ♗a5] **1 : 0 [Elizart Cardenas]**

6. MĂRTINUŞ – MATEI

1... ♖c3! 2. ♔c3 [2. gf5 ♕b4!! 3. ♔d1 ♖b3 4. ♖c1 ♖b2–+] **♘d4! 3. ♖hb1** [3. ♘d4 ♕c5 4. ♔b3 ♕d4 5. ♖ab1 ♕c3 6. ♔a2 ♕c2 7. ♔a3 ♗d4–+] **♕b4!! 4. ♔b4 ♘c2# 0 : 1 [Matei]**

7. NADANIAN – MARTIROSIAN

1. ♗h7! ♔h7 2. ♘g5 ♔g6 [2... ♔g8 3. ♕h3+–] **3. f5!** [3. ♕g3? f5; 3. ♕h3? ♖h8] **ef5** [3... ♔f5 4. ♖hf1 ♔g6 5. ♘f4 ♔h6 6. ♕h3+–] **4. ♘f4! ♔g5!** [4... ♔h6 5. ♕g3!+–] **5. ♕g3!** [5. ♘d5? ♔g6 6. ♘e7 ♘e7 7. ♕g3 ♔h5±] **♔h6 6. ♕h3 ♔g5 7. ♕h5! ♔f4 8. ♖he1!!** [△ g3#] **♘e4 9. ♖d5** [△ ♖f1+–] **♘e5 10. ♖f1 ♘f2** [10... ♔e3 11. ♖f3+–] **11. ♖f2 ♔e4 12. ♖d1** [△ ♕e2#] **♘g4** [12... f4 13. ♖e2#] **13. ♕f5 1 : 0 [Nadanian]**

8. PASCUAL PÉREZ – CRUZ-LIMA

1... g5! 2. fg5 hg5! [2... fg5? 3. ♔h5 △ 3... ♕h3? 4. ♕h3 ♔g7 5. ♖f1+–] **3. ♔h5 ♕h3!! 4. ♕h3 ♔g7!** [△ ♗f7#] **0 : 1 [Pascual Pérez]**

9. KOMLIAKOV – GADJILU

1. ♗h6! gh6 2. ♖h6 ♘h6 3. ♕h6 ♔g8 4. ♗c4! ♘e6 [4... ♔f7 5. ♘c7 ♘e6 6. ♕h7#; 4... ♖f7 5. ♘f6 ♗f6 6. ♖f6+–] **5. ♕g6 ♔h8 6. ♖f3 ♘g5 7. ♖h3!** [7... ♘h3 8. ♕h6 ♔g8 9. ♘f6#] **1 : 0 [Komliakov]**

10. M. KAMIŃSKI – STEFÁNSSON

1... ed3! 2. ♗a7 ♖b7!! 3. ♖b7 d2! 4. ♖d7 ♖d7 1/2 : 1/2 [Stefánsson]

11. ANDRÉS – LEBREDO

1... ♗f3!! 2. ♕f3□ [2. ♕b8? ♔f7 3. ♕c7 ♗e7 4. ♕g3 ♗d6!–+] **♗e5 3. ♔g1 ♕b1 4. ♔f2 ♕c2** [4... ♗d4 *a)* 5. ♔g3? ♕e1 6. ♔f4 (6. ♔h2 ♗g1–+) ♕d2! 7. ♔g3 ♗e5 8. ♔h4 ♕h6–+; *b)* 5. ♔e2 ♕c2 6. ♔f1□ (6. ♔e1 ♗c3! 7. ♔f1 ♕c1 8. ♔e2 ♕d2 9. ♔f1 ♕e1#) ♕c1 7. ♔e2=] **5. ♕e2** [5. ♔f1 ♕c1=] **♗d4 6. ♔f1** [6. ♔f3? ♕c3 7. ♔f4 ♗e5 8. ♔g5 ♕g3–+; 6. ♔e1 ♕c1 7. ♕d1 ♕e3=] **♕b1!** [6... ♕c1

7. ♕e1 ♕f4 8. ♔e2 ♕e3 9. ♔d1 ♕d3 10. ♕d2+−] **7. ♕e1 ♕d3** **1/2 : 1/2** **[Andrés]**

12. NISHIMURA – HSU LI YANG

1. ♘d7!! ♕h4? [1... ♕d7 2. ♖1a7 ♕a7 3. ♖a7 ♖c8 4. ♖a4±; 1... ♖a8 2. ♖a8 ♗f8 3. ♘f8 ♔g7 4. ♘e2!! ♘e2 (4... g5 5. ♘g3+−; 4... ♕f6 5. ♘d7+−; 4... ♕h4 5. ♘f4 ef4 6. ♗d4+−) 5. ♘e6! fe6 6. ♖a7±] **2. ♗f4 ef4 3. ♘h1 h5 4. ♘f8 ♗f8 5. gh5 g5** [6. ♖g1+−] **[Nishimura]**

13. ISTRĂŢESCU – BOGDAN

1. ♕g6! ed4 2. ♕h7 ♔f7 3. ♕h5 ♔e6 4. 0-0-0! [4. ♕g4 ♔f7 5. ♕h5=] **f5□ 5. ♖he1 ♔d6 6. ♘d5 ♔d5 7. ♕f3 ♔c5** [7... ♔d6 8. ♕g3+−] **8. ♖e6! ♖c8□** [8... ♕d7 9. b4! ♔b5 (9... ♔b4 10. ♖e7!! ♗h6 11. ♔b1+−) 10. ♕e2! ♔b4 11. c3 ♔b3 (11... ♔c5 12. b4 ♔d5 13. c4#) 12. ♕c2 ♔c4 13. cd4 ♔d5 14. ♕b3#] **9. c3!!+− ♔b5?** [⌓ 9... dc3 10. bc3 ♗c3!□ 11. ♖d8 ♖fd8 12. ♕f5 ♔b4 13. ♖e4 ♔b3 14. ♕e6 ♔a3 15. ♖c4+−] **10. ♕d3 ♔a5 11. ♔c2! 1 : 0** **[Istrăţescu]**

14. LANGIER – LIMA

1... ♘f2! 2. ♔f2 ♕h4 3. ♔g1 [3. ♔e3?? ♕f4 4. ♔d3 ♕d4#] **♕g3 4. ♔h1 ♕h3 5. ♔g1 ♕g3 6. ♔h1 ♗e6!? 7. ♘c3!** [7. d5? ♕h3 8. ♔g1 ♗c5−+; 7. ♗f3 e4 8. ♗g2 (8. ♗e4 ♕h4−+) ♗d6−+] **♕h4 8. ♔g2□** [8. ♔g1 ed4 9. ♘b5 ♕g3−+] **♗h3!** [8... ed4 9. ♕h1∓] **9. ♔h2 ed4 10. ♘b5 ♗e6 11. ♔g2□ ♕h3 12. ♔f2 ♕h2 13. ♔e1 ♗b4! 14. c3□** [14. ♗d2 ♕g3 15. ♔f1 ♗h3#] **dc3 15. bc3 ♕g3 16. ♔d2 ♖d8 17. ♔c2 ♖d1 18. ♗d1 ♗c5−+** **[Lima]**

15. MEŠJERINA – UMANSKAJA

1... ♗h3!! 2. ♔h3□ ♕g1 [△ ♕h1] **3. g4** [3. ♕c2 ♕f1 4. ♔h2 ♕f3−+] **♘c5!!** [△ ♘e6-f4−+] **4. gh5** [4. ♕e3 ♕f1 5. ♔g3 ♘e6 6. ♗c2 ♘f4 7. ♕f2 ♕h3#] **♘e6 5. hg6 fg6** [△ ♘f4] **0 : 1** **[Umanskaja]**

16. SHANTARAM – PRASAD

1... ♘c3! 2. ♗d1 [2. ♖c3 f6 3. ♖c8 fe5 4. ♖d8 ♕d8 5. ♘e5 ♕d5 6. ♗f3 ♕e5 7. ♗b7 ♕c3−+; 2. ♖ce1 ♘e2 3. ♖e2 ♗a6 4. b5 ♖c5−+; 2. ♘d4 ♖d5! 3. ♕f4 (3. ♘f5 ♘e2 △ ♕f8−+; 3. ♕g3 ♖d4 4. ♖c3 ♖c3−+; 3. ♕h2 e5−+) ♖d4 △ ♘e2−+] **♖d5 3. ♕h2□** [3. ♕g3 ♖d1 △ ♘e2−+] **♕d8! 4. ♘d4□ ♘d1** [5. ♖cd1 e5−+; 5. ♖c8 ♕c8 6. ♖d1 e5−+] **0 : 1** **[Prasad]**

17. STRIKOVIĆ – MARCOS

1. ♕d3! ♗f5 [1... ♗e6 2. ♕g6 ♗f7 3. ♕g7 ♔e8 4. ♕f8+−; 1... ♗h6 2. ♕g6 ♗g7 3. ♕h7+−] **2. ♕c3! ♘e5 3. ♘e5 ♗e6** [3... de5 4. ♕e5+−; 3... ♗h6 4. ♘g6+−] **4. ♘g6 ♔f7 5. ♕g7 ♔e8 6. ♕e7# 1 : 0** **[Striković]**

18. McCAMON – CARLIER

1. ♘f6! gf6 2. ef6 [2. ♗h6? h4!□ 3. ♕f3 f5□ 4. ♕f4 f6 5. ef6 ♔f7 6. ♕h4 ♕g8 (△ 7... ♔e8, 7... ♘d7) 7. ♗g7 ♔e8 △ ♔d7] **♕f8 3. ♕g3 ♔h8** [3... ♔h7 4. ♗f4 △ ♕d3+−] **4. ♗h6! ♕h6□ 5. ♕b8 ♔h7 6. ♖e1 ♕d2 7. ♕g3! ♕h6 8. ♕d3 1 : 0** **[McCamon]**

19. NIKOLAIDIS – GRIVAS

1. h4!!+− gh4□ 2. g5 ♗c7 3. f4 ♕b8 [3... ef4 4. gf6+−; 3... fg5 4. fe5+−; 3... ♕d6 4. ♕e1+−] **4. gf6 ♔f6 5. ♕f1! ♔g7** [5... ♔e7 6. ♕f2+− △ 7. ♕c5, 7. ♕h4] **6. fe5 ♗e5 7. ♕f4!! 1 : 0** **[Andrianov, Nikolaidis]**

20. N. VLASSOV – TH. MARTIN

1. g4! ♕g4 [1... ♕f3 2. ♖d7! ♔d7 3. ♗b5+−] **2. e6!! fe6** [2... ♗e6 3. ♗b5 ♔f8 4. ♕a5!+−] **3. ♖d7! ♔d7 4. ♗b5 ♘c6 5. ♗e5! ♖ac8** [5... ♖hc8 6. ♕d6 ♔e8 7. ♗c6 ♔f7 8. ♗a8 ♖c1 9. ♔d2 ♖h1 10. ♕d7+−] **6. ♕d6 ♔e8 7. ♗c6 ♖c6 8. ♕c6 ♔f7 9. ♕d7 1 : 0** **[N. Vlassov, Šipov]**

21. CORONA – STRIKOVIĆ

1. ♘g5?? [1. ♗h6! *a)* 1... gh6? 2. ♘f6 ♔f8 3. ♕h6 ♔e7 4. ♖ae1+−; *b)* 1... ♖e4 2. ♕g5 ♗e5 (2... f5 3. ♘f6 ♔f8□ 4. ♗g7 ♕g7 5. ♘e4+−; 2... ♖g4 3. ♘f6+−) 3. ♗g7! ♗g7□ (3... ♔h7 4. ♕h6 ♔g8 5. ♕h8#; 3... ♖g4 4. ♗e5 ♖g5 5. ♘f6! ♔g7 6. ♘e8 ♔g8 7. ♘c7+−) 4. ♘f6 ♔f8 5. ♘e4+−; *c)* 1... ♖e5 2. ♗g5! f6□ (2... ♖e4 3. ♘f6 gf6 4. ♗f6+−; 2... ♗f5 3. ♘f6+−; 2... f5 3. ♗d3 ♕f7 4. ♕f7 ♔f7 5. ♗f4+−) 3. f4! ♖e4□ 4. ♕g6! ♘d7 (4... ♕f7 5. ♘f6 ♔f8 6. ♕f7 ♔f7 7. ♘e4+−; 4... fg5 5. ♘f6 ♔f8 6. fg5+−; 4... ♖e7 5. ♘f6 ♔f8 6. ♘h7 ♔g8 7. ♗e7+−) 5. ♗f6 ♘f8□ (5... ♖e7 6. ♗e7 ♗e7 7. ♘g5 ♗g5 8. fg5 ♘f8 9. ♖f8 ♔f8 10. ♖f1 ♔g8 11. ♕e8 ♔h7 12. ♕h5 ♔g8 13. g6+−) 6. ♕e4 ♘h7 7. ♕e8+−] **♖e7 2. ♗d3 ♘d7 3. ♘e4 ♘c5=** **[Striković]**

22. ČELUŠKINA – PRUDNIKOVA

1. h5!! ♘g5 2. hg6 c4? [2... ♖e7□ 3. e3! (△ f4, ♖h5 ×f7; 3. gf7?! ♘f7?? 4. ♕h3 △ ♕h8#; 3... ♖f7!∞) ♕d7 (3... ♖d8 4. ♖h5+−) 4. dc5! (△ ♖d1) ♖c5 (4... ♕g4? 5. ♖c4 △ ♖ch4+−; 4... ♖d8 5. ♖d1+−; 4... ♘e6 5. gf7 ♔f7 6. ♕d3+−) 5. ♖c5 ♗c5 6. ♕c4 b6 7. ♖h5 ♘e6 8. gf7 ♔f7 9. ♕f4 ♔g8 10. ♕f5+−] **3. gf7 ♘f7 4. ♕f3** [4. ♕h3!! ♔f8 5. ♕f3 ♔e7 6. ♖c4+−] **♗d2 5. ♖c2 ♕f4 6. ♖d2 ♕f3 7. ef3±** **[Čeluškina, Jocić]**

23. G. ORLOV – LESKI

1... ♗e2! [1... ♘b4? 2. ♖a1 ♕a1 3. ♕a1 ♘c2 4. ♕c1 ♘e1 5. ♕e1 ♖e2 6. ♕d1 △ ♗f1+−] **2. ♖e2 ♖e2 3. bc6 bc6 4. ♖c6 ♕b2 5. ♗f1 ♖f2 6. ♕e1! ♖c2** [6... ♖h2?? 7. ♖c8! ♖c8 8. ♘e7 ♔h8 9. ♘c8 g6 10. ♘d6+−] **7. ♕e7 ♖f8 8. ♕d6?** [8. ♖c2□ ♕c2 9. ♕a7∓] **d3! 9. ♘e7 ♔h8 10. ♘g6 hg6 11. ♕f8 ♔h7 12. ♕d6** [12. ♖d6 ♕e5! 13. ♖d3 ♕f5−+] **♖c6 13. ♕c6 d2??** [13... ♕d4 14. ♔g2 d2 15. ♗e2 d1♕ 16. ♗d1 ♕d1−+] **14. ♕a4 ♕c1** **1/2 : 1/2** **[Donaldson, Leski]**

24. FAHNENSCHMIDT – ŠTOHL

1. ♖e5! fe5 [1... ♕e5 2. ♗f4 ♕c5 (2... ♕e7 3. ♖e1+−) 3. ♕d8 ♔f7 4. ♖d7! ♘d7 5. ♕d7 ♕e7□ (5... ♔f8 6. ♗d6+−) 6. ♗e6 ♔f8 7. ♗d6 ♖e8 8. ♕b7!+−; 1... ♔f8 2. ♕b4+−; 1... ♔f7 2. ♗e6 ♔e8 3. ♗b3 fe5 4. ♕d8+−] **2. ♗d8 ♕f7 3. ♕d6!** [△ 4. ♗e6, 4. ♗g5+−] **b6 4. ♗g5** [4... ♘a6 5. ♕d8 ♖d8 6. ♖d8#] **1 : 0** **[Štohl]**

25. EGIN – SERPER

1... ♘b2! [1... ♘e5? 2. de5 ♕e5 3. ♕d2=] **2. ♖d2** [△ 2... ♕g5? 3. f4!; 2. ♖f1 ♕g5 3. f3 ♖e5! 4. ♕g5 ♖g5 5. ♗c2 (5. ♖f2 ♘d1−+) ♖d5! 6. ♖b1 (6. ♗e4 ♖d7−+) ♖d4 7. ♖b2 ♖d2−+] **♕c6!!** [△ 3... ♕g2#, 3... ♕c1#; 3. ♘c6 ♖e1#] **0 : 1** **[Serper]**

26. G. M. TODOROVIĆ – TOŠIĆ

1. ♖d8! ♖d8 [1... ♔d8 2. ♖a7 *a)* 2... ♔e8 3. ♗a3 ♗d7 (3... ♕h4 4. ♘c4! ♗c4 5. ♕c6+−) 4. ♕d3 ♖d8 5. ♕d6 ♕h4 6. g3+−; *b)* 2... ♕e2 3. ♕d4 ♔e8 4. h3 ♕d3 (4... ♖d8 5. ♕c5 ♖d7 6. ♗a3! ♕e1 7. ♔h2 ♕h4 8. ♖a8 ♖d8 9. g3+−) 5. ♕c5 ♕d8 (5... ♗d7 6. ♗a3+−) 6. ♗a3 ♗d7 7. ♘c4+−] **2. ♗a3 ♕e2** [2... ♖d1 3. ♘d1 ♕d1 4. ♔f2+−] **3. h3 ♗d7** [⌓ 3... ♕e1 4. ♔h2 ♕a5 5. ♖e7 ♔f8 6. ♗b4 ♕a4 7. ♖d7 ♔e8 8. ♘f5!! ef5 (8... ♔d7 9. ♕b7+−; 8... ♗d7 9. ♘g7#; 8... ♖d7 9. ♕a8 ♖d8 10. ♘g7 ♔d7 11. ♕b7#; 8... ♕b4 9. ♘g7! ♔f8 10. ♘e6!+−) 9. ♖e7 ♔f8 10. ♕f5+−] **4. ♘f5! ♕d1 5. ♔h2 f6** [5... ef5 6. ♕b4+−] **6. ef6** [6... gf6 7. ♕e6! ♗e6 8. ♘g7#] **1 : 0** **[G. M. Todorović]**

27. RABIEGA – G. GEORGADZE

1... ♘f4! [1... ♗f2 2. ♗f2 ♘f4 3. ♘e5! ♖e5 4. ♕f3 ♖g5 5. ♘e3∞] **2. ♗f4 ♕g4** [2... ♗f2 3. ♔h1 ♕g4 4. ♗h2] **3. ♗g3 ♗g3** [3... ♘f2 4. ♘e5! ♖e5 5. ♔f2] **4. ♗g2□** [4. fg3 ♕g3 5. ♗g2□ ♕f2 6. ♔h1 ♔g7!−+] **♗f2 5. ♔f1 ♖f8 6. ♖a2 ♕g3!−+** [△ ♗d7-h3] **[G. Georgadze]**

registar • индекс • index • register • registre • registro • registro • register • 棋譜索引 • الفهرس

komentatori • комментаторы • commentators • kommentatoren • commentateurs • comentaristas • commentatori • kommentatorer • 棋譜解説 • المعلقون

završnice • окончания • endings • endspiele • finales • finales • finali • slutspel • 收 局 • المرحلة النهائية

klasifikacija • классификация • classification • klassifizierung • classification • clasificación • classificazione • klassifikation • 大分類 • التصنيف

♙	
♙ **0**	1, 2, 3 ‖ ♙ : ♔ 1 ♙ : 1 ♙ 2 ∞ ♙ : 2 ♙
♙ **1**	‖ 2 ♙ : 2 ♙
♙ **2**	3 ♙ : 3 ♙
♙ **3**	4 ♙ : 4 ♙ 5 ♙ : 5 ♙ 6 ♙ : 6 ♙ 7 ♙ : 7 ♙ 8 ♙ : 8 ♙
♙ **4**	2 ♙ : 1 ♙
♙ **5**	3 ♙ : 2 ♙
♙ **6**	4 ♙ : 3 ♙
♙ **7**	5 ♙ : 4 ♙
♙ **8**	6 ♙ : 5 ♙ 7 ♙ : 6 ♙ 8 ♙ : 7 ♙
♙ **9**	‖ ♙

♘♗	
♘♗ **0**	♘ : ♔ ♘ : ♙
♘♗ **1**	♗ : ♔ ♗ : ♙
♘♗ **2**	♘ : ♘
♘♗ **3**	♗ (∟ ♙) : ♘ (⅃ ♙) ♗ (⅃ ♙) : ♘ (∟ ♙)
♘♗ **4**	♗ (∟ ♙) : ♘ (∟ ♙) ∟ >
♘♗ **5**	♗ (∟ ♙) : ♘ (∟ ♙) ⅃ >
♘♗ **6**	♗ : ♗ ◻◼
♘♗ **7**	♗ : ♗ ◼◼
♘♗ **8**	♘♘/♘♗/♗♗ : ♔ ♘♘/♘♗/♗♗ : ♙ ♘♘/♘♗/♗♗ : ♘/♗
♘♗ **9**	‖ ♘♗

♖

♖ 0	♖ : ♔ ♖ : ♙
♖ 1	♖ : ♘
♖ 2	♖ : ♗
♖ 3	♖ (┘♙) : ♖ (┘♙) ♖ + 1 ♙ : ♖ (┘♙)
♖ 4	♖ + 2, 3, 4 ‖ ♙ : ♖ (┘♙)
♖ 5	♖ + 2 ♙ : ♖ + 1 ♙
♖ 6	‖ ♖ : ♖ └>
♖ 7	♖ (└♙) : ♖ (└♙) ┘>
♖ 8	♖ : ♘♘/♘♗/♗♗ ♖ : ♘♘♘/♘♘♗/♘♗♗/♗♗♗ ♖♘/♖♗ : ♙ ♖♘/♖♗ : ♘/♗ ♖♘/♖♗ : ♖
♖ 9	‖ ♖

♕

♕ 0	♕ : ♔ ♕ : ♙
♕ 1	♕ : ♘ ♕ : ♗
♕ 2	♕ : ♖
♕ 3	♕ (┘♙) : ♕ (┘♙) ♕ (└♙) : ♕ (┘♙)
♕ 4	♕ (└♙) : ♕ (└♙)
♕ 5	♕ : ♘♘/♘♗/♗♗ ♕ : ♖♘/♖♗
♕ 6	♕ : ♖♖ ♕ : ♘♘♘/♘♘♗/♘♗♗/♗♗♗ ♕ : ♖♘♘/♖♘♗/♖♗♗ ♕ : ♖♖♘/♖♖♗ ♕ : ♖♖♖
♕ 7	♕♘/♕♗ : ♙ ♕♘/♕♗ : ♘/♗ ♕♘/♕♗ : ♖ ♕♘/♕♗ : ♕
♕ 8	♕♘/♕♗ : ♘♘/♘♗/♗♗ ♕♘/♕♗ : ♖♘/♖♗ ♕♘/♕♗ : ♖♖ ♕♘/♕♗ : ♕♘/♕♗
♕ 9	‖ ♕

1. TABOROV 2380 – VOVK
Kiev 1993

♙ **3/b1**

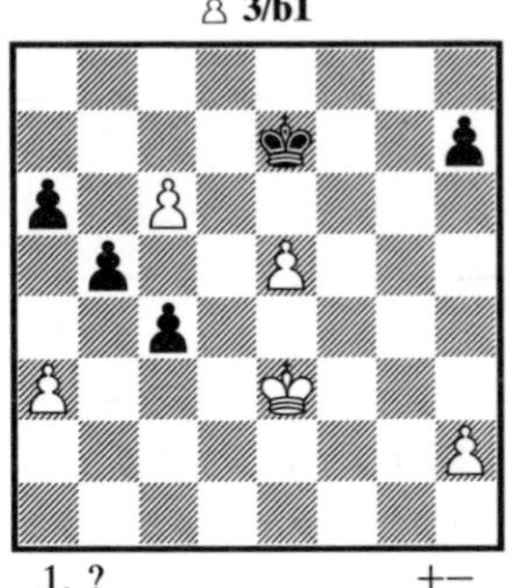

1. ? +–

2. S. VLAHOVIĆ 2225 – PIKULA 2330
Jugoslavija 1993

♙ **3/b2**

1... ? –+

3. D. RAJKOVIĆ 2450 – BOGDANOVSKI 2405
Star Dojran 1993

♘♗ **2/d**

1. ? =

4. EPIŠIN 2620 – RAZUVAEV 2525
Rostov na Donu 1993

♘♗ **2/d**

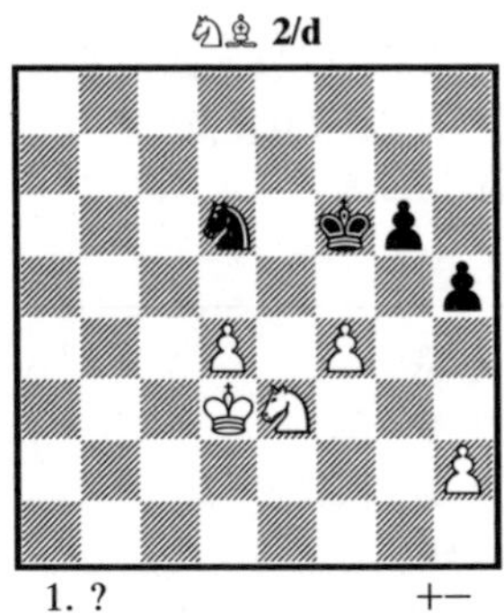

1. ? +–

5. M. KAMIŃSKI 2395 – MURREY 2530
Cappelle la Grande 1993

♘♗ **2/i**

1. ? +–

6. NOVIK 2430 – I. ALEKSANDROV 2380
Sankt-Peterburg 1993

♘♗ **4/d**

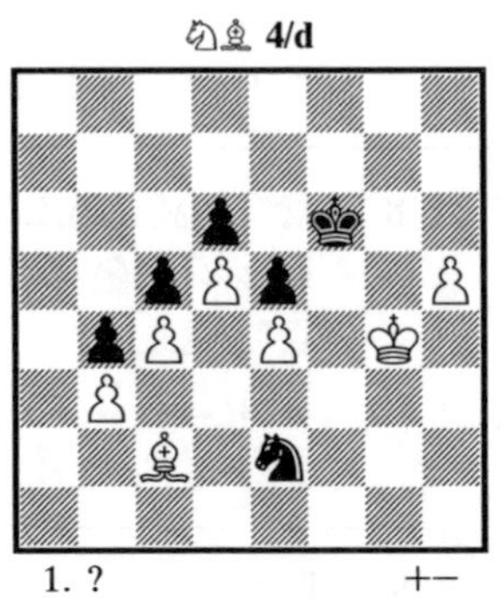

1. ? +–

7. N. VLASSOV 2385 – IL. BOTVINNIK 2395
Minsk 1993

♘♗ **4/g**

1. ? =

8. VOTAVA 2435 – SEREBRJANIK 2425
Israel 1992

♘♗ **5/e**

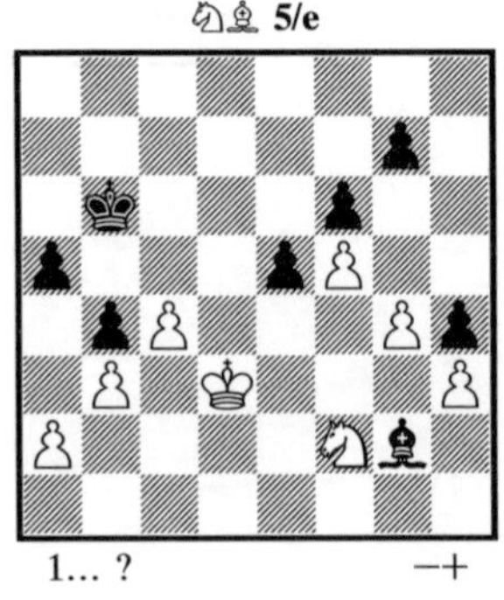

1... ? –+

9. CIEMNIAK 2440 – A. MIHAL'ČIŠIN 2520
Groningen (open) 1992

♘♗ **7/f**

1... ? +–

10. NADANIAN 2285 – ARAKELOV
Armenia 1993

♘♗ **7/k**

1. ? +–

11. RAECKIJ 2460 – PLETÁNEK 2320
Pardubice 1992

♘♗ **9/c**

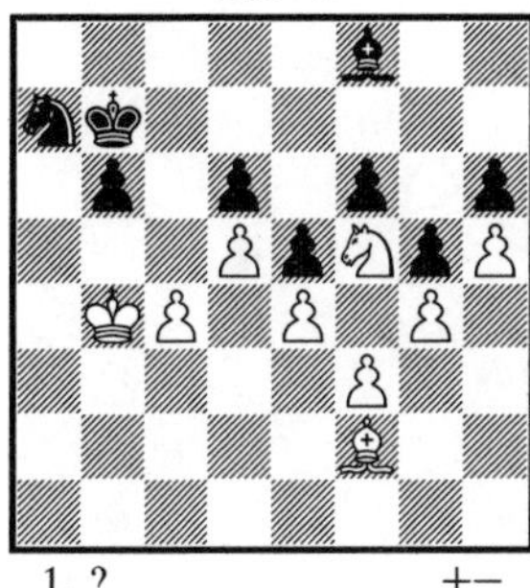

1. ? +–

12. ŠTOHL 2540 – LIPKA 2310
Slovensko 1993

♘♗ **9/d**

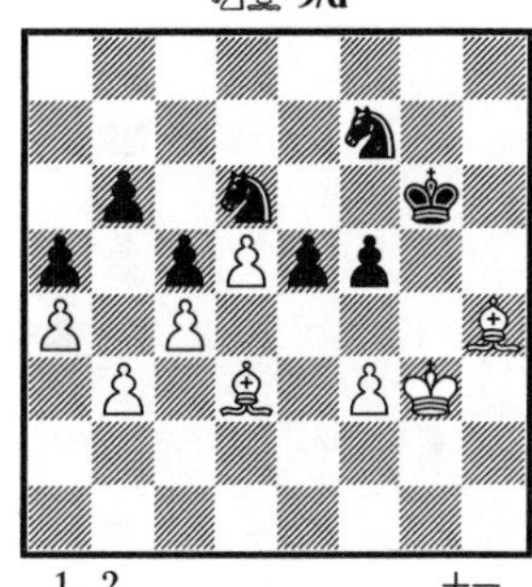

1. ? +–

13. SCHMITTDIEL 2450 – ROZENTALIS 2595
Deutschland 1993

♖ **2/j**

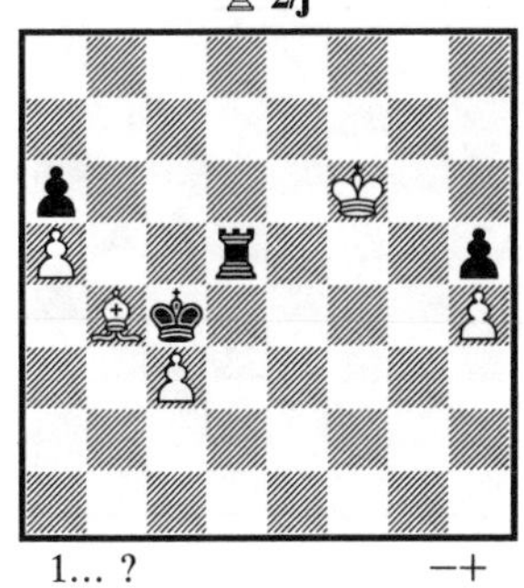

1... ? –+

14. AKOPIAN 2615 – A. N. PANČENKO 2460
Rostov na Donu (open) 1993

♖ **3/c3**

1... ? =

15. SAKAEV 2540 – HRÁČEK 2485
Brno 1992

♖ **4/d**

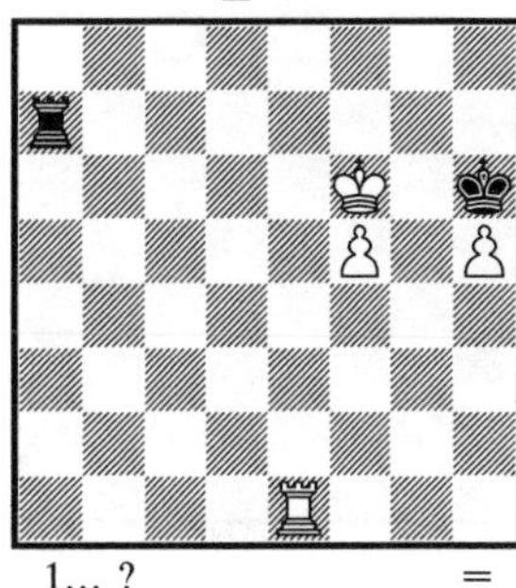

1... ? =

16. MAKAR'EV 2335 – GAVRILOV 2415
Rossija 1992

♖ **6/a**

1... ? –+

17. LUKIN 2445 – RODIN 2345
Rossija 1992

♖ **6/d**

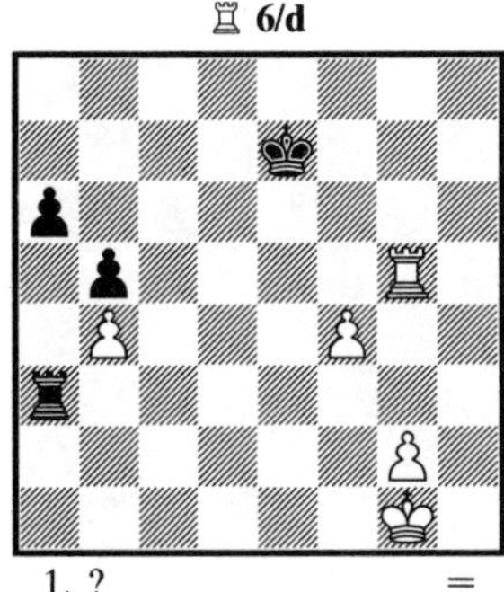

1. ? =

18. ŠAHOVIĆ 2385 – STRIKOVIĆ 2485
Jugoslavija 1993

♖ **7/f**

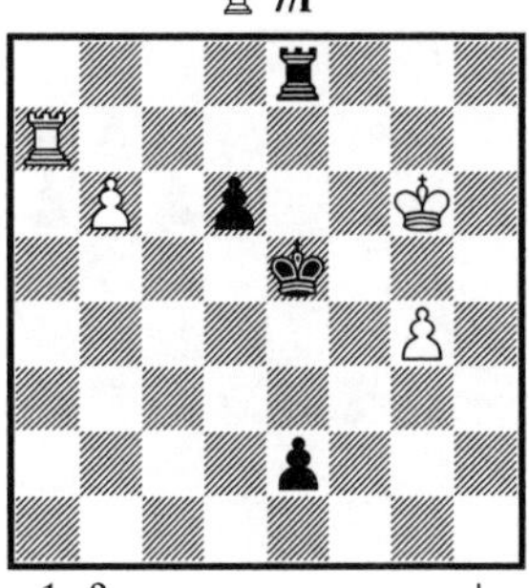

1. ? –+

19. VELIMIROVIĆ 2510 – D. SEKULIĆ 2410
Jugoslavija 1993

♖ **7/h**

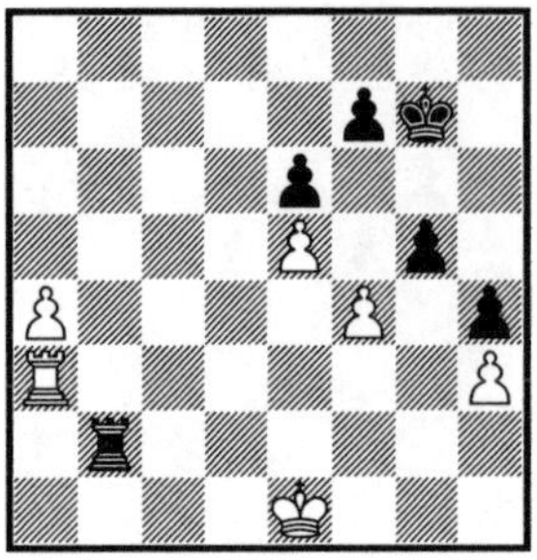

1. ? +–

20. G. GEORGADZE 2525
D. BERKOVIČ 2445
Podol'sk 1992

♖ **8/e**

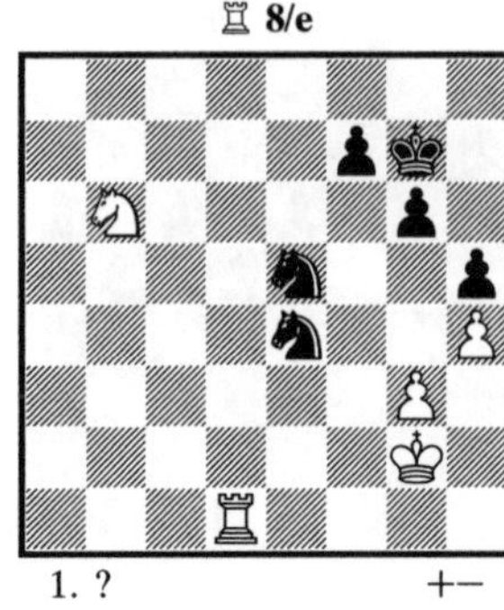

1. ? +–

21. J. BENJAMIN 2585 – A. FRIEDMAN 2325
Saint-Martin 1993

♖ **8/e**

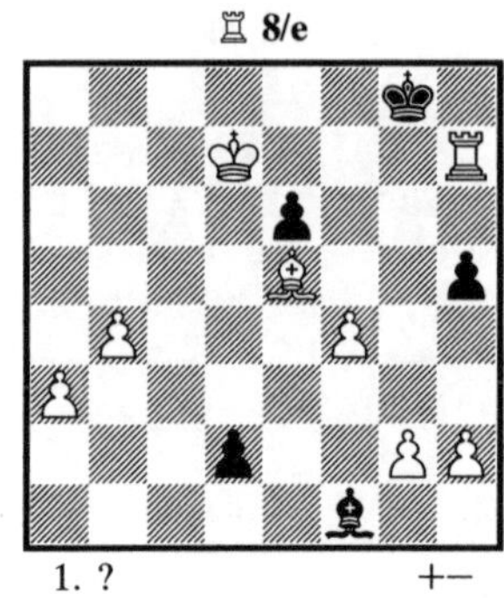

1. ? +–

22. D. LEKIĆ 2230 – B. MAKSIMOVIĆ 2325
Cetinje 1993

♖ **8/f4**

1... ? –+

23. IOSELIANI 2460 – ZSU. POLGÁR 2560
Monaco (m/4) 1993

♖ **8/g6**

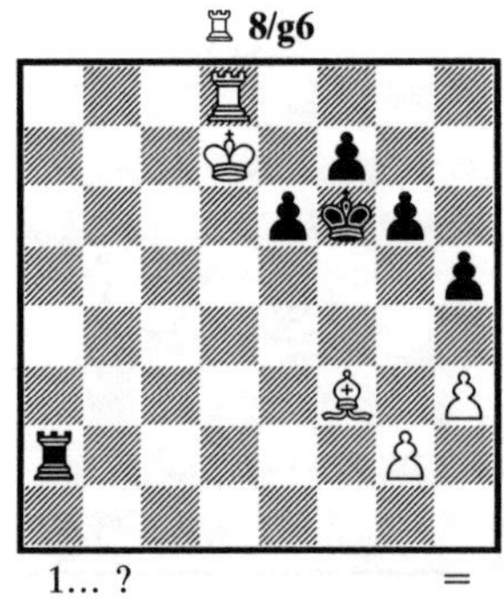

1... ? =

24. SERPER 2575 – ZAJCEV 2445
Moskva 1992

♖ **9/e**

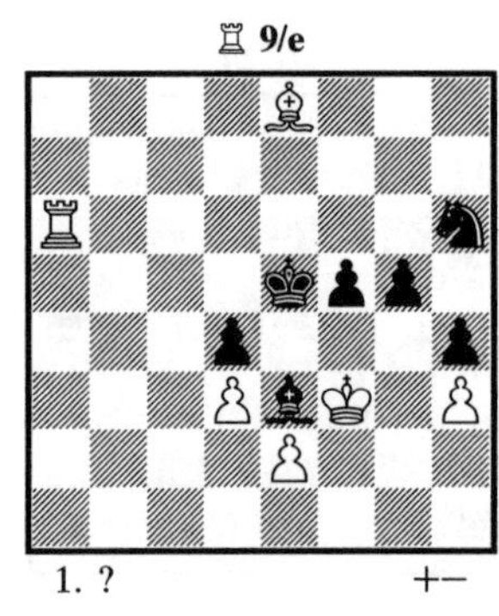

1. ? +–

25. TIMOŠENKO 2515 – SAVČENKO 2535
Alusta 1993

♖ **9/i**

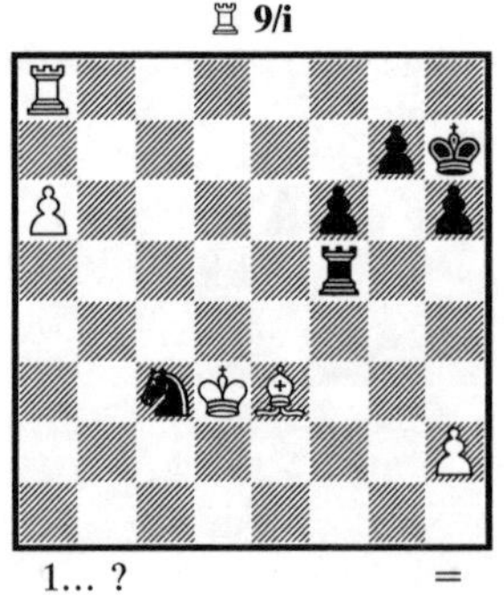

1... ? =

26. ISTRĂŢESCU 2470 – ZAJCEV 2450
Bucureşti 1993

♖ **9/k**

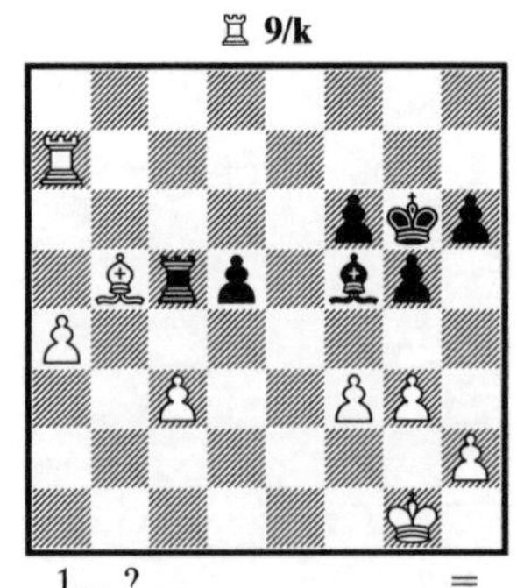

1... ? =

27. JAKOVIČ 2510 – SAVČENKO 2535
Rostov na Donu (open) 1993

♖ **9/k**

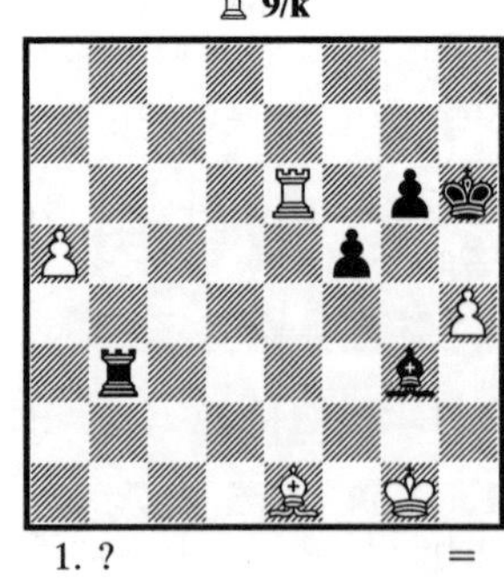

1. ? =

1. TABOROV – VOVK

1. ♔e4!+– [1. ♔d4?= a5! (1... ♔e6? 2. ♔c5 c3 3. c7 ♔d7 4. ♔b6 c2 5. e6 ♔c8 6. e7+–) 2. ♔c3 (2. a4 b4 3. ♔c4 ♔e6 4. ♔b3 ♔e7=) ♔e6 (2... ♔d8? 3. e6+–⊙) 3. ♔d4 ♔e7=] **♔e6** [1... a5 2. ♔d4!⊙ ♔e6 3. ♔c5+–] **2. ♔d4** [△ ♔c5] **♔e7□ 3. ♔c3 ♔e6** [3... a5 4. ♔d4!⊙ ♔e6 5. ♔c5+–] **4. ♔b4! ♔e7 5. ♔a5 c3 6. c7 ♔d7 7. ♔b6 c2 8. e6** [8... ♔c8 9. e7+–] **1 : 0**
[Taborov]

2. S. VLAHOVIĆ – PIKULA

1... ♔g5? [1... ♔e6! *a)* 2. g4 hg4 3. hg4 ♔f6 4. ♔f4 ♔g6 5. ♔f3 (5. g5 ♔h5 6. ♔f5 g6 7. ♔f6 b6–+) ♔g5 6. ♔g3 g6 7. ♔f3 ♔h4 8. ♔f4 g5 9. ♔f5 b6–+; *b)* 2. ♔d4 ♔f5 3. ♔d5 g6! (3... h4? 4. gh4 ♔f4 5. ♔e6=; 3... g5 4. ♔d4 △ 4... h4? 5. gh4 gh4 6. ♔e3! △ ♔f3-e3-f3=) 4. ♔d4 g5 5. ♔d3 (5. ♔d5 h4–+) ♔e5 6. ♔e3 ♔d5 7. ♔d3 (7. h4 gh4 8. gh4 ♔e5 9. ♔f3 ♔f5–+) b6 8. ♔e3 ♔c4 9. ♔d2 ♔d4 10. ♔e2 ♔e4 11. ♔f2 g4 12. hg4 hg4 13. ♔e2 b5–+; *c)* 2. ♔f4 ♔d5 3. ♔g5 (3. ♔e3 ♔c4 4. ♔d2 ♔d4!–+) ♔c4 4. ♔g6 (4. ♔h5 ♔b3 5. ♔g6 ♔b2 6. ♔g7 ♔a3 7. h4 ♔b4 8. h5 a3 9. h6 a2 10. h7 a1♕–+) ♔b3 5. ♔g7 ♔b2 6. g4 hg4 7. hg4 ♔a3 8. g5 ♔b4 9. g6 a3 10. ♔f8 (10. ♔h7 a2 11. g7 a1♕ 12. g8♕ ♕h1–+; 10. ♔f7 a2 11. g7 a1♕ 12. g8♕ ♕a2–+) a2 11. g7 a1♕ 12. g8♕ ♕a8–+; *d)* 2. h4 ♔f6 3. ♔f4 (3. g4 hg4 4. ♔f4 g3 5. ♔g3 ♔f5! 6. ♔f3 b5 7. ♔g3 ♔e4 8. ♔g4 ♔d3 9. ♔g5 ♔c2 10. ♔g6 ♔b2 11. ♔g7 ♔a3 12. h5 ♔b3 13. h6 a3 14. h7 a2 15. h8♕ a1♕–+) g5! (3... g6? 4. g4!=) 4. ♔e4 (4. hg5 ♔g6 5. g4 h4–+) b6! (4... ♔e6?? 5. hg5+–; 4... ♔g6?? 5. ♔e5+–; 4... gh4? 5. gh4 △ ♔f4-e4=) 5. hg5 (5. ♔f3 gh4 6. gh4 ♔f5–+) ♔g5 6. ♔f3 ♔f5 7. ♔e3 ♔g4 8. ♔f2 ♔h3 9. ♔f3 b5 10. ♔f2 ♔h2 11. ♔f3 ♔g1 12. ♔f4 (12. g4 h4–+) ♔f2 13. g4 hg4 14. ♔g4 ♔e2–+] **2. ♔e5 ♔g6 3. ♔e6 ♔g5 4. ♔f7 ♔h6 5. h4 ♔h7**
1/2 : 1/2 **[Cvetković]**

3. D. RAJKOVIĆ – BOGDANOVSKI

1. ♔a4 ♔c5 2. ♔a5 ♘e6 [2... ♔c4 3. ♔b6 d5 4. ♘g4! de4 5. ♘e5 ♔d4 6. ♘g4 ♘d5 7. ♔b5 ♘f6 8. ♘h6 ♔d3 (8... ♔e5 9. ♔c4 ♔f4 10. ♔c3 ♘g4 11. ♘f7 e3 12. ♔d3 ♔f3 13. ♘g5 ♔f2 14. ♘e4=) 9. ♘f5 ♘g4 10. ♔c5 ♘h6 11. ♘h4 e3 12. ♘g2=] **3. ♔a6! ♘g5 4. ♔b7 ♔c4 5. ♔c6 ♔d4 6. ♘d5! ♘e4 7. ♘c7 ♔c4 8. ♘d5 ♔d3** [8... ♘c3 9. ♔d6! e4 10. ♔e5!=] **9. ♘e7 ♔d4 10. ♘f5 ♔c4 11. ♘e7** [11... ♘g3 12. ♔d6 e4 13. ♘d5 ♔d4 14. ♘f4=] **1/2 : 1/2**
[D. Rajković]

4. EPIŠIN – RAZUVAEV

1. h4! ♘f7 2. d5 ♘d6 3. ♔d4 ♔e7 4. ♔c5 ♔d7 5. ♔d4 [5. ♘c4 ♘e4!□ 6. ♔d4 ♘g3 7. ♔e5 ♘f5 8. d6 ♘h4 9. ♔d5 ♘f5=] **♔e7 6. ♔e5 ♘f7 7. ♔e4! ♘d6 8. ♔d4 ♔d7 9. f5!!+– gf5 10. ♔e5 ♘e4 11. ♘f5 ♘f2 12. ♘e3 ♘h1 13. ♔f4 ♘f2 14. ♔g5 ♔d6 15. ♔h5 ♘d3 16. ♔g5** **1 : 0** **[Epišin]**

5. M. KAMIŃSKI – MURREY

1. ♘c2!⊙ [1. b5?! ♔c5 2. ♔g4 ♔d4! 3. b6 ♔e3 4. ♔h5□ f3=; 1. ♔g4 ♔e5 2. ♘f3 ♔e4 3. ♘g5 ♔e3 4. ♔h5 f3 5. ♘f3 ♔f3 6. b5 d4±] **♔e5** [1... ♔c6 2. ♔g4 ♘f6 3. ♔f4 ♔b5 4. ♔e5+–] **2. b5 ♘f6** [2... ♔d6 3. ♔g4 ♘f6 4. ♔f4 ♔c5 5. ♔f5 ♘e4 6. ♘a3+–] **3. ♘b4 ♘d7 4. h5 d4 5. ♘d3 ♔f5 6. ♘f4 ♘e5 7. ♔e2** [7. ♔g3? d3=] **♔g5 8. b6 d3 9. ♔d1 ♘d7 10. b7 ♘b8 11. ♔d2 ♘a6 12. ♔e3!** [12. ♔c3? ♔f4] **♔h6 13. ♘d3 ♔h5 14. ♔d4 ♔g6 15. ♘c5 ♘b4 16. ♔c4 ♘c6 17. ♔b5 ♘b8 18. ♔b6** **1 : 0**
[M. Kamiński]

6. NOVIK – I. ALEKSANDROV

1. ♗d1! ♘c3 [1... ♘d4 2. ♔h4+–⊙] **2. ♗f3** [△ h6-h7, ♔f5] **♘b1 3. h6! ♘d2 4. h7 ♔g7 5. ♗d1 ♔h7** [5... ♘e4 6. ♔f5 ♘c3 7. ♗c2! ♘e2 8. ♔e6 ♘d4 9. ♔d6 ♘c2 10. ♔e5 ♘d4 11. d6 ♘b3 12. d7 ♘a5 13. h8♕+–] **6. ♔f5 ♔g7 7. ♔e6 ♘e4 8. ♗c2 ♘d2!** [8... ♘f2 9. ♔d6 e4 10. ♔c5 e3 11. d6 e2 12. d7 e1♕ 13. d8♕+–] **9. ♔d6 e4 10. ♔c5!** [10. ♗e4? ♘e4 11. ♔e7 ♘d2 12. d6 ♘b3 13. d7 ♘a5 14. ♔d6 ♘b7 15. ♔c7 b3=] **e3 11. d6!** [11. ♗d1? ♘b3 12. ♔b4 ♘c1 13. ♔c5 ♔f7 14. ♔d6 e2 15. ♗e2 ♘e2 16. c5 ♘c3 17. c6 ♔e8 18. c7 ♘b5 19. ♔c6 ♘a7 20. ♔b7 ♔d7!=] **♔f7 12. ♔c6 ♘f3**

13. ♗d1 ♘d4 14. ♔b7!! [14. ♔c7 ♘b3! 15. ♗b3 (15. d7 ♘c5=) e2 16. d7 e1♕ 17. d8♕ ♕g3=] **e2** [14... ♔e6 15. c5+−] **15. ♗e2 ♘b3 16. d7 ♘c5 17. ♔c8 1 : 0 [Novik]**

7. N. VLASSOV − IL. BOTVINNIK

1. ♗f7? [1. ♔e4? ♔c5 2. ♔f4 a3 3. ♗f7 ♘c4−+; 1. ♗g6! a3 2. ♗f7! ♘d7 (2... ♔c6 3. ♗e8! ♔b7 4. ♔c5 b3 5. ♗f7 b2 6. ♗g6 ♘d7 7. ♔b4=) 3. ♗g8 ♘c5 (3... ♘e5 4. ♗d5? ♘d3! △ ♘c1, b3−+; 4. ♔e4!=) 4. ♔c4 b3 5. ♔b4! b2 6. ♗h7=] **a3!⊙ 2. ♗g8** [2. ♗e8 b3 3. ♗f7 b2 4. ♗g6 ♔c6 5. ♔c3 (5. ♗h7 ♘d7 △ ♘c5-b3−+) ♔c5 6. ♗h7 ♘c4 7. ♗f5 ♘e5 8. ♔b3 ♔d4 9. ♔a3 ♔c3−+] **♔c6! 3. ♗c4** [3. ♗f7 ♔b5 4. ♗e8 ♔a5 5. ♗f7 ♘a4 6. ♗b3 (6. ♔e5 ♘c3 7. ♔f4 ♘a2! 8. ♗a2 ♔a4−+) ♘c3 7. ♗f7 ♘b1! (△ ♘d2, b3) 8. ♗d5 ♔b5! (8... ♘d2 9. ♔d3!; 8... ♔b6 9. ♔c4!) 9. ♗c4 ♔b6 10. ♔d3 (10. ♗d5 ♘d2 11. ♔d3 ♔c5!−+) ♔c5 11. ♗f7 ♘c3 12. ♗b3 ♘b5 13. ♗f7 ♘d4−+] **♘a4 4. ♗d5 ♔d6** [⌓ 4... ♔b5 5. ♗f7 ♘c3 6. ♗e8 ♔a5 7. ♗f7 ♘b1!−+] **5. ♗g8 ♘c5?** [5... ♘b6? 6. ♗f7!=; 5... ♘c3? 6. ♗b3! ♔c6 7. ♔c4 ♘d5 8. ♗a4=; 5... ♘b2!□ 6. ♗b3 (6. ♗d5 ♘d3!−+) ♔c6 7. ♗e6 (7. ♔e4 ♔c5 8. ♔f4 ♘c4 △ ♘d2−+) ♔b5 △ ♘a4−+] **6. ♔c4 b3 7. ♔b4!** [7... b2 8. ♗h7=] **1/2 : 1/2 [N. Vlassov, Šipov]**

8. VOTAVA − SEREBRJANIK

1... a4! [1... ♗f1 2. ♔e4 ♔c6 3. ♔e3 a4 4. ♘d3 ♗h3 5. ♔f3] **2. ♔e2 a3 3. ♘d3** [3. ♔e3 ♗f1 △ ♗c4, b3] **♗h3 4. ♔f3 e4!** [4... ♔a5 5. ♘c5 ♗f1 6. ♔f2] **5. ♔e4 ♗g4 6. ♔f4 ♗d1 7. ♘b4 ♔c5 8. ♘d3 ♔d4 9. ♘b4 ♔c3! 10. ♘d5 ♔b2 11. c5 ♗b3! 12. ♘b6** [12. ♘b4!? ♗a4 13. c6 ♗c6 14. ♘c6 ♔a2 15. ♘b4 (15. ♔g4 ♔b3−+) ♔b3 16. ♘d3 a2 17. ♘c1 ♔b2 18. ♘a2 ♔a2 19. ♔g4 ♔b3 20. ♔h4 ♔c4 21. ♔h5 ♔d5 22. ♔g6 ♔e5−+] **h3 13. ♔g3** [13. c6 h2 14. c7 h1♕ 15. c8♕ ♕c1−+] **♗c2 0 : 1 [Serebrjanik]**

9. CIEMNIAK − A. MIHAL'ČIŠIN

1... h5 [1... ♗c1 2. g4 ♗g5 3. ♗e1 ♗f6 4. h4 △ g5+−] **2. ♗e5 c6 3. ♗b8 ♗h6 4. g3 ♗c1 5. ♗e5 ♗d2 6. h3 ♗g5 7. ♗f4 ♗f6 8. g4 hg4** [8... h4 9. g5 ♗g7 10. ♗e3 △ ♗d4+−] **9. hg4 ♗e7 10. g5 ♗a3 11. ♗e3 ♗d6** [11... ♗e7 12. g6 ♔f6 13. ♗g5!+−] **12. ♗d4 ♗c7 13. g6 ♗b8 14. ♔f3!** [14. g7 ♔f7 15. ♔f5 ♗c7 16. ♔g5 ♗d8 17. ♔h6 ♔g8 18. ♔g6 ♗c7 19. ♗f6 ♗a5=] **♗d6 15. ♔g4 ♗b4** [15... ♗e7 16. ♔h5 △ ♔h6-h7+−] **16. ♗e3** [16. ♔h5? ♗d2!] **♔f6 17. ♔h5 ♗f8 18. ♗c1!?** [18. ♗d4! ♔f5 19. c5! (19. g7? ♗g7 20. ♗g7 c5! △ ♔e4-d3=) ♔e4 20. g7+−] **♔e6 19. ♗h6 ♗a3 20. ♗f4 ♗f8 21. ♔g5 ♗g7 22. ♗g3 ♗f8 23. ♗e1!⊙ ♗g7** [23... ♔e5 24. ♗b4! c5 25. ♗c5+−] **24. ♗b4! ♗f6** [24... ♔d7 25. ♔f5 △ ♗d2-g5-f6+−] **25. ♔h6 ♔f5 26. ♗f8** [26. c5! ♔e6 27. ♔h7+−] **♔e4 27. c5!** [27. g7? ♗g7 28. ♔g7 c5!=] **1 : 0 [A. Mihal'čišin]**

10. NADANIAN − ARAKELOV

1. ♗d3!! ♔d8 [1... ♗g4 2. ♔b5 ♗f3 3. ♗c4+−] **2. ♗f5! ♗e8** [2... ♗f5 3. gf5 ♔c7 4. ♔b5 ♔b7 5. h5!+−] **3. h5! ♔e7** [3... ♔c7 4. g5!+−] **4. ♗c8!⊙ ♔f8** [4... ♔d8 5. g5! fg5 6. fg5 ♔e7 7. gh6 ♔f8 (7... ♔f6 8. ♗f5+−⊙) 8. h7 ♔g7 9. ♗f5 f6 10. h6 ♔h8 11. ♔c4 ♗f7 12. ♔b5! ♗d5 13. b4 ♗f7 14. ♔b6 ♗e8 (△ 15. b5?? ♗b5=) 15. ♔c7 (△ ♔d6-e7-f6) d5 16. ♔d6 d4 17. ♔c5 d3 18. ♗d3 ♗d7 19. ♔d6 ♗f5 20. ♗c4+− ♂b] **5. ♗b7** [△ ♗c6+−] **♗d7 6. ♗c6!** [6. f5? ♔e7 7. ♗c6 ♗c6 8. dc6 ♔d8 9. ♔c4 ♔c8! 10. b4 ♔c7=] **♗g4 7. ♔b5 ♗h5 8. ♔b6 ♗f3** [8... ♗d1 9. b4 h5 10. ♔c7 h4 11. ♗d7 ♔e7 12. b5 ♗f3 13. ♗c6! h3 14. b6 h2 15. b7 h1♕ 16. b8♕+−] **9. ♔c7! h5 10. ♔d6 f5** [10... h4 11. ♗d7 ♗g2 12. b4 h3 13. ♗h3 ♗h3 14. b5 ♔e8 15. b6 ♗c8 16. ♔c7 ♗a6 17. d6+−] **11. ♔c7 h4 12. d6 1 : 0 [Nadanian]**

11. RAECKIJ − PLETÁNEK

1. f4!! ♘c8 [1... gf4? 2. ♗h4 ♔c7 (2... f3 3. ♗f6 f2 4. ♘e3 △ ♗h4+−) 3. ♗f6 ♔d7 4. g5+−; 1... ef4 2. ♗d4 ♔c7 (2... f3? 3. ♗f6 f2 4. ♘g3 △ ♗d4+−) 3. ♗f6 ♔d7 4. ♔c3! (4. ♗g7?! ♗g7 5. ♘g7 f3 6. ♘f5 f2 7. ♘g3 ♔e7 8. ♔c3 ♔f6 9. ♔d4 b5!⇆) ♘c8 (4... b5? 5. ♗d4+−) 5. ♔d4! (5. ♗g7 ♗g7 6. ♘g7 ♘e7=) ♔c7 (5... ♔e8 6. ♗g7! ♗g7

7. ♘g7 △ ♘f5+−; 5… ♘a7 6. ♗g7 ♗g7 7. ♘g7 b5 8. ♘f5 bc4 9. ♔c4+−) 6. ♘g7 ♔d7 7. ♘e6 ♔e8 8. ♗g7! ♗g7 9. ♘g7 △ ♘f5+−] **2. fg5 fg5 3. ♗e3 ♘e7** [3… ♔c7 4. ♔b5! ♔b7 5. ♗g5!! hg5 6. h6 ♘e7 (6… ♗h6 7. ♘h6 ♘e7 8. ♘f7+−) 7. ♘d6 ♔c7 8. h7 ♘g6 9. ♘f7 ♗g7 10. d6 ♔d7 11. ♔b6 ♔e6 12. c5 ♔f7 13. c6 ♔e6 14. c7+−] **4. ♘d6 ♔c7 5. ♘b5 ♔d7 6. ♔c3+− ♘g8 7. ♗b6 ♘f6 8. ♔d3 ♘g4 9. c5 1 : 0 [Raeckij]**

12. ŠTOHL − LIPKA

1. f4! e4 2. ♗e2 ♘c8 3. ♔h3 ♘cd6 4. ♗e1! [△ ♗c3-e5] **♔h6 5. ♗c3 ♘c8 6. ♔h4 ♘fd6** [6… ♘cd6 7. ♗h5 △ ♗e5⊙] **7. ♗e5 ♔g6 8. ♗h5?!** [8. ♗d1! ♔h6 9. ♗h5⊙ e3 (9… ♘b7 10. ♗e8 ♘bd6 11. ♗d7+−) 10. ♗f3 ♘e4 (10… ♔g6 11. ♔g3 ♘e4 12. ♗e4 fe4 13. d6+−) 11. ♗e4 fe4 (11… e2 12. ♗c3 fe4 13. ♔g3 ♔g6 14. ♔f2 ♔f5 15. ♗e5+−) 12. ♔g3 ♘e7 13. d6 ♘f5 14. ♔g2+−] **♔h6 9. ♗f6?** [9. ♗d1 ♔g6 10. ♗e2 ♔h6 11. ♗h5+−⊙ − 8. ♗d1!] **e3! 10. ♗g5 ♔g7 11. ♔g3 ♘e4 12. ♔f3 ♘f6!=** [12… ♘d2? 13. ♔e3 ♘b3 14. ♗d8+−; 12… e2 13. ♗h4 ♘f6!=] **13. ♗f6 ♔f6 14. ♔e3 ♘d6 15. ♗e2 ♔g6 16. ♔f2 ♔h6 17. ♔g3 ♔g6 18. ♔h4 ♔h6 19. ♗h5 ♘c8 20. ♗d1** [20. ♗e8 ♘d6 21. ♗d7 ♔g6=] **1/2 : 1/2 [Štohl]**

13. SCHMITTDIEL − ROZENTALIS

1… ♔d3 2. ♔g6 ♖b5 3. ♔f6 ♔e4 4. ♔e6 ♖d5!⊙ 5. ♔f6 ♖f5! [5… ♔f4? 6. ♔e6 △ ♗d6, c4] **6. ♔e6 ♖f4! 7. ♗e7** [7. c4 ♔d3−+] **♔d3 8. ♗g5 ♖a4 9. ♗d8 ♖c4! 10. ♔f5 ♖c3 11. ♔g6 ♖c5 12. ♗g5 ♔e4!** [12… ♖a5 13. ♔h5=] **13. ♔h5 ♔f5 14. ♗d2 ♖c8 15. ♔h6□ ♖h8 16. ♔g7 ♖h4 17. ♗e3 ♖e4 18. ♗b6 ♖e6 19. ♔f7 ♔e5 20. ♗d4 ♔d5 21. ♗f2** [21. ♗b6 ♖b6 22. ab6 ♔c6 23. ♔e6 ♔b6 (23… a5? 24. b7!=) 24. ♔d5 ♔b5−+] **♖c6 22. ♗e3 ♔c4 23. ♗b6** [23. ♗c1 ♔b5 24. ♗d2 ♖c2 25. ♗e1 ♖c1 26. ♗d2 ♖d1 27. ♗c3 ♔c4 28. ♗e5 ♖d5−+] **♔b5** [24. ♗d8 ♖d6−+] **0 : 1 [Rozentalis]**

14. AKOPIAN − A. N. PANČENKO

1… ♖g1 2. ♔h4 ♖h1 3. ♔g3 ♖g1 4. ♔h2 [4. ♔f2 ♖g4 5. ♔f3 ♖g1 6. ♖a6 ♔e5=] **♖e1!** [4… ♖g4? 5. ♔h3 ♖g1 6. ♖a6! ♔e5 7. ♔h4 ♔f5 8. ♖f6+−] **5. ♔h3 ♖h1 6. ♔g2 ♖e1 7. ♖a6** [7. ♖f6 ♖e6=; 7. ♖g8 ♖e7! 8. ♔g3 ♔e6 9. ♖f8 ♖f7=] **♖e6!** [7… ♖e3? 8. g6 ♖e6 9. g7 ♖e8 10. ♖g6 ♖g8 11. ♔f3 ♔e5 12. ♔g4+−] **8. ♖a5 ♔d6 9. ♔f3** [9. ♔g3 ♔e7 10. ♖f5 ♖e4! 11. g6 ♖e6=] **♖e1!** [9… ♔e7? 10. ♖f5!+−] **10. ♔g4** [10. ♖f5 ♖g1! (10… ♔e6? 11. ♖f6 △ ♔g4+−) 11. ♔f4 ♔e7! 12. ♖f6 ♖f1=] **♔e6 11. ♖a7 ♖h1!= 12. ♖b7 ♖h2 1/2 : 1/2 [Akopian]**

15. SAKAEV − HRÁČEK

1… ♖b7!= [1… ♖a6 2. ♔f7 ♔g5 3. h6! ♖h6 4. ♔g7 ♖a6 5. f6+−] **2. ♖e8 ♖b6! 3. ♖e6 ♖b7!□ 4. ♖e2 ♖a7 5. ♔e6 ♔h5 6. ♔f6 ♖a6 7. ♖e6 ♖a7 8. ♖e7 ♖a6 9. ♔g7 ♔g5 10. ♖f7 ♖b6** [11. f6 ♖a6 12. ♖f8 ♖b6!=] **1/2 : 1/2 [Sakaev]**

16. MAKAR'EV − GAVRILOV

1… ♔b3! 2. ♖d3 [2. ♔c1 ♖c2 3. ♔b1 ♖c4 4. ♖d6 ♖b4−+] **♔c4 3. ♖d6** [♖ 5/a] **♔c5 4. ♖d3** [4. ♖h6 ♖e4 5. ♖h5 ♔c6 6. ♖h6 ♔b7 7. ♖h7 ♔a6−+] **♖e4 5. ♖c3□** [5. ♖a3 ♔b4 6. ♖a2 ♖e1−+] **♔d5!** [5… ♔b4? 6. ♖c6=; 5… ♖c4? 6. ♔b2! ♔d5 (6… ♔d4 7. ♖h3=) 7. ♖d3 ♖d4 (7… ♔c6 8. ♔a3=) 8. ♔c3!=] **6. ♖a3** [6. ♖b3 ♖b4−+; 6. ♖d3 ♔c4 7. ♖h3 ♔b4 8. ♖h6 ♔c5 9. ♖h5 ♔c6 10. ♖h6 ♔b7 11. ♖h7 ♔a6−+] **♔c4 7. ♔c2** [7. ♔b2 ♖e2 8. ♔c1 ♔b4−+] **♖e2 8. ♔d1 ♔b4! 9. ♖a1** [9. ♖h3 ♖e4 10. ♖h6 ♔c5−+] **♖b2! 10. ♔c1** [10. ♔e1 ♔c3 11. ♖c1 (11. ♔d1 ♖h2 12. ♖c1 ♔d3−+; 11. ♖a3 ♖b3 12. ♖a1 ♔b2 13. ♖d1 ♖b4−+) ♔b3 12. ♖a1 ♔c2 13. ♔e2 ♖b4 △ ♔b2−+] **♖h2** [11. ♖b1 ♔c3−+] **0 : 1 [Gavrilov]**

17. LUKIN − RODIN

1. ♔f2! [1. ♖g6?! ♖a4 2. g3 (2. ♔f2 ♖b4 3. ♔f3 a5 4. g4 a4 5. ♖a6 ♖b3 6. ♔e4 a3 7. ♔e5 ♖e3 8. ♔f5 b4 9. g5 ♖e2 10. g6 a2 11. g7 ♖g2 12. ♖a2 ♖g7=) ♖b4 3. ♖a6 ♖b2 4. ♖b6 ♔f7! (4… b4? 5. g4) 5. ♔f1 ♔e7 6. f5 ♖c2! 7. ♖b5 ♔f6=] **♖b3 2. ♖g7!** [2. ♖e5?! ♔d6! 3. g4 ♖b4 4. ♔f3 ♖b1=] **♔f6 3. ♖a7 ♔f5 4. g3 ♖b2** [4… ♖b4 5.

♖a6 ♖c4! 6. ♔g2 b4 7. ♖b6 *a)* 7... ♔e4? 8. ♖b5! ♔d3 (8... ♖d4 9. ♔h3 ♔f3 10. f5 ♖g4 11. f6 ♖g3 12. ♔h4 ♖g4 13. ♔h5 ♖f4 14. ♔g6+−) 9. f5 ♔c2 10. ♔f3 b3 11. g4 b2 12. ♖b2 ♔b2 13. f6 ♖c1 14. g5 ♖f1 15. ♔e4 ♔c3 16. ♔e5 ♖e1 17. ♔d6 ♖f1 18. ♔e6 ♖e1 19. ♔f7 ♔d4 20. g6 ♔e5 21. ♔g7!+−; *b)* 7... ♖c2! 8. ♔h3 ♖c4! 9. ♔h4 ♖d4! 10. ♔h5 (10. ♖b5 ♔f6! 11. ♔g4 ♖c4! 12. ♖b6 ♔e7 13. ♔g5 ♔d7 14. f5 ♔c7 15. ♖e6 b3 16. ♖e1 b2 17. ♖b1 ♖b4 18. ♔f6 ♔d8 19. ♔f7 ♖b7 20. ♔f8 ♔d7 21. g4 ♔d6 22. g5 ♔e5 23. f6 ♔f5 24. f7 ♔g6=) ♖c4 11. g4 (11. ♖b5 ♔f6! 12. f5 ♖c8! 13. ♔h4 ♖c1! 14. g4 ♖h1 15. ♔g3 ♔g5=) ♔f4 12. g5 ♔f5 13. g6 ♖c3! 14. ♔h6 b3=] **5. ♔f3 ♖b3 6. ♔g2 ♔g4 7. ♖g7 ♔f5 8. ♖g5 ♔f6** [8... ♔e4? 9. ♖e5 ♔d4 10. ♖e2! ♖b4 11. f5 ♖c4 12. f6 ♖c8 13. g4 b4 14. ♔g3 b3 15. g5+−] **9. ♖c5 ♖b4 10. ♖c6 ♔f5 11. ♖a6 ♖b2?** [11... ♖c4!=] **12. ♔h3+− ♖b1** [12... ♖c2 13. ♖b6] **13. ♖b6 b4** [13... ♖b2 14. ♖b8 ♖b1 15. ♖e8] **14. ♖b5 ♔e6 15. g4 b3** [15... ♔d6 16. ♔h4 ♔c6 17. ♖b8 ♔c7 18. ♖e8 b3 19. ♖e2! ♖c1 20. ♖b2 ♖c3 21. f5 ♔d7 22. ♔g5 ♔e7 23. ♔g6] **16. ♔h4**
1 : 0 **[Lukin]**

18. ŠAHOVIĆ – STRIKOVIĆ

1. ♔f7!□ [1. ♖a1? ♔f4−+] **e1♕** [1... ♖e6 2. b7 e1♕ 3. b8♕ ♕f1! (3... ♕f2 4. ♔g8) 4. ♔g8 (4. ♔g7? ♕f6−+) ♕c4 5. ♕b2!=] **2. ♔e8 ♔d5?** [2... ♔f4 3. ♔d7 ♕b4 4. ♔c7 ♕c5 5. ♔b7 d5 6. ♖a6 d4 7. ♔a8 d3 8. b7=; 2... ♔f6! 3. ♔d8 (3. ♔f8 ♕e6! 4. g5□ ♔g5 5. ♖g7 ♔f6 6. b7 ♕b3−+) ♕b4 4. ♔c7□ (4. b7 ♕b6−+; 4. ♖a6 ♕b5−+) ♕c5 5. ♔b7 ♔e6! (5... ♔g5 6. ♖a6 △ ♔a8, b7=) 6. ♖a6 ♔d7 7. ♔a8 (7. ♔b8 ♕b5 8. ♔b7□ d5 9. g5 d4 10. g6 d3 11. g7 ♕d5 12. ♔a7 d2 13. b7 d1♕ 14. b8♕ ♕1d4 15. ♕b6 ♕g7−+) ♕c6! (7... ♕b5 8. ♖a7 ♔e6 9. b7 ♕c6 10. ♖a5 △ ♔a7=) 8. ♔b8 (8. ♔a7 ♔c8−+) d5 9. ♖a7 ♔d6−+] **3. ♖e7! ♕b1** [3... ♕b4 4. b7 ♕g4 5. ♔d8 ♔c6 6. b8♕ (6. ♖c7 ♔d5 7. ♖e7=) ♕g8 7. ♖e8 ♕g5 8. ♖e7=; 3... ♕h4 4. b7 ♕h8 (4... ♕g4 5. ♔d8=) 5. ♔f7! △ g5=] **4. b7 ♔c6 5. ♔d8** [5. g5? ♕g6 6. ♔f8 ♕g5! 7. b8♕ ♕f6 8. ♔g8 ♕e7] **♕b2** [5... d5? 6. ♔c8; 5... ♕b6 6. ♔c8 ♕a6 7. g5] **6. ♖c7 ♔d5 7. ♖e7! 1/2 : 1/2** **[Mirković]**

19. VELIMIROVIĆ – D. SEKULIĆ

1. a5? [1. fg5! ♔g6 (1... ♖b6 2. a5 ♖a6 3. ♔f2 ♔g6 4. ♔f3 ♔g5 5. ♔e4 ♔h5 6. ♔f4 ♔g6 7. ♔g4 f6 8. ef6 ♔f6 9. ♔h4 ♔f5 10. ♔g3 ♔g5 11. ♔f3 ♔f5 12. ♔e3 ♔e5 13. ♔d3 ♔d5 14. h4+−) 2. a5 ♔g5 3. a6 ♖b8 4. a7 ♖a8 5. ♔f2 *a)* 5... f6 6. ef6 ♔f6 7. ♔f3 ♔f5 8. ♖a5 e5 9. ♔e3 ♔e6 10. ♔e4 ♔f6 11. ♖a1 ♔e6 12. ♖a2 ♔f6 13. ♖a5+−; *b)* 5... ♔f4 6. ♖a5 ♔e4 7. ♔e2 ♔f4 8. ♔d3 ♔f3 (8... ♔f5 9. ♔e3 ♔g5 10. ♔e4 ♔g6 11. ♔f4+− ×h4) 9. ♖a4! ♔g3 10. ♔e3 ♔g2 (10... ♔h3 11. ♔f2+−) 11. ♔f4 ♔h3 12. ♔f3+−; *c)* 5... ♔f5! 6. ♖a5 ♔f4! 7. ♔e2 ♔e4 8. ♔d2 ♔d4 9. ♔c2 ♔c4 10. ♔b2 ♔b4 11. ♖a1 ♔c4 12. ♖a4 ♔d5 (12... ♔b5 13. ♔b3 ♔c5 14. ♖a5 ♔d4 15. ♔b4 ♔e4 16. ♔c3 ♖c8 17. ♔d2 ♖a8 18. ♔e2+−⊙) 13. ♖a5 ♔c4 (13... ♔c6 14. ♔c3 ♔b6 15. ♔b4 ♖a7 16. ♖a7 ♔a7 17. ♔c5+−) 14. ♔a3 ♔c3 15. ♖a4 ♔d3 16. ♔b3 ♔e3 17. ♔c3+−] **gf4 2. a6 ♖b8 3. a7 ♖a8 4. ♔f2 f6!** [4... ♔g6 5. ♔f3 ♔f5 6. ♖a5!+−⊙] **5. ef6 ♔f6 6. ♔f3 e5 7. ♔g4 ♔g6 8. ♖a6 ♔g7 9. ♔h4 f3 1/2 : 1/2**
[G. M. Todorović]

20. G. GEORGADZE – D. BERKOVIČ

1. ♖e1! f5□ 2. ♘d5 ♘f7 3. ♖a1 ♘c5 4. ♖a7 ♘e6 5. ♖e7 ♘f8 6. ♔f3 ♘h7 7. ♘f4 ♘f8 8. ♔e3 ♔f6 9. ♖e8 ♔g7 10. ♔d4 ♘d6 11. ♖e7 ♔h6 [11... ♘f7? 12. ♔d5 ♔f6 13. ♖a7 ♘h6 14. ♖a8 ♔g7 15. ♔d6+−] **12. ♔e5 ♘e4 13. ♖f7 ♘h7 14. ♘e2 ♘f2 15. ♔e6 ♘e4** [△ ♘eg5] **16. ♖a7 ♘hf6 17. ♔f7 ♘g4 18. ♖a6 ♔h7□** [18... ♘e5 19. ♔g8 ♘g4 20. ♘f4 ♘gf6 21. ♔f7+−] **19. ♘f4 g5 20. ♘g6! ♘h6 21. ♔e8 ♔g7 22. hg5 ♘f7 23. ♘h4 ♘fg5 24. ♖g6! ♔h8** [24... ♔h7 25. ♔f8 ♔h8 26. ♖g8 ♔h7 27. ♖g7 ♔h8 28. ♘g6#] **25. ♔e7 ♘h7 26. ♘f5 ♘hg5 27. ♖h6 1 : 0** **[G. Georgadze]**

21. J. BENJAMIN – A. FRIEDMAN

1. ♖h6!! ♔f7 [1... d1♕ 2. ♔e7+−; 1... ♗d3 2. ♔e7 ♗h7 3. ♖f6 ♗d3 4. f5! ♗f5 (4... d1♕ 5. ♖f8 ♔h7 6. ♖h8#) 5. ♖f8 ♔h7 6. ♖d8+−] **2. ♖f6 ♔g8 3. ♔e7 ♔h7** [3... d1♕ 4. ♖h6+−] **4. ♖f7** [4. f5] **♔g6 5. f5 ef5** [5... ♔g5 6. ♖g7 ♔f5 7. ♖f7 ♔e5

8. ♖f1+−] **6. ♖f6** [6. ♖g7 ♔h6 7. ♔f6 h4 8. ♗f4 ♔h5 9. h3 d1♕ 10. ♖h7#] **♔g5 7. ♖d6 1 : 0 [J. Benjamin]**

22. D. LEKIĆ − B. MAKSIMOVIĆ

1... ♔h3! [♖ **1/i**; 1... ♖h3 2. e6 ♔f4 3. ♘g6! (3. e7 ♖e3 4. ♔f2 ♖e4−+) ♔e4 4. e7 ♖e3 5. ♔d2! ♔d4 6. ♘h4!!=] **2. e6 ♖a8!** [2... ♔g4 3. e7 ♖a8 4. ♘d7 △ ♘f6=; 2... ♔g3 3. e7 ♖a8 4. ♘g6 ♖e8 5. ♔e3 ♔g4 6. ♘e5 ♔h5 7. ♘c6 ♔g6 8. ♔d4=] **3. ♘h7** [3. e7 ♖e8! 4. ♘g6 ♔g4 5. ♔e3 ♔h5 6. ♘e5 ♖e7 7. ♔f3! (△ ♘c4-e3=) ♖c7!−+; 3. ♘g6 ♔g4! (3... ♖e8? 4. ♔f3 ♖e6 5. ♘e5!= △ ♘c4-e3) 4. ♔e3 ♖e8 5. e7 (5. ♘e5 ♔g3!−+) ♔h5 6. ♘e5 ♖e7 7. ♔f3 ♖c7−+] **♖e8?** [3... ♔g3! 4. ♔e3 ♖e8 5. ♘g5 ♖e7−+] **4. ♔f3! ♔h4 5. ♘f6 ♖e6 6. ♘d5!=** [△ ♘e3 ×f5] **[B. Maksimović]**

23. IOSELIANI − ZSU. POLGÁR

1... ♖d2! 2. ♔e8 ♖d8!! 3. ♔d8 [♘♗ **1/h**] **h4! 4. ♔e8 e5!= 5. ♔f8** [5. ♗d5 g5 6. ♗f7 g4!=] **g5 6. ♗h5 e4 7. ♔g8** [7. ♗f7 g4=] **e3 8. ♔f8 ♔e6 9. ♔g7 f5 10. ♔g6 g4 11. hg4 fg4 12. ♗g4 ♔e7! 13. ♔g7** [13. ♔g5 h3=] **♔e8 14. ♗e2 ♔e7 15. ♗b5 ♔e6 16. ♔g6 ♔e7 17. ♔g7 ♔e6 18. ♔g6 ♔e7 19. ♗c4 ♔f8 20. ♔h7 ♔e8 21. ♔g8 ♔e7 22. ♔g7 ♔e8 23. ♗e2 ♔e7 24. ♗f3 ♔e8 25. ♗g4 ♔e7 26. ♗h5 ♔e6 27. ♔g6 ♔e7 28. ♗f3 ♔f8 1/2 : 1/2 [Sakaev]**

24. SERPER − ZAJCEV

1. ♗d7!⊙ ♗d2 [1... ♔d5 2. ♖a5+−; 1... ♗c1 2. e4! fe4 3. de4 d3 4. ♖a5 ♔d4 5. ♖d5 ♔c3 6. e5+−] **2. e4!!** [△ ♖e6#] **fe4** [2... de3 3. ♖h6] **3. ♔e2! 1 : 0 [Serper]**

25. TIMOŠENKO − SAVČENKO

1... ♘d5□= [1... ♘b5 2. ♖c8 △ ♗c5, ♔c4+−] **2. a7** [2. ♗d4? ♘c7 3. ♖a7 ♘b5; 2. ♗g1 ♘c7 3. ♖a7 ♘a6=] **♘e3 3. ♖h8 ♔h8 4. a8♕ ♔h7 5. ♕e4** [5. ♔e3 ♖e5 △ h5=] **♔g8!** [5... ♔h8=; 5... g6? 6. ♕e7 ♔g8 7. ♕e8 ♔g7 8. ♕d7 ♔g8 9. ♔e3+−] **6. ♕e8 ♔h7 7. ♕e4** [7. ♕e3 ♖e5=] **1/2 : 1/2 [Savčenko]**

26. ISTRĂŢESCU − ZAJCEV

1... ♗c8!□ [1... h5? 2. ♗e8 ♔h6 3. ♖f7+−; 1... ♖c8? 2. ♖e7! h5 3. a5+−; 1... ♗e6? 2. ♖a6! △ ♖c6+−; 1... ♗c2? 2. g4! f5 3. ♖a6 ♔g7 4. ♖c6+−] **2. ♗e8** [2. g4 f5 3. ♗d3 ♖c3 4. gf5 ♔f6=] **♔f5 3. ♖a8** [3. ♖e7!? ♖c3 4. ♗h5 ♗a6! (4... d4? 5. ♖e4 △ g4+−) 5. ♗f7! ♗c4! (5... ♖f3?! 6. ♗e6! ♔g6□ 7. g4! ♗d3 8. ♗f7 ♔g7 9. ♗d5 ♔f8 10. ♖f7 ♔e8 11. ♗f3 ♔f7 12. a5 ♔e7 13. ♔f2±) 6. ♗g8!? (6. ♗e6 ♔e5=) ♖f3! 7. ♗e6 ♔g6□ 8. g4 f5! 9. ♗f5 ♔f6 10. ♖e6 ♔f7 11. ♖h6 ♗d3!=] **♔e5** [⌓ 3... ♗e6!? 4. a5 ♖c3 5. ♗h5 (5. a6 ♖f3!) ♔e5! 6. a6 ♖c8! (6... ♖a3!? 7. a7 d4! 8. ♗g6 f5! 9. ♗f5 ♗d5!=) 7. ♖c8 ♗c8 8. a7 ♗b7 9. ♔f2 ♔d4!=] **4. a5 ♖c3 5. a6 ♗h3!** [5... ♗e6 6. a7 ♖a3 7. ♗b5!⊙ ♗f7 (7... d4? 8. ♖e8 ♖a7 9. ♗c4+−; 7... ♖a2 8. f4! gf4 9. gf4 ♔f5 10. ♖e8 ♖a7 11. ♗d3±) 8. ♗d7! (△ ♖f8) ♗h5 9. g4 ♗g6 10. ♗e8! ♗d3 11. ♗c6 ♔d4 12. ♗d5!±] **6. ♗b5** [6. a7 ♔d4! 7. ♗b5 ♖c2! 7... ♖a3?! 8. g4! ♖a2 9. ♖h8! ♖g2 10. ♔f1! ♖a2 11. ♔e1 ♖a7 12. ♖h6 ♗g2 13. ♔f2 ♖a2 14. ♗e2±) 8. ♖d8 ♖g2 9. ♔h1 ♖c2 10. ♔g1 ♖g2=] **♖c8!** [6... ♖c2? 7. ♖e8 ♔d4 8. ♗e2 ♖a2 9. g4!±; 6... ♖a3?! 7. ♖e8 ♔d4 8. g4! f5 9. ♗e2 fg4 10. fg4 ♗g4 11. ♗g4 ♖a6 12. ♔f2±] **7. ♗c6!?** [7. ♖c8 ♗c8 8. ♔f2 ♔d4!=] **♖c6!** [7... ♖a8? 8. ♗a8+−; 7... ♖c7? 8. ♖e8 ♔d4 9. ♗b7 ♖c1 10. ♔f2 ♖a1 11. g4±] **8. ♖e8 ♔d4= 9. a7 ♖a6 10. a8♕ ♖a8 11. ♖a8 ♔e3 12. f4** [12. ♖a3 ♔e2] **d4 13. fg5 hg5 14. ♖e8 ♔f3 15. ♖d8 ♔e3 16. ♖e8 1/2 : 1/2 [Stoica]**

27. JAKOVIČ − SAVČENKO

1. ♔g2!□ [1. ♗d2 f4!? (1... ♔h5!? 2. a6 ♖a3 3. ♗e3 f4 4. ♗d4 f3 5. a7 ♖a2 6. ♖e8 ♖d2−+) 2. ♖e4 ♖b1 3. ♔g2 ♖b2 4. ♖e2 ♔h5−+; 1. ♖b6 ♖a3 2. ♗b4 ♖a2 △ ♗f2−+; 1. ♗g3 ♖g3 2. ♔f2 ♖a3 3. a6 ♔h5 4. ♔g2 ♖a4 5. ♔g3 ♖g4−+] **♗e1 2. ♖e1 ♖a3** [2... ♔h5 3. ♖a1=] **3. ♖g1!!□** [3. ♔h2 ♖a4! 4. ♔g3 ♔h5−+] **♖a5** [3... ♔h5 4. ♔h2 ♖a4 5. ♖g5 ♔h6 6. ♔h3=] **4. ♔h3 ♖a8 5. ♖g3 ♖e8** [5... ♖h8 6. ♖a3=] **6. ♖g1 ♖e6 7. ♖g3 ♖f6 8. ♖g2 ♖f8** [8... f4 9. ♔g4=] **9. ♖g1** [9. ♖g3?? f4−+] **f4 10. ♔g2! f3 11. ♔f2 ♖f5 12. ♖g4 ♔h5 13. ♖a4 1 : 0 [Jakovič]**

registar • индекс • index • register • registre • registro • registro • register • 棋譜索引 • الفهرس

komentatori • комментаторы • commentators • kommentatoren • commentateurs • comentaristas • commentatori • kommentatorer • 棋譜解説 • المعلقون

završnice u partijama • окончания из партий • endings in the games • endspiele in den partien • finales dans les parties • finales en las partidas • finali nelle partite • slutspelen från partierna • 收局索引 •
المرحلة النهائية للاشواط

turniri • турниры • tournaments • turniere • tournois • torneos • tornei • turneringar • 競技会 • دورة مباريات

CALCUTTA, II 1993
(76 players, 11 rounds)

1. Tivjakov 9, 2. Ju. Hodgson $8^1/_2$, 3—8. Murshed, Malanjuk, J. Hickl, Norwood, P. Thipsay, Prasad $7^1/_2$, 9—15. Gufel'd, Ermenkov, Murugan, Sahu, Kirov, S. Salov, King 7, 16—24. T. S. Ravi, Koshy, Prakash, Suvrajit Saha, Sanjeev Kumar, Sofieva, R. Singh, L. Ravi, Saravanan $6^1/_2$, etc.

BUDAPEST, II 1993 — cat. VIII (2432) g=9, m=$6^1/_2$

1—3. Bezold, Maiwald, I. Faragó $7^1/_2$, 4—6. S. Pedersen, Győrkös, Lyrberg $6^1/_2$, 7. B. Lengyel 6, 8—10. Pe. H. Nielsen, Wells, P. Lukács $5^1/_2$, 11—12. L. Lengyel, Dao Thien Hai 5, 13. J. Urban $3^1/_2$

BUCUREŞTI , II 1993 — cat. X (2480) g=$9^1/_2$, m=7

1—3. V. Neverov, Zajcev, V. Nevedničij $9^1/_2$, 4. Rogozenko 8, 5—7. S. Kiselëv, Marin, Istrăţescu $7^1/_2$, 8. Co. Ionescu 7, 9—10. Moldovan, Geo. Timošenko $6^1/_2$, 11—12. Marciano, Apicella 6, 13. Hauchard $5^1/_2$, 14. Ma. Tseitlin $4^1/_2$, 15. Gagarin 4

BERN, II 1993
(238 players, 9 rounds)

1—2. Epišin, Tukmakov $7^1/_2$, 3—10. Lerner, Razuvaev, van Wely, Conquest, Ward, Cvitan, Gallagher, Vyžmanavin 7, 11—23. Wojtkiewicz, N. Kelečević, Ėjngorn, van der Sterren, Landenbergue, I. Novikov, Dreev, Meyers, I. Ibragimov, Klovans, Robović, Hort, Schwägli $6^1/_2$, 24—38. Brunner, Marangunić, Ambrož, Cámpora, G. Flear, Blees, Reeh, Cladouras, A. Sokolov, Kohlweyer, Cuijpers, Polák, Steinbacher, Lukasiewicz, Nemet 6, etc.

CANNES, II 1993

			1	2	3	4	5	6	
KRAMNIK	g	2685	1	1	0	$^1/_2$	1	1	$4^1/_2$
LAUTIER	g	2645	0	0	1	$^1/_2$	0	0	$1^1/_2$

CANNES, II 1993
(138 players, 9 rounds)

1—5. K. Spraggett, Akopian, Howell, Ink'ov, Ragozin 7, 6—11. Dorfman, Palac, Wahls, Cebalo, Komarov, Löffler $6^1/_2$, 12—24. Dunnington, Godena, Galjamova, József Horváth, J.-R. Koch, Skembris, Velikov, V. Ikonnikov, Kr. Georgiev, Lanka, Dovžik, O. Renet, Chabanon 6, etc.

JAKARTA, II 1993 — cat. X (2478) g=6, m=$4^1/_2$

1. Handoko $7^1/_2$, 2—3. Ye Rongguang, Barcenilla 6, 4—5. Lin Weiguo, Torre $5^1/_2$, 6. Xu Jun 5, 7. Adianto 4, 8—9. Ginting, Nadera 2, 10. Sitanggang $1^1/_2$

KECSKEMÉT, II 1993 — cat. VII (2409) g=10, m=$7^1/_2$

1. Z. Almasi 10, 2. Luther $9^1/_2$, 3—4. Grószpéter, V. Loginov $8^1/_2$, 5—7. I. Almasi, Fogarasi, Vaulin $7^1/_2$, 8. Videki 6, 9—10. Vadász, Krizsany $5^1/_2$, 11. Stummer 5, 12. Stajčić $4^1/_2$, 13. Szalánczy $3^1/_2$, 14. Siklosi 2

MARIBOR, II 1993 — cat. VIII (2447) g=7, m=5

1. G. Mohr 7, 2–3. Kožul, Tolnai 6½, 4. Cebalo 5, 5–7. Barle, Sermek, Gostiša 4, 8. Danner 3, 9–10. A. Grosar, Riegler 2½

MONACO, II 1993

			1	2	3	4	5	6	7	8	9	10	11	12	
IOSELIANI	wg	2460	0	0	½	½	½	1	½	1	0	1	0	1	6
ZSU. POLGÁR	wg	2560	1	1	½	½	½	0	½	0	1	0	1	0	6

CAPPELLE LA GRANDE, II 1993
(415 players, 9 rounds)

1. Soloženkin, 7½, 2–9. Gofshtein, O. Danielian, Rausis, M. Kamiński, Čučelov, E. Geller, Jakovič, J. Gdański 7, 10–21. N. Mitkov, A. Šnejder, Kišnëv, G. Timoščenko, Jivaguinskij, Vaîsser, Th. Thorhallsson, Sadler, Luce, Fogarasi, M. Schlosser, Reinderman 6½, etc.

LINARES, II–III 1993 — cat. XVIII (2677) g=6½

				1	2	3	4	5	6	7	8	9	10	11	12	13	14		
1	KASPAROV	g	2805	●	1	1	½	½	½	½	½	1	1	½	1	1	1	10	1
2	AN. KARPOV	g	2725	0	●	½	½	½	1	½	1	1	½	1	0	1	1	8½	2–3
3	ANAND	g	2710	0	½	●	½	½	½	1	0	1	1	½	1	1	1	8½	2–3
4	ŠIROV	g	2670	½	½	½	●	1	0	½	0	1	1	½	½	1	1	8	4
5	KRAMNIK	g	2685	½	½	½	0	●	0	1	1	1	½	½	½	1	½	7½	5
6	V. SALOV	g	2660	½	0	½	1	1	●	0	½	½	1	½	½	½	0	6½	6–7
7	IVANČUK	g	2710	½	½	0	½	0	1	●	0	0	1	½	1	1	½	6½	6–7
8	BELJAVSKIJ	g	2610	½	0	1	1	0	½	1	●	0	0	½	1	½	0	6	8
9	KAMSKY	g	2655	0	0	0	0	0	½	1	1	●	½	1	1	0	½	5½	9–10
10	BAREEV	g	2670	0	½	0	0	½	0	0	1	½	●	½	1	½	1	5½	9–10
11	JUSUPOV	g	2645	½	0	½	½	½	½	½	½	0	½	●	0	½	½	5	11–12
12	TIMMAN	g	2635	0	1	0	½	½	½	0	0	0	0	1	●	½	1	5	11–12
13	B. GEL'FAND	g	2690	0	0	0	0	0	½	0	½	1	½	½	½	●	1	4½	13
14	LJUBOJEVIĆ	g	2605	0	0	0	0	½	1	½	1	½	0	½	0	0	●	4	14

PODGORICA, II–III 1993 — cat. X (2477) g=9, m=6½

1–3. M. Pavlović, Draško, F. Levin 9, 4. Damljanović 8½, 5–7. B. Ivanović, Vaulin, Poluljahov 7½, 8–9. M. Makarov, D. Kosić 6, 10. Abramović 5½, 11. I. Marinković 5, 12–13. Zontah, Mi. Lazić 4, 14. Kontić 2½

BUDAPEST, III 1993 — cat. VIII (2426) g=7½, m=5½

1. József Horváth 7, 2–3. P. Wells, Lékó 6½, 4–6. P. Lukács, Szalánczy, V. Loginov 6, 7. Šale 5½, 8–9. Zsó. Polgár, B. Lengyel 4, 10. S. Faragó 2½, 11. Arduman 1

LISBOA (zt), III 1993 — cat. VII (2415) m=6½

1. Illescas Córdoba 9, 2–3. Godena, Gómez Esteban 7½, 4. Ochoa de Echagüen 6½, 5. Damaso 6, 6–7. A. Fernandes, Arlandi 5½, 8. L. Galego 5, 9–10. Contin, F. Silva 4½, 11. A. P. Santos 2½, 12. Raul García 2

PROTVINO (zt), III 1993 — cat. X (2490) g=6, m=4

1. Lputian 6½, 2–3. Bagaturov, Nalbandian 5½, 4. Anastasian 5, 5. Sturua 4½, 6. O. Danielian 4, 7–10. Minasian, Ubilava, Supatashvili, Kacheishvili 3½

NIKOLAEV (zt), III 1993
(28 players, 11 rounds)

1. A. Aleksandrov 8½, 2. A. Frolov 8, 3–6. Savon, Savčenko, M. Brodskij, G. Kuz'min 7, 7–8. Borovikov, V. Neverov 6½, 9–10. S. Guliev, Kruppa 6, 11–18. Tukmakov, M. Golubev, Maksimenko, Rahmangulov, A. Fedorov, Lyecko, Bologan, V. Nevedničij 5½, etc.

VILNIUS (zt), III 1993 — cat. IX (2443) m=6½

1–2. Olls, Mališauskas 9, 3. Ruzele 8½, 4. Lanka 8, 5. Frídmans 7½, 6–7. Butnorjus, Žuravlovs 7, 8. A. Sokolovs 6, 9–11. J. Luckáns, Ryčagov, Sepp 5½, 12. Pešina 5, 13. Lauk 4, 14. V. Novikov 3½

BIŠKEK (zt), III 1993 cat. VII (2416) m=7½

1. Kakagel'dyev 9½, 2—3. Nesterov, Nenašev 9, 4—6. Vahidov, Nadirhanov, Jurtaev 8, 7. Serper 7½, 8—9. Kancler, Imanaliev 6½, 10. Ilinskij 4½, 11—13. Bajmurabov, Safin, Ajabbergenov 4, 14. Tumurhuyag 2½

GRAZ (zt), III 1993 cat. VIII (2445) g=9½, m=7

1. Lobron 10½, 2. Gostiša 9, 3. A. Grosar 8½, 4—6. R. Lau, Ch. Lutz, Ph. Schlosser 7½, 7. M. Wach 7, 8. Bönsch 6½, 9—10. Wirthensohn, Lendwai 5½, 11—12. Schroll, Hölzl 5, 13. Züger 4½, 14. R. Frick 1½

BUDAPEST (zt), III 1993

Group „A" cat. XI (2522) g=7, m=4½

				1	2	3	4	5	6	7	8	9	10	11	12		
1	KIR. GEORGIEV	g	2660	●	1	½	1	½	½	1	½	1	½	½	1	8	1
2	J. POLGÁR	g	2595	0	●	1	1	1	½	0	½	½	1	½	½	6½	2—5
3	J. GDAŃSKI	m	2480	½	0	●	½	½	1	0	1	½	1	1	½	6½	2—5
4	FTÁČNIK	g	2535	0	0	½	●	1	½	0	1	1	1	1	½	6½	2—5
5	WOJTKIEWICZ	g	2580	½	0	½	0	●	½	1	1	½	½	1	1	6½	2—5
6	ADORJÁN	g	2545	½	½	0	½	½	●	½	½	1	½	½	1	6	6
7	ŞUBĂ	g	2520	0	1	1	1	0	½	●	0	½	½	0	½	5	7—8
8	RÁŠIK	m	2405	½	½	0	0	0	½	1	●	0	1	1	½	5	7—8
9	ERMENKOV	g	2505	0	½	½	0	½	0	½	1	●	½	½	½	4½	9—10
10	AT. KOLEV	m	2510	½	0	0	0	½	½	½	0	½	●	1	1	4½	9—10
11	SAX	g	2570	½	½	0	0	0	½	1	0	½	0	●	1	4	11
12	COSMA	m	2365	0	½	½	½	0	0	½	½	½	0	0	●	3	12

Play off: cat. XII (2548)

				1	2	3	4		
1	J. POLGÁR	g	2595	● ●	1 1	0 ½	1 ½	4	1
2	FTÁČNIK	g	2535	0 0	● ●	½ 1	½ 1	3	2—3
3	WOJTKIEWICZ	g	2580	1 ½	½ 0	● ●	½ ½	3	2—3
4	J. GDAŃSKI	m	2480	0 ½	½ 0	½ ½	● ●	2	4

Group „B" cat. XI (2524) g=7, m=4½

				1	2	3	4	5	6	7	8	9	10	11	12		
1	TOPALOV	g	2635	●	½	½	½	½	1	1	½	½	½	1	1	7½	1—2
2	V. SPASOV	g	2520	½	●	0	½	½	½	1	1	½	1	1	1	7½	1—2
3	L. PORTISCH	g	2580	½	1	●	½	½	½	½	0	1	½	1	1	7	3
4	ŠTOHL	g	2540	½	½	½	●	½	½	1	½	½	1	1	0	6½	4—6
5	HÁBA	m	2485	½	½	½	½	●	½	½	½	½	½	1	1	6½	4—6
6	A. CHERNIN	g	2600	0	½	½	½	½	●	0	½	1	1	1	1	6½	4—6
7	ZSU. POLGÁR	g	2560	0	0	½	0	½	1	●	1	½	½	½	1	5½	7
8	ISTRĂŢESCU	m	2470	½	0	1	½	½	½	0	●	½	0	1	½	5	8
9	MARIŃ	m	2515	½	½	0	½	½	0	½	½	●	½	0	1	4½	9—10
10	KUCZYŃSKI	g	2525	½	0	½	0	½	0	½	1	½	●	½	½	4½	9—10
11	GAŽÍK	m	2425	0	0	0	0	0	0	½	0	1	½	●	1	3	11
12	A. SZNAPIK	m	2440	0	0	0	1	0	0	0	½	0	½	0	●	2	12

MINSK, III 1993 cat. IX (2468) g=8, m=5½

1. Dragomareckij 7½, 2—6. Dydyško, Kruppa, Maljutin, Pe. H. Nielsen, Golod 6½, 7—8. Šipov, A. Rotštejn 6, 9. Gipslis 5½, 10. Zajcev 3½, 11. Močalov 3, 12. Suėtin 2

CUXHAVEN, III 1993
(200 players, 9 rounds)

1—9. Čučelov, Dohojan, G. Georgadze, Glek, Ėjngorn, Kindermann, Ma. Schäfer, Kovalëv, Zapolskis 7, 10—13. Rabiega, Movsesian, Vasilčenko, Pašalić 6½, etc.

ZAGREB (zt), III 1993 cat. XI (2518) g=8½, m=6

				1	2	3	4	5	6	7	8	9	10	11	12	13	14		
1	KOŽUL	g	2550	●	½	½	½	½	1	1	0	1	1	1	1	1	1	10	1
2	SMIRIN	g	2590	½	●	½	½	½	½	0	1	1	1	1	½	1	1	9	2
3	CVITAN	g	2575	½	½	●	½	½	0	½	½	1	1	1	½	½	1	8	3
4	B. ALTERMAN	g	2600	½	½	½	●	½	½	0	½	1	½	1	½	1	½	7½	4
5	GOFSHTEIN	m	2560	½	½	½	½	●	½	½	1	0	0	1	1	½	½	7	5
6	PSAKHIS	g	2575	0	½	1	½	½	●	1	½	½	½	0	1	0	½	6½	6—7
7	HULAK	g	2540	0	1	½	1	½	0	●	0	½	0	½	1	1	½	6½	6—7
8	G. DIZDAR	g	2490	1	0	½	½	0	½	1	●	½	½	0	½	½	½	6	8—9
9	DIZDAREVIĆ	g	2540	0	0	0	0	1	½	½	½	●	1	½	1	½	½	6	8—9
10	N. NIKOLIĆ	m	2440	0	0	0	½	1	½	1	½	0	●	½	½	½	½	5½	10—11
11	KURAJICA	g	2535	0	0	0	0	0	1	½	1	½	½	●	½	1	½	5½	10—11
12	R. HAR-ZVI	m	2485	0	½	½	½	0	0	0	½	0	½	½	●	1	1	5	12
13	ROGIĆ		2280	0	0	½	0	½	1	0	½	½	½	0	0	●	1	4½	13
14	VLADO KOVAČEVIĆ	g	2485	0	0	0	½	½	½	½	½	½	½	½	0	0	●	4	14

BRAZILIA (zt), III 1993
(22 players, 9 rounds)

1. Granda Zuñiga 7, 2—4. Lima, Cámpora, Milos 6, 5. Sunye Neto 5½, 6—9. Slipak, Egger, R. Vásquez, Rubinetti 5, 10—11. Giardelli, H. van Riemsdijk 4½, 12—16. Catropa, Panno, Valiente, J. Silva, C. Braga 4, 17—19. Trindade, de Toledo, R. García 3½, 20—22. Mecking, Soppe, Izquierdo 3

HAFNARFJÖRDUR / KÖPAROGUR, III 1993

Ísland — France 49 : 51

BAD WÖRISHOFEN, III 1993
(217 players, 9 rounds)

1—2. Magerramov, Kohlweyer 7½, 3—11. Kengis, Ju. Hodgson, Jansa, I. Faragó, K. Bischoff, Brunner, Pähtz, Gallagher, Keitlinghaus 7, 12—18. Polák, Sermek, A. Bach, Schmaltz, W. Müller, Markus, Breustedt 6½, etc.

BEOGRAD, III 1993 cat. VII (2411) g=8½, m=6½

1—2. Poluljahov, M. Makarov 8½, 3—6. Velimirović, M. Knežević, N. Ostojić, Vaulin 6½, 7. V. Damjanović 6, 8—9. Ćirić, Zontah 5, 10. D. Nestorović 3½, 11. Radošević 2, 12. A. Arsović 1½

MONACO, III—IV 1993

Rapid chess (25-minute game):

1. Ljubojević 7½, 2. Ivančuk 7, 3—4. Kortchnoi, Seirawan 6½, 5. Je. Piket 6, 6—8. Anand, Zsu. Polgár, J. Polgár 5½, 9—10. An. Karpov, Polugaevskij 5, 11. L. Christiansen 4, 12. N. Short 2

Blindfold chess (25-minute game):

1—2. Anand, An. Karpov 8½, 3. Ljubojević 7, 4. J. Polgár 6½, 5—6. Ivančuk, Zsu. Polgár 5½, 7—9. L. Christiansen, N. Short, Kortchnoi 4½, 10—11. Je. Piket, Seirawan 4, 12. Polugaevskij 3

Combined:

1. Ljubojević 14½, 2. Anand 14, 3. An. Karpov 13½, 4. Ivančuk 12½, 5. J. Polgár 12, 6—7. Kortchnoi, Zsu. Polgár 11, 8. Seirawan 10½, 9. Je. Piket 10, 10. L. Christiansen 8½, 11. Polugaevskij 8, 12. N. Short 6½

BLED, III—IV 1993
(114 players, 9 rounds)

1. Sermek 7½, 2—5. Bukić, Meštrović, Kožul, Zelčić 7, 6—9. G. Mohr, Šer, Gostiša, B. Golubović 6½, 10—20. Mazi, Stajčić, Burović, Lužar, Z. Bašagić, Iz. Jelen, Kragelj, Soln, Lejlić, Tratar, Pavasović 6, etc.

STAR DOJRAN, III—IV 1993 cat. VII (2406) g=10, m=7½

1. Bogdanovski 10, 2. Poluljahov 9, 3—4. D. Rajković, Vaulin 8½, 5. Dimovski 7½, 6. Tringov 7, 7. Sofrevski 6½, 8—9. M. Knežević, Rama 6, 10. Mučo 5½, 11—12. Kiroski, T. Nedev 4½, 13. S. Georgievski 4, 14. O. Mitkovski 3½

TER APEL, III–IV 1993 cat. XIV (2579)

				1	2	3	4	5	6		
1	HALIFMAN	g	2630	●	½	½	½	1	1	3½	1–2
2	VAGANIAN	g	2615	½	●	0	1	1	1	3½	1–2
3	VAN WELY	g	2560	½	1	●	1	0	0	2½	3–4
4	CU. HANSEN	g	2610	½	0	0	●	1	1	2½	3–4
5	VAN DER WIEL	g	2555	0	0	1	0	●	½	1½	5–6
6	NIJBOER	g	2505	0	0	1	0	½	●	1½	5–6

BAGUIO CITY, III–IV 1993 cat. X (2482) g=6, m=4½

1. Antonio 6½, 2. Adianto 5½, 3–4. Liang Jinrong, Ye Rongguang 5, 5–6. Sitanggang, Lin Weiguo 4½, 7. Handoko 4, 8–9. Torre, Barcenilla 3½, 10. Nadera 3

DUBLIN (zt), IV 1993
(56 players, 11 rounds)

1. Adams 9, 2. Speelman 8½, 3–6. K. Arkell, Sadler, Levitt, Ju. Hodgson, 7½, 7–12. Howell, Parker, Crouch, P. Wells, McNab, Webster 7, 13–18. Kumaran, Miles, A.P. Smith, Barry, Ludgate, Rossiter 6½, etc.

SAN SEBASTIAN, IV 1993
(80 players, 9 rounds)

1–3. Kurajica, Izeta, Gómez Esteban 7, 4–7. Huzman, de la Villa García, Komljenović, Eslon 6½, 8–14. Magem Badals, Mellado, N. Mitkov, Alvarez Ibarra, Sánchez Almeyra, Pisá Ferrer, Solov'ev 6, 15–20. Franco, Ubilava, Sanz Alonso, Vehí Bach, Veingold, Pomes 5½, etc.

BUDAPEST, IV 1993 cat. VII (2421) g=8½, m=6½

1. Lékó 8½, 2. P. Lukács 7, 3–6. Zagrebel'nyj, Fogarasi, V. Loginov, Z. Varga 6½, 7–8. József Horváth, van Mil 5½, 9. B. Soos 4½, 10. Szalánczy 3½, 11. Körholz 3, 12. Dolgener 2½

NEW YORK, IV 1993
(143 players, 9 rounds)

1–7. J. Benjamin, A. Gol'din, Ehlvest, I. Gurevich, Alburt, Adianto, Hellers 7, 8–10. Kajdanov, van Wely, Minasian 6½, 11–23. Kudrin, Fedorowicz, Dzindzichashvili, Alexa. Ivanov, Epišin, D. Gurevich, de Firmian, B. Finegold, G. Georgadze, Bologan, Z. Almasi, Brenninkmeijer, Shirazi 6, 24–42. I. Novikov, Yermolinsky, Šabalov, V. Fedorov, A. Zapata, Fishbein, Braude, Bonin, Lesiège, Tolnai, Zlotnikov, Kelleher, Vučić, J. Fang, Southam, Laflair, Shaked, Belakovskaja, J. Friedman 5½, etc.

PLEASANTVILLE, IV 1993 cat. XIV (2559) g=5½, m=3

				1	2	3	4	5	6	7	8	9	10		
1	ŠABALOV	g	2575	●	½	½	½	½	1	½	1	1	1	6½	1
2	KAJDANOV	g	2620	½	●	0	½	1	½	1	½	1	1	6	2
3	J. BENJAMIN	g	2585	½	1	●	1	0	0	1	½	½	1	5½	3–4
4	WOJTKIEWICZ	g	2580	½	½	0	●	½	½	½	1	1	1	5½	3–4
5	YERMOLINSKY	g	2615	½	0	1	½	●	0	1	½	1	½	5	5
6	EHLVEST	g	2625	0	½	1	½	1	●	0	½	½	0	4	6–7
7	EDELMAN	f	2400	½	0	0	½	0	1	●	0	1	1	4	6–7
8	HELLERS	g	2565	0	½	½	0	½	½	1	●	0	0	3	8–9
9	A. GOL'DIN	g	2555	0	0	½	0	0	½	0	1	●	1	3	8–9
10	SHERZER	m	2465	0	0	0	0	½	1	0	1	0	●	2½	10

ZARAGOZA, IV 1993
(176 players, 9 rounds)

1–2. Vyžmanavin, Damljanović 7½, 3–7. Ju. Hodgson, Ubilava, Ulybin, Ochoa de Echagüen, de la Villa García 7, 8–18. García Palermo, Franco, García Ilundain, Nedobora, Miles, Eslon, Veingold, San Segundo, Tukmakov, O. Foişor, Narciso Dublan 6½, 19–33. de la Riva, Vojska, F. Braga, At. Kolev, Komljenović, Etchegaray, P. Aparicio, A. Hernando, Westerinen, Striković, Garza Marco, Vidarte, E. Ibañez, Carruez, V. Gallego 6, etc.

DORTMUND, IV 1993 cat. XVI (2637)

				1	2	3	4	5	6	7	8		
1	AN. KARPOV	g	2725	●	½	1	1	1	0	1	1	5½	1
2	KRAMNIK	g	2685	½	●	½	½	½	½	1	½	4	2–3
3	CH. LUTZ	g	2550	0	½	●	½	½	½	1	1	4	2–3
4	KAMSKY	g	2655	0	½	½	●	1	1	0	½	3½	4–5
5	DOLMATOV	g	2615	0	½	½	0	●	1	½	1	3½	4–5
6	LAUTIER	g	2645	1	½	½	0	0	●	½	½	3	6
7	SERPER	g	2600	0	0	0	1	½	½	●	½	2½	7
8	LOBRON	g	2620	0	½	0	½	0	½	½	●	2	8

DORTMUND (open), IV 1993
(164 players, 11 rounds)

1–2. R. Lau, Oniščuk 8½, 3–8. Malanjuk, Henkin, Razuvaev, A. Mihal'čišin, Kindermann, Šer 8, 9–17. K. Bischoff, Mandl, Schwartzman, Smagin, Podgaec, Nikitin, Bukal, Dinstuhl, G. Mainka 7½, etc.

ARANĐELOVAC, IV 1993 cat. IX (2452) g=9½, m=6½

1. M. Makarov 9½, 2. Cvetković 8½, 3–4. Velimirović, Miladinović 7½, 5–7. Tringov, Čabrilo, A. Kovačević 7, 8–11. Matulović, D. Kosić, J. Ivanov, Drozdov 6½, 12. Zontah 5½, 13. Ilinčić 5, 14. S. T. Jovanović ½

DOUAI, IV 1993
(106 players, 9 rounds)

1–4. Glek, Piskov, V. Ikonnikov, Budnikov 7, 5–7. Lanka, Gallagher, O. Todorov 6½, 8–13. Lëgky, Ph. Morris, Székely, McDonald, Salaun, Skomorohin 6, 14–28. Hector, Komarov, Conquest, Ciolac, Ohotnik, A. Rotštejn, Meyers, Safranska, Mollov, Klovans, Timmerman, Radu, Jankovskis, Delagontrié, Allouard 5½, etc.

PARIS, IV 1993
(110 players, 9 rounds)

1. Rublevskij 7½, 2–4. Soloženkin, R. Ščerbakov, N. Nikčević 7, 5–8. V. Milov, Dvojris, Naumkin, Ragozin 6½, 9–17. Ševelëv, G. Mohr, Plesec, Ch. Bernard, Sulipa, Satla, Giffard, Shabtai, Dunnington 6, etc.

BRUXELLES (zt), IV 1993
(36 players, 11 rounds)

1–2. van Wely, van der Sterren 8, 3. Vaïsser 7½, 4–6. van der Wiel, Nijboer, Bosboom 7, 7–12. Dorfman, Sosonko, Prié, Dutreeuw, Reinderman, A. David 6½, 13–17. Apicella, Bricard, Hauchard, Blees, Relange 6, etc.

BUENOS AIRES, IV 1993 cat. XIII (2571) g=6½, m=4

				1	2	3	4	5	6	7	8	9	10	11	12		
1	KAMSKY	g	2655	●	½	½	1	0	½	½	1	1	½	½	1	7	1–2
2	ŠIROV	g	2670	½	●	0	½	½	½	1	½	1	½	1	1	7	1–2
3	KORTCHNOI	g	2605	½	1	●	0	½	1	½	½	½	½	1	½	6½	3
4	B. LARSEN	g	2540	0	½	1	●	1	½	1	0	½	1	½	0	6	4–5
5	GRANDA ZUÑIGA	g	2590	1	½	½	0	●	½	½	1	½	0	1	½	6	4–5
6	ILLESCAS CÓRDOBA	g	2615	½	½	0	½	½	●	0	1	0	1	1	½	5½	6–8
7	MILOS	g	2560	½	0	½	0	½	1	●	0	1	½	½	1	5½	6–8
8	CÁMPORA	g	2550	0	½	½	1	0	0	1	●	0	½	1	1	5½	6–8
9	PANNO	g	2495	0	0	½	½	½	1	0	1	●	1	0	½	5	9
10	SPANGENBERG	f	2505	½	½	½	0	1	0	½	½	0	●	½	½	4½	10
11	SEIRAWAN	g	2595	½	0	0	½	0	0	½	0	1	½	●	1	4	11
12	ZARNICKI	m	2470	0	0	½	1	½	½	0	0	½	½	0	●	3½	12

KECSKEMÉT, IV–V 1993 cat. VII (2407) g=10, m=7½

1. Zagrebel'nyj 10, 2–3. Z. Almasi, Grószpéter 9½, 4. I. Csom 8½, 5–6. Gyimesi, Lékó 7½, 7–8. Mathe, Anká 6½, 9. Vadász 6, 10–11. Zak, Szalánczy 4½, 12–13. Stajčić, Ščipkov 4, 14. T. Farkas 2½

METZ, IV—V 1993
(128 players, 9 rounds)

1—3. Krasenkov, Henkin, Budnikov 7, 4—13. Eingorn, Pigusov, A. Rotštejn, Schwartzman, K. Spraggett, Sadler, Istrăţescu, M. Röder, Conquest, Klovans $6^1/_2$f, 14—22. Kohlweyer, Harlov, Galdunc, Martinović, Székely, Voskanian, Haïk, Nen. Ristić, E. L. Radu 6, etc.

GAUSDAL (open), IV—V 1993
(32 players, 9 rounds)

1—2. Skembris, Tivjakov $6^1/_2$, 3. Stefánsson 6, 4—11. Gausel, Grivas, Lyrberg, Fyllingeen, Tisdall, Degerman, Riemersma, Ward $5^1/_2$, 12. Jansa 5, 13—20. J. Bellin, Pe. H. Nielsen, Emms, Gullaksen, S. Pedersen, Elsness, Giddins, Gvein $4^1/_2$, etc.

LYON, IV—V 1993
(80 players, 9 rounds)

1—2. J.-R. Koch, A. Gol'din 7, 3—7. Lanka, Murey, Me. Sharif, Gallagher, Rausis $6^1/_2$, 8—15. N. Mitkov, Chabanon, Margolin, M. Lupu, Makarev, M. Mitkov, Plesec, Marzolo 6, 16—20. Anić, Hamdouchi, G. Mohr, Dunnington, Kosten $5^1/_2$, etc.

RENO, IV—V 1993
(301 players in 5 sections, 6 rounds)

1. Browne 5, 2—4. Kajdanov, G. Orlov, Leski $4^1/_2$, 5—16. de Firmian, Kudrin, I. Ivanov, Donaldson, McCambridge, J. Watson, E. Meyer, Piasetski, Silman, Fedorov, Peters, Saidy 4, etc.

DOS HERMANAS, IV—V 1993 cat. XIV (2582) g=5, m=3

				1	2	3	4	5	6	7	8	9	10		
1	AN. KARPOV	g	2725	●	1	$^1/_2$	$^1/_2$	$^1/_2$	1	1	1	1	1	$7^1/_2$	1
2	J. POLGÁR	g	2595	0	●	1	1	1	$^1/_2$	1	$^1/_2$	$^1/_2$	1	$6^1/_2$	2
3	HALIFMAN	g	2630	$^1/_2$	0	●	1	$^1/_2$	0	$^1/_2$	1	1	$^1/_2$	5	3—5
4	RIVAS PASTOR	g	2515	$^1/_2$	0	0	●	1	$^1/_2$	1	0	1	1	5	3—5
5	EPIŠIN	g	2620	$^1/_2$	0	$^1/_2$	0	●	$^1/_2$	$^1/_2$	1	1	1	5	3—5
6	JUDASIN	g	2610	0	$^1/_2$	1	$^1/_2$	$^1/_2$	●	0	$^1/_2$	0	1	4	6—7
7	MAGEM BADALS	m	2510	0	0	$^1/_2$	0	$^1/_2$	1	●	$^1/_2$	$^1/_2$	1	4	6—7
8	ADAMS	g	2630	0	$^1/_2$	0	1	0	$^1/_2$	$^1/_2$	●	$^1/_2$	$^1/_2$	$3^1/_2$	8
9	IZETA	m	2505	0	$^1/_2$	0	0	0	1	$^1/_2$	$^1/_2$	●	0	$2^1/_2$	9
10	FERNÁNDEZ GARCÍA	g	2475	0	0	$^1/_2$	0	0	0	0	$^1/_2$	1	●	2	10

SAINT-MARTIN, V 1993
(126 players, 9 rounds)

1. H. Ólafsson $7^1/_2$, 2—6. Pétursson, Yermolinsky, Ehlvest, Gulko, Šabalov 7, 7—13. Fedorowicz, Wojtkiewicz, J. Benjamin, Schmittdiel, Gamboa, Curdo, J. Árnason $6^1/_2$, 14—25. I. Gurevich, G. García, Vučić, Lein, Ashley, Thorsteins, A. Zapata, D. Gurevich, Henao, Giffard, Lukasiewicz, Peltrult 6, 26—37. Renet, Adianto, Waitzkin, Zaltsman, Burnett, Kotliar, Bec, Wheeler, Shmulevich, Chardin, Khatenamo, Trammel $5^1/_2$, etc.

GAUSDAL, V 1993 cat. X (2486) g=6, m=$4^1/_2$

1—3. B. Kristensen, Tisdall, Hellers 6, 4—5. Gausel, van Wely $5^1/_2$, 6. Rausis $4^1/_2$, 7. Skembris 4, 8. Baburin $3^1/_2$, 9. Djurhuus $2^1/_2$, 10. Engedal $1^1/_2$

CETINJE, V 1993
(54 players, 11 rounds)

1—8. Damljanović, Draško, Tošić, M. Vukić, D. Kosić, Ilinčić, Brenjo, Abramović $7^1/_2$, 9—10. Vujadinović, N. Kostić 7, 11—18. B. Maksimović, Zontah, Zd. Vuković, A. Kovačević, Nikač, D. Rajković, D. Blagojević, L. Grujić $6^1/_2$, 19—23. Kontić, D. Lekić, Drozdov, Č. Mićić, G. Stevanović 6, etc.

MAR DEL PLATA, V 1993
(215 players, 9 rounds)

1—2. B. Larsen, Granda Zuñiga $7^1/_2$, 3—10. Milos, Quinteros, Panno, Fiorito, Garbarino, de las Heras, Vasta, Llanos 7, 11—20. Gómez Baillo, Fraschini, Amura, Zarnicki, Ginzburg, Mendez, Disconzi, Quiroga, Mellano, Kanefsck $6^1/_2$, etc.

LEÓN, V 1993 cat. XIII (2556) g=5½, m=3½

				1	2	3	4	5	6	7	8	9	10		
1	JUDASIN	g	2610	•	½	½	½	½	1	1	1	1	1	7	1
2	VYŽMANAVIN	g	2620	½	•	½	½	½	½	1	1	½	1	6	2
3	AN. KARPOV	g	2725	½	½	•	½	½	½	1	½	½	1	5½	3—5
4	TOPALOV	g	2635	½	½	½	•	½	½	½	½	1	1	5½	3—5
5	LÉKÓ	m	2465	½	½	½	½	•	½	0	1	1	1	5½	3—5
6	MORÓVIĆ FERNÁNDEZ	g	2570	0	½	½	½	½	•	½	½	1	1	5	6
7	ILLESCAS CÓRDOBA	g	2615	0	0	0	½	1	½	•	1	1	½	4½	7
8	GARCÍA ILLUNDAIN	m	2475	0	0	½	½	0	½	0	•	½	½	2½	8
9	ROMERO HOLMES	m	2455	0	½	½	0	0	0	0	½	•	½	2	9
10	SIÓN CASTRO	m	2390	0	0	0	0	0	0	½	½	½	•	1½	10

AMSTERDAM, V 1993 cat. XVII (2663)

				1	2	3	4		
1	N. SHORT	g	2665	• •	0 1	½ 1	½ ½	3½	1—3
2	KRAMNIK	g	2685	1 0	• •	½ ½	½ 1	3½	1—3
3	ANAND	g	2710	½ 0	½ ½	• •	1 1	3½	1—3
4	JE. PIKET	g	2590	½ ½	½ 0	0 0	• •	1½	4

SAN MARTIN, V 1993 cat. VIII (2446) g=8, m=6

1. M. Sorokin 8, 2—4. Hoffman, Smyslov, Soppe 6½, 5—6. Rubinetti, Krogius 6, 7. H. van Riemsdijk 5½, 8—9. J. Szmetan, Spangenberg 5, 10—11. Scarella, An. Rodríguez 4½, 12. Schweber 2

SCHAAN, V 1993
(133 players, 9 rounds)

1. Adianto 8, 2. Davies 7½, 3—6. Tolnai, M. Kamiński, Conquest, Schmittdiel 7, 7—12. Baburin, I. Csom, Metz, Lane, Robović, Nykopp 6½, 13—25. Bancod, J. Hickl, Kelečević, Luther, Donev, Nemet, Szalánczy, Skomorohin, Ch. Foişor, S. Salov, Gärtner, Plieger, Mertens 6, etc.

ROSTOV NA DONU, V 1993 cat. XIV (2578) g=6, m=4

				1	2	3	4	5	6	7	8	9	10	11	12		
1	TIVJAKOV	g	2575	•	0	1	½	½	1	½	1	½	1	½	1	7½	1
2	PSAKHIS	g	2575	1	•	½	½	½	½	1	1	½	½	½	½	7	2—3
3	EPIŠIN	g	2620	0	½	•	½	½	1	½	½	½	1	1	1	7	2—3
4	DOLMATOV	g	2615	½	½	½	•	1	0	½	½	½	½	1	1	6½	4—5
5	SMIRIN	g	2590	½	½	½	0	•	½	½	½	1	½	1	1	6½	4—5
6	RAZUVAEV	g	2525	0	½	0	1	½	•	½	½	½	½	½	1	5½	6—8
7	VAGANIAN	g	2615	½	0	½	½	½	½	•	½	0	1	1	½	5½	6—8
8	TUKMAKOV	g	2605	0	0	½	½	½	½	½	•	1	½	1	½	5½	6—8
9	OLL	g	2585	½	½	½	½	0	½	1	0	•	0	1	½	5	9
10	SMYSLOV	g	2530	0	½	0	½	½	½	0	½	1	•	0	½	4	10
11	PUŠKOV	m	2485	½	½	0	0	0	½	0	0	0	1	•	½	3	11—12
12	LPUTIAN	g	2610	0	½	0	0	0	0	½	½	½	½	½	•	3	11—12

ROSTOV NA DONU (open), V 1993
(50 players, 9 rounds)

1. Savčenko 7, 2—5. Dreev, Krasenkov, Ceškovskij, Ionov 6½, 6—9. Akopian, Moskalenko, Anastasian, Matveeva 6, 10—13. Dvojris, Magerramov, Svešnikov, Lerner 5½, 14—18. Harlov, P. Svidler, Zvjagincev, Petrušin, Kahlian 5, etc.

BUDAPEST, V 1993 cat. VIII (2434) g=7½, m=5½

1. I. Faragó 7½, 2—3. Grószpéter, Z. Almasi 6½, 4—6. Danner, Dao Thien Hai, P. Lukács 5, 7—8. Holzke, Siebrecht 4½, 9—11. Dinstuhl, Lorincz, Contin 3½

MÜNCHEN, V 1993 cat. XVI (2628) g=5½

				1	2	3	4	5	6	7	8	9	10	11	12		
1	ŠIROV	g	2670	●	½	1	½	½	1	1	0	1	1	1	½	8	1
2	B. GEL'FAND	g	2690	½	●	½	½	1	½	1	1	½	½	1	½	7½	2
3	M. GUREVICH	g	2610	0	½	●	1	½	0	0	1	1	1	1	1	7	3
4	ADAMS	g	2630	½	½	0	●	1	½	1	1	½	½	½	½	6½	4—5
5	BAREEV	g	2670	½	0	½	0	●	1	1	½	0	1	1	1	6½	4—5
6	CH. LUTZ	g	2550	0	½	1	½	0	●	½	½	1	½	½	1	6	6
7	JUSUPOV	g	2625	0	0	1	0	0	½	●	1	½	½	½	1	5	7
8	HERTNECK	g	2575	1	0	0	0	½	½	0	●	½	½	½	1	4½	8—9
9	HÜBNER	g	2620	0	½	0	½	1	0	½	½	●	0	½	1	4½	8—9
10	LOBRON	g	2620	0	½	0	½	0	½	½	½	1	●	½	0	4	10
11	LAUTIER	g	2645	0	0	0	½	0	½	½	½	½	½	●	½	3½	11
12	HJARTARSON	g	2625	½	½	0	½	0	0	0	0	0	1	½	●	3	12

ISFAHAN (zt), V 1993
(18 players, 11 rounds)

1—3. Barua, Koshy, Murshed 8, 4—5. Refat, Al. Khateeb 7½, 6. Al Modiahki 7, 7—8. Ravi Hegde, P. Thipsay 6, etc.

EKSJÖ, V 1993

			1	2	3	4	5	6	
HELLERS	g	2565	½	1	½	½	½	½	3½
U. ANDERSSON	g	2625	½	0	½	½	½	½	2½

ALUSTA, V 1993 cat. X (2489) g=6, m=4½

1. Lazarev 6, 2—4. Gipslis, Morozevič, Timošenko 5, 5—7. I. Ibragimov, Savčenko, Moskalenko 4½, 8. Glejzerov 4, 9. Zločevskij 3½, 10. Dragomareckij 3

ALUSTA (open), V 1993
(42 players, 9 rounds)

1—3. Gufel'd, Fominyh, Starosek 6½, 4—8. Vaulin, Golod, Jandemirov, Kalegin, Varavin 6, 9—10. Suėtin, Rustemov 5½, etc.

ODORHEIU SECUIESC, V 1993 cat. XII (2526) g=7, m=4½

				1	2	3	4	5	6	7	8	9	10	11	12		
1	A. CHERNIN	g	2600	●	½	½	½	½	½	1	1	1	1	½	1	8	1
2	I. IBRAGIMOV	m	2540	½	●	½	½	1	1	0	1	½	½	1	1	7½	2
3	RIBLI	g	2620	½	½	●	½	½	½	1	½	½	½	1	½	6½	3
4	V. NEVEDNIČIJ	m	2495	½	½	½	●	½	1	½	1	½	0	0	1	6	4
5	V. NEVEROV	g	2550	½	0	½	½	●	½	1	½	½	1	½	0	5½	5—7
6	JÓZSEF HORVÁTH	g	2535	½	0	½	0	½	●	1	½	0	½	1	1	5½	5—7
7	ISTRĂŢESCU	m	2470	0	1	0	½	0	0	●	1	½	½	1	1	5½	5—7
8	SCHWARTZMAN	m	2455	0	0	½	0	½	½	0	●	1	½	1	1	5	8
9	MARIN	g	2515	0	½	½	½	½	1	½	0	●	½	0	½	4½	9—10
10	SAX	g	2570	0	½	½	1	0	½	½	½	½	●	0	½	4½	9—10
11	ROGOZENKO	m	2480	½	0	0	1	½	0	0	0	1	1	●	0	4	11
12	P. WELLS	m	2485	0	0	½	0	1	0	0	0	½	½	1	●	3½	12

NIJMEGEN, V 1993

			1	2	3	4	5	6	7	8	
KORTCHNOI	g	2605	½	½	1	1	½	1	1	½	6
JE. PIKET	g	2590	½	½	0	0	½	0	0	½	2

fide information

FIDE INTERNATIONAL RATING LIST, July 1, 1993

ALPHABETICAL LIST (MEN & WOMEN)

A

Title	Name	Games	Rating
	Aaberg, A. (SWE)	0	2265
	Aagaard, J. (DEN)	17	2255
	Aarland, S. A. (NOR)	0	2225
	Aban, E. (ARG)	0	2240
f	Abarca Aguirre, M. (CHI)	0	2360
	Abatino, M. (ITA)	0	2380
	Abbas, B. H. (IRQ)	0	2210
	Abbasi, R. (SYR)	0	2005
f	Abbou, M. (ALG)	0	2015
	Abdalrahim, M. (SYR)	6	2205
	Abdeldjebar, T. (ALG)	0	2110
m	Abdennabi, I. (EGY)	0	2375
	Abdul Karim, A.-A. (YEM)	0	2205
	Abdul Majeed, N. (IND)	0	2245
	Abdul Moula, S. (YEM)	0	2190
	Abdul Satar, M. A. (IRQ)	0	2240
	Abdul, M. (UAE)	0	2205
	Abdulghafour, Y. (QTR)	8	2190
	Abdulla, A. S. (UAE)	9	2105
	Abdulla, Ah. I. (QTR)	0	2240
	Abdullaeva, U. (AZE)	0	2090
	Abdullah, A. (IRQ)	0	2300
m	Abdullah, M. (UAE)	2	2290
	Abed, R. (JRD)	0	2205
m	Abel, L. (HUN)	84	2260
	Abhijit, K. (IND)	13	2205
f	Abibula, A. (ROM)	0	2280
	Abishova, A. (EST)	11	2010
	Abou el Zein, E. M. (EGY)	0	2325
	Abouchaaya, T. (AUS)	0	2215
g	Abramovic, B. (YUG)	69	2460
	Abramovic, D. (YUG)	10	2155
	Abramson, H. (ARG)	2	2215
f	Abravanel, Ch. (FRA)	9	2345
	Abregu, M. (ARG)	18	2280
m	Abreu, J. D. (DOM)	0	2385
	Absmaier, F. (GER)	0	2230
	Ac, M. (SVK)	0	2225
	Acebal, A. (ESP)	0	2280
f	Acevedo, A. (MEX)	2	2260
	Acevedo, H. (MEX)	0	2070
	Acha, J. (ARG)	0	2230
f	Acharya, Ch. K. (IND)	7	2270
	Acimovic, S. (YUG)	0	2350
	Ackermann, R. (SUI)	0	2280
	Acosta, A. (COL)	0	2325
	Acosta, T. (ARG)	0	2250
f	Acs, P. (HUN)	24	2245
	Ada, B. (CAN)	0	2225
	Adad, C. (ARG)	2	2205
	Adahl, M. (SWE)	0	2205
	Adam, M. (YUG)	13	2255
	Adamanova, L. (RUS)	0	2065
	Adamek, Z. (TCH)	2	2095
g	Adams, M. (ENG)	52	2630
m	Adamski, A. (POL)	16	2310
m	Adamski, J. (POL)	22	2430
	Adasiak, L. (POL)	12	2145
f	Adelman, Ch. D. (USA)	0	2220
	Ademi, S. (YUG)	0	2240
	Adhami, H. (PAL)	0	2195
g	Adianto, U. (INA)	52	2510
m	Adla, D. (ARG)	42	2435
	Adler, B. (SWE)	0	2235
f	Adler, J. (SUI)	4	2325
	Adler, V. (RUS)	0	2385
	Adoamnei, R. (ROM)	13	2065
g	Adorjan, A. (HUN)	35	2545
f	Adrian, C. (FRA)	13	2270
f	Ady, J. J. (ENG)	0	2300
f	Adzic, S. (YUG)	0	2265
m	Afek, Y. (ISR)	52	2430
m	Afifi, A. (EGY)	0	2395
	Afriany, V. (HAI)	0	2215
	Agababian, N. (MOL)	18	2195
	Agamaliev, Dj. (AZE)	0	2360
	Agamaliev, G. (AZE)	0	2425
	Agarwal, B. (IND)	0	2285
	Agdamus, J. L. (ARG)	0	2255
f	Agdestein, E. (NOR)	0	2330
g	Agdestein, S. (NOR)	8	2610
	Ageev, A. (RUS)	9	2325
	Ageichenko, G. A. (RUS)	0	2340
	Agh, M. (HUN)	0	2240
	Agistriotis, M. (GRE)	15	2135
	Agnello, G. (ITA)	0	2180
	Agnolin Diaz, A. (ARG)	0	2220
m	Agnos, D. (ENG)	32	2430
f	Agrawal, K. (IND)	15	2045
m	Agrest, E. (RUS)	25	2465
	Agudelo, A. (COL)	0	2355
	Aguera Naredo, J. (ESP)	0	2275
	Aguerreberry, C. (ARG)	0	2210
f	Aguila, G. (ARG)	14	2330
f	Aguilar, J. (PER)	0	2315
	Aguilera, J. (ESP)	0	2245
	Aguirre, P. J. (ESP)	1	2230
f	Agustsson, J. (ISD)	0	2315
f	Ahlander, B. (SWE)	0	2415
	Ahlberg, G. (GER)	0	2275
	Ahmed, F. M. (YEM)	0	2195
	Ahmed Saleh, B. (YEM)	0	2205
	Ahmed-Zaid, A. (ALG)	0	2255
	Ahmels, V. (GER)	0	2245
	Ahn, M. (BEL)	0	2245
	Ahrens, M. (GER)	19	2080
	Aidarov, N. (RUS)	0	2330
	Airapetian, S. H. (ARM)	9	2060
	Ajanski, J. S. (BUL)	0	2350
	Ajupbergenov, A. (KAZ)	13	2300
	Ajvazi, R. (YUG)	0	2225
	Akeel, M. (SYR)	0	2270
m	Akesson, R. (SWE)	0	2465
	Akhmadeev, V. (RUS)	12	2395
g	Akhsharumova, A. M. (USA)	0	2385
	Akintola, F. (NGR)	9	2260
g	Akopian, V. (ARM)	30	2600
	Akopov, R. (ARM)	0	2310
f	Al Hadarani, H. (YEM)	0	2315
	Al-Awadhi, K. (USA)	10	2200
	Al-Ghasra, A. (BRN)	8	2190
f	Al-Khateeb, A. (SYR)	17	2300
m	Al-Modiahki, M. (QTR)	19	2405
	Al-Othman, A. W. (KUW)	0	2240
	Alaa, E. (PAL)	0	2205
f	Alaan, V. (PHI)	0	2370
f	Aladjova, K. (AUS)	0	2145
	Alarcon, R. (CRC)	0	2230
	Alava, M. (FIN)	7	2290
f	Alawieh, A. (FRA)	12	2330
	Alayola, J. E. (MEX)	0	2225
f	Alber, H. (GER)	28	2340
	Albero Figueras, E. (ESP)	0	2225
	Albert, K. (HUN)	20	2105
	Albert, Th. (GER)	0	2275
	Albrecht, R. (GER)	0	2285
g	Albulet, M. (ROM)	0	2100
g	Alburt, L. O. (USA)	6	2545
f	Aldama, D. (CUB)	23	2460
	Alderete, R. (CUB)	0	2235
g	Alekhina, N. V. (RUS)	0	2230
	Aleksandrov, A. (BLA)	0	2530
	Aleksandrov, G. (BUL)	0	2235
	Alekseev, A. (RUS)	0	2340
	Alekseev, V. (BLA)	13	2355
	Aleksic, Milan (YUG)	5	2295
	Aleksic, Milo. (YUG)	0	2195
m	Aleksic, N. (YUG)	12	2405
	Aleksieva, S. (BUL)	18	2165
	Alet, J.-P. (FRA)	0	2265
	Alexakis, D. (GRE)	4	2220
	Alexandre, J. (POR)	0	2300
g	Alexandria, N. (GEO)	0	2295
	Alexandrou, A. (CYP)	0	2270
	Alexandrou, Th. (GRE)	9	2160
	Alexandrov, I. (RUS)	0	2380
	Alexanian, V. (ARM)	10	2240
	Alexeev, A. V. (RUS)	11	2365
	Alexopoulos, G. (GRE)	7	2255
	Alhousseyni, H. (MLI)	0	2205

	Name		
	Ali, G. M. (IRQ)	0	2380
	Alienkin, A. (RUS)	0	2415
f	Alieva, E. (AZE)	11	2185
	Aljamiat, R. W. (INA)	0	2110
	Aljautdinova, M. (RUS)	6	2095
	Alkaersig, O. (DEN)	7	2230
f	Allan, D. (CAN)	9	2275
	Allan, W. M. (JRD)	0	2195
f	Allegro, V. (SUI)	0	2270
	Allen, A. (AUS)	0	2170
f	Allen, B. L. (USA)	0	2325
	Allen, E. J. (USA)	0	2200
	Allen, K. (IRL)	0	2300
f	Almada, E. (SUI)	0	2345
	Almaguer, F. (CUB)	0	2215
m	Almasi, I. (HUN)	42	2400
m	Almasi, Z. (HUN)	73	2580
	Almeida Saenz, A. (MEX)	20	2325
	Almeida, C. (PAR)	0	2065
	Almeida, J. T. (POR)	0	2235
	Almeida, M. A. (ESP)	9	2235
	Almond, R. (ENG)	9	2115
	Alonso, C. (ESP)	0	2325
	Alonso, J. I. (ESP)	7	2295
m	Alonso, Re. (CUB)	22	2345
	Alonso, Ro. (ARG)	14	2170
	Alpern, A. (ARG)	6	2220
f	Alpern, D. (ARG)	0	2330
	Alperovich, A. (RUS)	15	2215
	Alsalati, A. H. (BRN)	0	2280
	Alsharfi, S. S. (YEM)	0	2205
	Alsharhan, F. (UAE)	0	2205
f	Alster, L. (TCH)	0	2235
	Altamirano, B. (ARG)	5	2245
g	Alterman, B. (ISR)	22	2585
	Alterman, L. (ISR)	16	2135
f	Alterman, V. I. (ISR)	9	2395
	Altgelt, A. (GER)	0	2220
	Altini, D. (ITA)	0	2255
	Alvarado, F. (ESP)	17	2140
	Alvarez Castillo, H. (ARG)	8	2220
m	Alvarez Ibarra, R. D. (ESP)	46	2440
	Alvarez, A. (COL)	11	2095
f	Alvarez, Fi. (CUB)	0	2275
	Alvarez, Fr. (DOM)	6	2250
	Alvarez, J. (CUB)	0	2240
	Alvas, P. (GRE)	8	2205
	Alvear, D. (CHI)	14	2050
f	Alvir, A. (BIH)	6	2290
m	Alzate, D. (COL)	0	2375
	Alzugaray, D. (CUB)	0	2205
	Amaral, N. (POR)	9	2225
	Ambarcumjan, A. (ARM)	0	2340
	Ambats, J. (USA)	0	2090
m	Ambroz, J. (TCH)	17	2420
	Amendola, K. (GRE)	9	2210
	Amer, S. (LBA)	0	2205
	Amil Meilan, H. (ARG)	0	2265
	Amit, Y. (ISR)	3	2230
	Amman, W. (SUI)	0	2335
f	Ammann, Ph. (SUI)	0	2250
	Amrein, R. (HUN)	9	2195
m	Amura, C. N. (ARG)	28	2365
m	An, Yangfeng (CHN)	0	2250
g	Anand, V. (IND)	19	2725
	Anapolsky, S. (UKR)	0	2385
m	Anastasian, A. (ARM)	36	2530
	Anceschi, V. (ITA)	0	2290
	Andersch, J. (GER)	0	2025
	Andersen, D. (DEN)	4	2245
	Andersen, I. (DEN)	0	2220
	Andersen, J. (GER)	0	2265
	Andersen, K. V. (DEN)	0	2295
f	Anderson, R. (USA)	24	2255
	Andersson, Be. (SWE)	0	2140
	Andersson, Bjorn (SWE)	0	2225

	Name		
f	Andersson, Bjorn (SWE)	0	2330
	Andersson, G. (SWE)	0	2235
g	Andersson, U. (SWE)	0	2625
	Anderton, D. W. (ENG)	0	2245
	Anderton, M. (ENG)	10	2155
	Andi, P. (HUN)	4	2245
m	Andonov, B. (BUL)	12	2365
f	Andonovski, Lj. (YUG)	16	2305
	Andrade, W. (BRA)	0	2275
	Andre, W. (GER)	0	2220
	Andreas, M. (GER)	9	2210
	Andreasen, J. H. (FAI)	9	2055
	Andreasen, P. (DEN)	0	2275
	Andreasson, I. (SWE)	0	2390
	Andreescu, N. A. (ROM)	23	2080
	Andreev, D. (BUL)	0	2240
	Andrei, G. (ROM)	9	2160
m	Andreieva, O. A. (UKR)	0	2250
	Andreoli, R. (ITA)	0	2200
m	Andres, M. (CUB)	0	2320
	Andresen, S. (GER)	24	2370
	Andrews, R. (USA)	0	2265
	Andriana, A. (ROM)	14	2020
m	Andrianov, N. (RUS)	8	2450
	Andriasian, A. (ARM)	9	2120
	Andrienko, A. (UKR)	0	2285
f	Andrijasevic, M. (YUG)	0	2315
m	Andrijevic, M. (YUG)	0	2355
m	Andruet, G. (FRA)	5	2360
	Andurkar, D. A. (IND)	0	2200
f	Anelli, A. (ARG)	14	2305
	Anetbaev, B. (KAZ)	0	2250
m	Angantysson, H. (ISD)	0	2295
	Angelis, M. (GRE)	5	2275
	Angelov, A. (BUL)	3	2275
	Angelov, E. (BUL)	0	2250
	Angelov, G. (BUL)	0	2200
m	Angelov, K. (BUL)	0	2300
	Angelov, R. (BUL)	0	2245
	Anglada, J. A. (ESP)	9	2190
	Angqvist, Th. (SWE)	4	2230
	Anguix Garrido, J. (ESP)	15	2340
	Angyal, F. (HUN)	0	2220
m	Anic, D. (FRA)	48	2440
m	Anikaev, Y. N. (RUS)	0	2420
	Anilkumar, N. R. (IND)	10	2315
	Anilkumar, O. T. (IND)	16	2225
	Anino, S. (ARG)	0	2275
m	Anitoaie, D. (ROM)	0	2350
	Anka, E. (HUN)	23	2395
	Ankerst, Ma. (SLO)	9	2210
	Ankerst, Mich. (GER)	14	2205
m	Ankerst, Mil. (SLO)	21	2130
m	Annageldiev, O. (TKM)	12	2420
	Annakov, B. (TKM)	27	2315
	Anokhin, V. (RUS)	0	2365
	Ansell, S. (ENG)	12	2290
f	Anselmo, A. (FRA)	19	2225
	Ansner, B. (SWE)	0	2110
	Anstad, T. (NOR)	0	2305
m	Antic, D. (YUG)	12	2380
	Antic, Z. (YUG)	0	2285
	Antkowiak, G. (POL)	0	2210
	Antollovich, A. (ARG)	0	2125
	Antonczyk, A. (POL)	0	2350
f	Antonic, D. (YUG)	0	2320
g	Antonio jr., R. (PHI)	18	2500
	Antonoff, G. (FRA)	14	2205
m	Antonov, V. (BUL)	0	2395
m	Antonsen, M. (DEN)	3	2385
	Antoshik, A. (TCH)	0	2245
g	Antoshin, V. S. (RUS)	0	2250
m	Antunes, A. (POR)	13	2425
	Aoiz, J. J. (ESP)	1	2310
	Aoldia, K. (ALG)	0	2210
f	Aparicio, A. (ARG)	2	2320
	Apatoczky, P. (HUN)	9	2190
	Apel, S. (GER)	6	2250

	Name		
m	Apicella, M. (FRA)	43	2475
	Apol, L. (FAI)	9	2130
f	Appel, R. (GER)	18	2430
	Appleberry, M. (USA)	2	2355
	Appolonov, S. (RUS)	5	2375
	Apro, A. (HUN)	9	2125
	Apsner, B. (GER)	0	2275
g	Arakhamia, K. (IM) (GEO)	13	2440
	Arancibia, E. (CHI)	20	2290
	Aranda Gonzales, J. (ESP)	0	2325
m	Arapovic, V. (BIH)	0	2380
	Araque, R. (COL)	11	2210
	Araros, H. (CHI)	0	2240
	Araslanov, F. (RUS)	0	2260
	Araya, C. (CRC)	0	2170
	Araya, G. (CHI)	9	2305
	Araya, M. (CHI)	27	2190
	Araya, R. (CHI)	20	2330
m	Arbakov, V. (RUS)	71	2460
	Arbanas, J. (CRO)	0	2170
	Arbatskaia, N. (RUS)	0	2230
f	Arbouche, M. (MAR)	0	2260
m	Arbunic Castro, G. B. (CHI)	0	2155
	Archangelsky, M. (RUS)	37	2275
f	Ardaman, M. (USA)	1	2390
f	Ardeleanu, A. (ROM)	24	2385
	Ardeleanu, C. (ROM)	0	2210
	Ardeleanu, S. (ROM)	0	2230
g	Ardiansyah, H. (INA)	0	2425
	Ardizzone, S. (ITA)	0	2225
f	Arduman, C. (TUR)	10	2355
m	Arencibia, J. J. (CUB)	0	2435
g	Arencibia, W. (CUB)	13	2485
	Ari, Z. (TUR)	0	2240
	Aria Nejad, H. (IRI)	6	2210
	Arias, R. (CRC)	11	2180
	Arikok, E. (SUI)	5	2200
	Arino, F. (FRA)	0	2210
	Arizaga Jasso, F. (MEX)	0	2280
m	Arkell, K. C. (ENG)	39	2460
g	Arkell, S. (ENG)	19	2335
	Arkhangelsky, B. (RUS)	0	2375
g	Arkhipov, S. (RUS)	54	2520
m	Arlandi, E. (ITA)	36	2440
	Arlt, R. (GER)	0	2240
	Armanda, I. (CRO)	12	2260
m	Armas, I. (FRA)	14	2410
m	Armas, J. (CUB)	13	2455
	Armenteros, N. (CUB)	0	2250
	Arnason, Ar. A. (ISR)	0	2165
	Arnason, As. T. (ISD)	0	2270
g	Arnason, J. L. (ISD)	24	2530
f	Arnason, Th. (ISD)	0	2290
	Arnaudov, P. (BUL)	13	2260
	Arndt, S. (GER)	0	2235
	Arne, M. (USA)	0	2400
	Arnett, D. A. (USA)	10	2335
f	Arnold, F. (HUN)	0	2325
	Arnold, K. N. (GER)	0	2100
f	Arnold, L. (GER)	8	2325
	Arokiaraj, P. S. (IND)	4	2185
	Arrata, P. (ECU)	0	2215
	Arregui, J. L. (ARG)	6	2360
m	Arribas, M. (CUB)	13	2215
	Arsic, S. (YUG)	0	2270
	Arsovic, A. (YUG)	11	2230
f	Arsovic, G. (YUG)	18	2380
f	Arsovic, Z. (YUG)	17	2290
	Artamonova, V. (UKR)	0	2115
	Arustamian, A. A. (RUS)	18	2320
	Arutyunyan, A. (ARM)	0	2155
m	Asanov, B. (KAZ)	37	2385
	Asaturoglu, R. (TUR)	0	2250
	Aschwanden, F.-B. (SUI)	0	2210
f	Ascic, A. (CRO)	0	2390
	Ascolese, P. (USA)	11	2220
g	Aseev, K. N. (RUS)	27	2490

	Name		
	Asseva, M. (RUS)	20	2090
	Asensio, E. (ARG)	11	2240
f	Asfora, M. (BRA)	0	2300
	Asfura, C. (CHI)	0	2225
	Ash, R. (USA)	13	2150
	Ashby, A.-M. (ENG)	3	2125
m	Ashley, M. (USA)	41	2435
	Asik, J. (YUG)	0	2225
m	Aslanian, L. K. (ARM)	13	2230
	Asmat Pacheco, J. (PER)	0	2205
	Assem, M. (EGY)	0	2310
	Assis, D. V. (BRA)	0	2320
f	Assmann, Th. (GER)	15	2355
	Astengo, C. (ITA)	3	2165
	Astolfi Perez, E. (FRA)	12	2040
	Astolfi, F. (FRA)	0	2240
f	Astrom, G. (SWE)	0	2290
f	Astrom, R. (SWE)	11	2335
m	Atalik, S. (TUR)	0	2535
f	Atanasijadis, A. (YUG)	0	2280
	Atanaskovic, P. (YUG)	0	2250
	Atanasov, G. (BUL)	0	2300
m	Atanasov, P. (BUL)	0	2365
	Atanasov, R. (BUL)	0	2250
	Ater, H. G. (IRQ)	0	2295
	Ater, I. (ISR)	0	2265
	Atia, J. A. (IRQ)	0	2240
	Atkinson, P. (WLS)	0	2215
	Atlas, D. (BLA)	8	2355
	Atlas, R. (USA)	0	2205
m	Atlas, V. (LIE)	15	2470
	Attard, W. (MLT)	0	2225
	Atutubo, R. (PHI)	0	2205
	Aubert, L. (FRA)	0	2275
	Auciello, S. (ARG)	1	2355
f	Auer, M. (GER)	0	2300
m	Augustin, J. (TCH)	0	2410
	Auletta, A. (ITA)	9	2220
	Aung, Th. (MYN)	0	2205
	Aurel, L. (FRA)	3	2200
	Aurell, B. (SWE)	0	2275
	Autowicz, B. (POL)	0	2025
	Autowicz, Z. (POL)	2	2225
g	Averbakh, Y. L. (RUS)	0	2445
m	Averkin, O. N. (RUS)	13	2500
f	Avni, A. (ISR)	9	2400
	Avrahami, R. (ISR)	0	2290
	Avramov, A. (BUL)	0	2235
	Avramovic, Z. (YUG)	0	2290
f	Avrukh, B. (KAZ)	26	2440
m	Avshalumov, A. (RUS)	0	2475
f	Awate, A. S. (IND)	0	2310
	Ayapbergenov, A. (KAZ)	14	2190
	Ayas, A. (ESP)	1	2310
	Ayaz, C. (TUR)	0	2290
	Aye, L. (MYN)	0	2360
	Ayelwin, M. (MYN)	0	2205
f	Ayza Ballester, J. (ESP)	0	2310
f	Azaric, S. (YUG)	5	2350
g	Azmaiparashvili, Z. (GEO)	41	2630

B

	Name		
	Babaeva, F. (AZE)	0	2055
	Babalola, B. (NGR)	9	2110
	Babar, F. (GER)	0	2230
f	Babar, M. (GER)	1	2310
f	Babault, P. (FRA)	0	2305
f	Babic, Drag. (YUG)	8	2315
f	Babic, Dras. (YUG)	0	2300
	Babic, M. (YUG)	0	2310
	Babik, T. (POL)	0	2235
	Babits, A. (HUN)	0	2265
	Babos, Cs. (ROM)	0	2220
	Babos, E. (HUN)	11	2105
	Babovic, Z. (YUG)	11	2105
	Babrikowski, P. (GER)	0	2265
m	Babu, S. N. (IND)	10	2380
m	Babula, M. (TCH)	3	2355
	Babula, V. (TCH)	6	2395
m	Baburin, A. (RUS)	24	2530
	Baccelliere Pena, M. E. (CHI)	0	2270
f	Bacetic, N. (YUG)	0	2330
f	Bach, A. (ROM)	18	2345
	Bach, E. (GER)	13	2245
f	Bach, M. (GER)	5	2300
	Bachilo, E. (BLA)	9	2100
	Bachler, R. (AUT)	13	2210
f	Bachmann, A. (GER)	0	2275
f	Bachmann, K.-H. (GER)	0	2325
	Bachmayr, P. (GER)	13	2270
	Baciu, S. (ROM)	11	2280
f	Baciu-Ionescu, O. (ROM)	39	2205
	Backe, P. (SWE)	0	2325
	Backelin, R. (SWE)	3	2290
	Backlund, A. (SWE)	0	2140
	Backstrom, M. (SWE)	0	2215
f	Backwinkel, P. (GER)	14	2410
	Bacrot, E. (FRA)	21	2230
f	Bacso, G. (HUN)	7	2230
f	Baczynskyj, B. (USA)	0	2285
	Badalova, T. (RUS)	0	2120
	Bade, H. (GER)	1	2020
	Bade, J. (GER)	0	2310
m	Badea, B. (ROM)	60	2340
	Bademian, J. (URU)	9	2195
	Badev, K. (BUL)	0	2250
	Badian, G. (HUN)	9	2180
f	Badii, M. (FRA)	9	2260
	Baert, A. (BEL)	0	2245
	Baerthel, J. (GER)	1	2205
	Bagakis, E. (GRE)	0	2200
m	Bagaturov, G. (GEO)	9	2495
m	Baginskaite, K. (LTU)	29	2325
g	Bagirov, V. (LAT)	23	2525
	Bagonyai, A. (HUN)	13	2245
	Bagrunov, V. (RUS)	0	2245
	Bahadur, S. (IND)	0	2030
	Baikov, V. A. (RUS)	38	2300
	Bailey, D. (CAN)	0	2210
	Baimuratov, S. (KAZ)	9	2335
	Baja, V. (USA)	0	2250
	Bajarany, I. Z. (AZE)	0	2260
	Bajkovic, N. (YUG)	21	2175
f	Bajovic, M. (YUG)	4	2290
	Bajusz, Gy. (HUN)	3	2240
f	Bakalar, P. (TCH)	0	2345
	Bakalarz, G. (GER)	3	2065
	Bakalarz, L. (POL)	5	2255
	Bakalarz, M. (GER)	0	2245
	Bakalova, I. (BUL)	0	2055
	Bakcsi, Gy. (HUN)	0	2220
	Baker, B. (USA)	0	2245
	Baker, Ch. W. (ENG)	0	2260
	Baker, M. D. (ENG)	10	2175
	Bakic, D. (YUG)	11	2345
f	Bakic, R. (YUG)	22	2400
	Baklan, N. (UKR)	16	2130
	Baklanova, T. (UKR)	11	2180
	Bako, V. (HUN)	3	2240
	Bakonyi, D. (HUN)	0	2250
	Bakus, M. (FRA)	19	2250
	Balaban, N. (YUG)	0	2040
	Balac, N. (YUG)	0	2295
g	Balashov, Y. S. (RUS)	28	2520
	Balaskas, P. (GRE)	0	2280
	Balasubramaniun, R. (IND)	14	2245
	Balazs jr., T. (HUN)	8	2250
	Balazs, A. (HUN)	2	2230
	Balazs, I. (HUN)	2	2200
f	Balcerowski, W. (POL)	0	2280
f	Baldauf, M. (GER)	0	2265
	Baldy, Ph. (FRA)	0	2265
f	Balenovic, Z. (CRO)	8	2270
	Balev, K. (BUL)	0	2295
	Bali, J. (HUN)	24	2235
g	Balinas, R. C. (PHI)	0	2350
	Balinov, I. (BUL)	0	2300
	Ballai, Zs. (HUN)	19	2225
	Ballester Sanz, J. (ESP)	4	2225
f	Ballicora, M. (ARG)	0	2245
f	Ballmann, M. (SUI)	4	2340
f	Ballon, G. J. (NED)	1	2200
f	Balogh, B. (HUN)	31	2255
	Balogh, P. (HUN)	0	2080
	Balogh, S. (HUN)	0	2325
	Balster, S. (GER)	0	2305
	Baltazar, R. (MEX)	0	2220
	Baltgailis, V. (CAN)	0	2005
	Balun, A. (POL)	0	2205
f	Baluta, C. (ROM)	11	2315
f	Balzar, A. (GER)	0	2330
f	Bammoune, A. E. (ALG)	6	2290
m	Banas, I. (SVK)	21	2380
	Banasik, H. (POL)	3	2240
	Banasik, M. (POL)	0	2270
	Bancel, G. (FRA)	1	2265
f	Bancod, R. (PHI)	11	2465
	Bandza, A. (LTU)	34	2350
	Bandziene, R. (LTU)	0	2100
f	Bang, A. (DEN)	0	2305
	Bangiev, A. (GER)	15	2385
	Banhazi, I. (HUN)	0	2210
	Banikas, H. (GRE)	10	2205
	Banjevic, S. (YUG)	0	2285
	Bank Friis, C. (DEN)	0	2245
	Banusic, Z. (YUG)	0	2315
m	Bany, J. (POL)	1	2420
	Baquero, L. A. (COL)	0	2365
	Barabas, A. (HUN)	7	2200
f	Baragar, F. (CAN)	0	2285
	Barahona, D. (CHI)	7	2250
	Barakat, R. (LEB)	0	2205
	Baranova, V. (UKR)	0	2085
	Baranyi, K. (HUN)	0	2315
	Barash, D. (ISR)	0	2260
f	Barbeau, S. (CAN)	0	2380
f	Barber, H. J. (AUS)	0	2310
	Barbera Estelles, R. (ESP)	1	2235
g	Barbero, G. F. (ARG)	13	2520
	Barbu, I. (ROM)	3	2290
	Barbu, N. (ROM)	0	2350
m	Barbulescu, D. (ROM)	0	2405
	Barbulescu, V. (ROM)	0	2200
	Barcelo, P. (ESP)	0	2280
m	Barcenilla, R. (PHI)	27	2465
g	Barczay, L. (HUN)	0	2380
	Bardel, S. (FRA)	0	2315
	Bardiani, D. (ARG)	19	2255
	Bardolf, G. (AUT)	9	2155
	Bardosi, J. (HUN)	18	2205
g	Bareev, E. (RUS)	38	2660
	Barenbaum, A. (ARG)	0	2225
	Bargad, A. (ARG)	0	2260
	Baric, D. (SLO)	9	2145
	Barillaro, L. (ITA)	0	2265
	Barishev, O. (RUS)	0	2330
	Barkhagen, J. (SWE)	13	2430
	Barkovsky, E. (RUS)	0	2295
	Barlay, I. (USA)	0	2235
m	Barle, J. (SLO)	17	2435
	Barletta, M. (ITA)	4	2210
	Barlocco, C. (ITA)	6	2290
g	Barlov, D. (YUG)	30	2495
	Baronets, I. (RUS)	0	2270
	Barredo, L. (CUB)	0	2260
m	Barreras, A. (CUB)	0	2315
	Barreto, L. N. M. (BRA)	0	2280
	Barria, D. (CHI)	18	2110
	Barrientos, V. (MEX)	0	2235
	Barrios Canseco, S. (ESP)	0	2285
	Barrios, F. (COL)	11	2250

	Name	Games	Rating
	Barrios, R. (MEX)	0	2080
	Barry, C. (IRL)	9	2295
	Barsegian, A. (ARM)	16	2330
	Barskij, V. (RUS)	42	2320
m	Barsov, A. (UZB)	49	2445
	Barta, S. (HUN)	0	2225
	Bartak, V. (TCH)	0	2305
	Bartek, L. (SVK)	5	2200
	Bartelborth, Th. (GER)	0	2250
	Bartels, F. (GER)	4	2305
f	Bartels, Ha. A. (NED)	0	2335
	Bartels, Ho. (GER)	11	2175
	Barth, R. (GER)	0	2285
	Bartha, A. (ROM)	8	2250
f	Bartha, S. (HUN)	24	2275
	Barthel, B. (GER)	3	2065
	Bartolini, T. (ITA)	7	2095
	Bartosik, O. (POL)	30	2085
	Bartosik, P. (POL)	11	2230
f	Bartsch, B. (GER)	9	2290
	Bartsch, S. (GER)	0	2310
g	Barua, D. (IND)	21	2510
m	Barus, C. (INA)	9	2405
	Barva, A. (HUN)	3	2235
f	Barwinski, D. (POL)	10	2310
g	Basagic, V. (BIH)	32	2360
m	Basagic, Z. (BIH)	15	2415
f	Basanta, G. (CAN)	0	2375
	Basart, J. M. (ESP)	6	2245
	Basener, W. (GER)	0	2200
m	Bashkov, V. (RUS)	29	2430
m	Basin, L. (RUS)	0	2425
m	Basman, M. J. (ENG)	6	2350
	Basoglu, Y. (TUR)	0	2200
f	Bass, A. (ARG)	7	2250
m	Bass, L. (USA)	0	2500
f	Basta, D. (YUG)	0	2340
	Basta-Sohair, F. (EGY)	0	2060
f	Bastian, H. (GER)	9	2300
	Bastian, M. (GER)	10	2255
	Batchinsky, S. (SUI)	0	2340
	Bates, L. (USA)	2	2235
	Bates, R. (ENG)	16	2235
	Bathie, N. (SCO)	0	2295
	Batkovic, R. (YUG)	20	2045
m	Bator, R. (SWE)	7	2380
f	Bator, Z. (SWE)	0	2345
	Batres, F. (NCA)	9	2180
	Batricevic, S. (YUG)	10	2240
	Batruch, K. (POL)	0	2245
	Battikhi, H. (JRD)	9	2205
	Baturin, M. (BLA)	18	2175
	Baudin, F. (FRA)	0	2260
f	Bauer, Ch. (FRA)	19	2485
	Bauer, E. (GER)	2	2300
	Bauer, M. (GER)	1	2250
f	Bauer, Peter (GER)	11	2295
	Bauer, Peter (HUN)	4	2210
f	Bauer, Re. (GER)	0	2310
	Bauer, Ri. N. (USA)	0	2235
f	Bauer, T. (HUN)	13	2395
	Bauert, R. (SUI)	0	2320
	Bauk, S. (CRO)	0	2330
f	Baum, B. (GER)	8	2305
f	Baumann, C. (SUI)	10	2070
f	Baumbach, F. (GER)	0	2345
	Baumegger, S. (AUT)	13	2260
f	Baumgartner, H. (AUT)	20	2300
m	Baumhus, R. (GER)	0	2360
m	Baumstark, G. (ROM)	1	2150
	Baury, G. (FRA)	9	2185
	Bauza, A. (URU)	11	2260
f	Bayer, E.-W. (GER)	0	2295
f	Bazaj, I. (CRO)	0	2345
f	Bazaj-Bockaj, S. (CRO)	18	2175
	Bazan, O. (ARG)	5	2280
	Bazant, P. (TCH)	0	2330
	Bazhin, A. (RUS)	15	2280
	Beade, C. (ESP)	0	2270
	Beake, B. (ENG)	0	2265
	Beaton, K. S. (SCO)	0	2115
	Beaumont, Ch. (ENG)	0	2365
	Bebcuk, E. (RUS)	7	2305
f	Becerra Rivero, J. (CUB)	32	2470
	Becher, H. (GER)	0	2305
	Bechkuis, G. (GER)	20	2300
	Beck, D. (GER)	0	2200
	Beck, G. (GER)	0	2255
	Beck, H. (AUT)	8	2285
m	Beckemeyer, W. (GER)	13	2390
	Becker, A. (USA)	0	2255
	Becker, Ma. (GER)	8	2380
f	Becker, Mi. (GER)	5	2305
	Beckhuis, G. (GER)	0	2195
	Beckman, Th. J. (USA)	8	2220
	Beckmann, K. (GER)	0	2285
f	Becx, C. (NED)	0	2260
	Bedic, Z. (CRO)	0	2270
	Bednar, J. (SVK)	4	2190
	Bednarek, S. (POL)	0	2310
f	Bednarska, M. (POL)	31	2200
m	Bednarski, J. B. (POL)	8	2300
	Bedolla, L. M. (MEX)	0	2040
	Bedos, M. (FRA)	0	2270
	Bee, M. (GER)	0	2310
f	Beelby, M. A. (USA)	35	2350
	Beggi, P. (ITA)	5	2235
	Begic, S. (BIH)	0	2270
	Beglerovic, J. (YUG)	0	2290
f	Begnis, N. (GRE)	0	2305
m	Begovac, F. (CRO)	6	2405
	Begun, S. M. (BLA)	2	2380
	Begunov, K. (RUS)	0	2340
	Behar, E. (ARG)	0	2210
f	Behle, K.-W. (GER)	0	2285
	Behnk, R. (GER)	12	2320
f	Behrens, H. (GER)	7	2285
f	Behrensen, J. (ARG)	0	2325
f	Behrhorst, F. (GER)	0	2260
	Beider, A. (RUS)	0	2305
m	Beikert, G. (GER)	19	2415
	Beikert, J. (GER)	0	2250
m	Beil, Z. (TCH)	0	2340
	Beilfuss, W. (GER)	8	2250
m	Beim, V. (ISR)	32	2500
	Beimfohr, U. (SUI)	9	2130
f	Beitar, H. (SYR)	0	2280
f	Bekefi, L. (HUN)	0	2300
g	Belakovskaja, A. (UKR)	5	2300
m	Belamaric, T. (CRO)	3	2155
	Belan, J. (SVK)	0	2230
	Belani, M. (CRO)	0	2245
	Belaska, P. (TCH)	2	2255
m	Belavenets, L. (RUS)	7	2175
	Belfiore, D. (ARG)	5	2195
g	Beliavsky, A. G. (UKR)	27	2635
	Belik, D. (TCH)	6	2325
m	Belikov, V. (RUS)	37	2450
	Belin, I. (AUS)	11	2310
	Belke, F. (GER)	0	2225
m	Belkhodja, S. (FRA)	3	2395
	Belkin, A. (UZB)	15	2160
	Bell, S. (ENG)	0	2385
m	Belle, E. (NED)	0	2095
	Bellemo, L. (ITA)	0	2220
	Bellet, G. (FRA)	0	2220
	Bellia, F. (ITA)	4	2280
g	Bellin, J. (ENG)	6	2195
m	Bellin, R. (ENG)	0	2395
	Bellini, F. (ITA)	2	2350
	Bellomo, F. (ITA)	0	2365
g	Bellon Lopez, J. M. (ESP)	6	2415
	Belmont, A. (MEX)	0	2250
f	Belopolsky, B. (USA)	10	2270
	Belotserkovsky, A. (RUS)	14	2285
m	Belotti, B. (ITA)	20	2410
m	Belov, I. (RUS)	22	2445
	Beltramini, J. M. (ARG)	9	2190
	Beltran, C. (COL)	0	2240
	Beltran, M. F. (MEX)	0	2035
	Beltran, S. (ESP)	0	2310
m	Beltz, M. (GER)	15	2185
	Ben-Menachem, I. (ISR)	0	2315
f	Bencze, L. (HUN)	2	2300
	Benderac, A. (YUG)	21	2125
	Benderac, S. (YUG)	6	2235
	Bener, A. (SWE)	5	2070
	Bengafer, M. (LBA)	0	2245
m	Benhadi, A. M. (ALG)	0	2225
	Benjamin, D. (USA)	10	2290
g	Benjamin, J. (USA)	69	2620
	Benko, F. (ARG)	16	2190
g	Benko, P. C. (USA)	10	2425
	Bennedik, M. (GER)	0	2035
	Bennett, A. (USA)	13	2285
	Bennett, Ch. (JAM)	0	2005
	Bennett, J. (ENG)	5	2205
f	Bennis, Z. (MAR)	10	2305
	Benno, P. (HUN)	0	2275
	Benoit, M. (FRA)	8	2245
	Benotman, A.-A. E. (LBA)	0	2205
	Bensch, P. (GER)	0	2260
m	Benschop, A. M. (NED)	0	2205
	Bense, J. (HUN)	1	2290
	Bentzen, E. (DEN)	0	2315
	Benz, R. (SUI)	11	2075
m	Berdichevski, I. (RUS)	11	2405
m	Berebora, F. (HUN)	18	2425
m	Berechet, O. (ROM)	0	2430
	Berecz, A. (HUN)	12	2215
	Berelovich, A. (UKR)	46	2510
	Berend, D. (ISR)	0	2260
f	Berend, F. (LUX)	16	2295
	Berenyi, G. (HUN)	15	2230
	Berenyi, T. (HUN)	9	2045
m	Berezina, I. (RUS)	12	2210
m	Berezjuk, S. (BLA)	16	2435
	Berezovics, A. (RUS)	6	2350
	Berg, D. (GER)	4	2345
	Berg, G. P. (USA)	11	2200
m	Berg, K. (DEN)	26	2390
	Berg, Michael (SWE)	5	2240
	Berg, Michael (GER)	0	2260
	Berg, S. (SWE)	14	2100
	Berg, Th. (GER)	0	2260
	Berger, G. (GER)	10	2095
	Berger, Th. (GER)	0	2275
	Berghoefer, G. (AUT)	0	2230
f	Bergsson, S. (ISD)	0	2265
m	Bergstrom, Ch. (SWE)	0	2420
	Bergstrom, P. (SWE)	0	2270
	Bergstrom, R. (SWE)	7	2255
f	Berkell, P. (SWE)	0	2315
m	Berkovich, D. (UKR)	49	2400
m	Berkovich, M. A. (ISR)	8	2425
	Bermejo Collado, J. (ESP)	0	2310
	Bermudez, S. (CRC)	19	2220
m	Bern, I. (NOR)	10	2370
	Bernal Caaman, J. L. (ESP)	0	2290
f	Bernal Moro, L. J. (ESP)	9	2385
	Bernal, E. (PHI)	0	2355
f	Bernard, Ch. (FRA)	14	2385
	Bernard, N. (BEL)	0	2210
f	Bernard, R. (POL)	0	2345
	Berndt, A. (GER)	0	2255
	Berndt, K. (GER)	0	2285
	Berndt, S. (GER)	2	2290
	Berndt, W. (GER)	0	2310
f	Bernei, A. (HUN)	11	2345
	Berntsen, P. (SWE)	0	2270
	Berntsen, Sh. (NOR)	10	2080
	Berovski, K. (BUL)	13	2315
f	Berrocal, J. (BOL)	0	2275

	Name	Games	Rating
f	Berry, J. (CAN)	0	2270
	Berry, S. (ENG)	5	2320
	Berset, Ph. (SUI)	16	2235
	Bersoult, F. (FRA)	1	2200
f	Bersutzki, G. (ISR)	1	2175
	Berta, K. (HUN)	6	2235
	Bertaccini, D. (ARG)	10	2225
f	Berthelot, Y. (FRA)	30	2300
f	Bertholee, R. (NED)	0	2350
m	Bertok, M. (CRO)	4	2310
	Bertona, F. (ARG)	24	2355
	Berube, R. (CAN)	6	2295
	Berzinsh, R. (LAT)	33	2370
m	Beshukov, S. (RUS)	83	2445
	Besvir, B. (CRO)	0	2250
	Besztercsenyi, T. (HUN)	13	2300
	Beszterczey, L. (HUN)	20	2210
	Betancort Curbelo, J. (ESP)	0	2255
	Betancourt, D. (COL)	11	2230
	Betkowski, A. (POL)	8	2255
	Bets, A. (RUS)	35	2330
	Beuchler, H. (GER)	10	2250
f	Beulen, M. (NED)	0	2310
	Beutel, H. (GER)	0	2270
	Bevan, P. M. (WLS)	9	2180
	Bevia, L. M. (ESP)	0	2230
f	Bewersdorff, O. (GER)	15	2300
	Bews, S. (SCO)	0	2295
	Bex, P.-A. (SUI)	4	2225
	Beyen, R. (BEL)	0	2275
	Beyer, H.-J. (GER)	0	2165
	Bezdan, T. (HUN)	13	2270
	Bezemer, A. (NED)	2	2235
	Bezgodov, A. (RUS)	33	2400
f	Bezold, M. (GER)	45	2490
	Bhagwat, M. (IND)	0	2205
	Bharathi, S. C. (IND)	7	2195
	Bhatt, P. R. (IND)	0	2215
	Bhattacharyya, P. (IND)	6	2190
	Bhave, R. (IND)	2	2250
m	Bhend, E. (SUI)	5	2280
	Bhowmik (IND)	0	2235
	Biaggi, E. (ARG)	1	2275
f	Bialas, W. (GER)	2	2310
f	Bialolenkier, P. (ARG)	2	2265
m	Bianchi, G. (ARG)	10	2425
	Bianco, V. (ITA)	13	2240
	Biancosino, R. (ARG)	1	2185
	Bibby, S. (ENG)	0	2290
	Bibik, J. (RUS)	3	2220
	Bibiloni, J. (ARG)	11	2245
f	Bichsel, W. (SUI)	7	2315
	Biebinger, G. (GER)	16	2310
	Biehler, Th. (GER)	0	2315
m	Bielczyk, J. (POL)	6	2375
	Bielicki, B. (GER)	2	2235
m	Bielicki, C. (ARG)	0	2320
	Bier, N. (GER)	0	2120
	Bierenbroodspot, P. (NED)	0	2280
	Bigier, H. (SUI)	0	2285
g	Bilek, I. (HUN)	26	2390
	Bilic, M. (CRO)	0	2295
	Bilinskas, R. (LTU)	18	2275
	Biliskov, V. (CRO)	11	2325
f	Bilobrk, F. (CRO)	0	2345
	Bilunov, B. (RUS)	0	2410
m	Bilunova, R. I. (RUS)	0	2155
	Binder, T. (HUN)	12	2255
	Bindu, S. K. (IND)	11	2105
m	Binham, T. F. (FIN)	0	2330
	Bintakies, M. (GER)	9	2260
	Biocanin, Goran (YUG)	0	2265
	Biocanin, Gord. (YUG)	0	2080
	Biolek, R. (TCH)	7	2415
	Bipin S., Sh. (IND)	10	2175
	Birer, A. (ISR)	4	2200
m	Biriescu, I. (ROM)	0	2340
	Biriukhatnikov, D. (RUS)	0	2355
	Biriukov, I. (RUS)	0	2370
	Birk, S. (GER)	2	2290
	Birke, M. (GER)	0	2275
f	Birmingham, E. (FRA)	7	2300
	Birnbaum, D. (FRA)	9	2185
m	Birnboim, N. (ISR)	44	2435
	Biro, J. (HUN)	0	2300
	Biro, K. (SVK)	0	2235
m	Biro, S. (ROM)	29	2285
	Birr, B. (GER)	0	2020
	Bischof, D. (GER)	7	2310
	Bischoff, D. (GER)	1	2240
g	Bischoff, K. (GER)	54	2515
g	Bisguier, A. B. (USA)	7	2365
f	Bistric, F. (BIH)	0	2400
m	Bistrikova, E. V. (RUS)	0	2115
	Biti, N. N. (ZIM)	0	2005
	Bitman, A. R. (RUS)	31	2205
	Bitran, D. (ISR)	0	2235
m	Bjarnason, S. (ISD)	0	2290
	Bjarnehag, P. (SWE)	0	2290
	Bjazevic Montalvo, P. (ECU)	0	2250
m	Bjelajac, M. (YUG)	5	2380
m	Bjelajac, O. (YUG)	13	2080
	Bjergtrup, M. (DEN)	0	2270
f	Bjerke, R. (NOR)	0	2265
f	Bjerring, K. (DEN)	26	2360
f	Bjork, C.-M. (SWE)	0	2310
	Bjornsson, B. (ISD)	0	2200
f	Bjornsson, T. (ISD)	2	2290
	Blackstock, L. S. F. (SCO)	0	2260
m	Blagojevic, D. (YUG)	36	2465
	Blagojevic, N. (YUG)	0	2300
	Blancke, S. (GER)	7	2275
f	Blanco Fernandez, A. (CUB)	0	2305
	Blandnet, M. J. (FRA)	8	2155
	Blank, O. (GER)	0	2225
f	Blasek, R. (GER)	7	2345
	Blaskowski, J. (GER)	0	2285
	Blasovszky, I. (HUN)	21	2230
	Blaszczuk, Z. (POL)	13	2210
f	Blatny, F. (TCH)	6	2365
g	Blatny, P. (TCH)	23	2510
f	Blauert, J. (GER)	22	2400
	Blazevic, Lj. (YUG)	9	2280
	Blazkova, P. (TCH)	0	2200
	Blazquez Gomez, J. C. (ESP)	0	2280
	Blazquez, D. (FRA)	0	2220
	Blazsik, Z. (HUN)	0	2065
	Blechzin, I. (RUS)	9	2350
	Blecken, V. (GER)	8	2215
m	Blees, A. (NED)	42	2415
	Blehm, P. (POL)	25	2160
f	Bletz, H. (GER)	5	2275
	Bleunven, A. (FRA)	14	2250
f	Blimke, D. (POL)	20	2030
	Bliumberg, V. (RUS)	28	2340
	Blizniuk, O. (UKR)	0	2045
m	Blocker, C. (USA)	0	2380
	Blodig, R. (GER)	0	2230
	Blodstein, A. (UZB)	10	2370
	Blodstein, B. (UZB)	15	2220
	Blokh, M. (RUS)	9	2355
f	Blokhuis, E. M. (NED)	0	2315
f	Blucha, D. (TCH)	0	2250
f	Bluhm, G. (GER)	1	2295
	Blum, G. (GER)	22	2245
	Blumel, O. (TCH)	0	2265
	Blumelova, Z. (TCH)	0	2045
f	Blumenfeld, R. (USA)	0	2370
	Bobic, Z. (YUG)	3	2220
	Bobras, P. (POL)	10	2225
	Bobrowska, M. (POL)	44	2180
	Bobu, A. (ROM)	10	2265
	Bobzin, P. (GER)	9	2205
	Bochev, K. (BUL)	2	2215
	Bochnon, A. (USA)	0	2285
	Bocina, D. (CRO)	2	2160
	Bock, J. (GER)	6	2230
	Bockius, A. (GER)	4	2215
	Bockowski, R. (POL)	0	2250
f	Bocksberger, S. (GER)	0	2340
	Boctor, W. (USA)	9	2265
	Bode, U. (GER)	8	2255
	Bode, W. (GER)	10	2365
f	Bodic, D. (YUG)	0	2295
	Bodiroga, P. (YUG)	7	2280
	Bodjanec, V. (CRO)	7	2290
	Bodo, N. (HUN)	5	2280
	Bodrogi, M. (HUN)	4	2245
	Boe, M. (DEN)	5	2270
	Boehle, L. (GER)	5	2340
f	Boehlig, H. (GER)	3	2310
	Boehm, H. (AUT)	0	2230
	Boehm, J. (GER)	0	2245
	Boehm, M. (GER)	9	2225
	Boenisch, A. (GER)	16	2160
f	Boenisch, M. (GER)	0	2315
g	Boensch, U. (GER)	48	2525
m	Boersma, P. A. (NED)	0	2365
	Boesken, C. P. (GER)	0	2270
m	Boey, J. (BEL)	0	2305
	Boeykens, M. (BEL)	0	2255
f	Bofill, A. (ESP)	0	2385
f	Bogaerts, J. (BEL)	0	2295
	Bogar, A. (HUN)	0	2295
	Bogdan, D. (ROM)	46	2295
	Bogdanos, A. (GRE)	11	2205
	Bogdanov, V. (UKR)	8	2450
m	Bogdanovic, R. (BIH)	0	2315
m	Bogdanovich, G. (RUS)	0	2425
m	Bogdanovski, V. (YUG)	74	2515
	Bogic, S. (YUG)	0	2245
	Bogicevic, A. (YUG)	0	2270
	Bogicevic, S. (YUG)	0	2275
	Bogner, H. (USA)	0	2235
	Bogo, S. (DEN)	0	2260
	Bogoevski, J. (YUG)	3	2255
	Bogumil, P. (RUS)	5	2355
	Bogumil, T. (RUS)	0	2050
	Boguslawsky, M. (RUS)	46	2290
m	Boguszlavszky, J. (HUN)	0	2350
	Bohak, J. (SLO)	4	2235
m	Bohm, H. (NED)	0	2390
	Bohn, Th. (GER)	9	2355
	Bohnsack, R. (GER)	0	2235
	Bohnstorff, M. (GER)	12	2250
	Boicu, N. (ROM)	3	2205
f	Boim, I. (ISR)	22	2340
m	Boissonet, C. P. (ARG)	0	2430
f	Bojczuk, Z. (POL)	2	2320
	Bojic, D. (YUG)	11	2290
g	Bojkovic, N. (YUG)	17	2365
f	Bojkovic, S. (YUG)	0	2365
	Bokan, D. (YUG)	5	2245
	Bokelbrink, U. (GER)	0	2275
	Bokor, I. (HUN)	9	2260
g	Bolbochan, J. (ARG)	0	2470
	Bolico, G. (PHI)	0	2040
	Boljsakov, M. (YUG)	0	2270
g	Bologan, V. (MOL)	22	2510
	Bolzoni, V.-A. (BEL)	0	2295
	Bombardiere Rosas, E. (CHI)	21	2305
	Bonaldi, P. (ARG)	0	2245
	Bonatti, W. (ARG)	2	2280
	Bonaveri, A. (ARG)	0	2180
	Bonchev, K. S. (BUL)	0	2315
	Bonchev, S. (BUL)	0	2220
	Bondarenko, V. (RUS)	2	2220

	Name		
	Bondarets, V. (YUG)	0	2315
	Bondoc, D. (ROM)	17	2310
m	Bonin, J. R. (USA)	47	2370
	Bonne, M. (BEL)	0	2250
f	Boog, A. (SUI)	10	2290
	Booij, J. (NED)	0	2275
	Booth, Step. A. (USA)	17	2265
	Booth, Stew. (AUS)	0	2280
	Borcsok, L. (HUN)	9	2290
	Borcz, J. (POL)	0	2240
	Bordas, Gy. (HUN)	20	2170
	Bordell Rosell, R. (ESP)	4	2260
	Bordoni, N. (ARG)	15	2150
f	Borek, J. (AUT)	10	2095
	Bores, R. (TCH)	0	2295
	Borg, A. (MLT)	0	2205
f	Borg, G. (MLT)	0	2355
m	Borge, N. (DEN)	21	2405
m	Borges Mateos, J. (CUB)	23	2400
	Borges, D. (PUR)	0	2010
f	Borghi, H. (ARG)	5	2335
f	Borgo, G. (ITA)	17	2370
	Borgstaedt, M. (GER)	0	2270
f	Boric, M. (BIH)	9	2305
	Boricsev, O. (UKR)	11	2325
m	Borik, O. (GER)	13	2415
g	Borisenko-Belova, V. (RUS)	0	2180
	Borisov, V. (RUS)	11	2270
m	Borisova, B. (SWE)	0	2155
f	Borkovic, V. (YUG)	5	2255
m	Borkowski, F. (POL)	9	2435
	Borloy, K. (HUN)	0	2225
	Borman, P. (GCI)	0	2205
	Born, M. (GER)	1	2220
	Borne, N. (FRA)	0	2275
	Bornemann, W. (GER)	5	2310
	Borner, D. (SUI)	2	2285
f	Borngaesser, R. (GER)	8	2360
	Borocz, I. (HUN)	26	2335
	Boronyak, A. (HUN)	21	2295
	Boros, D. (HUN)	11	2270
	Borovikov, V. (RUS)	0	2385
	Borozan, N. (YUG)	4	2075
m	Borriss, M. (GER)	35	2375
	Borsavolgyi, T. (HUN)	9	2265
	Borsi, I. (HUN)	13	2220
	Borsos, B. (UKR)	2	2350
	Borsuk, A. (UKR)	34	2230
m	Borulia, E. (UKR)	11	2300
	Borylia, E. (RUS)	0	2210
	Borysiak, B. (POL)	13	2280
	Bosbach, G. (GER)	7	2255
m	Bosboom, M. (NED)	28	2440
	Bosch, J. (NED)	0	2290
	Boschetti, C. (SUI)	2	2190
	Bosco, R. (ARG)	21	2235
f	Boshku, H. (ALB)	0	2325
	Boskovic, M. (YUG)	17	2100
	Boskovic, Z. (YUG)	0	2230
f	Bosman, M. (NED)	0	2285
	Bosnic, Lj. (BIH)	0	2030
	Bossert, Ch. (GER)	11	2305
m	Botan, M. S. (ROM)	0	2210
f	Botez, C. (ROM)	0	2300
	Both, A. (GER)	0	2065
	Botham, Ch. P. (ENG)	9	2065
	Boto, Z. (CRO)	8	2300
	Botos, F. (HUN)	11	2175
m	Botsari, A.-M. (GRE)	11	2245
	Botsaris, H.-D. (GRE)	0	2190
	Botvinnik, Il. (BLA)	37	2395
	Botvinnik, Ir. (BLA)	22	2080
	Bouah, L. (RSA)	0	2205
g	Bouaziz, S. (TUN)	13	2515
	Bouchaud, V. (FRA)	9	2235
m	Boudiba, M. (ALG)	0	2345
m	Boudre, J.-P. (FRA)	15	2380
m	Boudy, J. (CUB)	12	2300
	Bouhallel, R. (FRA)	9	2220
	Bouland, S. (FRA)	0	2265
	Boulard, E. (FRA)	0	2255
	Bourgoin, D. (FRA)	0	2195
	Bousbouras, S. (GRE)	0	2180
	Bousios, H. (GRE)	22	2285
	Bouton, Ch. (FRA)	8	2225
	Boutquin, P. (CAN)	0	2270
	Boutteville, C. (FRA)	0	2235
	Bouverot, O. (FRA)	16	2210
	Bouzoukis, Ch. (USA)	0	2285
	Bowden, K. (ENG)	3	2355
	Boyd, S. (CAN)	0	2245
	Bozanic, I. (CRO)	0	2235
	Bozek, A. (POL)	0	2360
	Bozic, Ma. (SLO)	10	2070
	Bozic, Mi. (YUG)	0	2250
	Bozovic, Ma. (YUG)	10	2045
	Bozovic, Mi. (YUG)	0	2235
	Bozovic, N. (YUG)	0	2300
	Bozzi, G. (ITA)	0	2305
	Bracken, C. (IRL)	0	2225
	Bradaric, R. (CRO)	0	2245
m	Bradbury, N. H. (ENG)	0	2335
f	Bradford, J. M. (USA)	0	2435
	Bradianu, I. (ROM)	0	2010
f	Brady, S. (IRL)	23	2320
f	Braeuning, R. (GER)	0	2305
f	Braga, C. (BRA)	23	2400
m	Braga, F. (ITA)	42	2455
	Bragin, A. (RUS)	10	2485
f	Brajovic, R. (YUG)	20	2300
	Braley, J. (USA)	0	2240
	Brameyer, H. (GER)	0	2285
	Brancaleoni, M. (ITA)	8	2195
	Brandauer, D. (GER)	9	2045
m	Brandics, J. (HUN)	96	2235
	Brandl, R. (AUT)	2	2275
	Brandner, S. (AUT)	0	2220
	Brankov, K. D. (BUL)	0	2315
f	Brasket, C. J. (USA)	16	2290
	Bratimirova, D. (BUL)	0	2080
	Bratu, N. (ROM)	0	2280
	Braude, M. (USA)	3	2490
	Brauer, Ch. (GER)	9	2190
	Braun, B. (HUN)	0	2040
f	Braun, G. (GER)	12	2335
	Braun, L. (USA)	5	2245
	Braun, M. (GER)	5	2345
f	Braun, W. (AUT)	1	2250
	Brautsch, S. (DEN)	0	2245
	Bravo, N. (ESP)	4	2290
	Brdicko, P. (TCH)	0	2250
f	Breahna, R. (ROM)	0	2335
	Breaz, M. (ROM)	0	2265
	Breja, S. (SVK)	0	2230
	Brekka, M. (FAI)	9	2165
	Brem, S. (GER)	5	2215
	Bremond, E. (FRA)	0	2300
f	Brendel, O. (GER)	14	2385
	Brenjo, S. (YUG)	17	2425
	Brenke, A. (GER)	0	2285
m	Brenninkmeijer, J. (NED)	14	2495
	Bresciani, N. (ITA)	0	2315
f	Brestak, J. (SVK)	0	2285
m	Brestian, E. (AUT)	19	2460
f	Bretsnajdr, V. (TCH)	0	2325
	Brettschneider, S. (GER)	0	2180
f	Breutigam, M. (GER)	23	2340
f	Breyther, R. (GER)	4	2315
f	Brglez, R. (SLO)	10	2310
	Brhlik, Gy. (HUN)	0	2205
m	Bricard, E. (FRA)	34	2440
	Briem, S. (ISD)	0	2205
	Briestensky, R. (SVK)	0	2215
	Briffel, F. (ANG)	0	2165
f	Brigljevic, M. (CRO)	2	2255
	Bril, L. (LAT)	11	2215
m	Brinck-Claussen, B. (DEN)	0	2385
	Brink, P. (NED)	15	2210
f	Brito, A. (ESP)	6	2375
	Brito, L. J. (BRA)	0	2370
f	Britton, R. (ENG)	10	2305
	Brkic, Dj. (YUG)	15	2230
m	Brkljaca, A. (YUG)	24	2375
	Brochet, Ph. (FRA)	9	2100
	Brod, M. (AUT)	0	2220
m	Brodskij, M. (UKR)	41	2515
	Brodsky, I. (RUS)	0	2360
m	Broeder, I. (GER)	0	2190
	Broemel, R. (GER)	0	2215
	Brondum, E. (DEN)	0	2225
	Bronnum, J. (DEN)	0	2220
g	Bronstein, D. I. (RUS)	13	2395
m	Bronstein, L. (ARG)	29	2420
	Brontz, A. (SWE)	0	2245
	Bronznik, V. (RUS)	0	2250
m	Brooks, M. A. (USA)	4	2440
	Broomes, M. (GUY)	0	2215
	Brown, D. (USA)	0	2240
	Brown, K. (JAM)	0	2205
	Brown, P. (FIJ)	0	2205
	Brown, S. D. (ENG)	0	2285
	Brown, T. G. (USA)	0	2230
g	Browne, W. S. (USA)	31	2515
	Brownescombe, T. (USA)	7	2315
	Bruch, I. (GER)	6	2305
	Bruch, J. (GER)	0	2285
f	Brueckner, Th. (GER)	2	2380
f	Brueggemann, J. (GER)	12	2335
f	Bruinenberg, C. (NED)	0	2100
	Brujic, B. (YUG)	3	2265
m	Bruk, O. (ISR)	20	2415
	Brull, C. (ESP)	0	2370
f	Brumen, D. (CRO)	1	2315
	Brumm, C. (GER)	3	2260
	Bruneau, L. (FRA)	0	2260
m	Brunner, L. (SUI)	45	2475
	Bruno, A. P. (ARG)	11	2320
	Bruno, F. (ITA)	0	2245
	Brunski, I. (CRO)	0	2210
	Brustkern, J. (GER)	25	2210
g	Brustman, A. (POL)	15	2280
	Brustman-Gawarecka, E. (POL)	0	2070
	Bryce, A. (ENG)	0	2225
f	Brychta, I. (TCH)	0	2300
	Brylev, I. (RUS)	0	2290
m	Brynell, S. (SWE)	6	2470
f	Bryson, D. M. (SCO)	8	2320
	Brzezicki, D. (POL)	0	2280
	Bubalovic, D. (CRO)	0	2285
	Bucan, D. (YUG)	6	2225
	Buch, C. (DEN)	0	2260
f	Buchal, S. (GER)	16	2305
	Buchanan, W. F. (SCO)	0	2155
	Buchenau, F. (GER)	6	2250
	Buchnicek, P. (TCH)	12	2180
	Buckley, G. (ENG)	26	2305
f	Buckmire, R. (BAR)	0	2305
f	Budde, V. (GER)	0	2300
	Buddensiek, U. (GER)	0	2260
	Budinszky, A. (HUN)	0	2260
m	Budnikov, A. (RUS)	30	2535
	Budovic, E. (UKR)	0	2230
	Budraitis, A. (LTU)	0	2275
	Buechle, R. (GER)	1	2015
f	Buecker, S. (GER)	23	2335
	Bueder, Th. (GER)	0	2250
	Buehler, B. (GER)	0	2160
f	Buela, D. V. (CUB)	0	2235
	Buenermann, V. (GER)	2	2240
m	Bueno-Perez, L. (CUB)	0	2240
	Buervenich, S. (GER)	6	2155
	Buescu, N. (ROM)	17	2250

Title	Name	Games	Rating
	Bugajski, R. (POL)	4	2360
	Bugariu, V. (ROM)	0	2205
	Bugyinszki, I. (HUN)	5	2305
	Buhr, C.-Ch. (GER)	0	2195
	Bujdoso, B. (HUN)	0	2035
f	Bujisic, V. (YUG)	12	2295
	Bujuklijev, E. (BUL)	0	2255
	Bujuklijev, N. (YUG)	11	2205
	Bujuklijski, A. (BUL)	0	2260
	Bujupi, B. (YUG)	0	2205
	Bujupi, F. (YUG)	0	2250
	Bukacek, E. (AUT)	12	2305
	Bukal jr., V. (YUG)	15	2280
m	Bukal, V. (CRO)	12	2405
	Bukanov, S. (RUS)	0	2340
m	Bukhman, E. (RUS)	0	2390
	Bukhtin, V. S. (RUS)	0	2305
g	Bukic, E. (SLO)	8	2450
	Bukowczyk, A. (POL)	0	2265
	Bukowska, K. (POL)	0	2090
	Bukvic, M. (YUG)	19	2275
	Bulajic, R. (YUG)	0	2270
f	Bulat, A. (CRO)	5	2365
	Bulatovic, D. (YUG)	5	2275
f	Bulcourf, C. (ARG)	28	2280
m	Buljovcic, I. (YUG)	0	2380
	Bunis, V. (BUL)	0	2285
m	Burchardt-Hofman, B. (GER)	5	2265
	Burczyk, E. (POL)	11	2045
	Burdio Gracia, D. (ESP)	2	2140
	Bures, M. (TCH)	0	2215
	Burgeois, W. (URU)	0	2160
m	Burger, K. (USA)	6	2320
f	Burgess, G. (ENG)	0	2300
	Burggraf, M. (GER)	9	2040
m	Burijovich, L. (ARG)	12	2230
	Burjan, A. (HUN)	14	2040
	Burkart, P. (GER)	10	2330
	Burkhardt, H. (GER)	0	2115
	Burlov, V. (RUS)	0	2335
m	Burmakin, V. (RUS)	17	2460
	Burman, A. (SWE)	0	2325
	Burnazovic, E. (BIH)	7	2390
	Burnett, K. (USA)	2	2285
f	Burnett, R. (USA)	3	2320
f	Burovic, I. (BIH)	11	2285
	Bursztyn, A. (ISR)	0	2260
m	Burtman, Sh. (USA)	0	2055
	Burwick, M. (SWE)	0	2225
	Burzynski, K. (POL)	0	2240
m	Bus, M. (POL)	11	2375
m	Busch, K. (GER)	21	2365
f	Busch, R. (GER)	0	2300
	Buscher, M. (GER)	7	2325
	Busisho, R. (FRA)	2	2070
f	Busquets, L. (USA)	5	2245
	Busse, K. (GER)	6	2190
	Bustelo, T. (URU)	9	2180
	Bustos, J. (CHI)	27	2255
	Butala, M. (SLO)	0	2280
f	Butnaru, C. (ROM)	0	2255
m	Butnorius, A. (LTU)	37	2450
	Butorac, I. (CRO)	0	2265
	Butt, C. (ROM)	0	2060
	Butunoi, A. (ROM)	0	2190
m	Buturin, V. (UKR)	11	2400
	Buymuratov, S. (KAZ)	13	2300
	Buza, A. (ROM)	0	2240
f	Buzbuchi, I. (GER)	0	2315
	Buzila, C. (ROM)	0	2330
	Byczynska, J. (POL)	0	2050
m	Bykhovsky, An. A. (RUS)	0	2420
g	Bykhovsky, Av. (RUS)	27	2470
	Bykov, V. (RUS)	0	2355
	Byrka, M. (POL)	0	2255
g	Byrne, R. E. (USA)	0	2460
	Bystrov, S. (RUS)	0	2375
f	Byway, P. (ENG)	0	2295
	Bzenic, D. (YUG)	0	2230
	Bzowski, B. (POL)	0	2260

C

Title	Name	Games	Rating
	Cabanna, D. (FRA)	11	2175
m	Cabarkapa, Mil. (YUG)	0	2290
f	Cabarkapa, Mio. (YUG)	10	2300
f	Cabarkapa, S. (YUG)	5	2300
	Cabarkapa, V. (YUG)	16	2225
	Cabrera Pelaez, E. (MEX)	0	2260
	Cabrera, G. (CUB)	0	2210
m	Cabrilo, G. (YUG)	37	2505
	Cacho, S. (ESP)	0	2360
	Cacic, S. (SLO)	0	2240
	Cacorin, S. (RUS)	0	2280
	Caels, V. (BEL)	0	2015
f	Caessens, R. (NED)	0	2260
	Caiafas, Th. (NGR)	9	2135
	Cajzler, H. (CRO)	0	2225
	Calcado, A. (BRA)	2	2240
f	Calderin, R. (CUB)	0	2430
	Calderwood, S. (ENG)	0	2230
f	Calinescu, G. (ROM)	0	2320
	Callergard, R. (SWE)	0	2315
m	Calvo Minguez, R. (ESP)	0	2355
	Calvo, J. M. (ESP)	0	2315
	Calzetta, M. (ESP)	0	2030
f	Camacho, R. (ESA)	0	2345
m	Camara, H. (BRA)	0	2335
	Camejo, R. (POR)	9	2275
	Cameron, A. (NED)	0	2015
	Cameron, P. (NED)	0	2015
	Caminade, Ch. (FRA)	0	2205
	Campa, K. (YUG)	14	2070
	Campanile, A. (ITA)	0	2245
	Campbell, B. G. (USA)	12	2155
	Campitelli, G. (ARG)	15	2215
	Campiz, L. (PUR)	1	2235
g	Campora, D. H. (ARG)	42	2540
m	Campos Lopez, M. (MEX)	0	2330
m	Campos Moreno, J. B. (CHI)	10	2450
f	Campos, Al. (MEX)	0	2315
	Campos, An. (ESP)	0	2215
	Campos, J. F. (ARG)	12	2255
	Campos, Luis F. (MEX)	0	2195
f	Campos, Luis M. (ARG)	7	2345
	Campos, M. (CUB)	0	2050
	Campos, R. (CRC)	9	2085
	Canalejo, P. (CUB)	0	2240
m	Canda, D. (NCA)	0	2320
m	Candea, G. (ROM)	0	2400
	Candela Perez, J. (ESP)	0	2315
	Cander, M. (SLO)	6	2245
m	Canela, T. (ESP)	0	2155
	Canfell, G. (AUS)	1	2295
	Cangiotti, C. (ITA)	2	2220
	Canic, T. (CRO)	0	2225
	Canina, J. A. (CUB)	9	2100
	Cantero, A. (ESP)	0	2285
	Cao, S. (VIE)	0	2195
	Capaccioli, J. (ARG)	0	2180
	Capek, I. (TCH)	0	2210
	Capella, R. (AHO)	0	2205
	Capit, F. (FRA)	3	2200
	Caplar, L. (ROM)	0	2045
	Capo Iturrieta, R. (CHI)	0	2280
f	Capo, J. (CHI)	9	2375
	Capo, O. (CHI)	0	2030
f	Caposciutti, M. (ITA)	4	2315
	Cappareli, G. (ARG)	0	2330
	Capuano, R. (ITA)	0	2235
	Car, T. (CRO)	0	2310
f	Carag, E. (PHI)	11	2350
f	Caravan, M. (ROM)	13	2065
	Carbajal, A. L. (CUB)	0	2085
	Carbonell, C. (ESP)	4	2340
	Carbonnel, P. (FRA)	0	2260
	Cardinali, M. (ITA)	3	2020
m	Cardon, H. (NED)	0	2375
m	Cardoso, R. (BRA)	0	2040
f	Carleson, C. (SWE)	0	2345
f	Carless, D. (HKG)	0	2265
	Carlhammar, M. (SWE)	0	2325
m	Carlier, B. (NED)	10	2360
	Carlin, A. B. (USA)	12	2215
f	Carlson, M. (SWE)	0	2305
	Carlsson, D. (SWE)	14	2120
	Carlsson, I. (SWE)	0	2250
	Carlsson, M. (SWE)	9	2015
f	Carmel, E. (ISR)	4	2295
	Carneiro, C. (POR)	3	2250
	Carnic, D. (YUG)	3	2195
f	Carnic, S. (YUG)	4	2295
	Carpintero, J. (ESP)	5	2285
f	Carr, N. L. (ENG)	0	2290
	Carranza Torres, Z. (MEX)	0	2120
	Carreras, F. (ESP)	0	2260
	Carrillo, A. (MEX)	0	2305
	Carrion, M. (DOM)	0	2210
f	Carstens, A. (GER)	6	2325
	Carton, N. (IRL)	4	2265
	Carton, P. (IRL)	6	2210
	Caruana Font, R. (ESP)	0	2205
	Caruhana, M. (MNC)	0	2210
	Caruso, A. (ITA)	0	2230
	Carvalho, G. (URU)	0	2175
	Carvalho, H. A. (BRA)	0	2220
	Casa, A. (FRA)	8	2220
f	Casafus, R. (ARG)	22	2430
f	Casagrande, H. (AUT)	18	2395
	Casangiu, P. H. (ROM)	11	2205
	Casas, F. (ARG)	0	2245
	Caselas, J. (ESP)	9	2310
	Caselli, L. (ITA)	0	2325
m	Casper, Th. (GER)	15	2440
	Cassai, P. (ITA)	0	2245
	Castagna, R. (SUI)	2	2265
	Castagnetta, G. (ITA)	0	2305
	Castaing, S. (FRA)	0	2010
	Castaneda, A. (MEX)	0	2245
	Castella, F. (CUB)	0	2310
	Castellano, J. (ESP)	12	2255
	Castellanos, B. (MEX)	0	2255
	Castellanos, C. (CUB)	0	2210
	Castellet, G. (ESP)	0	2360
	Castillo Castelan, M. (MEX)	10	2195
	Castillo, F. (VEN)	9	2045
	Castillo, J. (NCA)	0	2285
	Castillo, O. (GUA)	0	2210
m	Castro, O. H. (COL)	11	2410
	Cativelli, G. (ARG)	17	2225
	Catlow, J. (ENG)	3	2040
	Catropa, Dj. (BRA)	20	2375
	Cattoni, M. (FRA)	9	2145
	Cavalcanti, F. (BRA)	0	2260
f	Cavendish, J. (ENG)	0	2315
g	Cebalo, M. (CRO)	45	2510
f	Cecconi, G. A. (ITA)	4	2245
	Cech, P. (TCH)	0	2315
	Cechalova, E. (TCH)	0	2090
	Cecilia Ortiz, J. L. (ESP)	0	2285
	Cejkova, M. (TCH)	0	2060
	Ceko, J. (YUG)	0	2265
	Cekro, E. (BIH)	0	2415
	Celis Sanchez, C. (PER)	0	2395
	Celis, G. (ARG)	28	2255
	Celis, M. (PHI)	0	2005
	Cempel, J. (TCH)	0	2275
	Centgraf, J. (HUN)	0	2230
	Cepon, D. (SLO)	8	2205
	Cerf, M. (FRA)	0	2245

Title	Name	Games	Rating
f	Cerisier, Ph. (FRA)	6	2300
	Cernat, C. (ROM)	0	2150
	Cerovic, Z. (YUG)	18	2085
	Cersosico, F. (CRC)	8	2195
	Certek, P. (SVK)	0	2290
f	Certic, B. (YUG)	0	2395
f	Cesal, J. (TCH)	0	2320
	Cesareo, F. (SUI)	10	2070
f	Ceschia, I. (ITA)	0	2315
f	Ceteras, M. (ROM)	12	2330
	Cetkovic, B. (YUG)	0	2235
m	Cetkovic, Mi. (YUG)	11	2290
	Cetkovic, Mo. (YUG)	0	2335
m	Chabanon, J.-L. (FRA)	51	2415
	Chabris, Ch. (USA)	0	2270
	Chachaj, T. (POL)	0	2325
	Chachalev, J. (TCH)	0	2250
	Chachere, L. (USA)	13	2250
	Chachkarov, S. (BUL)	0	2220
	Chacon, J. A. (CUB)	0	2120
f	Chaivichit, S. (THA)	0	2330
	Chakravarti, K. (IND)	0	2230
	Chakurira, S. (ZIM)	0	2205
	Chalupnik, M. (POL)	2	2235
	Champion, O. (GER)	0	2065
f	Chan, P.-K. (SIN)	0	2300
g	Chandler, M. G. (ENG)	11	2565
	Chapa, E. (USA)	0	2235
	Chapurin, A. (RUS)	11	2360
	Charneira, H. (POR)	0	2245
	Charon, M. (CUB)	0	2300
	Charpenel Elorduy, M. (MEX)	0	2195
f	Charpentier, W. (CRC)	20	2330
	Chase, Ch. (USA)	10	2305
	Chatalbashev, B. (BUL)	24	2380
	Chatterjee, K. K. (IND)	2	2240
	Chattertee, L. (IND)	7	2270
	Chavarria, A. (CRC)	0	2275
m	Chaves, Jo. (BRA)	21	2025
m	Chaves, Ju. (BRA)	7	2140
	Chavez, M. (MEX)	0	2005
	Chavez, R. (BOL)	0	2220
f	Chaviano, M. (CUB)	0	2320
	Cheah, E. (MAS)	0	2255
	Checa, C. D. (ESP)	10	2265
	Chekaev, A. (RUS)	12	2340
g	Chekhov, V. A. (RUS)	19	2480
m	Chekhova-Kostina, T. M. (RUS)	14	2260
g	Chelushkina, I. (UKR)	39	2330
	Chemin, V. (BRA)	0	2245
f	Chen, De (CHN)	0	2325
	Chenski, D. (POL)	0	2295
	Chepukaitis, G. (RUS)	0	2235
	Chepurnaya, I. (RUS)	0	2050
	Cherati, M. (ARG)	0	2010
	Cherednichenko, A. (RUS)	0	2330
m	Cherepkov, A. V. (RUS)	0	2415
	Cherkasov, N. (RUS)	15	2325
	Cherniack, A. (USA)	14	2250
m	Cherniaev, A. (RUS)	46	2420
	Cherniak, L. (RUS)	0	2420
m	Chernikov, O. L. (RUS)	10	2395
	Chernikova, S. (RUS)	19	2160
g	Chernin, A. (HUN)	70	2615
	Chernin, O. (USA)	2	2265
	Chernosvitov, A. (RUS)	37	2380
	Chernov, V. (MOL)	11	2400
	Chernova, N. (RUS)	9	2240
	Chernyaev, A. (RUS)	0	2335
	Chernyshov, K. (RUS)	25	2400
	Cheron, M. (CUB)	0	2225
f	Cherrad, Z. (ALG)	0	2220
	Chervonenko, I. (ISR)	7	2135
	Chetverik, M. (RUS)	15	2290
	Cheutshenko, R. (EST)	0	2250
f	Chevalier, D. (FRA)	14	2290
	Cheymol, E. (FRA)	9	2200
f	Chia, A. (SIN)	0	2280
f	Chia, Ch.-S. (SIN)	0	2210
	Chiaudano, A. (USA)	0	2315
g	Chiburdanidze, M. (GM) (GEO)	0	2510
	Chidi, S. (NGR)	0	2005
m	Chilingirova, P. (BUL)	22	2265
	Chin, F. (MAS)	0	2275
f	Chinchilla, E. (CRC)	19	2305
f	Chiong, L. (PHI)	17	2390
	Chipashvili, M. (GEO)	0	2320
	Chipkin, L. (USA)	11	2225
m	Chiricuta Kantor, I. (ROM)	13	2165
	Chiricuta, M. (ROM)	0	2250
f	Chirila, R. (ROM)	2	2330
	Chis, E. (ROM)	0	2035
	Chiu, A. A. (MEX)	0	2225
	Chloupek, S. (TCH)	1	2295
	Chmelikova, M. (TCH)	0	2050
	Chmiel, P. (TCH)	0	2280
	Chmielarz, Z. (POL)	0	2225
	Chojnicki, Z. (POL)	0	2310
	Choleva, Z. (TCH)	0	2240
	Chomet, P. (FRA)	0	2275
	Chomu Clement, M. (KEN)	0	2210
	Chong, D. (SIN)	0	2210
	Choukralla, M. (LEB)	0	2205
f	Chow, A. (USA)	11	2285
f	Chow, R. (USA)	0	2335
	Chrapkowski, G. (POL)	0	2285
	Christ, R. (GER)	0	2240
	Christea, I. H. (ROM)	0	2170
	Christen, P. (SUI)	5	2255
	Christensen, B. G. (DEN)	12	2205
	Christensen, J. (DEN)	0	2240
	Christensen, L. (DEN)	0	2260
	Christensen, T. (DEN)	9	2375
	Christensen, W. (USA)	0	2140
	Christiansen, A. (DEN)	6	2250
	Christiansen, J. J. (DEN)	0	2270
g	Christiansen, L. M. (USA)	33	2555
	Christoffel, U. (GER)	0	2240
	Christopher, S. (ENG)	0	2095
	Chubinsky, P. (USA)	0	2315
m	Chuchelov, V. (RUS)	43	2510
	Chudinovskih, A. (RUS)	5	2310
	Chukhrova, N. (RUS)	0	2075
	Chuprikov, D. (RUS)	0	2365
	Chuprov, A. (RUS)	11	2405
	Chura, J. (TCH)	0	2200
	Churgulia, G. (GEO)	0	2295
	Chydzinski, Z. (POL)	12	2205
	Chytilek, R. (TCH)	0	2265
	Ciampi, V. (ITA)	9	2220
	Cianni, P. (ARG)	9	2310
	Cicak, S. (SWE)	0	2310
	Cichecki, H. (POL)	9	2005
f	Cichocki, A. (POL)	7	2355
	Cicmil, V. (YUG)	0	2215
	Cicovacki, J. (YUG)	0	2025
	Cicvaric, D. (YUG)	0	2280
m	Cid, M. A. (ARG)	23	2410
	Ciechocinska-Miecko, Z. (POL)	0	2055
	Ciechonski, P. (POL)	3	2215
m	Ciemniak, R. (POL)	61	2415
g	Cifuentes Parada, R. (NED)	29	2495
f	Cigan, S. (SLO)	0	2365
	Ciglic, B. (SLO)	4	2215
	Cilia Vincenti, V. (MLT)	0	2215
	Cimra, J. (SVK)	6	2235
	Cioara, A. N. (ROM)	13	2135
	Ciobanu, A. (ROM)	10	2280
m	Ciolac, G. (ROM)	10	2365
	Ciornei, D. (GER)	0	2275
	Cipa, M. (POL)	9	2225
f	Ciprianova-Kubikova, H. (TCH)	0	2165
	Cirabisi, F. (ITA)	8	2270
g	Ciric, D. M. (YUG)	17	2380
	Cirkvencic, F. (SLO)	4	2160
	Ciruk, J. (POL)	0	2235
	Cisneros, L. (ESP)	0	2335
	Ciszek, M. (POL)	0	2260
	Ciuksyte, D. (LTU)	14	2105
f	Ciurezu, M. (ROM)	0	2255
	Civric, Z. (YUG)	0	2235
f	Cizek, A. (TCH)	0	2340
	Claassen, J. (GER)	11	2105
m	Cladouras, P. (GER)	20	2345
	Claesen, P. (BEL)	0	2240
f	Clara, H. (GER)	1	2375
	Clarac, J.-M. (FRA)	10	2230
	Clarke, S. (ENG)	9	2285
	Clarke, Th. (IRL)	10	2225
f	Claus, C. (GER)	0	2135
	Clausen, S. (DEN)	0	2285
	Claussen, U. (GER)	13	2195
	Claverie, Ch. (FRA)	11	2245
	Clavijo, J. (COL)	0	2325
f	Clemance, Ph. A. (NZL)	0	2355
	Clement, J. (ESP)	0	2250
	Clever, G. (GER)	0	2385
f	Cmiel, Th. (GER)	0	2285
	Cnaan, M. (ISR)	5	2235
	Coakley, J. (CAN)	0	2210
	Cobb, Ch. (ENG)	8	2185
	Cobb, J. (ENG)	8	2280
	Cobben, J. M. (NED)	9	2135
	Cobic, V. (YUG)	0	2225
	Cochrane, J. M. (ZIM)	0	2190
f	Cocozza, M. (ITA)	0	2350
	Coenen, Norbert (GER)	0	2280
	Coenen, Norbert (GER)	0	2305
	Cohen, A. (ENG)	18	2190
	Cojocaru, C. (ROM)	15	2330
	Coklin, M. (SLO)	5	2225
	Colas, R. P. (ESP)	13	2305
	Colding, E. (USA)	2	2250
	Coleman, D. (ENG)	7	2260
	Colias, B. (USA)	0	2300
	Collado, J. (ESP)	0	2265
	Collantes, D. (ARG)	0	2205
	Collard, O. (FRA)	0	2240
	Collas, D. (FRA)	6	2260
	Collin, D. (FRA)	0	2265
f	Collinson, A. (ENG)	9	2360
	Colombo, P. (ITA)	11	2200
	Colovic, A. (YUG)	20	2235
	Colovic, D. (YUG)	16	2315
	Colure, Th. S. (USA)	5	2255
m	Comas Fabrego, L. (ESP)	9	2435
	Concepcion, L. (CUB)	0	2280
m	Condie, M. L. (SCO)	0	2455
	Connell, B. (ENG)	17	2230
f	Conover, W. (USA)	0	2310
g	Conquest, S. (ENG)	35	2485
	Constantin, A. (ROM)	0	2115
f	Contin, D. (ITA)	11	2385
	Contini, L. (ITA)	0	2320
	Contreras, H. (COL)	0	2265
	Converset, J. J. (ARG)	9	2335
	Cools, G. (BEL)	0	2275
m	Cooper, J. G. (WLS)	2	2375
f	Cooper, L. (ENG)	14	2310
	Coppini, G. (ITA)	0	2250
	Corbin, Ph. (BAR)	3	2250
	Cordara, M. (ITA)	4	2205
	Cordaro, J. (ISV)	0	2205
	Cordero, A. (ARG)	11	2280
f	Cordes, H.-J. (GER)	4	2320
f	Cording, H. (GER)	0	2310

Title	Name	Games	Rating
f	Cordovil, J. (POR)	9	2330
	Cordy, S. (WLS)	11	2255
	Coret Frasquet, J. (ESP)	5	2300
	Corgnati, M. (ITA)	3	2195
f	Corkett, A. (ENG)	4	2315
	Cornelison, P. (USA)	10	2245
f	Corral Blanco, J. A. (ESP)	0	2395
	Correa, A. A. (BRA)	11	2365
	Correa, J. (CHI)	2	2310
	Corrigan, F. (FRA)	9	2005
	Cortes Caceres, J. (CAN)	0	2030
	Cortes Moyano, J. (CHI)	0	2290
	Cortinas, V. (CUB)	0	2220
m	Cortlever, N. (NED)	0	2390
	Corvi, M. (ITA)	7	2205
	Corzo, A. (CUB)	0	2345
f	Cosic, M. (CRO)	3	2295
m	Cosma, I. (ROM)	46	2400
	Cosovic, M. (YUG)	4	2255
	Cosson, J. (FRA)	0	2195
m	Costa, J. L. (SUI)	0	2425
	Coste, Th. (FRA)	0	2210
	Costello, C. (ENG)	14	2135
	Costescu, M. (ROM)	13	2090
	Costianosky, R. (ARG)	4	2315
m	Costigan, R. (USA)	2	2280
m	Coudari, C. (CAN)	0	2325
	Coupet, P. (FRA)	0	2270
	Couppey, Ph. (FRA)	0	2245
	Courrier, A. (FRA)	9	2200
	Covic, D. (BIH)	0	2365
	Covini, C. A. (ARG)	19	2210
f	Cozianu, C. (ROM)	28	2295
m	Cramling, D. (SWE)	3	2420
g	Cramling, P. (GM) (SWE)	0	2525
f	Cranbourne, C. (ARG)	0	2290
m	Crawley, G. (ENG)	0	2400
	Crea, V. (ITA)	0	2195
	Cremades, J. (CUB)	0	2275
f	Crepan, M. (SLO)	2	2300
f	Crepinsek, Lj. (SLO)	0	2325
	Cretu, A. (ROM)	36	2020
m	Crisan, A. (ROM)	0	2480
	Crisan, I. (ROM)	0	2240
	Cristinacce, D. (ENG)	0	2115
	Cristobal, R. (ARG)	17	2250
	Crocker, M. (ENG)	6	2120
	Crocker, Ph. J. (ENG)	0	2225
	Cronick, S. (WLS)	9	2035
m	Crouch, C. S. (ENG)	29	2415
	Cruz Lopez, C. (ESP)	31	2290
f	Cruz-Lima, J. M. (CUB)	9	2300
	Csaba, A. (HUN)	7	2235
	Csaji, A. (HUN)	0	2220
f	Csala, I. (HUN)	0	2255
f	Csapo, Z. (HUN)	6	2275
	Csato, E. (HUN)	6	2050
	Cseh, A. (HUN)	8	2265
	Cseke, R. (HUN)	21	2260
	Cselotei, I. (HUN)	0	2250
g	Cseshkovsky, V. (RUS)	55	2495
	Csicsay, I. (HUN)	6	2250
	Csikar, B. (HUN)	0	2245
	Csillag, B. (HUN)	0	2310
	Csillik, I. (HUN)	3	2190
	Csiszar, Cs. (HUN)	21	2245
	Csizmadia, L. (HUN)	0	2065
m	Csoke, A. (HUN)	28	2235
	Csoke, K. (HUN)	21	2325
	Csom, E. (HUN)	1	2090
g	Csom, I. (HUN)	36	2475
	Csom, K. (HUN)	0	2070
	Csomos, R. (HUN)	19	2205
g	Csonkics, T. (HUN)	6	2330
f	Csulits, A. (GER)	1	2310
f	Cuadras, J. (ESP)	0	2305
m	Cuartas, C. (COL)	0	2335
	Cubar, V. (YUG)	0	2210
	Cubrilovic, N. (YUG)	0	2240
	Cudnik, A. (POL)	13	2190
f	Cuesta Navarro, S. (CUB)	0	2240
	Cueto, J. (BOL)	0	2170
m	Cuevas-Rodriguez, M. L. (ESP)	0	2240
	Cugini, W. (ITA)	0	2290
m	Cuijpers, F. A. (NED)	16	2425
	Culic, B. (CRO)	0	2220
f	Cullip, S. (ENG)	0	2300
	Cunha, E. A. (BRA)	0	2340
	Cunningham, R. (USA)	1	2330
f	Curdo, J. (USA)	11	2345
	Curien, N. (SUI)	0	2240
	Curione, F. (ITA)	11	2195
	Curtis, J. (AUS)	0	2290
	Cusi, R. (PHI)	0	2340
	Cutter, P. (GCI)	0	2205
m	Cvetkovic, S. (YUG)	38	2510
	Cvijanovic, V. (YUG)	12	2265
g	Cvitan, O. (CRO)	61	2550
f	Cvorovic, D. (CRO)	5	2400
	Cvorovic, M. (YUG)	0	2245
	Cybulak, A. (POL)	5	2300
	Cynolter-Bognarne, E. (HUN)	22	2040
	Czajka, Z. (POL)	1	2205
	Czaplak, T. (POL)	14	2225
	Czapp, J. (HUN)	21	2090
	Czarkowski, D. (POL)	0	2270
	Czarnik, D. (POL)	0	2210
	Czebe, A. (HUN)	38	2350
	Czebe, I. (HUN)	0	2265
	Czech, L. (GER)	1	2250
f	Czegledi, Zs. (HUN)	2	2230
	Czerniawski, M. (POL)	16	2260
	Czernicki, B. (POL)	13	2180
	Czerwonski, A. (POL)	18	2365
	Czibulka, Z. (HUN)	0	2215
	Czubak, M. (GER)	0	2235
	Czuczai, J. (HUN)	9	2240

D

Title	Name	Games	Rating
m	D'Amore, C. (ITA)	6	2415
	D'Apa, S. (ITA)	2	2225
f	D'Arruda, R. D. (ARG)	0	2335
	D'Israel, D. (ARG)	7	2285
	Da Costa, R. L. (BRA)	2	2300
	Dabek, M. (POL)	12	2095
f	Dabek, R. (POL)	7	2360
f	Dabetic, R. (YUG)	25	2325
m	Dabrowska, K. (POL)	15	2240
	Dabrowski, W. (POL)	3	2210
	Dachert, R. (GER)	9	2240
	Dada, B. (NGR)	0	2190
	Dadikina, A. (LAT)	19	2120
	Daemering, K. (GER)	13	2110
	Daeubler, H. (GER)	3	2195
m	Dahl, I. (NOR)	18	2130
	Dahlin, T. (SWE)	0	2295
f	Daillet, E. (FRA)	0	2315
	Dalponte, D. (ITA)	9	2295
	Daly, C. (IRL)	20	2260
f	Dam, R. (NED)	9	2255
	Damasco, R. (ITA)	0	2005
m	Damaso, R. (POR)	17	2425
	Dambrauskas, V. (LTU)	20	2360
	Dambravaite, A. (LTU)	9	2145
	Dambravaite, R. (LTU)	28	2180
	Damjanovic, D. (YUG)	5	2185
g	Damjanovic, M. (CRO)	0	2320
f	Damjanovic, V. (YUG)	35	2380
g	Damljanovic, B. (YUG)	62	2570
	Damm, F. (GER)	1	2220
	Damnjanovic, R. (YUG)	14	2240
m	Danailov, S. (BUL)	17	2440
f	Dancevski, O. (YUG)	32	2340
f	Danek, L. (TCH)	0	2355
	Dang, T. Th. (VIE)	0	2215
	Dang, D. V. (VIE)	0	2205
	Daniae, R. (ROM)	9	2310
f	Danielian, E. (ARM)	16	2205
	Danielian, M. (ARM)	0	2250
	Danielian, O. (ARM)	40	2460
m	Danielsen, H. (DEN)	18	2445
	Daniilidis, A. (GRE)	8	2325
	Daniliuk, S. (RUS)	21	2405
f	Danilov, V. (ROM)	12	2305
f	Danilovic, M. (YUG)	0	2340
f	Dankert, P. (GER)	6	2290
m	Danner, G. (AUT)	41	2385
	Dannevig, O. (NOR)	2	2300
	Danova, T. (BUL)	22	2135
	Danschczyk, Ch. (GER)	8	2305
	Dantas, B. S. (BRA)	2	2275
m	Dao, Th. H. (VIE)	27	2565
	Darakorn, P. (THA)	0	2230
f	Darchia, D. (GEO)	6	2040
f	Darcyl, T. (ARG)	1	2375
g	Darga, K. V. (GER)	0	2455
	Darnstaedt, F. (GER)	12	2360
	Dasaolu, R. (NGR)	9	2140
	Daskalova, M. (BUL)	0	2005
	Daudzvardis, J. (LAT)	9	2295
	Daugela, D. (LTU)	0	2270
	Daumens, M. (FRA)	0	2300
	Daurelle, H. (FRA)	18	2265
g	Dautov, R. (RUS)	0	2625
	Dauvergne, P. (CAN)	0	2270
	Davainis, M. (LTU)	10	2105
	Davcevski, D. (YUG)	11	2285
	Dave, K. (IND)	4	2260
	Daverkausen, B. (GER)	0	2290
f	David, Ad. (GER)	0	2305
f	David, Al. (LUX)	45	2380
	David, Ar. (HUN)	5	2210
	David, E. (NOR)	1	2150
m	David, P. (TCH)	12	2425
	David, V. (ROM)	0	2235
m	Davidovic, A. (AUS)	0	2410
m	Davies, N. R. (ENG)	38	2505
	Davila, C. (NCA)	22	2285
	Davila, E. (NCA)	22	2150
	Davila, J. (PUR)	0	2260
	Davin, P. (USA)	0	2225
	Davydiuk, S. (BLA)	2	2270
	Dawidow, J. (POL)	0	2355
m	Day, L. A. (CAN)	0	2355
m	De Armas, A. (CUB)	0	2150
	De Asa, J. (FIJ)	0	2205
	De Assis Dirceu, V. (BRA)	0	2400
	De Blasio, M. (ITA)	0	2250
m	De Boer, G.-J. (NED)	21	2435
	De Castro, A. (BRA)	0	2360
f	De Dovitiis, A. (ARG)	21	2355
f	De Eccher, S. (ITA)	0	2275
g	De Firmian, N. E. (USA)	18	2545
f	De Fotis, G. S. (USA)	0	2370
	De Francesco, K. (GER)	8	2245
m	De Greef, H. (NED)	16	2180
	De Gregorio, M. (ITA)	9	2070
m	De Guzman, R. (PHI)	0	2385
	De Jager, J. (NED)	0	2215
f	De Jong, T. (NED)	0	2330
f	De Jonghe, P. (BEL)	0	2295
m	De Kleuver, E. (NED)	21	2150
f	De La Cruz Lopez, J. (ESP)	0	2365
	De La Cruz, A. (CUB)	0	2205
	De La Garza, A. (MEX)	10	2230
	De La Paz, F. (CUB)	0	2210
	De La Riva, J. (ESP)	9	2265
	De La Riva, O. (ESP)	9	2400
f	De La Vega, H. (ARG)	0	2365
m	De La Villa Garcia, J. M. (ESP)	30	2440

Title	Name	Games	Rating
	De Las Heras, J. C. (ARG)	23	2335
	De Leon Medina, M. (MEX)	0	2035
	De Leon, A. (ARG)	2	2190
	De Leon, J. (PAN)	13	2145
	De Linde, A. (NOR)	0	2025
	De Needleman, C. (ARG)	0	2005
	De Oliveira, P. S. (BRA)	10	2165
	De Oliveira, R. M. (BRA)	0	2310
	De Prado, O. (ESP)	0	2295
	De San Mateo, F. (FRA)	15	2190
	De Sousa, J. (FRA)	11	2270
	De Souza, M. (BRA)	4	2300
	De Toledo, J. M. (BRA)	14	2290
	De Villiers, Ch. (RSA)	0	2315
	De Vries, E. (NED)	0	2235
m	De Vries, S. (NED)	14	2175
f	De Winter, W. (MEX)	0	2205
	De Wit, D. (NED)	0	2325
f	De Wit, J. S. (NED)	0	2410
f	De Wit, M. (NED)	0	2300
	De Wit, P. (NED)	0	2060
	Deak, L. (HUN)	0	2255
f	Deak, S. (HUN)	31	2330
	Deak, Z. (HUN)	0	2300
	Deantoni, V. (ITA)	0	2005
	Debard, M. (FRA)	7	2255
m	Debarnot, R. (ARG)	4	2360
	Debnar, L. (SVK)	0	2270
	Decroix, R. (FRA)	0	2220
	Dede, E. (HUN)	5	2265
f	Dedes, N. (GRE)	7	2245
m	Deev, A. (RUS)	0	2430
f	Defize, A. (BEL)	0	2295
	Degen, V. (GER)	0	2215
f	Degenhardt, H. (GER)	2	2335
m	Degerman, L. (SWE)	8	2460
m	Degraeve, J.-M. (FRA)	16	2465
f	Dehmelt, K. (USA)	0	2310
	Deich, J. (RUS)	0	2390
	Deiller, P. (FRA)	0	2175
	Dejeanne, F. (ARG)	0	2210
m	Dejkalo, S. (POL)	0	2395
	Dekany, L. (HUN)	0	2230
m	Dekar, L. (ALG)	8	2250
	Deker, G. (ARG)	9	2200
m	Dekic, B. N. (AUS)	12	2145
	Dekic, J. (YUG)	4	2260
	Dekker, A. (NED)	2	2205
	Dekker, Th. (NED)	2	2240
	Dekusar, M. (UKR)	0	2100
f	Del Castillo, G. (ARG)	2	2310
	Del Prado, C. (ESP)	0	2345
f	Del Rey, D. (ARG)	35	2400
	Del Rio, R. (GER)	5	2230
	Del Rio, S. G. (ESP)	0	2255
f	Delaney, J. (IRL)	0	2265
	Delanoy, A. (FRA)	18	2150
f	Delaune, R. K. (USA)	14	2390
	Delay, F. (SUI)	5	2275
m	Delchev, A. (BUL)	7	2480
	Delebarre, X. (FRA)	6	2265
	Delega, T. (POL)	9	2090
	Delekta, P. (POL)	0	2305
f	Deleyn, G. (BEL)	0	2320
	Delgado Cespedes, I. (CUB)	0	2270
	Delgado, E. (ESP)	0	2375
	Delgado, M. (CUB)	0	2095
	Delgado, V. (USA)	0	2370
	Delibasic, G. (YUG)	0	2230
	Delithanasis, D. (GRE)	1	2215
	Delitzsch, J. (GER)	0	2255
	Delmont, J. R. (FRA)	5	2165
	Delnef, A. (GER)	0	2235
	Delveborn, I. (SWE)	0	2240
m	Dely, P. (HUN)	11	2405
	Demarre, J. (FRA)	7	2265
	Demeny, A. (HUN)	0	2200
	Demeny, M.-N. (ROM)	16	2270
f	Demeter, I. (HUN)	3	2270
	Demeter, P. (SVK)	4	2325
	Demian, V. (ROM)	0	2230
	Demin, G. Y. (RUS)	0	2265
g	Demina, J. (RUS)	0	2365
	Demir, G. (TUR)	35	2165
	Demirel, T. (TUR)	0	2310
f	Den Boer, B. (NED)	0	2335
	Den Broeder, G. (NED)	0	2290
f	Dena, B. (CRO)	0	2260
m	Deng, Kongliang (CHN)	0	2430
	Dengel, J. (GER)	0	2115
	Dengler, P. (GER)	0	2330
f	Denijs, A. (BEL)	0	2285
	Denis, L. (FRA)	3	2245
	Denk, A. (AUT)	0	2265
g	Denker, A. S. (USA)	0	2275
f	Denny, K. (BAR)	8	2240
	Denoth, M. (SUI)	0	2260
	Denoyelle, A. (FRA)	1	2200
f	Depasquale, Ch. (AUS)	0	2270
	Depyl, P. (FRA)	0	2205
	Derera, M. (HUN)	0	2035
	Dereviagin, V. (RUS)	11	2305
f	Derikum, A. (GER)	5	2290
f	Derlich, K. (GER)	2	2130
	Derlukiewicz, J. (POL)	7	2235
f	Dermann, G. (GER)	9	2315
	Derrieux, Ch. (FRA)	12	2220
m	Desancic, M. (SUI)	0	2450
	Desbones, S. (FRA)	3	2265
	Deshmukh, A. (IND)	6	2265
	Desmoitier, J.-B. (FRA)	0	2245
m	Despotovic, M. (YUG)	0	2325
	Dessau, A. (FRA)	0	2230
	Deszczynski, A. (POL)	10	2235
	Detko, J. (POL)	0	2095
	Deumie, Ph. (FRA)	0	2045
	Deutsch, L. (AUT)	16	2220
	Devangshu, D. (IND)	10	2235
	Devcic, M. (ARG)	11	2300
	Devide, Z. (CRO)	0	2245
	Dextre, E. (FRA)	15	2195
	Dezan, P. (FRA)	12	2260
	Deze, V. (YUG)	5	2210
f	Dezelin, M. (YUG)	7	2335
	Dgebuadze, A. (GEO)	0	2400
	Dhar, S. (IND)	0	2050
	Di Donna, M. (ITA)	9	2235
	Di Paolo, R. (ITA)	8	2195
	Diaz Perez, J. D. (CUB)	0	2265
	Diaz, A. (CUB)	0	2285
	Diaz, Dag. (CUB)	0	2275
	Diaz, Dan. (URU)	9	2050
	Diaz, Ja. (COL)	0	2275
m	Diaz, Jo. C. (CUB)	13	2440
	Diaz, N. (ARG)	0	2180
	Diaz, R. (COL)	0	2370
	Dichev, N. (BUL)	6	2225
	Diek, H. (GER)	0	2270
	Dienavorian, M. (URU)	0	2280
f	Diesen, B. (NOR)	0	2275
	Dietrich, R. (GER)	11	2280
	Dietz, H. (GER)	1	2260
f	Dietz, J. (GER)	0	2320
	Dietze, F. (GER)	0	2225
f	Dietze, W. (GER)	2	2285
	Dietzsch, H. (GER)	0	2210
	Dieu, B. (FRA)	0	2330
	Dilip, P. (IND)	6	2240
	Dilley, J. (ENG)	0	2205
	Dimitar, P. (BUL)	0	2260
	Dimitriadi, A. (GRE)	0	2030
f	Dimitriadis, G. (GRE)	0	2305
f	Dimitriadis, K. (GRE)	2	2315
f	Dimitrijevic, D. (CRO)	0	2285
	Dimitrijevic, M. (YUG)	0	2325
m	Dimitrijevic, V. (USA)	2	2085
	Dimitrov, A. (BUL)	0	2290
	Dimitrov, I. L. (BUL)	0	2375
	Dimitrov, K. (BUL)	1	2210
	Dimitrov, Pe. (BUL)	0	2270
	Dimitrov, Pl. (BUL)	0	2255
g	Dimitrov, V. (BUL)	29	2525
	Dimitrova, L. (BUL)	26	2150
	Dimitrova, V. (BUL)	0	2095
	Dimov, D. (BUL)	8	2260
	Dimov, K. (BUL)	5	2310
m	Dimovski, N. (YUG)	13	2415
	Dinescu, A. (ROM)	11	2215
	Dinic, C. (CRO)	0	2225
f	Dinic, D. (YUG)	15	2250
	Dinis de Sousa, J. (POR)	0	2270
	Diniz, E. P. (BRA)	0	2270
	Dinov, Z. (YUG)	14	2290
f	Dinstuhl, V. (GER)	15	2365
	Dinu, G. (ROM)	3	2280
	Diozu, M. (MOL)	17	2065
	Dipanjan, D. (IND)	10	2170
	Dircks, J. (SWE)	9	2195
	Dirr, U. (GER)	19	2270
f	Dischinger, F. (GER)	11	2305
	Disconzi da Silva, R. (BRA)	25	2340
	Dishman, S. (ENG)	0	2310
	Disntuhl, B. (GER)	0	2335
f	Ditt, E. (GER)	6	2275
f	Dittmar, P. (GER)	16	2270
	Ditzler, J. (SUI)	2	2235
f	Dive, R. J. (NZL)	11	2315
	Divis, J. (TCH)	0	2265
g	Dizdar, G. (CRO)	34	2495
f	Dizdar, S. (BIH)	0	2330
g	Dizdarevic, E. (BIH)	25	2540
	Djafarov, M. (AZE)	12	2115
f	Djantar, Dj. (YUG)	0	2250
	Djeno, D. (BIH)	6	2205
	Djeno, M. (BIH)	21	2160
	Djerfi, K. (YUG)	4	2260
	Djexembinov, S. (RUS)	0	2140
	Djingarova, E. (BUL)	13	2050
	Djipa, N. (BIH)	0	2295
	Djokic, Neb. (YUG)	0	2265
f	Djokic, Nen. (YUG)	0	2295
	Djonev, S. (BUL)	0	2205
	Djordjevic, De. (YUG)	13	2255
	Djordjevic, Dr. (YUG)	3	2285
	Djordjevic, N. (YUG)	6	2225
f	Djoric, D. (YUG)	3	2350
	Djoric, G. (YUG)	0	2230
f	Djosic, S. (YUG)	5	2270
	Djubek, B. (SVK)	0	2280
	Djukic, M. (YUG)	0	2235
m	Djukic, Z. (YUG)	39	2370
	Djuran, N. (YUG)	0	2245
	Djurdjevic, P. M. (YUG)	0	2215
m	Djurhuus, R. (NOR)	18	2460
	Djuric, P. (YUG)	0	2170
g	Djuric, S. (YUG)	35	2495
	Djuric, V. (YUG)	0	2310
	Djuric, Zi. (YUG)	0	2235
	Djuric, Zo. (YUG)	11	2175
	Djurkovic, M. (YUG)	10	2120
f	Djurovic, D. (YUG)	0	2305
	Djurovic, S. (YUG)	0	2345
	Dlaykan, F. (COL)	0	2215
g	Dlugy, M. (USA)	12	2550
	Dluzniewski, M. (POL)	0	2225
	Dmitriev, I. (RUS)	34	2405
	Dobes, L. (TCH)	0	2145
m	Dobos, J. (HUN)	30	2350
f	Dobos, O. (HUN)	16	2050
m	Dobosz, H. (POL)	19	2430
	Dobosz, J. (POL)	9	2220

	Name		
	Dobrev, I. (BUL)	11	2345
m	Dobrev, N. (BUL)	24	2335
	Dobronauteanu, E. (ROM)	11	2220
	Dobronauteanu, I.-S. (ROM)	11	2265
	Dobrotka, M. (SVK)	0	2205
	Dobrowolski, P. (POL)	8	2240
m	Dobrowolsky, L. (TCH)	19	2390
f	Dobrzynski, W. (POL)	0	2275
	Dobson Aguilar, L. F. (CHI)	7	2220
	Dochev, D. (BUL)	14	2295
	Docx, S. (BEL)	0	2215
m	Doda, Z. (POL)	0	2345
f	Dodu, P. (ROM)	7	2290
	Doeres, H. J. (GER)	9	2240
	Doering, Th. (GER)	13	2225
m	Doery, J. (HUN)	10	2320
	Dogantug, I. (TUR)	0	2225
	Doghri, N. (TUN)	19	2320
	Dohr, A. (AUT)	12	2140
g	Dokhoian, Y. (RUS)	32	2550
	Dokuchaev, A. (RUS)	4	2400
f	Doleschall, Gy. (HUN)	0	2260
	Dolezal, C. (ARG)	5	2240
f	Dolezal, M. (TCH)	0	2275
	Dolezal, R. (TCH)	1	2260
	Dolgener, T. (GER)	25	2235
f	Dolgitser, K. (USA)	0	2260
f	Doljanin, T. (YUG)	3	2245
	Dolmadjan, A. (BUL)	0	2360
g	Dolmatov, S. (RUS)	52	2630
f	Dolovic, D. (YUG)	0	2300
	Domarkaite, L. (LTU)	9	2135
	Domazet, V. (YUG)	0	2215
	Domingo, M. (FRA)	0	2130
	Dominguez Rueda, J. (ESP)	0	2290
	Dominguez Sanz, J. P. (ESP)	0	2260
	Dominguez, H. (CHI)	9	2380
	Dominguez, R. (CUB)	0	2205
	Dominiguez, J. M. (DOM)	0	2265
f	Dominte, M. (ROM)	0	2350
	Dommes, V. M. (RUS)	3	2310
	Domnitz, Z. (ISR)	0	2275
f	Domont, A. (SUI)	6	2340
	Domosud, M. (POL)	0	2255
	Domuta, A. (ROM)	2	2050
m	Donaldson, J. W. (USA)	14	2425
g	Donaldson-Akhmilovskaya, E. (USA)	0	2405
	Donatti, A. (URU)	0	2265
m	Doncevic, D. (GER)	5	2370
	Donchenko, A. G. (RUS)	38	2410
	Donchenko, I. (RUS)	0	2110
g	Donchev, D. I. (BUL)	5	2485
	Doncheva, M. (BUL)	22	2095
m	Donev, I. H. (BUL)	4	2410
	Dongre, R. M. (IND)	11	2220
	Donguines, F. (PHI)	0	2380
	Doniec, A. (POL)	8	2195
f	Donka, P. (HUN)	21	2205
	Donnelly, R. A. (USA)	0	2030
	Donovan, N. (ENG)	9	2155
	Doornbos, Y. (FRA)	11	2260
	Dorenberg, G. (NED)	9	2345
g	Dorfman, J. D. (FRA)	39	2555
	Doric, N. (CRO)	3	2285
	Dorin, M. (ARG)	5	2300
	Dormann, L. (GER)	0	2290
f	Dorner, M. (GER)	0	2305
	Dornieden, M. (GER)	0	2265
f	Doroftei, N. (ROM)	11	2270
	Doroscenko, M. (MOL)	11	2310
	Doroshkievich, V. K. (RUS)	49	2405
	Dors, R. (POL)	0	2210
	Dorsch, Th. (USA)	19	2155
	Dos Santos, F. R. (ARG)	13	2325
	Dos Santos, H. C. (BRA)	0	2240
	Dos Santos, R. (ARG)	10	2340
	Dostan, J. (YUG)	5	2255
	Dostanic, M. (YUG)	0	2235
	Dotta, J. C. (ARG)	6	2235
m	Douven, R. C. (NED)	9	2405
	Dovat, S. (YUG)	0	2340
	Dovramadjiev, T. (BUL)	0	2270
	Dovramadjieva, H. (BUL)	0	2020
m	Dovzik, J. (UKR)	36	2370
	Down, N. (ENG)	0	2230
	Dozenko, V. (RUS)	10	2225
	Drabiniok, K. (POL)	5	2240
f	Draganov, R. (RUS)	0	2205
	Dragasevic, D. (YUG)	0	2295
m	Dragasevic-Georgieva, A. (YUG)	0	2205
	Dragiev, V. (BUL)	9	2280
	Dragiska, I. (BUL)	14	2035
m	Dragojlovic, A. (YUG)	5	2375
	Dragolov, T. (BUL)	0	2260
m	Dragomarezkij, E. (RUS)	65	2535
f	Dragomirescu, C. (ROM)	0	2230
	Dragonic, S. (CRO)	0	2285
	Dragos, D. (ROM)	0	2245
f	Dragovic, M. (YUG)	5	2410
	Drakeford, D. (IRL)	0	2185
	Dranov, A. (UKR)	8	2345
g	Drasko, M. (YUG)	67	2520
	Draskoczy, P. (HUN)	0	2235
	Draskovic, D. (YUG)	12	2265
m	Drazic, S. (YUG)	25	2400
	Drcelic, J. (CRO)	0	2330
	Drcelic, S. (YUG)	3	2245
g	Dreev, A. (RUS)	39	2570
	Drei, A. (ITA)	12	2255
	Drenchev, P. (BUL)	5	2205
f	Dresen, U. (GER)	0	2270
f	Drewes, M. (NED)	0	2100
f	Dreyer, Ma. (NZL)	0	2345
	Dreyer, Mi. (GER)	5	2220
	Dridi, A. (TUN)	0	2225
	Drill, F. (GER)	1	2200
m	Drimer, D. (ROM)	0	2345
f	Drlic, M. (CRO)	0	2315
	Droulers, D. (FRA)	0	2225
f	Drozd, R. (POL)	0	2230
	Drozdov, I. (UKR)	55	2445
	Drtina, M. (SVK)	0	2260
	Druckenthaner, A. (AUT)	9	2285
	Druon, R. (FRA)	3	2220
	Drygalski, W. (POL)	0	2265
	Drzemicki, D. (POL)	5	2300
	Du Chattel, Ph. J. (NED)	0	2260
	Du, Fengling (CHN)	0	2130
f	Duarte, M. R. (CHI)	3	2405
	Dubeck, L. (USA)	0	2335
	Dubeck, M. (GER)	4	2320
	Dubiel, J. (POL)	29	2285
	Dubinka, I. (UKR)	0	2140
f	Dubisch, R. (USA)	0	2300
f	Dubois, J.-M. (FRA)	9	2285
m	Dubois, M. (FRA)	12	2080
	Dubreuil, N. (FRA)	5	2240
	Duch, M. (POL)	0	2275
	Duchov, A. (RUS)	3	2460
f	Duckworth, M. (USA)	0	2310
	Duckworth, W. (USA)	13	2350
	Duda, A. (POL)	0	2240
	Dudakov, Sh. (ISR)	0	2230
	Dudas, I. (HUN)	0	2210
	Dudas, Jan (SVK)	0	2290
f	Dudas, Jano (HUN)	0	2305
	Dudek, A. (POL)	0	2215
	Dudek, R. (POL)	6	2280
m	Dueball, J. (GER)	8	2400
m	Dueckstein, A. (AUT)	12	2375
m	Duer, A. (AUT)	17	2415
	Duer, W. (AUT)	4	2300
	Dugandzic, B. (CRO)	0	2345
	Dugonjic, D. (YUG)	0	2310
	Duhayon, Y. (BEL)	0	2210
	Dujkovic, S. (YUG)	0	2315
m	Dukaczewski, P. (POL)	6	2215
	Duketic, N. (YUG)	0	2225
	Dulinski, J. (POL)	0	2240
f	Duminica, M. (ROM)	0	2130
m	Dumitrache, D. (ROM)	71	2425
	Dumitrache, S. (ROM)	11	2250
	Dumitrescu, D. (ROM)	17	2365
	Dumitrescu, V. (ROM)	0	2235
	Dumitriu, P. (ROM)	6	2240
f	Dumont, S. G. (BRA)	0	2340
f	Dumpor, A. (YUG)	0	2295
	Duncan, Ch. R. (ENG)	18	2280
	Dunn, A. (ENG)	5	2230
	Dunne, A. (USA)	0	2245
f	Dunne, D. J. (IRL)	0	2335
m	Dunnington, A. J. (ENG)	42	2415
f	Dunworth, Ch. (ENG)	15	2245
	Duong, Th. N. (CAN)	0	2335
	Dupsky, L. (HUN)	16	2235
m	Durao, J. (POR)	7	2215
	Durao, P. (POR)	0	2140
f	Durham, Da. (USA)	0	2240
	Durham, Di. G. (USA)	0	2025
	Duriga, S. (SVK)	0	2255
f	Dusper, H. (CRO)	0	2275
f	Dussol, P. (FRA)	7	2275
	Dusterwald, M. (GER)	0	2250
f	Dutreeuw, M. (BEL)	10	2455
	Dutschak, H. (GER)	8	2320
	Dutton, I. R. (ENG)	0	2215
g	Dvoirys, S. I. (RUS)	44	2590
m	Dvorietzky, M. I. (RUS)	0	2475
	Dworakowska, J. (POL)	32	2180
	Dworakowski, L. (POL)	22	2365
	Dyballa, M. (GER)	3	2320
f	Dybowski, J. (POL)	0	2360
m	Dydyshko, V. (BLA)	25	2525
	Dymerski, H. (POL)	7	2280
	Dzenic, D. (YUG)	0	2330
	Dzera, V. (CAN)	0	2220
m	Dzevlan, M. (YUG)	1	2395
	Dzhumaev, M. (UZB)	15	2385
	Dziadykiewicz, T. (POL)	13	2100
f	Dzieniszewski, A. (POL)	0	2350
	Dzierzak, B. (POL)	0	2230
g	Dzindzichashvili, R. (USA)	21	2535
	Dzuban, O. I. (KAZ)	26	2435

E

	Name		
	Eade, J. (USA)	18	2310
	Ebalard, M. (FRA)	0	2260
f	Ebeling, M. (FIN)	16	2375
	Ebenfelt, A. (SWE)	0	2305
	Eberle, J. (NED)	0	2215
f	Eberlein, W. (GER)	0	2260
	Ebner, H. (AUT)	6	2225
	Ebner, W. (AUT)	10	2245
	Echevarria, R. (CUB)	0	2235
f	Eckert, D. D. (USA)	0	2290
	Eckhardt, C. (GER)	9	2265
m	Edelman, D. (USA)	21	2415
	Edwards, P. (ENG)	0	2270
	Edzgveradze, N. (GEO)	12	2185
f	Effert, K. (GER)	0	2275
g	Efimov, I. (GEO)	13	2490
	Efler, D. (TCH)	0	2305
	Efler, L. (TCH)	0	2255
	Efstathiou, D. (GRE)	13	2195
	Efthimiatos, G. (GRE)	11	2215
f	Efthimiou, E. (GRE)	5	2255

Title	Name	Games	Rating
	Egartner, W. (AUT)	2	2215
f	Egedi, I. (HUN)	0	2290
m	Egerland, E. (HUN)	0	2265
f	Egger, J. (CHI)	31	2460
	Egger, Th. (GER)	0	2285
	Egiazarjan, A. (RUS)	0	2395
	Egiazaryan, N. (RUS)	0	2170
	Egin, V. (UZB)	0	2395
f	Eglezos, H. (GRE)	9	2250
	Egoroff, J. (BRA)	0	2280
	Egozi, N. (ISR)	4	2205
	Egri, L. (HUN)	15	2275
	Egyed, A. (HUN)	10	2235
	Ehab, M. A. (EGY)	15	2190
g	Ehlvest, J. (EST)	34	2620
f	Ehrenfeucht, W. (POL)	21	2350
m	Ehrke, A. D. (GER)	9	2200
	Ehrke, M. (GER)	11	2240
	Ehrler, E. (GER)	0	2210
	Eichner, A. (GER)	1	2010
m	Eidelson, R. (BLA)	70	2250
	Eilers, S. (GER)	0	2265
	Eilertsen, J. B. (NOR)	0	2240
	Einarsson, A. (ISD)	9	2265
f	Einarsson, H. (ISD)	0	2320
	Einersen, E. (DEN)	0	2240
g	Eingorn, V. S. (UKR)	24	2580
	Eisenbeis, N. (GER)	0	2240
f	Eising, J. (GER)	4	2310
	Eismont, O. (RUS)	23	2440
f	Eisterer, H. (AUT)	0	2355
	Ekic, O. (YUG)	0	2285
f	Eklund, L.-G. (SWE)	0	2300
	Eklund, M. (SWE)	0	2235
m	Ekstrom, R. (SUI)	0	2420
	El Arga, H. (SYR)	0	2205
m	El Arousy, A. H. (EGY)	0	2320
m	El Assiouti, Sh. (EGY)	1	2325
m	El Ghazali, Y. M. (EGY)	15	2345
m	El Taher, F. (EGY)	25	2415
	El-Mezwaghi, H. (LBA)	0	2205
f	Elbilia, J. (MAR)	26	2295
	Elenkova, L. (BUL)	5	2020
	Elgaard, B. (DEN)	9	2265
f	Elguezabal Varela, D. (ARG)	0	2300
	Eliet, N. (FRA)	14	2295
	Eliet, R. (FRA)	0	2225
	Elinson, E. (ISR)	0	2185
	Elizakov, A. (RUS)	0	2315
f	Elizart Cardenas, H. (CUB)	0	2305
	Eljanov, V. (UKR)	0	2350
	Elkuch, H. (LIE)	0	2205
	Ellenbroek, T. (NED)	11	2125
	Ellers, H. (GER)	21	2225
	Ellinger, H. (GER)	0	2300
	Elmquist, R. D. (USA)	0	2210
	Elsen, M. (GER)	0	2230
f	Elseth, R. (NOR)	0	2340
	Elsness, F. (NOR)	12	2300
	Elstner, H. (GER)	11	2235
	Elter, J. (HUN)	0	2285
	Elters, A. (URU)	0	2235
f	Elyoseph, H. (ISR)	0	2325
	Emelin, V. (RUS)	0	2345
	Emeljanov, A. (RUS)	0	2280
m	Emma, J. (ARG)	0	2405
m	Emms, J. M. (ENG)	40	2455
	Emodi, B. (HUN)	20	2260
f	Emodi, Gy. (HUN)	19	2345
	Emunds, H. G. (GER)	0	2275
	Enders, P. (GER)	10	2480
m	Eng, H. (GER)	4	2350
	Engedal, K. N. (NOR)	11	2240
	Engel, B. (GER)	15	2290
	Engel, M. (GER)	0	2255
	Engelbert, Ch. (GER)	0	2270
m	Engqvist, Th. (SWE)	12	2420
	Engsner, J. (SWE)	2	2240
	Engsner, N. (SWE)	13	2100
	Engstrom, K. (SWE)	0	2255
m	Eperjesi, L. (HUN)	33	2315
g	Epishin, V. (RUS)	64	2655
f	Eppinger, G. (GER)	1	2290
m	Epstein, E. (USA)	0	2255
m	Erdelyi, T. (HUN)	41	2350
m	Erdeus, G. (ROM)	21	2325
	Erdodi, G. (ROM)	18	2165
	Erdogan, H. (TUR)	0	2335
	Eremina, N. (LAT)	0	2050
g	Erenska-Radzewska, H. (POL)	22	2210
	Erenski, P. (POL)	0	2265
g	Eretova, K. (TCH)	11	2090
	Erikalov, A. (RUS)	0	2275
f	Eriksson, A. (SWE)	9	2355
	Eriksson, B. (SWE)	0	2335
	Eriksson, I. S. (SWE)	3	2075
	Eriksson, Joh. (SWE)	7	2305
	Eriksson, Jor. (SWE)	9	2195
	Eriksson, Mag. (SWE)	0	2365
	Eriksson, Mat. (SWE)	0	2225
	Erker, E. (GER)	0	2220
	Erlandsen, C. (DEN)	9	2225
	Ermeni, A. (YUG)	0	2230
g	Ermenkov, E. (BUL)	22	2495
g	Erneste, I. (LAT)	32	2325
f	Ernst, R. (GER)	3	2280
g	Ernst, Th. (SWE)	26	2480
	Ersek, E. (HUN)	0	2250
	Erskine, J. (USA)	0	2300
f	Ervin, R. C. (USA)	0	2395
	Esam, A. N. (EGY)	12	2305
f	Escandell, J. C. (ARG)	5	2290
	Escandon, F. (URU)	0	2120
	Escobar Forero, A. (COL)	0	2215
	Escobar, T. (ARG)	20	2260
	Escobedo Tinajero, A. (MEX)	10	2265
	Escofet, J. (URU)	9	2240
f	Escondrillas, C. (MEX)	0	2305
m	Eslon, J. (SWE)	38	2440
	Esmaeil, S. (IRI)	0	2205
f	Espig, G. (GER)	4	2135
g	Espig, L. (GER)	15	2455
	Espig, Th. (GER)	0	2310
	Espini, M. (CUB)	0	2240
f	Espinosa, J. (CUB)	12	2370
m	Espinoza, R. (MEX)	10	2460
	Essam, A. A. (EGY)	15	2320
m	Estevez, G. (CUB)	22	2335
	Estimo, N. (PHI)	0	2205
	Estival, A. (FRA)	11	2270
	Estrada, N. J. (MEX)	10	2230
	Estrella, J. (ESP)	0	2315
f	Estremera Panos, S. (ESP)	12	2365
f	Etchegaray, P. (FRA)	33	2410
	Etcheguia, T. (ARG)	9	2295
f	Etmans, M. D. (NED)	0	2230
	Etokowo, I. (NGR)	0	2005
	Euler, G. (GER)	3	2330
g	Evans, L. M. (USA)	0	2470
	Ezsol, M. (HUN)	11	2305

F

Title	Name	Games	Rating
	Fabbri, M. (ITA)	3	2215
	Fabiano, G. (ITA)	2	2245
	Fabisch, Ch. (AUT)	19	2325
	Fabre, M. (ESP)	0	2290
	Fabrega, E. (PAN)	10	2310
	Fabri, F. (HUN)	0	2265
	Fabris, A. (ITA)	0	2205
	Fabrowski, J. (POL)	0	2285
	Fadi, E. (LEB)	0	2205
f	Fahnenschmidt, G. (GER)	15	2395
	Fahrner, K. (AUT)	13	2290
	Faibisovich, V. Z. (RUS)	11	2445
	Fairclough, N. (JAM)	0	2210
	Fajdetic, H. (CRO)	1	2235
	Fakhirova, E. (GEO)	0	2080
	Falchetta, G. (ITA)	0	2210
	Faldt, M. (SWE)	12	2185
	Falk, U. (GER)	1	2225
m	Fancsy, I. (HUN)	40	2400
f	Fandino, R. (CUB)	0	2050
	Fang, Ch. (USA)	0	2220
f	Fang, J. (USA)	10	2385
g	Farago, I. (HUN)	60	2540
m	Farago, S. (HUN)	61	2375
	Farah, R. (ARG)	19	2245
	Faraoni, E. (ITA)	13	2150
	Fares, A.-G. (KUW)	0	2280
	Faria, P. R. M. (BRA)	3	2395
	Farias, L. (CHI)	11	2155
	Farias, S. A. (BRA)	0	2220
f	Farkas, Gy. (HUN)	10	2205
f	Farkas, J. (HUN)	0	2275
	Farkas, S. (HUN)	0	2225
	Farkas, Ti. (HUN)	40	2240
	Farkas, Tu. (HUN)	0	2050
	Farkas, Zs. (HUN)	13	2155
	Farkhutdinov, I. (RUS)	0	2240
	Farrel, N. R. (SCO)	5	2145
	Fasnacht, P. (GER)	0	2315
	Fassl, E. (AUT)	0	2245
g	Fatalibekova, E. (RUS)	11	2235
m	Fatin, T. (EGY)	0	2385
m	Fauland, A. (AUT)	19	2435
	Fauvel, Ph. (FRA)	4	2310
	Favaro, E. F. (BRA)	0	2295
	Fayard, A. (FRA)	0	2250
	Fecht, H.-P. (GER)	0	2240
m	Fedder, S. (DEN)	0	2380
f	Federau, J. M. (GER)	10	2305
	Federl, A. R. (USA)	0	2225
m	Fedorov, A. (BLA)	41	2490
m	Fedorov, V. (RUS)	18	2440
g	Fedorowicz, J. P. (USA)	61	2545
	Fedotov, A. (RUS)	0	2325
	Fedukin, A. (RUS)	9	2245
	Feher, A. (HUN)	3	2285
m	Feher, Gy. (HUN)	30	2380
	Feher, J. (HUN)	0	2240
	Fehling, M. (GER)	0	2260
	Feibert, F. (GER)	0	2335
f	Feick, S. (GER)	7	2230
	Feiff, T. (SWE)	3	2195
	Feigelson, J. (RUS)	0	2355
	Feistenauer, F. (AUT)	0	2300
	Fejzulahu, A. (YUG)	5	2285
	Fekete, A. (HUN)	0	2270
	Felber, J. J. (USA)	11	2180
	Feld, P. (TCH)	0	2390
	Feldman, A. (USA)	0	2210
	Feldman, S. (USA)	9	2275
	Feldmann, V. (AUS)	5	2315
f	Felegyhazi, L. (HUN)	9	2290
	Feletar, D. (CRO)	4	2300
	Felix, V. (TCH)	0	2255
	Felkai, A. (HUN)	0	2310
	Feller, J. (LUX)	12	2230
	Felmeri, J. (HUN)	0	2275
f	Felsberger, A. (AUT)	6	2360
	Feofanoviene, R. (LTU)	0	2040
f	Fercec, N. (CRO)	17	2380
	Ferenc, J. (POL)	0	2250
	Ferguson, M. (ENG)	3	2195
	Fernandes, Al. (POR)	0	2220
m	Fernandes, An. (POR)	17	2460
f	Fernandez Aguado, E. (ESP)	0	2360
	Fernandez Balague, L. (ARG)	9	2240

	Name	Games	Rating
	Fernandez Fernandez, A. (ESP)	0	2305
g	Fernandez Garcia, J. L. (ESP)	23	2445
	Fernandez L, F. (ESP)	1	2335
	Fernandez Lopez, J. (ESP)	0	2260
	Fernandez Murga, R. (ARG)	7	2245
m	Fernandez, A. (VEN)	11	2365
m	Fernandez, C. A. (CUB)	0	2290
	Fernandez, G. (CUB)	0	2260
	Fernandez, H. (ARG)	14	2225
	Fernandez, I. (ARG)	0	2260
	Fernandez, Jorge (ARG)	3	2240
	Fernandez, Jose (ARG)	3	2160
m	Fernandez, Juan C. (CUB)	0	2395
	Fernandez, Juan L. (ESP)	0	2285
	Fernandez, M. (ESP)	0	2280
	Fernandez, R. A. (BRA)	3	2355
	Ferraez, J. (MEX)	0	2230
f	Ferreira, A. (POR)	9	2335
m	Ferreira, N. (ANG)	0	2275
f	Ferreira, O. (PAR)	4	2295
	Ferrer, M. (ESP)	0	2270
m	Ferrer-Lucas, P. (ESP)	0	2120
	Ferrera, B. (MEX)	10	2225
	Ferretti, F. (ITA)	14	2295
f	Ferris, D. (AUS)	0	2325
	Ferron, C. (ESP)	7	2345
	Ferry, R. (FRA)	0	2225
	Fery, Ch. (FRA)	0	2260
f	Fette, M. (GER)	45	2330
	Feuerstein, A. (USA)	0	2235
f	Feustel, B. (GER)	6	2300
m	Feustel, P. (GER)	0	2250
	Fiala, J. (SVK)	0	2255
	Ficco, C. (ITA)	12	2195
m	Fichtl, J. (TCH)	0	2220
	Fico, M. (ITA)	0	2300
	Fieandt, J. (FIN)	0	2275
	Fiedler, T. (GER)	0	2330
	Fielding, P. (USA)	0	2250
	Fields, P. H. (USA)	0	2260
	Fievet, P. (FRA)	0	2265
	Figari, E. (PAR)	0	2015
	Figiel, M. (POL)	0	2360
	Filatov, M. (RUS)	14	2295
f	Filep, T. (HUN)	0	2240
	Filgueira, H. (ARG)	10	2290
m	Filguth, R. A. (BRA)	0	2410
	Filhol, L. (FRA)	0	2170
	Filichkina, S. (RUS)	0	2040
	Filip, H. (ROM)	0	2220
g	Filip, M. (TCH)	0	2465
	Filipenko, A. V. (RUS)	30	2435
	Filipovic, Bi. (YUG)	0	2125
m	Filipovic, Br. (YUG)	19	2400
	Filipovic, I. (YUG)	0	2015
	Filipovich, D. (CAN)	0	2215
m	Filipowicz, A. (POL)	0	2340
	Filippov, V. (RUS)	0	2400
f	Findlay, I. T. (CAN)	0	2335
m	Finegold, B. (USA)	25	2490
m	Finegold, G. L. (USA)	0	2115
f	Fink, P. (GER)	8	2095
	Fink, S. (USA)	1	2245
	Finkel, A. (ISR)	26	2370
	Finkenzeller, A. (GER)	0	2255
	Finn, S. (ENG)	0	2315
	Finnlaugsson, G. (SWE)	0	2210
f	Fioramonti, H. (SUI)	13	2385
	Fiore, M. (ITA)	0	2280
m	Fiorito, F. (ARG)	28	2435
	Fiorucci, M. (ARG)	2	2220
f	Firt, S. (TCH)	0	2380
m	Fischdick, G. (GER)	16	2290
f	Fischer, I. (GER)	0	2340
	Fischer, Johann (AUT)	3	2305
f	Fischer, Johanne (GER)	0	2340
	Fischer, Mark. (GER)	0	2290
	Fischer, Mart. (GER)	9	2260
	Fischer, S. (GER)	14	2215
	Fischer, Th. (GER)	0	2270
	Fischler, W. (AUT)	0	2370
	Fisekovic, M. (YUG)	0	2325
	Fish, G. (RUS)	9	2440
g	Fishbein, A. (USA)	15	2510
	Fising, R. (GER)	0	2235
	Fixter, N. (SCO)	0	2005
f	Flatow, A. (AUS)	0	2235
m	Flear, Ch. (FRA)	19	2170
g	Flear, G. C. (ENG)	27	2500
f	Fleck, J. (GER)	0	2380
	Fleger, H. (GER)	0	2260
	Fleischer, P. (GER)	0	2225
	Fleish, F. (ISR)	13	2280
	Fleuch, H.-J. (GER)	16	2155
f	Flis, J. (POL)	7	2340
	Flogel, U. (GER)	0	2275
	Florean, A. (ROM)	15	2155
	Floreen, D. (USA)	5	2310
	Flores, M. (NCA)	13	2130
	Flores, P. (CHI)	0	2230
	Florescu, C. (ROM)	41	2260
	Floresvillar, L. M. (MEX)	0	2240
	Florezabihi, A. (USA)	0	2235
	Florova, O. (RUS)	34	2195
f	Flueckiger, Ch. (SUI)	0	2240
	Fochtler, E. (GER)	0	2280
f	Fodre, S. (HUN)	13	2260
	Foessmeier, U. (GER)	7	2305
m	Fogarasi, T. (HUN)	58	2440
m	Foguelman, A. (ARG)	0	2320
	Fohler, C. (GER)	0	2350
	Foigel, I. (RUS)	11	2415
g	Foisor, Ch. A. (ROM)	33	2360
m	Foisor, O. (ROM)	13	2425
	Foister, S. (ENG)	0	2175
	Fokin, N. (ISR)	0	2005
	Fokin, S. (RUS)	21	2400
f	Foldi, I. (HUN)	13	2310
	Foldi, J. (HUN)	5	2245
	Folk, P. (TCH)	0	2285
	Foltz, Y. (RUS)	0	2375
m	Fomina, T. (EST)	24	2250
	Fong, J. M. (USA)	14	2185
	Fonseca, J. L. (NCA)	9	2290
	Fontaine, A. (MEX)	10	2180
	Fontaine, R. (FRA)	9	2150
	Fontana Sotomayour, J. (ESP)	4	2215
m	Fontanilla, G. (PHI)	0	2020
m	Forbes, C. (ENG)	0	2105
	Forchert, M. (GER)	2	2255
	Fordan, T. (HUN)	0	2225
	Forgacs, A. (HUN)	9	2180
	Forgacs, F. (HUN)	0	2205
m	Forgacs, Gy. (HUN)	2	2305
f	Forgacs, J. (HUN)	19	2320
m	Forgo, E. (HUN)	17	2250
g	Forintos, Gy. V. (HUN)	18	2410
m	Formanek, E. W. (USA)	24	2315
	Fornal, A. (POL)	5	2140
	Fornari, G. (ITA)	0	2240
	Forras, Cs. (HUN)	0	2305
f	Forster, M. (ENG)	0	2300
	Forster, R. (SUI)	25	2305
	Fossan, E. (NOR)	6	2315
f	Fossan, P. (NOR)	0	2315
	Foster, F. (NZL)	0	2020
	Foster, N. (ENG)	0	2290
	Fox, N. (ENG)	0	2210
	Foyo, R. (CUB)	0	2295
	Fraczek, D. (POL)	0	2270
	Fradkin, B. (RUS)	0	2385
m	Fraguela Gil, J. M. (ESP)	0	2260
g	Franco, Z. (PAR)	50	2480
	Francois, G. (FRA)	10	2255
	Francsics, E. (HUN)	9	2215
	Franczak, A. (POL)	0	2370
	Frangulea, A. (ROM)	10	2280
m	Franic, M. (CRO)	12	2395
	Frank, B. (GER)	1	2255
	Frank, Jozsef (HUN)	0	2335
	Frank, Jozsef (HUN)	6	2260
	Frank, M. (ARG)	0	2230
	Frank, V. (CRO)	0	2245
m	Franke, H. (GER)	2	2365
	Frankle, J. (USA)	0	2225
	Franklin, Ch. (ENG)	0	2250
f	Franklin, M. J. (ENG)	16	2275
	Fransson, P. (SWE)	0	2220
	Franz, K. (GER)	11	2150
m	Franzen, J. (SVK)	2	2310
m	Franzoni, G. (SUI)	6	2440
f	Fraschini, M. (ARG)	28	2345
	Fratila, G. (ROM)	9	2050
	Frauensohn, H. (FRA)	0	2225
	Frech, K. (HUN)	0	2260
	Freckmann, M. (GER)	8	2280
	Freeman, M. (SCO)	0	2205
	Freider, P. (RUS)	0	2255
	Freijedo Alvarez, S. (ESP)	0	2320
m	Freisler, P. (TCH)	0	2395
	Freitag, M. (AUT)	10	2275
	French, G. (USA)	9	2265
f	Frendzas, P. (GRE)	20	2345
f	Frenkel, V. (USA)	0	2070
	Freyre, J. (PUR)	0	2255
m	Frias, V. J. (USA)	13	2455
	Frick, Ch. (GER)	0	2250
	Frick, R. (LIE)	13	2195
	Fridbertsson, E. P. (ISD)	0	2200
	Fridh, A. (SWE)	0	2220
	Fridjonsson, J. (ISD)	0	2240
	Fridkin, J. (RUS)	0	2295
f	Fridman, D. (LAT)	29	2425
	Friedersdorff, F. (GER)	11	2250
f	Friedman, A. (ISR)	16	2300
	Friedman, E. (USA)	0	2290
	Friedman, J. (USA)	12	2320
f	Friedrich, N. (GER)	1	2330
m	Fries-Nielsen, J. O. (DEN)	9	2375
	Fries-Nielsen, N. J. (DEN)	9	2390
	Friesenhahn, H. (AUT)	0	2345
	Frink, F. (HUN)	7	2290
	Fritsch, R. (GER)	7	2215
	Fritsche, L. (GER)	14	2375
f	Fritz, R. (GER)	0	2320
	Fritze, B. (GER)	5	2290
	Froehlich, P. (GER)	11	2390
	Frog, I. (RUS)	49	2300
m	Frois, A. (POR)	27	2385
	Frolik, M. (TCH)	0	2285
m	Frolov, A. (UKR)	9	2535
	Frolov, Y. (RUS)	4	2350
	From, S. (DEN)	0	2285
m	Frometa, Z. (CUB)	13	2230
	Fromme, E. (GER)	0	2325
f	Fronczek, H. (POL)	0	2295
f	Frosch, E. (AUT)	11	2240
	Frumson, Y. (RUS)	0	2310
f	Fruteau, S. (FRA)	22	2185
	Frydman, I. (ARG)	0	2220
g	Ftacnik, L. (SVK)	41	2535
f	Fucak, E. (CRO)	11	2280
	Fuchs, B. (USA)	0	2230
	Fuentealba, J. (CHI)	13	2240
	Fuentes, A. (ARG)	17	2275
f	Fuentes, M. (CUB)	0	2355
	Fufuengmongkolkij, K. (THA)	0	2225
	Fugulyan, G. (ROM)	8	2260
	Fuhrmann, D. (GER)	11	2300

	Name	Games	Rating
	Fuksik, J. (TCH)	0	2210
f	Fulgenzi, E. (ARG)	4	2310
	Fulgsang, F. (DEN)	4	2260
	Fullbrook, N. (CAN)	0	2215
f	Fuller, M. L. (AUS)	2	2285
	Fulvi, F. (ITA)	0	2185
	Funes, A. (ARG)	24	2205
	Furdzik, R. (POL)	5	2215
	Furhoff, J. (SWE)	7	2285
	Furina, S. (RUS)	34	2165
	Furlan, M. (SLO)	12	2255
	Furmage, L. (WLS)	0	2005
	Furman, B. (RUS)	9	2235
	Fusi, Ch. (AUT)	4	2265
f	Fusthy, Zs. (HUN)	9	2320
	Fyllingen, R. (NOR)	8	2330

G

	Name	Games	Rating
	Gabaldon, M. (ESP)	0	2250
	Gabar, E. D. (ROM)	0	2075
	Gabdrakhmanov, R. (RUS)	7	2410
	Gabka, P. (POL)	14	2105
f	Gabler, B. (GER)	0	2315
	Gaborit, J.-P. (FRA)	10	2315
m	Gabriel, Ch. (GER)	35	2510
	Gabriel, J. (GER)	1	2240
	Gabriel, R. J. (GER)	2	2260
	Gachon, L. (FRA)	0	2275
	Gackic, B. (BIH)	0	2025
	Gacso, T. (HUN)	0	2255
	Gadjilu, R. (AZE)	5	2335
	Gaertner, G. (AUT)	15	2295
	Gaerts, R. (GER)	0	2325
	Gaffar, J. (BRN)	0	2205
m	Gagarin, V. (RUS)	14	2425
	Gagliardi, P. (ITA)	5	2215
	Gagloshvili, R. (RUS)	0	2160
	Gaidatzis, S. (GRE)	0	2220
	Gaika, P. (HUN)	0	2215
	Gajic, B. (YUG)	0	2255
f	Gajic, Dj. (YUG)	0	2335
f	Gajic, Z. (YUG)	0	2270
	Gal, A. (ISR)	0	2220
	Gal, Ja. (HUN)	13	2165
	Gal, Jo. (HUN)	27	2215
	Gal, K. (HUN)	0	2215
	Gal, S. (HUN)	2	2290
	Galakhov, S. (RUS)	15	2285
	Galandauer, J. (TCH)	0	2250
m	Galanov, B. (RUS)	3	2435
	Galat, A. (POL)	0	2265
m	Galdunts, S. (ARM)	10	2450
	Galeev, Sh. (RUS)	0	2280
m	Galego, L. (POR)	27	2390
	Galiana, J. R. (ESP)	0	2320
	Galic, K. (CRO)	3	2245
	Galic, V. (YUG)	0	2230
f	Galic, Z. (BIH)	0	2365
	Galindo, R. (ARG)	0	2275
g	Gallagher, J. G. (ENG)	58	2515
	Gallai, J. (HUN)	8	2290
m	Gallego Eraso, F. (ESP)	2	2385
	Gallego, J. (ESP)	0	2155
	Gallego, R. (AND)	0	2270
	Gallego, V. (ESP)	4	2365
	Gallegos, P. (USA)	1	2025
	Galleni, M. (ITA)	0	2135
g	Galliamova-Ivanchuk, A. (UKR)	30	2435
	Gallinnis, N. (GER)	3	2275
	Gallo, E. (ITA)	0	2225
	Gallo, J. (GER)	0	2240
	Galunov, T. (BUL)	0	2335
	Galyas, M. (HUN)	33	2230
f	Gamarra Caceres, C. (PAR)	0	2310
	Gamboa, N. (COL)	22	2405
	Gamundi, A. (ESP)	0	2440
	Ganaus, H. (AUT)	3	2295
	Ganchev, G. (BUL)	0	2315
f	Ganesan, S. (IND)	8	2320
	Gangler, Z. (HUN)	0	2260
	Ganguly, S. Sh. (IND)	7	2130
	Gant, Ch. (ENG)	2	2285
m	Gant, O. (GER)	0	2230
	Gantet, G. (FRA)	0	2235
m	Gaponenko, I. (UKR)	23	2290
g	Gaprindashvili, N. (GM) (GEO)	0	2375
f	Gara, Gy. (HUN)	9	2235
	Garabedian, V. (FRA)	4	2210
m	Garbarino, R. (ARG)	20	2410
f	Garber, S. (USA)	0	2375
f	Garbett, P. A. (NZL)	0	2310
	Garbisu, U. (ESP)	0	2255
	Garcia Ares, F. (ESP)	0	2305
f	Garcia Callejo, J. (ESP)	2	2265
	Garcia Espinoza, J. J. (MEX)	0	2035
f	Garcia Fernandez, C. (ESP)	13	2365
m	Garcia Ilundain, D. (ESP)	33	2480
	Garcia Larrouy, J. L. (ESP)	0	2240
f	Garcia Luque, A. (ESP)	0	2345
g	Garcia Martinez, S. (CUB)	0	2420
	Garcia Melgar, J. P. (ESP)	3	2290
	Garcia Molla, V. (ESP)	6	2280
	Garcia Munoz, J. J. (ESP)	0	2410
m	Garcia Padron, J. (ESP)	22	2465
g	Garcia Palermo, C. (ITA)	22	2455
	Garcia Trobat, F. (ESP)	13	2330
	Garcia, Alb. F. (ESP)	0	2330
	Garcia, Alv. (COL)	11	2295
g	Garcia, G. (COL)	21	2520
	Garcia, J. L. (ESP)	0	2270
	Garcia, Man. V. (BRA)	0	2295
	Garcia, Mar. (ESP)	9	2315
m	Garcia, N. (ESP)	9	2250
f	Garcia, Om. (CUB)	0	2310
	Garcia, Os. (CUB)	0	2270
	Garcia, P. J. (CUB)	0	2270
m	Garcia, Rai. (ARG)	15	2375
f	Garcia, Raul (AND)	11	2275
	Garcia, Ri. (ESP)	0	2275
m	Garkov, M. (BUL)	0	2250
	Garma, Ch. (PHI)	0	2380
	Garma, E. (PHI)	9	2375
	Garmendez Gonzalez, C. (MEX)	13	2210
f	Garmendez, F. (MEX)	12	2295
	Garner, P. (ENG)	0	2035
	Garrard, C. (ZIM)	0	2205
	Garrido, D. (FRA)	3	2200
	Garriga Nvalart, J. (ESP)	0	2385
f	Garwell, J. (WLS)	0	2170
	Gasic, B. (YUG)	11	2245
	Gasiorowski, R. (POL)	5	2255
	Gasiunas, N. (UKR)	5	2180
	Gaso, D. (BIH)	18	2055
	Gaspar, Z. (HUN)	3	2210
	Gaspariants, G. (RUS)	8	2260
	Gaspariants, V. (RUS)	0	2340
f	Gast, J. (SUI)	0	2255
	Gast, U. (SUI)	0	2255
	Gastgofer, V. (RUS)	24	2250
	Gatica, J. (CHI)	9	2270
	Gatine, A. (FRA)	18	2070
	Gattermayer, R. (AUT)	0	2025
	Gauche, Charles (BRA)	0	2295
	Gauche, Charles (BRA)	3	2340
	Gaughan, R. J. (ENG)	19	2085
m	Gauglitz, G. (GER)	13	2415
m	Gausel, E. (NOR)	26	2500
f	Gavela, D. (YUG)	2	2310
	Gavilan, M. S. (ESP)	4	2315
f	Gavilanes, A. (CUB)	0	2275
f	Gavric, M. (YUG)	4	2310
	Gavriel, T. (ENG)	2	2190
g	Gavrikov, V. (SUI)	21	2580
	Gavrila, E. (ROM)	0	2045
f	Gavrila, G. (ROM)	0	2275
m	Gavrilakis, N. (GRE)	5	2400
	Gavrilescu, C. (ROM)	0	2310
m	Gavrilov, A. (RUS)	47	2415
	Gavrilovic, V. (YUG)	0	2255
	Gawarecki, L. (POL)	0	2210
f	Gawehns, K. (GER)	9	2345
	Gawlinski, M. (POL)	0	2255
	Gawronski, M. (POL)	13	2255
	Gayson, P. (ENG)	0	2255
f	Gazarek, D. (CRO)	2	2340
	Gazda, I. (HUN)	0	2280
	Gazi, M. (SVK)	0	2250
m	Gazik, I. (SVK)	17	2410
	Gazis, E. (GRE)	0	2235
	Gazmaga, S. (GER)	2	2250
m	Gdanski, J. (POL)	35	2485
	Gdanski, P. (POL)	0	2310
	Gdovin, J. (TCH)	0	2265
	Gebhardt, U. (GER)	3	2240
f	Gedevanishvili, D. (AUS)	5	2365
f	Geenen, M. (BEL)	0	2320
	Geerlings, G. (GER)	0	2320
	Gefenas, V. (LTU)	10	2280
	Gefstein, G. (ISR)	7	2130
	Gegamian, A. (RUS)	0	2220
	Geiser, L. (SUI)	11	2180
f	Geisler, F. (GER)	0	2305
	Geisler, R. (GER)	2	2210
	Geissler, G. (GER)	0	2035
	Gekas, S. (GRE)	0	2245
f	Geleta, J. (YUG)	0	2310
g	Gelfand, B. (BLA)	35	2670
	Gelfand, D. (RUS)	14	2245
f	Gelfer, I. (ISR)	0	2350
	Gelle, I. (HUN)	6	2235
	Geller, A. (YUG)	13	2300
g	Geller, E. P. (RUS)	17	2505
	Gelman, A. (RUS)	15	2435
	Gelman, G. (USA)	7	2220
f	Gelpke, P. (NED)	0	2405
	Gemesi, A. (HUN)	9	2145
	Gemmell, P. (ENG)	0	2305
	Gempe, A. (GER)	11	2125
	Gempe, Th. (GER)	0	2225
	Gendelman, D. (ISR)	7	2210
	Genduso, G. (GER)	0	2220
	Genescu, C. (ROM)	12	2215
m	Genov, Petar (BUL)	8	2435
	Genov, Petko (BUL)	4	2310
m	Genova (Tsvetkova), R. (BUL)	13	2195
	Genovese, M. (ITA)	4	2255
f	Gentes, K. (CAN)	0	2325
	Gentil jr., L. (BRA)	12	2155
	Gentilleau, J.-Ph. (FRA)	7	2215
	Georg, H. (GER)	0	2235
	Georg, M. (SUI)	9	2225
m	Georgadze, G. (GEO)	27	2555
g	Georgadze, T. (GEO)	0	2530
f	Georgandzis, K. (GRE)	0	2275
	George T, M. (EGY)	0	2335
f	Georges, S. (SUI)	8	2310
f	Georgescu, Gabriel (ROM)	11	2375
	Georgescu, Gabriel II (ROM)	0	2210
	Georgescu, I. G. (ROM)	10	2345
	Georghiou, P. I. (ENG)	0	2225
	Georgi, P. (BUL)	0	2320
	Georgiakakis, I. (GRE)	13	2220
	Georgiev, B. (BUL)	0	2280

	Name		
	Georgiev, G. (BUL)	9	2240
g	Georgiev, Ki. (BUL)	11	2660
g	Georgiev, Kr. (BUL)	38	2475
	Georgiev, V. (BUL)	19	2430
	Georgieva, E. (BUL)	8	2070
	Georgievski, S. (YUG)	25	2325
	Georgievski, V. (YUG)	9	2255
	Gepstein, G. (RUS)	9	2065
f	Gerber, R. (SUI)	4	2320
	Gerencer, J. (SLO)	33	2230
	Gerer, J. (GER)	5	2220
	Gergel, V. P. (UKR)	0	2305
	Gerhold, M. (AUT)	0	2230
	Gerigk, E. (GER)	6	2270
	Gerlach, M. (GER)	3	2090
	German, G. (ARG)	12	2290
	German, P. (ARG)	16	2270
	Germanavicius, S. (LTU)	0	2360
	Gershon, A. (ISR)	9	2195
	Gerskovic, E. (UKR)	0	2330
f	Gerstner, W. (GER)	6	2355
m	Gerusel, M. (GER)	6	2320
f	Gervais, C. (FRA)	25	2215
f	Gervasi, G. (ITA)	0	2330
	Gervasio, R. (FRA)	7	2295
	Geselschap, J. (NED)	0	2305
	Gesicki, J. (POL)	0	2290
m	Gesos, P. (GRE)	3	2415
	Getta, M. (GER)	20	2070
f	Getz, Sh. D. (USA)	4	2320
f	Geveke, M. (GER)	10	2345
	Gevorgjan, K. (RUS)	21	2235
	Gezaljan, T. (ARM)	0	2320
	Ghada Ismail, M. (EGY)	0	2005
	Ghannoum, M. (CAN)	0	2240
	Ghassan, M. A. (IRQ)	0	2305
	Gheorghe, I. (ROM)	0	2295
	Gheorghe, M. (ROM)	0	2020
g	Gheorghiu, F. (ROM)	26	2460
	Ghervonenko, I. (ISR)	9	2120
	Ghijsen, P. (NED)	0	2220
m	Ghinda, E. (ROM)	0	2160
m	Ghinda, M.-V. (ROM)	11	2455
g	Ghitescu, Th. (ROM)	19	2415
	Ghosh, A. K. (IND)	9	2205
f	Giaccio, A. (ARG)	36	2350
	Giaccomazzi, D. (FRA)	3	2240
f	Giaidzi, A. (GRE)	13	2135
m	Giam, Ch.-K. (SIN)	0	2220
m	Giardelli, S. C. (ARG)	53	2475
	Gibert, R. (USA)	9	2190
	Gibiec, E. (TCH)	0	2255
	Gicev, B. (YUG)	2	2320
f	Giddins, S. (ENG)	14	2280
	Giemsa, S. (GER)	25	2275
	Giertz, N. (SUI)	7	2245
	Gietl, Th. (GER)	9	2240
m	Giffard, N. (FRA)	18	2380
	Gigerl, E. (AUT)	11	2345
	Gik, E. (RUS)	3	2355
f	Gil Gonzales, M. J. (ESP)	2	2355
m	Gil Reguera, J. C. (ESP)	5	2345
m	Gil, Ja. (ESP)	3	2425
	Gil, Jo. L. (CUB)	0	2150
	Gil, R. (ARG)	0	2245
	Gilbert, Ch. (FRA)	24	2090
f	Giles, M. (USA)	0	2360
	Gillen, A. (IRL)	5	2235
	Gilles, R. (FRA)	14	2250
	Gilruth, P. (USA)	0	2215
	Gimenez, I. (ARG)	0	2230
	Ginat, M. (AUS)	0	2225
	Gincomazzi, D. (FRA)	0	2275
	Ginsburg, G. (UKR)	8	2435
m	Ginsburg, M. (USA)	26	2380
m	Ginting, N. (INA)	9	2405
	Ginzburg, M. (ARG)	30	2375
g	Gipslis, A. (LAT)	40	2505
	Girinath, P. D. S. (IND)	19	2365
	Girkiyan, T. (KAZ)	5	2220
	Gislason, G. (ISD)	5	2270
	Giudici, E. (ARG)	11	2280
	Giulian, Ph. M. (SCO)	0	2275
	Giulian, R. (SCO)	0	2050
f	Giurumia, S. (ROM)	10	2230
f	Gizynski, T. (POL)	19	2350
	Gjergji, R. (ALB)	0	2055
	Gkogkas, D. (GRE)	4	2245
	Gladishev, O. (RUS)	0	2240
	Gladisheva, T. (RUS)	0	2115
	Gladyszew, O. (RUS)	0	2225
	Glaser, A. (GER)	9	2140
f	Glatt, G. (HUN)	9	2295
f	Glauser, H. (SUI)	0	2325
	Glavan, S. (BIH)	0	2210
f	Glavica, Z. (CRO)	0	2270
m	Glavina, P. (ARG)	15	2405
	Glavinits, Th. (AUT)	11	2125
m	Glaz, L. (ISR)	0	2200
	Gleizer, M. (ISR)	7	2305
g	Gleizerov, E. (RUS)	37	2525
g	Glek, I. V. (RUS)	61	2535
	Glettenberg, J. (GER)	10	2230
f	Glienke, M. (GER)	8	2270
g	Gligoric, S. (YUG)	0	2445
	Gligorovski, K. (YUG)	0	2265
m	Gliksman, Dar. (CRO)	0	2260
	Gliksman, Dav. N. (USA)	5	2255
	Glimbrant, T. (SWE)	4	2240
	Glisic, V. (YUG)	0	2220
f	Glodeanu, I. (ROM)	16	2360
	Gloria, E. (PHI)	14	2290
	Gluckman, D. (RSA)	0	2330
f	Glueck, D. (USA)	0	2320
m	Gluzman, M. (AUS)	7	2435
	Glyanets, A. (RUS)	16	2400
	Gmeiner, P. (GER)	6	2280
	Goban, M. (SVK)	0	2230
	Gobe, P. (FRA)	0	2235
m	Gobet, F. (SUI)	4	2385
	Gobrial, A. G. (EGY)	15	2295
	Gochev, M. (BUL)	0	2300
m	Gocheva, R. B. (BUL)	18	2200
	Goczan, L. (HUN)	6	2205
	Godard, M. (FRA)	0	2220
	Godel, R. (GER)	0	2205
m	Godena, M. (ITA)	47	2505
m	Godes, D. A. R. (RUS)	20	2430
	Godo, F. (CUB)	0	2295
	Godoy, C. (ARG)	5	2215
	Godoy, D. A. (CHI)	20	2325
f	Goehring, K.-H. (GER)	5	2310
	Goergens, M. (GER)	9	2225
	Goes, D. (BRA)	0	2335
	Goetz, R. (GER)	7	2350
m	Gofshtein, L. D. (ISR)	38	2540
	Gogalea, E. (ROM)	0	2055
	Gogichaishvili, G. (GEO)	0	2410
	Gohil, H. (GER)	0	2265
	Gohlke, H. (GER)	0	2300
	Goj, A. (POL)	9	2300
f	Gojkovic, P. (YUG)	5	2335
	Gokhale Jayant, S. (IND)	5	2330
m	Gokhale, A. (IND)	24	2200
	Gokhale, C. S. (IND)	0	2330
	Gokhale, R. V. (IND)	4	2200
f	Gola, M. (TCH)	3	2330
f	Goldberg, A. (GER)	12	2395
f	Goldberg, M. (USA)	0	2395
f	Goldenberg, R. (FRA)	0	2275
	Goldgewicht, L. (FRA)	27	2285
g	Goldin, A. (RUS)	34	2540
	Goldin, V. M. (RUS)	0	2345
	Goldschmidt, B. (ARG)	6	2185
	Goldsmith, A. (AUS)	0	2295
f	Goldstern, F. (NED)	0	2330
m	Golikov, A. (RUS)	0	2375
	Gollain, M. (FRA)	15	2265
	Gollewsky, P. (GER)	3	2070
m	Golod, V. (UKR)	11	2490
	Golovachov, S. (RUS)	0	2340
	Golovin, L. (RUS)	6	2415
	Golovko, S. (RUS)	4	2305
m	Golubev, M. (UKR)	19	2500
	Golubovic, B. (CRO)	4	2305
	Golubovic, Z. (YUG)	2	2310
m	Gomez Baillo, J. H. (ARG)	33	2415
m	Gomez Esteban, J. M. (ESP)	31	2450
	Gomez Jurado, L. A. (ESP)	14	2300
f	Gomez, A. (CUB)	0	2315
	Gomez, D. N. (ESP)	2	2210
f	Gomez, F. (CUB)	10	2310
	Gomez, J. (NCA)	0	2205
f	Gomez, Ju. (MEX)	0	2225
	Gon, Y. (MAS)	0	2205
	Goncalves, J. (POR)	0	2220
f	Gonsior, E. (TCH)	0	2315
	Gonzales Mata, J. (MEX)	0	2285
	Gonzales, E. (DOM)	0	2240
	Gonzales, Ga. J. (CUB)	0	2280
	Gonzales, Gu. (ESP)	0	2235
m	Gonzales, J. A. (COL)	13	2385
	Gonzales, R. (CUB)	0	2250
	Gonzalez Aguirre, L. (ESP)	0	2300
	Gonzalez Garcia, J. (MEX)	31	2380
	Gonzalez Perez, L. (ESP)	2	2370
f	Gonzalez Rabago, N. (CUB)	0	2310
f	Gonzalez, Be. (CRC)	41	2395
	Gonzalez, Bo. R. (BRA)	0	2320
f	Gonzalez, Juan C. (CUB)	32	2465
	Gonzalez, Juan D. (USA)	0	2225
	Gonzalez, M. (CUB)	0	2240
f	Gonzalez, R. (ARG)	0	2310
f	Gonzalez, S. (COL)	11	2315
	Goodwin, D. (ENG)	15	2180
f	Goormachtigh, J. (BEL)	0	2300
	Goossens, E. (BEL)	0	2075
	Gopal, K. N. (IND)	9	2220
	Gopalakrishna, K. (IND)	0	2230
	Gorbatow, A. (RUS)	45	2450
f	Gordan, N. (ROM)	11	2300
f	Goregliad, S. (USA)	10	2280
m	Gorelov, S. G. (RUS)	19	2505
	Gorgs, A. (GER)	0	2225
	Goric, E. (YUG)	0	2280
	Gorisnic, E. (ARG)	0	2240
	Gorjatschkin, W. (RUS)	0	2440
f	Gorman, D. (USA)	0	2330
	Gorniak, T. (POL)	0	2240
	Gosic, B. (YUG)	0	2310
	Gospodinov, I. (BUL)	0	2325
m	Gostisa, L. (SLO)	28	2470
	Gostomelski, V. (RUS)	0	2295
	Gostovic-Bozovic, M. (YUG)	0	2080
	Gosztola, I. (HUN)	9	2270
f	Gottesman, J. (USA)	0	2315
	Gountintas, A. (GRE)	0	2300
	Gouret, Th. (FRA)	12	2260
	Gouveia, C. (BRA)	0	2390
m	Govedarica, R. (YUG)	28	2395
	Govoni, F. (ITA)	0	2280
	Goy, U. (GER)	4	2210
	Grabarczyk, B. (POL)	5	2365
	Grabarczyk, M. (POL)	19	2470
	Grabarska, B. (POL)	3	2075
f	Grabert, R. (GER)	9	2245
	Grabher, H. (AUT)	11	2165
f	Grabics, M. (HUN)	27	2245

	Name		
	Grabliauskas, V. (LTU)	16	2300
	Grabow, G. (GER)	0	2330
	Grabowski, A. (POL)	0	2365
	Grabuzov, S. (RUS)	21	2370
m	Grabuzova, T. (RUS)	38	2275
	Gracin, D. (CRO)	0	2270
	Graef, S. (GER)	0	2255
	Graf, Ch. (GER)	6	2235
	Graf, G. (GER)	0	2240
m	Graf, J. (GER)	5	2440
	Graf, P. (POL)	5	2130
	Grafe, W. (GER)	9	2075
	Graff, G. (POL)	12	2340
	Graham, N. (USA)	11	2325
f	Gralka, J. (POL)	0	2300
	Gralka, P. (POL)	0	2280
	Gramer, K. (SWE)	0	2230
	Gramignani, R. (ITA)	0	2040
	Granados, R. (MEX)	4	2220
	Grancharov, G. (RUS)	0	2265
g	Granda Zuniga, J. E. (PER)	27	2605
	Graniou, M. (FRA)	4	2270
	Granovski, A. (KAZ)	24	2320
f	Gransky, M. (ISR)	0	2300
	Grant, J. (SCO)	12	2280
	Grassi, E. (SMR)	0	2210
f	Grathwohl, R. (GER)	0	2295
	Gratseas, S. (GRE)	0	2240
	Gratz, G. (USA)	10	2290
	Grbovic, V. (YUG)	0	2270
	Grdinic, Z. (CRO)	4	2405
	Greanias, S. (USA)	2	2365
f	Grebennikov, S. (RUS)	0	2385
	Grech, J. (MLT)	0	2205
	Grechinin, W. (RUS)	17	2170
	Green, P. (NZL)	0	2265
g	Greenfeld, A. (ISR)	34	2590
	Greer, K. (IRL)	5	2225
m	Grefe, J. A. (USA)	4	2400
	Greger, R. (DEN)	0	2275
	Gregor, J. (TCH)	0	2285
	Gregory, V. (MAS)	0	2235
f	Gretarsson, A. A. (ISD)	4	2310
f	Gretarsson, H. A. (ISD)	4	2365
	Grguric, D. (CRO)	0	2275
	Grguric, Z. (CRO)	0	2255
	Grichkevitch, G. (FRA)	0	2270
f	Griego, D. W. (USA)	3	2335
	Griffin, D. (SCO)	0	2275
	Griffiths, C. (WLS)	0	2005
	Griffiths, P. (ENG)	0	2240
m	Grigore, G. (ROM)	0	2455
	Grigorieva, A. (MOL)	4	2170
m	Grigorov, J. N. (BUL)	29	2375
	Grilc, S. (YUG)	11	2310
	Grillitsch, K. (AUT)	9	2270
f	Grimaldi, R. A. (ESA)	0	2270
f	Grimberg, G. (FRA)	9	2325
	Grimm, S. (GER)	8	2320
	Grinberg, N. (ISR)	5	2385
m	Grinchpun, E. (UZB)	26	2420
m	Grinfeld, A. B. (RUS)	14	2245
g	Grivas, E. (GRE)	38	2505
	Grizou, R. (FRA)	0	2215
	Groborz, M. (POL)	0	2240
m	Grochot, Cz. (POL)	19	2210
	Groenegress, W. (GER)	2	2210
	Groh, J. (TCH)	0	2145
	Gromada, A. (POL)	2	2055
	Gromczak, D. (POL)	0	2245
	Gronn, A. (NOR)	0	2325
m	Grooten, H. (NED)	21	2375
m	Grosar, A. (SLO)	29	2470
	Grosar, K. (SLO)	35	2145
m	Grosch, M. (HUN)	0	2135
f	Grosic, D. (CRO)	0	2290
	Gross, Dan. (USA)	11	2045
	Gross, Dav. (TCH)	3	2270
	Gross, G. (GER)	5	2295
m	Gross, S. (TCH)	13	2330
	Grosse-Kloenne, E. (GER)	15	2285
	Grossman, S. (RUS)	0	2115
	Grossmann, R. (POL)	0	2245
g	Groszpeter, A. (HUN)	58	2515
f	Grotnes, N. (NOR)	9	2330
	Grottke, H.-J. (GER)	0	2255
	Gruber, Th. (GER)	3	2220
	Grubisic, Z. (YUG)	0	2285
m	Gruchacz, R. (USA)	0	2335
m	Gruen, G.-P. (GER)	7	2370
m	Gruenberg, H.-U. (GER)	14	2460
f	Gruenberg, Ra. (GER)	0	2350
f	Gruenberg, Re. (GER)	0	2150
f	Gruenenwald, E. (SUI)	0	2115
f	Gruenenwald, J. (GER)	4	2325
g	Gruenfeld, Y. (ISR)	45	2535
	Gruia, A. (ROM)	11	2285
	Grujic, L. (YUG)	21	2375
	Grujic, N. (YUG)	14	2295
	Grujic, Z. (YUG)	17	2285
	Grunberg, M. (ROM)	6	2220
m	Grunberg, S. H. (ROM)	0	2345
	Grundherr, M. (GER)	0	2280
f	Grushka, C. (ARG)	0	2245
f	Gruszka, D. (POL)	0	2135
	Gruzmann, B. (RUS)	2	2260
	Gryciuk, W. (POL)	0	2245
	Gryczka, W. (POL)	12	2155
	Gryniakow, J. (POL)	0	2265
f	Grynszpan, M. (ARG)	0	2390
	Grzelak, A. (POL)	4	2255
	Grzelak, R. (POL)	6	2210
f	Grzesik, Th. (GER)	0	2285
m	Gschnitzer, O. (GER)	15	2460
	Guadalpi, D. (FRA)	12	2235
	Gual, A. (ESP)	8	2350
	Gubics, P. (HUN)	0	2215
	Gudat, A. (GER)	20	2125
	Gudmundsson, K. (ISD)	0	2255
	Gueci, R. (ITA)	0	2235
	Guedon, S. (FRA)	12	2220
	Gueler, S. (GER)	0	2245
	Guenther, A. (GER)	4	2035
	Guenther, C. (GER)	7	2265
f	Guenthner, O. (GER)	0	2260
	Guerra Bastida, D. (ESP)	0	2320
	Guerra, A. (ITA)	0	2205
f	Guerra, P. (CUB)	0	2355
	Guerra, U. (ITA)	0	2290
f	Guevara, M. (NCA)	22	2325
	Gueye, G. (SEN)	0	2215
g	Gufeld, E. (GEO)	31	2465
m	Guggenberger, I. D. (COL)	0	2055
	Gugler, E. (AUT)	0	2290
	Guglielmi, R. (ITA)	7	2210
	Guidez, Y.-M. (FRA)	7	2280
f	Guido, F. (ITA)	9	2280
	Guigonis, D. (FRA)	0	2280
f	Guimaraes, J. (POR)	3	2310
	Guimaraes, W. P. (BRA)	0	2290
g	Guimard, C. E. (ARG)	0	2345
	Guindy, E. (DEN)	9	2055
	Guispe, A. M. (BOL)	0	2005
	Gukasian, R. (RUS)	0	2290
	Gulakov, V. P. (UKR)	0	2435
	Guldner, K. (GER)	0	2290
	Gulicovski, K. (YUG)	10	2240
	Guliev, L. (AZE)	11	2315
m	Guliev, S. (AZE)	36	2465
g	Gulko, B. F. (USA)	30	2635
	Gullaksen, E. T. (NOR)	7	2390
	Gulshan, R. (BAN)	0	2005
	Guna, V. (ROM)	0	2205
m	Gunawan, Ro. (INA)	0	2420
f	Gunawan, Ru. (INA)	11	2295
	Gundersen, H. (NOR)	0	2255
	Gunnarson, A. (ISD)	0	2235
	Gupta, M. (GER)	17	2260
f	Gupta, R. S. (IND)	8	2245
	Gurcan, S. (TUR)	0	2205
g	Gurevich, D. (USA)	65	2575
	Gurevich, G. (ISR)	25	2355
m	Gurevich, I. (USA)	57	2575
g	Gurevich, M. (BEL)	47	2605
m	Gurevich, V. (UKR)	14	2420
g	Gurgenidze, B. (GEO)	0	2370
g	Gurieli, N. (GEO)	18	2355
	Guseinov, A. (AZE)	0	2395
	Gusev, V. A. (RUS)	0	2335
	Gusev, Y. S. (RUS)	0	2345
	Guskova, E. (RUS)	0	2130
	Gussjatinskij, A. (UKR)	0	2245
	Gutdeutsch, O. (AUT)	0	2265
	Gutierrez Torres, Ra. (MEX)	0	2255
	Gutierrez Torres, Ro. (MEX)	0	2220
	Gutierrez, J. (CRC)	0	2320
	Gutierrez, Ja. (ESP)	0	2290
m	Gutierrez, Jo. A. (COL)	11	2290
	Gutierrez, O. (NCA)	9	2020
	Gutin, D. (RUS)	0	2230
	Gutkin, B. (ISR)	0	2285
	Gutkina, E. (RUS)	0	2070
g	Gutman, L. (GER)	0	2450
	Gutop, Y. V. (RUS)	14	2325
	Gutzeit, A. (ISR)	9	2075
	Guy, D. (WLS)	9	2105
	Guyard, B. (FRA)	0	2180
f	Guyot, Ph. (FRA)	0	2295
	Guzijan, M. (YUG)	0	2355
	Guzkowska, M. (POL)	22	2080
	Guzman, E. (BOL)	0	2280
	Guzman, P. (DOM)	1	2010
	Gvein, K. (NOR)	11	2140
	Gyenes, I. (HUN)	12	2060
m	Gyimesi, Z. (HUN)	55	2390
	Gyorfi, L. (HUN)	0	2270
m	Gyorkos, L. (HUN)	58	2435
	Gyurkovics, M. (HUN)	13	2275

H

	Name		
m	Haag, E. (HUN)	10	2365
	Haag, G. (GER)	0	2215
	Haag, M. (GER)	0	2290
	Haag, W. (GER)	0	2290
	Haakert, J. (GER)	8	2335
	Haapasalo, J.-P. (FIN)	9	2235
	Haas, C. (ISR)	6	2235
	Haas, F. (GER)	0	2235
f	Haas, G. (LUX)	0	2290
	Haas, S. (GER)	0	2265
	Haas, W. (GER)	0	2245
m	Haba, P. (TCH)	26	2485
f	Habibi, A. (GER)	69	2310
	Habinak, T. (SVK)	0	2350
	Hacche, D. (AUS)	4	2255
	Hachaj, A. (POL)	0	2285
	Hachian, M. (RUS)	0	2415
	Hackel, M. (GER)	0	2340
	Hacker, Ch. (GER)	0	2220
	Hadjittofis, Y. (CYP)	0	2205
	Hadjiyiannis, C. (CYP)	0	2205
	Hadraba, V. (TCH)	0	2275
	Hadzidakis, M. (GRE)	10	2145
f	Hadzimanov, Lj. (YUG)	0	2265
	Hadzovic, I. (BIH)	0	2250
	Haessler, C. (USA)	5	2240
f	Hager, F. (AUT)	3	2275
	Hagermann, H. (GER)	0	2225
	Hagesaether, P. V. (NOR)	24	2125

	Name		
m	Haik, A. (FRA)	13	2400
	Haimovich, T. (ISR)	17	2270
	Haines, R. (USA)	0	2225
f	Haist, W. (GER)	0	2265
m	Hait, A. (RUS)	40	2360
	Hajdu, I. (HUN)	15	2170
f	Hajek, M. (TCH)	0	2285
	Hajkova, P. (TCH)	0	2080
m	Hajkova-Maskova, J. (TCH)	0	2220
m	Hakki, I. (SYR)	0	2320
f	Hakulinen, E.-M. (FIN)	24	2340
	Halac, M. (ARG)	7	2255
	Halaj, A. (HUN)	0	2180
	Halasz, A. (HUN)	0	2240
	Halasz, Cs. (HUN)	13	2215
	Halasz, S. (SVK)	0	2340
m	Halasz, T. (HUN)	9	2390
	Hald, J. E. (DEN)	0	2230
	Haldemann, P. (SUI)	11	2260
f	Haliamanis, G. (GRE)	3	2330
	Halilovic, H. (YUG)	0	2260
f	Hall, E. C. (USA)	0	2345
m	Hall, J. (SWE)	0	2450
	Halldorsson, G. (ISD)	0	2260
f	Hallebeek, F. (NED)	0	2320
	Hallerova, E. (GER)	0	2225
	Halpin, P. (AUS)	0	2270
	Halsegger, H. (AUT)	6	2195
	Haludrov, E. (RUS)	0	2265
	Hamacher, A. (GER)	0	2285
	Hamad, K. (SUD)	0	2205
	Hamadi, Dj. (ALG)	6	2160
	Hamadto, I. E. D. F. (SUD)	0	2205
m	Hamann, S. (DEN)	9	2355
	Hamdani (INA)	0	2285
m	Hamdouchi, H. (MAR)	8	2455
m	Hamed, A. (EGY)	0	2320
	Hamgokov, A. (RUS)	0	2325
m	Hamid, M. K. (YEM)	9	2305
m	Hamid, R. (BAN)	14	2170
f	Hamilton, R. (CAN)	0	2330
f	Hammar, B. (SWE)	0	2360
	Hammes, M. (GER)	1	2220
	Hamori, A. (HUN)	0	2225
	Han, H. (TUR)	4	2320
	Hana, A. (LAT)	4	2225
	Hanasz, W. (POL)	0	2270
	Hancas, M. (ROM)	0	2235
	Handa, R. (HUN)	0	2280
m	Handoko, E. (INA)	36	2520
f	Hanel, R. (AUT)	7	2365
	Hanemann, I. (GER)	0	2205
	Hanes, Madalina (ROM)	17	2105
	Hanes, Madalina (ROM)	10	2005
	Hangweyrer, M. (AUT)	0	2240
	Hanko, P. (SVK)	0	2225
	Hanks, J. (AUS)	4	2220
	Hanley, J. (USA)	8	2095
	Hannoun, N. (ALG)	0	2280
f	Hanreck, A. E. (ENG)	0	2255
f	Hansen, Ca. (DEN)	4	2290
	Hansen, Ch. J. (FAI)	0	2210
g	Hansen, Cu. (DEN)	25	2590
	Hansen, J. (DEN)	10	2135
	Hansen, Lars (DEN)	13	2275
	Hansen, Lars Be. (DEN)	0	2210
g	Hansen, Lars Bo (DEN)	30	2560
	Hansen, Ma. S. (DEN)	5	2310
	Hansen, Mo. (DEN)	9	2010
f	Hansen, So. B. (DEN)	0	2300
	Hansen, Sune (DEN)	10	2180
	Hansen, Sune B. (DEN)	9	2405
	Hansson, D. (ISD)	0	2250
	Hansson, H. (SWE)	0	2235
f	Happel, H. A. (NED)	3	2265
	Haque, N. (BAN)	0	2120
f	Haque, R. (BAN)	0	2225
m	Har-Zvi, R. (ISR)	33	2505
	Har-Zvi, Sh. (ISR)	0	2240
	Haragos, K. (HUN)	1	2175
	Harakis, A. (ENG)	1	2260
m	Harandi, K. (IRI)	6	2375
	Harari, Z. (USA)	7	2265
	Harasta, V. (SVK)	0	2220
f	Hardarson, R. (ISD)	10	2320
m	Hardicsay, P. (HUN)	11	2360
	Hardy, R. (ENG)	0	2100
	Harestad, Th. G. (NOR)	0	2270
	Hargens, Th. (GER)	6	2280
	Hargittai, S. (HUN)	17	2250
	Hariharan, V. (IND)	0	2215
f	Haritakis, Th. (GRE)	11	2265
	Harlamov, V. (RUS)	0	2375
f	Harley, A. (ENG)	1	2315
	Harlin, H. (FRA)	0	2215
	Harlov, A. (RUS)	0	2435
	Harmatosi, J. (HUN)	20	2260
	Harmon, C. (USA)	0	2235
m	Harmsen, J. (NED)	0	2170
	Harper, H. (ARG)	13	2200
	Harris, D. (USA)	0	2235
	Harris, M. (ENG)	0	2235
	Hart, C. (USA)	9	2345
	Hart, M. (USA)	0	2210
f	Hartereau, Ph. (FRA)	8	2315
	Hartlieb, J. (GER)	0	2245
m	Hartman, B. (CAN)	1	2390
m	Hartman, Ch. (SWE)	6	2365
	Hartmann, G. (GER)	0	2285
	Hartmans, E. (NED)	9	2250
m	Hartoch, R. G. (NED)	23	2345
	Hartung-Nielsen, J. (DEN)	0	2270
	Hartvig, O. W. (DEN)	11	2145
f	Harwar, J. (ENG)	0	2055
	Hasan, K. K. (BAN)	0	2275
	Hasan, N. F. (IRQ)	0	2370
f	Hasan, Y. (BAN)	0	2260
	Hasanov, M. (RUS)	5	2330
m	Hase, J. C. (ARG)	12	2345
f	Hasecic, S. (YUG)	0	2320
	Haselhorst, H. (GER)	0	2235
f	Hashim, A. A. (QTR)	8	2255
f	Haskamp, S. (GER)	0	2260
	Haslinger, C. (ENG)	0	2005
	Haslinger, G. (ENG)	0	2305
	Hass, R. (POL)	0	2330
	Hassabis, D. (ENG)	0	2260
	Hassan, M. (UAE)	0	2005
	Hassan, Mo. (IND)	7	2290
	Hassan, S. (EGY)	0	2205
	Hassan, Sa. B. (EGY)	15	2355
	Hassan, T. A. (EGY)	0	2260
	Hastings, J. (ENG)	3	2210
f	Hatlebakk, E. (NOR)	0	2300
	Haub, Th.-M. (GER)	16	2310
	Haubt, G. (GER)	13	2220
m	Hauchard, A. (FRA)	44	2450
m	Haugli, P. (NOR)	0	2395
	Hauke, Ch. (GER)	0	2235
	Hauschild, A. (GER)	4	2310
	Hausknecht, M. (GER)	9	2315
m	Hausner, I. (TCH)	19	2465
	Hausrath, D. (GER)	9	2280
	Havansi, E. E. T. (FIN)	4	2275
f	Havas, L. (CRO)	5	2290
	Havasi, J. (HUN)	8	2250
m	Hawelko, M. (POL)	0	2400
	Hawes, J. (GCI)	1	2070
m	Hawksworth, J. C. (ENG)	0	2355
	Hay, T. (AUS)	0	2310
	Hayoun, L. (FRA)	11	2395
	Hayward, K. (USA)	11	2285
m	Hazai, L. (HUN)	11	2465
	Hazelton, M. (ENG)	0	2205
	He, Tianjian (CHN)	0	2110
g	Hebden, M. (ENG)	52	2560
m	Hebert, J. (CAN)	0	2395
	Hebesberger, Th. (AUT)	9	2175
g	Hecht, H.-J. (GER)	1	2420
	Hecimovic, I. (CRO)	0	2220
	Heckler, M. (GER)	0	2285
g	Hector, J. (SWE)	33	2500
f	Hedke, F. (GER)	32	2345
f	Hedman Senarega, J. A. (CUB)	10	2320
	Hedman, E. (SWE)	11	2255
g	Heemskerk, F. (NED)	0	2005
f	Heemskerk, W. (NED)	0	2285
	Heer, S. (SUI)	9	2280
m	Hegde, R. G. (IND)	31	2330
f	Hegedus, I. (ROM)	0	2320
	Hegeler, F. (GER)	4	2195
f	Heidenfeld, M. (GER)	15	2315
	Heidl, G. (GER)	0	2400
f	Heidrich, M. (GER)	0	2335
	Heifez, E. (AUT)	0	2250
	Heigl, R. (GER)	0	2225
f	Heil, S. (GER)	0	2355
	Heilemann, M. (GER)	11	2285
	Heiligermann, G. (HUN)	15	2225
	Heim, B. (GER)	0	2205
	Heim, C. (ROM)	0	2270
	Heimrath, R. (GER)	2	2125
m	Heinatz, G. (GER)	16	2235
f	Heinatz, Th. (GER)	12	2380
m	Heinbuch, D. (GER)	7	2365
f	Heinemann, Th. (GER)	10	2380
f	Heinig, W. (GER)	7	2315
	Heinsohn, W. (GER)	0	2210
m	Heintze, M. (GER)	0	2235
	Heinz, J. (GER)	3	2270
	Heisel, G. (GER)	16	2255
	Heisman, D. (USA)	0	2285
	Heissler, J. (GER)	15	2425
	Helbig, P. (ENG)	0	2210
	Held, M. (GER)	15	2205
	Helenius, M. (FIN)	8	2290
f	Helgason, R. (SWE)	0	2340
	Helis, T. (POL)	17	2250
	Hellborg, T. (SWE)	0	2240
g	Hellers, F. (SWE)	30	2560
	Hellsten, J. (SWE)	17	2320
	Helmer, J. (ROM)	9	2225
	Helmrich, J. (HUN)	0	2315
	Hempson, P. W. (ENG)	0	2235
m	Henao, R. F. (COL)	23	2390
	Henc, R. (POL)	15	2125
	Hendriks, W. (NED)	0	2370
	Heng, D. (SIN)	0	2245
g	Henley, R. W. (USA)	0	2480
	Henni, M. (ALG)	6	2175
	Hennig, D. (GER)	1	2330
m	Hennigan, M. (ENG)	19	2415
m	Hennings, A. (GER)	5	2365
	Henrichsen, J. (DEN)	5	2185
	Henriksen, G. (NOR)	0	2250
f	Henriksson, Ch. (FIN)	17	2360
	Henriksson, J. (SWE)	0	2170
	Henris, L. (BEL)	4	2270
	Henry, R. (USA)	4	2220
	Henssler, J. (GER)	11	2230
f	Henttinen, M. I. O. (FIN)	0	2295
f	Hentunen, A. (FIN)	4	2315
	Hepworth, M. (ENG)	0	2080
f	Herb, P. (FRA)	0	2380
f	Herbrechtsmeier, Ch. (GER)	6	2285
m	Hergott, D. (CAN)	13	2430
	Hermaneck, H. (GER)	11	2155
m	Hermann, M. (GER)	16	2395
f	Hermansson, E. (SWE)	11	2205
	Hermansson, T. (ISD)	0	2260

Hermesmann, H. (GER) 6 2305
f Hermlin, A. (EST) 9 2365
Hernandez Deniz, R. (ESP) 0 2295
Hernandez Penna, S. (ARG) 7 2075
f Hernandez, Alb. (CUB) 0 2330
Hernandez, Alf. (MEX) 0 2185
Hernandez, Ama. (CUB) 0 2210
f Hernandez, Ame. (VEN) 0 2080
Hernandez, C. (MEX) 0 2245
Hernandez, E. (MEX) 0 2280
Hernandez, F. (CRC) 9 2210
Hernandez, Ge. (CUB) 0 2270
m Hernandez, Gi. (MEX) 13 2510
Hernandez, Gustavo (VEN) 0 2240
m Hernandez, Gustavo (DOM) 0 2340
f Hernandez, Je. (CUB) 0 2285
Hernandez, Ju. (CHI) 22 2290
Hernandez, P. (CUB) 0 2185
Hernandez, Rod. (CUB) 5 2200
g Hernandez, Rom. (CUB) 0 2450
f Hernandez, T. (CUB) 12 2220
Hernandez, Ya. (MEX) 13 2140
f Hernandez, Yu. (CUB) 12 2205
f Hernando Pertierra, J. C. (ESP) 4 2400
f Herndl, H. (AUT) 10 2310
Heroic, D. (CRO) 0 2275
Heron, H. (ENG) 0 2115
Herpai, J. (HUN) 0 2320
f Herrera Perez, J. (CUB) 0 2235
Herrera, F. (ARG) 4 2255
m Herrera, I. (CUB) 22 2365
Herrera, L. (ARG) 7 2030
Herrera, M. (MEX) 0 2355
f Herrmann, M. (GER) 0 2260
f Hertan, Ch. E. (USA) 7 2360
g Hertneck, G. (GER) 36 2555
f Hertzog, P. (GER) 0 2300
Heruti, O. (ISR) 9 2175
f Herzog, A. (AUT) 7 2350
Herzog, J. (SUI) 0 2285
Herzog, M. (SUI) 0 2265
Hess, Ch. (GER) 0 2250
Hess, M. (GER) 0 2110
m Hess, R. (GER) 12 2400
f Hesse, P. (GER) 4 2370
Hetenyi, G. (HUN) 0 2220
Hetey, L. (GER) 0 2285
Heuer, Th. (GER) 0 2305
Heuer, V. P. (EST) 0 2305
Heutschi, M. (ROM) 0 2200
f Hever, M. (HUN) 11 2330
Hevesi, Z. (HUN) 3 2230
Hewitt, W. (WLS) 9 2115
m Heyken, E. (GER) 22 2360
g Hickl, J. (GER) 42 2570
Hickl, Th. (GER) 0 2285
Hidalgo Mateos, J. J. (ESP) 0 2220
Hidalgo, A. (ESP) 9 2335
Hiderick, P. N. (BRA) 0 2305
Hidzos, G. (GRE) 0 2045
Hiebel, J. (GER) 8 2285
Hiermann, D. (AUT) 0 2115
Hifny, M. (EGY) 24 2365
Higatsberger, M. (AUT) 6 2185
Hill, R. (AUS) 0 2225
m Hill, Sh. M. (AUS) 0 2295
Hillarp Persson, T. (SWE) 8 2350
Hille, R. I. (GER) 5 2305
Hillermann, V. (GER) 3 2300
Hillery, J. (USA) 0 2275
Himmel, H. (GER) 9 2355
Hingst, S. (GER) 0 2245
Hinks-Edwards, Th. (ENG) 0 2205
Hinterberger, W. (AUT) 0 2175
Hintikka, E. (FIN) 2 2230
Hirht, U. (GER) 0 2170
Hirnik, H. (POL) 0 2275
Hirsch, J. (AUT) 0 2210
Hirtsgaard, N. (DEN) 0 2295
Hirzel, R. (SUI) 2 2215
Hj Kura, A. (BRU) 0 2205
g Hjartarson, J. (ISD) 25 2605
f Hjelm, N. (SWE) 0 2255
Hjelmas, L. (NOR) 0 2315
Hlavac, F. (TCH) 0 2245
Hlavnicka, J. (TCH) 0 2235
Hlian, E. (RUS) 9 2310
Hlusevich, S. (RUS) 0 2380
m Hmadi, S. (TUN) 9 2340
Hmelnicky, I. (RUS) 0 2345
Ho, V. H. (VIE) 0 2320
f Hoang Th., T. (VIE) 36 2300
Hobaica, J. P. (ARG) 9 2230
Hobuss, U. (GER) 0 2355
Hochgraefe, M. (GER) 0 2270
Hochreiter, J. (GER) 0 2335
Hodarkovski, M. (UKR) 0 2260
Hodgson, Jo. (ENG) 1 2240
g Hodgson, Ju. M. (ENG) 69 2625
Hodjko, V. (RUS) 0 2295
Hodot, Y. (FRA) 0 2180
Hoeckendorf, H. (GER) 0 2235
Hoefker, M. (GER) 0 2330
Hoehn, J. (GER) 2 2210
m Hoeksema, H. P. (NED) 0 2405
Hoellmann, L. (GER) 0 2260
Hoellrigl, W. (AUT) 0 2250
m Hoelzl, F. (AUT) 15 2390
f Hoen, R. (NOR) 0 2340
Hoenig, A. (GER) 0 2295
f Hoensch, M. (GER) 0 2325
Hoepfl, Th. (GER) 0 2240
Hofbauer, M. (AUT) 0 2265
Hofbauer, P. (AUT) 0 2215
Hoff, T. (NOR) 3 2040
m Hoffman, A. (ARG) 63 2440
Hoffman, R. (FRA) 0 2015
f Hoffmann, A. (USA) 3 2265
f Hoffmann, Ha. (GER) 4 2250
Hoffmann, He. (GER) 0 2195
m Hoffmann, M. (GER) 18 2455
Hoffmann, N. (GER) 11 2135
Hofman, R. (NED) 0 2235
Hofmann, Max (AUT) 0 2215
Hofmann, Mi. (SUI) 0 2250
Hogenacker, J. (GER) 0 2270
Hohelj, S. (UKR) 4 2305
f Hohler, P. (SUI) 0 2245
m Hoi, C. (DEN) 18 2400
m Hoiberg, N. (DEN) 9 2210
Hoidahl, E. (NOR) 0 2205
Hojman, A. (ARG) 9 2310
Holander, P. (ISR) 0 2240
Holderer, E. (GER) 0 2225
Holfelder, J. (GER) 0 2315
Holland, Ch. (ENG) 8 2230
Holland, E. (ENG) 5 2235
Holler, M. (GER) 11 2160
Hollermann, Th. (GER) 0 2265
Holm, M. (SWE) 0 2315
f Holmes, D. A. (SCO) 0 2300
Holmsgaard, H. (DEN) 4 2335
Holmsten, A. (FIN) 7 2285
m Holoubkova, M. (TCH) 16 2235
Holst, A. (DEN) 10 2330
Holst, C. (SWE) 18 2220
Holzapfel, D. (GER) 0 2285
Holzer, G. (AUT) 0 2230
f Holzhaeuer, M. (GER) 8 2355
Holzke, F. (GER) 18 2375
f Holzmann, H. (AUT) 9 2235
f Hon Kah Seng, Ch. (MAS) 0 2235
Hon, A. (ENG) 0 2300
Honfi, Gy. (HUN) 0 2240
m Honfi, Karoly (HUN) 26 2365
m Honfi, Karolyne (HUN) 0 2035
f Honos, A. (HUN) 8 2290
Honsch, P. (HUN) 9 2225
Hook, W. (IVB) 0 2205
Horak, Ji. (TCH) 0 2265
Horak, Jo. (TCH) 0 2360
Horak, M. (TCH) 6 2310
Horkai, A. (HUN) 4 2270
f Horn, P. (SUI) 0 2305
f Hornicek, J. (TCH) 0 2320
Hornung, H. (GER) 12 2220
Hornung, K. (AUS) 0 2260
Horodyski, R. (POL) 0 2320
Horoschavina, O. (UKR) 0 2120
f Horstmann, Ma. (GER) 0 2310
Horstmann, Mi. (GER) 0 2240
Horstmann, R. (GER) 0 2255
g Hort, V. (GER) 30 2530
f Horton, J. (CAN) 0 2325
Horvath, Ad. (HUN) 6 2095
Horvath, An. (HUN) 5 2290
m Horvath, Cs. (HUN) 20 2495
Horvath, D. (HUN) 0 2315
Horvath, Ga. (HUN) 9 2285
m Horvath, Gy. (HUN) 13 2450
f Horvath, Im. (HUN) 21 2400
Horvath, Is. (HUN) 17 2235
Horvath, Je. K. (HUN) 4 2210
g Horvath, Jozsef (HUN) 81 2545
Horvath, Jozsef M. (HUN) 10 2200
m Horvath, Ju. (HUN) 27 2245
Horvath, K. (HUN) 0 2280
f Horvath, Ma. (AUT) 10 2060
f Horvath, Miklos (HUN) 8 2275
f Horvath, Miklosne (HUN) 6 2165
f Horvath, Peter (HUN) 13 2390
Horvath, Peter (HUN) 10 2290
f Horvath, Sandor (HUN) 24 2325
Horvath, Sandor (HUN) 4 2215
m Horvath, Tamas (HUN) 13 2460
Horvath, Tamas I. (HUN) 4 2290
f Horvath, Z. (HUN) 9 2350
Hosek, M. (TCH) 0 2300
Hosticka, F. (TCH) 0 2240
Houser, P. (TCH) 0 2335
Houska, M. (ENG) 5 2300
Houston, D. (IRL) 0 2235
Hovanecz, L. (HUN) 5 2350
Hovde, F. (NOR) 0 2285
Hove, E. K. (DEN) 0 2275
Hove, J. B. (USA) 11 2245
Howell, Ch. (ENG) 9 2130
m Howell, J. C. (ENG) 44 2505
Hoyos-Millan, L. B. (COL) 15 2155
Hrabe, P. (TCH) 0 2330
m Hracek, Z. (TCH) 14 2510
f Hradeczky, T. (HUN) 1 2245
Hramtsov, A. (RUS) 14 2265
Hrapin, V. (RUS) 0 2265
Hrbolka, L. (TCH) 0 2260
m Hresc, V. (CRO) 5 2385
Hrisanthopoulos, D. (GRE) 0 2225
f Hristodorescu, D. (ROM) 29 2350
Hrivnak, V. (SVK) 0 2250
f Hsu, L. Y. (SIN) 38 2455
Huang, Zhengyuan (CHN) 0 2210
Huba, M. (SVK) 0 2195
Huber, A. (GER) 0 2310
Huber, G. (CAN) 0 2245
Huber, M. (GER) 0 2255
Hubert, R. (GER) 0 2385

	Huberty, M. (LUX)	0	2130
	Huda, N. (MAS)	12	2035
	Huda, R. (CAN)	0	2295
	Hudecek, J. (TCH)	6	2320
	Huebner, L. (GER)	0	2220
g	Huebner, R. (GER)	35	2605
	Huelsmann, J. (GER)	0	2225
	Huemmer, B. (GER)	4	2290
	Huenerkopf, H. (GER)	0	2295
f	Huergo, J. R. (CUB)	0	2335
m	Huerta, R. (CUB)	10	2320
	Hug, M. (SUI)	0	2235
m	Hug, W. (SUI)	0	2430
	Hugentobler, P. (SUI)	0	2260
	Hughes, Pe. (ENG)	0	2195
	Hughes, Ph. G. (ENG)	0	2220
	Hughes, S. (WLS)	9	2170
	Hugony, F. (ITA)	0	2255
	Huguet, B. (FRA)	0	2230
f	Huisl, W. (GER)	0	2325
	Huismann, Th. (BEL)	0	2225
	Hujo, J. (SVK)	0	2270
g	Hulak, K. (CRO)	31	2535
	Hulse, B. (USA)	8	2295
	Hultin, J. (SWE)	0	2285
	Huma, D. (ROM)	0	2255
f	Humer, W. (AUT)	9	2255
g	Hund, B. (SUI)	0	2250
f	Hund, I. (GER)	0	2115
	Hunt, A. (ENG)	9	2150
f	Hunt, H. (ENG)	26	2135
f	Hurme, H. M. (FIN)	4	2245
	Hurnik, Z. (POL)	0	2230
f	Hurtado, M. (MEX)	10	2285
	Husari, S. (SYR)	0	2275
	Husek, Z. (TCH)	0	2255
m	Huss, A. (SUI)	6	2410
	Hussein, H. A. (IRQ)	0	2430
	Hussein, N. A. (IRQ)	0	2305
	Hussein, Na. (YEM)	0	2195
	Huster, M. (GER)	6	2255
	Huszar, A. (HUN)	0	2205
	Hutcheson, J. (BOT)	0	2255
f	Hutchings, S. J. (WLS)	0	2325
	Hutter, O. (GER)	0	2220
m	Hutters, T. (DEN)	6	2430
g	Huzman, A. (UKR)	20	2520
	Hvenekilde, J. (DEN)	9	2320
	Hybl, J. (TCH)	0	2300
	Hyll, J. (TCH)	9	2100
	Hynes, K. A. (IRL)	4	2240

I

	Iacob, I. (ROM)	0	2280
	Iailian, M. (GEO)	0	2430
f	Iannacone, E. (ITA)	5	2395
f	Ianniello, R. (ITA)	4	2325
	Ianov, V. (RUS)	24	2295
m	Iashvili, A. (GEO)	5	2435
	Ibanez, D. (CUB)	0	2240
	Ibanez, F. (ARG)	4	2190
	Ibar, M. (ARG)	16	2300
	Ibragimov, A. (RUS)	0	2415
m	Ibragimov, I. (RUS)	60	2550
	Icklicki, W. (BEL)	0	2220
	Idelstein, M. (ISR)	7	2230
	Iglesias, Ale. (ARG)	4	2250
	Iglesias, Alf. (MEX)	0	2215
	Ignat, D. (ROM)	3	2055
	Ignatescu, Ra. (ROM)	11	2340
f	Ignatescu, Ru. (ROM)	13	2100
	Ignjatovic, G. (YUG)	5	2240
	Ikonic, B. (YUG)	0	2295
	Ikonnikov, D. (RUS)	0	2390
m	Ikonnikov, V. (RUS)	44	2485
	Ilandzis, S. (GRE)	0	2290
	Ilczuk, J. (POL)	0	2255
	Ilczuk, P. (POL)	3	2300
m	Ilic, Dragan (YUG)	8	2380
	Ilic, Dragan B. (YUG)	6	2260
	Ilic, G. (YUG)	12	2155
	Ilic, Ljubi. (YUG)	0	2330
f	Ilic, Ljubo. (YUG)	14	2275
	Ilic, St. M. (YUG)	0	2240
	Ilic, Sl. (YUG)	2	2270
	Ilic, V. (YUG)	0	2250
m	Ilic, Zoran (YUG)	0	2390
	Ilic, Zoran (YUG)	3	2240
	Ilieva, H. (BUL)	0	2140
f	Ilijć, M. (YUG)	0	2270
	Ilijev, M. (BUL)	0	2255
	Ilijevski, B. (YUG)	0	2225
f	Ilijevski, D. (YUG)	0	2310
m	Ilijin, N. (ROM)	4	2290
m	Ilincic, Z. (YUG)	58	2505
	Ilinsky, V. (KYR)	25	2355
	Iljikov, I. (BUL)	0	2245
g	Illescas Cordoba, M. (ESP)	52	2625
	Illetsko, J. (TCH)	0	2240
	Illi, H.-J. (SUI)	6	2185
	Illner, A. (GER)	11	2355
f	Imanaliev, T. (KYR)	13	2385
	Imocha, L. (IND)	0	2270
	Impris, O. (GER)	0	2345
m	Indjic, D. (YUG)	5	2385
f	Ingbrandt, J. (SWE)	0	2345
g	Inkiov, V. (BUL)	28	2485
	Inocencio, E. S. (USA)	10	2310
	Insam, H. (AUT)	0	2285
f	Ioakimidis, G. (GRE)	5	2305
	Ioffe, A. (RUS)	3	2320
	Iondescu-Brandis, I. (ROM)	44	2185
m	Ionescu, Co. (ROM)	60	2460
f	Ionescu, Cr. (ROM)	0	2275
	Ionescu, D. A. (ROM)	14	2270
	Ionescu, M. (ROM)	22	2255
	Ionescu, R. (ROM)	0	2275
m	Ionescu-Ilie, V. (ROM)	33	2160
f	Ionita, M. (ROM)	9	2115
m	Ionov, S. (RUS)	24	2495
	Iordache, C. B. (ROM)	0	2245
	Iordachescu, V. (MOL)	46	2375
g	Ioseliani, N. (GEO)	8	2470
f	Iosif, C. S. (ROM)	17	2210
	Iosif, M. (ROM)	10	2320
	Iotti, P. (ITA)	0	2300
	Ipek, A. (TUR)	4	2260
f	Ipek, N. (TUR)	0	2105
	Iruzubieta, J. M. (ESP)	28	2360
	Irzhanov, R. (KAZ)	14	2365
	Isaacs, R. (USA)	10	2225
	Isachievici, F. (ROM)	0	2220
	Isaev, A. (RUS)	0	2380
	Isaev, D. (TAJ)	0	2380
	Isepy, T. (HUN)	0	2245
m	Iskov, G. (DEN)	0	2320
	Isler, P. (SUI)	10	2185
	Ismai, H. (SYR)	0	2205
	Ismail, M. J. (IND)	8	2275
	Ismaitova, L. (AZE)	9	2155
	Issakainen, A. (FIN)	1	2245
m	Istratescu, A. (ROM)	64	2505
m	Istvandi, L. (HUN)	10	2355
	Istvanovszky, K. (HUN)	8	2300
	Isupov, V. (RUS)	10	2300
	Isusova, N. (BUL)	0	2045
	Itaas, S. (PHI)	0	2005
	Iten, P. (SUI)	0	2260
m	Itkis, B. (MOL)	59	2430
	Iuldachev, S. (UZB)	28	2445
	Ivacic, V. (SLO)	5	2295
	Ivan, A. (HUN)	0	2240
	Ivan, Z. (HUN)	0	2240
g	Ivanchuk, V. (UKR)	13	2705
	Ivancsics, M. (AUT)	0	2225
	Ivanenko, S. (RUS)	0	2300
m	Ivanisevic, Dusica (YUG)	12	2160
	Ivanisevic, Dusko (YUG)	12	2255
	Ivanisevic, I. (YUG)	0	2210
g	Ivanka-Budinsky, M. (HUN)	0	2260
	Ivankovic, G. (YUG)	5	2225
g	Ivanov, Alexa. V. (USA)	44	2535
m	Ivanov, Alexey (RUS)	23	2475
	Ivanov, An. (RUS)	0	2230
	Ivanov, E. (BUL)	0	2220
m	Ivanov, I. V. (USA)	63	2505
m	Ivanov, J. (BUL)	33	2425
	Ivanov, M. D. (RUS)	0	2285
g	Ivanov, Mi. M. (RUS)	0	2515
	Ivanov, O. (RUS)	6	2415
m	Ivanov, Se. (RUS)	27	2505
	Ivanov, Stoi. (BUL)	2	2170
	Ivanov, Stoj. (BUL)	0	2295
	Ivanov, T. (RUS)	42	2415
	Ivanov, V. I. (RUS)	4	2230
m	Ivanov, Vi. L. (RUS)	24	2410
g	Ivanovic, B. (YUG)	60	2475
	Ivanovic, M. (YUG)	4	2225
	Ivanovic, N. (YUG)	0	2225
f	Ivanovic, Z. (CRO)	0	2290
	Ivanyi, A. (HUN)	0	2275
f	Ivekovic, M. (CRO)	1	2310
g	Ivkov, B. (YUG)	0	2505
f	Ivkovic, D. (YUG)	0	2235
	Ivkovic, L. (YUG)	0	2230
	Ivkovic, S. (YUG)	0	2225
	Ivlev, V. (RUS)	11	2355
	Izaba, R. (NCA)	22	2110
	Izdebska, M. (POL)	11	2055
m	Izeta, F. (ESP)	35	2510
f	Izquierdo, D. (URU)	8	2315
m	Izrailov, I. (USA)	0	2195
f	Izsak, Gy. (HUN)	19	2385
	Izumikawa, B. (USA)	0	2365

J

	Jaaniste, K. (EST)	11	2090
	Jabir, S. (IRQ)	0	2125
f	Jablan, M. (YUG)	0	2270
	Jablonski, M. (POL)	0	2290
	Jablonski, Z. (POL)	0	2240
	Jachym, M. (FRA)	0	2250
m	Jacimovic, D. (YUG)	50	2375
	Jacimovic, S. (YUG)	7	2230
f	Jackelen, Th. (GER)	12	2425
	Jackson, A. (ENG)	0	2215
	Jackson, O. (ENG)	3	2235
	Jackson, R. (ISV)	0	2205
m	Jackson, Sh. (ENG)	14	2175
	Jacob, V. (GER)	0	2240
f	Jacobi, S. (USA)	0	2365
m	Jacobs, B. A. (ENG)	0	2300
	Jacobsen, B. (DEN)	11	2285
	Jacoby, F. (GER)	2	2240
	Jacoby, G. (GER)	0	2275
	Jacques, R. (FRA)	15	2160
m	Jadoul, M. (BEL)	0	2410
f	Jaeckle, M. (GER)	0	2320
	Jaeger, H. (GER)	0	2210
	Jaehnisch, O. (GER)	10	2280
	Jaeschke, B. (GER)	0	2235
	Jagicza, I. (HUN)	2	2320
	Jagicza, Zs. (HUN)	4	2280
	Jagodzinski, W. (POL)	0	2255
m	Jahn, C. (GER)	11	2195
	Jahn, G. (GER)	2	2075
	Jahr, U. (GER)	4	2190
	Jakob, S. (SUI)	3	2270
f	Jakobetz, L. (HUN)	8	2325
m	Jakobsen, O. (DEN)	11	2365

	Name		
	Jakobsen, P. (DEN)	0	2270
	Jakovljev, Z. (YUG)	0	2225
f	Jakovljevic, M. (YUG)	4	2340
	Jakovljevic, Vladan (YUG)	0	2230
	Jakovljevic, Vlado (YUG)	11	2290
	Jaksland, T. (DEN)	0	2245
	Jakubiec, A. (POL)	21	2355
	Jakubovics, N. (ENG)	8	2250
	Jakubowski, J. (POL)	0	2265
	Jakubowski, T. (POL)	11	2185
f	Jakus, K. (HUN)	0	2150
	Jalal, A. A. (IRQ)	0	2190
	Jaldin, J. (BOL)	0	2205
f	Jalowiec, H. (POL)	0	2145
	James, Dale R. (ENG)	0	2260
f	James, Dav. (WLS)	16	2255
m	Jamieson, R. M. (AUS)	7	2445
	Jamrich, Gy. (HUN)	6	2180
	Jamroz, Z. (POL)	0	2280
	Janachkov, A. (BUL)	0	2295
	Janahi, K. (BRN)	8	2250
f	Janahi, Z. (BRN)	0	2205
m	Janakiev, I. (BUL)	0	2325
	Janchev, P. (BUL)	0	2275
	Jancu, J.-M. (FRA)	0	2235
	Jandourek, L. (TCH)	0	2270
f	Janetschek, K. (AUT)	11	2325
	Janev, E. (BUL)	13	2395
m	Janjgava, L. (GEO)	0	2510
	Janjgava, N. (GEO)	0	2230
	Jankov, T. (BUL)	0	2305
f	Jankovec, I. (TCH)	0	2265
	Jankovic, M. (YUG)	4	2230
	Jankovskis, G. (LAT)	13	2310
	Jankowski, J. (POL)	0	2310
	Jankurova, J. (SVK)	0	2065
	Janocha, W. (POL)	9	2390
	Janoev, D. (GEO)	0	2385
	Janoschka, A. (GER)	13	2240
	Janosik, Gy. (HUN)	0	2235
	Janota, H. (POL)	8	2250
	Janov, V. (UKR)	8	2285
m	Janovsky, S. (RUS)	20	2445
g	Jansa, V. (TCH)	24	2500
	Jansen, A. (GER)	12	2310
	Jansen, P. (NED)	0	2045
f	Janssen, H. (NED)	0	2370
f	Jansson, J. (NOR)	0	2275
	Jantzen, H. (GER)	0	2295
	Janukovitch, A. (BLA)	9	2100
f	Janus, E. (GER)	2	2090
	Japaridze, D. (GEO)	0	2220
	Jaracz, P. (POL)	30	2345
m	Jarmolinskaia, M. (ISR)	26	2265
	Jarzynski, A. (POL)	0	2290
	Jashchenko, O. (RUS)	17	2195
	Jasinczuk, J. (FRA)	0	2330
m	Jasnikowski, Z. (POL)	42	2450
	Jaster, R. (GER)	0	2205
	Jaulin, M. (FRA)	8	2240
f	Jaworski, M. (POL)	3	2335
	Jazbinsek, S. (SLO)	9	2055
f	Jelen, Ig. (SLO)	14	2325
m	Jelen, Iz. (SLO)	5	2390
	Jelezov, S. (BUL)	0	2340
f	Jelic, G. (YUG)	10	2335
	Jell, K. (GER)	0	2210
m	Jelling, E. (DEN)	0	2400
	Jenal, J. (SUI)	2	2190
	Jenei, F. (HUN)	0	2215
	Jensen, A. (DEN)	0	2215
	Jensen, Ch. (DEN)	0	2015
	Jensen, F. (DEN)	10	2180
	Jensen, J. B. (DEN)	0	2255
	Jensen, R. (DEN)	0	2295
	Jensen, V. (DEN)	7	2235
	Jentsch, K. (GER)	9	2185
	Jepson, Ch. (SWE)	14	2295
	Jerabek, P. (TCH)	0	2230
	Jeraj, Z. (SLO)	7	2190
	Jeras, S. (YUG)	10	2130
	Jeremic, M. (YUG)	0	2330
f	Jeremic, S. (YUG)	0	2315
	Jerez, A. (ESP)	14	2270
f	Jeric, S. (SLO)	15	2365
	Jerimic, M. (YUG)	0	2250
	Jersblad, J. (SWE)	0	2090
	Jesenski, T. (YUG)	4	2245
	Jesic, D. (YUG)	0	2340
	Jeszenkovics, T. (HUN)	4	2250
	Jetzl, J. (AUT)	4	2255
f	Jevdjovic, M. (YUG)	0	2345
	Jevremovic, S. (YUG)	0	2225
	Jevtic, B. (YUG)	13	2040
f	Jevtic, Mio. (YUG)	21	2395
	Jevtic, Mir. (YUG)	0	2315
	Jezierski, P. (POL)	0	2310
	Jha, K. K. (IND)	0	2115
	Jhunjhnuwala, N. (HKG)	0	2240
	Jhunjhnuwala, R. (HKG)	0	2260
	Jiang, Chun (CHN)	0	2090
m	Jicman, L. (ROM)	36	2180
	Jimenez Frutos, F. (PAR)	0	2215
	Jimenez Morales, F. (ESP)	3	2220
	Jimenez Villena, F. J. (ESP)	3	2270
	Jimenez, A. (ESP)	0	2270
	Jiroveanu, G. (ROM)	10	2190
m	Jirovsky, M. (TCH)	5	2420
	Jirovsky, P. (TCH)	0	2290
	Jobe, M. (BOT)	0	2205
	Jochinger, F. (AUT)	2	2245
	Jocic, S. (YUG)	7	2265
	Jocovic, S. (YUG)	0	2295
f	Joecks, Ch. (GER)	12	2345
m	Johannessen, S. (NOR)	0	2330
f	Johannesson, L. (ISD)	0	2290
m	Johansen, D. K. (AUS)	14	2495
	Johansen, O. (NOR)	13	2325
	Johansen, T. O. (DEN)	0	2285
	Johansson, C. F. (SWE)	4	2220
	Johansson, G. (SWE)	0	2230
m	Johansson, J. (SWE)	2	2395
	Johansson, L.-E. (SWE)	0	2360
	Johansson, M. (SWE)	3	2270
	Johansson, Th. (SWE)	9	2110
	Johansson, U. (SWE)	0	2215
m	Johansson, V. (SWE)	13	2155
	Johnsen, Sv. (NOR)	0	2215
	Johnsen, Sy. (NOR)	9	2050
	Johnson, J. F. (USA)	0	2230
	Johnson, L. J. (USA)	11	2275
f	Johnstone, G. (CAN)	0	2305
	Johnstone, P. E. (ENG)	9	2280
f	Joita, P. (ROM)	0	2330
f	Jojic, M. (YUG)	0	2325
	Jojic, O. (FRA)	9	2235
	Jokic, I. (YUG)	0	2375
	Jokovic, D. (SLO)	0	2215
	Joksch, A. (GER)	3	2220
m	Joksic, S. (YUG)	0	2325
	Joksimovic, D. (YUG)	0	2315
f	Joksimovic, S. (YUG)	0	2295
f	Jolles, H. (NED)	0	2280
	Jolowicz, M. (GER)	0	2265
f	Jonasson, B. (ISD)	0	2280
	Jonczyk, W. (POL)	4	2230
	Jones, A. (WLS)	0	2295
	Jones, B. (AUS)	0	2280
	Jones, Ch. B. (USA)	4	2220
	Jones, Cu. (USA)	12	2380
	Jones, I. C. (WLS)	0	2235
	Jones, K. E. (USA)	0	2215
	Jongsma, W. (NED)	0	2185
	Jonker, M. (NED)	0	2325
	Jonkman, H. (NED)	8	2345
f	Jonsson, B. (ISD)	10	2405
f	Jonsson, H. (SWE)	1	2345
	Jonsson, L. (SWE)	15	2185
	Jonsson, M. (SWE)	11	2295
	Jooty, A. (MRI)	0	2205
	Jordan, W. (AUS)	0	2310
	Jorgensen, Brian (DEN)	0	2215
	Jorgensen, Brian J. (DEN)	0	2270
	Jorgensen, P. D. (DEN)	0	2295
	Jose, P. (FRA)	0	2235
f	Josenhans, D. (USA)	0	2245
	Joseph, S. (ENG)	0	2235
	Joseph, Y. (MNC)	0	2205
	Josephsen, N. (DEN)	0	2250
	Joshi, G. B. (IND)	7	2295
f	Joshi, S. J. (IND)	5	2310
f	Joshi, Sa (USA)	0	2405
f	Jost, C. (FRA)	2	2330
	Jouhki, Y. M. (FIN)	2	2230
	Joukl, Z. (TCH)	11	2170
	Jouravljev, A. (RUS)	4	2295
	Jovancic, M. (YUG)	3	2245
	Jovanovic, Bob. (YUG)	0	2250
	Jovanovic, Boj. (YUG)	13	2305
	Jovanovic, G. (YUG)	13	2090
	Jovanovic, J. (YUG)	24	2135
	Jovanovic, Mil. (YUG)	0	2330
	Jovanovic, Mir. (YUG)	0	2065
	Jovanovic, N. (YUG)	0	2325
	Jovanovic, Sanja (YUG)	24	2090
	Jovanovic, Sasa D. (CRO)	0	2290
f	Jovanovic, Sasa T. (YUG)	46	2300
	Jovanovic, Sr. (YUG)	0	2100
	Jovanovic, Z. (YUG)	26	2295
	Jovanovski, V. (YUG)	17	2340
	Jovcevska, P. (YUG)	0	2080
	Jovchev, A. (BUL)	18	2200
f	Jovcic, M. (YUG)	0	2285
	Jovcic, Z. (YUG)	0	2255
f	Jovic, A. (YUG)	1	2350
	Jovic, Dr. (YUG)	2	2315
	Jovic, Du. (YUG)	14	2315
m	Jovic, Lj. (YUG)	0	2345
	Jovic, S. (YUG)	5	2270
	Jovicevic, B. (YUG)	33	2280
m	Jovicic, M. (YUG)	0	2385
	Jovicic, R. (YUG)	0	2295
	Jovkova-Draganova, P. (BUL)	0	2055
	Jowett, P. (ENG)	9	2225
	Joyce, J. (IRL)	10	2185
	Joyner, L. (CAN)	0	2240
	Jozsa, Cs. (HUN)	10	2280
	Jozsa, Z. (HUN)	0	2120
m	Juarez Flores, C. A. (GUA)	0	2385
	Juarez Flores, G. E. (GUA)	0	2265
	Juarez Flores, J. G. (GUA)	0	2225
	Juarez Flores, R. (MEX)	0	2300
f	Juarez, A. (ARG)	20	2260
	Juarez, C. E. (ARG)	6	2285
	Judycki, W. (POL)	2	2205
	Juergen, D. (GER)	0	2270
	Juergens, P. (GER)	14	2235
	Juergensen, M. (GER)	0	2270
	Juhasz, B. (HUN)	18	2225
	Juhasz, J. (HUN)	8	2250
	Juhasz, L. (HUN)	0	2165
	Juhasz, M. (HUN)	0	2240
f	Juhnke, K. (GER)	0	2305
f	Jukic, B. (CRO)	6	2375
m	Jukic, M. (CRO)	5	2490
	Jukic, Z. (CRO)	0	2240
	Julia, E. (ARG)	1	2295
	Julve, Ph. (FRA)	0	2145
	Junco, C. (CUB)	0	2205
	Jung, K.-O. (GER)	4	2230

	Name	Games	Rating
f	Junge, R. (GER)	6	2355
	Juracsik, J. (HUN)	0	2215
	Juraczka, F. (AUT)	0	2290
m	Jurczynska, A. (POL)	5	2050
m	Jurek, J. (TCH)	20	2305
	Juric, S. (CRO)	0	2225
f	Jurka, M. (TCH)	4	2340
	Jurkiewicz, Krzyst. (POL)	0	2235
	Jurkiewicz, Krzysz. (POL)	8	2265
	Jurkovic, A. (CRO)	13	2290
	Jurkovic, H. (CRO)	0	2240
	Juroschkin, V. (RUS)	0	2350
	Juroszek, T. (POL)	0	2350
	Jusiak, G. (POL)	0	2335
	Jusic, Z. (CRO)	11	2335
	Just, G. (GER)	0	2070
	Justin, M. (SLO)	7	2385
f	Justo, D. (ARG)	13	2265
f	Juswanto, D. (INA)	9	2300
	Jzschenko, O. (BLA)	28	2220

K

	Name	Games	Rating
m	Kaabi, M. (TUN)	0	2315
	Kabatenski, A. (UKR)	9	2335
	Kabir, R. S. (BAN)	0	2145
	Kabisch, Th. (GER)	0	2290
	Kabli, M. A. (ALG)	6	2210
	Kabuye, E. (UGA)	0	2265
	Kacheisvili, G. (GEO)	9	2405
	Kachur, A. (UKR)	3	2295
	Kacirek, P. (TCH)	0	2190
m	Kaczorowska, B. (POL)	20	2230
	Kaczorowski, P. (POL)	6	2255
	Kaczynski, A. (POL)	0	2250
f	Kadar, G. (HUN)	8	2350
	Kadas, G. (HUN)	0	2275
m	Kadimova, I. (AZE)	24	2335
	Kadishev, L. (RUS)	2	2350
	Kadzinski, W. (POL)	5	2190
	Kaeding, R. (GER)	4	2245
	Kaelin, R. (SUI)	0	2185
f	Kaenel, H. (SUI)	5	2325
	Kaeser, U. (GER)	8	2275
	Kagan, Is. (AUS)	0	2285
	Kagan, It. (ISR)	0	2200
f	Kagan, N. (AUS)	0	2335
m	Kagan, Sh. (ISR)	0	2360
f	Kaganovski, M. (ISR)	0	2275
	Kaganski, M. (UKR)	20	2310
	Kagirov, R. (RUS)	19	2205
	Kagraminianz, V. (ARM)	0	2265
	Kahn, E. (HUN)	74	2390
	Kahn, M. (FRA)	13	2205
g	Kaidanov, G. S. (RUS)	43	2640
	Kaim, P. (POL)	14	2290
	Kaiser, D. (GER)	0	2260
f	Kaiser, W. (GER)	0	2355
m	Kaiszauri, K. (SWE)	6	2345
m	Kaiumov, D. D. (UZB)	15	2425
	Kajganovic, M. (YUG)	4	2300
	Kajnih, D. (SLO)	1	2240
	Kajumova, I. (UZB)	0	2060
	Kakabadze, R. (GEO)	0	2315
m	Kakageldyev, A. (TKM)	24	2465
g	Kakhiani, K. (GEO)	9	2410
	Kakuk, S. (HUN)	0	2295
	Kalantarian, N. (ARM)	7	2330
	Kalbermatter, H. (SUI)	11	2230
	Kalcheva, N. (BUL)	0	2070
m	Kaldor, A. (ISR)	0	2265
	Kaldus, A. (POL)	0	2210
	Kalegin, E. (RUS)	35	2445
m	Kalesis, N. (GRE)	30	2410
	Kalikova, J. (TCH)	0	2085
	Kaliksteyn, A. (USA)	16	2375
	Kalinichenko, Y. (UKR)	2	2270
m	Kalinichev, S. L. (RUS)	19	2480
	Kalinicheva, V. (RUS)	0	2165
	Kalinin, A. (RUS)	35	2390
	Kalinin, M. (GER)	8	2350
m	Kalinin, O. (UKR)	8	2420
	Kalinin, V. (WLS)	0	2275
	Kalinski, I. A. (UKR)	0	2220
	Kaliszewski, T. (POL)	11	2185
	Kalivoda, J. (TCH)	0	2250
f	Kalka, A. G. (GER)	9	2345
m	Kallai, G. (HUN)	31	2460
	Kallgren, M. (SWE)	0	2020
	Kalmar, K. (HUN)	15	2145
f	Kaloussis, E. (GRE)	0	2280
	Kamal, A. E. E. (EGY)	15	2115
	Kamaras, O. (HUN)	0	2240
	Kamaras, P. (HUN)	0	2245
	Kamath, R. C. (IND)	0	2115
	Kamath, S. J. (IND)	16	2250
f	Kamber, B. (SUI)	9	2325
	Kaminik, A. (UKR)	7	2200
f	Kaminker, H. (CAN)	0	2320
	Kaminski, J. (POL)	0	2235
m	Kaminski, M. (POL)	34	2450
m	Kaminski, U. (GER)	14	2385
f	Kaminsky, O. M. (USA)	0	2340
	Kamp, Ch. (GER)	9	2275
g	Kamsky, G. (USA)	34	2645
	Kamstra, C. (NED)	0	2240
	Kamuhangire, S. (UGA)	0	2190
	Kanamori, A. (USA)	0	2255
	Kandyba, L. (RUS)	16	2370
f	Kanefsck, G. (ARG)	32	2325
	Kanengoni, A. T. (ZIM)	0	2260
	Kania, A. (GER)	0	2285
	Kania, P. (POL)	6	2265
	Kanikevich, A. (AUS)	0	2410
f	Kanko, I. (FIN)	17	2330
m	Kanstler, B. (KYR)	13	2440
	Kantorik, M. (SVK)	0	2235
	Kantorovich, A. (RUS)	0	2060
	Kanya, Z. (HUN)	0	2050
f	Kapelan, M. (YUG)	0	2305
	Kapeljus, L. (RUS)	0	2370
m	Kapengut, A. Z. (BLA)	0	2450
m	Kapetanovic, A. (YUG)	9	2480
	Kapischka, J. (GER)	10	2290
	Kapitsyn, M. (RUS)	1	2330
	Kaplan, L. (USA)	3	2185
	Kaplivatski, A. (ISR)	3	2215
	Kaplun, L. I. (UKR)	6	2400
m	Kaposztas, M. (HUN)	20	2265
f	Kappler, J.-M. (FRA)	5	2325
	Kapstan, A. (CAN)	0	2210
	Kapu, J. (HUN)	3	2250
	Karabalis, H. (GER)	9	2225
	Karacsony, A. (HUN)	3	2250
	Karadag, C. (TUR)	0	2295
	Karadimov, M. (BUL)	0	2215
	Karagodin, V. A. (RUS)	0	2365
m	Karakashian, N. (ARM)	0	2190
m	Karaklajic, N. (YUG)	13	2380
	Karanfiloski, S. (YUG)	12	2135
	Karanikolas, K. (GRE)	1	2315
	Karapanos, N. (GRE)	2	2215
f	Karapchanski, D. (BUL)	0	2355
m	Karasev, V. I. (RUS)	15	2395
	Karason, A. O. (ISD)	0	2225
	Karavaev, V. (RUS)	12	2375
f	Karayannis, A. (GRE)	0	2280
	Karbowiak, A. (POL)	0	2265
	Karcz, R. (POL)	0	2215
	Kardkovacs, Zs. (HUN)	9	2140
	Kardys, Z. (POL)	0	2245
	Kargoll, B. (GER)	0	2350
	Kargoll, P. (GER)	0	2270
	Karhunen, K. (FIN)	9	2335
	Karibaev, B. (KAZ)	14	2110
	Karic, M. (YUG)	0	2275
	Karkalas, A. (LTU)	14	2340
f	Karkanaque, I. (ALB)	0	2355
f	Karklins, A. (USA)	16	2370
f	Karl, H. (SUI)	5	2280
	Karlik, J. (TCH)	0	2300
f	Karlik, V. (TCH)	2	2280
	Karlsson, A. S. (ISD)	0	2280
g	Karlsson, L. (SWE)	4	2505
	Karmachu (ROM)	0	2010
	Karmov, M. (RUS)	0	2235
m	Karner, H. (EST)	5	2345
	Karniewski, Z. (POL)	13	2185
	Karnik, P. (TCH)	0	2295
m	Karolyi jr., T. (HUN)	19	2395
f	Karolyi sr., T. (HUN)	0	2345
	Karp, M. (ISR)	13	2260
m	Karpatchev, A. (RUS)	70	2465
	Karpeshov, O. (RUS)	0	2365
	Karpik, T. (POL)	2	2245
m	Karpman, V. (UKR)	0	2425
	Karpov, Al. (RUS)	11	2370
g	Karpov, An. (RUS)	61	2760
m	Karsa, L. (HUN)	13	2410
	Karsai, I. (HUN)	0	2220
	Karwatt, L. (GER)	0	2250
m	Kas-Fromm, R. (GER)	10	2225
	Kasa, A. (HUN)	0	2295
	Kasi, A. L. (IND)	12	2195
	Kasimdzhanov, R. (UZB)	15	2360
f	Kasioura, F. (GRE)	18	2030
	Kasmiran (INA)	0	2110
m	Kasoshvili, Ts. (GEO)	0	2220
	Kasperek, R. (POL)	0	2325
f	Kaspret, G. (AUT)	10	2315
	Kasprzyk, T. (POL)	5	2150
f	Kassabe, E. (SYR)	0	2245
	Kassebaum, R. (GER)	8	2355
	Kastanieda, G. (RUS)	20	2305
	Kastek, Th. (GER)	0	2255
	Kastner, W. (AUT)	0	2205
	Kataev, S. (RUS)	7	2340
	Katalymov, B. N. (KAZ)	14	2430
	Katavic, B. (CRO)	0	2190
	Katdare, J. C. (IND)	0	2245
	Katishonok, N. (LAT)	0	2265
	Katona, F. (HUN)	10	2255
	Katona, J. (HUN)	0	2065
	Katona, M. (HUN)	18	2225
	Kaukiel, P. (POL)	0	2335
	Kaula, R. (POL)	0	2335
	Kaulfuss, H. (GER)	6	2195
	Kaunas, K. (LTU)	8	2350
	Kauschmann, H. (GER)	18	2200
f	Kaushansky, L. (USA)	3	2255
	Kausu, C. (ZAM)	0	2205
g	Kavalek, L. (USA)	0	2550
f	Kavnatsky, V. (USA)	0	2305
	Kawaciukova, Z. (TCH)	0	2085
	Kawczynski, L. (POL)	0	2290
	Kazak, V. (RUS)	0	2315
	Kazakov, D. (BUL)	4	2245
	Kazek, K. (POL)	17	2315
	Kazgaleev, M. (RUS)	19	2370
	Kazhdan, V. (ISR)	9	2010
	Kazhgaleyev, M. (KAZ)	11	2335
	Kazilaris, N. (GRE)	2	2280
	Kazmierska, M. (POL)	0	2015
	Kctrba, T. (TCH)	0	2225
	Kearns, J. (USA)	0	2275
	Kearns, Th. J. (USA)	11	2140
	Kebbekus, Th. (GER)	5	2230
	Keca, D. (YUG)	1	2260
	Kecic, S. (SLO)	0	2255
	Keck, D. (USA)	11	2180
	Keck, I. (GER)	9	2150
	Kecskes, G. (HUN)	38	2220
	Keen, E. (BER)	0	2190
f	Keglevic, P. (CRO)	7	2315

f	Keilhack, H. (GER)	0	2325
f	Keipo, G. (CUB)	0	2255
m	Keitlinghaus, L. (GER)	29	2485
f	Kekki, J. (FIN)	10	2295
f	Kekki, P. (FIN)	7	2285
	Kelecevic, M. (YUG)	0	2340
m	Kelecevic, N. (YUG)	14	2465
	Kelleher, W. (USA)	9	2335
	Keller, Ch. (FRA)	1	2285
m	Keller, D. (SUI)	0	2375
	Keller, M. (GER)	3	2220
	Keller, R. (SUI)	0	2285
	Keller, W. (GER)	1	2225
f	Kelson, R. (USA)	10	2315
	Kemp, P. (ENG)	2	2230
	Kempa, S. (POL)	9	2145
	Kemper, M. (GER)	9	2055
	Kempinski, R. (POL)	24	2370
	Kempinski, Z. (POL)	2	2240
	Kempter, R. (GER)	0	2250
f	Kempys, M. (POL)	0	2265
	Kende, Gy. (HUN)	2	2240
g	Kengis, E. (LAT)	34	2560
f	Kennaugh, Ch. (ENG)	0	2280
m	Kennedy, Sh. (USA)	0	2030
	Kenworthy, G. (ENG)	0	2285
	Keogh, E. (IRL)	11	2190
f	Ker, A. F. (NZL)	22	2325
	Kerecki, Lj. (YUG)	0	2225
	Kerek, Cs. (HUN)	9	2175
	Kerek, K. (HUN)	17	2185
	Kerekes, A. (HUN)	0	2240
	Kerekgyarto, J. (HUN)	3	2180
f	Kereszturi, S. (HUN)	10	2160
	Kerkhof, Ph. (BEL)	0	2245
	Kerkmeester, H. (NED)	0	2220
f	Kern, G. (GER)	16	2315
	Kern, J. (GER)	2	2270
	Kersten, U. (GER)	14	2350
m	Kertesz, A. (GER)	9	2375
f	Kertesz, F. (HUN)	2	2270
	Kertesz, Zs. (HUN)	6	2130
	Keschitz, Gy. (HUN)	32	2275
	Keserovic, M. (YUG)	0	2240
	Kesmaecker, Ph. (FRA)	0	2310
	Kessler, A. (GER)	0	2230
m	Kestler, H.-G. (GER)	2	2350
	Kevorkiants, S. (BLA)	4	2320
	Kgatshe, S. (BOT)	0	2205
	Khadempour, F. (GER)	0	2130
	Khakpoor, A. (IRI)	0	2205
	Khalafian, E. (ARM)	8	2100
	Khalgantian, G. (ARM)	9	2085
	Khalidhara, M. (YEM)	6	2205
g	Khalifman, A. (RUS)	42	2645
	Khalikian, O. (ARM)	0	2365
	Khalil, A. (YEM)	0	2205
	Khaludrov, E. (RUS)	0	2255
m	Khamdanov, S. (TAJ)	0	2210
	Khamraev, K. (KAZ)	9	2355
f	Khan, M. R. (IND)	0	2320
	Khandokar, H. K. (BAN)	0	2145
	Khanzhin, F. (RUS)	0	2290
	Khariton, L. (FRA)	0	2320
g	Kharitonov, A. Y. (RUS)	31	2530
m	Kharkova, E. (RUS)	11	2205
	Kharlamov, V. (RUS)	13	2380
g	Kharlov, A. (RUS)	34	2535
	Kharnak, D. (ISR)	12	2260
m	Khasin, A. (RUS)	13	2460
	Khavsky, G. (RUS)	0	2365
	Khavsky, S. V. (RUS)	0	2350
	Khechen, N. E. (LEB)	0	2225
	Khegai, A. (RUS)	0	2005
g	Khenkin, I. (ISR)	26	2570
	Khetsuriani, B. (GEO)	0	2340
	Khlgatian, G. (ARM)	0	2115
m	Khmelnitsky, I. N. (RUS)	10	2465
m	Khmiadashvili, T. (GEO)	0	2205
	Kholmogordva, S. (RUS)	0	2200
g	Kholmov, R. D. (RUS)	59	2455
	Khomullo, V. (RUS)	19	2370
	Khomyakov, V. (UKR)	18	2340
	Khoperia, Z. (GEO)	0	2320
	Khoroshavina, O. (RUS)	0	2040
f	Khorovets-Aiedinova, E. (BLA)	33	2230
	Khoze, E. (RUS)	9	2200
	Khropov, B. (RUS)	7	2235
	Khudgarian, N. (RUS)	11	2100
	Khudiakov, I. (RUS)	0	2410
m	Khurtsidze, N. (GEO)	29	2325
	Khurtsilava, I. (GEO)	9	2095
	Kibrik, T. (USA)	0	2130
m	Kiedrowicz, J. (POL)	18	2320
	Kiefer, G. (GER)	0	2255
	Kiefhaber, H. (GER)	0	2305
	Kielech, A. (POL)	0	2225
	Kienast, J. (GER)	0	2225
	Kientzler, I. (FRA)	2	2050
	Kiernan, M. (HKG)	0	2210
	Kiersz, L. (POL)	0	2230
	Kierzek, M. (GER)	7	2145
	Kies, M. (POL)	0	2205
	Kiese, M. (GER)	9	2135
	Kiesel, H. (GER)	0	2190
	Kievelitz, B. (GER)	4	2140
	Kiik, K. (EST)	10	2370
	Kikiani, T. (GEO)	0	2220
	Kilicaslan, H. (TUR)	0	2210
	Kim, N. (RUS)	14	2245
	Kim, O. (UZB)	0	2095
f	Kimpinsky, F. (GER)	2	2295
f	Kincs, I. (HUN)	20	2215
g	Kindermann, S. (GER)	57	2520
f	Kindl, P. (GER)	0	2335
	Kinez, I. (CRO)	0	2130
g	King, D. J. (ENG)	44	2455
	Kinin, M. (RUS)	0	2215
f	Kinsman, A. P. H. (ENG)	14	2370
	Kiran, P. R. (IND)	8	2245
	Kirchner, Th. (GER)	9	2270
	Kiriakov, P. (RUS)	10	2385
	Kirilov, R. (BUL)	0	2290
	Kirilov, V. (LAT)	6	2355
f	Kiroski, T. (YUG)	42	2235
g	Kirov, N. (BUL)	48	2485
	Kirpichnikov, V. S. (LAT)	0	2390
	Kirsanov, O. (RUS)	14	2375
	Kirszenberg, M. (FRA)	0	2230
	Kis, B. (HUN)	9	2110
	Kis, J. (HUN)	11	2275
	Kiselev, G. (RUS)	44	2455
	Kiselev, M. (RUS)	0	2360
m	Kiselev, S. (RUS)	52	2470
	Kiseleva, N. (RUS)	0	2170
m	Kishnev, S. (RUS)	28	2500
	Kislov, M. (RUS)	17	2370
m	Kislova, A. V. (RUS)	0	2165
m	Kiss, A. (HUN)	23	2345
	Kiss, F. (HUN)	27	2085
	Kiss, G. (HUN)	0	2160
f	Kiss, Istvan (HUN)	12	2265
	Kiss, Istvan I. (HUN)	0	2280
f	Kiss, Las. (HUN)	22	2260
f	Kiss, Lau. (ROM)	0	2290
	Kiss, M. (ROM)	0	2075
m	Kiss, P. (HUN)	42	2420
	Kiss, V. (HUN)	18	2110
	Kitchlew, A. (ENG)	0	2065
	Kitic, D. (YUG)	0	2265
	Kitte, S. (GER)	13	2240
	Kivipelto, K.-E. (FIN)	1	2270
	Kivisto, M. (FIN)	4	2285
	Kjeldsen, J. (DEN)	18	2375
	Kjurkchiiski, G. (BUL)	0	2295
	Kladiva, I. (HUN)	4	2135
f	Klarenbeek, H. (NED)	25	2425
f	Klarenbeek, M. (NED)	17	2405
g	Klaric, Z. (CRO)	2	2415
f	Klauser, M. (SUI)	14	2350
f	Klebel, M. (GER)	8	2420
	Kleeschaetzky, Rai. (GER)	7	2285
	Kleeschaetzky, Ralf (GER)	2	2305
	Kleff, A. (GER)	10	2170
	Klein, E. (USA)	6	2310
f	Klein, L. (USA)	0	2270
	Klein, M. G. (GER)	3	2290
	Klein, P. (SVK)	0	2260
	Kleinegger, F. (GER)	3	2295
f	Kleinplatz, S. (FRA)	9	2355
	Kleinscmidt, F. (GER)	1	2245
	Klemanic, E. (SVK)	0	2215
	Kleschtscov, J. (GER)	9	2100
	Klima, Ch. (AUT)	0	2205
	Klimaszewski, D. (POL)	0	2275
f	Klimes, J. (TCH)	0	2365
	Klimm, W. (GER)	9	2275
g	Klimova-Richtrova, E. (TCH)	0	2335
	Kling, A. (SWE)	0	2245
	Klingelhoefer, S. (GER)	8	2275
g	Klinger, J. (AUT)	26	2435
	Klinova, M. (RUS)	0	2115
f	Klip, H. (NED)	0	2340
	Kljako, D. (CRO)	15	2295
	Kloepfer, M. (GER)	1	2195
	Klopfenstein, G. (USA)	0	2225
	Klostermann, M. (GER)	3	2300
m	Klovans, J. (LAT)	44	2415
	Klovsky, R. (UKR)	6	2365
	Klubis, V. (RUS)	0	2250
	Klueners, J. (GER)	0	2205
m	Kluger, Gy. (HUN)	0	2250
	Kluger, N. (GER)	0	2220
m	Klundt, K. (GER)	8	2375
	Kluss, K. (GER)	2	2255
	Kluth, C. (GER)	0	2195
	Klykow, L. (POL)	1	2225
g	Knaak, R. (GER)	25	2525
	Knase, R. (USA)	11	2085
	Knazovcik, L. (TCH)	4	2280
f	Kneselac, A. (YUG)	0	2300
f	Knezevic, B. (YUG)	25	2320
g	Knezevic, M. (YUG)	68	2415
	Knizek, J. (TCH)	0	2215
	Knobel, R. (SUI)	0	2260
	Knoedler, D. (GER)	3	2255
f	Knoppert, E. G. J. (NED)	0	2375
f	Knott, S. J. B. (ENG)	0	2315
	Knowles, C. (ENG)	0	2210
	Knox, A. (IRL)	0	2005
	Knox, D. (ENG)	0	2210
f	Knox, V. W. (ENG)	0	2315
	Knudsen, K. V. (DEN)	2	2215
f	Knudsen, P. (DEN)	0	2330
	Knuth, H. (GER)	0	2360
	Koba, I. (RUS)	5	2340
	Kobaidze, Ts. (GEO)	0	2095
	Kobalija, M. (RUS)	14	2395
f	Kobas, A. (BIH)	0	2300
f	Kober, M. (CRO)	0	2320
	Kobese, W. (GER)	11	2270
	Kobylanski, J. (POL)	12	2175
	Koc, W. (POL)	0	2265
m	Koch, J.-R. (FRA)	33	2500
f	Koch, Th. (GER)	0	2315
	Koch, W. (GER)	0	2290
g	Kochyev, A. (RUS)	11	2475
f	Kock Hans, U. (GER)	0	2315
f	Kocovski, I. (YUG)	19	2305
	Kocsis, Gy. (HUN)	6	2265
	Kocsis, J. (ROM)	0	2275
	Kocsis, L. (ROM)	0	2265
	Kocur, A. (POL)	0	2280
	Kocwin, B. (POL)	6	2275
	Koczka, Zs. (HUN)	8	2285

Title	Name	Games	Rating
	Kodric, M. (SLO)	8	2255
	Koelle, A. (AUS)	0	2215
	Koeller, O. (GER)	0	2340
m	Koen, M. (BUL)	19	2215
	Koenig, D. (GER)	18	2265
	Koenig, W. (GER)	0	2295
	Koepcke, R. (USA)	0	2285
	Koepf, U. (GER)	0	2260
	Koerant, F. (GRE)	0	2175
	Koerholz, L. (GER)	19	2295
f	Kofidis, A. (GRE)	31	2400
	Kofidis, S. (GRE)	3	2255
f	Kogan, A. (ISR)	29	2340
f	Koglin, A. (GER)	10	2125
	Koh, K.-H. (SIN)	0	2285
	Kohalmi, E. (HUN)	0	2260
	Kohl, W. (GER)	0	2305
	Kohler, A. (NED)	0	2340
	Kohlman, R. (SVK)	0	2310
m	Kohlweyer, B. (GER)	36	2455
	Kohnert, A. (GER)	0	2220
m	Kojder, K. (POL)	0	2290
	Kokanovic, K. (YUG)	0	2175
f	Kokanovic, R. (YUG)	0	2310
	Kokeza, M. (YUG)	21	2280
	Kokkila, T. (FIN)	17	2320
	Kokowski, R. (GER)	0	2305
	Kolar, D. (YUG)	0	2250
	Kolar, J. (YUG)	0	2085
f	Kolar, S. (SLO)	13	2220
	Kolasinski, M. (POL)	4	2225
	Kolbert, E. (YUG)	0	2035
	Kolbus, D. (GER)	18	2365
	Kolcak, M. (SVK)	0	2285
	Kolchakova, J. (BUL)	0	2030
	Kolendo, F. (POL)	9	2140
f	Kolesar, M. (SVK)	0	2300
	Kolev, Al. (BUL)	11	2345
g	Kolev, At. (BUL)	23	2500
	Koller, H. (AUT)	9	2160
	Kolognat, P. (YUG)	5	2290
	Koltanyi, I. (HUN)	0	2140
m	Komarov, D. (UKR)	33	2525
	Komic, I. (YUG)	0	2265
	Komissarov, I. (RUS)	9	2380
m	Komliakov, V. (MOL)	33	2440
m	Komljenovic, D. (CRO)	42	2450
	Kommar, I. (HUN)	3	2210
f	Komnenic, B. (YUG)	0	2265
g	Konarkowska-Sokolov, H. (YUG)	11	2100
	Konate, I. (MLI)	0	2205
	Koncz, I. (HUN)	0	2210
	Kondenko, A. (RUS)	7	2255
m	Kondou, E. (GRE)	20	2215
f	Konguvel, P. (IND)	7	2375
	Konieczka, F. (GER)	0	2235
	Konig, B. (HUN)	0	2175
f	Konikowski, J. (GER)	1	2345
	Konings, L. (NED)	9	2230
f	Konjevic, Dj. (YUG)	0	2375
	Konnerth, E. (GER)	0	2240
m	Konopka, M. (SVK)	30	2425
g	Konopleva, N. (RUS)	0	2170
	Konrad, L. (GER)	0	2230
	Konstandinidis, H. (GRE)	9	2125
	Konstantinov, S. (RUS)	13	2370
f	Kontic, Dj. (YUG)	64	2365
m	Kopec, D. (USA)	0	2400
	Kopecky, P. (TCH)	0	2300
	Kopisch, M. (GER)	0	2265
	Kopjonkin, G. (RUS)	14	2390
f	Koploy, P. (USA)	0	2335
	Kopp, B. (GER)	1	2260
	Kopp, P. (GER)	20	2015
	Koppens, P. (NED)	0	2335
	Kopszorus, P. (HUN)	3	2265
	Kopylov, I. (RUS)	0	2380
	Koraksic, Lj. (YUG)	0	2230
	Korbela, L. (SVK)	0	2255
g	Korchnoi, V. (SUI)	42	2625
	Kordic, N. (YUG)	0	2205
	Korenek, P. (TCH)	0	2215
	Korenev, A. (RUS)	0	2250
	Korenika, M. (CRO)	0	2275
	Korjabkin, A. (RUS)	0	2330
m	Korkina, S. (RUS)	0	2255
f	Kormanyos, Z. (HUN)	3	2345
	Kornasiewicz, J. (POL)	0	2210
f	Kornasiewicz, S. (POL)	0	2315
m	Korneev, O. (RUS)	16	2475
	Korneeva, Z. (BLA)	0	2190
	Korneevets, A. (BLA)	0	2280
	Kornilovich, V. (BLA)	9	2240
	Korniukhin, G. (RUS)	0	2260
	Koronghy, Gy. (HUN)	0	2230
	Korosparti, S. (HUN)	4	2230
	Korotylev, A. (RUS)	14	2420
f	Korpics, Zs. (HUN)	26	2330
	Korsunsky, R. R. (AZE)	0	2300
m	Korsunsky, Y. (RUS)	14	2420
	Korte, M. (GER)	0	2240
	Koruchin, A. (RUS)	0	2370
	Korzubov, P. (BLA)	4	2460
	Kos, E. (YUG)	0	2210
	Kos, S. (GER)	0	2205
f	Kosa, L. (HUN)	0	2250
f	Kosanovic, D. (YUG)	10	2320
m	Kosanovic, G. A. (YUG)	25	2375
	Kosanovic, O. (YUG)	0	2050
m	Kosanski, S. (CRO)	22	2420
m	Kosashvili, Y. (ISR)	7	2500
	Kosc, R. (AUT)	10	2060
	Koscielski, J. (GER)	21	2215
	Kosciuk, J. (POL)	0	2295
	Kosebay, O. (TUR)	0	2215
	Kosec, T. (SLO)	0	2105
	Koshi, V. (IND)	29	2415
m	Kosic, D. (YUG)	66	2495
	Kosic, E. (CRO)	0	2300
	Kosikov, A. I. (UKR)	9	2430
	Kosir, P. (SLO)	9	2005
m	Koskela, N. (FIN)	3	2155
	Koski, A. (ISR)	0	2250
	Koskinen, H. (FIN)	22	2275
	Koskoska, G. (YUG)	9	2115
	Kosoric, A. (YUG)	12	2270
	Kosowski, T. (GER)	0	2240
	Kossobudzki, R. (POL)	0	2120
	Kostadin, B. (YUG)	0	2110
	Kostadinov, A. (BUL)	0	2245
	Kostadinov, R. (BUL)	17	2295
	Kostadinov, S. (BUL)	0	2220
	Kostadinov, T. (BUL)	0	2320
	Kostak, T. (UKR)	0	2075
	Kostakiev, D. (BUL)	0	2235
g	Kosten, A. C. (ENG)	17	2495
	Kostenko, I. (UKR)	12	2285
	Koster, A. (NED)	0	2030
f	Kostic, B. (YUG)	0	2305
	Kostic, J. (YUG)	16	2350
m	Kostic, Ne. (YUG)	47	2405
	Kostic, Ni. (YUG)	3	2245
f	Kostic, Vladimir V. (YUG)	4	2330
m	Kostic, Vladimir (YUG)	7	2410
	Kostov, G. (BUL)	0	2230
	Kostrov, A. (RUS)	4	2255
m	Kostyra, S. (POL)	35	2365
	Kosutic, V. (YUG)	0	2245
	Koszegi, L. (HUN)	0	2215
f	Kosztolanczi, Gy. (HUN)	10	2230
	Kot, J. (POL)	0	2280
	Kotan, L. (SVK)	4	2315
	Kotevski, D. (YUG)	0	2285
f	Kotliar, M. (ISR)	12	2300
	Kotlyar, G. (USA)	0	2350
	Kotlyar, S. (USA)	15	2115
	Kotok, A. (ISR)	9	2260
g	Kotronias, V. (GRE)	52	2590
	Kotsur, P. (KAZ)	37	2425
	Kotter, R. (GER)	0	2270
f	Kottke, U. (GER)	0	2305
	Kotwal, A. (IND)	0	2035
	Kotz, H. P. (AUT)	11	2225
g	Kouatly, B. (FRA)	10	2520
	Kourek, J. (TCH)	0	2295
f	Kourkounakis, I. (GRE)	9	2415
	Kourtesis, G. (GRE)	5	2280
	Koutsin, S. (UKR)	32	2420
	Kovac, B. (SLO)	0	2355
	Kovacevic, A. (YUG)	69	2390
	Kovacevic, B. (CRO)	6	2320
f	Kovacevic, D. (YUG)	0	2360
	Kovacevic, G. (YUG)	0	2230
f	Kovacevic, P. (YUG)	13	2405
	Kovacevic, R. (CRO)	2	2110
m	Kovacevic, S. (YUG)	25	2435
	Kovacevic, Ve. (CRO)	10	2355
	Kovacevic, Vladimir (YUG)	0	2265
g	Kovacevic, Vlado (CRO)	41	2475
	Kovacic, V. (YUG)	14	2105
	Kovacs, A. (HUN)	0	2365
	Kovacs, E. (HUN)	0	2240
	Kovacs, Gabor (HUN)	11	2190
	Kovacs, Gabor M. (HUN)	9	2295
	Kovacs, Istvan (HUN)	0	2240
	Kovacs, Istvan (HUN)	9	2240
f	Kovacs, J. (HUN)	28	2190
	Kovacs, Lajos (HUN)	9	2275
f	Kovacs, Lajos D. (HUN)	9	2215
m	Kovacs, Las. M. (HUN)	4	2340
	Kovacs, M. (HUN)	12	2275
	Kovacs, Z. (HUN)	8	2235
m	Kovacs-Pinter, M. (HUN)	11	2200
g	Kovalev, A. (BLA)	17	2545
f	Kovalevskaya, E. (RUS)	32	2290
	Kovalevsky, A. (RUS)	15	2255
	Kowalak, P. (POL)	4	2230
	Kowalczyk, L. (POL)	0	2245
f	Kowalska, E. (POL)	4	2065
	Kowalski, M. (POL)	0	2220
	Kowohl, A. (GER)	0	2125
	Kozak, M. (TCH)	0	2270
	Kozakov, M. (RUS)	0	2265
	Kozarov, P. (BUL)	0	2355
	Kozhevin, S. (RUS)	6	2320
	Kozirev, A. (RUS)	6	2360
m	Kozlov, O. (RUS)	17	2405
	Kozlov, Va. (RUS)	0	2340
	Kozlov, Vladimir E. (RUS)	0	2420
m	Kozlov, Vladimir N. (RUS)	82	2280
g	Kozlovskaya, V. (RUS)	0	2180
	Kozlowski, W. (POL)	0	2355
f	Kozma, E. (ROM)	12	2105
f	Kozma, K. (HUN)	9	2325
	Koznjak, M. (CRO)	0	2365
g	Kozul, Z. (BIH)	52	2595
	Kraai, J. (USA)	12	2280
	Kraehenbuehl, G. (SUI)	3	2240
	Kraeussling, A. (GER)	0	2270
	Kraft, V. (GER)	0	2250
	Kragelj, I. (SLO)	7	2305
g	Kraidman, Y. (ISR)	0	2355
	Krainski, A. (POL)	0	2260
	Krainski, S. (POL)	0	2225
	Krajina, A. (TCH)	0	2280
	Krajina, D. (YUG)	0	2275
	Krakops, M. (LAT)	17	2230
	Kral, P. (HUN)	8	2220
	Krallmann, M. (GER)	12	2255
	Kralovec, E. (AUT)	0	2270
	Kramadzjan, A. (RUS)	18	2390
	Kramer, M. (GER)	0	2215
g	Kramnik, V. (RUS)	61	2710
	Krancevic, M. (YUG)	0	2210
	Krant, R. (TCH)	22	2240

	Name	Games	Rating
	Kranyik, Gy. (HUN)	0	2215
f	Kranzl, P. (AUT)	23	2275
	Kraschl, J. (AUT)	5	2230
g	Krasenkov, M. (POL)	43	2595
	Krasenkova, I. (RUS)	17	2250
	Krasevec, A. (SLO)	3	2175
	Krasikov, N. (UKR)	0	2275
	Krasnov, S. (RUS)	11	2320
f	Krason, J. (POL)	0	2355
	Krastanov, G. (BUL)	0	2230
f	Kratochwil, Ch. (GER)	2	2310
	Kraus, O. (GER)	0	2025
	Krause, Ch. (GER)	0	2215
	Krause, U. (GER)	10	2285
	Krauss, Ha. -P. (GER)	0	2230
	Krauss, He. (GER)	0	2305
m	Kraut, R. (GER)	17	2425
	Krauze, D. (POL)	1	2305
	Krays, A. (ISR)	14	2330
	Krcmar, Z. (TCH)	0	2255
	Krebs, J. (AUT)	15	2085
	Kreckovic, M. (YUG)	11	2035
	Kreiman, B. (USA)	14	2400
	Krejic, I. (YUG)	0	2175
m	Kremenietsky, A. M. (RUS)	53	2350
	Kresojevic, V. (YUG)	8	2265
	Kretek, B. (TCH)	3	2275
	Kretz, J. (SWE)	10	2215
	Kreutzkamp, H.-R. (GER)	0	2220
	Kreuzer, M. (GER)	0	2300
	Kribben, J. (GER)	0	2255
	Kribben, M. (GER)	0	2240
	Krieger, H. (GER)	0	2280
m	Kristensen, B. (DEN)	32	2470
	Kristensen, J. J. (DEN)	0	2335
	Kristensen, K. (DEN)	0	2295
	Kristensen, L. (DEN)	0	2310
f	Kristiansen, E. (NOR)	0	2280
m	Kristiansen, J. (DEN)	9	2415
	Kristiansen, T. (NOR)	0	2235
	Kristjansson, O. (ISD)	0	2235
	Kristof, J. (FRA)	0	2230
m	Kristol, L. (ISR)	9	2225
	Kristovic, M. (CRO)	0	2280
	Krisztian, G. (HUN)	9	2105
	Krivodedov, E. (UKR)	9	2045
m	Krivonosov, O. (LAT)	45	2410
	Kriz, O. (SVK)	0	2230
m	Krizsany, L. (HUN)	53	2370
	Krmelj, N. (SLO)	19	2045
	Krnavek, L. (TCH)	0	2275
m	Krnic, Z. (YUG)	0	2425
	Krnjic, A. (CRO)	0	2345
	Krnjovsek, A. (SLO)	12	2075
	Krockenberger, M. (GER)	6	2305
	Kroencke, M. (GER)	0	2275
	Krogh, C. (DEN)	5	2280
g	Krogius, N. V. (RUS)	11	2465
	Krogulski, G. (POL)	15	2290
	Krojanski, H. G. (GER)	9	2320
	Kroll, O. (DEN)	0	2325
	Kron, V. (RUS)	0	2430
	Kroon, P. (RSA)	0	2330
	Kropff, R. (PAR)	0	2210
	Krouzel, J. (TCH)	0	2255
	Krsnik, B. (AUT)	0	2315
	Krstev, V. (YUG)	0	2245
	Krstic, M. (YUG)	0	2290
	Krstic, R. (YUG)	0	2260
	Krudde, F. (NED)	9	2255
	Krueger, K. (GER)	0	2305
	Krueger, R. (GER)	0	2255
	Krug, N. (GER)	12	2275
	Krumpacnik, D. (SLO)	16	2385
	Krupkova, P. (TCH)	9	2200
m	Kruppa, Y. (UKR)	20	2485
	Kruse, H. (GER)	10	2205
	Kruszyn, P. (POL)	12	2110
	Kruszynski, A. (POL)	12	2115
m	Kruszynski, W. (POL)	12	2390
	Krutti, V. (HUN)	26	2350
	Kruza, P. (POL)	0	2250
m	Krylov, S. (RUS)	9	2295
	Krynicka, J. (POL)	11	2115
	Kryzius, K. (LTU)	10	2070
	Krzisnik-Bukic, V. (SLO)	0	2175
	Krzywicki, D. (POL)	21	2320
	Krzyzanowska-Zadlo, L. (POL)	0	2015
m	Ksieski, Z. (POL)	0	2340
	Kubacsny, L. (HUN)	0	2320
	Kubala, M. (TCH)	0	2145
	Kuban, G. (GER)	0	2250
	Kube, H. (GER)	1	2050
f	Kubien, J. (POL)	0	2310
	Kubikova, H. (TCH)	9	2225
	Kucera, P. (TCH)	6	2345
m	Kuczynski, R. (POL)	59	2520
	Kudischewitsch, D. (RUS)	0	2380
	Kudriashov, A. A. (RUS)	0	2370
g	Kudrin, S. (USA)	44	2555
	Kuech, H. (GER)	9	2230
f	Kuenzner, F. (GER)	0	2300
m	Kuijf, M. (NED)	24	2445
	Kujala, A. (FIN)	3	2275
	Kujawa, J. (POL)	0	2085
	Kujawski, A. (POL)	0	2350
	Kujawski, R. (POL)	0	2275
f	Kuklin, A. (HUN)	1	2275
	Kuksov, V. (RUS)	0	2355
	Kukutanov, G. (YUG)	12	2250
f	Kula, R. (POL)	0	2280
	Kulagin, A. (RUS)	11	2265
	Kulak, D. (YUG)	8	2320
	Kulaots, K. (EST)	13	2330
f	Kulcsar, M. (HUN)	21	2250
	Kulcsar, T. (HUN)	2	2245
	Kulesza, K. (POL)	2	2225
g	Kuligowski, A. (POL)	0	2430
	Kulikov, O. (RUS)	0	2335
	Kulikov, V. (RUS)	14	2365
m	Kulish, I. (RUS)	15	2225
	Kuljic, G. (YUG)	0	2205
m	Kumaran, D. (ENG)	27	2425
	Kummer, H. (AUT)	12	2250
	Kummerow, H. (GER)	4	2240
	Kun, S. (HUN)	5	2250
	Kunovac, D. (YUG)	0	2255
f	Kunsztowicz, U. (GER)	0	2310
f	Kuntz, P. (FRA)	20	2200
	Kuntzig, W. (GER)	4	2250
f	Kunze, K. (GER)	0	2140
f	Kunze, M. (GER)	5	2310
	Kupfer, M. (GER)	0	2220
	Kupiec, A. (POL)	5	2225
f	Kupka, S. (TCH)	0	2365
m	Kuporosov, V. (RUS)	7	2500
f	Kupper, P. (SUI)	6	2295
g	Kupreichik, V. D. (BLA)	19	2535
	Kupruks, R. (LAT)	0	2175
g	Kurajica, B. (BIH)	64	2550
	Kuraszkiewicz, M. (GER)	3	2325
f	Kurcubic, A. (YUG)	0	2305
	Kure, A. (GER)	0	2240
	Kurkul, M. (LTU)	22	2170
	Kurlenda, A. (POL)	0	2210
	Kurochkin, V. (RUS)	0	2350
	Kurr, G. (GER)	0	2225
m	Kurtenkov, A. (BUL)	8	2425
	Kurth, J. (GER)	0	2305
	Kurtskhalia, I. (GEO)	0	2085
	Kurucsai, Istvan (HUN)	9	2155
	Kurucsai, Istvanne (HUN)	0	2080
f	Kurz, A. (GER)	3	2320
	Kurz, E. (GER)	0	2330
	Kushch, N. (UKR)	0	2360
	Kusina, J. (POL)	12	2205
	Kusmierz, M. (POL)	0	2205
	Kustar, S. (HUN)	23	2335
	Kut, M. (POL)	2	2215
	Kutnik, A. (ROM)	0	2230
	Kutschenko, R. (GER)	0	2215
f	Kutuzovic, B. (CRO)	2	2370
	Kuwaza, C. (ZIM)	0	2205
	Kuzev, B. (BUL)	0	2250
	Kuzev, J. (BUL)	0	2305
	Kuzmak, T. (UKR)	0	2255
	Kuzmanovic, M. (CRO)	0	2235
m	Kuzmin, A. (RUS)	0	2555
g	Kuzmin, G. P. (UKR)	16	2500
	Kuzmina, C. C. (RUS)	0	2170
f	Kuznecov, A. (CAN)	0	2310
	Kuznetsova, E. (RUS)	5	2180
	Kvamme, J. A. (NOR)	0	2240
g	Kveinys, A. (LTU)	35	2535
	Kvizhinadze, K. (GEO)	0	2190
	Kwasniewski, J. (GER)	0	2260
	Kwasniewski, Z. (POL)	0	2250
f	Kwatschewsky, L. (AUT)	11	2300
	Kwiatkowski, F. J. (ENG)	7	2250
	Kwiatkowski, L. (POL)	11	2285
	Kwiecien, Z. (POL)	0	2270
	Kwiecinski, R. (POL)	0	2250
	Kyas, J. (GER)	13	2265
	Kyhle, B. (SWE)	5	2235
	Kyriakides, S. (ZIM)	0	2240

L

	Name	Games	Rating
f	La Flair, R. (USA)	17	2330
	La Marca, E. N. (USA)	10	2080
	La Rosa, G. (VEN)	0	2005
f	La Rota, F. (COL)	5	2300
	Laato, A. (FIN)	0	2260
	Labahn, W. (GER)	7	2225
	Labollita, M. (ARG)	18	2275
	Laboranti, A. (ARG)	18	2160
	Labra, M. (CHI)	25	2165
	Labuckas, A. (LTU)	11	2255
	Labutin, S. (RUS)	0	2325
	Lacasa, J. A. (ESP)	2	2295
	Lacayo, R. (NCA)	13	2285
	Lacko, P. (SWE)	0	2245
	Laclau, D. (FRA)	0	2240
	Lacmanovic, S. (CRO)	0	2215
	Laco, G. (ITA)	3	2265
	Lacrosse, M. (BEL)	4	2230
	Lada, M. (POL)	10	2210
g	Ladanyike-Karakas, E. (HUN)	17	2125
	Ladines, S. (ARG)	3	2200
	Ladner, K. (AUT)	0	2070
	Lados, P. (POL)	0	2225
m	Laesson, T. (EST)	36	2265
	Lagopatis, N. (GRE)	0	2245
	Lagrotteria, S. (ITA)	4	2230
	Lagua, B. (PHI)	24	2295
	Lagumina, G. (ITA)	0	2275
m	Lagunov, A. (GER)	18	2420
	Lagvilava, G. (BLA)	47	2250
	Lahari, A. (IND)	2	2190
f	Lahav, E. (ISR)	0	2375
	Lahilhanne, Ph. (FRA)	0	2210
	Lahlum, H. O. (NOR)	14	2220
	Lahoz, J. A. (USA)	0	2255
	Lahtinen, M. (FIN)	3	2215
	Laine, H. (FIN)	3	2250
	Laine, P. (FIN)	8	2175
f	Laird, C. (AUS)	0	2270
	Lajos, J. (HUN)	3	2325
f	Lajthajm, B. (YUG)	0	2330
	Lakat, Gy. (HUN)	17	2150
f	Lakdawala, C. (USA)	0	2330
m	Laketic, G. (YUG)	9	2410
f	Lakic, N. (YUG)	0	2325

	Name		
f	Lako, L. (HUN)	0	2300
	Lakos, N. (HUN)	28	2230
	Lakunza, J. C. (ESP)	18	2265
m	Lalev, D. (BUL)	0	2425
g	Lalic, B. (CRO)	42	2520
f	Lalic, D. (YUG)	0	2325
f	Lalic, N. (BIH)	0	2385
	Lalova, V. (BUL)	0	2055
	Lamas, P. (URU)	9	2200
	Lamb, B. (CAN)	0	2120
	Lamford, P. A. (WLS)	0	2280
	Lamm, S. (GER)	0	2255
	Lammi, J. (FIN)	12	2265
f	Lamorelle, Y. (FRA)	3	2230
f	Lamoureux, Ch. (FRA)	63	2380
	Lamperti, J. F. (ARG)	0	2280
	Lamprecht, F. (GER)	0	2330
	Lamser, J. (TCH)	0	2295
f	Lamza, N. (CRO)	6	2300
	Lamza, Z. (POL)	11	2250
m	Lanc, A. (SVK)	0	2445
f	Lanchava, T. (GEO)	12	2165
m	Landa, K. (RUS)	19	2455
m	Landenbergue, C. (SUI)	47	2405
	Landry-Vuorenpaa, S. (FIN)	0	2025
m	Lane, G. W. (ENG)	8	2430
f	Lang, J. (GER)	4	2325
	Lang, M. (GER)	0	2220
	Lang, S. (GER)	9	2250
	Lang, T. (GER)	0	2055
m	Langeweg, K. (NED)	3	2380
f	Langier, D. (ARG)	28	2355
f	Langner, L. (TCH)	0	2345
	Langreck, J. (USA)	0	2245
g	Lanka, Z. (LAT)	38	2540
	Lantini, M. (ITA)	3	2190
f	Lanzani, M. (ITA)	6	2280
	Lanzendoerfer, J. (GER)	0	2230
	Lapicki, R. (ARG)	1	2250
	Lapienis, D. (LTU)	21	2315
	Laplaza, J. (ARG)	6	2225
	Lapshin, V. (RUS)	0	2265
	Lapshun, G. (USA)	10	2305
	Laptev, R. (RUS)	0	2310
	Laptos, K. (POL)	17	2265
	Laqua, Ch. (GER)	0	2210
f	Larduet, C. (CUB)	0	2335
	Lares, M. (MEX)	10	2210
m	Large, P. G. (ENG)	0	2335
	Larocca, H. (ARG)	0	2160
	Larrachea Formas, E. V. (CHI)	0	2030
	Larrachea, E. (CHI)	0	2275
	Larrosa, J. (ESP)	9	2315
g	Larsen, B. (DEN)	16	2555
f	Larsen, K. (USA)	4	2340
	Larsen, S. S. (DEN)	0	2280
f	Larsson, P. (SWE)	0	2355
	Larsson, T. (SWE)	0	2155
	Lastin, A. (RUS)	10	2335
	Lastovicka, J. (TCH)	0	2240
	Lastovicka, Z. (TCH)	0	2325
	Laszewicz, P. (POL)	0	2225
f	Laszlo, J. (HUN)	22	2280
f	Laszlop, F. (HUN)	0	2300
	Latas, B. (POL)	11	2285
	Latif, A. (EGY)	0	2280
	Latinov, G. (BUL)	0	2235
	Lau, C. (NCA)	0	2290
	Lau, D. (GER)	8	2205
	Lau, J. (GER)	10	2165
g	Lau, R. (GER)	57	2510
	Lau, U. (GER)	12	2260
	Laube, B. (AUT)	0	2250
	Lauferon, P. (BRA)	10	2230
	Lauk, U. (EST)	16	2360
	Lauren, M. (FIN)	6	2265
	Lauridsen, J. (DEN)	5	2205

	Name		
	Lauritsen, N. (UGA)	0	2295
m	Lauterbach, I. (GER)	12	2120
g	Lautier, J. (FRA)	44	2620
	Lauvas, D. (NOR)	0	2220
	Lauvsnes, A. (NOR)	0	2270
f	Laux, T. (GER)	0	2350
	Lava, G. (ITA)	5	2255
	Laven, R. (GER)	0	2315
	Lavie, A. (ISR)	0	2260
	Lavrov, A. (RUS)	20	2385
f	Law, A. P. (ENG)	0	2375
	Lawrenz, A. (GER)	7	2230
f	Lawson, D. (SCO)	5	2240
	Lazar, A. (HUN)	0	2220
f	Lazar, D. (ROM)	0	2240
	Lazar, I. (ROM)	0	2300
m	Lazarev, V. (RUS)	7	2440
g	Lazarevic, M. (YUG)	0	2205
	Lazarevic, S. (YUG)	20	2360
	Lazaridis, S. (GRE)	0	2270
	Lazic, D. (YUG)	0	2320
	Lazic, Lj. (YUG)	0	2220
	Lazic, Ma. (YUG)	15	2105
m	Lazic, Mi. (YUG)	53	2465
	Lazor, V. (YUG)	12	2180
f	Lazovic, G. (CRO)	0	2315
	Le Bellac, P. (FRA)	0	2215
	Le Bideau, A. (FRA)	10	2270
	Le Godec, D. (FRA)	0	2315
	Le Quang, K. (BEL)	16	2205
f	Leal, A. (MEX)	0	2270
	Lebedeva, T. (RUS)	12	2110
	Lebel, P. (FRA)	5	2210
m	Lebel-Arias, J. (FRA)	22	2050
m	Lebredo, G. (CUB)	0	2290
	Lebret, J.-M. (FRA)	0	2270
g	Lechtynsky, J. (TCH)	14	2405
	Leckel, H. (GER)	0	2230
f	Lecuyer, Ch. (FRA)	4	2270
	Lederer, Y. (ISR)	3	2300
m	Lederman, L. (ISR)	0	2345
f	Ledger, A. (ENG)	28	2375
	Ledger, D. (ENG)	21	2295
f	Ledic, T. (CRO)	0	2275
	Ledwon, E. (POL)	0	2275
	Lee, D. (USA)	29	2245
f	Lee, G. D. (ENG)	0	2345
	Lee, H. (USA)	0	2215
	Lee, O. (BRA)	0	2295
	Lee, W.-Sh. (SIN)	0	2290
	Legahn, D. (GER)	0	2250
	Legaspi, E. (PHI)	0	2155
m	Legky, N. A. (UKR)	41	2490
	Lehikoinen, P. I. (FIN)	0	2225
h	Lehmann, He. (GER)	19	2295
	Lehmann, Ho. (GER)	12	2105
	Lehmann, Ka. -H. (GER)	0	2285
f	Lehmann, Kl. (GER)	1	2315
	Lehmann, M. (GER)	0	2285
	Lehmann, Z. (HUN)	62	2300
f	Lehner, O. (AUT)	0	2300
	Lehri, Sh. (IND)	0	2190
	Lehtivaara, P. (FIN)	1	2275
f	Lehtivaara, R. (FIN)	0	2275
f	Lehto, V. (FIN)	0	2310
	Leiber, B. (GER)	0	2215
	Leikute, A. (LTU)	9	2160
g	Lein, A. (USA)	11	2465
	Leinov, G. (ISR)	0	2240
	Leira, J. (ESP)	9	2230
	Leiser, S. (GER)	9	2295
f	Leitao, R. D. (BRA)	13	2295
	Leito, P. (EST)	11	2205
	Lejeune, J.-P. (FRA)	0	2350
f	Lejlic, S. (BIH)	7	2420
	Lekander, R. (SWE)	0	2270
	Lekic, D. (YUG)	10	2265
	Lekic, M. (YUG)	0	2215
m	Leko, P. (HUN)	77	2555

	Name		
g	Lelchuk, Z. (UKR)	15	2340
g	Lematschko, T. (SUI)	0	2305
	Lemmers, O. (NED)	0	2385
	Lempereur, F. (FRA)	0	2275
m	Lempert, I. (RUS)	23	2455
	Len, K. (POL)	0	2055
f	Lenart, E. (HUN)	13	2305
	Lendvai, E. (HUN)	28	2095
	Lendvai, N. (HUN)	27	2105
m	Lendwai, R. (AUT)	34	2425
m	Lengyel, B. (HUN)	71	2420
f	Lengyel, F. (ROM)	9	2305
	Lengyel, La. (HUN)	10	2185
g	Lengyel, Le. (HUN)	25	2385
	Lenhart, Dj. (YUG)	0	2260
	Lentini, C. (ARG)	9	2085
f	Lentrodt, Th. (GER)	15	2320
	Lentze, I. (GER)	3	2250
f	Lenz, J. (GER)	0	2305
	Lenz, Th. (GER)	9	2285
	Leon, E. (CUB)	0	2065
	Leonardi, K. H. (GER)	0	2115
	Leonardo, J. (POR)	9	2255
	Leoncini, M. (ITA)	0	2250
	Leong, I. (SIN)	0	2225
m	Leow, L. M. (SIN)	0	2435
f	Lepelletier, B. (FRA)	0	2265
	Lerendegui, D. (ARG)	9	2200
	Leriche, E. (FRA)	0	2260
g	Lerner, K. Z. (UKR)	34	2530
	Lernik, M. (RUS)	0	2345
	Leroy, A. (FRA)	39	2345
	Lesic, G. (YUG)	0	2235
m	Lesiege, A. (CAN)	29	2485
m	Leski, M. (FRA)	7	2440
f	Leskovar, M. (ARG)	3	2365
	Leskur, D. (YUG)	5	2295
	Leszczynska, J. (POL)	0	2125
	Leszczynski, K. (POL)	0	2270
m	Leszner, L. (POL)	13	2190
	Leszner, M. (POL)	0	2240
f	Letay, Gy. (HUN)	14	2280
m	Letelier, R. (CHI)	13	2210
f	Letreguilly, O. (FRA)	9	2335
f	Letzelter, J.-C. (FRA)	2	2285
f	Leuba, D. (SUI)	5	2285
	Leustean, L. (ROM)	22	2220
	Leutwyler, M. (SUI)	13	2230
	Leuw, M. (NED)	0	2325
m	Lev, R. (ISR)	15	2465
m	Levacic, D. (FRA)	0	2385
	Levacic, P. (CRO)	20	2290
	Levchenkov, V. S. (LAT)	15	2300
f	Leveille, F. (CAN)	0	2345
m	Leventic, I. (CRO)	14	2390
	Leverett, B. W. (USA)	0	2230
f	Levi, E. (AUS)	5	2305
f	Levin, D. (USA)	8	2320
m	Levin, F. (UKR)	30	2510
	Levit, R. (USA)	9	2295
m	Levitan, Y. (USA)	11	2270
g	Levitina, I. S. (USA)	5	2425
m	Levitt, J. (ENG)	30	2455
	Levitt, M. (RSA)	14	2345
f	Levtchouk, G. (CAN)	0	2330
f	Levy, L. (USA)	0	2275
	Levy, R. (AUT)	0	2235
	Lewandowska, K. (POL)	29	2160
	Lewandowski, M. (POL)	2	2205
	Lewicka, S. (POL)	2	2035
	Lewicki, B. (POL)	0	2280
	Lewinski, D. (POL)	0	2260
f	Lewis, A. P. (ENG)	0	2330
	Lewis, J. E. (DOM)	0	2250
	Lex, Ch. (GER)	0	2245
f	Leyva, H. (CUB)	0	2355
	Leyva, R. (CUB)	0	2285
	Lezcano Jaen, P. (ESP)	18	2295
	Lhouvum, K. H. (IND)	0	2165

	Name		
	Li, Junyi (CHN)	0	2195
f	Li, M. (CUB)	10	2305
	Li, Wenliang (CHN)	0	2330
m	Li, Zunian (CHN)	0	2415
m	Liang, Jinrong (CHN)	18	2500
	Liang, Zhihua (CHN)	0	2230
m	Liao, Y. E. (DOM)	0	2425
	Liardet, F. (SUI)	10	2245
f	Libeau, R. (GER)	9	2425
	Libens, M. (FRA)	8	2230
	Liberus, M. (POL)	0	2235
g	Liberzon, V. M. (ISR)	0	2445
	Lichev, L. (BUL)	5	2250
	Licina, A. (SLO)	10	2135
	Licina, Z. (YUG)	0	2260
	Lida Garcia, F. (ARG)	7	2185
	Lida, F. E. (ARG)	0	2235
f	Lieb, H. (GER)	6	2295
	Liebau, A. (GER)	10	2220
m	Liebert, H. (GER)	5	2380
	Liebowitz, E. (USA)	0	2240
	Liedl, W. (AUT)	9	2215
	Liedtke, D. (GER)	0	2180
	Liedtke, M. (GER)	4	2295
	Lief, A. (USA)	0	2250
	Liemann, M. (GER)	5	2235
	Liepold, S. (GER)	0	2245
	Liesecke, A. (GER)	0	2070
m	Liew, Ch.-M.-J. (MAS)	0	2335
	Light, B. (DEN)	0	2300
m	Ligterink, G. (NED)	0	2435
	Liiva, R. (EST)	11	2360
	Likavsky, T. (SVK)	0	2240
	Lilja, R. (SWE)	10	2120
	Liljedahl, L. (SWE)	0	2325
	Lim, Ch.-L. (SIN)	0	2215
f	Lim, H.-Ch. (SIN)	0	2340
f	Lim, J. (SIN)	0	2300
	Lim, M. (SIN)	0	2255
m	Lima, D. (BRA)	20	2475
m	Limbach, R. (NED)	23	2180
	Limp, E. (BRA)	0	2290
m	Lin, T (CHN)	0	2410
m	Lin, Weiguo (CHN)	27	2540
	Linauskas, D. (LTU)	11	2340
	Lind, J.-O. (SWE)	4	2320
f	Lindberg, B. (SWE)	4	2335
	Lindberg, H. (SWE)	0	2180
	Lindemann, S. (SWE)	0	2255
	Lindfeldt, J. M. (DEN)	18	2185
	Lindgren, M. (SWE)	0	2250
m	Lindri, J. W. (INA)	14	2185
f	Lindsay, F. (USA)	3	2310
f	Lindstedt, J. (FIN)	6	2330
m	Lingnau, C. (GER)	27	2395
	Link, M. (GER)	7	2300
f	Linker, Th. (GER)	0	2300
	Linnanen, L. (FIN)	0	2225
	Linnemann, R. (GER)	1	2280
	Lipiniks, L. (PAR)	0	2240
	Lipka, J. (SVK)	0	2310
	Lipsanen, E. (FIN)	0	2240
	Lipski, T. (POL)	10	2200
m	Liptay, L. (HUN)	0	2410
m	Lirindzakis, T. (GRE)	25	2400
	Lisanti, A. (GER)	15	2345
	Lisek, J. (GER)	0	2280
	Lisenko, A. V. (RUS)	14	2410
	Lisica, A. (YUG)	0	2285
	Lisik, V. (RUS)	8	2440
f	Lisjak, Z. (CRO)	2	2345
	Lisko, F. (SVK)	0	2350
	Lisovskaja, A. (RUS)	9	2195
	Liss, A. (ISR)	0	2230
f	Liss, E. (ISR)	0	2405
	Liss, G. (ISR)	0	2205
m	Lissowska, A. (POL)	5	2175
g	Litinskaya-Shul, M. I. (UKR)	21	2305
	Litovicius, M. (ARG)	24	2300
	Littke, A. (USA)	7	2270
f	Littlewood, J. E. (ENG)	0	2320
m	Littlewood, P. E. (ENG)	0	2460
	Litus, V. (RUS)	50	2270
	Litvinov, V. (BLA)	8	2365
	Litvinyenko, A. (BLA)	2	2315
g	Liu, Shilan (CHN)	0	2230
m	Liu, Wenze (CHN)	0	2390
	Liu, Xin (CHN)	0	2095
f	Liverios, Th. (GRE)	0	2285
	Livshits, R. (CAN)	0	2310
	Livsitz, L. (UKR)	0	2420
	Ljangov, P. (BUL)	5	2205
	Ljavdansky, V. (RUS)	2	2285
	Ljubarskij, J. (RUS)	0	2305
	Ljubas, A. (YUG)	0	2255
	Ljubicic, F. (CRO)	5	2340
f	Ljubinkovic, M. (YUG)	12	2310
m	Ljubisavljevic, Z. (YUG)	4	2270
g	Ljubojevic, Lj. (YUG)	13	2595
f	Llanos, G. (ARG)	53	2405
	Llopis, M. (ESP)	0	2245
	Lloret Ramis, J. J. (ESP)	9	2285
	Lobach, P. V. (RUS)	6	2290
	Lobo, R. (ENG)	10	2295
g	Lobron, E. (GER)	68	2575
	Lobstein, A. (FRA)	15	2210
	Lochte, Th. (GER)	8	2265
	Lockl, L. (AUT)	0	2260
	Loebler, H. (AUT)	11	2290
m	Loeffler, S. (GER)	32	2460
	Loew, G. (GER)	4	2235
	Loffler, M. (GER)	0	2235
	Loftsson, H. (ISD)	0	2230
	Logdahl, H. (SWE)	0	2155
	Loginov, S. (RUS)	0	2285
g	Loginov, V. A. (UZB)	73	2505
	Loheac-Amoun, F. (LEB)	0	2225
	Loiterstein, M. (ARG)	6	2255
	Lokasto, A. (POL)	0	2370
	Lokotar, E. (EST)	0	2330
	Loktiev, I. (RUS)	11	2285
	Lomakina, O. (RUS)	4	2145
m	Lombard, A. (SUI)	0	2395
g	Lombardy, W. J. (USA)	0	2450
f	Lomineishvili, M. (GEO)	9	2090
	Loncar, R. (CRO)	13	2440
	Loncarevic, S. (YUG)	0	2270
m	London, D. (USA)	13	2405
	Long, P. (MAS)	0	2265
	Longren, W. B. (USA)	18	2295
	Lonoff, M. (USA)	3	2300
	Lont, A. (NED)	0	2335
	Lopatina, O. (RUS)	0	2105
	Lopez Izquierdo, A. (ESP)	0	2245
f	Lopez Jimenez, A. (CUB)	9	2265
	Lopez Trujillo, A. (COL)	0	2215
	Lopez Velasco, A. (MEX)	0	2210
	Lopez, C. M. (CUB)	0	2275
	Lopez, J. C. (ESP)	0	2250
	Lopez, Jor. (FRA)	0	2230
	Lopez, Jose L. (ESP)	10	2325
	Lopez, Man. (MEX)	0	2285
	Lopez, Marc. (BOL)	0	2230
	Lopez, Mario (CHI)	0	2240
	Lopez, R. (ARG)	6	2215
	Lorelli, C. (ARG)	6	2300
	Lorenc, M. (POL)	0	2270
	Lorenz, B. (GER)	0	2025
	Lorenz, G. (GER)	11	2235
	Lorenz, R. (GER)	0	2215
f	Lorenz, S. (GER)	8	2285
	Lorenzo, M. (ESP)	5	2165
f	Lorincz, I. (HUN)	11	2375
	Lorite, F. (ESP)	9	2270
f	Lorscheid, G. (GER)	22	2270
f	Los, S. (NED)	8	2335
	Losev, D. (RUS)	21	2365
	Lostuzzi, M. (ITA)	0	2335
	Lotzien, H. (GER)	0	2260
	Loureiro, L. (BRA)	0	2335
	Louvert, E. (FRA)	7	2160
	Lovas, D. (HUN)	0	2290
	Lovass, I. (HUN)	10	2220
	Love, A. J. (NZL)	11	2315
	Loven, A. (SWE)	0	2275
	Lovlu, S. (BAN)	0	2195
	Lovric, B. (CRO)	11	2300
	Low, P.-Y. (SIN)	0	2235
	Lower, S. (USA)	0	2240
	Lowy, M. (ISR)	0	2025
f	Lowy, W. (ISR)	6	2285
g	Lputian, S. G. (ARM)	41	2565
f	Lu, Xiaosha (CHN)	0	2260
	Lubarskaya, L. A. (RUS)	0	2145
	Lubos, A. (GER)	11	2150
	Lubosik, Z. (POL)	0	2200
	Lucaroni, M. (ITA)	6	2310
	Lucas, F. (FRA)	0	2260
	Lucasciuc, M. (ROM)	0	2255
m	Luce, S. (FRA)	14	2385
	Lucena, L. (BRA)	2	2235
	Luciani, C. (ITA)	0	2265
	Luco, A. (FRA)	1	2275
m	Luczak, A. (POL)	0	2365
	Ludgate, A. (IRL)	13	2275
	Ludvigsen, F. (NOR)	0	2330
	Ludvikow, T. (SWE)	1	2125
	Ludwikow, Th. (SWE)	12	2180
	Ludwikowski, D. (POL)	12	2245
m	Luecke, N. (GER)	40	2410
f	Luetke, J. (GER)	10	2315
	Luft, A. (GER)	0	2285
m	Lugo, B. (CUB)	0	2400
	Lugovoi, A. (RUS)	26	2390
	Luik, H. (EST)	9	2295
f	Luk, L.-W. (HKG)	0	2270
	Lukacs, Ja. (HUN)	0	2275
	Lukacs, Jo. (HUN)	0	2275
g	Lukacs, P. (HUN)	53	2485
f	Lukasiewicz, G. (POL)	13	2350
	Lukey, S. G. (NZL)	11	2330
f	Lukez, F. (SWE)	0	2320
f	Lukic, D. (YUG)	0	2305
	Lukic, M. (YUG)	0	2245
	Lukic, Z. (YUG)	0	2255
m	Lukin, A. M. (RUS)	23	2440
g	Lukov, V. (BUL)	8	2395
	Lukovnikov, A. (RUS)	2	2305
	Luminet, D. (BEL)	0	2310
m	Lumongdong, L. K. (INA)	14	2080
f	Lumper, Th. (GER)	0	2315
	Lund, B. D. (ENG)	0	2270
	Lundberg, O. (SWE)	0	2280
	Lundgren, B. (SWE)	19	2150
	Lundin, A. (SWE)	0	2270
	Lundkvist, D. (SWE)	0	2215
	Lungu, N. (ZAM)	0	2205
	Lunna, T. W. (USA)	0	2270
	Lupkowski, E. (POL)	7	2070
m	Lupu, M.-S. (ROM)	33	2400
m	Lupu, S. B. (ROM)	11	2145
	Lupu, T. (ROM)	0	2245
	Lurje, P. (SUI)	12	2100
	Lustenberger, D. (SUI)	0	2300
m	Luther, Th. (GER)	54	2480
	Lutskan, I. (LAT)	16	2345
	Lutskane, A. (LAT)	0	2085
g	Lutz, Ch. (GER)	57	2605
	Lutz, K.-J. (GER)	21	2325
	Lutzenberger, R. (GER)	0	2290
	Luyks, M. (POR)	0	2140
	Luzar, E. (YUG)	11	2300
	Ly, A. (MLI)	0	2205
	Lybin, D. (BLA)	18	2295
	Lyell, M. (ENG)	6	2235

	Name	Games	Rating
f	Lymar, I. (UKR)	11	2270
m	Lyrberg, P. (SWE)	28	2420
	Lys, J. (TCH)	0	2280
	Lytchak, A. (GER)	10	2255

M

	Name	Games	Rating
	Ma, Hongding (CHN)	0	2275
	Maahs, E. (GER)	17	2275
	Maass, A. (MEX)	0	2265
f	Maass, G. (MEX)	0	2275
	Mac Farland, J. (USA)	3	2155
	MacArthur, J. (USA)	0	2195
f	MacKay, I. D. (SCO)	0	2340
f	Macagno, S. (ARG)	0	2320
	Macanga, B. (YUG)	0	2250
f	Macarie, E. (ROM)	21	2175
	Maccagno, G. (ITA)	0	2280
	Macdonald, D. R. (ENG)	0	2275
m	Macek-Kalchbrenner, V. (CRO)	19	2250
	Mach, H. J. (GER)	0	2235
f	Machado, H. A. (BRA)	0	2310
	Machado, L. E. W. (BRA)	0	2305
	Machado, R. (CUB)	0	2240
	Machius, M. (GER)	0	2285
g	Machulsky, A. D. (RUS)	0	2535
f	Macieja, B. (POL)	22	2280
m	Maciejewski, A. (POL)	20	2360
f	Maciejewski, M. (POL)	6	2400
	Macionis, A. (LTU)	14	2335
	Mack, A. (ENG)	4	2250
f	Mack, P. (GER)	1	2285
	Mackic, Z. (YUG)	4	2340
	Mackowiak, M. (POL)	0	2245
f	Macles, J. (FRA)	0	2350
	Madebrink, L. (SWE)	0	2275
	Madeira, W. M. (BRA)	13	2250
	Madhavan, C. (MAS)	0	2225
	Madi, T. (HUN)	0	2320
	Madina, M. (ARG)	0	2260
g	Madl, I. (IM) (HUN)	8	2430
	Madsen, D. (NOR)	0	2310
	Madsen, P. (DEN)	0	2285
	Maduekwe, Ch. (NGR)	9	2235
f	Maeder, K.-H. (GER)	0	2335
f	Maeser, F. (SUI)	0	2295
	Maeurer, Ch. (GER)	0	2215
	Maga, M. (PHI)	0	2370
	Magamedov, M. (RUS)	0	2390
	Magar, Th. P. (USA)	0	2175
	Magbanua, R. (PHI)	0	2320
	Magdan, C. (ROM)	0	2235
m	Magem Badals, J. (ESP)	52	2505
g	Magerramov, E. (AZE)	25	2545
	Magg, Ch. (GER)	0	2290
	Magniea, H. (FRA)	10	2215
	Magnus, U. O. (ISD)	0	2260
f	Magnusson, J. (SWE)	0	2315
m	Magomedov, M. (TAJ)	11	2435
f	Magyar, O. (HUN)	22	2355
	Magyarosi, G. (HUN)	0	2245
	Mah, K. (ENG)	15	2115
	Mahayri, S. M. (SYR)	0	2205
m	Mahdi, A. S. (IRQ)	0	2220
	Mahdy, K. (EGY)	8	2420
f	Mahia, G. (ARG)	0	2380
	Mahmoud, P. (IRI)	0	2205
f	Mahmud, S. (INA)	0	2375
	Mai, Th. Th. H. (VIE)	0	2075
	Maia, J. E. (BRA)	0	2285
	Maidla, V. (EST)	3	2360
	Maier, A. (GER)	6	2250
f	Maier, Ch. (GER)	8	2365
	Maier, M. (GER)	0	2225
	Maika, B. (UKR)	0	2225
	Mailfert, J.-P. (FRA)	16	2115
	Mainka, G. (GER)	8	2385
g	Mainka, R. (GER)	53	2515
m	Maiwald, J.-U. (GER)	70	2430
	Majdanics, A. (HUN)	7	2240
	Majeed, M. (UAE)	0	2205
	Majer, D. (GER)	4	2230
f	Majeric, Z. (CRO)	0	2355
m	Majorovas, V. (LTU)	0	2435
	Majtyka, B. (POL)	0	2060
	Majul, I. (COL)	0	2075
	Majzik, L. (HUN)	9	2285
	Majzlan, I. (SVK)	0	2280
	Makarewicz, P. (POL)	5	2205
g	Makarichev, S. (RUS)	10	2540
	Makarjev, I. (RUS)	34	2345
m	Makarov, A. (RUS)	14	2465
	Makarov, G. (RUS)	0	2365
g	Makarov, M. (RUS)	61	2540
	Makarycheva-Ostrovskaya, M. (RUS)	5	2145
f	Maki, J. (USA)	3	2285
m	Maki, V. (FIN)	16	2405
	Maki-Uuro, M. (FIN)	18	2300
	Makoli, P. (YUG)	0	2235
	Makris, X. (GRE)	0	2240
m	Makropoulos, G. (GRE)	1	2405
g	Makropoulou, M. (GRE)	0	2270
m	Maksimenko, A. (UKR)	17	2440
m	Maksimovic, B. (YUG)	32	2370
	Maksimovic, D. (YUG)	6	2235
m	Maksimovic, S. (YUG)	25	2280
	Malachi, A. (ISR)	0	2230
f	Malachowski, M. B. (GER)	4	2165
	Malachowski, T. (POL)	0	2235
f	Malajovich, S. (ARG)	0	2130
g	Malaniuk, V. P. (UKR)	45	2635
f	Malbran, G. (ARG)	16	2355
	Malek, D. (ITA)	9	2165
f	Malek, F. (TUN)	0	2250
f	Malesevic, N. (YUG)	0	2285
	Malesevic, V. (YUG)	0	2340
	Maleska, A. (POL)	3	2060
	Malevinsky, A. A. (RUS)	0	2350
	Malfagia, A. (ITA)	0	2315
	Mali, S. (SLO)	3	2290
g	Malich, B. (GER)	7	2415
	Malin, U. (ISR)	0	2250
g	Malisauskas, V. (LTU)	45	2540
	Malisov, B. (ISR)	9	2225
	Malivanek, J. (TCH)	0	2195
m	Maljutin, E. (RUS)	59	2505
	Malloni, M. (ITA)	0	2235
	Malpert, R. (USA)	0	2315
	Maly, M. (AUT)	2	2245
	Malyakin, P. (RUS)	28	2350
m	Malysev, V. (RUS)	2	2400
	Mamadshoev, M. (TAJ)	0	2315
	Mamedova, R. (UZB)	0	2125
m	Mamombe, K. (ZIM)	14	2120
	Mamoulakis, E. (GRE)	2	2100
	Mamuzic, M. (YUG)	0	2245
	Man Yee, Ch. (BRA)	0	2260
	Managadze, N. (GEO)	0	2305
	Manakova, M. (RUS)	11	2175
	Manasterski, L. (POL)	0	2260
m	Manca, F. (ITA)	17	2390
	Mancebo Ibanez, F. (ESP)	0	2255
	Mancic, C. (YUG)	0	2205
	Mandecki, M. (POL)	12	2215
	Mandekic, I. (CRO)	3	2270
f	Mandel, A. (GER)	9	2370
	Mandelkow, H. (GER)	0	2230
	Mandic, S. (YUG)	0	2265
f	Mandl, Ro. (GER)	11	2420
	Mandl, Ru. (GER)	0	2260
	Manela, N. (ISR)	0	2235
	Manfred, J. (GER)	0	2205
	Mangal, P. (IND)	0	2085
	Mangrjan, M. A. (RUS)	0	2010
m	Manic, J. (YUG)	0	2325
	Manievich, V. (ISR)	9	2280
	Manik, M. (SVK)	27	2355
	Manikandaswamy, S. (IND)	0	2250
	Maniocha, A. (POL)	0	2305
	Manion, J. (USA)	10	2310
	Manish, M. (IND)	0	2205
	Manishi, K. (IND)	0	2220
	Manley, J. P. (ENG)	0	2200
m	Mann, Ch. (GER)	2	2455
	Mann, G. (HUN)	55	2130
	Manni, M. (FIN)	0	2240
f	Manninen, M. (FIN)	22	2355
f	Mannion, S. R. (SCO)	16	2390
	Mannke, M. (POL)	0	2230
	Manoj, V. (IND)	8	2210
	Manojlovic, Sa. (YUG)	5	2290
	Manojlovic, Se. (YUG)	2	2210
	Manojlovic, Z. (YUG)	0	2160
	Manolache, M. (ROM)	11	2325
	Manole, V. (ROM)	0	2270
m	Manolov, I. (BUL)	21	2360
m	Manor, I. (ISR)	0	2465
m	Manouck, Th. (FRA)	13	2305
	Mansoor, J. (MRI)	0	2205
	Mansson, P. (SWE)	9	2075
	Mansurov, V. (RUS)	8	2400
m	Mantovani, R. (ITA)	0	2380
	Manu, A. (ROM)	15	2015
	Manu, D. (ROM)	0	2075
f	Mar, C. (USA)	0	2420
m	Marangunic, S. (CRO)	5	2460
	Maras, M. (CRO)	0	2265
m	Marasescu, I. (ROM)	13	2340
	Marbach, J. (GER)	0	2245
f	Marcantoni, H. (FRA)	0	2305
	Marchand, F. (FRA)	18	2280
	Marcia, G. (ROM)	0	2265
m	Marciano, D. (FRA)	37	2410
	Marcinkowski, K. (POL)	4	2215
	Marcovici, A. (ISR)	17	2210
f	Marcus, J. (NED)	0	2300
	Marcussi, B. (ARG)	8	2280
	Marek, J. (TCH)	0	2280
	Mares, J. (TCH)	0	2305
	Margolin, B. (RUS)	59	2415
	Margot, F. (SUI)	2	2305
	Margulis, I. (USA)	18	2295
	Marholev, D. (BUL)	7	2270
	Mari Arul, S. (IND)	5	2245
m	Maria, L. R. S. (INA)	14	2190
	Mariano, Ch. R. (PHI)	12	2015
g	Maric, A. (IM) (YUG)	7	2405
f	Maric, D. (YUG)	5	2280
g	Maric, M. (YUG)	11	2305
	Maric, V. (YUG)	0	2285
g	Marin, M. (ROM)	49	2515
f	Marin-Ionescu, L. (ROM)	42	2160
f	Marinelli, T. (ITA)	19	2390
m	Marinello, B. M. (USA)	0	2160
m	Marinkovic, I. (YUG)	46	2455
f	Marinkovic, M. (YUG)	0	2310
	Marinkovic, R. (YUG)	0	2240
m	Marinkovic, S. (YUG)	42	2375
	Marinkovic, Z. (YUG)	0	2305
	Marinova, E. (BUL)	0	2075
	Marinovic, B. (YUG)	0	2380
	Marinsek, T. (SLO)	7	2210
g	Mariotti, S. (ITA)	0	2425
	Maris, I. (GRE)	0	2330
f	Marjanov, Z. (YUG)	0	2280
g	Marjanovic, S. (YUG)	0	2445
f	Markeluk, S. (ARG)	0	2355
	Markiewicz, J. (POL)	0	2315
	Markotic, B. (CRO)	0	2225
m	Markotic, G. (CRO)	12	2395
	Markov, J. (RUS)	4	2450
f	Markov, S. (YUG)	0	2115
f	Markov, V. (YUG)	11	2145
	Markovic, D. (YUG)	0	2240

m	Markovic, G. (YUG)	16	2240
	Markovic, Ig. (CRO)	5	2230
f	Markovic, Iv. (YUG)	0	2400
f	Markovic, L. (YUG)	2	2235
	Markovic, Milan (TCH)	0	2155
	Markovic, Milo. (YUG)	0	2265
f	Markovic, Mirol. (YUG)	0	2270
m	Markovic, Miros. (YUG)	4	2510
	Markovic, S. (YUG)	0	2280
f	Markovic, V. (YUG)	0	2305
	Markovic, Z. (YUG)	18	2385
	Markowski, D. (POL)	0	2265
m	Markowski, T. (POL)	46	2465
	Marks, Z. (POL)	0	2010
	Markun, B. (SLO)	0	2250
	Markus, J. R. (NED)	12	2235
f	Markzon, G. (USA)	30	2290
f	Maroja, H. (CRO)	0	2310
	Marosi, Cs. (HUN)	11	2270
f	Marosi, Gy. (HUN)	8	2290
	Maroto, J. L. (ESP)	0	2305
g	Marovic, D. (CRO)	0	2445
f	Marquet, G. (MEX)	0	2265
	Marquez Suarez, L. (MEX)	0	2015
	Marquez, R. (ECU)	4	2260
f	Marschner, J. (GER)	5	2295
f	Marszalek, R. (POL)	0	2265
	Marszk, K. (POL)	0	2225
m	Martens, M. (NED)	9	2430
	Marti, Gy. (HUN)	4	2375
f	Martic, Z. (CRO)	0	2280
f	Martidis, A. (CYP)	0	2360
	Martin Del Campo, A. (MEX)	0	2015
	Martin Del Campo, J. (MEX)	12	2200
m	Martin Del Campo, R. (MEX)	13	2420
m	Martin Gonzalez, A. (ESP)	6	2405
	Martin V., J. M. (ESP)	9	2085
m	Martin, A. D. (ENG)	23	2425
f	Martin, B. (NZL)	0	2410
	Martin, D. (WLS)	0	2045
	Martin, O. (CUB)	0	2255
	Martin, S. (GER)	2	2215
	Martin, Th. (GER)	4	2200
	Martine, J.-Ch. (FRA)	9	2190
	Martineau (HAI)	0	2210
	Martinez Garcia, J. J. (MEX)	0	2255
	Martinez Gonzalez, F. (ESP)	0	2295
	Martinez Medina, E. (ESP)	0	2235
	Martinez Otzeta, J. M. (ESP)	2	2275
	Martinez, A. (ARG)	0	2220
	Martinez, B. (CUB)	0	2285
f	Martinez, Ca. A. (BRA)	2	2290
	Martinez, Cr. (COL)	0	2320
	Martinez, D. (MEX)	0	2260
	Martinez, F. (ESP)	12	2160
	Martinez, G. (FRA)	0	2205
f	Martinez, I. (MEX)	12	2295
	Martinez, M. (ARG)	12	2310
	Martinez, N. (CUB)	0	2205
	Martinez, V. (MEX)	0	2025
	Martinidesz, D. (SUI)	4	2195
	Martinkus, R. (LTU)	16	2230
	Martinovic, M. (YUG)	9	2150
g	Martinovic, S. (YUG)	10	2465
f	Martinovsky, E. (USA)	19	2270
	Martins, J. F. P. (BRA)	0	2370
	Martiska, P. (SVK)	0	2220
	Marton, I. (HUN)	0	2245
f	Martorelli, A. (ITA)	11	2255
	Marttala, Th. (SWE)	0	2265
	Martynov, A. (RUS)	0	2360
m	Martynov, P. (RUS)	6	2430
	Marucha, W. (POL)	12	2020
	Marusenko, P. (UKR)	52	2370
	Marxen, P. (GER)	3	2250
	Maryasin, B. (ISR)	21	2380
	Marzano, C. (ITA)	5	2235
	Marzec, J. (POL)	3	2225
f	Marzoll, W. (GER)	9	2360
	Masango, M. (ZIM)	0	2205
	Masat, A. (HUN)	16	2245
	Mascarenhas, A. (BRA)	0	2285
m	Mascarinas, R. (PHI)	0	2420
	Masculo, J. (BRA)	0	2310
	Masenaite, I. (RUS)	0	2125
	Mashian, Y. (ISR)	0	2230
m	Masic, Lj. (YUG)	0	2295
	Masic, P. (YUG)	0	2240
	Masiyazi, R. (ZIM)	0	2005
	Maslanka, R. (POL)	0	2315
	Maslesa, B. (SLO)	0	2280
	Maslov, Y. (RUS)	3	2255
	Maslowski, T. (POL)	0	2265
	Masnjak, R. (CRO)	2	2035
	Massana, J. (PUR)	0	2240
	Massart, M. (FRA)	10	2240
	Massenzano, G. (ARG)	9	2190
	Masserey, Y. (SUI)	11	2320
	Masternak, A. (POL)	0	2220
	Masternak, G. (POL)	23	2350
f	Mastoras, I. (GRE)	13	2240
f	Mastrokoukos, G. (GRE)	20	2325
m	Matamoros, C. S. (ECU)	0	2410
	Matas, S. (SVK)	0	2210
f	Mate, L. (HUN)	22	2230
	Matei, F. (ROM)	5	2255
	Matejic, Z. (YUG)	0	2290
m	Mateo, R. (DOM)	0	2430
	Materzic, Ch. (CRO)	0	2175
m	Mateus, M. (ANG)	0	2220
	Matevzic, Ch. (AUT)	11	2360
	Mathe, A. (FRA)	6	2220
m	Mathe, G. (HUN)	15	2400
	Mathis, R. (SUI)	5	2145
f	Mathonia, C. (GER)	9	2220
	Matic, B. (YUG)	0	2245
	Matic, N. (YUG)	0	2220
	Matijasevic, M. (YUG)	0	2315
	Matijevic, H. (CRO)	2	2280
	Matjushina, Z. (UKR)	0	2150
f	Matkovic, T. (CRO)	2	2275
	Matlak, J. (POL)	0	2250
m	Matlak, M. (POL)	22	2430
	Matousek, M. (TCH)	0	2270
	Matovic, R. (YUG)	14	2165
	Matovu, G. (UGA)	0	2225
	Matros, A. (KAZ)	30	2345
	Matsuo, T. (JPN)	0	2205
	Matsuura, E. (BRA)	17	2290
	Matsuura, H. (BRA)	0	2230
	Matthaei, A. (GER)	19	2260
	Matthews, Sh. (JAM)	0	2265
	Matthias, H. (GER)	0	2335
	Mattick, L. (GER)	14	2250
g	Matulovic, M. (YUG)	18	2460
g	Matveeva, S. (KYR)	9	2395
	Matyszkiewicz, M. (POL)	13	2075
	Matzdorf, M. (GER)	0	2230
	Maung, H. D. (MYN)	0	2335
	Maurer, F. (SUI)	0	2285
	Mauro, A. (ITA)	11	2260
f	Maus, Si. (GER)	0	2305
m	Maus, So. (GER)	12	2415
	Mavrich, R. (ARG)	24	2215
	Maximenko, A. (RUS)	0	2430
f	Maxion, D. (GER)	6	2280
	Maya, H. (MEX)	0	2235
	Mayer, F. (GER)	0	2270
f	Mayer, I. (HUN)	6	2275
	Mayer, R. (ESP)	0	2235
	Mayers, D. E. (USA)	0	2240
	Maynard, F. (CRC)	9	2235
	Mazalon, M. (POL)	0	2225
m	Mazariego, C. (GUA)	0	2010
f	Mazi, L. (SLO)	18	2345
f	Mazul, W. (POL)	0	2345
	Mazuran, M. (CRO)	0	2255
	Mazurek, R. (POL)	0	2260
	Mazzoleni, J. (ARG)	5	2200
	Mazzoni, G. (FRA)	7	2220
	Mc Laren, L. (NZL)	0	2275
m	McCambridge, V. (USA)	5	2475
	McCamon, B. (SCO)	10	2300
	McCann, K. (IRL)	0	2235
	McCarthy, B. (USA)	25	2245
f	McCarthy, J. (USA)	3	2310
f	McClintock, D. (USA)	0	2390
	McCormick, J. (USA)	8	2235
m	McDonald, N. R. (ENG)	29	2395
	McDonnell, G. (USA)	1	2285
	McElligott, G. (IRL)	9	2260
	McEwan, K. B. (SCO)	3	2120
	McFarland, R. (ENG)	0	2290
	McHugh, K. (IRL)	12	2175
m	McKay, R. M. (SCO)	0	2375
	McKenna, J. (ENG)	0	2160
	McLure, A. (SCO)	0	2015
	McMahon, D. (IRL)	14	2275
	McMichael, R. (ENG)	3	2305
g	McNab, C. A. (SCO)	29	2490
	McTavish, D. (CAN)	0	2180
	Mctigue, J. (ISV)	0	2205
	Meazid, N. (BAN)	0	2055
	Mechkarov, V. (BUL)	0	2275
g	Mecking, H. (BRA)	8	2575
	Meczynski, W. (POL)	15	2180
f	Medak, D. (CRO)	4	2305
m	Medancic, R. (CRO)	9	2320
f	Medar, Z. (YUG)	10	2300
m	Medianikova, N. (RUS)	0	2145
f	Medic, M. (CRO)	7	2245
	Medina, J. (CUB)	0	2270
f	Medina, M. (CUB)	0	2245
	Medjedovic, J. (YUG)	31	2040
	Mednikova, S. (RUS)	23	2115
g	Mednis, E. J. (USA)	9	2440
g	Meduna, E. (TCH)	9	2470
	Medvedeva, E. (RUS)	0	2015
	Medvegy, N. (HUN)	32	2105
	Medvegy, Z. (HUN)	9	2285
	Meeres, M. (USA)	0	2300
	Meetei, A. B. (IND)	9	2290
	Mehaibia, A. (ALG)	0	2135
	Mehlhorn, U. (GER)	0	2125
	Mehrbrey, K. (GER)	0	2220
	Mehta, P. (IND)	2	2230
	Meier, Th. (GER)	7	2270
f	Meier, V. (GER)	13	2305
	Meins, G. (GER)	15	2430
f	Meinsohn, F. (FRA)	5	2235
f	Meinsohn, P. (FRA)	4	2365
	Meiser, M. (GER)	0	2260
	Meissner, B. (GER)	0	2285
	Meissner, H.-J. (GER)	6	2280
m	Meister, P. (GER)	4	2415
m	Meister, Y. (RUS)	19	2455
	Mejia, R. (COL)	0	2210
f	Mejic, P. (YUG)	0	2350
	Melashvili, K. (GEO)	0	2195
	Melashvili, N. (GEO)	0	2155
	Melaxasz, V. (HUN)	0	2225
m	Meleghegyi, Cs. (HUN)	0	2400
	Melendez Fierro, J. (ESP)	0	2330
	Melhuish, J. (CHI)	14	2270
	Melkumova, N. (RUS)	26	2130
m	Mellado, J. (ESP)	23	2415
	Mellano, S. (ARG)	26	2300
	Mellier, P. (SUI)	0	2210
	Melnic, V. (ROM)	0	2295
	Men, B. (USA)	15	2420
	Mena, Je. (MEX)	0	2185

	Name		
	Mena, Jo. (MEX)	10	2250
	Menacher, M. (GER)	2	2280
f	Mencinger, V. (SLO)	3	2360
	Mendez, E. (ARG)	29	2390
	Mendez, F. (ESP)	0	2315
	Mendez, G. (ARG)	16	2235
	Mendez, S. (MEX)	0	2250
	Mendoza, L. (ESP)	0	2285
	Mendoza, P. (MEX)	0	2005
	Mendoza, R. (COL)	11	2365
	Mendrinos, N. (GRE)	4	2255
	Menendez, D. (ARG)	1	2205
	Meneses, D. (COL)	0	2300
	Mengarini, A. (USA)	0	2255
	Menghi, C. (LUX)	0	2265
	Mensch, E. (FRA)	12	2210
	Menshikova, L. (RUS)	0	2080
	Mentov, S. (RUS)	0	2280
f	Menvielle Lacourrelle, A. (ESP)	9	2305
	Menyhart, T. (HUN)	11	2215
	Menzel, R. (GER)	0	2245
	Mercier, J.-P. (FRA)	0	2225
m	Merdinjan, A. (BUL)	0	2305
	Mereklishvili, Ts. (GEO)	0	2085
	Merino, M. (ESA)	0	2205
	Merriman, J. (ENG)	0	2235
	Mertens, K. (GER)	0	2195
	Mertins, K. (GER)	0	2230
	Meshjerina, T. (RUS)	0	2080
	Meshkov, Y. A. (RUS)	16	2250
	Meskhi, T. (GEO)	0	2175
	Mesropov, K. (RUS)	25	2370
m	Messa, R. (ITA)	0	2305
m	Messing, H. (CRO)	7	2355
	Messmer, M. (GER)	6	2315
g	Mestel, J. A. (ENG)	9	2520
f	Mester, Gy. (HUN)	32	2295
m	Mestrovic, Z. (BIH)	15	2450
m	Meszaros, A. (HUN)	29	2390
f	Meszaros, B. (YUG)	0	2330
	Meszaros, Gyo. (HUN)	8	2200
	Meszaros, Gyu. (HUN)	95	2465
	Metaxas, P. (GRE)	3	2225
	Metge, N. J. (NZL)	11	2100
	Metge, K. (NZL)	0	2005
	Metral, J.-P. (FRA)	8	2300
	Metrick, A. (USA)	0	2250
	Metz, H. (GER)	18	2275
f	Meulders, R. (BEL)	15	2310
	Meurrens, P. (BEL)	0	2265
	Mevel, A. (FRA)	5	2190
f	Meyer, C.-D. (GER)	9	2330
m	Meyer, E. B. (USA)	19	2480
	Meyer, F. (GER)	14	2300
f	Meyer, H. (GER)	9	2330
	Meyer, I. (GER)	0	2280
f	Meyer, J. C. (USA)	0	2345
	Meyer, L. (DEN)	9	2345
f	Meyer, P. (GER)	4	2360
m	Meyers, V. (LAT)	17	2415
	Mezentsev, V. (RUS)	11	2325
	Miana, E. (ARG)	0	2215
	Micalizzi, G. (ITA)	17	2250
m	Micayabas, M. (PHI)	0	2345
	Michael, M. (GER)	9	2305
m	Michaelsen, N. (GER)	26	2435
	Michalak, I. (POL)	4	2230
	Michalek, Ch. (GER)	8	2240
	Michalek, J. (TCH)	0	2300
	Michalet, G. (FRA)	14	2270
	Michalke, G. (GER)	15	2225
	Michalski, O. (POL)	4	2195
m	Michel Yunis, Ch. D. (CHI)	13	2340
	Michelakis, G. (RSA)	5	2355
f	Micheli, C. (ITA)	3	2300
f	Michenka, J. (TCH)	0	2405
	Micic, C. (YUG)	25	2315
m	Micic, J. (GER)	6	2280
f	Micic, S. (YUG)	17	2225
	Micov, V. (YUG)	0	2250
	Micu, I. (ROM)	0	2300
	Middelhoff, C. (GER)	0	2205
	Middendorf, F. (GER)	0	2250
	Midjord, J. P. (FAI)	32	2110
	Mielczarski, M. (POL)	0	2315
	Miezis, N. (LAT)	27	2410
	Mifsud, T. (MLT)	0	2205
	Migl, D. (GER)	9	2265
	Miguel, V. (ESP)	0	2300
	Mihai, N. (ROM)	10	2005
f	Mihajlovic, M. (YUG)	0	2270
	Mihalj, M. M. (YUG)	22	2200
m	Mihaljcisin, M. (YUG)	0	2280
	Mihalko, J. (HUN)	5	2285
f	Mihevc, N. (SLO)	18	2140
	Mihevic, I. (SLO)	0	2200
	Mihic, V. (YUG)	7	2205
	Mihojlic, M. (YUG)	0	2240
f	Mihok, L. (HUN)	0	2320
f	Mijailovic, Z. (YUG)	25	2335
	Mijatovic, A. (YUG)	0	2120
	Mijuskovic, B. (YUG)	0	2255
	Mijuskovic, N. (YUG)	4	2225
	Mika, J. (HUN)	0	2300
f	Mikac, M. (SLO)	10	2395
f	Mikac, T. (SLO)	1	2270
	Mikanovic, G. (YUG)	0	2275
	Mikanovic, M. (YUG)	0	2305
	Mikavica, M. (YUG)	11	2225
	Mikenas, A. (LTU)	0	2215
g	Mikhalchishin, A. (UKR)	30	2520
	Mikhalevski, A. (ISR)	19	2440
	Mikhalevski, V. (ISR)	28	2380
	Mikicic, D. (YUG)	0	2285
	Mikoleizig, E. (GER)	12	2290
	Mikulas, D. (SVK)	0	2300
	Mikulcik, L. (TCH)	0	2250
	Miladinov, M. (YUG)	0	2225
m	Miladinovic, I. (YUG)	39	2450
	Milanovic, D. (YUG)	0	2325
f	Milanovic, S. (YUG)	0	2250
f	Milanovic, V. (YUG)	4	2400
f	Milasin, M. (CRO)	11	2290
	Milasiute, V. (LTU)	9	2125
	Milenkovic, I. (YUG)	0	2255
	Milenkovic, J. (YUG)	0	2225
	Milenkovic, M. (YUG)	23	2215
g	Miles, A. J. (ENG)	38	2565
	Miletic, D. (YUG)	0	2215
	Mileto, G. (ITA)	0	2225
	Milic, N. (YUG)	10	2210
	Milic, S. (YUG)	0	2285
f	Milicevic, M. (YUG)	0	2295
	Milicevic, P. (YUG)	9	2345
	Milicic, T. (YUG)	22	2025
	Milicicevic, A. (YUG)	11	2250
	Milijanovic, G. (YUG)	13	2180
	Milivojevic, J. (YUG)	1	2280
f	Milivojevic, N. (SWE)	0	2205
	Milivojevic, S. (YUG)	7	2075
m	Miljanic, B. (YUG)	33	2370
f	Miljevic, B. (YUG)	0	2250
	Miller, R. (USA)	0	2330
	Milligan Scott, H. (SCO)	14	2035
	Mills, N. (AUS)	12	2010
f	Milocco, F. (ITA)	2	2365
	Milonjic, M. (YUG)	0	2215
g	Milos, G. (BRA)	27	2565
	Milosavac, Lj. (YUG)	0	2305
f	Milosavljevic, R. (YUG)	0	2280
	Milosevic, A. (YUG)	0	2255
m	Milosevic, G. (YUG)	0	2410
f	Milosevic, J. (YUG)	0	2360
	Milosevic, R. (SLO)	2	2225
	Milosevic, S. (YUG)	5	2315
f	Milosevic, V. (YUG)	0	2345
	Milosijev, T. (YUG)	6	2255
m	Milov, L. (UKR)	0	2480
m	Milov, V. (ISR)	43	2500
	Milovanovic, Ne. (YUG)	16	2215
	Milovanovic, Ni. (YUG)	0	2285
m	Milovanovic, R. (YUG)	0	2435
	Milovanovic, S. (YUG)	15	2265
f	Miltner, A. (GER)	6	2310
m	Milu, R. S. (ROM)	48	2400
	Milunovic, T. (YUG)	0	2345
f	Milut, M. (ROM)	0	2300
	Minarelli, G. (ITA)	0	2250
	Minasian, A. (ARM)	27	2220
g	Minasian, Ar. (ARM)	40	2535
f	Minaya, J. (COL)	0	2265
	Mincic, S. (YUG)	1	2355
	Mincsovics, M. (HUN)	8	2230
	Minero, B. P. (CRC)	9	2195
	Minero, C. (CRC)	7	2270
f	Minero, S. (CRC)	28	2415
	Minescu, D. O. (ROM)	0	2230
f	Minescu, I. K. (ROM)	0	2130
m	Minev, N. N. (USA)	0	2370
f	Miniboeck, G. (AUT)	0	2320
h	Minic, D. (CRO)	0	2355
	Minich, P. (SVK)	0	2215
	Minko, M. (RUS)	0	2335
	Minniti, V. (ITA)	0	2005
	Minnullin, A. (GER)	36	2300
m	Minogina, T. (RUS)	11	2230
	Minster, Y. (ISR)	0	2245
f	Minzer, C. J. (ARG)	25	2315
f	Mira, H. (AUT)	0	2085
	Mirable, T. (USA)	11	2180
	Miracca, J. (ARG)	0	2265
m	Miralles, G. (FRA)	0	2475
	Miranda, M. M. C. (BRA)	0	2265
	Miranovic, R. (YUG)	0	2365
	Mirchev, V. (BUL)	0	2265
	Mircov, N. (ROM)	12	2215
	Mirescu, R. (ROM)	0	2285
	Miricanac, A. (YUG)	0	2215
m	Mirkovic, S. (YUG)	26	2375
	Miron, T. (ROM)	0	2270
	Mironov, R. (EST)	25	2015
	Mironov, R.. (RUS)	14	2150
	Mirschinka, D. (GER)	6	2270
	Mirumian, V. (ARM)	20	2305
f	Misailovic, N. (YUG)	3	2420
f	Mischustov, M. (GER)	0	2370
	Miserendino, A. (ARG)	0	2260
m	Mishra, N.-K. (IND)	26	2375
	Mishuchkov, N. M. (RUS)	4	2370
	Misic, D. (YUG)	0	2235
	Misiuga, A. (POL)	0	2225
	Miskovic, P. (YUG)	2	2280
	Misojcic, M. (YUG)	5	2330
	Mistea, I. (ROM)	0	2260
m	Mitenkov, A. (RUS)	24	2430
	Mitescu, L. (ROM)	0	2015
f	Mitescu, N. (ROM)	0	2080
	Mitev, G. (BUL)	0	2310
f	Mithrakanth, P. (IND)	23	2355
f	Mititelu, G. (ROM)	0	2325
f	Mitkov, M. (YUG)	45	2370
g	Mitkov, N. (YUG)	51	2495
	Mitkovsky, K. (YUG)	8	2305
	Mitkovsky, O. (YUG)	28	2265
	Mitlashevsky, O. (RUS)	0	2220
	Mitov, B. (BUL)	0	2215
	Mitra, S. (IND)	13	2255
	Mitrandzas, A. (GRE)	14	2245
	Mitrovic, M. (YUG)	17	2085
	Mitrovic, P. (YUG)	0	2355
	Mitrovic, S. (YUG)	0	2240
	Mittelberger, P. (AUT)	0	2270
	Mittelman, G. (ISR)	0	2250
	Mittermayr, G. (AUT)	0	2250
	Mitura, V. (TCH)	0	2260

	Name		
f	Miulescu, G. (ROM)	28	2350
	Mladenov, S. (BUL)	0	2230
	Mlechev, H. (BUL)	0	2225
m	Mnatsakanian, E. A. (ARM)	8	2395
	Moatlhodi, K. (BOT)	0	2170
	Moberg, K. J. (SWE)	13	2285
	Moccero, E. (ARG)	21	2205
m	Mochalov, E. V. (BLA)	22	2420
f	Modr, B. (TCH)	10	2345
f	Modrova, H. (TCH)	7	2030
	Modzelan, A. (POL)	0	2230
f	Moe, M. (DEN)	0	2300
m	Moehring, G. (GER)	16	2345
	Moehrmann, M. (GER)	0	2235
	Moeldner, J. (GER)	0	2265
f	Moen, O.-Ch. (NOR)	0	2245
	Mogyorosi, F. (HUN)	1	2215
	Moh. Abdel, Z. (EGY)	15	2280
	Mohacsi, I. (HUN)	1	2245
	Mohamed, A. (PAL)	0	2205
f	Mohamed, F. A. (EGY)	15	2365
	Mohamed, M. M. (LBA)	0	2205
	Mohammed, A. (IRQ)	0	2200
	Mohammed, E. W. (IRQ)	0	2240
	Mohammed, K. (EGY)	24	2230
	Mohandessi, Sh. (BEL)	6	2280
	Mohanty, P. M. (IND)	0	2240
	Mohd, K. A. (MAS)	10	2195
	Mohebbi, J. (FRA)	8	2275
	Mohmed, K. (SYR)	0	2205
m	Mohr, G. (SLO)	62	2450
g	Mohr, S. (GER)	15	2455
m	Mohrlock, D. (GER)	7	2415
	Mohrmmad, A. R. (HUN)	6	2130
f	Moingt, J.-C. (FRA)	8	2200
	Moisan, F. (FRA)	0	2230
	Moise, D. (ROM)	0	2260
m	Moiseev, V. (RUS)	7	2450
	Mojzhess, I. (RUS)	11	2470
f	Mojzis, J. (TCH)	0	2230
	Mok, T.-M. (MAS)	10	2240
	Mokcsay, R. (HUN)	0	2265
g	Mokry, K. (SVK)	9	2515
	Moldobaev, E. (RUS)	0	2385
m	Moldovan, D. (ROM)	39	2415
	Moldoveanu, E. (ROM)	11	2270
	Moliboga, V. (RUS)	0	2330
	Molinaroli, M. (GER)	0	2295
m	Mollov, E. (BUL)	20	2385
	Molnar, B. (HUN)	11	2300
	Molnar, E. (HUN)	6	2195
	Molnar, J. (HUN)	9	2250
	Molnar, L. (HUN)	0	2240
	Molnar, V. (SVK)	0	2220
	Molnar, Z. (HUN)	0	2225
	Momeni, H. (IRI)	0	2350
	Momirovic, M. (YUG)	0	2275
	Mompo Ballest, V. (ESP)	5	2270
f	Monda, L. (HUN)	39	2170
	Mondaca, O. (ARG)	3	2155
	Monetti, C. (ARG)	9	2025
f	Monier, R. (ARG)	0	2360
	Monin, N. (RUS)	38	2400
	Monnard, L. (FRA)	2	2250
	Monori, Z. (HUN)	0	2145
	Monroy, E. (MEX)	0	2315
	Monte, P. (NED)	0	2190
f	Montecatine, R. (ESP)	5	2330
	Montell, J. C. (ESP)	0	2285
f	Montero Martinez, C. (CHI)	9	2250
	Montgomery, P. (USA)	1	2255
	Montiel, P. (CUB)	0	2285
	Monus, Z. (HUN)	0	2030
	Moore jr., B. G. (USA)	0	2275
	Moore, G. (ENG)	0	2210
	Moore, H. (CAN)	0	2280
	Moosa, I. (QTR)	0	2210
	Mora, F. (ITA)	0	2340
f	Mora, V. (FRA)	14	2165
	Moracchini, F. (FRA)	0	2260
	Morais, V. (POR)	0	2130
f	Morales, H. (MEX)	0	2275
	Morales, J. (ESP)	3	2220
f	Moran, A. (ECU)	19	2405
f	Moran, B. (ECU)	0	2290
	Morariu, I. (ROM)	5	2060
	Morawietz, D. (GER)	0	2385
	Moraza, M. (PUR)	0	2210
	Morchat, M. (POL)	0	2220
	Morcinek, M. (POL)	0	2290
	Mordhorst, H. (GER)	0	2310
	Mordue, T. A. (ENG)	0	2240
	Morella, J. (CUB)	0	2245
	Moreno Ruiz, J. (ESP)	0	2325
	Moreno, Alb. (PER)	0	2280
f	Moreno, Ale. (CUB)	9	2345
	Morgan, M. (USA)	10	2260
	Morgulov, A. M. (RUS)	0	2335
	Morin, Y. (CAN)	0	2205
	Morkisz, B. (POL)	2	2215
	Morosova, T. V. (UKR)	0	2140
g	Morovic Fernandez, I. (CHI)	27	2575
	Moroz, A. (UKR)	22	2445
m	Morozevich, A. (RUS)	19	2545
	Morozov, A. (RUS)	0	2280
	Morris, Ch. F. (WLS)	2	2195
	Morris, Co. (AUS)	0	2260
	Morris, M. (USA)	5	2325
m	Morris, Ph. (ENG)	15	2380
m	Morris, W. D. (USA)	0	2375
	Morrison, Ch. (SCO)	0	2225
f	Morrison, G. (SCO)	0	2325
	Morrison, L. G. P. (SCO)	0	2010
f	Mortazavi, A. (ENG)	0	2345
	Mortazavi, K. (IRI)	0	2230
	Mortensen, B. (DEN)	8	2095
m	Mortensen, E. (DEN)	28	2470
	Mortensen, H. (DEN)	3	2150
f	Morvay, M. (HUN)	7	2240
	Moscalic, A. (ROM)	0	2195
	Moscovich, F. (ARG)	0	2055
	Moser, G. (AUT)	11	2280
	Moser, K. (GER)	0	2285
g	Moskalenko, V. (UKR)	8	2555
	Moskalik, A. (POL)	2	2190
	Moskalj, N. (YUG)	0	2240
	Moskow, E. (USA)	38	2195
	Mosna, S. (ITA)	5	2225
	Moss, R. (ENG)	3	2285
	Mossong, H. (LUX)	0	2280
	Mostafavi-Kachani, K. (IRI)	9	2265
m	Mothersill, A. (ENG)	0	2045
	Mothes, H.-A. (FRA)	25	2195
	Mottas, Ch. (SUI)	9	2275
g	Motwani, P. (SCO)	0	2520
	Moukhbatt, J. (LEB)	0	2005
	Moulain, J.-P. (FRA)	0	2220
f	Moulin, P. (BEL)	12	2300
	Moulton, S. C. (IRL)	0	2040
	Moussa, A. (PAL)	9	2205
m	Moutousis, K. (GRE)	11	2425
	Movsesian, S. (GEO)	5	2380
m	Mowsziszian, K. (GER)	15	2480
	Moynihan, K. (IRL)	14	2065
	Moyse, N. (ITA)	0	2155
m	Mozes, E. (ROM)	27	2355
	Mozes, Z. (HUN)	9	2270
m	Mozetic, D. (YUG)	0	2580
f	Mozna-Hojdarova, E. (TCH)	0	2095
m	Mozny, M. (TCH)	5	2395
	Mravunac, D. (CRO)	15	2155
m	Mrdja, M. (CRO)	18	2355
	Mrkonjic, N. (CRO)	0	2225
f	Mrksic, B. (CRO)	6	2275
	Mrozek, P. (POL)	16	2160
	Mrsevic, M. (YUG)	8	2280
	Mrunalini, K. (IND)	11	2100
f	Mrva, M. (SVK)	5	2355
	Mrva, V. (SVK)	0	2305
	Mtine, J. (ZAM)	0	2005
	Mubarak, A. (QTR)	0	2205
	Muc, T. (POL)	0	2225
f	Muchnik, L. (UKR)	25	2230
m	Muco, F. (ALB)	13	2430
f	Mudelsee, M. (GER)	12	2275
f	Mudrak, J. (TCH)	0	2300
	Mudrochova, H. (SVK)	0	2190
	Muehlebach, F. (SUI)	9	2200
	Mueller, Ac. (GER)	8	2240
	Mueller, An. (GER)	9	2100
	Mueller, Ch. (GER)	9	2090
	Mueller, Ha. -G. (GER)	0	2270
f	Mueller, Hei. (GER)	0	2275
	Mueller, Helge (GER)	0	2295
	Mueller, Helm. (AUT)	9	2215
m	Mueller, K. (GER)	12	2480
	Mueller, L. (SUI)	13	2255
	Mueller, Mar. (GER)	0	2215
f	Mueller, Mat. (GER)	26	2350
	Mueller, Michael (GER)	8	2285
	Mueller, Michael (GER)	0	2315
f	Mueller, O. (GER)	11	2345
	Mueller, R. (GER)	0	2255
f	Mueller, Werner (GER)	5	2325
	Mueller, Werner (GER)	0	2215
f	Mufic, Go. (CRO)	4	2335
	Mufic, Gr. (CRO)	1	2020
	Mufics, I. (HUN)	2	2250
	Muhamedzjanov, N. (RUS)	12	2290
	Muharemagic, A. (YUG)	0	2235
	Muhtarov, L. (UKR)	24	2175
m	Muhutdinov, M. (RUS)	26	2480
	Muhvic, D. (CRO)	2	2230
m	Muir, A. J. (SCO)	0	2360
f	Mujagic, R. (YUG)	9	2295
f	Mujic, H. (YUG)	0	2230
	Mujica, L. (VEN)	0	2020
	Mujkic, N. (YUG)	0	2260
	Mukabi, J. (KEN)	0	2205
	Mukhametov, E. (RUS)	20	2405
	Mukhim, G. (RUS)	4	2395
f	Mukic, J. (YUG)	11	2285
	Mulet, P. (POL)	17	2315
	Muller, A. (FRA)	3	2015
	Mullner, I. (HUN)	2	2220
	Munck Mortensen, P. (DEN)	0	2245
	Munjiza, I. (CRO)	9	2035
	Munoz Agullo, F. (ESP)	0	2295
	Munoz Pantoja, M. (PER)	21	2295
	Munoz, F. J. (ESP)	1	2280
	Munoz, Fr. (COL)	0	2220
	Munoz, H. (ECU)	0	2205
	Munschi, S. (FRA)	2	2310
	Munteanu, A. (ROM)	24	2305
	Munzer, M. (GER)	0	2295
	Muralidharan, M. B. (IND)	21	2330
	Muratov, V. A. (RUS)	6	2405
	Murdzia, P. (POL)	37	2435
g	Muresan, M. (ROM)	13	2215
	Murgia, A. (ITA)	3	2255
f	Murillo, A. (CRC)	9	2335
	Murillo, M. (CRC)	9	2225
	Murin, J. (HUN)	5	2265
	Muron, M. (TCH)	0	2245
	Murray, G. (PUR)	0	2005
	Murray, J. (IRL)	0	2240
g	Murrey, J. (FRA)	28	2530
g	Murshed, N. (BAN)	31	2525
m	Murugan, K. (IND)	22	2430
	Murzin, L. (RUS)	16	2385
	Musat, A. (ROM)	26	2345

	Name	Games	Rating
	Muse, D. (GER)	18	2300
m	Muse, M. (GER)	19	2485
	Musil, M. (SLO)	0	2260
m	Musil, V. (SLO)	0	2340
	Musitz, L. (HUN)	0	2295
	Muslimova, A. E. (KAZ)	5	2235
	Mutschler, L. (HUN)	0	2240
	Muyambo, D. (ZIM)	0	2205
	Muziciuk, N. (RUS)	0	2080
	Myc, M. (POL)	9	2235
	Mydlarz, M. (ARG)	0	2290
	Myo, N. (MYN)	0	2205
	Myrvold, T. S. (NOR)	0	2330

N

	Name	Games	Rating
	Naberli, J. (SUI)	9	2240
	Nad, V. (YUG)	0	2245
	Nadanian, A. (RUS)	0	2285
	Nadera, B. A. (PHI)	18	2405
	Nadvesnik, V. (YUG)	11	2005
m	Nadyrhanov, S. (UZB)	37	2460
	Naeser, J. (SWE)	9	2015
	Nagatz, F. (GER)	4	2250
	Nagel, H. (AUT)	5	2270
f	Nagel, Y. (NED)	0	2100
	Nagendra, R. (IND)	6	2315
	Nagl, F. (AUT)	0	2235
	Nagrajsalovic, M. (CRO)	0	2320
f	Nagrocka, E. (GER)	5	2140
	Nagy, B. T. (HUN)	0	2110
m	Nagy, Ervin (HUN)	7	2305
f	Nagy, Ervinne (HUN)	0	2040
	Nagy, H. (HUN)	0	2090
	Nagy, I. (HUN)	0	2225
f	Nagy, J. (HUN)	13	2285
	Nagy, K. (HUN)	2	2235
	Nagy, L. (HUN)	0	2115
	Nagy, R. (HUN)	0	2225
	Nagy, S. I. (HUN)	0	2260
	Nagy, T. (HUN)	1	2215
	Nagy, Z. (HUN)	8	2305
	Nagyajtai, G. (HUN)	0	2290
	Naimanye, A. (UGA)	0	2370
	Nainapalert, T. (THA)	0	2185
g	Najdorf, M. (ARG)	0	2445
	Najer, E. (RUS)	14	2310
	Najjar, A. (LEB)	9	2290
	Najleti, E. (ARG)	0	2150
f	Nalbandian, T. (ARM)	37	2485
	Name, G. (BRA)	2	2240
	Namgilov, S. (RUS)	0	2440
	Namyslo, H. (GER)	9	2235
	Nandakumar, Y. (IND)	0	2230
f	Narandzic, V. (YUG)	0	2375
	Narayana, S. S. (IND)	0	2255
	Narciso, M. (ESP)	11	2300
	Nardini, D. (ARG)	0	2230
	Narodizki, E. (RUS)	0	2245
	Narva, J. (EST)	0	2305
m	Nascimento, A. (ANG)	0	2240
	Nasir Ali, S. (IND)	0	2325
	Nassr, N. (ALG)	6	2215
	Nasybullin, V. (KAZ)	37	2400
	Nataf, I.-A. (FRA)	17	2255
	Nathanail, E. (GRE)	0	2235
	Natri, A. (FIN)	7	2225
f	Naumann, F. (GER)	5	2250
g	Naumkin, I. (RUS)	35	2450
	Naung, K. Th. W. (VIE)	0	2120
f	Nautsch, W. (GER)	0	2300
m	Navarovszky, L. (HUN)	4	2320
m	Navarro, R. (MEX)	10	2410
	Navinsek, Th. (SLO)	0	2275
	Navratil, T. (YUG)	0	2240
m	Navrotescu, C. (ROM)	36	2390
	Naylor, J. (ENG)	0	2235
	Nazarko, Sh. (GER)	6	2325
	Nazarov, A. (TAJ)	0	2210

	Name	Games	Rating
f	Neamtu, S. (ROM)	0	2330
f	Nechifor, M. (ROM)	0	2135
m	Neckar, L. (TCH)	4	2360
m	Nedela, V. (TCH)	11	2400
	Nedeljkovic, A. (YUG)	0	2240
	Nedev, G. (BUL)	0	2340
	Nedev, T. (YUG)	24	2255
	Nedilko, V. (UKR)	0	2285
	Nedilsky, D. (ARG)	2	2230
m	Nedobora, M. (UKR)	19	2440
	Needleman, A. (ARG)	22	2355
	Neelakantan, N. (IND)	8	2245
m	Neely, E. (USA)	0	2110
	Negele, A. (GER)	0	2225
	Negi, V. S. (IND)	11	2230
	Negre, A. (FRA)	0	2215
f	Negri, S. (ARG)	10	2345
m	Negulescu, A. (ROM)	31	2435
	Negulescu-Dan, S. (ROM)	6	2020
m	Nei, I. (EST)	9	2405
f	Neidhardt, C. (GER)	8	2370
	Neil, D. (ENG)	0	2260
f	Neiman, E. (FRA)	0	2250
	Nekrasova, E. (UKR)	0	2065
	Nelis, J.-F. (FRA)	16	2215
	Nelson, A. (JAM)	0	2205
	Nemcova, V. (TCH)	0	2065
	Nemcova-Fialova, D. (TCH)	0	2085
	Neme, J. C. (ARG)	7	2190
	Nemec, P. (TCH)	0	2245
g	Nemet, I. (SUI)	18	2410
	Nemeth, A. (HUN)	8	2235
	Nemeth, F. (ROM)	12	2165
f	Nemeth, G. (HUN)	6	2260
f	Nemeth, M. (HUN)	11	2120
m	Nemeth, Z. (HUN)	21	2415
	Nemety, L. (FRA)	9	2240
	Nemirovski, S. (FRA)	0	2225
	Nemitz, K. (GER)	0	2175
	Nenadovic, Lj. (YUG)	0	2230
g	Nenashev, A. (UZB)	34	2580
	Nenkov, Lj. (BUL)	0	2295
m	Nepeina, M. (UKR)	17	2210
	Nepomiachty, A. (FRA)	9	2215
	Nepomnishay, M. I. (RUS)	5	2315
	Nerlev, C. (DEN)	0	2245
	Nesic, N. (YUG)	0	2220
	Nesterov, A. (RUS)	0	2205
m	Nesterov, J. (KAZ)	65	2485
	Nestorova-Petrova, L. (BUL)	0	2080
f	Nestorovic, D. (YUG)	59	2380
	Nestorovic, I. (YUG)	20	2020
	Nestorovic, V. (CRO)	0	2350
	Neto, H. (POR)	0	2175
	Netolitzky, G. (AUT)	0	2240
f	Netusil, M. (TCH)	0	2310
	Neubauer, M. (AUT)	9	2295
f	Neukirch, D. (GER)	3	2315
	Neulinger, M. (AUT)	11	2290
	Neumann, J. (GER)	0	2215
	Neumann, P. (TCH)	5	2190
	Neumark, Th. (GER)	0	2285
f	Neumeier, K. (AUT)	0	2330
	Neunhoeffer, H. (GER)	5	2295
	Neupauer, K. (HUN)	0	2280
f	Neurohr, S. (GER)	9	2310
	Neuschmied, S. (AUT)	6	2230
f	Nevanlinna, R. (FIN)	7	2290
	Nevednichy, B. M. (MOL)	32	2360
g	Nevednichy, V. (MOL)	51	2535
	Neven, K. (CAN)	0	2245
	Neverov, A. (RUS)	0	2305
g	Neverov, V. (UKR)	33	2535
	Nevostrujev, V. (RUS)	22	2445
	Newerovski, G. (RUS)	11	2360
	Ng, E. T. (MAS)	0	2190
	Ng, J. (SIN)	0	2205

	Name	Games	Rating
	Nguyen, K. D. (VIE)	0	2280
	Nguyen, Thi K. N. (VIE)	0	2055
f	Nguyen, Thi T. H. (VIE)	12	2140
f	Nicevski, D. (YUG)	0	2255
m	Nicevski, R. (YUG)	17	2380
f	Nicholson, J. G. (ENG)	0	2265
	Nickel, R. (GER)	9	2270
	Nickl, K. (AUT)	17	2220
m	Nickoloff, B. (CAN)	3	2390
f	Nicoara-Etchegaray, M. (FRA)	28	2140
f	Nicolaide, V. (ROM)	2	2350
	Nicolcea, C. (ROM)	14	2055
	Nicolescu, D. (ROM)	0	2250
f	Nicula, M. (ROM)	10	2295
f	Niedermaier, H. (GER)	9	2240
	Niedermayr, H. (AUT)	7	2240
	Niehaus, S. (GER)	0	2175
	Nielsen, Ja. (DEN)	10	2290
	Nielsen, Jo. (DEN)	0	2265
	Nielsen, L. A. (DEN)	0	2220
	Nielsen, N.-P. (DEN)	16	2245
	Nielsen, Pa. E. (DEN)	0	2235
m	Nielsen, Pe. H. (DEN)	61	2465
	Nielsen, Th. B. (DEN)	0	2290
	Nielsen, To. (DEN)	0	2190
f	Nielsen, U. V. (DEN)	0	2350
	Nieminen, K. (FIN)	6	2220
	Niering, M. (GER)	0	2240
	Niesel, M. (GER)	0	2280
f	Nieuwenhuis, P. (NED)	0	2315
g	Nijboer, F. (NED)	48	2555
	Nika, K. (GRE)	0	2025
	Nikac, P. (YUG)	31	2335
	Nikcevic, B. (YUG)	0	2220
m	Nikcevic, N. (YUG)	45	2405
	Nikitin, A. S. (RUS)	11	2430
	Niklasch, O. (GER)	0	2245
	Niklesova, H. (TCH)	0	2045
g	Nikolac, J. (CRO)	9	2435
	Nikoladze, S. (GEO)	12	2060
m	Nikolaev, S. (RUS)	0	2375
	Nikolaeva, N. (RUS)	23	2140
	Nikolaiczuk, L. (GER)	0	2280
	Nikolaidis, I. (GRE)	9	2440
	Nikolaidis, K. (GRE)	12	2315
m	Nikolenko, O. (RUS)	27	2475
f	Nikolic, B. (YUG)	10	2320
	Nikolic, Dragos. (YUG)	0	2290
	Nikolic, Dragov. (YUG)	0	2305
f	Nikolic, G. (YUG)	4	2360
	Nikolic, M. (YUG)	9	2145
m	Nikolic, N. (BIH)	30	2430
g	Nikolic, P. (BIH)	13	2625
f	Nikolic, Sa. N. (YUG)	0	2340
f	Nikolic, Si. (YUG)	0	2260
g	Nikolic, St. (YUG)	0	2325
f	Nikolic, V. (YUG)	0	2285
m	Nikolic, Zi. (YUG)	6	2480
	Nikolic, Zo. (YUG)	9	2210
	Nikolic-Kovacevic, D. (YUG)	0	2010
m	Nikolin, Z. (YUG)	18	2260
	Nikolov, N. (BUL)	0	2310
m	Nikolov, S. (BUL)	3	2350
	Nikontovic, S. (YUG)	0	2320
	Nikov, N. (BUL)	0	2295
	Nikovits, T. (HUN)	10	2230
	Nikuljshin, K. (RUS)	17	2385
	Nilssen, J. A. (FAI)	9	2265
	Nilsson, A. (SWE)	0	2290
	Nilsson, H. (SWE)	9	2220
	Nilsson, L. (DEN)	9	2260
	Nilsson, M. (SWE)	0	2175
	Nilsson, N. (DEN)	5	2245
	Nilsson, O. (SWE)	9	2225
	Nindl, G. (AUT)	0	2235
f	Ning, Chunhong (CHN)	0	2280
m	Ninov, K. (BUL)	15	2415

	Name		
m	Ninov, K. (BUL)	15	2415
	Ninov, N. (BUL)	0	2400
	Nishimura, H. (JPN)	11	2290
	Nisiochru, M. M. (IRL)	0	2085
f	Nisipeanu, D. (ROM)	43	2390
m	Nisman, B. I. (RUS)	0	2430
	Nissen, C. (GER)	0	2310
	Nizard, R. (FRA)	0	2150
	Nizhegorodova, M. (UKR)	0	2090
	Nizialek, R. (POL)	9	2210
	Nizynski, M. (POL)	0	2285
f	Noble, M. F. (NZL)	11	2290
	Noev, N. (BUL)	0	2225
	Nogly, Ch. (GER)	0	2240
	Nogradi, V. (HUN)	21	2280
	Nogueira, F. M. (BRA)	0	2270
	Nogueira, I. K. (BRA)	3	2195
g	Nogueiras, J. (CUB)	22	2580
	Nokka, R. (FIN)	0	2265
f	Nokso-Koivisto, A. (FIN)	8	2255
	Nolsoe, R. (FAI)	10	2200
	Nolte, R. (PHI)	0	2290
	Nolting, A. (GER)	0	2285
f	Nonnenmacher, E. (GER)	1	2295
	Noohu, M. J. (IND)	0	2255
	Nordahl, H. (NOR)	12	2265
f	Nordstrom, F. (SWE)	0	2210
	Norgaard, J. (DEN)	0	2320
	Noria, J. (ESP)	0	2305
	Norman, K. I. (ENG)	0	2220
	Norr, M. (DEN)	10	2135
	Norregaard, Ch. (DEN)	0	2235
f	Norri, J. (FIN)	29	2405
	Norris, D. C. (AUS)	14	2170
g	Norwood, D. (ENG)	25	2515
	Nory, P. (FRA)	0	2240
	Nosenko, A. (UKR)	0	2395
	Noskov, A. (KAZ)	0	2265
f	Notaros, K. (YUG)	8	2360
	Nothnagel, H. (GER)	0	2370
m	Notkin, M. (RUS)	63	2535
	Nouro, M. (FIN)	5	2230
	Novacan, M. (SLO)	0	2320
	Novak, D. (BIH)	0	2310
f	Novak, I. (SVK)	0	2280
	Novak, L. (HUN)	0	2205
f	Novakovic, D. (YUG)	0	2345
f	Novakovic, N. (YUG)	0	2345
f	Novicevic, M. (YUG)	0	2300
	Novichkov, V. (RUS)	14	2375
	Novik, M. (RUS)	20	2475
g	Novikov, I. A. (UKR)	20	2545
	Novikov, V. (LTU)	24	2315
	Novitzkij, D. (BLA)	11	2235
f	Novkovic, M. (YUG)	0	2370
m	Novoselski, Z. (YUG)	0	2370
	Novothny, A. (HUN)	0	2330
	Novotny, Ja. (TCH)	11	2315
	Novotny, Jo. (TCH)	4	2225
f	Nowak, I. (POL)	0	2395
	Nowak, J. (POL)	10	2035
	Nowak, R. (POL)	0	2250
	Nowicki, E. (GER)	4	2150
	Nowik, U. (POL)	0	2090
	Nowik, V. (GER)	0	2160
	Nowotny, H. (AUT)	0	2315
	Noyce, R. (ENG)	14	2230
f	Nuenchert, E. (GER)	3	2130
	Nukin, T. (KAZ)	14	2245
m	Nun, Ji. (TCH)	0	2435
m	Nun, Jo. (TCH)	0	2370
	Nunez Guzman, J. L. (MEX)	0	2295
	Nunez Vallina, J. A. (ESP)	0	2370
	Nunez, A. (AND)	0	2205
f	Nunez, An. (CUB)	10	2295
g	Nunn, J. D. M. (ENG)	32	2590
m	Nurkic, S. (BIH)	26	2395
	Nurkiewicz, M. (POL)	16	2155
	Nute, G. A. (USA)	0	2210
	Nutiu, H. (ROM)	0	2250
g	Nutu-Gajic, D. (ROM)	18	2340
	Nyaradi, S. (HUN)	0	2320
	Nykopp, J.-M. F. (FIN)	7	2245
	Nylen, A. (SWE)	9	2320

O

	Name		
	O'Brien, R. (IRL)	0	2240
	O'Cinneide, M. (IRL)	13	2225
	O'Connell, G. (IRL)	10	2145
	O'Connell, K. (IRL)	13	2360
	O'Donnell, M. (ISV)	0	2270
f	O'Donnell, T. (CAN)	0	2390
	O'Reilly, E. (IRL)	0	2240
	O'Shaughnessy, C. (IRL)	27	2340
	Oberfrank, I. (HUN)	5	2170
	Oberst, Th. (GER)	0	2285
	Obierak, W. (POL)	5	2170
m	Oblitas, C. (PER)	0	2425
	Obodchuk, A. (RUS)	33	2385
	Obradovic, A. (YUG)	0	2255
	Obradovic, B. (YUG)	0	2250
f	Obralic, E. (YUG)	0	2340
	Obrochta, B. (POL)	11	2140
	Obsivac, J. (TCH)	6	2310
m	Obukhov, A. (RUS)	55	2490
f	Ocampo, Raul (MEX)	10	2250
	Ocampo, Raul (ARG)	0	2315
	Ochkoos, J. (CAN)	0	2240
m	Ochoa De Echaguen, F. J. (ESP)	35	2450
	Ochs, H. (GER)	13	2190
	Ochsner, Th. (DEN)	0	2275
	Ocytko, A. (POL)	28	2260
	Odadzic, Z. (YUG)	0	2205
	Odeev, H. (RUS)	0	2405
	Odeeva, L. (TKM)	0	2135
	Odeh, K. (NGR)	16	2005
	Odendahl, R. (GER)	0	2295
m	Odendahl, S. M. (USA)	0	2425
	Oei, H. I. (NED)	19	2245
	Oepen, L. (GER)	0	2145
	Oesterle, P. (GER)	0	2375
	Ofek, R. (ISR)	0	2250
	Offinger, R. (GER)	0	2230
	Ofstad, P. (NOR)	0	2225
	Oganesian, S. (RUS)	11	2430
	Oggier, C. (ARG)	0	2225
	Ogloblina, L. (RUS)	0	2105
	Ohri, T. K. (IND)	0	2210
m	Ojanen, K. S. (FIN)	1	2345
m	Okhotnik, V. (UKR)	19	2395
	Okkes, M. (NED)	0	2285
	Okoth, J. (UGA)	0	2230
	Okrajek, A. (GER)	4	2270
	Okrucinski, T. (POL)	0	2260
	Okuniewski, B. (POL)	0	2235
	Olaffson, D. (ISD)	0	2270
g	Olafsson, Helgi (ISD)	21	2530
	Olafsson, Helgi (ISD)	0	2270
	Olah, P. (HUN)	0	2295
	Olah, Zs. (HUN)	0	2240
	Olarasu, I. (ROM)	0	2020
	Olausson, C. G. (SWE)	0	2265
	Olazarri, M. (URU)	18	2245
f	Olbrich, J. (GER)	1	2390
f	Olbrich, M. (GER)	0	2245
	Olcayoz, A. (TUR)	11	2245
	Olenderek, T. (POL)	10	2180
	Olesen, M. (DEN)	15	2340
	Olivares, D. (ARG)	17	2235
	Oliveira, A. (POR)	0	2290
	Oliver, C. (ESP)	1	2245
	Olivier, J.-Ch. (FRA)	0	2225
	Olivier, P. (FRA)	0	2230
	Olivieri, M. (ARG)	19	2270
	Oliwa, M. (POL)	11	2345
g	Oll, L. (EST)	58	2595

	Name		
	Olsen, H. (FAI)	32	2320
	Olsen, N. L. (DEN)	0	2285
	Olsen, P. E. (DEN)	6	2240
	Olson, K. (SWE)	0	2265
	Olsson, A. (SWE)	0	2270
	Olsson, K. (SWE)	11	2325
	Olsson, T. (SWE)	0	2110
	Olszewski, A. (POL)	0	2305
m	Oltean, D. (ROM)	0	2390
f	Oltean, L.-I. (ROM)	0	2350
f	Olteanu, G. (ROM)	0	2055
	Olthof, R. A. J. A. (NED)	0	2260
m	Oltra Caurin, R. (ESP)	14	2395
m	Onat, I. (TUR)	0	2350
f	Oney, F. (TUR)	0	2300
	Ong, A. (SIN)	0	2225
	Ong, Ch.-G. (SIN)	9	2265
f	Onischuk, A. (UKR)	34	2495
	Onoprienko, V. (RUS)	0	2290
	Opalka, J. (CHI)	0	2255
f	Opl, K. (AUT)	0	2270
	Oppitz, P. (GER)	1	2235
	Opravil, K. (TCH)	5	2120
	Orak, Lj. (CRO)	9	2350
f	Oral, T. (TCH)	9	2335
	Oratovsky, M. (ISR)	31	2420
	Orel, O. (SLO)	13	2335
	Orel, S. (SLO)	7	2050
	Oren, I. (ISR)	0	2295
	Oreopoulos, K. (GRE)	6	2255
m	Orev, P. (BUL)	0	2300
	Orfanos, L. (GRE)	14	2180
	Organdziev, O. (YUG)	13	2245
m	Orgovan, S. (HUN)	18	2340
	Orita, A.-M. (ROM)	3	2030
m	Orlov, G. (RUS)	14	2500
f	Orlov, K. (YUG)	0	2260
m	Orlov, P. (YUG)	0	2405
	Orlov, V. (RUS)	0	2280
	Orlov, Vs. (RUS)	0	2245
	Orlowski, J. (GER)	5	2255
	Ormos, G. (HUN)	5	2205
m	Ornstein, A. (SWE)	0	2440
	Orosz, A. (HUN)	0	2245
	Orpinas, C. (CHI)	0	2225
m	Orr, M. J. L. (IRL)	0	2345
f	Orsag, M. (TCH)	0	2390
f	Orso, J. (HUN)	0	2310
m	Orso, M. (HUN)	9	2330
	Ortega, A. (ESP)	0	2300
m	Ortega, L. (CUB)	15	2450
	Ortega-Nadera, L. (PHI)	0	2005
f	Ortel, E. (HUN)	11	2340
	Ortiz Aleman, J. C. (MEX)	0	2195
	Ortiz, M. (USA)	0	2305
	Orton, W. R. (USA)	2	2245
	Orzechowski, J. (POL)	3	2220
	Osiecki, S. (POL)	3	2220
f	Osieka, U. (GER)	8	2325
	Osipov, D. (RUS)	0	2395
	Osipow, N. (POL)	5	2240
	Oskulski, J. (POL)	0	2230
	Osman, G. A. (SUD)	0	2210
	Osman, M. (FRA)	12	2220
	Osmanbegovic, S. (SLO)	0	2355
m	Osmanovic, K. (BIH)	0	2340
m	Osnos, V. (RUS)	0	2440
	Osolin, M. (SLO)	0	2275
	Ospanov, A. (RUS)	16	2295
	Ossipova, V. (EST)	11	2095
	Ossowski, A. (POL)	0	2240
f	Ost-Hansen, J. (DEN)	0	2425
	Ostashinsky, B. (ISR)	9	2075
m	Ostenstad, B. (NOR)	0	2465
f	Ostergaard, D. (SWE)	18	2220
	Ostergaard, J. (DEN)	0	2290
	Osterman, G. (FIN)	0	2260
f	Osterman, R. (SLO)	0	2415
m	Ostermeyer, P. (GER)	8	2405

	Name	Games	Rating
f	Ostl, A. (GER)	8	2345
	Ostoja-Domaradzka, A. (POL)	0	2075
	Ostojic, D. (YUG)	0	2225
	Ostojic, G. (YUG)	0	2300
f	Ostojic, N. (YUG)	11	2450
g	Ostojic, P. (YUG)	0	2340
m	Ostos, J. (VEN)	0	2300
	Ostrovsky, A. (RUS)	0	2390
f	Ostrowski, L. (POL)	4	2340
m	Ostry, I. (KYR)	0	2240
	Oswald, G. (ENG)	0	2240
	Oswald, H.-J. (GER)	12	2305
f	Otero, E. (CUB)	21	2395
	Othman, M. A. (UAE)	0	2180
	Othman, R. (UAE)	0	2185
	Otman, V. (RUS)	0	2220
	Otovic, Lj. (YUG)	0	2040
	Ott, F. (GER)	0	2265
m	Ott, W. (GER)	0	2425
	Ottens, S. (GER)	0	2330
	Ottstadt, R. (GER)	0	2270
	Ouechtati, M. (TUN)	0	2280
	Ouseph, E. P. (IND)	0	2205
	Outerelo, M. (ESP)	0	2255
	Outulny, P. (TCH)	0	2240
	Ovchinikova, Y. (RUS)	0	2160
	Overgaard, Ch. M. (DEN)	0	2270
	Ovezova, M. (TKM)	0	2195
	Owosina, T. (NGR)	9	2135
	Oyeneyin, T. (NGR)	0	2205
	Ozgur, S. (TUR)	0	2185
f	Ozsvath, A. (HUN)	12	2285

P

	Name	Games	Rating
	Paal, A. (HUN)	0	2205
m	Paasikangas, J. (FIN)	17	2195
f	Paavilainen, J. (FIN)	7	2315
f	Pablo Marin, A. (ESP)	0	2375
	Pacal, M. (YUG)	0	2260
	Pacey, K. (CAN)	0	2285
	Pacheco, D. (ARG)	24	2305
g	Pachman, L. (TCH)	0	2370
f	Pachow, J. (GER)	10	2305
	Pacis, A. (PHI)	0	2290
	Packa, L. (SVK)	0	2230
	Packo, K. (POL)	0	2230
	Packroff, H. (GER)	0	2260
f	Pacl, V. (TCH)	1	2300
	Pacorro, F. (ESP)	2	2140
	Pacovsky, J. (TCH)	0	2320
f	Pacsay, L. (HUN)	5	2265
g	Padevsky, N. (BUL)	0	2385
g	Paehtz, Th. (GER)	10	2470
f	Paglietti, N. (ITA)	10	2325
m	Paglilla, C. (ARG)	24	2335
	Paidousis, A. (GRE)	0	2185
	Paige, W. (USA)	3	2240
	Pais, N. (HUN)	23	2225
	Paizis, A. (ITA)	0	2090
f	Pajkovic, V. (YUG)	2	2415
f	Pakkanen, J. (FIN)	9	2330
	Paksa, R. (HUN)	5	2255
	Paksi, Gy. (HUN)	15	2010
	Pal, G. (HUN)	6	2230
	Pal, I. (HUN)	0	2230
	Pala, L. (TCH)	0	2285
	Pala, V. (TCH)	8	2320
m	Palac, M. (CRO)	44	2485
f	Palacios De La Prida, E. (ESP)	2	2250
m	Palacios, A. (VEN)	0	2320
	Palacios, B. (CAN)	0	2240
	Palacios, L. F. (MEX)	0	2275
	Paladini, J.-M. (SUI)	0	2225
	Palamarek, D. (CAN)	0	2030
	Palanas, J. (ESP)	0	2290
m	Palao, M. (CUB)	0	2170
	Palatkova, E. (TCH)	0	2020
g	Palatnik, S. (UKR)	9	2500
	Paldanius, P. (FIN)	8	2260
f	Palermo, V. (ARG)	1	2235
	Palko, G. (HUN)	24	2040
m	Palkovi, J. (HUN)	10	2425
	Pallos, L. (HUN)	0	2250
	Pallova, M. (TCH)	0	2035
	Palm, N. (DEN)	5	2325
	Palma, J. A. (MEX)	0	2250
m	Palos, O. (BIH)	8	2390
f	Palosevic, A. (YUG)	0	2255
	Palosz, A. (POL)	3	2210
	Pamuk, M. (TUR)	0	2220
f	Panait, M. (ROM)	0	2290
	Panajotov, J. (BUL)	0	2245
m	Panbukchian, V. (BUL)	7	2415
m	Panchenko, Alexanda. G. (UKR)	9	2515
g	Panchenko, Alexande. N. (RUS)	41	2475
	Panchev, P. (BUL)	5	2320
	Pancu, G. (ROM)	0	2290
m	Panczyk, K. (POL)	0	2410
m	Pandavos, E. (GRE)	15	2335
m	Pandavos, P. (GRE)	26	2360
	Pandurevic, M. (CRO)	2	2220
m	Paneque, P. (CUB)	13	2425
	Pangrazzi, M. (ITA)	0	2250
	Panic, N. (YUG)	0	2250
	Panjkovic, A. (YUG)	11	2215
g	Panno, O. (ARG)	45	2505
	Pantaleev, D. (BUL)	13	2250
	Pantaleev, P. (BUL)	8	2180
	Pantaleoni, C. (ITA)	0	2225
	Pantev, V. (BUL)	0	2270
	Pantos, N. (YUG)	0	2265
	Pantovic, D. M. (YUG)	15	2220
	Panus, V. (MOL)	32	2175
f	Panzalovic, S. (YUG)	8	2390
m	Panzer, P. (GER)	43	2420
m	Paoli, E. (ITA)	2	2005
f	Papacek, S. (TCH)	0	2320
	Papagorasz, T. (HUN)	12	2270
	Papai, J. (HUN)	0	2230
f	Papaioannou, I. (GRE)	5	2385
f	Papanetz, P. (SVK)	0	2300
	Papastavropoulos, A. (GRE)	7	2195
	Papayanis, N. (GRE)	0	2220
	Papazov, I. (BUL)	0	2160
f	Pape, J. (GER)	0	2310
	Papp, L. (HUN)	17	2220
	Papp, N. (HUN)	16	2175
	Papp, Zs. (HUN)	2	2150
	Pappa, D. (ARG)	0	2220
	Pappaceno, M. (USA)	11	2085
	Parag, V. (IND)	0	2190
f	Paramentic, M. (YUG)	20	2090
m	Parameswaran, T. N. (IND)	28	2370
	Paraminski, A. (CRO)	9	2105
	Paramos, R. (ESP)	9	2375
	Parappalli, J. (IND)	5	2305
	Parcerias, P. (POR)	9	2270
	Pardic, O. (YUG)	6	2205
	Paredes, A. (ARG)	0	2200
	Parej, J. (HUN)	0	2200
	Pareja, J. (ESP)	0	2080
	Parera, J. (ESP)	0	2250
f	Pares Vives, J. (ESP)	0	2350
	Parezanin, D. (YUG)	7	2250
	Parfenova, O. (UZB)	0	2135
	Parkanyi, A. (HUN)	10	2290
f	Parker, J. (ENG)	20	2370
	Parmentier, X. (FRA)	0	2225
	Paronjan, A. (UZB)	28	2315
	Parr, D. (ENG)	8	2335
	Parr, F. (ENG)	3	2225
	Parsonage, I. (AUS)	9	2250
f	Parsons, D. (USA)	0	2310
	Partanen, J. (FIN)	5	2295
m	Partos, Ch. (SUI)	0	2385
	Parvanova, D. (BUL)	7	2025
	Parveen, S. Sh. (BAN)	16	2105
	Pasalic, H. (CRO)	0	2225
	Pasarelu, D. (ROM)	12	2215
	Paschall, W. (USA)	29	2215
	Pascua, R. (PHI)	0	2005
	Pasedag, P. (GER)	0	2330
	Pasic, E. (BIH)	0	2260
	Pasko, P. (SVK)	0	2220
	Passager, J.-P. (FRA)	0	2245
f	Passerotti, P. (ITA)	6	2335
	Passoni, C. (ITA)	0	2230
f	Pastircak, M. (TCH)	0	2385
	Pastivnychna, Z. (UKR)	9	2215
	Pastor Pons, C. (ESP)	5	2305
	Pastor jr., K. (TCH)	11	2180
f	Pastor, N. (ROM)	0	2260
	Pastor, P. (ESP)	12	2245
	Pastorini, M. (ITA)	8	2240
	Pastres, R. (ITA)	0	2225
	Pastukhova, L. (RUS)	1	2045
	Paszek, A. (POL)	2	2275
	Pasztor, F. (HUN)	24	2240
	Patrat, A. (FRA)	7	2200
	Patriarca, L. (PAR)	0	2295
	Patzl, K. (AUT)	0	2215
	Paulauskiene, V. (LTU)	0	2040
	Pauli, A. (GER)	3	2315
	Paulic, B. (YUG)	13	2240
f	Paulsen, D. (GER)	8	2330
m	Paunovic, D. (YUG)	5	2450
m	Paunovic, T. (YUG)	0	2425
	Paunovic, V. (YUG)	0	2345
f	Pavanasam, A. (IND)	21	2295
	Pavasovic, D. (SLO)	22	2295
	Pavicic, Z. (CRO)	0	2420
	Pavlenko, O. (AZE)	0	2295
	Pavlik, R. (YUG)	0	2230
f	Pavlin, V. (CRO)	0	2320
m	Pavlov, Mircea (ROM)	0	2385
	Pavlov, Miron (BUL)	0	2230
	Pavlov, N. (RUS)	2	2325
	Pavlova, M. (BUL)	0	2055
	Pavlovic, De. (YUG)	9	2405
f	Pavlovic, Dragan (YUG)	4	2295
	Pavlovic, Drago. (YUG)	24	2335
	Pavlovic, G. (YUG)	0	2335
m	Pavlovic, M. (YUG)	51	2455
	Pavlovic, R. (CRO)	3	2315
f	Pavlovic, S. (YUG)	0	2285
f	Payen, A. (FRA)	50	2285
	Paz, V. J. (ARG)	2	2240
	Pazdzior, J. (POL)	5	2205
m	Pazos, P. (ECU)	0	2290
	Pcola, P. (SVK)	0	2275
	Pe Japar, P. (BRU)	0	2205
	Peckford, W. (CAN)	0	2285
m	Pecorelli Garcia, H. (CUB)	13	2405
	Pedersen, B. (DEN)	0	2230
	Pedersen, D. V. (DEN)	25	2215
m	Pedersen, E. (DEN)	9	2400
	Pedersen, F. (DEN)	0	2270
	Pedersen, H. (DEN)	0	2245
	Pedersen, J. (DEN)	13	2305
	Pedersen, St. (DEN)	50	2385
	Pedersen, Sv. (DEN)	0	2250
	Pedersen, Th. S. (DEN)	0	2250
m	Pedzich, D. (POL)	19	2410
f	Peek, M. (NED)	0	2315
f	Peelen, P. (NED)	9	2375
m	Peev, P. (BUL)	31	2375
m	Peicheva-Hansen, E. (DEN)	18	2185
m	Peicheva-Juergens, V. (GER)	32	2350

	Name		
m	Pein, M. (ENG)	9	2420
	Peisser, M. (AUT)	0	2250
	Peist, J. (GER)	0	2260
f	Pejic, D. (YUG)	22	2090
	Pejic, M. (YUG)	0	2045
	Pekacki, S. (POL)	9	2205
m	Pekarek, A. (TCH)	15	2415
	Peker, O. (ISR)	12	2315
	Pekun, C. (TUR)	0	2205
	Pelaez, J. L. (CUB)	0	2240
	Pelc, Z. (POL)	0	2225
f	Pelech, L. (USA)	0	2220
	Pelikian, J. (BRA)	3	2285
	Pelitov, D. (BUL)	1	2275
	Pellant, T. (USA)	0	2265
	Pelletier, Y. (SUI)	21	2285
	Pelts, P. (USA)	0	2285
f	Pelts, R. (CAN)	0	2430
	Peng, Xiaomin (CHN)	0	2445
g	Peng, Zhaoqin (CHN)	0	2335
	Penson, Th. (BEL)	0	2295
	Penzias, M. (ISR)	6	2210
	Pepic, R. (YUG)	1	2280
m	Peptan, C. (ROM)	27	2310
f	Peralta, E. (PAR)	0	2290
	Peranic, D. (CRO)	13	2270
	Perchman, D. (URU)	9	2305
	Percze, J. (HUN)	0	2270
f	Perdek, M. (POL)	0	2315
	Peredy, F. (HUN)	18	2190
	Peregudov, N. (KAZ)	26	2460
	Pereira, A. (POR)	0	2295
	Pereira, F. (POR)	0	2275
	Pereira, J. (POR)	0	2250
	Pereira, S. C. (BRA)	2	2265
	Perelstein, M. (RUS)	0	2360
	Perera, P. (ESP)	0	2285
	Pereszupkin, A. (RUS)	0	2300
	Peretz, M. (ISR)	0	2295
	Perevertkin, V. (RUS)	4	2285
m	Perevoznic, M. (ROM)	4	2120
	Pereyra, D. (ARG)	15	2045
	Perez Fungueiro, M. A. (ESP)	0	2220
	Perez Garcia, H. (NED)	16	2215
f	Perez Pardo, J. C. (ESP)	10	2275
	Perez Pietronave, C. (ARG)	21	2235
	Perez, A. (CUB)	0	2285
	Perez, I. (CUB)	0	2250
	Perez, J. J. (VEN)	0	2245
f	Perez, Ju. C. (CUB)	0	2255
	Perez, Pedro (ESP)	0	2285
	Perez, Pedro T. (ESP)	18	2170
	Perez, Raul (CUB)	0	2245
	Perez, Raul (ARG)	6	2225
	Perez, Raul R. (ARG)	0	2225
f	Perez, Ro. (CUB)	0	2320
	Perez, S. (FRA)	12	2245
	Pergel, L. (HUN)	12	2030
f	Pergericht, D. (BEL)	0	2310
	Perhinig, R. (AUT)	0	2230
	Peric, Sl. (YUG)	39	2335
	Peric, St. (YUG)	4	2255
	Perifanis, G. (GRE)	10	2225
f	Perisic, R. (YUG)	4	2285
	Perkins, A. H. (ENG)	5	2280
	Perkovic, M. (YUG)	0	2220
	Permuy, C. (ESP)	9	2250
	Pernutz, H.-G. (GER)	3	2270
f	Perovic, D. (YUG)	0	2410
	Perovic, S. (YUG)	0	2020
	Persowski, S. (POL)	0	2220
	Persson, H. (SWE)	0	2235
	Pert, N. (ENG)	4	2065
	Perus, D. (SLO)	0	2345
f	Pervan, T. (YUG)	0	2340
f	Pesantes, C. (PER)	0	2335
	Peschel, A. (GER)	0	2240
f	Pesic, N. (YUG)	0	2355
	Pesiguna, S. (RUS)	23	2200
	Pesocki, V. (RUS)	0	2340
	Pesotsky, V. (UKR)	9	2410
f	Pessi, E. (ROM)	20	2310
	Pestov, S. (RUS)	0	2310
	Pesztericz, L. (HUN)	16	2280
	Petakov, U. (YUG)	0	2260
f	Pete, J. (YUG)	0	2275
	Petek, F. (SLO)	0	2035
m	Petek, M. (CRO)	14	2235
	Petek, P. (YUG)	12	2220
	Petelin, A. (RUS)	16	2375
	Peter, A. (HUN)	8	2285
	Petermann, H. (GER)	1	2230
	Peters, A. (GER)	8	2290
	Peters, C. (GER)	15	2285
m	Peters, J. A. (USA)	8	2465
	Petersen, F. P. (DEN)	10	2180
	Petersen, P. B. (DEN)	4	2210
	Petersen, S. B. (DEN)	0	2235
	Peterson, E. (GER)	7	2165
	Petievic, V. (RUS)	14	2115
	Petijevic, V. (YUG)	39	2295
	Petit, Eric (FRA)	22	2270
	Petit, Eric Th. (FRA)	0	2210
m	Petkevich, J. (LAT)	35	2445
	Petkov, V. (BUL)	7	2300
	Petkovic, P. (SWE)	16	2185
	Petkovic, R. (YUG)	5	2300
f	Petkovski, V. (YUG)	10	2275
	Petr, J. (TCH)	0	2250
	Petraki, M. (GRE)	20	2040
m	Petran, Pal (HUN)	44	2440
m	Petran, Pe. (SVK)	17	2435
	Petranovich, J. (USA)	3	2225
	Petrascu, R. (ROM)	0	2055
	Petre, M. (ROM)	13	2320
	Petre, N.-T. (ROM)	15	2185
	Petrenko, S. (MOL)	11	2080
	Petrescu, G. (ROM)	2	2110
f	Petrescu, I. C. (ROM)	5	2100
m	Petrienko, V. (RUS)	0	2440
f	Petrik, K. (SVK)	0	2265
	Petro, J. (HUN)	0	2265
	Petrone, D. (ITA)	0	2260
	Petrone, O. (ARG)	0	2280
m	Petronic, J. (YUG)	37	2445
f	Petronijevic, Z. (YUG)	7	2315
g	Petrosian, A. B. (ARM)	21	2485
	Petrosian, K. (RUS)	11	2410
	Petrov, J. (CRO)	4	2360
	Petrov, M. (BUL)	10	2340
	Petrov, V. (BUL)	0	2235
	Petrova-Kalmukova, M. (BUL)	20	2135
	Petrovic, Dj. (YUG)	5	2305
	Petrovic, Dr. (YUG)	0	2245
	Petrovic, Du. K. (YUG)	0	2250
m	Petrovic, Ma. (YUG)	37	2270
	Petrovic, Mi. (YUG)	11	2280
f	Petrovic, P. (YUG)	8	2295
f	Petrovic, Sla. (CRO)	0	2280
f	Petrovic, Slo. (YUG)	0	2300
	Petrovic, Vl. (YUG)	0	2230
f	Petrovic, Vo. (YUG)	0	2305
	Petrovic, Za. (YUG)	0	2210
	Petrovic, Zoran (YUG)	0	2250
	Petrovic, Zoran R. (YUG)	0	2250
f	Petrovic, Zv. (CRO)	6	2285
	Petrushin, A. I. (RUS)	26	2410
	Petrushina, N. (RUS)	0	2045
f	Petschar, K. (AUT)	9	2325
g	Petursson, M. (ISD)	46	2560
	Petyko, Z. (HUN)	0	2260
	Pevzner, A. (RUS)	7	2300
	Peyrat, O. (FRA)	0	2370
	Pezerovic, E. (BIH)	20	2400
f	Pfeifer, T. (HUN)	0	2315
f	Pfeiffer, H. (GER)	0	2275
g	Pfleger, H. (GER)	2	2485
	Pflichthofer, P. (GER)	0	2310
	Pfretzschner, R. (GER)	5	2285
f	Pfrommer, Ch. (GER)	0	2325
f	Pham, N. T. (VIE)	12	2150
	Phan, H. B. N. (VIE)	0	2025
	Phildius, B. (GER)	9	2320
g	Phominyh, A. (RUS)	25	2515
	Piankov, E. (UKR)	30	2395
m	Piarnpuu, L. (EST)	59	2140
m	Piasetski, L. (CAN)	10	2360
	Piazza, R. (GER)	0	2290
	Picanol, A. (ESP)	4	2220
	Picarda, L. (FRA)	4	2190
f	Piccardo, M. (ITA)	4	2220
m	Pichler, J. (GER)	5	2410
	Pickles, S. (AUS)	6	2235
	Piechocki, F. (POL)	14	2285
	Pielnik, R. (GER)	11	2280
	Pieniazek, An. (POL)	0	2240
m	Pieniazek, Ar. (POL)	13	2425
	Pienski, O. (GER)	3	2155
	Pieper, Th. (GER)	0	2225
m	Pieper-Emden, C. (GER)	8	2365
	Pierecker, M. (AUT)	0	2255
	Pieri, F. (ITA)	32	2215
f	Pierrot, F. (ARG)	10	2315
m	Piesina, G. (LTU)	50	2345
m	Pieterse, G. (NED)	0	2385
	Pietrusiak, B. (SWE)	0	2250
f	Pigott, J. C. (ENG)	0	2380
g	Pigusov, E. (RUS)	33	2585
m	Pihajlic, A. (YUG)	11	2120
g	Piket, Je. (NED)	34	2590
	Piket, Jo. J. (NED)	0	2245
f	Piket, M. (NED)	0	2350
	Pikula, D. (YUG)	4	2335
f	Pilardeu, G. (FRA)	9	2130
f	Pilarte, R. (NCA)	0	2215
	Pilczuk, A. (POL)	0	2290
	Pilgaard, K. (DEN)	0	2280
	Pilnick, C. (USA)	9	2185
	Pilotelle, B. (FRA)	0	2060
m	Pils, W. (AUT)	4	2360
	Pilz, D. (AUT)	0	2260
	Pimenta, A. (POR)	0	2220
f	Pina, A. (MEX)	0	2295
f	Pina, U. (CUB)	0	2305
m	Pinal, N. B. (CUB)	0	2315
	Pinard, A. (FRA)	7	2205
	Pinchuk, S. T. (UZB)	0	2405
	Pineau, J. (JPN)	0	2290
f	Pingas, B. (ARG)	8	2300
	Pingitzer, H. (AUT)	0	2260
f	Pinheiro, J. (POR)	0	2260
	Pinho, P. (POR)	0	2195
	Pink, S. (ENG)	9	2070
m	Pinkas, K. (POL)	21	2355
	Pinkus, L. (GER)	10	2265
	Pinnel, P. (GER)	7	2215
	Pinski, J. (POL)	10	2120
g	Pinter, J. (HUN)	11	2575
	Pinto, C. H. L. (BRA)	0	2375
	Pinto, Marc. (CHI)	0	2235
	Pinto, Mark (USA)	5	2225
	Pinus, R. (ARG)	0	2070
	Pioch, Th. (GER)	23	2190
	Pioch, Z. (POL)	16	2300
	Pionova, S. (BUL)	9	2115
	Piper, M. (ENG)	2	2250
	Piquemal, Ch. (FRA)	0	2055
f	Pira, D. (FRA)	10	2340
m	Pirisi, G. (HUN)	12	2400
	Piroska, I. (HUN)	0	2205
	Piroth, A. (HUN)	3	2230
m	Pirrot, D. (GER)	16	2400
f	Pirs, M. (SLO)	6	2340
f	Pirttimaki, T. (FIN)	3	2285

Title	Name	Games	Rating
m	Pisa Ferrer, J. (ESP)	5	2380
	Pisa, J. (CRO)	9	2250
	Pisarek, A. (POL)	8	2245
f	Piscicelli, D. (ARG)	2	2340
	Pisk, P. (TCH)	0	2340
g	Piskov, Y. (RUS)	24	2550
	Piskur, M. (SLO)	5	2265
	Pismany, V. (ISR)	0	2215
	Pismenny, A. (RUS)	2	2260
	Pisulinski, J. (POL)	7	2370
	Pitam, E. (ISR)	12	2085
	Pitic, J. (YUG)	0	2205
	Pitschka, C. (GER)	0	2255
	Piveny, I. (UKR)	5	2345
	Piwowarczyk, P. (POL)	0	2295
f	Piza, D. (ARG)	0	2280
	Piza, V. (TCH)	0	2275
	Pla, S. (ARG)	0	2240
g	Plachetka, J. (SVK)	27	2450
	Plank, F. (AUT)	0	2230
g	Plaskett, J. (ENG)	18	2470
	Platt, I. (ISR)	6	2225
	Playa, M. (ARG)	19	2380
f	Plesec, D. (SLO)	24	2380
	Plesek, J. (TCH)	0	2390
	Plesiuk, A. (POL)	0	2205
	Pletanek, J. (TCH)	0	2285
m	Pliester, L. (NED)	26	2420
	Plinta, E. (POL)	0	2285
	Ploetz, W. (GER)	4	2255
	Ploner, F. (AUT)	16	2255
f	Pocuca, B. (YUG)	0	2305
	Podat, V. (UKR)	0	2310
m	Podgaets, M. (UKR)	20	2465
	Podgurkii, S. (MOL)	13	2260
f	Podlesnik, B. (SLO)	8	2395
	Podobnik, M. (CRO)	0	2325
	Podolnjak, T. (YUG)	0	2160
m	Podrazhanskaya, O. (ISR)	4	2090
f	Podvrsnik, M. (SLO)	5	2215
m	Podzielny, K.-H. (GER)	15	2470
f	Poecksteiner, J. (AUT)	0	2225
	Poeltl, Th. (AUT)	0	2225
	Poesinger, A. (AUT)	19	2110
f	Pogats, J. (HUN)	12	2270
m	Pogorelov, R. (UKR)	25	2415
	Pogosian, G. (RUS)	11	2125
f	Pohl, J.-U. (GER)	12	2295
f	Pohla, H. (EST)	0	2340
	Pohlers, J. (GER)	2	2040
	Poitrac, L. (CAN)	0	2115
f	Pojedziniec, W. (POL)	0	2240
m	Pokojowczyk, J. (POL)	0	2340
f	Pokorny, Z. (TCH)	0	2310
	Polacek, J. (CAN)	0	2295
m	Polaczek, R. (BEL)	0	2415
m	Polajzer, D. (SLO)	0	2450
m	Polak, T. (TCH)	23	2410
f	Polakova-Kisova, P. (TCH)	3	2120
	Polaninov, A. (RUS)	0	2260
m	Polasek, J. (TCH)	0	2345
m	Poldauf, D. (GER)	22	2425
	Poleksic, M. (YUG)	0	2240
	Poley, V. (BLA)	11	2360
f	Polgar, I. (HUN)	0	2425
g	Polgar, J. (GM) (HUN)	40	2630
g	Polgar, S. (IM) (HUN)	30	2430
g	Polgar, Zs. (GM) (HUN)	19	2545
	Polgari, L. (SVK)	0	2050
	Poliakov, M. (RUS)	11	2415
	Poliakova, N. (RUS)	11	2095
g	Polihroniade, E. (ROM)	2	2220
	Politis, D. (GRE)	0	2195
	Poljak, S. (CRO)	9	2035
f	Pollard, A. (USA)	0	2290
m	Polnarieva, L. (RUS)	0	2205
	Polo, Vic. (COL)	11	2225
	Polo, Vin. (ESP)	0	2215
m	Poloch, P. (TCH)	0	2380
	Polovina, N. (YUG)	0	2205
m	Polovodin, I. A. (RUS)	24	2415
	Polster, W. (GER)	17	2370
g	Polugaevsky, L. (RUS)	14	2605
m	Poluljahov, A. (RUS)	88	2505
f	Polyak, I. (HUN)	2	2270
	Polyakova, N. (RUS)	15	2105
f	Polzin, R. (GER)	10	2380
g	Pomar Salamanca, A. (ESP)	0	2345
m	Pomes, J. (ESP)	13	2410
	Pomyjova-Chmielova, H. (TCH)	0	2065
f	Ponce, H. (CUB)	0	2335
	Ponceleusz, B. (POL)	15	2190
	Ponos, V. (CRO)	0	2290
	Pons, P. (ESP)	0	2275
	Pons, S. (ESP)	0	2305
	Ponyi, A. (HUN)	8	2080
	Poor, I. (HUN)	11	2280
	Poor, S. (HUN)	0	2230
	Popadic, D. (YUG)	5	2210
m	Popchev, M. (BUL)	19	2475
	Pope, J. (USA)	0	2255
	Popescu, C. (ROM)	11	2235
	Popescu, Dan (ROM)	9	2280
f	Popescu, Dani (ROM)	33	2380
	Popescu, F. (ROM)	0	2225
	Popescu, G. (ROM)	7	2235
	Popescu, L. (ROM)	0	2025
	Popiolek, H. (POL)	3	2210
	Popivoda, R. (RUS)	0	2135
	Popov, G. (FRA)	4	2370
	Popov, J. (YUG)	0	2185
m	Popov, L. (BUL)	0	2400
m	Popov, P. (BUL)	0	2345
	Popov, R. (YUG)	10	2020
f	Popov, Si. (YUG)	0	2310
f	Popov, St. (YUG)	12	2315
f	Popov, V. (YUG)	9	2340
	Popova, N. (BLA)	17	2065
	Popova, T. (RUS)	0	2170
	Popovic, B. (CRO)	0	2255
	Popovic, Da. (YUG)	12	2090
f	Popovic, Dj. (YUG)	5	2310
	Popovic, Do. (YUG)	0	2215
	Popovic, I. (CRO)	4	2195
f	Popovic, M. (YUG)	6	2320
g	Popovic, P. (YUG)	5	2520
	Popovic, Z. (YUG)	0	2245
	Popovici, D. (ROM)	13	2140
f	Popovych, O. (USA)	8	2245
f	Porfiriadis, S. (GRE)	12	2315
	Porjazov, P. (BUL)	0	2375
	Porkolab, Z. (HUN)	0	2215
m	Porper, E. (ISR)	15	2400
	Porsch, H. (GER)	0	2240
	Portenschlager, P. (AUT)	0	2230
	Porth, D. (GER)	3	2255
	Porth, H. (GER)	4	2260
m	Portisch, F. (HUN)	47	2405
f	Portisch, G. (HUN)	21	2305
g	Portisch, L. (HUN)	35	2585
	Portnoy, M. (BLA)	9	2050
	Porubszki, G. (GER)	15	2105
m	Porubszky-Angyalosine, M. A. (HUN)	16	2120
	Posa, N. (HUN)	0	2250
	Posch, W. (AUT)	17	2205
	Poseck, S. (GER)	0	2060
	Posharsky, V. (RUS)	0	2220
	Posnik, K. (POL)	0	2220
	Pospelov, E. (RUS)	0	2395
	Post, E. (USA)	3	2195
	Postl, A. (AUT)	11	2290
	Postler, R. (GER)	0	2350
	Poszpelov, J. (RUS)	0	2340
	Potapov, A. (RUS)	14	2365
	Potocnik, P. (SLO)	1	2225
	Potomak, V. (TCH)	0	2245
	Potterat, M. (SUI)	17	2185
	Potts, K. (USA)	0	2280
	Poulenard, R. (FRA)	0	2245
f	Poulsen, A. (DEN)	0	2320
	Poulton, J. (ENG)	12	2300
f	Pountzas, H. (GRE)	5	2285
	Powell, L. (WLS)	0	2010
	Powell, M. (JAM)	0	2030
	Powell, P. (USA)	0	2270
	Poyato, A. (CUB)	0	2230
	Pozarek, S. J. (USA)	0	2185
	Pozin, S. (RUS)	6	2340
	Pozzi, E. (ITA)	0	2225
	Prahov, V. (BUL)	0	2250
	Prakash, G. B. (IND)	23	2380
m	Prandstetter, E. (TCH)	0	2375
	Prangers, T. G. (NED)	0	2265
	Prantner jr., J. (HUN)	1	2300
m	Prasad, D. V. (IND)	24	2465
	Praszak, M. (POL)	3	2235
	Praud, J.-L. (FRA)	8	2195
f	Praznik, A. (SLO)	11	2305
	Predein, V. (RUS)	17	2315
	Preiss, M. (GER)	0	2235
f	Preissmann, E. (SUI)	6	2330
	Preker, H.-J. (GER)	0	2225
	Prentos, K. (GRE)	11	2285
	Preuschoff, M. (GER)	9	2260
m	Pribyl, J. (TCH)	8	2470
f	Pribyl, M. (TCH)	9	2300
m	Prie, E. (FRA)	44	2445
	Priedite, I. (LAT)	0	2225
m	Priehoda, V. (SVK)	7	2415
	Prieto, E. (COL)	0	2225
	Prieto, M. (ARG)	34	2175
	Primavera, R. (ITA)	1	2280
	Primiceri, N. (ITA)	11	2150
g	Prins, L. (NED)	0	2225
	Pripis, F. (RUS)	0	2315
m	Pritchett, C. W. (SCO)	14	2350
	Privman, B. (USA)	6	2260
f	Prizmic, M. (CRO)	7	2290
	Probst, D. (SUI)	14	2075
	Prochaska, J. (AUT)	0	2260
f	Prochazkova, D. (TCH)	0	2120
	Prochnow, M. (GER)	3	2285
	Prochownik, F. (POL)	5	2300
m	Prodanov, D. (BUL)	0	2325
	Prodanovic, S. (YUG)	10	2110
	Prohl, H. (GER)	13	2355
	Prohl, Th. (GER)	0	2120
	Prohorov, V. (YUG)	0	2230
	Prokopowicz, Cz. (LTU)	23	2140
	Proniuk, S. (GER)	1	2260
	Pronold, H. (GER)	0	2215
	Proost, D. (BEL)	0	2260
	Prosser, F. (ITA)	0	2245
f	Prosviriakov, V. (USA)	0	2310
	Protaziuk, A. (POL)	19	2025
	Protaziuk, G. (POL)	18	2215
g	Prudnikova, S. (RUS)	52	2385
	Prundeanu, H. (ROM)	0	2230
	Prymula, R. (TCH)	0	2275
	Przedmojski, R. (POL)	0	2310
	Przewoznik, D. (POL)	11	2275
m	Przewoznik, J. (POL)	19	2430
	Przybek, T. (POL)	0	2210
	Przybylka, D. (POL)	9	2280
g	Psakhis, L. (ISR)	44	2585
	Psaras, S. (GRE)	0	2210
	Psomiadis, S. (GRE)	4	2115
	Ptaschinski, D. (GER)	0	2210
	Pucarevic, M. (YUG)	1	2210
	Puchala, J. (POL)	0	2355
	Pucheta, R. (ARG)	0	2260
	Pudkova, T. N. (RUS)	0	2150
	Puelma, R. (CHI)	0	2250
	Pugachev, A. (RUS)	10	2470

	Name	Games	Rating
	Puhm, A. (FRA)	0	2220
	Pukshansky, M. B. (RUS)	0	2405
m	Puljek, Z. (CRO)	19	2230
	Pulkkinen, K. (FIN)	24	2315
f	Pupo, E. (CUB)	13	2355
	Pupols, V. (USA)	15	2270
	Puranen, J. (FIN)	2	2335
	Purdy, J. S. (AUS)	0	2225
	Purgin, N. (RUS)	7	2300
f	Puri, V. (CAN)	0	2260
	Puric, N. (YUG)	2	2285
	Purtov, A. (RUS)	9	2430
f	Puscasiu, O. (ROM)	0	2325
f	Puschmann, L. (HUN)	7	2335
m	Pushkov, N. (RUS)	75	2485
	Puszczewicz, K. (POL)	0	2170
	Putanec, V. (CRO)	0	2205
	Putenko, S. (RUS)	11	2455
	Putjatina, N. (RUS)	12	2200
f	Putzbach, G. (GER)	0	2275
	Puzic, S. (YUG)	0	2275
f	Pyda, Z. (POL)	6	2300
	Pyernik, M. (ISR)	0	2250
m	Pyhala, A. (FIN)	23	2380
	Pyka, R. (POL)	0	2220
	Pyrich, G. (SCO)	0	2005
m	Pytel, B. (FRA)	18	2115
m	Pytel, K. (FRA)	13	2425

Q

	Name	Games	Rating
m	Qi, Jingxuan (CHN)	0	2450
	Qian, Jifu (CHN)	0	2240
g	Qin, Kanying (CHN)	0	2410
	Quader, Z. (BAN)	9	2245
	Quatrini, A. (ARG)	11	2210
	Quek, S.-Sh. (SIN)	0	2230
	Quelle, H. (GER)	0	2230
	Quendro, L. (ALB)	0	2300
	Quillan, G. (ENG)	0	2300
	Quinn, M. (IRL)	16	2290
	Quinones, J. (CHI)	0	2135
	Quinonez Benitez, R. (MEX)	14	2125
	Quinteros, D. (ARG)	10	2295
g	Quinteros, M. A. (ARG)	19	2515
	Quiroga, F. (ARG)	17	2340
	Quiroga, S. (ARG)	5	2300
	Quiros, L. E. (CRC)	9	2130
	Quist, J. (NED)	0	2275
	Qvortrup, J. (NOR)	1	2220

R

	Name	Games	Rating
m	Raaste, E. J. (FIN)	4	2350
f	Rabelo Gil, E. (CUB)	10	2325
m	Rabiega, R. (GER)	28	2455
	Rabinovich, A. (USA)	3	2340
	Rabinovich, J. (RUS)	17	2320
	Rabl, J. (GER)	0	2215
	Rabovszky, Gy. (HUN)	15	2160
	Rabrenovic, V. (YUG)	0	2255
	Racasan, S. (ROM)	14	2210
m	Rachels, S. (USA)	15	2485
	Racherbaeumer, M. (GER)	0	2230
	Racz, A. (GER)	0	2230
	Racz, Z. (HUN)	0	2260
	Radakov, K. (YUG)	0	2280
	Radanska, V. (BUL)	22	2150
	Rade, M. (CRO)	11	2265
	Radecka, E. (POL)	0	2050
	Radenkovic, D. (YUG)	0	2250
m	Radev, N. (BUL)	3	2330
	Radha, S. R. (IND)	11	2050
f	Radibratovic, P. (YUG)	0	2340
	Radicevic, A. (YUG)	2	2005
	Radisavljevic, Z. (YUG)	0	2270
	Radlovacki, J. (YUG)	19	2385
f	Radnoti, B. (HUN)	0	2250
	Radnoti, G. (HUN)	9	2055
f	Radocaj, D. (CRO)	4	2345
	Radoja, Dj. (YUG)	4	2260
	Radojevic, Z. (YUG)	16	2300
	Radomskyj, P. (USA)	0	2245
f	Radonjanin, V. (YUG)	0	2350
	Radonjic, G. (YUG)	0	2220
f	Radosavljevic, S. (YUG)	18	2320
	Radosevic, N. (YUG)	11	2225
	Radovanovic, J. (YUG)	31	2230
m	Radovici, C. (ROM)	0	2370
	Radovszki, A. (RUS)	1	2345
m	Radu, E. L. (ROM)	44	2325
	Radu, M. (ROM)	25	2240
	Radu, S. (ROM)	0	2260
m	Radulescu, C. (ROM)	11	2305
	Radulov, D. (BUL)	0	2260
g	Radulov, I. (BUL)	16	2400
m	Radulovic, Dr. B. (YUG)	0	2300
	Radulovic, Du. (YUG)	0	2330
	Radulski, J. (BUL)	6	2360
f	Radusin, B. (YUG)	4	2300
	Radwan, L. (POL)	0	2205
f	Radziewicz, I. (POL)	26	2090
g	Radzikowska, K. (POL)	2	2060
	Raedecker, B. (GER)	9	2180
	Raedski, A. (RUS)	0	2390
m	Raetsky, A. (RUS)	55	2405
	Raeva, O. (BUL)	0	2055
	Raffalt, M. (AUT)	11	2280
	Raffay, G. (HUN)	0	2265
	Raghuve, S. (IND)	0	2120
m	Ragozin, E. (RUS)	30	2495
	Rahal, M. (ESP)	3	2310
	Rahimov, D. (UZB)	15	2310
	Rahls, P. (GER)	11	2315
	Rahman A, Y. (EGY)	15	2295
	Rahman, A. (BAN)	0	2180
	Rahman, J. (BAN)	0	2225
f	Rahman, T. (BAN)	0	2270
	Rahman, W. (ZIM)	0	2205
m	Rahman, Zia. (BAN)	11	2430
m	Rahman, Zil. (BAN)	17	2290
	Rahmani, Ch. (TUN)	6	2255
	Raiano, A. (ITA)	0	2230
f	Raicevic, I. (YUG)	16	2350
f	Raicevic, M. (YUG)	0	2365
g	Raicevic, V. (YUG)	11	2440
	Rainer, V. (CRO)	7	2095
	Raisa, U. (FIN)	7	2255
	Raj, S. (IND)	9	2165
	Rajcsanyi, Z. (HUN)	6	2145
	Rajevic, G. (YUG)	0	2280
	Rajic, D. (YUG)	0	2230
	Rajic, I. (YUG)	0	2210
	Rajiv, N. (IND)	5	2200
g	Rajkovic, D. (YUG)	31	2455
	Rajkovic, Ljubi. (YUG)	0	2295
	Rajkovic, Ljubo. (YUG)	0	2285
m	Rajna, G. (ISR)	0	2390
	Rajskij, E. (BLA)	0	2450
	Rakay, K. (SVK)	0	2205
	Rakhmangulov, A. (UKR)	0	2325
	Rakhmatullaeva, Sh. (RUS)	0	2005
	Rakib, I. S. (BAN)	0	2025
	Rakic, O. (YUG)	0	2055
m	Rakic, T. (YUG)	10	2375
f	Rakowiecki, T. (POL)	0	2325
	Ralavkakra (IND)	0	2015
	Ralis, P. (TCH)	0	2285
	Rama, F. (ALB)	13	2395
	Ramas, L. (CUB)	0	2240
m	Ramayrat, C. (PHI)	22	2365
	Ramdas, M. V. (IND)	5	2185
	Ramesh, R. B. (IND)	4	2200
	Ramic, F. (YUG)	3	2085
	Ramic, M. (YUG)	0	2055
	Ramik, Z. (TCH)	0	2315
	Ramirez, C. (COL)	11	2325
	Ramirez, Ed. (CRC)	0	2255
f	Ramirez, Em. (ARG)	0	2300
f	Ramirez, J. M. (MEX)	10	2220
	Ramis, J. (ARG)	10	2145
	Ramo Frontinan, C. (ESP)	1	2380
m	Ramon, V. (CUB)	0	2170
	Ramos Suria, F. (ESP)	2	2200
	Ramos, A. (ANG)	0	2205
m	Ramos, D. (PHI)	0	2335
	Ramos, S. L. (USA)	0	2250
	Ramos, V. (ESP)	0	2250
	Ramsingh, Y. (TRI)	0	2250
	Ramzina, N. (RUS)	0	2090
	Randjelovic, B. (YUG)	8	2270
	Ranganathan, K. (IND)	0	2275
m	Ranniku, M. (EST)	44	2180
	Ranola, Y. (PHI)	0	2325
g	Rantanen, Y. A. (FIN)	10	2350
f	Rao, V. (USA)	0	2420
	Rapatinski, K. (GER)	0	2240
	Rapp, R. (GER)	0	2300
	Rappa, D. (ARG)	0	2300
	Rasch, H. (GER)	11	2260
	Rasheed, A. A. (IRQ)	0	2430
g	Rashkovsky, N. N. (RUS)	17	2530
	Rasic, G. (YUG)	0	2225
	Rasidovic, S. (BIH)	0	2380
f	Rasik, V. (TCH)	11	2415
	Rasin, J. (RUS)	4	2355
	Rasmussen, C. (DEN)	5	2255
m	Rasmussen, K. (DEN)	9	2455
	Rasmussen, L. B. (LUX)	0	2240
	Rasmussen, P. (DEN)	19	2325
	Rasmussen, S. (FAI)	9	2210
	Rastenis, G. (LTU)	0	2265
	Raszka, J. (POL)	6	2275
	Raterman, L. (USA)	5	2215
	Rathore, S. K. (IND)	0	2215
	Ratkovic, M. (YUG)	10	2140
	Ratner, A. (UKR)	0	2080
	Ratolistka, J. (TCH)	6	2230
f	Ratti, R. (ITA)	0	2320
	Rattinger, F. (AUT)	0	2255
	Rattinger, Th. (AUT)	0	2300
	Ratzel, B. (GER)	9	2315
	Raubal, M. (AUT)	0	2225
	Rauch, F. (HUN)	1	2215
	Raud, R. (EST)	0	2375
f	Raupp, Th. (GER)	5	2360
	Rausch, R. (GER)	0	2250
f	Rausch, S. (GER)	4	2315
g	Rause, O. (LAT)	33	2335
g	Rausis, I. (LAT)	63	2575
	Rausz, A. (HUN)	0	2210
m	Ravi, L. (IND)	34	2415
f	Ravi, Th. Sh. (IND)	20	2370
	Ravia, M. (ISR)	12	2315
	Ravichandran, R. (IND)	0	2265
m	Ravikumar, V. (IND)	9	2355
m	Ravisekhar, R. (IND)	26	2380
	Ravishankar, S. N. (IND)	0	2205
	Rawski, S. (POL)	22	2220
	Ray, Ch. (ENG)	0	2190
	Rayner, F. (WLS)	17	2295
	Razinger, T. (SLO)	0	2010
g	Razuvaev, Y. S. (RUS)	39	2560
	Rea, A. (USA)	0	2195
	Readey, J. (USA)	1	2295
	Reales Murto, M. J. (ESP)	1	2280
	Rebb, R. (FRA)	0	2085
	Rebottaro, H. J. (ARG)	4	2310
f	Rechel, B. (GER)	0	2375
	Rechel, R. (GER)	7	2210
g	Rechlis, G. (ISR)	0	2510
f	Rechmann, P. (GER)	0	2360
	Rechner, K. (GER)	0	2255
f	Reddmann, H. (GER)	0	2290
	Redo, N. (ITA)	0	2210
	Redon, B. (FRA)	21	2230

	Name	Games	Rating
m	Redzepagic, R. (YUG)	16	2320
g	Ree, H. (NED)	0	2445
m	Reefschlaeger, H. (GER)	7	2390
m	Reeh, O. (GER)	21	2435
	Reepatbin, S. (BAN)	0	2210
	Reeve, J. (CAN)	0	2185
f	Regan, N. (ENG)	0	2140
	Rehbein, C. (GER)	2	2245
	Rehbein, D. (GER)	0	2275
	Rehorek, M. (TCH)	0	2335
f	Reich, Th. (GER)	14	2370
f	Reichenbach, W. (GER)	11	2260
f	Reicher, E. (ROM)	0	2300
m	Reicher, R. (ROM)	0	2060
	Reichmann, E. (AUT)	5	2280
	Reichstein, B. (USA)	11	2265
f	Reides, M. (ARG)	7	2285
f	Reilein, Ch. (GER)	0	2300
	Reilly, T. (AUS)	10	2315
	Reinartz, G. (GER)	0	2240
f	Reinderman, D. (NED)	46	2435
	Reinemer, F. (GER)	4	2265
	Reiner, S. (HUN)	0	2230
	Reinhardt, B. (GER)	0	2245
	Reis, G. (GER)	6	2235
	Reissman, W. (GER)	0	2265
	Reiter, L. (HUN)	12	2090
	Reiter, M. (GER)	9	2270
	Relange, E. (FRA)	35	2365
	Relic, R. (YUG)	10	2060
	Remizov, J. (RUS)	0	2150
	Remling, Ch. (GER)	12	2305
f	Remlinger, L. (USA)	37	2395
	Remmel, A. (EST)	6	2265
m	Remon, A. (CUB)	0	2355
	Renaudin, J.-Ph. (FRA)	0	2255
	Renaze, L. (FRA)	9	2260
	Rendon, M. L. (COL)	0	2010
	Rene, B. (FRA)	1	2225
	Renet, J. (BEL)	0	2300
g	Renet, O. (FRA)	50	2505
	Rengarajan, S. (IND)	3	2260
m	Renman, N.-G. (SWE)	0	2390
f	Renna, T. (USA)	0	2380
f	Renner, Ch. (GER)	16	2385
	Rentschler, J. (GER)	0	2265
	Repasi, Z. (HUN)	0	2315
m	Repkova, E. (SVK)	15	2320
	Reprintsev, A. (UKR)	0	2305
	Reprun, N. (UZB)	0	2115
f	Reschke, S. (GER)	24	2380
	Reschke, Th. (GER)	14	2230
f	Resende, A. C. (BRA)	4	2350
	Restas, P. (HUN)	20	2245
f	Restifa, H. (ARG)	22	2310
	Reuker, M. (GER)	0	2265
	Reuther, E. (GER)	0	2250
	Reutova, L. (RUS)	0	2115
	Revithis, I. (GRE)	0	2235
	Rewitz, P. (DEN)	7	2255
f	Rey, A. (ARG)	0	2320
m	Rey, G. (USA)	0	2355
	Reyes Najera, C. A. (GUA)	0	2275
m	Reyes, J. (PER)	7	2450
	Reyes, R. (PHI)	0	2245
	Reynaldo, J. (CUB)	0	2320
f	Reynolds, R. (USA)	0	2320
	Rezaei, R. (IRI)	0	2270
	Rezek, M. (CRO)	0	2240
	Rezonja, S. (SLO)	0	2270
	Rezsek, Gy. (HUN)	18	2125
	Rhodin, B. (GER)	3	2335
f	Rhodin, Ch. (GER)	8	2255
	Riabchonok, E. (RUS)	9	2415
	Riand, J.-Y. (SUI)	12	2030
	Ribac, D. (YUG)	4	2205
	Ribas, A. (URU)	11	2190
	Ribeiro, F. (POR)	16	2185
	Ribeiro, J.-M. (POR)	0	2280
m	Ribeiro, R. (BRA)	8	2080
g	Ribli, Z. (HUN)	35	2610
m	Ricardi, P. (ARG)	32	2470
	Ricci, M. (ITA)	10	2320
	Rice, Ch. (ENG)	14	2190
	Richard, R. (USA)	0	2210
	Richmond, P. (WLS)	0	2215
	Richter, G. (BEL)	0	2205
	Richter, K. (GER)	0	2240
	Richter, M. (GER)	0	2240
	Richter, R. (GER)	0	2280
	Richter, W. (GER)	10	2465
	Richtr, Z. (TCH)	0	2270
	Ridameya, J. (ESP)	9	2315
	Riebe, T. (GER)	0	2360
m	Riedel, A. (GER)	4	2155
	Riedel, H. (GER)	0	2210
f	Riedel, W. (GER)	8	2325
	Riedner, M. (AUT)	13	2175
	Riegler, P. (SLO)	17	2270
m	Riemersma, L. (NED)	8	2420
	Riemslag, A. (NED)	0	2080
	Riess, N. (GER)	5	2235
	Rifat, B. (BAN)	18	2420
	Rigan, J. (HUN)	6	2230
	Righi, E. (SMR)	0	2210
m	Rigo, J. (HUN)	13	2340
f	Riha, V. (TCH)	0	2310
	Rihterovic, M. (YUG)	5	2325
	Riipinen, J. (FIN)	0	2120
	Riline, A. (PAR)	0	2275
f	Rimawi, B. T. (JRD)	0	2265
m	Rind, B. (USA)	5	2365
	Riofrio, M. (ECU)	0	2005
	Rios Cabello, A. (MEX)	1	2220
	Rios, A. (COL)	0	2335
	Ris, B. (YUG)	13	2165
	Ristic, E. (YUG)	0	2095
	Ristic, Lj. (YUG)	11	2240
m	Ristic, Neb. (YUG)	17	2395
m	Ristic, Nen. (YUG)	10	2400
	Ristic, Slobodan B. (YUG)	0	2290
	Ristic, Slobodan M. (YUG)	0	2205
	Ristic, V. (YUG)	0	2230
	Ristoja, Th. W. (FIN)	1	2260
f	Ristovic, N. (YUG)	5	2255
	Rithnovszky, A. (HUN)	5	2245
	Ritova, M. (EST)	11	2095
	Ritova, R. (EST)	0	2070
	Ritter, G. (HUN)	0	2265
f	Ritter, M. (USA)	16	2400
	Rittiphunyawong, A. (THA)	0	2240
g	Rivas Pastor, M. (ESP)	9	2530
	Riveiro, J. (ARG)	9	2010
	Rivello, R. (ITA)	0	2235
m	Rivera, A. (CUB)	12	2375
f	Rivera, D. (URU)	23	2415
	Rivero, C. (CUB)	0	2020
	Rivero, J. L. (ARG)	25	2190
m	Rizzitano, J. (USA)	0	2395
f	Rizzo, M. (ARG)	0	2040
	Roa, S. (ESP)	7	2320
	Roach, Ph. (BAR)	0	2205
	Robak, Z. (POL)	0	2275
g	Robatsch, K. (AUT)	5	2410
	Robbiano Taboada, C. (PER)	0	2225
	Robert, A. (SUI)	3	2235
	Roberts, P. (SCO)	10	2195
	Robinson, C. (NGR)	9	2110
	Robledo, N. D. (ARG)	10	2305
	Robovic, S. (BIH)	33	2360
f	Roca, A. (ARG)	13	2365
	Roca, P. (PHI)	0	2350
m	Rocha, A. (BRA)	2	2300
	Rocha, S. (POR)	9	2310
	Rocha, W. C. (BRA)	0	2275
	Rocher, O. (FRA)	0	2195
	Rocio, J. (ECU)	0	2055
	Rockenschaub, M. (AUT)	10	2270
	Roder, P. (DEN)	9	2190
m	Rodgaard, J. (FAI)	0	2380
	Rodi, L. E. (ARG)	11	2225
f	Rodic, D. (YUG)	10	2310
	Rodic-Kures, G. (BIH)	0	2060
	Rodighiero, G. (ITA)	8	2190
	Rodin, M. (RUS)	10	2365
	Rodkin, R. (ISR)	11	2220
	Rodnishchev, S. (RUS)	2	2360
	Rodrigues, A. P. (BRA)	7	2285
	Rodrigues, J. (POR)	0	2040
f	Rodriguez Leon, A. (CUB)	0	2320
	Rodriguez Reinoso, V. (ESP)	0	2310
f	Rodriguez Talavera, J. C. (ESP)	19	2375
	Rodriguez Uria, J. A. (ESP)	0	2225
	Rodriguez, Ad. I. (ARG)	1	2260
f	Rodriguez, Al. (ARG)	0	2315
g	Rodriguez, Am. (CUB)	13	2490
	Rodriguez, Andres (ESP)	0	2350
m	Rodriguez, Andres (URU)	48	2405
f	Rodriguez, Ant. (ESP)	1	2300
	Rodriguez, Be. (CUB)	0	2230
	Rodriguez, Bo. (COL)	0	2260
	Rodriguez, C. (ESP)	2	2300
	Rodriguez, D. (VEN)	0	2270
f	Rodriguez, Jor. L. (ARG)	16	2370
	Rodriguez, Jose M. (ESP)	0	2240
	Rodriguez, Om. (CUB)	0	2205
g	Rodriguez, Or. (ESP)	6	2445
f	Rodriguez, P. (CUB)	0	2275
m	Rodriguez, R. (PHI)	10	2435
	Roe, S. J. (ENG)	0	2275
	Roeberg, F. (GER)	7	2305
f	Roeder, F. (GER)	36	2260
f	Roeder, G. (GER)	7	2255
m	Roeder, M. (GER)	29	2425
	Roederer, K. (GER)	2	2260
	Roehrich, S. (GER)	10	2230
f	Roemer, U. (GER)	5	2220
	Roepert, A. (GER)	0	2425
f	Roesch, A. (GER)	7	2375
f	Roeschlau, B. (GER)	2	2270
f	Roese, O. (GER)	0	2345
	Roesemann, R. (GER)	9	2200
	Roesler, M. (GER)	0	2240
	Roetteler, M. (GER)	0	2230
	Rogai, S. (ITA)	0	2015
	Rogalewicz, M. (POL)	23	2135
g	Rogers, I. (AUS)	19	2595
f	Rogers, J. (ENG)	0	2310
	Rogers, N. (USA)	9	2280
	Rogic, D. (CRO)	30	2385
	Rogovski, V. (UKR)	0	2420
	Rogovskoy, A. (RUS)	10	2280
	Rogowski, J. (POL)	0	2300
m	Rogozenko, D. (MOL)	38	2500
m	Rogulj, B. (CRO)	9	2405
g	Rohde, M. A. (USA)	15	2575
f	Rohde, U. (GER)	0	2285
	Roiz Baztan, D. (ESP)	4	2365
	Roj, M. (TCH)	0	2135
	Rojas Sepulveda, J. (CHI)	0	2210
	Rojas, L. (CHI)	41	2295
	Rojas, N. (ESP)	0	2295
	Rojo, G. (ESP)	2	2300
	Rojprapayont, V. (THA)	0	2205
	Rojzen, N. (MOL)	20	2255
	Roldan, A. (ARG)	0	2275
	Rolic, G. (YUG)	0	2240
	Roll, C. (USA)	3	2200
f	Rolletschek, H. (AUT)	19	2375
	Rolvag, M. (NOR)	0	2260
	Roman, F. (ARG)	10	2310
	Roman, O. (CHI)	14	2115
g	Romanishin, O. M. (UKR)	15	2615

	Romanowski, K. (POL)	0	2240
	Romantchouk, J. (FRA)	6	2230
	Rombaldoni, A. (ITA)	2	2260
f	Romero Gomez, J. C. (CUB)	0	2310
m	Romero Holmes, A. (ESP)	27	2440
	Romero, A. (ESP)	0	2210
	Romero, M. (ARG)	0	2225
	Romm, M. (ISR)	4	2270
	Ronin, V. (RUS)	0	2285
	Ronneland, D. (SWE)	0	2220
	Roofdhooft, M. (BEL)	0	2285
m	Roos, C. (FRA)	16	2170
m	Roos, D. (FRA)	7	2415
f	Roos, J.-L. (FRA)	13	2375
m	Roos, L. (FRA)	5	2445
f	Roos, Th. (GER)	15	2260
f	Roose, J. (BEL)	0	2335
m	Root, A. (USA)	0	2055
m	Root, D. (USA)	0	2470
	Rosa, C. R. (BRA)	0	2290
	Rosa, F. (CHI)	20	2200
f	Rosandic, D. (CRO)	9	2320
	Rosch, H. (PAN)	0	2205
	Roscin, A. V. (RUS)	0	2330
f	Roselli M, B. (URU)	11	2365
	Roselli, J. P. (URU)	0	2085
f	Rosen, B. (GER)	0	2295
	Rosen, W. (GER)	0	2265
	Rosenberg, A. (ISR)	9	2185
	Rosenberg, D. (ENG)	9	2210
f	Rosenberger, B. (GER)	0	2300
	Rosenlund, Th. (DEN)	0	2295
f	Rosenthal, D. (GER)	11	2325
	Rosenthal, J. (SUI)	0	2240
	Rosiak, A. (POL)	0	2370
	Rosiak, B. (POL)	0	2225
	Rosic, S. (YUG)	0	2315
	Rosican, B. (RUS)	0	2255
f	Rosino, A. (ITA)	0	2320
f	Rosito, J. (ARG)	24	2310
	Rositsan, M. (CAN)	0	2150
	Roska, B. (YUG)	0	2220
	Roski, F. (GER)	8	2295
f	Ross, D. (CAN)	0	2310
f	Ross, P. (CAN)	0	2300
g	Rossetto, H. (ARG)	11	2300
f	Rossi, C. (ITA)	5	2330
f	Rossiter, Ph. J. (ENG)	19	2330
f	Rossmann, H. (GER)	0	2265
	Rosta, S. (HUN)	13	2270
f	Rostalski, W. (GER)	0	2270
	Rostoll, D. (ARG)	9	2160
	Roth, Jo. (GER)	4	2190
	Roth, Ju. (GER)	0	2255
f	Roth, P. (AUT)	15	2290
f	Roth, R. (SUI)	0	2290
f	Rother, Ch. (GER)	0	2320
	Rotman, D. (ISR)	0	2205
	Rotshtein, E. (UKR)	4	2250
m	Rotstein, A. (UKR)	45	2470
	Rottstaedt, W. (GER)	0	2265
	Roumegous, E. (FRA)	8	2140
f	Rovid, K. (HUN)	30	2330
	Rovito, G. (ITA)	15	2210
f	Rowley, R. (USA)	0	2375
	Rowson, J. (SCO)	6	2325
	Rozenfeld, T. (UKR)	0	2080
g	Rozentalis, E. (LTU)	24	2600
	Rozgonyi, A. (HUN)	13	2170
	Rozovsky, G. A. (RUS)	0	2265
	Rozsa, S. (HUN)	5	2235
	Rozsnyai, T. (HUN)	2	2245
	Rozwarski, J. (POL)	0	2245
	Ruban, E. (BLA)	5	2325
g	Ruban, V. (RUS)	9	2590
	Rubenchik, R. (USA)	2	2225
	Rubenchik, V. (USA)	0	2310
m	Rubene, I. (LAT)	32	2220
m	Rubinetti, J. (ARG)	37	2455
	Rubingh, O. (NED)	8	2315
	Rubio Purrinos, H. (ESP)	0	2235
	Rubio, J. J. (ESP)	0	2275
m	Rublevsky, S. (RUS)	26	2525
	Ruby, T. (HUN)	0	2305
g	Rubzova, T. (RUS)	34	2275
	Rucci, M. (ARG)	10	2255
g	Ruchieva, N. (UKR)	11	2300
	Ruck, R. (HUN)	26	2415
	Ruck, T. (HUN)	5	2320
	Ruckschloss, K. (SVK)	0	2285
	Rudaityte, I. (LTU)	30	2140
	Rudikova-Prymulova, R. (TCH)	0	2055
	Rudnev, M. (BLA)	9	2095
	Rudolf, M. (POL)	13	2215
	Rueckleben, H. (GER)	0	2280
	Rueetschi, U. (SUI)	0	2265
f	Ruefenacht, M. (SUI)	0	2360
	Rueger, E. (GER)	0	2165
m	Ruf, M. (GER)	18	2430
	Ruggiero, P. (USA)	0	2060
	Ruiz Diez, J. C. (ESP)	9	2190
	Ruiz Gutierrez, M. (ESP)	3	2235
	Ruiz, A. (COL)	0	2295
	Ruiz, G. (MEX)	2	2245
	Ruiz, J. H. (ESP)	0	2270
	Ruiz, R. (FRA)	3	2220
	Rukavina, D. (CRO)	0	2330
m	Rukavina, J. (CRO)	0	2425
	Rumiancev, B. (LTU)	11	2285
	Rumiancev, G. (UKR)	0	2260
f	Runau, R. (GER)	0	2340
	Runic, Z. (YUG)	0	2240
	Rupell, B. (BRA)	10	2245
	Rupp, M. (GER)	0	2315
	Rusak, D. (POL)	6	2115
	Rusakov, J. (RUS)	3	2285
	Rusomanov, A. (YUG)	2	2215
	Russek, G. (MEX)	10	2335
	Russell, C. (USA)	0	2285
	Russo, G. M. (BRA)	1	2045
	Rustemov, A. (RUS)	32	2430
	Rustler, M. (GER)	0	2230
	Rusz, G. (HUN)	2	2250
	Ruta, G. (ROM)	0	2085
	Ruthenberg, H. (GER)	0	2275
	Rutman, A. (RUS)	0	2355
	Ruxton, K. (SCO)	0	2230
m	Ruzele, D. (LTU)	24	2500
	Ruzicka, P. (TCH)	0	2255
	Ryan, J. (IRL)	12	2250
	Rybak, M. (TCH)	0	2290
	Rybak, R. (TCH)	0	2290
	Rychagov, M. (RUS)	0	2430
	Rygaard, M. (SWE)	2	2230
	Rymaszewski, D. (POL)	0	2240
m	Ryskin, A. (BLA)	27	2515
m	Rytshagov, M. (EST)	38	2465
	Rzasa, J. (POL)	0	2270

S

	Saad, Z. B. (EGY)	15	2025
	Saavedra, C. (BOL)	0	2205
	Sabados, J. (YUG)	12	2075
	Sabani, A. (YUG)	0	2300
	Sabar, M. H. (MAS)	0	2205
	Sabas, J. (ARG)	0	2255
	Sabi, Y. (ISR)	0	2290
	Sabitov, O. (TAJ)	0	2235
	Saburova, T. (RUS)	0	2060
	Saccone, F. (ITA)	6	2200
	Sack, B. W. (GER)	2	2310
	Sacks, A. (USA)	9	2140
	Sader, M. (AUT)	0	2275
	Sadiku, B. (YUG)	0	2380
	Sadilkova, V. (TCH)	13	2135
m	Sadkiewicz, J. (POL)	0	2225
	Sadkowsky, D. (BEL)	0	2275
m	Sadler, M. (ENG)	41	2535
	Sadowski, M. (POL)	4	2195
	Sadunishvili, L. (GEO)	0	2155
	Saenz, J. J. (ESP)	9	2305
	Safin, S. (UZB)	13	2425
	Safiye, Y. (YUG)	0	2250
m	Safranska, A. (LAT)	30	2290
	Safyanovsky, M. (YUG)	4	2285
m	Sagalchik, G. (USA)	35	2545
	Sagall, R. (ENG)	11	2165
f	Sahlender, F. (GER)	5	2265
g	Sahovic, D. (YUG)	33	2420
m	Sahu, S. Ch. (IND)	23	2400
	Said, M. (PAL)	0	2245
	Saidova, T. (AZE)	0	2140
m	Saidy, A. F. (USA)	16	2405
	Sajko, Cz. (POL)	0	2250
	Sajter, Cs. (ROM)	0	2050
	Sakac, V. (YUG)	0	2270
g	Sakaev, K. (RUS)	34	2540
	Sakhatova, E. (KAZ)	9	2235
m	Sakhatova, G. (KAZ)	0	2325
	Sakurai, L. (ARG)	3	2270
	Salaba, J. (TCH)	0	2280
	Salac, J. (TCH)	0	2260
	Salagenu, G. (ROM)	0	2235
f	Salai, L. (SVK)	0	2390
	Salamon, F. (HUN)	9	2095
	Salamon, W. (AUT)	0	2255
	Salanki, E. (HUN)	4	2265
f	Salaun, Y. (FRA)	27	2300
m	Salazar, A. (COL)	0	2110
	Salazar, F. (NCA)	13	2120
m	Salazar, H. (CHI)	0	2370
	Salazar, P. (CRC)	9	2210
	Saldano, H. (ARG)	11	2300
	Sale, S. (CRO)	30	2405
	Saleh, Nab. (UAE)	0	2155
	Saleh, Nag. (UAE)	0	2215
	Salem, A. (ENG)	0	2295
	Saletovic, F. (YUG)	0	2210
	Salgado Allaria, C. (ESP)	8	2225
f	Salgado, R. R. (USA)	0	2305
	Salguero, F. (ARG)	0	2275
	Salisbury, M. (ENG)	9	2150
	Saljova, S. (TCH)	4	2095
f	Salman, N. (USA)	0	2280
	Salmon, J. (USA)	14	2260
	Salo, H. (FIN)	19	2240
	Salo, T. (FIN)	14	2330
	Salomon, M. (USA)	0	2315
	Salonen, J. (FIN)	2	2255
m	Salov, S. (RUS)	12	2280
g	Salov, V. (RUS)	23	2685
m	Saltaev, M. (UZB)	24	2450
	Salus, S. (FRA)	3	2260
	Salvatti, D. (ARG)	14	2215
f	Salvermoser, B. (GER)	0	2280
	Salvetti, A. (ITA)	0	2250
	Salzenberg, D. (GER)	0	2230
f	Samardzic, J. (CRO)	11	2150
	Samarin, I. (RUS)	32	2390
	Sambolec, Z. (YUG)	0	2245
	Samborski, H. (POL)	0	2240
	Samer, I. M. (IRQ)	0	2245
	Samimi, A. (USA)	0	2250
	Sammalvuo, T. (FIN)	23	2270
	Samoliuk, I. (RUS)	11	2260
f	Samovojska, D. (CRO)	3	2345
	Samuelsson, L. (SWE)	0	2005
	Samulevicius, T. (LTU)	10	2140
	Samur, A. (ARG)	3	2255
	San Claudio, F. (ESP)	0	2240
f	San Marco, B. (FRA)	4	2235
m	San Segundo, P. (ESP)	5	2440
m	Sanchez Almeyra, J. (ARG)	24	2435

	Name	Games	Rating
m	Sanchez Guirado, F. (ESP)	12	2330
	Sanchez, C. (VEN)	0	2340
	Sanchez, Ci. (CUB)	0	2045
	Sanchez, En. (NCA)	13	2015
	Sanchez, Ev. H. (ARG)	0	2210
	Sanchez, G. (USA)	0	2240
	Sanchis, A. (FRA)	16	2110
	Sand, R. (GER)	5	2125
	Sandager, S. (USA)	0	2325
	Sanden, S. (SWE)	2	2325
	Sander, J. (GER)	0	2285
f	Sandic, V. (YUG)	0	2325
	Sandien, M. (GER)	0	2305
	Sandler, L. (AUS)	4	2315
	Sandmeier, T. (GER)	7	2220
	Sandor, A. (HUN)	9	2095
	Sandor, Ch. (GER)	19	2305
	Sandor, J. (HUN)	0	2295
	Sandriev, R. (RUS)	0	2410
	Sands, D. (ENG)	0	2230
	Sandstrom, L. (SWE)	4	2300
	Sandu, Ma. S. (ROM)	0	2235
f	Sandu, Mi. (ROM)	14	2070
	Sanduleac, V. (MOL)	17	2325
	Sanetra, P. (POL)	12	2155
	Sanjeev, K. (IND)	11	2270
f	Sanna, G. (ITA)	0	2390
	Sansonetti, G. (ITA)	0	2205
	Santa Torres, J. (PUR)	0	2215
	Santa, L. A. (PUR)	0	2245
	Santa, R. (CRO)	0	2270
	Santacruz, C. S. (PAR)	0	2265
f	Santacruz, F. (PAR)	0	2310
	Santalla, A. (CUB)	10	2150
	Santamaria, V. (AND)	0	2220
	Santana, O. (PUR)	0	2255
	Santhosh, K. (IND)	0	2200
	Santl, A. (GER)	2	2265
m	Santo-Roman, M. (FRA)	13	2420
	Santolini, L. (ITA)	0	2240
	Santos, A. P. (POR)	16	2260
f	Santos, Ca. P. (POR)	0	2305
	Santos, Ch. (PHI)	0	2005
	Santos, E. (ANG)	0	2220
	Santos, Is. (POR)	0	2005
	Santos, Iz. F. (ESP)	0	2250
	Santos, Jose A. (POR)	0	2215
f	Santos, Jose P. (POR)	0	2375
	Santos, Ju. (POR)	9	2060
m	Santos, L. (POR)	0	2385
	Santos, R. A. (BRA)	5	2325
m	Sanz Alonso, F. J. (ESP)	15	2410
	Sanz Losada, V. (ESP)	0	2260
	Sapi, J. (HUN)	0	2240
m	Sapi, L. (HUN)	0	2300
m	Sapis, W. (POL)	30	2420
	Saradjen, J. (YUG)	10	2180
	Sarakauskas, G. (LTU)	10	2030
	Saraliev, V. (BUL)	0	2250
m	Sarapu, O. (NZL)	11	2295
	Saravanan, V. (IND)	17	2395
	Sareen, V. (IND)	8	2310
f	Saren, I. J. (FIN)	3	2350
f	Sarfati, J. D. (NZL)	11	2315
	Saric, I. (YUG)	6	2330
	Saric, N. (YUG)	4	2075
	Saric, P. (YUG)	0	2230
m	Sariego, W. (CUB)	24	2405
	Saripov, S. (RUS)	0	2350
m	Saritha, N. (IND)	15	2105
	Sarkany, P. (HUN)	0	2045
	Sarkosy, L. (SVK)	11	2330
	Sarlamanov, D. (YUG)	9	2270
	Sarmiento, B. A. (ESP)	5	2210
	Sarna, E. (POL)	0	2245
m	Sarno, S. (ITA)	22	2390
f	Sarosi, Z. (HUN)	9	2355
	Sarsam, S. A. (IRQ)	0	2365
	Sartori, S. (ITA)	0	2270
	Sarvari, R. (HUN)	0	2310
	Sarwat, W. (EGY)	15	2305
m	Sarwinski, M. (POL)	0	2390
	Sasaki, K. (JPN)	0	2210
	Saskowski, J. (POL)	0	2260
	Sass, V. (HUN)	9	2245
	Sasu-Ducsoara, A. (ROM)	26	2080
f	Sasvari, Z. (CRO)	0	2315
	Satchidanand, S. (IND)	0	2295
	Sather, Q. (NOR)	0	2150
	Satta, V. (ITA)	8	2340
	Sattar, R. (BAN)	0	2255
	Saucey, M. (FRA)	1	2245
	Saulin, D. (RUS)	14	2210
	Saunders, J. C. (ENG)	1	2245
	Saunier, S. (FRA)	9	2055
m	Saunina, L. (RUS)	8	2170
	Sautter, E. (GER)	0	2075
	Sauvin, J. (SUI)	11	2210
f	Savage, A. G. (USA)	2	2275
f	Savanovic, A. (YUG)	3	2320
	Savas, N. (TUR)	0	2230
g	Savchenko, S. (UKR)	16	2530
m	Savereide, D. (USA)	0	2250
	Savic, D. (YUG)	0	2260
	Savic, G. (YUG)	8	2145
	Savic, Mih. (YUG)	1	2210
	Savic, Mio. (YUG)	13	2215
	Savic, P. (YUG)	0	2265
	Savicevic, V. (YUG)	3	2295
f	Savin, D. (ROM)	0	2320
	Savko, A. (RUS)	15	2340
g	Savon, V. A. (UKR)	72	2450
m	Savova, S. (BUL)	13	2195
	Savtchour, F. (UKR)	0	2265
	Savva, P. (CYP)	0	2210
	Sawadkuhi, M.-A. (GER)	0	2270
	Sawatzki, F. (GER)	4	2240
g	Sax, Gy. (HUN)	46	2515
	Sazonov, A. (RUS)	7	2135
	Scafarelli, F. (ITA)	0	2300
f	Scarella, E. (ARG)	26	2410
f	Scekic, M. (YUG)	29	2315
	Scerbin, D. (RUS)	5	2345
	Scetinin, A. (RUS)	13	2330
f	Schaack, H. (GER)	1	2285
	Schabanel, S. (FRA)	8	2250
	Schadler, M. (LIE)	0	2205
f	Schaefer, A. (GER)	15	2125
m	Schaefer, Ma. (GER)	32	2455
	Schaefer, Mi. (GER)	6	2215
	Schaefer, N. (GER)	0	2265
	Schaefer, R. (GER)	0	2215
	Schaffarth, P. (GER)	0	2250
	Schain, R. (USA)	0	2240
	Schall, A. (FRA)	0	2200
m	Schandorff, L. (DEN)	18	2435
	Schaubmair, M. (AUT)	0	2280
f	Schaufelberger, H. (SUI)	0	2290
f	Schauwecker, M. (SUI)	0	2370
f	Schebler, G. (GER)	30	2315
	Scheck, R. (AUT)	3	2200
	Scheffner, A. (GER)	5	2275
f	Scheipl, R. (GER)	3	2265
	Schenker, M. (SUI)	0	2205
	Schenkerik, Cs. (HUN)	2	2230
	Schepel, K. (HKG)	0	2245
	Schepp, Z. (HUN)	12	2220
	Scherer, H. (GER)	0	2295
	Schettler, J. (GER)	8	2190
	Schienmann, B. (GER)	2	2250
	Schiff, A. (GER)	9	2265
f	Schiffer, K.-U. (GER)	9	2295
f	Schifferdecker, W. (GER)	0	2255
	Schild, H. (AUT)	0	2205
	Schiller, E. (USA)	7	2245
	Schiller, P. (SWE)	9	2280
	Schinayi (TUN)	0	2250
f	Schindler, W. (GER)	3	2295
	Schinis, M. (CYP)	0	2210
	Schipkov, B. (RUS)	47	2355
	Schirm, F. (GER)	12	2310
	Schischke, R. (GER)	0	2360
	Schlahetka, G. (HUN)	0	2305
	Schlamp, R. (GER)	0	2255
f	Schlehoefer, R. (GER)	0	2365
	Schleifer, M. (CAN)	0	2285
	Schleinkofer, K. (USA)	0	2280
f	Schlemermeyer, W. (GER)	12	2345
	Schlemmer, H. (GER)	0	2325
	Schlenker, Joc. (GER)	0	2210
	Schlenker, Joe. (GER)	0	2205
	Schlenker, R. (GER)	2	2255
	Schlesinger, O. (GER)	0	2275
	Schlichtmann, G. (GER)	0	2240
	Schlick, V. (GER)	8	2315
	Schliebener, S. (GER)	4	2300
	Schlindwein, R. (GER)	8	2345
	Schlingensiepen, Ch. (GER)	4	2330
f	Schlosser, H. (GER)	0	2345
m	Schlosser, M. (AUT)	18	2400
g	Schlosser, Ph. (GER)	48	2550
	Schlueter, W. (GER)	0	2245
	Schlusznyik, N. (HUN)	27	2095
	Schmall, J. (GER)	0	2340
f	Schmaltz, R. (GER)	20	2410
	Schmedders, H.-G. (GER)	7	2295
	Schmeidler, M. (GER)	0	2220
	Schmid, Ch. (SUI)	14	2210
f	Schmid, G. (GER)	0	2320
	Schmid, M. (GER)	5	2280
	Schmid, Si. (GER)	9	2265
	Schmid, St. (GER)	0	2285
f	Schmid, W. (GER)	2	2225
	Schmidt, Be. (GER)	11	2285
f	Schmidt, Bo. (GER)	14	2340
	Schmidt, E. (GER)	9	2315
	Schmidt, G. (GER)	5	2255
	Schmidt, K. (DEN)	0	2335
f	Schmidt, L. R. (JPN)	0	2340
	Schmidt, P. (GER)	20	2415
	Schmidt, R. (GER)	0	2180
	Schmidt, S. (GER)	7	2305
g	Schmidt, Wl. (POL)	26	2440
f	Schmidt, Wo. (GER)	0	2355
	Schmidt-Brauns, J. (GER)	13	2200
	Schmidt-Schaeffer, S. (GER)	12	2300
	Schmikli, L. (HUN)	10	2095
	Schmitt, An. (FRA)	0	2325
f	Schmitt, Ax. (GER)	3	2345
	Schmitt, Ch. (GER)	0	2230
m	Schmittdiel, E. (GER)	64	2410
	Schmitz, A. (GER)	0	2270
f	Schmitzer, H. (GER)	0	2305
f	Schmitzer, K. (GER)	13	2315
	Schnabel, R. (GER)	5	2230
	Schnaebele, U. (GER)	7	2245
m	Schneider, A. (HUN)	25	2390
m	Schneider, Bernd (GER)	0	2395
f	Schneider, Bernd (GER)	9	2280
	Schneider, Bernh. (GER)	0	2270
	Schneider, F. (GER)	0	2240
m	Schneider, L.-A. (SWE)	4	2455
	Schneider, S. (SWE)	23	2095
	Schneiders, A. (NED)	0	2230
	Schnelzer, R. (GER)	0	2285
	Schnitzspan, L. (GER)	6	2295
	Scho, Ch. (GER)	0	2135
	Schoebel, W. (GER)	7	2220
	Schoeber, P. (NED)	7	2270
	Schoeller, W. (GER)	0	2100
	Schoellmann, J. (GER)	11	2345
m	Schoen, W. (GER)	10	2375
f	Schoene, R. (GER)	14	2350

f Schoeneberg, M. (GER) 5 2340
f Schoentier, F. (GER) 0 2355
f Schoeppl, E. (AUT) 0 2305
f Scholseth, T. K. (NOR) 13 2305
Scholz, Ch. (GER) 0 2240
f Scholz, G. (FRA) 0 2345
Schoof, M. (GER) 0 2290
Schorr, L. (VEN) 0 2235
Schouten, N. (NED) 0 2265
Schramm, Ch. (GER) 0 2250
Schrancz, I. (HUN) 5 2265
Schratzenstaller, A. (GER) 0 2215
Schreiber, B. (HUN) 0 2310
Schreiber, E. (USA) 0 2025
Schreiner, R. (GER) 8 2215
Schrepp, M. (GER) 0 2240
Schroeder, Ch. (GER) 0 2270
Schroeder, S. (GER) 0 2075
Schroeder, W. (GER) 7 2270
m Schroer, J. (USA) 15 2320
m Schroll, G. (AUT) 31 2385
Schroter, Tamas (HUN) 7 2335
Schroter, Tamas (HUN) 11 2220
Schubert, H.-J. (AUT) 0 2195
Schueller, E. (AUT) 0 2265
Schuermann, Th. (GER) 0 2255
Schuermans, R. (BEL) 0 2235
f Schuetz, Th. (GER) 0 2295
f Schuh, F. (AUT) 0 2345
f Schuh, H. (GER) 8 2355
Schula, M. (TCH) 0 2270
Schulenburg, B. (GER) 12 2270
Schulenburg, P. (GER) 1 2290
Schuler, K. (GER) 0 2240
f Schulien, Ch. (USA) 0 2330
Schulman, J. (BLA) 14 2335
f Schulte, O. (GER) 0 2395
Schulte-Bartold, C. (GER) 0 2280
Schultz, J. (SWE) 0 2170
Schulz, J. (GER) 5 2255
f Schulz, Ka. (GER) 21 2330
m Schulz, Kl. -J. (GER) 15 2420
Schulz, M. (GER) 0 2335
Schulz, R. (GER) 11 2205
Schulz, W. (GER) 0 2135
Schulze, E. (GER) 3 2260
Schulze, Ha. (GER) 0 2215
Schulze, Hu. (GER) 0 2235
m Schulze, U. (GER) 8 2410
Schumacher, B. (GER) 12 2135
Schumacher, H. (BEL) 0 2205
Schumacher, N. (GER) 0 2300
Schumi, M. (AUT) 11 2255
Schunk, Th. (GER) 4 2210
f Schurade, M. (GER) 6 2360
Schuran, S. (GER) 0 2115
g Schussler, H. (SWE) 0 2465
Schuster, C. (ARG) 0 2275
Schuster, D. (USA) 0 2235
Schuster, K. (GER) 0 2205
Schuster, M. (AUT) 0 2205
Schuyler, J. (USA) 0 2315
Schwab, R. (AUT) 14 2280
Schwaegli, B. (SUI) 9 2295
Schwalfenberg, J. (GER) 0 2215
f Schwamberger, M. (GER) 6 2320
f Schwanek, C. (ARG) 0 2375
Schwartz, A. J. (NED) 0 2225
m Schwartzman, G. (ROM) 48 2480
Schwarz, A. (ISR) 0 2230
m Schwarz, M. (GER) 44 2405
f Schwarz, P. (GER) 16 2305
Schwarzkopf, Ch. (GER) 0 2220
m Schweber, S. (ARG) 28 2350
f Schweda, R. (AUT) 0 2305
Schweizer, M. (GER) 0 2200
Schwekendiek, U. (GER) 5 2310
Schwicker, F. (FRA) 0 2220
f Schwiep, J. (CUB) 0 2305
Sciborowski, M. (POL) 0 2245
Sciortino, M. (MLT) 0 2005
Scotto, M. (ITA) 13 2245
Seba, K. (ALG) 0 2245
Sebez, M. (YUG) 0 2235
m Sebih, K. (ALG) 6 2325
Secheli, G. (ROM) 0 2250
Seder, N. (ROM) 22 2195
Sederias, F. (ROM) 0 2025
Sedgwick, D. (ENG) 12 2165
m Sedina, E. (UKR) 11 2255
Sedlacek, O. (TCH) 0 2275
Sedlacek, P. (SVK) 0 2210
Sedlak, I. (YUG) 0 2240
Sedlakova, I. (SVK) 0 2015
Sedyshev, V. (RUS) 0 2340
Seeck, K. (GER) 9 2260
Seeger, W. (GER) 11 2205
f Seegers, H. (GER) 1 2320
Seet, C. (SIN) 0 2005
Seferjan, N. (RUS) 36 2405
m Segal, Al. S. (BRA) 15 2295
m Segal, Anna (ISR) 11 2175
Segal, N. (LAT) 0 2045
Seger, R. (GER) 10 2355
f Segi, L. (YUG) 0 2320
Seguera, R. (VEN) 0 2270
m Sehner, N. (GER) 7 2415
Sehovic, G. (YUG) 0 2290
f Seidemann, U. (GER) 0 2110
Seifarth, R. (TCH) 0 2260
f Seifert, H. (POL) 4 2255
f Seifert, M. (TCH) 0 2275
f Seils, J. (GER) 11 2355
g Seirawan, Y. (USA) 26 2575
f Seitaj, I. (ALB) 8 2410
Seitz, M. (GER) 2 2270
Sek, J. (POL) 4 2250
f Sek, Z. (POL) 7 2280
Sekanina, J. (TCH) 0 2160
Sekelj, G. (YUG) 0 2235
Sekerovic, M. (YUG) 0 2260
Seknadje, J. (FRA) 5 2185
Sekularac, P. (YUG) 15 2220
f Sekulic, D. (YUG) 50 2355
f Sekulic, V. (YUG) 0 2315
Sekulovic, D. (YUG) 0 2035
Sekulovska, V. (YUG) 2 2050
Sel, C. (TUR) 0 2265
Selivjorstov, A. (RUS) 3 2345
m Sellos, D. (FRA) 9 2435
Seltzer, R. (USA) 2 2265
Semakin, A. (RUS) 0 2345
Semakoff, A. (NOR) 0 2230
Semeniuk, A. A. (RUS) 17 2410
f Semenov, A. (YUG) 0 2355
Semenov, V. (UKR) 8 2325
Semenova, I. (RUS) 15 2105
g Semenova, L. K. (UKR) 20 2285
Semina, S. (RUS) 5 2180
Seminara, J. P. (ARG) 0 2185
m Semkov, S. (BUL) 24 2480
Senador, E. (PHI) 0 2365
Senchichin, J. (UKR) 0 2135
Sendera, J. (POL) 0 2290
Senez, Ch. (FRA) 0 2210
Senkiewicz, M. (IVB) 0 2205
Senner, P. (GER) 0 2215
Sentic, P. (YUG) 0 2270
Sepp, O. (EST) 16 2380
Seppelt, A. (GER) 0 2215
Sepulveda, J. (CHI) 11 2225
Sepulveda, L. (CHI) 0 2260
Sequera, J. (VEN) 0 2330
Serafimov, D. (BUL) 0 2305
Serafimov, T. (BUL) 2 2100
f Serban-Mitaru, D. (ROM) 32 2275
Serdarovic, M. (YUG) 0 2270
Serdean, P. D. (ROM) 0 2240
Serebrjanik, A. (RUS) 41 2415
Serebro, A. (UKR) 0 2225
Seredenko, V. (KAZ) 14 2365
Seres, B. (HUN) 0 2325
f Seres, L. (HUN) 15 2340
m Seret, J.-L. (FRA) 11 2450
Sergeev, Ve. (RUS) 11 2405
Sergeev, Vl. (UKR) 0 2440
Sergeeva, T. (KAZ) 5 2250
Sergejev, R. (EST) 11 2255
Sergienko, S. (RUS) 24 2430
m Sergievsky, V. D. (RUS) 11 2390
Sericano, C. (ITA) 0 2260
m Sermek, D. (SLO) 53 2460
Sermier, A. (FRA) 0 2245
Serotta, A. (USA) 0 2315
g Serper, G. (UZB) 20 2575
Serra Olives, T. (ESP) 0 2285
Serrano Marhuenda, S. (ESP) 0 2235
f Serrer, Ch. (GER) 19 2285
f Servat, R. (ARG) 27 2440
Servaty, R. (GER) 0 2290
Serwa, A. (POL) 12 2045
Sery, P. (FRA) 14 2090
Sestjakov, S. (RUS) 0 2345
f Seto, W. L. (MAS) 0 2020
f Setterqvist, K. (SWE) 0 2305
f Seul, G. (GER) 25 2425
Sevcik, V. (TCH) 0 2285
Sevic, S. (YUG) 0 2250
Sevillano, D. (ARG) 0 2265
m Sevillano, E. (PHI) 0 2375
f Seyb, D. (GER) 4 2290
Sferra, B. (USA) 0 2300
g Shabalov, A. (LAT) 62 2590
m Shabanov, Y. (RUS) 57 2410
Shaboian, V. (ARM) 0 2340
f Shabtai, R. (ISR) 19 2350
Shachar, E. (ISR) 10 2345
f Shadarevian, M. (SYR) 0 2375
Shadrina, T. (RUS) 24 2190
f Shahade, M. (USA) 4 2285
Shahal, N. (ISR) 0 2240
Shahid, A. (IND) 0 2100
Shahtahtinskij, A. (RUS) 0 2380
Shahul, H. (IND) 0 2205
Shaked, T. (USA) 13 2440
Shakhnazarov, O. (USA) 16 2295
Shalamberidze, A. (GEO) 0 2330
Shalnev, N. (UKR) 0 2285
g Shamkovich, L. (USA) 2 2410
Shani, A. (ISR) 15 2215
Shankar, R. (IND) 8 2275
f Shantharam, K. V. (IND) 11 2235
f Shapiro, D. E. (USA) 17 2310
m Sharif, Me. (FRA) 6 2425
Sharif, Mo. (UAE) 0 2235
Sharma, L. R. (IND) 0 2220
Sharma, La. (IND) 6 2250
Sharp, J. (ENG) 0 2265
Shashin, A. A. (RUS) 0 2350
Shaw, J. (SCO) 10 2270
m Shaw, T. I. (AUS) 0 2300
m Shchekachev, A. (RUS) 31 2475
Sheldon, R. (ENG) 17 2040
Shemer, Y. (ISR) 0 2265
Shepley, J. M. (ENG) 6 2205
g Sher, M. N. (RUS) 45 2535
g Sherbakov, R. (RUS) 33 2580
Sherbakov, V. (RUS) 0 2385
m Sheremetieva, M. (MOL) 29 2265
m Shereshevski, M. (BLA) 11 2470
Sherf, R. (ISR) 0 2205
Sherman, D. (USA) 14 2225
g Sherzer, A. (USA) 26 2500
Shestakov, S. S. (RUS) 2 2315
Shestoperov, A. (RUS) 22 2440
Shestoperova, A. (RUS) 0 2095

	Name	Games	Rating
	Shetty, R. (IND)	25	2405
	Shevelev, A. (ISR)	27	2325
m	Shevelev, S. (RUS)	32	2430
	Shibut, M. (USA)	4	2260
	Shifman, M. (ARG)	11	2185
	Shikerov, S. (BUL)	0	2260
m	Shikova, V. W. (BUL)	6	2115
	Shilov, S. (UKR)	0	2295
m	Shipman, W. (USA)	21	2345
m	Shipov, S. (RUS)	38	2500
m	Shirazi, K. (USA)	39	2380
g	Shirov, A. (LAT)	54	2685
	Shishkim, V. (RUS)	16	2220
	Shishkin, V. (UKR)	9	2410
	Shishkov, V. (RUS)	11	2170
	Shliahtin, I. E. (RUS)	16	2250
	Shmirin, A. (RUS)	0	2350
	Shmulevkh, M. (USA)	12	2160
m	Shmuter, L. (UKR)	14	2455
	Shnaider, D. (RUS)	0	2300
g	Shneider, A. (UKR)	27	2560
	Shocron, R. (USA)	0	2270
f	Short, Ph. M. (IRL)	14	2300
	Shour, J. (RUS)	34	2120
m	Shrentzel, I. (ISR)	11	2325
f	Shrentzel, M. (ISR)	9	2300
f	Shtern, I. (USA)	0	2255
m	Shtyrenkov, V. (RUS)	24	2435
	Shukin, E. (BUL)	0	2250
	Shulman, L. (RUS)	0	2280
	Shulman, V. (LAT)	0	2255
	Shulman, Y. (BLA)	29	2380
m	Shumiakina, T. (RUS)	31	2320
	Shur, G. (RUS)	0	2060
	Shur, M. (AZE)	25	2375
	Shuraev, A. A. (RUS)	4	2415
	Shure, G. (USA)	17	2260
	Shurmanov, A. (RUS)	0	2265
	Shurygin, S. (RUS)	0	2335
	Shushpanov, V. (RUS)	5	2275
	Shushpanova, N. (RUS)	9	2195
m	Shvedchikov, A. I. (RUS)	95	2460
m	Shvidler, E. (ISR)	19	2415
f	Sibarevic, M. (YUG)	14	2355
f	Sibilio, M. (ITA)	6	2320
	Sibriaev, A. (RUS)	7	2330
	Sicherl, P. (GER)	0	2230
f	Sick, O. (GER)	0	2335
	Sicker, R. (GER)	0	2240
	Sickles, D. N. (USA)	0	2215
m	Sideif-Sade, F. I. (AZE)	25	2405
	Sidelnikov, A. (USA)	0	2230
	Sidhoum, J. (FRA)	0	2245
	Sidorov, A. (RUS)	18	2390
f	Siebrecht, S. (GER)	8	2330
	Sieg, M. (GER)	3	2280
	Sieg, U. (GER)	7	2330
f	Siegel, G. (GER)	15	2335
f	Sieglen, J. (GER)	15	2415
	Siegmund, R. (GER)	2	2220
m	Sieiro-Gonzalez, L. (CUB)	23	2405
	Siekaczynski, R. (POL)	6	2240
	Siekaniec, J. (POL)	19	2245
	Siekanska, I. (POL)	6	2110
	Siekanski, J. (POL)	0	2295
	Siem, B.-Dj. (GER)	0	2220
	Sienczewski, Z. (POL)	0	2205
f	Siepelt, H. (GER)	7	2320
f	Siepenkoetter, A. (GER)	6	2125
f	Sievers, S. (GER)	10	2320
m	Sifrer, D. (SLO)	0	2440
	Sifres, P. (ARG)	19	2185
f	Sigfusson, S. (ISD)	0	2290
m	Siklosi, Z. (HUN)	111	2305
	Sikora, J. (TCH)	10	2145
m	Sikora-Gizynska, B. (POL)	5	2185
m	Sikora-Lerch, J. (TCH)	0	2395
	Silberman, J. (RUS)	0	2375
m	Silman, J. D. (USA)	21	2405
	Silseth, S. (SWE)	5	2285
	Silva Nazzari, R. (URU)	0	2205
	Silva, A. (POR)	0	2215
	Silva, C. (POR)	0	2005
m	Silva, F. (POR)	20	2355
	Silva, S. (CHI)	42	2380
	Silva-Morales, M. A. (COL)	0	2335
	Silveira, F. M. (BRA)	0	2385
	Simanjuntak, S. (INA)	0	2330
	Simeonov, A. (YUG)	9	2190
	Simeonov, S. (BUL)	5	2340
	Simic, Dr. (SLO)	4	2255
	Simic, Du. (YUG)	0	2245
	Simic, G. (YUG)	9	2235
	Simic, M. (YUG)	0	2205
g	Simic, R. (YUG)	27	2470
f	Simic, S. (YUG)	0	2295
	Simo, J. (HUN)	16	2035
f	Simon, R.-A. (GER)	2	2245
	Simon, S. (YUG)	0	2310
	Simonenko, S. (TKM)	11	2320
	Simonov, V. (RUS)	0	2315
f	Simonovic, A. (YUG)	6	2370
f	Simonyi, Z. (YUG)	0	2285
	Simpson, A. (BER)	0	2205
	Simpson, R. (USA)	0	2275
f	Sinadinovic, A. (YUG)	5	2315
m	Sinanovic, M. (CRO)	5	2405
m	Sindik, E. (CRO)	1	2325
	Singala, H. C. (IND)	0	2260
	Singer, Ch. (GER)	7	2225
f	Singer, H. (AUT)	0	2275
	Singer, R. (AUT)	3	2210
	Singh Sukh, J. (ENG)	0	2310
	Singh, J. (FIJ)	0	2200
	Singh, P. K. (IND)	15	2310
	Singh, Pr. (IND)	0	2305
	Singh, R. (IND)	11	2275
	Singh, S. D. (ENG)	0	2225
	Sinha, A. K. (IND)	0	2230
	Sinica, J. (POL)	0	2240
	Sinka, B. (HUN)	0	2035
	Sinka, I. (HUN)	0	2265
m	Sinkovics, P. (HUN)	18	2325
f	Sinowjew, J. (AUT)	8	2350
	Sinprayoon, P. (THA)	0	2245
	Sinz, B. (GER)	0	2090
m	Sion Castro, M. (ESP)	37	2385
	Sirias, D. (NCA)	0	2285
	Sirigos, N. (GRE)	11	2310
	Sirin, I. (RUS)	0	2375
	Siroker, J. (USA)	0	2245
	Sirotanovic, O. (YUG)	0	2240
g	Sisniega, M. (MEX)	0	2445
f	Sitanggang, S. (INA)	27	2390
	Sitnik, I. (YUG)	12	2230
m	Sitnikova, N. (RUS)	15	2225
	Situru, N. (INA)	0	2390
	Siva, M. (JAM)	0	2205
	Sivokho, S. (RUS)	3	2340
	Siwiec, B. (POL)	4	2270
	Sixtensson, M. (SWE)	0	2210
m	Sjoberg, M. (SWE)	0	2475
f	Sjodahl, P. (SWE)	0	2375
	Sjodin, B. (SWE)	2	2185
	Skacelikova, M. (TCH)	0	2090
f	Skacelova-Zahorovska, L. (TCH)	0	2075
	Skalik, P. (POL)	33	2345
m	Skalkotas, N. (GRE)	11	2330
f	Skalli, K. (MAR)	0	2235
	Skarica, A. (CRO)	0	2290
m	Skegina, K. (ISR)	4	2155
g	Skembris, S. (GRE)	53	2545
	Skiadopoulos, N. (GRE)	9	2265
	Skindzier, S. (POL)	3	2220
	Skogen, S. (NOR)	0	2220
	Skok, J. (SLO)	10	2150
	Skoko, Mil. (YUG)	8	2240
	Skoko, Mir. (YUG)	0	2250
m	Skomorokhin, R. (RUS)	39	2460
	Skora, W. (POL)	0	2250
	Skoularikis, F. (GRE)	0	2230
	Skousen, N. (DEN)	0	2205
	Skrebnevskis, R. (LTU)	10	2105
	Skribanek, L. (GER)	0	2315
f	Skripchenko, A. (MOL)	51	2165
	Skripova, T. (RUS)	12	2140
m	Skrobek, R. (POL)	0	2385
	Skrzypczak, J. (POL)	0	2245
	Skudnov, S. (RUS)	8	2395
	Skuinia, G. (LAT)	0	2090
	Slabek, A. (POL)	0	2160
	Slabek, G. (POL)	0	2240
	Sladkowski, S. (POL)	1	2210
	Slak, M. (SLO)	8	2220
	Slamar, V. (CRO)	0	2305
	Slanina, M. (TCH)	0	2210
	Slavin, G. (RUS)	0	2320
m	Slavotinek, A. (AUS)	0	2075
	Slavov, D. (BUL)	0	2260
	Sleisz, T. (HUN)	0	2215
	Slekys, E. (LTU)	23	2385
	Slezka, V. (TCH)	0	2380
	Slibar, M. (SLO)	0	2225
	Slingerland, C. (NED)	0	2140
	Slingerland, F. (NED)	0	2280
m	Slipak, S. (ARG)	64	2455
h	Sliwa, B. (POL)	0	2265
	Sljukic, M. (YUG)	4	2210
m	Slobodjan, R. (GER)	37	2435
	Slogar, D. (CRO)	3	2320
	Slonimskij, A. (RUS)	3	2210
f	Sloth, J. (DEN)	0	2370
	Sluckij, L. (RUS)	0	2375
	Slutzkin, U. (ISR)	10	2260
	Slutzky, L. M. (RUS)	0	2230
	Smagacz, D. (POL)	2	2250
g	Smagin, S. (RUS)	31	2550
	Smalara, K. (POL)	12	2085
	Small, G. (USA)	14	2235
	Small, S. (ENG)	0	2245
m	Small, V. A. (NZL)	11	2330
g	Smejkal, J. (TCH)	33	2515
	Smetana, J. (TCH)	0	2165
	Smida, J. (ROM)	0	2310
	Smiechowska, J. (POL)	0	2105
g	Smirin, I. (ISR)	68	2640
	Smirnov, V. (BLA)	12	2315
	Smith, Al. A. (ENG)	0	2265
	Smith, An. P. (ENG)	7	2290
	Smith, L. (AHO)	0	2205
	Smith, M. (AUS)	0	2320
	Smith, R. W. (NZL)	11	2255
	Smith, V. (NZL)	0	2035
	Smolenskaya, V. (ISR)	7	2045
f	Smolovic, M. (YUG)	13	2365
	Smuga, S. (POL)	0	2240
	Smuk, Z. (CRO)	0	2295
g	Smyslov, V. (RUS)	31	2520
	Soares, C. (BRA)	5	2305
	Sobek, J. (TCH)	0	2280
	Sobjerg, E. (DEN)	0	2270
	Sobolewski, P. (POL)	13	2250
	Sobrevia, L. (ESP)	0	2210
	Sobura, H. (POL)	0	2320
	Socha, Cz. (POL)	0	2235
f	Socha, K. (POL)	0	2305
f	Socko, B. (POL)	34	2325
	Socoteanu, M. (ROM)	0	2185
m	Soffer, R. (ISR)	32	2450
g	Sofieva, A. (AZE)	9	2390
	Sofrevska, L. (YUG)	0	2130
m	Sofrevski, J. (YUG)	54	2405

	Name		
	Sofrigin, A. (RUS)	0	2265
f	Sofronie, I. (ROM)	12	2315
	Sogaard, S. (DEN)	22	2280
	Soinski, K. (POL)	0	2195
	Sokalski, M. (POL)	9	2210
	Sokalsky, A. (UKR)	13	2255
	Sokolin, L. (RUS)	0	2430
	Sokolov, Al. (RUS)	9	2365
g	Sokolov, Andrei (RUS)	29	2525
m	Sokolov, Andrei (LAT)	57	2495
g	Sokolov, I. (BIH)	20	2610
	Sokolov, S. M. (RUS)	0	2370
	Sokolovic-Bertok, S. (CRO)	0	2025
	Sokolowski, R. (POL)	0	2240
	Sokolowski, S. (POL)	0	2265
	Solak, D. (YUG)	0	2195
	Solak, Z. (YUG)	0	2230
	Solakoglu, U. (TUR)	0	2320
f	Solana, E. (ESP)	27	2335
	Solanki, V. K. (IND)	13	2235
	Solano, A. (CRC)	10	2200
	Solbrand, S. (SWE)	7	2290
f	Solin, N. (SWE)	0	2265
	Solmundarson, M. (ISD)	0	2035
	Soln, P. (SLO)	13	2300
	Solomon, A. (ROM)	0	2265
	Solomon, D. (RSA)	0	2305
m	Solomon, S. J. (AUS)	0	2450
f	Solomunovic, I. (YUG)	3	2330
m	Solonar, S. (MOL)	50	2470
	Solorzano, R. (MEX)	0	2260
	Soloviov, S. (RUS)	4	2410
m	Solozhenkin, E. (RUS)	38	2515
	Solti, L. (HUN)	10	2025
g	Soltis, A. E. (USA)	13	2430
	Soltys, B. (POL)	0	2300
	Soluch, L. (AUT)	0	2215
	Solymosi, I. (HUN)	7	2285
	Solys, L. (LTU)	0	2325
	Somborski, N. (YUG)	0	2275
	Somlai, L. (HUN)	6	2380
	Sommaro, K. (GER)	0	2105
	Sommerbauer, N. (AUT)	9	2335
f	Somogyi, I. (HUN)	21	2305
	Son, I. (UKR)	6	2170
	Sondermann, J. (GER)	9	2015
	Song, P. (USA)	7	2245
	Sonnenberger, K. (GER)	0	2025
m	Sonntag, H.-H. (GER)	10	2405
	Soos, A. (HUN)	0	2315
m	Soos, B. (GER)	11	2365
	Soponyai, T. (HUN)	12	2135
m	Soppe, G. (ARG)	45	2460
	Soppela, J. (FIN)	0	2245
	Sopur, L. (POL)	0	2300
	Sorbucheva, I. (RUS)	15	2025
	Sorensen, B. (DEN)	0	2300
f	Sorensen, H. (DEN)	0	2220
m	Sorensen, J. (DEN)	0	2395
	Sorensen, T. (DEN)	0	2320
	Sorescu, M. (ROM)	0	2035
	Sorgic, D. (YUG)	0	2245
	Soriano, A. (PHI)	0	2205
m	Sorin, A. (ARG)	18	2435
	Sorokin, G. K. (RUS)	0	2425
g	Sorokin, M. (RUS)	52	2515
f	Sorri, K. J. (FIN)	1	2335
	Sosa Harrison, J. (PAR)	4	2300
	Sosa Macho, J. M. (URU)	16	2125
	Sosa, L. (PUR)	0	2245
	Soskic, B. (YUG)	0	2270
	Sosna, J. (TCH)	0	2375
	Sosnik, S. (POL)	0	2240
f	Sosnowska, E. (POL)	12	2095
g	Sosonko, G. (NED)	11	2525
	Sotnikov, I. (RUS)	9	2285
	Sotonyi, Zs. (HUN)	0	2065
	Souleidis, G. (GER)	25	2300
	Sousa, A. (ANG)	0	2245
	South, R. (CAN)	0	2240
	Southam, D. (CAN)	0	2215
f	Southam, T. (CAN)	5	2335
	Souza, I. (BRA)	0	2285
	Souza, M. A. (BRA)	2	2200
	Sowizdrzal, D. (POL)	0	2255
f	Sowray, P. J. (ENG)	0	2330
f	Soylu, S. (TUR)	11	2330
f	Spaan, M. (NED)	0	2315
m	Spacek, P. (TCH)	6	2385
	Spaete, U. (GER)	0	2080
	Spain, G. (NZL)	11	2235
	Spajic, L. (YUG)	16	2030
f	Spangenberg, H. (ARG)	67	2535
	Spanou, M. (GRE)	0	2010
	Sparic, N. (YUG)	8	2245
	Spasenovski, S. (YUG)	0	2275
	Spasic, B. (YUG)	11	2260
	Spasic, D. (YUG)	9	2080
f	Spasojevic, M. (YUG)	0	2375
	Spasojevic, Z. (YUG)	0	2300
g	Spasov, V. (BUL)	19	2540
g	Spassky, B. V. (FRA)	0	2565
g	Spassov, L. (BUL)	18	2435
	Speck, H. (SUI)	11	2275
	Speckner, R. (GER)	8	2260
g	Speelman, J. S. (ENG)	25	2605
	Speer, A. (GER)	0	2250
	Sperlich, O. (GER)	4	2265
	Spesny, J. (TCH)	2	2320
	Spicak, K. (POL)	12	2215
	Spice, A. (ENG)	6	2200
	Spiegel, S. (GER)	0	2265
	Spielmann, A. (FRA)	9	2240
f	Spielmann, J. (SUI)	9	2140
	Spiess, G. (GER)	5	2360
	Spinelli, D. (ITA)	11	2130
f	Spiric, I. (YUG)	4	2290
g	Spiridonov, N. (BUL)	9	2430
	Spiriev, P. (HUN)	0	2245
	Spirik, J. (TCH)	0	2260
	Spiro, B. (USA)	0	2220
	Spirov, T. (BUL)	0	2330
	Spisak, Cz. (POL)	17	2195
	Spitzlsperger, G. (GER)	0	2300
	Splane, M. (USA)	0	2120
	Sploshrov, S. (BLA)	9	2280
	Spodzieja, K. (POL)	0	2245
	Sponheim, O. (GER)	0	2280
	Spraggett, G. (CAN)	0	2280
g	Spraggett, K. (CAN)	38	2555
f	Sprecic, M. (BIH)	0	2330
	Spreng, S. (GER)	0	2255
	Sprotte, N. (GER)	0	2245
f	Spulber, C. (ROM)	28	2355
	Spyra, W. (POL)	13	2195
	Srch, J. (AUT)	0	2210
	Srdic, D. (YUG)	0	2250
	Srdjanov, S. (YUG)	5	2215
	Srebrnic, V. (SLO)	7	2240
	Srebrov, H. (BUL)	0	2210
	Sribar, P. (CRO)	0	2255
	Sridhar, C. S. (IND)	3	2255
	Srikanth, G. (IND)	19	2210
	Srinivasa, R. G. V. (IND)	5	2190
	Sriram, J. (IND)	0	2300
	Srivastava, Y. P. (IND)	9	2265
	Srivatsava, K. B. L. (IND)	0	2220
m	Srokowski, J. (UKR)	0	2425
	Ssentongo, E. (UGA)	0	2295
	Stabolewski, A. (GER)	7	2290
	Stadler, B. (CRO)	0	2095
g	Stadler, T. (YUG)	0	2175
	Stadtmuller, H. (GER)	8	2230
	Staflin, S. (SWE)	9	2020
	Staiger, F. (GER)	8	2305
m	Stajcic, N. (AUT)	88	2350
	Stajkov, K. (ROM)	0	2240
f	Staller, P. (GER)	12	2385
	Stalne, K. (SWE)	0	2105
	Stamatopoulos, I. (GRE)	6	2235
	Stambulin, A. (ARM)	11	2205
	Stamenkov, V. (YUG)	14	2330
f	Stamenkovic, Z. (YUG)	27	2425
	Stamnov, A. (YUG)	16	2285
m	Stanciu, G. (ROM)	32	2215
f	Stanciu, T. (ROM)	0	2315
f	Stanec, N. (AUT)	10	2440
	Stanetzek, C. (GER)	0	2200
	Stanev, V. (BUL)	0	2340
m	Stangl, M. (GER)	43	2525
	Stanic, J. (CRO)	13	2150
	Stanic, B. T. (YUG)	2	2225
	Stanic, Z. (CRO)	0	2200
f	Stanimirovic, A. (YUG)	0	2320
f	Stanisic, Lj. (YUG)	0	2270
	Stanisic, M. (YUG)	0	2245
m	Staniszewski, P. (POL)	7	2410
	Stanivukovic, D. (YUG)	4	2255
	Stanka, W. (AUT)	0	2330
	Stanke, J. (GER)	17	2320
	Stankov, G. (BUL)	7	2290
	Stankovac, D. (YUG)	0	2250
	Stankovic, B. (YUG)	0	2300
	Stankovic, De. (YUG)	1	2230
	Stankovic, Dragan (YUG)	6	2230
f	Stankovic, Dragan (YUG)	4	2290
	Stankovic, M. (YUG)	18	2110
f	Stanojevic, B. (YUG)	11	2345
f	Stanojoski, Z. (YUG)	34	2360
	Stanton, W. (ENG)	0	2165
f	Starcevic, G. (YUG)	0	2295
f	Starck, B. (GER)	0	2290
f	Starck, I. (GER)	0	2210
	Starke, D. (GER)	0	2280
	Starosek, K. (RUS)	9	2455
	Starosta, J. (HUN)	0	2215
m	Starr, N. (CAN)	0	2210
	Stasiunaite, L. (LTU)	9	2160
	Staskin, S. (RUS)	0	2330
	Staub, P. (FRA)	7	2200
	Stavanja, M. (SLO)	0	2260
	Stavrev, N. (BUL)	7	2245
	Stavru, A. (ITA)	0	2250
	Stawiarski, E. (FRA)	0	2270
	Stawizsinski, W. (GER)	14	2205
	Stayt, J. (ENG)	0	2120
	Stebbings, A. (ENG)	0	2250
	Stecki, W. (POL)	0	2230
f	Steckner, J. (GER)	5	2330
m	Steczkowski, K. (FRA)	0	2325
	Steer, J. (HUN)	0	2210
	Stefan, M. (ROM)	16	2285
	Stefanelli, L. (ITA)	0	2325
	Stefaniak, J. (POL)	0	2230
m	Stefanov, K. (BUL)	0	2380
m	Stefanov, P. (ROM)	23	2360
f	Stefanova, A. (BUL)	22	2215
	Stefanovic, Dj. (YUG)	0	2210
f	Stefanovic, Du. (YUG)	0	2340
g	Stefansson, H. (ISD)	35	2500
	Steffens, G. (GER)	5	2205
	Stefurak, D. L. (USA)	11	2290
	Steiger, B. (HUN)	0	2205
	Steil, J. J. (GER)	0	2245
	Stein, A. (USA)	4	2205
m	Stein, B. (GER)	19	2360
	Stein, K. W. (USA)	0	2320
f	Steinbacher, M. (GER)	43	2385
	Steiner, B. (AUT)	0	2200
f	Steiner, D. (SLO)	0	2305
	Steiner, G. (AUT)	0	2245
	Steiner, H. (AUT)	0	2180
f	Steiner, U. A. (AUT)	16	2185

	Name		
	Steinert, M. (GER)	6	2295
	Steinfl, A. (ITA)	5	2270
	Steingrimsson, H. (ISD)	10	2420
	Steinheimer, J. (GER)	0	2230
	Steinhoff, I. M. (BRA)	4	2210
	Steinmacher, J. (GER)	0	2030
	Stelting, Th. (GER)	0	2260
	Stempin, A. (POL)	0	2285
m	Stempin, P. (POL)	0	2435
	Stenner, P. (GER)	0	2265
	Stentebjerg-Hansen, P. (DEN)	0	2275
	Stenzel, H. (USA)	11	2215
f	Stepak, Y. (ISR)	14	2285
	Stepanov, P. (RUS)	0	2365
	Stepanov, V. (BLA)	5	2250
	Stephson, D. (AUS)	0	2240
	Stepite, I. (LAT)	0	2050
g	Stepovaia-Dianchenko, T. (RUS)	37	2285
	Sterin, I. (USA)	9	2305
f	Stern, R. (GER)	29	2385
	Sternina, V. E. (RUS)	0	2125
	Stertenbrink, G. (GER)	0	2285
	Stesser, C. (SWE)	9	2040
f	Stettler, M. (GER)	7	2370
	Steudtmann, Ch. (GER)	0	2295
	Stevanovic, G. (YUG)	14	2300
	Stevanovic, I. (GER)	10	2145
	Stevanovic, V. (YUG)	0	2315
	Stevens, L. (USA)	9	2240
	Stewart, D. (IRL)	0	2300
	Stewart, T. (DEN)	0	2090
	Sthalekar, V. G. (IND)	1	2260
	Stickler, A. (GER)	4	2245
	Stierhof, R. (GER)	0	2255
f	Stigar, P. (NOR)	0	2290
	Stillger, B. (GER)	9	2215
	Stimpel, F. (GER)	8	2255
f	Stipic, A. (CRO)	0	2275
	Stircz, Z. (ROM)	0	2070
	Stirling, B. I. (ENG)	0	2245
	Stisis, Y. (ISR)	17	2350
	Stjgkin, V. (RUS)	0	2375
f	Stobik, D. (GER)	0	2310
	Stocek, J. (TCH)	0	2210
	Stock, M. (GER)	0	2400
	Stockfleth, R. (GER)	3	2210
	Stocklin, C. (SUI)	15	2130
	Stodola, J. (TCH)	0	2230
	Stoeber, M. (GER)	0	2190
	Stoering, V. (GER)	8	2340
g	Stohl, I. (SVK)	29	2545
m	Stoica, V. (ROM)	0	2445
	Stoilov, A. (BUL)	0	2250
	Stoinev, M. (BUL)	4	2380
	Stoinov, I. (BUL)	0	2305
	Stoinov, J. (BUL)	0	2310
	Stoisavljevic, S. (YUG)	26	2150
f	Stojakovic, B. (CRO)	0	2305
	Stojanov, J. (YUG)	11	2150
	Stojanov, S. (BUL)	28	2300
	Stojanovic, Do. (YUG)	0	2325
f	Stojanovic, Dr. (YUG)	10	2300
	Stojanovic, Ma. (YUG)	0	2245
f	Stojanovic, Mih. (YUG)	0	2325
	Stojanovic, Mir. (YUG)	0	2245
	Stojanovic, S. (YUG)	0	2240
	Stojanovic, Z. (YUG)	10	2325
	Stojanovski, I. (YUG)	0	2260
	Stojkovic, M. (YUG)	0	2320
	Stokstad, P. G. (NOR)	0	2195
	Stoliar, E. S. (RUS)	0	2385
	Stoll, A. (GER)	0	2250
	Stoll, F. (GER)	10	2235
	Stolovitch, C. (FRA)	9	2055
	Stolz, M. (GER)	8	2280
f	Stone, R. (CAN)	15	2370
	Stopa, J. R. (USA)	0	2280
	Stopka, D. (GER)	0	2215
f	Stoppel, F. (AUT)	9	2250
	Storaas, J.-Th. (SWE)	13	2220
	Storga, D. (CRO)	2	2215
	Storland, K. H. (NOR)	0	2215
f	Storm, R. (GER)	0	2300
	Stornelli, V. (ITA)	9	2050
f	Stoyko, S. E. (USA)	0	2290
	Straat, E.-J. (NED)	1	2235
	Strachan, J. (SVK)	0	2250
	Straeter, T. (GER)	10	2355
	Strakos, D. (YUG)	9	2260
	Stranjakovitch, J. (FRA)	8	2245
	Stranz, R. (AUT)	0	2260
m	Stratil jr., L. (TCH)	0	2375
	Stratil, P. (TCH)	0	2270
	Strating, S. (NED)	0	2355
	Stratmann, B. (GER)	0	2220
	Stratta, R. (ARG)	9	2230
	Straub, P. (GER)	20	2155
	Strauss, A. (AUT)	9	2245
m	Strauss, D. J. (USA)	10	2435
f	Strausz, J. (FRA)	3	2285
	Strayer, G. (USA)	0	2360
	Streitberg, P. (TCH)	0	2260
	Strelets, I. (BLA)	9	2240
	Strenner, J. (HUN)	0	2235
	Strenner, Z. (HUN)	0	2235
	Strenzwilk, D. (USA)	16	2245
m	Strikovic, A. (YUG)	13	2465
m	Stripunsky, A. (UKR)	20	2490
f	Strizak, N. (YUG)	35	2220
	Strizhnev, P. (RUS)	0	2260
	Stroe, C. (FRA)	0	2345
	Strokov (RUS)	0	2235
	Stromberg, P. (SWE)	4	2220
	Stromer, A. (GER)	7	2245
	Strowsky, Y. (FRA)	19	2215
	Strozewski, F. (GER)	0	2295
	Strozyk, T. (POL)	0	2235
	Struc, M. (YUG)	0	2140
	Struchkova, S. (UKR)	0	2230
	Strugatsky, V. (USA)	0	2365
	Struk, J. (POL)	6	2160
m	Strutinskaya, G. N. (RUS)	0	2235
	Strzalka, J. (POL)	0	2065
	Strzelecki, K. (POL)	0	2345
	Stuart, P. (NZL)	11	2195
	Studenetzky, M. (ARG)	8	2195
	Stuhlik, M. (AUT)	8	2220
	Stulik, V. (TCH)	0	2290
	Stull, N. (LUX)	0	2245
f	Stummer, A. (AUT)	13	2305
	Stumpf, H. (GER)	3	2330
	Stupar, Sl. (CRO)	32	2185
	Stupar, Sz. (CRO)	9	2285
	Stupica, J. (SLO)	0	2290
g	Sturua, Z. (GEO)	18	2540
	Styblo, M. (TCH)	0	2310
	Stypka, M. (POL)	7	2245
	Suarez Roa, J. (ESP)	9	2295
f	Suarez, J. L. (ARG)	10	2280
g	Suba, M. (ROM)	27	2500
f	Subasic, I. (BIH)	0	2315
f	Subit, J. L. (CUB)	0	2340
	Subotic, M. (YUG)	0	2220
	Subramaniam, S. C. (IND)	7	2260
	Subramanian, S. (USA)	0	2225
	Subramanian, V. (IND)	8	2300
	Subrt, J. (TCH)	0	2205
	Suchorukow, A. (RUS)	26	2250
	Suciu, D.-S. (ROM)	2	2300
	Sudan, G. (SUI)	9	2065
	Suder, R. (POL)	11	2250
	Sudnikova, S. (BLA)	22	2040
	Sueess, M. (SUI)	0	2305
	Sueiro, J. (CUB)	0	2230
g	Suetin, A. S. (RUS)	34	2380
	Sugden, J. N. (ENG)	0	2240
	Suhail, A. (UAE)	0	2205
m	Suhendr, A. S. (INA)	0	2295
	Suhover, M. (RUS)	0	2035
	Sukatsch, M. (GER)	10	2025
f	Sula, Z. (ALB)	4	2350
m	Sulava, N. (CRO)	7	2430
	Suleimanov, S. (AZE)	0	2350
	Suleja, J. (POL)	13	2160
	Sulipa, A. (UKR)	20	2395
	Suljic, F. (YUG)	0	2220
	Suljovic, S. (YUG)	9	2265
	Sulkowska, M. (POL)	0	2015
f	Sulman, R. M. (USA)	4	2285
	Sulskis, S. (LTU)	27	2395
	Sulyok, S. (HUN)	0	2280
	Sulz, S. (CRO)	9	2035
f	Summermatter, D. (SUI)	7	2345
f	Summerscale, A. (ENG)	10	2355
	Sunil, L. (IND)	11	2135
f	Sunthornpongsathorn, V. (THA)	0	2325
g	Sunye Neto, J. (BRA)	20	2540
f	Supancic, D. (SLO)	0	2375
	Supatashvili, K. (GEO)	9	2440
	Supolo, J. (HUN)	4	2230
	Suprapto, B. (INA)	0	2060
	Suran, J. (TCH)	12	2200
	Suranyi, P. (HUN)	0	2205
	Sureshkumar, R. (IND)	3	2205
	Surinder, K. (IND)	0	2220
f	Sursock, S. (LEB)	0	2260
	Survila, R. (LTU)	10	2265
	Susnea, L. (ROM)	5	2060
	Susnik, M. (SLO)	5	2175
	Susnjar, M. (CRO)	0	2350
f	Susterman, A. (MOL)	16	2190
	Susterman, L. (RUS)	11	2295
	Suta, M. (ROM)	7	2235
	Sutkevicius, J. (LTU)	0	2115
	Sutor, M. (POL)	15	2115
m	Sutorikhin, V. (RUS)	47	2380
	Sutovskij, E. (ISR)	22	2410
	Sutter, O. (SUI)	17	2265
	Sutton, R. J. (NZL)	0	2275
	Suvrajit, S. (IND)	11	2390
	Suwarski, P. (POL)	15	2155
	Suzuki, H. (BRA)	0	2290
	Svatos, J. (TCH)	0	2320
	Svec, J. (GER)	0	2255
m	Svechnikova, M. (RUS)	15	2195
	Svedenborg, P. (NOR)	0	2255
f	Svenn, G. (SWE)	0	2350
	Svensk, I. (SWE)	0	2320
f	Svensson, B. (SWE)	0	2380
	Svensson, L. (SWE)	10	2235
g	Sveshnikov, E. (RUS)	39	2570
f	Svicevic, R. (YUG)	5	2270
m	Svidler, P. (RUS)	9	2495
	Svirin, O. (RUS)	19	2395
	Svistunov, K. (RUS)	11	2490
	Svitek, J. (TCH)	0	2180
	Svoboda, M. (TCH)	0	2250
	Swan, I. (SCO)	0	2275
	Swiatlowski, L. (POL)	0	2095
f	Swic, W. (POL)	0	2300
f	Swiecik, I. (NED)	17	2210
	Swierczewski, M. (POL)	0	2220
	Swol, M. (POL)	13	2205
m	Sydor, A. (POL)	0	2355
	Syeda, Sh. P. (BAN)	0	2205
m	Sygulski, A. (POL)	0	2360
m	Sygulski, B. (POL)	0	2345
	Sykora, R. (TCH)	0	2155
	Sylvan, J. (DEN)	0	2100
	Symbor, P. (POL)	5	2230
	Syre, Ch. (GER)	0	2275
	Syska, A. (GER)	4	2290

	Name		
	Szabo, E. (HUN)	7	2240
	Szabo, J. (HUN)	0	2235
	Szabo, Laslo (GER)	0	2300
g	Szabo, Laszlo (HUN)	0	2460
	Szabo, M. (HUN)	0	2260
	Szabo, P. (HUN)	11	2180
	Szabo, S. (HUN)	9	2110
	Szabo, Zo. (HUN)	6	2360
	Szabo, Zs. (HUN)	17	2280
m	Szabolcsi, J. (HUN)	23	2385
	Szacht, E. (POL)	0	2215
	Szafraniec, I. (POL)	11	2085
	Szajna, W. (POL)	0	2320
	Szakolczai, P. (HUN)	62	2265
	Szalajdewicz, J. (POL)	0	2290
m	Szalanczy, E. (HUN)	87	2360
	Szalay, S. (HUN)	0	2040
	Szanto, I. (HUN)	0	2210
	Szarvas, S. (HUN)	2	2275
	Szaszak, A. (HUN)	0	2280
	Szczep, Z. (POL)	15	2280
	Szczepanek, P. (POL)	19	2045
	Szczepanski, O. (GER)	0	2265
f	Szczygiel, A. (POL)	19	2085
	Szegedi, P. (HUN)	0	2270
m	Szekely, P. (HUN)	33	2425
	Szekeres, T. (HUN)	10	2200
f	Szeles, K. (HUN)	11	2335
f	Szell, L. (HUN)	13	2315
	Szemok, I. (HUN)	0	2205
	Szemzo, L. (HUN)	0	2240
	Szendrei, Cs. (HUN)	14	2265
	Szenetra, W. (GER)	1	2255
	Szep, A. (HUN)	12	2035
	Szepesvari, I. (HUN)	0	2220
f	Sziebert, A. (HUN)	33	2285
	Szigetvari, J. (HUN)	0	2225
m	Szilagyi, P. (HUN)	0	2400
	Szilardfy, Gy. (HUN)	14	2290
	Szili, I. (HUN)	0	2225
	Sziraki, T. (HUN)	16	2235
	Szirmai, E. (HUN)	19	2230
	Szirti, A. (HUN)	9	2195
	Szirti, L. (HUN)	0	2240
	Szitas, G. (HUN)	9	2275
	Szittar, A. (HUN)	0	2205
m	Sziva, E. (NED)	34	2235
	Szkatula, L. (POL)	0	2335
	Szlabey, G. (HUN)	0	2220
	Szlabey, K. (HUN)	1	2005
m	Szmacinska, G. (POL)	0	2260
m	Szmetan, J. (ARG)	40	2415
f	Szmetan, R. (ARG)	0	2300
	Szmigielska, A. (POL)	3	2120
m	Sznapik, A. (POL)	11	2420
	Sznapik, K. (POL)	9	2210
	Szobi, T. (HUN)	0	2280
	Szokacs, L. (HUN)	3	2250
	Szollosi jr., L. (HUN)	8	2345
	Szollosi sr., L. (HUN)	0	2255
	Szopieraj, D. (POL)	9	2145
	Szopka, D. (POL)	1	2300
	Sztercsco, S. (RUS)	0	2330
	Sztern, A. (AUS)	0	2190
	Szucs, G. (HUN)	0	2195
	Szucz, I. (YUG)	0	2195
	Szuhai, B. (HUN)	6	2205
	Szuhanek, R. (ROM)	13	2265
f	Szuk, B. (HUN)	21	2365
	Szulnis, M. (POL)	0	2065
	Szumilo, W. (POL)	0	2225
f	Szurovszky, E. (HUN)	9	2280
	Szydlowski, E. (POL)	0	2230
	Szymanski, A. (POL)	9	2250
m	Szymczak, Z. (POL)	11	2345
	Szyndler, A. (POL)	2	2210
m	Szypulski, A. (POL)	0	2390
	Szyszko, I. (POL)	0	2305
	Szyszko-Bohusz, A. (POL)	11	2235
	T		
	Tabakova, I. (BUL)	12	2080
m	Tabatadze, T. (GEO)	0	2425
	Tabdidishvili, M. (ISR)	0	2270
	Tabernig, B. (AUT)	9	2260
m	Tabor, J. (HUN)	0	2285
	Taborov, B. (UKR)	0	2380
	Tacu, V. (ROM)	0	2255
	Tadic, B. (YUG)	4	2230
f	Tadic, K. (YUG)	0	2235
f	Taeger, W. (GER)	7	2320
f	Taga, G. (ROM)	0	2310
f	Tagnon, N. (FRA)	36	2100
	Taha, M. (IRQ)	0	2365
	Taha, S. (IRQ)	0	2330
g	Taimanov, M. E. (RUS)	0	2500
	Tairi, F. (SWE)	0	2265
	Tajieva, LL. (KAZ)	0	2190
	Takac, Z. (CRO)	0	2265
f	Takacs, L. (HUN)	4	2305
	Takahashi, T. (JPN)	0	2205
f	Takemoto, N. (JPN)	12	2010
	Talanin, A. (RUS)	11	2260
	Taleb, M. (UAE)	0	2205
	Talic, E. (YUG)	0	2275
	Talla, V. (TCH)	0	2225
	Talos, J. (HUN)	0	2375
	Talpos, S. (ROM)	21	2095
	Tamai, R. (ITA)	0	2295
	Tamarkin, L. S. (USA)	10	2195
	Tamasi, A. (HUN)	0	2280
m	Tamin, U. D. (INA)	0	2140
	Tamm, U. (GER)	12	2240
	Tammela, K. (FIN)	1	2310
	Tammert, G. (GER)	0	2220
	Tan, Chengxuan (CHN)	1	2365
	Tan, Chin-Hoe (SIN)	0	2245
	Tan, J. (PHI)	0	2240
m	Tan, L.-A. (SIN)	0	2370
	Tan, O. (PHI)	7	2240
m	Tangborn, E. (USA)	0	2455
	Tanner, H. (SUI)	0	2255
	Tanner, P. (ARG)	36	2090
	Tansky, I. (RUS)	5	2390
	Tapaszto (VEN)	0	2240
	Tapper, L. (USA)	4	2255
	Tar, Cs. (HUN)	0	2295
	Tarasova, O. (RUS)	17	2140
	Tariq, A. (IRQ)	0	2305
	Tasic, B. (FRA)	5	2245
	Taskovits, I. (HUN)	10	2230
	Tataev, M. (RUS)	68	2395
m	Tatai, S. (ITA)	0	2440
	Tatar Kis, S. (HUN)	0	2235
	Tatari, E. A. (DEN)	0	2310
f	Tate, E. (USA)	11	2330
	Tatenhorst, V. (GER)	0	2250
	Tatisic, M. (YUG)	0	2230
	Tauber, M. (GER)	11	2215
	Tavadian, R. (ARM)	0	2295
	Tawakol, K. (GER)	10	2165
	Tawbeh, M. (LEB)	0	2160
	Tayeb, S. (UAE)	0	2205
f	Taylor, G. (CAN)	0	2335
	Taylor, S. (USA)	3	2230
m	Taylor, T. (USA)	0	2445
	Tazhieva, L. (KAZ)	5	2250
	Tchakov, P. (BUL)	11	2350
	Tchimino, J. (CHI)	0	2300
	Tchoubar, V. (UKR)	9	2395
m	Te, R. (RUS)	27	2240
f	Teaca, A. (ROM)	0	2300
m	Teasley, D. O. (USA)	0	2185
	Tebb, D. (ENG)	0	2290
	Teemae, U. (EST)	11	2080
	Tegzes, L. (HUN)	7	2260
f	Teichmann, E. O. (ENG)	0	2365
	Teixeira, R. S. (BRA)	0	2295
	Tejero, J. (ESP)	4	2300
	Telbis, G. (ROM)	0	2260
f	Telecki, I. (YUG)	0	2260
	Telfer, K. (AUS)	11	2245
	Telgeltia, B. (YUG)	0	2225
	Tellijohann, S. (GER)	22	2370
	Telman, V. (UKR)	0	2280
	Telo, S. (CUB)	0	2240
	Temanlis, Y. (ISR)	0	2285
m	Temirbaev, S. (KAZ)	37	2450
	Temkin, M. (USA)	10	2170
m	Tempone, M. (ARG)	22	2440
	Tengely, S. (HUN)	0	2210
	Tennant, S. (USA)	0	2235
	Tennstedt, A. (GER)	0	2320
	Tenyi, J. (HUN)	12	2200
	Teo, Kok Che (SIN)	0	2205
f	Teo, Kok-Siong (SIN)	0	2325
g	Teodorescu, M. (ROM)	4	2095
	Teodorescu, S. (ROM)	0	2235
	Teodoro, E. (CAN)	0	2215
	Teplicki, J. (RUS)	15	2345
	Tepper, F. (SVK)	0	2340
	Teran, I. (ESP)	9	2260
	Tereladze, S. (GEO)	0	2050
	Terentiev, S. (LAT)	0	2350
	Terentiev, V. G. (RUS)	6	2395
	Terhorst, J. (GER)	0	2220
	Termeulen, A. (NED)	0	2305
	Terraz, Ch. (SUI)	5	2205
f	Terreaux, G. (SUI)	0	2240
	Terrie, H. L. (USA)	0	2255
	Terterians, V. (RUS)	8	2380
f	Terzic, G. (YUG)	2	2315
	Terzic, I. (BIH)	0	2325
f	Terzic, S. (BIH)	3	2360
f	Tesic, D. (YUG)	5	2340
f	Tesic, M. (YUG)	0	2085
	Tesic, Z. (YUG)	0	2265
	Tesinszky, Gy. (HUN)	0	2215
m	Teske, H. (GER)	7	2475
	Teske, O. (GER)	0	2130
	Tesla, V. (YUG)	0	2300
	Testa, A. (ITA)	0	2210
	Teuton, F. L. (CAN)	0	2245
	Teyssou, D. (FRA)	0	2275
f	Thal, O. (GER)	0	2315
	Thaler, M. (SUI)	9	2140
	Thallinger, G. (AUT)	8	2195
	Theander, M. (DEN)	0	2025
	Thebault, B. (FRA)	0	2210
	Theissen, H. (GER)	8	2300
	Theodoulidis, Th. (GRE)	0	2205
m	Thesing, M. (GER)	20	2385
	Theuretzbacher, K. (AUT)	24	2245
	Thiede, L. (GER)	11	2280
f	Thiel, K. (GER)	0	2320
	Thiel, Th. (GER)	0	2265
	Thinius, M. (GER)	16	2300
f	Thinnsen, J. A. (USA)	3	2340
	Thipsay, A. M. (IND)	0	2230
m	Thipsay, B. S. (IND)	18	2175
m	Thipsay, P. M. (IND)	20	2465
	Thirunagalingam, M. (IND)	0	2240
	Thoeng, P. (BEL)	0	2260
	Thomas, H. (GER)	3	2240
m	Thomas, I. (ENG)	0	2365
	Thomsen, B. (FAI)	9	2090
	Thomsen, T. (FAI)	0	2180
f	Thomson, C. S. M. (SCO)	0	2335
	Thorhallsson, Gy. (ISD)	0	2295
m	Thorhallsson, Th. (ISD)	18	2440
f	Thorman, W. (GER)	0	2270
	Thorsson, O. (ISD)	0	2200
m	Thorsteins, K. (ISD)	17	2495
	Thorsteinsson, A. (ISD)	0	2250

	Name		
f	Thorsteinsson, Th. (ISD)	0	2300
	Thuesen, M. (DEN)	7	2280
m	Tibensky, R. (SVK)	0	2425
	Tiberkov, I. (BUL)	5	2300
	Tichelman, I. (NED)	0	2135
m	Tichy, V. (TCH)	0	2380
	Tichy-Racs, J. (HUN)	0	2215
	Tidoy, P. (PHI)	1	2305
	Tigau-Radu, S. (ROM)	0	2045
f	Tihonov, J. (BLA)	9	2220
	Tikkanen, K. (FIN)	4	2230
m	Tilak, Sh. S. (IND)	7	2355
	Tilmatine, A. (ALG)	6	2270
	Timanin, B. (UKR)	11	2345
	Timar, Zs. (HUN)	9	2235
	Timchenko, V. (RUS)	0	2335
g	Timman, J. H. (NED)	26	2620
f	Timmer, R. (NED)	7	2290
f	Timmerman, G. J. (NED)	6	2325
	Timmermans, I. (NED)	0	2295
g	Timoshchenko, G. A. (RUS)	24	2540
	Timoshchenko, V. I. (RUS)	0	2145
m	Timoshenko, G. (UKR)	26	2505
f	Timpel, K. (GER)	8	2300
	Tinkov, T. (BUL)	0	2310
	Tiomkin, T. (ISR)	14	2050
f	Tirabassi, M. (ITA)	0	2340
	Tirziu, M. (ROM)	0	2280
g	Tischbierek, R. (GER)	26	2480
	Tischendorf, M. (GER)	0	2225
f	Tischer, G. (GER)	0	2330
m	Tisdall, J. D. (NOR)	33	2465
	Titirisca, F. (ROM)	0	2260
	Titkos, J. (HUN)	0	2240
m	Titorenko, N. I. (RUS)	0	2100
m	Titov, G. (MOL)	13	2500
m	Titova-Boric, E. (UKR)	0	2260
f	Titz, H. (AUT)	18	2290
g	Tiviakov, S. (RUS)	59	2635
	Tjiam, D. (NED)	0	2290
	Tkachiev, V. (KAZ)	20	2455
	Tkebuchava, G. (GEO)	0	2375
	Tobyas, M. (TCH)	3	2285
f	Tocan, C. (ROM)	0	2305
	Tocchioni, D. (ITA)	9	2235
	Tockij, L. I. (RUS)	0	2390
	Toczek, G. (POL)	11	2280
	Todic, Z. (YUG)	0	2230
	Todirel, I. (ROM)	13	2050
	Todor, R. (ROM)	0	2305
g	Todorcevic, M. (YUG)	33	2480
	Todorov, Il. (BUL)	0	2345
	Todorov, Iv. (BUL)	0	2260
	Todorov, M. (BUL)	0	2295
m	Todorov, O. (BUL)	15	2380
	Todorov, T. (BUL)	6	2245
m	Todorovic, G. M. (YUG)	31	2475
f	Todorovic, G. N. (YUG)	14	2405
	Todorovic, J. (YUG)	6	2310
	Todorovic, M. (YUG)	3	2240
f	Todorovic, O. (YUG)	17	2105
	Todorovic, S. (YUG)	10	2020
	Todorovic, V. (YUG)	16	2050
	Todorovski, T. (YUG)	9	2205
	Todrovic, Z. (YUG)	3	2175
	Toh, T. (SIN)	9	2300
	Tokaji, N. Gy. (HUN)	0	2230
f	Tolgyi, V. (ROM)	0	2060
	Tolhuizen, L. (NED)	0	2270
f	Tolk, P. (NED)	0	2295
	Toll, J. (CUB)	0	2225
g	Tolnai, T. (HUN)	63	2490
	Toloza, P. (CHI)	11	2190
	Tolstikh, N. (RUS)	12	2380
f	Toma, D. (ROM)	0	2065
	Tomalczyk, T. (POL)	0	2210
	Tomasevic, S. (YUG)	0	2255
f	Tomasevic, T. (YUG)	20	2175
m	Tomaszewski, R. (POL)	0	2340
	Tomcsanyi, P. (HUN)	14	2290
f	Tomczak, R. (GER)	9	2350
f	Tomescu, V. (ROM)	33	2410
	Tomic, D. (GER)	8	2195
	Tomkins, K. (USA)	0	2350
	Tomovska, I. (BUL)	8	2075
m	Tompa, J. (HUN)	10	2445
m	Tonchev, M. (BUL)	0	2245
	Tondivar, B. (IRI)	9	2290
	Tong, Yuanming (CHN)	0	2355
	Tonkov, B. (BUL)	0	2335
	Tonoli, J. (BEL)	0	2245
f	Tonoli, W. (BEL)	0	2290
	Topakian, R. (AUT)	0	2280
g	Topalov, V. (BUL)	38	2650
	Topalovic, Z. (CRO)	0	2395
f	Tornai, I. (HUN)	12	2245
f	Tornblom, N. (SWE)	0	2255
	Toro, F. (CHI)	14	2270
	Torok, A. (HUN)	0	2230
	Torok, J. (HUN)	18	2290
g	Torre, E. (PHI)	27	2515
	Torrecillas, A. (ESP)	0	2350
	Torres Auro, A. (ARG)	0	2210
	Torres Flores, R. (MEX)	0	2145
	Torres, A. J. (CUB)	0	2220
	Torres, J. (USA)	37	2315
f	Torres, L. J. (PUR)	0	2310
	Tortarolo, M. (ITA)	6	2250
m	Toshkov, T. (BUL)	0	2455
m	Tosic, M. (YUG)	51	2465
	Tossutti, J. C. (ARG)	0	2235
	Totev, T. (BUL)	0	2220
	Toth G., G. (HUN)	0	2285
	Toth, A. (HUN)	0	2075
m	Toth, B. (ITA)	0	2390
f	Toth, Ch. E. (BRA)	13	2410
	Toth, Cs. (HUN)	0	2305
	Toth, I. (HUN)	0	2220
	Toth, J. (HUN)	10	2240
	Toth, Laszlo (HUN)	11	2275
	Toth, Laszlo (HUN)	0	2225
	Toth, Pal (HUN)	1	2130
	Toth, Pe. (BRA)	0	2230
	Totsky, L. (RUS)	34	2430
	Toulzac, P.-Y. (FRA)	9	2325
	Toure, A. (MLI)	0	2195
	Tourneur, J.-F. (FRA)	9	2250
	Touzane, O. (FRA)	34	2330
f	Tovillas, D. R. (ARG)	7	2335
f	Tozer, R. (ENG)	0	2300
f	Trabattoni, F. (ITA)	0	2335
m	Trabert, B. (GER)	20	2200
	Trajcevic, G. (YUG)	0	2105
	Trajkoski, S. (YUG)	24	2280
	Trajkovic, M. (YUG)	0	2265
	Trajkovic, P. (YUG)	0	2255
	Trajkovski, M. (YUG)	16	2235
	Tran, M. (VIE)	0	2005
m	Trapl, J. (TCH)	0	2375
f	Tratar, M. (SLO)	27	2290
f	Tratatovici, M. (ISR)	5	2245
	Traut, S. (GER)	0	2035
	Trauth, M. (GER)	11	2260
	Travenec, I. (SVK)	0	2235
	Travnicek, P. (TCH)	0	2270
	Treffert, P. (GER)	4	2290
	Trefny, V. (TCH)	0	2220
	Tregubov, A. (RUS)	0	2285
m	Tregubov, P. V. (RUS)	64	2475
m	Trepp, M. (SUI)	0	2375
f	Treppner, G. (GER)	6	2310
	Trettin, U. (GER)	0	2280
	Trevisani, B. (ITA)	0	2320
f	Treybal, D. (TCH)	0	2320
f	Trichkov, V. (BUL)	7	2395
	Trickovic, B. (YUG)	5	2280
	Trifan, V. (ROM)	0	2180
	Trifonas, S. (GRE)	9	2260
	Trifunov, D. (BUL)	0	2420
	Trifunov, M. (YUG)	0	2250
	Trifunovic, A. (ENG)	23	2195
f	Trifunovic, M. (YUG)	0	2330
	Trigueros, G. (CRC)	18	2315
f	Trikaliotis, G. (GRE)	17	2270
f	Trincado, J. F. (ARG)	10	2315
m	Trindade, S. (BRA)	23	2345
g	Tringov, G. P. (BUL)	80	2450
f	Trisa-Ard, N. (THA)	0	2265
	Trisic, A. (GER)	3	2185
	Trkaljanov, V. (YUG)	0	2270
	Trkulja, G. (YUG)	0	2265
	Trochimczuk, R. (POL)	0	2255
	Troeger, P. (GER)	0	2225
m	Trois, F. R. T. (BRA)	2	2350
	Trojan, L. (TCH)	0	2250
f	Troltenier, D. (GER)	0	2290
	Trombik, K. (TCH)	0	2215
	Trommsdorf, F. (FRA)	16	2195
	Trosic, G. (YUG)	3	2035
f	Troyke, Ch. (GER)	34	2395
	Trpkovic, M. (YUG)	4	2110
	Truelson, N. W. (USA)	11	2245
	Trujillo, I. (ESP)	27	2165
	Trumic, E. (YUG)	0	2235
f	Truong, H. (USA)	0	2335
f	Truta, S. (SLO)	26	2270
	Trylski, A. (POL)	12	2230
	Trzaska, P. (GER)	4	2245
	Tsang, H. (ENG)	0	2205
	Tsarev, V. (RUS)	0	2300
	Tsarouhas, K. (GRE)	3	2275
	Tscharotschkin, M. (GER)	5	2180
m	Tseitlin, Ma. D. (ISR)	26	2430
g	Tseitlin, Mi. S. (RUS)	29	2430
	Tseleng, E. (BOT)	0	2210
	Tsemekhman, V. (USA)	3	2350
m	Tsesarsky, I. (ISR)	5	2450
	Tsevremes, I. (GRE)	0	2175
	Tsifanskaya, L. A. (ISR)	29	2205
m	Tsiganova, M. (EST)	50	2300
	Tsiolakidis, A. (GRE)	2	2375
f	Tsomis, D. (GRE)	11	2295
f	Tsorbatzoglou, Th. (GRE)	10	2290
f	Tsuboi, E. K. (BRA)	15	2325
	Tsvetkov, G. (BUL)	0	2270
	Tsvetkov, I. (BUL)	0	2320
m	Tu, H. Th. (VIE)	9	2430
	Tuchenhagen, A. (GER)	0	2195
	Tucker, A. (ENG)	4	2215
	Tudorache, R. (ROM)	19	2270
	Tufa, M. (ROM)	11	2285
	Tugui, A. (ROM)	0	2210
g	Tukmakov, V. B. (UKR)	56	2600
	Tun, A. (RUS)	0	2285
m	Tunik, G. (RUS)	72	2490
	Tuomala, T. (FIN)	1	2215
	Turauskiene, R. (LTU)	0	2220
	Turcan, M. (TCH)	12	2210
	Turci, S. (ITA)	0	2230
	Turczynowicz, J. (POL)	0	2115
	Turebaeva, A. (KAZ)	17	2065
	Turgut, T. (TUR)	2	2250
	Turian, H. (AUT)	4	2265
	Turikov, V. (RUS)	4	2290
f	Turner, M. (ENG)	14	2400
	Turudic, N. (YUG)	0	2285
f	Turunen, E. O. (FIN)	0	2240
	Turzo, A. (HUN)	29	2230
	Tust, D. (POL)	13	2100
	Tuteja, A. (IND)	0	2285
m	Tverskaya, J. (USA)	0	2090
f	Twardon, M. (POL)	10	2370
	Tyehimba, B. (USA)	0	2235

	Name	Games	Rating
	Tyni, J.-P. (FIN)	4	2265
m	Typek, K. (POL)	9	2410
	Tyrant, P. (FRA)	0	2210
	Tyrtania, M. (GER)	4	2240
	Tyszkiewicz, Z. (POL)	0	2265
	Tzermiadianos, A. (GRE)	13	2315
f	Tzoumbas, A. (GRE)	6	2215

U

	Name	Games	Rating
	Ubach, M. (ESP)	9	2295
	Ubezio, M. (ITA)	10	2200
g	Ubilava, E. (GEO)	42	2530
	Uddenfeldt, D. (SWE)	0	2385
	Udvari, T. (HUN)	0	2240
	Ueter, H.-D. (GER)	0	2265
	Ueti, S. (BRA)	0	2290
	Ugalde, R. (CRC)	9	2225
g	Uhlmann, W. (GER)	34	2510
	Uhmann, J. (TCH)	0	2220
	Ujhazi, D. (YUG)	23	2040
f	Ujhazi, I. (YUG)	17	2275
	Ujma, J. (POL)	1	2200
	Ulak, S. (POL)	5	2220
g	Ulibin, M. (RUS)	53	2560
	Ulloa, L. (CHI)	14	2115
	Ullrich, F.-R. (GER)	0	2255
	Ulms, S. (GER)	14	2160
f	Ulrichsen, J. H. (NOR)	0	2290
	Ulucan, T. (TUR)	0	2185
m	Umanskaya, I. (RUS)	56	2305
	Umanski, V. (RUS)	0	2265
	Umansky, M. (RUS)	0	2445
	Umezinwa, G. (USA)	18	2290
	Umnov, K. (RUS)	0	2360
	Unding, H. (PHI)	0	2305
	Unger, M. (GER)	0	2205
f	Ungur, O. (ROM)	0	2325
	Ungure, L. (LAT)	3	2145
m	Ungureanu, E. (ROM)	8	2305
	Unni, C. S. (IND)	6	2235
m	Unni, V. (IND)	11	2120
	Unrath, H. (GER)	0	2320
	Unterfrauner, A. (ITA)	0	2270
	Unzicker, F. (GER)	0	2335
g	Unzicker, W. (GER)	7	2450
	Uogele, A. (LTU)	11	2285
	Upadhayay, R. (IND)	0	2195
	Upliger, M. (GER)	0	2245
	Upton, I. J. (ENG)	0	2245
f	Upton, T. J. (SCO)	4	2245
	Uralbaev, A. (KAZ)	14	2245
m	Urban, J. (GER)	43	2340
m	Urban, K. (POL)	30	2440
	Urban, M. (GER)	12	2210
	Urban, R. (GER)	9	2250
	Urbaneja, J. C. (VEN)	0	2225
	Urbina, J. (COL)	0	2205
g	Urday, H. (PER)	33	2455
f	Urosevic, R. (YUG)	3	2245
	Urosevic, Z. (YUG)	0	2300
	Ursuleac, V. (ROM)	10	2140
m	Urzica, A. (ROM)	0	2370
	Urzica-Carmaciu, L. (ROM)	0	2025
	Usachiy, V. (UKR)	3	2285
	Usachyi, M. (UKR)	4	2305
	Ushakova, I. (RUS)	12	2205
m	Uskova, F. (KAZ)	5	2260
	Usov, A. (RUS)	0	2340
	Utemov, V. (RUS)	14	2410
	Utman, C. (CHI)	20	2110
	Uzuner, C. T. (TUR)	0	2115

V

	Name	Games	Rating
f	Vachev, V. (BUL)	0	2265
	Vaczi, I. (HUN)	0	2265
g	Vadasz, L. (HUN)	60	2400
	Vadla, Z. (CRO)	8	2255
	Vagalinski, S. (BUL)	0	2270
g	Vaganian, R. A. (ARM)	42	2615
	Vagapov, A. (RUS)	14	2195
	Vager, B. (RUS)	0	2280
m	Vaidya, A. B. (IND)	33	2300
	Vainerman, I. (UKR)	0	2400
	Vainshtein, V. (ISR)	11	2375
m	Vaisman, V. (FRA)	9	2390
g	Vaisser, A. (FRA)	38	2580
	Vajda, A. (ROM)	41	2345
	Vajda, L. (ROM)	15	2135
f	Vajda, S. (ROM)	34	2145
	Vajdic, N. (YUG)	0	2215
m	Vakhidov, T. (UZB)	28	2470
	Vakulienko, V. (BLA)	9	2330
f	Valdes, L. E. (CUB)	9	2315
f	Valdes, M. (POR)	0	2125
f	Valdes-Castillo, A. (CUB)	0	2225
	Valdettaro, N. (ITA)	0	2230
f	Valdivia, M. (CUB)	0	2265
	Valensi, B. (TUR)	0	2200
	Valenti, G. (ITA)	14	2260
	Valenti, R. (FRA)	0	2260
f	Valerga, D. (ARG)	38	2365
	Valet, R. (GER)	0	2190
f	Valiente R, C. (PAR)	23	2375
	Valis, J. (HUN)	0	2205
m	Valkesalmi, K. (FIN)	6	2345
	Valle, A. (BRA)	1	2220
f	Vallifuoco, Gia. (ITA)	0	2380
	Vallifuoco, Gio. (ITA)	0	2260
m	Valvo, M. J. (USA)	11	2365
	Vamos, V. (HUN)	9	2190
	Van Amerongen, M. (NED)	5	2070
f	Van Baarle, J. C. (NED)	0	2325
	Van Beers, E. (BEL)	0	2175
f	Van Buskirk, Ch. (USA)	3	2285
	Van De Berkmortel, Th. (NED)	0	2295
	Van De Bourry, D. (BEL)	0	2215
	Van De Mortel, J. (NED)	4	2300
f	Van De Oudeweetering, A. (NED)	7	2335
	Van De Plassche, B. (NED)	0	2275
	Van Den Berg, J. (NED)	0	2230
	Van Den Broeck, H. (BEL)	0	2230
f	Van Der Griendt, J. W. (NED)	0	2400
	Van Der Linde, M. (NED)	0	2260
g	Van Der Mije, A. (NED)	0	2180
	Van Der Poel, H. (NED)	0	2365
g	Van Der Sterren, P. (NED)	33	2525
	Van Der Veen, H. (GER)	0	2225
	Van Der Vorm, T. (NED)	0	2370
	Van Der Weide, P. (NED)	0	2235
	Van Der Weij, A. (NED)	0	2305
m	Van Der Werf, M. (NED)	21	2405
g	Van Der Wiel, J. T. H. (NED)	40	2565
	Van Der Wijk, W. (NED)	0	2210
	Van Dijk, B. (NED)	6	2265
	Van Doeland, J. (NED)	0	2290
	Van Dongen, P. (FRA)	11	2185
	Van Egmond, R. M. (NED)	0	2315
	Van Elst, M. (NED)	0	2020
	Van Gaalen, B. (NED)	0	2390
m	Van Geet, D. D. (NED)	7	2320
f	Van Gisbergen, S. (NED)	9	2385
	Van Hasselt, F. (HKG)	0	2210
	Van Heirzeele, D. (BEL)	0	2230
	Van Herck, M. (BEL)	0	2210
	Van Hoolandt, P. (BEL)	0	2110
	Van Houtte, Th. (BEL)	0	2220
f	Van Laatum, G. (NED)	9	2400
	Van Leeuwen, E. (BEL)	0	2075
m	Van Mil, J. A. J. (NED)	34	2435
f	Van Parreren, H. (NED)	16	2175
	Van Riemsdijk, D. D. (BRA)	0	2240
m	Van Riemsdijk, H. C. (BRA)	42	2405
	Van Schaardenburg, M. (NED)	8	2285
m	Van Scheltinga, Th. D. (NED)	0	2300
	Van Steenis, J. (NED)	0	2280
f	Van Tilbury, C. (ISV)	1	2290
	Van Voorthuijsen, P. W. (NED)	0	2290
g	Van Wely, L. (NED)	79	2585
	Van, Z. (NED)	9	2135
	Vancini, E. (ITA)	3	2300
	Vancsura, V. (HUN)	1	2195
	Vancsura, Z. (HUN)	0	2240
	Vanczak, A. (HUN)	1	2230
f	Vanderwaeren, S. (BEL)	0	2300
	Vandevoort (BEL)	10	2070
	Vandevoort, P. (BEL)	0	2310
	Vandoros, D. (GRE)	7	2270
f	Vandrey, W. (GER)	11	2305
	Vanecek, J. (TCH)	0	2030
	Vanek, P. (TCH)	0	2220
m	Vanheste, J. (NED)	0	2410
	Vaniuschkina, N. (UKR)	0	2120
	Vanjshkina, N. (UKR)	0	2125
	Vanka, M. (TCH)	0	2260
	Varaljai, A. (HUN)	0	2270
	Varas, C. (CHI)	0	2210
m	Varasdy, I. (HUN)	1	2380
m	Varavin, V. (RUS)	8	2465
	Varbanov, T. (BUL)	0	2240
	Varbanov, V. (BUL)	0	2150
	Varberg, K. (DEN)	0	2260
	Vardhana, T. K. (IND)	0	2220
	Vardi, Sh. (ISR)	0	2020
f	Vareille, F. (FRA)	0	2315
	Varejcko, J. (TCH)	0	2300
	Varga, K. (HUN)	0	2305
	Varga, L. (HUN)	0	2160
f	Varga, M. (ARG)	0	2275
	Varga, P. (HUN)	22	2320
	Varga, S. (HUN)	16	2250
	Varga, Za. (HUN)	1	2275
m	Varga, Zo. (HUN)	58	2475
	Vargas, A. (CRC)	0	2220
f	Vargic, D. (CRO)	0	2290
	Vargyas, Z. (HUN)	9	2275
	Varhegyi, M. (HUN)	17	2210
	Varlamov, V. (RUS)	0	2305
	Varlan, H. (ROM)	0	2255
	Varley, P. (WLS)	0	2225
f	Varnusz, E. (HUN)	0	2345
	Vas, P. (HUN)	0	2195
	Vasallo, M. (ARG)	5	2325
	Vasconcellos, J. (FRA)	9	2210
	Vasicek, M. (TCH)	0	2135
f	Vasiesu, D. (ROM)	0	2330
	Vasilchenko, O. (RUS)	20	2425
	Vasile, B. (ROM)	0	2280
f	Vasile, C. (ROM)	0	2270
m	Vasilescu, L. (ROM)	13	2400
	Vasilev, M. (BUL)	3	2115
	Vasilev, N. (BUL)	0	2305
	Vasilev, V. (BUL)	0	2255
f	Vasilevich, T. (UKR)	14	2250
	Vasiliev, R. N. (RUS)	4	2380
	Vasiliev, V. (RUS)	4	2265
	Vasiljevic, B. (YUG)	17	2280
m	Vasiljevic, D. (YUG)	13	2405
	Vasilyev, M. (UKR)	17	2335
g	Vasiukov, E. (RUS)	0	2495

	Name		
f	Vasovski, N. (YUG)	16	2290
	Vasquez, F. (ESP)	0	2250
m	Vasquez, R. (CHI)	36	2500
f	Vasta, E. (ARG)	24	2400
	Vasudevan, S. (IND)	0	2270
m	Vatnikov, J. E. (RUS)	8	2425
f	Vatter, H.-J. (GER)	10	2320
m	Vaulin, A. (RUS)	71	2500
	Vavpetic, V. (SLO)	3	2210
	Vavpotic-Kosanski, T. (SLO)	0	2065
	Vavra, P. (TCH)	0	2350
	Vavruska, A. (TCH)	0	2280
	Vavruska, D. (TCH)	0	2265
	Vaysman, A. (UKR)	0	2355
	Vazquez Toledo, E. (MEX)	10	2175
f	Veach, J. (USA)	0	2295
f	Vebic, K. (YUG)	5	2240
	Vechet, S. (TCH)	0	2225
	Vedder, H. (NED)	14	2385
	Veerman, J. (NED)	8	2230
	Vega Holm, F. (ESP)	12	2385
	Vega, J. (MEX)	2	2370
m	Vegh, E. (HUN)	29	2380
m	Vehi Bach, V. M. (ESP)	14	2380
	Vehreschild, A. (GER)	9	2120
f	Veinger, I. (ISR)	22	2340
m	Veingold, A. (EST)	37	2465
	Vekshenkov, N. (RUS)	2	2375
	Velandia, N. (COL)	0	2245
	Velasco Sotomayor, G. (MEX)	0	2015
	Velasquez, C. (CHI)	25	2315
	Velcev, N. (BUL)	3	2300
	Velcheva, M. (BUL)	32	2120
	Velea, P. (ROM)	0	2285
m	Velez, N. (CUB)	10	2270
m	Velicka, P. (TCH)	5	2420
	Velickovic, Lj. (YUG)	0	2270
m	Velickovic, S. (YUG)	15	2375
	Velickovic, Z. (SLO)	0	2285
	Velickovski, M. (YUG)	20	2150
m	Velikhanli, F. (AZE)	11	2320
g	Velikov, P. (BUL)	17	2460
g	Velimirovic, D. (YUG)	30	2505
	Veliova, I. (YUG)	11	2095
	Velitshko, J. (EST)	0	2250
	Veljkovic, M. (YUG)	11	2280
m	Velvart, P. (HUN)	14	2155
f	Vencl, R. (YUG)	0	2300
f	Venegas Ocampo, E. N. (MEX)	0	2015
	Venkata Ramana, J. (IND)	1	2255
	Venkataramanan, T. S. (IND)	0	2285
	Ventura, G. (ITA)	9	2030
f	Vepkhvishvili, V. (GEO)	0	2330
g	Vera, R. (CUB)	22	2525
	Verat, L. (FRA)	17	2315
	Verdihanov, V. A. (AZE)	18	2365
	Verdonk, R. (NED)	16	2265
m	Verduga, D. (MEX)	10	2355
	Vere, J. (ENG)	0	2185
	Veremeichik, V. (BLA)	4	2335
	Veres, I. (HUN)	4	2060
	Veres, R. (SVK)	0	2270
	Veresagin, J. (RUS)	5	2360
	Verner, A. (RUS)	0	2385
	Vernersson, P. (SWE)	0	2310
g	Veroci, Zs. (HUN)	25	2325
	Verrascina, R. (ITA)	1	2225
	Vertkin, S. (RUS)	0	2295
f	Verus, B. (YUG)	0	2150
	Vescovi, G. (BRA)	17	2340
m	Veselovsky, S. (RUS)	32	2440
	Veselsky, J. (SVK)	0	2270
	Vesin, J.-R. (FRA)	0	2295
	Vesovski, J. (YUG)	0	2280
f	Vetemaa, Y. (EST)	0	2385
	Vetrovsky, M. (TCH)	0	2240
	Veverita, D. (ROM)	0	2285
	Vez, D. R. (POR)	0	2345
	Vezzani, S. (ITA)	0	2230
f	Vezzosi, P. (ITA)	15	2280
	Vial, P. (FRA)	0	2280
	Vianin, P. (SUI)	0	2180
	Vickery, J. (ENG)	0	2260
	Vida, J. (SLO)	9	2040
	Vidal, J. R. (ARG)	34	2305
	Vidal, T. (CHI)	0	2380
f	Vidarsson, J. G. (ISD)	0	2325
m	Videki, S. (HUN)	50	2385
	Videkovic, M. (CRO)	12	2145
	Vidoniak, N. (UKR)	21	2225
	Vidoniak, R. (UKR)	11	2360
	Vieira, I. A. G. (BRA)	0	2285
	Vigfusson, Th. (ISD)	0	2260
m	Vigh, B. (HUN)	10	2410
	Vigus, J. (ENG)	7	2095
	Vijayakumar, G. (IND)	1	2270
	Vijila, C. (ROM)	21	2255
	Viksni, I. (RUS)	0	2285
	Vila, A. (ESP)	2	2315
	Viland, B. (CRO)	0	2230
	Vilar, M. (ESP)	2	2135
	Vilas Boas, L. (POR)	0	2005
f	Vilaseco, F. (CUB)	0	2325
	Vilceanu, M. (ROM)	0	2215
m	Vilela, J. L. (CUB)	13	2415
	Villabrille, R. (ARG)	0	2210
	Villalba, H. (ARG)	0	2220
	Villarreal, H. (ARG)	16	2265
m	Villarreal, J. (MEX)	0	2390
f	Villavicencio, A. (ESP)	0	2360
	Villegas, S. (ARG)	0	2030
m	Villeneuve, A. (FRA)	0	2340
	Villing, D. (GER)	0	2280
	Vincent, S. (FRA)	0	2270
f	Vincze, I. (HUN)	8	2350
	Viner, Ph. (AUS)	2	2210
m	Vinje-Gulbrandsen, A. (NOR)	0	2335
	Vinke, D. (GER)	0	2275
	Vinogradov, O. (RUS)	0	2210
	Viot, A. (FRA)	7	2185
	Visek, P. (TCH)	0	2355
f	Visier Segovia, F. (ESP)	3	2320
	Viskic, P. (CRO)	6	2235
f	Visser, Y. (NED)	8	2335
	Vistinietzki, I. (ISR)	0	2290
	Viswanathan, V. N. (IND)	0	2245
	Vitalijic, N. (YUG)	0	2245
	Vitaljic, N. (CRO)	8	2220
	Vitanova, R. (BUL)	0	2075
	Vitic, I. (CRO)	0	2230
m	Vitolinsh, A. (LAT)	0	2435
	Vitor, A. (POR)	0	2170
m	Vizantidis, L. (GRE)	0	2220
m	Vlad, D. (ROM)	34	2365
m	Vladimirov, B. T. (RUS)	0	2405
g	Vladimirov, E. (KAZ)	7	2585
	Vlahos, A. (GRE)	7	2055
	Vlahov, D. (CRO)	0	2275
	Vlahovic, B. (YUG)	0	2235
	Vlahovic, S. (YUG)	4	2230
	Vlajkovic, S. (YUG)	0	2245
	Vlam, H. (NED)	0	2235
f	Vlaovic, Dj. (YUG)	0	2300
	Vlasak, R. (AUT)	0	2220
f	Vlasic, N. (CRO)	0	2315
	Vlasov, I. (RUS)	0	2345
	Vlassis, P. (GRE)	10	2185
	Vlassov, N. (RUS)	16	2380
f	Vlatkovic, S. (YUG)	4	2340
	Voboril, P. (TCH)	0	2225
	Vodep, O. (AUT)	4	2230
	Vodicka, V. (TCH)	2	2355
	Vodopija, G. (CRO)	0	2270
f	Voekler, B. (GER)	25	2335
f	Vogel, J. (NED)	0	2300
f	Vogel, R. (GER)	13	2335
	Vogler, T. (GER)	0	2295
g	Vogt, L. (GER)	25	2495
	Voiculescu, P. (ROM)	0	2260
	Voigt, M. (GER)	0	2305
	Voinescu, G. (ROM)	0	2040
g	Voiska, M. (BUL)	39	2345
	Voitsekhovsky, S. (RUS)	14	2385
	Vojan, I. (HUN)	0	2235
	Vojinovic, G. (YUG)	6	2335
m	Vokac, M. (TCH)	19	2465
	Vokoun, J. (TCH)	0	2265
m	Volke, K. (GER)	32	2470
	Volkmann, F. (AUT)	8	2320
	Volkmer, A. (GER)	0	2265
	Volkov, N. (RUS)	77	2145
	Volman, H. (ISR)	1	2235
m	Vologyin, V. (RUS)	13	2375
m	Voloshin, L. (RUS)	28	2410
	Voloshin, V. (RUS)	0	2360
	Volosin, V. (RUS)	13	2285
f	Volovich, A. A. (USA)	0	2390
	Voltolini, G. (ITA)	0	2325
	Volzhin, A. (RUS)	20	2410
	Vombek, D. (SLO)	0	2270
	Von Allmen, A. (SUI)	0	2275
	Von Alvensleben, W. (GER)	6	2235
	Von Buelow, G. (GER)	11	2240
f	Von Der Weth, C. M. (GER)	0	2110
	Von Gleich, A. (GER)	22	2315
	Von Herman, U. (GER)	7	2280
	Vonthron, H. (GER)	7	2355
	Vooremaa, A. (EST)	8	2320
	Voormans, J. (NED)	0	2230
	Voronov, V. (RUS)	0	2290
m	Voronova, T. (LAT)	25	2240
	Vorontsov, N. (RUS)	32	2355
m	Vorotnikov, V. V. (RUS)	19	2465
f	Voscilla, A. (CRO)	0	2320
	Voskanian, V. (RUS)	8	2275
	Vospernik, A. (SLO)	9	2185
	Vospernik, M. (SLO)	2	2120
	Voss, I. (GER)	0	2250
	Vosselman, J. (NED)	0	2305
m	Votava, J. (TCH)	19	2425
f	Votruba, P. (TCH)	9	2370
	Vouldis, A. (GRE)	15	2285
	Vovinkina, N. (BLA)	13	2090
f	Vragoteris, A. (GRE)	19	2290
	Vrana, F. (TCH)	0	2250
m	Vranesic, Z. (CAN)	0	2315
f	Vratonjic, S. (YUG)	28	2400
	Vrbata, Z. (TCH)	0	2325
h	Vreeken, C. (NED)	0	2135
	Vrekalo, M. (CRO)	0	2150
	Vreljanski, D. (YUG)	1	2275
	Vrona, M. (HUN)	6	2260
	Vucenovic, D. (SUI)	0	2285
m	Vucic, M. (USA)	35	2425
	Vucicevic, M. (YUG)	0	2355
f	Vucinic, P. (YUG)	1	2325
	Vuckovic, A. (GER)	11	2300
f	Vujacic, B. (YUG)	0	2315
m	Vujadinovic, G. (YUG)	56	2335
m	Vujakovic, B. (CRO)	0	2375
	Vujanovic, B. (YUG)	0	2225
	Vujanovic, T. (YUG)	0	2080
	Vujatovic, R. (ENG)	0	2270
	Vuji, A. (ALB)	0	2135
	Vujic, B. (YUG)	0	2205

	Name		
	Vujic-Katanic, B. (YUG)	9	2190
f	Vujicic, M. (YUG)	0	2340
	Vujmilovic, N. (YUG)	0	2205
	Vujosevic, G. (YUG)	0	2215
m	Vujosevic, S. (CAN)	0	2075
m	Vujosevic, V. (YUG)	47	2355
m	Vujovic, M. (YUG)	10	2280
	Vujovic, P. (YUG)	0	2225
	Vukajlovic, B. (YUG)	0	2265
	Vukanovic, S. (YUG)	16	2355
	Vukelic, Dj. (YUG)	0	2295
	Vukelic, T. (YUG)	0	2360
	Vukic, A. (YUG)	0	2220
g	Vukic, M. I. (YUG)	38	2460
	Vukic, R. (YUG)	0	2310
f	Vukoje, V. (CRO)	0	2290
	Vukosavljevic, Lj. (YUG)	0	2195
f	Vukovic, I. (CRO)	0	2290
	Vukovic, M. (YUG)	0	2260
	Vukovic, V. (YUG)	0	2260
m	Vukovic, Zd. (YUG)	32	2440
	Vukovic, Ze. (CRO)	2	2050
m	Vuksanovic, S. (YUG)	38	2260
	Vul, A. E. (RUS)	27	2375
	Vuletic, P. (YUG)	0	2265
f	Vulevic, V. (SUI)	0	2325
	Vulfson, V. (RUS)	14	2430
	Vulicevic, B. (YUG)	3	2295
	Vulicevic, N. (YUG)	47	2270
	Vulovic, D. (YUG)	0	2030
	Vulovic, R. (YUG)	0	2235
f	Vuruna, M. (YUG)	0	2255
	Vutov, M. M. (BUL)	6	2250
	Vybiral, Z. (TCH)	0	2255
	Vydeslaver, A. (ISR)	15	2290
	Vykydal, F. (TCH)	0	2235
	Vysoglad, P. (TCH)	0	2150
g	Vyzmanavin, A. (RUS)	51	2605
	W		
	Waagener, U. (GER)	0	2290
f	Wach, M. (AUT)	24	2345
	Wach, S. (POL)	3	2260
f	Wachinger, G. (GER)	0	2260
	Wacker, P. (GER)	2	2300
	Wada, R. D. (USA)	0	2280
m	Wade, R. G. (ENG)	0	2290
	Wademark, H. (SWE)	0	2210
	Wademark, O. (SWE)	0	2270
	Wagenmakers, E.-J. (NED)	0	2220
	Wagh, G. M. (IND)	8	2205
f	Wagman, S. (USA)	17	2225
	Wagner, A. (GER)	9	2340
f	Wagner, C. (FRA)	9	2315
f	Wagner, H. (GER)	4	2275
m	Wagner-Michel, A. (GER)	2	2180
g	Wahls, M. (GER)	44	2480
	Waitzkin, J. (USA)	49	2370
	Wajih, N. (IND)	0	2295
	Walach, M. (POL)	24	2305
	Waldhorn, T. (SUI)	0	2280
	Waldmann, H. J. (GER)	0	2395
f	Waldmann, I. (HUN)	1	2295
	Walek, M. (TCH)	12	2320
	Walicki, D. (ARG)	0	2285
	Walid, R. M. (YEM)	0	2205
	Walker, B. (CAN)	0	2265
f	Walker, D. (ENG)	0	2305
	Walker, M. (ENG)	1	2230
	Walkusz, Ma. (POL)	41	2005
	Walkusz, Mi. (POL)	24	2215
	Walkusz, W. (POL)	16	2230
	Wall, G. (ENG)	8	2295
	Wall, T. (ENG)	0	2230
	Wallace, J. P. (AUS)	6	2285
f	Waller, H. (AUT)	16	2170
	Wallinger, M. (GER)	5	2200
	Wallner, A. (AUT)	0	2215
	Wallner, W. (AUT)	11	2205
	Wallyn, A. (FRA)	10	2235
	Walsh, C. (WLS)	9	2180
	Walter, G. (AUT)	0	2220
	Walter, K. (GER)	13	2105
	Walther, C. (GER)	9	2260
	Walther, G. (GER)	0	2275
	Walti, R. (SUI)	0	2275
	Walton, J. S. (ENG)	12	2260
f	Wang, Le (CHN)	0	2245
f	Wang, Miao (CHN)	0	2185
g	Wang, Pi (CHN)	0	2335
	Wang, Ya (CHN)	0	2055
m	Wang, Zili (CHN)	0	2515
	Waniek, A. (POL)	3	2090
	Wanke, R. (GER)	0	2205
m	Ward, Ch. (ENG)	29	2460
	Warren, A. (ENG)	2	2005
	Warwaszynski, Z. (POL)	0	2270
	Wasmuth, M. (GER)	0	2225
	Wasnetsky, U. (GER)	0	2090
m	Watanabe, R. (BRA)	0	2380
	Waters, M. (IRL)	8	2110
	Watesnik, M. (GER)	9	2085
m	Watson, J. L. (USA)	12	2390
g	Watson, W. N. (ENG)	5	2550
f	Watzka, H. (AUT)	6	2320
	Wauters, A. (FRA)	1	2210
	Wavresky, P. (FRA)	8	2150
	Wawrowski, Z. (POL)	0	2235
	Waxman, J. L. (USA)	0	2235
	Wayne, B. (CAN)	0	2215
	Webb, L. (ENG)	0	2260
m	Webb, S. (ENG)	0	2420
	Weber, L. (LUX)	0	2205
f	Weber, M. (GER)	4	2290
	Weber, P. (GER)	0	2205
f	Weber, S. (GER)	6	2290
	Weber, U. (GER)	0	2320
m	Webster, A. (ENG)	29	2410
m	Wedberg, T. (SWE)	5	2460
	Weeks, M. (USA)	0	2235
m	Weemaes, R. (BEL)	3	2335
	Wegener, D. (GER)	50	2295
	Wegerer, F. (AUT)	26	2305
	Weglarz, L. (POL)	0	2360
m	Wegner, H. (GER)	19	2390
f	Wehmeier, S. (GER)	8	2310
	Weide, J. (NED)	0	2340
	Weidemann, Ch. (GER)	9	2195
f	Weidemann, J. (GER)	8	2285
	Weider, D. (POL)	0	2220
	Weierman, A. (GER)	5	2275
	Weigel, H. (GER)	10	2290
f	Weigel, R. (GER)	0	2245
	Weil, V. (GER)	0	2240
	Weiler, D. (GER)	0	2225
	Weill, R. (FRA)	9	2260
f	Weinberger, T. (USA)	6	2235
f	Weindl, A. (GER)	14	2335
	Weiner, O. (GER)	0	2245
	Weinstock, D. (USA)	0	2280
	Weinstock, S. (USA)	10	2245
f	Weinzettl, E. (AUT)	0	2330
	Weis, R. (GER)	7	2285
	Weisbuch, U. (ISR)	9	2210
	Weischede, Th. (GER)	1	2335
	Weiss, Ch. (AUT)	5	2225
	Weiss, M. (USA)	0	2250
	Weiss, R. (GER)	0	2275
	Weiss, U. (AUT)	0	2040
	Weiss-Nowak, Ch. (GER)	0	2245
	Weisse, M. (GER)	0	2230
	Weiszhaupt, R. (GER)	13	2145
	Weitzer, S. (GER)	11	2240
f	Weldon, Ch. (USA)	10	2305
m	Welin, Th. (SWE)	0	2375
m	Welling, G. (NED)	5	2400
m	Wells, P. K. (ENG)	60	2455
	Welz, P. (GER)	11	2325
	Welz, Th. (GER)	1	2330
	Wendel, S. (GER)	0	2245
f	Wendt, R. (GER)	5	2300
	Wenzel, R. (GER)	6	2165
	Wenzel, S. (GER)	1	2050
	Werbeck, T. (GER)	0	2265
	Werner, C. (GER)	11	2305
m	Werner, D. (GER)	8	2375
	Werner, G. (GER)	10	2135
	Werner, I. (GER)	9	2220
f	Werner, M. (GER)	20	2335
	Werner, P. (GER)	0	2335
	Werner, V. (GER)	16	2175
	Werther, T. (ITA)	0	2325
f	Wesolowska, H. (POL)	3	2080
f	Wesseln, K. (GER)	9	2350
m	Wessman, R. (SWE)	9	2425
m	West, G. (AUS)	7	2410
	West, J. R. (USA)	3	2225
g	Westerinen, H. M. J. (FIN)	40	2385
	Westphal, M. (GER)	0	2310
	Wetscherek, G. (AUT)	0	2205
f	Weyrich, M. (GER)	2	2365
	Wharton, W. (USA)	0	2305
m	Whitehead, J. E. (USA)	0	2410
m	Whiteley, A. J. (ENG)	5	2315
	Wiander, M. (SWE)	0	2275
	Wians, C. (LUX)	19	2250
m	Wibe, T. (NOR)	0	2310
	Wichmann, C. (GER)	3	2215
f	Wicker, K. J. (ENG)	0	2275
	Widera, J. (POL)	11	2150
	Wiech, G. (POL)	17	2260
	Wieckiewicz, K. (USA)	0	2020
	Wieczorek, Z. (POL)	21	2325
m	Wiedenkeller, M. (SWE)	0	2450
	Wiedner, R. (AUT)	16	2245
	Wielecki, Z. (POL)	3	2230
	Wiemer, P. (GER)	10	2195
f	Wiemer, R. (GER)	7	2300
	Wiens, H. (GER)	0	2255
	Wierzbicka, E. (POL)	0	2020
	Wierzbiczki, J. (GER)	3	2055
m	Wiese-Jozwiak, M. (POL)	0	2205
	Wiesniak, T. (POL)	0	2205
	Wikner, A. (SWE)	19	2215
	Wild, R. (GER)	0	2265
	Wilde, P. (GER)	9	2295
g	Wilder, M. (USA)	0	2540
	Wildi, M. (SUI)	17	2310
	Wiley, T. E. (ENG)	0	2250
	Wiliczkiewicz, I. (POL)	0	2140
	Wiliczkiewicz, Z. (POL)	8	2015
	Wilke, M. (GER)	0	2205
f	Willemsen, J. (NED)	0	2280
f	Williams, A. H. (WLS)	3	2335
	Williams, S. (ENG)	9	2255
	Williams, W. (SIN)	0	2220
	Willke, H. (GER)	0	2270
	Willmoth, R. (ENG)	0	2225
	Wilson, B. (USA)	0	2230
	Wilson, J. (ENG)	8	2225
	Wimmer, H. (GER)	0	2270
m	Winants, L. (BEL)	19	2490
	Wind, L. (GER)	0	2320
f	Wind, M. A. (NED)	0	2345
	Winge, S. (SWE)	2	2275
	Winiwarter, F. (AUT)	3	2240
f	Winkler, G. (FRA)	3	2120
m	Winslow, E. C. (USA)	18	2320
m	Winsnes, R. (SWE)	8	2405
	Winter, I. (GER)	0	2010
f	Winterstein, W. (GER)	13	2305
f	Wintzer, J. (GER)	8	2300